UNDER THE ADVISORY EDITORSHIP OF

GORDON WRIGHT

Professor of History, Stanford University

THE WESTERN WORLD

Volume II: From 1700

THE
WESTERN
WORLD

NEW YORK   HAGERSTOWN   SAN FRANCISCO   LONDON

Volume II: From 1700

WALLACE E. ADAMS
RICHARD B. BARLOW
GERALD R. KLEINFELD
RONALD D. SMITH
WILLIAM W. WOOTTEN
Arizona State University

Harper & Row, Publishers

THE WESTERN WORLD: Volume II—From 1700

Library of Congress Catalog Card Number: 68-16192
Standard Book Number: 06-040166-4

ACKNOWLEDGMENTS FOR VOLUMES I AND II

George Allen & Unwin, Ltd., for *The Meaning of the Glorious Koran,* Marmaduke Pickthall, trans.; Friedrich Nietzsche, *The Will To Power,* Anthony M. Ludovici, trans.; G. Bernard Shaw, ed., *Fabian Essays in Socialism;* José Ortega y Gasset, *The Revolt of the Masses;* Sir Arthur Salter, *et al., The World's Economic Crisis and the Way of Escape;* Georges Sorel, *Reflections on Violence,* T. E. Hulme and J. Roth, trans. **The American-Scandinavian Foundation,** for *Three Icelandic Sagas,* M. H. Scargill and Margaret Schlauch, trans. **Edward Arnold (Publishers) Ltd.,** for Friedrich von Bernhardi, *Germany and the Next War,* Allen H. Powles, trans. **Basic Books, Inc.,** for *Voltaire's Philosophical Dictionary,* Peter Gay, trans., © 1962 by Basic Books Publishing Co., Inc. **Beacon Press,** for Roland H. Bainton, *The Life and Death of Michael Servetus,* copyright © 1953 by the Beacon Press. **C. H. Beck'sche Verlagsbuchhandlung,** for Hajo and Annemarie Holborn, eds., *D. Erasmus Roterodamus Ausgewahlte Werke,* reprinted in 1964. **G. Bell & Sons, Ltd.,** for Ernest F. Henderson, ed. and trans., *Select Documents of the Middle Ages;* Charles Heron Wall, ed. and trans., *The Dramatic Works of Molière,* Vol. II; Arthur Young, *Travels in France During the Years 1787, 1788, 1789: The Works of Edmund Burke,* Vol. II. **Ernest Benn Limited,** for Nikolai Gogol, *Dead Souls;* Paul Miliukov, *Russia and Its Crisis.* **Walter J. Black, Inc.,** for Thomas à Kempis, *The Imitation of Christ.* **Basil Blackwell & Mott Ltd.,** for A. P. D'Entrèves, ed., *Aquinas: Selected Political Writings;* Michael Oakeshott, ed., Thomas Hobbes, *Leviathan;* Thomas Mun, *England's Treasure by Forraign Trade;* J. M. Thompson, ed., *Napoleon's Letters.* **The Bodley Head,** for Houston Stewart Chamberlain, *Foundations of the Nineteenth Century,* John Lees, trans. **Burns & Oates, Ltd.,** for Sidney Z. Ehler and John B. Morall, eds., *Church and State Through the Centuries.* **Cambridge University Press,** for J. L. I. Fennell, trans., *The Correspondence Between Prince A. M. Kurbsky and Tsar Ivan IV of Russia, 1564–1579;* Leonard Forster, ed. and trans., *Selections from Conrad Celtis, 1459–1508.* **Carnegie Endowment for International Peace,** for Samuel von Pufendorf, *Two Books on the Duty of Man and Citizen According to the Natural Law,* Frank G. Moore, trans.; *The Treaties of Peace, 1919–1923.* **Catholic Truth Society, Inc.,** for Leo XIII, *The Pope and the People: Select Letters and Addresses.* **The Catholic University of American Press,** for *Tertullian: Apologetical Works and Minucius Felix: Octavius,* in Vol. 10 of *Fathers of the Church.* **Chatto & Windus, Ltd.,** for *Epistolae Obscurorum Virorum,* Francis Griffin Stokes, trans.; Alexander Herzen, *The Memoirs of My Past and Thoughts,* Constance Garnett, trans. Reprinted by permission of Chatto & Windus, Ltd., and David Garnett. **The Clarendon Press, Oxford,** for Aristotle, "Politics," and "Nicomachaean Ethics" from the *Oxford Translation of Aristotle:* Epicurus, "Letter to Menoeceus" and "Fragments", in Whitney J. Oates, ed., *The Stoic and Epicurean Philosophers,* C. Bailey, trans.; Epictetus, "The Discourses of Epictetus," in Whitney J. Oates, ed., *The Stoic and Epicurean Philosophers,* P. E. Matheson, trans.; Plato, "Republic," and "Crito," in *The Dialogues of Plato,* B. Jowett, trans.; B. J. Kidd, ed., *Documents of the Continental Reformation;* A. J. Whyte, *The Political Life and Letters of Cavour;* A. C. Fraser, ed., John Locke, *An Essay Concerning Human Understanding;* Adam Smith, *An Inquiry into the Nature and Causes of the Wealth of Nations;* Jeremy Bentham, *Principles of Morals and Legislation.* **Columbia University Press,** for Naphtali Lewis and Meyer Reinhold, eds., *Roman Civilization:* Gregory of Tours, *History of the Franks,* Ernest Brehaut, trans.; *Medieval Russian Laws,* George Vernadsky, trans.; William of Tyre, *A History of Deeds Done Beyond the Sea,* Emily Atwater Babcock and A. C. Krey, trans.; Desiderius Erasmus, *The Education of a Christian Prince,* Lester K. Born, trans.; Philip K. Hitti, *The Origins of the Islamic State;* Beatrice F. Hyslop, *A Guide to the General Cahiers of 1789.* **Constable and Com-**

pany, Limited, for John A. Hobson, *Imperialism, A Study;* Heinrich von Treitschke, *Politics,* Blanche Dugdale and Torbe de Bille, trans. J. M. Dent & Sons Ltd., for John Stuart Mill, *Utilitarianism, Liberty and Representative Government;* Robert Owen, *A New View of Society and Other Writings;* E. H. Blackeney, ed., *Tacitus: Historical Works.* Everyman's Library Edition; Thucydides, *History of the Peloponnesian War,* Richard Crawley, trans. Everyman's Library; de Villehardouin and de Joinville, *Memoirs of the Crusades,* Sir Frank T. Marzials, trans.; Geoffrey of Monmouth, *History of the Kings of Britain* (the Sebastian Evans translation revised by Charles W. Dunn), Everyman's Library text. The Devin Adair Company, for George Rotvand, *Franco Means Business,* Reginald Dingle, trans. E. P. Dutton & Co., Inc., for *Historical Works of Tacitus,* Arthur Murphy, trans., Vol. II, Everyman's Library Edition; Thucydides, *History of the Peloponnesian War,* Richard Crawley, trans., Everyman's Library; de Villehardouin and de Joinville, *Memoirs of the Crusades,* Sir Frank T. Marzials, trans., Dutton Paperback series; Geoffrey of Monmouth, *History of the Kings of Britain.* The Sebastian Evans translation revised by Charles W. Dunn, copyright © 1958. Dutton Paperback Series; Hans Jacob Christoph von Grimmelshausen, *The Adventurous Simplicissimus,* A. T. S. Goodrick, trans.; Robert Owen, *A New View of Society and Other Writings,* Everyman's Library Edition; John Stuart Mill, *Utilitarianism; On Liberty;* and *Representative Government.* Everyman's Library Edition. Faber and Faber, Ltd., for T. S. Eliot, *Collected Poems, 1909–1962.* Farrar, Straus & Giroux, Inc., for *Hitler's Secret Conversations, 1941–1944,* Norman Cameron and R. H. Stevens, trans., Trevor Roper, ed., copyright 1953 by Farrar, Straus & Young, Inc. "Foreign Affairs," for André Tardieu, "The Policy of France," excerpted by special permission from *Foreign Affairs,* September 1922. Copyright by the Council on Foreign Relations, Inc., New York. Fortress Press, for Harold J. Grimm, ed., *Luther's Works,* Vol. 31; George W. Forell, ed., *Luther's Works,* Vol. 32; Martin Luther, *Three Treatises.* Éditions Garnier Frères, for Émile Ollivier, *L'Empire Liberal.* Ginn and Company, for James Harvey Robinson, *Readings in European History.* Victor Gollancz, Ltd., for Léon Blum, *For All Mankind.* Hafner Publishing Company, for Jean-Jacques Rousseau, *The Social Contract,* Charles Frankel, trans. Hamish Hamilton, Ltd., for *Saint-Simon at Versailles,* Lucy Norton, trans., copyright 1958; Albert Camus, *The Rebel,* Anthony Bower, trans. Harcourt, Brace & World, Inc., for Walter Görlitz, ed., *The Kaiser and his Court: The Diaries, Notebooks and Letters of Admiral Georg Alexander von Müller, Chief of the Naval Cabinet, 1914–1918,* Mervyn Savill, trans., © 1959 by Musterschmidt-Verlag, Frankfurt, English translation © 1961 by Macdonald & Co. (Publishers) Ltd.; T. S. Eliot, *Collected Poems 1909–1962,* copyright 1936 by Harcourt, Brace & World, Inc.; copyright © 1963, 1964, by T. S. Eliot; John Maynard Keynes, *The Economic Consequences of the Peace,* copyright 1925 by Harcourt, Brace & World, Inc., renewed 1963 by R. F. Kahn. Harper & Row, Publishers, Inc., for *Saint-Simon at Versailles,* Lucy Norton, trans., copyright © 1958 by Hamish Hamilton, Ltd. and Harper & Row, Publishers Incorporated; Samuel Smiles, *Self Help;* Otto von Bismarck, *Bismarck the Man and the Statesman,* A. J. Butler, trans.; Ernst Haeckel, *The Riddle of the Universe at the Close of the Nineteenth Century,* Joseph McCabe, trans.; Henry W. Nevinson, *The Dawn in Russia.* Harvard University Press, for Richard Pipes, *Karamzin's Memoir on Ancient and Modern Russia,* copyright 1959 by the President and Fellows of Harvard College; Charles Homer Haskins, *The Renaissance of the Twelfth Century,* copyright 1927 by the President and Fellows of Harvard College, 1955 by Clare Allen Haskins; Gertrude Richards, *Florentine Merchants in the Age of the Medici;* C. H. McIlwain, *The Political Writings of James I;* A. E. R. Boak, *Journal of Economic and Business History,* Vol. I. The following selections are reprinted by permission of the publishers and the Loeb Classical Library: Cicero, *De Officiis,* Walter Miller, trans.; Cicero, *The Verrine Orations,* L. H. G. Greenwood, trans.; Velleius Paterculus, *Res Gestae Divi Augusti,* F. Shipley, trans.; Petronius, *Satyricon,* Michael Haseltine, trans.; Tacitus, *Annals,* John Jackson, trans.; Eusebius, *Ecclesiastical History,* J. E. L. Oulton, trans.; Procopius, *Anecdota or Secret History,* H. B. Dewing, trans.; Xenophon, *Scripta Minora,* E. C. Marchant, trans.; Aristotle, *Athenian Constitution, etc.,* H. Rackham, trans.; Arrian, E. I. Robson, trans. William Heinemann, Ltd., for Hans J. C. von Grimmelshausen, *The Adventurous Simplicissimus,* A. T. S. Goodrick, trans.; Arthur Koestler, *Dialogue With Death,* Trevor and Phyllis Blewitt, trans. Her Majesty's Stationery Office, for *Collected Diplomatic Documents Relating to the Outbreak of the European War;* C. H. Firth and R. S. Rait, eds., *Acts and Ordinances of the Interregnum, 1642–1660.* Hodder and Stoughton Limited, for Philipp Scheidemann, *Memoirs of a Social Democrat,* J. E. Michell, trans. The Hogarth Press, Ltd., for *The Standard Edition of the Complete Psychological Works of Sigmund Freud,* volume 21. Sigmund Freud copyright Ltds., the Estate of Mr. James Strachey, and the Hogarth Press, Ltd.; Benito Mussolini, *The Political and Social Doctrine of Fascism,* Jane Soames, trans. Houghton Mifflin Company, for "Prometheus Bound," Paul Elmer More, trans., in Whitney J. Oakes, ed., *Seven Famous Greek Plays;* R. M. Johnston, ed., *The Corsican: A Diary of Napoleon's Life in his own words;* Adolf Hitler, *Mein Kampf.* Copyright 1939. John Howell, Books, for *Laws of Burgos,* Lesley Byrd Simpson, trans. Independent Labour Party, for Eduard Bernstein, *Evolutionary Socialism: A Criticism and an Affirmation.* Jackson Son & Co. (Booksellers) Ltd., for Richard Hakluyt, *The Principal Navigations, Voyages, Traffiques, and Discoveries of the English Nation. Augustus M. Kelley Publishers,* for Friedrich List, *The National System of Political Economy.* Alfred A. Knopf, Inc., for Alexander Herzen, *The Memoirs of my Past and Thoughts,* trans. by Constance Garnett and revised by Humphrey Higgins, © Copyright 1968 by Chatto and Windus, Ltd., reprinted by permission of Alfred A. Knopf, Inc. Albert Camus, *The Rebel,* Anthony Bower, trans. Copyright 1956 by Alfred A. Knopf, Inc.; *The Trial* by Franz Kafka, trans. by Willa and Edna Muir, copyright 1937 and renewed 1964 by Alfred A. Knopf, Inc. Verlag W. Kohlhammer GmbH, for Ernst Rudolf Huber, ed., *Dokumente zur Deutschen Verfassungsgeschichte.* Longmans, Green & Co., Limited, for Benjamin Disraeli, *Selected Speeches of the Earl of Beaconsfield,* Vol. II; *The Institutes of Justinian,* Thomas C. Sanders, trans.; Henry Thomas Riley, ed., *Memorials of London and London Life, A.D. 1276-1419; The Annual Register* for the years: 1772, 1789, 1849, 1859. David McKay Company, Inc., for *The Song of Roland,* Merriam Sherwood, trans., copyright 1938, renewed 1966 by Penelope Sherwood; Friedrich von Bernhardi, *Germany and the Next War,* Allen H. Powles, trans. Macdonald & Co. (Publishers) Ltd., for Walter Görlitz, ed., *The Kaiser and his Court: The Diaries, Note Books and Letters of Admiral Georg Alexander von Müller, Chief of the Naval Cabinet, 1914-1918,* Mervyn Savill, trans. The Macmillan Company—Free Press of Glencoe, for George Sorel, *Reflections on Violence,* T. E. Hulme and J. Roth, trans., copyright 1950 by The Free Press, a Corporation; Ferenc Nagy, *The Struggle Behind the Iron Curtain,* Stephen K. Swift, trans., copyright 1948 by Ferenc Nagy; Arthur Koestler, *Dialogue With Death,* first published in the U.S. by The Macmillan Company in 1942; John Hall Stewart, ed., *A Documentary Survey of the French Revolution* copyright 1951 by The Macmillan Company; Heinrich von Treitschke, *Politics,* Blanche Dugdale and Torben de Bille, trans., copyright 1916 by The Macmillan Company. Macmillan & Co., Ltd., for John Maynard Keynes, *The Economic Consequences of the Peace,* reprinted by permission of the Trustees of the Estate of the late Lord Keynes, The Macmillan Company of Canada Ltd., and Macmillan & Co., Ltd., London; *The Histories of Polybius,* Evelyn S. Shuckburgh, trans.; Benedict de Spinoza, *Ethics Demonstrated in Geometrical Order,* W. Hale White and Amelia H. Sterling, trans.; A. R. Jacques Turgot, *Reflections on the Formation and Distribution of Riches;* John Bright and James E. Thorold Rogers, eds., Richard Cobden, *Speeches on Questions of Public Policy.* The Mediaeval Academy of America, for *The Russian Primary Chronicle,* Samuel H. Cross and Olgerd P. Sherbowitz-Wetzor, trans. Methuen & Co., Ltd., Publishers, for R. G. D. Laffan, ed., *Select Documents of European History.* John Murray, for *The History of Herodotus,* George Rawlinson, trans.; Charles W. Vane, ed., *Correspondence, Despatches, and Papers of Viscount Castlereagh, Second Marquess of Londonderry,* Vol. XII. National Council of the Churches of Christ, Division of Christian Education, for *Revised Standard Version of the Bible,* copyrighted 1946 and 1952 by the Division of Christian Education, National Council of Churches. New Directions Publishing Corp., George F. Whicher, *The Goliard Poems,* copyright 1949 by George F. Whicher. The New York Times, for June 5, 1956, pp. 13–16, copyright © 1956 by The New York Times Company. Martinus Nijhoff, Publisher and Bookseller, for W. K. Ferguson, ed., *Erasmi Opuscula.* W. W. Norton & Company, Inc., for Sigmund Freud, *Civilization and Its Discontents,* James Strachey, ed. and trans., copyright © 1961 by James Strachey; José Ortega y Gasset, *The Revolt of the Masses,* copyright 1932, W. W. Norton & Co., Inc., copyright © 1960 by Teresa Carey. Oliver & Boyd, Ltd., for *Studies of Wolfram von Eschenbach,* Margaret F. Richey, trans. Oxford University Press, for *The New English Bible: New Testament,* © The Delegates of the Oxford University Press and The Syndics of Cambridge University Press 1961; Jane Degras, ed., *Soviet Documents on Foreign Policy,* Vol. III, published by Oxford University Press under the auspices of the Royal Institute of International Affairs; *The Odyssey of Homer,* T. E. Shaw, trans., copyright 1932 by Bruce Rogers, renewed 1960 by A. W. Lawrence; Henry Bettenson, ed., *Documents of the Christian Church,* copyright 1947 by Oxford University Press; William Huse Hunham, Jr. and Stanley Pargellis, eds., *Complaint and Reform in England,* copyright 1938 by Oxford University Press, renewed 1966 by the authors; Andrew Browning, ed., *English Historical Documents, 1660-1714,* Vol. VIII; Mark DeWolfe Howe, ed., *The Holmes-Laski Letters, 1916-1935.* Paulist-Newman Press, for Sidney Z. Ehler and John B. Morrall, eds., *Church and State Through the Centuries.* Frederick A. Praeger, Inc., for Gerhard Ritter, *The Schlieffen Plan: Critique of a Myth,* Andrew and Eva Wilson, trans.; Milovan Djilas, *The New Class.* Princeton University Press, for James B. Pritchard, ed., *Ancient Near Eastern Texts Relating to the Old Testament* (rev. ed., 1955); *The Chief Plays of Pierre Corneille,* Lacy Lockert, trans. G. P. Putnam's Sons, for Sir Leslie Stephen, *An Agnostic' Apology and other Essays;* Leo Wiener, *Anthology of Russian Literature from the Earliest Period to the Present Time.* Random House, Inc., for Saint Augustine, *The City of God,* Marcus Dodds, trans.; Richard McKeon, ed., *The Basic Works of Aristotle,* copyright 1941 by Random House, Inc.; Francis R. B. Godolphin, ed., *The Greek Historians* (2 vols.), copyright 1942 by Random House, Inc.; Whitney J. Oates and Eugene O'Neill, Jr., eds., *Seven Famous Greek Plays,* copyright 1940 by Random House, Inc.; Whitney J. Oates, ed., *The Stoic and Epicurean Philosophers,* copyright 1940 by Random House, Inc., reprinted by permission of Random House, Inc., and The Clarendon Press, Oxford; Anton C. Pegis, ed., *Basic Writings of Saint Thomas Aquinas* (2 vols.), copyright 1945 by Random House, Inc.; Dante Alighieri, *Divine Comedy,* Lawrence Grant White, trans., copyright

1948 by Pantheon Books, reprinted by permission of Random House, Inc. Routledge & Kegan Paul Ltd., for *The Works of Liudprand of Cremona*, F. A. Wright, trans.; Henry Morley, ed., *The Decameron of Giovanni Boccacio;* Auguste Comte, *A General View of Positivism*, J. H. Bridges, trans. Royal Historical Society, for *Transactions of the Royal Historical Society*, Vol. VI, (1901). Russell & Russell Publishers, for Friedrich Nietzsche, *The Will to Power* (2 vols.), Anthony M. Ludovici, trans., in *The Complete Works of Friedrich Nietzsche*, trans. under the General Editorship of Oscar Levy (18 vols.) [1909–1911], New York: Russell & Russell, 1964. Rutgers University Press, for Louis L. Snyder, ed., *Documents of German History;* Hans Kohn, *The Mind of Modern Russia*. Charles Scribner's Sons, Publishers, for Richard McKeon, ed., *Selections from Medieval Philosophers*, Vol. I, copyright 1929 Charles Scribner's Sons renewal copyright © 1957; Oliver J. Thatcher and Edgar H. McNeal, *A Source Book for Medieval History;* Baldassare Castiglione, *The First Book of The Courtier*, Leonard E. Opdyke, trans. Schocken Books, Inc., for Eduard Bernstein, *Evolutionary Socialism: A Criticism and an Affirmation*. Martin Secker & Warburg Limited, for Franz Kafka, *The Trial*, Willa and Edwin Muir, trans. Stanford University Press, for *The Complete Essays of Montaigne*, Donald M. Frame, trans., © copyright 1948, 1957, 1958 by the Board of Trustees of the Leland Stanford Junior University. The Times Publishing Company Limited (London), for issues of: 29 Feb. 1884; 31 July 1909; 10 Feb. 1912; 1 Oct. 1938; 3 Oct. 1938. Union Générale d'éditions, for Maximilien Robespierre, *Discours et Rapports à la Convention*. University of California Press, for Sir Isaac Newton, *The Mathematical Principles of Natural Philosophy*, Florian Cajori, trans. The University of Chicago Press, for Sophocles, *Antigone*, Elizabeth Wyckoff, trans., in David Greene and Richard Lattimore, eds., *The Complete Greek Tragedies*, copyright © 1954, 1959; Ernst Cassirer, *et al.*, eds., *The Renaissance Philosophy of Man*, copyright 1948; Paul N. Milyoukov, *Russia and Its Crisis;* Karl Jaspers, *The Future of Mankind*, E. B. Ashton, trans., © 1961. The University of Michigan Press, for Konstantin Petrovich Pobedonostsev, *Reflections of a Russian Statesman*, Robert Crozier Long, trans. University of Notre Dame Press, for Hans Kohn, *Pan-Slavism: Its History and Ideology*. University of Pennsylvania History Department, for *Translations and Reprints from the Original Sources of European History*. 6 vols. University of Toronto Press, for Karl Jaspers, *The Future of Mankind*, E. B. Ashton, trans. D. Van Nostrand, Inc., for Philip K. Hitti, *Islam and the West*. The Viking Press, Inc., for Léon Blum, *For All Mankind*, copyright 1946 by Léon Blum; J. B. Ross and M. M. McLaughlin, eds., *The Portable Renaissance Reader*. Wahr's University Bookstore, for James H. Meisel and Edward S. Kozera, eds., *Materials for the Study of the Soviet System*. Washington Square Press, Inc., John R. Hale, ed., *Guicciardini: History of Italy and the History of Florence*, Cecil Grayson, trans. Copyright © 1964, Washington Square Press, Inc. George Weidenfeld & Nicolson Limited, for *Hitler's Secret Conversations, 1941–1944*, Norman Cameron and R. H. Stevens, trans. Dr. Herbert Wendler & Co., for Dr. Johannes Hohlfeld, *Dokumente der Deutschen Politik und Geschicte*, Band IV. The H. W. Wilson Company, for Frank Maloy Anderson, ed., *The Constitutions and Other Select Documents Illustrative of the History of France, 1789–1907*. Yale University Press, for Edward Surtz, ed., St. Thomas More, *Utopia*.

Preface

ALMOST three centuries ago the Baron de Montesquieu asserted:

> There is no class of authors I despise more than I do compilers, who come from every side to search for the fragments of other men's works. . . . I would have original works respected. It is a kind of profanation to tear from them the parts of which they are composed, as if from a sanctuary, and thereby expose them to a concept they do not deserve. . . . [*Persian Letters*]

The western world has changed drastically in habits and educational approach since the outspoken French aristocrat expressed his views, and there is no need to defend the publication of a collection of historical sources. Nevertheless, Montesquieu's words of caution to the editors of collected readings are as appropriate in the twentieth century as they were in the eighteenth. The editors of this collection have labored at all times to respect the original language and central points of the works selected, thus answering Montesquieu's objections in large measure.

In planning the form and scope of the two volumes of *The Western World*, the editors have relied on their classroom experiences of the past decade. While recognizing the importance of historical interpretation, we believe that students ought first be exposed to a broad panorama of original sources. Therefore, we have left interpretation, insofar as it does not arise from the documents themselves, to the professor in class and to narrative texts. An encounter with the actual documents provides a drama and a flavor rarely matched by works written about them, and the editors believe that beginning students should have an opportunity to read and work with the raw materials of history.

No two-volume collection of readings can be comprehensive enough to more than scan the vast canvas of historical evolution. In choosing materials to represent the changing ideas and institutions of western man, the editors have grouped their selections in a roughly chronological order. Further, because political, social, economic, and cultural issues cut across every dimension of history, we have avoided the "problem" approach of grouping sources into a narrow or pre-fixed pattern which would sharply limit the student's horizon. Continuity in history is as significant as the attempt to isolate given issues at a precise moment in the past, and we have attempted to provide instructors with a wide variety of significant materials which can be grouped to emphasize a particular approach to western civilization.

We have employed two types of introductions to the reading selections. On the assumption that these volumes ordinarily will be used in conjunction with a narrative text, chapter introductions are designed to establish only a general framework for the documents in a given historical period. Introductions to specific selections furnish basic information to clarify the source while still allowing each document to stand on its own merits. The questions used to conclude selection introductions suggest some profitable lines of inquiry into significant ideas or issues presented by the source. We have found such questions useful as starting points for classroom discussion, but each instructor doubtless will adapt them to suit his own objectives. In no sense do the questions asked purport to exhaust the significance of each selection.

These two volume divide at approximately 1700, with the final chapter of Volume I and the first chapter of Volume II overlapping chronologically. The editors believe that the new philosophic and scientific ideas contributed by seventeenth-century thinkers can be most usefully explored in conjunction with the eighteenth-century Enlightenment. Thus, Volume I concludes with political, economic, and literary sources from the seventeenth century; Chapter One of Volume II begins with philosophic and scientific documents from the seventeenth century and concludes with the political thought of the Enlightenment.

A large number of selections focus on the ideas and institutions of central and eastern Europe. Such readings are designed to complement the better known materials relating to England, France, Italy, and their neighbors. The editors have also revised a number of antiquated translations, modernized the spelling of a few selections, and provided an original translation when no satisfactory version was available in English. Our purpose throughout has been to present a collection of documents characterized by breadth and accuracy.

Many selections in this publication have been used by our classes in an experimental form and we wish to thank students at Arizona State University who offered constructive comments and criticisms. The Department of History has also been most considerate in providing office space and facilities, while our colleagues have graciously tolerated the distracted behavior which characterized five of their number during the final stages of completing these volumes. For assistance in typing the final manuscript we are indebted to Mrs. Grace Skinaway, Miss Estella Aguon, and Miss Sheryl Hankins. Professors John C. Ellis, Edwin P. Grobe, Judith J. Radke, E. Bernell McIntyre and Mr. James Malcomson supplied a number of the translations produced in this publication, and the staff of Hayden Library at Arizona State University proved most helpful at all times. We also owe special thanks to Professor Lawrence Steefel for reading the draft manuscript and to Professor Gordon Wright for his enthusiastic interest and valuable criticism. Mr. Philip Winsor and Mrs. Genia Graves of Dodd, Mead & Company offered many valuable suggestions as the manuscript reached its final form. Finally, the patience, help, and encouragement provided by Nan Adams, Barbara Smith, and Ruth Wootten were essential contributions to the completion of these volume.

THE EDITORS

Contents

CHAPTER THREE. REACTION AND REVOLUTION, 1815–1848   125

CHAPTER FOUR. THE EARLY IMPACT
OF INDUSTRIALISM   184

INDUSTRIALIZATION AND ECONOMIC LIBERALISM

UTOPIAN AND SCIENTIFIC SOCIALISM

CHAPTER FIVE. THE POLITICAL
REORIENTATION OF EUROPE   239

ENGLAND: THE VICTORIAN COMPROMISE

FRANCE: THE SECOND EMPIRE

THE UNIFICATION OF ITALY AND GERMANY

TSARIST RUSSIA

CHAPTER NINE. THE SECOND WORLD WAR AND AFTER   586

Chapter One

THE SCIENTIFIC REVOLUTION AND THE EIGHTEENTH-CENTURY ENLIGHTENMENT

BY mid-eighteenth century a number of European intellectuals believed that they had found techniques to overcome man's timeless moral, political, and economic difficulties. Their views reflected a revolution in men's minds which began in the late Middle Ages and came to fruition in the eighteenth-century Enlightenment.

The majority of western scholars, as late as the Reformation, still sought knowledge by examining the teachings of traditional authorities rather than by employing the methods of experimental science. Aristotle's concept of motion and his insistence that bodies fall faster or slower according to their weight were almost universally accepted. The Holy Inquisition, in 1616, made a definitive pronouncement that it was unscriptural and therefore untrue to say that the earth was not the center of the universe and that Jerusalem was not the center of the earth. Such non-scientific views, based neither upon observation nor experimentation, were an important part of the impressive body of thought upon which the European world was based.

Nevertheless, the classical concept of the relationship between the earth, the sun, and the stars gradually faded from men's minds as mathematicians and astronomers like Johannes Kepler (1571–1630) and Galileo Galilei (1564–1642) studied the physical features of the universe. Despite fulminations from conservative ecclesiastical authorities, a growing body of scientific knowledge was accumulated. In England, Sir Francis Bacon (1561–1626) defended the principles of inductive reasoning (*i.e.,* forming conclusions from specific examples). Man's confidence in the power of reason was given even greater impetus by the Frenchman, René Descartes (1596–1650). To distinguish between fact and fancy, Descartes advocated the method of doubting everything that could be doubted He concluded that the only thing which could not be doubted was the existence of one's own doubting mind (*Dubito, ergo sum*). Having verified, to his own

1

satisfaction, the existence of his mind and hence of the whole real world, Descartes was prepared to subject all phenomena of experience to precise and logical examination in the supreme court of human reason. Long after the seventeenth century the technique of "Cartesian doubt" exerted a strong influence upon European intellectual life.

Benedict Spinoza (1632–77) was a brilliant rationalist philosopher who, like Descartes, looked on the universe as a vast machine ordered by mathematical principles which could be measured and explained by the laws of physics. Both Descartes and Spinoza refused to mix science with theology. Miracles, therefore, were mere figments of the imagination and played no part in the operation of a universe based on the principles of invariable natural law. Utilizing the approach of seventeenth-century science and mathematics, they helped to enthrone natural law and human reason.

The scientific upheaval which had begun with Copernicus' heliocentric astronomy continued with Sir Isaac Newton's *Philosophiae Naturalis Principia* (1687), a landmark in the history of applied mathematics. Newton provided the most forceful arguments for the new faith in natural law by synthesizing scientific concepts and offering a basis for new philosophical speculations. He explained the movement of all bodies, both celestial and terrestrial, on the basis of mechanical and mathematical principles. Man was thus a creature dwarfed by the immense machine that was the universe. The fundamental features of Newton's universe were numbers, mathematical quantities, and invariable natural laws valid for all times and places. Gone forever were the spirits and intelligences thought necessary to push the skies around the earth every day. With supreme faith in the sovereign power of Natural Law and man's ability to interpret it, the poet Alexander Pope asserted:

> Nature and Nature's laws lay hid in night;
> God said: "Let Newton be!" and there was light.

The new scientific method was quickly applied to political, social, and economic institutions. The success of the bloodless English Revolution of 1688, which established parliamentary rule, a considerable degree of religious toleration, equality before the law, and freedom of speech, drew attention to the writings of its eloquent oracle, John Locke (1632-1704). Locke's works contained the essence of the eighteenth-century Enlightenment, for underlying all of his thought was the belief that human reason, if applied resolutely and dispassionately, could eradicate every element of medieval obscurantism and social injustice and make way for a happier future where continued progress and enlightenment would be in store for all men

In France, under the original inspiration of Newtonian physics and Lockean philosophy, there developed a loosely knit group of thinkers and writers known as *les philosophes* (the philosophers). Despite many personal differences and jealousies, men like Fontenelle, Montesquieu, Voltaire, Diderot, Turgot, Buffon, Quesnay, Helvétius, and Rousseau believed in the sovereign power of human reason. They idealized the order they saw in nature, believed in the essential goodness of humanity, and were confident that human progress was inevitable.

Few *philosophes* believed in democracy. To remedy political ills they looked for an enlightened despot—a beneficent, all-wise lawgiver who (no doubt aided by *les philosophes* themselves) would sweep aside medieval anachronisms. Claude Adrien Helvétius (1715-71) summed up the basic political principles of his contemporaries when he wrote: "It is the wise lawgiver who creates the good citizen." Only Jean Jacques Rousseau (1712-78), among eminent eighteenth-century French thinkers before the Revolution of 1789, spoke out for the sovereignty of the people.

The enlightened despots of eighteenth-century Europe claimed to be disciples of the *philosophes,* priding themselves in their devotion to principles of rational government. In Prussia, Frederick the Great (r. 1740-86) agreed that "the monarch exists for the sake of the people and not the people for the sake of the monarch." After 1763, through the rigorous practice of royal paternalism, he sought to provide an efficient government characterized by uniformity of law, a degree of religious toleration, and a strictly regulated economy for the benefit of the state. Catherine the Great, Empress of Russia (r. 1762-96), maintained a lively correspondence with several *philosophes*. In Austria, Joseph II, upon the death of his mother the Empress Maria Theresa in 1780, tried to "make philosophy the ruler of Austria." His hundreds of decrees and royal edicts, however, which aimed to centralize the administration of his inchoate dynastic inheritance, stirred up local rebellions—particularly in Belgium and Hungary. By the time of his death in 1790, Joseph had been forced to withdraw every decree except the edicts which applied to the abolition of serfdom. Gustavus III of Sweden (r. 1771-92) more successfully pared away the privileges of his feudal nobility in the interests of a centralized monarchy.

The century which ended with the French Revolution of 1789 was an age of privilege and tradition, known in France as the *ancien régime*. Countries were still treated as hereditary property, and their destinies were determined by the principle of dynastic kingship. Royal marriages were the basic means by which alliances were sealed and by which lands were divided, with utter disregard for the principle of nationality. The First Partition of Poland among Frederick II of Prussia, Catherine II of Russia, and Maria Theresa of Austria in 1772 was a particularly glaring example of how eighteenth-century monarchs carved up territories without regard for the wishes of the inhabitants.

One major event in European history which denied the right of established governments to rule as they pleased, without popular sanction, was the American Revolution. The Declaration of Independence of the Thirteen British Colonies in North America claimed that men were "endowed with inalienable rights." Thomas Jefferson and other revolutionists thus struck at the very heart of kingship "by the Grace of God." Since all political structures were created for man's convenience, leaders of the American Revolution asserted that governments could be unmade for the same purpose. They leaned heavily upon the abstract reasoning of Locke and Rousseau, and their philosophical speculations became basic principles of American constitutional law. Defenders of absolute monarchy in Europe might well have trembled before the example of the infant United States of America—a government actually functioning upon principles which constituted a solemn mockery of all that the *ancien régime* represented.

SCIENCE AND PHILOSOPHY

1. RENÉ DESCARTES: DISCOURSE ON METHOD*

René Descartes (1596–1650) was educated in the Jesuit school at La Flèche and at the University of Poitiers. After traveling extensively in southern Germany, where he served in the army of Prince Maurice of Nassau, Descartes lived for a time in Paris; in 1628 he retired to Holland where he completed his most significant work, *Discourse on the Method of Rightly Conducting the Reason and Seeking Truth in the Sciences* (1637). In his *Discourse* he described his disillusionment with scholastic education and related how he came to abandon the study of letters to seek knowledge in "the great book of the universe." Descartes also wrote essays on optics, astronomy, music, physiology, physics, analytical geometry, and algebra, all of which made significant contributions to the philosophical application of scientific discoveries.

Mathematics was Descartes' greatest interest, and it was his attempt to extend mathematical methods to all fields of human knowledge that led him to discard the authoritative system of the scholastics and to test everything in human experience by his formula of universal doubt. What specific steps did Descartes believe would lead the individual thinker to true knowledge? Did he advocate scientific experiments based upon inductive reasoning, or did he emphasize deductive methods as a guide to truth? Why is Cartesian philosophy classified as dualistic, and on what grounds could Descartes claim that his method of reasoning in no way challenged traditional religious dogma?

But like one walking alone and in the dark, I resolved to proceed so slowly and with such circumspection, that if I did not advance far, I would at least guard against falling. I did not even choose to dismiss summarily any of the opinions that had crept into my belief without having been introduced by Reason, but first of all took sufficient time carefully to satisfy myself of the general nature of the task I was setting myself, and ascertain the true Method by which to arrive at the knowledge of whatever lay within the compass of my powers.

Among the branches of Philosophy, I had, at an earlier period, given some attention to Logic, and among those of the Mathematics to Geometrical Analysis and Algebra,—three Arts or Sciences which ought, as I conceived, to contribute something to my design. But, on examination, I found that, as for Logic, its syllogisms and the majority of its other precepts are of avail rather in the communication of what we already know, or even as the Art of Lully, in speaking without judgment of things of which we are ignorant, than in the investigation of the unknown; and although this Science contains indeed a number of correct and very excellent precepts, there are, nevertheless, so many others, and these either injurious or superfluous, mingled with the former, that it is almost quite as difficult to effect a severance of the true from the false as it is to extract a Diana or a Minerva from a rough block of marble. Then as to the Analysis of the ancients and the Algebra of the moderns, besides that they embrace only

* René Descartes, *Discourse on Method and Meditations*, trans. John Vietch (Washington, D.C.: M. Walter Dunne, 1901), pp. 160–62, 170–74, 176–77.

matters highly abstract, and, to appearance, of no use, the former is so exclusively restricted to the consideration of figures, that it can exercise the Understanding only on condition of greatly fatiguing the Imagination; and, in the latter, there is so complete a subjection to certain rules and formulas, that there results an art full of confusion and obscurity calculated to embarrass, instead of a science fitted to cultivate the mind. By these considerations I was induced to seek some other Method which would comprise the advantages of the three and be exempt from their defects. And as a multitude of laws often only hampers justice, so that a state is best governed when, with few laws, these are rigidly administered; in like manner, instead of the great number of precepts of which Logic is composed, I believed that the four following would prove perfectly sufficient for me, provided I took the firm and unwavering resolution never in a single instance to fail in observing them.

The FIRST was never to accept anything for true which I did not clearly know to be such; that is to say, carefully to avoid precipitancy and prejudice, and to comprise nothing more in my judgment than what was presented to my mind so clearly and distinctly as to exclude all ground of doubt.

The SECOND, to divide each of the difficulties under examination into as many parts as possible, and as might be necessary for its adequate solution.

The THIRD, to conduct my thoughts in such order that, by commencing with objects the simplest and easiest to know, I might ascend by little and little, and, as it were, step by step, to the knowledge of the more complex; assigning in thought a certain order even to those objects which in their own nature do not stand in a relation of antecedence and sequence.

At the LAST, in every case to make enumerations so complete, and reviews so general, that I might be assured that nothing was omitted.

The long chains of simple and easy reasonings by means of which geometers are accustomed to reach the conclusions of their most difficult demonstrations, had led me to imagine that all things, to the knowledge of which man is competent, are mutually connected in the same way, and that there is nothing so far removed from us as to be beyond our reach, or so hidden that we cannot discover it, provided only we abstain from accepting the false for the true, and always preserve in our thoughts the order necessary for the deduction of one truth from another. And I had little difficulty in determining the objects with which it was necessary to commence, for I was already persuaded that it must be with the simplest and easiest to know, and considering that of all those who have hitherto sought truth in the Sciences, the mathematicians alone have been able to find any demonstrations, that is, any certain and evident reasons, I did not doubt but that such must have been the rule of their investigations. I resolved to commence, therefore, with the examination of the simplest objects, not anticipating, however, from this any other advantage than that to be found in accustoming my mind to the love and nourishment of truth, and to a distaste for all such reasonings as were unsound. . . .

I am in doubt as to the propriety of making my first meditations, in the place above mentioned, matter of discourse; for these are so metaphysical, and so uncommon, as not, perhaps, to be acceptable to everyone. And yet, that it may be determined whether the foundations that I have laid are sufficiently secure, I find myself in a measure constrained to advert to them. I had long before remarked that, in relation to practice, it is sometimes necessary to adopt, as if above doubt, opinions which we discern to be highly uncertain, as has been already said; but as I then desired to give my attention solely to the search after truth, I thought that a procedure exactly the opposite was called for, and that I ought to reject as absolutely false all opinions in regard to which I could suppose the least ground for doubt, in order to ascertain whether after that there remained aught in my belief that was wholly indubitable. Accordingly, seeing that our senses sometimes deceive us, I was willing to suppose that there existed nothing really such as they presented to us; and because some men err in reasoning, and fall into paralogisms, even on the simplest matters of Geometry, I, convinced that I was as open to error as any other, rejected as false all the reasonings I had hitherto taken for demonstrations; and finally, when I considered that the very same thoughts (presentations) which we experience when awake may also be experienced when we are asleep, while there is at that time not one of them true, I supposed that all the objects (presentations) that had ever entered into my mind when awake, had in them no more truth than the illusions of my dreams. But immediately upon this I observed that, whilst I thus wished to think that all was false, it was absolutely necessary that I, who thus thought, should be something; and as I observed that this truth, I THINK, HENCE I AM, was so certain and of such evidence, that no ground of doubt, however extravagant, could be alleged by the Sceptics capable of shaking it, I concluded that I might, without scruple, accept it as the first principle of the Philosophy of which I was in search. . . .

In the next place, from reflecting on the circumstance that I doubted, and that consequently my being was not wholly perfect (for I clearly saw that it was a greater perfection to know than to doubt), I was led to inquire whence I had learned to think of something more perfect than myself; and I clearly recognized that I must hold this notion from some Nature which in reality was more perfect. As for the thoughts of many other objects external to me, as of the sky, the earth, light, heat, and a thousand more, I was less at a loss to know whence these came; for since I remarked in them nothing which seemed to render them superior to myself, I could believe that, if these were true, they were dependencies on my own nature, in so far as it possessed a certain perfection, and, if they were false, that I held them from nothing, that is to say, that they were in me because of a certain imperfection of my nature. But this could not be the case with the idea of a Nature more perfect than myself; for to receive it from nothing was a thing manifestly impossible; and, because it is not less repugnant that the more perfect should be an effect of, and dependence on the less perfect, than that something should proceed from nothing, it was equally impossible that I could hold it from myself: accordingly, it but remained that it had been placed in me by a Nature which was in reality more perfect than mine, and which even possessed within itself all the perfections of which I could form any idea: that is to say, in a single word, which was God. . . .

. . . Recurring to the examination of the idea of a Perfect Being, I found that the existence of the Being was comprised in the idea in the same way that the equality of its three angles to two right angles is comprised in the idea of a triangle, or as in the idea of a sphere, the equidistance of all points on its surface from the center, or even still more clearly; and that consequently it is at least as certain that God, who is this Perfect Being, is, or exists, as any demonstration of Geometry can be. . . .

. . . For, in fine, whether awake or asleep, we ought never to allow ourselves to be persuaded of the truth of anything unless on the evidence of our Reason. And it must be noted that I say of our REASON, and not of our imagination or of our senses: thus, for example, although we very clearly see the sun, we ought not therefore to determine that it is only of the size which our sense of sight presents; and we may very distinctly imagine the head of a lion joined to the body of a goat, without being therefore shut up to the conclusion that a chimera exists; for it is not a dictate of Reason that what we thus see or imagine is in reality existent; but it plainly tells us that all our ideas or notions contain in them some truth; for otherwise it could not be that God, who is wholly perfect and veracious, should have placed them in us. And because our reasonings are never so clear or so complete during sleep as when we are awake, although sometimes the acts of our imagination are then as lively and distinct, if not more so than in our waking moments, Reason further dictates that, since all our thoughts cannot be true because of our partial imperfection, those possessing truth must infallibly be found in the experience of our waking moments rather than in that of our dreams. . . .

2. BENEDICT SPINOZA: GEOMETRICAL PRINCIPLES OF ETHICS*

Benedict Spinoza (1632–77) was by descent a Portuguese Jew whose ancestors had fled from the Catholic Inquisition and settled in Holland. Expelled from the Amsterdam Synagogue as an atheist at the age of twenty-four, Spinoza changed his name from Baruch to Benedict and continued his philosophical studies while he earned a modest living by grinding lenses for the newly invented telescope and microscope. In 1663 he published a *Geometric Version* of Descartes' philosophy, followed by a *Treatise on Religion and Political Philosophy* which aroused a storm of condemnation and was labeled a sacrilegious and atheistic work. Because of official censorship, his most important study, the *Ethics Demonstrated in Geometrical Order,* was not published until after his death. Why was this work also generally regarded as sacrilegious? Was Spinoza an atheist? What was his attitude toward miracles? How did Spinoza's methods differ from Descartes', and what specific criticism did he level against the great French philosopher? Why has Spinoza's system been classified as monistic in contrast to Descartes' dualism? Can it be held that Spinoza believed in predestination and determinism as fully as John Calvin, but on different grounds? Why?

OF GOD

Nothing . . . comes to pass in nature in contravention to her universal laws; no, everything agrees with them and follows from them, for whatever comes to pass occurs by the will and eternal decree of God; that is, as we have just

---

* Benedict de Spinoza, *Ethics Demonstrated in Geometrical Order,* trans. W. Hale White and Amelia H. Sterling (New York: Macmillan, 1894), pp. 33, 35, 38–43, 104–5. Translation revised by the editors.

pointed out, whatever comes to pass, occurs according to laws and rules which involve eternal necessity and truth. Nature therefore always observes laws and rules which involve eternal necessity and truth, although they may not be known to us, and therefore she keeps a fixed and immutable order. Nor is there any sound reason for limiting the power and efficacy of nature, and asserting that her laws are fit for certain purposes but not for all; for as the efficacy and power of nature are the very efficacy and power of God, and as the laws and rules of nature are the decrees of God, it is in every way to be believed that the power of nature is infinite, and that her laws are broad enough to embrace everything conceived by the Divine intellect. The only alternative is to assert that God has created nature so weak and has ordained for her laws so barren that He is repeatedly compelled to come afresh to her aid if He wishes that she should be preserved and that things should happen as He desires—a conclusion in my opinion very far removed from reason. Furthermore, as nothing happens in nature which does not follow from her laws, and as her laws embrace everything conceived by the Divine intellect, and lastly, as nature preserved a fixed and immutable order, it most clearly follows that miracles are only intelligible in relation to human opinions and merely mean events of which the natural cause cannot be explained by reference to any ordinary occurrence, either by us or by the writer and narrator of the miracle. . . .

I have now explained the nature of God and its properties. . . . Moreover, wherever an opportunity was afforded, I have tried to remove prejudices which might hinder the perception of the truth of what I have demonstrated; but because not a few prejudices still remain . . . I have thought it worthwhile to call them up to be examined by reason.

All such prejudices spring from the opinion commonly held that all things in nature act as men themselves act. Indeed, it is accepted as certain that God himself directs all things toward some sure end, for it is said that God made all things for man, and man that he might worship God. I will therefore consider this opinion, asking first why it obtains general credence and why all men are so naturally prone to adopt it. I shall then show its falsity. . . .

Men do all things for an end, namely, that which is useful to them. . . . So it happens that they attempt to discover merely the final causes of events, and when these are learned, they are satisfied because there is no longer any need for further uncertainty. If they cannot learn such causes from external sources, they are compelled to turn inward and reflect what end would have induced them personally to bring about the given event, and thus they necessarily judge other natures by their own. Moreover, as they discover both within and outside of themselves a multitude of means which contribute not a little in their search for what is useful—for example, the eyes for seeing, teeth for chewing, plants and animals for food, the sun for giving light, the sea for breeding fish—it comes to pass that all natural objects are considered as a means for obtaining what is profitable. As men are aware that they found these conveniences and did not make them, they have cause for believing that some other being exists who has prepared them for man's use. Since they look upon things as means, they cannot believe them to be self-created; but, judging from the means which they are accustomed to prepare for themselves, they are bound to believe in some ruler or rulers of the universe endowed with human freedom who have arranged and adapted everything for man's use. Since they never heard anything about the mind of these rulers, men are compelled to judge it from their own, and hence they affirm that the gods direct everything for man's advantage in order that he may be bound to them and hold them in highest honor. This is the reason why each man devises for himself, out of his own brain, a different mode of worshipping God, so that God may love him above all others, and direct all nature to the service of his blind cupidity and insatiable avarice.

Thus has this prejudice been turned into a superstition and has driven deep roots into the mind—a prejudice which explains the reason why every one has so eagerly tried to discover and account for the final causes of things. The attempt, however, to show that nature does nothing in vain (that is to say, nothing which is not profitable to man) seems to end in showing that nature, the gods, and man are all alike mad.

Observe, I pray you, the result: Amid so much in nature that is beneficial, not a few things must be observed which are injurious, such as storms, earthquakes, and diseases; but it is affirmed that these things happen either because the gods are angry at wrongs which have been inflicted on them by man, or because of sins committed in the method of worshipping them. Although experience daily contradicts such notions and shows by an infinity of examples that both the beneficial and the injurious are indiscriminately bestowed on the pious and the impious, the inveterate prejudices on this point have not been abandoned. It has been easier for men to classify such contradictions among other unknown things of which they are ignorant, and thus to retain their actual and innate condition of ignorance, than to destroy the whole fabric of their reasoning and to start afresh. Men therefore lay down as an axiom the doctrine that God's judgments far transcend human understanding. Such a doctrine might well have sufficed to conceal the truth from mankind for all eternity, if mathematics had not furnished another standard of truth in considering solely the essence and properties of forms without regard to their final causes. . . .

I have thus sufficiently explained what I promised in the first place to explain. There will be no need now of many words to show that nature has set no end before herself, and that all final causes are nothing but human fictions. . . . Nevertheless, I will stress that this doctrine concerning an end altogether contravenes nature. . . . In fact, it does away with God's perfection. For if God works to obtain an end, He necessarily seeks something which He lacks. Although theologians and metaphysicians distinguish between the object of want and the object of assimilation [*finem indigentiae et finem assimilationis*] still they confess that God made all things for the sake of creation. They are unable to point to anything prior to creation except God himself as an object for which God should act, and are therefore driven to admit that God stood in need of and desired those ends for which he determined to create means.

Nor is it here to be overlooked that the adherents of this doctrine, who have found pleasure in displaying their ingenuity in assigning the ends [final causes] of things, have introduced a new species of argument to prove their position— a reduction, not to the impossible, but to ignorance—which shows that they have no other method of defence. For example, if a stone falls from a roof on someone's head and kills him, they will demonstrate by their method that the stone fell in order to kill the man. For if it did not fall for that purpose by the will of God, how could so many circumstances concur through chance (and a number often simultaneously do concur)? You will answer, perhaps, that the event happened because the wind blew and the man was passing that way. But, they will argue: "Why did the wind blow at that time, and why did the man pass that way precisely at the same moment?" If you again reply that the wind rose then because the sea on the preceding day began to be stormy, the weather before then having been calm, and that the man had been invited by a friend, they will argue again, because there is no end of questioning: "But why was the sea agitated? Why was the man invited at that time?" And so they will not cease from asking the causes of causes, until at last you take refuge in the will of God, the refuge for ignorance.

So also, when they behold the structure of the human body, they are amazed; and, because they are ignorant of the causes of such an art, they conclude that the body was made not by mechanical but by a supernatural or divine art, and has been formed in such a way so that the one part may not injure the other. So it happens that the man who endeavors to find out the true causes of miracles, and who desires as a wise man to understand nature, and not to gape at it like a fool, is generally considered to be a heretic and impious by those whom the vulgar worship as the interpreters both of nature and the gods. For these men know that if ignorance is removed, then amazed stupidity, the sole ground on which they rely in arguing or in defending their authority, is taken away also....

OF THE EMOTIONS

Most people who have written about the emotions and man's conduct in life seem to discuss not the natural things which follow the common laws of nature, but things which are outside her. They seem indeed to consider man in nature as a kingdom within a kingdom. For they believe that man disturbs rather than follows her order, that he has an absolute power over his own actions, and that he is altogether self-determined. They then proceed to attribute the cause of human weakness and changeableness, not to the common power of nature, but to some vice of human nature, which they therefore bewail, laugh at, mock, or, as is more generally the case, detest—while he who knows how to revile most eloquently or subtilely the weaknesses of the mind is looked upon as divine. It is true that very eminent men have not been wanting, to whose labor and industry we confess ourselves much indebted, who have written many excellent things about the right conduct of life, and who have given to mortals counsels full of prudence, but no one so far as I know has determined the nature and strength of the emotions, and what the mind is able to do toward controlling them. I remember, indeed, that the celebrated Descartes, although he believed that the mind is absolute master over its own actions, tried nevertheless to explain human emotions by their first causes and at the same time to show the way by which the mind could obtain absolute power over the emotions. But in my opinion he has shown nothing but the acuteness of his great intellect, as I shall make evident in the proper place, for I wish to return to those who prefer to detest and scoff at human emotions and actions than to understand them.

To such people it will doubtless seem a strange procedure for me to attempt to treat by a geometrical method the vices and follies of men, and to desire by a sure method to demonstrate those things which these men cry out against as being opposed to reason, or as being vanties, absurdities, and monstrosities. The following is my reason for so doing. Nothing happens in nature which can be attributed to any vice of nature, for she is always the same and everywhere one. Her virtue is the same, and her power of acting—that is to say her laws and rules, according to which all things exist and are changed from form to form—are everywhere and always the same; so there must also be one and the same method of understanding the nature of all things whatsoever, that is to say, by the universal laws and rules of nature. The emotions, therefore, of hatred, anger, envy, considered in themselves, follow from the same necessity and virtue of nature as other individual things. They have therefore certain causes through which they are to be understood, and certain properties which are just as worthy of being known as the properties of any other thing in the contemplation of which we find pleasure. I shall, therefore, pursue the same method in considering the nature and strength of the emotions and the power of the mind over them which I pursued in our previous discussion of God and the mind, and I shall consider human actions and passions just as if I were considering lines, planes, or bodies.

3. JOHN LOCKE: AN ESSAY CONCERNING HUMAN UNDERSTANDING*

John Locke (1632–1704), the founder of British empiricism, was educated at Oxford, where he lectured in philosophy and studied medicine. His familiarity with practical scientific discoveries stimulated him to probe the realms of politics, economics, and theology, as well as epistemology, in a manner which set a pattern for eighteenth-century thinkers. Locke's best known work, *An Essay Concerning Human Understanding* (1690), attracted immediate attention because it sharply rejected scholastic and Aristotelian theories of knowledge. How did Locke's thesis that all knowledge derives ultimately from sense perceptions differ from the views of Descartes and Spinoza? Why was Locke's approach to knowledge more favorable toward the encouragement of scientific experiments? How did Locke define "reason," and what was the role of reason in questions of religious dogma? On what grounds could Locke claim to be an orthodox Christian?

It is an established opinion amongst some men that there are in the understanding certain *innate principles;* some primary notions, . . . characters, as it were, stamped upon the mind of man; which the soul receives in its very first being, and brings into the world with it. It would be sufficient to convince unprejudiced readers of the falseness of this supposition, if I should only show

* John Locke, *An Essay Concerning Human Understanding,* collated and annotated by A. C. Fraser (2 vols.; Oxford: The Clarendon Press, 1894), I, 37–38, 121–22, II, 386–88, 412–14.

(as I hope I shall in the following parts of this Discourse) how men, barely by the use of their natural faculties, may attain to all the knowledge they have, without the help of any innate impressions; and may arrive at certainty, without any such original notions or principles. . . .

Let us then suppose the mind to be, as we say, white paper, void of all characters, without any ideas:—How comes it to be furnished? Whence comes it by that vast store which the busy and boundless fancy of man has painted on it with an almost endless variety? Whence has it all *materials* of reason and knowledge? To this I answer, in one word, from EXPERIENCE. In that all our knowledge is founded; and from that it ultimately derives itself. Our observation employed either, about external sensible objects, or about the internal operations of our minds perceived and reflected on by ourselves, is that which supplies our understandings with all the *materials* of thinking. These two are the fountains of knowledge, from whence all the ideas we have, or can naturally have, do spring. . . .

OF REASON

If general knowledge, as has been shown, consists in a perception of the agreement or disagreement of our own ideas, and the knowledge of the existence of all things without us . . . be had only by our senses, what room is there for the exercise of any other faculty but *outward sense* and *inward perception?* What need is there of *reason?* Very much: both for the enlargement of our knowledge and regulating our assent. For it hath to do both in knowledge and opinion, and is necessary and assisting to all our other intellectual faculties, and indeed contains two of them, . . . *sagacity* and *illation.* By the one it finds out; and by the other it so orders the intermediate ideas as to discover what connexion there is in each line of the chain whereby the extremes are held together; and thereby, as it were, to draw into view the truth sought for, which is that which we call *illation* or *inference,* and consists in nothing but the perception of the connexion there is between the ideas, in each step of the deduction; whereby the mind comes to see, either the certain agreement or disagreement of any two ideas, as in demonstration, in which it arrives at *knowledge;* or their probable connexion, on which it gives or withholds its assent, as in *opinion.* Sense and intuition reach but a very little way. The greatest part of our knowledge depends upon deductions and intermediate ideas: and in those cases where we are fain to substitute assent instead of knowledge, and take propositions for true, without being certain they are so, we have need to find out, examine, and compare the grounds of their probability. In both these cases, the faculty which finds out the means, and rightly applies them, to discover certainty in the one, and probability in the other, is that which we call *reason.* For, as reason perceives the necessary and indubitable connexion of all the ideas or proofs one to another, in each step of any demonstration that produces knowledge; so it likewise perceives the probable connexion of all the ideas or proofs one to another, in every step of a discourse, to which it will think assent due. This is the lowest degree of that which can be truly called reason. For where the mind does not perceive this probable connexion, where it does not discern whether there be any such connexion or no; there men's opinions are not the product of judgment, or the consequence of reason, but the effects of chance and hazard, of a mind floating at all adventures, without choice and without direction. . . .

FAITH AND REASON

By what has been before said of reason, we may be able to make some guess at the distinction of things, into those that are according to, above, and contrary to reason. (1) *According to reason* are such propositions whose truth we can discover by examining and tracing those ideas we have from sensation and reflection; and by natural deduction find to be true or probable. (2) *Above reason* are such propositions whose truth or probability we cannot by reason derive from those principles. (3) *Contrary to reason* are such propositions as are inconsistent with or irreconcilable to our clear and distinct ideas. Thus the existence of one God is according to reason; the existence of more than one God, contrary to reason; the resurrection of the dead, above reason. . . .

There is another use of the word *reason,* wherein it is *opposed to faith:* which, though it be in itself a very improper way of speaking, yet common use has so authorized it, that it would be folly either to oppose or hope to remedy it. Only I think it may not be amiss to take notice, that, however faith be opposed to reason, faith is nothing but a firm assent of the mind: which, if it be regulated, as is our duty, cannot be afforded to anything but upon good reason; and so cannot be opposite to it. He that believes without having any reason for believing, may be in love with his own fancies; but neither seeks truth as he ought, nor pays the obedience due to his Maker, who would have him use those discerning faculties he has given him, to keep him out of mistake and error. He that does not this to the best of his power, however he sometimes lights on truth, is in the right but by chance; and I know not whether the luckiness of the accident will excuse the irregularity of his proceeding. This at least is certain, that he must be accountable for whatever mistakes he runs into: whereas he that makes use of the light and faculties God has given him, and seeks sincerely to discover truth by those helps and abilities he has, may have this satisfaction in doing his duty as a rational creature, that, though he should miss truth, he will not miss the reward of it. For he governs his assent right, and places it as he should, who, in any case or matter whatsoever, believes or disbelieves according as reason directs him. He that doth otherwise, transgresses against his own light, and misuses those faculties which were given to him to no other end, but to search and follow the clearer evidence and greater probability. . . .

4. ISAAC NEWTON: PRINCIPIA*

Sir Isaac Newton (1642–1727), Professor of Mathematics at Cambridge University, synthesized the scientific discoveries of his century and concluded that the universe must have been designed by a God who was a mathematician. In his *Mathematical Principles of Natural Philosophy* (1687), Newton created the science of dynamics and applied his theorems to the movement of the heavenly

* Sir Isaac Newton, *Mathematical Principles of Natural Philosophy and His System of the World,* rev. ed. by Florian Cajori of the 1729 translation (Berkeley: University of California Press, 1934), pp. 398–400. Reprinted by permission.

bodies, developing the theory of gravitation. Compare Newton's rules for arriving at knowledge with Descartes' philosophical method. Did Newton advocate an inductive method, a deductive method, or both? What importance did Newton's views have for areas of intellectual endeavor not directly related to mathematics?

RULES OF REASONING IN PHILOSOPHY

RULE I: *We are to admit no more causes of natural things than such as are both true and sufficient to explain their appearances.*

To this purpose the philosophers say that Nature does nothing in vain, and more is in vain when less will serve; for Nature is pleased with simplicity, and affects not the pomp of superfluous causes.

RULE II: *Therefore to the same natural effects we must, as far as possible, assign the same causes.*

As to respiration in a man and in a beast; the descent of stones in *Europe* and in *America;* the light of our culinary fire and of the sun; the reflection of light in the earth, and in the planets.

RULE III: *The qualities of bodies, which admit neither intensification nor remission of degrees, and which are found to belong to all bodies within the reach of our experiments, are to be esteemed the universal qualities of all bodies whatsoever.*

For since the qualities of bodies are only known to us by experiments, we are to hold for universal all such as universally agree with experiments; and such as are not liable to diminution can never be quite taken away. We are certainly not to relinquish the evidence of experiments for the sake of dreams and vain fictions of our own devising; nor are we to recede from the analogy of Nature, which is wont to be simple, and always consonant to itself. We no other way know the extension of bodies than by our senses, nor do these reach it in all bodies; but because we perceive extension in all that are sensible, therefore we ascribe it universally to all others also. That abundance of bodies are hard, we learn by experience; and because the hardness of the whole arises from the hardness of the parts, we therefore justly infer the hardness of the undivided particles not only of the bodies we feel but of all others. That all bodies are impenetrable, we gather not from reason, but from sensation. The bodies which we handle we find impenetrable, and thence conclude impenetrability to be an universal property of all bodies whatsoever. That all bodies are movable, and endowed with certain powers (which we call the inertia) of persevering in their motion, or in their rest, we only infer from the like properties observed in the bodies which we have seen. The extension, hardness, impenetrability, mobility, and inertia of the whole, results from the extension, hardness, impenetrability, mobility, and inertia of the parts; and hence we conclude the least particles of all bodies to be also all extended, and hard and impenetrable, and movable, and endowed with their proper inertia. And this is the foundation of all philosophy. Moreover, that the divided but contiguous particles of bodies may be separated from one another, is matter of observation; and, in the particles that remain undivided, our minds are able to distinguish yet lesser parts, as is mathematically demonstrated. But whether the parts so distinguished, and not yet divided, may, by the powers of Nature, be actually divided and separated from one another, we cannot certainly determine. Yet, had we the proof of but one experiment that any undivided particle, in breaking a hard and solid body, suffered a division, we might by virtue of this rule conclude that the undivided as well as the divided particles may be divided and actually separated to infinity.

Lastly, if it universally appears, by experiments and astronomical observations, that all bodies about the earth gravitate towards the earth, and that in proportion to the quantity of matter which they severally contain; that the moon likewise, according to the quantity of its matter, gravitates towards the earth; that, on the other hand, our sea gravitates towards the moon; and all the planets one towards another; and the comets in like manner towards the sun; we must, in consequence of this rule, universally allow that all bodies whatsoever are endowed with a principle of mutual gravitation. For the argument from the appearances concludes with more force for the universal gravitation of all bodies than for their impenetrability; of which, among those in the celestial regions, we have no experiments, nor any manner of observation. Not that I affirm gravity to be essential to bodies: by their *vis insita* I mean nothing but their inertia. This is immutable. Their gravity is diminished as they recede from the earth.

RULE IV: *In experimental philosophy we are to look upon propositions inferred by general induction from phenomena as accurately or very nearly true, notwithstanding any contrary hypotheses that may be imagined, till such time as other phenomena occur, by which they may either be made more accurate, or liable to exceptions.*

This rule we must follow, that the argument of induction may not be evaded by hypotheses.

5. BERNARD DE FONTENELLE: CONVERSATIONS ON THE PLURALITY OF WORLDS*

Bernard de Fontenelle (1657–1757), nephew of the playwright Pierre Corneille, was himself a gifted and versatile writer who composed poems, operas, tragedies, and histories. In 1697 Fontenelle became permanent secretary of the French Academy of Sciences. Although Fontenelle made no original contributions to experimental science, he possessed an extraordinary talent for popularizing the new science of the seventeenth century. His *Considerations on the Ancients and the Moderns* (1688) emphasized the idea of the progress of knowledge; his *Eulogies of Scientists* (1708–19) showed the growing prestige of science and scientists.

Fontenelle's *Conversations on the Plurality of Worlds* (1686) was a popular treatise which sought to explain the nature of the universe as revealed by the new science. It took the form of a dialogue between Fontenelle and a fashionable *Marquise* who postponed love-making in order to discuss philosophy. In what ways did Fontenelle contrast the world view of the Ancients with the world view of the Moderns? How did he characterize the "new philosophy"?

* Bernard de Fontenelle, "Conversations on the Plurality of Worlds," in *Oeuvres choisies* (Paris: La Renaissance du livre [1910]), pp. 16, 20–24. Translated by the editors.

I will not waste time in saying that I have selected from the world of philosophy those things most likely to excite curiosity. It seems that nothing should interest us more than to know how this world we inhabit is made, and if there are other similar worlds which might also be inhabited; . . .

I have put in these *Entretiens* [conversations] a woman who is being enlightened and has never heard of such things. I believe that such a literary device will be useful both to make the work more pleasing and to encourage other ladies by the example of a woman . . . who has not even a smattering of knowledge about science nevertheless being able to understand what one explains to her. . . .

We went, then, one evening after dining, to take a walk in the park. It was a delightfully cool and refreshing evening, which compensated for the very hot day we had endured. The moon had risen perhaps an hour before and its light, which shone on us here and there between the branches of trees, made an agreeable pattern of light and shadow. There wasn't a single cloud to obscure the stars; they were of a dazzling, pure gold, set off by the deep blue of their firmament. The spectacle made me dream, and perhaps without the *Marquise* I would not have stayed so long; but the presence of such a friendly lady would not permit me to leave the moon and the stars. . . .

"I love the stars and I complain of the sun when it hides them," she said.

"Ah," I cried. "I cannot forgive the sun for making me lose sight of all the other worlds."

"What do you call all those worlds?" she asked, . . .

"I ask your pardon," I replied, "you have started me on my favorite subject and my imagination immediately takes flight."

"What do you mean?" she continued.

"Alas!" I replied, "I am ashamed to admit it to you. I have it in my head that each star could well be another world. I would not swear that my idea is true; but I take it for truth because I am pleased to believe it. . . .

"Well," she replied, "since your mania is so agreeable, let me share it. I believe there is on the stars all that you say, providing I find pleasure in it."

"Ah, Madame," I answered quickly, "it is not a pleasure such as you would find in one of Molière's comedies. It is found—I don't know where—in the reason, and makes only the spirit laugh."

"Well, then!" she responded, "do you believe that one might be incapable of pleasures which are only of the reason . . . ; teach me about your stars."

. . . I found I didn't know where to begin my discourse: with a person who knew nothing of the subject of physics it was necessary to start at the beginning in order to prove to her that the earth could be a planet and the planets so many lands, and all the stars so many suns which light up other worlds. I kept interrupting my discourse to tell her it would be better to make small talk as all sensible people would have done in our place. Finally, however, to give her a general idea of philosophy, this is how I began.

"All philosophy," I said to her, "is founded on only two things: on the extent to which one has a spirit of curiosity and poor eyes; for if your eyes were better than they are, you would see for yourself whether or not the stars are suns which light as many other worlds; and if, on the other hand, you were less curious, you would not worry about knowing it, which comes to the same thing. But one wants to know more than only what one can see, and that is the difficulty. Furthermore, if one saw clearly everything that one sees, that would be much more than is known for certain, for one sees everything differently than it really is. Thus, true philosophers spend their lives not believing what they see, and trying to guess what they can't see at all, . . .

"On that subject I always imagine nature as a great spectacle which resembles the opera. From where you sit, you don't see the theater as it really is; the decorations and the machinery have been placed to create a pleasing effect from afar, and all the wheels and counterweights which make everything on the stage function are hidden from view. Just so, in the same way, don't worry your head about how it is all done. [But imagine] a mechanically inclined observer hidden in the pit of the theater who worries about what seems to him extraordinary, and who absolutely must unravel how the performance was accomplished. You can readily see that the questioner is then made from the same mold as the philosopher. What makes it more difficult for the philosopher is that in the machinery nature shows to us the strings are completely hidden from view, so completely hidden that man has been trying for a long time to guess what caused the movements of the universe. Think of all the wise men attending the opera—the Pythagorases, the Platos, the Aristotles—and all those men whose names still sound in our ears. Suppose they were to see the flight of *Phaéton,* whom the winds carried off, and that they could not see the ropes and wires and they didn't know how the backstage of a theater is arranged. One of them would say, '*Phaéton* is composed of certain numbers which cause him to rise.' Another, '*Phaéton* has a certain attraction for the ceiling of the theater; he is not at ease unless he is there.' Another, '*Phaéton* is not made to fly, but he prefers to fly rather than to leave the top of the theater empty,' and a hundred other theories would be advanced. . . . Finally Descartes and some other moderns came along and said, '*Phaéton* rises because he is pulled by ropes and because a weight heavier than he is pulling down.' Thus one no longer believes a body moves by itself if it is not pulled, or pulled by another body; one no longer believes that it rises or descends, unless it is the result of a counterweight or spring, and he who would see nature as she really is would see only the backstage of the theater or the opera." . . .

"In that case," said the *Marquise,* "philosophy has become quite mechanical?"

"So mechanical," I replied, "that I fear that one may soon be ashamed of it. One wishes that the universe would be something more than a large-scale watch where everything runs itself by regular movements which depend on the arrangement of the parts. Admit it! Haven't you sometimes had a more sublime idea than that of the universe? And haven't you accorded it more honor than it merited? I have known people who value the universe less after knowing it better."

"And I," she replied, "I value it more after learning that it resembles a watch: it is surprising that the order of nature, admirable as it is, turns on such simple things."

"I don't know," I answered her, "who has given you such healthy ideas; but, truthfully, it is not too common to have such ideas. Many people have in their heads a false wonder [of the universe], wrapped in an obscurity which they hold in respect. They admire nature only because they believe it to be a kind of magic of which they understand nothing; it is certain that for them everything is spoiled as soon as it is understood. But Madame," I continued, "you are so ready to entertain all that I say to you that I believe I have but to pull the curtain and show you the world. . . ."

6. MIKHAIL LOMONOSOV: EVENING MEDITATIONS ON SEEING THE AURORA BOREALIS*

One of the first Russian intellectuals to study abroad, Mikhail Vasilievich Lomonosov (1711–65) was trained in metallurgy and chemistry at the University of Marburg and became professor of chemistry at St. Petersburg upon his return to Russia. He conducted significant experiments in physics, chemistry, and optics and seemed particularly fascinated by the power of electricity, duplicating by coincidence several of Benjamin Franklin's experiments with lightning conductors. Nevertheless, Lomonosov's scientific achievements attracted little attention in eighteenth-century Russia; rather, he achieved fame as a poet and philologist. His monumental *Russian Grammar* (1755) succeeded in molding his native tongue into a literary language by charting a middle course between the complex old Slavonic used in church services and contemporary Russian as it was spoken by the people. In what ways did the following poem reflect Lomonosov's interest in science? Compare his views with the attitudes of Fontenelle and other thinkers in western Europe.

The day retires, the mists of night are spread
Slowly o'er nature, darkening as they rise;
The gloomy clouds are gathering round our heads,
And twilight's latest glimmering gently dies:
The stars awake in heaven's abyss of blue;
Say, who can count them?—Who can sound it?—Who?

Even as a sand in the majestic sea,
A diamond-atom on a hill of snow,
A spark amidst a Hecla's majesty,
An unseen mote where maddened whirlwinds blow,
And I midst scenes like these—the mighty thought
O'erwhelms me—I am nought, or less than nought.

And science tells me that each twinkling star
That smiles above us is a peopled sphere,
Or central sun, diffusing light afar;
A link of nature's chain:—and there, even there,
The Godhead shines displayed—in love and light,
Creating wisdom—all-directing might.

* Leo Wiener, *Anthology of Russian Literature from the Earliest Period to the Present Time* (2 vols.; New York: G. P. Putnam's Sons, 1902), I, 253–54.

Where are thy secret laws, O Nature, where?
In wintry realms thy dazzling torches blaze,
And from thy icebergs streams of glory there
Are poured, while other suns their splendent race
In glory run: from frozen seas what ray
Of brightness?—From yon realms of night what day?

Philosopher, whose penetrating eye
Reads nature's deepest secrets, open now
This all-inexplicable mystery:
Why do earth's darkest, coldest regions glow
With lights like these?—Oh, tell us, knowing one,
For thou dost count the stars, and weigh the sun!

Whence are these varied lamps all lighted round?—
Whence all the horizon's glowing fire?—The heaven
Is splendent as with lightning—but no sound
Of thunder—all as calm as gentlest even;
And winter's midnight is as bright, as gay,
As the fair noontide of a summer's day.

What stores of fire are these, what magazine,
Whence God from grossest darkness light supplies?
What wondrous fabric which the mountains screen,
Whose bursting flames above those mountains rise;
Where rattling winds disturb the mighty ocean,
And the proud waves roll with eternal motion?

Vain is the inquiry—all is darkness, doubt:
This earth is one vast mystery to man.
First find the secrets of this planet out,
Then other planets, other systems scan!
Nature is veiled from thee, presuming clod!
And what canst thou conceive of Nature's God?

THE AGE OF REASON—THE *PHILOSOPHES*

7. BARON DE MONTESQUIEU: THE PERSIAN LETTERS*

Charles de Secondat, Baron de Montesquieu (1689–1755), became famous almost overnight with the publication of his satirical *Persian Letters* in 1721. The first edition sold out rapidly and irritated almost as many readers as it entertained. Montesquieu never fully accepted or disowned the reputation created by his *Persian Letters,* but paid a price for his literary triumph. When

* Baron de Montesquieu, *The Persian Letters* (New York: Athenaeum Publishing Co., 1897 [London: Printed for Subscribers Only, 1901]), pp. 45–46, 55–57, 100–102, 119–20, 181–83.

a seat in the French Academy became vacant in 1726, offended clerics succeeded in temporarily barring Montesquieu from membership.

Montesquieu's literary device was simple and effective. Two fictional Persians arrived in Paris to study European manners and institutions, and their letters back to Persia were full of seemingly naïve, but barbed comments on contemporary French customs and mores. Montesquieu exposed and held up to ridicule the vices, stupidities, and foibles of the monarchy, the Church, and the notables of France. Although written in a light vein, the *Persian Letters* constituted the first great eighteenth-century criticism of the *ancien régime*. Did Montesquieu voice the same criticisms of non-aristocrats as those of his contemporary, Saint-Simon? What were Montesquieu's criticisms of the Crown and the Church? Why, when the author was on his deathbed, did Jesuit priests attempt to gain a retraction of the *Persian Letters* while the Encyclopedists tried to block such a retraction?

We have been a month in Paris, and have never had a moment's rest. . . . The King of France [Louis XIV] is the most powerful prince in Europe. He has no gold mines like his neighbor the King of Spain; but he is far richer than he, because he can draw his wealth from the vanity of his subjects, and that is more inexhaustible than all the mines in the world. He has undertaken or sustained great wars without other resources than the titles of honor he had for sale, and this marvellous example of human pride has enabled him to pay his troops, fortify his cities, and equip his fleet.

Moreover, this king is a great magician; even the minds of his subjects are subject to his dominion; he makes them think what he wishes. If he has only a million crowns in his treasury, he has but to persuade them that one crown is worth two, and they believe him. If he has to carry on a costly war, and is without money for the purpose, all he need do is to insinuate that a bit of paper is money, and they are all convinced that such is the case on the spot. He has even succeeded in making them believe that his mere touch cures all manner of diseases, so great is the strength and power he exercises over their minds.

Nor ought you to be astonished at the account I give of this prince; there is another magician whose control over the mind of this sovereign is as absolute as that of the latter is over his own subjects. This magician is called the Pope: at one time, he persuades the prince that three are really one; at another, that the bread he eats is not bread, or that the wine he drinks is not wine, and a thousand other such things. . . .

The Pope is the head of the Christians. He is an old idol to which incense is offered from habit. At one time he was formidable even to princes, for he deposed them with as much ease as our magnificent sultans depose [the kings of our land]. But he is feared no longer. He proclaims himself to be the successor of one of the first Christians, called Saint Peter; and certainly his inheritance is a rich one, for he has immense treasures, and a large extent of territory is under his dominion.

The bishops are jurists of a certain character; they are subordinates of the Pope, and exercise two very different functions under his authority. When they are gathered together, they can, like him, decree articles of faith; while in their individual capacity, they have hardly any other function than that of dispensing with the law. For you must understand that the Christian religion is burdened with an immense number of customs that are very hard to observe; and, as it has been judged that it is less easy to observe these customs than to have bishops who can dispense from their observance, these functionaries have been appointed in the interests of the public. Thus, if a person . . . desires to have the customary formalities in marriage omitted, or to break his vows, or to marry within the forbidden degrees of kindred, or sometimes, to be released from his oath, application is made to the bishop or to the Pope, who gives a dispensation at once. . . .

Those who startle the world with some new proposition are at first called heretics. Every heresy has its own particular name, which becomes the rallying-cry of its adherents. But no one need be a heretic unless he is perfectly willing to be so: all he has to do is to split a hair with his adversaries; to propound some subtle distinction for the benefit of his accusers; and whether his distinction be intelligible or not, it renders our logician as white as snow, and he may now insist on being called orthodox.

All I have mentioned holds good for France and Germany, for I have been told that in Spain and Italy there are certain dervishes who do not understand a joke, and who burn a man, just as if he were so much straw. Whoever falls into the hands of these people may account himself happy if he has always prayed to God with little wooden beads in his hand, or has worn two pieces of cloth tied with two ribbons, or has gone to a place they call Galicia! A poor devil who cannot advance any of these proofs of his innocence finds himself in terrible trouble indeed! Though he swear like any pagan that he is orthodox, they will very likely refuse to be moved by his protestations, and will roast him as a heretic. His distinctions may be in the subtlest vein—they will have none of them; he will be ashes before they have heard him to the end. . . .

The French never speak of their wives; the reason is, they are afraid to speak about them before persons who are better acquainted with them than they are themselves. . . .

Consequently, there is no country in the world where the number of jealous husbands is so small as in France. Their tranquility is not based on the confidence they have in their wives; it is, on the contrary, based on the ill opinion they have of them. . . . Husbands accept their appointed destiny with a good grace, and regard the infidelities of their wives as mishaps decreed by the higher powers. A husband who wished to possess his wife to the exclusion of everybody else would be considered a disturber of the public happiness, a madman, who desired to deprive others of the light of the sun that he might enjoy it alone.

Here, if a husband loves his wife, it is a proof that he has not sufficient merit to win the love of another woman; who abuses the power given him by the law to supply those pleasures he cannot otherwise obtain; who avails himself of all his advantages to the prejudice of society at large; who appropriates to his own use what has been only given him as a pledge, and who does everything in his power to upset a tacit convention essential to the happiness of both sexes. The reputation of having a handsome wife, which is so carefully concealed in Asia, is borne here without any anxiety: there is always the satisfaction of being able to make an attack in some other quarter. A prince consoles himself for the loss of one fortress by the capture of another. . . .

As a rule, the man who bears patiently the infidelities of his wife is not regarded with disapproval; on the contrary, he is praised for his prudence; only in certain peculiar cases is he felt to have incurred any reproach.

It is not that there are no virtuous women; there are, and they are persons of much distinction also; my friendly guide always pointed them out to me; but they were all so ugly that one would have to be a saint not to hate virtue.

After all I have told you about the morals of this country, you can easily imagine the French do not pride themselves on their constancy: they believe that it is as ridiculous to swear eternal devotion to a woman, as it is to insist that health and happiness are going to last forever. When they promise a woman that they will always love her, they do so with the proviso that she must be always lovable; and, if she breaks her word, they do not think they are bound to keep theirs. . . .

Although people are very much devoted to science in these quarters, I am rather inclined to doubt as to the extent of their learning. The man who is sceptical about everything as a philosopher does not venture to deny anything as a theologian; such a contradictory personage is quite satisfied with himself, if you grant him the privilege of making certain distinctions. The passion of most Frenchmen is to be thought wits; and the passion of those who wish to be thought wits is to write books.

It is impossible to imagine a more unfortunate mania: nature has wisely provided that the follies of men should be ephemeral; but, unhappily, these very follies are immortalized in books. A fool ought to have been satisfied with boring all those who have lived with him; yet he insists on torturing future races; he is determined that his folly shall triumph over the oblivion in which he ought to have been able to find as much enjoyment as he does in his last slumber; he wishes posterity to know that he has lived, and remember forever that he was a fool. . . .

The caprices of fashion among the French are really astonishing. They have forgotten how they were dressed last summer, they have still less knowledge as to how they will be dressed this winter; but, above all, you would never have any idea of how much it costs a husband to have his wife in the fashion. What would be the use of me describing to you their habiliments and adornments? A new fashion would come and destroy all my work, as it does that of their workwoman, and, before you had received my letter, all would be changed.

A woman who has stayed six months in the country returns from it almost as much of an antique as if she had lived there thirty years. The son does not recognize his mother's portrait, so strange does the dress in which she was painted appear to him; he imagines it is some fair American that is represented there, or else the painter has tried to express some fancy of his own.

Sometimes the coiffures go up slowly and come down suddenly—there has been a revolution! There was a time when their immense height placed the face of a woman in her middle; there was another when it was the feet that were in this position. The heels formed a pedestal that held them suspended. Would you believe it? Architects have been obliged to raise or lower or widen doors, to keep up with the changes in the dresses of the women, and the rules of their art had to bend to such freaks. Sometimes a prodigious quantity of patches is seen on a face; look for them the next day and they are all gone. Formerly women had figures and teeth; today you don't see either. In this changing nation, the daughters are differently made from their mothers, whatever critics may say to the contrary.

What I have said of their fashions may also be said of their manners and style of living. The French change their manners with the age of their king. The monarch could succeed even in making this people serious, if he chose to undertake the task. The prince impresses his mental characteristics on the court, the court on the city, and the city on the provinces. The soul of the sovereign is a mould in which all are formed.

I spoke to you the other day of the extraordinary fickleness of the French as to their fashions. The obstinacy with which they cling to them is inconceivable. The laws of fashion determine their opinion of other nations; to this standard everything is referred. All that swerves from it always appears to them ridiculous. I confess I cannot reconcile this furious devotion to fashion with the inconstancy which makes them change it every day.

When I told you they despised everything foreign I should have added that this is so only in the case of trifling matters; for, in important ones, they seem to want confidence in themselves so much as almost to be open to the charge of self-degradation.

They acknowledge cheerfully that other nations are wiser, provided it be granted that they are better dressed. They would willingly agree to accept the laws of a foreign nation if French wig-makers were in turn to legislate on the form of foreign wigs. Nothing makes them feel so proud as the spectacle of their cooks reigning from north to south, and their hair-dressers having the *entrée* into every dressing room in Europe.

With these noble advantages, what does it matter if common-sense comes to them from other quarters, and if they borrow from their neighbors everything of importance in their political and civil government? . . .

8. BARON DE MONTESQUIEU: SPIRIT OF THE LAWS*

Montesquieu labored for twenty years on the *Spirit of the Laws,* working and reworking the text until he had completed a terse, almost epigrammatic, survey of government and law. His sociological approach to the variations of government in time and place was the first great study of comparative governments in modern western history. In only eighteen months *Spirit of the Laws* had to

* Baron de Montesquieu, *The Spirit of Laws,* trans. Thomas Nugent (rev. ed.; New York: P. F. Collier and Son, 1900), I, 1, 3–4, 6–10, 149–52, 154–55.

be reissued twenty-two times. Montesquieu was an atypical *philosophe*. He believed in the importance of human reason, but without becoming dogmatic, and
was sharply aware of the relevance of the past to the present. In his view, governments and societies naturally differed from area to area because they had been
shaped by variations in race, customs, morals, commerce, and climate.

Montesquieu's personal preference centered on a system of government with
shared authority. As a member of the French aristocracy and, briefly, chief
justice of the *parlement* of Bordeaux, he was sensitive to the deterioration of
aristocratic political authority under successive French monarchs and admired
the British government as an example of shared power. Although Montesquieu
misunderstood the British governmental system and the way it had evolved, his
conclusions would have a profound impact on the writers of the Constitution of
the United States. What did Montesquieu mean by liberty? What distinguished
republican, monarchical, and despotic governments from one another? Could
people be trusted to govern themselves? Which elements of Montesquieu's
thoughts seem most directly relevant to the governmental structure of the United
States?

OF THE RELATION OF LAWS TO DIFFERENT BEINGS

Laws, in their most general signification, are the necessary relations arising
from the nature of things. In this sense all beings have their laws: the Deity His
laws, the material world its laws, the intelligences superior to man their laws,
the beasts their laws, man his laws.

They who assert that a blind fatality produced the various effects we behold
in this world talk very absurdly; for can anything be more unreasonable than
to pretend that a blind fatality could be productive of intelligent beings?

There is, then, a prime reason; and laws are the relations subsisting between
it and different beings, and the relations of these to one another. . . .

Man, as a physical being, is like other bodies governed by invariable laws. As
an intelligent being, he incessantly transgresses the laws established by God,
and changes those of his own instituting. He is left to his private direction,
though a limited being, and subject, like all finite intelligences, to ignorance
and error: even his imperfect knowledge he loses; and as a sensible creature, he
is hurried away by a thousand impetuous passions. Such a being might every
instant forget his Creator; God has therefore reminded him of his duty by the
laws of religion. Such a being is liable every moment to forget himself; philosophy has provided against this by the laws of morality. Formed to live in society,
he might forget his fellow-creatures; legislators have, therefore, by political and
civil laws, confined him to his duty.

OF THE LAWS OF NATURE

Antecedent to the above-mentioned laws are those of nature, so called, because
they derive their force entirely from our frame and existence. . . . Man in a
state of nature would have the faculty of knowing, before he had acquired any
knowledge. . . .

In this state every man, instead of being sensible of his equality, would fancy
himself inferior. There would, therefore, be no danger of their attacking one
another; peace would be the first law of nature. . . .

OF POSITIVE LAWS

Law in general is human reason, inasmuch as it governs all the inhabitants of the earth: the political and civil laws of each nation ought to be only the particular cases in which human reason is applied.

They should be adapted in such a manner to the people for whom they are framed that it should be a great [coincidence] if those of one nation suit another.

They should be in relation to the nature and principle of each government: whether they form it, as may be said of politic laws; or whether they support it, as in the case of civil institutions.

They should be in relation to the climate of each country, to the quality of its soil, to its situation and extent, to the principal occupation of the natives, whether husbandmen, huntsmen, or shepherds: they should have relation to the degree of liberty which the constitution will bear; to the religion of the inhabitants, to their inclinations, riches, numbers, commerce, manners, and customs. In fine, they have relations to each other, as also to their origin, to the intent of the legislator, and to the order of things on which they are established; in all of which different lights they ought to be considered.

This is what I have undertaken to perform in the following work. These relations I shall examine, since all these together constitute what I call the Spirit of Laws. . . .

OF THE NATURE OF THREE DIFFERENT GOVERNMENTS

There are three species of government: republican, monarchial, and despotic. . . . A republican government is that in which the body, or only a part of the people, is possessed of the supreme power; monarchy, that in which a single person governs by fixed and established laws; a despotic government, that in which a single person directs everything by his own will and caprice. . . .

OF THE REPUBLICAN GOVERNMENT, AND THE LAWS IN RELATION TO DEMOCRACY

In a democracy the people are in some respects the sovereign, and in others the subject. There can be no exercise of sovereignty but by their suffrages, which are . . . fundamental to this government. And indeed it is as important to regulate in a republic, in what manner, by whom, to whom, and concerning what suffrages are to be given, as it is in a monarchy to know who is the prince, and after what manner he ought to govern. . . .

It is an essential point to fix the number of citizens who are to form the public assemblies; otherwise it would be uncertain whether the whole or only a part of the people had given their votes. . . . Rome, I say, never fixed the number; and this was one of the principal causes of her ruin.

The people, in whom the supreme power resides, ought to have the management of everything within their reach: that which exceeds their abilities must be conducted by their ministers. . . .

The people are extremely well qualified for choosing those whom they are to intrust with part of their authority. . . . They can tell when a person has fought many battles, and been crowned with success; . . . They can tell when a judge is assiduous in his office, gives general satisfaction, and has never been charged with bribery. . . . But are they capable of conducting an intricate affair, of seizing and improving the opportunity and critical moment of action? No; this surpasses their abilities. . . .

As most citizens have sufficient ability to choose, though unqualified to be chosen, so the people, though capable of calling others to an account for their administration, are incapable of conducting the administration themselves. . . .

DIFFERENT SIGNIFICATIONS OF THE WORD LIBERTY

There is no word that admits of more various significations, and has made more varied impressions on the human mind, than that of Liberty. . . . It is true that in democracies the people seem to act as they please; but political liberty does not consist in an unlimited freedom. In governments, that is, in societies directed by laws, liberty can consist only in the power of doing what we ought to will, and in not being constrained to do what we ought not to will.

We must have continually present to our minds the difference between independence and liberty. Liberty is a right of doing whatever the laws permit, and if a citizen could do what they forbid he would be no longer possessed of liberty, because all his fellow-citizens would have the same power.

Democratic and aristocratic states are not in their own nature free. Political liberty is to be found only in moderate governments; and even in these it is not always found. It is there only when there is no abuse of power. But constant experience shows us that every man invested with power is apt to abuse it, and to carry his authority as far as it will go. Is it not strange, though true, to say that virtue itself has need of limits?

To prevent this abuse, it is necessary from the very nature of things that power should be a check to power. A government may be so constituted, as no man shall be compelled to do things to which the law does not oblige him, nor forced to abstain from things which the law permits. . . .

In every government there are three sorts of power: the legislative; the executive in respect to things dependent on the law of nations; and the executive in regard to matters that depend on the civil law.

By virtue of the first, the prince or magistrate enacts temporary or perpetual laws, and amends or abrogates those that have been already enacted. By the second, he makes peace or war, sends or receives embassies, establishes the public security, and provides against invasions. By the third, he punishes criminals, or determines the disputes that arise between individuals. The latter we shall call the judiciary power, and the other simply the executive power of the state.

The political liberty of the subject is a tranquillity of mind arising from the opinion each person has of his safety. In order to have this liberty, it is requisite the government be so constituted as one man need not be afraid of another.

When the legislative and executive powers are united in the same person, or in the same body of magistrates, there can be no liberty; because apprehensions may arise, lest the same monarch or senate should enact tyrannical laws, to execute them in a tyrannical manner.

Again, there is no liberty if the judiciary power be not separated from the legislative and executive. Were it joined with the legislative, the life and liberty of the subject would be exposed to arbitrary control; for the judge would be then the legislator. Were it joined to the executive power the judge might behave with violence and oppression.

There would be an end of everything, were the same man or the same body, whether of the nobles or of the people, to exercise those three powers, that of enacting laws, that of executing the public resolutions, and of trying the causes of individuals. . . .

. . . in a country of liberty, every man who is supposed a free agent ought to be his own governor; the legislative power should reside in the whole body of the people. But since this is impossible in large states, and in small ones is subject to many inconveniences, it is fit the people should transact by their representatives what they cannot transact by themselves.

The inhabitants of a particular town are much better acquainted with its wants and interests than with those of other places; and are better judges of the capacity of their neighbors than of that of the rest of their countrymen. The members, therefore, of the legislature should not be chosen from the general body of the nation; but it is proper that in every considerable place a representative should be elected by the inhabitants.

The great advantage of representatives is their capacity of discussing public affairs. For this the people collectively are extremely unfit, which is one of the chief inconveniences of a democracy. . . .

All the inhabitants of the several districts ought to have a right of voting at the election of a representative, except such as are in so mean a situation as to be deemed to have no will of their own. . . . [The people] ought to have no share in the government but for the choosing of representatives, which is within their reach. For though few can tell the exact degree of men's capacities, yet there are none but are capable of knowing in general whether the person they choose is better qualified than most of his neighbors. . . .

9. VOLTAIRE: THE PHILOSOPHICAL DICTIONARY*

The wittiest and most pungent of the *philosophes* was François Marie Arouet (1694–1778), who assumed the name Voltaire. Voltaire was an enthusiastic partisan of liberty and threw his sharpest barbs at what he considered the anachronistic institutions of his age. Above all, he was a critic of organized religion, with the Catholic Church as his main target. He also attacked Protestants, Buddhists, Muslims, and Jews. Voltaire was not an atheist, as many of his critics charged, for he believed in a God of humanity. But his ideas did tend to neutralize God, and Voltaire refused to accept Christianity or any other religion as the universal voice of true moral and religious dogma. Further, he felt that Christianity, like all organized institutions which promote their own objectives, generated fanaticism and strife, and curbed man's power to reason.

Voltaire never offered a full program of reform. He embodied a spirit of reform and relied on enlightened despots to effect the necessary programs. He was not a revolutionary and had little faith in the unenlightened masses; he never saw the masses as an alternative to royal despotism. His criticisms of the old

* Voltaire, *Philosophical Dictionary*, trans. Peter Gay (2 vols.; New York: Basic Books, Inc., 1962), I, 158–60, 245–47; II, 377–80, 463–66, 475–78. Reprinted by permission.

order were designed to promote reason and naturalness, and he remained a crusader for civil liberty without urging political liberty.

Voltaire's *Philosophical Dictionary* was begun in 1750, and the first volume was published in 1764. None of his brief, light, and satirical essays had the philosophical depth of a work by Descartes or the historical sense of a Gibbon, but Voltaire's arguments were direct, simple, and clear. In the following selections, which religious sect did Voltaire find most tolerable? What, in his opinion, were the basic flaws in Christianity? Did Voltaire believe in the natural goodness of man? Why, or why not? Which superstitions were least acceptable to Voltaire?

CERTAIN, CERTAINTY

"How old is your friend Christopher?" "Twenty-eight; I have seen his marriage contract, his baptismal certificate; I have known him since his childhood; he is twenty-eight, I am certain, absolutely certain of it."

I have hardly heard the reply of this man who is so sure of what he says, and the replies of twenty others saying the same thing, when I learn that for secret reasons, and by a strange trick, Christopher's baptismal certificate had been antedated. Those I talked to don't know anything about it yet; nevertheless they continue to be certain about something that is not so.

If you had asked the whole world before the time of Copernicus: "Did the sun rise today? Did it set?" all men would have answered you: "We are absolutely certain of it." They were certain, and they were wrong.

Witchcraft, divinations, possessions, were for a long time the most certain things in the world in the eyes of all nations. What an innumerable crowd of people who saw all these fine things, who were certain of them! Today that certainty has diminished a little.

A young man beginning to study geometry sought me out; he had only reached the definition of triangles. "Aren't you certain," I asked him, "that the three angles of a triangle are equal to two right angles?" He answered me that he was not only uncertain of it, but that he didn't even have a clear idea of the proposition. I demonstrated it to him; he then became quite certain of it, and will be so all his life.

This is a certainty very different from the others: they were nothing but probabilities, and, once examined, became errors; but mathematical certainty is immutable and eternal.

I exist, I think, I feel pain; is all this as certain as a geometric truth? Yes. Why? Because these truths are proved by the same principle that a thing cannot be and not be at the same time. I can't exist and not exist, feel and not feel, at the same time. A triangle can't have a hundred and eighty degrees, which is the sum of two right angles, and at the same time not have them.

The physical certainty of my existence and of my feeling are thus of the same value as mathematical certainty, although they are different in kind.

The same is not true of certainty founded on appearances, or on unanimous reports that men draw up for us.

"But look!" you say to me, "aren't you certain that Peking exists? Don't you have cloth from Peking in your houses? Haven't men of different countries, different opinions, who wrote violently against each other while they were all preaching the truth in Peking—haven't they all assured you of the existence of the town?" I reply that it seems extremely probable to me that there was a city of Peking at that time; but I wouldn't want to bet my life that the town exists; and I would bet my life at any time that the three angles of a triangle are equal to two right angles. . . .

What does a dog owe to a dog, and a horse to a horse? Nothing. No animal depends on his kind; but since man has received the gleam of divinity called *reason,* what is the result? He becomes a slave almost everywhere in the world.

If this world were what it seems it should be, that is, if man found easy and assured subsistence everywhere, and a climate congenial to his nature, it is clear that one man couldn't possibly have enslaved another. If this globe were covered with wholesome fruits; if the air which should contribute to our life gave us neither diseases nor death; if man needed no other lodging and no other bed than do deer and roe; then the Genghis Khans and Tamerlanes would have no valets but their children, who would be people good enough to help them in their old age. . . .

Thus all men would necessarily be equal, if they were without needs. It is the misery attached to our species that subordinates one man to another; it is not inequality which is the real evil, it is dependence. It matters very little if some man is called His Highness, and another, His Holiness; but it is hard to have to serve one or the other.

A numerous family cultivates good soil; two small neighboring families till sterile and obstinate fields: the two poor families must either serve the opulent family or cut its collective throat; there's no problem about that. One of the two poor families offers its services to the rich one so it may have bread; the other attacks the rich family and is beaten. In the serving family we see the origin of domestics and laborers; in the beaten family the origin of slaves.

On our miserable globe it is impossible for men living in society not to be divided into two classes, one the rich who command, the other the poor who serve; and these two subdivide themselves into a thousand, and these thousand have still several further divisions.

All the poor are not absolutely miserable. Most of them are born in that condition, and continual labor prevents them from feeling their situation too keenly; but when they do feel it, then you see wars, like that of the popular party against the senatorial party in Rome, or the peasant wars in Germany, England, and France. Sooner or later all these wars end with the enslavement of the people, because the powerful have money, and within a state money is the master of all: I say within a state, because the same is not true between nation and nation. The nation that puts the sword to the best use will always subjugate the one that has more gold and less courage.

Every man is born with a powerful urge toward domination, wealth, and pleasures, and with a strong taste for laziness; consequently every man would like the money and the women or the girls of others, to be their master, to subject them to all his caprices, and to do nothing, or at least to do only the very agreeable things. . . .

Mankind, such as it is, cannot go on existing unless there is an infinite number of useful men who possess nothing at all; for surely a man who is well off will not leave his land to labor on yours; and if you need a pair of shoes, it won't be a *maître des requêtes* who'll make them for you. Thus, equality is at once the most natural and at the same time the most chimerical of things.

Since men go to excess in everything whenever they can, they have exaggerated this inequality; in some countries they maintain that a citizen is not permitted to leave the country in which he was born by chance; obviously the meaning of this law is: *This country is so bad, and so badly governed, that we forbid every individual to leave it, lest everybody leave it.* Do better: create in all your subjects the desire to remain at home, and in foreigners, the desire to come there.

In his heart of hearts every man has the right to think himself entirely equal to other men; it doesn't follow from this that a cardinal's cook should order his master to cook him a dinner; but the cook can say: "I am a man like my master, like him I was born crying; like me, he will die in anguish, with the same ceremonies. . . . If the Turks took Rome and I became a cardinal and my master a cook, I should take him into my service." This whole speech is reasonable and right; but while he waits for the Grand Turk to take Rome, the cook must do his duty, or human society is perverted. . . .

EVIL

People clamor that human nature is essentially perverse, that man is born the child of the devil, and of evil. Nothing is more ill-advised; for, my friend, in preaching at me that everybody is born perverse, you warn me that you were born that way, that I must distrust you as I would a fox or a crocodile. . . . It would be much more reasonable, much nobler, to say to me: "You were all born good; see how frightful it would be to corrupt the purity of your being." We should treat mankind as we should treat all men individually. . . .

Man is not born evil; he becomes evil, as he becomes sick. . . . Gather together all the children of the universe; you will see in them nothing but innocence, gentleness, and fear; . . . Man, then, is not born evil. Why then are some of them infected with this plague of malevolence? It's because those who are at their head have the malady and communicate it to the rest of mankind, just as a woman attacked by the sickness Christopher Columbus brought back from America spread that poison from one end of Europe to the other. The first ambitious man corrupted the earth. . . .

If men were essentially evil, if they were all born the subjects of a being as malevolent as it is unhappy, who inspired them with all this frenzy to avenge his own torment, we would see husbands murdered by their wives, and fathers by their children every morning. . . .

If there are a billion human beings in the world, that's a great deal. That would make about five hundred million women who sew, spin, nourish their little ones, keep the house or cabin neat, and slander their neighbors a little. I don't know what great harm these poor innocent women do in the world. With that number of inhabitants on the globe, there are at least two hundred million children, and of course they neither kill nor rob; and about as many old people who don't have the strength. There remain at the most a hundred million young men, robust and capable of crime. Of these hundred million, ninety are steadily occupied with breaking the ground, by prodigious labor, to furnish themselves with nourishment and clothing; they hardly have any time to do evil.

The ten million who remain include idle, well-bred gentlemen, who wish to enjoy themselves in peace; men of talent, busy with their professions; magistrates, priests, obviously interested in living a pure life, at least in appearance. Then the only truly evil men remaining are a few politicians, whether secular or religious, who perpetually seek to stir up trouble, and a few thousand vagabonds who hire out their services to these politicians. Now, there has never been a million of these ferocious beasts at work all at once; and I count highway robbers in this group. Then you have at most one man out of a thousand, in the stormiest of times, whom you can call evil: and even he isn't always evil.

There is, then, infinitely less evil in this world than people say and believe. To be sure, there is still too much: we see horrible misfortunes and crimes; but the pleasure of complaining and exaggerating is so great that at the slightest scratch you cry out that the world runs over with blood. Have you been deceived? Then all men are perjurers. A melancholy soul who has suffered some injustice sees the universe covered with the damned, ...

SECT

Every sect, of whatever kind, is the rallying point for doubt and error. Scotists, Thomists, Realists, Nominalists, Papists, Calvinists, Molinists, Jansenists, are nothing but assumed names.

There are no sects in geometry; we don't say, an Euclidian, an Archimedian. When the truth is evident, it is impossible for parties and factions to arise. People have never argued over whether it was daytime at noon.

Once the part of astronomy which determines the course of the stars and the recurrence of eclipses was known, there were no longer any disputes among astronomers.

People don't say in England: "I am a Newtonian, I am a Lockian, Halleyian"; why? Because whoever has done some reading cannot refuse his assent to truths taught by these three great men. The more Newton is revered, the less people call themselves Newtonians; this word would suggest that there are anti-Newtonians in England. Perhaps we still have some Cartesians in France; that's simply because the system of Descartes is a tissue of erroneous and ridiculous fancies.

The same thing holds true of the small number of truths of fact which are well established. ... You are a Mahometan, hence there are people who are not, hence you might be wrong. Which would be the true religion if Christianity didn't exist? The one in which there were no sects; the one about which all minds would inevitably agree.

Now on what dogma do all minds agree? On the worship of a God, and on probity. All the philosophers on earth who had a religion have said at all times: "There is a God, and men must be just." This, then, is the universal religion established in all times and for all men.

Hence, the point on which they all agree is true, and hence the systems by which they disagree are false. ... Now who will judge this contest? ... The man who is reasonable, impartial, learned in a science which is not merely verbal, the man liberated from prejudices, and a lover of truth and justice; in a word, the man who is not a beast and doesn't think he is an angel.

SUPERSTITION

. . . The most superstitious ages have always been the ages of the most horrible crimes. The superstitious man is to the rascal what the slave is to the tyrant. Indeed, more: the superstitious man is ruled by the fanatic, and turns into one. Superstition, born in paganism, adopted by Judaism, infected the Christian Church from the beginning. All the Fathers of the Church without exception believed in the power of magic. The Church always condemned magic, but it always believed in it: it didn't excommunicate sorcerers as madmen who were deceived, but as men who really had intercourse with devils.

Today half of Europe believes that the other half has long been and still is superstitious. The Protestants regard relics, indulgences, macerations, prayers for the dead, holy water, and almost all the rites of the Roman Church as superstitious lunacy. According to them, superstition consists of taking useless practices for necessary practices. Among the Roman Catholics there are men, more enlightened than their ancestors, who have renounced many practices that were once held sacred; and they defend the others by saying: "They are unimportant, and what is only unimportant cannot be an evil."

It is hard to mark out the boundaries of superstition. . . . The archbishop of Canterbury claims that the archbishop of Paris is superstitious; the Presbyterians levy the same reproach against his Grace of Canterbury, and are in their turn called superstitious by the Quakers, who are the most superstitious of men in the eyes of other Christians.

Thus there is no agreement in Christian societies about what superstition is. . . . Can there be a nation free from all superstitious prejudices? That's like asking: Can there be a nation of philosophers? [To summarize,] in a word, the fewer superstitions, the less fanaticism; and the less fanaticism, the fewer calamities.

10. DENIS DIDEROT: DEFINITION OF A PHILOSOPHER*

Although Denis Diderot (1713–84) was a novelist, a satirist, and a playwright, his fame as a *philosophe* stemmed mainly from his work as editor-in-chief of the famous *Encyclopedia of Arts and Sciences.* Between 1751 and 1772, defying all threats of censorship, Diderot published his *Encyclopedia* in twenty-eight volumes. He enlisted most of the important writers of his time in the project and succeeded in producing a compendium of human knowledge which was a clear statement of nature worship and faith in human perfectibility. How did Diderot define a philosopher in the Encyclopedia? What was the purpose of philosophy?

There is nothing which costs less to acquire nowadays than the name of *Philosopher;* an obscure and retired life, some outward signs of wisdom, with a little reading, suffice to attach this name to persons who enjoy the honor without meriting it.

* Denis Diderot, "The Philosopher," *Encyclopedia* in Merrick Whitcomb, ed., *Translations and Reprints from the Original Sources of European History* (Philadelphia: University of Pennsylvania, 1899) vol. VI, no. 1, pp. 20–23.

Others in whom freedom of thought takes the place of reasoning, regard themselves as the only true philosophers, because they have dared to overturn the consecrated limits placed by religion, and have broken the fetters which faith laid upon their reason. Proud of having gotten rid of the prejudices of education, in the matter of religion, they look upon others with scorn as feeble souls, servile and pusillanimous spirits, who allow themselves to be frightened by the consequences to which irreligion leads, and who, not daring to emerge for an instant from the circle of established verities, nor to proceed along unaccustomed paths, sink to sleep under the yoke of superstition. But one ought to have a more adequate idea of the philosopher, and here is the character which we give him:

Other men make up their minds to act without thinking, nor are they conscious of the causes which move them, not even knowing that such exist. The philosopher, on the contrary, distinguishes the causes to what extent he may, and often anticipates them, and knowingly surrenders himself to them. In this manner he avoids objects that may cause him sensations that are not conducive to his well being or his rational existence, and seeks those which may excite in him affections agreeable with the state in which he finds himself. Reason is in the estimation of the philosopher what grace is to the Christian. Grace determines the Christian's action; reason the philosopher's.

Other men are carried away by their passions, so that the acts which they produce do not proceed from reflection. These are the men who move in darkness; while the philosopher, even in his passions, moves only after reflection. He marches at night, but a torch goes on ahead.

The philosopher forms his principles upon an infinity of individual observations. The people adopt the principle without a thought of the observations which have produced it, believing that the maxim exists, so to speak, of itself; but the philosopher takes the maxim at its source, he examines its origin, he knows its real value, and only makes use of it, if it seems to him satisfactory.

Truth is not for the philosopher a mistress who vitiates his imagination, and whom he believes to find everywhere. He contents himself with being able to discover it wherever he may chance to find it. He does not confound it with its semblance; but takes for true that which is true, for false that which is false, for doubtful that which is doubtful, and for probable that which is only probable. He does more—and this is the great perfection of philosophy; that when he has no real grounds for passing judgment, he knows how to remain undetermined.

The world is full of persons of understanding, even of much understanding, who always pass judgment. They are guessing always, because it is guessing to pass judgment without knowing when one has proper grounds for judgment. They misjudge of the capacity of the human mind; they believe it is possible to know everything, and so they are ashamed not to be prepared to pass judgment, and they imagine that understanding consists in passing judgment. The philosopher believes that it consists in judging well: he is better pleased with himself when he has suspended the faculty of determining, than if he had determined before having acquired proper grounds for his decision. . . .

The philosophic spirit is then a spirit of observation and of exactness, which refers everything to its true principles; but it is not the understanding alone which the philosopher cultivates; he carries further his attention and his labors.

Man is not a monster, made to live only at the bottom of the sea or in the depths of the forest; the very necessities of his life render intercourse with others necessary; and in whatsoever state we find him, his needs and his well-being lead him to live in society. To that reason demands of him that he should know, that he should study and that he should labor to acquire social qualities.

Our philosopher does not believe himself an exile in the world; he does not believe himself in the enemy's country; he wishes to enjoy, like a wise economist, the goods that nature offers him; he wishes to find his pleasure with others; and in order to find it, it is necessary to assist in producing it; so he seeks to harmonize with those with whom chance or his choice has determined he shall live; and he finds at the same time that which suits him: he is an honest man who wishes to please and render himself useful. . . .

The philosopher is then an honest man, actuated in everything by reason, one who joins to the spirit of reflection and of accuracy the manners and qualities of society.

With this idea in mind, it is easy to see what gulf divides the wise insensibility of the stoics from the ideal of our philosopher. Such a philosopher is a man, and their sage is no more than a phantom. They blush before humanity, and glory in the fact; they foolishly wish to annihilate the passions and to elevate us above our nature by a chimerical insensibility. As for our philosopher, he pretends to no empty honor in the destruction of his passions, because that is impossible; but he seeks to escape their tyranny, to turn them to his profit, to make a reasonable use of them, because that is possible, and reason so ordains.

The philosophic spirit is a gift of nature, perfected by effort, art and usage, for judging sanely of all things. When one possesses in an exceptional degree this spirit, it produces a marvelous intelligence, a force of reasoning, an accurate and reflective taste in that which there is of good and bad in the world; it is the criterion of the true and beautiful. There is nothing estimable in the various works that issue from the hands of man that is not animated with this spirit. On it depends, in an especial measure, the glory of literature; but since it is the portion of very few among the learned, and it is neither possible nor necessary for the success of letters that a talent so rare should be found in all those who cultivate this art, it is sufficient for a nation that certain great spirits shall possess it to an eminent degree, and that the superiority of their judgment shall render them arbiters of taste, oracles of criticism, dispensers of literary glory.

11. JEAN JACQUES ROUSSEAU: THE SOCIAL CONTRACT*

The trinity of faiths so important to the *philosophes*—reason, nature, and progress—were largely disregarded by the most original thinker of the French Enlightenment, Jean Jacques Rousseau (1712–78). Rousseau sought a deeper truth than reason could provide by glorifying the insights of human sentiment and of the human heart. He urged a return to nature and trusted in the instinctive goodness of man.

---

* Jean Jacques Rousseau, *The Social Contract*, ed. and trans. Charles Frankel (New York: Hafner Publishing Co., 1947), pp. 5–6, 14–19, 21–24, 26–27. Reprinted by permission.

Rousseau was a champion of equality. He believed that man had been corrupted by society and could regain part of his natural goodness if the artificial restrictions imposed by society could be removed. He advocated the improvement of education and argued for marriage based on love rather than parental convenience. Above all, Rousseau raised important questions involving the individual and the state. How could liberty and equality be reconciled, and how could both the rights of the individual and the rights of the community be preserved in a free society? The idea of popular sovereignty, a revolutionary concept in the eighteenth century, was developed by Rousseau in his most important political work, *The Social Contract* (1762). What did Rousseau mean by individual liberty? When was man most truly free? Could a man be compelled to be free? Did *The Social Contract* give subjects the right to revolt against tyranny? When did the individual surrender his rights to the general will? In what ways might the concept of an all-powerful general will open the door to either tyranny or liberty?

Man is born free, and yet we see him everywhere in chains. Those who believe themselves the masters of others cease not to be even greater slaves than the people they govern. How this happens I am ignorant; but, if I am asked what renders it justifiable, I believe it may be in my power to resolve the question.

If I were only to consider force, and the effects of it, I should say, "When a people is constrained to obey, and does obey, it does well; but as soon as it can throw off its yoke, and does throw it off, it does better: for a people may certainly use, for the recovery of their liberty, the same right that was employed to deprive them of it: it was either justifiably recovered, or unjustifiably torn from them." But the social order is a sacred right which serves for the basis of all others. Yet this right comes not from nature; it is therefore founded on conventions. The question is, what those conventions are. . . .

OF THE SOCIAL COMPACT

I will suppose that men in the state of nature are arrived at that crisis when the strength of each individual is insufficient to overcome the resistance of the obstacles to his preservation. This primitive state can therefore subsist no longer; and the human race would perish unless it changed its manner of life.

As men cannot create for themselves new forces, but merely unite and direct those which already exist, the only means they can employ for their preservation is to form by aggregation an assemblage of forces that may be able to overcome the resistance, to be put in motion as one body, and to act in concert.

This assemblage of forces must be produced by the concurrence of many; but as the force and the liberty of each man are the chief instruments of his preservation, how can he engage them elsewhere without danger to himself, and without neglecting the care which is due himself? This difficulty, which leads directly to my subject, may be expressed in these words:

"Where shall we find a form of association which will defend and protect with the whole common force the person and the property of each associate, and by which every person, while uniting himself with all, shall obey only himself and remain as free as before?" Such is the fundamental problem of which the Social Contract gives the solution.

The articles of this contract are so unalterably fixed by the nature of the act that the least modification renders them vain and of no effect; so that they are the same everywhere, and are everywhere tacitly understood and admitted, even though they may never have been formally announced; until, the social compact being violated, each individual is restored to his original rights, and resumes his native liberty, while losing the conventional liberty for which he renounced it.

The articles of the social contract will, when clearly understood, be found reducible to this single point: the total alienation of each associate, and all his rights, to the whole community; for, in the first place, as every individual gives himself up entirely, the condition of every person is alike; and being so, it would not be to the interest of any one to render that condition offensive to others.

Nay, more than this, the alienation being made without any reserve, the union is as complete as it can be, and no associate has any further claim to anything: for if any individual retained rights not enjoyed in general by all, as there would be no common superior to decide between him and the public, each person being in some points his own judge, would soon pretend to be so in everything; and thus would the state of nature be continued and the association necessarily become tyrannical or be annihilated.

Finally, each person gives himself to all, and so not to any one individual; and as there is no one associate over whom the same right is not acquired which is ceded to him by others, each gains an equivalent for what he loses, and finds his force increased for preserving that which he possesses.

If, therefore, we exclude from the social compact all that is not essential, we shall find it reduced to the following terms: *Each of us places in common his person and all his power under the supreme direction of the general will; and as one body we all receive each member as an indivisible part of the whole.*

From that moment, instead of as many separate persons as there are contracting parties, this act of association produces a moral and collective body, composed of as many members as there are votes in the assembly, which from this act receives its unity, its common self, its life, and its will. This public person, which is thus formed by the union of all other persons, took formerly the name of "city," and now takes that of "republic," or "body politic." It is called by its members "State" when it is passive, "Sovereign," when in activity, and, whenever it is compared with other bodies of a similar kind, it is denominated "power." The associates take collectively the name of "people," and separately, that of "citizens," as participating in the sovereign authority, and of "subjects," because they are subjected to the laws of the State. . . .

OF THE SOVEREIGN

It appears from this formula that the act of association contains a reciprocal engagement between the public and individuals, . . . The body politic, or the Sovereign [authority], which derives its existence from the sacredness of the contract, can never bind itself, even towards outsiders, in anything that would derogate from the original act, such as alienating any portion of itself, or submitting to another Sovereign. To violate the contract by which it exists would be to annihilate itself; and that which is nothing can produce nothing.

As soon as this multitude is united in one body, you cannot offend one of its members without attacking the body; much less can you offend the body without incurring the resentment of all the members. Thus duty and interest equally oblige the two contracting parties to lend aid to each other; and the same men must endeavour to unite under this double character all the advantages which attend it.

Further, the Sovereign, being formed only of the individuals who compose it, neither has, nor can have, any interest contrary to theirs; consequently, the sovereign power need give no guarantee to its subjects, because it is impossible that the body should seek to injure all its members; and we shall see presently that it can do no injury to any individual in particular. The Sovereign, by its nature, is always everything it ought to be. . . .

In fact, each individual may, as a man, have a private will, dissimilar or contrary to the general will which he has as a citizen. His own private interest may dictate to him very differently from the common interest; his absolute and naturally independent existence may make him regard what he owes to the common cause as a gratuitous contribution, the omission of which would be less injurious to others than the payment would be burdensome to himself; and considering the moral person which constitutes the State as a creature of the imagination, because it is not a man, he may wish to enjoy the rights of a citizen without being disposed to fulfill the duties of a subject. Such an injustice would in its progress cause the ruin of the body politic.

In order, therefore, to prevent the social compact from becoming an empty formula, it tacitly comprehends the engagement, which alone can give effect to the others—that whoever refuses to obey the general will shall be compelled to it by the whole body: this in fact only forces him to be free; for this is the condition which, by giving each citizen to his country, guarantees his absolute personal independence, a condition which gives motion and effect to the political machine. This alone renders all civil engagements justifiable, and without it they would be absurd, tyrannical, and subject to the most enormous abuses.

OF THE CIVIL STATE

The passing from the state of nature to the civil state produces in man a very remarkable change, by substituting justice for instinct in his conduct, and giving to his actions a moral character which they lacked before. It is then only that the voice of duty succeeds to physical impulse, and a sense of what is right, to the incitements of appetite. Man, who had till then regarded none but himself, perceives that he must act on other principles, and learns to consult his reason before he listens to his inclinations. Although he is deprived in this new state of many advantages which he enjoyed from nature, he gains in return others so great, his faculties so unfold themselves by being exercised, his ideas are so extended, his sentiments so exalted, and his whole mind so enlarged and refined, that if, by abusing his new condition, he did not sometimes degrade it even below that from which he emerged, he ought to bless continually the happy moment that snatched him forever from it, and transformed him from a circumscribed and stupid animal to an intelligent being and a man.

In order to draw a balance between the advantages and disadvantages attending his new situation, let us state them in such a manner that they may be easily compared. Man loses by the social contract his *natural* liberty, and an unlimited right to all which tempts him, and which he can obtain; in return he acquires *civil* liberty, and proprietorship of all he possesses. That we may not be deceived in the value of these compensations, we must distinguish natural liberty, which knows no bounds but the power of the individual, from civil liberty, which is limited by the general will; and between possession, which is only the effect of force or of the right of the first occupant, from property, which must be founded on a positive title. In addition we might add to the other acquisitions of the civil state that of moral liberty, which alone renders a man master of himself; for it is *slavery* to be under the impulse of mere appetite, and *freedom* to obey a law which we prescribe for ourselves. . . .

OF REAL PROPERTY

Each member of the community, at the moment of its formation, gives himself up to it just as he is: himself and all his forces, of which his wealth forms a part. . . .

It may also happen that men begin to associate before they have any possessions, and that, spreading afterwards over a country sufficient for them all, they may either enjoy it in common, or part it between them equally, or in such proportions as the Sovereign shall direct. In whatever manner the acquisition is made, the right which each individual has over his own property is always subordinate to the right which the community has over all; . . . The basis of the whole social system is that instead of destroying the natural equality of mankind, the fundamental compact substitutes, on the contrary, a moral and legal equality for that physical inequality which nature placed among men, and that, let men be ever so unequal in strength or in genius, they are all equalized by convention and legal right. (Under bad governments this equality is but an illusive appearance, which only serves to keep the poor in misery, and support the rich in their usurpations. In fact, laws are always useful to those who have abundance, and injurious to those who have nothing: from whence it follows that the social state is only advantageous to men when every individual has some property, and no one has too much.)

THAT SOVEREIGNTY IS INALIENABLE

The first and most important consequence of the principles already established is that the general will alone can direct the forces of the State agreeably to the end of its institution, which is the common good; for if the clashing of private interests has rendered the establishing of societies necessary, the agreement of the same interests has made such establishments possible. It is what is common in these different interests that forms the social bond; and if there was not some point in which they all unanimously centered, no society could exist. It is on the basis of this common interest alone that society must be governed.

I say, therefore, that sovereignty, being only the exercise of the general will, can never alienate itself, and that the Sovereign, which is only a collective being, cannot be represented but by itself: the *power* may well be transmitted but not the *will*. ...

THAT SOVEREIGNTY IS INDIVISIBLE

For the same reason that sovereignty is inalienable, it is indivisible. For the will is general or it is not; it is either the will of the whole body of the people, or only of a part. In the first case, this declared will is an act of sovereignty and constitutes law; in the second, it is but a private will or an act of magistracy, and is at most but a decree. ...

WHETHER THE GENERAL WILL CAN ERR

It follows from what has been said that the general will is always right and tends always to the public advantage; but it does not follow that the deliberations of the people have always the same rectitude. Our will always seeks our own good, but we do not always perceive what it is. The people are never corrupted, but they are often deceived, and only then do they seem to will what is bad.

There is frequently much difference between the *will of all* and the *general will*. The latter regards only the common interest; the former regards private interest, and is indeed but a sum of private wills: but remove from these same wills the pluses and minuses that cancel each other, and then the general will remains as the sum of the differences.

If, when the people, sufficiently informed, deliberated, there was to be no communication among them, from the grand total of trifling differences the general will would always result, and their resolutions be always good. But when cabals and partial associations are formed at the expense of the great association, the will of each such association, though *general* with regard to its members, is *private* with regard to the State: it can then be said no longer that there are as many voters as men, but only as many as there are associations. By this means the differences being less numerous, they produce a result less general. Finally, when one of these associations becomes so large that it prevails over all the rest, you have no longer the sum of many opinions dissenting in a small degree from each other, but one great dictating dissentient; from that moment there is no longer a general will, and the predominating opinion is only an individual one.

It is therefore of the utmost importance for obtaining the expression of the general will, that no partial society should be formed in the State, and that every citizen should speak his opinion entirely from himself: such was the unique and sublime system of the great Lycurgus. When there are partial societies, it is politic to multiply their number, that they may be all kept on an equality. This method was pursued by Solon, Numa, and Servius. These are the only precautions that can be taken to make the general will always intelligent, and prevent the people from being deceived. ...

12. THOMAS JEFFERSON: DECLARATION OF INDEPENDENCE*

The American Declaration of Independence was the first historical document which sought to put the "natural rights" theories of the Enlightenment into practical effect. As such, its publication produced a dramatic sensation among the political thinkers of Europe. Essentially a partisan document, the Declaration begins by stating its purpose and then expounds a general theory of government.

The Declaration was the work of Thomas Jefferson (1743–1826), an apostle of agrarian democracy. Jefferson was educated at the College of William and Mary (Virginia) where he made a thorough study of political philosophies. He served in the Virginia House of Burgesses from 1769 to 1775, joining the patriot faction in protest against British procedures of taxation. In his *Summary of the Rights of British America* (1774), Jefferson gave a lucid explanation of the view that Parliament had no authority in the colonies and that the only bond with England was allegiance to a common monarch whose proper function was to respect the legislative and fiscal authority of the colonial assemblies. Jefferson served as a member of the Continental Congresses of 1775 and 1776 and was entrusted with the task of drafting the Declaration of Independence. What particularly original or novel thoughts were presented by Jefferson in the Declaration? Compare the theory of government defended in the Declaration with the doctrines of Hobbes, Locke, Montesquieu, and Rousseau. To which is it closer and why? What is the proper function of government, according to the Declaration, and why had George III violated his right to rule over the American colonies?

THE UNANIMOUS DECLARATION OF THE THIRTEEN UNITED STATES OF AMERICA

When in the Course of human events, it becomes necessary for one people to dissolve the political bands which have connected them with another, and to assume among the powers of the earth, the separate and equal station to which the Laws of Nature and of Nature's God entitle them, a decent respect to the opinions of mankind requires that they should declare the causes which impel them to the separation.

We hold these truths to be self-evident, that all men are created equal, that they are endowed by their Creator with certain unalienable Rights, that among these are Life, Liberty and the pursuit of Happiness. That to secure these rights, Governments are instituted among Men, deriving their just powers from the consent of the governed,—That whenever any Form of Government becomes destructive of these ends, it is the Right of the People to alter or to abolish it, and to institute new Government, laying its foundation on such principles and organizing its powers in such form, as to them shall seem most likely to effect their Safety and Happiness. Prudence, indeed, will dictate that Governments long established should not be changed for light and transient causes; and accordingly all experience hath shown, that mankind are more disposed to suffer, while evils are sufferable, than to right themselves by abolishing the forms to which they are accustomed. But when a long train of abuses and usurpations, pursuing invariably the same Object evinces a design to reduce them under absolute Despotism, it is their right, it is their duty, to throw off

* "Declaration of American Independence" in *United States Code* (1964 ed., 14 vols.; Washington, 1965), I, xxvii–xxix.

such Government, and to provide new Guards for their future security.—Such has been the patient sufferance of these Colonies; and such is now the necessity which constrains them to alter their former Systems of Government. The history of the present King of Great Britain is a history of repeated injuries and usurpations, all having in direct object the establishment of an absolute Tyranny over these States. To prove this, let Facts be submitted to a candid world.

He has refused his Assent to Laws, the most wholesome and necessary for the public good. He has forbidden his Governors to pass Laws of immediate and pressing importance, unless suspended in their operation till his Assent should be obtained; and when so suspended, he has utterly neglected to attend to them.

He has refused to pass other Laws for the accommodation of large districts of people, unless those people would relinquish the right of Representation in the Legislature, a right inestimable to them, and formidable to tyrants only.

He has called together legislative bodies at places unusual, uncomfortable, and distant from the depository of their Public Records, for the sole purpose of fatiguing them into compliance with his measures.

He has dissolved Representative Houses repeatedly, for opposing with manly firmness his invasions on the rights of the people.

He has refused for a long time, after such dissolutions, to cause others to be elected; whereby the Legislative Powers, incapable of Annihilation, have returned to the People at large for their exercise; the State remaining, in the mean time, exposed to all the dangers of invasion from without and convulsions within.

He has endeavoured to prevent the population of these States; for that purpose obstructing the Laws for Naturalization of Foreigners; refusing to pass others to encourage their migration hither, and raising the conditions of new Appropriations of Lands.

He has obstructed the Administration of Justice, by refusing his Assent to Laws for establishing Judiciary powers.

He has made Judges dependent on his Will alone, for the tenure of their offices, and the amount and payment of their salaries.

He has erected a multitude of New Offices, and sent hither swarms of Officers to harass our People, and eat out their substance.

He has kept among us, in times of peace, Standing Armies without the Consent of our legislatures.

He has affected to render the Military independent of and superior to the Civil power.

He has combined, with others, to subject us to a jurisdiction foreign to our constitution, and unacknowledged by our laws; giving his Assent to their acts of pretended legislation:

For quartering large bodies of armed troops among us:

For protecting them, by a mock Trial, from Punishment for any Murders which they should commit on the Inhabitants of these States:

For cutting off our Trade with all parts of the world:

For imposing Taxes on us without our Consent:

For depriving us in many cases, of the benefits of Trial by Jury:

For transporting us beyond Seas to be tried for pretended offences:

For abolishing the free System of English Laws in a neighbouring Province, establishing therein an Arbitrary government, and enlarging its Boundaries so as to render it at once an example and fit instrument for introducing the same absolute rule into these Colonies:

For taking away our Charters, abolishing our most valuable Laws, and altering fundamentally the Forms of our Governments:

For suspending our own Legislatures, and declaring themselves invested with Power to legislate for us in all cases whatsoever.

He has abdicated Government here, by declaring us out of his Protection and waging War against us.

He has plundered our seas, ravaged our Coasts, burnt our towns, and destroyed the lives of our people.

He is at this time transporting large armies of foreign mercenaries to complete the works of death, desolation and tyranny, already begun with circumstances of Cruelty and perfidy scarcely paralleled in the most barbarous ages, and totally unworthy the Head of a civilized nation.

He has constrained our fellow Citizens, taken Captive on the high Seas, to bear Arms against their Country, to become the executioners of their friends and Brethren, or to fall themselves by their Hands.

He has excited domestic insurrections amongst us, and has endeavoured to bring on the inhabitants of our frontiers, the merciless Indian Savages, whose known rule of warfare, is an undistinguished destruction of all ages, sexes and conditions.

In every stage of these Oppressions We have Petitioned for Redress in the most humble terms: Our repeated Petitions have been answered only by repeated injury. A Prince, whose character is thus marked by every act which may define a Tyrant, is unfit to be the ruler of a free People.

Nor have We been wanting in attentions to our British brethren. We have warned them from time to time of attempts by their legislature to extend an unwarrantable jurisdiction over us. We have reminded them of the circumstances of our emigration and settlement here. We have appealed to their native justice and magnanimity, and we have conjured them by the ties of our common kindred to disavow these usurpations, which would inevitably interrupt our connections and correspondence. They too have been deaf to the voice of justice and of consanguinity. We must, therefore, acquiesce in the necessity, which denounces our Separation, and hold them, as we hold the rest of mankind, Enemies in War, in Peace Friends.

We, therefore, the Representatives of the united States of America, in General Congress, Assembled, appealing to the Supreme Judge of the world for the rectitude of our intentions, do, in the Name, and by Authority of the good People of these Colonies, solemnly publish and declare, That these United Colonies are, and of Right ought to be Free and Independent States; that they are Absolved from all Allegiance to the British Crown, and that all political connection between them and the State of Great Britain, is and ought to be totally dissolved; and that as Free and Independent States, they have full Power to levy War, conclude Peace, contract Alliances, establish Commerce, and to do all other Acts and Things which Independent States may of right do. And for the support of this Declaration, with a firm reliance on the Protection of Divine Providence, we mutually pledge to each other our Lives, our Fortunes and our sacred Honor.

13. JACQUES TURGOT: REFLECTIONS ON THE FORMATION AND THE DISTRIBUTION OF RICHES*

Like the *philosophes,* the Physiocrats were deeply influenced by the new science and the confidence in human reason which characterized the Enlightenment. Physiocrats attempted to treat the subject of economics scientifically and visualized the flow of goods and services as part of a natural economic order which must be exempt from artificial restrictions. The mercantilist belief in state control and regulation was decried, and *laisser-faire, laisser-passer* became the creed of the Physiocrats. Further, the mercantilist concept of increasing wealth through trade and the accumulation of bullion was discarded. Wealth, the Physiocrats insisted, was the product of productive labor which could be found only in agriculture.

Physiocracy was replete with contradictions. Physiocrats argued against state intervention on behalf of trade and industry while calling on the state to support the right of the individual to enjoy the benefits of property; property rights had to be maintained to keep society in tune with the "natural economic order." They fought a rear-guard action in support of the landed order while arguing production in capitalistic terms, a dilemma seen by two later economists who were influenced by the Physiocrats—Adam Smith and Karl Marx.

The leader of the Physiocrats was François Quesnay (1694–1774), but the first Physiocrat to hold an important state position in France was Anne Robert Jacques Turgot, baron d'Aulne (1727–81), who was appointed *Contrôleur Général des Finances* in 1774. For two years Turgot attempted far-reaching fiscal reforms, though he managed only to take important first steps in the revamping of France's financial and economic structure. Turgot's proposals aroused loud and intensive opposition from special-interest groups, especially among the nobility. When he proposed a widening of the tax base to include the privileged classes, Louis XVI bowed to pressure from the Queen and members of the court. Turgot was dismissed, and succeeding ministers failed to solve the problems he had skillfully diagnosed.

Turgot's brief ministry was the zenith, as well as the beginning of the end, for French Physiocracy. Quesnay died in 1774, and Physiocratic publications appealed to a diminishing number of readers. The appearance of Adam Smith's *Wealth of Nations* in 1776 helped to render Physiocratic doctrines obsolete.

Turgot's *Reflections on the Formation and the Distribution of Riches* was published in 1770. It was written for two young Chinese students returning home after being educated in France. In the *Reflections,* Turgot repeated the basic principles advanced by Quesnay, but clarified Physiocratic concepts by using a narrative rather than a statistical format to make his main points. According to Turgot, was the division of society into productive and non-productive classes a natural development? Why, or why not? What justified the existence of a proprietor class? Why was the labor of the artisan non-productive?

* A. R. Jacques Turgot, *Reflections on the Formation and the Distribution of Riches* (London: The Macmillan Co., 1898), pp. 5, 6–17.

The products of the land require preparations long & difficult, in order to render them fit to satisfy the wants of man.

The crops which the land produces to satisfy the different wants of man cannot serve that purpose, for the most part, in the state in which nature gives them; they must undergo various changes and be prepared by art. Wheat must be converted into flour and then into bread; hides must be tanned or dressed; wool and cotton must be spun; silk must be drawn from the cocoons; hemp and flax must be soaked, peeled, and spun; next, different textures must be made from them; and then they must be cut and sewn into garments, foot-gear, etc. If the man who causes his land to produce all these different things and uses them to supply his wants were himself obliged to put them through all these intermediate stages, it is certain that he would succeed very badly. The greater part of these preparations demand an amount of care, of attention, of long experience, such as are only to be acquired by working continuously and on a great quantity of materials. . . .

The necessity of these preparations brings about the exchange of produce for labour.

The same motive which has established the exchange of crop for crop between the Cultivators of different kinds of soil must, then, have necessarily brought about the exchange of crop for labour between the Cultivators and another part of the society, which shall have preferred the occupation of preparing and working up the produce of the land to that of growing it. Everyone profited by this arrangement, for each by devoting himself to a single kind of work succeeded much better in it. The Husbandman obtained from his field the greatest amount of produce possible, and procured for himself much more easily all the other things he needed by the exchange of his surplus than he would have done by his own labour. The Shoemaker, by making shoes for the Husbandman, obtained for himself a part of the latter's harvest. Each workman laboured to satisfy the wants of the workmen of all the other kinds, who, on their side, all laboured for him.

Pre-eminence of the Husbandman who produces over the Artisan who works up materials. The Husbandman is the first mover in the circulation of labours; it is he who causes the land to produce the wages of all the Artisans.

It must however be observed that the Husbandman, furnishing all with the most important and most considerable article of their consumption, (I mean their food and also the materials of almost every industry) has the advantage of a greater independence. His labor, in the sequence of the labors divided among the different members of the society, retains the same primacy, the same pre-eminence, as the labor which provided his own food had among the different kinds of labor which, when he worked alone, he was obliged to devote to his different kinds of wants. We have here neither a primacy of honor nor of dignity; it is one of *physical necessity*. The Husbandman, we may say in general terms, can get on without the labor of the other workmen, but no workman can labor if the Husbandman does not enable him to live. In this circulation, which, by the reciprocal exchange of wants, renders men necessary to one another and forms the bond of the society, it is, then, the labor of the Husbandman which imparts the first impulse. What his labor causes the land to produce beyond his personal wants is the only fund for the wages which all the other members of the society receive in exchange for their labor. The latter, in making use of the price of this exchange to buy in their turn the products of the Husbandman, only return to him exactly what they have received from him. We have here a very essential difference between these two kinds of labors, upon which it is necessary to lay stress in order to be well assured of the evidence on which it rests, before we accept the innumerable consequences which flow from it.

The wages of the Workman are limited to his subsistence by the competition among the Workmen. He gets only his livelihood.

The mere Workman, who has only his arms and his industry, has nothing except in so far as he succeeds in selling his toil to others. He sells it more or less dear; but this price, more or less high as it may be, does not depend upon himself alone: it results from the agreement which he makes with him who pays his labour. The latter pays him as little as he can; as he has the choice among a great number of Workmen, he prefers the one who works cheapest. The Work-men are therefore obliged to lower the price, in competition with one another. In every kind of work it cannot fail to happen, and as a matter of fact it does happen, that the wages of the workman are limited to what is necessary to procure him his subsistence.

The Husbandman is the only person whose labour produces something over and above the wages of the labour. He is therefore the sole source of all wealth.

The position of the Husbandman is very different. The land pays him directly the price of his labour, independently of any other man or any agreement. Nature does not bargain with him to oblige him to content himself with what is absolutely necessary. What she grants is proportioned neither to his wants, nor to a contractual valuation of the price of his days of labour. It is the physical result of the fertility of the soil, and of the wisdom, far more than of the laboriousness, of the means which he has employed to render it fertile. As soon as the labour of the Husbandman produces more than his wants, he can, with this superfluity that nature accords him as a pure gift, over and above the wages of his toil, buy the labour of the other members of the society. The latter, in selling to him, gain only their livelihood; but the Husbandman gathers, beyond his subsistence, a wealth which is independent and disposable, which he has not bought and which he sells. He is, therefore, the sole source of the riches, which, by their circulation, animate all the labours of the society; because he is the only one whose labour produces over and above the wages of the labour.

First division of the society into two classes: the one productive, *or that of the Cultivator; the second* stipendiary, *or that of the Artisans.*

Here then we have the whole society divided, by a necessity founded on the nature of things, into two classes: equally industrious. But one of these by its labor produces, or rather draws from the land, riches which are continually springing up afresh, and which supply the whole society with its subsistence and with the materials for all its needs. The other, occupied in giving to materials thus produced the preparations and the forms which render them suitable for the use of man, sells its labor to the first class, and receives in exchange its subsistence. The first may be called the *productive* class, and the second the *stipendiary* class.

Up to this point we have not yet distinguished the Husbandman from the Proprietor of the lands; and in fact they were not originally distinct. It is by the labor of those who have been the first to till the fields, and who have enclosed them, in order to secure to themselves the harvest, that all the lands have ceased to be common to all, and that landed properties have been established. . . .

Progress of the society; all the lands have a master.

But the land filled up, and was more and more cleared. The best lands at length came to be all occupied. There remained for the last comers only the sterile soils rejected by the first. But in the end all land found its master, and those who could not have properties had at first no other resource than that of exchanging the labor of their arms, in the employments of the stipendiary class, for the superfluous portion of the crops of the cultivating Proprietor. . . .

Inequality in the division of properties: causes which render that inevitable.

The original Proprietors at first occupied, as has been already said, as much of the ground as their forces permitted them to cultivate with their family. A man of greater strength, more industrious, more anxious about the future, took more of it than a man of a contrary character. He whose family was more numerous, as he had more needs and more hands at his disposal, extended his possessions further: here was already a first inequality. All pieces of ground are not equally fertile: two men, with the same extent of ground and the same labour, could obtain a very different produce from it: second source of inequality. Properties, in passing from fathers to children, are divided into portions more or less small, according as the families are more or less numerous; as generations succeed one another, sometimes the inheritances are still further subdivided, sometimes they are reunited again by the extinction of some of the branches: third source of inequality. The contrast between the intelligence, the activity, and, above all, the economy of some and the indolence, inaction and dissipation of others, was a fourth principle of inequality and the most powerful of all. The negligent and improvident Proprietor, who cultivates badly, who, in abundant years, consumes the whole of his superfluity in frivolities, finds himself reduced, on the least accident, to request assistance from his neighbour who has been more prudent, and to live by borrowing. If, by new accidents, or through a continuance of his neglect, he finds himself not in a condition to repay, if he is obliged to have recourse to new loans, he will at last have no other resource than to abandon a part or even the whole of his estate to his creditor, who will take it as an equivalent; or to assign it to another, in exchange for other values wherewith he will discharge his obligation to his creditor.

Consequence of this inequality: the Cultivator distinguished from the Proprietor.

Here, then, we have landed properties as objects of commerce, and bought and sold. The portion of the extravagant or unfortunate Proprietor serves for the increase of that of the Proprietor who has been more fortunate or less prudent; and, in this infinitely varied inequality of possessions, it is impossible but that many Proprietors should have more than they can cultivate. Besides, it is natural enough that a rich man should wish to enjoy his wealth in tranquility, and that instead of employing his whole time in toilsome labors, he should prefer to give a part of his superfluity to people who will work for him.

Division of the produce between the Cultivator & the Proprietor. Net produce *or revenue.*

By this new arrangement the produce of the land is divided into two parts. The one includes the subsistence and the profits of the Husbandman, which are the reward of his labour and the condition upon which he undertakes to cultivate the field of the Proprietor. What remains is that independent and disposable part which the land gives as a pure gift to him who cultivates it, over and above his advances and the wages of his trouble; and this is the portion of the Proprietor, or the *revenue* with which the latter can live without labour and which he carries where he will.

New division of the Society into three classes, of Cultivators, of Artisans & of Proprietors; or the productive *class, the* stipendiary *class and the* disposable *class.*

Here then we have the Society divided into three classes; the class of Husbandmen, for which we may keep the name of *productive class;* the class of Artisans and others who *receive stipends* from the produce of the land; and the class of Proprietors, the only one which, not being bound by the need of subsistence to a particular labour, can be employed for the general needs of the Society, such as war and the administration of justice, either by a personal service, or by the payment of a part of their revenue with which the State or the Society may engage men to discharge these functions. The name which, for this reason, suits it the best is that of *disposable class.*

Resemblances between the two working or non-disposable classes.

The two classes of the Cultivators and the Artisans resemble each other in many respects, and above all in this, that those who compose them possess no revenue and live equally on wages, which are paid them out of the produce of the land. Both have also this in common, that they get nothing but the price of their labour and of their advances, and this price is nearly the same in the two classes; the Proprietor bargaining with those who cultivate the land to yield to them as small a part of the produce as possible, in the same way as he chaffers with his Shoemaker to buy his shoes as cheaply as possible. In a word, the Cultivator and the Artisan receive, neither of them, more than the recompense of their labour.

Essential difference between the two working classes.

But there is this difference between the two kinds of labours, that the labour of the Cultivator produces his own wages, and, in addition, the revenue which serves to pay the whole class of Artisans and other stipendiaries; while the Artisans receive simply their wages; that is to say their part of the produce of the land in exchange for their labour, and do not produce any revenue. The Proprietor has nothing except through the labour of the Cultivator; he receives from him his subsistence, and that wherewith he pays the labours of the other stipendiaries. He has need of the Cultivator through the necessity of the physical order, in virtue of which the land produces nothing without labour; but the Cultivator has need of the Proprietor only by virtue of the human conventions and the civil laws which have been obliged to guarantee to the first Cultivators and to their heirs the ownership of the grounds which they have occupied even after they ceased to cultivate them. But these laws could guarantee to the man who took no part in the work himself only that portion of the produce which the land gives over and above the recompense due to the Cultivators. The Proprietor is obliged to give up this latter, on pain of losing the whole. The Cultivator, confined though he is to the recompense of his labour, thus preserves that natural and physical primacy which renders him the first mover of the whole machine of the Society and which causes his own subsistence as well as the wealth of the Proprietor and the wages of all the other labours to depend upon his labour alone. The Artisan, on the contrary, receives his wages, whether it be from the Proprietor or from the Cultivator, and gives them, in exchange for his labour, only the equivalent of these wages and nothing more.

Thus, although neither the Cultivator nor the Artisan gains more than the recompense of his labour, the Cultivator causes, over and above that recompense, the revenue of the Proprietor to come into existence; and the Artisan causes no revenue to come into existence either for himself or for others.

This difference justifies their being distinguished as productive & barren *class respectively.*

We can then distinguish the two non-disposable classes as the *productive class,* which is that of the Cultivators, and the *barren class,* which includes all the other stipendiary members of the Society. . . .

ENLIGHTENED DESPOTISM

14. FREDERICK II: MEMOIRS AND LETTERS*

In the years immediately preceding his accession to the Prussian throne in 1740, Frederick the Great (r. 1740–86) had mastered the ideas of the leading

---

* The memoirs are from *Posthumous Works of Frederick II, King of Prussia. Memoirs from the Peace of Hubertsburg, to the Partition of Poland, and of the Bavarian War,* trans. Thomas Holcroft (London, 1789) IV, 119–121, 381–86. The letters are from *Letters Between Frederick II and M. De Voltaire,* trans. Thomas Holcroft (London, 1789), pp. 32–33, 285–86.

authors of his time. He had corresponded with Voltaire and had also written in French (pronouncing that German was a language fit only for soldiers and horses) a refutation of Machiavelli's thesis that for rulers the end justifies the means. Consequently, European intellectuals looked forward with enthusiasm to the accession of such an enlightened prince to absolute power. But, contrary to the hopes of the *philosophes,* Frederick had every intention of using the magnificently trained Prussian army as an instrument for the extension of his dynastic inheritance. Taking advantage of the death of the Emperor Charles VI in October 1740, and of the fact that the heir to the conglomerate Habsburg realms was a woman (Maria Theresa), Frederick precipitated a general European war (The War of the Austrian Succession, 1740–48) by seizing the rich Austrian province of Silesia, cynically justifying his action through vague sixteenth-century Hohenzollern claims to the area. Fearing that Maria Theresa would be able to wrest Silesia from him through a Franco-Russian-Austrian alliance, Frederick for the second time plunged Europe into a general war (The Seven Years' War, 1756–63).

The following selections from Frederick's writings reflect his philosophical and political views over nearly a half century. What were Frederick's views on the proper duties and functions of a monarch? Did he regard himself as a philosopher-king? What was his attitude toward religious questions? What program did he advocate for the economic prosperity of his realms, and to what school of economic thought did he belong? What views did he express about the level of German culture and the means by which it might be advanced? How did Frederick's theories of the good ruler compare with his actual conduct as King of Prussia?

CONSIDERATIONS ON THE PRESENT STATE OF THE BODY-POLITIC IN EUROPE

From what has been said, it will be easy to perceive that the political body of Europe is in a perilous situation. It is deprived of its due equilibrium, and is in a state in which it cannot long remain, without great risk. The political resembles the human body, which can only subsist by a mixture of equal quantities of the acid and the alkali. Whenever one of these two substances predominates, the body is made sensible of it, and the health is considerably injured: should that substance continue to increase, it may finally cause the destruction of the machine. Thus, whenever the policy and prudence of the princes of Europe lose sight of the maintenance of a just balance, between the principal powers, it is felt by the constitution of the whole body-politic. Violence on the one side, weakness on the other; the desire of invading on the one, and on the other the inability to prevent invasion. The most puissant gives law, and the feeble are under the necessity of adding their signature. All finally concur in augmenting disorder and confusion. Force acts like an impetuous torrent, passes its bounds, carries everything with it, and exposes this unfortunate body-politic to the most fatal revolutions. . . .

. . . I will venture to probe the wound of this body-politic still deeper, and exert myself to discover its most secret causes. Should my reflections fortunately come to the ears of some princes, they will there find truths which they never would have learned from the mouth of their courtiers, and their parasites. Perhaps they will even be astonished to perceive these truths arranging themselves around the throne. Let them be taught, therefore, that their own false principles are the most poisonous source of the misfortunes of Europe.

The error of most of these princes is they imagine God has expressly created, out of particular attention to their grandeur their felicity and their pride, that multitude of men, the prosperity of whom is committed to their charge; and that their subjects are destined only to be their instruments, and the ministers of their ungoverned passions. Whenever first principles are founded in error, the consequences deduced must continually be vicious. . . .

Were princes to reject these erroneous ideas, were they desirous of inquiring into the end of their institution, they would then perceive that the rank of which they are so vain, and their elevation, is the work of the people; that the millions of men over whom they are to watch did not all yield themselves up as the slaves of an individual, in order to render him more formidable and more puissant, and that they did not subject themselves to a fellow citizen to fall the martyrs of his caprices, and to be made the sport of his whims, but that they chose the person among them whom they supposed the most just as their governor, that he might be to them a father; the most humane, that he might compassionate and alleviate their misfortunes; the most valiant, that he might defend them against their enemies; the most wise, that he might not insensibly plunge them into ruinous and destructive wars; and, in fine, the man who most effectively could represent the embodied states, and in whom foreign power might be the support of justice and the laws, and not the instrument of committing crimes with impunity, and of exercising tyranny.

This principle being established, princes would consistently avoid the two rocks which in all ages have occasioned the ruin of empires, and the world's confusion; that is to say immeasurable ambition, and cowardly indolence. Instead of incessantly projecting conquests, these gods of the earth would labour only to secure happiness to their people; would wholly employ themselves to relieve the miserable, and to render their government mild and salutary. It is necessary that the benefits they should bestow should inspire men with a wish to have been born their subjects; that a general rivalship should reign among them, each endeavoring to surpass the other in bounty and clemency; that they should be convinced the true glory of monarchs does not consist in oppressing their neighbors, nor in augmenting the number of their slaves, but in fulfilling the duties of their offices, and in perfectly corresponding to the intention of those by whom they have been clothed with power, and from whom they hold supreme grandeur.

Yes, sovereigns ought to remember that ambition and vain glory are vices which are severely punished in private persons, and held in abhorrence when discovered in a prince.

Neither would those kings who should unceasingly reflect on their duties neglect to perform those duties, or hold them to be occupations unworthy of their splendor. They would not blindly commit the welfare of their people to a minister who might be corrupted, who might be deficient in talents, and who is generally less interested in the public welfare than the sovereign. . . .

In a word, to lose provinces is opprobrious and ignominious; and to conquer those over which we have no legal claim is unjust and criminal rapacity.

LETTERS TO VOLTAIRE

Breslau, 1 September 1766

You will have read in my preceding letter that peaceable philosophers may expect to be well received in my states. I have not seen the son of the modern Hippocrates, nor have I spoken to him. [Possibly, Frederick was referring to a son of François Quesnay, the physician and economist, whom he had invited to visit Prussia.] I know not what can have transpired of the design of your philosophers; I wash my hands of it. I am here in a province where physics are preferred to metaphysics. The people cultivate their lands; they have rebuilt eight hundred houses and they bring forth some thousands of children annually to replace those which the frenzy of politics and of war caused to perish.

I know not whether, all things considered, it be not more advantageous to labor at population than to write bad arguments. The lord and the peasant, occupied in their own re-establishment, live in peace; and they are so busied by their work that no person pays attention to the religion of his neighbor. . . . Believe me, indolence gives birth to most disputes. That such may be extinguished in France, you need but renew the times of the defeats of Poitiers and Agincourt. Your ecclesiastics and your *parlements,* busily employed in their own affairs, would think on them only, and would leave both the public and the government in peace. This is a proposition which may be made to these gentlemen; but I doubt much of their approbation.

Your works are common here; they are in the hands of everybody. There is no region, no nation, that has not heard your name; nor is there any polished society in which your fame is not resplendent. Enjoy this fame and enjoy it long!

Potsdam, 24 October 1773

I have been returned from my journeys more than a month. I have travelled into Prussia to abolish servitude, reform barbarous laws, promulgate others more rational, open a canal by which the Vistula, the Strez, the Wartha, the Oder, and the Elbe have a communication, rebuild towns that have lain in ruins ever since the plague of 1760, drain twenty miles of marshy land, and establish a police in a country where the name had before been unknown.

I thence went to Silesia to console my poor Jesuits for the rigors of the court of Rome.[1] My purpose is to corroborate their order, and to form a corps through diverse provinces in which I preserve them, thus to render them useful to the country by placing them over schools for the instruction of youth, to which occupation I wish them to be entirely confined.

I have beside ordered sixty villages to be built in Upper Silesia where there was land still uncultivated, each village to consist of twenty families. I have caused high roads to be made among the mountains for the facility of trade,

1. Under pressure from the Bourbon kings of France, Spain, and Naples, Pope Clement XIV had issued the Bull *Dominus ac Redemptor* (April 1773) which accused the Jesuits of meddling in politics contrary to their own Constitution and declared the Society abolished. But the Order, ignoring its own law of absolute obedience, refused to die. It took refuge in Prussia and Russia, arguing that papal bulls were not binding in the territory of any sovereign who did not authorize their publication. The Papacy did not lift its ban against the Jesuits until the turn of the century.

and two towns that had been burnt to be rebuilt. Their houses were of wood; they are to be of brick, and even of hewn stone, brought from the mountains.

I shall not speak to you of the troops; that is a subject too severely prohibited at Ferney [Voltaire's residence] for me to touch upon. . . . But, you will perceive, while doing all these things, I have not remained with folded arms.

Neither I nor the Emperor shall interfere with the Crescent: there are no more relics to be recovered from Jerusalem. We hope that peace will perhaps be made this winter: not to mention that we love the proverb which says—"Live and let live." The peace has scarcely continued ten years and ought to be preserved as long as possible without risk; still neither more nor less continuing to put ourselves in such a condition as not to be taken unprovided by some chief of banditti, the leader of hireling murderers.

This system is neither that of Richelieu nor of Mazarin; but is that of the good of the people who ought to form the principal object of the magistrate's care by whom they are governed.

Potsdam, 8 September 1775

You may well say that our good Germans are still in the twilight of knowledge. Germany is now, relatively to the fine arts, what your country was under Francis I. The arts are loved and sought after; foreigners transplant them among us, but the soil is not sufficiently prepared to be self-productive. The Thirty Years War was more injurious to Germany than foreigners have imagined. It was necessary to begin by cultivating the land, next to apply to manufactures, and finally to obtain some trifling commerce. In preparation as these plans gain strength a degree of welfare springs up which is followed by increasing opulence, without which the arts cannot prosper. It is the will of the Muses that the waters of Pactolus should wash the feet of the Parnassian mount. We must first be at our ease before we can gain knowledge and think freely. Thus Athens was superior to Sparta in what related to science and the fine arts.

Taste will not extend itself through Germany till the classic authors: Greek, Roman, and French shall have been maturely studied. Two or three men of genius will correct the language, will render it less barbarous, and will naturalize those masterpieces of literature which other nations have produced.

For my part, my end approaches, and I shall never see these fortunate times. Much would I have contributed to their birth; but what could a being effect, who, during three parts of his career, was disturbed by continual wars, was obliged to repair the evils these wars had occasioned, and who was born with talents insufficient for enterprises so great? Philosophy has descended to us from Epicurus, and has been improved by Gassendi, Newton, and Locke. I do myself the honor of being their disciple, but nothing more:

> On blindness and a world of night
> You pour a splendid flood of light.
> From fears which bigot fools receive,
> Poor trembling mortals you relieve;
> And wield the sword of truth so well
> That error and her crew you quell.

It is to your precursor, [Pierre] Bayle, and to yourself, indubitably, that the glory is due of the revolution which has been effected in the human mind. But let us confess the truth—this revolution is not complete; the bigots have their partisans: and it never will be completed, except by superior force. The sentence which must crush the *infamous*—must be pronounced by government. Enlightened ministers may greatly contribute, but the will of the sovereign must be added. This no doubt will happen in time, but neither you nor I will be the spectators of the so much wished for moment.

Potsdam, 5 September 1777

I am returned from Silesia where I have been very well satisfied. Agriculture is making a very sensible progress there, and manufactures prosper. We have exported linens to the amount of five millions and cloths to the amount of one million two hundred thousand crowns. A cobalt mine has been discovered among the mountains which will supply all Silesia. We make vitriol equal to that which is imported, and a very industrious man there manufactures indigo not inferior to that which is brought from India. An excellent method is found for the hardening of steel, and one much more simple than that proposed by Reaumur. Since the year 1756, which was the year before the war, our population has increased one hundred and eighty thousand souls. In fine, all the scourges which had laid this poor country desolate are vanished as if they had never been, and I own I feel a sweet satisfaction in seeing a province recover from such distress.

MEMOIRS FOR THE YEAR 1774

When a country has but few products to export and is obliged to have recourse to the industry of its neighbors, the balance of trade must necessarily be unfavorable to such a country; it must pay more money to foreigners than it receives; and, if the practice is continued, it will necessarily, after a certain number of years, find itself destitute of specie. If money be daily taken out of a purse into which money is not again returned it must soon be emptied. . . .

To obviate the inconveniency there were no other means than those of increasing the manufactures. The peculiar products of any country are wholly gain, and the price of workmanship, at the least, is gained from foreigners. These maxims, as true as they are palpable, served as principles to the government [of Prussia], and according to these were all the operations of trade directed. Thus, in the year 1773, there were two hundred and sixty-four new manufactories. Among others, there were a porcelain manufactory established at Berlin, the workmanship of which, while it afforded subsistence to five hundred persons, soon surpassed the Saxon porcelain. A snuff manufactory was formed, which was put under the direction of a company. This company had warehouses in all the provinces, which supplied the consumption of those provinces, and gained by the sale of leaf tobacco, which must have been purchased from Virginia, from foreigners. The revenues of the crown were increased and the proprietors were paid ten percent for their capitals.

15. GUSTAVUS III: SPEECH TO THE SWEDISH RIKSDAG*

Gustavus III (r. 1771–92), son of Adolphus Frederick, King of Sweden, and Queen Ulrica Eleanore (sister of Frederick the Great) was a high-spirited and intelligent prince. He spoke French as a second language, corresponded with the encyclopedists, and wrote a number of plays and poems. Gustavus' cultural pursuits seemed ill-calculated to prepare him for political intrigue in Stockholm. The Swedish parliament (*Riksdag*) was dominated by the higher nobility which had gained so much political control that they were accustomed to use a metal stamp of the King's signature without even making a pretense of gaining his approval for decrees. It was rumored, quite correctly, that Frederick of Prussia and Catherine of Russia had signed a secret agreement to preserve the weak Swedish constitution which facilitated political decentralization. The two monarchs could thus hope to pursue their own policies in the Baltic area with little interference.

In view of the dismemberment of Poland, many Swedes hoped for another Gustavus Vasa or Gustavus Adolphus to pull the nation together under a strong monarch before Swedish territory was also partitioned. On August 19, 1772, with the help of his brothers and a group of army officers, Gustavus III staged a military coup d'état. The King's action in overthrowing the corrupt regime of squabbling nobles was warmly and enthusiastically endorsed by the army and the general populace. Taken by surprise, the nobility was unable to resist the pressure of public opinion. Gustavus III re-established the authority of the Swedish Crown. Fortunately for the new monarch, both Frederick and Catherine were too involved in Poland to take military action against him. They were forced to content themselves with letters of protest which Gustavus ignored. In the following speech to the *Riksdag* on August 21, 1772, what reasons did King Gustavus give for the necessity of altering the constitution of Sweden? What charges did he level against the Swedish nobility? What views of monarchy and patriotism did he express? Compare his ideas with the political thought of his uncle, Frederick the Great.

Nobles and People of Sweden: . . .

It is a melancholy but well-known truth that hatred and discord have torn the realm: the people have been for a long time severed by two parties, divided as it were into two separate nations, united only in the mangling of their parent country. You know how this discord has produced rancour, rancour revenge, revenge persecution, and persecution new revolutions, which grew at last into a periodical disease, disfiguring and humiliating the whole commonwealth. Such commotions have shaken the realm for the sake of a few people's ambition; streams of blood have flowed, poured out sometimes by one party, and sometimes by another; and always the people have been sacrificed to quarrels. . . . The only end of the rulers has been to fortify their own power: all has of necessity been adapted to that purpose often at the expense of their fellow citizens, always at that of the country. Where the law was clear, the letter of it has been perverted; where it was palpably repugnant, it has been broken through. Nothing has been sacred to a people inflamed with hatred and re-

* *The Annual Register for the Year 1772* (London, 1773), pp. 243–46.

venge; and the seeds of confusion have in the end spread so far, it has become a declared opinion that a majority [in the *Riksdag*] is above [the] law and owns no restraint but its own pleasure.

Thus liberty, the noblest of the rights of men, has been transformed into an insupportable aristocratical tyranny in the hands of the ruling party which was itself enslaved and led at pleasure by a very small number of its body. The notice of a new assembly of the states has made every one tremble: far from considering how the affairs of the nation might best be transacted, they have been only busied in getting together a majority for their party, that they might be screened from the insolence and lawless violence of the other. If the interior situation of the realm stood thus endangered, how hideous was its external aspect! I blush to speak about it. Born a Swede and a king of Sweden it should be an impossibility for me to believe that foreign schemes could govern Swedish men; nay more, that the very basest means should have been employed for that purpose. You know what it is I mean. My blushes ought to make you deeply sensible into what contempt the kingdom has been thrown by your quarrels.

Such was the situation wherein I found this kingdom when I received by the decrees of the Divine Providence the Swedish scepter. Your heart will tell you I have spared no pains to unite you: in all my speeches from the throne and on all other occasions I have insisted upon concord and submission to the law: I have given up as well what might concern me as a man as what might be dear to me as a king. I have held no obligation too difficult to submit to, no steps too rugged to pass in order to reach an end so valuable to my parent country. If there be one among you who can deny this solemn truth, let him freely stand up and speak.

I formed a hope that these endeavours on my part would have released you from those chains which foreign gold, intestine hatred, and avowed licentious-ness were on the point to fix on you; and that the hideous examples of other countries thus enslaved might have afforded you a threatening warning: but all has been in vain. You have been misguided on one part by your leaders, and on the other inflamed by your private animosities. All senses have been trampled to the earth, all stipulations broken; licentiousness has had its free course and has run on with the more violence. . . . The most virtuous, the most deserving, the first, and highest of your fellow citizens have been sacrificed; veterans in office, men of known capacity and long-tried faith have been de-graded; whole magistracies have been suspended; nay, even the people crushed: their just complaints have been tortured into sedition and liberty itself at length transformed into an aristocratic yoke no Swede can bear. Even the most High has appeared in anger at the unrighteousness of those who governed; the earth refused its natural increase and famine and distress fell heavy on the whole country. Yet even then, far from endeavouring at a timely remedy, when I insisted on such measures, you appeared more attentive to exert your own vengeances than to find measures of relief for your constituents: nor could neces-sity itself oblige you to look into the distress of a miserable people till it was very, very near too late. In this manner was a whole year spent under one diet, burdensome to the country, yet destitute of any good effect. My representations to you proved all in vain, all my endeavours fruitless. I waited in silence, full of grief for the distress of my country, to see what the nation would think of this conduct of its representatives toward me and toward themselves. Part have submitted to the tyranny with sighs; but in silence, not knowing where help could be found, or by what means to seek it, despair has seized one corner of the kingdom and there they have taken up arms. In this situation, when the whole country, when true liberty and just security (not to speak of the danger of my own life), when all was thus at stake, I saw no other way, next after the assistance of the Divine Providence, but to apply to those measures which have freed other generous and resolute nations, and which formerly freed Sweden herself from unsufferable oppression, under the conduct of Gustavus Vasa. God has been pleased to bless my undertaking. . . . All has succeeded happily and I have saved my parent country and myself without injury to one single fellow citizen.

You are greatly mistaken if you believe that there has been any other aim but liberty and law. I have promised to govern a free people; this vow is more sacred as it was voluntary and what has happened shall never lead me from a purpose which was not founded merely on necessity, but also on conviction. Far from affecting liberty, it is licentiousness I shall destroy, and with it that arbitrary sway with which this country has been ruled, transforming all into an orderly and settled government such as the ancient Swedish laws establish and such as Sweden before enjoyed under my greatest predecessors.

This is the purpose I have had . . . to establish a true liberty which alone can render you, my dear subjects, a happy people; by security under the law, and by the law in all your possessions, by the exercise of all honest professions, by an impartial distribution of justice, by regular order in cities and throughout the country, by careful endeavours to promote the common good, by giving to every one the enjoyment of it in peace and safety, and, to crown all, by a true piety free from hypocrisy and superstition. All this can be obtained alone by establishing for the government of the kingdom a fixed, unalterable law whose very letter must not be perverted, which must bind not the king alone but must bind in the same manner also the states, and which must be incapable of being repealed or altered otherwise than by the free consent of both: which shall permit a sovereign, zealous for the prosperity of his country to confer with the states without their looking on him as an object of terror, and which shall finally unite together the king and the states in one common interest, the welfare of the kingdom. . . .

16. FREDERICK II: MEMOIRS ON THE PARTITION OF POLAND*

The partition of Poland stands out as a cynical piece of international knavery even for the eighteenth century. The first division of Polish territory among the three rapacious sovereigns was signed in August 1772, "in the Name of the Holy and Most Sacred Trinity," for the pious purpose of "preserving the

---

* *Posthumous Works of Frederick II, King of Prussia. Memoirs from the Peace of Hubertusburg, to the Partition of Poland, and of the Bavarian War*, trans. Thomas Holcroft (London, 1789), IV, 45–47, 57–61, 85–88.

Polish State." The ruling class in the Polish Republic consisted of nobles—magnates and *szlachta* (gentry)—who dominated the burghers and peasants. Consisting of about 10 per cent of the total population, the nobles elected and controlled the Polish kings through a sovereign Diet. The nobility clung so tenaciously to their notions of equality that a single factious member could exercise veto power (*liberum veto*) and "explode" the Diet. Under such an anarchical constitution, the elected kings of the Polish Republic stood little chance of wielding effective authority, and the country was helpless in the face of greedy neighbors who, quite naturally, took delight in pledging to preserve the constitution in its traditional form.

Frederick the Great made no effort to conceal his true motives when he marked the successful conclusion of negotiations among Russians, Prussians, and Austrians with a blasphemous jest: "This will unite three religions [Orthodox, Lutheran, and Catholic]. We communicate in the Eucharistic Body of Poland; and if it is not for the good of our souls, it is for the good of our countries." Frederick took Polish Prussia, minus Danzig and Thorn, with perhaps a million inhabitants; Catherine took White Russia with a population of about two million; and Maria Theresa absorbed Galicia and its three million people. What, in Frederick's view, were the underlying causes for the partition, and what purposes did it serve? Why did the court of Vienna initially hesitate to join the Russians and Prussians? By what diplomatic means did Frederick attempt to cement his alliance with the Russians? What pressures were employed to persuade the Polish Diet to ratify the partition treaty?

While Vienna abounded in projects, and Hungary in armed men, an Austrian corps entered Poland and seized on the lordship of Zips, on which the court had pretended claims. A step so daring astonished the court of Petersburg; and it was this which most promoted the partition treaty, which afterward was concluded between the three powers. The principal reason was that of avoiding a general war, which was on the eve of bursting forth; beside which it was necessary to maintain a balance of power between three such near neighbors; and, as the court of Vienna sufficiently gave it to be understood that she meant to profit by the present troubles, to effect her own aggrandisement, the King was under the necessity of following her example.

Irritated that any troops except her own should dare to give law to Poland, the Empress of Russia informed Prince Henry [Frederick's brother and representative at St. Petersburg] that, if it were the purpose of the court of Vienna to dismember Poland, the other neighbors of that kingdom had a right to do the same. The overture was made a-propos; for, all circumstances examined, this was the only remaining mode of avoiding new troubles, and giving everyone satisfaction. Russia might indemnify herself for the expenses of her war with the Turks; and, instead of Wallachia and Moldavia, which she could only hope to possess after having been as victorious over the Austrians as she had been over the Ottomans, [Wallachia and Moldavia, part of present-day Rumania, controlled the mouths of the river Danube and hence were of great interest to Austria], she had only to choose a province of Poland, such as might please her, and in which choice she would encounter no new perils. To the Empress-Queen a province in the vicinity of Hungary might be assigned; and to the King, that part of Polish Prussia which separated the states of Prussia-royal; while, by this equilibruim of the political balance, the three powers would remain in a nearly equivalent state of strength. . . .

Though every court was active, the dilatoriness and irresolution of the Russians retarded the conclusion of the treaty of dismemberment. The negotiation chiefly stopped at the possession of the city of Danzig. The Russians pretended that they had guaranteed the freedom of this petty republic; but in reality it was the English who, jealous of the Prussians, protected the liberties of that maritime town; and who encouraged the Empress of Russia in refusing her consent to the demands of his Prussian majesty. It was nevertheless necessary for the King to determine; and, as it was evident that the possession of the Vistula, and the port of Danzig, would in time also subject the city, it was thought proper not to delay a negotiation so important for an advantage which, in reality, was but deferred; for which reason his majesty desisted from his demand.

After much lingering, the ultimatum of the court of Petersburg was received (January the 12th). The Russians continued to insist on the considerable concessions which they demanded from the Prussians, should the Austrians declare war. However offensive such inequalities were, however disproportionate to the aid which allies in reality mutually owe each other, as the Empress-Queen was known at the time to be in a more favorable and pacific temper than she had been, these considerations ceased to continue of importance, when a treaty so advantageous was to be concluded; and the Russians were promised concessions which, after such a treaty, never could be called in question.

(February 17th) Obstacles so numerous being removed, the secret convention was at length signed at Petersburg. The Russian acquisitions were such as we have described them; the cities of Danzig and Thorn, and their territories excepted. By this partition, the court of Petersburg acquired a very considerable district in Poland, extending along its ancient frontiers, from the Dvina as far as the Dniester. The time fixed on for taking possession was the month of June; and it was agreed to invite the Empress-Queen to join the two contracting powers, and to make herself a party in the dismemberment. Russia and Prussia guaranteed their respective acquisitions, and promised to act in concert at the diet of Warsaw, that they might obtain the consent of the republic to all these concessions. The King further engaged, by a secret article, to send twenty thousand men into Poland, who were to join the Russians, should the war become general. His majesty further pledged himself openly to declare against the house of Austria, if this should not be found sufficient. . . . Russia also agreed to maintain an army of fifty thousand men in Poland, in order to assist the King with all her powers, after the war with the Ottomans should be terminated; and in fine to continue this aid till such time as, by a general pacification, a suitable compensation could be procured for Prussia. A separate convention was added to all these articles to regulate the reciprocal maintenance of the auxiliary troops.

This work, which was to serve as a basis to the projects that were to ensue, being terminated, it now remained to persuade the court of Vienna to join the two contracting powers. There were three parties formed in that court, and which were of three different opinions. The Emperor was desirous of regaining in Hungary those provinces which his ancestors had lost by the peace of Belgrade. The Empress, his mother, no longer possessed of that energy and fortitude of which she had given so many examples in her youth and who began to addict herself to mystical devotion, reproached herself with the blood which her past wars had shed. She detested war, and wished to purchase peace, be the price what it might. Prince Kaunitz, endowed with an accurate judgment, who wished to unite the interests of the monarchy with the inclination of his mistress, consequently found himself obliged to choose between war or the dismemberment of Poland; and had further to dread that, should he determine on the latter, the union between the houses of Bourbon and Austria, which he regarded as his masterpiece would have an end. On one side, the Prussian cavalry, remounted with such promptitude, gave him cause to understand that the King was decisive in his measures; on the other, he saw his majesty was desirous of a general pacification, to effect which he ardently labored.

In fine the King told the Austrian envoy, during a conference between them, that his majesty congratulated the Empress-Queen for having at that moment the destiny of Europe in her power; because that, in reality, peace or war, under the present circumstances, depended on her actions. . . .

. . . It was the King who, by his efforts, occasioned the choice which the Empress (Catherine of Russia) made of a daughter-in-law to alight on the princess of Darmstadt, own sister to the princess of Prussia. If influence was to be preserved in Russia, it was necessary persons should reside there who were connected with Prussia. When the prince of Prussia should ascend the throne, it was to be hoped he might hence derive great advantages. M. von Asseburg, a subject of the King, and who had passed into the service of the Empress, was commissioned to make a tour through the courts of Germany, in which there were marriageable princesses, and to give in his report. He chose the princess of Darmstadt, who was designed for the consort of the grand duke.

While the marriage festivals were celebrating in the city of Petersburg, the diet of Poland assembled at Warsaw. The three courts there published a manifesto, with a deduction of their claims. They demanded that the King (of Poland) and the Republic should: (1.) Sign the treaty of cession in favor of the three courts. (2.) The pacification of Poland. (3.) Set apart a fixed sum for the support of their king. (4.) Should establish a permanent council. (5.) Appoint a stable fund by which the Republic might maintain thirty thousand men.

At the same time each power sent a corps of ten thousand men into Poland. Each, in like manner, sent a general to Warsaw. The name of the Austrian general was Richecourt, of the Russian Bibikow, of the Prussian Lentulus. They had orders to act in concert, and to chastize the grandees who should attempt to cabal, or be any let to the innovations which were intended to be made on their country.

At the beginning the Poles were [obstinate]; they treated whatever was proposed with repugnance, and the nuncios from the palatinates did not arrive at Warsaw. Fatigued by these delays and this obstinacy, the court of Vienna proposed to fix a day for the assembling of the diet, with a menace that, if the nuncios should fail to be present, the three courts, without further loss of time, would dismember the whole kingdom. But it was likewise added that, out of regard to them, if they should give indications of their docility, as soon as the act of cession should be signed, the three powers would withdraw their troops from the territories of the Republic.

Scarcely was this declaration published before all acted as if there had been no constraint. The diet assembled on the 19th of April; the treaty of cession was approved and signed first with the Austrian, afterward with the Russians, and that of Prussia on the 18th of September. It was agreed that commissaries should be sent to regulate the frontiers. The Republic in favor of his majesty renounced its right to the reversion of the kingdom of Prussia, and on the fiefs of Lauenburg, Butow, and Draheim. Several articles of the treaty of Welau were abolished, and all the remaining provinces were guaranteed to Poland. The King further promised to preserve the Catholic religion, in his portion of the dismemberment, in the state in which he found it; and the articles which related to trade were referred to separate acts. This treaty, and those of the other courts, were at first only signed by the two marshals of the confederation, the president of the delegation, and the ambassadors of the three powers. These ambassadors began afterward to treat with the members of the delegation. The creation of a permanent council was agreed on, but the discussions concerning it, which must necessarily be long and circumstantial, were remitted to succeeding assemblies. . . .

17. PRINCESS DE LAMBALLE: SECRET MEMOIRS*

The Princess de Lamballe (1749–92) was the devoted friend of the future queen of France, Marie Antoinette, whom she served first as lady-in-waiting and eventually as superintendant of the royal household after 1774. Familiar with court life at both Vienna and Paris, the Princess kept a detailed diary about the events of her time and the personalities whom she met. What major tool of diplomacy was employed by the Empress-Queen? What was the Princess de Lamballe's opinion of Maria Theresa's policies?

The character of Maria Theresa, the Empress-mother of Maria Antoinette, is sufficiently known. The same spirit of ambition and enterprise which had already animated her contentions with France in the latter part of her career impelled her to wish for its alliance. In addition to other hopes, she had been encouraged to imagine that Louis XV might one day aid her in recovering the provinces which the King of Prussia had violently wrested from her ancient dominions. She felt the many advantages to be derived from a union with her ancient enemy, and she looked for its accomplishment by the marriage of her daughter.

Policy, in sovereigns, is paramount to every other consideration. They regard beauty as a source of profit, like managers of theaters, who, when a female candidate is offered, ask whether she is young and handsome—not whether she has talent. Maria Theresa believed that her daughter's beauty would have proved more powerful over France than her own armies. Like Catherine II, her

* Princess de Lamballe, *Secret Memoirs* (Washington: M. Walter Dunne, 1901), pp. 15–18.

envied contemporary, she consulted no ties of nature in the disposal of her children; a system more in character where the knout is the logician than among nations boasting higher civilization: indeed her rivalry with Catherine even made her grossly neglect their education. Jealous of the rising power of the North, she saw that it was the purpose of Russia to counteract her views in Poland and Turkey through France, and so totally forgot her domestic duties in the desire to thwart the ascendency of Catherine that she often suffered eight or ten days to go by without even seeing her children, allowing even the essential sources of instruction to remain unprovided. . . .

The Archduchess Carolina . . . when deemed adequately qualified was sent to Naples, where she certainly never forgot she was an Austrian nor the interest of the Court of Vienna. One circumstance concerning her and her mother fully illustrates the character of both. On the marriage, the Archduchess found that Spanish etiquette did not allow the Queen to have the honor of dining at the same table as the King. She apprised her mother. Maria Theresa instantly wrote to the Marchese Tonucei, then Prime Minister at the Court of Naples, to say that if her daughter, now Queen of Naples, was to be considered less than the King, her husband, she would send an army to fetch her back to Vienna, and the King might purchase a Georgian slave, for an Austrian princess should not be thus humbled. Maria Theresa need not have given herself all this trouble, for before the letter arrived the Queen of Naples had dismissed all the ministry, upset the cabinet of Naples, and turned out even the King himself from her bedchamber! So much for the overthrow of Spanish etiquette by Austrian policy. The King of Spain became outraged at the influence of Maria Theresa, but there was no alternative.

The other daughter of the Empress was married, as I have observed already, to the Duke of Parma, for the purpose of promoting the Austrian strength in Italy against that of France, to which the Court of Parma, as well as that of Modena, had been long attached.

The fourth Archduchess [the other one, Josepha, had died of smallpox] Maria Antoinette, being the youngest and most beautiful of the family, was destined for France. There were three other than Marie Antoinette; but she, being much lovelier than her sisters, was selected on account of her charms. Her husband was never considered by the contrivers of the scheme: he was known to have no say whatever, not even in the choice of his own wife! But the character of Louis XV was recollected, and calculations drawn from it upon the probable power which youth and beauty might obtain over such a King and Court. . . .

Chapter Two

AN ERA OF REVOLUTION

THE crackle of muskets at Lexington-Concord signified the beginning of a new relationship between Britain and her American colonies, but the crash of falling masonry at the Paris Bastille in 1789 more dramatically symbolized the changes sweeping across late eighteenth-century Europe. Few events have so thoroughly captured the public imagination as the French Revolution (1789–99) and its Napoleonic postscript (1799–1815). Perhaps because Western man's ideals, passions, and frailties seemed to be dramatized in capsule form throughout that quarter-century, the date 1789 has often been used as a dividing line between historical epochs.

Nineteenth-century scholars tended to see the French Revolution either as an example of oppressed masses rising in revolt against tyrannical masters, or as a case study of senseless rebellion destroying the old order without being able to provide a workable replacement. After nearly two centuries of debate and investigation, there exist no universally satisfying explanations of why the Revolution began and what it meant to the future of Europe. Clearly, revolutions of such dimensions are highly complex from beginning to end, often effecting sweeping changes with little regard for long-range consequences.

By the middle of the eighteenth century, voices of dissent could be heard in France. The governments of Louis XV (r. 1715–74) and Louis XVI (r. 1774–92) vacillated between the extremes of tyranny and enlightened despotism, and a growing body of critics urged reforms which would benefit their special interests. The French aristocracy became increasingly aggressive in the 1770's in their attempt to regain some of the political power which they had gradually lost to the central government in the seventeenth and eighteenth centuries. The prosperous bourgeoisie, who had traditionally sought to use its wealth to join the privileged classes, found that social mobility seemed to disappear after mid-century and became increasingly restive. The major ideas of the *philosophes* had been published by the 1760's and a portion of the bourgeoisie gradually became more receptive to the abstract criticisms of the *ancien régime* proffered by intellectuals.

The French economy was relatively prosperous. Nevertheless, the national wealth was unevenly shared, and the economy went through cyclical slumps which laid hardships on both the privileged and non-privileged classes. The government of Louis XVI, plagued by military expenses and a hopelessly inadequate tax system, fumbled for new solutions to old problems. Successive ministers urged the Crown to broaden the tax base by taxing the privileged classes, a proposal resisted by both clergy and aristocracy. Finally, as the nation's temper grew more bitter, and in the face of mounting fiscal problems, Louis XVI agreed to call a meeting of the almost forgotten Estates-General (which had last met in 1614). The air of gloom and hostility which had hovered over France seemed to dissipate in the winter of 1788–89 as the nation turned to the first election of an Estates-General in 175 years.

Following the selection of deputies, often through complicated electoral procedures, the three estates came together in the late spring of 1789. An immediate squabble over voting procedures laid bare a power struggle among the estates which reached a climax with the formation of a National Assembly dominated by the Third Estate along with a few sympathizers from the other orders. Louis XVI, in agreeing to a meeting of the Estates-General, had assumed that the purpose of the assembly would be to supply revenues needed to restore financial solvency to the royal treasury; the aristocracy had assumed that it would speak for the nation and for the other estates, bargaining increased taxation for a share of political authority. Neither assumption was correct, and the National Assembly found itself in the process of writing a constitution for France—a reflection of the Crown's inability to direct or lead the Assembly.

Between 1792 and 1815 the French Revolution passed through several phases against a background of continuous wars that mingled the joyous refrains of the "Marseillaise" with the piteous cries of the dying. A constitutional monarchy, the seeming embodiment of the finest ideals of the *philosophes,* gave way in 1792 to a republic charged with revolutionary fervor and pressed by threats of invasion from without and treason from within. Although republican leaders succeeded in ending the danger of foreign invasion, and the domestic threat became increasingly obscure, a Reign of Terror carried the Revolution to new extremes. Then, with little security left even for supporters of the Terror, a counterrevolution occurred. A moderate republican interlude known as the Directory (1795–99) muddled along until General Napoleon Bonaparte seized power.

The Directory was replaced by the Consulate, a thinly disguised military dictatorship dominated by Napoleon as First Consul. In 1802, at Napoleon's suggestion, the Senate made him Consul for life. France had again fallen under an authoritarian regime, even if most Frenchmen were not yet aware of the fact, and it was a simple matter for Bonaparte to consign the Consulate to oblivion and rule openly as Emperor after 1804. At home Napoleon moved with speed and confidence. His able bureaucracy put France on a new foundation, establishing a more satisfactory relationship between Church and State, economic stability and a solid currency, equality before the law through codification of the law, and educational reforms. Ruling with a tight rein and a strong hand, Napoleon was confident of general public support.

Domestic reforms were Napoleon's greatest contribution to the future of France, but it was in the realm of foreign policy and war that he made a lasting impression on Europe. Like Charlemagne before him, and Adolf Hitler more than a century later, the French Emperor saw his authority expand in seemingly endless waves until virtually the whole of Europe lay at his feet. Only England, Spain, and finally, Russia, seemed able to resist Napoleon's legions. Finally, however, the combined armies of the continental powers and Britain defeated him in 1813–14. Returning from exile to seize power briefly in 1815, Napoleon was again defeated, and a Bourbon monarchy was restored in France.

The impact on Europe of events in tumultuous France between 1789 and 1815 varied from country to country. In the beginning, there was a tendency outside France to see a Jacobin under every bush and bed, yet many intellectuals and members of the bourgeoisie welcomed the Revolution. To conservative and reactionary monarchs, the revolutionary slogan of Liberty, Equality, and Fraternity was a dangerous threat to the status quo, but to many of their subjects it was a call for the end of feudal privilege and of ancient and outmoded institutions. Few French agents were actually sent to stir revolutionary action in foreign lands, but French armies carried the seeds of change across the Continent. Napoleon, who reorganized the Germanies, found that he had helped to stimulate German nationalism among the very people to whom he had brought the enlightened administration of the French imperial system. Spanish nationalism made the Iberian peninsula a difficult battleground for French armies and helped to spearhead the Emperor's defeat. The general reaction to two decades of war also contributed to a momentary decline in revolutionary enthusiasm. Even before the decisive events of 1812–15, the popularity of peace was a counterbalance to revolutionary promises.

In retrospect, the French Revolution was not as unique as contemporary observers believed. It was the most dramatic and far-reaching movement for reform and change in the eighteenth century, but it was only a part of the new ideas, changing economic patterns, and altered political concepts sweeping the Western world.

A DECADE OF REVOLUTION

1. PROTEST OF THE COUR DES AIDES, MAY 6, 1775*

The crisis of 1789 had been brewing for decades. Protests and proposals for reform appeared with increasing frequency after the death of Louis XIV. Such complaints were usually framed by the most aggressive segment of the French society, the aristocracy. Concerned with its loss of political authority, and often looking back to the glory of feudalism in an age when industrialization was beginning to change the face of western Europe, the French nobility considered itself the voice of the nation in treating with the Crown.

During the reign of Louis XVI (r. 1774–92), the *Parlement* of Paris (a semi-judicial body with the traditional power of approving royal decrees) frustrated attempts by royal ministers to revamp the tax structure. The *Parlement* insisted

---

* "Protest of the Cour des aides of Paris, April 10, 1775," trans. Grace Reade Robinson in James Harvey Robinson, ed., *Translations and Reprints from the Original Sources of European History* (Philadelphia: University of Pennsylvania, 1899), vol. V, no. 2, pp. 77–83, 86–87, 92–93, 98–100, 105, 145.

that taxing the privileged classes was a violation of French liberty and constitutional rights and that the nation as a whole had to be consulted before such a drastic step as broadening the tax base could be enacted into law. The nobility eventually paid with its titles and lands and special privileges for its assumption that the first and third estates would follow aristocratic leadership in 1789.

In the spring of 1775 the *Cour des aides* in Paris presented the king with a detailed exposé of abuses in legal practice and taxation. The *Cour des aides*, a tribunal which dated back at least to the fifteenth century, was responsible for trying lawsuits involving the tax farmers as well as cases concerning the exemptions and privileges of nobility and clergy in tax questions.

The farming of taxes was a practice whereby the government sold the right to collect taxes to individuals or corporations in return for a guaranteed sum paid to the national treasury, and the Farmers-General then sublet the bill to be collected to agents. There was a sharp difference between the amount of taxes collected and the amount of moneys received by the royal treasury. What specific criticisms were leveled against "farmed taxes" in the protest? What was a *lettre de cachet*, and how might it be abused?

MOST HUMBLE AND MOST RESPECTFUL PROTEST

*Presented to the King, our most honored Sovereign and
Lord, by those who hold his Cour des aides at Paris
Paris, May 6, 1775*

Sire:

1. . . . It is the cause of the people which we must now plead before the tribunal of your Majesty. We must present a faithful picture to you of the taxes and dues which are levied in your kingdom, and which constitute the subject-matter of the jurisdiction confided to us; we must make known to your Majesty at the beginning of your reign the real condition of the people, whom the spectacle of a brilliant court can never call to your mind. . . . Our Nation, Sire, has always proved its devotion to its masters by its strenuous efforts to maintain the splendor of their throne; but Your Majesty should at least know what these enormous contributions are costing the unhappy people.

2. A careful examination of all the taxes would, however, involve an infinite amount of labor, which your Majesty cannot yourself undertake. We will therefore submit special communications on each subject, and your Majesty may hand them over for consideration to those whom you may choose to honor with your confidence. . . .

6. The first matter which we have to lay before your Majesty is that class of imposts known as the "farmed taxes." We are not imparting anything new to you, Sire, when we assert that these taxes are not so onerous by reason of the actual sums paid by the people into the royal treasury, as on account of the cost of administration and the profits of the Farmers of the revenue, which are assuredly too great, since the Ministers of the previous reign were able to appropriate a part of this profit, not indeed for the benefit of Your Majesty, but in order to bestow it upon their favorites. This fact, which is in everybody's mouth, cannot be unknown to your Majesty.

7. You are aware also that aside from the money taken from your subjects

the State is deprived, through the farming of the taxes, of the services of a large number of citizens, part of whom are occupied in perpetrating frauds, and the rest in trying to prevent them. . . .

8. Neither can your Majesty be unaware that in addition to the taxation of individual commodities the production of certain of them is either forbidden or embarrassed throughout the country in the interest of the Farm. . . .

11. But there is still another sort of tyranny, of which it is possible that your Majesty has never heard. Although it does not afford so cruel a spectacle as that of which we have been speaking, . . . it affects all the citizens of the lowest class, those who live quietly by labor or trade. It is due to the circumstance that every man belonging to the people is forced to submit daily to the caprices, the insolence, even the insults of the minions of the Tax-farmer. This particular kind of annoyance has never received much attention, because it is only experienced by the obscure and unknown . . . it is precisely by means of this consideration for the Great that the Farm has been able to subject the defenceless people to an unrestrained and unlimited despotism. Yet this unprotected class is the largest in your realm, and the defenceless certainly have the first claim to the direct protection of your Majesty.

12. It devolves upon us, therefore, to explain to your Majesty the real cause of the servitude to which the people are reduced throughout the provinces. That cause, Sire, is to be sought in the nature of the power exercised by the officers of the Farm—a power arbitrary in many respects, which makes it only too easy for them to render themselves formidable.

13. In the first place, the General Farm has an enormous body of rules and regulations, which have never been collected and codified. It is an occult science which no one except the Financiers themselves has studied, or can study, so that the individual against whom action is brought can neither know the law himself nor consult any one else; he is obliged to rely on the very same Clerk who is his enemy and persecutor. How can a laborer or an artisan help trembling and humbling himself continually before an adversary who has such terrible weapons to turn against him? . . .

18. . . . What we denounce to your Majesty is the arbitrary system of justice under which the people have groaned for a century past, and must continue to groan if protests are made only when the power is in the hands of those who have the will to abuse it. . . .

24. You will learn . . . to what extent the Financiers have abused their arbitrary power. . . . You will find that all such as come under the head of registration fees and the tax of the *centième denier* [a tax on real estate sales], taxes which are levied upon every contract entered into between citizens, are determined according to the fancy of the Farmer and his agents; that the supposed laws on these matters are so obscure and fragmentary that he who pays can never know what he really owes, that often the agent himself knows no more about it than the taxpayer, and interprets the law more or less rigorously according as he is more or less greedy; and that it is notorious that all these taxes may receive an extension under one Farmer and not under the others, from which it is evident that the Farmer is the sovereign legislator in matters where his own personal interests are concerned. . . .

25. Your Majesty will be aware that these extensions have of late been carried to an excess hitherto unknown; that the Farmer is no longer satisfied with learning the family secrets recorded in the legal documents which are drawn up from day to day, but pries into the records of the last twenty years on the pretext that the dues have not been exacted with the requisite strictness. . . .

27. The right of franc-fief—which is also called a domain due—is a due exacted from commoners or non-nobles for the fiefs they hold; it, too, has been included in the arbitrary system of justice. It consists of a year's revenue, which one pays every twentieth year in order to be left in peace for the other nineteen. But when there is a transfer during the twenty years the new possessor is obliged to pay the tax, although the former owner is given no indemnity for the years of exemption which he paid for and has not enjoyed—a usage which may now be sanctioned by some regulation, but which was certainly in the beginning an extortion. . . .

45. France . . . is crushed under the weight of taxes, and the rivalry of the Powers has led them to vie with each other in the enormous expenses which have rendered these taxes necessary; expenses are moreover doubled by a huge national debt contracted under previous reigns. Your Majesty must therefore remember that although your ancestors covered themselves with glory, that glory is being paid for by the present generation; that while they captivated all hearts by their liberality, and astonished Europe by their magnificence, that magnificence and that liberality were the origin of taxes and debts which still exist today. . . .

49. For the present, Sire, without venturing to propose to your Majesty a general reformation of the farmed taxes, special memoirs may be presented to you on various subjects, which may be discussed with your Ministers, . . . What we do ask at present of your Majesty personally is to institute an investigation into the manner in which all taxes were extended under the last ministry, . . .

64. Our hopes carry us still farther; for if your Majesty decides to have this investigation made, we do not doubt that you will improve the opportunity to establish certain principles in this matter where none have been recognized before. One thing at least will become apparent, that orders affecting the personal liberty of citizens should never be granted to private individuals, either for their personal interest or to avenge their private injuries; for in a country where there are laws individuals should have no need of extra-judicial orders; and, moreover, such orders granted to the powerful against the weak, with no chance of redress, constitute the worst form of injustice.

65. It may perhaps be thought that there are certain exceptional cases in which the public good requires acts of authority that are not clothed with the ordinary formalities of justice. It will be urged that it is sometimes desirable to furnish a substitute for the tardy course of justice, which might allow criminals to escape; that police control and the public safety in great cities make it necessary to keep some hold upon suspected persons, and that often public and family interest are at one in requiring the separation from society of an individual who might cause annoyance, and against whom there are no other proofs than those which are controlled by the family itself which is seeking to protect itself from the ignominy of a public trial.

66. But when all these considerations have been discussed in your presence, and all these abuses have been brought to your attention, you will see, Sire, that these are mere pretexts, which could never have furnished a sufficient justification for permitting the liberty of the citizen to be subjected to arbitrary authority, or that, at least, the right of protesting against wrongs should be secured to the oppressed. . . .

68. You will perceive that if the public safety demands that some hold shall be kept upon a person who has given just cause for suspicion, the legitimacy of these suspicions should be formally verified, in order that an innocent victim of such precautions may demand and obtain indemnity, or that he may at least know why, and by whom, these violent measures have been taken. . . .

70. The prisoner, whatever his crime, should be permitted to present his defense, and even to demand that the reasons for this severe order should be examined afresh by others than those who have issued it, and be reported upon anew to the King, who would naturally choose for this examination men of the most assured and unassailable reputation. But since it is very difficult and often impossible for a prisoner to reach the King himself, it would be necessary, from time to time, that all the royal prisons should be visited and all the existing *lettres de cachet*[1] reviewed by persons unconnected with the administration and of acknowledged integrity. . . .

89. General assemblies of the Nation have not been convened for a hundred and sixty years, and for a long time before that they were very infrequent, and, we venture to say, almost useless, since what should have rendered their presence especially necessary, namely, the fixing of the taxes, was accomplished without them. . . .

236. In regard to all these questions, Sire, there are necessarily two parties in the kingdom; all those, on the one hand, who are privileged to approach their Sovereign, and on the other, the rest of the Nation. Consequently, a King who loves justice must seek his motives in his own heart, and enlightenment in the hearts of the Nation. . . .

2. CAHIER OF THE THIRD ESTATE OF THE BAILLIAGE D'ÉTAIN*

In the summer of 1788 Louis XVI agreed to convoke a meeting of the Estates-General. The election of deputies began in February 1789, amid mounting confusion as to the objective of the assembly. Election practices were not uniform, though literally every Frenchman over twenty-five whose name was on the tax rolls was eligible to vote. Delegates of the First and Second Estates generally were elected directly by a meeting of members of their order in a particular

* "Cahier of the Third Estate of the Bailliage of Étain" in Beatrice F. Hyslop, *A Guide to the General Cahiers of 1789* (New York: Columbia University Press, 1936), pp. 297–301. Translated by the editors.

1. A *lettre de cachet* could authorize an arrest in the king's name, and could be used and abused quite arbitrarily. The most famous case, preceding the *Cour des aides* protest of 1775, involved the arrest of a merchant named Monnerat who was accused of smuggling. He was chained by his neck to the wall in a completely dark cell for a month, and then kept in a slightly better cell for a year and a half. Only then was it discovered that the wrong man had been arrested, and he was released. All attempts to receive an indemnity failed, however, as the tax farmers who had caused the arrest were able to block Monnerat's suit for damages.

district. But the election of Third Estate deputies was usually indirect, with the bourgeoisie often able to screen candidates and elect men of their own choice. As a result, the deputies of the Third Estate included many of the most talented and articulate members of the middle class; more than half were lawyers.

In addition to the election of deputies in 1789, a list of grievances (*Cahiers*), specifying both local and national complaints, was drawn up in each electoral district. The *Cahiers* of the clergy (First Estate) were generally reactionary, though some lists revealed a clash of views between the lower, more liberal, clergy and the more conservative clerical hierarchy. The *Cahiers* of the nobility (Second Estate) voiced criticisms of the Crown, the clergy, and even of the "nobles of the robe" who had achieved entry into the aristocracy comparatively recently. The following *Cahier* is typical of many drawn up by the Third Estate. What reforms did the *Cahier* recommend? Was the Third Estate urging revolution? Was the *Cahier* a revolutionary document?

CAHIER OF COMPLAINTS, GRIEVANCES, AND REMONSTRANCES OF THE THIRD ESTATE OF THE BAILLIAGE D'ÉTAIN TO BE CARRIED BEFORE THE ASSEMBLY WHICH WILL MEET AT BAR [-LE-DUC] ON MARCH 31, [1789], AND TO HIS MAJESTY AT THE ESTATES-GENERAL WHICH WILL MEET AT VERSAILLES IN APRIL.

Our complaints are great, but they are known; and because your Majesty wishes to search for the source, in order to rectify the situation, one must look to the subjects on whom will fall the following requests which we charge the deputies who represent us at the Estates-General to present for us, with confidence that they will do their utmost [in our behalf], and that they will be heard favorably by our good King.

They will ask, therefore, in the name of the *Bailliage d'Étain*

ARTICLE 1: That it [the Estates-General] proceed first to the drafting of Constitutional Laws.

ARTICLE 2: That the Estates-General continue to hold meetings periodically, as will be determined.

ARTICLE 3: That at the Estates-General the Third Estate be represented only by members of its own order.

ARTICLE 4: That the votes not be taken by head unless the deputies of the Third Estate outnumber those of the clergy and nobility combined, . . .

ARTICLE 6: That henceforth elevation to the Nobility shall be accorded solely for distinguished merit and not for money, and that governmental offices which carry noble rank be abolished as they become vacant, . . .

ARTICLE 7: That all laws which exclude the Third Estate from certain occupations or high church positions, civil or military, be abolished as unjust and injurious; . . .

ARTICLE 8: That members of the Third Estate be admitted, in such numbers as His Majesty deems proper, to all parts of the administration and even in the High Courts.

ARTICLE 9: That all forced labor such as [*corvées*] [a peasant tax involving forced labor on roads, the *corvée* was suppressed by Turgot in 1776 but revived generally as a money payment; the tax involved about thirty days of labor a year, with the peasants having to provide their own tools] . . . be abolished, or at least subject to purchase.

ARTICLE 11: That no *lettre de cachet* be granted without full deliberation.

ARTICLE 12: That, in all other cases, every citizen arrested must be taken before the proper judicial officials within twenty-four hours.

ARTICLE 13: That no assessments or new taxes be established without the consent of the Estates-General.

ARTICLE 14: That government Ministers be obliged to render an account for their use of public funds to His Majesty in the Estates-General.

ARTICLE 16: That no new pensions or gratuities be granted without the consent of the Estates-General.

ARTICLE 17: That the press shall be free.

ARTICLE 18: That the impositions of all kinds which fall only on the Third Estate [*Tailles, Corvées,* etc.], which are unnaturally heavy, be abolished.

ARTICLE 19: That all other taxes which do not fall equally and without discrimination on the three orders, . . . such as the *vingtième* tax, etc., be abolished.

ARTICLE 20: That hidden taxes, which fall only on the Third Estate, such as the charges of the *franc-fief,* etc., be abolished.

ARTICLE 21: That all taxes, disguised or not, under whatever name, which hinder commerce and distress the population, such as those included in the *ferme Générale,* the monopoly on Salt, Tobacco, etc., etc., . . . be suppressed.

ARTICLE 28: That neither under the pretext of annates, or other laws, shall money continue to be sent to Rome.

ARTICLE 30: That the Clergy take the necessary steps to eliminate the existing disparity between incomes from similar benefices, and that after having provided adequately for each according to their needs and the dignity of their rank, the remainder be applied to the needs of the State so long as no *curé* of the Kingdom receives less than 1200 *Livres* in income; . . .

ARTICLE 33: That all taxes necessary to carry out the responsibilities of the Kingdom be imposed without discrimination on the members of the Three Orders, proportionate to their means and ability to pay, and on all real estate without exception.

ARTICLE 40: That all exclusive privileges in industry and commerce be abolished.

ARTICLE 44: That all Offices which manifestly are a burden on the people and which serve no useful purpose, . . . be abolished.

ARTICLE 49: That there be but one standard system of weights and measurements, and but one denomination of money for all the Kingdom.

ARTICLE 52: That there shall be a uniform code of law for all the Kingdom.

ARTICLE 54: That the procedures of civil law be simplified and abbreviated. . . .

3. ABBÉ SIEYÈS: WHAT IS THE THIRD ESTATE?*

Convocation of the Estates-General was the beginning of Act One of the French Revolution, and among the many individuals who played key roles in the unfolding drama was an obscure clergyman, Emmanuel Joseph Sieyès (1748–1836). Part deist, part agnostic, more committed to reason and humanity than

* Abbé Sieyès, "What Is the Third Estate?" in John Hall Stewart, ed., *A Documentary Survey of the French Revolution* (New York: The Macmillan Co., 1951), pp. 42–44, 46, 51–52. Reprinted by permission.

to orthodox Christianity, Abbé Sieyès had been frustrated by his failure to rise in church ranks. He was preparing to leave France for America when the meeting of the Estates-General was called. Sieyès was elected as a representative of the Third Estate rather than his own order. In January 1789 the Abbé unleashed a storm by publishing a small pamphlet entitled *What Is the Third Estate?* It was an immediate best seller and gave the bourgeois leaders of the Third Estate a rallying cry and a program.

Because the Estates-General had not met since 1614, lawyers had been forced to dig into royal archives to discover precisely how the nation should be represented and how the three orders should vote when in session. The aristocratic *Parlement* of Paris ruled that each of the Estates should have the same number of deputies and that each order should vote separately. Consistent with the *Parlement*'s intentions in urging a meeting of the Estates, the privileged classes were to have a majority and could veto any measures proposed by the Third Estate. Almost overnight, the popularity of the *Parlement* dropped to zero, and Sieyès' pamphlet (published only one month before the election of deputies commenced) cut to the heart of the vital question of representation and voting procedures. Contrast the tone of Sieyès' demands with the *Cahier*. What degree of "parity" did Sieyès ask for the Third Estate? On what grounds did he base his demand?

The plan of this pamphlet is very simple. We have three questions to ask:
1st. What is the third estate? Everything.
2nd. What has it been heretofore in the political order? Nothing.
3rd. What does it demand? To become something therein.

We shall see if the answers are correct. Then we shall examine the measures that have been tried and those which must be taken in order that the third estate may in fact become *something*. Thus we shall state:
4th. What the ministers have *attempted,* and what the privileged classes themselves *propose* in its favor.
5th. What *ought* to have been done.
6th. Finally, what *remains* to be done in order that the third estate may take its rightful place. . . .

It suffices here to have revealed that the alleged utility of a privileged order to public service is only a chimera; that without it, all that is arduous in such service is performed by the third estate; that without it, the higher positions would be infinitely better filled; that they naturally ought to be the lot of and reward for talents and recognized services; and that if the privileged classes have succeeded in usurping all the lucrative and honorary positions, it is both an odious injustice to the majority of citizens and a treason to the commonwealth.

Who, then, would dare to say that the third estate has not within itself all that is necessary to constitute a complete nation? It is the strong and robust man whose one arm remains enchained. If the privileged order were abolished, the nation would be not something less but something more. Thus, what is the third estate? Everything; but an everything shackled and oppressed. What would it be without the privileged order? Everything; but an everything free and flourishing. Nothing can progress without it; everything would proceed infinitely better without the others . . . the privileged classes, far from being useful to the nation, can only enfeeble and injure it; . . . moreover, the nobility does not belong to the social organization at all; indeed, it may be a *burden* upon the nation. . . .

What is a nation? a body of associates living under a *common* law and represented by the same *legislature*.

Is it not exceedingly clear that the noble order has privileges, exemptions, even rights separate from the rights of the majority of citizens? Thus it deviates from the common order, from the common law. Thus its civil rights already render it a people apart in a great nation. It is indeed *imperium in imperio*.

Also, it enjoys its political rights separately. It has its own representatives, who are by no means charged with representing the people. Its deputation sits apart; and when it is assembled in the same room with the deputies of ordinary citizens, it is equally true that its representation is essentially distinct and separate; it is foreign to the nation in principle, since its mandate does not emanate from the people, and in aim, since its purpose is to defend not the general but a special interest.

The third estate, then, comprises everything appertaining to the nation; and whatever is not the third estate may not be regarded as being of the nation. What is the third estate? Everything! . . .

. . . The true petitions of [the third estate] may be appreciated only through the authentic claims directed to the government by the large municipalities of the kingdom. What is indicated therein? That the people wishes to be *something,* and, in truth, the very least that is possible. It wishes to have real representatives in the Estates General, that is to say, deputies *drawn from its order,* who are competent to be interpreters of its will and defenders of its interests. But what will it avail it to be present at the Estates General if the predominating interest there is contrary to its own! Its presence would only consecrate the oppression of which it would be the eternal victim. Thus, it is indeed certain that it cannot come to vote at the Estates General unless it is to have in that body *an influence at least equal to that of the privileged classes;* and it demands a number of representatives equal to that of the first two orders together. Finally, this equality of representation would become completely illusory if every chamber voted separately. This third estate demands, then, that votes be taken *by head and not by order.* This is the essence of those claims so alarming to the privileged classes, because they believed that thereby the reform of abuses would become inevitable. The real intention of the third estate is to have an influence in the Estates General equal to that of the privileged classes. I repeat, can it ask less? And is it not clear that if its influence therein is less than equality, it cannot be expected to emerge from its political nullity and become *something?* . . .

The third estate awaits, to no purpose, the meeting of all classes, the restitution of its political rights, and the plenitude of its civil rights; the fear of seeing abuses reformed alarms the first two orders [clergy and aristocracy] far more than the desire for liberty inspires them. Between liberty and some odious privileges, they have chosen the latter. Their soul is identified with the favors of servitude. Today they dread this Estates General which but lately they invoked so ardently. . . .

The third estate must perceive in the trend of opinions and circumstances that it can hope for nothing except from its own enlightenment and courage. Reason and justice are in its favor; ... there is no longer time to work for the conciliation of parties. What accord can be anticipated between the energy of the oppressed and the rage of the oppressors?

They have dared pronounce the word secession. They have menaced the King and the people. Well! Good God! How fortunate for the nation if this so desirable secession might be made permanently! How easy it would be to dispense with the privileged classes! How difficult to induce them to be citizens! ...

In vain would they close their eyes to the revolution which time and force of circumstances have effected; it is none the less real. Formerly the third estate was serf, the noble order everything. Today the third estate is everything, the nobility but a word. ...

In such a state of affairs, what must the third estate do if it wishes to gain possession of its political rights in a manner beneficial to the nation? There are two ways of attaining this objective. In following the first, the third estate must assemble apart: it will not meet with the nobility and the clergy at all; it will not remain with them, either by *order* or by *head*. I pray that they will keep in mind the enormous difference between the assembly of the third estate and that of the other two orders. The first represents 25,000,000 men, and deliberates concerning the interests of the nation. The two others, were they to unite, have the powers of only about 200,000 individuals, and think only of their privileges. The third estate alone, they say, cannot constitute the *Estates General*. Well! So much the better! It will form a *National Assembly*. ...

4. ARTHUR YOUNG: TRAVELS IN FRANCE*

Few visitors to France immediately before and during the Revolution were as sensitive and acute as the British agriculturist Arthur Young (1741–1820). Because he believed that "the clouds have indicated a change in the political sky of France," and in order to see the French nation prior to such change, Young traveled through France in 1787, 1788, and 1789. His travel diary was alternately terse and rambling, jotted down in haste, as he walked or rode from village to village. On his last trip he witnessed the momentous changes taking place through the Estates-General; he concluded his *Travels* with an overview of France entitled *General Observations,* from which the following selections have been taken. Young was in sympathy with the revolutionary changes of 1789, but became an outspoken critic of developments in France as the Revolution gained momentum. In June 1789, he erroneously noted that "the whole business is over" and left Paris; thereafter, his disgust with the policies of the popular assembly mounted, for those policies ran counter to his own ideas of economic reform. What specific abuses did Young see as responsible for the rise of a revolutionary spirit in France? How did he justify the peasant uprising (Great Fear) of 1789? Could the Revolution, in his view, have been avoided?

The gross infamy which attended *lettres de cachet* [was thought of by many] as the most prominent feature of the despotism of France. They were certainly carried to an access [excess] hardly credible; to the length of being sold, with blanks to be filled up with names at the pleasure of the purchaser; who was

* Arthur Young, *Travels in France During the Years 1787, 1788, 1789* (London: G. Bell & Sons, Ltd., 1892), pp. 313–24.

thus able, in the gratification of private revenge, to tear a man from the bosom of his family, and bury him in a dungeon, where he would exist forgotten, and die unknown!—But such excesses could not be common in any country; and they were reduced almost to nothing, from the accession of the present King [Louis XVI]. The great mass of the people, by which I mean the lower and middle ranks, could suffer very little from such engines, . . . had there been nothing else to complain of, it is not probable they would ever have been brought to take arms. The abuses attending the levy of taxes were heavy and universal. The kingdom was parcelled into generalities, with an intendant at the head of each, into whose hands the whole power of the crown was delegated for every thing except the military authority; but particularly for all affairs of finance. The generalities were subdivided into elections, at the head of which was a *sub-delegué,* appointed by the intendant. The rolls of the *taille, capitation, vingtièmes,* and other taxes, were distributed among districts, parishes, and individuals, at the pleasure of the intendant, who could exempt, change, add, or diminish, at pleasure. Such an enormous power, constantly acting, and from which no man was free, might in the nature of things, degenerate in many cases into absolute tyranny. . . . Instances, and even gross ones, have been reported to me in many parts of the kingdom, that made me shudder at the oppression to which numbers must have been condemned, by the undue favours granted to such crooked influence. But, without recurring to such cases, what must have been the state of the poor people paying heavy taxes, from which the nobility and clergy were exempted? A cruel aggravation of their misery, to see those who could best afford to pay exempted. . . . The *corvées* or police of the roads, were annually the ruin of many hundreds of farmers; more than 300 were reduced to beggary in filling up one vale in Lorraine: all these oppressions fell on the *tiers état* [Third Estate] only; the nobility and clergy having been equally exempted from *tailles,* militia, and *corvées.* The penal code of finance makes one shudder at the horrors of punishment inadequate to the crime. A few features will sufficiently characterize the old government of France.

1. Smugglers of salt,[2] armed and assembled to the number of five, in Provence, *a fine of* 500 livres *and nine years gallies;*—in all the rest of the kingdom, *death.*

2. Smugglers armed, assembled, but in number under five, *a fine of* 300 livres *and three years gallies.* Second offence, *death.*

3. Smugglers, without arms, but with horses, carts, or boats; *a fine of* 300 livres *if not paid, three years gallies.* Second offence, 400 livres *and nine years gallies.*—In Dauphiné, second offence, *gallies for life.* In Provence, *five years gallies.* . . .

5. Women, married and single, smugglers, first offence, *a fine of* 100 livres. Second, 300 livres. Third, *flogged, and banished the kingdom for life. Husbands responsible both in fine and body.*

6. Children smugglers, the same as women.—*Fathers and mothers responsible; and for defect of payment flogged.* . . .

. . . Such were [some of] the exertions of arbitrary power which the lower orders felt directly from the royal authority; but, heavy as they were, it is a

---

2. Commerce in salt was a government monopoly.

question whether the others, suffered circuitously through the nobility and the clergy, were not yet more oppressive? Nothing can exceed the complaints made in the *cahiers* under this head. They speak of the dispensation of justice in the manorial courts, as comprizing every species of despotism: the districts indeterminate—appeals endless—irreconcilable to liberty and prosperity—augmenting litigations—favouring every species of chicane—ruining the parties—not only by enormous expences on the most petty objects, but by a dreadful loss of time. The judges commonly ignorant pretenders, who hold their courts in *cabarets,* and are absolutely dependent on the seigneurs, in consequence of their feudal powers. . . . The countryman is tyrannically enslaved by [feudal power]. Fixed and heavy rents; vexatious processes to secure them; appreciated unjustly to augment: rents, *solidaires,* and *revenchables; rents, chéantes,* and *levantes, fumages.* Fines at every change of the property, in the direct as well as collateral line; feudal redemption (*retraite*); fines on sale, to the 8th and even the 6th penny; redemptions (*rachats*) injurious in their origin, and still more so in their extension; . . . *corveés* by custom; *corveés* by usage of the fief; *corveés* established by unjust decrees; *corveés* arbitrary, and even phantastical; servitudes; collections by assessments incollectible; litigations ruinous and without end: the rod of seigneural finance for ever shaken over our heads; vexation, ruin, outrage, violence, and destructive servitude, under which the peasants, almost on a level with Polish slaves, can never but be miserable, vile, and oppressed. . . . In passing through many of the French provinces, I was struck with the various and heavy complaints of the farmers and little proprietors of the feudal grievances, . . . but I could not then conceive the multiplicity of the shackles which kept them poor and depressed. I understood it better afterwards, from the conversation and complaints of some grand seigneurs, as the revolution advanced; and I then learned, that the principal rental of many estates consisted in services and feudal tenures; by the baneful influence of which the industry of the people was almost exterminated. . . .

. . . But these were not all the evils with which the people struggled. The administration of justice was partial, venal, infamous. . . . The conduct of the parliaments [parlements] was profligate and atrocious. Upon almost every cause that came before them, interest was openly made with the judges; and woe betided the man who, with a cause to support, had no means of conciliating favour, either by the beauty of a handsome wife, or by other methods. . . . To reflecting minds, the cruelty and abominable practice attending such courts are sufficiently apparent. There was also a circumstance in the constitution of these parliaments, but little known in England, and which, under such a government as that of France, must be considered as very singular. They had the power, and were in the constant practice of issuing decrees, without the consent of the crown and which had the force of laws through the whole of their jurisdiction; and of all other laws, these were sure to be the best obeyed; for as all infringements of them were brought before sovereign courts, composed of the same persons who had enacted these laws (a horrible system of tyranny!) they were certain of being punished with the last severity. It must appear strange, in a government so despotic in some respects as that of France, to see the parliaments [parlements] in every part of the kingdom making laws without the King's consent, and even in defiance of his authority. . . .

It is impossible to justify the excesses of the people on their taking up arms [in the *Great Fear*] they were certainly guilty of cruelties; it is idle to deny the facts, for they have been proved too clearly to admit of a doubt. But is it really the people to whom we are to impute the whole?—Or to their oppressors who had kept them so long in a state of bondage? He who chooses to be served by slaves, and by ill-treated slaves, must know that he holds both his property and life by a tenure far different from those who prefer the service of well treated freemen; and he who dines to the music of groaning sufferers, must not, in the moment of insurrection, complain that his daughters are ravished, and then destroyed; and that his sons' throats are cut. When such evils happen, they surely are more imputable to the tyranny of the master, than to the cruelty of the servant. The analogy holds with the French peasants—the murder of a seigneur, or a chateau in flames, is recorded in every newspaper; the rank of the person who suffers, attracts notice; but where do we find the register of that seigneur's oppressions of his peasantry, and his exactions of feudal services, from those whose children were dying around them for want of bread? Where do we find the minutes that assigned these starving wretches to some vile petty-fogger, to be fleeced by impositions, and a mockery of justice, in the seigneural courts? Who gives us the awards of the intendant and his *sub-delegués,* which took off the taxes of a man of fashion, and laid them with accumulated weight, on the poor, who were so unfortunate as to be his neighbours? Who has dwelt sufficiently upon explaining all the ramifications of despotism, regal, aristocratical, and ecclesiastical, pervading the whole mass of the people; reaching, like a circulating fluid, the most distant capillary tubes of poverty and wretchedness? In these cases, the sufferers are too ignoble to be known; and the mass too indiscriminate to be pitied. . . . The true judgment to be formed of the French revolution, must surely be gained, from an attentive consideration of the evils of the old government: when these are well understood—and when the extent and universality of the oppression under which the people groaned—oppression which bore upon them from every quarter, it will scarcely be attempted to be urged, that a revolution was not absolutely necessary to the welfare of the kingdom. Not one opposing voice can, with reason, be raised against this assertion: abuses ought certainly to be corrected, and corrected effectually: this could not be done without the establishment of a new form of government; whether the form that has been adopted were the best, is another question absolutely distinct. . . .

5. DECLARATION OF THE RIGHTS OF MAN AND OF THE CITIZEN*

The Estates-General was transformed into a National Assembly by June 1789. As the deputies began to undertake their self-appointed task of drafting a formal constitution for France, they were unable to escape the pressure of events. The Bastille fell to a Paris mob on July 14, and peasants rioted in rural areas of the kingdom during August, an uprising called the Great Fear. Reacting quickly, the National Assembly abolished feudalism, enacted a declaration of rights, and later limited the king to a suspensive veto over legislation.

*The Annual Register for the Year 1789 (London, 1792), pp. 332–33.

The Declaration of the Rights of Man and of the Citizen gave the deputies of 1789 a creed and a statement of ideals. Strongly influenced by complaints in the *Cahiers,* the Declaration was an idealistic, yet reasonably practical document. The Declaration recognized that basic human rights were older than any society and insisted that the state must defend individual freedoms. Rights were coupled to duties, state power limited in scope, and government held accountable for its actions. Passed on August 27, the Declaration became the preamble to the Constitution of 1791. Compare the French Declaration of Rights with the American Declaration of Independence. Was the Declaration of Rights closer to the concepts of John Locke or Jean Jacques Rousseau? Why? Did it reflect the desires and views of all social classes?

THE DECLARATION OF RIGHTS, WHICH HAS BEEN AGREED TO BY THE NATIONAL ASSEMBLY OF FRANCE, AND SANCTIONED BY THE KING, AND WHICH FORMS THE BASIS OF THE NEW CONSTITUTION OF FRANCE.

The representatives of the people of France, formed into a national assembly, considering that ignorance, neglect, or contempt of human rights, are the sole causes of public misfortunes and corruptions of government, have resolved to set forth, in a solemn declaration, these natural, imprescriptible, and unalienable, rights: that this declaration being constantly present to the minds of the members of the body social, they may be ever kept attentive to their rights and their duties: that the acts of the legislative and executive powers of government being capable of being every moment compared with the end of political institutions, may be more respected; and also, that the future claims of the citizens, being directed by simple and incontestable principles, may always tend to the maintenance of the constitution, and the general happiness.

For these reasons the national assembly doth recognize and declare, in the presence of the Supreme Being, and with the hope of his blessing and favour, the following sacred rights of men and of citizens.

I. Men were born and always continue free, and equal in respect of their rights. Civil distinctions, therefore, can be founded only on public utility.

II. The end of all political associations is the preservation of the natural and imprescriptible rights of man; and these rights are liberty, property, security, and resistance of oppression.

III. The nation is essentially the source of all sovereignty; nor can any individual, or any body of men, be entitled to any authority which is not expressly derived from it.

IV. Political liberty consists in the power of doing whatever does not injure another. The exercise of the natural rights of every man, has no other limits than those which are necessary to secure to every other man the free exercise of the same rights; and these limits are determinable only by the law.

V. The law ought to prohibit only actions hurtful to society. What is not prohibited by the law should not be hindered; nor should any one be compelled to that which the law does not require.

VI. The law is an expression of the will of the community. All citizens have a right to concur, either personally or by their representatives, in its formation. It should be the same to all, whether it protects or punishes; and all being equal in its sight, are equally eligible to all honours, places, and employments, according to their different abilities, without any other distinction than that created by their virtues and talents.

VII. No man should be accused, arrested, or held in confinement, except in cases determined by the law, and according to the forms which it has prescribed. All who promote, solicit, execute, or cause to be executed, arbitrary orders, ought to be punished: and every citizen called upon or apprehended by virtue of the law, ought immediately to obey, and renders himself culpable by resistance.

VIII. The law ought to impose no other penalties than such as are absolutely and evidently necessary; and no one ought to be punished but in virtue of a law promulgated before the offence, and legally applied.

IX. Every man being presumed innocent till he has been convicted, whenever his detention becomes indispensable, all rigour to him, more than is necessary to secure his person, ought to be provided against by the law.

X. No man ought to be molested on account of his opinions, not even on account of his religious opinions, provided his avowal of them does not disturb the public order established by the law.

XI. The unrestrained communication of thoughts and opinions being one of the most precious rights of man, every citizen may speak, write, and publish freely, provided he is responsible for the abuse of this liberty in cases determined by the law.

XII. A public force being necessary to give security to the rights of men and of citizens, that force is instituted for the benefit of the community, and not for the particular benefit of the persons to whom it is entrusted.

XIII. A common contribution being necessary for the support of the public force, and for defraying the other expenses of government, it ought to be divided equally among the members of the community, according to their abilities.

XIV. Every citizen has a right, either by himself or his representative, to a free voice in determining the necessity of public contributions, the appropriation of them, and their amount, mode of assessment, and duration.

XV. Every community has a right to demand of all its agents an account of their conduct.

XVI. Every community in which a separation of powers and a security of rights is not provided for, wants a constitution.

XVII. The right to property being inviolable and sacred, no one ought to be deprived of it, except in cases of evident public necessity legally ascertained, and on condition of a previous just indemnity.

6. THE CIVIL CONSTITUTION OF THE CLERGY*

The oldest institution in France was the Catholic Church. Subjected to criticism by the *philosophes* prior to the Revolution, the Church nevertheless retained a deep hold on the French masses. The Church was also wealthy, controlling

* "The Civil Constitution of the Clergy" in Frank Maloy Anderson, *The Constitutions and Other Select Documents Illustrative of the History of France, 1789–1907* (Minneapolis: The H. W. Wilson Co., 1908), pp. 16–22.

vast lands and revenues; one out of every fifty adults was a monk, nun, or priest. By 1789 a reform movement had developed within the Church, but it was led mainly by parish priests and had yet had little effect on the aristocratic hierarchy.

Abolition of feudalism had cleared the ground for clerical reform, and the wealth of the Church was attractive to a National Assembly unable to provide financial stability to the nation. The Civil Constitution of the Clergy of July 12, 1790, reorganized the Church without directly altering matters of faith. Convinced that the assembly had the right to make such changes as it felt necessary, most deputies failed to comprehend the potential consequences of their decision. The Papacy and most French clergymen refused to accept the Civil Constitution, precipitating a decade of Church-State antagonism. King Louis XVI, who had failed to lead the Assembly during the critical months of 1789, stiffened in his opposition to the actions of the deputies and only very reluctantly gave final approval to the Civil Constitution in December 1790. The King's sympathies obviously were with Pope Pius VI who shortly issued a bull condemning the Civil Constitution. Louis was thus further alienated from the Assembly. According to the Civil Constitution, how were members of the clergy to be named to their office? In what ways was the clergy's freedom of movement restricted? What oath was required of the clergy?

The National Assembly, after having heard the report of the Ecclesiastical Committee, has decreed and does decree the following as constitutional articles:—

TITLE I. OF THE ECCLESIASTICAL OFFICES

1. Each department shall form a single diocese, and each diocese shall have the same extent and the same limits as the department.

2. The seats of the bishoprics of the eighty-three departments of the kingdom shall be established as follows: [The names of the episcopal sees follow in the text, but are omitted here.]

All other bishoprics in the eighty-three departments of the kingdom, which are not included by name in the present article, are and forever shall be abolished. . . .

4. No church or parish of France nor any French citizen may acknowledge upon any occasion or upon any pretext whatsoever, the authority of an ordinary bishop or of an archbishop whose see shall be under the supremacy of a foreign power, nor that of their representatives residing in France or elsewhere; without prejudice, however, to the unity of the faith and the intercourse which shall be maintained with the visible head of the universal church, as hereinafter provided.

20. All titles and offices other than those mentioned in the present constitution, *dignités,* canonries, prebends, half-prebends, chapels, chaplainships, both in cathedral and collegiate churches, all regular and secular chapters for either sex, abbacies and priorships, both regular and *in commendam,* for either sex, as well as all other benefices and prestimonies in general, of whatever kind or denomination, are from the day of this decree extinguished and abolished and shall never be re-established in any form.

TITLE II. APPOINTMENTS TO BENEFICES

1. Beginning with the day of publication of the present decree there shall be but one mode of choosing bishops and *curés,* namely that of election. . . .

2. All elections shall be by ballot and shall be decided by the majority of the votes.

3. The election of bishops shall take place according to the forms and by the electoral body designated in the decree of December 22, 1789, for the election of members of the departmental assembly.

6. The election of a bishop can only take place or be undertaken upon Sunday, in the principal church of the chief town of the department, at the close of the parish mass, at which all the electors are required to be present.

7. In order to be eligible to a bishopric, one must have fulfilled for fifteen years at least the duties of the church ministry in the diocese as a parish priest, officiating minister or curate, or as superior, or as directing vicar of the seminary.

19. The new bishop shall not apply to the Pope for any form of confirmation, but shall write to him as the Visible Head of the Universal Church, as a testimony to the unity of faith and communion maintained with him. . . .

21. Before the ceremony of consecration begins, the bishop-elect shall take a solemn oath in the presence of the municipal officers, the people and the clergy, to guard with care the faithful of his diocese who are confided to him, to be loyal to the nation, the law and the king, and to support with all his power the constitution decreed by the National Assembly and accepted by the king.

40. Bishoprics and *curés* shall be looked upon as vacant until those elected to fill them shall have taken the oath above mentioned.

TITLE III. SALARIES OF THE MINISTERS OF RELIGION

2. Every bishop, priest and officiating clergyman in a chapel of ease, shall be furnished with a suitable dwelling, on condition, however, that the occupant shall make all the necessary current repairs. This shall not affect, at present, in any way, those parishes where the priest now receives a money equivalent instead of his dwelling. The departments shall, moreover, have cognizance of suits arising in this connection, brought by the parishes and by the priests. Salaries shall be assigned to each, as indicated below.

7. The salaries *in money* of the ministers of religion shall be paid every three months, in advance, by the treasurer of the district.

12. In view of the salary which is assured to them by the present constitution, the bishops, *curés,* and curates shall perform the episcopal and priestly functions gratis.

TITLE IV. OF THE LAW OF RESIDENCE

1. The law of residence shall be strictly observed, and all vested with an ecclesiastical office or function shall be subject thereto without any distinction or exception.

2. No bishop shall absent himself from his diocese more than fifteen days consecutively during the year, except in case of real necessity, and with the consent of the directory of the department in which his see is situated.

3. In the same manner the *curés* and the curates may not absent themselves from the place of their duties beyond the term fixed above, except for weighty reasons, and even in such cases the *curés* must obtain the permission both of their bishop and of the directory of their district, and the curates that of their *curés*.

6. Bishops, *curés* and curates may, as active citizens, be present at the primary and electoral assemblies, they may be chosen electors or as deputies to the legislative body, or as members of the general council of the communes or of the administrative councils of their districts or departments; but their duties are declared incompatible with those of mayor and other municipal offices and those of the members of the directories of the district and of the department; and if elected to one of these last mentioned offices they must make a choice between it and their ecclesiastical position.

7. THE "CHAPELIER" LAW*

Continuing disturbances in Paris, stemming in part from opposition to the moderate course of the Revolution, prompted the National Assembly to outlaw workers' associations. The "Chapelier" Law of June 14, 1791, was named for the deputy who sponsored the decree, and later in 1791 a similar measure was applied to agricultural workers. The "Chapelier" Law remained a fixture of French legislation through the middle of the nineteenth century and helped to stifle the growth of trade unions. How complete were the antiassociation strictures of the law? As similar legislation was not passed against employers' associations, which sector of the Assembly was responsible for approval of the "Chapelier" Law? Did the law clash with any of the principles of the Declaration of Rights?

1. Since the abolition of all kinds of corporations of citizens of the same occupation and profession is one of the fundamental bases of the French Constitution, re-establishment thereof under any pretext or form whatsoever is forbidden.

2. Citizens of the same occupation or profession, *entrepreneurs,* those who maintain open shop, workers, and journeymen of any craft whatsoever may not, when they are together, name either president, secretaries, or trustees, keep accounts, pass decrees or resolutions, or draft regulations concerning their alleged common interests.

3. All administrative or municipal bodies are forbidden to receive any address or petition in the name of an occupation or profession, or to make any response thereto; and they are enjoined to declare null whatever resolutions have been made in such manner, and to make certain that no effect or execution be given thereto.

4. If, contrary to the principles of liberty and the Constitution, some citizens associated in the same professions, arts, and crafts hold deliberations or make agreements among themselves tending to refuse by mutual consent or to grant only at a determined price the assistance of their industry or their labor, such deliberations and agreements, whether accompanied by oath or not, are de-

* "The 'Chapelier' Law" in John Hall Stewart, ed., *A Documentary Survey of the French Revolution* (New York: The Macmillan Co., 1951), pp. 165–66. Reprinted by permission.

clared unconstitutional, in contempt of liberty and the Declaration of the Rights of Man, and noneffective; administrative and municipal bodies shall be required so to declare them. The authors, leaders, and instigators who have provoked, drafted, or presided over them shall be cited before the police court, at the request of the communal attorney, each condemned to a fine of 500 *livres,* and suspended for a year from the enjoyment of all rights of active citizenship and from admittance to the primary assemblies.

6. If the said deliberations or convocations, posted placards, or circular letters contain any threats against *entrepreneurs,* artisans, workers, or foreign day laborers working there, or against those who are satisfied with a lower wage, all authors, instigators, and signatories of such acts or writings shall be punished with a fine of 1,000 *livres* each and imprisonment for three months.

7. Those who use threats or violence against workers who are utilizing the liberty granted to labor and to industry by the constitutional laws shall be subject to criminal prosecution, and shall be punished according to the rigor of the laws as disturbers of the public peace.

8. All assemblies composed of artisans, workers, journeymen, day laborers, or those incited by them against the free exercise of industry and labor appertaining to every kind of person and under all circumstances arranged by private contract, or against the action of police and the execution of judgments rendered in such connection, as well as against public bids and auctions of divers enterprises, shall be considered as seditious assemblies, and as such shall be dispersed by the depositaries of the public force, upon legal requisitions made thereupon, and shall be punished according to all the rigor of the laws concerning authors, instigators, and leaders of the said assemblies, and all those who have committed assaults and acts of violence.

8. THE BRUNSWICK MANIFESTO*

With the outbreak of war in April 1792, radical sentiment in Paris became more vocal. Abroad, the *émigrés* grew desperate and continued to urge foreign monarchs to protect Louis XVI. The Brunswick Manifesto was issued on July 25, 1792, under the signature of the Commander of allied armies invading France, but was composed by disgruntled *émigrés* attached to his forces. The timing of the Manifesto could scarcely have been less appropriate, for agitation against the King in Paris was approaching a climax. The Manifesto galvanized anti-royalist emotions and contributed to the riots of August 10, 1792. In what ways could republicans find proof of royal treachery in the Manifesto? What threats were made against Paris and those Frenchmen who might harm the King?

Their Majesties, the Emperor and the King of Prussia, having committed to me the command of the united armies which they have caused to assemble on the frontiers of France, I have wished to announce to the inhabitants of this kingdom, the motives which have determined the measures of the two sovereigns and the intentions which guide them.

* "The Duke of Brunswick's Manifesto" in Frank Maloy Anderson, *The Constitutions and Other Select Documents Illustrative of the History of France, 1789–1907* (Minneapolis: The H. W. Wilson Co., 1908), pp. 119–22.

After having arbitrarily suppressed the rights and possessions of the German princes in Alsace and Lorraine, disturbed and overthrown good order and legitimate government in the interior, exercised against the sacred person of the king and his august family outrages and brutalities which are still carried on and renewed day by day, those who have usurped the reins of the administration have at last completed their work by declaring an unjust war against His Majesty the Emperor and by attacking his provinces situated in the Low Countries. Some of the possessions of the Germanic Empire have been enveloped in this oppression, and several others have only escaped the same danger by yielding to the imperious threats of the dominant party and of its emissaries.

His Majesty the King of Prussia, united with his Imperial Majesty by the bonds of a strict defensive alliance and himself the preponderant member of the Germanic body, could not excuse himself from marching to the help of his ally and his co-state; and it is under this double relationship that he takes up the defence of this monarch and of Germany.

To these great interests is added another aim equally important and very dear to the two sovereigns; it is to put an end to the anarchy in the interior of France, to stop the attacks carried on against the throne and the altar, to re-establish the legal power, to restore to the king the security and liberty of which he is deprived, and to put him in a position to exercise the legitimate authority which is his due.

Convinced that the sound part of the French nation abhors the excesses of a faction which dominates it, and that the greatest number of the inhabitants look forward with impatience to the moment of relief to declare themselves openly against the odious enterprises of their oppressors, His Majesty the Emperor and His Majesty the King of Prussia, call upon them and invite them to return without delay to the ways of reason, justice, order and peace. It is in accordance with these views, that I, the undersigned, the General, commanding in chief the two armies, declare:

1. That, drawn into the present war by irresistible circumstances, the two allied courts propose to themselves no other aim than the welfare of France and have no intention of enriching themselves by conquests;

2. That they do not intend to meddle with the internal government of France, but that they merely wish to deliver the king, the queen and the royal family from their captivity, and to procure for His Most Christian Majesty the necessary security that he may make without danger or hindrance the conventions which he shall judge suitable and may work for the welfare of his subjects, according to his promises and as far as it shall depend upon him;

3. That the combined armies will protect the towns, boroughs and villages and the persons and goods of those who shall submit to the king and who shall co-operate in the immediate re-establishment of order and of the police in the whole of France;

4. That the national guard will be called upon to watch provisionally over the peace of the towns and country districts, the security of the persons and goods of all Frenchmen, until the arrival of the troops of their Imperial and Royal Majesties, or until otherwise ordered, under pain of being personally responsible; that on the contrary, those of the national guard who shall fight against

the troops of the two allied courts, and who shall be taken with arms in their hands, will be treated as enemies and punished as rebels to their king and as disturbers of the public peace.

5. That the generals, officers, under officers, and troops of the French line are likewise summoned to return to their former fidelity and to submit themselves at once to the king, their legitimate sovereign;

6. That the members of the departments, of the districts and municipalities shall likewise answer with their heads and their goods for all offences, fires, murders, pillaging, and acts of violence, which they shall allow to be committed, or which they have not manifestly exerted themselves to prevent within their territory; that they shall likewise be required to continue their functions provisionally, until His Most Christian Majesty, being once more at liberty, may have provided for them subsequently or until it shall have been otherwise ordained in his name in the meantime;

7. That the inhabitants of the towns, boroughs and villages who may dare to defend themselves against the troops of their Imperial and Royal Majesties and fire on them either in the open country, or through the windows, doors and openings of their houses, shall be punished immediately according to the strictness of the law of war, and their houses destroyed or burned. On the contrary, all the inhabitants of the said towns, boroughs and villages, who shall submit to their king, opening their doors to the troops of their Majesties, shall at once be placed under their immediate protection; their persons, their property, and their effects shall be under the protection of the laws, and the general security of all and each of them shall be provided for;

8. The city of Paris and all its inhabitants without distinction shall be required to submit at once and without delay to the king, to put that prince in full and perfect liberty, and to assure him as well as the other royal personages the inviolability and respect which the law of nations and men requires of subjects toward their sovereigns; their Imperial and Royal Majesties declare personally responsible with their lives for all events, to be tried by military law and without hope of pardon, all the members of the National Assembly, of the department, district, municipality and national guard of Paris, the justices of the peace and all others that shall be concerned; their said Majesties also declare on their honor and on their word as Emperor and King, that if the chateau of the Tuileries be entered by force or attacked, if the least violence or outrage be offered to their Majesties, the king, queen, and royal family, if their preservation and their liberty be not immediately provided for, they will exact an exemplary and ever-memorable vengeance, by delivering the city of Paris over to a military execution and to complete ruin, and the rebels guilty of these outrages to the punishments they shall have deserved. Their Imperial and Royal Majesties, on the contrary, promise the inhabitants of Paris to employ their good offices with His Most Christian Majesty to obtain pardon for their misdeeds and errors, and to take the most vigorous measures to assure their lives and property, if they obey promptly and exactly all the above mentioned orders.

Finally, their Majesties being able to recognize as laws in France only those which shall emanate from the king, in the enjoyment of a perfect liberty, protest beforehand against the authenticity of any declarations which may be made in the name of His Most Christian Majesty, so long as his sacred person, that of the queen, and those of the royal family shall not be really in security, for the effecting of which their Imperial and Royal Majesties beg His Most Christian Majesty to appoint the city in his kingdom nearest the frontiers, to which he would prefer to retire with the queen and his family under good and sufficient escort, which will be furnished him for this purpose, so that his most Christian Majesty may in all security summon such ministers and councillors as he may see fit, hold such meetings as he deems best, provide for the re-establishment of good order and regulate the administration of his kingdom.

Finally, I declare and bind myself, moreover, in my own private name and in my above capacity, to cause the troops entrusted to my command to observe a good and exact discipline, promising to treat with kindness and moderation all well intentioned subjects who show themselves peaceful and submissive, and only to use force against those who shall make themselves guilty of resistance and ill-will.

It is for these reasons that I call upon and exhort all the inhabitants of the kingdom in the strongest and most urgent manner not to oppose the march and the operations of the troops which I command, but rather to grant them everywhere a free passage and with every good will to aid and assist as circumstances shall require.

Given at the head-quarters at Coblentz, July 25, 1792.

Signed, Charles-William Ferdinand,
Duke of Brunswick-Lunebourg

9. CONVENTION FOREIGN POLICY*

The National Convention, inheriting a war with Austria and Prussia, pressed for the transformation of the ideals and goals of the French Revolution into a program for all peoples. By the fall of 1792 foreign armies had been forced into retreat, the nation had become a republic, and leaders in the Convention promoted and enforced wartime emergency measures. A military victory in Belgium early in November 1792 aroused further enthusiasm in the Convention, and the shift from defensive to offensive military operations turned the French Revolution into a crusade. Because European states were alarmed by French expansionism, and because not all neighboring areas wanted to be "liberated" by French armies, the following propaganda decrees were an attempt to explain the Convention's position. What changes were proposed for areas occupied by French armies? Were conquered areas to be annexed by France? What arguments were advanced to justify French conquest and occupation?

DECLARATION FOR ASSISTANCE AND FRATERNITY TO FOREIGN PEOPLES,
NOVEMBER 19, 1792

The National Convention declares, in the name of the French people, that it will accord fraternity and assistance to all peoples who shall wish to recover their liberty, and charges the executive power to give to the generals the neces-

* "Documents upon the Convention and Foreign Policy" in Frank Maloy Anderson, *The Constitutions and Other Select Documents Illustrative of the History of France, 1789–1907* (Minneapolis: The H. W. Wilson Co., 1908), pp. 130–34.

sary orders to furnish assistance to these peoples and to defend the citizens who may have been or who may be harassed for the cause of liberty. The present decree shall be translated and printed in all languages.

DECREE FOR PROCLAIMING THE LIBERTY AND SOVEREIGNTY OF ALL PEOPLES,
DECEMBER 15, 1792

The National Convention, after having heard the report of its united committees of finances, war, and diplomacy, faithful to the principles of the sovereignty of the people, which do not permit it to recognize any of the institutions that constitute an attack thereon, and wishing to settle the rules to be followed by the generals of the armies of the Republic in the countries where they shall carry its arms, decrees:

1. In the countries which are or shall be occupied by the armies of the Republic, the generals shall proclaim immediately, in the name of the French nation, the sovereignty of the people, the suppression of all the established authorities and of the existing imposts and taxes, the abolition of the tithe, of feudalism, of seignioral rights, both feudal and *censuel,* fixed or precarious, of *banalités,* of real and personal servitude, of the privileges of hunting and fishing, of *corvées,* of the nobility, and generally of all privileges.

2. They shall announce to the people that they bring them peace, assistance, fraternity, liberty and equality, and that they will convoke them directly in primary or communal assemblies in order to create and organize an administration and a provisional judiciary; they shall look after the security of persons and property; they shall cause the present decree and the proclamation herewith annexed to be printed in the language or idiom of the country, and to be posted and executed without delay in each commune.

3. All the agents and civil and military officers of the former government, as well as the persons formerly reputed noble, or the members of any formerly privileged corporation, shall be, for this time only, inadmissible to vote in the primary or communal assemblies, and they shall not be elected to administrative positions or to the provisional judicial power.

4. The generals shall directly place under the safeguard and protection of the French Republic all the movable and immovable goods belonging to the public treasury, to the prince, to his abettors, adherents and voluntary satellites, to the public establishments, to the lay and ecclesiastical bodies and communities; they shall cause to be prepared without delay a detailed list thereof which they shall dispatch to the executive council, and shall take all the measures which are in their power that these properties may be respected.

5. The provisional administration selected by the people shall be charged with the surveillance and control of the goods placed under the safeguard and protection of the French Republic; it shall look after the security of persons and property; it shall cause to be executed the laws in force relative to the trial of civil and criminal suits and to the police and the public security; it shall be charged to regulate and to cause the payment of the local expenses and those which shall be necessary for the common defence; it may establish taxes, provided, however, that they shall not be borne by the indigent and laboring portion of the people. . . .

11. The French nation declares that it will treat as enemies the people who, refusing liberty and equality, or renouncing them, may wish to preserve, recall, or treat with the prince and the privileged castes; it promises and engages not to subscribe to any treaty, and not to lay down its arms until after the establishment of the sovereignty and independence of the people whose territory the troops of the Republic have entered upon and who shall have adopted the principles of equality, and established a free and popular government.

12. The executive council shall dispatch the present decree by extraordinary couriers to all the generals and shall take the necessary measures to assure the execution of it.

DECREE UPON NON-INTERVENTION, APRIL 13, 1793

The National Convention declares, in the name of the French people, that it will not interfere in any manner in the government of the other powers; but it declares at the same time, that it will sooner be buried under its own ruins than suffer that any power should interfere in the internal regime of the Republic, or should influence the creation of the constitution which it intends to give itself.

The National Convention decrees the penalty of death against anyone who may propose to negotiate or treat with the hostile powers which may not have previously recognized in a solemn manner the independence of the French Republic, its sovereignty, and the indivisibility and unity of the Republic, founded upon liberty and equality.

10. DECREES AGAINST THE ÉMIGRÉS*

A few members of the nobility left France immediately after the fall of the Bastille, and the number of *émigrés* mounted as the Assembly passed various decrees affecting the social order. The *émigrés* were bitter and resentful at the course of the changes in France and often spoke out against the Revolution from the security of their exile. As a result, the Legislative Assembly (convened according to the new Constitution on October 1, 1791) looked with growing suspicion on the activities of the aristocratic *émigrés* and voted a decree on November 9, 1791, ordering them to return to France or be declared antirevolutionary conspirators. Louis XVI used his constitutional veto to halt the decree and, though the King's action was legal, many members of the Assembly were irritated. They believed that the Crown was working with the *émigrés* to destroy the Revolution. The rejected decree thus contributed to a French declaration of war on Austria in April 1792 and to the overthrow of the monarchy.

After the establishment of the First Republic, the more radical National Convention consolidated earlier legislative measures and on March 28, 1793, passed a broad condemnation of *émigrés*. The measure reflected both the Convention's concern with counterrevolutionary movements and the desire of many Frenchmen to take over the confiscated property of the *émigrés*. Who, according to the decree of March 28, 1793, were defined as *émigrés*? What penalties were leveled against them? What distinction was made between nobles, clergymen, and

* "Decree Against the Émigrés" in Frank Maloy Anderson, *The Constitutions and Other Select Documents Illustrative of the History of France, 1789–1907* (Minneapolis: The H. W. Wilson Co., 1908), pp. 98, 147–48.

members of the bourgeoisie who had gone into exile? Why, or why not, would such a distinction be made by 1793?

THE REJECTED DECREE OF NOVEMBER 9, 1791

The National Assembly, considering that the tranquillity and security of the kingdom require it to take prompt and effective measures against Frenchmen who, despite the amnesty, do not cease to plot abroad against the French constitution, and that it is time finally to repress severely those whom indulgence has not been able to reclaim to the duties and sentiments of free citizens, has declared that there is urgency for the following decree, and the decree of urgency being previously rendered, has decreed as follows:

1. The Frenchmen mustered beyond the frontiers of the kingdom are from this moment declared suspects for conspiracy against the fatherland.

2. If on the 1st of January next they are still in a state of muster, they shall be declared guilty of conspiracy, they shall be prosecuted as such and punished with death.

3. As to the French princes and public functionaries, civil and ecclesiastical, and those who were such at the date of their departure from the kingdom, their absence at the above cited date of the 1st of January, 1792, shall make them guilty of the same crime of conspiracy against the fatherland; they shall be punished with the penalty provided in the preceding article. . . .

5. The incomes of the conspirators condemned in contumacy shall be collected during their lifetime for the benefit of the nation, without prejudice to the rights of their wives, children, and lawful creditors. . . .

14. The National Assembly charges its diplomatic committee to propose to it the measures which the king shall be requested to take in the name of the nation with respect to the adjacent foreign powers which permit upon their territories the musters of French fugitives. . . .

DECREE AGAINST THE ÉMIGRÉS, MARCH 28, 1793.

1. The *émigrés* are forever banished from French territory; *they are civilly dead;* their estates are acquired by the Republic.

2. Infraction of the banishment pronounced by article 1 shall be punished by death. . . .

6. *Émigrés* are:

1st. Every Frenchman of either sex who, after having left the territory of the Republic since July 1, 1789, has not made proof of his return to France within the periods fixed by the decree of March 30–April 8, 1792. The said decree shall continue to be executed in that which has to do with the pecuniary penalties pronounced against those who shall have returned within the period which it has prescribed;

2d. Every Frenchman of either sex, absent from the place of his domicile, who shall not prove, in the form which is about to be prescribed, an uninterrupted residence in France since May 9, 1792;

3d. Every Frenchman of either sex who, although actually present, has been absent from the place of his domicile and shall not make proof of an uninterrupted residence in France since May 9, 1792;

4th. Those who shall leave the territory of the Republic without fulfilling the formalities prescribed by the decree;

5th. Every agent of the government who, having been charged with a mission to foreign powers, has not returned to France within three months from the day of notification of his recall;

6th. Every Frenchman of either sex who, during invasion made by foreign armies, has left non-invaded French territory in order to reside upon territory occupied by the enemy;

7th. Those who, although born in foreign countries, have exercised the rights of citizens in France, or who, having a double domicile, to wit, one in France and the other in foreign countries, shall not make proof of an uninterrupted residence in France since May 9, 1792. . . .

11. DECREE ON THE FORMATION OF A COMMITTEE OF PUBLIC SAFETY*

In response to the dual threats of foreign war and internal dissension, the beleaguered National Convention proclaimed the Republic in danger and established an extraordinary authority—the Committee of Public Safety (April 6, 1793), responsible directly to the Convention. The Committee served as a cabinet. Although other administrative committees were formed, the Committee of Public Safety dominated them as well as the Convention which had created it. Under Jacobin control, with its membership raised to twelve, the Committee of Public Safety became the administrative organ of the Terror (1793–94). How extensive were the initial powers of the Committee? How long was the Committee supposed to stay in existence? What pressures enabled it to prolong its role?

The National Convention decrees:

1. A Committee of Public Safety, composed of nine members of the National Convention, shall be formed by roll call.

2. The committee shall deliberate in secret; it shall be responsible for supervising and accelerating the work of administration entrusted to the provisional Executive Council, the decrees of which it may even suspend when it believes them contrary to the national interest, upon condition that it inform the Convention thereof without delay.

3. Under critical circumstances it is authorized to take measures of general defence, both internal and external; and the orders signed by the majority of its deliberating members, which may not be less than two-thirds, shall be executed without delay by the provisional Executive Council. In no case may it issue warrants of arrest, except against executive agents, and upon condition of rendering account thereof, without delay, to the Convention.

4. The National Treasury shall hold at the disposal of the Committee of Public Safety for secret expenditures funds to the amount of 100,000 *livres,* which shall be issued by the committee, and paid upon orders which shall be signed as are decrees.

* "Decree on the Formation of a Committee of Public Safety" in John Hall Stewart, ed., *A Documentary Survey of the French Revolution* (New York: The Macmillan Co., 1951), pp. 424–25. Reprinted by permission.

5. It shall make a weekly general report, in writing, of its activities and of the state of the Republic.

6. A register of all its deliberations shall be kept.

7. The aforementioned committee is established for only one month.

8. The National Treasury shall remain independent of the executive committee and subject to the immediate supervision of the Convention, according to the manner established by decrees.

12. CONSTITUTION OF THE YEAR I*

A National Convention had been elected after the execution of Louis XVI and the overthrow of the monarchical constitution. While fighting a war and governing France in the interim, the Convention assumed the primary function of drafting a republican constitution. The Constitution of 1793 (Year I in the new republican calendar) promulgated on June 24, 1793, emphasized political democracy while still assuring the bourgeoisie their property rights. Emergency conditions, however, persuaded the Convention that the new constitution (which would have demanded the election of another new legislative body) should not take effect until the end of the war. Temporary suspension became permanent, and a more moderate constitution was substituted in 1795 (Constitution of the Year III). The following selection is the preamble to the Constitution of 1793. Contrast the 1793 Declaration of Rights with the Declaration of 1789. In what respects was the 1793 preamble more radical? What additional responsibilities were given to the state? What rights were guaranteed the individual?

DECLARATION OF THE RIGHTS OF MAN AND CITIZEN

The French people, convinced that forgetfulness and contempts of the natural rights of man are the sole causes of the miseries of the world, have resolved to set forth in a solemn declaration these sacred and inalienable rights, in order that all the citizens, being able to compare unceasingly the acts of the government with the aim of every social institution, may never allow themselves to be oppressed and debased by tyranny; and in order that the people may always have before their eyes the foundations of their liberty and their welfare, the magistrate the rule of his duties, and the legislator the purpose of his commission.

In consequence, it proclaims in the presence of the supreme being the following declaration of the rights of man and citizen.

1. The aim of society is the common welfare.

Government is instituted in order to guarantee to man the enjoyment of his natural and imprescriptible rights.

2. These rights are equality, liberty, security, and property.

3. All men are equal by nature and before the law.

4. Law is the free and solemn expression of the general will; it is the same for all, whether it protects or punishes; it can command only what is just and useful to society; it can forbid only what is injurious to it.

* "Constitution of the Year I" in Frank Maloy Anderson, *The Constitutions and Other Select Documents Illustrative of the History of France, 1789–1907* (Minneapolis: The H. W. Wilson Co., 1908), pp. 171–74.

5. All citizens are equally eligible to public employments. Free peoples know no other grounds for preference in their elections than virtue and talent.

6. Liberty is the power that belongs to man to do whatever is not injurious to the rights of others; it has nature for its principle, justice for its rule, law for its defence; its moral limit is in this maxim: Do not do to another that which you do not wish should be done to you.

7. The right to express one's thoughts and opinions by means of the press or in any other manner, the right to assemble peaceably, the free pursuit of religion, cannot be forbidden.

8. Security consists in the protection afforded by society to each of its members for the preservation of his person, his rights, and his property.

9. The law ought to protect public and personal liberty against the oppression of those who govern.

10. No one ought to be accused, arrested, or detained except in the cases determined by law and according to the forms that it has prescribed. Any citizen summoned or seized by the authority of the law, ought to obey immediately; he makes himself guilty by resistance.

11. Any act done against man outside of the cases and without the forms that the law determines is arbitrary and tyrannical; the one against whom it may be intended to be executed by violence has the right to repel it by force.

12. Those who may incite, expedite, subscribe to, execute or cause to be executed arbitrary legal instruments are guilty and ought to be punished.

13. Every man being presumed innocent until he has been pronounced guilty, if it is thought indispensable to arrest him, all severity that may not be necessary to secure his person ought to be strictly repressed by law.

14. No one ought to be tried and punished except after having been heard or legally summoned, and except in virtue of a law promulgated prior to the offence. The law which would punish offences committed before it existed would be a tyranny: the retroactive effect given to the law would be a crime.

15. The law ought to impose only penalties that are strictly and obviously necessary: the punishments ought to be proportionate to the offence and useful to society.

16. The right of property is that which belongs to every citizen to enjoy, and to dispose at his pleasure of his goods, income, and of the fruits of his labor and his skill.

17. No kind of labor, tillage, or commerce can be forbidden to the skill of the citizens.

18. Every man can contract his services and his time, but he cannot sell himself nor be sold: his person is not an alienable property. The law knows of no such thing as the status of servant; there can exist only a contract for services and compensation between the man who works and the one who employs him.

19. No one can be deprived of the least portion of his property without his consent, unless a legally established public necessity requires it, and upon condition of a just and prior compensation.

20. No tax can be imposed except for the general advantage. All citizens have the right to participate in the establishment of taxes, to watch over the employment of them, and to cause an account of them to be rendered.

21. Public relief is a sacred debt. Society owes maintenance to unfortunate citizens, either in procuring work for them or in providing the means of existence for those who are unable to labor.

22. Education is needed by all. Society ought to favor with all its power the advancement of the public reason and to put education at the door of every citizen.

23. The social guarantee consists in the action of all to secure to each the enjoyment and the maintenance of his rights: this guarantee rests upon the national sovereignty.

24. It cannot exist if the limits of public functions are not clearly determined by law and if the responsibility of all the functionaries is not secured.

25. The sovereignty resides in the people; it is one and indivisible, imprescriptible, and inalienable.

26. No portion of the people can exercise the power of the entire people; but each section of the sovereign, in assembly, ought to enjoy the right to express its will with entire freedom.

27. Let any person who may usurp the sovereignty be instantly put to death by free men.

28. A people has always the right to review, to reform, and to alter its constitution. One generation cannot subject to its law the future generations.

29. Each citizen has an equal right to participate in the formation of the law and in the selection of his mandatories or his agents.

30. Public functions are necessarily temporary; they cannot be considered as distinctions or rewards, but as duties.

31. The offences of the representatives of the people and of its agents ought never to go unpunished. No one has the right to claim for himself more inviolability than other citizens.

32. The right to present petitions to the depositories of the public authority cannot in any case be forbidden, suspended, nor limited.

33. Resistance to oppression is the consequence of the other rights of man.

34. There is oppression against the social body when a single one of its members is oppressed: there is oppression against each member when the social body is oppressed.

35. When the government violates the rights of the people, insurrection is for the people and for each portion of the people the most sacred of rights and the most indispensable of duties.

13. DECREE ESTABLISHING THE LEVY EN MASSE*

Under the impact of war and political factionalism, nationalism and patriotism became increasingly important stimulants to the nation between 1781 and 1793. Through the following decree of August 23, 1793, France mobilized her strength and turned defense of the nation into a force for expansion. With the nation secure, spirited and aggressive French forces swarmed across the frontier to

* "Decree Establishing the Levy *en masse*" in John Hall Stewart, ed., *A Documentary Survey of the French Revolution* (New York: The Macmillan Co., 1951), pp. 472–74. Reprinted by permission.

become "liberating" armies. What was the levy *en masse,* and how did it differ from methods of forming armies in other European countries? Was there any historical precedent for a national mobilization so complete? What role did the Committee of Public Safety play in the administration of the decree?

1. Henceforth, until the enemies have been driven from the territory of the Republic, the French people are in permanent requisition for army service.

The young men shall go to battle; the married men shall forge arms and transport provisions; the women shall make tents and clothes, and shall serve in the hospitals; the children shall turn old linen into lint; the old men shall repair to the public places, to stimulate the courage of the warriors and preach the unity of the Republic and hatred of kings.

2. National buildings shall be converted into barracks; public places into armament workshops; the soil of cellars shall be washed in lye to extract saltpeter therefrom.

3. Arms of caliber shall be turned over exclusively to those who march against the enemy; the service of the interior shall be carried on with fowling pieces and sabers.

5. The Committee of Public Safety is charged with taking all measures necessary for establishing, without delay, a special manufacture of arms of all kinds, in harmony with the *élan* and the energy of the French people. Accordingly, it is authorized to constitute all establishments, manufactories, workshops, and factories deemed necessary for the execution of such works, as well as to requisition for such purpose, throughout the entire extent of the Republic, the artists and workmen who may contribute to their success. For such purpose a sum of 30,000,000, taken from the 498,200,000 livres in *assignats* in reserve in the "Fund of the Three Keys," shall be placed at the disposal of the Minister of War. The central establishment of said special manufacture shall be established at Paris.

6. The representatives of the people dispatched for the execution of the present law shall have similar authority in their respective *arrondissements,* acting in concert with the Committee of Public Safety; they are invested with the unlimited powers attributed to the representatives of the people with the armies.

7. No one may obtain a substitute in the service to which he is summoned. The public functionaries shall remain at their posts.

8. The levy shall be general. Unmarried citizens or childless widowers, from eighteen to twenty-five years, shall go first; they shall meet, without delay, at the chief town of their districts, where they shall practice manual exercise daily, while awaiting the hour of departure.

11. The battalion organized in each district shall be united under a banner bearing the inscription: *The French people risen against tyrants.*

13. In order to collect supplies in sufficient quantity, the farmers and managers of national property shall deposit the produce of such property, in the form of grain, in the chief town of their respective districts. . . .

14. THE LAW OF SUSPECTS*

Revolt in the Vendée, where the anticlerical and antiroyalist measures of the Paris Assembly had never been accepted, infighting between Jacobins and Girondins, and the threat of foreign invasion created a national atmosphere of suspicion. Emergency measures such as the so-called Law of Suspects marked the beginning of the Reign of Terror. What was the purpose of the Law? Which individuals were automatically labeled as suspects? To what extent were the terms of the Law so vague as to render abuses inevitable? Which committee was charged with administration of the Law? What protections were left to the individual?

1. Immediately after the publication of the present decree all the suspect-persons who are in the territory of the Republic and who are still at liberty shall be placed under arrest.

2. These are accounted suspect-persons: (1st) those who by their conduct, their connections, their remarks, or their writings show themselves the partisans of tyranny or federalism and the enemies of liberty; (2d) those who cannot, in the manner prescribed by the decree of March 21st last, justify their means of existence and the performance of their civic duties; (3d) those who have been refused certificates of civism; (4th) public functionaries suspended or removed from their functions by the National Convention or its commissioners and not reinstated, especially those who have been or shall be removed in virtue of the decree of August 14th last; (5th) those of the former nobles, all of the husbands, wives, fathers, mothers, sons or daughters, brothers, or sisters, and agents of the *émigrés* who have not constantly manifested their attachment to the revolution; (6th) those who have emigrated from France in the interval from July 1, 1789, to the publication of the decree of March 30–April 8, 1792, although they may have returned to France within the period fixed by that decree or earlier.

3. The committees of surveillance established according to the decree of March 21st last, or those which have been substituted for them, either by the orders of the representatives of the people sent with the armies and into the departments, or in virtue of special decrees of the National Convention, are charged to prepare, each in its district, the list of suspect-persons, to issue warrants or arrest against them, and to cause seals to be put upon their papers. The commanders of the public force to whom these warrants shall be delivered shall be required to put them into execution immediately, under penalty of removal.

4. The members of the committee, without being seven in number and [having] an absolute majority of votes, cannot order the arrest of any person.

5. The persons arrested as suspects shall be first conveyed to the jail of the place of their imprisonment: in default of jails, they shall be kept from view in their respective dwellings. . . .

8. The expenses of custody shall be at the charge of the prisoners and shall be divided among them equally; this custody shall be confided preferably to the fathers of families and the parents of the citizens who are upon or shall go

---

* "The Law of Suspects" in Frank Maloy Anderson, *The Constitutions and Other Select Documents Illustrative of the History of France,* 1789–1907 (Minneapolis: The H. W. Wilson Co., 1908), pp. 186–87,

to the frontiers. The salary for it is fixed for each man of the guard at the value of a day and a half of labor.

9. The committees of surveillance shall send without delay to the committee of general security of the National Convention the list of the persons whom they shall have caused to be arrested, with the reasons for their arrest and the papers which shall have been seized with them as suspect-persons.

10. The civil and criminal tribunals can, if there is need, cause to be arrested and sent into the above-mentioned jails persons accused of offences in respect of whom it may have been declared that there was no ground for accusation, or who may have been acquitted of the accusations brought against them.

15. MAXIMILIEN ROBESPIERRE: ON POLITICAL MORALITY*

The embodiment of the Terror, and perhaps of the entire Revolution, was Maximilien Robespierre (1758–94). A provincial lawyer before 1789, he was more admired and less liked than any other member of the Convention. He was known as the "Incorruptible," and lived the life of an austere fanatic. It was a steadfast belief in his own views that slowly pushed Robespierre to the forefront as a Jacobin leader, for he was a paradox in many ways. He opposed capital punishment as a young lawyer, but guided the Reign of Terror; he was raised by Jesuits, but valued religion only as a bond to hold citizens together. Strongly influenced by the writings of Rousseau, Robespierre was unable to understand how any other person or party could be even partly correct when their views did not concur with his own.

Robespierre's democracy, based on public virtue and enforced by representatives of the people, had a brief existence. It became clear to the remaining deputies in the Convention that the Republic of Virtue had a Grand Inquisitor and that no one was secure from the finger of accusation. Conspiracies against Robespierre began to take form, and the "Incorruptible" took his place in the long line to the guillotine.

This selection, from a speech by Robespierre to the National Convention on February 5, 1794, presents the essence of his political philosophy. According to Robespierre, what was the purpose of the Revolution? How did he define liberty and equality? What was democracy? What was a Republic of Virtue? How did he defend the Reign of Terror?

ON THE PRINCIPLES OF POLITICAL MORALITY WHICH SHOULD GUIDE THE
NATIONAL CONVENTION IN THE DOMESTIC ADMINISTRATION OF THE REPUBLIC

(REPORT PRESENTED IN THE NAME OF THE COMMITTEE OF PUBLIC SAFETY)
(18 PLUVIÔSE YEAR II. 5 FEBRUARY 1794)

Citizen representatives of the people; . . .

It is time to define clearly the goal of the Revolution and the end which we wish to reach; it is time that we ourselves understand both the obstacles which keep us from it and the means we ought to adopt to attain it: a simple and important idea which seems never to have been perceived. Well, how could a cowardly and corrupt government have dared realize it? A king, a vain sen-

* Maximilien Robespierre, *Discours et Rapports à la Convention* (Paris: Union Générale d'Editions, 1965), pp. 209–19, 221–23, 225–26. Translated for this volume by Judith Radke.

ate, a Caesar, a Cromwell must above all cover their plans with a religious veil, compromise with all the vices, caress all parties, crush the party of virtuous men, oppress or deceive the people, in order to achieve the goal of their perfidious ambition. If we had not had a greater task to fulfill, if it were here only a question of the interests of a faction or a new aristocracy, we might have believed, as do certain writers, even more ignorant than vicious, that the plan of the French Revolution was written out in full in the books of Tacitus and of Machiavelli, and we might have sought the duties of the people's representatives in the history of Augustus, of Tiberius or of Vespasian, or even in that of certain French legislators; for, with a few minor distinctions of perfidy or cruelty, all tyrants resemble one another.

As for us, we come today to confide your political secrets to the universe, so that all the friends of the country can rally to the voice of reason and of public interest; so that the French nation and its representatives will be respected in all the countries of the universe where knowledge of their true principles may reach; so that the schemers who always seek to replace other intriguers, may be judged by public opinion, according to sure and easy rules.

It is necessary to take precautions in advance in order to place the destinies of liberty in the hands of the truth which is eternal, rather than in those of passing men, so that if the government were to forget the interests of the people, or if it were to fall into the hands of corrupt men, according to the natural order of things, the light of recognized principles would reveal its betrayals, and every new faction would find death in even the thought of crime.

Happy the people which can come to this! For, whatever new outrages may be prepared for it, how great are the resources in an order of things where public reason is the guarantee of liberty!

What is the goal toward which we strive? The peaceful enjoyment of liberty and equality; the reign of that eternal justice, whose laws are engraved neither in marble nor in stone, but in the hearts of all men, even in the heart of the slave who forgets them, and of the tyrant who denies them.

We wish an order of things where all the base and cruel passions are chained, all generous and beneficent passions aroused by the laws; where ambition is the desire to merit glory and to serve the country; where distinctions are born only of equality itself; where the citizen is obedient to the magistrate, the magistrate to the people, and the people to justice; where the country assures the well-being of each individual, and where each individual enjoys with pride the prosperity and the glory of the country, in which all souls become richer by the continual communication of republican sentiments and by the need to merit the esteem of a great people; where the arts are ornaments of the liberty which ennobles them, commerce the source of public wealth and not just of the monstrous opulence of a few families.

We want to substitute, in our country, morality for egoism, probity for honor, principles for customs, duties for proprieties, the rule of reason for the tyranny of fashion, the scorn of vice for the scorn of misfortune, pride for insolence, greatness of soul for vanity, the love of glory for the love of money, goodhearted people for the well-bred, merit for intrigue, genius for wit, truth for ostentation, the charm of happiness for the ennuis of sensual pleasure, the grandeur of mankind for the pettiness of great men, a magnanimous, powerful, happy people for an amiable, frivolous, miserable one, that is to say all the miracles and virtues of the Republic for all the vices and all the ridicules of the monarchy.

We wish, in a word, to fulfill the desires of nature, to accomplish the destinies of humanity, to keep the promises of philosophy, to release providence from the long reign of crime and tyranny. May France, once illustrious among slave nations, eclipsing the glory of all free peoples who have existed, become the model of nations, the terror of oppressors, the consolation of the oppressed, the ornament of the universe, and by sealing our work with our blood, may we at least see the dawn of universal felicity. . . . That is our ambition, that is our goal.

What kind of government can realize these wonders? Only a democratic or republican government: these two words are synonymous, in spite of the abuses of popular usage; . . . Democracy is not a state where the people, in continual assembly, settles by itself all public affairs; even less is it one where a hundred thousand fractions of the people, by isolated, hasty and contradictory measures, would decide the fate of the entire society: such a government has never existed, and if it were to exist, it would only lead the people back to despotism.

Democracy is a state where the sovereign people, guided by laws which are its work, does itself all which it can do well, and through delegates all which it cannot do itself.

It is then in the principles of democratic government that you must seek the rules of your political conduct.

But, in order to establish and consolidate democracy in our country, in order to arrive at the peaceful reign of constitutional laws, it is necessary to bring to an end the war of liberty against tyranny and to pass through the storms of the Revolution successfully: such is the goal of the revolutionary system which you have regularized. You must, then, base your conduct upon the stormy circumstances in which the Republic finds itself; and the plan of your administration must be the result of the spirit of revolutionary government, combined with the general principles of democracy.

For, what is the fundamental principle of democratic or popular government, . . ? It is virtue; I speak of the public virtue which produced so many marvels in Greece and Rome, and which ought to produce even more astonishing ones in republican France; of that virtue which is nothing else but love of the country and of its laws.

But since the essence of the Republic or of democracy is equality, it follows that love of country embraces necessarily love of equality.

It is also true that this sublime sentiment supposes the preference of the public interest to all private interests; from which it follows that love of country supposes or produces all virtues; for are virtues anything else but the strength of spirit which makes one capable of these sacrifices? And how could the slave of avarice or ambition, for example, sacrifice his idol to his country?

Not only is virtue the soul of democracy, but it can exist only in this government. In the monarchy, I know of only one individual who can love the country, and who, in order to do so, has no need of virtue; that is the monarch. The reason for that is that of all the inhabitants of his realm, the monarch is the only one who has a country. Is he not the sovereign power, at least in fact? Does he not take the place of the people? And what is country, if it is not the land where one is a citizen and a member of the sovereign power?

As a consequence of the same principle, in aristocratic states, the word *patrie* means something only to the patrician families which exercise the sovereignty.

Only in a democracy is the state truly the country of all the individuals which comprise it and can the state count as many defenders interested in its cause as its citizens. That is the source of the superiority of free peoples over others. If Athens and Sparta triumphed over the tyrants of Asia, and the Swiss over the tyrants of Spain and Austria, there is no other reason for their triumphs.

But the French are the first people in the world who have established true democracy, by giving equality and full rights of citizenship to all men; and that is, in my opinion, the true reason that all tyrants in league against the Republic will be vanquished. . . .

Since the soul of the Republic is virtue and equality, and since our goal is to found, to consolidate the Republic, it follows that the first rule of your political conduct ought to be to relate all your operations to the maintenance of equality and to the development of virtue; for the first concern of the legislator must be to strengthen the principle of the government. Thus, everything which tends to stimulate love of country, to purify manners, to elevate spirits, to direct the passions of the human heart toward the public interest, must be adopted or established by you. Everything that tends to concentrate the passions upon the abject personal ego, to arouse an enthusiasm for petty things and scorn of great concerns, must be rejected or repressed by you. In the system of the French Revolution, what is immoral is impolitic, what is corrupting is counter-revolutionary. Weakness, vices, prejudices are the way of royalty. Swayed too often perhaps by the weight of our former habits, as well as by the imperceptible bent of human weakness, toward false ideas and faint-hearted sentiments, we must refrain much less from too much energy than from too much weakness. Perhaps the greatest danger which we have to avoid is not the fervor of zeal, but rather the lassitude of good works, and fear of our own courage. Wind up the sacred spring of republican government continually instead of letting it run down. Needless to say, I do not wish to justify any excess. The most sacred principles are abused; it is up to the wisdom of the government to consider the circumstances, to decide on the right moment, to choose the means; for the manner of preparing great things is an essential part of the talent for bringing them to pass, as wisdom is itself a part of virtue. . . .

Republican virtue can be considered in relation to the people and in relation to the government: it is necessary to both of them. When the government alone is deprived of it, there remains a resource in the virtue of the people; but, when the people itself is corrupt, liberty is already lost. . . .

But, when, by prodigious efforts of courage and reason, a people breaks the chains of despotism to make trophies for liberty out of them; when by the force of its moral temperament, it escapes, in a way of speaking, from the arms of death to reassume all the vigor of its youth; when, in turn sensitive and proud, intrepid and docile, it can be stopped neither by the impregnable ramparts nor by the innumerable armies of the tyrants armed against it, and when it stops of its own accord before the image of the law; it does not then thrust rapidly to the height of its destinies, that could only be the fault of those who govern it. . . .

If the force of popular government in peace is virtue, that of popular government in revolution is both *virtue and terror;* virtue, without which terror is deadly; terror, without which virtue is powerless. Terror is nothing but prompt, severe, inflexible justice; it is then an emanation of virtue; it is less a particular principle than a consequence of the general principle of democracy, applied to the most pressing needs of the country. *Mao - "friends and enemies, up treatment of enemies*

It has been said that terror was the basic weapon of despotic government. Does your government then resemble a despotism? Yes, just as the sword which shines in the hands of the heroes of liberty resembles the one with which the satellites of tyranny are armed. Let the despot govern his brutalized subjects by terror; he is right to do, as a despot: subdue by terror the enemies of liberty and you will be right, as founders of the Republic. The government of the Revolution is the despotism of liberty over tyranny. Was force created only to protect crime? And is it not the destiny of lightning to strike proud heads?

Nature imposes upon every physical and moral being the law of self-preservation; crime butchers innocence in order to rule, and innocence struggles with all its might in the hands of crime. If tyranny reigns a single day, the following day there will be not one patriot left. How long will the despot's fury be called justice, and the justice of the people, barbarity or rebellion? How gentle they are with the oppressors, and how inexorable for the oppressed! Nothing is more natural than this: whosoever does not hate crime, cannot love virtue. . . .

When it is a question of the salvation of the country, the testimony of the universe cannot take the place of the truth attested to by witnesses, nor evidence itself be a substitute for literal proof.

The slowness of the trials is equivalent to impunity; the uncertainty of punishment encourages all the guilty; and yet they complain of the severity of justice; they complain of the detention of the enemies of the Republic. They seek their examples in the history of tyrants, because they do not wish to choose them from the history of the people, nor to draw them from the spirit of threatened liberty. In Rome, when the consul discovered conspiracy and stifled it instantly by the death of the accomplices of Catiline, he was accused of having violated methods of procedure. By whom? By the ambitious Caesar, who wished to add the horde of conspirators to his party, . . . and all the evil citizens who feared on their own behalf the virtue of a true Roman and the severity of the laws.

To punish humanity's oppressors is clemency; to pardon them is barbarousness. The severity of tyrants has as its principle severity alone: the severity of republican government has its source in beneficence. . . .

16. MAXIMILIEN ROBESPIERRE: ESTABLISHMENT OF THE WORSHIP OF A SUPREME BEING*

The climax to the Reign of Terror was an attempt to turn France into a Republic of Virtue in order to achieve the utopia of absolute equality which philosophers such as Rousseau had idealized. For Robespierre and his supporters the Age of Reason had arrived, and it was logical that the state should exercise its authority on behalf of the souls of the people. In less than half a decade the ecclesiastical organization of religion had been thoroughly transformed, and the de-Christianizing process finally saw the cathedral of Notre Dame used for services in honor of Reason. In the following address to the Committee of Public Safety, what arguments did Robespierre offer in defense of legislation to establish the worship of a Supreme Being? How did he define "fanaticism," and why, in his view, were all enemies of the Republic subject to the charge of fanaticism and corruption? What remnants of traditional Christianity were retained in the decree proposed by Robespierre and enacted on May 7, 1794, by the National Convention to establish the worship of a Supreme Being? Was the decree essentially political or theological? In what ways?

[ADDRESS BY ROBESPIERRE READ TO THE COMMITTEE OF
PUBLIC SAFETY, MAY 7, 1794]

Citizens: Every doctrine which consoles and elevates the mind ought to be received; reject all those which tend to degrade it and corrupt it. Reanimate—exalt—every generous sentiment and those great moral truths which some have attempted to extinguish. . . .

The idea of the Supreme Being and of the immortality of the soul is a continual appeal to justice: this idea is then social and republican. I know of no legislator who ever attempted to nationalize atheism . . . [and] you are fortunate in living in an age and in a country whose enlightenment leaves us no other task to fulfil than to recall men to nature and to truth. Be very cautious not to sever the sacred bond which unites men to the Author of their being. . . .

Let us learn the lessons of history. . . . Among those . . . at the time of which I speak, . . . one man, Rousseau, by the elevation of his mind and the grandeur of his character, showed himself worthy of being the preceptor of the human race. He openly attacked tyranny. He spoke with the enthusiasm of the Divinity; his masculine and virtuous eloquence painted in glowing colors the charms of virtue; it defended those consolatory dogmas with which reason supports the human heart. . . . Ah, if he had witnessed this Revolution, of which he was the precursor, who can doubt that his generous soul would have embraced with transport the cause of justice and equality? . . .

. . . Fanatics, hope nothing from us! To recall men to the pure worship of the Supreme Being is to give a mortal blow to fanaticism. All fiction disappears before truth, and every folly falls before reason. . . . Ambitious priests, do not expect that we shall re-establish your empire! . . . You have destroyed yourselves. And, besides, what is there in common between the priests and God? How different is the God of nature from the God of priests? Priests have so disfigured

* Maximilien Robespierre, "Address to the Committee of Public Safety" in Mayo W. Hazeltine, ed., *Orations* (25 vols.; New York: P. F. Collier and Son, 1902), VIII, 3300–3305.

the Supreme Being that they have done their best to destroy the idea; they have made him sometimes a globe of fire, sometimes an ox, sometimes a tree, sometimes a man, and sometimes a king. Priests created a God in their own image— they made him jealous, capricious, covetous, cruel, and implacable. . . . The true priest of the Supreme Being is nature; his temple the universe; his religion virtue; his *fêtes* the joy of a great people assembled under his eyes, to draw closer the sweet bonds of universal fraternity, and to present to him the homage of pure and sensitive hearts. . . .

The enemies of the Republic are all corrupt men. The patriot is in every sense an honest and magnanimous man. It is little to annihilate kings; we must make every nation respect the character of the French people. It is useless to bear to the end of the universe the renown of our arms, if very passion tears with impunity the bosom of our own country. Let us beware of the intoxication of success! Let us be terrible in reverses, modest in triumph, and let us secure peace and happiness by wisdom and morality. That is the true aim of our labors— that our heroic and difficult task. We believe we shall achieve this aim by proposing the following decree*:

1. The French people recognize the existence of the Supreme Being and the immortality of the soul.
2. They recognize that the worship worthy of the Supreme Being is the practice of the duties of man.
3. They place in the first rank of these duties, to detest bad faith and tyranny, to punish tyrants and traitors, to relieve the unfortunate, to respect the weak, to defend the oppressed, to do to others all the good that is possible and not to be unjust to anyone.
4. Festivals shall be instituted to remind man of the thought of the divinity and of the dignity of his being.
5. They shall take their names from the glorious events of our revolution, from the virtues most cherished and most useful to man, and from the great gifts of nature.
6. The French Republic shall celebrate every year the festival of July 14, 1789, August 10, 1792, January 21, 1793, and May 31, 1793.
7. It shall celebrate on the days of *décadi* [The months in the new republican calendar were divided into three equal parts of ten days each called *décades,* the 10th days termed *décadi*] the list of festivals that follows: to the supreme being and to nature; to the human race; to the French people; to the benefactors of humanity; to the martyrs of liberty; to liberty and equality; to the republic; to the liberty of the world; to the love of the fatherland; to the hatred of tyrants and of traitors; to truth; to justice; to modesty; to glory and immortality; to friendship; to frugality; to courage; to good faith; to heroism; to disinterestedness; to stoicism; to love; to conjugal love; to paternal love; to maternal tenderness; to filial affection; to childhood; to youth; to manhood; to old age; to misfortune; to agriculture; to industry; to our forefathers; to posterity; to happiness. . . .

* "Decree for Establishing the Worship of the Supreme Being" in Frank Maloy Anderson, *The Constitutions and Other Select Documents Illustrative of the History of France, 1789–1907* (Minneapolis: The H. W. Wilson Co., 1908), pp. 137–39.

9. The National Convention summons all the talents worthy to serve the cause of humanity to the honor of contributing to its establishment by hymns and patriotic songs and by all the means which can enhance its beauty and utility.

10. The Committee of Public Safety shall confer distinction upon those works which seem the best adapted to carry on these purposes and shall reward their authors.

11. Liberty of worship is maintained, in conformity with the decree of 18 Frimaire.

12. Every gathering that is aristocratic and contrary to public order shall be suppressed.

13. In case of disturbances of which any worship whatsoever may be the occasion or motive, those who may excite them by fanatical preaching or by counter-revolutionary insinuations, those who may provoke them by unjust and gratuitous violence, shall likewise be punished with all the severity of the law. . . .

17. THE REIGN OF TERROR—MEMOIRS OF A PRISONER*

The Reign of Terror was widespread, but was intended to operate more against members of the government than against the people as a whole. It called for a policy of intimidation against spies (real and suspected), aristocrats, royalists, non-juring priests, profiteers, hoarders, ineffective generals, corrupt government officials, and all other counterrevolutionary persons. Because excessive power was given to local revolutionary committees, however, the process of denunciation, conviction, and execution rapidly was abused, and the innocent and the guilty followed one another to the guillotine. The final product was an air of suspicion and fear rather than a spirit of virtue. Nevertheless, the total number of victims hardly compared with the casualties inflicted in a Napoleonic campaign, and the government's control of the populace did not match the practices of modern totalitarian states.

The Girondins were a loose coalition of deputies mainly from provincial districts and named for the province of *Gironde* in the south of France. As losers in a power struggle with the Jacobins, many Girondins later paid the supreme price. The following account was written by a Girondin sympathizer who suffered arrest and imprisonment but was not executed. Who was blamed for the Reign of Terror? On what grounds? What was meant by the charge of "federalism"?

The month of October, 1793, will be for ever remarkable for the innumerable arrests which were made by the then superior powers through France. The whole country bent beneath the tyrannic yoke of the faction headed by Robespierre, which triumphed on all sides, and reaped the fruits of the victory which it had gained on the 31st of May. His usurpation was assuming an organized

* "Memoirs of a Prisoner" in *The Reign of Terror; A Collection of Authentic Narratives of the Horrors Committed by the Revolutionary Government of France Under Marat and Robespierre. Written by Eye-Witnesses of the Scenes* (2 vols.; London, 1826), I, 263–64, 269–73, 275–76, 279, 282–84, 287, 290–91, 292–94, 297–99, 326–30.

form: the efforts of the upright citizens, being without connection, without force, and without any central point of union, . . . only served to mark out more distinctly for the vengeance of the tyrant, all the enlightened and energetic members of the republic. The accusation of federalism was a vast snare against all the members of the administration who were worthy of their posts, and against the liberty of many worthy men. An entire generation, the true disciples of the Jean Jacqueses, the Voltaires, and the Diderots, was exposed to destruction, and was partly destroyed under that horrible pretext. It is melancholy to think of the hopes of the country thus destroyed by a tyrant, and abandoned to the ferocious fury of the Jacobins, his satellites. At this time France presented the picture of a country conquered by savages, whose ravaging and destructive hands were directed by their leader against all that was enlightened and honest. In this disastrous state of things, the town of Bordeaux had its share in the common misfortune. The opportunity presented itself of accusing it of federalism, and it was not suffered to escape. . . .

. . . A body of National Guards, chosen from among the lowest and most ignorant people, took possession of the city as of a place which had been carried by assault. There no longer appeared any traces of liberty in Bordeaux. Bodies of hired brigands spread terror in every house, and carried off a number of citizens during the night. Not a single inhabitant could now enjoy a moment of repose. The report of the arrests which had taken place during the night was spread around in the morning, and filled all quarters of the city with stupor and alarm. The upright magistrates were deposed, forced to fly, or arrested. An invisible evil genius appeared to hover over the city, and to take pleasure in striking his blows in the dark. In the midst of these circumstances, suddenly appeared the bust of Marat, covered with a red cap, and carried through the streets by an actor of the Vaudeville, followed by a crowd of men whose features were entirely unknown. These frightful presages, which were called a *fête,* increased the general anxiety. . . . The city was filled with the emissaries and spies of the Jacobin party. It was then that the agents of the tyrant entered as conquerors into Bordeaux; and they organized a new and dreadful system of tactics, which united treachery to crime, in which villainy and hypocrisy were alone of importance, and by which the general and the soldiers only appeared in order to pillage and prescribe. I was not myself a witness of these horrors; I was destined to behold others still more atrocious. Although I was not present at the devastation of Bordeaux, and although I did not see the torrents of blood which flowed within its walls, I beheld its deputies massacred; the most enlightened men, the most eloquent and the most virtuous members of the republic, only survived a few days the liberty of the city which they represented, and whose glory they maintained, even upon the scaffold.

Such was the deplorable state of Bordeaux, when I was arrested there, on the 4th of October, 1793, at three o'clock in the morning, . . . I had never in my life appeared before any magistrate; I had never been cited before any tribunal; and I think I may say that my independence had been, until then, as great and as complete as any individual had ever enjoyed. I actually had no idea of the nature of a prison or of fetters. . . . It was in this state of primitive independence.

if I may so express myself, that I was suddenly plunged into captivity, and loaded with irons. My situation at first appeared to me like a dream—I expected every moment to awake and find myself at liberty.

I was carried before the revolutionary committee. . . . It was composed of clubists [Jacobins], and presided over by the emissaries of the tyrant. . . . A Spaniard had been arrested at the same time with me. He had come into France in pursuit of liberty, under the guarantee of national faith. Being persecuted by the religious inquisition of his own country, he had fallen, in France into the hands of the political inquisition of the revolutionary committee. I doubt whether there ever existed a soul more strongly or more sincerely imbued with a love of liberty, or more worthy of enjoying it. It was his fate to be always persecuted for that sacred cause, and yet his love for it increased. To relate my own misfortunes is to relate his: our persecution proceeded from the same causes: the same iron chained us to the ground, the same dungeon inclosed us, and the same unhappy fate appeared to await us. . . . I was indignant enough on my own account, but was much more so when I beheld the representative, Duchâtel, with his head uncovered, pressed by the questions of these satellites. . . . They had the impudence to interrogate him. . . . I felt as if I beheld the whole French nation outraged in his person. At the end of three hours we were informed that Duchâtel, the Spaniard, and I were to be immediately sent forward to La Reote, to undergo [further] examination. . . .

We were each of us thrown into a carriage. . . . I had four citizens in my carriage, without reckoning those who were on the coach-box, and on the roof. . . . At our first pause, in order to take supper, I could not restrain my indignation: the Spaniard and I were not bound; but Duchâtel was. An innocent man, a representative of the people—any man in such a state thus insulted and abused, made the blood boil in my veins. . . . I seized, without perceiving it, a bottle, in the attitude of a person who intended to throw it. Nothing more was necessary: three gendarmes immediately seized me. . . . In about a quarter of an hour I was tied hand and foot, like my unhappy companion of misfortune, and continued so during the remainder of our journey to Paris. . . . Upon our arrival at La Reote, I was locked up alone in a dungeon, under pretence of my having mutinied. . . . [After further interrogation] we were at length sent to Paris, under the guard of two gendarmes, who made a speculation of us, and famished us during our journey. . . . We performed the journey without once getting out of the carriages, or taking any rest, and were forced to remain for a hundred and forty-nine hours seated in the back of a very inconvenient cabriolet. . . . At Agen [our guards] riveted on the legs of the Spaniard and myself a bar-shot of eighty pounds weight. Our hands being tied, and our bodies bound with a triple rope, did not appear to them sufficient precautions: we were loaded during the remainder of our journey with this weight of iron, which was so heavy, that, had the carriage fallen on one side, we should inevitably have had a leg broken. . . .

We arrived at Paris on the 16th of October. Here a new scene began to open. Behold us three cast into that abyss of the living, into the *Conciergerie* of Paris, still dyed with the blood of the victims of the 2d of September, and in which the revolutionary tribunal, by its conduct, exceeded all former instances of ferocity and crime. We were carried to all the prisons of Paris, one after another, from the *Luxembourg* to *La Force,* and from *La Force* to the prison of *L'Abbaye,* and from thence to the Conciergerie, where we were carried into the first ward-room, and a blacksmith was sent for to unrivet my irons, and those of the Spaniard. I was first put into an arm-chair; but this posture not appearing convenient to the workman, I was stretched on the ground, where I lay like an animal offered for sale, and exposed to their insulting ridicule. [After a hundred and forty-nine hours in the carriage] I could not support my steps. No hand was held out to assist me. I was pushed about from one to another like a drunken man who is made the sport of the mob. . . . I was soon separated from my companions, and plunged, under the pretence of secrecy, into the most loathsome dungeon in the prison. . . . It was at the utmost not more than twelve feet square. My companions were to the number of three. . . .

Such were the individuals whom I discovered around me [an accused murderer, a forger, and another political prisoner], because I was suspected of being a *brissotine.* They were clothed in rags, and their professions were written in their features. . . .

I remained in this dungeon thirteen days. . . . During all this time, I scarcely ever knew one of my companion to feel any other remorse than that of having let himself be taken. . . . I was overwhelmed with melancholy, in the midst of these robbers. I could find no connection between my pretended *girondisme* and their crimes. Deprived of light—the air charged with a most loathsome smell—covered with filth—confined in a hole only twelve feet square, in which up to seven of us were heaped together, and those the very refuse of mankind—my wretched situation may be easily conceived. . . . I was in complete ignorance of what was going on in the rest of the world. I was kept in the most rigorous confinement, without any news of my companions in misfortune, and without even being examined. . . .

About eleven o'clock one morning the bolts resounded; the door of our cell was opened, and Lebeau, the keeper of the Prison, made his appearance. He came in person to lead me to be examined. . . . Pale and exhausted, with a long and filthy beard, and my clothes covered with the chopped straw which had composed my bed for thirteen days—I sustained a long interrogatory, and was not treated with the indulgence that was due to the state in which I was.

I was confined in another part of the Conciergerie, and entered the temple of persecuted virtue. Vergniaux, Gonsonné, Brissot, Ducos, Fongrede, Valazé, Duchâtel, and their colleagues, were the inmates whom I found installed in my new dwelling. . . . Curiosity will be awakened at the mention of these celebrated names, but I have but little means of satisfying it; I arrived among them two days before their condemnation, and as if to be a witness of their death. France and all Europe are acquainted with the particulars of their trial, if that name can be given to the most atrocious proscription; it was all through a most solemn violation of every right, even of that of defending themselves. . . .

They were condemned to death on the night of the 30th of October at about eleven o'clock. They all received the same sentence; . . . This was the first time that so many extraordinary men had been massacred in a body. Youth, beauty, genius, virtue, talents, everything that was interesting in man, was cut off by a single stroke; if cannibals had been their judges, they would not have committed such a horror. Our minds were so exalted by their courage, that it was not for a considerable time after the blow was struck, that we began to feel its effects. . . .

Oh you, the first of our citizens, your only crimes were your being born in an age of villany [*sic*], and your having felt the courage of virtue in the most abandoned of cities! In vain will that city erect statues to your honour, and endeavour to conceal, under their foundations, the spot on which you were immolated, which it will do, if it is its destiny to become free once more; it never will efface the marks of your blood, which will depose against it in the eyes of the universe and of posterity. You have died like men who founded the liberty of the republic, and with the fall of which our own was connected. . . .

A hundred thousand Frenchmen were immolated on your tomb; social order fell to the ground, and tyranny reigned over the dead; our finest cities were destroyed or ravaged; a year of horrors, hitherto unexampled in the history of the world, followed your destruction, and has engraved your vindication on the tablets of history. . . .

Victims were thrown into the Conciergerie from all parts of the country. It was filled incessantly by the crowds sent from the departments, and was emptied as soon by the daily massacres, and the transfers to other prisons. . . . Thus, the daily distribution of these death-warrants, which were destined for sixty or eighty persons, filled with terror the hearts of at least six hundred. . . .

They began to heaping fifteen persons together in the fatal cart. They soon put thirty, and at length went as far as eighty-four: and the day that the death of Robespierre rescued the human race from their fury, they had everything prepared for sending a hundred and fifty persons together to the place of execution. An immense aqueduct had already been dug in the *Place St. Antoine,* for the purpose of carrying away the blood, and, I tremble as I mention the dreadful fact . . . the blood of the unfortunate victims was spilled each day in buckets, and four men were occupied, at the moment of execution, in emptying them into this aqueduct.

. . . I have seen forty-five magistrates of the Parliament of Paris, the thirty-three of the Parliament of Toulouse, walking forth to death with the same air with which they formerly followed in the public processions. I have seen thirty farmers-general pass by with a calm and firm step; . . . Yes, I have absolutely seen these men led to the scaffold, like droves of cattle to the slaughterhouse. . . . These bodies of victims, to which they gave the name of batches, were composed of men the most diametrically opposite in principles and parties. . . . Entire generations have literally been swept away in one day. The venerable Malesherbes was dragged to the scaffold, at the head of his whole family. . . . Fourteen young girls of Verdun, who appeared like virgins dressed out for a public *fête,* were led out together to the scaffold. . . . Twenty women from Poitou, the greater part of whom were peasant girls, were also butchered together. . . . They were all executed a few days after their arrival. At the moment of her mounting the scaffold, they tore, from the breast of one of these unfortunate females, the child she was suckling, and which was, at that very moment, imbibing a nourishment of which the executioner was going to destroy the source. . . . Several of the others died in the cart, on the way to the scaffold, but their dead bodies were guillotined. . . . And those who acted thus were men, were Frenchmen, to whom the most eloquent philosophers have been preaching humanity and tolerance for sixty years back. . . . If a stop had not been put to this deluge of human blood, I have no doubt that we should soon have seen men voluntarily precipitate themselves under the edge of the guillotine. . . .

THE NAPOLEONIC ERA

18. NAPOLEON BONAPARTE: PROCLAMATION TO THE ARMY OF ITALY*

The conspirators who overthrew Robespierre did not intend to halt the Reign of Terror, but the nation was in no mood to continue the emergency measures initiated in 1793–94. The Directory, which replaced the Convention, was continuously harried by dissident political factions at home while waging an aggressive war abroad. A planned military campaign against Austria in 1796 envisaged French armies pushing across the Rhine through the Germanies while a diversionary attack in the south tied up as many Austrian troops as possible. The young General Napoleon Bonaparte, who had defended the Convention against Parisian rioters in its final days on the 13th Vendémiaire (October 5, 1795), was placed in command of the Army of Italy. Although they were veterans, the soldiers of the Army of Italy suffered from low morale under the Directory until Napoleon took command. What did Napoleon offer to spur his army forward in his Proclamation of March 27, 1796? In what ways did his Proclamation demonstrate statesmanship?

7 Germinal, Year IV (March 27, 1796)

Soldiers, you are naked, ill fed! The Government owes you much; it can give you nothing. Your patience, the courage you display in the midst of these rocks, are admirable; but they procure you no glory, no fame is reflected upon you. I seek to lead you into the most fertile plains in the world. Rich provinces, great cities will be in your power. There you will find honor, glory, and riches. Soldiers of Italy, would you be lacking in courage or constancy?

7 Floréal, Year IV (April 26, 1796)

Soldiers:

In a fortnight you have won six victories, taken twenty-one standards, fifty-five pieces of artillery, several strong positions, and conquered the richest part of Piedmont; you have captured 15,000 prisoners and killed or wounded more than 10,000 men.

Heretofore you fought for sterile rocks, made famous by your prowess, but useless to the *Patrie;* today, by your accomplishments you equal the armies of Holland and the Rhine. Destitute of everything, you have supplied everything. You have won battles without cannon, crossed rivers without bridges, made

* "Bonaparte's Proclamation to the Army of Italy" in John Hall Stewart, ed., *A Documentary Survey of the French Revolution* (New York: The Macmillan Co., 1951), pp. 672–73. Reprinted by permission.

forced marches without shoes, camped without brandy and often without bread. Soldiers of liberty, only republican phalanxes could have endured what you have endured. Soldiers, you have our thanks! The grateful *Patrie* will owe its prosperity to you; and if, as conquerors of Toulon, you foreshadowed the immortal campaign of 1794, your present victories presage a still greater one.

The two armies which but recently attacked you with audacity are fleeing before you in terror; the wicked men who laughed at your misery and rejoiced at the thought of the triumphs of your enemies are confounded and trembling.

But, soldiers, as yet you have done nothing compared with what remains to be done. . . . Undoubtedly the greatest obstacles have been overcome; but you still have battles to fight, cities to capture, rivers to cross. Is there one among you whose courage is abating? . . . No. . . . All of you are consumed with a desire to extend the glory of the French people; all of you long to humiliate those arrogant kings who dare to contemplate placing us in fetters; all of you desire to dictate a glorious peace, one which will indemnify the *Patrie* for the immense sacrifices it has made; all of you wish to be able to say with pride as you return to your villages, "I was with the victorious army of Italy!"

Friends, I promise you this conquest; but there is one condition you must swear to fulfill—to respect the people whom you liberate, to repress the horrible pillaging committed by scoundrels incited by our enemies. Otherwise you would not be the liberators of the people; you would be their scourge; . . . Plunderers will be shot without mercy; already, several have been. . . .

Peoples of Italy, the French army comes to break your chains; the French people is the friend of all peoples; approach it with confidence; your property, your religion, and your customs will be respected.

We are waging war as generous enemies, and we wish only to crush the tyrants who enslave you.

19. LOUIS DE BOURRIENNE: MEMOIRS OF NAPOLEON BONAPARTE*

Louis de Bourrienne (1769–1834) served as Napoleon's private secretary from 1797 until he was dismissed in 1802. Perhaps because of the close association between the two men, Bourrienne's views of Napoleon were colored by two facts: envy of a man whom, in their school days, Bourrienne had considered inferior to himself, and pique at being dismissed from his official position because of a financial misadventure. Still, when Bourrienne's *Memoirs* were first published in 1829 they were generally received as the most truthful account of the Corsican yet to appear. According to Bourrienne's *Memoirs* did Napoleon appear to have been a secure, well-balanced, gregarious person, living and working for the long-range welfare of France, or was he insecure, vain, and unconcerned with history? How did Bourrienne view Napoleon's allegiance to liberty?

At this period, 1797, Napoleon was still swayed by the impulse of the age. He thought of nothing but representative governments. Often has he said to me, "I should like the era of representative governments to be dated from my

* Louis Antoine Fauvelet de Bourrienne, *Memoirs of Napoleon Bonaparte*, trans. R. W. Phipps (4 vols., rev. ed.; New York: Charles Scribner's Sons, 1891), I, 112, 306–8, 313–17, 338.

time." His conduct in Italy and his proclamations ought to give, and in fact do give, weight to this account of his opinion. But there is no doubt that this idea was more connected with lofty views of ambition than a sincere desire for the benefit of the human race; for, at a later period, he adopted this phrase: "I should like to be the head of the most ancient of the dynasties of Europe." What a difference between Bonaparte, . . . the subduer of royalism at Toulon, . . . the fortunate conqueror of the 13th Vendémiaire, the instigator and supporter of the revolution of Fructidor, and the founder of the Republics of Italy, the fruits of his immortal victories,—and Bonaparte, First Consul in 1800, Consul for life in 1802, and, above all, Napoleon, Emperor of the French in 1804, and King of Italy in 1805.

Bonaparte was now, 1800, in the prime of life, and about thirty. . . . His finely-shaped head, his superb forehead, his pale countenance and his usual meditative look, have been transferred to the canvas; but the versatility of his expression was beyond the reach of imitation. All the various workings of his mind were instantaneously depicted in his countenance; and his glance changed from mild to severe, and from angry to good-humoured, almost with the rapidity of lightning. It may truly be said that he had a particular look for every thought that arose in his mind.

Bonaparte had beautiful hands, and he was very proud of them; while conversing he would often look at them with an air of self-complacency. He also fancied he had fine teeth, but his pretension to that advantage was not so well founded as his vanity on the score of his hands.

When walking, either alone or in company with any one, in his apartments or in his gardens, he had the habit of stooping a little, and crossing his hands behind his back. He frequently gave an involuntary shrug of his right shoulder, which was accompanied by a movement of his mouth from left to right. This habit was always most remarkable when his mind was absorbed in the consideration of any profound subject. It was often while walking that he dictated to me his most important notes. He could endure great fatigue, not only on horseback but on foot; he would sometimes walk for five or six hours in succession without being aware of it. . . .

Bonaparte had two ruling passions, glory and war. He was never more gay than in the camp, and never more morose than in the inactivity of peace. Plans for the construction of public monuments also pleased his imagination, and filled up the void caused by the want of active occupation. He was aware that monuments from part of the history of nations, of whose civilisation they bear evidence for ages after those who created them have disappeared from the earth, and that they likewise often bear false witness to remote posterity of the reality of merely fabulous conquests. Bonaparte was, however, mistaken as to the mode of accomplishing the object he had in view. His ciphers, his trophies, and subsequently his eagles, splendidly adorned the monuments of his reign. But why did he wish to stamp false initials on things with which neither he nor his reign had any connection; as, for example the old Louvre? Did he imagine that the letter "N," which everywhere obtruded itself on the eye, had in it a charm to controvert the records of history, or alter the course of time?

His sentiments towards France now differed widely from what I had known them to be in his youth . . . and it might be said that he now ardently loved

France. His imagination was fired by the very thought of seeing her great, happy, and powerful, and, as the first nation in the world, dictating laws to the rest. He fancied his name inseparably connected with France, and resounding in the ears of posterity. In all his actions he lost sight of the present moment, and thought only of futurity; so, in all places where he led the way to glory, the opinion of France was ever present in his thoughts. . . . He had it in his power to do much, for he risked everything and spared nothing. His inordinate ambition goaded him on to the attainment of power; and power when possessed served only to augment his ambition. Bonaparte was thoroughly convinced of the truth that trifles often decide the greatest events; therefore he watched rather than provoked opportunity, and when the right moment approached, he suddenly took advantage of it. It is curious that, amidst all the anxieties of war and government, the fear of the Bourbons incessantly pursued him, and the Faubourg St. Germain was to him always a threatening phantom.

He did not esteem mankind, whom, indeed, he despised more and more in proportion as he became acquainted with them. In him this unfavourable opinion of human nature was justified by many glaring examples of baseness, and he used frequently to repeat, "There are two levers for moving men,—interest and fear." . . .

One of Bonaparte's greatest misfortunes was, that he neither believed in friendship nor felt the necessity of loving. How often have I heard him say, "Friendship is but a name; I love nobody. I do not even love my brothers. Perhaps Joseph, a little, from habit and because he is my elder: and Duroc,[3] I love him too. But why? Because his character pleases me. He is stern and resolute; and I really believe the fellow never shed a tear. For my part, I know very well that I have no true friends. As long as I continue what I am, I may have as many pretended friends as I please. Leave sensibility to women; it is their business. But men should be firm in heart and in purpose, or they should have nothing to do with war or government. . . ."

He was then, if I may use the expression, two individuals in one: the Republican general, who was obliged to appear the advocate of liberty and the principles of the Revolution; and the votary of ambition, secretly plotting the downfall of that liberty and those principles.

I often wondered at the consummate address with which he contrived to deceive those who were likely to see through his designs. This hypocrisy, which some perhaps, may call profound policy, was indispensable to the accomplishment of his projects; and sometimes as if to keep himself in practice, he would do it in matters of secondary importance. For example, his opinion of the insatiable avarice of Sieyès is well known; yet when he proposed, in his message to the Council of Ancients, to give his colleague, under the title of national recompense, the price of his obedient secession, it was, in the words of the message, a recompense worthily bestowed on his *disinterested virtues*.

While at the Luxembourg Bonaparte showed, by a Consular act, his hatred of the liberty of the press above all liberties, for he loved none. . . .

---

3. General Geraud Duroc (1772–1813) was one of Napoleon's few close personal friends.

20. ORDER REGULATING THE NEWSPAPERS*

Between 1789 and 1799 the press had played a major role in stirring and shaping public emotions. The Consulate, which was a disguised dictatorship even though most Frenchmen were not immediately aware of that fact, took steps to prevent criticism and agitation by effectively muzzling the French press in an Order of January 17, 1800. On what grounds did the consuls justify their restrictions on freedom of publication? How much freedom was left to the press? What types of foreign news could be printed?

The consuls of the Republic, considering that a part of the newspapers which are printed in the department of the Seine are instruments in the hands of the enemies of the Republic; that the government is particularly charged by the French people to look after their security, orders as follows:

1. The minister of police shall permit to be printed, published, and circulated during the whole course of the war only the following newspapers: . . . [Here follows the names of thirteen newspapers], and newspapers devoted exclusively to science, arts, literature, commerce, announcements and notices.

2. The minister of the general police shall immediately make a report upon all the newspapers that are printed in the other departments.

3. The minister of the general police shall see that no new newspaper be printed in the department of the Seine, as well as in all the other departments of the Republic.

4. The proprietors and editors of the newspapers preserved by the present order shall present themselves to the minister of the police in order to attest their character as French citizens, their residences and signatures, and they shall promise fidelity to the constitution.

5. All newspapers which shall insert articles opposed to the respect that is due to the social compact, to the sovereignty of the people and the glory of the armies, or which shall publish invectives against the governments and nations who are the friends or allies of the Republic, even when these articles may be extracts from foreign periodicals, shall be immediately suppressed.

6. The minister of the general police is charged with the execution of the present order, which shall be inserted in the *Bulletin of the Laws*.

21. LAW RE-ESTABLISHING SLAVERY IN THE FRENCH COLONIES†

Revolutionary enthusiasm for human liberty had led the Convention to abolish Negro slavery in all French colonies in 1794. Napoleon, however, planned to re-create the prerevolutionary French empire, and the re-establishment of slavery was viewed as a necessary step in affirming complete governmental control in the colonies. In 1795, France, which already owned Haiti,

* "Order for Suppressing the Newspapers" in Frank Maloy Anderson, *The Constitutions and Other Select Documents Illustrative of the History of France, 1789–1907* (Minneapolis: The H. W. Wilson Co., 1908), p. 282.

† "Law for Re-establishing Slavery in the French Colonies" in Frank Maloy Anderson, *The Constitutions and Other Select Documents Illustrative of the History of France, 1789–1907* (Minneapolis: The H. W. Wilson Co., 1908), p. 339.

assumed control of the Spanish half of the island of Santo Domingo. The island was in a state of revolt and became a principal area of conflict when slavery was re-established. Napoleon's Proclamation of May 20, 1802 intensified native opposition to French rule and contributed to the sharp defeat of French forces in the West Indies—the only substantial reversal suffered by Napoleon during the Consulate. Can the Proclamation of 1802 be reconciled with the revolutionary ideals of 1789? Which colonies were exempt from the proclamation?

1. In the colonies restored to France in fulfillment of the treaty of Amiens of 6 Germinal, Year X, slavery shall be maintained in conformity with the laws and regulations in force prior to 1789.

2. The same shall be done in the other French colonies beyond the Cape of Good Hope.

3. The trade in the blacks and their importation into the said colonies shall take place in conformity with the laws and regulations existing prior to the said date of 1789.

4. Notwithstanding all previous laws, the government of the colonies is subject for ten years to the regulations which shall be made by the government.

22. IMPERIAL CATECHISM*

Church-State relations in France began to deteriorate in 1790 and reached a level of open hostility under the National Convention. A few of the open wounds were partially salved by the Directors, but full reconciliation of Church and State was not achieved until the Napoleonic era. The new direction in Church-State relations was only one of Napoleon's rapid moves to reconstruct France. His motives were political rather than theological. In 1801 Napoleon persuaded Pope Pius VII to accept a concordat, with the French government retaining the right to regulate any differences in interpretation which might arise. Through the concordat the Church regained a privileged position in French life, but only at the cost of abandoning property lost during the Revolution and of subjecting itself to constant governmental interference. Without consulting the Holy See, Napoleon's rubber-stamp legislature passed Organic Laws in 1802 which outlined the limited privileges of both Catholicism and Protestantism and which subordinated the clergy to the state. The Imperial Catechism of April 4, 1807, extracted from a church-school textbook, revealed how thoroughly the Church had been subordinated to the imperial will. What religious sanctions for emperor worship were given in the Catechism? What penalty awaited those who failed to obey the emperor?

LESSON VII. CONTINUATION OF THE FOURTH COMMANDMENT

QUESTION: What are the duties of Christians with respect to the princes who govern them, and what in particular are our duties towards Napoleon I, our Emperor?

ANSWER: Christians owe to the princes who govern them, and we owe in particular to Napoleon I, our Emperor, *love, respect, obedience, fidelity, military service* and the tributes laid for the preservation and defence of the Empire and

* "Imperial Catechism" in Frank Maloy Anderson, *The Constitutions and Other Select Documents Illustrative of the History of France, 1789–1907* (Minneapolis: The H. W. Wilson Co., 1908), pp. 312–13.

of his throne; we also owe to him fervent prayers for his safety and the spiritual and temporal prosperity of the state.

QUESTION: Why are we bound to all these duties towards our Emperor?

ANSWER: First of all, because God, who creates empires and distributes them according to His will, in loading our Emperor with gifts, both in peace and in war, has established him as our sovereign and has made him the minister of His power and His image upon the earth. *To honor and to serve our Emperor is then to honor and to serve God himself.* Secondly, because our Lord Jesus Christ by his doctrine as well as by His example, has Himself taught us what we owe to our sovereign: He was born the subject of Caesar Augustus; He paid the prescribed impost; and just as He ordered to render to God that which belongs to God, so He ordered to render to Caesar that which belongs to Caesar.

QUESTION: Are there not particular reasons which ought to attach us more strongly to Napoleon I, our Emperor?

ANSWER: Yes; for it is he whom God has raised up under difficult circumstances to re-establish the public worship of the holy religion of our fathers and to be the protector of it. He has restored and preserved public order by his profound and active wisdom; he defends the state by his powerful arm; he has become the anointed of the Lord through the consecration which he received from the sovereign pontiff, head of the universal church.

QUESTION: What ought to be thought of those who may be lacking in their duty towards our Emperor?

ANSWER: According to the apostle Saint Paul, they would be resisting the order established by God himself and would render themselves *worthy of eternal damnation.*

QUESTION: Will the duties which are required of us towards our Emperor be equally binding with respect to his lawful successors in the order established by the constitution of the Empire?

ANSWER: Yes, without doubt; for we read in the holy scriptures, that God, Lord of heaven and earth, by an order of His supreme will and through His providence, gives empires not only to one person in particular, but also to his family.

23. AN ENGLISH TRAVEL GUIDE TO FRANCE*

To establish his authority inside France more completely, Napoleon needed an end to the ceaseless wars which had racked Europe for a decade. In 1802 peace was concluded between England and France in the Treaty of Amiens. However, little more than a year later the two nations were again at war, largely because Napoleon would not abide by the spirit of the agreement. During the brief interval of peace the Continent was open to British travelers. A contemporary English *Travel Guide* of 1802, from which the following excerpts are taken, provided prospective visitors to France with a detailed description of the Republic under the Consulate. In the British view, what kind of a person and leader was Napoleon? Was the English opinion of Bonaparte hostile or sympathetic? In what ways?

* *A Practical Guide During a Journey from London to Paris; with a Correct Description of all the Objects Deserving of Notice in the French Metropolis* (London: Lewis and Co., 1802), pp. 2-3, 37-38, 109-10, 131-34, 136.

The following pages have been compiled by a gentleman lately resident in Paris. His object has been to compress into a small compass, every fact which can be useful to his numerous countrymen, who may be tempted to visit that gay metropolis, in consequence of the wonderful events of which it has lately been the scene, and of the restraint which a war of ten years has imposed upon their curiosity. . . .

The information throughout the Work, refers to the state of Paris in the months of March and April, 1802, and for any changes which may have taken place, the candid reader will not consider him to be accountable. . . .

London, June 25, 1802.

THE GOVERNMENT

First Consul—Bonaparte (The following description of this extraordinary man has been communicated to the editor, by a person who has had frequent opportunities of seeing him, and whose information is unquestionable.) His hair is of a dark brown colour, cut short, and without powder; forehead high and narrow; eye-brows thin, arched a little, and low; eyes large, of a dark grey colour, and well-formed; his skin is of a yellow hue; nose large, regular, and approaching to the Grecian; upper lip very short, turned up a little at its extremity; mouth large; lips thin and pallid; his stature does not exceed five feet six inches; thin, but muscular and well-proportioned; his countenance is rather expressive of melancholy and dejection, and is only animated by his dark, piercing eyes: it impresses one with the idea that it has never known the sweet relaxation of a smile.

(The exalted situation which he fills, has scarcely produced any change in his character or manners. He is, as formerly, reserved to strangers, but affable, condescending, and familiar, to his friends. When a person with whom he is acquainted is admitted to an audience with him, it is usual for the Consul to walk up and down the room, holding, with the engaging ease of friendship or personal kindness, the arm of the man with whom he converses. His memory is uncommonly retentive; he is equally beloved by the soldiers and the officers of the army, who speak of him in terms of almost idolatrous admiration. In private life, Bonaparte is regular and abstemious; indulging in no expensive pleasures, and sternly discountenancing all irregularity of manners. As to his religious opinions, it is generally thought that the existence of a Supreme Being is a belief finally established in his mind.)

PUBLIC BUILDINGS

Les Tuileries: . . . This palace is inhabited by the three consuls. Upon the dome in the centre, is inscribed in large golden letters, République Française, above which there is a clock, divided according to the numeration now in vogue, namely into decimal instead of duodecimal parts. . . .

The First Consul holds a parade on every decade, in the court of the Tuileries. No one can enter the palace on this occasion, without a ticket of admission. The court-yard is then filled with field-officers and generals, the flower of the French commanders, many of whom bear, on their undaunted brows, the most honourable evidence of their valour in the day of battle. Their military dresses are remarkable for their variety and richness. Among the superior officers, not merely the caps, coats, and belts, but the pantaloons, the Hessian boots and spurs, are many of them richly wrought with gold and silver. The approach of the French colours is announced by the Marsellois [*sic*] hymn, which the band in the court-yard play with considerable effect. The colours are conducted by the body-guard of the First Consul, through the ante-chamber, into the room of audience; they are saluted by the soldiers on guard, who open an instant passage to the procession. Soon after, the folding-doors of the audience-room are thrown open, and the colours return, preceding the *Great Warrior* and the *Great Pacificator,* down to the court, where he mounts a milk-white charger, and inspects the troops, consisting of horse, foot, and artillery. He is attended by some general officers, mounted on chargers, richly caparisoned. The parade is conducted in a manner very inferior to what may be seen almost every day in England. The discipline appears altogether very lax and unwarlike. The heavy black horses seem to be powerful animals, and are kept in high condition; but the light-horse, are of all colours, mean and unmartial in their appearance, but capable, it is said, of enduring great fatigue. . . .

SOME IDEAS OF THE MANNERS OF MODERN PARIS

No one, from the general manners of the Parisian people, will suspect them of having committed, or even suffered, the commission of those horrible enormities, which have stained with so indelible a die, the history of their revolution. Brutal battles, quarrels, and noisy drunken fellows, are disturbances seldom to be met with in Paris. The lower class of people behave to each other with a surprising degree of civility. The unhappy females, who roam the streets at night, are neither obtrusive, rude, nor riotous. . . . Politeness and good manners may be traced, though in different proportions, through every rank. This, however, does not form a more remarkable and distinguishing feature in the French national character, than the vivacity, impetuousity, and fickleness, for which the ancient as well as the modern inhabitants of Paris, have been noted. . . .

To a person who compares Paris as it now is, with what it was during the early period of the war, nothing can present a more abrupt contrast. There is a marked difference between the Parisian of 1793, and the inhabitant of the metropolis in 1802. In dress, in manners, and in opinion, the transmutation seems to be complete. In the infancy of the republic, the Parisian took all his models from Rome and Sparta; these are become antiquated, and what is left of them, appears only in the style of the furniture, and in the dress of the female part of his family. The new-fangled republican modes and terms are fallen into disuse; the streets, which had undergone a kind of revolutionary baptism, are now known only by their former titles; the term *citoyen* [citizen] is become a mere *mot de bureau;* and, if addressed to any person in private society, would be almost an insult. Pomp and royal splendour are now the order of the day. No one of the family of the consuls now appears in public without three footmen behind their carriage, who, with the coachmen and out-riders, are all habited in dark green liveries, richly embroidered with gold. . . .

It is but just to say, that the present government is actively and usefully employed in promoting the moral and intellectual improvements of the people. We shall only express our wish, that the great man who has done so much for

France and mankind may moderate his ambition, and make the illustrious WASHINGTON the model of his political life, bequeathing to France the same degree of civil liberty which that matchless character bestowed, under similar circumstances, upon America.

24. NAPOLEON: THE BERLIN DECREE*

Attempts to prevent British trade with the Continent were broadened by Napoleon on November 21, 1806, into a Continental System which attempted to close every European port to English ships and goods. Convinced that the British could be broken financially once they were isolated from European markets, the Emperor believed he could then force England to sue for peace. Peace between France and Russia (1807) finally seemed to make Napoleon's plan feasible, but without an effective navy to support the Continental System Napoleon's hopes were frustrated. The British found new markets, especially in America, and effective smuggling networks carried increasingly large cargoes of British products to continental nations after 1810. What justification did Napoleon offer for the issuance of the Berlin Decree? How complete was the Continental System?

From our Imperial Camp at Berlin, November 21, 1806.

Napoleon, Emperor of the French and King of Italy, in consideration of the fact:

1. That England does not recognize the system of international law universally observed by all civilized nations;

2. That she regards as an enemy every individual belonging to the enemy's state, and consequently makes prisoners of war not only of the crews of armed ships of war but of the crews of ships of commerce and merchantmen, and even of commercial agents and of merchants travelling on business;

3. That she extends to the vessels and commercial wares and to the property of individuals the right of conquest, which is applicable only to the possessions of the belligerent power;

4. That she extends to unfortified towns and commercial ports, to harbors and the mouths of rivers, the right of blockade, which, in accordance with reason and the customs of all civilized nations, is applicable only to fortified places;

That she declares places in a state of blockade, before which she has not even a single ship of war, although a place may not be blockaded except it be so completely guarded that no attempt to approach it can be made without imminent danger. That she declares also in a state of blockade places which all her united forces would be unable to blockade, such as entire coasts and the whole of an empire.

5. That this monstrous abuse of the right of blockade has no other aim than to prevent communication among the nations and to raise the commerce and the industry of England upon the ruins of that of the continent.

* "The Berlin Decree" in Frank Maloy Anderson, *The Constitutions and Other Select Documents Illustrative of the History of France, 1789–1907* (Minneapolis: The H. W. Wilson Co., 1908), pp. 385–87.

6. That, since this is the obvious aim of England, whoever deals on the continent in English goods, thereby favors and renders himself an accomplice of her designs.

7. That this policy of England, worthy of the earliest stages of barbarism, has profited that power to the detriment of every other nation.

8. That it is a natural right to oppose such arms against an enemy as he makes use of, and to fight in the same way that it fights; when it disregards all ideas of justice and every high sentiment, due to the civilization among mankind.

We have resolved to apply to her the usages which she has sanctioned in her maritime legislation.

The provisions of the present decree shall continue to be looked upon as embodying the fundamental principles of the Empire until England shall recognize that the law of war is one and the same on land and sea, and that the rights of war cannot be extended so as to include private property of any kind or the persons of individuals unconnected with the profession of arms, and that the right of blockade should be restricted to fortified places actually invested by sufficient forces.

We have consequently decreed and do decree that which follows:

1. The British Isles are declared to be in a state of blockade.

2. All commerce and all correspondence with the British isles are forbidden. Consequently letters or packages directed to England or to an Englishman or written in the English language shall not pass through the mails and shall be seized.

3. Every individual who is an English subject, of whatever state or condition he may be, who shall be discovered in any country occupied by our troops or by those of our allies, shall be made a prisoner of war.

4. All warehouses, merchandise or property of whatever kind belonging to a subject of England shall be regarded as lawful prize.

5. Trade in English goods is prohibited, and all goods belonging to England or coming from her factories or her colonies are declared lawful prize.

6. Half of the product resulting from the confiscation of the goods and possessions declared lawful prize by the preceding articles shall be applied to indemnify the merchants for the losses they have experienced by the capture of merchant vessels taken by English cruisers.

7. No vessel coming directly from England or from the English colonies or which shall have visited these since the publication of the present decree shall be received in any port.

8. Any vessel contravening the above provision by a false declaration shall be seized, and the vessel and cargo shall be confiscated as if it were English property.

9. Our court of prizes at Paris shall pronounce final judgment in all cases arising in our Empire or in the countries occupied by the French army relating to the execution of the present decree. Our court of prizes at Milan shall pronounce final judgment in the said cases which may arise within our Kingdom of Italy.

10. The present decree shall be communicated by our minister of foreign affairs to the kings of Spain, of Naples, of Holland and of Etruria, and to our

other allies whose subjects, like ours, are the victims of the unjust and barbarous maritime legislation of England.

11. Our ministers of foreign affairs, of war, of the navy, of finance and of the police and our directors-general of the port are charged with the execution of the present decree so far as it affects them.

Signed, NAPOLEON.

25. NAPOLEON: INSTRUCTIONS TO JEROME, KING OF WESTPHALIA*

As the Napoleonic Empire expanded, members of Napoleon's family became rulers of old states such as Naples and Holland or of new states like Westphalia. Napoleon repeatedly admonished his family to conform to his own policies and his own views on government. The following messages to Jerome, King of Westphalia, suggest how closely the Emperor attempted to supervise his relatives. How much independence was left to Jerome? Was Napoleon's advice idealistic or utilitarian?

Fontainebleau, 15th November 1807

I enclose the constitution for your Kingdom. It embodies the conditions on which I renounce all my rights of conquest, and all the claims I have acquired over your state. You must faithfully observe it. I am concerned for the happiness of your subjects, not only as it affects your reputation, and my own, but also for its influence on the whole European situation. Don't listen to those who say that your subjects are so accustomed to slavery that they will feel no gratitude for the benefits you give them. There is more intelligence in the Kingdom of Westphalia than they would have you believe; and your throne will never be firmly established except upon the trust and affection of the common people. What German opinion impatiently demands is that men of no rank, but of marked ability, shall have an equal claim upon your favour and your employment, and that every trace of serfdom, or of a feudal hierarchy between the sovereign and the lowest class of his subjects, shall be done away with. The benefits of the Code Napoleon, public trial, and the introduction of juries, will be the leading features of your government. And to tell you the truth, I count more upon their effects, for the extension and consolidation of your rule, than upon the most resounding victories. I want your subjects to enjoy a degree of liberty, equality, and prosperity hitherto unknown to the German people. I want this liberal regime to produce, one way or another, changes which will be of the utmost benefit to the system of the Confederation, and to the strength of your monarchy. Such a method of government will be a stronger barrier between you and Prussia than the Elbe, the fortresses, and the protection of France. What people will want to return under the arbitrary Prussian rule, once it has tasted the benefits of a wise and liberal administration? In Germany, as in France, Italy, and Spain, people long for equality and liberalism. I have been managing the affairs of Europe long enough now to know that the burden of the privileged

*J. M. Thompson, ed., *Napoleon's Letters* (London: J. M. Dent and Sons, Ltd., 1954), pp. 190–91, 202. Reprinted by permission of the publisher and Mrs. M. Thompson.

classes was resented everywhere. Rule constitutionally. Even if reason, and the enlightenment of the age, were not sufficient cause, it would be good policy for one in your position; and you will find that the backing of public opinion gives you a great natural advantage over the absolute kings who are your neighbours.

[NAPOLEON]

Bayonne, 16th July 1808

You owe the bank two millions. You allow your notes to be repudiated. It is thoroughly dishonest of you. I will not be let down like this. You must sell your diamonds and your plate. There must be an end to the mad extravagance which already makes you the laughing-stock of Europe, and will end by rousing the indignation of your subjects. Sell your furniture, sell your horses, sell your jewelry, and pay your debts. Honour is the best currency. It is bad form to leave your debts unpaid, whilst everyone can see the kind of presents you give. The luxury you indulge in bewilders and shocks your subjects. You are young and light-headed, and care nothing for the value of money—and that at a time when your people are suffering from the after-effects of war.

[NAPOLEON]

26. NAPOLEON: LETTERS ON FOREIGN POLICY*

Napoleon's correspondence, as a whole, reveals the Emperor's ideas more vividly and concisely than the countless memoirs and biographies penned by his contemporaries. The following selections on foreign affairs are drawn from Napoleon's correspondence between 1802 and 1814. What was Napoleon's attitude toward other European powers and traditional diplomacy? Contrast the image of Napoleon revealed in his own writings with the account of Bourrienne.

TO HIS HOLINESS THE POPE

Paris, 28th August 1802

Holy Father, I have read with the greatest attention the letter that Your Holiness was good enough to write me, dated 18th August. I cannot but express my approval of Your Holiness' intention to nominate one of my subjects to the Grand Mastership of Malta.

I observe with some anxiety that Your Holiness does not think it proper to agree to a concordat with the Italian Republic. If your mind is made up on this point, I beg you to empower the cardinal-legate to regulate with me . . . the various religious questions in the Italian Republic. . . .

The cardinals I would propose to Your Holiness are the Archbishops of Paris and Lyons, and the Bishops of Troyes and Autun. The Archbishop of Paris . . . is full of virtue and though he is ninety-three, he still retains his memory and his physical powers. The Archbishop of Lyons is a young man with fewer

* J. M. Thompson, ed., *Napoleon's Letters* (London: J. M. Dent and Sons, Ltd., 1954), pp. 94–96, 127, 153–55, 281–82, 291–92, 299–300. Reprinted by permission of the publisher and Mrs. M. Thompson.

claims, but he is marked out by his high moral character, and by my special regard for him, as a near relation of my own. . . .

Your Holiness will see that I have not put forward the Bishop of Orléans. I will say quite frankly that I should like you to tell him that you will nominate him on the first opportunity: but I do not think it in the best interests of religion to give a cardinal's hat at this moment to a man who has indeed been of great service to us, but who, in those unhappy times, took too prominent a part in the civil war. The government would derive more embarrassment than benefit, at the present moment, from his promotion. As, however, I gave him a sort of promise that I would some day ask Your Holiness to give him this appointment, you will be able to nominate him to the first vacancy; and it cannot be long coming, since three out of the four candidates I have put forward are over eighty years old.

I hear from indirect sources that Your Holiness has experienced considerable difficulty in your relations with Russia. I think that, in dealing with this power, you should play for time as much as possible. The emperor really pays no attention to requests that come to him through his Cabinet; so that, if Your Holiness has to answer him, it is better that you should do so yourself, by a brief addressed to the emperor personally, than by a note from one Cabinet to the other. The Emperor Alexander is fair-minded, honest, and peaceable; his Cabinet is unprincipled, quarrelsome, and presumptuous. This, as Your Holiness will realize, is for your ears alone.

I must inform Your Holiness that I have just induced the Bey of Algiers to release a large number of Christians, many of whom are Your Holiness' subjects: it was part of the satisfaction demanded from the Bey for an insult to the French flag.

I have placed the Holy Sepulchre and the Syrian Christians once more under French protection, . . . with all the churches in Constantinople. . . .

TO M. LEBRUN

Boulogne Camp, 11th August 1805

I was sorry to see your decree forbidding the recruitment of sailors at Genoa. No doubt it is a way of making yourself very popular; but it is also a serious blow to the efficiency of the navy. I mobilized the fleet at Genoa just in order to get sailors. . . . Why do you suppose I annexed Genoa, and admitted her to the many great advantages she gains by membership in my Empire? It was not for the money I can get out of her, nor for the reinforcements she provides for my armies on land: my only object was to have 15,000 more sailors. It is therefore contravening the whole spirit of the annexation to pass a decree disavowing naval recruitment. I cannot imagine anything more impolitic. . . . Genoa will never be French until it has 6,000 men serving in my fleets. I want you, then, to set yourself seriously to procure sailors. Make it understood . . . that this is the only way in which the Genoese can help me. . . . I repeat it: these people will never be really gallicized until I have their sailors on board my ships. . . . I'm afraid you have been influenced, in your management of this business, by the fear of offending the Genoese. Never mind about that. Whether they wish it or not, I must have them on my vessels; . . . Nations cannot be governed by weakness: it only does them harm. I am afraid you have been displaying more of it than is warranted by your character. Did you really expect to manage people without making yourself unpopular? . . . But let sailors be the one object of your day's work. Dream of nothing but sailors. Say anything you like on my behalf, but say that I must have sailors.

TO M. DE TALLEYRAND, PRINCE OF BENEVENTO,
MINISTER FOR FOREIGN AFFAIRS

Saint-Cloud, 12th September, 1806

Note on the Present Situation

It is not in my interest to trouble the peace of the continent. Austria is not in a position to attempt anything. Russia and Prussia are kept apart by every kind of rivalry and dislike. Austria's wounds are still unhealed. It may be assumed that no considerable force of Russians can appear in Europe just yet. They might go to some lengths to attack the Porte: they might keep reserves in Poland: but I don't think they will again run the risks of sending 100,000 men into Germany.

The idea that Prussia could take me on single-handed is too absurd to merit discussion. It is impossible for me to have a genuine alliance with any of the great European powers: Prussia is only my ally through fear. Her Cabinet is so contemptible, her king so weak, and her court so dominated by young officers in search of adventure, that no one can depend upon her. She will go on acting as she has acted—arming today, disarming tomorrow; standing by, sword in hand, while the battle is fought, and then making terms with the conqueror.

The fact that Prussia should be arming at this moment astonishes all Europe: yet the motive is the same as it has been at any time during the last twelve years. That being so, we must give her plenty of time to regain confidence, and to disarm again peacefully. All the same, it might so happen that, after arming from the fear of me, and regaining confidence through my kindness, Prussia might become alarmed on her own account, and make alliances with the other European powers—flimsy alliances, no doubt, but I shall have to keep my eyes open.

Two courses are open: first, to reassure Prussia, and to look for the easiest means to restore her previous peacefulness; or secondly, to do anything I can to reinforce my German armies with men and arms. But these two courses are incompatible. If Prussia is already afraid of my army, she will be still more so when it is reinforced. She must therefore disarm in a mood of reassurance touched with fear. That is the language she understands. That is the only form of appeal that really moves her.

My object, in this *démarche,* is to change my tone. Instead of saying: "Disarm or fight," which Prussia might still find rather alarming, I shall say: "Disarm, if you don't want me to reinforce." This way of putting it is a little more reassuring: there is even a touch of friendliness in it. It suggests no hostile intention against Prussia. It makes the French moves dependent on the Prussian. This procedure is half encouragement and half threat. The first part puts fear to sleep: the second wakes it up ever so little. Such half-and-half measures are just the medicine Prussia needs.

Newmarkt, 2nd July 1813

I sent you a special messenger yesterday; I am sending a second today, and I will send a third as soon as the armistice is signed. I do not mind telling you that what has induced me to arrest my victorious course is the arming of Austria, and the desire to gain time for your army to encamp at Laybach, whilst I have two armies, one camped on the Regnitz and the other at Pirna. There is no end to the insolence of Austria. In honeyed, almost sentimental phrases, she proposes to deprive me of Dalmatia, Istria, and perhaps even more territory, right up to the Isonzo. She would like to break up the Bavarian frontier, recover the left bank of the Inn, and take back the part of Galicia which she gave up by the peace of Vienna. These people are mad, and hopelessly out in their reckoning. No court could be more treacherous. If one were to give them what they ask now, they would soon be wanting Italy and Germany. Assuredly they will get nothing from me.

. . . I hope that early in July you will be able to encamp at Laybach with fifty thousand men and a hundred guns. . . . When Austria sees these three armies ready to attack her, she will begin to realize the ridiculous folly of her demands.

TO GENERAL CAULAINCOURT, DUKE OF VICENZA,
MINISTER FOR FOREIGN AFFAIRS

Paris, 4th January 1814

. . . I think it is doubtful whether the Allies are honest, or whether England desires peace. I desire peace, but it must be substantial and honourable. A France without her natural frontiers, without Ostend, and without Antwerp, would lose touch with the other states of Europe. The natural frontiers were recognized by England and all the powers at Frankfurt. The French conquests up to the Rhine and the Alps do not balance all the territory that Austria, Russia, and Prussia have acquired in Poland and Finland, and that England has overrun in Asia. Austria will be influenced by English policy, and by the resentment of the Russian emperor. I accepted the principles proposed at Frankfurt: but it is unlikely that they represented the Allies' real ideas; they were only a mask. Once negotiations are allowed to be influenced by changes in the military situation, a system is admitted whose results cannot be foreseen. . . .

. . . You must try to find out what the Allies' views are . . . Do they want to reduce France to her ancient frontiers? It would be an insult. They are vastly mistaken if they suppose the misfortunes of war reconcile us to such a peace as that. In six months' time there would not be a man in France who failed to feel the indignity of such terms, or to reproach a Government which had been so cowardly as to accept them. . . .

TO FRANCIS II, EMPEROR OF AUSTRIA

Headquarters, Nogent-sur-Seine,
21st February, 1814

. . . Things being so, I propose to your Majesty that peace should be signed, without delay, upon the principles laid down by yourself at Frankfurt, and adopted by myself and the French people as the utmost we can concede. I will go further, and say that these principles alone can re-establish the equilibrium of Europe.

I will never give up Antwerp and Belgium. A peace on the lines of Frankfurt can be honestly enforced, and will enable France to turn all her attention to rebuilding her fleet, and re-establishing her commerce. Nothing else can. If your Majesty persists in sacrificing your own interests to the selfish policy of England, or the resentment of Russia; if you will not lay down arms except upon the frightful conditions proposed at the Congress: then Providence and the genius of France will be on our side. . . .

One word from your Majesty would end the war, secure the happiness of Austria and of Europe, safeguard you against fickleness of fortune, and put an end to the miseries of a people which is the victim of no ordinary ills, but of the crimes of desert Tartars, scarcely deserving the name of men.

27. NAPOLEON: DIARY*

Napoleon's *Diary*, compiled after his deportation to St. Helena, was intended by the former Emperor to justify his role in European affairs. Napoleon's interpretation of Napoleon was less than objective truth, but did provide some insights into his character and personality. How did Napoleon view his own character? How did Napoleon evaluate his contribution to France and Europe?

May 1, 1816: They may change, and chop, and suppress, but after all they will find it pretty difficult to make me disappear altogether. A French historian cannot very easily avoid dealing with the Empire; and, if he has a heart, he will have to give me back something of my own. I sealed the gulf of anarchy, and I unravelled chaos. I purified the revolution, raised the people, and strengthened monarchy. I stimulated every ambition, rewarded every merit, and pushed back the bounds of glory! All that amounts to something!

June 1, 1816: When any one of my ministers, or other high personages, had blundered badly, and it was necessary to get annoyed, really angry, furious, I always took care to have a third party present at the scene; my rule was that when I had decided to strike, the blow should fall on a good many; the one on whom it fell was neither more nor less resentful; while the witness, whose face and embarrassment were worth seeing, would go off and discreetly spread far and wide what he had seen and heard: a healthy terror circulated through the veins of the social body. Things went better; I had to punish less frequently; I profited much and without doing much harm.

September 24, 1816: My force of character has often been praised; yet for my own family I was nothing but a mollycoddle, and they knew it. The first storm over, their perseverance, their obstinacy, always carried the day; and, from sheer lassitude, they did what they liked with me. I made some great errors there. I did not have the luck Genghis Khan had with his four sons, who knew no emulation save that of serving him well. When I created a king, he at once

* R. M. Johnston, ed., *The Corsican: A Diary of Napoleon's Life in His Own Words* (Boston. Houghton Mifflin Co., 1910), pp. 475, 479, 485–87. Reprinted by permission.

considered himself by the grace of God. A delusion seized all of them that they were adored, preferred to me.

September 27, 1816: That's it; work is my element; I was born, I was made for work. I have reached the limit with my legs; I have reached the limit with my eyes; but never in my work. And so I almost killed poor Méneval; I had to relieve him and put him out as a convalescent with Maria Louisa, with whom his duties were a real sinecure.

September 29, 1816: You want to know the treasures of Napoleon? They are enormous, it is true, but in full view. Here they are: the splendid harbour of Antwerp, that of Flushing, capable of holding the largest fleets; the docks and dykes of Dunkirk, of Havre, of Nice; the gigantic harbour of Cherbourg; the harbour works at Venice; the great roads from Antwerp to Amsterdam, from Mainz to Metz, from Bordeaux to Bayonne; the passes of the Simplon, of Mont Cenis, of Mont Genèvre, of the Corniche, that give four openings through the Alps; in that alone you might reckon 800 millions. The roads from the Pyrenees to the Alps, from Parma to Spezzia, from Savona to Piedmont; the bridges of Jena, of Austerlitz, of the Arts, of Sèvres, of Tours, of Lyons, of Turin, of the Isère, of the Durance, of Bordeaux, of Rouen; the canal from the Rhine to the Rhône, joining the waters of Holland to the Mediterranean; the canal that joins the Scheldt and the Somme, connecting Amsterdam and Paris; that which joins the Rance and the Vilaine; the canal of Arles, of Pavia, of the Rhine; the draining of the marshes of Bourgoing, of the Cotentin, of Rochefort; the rebuilding of most of the churches pulled down during the Revolution, the building of new ones; the construction of many industrial establishments for putting an end to pauperism; the construction of the Louvre, of the public granaries, of the Bank, of the canal of the Ourcq; the water system of the city of Paris, the numerous sewers, the quays, the embellishments and monuments of that great city; the public improvements of Rome; the reëstablishment of the manufactories of Lyons. Fifty millions spent on repairing and improving the Crown residences; sixty millions' worth of furniture placed in the palaces of France and Holland, at Turin, at Rome; sixty millions' worth of Crown diamonds, all of it the money of Napoleon; even the Regent, the only missing one of the old diamonds of the Crown of France, purchased from Berlin Jews with whom it was pledged for three millions; the Napoleon Museum, valued at more than 400 millions.

These are monuments to confound calumny! History will relate that all this was accomplished in the midst of continuous wars, without raising a loan, and with the public debt actually decreasing day by day.

Chapter Three

REACTION AND REVOLUTION, 1815-1848

THE Battle of Waterloo in 1815, which shattered Napoleon's hastily assembled army, marked the final overthrow of the French Empire and the end of France's bid for European hegemony. Between the defeat of Napoleon and the Revolutions of 1848 Europe experienced three decades of enforced harmony and conservative reaction, interrupted sporadically by fitful bursts of revolt—an age dominated by the serene, charming, and slightly vacant face of the Austrian Chancellor, Prince Klemens von Metternich, the personification of conservative restoration.

With the collapse of Napoleon's Empire, representatives of the victorious Allies assembled at Vienna to redraw the map of Europe. Defeated France, restored to Bourbon rule, was also invited to participate in the deliberations. The prevailing tone of this Congress of Vienna was one of reaction prompted by a desire to re-establish the social, political, and international order that had been threatened and upset by twenty years of war. Amid panoply and pomp, the sovereigns of Europe and their representatives were wined and dined by their Austrian hosts as they negotiated and apportioned territories. A complete resurrection of the social and political order of 1788 was impossible, but the assembled monarchs and their ministers had little use for the slogan of Liberty, Equality, and Fraternity. They sought to strangle the revolutionary doctrines of liberalism and nationalism by concerted action.

As a result of decisions made at the Congress of Vienna, a European balance of power was restored and France was ringed by buffer states to prevent further aggression. The English Foreign Minister, Lord Castlereagh, successfully warded off a collision of interests over Poland and Saxony and thus emphasized the traditional British role as an aloof, if not isolated, mediator of continental rivalries. France was readmitted to the European international community, partly through the machinations of Prince Talleyrand. Austria and Prussia were neatly balanced in the German Confederation, while Prince Metternich secured Austrian dominance in divided Italy. Tsar Alexander was confirmed in his control of the major part of Poland. Though no power was completely satisfied, concerted agreement had restored stability. The conservative social order was reinstated in Germany and Italy, and the doctrines of liberalism and nationalism were officially banished.

To maintain the decisions made at Vienna, the five major powers (England, Austria, Russia, Prussia, and France) agreed to act in concert as the Quintuple Alliance and to hold regular congresses. In British eyes, however, once the reconstruction of Europe had been accomplished, it was inadvisable to use the European Concert to repress constitutional and liberal developments on the Continent, and Britain gradually withdrew from the Concert. Metternich then emerged as the leading symbol of a conservative alliance embracing Austria, Prussia, Russia, and, ever more reluctantly, France. The Carlsbad Decrees (1819) and the "congresses" at Troppau (1820) and Laibach (1821) marked the apogee of the Concert's unity and authority. Revolutions destroyed the carefully built edifice almost before Napoleon's body had grown cold in the barren soil of St. Helena.

The Revolution of 1789, indebted to the ideals of the Enlightenment, had spurred both the development of European liberalism and an anti-liberal reaction which embraced a variety of conservative philosophies. The most articulate and thoughtful spokesman for political conservatives was Edmund Burke (1729-97) who, as early as 1790, had condemned the excesses of the French Revolution. Proud and confident in England's constitutional past, Burke profoundly influenced the development of British and American conservatism through his *Reflections on the Revolution in France.* In the years immediately following the Congress of Vienna, continental reactionaries sought to justify a return to the political situation of 1788, while conservatives attempted to fashion a philosophical basis for the social and political order which they intended to defend. An alliance of throne and altar bolstered the continental monarchies. Traditions of absolutism, blended with newly triumphant Romanticism, deeply influenced the conservative philosophy of Georg W. F. Hegel who won laurels from a grateful king in Prussia. In central and eastern Europe, the nobility, gathered around absolute sovereigns, sought to defend their prerogatives while influencing the course of government. The middle classes were denied any significant political function.

Romanticism was also a reaction against the excessive mechanistic and rationalistic tendencies of the Enlightenment. The Romantic Movement was not created by reaction to the Revolution, but grew slowly until it welled up and flooded across Europe in the last decade of the eighteenth century. Jean Jacques Rousseau had drawn attention to the importance of sentiment and beauty; English Methodists and German Pietists had also rejected the basic premises of the Age of Reason. With a devotion to spirit, beauty, fantasy, and emotion, with an appeal to a world of unities as opposed to a world of finite particles, Romantics spun poetry, novels, and political philosophy based upon sensibility and passion. Romantics looked backward to an idyllic past and forward toward a utopian future; they appealed to conservatives and radical revolutionists alike, depending upon what feelings were emphasized. Metternich himself, with his emphasis upon virtues of stability inherent in the medieval institutions of Austria, was strongly influenced by the conservative aspect of Romanticism.

Especially in Germany, the Romantic Movement became closely identified with new nationalistic feelings. The Romantic concept of a *Volk,* or nation, ideally suited the needs of Germans seeking unity in the fragmented German Confederation. The concept of national history, as the history of a people, was born. Romantic nationalism became a powerful weapon against the Metternichian system; its influence can be plainly detected in the writings of German revolutionaries like Carl Schurz.

Even before mid-century, it was clear to many Europeans that the conservative order could not be maintained. The Napoleonic Wars had unleashed nationalism in central Europe, and Germans, Italians, Poles, and Hungarians grew increasingly restless under an antinational political system that they despised. Leaders among the emergent middle classes of central Europe, learning from France, burned to achieve constitutional rule. In France, the folly of Bourbon kings was matched only by the increasing dissatisfaction of the bourgeoisie and the new industrial workers. There were sporadic revolutions across Europe after 1815, and cracks in the Metternichian order appeared in Belgium, Italy, and Greece. The final crisis came in 1848.

The Revolutions of 1848 toppled the Orléans dynasty in France and spread to Vienna, Prague, Budapest, throughout Germany and the Italian peninsula, sending Metternich in flight to England. Rebels proclaimed German and Italian unity, and a new French Republic granted universal suffrage. Eventually, loyal troops were able to crush the revolution in Austria and Hungary, and the feeble attempt at German unification collapsed ingloriously. The Tsar helped the Austrian Emperor to defeat the Hungarians, while Austrian troops destroyed the Italian revolution. The social and economic overtones of the revolution in France shocked the bourgeoisie and encouraged the conservatism of the peasantry. When the French elected Louis Napoleon Bonaparte as President of the Second Republic, in December 1848, the revolution had run its course in that country as well.

The Europe of Metternich was shaken to its foundations by the Revolutions of 1848, but the old system was not completely destroyed. The European unity and balance displayed at the Congress of Vienna, and given a wider meaning by the universality of the Romantic Movement, was not immediately overthrown. Liberalism was profoundly affected by the failures of 1848, while industrialization, materialism, socialism, nationalism, and political realism became forces of change that succeeded in burying the old order during the second half of the century.

THE CONCERT OF EUROPE

1. REPORT OF LORD CASTLEREAGH'S SPEECH IN PARLIAMENT ON THE CONGRESS OF VIENNA*

Lord Castlereagh (1769–1822), Foreign Minister and principal British representative at the Congress of Vienna, faced an uncomfortable and difficult task. Tsar Alexander of Russia believed that Russian troops had played the major role in the overthrow of Napoleon. He liked to look upon himself as the liberator of

* William Cobbett, ed., *Parliamentary History* (London, 1815), vol. XXX, col. 288–304.

Europe and, while toying with liberal ideas, nevertheless sought the extension of
Russian power. The Tsar desired to rule the whole of Poland, promising a
constitution for the Poles, and to retain influence in Germany as well. Nor could
Alexander understand why his magnanimity, his generosity, and his power
called forth so much suspicion from his allies. Frederick William III, King of
Prussia, wanted to annex Saxony to assure the revival of Prussian strength. He
allowed himself to be persuaded to join with Alexander, each supporting the
other's claims. Metternich, as Austrian Chancellor, could hardly permit such an
increase in Prussian strength, directly across his border. He also objected to the
expansion of Russia in Europe. Talleyrand exploited the division among the
allies and sought to recover French influence.

It remained to Castlereagh to smooth over the differences among the powers,
and to arrange a compromise. Sensitive British morals were offended by the
apparent willful transfer of populations from one sovereign to another, and the
Foreign Minister was attacked vigorously in the House of Commons. According
to Lord Castlereagh, what principles guided the Congress? What were British
objectives at Vienna? What was Castlereagh's German policy, and why? How
did he defend the treatment of the Poles? Why did Castlereagh defend the
Bourbon restoration in France? Was Castlereagh correct in his assessment of
the Vienna settlement?

The House were aware that the object of the Congress was to carry into
effect the Treaty of Paris. The fair question, therefore, was, taking that Treaty
as the foundation of their proceedings, whether the Allied Governments had
fairly and honourably executed the task which they had prescribed to themselves. . . . In considering the recent transactions, the House would not expect
to find that in such an assembly of sovereigns and ministers, no clashing of
interests had occurred, no differences of opinion had existed. Such an entire
unanimity would have been contrary to the feelings of human nature, and of
that independence which the destruction of the tyrant-mind had happily permitted in the different states of Europe. The question which the House would
have to decide was, whether a system had been created under which all countries might live in that peace which it was the great object of the confederacy
to establish. A difference of sentiment on some points of the arrangements could
be no impeachment of the wisdom of the whole. Perfection belonged to no work
of human beings, even when many years were devoted to it; much less when
its completion was accelerated by the necessity of circumstances. On this general
principle he [Castlereagh] applauded and was prepared to maintain the proceedings of the Congress at Vienna.

On this general principle he protested against the observations made by the
hon. gentleman [a previous speaker for the Opposition] on the conduct of the
allied sovereigns. If they had issued a declaration that all the governments of
Europe, which had been swept away during the late convulsions, should be
revived, without considering the tendency of that revival to recreate the dangers
from which Europe had so happily escaped, and without providing any safe-
guards against their recurrence; if that was the way in which their declaration
was to be understood, he should be ashamed that Great Britain belonged to a
confederacy formed on a system of such imbecility. But parliament had to
inquire first whether or not the principle on which the Congress had proceeded

was unsound, and if not so, then whether by departing from that principle in execution they had betrayed the trust which the confidence of Europe had reposed in them.

On these grounds he was ready to refute the hon. gentleman. The excellence of the principles on which they had set out . . . in the Treaty of Paris, the hon. gentleman had already acknowledged, and it would be found that from those principles no departure had been made. It was perfectly understood during the whole of the negotiations for the general peace, that the great object of the sovereigns of Europe was the re-establishment and the re-organization of those two great monarchies, which, to all practical purposes, had been destroyed during the war—Austria and Prussia. To do this it became necessary to establish a security for the flanks of those monarchies: a power between the north of Germany and France, and a power acting as a barrier between Italy and France, to prevent them from coming into contact. It was necessary also to maintain the independence of Switzerland, and to restore the constitution of the German states. The question was, whether the arrangements which had been made were calculated to effect these great objects—whether the assembled powers had endeavoured unduly to aggrandize themselves, or faithfully to execute their trust. The hon. gentleman had alluded to the letter of the minister of France, protesting against throwing the whole population of Europe into a general fund, and then drawing it out again in different portions, for the advantage of particular sovereigns. If that letter were written against the annexation of Saxony to Prussia, and if that annexation were not called for by all the circumstances of the case, and justified by every consideration of the law of nations and of a wise policy, the argument would be cogent. But while he admitted the truth of the general principle, which it involved, he denied its application in the present case. The object was to give Prussia additional force, and increased population was that force.

. . . With regard to Poland, his lordship had interested himself as much as possible, to procure a determination that would be equally satisfactory to all parties; and whatever might be the particular arrangements that the separate powers might adopt, they would all be dictated by the same spirit of liberality and justice that had governed the great states in all arrangements. The main object of conciliating the people would not be lost sight of, and they would be relieved from those local difficulties and personal disqualifications under which they formerly laboured. Whatever system of policy might formerly exist, the Poles would now be governed as Poles; and with regard to territorial arrangement, and to the particular form of government that each possessor would establish, he wished the House to suspend any opinion until more detailed information was supplied. In erecting them into a separate kingdom, hon. gentlemen would not forget the many difficulties that must be encountered, not merely in procuring the assent of the monarchs who were interested, but in severing immense tracts of territory bound to its neighbour during a long course of years, until at length they had grown, as it were, into each other, and were sometimes incapable of separate existence.

In calling the attention of Parliament to those parts of the arrangements that more peculiarly regarded this country, he should have had less satisfaction if, during the course of his mission, he had employed himself in obtaining concessions, the objects of which were merely the separate aggrandizement and interest of Great Britain; but in the case of Holland, in whose establishment under the present system, we were individually dearly interested, the allied powers had felt, as they must feel, that they were all gaining an equivalent advantage. If it were impolitic for this country, as no one would deny, that France should in future possess the large naval resources supplied by a long line of coast from the Pyrenees to the Texel, it was not less the interest of the other states of Europe to prevent the application of such means; and at the same time, by erecting Holland into a powerful and independent kingdom, under the House of Orange, by the annexation of territory formerly belonging to Austria, an essential service was rendered to all the continental powers. It was but a tribute due to the sovereign now reigning, to say, that none of the high individuals had been more successful in gaining the confidence of his subjects, by persevering endeavours for their benefit, by liberality in the exercise of his authority, and by a happy talent of drawing resources equally from all parts of the dominions so recently placed in his hands. What he had said of Holland would apply equally to Hannover. . . .

. . . It was not merely a question whether the Bourbon family, which had already given so many benefits to France, and among them, that best of all benefits, peace, should continue to reign in France, but whether tyranny and despotism should again reign over the independent nations of the continent. Whether as applied to this country, we should enjoy the happy state that we had bought with our blood after a long struggle, or whether we should once more revert to that artificial system which, during that struggle, we were compelled to maintain? Upon these points there could exist only one feeling, and his lordship trusted that Providence would ordain only one result. After referring again to the efforts made by the King of France to give a free constitution to that country, and the success with which the experiment had been attended during the sitting of the legislature for five or six months, his lordship concluded by justifying himself for not having, as much as might be wished by some, endeavoured abroad to introduce the free principles of the British constitution; he had not, like a missionary, gone about to preach to the world its excellency and its fitness, because he by no means felt convinced, that in countries yet in a state of comparative ignorance, and brought up under a system so diametrically opposite, it could be advantageously introduced. A great deal had been done to promote the happiness of nations, and if Buonaparte was not permitted to intercept the prospects which were arising, never could Europe look forward to brighter days than those which it might now anticipate. The noble lord sat down amidst loud and repeated cheers.

2. FRIEDRICH VON GENTZ: ON THE CONGRESS OF VIENNA*

During the Napoleonic ascendancy in divided Germany, a number of German publicists warned the people about the dangers of French rule for the future of the German nation. Some, like Friedrich von Gentz (1764–1832), were also

---

* Prince Richard Metternich, ed., *Memoirs of Prince Metternich, 1773–1815*, trans. Mrs. Alexander Napier (5 vols.; New York: Charles Scribner's Sons, 1880), II, 553–59, 561–63.

genuine conservatives appalled by the revolutionary doctrines of Napoleonic France. Gentz translated Edmund Burke's *Reflections on the Revolution in France* into German and eventually took service at the Austrian court in Vienna. In that capacity, close to Prince Metternich, Gentz acted as secretary to the Congress of Vienna. In his *Memoir,* written during the Congress, Gentz revealed a marked pro-Austrian bias. Compare Gentz's assessment of the position of the major powers with the evaluation presented in Castlereagh's speech. Was Gentz's judgment of Britain justified?

Those who at the time of the assembling of the Congress at Vienna had thoroughly understood the nature and objects of this Congress, could hardly have been mistaken about its course, whatever their opinion about its results might be. The grand phrases of "reconstruction of social order," "regeneration of the political system of Europe," "a lasting peace founded on a just division of strength," &c., &c., were uttered to tranquillise the people, and to give an air of dignity and grandeur to this solemn assembly; but the real purpose of the Congress was to divide amongst the conquerors the spoils taken from the vanquished. The comprehension of this truth enables us to foresee that the discussions of this Congress would be difficult, painful, and often stormy. But to understand how far they have been so, and why the hopes of so many enlightened men, but more or less ignorant of cabinet secrets, have been so cruelly disappointed, one must know the designs which the principal Powers had in presenting themselves on this great battle-field, and the development which particular circumstances and personal relations have given to these designs. The following observations will serve to characterise them.

DESIGNS OF THE POWERS AT THE OPENING OF THE CONGRESS

The Emperor of Russia has come to Vienna, in the first place to be admired (which is always the principal thing in his thoughts), and next to direct personally the important arrangements which should fix the boundaries and future position of the many states who claim their share of the immense spoil which is placed at the disposal of the Allies, by their success against the common enemy. The three principal objects of the Emperor Alexander were: 1st, to take possession for ever of the whole, or almost the whole, of the Duchy of Warsaw, with the exception of some small portions, which he would give to the two neighbouring powers; 2nd, to prevent Austria from profiting too much by the advantages of her new position; 3rd, to enrich Prussia as much as possible, not only to compensate her for her ancient Polish provinces, which he had carried away from her by surprise, and which he retained because it pleased him to do so, but also to make her a useful and powerful ally, the only one on whom he could rely in the future. Such were the *real* objects he had in view; the *ostensible* object was to mingle in all the affairs of Europe, and to pass as the arbiter of their destinies.

On arriving at Vienna the Emperor was already more or less embroiled with Austria, England, and France. His displeasure with Austria was chiefly on account of the many and deep grievances which he had, or pretended to have, against Prince Metternich. The first and true origin of these grievances dated from the opposition of that minister to the Emperor's proposal to become himself the commander-in-chief of the allied armies. . . . Since that moment there has been no return of harmony. Angry and bitter discussions took place almost every day during the last part of the campaign, and by the time the Allies reached Paris they preserved, with difficulty, the outward appearance of a friendliness which had no longer any foundation. The Emperor accustomed himself to look on M. de Metternich only as a permanent obstacle to his designs, as a man occupied without intermission in opposing and thwarting him; at last, as a sworn enemy. The calmness and serenity which M. de Metternich always opposed to these prejudices, instead of softening the Emperor, appeared only to embitter him the more; private feelings, above all a strong jealousy of M. de Metternich's success, both in politics and society, increased this irritation. . . .

His relations with England (a Power which he had always cordially detested, and which he only cultivated either from interest or fear) have been sensibly disturbed since his visit to London. Lord Castlereagh was particularly disagreeable to him; he called him cold and pedantic, and there were moments in Vienna when he would have treated him as he did M. de Metternich, if extreme fear of openly compromising himself with the British Government (the only one before whom he trembled) had not forced him to dissimulate. Neither was the Emperor inclined to friendly relations with France. He had not pardoned the King for having adopted a system of government contrary to the advice which he had wished to give him; he was furious against Prince Talleyrand, who, at the time of the Allies entering Paris, had appeared to recognise no law but the will of the Russian Emperor, and who, four weeks afterwards, had found the means of rendering himself independent. . . .

Prussia only brought to the Congress an immoderate desire for extending her possessions at the expense of all the world, and without regard to any principle of justice or even of decency. This passion for conquest had its origin neither in the character of the King nor of his Prime Minister; for the King, although below mediocrity in intellect and judgment, is yet at bottom a good sort of man, and Chancellor Hardenberg one of the best that ever existed. . . .

. . . England appeared at Vienna with all the brilliancy which she owes to her immense successes, the prominent part which she had played in the coalition, to her influence without limits, to a condition of strength and solid prosperity which no other Power has attained in these days, and lastly to the respect and fear which she inspires and which govern her relations with all the other governments. In profiting by these advantages, England could have given the law to all Europe; by making common cause with Austria, whose interests were also hers, she might have prevented the aggrandisement of Russia, made Prussia fall back within her own boundaries, re-established a true equilibrium in Germany, and guaranteed for a long time the repose of Europe. . . . It is true, Lord Castlereagh for some time resisted the ambitious schemes of Russia, but he ended by abandoning this opposition. Guided by the purest intentions, but with some radically false views, he first supported Prussia's designs on Saxony to their utmost extent, returned later to a course more in conformity with just principles, and more favourable to Austria, but, stopping half way, he finally only saved a part of Saxony by a thoroughly bad arrangement. He observed in all the other questions (with the exception of those directly concerning England, such as the establishment of the House of Orange, the slave treaty, &c.) a neutrality often astonishing. But, though capable of being the arbiter for Europe, he gave her only weak and partial support. This was, without doubt, the principal cause of the unsatisfactory issue of the Congress.

The part of the French Ministers at this Congress was decidedly the most simple and agreeable of all. Everything relating to France having been regulated by the Treaty of Paris, they had nothing to demand for themselves, and could confine themselves to watching the conduct of others. Defending the feeble against the strong restrains each Power within its proper limits, and to working in good faith for the re-establishment of political equilibrium. To do them justice, their general course has been in accordance with these principles, for they have made no proposal, started no scheme tending directly or indirectly to the least change in the stipulations of the Treaty of Paris, to the slightest extension of their frontiers, or to any pretension whatever, incompatible with the rights of their neighbours or general tranquillity. . . .

Austria found herself, between these four Powers, in the most embarrassing position. She could not look on the Emperor Alexander, in spite of all his protestations of friendship for the Emperor [Francis I of Austria], but as a declared enemy, and Prussia, always carried away by her own rapacity and ambition, as the inseparable ally of this enemy. She was deterred from too great a friendship with France, not by any reason of direct repugnance or distrust, for she was perfectly convinced of her loyal and friendly disposition, but by what is called respect of mankind, that is to say, by the fear of lowering herself in public opinion, by leaguing herself openly with a Power which had formerly been the common enemy of Europe, and which still preserved its bad reputation in the minds of the multitude, led away by the hypocritical declarations of the Russian and Prussian party. . . .

. . . There remained then only England as any support to Austria; but England wished for peace, peace before everything, peace—I am sorry to say it—at any price and almost on any conditions. Thus Austria was absolutely in the position of having to rely on herself alone, against Russia and Prussia united; she had but one ally, who would follow her at the first call, Bavaria; if war broke out, she could rely on the help of France; but this help would be tardy and constrained, and would turn the opinion of all the rest of Germany still more against her. . . . By reflecting on this *ensemble,* you will understand the course of the negotiations. . . .

3. THE CARLSBAD DECREES*

Napoleon aroused nascent German nationalism by annexing German territory and by inflicting a series of humiliating military defeats on Austria and Prussia. Growing nationalist exuberance assisted in the final defeat of the French Emperor even though it was still confined to a narrow segment of the German people, particularly the middle class and university students. Many nationalists were disenchanted, however, when the Congress of Vienna failed to create a unified Germany and established a conservative, weak, and antinational German

* "Decrees Based upon the Resolutions of Carlsbad" in James Harvey Robinson, ed., *Translations and Reprints from the Original Sources of European History* (Philadelphia: University of Pennsylvania, 1902), vol. I, no. 3, pp. 16 19.

Confederation dominated by Austria. The lingering opposition to the Vienna settlement was revealed openly when several hundred university students gathered at Wartburg Castle in Saxe-Weimar on October 17, 1817, to celebrate the fourth anniversary of Napoleon's defeat at the Battle of Leipzig and the 300th anniversary of Luther's Ninety-five Theses. The Wartburg Festival was climaxed by an enormous bonfire, in which the students burned various symbols of the conservative military establishment. A number of German princes were worried by the revolutionary implications of this display, but Metternich was not sufficiently disturbed to take action. In March 1819, however, a fanatical student named Karl Sand assassinated August Kotzebue, a well-known reactionary publicist in the employ of Tsar Alexander I. Metternich responded by formulating the Carlsbad Decrees, which were then immediately rammed through the Diet of the Confederation by joint Austro-Prussian efforts. What specific means were employed by the Carlsbad Decrees to curtail nationalist sentiment? To what extent did the Decrees limit the academic freedom of students and professors?

PROVISIONAL DECREE RELATING TO THE UNIVERSITIES, UNANIMOUSLY ADOPTED SEPTEMBER 20, 1819

Decreed that, with a view to the fundamental improvement of the whole system of schools and universities a series of provisional measures shall, pending further deliberations of the Diet, be adopted without delay, for remedying the defects of the same. For this purpose the draft in question shall be adopted. This law of the Confederation shall, in accordance with its provisions, go into force immediately in all the states of the Union.

1. A special representative of the ruler of each state shall be appointed for each university with appropriate instructions and extended powers, and who shall reside in the place where the university is situated. This office may devolve upon the existing Curator or upon any other individual whom the government may deem qualified.

The function of this agent shall be to see to the strictest enforcement of existing laws and disciplinary regulations; to observe carefully the spirit which is shown by the instructors in the university in their public lectures and regular courses, and, without directly interfering in scientific matters or in the methods of teaching, to give a salutary direction to the instruction, having in view the future attitude of the students. Lastly, they shall devote unceasing attention to everything that may promote morality, good order and outward propriety among the students.

The relation of these special agents to the Senate of the university, as well as all details relating to the extent of their duties and to their manner of action, shall be included in the instructions furnished by the superior government officials. These instructions shall be as precise as the circumstances which have dictated the appointment of the agents in question shall permit.

2. The confederated governments mutually pledge themselves to remove from the universities or other public educational institutions all teachers who, by obvious deviation from their duty or by exceeding the limits of their functions, or by the abuse of their legitimate influence over the youthful minds, or by propagating harmful doctrines hostile to public order or subversive of exist-

ing governmental institutions, shall have unmistakably proved their unfitness for the important office intrusted to them. No obstacle whatever shall prevent the execution of this provision so long as it shall remain in force and until such time as this matter shall be definitely regulated. Removals of this character shall however, never be made except upon the recommendation, accompanied with full reasons, of the aforesaid special agent of the government at the university or in view of a report previously required from him.

No teacher who shall have been removed in this manner shall be again appointed to a position in any public institution of learning in another state of the Union.

3. Those laws which have for a long period been directed against secret and unauthorized societies in the universities, shall be strictly enforced. These laws apply especially to that association established some years since under the name Universal Students' Union (*Allegmeine Burschenschaft*), since the very conception of the society implies the utterly unallowable plan of permanent fellowship and constant communication between the various universities. The duty of especial watchfulness in this matter should be impressed upon the special agents of the government.

The governments mutually agree that such persons as shall, after the publication of the present decree, be shown to have remained in secret or unauthorized associations or shall have entered such associations, shall not be admitted to any public office.

4. No student, who shall be expelled from a university by a decision of the University Senate, which was ratified or prompted by the agent of the government, or who shall have left the institution in order to escape expulsion, shall be received in any other university. Nor, in general, shall any student be admitted to another university without a satisfactory certificate of his good conduct at the university he has left.

PRESS LAWS FOR FIVE YEARS

1. So long as this decree shall remain in force no publication which appears in the form of daily issues or as a serial not exceeding twenty sheets of printed matter shall go to press in any state of the Union without the previous knowledge and approval of the state officials.

Writings which do not belong to one of the above-mentioned classes shall be treated according to the laws now in force or which may be enacted in the individual states of the Union. If such publications shall, however, give rise to a complaint upon the part of any state of the Union, proceedings against the author or publisher of the obnoxious publication shall be conducted in the name of the government to which the complaint was directed and with the forms prevailing in the several states of the Union.

2. The details of means and provisions necessary for the enforcement of this decree shall be left to the several governments. These must, however, be of such a character as fully to carry out the purpose and aim of the main provisions of Section 1.

3. Since the present decree has been called forth by the necessity which is recognized under the existing circumstances by the confederated governments,

of preventative measures against the abuse of the press, the existing laws aiming at the judicial prosecution and punishment of offences actually committed in the way of publication, shall not, so long as this decree remains in force, be deemed sufficient in any state of the Union, in so far as their provisions relate to the classes of publication mentioned in Section 1.

4. Each state of the Union is responsible not only to the state against which the offence is directly committed, but to the whole Confederation for every publication appearing under its supervision (and consequently for all publications included in Section 1) in which the honor or security of other states is infringed or their constitution or administration attacked.

6. . . . The Diet shall have the right, moreover, to suppress on its own authority, without being petitioned, such writings included in Section 1, in whatever German state they may appear, as in the opinion of a commission appointed by it, are inimical to the honor of the Union, the safety of individual states or the maintenance of peace and quiet in Germany. There shall be no appeal from such decisions and the governments involved are bound to see that they are put into execution.

7. When a newspaper or periodical is suppressed by a decision of the Diet the editor thereof may not, within a period of five years, edit a similar publication in any state of the Union. The writers, publishers and dealers in publications included in Section 1 shall be free from all further responsibility if they have complied with the requirements of this decree. The decisions of the Diet provided for in Section 6 shall be directed exclusively against publications, never against persons.

10. The present provisional decree shall remain in force during a period of five years from this day. Before the expiration of this period the Diet shall take into careful consideration in what manner measures may best be taken for establishing the uniform regulations mentioned in Article 18 of the Act of Confederation in regard to the freedom of the press, and thus secure a permanent law fixing the proper limits of the freedom of the press in Germany.

4. CLEMENS VON METTERNICH: MEMOIR ON THE CONCERT OF EUROPE*

The three eastern powers—Austria, Prussia, and Russia—formed the core of the European Concert, and Prince Metternich (1773–1859) was its chief spokesman. The Austrian Chancellor worked jointly with Prussia in Germany and exerted a profound influence over the unstable Tsar Alexander I of Russia, a mystic who had earlier been attracted to liberal ideas. Prince Metternich had definite ideas about the goals of the Concert, and he besieged the troubled Alexander with memoranda designed to hold the Tsar in line. In the Austrian Chancellor's view, what threat menaced the sovereigns of Europe, and how had the problem arisen? What measures were necessary to control it? Did the views expressed by Metternich reveal him to have been a statesman of Romantic, mystical, or pragmatic qualities? Compare Metternich's view of human nature with the concepts of Locke and Rousseau. Would it be fair to accuse Metternich

* Prince Richard Metternich, ed., *Memoirs of Prince Metternich, 1773–1815,* trans. Mrs. Alexander Napier (5 vols.; New York: Charles Scribner's Sons, 1880), III, 454–62, 467–71.

of being bewildered by the Romantic movement because he could not tell whether it moved forward or backward? Why or why not?

Kings have to calculate the chances of their very existence in the immediate future; passions are let loose, and league together to overthrow everything which society respects as the basis of its existence; religion, public morality, laws, customs, rights, and duties, all are attacked, confounded, overthrown, or called in question. The great mass of the people are tranquil spectators of these attacks and revolutions, and of the absolute want of all means of defence. A few are carried off by the torrent, but the wishes of the immense majority are to maintain a repose which exists no longer, and of which even the first elements seem to be lost.

What is the cause of all these evils? By what methods has this evil established itself, and how is it that it penetrates into every vein of the social body?

. . . Man's nature is immutable. The first needs of society are and remain the same, and the differences which they seem to offer find their explanation in the diversity of influences, acting on the different races by natural causes, such as the diversity of climate, barrenness or richness of soil, insular or continental position, etc., etc. These local differences no doubt produce effects which extend far beyond purely physical necessities; they create and determine particular needs in a more elevated sphere; finally, they determine the laws, and exercise and influence even on religions.

It is, on the other hand, with institutions as with everything else. Vague in their origin, they pass through periods of development and perfection, to arrive in time at their decadence; and, conforming to the laws of man's nature, they have, like him, their infancy, their youth, their age of strength and reason, and their age of decay.

Two elements alone remain in all their strength, and never cease to exercise their indestructible influence with equal power. These are the precepts of morality, religious as well as social, and the necessities created by locality. From the time that men attempt to swerve from these bases, to become rebels against these sovereign arbiters of their destinies, society suffers from a malaise which sooner or later will lead to a state of convulsion. The history of every country, in relating the consequences of such errors, contains many pages stained with blood; but we dare to say, without fear of contradiction, one seeks in vain for an epoch when an evil of this nature has extended its ravages over such a vast area as it has done at the present time.

. . . Having now thrown a rapid glance over the first causes of the present state of society, it is necessary to point out in a more particular manner the evil which threatens to deprive it, at one blow, of the real blessings, the fruits of genuine civilisation, and to disturb it in the midst of its enjoyments. This evil may be described in one word—presumption; the natural effect of the rapid progression of the human mind towards the perfecting of so many things. This it is which at the present day leads so many individuals astray, for it has become an almost universal sentiment.

Religion, morality, legislation, economy, politics, administration, all have become common and accessible to everyone. Knowledge seems to come by inspiration; experience has no value for the presumptuous man; faith is nothing to him; he substitutes for it a pretended individual conviction, and to arrive at this conviction dispenses with all inquiry and with all study; for these means appear too trivial to a mind which believes itself strong enough to embrace at one glance all questions and all facts. Laws have no value for him, because he has not contributed to make them, and it would be beneath a man of his parts to recognise the limits traced by rude and ignorant generations. Power resides in himself; why should he submit himself to that which was only useful for the man deprived of light and knowledge? That which, according to him, was required in an age of weakness cannot be suitable in an age of reason and vigour, amounting to universal perfection, which the German innovators designate by the idea, absurd in itself, of the Emancipation of the People! Morality itself he does not attack openly, for without it he could not be sure for a single instant of his own existence; but he interprets its essence after his own fashion, and allows every other person to do so likewise, provided that other person neither kills nor robs him.

In thus tracing the character of the presumptuous man, we believe we have traced that of the society of the day, composed of like elements, if the denomination of society is applicable to an order of things which only tends in principle towards individualising all the elements of which society is composed. Presumption makes every man the guide of his own belief, the arbiter of laws according to which he is pleased to govern himself, or to allow someone else to govern him and his neighbours; it makes him, in short, the sole judge of his own faith, his own actions, and the principles according to which he guides them.

. . . It is sufficient to cast a glance on the course which the Governments followed during the eighteenth century, to be convinced that not one among them was ignorant of the evil or of the crisis towards which the social body was tending. There were, however, some men, unhappily endowed with great talents, who felt their own strength, and were not slow to appraise the progressive course of their influence, taking into account the weakness or the inertia of their adversaries; and who had the art to prepare and conduct men's minds to the triumph of their detestable enterprise—an enterprise all the more odious as it was pursued without regard to results, simply abandoning themselves to the one feeling of hatred of God and of His immutable moral laws.

France had the misfortune to produce the greatest number of these men. It is in her midst that religion and all that she holds sacred, that morality and authority, and all connected with them, have been attacked with a steady and systematic animosity, and it is there that the weapon of ridicule has been used with the most ease and success.

. . . It would be difficult not to pause here to consider the influence which the example of England had for a long time exercised on France. England is herself placed in such a peculiar situation that we believe we may safely say that not one of the forms possible to that State, not one of its customs or institutions, would suit any Continental State, and that where we might wish to take them for models, we should only obtain inconvenience and danger, without securing a single one of the advantages which accompany them.

. . . Nevertheless the revolutionary seed had penetrated into every country and spread more or less. It was greatly developed under the regime of the military despotism of Bonaparte. His conquests displaced a number of laws, institutions, and customs; broke through bonds sacred among all nations, strong enough to resist time itself; which is more than can be said of certain benefits conferred by these innovators. From these perturbations it followed that the revolutionary spirit could in Germany, Italy, and later on in Spain, easily hide itself under the veil of patriotism.

Prussia committed a grave fault in calling to her aid such dangerous weapons as secret associations always will be: a fault which could not be justified even by the deplorable situation in which that Power then found itself. This it was that first gave a strong impulse to the revolutionary spirit in her States, and this spirit made rapid progress, supported as it was in the rest of Germany by the system of foreign despotism which since 1806 has been there developed. Many Princes of the Rhenish Confederation were secretly auxiliaries and accomplices of this system, to which they sacrificed the institutions which in their country from time immemorial had served as a protection against despotism and democracy.

... There is besides scarcely any epoch which does not offer a rallying cry to some particular faction. This cry, since 1815, has been Constitution. But do not let us deceive ourselves: this word, susceptible of great latitude of interpretation, would be but imperfectly understood if we supposed that the factions attached quite the same meaning to it under the different regimes. Such is certainly not the case. In pure monarchies it is qualified by the name of "national representation." In countries which have lately been brought under the representative regime it is called "development," and promises charters and fundamental laws. In the only State which possesses an ancient national representation it takes "reform" as its object. Everywhere it means change and trouble.

... The evil is plain; the means used by the faction which causes these disorders are so blameable in principle, so criminal in their application, and expose the faction itself to so many dangers, that what men of narrow views (whose head and heart are broken by circumstances stronger than their calculations or their courage) regard as the end of society may become the first step towards a better order of things. These weak men would be right unless men stronger than they are come forward to close their ranks and determine the victory.

We are convinced that society can no longer be saved without strong and vigorous resolutions on the part of the Governments still free in their opinions and actions.

We are also convinced that this may yet be, if the Governments face the truth, if they free themselves from all illusion, if they join their ranks and take their stand on a line of correct, unambiguous, and frankly announced principles.

... There is a rule of conduct common to individuals and to States, established by the experience of centuries as by that of everyday life. This rule declares "that one must not dream of reformation while agitated by passion; wisdom directs that at such moments we should limit ourselves to maintaining."

Let the monarchs vigorously adopt this principle; let all their resolutions bear the impression of it. Let their actions, their measures, and even their words announce and prove to the world this determination—they will find allies everywhere. The Governments, in establishing the principle of stability, will in no wise exclude the development of what is good, for stability is not immobility. But it is for those who are burdened with the heavy task of government to augment the well-being of their people! It is for Governments to regulate it according to necessity and to suit the times. It is not by concessions, which the factious strive to force from legitimate power, and which they have neither the right to claim nor the faculty of keeping within just bounds, that wise reforms can be carried out. That all the good possible should be done is our most ardent wish; but that which is not good must never be confounded with that which is, and even real good should be done only by those who unite to the right of authority the means of enforcing it. Such should be also the sincere wish of the people, who know by sad experience the value of certain phrases and the nature of certain caresses.

Respect for all that is; liberty for every Government to watch over the well-being of its own people; a league between all Governments against factions in all States; contempt for the meaningless words which have become the rallying cry of the factious; respect for the progressive development of institutions in lawful ways; refusal on the part of every monarch to aid or succour partisans under any mask whatever—such are happily the ideas of the great monarchs: the world will be saved if they bring them into action—it is lost if they do not.

5. LORD CASTLEREAGH ON THE EUROPEAN CONCERT*

Early in 1820 an uprising broke out in Spain against the incompetent Ferdinand VII, who was attempting to collect troops for the reconquest of Latin America. The Spanish crisis was more of a military revolt than a political revolution, but Tsar Alexander was apprehensive. Despite warnings from Lord Castlereagh, the Tsar insisted that the Quadruple Alliance (the instrument of the European Concert) take action. In July, another revolution, with obvious liberal overtones, forced the King of Naples to grant his people a constitution, and revolution broke out in Portugal in August. The three eastern monarchies were greatly disturbed, almost terrified, and another European congress was called for October in Troppau, Austria. In accordance with decisions reached by representatives of Austria, Russia, and Prussia at Troppau (1820) and a later meeting at Laibach (1821), an Austrian army marched into Naples, overthrew the constitution, and restored the king as an absolute monarch. The French, in their only action in solid support of the Concert, were finally persuaded to send troops to Spain to assist Ferdinand VII.

Lord Castlereagh refused to attend the conferences at Troppau and Laibach, making the British position clear in the following letter to Lord Charles Stewart, his half-brother, British ambassador to Vienna. How did Castlereagh interpret the Quadruple Alliance? On what grounds did Great Britain refuse to intervene in the Neapolitan revolution? What traditional principle of British foreign policy did Castlereagh's views represent? What were the obvious weaknesses within the Alliance?

. . . With all the respect and attachment which I feel for the system of the Alliance, as regulated by the transactions of Aix-la-Chapelle, I should much question the prudence, or, in truth, the efficacy, of any formal exercise of its forms and provisions on the present occasion.

If the existing danger arose from any obvious infraction of the stipulations of our treaties, an extraordinary reunion of Sovereigns and of their Cabinets would be a measure of obvious policy; but when the danger springs from the internal convulsions of independent States, the policy of hazarding such a step is much more questionable: and when we recollect to what prejudicial misconceptions and popular irritation the conferences at Pilnitz and the declaration of the Duke of Brunswick, at the commencement of the late revolutionary war, gave occasion, it may well suggest the expediency that whatever ought or can be done for the general safety against the insurrectionary movements of conspiring and rebellious troops should be undertaken, after full deliberation, in the manner which will afford the least handle for misrepresentation and excitement, and which may give the effort to be made the fullest justification of a local and specific necessity arising out of the particular case.

I therefore hope that the Emperor of Russia will be content to confine the interview at Troppau within the prudent limits proposed by his Ally the Emperor of Austria, that whatever Ministerial conferences may be held may be regarded as only adding to our other means of confidential explanation, and that whatever is done shall be upon the particular case, without hazarding general declarations, containing universal pledges that cannot be redeemed, and which, from the first, will be seen through and despised. Dissertations on abstract principles will do nothing in the present day, unless supported.

. . . Now, this is a concert which the British Government cannot enter into.

1st. Because it binds them to engagements which they could not be justified in taking without laying the whole before Parliament.

2ndly. It creates a league which at any moment may involve them in the necessity of using force: for it is clear the *de facto* Government of Naples, upon such an act being agreed to by us, might, according to the ordinary laws of nations, without further notice, sequester all British property at Naples, and at once shut their ports against British commerce; and it further makes the continuance of that league dependent upon the common deliberation of all the Powers composing it.

3rdly. It is further inconsistent with the principles of the neutrality which this Government, with a view to the security of the royal family of Naples, has been induced to authorize Sir William à Court to declare and to act upon.

4thly. Such a league would render the British Government, both morally and in a parliamentary sense, responsible for all the future acts of the league; and, consequently, if Austria should move forward her army into the Neapolitan territory; for the acts of a Power, over whose councils in the execution of her intended measures they could not and ought not to have that species of detailed control which would justify such a responsibility.

5thly. Before such a power could in reason be delegated by the Alliance to Austria, the whole course of measures must previously be settled by common consent, which is, from the very nature of the case, impracticable, or the Austrian Commander, in the execution of the service, must be saddled with and act under the direction of a Council of Regency of the Allied Ministers residing at head-quarters, which is equally impracticable and inexpedient.

6thly. Such a league would most certainly be disapproved by our Parliament; and even could it be sustained, it is obvious that, from that moment, every act of the Austrian army in the kingdom of Naples would fall as much under the immediate cognizance and jurisdiction of the British Parliament, and be canvassed as freely and fully, as if it was the act of a British army and Commander-in-Chief.

The natural result of this seems to be, that Austria must, at least as far as we are concerned, make the measure, whatever it is, her own; that she may, by previous and confidential intercourse, collect the sentiments of her Allies, and thereby satisfy herself that she is not likely to incur their disapprobation, or be disavowed by them in what she proposes to attempt; but she must adopt it upon her own responsibility, and in her own name, and not in that of the five Powers, and she must be satisfied to justify it upon the grounds that decide her to act, receiving such an acquiescence or such an approbation from the other Powers as they may be prepared to afford to her.

Before such acquiescence or approbation can be expected, Austria must, however, be prepared to satisfy her Allies that she engages in this undertaking with no views of aggrandizement; that she aims at no supremacy in Italy incompatible with existing treaties; in short, that she has no interested views; that her plans are limited to objects of self defence; and that she claims no more from the country she proposes to enter, than having her army sustained in the usual manner, whilst necessarily stationed beyond her own frontier.

Prince Metternich, I have no doubt, really means so to limit his views; but, to inspire the confidence necessary to his own purpose, and to protect himself against the jealousy of other States, he must explain himself more explicitly than he has done in the Memoir in question. This being done, whatever hesitation particular Powers may have with respect to their own line of policy, none, I apprehend, will feel themselves disposed or entitled to impede or embarrass Austria in the course she may feel it necessary to pursue for her own security and that of her Italian States. . . .

For these reasons you will see that engagements of such a nature, at least on our part, are out of the question. We desire to leave Austria unembarrassed in her course; but we must claim for ourselves the same freedom of action. It is for the interest of Austria that such should be our position. It enables us, in our Parliament, to consider, and consequently to respect her measures as the acts of an independent State—a doctrine which we could not maintain, if we had rendered ourselves, by a previous concert, parties to those acts; and it places us in a situation to do justice in argument to the considerations which may influence her counsels, without, in doing so, being thrown upon the defence of our own conduct. Austria must, as I conceive, be contented to find in these Conferences the facilities for pursuing what she feels to be her own necessary policy; but she must not look to the involving by this expedient other Powers in a completely common interest and a common responsibility. The consequence of so doing would be to fetter her own freedom of action. She must preserve to herself the power of pursuing with rapidity and effect her immediate views of security; and the other Allied States must reserve to themselves the faculty of interposing, if they see cause for doing so.

CONSERVATISM AND ROMANTICISM

6. EDMUND BURKE: REFLECTIONS ON THE REVOLUTION IN FRANCE*

Edmund Burke (1729–97), an English Whig, was as a member of Parliament and a political propagandist. He expressed strong views in Parliament on leading domestic and foreign issues, including the revolutions in America and France. A firm believer in the fundamental tradition of British constitutional liberties, Burke was a consistent parliamentary champion of evolved rights. Defending tradition and proved historical standards, he mistrusted individual men and the whims of the masses. Burke's *Reflections on the Revolution in France* provided a model for conservative political arguments long after it first appeared in 1790. In Burke's view, what were the essential qualities of an enduring constitution? Why was he opposed to political authority residing with the masses? Why was Burke opposed to the concept of equality, and what did he claim were the basic qualifications for participation in government? Burke approved of the American Revolution and condemned the French Revolution. Which of his ideas explain this seeming contradiction?

You will observe, that from Magna Charta to the Declaration of Right, it has been the uniform policy of our constitution to claim and assert our liberties, as an *entailed inheritance* derived to us from our forefathers, and to be transmitted to our posterity; as an estate specially belonging to the people of this kingdom, without any reference whatever to any other more general or prior right. By this means our constitution preserves a unity in so great a diversity of its parts. We have an inheritable crown; an inheritable peerage; and a House of Commons and a people inheriting privileges, franchises, and liberties, from a long line of ancestors.

This policy appears to me to be the result of profound reflection; or rather the happy effect of following nature, which is wisdom without reflection, and above it. A spirit of innovation is generally the result of a selfish temper, and confined views. People will not look forward to posterity, who never look backward to their ancestors. Besides, the people of England well know, that the idea of inheritance furnishes a sure principle of conservation, and a sure principle of transmission; without at all excluding a principle of improvement. It leaves acquisition free; but it secures what it acquires. Whatever advantages are obtained by a state proceeding on these maxims, are locked fast as in a sort of family settlement; grasped as in a kind of mortmain forever. By a constitutional policy, working after the pattern of nature, we receive, we hold, we transmit our government and our privileges, in the same manner in which we enjoy and transmit our property and our lives. The institutions of policy, the goods of fortune, the gifts of providence, are handed down to us, and from us, in the same course and order. Our political system is placed in a just correspondence and symmetry with the order of the world, and with the mode of existence

* *The Works of Edmund Burke* (5 vols.; London: George Bell and Sons, 1901), II, 306–7, 323–24, 332–34.

decreed to a permanent body composed of transitory parts; wherein, by the disposition of a stupendous wisdom, moulding together the great mysterious incorporation of the human race, the whole, at one time is never old, or middle-aged, or young, but, in a condition of unchangeable constancy, moves on through the varied tenor of perpetual decay, fall, renovation, and progression. Thus, by preserving the method of nature in the conduct of the state, in what we improve, we are never wholly new; in what we retain, we are never wholly obsolete. By adhering in this manner and on those principles to our forefathers, we are guided not by the superstition of antiquarians, but by the spirit of philosophic analogy. In this choice of inheritance we have given to our frame of polity the image of a relation in blood; binding up the constitution of our country with our dearest domestic ties; adopting our fundamental laws into the bosom of our family affections; keeping inseparable, and cherishing with the warmth of all their combined and mutually reflected charities, our state, our hearths, our sepulchres, and our altars. . . .

I do not, my dear Sir, conceive you to be of that sophistical, captious spirit, or of that uncandid dullness, as to require, for every general observation or sentiment, an explicit detail of the correctives and exceptions, which reason will presume to be included in all the general propositions which come from reasonable men. You do not imagine, that I wish to confine power, authority, and distinction to blood, and names, and titles. No, Sir. There is no qualification for government but virtue and wisdom, actual or presumptive. Wherever they are actually found, they have, in whatever state, condition, profession, or trade, the passport of Heaven to human place and honour. Woe to the country which would madly and impiously reject the service of the talents and virtues, civil, military, or religious, that are given to grace and to serve it; and would condemn to obscurity everything formed to diffuse lustre and glory around a state! Woe to that country too, that, passing into the opposite extreme, considers a low education, a mean contracted view of things, a sordid, mercenary occupation, as a preferable title to command! Everything ought to be open; but not indifferently to every man. No rotation; no appointment by lot; no mode of election operating in the spirit of sortition, or rotation, can be generally good in a government conversant in extensive objects. Because they have no tendency, direct or indirect, to select the man with a view to the duty or to accommodate the one to the other. I do not hesitate to say, that the road to eminence and power, from obscure condition, ought not to be made too easy, nor a thing too much of course. If rare merit be the rarest of all rare things, it ought to pass through some sort of probation. The temple of honour ought to be seated on an eminence. If it be opened through virtue, let it be remembered too, that virtue is never tried but by some difficulty and some struggle.

Nothing is a due and adequate representation of a state, that does not represent its ability, as well as its property. But as ability is a vigorous and active principle, and as property is sluggish, inert, and timid, it never can be safe from the invasions of ability, unless it be, out of all proportion, predominant in the representation. It must be represented too in great masses of accumulation, or it is not rightly protected. The characteristic essence of property, formed out of the combined principles of its acquisition and conservation, is to be *unequal*.

The great masses therefore which excite envy, and tempt rapacity, must be put out of the possibility of danger. Then they form a natural rampart about the lesser properties in all their gradations. The same quantity of property, which is by the natural course of things divided among many, has not the same operation. Its defensive power is weakened as it is diffused. In this diffusion each man's portion is less than what, in the eagerness of his desires, he may flatter himself to obtain by dissipating the accumulations of others. The plunder of the few would indeed give but a share inconceivably small in the distribution to the many. But the many are not capable of making this calculation; and those who lead them to rapine never intend this distribution. . . .

If civil society be the offspring of convention, that convention must be its law. That convention must limit and modify all the descriptions of constitution which are formed under it. Every sort of legislative, judicial, or executory power are its creatures. They can have no being in any other state of things; and how can any man claim under the conventions of civil society, rights which do not so much as suppose its existence? Rights which are absolutely repugnant to it? One of the first motives to civil society, and which becomes one of its fundamental rules, is, *that no man should be judge in his own cause*. By this each person has at once divested himself of the first fundamental right of un-covenanted man, that is, to judge for himself, and to assert his own cause. He abdicates all right to be his own governor. He inclusively, in a great measure, abandons the right of self-defence, the first law of nature. Men cannot enjoy the rights of an uncivil and of a civil state together. That he may obtain justice, he gives up his right of determining what it is in points the most essential to him. That he may secure some liberty, he makes a surrender in trust of the whole of it.

Government is not made in virtue of natural rights, which may and do exist in total independence of it; and exist in much greater clearness, and in a much greater degree of abstract perfection: but their abstract perfection is their practical defect. By having a right to everything they want everything. Government is a contrivance of human wisdom to provide for human *wants*. Men have a right that these wants should be provided for by this wisdom. Among these wants is to be reckoned the want, out of civil society, of a sufficient restraint upon their passions. Society requires not only that the passions of individuals should be subjected, but that even in the mass and body, as well as in the individuals, the inclinations of men should frequently be thwarted, their will controlled, and their passions brought into subjection. This can only be done *by a power out of themselves;* and not, in the exercise of its function, subject to that will and to those passions which it is its office to bridle and subdue. In this sense the restraints on men, as well as their liberties, are to be reckoned among their rights. But as the liberties and the restrictions vary with times and circumstances, and admit of infinite modifications, they cannot be settled upon any abstract rule; and nothing is so foolish as to discuss them upon that principle.

The moment you abate anything from the full rights of men, each to govern himself, and suffer any artificial, positive limitation upon those rights, from that moment the whole organization of government becomes a consideration of convenience. This it is which makes the constitution of a state, and the due distribution of its powers, a matter of the most delicate and complicated skill. It requires a deep knowledge of human nature and human necessities, and of the things which facilitate or obstruct the various ends, which are to be pursued by the mechanism of civil institutions. The state is to have recruits to its strength, and remedies to its distempers. What is the use of discussing a man's abstract right to food or medicine? The question is upon the method of procuring and administering them. In that deliberation I shall always advise to call in the aid of the farmer and the physician, rather than the professor of metaphysics.

The science of constructing a commonwealth, or renovating it, or reforming it, is, like every other experimental science, not to be taught *a priori*. Nor is it a short experience that can instruct us in that practical science: because the real effects of moral causes are not always immediate: but that which in the first instance is prejudicial may be excellent in its remoter operation; and its excellence may arise even from the ill effects it produces in the beginning. The reverse also happens: and very plausible schemes, with very pleasing commencements, have often shameful and lamentable conclusions. In states there are often some osbcure and almost latent causes, things which appear at first view of little moment, on which a very great part of its prosperity or adversity may most essentially depend. The science of government being therefore so practical in itself and intended for such practical purposes, a matter which requires experience, and even more experience than any person can gain in his whole life, however sagacious and observing he may be, it is with infinite caution that any man ought to venture upon pulling down an edifice, which has answered in any tolerable degree for ages the common purposes of society, or on building it up again, without having models and patterns of approved utility before his eyes. . . .

7. JOSEPH DE MAISTRE: A DEFENSE OF THE OLD ORDER*

One of the harshest critics of revolution and of Enlightenment thought was Count Joseph de Maistre (1753–1821). De Maistre was driven out of his native Savoy by invading French troops and chose to await the defeat of Napoleon before returning to claim his estates. The thirteen volumes of de Maistre's collected works, composed between 1791 and 1821, are filled with bitter attacks against revolutionaries as well as a general defense of the authority of kings and popes. Although de Maistre distorted history to fit his own ideas, his exposition of the superficialities of eighteenth-century rationalism appealed widely to those seeking a status quo in the aftermath of Napoleon. In his *Essay on the Generative Principle of Political Constitutions* (1810) what did de Maistre hold to be the main political folly of his age? On what grounds did de Maistre justify his interpretation of papal authority?

One of the grand errors of an age, which professed them all, was, to believe that a political constitution could be written and created *a priori;* whilst reason and experience unite in establishing, that a constitution is a Divine work, and

* Joseph de Maistre, *Essay on the Generative Principle of Political Constitutions* (Boston: Little and Brown, 1847), pp. 25–26, 29–31, 41–42, 48, 56–59, 73–77.

that which is most fundamental, and most essentially constitutional, in the laws of a nation, is precisely what cannot be written. . . .

Hence it is that the good sense of antiquity, happily anterior to sophisms, has sought, on every side, the sanction of laws, in a power above man, either in recognizing that sovereignty comes from God, or in revering certain unwritten laws as proceeding from him.

The compilers of the Roman laws have placed, unpretendingly, in the first chapter of their collection, a very remarkable fragment of Greek jurisprudence. Among the laws which govern us, says this passage, some are written, others are unwritten. Nothing can be more simple or profound. Is there any Turkish law which expressly permits the sovereign to pass sentence of death upon a man immediately, without the decision of an intermediate tribunal? Are we acquainted with any written law, even religious, which prohibits the sovereigns of Christian Europe from doing this? Yet the Turk is no more surprised at seeing his master pass sentence of immediate death upon a man, than at seeing him go to the mosque. He believes with all Asia, and even with all antiquity, that the right to inflict death immediately, is a legitimate appendage of the sovereignty. But our princes would tremble at the bare idea of condemning a man to death; for, according to our view, this condemnation would be an atrocious murder. And yet, I doubt whether it would be possible to prohibit them from doing this by a fundamental written law, without producing greater evils than those we might wish to prevent. . . .

The more we examine the influence of human agency in the formation of political constitutions, the greater will be our conviction that it enters there only in a manner infinitely subordinate, or as a simple instrument; and I do not believe there remains the least doubt of the incontestable truth of the following propositions:—

1. That the fundamental principles of political constitutions exist before all written law.

2. That a constitutional law is, and can only be, the development or sanction of an unwritten pre-existing right.

3. That which is most essential, most intrinsically constitutional, and truly fundamental, is never written, and could not be, without endangering the state.

4. That the weakness and fragility of a constitution are actually in direct proportion to the multiplicity of written constitutional articles. . . .

Now since these elements, thus projected into space, have arranged themselves in such beautiful order, without a single man, among the innumerable multitude who have acted in this vast field, having ever known what he had done relatively to the whole, nor foreseen what would happen, it follows, inevitably, that these elements were guided in their fall by an infallible hand, superior to man. The greatest folly, perhaps, in an age of follies, was in believing that fundamental laws could be written *a priori,* whilst they are evidently the work of a power above man; and whilst the very committing them to writing, long after, is the most certain sign of their nullity. . . .

. . . I should be glad to see the *Confessions of Augsburg,* or the *Thirty-nine Articles,* set to music; this would be diverting.

The first symbols are far from containing the announcement of all our dogmas; on the contrary, Christians then would have regarded the announcement of them all as a great sin. The same is true of the Holy Scriptures; there never was an idea more shallow than that of seeking in them for the totality of the Christian doctrines; there is not a line in these writings which declares, or even allows us to discover, the design of making from them a code or dogmatic declaration of all the articles of faith.

More than this: if a people possess one of these codes of belief, we may be sure of three things:

1. That the religion of this people is false.

2. That it has written its religious code in a paroxysm of fever.

3. That this code will be ridiculed in a little while among this very nation, and that it will possess neither power nor durability. Such are, for example, those famous ARTICLES, which are signed by more than read, and read by more than believe them. Not only is this catalogue of dogmas counted for nothing, or next to nothing, in the country which gave them birth; but furthermore, it is manifest, even to a foreign eye, that the illustrious possessors of this sheet of paper are greatly embarrassed with it. In fact, they wish themselves well rid of it, because the national mind, enlightened by time, has grown weary of it; and besides it recalls to them an unhappy origin: but the constitution is written.

The English doubtless, would never have asked for the Great Charter, had not the privileges of the nation been violated; nor would they have asked for it, if these privileges had not existed before the Charter. What is true of the State, in this respect, is also true of the Church: if Christianity had never been attacked, there never would have been any writings to settle the dogmas; nor would the dogmas have been settled by writing, had they not pre-existed in their natural state, which is the oral.

The real authors of the Council of Trent were the two grand innovators of the sixteenth century. Their disciples having become more calm, have since proposed to us to expunge this fundamental law, because it contains some hard words for them; and they have endeavoured to tempt us, by indicating to us the possibility of a reunion, on that condition, which would make us accomplices instead of rendering us friends; but this demand is neither theological nor philosophical. They themselves formerly introduced into religious language those words which now weary them. Let us desire that they should now learn to pronounce them. . . .

Every right mind will convince itself on this point, by a little reflection upon an axiom equally striking by its importance and by its universality. It is this, THAT NOTHING GREAT HAS GREAT BEGINNINGS. There will not be found in the history of all ages a single exception to this law. *Crescit occulto velut arbor ævo,* is the immortal device of every great institution; and hence it is, that every false institution writes much, because it feels its weakness, and seeks support. From the truth just expressed, follows the unalterable consequence, that no institution, truly great and real, could be founded on a written law, since the men themselves, the successive instruments of its establishment, know not what it will become, and since insensible growth is the true sign of durability, in every possible order of things. A remarkable example of this kind, may be found in the power of the sovereign Pontiffs, which I do not intend to consider here in a dogmatic way. A multitude of able writers, since the sixteenth century, have employed a prodigious amount of learning, in order to establish, by going back to the cradle of Christianity, that the Bishops of Rome were not, in the first centuries, what they afterwards became; thus supposing, as a point conceded, that every thing which is not found in primitive times, is an abuse. Now I say, without the least spirit of contention, and without the design of offending any body, they manifest in this as much philosophy and true knowledge, as they would do in seeing, in an infant in swaddling clothes, the true dimensions of a full-grown man. The sovereignty, of which I am speaking at this moment, was born like others, and has grown like others. It is lamentable to see excellent minds taking such immense pains, to prove by infancy that manhood is an abuse; whilst any institution whatever, adult at birth, would be the grossest of absurdities, a true logical contradiction. If the enlightened and generous enemies of this power (and there are undoubtedly many of this class) will examine the question in this point of view, as I affectionately pray them to do, I do not doubt that all these objections, drawn from antiquity, will disappear as a light mist from before their eyes.

Concerning abuses, I ought not to employ myself here. I will say, however, since I have already had occasion to refer to them, that there is much to abate the declamatory invectives which the last century has compelled us to read on this great subject. A time will come, when the Popes, against whom the most clamour has been made, such as Gregory VII, for example, will be regarded, in every country, as the friends, guardians, and saviours of the human race,—as the true constitutive geniuses of Europe.

No person will doubt it, when learned Frenchmen shall be Christians, and when learned Englishmen shall be Catholics;—which will yet come to pass.

8. GEORG W. F. HEGEL: PHILOSOPHY OF HISTORY*

The rationalism of the Enlightenment encouraged a view of history which rejected the past as a time of oppression when reason had not prevailed. The *ancien régime,* a creature of historical development, was excoriated as anachronistic and antirational. The excesses of the Revolution in France, however, and the Napoleonic Wars, cast doubts on man's capacity to construct a rational society based upon the principles of the *philosophes*. Romanticism, with its emphasis upon the whole—society as opposed to the individual—its emphasis upon the ideal, and its yearning for a beautiful past out of a brutal and terrible present, sought a new view of history. Georg W. F. Hegel (1770–1831) was the most important of nineteenth-century idealistic philosophers and the most influential single philosopher of the century. As Romanticism itself, Hegel's philosophy has been interpreted in a variety of ways and has stimulated conservative as well as radical thought.

For Hegel, history was not a disjointed series of disconnected events, but a path toward a goal. History was dynamic; it proceeded according to a pattern (which Hegel called the Idea); it progressed by means of a conflict. The conflict was not of material things, but of ideas. It was a dialectic wherein a thesis

* Georg William Friedrich Hegel, *The Philosophy of History,* trans. J. Sibree (rev. ed.; New York: P. F. Collier and Son, 1900), pp. 64–84, 86–90, 95–97. Reprinted by permission.

(representing an imperfect manifestation of ultimate truth at any particular time) gave rise to a contradictory idea, the antithesis. Out of the conflict between the two arose a synthesis, which combined the highest features of each and which in turn became a new thesis, continuing the dialectic. Progress, through the conflict represented by the dialectic, is thus inherent in history.

The following selection is drawn from Hegel's *Philosophy of History*. What is the goal of history? What is the goal of philosophy? What is the nature of the state, and what is the relationship of the individual to the state? What, in Hegel's view, is freedom, and how is it to be achieved? Compare the idealism of Hegel with the concepts of Locke and Rousseau.

The destiny of the Spiritual World, . . . *the final cause of the World at large,* we allege to be the *consciousness* of its own freedom on the part of Spirit, and *ipso facto,* the *reality* of that freedom. . . .

. . . The insight then to which—in contradistinction from those ideals—philosophy is to lead us, is, that the real world is as it ought to be—that the truly good—the universal divine reason—is not a mere abstraction, but a vital principle capable of realizing itself. This *Good,* this *Reason,* in its most concrete form, is God. God governs the world: the actual working of his government—the carrying out of his plan—is the History of the World. This plan philosophy strives to comprehend; for only that which has been developed as the result of it, possesses *bona fide* reality. That which does not accord with it, is negative, worthless existence. Before the pure light of this Divine Idea—which is no mere Ideal—the phantom of a world whose events are an incoherent concourse of fortuitous circumstances, utterly vanishes. Philosophy wishes to discover the substantial purport, the real side, of the Divine Idea, and to justify the so much despised Reality of things; for Reason is the comprehension of the Divine work. . . .

. . . The Idea is the inner spring of action; the State is the actually existing, realized moral life. For it is the Unity of the universal, essential Will, with that of the individual; and this is "Morality." The Individual living in this unity has a moral life; possesses a value that consists in this substantiality alone. Sophocles in his Antigone, says, "The divine commands are not of yesterday, nor of today; no, they have an infinite existence, and no one could say whence they came." The laws of morality are not accidental, but are the essentially Rational. It is the very object of the State that what is essential in the practical activity of men, and in their dispositions, should be duly recognized; that it should have a manifest existence, and maintain its position. It is the absolute interest of Reason that this moral Whole should exist; and herein lie the justification and merit of heroes who have founded states—however rude these may have been. In the history of the World, only those peoples can come under our notice which form a state. For it must be understood that this latter is the realization of Freedom, *i.e.* of the absolute final aim, and that it exists for its own sake. It must further be understood that all the worth which the human being possesses—all spiritual reality, he possesses only through the State. For his spiritual reality consists in this, that his own essence—Reason—is objectively present to him, that it possesses objective immediate existence for him. Thus only is he fully conscious; thus only is he a partaker of morality—of a just and moral social and political life. For Truth is the Unity of the universal and subjective Will; and the Universal is to be found in the State, in its laws, its universal and rational arrangements. The State is the Divine Idea as it exists on Earth. We have in it, therefore, the object of History in a more definite shape than before; that in which Freedom obtains objectivity, and lives in the enjoyment of this objectivity. For Law is the objectivity of Spirit; volition in its true form. Only that will which obeys law, is free; for it obeys itself—it is independent and so free. When the State of our country constitutes a community of existence; when the subjective will of man submits to laws—the contradiction between Liberty and Necessity vanishes. The Rational has necessary existence, as being the reality and substance of things, and we are free in recognizing it as law, and following it as the substance of our own being. The objective and the subjective will are then reconciled, and present one identical homogeneous whole. . . .

. . . When man is spoken of as "free by Nature," the mode of his existence as well as his destiny is implied. His merely natural and primary condition is intended. In this sense a "state of Nature" is assumed in which mankind at large are in the possession of their natural rights with the unconstrained exercise and enjoyment of their freedom. This assumption is not indeed raised to the dignity of the historical fact; it would indeed be difficult, were the attempt seriously made, to point out any such condition as actually existing, or as having ever occurred. Examples of a savage state of life can be pointed out, but they are marked by brutal passions and deeds of violence; while, however rude and simple their conditions, they involve social arrangements which (to use the common phrase) *restrain* freedom. That assumption is one of those nebulous images which theory produces; an idea which it cannot avoid originating, but which it fathers upon real existence, without sufficient historical justification.

What we find such a state of Nature to be in actual experience, answers exactly to the Idea of a *merely* natural condition. Freedom as the *ideal* of that which is original and natural, does not exist *as original and natural*. Rather must it be first sought out and won; and that by an incalculable medial discipline of the intellectual and moral powers. The state of Nature is, therefore, predominantly that of injustice and violence, of untamed natural impulses, of inhuman deeds and feelings. Limitation is certainly produced by Society and the State, but it is a limitation of the mere brute emotions and rude instincts; as also, in a more advanced stage of culture, of the premeditated self-will of caprice and passion. This kind of constraint is part of the instrumentality by which only the consciousness of Freedom and the desire for its attainment, in its true—that is Rational and Ideal—form can be obtained. To the Ideal of Freedom, Law and Morality are indispensably requisite; and they are in and for themselves, universal existences, objects and aims; which are discovered only by the activity of thought, separating itself from the merely sensuous, and developing itself, in opposition thereto; and which must, on the other hand, be introduced into and incorporated with the originally sensuous will, and that contrarily to its natural inclination. The perpetually recurring misapprehension of Freedom consists in regarding that term only in its *formal,* subjective sense, abstracted from its essential objects and aims; thus a constraint put upon impulse, desire, passion—pertaining to the particular individual as such—a limitation of caprice and self-will is regarded as a fettering of Freedom. We should on the contrary look upon such limitation as the indispensable proviso of emancipation. Society and the State are the very conditions in which Freedom is realized. . . .

A State is an individual totality, of which you cannot select any particular side, although a supremely important one, such as its political constitution; and deliberate and decide respecting it in that isolated form. Not only is that constitution most intimately connected with and dependent on those other spiritual forces; but the form of the entire moral and intellectual individuality —comprising all the forces it embodies—is only a step in the development of the grand Whole—with its place preappointed in the process; a fact which gives the highest sanction to the constitution in question, and establishes its absolute necessity.—The origin of a state involves imperious lordship on the one hand, instinctive submission on the other. But even obedience—lordly power, and the fear inspired by a ruler—in itself implies some degree of voluntary connection. Even in barbarous states this is the case; it is not the isolated will of individuals that prevails; individual pretensions are relinquished, and the general will is the essential bond of political union. This unity of the general and the particular is the Idea itself, manifesting itself as a *state,* and which subsequently undergoes further development within itself. The abstract yet necessitated process in the development of truly independent states is as follows:—They begin with regal power, whether of patriarchal or military origin. In the next phase, particularity and individuality assert themselves in the form of Aristocracy and Democracy. Lastly, we have the subjection of these separate interests to a single power; but which can be absolutely none other than one outside of which those spheres have an independent position, viz. the Monarchical. Two phases of royalty, therefore, must be distinguished—a primary and a secondary one. This process is necessitated, so that the form of government assigned to a particular stage of development *must* present itself: it is therefore no matter of choice, but is that form which is adapted to the spirit of the people.

In a Constitution the main feature of interest is the self-development of the *rational,* that is, the *political* condition of a people; the setting free of the successive elements of the Idea: so that the several powers in the State manifest themselves as separate—attain their appropriate and special perfection—and yet in this independent condition, work together for one object, and are held together by it—*i.e.* form an organic whole. The State is thus the embodiment of rational freedom, realizing and recognizing itself in an objective form. For its objectivity consists in this—that its successive stages are not merely ideal, but are present in an appropriate reality; and that, in their separate and several working, they are absolutely merged in that agency by which the totality—the soul—the individuate unity—is produced, and of which it is the result.

The State is the Idea of Spirit in the external manifestation of human Will and its Freedom. It is to the State, therefore, that change in the aspect of History indissolubly attaches itself; and the successive phases of the Idea manifest themselves in it as distinct political *principles.* The Constitutions under which World-Historical peoples have reached their culmination are peculiar to them; and therefore do not present a generally applicable political basis. Were it otherwise, the differences of similar constitutions would consist only in a peculiar method of expanding and developing that generic basis; whereas they really originate in diversity of principle. . . .

9. ALEXIS DE TOCQUEVILLE: DEMOCRACY IN AMERICA*

Alexis Henri Charles Maurice Clerel, Comte de Tocqueville (1805–59) was a French aristocrat of liberal views who traveled to the United States in 1831 for the purpose of studying penal institutions. During his travels de Tocqueville became intrigued by the questions of whether American democracy had an applicability to Europe, and particularly to France. His conclusions were published under the title *Democracy in America* (1835–40) and formed a scientific analysis of American social and political institutions. In the course of his study, de Tocqueville justified democracy and predicted its ultimate triumph in Europe. He concluded his researches by observing: "The nations of our time cannot prevent the conditions of men from becoming equal; but it depends upon themselves whether the principle of equality is to lead them to servitude or to freedom, to knowledge or barbarism, to prosperity or to wretchedness."

On what grounds did de Tocqueville believe that "the species of oppression by which democratic nations are menaced is unlike anything which ever before existed in the world"? What, for him, was the most dangerous of all the forms which "democratic despotism" might assume? Why did democratic societies tend to show greater concern for equality than for liberty? Compare de Tocqueville's political views with the opinions of Robespierre, Burke, and de Maistre.

WHAT SORT OF DESPOTISM DEMOCRATIC NATIONS HAVE TO FEAR

I had remarked during my stay in the United States, that a democratic state of society, similar to that of the Americans, might offer singular facilities for the establishment of despotism; and I perceived, upon my return to Europe, how much use had already been made by most of our rulers, of the notions, the sentiments, and the wants engendered by this same social condition, for the purpose of extending the circle of their power. This led me to think that the nations of Christendom would perhaps eventually undergo some sort of oppression like that which hung over several of the nations of the ancient world. A more accurate examination of the subject, and five years of further meditations, have not diminished my apprehensions, but they have changed the object of them. No sovereign ever lived in former ages so absolute or so powerful as to undertake to administer by his own agency, and without the assistance of intermediate powers, all the parts of a great empire: none ever attempted to subject all his subjects indiscriminately to strict uniformity of regulation, and personally to tutor and direct every member of the community. The notion of such an undertaking never occurred to the human mind; and if any man had conceived it, the want of information, the imperfection of the administrative system, and above all, the natural obstacles caused by the inequality of conditions, would speedily have checked the execution of so vast a design. When the Roman

* Alexis de Tocqueville, *Democracy in America* [iv. 6], trans. Henry Reeve (New York: The Colonial Press, 1899), II, 330–35.

emperors were at the height of their power, the different nations of the empire still preserved manners and customs of great diversity; although they were subject to the same monarch, most of the provinces were separately administered; they abounded in powerful and active municipalities; and although the whole government of the empire was centred in the hands of the emperor alone, and he always remained, upon occasions, the supreme arbiter in all matters, yet the details of social life and private occupations lay for the most part beyond his control. The emperors possessed, it is true, an immense and unchecked power, which allowed them to gratify all their whimsical tastes, and to employ for that purpose the whole strength of the State. They frequently abused that power arbitrarily to deprive their subjects of property or of life: their tyranny was extremely onerous to the few, but it did not reach the greater number; it was fixed to some few main objects, and neglected the rest; it was violent, but its range was limited.

But it would seem that if despotism were to be established amongst the democratic nations of our days, it might assume a different character; it would be more extensive and more mild; it would degrade men without tormenting them. I do not question, that in an age of instruction and equality like our own, sovereigns might more easily succeed in collecting all political power into their own hands, and might interfere more habitually and decidedly within the circle of private interests, than any sovereign of antiquity could ever do. But this same principle of equality which facilitates despotism, tempers its rigor. We have seen how the manners of society become more humane and gentle in proportion as men become more equal and alike. When no member of the community has much power or much wealth, tyranny is, as it were, without opportunities and a field of action. As all fortunes are scanty, the passions of men are naturally circumscribed—their imagination limited, their pleasures simple. This universal moderation moderates the sovereign himself, and checks within certain limits the inordinate extent of his desires.

Independently of these reasons drawn from the nature of the state of society itself, I might add many others arising from causes beyond my subject; but I shall keep within the limits I have laid down to myself. Democratic governments may become violent and even cruel at certain periods of extreme effervescence or of great danger: but these crises will be rare and brief. When I consider the petty passions of our contemporaries, the mildness of their manners, the extent of their education, the purity of their religion, the gentleness of their morality, their regular and industrious habits, and the restraint which they almost all observe in their vices no less than in their virtues, I have no fear that they will meet with tyrants in their rulers, but rather guardians. I think then that the species of oppression by which democratic nations are menaced is unlike anything which ever before existed in the world: our contemporaries will find no prototype of it in their memories. I am trying myself to choose an expression which will accurately convey the whole of the idea I have formed of it, but in vain; the old words "despotism" and "tyranny" are inappropriate: the thing itself is new; and since I cannot name it, I must attempt to define it.

I seek to trace the novel features under which despotism may appear in the world. The first thing that strikes the observation is an innumerable multitude of men all equal and alike, incessantly endeavoring to procure the petty and paltry pleasures with which they glut their lives. Each of them, living apart, is as a stranger to the fate of all the rest—his children and his private friends constitute to him the whole of mankind; as for the rest of his fellow-citizens, he is close to them, but he sees them not—he touches them, but he feels them not; he exists but in himself and for himself alone; and if his kindred still remain to him, he may be said at any rate to have lost his country. Above this race of men stands an immense and tutelary power, which takes upon itself alone to secure their gratifications, and to watch over their fate. That power is absolute, minute, regular, provident, and mild. It would be like the authority of a parent, if, like that authority, its object was to prepare men for manhood; but it seeks on the contrary to keep them in perpetual childhood: it is well content that the people should rejoice, provided they think of nothing but rejoicing. For their happiness such a government willingly labors, but it chooses to be the sole agent and the only arbiter of that happiness: it provides for their security, foresees and supplies their necessities, facilitates their pleasures, manages their principal concerns, directs their industry, regulates the descent of property, and subdivides their inheritances—what remains, but to spare them all the care of thinking and all the trouble of living? Thus it every day renders the exercise of the free agency of man less useful and less frequent; it circumscribes the will within a narrower range, and gradually robs a man of all the uses of himself. The principle of equality has prepared men for these things: it has predisposed men to endure them, and oftentimes to look on them as benefits.

After having thus successively taken each member of the community in its powerful grasp, and fashioned them at will, the supreme power then extends its arm over the whole community. It covers the surface of society with a network of small complicated rules, minute and uniform, through which the most original minds and the most energetic characters cannot penetrate, to rise above the crowd. The will of man is not shattered, but softened, bent, and guided: men are seldom forced by it to act, but they are constantly restrained from acting: such a power does not destroy, but it prevents existence; it does not tyrannize, but it compresses, enervates, extinguishes, and stupefies a people, till each nation is reduced to be nothing better than a flock of timid and industrious animals, of which the government is the shepherd.

I have always thought that servitude of the regular, quiet, and gentle kind which I have just described, might be combined more easily than is commonly believed with some of the outward forms of freedom; and that it might even establish itself under the wing of the sovereignty of the people. Our contemporaries are constantly excited by two conflicting passions; they want to be led, and they wish to remain free: as they cannot destroy either one or the other of these contrary propensities, they strive to satisfy them both at once. They devise a sole, tutelary, and all-powerful form of government, but elected by the people. They combine the principle of centralization and that of popular sovereignty; this gives them a respite; they console themselves for being in tutelage by the reflection that they have chosen their own guardians. Every man allows himself to be put in leading-strings, because he sees that it is not a person or a class of persons, but the people at large that holds the end of his chain. By this system the people shake off their state of dependence just long enough to select their master, and then relapse into it again. A great many persons at the present day are quite contented with this sort of compromise between administrative despotism and the sovereignty of the people; and they think they have done enough for the protection of individual freedom when they have surrendered it to the power of the nation at large. This does not satisfy me: the nature of him I am to obey signifies less to me than the fact of extorted obedience.

I do not however deny that a constitution of this kind appears to me to be infinitely preferable to one, which, after having concentrated all the powers of government, should vest them in the hands of an irresponsible person or body of persons. Of all the forms which democratic despotism could assume, the latter would assuredly be the worst. When the sovereign is elective, or narrowly watched by a legislature which is really elective and independent, the oppression which he exercises over individuals is sometimes greater, but it is always less degrading; because every man, when he is oppressed and disarmed, may still imagine, that whilst he yields obedience it is to himself he yields it, and that it is to one of his own inclinations that all the rest give way. In like manner I can understand that when the sovereign represents the nation, and is dependent upon the people, the rights and the power of which every citizen is deprived, not only serve the head of the State, but the State itself; and that private persons derive some return from the sacrifice of their independence which they have made to the public. To create a representation of the people in every centralized country is, therefore, to diminish the evil which extreme centralization may produce, but not to get rid of it. I admit that by this means room is left for the intervention of individuals in the more important affairs; but it is not the less suppressed in the smaller and more private ones. It must not be forgotten that it is especially dangerous to enslave men in the minor details of life. For my own part, I should be inclined to think freedom less necessary in great things than in little ones, if it were possible to be secure of the one without possessing the other. Subjection in minor affairs breaks out every day, and is felt by the whole community indiscriminately. It does not drive men to resistance, but it crosses them at every turn, till they are led to surrender the exercise of their will. Thus their spirit is gradually broken and their character enervated; whereas that obedience, which is exacted on a few important but rare occasions, only exhibits servitude at certain intervals, and throws the burden of it upon a small number of men. It is in vain to summon a people, which has been rendered so dependent on the central power, to choose from time to time the representatives of that power; this rare and brief exercise of their free choice, however important it may be, will not prevent them from gradually losing the faculties of thinking, feeling, and acting for themselves, and thus gradually falling below the level of humanity. I add that they will soon become incapable of exercising the great and only privilege which remains to them. The democratic nations which have introduced freedom into their political constitution, at the very time when they were augmenting the despotism of their administrative constitution, have been led into strange paradoxes. To manage those minor affairs in which good sense is all that is wanted—the people are held to be unequal to the task, but when the government of the country is at stake, the people are invested with immense powers; they are alternately made the playthings of their ruler, and his masters —more than kings, and less than men. After having exhausted all the different modes of election, without finding one to suit their purpose, they are still amazed, and still bent on seeking further; as if the evil they remark did not originate in the constitution of the country far more than in that of the electoral body. It is, indeed, difficult to conceive how men who have entirely given up the habit of self-government should succeed in making a proper choice of those by whom they are to be governed; and no one will ever believe that a liberal, wise, and energetic government can spring from the suffrages of a subservient people. A constitution, which should be republican in its head and ultra-monarchical in all its other parts, has ever appeared to me to be a short-lived monster. The vices of rulers and the ineptitude of the people would speedily bring about its ruin; and the nation, weary of its representatives and of itself, would create freer institutions, or soon return to stretch itself at the feet of a single master.

10. FRANÇOIS RENÉ DE CHATEAUBRIAND: THE GENIUS OF CHRISTIANITY*

After serving in the French army under Louis XVI, François René de Chateaubriand (1768–1848) traveled to America during the early stages of the French Revolution. Opposed to the stream of events in his native country, he supported the royalist cause after his return in 1792 and was wounded in battle. He fled to England, where he lived in poverty for years. After the rise of Napoleon Chateaubriand served the French Empire in Rome (1803–6), although his sympathies lay with the supporters of the exiled Bourbon dynasty. With the restoration of Louis XVIII, Chateaubriand became a leader in the ultra-rightist party and, as Foreign Minister, presided over the French intervention in Spain.

In 1802 Chateaubriand wrote *The Genius of Christianity,* a vigorous defense of Christianity against the *philosophes* and the secularized philosophy of the eighteenth century. His enthusiasm was echoed by Romantic writers who created an idealized and often idyllic view of the past, especially the Middle Ages, when the Universal Church had been dominant. What specific influences had Christianity exerted upon the nations of Europe? Upon what grounds did Chateaubriand base his defense of Christianity? Compare his philosophy of history with the views of Burke, de Maistre, and Hegel.

If we consult the history of our states-general, we shall find that the clergy always acted the admirable part of moderators. They pacified, they soothed the minds of men, and prevented their rushing to extremities. The Church alone possessed information and experience when haughty barons and ignorant commoners knew nothing but factions and absolute obedience. She alone, from the habit of holding synods and councils, understood the art of public speaking and debate. She alone had dignity when it was wanting in all around her. We behold her alternately opposing the excesses of the people, remonstrating freely with the sovereign, and defying the anger of the nobles. Her superior knowl-

* Viscount de Chateaubriand, *The Genius of Christianity* (Baltimore: John Murphy and Co., 1856), pp. 658–61, 663, 667–68, 679.

edge, her conciliatory spirit, her mission of peace, the very nature of her interests, could not fail to inspire her with generous ideas in politics, which were not to be found in the two other orders. Placed between these, she had everything to fear from the nobility and nothing from the commons, of whom, for this very reason, she became the natural protector. Accordingly, we see her in times of disturbance voting in preference with the latter. The most dignified spectacle which our old states-general exhibited was that bench of aged prelates who, with the mitre on their heads and the crosier in their hands, alternately pleaded the cause of the people against the great, and of the sovereign against his factious nobility.

These prelates frequently fell victims to their devotedness. At the beginning of the thirteenth century, such was the hatred of the nobles against the clergy, that St. Dominic was necessitated to preach a kind of crusade to wrest the possessions of the Church from the barons, by whom they had been seized. Several bishops were murdered by the nobles or imprisoned by the court. They experienced by turns the vengeance of the monarch, of the aristocracy, and of the people.

If you take a more extensive view of the influence of Christianity on the political existence of the nations of Europe, you will see that it prevented famines, and saved our ancestors from their own fury, by proclaiming those intervals of peace denominated the peace of God, during which they secured the harvest and the vintage. In popular commotions the popes often appeared in public like the greatest princes. By rousing sovereigns, sounding the alarm, and forming leagues, they prevented the West from falling a prey to the Turks. This service alone rendered to the world by the Church would entitle her to a religious veneration.

Men unworthy of the name of Christians slaughtered the people of the New World, and the Court of Rome fulminated its bulls to prevent these atrocities. Slavery was authorized by law, and the Church acknowledged no slaves among her children. The very excesses of the Court of Rome have served to diffuse the general principles of the law of nations. When the popes laid kingdoms under an interdict—when they made emperors account for their conduct to the Holy See—they arrogated a power of which they were not possessed; but in humbling the majesty of the throne they perhaps conferred a benefit on mankind. Kings became more circumspect. They felt that they had a curb, and the people a protector. The papal rescripts never failed to mingle the voice of nations and the general interests of humanity with particular complaints. We have been informed that Philip, Ferdinand, or Henry, oppresses his people, etc. Such was the exordium of almost all those decrees of the Court of Rome.

If there existed in Europe a tribunal to judge nations and monarchs in the name of God, and to prevent wars and revolutions, this tribunal would doubtless be the masterpiece of policy and the highest degree of social perfection. The popes, by the influence which they exercised over the Christian world, were on the point of effecting this object.

Montesquieu has ably proved that Christianity is hostile, both in spirit and counsel, to arbitrary power; and that its principles are more efficacious than honor in monarchies, virtue in republics, and fear in despotic states. . . .

Upon the whole, Christianity is peculiarly admirable for having transformed the physical man into the moral man. All the great principles of Greece and Rome, such as equality and liberty, are to be found in our religion, but applied to the mind and considered with reference to the most sublime objects.

The counsels of the gospel form the genuine philosopher and its precepts the genuine citizen. There is not a petty Christian state under which a person may not live more agreeably, than he could have done among the most renowned people of antiquity, excepting Athens, which was attractive, but horridly unjust. Among modern nations there is an internal tranquillity, a continual exercise of the most peaceful virtues, which never prevailed on the banks of the Ilissus and the Tiber. If the republic of Brutus or the monarchy of Augustus were all at once to rise from the dust of ages, we should be shocked at the life of the Romans. Picture to yourself the games of the goddess Flora and the continual slaughter of gladiators, and you will be convinced of the prodigious difference which the gospel has made between us and the Pagans. The meanest of Christians, if a virtuous man, is more moral than was the most eminent of the philosophers of antiquity. . . .

We must repeat, as we have shown, that to the Church we owe the revival of the arts and sciences and of letters; that to her are due most of the great modern discoveries, as gunpowder, clocks, the mariner's compass, and, in government, the representative system; that agriculture and commerce, the laws and political science, are under innumerable obligations to her; that her missions introduced the arts and sciences among civilized nations and laws among savage tribes; that her institution of chivalry powerfully contributed to save Europe from an invasion of new barbarians; that to her mankind is indebted for

The worship of one only God;

The more firm establishment of the belief in the existence of that Supreme Being;

A clearer idea of the immortality of the soul, and also of a future state of rewards and punishments;

A more enlarged and active humanity;

A perfect virtue, which alone is equivalent to all the others—Charity.

A political law and the law of nations, unknown to the ancients, and, above all, the abolition of slavery.

Who is there but must be convinced of the beauty and the grandeur of Christianity? Who but must be overwhelmed with this stupendous mass of benefits? . . .

The gospel has changed mankind in every respect and enabled it to take an immense step toward perfection. If you consider it as a grand religious institution, which has regenerated the human race, then all the petty objections, all the cavils of impiety, fall to the ground. It is certain that the pagan nations were in a kind of moral infancy in comparison to what we are at the present day. A few striking acts of justice exhibited by a few of the ancients are not sufficient to shake this truth or to change the general aspect of the case.

Christianity has unquestionably shed a new light upon mankind. It is the religion that is adapted to a nation matured by time. It is, if we may venture to use the expression, the religion congenial to the present age of the world, as the reign of types and emblems was suited to the cradle of Israel. In heaven it has placed one only God; on earth it has abolished slavery. On the other hand, if you consider its mysteries (as we have done) as the archetype of the laws of nature, you will find nothing in them revolting to a great mind. The truths of Christianity, so far from requiring the submission of reason, command, on the contrary, the most sublime exercise of that faculty.

THE REVOLUTIONS OF 1848

11. ALPHONSE DE LAMARTINE: ON THE OVERTHROW OF LOUIS PHILIPPE*

Revolutionaries in Paris rose in 1830 against the ultra-royalist regime of Charles X and succeeded in placing Louis Philippe d'Orléans on the throne as a constitutional monarch. Louis Philippe was King of the French, not merely King of France, and successive ministries unhurriedly ruled the nation in the interest of the upper bourgeoisie. In the 1840's, badly advised by ministers like the historian François Guizot, opposition to the so-called July Monarchy grew, and neither the king nor his ministers properly assessed the changing mood of the nation. Opposition leaders, forbidden the right to public displays, held great open "banquets" as a means of rallying support. Guizot, however, held steadfast against opposition and reform with a determination that revealed him as the master of a regime characterized "not by the stability of firm purpose but of creeping paralysis."

By February 1848 the mood of discontent had become more open. When the government prohibited a scheduled public banquet, barricades began to spring up. The King dismissed Guizot and tried to save his throne by appointing a new ministry, but Louis Philippe had reacted too slowly—he shortly followed the route of his predecessors into exile in England.

In the provisional government which followed the overthrow of the July Monarchy, Alphonse de Lamartine (1790–1869), poet, historian, and outspoken republican, helped guide France in a new direction. Lamartine pressed for a constitution with an elected presidency, and the short-lived Second Republic was born. Why, according to Lamartine, was Louis Philippe overthrown?

Louis Philippe of Orléans was of a revolutionary race, though a prince of the blood. His father had plunged into the most deplorable excesses of the Convention. He had made himself popular, not through the glory, but the atrocity, of this epoch; and the faults of the father were the pledges of the son in the eyes of the revolution of 1830.

Still Louis Philippe was too honest and adroit a man to redeem the sanguinary promise of his name to the revolution which proclaimed him king. Nature had made this prince a man of probity and moderation; exile and experience had made him a politician. The difficulty of his part, as a prince among democrats and democrat among princes, in the commencement of his life, had rendered him supple to circumstances, patient in events, and temporizing with fortune. He seemed to foresee that destiny owed him a throne. In the mean while, he

* Alphonse de Lamartine, *History of the French Revolution of 1848*, trans. Francis A. Durivage and William S. Chase (Boston: Phillips, Sampson and Co., 1849), pp. 4–7.

enjoyed the pleasures and virtues of family relations in a retired, modest, and irreproachable domestic life. He had always a tribute of respect for the reigning monarch, and a smile of intelligence for the opposition, without, however, encouraging them by any criminal complicity. Studious, thoughtful, and exceedingly well informed on all points touching the interior administration of empires; profoundly versed in history; a diplomatist equal to Mazarin or Talleyrand; possessed of a fluent and inexhaustible elocution, which resembled eloquence as much as conversation can resemble oratory; a model for husbands, an example for fathers, in the midst of a nation which loves to see good morals seated on the throne; gentle, humane and peaceable; brave by birth but abhorring bloodshed; it might be said that nature and art had endowed him with all the qualities which make up a popular king, with one exception:—greatness. . . .

Such was Louis Philippe at the commencement of the year 1848. This whole perspective was reality. His enemies acknowledged themselves vanquished. Parties adjourned their hopes to the day of his death. Reflection was overwhelmed in contemplating a wisdom so profound, and a fortune so constant. But to this wisdom and to this fortune a broader basis was wanting—the people.

Louis Philippe had not comprehended all the democracy in his views. Served by ministers, skillful and eloquent indeed, but rather members of parliament than statesmen, he had restricted the democracy to the proportions of an elected dynasty, with the chambers and three hundred thousand electors. He had left beyond the pale of rights and political action all the rest of the nation. He had made of a pecuniary quitrent the sign and material title of sovereignty, instead of recognizing and establishing this sovereignty by the divine right of man—a creature capable of rights, of discernment, and of will. In a word, he and his short-sighted ministers had put their faith in an oligarchy, instead of founding it on unanimity. There were no longer slaves, but there was an entire people condemned to see themselves governed by a handful of electoral dignitaries, and these electors alone were legal men. The masses were only masses sustaining the government without sharing in it. Such a government could not fail to become selfish—such masses could not fail to become disaffected.

Other great faults, produced by the natural intoxication of a mind which had commanded constant success, had contributed insensibly to alienate these masses from the throne. The people have not the science, but they have a confused perception of politics. It was soon seen that the nation was sacrificed to the interests of the strengthening and aggrandizement of the dynasty into our relations with foreign powers; that Louis Philippe degraded peace; that his alliance at whatever price with London sometimes gave him the attitude of an English viceroy on the continent; that the treaties of 1815, the natural but temporary reaction of the unjust conquests of the empire, would become, under his dynasty, the regular and definitive state of the continent for France; that England, Russia, Austria and Prussia, assuming annually immense dimensions on the seas, in the east, in Poland, in Italy, in Germany, on the lower Danube, beyond the Caucasus, and on the side of Turkey,—France, forbidden to increase on the sea, in territory and in influence, was proportionately diminishing in the family of nations, and found herself insensibly and comparatively reduced to the condition of a secondary power. The unuttered or articulated opinion of the masses also reproached the reign of Louis Philippe with betraying the revolution internally, by resuming one by one the traditions of the monarchy of divine right, instead of conforming to the democratic spirit of the elective monarchy of 1830.

12. THE WORKERS OF PARIS AND THE "JUNE DAYS"*

The overthrow of Louis Philippe in February 1848 led to political democracy in France, but the social and economic goals of many who had participated in the revolution were not achieved. The working classes were quickly disappointed and disillusioned and felt cheated of their apparent victory. A growing sense of despair and anger permeated the working-class sections of Paris as unemployment mounted precipitously through the early months of 1848.

During the last years of the July Monarchy a French utopian Socialist, Louis Blanc, had advanced a plan for national workshops designed to promote industrial harmony. The provisional government did establish workshops, but along drastically different lines from Blanc's original proposal. The workshops soon became nothing more than a means for distributing a dole, and the provisional government, as soon as it felt strong enough, moved to dissolve the workshops. Thus provoked, the workers rose in revolt, and Paris erupted in civil war. The bloody "June Days" alienated the workers from the Republic and helped to pave the way for Louis Napoleon Bonaparte's election as President of the Republic in December 1848. On what grounds did the provisional government believe its national-workshops program would solve the problem of unemployment? Why did the government dissolve the workshops? What traditional revolutionary action did the working classes take, and how did the government react?

Orders were given to resume the public works which were in progress at the outbreak of the Revolution; and decrees full of cajolery and flattery to the working classes were issued from the prolific mint of the Provisional Government. One of them ran as follows:

"From Wednesday March 1, important works will be organized on different points. All workmen who wish to take part in them should apply to one of the mayors of Paris, who will receive their applications, and direct them without delay to the different workyards.

"*Workmen of Paris,* you wish to live honourably by labour; all the efforts of the Provisional Government will, you may rely on it, be directed to assist you in the accomplishment of that wish. The Republic has a right to expect, and it does expect, from the patriotism of all its citizens, that the example it gives may be followed. In that manner the extent of the works may be increased. Let labour, therefore, everywhere resume its wonted activity. Workmen, after victory, labour is a fine example which you have to give to the world, and you will give it."

Another was still more explicit and magnificent in its promises.

"Considering that the Revolution made by the people ought to be made *for* them;

"That it is time to put an end to the long and iniquitous sufferings of workmen;

"That the labour question is one of supreme importance;

* *The Annual Register for the Year 1848* (London, 1849), pp. 252–54, 259–60, 282–86, 288.

"That there is no other more high or more worthy of the consideration of a Republican Government;

"That it belongs to France to study ardently, and to resolve a problem submitted at present to all the industrial nations of Europe;

"The Provisional Government of the Republic decrees a permanent commission, which shall be named *Commission de Gouvernment pour les Travailleurs,* is about to be nominated, with the express and special mission of occupying themselves with their lot.

"To show how much importance the Provisional Government of the Republic attaches to the solution of this great problem, it nominates President of the Commission of Government for Workmen one of its members, M. Louis Blanc, and for Vice-President another of its members, M. Albert, workman.

"Workmen will be invited to form part of the committee.

"The seat of the committee will be at the Palace of the Luxembourg."

These doctrines were of course highly acceptable to the labouring classes, and they determined to give them practical effect. Large bodies proceeded to the Hôtel de Ville, and demanded that the period of labour should be reduced to ten hours a day; a minimum rate of wages established; and the system of employing middlemen abolished. And one of the first acts of the new Commission was to decree that:

"Considering that the intention of the Provisional Government, such as it appears from the very terms of the decree, has been to spare the strength of the operatives, and to leave a portion of their time for their intelligence;

"The duration of effective labour in Paris and in the suburbs is fixed at ten hours, for all professions."

In order to find occupation for the dangerous class of unemployed workmen, national workshops called *ateliers* were opened by the Government, where two francs a day were paid to those who were engaged; and, as it was impossible to employ all, who applied in crowds for admission, one franc a day was in the mean time doled out to those to whom work could not immediately be given. This, however, produced a very evil effect. The operatives preferred the smaller pay and idleness to higher wages and work, and their minds had become so unsettled by the events in which they had played such a prominent part, that they were disinclined to return to habits of steady industry. This produced a remonstrance from Marie, the Minister of Public Works, who thus addressed the *ouvriers* of Paris.

"*Citizens,* you demanded that the terms on which you labour should be ameliorated, and your demands were satisfied. All intermediaries between the master and operative have been removed by common accord, and the period of the day's work has been fixed at ten hours. Nevertheless, for some days past the great workshops opened by the state or by manufacturers, whom the difficulty of circumstances and the financial crisis have not a moment discouraged, have again been abandoned, or are menaced with being so. Citizens, you are men of industry, and you are proud of your condition—and you are right, for industry is the true source of happiness, for man, for his family, and for all society, for in that alone consists true independence and true liberty. Return, then, to your workshops, resume that active and laborious life which is an honour to you, and a subject of hope for the country." . . .

Besides this, M. Louis Blanc declared that it would be necessary to unite workshops belonging to the same branch of industry; to unite all the workshops of different branches of industry, but placed in the same condition; and to guarantee the interests of the consumer as regarded the quality and the lowest possible price of the produce.

"The plan is, that a Council of Administration should be placed at the head of all the *ateliers,* in whose hands would be united the guidance of all the industries, in the same way that the direction of each particular industry would be placed in the hands of an engineer. The State would arrive at the realization of this plan by successive measures. No one is to have violence done to him. The State intends to establish a model, by the side of which the private associations and the present economical system may live."

As a practical commentary upon these doctrines, we may mention that the conductors of the Paris omnibuses assembled, and ordered all the vehicles, without exception, to stop running: they sent them off their stands, forcibly stopped them in the streets, and compelled the passengers to evacuate them, and carried away the wooden houses (*bureaux de contrôle*) erected on the Boulevards. They thus forced the public to submit to a higher rate of fares.

The case was taken into consideration by the conclave at the Luxembourg, and M. Louis Blanc fixed the salaries of the drivers and conductors of omnibuses at 3f. 50c. per day. He also considerably reduced the amount of the fines to which they were liable, and decided that their proceeds should in future specially belong to the conductors and drivers, and form a fund for the benefit of the sick and wounded, their widows and families.

Hitherto all had gone on smoothly, but there was an undercurrent of discontent at work which was destined to convulse the capital, and endanger the existence of the Republic as it had been accepted by the nation. There was a dangerous class of men called *Communistes* or *Socialists,* in whose eyes the possession of property was a crime, and whose untiring object it was, and still is, to overthrow all existing institutions, and establish the dominion of an unchecked and unbridled democracy in its wildest and most licentious form. This party had been gradually growing in numbers and strength, and to them the Revolution seemed to be only half accomplished, while the rights of property were respected, and a curb was placed upon disorder. Those of their most prominent leaders were MM. Blanqui, Cabet, and Raspail, and the former had convoked a meeting of his associates in the Champs Élysées for the 16th of April, without specifying the object for which they were summoned. The Government, however, took the alarm, and on that day the *rappel* was beaten throughout Paris, and the streets were filled with upwards of 200,000 National Guards. The meeting convened by M. Blanqui was held, and, after some violent speeches, the crowd, about 5000 in number, resolved to march to the Hôtel de Ville, and demand the dismissal of the more moderate Members of the Provisional Government.

When they arrived at the *Pont Neuf,* they found the bridge occupied by troops, and cries of "À bas les communistes!" "À bas Blanqui!" rent the air. Finding that the attempt to proceed was vain, and that if they ventured to provoke a collision they must be overpowered and destroyed, they at last disbanded and dispersed. ...

M. Trélat, Minister of Public Works, said that many labourers had already been formed into brigades, and would leave in a few days for the canal of the Marne, the Upper Marne, the Upper Seine, and the Tours and Nantes Railroad. Their number was about 14,000. M. Trélat regretted the anxiety evinced by the committees of the Assembly to destroy these workshops. For his part he would never consent to it, nor would he adopt hasty measures when the interests of his fellow-creatures were at stake. He could understand the surprise of the Assembly at finding that the working of these establishments continued the same, notwithstanding all the activity and zeal he had displayed to reform the abuse.

This question of the removal of the workmen became the pretext for a terrible explosion, and revealed the existence of a dark and deep-seated conspiracy to deliver up the capital and France to all the horrors of anarchy, by establishing the triumph of the Red Republicans.

The masses of unemployed workmen in Paris, who must either support themselves on the pittance doled out in the *Ateliers Nationaux* or starve, were ripe for a revolt; and the specious doctrines of the Communists and Socialists, who were actively employed in disseminating them, found a ready reception with them, while they were in a state of idleness and hunger. During the few days before the eventful 23rd of June, the condition of the lower classes had been the subject of frequent comment in the National Assembly. M. Victor Hugo, the well-known novelist, said with reference to the *ateliers,* that he admitted that those establishments had been at first a necessity, but it was now full time to remedy an evil of which the least inconvenience was to squander uselessly the resources of the country. What, he asked, had they produced in the course of four months? Nothing. They had degraded the vigorous children of labour, deprived them of all taste for labour, and demoralized them to such a degree that they no longer blushed to beg in the streets. The Monarchy had its idlers; the Republic its vagabonds. He thought, however, that the enemies of the country would not succeed in converting the Parisian labourers, formerly so virtuous, into lazzaroni and janissaries, or prætorians of *émeute,* at the service of a dictatorship. M. Hugo then drew a gloomy picture of the financial and commercial situation of France, and, appealing to the Socialists, he summoned them in the name of humanity to cease to préach their anarchial doctrines. At the moment that Paris struggled in a paroxysm which was regarded by its neighbours as an agony, London, he said, rejoiced, and its industry and commerce had trebled. Those who excited the people to revolt were most culpable, for they created distrust, and obliged capital to fly. When they agitated Paris, they asserted the power, grandeur, wealth, prosperity, and preponderance of England. The misery of the rich constituted at no time the wealth of the poor. The Socialists should consider that civil war was a servile war; and he entreated them to suspend their declamations against family and property, the basis of all society.

M. Leon Faucher complained of the little attention paid by the Government to the question of the national workshops, and of its allowing the numbers of individuals employed in them to increase from 13,000 to 120,000. Misery, he maintained, was extending to all classes of society. Very soon not a single manufacture would be in operation in Paris; the shops would by degrees be closed, and the contagion soon reach the provinces. M. Faucher felt fully justified in stating that one half of Paris was relieved by the other half. It would be far preferable to destroy those national workshops altogether, and to employ the funds in distributing alms to the indigent.

In order to diminish the danger which threatened the peace of the metropolis, the Government determined to reduce the number of *ouvriers* who were receiving relief there, and on the 22nd of June an order was issued that 3000 of those who came from the provinces should quit Paris, and return to their respective homes. They were supplied with money, and tickets, to enable them to procure provisions and lodgings on the road. They left the capital in sullen discontent, but halted after they had passed the barriers, and a body of 400 of them returned, under a pretext of wishing to have an interview with the Executive Committee, at the palace of Luxembourg. A deputation of four was admitted to the presence of M. Marie, to whom they detailed their grievances. Some expressions of his were misinterpreted, and, on the return of the delegates to their comrades, they marched along the streets, shouting, "Down with the Executive Commission!" "Down with Assembly!" Their numbers rapidly increased, and different divisions of workmen poured through the streets converging on the Hôtel de Ville, where they assembled in a tumultuous crowd. No act of violence however yet took place, and they separated in the direction of the different Faubourgs, where the plan of insurrection was already fully organized. In the meantime the Government was not idle, and large bodies of troops were concentrated upon the different points where it was thought probable that attacks might be made. Some companies of the line and National Guards bivouacked in the Place de Grove, and the Hall of the Assembly was filled with troops. Although noisy and disorderly crowds of workmen congregated in different parts until late in the evening, no collision happened, and the night was passed in uneasy expectation of the struggle which seemed inevitable on the morrow.

In the morning, the sound of the *rappel* was everywhere heard, but this was soon changed for the more ominous beat of the *générale,* and the National Guard appeared in great force in the streets. About 9 o'clock the insurgents began to erect barricades at the Porte St. Denis and the Porte St. Martin, and in those Faubourgs, as well in the notorious Faubourg St. Antoine, so famous in the history of Parisian disturbances. The conflict first commenced at the Porte St. Denis. Here a small party of National Guards was stopped by the barricade, and immediately attacked it; but the resistance was obstinate, and it was only after a severe struggle, in which the assailants were obliged twice to retreat, and some lives were lost, that the barricade was carried. A similar contest took place at the Porte St. Martin, with a like result, and many barricades were taken in the course of the day. The plan of the insurgents seemed to be to defend desperately these barricades as long as they were tenable, and then suddenly abandoning them to fall back upon other positions, fortified in the same rapid and extempore manner. But as soon as the post was taken by the troops, and they attempted to follow the rebels through the streets, they were received by a galling fire from the houses, which were prepared in a manner that proved how skillfully and deliberately the revolt had been concerted. They were pierced with loop-holes, and passages were cut through the party walls, so that as fast as one was taken the inmates retired to the next house, and there continued their unfaltering resistance. In fact, in some quarters the houses might be compared to a rabbit warren, full of holes and galleries, through which the National Guards had to pursue an invisible but deadly foe. Mattresses were placed against the windows, behind which marksmen were posted, who could thus take secure aim; and women were actively employed in casting bullets, supplying arms, and tending to the wounded. The Garde Mobile behaved admirably. Doubts of its fidelity were entertained, as its ranks were composed of the same class as the men against whom it was employed; but it displayed the most brilliant courage, and fought with determined zeal by the side of the troops of the line and the National Guards. In the course of the afternoon General Cavaignac, the Minister of War, was invested with the command of the whole of the armed force at the disposal of the Government in Paris, and the roar of cannon was heard in the streets before nightfall, as it was found impossible to penetrate some of the barricades without artillery. Over all these formidable structures, behind which the insurgents had intrenched themselves, the red flag waved, and heaps of dead bodies lay by their side attesting the fierce nature of the strife which was raging. . . .

In the course of the morning the Executive Committee resigned their functions, and the National Assembly voted a decree, whereby Paris was declared to be in a state of siege, and all the Executive powers were delegated to General Cavaignac. Thus was the usual destiny of popular revolutions accomplished, and France saw itself once more under the sway of a military dictator. In the meantime immense numbers of Provincial National Guards had poured into Paris from Rouen, Amiens, Beauvais, Clermont, Poissy, Chaten, Carrière, Mendon, Senlis, Meaux, Melun, and other places; but the rebels had made themselves masters of four pieces of artillery on their way from Vincennes, and General Cavaignac issued the following notice:—

"If at noon the barricades are not removed, mortars and howitzers will be brought, by which shells will be thrown, which will explode behind the barricades and in the apartments of the houses occupied by the insurgents."

This threat, however, had no effect, and in the afternoon the roar of cannon announced that the combat was maintained with undiminished vigour. Many of the Members of the National Assembly distinguished themselves by the courage with which they approached the barricades, and, after in vain endeavouring to induce the misguided multitude to yield, fought gallantly with the troops. During the day M. Bixio, a representative, was killed, and General Bédeaux, M. Clement Thomas, and M. Dornès were severely wounded. . . .

General Lamoricière, who directed in person the operations of the troops, ordered cannon and mortars to be brought up, and after the heavy artillery had made a clear breach through the formidable barrier, and reduced many of the adjacent houses to a heap of ruins, the soldiers rushed in and put to the sword all whom they found with arms in their hands on the other side. The next point of attack was the Faubourg St. Antoine, which was surrounded by troops on all sides within the city, and it was thought that this focus and stronghold of revolutionary fury would only yield after a severe bombardment. The artillery was placed in position, and General Lamoricière was about to begin the cannonade, when General Cavaignac ordered that a summons should be sent to the infatuated inhabitants to surrender before opening the fire. A certain time was given, and when this had passed the attack began. Soon, however, an individual appeared with a flag of truce, and stated to General Lamoricière, on behalf of the Insurgents, that they were willing to surrender on the terms proposed by General Cavaignac. Some delay and misunderstanding at first took place, and the combat was partially renewed; but a second negotiation was opened, and the Faubourg finally capitulated, and was, without any further resistance, taken possession of by the troops. About the hour of noon the following letter from Gen. Cavaignac announced to the National Assembly the final suppression of the insurrection:—

"Citizen President, Thanks to the attitude of the National Assembly, and the devotion and courage of the National Guard and army, the revolt has been suppressed. The struggle has completely ceased in Paris. The moment I am assured that the powers confided to me by the National Assembly are no longer necessary for the salvation of the Republic, I will respectfully resign them into its hands."

13. KARL MARX: CLASS STRUGGLES IN FRANCE*

Born in Rhenish Prussia of German-Jewish parents who had been converted to Christianity, Karl Marx (1818–83) earned a doctorate at the University of Berlin after studying Hegelian philosophy. The Prussian government harassed Marx for his radical views and blocked the road to a university appointment, forcing him to earn a precarious living as a journalist. In 1843 he fled to Paris where he came into intimate contact with the Socialist and Anarchist views of Louis Blanc, Pierre Proudhon, and the Comte de Saint-Simon. Marx also began his lifelong friendship and literary collaboration with Friedrich Engels in Paris. Leaving France in 1845, Marx resided temporarily in Brussels. He returned to Germany during the Revolutions of 1848 and then took up permanent residence in London after the German revolution failed in 1849.

Because Marx believed that his own Socialist concept was the only truly scientific, and hence historically realistic, Socialist philosophy, he criticized bitterly all other Socialist movements in Europe and America. Primarily concerned with class struggle, Marx presented in his *Class Struggles in France* (1850) a brilliant social analysis of the forces which contributed to the downfall of the July Monarchy. According to Marx, what portion of the French population played a significant role in the political and economic organization of the French state? By what means did a minority of the population profit from public financing and public indebtedness? What role did the working class play in the 1848 Revolution, and how did that role change with the advent of the June Days?

It was not the French bourgeoisie that ruled under Louis Philippe, but a *fraction* of it, bankers, stock exchange kings, railway kings, owners of coal and

* Karl Marx, "The Class Struggles in France" in *Selected Works,* ed. V. Adoratsky (2 vols.; Moscow: Co-operative Publishing Society of Foreign Workers in the U.S.S.R., 1935), II, 193–203, 221.

iron works and forests, a part of the landed proprietors that rallied round them —the so-called *finance aristocracy*. It sat on the throne, it dictated laws in the Chambers, it conferred political posts from cabinet portfolios to the tobacco bureau.

The real *industrial bourgeoisie* formed part of the official opposition, *i.e.*, it was represented only as a minority in the Chambers. Its opposition was expressed all the more decisively, the more unalloyed the autocracy of the finance aristocracy became, and the more it itself imagined that its domination over the working class was ensured after the mutinies of 1832, 1834 and 1839, which had been drowned in blood. . . .

The *petty bourgeoisie* of all degrees, and the *peasantry* also, were completely excluded from political power. Finally, in the official opposition or entirely outside the *pays légal,* there were the *ideological* representatives and spokesmen of the above classes, their savants, lawyers, doctors, etc., in a word: their so-called *talents.*

The July monarchy, owing to its financial need, was dependent from the beginning on the big bourgeoisie, and its dependence on the big bourgeoisie was the inexhaustible source of a growing financial need. It was impossible to subordinate state administration to the interests of national production without balancing the budget, establishing a balance between state expenses and income. And how was this balance to be established, without limiting state expenditure, *i.e.*, without encroaching on interests which were so many supports of the ruling system, and without redistributing taxes, *i.e,* without putting a considerable share of the burden of taxes on the shoulders of the big bourgeoisie itself?

Moreover the fraction of the bourgeoisie that ruled and legislated through the Chambers had a *direct interest* in *state indebtedness*. The *state deficit* was even the main object of its speculation and played the chief role in its enrichment. At the end of each year a new deficit. After expiry of four or five years a new loan. And every new loan offered new opportunities to the finance aristocracy for defrauding the state which was kept artificially on the verge of bankruptcy —it had to contract with the bankers under the most unfavourable conditions. Each new loan gave a further opportunity for plundering the public, that had invested its capital in state bonds, by stock exchange manipulations into the secrets of which the government and the majority in the Chambers were admitted. In general, the fluctuation of state credits and the possession of state secrets gave the bankers and their associates in the Chambers and on the throne the possibility of evoking sudden, extraordinary fluctuations in the quotations of state bonds, the result of which was always bound to be the ruin of a mass of smaller capitalists and the fabulously rapid enrichment of the big gamblers. If the state deficit was in the direct interest of the ruling fraction of the bourgeoisie, then it is clear why the *extraordinary* state expenditure in the last years of Louis Philippe's government was far more than double the extraordinary state expenditure under Napoleon, indeed reached a yearly sum of nearly 400,000,000 francs, whereas the whole annual export of France seldom attained a volume amounting to 750,000,000 francs. The enormous sums which, in this way, flowed through the hands of the state facilitated, moreover, swindling contracts for deliveries, bribery, defalcations and all kinds of roguery. The defrauding of the state, just as it occurred on a large scale in connection with loans, was repeated in detail, in the state works. The relationship between Chamber and government multiplied itself as the relationship between individual departments and individual *entrepreneurs*.

In the same way as the ruling class exploited state expenditure in general and state loans, they exploited the *building of railways*. The Chambers piled the main burdens on the state, and secured the golden fruits to the speculating finance aristocracy. One recalls the scandals in the Chamber of Deputies, when by chance it came out that all the members of the majority, including a number of ministers, had taken part as shareholders in the very railway construction which as legislators they caused to be carried out afterwards at the cost of the state.

On the other hand, the smallest financial reform was wrecked by the influence of the bankers. For example, the *postal reform*. Rothschild protested. Was it permissible for the state to curtail sources of income out of which interest was to be paid on its ever increasing debt?

The July monarchy was nothing other than a joint stock company for the exploitation of French national wealth, the dividends of which were divided among ministers, Chambers, 240,000 voters and their adherents. Louis Philippe was the director of this company—...

The eruption of the general discontent was finally accelerated and the sentiment for revolt ripened by *two economic world events*.

The *potato blight* and the *bad harvests* of 1845 and 1846 increased the general ferment among the people. The high cost of living of 1847 called forth bloody conflicts in France as well as the rest of the Continent. As against the shameless orgies of the finance aristocracy, [there was] the struggle of the people for the first necessities of life!...

The second great economic event which hastened the outbreak of the revolution was a *general commercial and industrial crisis* in England. Already heralded in the autumn of 1845 by the wholesale reverses of the speculators in railway shares, delayed during 1846 by a number of incidents such as the impending abolition of the corn duties, in the autumn of 1847 the crisis finally burst forth with the bankruptcy of the London grocers, on the heels of which followed the insolvencies of the land banks and the closing of the factories in the English industrial districts. The after effect of this crisis on the Continent had not yet spent itself when the February Revolution broke out. . . .

The *Provisional Government* which emerged from the February barricades necessarily mirrored in its composition the different parties which shared in the victory. It could not be anything but a *compromise between the different classes* which together had overturned the July throne, but whose interests were mutually antagonistic. The great *majority* of its members consisted of representatives of the bourgeoisie. The republican petty bourgeoisie were represented by Ledru-Rollin and Flocon, the republican bourgeoisie by the people from the *National*, the dynastic opposition by Cremieux, Dupont de l'Eure, etc. The working class had only two representatives, Louis Blanc and Albert. Finally, Lamartine as a member of the Provisional Government; this was actually no real interest, no definite class, this was the February Revolution itself, the common uprising with its illusions, its poetry, its imagined content and its phrases. For the rest, the spokesman of the February Revolution, by his position and his views, belonged to the *bourgeoisie*.

If Paris, as a result of political centralisation, rules France, the workers, in moments of revolutionary earthquakes, rule Paris. The first act in the life of the Provisional Government was an attempt to escape from this overpowering influence, by an appeal from intoxicated Paris to sober France. Lamartine disputed the right of the barricade fighters to proclaim the republic, on the ground that only the majority of Frenchmen had that right; they must await their votes, the Parisian proletariat must not besmirch its victory by a usurpation. The bourgeoisie allowed the proletariat only *one* usurpation—that of fighting.

Up to noon on February 25, the republic had not yet been proclaimed; on the other hand, the whole of the Ministries had already been divided among the bourgeois elements of the Provisional Government and among the generals, bankers and lawyers of the *National*. But the workers were this time determined not to put up with any swindling like that of July 1830. They were ready to take up the fight anew and to enforce the republic by force of arms....

Even the memory of the limited aims and motives which drove the bourgeoisie into the February Revolution was extinguished by the proclamation of the republic on the basis of universal suffrage. Instead of a few small fractions of the bourgeoisie, whole classes of French society were suddenly hurled into the circle of political power, forced to leave the boxes, the stalls and the gallery and to act in person upon the revolutionary stage! With the constitutional monarchy the semblance of a state power independently confronting bourgeois society also vanished, as well as the whole series of subordinate struggles which this semblance of power called forth!

The proletariat, by dictating the republic to the Provisional Government and through the Provisional Government to the whole of France, stepped into the foreground forthwith as an independent party, but at the same time challenged the whole of bourgeois France to enter the lists against it. What it won was the terrain for the fight for its revolutionary emancipation, but in no way this emancipation itself!

The first thing that the February republic had to do was rather to *complete the rule of the bourgeoisie* by allowing, besides the finance aristocracy, *all the propertied classes* to enter the circle of political power.... The February republic finally brought the rule of the bourgeoisie clearly into prominence, since it struck off the crown behind which capital kept itself concealed.

Just as the workers by fighting in the July days had won the *bourgeois monarchy,* so by fighting in the February days they won the *bourgeois republic.* Just as the July monarchy had to proclaim itself as a monarchy *surrounded by republican institutions* so the February republic was forced to proclaim itself a republic *surrounded by social institutions.* The Parisian proletariat *compelled* this concession, too....

In common with the bourgeoisie the workers had made the February Revolution, and *alongside* the bourgeoisie they sought to put through their interests, just as they had installed a worker in the Provisional Government itself alongside the bourgeois majority. *Organisation of labour!* But wage labour is the existing, bourgeois organisation of labour. Without it there is no capital, no bourgeoisie, no bourgeois society. . . . Just as the workers thought to emancipate themselves side by side with the bourgeoisie, so they thought they would be able to consummate a proletarian revolution within the national walls of France, side by side with the remaining bourgeois nations. . . .

February 25, 1848, had granted the *republic* to France, June 25 thrust the *revolution* on her. And revolution, after June, meant: *overthrow of bourgeois society*, whereas, before February, it had meant *overthrow of the form of state*.

The June fight had been led by the republican fraction of the bourgeoisie; with victory, the state power inevitably fell to its share. The state of siege laid Paris, gagged, unresisting at its feet, and in the provinces there was a moral state of siege, the threatening, brutal arrogance of the victorious bourgeoisie and the unleashed property fanaticism of the peasants. No danger, therefore, from below!

14. CARL SCHURZ: REMINISCENCES*

While still a student at the University of Bonn, Carl Schurz (1829–1906) played a minor role in the Revolution of 1848 in Germany. Schurz emigrated to the United States when the revolution proved unsuccessful and became active in American politics. He helped organize the Republican party in Wisconsin, served as American Minister to Spain, became a Union general during the Civil War, was elected United States Senator from Missouri, and was appointed Secretary of the Interior by President Rutherford B. Hayes. In what ways did Schurz's account of 1848 reflect the lack of political experience among German university students? What did Schurz mean by the "elemental forces" that expressed the "feelings of the people"? On what grounds did German liberals hope that the overthrow of Louis Philippe in France would lead to beneficial results in their own country?

Frederick William IV was possessed of a mystical faith in the absolute power of kings "by the grace of God." He indulged himself in romantic imaginings about the political and social institutions of the Middle Ages, which had for him greater charm than those befitting the nineteenth century. He had sudden conceits, but no convictions; whims, but no genuine force of will; wit, but no wisdom. He possessed the ambition to do something great and thus to engrave his name upon the history of the world; but he wished at heart to leave everything substantially as it had been. He thought he could satisfy the people with an appearance of participation in the government without however in the least limiting the omnipotence of the crown. But these attempts ended like others made by other monarchs in other times. The merely ostensible and insufficient things he offered served only to strengthen and inflame the popular demand for something substantial and effective. Revolutions often begin with apparent but unreal reforms. He called "provincial diets," assemblies of local representative bodies, with the expectation that they would modestly content themselves with the narrow functions he prescribed for them. But they petitioned vehemently for a great deal more. The experiment of appearing to give and of really

* *The Reminiscences of Carl Schurz* (2 vols.; New York: The McClure Co., 1907), I, 106–14.

withholding everything was bound to fail miserably. The petitions of the provincial diets for freedom of the press, for trial by jury, and a liberal constitution, became more and more pressing. The discontent gradually grew so general, the storm of petitions so violent, the repugnance of the people to the police-despotism so menacing, that the old parade of the absolute kingly power would no longer suffice, and some new step in the direction of liberal innovations seemed imperatively necessary.

At last Frederick William IV. decided to convoke the so-called "United Diet," an assembly consisting of the members of all the provincial diets, to meet on April 11, 1847, in Berlin. But it was the old game over again. This assembly was to have the look of a parliament and yet not to be one. Its convocation was always to depend upon the pleasure of the king. Its powers were circumscribed within the narrowest limits. It was not to make laws nor to pass binding resolutions. It was to serve only as a sort of privy council to the king, to assist him in forming his decisions, its wishes to be presented to him only by way of petition. In the speech with which the king opened the United Diet, he declared with emphasis that this was now the utmost concession to which he would ever consent; he would never, never permit a piece of paper, meaning a written constitution, to be put between the prince and his people; the people themselves, he claimed, did not desire a participation of their representatives in the government; the absolute power of the king must not be broken; "the crown must reign and govern according to the laws of God and of the country and according to the king's own resolutions"; he could not, and must not, "govern according to the will of majorities"; and he, the king, "would never have called this assembly had he ever suspected in the slightest degree that its members would try to play the part of so-called representatives of the people." This was now, he said, the fulfillment, and "more than the fulfillment," of the promises made in the time of distress in 1813, before the expulsion of the French.

General disappointment and increasing discontent followed this pronouncement. But the concession made by the king in fact signified more than he had anticipated. A king who wishes to govern with absolute power must not permit a public discussion of the policy and of the acts of the government by men who stand nearer to the people than he does. The United Diet could indeed not resolve, but only debate and petition. But that it could debate, and that its debates passed through faithful newspaper reports into the intelligence of the country—that was an innovation of incalculable consequence.

The bearing of the United Diet, on the benches of which sat many men of uncommon capacity and liberal principles, was throughout dignified, discreet and moderate. But the struggle against absolutism began instantly, and the people followed it with constantly increasing interest. What has happened in the history of the world more than once happened again. Every step forward brought to the consciousness of the people the necessity of further steps forward. And now, when the king endeavored to stem the growing commotion, repelled the moderate demands made by the United Diet with sharp words, and dismissed that assembly "ungraciously," then the public mind was, by the government itself, dragged into that channel of thought in which revolutionary sentiments grow.

There had indeed long been some revolutionary agitators who, in their isolation, had passed for dreamers and could win but a slim following. But now the feeling began to spread in large circles that the real thunder-storm was coming, although hardly anybody anticipated how soon it would come. In former days people had excited themselves about what Thiers and Guizot had said in the French chambers, or Palmerston and Derby in the English parliament, or even what Hecker, Rotteck and Welker had said in the little Diet of the grand duchy of Baden. But now everybody listened with nervous eagerness to every word that in the United Diet of the most important of German states had fallen from the lips of Camphausen, Vincke, Beckerath, Hansemann and other liberal leaders. There was a feeling in the air as if this United Diet, in its position and the task to be performed by it, was not at all unlike the French assembly of the year 1789.

We university students watched these events with perhaps a less clear understanding, but with no less ardent interest, than our elders. As I have already mentioned, the "Burschenschaft" had its political traditions. Immediately after the wars of liberation—1813 to 1815—it had been among the first in line to raise the cry for the fulfillment of the pledges given by the princes. It had cultivated the national spirit with zeal, although sometimes with exaggerated demonstrations. It had furnished many victims in the persecutions of so-called demagogues. The political activity of the old Burschenschaft had indeed not been continued by the younger associations; but "God, Liberty, Fatherland," had still remained the common watchword; we still wore the prohibited black-red-golden ribbon under our coats, and very many members of the new Burschenschaft societies still recognized it as their duty to keep themselves well informed of what happened in the political world and to devote to it as active an interest as possible. Thus the liberal currents of our time found among us enthusiastic partisans, although we young people could not give a very definite account of the practical steps to be taken.

In the prosecution of my studies I had taken up with ardor the history of Europe at the period of the great Reformation. I expected to make this my specialty as a professor of history. The great characters of that period strongly attracted me and I could not resist the temptation to clothe some of them in dramatic form. So I planned a tragedy, the main figure of which was to be Ulrich von Hutten, and I began to elaborate some scenes in detail. At the beginning of the winter semester of 1847-48 I had made the acquaintance of a young student from Detmold, who became not indeed a member, but a guest of the Franconia. His name was Friedrich Althaus. More than any young man of my acquaintance he responded to the ideal of German youth. His was a thoroughly pure and noble nature and richly endowed with mental gifts. As we pursued similar studies we easily became intimates, and this friendship lasted with undiminished warmth long beyond the university years. To him I confided my Hutten secret, and he encouraged me to carry out my plan. Happy were the hours when I read to him what I had written and he gave me his judgment, which usually was altogether too favorable. Thus passed the larger part of the winter in useful and enjoyable occupations. Then fate broke in with the force of a mighty hurricane, which swept me, as well as many others, with irresistible power out of all life-plans previously designed and cherished....

One morning, toward the end of February, 1848, I sat quietly in my attic-chamber, working hard at my tragedy of "Ulrich von Hutten," when suddenly a friend rushed breathlessly into the room, exclaiming: "What, you sitting here! Do you not know what has happened?"

"No; what?"

"The French have driven away Louis Philippe and proclaimed the republic."

I threw down my pen—and that was the end of "Ulrich von Hutten." I never touched the manuscript again. We tore down the stairs, into the street, to the market-square, the accustomed meeting-place for all the student societies after their midday dinner. Although it was still forenoon, the market was already crowded with young men talking excitedly. There was no shouting, no noise, only agitated conversation. What did we want there? This probably no one knew. But since the French had driven away Louis Philippe and proclaimed the republic, something of course must happen here, too. Some of the students had brought their rapiers along, as if it were necessary at once to make an attack or to defend ourselves. We were dominated by a vague feeling as if a great outbreak of elemental forces had begun, as if an earthquake was impending of which we had felt the first shock, and we instinctively crowded together. Thus we wandered about in numerous bands—to the "Kneipe," where our restlessness, however, would not suffer us long to stay; then to other pleasure resorts, where we fell into conversation with all manner of strangers, to find in them the same confused, astonished and expectant state of mind; then back to the market-square, to see what might be going on there; then again somewhere else, and so on, without aim and end, until finally late in the night fatigue compelled us to find the way home.

The next morning there were the usual lectures to be attended. But how profitless! The voice of the professor sounded like a monotonous drone coming from far away. What he had to say did not seem to concern us. The pen that should have taken notes remained idle. At last we closed with a sigh the note-book and went away, impelled by a feeling that now we had something more important to do—to devote ourselves to the affairs of the fatherland. And this we did by seeking as quickly as possible again the company of our friends, in order to discuss what had happened and what was to come. In these conversations, excited as they were, certain ideas and catchwords worked themselves to the surface, which expressed more or less the feelings of the people. Now had arrived in Germany the day for the establishment of "German Unity," and the founding of a great, powerful national German Empire. In the first line the convocation of a national parliament. Then the demands for civil rights and liberties, free speech, free press, the right of free assembly, equality before the law, a freely elected representation of the people with legislative power, responsibility of ministers, self-government of the communes, the right of the people to carry arms, the formation of a civic guard with elective officers, and so on—in short, that which was called a "constitutional form of government on a broad democratic basis." Republican ideas were at first only sparingly expressed. But the word democracy was soon on all tongues, and many, too, thought it a matter of course that if the princes should try to withhold from the people the rights and liberties demanded, force would take the place of mere petition. Of course the regeneration of the fatherland must, if possible, be accomplished by peaceable means. A few days after the outbreak of this commotion I reached my nineteenth birthday. I remember to have been so entirely absorbed by what was happening that I could hardly turn my thoughts to anything else. Like many of my friends, I was dominated by the feeling that at last the great opportunity had arrived for giving to the German people the liberty which was their birthright and to the German fatherland its unity and greatness, and that it was now the first duty of every German to do and to sacrifice everything for this sacred object. We were profoundly, solemnly in earnest.

15. FREDERICK WILLIAM IV: ON CONSTITUTIONAL GOVERNMENT IN PRUSSIA*

In 1848 the German liberal nationalists who sought the unification of their fatherland through the deliberations of the Frankfurt assembly looked to Prussia as the nucleus around which a German national state could be formed. Austria could elect to join or remain outside the future German state, but a Germany without Prussia was inconceivable.

The King of Prussia, Frederick William IV (r. 1840–61), was a dreamy, conservative monarch who mistrusted constitutionalists and firmly opposed liberal ideas. Shocked when his own Berliners revolted in 1848, he reluctantly flew the German tricolor from his royal palace and proclaimed that "Prussia is merged into Germany." The private feelings of the King, however, were revealed to his confidants and friends among the Junker aristocracy which traditionally surrounded and served the kings of Prussia. The following letter, written by Frederick William IV to his friend and adviser Josef Maria von Radowitz (1797–1853), revealed the monarch's personal views. To what extent did Frederick William understand the liberal and constitutional aspirations of Germans such as Carl Schurz? Why were the Frankfurt parliamentarians ill-advised to place their trust in Frederick William IV?

Many heartfelt thanks, my dearest Radowitz, for your report concerning your election to Frankfurt. I fear, however, that you are wasted there. Satan and Adramelech have their headquarters in that place! Here I will open the fateful Diet [Prussian parliament] on the morrow. I have summoned them to the Royal Castle, but a significant number of members has protested and wants me to come to the assembly in the Berlin Choral Academy Hall. You need not doubt how I take such insolence. If they do not follow the summons of the Cabinet tomorrow, then I shall command them to do so on the next day as their king and lord. And if then they do not come, then I will dissolve the Assembly and call the old United Diet again.[1] That is, in so far as my Cabinet *does not leave me in the lurch*. The government has put together a draft constitution that would shame a sixth-grade student and that could be described by a fifth-grader as "not bad." The discussion of the draft was the most horrible hour of my life! . . . Now, listen to my resolutions. I confess that your counsel, my dearest friend, can change them. Still, I hope that you agree. There are three eventualities that *I do not intend to tolerate:*

* W. Möring, *Jos. von Radowitz Nachgelassene Briefe und Aufzeichnungen zur Geschichte der Jahre 1848–1853* (Stuttgart, 1922), pp. 46–48. Translated by the editors.
1. The semi-feudal Diet of 1847.

1. If the Prussian Diet puts through a law establishing the sovereignty of the people [with a majority].

2. If they protest [Crown] Prince William's return [to Berlin] and thus directly or indirectly bring the matter of succession to the throne before their forum.

3. If, either freely or under pressure by masses of rabble, they proclaim the republic.

Then, I will toss the assembly to the devil, . . . Dear Radowitz, what do you think the effect of such an act would be on the Frankfurt Assembly and southwest Germany? I need your counsel again. If it comes to such extremes, then you are hereby called to my side. I need you. If any serious resistance shows itself in the eastern part of the monarchy, must I immediately call upon Russia for help? Naturally, I am concentrating everything that I can of regulars and militia, namely the troops at Bamberg, those from Prussia, those I can spare from Posen and Silesia . . . etc., etc. What I hear of the temper of the country outside of the Rhine Province gives me fresh courage to hazard such a course. Also, for further eventualities, I am hoping for [assistance from] Hanover and Bavaria. May God's grace allow that the critical turn for the better in Vienna is not again reversed! If only the Emperor and his family do not return [to be captured]!!! or [better yet, return] with 10,000 Tyrolean sharpshooters. . . .

You will soon read in the newspapers the abomination that is the draft constitution. I have done everything that a man can do in order to get myself away from this coarsest filth—but completely in vain!!!!!! The day before yesterday in the meetings of the Cabinet, I thought that I would die of pain, mortification, and indignation! Pray for me, dearest Friend. . . .

16. THE FRANKFURT CONSTITUTION*

The German National Assembly met at St. Paul's Church in Frankfurt on May 18, 1848. Professional men—lawyers, university professors, doctors, and businessmen—comprised the majority of the delegates, and the proceedings were characterized by an emphasis on order, moderate liberalism, and fervent nationalism. Conservatives and members of the lower classes exerted little direct influence on the work of the Assembly. The smaller German states were overrepresented, whereas Prussia and, to a greater degree, Austria, were underrepresented. After ten months of debate, during which the Frankfurt Assembly sanctioned a nationalist war against Denmark and was almost routed from its host city by a local uprising (which had to be put down by Prussian troops), the delegates belatedly produced in 1849 a constitution for a unified Germany. The King of Prussia, Frederick William IV, was elected hereditary emperor. When informed of his election Frederick William declined the crown, privately expressing his contempt for the work of the Assembly. In the abortive Frankfurt constitution what provisions ensured a federal structure for the German Empire? What were the boundaries of the new state? In what ways was the constitution liberal or democratic? Compare the "Fundamental Rights of the German People" with the earlier French "Declaration of the Rights of Man and the Citizen."

* "Die Frankfurter Reichsverfassung" in Ernst Rudolf Huber, ed., Dokumente zur Deutschen Verfassungsgeschichte (2 vols.; Stuttgart: W. Kohlhammer, 1961), I, 304–24. Translated by the editors.

Article I

1. The German Reich consists of the territory of the former German Confederation. . . .

2. If a German state has the same Chief of State as a non-German state [in other words, if a monarch ruled both German and non-German lands], then the German state must have its own constitution, government, and administration, separate from the non-German state. Only German citizens may serve in the government and administration of the German state . . . [and if the monarch lives in the non-German part of his territories, then he must appoint a German citizen as regent for his German lands]. . . .

Article II

10. The right of war and peace is the exclusive authority of the Reich. . . . [*Further paragraphs provided that the Reich Army was to consist of the armed forces of the individual states. The Reich legislated for the armed forces, but the legislation was implemented by the states under Reich supervision. The states had authority over their forces while they were not needed by the Reich. All troops took a principal oath of allegiance first to the Emperor and the Reich Constitution.*]

Article VII

33. The German Reich shall form a single customs and trade community, with common customs regulations; tariff barriers within the Reich are eliminated. [*Various other articles provided that the Reich had authority over rivers and waterways, railroads, etc. as well as supervision over postal service, etc. The Reich had authority to introduce a common coinage for Germany.*]

71. The Chief of State bears the title: Emperor of the Germans . . . The Emperor exercises the power entrusted to him through responsible ministers named by him.

76. The Emperor declares war and concludes peace.

79. The Emperor convenes and closes the Reichstag; he has the right to dissolve the House of the People [*Volkshaus*].

85. The Reichstag consists of two houses, the House of States [*Staatenhaus*] and the House of the People [*Volkshaus*].

[*Further articles in this section outline the election and responsibility of the two houses. The Staatenhaus was to have members apportioned to the states on the basis of relative size and population, half of the members of each state to be elected by the state parliament and half by the state government (ministry). Half of the Staatenhaus was to be subject to election every three years. The*

Volkshaus was to be elected directly by the people, for a term of three years. Representatives were to be paid, and to have freedom from arrest during the sessions.]

SECTION VI: THE FUNDAMENTAL RIGHTS OF THE GERMAN PEOPLE

130. The German people shall possess the following fundamental rights. These rights shall serve as a standard for the constitutions of the individual German states, and no constitution or legislation of a German state shall abolish or limit them.

Article I

131. The German people consists of the citizens of the states which form the German Reich.

132. Every German has the right of citizenship in the Reich. He can exercise this right in every German state. . . .

133. Every German has the right to live or reside in any part of the Reich territory, to acquire and dispose of all kinds of property, to pursue his livelihood, and to win the right of communal citizenship. The conditions for living and residence shall be established by a law effected by the administration of the Reich for all Germany. The same shall be true with respect to trade and industry regulations.

134. No German state may make a distinction between its citizens and other Germans in civil, criminal, and litigation matters which tend to place the latter in the position of foreigners.

Article II

137. There are no class differences before the law. The rank of nobility is abolished.

All special class privileges are abolished.

All Germans are equal before the laws.

All titles, insofar as they are not bound with an office, are abolished and may not be introduced again.

Public office shall be equally open to all men on the basis of ability.

All citizens are equally subject to military service; there shall be no substitutions in the draft.

Article III

138. The freedom of man is inviolable.

The arrest of a person, except in the case of being caught in the act, may take place only under a legally executed warrant. . . .

139. Capital punishment . . . is abolished. . . .

Article IV

143. Every German shall have the right freely to express his opinion through speech, writing, publication, and illustration.

Freedom of the press may not be suspended or abolished under any circumstances or in any way by means of preventive measures, namely, censorship, concessions, security orders, . . .

Article V

144. Every German has complete freedom of religion and conscience. No one is required to reveal his religious convictions.

145. Every German possesses the unlimited right of private and public exercise of his religion.

Crimes and transgressions which prevent the exercise of this freedom are punishable by law.

[*Other articles provided for free public education and freedom of assembly, and equality of taxation.*]

Article IX

164. Property is inviolable. . . .

Article XII

186. Every German state shall have a constitution providing for representation of the people. The ministers are responsible to the people's representatives.

Article XIII

188. The non-German-speaking people of Germany are guaranteed their national development, namely equal rights for their languages, insofar as they exist in their territories, in ecclesiastical matters, in local administration, and in the law.

17. FRANTIŠEK PALACKÝ: LETTER TO THE GERMAN NATIONAL ASSEMBLY*

The conglomerate empire of the Habsburgs included peoples of many nationalities: approximately one-fourth of the Emperor's subjects were Germans, one-fourth were Magyars, and half were Slavs. Czechs, Poles, Croats, Slovenes, Ruthenians, and others had achieved varying stages of national awakening by 1848, and many Slavs were stirred by the same currents that moved Germans and Magyars. When the Frankfurt Assembly proposed that the parts of Austria formerly within the German Confederation join the proposed German Empire, the Czechs, whose Bohemian homeland had been part of the medieval Holy Roman Empire and subsequently of the German Confederation, demurred. From Prague, the noted Czech historian František Palacký (1798–1876) replied to the invitation, firmly announcing the arrival of Czech nationalism on the European scene. On June 22, 1848, a Slav Congress, representing most of the Austrian Slavic peoples, opened in Prague at the invitation of Czech leaders. For a time during 1848–49 it seemed that the Austrian Empire was on the verge of disintegration.

Although the Empire survived 1848, her sovereigns did not alter their monarchy to conform with Palacký's wishes—nor could they. They were forced to watch, in later years, while the Slavic nationalism kindled in 1848 spread across the Habsburg Empire and throughout eastern Europe, where it conflicted with German, Magyar, and Russian nationalism. Why did Palacký reject participation in the German National Assembly? What special role had the Habsburg monarchy played up to 1848? What constitutional form did Palacký envisage as essential for the Austrian Empire? What was Palacký's attitude toward Russians and Magyars? Why?

. . . I am a Czech of Slav descent and with all the little I own and possess I have devoted myself wholly and for ever to the service of my nation. That nation is small, it is true, but from time immemorial it has been an independent

* Hans Kohn, *Pan-Slavism: Its History and Ideology* (Notre Dame, Ind.: University of Notre Dame Press, 1953), pp. 65–69. Reprinted by permission.

nation with its own character; its rulers have participated since old times in the federation of German princes, but the nation never regarded itself nor was it regarded by others throughout all the centuries, as part of the German nation. The whole union of the Czech lands first with the Holy German Empire and then with the German Confederation was always a purely dynastic one of which the Czech nation, the Czech Estates, hardly wished to know and which they hardly noticed. . . . If anyone asks that the Czech nation should now unite with the German nation, beyond this heretofore existing federation between princes, this is then a new demand which has no historical legal basis, a demand to which I personally do not feel justified in acceding until I receive an express and valid mandate for it. The second reason which prevents me from participating in your deliberations is the fact that from all that has been so far publicly announced of your aims and purposes you irrevocably are, and will be, aiming to undermine Austria forever as an independent empire and to make its existence impossible—an empire whose preservation, integrity and consolidation is, and must be, a great and important matter not only for my own nation but for the whole of Europe, indeed for mankind and civilization itself. Allow me kindly to explain myself briefly on this point.

You know, gentlemen, what power it is that holds the whole great eastern part of our continent; you know that this power which now already has grown to vast dimensions, increases and expands by its own strength every decade to a far greater extent than is possible in the Western countries; that being inaccessible at its own center to almost every attack, it has become, and has for a long time been, a threat to its neighbours; and that, although it has an open access to the north, it is nevertheless always seeking, led by natural instinct, to expand southwards and will continue to do it; that every further step which it will take forward on this path threatens at an ever accelerated pace to produce and found a *universal monarchy,* that is to say, an infinite and inexpressible evil, a misfortune without measure or bound which I, though heart and soul a Slav, would nonetheless deeply regret for the good of mankind even though that monarchy proclaimed itself a Slav one. Many people in Russia call and regard me as an enemy of the Russians, with as little justice as those who among the Germans regard me as an enemy of the Germans. I proclaim loudly and publicly that I am in no way an enemy of the Russians: on the contrary, I observe with joyful sympathy every step by which this great nation within its natural borders progresses along the road of civilization: but with all my ardent love of my nation I always esteem more highly the good of mankind and of learning than the good of the nation; for this reason the bare possibility of a Russian universal monarchy has no more determined opponent or adversary than myself, not because that monarchy would be Russian but because it would be universal.

You know that in south-east Europe, along the frontiers of the Russian empire, there live many nations widely different in origin, language, history and habits—Slavs, Rumanians, Magyars and Germans, not to speak of Greeks, Turks and Albanians—none of whom is strong enough by itself to be able to resist successfully for all time the superior neighbour to the east; they could do it only if a close and firm tie bound them all together. The vital artery of this necessary union of nations is the Danube; the focus of its power must never be removed far from this river, if the union is to be effective at all and to remain so. Certainly, if the Austrian state had not existed for ages, we would be obliged in the interests of Europe and even of mankind to endeavor to create it as fast as possible.

But why have we seen this state, which by nature and history is destined to be the bulwark and guardian of Europe against Asiatic elements of every kind —why have we seen it in a critical moment helpless and almost unadvised in the face of the advancing storm? It is because in an unhappy blindness which has lasted for very long, Austria has not recognized the real legal and moral foundation of its existence and has denied it: the fundamental rule that all the nationalities united under its scepter should enjoy complete equality of rights and respect. The right of nations is truly a natural right; no nation on earth has the right to demand that its neighbour should sacrifice itself for its benefit, no nation obliged to deny or sacrifice itself for the good of its neighbour. Nature knows neither ruling nor subservient nations. If the union which unites several different nations is to be firm and lasting, no nation must have cause to fear that by that union it will lose any of the goods which it holds most dear; on the contrary each must have the certain hope that it will find in the central authority defense and protection against possible violations of equality by neighbours; then every nation will do its best to strengthen that central authority so that it can successfully provide the aforesaid defense. I am convinced that even now it is not too late for the Austrian empire to proclaim openly and sincerely this fundamental rule of justice, the *sacra ancora* for a ship in danger of floundering, and to carry it out energetically in common and in every respect: but every moment is precious; for God's sake do not let us delay another hour with this! . . .

When I look behind the Bohemian frontiers, then natural and historical reasons make me turn not to Frankfurt but to Vienna to seek there the center which is fitted and destined to ensure and defend the peace, the liberty and the right of my nation. Your efforts, gentlemen, seem to me now to be directed as I have already stated, not only towards ruinously undermining, but even utterly destroying that center from whose might and strength I expect the salvation not only of the Czech land. Or do you think that the Austrian state will continue to exist when you forbid it to maintain an army in its own hereditary lands, independent of Frankfurt as the joint head? Do you think that the Austrian emperor or any succeeding sovereign will be able to maintain his position if you impose upon him the duty of accepting all the more important laws from your committee, and thus make the institutions of the imperial Austrian parliament and the historical Diets of the united Kingdoms mere shadows without substance and power? And if then Hungary following its instincts severs its connections with the state or, what would amount almost to the same, concentrates within itself—will then Hungary which does not wish to hear of national equality within its borders be able to maintain itself free and strong in the future? Only the just is truly free and strong. A voluntary union of the Danubian Slavs and Rumanians, or even of the Poles themselves, with such a state which declares that a man must first be a Magyar before he can be a human being is entirely out of question; and even less thinkable would be a compulsory union of this kind. For the sake of Europe, Vienna must not sink to the role of a provincial town. If there are in Vienna itself such people who demand to have your Frankfurt as their capital, then we must cry: Lord, forgive them, for they know not what they ask!

Finally, there is a third reason for which I must decline to take part in your councils: I regard all the attempts made so far to give to the German Empire a new constitution based on the will of the people as impossible of achievement and as unstable for the future, unless you decide upon a real life-or-death operation; by this I mean the proclamation of a German Republic. . . . I must, however, reject in advance energetically and emphatically every idea of a republic within the frontiers of the Austrian empire. Think of the Austrian empire divided up into a number of republics and dwarf republics—what a delightful basis for a universal Russian monarchy.

In conclusion, to end these lengthy but rapidly drawn-up remarks, I must briefly express my conviction that those who ask that Austria (and with it Bohemia) should unite on national lines with the German empire, demand its suicide, which is morally and politically meaningless; on the contrary it would be much more meaningful to demand that Germany should unite with the Austrian empire, that is, that it should accede to the Austrian state under the conditions above mentioned. As that, however, does not accord with German national sentiment and opinion, nothing remains for the two powers, the Austrian and German Empires, but to organize themselves side by side on a footing of equality, to convert the existing ties into a permanent alliance of defense and defiance, and should it be advantageous to both sides perhaps to create also a customs union. I am ready at every moment gladly to give a helping hand in all activities which do not endanger the independence, integrity and growth in power of the Austrian empire.

Chapter Four

THE EARLY IMPACT
OF INDUSTRIALISM

GRADUALLY but radically the general conditions of life in western
Europe were altered between 1720 and 1820. There was a thorough transformation of agricultural techniques, which provided increased quantities of food and
allowed for a rapid growth of population. Cultivated strips, previously separated
by hedges, were enclosed and given over to capitalistic methods of farming.
Improved methods of land cultivation were introduced and were combined
with better crop rotation, employment of fertilizers, and use of farm machinery.
Many landowners began to experiment in stock breeding, increasing the size
and fleshy girth of animals. With fewer laborers required to till the soil, an
increase in food production, and an unprecedented growth in the population,
a base was provided for the Industrial Revolution.

The Industrial Revolution was characterized by the adaptation of new
forms of energy to manufacturing and production, thus enhancing the multiplication of consumer and capital goods. Several elements combined to bring
about industrialization: the development of machinery, the increased availability of capital through banks and stock companies, and a series of timely
and resourceful inventions. Continued commercial expansion and access to
large quantities of raw materials contributed to the industrialization of England,
particularly to the growth of cotton mills in the eighteenth century. The factory
system began in the textile industry, and thousands of workers swelled the size
of English cities, placing England generations ahead of the rest of Europe in
economic development.

The more sophisticated capitalistic system which accompanied the Industrial
Revolution encouraged a drive for larger profits with which to expand capital
investment. A strong competitive spirit soon confronted and eventually assaulted
the principles of seventeenth- and eighteenth-century mercantilism. Governments had always been influenced by economic power and wealth, either
through fiscal needs or general national interest, and it was inevitable that
prosperous industrial leaders brought pressures upon and sought to mold the
policies of respective European states.

Through corporate business organization, industrial capitalism promoted
the triumph of the middle classes and their economic philosophy—laissez faire.
The textbook for this philosophy was Adam Smith's *Wealth of Nations,* which

postulated that every individual pursued his own best interests financially, and that complete business freedom benefited the public good. The essence of laissez faire liberalism was expressed by Lord Macaulay, who wrote that "our rulers will best promote the improvement of the nation by strictly confining themselves to their own legitimate duties, by leaving capital to find its most lucrative course, . . . industry and intelligence their natural reward, idleness and folly their natural punishment." Macaulay's emphasis upon natural reward and punishment revealed his *a priori* assumption that specific laws, which dictated free choice, governed economics.

Economic liberalism led to the conclusion that nothing could or should be done to correct the social evils which resulted from industrialization. Among the gloomier observers of economic circumstances was Thomas Malthus (1766–1834), an English clergyman whose reputation rested upon his *Essay on Population*. Malthus asserted that population always outran the food supply and that any intervention by governmental agencies or charitable institutions merely increased and prolonged a misery which was natural. The English economist David Ricardo (1772–1823) reached similar conclusions regarding wages for labor, which he held would always remain at a bare subsistence level because of an ironclad law that labor is always more readily available than capital.

Among the writers who helped popularize the doctrine of laissez faire liberalism were Jeremy Bentham (1748–1832) and John Stuart Mill (1806–73). Bentham devised a doctrine called utilitarianism or "philosophical radicalism," based on the concept of utility and happiness. Utility was a yardstick for measuring the validity of institutions and legislation. Happiness, Bentham believed, resulted from the greatest degree of individual freedom. It was the chief function of government to secure and guarantee freedom for every man. Mill, though his education bore the indelible stamp of Benthamite ideas, chose to deviate from his mentors where economic practices were concerned. He believed in guaranteeing the greatest degree of personal liberty for the individual and agreed that the basic interests of all people were the same. However, Mill took issue with the utilitarians by claiming that unlimited competition and unrestricted property rights could endanger the personal and political liberty of the non-propertied classes. For Mill, distribution of wealth depended upon law and customs of society, and these could be changed by the will of men. As a doubter of the natural absolutes of utilitarianism, Mill presented a transitional view which prophesied the political victory of the laboring masses and the economic struggles which would characterize the late nineteenth and early twentieth centuries.

On paper, the laissez faire philosophy seemed a practical and positive aid to social and economic progress. But a divergence between theory and practice was soon revealed in the form of monopolistic activities and business collusion which often precluded a guarantee of fair prices. The scrupulous industrialist often succumbed to the competition of the unscrupulous, the ethical to the underhanded. It became difficult to reconcile the growing wealth of the few with the burden of poverty carried by the many.

Western European intellectuals were appalled by the misery which accompanied the Industrial Revolution, and they soon articulated their sentiments in a variety of forms. In England, Charles Dickens, Benjamin Disraeli, Thomas

Carlyle, and John Ruskin exposed the ugliness and drudgery which characterized life in industrial society. In France, the celebrated authoress George Sand
wrote sympathetically about the condition of impoverished workers, while
Honoré Daumier devoted dozens of his lithographs to the critical contrast
between gluttonous bourgeoisie and earnest but shabby workingmen. Political
leaders, responding to such protests, enacted reforms which were philanthropic
and remedial in character and tended to treat the serious problems of industrialization as though they were casual rather than chronic.

More realistic and practical dissent from the tenets of nineteenth-century
liberalism was provided by the Socialists—utopian or scientific. Most Utopian
Socialists believed firmly in the Enlightenment doctrines of human perfectibility and progress; they sought to deliver the benefits of industrial and material
advances to all of society on an equitable basis. The Comte de Saint-Simon
(1760–1825) called for a planned industrial society ruled by benevolent and
paternalistic despots drawn from the ranks of scientists, technicians, and captains
of industry. While Saint-Simon tried to organize industrialization for the
benefit of society, his contemporary, Charles Fourier (1772–1837) urged the
abandonment of industrialization and the formation of agrarian communities
called *phalansteries*. He envisaged such communities as voluntary and co-
operative, self-sufficient economic units run by and for agrarians, mechanics,
and artisans. A slightly more practical, but nonetheless utopian, Robert Owen
(1771–1858) experimented with a program for a model community at his
textile mills in New Lanark, Scotland. The productive profits of the mills
provided housing, garbage collection, sanitation, adequate diet, clothing, and
free education for the children of the workers. Such utopian communities were
ephemeral and failed to cope with the large-scale problems of industrialization.

By mid-century, a new and more vigorous form of socialism had emerged.
Karl Marx (1818–83), who derided earlier Socialists as utopian, believed that
control was the key to the future of society. Marx postulated the eventual
demise of bourgeois capitalism through an inevitable proletarian revolution,
resulting in the establishment of a Communist society. He saw all human
history in terms of a struggle between classes, classes which had always had a
direct relationship to control of the means of production. By applying the
dialectic formula of G. W. F. Hegel to his own thesis of historical development
through class struggle, Marx concluded that a classless, or Communist, society
would be the end result of the operation of the dialectic through historical
materialism. Proletarian victory in the class struggle was not only inevitable,
it was inherent in the social process.

Marxism had an immeasurable impact upon the nineteenth and twentieth
centuries. Not only did the response of Marx's protagonists reflect the influence
and spread of his ideas and formulas, but most western European nations by
the 1890's witnessed the development of sizable and articulate parties founded
on Marxian principles.

INDUSTRIALISM AND ECONOMIC LIBERALISM

1. ADAM SMITH: WEALTH OF NATIONS*

The rapid and continued growth of British power in the nineteenth century was based upon the country's commercial leadership, industrial development, and imperial expansion. Great Britain demonstrated the political implications of her economic prosperity by financing several coalitions against Napoleon. The advance of commerce and manufacturing, which contributed to Britain's invulnerability and power, had been accomplished with a minimum of government participation. Moreover, by the last quarter of the eighteenth century, many British merchants had come to believe that the remnants of mercantilism were a serious obstacle to further commercial growth.

In his *Wealth of Nations* (1776), Adam Smith (1723-90), Professor of Moral Philosophy at Glasgow, proposed a new synthesis of economic thought concerning natural laws which shaped and governed commerce and industry. Smith's concepts became a foundation for classical economic theory, influencing also the thought of Karl Marx. In Smith's view, what motives dictated an individual's behavior in commerce and industry? What was the relationship of capital to wealth? How did society benefit through the economic activity of individuals? In what ways can Smith's views on government intervention in economic affairs be described as dogmatic?

That [a] monopoly of the home market frequently gives great encouragement to that particular species of industry which enjoys it, and frequently turns towards that employment a greater share of both the labour and stock of the society than would otherwise have gone to it, cannot be doubted. But whether it tends either to increase the general industry of the society, or to give it the most advantageous direction, is not, perhaps, altogether so evident.

The general industry of the society never can exceed what the capital of the society can employ. As the number of workmen that can be kept in employment by any particular person must bear a certain proportion to his capital, so the number of those that can be continually employed by all the members of a great society, must bear a certain proportion to the whole capital of that society, and never can exceed that proportion. No regulation of commerce can increase the quantity of industry in any society beyond what its capital can maintain. It can only divert a part of it into a direction into which it might not otherwise have gone; and it is by no means certain that this artificial direction is likely to be more advantageous to the society than that into which it would have gone of its own accord.

Every individual is continually exerting himself to find out the most advantageous employment for whatever capital he can demand. It is his own advantage, indeed, and not that of the society, which he has in view. But the study of his own advantage naturally or rather necessarily, leads him to prefer that employment which is most advantageous to the society.

* Adam Smith, *An Inquiry into the Nature and Causes of the Wealth of Nations* (Oxford: The Clarendon Press, 1880), pp. 25-26, 28-30, 35-36.

First, every individual endeavours to employ his capital as near home as he can, and consequently as much as he can in the support of domestic industry; provided always that he can thereby obtain the ordinary, or not a great deal less than the ordinary, profits of stock. . . .

Secondly, every individual who employs his capital in the support of domestic industry, necessarily endeavours so to direct that industry, that its produce may be of the greatest possible value.

The produce of industry is what it adds to the subject or materials upon which it is employed. In proportion as the value of this produce is great or small, so will likewise be the profits of the employer. But it is only for the sake of profit that any man employs a capital in the support of industry; and he will always, therefore, endeavour to employ it in the support of that industry of which the produce is likely to be of the greatest value, or to exchange for the greatest quantity either of money or of other goods.

But the annual revenue of every society is always precisely equal to the exchangeable value of the whole annual produce of its industry, or rather is precisely the same thing with that exchangeable value. As every individual, therefore, endeavours as much as he can both to employ his capital in the support of domestic industry, and so to direct that industry that its produce may be of the greatest value, every individual necessarily labours to render the annual revenue of the society as great as he can. He generally, indeed, neither intends to promote the public interest, nor knows how much he is promoting it. By preferring the support of domestic to that of foreign industry, he intends only his own security; and by directing that industry in such a manner as its produce may be of the greatest value, he intends only his own gain, and he is in this, as in many other cases, led by *an invisible hand* to promote an end which was no part of his intention. Nor is it always the worse for the society that it was no part of it. By pursuing his own interest he frequently promotes that of the society more effectually than when he really intends to promote it. I have never known much good done by those who affected to trade for the public good. It is an affectation, indeed, not very common among merchants, and very few words need be employed in dissuading them from it.

What is the species of domestic industry which his capital can employ, and of which the produce is likely to be of the greatest value, every individual, it is evident, can, in his local situation, judge much better than any statesman or lawgiver can do for him. The statesman, who should attempt to direct private people in what manner they ought to employ their capitals, would not only load himself with a most unnecessary attention, but assume an authority which could safely be trusted, not only to no single person, but to no council or senate whatever, and which would nowhere be so dangerous as in the hands of a man who had folly and presumption enough to fancy himself fit to exercise it.

To give the monopoly of the home market to the produce of domestic industry, in any particular art or manufacture, is in some measure to direct private people in what manner they ought to employ their capitals, and must, in almost all cases, be either a useless or a hurtful regulation. If the produce of domestic [industry] can be brought there as cheap as that of foreign industry, the regulation is evidently useless. If it cannot, it must generally be hurtful. It is the maxim of every prudent master of a family, never to attempt to make at home what it will cost him more to make than to buy. The tailor does not attempt to make his own shoes, but buys them of the shoemaker. The shoemaker does not attempt to make his own clothes, but employs a tailor. The farmer attempts to make neither the one nor the other, but employs those different artificers. All of them find it for their interest to employ their whole industry in a way in which they have some advantage over their neighbours, and to purchase with a part of its produce, or, what is the same thing, with the price of a part of it, whatever else they have occasion for.

What is prudence in the conduct of every private family, can scarce be folly in that of a great kingdom. If a foreign country can supply us with a commodity cheaper than we ourselves can make it, better buy it of them with some part of the produce of our own industry, employed in a way in which we have some advantage. The general industry of the country, being always in proportion to the capital which employs it, will not thereby be diminished, no more than that of the above-mentioned artificers, but only left to find out the way in which it can be employed with the greatest advantage. It is certainly not employed to the greatest advantage, when it is thus directed towards an object which it can buy cheaper than it can make. The value of its annual produce is certainly more or less diminished, when it is thus turned away from producing commodities evidently of more value than the commodity which it is directed to produce. According to the supposition, that commodity could be purchased from foreign countries cheaper than it can be made at home. It could, therefore, have been purchased with a part only of the commodities, or, what is the same thing, with a part only of the price of the commodities, which the industry employed by an equal capital would have produced at home, had it been left to follow its natural course. The industry of the country, therefore, is thus turned away from a more to a less advantageous employment, and the exchangeable value of its annual produce, instead of being increased, according to the intention of the lawgiver, must necessarily be diminished by every such regulation.

By means of such regulations, indeed, a particular manufacture may sometimes be acquired sooner than it could have been otherwise, and after a certain time may be made at home as cheap or cheaper than in the foreign country. But though the industry of the society may be thus carried with advantage into a particular channel sooner than it could have been otherwise, it will by no means follow that the sum total, either of its industry or of its revenue, can ever be augmented by any such regulation. The industry of the society can augment only in proportion as its capital augments, and its capital can augment only in proportion to what can be gradually saved out of its revenue. But the immediate effect of every such regulation is to diminish its revenue, and what diminishes its revenue is certainly not very likely to augment its capital faster than it would have augmented of its own accord, had both capital and industry been left to find out their natural employments.

Though for want of such regulations the society should never acquire the proposed manufacture, it would not, upon that account, necessarily be the poorer in any one period of its duration. In every period of its duration its whole capital and industry might still have been employed, though upon different objects, in the manner that was most advantageous at the time. In every period its revenue might have been the greatest which its capital could afford, and both capital and revenue might have been augmented with the greatest possible rapidity. . . .

To prohibit by a perpetual law the importance of foreign corn and cattle is, in reality, to enact that the population and industry of the country shall at no time exceed what the rude produce of its own soil can maintain.

There seem, however, to be cases in which it will generally be advantageous to lay some burden upon foreign for the encouragement of domestic industry.

. . . The defence of Great Britain, for example, depends very much upon the number of its sailors and shipping. The Act of Navigation, therefore, very properly endeavours to give the sailors and the shipping of Great Britain the monopoly of the trade of their own country, in some cases by absolute prohibitions, and in others by heavy burdens upon the shipping of foreign countries. . . .

2. THOMAS MALTHUS: ESSAY ON POPULATION*

The views of the Physiocrats and Adam Smith were reshaped by the Reverend Thomas Malthus (1766–1834). In his *Essay on Population,* published in 1798, Malthus laid down a rigid formula describing why population growth inevitably exceeds food supply. He concluded that population growth was responsible for the condition of Europe's depressed masses and that any attempt to reform society and the condition of the masses was foredoomed to failure. The plight of the working classes was thus not the result of industrialization. The Malthusian tradition influenced the nineteenth-century school of English economic thought known as philosophical radicalism. Why was the indefinite multiplication of population an impossibility? What natural occurrences operated to restrict, partially or temporarily, the growth of population? Since Malthus was a laissez-faire liberal, what other checks might he have condoned as a supplement to these natural regulators? From what point of view might it be argued that Malthus was a humanitarian?

CHAPTER I. STATEMENT OF THE SUBJECT.
RATIOS OF THE INCREASE OF POPULATION AND FOOD

In an inquiry concerning the improvement of society, the mode of conducting the subject which naturally presents itself, is—

1. To investigate the causes that have hitherto impeded the progress of mankind towards happiness; and,

2. To examine the probability of the total or partial removal of these causes in future.

To enter fully into this question, and to enumerate all the causes that have hitherto influenced human improvement, would be much beyond the power of an individual. The principal object of the present essay is to examine the effects of one great cause intimately united with the very nature of man; which, though it has been constantly and powerfully operating since the commencement of society, has been little noticed by the writers who have treated this subject. The facts which establish the existence of this cause have, indeed, been

* T. R. Malthus, *An Essay on the Principle of Population* (8th ed.; London: Reeves and Turner, 1878), pp. 1–3, 6–9, 12–13.

repeatedly stated and acknowledged; but its natural and necessary effects have been almost totally overlooked; though probably among these effects may be reckoned a very considerable portion of that vice and misery, and of that unequal distribution of the bounties of nature, which it has been the unceasing object of the enlightened philanthropist in all ages to correct. . . .

This is incontrovertibly true. Throughout the animal and vegetable kingdoms Nature has scattered the seeds of life abroad with the most profuse and liberal hand; but has been comparatively sparing in the room and the nourishment necessary to rear them. The germs of existence contained in this earth, if they could freely develop themselves, would fill millions of worlds in the course of a few thousand years. Necessity, that imperious, all-pervading law of nature, restrains them within the prescribed bounds. The race of plants and the race of animals shrink under this great restrictive law; and man cannot by any efforts of reason escape from it.

In plants and irrational animals, the view of the subject is simple. They are all impelled by a powerful instinct to the increase of their species, and this instinct is interrupted by no doubts about providing for their offspring. Wherever, therefore, there is liberty, the power of increase is exerted, and the superabundant effects are repressed afterwards by want of room and nourishment.

The effects of this check on man are more complicated. Impelled to the increase of his species by an equally powerful instinct, reason interrupts his career, and asks him whether he may not bring beings into the world for whom he cannot provide the means of support. If he attend to this natural suggestion, the restriction too frequently produces vice. If he hear it not, the human race will be constantly endeavouring to increase beyond the means of subsistence. But as, by that law of our nature which makes food necessary to the life of man, population can never actually increase beyond the lowest nourishment capable of supporting it, a strong check on population, from the difficulty of acquiring food, must be constantly in operation. This difficulty must fall somewhere, and must necessarily be severely felt in some or other of the various forms of misery, or the fear of misery, by a large portion of mankind.

That population has this constant tendency to increase beyond the means of subsistence, and that it is kept to its necessary level by these causes, will sufficiently appear from a review of the different states of society in which man has existed. But, before we proceed to this review, the subject will perhaps be seen in a clearer light, if we endeavour to ascertain what would be the natural increase of population, if left to exert itself with perfect freedom; and what might be expected to be the rate of increase in the productions of the earth, under the most favourable circumstances of human industry. . . .

The necessary effects of these two different rates of increase, when brought together, will be very striking. Let us call the population of this island eleven millions; and suppose the present produce equal to the easy support of such a number. In the first twenty-five years the population would be twenty-two millions, and the food being also doubled, the means of subsistence would be equal to this increase. In the next twenty-five years, the population would be forty-four millions, and the means of subsistence only equal to the support of thirty-three millions. In the next period the population would be eighty-eight millions, and the means of subsistence just equal to the support of half that number. And, at the conclusion of the first century, the population would be a hundred and seventy-six millions, and the means of subsistence only equal to the support of fifty-five millions, leaving a population of a hundred and twenty-one millions totally unprovided for.

Taking the whole earth, instead of this island, emigration would of course be excluded; and, supposing the present population equal to a thousand millions, the human species would increase as the numbers, 1, 2, 4, 8, 16, 32, 64, 128, 256; and subsistence as 1, 2, 3, 4, 5, 6, 7, 8, 9. In two centuries the population would be to the means of subsistence as 256 to 9; in three centuries as 4096 to 13, and in two thousand years the difference would be almost incalculable.

In this supposition no limits whatever are placed to the produce of the earth. It may increase for ever, and be greater than any assignable quantity; yet still the power of population being in every period so much superior, the increase of the human species can only be kept down to the level of the means of subsistence by the constant operation of the strong law of necessity, acting as a check upon the greater power.

CHAPTER II. OF THE GENERAL CHECKS TO POPULATION, AND THE MODE OF THEIR OPERATION

The ultimate check to population appears then to be a want of food, arising necessarily from the different ratios according to which population and food increase. But this ultimate check is never the immediate check, except in cases of actual famine.

The immediate check may be stated to consist in all those customs, and all those diseases, which seem to be generated by a scarcity of the means of subsistence; and all those causes, independent of this scarcity, whether of a moral or physical nature, which tend prematurely to weaken and destroy the human frame.

These checks to population, which are constantly operating with more or less force in every society, and keep down the number to the level of the means of subsistence, may be classed under two general heads—the preventive and the positive checks.

The preventive check, as far as it is voluntary, is peculiar to man, and arises from that distinctive superiority in his reasoning faculties which enables him to calculate distant consequences. The checks to the indefinite increase of plants and irrational animals are all either positive or, if preventive, involuntary. But man cannot look around him, and see the distress which frequently presses upon those who have large families; he cannot contemplate his present possessions or earnings, which he now nearly consumes himself, and calculate the amount of each share, when with very little addition they must be divided, perhaps, among seven or eight, without feeling a doubt whether, if he follow the bent of his inclinations, he may be able to support the offspring which he will probably bring into the world. In a state of equality, if such can exist, this would be the simple question. In the present state of society other considerations occur. Will he not lower his rank in life, and be obliged to give up in great measure his former habits? Does any mode of employment present itself by which he may reasonably hope to maintain a family? Will he not at any rate subject himself to greater difficulties, and more severe labour, than in his single state? Will he not be unable to transmit to his children the same advantages of education and improvement that he had himself possessed? Does he even feel secure that, should he have a large family, his utmost exertions can save them from rags and squalid poverty, and their consequent degradation in the community? And may he not be reduced to the grating necessity of forfeiting his independence, and of being obliged to the sparing hand of charity for support?

These considerations are calculated to prevent, and certainly do prevent, a great number of persons in all civilised nations from pursuing the dictate of nature in an early attachment to one woman.

If this restraint do not produce vice, it is undoubtedly the least evil that can arise from the principle of population. Considered as a restraint on a strong natural inclination, it must be allowed to produce a certain degree of temporary unhappiness; but evidently slight, compared with the evils which result from any of the other checks to population; and merely of the same nature as many other sacrifices of temporary to permanent gratification, which it is the business of a moral agent continually to make. . . .

The positive checks to population are extremely various, and include every cause, whether arising from vice or misery, which in any degree contribute to shorten the natural duration of human life. Under this head, therefore, may be enumerated all unwholesome occupations, severe labour and exposure to the seasons, extreme poverty, bad nursing of children, large towns, excesses of all kinds, the whole train of common diseases and epidemics, wars, plague, and famine.

On examining these obstacles to the increase of population which are classed under the heads of preventive and positive checks, it will appear that they are all resolvable into moral restraint, vice, and misery.

Of the preventive checks, the restraint from marriage which is not followed by irregular gratifications may properly be termed moral restraint.

Promiscuous intercourse, unnatural passions, violations of the marriage bed, and improper arts to conceal the consequences of irregular connections, are preventive checks that clearly come under the head of vice.

Of the positive checks, those which appear to arise unavoidably from the laws of nature, may be called exclusively misery; and those which we obviously bring upon ourselves, such as wars, excesses, and many others which it would be in our power to avoid, are of a mixed nature. They are brought upon us by vice, and their consequences are misery.

The sum of all these preventive and positive checks, taken together, forms the immediate check to population; and it is evident that, in every country where the whole of the procreative power cannot be called into action, the preventive and the positive checks must vary inversely as each other; that is, in countries either naturally unhealthy, or subject to a great mortality, from whatever cause it may arise, the preventive check will prevail very little. In those countries, on the contrary, which are naturally healthy, and where the preventive check is found to prevail with considerable force, the positive check will prevail very little, or the mortality be very small. . . .

In savage life, where there is no regular price of labour, it is little to be doubted that similar oscillations take place. When population has increased nearly to the utmost limits of the food, all the preventive and the positive checks will naturally operate with increased force. Vicious habits with respect to the sex will be more general, the exposing of children more frequent, and both the probability and fatality of wars and epidemics will be considerably greater; and these causes will probably continue their operation till the population is sunk below the level of the food; and then the return to comparative plenty will again produce an increase, and, after a certain period, its further progress will again be checked by the same causes.

But without attempting to establish these progressive and retrograde movements in different countries, which would evidently require more minute histories than we possess, and which the progress of civilisation naturally tends to counteract, the following propositions are intended to be proved:—

1. Population is necessarily limited by the means of subsistence.

2. Population invariably increases where the means of subsistence increase, unless prevented by some very powerful and obvious checks.

3. These checks, and the checks which repress the superior power of population, and keep its effects on a level with the means of subsistence, are all resolvable into moral restraint, vice, and misery. . . .

3. JEREMY BENTHAM: PRINCIPLES OF MORALS AND LEGISLATION*

Although problems of social reform began to receive increasing attention during the last half of the eighteenth century, Jeremy Bentham (1748-1832) was the first to offer a systematic formula for the appreciation and understanding of the problems accompanying industrialism. Bentham was little interested in the past and much concerned with contemporary social evils; his philosophy was constructed upon a general principle of utility. According to Bentham, all laws must follow a formula of pleasure and pain in order to promote the greatest benefit for the greatest number of people.

Benthamite utilitarianism inspired English radicals and provided an intellectual premise for such legislation as the charter of the University of London, the Reform Act of 1832, the Poor Law of 1834, and the Municipal Corporations Act of 1835. What did Bentham mean by a scientific system of measurement based upon the principles of pleasure and pain? Was Bentham an individualist, or did he view society in the collective or organic sense? How would Bentham apply his utilitarian principles to such problems as franchise variations from county to county, a privileged position for one church, anomalies in civil and criminal law, the selection of civil servants, and admittance to educational institutions?

Nature has placed mankind under the governance of two sovereign masters, *pain* and *pleasure*. It is for them alone to point out what we ought to do, as well as to determine what we shall do. On the one hand the standard of right and wrong, on the other the chain of causes and effects, are fastened to their throne. They govern us in all we do, in all we say, in all we think: every effort we can make to throw off our subjection, will serve but to demonstrate and confirm it. In words a man may pretend to abjure their empire: but in reality he will

* Jeremy Bentham, *An Introduction to The Principles of Morals and Legislation* (New York: Hafner Publishing Co., 1948 [Reprint of the 1823 edition]), pp. 1-4, 13-17, 24-26. Reprinted by permission.

remain subject to it all the while. The *principle of utility* recognises this subjection, and assumes it for the foundation of that system, the object of which is to rear the fabric of felicity by the hands of reason and of law. Systems which attempt to question it, deal in sounds instead of sense, in caprice instead of reason, in darkness instead of light.

But enough of metaphor and declamation: it is not by such means that moral science is to be improved.

The principle of utility is the foundation of the present work: it will be proper therefore at the outset to give an explicit and determinate account of what is meant by it. By the principle of utility is meant that principle which approves or disapproves of every action whatsoever, according to the tendency which it appears to have to augment or diminish the happiness of the party whose interest is in question: or, what is the same thing in other words, to promote or to oppose that happiness. I say of every action whatsoever; and therefore not only of every action of a private individual, but of every measure of government.

By utility is meant that property in any object, whereby it tends to produce benefit, advantage, pleasure, good, or happiness, (all this in the present case comes to the same thing) or (what comes again to the same thing) to prevent the happening of mischief, pain, evil, or unhappiness to the party whose interest is considered: if that party be the community in general, then the happiness of the community: if a particular individual, then the happiness of that individual.

The interest of the community is one of the most general expressions that can occur in the phraseology of morals: no wonder that the meaning of it is often lost. When it has a meaning, it is this. The community is a fictitious *body*, composed of the individual persons who are considered as constituting as it were its *members*. The interest of the community then is, what? the sum of the interests of the several members who compose it.

It is in vain to talk of the interest of the community, without understanding what is the interest of the individual. A thing is said to promote the interest, or to be *for* the interest, of an individual, when it tends to add to the sum total of his pleasures: or, what comes to the same thing, to diminish the sum total of his pains.

An action then may be said to be conformable to the principle of utility, or, for shortness sake, to utility, (meaning with respect to the community at large) when the tendency it has to augment the happiness of the community is greater than any it has to diminish it.

A measure of government (which is but a particular kind of action, performed by a particular person or persons) may be said to be conformable to or dictated by the principle of utility, when in like manner the tendency which it has to augment the happiness of the community is greater than any which it has to diminish it.

When an action, or in particular a measure of government, is supposed by a man to be conformable ot the principle of utility, it may be convenient, for the purposes of discourse, to imagine a kind of law or dictate, called a law or dictate of utility: and to speak of the action in question, as being conformable to such law or dictate.

A man may be said to be a partizan of the principle of utility, when the approbation or disapprobation he annexes to any action, or to any measure, is determined by and proportioned to the tendency which he conceives it to have to augment or to diminish the happiness of the community: or in other words, to its conformity or unconformity to the laws or dictates of utility.

Of an action that is conformable to the principle of utility one may always say either that it is one that ought to be done, or at least that it is not one that ought not to be done. One may say also, that it is right it should be done; at least that it is not wrong it should be done: that it is a right action; at least that it is not a wrong action. When thus interpreted, the words *ought,* and *right* and *wrong,* and others of that stamp, have a meaning: when otherwise, they have none. . . .

The principle of utility is capable of being consistently pursued; and it is but tautology to say, that the more consistently it is pursued, the better it must ever be for human-kind. The principle of asceticism never was, nor ever can be, consistently pursued by any living creature. Let but one tenth part of the inhabitants of this earth pursue it consistently, and in a day's time they will have turned it into a hell.

Among principles adverse to that of utility, that which at this day seems to have most influence in matters of government, is what may be called the principle of sympathy and antipathy. By the principle of sympathy and antipathy, I mean that principle which approves or disapproves of certain actions, not on account of their tending to augment the happiness, nor yet on account of their tending to diminish the happiness of the party whose interest is in question, but merely because a man finds himself disposed to approve or disapprove of them: holding up that approbation or disapprobation as a sufficient reason for itself, and disclaiming the necessity of looking out for any extrinsic ground. Thus far in the general department of morals: and in the particular department of politics, measuring out the quantum (as well as determining the ground) of punishment, by the degree of the disapprobation.

It is manifest, that this is rather a principle in name than in reality: it is not a positive principle of itself, so much as a term employed to signify the negation of all principle. What one expects to find in a principle is something that points out some external consideration, as a means of warranting and guiding the internal sentiments of approbation and disapprobation: this expectation is but ill fulfilled by a proposition, which does neither more nor less than hold up each of those sentiments as a ground and standard for itself.

In looking over the catalogue of human actions (says a partizan of this principle) in order to determine which of them are to be marked with the seal of disapprobation, you need but to take counsel of your own feelings: whatever you find in yourself a propensity to condemn, is wrong for that very reason. For the same reason it is also meet for punishment: in what proportion it is adverse to utility, or whether it be adverse to utility at all, is a matter that makes no difference. In that same *proportion* also is it meet for punishment: if you hate much, punish much: if you hate little, punish little: punish as you hate. If you hate not at all, punish not at all: the fine feelings of the soul are not to be overborne and tyrannized by the harsh and rugged dictates of political utility. . . .

It has been shown that the happiness of the individuals, of whom a community is composed, that is their pleasures and their security, is the end and the sole end which the legislator ought to have in view: the sole standard, in conformity to which each individual ought, as far as depends upon the legislator, to be *made* to fashion his behaviour. But whether it be this or any thing else that is to be *done,* there is nothing by which a man can ultimately be *made* to do it, but either pain or pleasure. Having taken a general view of these two grand objects (*viz.* pleasure, and what comes to the same thing, immunity from pain) in the character of *final* causes; it will be necessary to take a view of pleasure and pain itself, in the character of *efficient* causes or means.

There are four distinguishable sources from which pleasure and pain are in use to flow: considered separately, they may be termed the *physical*, the *political*, the *moral*, and the *religious*: and inasmuch as the pleasures and pains belonging to each of them are capable of giving a binding force to any law or rule of conduct, they may all of them be termed *sanctions.*

If it be in the present life, and from the ordinary course of nature, not purposely modified by the interposition of the will of any human being, nor by any extraordinary interposition of any superior invisible being, that the pleasure or the pain takes place or is expected, it may be said to issue from or to belong to the *physical sanction.* . . .

Pleasures or pains which may be expected to issue from the *physical, political*, or *moral* sanctions, must all of them be expected to be experienced, if ever, in the *present* life: those which may be expected to issue from the *religious* sanction, may be expected to be experienced either in the *present* life or in a *future.*

Those which can be experienced in the present life, can of course be no others than such as human nature in the course of the present life is susceptible of: and from each of these sources may flow all the pleasures or pains of which, in the course of the present life, human nature is susceptible. With regard to these then (with which alone we have in this place any concern) those of them which belong to any one of those sanctions, differ not ultimately in kind from those which belong to any one of the other three: the only difference there is among them lies in the circumstances that accompany their production. A suffering which befalls a man in the natural and spontaneous course of things, shall be styled, for instance, a *calamity;* in which case, if it be supposed to befall him through any imprudence of his, it may be styled a punishment issuing from the physical sanction. Now this same suffering, if inflicted by the law, will be what is commonly called a *punishment;* if incurred for want of any friendly assistance, which the misconduct, or supposed misconduct, of the sufferer has occasioned to be withholden, a punishment issuing from the *moral* sanction; if through the immediate interposition of a particular providence, a punishment issuing from the religious sanction. . . .

4. THE SADLER REPORT—FACTORY CONDITIONS AT LEEDS*

Industrialization and the factory system, which spread rapidly across the English midlands by the early nineteenth century, brought a swift growth of cities. Many of the early factories and factory towns were characterized by

* Charles Wing, *Evils of the Factory System* (London: Saunders and Otley, 1837), pp. 9–10.

appalling squalor, poor working conditions, and uncontrolled human exploitation. Humanitarians and some of the leading figures in English society strove
to improve the desperate conditions in industrial communities. In 1832 a royal
commission concluded an investigation of conditions in English textile factories
with a series of hearings before a parliamentary committee headed by Michael
Sadler. The published report of the Committee's findings revealed the abuses of
the factory system in such graphic terms that few members of Parliament
could fail to recognize the necessity of reform. By the end of the nineteenth
century, child labor had been prohibited and adolescent employment had been
reduced to a ten-hour day. In the selection which follows, what particular
dilemma did Miss Elizabeth Bentley face at age twenty-three? What were the
most degrading aspects of textile work? What methods were employed by the
overlooker in order to maintain production quotas?

[ABRIDGMENT OF EVIDENCE]

BENTLEY, ELIZABETH, age 23,—examined, 4th June, 1832,—as doffer, began to
work, when six years old, in a flax mill, at Leeds.

1. What were your hours of labour? — From five in the morning, till nine at
night, when they were thronged.

2. For how long a time together have you worked that excessive length of
time? — For about half a year.

3. What were your usual hours of labour, when you were not so thronged?
— From six in the morning, till seven at night.

4. What time was allowed for your meals? — Forty minutes at noon.

5. Had you any time to get your breakfast, or drinking? — No, we got it as
we could.

6. And when your work was bad, you had hardly any time to eat it at all?
— No; we were obliged to leave it or to take it home, and when we did not
take it, the overlooker took it, and gave it to his pigs.

7. Do you consider doffing a laborious employment? — Yes; when the
frames are full, they have to stop the frames, and take the flyers off, and take the
full bobbins off, and carry them to the roller, and then put empty ones on, and
set the frames going again.

8. Does that keep you constantly on your feet? — Yes; there are so many
frames, and they run so quick.

9. Suppose you flagged a little, or were too late, what would they do? —
Strap us.

10. Girls as well as boys? — Yes.

11. Have you ever been strapped? — Yes, severely.

12. Were you strapped if you were too much fatigued to keep up with the
machinery? — Yes; the overlooker I was under was a very severe man, and
when we have been fatigued, and worn out, and had not baskets to put the
bobbins in, we used to put them in the window bottoms, and that broke the
panes sometimes, and I broke one one time, and the overlooker strapped me on
the arm, and it rose a blister, and I ran home to my mother.

13. How long were you in your first situation? — Three or four years.

14. Where did you go then? — To Benyon's factory.

15. What were you there? — A weigher in the card-room.

16. How long did you work there? — From half-past five, till eight at night.

17. The carding-room is more oppressive than the spinning department? — Yes, it is so dusty; they cannot see each other for dust.

18. Did working in the card-room affect your health? — Yes; it was so dusty, the dust got up my lungs, and the work was so hard; I was middling strong when I went there, but the work was so bad; I got so bad in health, that when I pulled the baskets down, I pulled my bones out of their places.

19. You are considerably deformed in your person in consequence of this labour? — Yes, I am.

20. At what time did it come on?— I was about thirteen years old when it began coming, and it has got worse since; it is five years since my mother died, and my mother was never able to get me a pair of good stays to hold me up; when my mother died, I had to do for myself, and got me a pair.

21. Were you straight till you were thirteen? — Yes, I was.

22. Have you been attended to by any medical gentleman at Leeds, or the neighbourhood? — Yes, I have been under Mr. Hares.

23. To what did he attribute it? — He said it was owing to hard labour, and working in the factories.

24. Where are you now? — In the poor house.

25. Do any of your former employers come to see you? — No.

26. Did you ever receive anything from them when you became afflicted? — When I was at home, Mr. Walker made me a present of 1s. or 2s.; but since I have left my work and gone to the poor house, they have not come nigh me.

27. You are supported by the parish? — Yes.

28. You are utterly incapable now of any exertion in the factories? — Yes.

29. You were very willing to have worked as long as you were able, from your earliest age? — Yes.

30. And to have supported your widowed mother as long as you could? — Yes. . . .

5. BENJAMIN DISRAELI: SYBIL*

The active political career of Benjamin Disraeli (1804–81) began during the period of expanding industrialism, Chartist agitation, and the anti-Corn Law movement and closed amid militant unionism, imperialist upsurge, and the controversy over Irish Home Rule. He served in three cabinets and was Prime Minister in two others. Two years before entering the House of Commons in 1837 Disraeli published his *Vindication of the British Constitution,* in which he subscribed to the Burkean tradition as the best guide for England's future development. In addition to his political activities, Disraeli wrote eight novels and established a reputation of respectable literary merit. His best known novel, *Sybil* (1845), was rich with the political-economic philosophy expressed by a group of Tory aristocrats generally referred to as Young England. Disraeli called for a fulfillment of what he conceived as the aristocratic mission to serve the needs of the masses, a goal which he believed the Whigs could not achieve because of their classical liberal doctrines.

In the passages below, Disraeli provided a description of the rural town of Marney and depicted the drudgery of mining life. What were the most serious

* Benjamin Disraeli, *Sybil* (London: R. Brimley Johnson, 1904), pp. 69–71, 184–86, 86–88.

or detrimental aspects of rural town life? What most disturbed Disraeli about working conditions in the mines? What did the dialogue imply regarding contemporary English economic development and the concept of civic or community pride?

The situation of the rural town of Marney was one of the most delightful easily to be imagined. In a spreading dale, contiguous to the margin of a clear and lively stream, surrounded by meadows and gardens, and backed by lofty hills, undulating and richly wooded, the traveller on the opposite heights of the dale would often stop to admire the merry prospect that recalled to him the traditional epithet of his country.

Beautiful illusion! For behind that laughing landscape, penury and disease fed upon the vitals of a miserable population.

The contrast between the interior of the town and its external aspect was as striking as it was full of pain. With the exception of the dull High street, which had the usual characteristics of a small agricultural market town, some sombre mansions, a dingy inn, and a petty bourse, Marney mainly consisted of a variety of narrow and crowded lanes formed by cottages built of rubble, or unhewn stones without cement, and, from age or badness of the material, looking as if they could scarcely hold together. The gaping chinks admitted every blast; the leaning chimneys had lost half their original height; the rotten rafters were evidently misplaced; while in many instances the thatch, yawning in some parts to admit the wind and wet, and in all utterly unfit for its original purpose of giving protection from the weather, looked more like the top of a dunghill than a cottage. Before the doors of these dwellings, and often surrounding them, ran open drains full of animal and vegetable refuse, decomposing into disease, or sometimes in their imperfect course filling foul pits or spreading into stagnant pools, while a concentrated solution of every species of dissolving filth was allowed to soak through, and thoroughly impregnate, the walls and ground adjoining.

These wretched tenements seldom consisted of more than two rooms, in one of which the whole family, however numerous, were obliged to sleep, without distinction of age, or sex, or suffering. With the water streaming down the walls, the light distinguished through the roof, with no hearth even in winter, the virtuous mother in the sacred pangs of childbirth, gives forth another victim to our thoughtless civilization; surrounded by three generations whose inevitable presence is more painful than her sufferings in that hour of travail; while the father of her coming child, in another corner of the sordid chamber, lies stricken by that typhus which his contaminating dwelling has breathed into his veins, and for whose next prey is perhaps destined his new-born child. These swarming walls had neither windows nor doors sufficient to keep out the weather, or admit the sun, or supply the means of ventilation; the humid and putrid roof of thatch exhaling malaria like all other decaying vegetable matter. The dwelling rooms were neither boarded nor paved; and whether it were that some were situate in low and damp places, occasionally flooded by the river, and usually much below the level of the road; or that the springs, as was often the case, would burst through the mud floor; the ground was at no time better than so much clay, while sometimes you might see little channels cut from the centre under the doorways to carry off the water, the door itself removed from its hinges: a resting place for infancy in its deluged home. These hovels were in many instances not provided with the commonest conveniences of the rudest police; contiguous to every door might be observed the dung-heap on which every kind of filth was accumulated, for the purpose of being disposed of for manure, so that, when the poor man opened his narrow habitation in the hope of refreshing it with the breeze of summer, he was met with a mixture of gases from reeking dunghills. . . .

The last rays of the sun, contending with clouds of smoke that drifted across the country, partially illumined a peculiar landscape. Far as the eye could reach, and the region was level, except where a range of limestone hills formed its distant limit, a wilderness of cottages, or tenements that were hardly entitled to a higher name, were scattered for many miles over the land; some detached, some connected in little rows, some clustering in groups, yet rarely forming continuous streets, but interspersed with blazing furnaces, heaps of burning coal, and piles of smouldering ironstone; while forges and engine chimneys roared and puffed in all directions, and indicated the frequent presence of the mouth of the mine and the bank of the coal-pit. Notwithstanding the whole country might be compared to a vast rabbit warren, it was nevertheless intersected with canals crossing each other at various levels, and though the subterranean operations were prosecuted with so much avidity that it was not uncommon to observe whole rows of houses awry, from the shifting and hollow nature of the land, still, intermingled with heaps of mineral refuse or of metallic dross, patches of the surface might here and there be recognised, covered, as if in mockery, with grass and corn, looking very much like those gentlemen's sons that we used to read of in our youth, stolen by the chimney-sweeps and giving some intimations of their breeding beneath their grimy livery. But a tree or a shrub—such an existence was unknown in this dingy rather than dreary region.

It was the twilight hour; the hour at which in southern climes the peasant kneels before the sunset image of the blessed Hebrew maiden; when caravans halt in their long course over vast deserts, and the turbaned traveller, bending in the sand, pays his homage to the sacred stone and the sacred city; the hour, not less holy, that announces the cessation of English toil, and sends forth the miner and the collier to breathe the air of earth, and gaze on the light of heaven.

They come forth: the mine delivers its gang and the pit its bondsmen; the forge is silent and the engine is still. The plain is covered with the swarming multitude: bands of stalwart men, broad-chested and muscular, wet with toil, and black as the children of the tropics; troops of youth—alas! of both sexes—though neither their raiment nor their language indicates the difference; all are clad in male attire; and oaths that men might shudder at issue from lips born to breathe words of sweetness. Yet these are to be—some are—the mothers of England! But can we wonder at the hideous coarseness of their language, when we remember the savage rudeness of their lives? Naked to the waist, an iron chain fastened to a belt of leather runs between their legs clad in canvas trousers, while on hands and feet an English girl, for twelve, sometimes for sixteen hours a-day, hauls and hurries tubs of coals up subterranean roads, dark, precipitous, and plashy: circumstances that seem to have escaped the notice of the Society for the Abolition of Negro Slavery. Those worthy gentlemen too appear to have been singularly unconscious of the sufferings of the Little Trappers, which was remarkable, as many of them were in their own employ.

See, too, these emerge from the bowels of the earth! Infants of four and five years of age, many of them girls, pretty and still soft and timid; entrusted with the fulfillment of most responsible duties, and the nature of which entails on them the necessity of being the earliest to enter the mine and the latest to leave it. Their labour indeed is not severe, for that would be impossible, but it is passed in darkness and in solitude. They endure that punishment which philosophical philanthropy has invented for the direst criminals, and which those criminals deem more terrible than the death for which it is substituted. Hour after hour elapses, and all that reminds the infant trappers of the world they have quitted and that which they have joined, is the passage of the coal-waggons for which they open the air-doors of the galleries, and on keeping which doors constantly closed, except at this moment of passage, the safety of the mine and the lives of the persons employed in it entirely depend. . . .

"There is so much to lament in the world in which we live," said the younger of the strangers, "that I can spare no pang for the past."

"Yet you approve of the principle of their society; you prefer it, you say, to our existing life."

"Yes; I prefer association to gregariousness."

"That is a distinction," said Egrement, musingly.

"It is a community of purpose that constitutes society," continued the younger stranger; "without that, men may be drawn into contiguity, but they still continue virtually isolated."

"And is that their condition in cities?"

"It is their condition everywhere; but in cities that condition is aggravated. A density of population implies a severe struggle for existence, and a consequent repulsion of elements brought into too close contact. In great cities men are brought together by the desire of gain. They are not in a state of co-operation, but of isolation, as to the making of fortunes; and for all the rest they are careless of neighbours. Christianity teaches us to love our neighbour as ourself; modern society acknowledges no neighbour."

"Well, we live in strange times," said Egremont, struck by the observation of his companion, and relieving a perplexed spirit by an ordinary exclamation, which often denotes that the mind is more stirring than it cares to acknowledge, or at the moment is capable to express.

"When the infant begins to walk, it also thinks that it lives in strange times," said his companion.

"Your inference?" asked Egremont.

"That society, still in its infancy, is beginning to feel its way."

"This is a new reign," said Egremont, "perhaps it is a new era."

"I think so," said the younger stranger.

"I hope so," said the elder one.

"Well, society may be in its infancy," said Egremont slightly smiling; "but, say what you like, our Queen reigns over the greatest nation that ever existed."

"Which nation?" asked the younger stranger, "for she reigns over two."

The stranger paused; Egremont was silent, but looked inquiringly.

"Yes," resumed the younger stranger after a moment's interval. "Two nations; between whom there is no intercourse and no sympathy; who are as ignorant of each other's habits, thoughts, and feelings, as if they were dwellers in different zones, or inhabitants of different planets; who are formed by a different breeding, are fed by a different food, are ordered by different manners, and are not governed by the same laws."

"You speak of—" said Egremont, hesitatingly.

"The RICH and the POOR."

6. SAMUEL SMILES: SELF-HELP*

root of many beliefs "conservative"

Samuel Smiles (1812–1904) was a physician who practiced medicine in the factory town of Leeds. His observations of working-class behavior led him to the conviction that each individual was morally responsible for his own material welfare. Although Smiles confused moral judgments with opportunities for employment, he nevertheless blindly insisted that advancement and self-betterment were possible for all men. As a popularizer of individual virtue, Smiles saw his major literary work, *Self-Help*, translated into many languages and enthusiastically accepted by the prosperous middle classes of the Western world. What was the central thesis of *Self-Help?* How did Smiles support his assertions? According to Smiles, in what ways was government to help the individual to improve his material position? Contrast the essential emphasis of Smiles's argument with Bentham's concept of the greatest good for the greatest number.

"Heaven helps those who help themselves" is a well-tried maxim, embodying in a small compass the results of vast human experience. The spirit of self-help is the root of all genuine growth in the individual; and, exhibited in the lives of many, it constitutes the true source of national vigor and strength. Help from without is often enfeebling in its effects, but help from within invariably invigorates. Whatever is done *for* men or classes, to a certain extent takes away the stimulus and necessity of doing for themselves; and where men are subjected to overguidance and over-government, the inevitable tendency is to render them comparatively helpless.

Even the best institutions can give a man no active help. Perhaps the most they can do is, to leave him free to develop himself and improve his individual condition. But in all times men have been prone to believe that their happiness and well-being were to be secured by means of institutions rather than by their own conduct. Hence the value of legislation as an agent in human advancement has usually been much over-estimated. To constitute the millionth part of a Legislature, by voting for one or two men once in three or five years, however conscientiously this duty may be performed, can exercise but little active influence upon any man's life and character. Moreover, it is every day becoming

* Samuel Smiles, *Self-Help, with Illustrations of Character, Conduct, and Perseverance* (New York: Harper and Brothers, 1874), pp. 21–23, 25–27.

more clearly understood, that the function of Government is negative and restrictive, rather than positive and active; being resolvable principally into protection—protection of life, liberty, and property. Laws, wisely administered, will secure men in the enjoyment of the fruits of their labor, whether of mind or body, at a comparatively small personal sacrifice; but no laws, however stringent, can make the idle industrious, the thriftless provident, or the drunken sober. Such reforms can only be effected by means of individual action, economy, and self-denial; by better habits, rather than by greater rights.

The Government of a nation itself is usually found to be but the reflex of the individuals composing it. The Government that is ahead of the people will inevitably be dragged down to their level, as the Government that is behind them will in the long run be dragged up. In the order of nature, the collective character of a nation will as surely find its befitting results in its law and government, as water finds its own level. The noble people will be nobly ruled, and the ignorant and corrupt ignobly. Indeed, all experience serves to prove that the worth and strength of a State depend far less upon the form of its institutions than upon the character of its men. For the nation is only an aggregate of individual conditions, and civilization itself is but a question of the personal improvement of the men, women, and children of whom society is composed.

National progress is the sum of individual industry, energy, and uprightness, as national decay is of individual idleness, selfishness, and vice. What we are accustomed to decry as great social evils, will for the most part be found to be but the outgrowth of man's own perverted life; and though we may endeavor to cut them down and extirpate them by means of Law, they will only spring up again with fresh luxuriance in some other form, unless the conditions of personal life and character are radically improved. If this view be correct, then it follows that the highest patriotism and philanthropy consists, not so much in altering laws and modifying institutions, as in helping and stimulating men to elevate and improve themselves by their own free and independent individual action.

It may be of comparatively little consequence how a man is governed from without, whilst every thing depends upon how he governs himself from within. The greatest slave is not he who is ruled by a despot, great though that evil be, but he who is the thrall of his own moral ignorance, selfishness, and vice. Nations who are thus enslaved at heart can not be freed by any mere changes of masters or of institutions; and so long as the fatal delusion prevails, that liberty solely depends upon and consists in government, so long will such changes, no matter at what cost they may be effected, have as little practical and lasting result as the shifting of the figures in a phantasmagoria. The solid foundation of liberty must rest upon individual character; which is also the only sure guaranty for social security and national progress. John Stuart Mill truly observes that "even despotism does not produce its worst effects so long as individuality exists under it; and whatever crushes individuality is despotism, by whatever name it be called." . . .

The spirit of self-help, as exhibited in the energetic action of individuals, has in all times been a marked feature in the English character, and furnishes the true measure of our power as a nation. Rising above the heads of the mass, there were always to be found a series of individuals distinguished beyond others, who commanded the public homage. But our progress has also been owing to multitudes of smaller and less known men. Though only the generals' names may be remembered in the history of any great campaign, it has been in a great measure through the individual valor and heroism of the privates that victories have been won. And life, too, is "a soldier's battle"—men in the ranks having in all times been amongst the greatest of workers. Many are the lives of men unwritten, which have nevertheless as powerfully influenced civilization and progress as the more fortunate Great whose names are recorded in biography. Even the humblest person, who sets before his fellows an example of industry, sobriety, and upright honesty of purpose in life, has a present as well as a future influence upon the well-being of his country; for his life and character pass unconsciously into the lives of others, and propagate good example for all time to come. . . .

Biographies of great, but especially of good men, are nevertheless most instructive and useful, as helps, guides, and incentives to others. Some of the best are almost equivalent to gospels—teaching high living, high thinking, and energetic action for their own and the world's good. The valuable examples which they furnish of the power of self-help, of patient purpose, resolute working, and steadfast integrity, issuing in the formation of truly noble and manly character, exhibit in language not to be misunderstood, what it is in the power of each to accomplish for himself; and eloquently illustrate the efficacy of self-respect and self-reliance in enabling men of even the humblest rank to work out for themselves an honorable competency and a solid reputation.

Great men of science, literature, and art—apostles of great thoughts and lords of the great heart—have belonged to no exclusive class or rank in life. They have come alike from colleges, workshops, and farm-houses—from the huts of poor men and the mansions of the rich. Some of God's greatest apostles have come from "the ranks." The poorest have sometimes taken the highest places, nor have difficulties apparently the most insuperable proved obstacles in their way. Those very difficulties, in many instances, would even seem to have been their best helpers, by evoking their powers of labor and endurance, and stimulating into life faculties which might otherwise have lain dormant. The instances of obstacles thus surmounted, and of triumphs thus achieved, are indeed so numerous, as almost to justify the proverb that "with Will one can do any thing." . . .

7. RICHARD COBDEN: ON FREE TRADE*

The influence of British utilitarians and philosophical radicals in the Whig party was demonstrated by the passage of the Parliamentary Reform Bill in 1832. But the Whig leadership soon lost its enthusiasm for further and more far-reaching reform. Representatives of the new manufacturing and business interests gradually assumed leadership in the Whig party by the later 1830's. Calling themselves Free Traders, though better known generally as the Man-

* Richard Cobden, *Speeches on Questions of Public Policy,* eds. John Bright and James E. Thorold Rogers (2 vols.; London: Macmillan and Co., 1870), I, 6–7, 113–14, 116–18.

chester School, these middle-class advocates of laissez faire stimulated the Anti-Corn Law League. The goal of the League was to remove protective tariffs from agricultural products. Between 1838 and 1846 numerous torchlight parades, mass gatherings, and the distribution of a vast number of pamphlets indicated a growing sentiment for repeal of the Corn Laws. Richard Cobden (1804–65), a Lancashire manufacturer, was one of the most articulate voices for this cause, both in and outside of Parliament. An expert on economic conditions in Germany and the United States and a self-made man of great wealth, Cobden devoted himself to repeal of the Corn Laws and to other efforts to promote free trade.

According to the following excerpts from a speech delivered to his constituents, on what grounds did he argue that "the rate of wages has no more connection with the price of food than with the moon's changes"? What conditions did he claim regulated wages? Who were "the selfish oligarchy of the sugar-hogshead and the flour-sack" whom Cobden attacked? Why did he hold that protective tariffs on all commodities—agricultural and manufactured—were equally harmful to British economic growth?

There is another stage in the labour market—I refer to labourers in the agricultural districts—where the amount of wages has reached the very minimum, according to their habits of life. These unfortunate men are told that their wages will rise as the price of provisions advances. Why? Is it because the high price of provisions increases the demand for labour, or is it done from pure charity? But I come to that state of the labour market under which—and God knows how long it will continue under such legislation—the various products of our manufacturing industry are called into existence, and there, I assert, without fear of contradiction, that the rate of wages has no more connection with the price of food than with the moon's changes. There it depends entirely on the demand for labour; there the price of food never becomes an ingredient in testing the value of labour. There the labour market is, happily, elastic, and will become more so, if you leave it unfettered. But if you continue to legislate in the spirit by which you have so long been animated, you will succeed at least in bringing our commercial and manufacturing population down to the same pitch to which you have reduced our agriculturists, and then these merchants and manufacturers may come forward and give alms to the wretched men in the employment; then it will perhaps be said that "with the increase in the price of food arises an increase in the rate of wages." It will be doled out as an alms, as a mere act of charity, and not because the working man, as a free agent, is entitled, in return for his labour, to a decent subsistence. . . .

. . . Now, we are "Free Traders;" and what is Free Trade? Not the pulling down of all custom-houses, as some of our wise opponents the dukes and earls have lately been trying to persuade the agricultural labourers; I should think it would do with nobody else. By Free Trade we mean the abolition of all protective duties. It is very possible that our children, or at all events their offspring, may be wise enough to dispense with custom-house duties altogether. They may think it prudent and economical to raise their revenues by direct taxation, without circumventing their foreign trade. We do not propose to do that; but there are a class of men who have taken possession of the Custom-house, and have installed their clerks there, to collect revenue for their own particular benefit, and we intend to remove them out of the Custom-house.

Now, I want to impress on our new friends, these students in Free Trade, to remind them of that which I have frequently dwelt upon, and which cannot be too often repeated, that this system of monopoly is analogous in every respect to that which existed 250 years ago under the Tudors and the Stuarts, when sovereigns granted monopolies to the creatures of their courts for the exclusive sale of wine, leather, salt, and other things, and which system our forefathers, at great labour and heavy sacrifice, utterly extirpated. One by one these monopolies were abolished; and, not content with destroying the existing monopolies, they passed a law, which became, as it were, a fundamental principle in our Constitution, that no sovereign, thenceforth or for ever, should have the power of granting a monopoly to anybody for the exclusive sale of any necessary commodity of life. Now, what I want to impress on our young learners is this, that that which sovereigns cannot do, a band of men united together—the selfish oligarchy of the sugar-hogshead and the flour-sack—have done. They have got together in the House of Commons, and by their own Acts of Parliament have appropriated to their own classes the very privileges, the self-same monopolies, or monopolies as injurious in every respect to the interests of the people as those monopolies were which our forefathers abolished two centuries and a half ago. . . .

Now, what are the objections alleged against the adoption of Free-trade principles? First of all, take the most numerous body—the working class—by far the most important in the consideration of this question: for probably nine-tenths of all the population of this country are dependent on labour, either the hard work of hands, or the equally hard toil of heads. I say, take their case first. We are told this system of restriction is for the benefit of the labourers. We are informed by the earls, dukes, and the squires, that the price of corn regulates the rate of wages; and that, if we reduce the price of corn by a free trade in that article, we shall only bring down the rate of wages. Now, I see a good many working people in this assembly, and would ask them whether, in any bargain ever made for labour in London, the question of corn or its price was ever made an element in that agreement? Why, look at your hackney-coach and watermen's fares, and at your ticket-porters' charges. Your own Corporation, in their by-laws and Acts of Parliament regulating the wages of a variety of labourers in this metropolis, have been strangely oblivious of this sliding scale of corn, when they have fixed a permanent rate of wages. . . .

Now, the first and greatest count in my indictment against the Corn-law is, that it is an injustice to the labourers of this and every other country. My next charge is, that it is a fraud against every man of capital engaged in any pursuit, and every person of fixed income not derived from land. I will take the trader. I am a manufacturer of clothing, and I do not know why, in this climate, and in the artificial state of society in which we live, the making of clothes should not be as honourable—because it is pretty near as useful—a pursuit as the manufacture of food. Well, did you ever hear any debates in the House to fix the price of my commodities in the market? Suppose we had a majority of cotton-printers (which happens to be my manufacture) in the House; and if we had a majority I have no doubt we should find Sir Robert Peel quite willing to do our work for us: he is the son of a cotton-printer, and I dare say he would do it for us as well as any one else. Let us suppose that you were reading the newspaper some fine morning, and saw an account of a majority of the House having been engaged the night before in fixing the price at which yard-wide prints should be sold: "Yard-wide prints, of such a quality, 10d., a yard; of such a quality, 9d.; of such a quality, 8d.; of such a quality, 7d.," and so on. Why, you would rub your eyes with astonishment! You would clear your spectacles, if you wore any, and you would doubt your own senses! The very boys in the streets leading to Parliament, and the cabmen and omnibus-drivers, would hoot and hiss us out of the metropolis! Now, did it ever occur to you that there is no earthly difference between a body of men, manufacturers of corn, sitting down in the House, and passing a law enacting that wheat shall be so much, barley so much, beans so much, and oats so much? . . .

8. FRIEDRICH LIST: THE NATIONAL SYSTEM OF POLITICAL ECONOMY*

The economist Friedrich List (1789–1846), a south German radical, devoted his energies during the post-1815 era to the cause of commercial union for all Germany. In the fragmented world of thirty-nine German states, advocates of commercial union were frequently allied with liberal proponents of political unification. Such radicals were often in conflict with the conservative policies of Austria and Prussia and went into exile. List fled to the United States in 1825 and became an active participant in the American tariff controversy with Great Britain. He returned to Europe in 1832 as American consul at Leipzig and immediately began to develop the main lines of his major economic work, *The National System of Political Economy*. Did List attempt to refute the general validity of laissez faire or classical economic arguments? What essential shortcomings did he find in the views of Adam Smith and the Physiocrats? Why did List believe universal laissez faire principles were more beneficial to Great Britain than to other nations? Why did he hold Alexander Hamilton, Secretary of the Treasury under President George Washington, in such high esteem as a statesman? How can it be argued that List's views place him within the Hegelian tradition?

POLITICAL AND COSMOPOLITICAL ECONOMY

Before Quesnay and the French economists there existed only a *practice* of political economy which was exercised by the State officials, administrators, and authors who wrote about matters of administration, occupied themselves exclusively with the agriculture, manufactures, commerce, and navigation of those countries to which they belonged, without analysing the causes of wealth, or taking at all into consideration the interests of the whole human race.

Quesnay (from whom the idea of universal free trade originated) was the first who extended his investigations to the whole human race, without taking into consideration the idea of the nation. He calls his work "Physiocratie, ou du

* Friedrich List, *The National System of Political Economy* (New York: Augustus M. Kelley, Reprints of Economic Classics, 1966), pp. 119–20, 122–23, 130, 174–78. Reprinted by permission.

Gouvernement le plus avantageux au Genre Humain," his demands being that we must imagine that *the merchants of all nations formed one commercial republic.* Quesnay undoubtedly speaks of *cosmopolitical* economy, *i.e.* of that science which teaches how the entire human race may attain prosperity; in opposition to political economy, or that science which limits its teaching to the inquiry how a *given nation* can obtain (under the existing conditions of the world) prosperity, civilisation, and power, by means of agriculture, industry, and commerce.

Adam Smith treats his doctrine in a similarly extended sense, by making it his task to indicate the cosmopolitical idea of the absolute freedom of the commerce of the whole world in spite of the gross mistakes made by the physiocrates against the very nature of things and against logic. Adam Smith concerned himself as little as Quesnay did with true political economy, *i.e.* that policy which each separate nation had to obey in order to make progress in its economical conditions. He entitles his work, "The Nature and Causes of the Wealth of Nations" (*i.e.* of all nations of the whole human race). He speaks of the various systems of political economy in a separate part of his work solely for the purpose of demonstrating their non-efficiency, and of proving that "political" or *national* economy must be replaced by "cosmopolitical or world-wide economy." Although here and there he speaks of wars, this only occurs incidentally. The idea of a perpetual state of peace forms the foundation of all his arguments. Moreover, according to the explicit remarks of his biographer, Dugald Stewart, his investigations from the commencement are based upon the principle that "most of the State regulations for the promotion of public prosperity are unnecessary, and a nation in order to be transformed from the lowest state of barbarism into a state of the highest possible prosperity needs nothing but bearable taxation, fair administration of justice, and *peace.*" Adam Smith naturally understood under the word "peace" the "perpetual universal peace" of the Abbé St. Pierre. . . .

For our own part, we are far from rejecting the theory of *cosmopolitical* economy, as it has been perfected by the prevailing school; we are, however, of opinion that political economy, or as [J. B.] Say calls it "économie publique," should also be developed scientifically, and that it is always better to call things by their proper names than to give them significations which stand opposed to the true import of words.

If we wish to remain true to the laws of logic and of the nature of things, we must set the economy of individuals against the economy of societies, and discriminate in respect to the latter between true political or national economy (which, emanating from the idea and nature of the nation, teaches how a given *nation* in the present state of the world and its own special national relations can maintain and improve its economical conditions) and cosmopolitical economy, which originates in the assumption that all nations of the earth form but one society living in a perpetual state of peace.

If, as the prevailing school requires, we assume a universal union or confederation of all nations as the guarantee for an everlasting peace, the principle of international free trade seems to be perfectly justified. The less every individual is restrained in pursuing his own individual prosperity, the greater the number and wealth of those with whom he has free intercourse, the greater the area over which his individual activity can exercise itself, the easier it will be for him to utilise for the increase of his prosperity the properties given him by nature, the knowledge and talents which he has acquired, and the forces of nature placed at his disposal. As with separate individuals, so is it also the case with individual communities, provinces, and countries. A simpleton only could maintain that a union for free commercial intercourse between themselves is not as advantageous to the different states included in the United States of North America, to the various departments of France, and to the various German allied states, as would be their separation by internal provincial customs tariffs.

In the union of the three kingdoms of Great Britain and Ireland the world witnesses a great and irrefragable example of the immeasurable efficacy of free trade between united nations. Let us only suppose all other nations of the earth to be united in a similar manner, and the most vivid imagination will not be able to picture to itself the sum of prosperity and good fortune which the whole human race would thereby acquire.

Unquestionably the idea of a universal confederation and a perpetual peace is commended both by common sense and religion. If single combat between individuals is at present considered to be contrary to reason, how much more must combat between two nations be similarly condemned? The proofs which social economy can produce from the history of the civilisation of mankind of the reasonableness of bringing about the union of all mankind under the law of right, are perhaps those which are the clearest to sound human understanding. . . .

We have shown into what errors the school has fallen by judging the productive forces of the human race from a political point of view; we have now also to point out the mistakes which it has committed by regarding the separate interests of nations from a cosmopolitical point of view.

If a confederation of all nations existed in reality, as is the case with the separate states constituting the Union of North America, the excess of population, talents, skilled abilities, and material capital would flow over from England to the Continental states, in a similar manner to that in which it travels from the eastern states of the American Union to the western, provided that in the Continental states the same security for persons and property, the same constitution and general laws prevailed, and that the English Government was made subject to the united will of the universal confederation. Under these suppositions there would be no better way of raising all these countries to the same stage of wealth and cultivation as England than free trade. This is the argument of the school. But how would it tally with the actual operation of free trade under the existing conditions of the world? . . .

NATIONALITY AND THE ECONOMY OF THE NATION

The system of the school suffers, as we have already shown in the preceding chapters, from three main defects: firstly, from boundless *cosmopolitanism*, which neither recognises the principle of nationality, nor takes into consideration the satisfaction of its interests; secondly, from a dead *materialism*, which everywhere regards chiefly the mere exchangeable value of things without taking into consideration the mental and political, the present and the future interests, and the productive powers of the nation; thirdly, from a *disorganising particularism* and *individualism,* which, ignoring the nature and character of social labour and the operation of the union of powers in their higher consequences, considers private industry only as it would develop itself under a state of free interchange with society (*i.e.* with the whole human race) were that race not divided into separate national societies.

Between each individual and entire humanity, however, stands THE NATION, with its special language and literature, with its peculiar origin and history, with its special manners and customs, laws and institutions, with the claims of all these for existence, independence, perfection, and continuance for the future, and with its separate territory; a society which, united by a thousand ties of mind and of interests, combines itself into one independent whole, which recognises the law of right for and within itself, and in its united character is still opposed to other societies of a similar kind in their national liberty, and consequently can only under the existing conditions of the world maintain self-existence and independence by its own power and resources. As the individual chiefly obtains by means of the nation and in the nation mental culture, power of production, security, and prosperity, so is the civilisation of the human race only conceivable and possible by means of the civilisation and development of the individual nations.

Meanwhile, however, an infinite difference exists in the condition and circumstances of the various nations: we observe among them giants and dwarfs, well-formed bodies and cripples, civilised, half-civilised, and barbarous nations; but in all of them, as in the individual human being, exists the impulse of self-preservation, the striving for improvement which is implanted by nature. It is the task of politics to civilise the barbarous nationalities, to make the small and weak ones great and strong, but, above all, to secure to them existence and continuance. It is the task of national economy to accomplish *the economical development of the nation,* and to prepare it for admission into the universal society of the future.

A nation in its normal state possesses one common language and literature, a territory endowed with manifold natural resources, extensive, and with convenient frontiers and a numerous population. Agriculture, manufactures, commerce, and navigation must be all developed in it proportionately; arts and sciences, educational establishments, and universal cultivation must stand in it on an equal footing with material production. Its constitution, laws, and institutions must afford to those who belong to it a high degree of security and liberty, and must promote religion, morality, and prosperity; in a word, must have the well-being of its citizens as their object. It must possess sufficient power on land and at sea to defend its independence and to protect its foreign commerce. It will possess the power of beneficially affecting the civilisation of less advanced nations, and by means of its own surplus population and of their mental and material capital to found colonies and beget new nations.

A large population, and an extensive territory endowed with manifold national resources, are essential requirements of the normal nationality; they are the fundamental conditions of mental cultivation as well as of material development and political power. A nation restricted in the number of its population and in territory, especially if it has a separate language, can only possess a crippled literature, crippled institutions for promoting art and science. A small State can never bring to complete perfection within its territory the various branches of production. In it all protection becomes mere private monopoly. Only through alliances with more powerful nations, by partly sacrificing the advantages of nationality, and by excessive energy, can it maintain with difficulty its independence.

A nation which possesses no coasts, mercantile marine, or naval power, or has not under its dominion and control the mouths of its rivers, is in its foreign commerce dependent on other countries; it can neither establish colonies of its own nor form new nations; all surplus population, mental and material means, which flows from such a nation to uncultivated countries, is lost to its own literature, civilisation and industry, and goes to the benefit of other nationalities.

A nation not bounded by seas and chains of mountains lies open to the attacks of foreign nations, and can only by great sacrifices, and in any case only very imperfectly, establish and maintain a separate tariff system of its own.

Territorial deficiencies of the nation can be remedied either by means of hereditary succession, as in the case of England and Scotland; or by purchase, as in the case of Florida and Louisiana; or by conquests, as in the case of Great Britain and Ireland.

In modern times a fourth means has been adopted, which leads to this object in a manner much more in accordance with justice and with the prosperity of nations than conquest, and which is not so dependent on accidents as hereditary succession, namely, the union of the interests of various States by means of free conventions.

By its Zollverein, the German nation first obtained one of the most important attributes of its nationality. But this measure cannot be considered complete so long as it does not extend over the whole coast, from the mouth of the Rhine to the frontier of Poland, including *Holland* and *Denmark*. A natural consequence of this union must be the admission of both these countries into the German Bund, and consequently into the German nationality, whereby the latter will at once obtain what it is now in need of, namely, fisheries and naval power, maritime commerce and colonies. Besides, both these nations belong, as respects their descent and whole character, to the German nationality. The burden of debt with which they are oppressed is merely a consequence of their unnatural endeavours to maintain themselves as independent nationalities, and it is in the nature of things that this evil should rise to a point when it will become intolerable to those two nations themselves, and when incorporation with a larger nationality must seem desirable and necessary to them.

Belgium can only remedy by means of confederation with a neighbouring larger nation her needs which are inseparable from her restricted territory and population. *The United States* and *Canada,* the more their population increases, and the more the protective system of the United States is developed, so much the more will they feel themselves drawn towards one another, and the less will it be possible for England to prevent a union between them.

As respects their economy, nations have to pass through the following stages of development: original barbarism, pastoral condition, agricultural condition, agricultural-manufacturing condition, and agricultural-manufacturing-commercial condition.

The industrial history of nations, and of none more clearly than that of England, proves that the transition from the savage state to the pastoral one, from the pastoral to the agricultural, and from agriculture to the first beginnings in manufacture and navigation, is effected most speedily and advantageously by means of free commerce with further advanced towns and countries, but that a perfectly developed manufacturing industry, an important mercantile marine, and foreign trade on a really large scale, can only be attained by means of the interposition of the power of the State. . . .

9. VICTOR HUGO: LES MISÉRABLES*

Victor Hugo (1802–85) entered the French literary world as a friend of the Restoration and an ardent Romantic. Shifting emphasis during the July Monarchy of Louis Philippe, he idealized and romanticized the republican tradition. With the coup d'état of Louis Napoleon, Hugo fled into exile and used his powerful literary talents to ridicule the Second Empire. Finally he returned to France to reign as a kind of senior literary laureate during the early years of the Third Republic.

Hugo's most important contribution to an understanding of nineteenth-century France was his description of contemporary economic and social problems. His sympathies poured out to those most abused by industrialization, hypocritical standards, and social injustices. In the selection from *Les Misérables* (1862) which follows, the heroine (Fantine) was a victim of brutal injustices which were characteristic of a society void of humanitarianism. In what ways did Hugo make it clear that he was describing more than the plight of a single young woman? In what ways was society responsible for the physical and psychological destruction of Fantine? What indictment did Hugo level against the police for these activities?

She had been dismissed towards the end of the winter; the summer passed, but winter came again. Short days, less work. Winter: no warmth, no light, no noonday, the evening joining on to the morning, fogs, twilight; the window is gray; it is impossible to see clearly at it. The sky is but a vent-hole. The whole day is a cavern. The sun has the air of a beggar. A frightful season! Winter changes the water of heaven and the heart of man into a stone. Her creditors harassed her.

Fantine earned too little. Her debts had increased. The Thénardiers, who were not promptly paid, wrote to her constantly letters whose contents drove her to despair, and whose carriage ruined her. One day they wrote to her that her little Cosette [Fantine's illegitimate child] was entirely naked in that cold weather, that she needed a woollen skirt, and that her mother must send at least ten francs for this. She received the letter, and crushed it in her hands all day

* Victor Hugo, "Fantine," in *Les Misérables*, trans. Isabel F. Hapgood (New York: Thomas Y. Crowell and Co., 1887), pp. 173–78, 180–83.

long. That evening she went into a barber's shop at the corner of the street, and pulled out her comb. Her admirable golden hair fell to her knees.

"What splendid hair!" exclaimed the barber.

"How much will you give me for it?" said she.

"Ten francs."

"Cut it off."

She purchased a knitted petticoat and sent it to the Thénardiers. This petticoat made the Thénardiers furious. It was the money that they wanted. They gave the petticoat to Éponine. The poor Lark continued to shiver.

Fantine thought: "My child is no longer cold. I have clothed her with my hair." She put on little round caps which concealed her shorn head, and in which she was still pretty. . . .

She took a lover, the first who offered, a man whom she did not love, out of bravado and with rage in her heart. He was a miserable scamp, a sort of mendicant musician, a lazy beggar, who beat her, and who abandoned her as she had taken him, in disgust.

She adored her child.

The lower she descended, the darker everything grew about her, the more radiant shone that little angel at the bottom of her heart. She said, "When I get rich, I will have my Cosette with me;" and she laughed. Her cough did not leave her, and she had sweats on her back.

One day she received from the Thénardiers a letter couched in the following terms: "Cosette is ill with a malady which is going the rounds of the neighborhood. A miliary fever, they call it. Expensive drugs are required. This is ruining us, and we can no longer pay for them. If you do not send us forty francs before the week is out, the little one will be dead."

She burst out laughing, and said to her old neighbor: "Ah! they are good! Forty francs! the idea! That makes two napoleons! Where do they think I am to get them? These peasants are stupid, truly."

Nevertheless she went to a dormer window in the staircase and read the letter once more. Then she descended the stairs and emerged, running and leaping and still laughing. . . .

As she crossed the square, she saw a great many people collected around a carriage of eccentric shape, upon the top of which stood a man dressed in red, who was holding forth. He was a quack dentist on his rounds, who was offering to the public full sets of teeth, opiates, powders, and elixirs.

Fantine mingled in the group, and began to laugh with the rest at the harangue, which contained slang for the populace and jargon for respectable people. The tooth-puller espied the lovely, laughing girl, and suddenly exclaimed: "You have beautiful teeth, you girl there, who are laughing; if you want to sell me your palettes, I will give you a gold napoleon apiece for them."

"What are my palettes?" asked Fantine.

"The palettes," replied the dental professor, "are the front teeth, the two upper ones."

"How horrible!" exclaimed Fantine.

"Two napoleons!" grumbled a toothless old woman who was present. "Here's a lucky girl!"

Fantine fled and stopped her ears that she might not hear the hoarse voice of the man shouting to her: "Reflect, my beauty! two napoleons; they may prove of service. If your heart bids you, come this evening to the inn of the *Tillac d'Argent;* you will find me there."

Fantine returned home. She was furious, and related the occurrence to her good neighbor Marguerite: "Can you understand such a thing? Is he not an abominable man? How can they allow such people to go about the country! Pull out my two front teeth! Why, I should be horrible! My hair will grow again, but my teeth! Ah! what a monster of a man! I should prefer to throw myself head first on the pavement from the fifth story! He told me that he should be at the *Tillac d'Argent* this evening."

"And what did he offer?" asked Marguerite.

"Two napoleons."

"That makes forty francs."

"Yes," said Fantine; "that makes forty francs."

She remained thoughtful, and began her work. At the expiration of a quarter of an hour she left her sewing and went to read the Thénardiers' letter once more on the staircase.

On her return, she said to Marguerite, who was at work beside her:—

"What is a miliary fever? Do you know?"

"Yes," answered the old spinster; "it is a disease."

"Does it require many drugs?"

"Oh! terrible drugs."

"How does one get it?"

"It is a malady that one gets without knowing how."

"Then it attacks children?"

"Children in particular."

"Do people die of it?"

"They may," said Marguerite.

Fantine left the room and went to read her letter once more on the staircase.

That evening she went out, and was seen to turn her steps in the direction of the Rue de Paris, where the inns are situated.

The next morning, when Marguerite entered Fantine's room before daylight, —for they always worked together, and in this manner used only one candle for the two,—she found Fantine seated on her bed, pale and frozen. She had not lain down. Her cap had fallen on her knees. Her candle had burned all night, and was almost entirely consumed. Marguerite halted on the threshold, petrified at this tremendous wastefulness, and exclaimed:—

"Lord! the candle is all burned out! Something has happened."

Then she looked at Fantine, who turned toward her, her head bereft of its hair.

Fantine had grown ten years older since the preceding night.

"Jesus!" said Marguerite, "what is the matter with you, Fantine?"

"Nothing," replied Fantine. "Quite the contrary. My child will not die of that frightful malady, for lack of succor. I am content."

So saying, she pointed out to the spinster two napoleons which were glittering on the table.

"Ah! Jesus God!" cried Marguerite. "Why, it is a fortune! Where did you get those louis d'or?"

"I got them," replied Fantine.

At the same time she smiled. The candle illuminated her countenance. It was a bloody smile. A reddish saliva soiled the corners of her lips, and she had a black hole in her mouth.

The two teeth had been extracted.

She sent the forty francs to Monfermeuil.

After all it was a ruse of the Thénardiers to obtain money. Cosette was not ill.

Fantine threw her mirror out of the window. She had long since quitted her cell on the second floor for an attic with only a latch to fasten it, next the roof; one of those attics whose extremity forms an angle with the floor, and knocks you on the head every instant. The poor occupant can reach the end of his chamber as he can the end of his destiny, only by bending over more and more.

She had no longer a bed; a rag which she called her coverlet, a mattress on the floor, and a seatless chair still remained. A little rosebush which she had, had dried up, forgotten, in one corner. In the other corner was a butter-pot to hold water, which froze in winter, and in which the various levels of the water remained long marked by these circles of ice. She had lost her shame; she lost her coquetry. A final sign. She went out, with dirty caps. Whether from lack of time or from indifference, she no longer mended her linen. As the heels wore out, she dragged her stockings down into her shoes. This was evident from the perpendicular wrinkles. She patched her bodice which was old and worn out, with scraps of calico which tore at the slightest movement. The people to whom she was indebted made "scenes" and gave her no peace. She found them in the street, she found them again on her staircase. She passed many a night weeping and thinking. Her eyes were very bright, and she felt a steady pain in her shoulder towards the top of the left shoulder-blade. She coughed a great deal. She deeply hated Father Madeleine, but made no complaint. She sewed seventeen hours a day; but a contractor for the work of prisons, who made the prisoners work at a discount, suddenly made prices fall, which reduced the daily earnings of working-women to nine sous. Seventeen hours of toil, and nine sous a day! Her creditors were more pitiless than ever. The second-hand dealer, who had taken back nearly all his furniture, said to her incessantly "When will you pay me, you hussy?" What did they want of her, good God! She felt that she was being hunted, and something of the wild beast developed in her. About the same time, Thénardier wrote to her that he had waited with decidedly too much amiability and that he must have a hundred francs at once; otherwise he would turn little Cosette out of doors, convalescent as she was from her heavy illness, into the cold and the streets, and that she might do what she liked with herself, and die if she chose. "A hundred francs," thought Fantine. "But in what trade can one earn a hundred sous a day?"

"Come!" said she, "let us sell what is left."

The unfortunate girl became a woman of the town.

What is this history of Fantine? It is society purchasing a slave.

From whom? From misery.

From hunger, cold, isolation, destitution. A dolorous bargain. A soul for a morsel of bread. Misery offers; society accepts.

The sacred law of Jesus Christ governs our civilization, but it does not, as yet, permeate it; it is said that slavery has disappeared from European civilization. This is a mistake. It still exists; but it weighs only upon the woman, and it is called prostitution.

It weighs upon the woman, that is to say, upon grace, weakness, beauty, maternity. This is not one of the least of man's disgraces.

At the point in this melancholy drama which we have now reached, nothing is left to Fantine of that which she had formerly been.

She has become marble in becoming mire. Whoever touches her feels cold. She passes; she endures you; she ignores you; she is the severe and dishonored figure. Life and the social order have said their last word for her. All has happened to her that will happen to her. She has felt everything, borne everything, experienced everything, suffered everything, lost everything, mourned everything. She is resigned, with that resignation which resembles indifference, as death resembles sleep. She no longer avoids anything. Let all the clouds fall upon her, and all the ocean sweep over her! What matters it to her? She is a sponge that is soaked. . . .

It was the period of the conflict of the republics of South America with the king of Spain, of Bolivar against Morillo. Narrow-brimmed hats were royalist, and were called *morillos;* liberals wore hats with wide brims, which were called *bolivars.*

Eight or ten months, then, after that which is related in the preceding pages, towards the first of January, 1823, on a snowy evening, one of these dandies, one of these unemployed, a "right thinker," for he wore a morillo, and was, moreover, warmly enveloped in one of those large cloaks which completed the fashionable costume in cold weather, was amusing himself by tormenting a creature who was prowling about in a ball-dress, with neck uncovered and flowers in her hair, in front of the officers' café. This dandy was smoking, for he was decidedly fashionable.

Each time that the woman passed in front of him, he bestowed on her, together with a puff from his cigar, some apostrophe which he considered witty and mirthful, such as, "How ugly you are!—Will you get out of my sight?— You have no teeth!" etc., etc. This gentleman was known as M. Bamatabois. The woman, a melancholy, decorated spectre which went and came through the snow, made him no reply, did not even glance at him, and nevertheless continued her promenade in silence, and with a sombre regularity, which brought her every five minutes within reach of this sarcasm, like the condemned soldier who returns under the rods. The small effect which he produced no doubt piqued the lounger; and taking advantage of a moment when her back was turned, he crept up behind her with the gait of a wolf, and stifling his laugh, bent down, picked up a handful of snow from the pavement, and thrust it abruptly into her back, between her bare shoulders. The woman uttered a roar, whirled round, gave a leap like a panther, and hurled herself upon the man, burying her nails in his face, with the most frightful words which could fall from the guard-room into the gutter. These insults, poured forth in a voice roughened by brandy, did, indeed, proceed in hideous wise from a mouth which lacked its two front teeth. It was Fantine.

At the noise thus produced, the officers ran out in throngs from the café, passers-by collected, and a large and merry circle, hooting and applauding, was formed around this whirlwind composed of two beings, whom there was some difficulty in recognizing as a man and a woman: the man struggling, his hat on the ground; the woman striking out with feet and fists, bareheaded, howling, minus hair and teeth, livid with wrath, horrible.

Suddenly a man of lofty stature emerged vivaciously from the crowd, seized the woman by her satin bodice, which was covered with mud, and said to her, "Follow me!"

The woman raised her head; her furious voice suddenly died away. Her eyes were glassy; she turned pale instead of livid, and she trembled with a quiver of terror. She had recognized Javert.

The dandy took advantage of the incident to make his escape.

Javert thrust aside the spectators, broke the circle, and set out with long strides towards the police station, which is situated at the extremity of the square, dragging the wretched woman after him. She yielded mechanically. Neither he nor she uttered a word. The cloud of spectators followed, jesting, in a paroxysm of delight. Supreme misery an occasion for obscenity.

On arriving at the police station, which was a low room, warmed by a stove, with a glazed and grated door opening on the street, and guarded by a detachment, Javert opened the door, entered with Fantine, and shut the door behind him, to the great disappointment of the curious, who raised themselves on tiptoe, and craned their necks in front of the thick glass of the station-house, in their effort to see. Curiosity is a sort of gluttony. To see is to devour.

On entering, Fantine fell down in a corner, motionless and mute, crouching down like a terrified dog.

The sergeant of the guard brought a lighted candle to the table. Javert seated himself, drew a sheet of stamped paper from his pocket, and began to write.

This class of women is consigned by our laws entirely to the discretion of the police. The latter do what they please, punish them, as seems good to them, and confiscate at their will those two sorry things which they entitle their industry and their liberty. Javert was impassive; his grave face betrayed no emotion whatever. Nevertheless, he was seriously and deeply preoccupied. It was one of those moments when he was exercising without control, but subject to all the scruples of a severe conscience, his redoubtable discretionary power. At that moment he was conscious that his police agent's stool was a tribunal. He was entering judgment. He judged and condemned. He summoned all the ideas which could possibly exist in his mind, around the great thing which he was doing. The more he examined the deed of this woman, the more shocked he felt. It was evident that he had just witnessed the commission of a crime. He had just beheld, yonder, in the street, society, in the person of a freeholder and an elector, insulted and attacked by a creature who was outside all pales. A prostitute had made an attempt on the life of a citizen. He had seen that, he, Javert. He wrote in silence.

When he had finished he signed the paper, folded it, and said to the sergeant of the guard, as he handed it to him, "Take three men and conduct this creature to jail."

Then, turning to Fantine, "You are to have six months of it." The unhappy woman shuddered.

"Six months! six months of prison!" she exclaimed. "Six months in which to earn seven sous a day! But what will become of Cosette? My daughter! my daughter! But I still owe the Thénardiers over a hundred francs; do you know that, Monsieur Inspector?"

She dragged herself across the damp floor, among the muddy boots of all those men, without rising, with clasped hands, and taking great strides on her knees.

"Monsieur Javert," said she, "I beseech your mercy. I assure you that I was not in the wrong. If you had seen the beginning, you would have seen. I swear to you by the good God that I was not to blame! That gentleman, the bourgeois, whom I do not know, put snow in my back. Has any one the right to put snow down our backs when we are walking along peaceably, and doing no harm to any one? I am rather ill, as you see. And then, he had been saying impertinent things to me for a long time: 'You are ugly! you have no teeth!' I know well that I have no longer those teeth. I did nothing; I said to myself, 'The gentleman is amusing himself.' I was honest with him; I did not speak to him. It was at that moment that he put the snow down my back. Monsieur Javert, good Monsieur Inspector! is there not some person here who saw it and can tell you that this is quite true? Perhaps I did wrong to get angry. You know that one is not master of one's self at the first moment. One gives way to vivacity; and then, when some one puts something cold down your back just when you are not expecting it! I did wrong to spoil that gentleman's hat. Why did he go away? I would ask his pardon. Oh, my God! It makes no difference to me whether I ask his pardon. Do me the favor to-day, for this once, Monsieur Javert. Hold! you do not know that in prison one can earn only seven sous a day; it is not the government's fault, but seven sous is one's earnings; and just fancy, I must pay one hundred francs, or my little girl will be sent to me. Oh, my God! I cannot have her with me. What I do is so vile! Oh, my Cosette! Oh, my little angel of the Holy Virgin! what will become of her, poor creature? I will tell you: it is the Thénardiers, inn-keepers, peasants; and such people are unreasonable. They want money. Don't put me in prison! You see, there is a little girl who will be turned out into the street, to get along as best she may, in the very heart of the winter, and you must have pity on such a being, my good Monsieur Javert. If she were older, she might earn her living; but it cannot be done at that age. I am not a bad woman at bottom. It is not cowardliness and gluttony that have made me what I am. If I have drunk brandy, it was out of misery. I do not love it; but it benumbs the senses. When I was happy, it was only necessary to glance into my closets, and it would have been evident that I was not a coquettish and untidy woman. I had linen, a great deal of linen. Have pity on me, Monsieur Javert!"

She spoke thus, rent in twain, shaken with sobs, blinded with tears, her neck bare, wringing her hands, and coughing with a dry, short cough, stammering softly with a voice of agony. Great sorrow is a divine and terrible ray, which transfigures the unhappy. At that moment Fantine had become beautiful once more. From time to time she paused, and tenderly kissed the police agent's coat. She would have softened a heart of granite; but a heart of wood cannot be softened.

"Come!" said Javert, "I have heard you out. Have you entirely finished? You will get six months. Now march! The Eternal Father in person could do nothing more."

At these solemn words, *"the Eternal Father in person could do nothing more,"* she understood that her fate was sealed. She sank down, murmuring, "Mercy!"

Javert turned his back.

The soldiers seized her by the arms.

UTOPIAN AND SCIENTIFIC SOCIALISM

10. HENRI DE SAINT-SIMON: ON THE IMPLICATIONS OF INDUSTRIALIZATION*

Claude Henri Comte de Saint-Simon (1760–1825), the so-called father of Utopian Socialism, was a social philosopher who urged industrial leaders and scientists to pool their resources in reorganizing society for the purpose of improving the living conditions of even the poorest classes. In 1790 Saint-Simon renounced his title of nobility and supported the French Revolution. After the Revolution had run its course, he spent the rest of his life spreading his gospel of social improvement and attempting to persuade the restored French monarchy to accept his ideas. The following excerpts have been translated from two of Saint-Simon's major works: *Système industriel* (1821) and *Catéchisme des industriels* (1823). Who, in Saint-Simon's view, were the parasitic classes, and what group should replace them? What was his definition of an industrialist? How did Saint-Simon's economic views compare with the doctrines of the Physiocrats and Adam Smith?

AGAINST THE PARASITES

The existing political struggle since the revolution has only now assumed its true character; it is the fundamental cause of all troubles which disturb kings and peoples. Up to the present the struggle has been illegitimate, for it existed essentially only among the idle rich and parasitic classes of society. It had no other object than to determine whether abusive exploitation should continue to belong by privilege to the gentry and priesthood, or whether such privileges should be extended by equal legal rights to the military caste and to lawyers and do-nothing propertied groups who are not a part of the nobility. The great body of the nation, that is to say the producers, have not yet taken any direct and definite part in the debates. It has remained outside of the struggle, or at least it has entered only in auxiliary fashion summoned by ineffective leaders. Such is the true state of things not only in France, but in Italy and generally throughout all western Europe.

This false and illegitimate situation clearly cannot endure. The producers attach no more importance to being pillaged by one parasitic class than another. It is clear that the final struggle for existence between the entire parasitic class on the one hand and the mass of producers on the other will determine whether the producers will continue to be the prey of the ruling class, or whether the

* *L'Oeuvre d'Henri de Saint-Simon, Textes choisies* (Paris: Libraire Félix Alcan, 1925), pp. 149–59. Translated by the editors.

producers will be able to obtain control of a society of which today they compose the essential part. This question will be resolved as soon as it is posed in a direct and clear manner accompanied by the immense superiority of the producing class over the non-producers.

The point at which the struggle must assume its true character has actually arrived. The cause of the producers cannot be postponed or thwarted. And even among some whom birth has placed in the parasitic class there are those who have committed themselves in soul and spirit to the burgeoning sentiment for improvement that is the only honorable course of action, which they today judge to consist of employing all means to encourage producers to enter the political arena. They seek to aid the workers in gaining a position in general affairs—a position consistent with the preponderance they have achieved in society.

WHAT WILL HAPPEN

What is fundamental to you? What do you most want to know? What I propose to teach you is *what will happen*. Very well, gentlemen, I am going to explain myself in the most categorical manner. I am going to tell you what will come to pass and what course it will take. I am going to pose successively the three questions which I have just enunciated; I shall answer separately each one of the questions and at the conclusion of each answer I shall add the reasons upon which I base my opinions.

The first question: What are the principal political changes which will be accomplished during the fourth Christian era? My response: I believe that during this fourth era there will be an organized spiritual authority and a new temporal authority.

I believe that the new spiritual authority will be composed, in its origin, of all the academies of sciences existing in Europe and of all the persons who merit admission into these scientific bodies. I believe that this nucleus, once formed, will manage its own internal organization. I believe that the direction of education as well as the direction of public instruction will be entrusted to a new spiritual élite. I believe that the simple purity of holy scripture will serve as the basis for the new public instruction and that the new morality will be dispersed as widely as possible. . . . Finally, I believe that the new spiritual élite will settle a more or less large number of its members in every community, and that these detached intellectuals will have as their primary function the task of inspiring their spiritual charges with passion for the public good.

I believe that in each European nation the administration of temporal affairs will be relegated to businessmen of peaceful occupations who will supervise the large majority of people. I am convinced that this administration, as a consequence of the leaders' natural interests, will make its first concern the keeping of peace between nations, and then the reduction as much as possible of tariffs, with the aim of gaining from such a system the products most essential to community needs. Here are the reasons on which I base this opinion:

1. The new basis of social organization, conforming directly to the interests of the large majority of the population, must be considered as a general political consequence emanating from the principle of divine ethics. All men must look upon one another as brothers; they must love one another and help one another.

Thus in the present state of civilized human beings God evidently wills that Christian society be constituted in such a fashion.

2. Speaking in human terms, and without placing ourselves beyond the bounds of scientific methods, the construction of a Christian society is the natural end and the immediate result of the destruction of slavery, as well as the superiority of the science of observation over theology and over other branches of metaphysics.

3. While limiting ourselves to political considerations, it is evident that the progress of civilization will bring about this result; for the positive forces of today, intellectual as well as material, reside in the hands of those who practice the sciences of observation and those who undertake and direct industrial pursuits. It is only through ancient habits and customs that society bares the yoke of nobles and theologians. History has proved that society has always rid itself of acquired customs whenever such customs became detrimental to its interests, and found new methods for satisfying its needs. It is therefore beyond all doubt that the institutions of clergy and nobility will be abandoned by society. It is also beyond doubt that the political power will pass into the hands of those who already possess nearly the sum total of all social forces. . . .

THE INDUSTRIALISTS' CATECHISM

QUESTION: What is an industrialist?

ANSWER: An industrialist is a man who works to produce or to put at the disposal of different members of society one or several material means which can satisfy their needs or their physical appetites. Thus, a farmer who sows wheat, who raises poultry or stock animals, is an industrialist; a wheelwright, a blacksmith, a locksmith, all are industrialists; a cobbler, a hatter, a linen maker, a draper, a sweater maker, each is equally an industrialist; a merchant, a printer, a sailor employed on merchant ships, are industrialists. All industrialists work in unity to produce and to provide for the members of society all the material means to satisfy their needs and physical tastes, and they constitute three great classes which are known as cultivators, manufacturers, and merchants.

QUESTION: What rank must these industrialists occupy in society?

ANSWER: The industrial class must occupy the first ranks in society because they are most important of all, because they can surpass all of the others and because no other one can surpass them, because they subsist through proper functions by their personal toil. The other classes should work for the industrial class, for it is that class which has created the means by which the others maintain their existence. In a word, everything is done by industry; everything must be done for it.

QUESTION: What rank does the industrial class currently hold in society?

ANSWER: The industrial class actually constitutes the lowest class in the present social order. The social organization presently accords greater considerations to the secondary workers, even to the idle, than to workers who perform the most useful functions.

QUESTION: Why does the industrial class, which should occupy the first position, find itself placed at the bottom? Why are those who constitute, in fact, the first actually in the position of the last?

ANSWER: We shall explain such an anomaly in the following discussion of this catechism.

QUESTION: What must the industrial class do in order to move from the lower position in which they have been placed to the superior one which they should occupy?

ANSWER: We will explain in the catechism the manner in which that class must conduct itself in order to bring improvement to its social status.

QUESTION: Then what is the nature of the task you must undertake? In a word, what are the purposes of the catechism?

ANSWER: We propose to indicate to the industrialists the means to render possible their well-being. We propose to teach them the general procedures which they should employ in order to realize their social importance.

QUESTION: What means must be employed to attain such an objective?

ANSWER: In the first place we will give to the industrialists a clear outline of their true social situation. We will make them see that it is a situation entirely substandard, and as a consequence very inferior to what it should be, even though they are the most capable and useful class in society. On the other hand, we will even trace for them the course which they must follow in order to bring themselves to the first rank in society. . . .

QUESTION: You will preach, then, in the catechism, insurrection and revolt, because the classes which are currently invested with authority and special consideration will not renounce voluntarily the advantages which they enjoy?

ANSWER: Rather than preaching insurrection and revolution, we will present the only means of preventing the acts of violence which will menace society and from which it can not escape so long as the industrial authority continues to remain passive amid the factions which compete for power. The public tranquility can not remain stable as long as the most important industrialists are not charged with direction and administration of public property.

QUESTION: Explain and tell us why the public tranquility will be disturbed if the leaders of the industrialist class do not gain control of public property.

ANSWER: The reason is very simple. The general inclination of the immense majority of society is to be governed under the best possible consensus, to be governed as little as possible, to be governed by the most capable and talented men who guarantee complete public tranquility. The only means of satisfying, under these circumstances, the desires of the majority is to place the public fortunes under the direction of the industrialists, for it is the industrialists who are the most interested in maintaining the public order. They are the ones interested in maintaining public peace; they are the ones interested in economizing in public expenditures; they are, moreover, the ones most interested in limiting arbitrary authority. Finally, they are, of all the members of society, the ones who have proved to exhibit the greatest capacity for positive administration through the achievements in their own special fields of enterprise and special skills. . . .

11. ROBERT OWEN: ON SOCIETY AND PRODUCTION*

Utopian Socialism is most often connected with the name of the self-made British businessman, Robert Owen (1771–1858). As a young man, Owen criticized English industrial management which did not consider the health and happiness of factory workers, and he sought to develop a proposal for the elimination of the evils of industrialism. After he had taken charge of a large cotton-mill complex at New Lanark, Scotland, Owen launched an experimental program to ameliorate the general state of his employees. Healthier working conditions were introduced along with shorter hours, better pay, cleaner housing, and practical education for workers' children. Owen's ideas carried the impress of John Locke and Jean Jacques Rousseau. He believed that the general ailments of industrial society could be cured through education and that the gloomy prophecies of Thomas Malthus could be thwarted. Despite the success of his own philanthropic and paternalistic experiment at New Lanark, other businessmen failed to follow Owen's lead. But he never relented in enthusiasm; he not only devoted considerable efforts to writing and speaking in behalf of his theories but also attempted to organize a national union of all British laborers.

The following selection expresses Owen's philosophic reflections on mankind in general and contains some of his specific recommendations for economic planning. What role did Owen assign to environment in man's development, and in what ways was that role central to Owen's thesis on progress and reform? What type of legislation would be required to implement Owen's proposals for land ownership and use? To what extent would such legislation have changed contemporary English social structures?

Those who have duly reflected on the nature and extent of the mental movements of the world for the last half-century, must be conscious that great changes are in progress; that man is about to advance another important step towards that degree of intelligence which his natural powers seem capable of attaining. Observe the transactions of the passing hours; see the whole mass of mind in full motion; behold it momentarily increasing in vigour, and preparing ere long to burst its confinement. But what is to be the nature of this change? A due attention to the facts around us, and to those transmitted by the invention of printing from former ages, will afford a satisfactory reply.

From the earliest ages it has been the practice of the world to act on the supposition that each individual man forms his own character, and that therefore he is accountable for all his sentiments and habits, and consequently merits reward for some and punishment for others. Every system which has been established among men has been founded on these erroneous principles. When, however, they shall be brought to the test of fair examination, they will be found not only unsupported, but in direct opposition to all experience, and to the evidence of our senses.

This is not a slight mistake, which involves only trivial consequences; it is a fundamental error of the highest possible magnitude; it enters into all our proceedings regarding man from his infancy; and it will be found to be the true

* Robert Owen, *A New View of Society and Other Writings*, ed. Ernest Rhys (London: J. M. Dent and Sons, Ltd., 1927), pp. 44–46, 266–68. Reprinted by permission of J. M. Dent and Sons, Ltd., and E. P. Dutton, Inc.

and sole origin of evil. It generates and perpetuates ignorance, hatred, and revenge, where, without such error, only intelligence, confidence, and kindness would exist. It has hitherto been the Evil Genius of the world. It severs man from man throughout the various regions of the earth; and makes enemies of those who, but for this gross error, would have enjoyed each other's kind offices and sincere friendship. It is, in short, an error which carries misery in all its consequences.

This error cannot much longer exist; for every day will make it more and more evident that the character of man is, without a single exception, always formed for him; that it may be, and is, chiefly, created by his predecessors; that they gave him, or may give him, his ideas and habits, which are the powers that govern and direct his conduct. Man, therefore, never did, nor is it possible he ever can, form his own character.

The knowledge of this important fact has not been derived from any of the wild and heated speculations of an ardent and ungoverned imagination; on the contrary, it proceeds from a long and patient study of the theory and practice of human nature, under many varied circumstances; it will be found to be a deduction drawn from such a multiplicity of facts, as to afford the most complete demonstration.

Had not mankind been misintructed from infancy on this subject, making it necessary that they should unlearn what they have been taught, the simple statement of this truth would render it instantly obvious to every rational mind. Men would know that their predecessors might have given them the habits of ferocious cannibalism, or of the highest known benevolence and intelligence; and by the acquirement of this knowledge they would soon learn that, as parents, preceptors, and legislators united, they possess the means of training the rising generations to either of those extremes; that they may with the greatest certainty make them the conscientious worshippers of Juggernaut, or of the most pure spirit, possessing the essence of every excellence which the human imagination can concieve; that they may train the young to become effeminate, deceitful, ignorantly selfish, intemperate, revengeful, murderous,—of course ignorant, irrational, and miserable; or to be manly, just, generous, temperate, active, kind, and benevolent,—that is, intelligent, rational, and happy. The knowledge of these principles having been derived from facts which perpetually exist, they defy ingenuity itself to confute them; nay, the most severe scrutiny will make it evident that they are utterly unassailable. . . .

REPORT TO LANARK

Recommending, then, from 300 to 2,000, according to the localities of the farm or village, as the number of persons who should compose the associations for the new system of spade husbandry, we now proceed to consider— . . . the extent of land to be cultivated by such association.

This will depend upon the quality of the soil and other local considerations. Great Britain and Ireland, however, do not possess a population nearly sufficient to cultivate our best soils in the most advantageous manner. It would therefore be nationally impolitic to place these associations upon inferior lands, which, in consequence, may be dismissed from present consideration.

II. It is high time that Communists should openly, in the face of the whole world, publish their views, their aims, their tendencies, and meet this nursery tale of the spectre of communism with a manifesto of the party itself.

To this end, Communists of various nationalities have assembled in London, and sketched the following manifesto, to be published in the English, French, German, Italian, Flemish and Danish languages.

BOURGEOIS AND PROLETARIANS

The history of all hitherto existing society is the history of class struggles.

Freeman and slave, patrician and plebeian, lord and serf, guild-master and journeyman, in a word, oppressor and oppressed stood in constant opposition to one another, carried on an uninterrupted, now hidden, now open fight, a fight that each time ended, either in a revolutionary reconstitution of society at large, or in the common ruin of the contending classes.

In the earlier epochs of history, we find almost everywhere a complicated arrangement of society into various orders, a manifold gradation of social rank. In ancient Rome we have patricians, knights, plebeians, slaves; in the Middle Ages, feudal lords, vassals, guild-masters, journeymen, apprentices, serfs; in almost all of these classes, again, subordinate gradations.

The modern bourgeois society that has sprouted from the ruins of feudal society has not done away with class antagonisms. It has but established new classes, new conditions of oppression, new forms of struggle in place of the old ones.

Our epoch, the epoch of the bourgeoisie, possesses, however, this distinctive feature: It has simplified the class antagonisms. Society as a whole is more and more splitting up into two great hostile camps, into two great classes directly facing each other—bourgeoisie and proletariat.

From the serfs of the Middle Ages sprang the chartered burghers of the earliest towns. From these burgesses the first elements of the bourgeoisie were developed.

The discovery of America, the rounding of the Cape, opened up fresh ground for the rising bourgeoisie. The East-Indian and Chinese markets, the colonisation of America, trade with the colonies, the increase in the means of exchange and in commodities generally, gave to commerce, to navigation, to industry, an impulse never before known, and thereby, to the revolutionary element in the tottering feudal society, a rapid development.

The feudal system of industry, in which industrial production was monopolised by closed guilds, now no longer sufficed for the growing wants of the new markets. The manufacturing system took its place. The guild-masters were pushed aside by the manufacturing middle class; division of labour between the different corporate guilds vanished in the face of division of labour in each single workshop.

Meantime the markets kept ever growing, the demand ever rising. Even manufacture no longer sufficed. Thereupon, steam and machinery revolutionised industrial production. The place of manufacture was taken by the giant, modern industry, the place of the industrial middle class by industrial millionaires, the leaders of whole industrial armies, the modern bourgeois.

Modern industry has established the world market, for which the discovery of America paved the way. This market has given an immense development to commerce, to navigation, to communication by land. This development has, in its turn, reacted on the extension of industry; and in proportion as industry, commerce, navigation, railways extended; in the same proportion the bourgeoisie developed, increased its capital, and pushed into the background every class handed down from the Middle Ages.

We see, therefore, how the modern bourgeoisie is itself the product of a long course of development, of a series of revolutions in the modes of production and of exchange.

Each step in the development of the bourgeoisie was accompanied by a corresponding political advance of that class. An oppressed class under the sway of the feudal nobility, an armed and self-governing association in the mediæval commune; here independent urban republic (as in Italy and Germany), there taxable "third estate" of the monarchy (as in France); afterwards, in the period of manufacture proper, serving either the semi-feudal or the absolute monarchy as a counterpoise against the nobility, and, in fact, corner-stone of the great monarchies in general—the bourgeoisie has at last, since the establishment of modern industry and of the world market, conquered for itself, in the modern representative state, exclusive political sway. The executive of the modern state is but a committee for managing the common affairs of the whole bourgeoisie.

The bourgeoisie, historically, has played a most revolutionary part.

The bourgeoisie, wherever it has got the upper hand, has put an end to all feudal, patriarchal, idyllic relations. It has pitilessly torn asunder the motley feudal ties that bound man to his "natural superiors," and has left no other nexus between man and man than naked self-interest, than callous "cash payment." It has drowned the most heavenly ecstasies of religious fervour, of chivalrous enthusiasm, of philistine sentimentalism, in the icy water of egotistical calculation. It has resolved personal worth into exchange value, and in place of the numberless indefeasible chartered freedoms, has set up that single, unconscionable freedom—Free Trade. In one word, for exploitation, veiled by religious and political illusions, it has substituted naked, shameless, direct, brutal exploitation.

The bourgeoisie has stripped of its halo every occupation hitherto honoured and looked up to with reverent awe. It has converted the physician, the lawyer, the priest, the poet, the man of science, into its paid wage labourers.

The bourgeoisie has torn away from the family its sentimental veil, and has reduced the family relation to a mere money relation.

The bourgeoisie has disclosed how it came to pass that the brutal display of vigour in the Middle Ages, which reactionaries so much admire, found its fitting complement in the most slothful indolence. It has been the first to show what man's activity can bring about. It has accomplished wonders far surpassing Egyptian pyramids, Roman aqueducts, and Gothic cathedrals; it has conducted expeditions that put in the shade all former exoduses of nations and crusades.

The bourgeoisie cannot exist without constantly revolutionising the instruments of production, and thereby the relations of production, and with them the whole relations of society. Conservation of the old modes of production in unaltered form, was, on the contrary, the first condition of existence for all earlier industrial classes. Constant revolutionising of production, uninterrupted disturbance of all social conditions, everlasting uncertainty and agitation distinguish the bourgeois epoch from all earlier ones. All fixed, fast frozen relations, with their train of ancient and venerable prejudices and opinions, are swept away, all new-formed ones become antiquated before they can ossify. All that is solid melts into air, all that is holy is profaned, and man is at last compelled to face with sober senses his real conditions of life and his relations with his kind.

The need of a constantly expanding market for its products chases the bourgeoisie over the whole surface of the globe. It must nestle everywhere, settle everywhere, establish connections everywhere.

The bourgeoisie has through its exploitation of the world market given a cosmopolitan character to production and consumption in every country. To the great chagrin of reactionaries, it has drawn from under the feet of industry the national ground on which it stood. All old-established national industries have been destroyed or are daily being destroyed. They are dislodged by new industries, whose introduction becomes a life and death question for all civilised nations, by industries that no longer work up indigenous raw material, but raw material drawn from the remotest zones; industries whose products are consumed, not only at home, but in every quarter of the globe. In place of the old wants, satisfied by the production of the country, we find new wants, requiring for their satisfaction the products of distant lands and climes. In place of the old local and national seclusion and self-sufficiency, we have intercourse in every direction, universal inter-dependence of nations. And as in material, so also in intellectual production. The intellectual creations of individual nations become common property. National one-sidedness and narrow-mindedness become more and more impossible, and from the numerous national and local literatures there arises a world literature.

The bourgeoisie, by the rapid improvement of all instruments of production, by the immensely facilitated means of communication, draws all, even the most barbarian, nations into civilisation. The cheap prices of its commodities are the heavy artillery with which it batters down all Chinese walls, with which it forces the barbarians' intensely obstinate hatred of foreigners to capitulate. It compels all nations, on pain of extinction, to adopt the bourgeois mode of production; it compels them to introduce what it calls civilisation into their midst, i.e., to become bourgeois themselves. In one word, it creates a world after its own image.

The bourgeois has subjected the country to the rule of the towns. It has created enormous cities, has greatly increased the urban population as compared with the rural, and has thus rescued a considerable part of the population from the idiocy of rural life. Just as it has made the country dependent on the towns, so it has made barbarian and semi-barbarian countries dependent on the civilised ones, nations of peasants on nations of bourgeois, the East on the West.

The bourgeoisie keeps more and more doing away with the scattered state of the population, of the means of production, and of property. It has agglomerated population, centralised means of production, and has concentrated property in a few hands. The necessary consequence of this was political centralisation. Independent, or but loosely connected provinces, with separate interests, laws, governments and systems of taxation, became lumped together into one nation, with one government, one code of laws, one national class interest, one frontier and one customs tariff.

The bourgeoisie, during its rule of scarce one hundred years, has created more massive and more colossal productive forces than have all preceding generations together. Subjection of nature's forces to man, machinery, application of chemistry to industry and agriculture, steam navigation, railways, electric telegraphs, clearing of whole continents for cultivation, canalisation of rivers, whole populations conjured out of the ground—what earlier century had even a presentiment that such productive forces slumbered in the lap of social labour? . . .

A similar movement is going on before our own eyes. Modern bourgeois society with its relations of production, of exchange and of property, a society that has conjured up such gigantic means of production and of exchange, is like the sorcerer who is no longer able to control the powers of the nether world whom he has called up by his spells. For many a decade past the history of industry and commerce is but the history of the revolt of modern productive forces against modern conditions of production, against the property relations that are the conditions for the existence of the bourgeoisie and of its rule. It is enough to mention the commercial crises that by their periodical return put the existence of the entire bourgeois society on its trial, each time more threateningly. In these crises a great part not only of the existing products, but also of the previously created productive forces, are periodically destroyed. In these crises there breaks out an epidemic that, in all earlier epochs, would have seemed an absurdity—the epidemic of over-production. Society suddenly finds itself put back into a state of momentary barbarism; it appears as if a famine, a universal war of devastation had cut off the supply of every means of subsistence; industry and commerce seem to be destroyed. And why? Because there is too much civilisation, too much means of subsistence, too much industry, too much commerce. The productive forces at the disposal of society no longer tend to further the development of the conditions of bourgeois property; on the contrary, they have become too powerful for these conditions, by which they are fettered, and so soon as they overcome these fetters, they bring disorder into the whole of bourgeois society, endanger the existence of bourgeois property. The conditions of bourgeois society are too narrow to comprise the wealth created by them. And how does the bourgeoisie get over these crises? On the one hand, by enforced destruction of a mass of productive forces; on the other, by the conquest of new markets, and by the more thorough exploitation of the old ones. That is to say, by paving the way for more extensive and more destructive crises, and by diminishing the means whereby crises are prevented.

The weapons with which the bourgeoisie felled feudalism to the ground are now turned against the bourgeoisie itself.

But not only has the bourgeoisie forged the weapons that bring death to itself; it has also called into existence the men who are to wield those weapons—the modern working class—the proletarians.

In proportion as the bourgeoisie, *i. e.,* capital, is developed, in the same proportion is the proletariat, the modern working class, developed—a class of labourers, who live only so long as they find work, and who find work only so long as their labour increases capital. These labourers, who must sell themselves piecemeal, are a commodity, like every other article of commerce, and are consequently exposed to all the vicissitudes of competition, to all the fluctuations of the market.

Owing to the extensive use of machinery and to division of labour, the work of the proletarians has lost all individual character, and, consequently, all charm for the workman. He becomes an appendage of the machine, and it is only the most simple, most monotonous, and most easily acquired knack, that is required of him. Hence, the cost of production of a workman is restricted, almost entirely, to the means of subsistence that he requires for his maintenance, and for the propagation of his race. But the price of a commodity, and therefore also of labour, is equal to its cost of production. In proportion, therefore, as the repulsiveness of the work increases, the wage decreases. Nay more, in proportion as the use of machinery and division of labour increases, in the same proportion the burden of toil also increases, whether by prolongation of the working hours, by increase of the work exacted in a given time, or by increased speed of the machinery, etc.

Modern industry has converted the little workshop of the patriarchal master into the great factory of the industrial capitalist. Masses of labourers, crowded into the factory, are organised like soldiers. As privates of the industrial army they are placed under the command of a perfect hierarchy of officers and sergeants. Not only are they slaves of the bourgeois class, and of the bourgeois state; they are daily and hourly enslaved by the machine, by the overlooker, and, above all, by the individual bourgeois manufacturer himself. The more openly this despotism proclaims gain to be its end and aim, the more petty, the more hateful and the more embittering it is.

The less the skill and exertion of strength implied in manual labour, in other words, the more modern industry becomes developed, the more is the labour of men superseded by that of women. Differences of age and sex have no longer any distinctive social validity for the working class. All are instruments of labour, more or less expensive to use, according to their age and sex.

No sooner is the exploitation of the labourer by the manufacturer, so far at an end, that he receives his wages in cash, than he is set upon by the other portions of the bourgeoisie, the landlord, the shopkeeper, the pawnbroker, etc.

The lower strata of the middle class—the small tradespeople, shopkeepers, and retired tradesmen generally, the handicraftsmen and peasants—all these sink gradually into the proletariat, partly because their diminutive capital does not suffice for the scale on which modern industry is carried on, and is swamped in the competition with the large capitalists, partly because their specialised skill is rendered worthless by new methods of production. Thus the proletariat is recruited from all classes of the population.

The proletariat goes through various stages of development. With its birth begins its struggle with the bourgeoisie. At first the contest is carried on by individual labourers, then by the work people of a factory, then by the operatives of one trade, in one locality, against the individual bourgeois who directly exploits them. They direct their attacks not against the bourgeois conditions of production, but against the instruments of production themselves; they destroy imported wares that compete with their labour, they smash to pieces machinery, they set factories ablaze, they seek to restore by force the vanished status of the workman of the Middle Ages.

At this stage the labourers still form an incoherent mass scattered over the whole country, and broken up by their mutual competition. If anywhere they unite to form more compact bodies, this is not yet the consequence of their own active union, but of the union of the bourgeoisie, which class, in order to attain its own political ends, is compelled to set the whole proletariat in motion, and is moreover yet, for a time, able to do so. At this stage, therefore, the proletarians do not fight their enemies, but the enemies of their enemies, the remnants of absolute monarchy, the landowners, the non-industrial bourgeois, the petty bourgeoisie. Thus the whole historical movement is concentrated in the hands of the bourgeoisie; every victory so obtained is a victory for the bourgeoisie.

But with the development of industry the proletariat not only increases in number; it becomes concentrated in greater masses, its strength grows, and it feels that strength more. The various interests and conditions of life within the ranks of the proletariat are more and more equalised, in proportion as machinery obliterates all distinctions of labour, and nearly everywhere reduces wages to the same low level. The growing competition among the bourgeois, and the resulting commercial crises, make the wages of the workers ever more fluctuating. The unceasing improvement of machinery, ever more rapidly developing, makes their livelihood more and more precarious; the collisions between individual workmen and individual bourgeois take more and more the character of collisions between two classes. Thereupon the workers begin to form combinations (trades unions) against the bourgeois; they club together in order to keep up the rate of wages; they found permanent associations in order to make provision beforehand for these occasional revolts. Here and there the contest breaks out into riots.

Now and then the workers are victorious, but only for a time. The real fruit of their battles lies, not in the immediate result, but in the ever expanding union of the workers. This union is helped on by the improved means of communication that are created by modern industry, and that places the workers of different localities in contact with one another. It was just this contact that was needed to centralise the numerous local struggles, all of the same character, into one national struggle between classes. But every class struggle is a political struggle. And that union, to attain which the burghers of the Middle Ages, with their miserable highways, required centuries, the modern proletarians, thanks to railways, achieve in a few years.

This organisation of the proletarians into a class, and consequently into a political party, is continually being upset again by the competition between the workers themselves. But it ever rises up again, stronger, firmer, mightier. It compels legislative recognition of particular interests of the workers, by taking advantage of the divisions among the bourgeoisie itself. Thus the ten-hours' bill in England was carried. . . .

Finally, in times when the class struggle nears the decisive hour, the process of dissolution going on within the ruling class, in fact within the whole range of old society, assumes such a violent, glaring character, that a small section of the ruling class cuts itself adrift, and joins the revolutionary class, the class that holds the future in its hands. Just as, therefore, at an earlier period, a section of the nobility went over to the bourgeoisie, so now a portion of the bourgeoisie goes over to the proletariat, and in particular, a portion of the bourgeois ideologists, who have raised themselves to the level of comprehending theoretically the historical movement as a whole.

Of all the classes that stand face to face with the bourgeoisie today, the proletariat alone is a really revolutionary class. The other classes decay and finally disappear in the face of modern industry; the proletariat is its special and essential product.

The lower middle class, the small manufacturer, the shopkeeper, the artisan, the peasant, all these fight against the bourgeoisie, to save from extinction their existence as fractions of the middle class. They are therefore not revolutionary, but conservative. Nay more, they are reactionary, for they try to roll back the wheel of history. If by chance they are revolutionary, they are so only in view of their impending transfer into the proletariat; they thus defend not their present, but their future interests; they desert their own standpoint to place themselves at that of the proletariat. . . .

In the conditions of the proletariat, [the social conditions no longer exist]. The proletarian is without property; his relation to his wife and children has no longer anything in common with the bourgeois family relations; modern industrial labour, modern subjection to capital, the same in England as in France, in America as in Germany, has stripped him of every trace of national character. Law, morality, religion, are to him so many bourgeois prejudices, behind which lurk in ambush just as many bourgeois interests. . . .

All previous historical movements were movements of minorities, or in the interest of minorities. The proletarian movement is the self-conscious, independent movement of the immense majority, in the interest of the immense majority. The proletariat, the lowest stratum of our present society, cannot stir, cannot raise itself up, without the whole superincumbent strata of official society being sprung into the air. . . .

Hitherto, every form of society has been based, as we have already seen, on the antagonism of oppressing and oppressed classes. But in order to oppress a class, certain conditions must be assured to it under which it can, at least, continue its slavish existence. The serf, in the period of serfdom, raised himself to membership in the commune, just as the petty bourgeois, under the yoke of feudal absolutism, managed to develop into a bourgeois. The modern labourer, on the contrary, instead of rising with the progress of industry, sinks deeper and deeper below the conditions of existence of his own class. He becomes a pauper, and pauperism develops more rapidly than population and wealth. And here it becomes evident, that the bourgeoisie is unfit any longer to be the ruling class in society, and to impose its conditions of existence upon society as an overriding law. It is unfit to rule because it is incompetent to assure an existence to its slave within his slavery, because it cannot help letting him sink into such a state, that it has to feed him, instead of being fed by him. Society can no longer live under this bourgeoisie, in other words, its existence is no longer compatible with society.

The essential condition for the existence and for the sway of the bourgeois class, is the formation and augmentation of capital; the condition for capital is wage labour. Wage labour rests exclusively on competition between the labourers. The advance of industry, whose involuntary promoter is the bour-geoisie, replaces the isolation of the labourers, due to competition, by their revolutionary combination, due to association. The development of modern industry, therefore, cuts from under its feet the very foundation on which the bourgeoisie produces and appropriates products. What the bourgeoisie therefore produces, above all, are its own grave-diggers. Its fall and the victory of the proletariat are equally inevitable.

PROLETARIANS AND COMMUNISTS

In what relation do the Communists stand to the proletarians as a whole?

The Communists do not form a separate party opposed to other working class parties.

They have no interests separate and apart from those of the proletariat as a whole.

They do not set up any sectarian principles of their own, by which to shape and mould the proletarian movement.

The Communists are distinguished from the other working class parties by this only: 1. In the national struggles of the proletarians of the different coun-tries, they point out and bring to the front the common interests of the entire proletariat, independently of all nationality. 2. In the various stages of develop-ment which the struggle of the working class against the bourgeoisie has to pass through, they always and everywhere represent the interests of the movement as a whole.

The Communists, therefore, are on the one hand, practically, the most advanced and resolute section of the working class parties of every country, that section which pushes forward all others; on the other hand, theoretically, they have over the great mass of the proletariat the advantage of clearly under-standing the line of march, the conditions, and the ultimate general results of the proletarian movement.

The immediate aim of the Communists is the same as that of all the other proletarian parties: Formation of the proletariat into a class, overthrow of the bourgeois supremacy, conquest of political power by the proletariat.

The theoretical conclusions of the Communists are in no way based on ideas or principles that have been invented, or discovered, by this or that would-be universal reformer.

They merely express, in general terms, actual relations springing from an existing class struggle, from a historical movement going on under our very eyes. The abolition of existing property relations is not at all a distinctive feature of communism.

All property relations in the past have continually been subject to historical change consequent upon the change in historical conditions.

The French Revolution, for example, abolished feudal property in favour of bourgeois property.

The distinguishing feature of communism is not the abolition of property generally, but the abolition of bourgeois property. But modern bourgeois private property is the final and most complete expression of the system of producing and appropriating products that is based on class antagonisms, on the exploitation of the many by the few.

In this sense, the theory of the Communists may be summed up in the single sentence: Abolition of private property. . . .

To be a capitalist, is to have not only a purely personal, but a social, *status* in production. Capital is a collective product, and only by the united action of many members, nay, in the last resort, only by the united action of all members of society, can it be set in motion.

Capital is therefore not a personal, it is a social power.

When, therefore, capital is converted into common property, into the property of all members of society, personal property is not thereby transformed into social property. It is only the social character of the property that is changed. It loses its class character. . . .

You are horrified at our intending to do away with private property. But in your existing society, private property is already done away with for nine-tenths of the population; its existence for the few is solely due to its non-existence in the hands of those nine-tenths. You reproach us, therefore, with intending to do away with a form of property, the necessary condition for whose existence is the non-existence of any property for the immense majority of society.

In one word, you reproach us with intending to do away with your property. Precisely so; that is just what we intend. . . .

Communism deprives no man of the power to appropriate the products of society; all that it does is to deprive him of the power to subjugate the labour of others by means of such appropriation. . . .

Abolition of the family! Even the most radical flare up at this infamous proposal of the Communists.

On what foundation is the present family, the bourgeois family, based? On capital, on private gain. In its completely developed form this family exists only among the bourgeoisie. But this state of things finds its complement in the practical absence of the family among the proletarians, and in public prostitution.

The bourgeois family will vanish as a matter of course when its complement vanishes, and both will vanish with the vanishing of capital.

Do you charge us with wanting to stop the exploitation of children by their parents? To this crime we plead guilty. . . .

The bourgeois claptrap about the family and education, about the hallowed correlation of parent and child, becomes all the more disgusting, the more, by the action of modern industry, all family ties among the proletarians are torn asunder, and their children transformed into simple articles of commerce and instruments of labour.

But you Communists would introduce community of women, screams the whole bourgeoisie in chorus.

attitudes of the time ?

The bourgeois sees in his wife a mere instrument of production. He hears that the instruments of production are to be exploited in common, and, naturally, can come to no other conclusion than that the lot of being common to all will likewise fall to the women.

He has not even a suspicion that the real point aimed at is to do away with the status of women as mere instruments of production.

For the rest, nothing is more ridiculous than the virtuous indignation of our bourgeois at the community of women which, they pretend, is to be openly and officially established by the Communists. The Communists have no need to introduce a community of women; it has existed almost from time immemorial.

Our bourgeois, not content with having the wives and daughters of their proletarians at their disposal, not to speak of common prostitutes, take the greatest pleasure in seducing each other's wives. *sex ploitation of*

Bourgeois marriage is in reality a system of wives in common and thus, at *women !* the most, what the Communists might possibly be reproached with is that they *How* desire to introduce, in substitution for a hypocritically concealed, an openly *backward* legalised community of women. For the rest, it is self-evident, that the abolition *!* of the present system of production must bring with it the abolition of the community of women springing from that system, *i.e.*, of prostitution both public and private.

The Communists are further reproached with desiring to abolish countries and nationality.

The workingmen have no country. We cannot take from them what they have not got. Since the proletariat must first of all acquire political supremacy, must rise to be the leading class of the nation, must constitute itself *the* nation, it is, so far, itself national, though not in the bourgeois sense of the word. . . .

In proportion as the exploitation of one individual by another is put an end to, the exploitation of one nation by another will also be put an end to. In proportion as the antagonism between classes within the nation vanishes, the hostility of one nation to another will come to an end. . . .

. . . In the most advanced countries, the following will be pretty generally applicable.

1. Abolition of property in land and application of all rents of land to public purposes.

2. A heavy progressive or graduated income tax.

3. Abolition of all right of inheritance.

4. Confiscation of the property of all emigrants and rebels.

5. Centralisation of credit in the hands of the state, by means of a national bank with state capital and an exclusive monopoly.

6. Centralisation of the means of communication and transport in the hands of the state.

7. Extension of factories and instruments of production owned by the state; the bringing into cultivation of waste lands, and the improvement of the soil generally in accordance with a common plan.

8. Equal obligation of all to work. Establishment of industrial armies, especially for agriculture. *even women; children ?*

9. Combination of agriculture with manufacturing industries; gradual aboli-

tion of the distinction between town and country, by a more equable distribution of the population over the country.

10. Free education for all children in public schools. Abolition of children's factory labour in its present form. Combination of education with industrial production, etc.

When, in the course of development, class distinctions have disappeared, and all production has been concentrated in the hands of a vast association of the whole nation, the public power will lose its political character. Political power, properly so called, is merely the organised power of one class for oppressing another. If the proletariat during its contest with the bourgeoisie is compelled, by the force of circumstances, to organise itself as a class; if, by means of a revolution, it makes itself the ruling class, and, as such, sweeps away by force the old conditions of production, then it will, along with these conditions, have swept away the conditions for the existence of class antagonisms and of classes generally, and will thereby have abolished its own supremacy as a class.

how?

In place of the old bourgeois society, with its classes and class antagonisms, we shall have an association, in which the free development of each is the condition for the free development of all. . . .

The Communists disdain to conceal their views and aims. They openly declare that their ends can be attained only by the forcible overthrow of all existing social conditions. Let the ruling classes tremble at a communist revolution. The proletarians have nothing to lose but their chains. They have a world to win.

Workingmen of all countries, unite!

Questions

role of peasants – proletarian ?
"   "   women –
distribution — land, goods.
taxes

(not yet "evolutionary" . . . 1859.)

Chapter Five

THE POLITICAL
REORIENTATION
OF EUROPE

EUROPE returned to an uneasy stability after the failure of the nationalist and liberal revolts of 1848. The idealistic aspirations of revolutionaries and reformers were submerged in a revival of state power and political reaction in France, Italy, and the Germanies. In the mid-1850's the peaceful calm of the European Concert was finally shattered by the Crimean War, which pitted Great Britain, France, Piedmont-Sardinia, and Turkey against Russia. The Russian defeat, especially galling to the tsar because of Austria's refusal to come to his assistance, destroyed the traditional conservative alliance of Austria, Russia, and Prussia, leaving Austria effectively isolated and temporarily curbing Russia's imperialistic ambitions. France, under Napoleon III, revived her claim to continental leadership; Germany and Italy were unified and emerged as new major powers. Serene and powerful, Britain stood aloof from European alliances.

The death in 1837 of King William IV, the last of George III's sons, and the accession of the young Queen Victoria gave Great Britain a public symbol of prosperity, confidence, and power. Nevertheless, serious social problems accompanied Britain's rapid economic growth. The Reform Bill of 1832 gave the franchise to the upper middle classes, bringing them into a vague political partnership with the aristocracy and landed gentry. Britain's undoubted mastery of the seas and her unrivaled commercial and industrial superiority, enhanced by the free-trade policies that followed the repeal of the Corn Laws in 1846, lent a superficial calm to the domestic scene. Both houses of Parliament remained elite political clubs dominated by many groups of businessmen, gentry, and nobility who nevertheless represented the most advanced combination of aristocracy and democracy among the major European powers. The apparent harmony of those mid-century decades of economic growth and tempered reform has often been called the Victorian Compromise.

Across the channel, Prince Louis Napoleon Bonaparte moved quickly to consolidate his power following his election as President of the Second French

Republic in December 1848. In December 1852, the Prince-President had himself proclaimed Napoleon III, Emperor of the French, and institutionalized his version of Bonapartism as the Second Empire. Allied at home with the Church and the peasantry, while undertaking a paternalistic program on behalf of the working classes, the Emperor carried out an ambitious foreign policy designed to enhance French prestige. In an effort to bolster his popularity and to pacify dissident elements in French society, Napoleon III liberalized his regime in the 1860's. Thus, the Emperor was gradually forced toward a fateful decision between constitutional government and authoritarian rule when disaster struck. Seriously ill, Napoleon III was badly outmaneuvered in diplomatic discussions with Prussia and committed a fatal series of errors in foreign policy which ended with a disastrous French defeat in the Franco-Prussian War.

Austria was the principal obstacle to a united Italy. Her diplomatic isolation after the Crimean War gave hope to Italian nationalists who believed their nation too weak to oppose the Austrians in battle and were anxiously seeking foreign support. There were three possible courses open to the nationalists: first, a popular uprising culminating in the establishment of an Italian Republic; second, a federation of Italian states could be formed under the presidency of the pope; third, the creation of an Italian kingdom under the rule of the king of Piedmont-Sardinia, the only "Italian" ruler of an Italian state. Through shrewd and careful diplomacy Count Camillo di Cavour, Premier of Piedmont, secured an alliance with Napoleon III. The French Emperor was anxious to seem to be a supporter of nationalist movements. In return for French annexation of two Piedmontese territories—Nice and Savoy—Napoleon III agreed to support Piedmont if she were attacked by Austria. In 1859 Cavour provoked an Austrian attack, and French armies assisted the Piedmontese in forcing the Austrians to retreat toward the Alps. In the peace negotiations Cavour managed to extract Lombardy from the Austrians. Piedmont also succeeded in absorbing several of the other Italian states in 1860, and in 1861 the King of Piedmont was proclaimed King of Italy. When Cavour died in 1861 a unified Italy was closer to realization than at any time since the sixth century. Austria's defeat in the Austro-Prussian War of 1866 enabled the young Kingdom of Italy to acquire Venetia, while France's defeat in the Franco-Prussian War of 1870–71 withdrew the protective shield of French troops around Rome and the Papacy. With the addition of Rome, the *Risorgimento*—Italy's triumphant resurgence—culminated in the union of most Italians. Only the Trentino and a few small lands in the north remained as *Italia irredenta*—unredeemed Italy.

The failure of liberal revolution represented by the Frankfurt parliament in 1848 left unresolved the question of a future Austrian role in a united Germany. Unification without Prussia was impossible, but the constitutional conflict that arose in Berlin during the 1860's depressed liberal hopes for enlightened Prussian leadership in the likely duel with Austria. The Prussian Minister-President, Otto von Bismarck, surprised Europe by riding roughshod over parliament and by propelling Prussia through three successive wars—in 1864 allied with Austria against Denmark, in 1866 allied with Italy against Austria, and in 1870–71 allied with southern German states against France. Although Bismarck had not originally planned to unify Germany, he quickly grasped the possibility offered by the Austrian defeat in 1866. German liberals quickly forgot their earlier antipathy to his unconstitutional policies and joined in a general chorus of praise when the German Empire was proclaimed in January 1871 at Versailles. A shrewd practitioner of *Realpolitik,* Bismarck had united Germany by Prussian might, pushing Austria out of German affairs without destroying the Habsburg monarchy.

Under Nicholas I (1825–55), dubbed the Iron Tsar, Russia was the paramount continental symbol of conservatism. The Tsar, brought up in a military environment, refused to countenance liberal or western ideas and rigorously suppressed a national uprising in Poland in 1830. With the heavy hand of imperial authority set against change, Russia moved slowly into the modern world. Her agriculture and industry were still hampered by serfdom, by her vast distances, and by her backwardness. A growing circle of writers turned to a serious discussion of the future of their nation, languishing as "Frozen Russia" under the firm rule of Nicholas I. Those who urged a western course for Russia, who sought the importation of western European ideas and technology, were called "westernizers"; they clashed bitterly with Slavophils, who emphasized the peculiar nature of Russian history and searched for a "Russian" path to the future. But to all, the greatest problem of the day was serfdom. Not until the death of Nicholas I, and the Russian defeat in the Crimean War, did the government summon the courage to tackle this enormous problem. Finally, in 1861, Tsar Alexander II issued his Emancipation Manifesto, and Russia, too, seemed ready to break with the past.

The middle years of the nineteenth century were decades of swift change encompassing all facets of human existence. Economic advance created new wealth; political and nationalist pressure created new tensions; and the formation of united Italy and unified Germany destroyed the old balance of power.

ENGLAND: THE VICTORIAN COMPROMISE

1. "THE ANNUAL REGISTER"—REPORT ON DOMESTIC AFFAIRS IN ENGLAND, 1848*

The conservative *Annual Register* came out in solid opposition to the demands of Chartist petitioners who sought to bring political power to the masses through popular democratic practices. Annual parliaments, universal suffrage, equal electoral districts, no property qualifications for voting, and payment of the members of Parliament were the five demands which followers of the Chartist movement presented to the House of Commons in 1848. Although all Chartist demands except the insistence upon annual parliaments ultimately became a part of the British constitution, none were realized during the lifetime of the movement. The general period of prosperity which extended from the 1840's to the 1870's did much to dampen an effective interest in such goals.

Nevertheless, Chartist demands and criticisms provoked a sharp debate in the House of Commons which the *Annual Register* covered with great interest. To

* *The Annual Register for 1848* (London, 1849), pp. 124-25, 142-51.

what extent was the anonymous reporter in the *Annual Register* a disciple of Edmund Burke's views on the English constitution? On what specific grounds did he criticize the Chartists? What arguments did Mr. Joseph Hume use to convince the Commons that "this House . . . does not fairly represent the population, the property, and the industry of this country"? Why did Hume argue that his proposals for reform would impose no harmful or revolutionary changes? In his reply for the government, why did Lord John Russell oppose Mr. Hume's proposals? On what grounds did he assert that the House of Commons "represented the nation fairly" and that the House was by no means a "mere servant of aristocracy"? What arguments did Benjamin Disraeli offer against Mr. Hume's motion for reform, and what alternative course of action did he propose?

The security which under the protection of Providence this country derives from its free and popular constitution was never more signally exemplified than during the year of political agitation and disorder of which the memorable events are commemorated in this volume. While almost every throne on the Continent was emptied or shaken by revolution, the English monarchy, strong in the loyal attachment of the people, not only stood firm in the tempest, but appeared even to derive increased stability from the events that convulsed foreign kingdoms. In the most perfect constitution of society indeed, as it is impossible to extirpate the passions and vices of our common nature, disaffection, in a more or less degree, is always latent; and, as often as circumstances present the occasions of disorder, there will be found no lack of turbulent and unruly spirits to take advantage of them. It is at such periods that the soundness of a nation's political sentiments and the reality of its attachment to the constituted authorities is brought to a searching trial. A system which has been supported only by the strong hand of power, or by that allegiance which is the creature of habit rather than of reflection, is unable to withstand that contagious fever of innovation which spreads from country to country, under the impulse of any extraordinary movement in the human mind. On the other hand, a loyalty, based on reason and conviction, and an enlightened appreciation of the benefits derived from well-tried institutions, proves a sure bulwark in the hour of trial against the machinations of conspirators and anarchists. Such was the lesson exhibited by England in the revolutionary era of 1848. The agitation which derived its impulse from the convulsions of the Continent prevailed only so far as to disturb for a moment the serenity of her political atmosphere. Awed by the overwhelming strength and imposing attitude of the friends of order, the mischief subsided almost as soon as it appeared, and the cause of rational freedom was materially strengthened by the futile efforts made to undermine it. When a knot of obscure and ill-disposed malcontents would fain have played off in our metropolis the scenes which had been enacted with such sanguinary effects in Paris and Vienna, their insignificance was demonstrated, and their menaces rendered impotent by the firm and imposing attitude of the loyal and well-affected inhabitants arrayed in the defence of peace, property, and order.

The 10th of April was the day which the disciples of physical force, organized under the banner of Chartism, had announced for a grand display of their strength and numbers; a demonstration by which it was intended to overawe the Government into a concession of their demands, as the only means of averting a violent revolution. But the day which was to have been signalized by the jubilee of democratic licence terminated in the most decisive triumph of the Throne and Constitution. Without the slightest collision between the authorities and the people, without a blow struck, or a drop of blood shed, nay without the appearance of a single soldier in the streets of London, uninterrupted peace and order were maintained, and the vaunted demonstration passed off quietly and safely. The result was not only to reassure all those persons who had trembled for the stability of the social fabric at home, but to strengthen the cause of constitutional liberty all over the world, and to accelerate that reaction in favour of moderate and sober counsels, which naturally succeeds to a revolutionary ebullition. But, although all danger to the institutions of this country was shown to be at an end, it was in the power of the mischievous and ill-disposed, availing themselves of the general excitement of the times, to give some trouble and annoyance to the Government. Meetings were held for the promotion of the so-called People's Charter, at which a great deal of seditious and revolutionary language was spoken; and, if these efforts to excite the ignorant and misguided failed of their effect, it was certainly not from any want of will in the turbulent demagogues who took the part of leaders. Nor was the mischief confined to mere speech-making and seditious publications. Tumultuous assemblies, consisting for the most part of the refuse of a crowded city, thieves, pickpockets, and other disorderly characters, took place in some parts of the metropolis; windows were broken, some shops plundered, the police were assailed with abuse, stones and missiles, and the peaceable inhabitants put in terror for their safety. Although the civil force always proved a more than sufficient match for these riotous mobs, it was not always in its power to prevent the destruction of property, and the suspension of business, occasioned by such disturbances, while the necessity of constant vigilance in several quarters of the metropolis at once proved very harassing to the police. The contagion spread to some of the large manufacturing towns both in England and Scotland, and in some parts of the country the Chartist gatherings and demonstrations created a good deal of apprehension. Happily, however, all these commotions passed off without any serious explosion. The Government meanwhile kept a careful watch upon the progress of the movement. A few of the more violent leaders and speech-makers were arrested and committed for trial, and every preparation was made for vigorous action in the event of an outbreak taking place. . . .

It was the opinion of a certain class of politicians, at this crisis, that the true remedy for the dangers and discontents which prevailed was to be found in a larger concession of popular claims, and that the constitution would be most effectually strengthened by widening the basis of representation in Parliament. The veteran Reformer, once Member for Middlesex and now for Montrose, Mr. Joseph Hume, took the lead in this new movement, and at some large public meetings, which took place about this time, he expressed in strong terms his sense of the expediency of a wide extension of the elective franchise. Associations were formed and meetings held in various parts of the kingdom for the promotion of this object, and Mr. Hume undertook to bring the question to a test by a formal motion in the House of Commons. The day fixed for the debate was the 21st June, when, after several numerously signed petitions had been presented in favour of Mr. Hume's object, that gentleman rose to move a resolution in the following terms:—

"That this House, as at present constituted, does not fairly represent the population, the property, or the industry of the country; whence has arisen great and increasing discontent in the minds of a large portion of the people: and it is therefore expedient, with a view to amend the national representation, that the elective franchise shall be so extended as to include all householders; that votes shall be taken by ballot; that the duration of Parliaments shall not exceed three years; and that the apportionment of Members to population shall be made more equal."

Mr. Hume began by referring to the numerous petitions which had been presented upon that and previous days, denying that they had been concocted by any undue influence or organized confederacy.

He glanced at the state of public feeling in this country—the general disposition, amid the disturbance of Europe, to maintain order, and especially the maintenance of peace on the 10th of April last. It was for the House, however, to consider whether those who had manifested at that crisis such a determination to obtain an extension of the suffrage, had just cause of complaint. He believed that if the Reform Bill had not been granted, much more serious disturbances would have happened. Our position, however, had materially altered within the last three or four years; events had changed the condition and relative situation of the working classes with other classes in this country. We formerly boasted, that, while in other countries despots maintained themselves by large armies, we could maintain the peace and welfare of the country by the agency of Parliament, without the aid of military measures. But whereas we were formerly a civil nation, we had now become a military nation, with a great expenditure; and the discontent in the country had become general. It was upon that ground that he felt it to be his duty to submit to the House what he thought would be a remedy for existing evils.

Reverting to the Reform Act of 1832, he contended that it had failed to answer all the purposes for which it was intended. "Parliament purports to be an engine for governing a constitutional country, all classes being represented: is that so now? Taxation and representation should go together. Every man should have his share in sanctioning the laws by which he is governed—the sole difference between a freeman and a slave. The Crown, Lords, and Commons, form the best method of giving effect to that constitutional government: the House of Commons, therefore, ought to be invested with the highest authority and influence in the country: no act of the Crown ought to be valid without its sanction; and the large classes of the community ought to be represented. But what is the fact? Five out of every six male adults in this country are without any voice in the election of the representatives to that House. The population of Great Britain was 18,500,000 in 1841; out of the male adults above twenty-one, taking the average—some individuals being registered for three, four, or five different places—the number of registered electors does not amount to more than from 800,000 to 850,000. The rest of the 5,000,000 or 6,000,000 adults who have not this privilege are placed in an inferior situation, and deprived of that *right* which by the constitution they are entitled to enjoy. At eighteen, or even sixteen years of age, a man can be drawn for the militia and called out to quell riots. Yet classes of workmen distinguished for their industry, intelligence, and ability, are excluded from the franchise." Mr. Hume cited the oath taken by Cabinet Ministers to maintain the peace of the country, and, quoting the words of Earl Grey when introducing the Reform Bill in 1831, maintained that the way to do so is by giving to the people "a full, vigorous, and efficient" representation. . . .

. . . He then quoted a number of statistical details from various sources, showing how partially and unequally the franchise is distributed. Huntingdon, Westmoreland, and Rutland, with 26,000 adult males and 9,000 electors, returned 6 Members, and thus neutralized the 6 Members of Middlesex, West Yorkshire, and South Lancashire, with a population of 316,000 adult males and 73,000 electors. The Tower Hamlets, with a population of 400,000, were neutralized by Harwich, with a population of 3,700. Some large towns had no representatives. Mr. Hume cited statistics adduced by the late Mr. O'Connell, showing the scanty representation of Ireland; and others from a pamphlet recently published, illustrating the general inequality. To prove how unequally different interests and populations are balanced in the House of Commons, he took twenty-two boroughs, the aggregate population of which was but a fraction above 100,000, and found that they had 42 representatives in the House of Commons,—that is to say, one Member for every 2,390 persons; while twenty other cities and boroughs, with an aggregate population of 3,780,000, also returned 42 Members, being one Member for about every 90,000 persons. The Metropolis, including all its Parliamentary districts, with a population of 2,000,000, was represented by 16 Members in Parliament. The eight boroughs of Bridgenorth, Honiton, Harwich, Thetford, Richmond (Yorkshire), Totness, Stafford, and Lymington, with an aggregate population falling short of 40,000, returned the same number of Members.

Another evil was the great diversity of the franchise. Although the ten-pound rental was the standard for boroughs, and the forty-shilling freehold the standard for counties, there were, in truth, no fewer than eighty-five different kinds of franchise. It was scarcely possible to appreciate the confusion, the delay, and the expense that such a system produces. What the House ought to do, was to render the suffrage as simple, as general, as easily obtained, and as easily defended as possible. Mr. Hume enumerated many varieties of the franchise,— by estate in fee, occupation, marriage settlement, joint tenancy, promotion to a benefice, lease-holding, corporate right, &c.

He argued that want of confidence in the representation made the people indifferent to the acts of the Legislature; and with that indifference the public expenditure was increasing.

He then explained, that in his notice the word "all" was unintentionally omitted; and he now supplied this definition of household suffrage—"That every such person of full age, and not subject to any mental or legal incapacity, who shall have occupied a house, or part of a house, for twelve months, and shall have been rated to the poor for that period, shall be registered as an elector; and every lodger shall have the right to claim to be rated to the poor, and after

such rating and residence for twelve months he shall be registered as an elector."
There would be no difficulty in carrying out this object. The apparatus all
existed. By the present law, every house was rated to the poor; and the Act
conferring this suffrage would provide that every man who so desired might,
upon entering upon the occupation of part of a house, have a right to be rated
for a portion, whatever it might be, of the poor rate assessed upon that house.
Thus registration and residence, both of which were important, would be
secured, and a line would be drawn between the mere vagrant and the worthy
and educated man who was now excluded from the suffrage merely on account
of the nature of his occupation. It might be argued that this proposal would not
keep up the distinction between personal rights and property. He did not wish
to draw that distinction too tight; but he must say, that by the law as it stood
too much attention had been paid to bricks and mortar and too little to brains,
and the time has now come when common sense should prevail.

Mr. Hume then went over all the several parts of his proposition, maintaining
that each was proper and expedient. Not desiring change for the sake of change,
he would not cut up the country into electoral districts, and he would not disturb the distribution of Members for England, Ireland, and Scotland. He
thought that the duration of Parliaments for three years would afford sufficient
control over Members. There was no property qualification in Scotland, and he
did not see any reason why England and Ireland should not be put on the same
footing. He quoted copiously from Lord John Russell's speech on the 1st of
March, 1831, introducing the Reform Bill. Lord John then held that it was
necessary to re-establish confidence and sympathy between the House and its
constituents; not wishing to encumber that particular measure with other matters, he left such questions as ballot and the duration of Parliaments to future
consideration; and he closed his speech with this declaration—"It is the only
way calculated to insure permanency to that constitution which has so long been
the admiration of foreign nations, on account of its popular spirit; but that
admiration cannot continue to exist much longer, unless, by an infusion of new
popular spirit, you show that you are determined not to be the representatives
of small classes or particular interests, but that you will form a body which,
representing the people—which, springing from the people—which, sympathiz-
ing with the people—can fairly call upon the people to support any future
burdens, and to struggle with any future difficulties you may have to encounter,
confident that those who ask them so to do are united heart and hand with
them, and look only, like themselves, to the glory and welfare of England. . . ."

Lord John Russell rose early in the debate, because he thought the House was
entitled to an early explanation of his views, not only with regard to this motion,
but to other questions akin to it. After referring briefly to the petitions which
had been presented, and vindicating some expressions recently used by himself,
which had been perverted by speakers at public meetings into a declaration of
his belief that the people desired no further reforms, the noble Lord proceeded
to combat the views advocated by the mover of the resolution. He accepted Mr.
Hume's admission that the Reform Act had been mainly instrumental in maintaining the peace of the country during the recent excitement as a proof that it
had averted disorder and conferred benefit on the country. If Mr. Hume's

assertion were correct, that every man who contributed to the taxes had a right to a vote, there was an end to the question, and there was no occasion for the restrictions and qualifications with which Mr. Hume was now going to encumber that pretended right. If every man had that right, what did Mr. Hume mean by now restricting it to all householders? Even under his definition of household suffrage some two or three millions of adult males would be excluded from the representation, and thus the universal content which he wished to introduce would not be obtained. He differed from Mr. Hume as to the basis of his proposed representation. That which every man of full age had a right to was the best possible government and the best representative system which the Legislature could form. If universal suffrage would give the best representative system, the best laws, and the best government, the people would have a right to it; but, if universal suffrage would not give this, then it was mere idle pedantry to say that every man had a right to a vote and was entitled to share in legislation. In considering this question, he could not but recollect that ours was a mixed constitution, that we had a Sovereign and a House of Lords, and that they were not evils to be endured, but institutions to be proud of. Tacitus had said that every government was formed of monarchy, aristocracy, or democracy—that a government formed out of the three might be easily conceived, but could not easily be brought to pass, and that, if it could be brought to pass, it could not be durable. That sentiment had been justified by the experience of all the modern nations of the world, save one, and that one was England. We, therefore, ought to apply ourselves with the greatest caution and anxiety to any plan which would alter in any way the adjustment of the different powers of the constitution, as this plan would do in regard to our whole representative system. The noble Lord then entered into a long argument to prove that a Parliament elected by householders and lodgers would not be a better Parliament than the present. If such a representative system were adopted, it would render it necessary to adopt such a division of the country into electoral districts as was contemplated in the so-called People's Charter. Having shown that such a division would not be conducive to the interests of the people, he next proceeded to argue that the apportionment of the representation to the population would lead to such collisions of opinion between the representatives of the town and country districts as would be injurious to its future tranquillity. He declined to enter into any long argument as to the vote by ballot, though he was of opinion that it would be no remedy against intimidation. He also declared himself satisfied with the present duration of Parliament, and should not give his vote for any change in it. He then proceeded to defend the Reform Act, by showing that since it was passed the House had not been the mere servant of the aristocracy, or the bigoted opponent of all plans of amelioration. No one who considered the changes which had been made since 1832 could say that the House of Commons had not responded quickly and readily to public opinion. He then recapitulated the great measures which it had passed in that interval, as, for instance, the abolition of slavery, the opening of the China trade, the commutation of tithes, the remedy of the grievances of Dissenters as to births and marriages, the reform of the municipal corporations in England, Scotland, and Ireland, the alterations in the tariff, the alterations in the postage system, and, lastly, the total repeal of the Corn Laws, which proved that the House was not under the rule and dominion of the landed aristocracy. Thinking as he did that the Reform Act was an improvement on our old representative system, still he had always been of opinion that it would admit of improvement from time to time. When he had been most attacked for finality, he had proposed, in his letter to the electors of Stroud, in 1839, either to disfranchise the freemen or to make them the representatives of the industrious mechanics in our large manufacturing towns who were not entitled to vote at present. He had also said that the 10*l.* franchise was too much fettered by restriction, and that the system of registration was complicated and vexatious. From 1839 to the present day neither Mr. Hume nor his colleagues had brought forward any proposition for the reconstruction of the House of Commons. Nor had he (Lord J. Russell). Yet it appeared to him that the public mind was now turned to the subject, and that the time was at hand, if it had not already come, when some reforms of the nature to which he had just alluded must be made in the representative system. The inquiries which the House was then making into the proceedings of some corrupt boroughs would give it further information, and then it would know whether it should disfranchise those boroughs or only the freemen of them. The great defect in the Reform Act appeared to him to be that it had reduced too much the varieties of the right of voting under the old constitution. He thought that by some variety of suffrage, such as by making the freemen the representatives of our industrial classes in the large towns, or by making the right depend upon accumulations in the savings' banks, or by some other mode of the same kind, we might extend the franchise without injuring the basis of our representation. He was, therefore, not disposed to say that you could not beneficially alter or improve the Reform Act; but he was not prepared at present to introduce Bills to carry the amendments which he had mentioned into effect. This was not the moment, when such dangerous opinions respecting capital, and wages, and labour were afloat, to make great and extensive changes in the construction of the House of Commons, which, he believed, represented the nation fairly. The advantages of our constitution were to ourselves invaluable. The stability of our institutions amid the existing convulsions of the world had excited the admiration of every lover of peace and order in every nation, and therefore he hoped that the House would do nothing to diminish that admiration or forfeit that respect. He trusted that the House would not select the present as the time for making a reform, which stopped, indeed, short of the Charter, but which must ultimately terminate in it; but that it would think it due to the other branches of the Legislature and to that great people of which it was the representative, to give a decided negative to this resolution. . . .

Mr. Disraeli opposed the motion in a speech of very felicitous effect. . . .

Mr. Hume's advocacy of his new franchise went to the extent of universal suffrage. Every Englishman had a right to vote, as Mr. Hume contended; if so, why was he to be required to live in a house to exercise that right? If in any one point more than another the act of 1832 was objectionable, it was in its too rigid adoption of the qualification from property; but the proposed franchise recognised property alone as its basis. The second point—the voting by ballot—could not be effected except by making or following a complete change of the character and habits of the people; sufficient reason against it on this occasion. The third point—the legal duration of Parliament—was taken from the old Tory creed and system, which Mr. Disraeli had ever supported: he would support it himself if any manifest benefit could be adduced; but no sensible man could believe that the policy or legislation of Parliament would be affected by such a change if it were now made. The fourth point was one that based the representation of England solely on population. (*Dissent from Mr. Hume.*) Mr. Disraeli went into a detailed development of the working of this plan, taking Buckinghamshire, London, Glasgow, Dublin, and other leading instances as his illustrations, and making dexterous use of the results. On a population basis, London would have as many members as all Scotland. He humorously sketched the origin of Mr. Hume's Reform movement, from the day of the meeting of a few veteran League agitators at their rooms—never permanently deserted—in Newall's Buildings, Manchester. We had lived to see the origin of a new profession in England. "An honourable gentleman the other night said that diplomacy was going out of fashion. Possibly it may be: many people think lawyers useless—they make their own wills and die; there are those who think doctors good for nothing—they take quack medicines, and die also; and there may be Ministers of State who think that they can dispense with the services of ambassadors and envoys. But those who are interested in finding employment for the rising generation will be glad to learn that a new profession has been discovered, and that is the profession of agitation." (*Cheers and laughter*) . . . Completing his sketch of the movement to the present time, Mr. Disraeli observed—"The remarkable circumstance is this, that the present movement has not in the slightest degree originated in any class of the people, even if the people had been misled. It is possible that there might be a popular movement and yet erroneous; but this is erroneous and yet not popular. (*Cheers and laughter*) But the moral I draw from all this—from observing this system of organized agitation, this playing and paltering with popular passions for the aggrandizement of one too ambitious class—the moral I draw and the question I ask is this—why are the people of England forced to find leaders among these persons? Their proper leaders are the gentry of England; and if they are not the leaders of the people, it is because the gentlemen of England have been so negligent of their duties and so unmindful of their station, that this system of professional agitation, so ruinous to the best interests of the country, has arisen in England."

2. JOHN STUART MILL: ON LIBERTY AND ON REPRESENTATIVE GOVERNMENT*

Most historians view John Stuart Mill (1806–73) as an intellectual mentor of the Victorian Compromise. Although not a politician, Mill expressed strong views on the significant political issues in Victorian England and exerted a great influence upon the thinking of the British upper classes. In 1865 he was elected to Parliament and championed such liberal causes as Irish Home Rule and the

* John Stuart Mill, *Utilitarianism, Liberty, and Representative Government* (London: J. M. Dent and Sons, Ltd., 1910), pp. 111–13, 193, 207–8, 239–41, 243, 256–57, 280–82. Reprinted by permission.

extension of suffrage to the working classes and to women. At the same time, Mill opposed both the use of the secret ballot and salaries for members of Parliament. His essay *On Liberty* (1859) contained a cogent philosophical defense of free speech, and his *Considerations on Representative Government* (1861) examined the difficult interrelationships among individual freedom, governmental power, and the position of minorities under conditions of political democracy.

In Mill's view why was freedom of speech and opinion necessary to "the mental well-being of mankind"? To what extent should unpopular opinions be tolerated? According to Mill what constituted the essence of good government? What qualifications for suffrage did Mill advocate for all citizens? What, in Mill's view, was meant by representative government? What possible evils or dangers were to be found in representative government, and by what techniques might such evils be curtailed? Compare Mill's views on government with the political doctrines of Edmund Burke and with the opinions expressed in the House of Commons debate on Parliamentary reform (1848).

ON LIBERTY

I do not pretend that the most unlimited use of the freedom of enunciating all possible opinions would put an end to the evils of religious or philosophical sectarianism. Every truth which men of narrow capacity are in earnest about, is sure to be asserted, inculcated, and in many ways even acted on, as if no other truth existed in the world, or at all events none that could limit or qualify the first. I acknowledge that the tendency of all opinions to become sectarian is not cured by the freest discussion, but is often heightened and exacerbated thereby; the truth which ought to have been, but was not, seen, being rejected all the more violently because proclaimed by persons regarded as opponents. But it is not on the impassioned partisan, it is on the calmer and more disinterested bystander, that this collision of opinions works its salutary effect. Not the violent conflict between parts of the truth, but the quiet suppression of half of it, is the formidable evil; there is always hope when people are forced to listen to both sides; it is when they attend only to one that errors harden into prejudices, and truth itself ceases to have the effect of truth, by being exaggerated into falsehood. And since there are few mental attributes more rare than that judicial faculty which can sit in intelligent judgment between two sides of a question, of which only one is represented by an advocate before it, truth has no chance but in proportion as every side of it, every opinion which embodies any fraction of the truth, not only finds advocates, but is so advocated as to be listened to.

We have now recognised the necessity to the mental well-being of mankind (on which all their other well-being depends) of freedom of opinion, and freedom of the expression of opinion, on four distinct grounds; which we will now briefly recapitulate.

First, if any opinion is compelled to silence, that opinion may, for aught we can certainly know, be true. To deny this is to assume our own infallibility.

Secondly, though the silenced opinion be an error, it may, and very commonly does, contain a portion of truth; and since the general or prevailing opinion on any subject is rarely or never the whole truth, it is only by the collision of adverse opinions that the remainder of the truth has any chance of being supplied.

Thirdly, even if the received opinion be not only true, but the whole truth; unless it is suffered to be, and actually is, vigorously and earnestly contested, it will, by most of those who receive it, be held in the manner of a prejudice, with little comprehension or feeling of its rational grounds. And not only this, but, fourthly, the meaning of the doctrine itself will be in danger of being lost, or enfeebled, and deprived of its vital effect on the character and conduct: the dogma becoming a mere formal profession, inefficacious for good, but cumbering the ground, and preventing the growth of any real and heartfelt conviction, from reason or personal experience.

Before quitting the subject of freedom of opinion, it is fit to take some notice of those who say that the free expression of all opinions should be permitted, on condition that the manner be temperate, and do not pass the bounds of fair discussion. Much might be said on the impossibility of fixing where these supposed bounds are to be placed; for if the test be offence to those whose opinions are attacked, I think experience testifies that this offence is given whenever the attack is telling and powerful, and that every opponent who pushes them hard, and whom they find it difficult to answer, appears to them, if he shows any strong feeling on the subject, an intemperate opponent. But this, though an important consideration in a practical point of view, merges in a more fundamental objection. Undoubtedly the manner of asserting an opinion, even though it be a true one, may be very objectionable, and may justly incur severe censure. But the principal offences of the kind are such as it is mostly impossible, unless by accidental self-betrayal, to bring home to conviction. The gravest of them is, to argue sophistically, to suppress facts or arguments, to misstate the elements of the case, or misrepresent the opposite opinion. But all this, even to the most aggravated degree, is so continually done in perfect good faith, by persons who are not considered, and in many other respects may not deserve to be considered, ignorant or incompetent, that it is rarely possible, on adequate grounds, conscientiously to stamp the misrepresentation as morally culpable; and still less could law presume to interfere with this kind of controversial misconduct. With regard to what is commonly meant by intemperate discussion, namely invective, sarcasm, personality, and the like, the denunciation of these weapons would deserve more sympathy if it were ever proposed to interdict them equally to both sides; but it is only desired to restrain the employment of them against the prevailing opinion: against the unprevailing they may not only be used without general disapproval, but will be likely to obtain for him who uses them the praise of honest zeal and righteous indignation. Yet whatever mischief arises from their use is greatest when they are employed against the comparatively defenceless; and whatever unfair advantage can be derived by any opinion from this mode of asserting it, accrues almost exclusively to received opinions. The worst offence of this kind which can be committed by a polemic is to stigmatise those who hold the contrary opinion as bad and immoral men. To calumny of this sort, those who hold any unpopular opinion are peculiarly exposed, because they are in general few and uninfluential, and nobody but themselves feels much interested in seeing justice done them; but this weapon is, from the nature of the case, denied to those who attack a prevailing opinion: they can neither use it with safety to themselves, nor, if they could, would it do anything but recoil on their own cause. In general, opinions contrary to those commonly received can only obtain a hearing by studied moderation of language, and the most cautious avoidance of unnecessary offence, from which they hardly ever deviate even in a slight degree without losing ground: while unmeasured vituperation employed on the side of the prevailing opinion really does deter people from professing contrary opinions, and from listening to those who profess them. For the interest, therefore, of truth and justice, it is far more important to restrain this employment of vituperative language than the other; and, for example, if it were necessary to choose, there would be much more need to discourage offensive attacks on infidelity than on religion. It is, however, obvious that law and authority have no business with restraining either, while opinion ought, in every instance, to determine its verdict by the circumstances of the individual case; condemning every one, on whichever side of the argument he places himself, in whose mode of advocacy either want of candour, or malignity, bigotry, or intolerance of feeling manifest themselves; but not inferring these vices from the side which a person takes, though it be the contrary side of the question to our own; and giving merited honour to every one, whatever opinion he may hold, who has calmness to see and honesty to state what his opponents and their opinions really are, exaggerating nothing to their discredit, keeping nothing back which tells, or can be supposed to tell, in their favour. This is the real morality of public discussion: and if often violated, I am happy to think that there are many controversialists who to a great extent observe it, and a still greater number who conscientiously strive towards it.

REPRESENTATIVE GOVERNMENT

There is no difficulty in showing that the ideally best form of government is that in which the sovereignty, or supreme controlling power in the last resort, is vested in the entire aggregate of the community; every citizen not only having a voice in the exercise of that ultimate sovereignty, but being, at least occasionally, called on to take an actual part in the government, by the personal discharge of some public function, local or general.

To test this proposition, it has to be examined in reference to the two branches into which, as pointed out in the last chapter, the inquiry into the goodness of a government conveniently divides itself, namely, how far it promotes the good management of the affairs of society by means of the existing faculties, moral, intellectual, and active, of its various members, and what is its effect in improving or deteriorating those faculties.

Its superiority in reference to present well-being rests upon two principles, of as universal truth and applicability as any general propositions which can be laid down respecting human affairs. The first is, that the rights and interests of every or any person are only secure from being disregarded when the person interested is himself able, and habitually disposed, to stand up for them. The second is, that the general prosperity attains a greater height, and is more widely diffused, in proportion to the amount and variety of the personal energies enlisted in promoting it. . . .

Instead of the function of governing, for which it is radically unfit, the proper office of a representative assembly is to watch and control the government: to throw the light of publicity on its acts: to compel a full exposition and justification of all of them which any one considers questionable; to censure them if found condemnable, and, if the men who compose the government abuse their trust, or fulfill it in a manner which conflicts with the deliberate sense of the nation, to expel them from office, and either expressly or virtually appoint their successors. This is surely ample power, and security enough for the liberty of the nation. In addition to this, the Parliament has an office, not inferior even to this in importance; to be at once the nation's Committee of Grievances, and its Congress of Opinions; an arena in which not only the general opinion of the nation, but that of every section of it, and as far as possible of every eminent individual whom it contains, can produce itself in full light and challenge discussion; where every person in the country may count upon finding somebody who speaks his mind, as well or better than he could speak it himself—not to friends and partisans exclusively, but in the face of opponents, to be tested by adverse controversy; where those whose opinion is overruled, feel satisfied that it is heard, and set aside not by a mere act of will, but for what are thought superior reasons, and commend themselves as such to the representatives of the majority of the nation; where every party or opinion in the country can muster its strength, and be cured of any illusion concerning the number or power of its adherents; where the opinion which prevails in the nation makes itself manifest as prevailing, and marshals its hosts in the presence of the government, which is thus enabled and compelled to give way to it on the mere manifestation, without the actual employment, of its strength; where statesmen can assure themselves, far more certainly than by any other signs, what elements of opinion and power are growing, and what declining, and are enabled to shape their measures with some regard not solely to present exigencies, but to tendencies in progress.

It is for want of this judicious reserve that popular assemblies attempt to do what they cannot do well—to govern and legislate—and provide no machinery but their own for much of it, when of course every hour spent in talk is an hour withdrawn from actual business. But the very fact which most unfits such bodies for a Council of Legislation qualifies them the more for their other office—namely, that they are not a selection of the greatest political minds in the country, from whose opinions little could with certainty be inferred concerning those of the nation, but are, when properly constituted, a fair sample of every grade of intellect among the people which is at all entitled to a voice in public affairs. Their part is to indicate wants, to be an organ for popular demands, and a place of adverse discussion for all opinions relating to public matters, both great and small; and, along with this, to check by criticism, and eventually by withdrawing their support, those high public officers who really conduct the public business, or who appoint those by whom it is conducted. . . .

The positive evils and dangers of the representative, as of every other form of government, may be reduced to two heads: first, general ignorance and incapacity, or, to speak more moderately, insufficient mental qualifications, in the controlling body; secondly, the danger of its being under the influence of interests not identical with the general welfare of the community. . . .

... We have next to consider how far it is possible so to organise the democracy as, without interfering materially with the characteristic benefits of democratic government, to do away with those two great evils, or at least to abate them, in the utmost degree attainable by human contrivance.

The common mode of attempting this is by limiting the democratic character of the representation, through a more or less restricted suffrage. But there is a previous consideration which, duly kept in view, considerably modifies the circumstances which are supposed to render such a restriction necessary. A completely equal democracy, in a nation in which a single class composes the numerical majority, cannot be divested of certain evils; but those evils are greatly aggravated by the fact that the democracies which at present exist are not equal, but systematically unequal in favour of the predominant class. Two very different ideas are usually confounded under the name democracy. The pure idea of democracy, according to its definition, is the government of the whole people by the whole people, equally represented. Democracy as commonly conceived and hitherto practised is the government of the whole people by a mere majority of the people, exclusively represented. The former is synonymous with the equality of all citizens; the latter, strangely confounded with it, is a government of privilege, in favour of the numerical majority, who alone possess practically any voice in the State. This is the inevitable consequence of the manner in which the votes are now taken, to the complete disfranchisement of minorities. . . .

There are, however, certain exclusions, required by positive reasons, which do not conflict with this principle, and which, though an evil in themselves, are only to be got rid of by the cessation of the state of things which requires them. I regard it as wholly inadmissible that any person should participate in the suffrage without being able to read, write, and, I will add, perform the common operations of arithmetic. Justice demands, even when the suffrage does not depend on it, that the means of attaining these elementary acquirements should be within the reach of every person, either gratuitously, or at an expense not exceeding what the poorest who earn their own living can afford. If this were really the case, people would no more think of giving the suffrage to a man who could not read, than of giving it to a child who could not speak; and it would not be society that would exclude him, but his own laziness. When society has not performed its duty, by rendering this amount of instruction accessible to all, there is some hardship in the case, but it is a hardship that ought to be borne. If society has neglected to discharge two solemn obligations, the more important and more fundamental of the two must be fulfilled first: universal teaching must precede universal enfranchisement. . . . It is better that the suffrage should be conferred indiscriminately, or even withheld indiscriminately, than that it should be given to one and withheld from another at the discretion of a public officer. In regard, however, to reading, writing, and calculating, there need be no difficulty. It would be easy to require from every one who presented himself for registry that he should, in the presence of the registrar, copy a sentence from an English book, and perform a sum in the rule of three; and to secure, by fixed rules and complete publicity, the honest application of so very simple a test. This condition, therefore, should in all cases accompany universal suffrage; and it would, after a few years, exclude none but those who cared so little for the privilege, that their vote, if given, would not in general be an indication of any real political opinion.

It is also important, that the assembly which votes the taxes, either general or local, should be elected exclusively by those who pay something towards the taxes imposed. Those who pay no taxes, disposing by their votes of other people's money, have every motive to be lavish and none to economise. As far as money matters are concerned, any power of voting possessed by them is a violation of the fundamental principle of free government; a severance of the power of control from the interest in its beneficial exercise. It amounts to allowing them to put their hands into other people's pockets for any purpose which they think fit to call a public one; which in some of the great towns of the United States is known to have produced a scale of local taxation onerous beyond example, and wholly borne by the wealthier classes. That representation should be co-extensive with taxation, not stopping short of it, but also not going beyond it, is in accordance with the theory of British institutions. But to reconcile this, as a condition annexed to the representation, with universality, it is essential, as it is on many other accounts desirable, that taxation, in a visible shape, should descend to the poorest class. In this country, and in most others, there is probably no labouring family which does not contribute to the indirect taxes, by the purchase of tea, coffee, sugar, not to mention narcotics or stimulants. But this mode of defraying a share of the public expenses is hardly felt: the payer, unless a person of education and reflection, does not identify his interest with a low scale of public expenditure as closely as when money for its support is demanded directly from himself; and even supposing him to do so, he would doubtless take care that, however lavish an expenditure he might, by his vote, assist in imposing upon the government, it should not be defrayed by any additional taxes on the articles which he himself consumes. It would be better that a direct tax, in the simple form of a capitation, should be levied on every grown person in the community; or that every such person should be admitted an elector on allowing himself to be rated *extra ordinem* to the assessed taxes; or that a small annual payment, rising and falling with the gross expenditure of the country, should be required from every registered elector; that so every one might feel that the money which he assisted in voting was partly his own, and that he was interested in keeping down its amount. . . .

FRANCE: THE SECOND EMPIRE

3. LOUIS NAPOLEON: PROCLAMATION TO THE FRENCH PEOPLE*

France lived through ten hectic months of dissension and unrest following the revolution of February 1848. When voters finally went to the polls in December to elect a president of the new French Republic, they ignored Lamartine and other revolutionary leaders and overwhelmingly elected a dark horse with a famous name—Louis Napoleon Bonaparte. Like his uncle, Louis Napo-

* "Documents upon the Coup d'État of December 2, 1851" in Frank Maloy Anderson, *The Constitutions and Other Select Documents Illustrative of the History of France, 1789–1907* (Minneapolis: The H. W. Wilson Co., 1908), pp. 538–40.

leon appealed to a broad cross-section of French society. He carefully avoided all major issues and succeeded in becoming all things to all people in the presidential campaign. Three years later, having failed to persuade the Chamber of Deputies to amend the constitution so that he could run for re-election, Louis Napoleon engineered a coup d'état under the code name Rubicon. The date of the coup d'état, December 2, 1851, was the anniversary of Napoleon I's earlier victory at Austerlitz. Few Frenchmen were willing to fight for the Second Republic and the men who opposed the coup d'état fell victim to Louis Napoleon's planning. Republicans found it impossible to marshal public sentiment against the new Bonaparte regime. What arguments did Louis Napoleon use to justify his unconstitutional acts? In what ways did Louis Napoleon's outline for a new constitution preclude the conditions of representative government?

PROCLAMATION TO THE PEOPLE
DECEMBER 2, 1851

FRENCHMEN!

The present situation cannot last much longer. Each day that passes increases the dangers of the country. The assembly, which ought to be the firmest support of order, has become a centre of conspiracies. The patriotism of three hundred of its members could not arrest its fatal tendencies. Instead of making laws in the general interest, it forges weapons for civil war; it makes an attack upon the authority that I hold directly from the people; it encourages all the evil passions; it puts in jeopardy the repose of France: I have dissolved it, and I make the whole people judge between it and me. . . .

Persuaded that the instability of the executive authority and the preponderance of a single assembly are permanent causes of trouble and discord, I submit to you the following fundamental bases of a constitution which the assemblies will develop later.

1st. A responsible chief selected for ten years;

2nd. Ministers dependent upon the executive power alone;

3rd. A council of state composed of the most distinguished men to prepare the laws and to discuss them before the legislative body;

4th. A legislative body to discuss and vote the laws, elected by universal suffrage. . . .

5th. A second assembly, composed of all the illustrious persons of the country [as] guardian of the fundamental compact and of the public liberties.

4. NAPOLEON III: SPEECH TO THE LEGISLATIVE CHAMBERS*

Louis Napoleon Bonaparte was officially proclaimed Emperor of the French in December 1852. As Emperor, Napoleon III displayed a curious mixture of personal idealism and hardheaded realism. In what ways did the following speech of January 18, 1858, illustrate the Emperor's awareness of factions which pulled France in different directions? What methods did he employ in attempting to gain the support of all citizens for his regime, and how did he define the purpose of his Second Empire? In the last analysis, on what arguments did his authority rest? Compare the programs and purposes of Napoleon III with the career of his uncle, Napoleon I.

* The Annual Register for 1858 (London, 1859), pp. 222–24.

Gentlemen, Senators, and Deputies—At the annual meeting of the Chambers, I render you an account of what has taken place during your absence, and I ask your support for the measures to be taken.

Since last year, the Government has followed its regular and progressive march, exempt from all vain ostentation. It has often been pretended that to govern France it was necessary continually to keep the public mind alive with some great theatrical display. I think, on the contrary, that it suffices to endeavour exclusively to do good to deserve the confidence of the country. The action of the Government has consequently been confined to doing what was most necessary in the different branches of the administration.

In the interests of agriculture, the exportation of the distillation from grain has again been authorised, and the support of the Bank has given support to the landed interest. The cultivation of the *landes* has commenced.

In public works, the most important results are 1330 kilometres of railway, thrown open in 1857 to traffic, and 2600 kilometres of new lines granted for construction; the floating-dock of St. Nazaire, and the canal from Caen to the sea thrown open to navigation; careful surveys made to prevent the scourge of inundations; improvements of our ports, and among others of Havre, Marseilles, Toulon, and Bayonne; in the North and in the East of France the working of new coal-mines; at Paris the inauguration of the Louvre and of a wing of Vincennes; finally, in the capital, as at Lyons, quarters thrown open for the first time since centuries to the light of day, and throughout France religious edifices are being constructed or restored.

Public instruction, protected by the State, is being developed by the side of free education honourably protected. The number of colleges has been increased by 1500. Education has become more moral and religious, with a tendency towards sound humanities and useful sciences. The College of France has been reorganized; elementary instruction is spreading far. It is the wish of the Government that the principle of freedom of worship shall be sincerely admitted, without forgetting that the Roman Catholic religion is that of the great majority of Frenchmen. Therefore, this religion has never been more respected nor more unshackled.

The Municipal Councils meet without hinderance; and the bishops enjoy the full plenitude of their sacred office; the Lutheran, Protestant, and Jewish confessions, pay their just proportion of taxes to the State, and are equally protected.

The increase in the price of all necessaries has compelled us since last year to augment the salaries of the lesser functionaries; the rations of the soldiers have been improved, and the pay of subalterns increased.

The budget of 1859 provides for better payment for teachers and professors, and for magistrates. I may point out an increase of charitable societies—in the country those of the medical corporations, and in the towns the establishment of soup-kitchens. One million has been distributed in relief of the populations which have suffered most from want of work.

Algeria, connected with France by the electric wire, has afforded new glory to our troops by the submission of Kabylia. That expedition, skillfully planned and vigorously executed, has completed our domination. The army, which has no more enemies to overcome, will have to struggle against new difficulties in constructing railways, so necessary for the development of the prosperity of our colony.

The relations of France with Foreign Powers were never on a better footing. Our ancient allies, true to the sentiments which sprang from a common cause, give us the same confidence as usual, and our new allies, by their straightforward and loyal conduct in all great questions, make us almost regret that we ever were their foes. I had the opportunity of satisfying myself at Osborne, as well as at Stuttgart, that my desire to keep up the intimacy of old relations, as well as to form new ones, was equally shared by the chiefs of two great empires. If the policy of France is appreciated as it deserves to be in Europe, it is because we have the common sense only to deal with questions which concern ourselves directly, either as a nation or as a great European Power. . . .

What is the Empire? Is it a retrograde government, an enemy of progress, desirous of suppressing generous impulses, and of impeding the specific extension of the great and civilizing principles of 1789? No; the Empire inscribes these principles as the motto of its constitution. It frankly adopts everything of a nature to ennoble the heart or exalt the mind for what is good; but it is also the enemy of every abstract theory. It seeks a strong power, capable of overcoming the obstacles which might stop its advance, for—let us not forget it—the advance of every new power is a long struggle. Moreover, there is a truth inscribed upon every page of the history of France and of England—namely, that liberty without obstacles is impossible as long as there exists in a country a faction which obstinately disowns the fundamental bases of the government; for then liberty, instead of enlightening, controlling, ameliorating, is nothing else but in the hands of factions, but a weapon of destruction. Therefore, as I did not accept the power of the nation with the view to acquire that ephemeral popularity, the paltry prize of concessions exacted from weakness, but with a view one day to deserve the approbation of posterity by founding something lasting in France, I do not fear to declare to you to-day that the danger, no matter what is said to the contrary, does not exist in the excessive prerogatives of power, but rather in the absence of repressive laws. Thus, the last elections, despite their satisfactory result, offered, in many localities, a sad spectacle. Hostile parties took advantage of it to create agitation in the country; and some men had the boldness openly to declare themselves the enemies of the national institutions, deceived the electors by false promises, and, having gained their votes, then spurned them with contempt. You will not allow a renewal of such a scandal, and you will compel every elector to take an oath to the Constitution before presenting himself as a candidate.

As the quiet of the public mind ought to be the constant object of our efforts, you will assist me in finding the means to silence extreme and annoying oppositions. In fact, is it not too sad to behold in a quiet, prosperous country, which is respected in Europe, on the one hand, men crying down a government to which they are indebted for the security which they enjoy, while others only take advantage of the free exercise of their political rights to undermine the existing institutions? I welcome heartily, without inquiring into their antecedents, all those who recognize the national will. As regards the originators of disturbances and conspiracies, let them understand that their day has gone by. . . .

5. VICTOR HUGO: NAPOLÉON LE PETIT*

Among the political casualties of the Napoleonic coup d'état in 1851 was a large number of intellectuals and politicians devoted to the republican ideal. Those who escaped arrest and prison, but were unable to tolerate the new strongman regime, often chose voluntary exile. One literary supporter of the fallen Republic was Victor Hugo. As a result of his views, Hugo spent nearly two decades in exile on the island of Guernsey off the English coast. Though his Romantic tendencies made it difficult for him to write serious political prose, one of Hugo's political tracts—*Napoléon le petit*—became a classic in anti-Bonaparte circles. How did Hugo characterize the Emperor's political motives or aims? Why was Napoleon III only half a Caesar?

Before the 2d of December [1851], it was a common saying among the leaders of the Right with regard to Louis Bonaparte: "He is an idiot." They were mistaken. Certainly that brain of his is muddy, has gaps here and there; but thoughts logically connected and interlinked may, to some extent, be discerned in places. It is a book from which certain pages have been torn out. Louis Bonaparte is a man of one fixed idea, but a fixed idea is not idiocy. He knows what he wants, and marches to his aim. Over justice, over law, over reason, honour, and humanity, if you will, he still marches to his aim.

He is not an idiot. He is a man of other times than ours. He seems absurd and mad because he has no counterpart. Transport him to Spain in the sixteenth century, and Philip II. will recognize him; to England, and Henry VIII. will smile on him; to Italy, and Cæsar Borgia will throw his arms about his neck. Or even confine yourself to placing him outside of European civilization; drop him at Yanina in 1817, Ali Tepelini will tender him his hand. . . .

When the man is measured and found so little, and his success is measured and found so enormous, it is impossible for the mind not to experience some surprise. We ask ourselves: How has he done it? We analyze the adventure and the adventurer, and, laying aside the advantage he derives from his name, and certain facts which aided him in scaling the ramparts, we can discover nothing at the bottom of the man and of his actions but these,—craft and money. . . .

Is Monsieur Bonaparte a dictator? We see no impropriety in answering yes. *Prætor maximus,*—commander-in-chief? The flag salutes him. *Magister populi* —master of the people? Ask the cannon levelled on the public squares. *Pro numine observatum,*—considered a god? Inquire of M. Troplong. He has named the Senate, he has instituted holy days; he has provided for the "safety of society"; he has driven a sacred nail into the wall of the Pantheon, and on this nail has hung his *coup d'état*. He even makes and unmakes laws at his good pleasure, rides without asking permission, and as to the six months, he takes a little longer time. Cæsar took five years; he takes double that. It is quite proper. Julius Cæsar five, Monsieur Louis Bonaparte ten; the proportion is observed. . . .

* Victor Hugo, "Napoleon the Little" in *The History of a Crime* (Édition de Luxe, 2 vols.; Boston: Estes and Lauriat [1891]), II, 189, 196, 225, 236.

Does the dictator smell the incense; does he smell the tobacco? Find out. He smells the tobacco and the incense. O France! what a government! The soutane covers the spurs. The *Coup d'État* goes to Mass, cudgels the cockneys, reads its breviary, cuddles Catin, tells its beads, empties the pitchers, and goes to its Easter duty. The *Coup d'État* affirms that we have returned to the age of the Jacqueries; this may be doubtful, but it is clear enough that it is leading us back to the time of the crusades. Cæsar has taken the cross for the Pope. *Deus lo vult*. The Elysée has the Templar's faith, and his thirst as well.

To enjoy life to the utmost; to devour the budget; to believe nothing, and turn everything to account; to compromise at the same time two sacred things, military honour and religious faith; to stain the altar with blood, and the flag with the holy-water sprinkler; to render the soldier ridiculous and the priest just a little savage; to mingle the Church and the Nation, the Catholic conscience and the patriotic conscience, in the gigantic political swindle which he calls his power,—such is the method of Bonaparte the Little. . . .

THE UNIFICATION OF ITALY AND GERMANY

6. GIUSEPPE MAZZINI: INSTRUCTIONS FOR YOUNG ITALY*

Austrian opposition to any form of liberalism or to any nationalist movement was often demonstrated in post-Napoleonic Italy. Not even the southern part of the peninsula was beyond the reach of Austrian troops. Secret societies, such as the *Carbonari* (charcoal burners), sought both to awaken the Italian people to hatred of the Austrians and to rouse them to action. Giuseppe Mazzini (1805–72), humanitarian, idealist, journalist, and one of the foremost Italian nationalist leaders, saw the future of Italy in terms of a wider struggle of European peoples for freedom and national unity. While a young man, he joined the *Carbonari* and helped to spark the revolutions of 1834 and 1848. Both failed, and it was apparent that Italian unity required a stronger force than domestic revolution. Moreover, Mazzini's fervent republicanism did not appeal to all nationalists. He fled abroad and lived in exile for most of the remainder of his life. Mazzini returned to the Kingdom of Italy after unification had been achieved in the 1860's, but he refused to compromise his republican principles even then. He died at Pisa in 1872.

Mazzini always had a considerable following, in other nations as well as among Italians, and he played the dual role of stimulating nationalism and helping to awaken foreign sympathy for the goals of his own people. He became a symbol of resistance to oppression and of the common bond that united the people of Europe. Compare the nationalistic idealism of Mazzini with the doctrines of French revolutionaries in the Declaration of the Rights of Man. What were the aims of Young Italy, and what specific steps was the society to follow in the achievement of its purposes? What role could the ordinary citizen play in the struggle for national unity? Why did Mazzini insist that "the inevitable tendency of the series of progressive transformations taking place in Europe is towards the enthronement of the republican principle," and why did he assert

* *Life and Writings of Joseph Mazzini* (6 vols.; London: Smith, Elder, and Co., 1890), I, 96–113.

that monarchical government was unsuited to Italy? Why did he maintain that "insurrection by means of guerrilla bands is the true method of warfare for all nations desirous of emancipating themselves from a foreign yoke"?

GENERAL INSTRUCTIONS FOR THE MEMBERS OF YOUNG ITALY

Young Italy is a brotherhood of Italians who believe in a law of Progress and Duty, and are convinced that Italy is destined to become one nation— convinced also that she possesses sufficient strength within herself to become one, and that the ill success of her former efforts is to be attributed not to the weakness, but to the misdirection of the revolutionary elements within her— that the secret of force lies in constancy and unity of effort. They join this association in the firm intent of consecrating both thought and action to the great aim of re-constituting Italy as one independent sovereign nation of free men and equals.

By Italy we understand—1. Continental and peninsular Italy, bounded on the north by the upper circle of the Alps, on the south by the sea, on the west by the mouths of the Varo, and on the east by Trieste; 2. The islands proved Italian by the language of the inhabitants, and destined, under a special administrative organization, to form a part of the Italian political unity.

By the nation we understand the universality of Italians bound together by a common Past, and governed by the same laws. . . .

Whosoever would assume the position of initiator in the transformation of a nation—whether individual or association—must know clearly to what the proposed changes are to lead. Whosoever would presume to call the people to arms, must be prepared to tell them wherefore. Whosoever would undertake a work of regeneration, must have a faith; if he have it not, he can but create enemies, nothing more, and become the author of an anarchy he is neither able to remedy nor overcome. For, indeed, no whole nation ever rises to battle in ignorance of the aim to be achieved by victory.

For these reasons the members of Young Italy make known to their fellow-countrymen, without reserve, the programme in the name of which they intend to combat.

The aim of the association is revolution; but its labours will be essentially educational, both before and after the day of revolution; and it therefore declares the principles upon which the national education should be conducted, and from which alone Italy may hope for safety and regeneration.

By preaching exclusively that which it believes to be truth, the association performs a work of duty, not of usurpation.

By inculcating before the hour of action by what steps the Italians must achieve their aim, by raising its flag in the sight of Italy, and calling upon all those who believe it to be the flag of national regeneration, to organize themselves beneath its folds—the association does not seek to substitute that flag for the banner of the future nation.

When once the nation herself shall be free, and able to exercise that right of sovereignty which is hers alone, she will raise her own banner, and make known her revered and unchallenged will as to the principle and the fundamental law of her existence.

Young Italy is Republican and Unitarian.

Republican—because theoretically every nation is destined, by the law of God and humanity, to form a free and equal community of brothers; and the republican is the only form of government that insures this future.

Because all true sovereignty resides essentially in the nation, the sole progressive and continuous interpreter of the supreme moral law.

Because, whatever be the form of privilege that constitutes the apex of the social edifice, its tendency is to spread among the other classes, and by undermining the equality of the citizens, to endanger the liberty of the country.

Because, when the sovereignty is recognised as existing not in the whole body, but in several distinct powers, the path to usurpation is laid open, and the struggle for supremacy between these powers is inevitable; distrust and organized hostility take the place of harmony, which is society's law of life.

Because the monarchical element being incapable of sustaining itself alone by the side of the popular element, it necessarily involves the existence of the intermediate element of an aristocracy—the source of inequality and corruption to the whole nation.

Because both history and the nature of things teach us that elective monarchy tends to generate anarchy; and hereditary monarchy tends to generate despotism.

Because the inevitable tendency of the series of progressive transformations taking place in Europe, is towards the enthronement of the republican principle, and because the inauguration of the monarchical principle in Italy would carry along with it the necessity of a new revolution shortly after.

Because when monarchy is not—as in the middle ages—based upon the belief now extinct in right divine, it becomes too weak to be a bond of unity and authority in the state.

Young Italy is republican, because practically there are no monarchical elements in Italy. We have no powerful and respected aristocracy to take the intermediate place between the throne and the people; we have no dynasty of Italian princes possessing any tradition either of glory or of important services rendered to the development of the nation, and commanding the affection and sympathy of the various states.

Because our Italian tradition is essentially republican; our great memories are republican; the whole history of our national progress is republican; whereas the introduction of monarchy amongst us was coeval with our decay, and consummated our ruin by its constant servility to the foreigner, and antagonism to the people, as well as to the unity of the nation.

Because, while the populations of the various Italian states would cheerfully unite in the name of a principle which could give no umbrage to local ambition, they would not willingly submit to be governed by a man—the offspring of one of those states; and their several pretensions would necessarily tend to federalism.

Because, if monarchy were once set up as the aim of the Italian insurrection, it would, by logical necessity, draw along with it all the obligations of the monarchical system; concessions to foreign courts; trust in and respect for diplomacy, and the repression of that popular element by which alone our salvation can be achieved and, by entrusting the supreme authority to monarchists, whose interest it would be to betray us, we should infallibly ruin the insurrection. . . .

Young Italy is Unitarian—

Because, without unity, there is no true nation.

Because without unity, there is no real strength and Italy, surrounded as she is by powerful, united, and jealous nations, has need of strength before all things.

Because federalism, by reducing her to the political impotence of Switzerland, would necessarily place her under the influence of one of the neighbouring nations.

Because federalism, by reviving the local rivalries now extinct, would throw Italy back upon the middle ages.

Because federalism, by destroying the unity of the great Italian family, would strike at the root of the great mission Italy is destined to accomplish towards humanity.

Because Europe is undergoing a progressive series of transformations, which are gradually and irresistibly guiding European society to form itself into vast and united masses. . . .

National unity, as understood by Young Italy, does not imply the despotism of any, but the association and concord of all. The life inherent in each locality is sacred. Young Italy would have the administrative organization designed upon a broad basis of religious respect for the liberty of each commune, but the political organization, destined to represent the nation in Europe, should be one and central.

Without unity of religious belief, and unity of social pact; without unity of civil, political, and penal legislation, there is no true nation.

These principles, which are the basis of the association, and their immediate consequences, set forth in the publications of the association, form the creed of Young Italy; and the society only admits as members those who accept and believe in this creed. . . .

Both initiators and initiated must never forget that the moral application of every principle is the first and the most essential; that without morality there is no true citizen; that the first step towards the achievement of a holy enterprise is the purification of the soul by virtue; that, where the daily life of the individual is not in harmony with the principles he preaches, the inculcation of those principles is an infamous profanation and hypocrisy; that it is only by virtue that the members of Young Italy can win over others to their belief; that if we do not show ourselves far superior to those who deny our principles, we are but miserable sectarians; and that Young Italy must be neither a sect nor a party, but a faith and an apostolate. As the precursor of Italian regeneration, it is our duty to lay the first stone of its religion.

The means by which Young Italy proposes to reach its aim are—education and insurrection, to be adopted simultaneously, and made to harmonize with each other.

Education must ever be directed to teach by example, word, and pen, the necessity of insurrection. Insurrection, whenever it can be realised, must be so conducted as to render it a means of national education.

Education, though of necessity secret in Italy, will be public out of Italy.

The members of Young Italy will aid in collecting and maintaining a fund for the expenses of the printing and diffusion of the works of the association.

The mission of the Italian exiles is to constitute an apostolate.

The instructions and intelligence indispensable as preparatory to action will be secret, both in Italy and abroad. . . .

Young Italy is aware that revolutionary Europe awaits a signal, and that this signal may be given by Italy as well as by any other nation. It knows that the ground it proposes to tread is virgin soil; and the experiment untried. Foregone insurrections have relied upon the forces supplied by one class alone, and not upon the strength of the whole nation.

The one thing wanting to twenty millions of Italians, desirous of emancipating themselves, is not power, but faith.

Young Italy will endeavour to inspire this faith,—first by its teachings, and afterwards by an energetic initiative.

Young Italy draws a distinction between the period of insurrection, and that of revolution. The revolution begins as soon as the insurrection is triumphant.

Therefore, the period which may elapse between the first initiative and the complete liberation of the Italian soil, will be governed by a provisional dictatorial power, concentrated in the hands of a small number of men.

The soil once free, every authority will bow down before the National Council, the sole source of authority in the State.

Insurrection—by means of guerrilla bands—is the true method of warfare for all nations desirous of emancipating themselves from a foreign yoke. This method of warfare supplies the want—inevitable at the commencement of the insurrection—of a regular army; it calls the greatest number of elements into the field, and yet may be sustained by the smallest number. It forms the military education of the people, and consecrates every foot of the native soil by the memory of some warlike deed.

Guerrilla warfare opens a field of activity for every local capacity; forces the enemy into an unaccustomed method of battle; avoids the evil consequences of a great defeat; secures the national war from the risk of treason, and has the advantage of not confining it within any defined and determinate basis of operations. It is invincible, indestructible.

The regular army, recruited with all possible solicitude, and organized with all possible care, will complete the work begun by the war of insurrection.

All the members of Young Italy will exert themselves to diffuse these principles of insurrection. The association will develop them more fully in its writings, and explain from time to time the ideas and organization which should govern the period of insurrection. . . .

7. CAMILLO DI CAVOUR: DIPLOMACY AND ITALIAN UNIFICATION*

Count Camillo di Cavour (1810–61), a patriot who believed in monarchy as a stabilizing national force, was the leading statesman of Italian unification. A liberal parliamentarian, Cavour became Prime Minister of Piedmont-

* A. J. Whyte, The Political Life and Letters of Cavour, 1848–1861 (Oxford: The Oxford University Press, 1930), pp. 222–23. Reprinted by permission.

Sardinia in 1852 shortly after the disastrous Piedmontese attempt to unify Italy in 1848–49. When Britain and France declared war on Russia in 1854, joining Turkey in the Crimean War, Cavour took Piedmont into the conflict on the side of the allies. Later, he maneuvered Austria into the Austro-Sardinian War, unleashing the forces which led to Italian unification in the 1860's. The establishment of the Kingdom of Italy, shortly after Cavour's death in 1861, carried his dreams to fruition.

In the following speech to the Piedmontese Parliament, Cavour defended his country's participation in the Crimean War and in the Peace Congress of Paris. The speech indicates Cavour's awareness of the delicate diplomatic position of Piedmont in 1856. Contrast the attitudes of Cavour and Mazzini in terms of *Realpolitik*. What advantages did Cavour obtain for Italy by Piedmontese participation in the Congress of Paris?

The great solutions are not carried into effect with the pen. Diplomacy is powerless to change the condition of a nation. At most, it can but sanction completed facts and give them legal form. What benefit then has Italy obtained from the Congress? We have gained two things; first, that the anomalous and unhappy condition of Italy has been proclaimed to Europe, not by demagogues, or revolutionaries, excited journalists, or party men, but by representatives of the greatest nations in Europe; by statesmen at the head of their countries' Governments; by distinguished men accustomed to consult the dictates of reason rather than the impulse of emotion. That is the first fact, which I consider of the greatest value. The second is that these same powers have declared that, not only in the interests of Italy herself, but in the interests of Europe, a remedy must be found for the evils from which Italy is suffering. I cannot believe that the sentiments expressed and the advice given by such nations as France and England can remain for long, sterile of results. . . .

Truly if from one side we may congratulate ourselves on this result, on the other, we have to recognize that our position is not without difficulties and dangers. It is certain, gentlemen, that the negotiations conducted in Paris have not improved our relations with Austria. We have to confess that the Plenipotentiaries of Sardinia and Austria, after having sat for two months side by side, and after having co-operated together in the greatest political task of the last forty years, have parted without any personal animosity but with the profound conviction that the political position of the two countries is farther than ever from any common accord, the political principles of the two countries being irreconcilable. This fact, gentlemen, it has to be admitted, is grave; this fact may arouse difficulties and dangers, but it is an inevitable, a fatal, consequence of that loyal, liberal, and decided system initiated by King Victor Emmanuel when he ascended the throne, of which the government of the King has always sought to be the interpreter, and to which you have always lent a firm and consistent support. Nor do I believe that in face of these difficulties and dangers you would wish to advise the King to change his policy. As a result of the policy pursued during these last few years we have taken a great step forward; for the first time in our history the Italian question has been brought forward and discussed before a European Congress, not as at Laibach and Verona with a view to aggravating the evils of Italy and riveting more tightly her chains, but with the manifest intention of bringing some remedy to her wounds and of expressing strongly the sympathy felt for her by the Great Powers. The Congress over, the cause of Italy is now carried before the bar of public opinion; before that tribunal which, in the memorable words of the French Emperor, must deliver the final verdict and proclaim the ultimate victory. The struggle may be long, the fluctuations of fortune, perchance, many; but we, trusting in the righteousness of our cause, await with confidence the final issue.

8. OTTO VON BISMARCK: MEMOIRS*

When Otto von Bismarck (1815–98) was appointed Minister-President of Prussia, he was charged by King William I with the task of forcing the Prussian Diet to accept a royal budget which included an army reform measure. The Diet, with a Liberal majority, refused. Irritated, Bismarck implemented the budget without parliamentary approval, and sanctioned the army reform. To the Budget Committee of the Diet he insisted: "Germany does not look to Prussia's liberalism, but to her power; Bavaria, Württemberg, and Baden may indulge in liberalism, and no one will expect them to play Prussia's role; . . . not with speeches and majority decisions will the great problems of the day be decided—that was the great mistake of 1848 and 1849—but with iron and blood."

A strong, deliberate, and effective foreign policy soon led to wars with Denmark, Austria, and France, culminating in the creation of the German Empire in 1871. German liberals and nationalists alike praised Bismarck for achieving German unification, and the Prussian Diet voted retroactively to exonerate him for his extra-constitutional budgetary action. In his memoirs, the "Iron Chancellor," as he was called, commented upon his treatment of Austria in 1866 and on the parliamentary situation in the North German Confederation in 1867. Why did Bismarck insist that Austria be treated leniently in 1866? Who opposed him? What did Bismarck claim as his goal in 1866? What was his attitude toward France? Italy? Russia? England? Why have historians regarded Bismarck as a practitioner of *Realpolitik?* Why did the Iron Chancellor insist on universal suffrage, and what qualifications did he insist upon?

We had to avoid wounding Austria too severely; we had to avoid leaving behind in her any unnecessary bitterness of feeling or desire for revenge; we ought rather to reserve the possibility of becoming friends again with our adversary of the moment, and in any case to regard the Austrian state as a piece on the European chessboard and the renewal of friendly relations with her as a move open to us. If Austria were severely injured, she would become the ally of France and of every other opponent of ours; she would even sacrifice her anti-Russian interests for the sake of revenge on Prussia.

On the other hand, I could not see any guarantee for us in the future of the countries constituting the Austrian monarchy, in case the latter were split up by risings of the Hungarians and Slavs or made permanently dependent on those peoples. What would be put in that portion of Europe which the Austrian

* Bismarck, the Man and the Statesman. Being the Reflections and Reminiscences of Otto, Prince von Bismarck, Written and Dictated by Himself after his Retirement from Office, trans. A. J. Butler (2 vols.; New York: Harper and Brothers, 1899), II, 50–52, 59–63, 65–67.

state from Tyrol to the Bukowina had hitherto occupied? Fresh formations on this surface could only be of a permanently revolutionary nature. German Austria we could neither wholly nor partly make use of. The acquisition of provinces like Austrian Silesia and portions of Bohemia could not strengthen the Prussian state; it would not lead to an amalgamation of German Austria with Prussia, and Vienna could not be governed from Berlin as a mere dependency.

If the war continued, the probable theatre would be Hungary. The Austrian army which, if we crossed the Danube at Pressburg, would not be able to hold Vienna, would scarcely retreat southwards, where it would be caught between the Prussian and Italian armies, and, by its approach to Italy, once more revive the military ardour of the Italians which, already depressed, had been restricted by Louis Napoleon; it would retreat towards the east, and continue its defence in Hungary—if only in the expectation of the prospective intervention of France and the weakening of Italy's interest in the matter, through France's agency. Moreover I held, even from a purely military standpoint, and according to my knowledge of Hungarian territory, that a prosecution of the war there would not repay us, and that the successes to be won there would be out of all proportion to the victories we had hitherto gained, and consequently be calculated to diminish our prestige—quite apart from the fact that the prolongation of the war would pave the way for a French intervention. We must finish off rapidly; before France won time to bring further diplomatic action to bear upon Austria.

To all this the King raised no objection, but declared the actual terms as inadequate, without, however, definitely formulating his own demands. Only so much was clear, that his claims had grown considerably since July 4. He said that the chief culprit could not be allowed to escape unpunished, and that justice once satisfied, we could let the misled backsliders off more easily, and he insisted on the cessions of territory from Austria which I have already mentioned. I replied that we were not there to sit in judgment, but to pursue the German policy. Austria's conflict in rivalry with us was no more culpable than ours with her; *our task was the establishment or initiation of a German national unity under the leadership of the King of Prussia.*

Passing on to German states, he spoke of various acquisitions by cutting down the territories of all our opponents. I repeated that we were not there to administer retributive justice, but to pursue a policy; that I wished to avoid, in the German federation of the future, the sight of mutilated territories, whose princes and peoples might very easily (such is human weakness) retain a lively wish to recover their former possessions by means of foreign help; such allies would be very unreliable. The same would be the case if, for the purpose of compensating Saxony, Würtzburg or Nuremburg were demanded of Bavaria, a plan, moreover, which would interfere with the dynastic prejudice of his Majesty in favour of Anspach. I had also to resist plans which were aimed at an enlargement of the Grand Duchy of Baden, the annexation of the Bavarian Palatinate, and an extension in the region of the lower Main. . . .

I at no time regarded a war with France as a simple matter, considered quite apart from the possible allies that France might find in Austria's thirst for revenge, or in Russia's desire for a balance of power. My strenuous efforts to postpone the outbreak of war until the effect of our military legislation and our military training could be thoroughly developed in all portions of the country which had been newly joined to Prussia, were therefore quite reasonable; and this aim of mine was not even approximately reached in the Luxembourg question in 1867. Each year's postponement of the war would add 100,000 trained soldiers to our army. In the attitude I took up towards the King on the question of the bill of Indemnity, and in dealing wih the question of the constitution in the Prussian Diet, I felt the urgent necessity of letting other countries see no trace of actual or prospective obstacles consequent on our internal condition; I wished to offer them the spectacle of a united national sentiment; and the more so inasmuch as it was impossible to judge what allies France would have on her side in a war against us. The negotiation and *rapprochements* between France and Austria soon after 1866, at Salzburg and elsewhere, under the direction of Herr von Beust [Austrian foreign minister], might prove successful; and the very appointment of that Saxon Minister in a bad temper to the control of Viennese policy already pointed to the probability that it would take the direction of revenge.

Italy's attitude was not to be reckoned upon as soon as French pressure was applied, as we discovered by her submissiveness to Napoleon in 1866. During a conference I had with General Govone in Berlin, in the early part of 1866, he was horrified when I expressed the wish that he should inquire at home if we could rely on Italy's loyalty to her engagements even against Napoleonic ill-humor. He replied that a question of this kind would be telegraphed to Paris the very same day with the question: "What answer shall be given?" To judge by the attitude of Italian policy during the war, I could not place any definite reliance on public opinion in Italy, not only on the ground of Victor Emmanuel's personal friendship to Louis Napoleon, but also by the standard of the partisanship announced by Garibaldi in the name of Italian public opinion. Not only my apprehensions, but the public opinion of Europe considered that a league of Italy with France and Russia was not outside the bounds of probability.

. . . By the influence which during the time of the Crimean war I had been able to exercise in favour of Russia on the resolutions of King Frederick William IV, I had gained for myself the goodwill of the Emperor Alexander, and his confidence in me was strenghtened during my residence as ambassador in St. Petersburg. Meanwhile, in the Russian Cabinet, under the leadership of Gortchakoff [Russian foreign minister], the doubt as to the advantage for Russia of so important an increase of Prussian power began to outweigh the Emperor's friendship for King William and his gratitude for our policy during the Polish question of 1863. If the communication be accurate which was made by Drouyn de Lhuys to Count Vitzthum von Eckstadt, then in July, 1866, Gortchakoff invited France to a common protest against the overthrow of the German confederation, and experienced a rebuff. In his first feeling of surprise, immediately upon the dispatch of Manteuffel to St. Petersburg, the Emperor Alexander had acquiesced in the result of the Nikolsburg preliminaries in general and *obiter*. At first the hatred against Austria, which, since the time of the

Crimean war, had dominated the public opinion of Russian "society," had found satisfaction in the defeat of Austria; this feeling, however, was opposed to Russian interests which were connected with the Czar's influence in Germany and the dangers with which it was threatened by France.

I took it indeed for granted that we could count on Russian support against any coalition that France might form against us; but that we should not receive it till we had the misfortune to suffer defeats, by which the question whether Russia could tolerate the proximity of a victorious Franco-Austrian coalition on her Polish frontiers would be brought nearer. The inconvenience of such a neighbour would perhaps be increased if, instead of the anti-papal kingdom of Italy, the Papacy itself were to become a third in the league of the two great Catholic Powers. I considered it, however, probable, that until the nearer approach of a danger such as would result from Prussian defeat, Russia would not be displeased, or at all events would offer no interference, if a numerically superior coalition had poured a little water into our wine of 1866.

From England we certainly could rely on no active support against the Emperor Napoleon, although English policy required a strong and friendly continental power with many battalions, and this necessity had been attended to under the Pitts, father and son, to the advantage of Prussia, later to that of Austria, then under Palmerston until the Spanish marriages, and afterwards again under Clarendon, in favour of France. The requirement of England's policy was either an *entente cordiale* with France, or the possession of a strong ally against the enmity of France. England is, indeed, ready to accept the stronger German-Prussia in place of Austria; and during the situation of the autumn of 1866 we could in any case count upon platonic goodwill and didactic newspaper articles from over there; but this theoretical sympathy would scarcely have condensed itself into an active support by land and by sea. The occurrences of 1870 have shown my estimation of England to have been correct. The representation of France in North Germany was undertaken in London with a readiness which was at least mortifying to us; and during the war England never compromised herself so far in our favour as thereby to endanger her friendship with France: on the contrary.

It was chiefly under the influence of these reflections in the sphere of our foreign policy, that I determined to regulate the movements of our home policy in accordance with the question, whether it would support or injure the impression of the power and coherence of the state. I argued to myself that our first great aim must be our independence and security in our foreign relations; that to this and not only actual removal of internal dissensions was requisite, but also any appearance of such a thing must be avoided in the sight of the foreign Powers and of Germany; that, if we first gained independence of foreign influence, we should then be able to move freely in our internal development, and to organise our institutions in as liberal or reactionary a manner as should seem right and fitting; that we might adjourn all domestic questions until we had secured our national aims abroad. I never doubted the possibility of giving to the royal power the strength necessary in order that our clock should be correctly set at home, provided that we first secured the necessary freedom from without to live as an independent great nation. Until that should be accomplished I was ready, if necessary, to pay "black-mail" to the opposition, in order to be in a position in the first place to throw into the scale our full power, and diplomatically to use the appearance of this united power and, in case of need, even to have the possibility of letting loose national revolutionary movements against our enemies. . . .

With respect to the necessity, in a fight against an overwhelming foreign power, of being able, in extreme need, to use even revolutionary means, I had no hesitation whatever in throwing into the frying-pan of the circular dispatch of June 10, 1866, the most powerful ingredient known at that time to liberty-mongers, namely, universal suffrage, by means so as to frighten off foreign monarchies from trying to stick a finger into our national omelette. I never doubted that the German people would be strong and clever enough to free themselves from the existing suffrage as soon as they realised that it was a harmful institution. If it cannot, then my saying that Germany can ride when once it has got into the saddle was erroneous. The acceptance of universal suffrage was a weapon in the war against Austria and other foreign countries, in the war for German Unity, as well as a threat to use the last weapons in a struggle against coalitions. In a war of this sort, when it becomes a matter of life and death, one does not look at the weapons that one seizes, nor the value of what one destroys in using them: one is guided at the moment by no other thought than the issue of the war, and the preservation of one's external independence; the settling of affairs and reparation of the damage has to take place after the peace. Moreover, I still hold that the principle of universal suffrage is a just one, not only in theory but also in practice, provided always that voting be not secret, for secrecy is a quality that is indeed incompatible with the best characteristics of German blood.

The influences and the dependence on others that the practical life of man brings in its train are God-given realities which we cannot and must not ignore. If we refuse to transfer them to political life, and base the public life of the country on the belief in the secret insight of all, we fall into a contradiction between public law and the realities of human life which practically leads to constant frictions, and finally to an explosion, and to which there is no theoretical solution except in the way of the insanities of social-democracy, the support given to which rests on the fact that the judgment of the masses is sufficiently stultified and undeveloped to allow them, with the assistance of their own greed, to be continually caught by the rhetoric of clever and ambitious leaders.

The counterpoise to this lies in the influence of the educated classes, which would be greatly strengthened if voting were public, as for the Prussian Diet. It may be that the greater discretion of the more intelligent classes rests on the material basis of the preservation of their possessions. The other motive, the struggle for gain, is equally justifiable; but a preponderance of those who represent property is more serviceable for the security and development of the state. A state, the control of which lies in the hands of the greedy, of the *novarum rerum cupidi,* and of orators who have the capacity for deceiving the unreasoning masses in a higher degree than others, will constantly be doomed to a restlessness of development, which so ponderous a mass as the commonwealth of the state cannot follow without injury to its organism. Ponderous masses, and among these the life and development of great nations must be reckoned, can only move with caution, since the road on which they travel to an unknown future has no smooth iron rails. Every great state-commonwealth that loses the prudent and restraining influence of the propertied class, whether that influence rests on material or moral grounds, will always end by being rushed along at a speed which must shatter the coach of state, as happened in the development of the French Revolution. The element of greed has the preponderance arising from the large masses which in the long run must make its way. It is in the interests of the great mass itself to wish decision to take place without dangerous acceleration of the speed of the coach of state, and without its destruction. If this should happen, however, the wheel of history will revolve again, and always in a proportionately shorter time to dictatorship, to despotism, to absolutism, because in the end the masses yield to the need of order; if they do not recognise this need *a priori*, they always realise it eventually after manifold arguments *ad hominem*; and in order to purchase order from a dictatorship and Caesarism they cheerfully sacrifice that justifiable amount of freedom which ought to be maintained, and which the political society of Europe can endure without ill-health. . . .

9. THE EMS DISPATCH*

In 1868 Napoleon III was still smarting over his failure to win compensation for France after Prussia had defeated Austria and reorganized Germany. The North German Confederation, created in 1867, was dominated by Prussia and bound by alliances to the four remaining southern German states. Amid an already upset balance of power a new diplomatic crisis in Spain intensified Franco-German tensions. A military coup overthrew Queen Isabella II, and Bismarck secretly pressed the candidacy of a Hohenzollern prince (Leopold of Hohenzollern-Sigmaringen) for the vacant throne of Spain. The Hohenzollern candidacy unexpectedly was made public early in 1870. The French government angrily objected, and Leopold withdrew his candidacy. Napoleon III, pressed by his cabinet and the Empress for further concessions, sent the French ambassador, Vincent Benedetti, to visit King William at Ems.

The Ems Dispatch, a telegraphic report of the meeting sent to Bismarck, is one of the fateful documents of modern history. Bismarck edited the dispatch and had his version published in the press. French officials, incensed by the treatment accorded their ambassador, pressed Napoleon III to declare war in 1870. In what ways did Bismarck distort the original dispatch?

THE ORIGINAL TEXT

Ems, July 13, 1870.

To the Federal Chancellor, Count Bismarck, No. 27, No. 61 *eod.* 3:10 P.M. (*Station Ems*: Rush!)

His Majesty the King writes to me:

"M. Benedetti intercepted me on the Promenade in order to demand of me most insistently that I should authorize him to telegraph immediately to Paris that I shall obligate myself for all future time never again to give my approval

* *Propylaear Weltgeschichte* [VIII, 248] in Louis L. Snyder, ed. and trans., *Documents of German History* (New Brunswick, N.J.: Rutgers University Press, 1958), pp. 215–16. Reprinted by permission.

to the candidacy of the Hohenzollerns should it be renewed. I refused to agree to this, the last time somewhat severely, informing him that one dare not and cannot assume such obligations *à tout jamais*. Naturally, I informed him that I had received no news as yet, and since he had been informed earlier than I by way of Paris and Madrid, he could easily understand why my government was once again out of the matter."

Since then His Majesty has received a dispatch from the Prince [Charles Anthony]. As His Majesty has informed Count Benedetti that he was expecting news from the Prince, His Majesty himself, in view of the above-mentioned demand and in consonance with the advice of Count Eulenburg and myself, decided not to receive the French envoy again but to inform him through an adjutant that His Majesty had now received from the Prince confirmation of the news which Benedetti had already received from Paris, and that he had nothing further to say to the Ambassador. His Majesty leaves it to the judgment of Your Excellency whether or not to communicate at once the new demand by Benedetti and its rejection to our ambassadors and to the press.

BISMARCK'S EDITED VERSION

After the reports of the renunciation by the hereditary Prince of Hohenzollern had been officially transmitted by the Royal Government of Spain to the Imperial Government of France, the French Ambassador presented to His Majesty the King at Ems the demand to authorize him to telegraph to Paris that His Majesty the King would obligate himself for all future time never again to give his approval to the candidacy of the Hohenzollerns should it be renewed.

His Majesty the King thereupon refused to receive the French envoy again and informed him through an adjutant that His Majesty had nothing further to say to the Ambassador.

TSARIST RUSSIA

10. NIKOLAI KARAMZIN: MEMOIR ON ANCIENT AND MODERN RUSSIA*

Nikolai Karamzin (1766–1826) was appointed official historiographer of Russia in 1803. As a patriot Karamzin saw no great advantage for Russia in borrowing heavily from the West. He criticized the work of Tsar Peter the Great, who, after "seeing Europe, wanted to make Russia into Holland." When Alexander I contemplated the introduction of liberal reforms recommended by his friend, Michael Speransky, Karamzin protested. Strongly conservative, the historian took exception to Speransky's plans to ameliorate the condition of the peasantry and wrote the Tsar a lengthy *Memorandum on Ancient and Modern Russia* (1811). Why did Karamzin oppose the abolition of serfdom? What moral arguments did he use to justify his position?

. . . We have heard of monstrous landowners who engaged in an inhuman traffic with people. Having purchased a village, these men picked the peasants

* *Karamzin's Memoir on Ancient and Modern Russia*, trans. Richard Pipes (Cambridge: Harvard University Press, 1959), pp. 162–67. Reprinted by permission.

fit for military service, and then sold them without land. Let us assume that there still are such beasts today. Trade of this kind should then be outlawed by a strict decree, containing a proviso that the estates of the unworthy landowners engaging in it are to be placed under guardianship. The enforcement of such a law could be entrusted to the governors. Instead of doing this, the government outlaws the sale and purchase of recruits. In the past, the better farmer toiled gladly for ten, twenty years in order to accumulate 700 or 800 rubles with which to purchase a recruit, so as to keep his family intact. Now he has lost his most powerful incentive to engage in beneficent hard work and stay sober. Of what use is wealth to a parent if it cannot save his beloved son? Yes, inn-keepers rejoice, but the heads of families weep. The state must have its recruits—it is better to draw them from miserable than from happy people, for the latter are incomparably worse off in the army than they were before. I would like to ask whether the peasants of a tyrannical landlord—one whose greed is such that he would be capable of selling them as recruits—prosper from the prohibition of such sales? If anything, their lot may be less miserable in the regiments! But as for the landowners of modest means, they have now lost an opportunity of ridding themselves of unsatisfactory peasants or household serfs, to their own and to society's benefit; under the old system the lazy, intemperate peasant would mend his ways in the strict military school, while the diligent, sober one would remain behind the plow. Moreover, the example itself exercised a salutary effect, and other peasants swore off the bottle knowing the master's rights to sell them as recruits. What means has a petty landowner nowadays with which to frighten his dissolute peasants when it is not his turn to furnish recruits? The cane? Backbreaking labor? Is it not more useful to have them frightened of the cane in the ranks of the military company? One may argue that our soldiers have improved as a result of this decree, but have they indeed? I inquired of generals—they have not noticed it. At any rate, it is true that the village peasants have deteriorated. The father of three or even two sons readies in good time one of them for the draft, and keeps him unmarried; the son, knowing what awaits him, drinks, because good behavior will not save him from military service. The legislator should view things from a variety of angles and not merely from one; or else, extirpating one evil, he may occasion yet greater evil.

Thus we are told that the present government had the intention of emancipating proprietary serfs. One must know the origins of this bondage. In Russia in the ninth, tenth, and eleventh centuries the only bondmen were the *kholopy,* *i.e.,* either foreigners captured in war or purchased, or criminals deprived by law of citizenship, together with their descendants. But rich men, disposing of a multitude of *kholopy,* populated their lands with them, and in this manner arose the first serf villages in the modern sense of the word. Furthermore, proprietors also admitted into servitude free peasants on terms which more or less constrained the latter's natural and civil liberties; some of these peasants, upon receipt of land from the proprietor, committed themselves and the children to serve him forever. This was the second source of slavery in the countryside. Other peasants—and they constituted the majority—rented land from the owners in return for a payment consisting only of money or a set quantity of cereals, while retaining the right to move on elsewhere after the expiration of a fixed period of time. These free movements, however, had their drawbacks, for great lords and wealthy men lured free peasants away from weak landlords, and the latter, left with deserted fields, were unable to meet their state obligations. Tsar Boris was the first to deprive all peasants of this freedom to move from place to place, that is, he bound them to their masters. . . . I do not want to pursue this controversy further, but I should like to point out that as far as the state is concerned, natural law yields to civil law, and that the prudent autocrat abrogates only those laws which have become harmful or inadequate, and which can be replaced by superior ones.

What does the emancipation of serfs in Russia entail? That they be allowed to live where they wish, that their masters be deprived of all authority over them, and that they come exclusively under the authority of the state. Very well. But these emancipated peasants will have no land, which—this is incontrovertible—belongs to the gentry. They will, therefore, either stay on with their present landlords, paying them quitrent, cultivating their fields, delivering bread where necessary—in a word, continuing to serve them as before; or else, dissatisfied with the terms, they will move to another, less exacting landlord. In the first case, is it not likely that the masters, relying on man's natural love for his native soil, will impose on the peasants the most onerous terms? Previously they had spared them, seeing in the serfs their own property, but now the greedy among them will try to exact from the peasants all that is physically possible. The landlords will draw up a contract, the tiller will renege—and there will be lawsuits, eternal lawsuits! In the second case, with the peasant now here, now there, won't the treasury suffer losses in the collection of the soul-tax and other revenues? Will not agriculture suffer as well? Will not many fields lie fallow, and many granaries stay empty? After all, the bread on our markets comes, for the most part, not from the free farmers but from the gentry. And here is one more evil consequence of emancipation: the peasants, no longer subjected to seignorial justice from which there is no appeal and which is free of charge, will take to fighting each other and litigating in the city—what ruin! . . . Freed from the surveillance of the masters who dispose of their own *zemskaia isprava,* or police, which is much more active than all the Land Courts, the peasants will take to drinking and villainy—what a gold mine for taverns and corrupt police officials, but what a blow to morals and to the security of the state! In short, at the present time, the gentry, dispersed throughout the realm, assist the monarch in the preservation of peace and order; by divesting them of this supervisory authority, he would, like Atlas, take all of Russia upon his shoulders. Could he bear it? A collapse would be frightful. The primary obligation of the monarch is to safeguard the internal and external unity of the state; benefiting estates and individuals comes second. Alexander wishes to improve the lot of the peasants by granting them freedom; but what if this freedom should harm the state? And will the peasants be happier, freed from their masters' authority, but handed over to their own vices, to tax farmers, and to unscrupulous judges? There can be no question that the serfs of a sensible landlord, one who contends himself with a moderate quitrent, or with labor on a *desiatina* of plowland for each household, are happier than state peasants, for they have in him a vigilant protector and defender. Is it not better quietly to take measures to bridle cruel landlords? These men are known to the governors. If the latter faithfully fulfill their obligations, such landlords will promptly become a thing of the past; and unless Russia has wise and honest governors, the free peasants will not prosper either. I do not know whether Godunov did well in depriving the peasants of their freedom since the conditions of that time are not fully known. But I do know that this is not the time to return it to them. Then they had the habits of free men—today they have the habits of slaves. It seems to me that from the point of view of political stability it is safer to enslave men than to give them freedom prematurely. Freedom demands preparation through moral improvement—and who would call our system of wine-farming and the dreadful prevalence of drunkenness a sound preparation for freedom? In conclusion, we have this to say to the good monarch: "Sire! history will not reproach you for the evil which you have inherited (assuming that serfdom actually is an unequivocal evil), but you will answer before God, conscience, and posterity for every harmful consequence of your own statutes." ...

11. VISSARION BELINSKY: RUSSIA AND THE SLAVOPHILS*

The imperious figure of Tsar Peter the Great (r. 1682–1725), an innovator who borrowed freely and consciously from western technology, was the inspiration of a considerable segment of Russian intelligentsia known as the "westerners." To this group of scholars, success and progress for Russia were to be achieved by borrowing ideas and technology from western Europe and casting out the backwardness, traditions, and old customs that shackled the Russian people. Their opponents, known as "Slavophils," insisted upon the differences between Russia and Europe and sought to emphasize native Russian traditions. To them Tsar Peter had been an evil genius who had attempted to drive Russia along the wrong path.

Vissarion Belinsky (1811–48) was a literary critic, journalist, and philosopher. He argued sharply against serfdom, condemned the Russia of Nicholas I (r. 1825–55) severely in a famous letter to the writer Gogol (the letter was circulated widely in handwritten copies since censorship prevented its publication), and was the idol of a generation of radical youth. Leaning toward socialism and the social purpose of literature, Belinsky was Russia's leading westernizer.

Belinsky's pride in Russia and his efforts to encourage the development of Russian literature marked him as a patriot. As a westernizer, however, he resisted the spread of Slavophil doctrines. What, according to Belinsky, was Slavophilism? With which presuppositions of Slavophilism was Belinsky in sympathy? Why did he assert that "the Russian to himself is still a riddle"? What destiny did Belinsky advocate for Russia?

The influence of Karamzin through his *History of the Russian State* is still very conspicuous. This is best evidenced by the so-called Slavophil party. We know that in Karamzin's eyes Ivan III stood higher than Peter the Great, and pre-Petrine Russ was better than the new Russia. Here you have the origin of the so-called Slavophil movement, which, by the way, we regard in many

* V. Belinsky, "Russia and the Slavophils" in Hans Kohn, ed., *The Mind of Modern Russia* (New Brunswick, N.J.: Rutgers University Press, 1955), pp. 133–35. Reprinted by permission.

respects as a very important phenomenon. It proves that the adult and mature period of our literature is close at hand. During the infancy of literature all men are engaged with problems which, though they may be important in themselves, have no practical bearing on life. Slavophilism without doubt has a vital bearing on the most important aspects of our public life.

Slavophilism is first of all a conviction. Like all convictions, it merits our utmost respect, even though we may entirely disagree with it. We have many Slavophils, and their number is steadily growing.

The positive side of their doctrine consists of some sort of nebulous, mystical presentiment of the victory of the East over the West. The Slavophil fallacy is all too clearly exposed by the facts of reality. The negative side of the Slavophil creed, however, deserves much more attention, not in that it falls foul of the allegedly decaying West—the Slavophils are absolutely unable to understand the West because they measure it with an Eastern yardstick—but in that it falls foul of Russian Europeanism. They have a good deal to say of it, which is pertinent. One cannot help at least half-agreeing with some of their contentions, for instance that there is a sort of duality in Russian life and consequently a lack of moral unity; that this deprives us of a clearly defined national character such as distinguishes, to their credit, all the European nations; that this makes a kind of nonesuch out of us, well able to think in French, German, and English, but unable to think in Russian; and that the cause for all this lies in the reforms of Peter the Great.

To some extent, all this is correct. We must not, however, confine ourselves to such an admission; we must investigate the causes in the hope of discovering, within the evil itself, a way out of it. This the Slavophils have not done; but this is what they have made their opponents, if not accomplish, then at least attempt to do. Herein lies the true service which they have rendered. It is equally fruitless and harmful to fall asleep in ambitious dreams, whether of our national glory or of our Europeanism. Sleep is not life, but merely a realm of fancies, and we cannot but be grateful to him who breaks such a sleep. Indeed, never before has the study of Russian history assumed such a serious character as lately. We probe and question the past for an explanation of our present and a hint as to our future. We seem to have taken alarm for our life, for our significance, for our past and future, and are in a hurry to solve the great problem of to be or not to be. . . .

Russia should not be compared to the old states of Europe. Their history followed a course diametrically opposed to ours, and has long since yielded both its blossom and its fruit. Without doubt it is easier for a Russian to adopt the view of a Frenchman, Englishman, or German than to think independently in Russian, for the first way presents a ready-made view the acquaintance with which is rendered easy both by science and by present-day realities. To think in Russian is much more difficult, because the Russian to himself is still a riddle, and the significance and destiny of his native land, where everything is embryonic and incipient and nothing is determinate, fully evolved, and formed, are likewise a riddle to him. To be sure, there is something sad in it, but still more something that is comforting. The oak grows slowly, but then it lives for centuries. It is natural for man to wish the speedy fulfillment of his desires, but precocity is unreliable: we more than anybody else should have convinced ourselves of this truth. . . .

We Russians need have no doubts as to our . . . political significance: we alone, of all the Slav peoples, have formed a strong and powerful state, and have, both before and ever since the time of Peter the Great, come through many a severe ordeal with flying colors. We often stood on the brink of ruin, and yet we invariably rode out the storm to reappear on its crest in new and greater vigor and strength. A nation incapable of internal growth could not possess such strength and vigor. Yes, we have the national life in us, we are destined to give our message and our thought to the world; but it is too early yet to conjecture what that message or thought will be. Our grandchildren or great-grandchildren will earn it without any effort at hard guessing, because that message and that thought will be uttered by them. . . .

12. ALEXANDER HERZEN: MY PAST AND THOUGHTS*

Alexander Herzen (1812–70) was Russia's first revolutionary in exile. A westerner by instinct, he also sympathized with the Slavophils because of their patriotism. Herzen despised the oppressive regime of Tsar Nicholas I, especially because the Tsar sponsored an "official nationalism" under which the Imperial Government promoted orthodoxy and nationalism for the benefit of the autocracy. In 1847 Herzen fled abroad, eventually to settle in London, where he lived comfortably (thanks to a large fortune left him by his father), financed revolutionaries, and published newspapers which were smuggled into Russia. The most famous of his journals was *Kolokol* (the Bell). Herzen advocated a nebulous form of socialism, which he based on the native Russian peasant commune, the *mir*. He urged the emancipation of the serfs and applauded the efforts of Tsar Alexander II (r. 1855–81) to liberate them. By the time of his death in 1870, however, a new generation of younger revolutionaries began to advance sharply different doctrines. To that new generation of revolutionaries, radicalism and terror were essential instruments for the destruction of the Russian autocracy; Herzen and his ideas seemed "quaint" to them. What features of Slavophilism attracted Herzen? How did Herzen use history to demonstrate that Russian culture was unique?

. . . Beside our circle were our opponents, *nos amis les ennemis,* or more correctly, *les ennemis nos amis*—the Moscow Slavophils.

The conflict between us ended long ago and we have held out our hands to each other; but in the early forties we could not but be antagonistic—without being so we could not have been true to our principles. We might not have quarrelled with them over their childish homage to the childhood of our history; but accepting their orthodoxy as meant in earnest, seeing their ecclesiastical intolerance on both sides—in relation to learning and in relation to sectarianism—we were bound to take up a hostile attitude to them. We saw in their doctrines fresh oil for anointing the Tsar, new chains laid upon thought, new subordination of conscience to the slavish Byzantine Church.

The Slavophils are to blame for our having so long failed to understand the

* Alexander Herzen, *The Memoirs of My Past and Thoughts,* trans. Constance Garnett (6 vols.; London: Chatto and Windus, 1924), II, 254–60, 263, 271–75. Reprinted by permission.

Russian people and its history; their ikon-painter's ideals and incense smoke hindered us from seeing the realities of the people's existence and the foundations of village life.

The orthodoxy of the Slavophils, their historical patriotism and oversensitive, exaggerated feeling of nationality were called forth by the extremes on the other side. The importance of their outlook, what was true and essential in it, lay not in orthodoxy, and not in exclusive nationalism, but in those elements of Russian life which they unearthed from under the manure of civilisation.

The idea of nationality is in itself a conservative idea—the demarcation of one's rights, the opposition of self to another; it includes both the Judaic conception of superiority of race, and the aristocratic claim to purity of blood, and right to ascendancy. Nationalism as a standard, as a war-cry, is only surrounded with the halo of revolution when a people is fighting for its independence, when it is throwing off a foreign yoke. That is why national feeling with all its exaggerations is full of poetry in Italy and in Poland, while it is vulgar in Germany.

For us to display our nationalism would be even more absurd than it is for the Germans; even those who abuse us do not doubt it; they hate us from fear, but they do not refuse to recognise us, as Metternich did Italy. We have had to set up our nationalism against the Germanised government and its renegades. . . .

Our Slavophils took sympathy with the western Panslavists for identity of cause and policy, forgetting that their exclusive nationalism was at the same time the cry of a people oppressed by a foreign yoke. Western Panslavism on its first appearance was taken by the Austrian government itself for a conservative movement. It developed at the melancholy epoch of the Congress of Vienna. It was a period of restorations and resurrections of all sorts, a period when every kind of Lazarus, fresh and decayed rose up from the dead. Together with *Teutschthum,* which looked for the renaissance of the *happy days* of Barbarossa and the Hohenstaufens, Czech Panslavism made its appearance. The governments were pleased with this movement and at first encouraged the development of international hatreds; the masses rallied again round the idea of racial kinship, the bond of which was drawn tighter, and were again turned aside from general demands for the improvement of their lot. Frontiers became more impassable, ties and sympathies between peoples were broken. It need hardly be said that only among apathetic and feeble peoples was nationalism allowed to develop, and only so long as it confined itself to archaeological and linguistic disputes. In Milan and in Poland where nationalism was not confined to grammar, a tight rein was kept upon it.

The Czech Panslavism provoked Slavonic sympathies in Russia.

Slavism or Russianism, not as a theory, not as a doctrine, but as a wounded national feeling, as an obscure tradition and a true instinct, as antagonism to an exclusively foreign influence, has existed ever since Peter the Great cut off the first Russian beard.

There has never been any interval in the resistance to the Petersburg forcible imposition of culture; it reappears in the form of the mutinous Stryeltsl, punished, quartered, hanged on the walls of the Kremlin and there shot by Menshikov and other favourites of the Tsar, in the form of the Tsarevitch Alexis poisoned in the dungeon of the Petersburg fortress, as the party of the *Dolgorukys* in the reign of Peter III, as the hatred for the Germans in the time of Biron, as Pugatchov in the time of Catherine II, as Catherine herself, the Orthodox German in the reign of the Russian Holsteiner Peter III, as Elizabeth who ascended the throne through the support of the Slavophils of those days (the people in Moscow expected all the Germans to be massacred at her coronation).

All the dissenters are Slavophils.

All the clergy, both white and black, are Slavophils of another sort.

The soldiers who demanded the removal of Barclay de Tolly on account of his German name were the precursors of Homyakov and his friends. The war of 1812 greatly developed the national consciousness and love for the Fatherland. . . .

In the reign of Nicholas patriotism became something associated with the knout, with the police, especially in Petersburg, where the savage government ended, in harmony with the cosmopolitan character of the town, by the invention of a national hymn after Sebastian Bach and in Prokopy Lyapunov—after Schiller!

To cut himself off from Europe, from enlightenment, from the revolution of which he had been terrified since the Fourteenth of December, Nicholas on his side raised the banner of orthodoxy, autocracy, and nationalism, remodelled after the fashion of the Prussian standard and supported by anything that came to hand—the barbaric romances of Zagoskin, barbaric ikon-painting, barbaric architecture, by Uvarov, by the persecution of the Uniats and by "The Hand of the Most High saved the Fatherland."

The existence of the Petersburg Slavophilism of Nicholas was very fortunate for the Moscow Slavophils. Nicholas was simply flying to nationalism and orthodoxy to escape from revolutionary ideas. The Slavophils had nothing in common with him but words. . . .

Long cut off from the people, part of Russia had been suffering in silence under the most stupid and prosaic yoke, which gave them nothing in return. Every one felt the oppression of it, every one had something weighing on his heart, and yet all were silent; at last a man had come who in his own way told them what it was. He spoke only of pain, there was no ray of light in his words, nor indeed in his view. Tchaadayev's letter was a merciless cry of reproach and bitterness against Russia; it deserved the indictment; had it shown pity or mercy to the author or any one else? . . .

But it did not pass unnoticed; for a minute all, even the drowsy and the crushed, were roused, alarmed by this menacing voice. . . .

Nothing in the world could be more opposed to the Slavophils than the hopeless pessimism which was Tchaadayev's vengeance on Russian life, the deliberate curse wrung out of him by suffering, with which he summed up his melancholy existence through a whole period of Russian history. He could not but awaken intense opposition in them; with bitterness and weary malice he insulted all that was precious to them, from Moscow downwards.

"In Moscow," Tchaadayev used to say, "every foreigner is taken to look at the great cannon and the great bell—the cannon which can never be fired and the bell which fell down before it was rung. It is a strange town in which the objects of interest are distinguished by their absurdity; or perhaps that great bell without a tongue is a hieroglyph symbolic of that immense dumb land, inhabited by a race calling themselves Slavs as though surprised at the possession of human speech."

Tchaadayev and the Slavophils alike stood facing the unsolved Sphinx of Russian life, the Sphinx sleeping under the overcoat of the soldier and the watchful eye of the Tsar; they alike were asking: "What will come of it? To live like this is impossible: the oppressiveness and absurdity of the present position is obvious and unendurable—where is the way out?"

"There is none," answered the man of the Petersburg period of exclusively Western civilisation, who, in Alexander's reign, had believed in the European future of Russia. He mournfully pointed out to what the efforts of a whole age had led. Culture had only given new methods of oppression, the church had become a mere shadow under which the police lay hidden; the people bore all, endured all, the government crushed all, oppressed all. "The history of other nations is the story of their emancipation. Russian history is the development of serfdom and autocracy." Peter the Great's upheaval had made us into the worst that men can be made into—enlightened slaves. We had suffered enough, in this oppressive, troubled moral state, misunderstood by the people, struck down by the government—it was time to find rest, time to find peace for the soul, to find support in something . . . this almost meant "time to die," and Tchaadayev thought to find in the Catholic Church the peace promised to all who are weary and heavy-laden.

From the point of view of Western civilisation in the form in which it found expression at the time of the restoration, from the point of view of the Russia of the Petersburg period, this attitude was completely justified.

The Slavophils solved the question in a different way.

Their solution implied a true recognition of the living soul in the people; their instinct was more penetrating than their reasoning. They saw that the existing condition of Russia, however oppressive, was not a moral disease. And while Tchaadayev had a faint glimmer of the possibility of saving individuals but not the people, the Slavophils had a clear perception of the ruin of individuals in the grip of the existing order and faith in the salvation of the people.

"The way out is with us," said the Slavophils, "the way out lies in renouncing the Petersburg period, in going back to the people from whom we have been cut off by foreign education and foreign government; let us return to the old ways!"

But history does not turn back; life is rich in materials, it has no need to remake old clothes. All renaissances, all restorations have been masqueraders. We have seen two; the Legitimists did not go back to the days of Louis XIV, nor the Republicans to the 8th of Thermidor. What has once happened is stronger than anything written; no axe can hew it away.

Moreover, we have nothing to which to go back. The political life of Russia before Peter the Great was grotesque, poor, savage, yet it was to this that the

Slavophils wanted to return, though they did not admit the fact; how else are we to explain all their antiquarian revivals, their worship of the manners and customs of old days, and their attempts to return, not to the existing (and excellent) dress of the peasants but to the old-fashioned and clumsy costumes?

In all Russia no one wears the *murmolka* but the Slavophils. K. S. Aksakov wore a dress so national that the peasants in the street took him a Persian, as Tchaadayev used to tell as a joke.

They took the going back to the people in a very crude sense too, as the majority of Western democrats did also, accepting the people as something complete and finished. They imagined that to share the superstitions of the people means being at one with them, that it was a great act of humility to sacrifice one's reason instead of developing reason in the people. This led to an affectation of devoutness, the observance of rites which are touching when there is a naive faith in them and insulting where an ulterior motive can be discerned. The best proof of the lack of reality in the Slavophils' return to the people lies in the fact that they did not arouse the slightest sympathy in the people. Neither the Byzantine Church nor the *Granovitaya Palata* will do anything more for the future development of the Slav world. To go back to the village, to the workmen's guild, to the meeting of the mir, to the Cossack system is a different matter; but we must return to them not in order to strengthen them in immovable Asiatic crystallisations but to develop and set free the elements on which they were founded, to purify them from all that is extranaeous and distorting, from the rank growths with which they are overgrown—that, of course, is what we are called to do. But we must make no mistake, all this lies outside the sphere of the State: the Moscow period is of as little use here as the Petersburg, indeed it was at no time better. The Novogorod bell which used to call the citizens to their ancient mote was merely melted into a cannon by Peter, but had been taken down from the belfry by Ivan III; serfdom was only confirmed by the census under Peter but was introduced by Boris Godunov; in the *Ulozhenie* there is no mention of sworn witnesses, and the knout, the reds, and the lash made their appearance long before the day of *Spitzruten* and *Fuchtein*.

The mistake of the Slavophils lies in their imagining that Russia once had an individual culture, obscured by various events and finally by the Petersburg period. Russia never had this culture, never could have had it. That which is only now reaching our consciousness, that of which we are beginning to have a presentiment, a glimmer in our thoughts, that which existed unconsciously in the peasants' hut and in the open country, is only now beginning to grow in the fields of history, enriched by the blood, the tears, the sweat of twenty generations.

The foundations of our life are not memories, they are the living elements, existing not in chronicles but in the actual present; but they have merely survived under the hard historical process of building up a single state and under the yoke of the state they have only been preserved not developed. I doubt, indeed, whether the inner strength for their development would have been found without the Petersburg period, without the period of European culture.

The primitive foundations of our life are insufficient. In India there has existed for ages and exists to this day a village commune very like our own and founded on a division of fields; yet the people of India have not gone very far, even with it.

Only the mighty thought of the West to which all its long history has led up is able to fertilise the seeds slumbering in the patriarchal mode of life of the Slavs. The workmen's guild and the village commune, the sharing of profits and the division of fields, the *mir* meeting and the union of villages into self-governing *volosts,* are all the corner-stones on which the temple of our future, freely communal existence will be built. But these corner-stones are only stones . . . and without the thought of the West our future cathedral will not rise above its foundations.

13. NIKOLAI GOGOL: DEAD SOULS*

Palace revolts had overthrown or determined the succession of most Russian emperors and empresses of the eighteenth century. In spite of their participation in these revolts, the Russian nobility failed to seize political power, and each new tsar remained absolute. Catherine the Great, in part to protect herself against a palace revolt, confirmed the nobles in the extraordinary rights and privileges which gave them virtually unlimited power on their private estates. In the provinces, far from cities and the court, many nobles lived in a backward, agrarian world. The great Russian writer, Nikolai Gogol (1809–52), deplored the stagnant society of the vast countryside. One of the founders of Russian realistic literature, Gogol depicted the decadence of the provincial nobility and bureaucracy in his novel *Dead Souls* (1842). The following excerpts present character sketches of two Russian landlords (*boyars*)—Nozdreff and Pliushkin. What were the attitudes of Gogol's characters toward their peers, their property, and their serfs? Contrast the economic, social, and cultural interests of Gogol's landlords with the interests and political involvement displayed by the British aristocrats in the House of Commons debate on Parliamentary reform in 1848. What specific illustrations did Gogol use to show the lack of culture and knowledge of world affairs among Russian *boyars* and bureaucrats?

NOZDREFF

On reaching the inn Tchitchikoff commanded a halt for two reasons: on the one hand, to give the horses an opportunity to rest, and, on the other, to get something to eat for himself.

The wooden inn, darkened with age, received Tchitchikoff beneath its narrow but hospitable verandah, supported on turned wooden columns, which resembled ancient ecclesiastical candlesticks. The inn was somewhat like an *izbà* (cabin), but of rather larger dimensions. The carving on the cornice round the windows and door gave it a tolerably artistic appearance, which was heightened by some jugs and flowers painted on the shutters.

Ascending the narrow wooden staircase which led up-stairs into a spacious vestibule, Tchitchikoff encountered a door which opened with a squeak, and beheld a fat old woman in a motley chintz gown, who addressed him with, "This way, if you please."

* Nikolai Gogol, *Dead Souls* (London: T. Fisher Unwin, 1893), pp. 54–61, 98–103. Reprinted by permission of Ernest Benn, Ltd.

"Do you happen to have a roast suckling-pig?" Tchitchikoff asked in reply to her greeting.

"Yes."

"With horse-radish and sour cream?"

"Yes, with both."

"Fetch it here, then."

The old woman went to get it, and brought a plate, and a napkin which was starched to such a point that it stood on one end like a dry crust; then she brought a knife with a yellow bone handle and a blade as thin as a penknife, a two-pronged fork, and a salt-cellar which could not be induced to stand straight on the table.

Our hero, according to his custom, immediately entered into conversation with the landlady, and inquired whether she kept the inn herself, or whether there was a landlord, and how much money the inn brought in each year, and whether her sons lived with her, and whether the eldest one was married or unmarried, what sort of a wife he had, whether she had brought him a large dowry or not, and whether the bride's father was satisfied, or whether he had been angry at receiving only a few presents at the wedding; in short, he omitted nothing. Of course it is understood that he inquired what landowners there were in the vicinity; and he found out that there were several, named Blokhin, Potchitaeff, Muilnoi, Tcheprakoff, and Sobakevitch. "Ah! do you know Sobakevitch?" he asked, and he immediately learnt that the old woman knew not only Sobakevitch, but Maniloff also. She declared, too, that Maniloff was *more exacting* than Sobakevitch: "He immediately orders a chicken to be boiled, asks for some veal," she said; "and if there is any roast mutton, he asks for that also—indeed he tries everything; but Sobakevitch only asks for one thing, eats it all up, and then wants a second helping without extra charge."

While Tchitchikoff thus was conversing and eating the roast suckling-pig, the rumble of an approaching carriage became audible. Peeping through the window he perceived a light britchka, attached to a troika of three fine horses, halting before the door of the inn. Two men descended from the britchka. One of them was fair-haired and of lofty stature; the other somewhat shorter and of dark complexion. The fair man wore a dark-blue Hungarian coat, the dark one a simple striped summer jacket. In the distance an empty calash was coming along, drawn by four long-maned horses with frayed collars and some rope harness. The fair-haired man immediately walked up-stairs, while the dark one remained fumbling for something in the britchka, talking to the servant and pointing to the advancing calash. His voice struck Tchitchikoff as familiar to him in some way or other. While he was still gazing out of the window the fair-haired man had succeeded in opening the door of the room. He was of lofty stature, with a thin, or what is called a worn face, and a reddish moustache. It might be surmised from his brown cheeks that he knew what smoke was, if not the smoke of powder, at least that from tobacco. He bowed courteously to Tchitchikoff, and the latter responded in the same way. Then the dark-complexioned man entered, flinging his cap from his head upon the table, and jauntily passing his fingers through his thick black hair. He was a well-built young man of medium height, with full red cheeks, teeth as white as snow, and whiskers as black as pitch. He looked as fresh as blood and milk; his face was radiant with health.

"Bah, bah, bah!" he exclaimed all at once, flinging both arms about as he caught sight of Tchitchikoff. "How did you come here?"

Tchitchikoff now recognised Nozdreff, the same person in whose company he had dined at the procurator's, and now, in the course of a very few minutes, had got upon a very intimate footing with him.

"Where have you been?" resumed Nozdreff; and without awaiting a reply, he went on. "For myself I have been to the fair, my dear fellow. And now congratulate me! I'm totally ruined! Would you believe it? I was never so completely plucked in all my life! Why, I am travelling with peasants' horses! Just look out of the window!" Hereupon he bent Tchitchikoff's head so that it almost came in violent contact with the window sash. "Do you see what wretched beasts they are?" he continued. "It was with difficulty that they dragged me along, the cursed animals! I had to get into his britchka." So saying, Nozdreff pointed to his comrade. "By the way, you are not already acquainted? This is my brother-in-law, Mizhueff. We were talking about you this morning. 'See, now,' said I, 'we must find Tchitchikoff!' But oh! my friend, if you only knew how completely ruined I am! Will you believe it? I not only lost four trotters, but everything else besides! Why, I haven't either a watch or a chain about me!"

Tchitchikoff now looked at Nozdreff, and perceived that he had neither watch nor chain. It even struck him that one of his whiskers was smaller and thinner than the other.

"If I only had had twenty roubles in my pocket," continued Nozdreff, "only just twenty, I could have won everything back; that is to say, I could have won that and thirty thousand roubles besides, and have immediately put them into this pocket-book, like an honourable man."

"But that was what you said at the time," replied the fair-haired man; "and when I gave you fifty roubles, you lost them too."

"I did not mean to lose them: by heavens, I didn't mean to! If I had not committed a mistake I should not have lost them. If I hadn't staked three to two on that cursed seven after the king, I might have broken the bank."

"But you didn't break it," said the fair-haired man.

"I did not break it because I played too soon. But do you think that your major plays well?"

"Whether he plays well or not, he outplayed you."

"Much that amounts to!" said Nozdreff. "I'll win some cash from him in the same way. Yes, just let him play with me again, then we'll see, we'll see what sort of a player he is. Ah! how jolly we were in town, friend Tchitchikoff! Really, the fair was capital. The merchants themselves declared that there never was such a concourse of people. Everything which I had brought up from the country sold at the most favourable prices. Ah, my friend, what a carouse we had! Even now when I think of it—deuce take it—that is, it is such a pity you were not there. Just imagine, a regiment of dragoons was stationed at three versts from the town. Every one of the officers—and there were forty of them—came to town; and then we began to drink, brother, with the staff cavalry captain, Potzyelueff, such a splendid fellow he is! such a moustache he has, brother! He calls Bordeaux 'burdashki.' 'Bring some burdashki, my good fellow,' says he. Then Lieutenant Kuvshinnikoff—ah, my friend, what a charming man he is! And I may say that the carouse was managed according to rule. We were all together, and what wine Ponomareff gave us! He is a rascal though, and you mustn't purchase anything in his shop: he mixes all sorts of rubbish in his wine—sandal-wood, burnt cork, and he even colours it with elderberry, the villain; but after all if he brings a little bottle from the cellar which he calls his own sanctum, then truly, my friend, you find yourself in the empyrean. Our champagne was so good that the governor's is nothing to it, simply kvas.[1] Fancy, not only real Cliquot, but a special sort of Cliquot—double-distilled Cliquot. And then I got one little bottle of a French wine called "Bonbon," with a perfume. Ah! roses and everything you like. But what a carouse we did have! After us came some prince or other, and he sent to the shop for champagne; but no, there wasn't a single bottle left in the whole city, the officers had drunk it all up. Just think, I alone drank seventeen bottles in the course of the dinner."

"Come, now, you can't drink seventeen bottles," remarked the fair-haired man.

"On the word of an honest man, I say that I did drink them," replied Nozdreff.

"You can say what you like, but I assert that you cannot drink ten."

"Come, will you not bet that I can't drink them?"

"What's the use of betting?"

"Come, now, wager that gun which you bought in town."

"No, I won't."

"Come wager it, try it."

"I don't want to try it."

"Yes, you would be left without a gun as you are left without a hat. Ah, Friend Tchitchikoff, how sorry I am that you were not there. I know that you could not have parted from Kuvshinnikoff. How well you would have agreed with each other! He's not at all like the procurator and all those government misers who tremble over every copeck. He can play at *galbik*, faro, or anything you wish. Ah, Tchitchikoff! Now, what would it cost you to come? Truly, you are a dirty pig for not coming, a thorough lout. Kiss me, my soul; death, but I love you! Look, Mizhueff! fate has brought us together. Now, what is he to me, or what am I to him? He has come here, God knows whence, and we also have come here. But, I say, how many carriages there were, my friend, at the fair, and all on such a grand scale! I tried my luck at the wheel of fortune, and won two boxes of pomatum, a porcelain cup, and a guitar: then I staked once more, and gave the thing a twist, and lost more than six roubles, dash it! But I say, if you only knew what a wild fellow Kuvshinnikoff is! We went to nearly all the balls together. There was such a woman at one of them, with hardly anything on her back. She was nearly naked, and I thought to myself, 'Devil take it!' But Kuvshinnikoff—he's such a brute!—he just seated himself

---

1. A sourish beer made from rye meal and malt.

beside her, and paid her such compliments in French. I assure you, he didn't miss flirting with any of the women. That's what he calls 'making the most of the strawberries.' By the way one dealer at the fair sold such wonderful fish and slices of dried sturgeon. I have brought some with me—lucky I thought of buying them while I still had some money left. But, I say, where are you going now?"

"To see a man I have to deal with," said Tchitchikoff.

"Oh, dash the man! let him alone; come to my house."

"Impossible, impossible! I have some business to transact with him."

"Well, that's a nice story to invent. Ah, you Opodeldok Ivanovitch, you're deceiving us!"

"Really, I have some business to attend to, and very important business too."

"I'll bet that you are lying! Come, tell me to whose house you are going."

"Well, then, to Sobakevitch's."

On hearing this Nozdreff burst into such a resounding laugh as only a fresh, healthy man can give vent to, displaying all his sugar-white teeth, and his cheeks quivering and leaping. A traveller in an adjoining room who was abruptly aroused from his slumbers, stared round, wondering what was happening, and finally ejaculated,

"Eh, what! has the house tumbled down?"

"What is there ridiculous in what I said?" said Tchitchikoff, somewhat offended by Nozdreff's laugh.

But Nozdreff continued laughing at the top of his voice, and even shouted at intervals, "Oh, mercy! I shall burst."

"But there's nothing to laugh at. I promised Sobakevitch to go and see him," said Tchitchikoff.

"You'll be sorry when you reach his house, he's a downright niggard! Ah! I know your character; you'll be mightily disappointed if you think you'll find a faro bank and a good bottle of 'bonbon' there. Listen, my dear fellow; let Sobakevitch go to the devil, and come with me. What dried sturgeon I'll treat you to! Ponomareff bowed to me when I bought it and said, 'It's only for you; you may search through the whole fair, and you won't find any such dried sturgeon.' But he's a frightful scamp, and I said so to his face. 'You,' said I, 'and our brandy farmers are the biggest rascals we have.' The beast laughed, and stroked his beard. Kuvshinnikoff and I breakfasted at his place every day. Ah, my dear fellow, I forgot to tell you. But I've got something which I wouldn't sell for ten thousand roubles. Hey, there, Porfiriy!" he shouted to his man, who was holding in one hand a knife, and in the other a crust of bread with a bit of sturgeon, which he had succeeded in slicing off on the sly. "Hey, there, Porfiriy!" shouted Nozdreff, "bring that puppy here. Such a dog!" he continued, turning to Tchitchikoff. "I didn't buy it, I stole it; the owner wouldn't give it up of his own free will. I offered him a chestnut horse: you remember it—the one I won from Khvostuireff?"

As it happened, Tchitchikoff had never seen either the chestnut horse nor Khvostuireff in his life.

"Won't you have something to eat, master, now?" said the old woman, approaching Nozdreff.

"No, nothing. Ah, my dear Tchitchikoff, how we did carouse! However, woman, give me a glass of vodka. What kind have you got?"

"Aniseed," replied the old woman.

"Well, fetch your aniseed," said Nozdreff.

"Give me a glass too," said the fair-haired man.

"There was an actress at the theatre who sang like a canary," now resumed Nozdreff. "Kuvshinnikoff, who sat beside me, said, 'There, my dear fellow, we must make the most of the strawberries with her.' I think there were at least fifty booths at the fair. A fellow named Fenardi turned somersets for four hours." Here he took a glass of aniseed from the old woman, who made a low reverence to him. "Bring it here!" he next cried, catching sight of Porfiriy entering with the puppy.

Porfiriy was dressed like his master, in a dirty wadded *arkhaluk* [a long, straight coat reaching to the knees]. He set the puppy on the floor; the animal stretched itself out, and then began to sniff and smell.

"There's a pup," said Nozdreff, grasping it by the back, and lifting it up, whereupon it emitted a very pitiful howl. "But you haven't done as I told you," resumed Nozdreff, turning to Porfiriy, and examining the dog's belly attentively. "You have not combed him."

"Yes, I did comb him."

"Then where have all those fleas come from?"

"I can't tell. Perhaps they crawled on to him from the britchka."

"You lie! you lie! and you never meant to comb him. I believe, you fool, that you have given him some of your own fleas. Look here, Tchitchikoff, look what ears he has! just feel them with your hand."

"Oh, I can see them; he's of a good breed," replied Tchitchikoff.

"No, but take hold of him; feel his ears."

Tchitchikoff, to please Nozdreff, felt the animal's ears, and then remarked, "Yes, he will be a good dog."

"And do you feel how cold his nose is? Take it in your hand."

Not wishing to offend him, Tchitchikoff touched the dog's snout also, saying, "Good scent."

"A genuine bull-dog," went on Nozdreff. "I confess that I had for a long time been whetting my teeth for a bull-dog. Here, Porfiriy, take him away."

Porfiriy took hold of the dog, and carried him off to the britchka.

"Listen, Tchitchikoff," continued Nozdreff, "you certainly must come to my house; it's only five versts away; we shall be there in no time, and then you can go to Sobakevitch's, if you like."

"Why not?" said Tchitchikoff to himself. "I will go to Nozdreff's, after all. He isn't any worse than the others. He's like everybody else; and, besides, he's just been losing money. He has plenty of everything, evidently; and I might ask him to give me something without payment." "I'll go, if you like," he now added aloud; "but don't detain me long; time is of value to me just now."

"Ah! that's right! that's good! Wait, I'll kiss you for that." Here Nozdreff and Tchitchikoff embraced each other. "That's glorious!" added the former; "we'll all three ride together."

"No, you must let me leave you," said the fair-haired man. "I must go home."

"Nonsense, nonsense, my dear fellow! I won't let you go."

"But really, my wife will be angry; you can get into the other britchka now."

"Ni, ni, ni, don't think of it."

The fair-haired man was one of those individuals who, at first sight, seem to have a stubborn character. Before you have succeeded in opening your mouth they are ready to dispute, and it seems as if they would never agree with any-one. However, it always ends by their betraying some weakness, and consenting to the very thing they had opposed.

"Nonsense!" said Nozdreff, in answer to some objection made by his brother-in-law. Then he set the latter's cap on his head, and the fair-haired fellow followed his companions.

"You haven't paid for your aniseed, master," now said the landlady.

"Oh, very well, very well, my good woman! I say, brother-in-law, pay, if you please. I haven't a copeck left in my pocket."

"How much do you want?" asked his brother-in-law.

"Why, twenty copecks in all," said the old woman.

"She's mad! Give her ten; that's more than enough."

"It's but little, master," said the old woman. However, she took the money gratefully, and hastily went to open the door for them. She had lost nothing, as she had asked four times the worth of the vodka. . . .

A VISIT TO PLIUSHKIN'S MANOR HOUSE

Upon the walls several pictures were suspended close together, and without any attempt at arrangement; there was a long, yellow engraving of some bat-tle, with huge drums, shouting soldiers, three-cornered hats, and prancing horses. This lacked a glass, and was mounted in a dilapidated mahogany frame. On a line with this a huge oil painting, which represented some flowers and fruits, with a boar's head, and a duck hanging head downwards, monopolised half the wall. From the middle of the ceiling hung a chandelier enveloped in a linen bag, to which the accumulated dust gave the aspect of a silkworm's cocoon with the worm in it; and in one corner of the room various things not worthy to lie upon the table were piled up in a heap. It would have been impos-sible to affirm that a living being inhabited this apartment, had not an ancient, threadbare nightcap, which lay upon the table, borne witness to the fact. While Tchitchikoff was still engaged in surveying the place, a side-door opened, and the same housekeeper whom he had encountered in the yard entered the room. But he now became aware that this person was rather a steward than a house-keeper; a housekeeper, at all events, does not shave, whereas this person, on the contrary, shaved every now and then, for his chin and all the lower portion of his cheeks resembled one of those currycombs made of iron wire, with which horses are cleaned down in the stable. Tchitchikoff, imparting an inquiring expression to his countenance, waited impatiently to hear what the steward would say to him. The steward, on his side, waited for Tchitchikoff to speak. At length, our hero, surprised by such strange indecision, made up his mind to inquire,—

"Where is your master? Is he at home?"

"Yes, he is here," said the steward.

"Where?" repeated Tchitchikoff.

"What, my good fellow, are you blind?" said the steward. "At home, indeed! I am the master!"

Here our hero involuntarily stepped back, and looked more attentively at this person. It had been his lot to see many sorts of people—even people such as the author and the reader have never beheld—but such an individual as this one he had never yet looked upon. His face was like that of many gaunt old men, only his chin projected so much that every time he wanted to spit he had to cover it with his handkerchief, in order not to spit upon it; his small eyes were still bright, and they darted about beneath his lofty, bushy brows like mice when they thrust their pointed noses out of their dark holes, prick up their ears, and peer about to see whether a cat, or some scamp of a boy, is not hidden somewhere. His attire was even more worthy of remark. It was difficult to tell of what material his dressing-gown was made; the sleeves and the upper portions of the skirts were greasy and shiny to such a degree that they resembled the Russia leather of which boots are made; behind there were four tails instead of two, from between which protruded some checked cotton. Something, also impossible to distinguish, either a stocking or a belt, but certainly not a neckerchief, was knotted about his neck. In short, if Tchitchikoff had encountered this landowner, thus arrayed, at the door of a church, he would probably have bestowed a copper groschen upon him; for it must be stated, to our hero's credit, that he had a compassionate heart, and could not refrain from giving a copper groschen to a poor man.

However, it was not a beggar, but a landowner, who stood before him. This proprietor possessed over a thousand souls: and one might have searched a long while for a person having so much wheat, flour, and so forth, in his storehouse, or possessing so many storerooms, barns, and drying-houses, filled with sheepskins, both dressed and tanned; and having such quantities of linen, cloth, dried fish, and dried vegetables at his disposal. If any one had peeped in upon him in his yard, where stores of wood and utensils were accumulated, it would have seemed to him that he had, by some means, come upon the "shavings market" at Moscow, where wooden vessels are sold, and where clever mothers-in-law betake themselves daily, followed by their cooks to purchase household requisites. At Pliushkin's one found every sort of article in wood, turned, fitted together, and plaited,—casks, half-casks, buckets with handles and without handles, tar-barrels, the tubs in which women soak flax and dirty clothes; baskets, made of thin strips of ash; oval boxes of plaited birch-bark, with wooden bottoms and covers; and many other things of various sorts which are of service to the Russians both rich and poor.

But what was the use of all these things to Pliushkin? Two such estates as his could not have used them up in a lifetime, though that seemed to make no difference to him. Not content with what he had, he rambled about the streets of his village, peering beneath the bridges and the planks thrown across the gutters, and everything he came across, whether it was the old sole of a shoe, a woman's discarded rag, an iron nail, or a piece of a broken earthenware pot, he carried it all home with him, and threw it upon the heap which Tchitchikoff had observed in the corner of the room. "There's the old fisherman out on his ramble," the moujiks would say, when they spied him searching after his booty. And, in fact, there was no need of sweeping the streets after he had gone on his rounds; if a passing officer chanced to lose a spur, the spur was forthwith transferred to the familiar heap; if a woman gaped over the well, and forgot her pail, Pliushkin carried off the pail. However, whenever a moujik caught him in the act, he never disputed, but immediately surrendered the stolen article; though if it once fell upon his heap, that was the end of it: he swore that it was his own, that he had bought it at such and such a time, of such or such a person, or that he had inherited it from his grandfather. In his own room he picked up everything he saw—a bit of sealing-wax, a scrap of paper, or a tiny feather—and stuffed everything away in his desk, or on the window-ledge.

Of course, there had been a time when he had simply been a careful manager, when he had been a married family man, and when his neighbours had been in the habit of coming to dine with him, and listening to him, and taking lessons from him in wise economy. Everything then went on briskly: grain-mills and fulling-mills were in operation, cloth-mills were running, carpenters' shops and spinning-rooms were at work; the searching glance of the master penetrated everywhere and into everything; and carefully, but assiduously, like an industrious spider, did he run about attending to domestic matters. In those times his courteous and talkative wife was renowned for her hospitality; two charming daughters, both fair and as fresh as roses, came to greet the guests: the son, a fine, vivacious little boy, ran out and kissed everybody. All the windows in the house were open then: there was a French tutor, who was a great sportsman, and who was always bringing home partridges or ducks for dinner. And there was also a governess for the little girls. But the good housewife died. Pliushkin became restless, and, like all widowers, suspicious and saving. He did not place full confidence in his eldest daughter, Alexandra Stepanovna, and he was right; for Alexandra Stepanovna soon eloped with a staff-captain, belonging to God knows what regiment of cavalry, and she married him in haste in some village church, although she knew that her father did not like officers, on account of a strange, prejudiced belief of long standing, that they were all gamblers and spendthrifts. Her father sent his curse after her, and then the house grew more desolate, its owner became more and more miserly. The French tutor was dismissed, because the time had arrived for the son to enter the civil service; the governess was sent about her business, because it appeared that she was not free from guilt in the matter of Alexandra Stepanovna's elopement; the son, on being despatched to the chief town of the government, in order to learn official routine, according to his father's wish, enlisted in a regiment instead, and wrote to his father immediately afterwards, asking for some money. Very naturally, he received in reply what the common people call a *shish*.[2] Finally, the last daughter, who had remained at home with the father, died, and the old man found himself the sole guardian, protector, and owner of his wealth.

His lonely life then made him yet more miserly, and as though for the express purpose of confirming him in his opinion of military men, his son ruined himself at cards: he sent him a hearty paternal curse, and never troubled himself

2. Literally, an insulting sign, made with the finger.

afterwards to inquire whether he still existed in the world or not. More windows were shut up every year in the house, until at last only two remained to admit any light, one of which, as the reader has already seen, was pasted up with blue paper. As time went on he paid less and less attention to domestic management, busying himself more about the scraps of paper and feathers which he collected in his room; he became more and more crusty with the people who came to buy the products of his estate; the dealers grew disgusted with him, and finally abandoned him altogether, saying that he was a devil, and not a man; his hay and grain rotted; his ricks and stores of all sorts turned into manure, pure and simple, so that cabbages might have been grown upon them; the flour in his vaults turned to stone, and had to be chopped up: it was terrible to touch the linen, the cloth, and other materials of domestic manufacture; they turned to dust under the hand. He himself had already forgotten what he possessed of any given article. He only remembered the sideboard which contained his decanters of brandy, upon which he had made a mark, in order that no one might thievishly drink the liquor. Meanwhile, however, the revenues of the estate were collected as before: the moujiks had to bring as much obrok as usual, the same tribute of nuts was imposed upon every housewife, and the weaving women were obliged to furnish the same number of webs of linen. Everything finally was piled away in the storerooms and rotted, and he himself became at last scarcely human. His daughter, Alexandra Stepanovna, came a couple of times with her little son, to try whether she could not obtain something: it was evident that wandering life with a cavalry captain was not so attractive as it had appeared before marriage. However, Pliushkin forgave her, and allowed the little boy to play with a button which was lying on the table, but he gave her no money. On another occasion, Alexandra Stepanovna came with two children, and brought her father an Easter-cake to eat with his tea, and also a new dressing-gown; for the one which he was wearing was in such a state that it made her both confused and ashamed to look at it. Pliushkin caressed both of his grandchildren, and placing them, one on his right knee and the other on his left, he trotted them exactly as though they had been riding on horses; he also accepted the Easter-cake and the dressing-gown, but he gave his daughter absolutely nothing, whereupon Alexandra Stepanovna took her departure.

But we must return to our hero. Pliushkin had been standing in front of him for several minutes without uttering a word; and Tchitchikoff was still utterly incapable of beginning the conversation, distracted as he was by the sight of the master himself, as well as by all that was in the room. For a long time he could not think how to explain the reason of his visit. He was on the point of expressing himself to the effect that, having heard of Pliushkin as a public benefactor, he had considered it his duty to pay him a personal tribute of respect; but he felt that that would be too much. On casting one more stealthy glance on all that was in the room, he became conscious that the expression *public benefactor* might be successfully replaced by the words *economy* and *order*: so, having reconstructed his sentence on that pattern, he said that, having heard of his economy and rare skill in managing his estate, he had regarded it as his duty to make his acquaintance and offer his respects in person. He certainly might have alleged some other and better reason, but none occurred to him.

To this, Pliushkin mumbled some reply between his lips, for he had no teeth. What it was exactly is not known, but in all probability, the sense was as follows: "May the deuce take you and your respects!" However, since hospitality is in such repute all over Russia that even a miser cannot ignore its laws, he added a little more distinctly, "I beg you most humbly to take a seat. I have not been in the habit of receiving guests for a long time, and I must confess that I perceive but very little use in them. A strange custom has sprung up, of going about to visit peoples' estates to the neglect of domestic affairs. However, I can't offer you anything, for I dined long ago: and my kitchen is very mean and poor, and the chimneys are in a state of utter ruin; if you try to heat the stove, you will certainly set the house on fire."

"So that's the kind of man he is!" said Tchitchikoff to himself. "It's lucky that I dined at Sobakevitch's and tucked into that breast of mutton."

"And it is a most unfortunate circumstance but there is hardly a wisp of hay for your horses in the whole establishment," proceeded Pliushkin. "Yes, and where is there any to be had? The farm is small and barren: the peasants are lazy; they are not fond of working; they only think of getting away to the pot-house. As you know, people are thrown on the world in their old age."

"But I was told," said Tchitchikoff modestly, "that you had over a thousand souls."

"Why! who said that? My good fellow, you should have spit in the eye of the person who told you that! He was a jester: he evidently wanted to make fun of you. That is the way people talk; but for the last three years a cursed fever has been killing off my serfs in swarms."

"You don't say so! And have many really died?" exclaimed Tchitchikoff sympathetically.

"Yes; a great many have been carried off."

"Will you permit me to inquire the number?"

"Fully eighty souls."

"No, really?"

"I am not in the habit of lying, my good fellow."

"Permit me to ask another question: I assume that you are reckoning these souls from the time when the last census was taken?"

"Glory to God if it were only that!" said Pliushkin; "but since the last census I must have lost fully one hundred and twenty souls."

"Really? fully one hundred and twenty?" exclaimed Tchitchikoff, and he even dropped his jaw somewhat with amazement.

"I am rather old to lie, my good fellow: I have lived seventy years," said Pliushkin, who seemed to have taken offence at our hero's almost joyous exclamation.

Tchitchikoff perceived that such a want of sympathy in another's woe had really been extremely impolite; so he immediately sighed, and said that he felt very sorry.

"Yes, but your sorrow won't put anything in my pocket," said Pliushkin. . . .

Chapter Six

THE APOGEE OF EUROPE

BETWEEN 1848 and 1914 European influence on world affairs reached new heights. Nevertheless, beneath the surface of what seemed a Golden Age to those who enjoyed the political and economic fruits of the nineteenth century, unresolved internal problems impelled Europe toward future revolutionary upheavals. The assurance which superficially characterized the "Europeanization of the world" only created a myth which glamorized an era of bewildering dilemmas.

The Revolutions of 1848 had been hailed by millions as the cataclysm that would usher in a new age, but liberalism was everywhere suppressed by force. The dreams failed to come true; the utopias were discredited. Imaginative idealists lost faith in their own abilities, and a mood of pessimism possessed the minds of most reformers.

A new spirit which emphasized "nature red in tooth and claw" inspired journalists and educators to dramatize the struggle for life and the survival of the fittest, preparing the way for politicians who despised abstract idealism, boasted of their realism, and deified power. The supremacy of a new cult of force was illustrated by the sudden revival of warfare. From Waterloo to mid-century, Europe had been relatively free from war, but the twenty years after 1850 were disturbed by a steady stream of localized conflicts. Napoleon III, Bismarck, and Cavour each defended war as an instrument of national policy, while Lord Palmerston bullied all of Europe with the might of Britain's naval power.

Many Europeans also began to adopt the attitudes of *Realpolitik* in their evaluations of the physical and material world. By 1870, when the statesmen of *Realpolitik* were reaching the height of their greatness, most of Europe's intelligentsia believed that they had found in science an infallible guide through the misty marshes of speculative thought. Their consensus was that the intellectual leadership of European society should be awarded to natural scientists, who concerned themselves not with utopias but with plants and animals, matter and energy—objects that were measurably real. In contrast to the vapid speculations of Romantic idealists in the 1840's, the methods of natural science seemed sharp and clear. Scientists gratified the popular demand for certainty by declaring that knowledge was power and that they alone possessed the key to truth.

The political events of 1870 were a tremendous aid to promoters of the new faith in science. In intellectual circles and among broad segments of the German population the military victories of that year were followed by a great outburst of enthusiasm for applied science. On the other hand, the humiliation of defeat stimulated Frenchmen to embrace science in an effort to retrieve their country's eminence. In the words of Émile Zola: "Today we need the strength of truth, if we are to be glorious in the future as we have been in the past. It is by applying the scientific formula that our sons will some day regain Alsace and Lorraine."

The doctrine of organic evolution demonstrated the part played by scientific discovery in bringing about a new frame of mind. The evidence which Charles Darwin (1809–82) mustered in his *Origin of the Species* (1859) and *Descent of Man* (1871) to prove that men were descended from lower orders of animals shocked the general public. Nevertheless, through the efforts of writers like Herbert Spencer and Ernst Haeckel, it became apparent that Darwin's views were only a new version of the eighteenth-century doctrine of progress. Men had not progressed merely from savagery, but from the lowest forms of life; in popular opinion men had clearly "ascended." The theory of "survival of the fittest" was in harmony with the spirit of the times and was profoundly flattering to the survivors. During the 1870's and 1880's the middle classes of Europe were experiencing generally higher levels of income than ever before; the yearning for reform which had dominated Western thought in 1848 had been somewhat diminished by the economic prosperity of the 1860's and by the political triumphs of the 1870's. The middle and upper classes tended to be well satisfied with their material achievements, and they rarely objected when science told them that they were the supreme creation of nature.

Between 1870 and 1900 the most vociferous dissenters from the teachings of the new science were Protestant theologians, who viewed such materialistic explanations of human origins as contrary to divine revelation. Most unwisely, many theologians attempted to argue science with trained scientists. The result found the theologians outmaneuvered at every turn; the warfare between science and theology ended with complete discomfiture for the theologians. Moreover, many leading thinkers of the last quarter of the nineteenth century declared themselves agnostic in religious matters, professing their doubts about God, immortality, and other theological doctrines, and asserting that it was impossible for man to know anything about such matters.

Although reverence for the methods of natural science largely set the intellectual tone of late nineteenth-century Europe, social reformers continued to strive for public acceptance of their increasingly radical theories. The pressures for political democracy kept demands for social reforms before the middle classes. Not all patriotic thinkers followed the German historian Heinrich von Treitschke (1834–96) in portraying the state as a mystical entity with a *Geist* (spirit) of its own. They often united democratic idealism to their patriotism, devoting their enthusiasm not to the state but to the people. Journalists and essayists pointed out that the state could be strong only if its citizens were well developed physically, culturally, and spiritually—if the people were made to realize that the government was really theirs by being given a part in it—and if they enjoyed a high level of economic prosperity. In accordance with Prussian tradition, Otto von Bismarck was prepared to admit that the greatness of a nation and the well-being of its citizens must go hand-in-hand, although his social reforms of the 1880's were specifically designed to curb the growth of the Social Democratic party. Agitation for democracy and reform in Great Britain was renewed during the Liberal Prime Minister William Gladstone's "Great Ministry" (1868–74), when a series of statutes liberalized the civil service and guaranteed a public primary education to all Englishmen. Gladstone's career culminated in his successful support of the Reform Bill of 1884–85, which added two million voters to the electoral rolls.

Orthodox Marxists and their rivals competed for the support of the masses by urging extreme measures of political and social change. The most extreme of Marx's critics, Michael Bakunin (1814–76), voiced only contempt for the "evolutionary and tame" methods of scientific socialism. Bakunin declared himself a realist and opposed all idealistic concepts such as God and the State. He spent his life preaching the immediate and violent overthrow of existing society, advocating the "propaganda of the deed," and urging assassinations and other acts of violence as a means of advertising the revolutionary movement.

The work of Bakunin in spreading Anarchist doctrine was continued by another Russian of vastly different temperament. Prince Peter Kropotkin (1842–1921) had become interested in a group of Russian agitators known as *Narodniki,* or Populists, during the 1870's and gave up his title in order to join them. Arrested by the tsarist police for his radical views, Kropotkin escaped from prison and eventually settled in England, where he remained until returning to Russia after the Revolution of 1917. In England he published a series of articles attacking the doctrines of "struggle for life" and "survival of the fittest," maintaining that mutual aid of different members of the same species was the most powerful element in evolution and human progress. Carrying these views into the realm of social development, Kropotkin dreamed of a purely voluntary society based on the cooperation of its members, but with all violence and all government eliminated. Like Bakunin he was also an ardent revolutionist, organizing societies of workers to reform existing conditions, but opposed to Bakunin's views on violence.

Anarchist attacks upon European society were augmented by the vigorous anti-Christian arguments of a German intellectual who exerted a profound influence on early twentieth-century thought. Pronouncing that "God is dead," Friedrich Nietzsche (1844–1900) denounced all efforts to alleviate the condition of the poor and the unfortunate as tending to perpetuate weaklings and those who had been worsted in the struggle for life. Indeed, from the doctrine of evolution, he concluded that just as men represented an evolution from lower forms of life, so after them there must appear a different and still higher form —the superman (*Übermensch*). In Nietzsche's view, such a man must constitute a higher order of being. Thus, he condemned traditional moral values, humility, democracy, and piety of any kind. Man must respect the life-process and the human "will to power."

Nietzsche was a pioneer in probing the unconscious motivations of human behavior. Along with other rebels near the turn of the century, Nietzsche rejected the premises of rationalism and nineteenth-century positivism. Most young intellectuals, however, continued to devote themselves to science, and some of the most brilliant thinking accomplished between 1890 and 1914 was done by natural scientists. Radium, X-rays, and wireless waves were discovered, followed by new theories on the ultimate nature of matter and culminating in Albert Einstein's (1879–1955) theory of relativity, which was first stated in 1905. Physics and chemistry were not the only fields of human knowledge to be revolutionized in the closing years of the nineteenth century. Biology was fundamentally altered by new theories of heredity which held that evolution had not been a slow process, as Darwin taught, but a series of sudden mutations or changes. Applied science also kept pace with the theoreticians, and the generation before 1914 witnessed all the wonders of a new electrical age which revolutionized transportation, communications, and household gadgetry.

Social reformers during the closing years of the nineteenth century expressed themselves through large numbers of problem plays, novels, and newspaper editorials. Writers like Henrik Ibsen, G. B. Shaw, H. G. Wells, and John Galsworthy criticized fundamental social abuses of the day, reaching a far broader audience than had critics of an earlier generation. Nevertheless, the call for social reform was mild compared to the shriek of virulent nationalists.

Especially after 1870 the responsibilities of patriotism were drummed into the minds of European youth. Newspaper editors found it profitable to play upon the patriotic emotions of their readers, and politicians began to exploit the patriotism of their followers to an unprecedented degree. Extreme nationalists believed that all other feelings, hopes, and ambitions were secondary to national interests. For the true patriot his country came before all; in the phrases of popular songs, "Brittania Rules the Waves," and "Deutschland über alles!" A tremendous wave of patriotic monomania swept over Europe before 1914, and chauvinism took on the character of a religion, replacing, in part, older Christian values which had been discredited in the eyes of many by modern science. All chauvinists were firmly convinced that their own country was pre-eminent in the noble things of life. Some attributed this superiority to *Kultur,* others to political institutions, still others to language, and in many cases, to racial characteristics. Each nation—whether Slav, German, or Anglo-Saxon—was proclaimed superior to all others, and a political union of all similar peoples under one flag was demanded.

Historians have advanced many explanations for the popularity of the new imperialism of the 1880's and 1890's. In those decades, European states staked out their claims for the last remaining bits of Africa and clashed over the partition of Asia. Humanitarianism, the economic needs of capitalism, and the expansion of the balance of power were decisive elements in the activities of the imperialists. Most of the intellectual, spiritual, and moral attitudes which justified the new imperialism were provided by late nineteenth-century chauvinists. With the superiority of their own race firmly established, many chauvinists considered the steps they might take to share their magnificent institutions with outsiders. Most Europeans considered that the backward races ought to be civilized even at considerable cost and sometimes referred to the duty of spreading their civilization among black, brown, and yellow people as "the white man's burden." No writer advocated such views more eloquently than Rudyard Kipling (1865–1936), whose many books left a portrait of the British Empire at the pinnacle of its power. Kipling's readers could not fail to see that their country had fulfilled a glorious mission in helping inferior men to model themselves after British ideals. Christian missionaries also aided the cause and profited by it, for they no longer confined themselves to preaching the Gospel. Wherever they went they established schools, hopsitals, and orphanages for the purpose of making the people over into good Europeans.

Like President Theodore Roosevelt, a typical statesman of his age, many Europeans justified their imperialistic activities by extolling the virtues of competition among nations. Returning from a year of hunting big game in Africa after his second term in the White House, Roosevelt stopped off at London in 1910 to attend the coronation of King George V and prepared a speech likening each of the great European states to one of the animals whose habits he had studied. His point was that just as wild animals throve on competition, so states needed the "athletic exercise" of occasional military clashes. But Roosevelt and other contemporary statesmen were apparently naïve enough to believe that such disputes would always be localized by a balance of power under which the contestants, after getting some exercise, would soon find it necessary to settle matters at the conference table. Indeed, most western men seemed to share a common faith in unlimited progress through science. They saw the ecstatic vision of a better world: the Messiah was about to come, and the Kingdom of Heaven would soon be realized on earth. Instead, in 1914, Europe erupted in an orgy of mass destruction in which the technological advances of preceding decades consumed a generation of young Russians, Germans, Frenchmen, Italians, and Englishmen.

MAN AND SOCIETY

1. AUGUSTE COMTE: A GENERAL VIEW OF POSITIVISM*

Isidore Auguste Marie François Xavier Comte (1798–1857) was educated at the École Polytechnique in Paris. Stimulated by the ideas of Saint-Simon, Comte devoted himself to what he called "the social regeneration of Western Europe." He began to expound a "Positive Philosophy" through a series of lectures and articles in the 1820's and published his *Cours de philosophie positive* in installments between 1830 and 1842. Finally, he summarized his views in *A General View of Positivism* (1848). Comte believed that through a study of history he had discovered a formula which accounted for the intellectual advances of humanity through a theological stage, a metaphysical stage, and a scientific or positive stage. Positivism, in Comte's view, meant the application of scientific principles to the study of human behavior and made possible the "science" of sociology (a term which he himself coined). How did Comte define the nature and goals of Positivism? To what extent did Comte's Positivism reflect the influence of Saint-Simon? Compare Comte's method of analyzing social prob-

* Auguste Comte, *A General View of Positivism*, trans. J. H. Bridges (London: George Routledge and Sons, 1903), pp. 1–4, 363–65.

lems and proposing solutions for them with the "scientific socialism" of Karl Marx. On what points would Marx and Comte, as social analysts, find common grounds for agreement, and on what issues would they quarrel? Did Comte or Marx show more clearly the influence of eighteenth-century Enlightenment *philosophes,* and in what ways? Would orthodox theologians find the doctrines of both Comte and Marx equally heretical? Why?

Positivism consists essentially of a Philosophy and a Polity. These can never be dissevered; the former being the basis and the latter the end of one comprehensive system in which our intellectual faculties and our social sympathies are brought into close correlation with each other. For, in the first place, the science of Society, besides being more important than any other, supplies the only logical and scientific link by which all our varied observations of phenomena can be brought into one consistent whole. Of this science it is even more true than of any of the preceding sciences that its real character cannot be understood without explaining its exact relation in all general features with the art corresponding to it. Now here we find a coincidence which is assuredly not fortuitous. At the very time when the theory of society is being laid down, an immense sphere is opened for the application of that theory; the direction, namely, of the social regeneration of Western Europe. For, if we take another point of view and look at the great crisis of modern history as its character is displayed in the natural course of events, it becomes every day more evident how hopeless is the task of reconstructing political institutions without the previous remodeling of opinion and of life. To form then a satisfactory synthesis of all human conceptions is the most urgent of our social wants: and it is needed equally for the sake of Order and of Progress. During the gradual accomplishment of this great philosophical work, a new moral power will arise spontaneously throughout the West, which, as its influence increases, will lay down a definite basis for the reorganization of society. It will offer a general system of education for the adoption of all civilized nations, and by this means will supply in every department of public and private life fixed principles of judgment and conduct. Thus the intellectual movement and the social crisis will be brought continually into close connexion with each other. Both will combine to prepare the advanced portion of humanity for the acceptance of a true spiritual power, a power more coherent, as well as more progressive, than the noble but premature attempt of medieval Catholicism.

The primary object of Positivism, then, is twofold: to generalize our scientific conceptions and to systematize the art of social life. These are but two aspects of one and the same problem. They will form the subjects of the first two chapters of this work. I shall first explain the general spirit of the new philosophy. I shall then show its necessary connexion with the whole course of that vast revolution which is now about to terminate under its guidance in social reconstruction.

This will lead us naturally to another question. The regenerating doctrine cannot do its work without adherents; in what quarter should we hope to find them? Now, with individual exceptions of great value, we cannot expect the adhesion of any of the upper classes in society. They are all more or less under the influence of baseless metaphysical theories, and of aristocratic self-seeking.

They are absorbed in blind political agitation and in disputes for the possession of the useless remnants of the old theological and military system. Their action only tends to prolong the revolutionary state indefinitely, and can never result in true social renovation.

Whether we regard its intellectual character or its social objects, it is certain that Positivism must look elsewhere for support. It will find a welcome in those classes only whose good sense has been left unimpaired by our vicious system of education, and whose generous sympathies are allowed to develop themselves freely. It is among women, therefore, and among the working classes that the heartiest supporters of the new doctrine will be found. It is intended, indeed, ultimately for all classes of society. But it will never gain much real influence over the higher ranks till it is forced upon their notice by these powerful patrons. When the work of spiritual reorganization is completed, it is on them that its maintenance will principally depend; and so too, their combined aid is necessary for its commencement. Having but little influence in political government, they are the more likely to appreciate the need of a moral government, the special object of which it will be to protect them against the oppressive action of the temporal power. . . .

All essential phases in the evolution of society answer to corresponding phases in the growth of the individual, whether it has proceeded spontaneously or under systematic guidance, supposing always that his development be complete. But it is not enough to prove the close connexion which exists between all modes and degrees of human regeneration. We have yet to find a central point round which all will naturally meet. In this point consists the unity of Positivism as a system of life. Unless it can be thus condensed, round one single principle, it will never wholly supersede the synthesis of Theology, notwithstanding its superiority in the reality and stability of its component parts, and in their homogeneity and coherence as a whole. There should be a central point in the system toward which Feeling, Reason, and Activity alike converge. The proof that Positivism possesses such a central point will remove the last obstacles to its complete acceptance as the guide of private or of public life.

Such a centre we find in the great conception of Humanity toward which every aspect of Positivism naturally converges. By it the conception of God will be entirely superseded, and a synthesis be formed more complete and permanent than that provisionally established by the old religions. Through it the new doctrine becomes at once accessible to men's hearts in its full extent and application. From their heart it will penetrate their minds, and thus the immediate necessity of beginning with a long and difficult course of study is avoided, though this must of course be always indispensable to its systematic teachers.

This central point of Positivism is even more moral than intellectual in character: it represents the principle of Love upon which the whole system rests. It is the peculiar characteristic of the Great Being who is here set forth, to be compounded of separable elements. Its existence depends therefore entirely upon mutual Love knitting together its various parts. The calculations of self-interest can never be substituted as a combining influence for the sympathetic instincts.

Yet the belief in Humanity, while stimulating Sympathy, at the same time enlarges the scope and vigour of the Intellect. For it requires high powers of generalization to conceive clearly of this vast organism, as the result of spontaneous co-operation, abstraction made of all partial antagonisms. Reason, then, has its part in this central dogma as well as Love. It enlarges and completes our conception of the Supreme Being by revealing to us the external and internal conditions of its existence.

Lastly, our active powers are stimulated by it no less than our feelings and our reason. For since Humanity is so far more complex than any other organism, it will react more strongly and more continuously on its environment, submitting to its influence and so modifying it. Hence results Progress which is simply the development of Order under the influence of Love.

Thus, in the conception of Humanity, the three essential aspects of Positivism, its subjective principle, its objective dogma, and its practical object, are united. Towards Humanity, who is for us the only true Great Being, we, the conscious elements of whom she is composed, shall henceforth direct every aspect of our life, individual or collective. Our thoughts will be devoted to the knowledge of Humanity, our affections to her love, our actions to her service.

Positivists then may, more truly than theological believers of whatever creed, regard life as a continuous and earnest act of worship; worship which will elevate and purify our feelings, enlarge and enlighten our thoughts, ennoble and invigorate our actions. It supplies a direct solution, so far as a solution is possible, of the great problems of the Middle Ages, the subordination of Politics to Morals. For this follows at once from the consecration now given to the principle that social sympathy should preponderate over self-love.

Thus Positivism becomes, in the true sense of the word, a Religion: the only religion which is real and complete; destined therefore to replace all imperfect and provisional systems resting on the primitive bias of theology.

2. CHARLES DARWIN: THE DESCENT OF MAN*

Charles Darwin (1809–82), the greatest naturalist of the nineteenth century, studied at the University of Cambridge where he formed a close friendship with John Henslow, Professor of Botany. Through Henslow's recommendation Darwin gained an appointment as official naturalist aboard H. M. S. "Beagle," a ten-gun brig of 235 tons which had been authorized by the British Admiralty to conduct a survey of the coastline of South America and "to carry a chain of chronometrical measurements round the world." Darwin returned from the five-year voyage (1831–36) full of thoughts on evolution impressed upon his mind by South American fossils, Galapagos birds, and by observations of the complex interdependence of the varied living creatures which he had studied. By 1844 he had published several monographs on "The Zoology of the Voyage of the Beagle," and in the intervening years between 1844 and 1858, when he wrote *The Origin of the Species,* Darwin read whole series of periodicals, books on travel, natural history, horticulture, and the breeding of animals to muster evidence for his theory of evolution.

The Origin of the Species, published in 1859, contained a wealth of lucid detail in support of evolution, and *The Descent of Man* (1871) presented Darwin's final conclusions on the subject. What evidence did Darwin present in

* Charles Darwin, *The Descent of Man and Selection in Relation to Sex* (New York: D. Appleton and Co., 1897), pp. 606–13, 618–19.

defense of his thesis that "man is descended from some less highly organized form"? Why did he assert that "the grounds upon which this conclusion rests will never be shaken"? What did Darwin mean by "the work of natural selection," and how did the operation of such a principle explain racial differences? How did he account for the development of moral qualities in man, and what explanation did he offer for belief in "a universal and beneficent Creator"? Why did Darwin assert that it was just as morally edifying to teach that man was descended from a "heroic little monkey" as from a primitive savage who lived according to the law of his tribe?

A brief summary will be sufficient to recall to the reader's mind the more salient points in this work. Many of the views which have been advanced are highly speculative, and some no doubt will prove erroneous; but I have in every case given the reasons which have led me to one view rather than to another. It seemed worth while to try how far the principle of evolution would throw light on some of the more complex problems in the natural history of man. False facts are highly injurious to the progress of science, for they often endure long; but false views, if supported by some evidence, do little harm, for every one takes a salutary pleasure in proving their falseness; and when this is done, one path towards error is closed and the road to truth is often at the same time opened.

The main conclusion here arrived at, and now held by many naturalists who are well competent to form a sound judgment, is that man is descended from some less highly organised form. The grounds upon which this conclusion rests will never be shaken, for the close similarity between man and the lower animals in embryonic development, as well as in innumerable points of structure and constitution, both of high and of the most trifling importance,—the rudiments which he retains, and the abnormal reversions to which he is occasionally liable,—are facts which cannot be disputed. They have long been known, but until recently they told us nothing with respect to the origin of man. Now when viewed by the light of our knowledge of the whole organic world, their meaning is unmistakable. The great principle of evolution stands up clear and firm, when these groups of facts are considered in connection with others such as the mutual affinities of the members of the same group, their geographical distribution in past and present times, and their geological succession. It is incredible that all these facts should speak falsely. He who is not content to look, like a savage, at the phenomena of nature as disconnected, cannot any longer believe that man is the work of a separate act of creation. He will be forced to admit that the close resemblance of the embryo of man to that, for instance, of a dog— the construction of his skull, limbs and whole frame on the same plan with that of other mammals, independently of the uses to which the parts may be put—the occasional re-appearance of various structures, for instance of several muscles, which man does not normally possess, but which are common to the Quadrumana—and a crowd of analogous facts—all point in the plainest manner to the conclusion that man is the co-descendant with other mammals of a common progenitor.

We have seen that man incessantly presents individual differences in all parts of his body and in his mental faculties. These differences or variations seem to be induced by the same general causes, and to obey the same laws as with the lower animals. In both cases similar laws of inheritance prevail. Man tends to increase at a greater rate than his means of subsistence; consequently he is occasionally subjected to a severe struggle for existence, and natural selection will have effected whatever lies within its scope. A succession of strongly-marked variations of a similar nature is by no means requisite; slight fluctuating differences in the individual suffice for the work of natural selection; not that we have any reason to suppose that in the same species, all parts of the organisation tend to vary to the same degree. We may feel assured that the inherited effects of the long-continued use or disuse of parts will have done much in the same direction with natural selection. Modifications formerly of importance, though no longer of any special use, are long-inherited. When one part is modified, other parts change through the principle of correlation, of which we have instances in many curious cases of correlated monstrosities. Something may be attributed to the direct and definite action of the surrounding conditions of life, such as abundant food, heat or moisture; and lastly, many characters of slight physiological importance, some indeed of considerable importance, have been gained through sexual selection. . . .

Through the means just specified, aided perhaps by others as yet undiscovered, man has been raised to his present state. But since he attained to the rank of manhood, he has diverged into distinct races, or as they may be more fitly called, sub-species. Some of these, such as the Negro and European, are so distinct that, if specimens had been brought to a naturalist without any further information, they would undoubtedly have been considered by him as good and true species. Nevertheless all the races agree in so many unimportant details of structure and in so many mental peculiarities, that these can be accounted for only by inheritance from a common progenitor; and a progenitor thus characterised would probably deserve to rank as man.

It must not be supposed that the divergence of each race from the other races, and of all from a common stock, can be traced back to any one pair of progenitors. On the contrary, at every stage in the process of modification, all the individuals which were in any way better fitted for their conditions of life, though in different degrees, would have survived in greater numbers than the less well-fitted. The process would have been like that followed by man, when he does not intentionally select particular individuals, but breeds from all the superior individuals, and neglects the inferior. He thus slowly but surely modifies his stock, and unconsciously forms a new strain. So with respect to modifications acquired independently of selection, and due to variations arising from the nature of the organism and the action of the surrounding conditions, or from changed habits of life, no single pair will have been modified much more than the other pairs inhabiting the same country, for all will have been continually blended through free intercrossing.

By considering the embryological structure of man,—the homologies which he presents with the lower animals,—the rudiments which he retains,—and the reversions to which he is liable, we can partly recall in imagination the former condition of our early progenitors; and can approximately place them in their proper place in the zoological series. We thus learn that man is descended from a hairy, tailed quadruped, probably arboreal in its habits, and an inhabitant of the Old World. This creature, if its whole structure had been examined by a naturalist, would have been classed amongst the Quadrumana, as surely as the still more ancient progenitor of the Old and New World monkeys. The Quadrumana and all the higher mammals are probably derived from an ancient marsupial animal, and this through a long line of diversified forms, from some amphibian-like creature, and this again from some fish-like animal. In the dim obscurity of the past we can see that the early progenitor of all the Vertebrate must have been an aquatic animal, provided with branchiæ, with the two sexes united in the same individual, and with the most important organs of the body (such as the brain and heart) imperfectly or not at all developed. This animal seems to have been more like the larvae of the existing marine Ascidians than any other known form.

The high standard of our intellectual powers and moral disposition is the greatest difficulty which presents itself, after we have been driven to this conclusion on the origin of man. But every one who admits the principle of evolution, must see that the mental powers of the higher animals, which are the same in kind with those of man, though so different in degree, are capable of advancement. Thus the interval between the mental powers of one of the higher apes and of a fish, or between those of an ant and scale-insect, is immense; yet their development does not offer any special difficulty; for with out domesticated animals, the mental faculties are certainly variable, and the variations are inherited. No one doubts that they are of the utmost importance to animals in a state of nature. Therefore the conditions are favourable for their development through natural selection. The same conclusion may be extended to man; the intellect must have been all-important to him, even at a very remote period, as enabling him to invent and use language, to make weapons, tools, traps, etc., whereby with the aid of his social habits, he long ago became the most dominant of all living creatures. . . .

The development of the moral qualities is a more interesting problem. The foundation lies in the social instincts, including under this term the family ties. These instincts are highly complex, and in the case of the lower animals give special tendencies towards certain definite actions; but the more important elements are love, and the distinct emotion of sympathy. Animals endowed with the social instincts take pleasure in one another's company, warn one another of danger, defend and aid one another in many ways. These instincts do not extend to all the individuals of the species, but only to those of the same community. As they are highly beneficial to the species, they have in all probability been acquired through natural selection.

A moral being is one who is capable of reflecting on his past actions and their motives—of approving of some and disapproving of others; and the fact that man is the one being who certainly deserves this designation, is the greatest of all distinctions between him and the lower animals. But in the fourth chapter I have endeavored to show that the moral sense follows, firstly, from the enduring and ever-present nature of the social instincts; secondly, from man's appreciation of the approbation and disapprobation of his fellows; and thirdly, from the high activity of his mental faculties, with past impressions extremely vivid; and in these latter respects he differs from the lower animals. Owing to this condition of mind, man cannot avoid looking both backwards and forwards, and comparing past impressions. Hence after some temporary desire or passion has mastered his social instincts, he reflects and compares the now weakened impression of such past impulses with the ever-present social instincts; and he then feels that sense of dissatisfaction which all unsatisfied instincts leave behind them, he therefore resolves to act differently for the future,—and this is conscience. Any instinct, permanently stronger or more enduring than another, gives rise to a feeling which we express by saying that it ought to be obeyed. A pointer dog, if able to reflect on his past conduct, would say to himself, I ought (as indeed we say of him) to have pointed at that hare and not have yielded to the passing temptation of hunting it. . . .

The belief in God has often been advanced as not only the greatest, but the most complete of all the distinctions between man and the lower animals. It is however impossible, as we have seen, to maintain that this belief is innate or instinctive in man. On the other hand a belief in all-pervading spiritual agencies seems to be universal; and apparently follows from a considerable advance in man's reason, and from a still greater advance in his faculties of imagination, curiosity and wonder. I am aware that the assumed instinctive belief in God has been used by many persons as an argument for His existence. But this is a rash argument, as we should thus be compelled to believe in the existence of many cruel and malignant spirits, only a little more powerful than man; for the belief in them is far more general than in a beneficent Deity. The idea of a universal and beneficent Creator does not seem to arise in the mind of man, until he has been elevated by long-continued culture.

He who believes in the advancement of man from some low organised form, will naturally ask how does this bear on the belief in the immortality of the soul. The barbarous races of man, as Sir J. Lubbock has shown, possess no clear belief of this kind but arguments derived from the primeval beliefs of savages are as we have just seen, of little or no avail. Few persons feel any anxiety from the impossibility of determining at what precise period in the development of the individual, from the first trace of a minute germinal vesicle, man becomes an immortal being; and there is no greater cause for anxiety because the period cannot possibly be determined in the gradually ascending organic scale.

I am aware that the conclusions arrived at in this work will be denounced by some as highly irreligious; but he who denounces them is bound to show why it is more irreligious to explain the origin of man as a distinct species by descent from some lower form, through the laws of variation and natural selection, than to explain the birth of the individual through the laws of ordinary reproduction. The birth both of the species and of the individual are equally parts of that grand sequence of events, which our minds refuse to accept as the result of blind chance. The understanding revolts at such a conclusion, whether or not we are able to believe that every slight variation of structure,—the union of each pair in marriage,—the dissemination of each seed,—and other such events, have all been ordained for some special purpose. . . .

The main conclusion arrived at in this work, namely that man is descended from some lowly organised form, will, I regret to think, be highly distasteful to many. But there can hardly be a doubt that we are descended from barbarians. The astonishment which I felt on first seeing a party of Fuegians on a wild and broken shore will never be forgotten by me, for the reflection at once rushed into my mind—such were our ancestors. These men were absolutely naked and bedaubed with paint, their long hair was tangled, their mouths frothed with excitement, and their expression was wild, startled, and distrustful. They possessed hardly any arts, and like wild animals lived on what they could catch; they had no government, and were merciless to everyone not of their own small tribe. He who has seen a savage in his native land will not feel much shame, if forced to acknowledge that the blood of some more humble creature flows in his veins. For my own part I would as soon be descended from that heroic little monkey, who braved his dreaded enemy in order to save the life of his keeper, or from that old baboon, who descending from the mountains, carried away in triumph his young comrade from a crowd of astonished dogs—as from a savage who delights to torture his enemies, offers up bloody sacrifices, practises infanticide without remorse, treats his wives like slaves, knows no decency, and is haunted by the grossest superstitions.

Man may be excused for feeling some pride at having risen, though not through his own exertions, to the very summit of the organic scale; and the fact of his having thus risen, instead of having been aboriginally placed there, may give him hope for a still higher destiny in the distant future. But we are not here concerned with hopes or fears, only with the truth as far as our reason permits us to discover it; and I have given the evidence to the best of my ability. We must, however, acknowledge, as it seems to me, that man with all his noble qualities, with sympathy which feels for the most debased, with benevolence which extends not only to other men, but to the humblest living creature, with his god-like intellect which has penetrated into the movements and constitution of the solar system—with all these exalted powers—Man still bears in his bodily frame the indelible stamp of his lowly origin.

3. HERBERT SPENCER: PRINCIPLES OF SOCIOLOGY*

Herbert Spencer (1820–1903) was not a trained scientist, but his command of scientific facts and his skill in the use of illustrations enabled him to become a leading popularizer of Darwin's ideas. After serving as subeditor of *The Economist* during the 1840's and developing his journalistic skills, Spencer planned a series of volumes which would bring the achievements of nineteenth-century science within the grasp of the general reading public. In the first of his major works, *Social Statics* (1851), Spencer, like Comte, proclaimed the principle of social evolution and confidently asserted that human progress was not an accident but a necessity: "The changes that constitute progress are the successive steps of transition (adaptation to nature). And the belief in human perfectibility merely amounts to the belief that in virtue of this process man will eventually be completely suited to his mode of life." In 1860 Spencer made public his "synthetic system of philosophy" which he expounded in several multi-volume works eventually published under the titles: *First Principles* (1862),

* Herbert Spencer, *The Principles of Sociology* (2 vols., New York: D. Appleton and Co., 1897), II:3, pp. 590, 608-11.

Principles of Biology (1864), *Principles of Psychology* (1871), *Principles of Sociology* (1876), *Principles of Ethics* (1879). Throughout his extensive writings Spencer attempted to apply the doctrine of organic evolution to all phases of life in the universe. Compare Spencer's views on a "science of society" with Comte's. What did he mean by advocating a "relative optimism" about the evolutionary process? What parallels did he draw between organic and social evolution? Why did he believe that integration was "the primary process of evolution," and what results did he foresee from the achievement of a "final stage" in human development?

. . . It may fairly be said that the study of sociology is useless if, from an account of what has been, we cannot infer what is to be—that there is no such thing as a science of society unless its generalizations concerning past days yield enlightenment to our thoughts concerning days to come, and consequent guidance to our acts. So that, willingly as I would have avoided the making of forecasts, there is for me no defensible alternative. . . .

How long this phase of social life to which we are approaching will last, and in what way it will come to an end, are of course questions not to be answered. Probably the issue will be here of one kind and there of another. A sudden bursting of bonds which have become intolerable may in some cases happen: bringing on a military despotism. In other cases practical extinction may follow a gradual decay, arising from abolition of the normal relation between merit and benefit, by which alone the vigour of a race can be maintained. And in yet further cases may come conquest by peoples who have not been emasculated by fostering their feebles—peoples before whom the socialistic organization will go down like a house of cards, as did that of the ancient Peruvians before a handful of Spaniards.

But if the process of evolution which, unceasing throughout past time, has brought life to its present height, continues throughout the future, as we cannot but anticipate, then, amid all the rhythmical changes in each society, amid all the lives and deaths of nations, amid all the supplantings of race by race, there will go on that adaptation of human nature to the social state which began when savages first gathered together into hordes for mutual defence—an adaptation finally complete. Many will think this a wild imagination. Though everywhere around them are creatures with structures and instincts which have been gradually so moulded as to subserve their own welfares and the welfares of their species, yet the immense majority ignore the implication that human beings, too, have been undergoing in the past, and will undergo in the future, progressive adjustments to the lives imposed on them by circumstances. But there are a few who think it rational to conclude that what has happened with all lower forms must happen with the highest form—a few who infer that among types of men those most fitted for making a well-working society will, hereafter as heretofore, from time to time emerge and spread at the expense of types less fitted, until a fully fitted type has arisen.

The view thus suggested must be accepted with qualifications. If we carry our thoughts as far forward as palæolithic implements carry them back, we are introduced, not to an absolute optimism but to a relative optimism. The cosmic process brings about retrogression as well as progression, where the conditions favour it. Only amid an infinity of modifications, adjusted to an infinity of changes of circumstances, do there now and then occur some which constitute an advance: other changes meanwhile caused in other organisms, usually not constituting forward steps in organization, and often constituting steps backwards. Evolution does not imply a latent tendency to improve, everywhere in operation. There is no uniform ascent from lower to higher, but only an occasional production of a form which, in virtue of greater fitness for more complex conditions, becomes capable of a longer life of a more varied kind. And while such higher type begins to dominate over lower types and to spread at their expense, the lower types survive in habitats or modes of life that are not usurped, or are thrust into inferior habitats or modes of life in which they retrogress.

What thus holds with organic types must hold also with types of societies. Social evolution throughout the future, like social evolution throughout the past, must, while producing step after step higher societies, leave outstanding many lower. Varieties of men adapted here to inclement regions, there to regions that are barren, and elsewhere to regions unfitted, by ruggedness of surface or insalubrity, for supporting large populations, will, in all probability, continue to form small communities of simple structures. Moreover, during future competitions among the higher races there will probably be left, in the less desirable regions, minor nations formed of men inferior to the highest; at the same time that the highest overspread all the great areas which are desirable in climate and fertility. But while the entire assemblage of societies thus fulfils the law of evolution by increase of heterogeneity,—while within each of them contrasts of structure, caused by differences of environments and entailed occupations, cause unlikenesses implying further heterogeneity; we may infer that the primary process of evolution—integration—which up to the present time has been displayed in the formation of larger and larger nations, will eventually reach a still higher stage and bring yet greater benefits. As, when small tribes were welded into great tribes, the head chief stopped inter-tribal warfare; as, when small feudal governments became subject to a king, feudal wars were prevented by him; so, in time to come, a federation of the highest nations, exercising supreme authority (already foreshadowed by occasional agreements among "the Powers"), may, by forbidding wars between any of its constituent nations, put an end to the re-barbarization which is continually undoing civilization.

When this peace-maintaining federation has been formed, there may be effectual progress towards that equilibrium between constitution and conditions —between inner faculties and outer requirements—implied by the final stage of human evolution. Adaptation to the social state, now perpetually hindered by anti-social conflicts, may then go on unhindered; and all the great societies, in other respects differing, may become similar in those cardinal traits which result from complete self-ownership of the unit and exercise over him of nothing more than passive influence by the aggregate. On the one hand, by continual repression of aggressive instincts and exercise of feelings which prompt ministration to public welfare, and on the other hand by the lapse of restraints, gradually becoming less necessary, there must be produced a kind of man so constituted that while fulfilling his own desire he fulfils also the social needs. Already, small groups of men, shielded by circumstances from external antagonisms, have been moulded into forms of moral nature so superior to our own, that, as said of the Let-htas, the account of their goodness "almost savours of romance"; and it is reasonable to infer that what has even now happened on a small scale, may, under kindred conditions, eventually happen on a large scale. Long studies, showing among other things the need for certain qualifications above indicated, but also revealing facts like that just named, have not caused me to recede from the belief expressed nearly fifty years ago that—"The ultimate man will be one whose private requirements coincide with public ones. He will be that manner of man who, in spontaneously fulfilling his own nature, incidentally performs the functions of a social unit; and yet is only enabled so to fulfil his own nature by all others doing the like."

4. ERNST HAECKEL: THE RIDDLE OF THE UNIVERSE*

Ernst Haeckel (1834–1919) was Professor of Zoology at the University of Jena. Through his lectures and writings he popularized Darwin's ideas in Germany as Herbert Spencer and Thomas Huxley, his older contemporaries, had done in England. Haeckel defended a theory of monism which posited the unity of organic and inorganic substances. He concluded that everything—including life itself—had its origin in the properties of carbon atoms. For what specific historical reasons did Haeckel assert that "eternal iron laws of nature" had completely obliterated any "anthropomorphic notion of a deliberate architect and ruler of the world" among nineteenth-century scientists? How, according to Haeckel, had Charles Darwin furnished the answer to the fundamental riddle which no philosopher had been able to solve: "How can purposive contrivances be produced by a purely mechanical process without design?" Why were historians foolish to look for a "moral order in the universe"? Why have "the victors in the struggle for life" not always been "the noblest or most perfect forms in the moral sense"? What was Haeckel's personal explanation of the manner in which chance could be combined with the operations of an overarching scientific law?

Since Newton (1682) formulated the law of gravitation, and Kant (1755) established "the constitution and mechanical origin of the entire fabric of the world on Newtonian laws," and Laplace (1796) provided a mathematical foundation for this law of cosmic mechanicism, the whole of the inorganic sciences have become purely *mechanical,* and at the same time purely *atheistic.* Astronomy, cosmogony, geology, meteorology, and inorganic physics and chemistry are now absolutely ruled by mechanical laws on a mathematical foundation. The idea of "design" has wholly disappeared from this vast province of science. At the close of the nineteenth century, now that this monistic view has fought its way to general recognition, no scientist ever asks seriously of the "purpose" of any single phenomenon in the whole of this great field. Is any astronomer likely to inquire seriously to-day into the purpose of planetary motion, or a mineralogist to seek design in the structure of a crystal? Does the physicist

* Ernst Haeckel, *The Riddle of the Universe at the Close of the Nineteenth Century,* trans. Joseph McCabe (New York: Harper and Brothers, 1900), pp. 260–64, 269–74.

investigate the purpose of electric force, or the chemist that of atomic weight? We may confidently answer in the negative—certainly not, in the sense that God, or a purposive natural force, had at some time created these fundamental laws of the mechanism of the universe with a definite design, and causes them to work daily in accordance with his rational will. The anthropomorphic notion of a deliberate architect and ruler of the world has gone forever from this field; the "eternal, iron laws of nature" have taken his place.

But the idea of design has a very great significance and application in the *organic* world. We do undeniably perceive a purpose in the structure and in the life of an organism. The plant and the animal seem to be controlled by a definite design in the combination of their several parts, just as clearly as we see in the machines which man invents and constructs; as long as life continues the functions of the several organs are directed to definite ends, just as is the operation of the various parts of a machine. Hence it was quite natural that the older naïve study of nature, in explaining the origin and activity of the living being, should postulate a creator who had "arranged all things with wisdom and understanding," and had constructed each plant and animal according to the special purpose of its life. The conception of this "almighty creator of heaven and earth" was usually quite anthropomorphic; he created "everything after its kind." As long as the creator seemed to man to be of human shape, to think with his brain, see with his eyes, and fashion with his hands, it was possible to form a definite picture of this "divine engineer" and his artistic work in the great workshop of creation. This was not so easy when the idea of God became refined, and man saw in his "invisible God" a creator without organs—a gaseous being. Still more unintelligible did these anthropomorphic ideas become when physiology substituted for the conscious, divine architect an unconscious, creative "vital force"—a mysterious, purposive, natural force, which differed from the familiar forces of physics and chemistry, and only took these in part, during life, into its service. This vitalism prevailed until about the middle of the nineteenth century. Johannes Müller, the great Berlin physiologist, was the first to menace it with a destructive dose of facts. It is true that the distinguished biologist had himself (like all others in the first half of the century) been educated in a belief in this vital force, and deemed it indispensable for an elucidation of the ultimate sources of life; nevertheless, in his classical and still unrivalled *Manual of Physiology* (1833) he gave a demonstrative proof that there is really nothing to be said for this vital force. Müller himself, in a long series of remarkable observations and experiments, showed that most of the vital processes in the human organism (and in the other animals) take place according to physical and chemical laws, and that many of them are capable of mathematical determination. That was no less true of the animal functions of the muscles and nerves, and of both the higher and the lower sense-organs, than of the vegetal functions of digestion, assimilation, and circulation. Only two branches of the life of the organism, mental action and reproduction, retained any element of mystery, and seemed inexplicable without assuming a vital force. But immediately after Müller's death such important discoveries and advances were made in these two branches that the uneasy "phantom of vital force" was driven from its last refuge. By a very remarkable coincidence Johannes Müller died in the year 1858, which saw the publication of Darwin's first communication concerning his famous theory. The theory of selection solved the great problem that had mastered Müller—the question of the origin of orderly arrangements from purely mechanical causes.

Darwin, as we have often said, had a twofold immortal merit in the field of philosophy—firstly, the reform of Lamarck's theory of descent, and its establishment on the mass of facts accumulated in the course of the half-century; secondly, the conception of the theory of selection, which first revealed to us the true causes of the gradual formation of species. Darwin was the first to point out that the "struggle for life" is the unconscious regulator which controls the reciprocal action of heredity and adaptation in the gradual transformation of species; it is the great "selective divinity" which, by a purely "natural choice," without preconceived design, creates new forms, just as selective man creates new types by an "artificial choice" with a definite design. That gave us the solution of the great philosophic problem: "How can purposive contrivances be produced by purely mechanical processes without design?" Kant held the problem to be insoluble, although Empedocles had pointed out the direction of the solution two thousand years before. His principle of "teleological mechanism" has become more and more accepted of late years, and has furnished a mechanical explanation even of the finest and most recondite processes of organic life by "the functional self-production of the purposive structure." Thus have we got rid of the transcendental "design" of the teleological philosophy of the schools, which was the greatest obstacle to the growth of a rational and monistic conception of nature. . . .

In the philosophy of history—that is, in the general reflections which historians make on the destinies of nations and the complicated course of political evolution—there still prevails the notion of a "moral order of the universe." Historians seek in the vivid drama of history a leading design, an ideal purpose, which has ordained one or other race or state to a special triumph, and to dominion over the others. This teleological view of history has recently become more strongly contrasted with our monistic view in proportion as monism has proved to be the only possible interpretation of inorganic nature. Throughout the whole of astronomy, geology, physics, and chemistry there is no question to-day of a "moral order," or a personal God, whose "hand hath disposed all things in wisdom and understanding." And the same must be said of the entire field of biology, the whole constitution and history of organic nature, if we set aside the question of man for the moment. Darwin has not only proved by his theory of selection that the orderly processes in the life and structure of animals and plants have arisen by mechanical laws without any preconceived design, but he has shown us in the "struggle for life" the powerful natural force which has exerted supreme control over the entire course of organic evolution for millions of years. It may be said that the struggle for life is the "survival of the fittest" or the "victory of the best"; that is only correct when we regard the strongest as the best (in a moral sense). Moreover, the whole history of the organic world goes to prove that, besides the predominant advance towards perfection, there are at all times cases of retrogression to lower stages. Even [Carl Ernst] Baer's notion of "design" has no moral feature whatever.

Do we find a different state of things in the history of peoples, which man, in his anthropocentric presumption, loves to call "the history of the world"? Do we find in every phase of it a lofty moral principle or a wise ruler, guiding the destinies of nations? There can be but one answer in the present advanced stage of natural and human history: No. The fate of those branches of the human family, those nations and races which have struggled for existence and progress for thousands of years, is determined by the same "eternal laws of iron" as the history of the whole organic world which has peopled the earth for millions of years.

Geologists distinguish three great epochs in the organic history of the earth, as far as we can read it in the monuments of the science of fossils—the primary, secondary, and tertiary epochs. According to a recent calculation, the first occupied at least thirty-four million, the second eleven million, and the third three million years. The history of the family of vertebrates, from which our own race has sprung, unfolds clearly before our eyes during this long period. Three different stages in the evolution of the vertebrate correspond to the three epochs; the *fishes* characterized the primary (palæozoic) age, the *reptiles* the secondary (mesozoic), and the *mammals* the tertiary (cænozoic). Of the three groups the fishes rank lowest in organization, the reptiles come next, and the mammals take the highest place. We find, on nearer examination of the history of the three classes, that their various orders and families also advanced progressively during the three epochs towards a higher stage of perfection. May we consider this progressive development as the outcome of a conscious design or a moral order of the universe? Certainly not. The theory of selection teaches us that this organic progress, like the earlier organic differentiation, is an inevitable consequence of the struggle for existence. Thousands of beautiful and remarkable species of animals and plants have perished during those forty-eight million years, to give place to stronger competitors, and the victors in this struggle for life were not always the noblest or most perfect forms in a moral sense.

It has been just the same with the history of humanity. The splendid civilization of classical antiquity perished because Christianity, with its faith in a loving God and its hope of a better life beyond the grave, gave a fresh, strong impetus to the soaring human mind. The Papal Church quickly degenerated into a pitiful caricature of real Christianity, and ruthlessly scattered the treasures of knowledge which the Hellenic philosophy had gathered; it gained the dominion of the world through the ignorance of the credulous masses. In time the Reformation broke the chains of this mental slavery, and assisted reason to secure its right once more. But in the new, as in the older, period the great struggle for existence went on in its eternal fluctuation, with no trace of a moral order.

And it is just as impossible for the impartial and critical observer to detect a "wise providence" in the fate of individual human beings as a moral order in the history of peoples. Both are determined with iron necessity by a mechanical causality which connects every single phenomenon with one or more antecedent causes. Even the ancient Greeks recognized *ananke,* the blind *heimarmene,* the fate "that rules gods and men," as the supreme principle of the universe. Christianity replaced it by a conscious Providence, which is not blind, but sees, and which governs the world in patriarchal fashion. The anthropomorphic character of this notion, generally closely connected with belief in a personal God, is quite obvious. Belief in a "loving Father," who unceasingly guides the destinies of one billion five hundred million men on our planet, and is attentive at all times to their millions of contradictory prayers and pious wishes, is absolutely impossible; that is at once perceived on laying aside the colored spectacles of "faith" and reflecting rationally on the subject.

As a rule, this belief in Providence and the tutelage of a "loving Father" is more intense in the modern civilized man—just as in the uncultured savage—when some good fortune has fallen him: an escape from peril of life, recovery from a severe illness, the winning of the first prize in a lottery, the birth of a long-delayed child, and so forth. When, on the other hand, a misfortune is met with, or an ardent wish is not fulfilled, "Providence" is forgotten. The wise ruler of the world slumbered—or refused his blessing.

In the extraordinary development of commerce of the nineteenth century the number of catastrophes and accidents has necessarily increased beyond all imagination; of that the journal is a daily witness. Thousands are killed every year by shipwreck, railway accidents, mine accidents, etc. Thousands slay each other every year in war, and the preparation for this wholesale massacre absorbs much the greater part of the revenue in the highest civilized nations, the chief professors of "Christian charity." And among these hundreds of thousands of annual victims of modern civilization strong, industrious, courageous workers predominate. Yet the talk of a "moral order" goes on.

Since impartial study of the evolution of the world teaches us that there is no definite aim and no special purpose to be traced in it, there seems to be no alternative but to leave everything to "blind chance." This reproach has been made to the transformism of Lamarck and Darwin, as it had been to the previous systems of Kant and Laplace; there are a number of dualist philosophers who lay great stress on it. It is, therefore, worth while to make a brief remark upon it.

One group of philosophers affirms, in accordance with its teleological conception, that the whole cosmos is an orderly system, in which every phenomenon has its aim and purpose; there is no such thing as chance. The other group, holding a mechanical theory, expresses itself thus: The development of the universe is a monistic mechanical process, in which we discover no aim or purpose whatever; what we call design in the organic world is a special result of biological agencies; neither in the evolution of the heavenly bodies nor in that of the crust of our earth do we find any trace of a controlling purpose—all is the result of chance. Each party is right—according to its definition of chance. The general law of causality, taken in conjunction with the law of substance, teaches us that every phenomenon has a mechanical cause; in this sense there is no such thing as chance. Yet it is not only lawful, but necessary, to retain the term for the purpose of expressing the simultaneous occurrence of two phenomena, which are not causally related to each other, but of which each has its own mechanical cause, independent of that of the other. Everybody knows that chance, in its monistic sense, plays an important part in the life of man and in the universe at large. That, however, does not prevent us from recognizing in each "chance" event, as we do in the evolution of the entire cosmos, the universal sovereignty of nature's supreme law, *the law of substance.* [*I.e.,* the unity of organic and inorganic matter in the properties of carbon.]

5. LESLIE STEPHEN: AN AGNOSTIC'S APOLOGY*

Sir Leslie Stephen (1832–1904) was a prominent English philosopher and literary critic. His family background afforded him every educational advantage. After attending Eton and King's College, London, Stephen continued his studies at Trinity Hall, Cambridge, where he was elected to a fellowship in 1854 and a tutorship in 1856. He had been ordained to the Anglican ministry in 1855, but his philosophical studies and his deep interest in the controversy over Darwin's *Origin of the Species* undermined his religious faith. In 1862 Stephen resigned his positions at Cambridge and moved to London, where he devoted himself to literary criticism and to the study of philosophy, producing his monumental *History of English Thought in the Eighteenth Century* (1876). In 1882 he published a major philosophical contribution to skepticism, *The Science of Ethics.*

What, according to Stephen, was the fundamental dogma of agnosticism? What did he assert was the most troublesome problem which both determinist theologians and believers in free will had failed to answer? Why, in his view, was the problem beyond the bounds of human knowledge? Did Stephen's approach to theological problems leave any room for belief in traditional Christian doctrines?

You tell us to be ashamed of professing ignorance. Where is the shame of ignorance in matters still involved in endless and hopeless controversy? Is it not rather a duty? Why should a lad who has just run the gauntlet of examinations and escaped to a country parsonage be dogmatic, when his dogmas are denounced as erroneous by half the philosophers of the world? What theory of the universe am I to accept as demonstrably established? At the very earliest dawn of philosophy men were divided by earlier forms of the same problems which divide them now. Shall I be a Platonist or an Aristotelian? Shall I admit or deny the existence of innate ideas? Shall I believe in the possibility or in the impossibility of transcending experience? Go to the mediæval philosophy, says one controversialist. To which mediæval philosophy, pray? Shall I be a nominalist or a realist? And why should I believe you rather than the great thinkers of the seventeenth century, who agreed with one accord that the first condition of intellectual progress was the destruction of that philosophy? There would be no difficulty if it were a question of physical science. I might believe in Galileo and Newton and their successors down to Adams and Leverrier without hesitation, because they all substantially agree. But when men deal with the old problems there are still the old doubts. Shall I believe in Hobbes or in Descartes? Can I stop where Descartes stopped, or must I go on to Spinoza? Or shall I follow Locke's guidance, and end with Hume's scepticism? Or listen to Kant, and, if so, shall I decide that he is right in destroying theology, or in reconstructing it,

---

* Leslie Stephen, *An Agnostic's Apology and Other Essays* (2d ed.; New York: G. P. Putnam's Sons, 1903), pp. 13–16, 23–24, 37–41.

or in both performances? Does Hegel hold the key of the secret, or is he a mere spinner of jargon? May not Feuerbach or Schopenhauer represent the true development of metaphysical inquiry? Shall I put faith in Hamilton and Mansel, and, if so, shall I read their conclusions by the help of Mr. Spencer, or shall I believe in Mill or in Green? State any one proposition in which all philosophers agree, and I will admit it to be true; or any one which has a manifest balance of authority, and I will agree that it is probable. But so long as every philosopher flatly contradicts the first principles of his predecessors, why affect certainty? The only agreement I can discover is, that there is no philosopher of whom his opponents have not said that his opinions lead logically either to Pantheism or to Atheism.

When all the witnesses thus contradict each other, the *primâ facie* result is pure scepticism. There is no certainty. Who am I, if I were the ablest of modern thinkers, to say summarily that all the great men who differed from me are wrong, and so wrong that their difference should not even raise a doubt in my mind? From such scepticism there is indeed one, and, so far as I can see, but one, escape. The very hopelessness of the controversy shows that the reasoners have been transcending the limits of reason. They have reached a point where, as at the pole, the compass points indifferently to every quarter. Thus there is a chance that I may retain what is valuable in the chaos of speculation, and reject what is bewildering by confining the mind to its proper limits. But has any limit ever been suggested, except a limit which comes in substance to an exclusion of all ontology? In short, if I would avoid utter scepticism, must I not be an Agnostic? ...

The ancient difficulty which has perplexed men since the days of Job is this: Why are happiness and misery arbitrarily distributed? Why do the good so often suffer, and the evil so often flourish? The difficulty, says the determinist, arises entirely from applying the conception of justice where it is manifestly out of place. The advocate of free-will refuses this escape, and is perplexed by a further difficulty. Why are virtue and vice arbitrarily distributed? Of all the puzzles of this dark world, or of all forms of the one great puzzle, the most appalling is that which meets us at the corner of every street. Look at the children growing up amidst moral poison; see the brothel and the public-house turning out harlots and drunkards by the thousand; at the brutalised elders preaching cruelty and shamelessness by example; and deny, if you can, that lust and brutality are generated as certainly as scrofula and typhus. Nobody dares to deny it. All philanthropists admit it; and every hope of improvement is based on the assumption that the moral character is determined by its surroundings. What does the theological advocate of free-will say to reconcile such a spectacle with our moral conceptions? Will God damn all these wretches for faults due to causes as much beyond their power as the shape of their limbs or as the orbits of the planets? Or will He make some allowance, and decline to ask for grapes from thistles, and exact purity of life from beings born in corruption, breathing corruption, and trained in corruption? ...

In any case the real appeal must be to experience. Ontologists may manufacture libraries of jargon without touching the point. They have never made.

or suggested the barest possibility of making, a bridge from the world of pure reason to the contingent world in which we live. To the thinker who tries to construct the universe out of pure reason, the actual existence of error in our minds and disorder in the outside world presents a difficulty as hopeless as that which the existence of vice and misery presents to the optimist who tries to construct the universe out of pure goodness. To say that misery does not exist is to contradict the primary testimony of consciousness; to argue on *a priori* grounds that misery or happiness predominates, is as hopeless a task as to deduce from the principle of the excluded middle the distance from St. Paul's to Westminster Abbey. Questions of fact can only be solved by examining facts. Perhaps such evidence would show—and if a guess were worth anything, I should add that I guess that it would show—that happiness predominates over misery in the composition of the known world. I am, therefore, not prejudiced against the Gnostic's conclusion; but I add that the evidence is just as open to me as to him. The whole world in which we live may be an illusion—a veil to be withdrawn in some higher state of being. But be it what it may, it supplies all the evidence upon which we can rely. If evil predominates here, we have no reason to suppose that good predominates elsewhere. All the ingenuity of theologians can never shake our conviction that facts are what we feel them to be, nor invert the plain inference from facts; and facts are just as open to one school of thought as to another.

What, then, is the net result? One insoluble doubt has haunted men's minds since thought began in the world. No answer has ever been suggested. One school of philosophers hands it to the next. It is denied in one form only to reappear in another. The question is not which system excludes the doubt, but how it expresses the doubt. Admit or deny the competence of reason in theory, we all agree that it fails in practice. Theologians revile reason as much as Agnostics; they then appeal to it, and it decides against them. They amend their plea by excluding certain questions from its jurisdiction, and those questions include the whole difficulty. They go to revelation, and revelation replies by calling doubt, mystery. They declare that their consciousness declares just what they want it to declare. Ours declares something else. Who is to decide? The only appeal is to experience, and to appeal to experience is to admit the fundamental dogma of Agnosticism.

Is it not, then, the very height of audacity, in face of a difficulty which meets us at every turn, which has perplexed all the ablest thinkers in proportion to their ability, which vanishes in one shape only to show itself in another, to declare roundly, not only that the difficulty can be solved, but that it does not exist? Why, when no honest man will deny in private that every ultimate problem is wrapped in the profoundest mystery, do honest men proclaim in pulpits that unhesitating certainty is the duty of the most foolish and ignorant? Is it not a spectacle to make the angels laugh? We are a company of ignorant beings, feeling our way through mists and darkness, learning only by incessantly-repeated blunders, obtaining a glimmering of truth by falling into every conceivable error, dimly discerning light enough for our daily needs, but hopelessly differing whenever we attempt to describe the ultimate origin or end of our paths; and yet, when one of us ventures to declare that we don't know the map of the universe as well as the map of our infinitesimal parish, he is hooted, reviled, and perhaps told that he will be damned to all eternity for his faithlessness. Amidst all the endless and hopeless controversies which have left nothing but bare husks of meaningless words, we have been able to discover certain reliable truths. They don't take us very far, and the condition of discovering them has been distrust of *a priori* guesses, and the systematic interrogation of experience. Let us, say some of us, follow at least this clue. Here we shall find sufficient guidance for the needs of life, though we renounce for ever the attempt to get behind the veil which no one has succeeded in raising; if, indeed, there be anything behind. You miserable Agnostics! is the retort; throw aside such rubbish, and cling to the old husks. Stick to the words which profess to explain everything; call your doubts mysteries, and they won't disturb you any longer; and believe in those necessary truths of which no two philosophers have ever succeeded in giving the same version.

Gentlemen, we can only reply, wait till you have some show of agreement amongst yourselves. Wait till you can give some answer, not palpably a verbal answer, to some one of the doubts which oppress us as they oppress you. Wait till you can point to some single truth, however trifling, which has been discovered by your method, and will stand the test of discussion and verification. Wait till you can appeal to reason without in the same breath vilifying reason. Wait till your Divine revelations have something more to reveal than the hope that the hideous doubts which they suggest may possibly be without foundation. Till then we shall be content to admit openly, what you whisper under your breath or hide in technical jargon, that the ancient secret is a secret still; that man knows nothing of the Infinite and Absolute; and that, knowing nothing, he had better not be dogmatic about his ignorance. And, meanwhile, we will endeavour to be as charitable as possible, and whilst you trumpet forth officially your contempt for our scepticism, we will at least try to believe that you are imposed upon by your own bluster.

6. PIUS IX: SYLLABUS OF ERRORS*

The thirty-two year reign of Pope Pius IX (r. 1846–78) was one of the longest in papal history. Pius began his pontificate by adopting a moderately liberal policy. He granted a limited constitution for the Papal States, which were clamoring for greater self-government. But when the revolutionary germs of 1848 infected his realms and rioting drove him from Rome to Gaeta, the Pope became staunchly conservative and in some matters even reactionary. He was able to return to Rome in 1850 and remained there only by the continued support of French troops. With the collapse of Napoleon III and the withdrawal of his troops in 1870, Italian nationalists took possession of Rome. As a result, the Pope's temporal authority was for all practical purposes restricted to the tiny area of a few palaces in the Vatican. Pius IX and his successors refused to recognize Italian annexation of Rome until the Lateran Treaty of 1929. The invading Italian troops dispersed Vatican Council I which had just declared the dogma of

---

* "Pope Pius IX: Political Sections of the 'Syllabus errorum,' December 8, 1864" in Sidney Z. Ehler and John B. Morrall, eds., *Church and State Through the Centuries* (London: Burns and Oates, 1954), pp. 282–85. Reprinted by permission.

the Immaculate Conception of the Blessed Virgin Mary and promulgated the doctrine of papal infallibility.

In 1864, with a view to combating recently formulated theories on the nature of man and on man's place in society, Pius IX issued the *Syllabus of Errors.* What specific assertions of secular authority did Pius IX condemn? What actions of an absolute ruler like Napoleon Bonaparte would the Pope have found most objectionable? To what extent did the old medieval investiture controversy remain a significant issue in the *Syllabus?* How did the influence of new philosophical and scientific ideas register themselves in the *Syllabus?* With what justification can it be argued that the *Syllabus* condemned religious toleration? What was the Pope's opinion on the separation of Church and State? Why have some argued that the *Syllabus* constituted a fundamental barrier to all future growth or progress in the Church?

ERRORS CONCERNING THE CIVIL SOCIETY, CONSIDERED BOTH IN ITSELF AND IN ITS RELATION TO THE CHURCH

The secular commonwealth, since it is the origin and source of all laws, is possessed of a type of law which can be circumscribed by no limits.

The doctrine of the Catholic Church is inimical to the good and well-being of human society.

To the civil power, when exercised by an unbelieving ruler, belongs an indirect negative authority in religious matters; so that there belongs to it not only the right known as "exequatur," but also the right known as "appeal from abuse."

In a legal conflict between either authority, civil law should have precedence.

The secular power has authority to rescind and declare and make void solemn undertakings (commonly called Concordats) entered into with the Apostolic See concerning the functioning of laws dealing with the immunity of the Church, without the consent of that See; or even in spite of its protests against such action.

The civil authority can intervene in matters which pertain to religion, morals and spiritual discipline. Hence, it can decide concerning the instructions which the clergy of the Church issue, as part of their duty, for the regulation of consciences, and it can even reach decisions on the administration of the Divine Sacraments and the dispositions necessary for their reception.

The whole administration of public schools, in which the youth of any Christian State is educated, can and should be placed in the hands of the civil authority, with the sole exception, for a good reason, of episcopal seminaries; it should be so placed in the hands of that authority, that there may be recognized to no other authority whatever any right of intervention in the administration of the schools, the arrangement of studies, the conferring of degrees, or the choice of approval of teachers.

Even in clerical seminaries, the programme of studies is subject to addition by the civil authority.

The best interest of civil society requires that the popular schools, which are open to all children from any class of the people, and which are publicly endowed everywhere and intended for the transmission of humane and more advanced disciplines, should be withdrawn from any control, directive power or supervision of the Church; and being at the complete discretion of the civil and political authority, they may be subjected to the will of the rulers according to the common opinions of the age.

Reason can prove for Catholic men, concerned with the education of youth, what may be separated from the Catholic faith and the authority of the Church, and those things which pertain merely to the knowledge of natural things and the ends of temporal social life either wholly or at least primarily.

The civil authority can impose restrictions in order that the clergy and faithful laity may not freely and mutually communicate with the Roman Pontiff.

The secular authority has in itself the right of "presenting" bishops and can insist that they enter upon the administration of their dioceses before receiving canonical institution by the Holy See and Apostolic Letters.

Furthermore, the secular government has the right to depose bishops from the exercise of their pastoral ministry, and it is not bound to obey the Roman Pontiff in those things which concern the institution of bishops and bishoprics.

The government can, by its own law, change the age laid down by the Church for religious profession of men and women, and can direct all religious congregations not to admit anyone to the taking of solemn vows without the government's permission.

The laws which pertain to preserving the status of religious congregations and their rules and functions are to be abolished; in addition, the civil government can furnish aid to all those who wish to desert the practice of the religious life which they have taken up and to break their solemn vows; equally it can, in like manner, completely suppress religious congregations, collegiate churches and simple benefices, even those which have legal patronage, and claim their goods and revenues to be subject to the administration and disposal of the civil power.

Not only are kings and princes free from the jurisdiction of the Church, but they are even superior to the Church in deciding questions of jurisdiction.

The Church should be separated from the State and the State from the Church.

ERRORS CONCERNING NATURAL AND CHRISTIAN ETHICS

Moral laws lack Divine sanction, and there is no need for human laws to conform to the Natural Law or to receive obligatory force from God.

The knowledge of philosophical matters, ethics and civil laws can and should be divorced from Divine and ecclesiastical authority.

No forces other than material ones are to be recognized and all moral discipline and goodness ought to aim at the enlargement and increase of wealth by every possible means and at the fulfilment of pleasure.

Law consists in material fact; all human positions are empty titles, and all human deeds have the force of law.

Authority is nothing other than a number and total of material forces. . . .

The principle known as that of "non-intervention" [i.e. of the Church in political affairs] is to be proclaimed and observed.

It is lawful to take away obedience from legitimate princes and even to rebel against them.

The violation of the most solemn oath or the commission of the most sinful and depraved action imaginable is not only free from blame, but is even to be regarded as lawful and extremely praiseworthy in every way, when it is performed for the sake of patriotism.

ERRORS CONCERNING THE CIVIL GOVERNMENT OF THE ROMAN PONTIFF

Children of the Christian and Catholic Church may differ in their opinions about the compatibility of the temporal with the spiritual power.

The abolition of the temporal power possessed by the Apostolic See would promote, in the highest degree, the liberty and happiness of the Church.

ERRORS WHICH REFER TO CONTEMPORARY LIBERALISM

In this age of ours it is no longer expedient that the Catholic religion should be treated as the sole State religion and that any other forms of religious worship should be excluded.

Hence those States, nominally Catholic, who have legally enacted that immigrants be permitted to have free exercise of their own particular religion, are to be praised.

Similarly, it is not true that civil liberty for any religious sect whatever and the granting to all of full right to express any kind of opinion and thought whatever, openly and publicly, conduces to the easier corruption of the morals and minds of peoples and the spread of the disease of indifferentism.

The Roman Pontiff can and should reconcile himself and reach agreement with "progress," Liberalism and recent departures in civil society.

7. LEO XIII: RERUM NOVARUM*

The negative and fundamentally reactionary nature of the *Syllabus of Errors* rendered more positive statements on man's place in modern society a necessary task for the Papacy. Pope Leo XIII (r. 1878–1903) fulfilled this need in his encyclical letters on political, moral, and economic problems facing modern industrial states. Excerpts from his most famous encyclical, *Rerum Novarum* (1891), are printed below. To what extent was Leo XIII prepared to condemn the practices of nineteenth-century industrial capitalism? With what essential doctrines of socialism did the Pope take issue? Why? How did Leo XIII's views on "stable and permanent possession," his pronouncement that man was "master of his own acts," and his assertion of a "Providence governing all things," compare with Charles Darwin's view of man and his place in the universe? Under what circumstances did the Pope assert that the state had a right to intervene in family affairs? Did *Rerum Novarum* allow a wider range of secular authority than the *Syllabus of Errors?* In what specific ways? How extensive a program of social legislation would Pope Leo have favored? Why did he recognize the validity of labor unions? In what ways did Leo XIII attempt to adapt the views of St. Thomas Aquinas to the problems of modern industrial society? What action did he recommend to Catholics in dealing with problems of modern industrialism?

* Leo XIII, *The Pope and the People: Select Letters and Addresses* (London: Catholic Truth Society, 1903), pp. 1–6, 9–10, 13–15, 24–25, 28–29, 38–40, 42–43. Reprinted by permission.

Encyclical Letter, May 15, 1891

That the spirit of revolutionary change, which has long been disturbing the nations of the world, should have passed beyond the sphere of politics and made its influence felt in the cognate sphere of practical economics is not surprising. The elements of the conflict now raging are unmistakable, in the vast expansion of industrial pursuits and the marvellous discoveries of science; in the changed relations between masters and workmen; in the enormous fortunes of some few individuals, and the utter poverty of the masses; in the increased self-reliance and closer mutual combination of the working classes; as also, finally, in the prevailing moral degeneracy. The momentous gravity of the state of things now obtaining fills every mind with painful apprehension; wise men are discussing it; practical men are proposing schemes; popular meetings, legislatures, and rulers of nations are all busied with it—and actually there is no question which has taken a deeper hold on the public mind.

Therefore, Venerable Brethren, as on former occasions when it seemed opportune to refute false teaching, . . . so have we thought it expedient now to speak ON THE CONDITION OF THE WORKING CLASSES. . . . It is no easy matter to define the relative rights and mutual duties of the rich and of the poor, of Capital and of Labour. And the danger lies in this, that crafty agitators are intent on making use of these differences of opinion to pervert men's judgments and to stir up the people to revolt.

But all agree, and there can be no question whatever, that some remedy must be found, and found quickly, for the misery and wretchedness pressing so heavily and unjustly at this moment on the vast majority of the working classes.

For the ancient working-men's Guilds were abolished in the last century, and no other organisation took their place. Public institutions and the very laws have set aside the ancient religion. Hence by degrees it has come to pass that working-men have been surrendered, all isolated and helpless, to the hard-heartedness of employers and the greed of unchecked competition. The mischief has been increased by rapacious usury, which, although more than once condemned by the Church, is nevertheless, under a different guise, but with the like injustice, still practised by covetous and grasping men. To this must be added the custom of working by contract, and the concentration of so many branches of trade in the hands of a few individuals; so that a small number of very rich men have been able to lay upon the teeming masses of the labouring poor a yoke little better than that of slavery itself.

To remedy these wrongs the Socialists, working on the poor man's envy of the rich, are striving to do away with private property, and contend that individual possessions should become the common property of all, to be administered by the State or by municipal bodies. They hold that by thus transferring property from private individuals to the community, the present mischievous state of things will be set to rights, inasmuch as each citizen will then get his fair share of whatever there is to enjoy. But their contentions are so clearly powerless to end the controversy that were they carried into effect the working-man himself would be among the first to suffer. They are moreover emphatically unjust, because they would rob the lawful possessor, bring State action into a sphere not within its competence, and create utter confusion in the community.

It is surely undeniable that, when a man engages in remunerative labour, the impelling reason and motive of his work is to obtain property, and thereafter to hold it as his very own. If one man hires out to another his strength or skill, he does so for the purpose of receiving in return what is necessary for sustenance and education; he therefore expressly intends to acquire a right full and real, not only to the remuneration, but also to the disposal of such remuneration, just as he pleases. Thus, if he lives sparingly, saves money, and, for greater security, invests his savings in land, the land, in such case, is only his wages under another form; and, consequently, a working-man's little estate thus purchased should be as completely at his full disposal as are the wages he receives for his labour. But it is precisely in such power of disposal that ownership obtains, whether the property consist of land or chattels. Socialists, therefore, by endeavouring to transfer the possessions of individuals to the community at large, strike at the interests of every wage-earner, since they would deprive him of the liberty of disposing of his wages, and thereby of all hope and possibility of increasing his stock and of bettering his condition in life.

What is of far greater moment, however, is the fact that the remedy they propose is manifestly against justice. For every man has by nature the right to possess property as his own. This is one of the chief points of distinction between man and the animal creation, for the brute has no power of self-direction, but is governed by two main instincts, which keep his powers on the alert, impel him to develop them in a fitting manner, and stimulate and determine him to action without any power of choice. One of these instincts is self-preservation, the other the propagation of the species. Both can attain their purpose by means of things which lie within range; beyond their verge the brute creation cannot go, for they are moved to action by their senses only, and in the special direction which these suggest. But with man it is wholly different. He possesses, on the one hand, the full perfection of the animal being, and hence enjoys, at least as much as the rest of the animal kind, the fruition of things material. But animal nature, however perfect, is far from representing the human being in its completeness, and is in truth but humanity's humble handmaid, made to serve and to obey. It is the mind, or reason, which is the predominant element in us who are human creatures; it is this which renders a human being human, and distinguishes him essentially and generically from the brute. And on this very account—that man alone among the animal creation is endowed with reason—it must be within his right to possess things not merely for temporary and momentary use, as other living things do, but to have and to hold them in stable and permanent possession; he must have not only things that perish in the *"user"* but those also which, though they have been reduced into use, continue for further use in after time.

This becomes still more clearly evident if man's nature be considered a little more deeply. For man, fathoming by his faculty of reason matters without number, and linking the future with the present, becoming, furthermore, by taking enlightened forethought, master of his own acts, guides his ways under the eternal law and the power of God, Whose Providence governs all things. Wherefore it is in his power to exercise his choice not only as to matters that regard his present welfare, but also about those which he deems may be for his advantage in time yet to come. Hence man not only can possess the fruits of the earth, but also the very soil, inasmuch as from the produce of the earth he has to lay by provision for the future. Man's needs do not die out, but recur; although satisfied to-day, they demand fresh supplies for tomorrow. . . .

Neither do we, at this stage, need to bring into action the interference of the State. Man precedes the State, and possesses, prior to the formation of any State, the right of providing for the sustenance of his body. . . .

. . . Inasmuch as the domestic household is antecedent, as well in idea as in fact, to the gathering of men into a community, the family must necessarily have rights and duties which are prior to those of the Community, and founded more immediately in nature. If the citizens of a State—in other words the families—on entering into association and fellowship, were to experience at the hands of the State hindrance instead of help, and were to find their rights attacked instead of being upheld, such association should be held in detestation, rather than be an object of desire.

The contention, then, that the civil government should at its option intrude into and exercise intimate control over the Family and the household, is a great and pernicious error. True, if a family finds itself in exceeding distress, utterly deprived of the counsel of friends, and without any prospect of extricating itself, it is right that extreme necessity be met by public aid, since each family is a part of the commonwealth. In like manner, if within the precincts of the household there occur grave disturbance of mutual rights, public authority should intervene to force each party to yield to the other its proper due; for this is not to deprive citizens of their rights, but justly and properly to safeguard and strengthen them. But the rulers of the State must go no further: here nature bids them stop. Paternal authority can be neither abolished nor absorbed by the State; for it has the same source as human life itself. . . . The Socialists, in setting aside the parent and setting up a State supervision, act *against natural justice,* and break into pieces the stability of all family life. . . .

The great mistake made in regard to the matter now under consideration, is to take up with the notion that class is naturally hostile to class, and that the wealthy and the working-men are intended by nature to live in mutual conflict. So irrational and so false is this view, that the direct contrary is the truth. Just as the symmetry of the human frame is the resultant of the disposition of the bodily members, so in a State is it ordained by nature that these two classes should dwell in harmony and agreement, and should, as it were, groove into one another, so as to maintain the balance of the body politic. Each needs the other: Capital cannot do without Labour, nor Labour without Capital. Mutual agreement results in pleasantness of life and the beauty of good order; while perpetual conflict necessarily produces confusion and savage barbarity. Now, in preventing such strife as this, and in uprooting it, the efficacy of Christian institutions is marvellous and manifold.

First of all, there is no intermediary more powerful than Religion (whereof the Church is the interpreter and guardian) in drawing the rich, and the poor bread-winners, together, by reminding each class of its duties to the other, and especially of the obligations of justice. Thus Religion teaches the labouring man and the artisan to carry out honestly and fairly all equitable agreements freely entered into; never to injure the property, nor to outrage the person, of an employer; never to resort to violence in defending their own cause, nor to engage in riot or disorder; and to have nothing to do with men of evil principles, who work upon the people with artful promises, and excite foolish hopes which usually end in useless regrets, followed by insolvency. Religion teaches the wealthy owner and the employer that their work-people are not to be accounted their bondsmen; that in every man they must respect his dignity and worth as a man and as a Christian; that labour is not a thing to be ashamed of, if we lend ear to right reason and to Christian philosophy, but is an honourable calling, enabling a man to sustain his life in a way upright and creditable; and that it is shameful and inhuman to treat men like chattels to make money by, or to look upon them merely as so much muscle or physical power. Again, therefore, the Church teaches that, as Religion and things, spiritual and mental, are among the working-man's main concerns, the employer is bound to see that the worker has time for his religious duties; that he be not exposed to corrupting influences and dangerous occasions; and that he be not led away to neglect his home and family, or to squander his earnings. Furthermore, the employer must never tax his work-people beyond their strength, or employ them in work unsuited to their sex or age. His great and principal duty is to give every one a fair wage. . . .

. . . The foremost duty, therefore, of the rulers of the State should be to make sure that the laws and institutions, the general character and administration of the commonwealth, shall be such as of themselves to realise public well-being and private prosperity. This is the proper scope of wise statesmanship and is the work of the heads of the State. Now, a state chiefly prospers and thrives through moral rule, well-regulated family life, respect for religion and justice, the moderation and equal allocation of public taxes, the progress of the arts and of trade, the abundant yield of the land—through everything, in fact, which makes the citizens better and happier. Hereby, then, it lies in the power of a ruler to benefit every class in the State, and amongst the rest to promote to the utmost the interests of the poor; and this in virtue of his office, and without being open to any suspicion of undue interference—since it is the province of the State to consult the common good. And the more that is done for the benefit of the working classes by the general laws of the country, the less need will there be to seek for special means to relieve them. . . .

Whenever the general interest or any particular class suffers, or is threatened with mischief which can in no other way be met or prevented, the public authority must step in to deal with it. Now, it interests the public, as well as the individual, that peace and good order should be maintained; that family life should be carried on in accordance with God's laws and those of nature; that Religion should be reverenced and obeyed; that a high standard of morality should prevail, both in public and private life; that the sanctity of justice should be respected, and that no one should injure another with impunity; that the members of the commonwealth should grow up to man's estate strong and robust, and capable, if need be, of guarding and defending their country. If by a strike, or other combination of workmen, there should be imminent danger of disturbance to the public peace; or if circumstances were such as that among the labouring population the ties of family life were relaxed; if Religion were found to suffer through the operatives not having time and opportunity afforded them to practise its duties; if in workshops and factories there were danger to morals through the mixing of the sexes or from other harmful occasions of evil; . . . in such cases, there can be no question but that, within certain limits, it would be right to invoke the aid and authority of the law. The limits must be determined by the nature of the occasion which calls for the law's interference —the principle being that the law must not undertake more, nor proceed further, than is required for the remedy of the evil or the removal of the mischief. . . .

The most important of all are Working-men's Unions; for these virtually include all the rest. History attests what excellent results were brought about by the Artificers' Guilds of olden times. They were the means of affording not only many advantages to the workmen, but in no small degree of promoting the advancement of art, as numerous monuments remain to bear witness. Such Unions should be suited to the requirements of this our age—an age of wider education, of different habits, and of far more numerous requirements in daily life. It is gratifying to know that there are actually in existence not a few Associations of this nature, consisting either of workmen alone, or of workmen and employers together; but it were greatly to be desired that they should become more numerous and more efficient. We have spoken of them more than once; yet it will be well to explain here how notably they are needed, to show that they exist of their own right, and what should be their organisation and their mode of action. . . . *A brother that is helped by his brother is like a strong city*. It is this natural impulse which binds men together in civil society; and it is likewise this which leads them to join together in associations of citizen with citizen; associations which, it is true, cannot be called societies in the full sense of the word, but which, notwithstanding, *are* societies.

These lesser societies and the society which constitutes the State differ in many respects, because their immediate purpose and aim is different. Civil society exists for the common good, and hence is concerned with the interests of all in general, albeit with individual interests also in their due place and degree. It is therefore called *public* society, because by its agency, as St. Thomas of Aquin says, "Men establish relations in common with one another in the setting up of a commonwealth." But societies which are formed in the bosom of the State are styled *private,* and rightly so, since their immediate purpose is the private advantage of the associates. "Now a private society," says St. Thomas again, "is one which is formed for the purpose of carrying out private objects; as when two or three enter into partnership with the view of trading in common." Private societies, then, although they exist within the State, and are severally part of the State, cannot nevertheless be absolutely, and as such, prohibited by the State. For to enter into a "society" of this kind is the natural right of man; and the State is bound to protect natural rights, not to destroy them; and if it forbid its citizens to form associations, it contradicts the very principle of its own existence; for both they and it exist in virtue of the like principle, namely, the natural tendency of man to dwell in society.

There are occasions, doubtless, when it is fitting that the law should intervene to prevent association; as when men join together for purposes which are evidently bad, unlawful, or dangerous to the State. In such cases public authority may justly forbid the formation of associations, and may dissolve them if they already exist. But every precaution should be taken not to violate the rights of individuals and not to impose unreasonable regulations under pretence of public benefit. For laws only bind when they are in accordance with right reason, and hence with the eternal law of God. . . .

Those Catholics are worthy of all praise—and they are not a few—who, understanding what the times require, have striven, by various undertakings and endeavours, to better the condition of the working-class without any sacrifice of principle being involved. They have taken up the cause of the workingman, and have spared no efforts to better the condition both of families and individuals; to infuse a spirit of equity into the mutual relations of employers and employed; to keep before the eyes of both classes the precepts of duty and the laws of the Gospel—that Gospel which, by inculcating self-restraint, keeps men within the bounds of moderation, and tends to establish harmony among the divergent interests, and the various classes which compose the State. It is with such ends in view that we see men of eminence meeting together for discussion, for the promotion of concerted action, and for practical work. Others, again, strive to unite working-men of various grades into Associations, help them with their advice and means, and enable them to obtain fitting and profitable employment. The Bishops, on their part, bestow their ready goodwill and support; and with their approval and guidance many members of the clergy, both secular and regular, labour assiduously in behalf of the spiritual and mental interests of the members of such Associations. . . .

8. FRIEDRICH NIETZSCHE: THE WILL TO POWER*

Friedrich Nietzsche (1844–1900) has been one of the most widely misinterpreted of German philosophers. Partly because he died insane, and because his sister assiduously devoted her life to the fabrication of a Nietzsche legend which somewhat distorted the philosopher's intentions, Nietzsche has left a mixed legacy. A good European, he has been derided as a prophet of supermen, of strident chauvinism, and of Nazism; yet the philosopher would have been the first to condemn the Third Reich of Adolf Hitler. Nietzsche himself was partly responsible for the apparent contradictions and lack of clarity of his philosophy. He did not seek to construct a systematic body of doctrine, and his style suggests that his books were written in a fury of ecstasy. Although the aphorisms of *Thus Spake Zarathustra* do not display crisp clarity, Nietzsche was a master of epigrammatic prose.

Nietzsche was a trenchant critic of nineteenth-century society. He attacked Christianity, trumpeting that "God is dead," and called for the creation of a new set of values to replace the old. The state was the enemy of culture. Hypocrisy, the mass culture of Germany, chauvinistic arrogance, and the influence of the massman were attacked with a venomous pen. Nietzsche called for a

* Friedrich Nietzsche, *The Will to Power*, trans. Anthony M. Ludovici (2 vols.; London: George Allen and Unwin, Ltd., 1924), I, 228–29, 236–37, 291; II, 110, 124, 130, 184–86, 205–7, 225–27, 295–99, 312–13, 361–65. Reprinted by permission.

"transvaluation of values," for a new breed of supermen who would recognize the irrational of the universe and would master themselves. What was the herd? What was the herd instinct? Why did Nietzsche attack Christianity? What was the "will to power"? In what ways were Nietzsche's views on racism unique? Why did he make the bold-faced assertion that "it is necessary for higher men to declare war upon the masses"? What did he mean by the "terrible consequences of equality"? In what ways did Nietzsche both reflect and contradict major philosophies and scientific trends of late nineteenth-century thought? What specific process was involved in the realization of Nietzsche's "transvaluation of values"? Why did such a process appeal to large numbers of the younger generation before World War I?

The whole of the morality of Europe is based upon the values *which are useful to the herd:* the sorrow of all higher and exceptional men is explained by the fact that everything which distinguishes them from others reaches their consciousness in the form of a feeling of their own smallness and egregiousness. It is the virtues of modern men which are the causes of pessimistic gloominess; the mediocre, like the herd, are not troubled much with questions or with conscience—they are cheerful. (Among the gloomy strong men, Pascal and Schopenhauer are noted examples.)

The more dangerous a quality seems to the herd, the more completely it is condemned. . . .

The mortal enmity of the herd towards all *order of rank:* its instinct is in favour of the *leveller* (Christ). Towards all *strong individuals* (the sovereigns) it is hostile, unfair, intemperate, arrogant, cheeky, disrespectful, cowardly, false, lying, pitiless, deceitful, envious, revengeful.

My teaching is this, that the herd seeks to maintain and preserve one type of man, and that it defends itself on two sides—that is to say, against those which are decadents from its ranks (criminals, etc.), and against those who rise superior to its dead level. The instincts of the herd tend to a stationary state of society; they merely preserve. They have no creative power. . . .

My philosophy aims at a new *order or rank:* not at an individualistic morality. The spirit of the herd should rule within the herd—but not beyond it: the leaders of the herd require a fundamentally different valuation for their actions, as do also the independent ones or the beasts of prey, etc. . . .

I have declared war against the anaemic Christian ideal (together with what is closely related to it), not because I want to annihilate it, but only to put an end to its *tyranny* and clear the way for other *ideals,* for more *robust* ideals.

. . . The *continuance* of the Christian Ideal belongs to the most desirable of desiderata: if only for the sake of the ideals which wish to take their stand beside it and perhaps above it—they must have opponents, and strong ones too, in order to grow *strong* themselves. That is why we immoralists require the *power* of *morality:* our instinct of self-preservation insists upon our opponents maintaining their strength—all it requires is to *become master of them.* . . .

The triumphant concept *"energy,"* with which our physicists created God and the world, needs yet to be completed: it must be given an inner will which I characterise as the *"Will to Power"*—that is to say, as an insatiable desire to manifest power; or the application and exercise of power as a creative instinct, etc. . . .

The Will to Power *interprets* (an organ in the process of formation has to be interpreted): it defines, it determines gradations, differences of power. Mere differences of power could not be aware of each other as such: something must be there which will grow, and which interprets all other things that would do the same, according to the value of the latter. . . .

The will to power can manifest itself only against *obstacles;* it therefore goes in search of what resists it—this is the primitive tendency of the protoplasm when it extends its *pseudopodia* and feels about it. . . .

The State, or *unmorality* organised, is from within—the police, the penal code, status, commerce, and the family; and from without, the will to war, to power, to conquest and revenge. . . .

Everything that a man does in the service of the State is against his own nature. . . .

Man has one terrible and fundamental wish; he desires power, and this impulse, which is called freedom, must be the longest restrained. Hence ethics has instinctively aimed at such an education as shall restrain the desire for power; thus our morality slanders the would-be tyrant, and glorifies charity, patriotism, and the ambition of the herd. . . .

According as to whether a people feels: "the rights, the keenness of vision, and the gifts of leading, etc., are with the few" or "with the many"—it constitutes an oligarchic or a democratic community.

Monarchy represents the belief in a man who is completely superior—a leader, a saviour, a demigod.

Aristocracy represents the belief in a chosen few—in a higher caste.

Democracy represents the disbelief in all great men and in all elite societies: everybody is everybody else's equal. "At bottom we are all herd and mob."

I am opposed to Socialism because it dreams ingenuously of "goodness, truth, beauty, and equal rights" (anarchy pursues the same ideal, but in a more brutal fashion).

I am opposed to parliamentary government and the power of the press, because they are the means whereby cattle become masters.

The arming of the people means in the end the arming of the mob.

Socialists are particularly ridiculous in my eyes, because of their absurd optimism concerning the "good man" who is supposed to be waiting in their cupboard, and who will come into being when the present order of society has been overturned and has made way for natural instincts. But the opposing party is quite as ludicrous, because it will not see the act of violence which lies beneath every law, the severity and egoism inherent in every kind of authority. "I and my kind will rule and prevail. Whoever degenerates will be either expelled or annihilated." This was the fundamental feeling of all ancient legislation. The idea of a higher order of man is hated much more profoundly than monarchs themselves. Hatred of aristocracy always uses hatred of monarchy as a mask. . . .

The two traits which characterise the modern European are apparently antagonistic—*individualism and the demand for equal rights:* this I am at last beginning to understand. The individual is an extremely vulnerable piece of vanity: this vanity, when it is conscious of its high degree of susceptibility to pain, demands that every one should be made equal; that the individual should only stand *inter pares.* But in this way a social race is depicted in which, as a matter of fact, gifts and powers are on the whole equally distributed. The pride which would have loneliness and but few appreciators is quite beyond comprehension: really "great" successes are only attained through the masses—indeed, we scarcely understand yet that a mob success is in reality only a small success. . . .

No morality will countenance order of rank among men, and the jurists know nothing of a communal conscience. The principle of individualism rejects *really great* men, and demands the most delicate vision for, and the speediest discovery of, a talent among people who are almost equal; and inasmuch as every one has some modicum of talent in such late and civilised cultures (and can, therefore, expect to receive his share of honour), there is a more general buttering-up of modest merits to-day than there has ever been. This gives the age the appearance of *unlimited justice.* Its want of justice is to be found not in its unbounded hatred of tyrants and demagogues, even in the arts; but in its detestation of noble natures who scorn the praise of the many. The demand for equal rights (that is to say, the privilege of sitting in judgment of everything and everybody) is anti-aristocratic.

This age knows just as little concerning the absorption of the individual, of his mergence into a great type of men who do not want to be personalities. It was this that formerly constituted the distinction and the zeal of many lofty natures (the greatest poets among them); or of the desire to be a *polis,* as in Greece; or of Jesuitism or of the Prussian Staff Corps, and bureaucracy; or of apprenticeship and a continuation of the tradition of great masters: to all of which things, non-social conditions and the absence of *petty vanity* are necessary.

Individualism is a modest and still unconscious form of will to power; with it a single human unit seems to think it sufficient to free himself from the preponderating power of society (or of the State or Church). He does not set himself up in opposition as a *personality,* but merely as a unit; he represents the rights of all other individuals as against the whole. That is to say, he instinctively places himself on a level with every other unit: what he combats he does not combat as a person, but as a representative of units against a mass. . . .

In this age of universal suffrage, in which everybody is allowed to sit in judgment upon everything and everybody, I feel compelled to re-establish the order of rank.

Quanta of power alone determine rank and distinguish rank: nothing else does.

The will to power.—How must those men be constituted who would undertake this transvaluation? The order of rank as the order of power: war and danger are the prerequisites which allow of a rank maintaining its conditions. The prodigious example; man in Nature—the weakest and shrewdest creature making himself master, and putting a yoke upon all less intelligent forces.

I distinguish between the type which represents ascending life and that which represents decay, decomposition and weakness. Ought one to suppose that the question of rank between these two types can be at all doubtful?

The modicum of power which you represent decides your rank; all the rest is cowardice.

The advantages of standing detached from one's age.—Detached from the two movements, that of individualism and that of collectivist morality; for even the first does not recognise the order of rank, and would give one individual the same freedom as another. My thoughts are not concerned with the degree of freedom which should be granted to the one or to the other or to all, but with the degree of power which the one or the other should exercise over his neighbour or over all; and more especially with the question to what extent a sacrifice of freedom, or even enslavement, may afford the basis for the cultivation of a *superior* type. In plain words: *how could one sacrifice the development of mankind* in order to assist a higher species than man to come into being.

Concerning rank,—the terrible consquences of "equality"—in the end everybody thinks he has the right to every problem. All order of rank has vanished.

It is necessary for *higher* men to declare war upon the masses! In all directions mediocre people are joining hands in order to make themselves masters. Everything that pampers, that softens, and that brings the "people" or "woman" to the front, operates in favour of universal suffrage—that is to say, the dominion of *inferior* men. But we must make reprisals, and draw the whole state of affairs (which commenced in Europe with Christianity) to the light of day and to judgment.

A teaching is needed which is strong enough to work in a *disciplinary* manner; it should operate in such a way as to strengthen the strong and to paralyse and smash up the world-weary.

The annihilation of declining races. The decay of Europe. The annihilation of slave-tainted valuations. The dominion of the world as a means to the rearing of a higher type. The annihilation of the humbug which is called morality (Christianity as a hysterical kind of honesty in this regard: Augustine, Bunyan). The annihilation of universal suffrage—that is to say, that system by means of which the lowest natures prescribe themselves as a law for higher natures. The annihilation of mediocrity and its prevalence. (The one-sided, the individuals—peoples; constitutional plenitude should be aimed at by means of the coupling of opposites; to this end race-combinations should be tried.) The new kind of courage—no *a priori* truths (those who were accustomed to believe in something sought such truths!), but *free* submission to a ruling thought, which has its time; for instance, time conceived as the quality of space, etc.

The notion, "strong and weak man," resolves itself into this, that in the first place much strength is inherited—the man is a total sum: in the other, *not yet enough* (inadequate inheritance, subdivision of the inherited qualities). Weakness may be a starting phenomenon: *not yet enough:* or a final phenomenon: "no more."

The determining point is there where great strength is present, or where a great amount of strength can be discharged. The mass, as the sum-total of the *weak,* reacts *slowly;* it defends itself against much for which it is too weak,—against that for which it has no use; it *never* creates, it *never* takes a step forward. This is opposed to the theory which denies the strong individual and would maintain that the "masses do everything." The difference is similar to that which obtains between separated generations: four or even five generations may lie between the masses and him who is the moving spirit—it is a *chronological* difference.

The *values of the weak* are in the van, because the strong have adopted them in order to *lead* with them. . . .

The degeneration of the ruler and of the ruling classes has been the cause of all the great disorders in history! Without the Roman Caesars and Roman society, Christianity would never have prevailed.

When it occurs to inferior men to doubt whether higher men exist, then the danger is great! It is then that men finally discover that there are virtues even among inferior, suppressed, and poor-spirited men, and that everybody is equal before God: which is the *non plus ultra* of all confounded nonsense that has ever appeared on earth! For in the end higher men begin to measure themselves according to the standard of virtues upheld by the slaves—and discover that they are "proud," *etc.,* and that all their *higher* qualities should be condemned.

When Nero and Caracalla stood at the helm, it was then that the paradox arose: "The lowest man is of more value than that one on the throne!" And thus the path was prepared for an *image of God* which was as remote as possible from the Image of the mightiest,—God on the Cross! ...

The aspect of the European of to-day makes me very hopeful. A daring and ruling race is here building itself up upon the foundation of an extremely intelligent, gregarious mass. ...

The question, and at the same time the task, is approaching with hesitation, terrible as Fate, but nevertheless inevitable: how shall the earth as a whole be ruled? And to what end shall man as a whole—no longer as a people or as a race—be reared and trained?

Legislative moralities are the principal means by which one can form mankind, according to the fancy of a creative and profound will: provided, of course, that such an artistic will of the first order gets the power into its own hands, and can make its creative will prevail over long periods in the form of legislation, religions, and morals. At present, and probably for some time to come, one will seek such colossally creative men, such really great men, as I understand them, in vain: they will be lacking, until, after many disappointments, we are forced to begin to understand why it is they are lacking, and that nothing bars with greater hostility their rise and development, at present and for some time to come, than that which is now called *the* morality in Europe. Just as if there were no other kind of morality, and could be no other kind, than the one we have already characterised as herd-morality. It is this morality which is now striving with all its power to attain to that green-meadow happiness on earth, which consists in security, absence of danger, ease, facilities for livelihood, and, last but not least, "if all goes well," even hopes to dispense with all kinds of shepherds and bell-wethers. The two doctrines which it preaches most universally are "equality of rights" and "pity for all sufferers"— and it even regards suffering itself as something which must be got rid of absolutely. That such ideas may be modern leads one to think very poorly of modernity. He, however, who has reflected deeply concerning the question, how and where the plant man has hitherto grown most vigorously, is forced to believe that this has always taken place under the opposite conditions; that to this end the danger of the situation has to increase enormously, his inventive faculty and dissembling powers have to fight their way up under long oppression and compulsion, and his will to life has to be increased to the unconditioned will to power, to over-power: he believes that danger, severity, violence, peril in the street and in the heart, inequality of rights, secrecy, stoicism, seductive art, and devilry of every kind—in short, the opposite of all gregarious desiderata—are necessary for the elevation of man. Such a morality with opposite designs, which would rear man upwards instead of to comfort and mediocrity; such a morality, with the intention of producing a ruling caste—the future lords of the earth— must, in order to be taught at all, introduce itself as if it were in some way correlated to the prevailing moral law, and must come forward under the cover of the latter's words and forms. But seeing that, to this end, a host of transitionary and deceptive measures must be discovered, and that the life of a single individual stands for almost nothing in view of the accomplishment of such lengthy tasks and aims, the first thing that must be done is to rear *a new kind of man* in whom the duration of the necessary will and the necessary instincts is guaranteed for many generations. This must be a new kind of ruling species and caste—this ought to be quite as clear as the somewhat lengthy and not easily expressed consequences of this thought. The aim should be to prepare a *transvaluation of values* for a particularly strong kind of man, most highly gifted in intellect and will, and, to this end, slowly and cautiously to liberate in him a whole host of slandered instincts hitherto held in check: whoever meditates about this problem belongs to us, the free spirits—certainly not to that kind of "free spirit" which has existed hitherto: for these desired practically the reverse. To this order, it seems to me, belong, above all, the pessimists of Europe, the poets and thinkers of a revolted idealism, in so far as their discontent with existence in general must *consistently* at least have led them to be dissatisfied with the man of the present; the same applies to certain insatiably ambitious artists who courageously and unconditionally fight against the gregarious animal for the special rights of higher men, and subdue all herd-instincts and precautions of more exceptional minds by their seductive art. Thirdly and lastly, we should include in this group all those critics and historians by whom the discovery of the Old World, which has begun so happily—this was the work of the *new* Columbus, of German intellect—will be courageously *continued* (for we still stand in the very first stages of this conquest). For in the Old World, as a matter of fact, a different and more lordly morality ruled than that of to-day; and the man of antiquity, under the educational ban of his morality, was a stronger and deeper man than the man of to-day—up to the present he has been the only well-constituted man. The temptation, however, which from antiquity to the present day has always exercised its power on such lucky strokes of Nature, *i.e.* on strong and enterprising souls, is, even at the present day, the most subtle and most effective of anti-democratic and anti-Christian powers, just as it was in the time of the Renaissance.

I am writing for a race of men which does not yet exist: for "the lords of the earth." ...

9. HOUSTON STEWART CHAMBERLAIN: FOUNDATIONS OF THE NINETEENTH CENTURY*

The expansion of scientific horizons and the spread of nationalism in Europe encouraged philosophical speculations which gave a new twist to an old theory. Pseudo-science, nationalism, and Romanticism inspired a number of racial theorists to publicize their views. Arthur, Comte de Gobineau (1816–1882) published an *Essay on the Inequality of the Human Races* (1853), in which he concluded that racial purity must be maintained in order to assure the preservation of civilization. Gobineau's ideas did not spread widely, but toward the end of the nineteenth century an Englishman who later became a naturalized German, Houston Stewart Chamberlain (1855–1927), popularized racist theories in the German Empire.

Chamberlain attempted a monumental analysis of the development of civilization and published *The Foundations of the Nineteenth Century* in 1900. The book was an immediate popular success. Racism, in Chamberlain's thought, was the most important aspect of civilization and the hope of mankind. His literary tour de force attempted to Germanize Christianity and to explain the importance of race for civilization. As a result, he managed to lend an outwardly respectable cloak to racist theory, and Kaiser Wilhelm II was a conspicuous supporter of Chamberlain's thesis. Similar racist philosophies were more or less popular in England, France, and Russia, but the appeal of Chamberlain's ideas made racism more prominent in Germany than elsewhere.

In Chamberlain's view, what was the historic importance of race? What evidence did Chamberlain muster to support his belief that the "Germanic race" was morally and culturally superior to all others? What peoples qualified for inclusion in the Teutonic race? Wilhelm II ordered that a copy of *The Foundations of the Nineteenth Century* be presented to every officer in the German army. What specific assertions in the following selection might have prompted the Kaiser's action? How did Chamberlain contrast freedom and loyalty? What was "mongrelization"?

Let us attempt a glance into the depths of the soul. What are the specific intellectual and moral characteristics of this Germanic race? Certain anthropologists would fain teach us that all races are equally gifted; we point to history and answer: that is a lie! The races of mankind are markedly different in the nature and also in the extent of their gifts, and the Germanic races belong to the most highly gifted group, the group usually termed Aryan. Is this human family united and uniform by bonds of blood? Do these stems really all spring from the same root? I do not know and I do not much care; no affinity binds more closely than elective affinity, and in this sense the Indo-European Aryans certainly form a family. In his *Politics* Aristotle writes [i. 5]: "If there were men who in physical stature alone were so pre-eminent as the representatives of the Gods, then every one would admit that other men by right must be subject unto them. If this, however, is true in reference to the body, then there is still greater justification for distinguishing between pre-eminent and common-place souls." Physically and mentally the Aryans are pre-eminent among all

---

* Houston Stewart Chamberlain, *Foundations of the Nineteenth Century*, trans. John Lees (London: John Lane, The Bodley Head, 1913), I, 542–50. Reprinted by permission.

peoples; for that reason they are by right, as the Stagirite expresses it, the lords of the world. Aristotle puts the matter still more concisely when he says, "Some men are by nature free, others slaves"; this perfectly expresses the moral aspect. For freedom is by no means an abstract thing, to which every human being has fundamentally a claim; a right to freedom must evidently depend upon capacity for it, and this again presupposes physical and intellectual power. One may make the assertion, that even the mere conception of freedom is quite unknown to most men. Do we not see the *homo syriacus* develop just as well and as happily in the positions of slave as of master? Do the Chinese not show us another example of the same nature? Do not all historians tell us that the Semites and half-Semites, in spite of their great intelligence, never succeeded in founding a State that lasted, and that because every one always endeavoured to grasp all power for himself, thus showing that their capabilities were limited to despotism and anarchy, the two opposites of freedom? And here we see at once what great gifts a man must have in order that one may say of him, he is "by nature free," for the first condition of this is the power of creating. Only a State-building race can be free; the gifts which make the individual an artist and philosopher are essentially the same as those which, spread through the whole mass as instinct, found States and give to the individual that which hitherto had remained unknown to all nature: the idea of freedom. As soon as we understand this, the near affinity of the Germanic peoples to the Greeks and Romans strikes us, and at the same time we recognise what separates them. In the case of the Greeks the individualistic creative character predominates, even in the forming of constitutions; in the case of the Romans it is communistic legislation and military authority that predominate; the Germanic races, on the other hand, have individually and collectively perhaps less creative power, but they possess a harmony of qualities, maintaining the balance between the instinct of individual freedom, which finds its highest expression in creative art, and the instinct of public freedom which creates the State; and in this way they prove themselves to be the equals of their great predecessors. Art more perfect in its creations, so far as form is concerned, there may have been, but no art has ever been more powerful in its creations than that which includes the whole range of things human between the winged pen of Shakespeare and the etching-tool of Albrecht Dürer, and which in its own special language—music—penetrates deeper into the heart than any previous attempt to create immortality out of that which is mortal—to transform matter into spirit. And in the meantime the European States, founded by Germanic peoples, in spite of their, so to speak, improvised, always provisional and changeable character —or rather perhaps thanks to this character—proved themselves to be the most enduring as well as the most powerful in the world. In spite of all storms of war, in spite of the deceptions of that ancestral enemy, the chaos of peoples, which carried its poison into the very heart of our nation, Freedom and its correlative, the State, remained, through all the ages the creating and saving ideal, even though the balance between the two often seemed to be upset: we recognise that more clearly to-day than ever.

In order that this might be so, that fundamental and common "Aryan" capacity of free creative power had to be supplemented by another quality, the

incomparable and altogether peculiar Germanic loyalty [*Treue*]. If that intellectual and physical development which leads to the idea of freedom and which
produces on the one hand art, philosophy, science, on the other constitutions (as
well as all the phenomena of culture which this word implies), is common to
the Hellenes and Romans as well as to the Germanic peoples, so also is the
extravagant conception of loyalty a specific characteristic of the Teuton. As the
venerable Johann Fischart sings:

> Standhaft und treu, und treu und standhaft,
> Die machen ein recht teutsch Verwandtschaft!

Julius Cæsar at once recognised not only the military prowess but also the
unexampled loyalty of the Teutons and hired from among them as many
cavalrymen as he could possibly get. In the battle of Pharsalus, which was so
decisive for the history of the world, they fought for him; the Romanised Gauls
had abandoned their commander in the hour of need, the Germanic troops
proved themselves as faithful as they were brave. This loyalty to a master chosen
of their own free will is the most prominent feature in the Germanic character;
from it we can tell whether pure Germanic blood flows in the veins or not.
The German mercenary troops have often been made the object of ridicule, but
it is in them that the genuine costly metal of this race reveals itself. The very
first autocratic Emperor, Augustus, formed his personal bodyguard of Teutons;
where else could he have found unconditional loyalty? During the whole time
that the Roman Empire in the east and the west lasted, this same post of honour
was filled by the same people, but they were always brought from farther and
farther north, because with the so-called "Latin culture" the plague of disloyalty had crept more deeply into the country; finally, a thousand years after
Augustus, we find Anglo-Saxons and Normans in this post, standing on guard
around the throne of Byzantium. Hapless Germanic Lifeguardsman! Of the
political principles, which forcibly held together the chaotic world in a semblance of order, he understood just as little as he did of the quarrels concerning
the nature of the Trinity, which cost him many a drop of blood: but one thing
he understood: to be loyal to the master he had himself chosen. When in the
time of Nero the Frisian delegates left the back seats which had been assigned
to them in the Circus and proudly sat down on the front benches of the senators
among the richly adorned foreign delegates, what was it that gave these poor
men, who came to Rome to beg for land to cultivate, such a bold spirit of independence? Of what alone could they boast? "That no one in the world surpassed the Teuton in loyalty." Karl Lamprecht has written so beautifully about
this great fundamental characteristic of loyalty in its historical significance that
I should reproach myself if I did not quote him here. He has just spoken of the
"retainers" who in the old German State pledge themselves to their chief to be
true unto death and prove so, and then he adds: "In the formation of this body
of retainers we see one of the most magnificent features of the specifically
Germanic view of life, the feature of loyalty. Not understood by the Roman
but indispensable to the Teuton, the need of loyalty existed even at that time,
that ever-recurring German need of closest personal attachment, of complete
devotion to each other, perfect community of hopes, efforts and destinies.

Loyalty never was to our ancestors a special virtue, it was the breath of life of everything good and great; upon it rested the feudal State of the Early and the co-operative system of the Later Middle Ages, and who could conceive the military monarchy of the present day without loyalty? . . . Not only were songs sung about loyalty, men lived in it. The retinue of the King of the Franks, the courtiers of the great Karolingians, the civil and military ministers of our mediæval Emperors, the officials of the centres of administration under our Princes since the fourteenth and the fifteenth centuries are merely new forms of the old Germanic conception. For the wonderful vitality of such institutions consisted in this, that they were not rooted in changing political or even moral conditions, but in the primary source of Germanicism itself, the need of loyalty."

However true and beautiful every word that Lamprecht has here written, I do not think that he has made quite clear the "primary source." Loyalty, though distinguishing the Teutons from mongrel races, is not altogether a specific Germanic trait. One finds it in almost all purely bred races, nowhere more than among the negroes, for example, and—I would ask—what man could be more faithful than the noble dog? No, in order to reveal that "primary source of Germanicism," we must show what is the nature of this Germanic loyalty, and we can only succeed in doing so if we have grasped the fact that freedom is the intellectual basis of the whole Germanic nature. For the characteristic feature of this loyalty is its free self-determination. The human character resembles the nature of God as the theologians represent it: complex and yet indiscernible, an inseparable unity. This loyalty and this freedom do not grow the one out of the other, they are two manifestations of the same character which reveals itself to us on one occasion more from the intellectual on another more from the moral side. The negro and the dog serve their masters, whoever they may be: that is the morality of the weak, or, as Aristotle says, of the man who is born to be a slave; the Teuton chooses his master, and his loyalty is therefore loyalty to himself: that is the morality of the man who is born free. But loyalty as displayed by the Teuton was unexampled. The disloyalty of the extravagantly gifted proclaimer of poetical and political freedom, i.e., of the Hellene, was proverbial from time immemorial; the Roman was loyal only in the defence of his own, German loyalty remained, Lamprecht says, "incomprehensible to him"; here, as everywhere in the sphere of morals, we see an affinity with the Indo-Aryans; but these latter people so markedly lacked the artistic sense which urges men on to adventure and to the establishment of a free life, that their loyalty never reached that creative importance in the world's history which the same quality attained under the influence of the Germanic races. Here again, as before, in the consideration of the feeling of freedom, we find a higher harmony of character in the Teuton; hence we may say that no one in the world, not even the greatest, has surpassed him. One thing is certain: if we wish to sum up in a single word the historic greatness of the Teuton—always a perilous undertaking, since everything living is of Protean nature—we must name his loyalty. That is the central point from which we can survey his whole character, or better, his personality. But we must remember that this loyalty is not the primary source, as Lamprecht thinks, not the root but the blossom—the fruit by which we recognise the tree. Hence it is that this loyalty is the finest touchstone for distinguishing between genuine and false Germanicism; for it is not by the roots but by the fruit that we distinguish the species; we should not forget that with unfavourable weather many a tree has no blossoms or only poor ones, and this often happens in the case of hard-pressed Teutons. The root of their particular character is beyond all doubt that power of imagination which is common to all Aryans and peculiar to them alone and which appeared in greatest luxuriance among the Hellenes. I spoke of this in the beginning of the chapter on Hellenic art and philosophy; from that root everything springs, art, philosophy, politics, science; hence, too, comes the peculiar sap which tinges the flower of loyalty. The stem then is formed by the positive strength—the physical and the intellectual, which can never be separated; in the case of the Romans, to whom we owe the firm bases of family and State, this stem was powerfully developed. But the real blossoms of such a tree are those which mind and sentiment bring to maturity. Freedom is an expansive power which scatters men, Germanic loyalty is the bond which by its inner power binds men more closely than the fear of the tyrant's sword: freedom signifies thirst after direct self-discovered truth, loyalty the reverence for that which has appeared to our ancestors to be true; freedom decides its own destiny and loyalty holds that decision unswervingly and for ever. Loyalty to the loved one, to friend, parents, and fatherland we find in many places; but here, in the case of the Teuton, something is added, which makes the great instinct become a profoundly deep spiritual power, a principle of life. Shakespeare represents the father giving his son as the best advice for his path through life, as the one admonition which includes all others, these words:

This above all: to thine own self be true!

The principle of Germanic loyalty is evidently not the necessity of attachment, as Lamprecht thinks, but on the contrary the necessity of constancy within a man's own autonomous circle; self-determination testifies to it; in it freedom proves itself; by it the vassal, the member of the guild, the official, the officer asserts his independence. For the free man, to serve means to command himself. "It was the Germanic races who first introduced into the world the idea of personal freedom," says Goethe. What in the case of the Hindoos was metaphysics and in so far necessarily negative, seclusive, has been here transferred to life as an ideal of mind, it is the "breath of life of everything great and good," a star in the night, to the weary a spur, to the storm-tossed an anchor of safety. In the construction of the Germanic character loyalty is the necessary perfection of the personality, which without it falls to pieces. Immanuel Kant has given a daring, genuinely Germanic definition of personality: it is, he says, "freedom and independence of the mechanism of all nature"; and what it achieves he has summed up as follows: "That which elevates man above himself (as part of the world of sense), attaches him to an order of things which only the understanding can conceive, and which has the whole world of sense subject to it, is Personality." But without loyalty this elevation would be fatal: thanks to it alone the impulse of freedom can develop and bring blessing instead of a curse. Loyalty in this Germanic sense cannot originate without freedom, but it is impossible to see how an unlimited, creative impulse to freedom could exist without loyalty. Childish attachment to nature is a proof of loyalty: it enables man to raise himself above nature, without falling shattered to the ground, like the Hellenic Phaethon. Therefore it is that Goethe writes: "Loyalty preserves personality!" Germanic loyalty is the girdle that gives immortal beauty to the ephemeral individual, it is the sun without which no knowledge can ripen to wisdom, the charm which alone bestows upon the free individual's passionate action the blessing of permanent achievement.

ANARCHISM, SYNDICALISM, AND REVISIONARY MARXISM

10. PIERRE JOSEPH PROUDHON: ON PROPERTY AND ANARCHY*

Pierre Joseph Proudhon (1809–65), often labeled the "father of anarchism," was a fanatical libertarian who believed that power, regardless of its source, always led to corruption. Like Marx, he rejected capitalism and accepted the existence of class inequalities; yet Proudhon was basically suspicious of a Marxian future, fearing that Marxists in power would be content with power itself.

As an advocate of social justice Proudhon rejected the state, private property, industrial capitalism, centralized government, and all other sources of real or potential coercion. His ideal was a society centered upon spontaneous, voluntarily operated producers' cooperatives which would leave men free and allow the best in human nature to rise to the surface. Above all, Proudhon saw the maldistribution of property as the basic source of nineteenth-century social evils. Because "property is theft," nothing less than the abolition of private property, as well as the centralized bourgeois governments which protected private property, would free mankind from its traditional fetters. Anarchy, for Proudhon, was not a world of turbulence and confusion, but rather a society of free spirits. In the following selections, taken from *On Property* (1840) and *The General Idea of of the Revolution* (1851), on what grounds did Proudhon condemn private property? How did he explain the evolution of society to its present state of development? What description did Proudhon offer of life in an anarchistic society?

PROPERTY

If I were asked to answer the following question: *What is slavery?* and I should answer in one word, *It is murder,* my meaning would be understood at once. No extended argument would be required to show that the power to take from a man his thought, his will, his personality, is a power of life and death; and that to enslave a man is to kill him. Why, then, to this other question: *What is property?* may I not likewise answer, *It is robbery,* without the certainty of being misunderstood; the second proposition being no other than a transformation of the first? . . .

But murmurs arise!

* "Property" from Pierre Joseph Proudhon, *What Is Property?*, trans. Benjamin R. Tucker (New York: Howard Fertig, 1966 [reprinted from 1890 edition]), pp. 11–12, 92, 94–95, 209–10, 247–49, 279–80. Reprinted by permission of Howard Fertig, Inc. "Anarchy" from P. J. Proudhon, *General Idea of the Revolution in the Nineteenth Century*, trans. John Beverley Robinson (London: Freedom Press, 1923), pp. 195, 290–92, 294. Reprinted by permission.

Property is robbery! That is the war-cry of '93! That is the signal of revolutions!

Reader, calm yourself: I am no agent of discord, no firebrand of sedition. I anticipate history by a few days; I disclose a truth whose development we may try in vain to arrest; I write the preamble of our future constitution. This proposition which seems to you blasphemous—*property is robbery*—would, if our prejudices allowed us to consider it, be recognized as the lightning-rod to shield us from the coming thunderbolt; but too many interests stand in the way! . . . Alas! philosophy will not change the course of events: destiny will fulfill itself regardless of prophecy. Besides, must not justice be done and our education be finished? . . .

From whatever point we view this question of property—provided we go to the bottom of it—we reach equality. I will not insist farther on the distinction between things which can, and things which cannot, be appropriated. On this point, economists and [lawyers] talk worse than nonsense. . . .

Prescription gives no Title to Property.

The right of property was the origin of evil on the earth, the first link in the long chain of crimes and misfortunes which the human race has endured since its birth. The delusion of prescription is the fatal charm thrown over the intellect, the death sentence breathed into the conscience, to arrest man's progress towards truth, and bolster up the worship of error.

The Code defines prescription thus: "The process of gaining and losing through the lapse of time." In applying this definition to ideas and beliefs, we may use the word *prescription* to denote the everlasting prejudice in favor of old superstitions, whatever be their object; the opposition, often furious and bloody, with which new light has always been received, and which makes the sage a martyr. Not a principle, not a discovery, not a generous thought but has met, at its entrance into the world, with a formidable barrier of preconceived opinions, seeming like a conspiracy of all old prejudices. Prescriptions against reason, prescriptions against facts, prescriptions against every truth hitherto unknown,—that is the sum and substance of the *status quo* philosophy, the watchword of conservatives throughout the centuries. . . .

Property is impossible, because, in consuming its Receipts, it loses them; in hoarding them, it nullifies them; and in using them as Capital, it turns them against Production.

If, with the economists, we consider the laborer as a living machine, we must regard the wages paid to him as the amount necessary to support this machine, and keep it in repair. The head of a manufacturing establishment—who employs laborers at three, five, ten, and fifteen francs per day, and who charges twenty francs for his superintendence—does not regard his disbursements as losses, because he knows they will return to him in the form of products. Consequently, *labor* and *reproductive consumption* are identical.

What is the proprietor? He is a machine which does not work; or, which working for its own pleasure, and only when it sees fit, produces nothing.

What is it to consume as a proprietor? It is to consume without working, to consume without reproducing. For, once more, that which the proprietor con-sumes as a laborer comes back to him; he does not give his labor in exchange for his property, since, if he did, he would thereby cease to be a proprietor. In consuming as a laborer, the proprietor gains, or at least does not lose, since he recovers that which he consumes; in consuming as a proprietor, he impoverishes himself. To enjoy property, then, it is necessary to destroy it; to be a real pro-prietor, one must cease to be a proprietor.

The laborer who consumes his wages is a machine which destroys and repro-duces; the proprietor who consumes his income is a bottomless gulf,—sand which we water, a stone which we sow. So true is this, that the proprietor—neither wishing nor knowing how to produce, and perceiving that as fast as he uses his property he destroys it for ever—has taken the precaution to make some one produce in his place. That is what political economy, speaking in the name of eternal justice, calls *producing by his capital,—producing by his tools.* And that is what ought to be called *producing by a slave,—producing as a thief and as a tyrant.* He, the proprietor, produce! . . . The robber might say, as well: "I produce." . . .

Equality of conditions has never been realized, thanks to our passions and our ignorance; but our opposition to this law has made it all the more a neces-sity. To that fact history bears perpetual testimony, and the course of events reveals it to us. Society advances from equation to equation. To the eyes of the economist, the revolutions of empires seem now like the reduction of algebraical quantities, which are inter-deducible; now like the discovery of unknown quan-tities, induced by the inevitable influence of time. Figures are the providence of history. Undoubtedly there are other elements in human progress; but in the multitude of hidden causes which agitate nations, there is none more powerful or constant, none less obscure, than the periodical explosions of the proletariat against property. Property, acting by exclusion and encroachment, while popula-tion was increasing, has been the life-principle and definitive cause of all revo-lutions. Religious wars, and wars of conquest, when they have stopped short of the extermination of races, have been only accidental disturbances, soon repaired by the mathematical progression of the life of nations. The downfall and death of societies are due to the power of accumulation possessed by property. . . .

Here my task should end. I have proved the right of the poor; I have shown the usurpation of the rich. I demand justice; it is not my business to execute the sentence. If it should be argued—in order to prolong for a few years an illegitimate privilege—that it is not enough to demonstrate equality, that it is necessary also to organize it, and above all to establish it peacefully, I might reply: The welfare of the oppressed is of more importance than official com-posure. Equality of conditions is a natural law upon which public economy and jurisprudence are based. The right to labor, and the principle of equal distribu-tion of wealth, cannot give way to the anxieties of power. It is not for the prole-taire to reconcile the contradictions of the codes, still less to suffer for the errors of the government. On the contrary, it is the duty of the civil and administrative power to reconstruct itself on the basis of political equality. An evil, when known, should be condemned and destroyed. The legislator cannot plead ig-norance as an excuse for upholding a glaring iniquity. Restitution should not be delayed. Justice, justice! recognition of right! reinstatement of the proletaire! —when these results are accomplished, then, judges and consuls, you may attend to your police, and provide a government for the Republic! . . .

The proprietor, the robber, the hero, the sovereign—for all these titles are synonymous—imposes his will as law, and suffers neither contradiction nor control; that is, he pretends to be the legislative and the executive power at once. Accordingly, the substitution of the scientific and true law for the royal will is accomplished only by a terrible struggle; and this constant substitution is, after property, the most potent element in history, the most prolific source of political disturbances. Examples are too numerous and too striking to require enumeration.

Now, property necessarily engenders despotism,—the government of caprice, the reign of libidinous pleasure. That is so clearly the essence of property that, to be convinced of it, one need but remember what it is, and observe what happens around him. Property is the right to *use* and *abuse*. If, then, government is economy,—if its object is production and consumption, and the distribution of labor and products,—how is government possible while property exists? And if goods are property, why should not the proprietors be kings, and despotic kings—kings in proportion to their *facultés bonitaires?* And if each proprietor is sovereign lord within the sphere of his property, absolute king throughout his own domain, how could a government of proprietors be any thing but chaos and confusion? . . .

ANARCHY

Through the land the plundering of man began, and in the land it has rooted its foundations. The land is the fortress of the modern capitalist, as it was the citadel of feudalism, and of the ancient patriciate. Finally, it is the land which gives authority to the governmental principle, an ever-renewed strength, whenever the popular Hercules overthrows the giant.

To-day the stronghold, attacked upon all the secret points of its bastions, is about to fall before us, as fell, at the sound of Joshua's trumpets, the walls of Jericho. . . .

From the origin of societies, the spirit of man, confined and enveloped by the theologico-political system, shut up in a hermetically closed box, of which Government is the bottom and Religion the top, has taken the limits of this narrow horizon for the limits of a rational society. God and King, Church and State, twisted in every way, worked over to infinity, have been his Universe. For a long time he has known nothing, imagined nothing beyond. At last, the circle has been traversed; the excitement of the systems suggested by this has exhausted him; philosophy, history, political economy, have completed the triangulation of this inner world; the map of it has been drawn; and it is known that the supernatural scheme which humanity contemplates as its horizon, and its limit, is but itself; that, far as humanity may look into the depths of its consciousness, it sees but itself; that this God, source of all power, origin of all causality, of which humanity makes its sun, is a lamp in a cavern, and all these governments made in his image are but grains of sand that reflect the faint light.

These religions, these legislations, these empires, these Governments, this wisdom of State, this virtue of Pontiffs, all are but a dream and a lie, which all hang upon one another and converge toward a central point, which itself has no reality. If we want to get a more correct idea of things, we must burst this crust and get out of this inferno, in which man's reason will be lost, and he will become an idiot. . . .

When society has turned from within to without, all relations are overturned. Yesterday we were walking with our heads downwards: to-day we hold them erect, without any interruption to our life. Without losing our personality, we change our existence. Such is the nineteenth century Revolution.

The fundamental, decisive idea of this Revolution is it not this: NO MORE AUTHORITY, neither in the Church, nor in the State, nor in land, nor in money?

No more Authority! That means something we have never seen, something we have never understood; the harmony of the interest of one with the interest of all; the identity of collective sovereignty and individual sovereignty.

No more Authority! That means debts paid, servitude abolished, mortgages lifted, rents reimbursed, the expense of worship, justice, and the State suppressed; free credit, equal exchange, free association, regulated value, education, work, property, domicile, low price, guaranteed: no more antagonism, no more war, no more centralization, no more governments, no more priests. Is not that Society emerged from its shell and walking upright?

No more Authority! That is to say further: free contract in place of arbitrary law; voluntary transactions in place of the control of the State; equitable and reciprocal justice in place of sovereign and distributive justice; rational instead of revealed morals; equilibrium of forces instead of equilibrium of powers; economic unity in place of political centralization. Once more, I ask, is not this what I may venture to call a complete reversal, a turn-over, a Revolution? . . .

. . . To be GOVERNED is to be kept in sight, inspected, spied upon, directed, law-driven, numbered, enrolled, indoctrinated, preached at, controlled, estimated, valued, censured, commanded, by creatures who have neither the right, nor the wisdom, nor the virtue to do so. . . . To be GOVERNED is to be at every operation, at every transaction, noted, registered, enrolled, taxed, stamped, measured, numbered, assessed, licensed, authorized, admonished, forbidden, reformed, corrected, punished. It is, under pretext of public utility, and in the name of the general interest, to be placed under contribution, trained, ransomed, exploited, monopolized, extorted, squeezed, mystified, robbed; then, at the slightest resistance, the first word of complaint, to be repressed, fined, despised, harassed, tracked, abused, clubbed, disarmed, choked, imprisoned, judged, condemned, shot, deported, sacrificed, sold, betrayed; and, to crown all, mocked, ridiculed, outraged, dishonored. That is government; that is its justice; that is its morality. . . .

11. PETER KROPOTKIN: ON THE ORIGIN OF ANARCHISM*

The Anarchist-Socialists concurred with Marxian dogma in their criticisms of existing society. But they rejected the traditionalist Socialist concept of expanded state authority and launched an attack upon both capitalism and governmental power. Government was evil, and true freedom could not exist until the past

* Peter Kropotkin, *Modern Science and Anarchism* (London: Freedom Press, 1912), pp. 1–5, 38, 45–46. Reprinted by permission.

was destroyed; the possibility of reforming the old state structure seemed so remote that Anarchists insisted the structure itself must be demolished.

Prince Peter Kropotkin (1842–1921) was a geographer, social philosopher, and enthusiastic revolutionary. He was a member of the International Working-men's Association, but his extreme views kept him on the fringe of that Marxian organization. Forced to move from country to country because of his views and his revolutionary writings, Kropotkin documented his active life in *Memoirs of a Revolutionist* (1899). The selection below is drawn from one of his later works, *Modern Science and Anarchism,* first published in 1903. How did Kropotkin explain the history of anarchism? What links existed between anarchism and socialism? Why was anarchism different from other utopian concepts of the nineteenth century?

Anarchy does not draw its origin from any scientific researches, or from any system of philosophy. . . . Like Socialism in general, and like all other social movements, Anarchism originated among the people, and it will preserve its vitality and creative force so long only as it remains a movement of the people. . . .

It is evident that Anarchy represents . . . the creative constructive force of the masses, who elaborated common-law institutions in order to defend themselves against a domineering minority. It is also by the creative and constructive force of the people, aided by the whole strength of modern science and technique, that today Anarchy strives to set up institutions that are indispensable to the free development of society, in opposition to those who put their hope in laws made by governing minorities.

We can therefore say that from all times there have been Anarchists and Statists.

Moreover, we always find that institutions, even the best of them, that were built up to maintain equality, peace, and mutual aid, become petrified as they grow old. They lose their original purpose, they fall under the domination of an ambitious minority, and gradually they become an obstacle to the ulterior development of society. Then individuals, more or less isolated, rebel against these institutions. . . . There were Revolutionists in all times known to history. . . .

Formidable popular movements, stamped with the character of Anarchism, took place several times in the past. Villages and cities rose against the principle of government, against the supporters of the State, its tribunals, its laws, and they proclaimed the sovereignty of the rights of man. They denied all written law, and asserted that every man should govern himself according to his conscience. They thus tried to found a new society, based on the principles of equality, full liberty, and work. In the Christian movement in Judea, under Augustus, against the Roman law, the Roman state, and the morality, or rather the immorality, of that epoch, there was unquestionably much Anarchism. Little by little this movement degenerated into a Church movement, fashioned after the Hebrew Church and Imperial Rome itself, which naturally killed all that Christianity possessed of Anarchism at its outset, gave the Christian teachings a Roman form, and soon made of it the mainstay of authority, State, slavery, and oppression. The first seeds of "Opportunism" introduced into Christianity are already strong in the four Gospels and the Acts of the Apostles—or, at least, in the versions of the same that are incorporated in the New Testament.

The Anabaptist movement of the sixteenth century, which in the main inaugurated and brought about the Reformation, also had an Anarchist basis. But, crushed by those Reformers who, under Luther's rule, leagued with princes against the rebellious peasants, the movement was suppressed by the great massacre of peasants and the poorer citizens of the towns. Then the right wing of the Reformers degenerated little by little, till it became the compromise between its own conscience and the State which exists today under the name of Protestantism.

Thus, to summarise: Anarchism had its origin in the same creative, constructive activity of the masses which has worked out in times past all the social institutions of mankind—and in the revolts of both the individuals and the nation against the representatives of force, external to these social institutions, who had laid their hands upon these institutions and used them for their own advantage. Those of the rebels whose aim was to restore to the creative genius of the masses the necessary freedom for its creative activity, so that it might work out the required new institutions, were imbued with the Anarchist spirit.

In our times, Anarchy was brought forth by the same critical and revolutionary protest which gave rise to Socialism in general. However, one portion of the Socialists, after having reached the negation of Capitalism and of society based on the subjection of labour to capital, stopped in its development at this point. They did not declare themselves against what constitutes the real strength of Capitalism: the State and its principal supports—centralisation of authority, law, always made by a minority for its own profit, and a form of justice whose chief aim is to protect Authority and Capitalism. As to Anarchism, it did not stop in its criticism before these institutions. It lifted its sacrilegious arm, not only against Capitalism, but also against these pillars of Capitalism: Law, Authority, and the State. . . .

. . . Anarchism is a conception of the Universe based on the mechanical (it would have been better to say "kinetic" but this expression is less known) interpretation of phenomena, which comprises the whole of Nature, including the life of human societies and their economic, political, and moral problems. Its method is that of natural sciences, and every conclusion it comes to must be verified by this method if it pretends to be scientific. Its tendency is to work out a synthetic philosophy which will take in all facts of Nature, including the life of societies, without, however, falling into the errors of Comte and Spencer, . . .

It is evident that on this account Anarchism necessarily has to give its own answers to all questions put before us by modern life, and it unavoidably takes up an attitude with regard to them quite different from that of all political parties, as also, up to a certain point, of the Socialist parties, which have not yet freed themselves from old metaphysical fictions. . . .

It is seen from the foregoing that a variety of considerations, historical, ethnological, and economical, have brought the Anarchists to conceive a society, very different from what is considered as its ideal by the authoritarian political parties. The Anarchists conceive a society in which all the mutual relations of its members are regulated, not by laws, not by authorities, whether self-imposed or elected, but by mutual agreements between the members of that society, and by a sum of social customs and habits—not petrified by law, routine, or superstition, but continually developing and continually readjusted, in accordance with the ever-growing requirements of a free life, stimulated by the progress of science, invention, and the steady growth of higher ideals.

No ruling authorities, then. No government of man by man; no crystallisation and immobility, but a continual evolution—such as we see in Nature. Free play for the individual, for the full development of his individual gifts—*for his individualisation*. In other words, no actions are *imposed* upon the individual by a fear of punishment; none is required from him by society, but those which receive his free acceptance. *In a society of equals* this would be quite sufficient for preventing those unsociable actions that might be harmful to other individuals and to society itself, and for favouring the steady moral growth of that society.

This is the conception developed and advocated by the Anarchists.

Of course, up till now no society has existed which would have realised these principles in full, although the striving towards a partial realisation of such principles has always been at work in mankind. We may say, therefore, that Anarchism is a certain *ideal* of society, and that this ideal is different from the ideal of society which has hitherto been advocated by most philosophers, scientists, and leaders of political parties, who pretended to rule mankind and to govern men.

But it would not be fair to describe such a conception as a *Utopia,* because the word "Utopia" in our current language conveys the idea of something that *cannot* be realised.

Taken in its usual current sense, therefore, the word "Utopia" ought to be limited to those conceptions only which are based on merely theoretical reasonings as to what is *desirable* from the writer's point of view, but not on what *is already developing* in human agglomerations. Such were, for instance, the Utopias of the Catholic Empire of the Popes, the Napoleonic Empire . . . and so on. But it cannot be applied to a conception of society which is based, as Anarchism is, on an analysis of *tendencies of an evolution that is already going on in society,* and on *inductions* therefrom as to the future—those tendencies which have been, . . . for thousands of years the mainsprings for the growth of sociable habits and customs, known in science under the name of Customary Law, and which affirm themselves more and more definitely in modern society. . . .

12. GEORGES SOREL: REFLECTIONS ON VIOLENCE*

Georges Sorel (1847–1922) was a leading figure among the intellectual rebels who believed Western man was being crushed by mediocrity and decadence in the early twentieth century. He understood more clearly than most of his col-

* Georges Sorel, *Reflections on Violence,* trans. T. E. Hulme and J. Roth (Glencoe, Ill.: The Free Press, 1950), pp. 104–6, 136–40, 142–45, 167–68, 301–2. Reprinted by permission.

leagues the nature of political currents gathering force before World War I. Sorel was primarily an observer and a moralist, and offered neither a comprehensive philosophical system (in the Marxian sense) nor a future utopian society. His most direct impact was on syndicalism,[1] for Sorel feared that workers' associations were becoming as decadent as the bourgeoisie. Denouncing bourgeois democracy as synonymous with mediocrity, Sorel explained the virtues of the violent general strike in *Reflections on Violence* (1908).

In Sorel's view the masses might be incited to revolutionary action through a device which he labeled "myth." As the motivating force behind mass action, myth emphasized the non-rational characteristics of human behavior, and thus forecast the nature of twentieth-century propaganda techniques. Myths were not what did or did not happen in fact, but rather what people *believed* had happened. Myth was truer than truth itself, encouraging people to respond to their emotional beliefs rather than to facts that might be raised in calm deliberation or rational inquiry. Thus, each nation required historical myths to promote patriotism and cohesion. Why, according to Sorel, was "violence" virtuous? In what ways was the concept of "myth" similar to the "big-lie" techniques of contemporary propaganda? Why did Sorel denounce "bourgeois democracy"? Why, in Sorel's view, was Marxism an inadequate solution to the problems of the working class?

It is often urged, in objection to the people who defend the Marxian conception, that it is impossible for them to stop the movement of degeneration which is dragging both the middle class and the proletariat far from the paths assigned to them by Marx's theory. They can doubtless influence the working classes, and it is hardly to be denied that strike violences do keep the revolutionary spirit alive; but how can they hope to give back to the middle class an ardour which is spent?

It is here that the rôle of violence in history appears to us as singularly great, for it can, in an indirect manner, so operate on the middle class as to awaken them to a sense of their own class sentiment. Attention has often been drawn to the danger of certain acts of violence which compromised *admirable social works,* disgusted employers who were disposed to arrange the happiness of their workmen, and developed egoism where the most noble sentiments formerly reigned.

To repay with *black ingratitude* the *benevolence* of those who would protect the workers, to meet with insults the homilies of the defenders of human fraternity, and to reply by blows to the advances of the propagators of social peace —all that is assuredly not in conformity with the rules of the fashionable Socialism of M. and Mme. Georges Renard, but it is a very practical way of indicating to the middle class that they must mind their own business and only that.

I believe also that it may be useful to thrash the orators of democracy and the representatives of the Government, for in this way you insure that none shall retain any illusions about the character of acts of violence. But these acts can

---

1. Syndicalism was an ideology of direct action which urged workers to take control of factories and other production sources through general strikes. Syndicalism was a sharper break from the past than Marxism, for it was anti-intellectual in tone and rejected most contemporary institutions and channels of communication. With variations in time and place, syndicalism was most sharply felt in France, Italy, and Spain.

have historical value only if they are the *clear and brutal expression of the class war:* the middle classes must not be allowed to imagine that, aided by cleverness, social science, or high-flown sentiments, they might find a better welcome at the hands of the proletariat.

The day on which employers perceive that they have nothing to gain by works which promote social peace, or by democracy, they will understand that they have been ill-advised by the people who persuaded them to abandon their trade of creators of productive forces for the noble profession of educators of the proletariat. Then there is some chance that they may get back a part of their energy, and that moderate or conservative economics may appear as absurd to them as they appeared to Marx. In any case, the separation of classes being more clearly accentuated, the proletarian movement will have some chance of developing with greater regularity than to-day.

The two antagonistic classes therefore influence each other in a partly indirect but decisive manner. Capitalism drives the proletariat into revolt, because in daily life the employers use their force in a direction opposed to the desire of their workers; but the future of the proletariat is not entirely dependent on this revolt; the working classes are organised under the influence of other causes, and Socialism, inculcating in them the revolutionary idea, prepares them to suppress the hostile class. . . .

Proletarian violence not only makes the future revolution certain, but it seems also to be the only means by which the European nations—at present stupefied by humanitarianism—can recover their former energy. . . .

Every time that we attempt to obtain an exact conception of the ideas behind proletarian violence we are forced to go back to the notion of the general strike; . . .

The revolutionary Syndicates argue about Socialist action exactly in the same manner as military writers argue about war; they restrict the whole of Socialism to the general strike; they look upon every combination as one that should culminate in this catastrophe; they see in each strike a reduced facsimile, an essay, a preparation for the great final upheaval.

The *new school,* which calls itself Marxist, Syndicalist, and revolutionary, declared in favour of the idea of the general strike as soon as it became clearly conscious of the true sense of its own doctrine, of the consequences of its activity, and of its own originality. It was thus led to leave the old official, Utopian, and political tabernacles, which hold the general strike in horror, and to launch itself into the true current of the proletarian revolutionary movement; for a long time past the proletariat had made adherence to the principle of the general strike the test by means of which the Socialism of the workers was distinguished from that of the amateur revolutionaries.

Parliamentary Socialists can only obtain great influence if they can manage, by the use of a very confused language, to impose themselves on very diverse groups; for example, they must have working-men constituents simple enough to allow themselves to be duped by high-sounding phrases about future collectivism; they are compelled to represent themselves as profound philosophers to stupid middle-class people who wish to appear to be well informed about social questions; it is very necessary also for them to be able to exploit rich people who think that they are earning the gratitude of humanity by taking shares in the enterprises of Socialist politicians. This influence is founded on balderdash, and our bigwigs endeavour—sometimes only too successfully—to spread confusion among the ideas of their readers; they detest the general strike because all propaganda carried on from that point of view is too socialistic to please philanthropists.

In the mouths of these self-styled representatives of the proletariat all socialistic formulas lose their real sense. The class war still remains the great principle, but it must be subordinated to national solidarity. Internationalism is an article of faith about which the most moderate declare themselves ready to take the most solemn oaths; but patriotism also imposes sacred duties. The emancipation of the workers must be the work of the workers themselves— . . .

Against this noisy, garrulous, and lying Socialism, which is exploited by ambitious people of every description, which amuses a few buffoons, and which is admired by decadents—revolutionary Syndicalism takes its stand, and endeavours, on the contrary, to leave nothing in a state of indecision; its ideas are honestly expressed, without trickery and without mental reservations; no attempt is made to dilute doctrines by a stream of confused commentaries. Syndicalism endeavours to employ methods of expression which throw a full light on things, which put them exactly in the place assigned to them by their nature, and which bring out the whole value of the forces in play. Oppositions, instead of being glozed over, must be thrown into sharp relief if we desire to obtain a clear idea of the Syndicalist movement; the groups which are struggling one against the other must be shown as separate and as compact as possible; in short, the movements of the revolted masses must be represented in such a way that the soul of the revolutionaries may receive a deep and lasting impression.

These results could not be produced in any very certain manner by the use of ordinary language; use must be made of a body of images which, *by intuition alone,* and before any considered analyses are made, is capable of evoking as an undivided whole the mass of sentiments which corresponds to the different manifestations of the war undertaken by Socialism against modern society. The Syndicalists solve this problem perfectly, by concentrating the whole of Socialism in the drama of the general strike; there is thus no longer any place for the reconciliation of contraries in the equivocations of the professors; everything is clearly mapped out, so that only one interpretation of Socialism is possible. This method has all the advantages which "integral" knowledge has over analysis, according to the doctrine of Bergson;[2] and perhaps it would not be possible to cite another example which would so perfectly demonstrate the value of the famous professor's doctrines. . . .

And yet without leaving the present, without reasoning about this future, which seems for ever condemned to escape our reason, we should be unable to act at all. Experience shows that the *framing of a future, in some indeterminate time,* may, when it is done in a certain way, be very effective, and have very

2. Henri Bergson (1859–1941), a French philosopher and professor, was a leader among intellectuals seeking a deeper understanding of the non-rational characteristics of human behavior.

few inconveniences; this happens when the anticipations of the future take the form of those myths, which enclose with them, all the strongest inclinations of a people, of a party or of a class, inclinations which recur to the mind with the insistence of instincts in all the circumstances of life; and which give an aspect of complete reality to the hopes of immediate action by which, more easily than by any other method, men can reform their desires, passions, and mental activity. We know, moreover, that these social myths in no way prevent a man profiting by the observations which he makes in the course of his life, and form no obstacle to the pursuit of his normal occupations.

The truth of this may be shown by numerous examples.

The first Christians expected the return of Christ and the total ruin of the pagan world, with the inauguration of the kingdom of the saints, at the end of the first generation. The catastrophe did not come to pass, but Christian thought profited so greatly from the apocalyptic myth that certain contemporary scholars maintain that the whole preaching of Christ referred solely to this one point. The hopes which Luther and Calvin had formed of the religious exaltation of Europe were by no means realised; these fathers of the Reformation very soon seemed men of a past era; for present-day Protestants they belong rather to the Middle Ages than to modern times, and the problems which troubled them most occupy very little place in contemporary Protestantism. Must we for that reason deny the immense result which came from their dreams of Christian renovation? It must be admitted that the real developments of the Revolution did not in any way resemble the enchanting pictures which created the enthusiasm at its first adepts; but without those pictures would the Revolution have been victorious? Many Utopias were mixed up with the Revolutionary myth, because it had been formed by a society passionately fond of imaginative literature, full of confidence in the "science," and very little acquainted with the economic history of the past. These Utopias came to nothing; but it may be asked whether the Revolution was not a much more profound transformation than those dreamed of by the people who in the eighteenth century had invented social Utopias. In our own times Mazzini pursued what the wiseacres of his time called a mad chimera; but it can no longer be denied that, without Mazzini, Italy would never have become a great power, and that he did more for Italian unity than Cavour and all the politicians of his school.

A knowledge of what the myths contain in the way of details which will actually form part of the history of the future is then of small importance; they are not astrological almanacs; it is even possible that nothing which they contain will ever come to pass,—as was the case with the catastrophe expected by the first Christians. In our own daily life, are we not familiar with the fact that what actually happens is very different from our preconceived notion of it? And that does not prevent us from continuing to make resolutions. Psychologists say that there is heterogeneity between the ends in view and the ends actually realised: the slightest experience of life reveals this law to us, which Spencer transferred into nature, to extract therefrom his theory of the multiplication of effects.

The myth must be judged as a means of acting on the present; any attempt to discuss how far it can be taken literally as future history is devoid of sense. *It is the myth in its entirety which is alone important:* its parts are only of interest in so far as they bring out the main idea. No useful purpose is served, therefore, in arguing about the incidents which may occur in the course of a social war, and about the decisive conflicts which may give victory to the proletariat; even supposing the revolutionaries to have been wholly and entirely deluded in setting up this imaginary picture of the general strike, this picture may yet have been, in the course of the preparation for the Revolution, a great element of strength, if it has embraced all the aspirations of Socialism, and if it has given to the whole body of Revolutionary thought a precision and a rigidity which no other method of thought could have given.

To estimate, then, the significance of the idea of the general strike, . . . We know that the general strike is indeed what I have said: the *myth* in which Socialism is wholly comprised, *i.e.* a body of images capable of evoking instinctively all the sentiments which correspond to the different manifestations of the war undertaken by Socialism against modern society. Strikes have engendered in the proletariat the noblest, deepest, and most moving sentiments that they possess; the general strike groups them all in a co-ordinated picture, and, by bringing them together, gives to each one of them its maximum of intensity; appealing to their painful memories of particular conflicts, it colours with an intense life all the details of the composition presented to consciousness. . . .

Socialism is necessarily very obscure, since it deals with production, *i.e.* with the most mysterious part of human activity, and since it proposes to bring about a radical transformation of that region which it is impossible to describe with the clearness that is to be found in more superficial regions. No effort of thought, no progress of knowledge, no rational induction will ever dispel the mystery which envelops Socialism; and it is because the philosophy of Marx recognised fully this feature of Socialism that it acquired the right to serve as the starting-point of Socialist inquiry.

But we must hasten to add that this obscurity lies only in the language by which we endeavour to describe the methods of realising Socialism; this obscurity may be said to be scholastic only; it does not in the least prevent us picturing the proletarian movement in a way that is exact, complete, and striking, and this may be achieved by the aid of that powerful construction which the proletarian mind has conceived in the course of social conflicts, and which is called the "general strike." It must never be forgotten that the perfection of this method of representation would vanish in a moment if any attempt were made to resolve the general strike into a sum of historical details; *the general strike must be taken as a whole and undivided, and the passage from capitalism to Socialism conceived as a catastrophe, the development of which baffles description.* . . .

It is in strikes that the proletariat assert its existence. I cannot agree with the view which sees in strikes merely something analogous to the temporary rupture of commercial relations which is brought about when a grocer and the wholesale dealer from whom he buys his dried plums cannot agree about the price. The strike is a phenomenon of war. It is thus a serious misrepresentation to say that violence is an accident doomed to disappear from the strikes of the future.

The social revolution is an extension of that war in which each great strike is an episode; this is the reason why Syndicalists speak of that revolution in the language of strikes; for them Socialism is reduced to the conception, the expectation of, and the preparation for the general strike, which, like the Napoleonic battle, is to completely annihilate a condemned *régime*. . . .

It would serve no purpose to explain to the poor that they ought not to feel sentiments of jealousy and vengeance against their masters; these feelings are too powerful to be suppressed by exhortations; it is on the widespread prevalence of these feelings that democracy chiefly founds its strength. Social war, by making an appeal to the honour which develops so naturally in all organised armies, can eliminate those evil feelings against which morality would remain powerless. If this were the only reason we had for attributing a high civilising value to revolutionary Syndicalism, this reason alone would, it seems to me, be decisive in favour of the apologists for violence.

The conception of the general strike, engendered by the practice of violent strikes, admits the conception of an irrevocable overthrow. There is something terrifying in this which will appear more and more terrifying as violence takes a greater place in the mind of the proletariat. But, in undertaking a serious, formidable, and sublime work, Socialists raise themselves above our frivolous society and make themselves worthy of pointing out new roads to the world. . . . What will remain of the present Socialist movement will be the epic of the strikes.

13. EDUARD BERNSTEIN: EVOLUTIONARY SOCIALISM*

The impact of Marxian concepts on Western society can be measured not only by the sharp response of business leaders and politicians who steadfastly opposed such doctrines, but also by the appearance of new variations of Marxism in the late nineteenth century. The most important of the "revisionary Marxists" was a German Socialist, Eduard Bernstein (1850–1932).

Karl Marx had considered Germany the nation most ripe for a proletarian revolution. Industry had expanded rapidly through the last half of the nineteenth century; trade unions were strong and well organized; and the landless proletariat had multiplied in the growing cities of the German Empire. Nevertheless, viewing Germany near the end of the century, Bernstein realized that the economic crisis which Marx had predicted would bring revolution had failed to occur and was unlikely to occur in the near future. Convinced that he was not destroying, but merely facing reality and improving Marxian doctrine through his alterations, Bernstein urged his fellow Socialists to abandon the idea of forceful revolution in favor of transforming the state to a Socialist mold through legal means. Because Bernstein argued that Marxism must adjust to meet changing conditions, even at the price of correcting Marx, he came under sharp attack from more orthodox Socialists. His revisionary adjustments served to divide German Socialists and foreshadowed the twentieth-century cleavage between Communist and parliamentary Socialist parties. The following selection is from the preface to Bernstein's most famous work, *Evolutionary Socialism*, written in 1899. Which aspects of Marx's thought did Bernstein praise and condemn? What did he mean by "social democracy"? How did Bernstein defend himself against charges pressed by other Marxists?

* Eduard Bernstein, *Evolutionary Socialism: A Criticism and an Affirmation,* trans. Edith C. Harvey (London: Independent Labour Party, 1909), pp. x–xvii.

It has been maintained in a certain quarter that the practical deductions from my treatises would be the abandonment of the conquest of political power by the proletariat organised politically and economically. That is quite an arbitrary deduction, the accuracy of which I altogether deny.

I set myself against the notion that we have to expect shortly a collapse of the bourgeois economy, and that social democracy should be induced by the prospect of such an imminent, great, social catastrophe to adapt its tactics to that assumption. That I maintain most emphatically.

The adherents of this theory of a catastrophe, base it especially on the conclusions of the *Communist Manifesto*. This is a mistake in every respect.

The theory which the *Communist Manifesto* sets forth of the evolution of modern society was correct as far as it characterised the general tendencies of that evolution. But it was mistaken in several special deductions, above all in the estimate of the *time* the evolution would take. The last has been unreservedly acknowledged by Friedrich Engels, the joint author with Marx of the *Manifesto,* in his preface to the *Class War in France*. But it is evident that if social evolution takes a much greater period of time than was assumed, it must also take upon itself *forms* and lead to forms that were not foreseen and could not be foreseen then.

Social conditions have not developed to such an acute opposition of things and classes as is depicted in the *Manifesto*. It is not only useless, it is the greatest folly to attempt to conceal this from ourselves. The number of members of the possessing classes is to-day not smaller but larger. The enormous increase of social wealth is not accompanied by a decreasing number of large capitalists but by an increasing number of capitalists of all degrees. The middle classes change their character but they do not disappear from the social scale. . . .

In all advanced countries we see the privileges of the capitalist bourgeoisie yielding step by step to democratic organisations. Under the influence of this, and driven by the movement of the working classes which is daily becoming stronger, a social reaction has set in against the exploiting tendencies of capital, a counteraction which, although it still proceeds timidly and feebly, yet does exist, and is always drawing more departments of economic life under its influence. Factory legislation, the democratising of local government, and the extension of its area of work, the freeing of trade unions and systems of co-operative trading from legal restrictions, the consideration of standard conditions of labour in the work undertaken by public authorities—all these characterise this phase of the evolution.

But the more the political organisations of modern nations are democratised the more the needs and opportunities of great political catastrophes are diminished. He who holds firmly to the catastrophic theory of evolution must, with all his power, withstand and hinder the evolution described above, which, indeed, the logical defenders of that theory formerly did. But is the conquest of political power by the proletariat simply to be by a political catastrophe? Is it to be the appropriation and utilisation of the power of the State by the proletariat exclusively against the whole non-proletarian world?

He who replies in the affirmative must be reminded of two things. In 1872 Marx and Engels announced in the preface to the new edition of the *Commu-*

nist Manifesto that the Paris Commune had exhibited a proof that "the working classes cannot simply take possession of the ready-made State machine and set it in motion for their own aims." And in 1895 Friedrich Engels stated in detail in the preface to *War of the Classes* that the time of political surprises, of the "revolutions of small conscious minorities at the head of unconscious masses" was to-day at an end, that a collision on a large scale with the military would be the means of checking the steady growth of social democracy and of even throwing it back for a time—in short, that social democracy would flourish far better by lawful than by unlawful means and by violent revolution. And he points out in conformity with this opinion that the next task of the party should be "to work for an uninterrupted increase of its votes" or to carry on a slow *propaganda of parliamentary activity. . . .*

If not, and if one subscribes to his conclusions, one cannot reasonably take any offence if it is declared that for a long time yet the task of social democracy is, instead of speculating on a great economic crash, "to organise the working classes politically and develop them as a democracy and to fight for all reforms in the State which are adapted to raise the working classes and transform the State in the direction of democracy."

That is what I have said in my impugned article and what I still maintain in its full import. As far as concerns the question propounded above it is equivalent to Engel's dictum, for democracy is, at any given time, as much government by the working classes as these are capable of practising according to their intellectual ripeness and the degree of social development they have attained. . . .

No one has questioned the necessity for the working classes to gain the control of government. The point at issue is between the theory of a social cataclysm and the question whether with the given social development in Germany and the present advanced state of its working classes in the towns and the country, a sudden catastrophe would be desirable in the interest of the social democracy. I have denied it and deny it again, because in my judgment a greater security for lasting success lies in a steady advance than in the possibilities offered by a catastrophic crash.

And as I am firmly convinced that important periods in the development of nations cannot be leapt over I lay the greatest value on the next tasks of social democracy, on the struggle for the political rights of the working man, on the political activity of working men in town and country for the interests of their class, as well as on the work of the industrial organisation of the workers.

In this sense I wrote the sentence that the movement means everything for me and that what is *usually* called "the final aim of socialism" is nothing; and in this sense I write it down again to-day. . . .

The conquest of political power by the working classes, the expropriation of capitalists, are no ends in themselves but only means for the accomplishment of certain aims and endeavours. As such they are demands in the programme of social democracy and are not attacked by me. Nothing can be said beforehand as to the circumstances of their accomplishment; we can only fight for their realisation. But the conquest of political power necessitates the possession of political *rights;* and the most important problem of tactics which German social democracy has at the present time to solve, appears to me to be to devise the best ways for the extension of the political and economic rights of the German working classes.

The following work has been composed in the sense of these conclusions.

I am fully conscious that it differs in several important points from the ideas to be found in the theory of Karl Marx and Engels—men whose writings have exercised the greatest influence on my socialist line of thought, . . .

. . . I have now a controversy with socialists who, like me, have sprung from the Marx-Engels school; and I am obliged, if I am to maintain my opinions, to show them the points where the Marx-Engels theory appears to me especially mistaken or to be self-contradictory.

I have not shirked this task. . . .

14. SIDNEY WEBB: FABIAN ESSAYS*

Bernstein and Jean Jaurès (1859–1914), the leading French revisionist, stripped much of the revolutionary fervor of Marx from German and French socialism. The Fabian Society,[3] composed of a group of intellectuals closer to the long tradition of reform than to the doctrines of Marx, exemplified British socialism late in the nineteenth century. Spearheaded by George Bernard Shaw, Sidney and Beatrice Webb, and H. G. Wells, the Fabians urged far-reaching political, economic, and social reforms on behalf of the public welfare but insisted that such reforms must remain within the realm of British constitutionalism. They believed that mass democracy was the unchangeable trend of the future and that control of the means of production could not remain in the hands of a few capitalists who reaped profits at the public expense. Although they agreed with many of Marx's criticisms of capitalism, the Fabians rejected the concept of class war and attempted to promote their program through educational and democratic channels.

The following selection was written by Sidney Webb (1859–1947), later Lord Passfield, as one of a group of *Fabian Essays* first published in 1889 and frequently reprinted through the twentieth century. How did Webb attempt to show that British history had steadily pushed toward socialism? In what ways had socialism unconsciously crept into British life and government? Who was responsible for that development? Why was socialism held to be inevitable? Why have Fabian views sometimes been described as "Marx and water"?

In discussing the historic groundwork of Socialism, it is worth remembering that no special claim is made for Socialism in the assertion that it possesses a basis in history. Just as every human being has an ancestry, unknown to him though it may be; so every idea, every incident, every movement has in the past its own long chain of causes, without which it could not have been. . . . The record of the century in English social history begins with the trial and hopeless failure of an almost complete industrial individualism, in which, however, unrestrained private ownership of land and capital was accompanied by subjec-

---

* G. Bernard Shaw, Sidney Webb et al., *Fabian Essays in Socialism,* ed. G. Bernard Shaw (London: The Fabian Society, 1889), pp. 30–35, 47–50, 60–61. Reprinted by permission of George Allen and Unwin, Ltd.

3. The Fabian Society adopted its name from Q. Fabius Maximus (died 203 B.C.), known as the "delayer" because of the military strategy he employed against Hannibal and the Carthaginians—harassing and wearing down Hannibal's strength while avoiding a decisive battle.

tion to a political oligarchy. So little element of permanence was there in this individualistic order that, with the progress of political emancipation, private ownership of the means of production has been, in one direction or another, successively regulated, limited and superseded, until it may now fairly be claimed that the Socialist philosophy of to-day is but the conscious and explicit assertion of principles of social organization which have been already in great part unconsciously adopted. The economic history of the century is an almost continuous record of the progress of Socialism.

Socialism too, has in the record of its internal development a history of its own. Down to the present generation, the aspirant after social regeneration naturally vindicated the practicability of his ideas by offering an elaborate plan with specifications of a new social order from which all contemporary evils were eliminated. Just as Plato had his Republic and Sir Thomas More his Utopia, so Babœuf had his Charter of Equality, Cabet his Icaria, St. Simon his Industrial System, and Fourier his ideal Phalanstery. Robert Owen spent a fortune in pressing upon an unbelieving generation his New Moral World; and even Auguste Comte, superior as he was to many of the weaknesses of his time, must needs add a detailed Polity to his Philosophy of Positivism.

The leading feature of all these proposals was what may be called their statical character. The ideal society was represented as in perfectly balanced equilibrium, without need or possibility of future organic alteration. Since their day we have learned that social reconstruction must not be gone at in this fashion. Owing mainly to the efforts of Comte, Darwin, and Herbert Spencer, we can no longer think of the ideal society as an unchanging State. The social ideal from being static has become dynamic. The necessity of the constant growth and development of the social organism has become axiomatic. No philosopher now looks for anything but the gradual evolution of the new order from the old, without breach of continuity or abrupt change of the entire social tissue at any point during the process. The new becomes itself old, often before it is consciously recognized as new; and history shows us no example of the sudden substitutions of Utopian and revolutionary romance.

Though Socialists have learnt this lesson better than most of their opponents, the common criticism of Socialism has not yet noted the change, and still deals mainly with the obsolete Utopias of the pre-evolutionary age. Parodies of the domestic details of an imaginary Phalanstery, and homilies on the failure of Brook Farm or Icaria, may be passed over as belated and irrelevant now that Socialists are only advocating the conscious adoption of a principle of social organization which the world has already found to be the inevitable outcome of Democracy and the Industrial Revolution. For Socialism is by this time a wave surging throughout all Europe; and for want of a grasp of the series of apparently unconnected events by which and with which it has been for two generations rapidly coming upon us—for want, in short, of knowledge of its intellectual history, we in England to-day see our political leaders in a general attitude of astonishment at the changing face of current politics; both great parties drifting vaguely before a nameless undercurrent which they fail utterly to recognize or understand. With some dim impression that Socialism is one of the Utopian dreams they remember to have heard comfortably disposed of in their academic youth as the impossible ideal of Humanity-intoxicated French-men, they go their ways through the nineteenth century as a countryman blunders through Cheapside. One or two are history fanciers, learned in curious details of the past: the present eludes these no less than the others. They are so near to the individual events that they are blind to the onward sweep of the column. They cannot see the forest for the trees. . . .

The main stream which has borne European society towards Socialism during the past 100 years is the irresistible progress of Democracy. De Tocqueville drove and hammered this truth into the reluctant ears of the Old World two genera-tions ago; and we have all pretended to carry it about as part of our mental furniture ever since. But like most epigrammatic commonplaces, it is not generally realized; and De Tocqueville's book has, in due course, become a classic which everyone quotes and nobody reads. . . .

In the present Socialist movement two streams are united: advocates of social reconstruction have learnt the lesson of Democracy, and know that it is through the slow and gradual turning of the popular mind to new principles that social reorganization bit by bit comes. All students of society who are abreast of their time, Socialists as well as Individualists, realize that important organic changes can only be (1) democratic, and thus acceptable to a majority of the people, and prepared for in the minds of all; (2) gradual, and thus causing no dislocation, however rapid may be the rate of progress; (3) not regarded as immoral by the mass of the people, and thus not subjectively demoralizing to them; and (4) in this country at any rate, constitutional and peaceful. Socialists may therefore be quite at one with Radicals in their political methods. Radicals, on the other hand, are perforce realizing that mere political levelling is insufficient to save a State from anarchy and despair. Both sections have been driven to recognize that the root of the difficulty is economic; and there is every day a wider consensus that the inevitable outcome of Democracy is the control by the people themselves, not only of their own political organization, but, through that, also of the main instruments of wealth production; the gradual substitution of organized co-operation for the anarchy of the competitive struggle; and the consequent recovery, in the only possible way, of what John Stuart Mill calls "the enormous share which the possessors of the instruments of industry are able to take from the produce." The economic side of the democratic ideal is, in fact, Socialism itself. . . .

. . . The theorists who denounce the taking by the community into its own hands of the organization of its own labor as a thing economically unclean, repugnant to the sturdy individual independence of Englishmen, and as yet outside the sphere of practical politics, seldom have the least suspicion of the extent to which it has already been carried. Besides our international relations and the army, navy, police and the courts of justice, the community now carries on for itself, in some part or another of these islands, the post office, telegraphs, carriage of small commodities, coinage, surveys, the regulation of the currency and note issue, the provision of weights and measures, the making, sweeping, lighting, and repairing of streets, roads, and bridges, life insurance, the grant of annuities, shipbuilding, stockbroking, banking, farming, and money-lending.

It provides for many thousands of us from birth to burial—midwifery, nursery, education, board and lodging, vaccination, medical attendance, medicine, public worship, amusements, and interment. It furnishes and maintains its own museums, parks, art galleries, libraries, concert-halls, roads, streets, bridges, markets, slaughter-houses, fire-engines, lighthouses, pilots, ferries, surfboats, steamtugs, lifeboats, cemeteries, public baths, washhouses, pounds, harbours, piers, wharves, hospitals, dispensaries, gasworks, waterworks, tramways, telegraph cables, allotments, cow meadows, artizans' dwellings, schools, churches, and reading-rooms. It carries on and publishes its own researches in geology, meteorology, statistics, zoology, geography, and even theology. . . . Every one of these functions, with those of the army, navy, police, and courts of justice, were at one time left to private enterprise, and were a source of legitimate individual investment of capital. Step by step the community has absorbed them, wholly or partially; and the area of private exploitation has been lessened. Parallel with this progressive nationalization or municipalization of industry, there has gone on the elimination of the purely personal element in business management. The older economists doubted whether anything but banking and insurance could be carried on by joint stock enterprise: now every conceivable industry, down to baking and milk-selling, is successfully managed by the salaried officers of large corporations of idle shareholders. More than one-third of the whole business of England, measured by the capital employed, is now done by joint stock companies, whose shareholders could be expropriated by the community with no more dislocation of the industries carried on by them than is caused by the daily purchase of shares on the Stock Exchange. . . .

Even in the fields still abandoned to private enterprise, its operations are thus every day more closely limited, in order that the anarchic competition of private greed, which at the beginning of the century was set up as the only infallibly beneficent principle of social action, may not utterly destroy the State. All this has been done by "practical" men, ignorant, that is to say, of any scientific sociology, believing Socialism to be the most foolish of dreams, and absolutely ignoring, as they thought, all grandiloquent claims for social reconstruction. Such is the irresistible sweep of social tendencies, that in their every act they worked to bring about the very Socialism they despised; and to destroy the Individualist faith which they still professed. They builded better than they knew. . . .

The general failure to realize the extent to which our unconscious Socialism has already proceeded—a failure which causes much time and labor to be wasted in uttering and elaborating on paper the most ludicrously unpractical anti-socialist demonstrations of the impossibility of matters of daily occurrence—is due to the fact that few know anything of local administration outside their own town. It is the municipalities which have done most to "socialize" our industrial life; and the municipal history of the century is yet unwritten. . . .

. . . With the masses painfully conscious of the failure of Individualism to create a decent social life for four-fifths of the people, it might have been foreseen that Individualism could not survive their advent to political power. If private property in land and capital necessarily keeps the many workers permanently poor (through no fault of their own) in order to make the few idlers rich (from no merit of their own), private property in land and capital will inevitably go the way of the feudalism which it superseded. The economic analysis confirms the rough generalization of the suffering people. The history of industrial evolution points to the same result; and for two generations the world's chief ethical teachers have been urging the same lesson. No wonder the heavens of Individualism are rolling up before our eyes like a scroll. . . .

THE GROWTH OF DEMOCRACY IN WESTERN EUROPE

15. WILLIAM GLADSTONE: REPRESENTATION OF THE PEOPLE BILL*

William E. Gladstone's (1809–98) political career and the programs associated with him represented some of the more typical values of gentlemen-statesmen during the Victorian era. As a firm evangelical Christian, Gladstone believed in peace and reform as moral imperatives. Retrenchment and frugality in government were also firm public obligations, in his view. Most of Gladstone's struggles against Conservative opponents in the Commons resulted from his support of democratic reforms and his concerted efforts to maintain laissez faire liberalism as a standard of good policy during a period of imperialist clamor. The secret ballot, reformed judicial processes, legal status for unions, a merit system for the civil service, and public education were measures which Parliament passed into law during his first ministry (1868–74). In foreign affairs Gladstone settled the Alabama Claims with the United States through an impartial international tribunal. His second ministry was plagued by violence in Ireland and attacks on British policies in Egypt, but Gladstone managed to achieve the passage of a major reform bill in 1884.

The following selection was taken from one of the Prime Minister's speeches during debate on his proposed Representation of the People Bill. In Gladstone's view, what basic elements constituted strength and stability in a modern state? Who, according to the Prime Minister, were capable citizens? What proposals were made to meet the needs of a mobile labor force? Which individuals were still excluded from voting?

Sir, I shall try to dismiss altogether from my mind any memory of the conversation, or nearly the whole of the conversation, of the last three-quarters of an hour, and shall proceed to address myself to the object which a large portion of this House at least believes to be of vital importance, in that full reliance upon the indulgence of the House which my experience assures me I may very safely anticipate. It naturally happens that with regard to these large Constitutional questions—and it is well that it should so happen—before they are proposed upon the responsibility of the Queen's Government, they have attained to an advanced stage of progress in the public mind through discussion out of doors. And, in consequence, it is not necessary very long to detain the

* The Times (London), February 28, 1884, p. 7.

House with the general arguments which, if they were entirely new, would undoubtedly be requisite for the introduction of a Bill. On that part of the subject, therefore, I shall be very brief. But a few words I must necessarily say.

I conceive that this proposition may be presented to the House under any one, and, indeed, under all of three distinct and several aspects. In the first place, it is on our part the redemption of a pledge, because, although I do not use the word in its more narrow and objectionable sense, there is no doubt, as regards the persons prominently concerned in conducting the affairs of the country in conjunction with the Liberal party, that, before as well as since the last election, they have constantly assured the country that they regarded the work of Parliamentary reform as a proper and vital part of the mission, so to speak, of the present Parliament. (*Hear, hear.*) It may be regarded secondly, as intended to satisfy a desire, for they believe that a desire for the extension of household suffrage in counties is widely and generally entertained among the classes which are to be affected by that extension. (*Hear, hear.*) But there is another aspect, in which I for one hope that it will still more pointedly and constantly be viewed. If it is a proposal in satisfaction of a pledge, if it is a proposal to meet a desire, it is also a proposal in my view—I think I may say in our view—to add strength to the State. (*Cheers.*)

I am not prepared to discuss admission to the franchise now as it was discussed 50 years ago, when Lord J. Russell had to state, with almost bated breath, that he expected to add in the three kingdoms half a million to the constituencies. It is not now a question of nicely-calculated less or more. I take my stand upon the broad principle, that the enfranchisement of capable citizens, be they few or be they many—and if they be many so much the better (*cheers*)—is an addition to the strength of the State. (*Hear, hear.*) The strength of the modern State lies in the representative system. I rejoice to think that in this happy country, and in this happy Constitution, we have other sources of strength in the respect paid to the various orders of the State, in the authority they enjoy, and in the unbroken course which has been allowed to most of our national traditions. But still, in the main, it is the representative system which is the strength of the modern State in general, and of the State in this country in particular. (*Hear, hear.*)

I may say—and it is an illustration which will not keep me more than a moment—that I believe that never has this great truth been so vividly illustrated as in the recent war in the American Republic. The convulsion of that country between 1861 and 1865 was probably the most frightful which ever assailed a national existence. (*Hear, hear.*) The efforts which were made on both sides, and the exertion by which alone the movement was put down, were not only extraordinary; they were what antecedently would have been called impossible (*hear, hear*), and they were only rendered possible by the fact that they proceeded from a nation where every capable citizen was enfranchised and had a direct and energetic interest in the unity and well-being of the State. (*Cheers.*)

Sir, the only question that arises in the general argument is, who are capable citizens? And, fortunately, this is a question which, on the present occasion, need not be answered at length, for it has been already settled. It has been conceded in the first place by a solemn legislative judgment, acquiesced in by both parties in the State (*hear, hear*); and, in the second place, it has been settled by the experience of the last more than 15 years. Who are the capable citizens of the State whom it is proposed to enfranchise? It is proposed in the main to enfranchise the county population upon the footing of a measure that has been already administered to the population in the towns. (*Hear, hear.*) What are the main constituents of the county population? First of all, they are the minor tradesmen of the country and the skilled labourers and artisans in all the common arts of life, and especially in connexion with our great mining industry. (*Hear, hear.*) Is there any doubt that these are capable citizens? You have yourselves asserted it by enfranchising them in the towns, and I can only say that we heartily subscribe to the assertion. But besides the artisans and the smaller tradesmen scattered throughout our rural towns, we have also to deal with the peasantry of the country. Is there any doubt that the peasantry of this country are capable citizens, qualified for enfranchisement, qualified to make good use of their power as voters? Can this be questioned which has been solved for us by the first and the second Reform Bill, because many places which, under the name of towns, are now represented in this House are really rural communities (*hear, hear*), based upon a peasant constituency?

For my own part, I should be quite ready to fight the battle of the peasant upon general argumentative grounds. I believe the peasant to be, not in the highest sense, but in a very real sense, a skilled labourer. The peasant is not a man tied down to one mechanical exercise of his physical powers. He is a man who must do many things, and many things which require in him the possession of native intelligence. It is not necessary to argue in his behalf, because, in the first place, he has got his friends opposite (*cheers*), to whom we must attribute great zeal for his enfranchisement; and secondly, because the question has been settled by legislative authority in the towns to which I have referred and by practical experience. And if he has a defect, it is that he is too ready to work with and under the influence of his superiors, at least in one respect. (*Cheers.*) But that is the last defect you will be disposed to plead against him, and it is a defect which I do not think others are entitled to plead in bar to his claim. We are ready, and, much more, we are joyful to bring him within reach of the last and highest privilege of the Constitution. (*Cheers.*)

Only one word more on this part of the subject. The present condition of the franchise is one of greater and grosser anomaly than any in which it had been left hitherto, because persons are excluded in one place where the same persons have been admitted in another. (*Hear, hear.*) I wish to call the attention of the House to an important fact connected with this part of the question, and it is one of frequent occurrence. It is a thing which the House detests, and which we, in this Bill, shall endeavour to avoid—namely, the infliction of personal disfranchisement. (*Hear, hear.*) Observe how the present state of the law brings this about. It is well known and understood that the labourer must follow his labour; where his work goes he is bound to follow. He cannot remain at a great distance.

I will give you an instance which has been mentioned to me. I do not know it myself, but there is no doubt of the fact, and it is singularly applicable. It has been especially going on with respect to the shipbulding works upon the Clyde. These works were within the precincts of the city of Glasgow, and being within the precincts of the city of Glasgow the persons who laboured on them were able to remain within the city, being near their work, and at the same time to enjoy the franchise. But the marvelous enterprise of Glasgow, which has made that city the centre and crown of the shipbuilding business of the world, would not allow it to be confined within the limits of the city of Glasgow and it moved down the river. As the trade moves down the river the artisans require to move down with it. That is a matter of necessity and involves wholesale disfranchisement under the present law.

That is an argument which is sufficient for disposing of the general question. The whole population, we rejoice to think, have liberty of speech and liberty of writing; they have liberty of meeting in public, they have liberty of private association, they have liberty of petitioning Parliament. (*Cheers.*) All these privileges are not privileges taken away from us, diminishing our power and security; they are all of them privileges on the existence of which our security depends. (*Cheers.*) Without them we could not be secure. I ask you to confer upon the very same classes that crowning privilege, the vote for a representative in Parliament; and then I say we, who are strong now as a nation and a State, will, by virtue of that change, be stronger still. (*Cheers.*)

I shall be obliged from the circumstances in which I stand to deal with this subject on its affirmative and on its negative side. I shall endeavour to explain to the House, without undue detail and without affecting too much of legal and technical precision, what are the provisions contained in the Bill that I propose, on the part of the Government, to introduce. But it will be equally necessary for me to dwell upon those proposals which some have expected and some have desired, but which the Bill does not contain, because what I have to say upon that subject is vital to all hope of carrying what is contained in the Bill. I have considered what is the most convenient course of exposition for the House, and I have arrived at this conclusion.

I wish, in the first place, to fasten your attention upon the borough franchise as it exists in England, because the borough franchise as it exists in England, with the modifications which we propose to introduce into it and which I will immediately proceed to explain, is the hinge of the whole Bill. Upon that borough franchise the entire structure holds as respects not only England, but also as respects Scotland and Ireland. The borough franchise as it is is threefold. I ought to say that I put entirely out of sight what is sometimes called the ancient-right franchise—the cases of freemen, of liverymen, and of burgess tenure—and of whatever miscellaneous franchises may have survived under the old system. These I set aside because they are not touched by the Bill, for reasons I will afterwards explain. Setting these aside, then, the borough franchise is threefold. It consists, in the first place, of enfranchised occupiers of buildings of £10 clear annual value with or without land. That was the franchise established by the Act of 1832. It consists, in the second place, of inhabiting occupiers of rated dwelling houses. That was the franchise established and extended by the Acts of 1867, 1868, and 1869, and is the principal borough franchise of the country. The third branch of the borough franchise is the lodger franchise. So much for the present borough franchise in England.

Now I come to the true borough franchise which we propose. First, as I have already said, we leave the ancient-right franchises exactly as they are and touch them in no way. We leave the household franchise proposed and established by the Act of 1867 exactly as it is now, and we leave the lodger franchise exactly as it is now. But we do two things notwithstanding. First of all, for reasons which are partly of principle and partly with a view of unity, we extend the £10 clear yearly value franchise to cases where the occupation is of land without houses or buildings. At present it may be for houses or buildings alone, or houses and buildings with land. We extend it to land alone, without houses or buildings.

There is a more important change which we propose to introduce and which is also in the direction of extension. We propose to establish a new franchise, which I shall call, until a better phrase is discovered, a service franchise. It will be given to persons who are inhabitants and, in the sense of inhabitancy, who are occupiers. The present law restricts, I believe, the signification of the term occupiers to those who are either owners or tenants. Our object is to provide a franchise for those inhabitants who are neither owners nor tenants (*cheers*); but they must be householders in this sense—either, in the first place, that they are actual inhabitants, or, in the second place, that there is no other inhabitant with them superseding them or standing in the same position with them. . . .

16. DAVID LLOYD GEORGE: THE "PEOPLES' BUDGET" OF 1909*

During the nineteenth century, British radicalism had generally found political expression within the framework of the Whig-Liberal party. The reform bills of 1832, 1867, and 1884, the social measures of Gladstone's "Great Ministry" and the influence of radicalism in Tory circles testified to the strength and breadth of radical sentiment. Toward the turn of the century a minority of liberals promoted radical programs under the banner of what they described as a "new liberalism." Loudest and most effective of them was the Liberal party leader, David Lloyd George (1863–1945), who became Chancellor of the Exchequer in 1908. The Liberal cabinet had been deeply committed to extensive and expensive reform programs. Having pledged his government to public education, pensions, and insurance, Lloyd George faced the dilemma of financing not only domestic legislation but also an expanding navy. His solution was to maintain Liberal domestic programs by shifting the burden of taxation to the possessors of wealth. The proposed budget of 1909 created a constitutional crisis. What class or group in Britain was most affected by the "Peoples' Budget"? Where was the legislative power of this class or group concentrated, and why would their opposition create a constitutional crisis? In what ways did Lloyd George demonstrate a close knowledge of economic growth, productivity, and social change? Why did he insist that his budget aimed only at unearned wealth?

A few months ago a meeting was held not far from this hall, in the heart of the City of London, demanding that the Government should launch into enormous expenditure on the Navy. That meeting ended up with a resolution promising that those who passed that resolution would give financial support to the Government in their undertaking. There have been two or three meetings held in the City of London since, attended by the same class of people, but not ending up with a resolution promising to pay. On the contrary, we are spending

* *The Times* (London), July 31, 1909, p. 9.

the money, but they won't pay. What has happened since to alter their tone? Simply that we have sent in the bill. We started our four "Dreadnoughts." They cost eight millions of money. We promised them four more; they cost another eight millions. Somebody has to pay, and then these gentlemen say, "Perfectly true; somebody has to pay, but we would rather that somebody were somebody else." We started building; we wanted money to pay for the building; so we sent the hat round. We sent it round amongst workmen, and the miners and weavers of Derbyshire and Yorkshire, and the Scotchmen of Dumfries, who, like all their countrymen, know the value of money; they all dropped in their coppers. We went round Belgravia, and there has been such a howl ever since that it has well-nigh deafened us.

But they say, "It is not so much the 'Dreadnoughts' we object to, it is pensions." If they objected to pensions why did they promise them? They won elections on the strength of their promises. It is true they never carried them out. Deception is always a pretty contemptible vice, but to deceive the poor is the meanest of all. They go on to say, "When we promised pensions we meant pensions at the expense of the people for whom they were provided. We simply meant to bring in a Bill to compel workmen to contribute to their own pensions." If that is what they meant, why did they not say so? The Budget, as your chairman has already so well reminded you, is introduced not merely for the purpose of raising barren taxes, but taxes that are fertile, taxes that will bring forth fruit—the security of the country which is paramount in the minds of all. The provision for the aged and deserving poor—was it not time something was done? It is rather a shame that a rich country like ours—probably the richest in the world, if not the richest the world has ever seen—should allow those who have toiled all their days to end in penury and possibly starvation. It is rather hard that an old workman should have to find his way to the gates of the tomb, bleeding and footsore, through the brambles and thorns of poverty. We cut a new path for him—an easier one, a pleasanter one, through fields of waving corn. We are raising money to pay for the new road—aye, and to widen it so that 200,000 paupers shall be able to join in the march. There are many in the country blessed by Providence with great wealth, and if there are amongst them men who grudge out of their riches a fair contribution towards the less fortunate of their fellow-countrymen they are very shabby rich men.

We propose to do more by means of the Budget. We are raising money to provide against the evils and sufferings that follow from unemployment. We are raising money for the purpose of assisting our great friendly societies to provide for the sick and the widows and orphans. We are providing money to enable us to develop the resources of our own land. I do not believe any fairminded man would challenge the justice and the fairness of the objects which we have in view in raising this money.

Some of our critics say, "The taxes themselves are unjust, unfair, unequal, oppressive—notably so the land taxes." They are engaged, not merely in the House of Commons, but outside the House of Commons, in assailing these taxes with a concentrated and a sustained ferocity which will not allow even a comma to escape with its life. Now, are these taxes really so wicked? Let us examine them; because it is perfectly clear that the one part of the Budget that attracts all this hostility and animosity is that part which deals with the taxation of land. Well, now let us examine it. I do not want you to consider merely abstract principles. I want to invite your attention to a number of concrete cases; fair samples to show you how in these concrete illustrations our Budget proposals work. Let us take them. Let us take first of all the tax on undeveloped land and on increment.

Not far from here, not so many years ago, between the Lea and Thames, you had hundreds of acres of land which was not very useful even for agricultural purposes. In the main it was a sodden marsh. The commerce and the trade of London increased under Free Trade, the tonnage of your shipping went up by hundreds of thousands of tons and by millions; labour was attracted from all parts of the country to cope with all this trade and business which was done here. What happened? There was no housing accommodation. This Port of London became overcrowded, and the population overflowed. That was the opportunity of the owners of the marsh. All that land became valuable building land, and land which used to be rented at £2 or £3 an acre has been selling within the last few years at £2,000 an acre, £3,000 an acre, £6,000 an acre, £8,000 an acre. Who created that increment? Who made that golden swamp? Was it the landlord? Was it his energy? Was it his brains—a very bad lookout for the place if it were—his forethought? It was purely the combined efforts of all the people engaged in the trade and commerce of the Port of London— trader, merchant, shipowner, dock labourer, workman—everybody except the landlord. Now, you follow that transaction. Land worth £2 or £3 an acre running up to thousands. During the time it was ripening the landlord was paying his rates and his taxes not on £2 or £3 an acre. It was agricultural land, and because it was agricultural land a munificent Tory Government voted a sum of two millions to pay half the rates of those poor distressed landlords, and you and I had to pay taxes in order to enable those landlords to pay half their rates of agricultural land, while it was going up every year by hundreds of pounds through your efforts and the efforts of your neighbours.

That is now coming to an end. On the walls of Mr. Balfour's meeting last Friday were the words, "We protest against fraud and folly." So do I. These things I tell you of have only been possible up to the present through the "fraud" of the few and the "folly" of the many. What is going to happen in the future? In future those landlords will have to contribute to the taxation of the country on the basis of the real value—only one halfpenny in the pound! Only a halfpenny! And that is what all the howling is about.

There is another little tax called the increment tax. For the future what will happen? We mean to value all the land in the kingdom. And here you can draw no distinction between agricultural land and other land, for the simple reason that East and West Ham was agricultural land a few years ago. And if land goes up in the future by hundreds and thousands an acre through the efforts of the community, the community will get 20 per cent of the increment. Ah! what a misfortune it is that there was not a Chancellor of the Exchequer to do this thirty years ago! We should now have been enjoying an abundant revenue from this source. . . .

There are many cases where landlords take advantage of the needs of municipalities and even of national needs and of the monopoly which they have got in land in a particular neighbourhood in order to demand extortionate prices.

Take the very well-known case of the Duke of Northumberland, when a county council wanted to buy a small plot of land as a site for a school to train the children who in due course would become the men labouring on his property. The rent was quite an insignificant thing; his contribution to the rates I think was on the basis of 30*s* an acre. What did he demand for it for a school? £900 an acre. All we say is this—if it is worth £900, let him pay taxes on £900. . . .

I do not want to weary you with these cases. But I could give you many. I am a member of a Welsh county council, and landlords even in Wales are not more reasonable. The police committee the other day wanted a site for a police station. Well, you might have imagined that if a landlord sold land cheaply for anything it would have been for a police station. The housing of the working classes—that is a different matter. But a police station means security for property. Not at all. The total population of Carnarvonshire is not as much—I am not sure it is as great—as the population of Limehouse alone. It is a scattered area; no great crowded populations there. And yet they demanded for a piece of land which was contributing 2*s*. a year to the rates, £2,500 an acre! All we say is, "If their land is as valuable as all that, let it have the same value in the assessment book as it seems to possess in the auction-room."

Now, all we say is this: "In future you must pay one halfpenny in the pound on the real value of your land. In addition to that, if the value goes up, not owing to your efforts—if you spend money on improving it we will give you credit for it—but if it goes up owing to the industry and the energy of the people living in that locality, one-fifth of that increment shall in future be taken as a toll by the State." They say: "Why should you tax this increment on landlords and not on other classes of the community?" They say: "You are taxing the landlord because the value of his property is going up through the growth of population, through the increased prosperity of the community. Does not the value of a doctor's business go up in the same way?"

Ah, fancy their comparing themselves for a moment! What is the landlord's increment? Who is the landlord? The landlord is a gentleman—I have not a word to say about him in his personal capacity—the landlord is a gentleman who does not earn his wealth. He does not even take the trouble to receive his wealth. He has a host of agents and clerks to receive it for him. He does not even take the trouble to spend his wealth. He has a host of people around him to do the actual spending for him. He never sees it until he comes to enjoy it. His sole function, his chief pride is stately consumption of wealth produced by others. What about the doctor's income? How does the doctor earn his income? The doctor is a man who visits our homes when they are darkened with the shadow of death; who, by his skill, his trained courage, his genius, wrings hope out of the grip of despair, wins life out of the fangs of the Great Destroyer. All blessings upon him and his divine art of healing that mends bruised bodies and anxious hearts. To compare the reward which he gets for that labour with the wealth which pours into the pockets of the landlord purely owing to the possession of his monopoly is a piece—if they will forgive me for saying so—of insolence which no intelligent man would tolerate.

So much then for the halfpenny tax on unearned increment. Now I come to the reversion tax. What is the reversion tax? You have got a system in this country which is not tolerated in any other country in the world, except, I believe, Turkey—a system whereby landlords take advantage of the fact that they have got complete control over the land to let it for a term of years, spend money upon it in building, and year by year the value passes into the pockets of the landlord, and at the end of 60, 70, 80, or 90 years the whole of it passes away to the pockets of a man who never spent a penny upon it. In Scotland they have a system of 999 years lease. The Scotsmen have a very shrewd idea that at the end of 999 years there will probably be a better land system in existence, and they are prepared to take their chance of the millennium coming round by that time. But in this country we have 60 years leases. I know districts—quarry districts—in Wales where a little bit of barren rock on which you could not feed a goat, where the landlord could not get a shilling an acre for agricultural rent, is let to quarrymen for the purpose of building houses at a ground rent of 30s. or £2 a house. The quarryman builds his house. He goes to a building society to borrow money. He pays out of his hard-earned weekly wage contributions to the building society for 10, 20, or 30 years. By the time he becomes an old man he has cleared off the mortgage, and more than half the value of the house has passed into the pockets of the landlord. . . .

The ownership of land is not merely an enjoyment, it is a stewardship. It has been reckoned as such in the past, and if the owners cease to discharge their functions in seeing to the security and defence of the country, in looking after the broken in their villages and in their neighbourhoods, the time will come to reconsider the conditions under which land is held in this country. No country, however rich, can permanently afford to have quartered upon its revenue a class which declines to do the duty which it was called upon to perform since the beginning.

I do not believe in their threats. They have threatened and menaced like this before, but in good time they have seen it is not to their interest to carry out their futile menaces. They are now protesting against paying their fair share of the taxation of the land, and they are doing so by saying: "You are burdening industry; you are putting burdens upon the people which they cannot bear." Ah! they are not thinking of themselves. Noble souls! It is not the great dukes they are feeling for, it is the market gardener, it is the builder, and it was, until recently, the small holder. In every debate in the House of Commons they said: "We are not worrying for ourselves. We can afford it, with our broad acres"; but just think of the little man who has only got a few acres"; and we were so much impressed by this tearful appeal that at last we said: "We will leave him out." And I almost expected to see Mr. Pretyman jump over the table when I said it—fall on my neck and embrace me. Instead of that, he stiffened up, his face wreathed with anger, and he said, "The Budget is more unjust than ever." . . .

17. LÉON GAMBETTA: BELLEVILLE MANIFESTO*

Léon Gambetta (1838–82) was a militant radical republican who spearheaded the establishment of the Third French Republic in 1870. Though crude in appearance and eccentric in habits, Gambetta gained prominence as an orator

* Léon Gambetta, "Belleville Manifesto" in Émile Ollivier, *L'empire libéral* (Paris: Garnier Frères, 1918), pp. 497–98. Translated for this volume by John V. Gormley.

and spokesman for French radicalism. Like Jules Ferry and Georges Clemenceau, Gambetta was one of the new breed of tough-minded young radicals who attracted public attention as opponents of Napoleon III's Second French Empire. When Prussian troops defeated the French armies and captured Napoleon III in 1870, Gambetta roused the citizens of Paris to proclaim a republic. As Paris fell under siege, Gambetta organized a last-ditch defense of the French capital and then attempted to raise relieving armies in the south of France.

After the capitulation of 1871, Gambetta stood aside from both the Commune uprising and the new leadership of the royalist-dominated National Assembly. Jealous of his popular appeal and overemphasizing his extreme radical views, Gambetta's fellow republicans attempted to shunt him to the sidelines and to deny him national leadership. As a result, Gambetta led only one brief ministry prior to his death in 1882. Nevertheless, Gambetta had contributed far more than his contemporaries realized to the future stability of the Third Republic by persuading his followers to accept moderate republican leadership. What were the essential features of Gambetta's radicalism? In what ways did his program reflect the French revolutionary tradition?

"In the name of universal suffrage, the foundation of all political and social organization, let us give a mandate to our deputy to affirm the principles of radical democracy and to reclaim energetically; the most radical application of universal suffrage, as much for the election of mayors and municipal officials, without regional distinctions, as for the election of deputies;—the distribution based upon the actual number of legal voters, and not on the number of registered voters;—individual liberty henceforth placed under the protection of the laws, and not at the whim of arbitrary administrative action;—the abrogation of the law of general security;—the suppression of article 75 of the Constitution of the Year VIII and the direct responsibility of all civil servants;—the political offenses of all kinds submitted to jury trial;—the freedom of the press in all its ramifications free from licensing and regulation;—the suppression of printing and book-selling permits;—the freedom of assembly without obstruction and entrapment, with the right to discuss all religious, philosophical, political and social affairs;—the abrogation of Article 291 of the penal code;—unlimited freedom of association;—the suppression of funds employed for religious groups, and the separation of church and state;—elementary secular education, free and mandatory, with admission to advanced studies also free and based upon competitive examination:—the suppression of all municipal customs and tariffs, the suppression of exorbitant salaries and the holding of several offices, and the modification of our tax system;—the nomination of all public officials by election;—the suppression of standing armies, responsible for ruining the finances and stability of the nation, the source of hatred among the people and domestic defiance;—abolition of privileges and monopolies, that we define in these words: "propagator of indolence";—the economic reforms, which touch upon the social problem, and whose solution, even though dependent upon political change, should be constantly studied and reevaluated in the name of justice and social equality. This principle, expanded and applied, alone can dispel social antagonism and completely bring realization to our motto: LIBERTY, EQUALITY, FRATERNITY."

—"Voting citizens, I accept this mandate; on these conditions I will be especially proud to represent you, because this election will be carried out in conformity with the two principles of universal suffrage; the electors will be able to decide the political program of their representatives; this method seems to me to conform both to the law and the tradition of the early days of the French Revolution. And so, I subscribe willingly to the declaration of principles and to the reaffirmation of the laws whose demands you have commissioned me to seek in the public forum. I do more than consent! This is my vow: I swear obedience to the present contract and fidelity to the sovereign people."

Léon Gambetta
Radical Candidate

18. ÉMILE ZOLA: APPEAL FOR DREYFUS*

In 1894 an officer assigned to the French General Staff, Captain Alfred Dreyfus (1859–1935), was accused of selling military secrets to Germany and convicted of treason. After being degraded, he was sent to Devil's Island off the coast of French Guiana. The twelve years that followed included a reopening of the case, a retrial, the reconviction of Dreyfus, and a government pardon. The case was again reopened in 1906 and Dreyfus was finally exonerated. The Dreyfus Affair acted as a catalyst, laying bare the political, economic, and social weaknesses of the French Republic and, since Dreyfus was a Jew, uncovered the strength of anti-Semitism in the army. Slowly roused to face the critical issues of the Dreyfus Affair, many Frenchmen finally realized that the army, in its conviction of Dreyfus, had placed itself above the law and that an individual had been persecuted in the name of national security. By 1898 the nation was beginning to divide into Dreyfusard and anti-Dreyfusard camps, each attacking the other. Dreyfus the man became subordinated to more vocal and emotional issues such as racism, militarism, anticlericalism and ultramontanism, distorted out of proportion by a scurrilous press.

Among the early defenders of Dreyfus was a small group of intellectuals including Georges Clemenceau, who edited the newspaper *L'Aurore*. Suspecting that the real traitor was another army officer, Major Walsin-Esterhazy, the Dreyfusards sought a dramatic ploy to center public attention upon the miscarriage of justice. In January 1898 the widely known author Émile Zola (1840–1902) wrote an open letter to the President of the Republic. The letter was published in *L'Aurore*, under the title *"J'Accuse."* Zola was instantly sued for libel. At his trial Zola delivered an impassioned plea for Dreyfus. Why did Zola provoke the libel suit? What was the role of the army in the Dreyfus case? What was the larger issue to which Zola referred in his defense?

February 22, 1898.

In the Chamber at the sitting of January 22, M. Méline, the Prime Minister, declared, amid the frantic applause of his complaisant majority, that he had confidence in the twelve citizens to whose hands he intrusted the defence of the army. It was of you, gentlemen, that he spoke. And just as General Billot dictated its decision to the court-martial intrusted with the acquittal of Major

* Émile Zola, "His Appeal for Dreyfus" in Mayo W. Hazeltine, ed., *Orations* (New York: P. F. Collier and Son, 1902), XXIV, 10330–10339.

Esterhazy, by appealing from the tribune for respect for the *chose jugée,* so likewise M. Méline wished to give you the order to condemn me "out of respect for the army," which he accuses me of having insulted!

I denounce to the conscience of honest men this pressure brought to bear by the constituted authorities upon the justice of the country. These are abominable political practices which dishonor a free nation. We shall see, gentlemen, whether you will obey.

. . . If I am before you, it is because I wished it. I alone decided that this obscure, this abominable affair, should be brought before your jurisdiction, and it is I alone of my free will who chose you, you, the loftiest, the most direct emanation of French justice, in order that France, at last, may know all, and give her decision. My act had no other object, and my person is of no account. I have sacrificed it in order to place in your hands, not only the honor of the army, but the imperilled honor of the nation.

It appears that I was cherishing a dream in wishing to offer you all the proofs, considering you to be the sole worthy, the sole competent judge. They have begun by depriving you with the left hand of what they seemed to give you with the right. They pretended, indeed, to accept your jurisdiction, but if they had confidence in you to avenge the members of the court-martial, there were still other officers who remained superior even to your jurisdiction. Let who can understand. It is absurdity doubled with hypocrisy, and it shows clearly that they dreaded your good sense—that they dared not run the risk of letting us tell all and of letting you judge the whole matter. They pretend that they wished to limit the scandal. What do you think of this scandal—of my act which consisted in bringing the matter before you—in wishing the people, incarnate in you, to be the judge? They pretend also that they could not accept a revision in disguise, thus confessing that in reality they have but one fear, that of your sovereign control. The law has in you its complete representation, and it is this chosen law of the people that I have wished for—this law which, as a good citizen, I hold in profound respect, and not the suspicious procedure by which they hoped to make you a laughing-stock.

I am thus excused, gentlemen, for having brought you here from your private affairs without being able to inundate you with the full flood of light of which I dreamed. The light, the whole light—this was my sole, my passionate desire! And this trial has just proved it. We have had to fight step by step against an extraordinarily obstinate desire for darkness. A battle has been necessary to obtain every atom of truth. Everything has been refused us. Our witnesses have been terrorized in the hope of preventing us from proving our case. And it is on your behalf alone that we have fought, that this proof might be put before you in its entirety, so that you might give your opinion on your consciences without remorse. I am certain, therefore, that you will give us credit for our efforts, and that, I feel sure, too, that sufficient light has been thrown upon the affair.

You have heard the witnesses; you are about to hear my counsel, who will tell you the true story, the story that maddens everybody and that everybody knows. I am, therefore, at my ease. You have the truth at last, and it will do its work. M. Méline thought to dictate your decision by intrusting to you the honor of the army. And it is in the name of the honor of the army that I too appeal to your justice. . . .

I am not defending myself, moreover. I leave history to judge my act, which was a necessary one; but I affirm that the army is dishonored when gendarmes are allowed to embrace Major Esterhazy after the abominable letters written by him. I affirm that that valiant army is insulted daily by the bandits who, on the plea of defending it, sully it by their degrading championship—who trail in the mud all that France still honors as good and great. I affirm that those who dishonor that great national army are those who mingle cries of "Vive l'armée!" with those of "À bas les juifs!" and "Vive Esterhazy!" Grand Dieu! the people of Saint Louis, of Bayard, of Condé, and of Hoche, the people which counts a hundred great victories, the people of the great wars of the Republic and the Empire, the people whose power, grace, and generosity have dazzled the world, crying "Vive Esterhazy!" It is a shame the stain of which our efforts on behalf of truth and justice can alone wipe out!

You know the legend which has grown up: Dreyfus was condemned justly and legally by seven infallible officers, whom it is impossible even to suspect of a blunder without insulting the whole army. Dreyfus expiates in merited torments his abominable crime, and as he is a Jew, a Jewish syndicate is formed, an international sans patrie syndicate disposing of hundreds of millions, the object of which is to save the traitor at any price, even by the most shameless intrigues. And thereupon this syndicate began to heap crime on crime, buying consciences, precipitating France into a disastrous tumult, resolved on selling her to the enemy, willing even to drive all Europe into a general war rather than renounce its terrible plan.

It is very simple, nay childish, if not imbecile. But it is with this poisoned bread that the unclean press has been nourishing our poor people now for months. And it is not surprising if we are witnessing a dangerous crisis; for when folly and lies are thus sown broadcast, you necessarily reap insanity. . . .

The Dreyfus case, gentlemen, has now become a very small affair. It is lost in view of the formidable questions to which it has given rise. There is no longer a Dreyfus case. The question now is whether France is still the France of the rights of man, the France which gave freedom to the world, and ought to give it justice. Are we still the most noble, the most fraternal, the most generous of nations? Shall we preserve our reputation in Europe for justice and humanity? Are not all the victories that we have won called in question? Open your eyes, and understand that, to be in such confusion, the French soul must have been stirred to its depths in face of a terrible danger. A nation cannot be thus moved without imperilling its moral existence. This is an exceptionally serious hour; the safety of the nation is at stake. . . .

Dreyfus is innocent. I swear it! I stake my life on it—my honor! At this solemn moment, in the presence of this tribunal which is the representative of human justice, before you, gentlemen, who are the very incarnation of the country, before the whole of France, before the whole world, I swear that Dreyfus is innocent. By my forty years of work, by the authority that this toil may have given me, I swear that Dreyfus is innocent. By all I have now, by the name I have made for myself, by my works which have helped for the expansion of French literature, I swear that Dreyfus is innocent. May all that melt away, may my works perish if Dreyfus be not innocent! He is innocent. All seems against me—the two Chambers, the civil authority, the most widely-circulated journals, the public opinion which they have poisoned. And I have for me only an ideal of truth and justice. But I am quite calm; I shall conquer. I was determined that my country should not remain the victim of lies and injustice. I may be condemned here. The day will come when France will thank me for having helped to save her honor.

CENTRAL EUROPE: GERMANY

19. HEINRICH VON TREITSCHKE: POLITICS*

After the failure of the Revolutions of 1848, German liberals turned increasingly to aggressive nationalism, a transition clearly reflected in the career of the Prussian historian Heinrich von Treitschke (1834–96). Prior to the proclamation of the German Empire on January 18, 1871, Treitschke had become a most effective herald of unity and the creation of a power state on the foundation of Prussian military might and administrative efficiency. After the formation of the Empire, he directed his efforts as Professor of History at the University of Berlin to teaching a single-minded devotion to the state and eulogizing the Prussian authoritarian tradition.

Although many German historians criticized his approach to history, Treitschke was able to influence young Germans through his course on politics at the University and through his best-selling *History of Germany in the Nineteenth Century*. The selection below is taken from *Politics*, compiled from students' lecture notes and published after Treitschke's death. According to Treitschke, what unique elements distinguished the German Imperial Constitution? In what specific ways did the new Reich differ from such federal republics as Switzerland and the United States? How had Prussian organizational and administrative genius served as the major determining force in molding the Imperial Constitution?

In order to understand the difference between our own Empire and the republican Federations which we have been considering in the foregoing chapters we must retrace the history of the various developments of these States, and doing so, we discover a contrast of the sharpest possible kind. We have seen how, in the case of Switzerland, the separate provinces were gradually drawn more closely to each other by the common struggle for independence against their powerful neighbours, and how this military alliance in process of time became a firmer federative bond. In America we have seen the same kind of military union gradually forging a link between the colonies which had nothing in common except their origin, and a more or less nominal dependence upon the British Crown; it has been said that that they were sisters only through their mother-country. These processes are obvious and normal, but who can discover any analogous federalistic development in the history of our own Fatherland? What

---

* Heinrich von Treitschke, *Politics*, trans. Blanche Dugdale and Torben de Bille (2 vols.; New York: The Macmillan Co., 1916), II, 358–59, 361–68, 373–75, 381–83. Reprinted by permission.

has Germany been these thousand years? Always an Empire, always a Monarchy, with the exception of sixty years of a shameful federal anarchy, for which we have Napoleon to thank. Is the history of ten centuries to be estimated by this one exception to it?

Germany has been a monarchy since the Treaty of Verdun, although it was feudally constituted and prone therefore to disruption. . . .

The only real force which was capable of surviving this chaos lay undoubtedly in the secular principalities. Their particularism shone out as relatively the healthiest influence in the welter of territories held by Church or town, noble or princely Houses. They had the vigour which the crumbling national monarchy had lost and which the Federalistic tendencies failed to grip. . . . The die was cast in favour of the German princes when they earned, in the days of Luther, their undying honour as protectors of the Reformation, and showed that the territorial principalities of Germany were destined to rise above the chaos. The only question was which of them would succeed in establishing a government strong and noble enough to make his province the cradle of a new movement for German unity, to fill the Imperial throne, and thus re-create the monarchy from the heart of the nation itself.

. . . It seemed for a time as if the gifted Palatine might build up some such State. But it came to nought, and with the Great Elector the race of Hohenzollern began to rise, greater and more fortunate than all its rivals, in Brandenburg-Prussia. The Hohenzollerns thrust their State so far into the van of the national life that from the reign of Frederick II it was clear that Prussia must either rule Germany or perish. Frederick the Great did not create German dualism, for it had existed since the days of Luther. The huge hypocrisy of the "Reichsrecht" had become absolutely ridiculous since Germany had become a Protestant country to such an extent that all the most characteristic productions of our national intellect, and the whole of our art and literature, were Protestant through and through. Yet still the native land of Luther remained politically Roman Catholic, ruled by an Emperor who was a Deacon of the Church of Rome, for he was chosen by an Electoral College where Catholic priests and their co-religionists held a majority. A Catholic State and a Protestant people—here was the great lie in the Constitution of the Empire, which Hegel called "unreason legalized. . . ."

Only hypocrites can deny that it had now become the sacred duty of Germany to complete by her own exertions the necessary and life-giving process of simplifying her territorial conditions. Unfortunately this could not be accomplished without the intervention of a foreign Power. . . . It was France who finally dissolved the chaos of ecclesiastical States in the revolutionary wars. Next came the Act of the Diet which dissolved the Empire (*Reichsdeputationshauptschluss*) in 1803, and crystallized the result of all that had gone before. It was a revolution from above, than which a baser has been seldom seen. No glimmer of patriotism animated the politicians who made it, not one of them spared a thought for their great Fatherland out of the greed which utterly possessed them. Nevertheless this revolution was a pure benefit politically, for it only accomplished what was necessary and should long ago have been done. With one stroke it swept away all the dirty little States of the Roman Church, which existed to give fat livings to the Catholic nobility. The year 1806 brought the downfall of the Holy Roman Empire, and the last division of territory was taken in hand. . . .

When we call to mind the endless fluctuations of frontier which conquests and secularizations have brought about in Germany, we are bound to admit that the respect for existing boundaries which we have perceived in the Federal States of Switzerland and North America has been totally lacking. For the last three hundred years our history has recorded an unceasing series of annexations, which have made it impossible for any German to feel the federative instinct for law which rightly characterizes the Swiss. . . .

It has therefore been impossible for us to breathe that federalistic atmosphere which emanates from the political forms of Switzerland and America. The result of our whirlpool of contending forces has rather been to give prominence to the one among them all which was real and living—the Prussian State. No unprejudiced person can deny that the whole political history of Germany has been centred in Prussia ever since the days of the Great Elector. Through her was won back every clod of the land which the sins of the ancient Empire had let slip. Thenceforward she became the pivot of the political strength of the German nation, as surely as she had ignored and even repelled its intellectual forces. After the tumults of the war of liberation the new Germany was at first nothing but a flimsy agglomeration of the little monarchical States which had survived the gigantic upheaval. Once again Prussia set to work upon her task of creation. In her were gathered all the real political threads of the Confederation's history. Upon her soil grew the nation in arms which was later to become the possession of all Germany, and with its growth her eight provinces were welded into one whole. She was the living proof that a Government which could bind Treves and Tilsit in an inward harmony could also unite all Germany under her protecting wing. Already the Prussian Zollverein began to mark the true frontier between Germany and the world beyond, and the black and yellow boundary posts, with their profligate Double Eagle atop, [i.e., Austrian] remained beyond the pale. For many centuries it had been our misfortune that Germany's limits had never been clearly defined. Now at last came the triumph of the old Emperor's one-headed eagle, the insignia to which East Prussia alone had held fast, over the Double Eagle which had wrought us so much injury and shame.

In the march of these events we see the secret forces of Nature themselves at work, for Prussia's Crown was not always a willing agent. Nothing lay further from the thoughts of Frederick William III than that his Customs Union should pave the way to separation from Austria, for in dualism he saw only benefit to his Fatherland. The final result was brought about by the very nature of things, and it produced a real Germany, united by common economic interests, while Frankfort, like Regensburg in earlier days, was ruled by the mere phrases of politicians. The Austrian leanings of Frederick William IV were even more pronounced than his predecessor's, for he displayed greater enthusiasm for Austria than for his own State, and yet, despite all this, the amalgamation of Prussian interests went on and could not be checked. Although the Central States would have gladly destroyed Prussia after 1851, not one of them dared disturb the Zollverein, which held them without possibility of escape.

At last the men of genius arose who were able to read the signs of the times —William I, Bismarck, and Roon, and the decisive struggle of 1866 began. How did it end? Against the will of all Germany the Prussian State carved out with its good sword a Constitution which, even if couched in mild and friendly forms, could naturally be nothing but a complete subordination of the smaller States, a submission of the vanquished to the victor. Here was no realization of the dream of 1848, of a German nation elevating Prussia almost against her own will to become part of a united Germany. Thus did 1848 envisage the situation; Prussia was a so-called German State, and so was Schwarzburg-Sondershausen. The future Empire of Germany was to be the framework for Prussia's rise as much as of Schwarzburg's fall. These were the visions which inspired the makers of the Frankfort Constitution. But Prussia was totally unlike the other States, not only in size but in her nature as well. She was a living entity, not depending for her existence merely upon her share in the common life of Germany, but boasting a glorious history of her own. 1866 was to prove the reality of her individuality. Prussia was not swallowed up in Germany, although this phrase is sometimes used to this day in flat contradiction of the visible facts. Prussia extended her own institutions over the rest of Germany. . . .

All these are characteristics which our Empire has in common with both the Federal Republics, and they are enough for most teachers of constitutional law; but we historians have to consider the historical foundations and the living spirit of Imperial politics, and then it becomes clear as day that our Empire rests upon a principle exactly opposed to that of these Federal States. They are obliged to smooth over as far as possible the inequalities among their members, while our Empire is founded upon this very inequality, and upon the leadership of one State which has subordinated all the others to itself in a Federal bond. What would happen to Germany if Prussia should cease to be? There could be no more German Empire. Out of this follows a truth, unpleasant to most people, but which contains no insult to a non-Prussian—namely that Prussia is the only one of the former States within the German Empire who has preserved her sovereignty. She has not lost the right of arms, nor is she compelled to make her supreme authority conform to the will of others. The German Emperor is also King of Prussia; he is the leader of the nation in war, and it is only an empty quibble to imagine cases in which conflict might arise between the Emperor of Germany and the King of Prussia. We sink to the level of the silly joke which runs, "I would not advise the German Emperor to meddle with the Prussian King." We may leave it to theorizing professors to talk about the "war-lordship in peace time," which our lesser kings still vaunt, and which foreigners smile at. No doubt the outward forms of it are treated with all manner of consideration. Even the Prince of Reuss may boast of his army on paper, and a courtly myth maintains that this battalion is the Reussian army. Indulgence in these matters has been pushed only too far, but the fact remains that in spite of political provisos neither the King of Bavaria nor the King of Saxony are able to set a single man in the field. In war, the German Emperor is the war-lord; the right of arms has passed to the Empire, and in the person of its bearer the Empire is identical with the State of Prussia. . . .

The historical and political foundations of the whole Empire rest upon the actual and formal preponderance of Prussia, or upon "Prussia extended," as the Emperor William once remarked to Bismarck. What is the German army but the army of Prussia, constituted in 1814 as the nation in arms, and then expanded over the Empire. The Imperial Posts and Telegraphs and the Imperial Bank (*Reichsbank*) are all old Prussian institutions. This is all as it should be. Every Prussian will rejoice that the best political institutions should be spread over the rest of Germany, and every reasonable non-Prussian must be glad that Prussia should bring honour to the German name once more. Matters are so arranged that the will of the Empire, in the last resort, cannot be anything but the will of Prussia. . . .

Thus conditions have arisen amongst us which are obviously quite different from those of all Federal Republics. The divergence can be traced in the whole spirit of our legislation. Federal States are usually very averse to change in their law-giving, for nothing but a strict conservatism will carry them over the difficulties which beset them. In a hundred years America has only made one quite unimportant change in her Constitution. The legislative activity of the German Empire, on the contrary, has become almost feverishly great, for the new Empire is a growing monarchy, even as the old Empire was a declining one. Like a ball set upon a steep slope where it must roll without possibility of pause, our Empire is destined to travel more and more towards a firm centralization. . . .

A real capital city was the first demand of the Empire's need of centralization, while the Federal Republics, as we have seen, display the very reverse of this requirement. Even although the Berliner is the most insupportable person in all Germany, Berlin must still grow larger, and draw more of the national forces into itself. Before 1866 there were many sturdy patriots who were sincerely in favour of German unity, but whose understandable dislike of Berlin prompted them to wish to make Brunswick or Nuremberg or Hildesheim the capital of the Empire. Such mistakes seem inexplicable nowadays, but at that time they were very firmly rooted. The headquarters of Jewish journalism could certainly never become the centre of the national life of Germany, and, moreover, the atmosphere of Berlin is too unaesthetic ever to allow the noblest artistic achievements of the German people to spring from there, for it can be no home for any true artist. It has always been incomprehensible to me how a man can be a poet and settle in Berlin. Towns like Munich and Dresden will always offer greater stimulus to the artistic spirit than Berlin ever can. This is one of the reasons why the Empire has always shown a justifiable particularism in matters aesthetic, and has left them in charge of the individual States, thereby upon the whole benefiting art itself.

For the rest it is evident that once the capital is recognized it must be enriched by every possible intellectual force. Federal policy made a grave mistake, which, unfortunately, is now irreparable, when it transferred the Supreme Court of the Empire to Leipsig. Every advocate pleading in that Court feels like a fish out of water there. In all truly single States the seat of the supreme Court has always been also the capital. An increasing centralization in Berlin is also unavoidable for our commercial life, for it is obvious what power of attraction is wielded by the Reichsbank and the other Berlin banks. No change is possible. If Germany is to become a true monarchy, the capital city of its Emperor must also be the capital city of the nation; and this centralization is in the nature of things.

20. FRIEDRICH VON BERNHARDI: GERMANY AND THE NEXT WAR*

By the turn of the century many Europeans and Americans looked upon the German Empire as a militaristic state. The Prussian military tradition seemed all-pervasive in German life, and the army's influence was never effectively challenged even in peacetime. Foreign fears of an aggressive Germany were intensified when General Friedrich von Bernhardi (1849–1930), military historian to the German General Staff, published *Germany and the Next War* in 1912. What was Bernhardi's view of war? What did he believe were the advantages of war? In what ways could Bernhardi be labeled a "military Darwinist"? On what grounds did he claim that his views were truly Christian? Compare Bernhardi's view of the state with Treitschke's doctrines on the unique qualities of the German Reich.

Everyone will, within certain limits, admit that the endeavours to diminish the dangers of war and to mitigate the sufferings which war entails are justifiable. It is an incontestable fact that war temporarily disturbs industrial life, interrupts quiet economic development, brings widespread misery with it, and emphasizes the primitive brutality of man. It is therefore a most desirable consummation if wars for trivial reasons should be rendered impossible, and if efforts are made to restrict the evils which follow necessarily in the train of war, so far as is compatible with the essential nature of war. All that the Hague Peace Congress has accomplished in this limited sphere deserves, like every permissible humanization of war, universal acknowledgment. But it is quite another matter if the object is to abolish war entirely, and to deny its necessary place in historical development.

This aspiration is directly antagonistic to the great universal laws which rule all life. War is a biological necessity of the first importance, a regulative element in the life of mankind which cannot be dispensed with, since without it an unhealthy development will follow, which excludes every advancement of the race, and therefore all real civilization. "War is the father of all things." The sages of antiquity long before Darwin recognized this.

The struggle for existence is, in the life of Nature, the basis of all healthy development. All existing things show themselves to be the result of contesting forces. So in the life of man the struggle is not merely the destructive, but the life-giving principle. "To supplant or to be supplanted is the essence of life," says Goethe, and the strong life gains the upper hand. The law of the stronger

*General Friedrich von Bernhardi, *Germany and the Next War*, trans. Allen H. Powles (New York: Longmans Green and Co., 1914), pp. 18–19, 25–29. Reprinted by permission of David McKay Company, Inc. and Edward Arnold Ltd.

holds good everywhere. Those forms survive which are able to procure them-selves the most favourable conditions of life, and to assert themselves in the universal economy of Nature. The weaker succumb. This struggle is regulated and restrained by the unconscious sway of biological laws and by the interplay of opposite forces. In the plant world and the animal world this process is worked out in unconscious tragedy. In the human race it is consciously carried out, and regulated by social ordinances. The man of strong will and strong intellect tries by every means to assert himself, the ambitious strive to rise, and in this effort the individual is far from being guided merely by the consciousness of right. The life-work and the life-struggle of many men are determined, doubt-less, by unselfish and ideal motives, but to a far greater extent the less noble passions—craving for possessions, enjoyment and honour, envy and the thirst for revenge—determine men's actions. Still more often, perhaps, it is the need to live which brings down even natures of a higher mould into the universal struggle for existence and enjoyment.

There can be no doubt on this point. The nation is made up of individuals, the State of communities. The motive which influences each member is promi-nent in the whole body. It is a persistent struggle for possessions, power, and sovereignty, which primarily governs the relations of one nation to another, and right is respected so far only as it is compatible with advantage. So long as there are men who have human feelings and aspirations, so long as there are nations who strive for an enlarged sphere of activity, so long will conflicting interests come into being and occasions for making war arise.

"The natural law, to which all laws of Nature can be reduced, is the law of struggle. All intrasocial property, all thoughts, inventions, and institutions, as, indeed, the social system itself, are a result of the intrasocial struggle, in which one survives and another is cast out. The extrasocial, the supersocial, struggle which guides the external development of societies, nations, and races, is war. The internal development, the intrasocial struggle, is man's daily work—the struggle of thoughts, feelings, wishes, sciences, activities. The outward develop-ment, the supersocial struggle, is the sanguinary struggle of nations—war. In what does the creative power of this struggle consist? In growth and decay, in the victory of the one factor and in the defeat of the other! This struggle is a creator, since it eliminates." [Clauss Wagner, "Der Krieg als schaffendes Welt-prinzip."] ...

This highest expansion can never be realized in pure individualism. Man can only develop his highest capacities when he takes his part in a community, in a social organism, for which he lives and works. He must be in a family, in a society, in the State, which draws the individual out of the narrow circles in which he otherwise would pass his life, and makes him a worker in the great common interests of humanity. The State alone, so Schleiermacher once taught, gives the individual the highest degree of life.

War, from this standpoint, will be regarded as a moral necessity, if it is waged to protect the highest and most valuable interests of a nation. As human life is now constituted, it is political idealism which calls for war, while materialism —in theory, at least—repudiates it.

If we grasp the conception of the State from this higher aspect, we shall soon see that it cannot attain its great moral ends unless its political power increases. The higher object at which it aims is closely correlated to the advancement of its material interests. It is only the State which strives after an enlarged sphere of influence that creates the conditions under which mankind develops into the most splendid perfection. The development of all the best human capabilities and qualities can only find scope on the great stage of action which power creates. But when the State renounces all extension of power, and recoils from every war which is necessary for its expansion; when it is content to exist, and no longer wishes to grow; when "at peace on sluggard's couch it lies," then its citizens become stunted. The efforts of each individual are cramped, and the broad aspect of things is lost. This is sufficiently exemplified by the pitiable existence of all small States, and every great Power that mistrusts itself falls victim to the same curse. . . .

War, in opposition to peace, does more to arouse national life and to expand national power than any other means known to history. It certainly brings much material and mental distress in its train, but at the same time it evokes the noblest activities of the human nature. This is especially so under present-day conditions, when it can be regarded not merely as the affair of Sovereigns and Governments, but as the expression of the united will of a whole nation.

All petty private interests shrink into insignificance before the grave decision which a war involves. The common danger unites all in a common effort, and the man who shirks this duty to the community is deservedly spurned. This union contains a liberating power which produces happy and permanent results in the national life. We need only recall the uniting power of the War of Liberation or the Franco-German War and their historical consequences. The brutal incidents inseparable from every war vanish completely before the idealism of the main result. All the sham reputations which a long spell of peace undoubtedly fosters are unmasked. Great personalities take their proper place; strength, truth, and honour come to the front and are put into play. "A thousand touching traits testify to the sacred power of the love which a righteous war awakes in noble nations."

Frederick the Great recognized the ennobling effect of war. "War," he said, "opens the most fruitful field to all virtues, for at every moment constancy, pity, magnanimity, heroism, and mercy, shine forth in it; every moment offers an opportunity to exercise one of these virtues."

"At the moment when the State cries out that its very life is at stake, social selfishness must cease and party hatred be hushed. The individual must forget his egoism, and feel that he is a member of the whole body. He should recognize how his own life is nothing worth in comparison with the welfare of the community. War is elevating, because the individual disappears before the great conception of the State. The devotion of the members of a community to each other is nowhere so splendidly conspicuous as in war. . . . What a perversion of morality to wish to abolish heroism among men!"

Even defeat may bear a rich harvest. It often, indeed, passes an irrevocable sentence on weakness and misery, but often, too, it leads to a healthy revival, and lays the foundation of a new and vigorous constitution. "I recognize in the effect of war upon national character," said Wilhelm von Humboldt, "one of the most salutary elements in the moulding of the human race."

The individual can perform no nobler moral action than to pledge his life on his convictions, and to devote his own existence to the cause which he serves, or even to the conception of the value of ideals to personal morality. Similarly, nations and States can achieve no loftier consummation than to stake their whole power on upholding their independence, their honour, and their reputation.

Such sentiments, however, can only be put into practice in war. The possibility of war is required to give the national character that stimulus from which these sentiments spring, and thus only are nations enabled to do justice to the highest duties of civilization by the fullest development of their moral forces. An intellectual and vigorous nation can experience no worse destiny than to be lulled into a Phæacian existence by the undisputed enjoyment of peace.

From this point of view, efforts to secure peace are extraordinarily detrimental to the national health so soon as they influence politics. The States which from various considerations are always active in this direction are sapping the roots of their own strength. The United States of America, e.g., in June, 1911, championed the ideas of universal peace in order to be able to devote their undisturbed attention to money-making and the enjoyment of wealth, and to save the three hundred million dollars which they spend on their army and navy; they thus incur a great danger, not so much from the possibility of a war with England or Japan, but precisely because they try to exclude all chance of contest with opponents of their own strength, and thus avoid the stress of great political emotions, without which the moral development of the national character is impossible. If they advance farther on this road, they will one day pay dearly for such a policy.

Again, from the Christian standpoint we arrive at the same conclusion. Christian morality is based, indeed, on the law of love. "Love God above all things, and thy neighbour as thyself." This law can claim no significance for the relations of one country to another, since its application to politics would lead to a conflict of duties. The love which a man showed to another country as such would imply a want of love for his own countrymen. Such a system of politics must inevitably lead men astray. Christian morality is personal and social, and in its nature cannot be political. Its object is to promote morality of the individual, in order to strengthen him to work unselfishly in the interests of the community. It tells us to love our individual enemies, but does not remove the conception of enmity. Christ Himself said: "I am not come to send peace on earth, but a sword." His teaching can never be adduced as an argument against the universal law of struggle. There never was a religion which was more combative than Christianity. Combat, moral combat, is its very essence. If we transfer the ideas of Christianity to the sphere of politics, we can claim to raise the power of the State—power in the widest sense, not merely from the material aspect—to the highest degree, with the object of the moral advancement of humanity, and under certain conditions the sacrifice may be made which a war demands. Thus, according to Christianity, we cannot disapprove of war in itself, but must admit that it is justified morally and historically. . . .

21. PHILLIPP SCHEIDEMANN: MEMOIRS OF A SOCIAL DEMOCRAT*

Philipp Scheidemann (1865-1939) was a major force within the German Social Democratic party in Imperial Germany. He was a brilliant orator and was often sent by his party to campaign in peasant districts, where crusty farmers formed an unreceptive audience. Largely through the efforts of such indefatigable workers and political organizers as Scheidemann, as well as through the popular appeal of its program, the Social Democratic party gained strength in almost every Reichstag election. The anti-Socialist laws of the Bismarckian era were swept away by an avalanche of votes, and by 1911 the Social Democratic party was the largest in the Reichstag. Derided as *Reichsfeinde* (enemies of the Reich), they had already modified their tone, and the forces of revisionism were strong in the Socialist ranks. The following selection from Scheidemann's *Memoirs* describes one of his experiences in the Imperial Reichstag. What effect did the fact that Reichstag members were not paid have upon the members and their conduct? What steps did the Social Democratic party take to provide for the support of Socialist members? Was the Social Democratic party the monolithic organization it appeared to its enemies? Did Scheidemann's speech indicate that he was speaking for *Reichsfeinde*? Compare parliamentary procedure in the Reichstag with procedure in the British House of Commons.

Eighty-one men strong, we Socialists marched into the Reichstag on 3rd December after the elections in June 1903. A feeling of heavy responsibility came over me when I took part for the first time in a Party committee meeting on the top floor, Room 20. The furniture of the room had been taken from the former Conference Hall of the old Federal Council. The armchair in which Singer was sitting was formerly Bismarck's seat. Next to Singer sat [August] Bebel, and then came all the champions, some of whom I knew personally from old Party Congress days, and all the others by name and from the reports of their speeches in the Reichstag. . . . The list of colleagues of those days whom death has called away is a long one. Singer and Bebel welcomed the new-comers and gave them all sorts of hints; senior colleagues showed us the numerous halls and antechambers. The House was only well filled on the first days of the session, and then became emptier and emptier, and finally only a small group of regular *habitués* were visible. Out of 397 members not more than 150 at the most were regularly in the House, so there was plenty of room to work in. The bad attendance was due to the members not being paid. The privilege of sitting in the Imperial Parliament, with its universal, free, direct and secret franchise, should be entirely reserved, in the opinion of the "powers that be," for those who could afford to live in Berlin without any special allowances. The Prussian Diet, with its pitiable Three-Class franchise, was pretty safe from having paupers elected to it. In consequence, its members, who were to a great extent magistrates, Government officials and big industrials, received 15 marks a day. In the Reichstag, as aforesaid, no one got a farthing. The Social Democratic Party therefore had to give their members, if they were to come to Berlin at all, fixed allowances from the Party chest. These allowances were very small, and

*Philipp Scheidemann, *Memoirs of a Social Democrat,* trans. J. E. Michell (2 vols.; London: Hodder and Stoughton, Ltd., 1929), I, 126-33, 138-40. Reprinted by permission.

amounted to from 3 to 7 marks a day, according to the member's income. With this, members of the Social Democratic Party had to be content. Those who had to rent a room in Berlin received a small rent allowance every month.

To spare the Party chest as much as possible, the Party treasurer, Hein Meister, had to see to it that no member who was not indispensable should ever come to Berlin at all. Any member who had been in Berlin for more than three or four days in the week for any reason whatsoever had to pick a big bone with Hein before he received his daily allowances. Payment was made on Friday afternoons, generally in what is now the Zeppelin Room. Hein Meister, who wore an eyeglass and spoke with a stammer, though he could talk freely enough when required, had at the time one of the stingiest of colleagues sitting alongside him. The two spat like cats at anyone who claimed more than a three-days' allowance, as if he were asking for a huge amount. While Hein's assistant, Frederick Brühne of Frankfurt, an honest fellow, long employed at the job, cross-examined the member demanding his dole and got the receipts duly signed, Hein himself, growling perpetually, would stick a long stocking-needle with a long thread attached through the receipts. Pay day was invariably a great rag, for everybody knew that though Hein and his assistant were the best fellows in the world, they would be terribly keen on saving the chest any and every expense. If a member got his allowance for four days in the week and had not been summoned for an important division, he was told off in these words: "Well, don't let me see you again for four weeks; if you do, you won't get a copper." The non-payment of members had the most shocking effects. Count Posadowsky, then Secretary of State for the Home Department, had often to attend and protest in the Reichstag for three weeks running before his salary was paid him.

The House had never been competent to pass resolutions, and only when we Social Democrats took the members of the Government most seriously to task did we force a division without threatening to raise the question of competence.

The other Parties suffered just as much under these conditions: they too only whipped up their members by urgent telegrams for important divisions. In the Committees this non-payment of members was likewise very unpleasant. The whole of the Parliamentary business was transacted in each Committee. A few specially appointed members did everything, while the herd in the true sense of the word were "voting sheep" who were summoned by wire when wanted. For eight years, till I was elected on the Executive in 1911, I did all the political work of all the papers I managed. As the journalistic work of the Social Democratic organs then was—without wireless, telephones and correspondence bureaux—everything went swimmingly. . . .

The Reichstag that had been elected on 16th June—the first of the twentieth century, as President [of the Reichstag] von Ballestrem once said—assembled for the first time on 3rd December, 1903. We young bloods often sat on hot bricks at the full sitting when a debate did not go as we expected or wished. At any ordinary meeting we should have jumped up and asked to speak. Here only special speakers appointed by the Sections spoke. The President determined the order in which they should speak. Strict discipline prevailed in the Reichstag. The worst of calumnies against our Party could not be refuted at once. Everything was done in strict order. The President was Count von Ballestrem (Centre), an extraordinarily firm and clever man with lots of humour. To be able to say anything personal was an art that many members never learnt. I kept my ears open like a sporting dog, so as not to get off the rails should I ever happen to excite attention.

At the twenty-seventh sitting of the new Reichstag, 8th November, 1904, I delivered my maiden speech. Another speech I had carefully prepared I could only deliver half an hour later in the High Court of Parliament. I therefore spoke twice at the same sitting, and, much to the surprise of the House, had excited some attention by my first speech. I could truly say, as they say in Berlin: "Unaccustomed as I am . . ." This speech came about in the following way. The sitting had opened with a debate on the agenda, in which Bebel took part and over which he lost his temper. As everything went differently from what he expected—*e.g.* prescribed subjects being shelved and others brought forward for which no speaker had been announced by the Section, Bebel said to me, sitting by chance beside him, "This is about the limit; we haven't even announced one speaker to the Ministry of Health; usually a full dozen come forward." I asked him diffidently if he wanted me "to let drive"; I had, I said, investigated the question of well-founded complaints about the stench from the Wupper, and though not really prepared could talk on the question. "If you are sure of your ground, get up." At the same moment the name of Paasche, a member of the Reichstag, was called upon to speak. He was not in the hall, and lo and behold, I was standing on the rostrum, having had barely time to snatch from my drawer an envelope containing cuttings and official papers. The President then announced, "Scheidemann, member of the Reichstag."

Ha, a maiden speech! Most of the members were curious; many were even eager to embarrass a man speaking for the first time with interruptions. Nothing of the sort happened to me: I had at once the ear of the House. I referred to petitions protesting against the foulness of rivers. Real relief could only be obtained by an Act of Parliament. To get such powers was certainly a difficult business, for by Article 65 of the Transport Bill (Civil Legislation) the waterways were withdrawn expressly from the Reichstag and handed over to the Board of Agriculture. But I thought, "Where there's a will, there's a way." I gave two examples of the necessity for finding such a way—one from the division I had the honour to represent, that concerned the Wupper, and a second from my home in Offenbach, that concerned the Main. Dr. Wolf, the Prussian technical inspector, had already reported most unfavourably on the Wupper in 1885. "He calculated that the tiny Wupper brings down 150 tons of mud, etc., a day, and that these 150 tons of mud are the cause of a huge stench and poison the whole neighbourhood; that they flood the banks, thereby damaging the fields, and are a very grave nuisance to the public. I think you gentlemen on the Right should take up the question, as land cultivation is injured. When these masses of filth come over the banks tillage is an impossibility. The health of the district is also imperilled—that is obvious, if a river brings down such quantities of foul matter. Dr. Wolf proved eighteen years ago that, owing to the fouling of the river and the stench, in Elberfeld alone compared with other towns 12.8 per cent. of deaths were due to infectious disease, whereas in Düsseldorf and Cologne on the Rhine the death rate was less by a half. Dr. Wolf said: 'I will only allude to the dangers to which the inhabitants of the lower and middle Wupper would be exposed in case of an outbreak of cholera. The bed of the Wupper, with its filth, impregnated with dung and other animal excrescences, is just the right sub-soil for the spreading and development of the plague. My view is that steps must be at once taken to abate the nuisance.'

"Eighteen years have gone by, and nothing has been done. The Wupper, a fine German river, formerly abounding with fish, has had none for many years. Water rats are now the only living things in it. When you approach the fine uplands of the Wupper near Solingen and adjoining Müngsten, where German engineering skill has constructed the fine Müngsten bridge over the Wupper, and see what our technical skill can do and produce, and how it can correct the apparent ugliness of Nature, your heart leaps with joy, but a painful impression is at once created when you see the black, inky waters of the river flowing under this fine structure. The same technical skill, the same industry that improved Nature in such a striking way, has also spoilt the beauties of Nature. That should make us think; it should not be possible for industry to destroy our beautiful countryside in this way."

I answered interruptions by saying: "The Wupper below Solingen is so black, as a matter of fact, that if you were to duck a National Liberal in it you would be able to pull him out as a member of the Centre."

At first this disparaging remark in a maiden speech struck the House as something quite out of the common, but the tension was relieved by a roar of laughter, and I was soon able to resume my speech to an attentive audience.

Count Posadowsky rose immediately afterwards to say that here was a question that was becoming every day more important in view of the progress industry was making. He mentioned what had happened and must happen in this field, and ended with these words: "I am resolved to give this matter my earnest attention and insist on a gradual improvement of present conditions." The members of the Section were satisfied with my maiden speech, and congratulated me. In course of a remarkable sitting, Rettich, a Conservative member, seized the opportunity of touching on the Meat Inspection Act and ventilating a question that I had thoroughly studied in all its phases and should have discussed in my maiden speech. In agreement with Bebel, I forthwith got on my legs again and spoke—I am sorry to say—for an hour and a half on this uncommonly important food question. Later I frequently discussed it in "Supply" and in interpellations by members of the Section; my object was to prove that many of the Public Health regulations were only a blind, and their chief concern was to stop the importation of cattle and meat and other meat products, as far as possible, so that foreign competition, so inconvenient to our cattle dealers and farmers, might be arrested in order that these fellows might force up prices whenever they liked.

Questions on agriculture and cattle-breeding were for years my special province. My five years' experience in Giessen came in quite handly, as I had had there to study these subjects pretty thoroughly. Without this knowledge I could never have faced the small country farmer. Great amusement was caused in the Section, when the Foot and Mouth Bill was discussed, by my volunteering to act as its spokesman. My colleague, Stücklen, likewise volunteered out of friendship for me. We two worked very hard in Committee, and sometimes caused obstruction off our own bats. And we had fine opportunities, as in Committee every sort of animal disease was discussed. I remember with great pleasure a debate on "foul brood" in bees. According to experts, especially those from the Public Health office, it seemed well-nigh impossible to combat this devilish disease. I asked, with the solemnest face in the world, whether any special treatment of the microbe was being attempted, when whole nations could not be made healthy.

We were a sporting lot on Committees, in spite of lively disagreements. The gentlemen on the Right got very angry, certainly, when, according to the last section of the Act, it was stated that the Export regulations had to be made by the Provincial Governments. Stücklen and I, with very earnest faces, suggested that the Export regulations should be formulated by the Federal Government, which should introduce as soon as possible a universal equal, direct and secret franchise Bill. Unfortunately, our effort—it was naturally no formal proposal— to drag in the Prussian method of voting via the Foot and Mouth Disease Act was unsuccessful. . . .

The Social Democratic Section numbered forty-three members in 1907. One half of it was Radical, the other Revisionist. Both parts held separate meetings before the Section assembled. At these irregular sittings the two halves settled who of the section should speak on the various questions, what motions should be brought forward, accepted or rejected, and who should be told off to speak on especial points in the agenda at the plenary sitting of the House. Both halves naturally tried to keep their meetings a secret. The whole situation was extremely uncomfortable for me. I did not, in fact, fit into either, but the standoffish way in which my Revisionistic colleagues in the Section treated those of the other persuasion annoyed me so intensely that I went over to the Radical camp. It did no harm to the Section, and I can rejoice even to-day at having been able on repeated occasions to stop proposals that seemed to me foolish, and in the end to break up the separate sittings of the Radicals altogether. That occurred directly I saw that this nonsense was clearly dangerous both to the Section and the Party.

As not more than thirty-four or thirty-five of the forty-three members of the Section could be in Berlin, the majority of those who could carry a motion in the Section numbered eighteen or nineteen. As also the separate sittings were never attended by all members either of the Right or Left, the motions to be brought before the Section were sometimes settled at the separate meetings by quite a small number of members. This must be made quite clear in order to show the utter worthlessness, from a practical standpoint, of these separate meetings of the Section. Let us say that out of twenty members of each group nine or ten were present; then six of these had virtually the decision in their hands, for the majority naturally decided not only in and for the Section, but the decision of the majority then taken was binding on all members attached to the group. The Radical half was dominated by Ledebour. But Ledebour did not hunt round for four or six supporters in the Section beforehand to get a majority, but buttonholed in the Reichstag this or that member whose support he made sure of; in other words, this man was supreme in the Section for a long time, as the great men, Bebel and Singer, though not officially, were on the Radical side. Neither of them ever attended the meetings of the group, but both were always informed of what occurred. . . .

RUSSIA UNDER THE LAST ROMANOV

22. P. N. MILIUKOV: THE PLIGHT OF THE PEASANT IN RUSSIA*

Pavel Nikolaevich Miliukov (1859–1943) was a historian and member of the Constitutional Democratic party (Kadets). The Kadet party was active before the Revolution of 1905 and was represented in the various dumas from 1906 until the February Revolution in 1917. Miliukov served as Foreign Minister in the Provisional Government after the collapse of the Romanov dynasty in 1917. Pressure from the Petrograd Soviet forced him to resign in May, 1917.

Between 1902 and 1904 Miliukov traveled to western Europe and the United States. The following selection is taken from a lecture which he delivered during a trip through America. According to Miliukov, had the emancipation of the serfs been of economic benefit to the Russian peasantry? Why was Russia suffering an agrarian crisis? Contrast Miliukov's view of the Russian agrarian crisis with Arthur Young's description of France on the eve of the Revolution of 1789.

Briefly stated, the agrarian crisis in Russia is the necessary consequence of two agents: the elementary state of public economy, and the increased strain exerted on it by the demand of the state and by the changed conditions of life. As a result, private expenditures have greatly increased, while private incomes have remained the same as before, or have even diminished, owing to the exhaustion of the natural resources, the increase of population, the condition of the foreign market, etc. Hence the balance between revenue and expense has been quite disturbed. This is the crisis reduced to its simplest terms. Let us proceed to a more detailed explanation.

Prior to the emancipation of the peasants, forty years ago, economic life in Russia still preserved its mediæval character. It was based on home production for home consumption—at least so far as peasant life was concerned. The outlay for food, lodging, clothing, fuel, and light—in short, for all the chief items of the family budget—was practically naught. A man paid nothing for his own hovel; he fed on the products of his own field and garden; he was amply supplied with homespun clothing made of the wool of his own sheep and of the fiber of his own flax; he did not spare the wood to keep hot the old-fashioned, enormous oven which filled a quarter of the house, and which during the long winter months turned it into a bathhouse; nor did he spare his eyes, for he lit the interior of the hut with thin chips constantly renewed in a stand of prehistoric shape, during the long winter evenings while the women spun threads on their

* Paul Miliukov, *Russia and Its Crisis* (Chicago: The University of Chicago Press, 1906), pp. 439–43.

distaffs and spindles. Now, however, all this had changed. Wooden chips have given way to a kerosene "smoker;" homespun linen has been superseded by calicoes, while woolen stuffs have disappeared without a substitute; fuel has become very scarce and expensive. Food—which consists of vegetable products alone—is insufficiently supplied; too often it has to be bought by the grain-producers themselves; in fact, so often that the question has seriously been raised, and has been answered in the affirmative by a body of learned economists, whether it is not better for the Russian producers to have low grain prices.

Why have the conditions of life thus changed? In Russia you may sometimes hear the explanation, on the part of the former landlords, that it is because the Russian peasant has become lazy; that he is now a spendthrift, since nobody is there to take care of him. This is adduced as a reason why the peasant prefers the factory products to those of his own making. The fact is that the peasant now is too poor to utilize his and his family's work for himself; and, at the same time, he has no more raw material for his home industry. He can no longer have his clothes prepared by the women of his own family, because he has no more wool or linen to spare. His new expenses for the factory calico are certainly not inspired by any taste for fancy articles, but by mere necessity; and his purchases are generally cheap and of inferior quality. He can hardly be accused of lavishness on the ground that he has to buy some food in the market, since the fact is that on an average his yearly consumption is still below the necessary minimum. He gets only about twenty-three to twenty-six Russian *poods* of grain, and sometimes even as little as fifteen, while the soldiers are entitled to not less than twenty-nine *poods*. Moreover, the Russian peasant does not eat wheat, which he produces for sale only, but rye or, more frequently, potatoes. While the production of grain in general is now only 88 per cent. of what it was forty years ago, the potato crop is more than three times as large. Thus, his buying of grain in the market only shows that the Russian peasant is obliged to sell the better sorts to cover other necessary expenses; or that he is compelled to sell at one time in order to buy at another (and this at a loss); or that upon his holdings he is unable to produce even the necessary minimum of food. To be sure, he will not be found buying meat, because on the average he eats meat only four times a year. If he still finds money to buy alcohol—the famous *vodka*—it is not because he is a drunkard, but because *vodka* is considered by the Russian to be as necessary for social entertainment as soda and whisky in the American clubs. And yet the consumption of alcohol is lower in Russia than in any other civilized country, and, as we have seen, is still decreasing.

Thus, such purchases in the market as we have enumerated are absolutely compulsory. The increase in the peasant's cash expenditure for food, clothing, light, etc., does not at all signify any rise in his standard of life or any enhancement of his material well-being; on the contrary, it is a symptom of the deterioration of his condition. This will become still more evident upon a closer examination of that most important item of the peasant's expenditure, the one which conditions all other; namely, his payment of taxes.

If the Russian peasant has no time to work for himself; if he is fatally underfed and underclothed; if he needs money badly, it is, first and foremost, because he is compelled to perform his functions as a taxpayer. He does his best to pay his taxes; and if, in spite of all his exertions, he accumulates arrears upon arrears, it is not because he will not, but because he cannot, pay. In the decade 1883–92, while the population increased 16 per cent., taxation increased 29 per cent.; *i.e.*, nearly twice as much; and in the following decade, 1893–1902, while the growth of the exhausted population still further fell off, the increase being only 13 per cent., taxation took an unheard-of upward leap, showing an increase of 49 per cent., or nearly four times as much. No wonder then that, while in 1871–80 every *dessyatin* (2.70 acres) of the land owned by the peasant owed to the state 19 cents in arrears, in 1881–90 this debt had increased to 24 cents, and in 1891–1900 to 54 cents. . . . Thus the peasantry is reduced to a state of chronic insolvency, and finally grows quite apathetic. . . .

23. KONSTANTIN P. POBEDONOSTSEV: REFLECTIONS OF A RUSSIAN STATESMAN*

Konstantin Petrovich Pobedonostsev (1827–1907) was a professor of civil law and an influential adviser to three tsars. He helped write judicial legislation for Tsar Alexander II (r. 1855–81) and served as tutor to the future tsars Alexander III (r. 1881–94) and Nicholas II (r. 1894–1917). He was procurator of the Holy Synod from 1880 to 1905, which gave him a powerful position in the official Russian Orthodox Church. A conservative nationalist, Pobedonostsev thought of Moscow as the Third Rome in the tradition of the theocratic, imperial, and Russian Orthodox pretensions that had evolved since the reign of Ivan III (grand duke of Muscovy, 1462–1505). Pobedonostsev, who maintained his posi-tion as adviser to the crown until 1905, despised western European ideas, espe-cially democracy, and fought against freedom of the press and trial by jury. He used all of his persuasive abilities to urge Tsar Nicholas II to stand fast against concessions to the people.

What were Pobedonostsev's objections to democracy? On what grounds did he assert that democracy in theory and democracy in practice could never be reconciled? How did he use history to uphold his thesis?

That which is founded on falsehood cannot be right. Institutions founded on false principles cannot be other than false themselves. This truth has been demonstrated by the bitter experience of ages and generations.

Among the falsest of political principles is the principle of the sovereignty of the people, the principle that all power issues from the people, and is based upon the national will—a principle which has unhappily become more firmly established since the time of the French Revolution. Thence proceeds the theory of Parliamentarism, which, up to the present day, has deluded much of the so-called "intelligence," and unhappily infatuated certain foolish Russians. It continues to maintain its hold on many minds with the obstinacy of a narrow fanaticism, although every day its falsehood is exposed more clearly to the world.

In what does the theory of Parliamentarism consist? It is supposed that the people in its assemblies makes its own laws, and elects responsible officers to

* Konstantin Petrovich Pobedonostsev, *Reflections of a Russian Statesman,* trans. Robert Crozier Long (Ann Arbor, Mich.: University of Michigan Press, 1965), pp. 32–37, 44–46. Reprinted by permission.

execute its will. Such is the ideal conception. Its immediate realisation is impossible. The historical development of society necessitates that local communities increase in numbers and complexity; that separate races be assimilated, or, retaining their polities and languages, unite under a single flag, that territory extend indefinitely: under such conditions direct government by the people is impracticable. The people must, therefore, delegate its right of power to its representatives, and invest them with administrative autonomy. These representatives in turn cannot govern immediately, but are compelled to elect a still smaller number of trustworthy persons—ministers—to whom they entrust the preparation and execution of the laws, the apportionment and collection of taxes, the appointment of subordinate officials, and the disposition of the militant forces.

In the abstract this mechanism is quite symmetrical: for its proper operation many conditions are essential. The working of the political machine is based on impersonal forces constantly acting and completely balanced. It may act successfully only when the delegates of the people abdicate their personalities; when on the benches of Parliament sit mechanical fulfillers of the people's behests; when the ministers of State remain impersonal, absolute executors of the will of the majority; when the elected representatives of the people are capable of understanding precisely, and executing conscientiously, the programme of activity, mathematically expressed, which has been delivered to them. Given such conditions the machine would work exactly, and would accomplish its purpose. The law would actually embody the will of the people; administrative measures would actually emanate from Parliament; the pillars of the State would rest actually on the elective assemblies, and each citizen would directly and consciously participate in the management of public affairs.

Such is the theory. Let us look at the practice. Even in the classic countries of Parliamentarism it would satisfy not one of the conditions enumerated. The elections in no way express the will of the electors. The popular representatives are in no way restricted by the opinions of their constituents, but are guided by their own views and considerations, modified by the tactics of their opponents. In reality, ministers are autocratic, and they rule, rather than are ruled by, Parliament. They attain power, and lose power, not by virtue of the will of the people, but through immense personal influence, or the influence of a strong party which places them in power, or drives them from it. They dispose of the force and resources of the nation at will, they grant immunities and favours, they maintain a multitude of idlers at the expense of the people, and they fear no censure while they enjoy the support in Parliament of a majority which they maintain by the distribution of bounties from the rich tables which the State has put at their disposal. In reality, the ministers are as irresponsible as the representatives of the people. Mistakes, abuse of power, and arbitrary acts, are of daily occurrence, yet how often do we hear of the grave responsibility of a minister? It may be once in fifty years a minister is tried for his crimes, with a result contemptible when compared with the celebrity gained by the solemn procedure.

Were we to attempt a true definition of Parliament, we should say that Parliament is an institution serving for the satisfaction of the personal ambition, vanity, and self-interest of its members. The institution of Parliament is indeed one of the greatest illustrations of human delusion. Enduring in the course of centuries the tyranny of autocratic and oligarchical governments, and ignoring that the evils of autocracy are the evils of society itself, men of intellect and knowledge have laid the responsibility for their misfortunes on their rulers and on their systems of government, and imagined that by substituting for these systems government by the will of the people, or representative government, society would be delivered from all the evils and violence which it endured. What is the result? The result is that . . . all has remained essentially as before, and men, retaining the weaknesses and failings of their nature, have transfused in the new institutions their former impulses and tendencies. As before, they are ruled by personal will, and in the interests of privileged persons, but this personal will is no longer embodied in the person of the sovereign, but in the person of the leader of a party; and privilege no longer belongs to an aristocracy of birth, but to a majority ruling in Parliament and controlling the State.

On the pediment of this edifice is inscribed: "All for the Public Good." This is no more than a lying formula: Parliamentarism is the triumph of egoism— its highest expression. All here is calculated to the service of the ego. In the Parliamentary fiction, the representative, as such, surrenders his personality, and serves as the embodiment of the will and opinions of his constituents; in the reality, the constituents in the very act of election surrender all their rights in favour of their representative. In his addresses and speeches the candidate for election lays constant emphasis upon this fiction; he reiterates his phrases about the public welfare; he is nothing but a servant of the people; he will forget himself and his interests for its sake. But these are words, words, words, alone— temporary steps of the staircase by which he casts away when he needs them no longer. Then, so far from beginning to work for society, society becomes the instrument of his aims. To him his constituents are a herd, an aggregation of votes, and he, as their possessor, resembles those rich nomads whose flocks constitute their whole capital—the foundation of their power and eminence in society. Thus is developed to perfection the art of playing on the instincts and passions of the mass, in order to attain the personal ends of ambition and power. The people loses all importance for its representative, until the time arrives when it is to be played upon again; then false and flattering and lying phrases are lavished as before; some are suborned by bribery, others terrified by threats —the long chain of manoeuvres spun which forms an invariable factor of Parliamentarism. Yet this electoral farce continues to deceive humanity, and to be regarded as an institution which crowns the edifice of State. Poor humanity! . . .

Thus the representative principle works in practice. The ambitious man comes before his fellow-citizens, and strives by every means to convince them that he more than any other is worthy of their confidence. What motives impel him to this quest? It is hard to believe that he is impelled by disinterested zeal for the public good.

In our time, nothing is so rare as men imbued with a feeling of solidarity with the people, ready for labour and self-sacrifice for the public good; this is the ideal nature, but such natures are little inclined to come into contact with the baseness of the world. He who, in the consciousness of duty, is capable of disinterested service of the community does not descend to the soliciting of votes, or the crying of his own praise at election meetings in loud and vulgar phrases. Such men manifest their strength in their own work, in a small circle of congenial friends, and scorn to seek popularity in the noisy market place. If they approach the crowd, it is not to flatter it, or to pander to its basest instincts and tendencies, but to condemn its follies and expose its depravity. To men of duty and honour the procedure of elections is repellent; the only men who regard it without abhorrence are selfish, egoistic natures, which wish thereby to attain their personal ends.

24. H. W. NEVINSON: THE DAWN IN RUSSIA*

Henry W. Nevinson (1856–1941), a British journalist, was in Russia during the Russo-Japanese War and the Revolution of 1905. The war was not popular with the Tsar's subjects, who refused to be impressed by the government's imperialistic projects in Asia and were more concerned with serious economic and political problems at home. The imperial government, which had hoped that the war would unite the people and divert public attention from domestic concerns, was dismayed by the destruction of two Russian fleets by the Japanese navy and by the failure of the Russian army to dislodge the Japanese from Manchuria. Domestic discontent erupted into open rebellion after police fired on a workers' procession in St. Petersburg in January 1905, and for several months the vast Russian Empire was convulsed by revolution. Peasants rioted in the countryside, and workers established soviets (workers' councils) in the chief cities. Finally Tsar Nicholas II reluctantly bowed to the public clamor and conceded a National Assembly (Duma) in October 1905. What attitude did "comfortable people" take toward returning veterans of the Russo-Japanese War? According to Nevinson, what role did Socialist groups play in the events of 1905?

These were the soldiers returning from the [Russo-Japanese] war, the van and first instalment of that great and ruined army coming home. At last they had completed the 5000 or 6000 miles of their journey from the starving East, across the frozen lake, and through the long Siberian plains, and were alive in the heart of their own country again. And this was how they were received. Certainly, the Moscow municipality had intended to arrange some sort of festivities at the station. They had intended to give little presents to the men— something in the shape of chocolates and cigarettes that comfort the hearts of heroes. They had prepared little decorations for the officers, with the inscription, "To the defenders of the country." But whether these festivities were ever held and these little presents given, no one could tell me. The papers had announced that the army from the Far East would begin to arrive on the Sunday. The paternal Government took care that they should arrive on the Saturday.

Probably the town officials retained for themselves their little offerings to patriotism, and will wear the war decorations with pride at family parties. So

* Henry W. Nevinson, *The Dawn in Russia: Or Scenes in the Russian Revolution* (New York: Harper and Brothers, 1906), pp. 98–110.

little interest was taken in the whole thing that the evening papers continued to announce that the army would begin to arrive on the morrow. The market people and cabdrivers stopped for a moment to look at them before hurrying on through the snow, and no further notice of any kind was taken of the defenders of the country.

So they drifted westward, down the dirty streets, and disappeared. On reaching the barracks, the Reservists among them were discharged, and the crowds of beggars who, with threats and curses, violently demanded the milk of human kindness at every corner, were increased by many tattered figures. They limped about in traces of departed uniforms, and as they passed, people said, "A soldier from the war." One night I saw two or three of them seated on a curbstone beside a fire which had been lighted in a street. One was swaying gently backwards and forwards and continually repeating, "At home and alive! at home and alive!" The others took no notice, but stared like imbeciles into the flames.

Some were drafted back by rail to their villages, and the terror of comfortable people was that they would there spread the tale of mismanagement, corruption, and misery till all the peasants would rise in fury and sweep upon the cities in ravenous and overwhelming hordes. Sometimes a dim rumour reached us from the Far East of a distracted army, mutinous and starving; maddened with hardship and the longing for home, but unable to crowd into the worn-out trains that crept along those thousands of miles of single line, choked with stores and blocked by continual accidents and strikes. If they should all come home— all the 500,000 or 600,000 of them at once? The comfortable citizens—and even in Moscow there were such people—shuddered in their furs and thanked Heaven for the difficulties of that narrow road.

On the other hand, a big manufacturer told me he was delighted to see the army returning. "For now," he said, "the Reservists on garrison duty here will be dismissed, and we can always trust the Line to obey their officers and shoot in defence of law and order." At the time I hoped he was oversanguine. In Russia there is no caste of soldiers as with us. All come from the people, and in a year or two will return to the people. The Line are exactly the same kind of men as the Reservists, only younger. . . .

There were rumours about the disaffection of a good many battalions. The Rostoff regiment got up a little mutiny on its own account one day, and planted guns at the corners of their barracks, but they were soon won back by promises of bodily comfort. For the rest, the troops patrolled the streets in mounted and unmounted parties day and night, but no one knew whether they represented a Government or not. Their chief duties were concentrated round the great block of Post Office buildings. For all day long large groups of postal clerks and officials on strike were gathered upon the pavements there, like working bees around a ruined hive, and in the neighbouring boulevard gardens, where girls and children skated, they assembled in eager controversy.

On the Monday morning (December 11th), I saw there a feeble little attempt to rush a mail-cart starting for the provinces, or for the St. Petersburg station, under mounted escort. In a moment two Cossack patrols wheeled round and dashed at full gallop into the crowd, striking blindly at the nearest heads with the terrible nagaikas or loaded whips which I described before. Where the patrols had passed, men, women, and little girls, lay felled to the ground or stood screaming with pain while blood ran down their faces. Pushing, stumbling, and scrambling for life, the crowd fled in panic before the stroke of the hoofs and the whirling whips. Then I knew that until they could face violence with some sort of organized front, the revolutionists had better stay at home. Against twenty men in uniform, five hundred had no chance. . . .

In the ordinary affairs of life we enjoyed liberty tempered by assassination. The advance from tyranny supported by execution was immeasurable, and it had all been accomplished in about six weeks. In that old city, the natural centre of Russian life both by position and trade, were gathered some 1,100,000 souls who had never known liberty before, either in politics, economics, or thought. It was very natural that they should not know exactly what to make of the change at first. The surprising thing was to see how rapidly their instinct for organization and self-government developed, especially in the working classes. . . .

Every one was then waiting for the next step in history, and the wildest rumours flew. At every corner and in every restaurant stood prophets foretelling the fates, and winning the momentary applause of delight or terror. But, except for such rewards, the time of prophets was not more valuable than usual, and for ordinary people, whose perceptions are blind to futurity, the real points of interest were still the postal strike and the rapid formation of unions. The loss to friendship and business owing to the cessation of letters was so severe, that the leaders of finance and commerce in Moscow drew up a petition to Witte and Durnovo, urging them to grant the economic demands, especially the right of union, even if no political demands were considered. The Government replied with a manifesto dismissing one thousand of the postal strikers offhand, and making all strikes among Government servants a criminal offence.

The hardship was great. Many of the strikers had served fifteen years or more, and were entitled to pensions, which they now lost. Many lived in Government quarters, from which they were now evicted. The Progressives certainly did all that they could to assist them. At all lectures and meetings, such as were held in various parts of the city every night, the bag was sent round for aid to the strikers. At one lecture I counted seven bags—chiefly students' caps—going round for various righteous causes. In one of the most moderate of all Liberal papers—the *Russian News*—a strike fund was organized for the women and children, and it reached about £5000 before the Government clutched it and put it in its own pocket. In all Progressive papers you read advertisements that Mr. or Mrs. So-and-So would undertake to feed so many strikers for so many days, or to house the children. I knew three Socialist families of quite poor people who took in one or two children of strikers every day to share their dinner. The noticeable thing was that the children were fed, no matter what party of Socialism their parents belonged to. All the workers knew that the strike so far had been the people's only weapon. The Government had two— hunger and the rifle.

Nearly every night meetings were held for the new unions which were springing up on every side. The whole of Moscow, which is built in concentric circles round the Kremlin or eminent citadel overhanging the little river, had been divided off into wedges, or "rays," as they were called, and each ray sent so many delegates to the central committee—corresponding to the Council of Labour Delegates in St. Petersburg—which superintended the whole labour question, and had to decide the moment for strikes. But besides the central organizations, almost every trade was forming its own union of defence.

First came the great Railway Union, which controlled the powerful instrument of the railway strikes, and had its headquarters in Moscow, because the city is the obvious centre of all Russian railways. Perhaps next in size, though hardly in importance, came the peculiar union of Floor Polishers—a class of workers unknown in England, because we are not clean enough to have parquetted floors. But in Moscow they were said to number thirty thousand in the union. There were other large unions besides—the tailors', the metal-workers', the waiters', the jewellers', and a very strong printers' union called "The Society of the Printed Word," said to be the oldest in Russia, and rising almost to the dignity of a knightly order by its title. . . .

One evening I was present at the formation of two new unions in very different classes of labour. First I went to an immense meeting of tea-packers in a summer theatre, attached to the Aumont, a music hall of easy virtue. But the theatre had now been boarded up into a meeting-house as more suitable for the times. Packers of the Chinese tea that comes overland are naturally a large class in Moscow, for the tea is still the Russian national drink, in spite of the deadly blend from Ceylon which is slowly being introduced. The packers are said to number about six thousand, and forty companies sent deputies to the meeting, though some of the companies employed only eight or ten hands. It is an unhealthy trade, the dust leading to consumption; and of all the many meetings I attended it was only here that I found the voices feeble and toneless. Wages run from half a crown a week for boys and girls up £1 a week for the best men. But in the trade there is an ancient peculiarity that the wife of the owner or manager has to supply a free midday dinner for the hands, and, as one of the delegates said, "Apparently she cooks it in hell."

The other new union was formed at a meeting of shop assistants, conducted with that suavity and grandeur of manner which one always notices at meetings of this class. It comes from watching the grace of the shopwalkers, who alone carry the dignified and charming traditions of the old noblesse into modern life. The meeting was occupied for many hours in discussing whether the union should attend only to the assistants' interests, or should enter into wider life as a political force. The Social Democrats urged them to be bold, and, as usual, they had their way. They were far the most strongly organized party; they had their speakers ready at every meeting, and they played their "minimum programme" of quietly progressive measures with great effect. Their opponents were unprepared, and on this occasion were almost too polite to argue. I came away soon after midnight, but it was obvious that the Shop Assistants' Union would be a Social Democratic force before dawn.

Mid-winter is the height of the season for learning, art, and pleasure, but Moscow was neither gay nor learned. Reading and fiddling seemed equally irrelevant. So were painting, poetry, love-making, and all the other pleasant arts. In the big restaurant of the Métropole, it is true, an orchestra still maintained a pretence of joy, and poured out its vapid tunes to the rare guests who sat like shipwrecked sailors scattered on a vasty deep, and struggled to be gay. But, like a middle-aged picnic on the Thames, the thing was too deliberate a happiness, and too conscious of its failure. "We must keep our spirits up, you know," I heard a youth say to an elderly gentleman as he poured out the champagne. But it was no good. The elderly gentleman had obviously dined well daily for many years, and was overwhelmed at the solemn thought that at any moment dinners might end for ever. Day and night he was living in "the haggard element of fear."

The University was closed. Her seven thousand students were scattered, some to their homes, some to their lodgings in the city, where for the most part they swelled the army of the Social Democrats, and spent their time discussing maximum and minimum programmes and the socialization of productivity. They were also collecting arms. . . .

Another evening, in one of those dubious theatres which had just been converted to decent use, I heard a Professor deliver an immense discourse upon the first principles of Social Democracy before an audience half composed of working people. They also listened patiently, but the moment of real excitement came when the lecturer ceased, and three young soldiers sprang upon the stage and shouted that, on the highest economic principles, they too had struck, and would Cossack it no more. "I have flung away the uniform!" shouted one, who was apparelled in a long dressing-gown. "No more fools of officers over me!" shouted another. "And they fed us like swine!" shouted the third, who was just economically drunk. The applause that rocked the audience was one of the grandest noises I have ever heard. If only all the army would follow the example of those three gallant musketeers! But that night they vanished from the blaze of glory, and I heard of them no more. . . .

25. SERGEI WITTE: ON THE OCTOBER MANIFESTO*

Count Sergei Witte (1849–1915) became Minister of Finance in August 1892 and immediately began to promote the industrialization of Russia. By broadening the protective tariff and encouraging foreign investments, he pulled the Russian economy into the twentieth century. Witte also pressed for the completion of the Trans-Siberian Railroad in order to accelerate the economic development of Siberia and to facilitate Russian imperialistic designs in Asia.

Despite Witte's aggressive championship of modernization, the minister was personally disliked by both the Tsar and the Tsarina. In 1903 he was dismissed and appointed to an honorific sinecure. When revolution broke out in 1905 Witte was recalled. He wrote the Tsar's Manifesto of October 17 which transformed Russia into a semiconstitutional monarchy. Tsar Nicholas appointed him President of the Council of Ministers, and Witte negotiated the Treaty of Portsmouth which ended the Russo-Japanese War in 1907. Nevertheless, Witte was again dismissed as soon as Tsar Nicholas believed that he could dispense with the ambitious minister. The following selection is drawn from Witte's highly

* Sergei Witte, *The Memoirs of Count Witte,* trans. Avrahm Yarmolinsky (London: William Heinemann, 1921), pp. 257–61, 263–69, 310–12. Reprinted by permission of Avrahm Yarmolinsky.

outspoken *Memoirs.* What was the attitude of the Russian imperial government toward national minorities? Why, according to Witte, was Russia in a revolutionary situation? Why was Witte opposed to the publication of a constitutional manifesto? In what ways could Witte be compared with Turgot, the reforming French Finance Minister of Louis XVI's reign?

What prevented the Government from coping promptly and successfully with the revolutionary outbreaks was the lethargy, incompetence and timidity prevalent among executive and administrative officers. To begin with, the Minister of the Interior, Bulygin, was altogether apathetic because he was aware that in reality not he, but General Trepov, ruled. In his turn, Trepov was almost out of his mind. He worked in starts and fits and writhed with apprehension as he saw the storm come sweeping on. Broken in health and spirit, he longed to escape from the whole incomprehensible nightmare. He told me that he could stay no longer at his post of Associate Minister of the Interior, actually a position of dictatorship, which he had created for himself. Indeed, the desire to retire from the places of responsibility was very common at this time. The sagacious and skeptical K. P. Pobiedonostzev, for instance, abandoned the whole business except that he corresponded with the Emperor. The rest of the ministers, a colourless insignificant lot, Kokovtzev, Schwanebach, General Glazov, and General Rediger, kept silent and did nothing.

The revolution made its appearance first in the border territories, the Baltic provinces being the earliest to show signs of deep unrest. In that region it took the form of agrarian disturbances. The chief reason for this was the policy of Russification which the Government pursued in that territory. The lower classes of the population of the Baltic provinces consist, as is known, of Letts, while the upper class is made up of Germans. In trying to Russify the region, our Government has succeeded, during the last several decades, in destroying the elements of culture which the German masters had forced upon the Letts. This was done through the instrumentality of the Russian school, with its liberal spirit, so thoroughly opposed to the mediæval traditions in which the German nobility educated the Lettish peasant. As a result, the effect of the Russification policy was to pit the Lettish plebeian against the German aristocrat. Small wonder that, when the revolutionary wave reached the narrow-minded, staunch Letts, they responded to it by a veritable orgy of burning and looting the German landowners' property. In consequence, the leaders of the Baltic nobility, for instance, Budberg and Richter, the President of the Court of Appeals, urged the Government to establish military rule in that territory. As a matter of fact, at Mitau and in the southern districts adjacent to that city there was already something in the nature of martial law. I did not wish, however, to grant the desire of the Baltic barons. . . .

As early as the beginning of 1905, Finland was in a state of latent conflagration. Upon ascending the throne, Nicholas II by a special manifesto solemnly proclaimed his intention to respect the privileges granted to Finland by his predecessors. Such was indeed his sincere desire. During the first year of his reign he expressed his willingness to permit the Finns to establish a direct connection between the Finnish and Swedish railroads, although I pointed out to him that his most august father was opposed to that measure for strategic reasons. He did not doubt, he said, the loyalty of his Finnish subjects, and he had complete confidence in them.

When General Kuropatkin became Minister of War, he raised the question of Russifying Finland. He wished to distinguish himself. As long as Count Heyden, the Finnish Governor-General, was alive he held Kuropatkin's zeal in check. But soon the count died, and General Bobrikov was appointed to succeed him. When I congratulated him upon his nomination, he remarked that his mission in Finland was analogous to that of Count Muraviov in Poland. The comparison was rather unexpected, and I could not refrain from observing that while Count Muraviov had been appointed to suppress a rebellion, he was apparently commissioned to create one. . . . That was our last friendly conversation. . . .

Soon afterwards Kuropatkin hatched a project of a military reform in Finland. Simultaneously an Imperial manifesto was issued decreeing that all the legislative matters affecting the interests of the Empire should be passed upon by the Imperial Council. This was a violation of the Finnish constitution granted by His Majesty's predecessors and confirmed by himself. Kuropatkin laid his project before the Council, in the hope that this body would pass it, in spite of the opposition of the Finnish Diet. I vigorously opposed the reform as the Minister of War conceived it, and I drafted what I considered to be an acceptable version of the project. I had behind me the majority of the Imperial Council and also the public opinion of Finland. Nevertheless, the Emperor sanctioned Kuropatkin's project, which was naturally supported by Bobrikov and Plehve.

In the meantime, the Russification of Finland was being carried into effect. The Russian authorities took a number of measures, which from the Finnish standpoint were clearly and aggressively illegal. The Russian language was forced upon the Finnish schools, the country was flooded with Russian secret agents, Finnish senators were dismissed and replaced by men who had nothing in common with the people, and those who protested were deported from the country. As a result Bobrikov was assassinated, the terroristic act being committed not by anarchists but by Finnish nationalists, and the country became a hotbed of unrest.

In consequence, the outbreak of the revolution in Central Russia was a signal for the beginning of the revolution in Finland. Prince Obolensky, the Governor-General, immediately gave up the struggle and after a while resigned. I was aware that a Finnish insurrection would greatly complicate the revolutionary chaos in Russia. On the other hand, I was always opposed to the policy of persecution inaugurated in Finland by Nicholas II. Therefore, when the Finnish representatives came to me and assured me that the Finns would forget all their grievances and quiet down, if the Russian Government would conscientiously observe the privileges granted to the duchy by the Emperor Alexander I and Alexander II,—I, on my part, expressed my conviction to His Majesty that it was imperative to revert to the Finnish policy of his predecessors. I pointed out to him that the Finns had always been loyal as long as they were treated decently, and that it was highly dangerous to create a second Poland close by the gates of St. Petersburg. I urged His Majesty to respect the liberties granted to the Finns by Emperors Alexander I and Alexander II. At my recommendation, the Emperor appointed Gerard as Governor-General of Finland, to succeed Prince Obolensky, who had tendered his resignation. Upon Gerard's appointment, Finland ceased to be the stage for the rehearsal of revolutionary tragedies intended for Russia. At present, it seems, Russian militant chauvinism is again turning against Finland, in the hope of making trouble. It is noteworthy that the Empress Dowager Maria Fiodorovna was completely out of sympathy with Bobrikov's policy. She repeatedly intervened before the Emperor in behalf of the persecuted Finns.

At this juncture Poland was also permeated with a spirit of revolt, but the malcontents were forced to keep under cover and disturbances occurred only sporadically because of the comparatively large army stationed there. It was commanded by Governor-General Skalon, who, while not a marvel, was at least a brave, straightforward man. He had been chosen shortly before when his predecessor, General Maximovich, a petty character, appointed on the recommendation of the Court Minister, Baron Frederichs, was removed because he deserted to his country villa near Warsaw, whence he did not emerge till after the storm had blown over. He had been recommended merely in return for a favour rendered to Baron Frederichs at the time of the latter's marriage, which was a misalliance.

When I became President of the Cabinet of Ministers, in October, 1905, I found Poland in a state of complete anarchy, assassinations and other terroristic acts happening daily. The disturbances were partly agrarian, partly industrial, in character. The situation was complicated by the nationalistic movement which united all classes of the population by a common aspiration for national independence, some dreaming of a separate Polish kingdom united to the Empire only in the person of the monarch, but most hoping for local autonomy.

Odessa, too, was seething with rebellion. There were two special causes for the extreme disorder in this city. In the first place, the Jews, who formed a large proportion of its inhabitants, supposed that, by taking advantage of the general confusion and the undermining of the Government's prestige, they would be able to obtain equal rights through revolution. At this time only a comparatively small number of the Jews were active, but the overwhelming majority, having lost patience long before by reason of the many injustices practised against them, sympathized with the so-called emancipatory movement, which was now adopting revolutionary tactics. In the second place, the uprising was largely provoked by the brutality of the Municipal Governor, Neidhart, who was bitterly hated by most of the inhabitants. Fitted neither by education nor by experience for such an important position, he had been appointed simply because he was Stolypin's brother-in-law, the same reason for which he was later made senator. The appointment may also have been due partly to the fact that the Czar had taken a liking to Neidhart as the buffoon officer of the Preobrazhensky regiment, in which His Majesty served during his youth. Neidhart, though not stupid, was very superficial and ignorant, but he had a high opinion of himself and excited such hostility by his arrogance and harshness toward his subordinates and the people that I had to remove him soon after the 17th of October, an action for which he and his sister, Premier Stolypin's wife, have been my enemies ever since.

In the southeastern territory, Governor-General Kleigels had become inactive and when the October days came, he abandoned his post altogether. Previously he had been Governor of St. Petersburg. He was a dull-witted individual, but the Emperor liked him very much, wholly, I imagine, because of his knightly appearance and his imperturbable demeanour. As police chief, Kleigels was perhaps in the right place, but he was totally unfit to occupy such an important place as the governor-generalship of Kiev; and when the Emperor appointed him, all who had not given up the attempt to follow the course of events were greatly astonished.

In the Caucasus both the country districts and the towns were in full blaze, and all sorts of excesses were committed daily. The lieutenant, Count Vorontzov-Dashkov, tried to pursue a policy of conciliation, but all he actually put into practice was a perpetual interchange of liberal and reactionary measures. On the whole, the count, though not very intelligent, meant well and was endowed with common sense, but he failed principally on account of his inability to choose capable subordinates.

The whole of Siberia was in a terrible turmoil. This was due to the fact that this territory had been for a long time, as it still is, a reservoir for criminals, exiles and restless people generally. Furthermore, being nearer to the theatre of war, Siberia felt its shame more keenly, and having witnessed the traffic to and from the battlefields, was more deeply horrified at its disasters. Besides, here, too, the situation was aggravated by the presence of an inefficient governor-general. Kutaisov, who held the office and had his headquarters at Irkutsk, did not lack intelligence, but he was not a man of action and wasted his time in talking continually and to no purpose. It was said that he had been appointed merely to satisfy the wish of the Empress, Alexandra Fyodorovna, who, as a girl, while visiting her grandmother, Queen Victoria, had become acquainted with Kutaisov during the time that he was our military attaché in London. The administration's power in Siberia was also impaired by the frequent disputes between Kutaisov and Sukhotin, the Governor-General at Omsk, who was dependable, straightforward and clever, but somewhat irascible.

The border provinces were clearly taking advantage of the weakening of Central Russia to show their teeth. They began to retaliate for the age-long injustices which had been inflicted upon them and also for the measures which, although correct, outraged the national feeling of the peoples which we had conquered but not assimilated. They were ardently waiting for what appeared to them as their deliverance from the Russo-Mongolian yoke. For this situation we alone were to blame. . . .

A general feeling of profound discontent with the existing order was the most apparent symptom of the corruption with which the social and political life of Russia was infested. It was this feeling that united all the classes of the population. They all joined in a demand for radical political reforms, but the manner in which the different social groups visioned the longed-for changes varied with each class of people.

The upper classes, the nobility, were dissatisfied and impatient with the Government. They were not averse to the idea of limiting the Emperor's autocratic powers, but with a view to benefiting their own class. Their dream was an aristocratic constitutional monarchy. The merchants and captains of industry, the rich, looked forward to a constitutional monarchy of the burgeois type and dreamed of the leadership of capital and of a mighty race of Russian Rothschilds. The "intelligentzia," *i.e.,* members of various liberal professions, hoped for a constitutional monarchy, which was eventually to result in a bourgeois republic modelled upon the pattern of the French State. The students, not only in the universities, but in the advanced high school grades, recognized no law, —except the word of those who preached the most extreme revolutionary and anarchistic theories. Many of the officials in the various governmental bureaus were against the régime they served, for they were disgusted with the shameful system of corruption which had grown to such gigantic proportions during the reign of Nicholas II. The zemstvo and municipal workers had long before declared that safety lay in the adoption of a constitution. As for the workmen, they were concerned about filling their stomachs with more food than had been their wont. For this reason they revelled in all manner of socialistic schemes of state organization. They fell completely under the sway of the revolutionists and rendered assistance without stint wherever there was need of physical force.

Finally, the majority of the Russian people, the peasantry, were anxious to increase their land holdings and to do away with the unrestrained arbitrary actions on the part of the higher landed class and of the police throughout the extent of its hierarchy, from the lowest gendarme to the provincial governor. The peasant's dream was an autocratic Czar, but a people's Czar, pledged to carry out the principle proclaimed in the reign of Emperor Alexander II, to wit, the emancipation of the peasants with land in violation of the sacredness of property rights. The peasants were inclined to relish the idea of a constitutional monarchy and the socialistic principles as they were formulated by the labourite party, which party emphasized labour and the notion that labour alone, especially physical labour, is the foundation of all right. The peasants, too, were ready to resort to violence in order to obtain more land and, in general, to better their intolerable condition.

It is noteworthy that the nobility was willing to share the public pie with the middle class, but neither of these classes had a sufficiently keen eye to notice the appearance on the historical stage of a powerful rival, who was numerically superior to both and possessed the advantage of having nothing to lose. No sooner did this hitherto unnoticed class, the proletariat, approach the pie than it began to roar like a beast which stops at nothing to devour its prey. . . .

Anarchistic attacks directed against the lives of government officials; riots in all the institutions of higher learning and even in the secondary schools, which were accompanied by various excesses; trouble in the army; disturbances among peasants and workmen, involving destruction of property, personal injury and loss of life; and finally strikes,—such were the main conditions with which the authorities had to cope. On October 8, 1905, traffic on the railroads adjoining Moscow ceased completely. It took the railway strike but two days to spread to the Kharkov railroad junction, and on October 12th, the St. Petersburg junction was tied up. In the subsequent days traffic ceased on the remaining railroads. By October 17th, nearly the entire railway net and the telegraph were in a state of complete paralysis. About the same time almost all the factories and mills in the large industrial centres of Russia came to a stand-still. In St. Petersburg the strike in the factories and mills began on the 12th day of October, and on the 15th the business life of the capital was completely tied up.

Thus all these ills came to afflict the land at one and the same time and such terrible confusion resulted that one can truthfully say that Russia's soul cried out in agony. . . .

The manifesto [of October 17, 1905] was drawn up hastily and until the last moment I did not know whether His Majesty would sign it. Had it not been for Grand Duke Nikolai Nikolaievich, he would not perhaps have done it. It is noteworthy that immediately upon the promulgation of the manifesto the Grand Duke embraced the creed of the Black Hundreds. Prince A. D. Obolensky, one of the authors of the manifesto, was in a state of neurasthenia at the time when he took part in its composition. Several days after the publication of the act this earnest advocate of the manifesto declared to me that his participation in the movement for the manifesto had been the greatest sin of his life. In the days immediately preceding the publication of the manifesto, His Majesty conducted two parallel sets of conferences. I participated in one, Goremykin—in the other. This extreme duplicity at such a critical time greatly discouraged me.

As a matter of fact, I was rather opposed to the publication of a constitutional manifesto, and I gave much thought to the alternative plan of setting up a military dictatorship. The original text of the document was drafted against my will and behind my back. Seeing, however, that the high spheres were intent upon issuing the manifesto, I insisted that my own version of it should be adopted, if I was to be appointed Prime Minister.

The effect of the act of October 17th was in many respects salutary. Thus, for instance, the manifesto destroyed that unity of front which made the camp of the opposition so formidable. It sobered the country down, so that the voice of patriotism was heard in the land again, and the propertied people girt their loins and arose in defence of their possessions. But it also had its serious drawbacks. The manifesto came as a bolt from the blue. Most of the provincial authorities did not understand what happened, and many were clearly out of sympathy with the new course of policy. As the manifesto came unexpectedly, the regions which had already been in a state of tension were thrown into a fever by its sudden appearance. Violent outbreaks, both revolutionary and counter-revolutionary, took place all over the country, the reactionary manifestations involving, of course, pogroms. The latter were organized or, at least, encouraged by the local authorities. Thus the manifesto actually stimulated disorder. That was what I feared, and that was why I opposed the idea of issuing a manifesto. Furthermore, it laid the imprint of undue haste upon all the other acts of the Government.

I did not for a moment doubt the necessity of a parliamentary régime for the country. In those days even the conservatives advocated a constitution. In fact, there were no conservatives in Russia on the eve of October 17, 1905. The manifesto cut Russia's past from her present as with a knife. The historical operation was surely necessary, but it should have been performed with greater care and more precautions. Yet, I thank the Lord that the constitution has been granted.

It is far better that the past has been cut off, even though somewhat roughly and hurriedly, than if it had been slowly sawed off with a blunt saw wielded by a bungling surgeon.

Everybody understood that the act of October 17th marked an historical turning-point of great significance. The truly enlightened element, which had preserved its faith in the political decency of the ruling powers, perceived that the dream of several generations, to which, beginning with the Decembrists, so many noble lives were sacrificed, had come true. As for the embittered and the unbalanced, they felt that the chief representatives of the old order, above all the Monarch himself, should have gone into the scrapheap with the ancient régime. For did not Nicholas II actually ruin Russia and cast her off the pedestal on which she had stood? Many also suspected—and their suspicions proved eminently true—that the constitution had been granted by the Emperor in a fit of panic and that as soon as his position improved he would so manipulate the constitution as to annul it and turn it into a ghastly farce. . . .

IMPERIALISM

26. BENJAMIN DISRAELI: CRYSTAL PALACE SPEECH*

With the possible exception of Lord Palmerston, Benjamin Disraeli (1804–81) was the most outspoken exponent of imperialism among nineteenth-century British prime ministers. He defended the expansion of British authority in South Africa, Afghanistan, India, Egypt, and Cyprus. Critics of his ministry coined the term imperialism to describe Disraeli's policies, and the Prime Minister gladly accepted this label. In 1872, two years before his second ministry (1874–80), Disraeli outlined his concept of imperialism in a speech delivered at the Crystal Palace in London. According to Disraeli, why was the British Empire on the verge of dissolution in 1872? Was Disraeli sympathetic or unsympathetic to laissez faire liberalism? Why? What was Disraeli's attitude toward self-government in the colonies?

Gentlemen, there is another and second great object of the Tory party. If the first is to maintain the Institutions of the country, the second is, in my opinion, to uphold the Empire of England. If you look to the history of this country since the advent of Liberalism—forty years ago—you will find that there has been no effort so continuous, so subtle, supported by so much energy, and carried on with so much ability and acumen, as the attempts of Liberalism to effect the disintegration of the Empire of England.

And, gentlemen, of all its efforts, this is the one which has been the nearest to success. Statesmen of the highest character, writers of the most distinguished ability, the most organised and efficient means, have been employed in this endeavour. It has been proved to all of us that we have lost money by our colonies. It has been shown with precise, with mathematical demonstration, that there never was a jewel in the Crown of England that was so truly costly as the possession of India. How often has it been suggested that we should at once

* Benjamin Disraeli, *Selected Speeches of the Earl of Beaconsfield* (London: Longmans Green and Co., 1882), II, 529–31, 534–35.

emancipate ourselves from this incubus. Well, that result was nearly accomplished. When those subtle views were adopted by the country under the plausible plea of granting self-government to the Colonies, I confess that I myself thought that the tie was broken. Not that I for one object to self-government. I cannot conceive how our distant colonies can have their affairs administered except by self-government. But self-government, in my opinion, when it was conceded, ought to have been conceded as part of a great policy of Imperial consolidation. It ought to have been accompanied by an Imperial tariff, by securities for the people of England for the enjoyment of the unappropriated lands which belonged to the Sovereign as their trustee, and by a military code which should have precisely defined the means and the responsibilities by which the colonies should be defended, and by which, if necessary, this country should call for aid from the colonies themselves. It ought, further, to have been accompanied by the institution of some representative council in the metropolis, which would have brought the Colonies into constant and continuous relations with the Home Government. All this, however, was omitted because those who advised that policy—and I believe their convictions were sincere—looked upon the Colonies of England, looked upon our connection with India, as a burden upon this country, viewing everything in a financial aspect, and totally passing by those moral and political considerations which make nations great, and by the influence of which alone men are distinguished from animals.

Well, what has been the result of this attempt during the reign of Liberalism for the disintegration of the Empire? It has entirely failed. But how has it failed? Through the sympathy of the Colonies with the Mother Country. They have decided that the Empire shall not be destroyed, and in my opinion no minister in this country will do his duty who neglects any opportunity of reconstructing as much as possible our Colonial Empire, and of responding to those distant sympathies which may become the source of incalculable strength and happiness to this land. Therefore, gentlemen, with respect to the second great object of the Tory party also—the maintenance of the Empire—public opinion appears to be in favour of our principles—that public opinion which, I am bound to say, thirty years ago, was not favourable to our principles, and which, during a long interval of controversy, in the interval had been doubtful. . . . When you return to your counties and to your cities, you must tell to all those whom you can influence that the time is at hand, that, at least, it cannot be far distant, when England will have to decide between national and cosmopolitan principles. The issue is not a mean one. It is whether you will be content to be a comfortable England, modelled and moulded upon Continental principles and meeting in due course an inevitable fate, or whether you will be a great country,—an Imperial country—a country where your sons, when they rise, rise to paramount positions, and obtain not merely the esteem of their countrymen, but command the respect of the world.

Upon you depends the issue. Whatever may be the general feeling, you must remember that in fighting against Liberalism or the Continental system you are fighting against those who have the advantage of power—against those who have been in high places for nearly half a century. You have nothing to trust to but your own energy and the sublime instinct of an ancient people. You must act as if everything depended on your individual efforts. The secret of success is constancy of purpose. Go to your homes, and teach there these truths, which will soon be imprinted on the conscience of the land. Make each man feel how much rests on his own exertions. The highest, like my noble friend the chairman, may lend us his great aid. But rest assured that the assistance of the humblest is not less efficient. Act in this spirit, and you will succeed. You will maintain your country in its present position. But you will do more than that—you will deliver to your posterity a land of liberty, of prosperity, of power, and of glory.

27. RUDYARD KIPLING: THE WHITE MAN'S BURDEN*

Among the many complex and varied explanations for imperialism offered by apologists and critics was a modification of social Darwinian theory—the white man's burden. Rudyard Kipling (1865–1936), one of the most widely acclaimed British poets at the turn of the century, helped to mold the popular concept of imperialism in his *White Man's Burden* (1899). The son of a British civil servant in India, Kipling took the whole of the British Empire as his literary province. The garrisoned soldier was his hero, and the romantic and evangelical trappings of empire his perennial theme. According to Kipling, what was the "White Man's Burden"? How was it inescapable and noble and justified?

> Take up the White Man's burden—
>   Send forth the best ye breed—
> Go, bind your sons to exile
>   To serve your captives' need;
> To wait, in heavy harness,
>   On fluttered folk and wild—
> Your new-caught sullen peoples,
>   Half devil and half child.
>
> Take up the White Man's burden—
>   In patience to abide,
> To veil the threat of terror
>   And check the show of pride;
> By open speech and simple,
>   An hundred times made plain,
> To seek another's profit
>   And work another's gain.
>
> Take up the White Man's burden—
>   The savage wars of peace—
> Fill full the mouth of Famine,
>   And bid the sickness cease;
> And when your goal is nearest
>   (The end for others sought)
> Watch sloth and heathen folly
>   Bring all your hope to nought.

* Rudyard Kipling, "The White Man's Burden," *McClure's Magazine*, Vol. XII, No. 4 (February 1899), pp. 290–91.

Take up the White Man's burden—
 No iron rule of kings,
But toil of serf and sweeper—
 The tale of common things.
The ports ye shall not enter,
 The roads ye shall not tread,
Go, make them with your living
 And mark them with your dead.

Take up the White Man's burden,
 And reap his old reward—
The blame of those ye better
 The hate of those ye guard—
The cry of hosts ye humour
 (Ah, slowly!) toward the light:—
"Why brought ye us from bondage,
 Our loved Egyptian night?"

Take up the White Man's burden—
 Ye dare not stoop to less—
Nor call too loud on Freedom
 To cloke your weariness.
By all ye will or whisper,
 By all ye leave or do,
The silent sullen peoples
 Shall weigh your God and you.

Take up the White Man's burden!
 Have done with childish days—
The lightly-proffered laurel,
 The easy ungrudged praise:
Comes now, to search your manhood
 Through all the thankless years,
Cold, edged with dear-bought wisdom,
 The judgment of your peers.

28. J. A. HOBSON: IMPERIALISM*

Among the contemporary economists who sought to offer an analysis of imperialism, John A. Hobson (1858–1940) wrote a prodigious number of books and articles which carried his views to millions of readers. *Imperialism: A Study* (1902) became a classic expression of anti-imperialist thought. Hobson's interpretation has often been employed by historians as a basis for further analysis and as substance for rebuttal—a significant acknowledgment by present-day writers of Hobson's great insight into the nature of imperialism. Even the broody, con-

* John A. Hobson, *Imperialism: A Study* (London: A. Constable and Co., 1905), pp. 25, 42–43, 53–55, 216–18. Reprinted by permission.

trasting conclusions of Lenin are supported with generous quotations gleaned from Hobson.

According to Hobson, what were the motives behind imperialistic expansion? How did the terms rational and irrational apply to imperialism? What was the true "motor power" of imperialism, and how was it to be distinguished from the engine? How might Hobson be contrasted with Kipling on the question of native races?

The absorption of so large a proportion of public interest, energy, blood and money in seeking to procure colonial possessions and foreign markets would seem to indicate that Great Britain obtains her chief livelihood by external trade. Now this is not the case. Large as is our foreign and colonial trade in volume and in value, essential as is much of it to our national well-being, nevertheless it furnishes a small proportion of the total industry of the nation.

According to the conjectural estimate of the Board of Trade "the proportion of the total labour of the British working classes which is concerned with the production of commodities for export (including the making of the instruments of this production and their transport to the ports) is between one-fifth and one-sixth of the whole."

If we suppose the profits, salaries, etc., in connexion with export trade to be at the same level with those derived from home trade, we may conclude that between one-fifth and one-sixth of the income of the nation comes from the production and carriage of goods for export trade. . . .

Seeing that the Imperialism of the last three decades is clearly condemned as a business policy, in that at enormous expense it has procured a small, bad, unsafe increase of markets, and has jeopardised the entire wealth of the nation in rousing the strong resentment of other nations, we may ask, "How is the British nation induced to embark upon such unsound business?" The only possible answer is that the business interests of the nation as a whole are subordinated to those of certain sectional interests that usurp control of the national resources and use them for their private gain. This is no strange or monstrous charge to bring; it is the commonest disease of all forms of government. The famous words of Sir Thomas More are as true now as when he wrote them: "Everywhere do I perceive a certain conspiracy of rich men seeking their own advantage under the name and pretext of the commonwealth."

Although the new Imperialism has been bad business for the nation, it has been good business for certain classes and certain trades within the nation. The vast expenditure on armaments, the costly wars, the grave risks and embarrassments of foreign policy, the stoppage of political and social reforms within Great Britain, though fraught with great injury to the nation, have served well the present business interests of certain industries and professions.

It is idle to meddle with politics unless we clearly recognise this central fact and understand what these sectional interests are which are the enemies of national safety and the commonwealth. We must put aside the merely sentimental diagnosis which explains wars or other national blunders by outbursts of patriotic animosity or errors of statecraft. Doubtless at every outbreak of war not only the man in the street but the man at the helm is often duped by the cunning with which aggressive motives and greedy purposes dress themselves in defensive clothing. There is, it may be safety asserted, no war within memory, however nakedly aggressive it may seem to the dispassionate historian, which has not been presented to the people who were called upon to fight as a necessary defensive policy, in which the honour, perhaps the very existence, of the State was involved.

The disastrous folly of these wars, the material and moral damage inflicted even on the victor, appear so plain to the disinterested spectator that he is apt to despair of any State attaining years of discretion, and inclines to regard these natural cataclysms as implying some ultimate irrationalism in politics. But careful analysis of the existing relations between business and politics shows that the aggressive Imperialism which we seek to understand is not in the main the product of blind passions of races or of the mixed folly and ambition of politicians. It is far more rational than at first sight appears. Irrational from the standpoint of the whole nation, it is rational enough from the standpoint of certain classes in the nation. A completely socialist State which kept good books and presented regular balance-sheets of expenditure and assets would soon discard Imperialism; an intelligent *laissez-faire* democracy which gave duly proportionate weight in its policy to all economic interests alike would do the same. But a State in which certain well-organised business interests are able to outweigh the weak, diffused interest of the community is bound to pursue a policy which accords with the pressure of the former interests. . . .

In view of the part which the non-economic factors of patriotism, adventure, military enterprise, political ambition, and philanthropy play in imperial expansion, it may appear that to impute to financiers so much power is to take a too narrowly economic view of history. And it is true that the motor-power of Imperialism is not chiefly financial: finance is rather the governor of the imperial engine, directing the energy and determining its work: it does not constitute the fuel of the engine, nor does it directly generate the power. Finance manipulates the patriotic forces which politicians, soldiers, philanthropists, and traders generate; the enthusiasm for expansion which issues from these sources, though strong and genuine, is irregular and blind; the financial interest has those qualities of concentration and clear-sighted calculation which are needed to set Imperialism to work. An ambitious statesman, a frontier soldier, an overzealous missionary, a pushing trader, may suggest or even initiate a step of imperial expanson, may assist in educating patriotic public opinion to the urgent need of some fresh advance, but the final determination rests with the financial power. The direct influence exercised by great financial houses in "high politics" is supported by the control which they exercise over the body of public opinion through the Press, which, in every "civilised" country, is becoming more and more their obedient instrument. While the specifically financial newspaper imposes "facts" and "opinions" on the business classes, the general body of the Press comes more and more under the conscious or unconscious domination of financiers. . . .

Such is the array of distinctively economic forces making for Imperialism, a large loose group of trades and professions seeking profitable business and lucrative employment from the expansion of military and civil services, and from the expenditure on military operations, the opening up of new tracts of territory and trade with the same, and the provision of new capital which these operations require, all these finding their central guiding and directing force in the power of the general financier.

The play of these forces does not openly appear. They are essentially parasites upon patriotism, and they adapt themselves to its protecting colours. In the mouths of their representatives are noble phrases, expressive of their desire to extend the area of civilisation, to establish good government, promote Christianity, extirpate slavery, and elevate the lower races. Some of the business men who hold such language may entertain a genuine, though usually a vague, desire to accomplish these ends, but they are primarily engaged in business, and they are not unaware of the utility of the more unselfish forces in furthering their ends. Their true attitude of mind is expressed by Mr. Rhodes in his famous description of "Her Majesty's Flag" as "the greatest commercial asset in the world." . . .

The widest and ultimately the most important of the struggles in South Africa is that between the policy of Basutoland and that of Johannesburg and Rhodesia; for there, if anywhere, we lay our finger on the difference between a "sane" Imperialism, devoted to the protection, education, and self-development of a "lower race," and an "insane" Imperialism, which hands over these races to the economic exploitation of white colonists who will use them as "live tools" and their lands as repositories of mining or other profitable treasure.

It is impossible to ignore the fact that this "saner" Imperialism has been vitiated in its historic origins in almost every quarter of the globe. Early Imperialism had two main motives, the lust of "treasure" and the slave trade. . . .

Now modern Imperialism in its bearing on the "lower races" remains essentially of the same type: it employs other methods, other and humaner motives temper the dominance of economic greed, but analysis exposes the same character at bottom. Wherever white men of "superior races" have found able-bodied savages or lower races in possession of lands containing rich mineral or agricultural resources, they have, whenever strong enough, compelled the lower race to work for their benefit, either organizing their labour on their own land, or inducing them to work for an unequal barter, or else conveying them as slaves or servants to another country where their labour-power could be more profitably utilized. The use of imperial force to compel "lower races" to engage in trade is commonly a first stage of Imperialism; China is here the classic instance of modern times, exhibiting the sliding scale by which sporadic trade passes through "treaties," treaty ports, customs control, rights of inland trading, mining and railway concession, towards annexation and general exploitation of human and natural resources. . . .

29. V. I. LENIN: IMPERIALISM*

Nikolai Lenin (Vladimir Ilyich Ulyanov, 1870–1924), who founded the Communist régime in Russia, was an important economic theorist and interpreter of Marxist doctrine in his own right. Condemning the Russo-Japanese War (1904–5) and the other wars of the early twentieth century which culminated

* V. I. Lenin, "Imperialism, The Highest Stage of Capitalism," trans. Yuri Sdobnikov in George Hanna, ed., Collected Works (Moscow: Progress Publishers, 1964), XXII, 265–69, 298–300.

in the First World War, Lenin promulgated a doctrine of imperialism which he reconciled with Marxism. He published his analysis in *Imperialism: The Highest Stage of Capitalism* in 1916. Why did Lenin view imperialism as the highest stage of capitalism? Upon what interest groups did he place the responsibility for expanding colonialism?

We must now try to sum up, put together, what has been said above on the subject of imperialism. Imperialism emerged as the development and direct continuation of the fundamental characteristics of capitalism in general. But capitalism only became capitalist imperialism at a definite and very high stage of its development, when certain of its fundamental characteristics began to change into their opposites, when the features of the epoch of transition from capitalism to a higher social and economic system had taken shape and revealed themselves all along the line. Economically, the main thing in this process is the displacement of capitalist free competition by capitalist monopoly. Free competition is the fundamental characteristic of capitalism, and of commodity production generally; monopoly is the exact opposite of free competition, but we have seen the latter being transformed into monopoly before our eyes, creating large-scale industry and forcing out small industry, replacing large-scale by still larger-scale industry, and carrying concentration of production and capital to the point where out of it has grown and is growing monopoly: cartels, syndicates and trusts, and merging with them, the capital of a dozen or so banks, which manipulate thousands of millions. At the same time the monopolies, which have grown out of free competition, do not eliminate the latter, but exist over it and alongside of it, and thereby give rise to a number of very acute, intense antagonisms, frictions and conflicts. Monopoly is the transition from capitalism to a higher system.

If it were necessary to give the briefest possible definition of imperialism we should have to say that imperialism is the monopoly stage of capitalism. Such a definition would include what is most important, for, on the one hand, finance capital is the bank capital of a few very big monopolist banks, merged with the capital of the monopolist combines of industrialists; and, on the other hand, the division of the world is the transition from a colonial policy which has extended without hindrance to territories unseized by any capitalist power, to a colonial policy of monopolistic possession of the territory of the world which has been completely divided up.

But very brief definitions, although convenient, for they sum up the main points, are nevertheless inadequate, since very important features of the phenomenon that has to be defined have to be especially deduced. And so, without forgetting the conditional and relative value of all definitions in general, which can never embrace all the concatenations of a phenomenon in its complete development, we must give a definition of imperialism that will include the following five of its basic features: 1) the concentration of production and capital has developed to such a high stage that it has created monopolies which play a decisive role in economic life; 2) the merging of bank capital with industrial capital, and the creation, on the basis of this "finance capital," of a financial oligarchy; 3) the export of capital as distinguished from the export of commodities acquires exceptional importance; 4) the formation of international monopolist capitalist combines which share the world among themselves, and 5) the territorial division of the whole world among the biggest capitalist powers is completed. Imperialism is capitalism in that stage of development in which the dominance of monopolies and finance capital has established itself; in which the export of capital has acquired pronounced importance; in which the division of the world among the international trusts has begun; in which the division of all territories of the globe among the biggest capitalist powers has been completed.

We shall see later that imperialism can and must be defined differently if we bear in mind, not only the basic, purely economic concepts—to which the above definition is limited—but also the historical place of this stage of capitalism in relation to capitalism in general, or the relation between imperialism and the two main trends in the working-class movement. The point to be noted just now is that imperialism, as interpreted above, undoubtedly represents a special stage in the development of capitalism. . . .

. . . The characteristic feature of imperialism is *not* industrial *but* finance capital. It is not an accident that in France it was precisely the extraordinarily rapid development of *finance* capital, and the weakening of industrial capital, that, from the 'eighties onwards, gave rise to the extreme intensification of annexationist (colonial) policy. The characteristic feature of imperialism is precisely that it strives to annex *not only* agrarian territories, but even most highly industrialized regions (German appetite for Belgium; French appetite for Lorraine), because 1) the fact that the world is already divided up obliges those contemplating a *redivision* to reach out for *every kind* of territory, and 2) an essential feature of imperialism is the rivalry between several Great Powers in the striving for hegemony, *i.e.,* for the conquest of territory, not so much directly for themselves as to weaken the adversary and undermine *his* hegemony. (Belgium is particularly important for Germany as a base for operations against England; England needs Bagdad as a base for operations against Germany, etc.) . . .

We have seen that in its economic essence imperialism is monopoly capitalism. This in itself determines its place in history, for monopoly that grows out of the soil of free competition, and precisely out of free competition, is the transition from the capitalist system to a higher social-economic order. We must take special note of the four principal types of monopoly, or principal manifestations of monopoly capitalism, which are characteristic of the epoch we are examining.

Firstly, monopoly arose out of a very high stage of development of the concentration of production. This refers to the monopolist capitalist combines, cartels, syndicates and trusts. We have seen the important part these play in present-day economic life. At the beginning of the twentieth century, monopolies had acquired complete supremacy in the advanced countries, and although the first steps towards the formation of the cartels were first taken by countries enjoying the protection of high tariffs (Germany, America), Great Britain, with her system of free trade, revealed the same basic phenomenon, only a little later, namely, the birth of monopoly out of the concentration of production.

Secondly, monopolies have stimulated the seizure of the most important sources of raw materials, especially for the basic and most highly cartelized industries in capitalist society: the coal and iron industries. The monopoly of the most important sources of raw materials has enormously increased the power of big capital, and has sharpened the antagonism between cartelized and non-cartelized industry.

Thirdly, monopoly has sprung from the banks. The banks have developed from humble middlemen enterprises into the monopolists of finance capital. Some three to five of the biggest banks in each of the foremost capitalist countries have achieved the "personal union" of industrial and bank capital, and have concentrated in their hands the control of thousands upon thousands of millions which form the greater part of the capital and income of entire countries. A financial oligarchy, which throws a close network of dependence relationships over all the economic and political institutions of present-day bourgeois society without exception—such is the most striking manifestation of this monopoly.

Fourthly, monopoly has grown out of colonial policy. To the numerous "old" motives of colonial policy, finance capital has added the struggle for the sources of raw materials, for the export of capital, for "spheres of influence," *i.e.*, for spheres for profitable deals, concessions, monopolist profits and so on, and finally, for economic territory in general. When the colonies of the European powers in Africa, for instance, comprised only one-tenth of that territory (as was the case in 1876), colonial policy was able to develop by methods other than those of monopoly—by the "free grabbing" of territories, so to speak. But when nine-tenths of Africa had been seized (by 1900), when the whole world had been divided up, there was inevitably ushered in the era of monopoly ownership of colonies and, consequently, of particularly intense struggle for the division and the redivision of the world.

The extent to which monopolist capital has intensified all the contradictions of capitalism is generally known. It is sufficient to mention the high cost of living and the tyranny of the cartels. This intensification of contradictions constitutes the most powerful driving force of the transitional period of history, which began from the time of the final victory of world finance capital.

Monopolies, oligarchy, the striving for domination instead of striving for liberty, the exploitation of an increasing number of small or weak nations by a handful of the richest or most powerful nations—all these have given birth to those distinctive characteristics of imperialism which compel us to define it as parasitic or decaying capitalism. More and more prominently there emerges, as one of the tendencies of imperialism, the creation of the "rentier state," the usurer state, in which the bourgeoisie to an ever increasing degree lives on the proceeds of capital exports and by "clipping coupons." It would be a mistake to believe that this tendency to decay precludes the rapid growth of capitalism. It does not. In the epoch of imperialism, certain branches of industry, certain strata of the bourgeoisie and certain countries betray, to a greater or lesser degree, now one and now another of these tendencies. On the whole, capitalism is growing far more rapidly than before; but this growth is not only becoming more and more uneven in general, its unevenness also manifests itself, in particular, in the decay of the countries which are richest in capital (Britain). . . .

Chapter Seven

THE FIRST WORLD WAR

WITH a profound faith in science and the future of Western man, a proud and self-confident Europe entered the twentieth century. The power of Europe, the productive capacity of her industry, the scholarly output of her universities, the glamor of her empires, and the complacency of her cultured society stimulated a euphoria which masked the serious maladjustments in European life.

The balance of power, precariously maintained from the Congress of Vienna until the unifications of Germany and Italy, and artificially revived by Bismarck, had become a rigid structure which lacked flexibility. Prince von Bismarck, in his efforts to gain security for the new German Empire, had forged a system of alliances which confounded his successors and proved less permanent than the Iron Chancellor had hoped. The Triple Alliance of Germany, Austria-Hungary, and Italy which emerged from the Bismarckian era soon faced the threat of a Franco-Russian entente with Great Britain. Reappraising her diplomatic position, Italy cautiously mended her bridges to the entente powers. Germany was confronted by a competitive alliance grouping that presented an ominous challenge to her Bismarckian pre-eminence on the European Continent. Thus, the Triple Alliance (with Italy's allegiance somewhat tenuous) faced the Triple Entente of Great Britain, France, and Russia in 1907.

A series of international crises occurred after the turn of the century, heightening the general tension and encouraging an arms race among the major powers: the Russo-Japanese War in 1904–5, the first Morocco crisis in 1905, the Bosnian crisis in 1908, the Italo-Turkish War in 1911, the second Morocco crisis in 1911, and the Balkan Wars in 1912 and 1913. With all the great powers committed to alliance arrangements, Europe uncomfortably faced the prospect of general war for the first time since Napoleon.

Historians have debated the origins of World War I for decades, but they are far more united in an assessment of the causes behind the conflict than in the assignment of "guilt" for its outbreak. Nationalism, the system of entangling alliances, the arms race, the influence of military establishments, the overconfidence and insecurity, and the imperialist rivalries all played a role in causing the war. Nevertheless, the fatal crisis of 1914, provoked by the assassination of the heir to the Austro-Hungarian throne by a south-Slav nationalist, need not have meant war. The "guilt" for World War I has been variously fixed, and a final judgment is not likely to be made, since major statesmen of the great powers shared responsibility.

The great conflict which began on August 1, 1914, lasted for four years, far longer than most Europeans expected when it began. It was brutal, bloody, and destructive. Four years of wavering trench warfare in western Europe swallowed millions of lives and with them the *élan,* the confidence, the pride, and the optimism of nineteenth-century Europe. The seesaw battles of the eastern front, no less bloody, strained the resources of four huge empires and ultimately helped to produce revolutions in each of them.

The long-awaited revolution in Russia swept away tsarist authority quickly and without a struggle. In March 1917, strikers initiated the revolt in Petrograd. Tsar Nicholas II was at the front and refused at first to comprehend the seriousness of the situation. When he tried to take action the monarchy was already doomed. Unable to reach the capital, the Tsar abdicated and the Romanov dynasty collapsed. A Provisional Government, dominated at first by liberals, grasped at the shreds of bureaucratic power. The peasants, who were probably more impressed by the Socialist Revolutionaries than by the liberals, had only two thoughts—land and peace. Factory workers in the cities immediately formed *soviets* (workers' councils), which threatened the authority of the Provisional Government from the outset. In the months that followed, the Provisional Government lost strength. It failed to call a constituent assembly quickly, continued the war in the face of public clamor for peace, refused to sanction the seizure of land by peasants, and was unable to cope with mounting economic and political unrest. Allied diplomacy helped to weaken the Provisional Government by insisting on further Russian commitments to the war effort.

Meanwhile, the Germans were faced with a grim war on two fronts and the entrance of the United States of America into the conflict on the side of the Allies. They therefore facilitated the passage of Lenin from Switzerland to Russia in the hope that he would be able to destroy the Russian will to fight. Lenin, leader of the Bolshevik wing of the Russian Social Democrats, arrived in Russia in April 1917, and preached immediate withdrawal of Russia from the war. From April to November the fortunes of the Bolshevik party (the name of the party was soon changed to Communist) rose and fell, but Lenin finally galvanized the party leadership and, together with Leon Trotsky, secured the party's approval for a coup d'état. Trotsky captured control of the Petrograd Soviet and played a major role in the coup that followed. The Bolsheviks struck on November 7, 1917, overthrew the Provisional Government, and seized power in Petrograd. Within weeks they controlled a number of cities, but years of struggle and civil war delayed their final control of the vast Russian Empire until 1921.

Although Lenin pulled Russia out of World War I in January 1918, with the Treaty of Brest-Litovsk which he signed with the Central Powers, Germany was unable to turn the tide. American intervention secured a final Allied victory in the fall of 1918, and Germany signed an armistice on November 11. Her allies had already surrendered.

The triumphant victors not only achieved an end to the hostilities but also witnessed revolutions in Germany, Austria-Hungary, and Turkey as well as in

Russia. Austria-Hungary disintegrated into smaller national states. Poland was formed from parts of Russia, Germany, and Austria. Czechoslovakia emerged from Austria and Hungary. Rumania added new territory. Serbia absorbed the South-Slav territories of Austria-Hungary. Estonia, Latvia, Lithuania, and Finland secured their independence from a weak Russia. All of these successor states sought representation in the peace conference which assembled at Paris to redraw the map of Europe and to guarantee peace for the future.

The Paris Peace Conference was dominated by four men—the President of the United States (Woodrow Wilson) and the Prime Ministers of Great Britain, France, and Italy (David Lloyd George, Georges Clemenceau, and Vittorio Orlando). Since the Allies had formulated few definite peace plans during the war and were totally unprepared for the disintegration of the empires of eastern Europe, a monumental task of negotiation awaited them. Wilson had stated his general principles in the Fourteen Points and had urged the formation of a League of Nations. His allies had not completely accepted the Fourteen Points and were bound by their own special interests and secret treaties.

The Peace Conference labored with a growing mass of data assembled by diplomats, geographers, demographers, politicians, generals, and experts of all kinds. Several treaties emerged—the Treaty of Versailles with Germany, the Treaty of Saint-Germain with Austria, the Treaty of Trianon with Hungary, the Treaty of Neuilly with Bulgaria, and the Treaty of Sèvres with Turkey. Wilson's principle of self-determination, whereby a people had the right to determine the nation-state which it wished to join, was applied in many cases. But idealism did not dominate the Conference, and historical tradition, economic necessity, and need for security were as strong as President Woodrow Wilson's Fourteen Points.

Austria-Hungary had ceased to exist. Russia had withdrawn from Europe and was in the throes of civil strife. Germany was weakened and defeated. Thus, France was left as the pre-eminent continental power. To ensure her security and to construct a system for the preservation of her hegemony, France concluded a series of alliances with many of the new states of eastern Europe after the Peace Conference adjourned. The First World War, however, did more than destroy boundaries and rearrange nationalities. It heralded the end of an age. The nineteenth century—optimism, power, world empires, faith in science—died on the battle fields. Even Wilsonian idealism seemed checkmated by the dark evils of man's nature and, though the American President succeeded in establishing a new hope for mankind in the League of Nations, he was denied the essence of his victory. The United States Senate refused to ratify American participation in the League. Europe, bleeding and gasping in its great war, had found peace through American intervention, a sign indicating that the end of Europe's dominion over the world was at hand.

REALPOLITIK—THE SYSTEM OF ALLIANCES

1. THE TRIPLE ALLIANCE*

Prince von Bismarck sought to guarantee the security of the German Empire after the defeat of France in 1871 and to provide a stability in Europe which would assure the preservation of German power. For these purposes, he constructed a delicate series of alliances based upon the isolation of France and German mediation of Austro-Russian conflicts in the Balkans. The Three Emperors' League, beginning in 1872, brought Austria-Hungary, Germany, and Russia into a mutual pact which might have prevented a great clash in the Balkans. When the strain on that rather loose arrangement proved too great during the Russo-Turkish War (1877–78), a defensive alliance was negotiated with Austria-Hungary to checkmate any future Russian aggression. In 1882 Italy joined Germany and Austria, signing the treaty of the Triple Alliance which superseded but did not replace the Dual Alliance. French expansion in Tunis threatened to block Italian imperialism in North Africa and had prompted the Italian government to seek Germany's support.

Although the Triple Alliance remained in force until 1915, Italy remained a hesitating ally of Germany, and continued to seek a *modus vivendi* with France. Under what conditions were the contracting powers obligated to go to war on one another's behalf? Was the Triple Alliance essentially offensive or defensive?

Their Majesties the Emperor of Austria, King of Bohemia, *etc.*, and Apostolic King of Hungary, the Emperor of Germany, King of Prussia, and the King of Italy, animated by the desire to increase the guaranties of the general peace, to fortify the monarchical principle and thereby to assure the unimpaired maintenance of the social and political order in Their respective States, have agreed to conclude a Treaty which, by its essentially conservative and defensive nature, pursues only the aim of forestalling the dangers which might threaten the security of Their States and the peace of Europe. . . .

ARTICLE I. The High Contracting Parties mutually promise peace and friendship, and will enter into no alliance or engagement directed against any one of Their States.

They engage to proceed to an exchange of ideas on political and economic questions of a general nature which may arise, and they further promise one another mutual support within the limits of their own interests.

ARTICLE II. In case Italy, without direct provocation on her part, should be attacked by France for any reason whatsoever, the two other Contracting Parties shall be bound to lend help and assistance with all their forces to the Party attacked.

This same obligation shall devolve upon Italy in case of any aggression without direct provocation by France against Germany.

* "First Treaty of Alliance. Austria, Germany, and Italy. May 20, 1882" in George B. Manhart, *Alliance and Entente, 1871–1914* (New York: F. S. Crofts and Co., 1932), pp. 15–16. Reprinted by permission.

ARTICLE III. If one, or two, of the High Contracting Parties, without direct provocation on their part, should chance to be attacked and to be engaged in a war with two or more Great Powers nonsignatory to the present Treaty, the *casus foederis* will arise simultaneously for all the High Contracting Parties.

ARTICLE IV. In case a Great Power nonsignatory to the present Treaty should threaten the security of the states of one of the High Contracting Parties, and the threatened Party should find itself forced on that account to make war against it, the two others bind themselves to observe towards their Ally a benevolent neutrality. Each of them reserves to itself, in this case, the right to take part in the war, if it should see fit, to make common cause with its Ally. . . .

ARTICLE VI. The High Contracting Parties mutually promise secrecy as to the contents and existence of the Present Treaty. . . .

2. THE ENTENTE CORDIALE*

Following the resignation of Prince von Bismarck in 1890, the German government did not renew its Reinsurance Treaty with Russia. Cut adrift by the German action, Russia negotiated a defensive alliance with France, which came into effect in 1894. Thus, two alliance camps faced one another— the Triple Alliance versus the Franco-Russian alliance. For a number of years Great Britain continued in isolation, finally concluding a treaty with Japan in 1902 by which the two countries recognized their mutual interests. Continuing to feel insecure in her policy of isolation in Europe, Britain concluded the *Entente Cordiale* with France in 1904. Was the *Entente Cordiale* a firm military commitment like the Triple Alliance? What specific Anglo-French differences was the Entente designed to resolve? Why did the Germans claim that the *Entente Cordiale* completed the "encirclement" of Germany?

ARTICLE I. His Britannic Majesty's Government declare that they have no intention of altering the political status of Egypt.

The Government of the French Republic, for their part, declare that they will not obstruct the action of Great Britain in that country by asking that a limit of time be fixed for the British occupation or in any other manner. . . .

It is agreed that the post of Director-General of Antiquities in Egypt shall continue, as in the past, to be entrusted to a French *savant*.

The French schools in Egypt shall continue to enjoy the same liberty as in the past.

ARTICLE II. The Government of the French Republic declare that they have no intention of altering the political status of Morocco.

His Britannic Majesty's Government, for their part, recognise that it appertains to France, more particularly as a Power whose dominions are conterminous for a great distance with those of Morocco, to preserve order in that country, and to provide assistance for the purpose of all administrative, economic, financial, and military reforms which it may require.

They declare that they will not obstruct the action taken by France for this purpose, provided that such action shall leave intact the rights which Great

---

* "Declaration between the United Kingdom and France Respecting Egypt and Morocco. April 8, 1904" in George B. Manhart, *Alliance and Entente, 1871–1914* (New York: F. S. Crofts and Co., 1932), pp. 38–39. Reprinted by permission.

Britain, in virtue of Treaties, Conventions, and usage, enjoys in Morocco, including the right of coasting trade between the ports of Morocco, enjoyed by British vessels since 1901.

ARTICLE III. His Britannic Majesty's Government, for their part, will respect the rights which France, in virtue of Treaties, Conventions, and usage, enjoys in Egypt, including the right of coasting trade between Egyptian ports accorded to French vessels.

ARTICLE IV. The two Governments, being equally attached to the principle of commercial liberty both in Egypt and Morocco, declare that they will not, in those countries, countenance any inequality either in the imposition of customs duties or other taxes, or of railway transport charges . . .

Nevertheless, the Government of the French Republic reserve to themselves in Morocco, and his Britannic Majesty's Government reserve to themselves in Egypt, the right to see that the concessions for roads, railways, ports, etc., are only granted on such conditions as will maintain intact the authority of the State over these great undertakings of public interest. . . .

3. WINSTON CHURCHILL: GLASGOW SPEECH ON THE GERMAN FLEET*

Kaiser Wilhelm II and his Minister of Marine, Alfred von Tirpitz, were among the world leaders impressed by Admiral Alfred Mahan's book on *The Influence of Sea Power on History*. Believing that Germany's new imperial interests, continental power, prestige, and future greatness required a high-seas fleet, the Kaiser and Tirpitz undertook an ambitious program of naval construction. Although Tirpitz insisted that a powerful German fleet would render the British more docile and friendly, the British reaction was to build more ships and thus guarantee British naval supremacy. By 1906 Great Britain and Germany were locked in a naval race which was aggravated by the Kaiser's personal attitude, a belligerent press in both countries, and the requirements of national chauvinism.

Prime Minister Asquith's Liberal government, already pressed to pay for new social legislation and embroiled in a struggle to revise the constitutional position of the House of Lords, was forced to order six additional battleships of the dreadnought class for 1909. Winston Churchill, who became First Lord of the Admiralty in October 1911, vociferously supported the British naval program. Provoked by the Agadir crisis, when the Germans reopened the Morocco question, Churchill delivered a speech at Glasgow on the state of the British fleet. The speech was also intended for German ears, and the reported response of Kaiser Wilhelm was that Churchill's words demonstrated an "arrogance demanding of an apology." What truth was there in the Kaiser's allegation? On what grounds did Churchill claim that Britain's fleet was a necessity while the German navy was a luxury?

. . . I can give you a very good account of the British Navy. In ships, it is possible to watch every other type of ship in the world and show a clear superiority ship for ship. The relative numbers can be computed from the public returns. In guns, I think, there is no doubt that we possess in the latest 13.5 one

*Winston Churchill, "Supremacy of the Navy," in *The Times* (London), February 10, 1912, pp. 9–10. Reprinted by permission.

of the finest weapons that the British Navy ever possessed. . . . The rumors which have filled some of the newspapers during the last two months that the Navy was last year unprepared are absolutely baseless, and we hope that the creation of a Naval War Staff will tend to render the propagation of such rumors absolutely impossible in the future. (*Cheers.*) . . .

You all realise, but it is our duty to affirm, that the purposes of British Naval power are essentially defensive. (*Cheers.*) We have no thoughts, and we have never had any thoughts, of aggression—and we attribute no such thoughts to other Great Powers. There is, however, this difference between the British naval power and the naval power of the great and friendly Empire—and I trust it may long remain the great and friendly empire—of Germany. The British Navy is to us a necessity and, from some points of view, the German Navy is to them more in the nature of a luxury. Our naval power involves British existence. It is existence to us; it is expansion to them. We cannot menace the peace of a single Continental hamlet, nor do we wish to do so no matter how great and supreme our Navy may become. But, on the other hand, the whole fortunes of our race and Empire, the whole treasure accumulated during so many centuries of sacrifice and achievement would perish and be swept utterly away if our naval supremacy were to be impaired.

It is the British Navy which makes Great Britain a Great Power. But Germay was a Great Power, respected and honored all over the world, before she had a single ship.

Those facts ought clearly to be stated because there is no doubt that there is a disposition in some quarters to suppose that Great Britain and Germany are on terms of equality so far as naval risks are concerned. Such a supposition is utterly untrue. (*Cheers.*) The Government is resolved to maintain the naval supremacy which this country enjoys. . . .

We now see, so far as public prints inform us, that there are prospects of further naval increases among the Powers of the European Continent, and that is a very serious matter, because, not only are navies increasing in size, but everything connected with navies is increasing in cost. Ships are getting larger, longer and broader. Appliances with which they are provided are becoming every day more complicated and more expensive. The means of repairing these ships require every day more elaborate and more costly machinery. The accommodation for docking these vessels involves every year a provision of docks on a scale and of dimensions not hitherto foreseen. The size of the guns increases the size of the ammunition and the expense both of armament and ammunition. The increasing horsepower of the new vessels now being added to the fleets means a greater consumption of coal and oil. Altogether there is no doubt that the nations of Europe are at the present time pressing forward, and pressing each other forward, into an avenue of almost indefinite naval expansion and expense. (*Hear Hear.*) We may have our own opinion as to how far future generations will compliment the present age upon the wisdom, the Christianity, and the civilization which have made that sterile and dangerous competition so large a feature of our lives. . . .

There is no chance whatever of our being overtaken in naval strength unless we want to be. We think that we can build as well and as good ships as any other constructors in the world. I could put it higher, but, as Dr. Pangloss observes, ". . . on their own merits modest men are dumb." (*Laughter and cheers.*) But we know, whatever may be said about quality, that we can build as fast, and faster, cheaper, and on a far larger scale than any other Power in the world. (*Cheers.*)...

4. ALFRED VON SCHLIEFFEN: MEMORANDUM ON A WAR WITH FRANCE AND RUSSIA*

All of the great powers had war plans, prepared by their general staffs, for use in the event of an outbreak of hostilities. These plans were prepared with specific reference to possible enemies and incorporated as wide a knowledge of the prospective enemy's strength and disposition as was available. The military planners, concerned that their strategic observations be accepted by civilian authorities, often pressed for official recognition of the necessity of relating diplomatic policy to war plans. Thus, military leaders sought to influence government policy.

The German war plan, usually known as the Schlieffen Plan, was widely criticized during and after World War I for its rigid insistence on an attack upon France through Belgium if war seemed unavoidable. Rather than attack Russia, France's ally, the German Chief of Staff, Count Alfred von Schlieffen (1833–1913), proposed to destroy the French first. His recommendations, modified by his successors after his retirement in 1905, greatly influenced Germany's decision to declare war on France after Russia began to mobilize in the fatal last days of July 1914. The plan itself was a bold gamble, and its importance lay partly in the momentum which it gave to German diplomacy in the final crisis which led to war. The following selection is an excerpt from Field Marshal Count von Schlieffen's memorandum of December 28, 1912, which embodied his final recommendations just before his death in 1913. How did Schlieffen's memorandum reveal the fears generated by the legacy of the Bismarckian alliance system and by the role of a united Germany in the European balance of power? Why did Schlieffen insist upon a violation of Belgian neutrality?

The Triple Alliance developed out of an alliance between Germany and Austria-Hungary. Both Powers felt threatened by Russia: [Austria due to serious political differences which could easily have led to a war, Germany because of personal irritations which might nevertheless soon have given way to traditional friendship again, had they not been aggravated by the signing of a treaty with Russia's enemy.] The alliance was conceived defensively, but in case of war was to be carried into effect offensively.

At that time the Russian army was distributed throughout the vast expanse of the empire, and the Russian railway system was altogether inadequate. Therefore in the first stages of a war it would only have been possible to assemble a part of the army in Poland right of the Vistula. Against this part the allies intended to advance from north and south in order to crush the enemy in the middle of the country.

While the two allies were still enjoying this pleasant prospect, rumours got about that Russia was pulling her corps stationed in the East westwards and preparing to assemble an army on the Niemen, on the Germans' left flank, and

* Gerhard Ritter, *The Schlieffen Plan: Critique of a Myth,* trans. Andrew and Eva Wilson (New York: Praeger, 1958), pp. 169–73, 176. Reprinted by permission.

on the eastern frontier of Galicia, the Austrians' right flank. Austria intended to clear her flank first and postpone the offensive into Poland until this was done. Unless Germany were prepared to invade Poland alone, she had no choice but to follow her ally's example. Thus two quite separate prospective theatres of war were created: one in Eastern Galicia, the other in East Prussia, each with its adjoining Russian provinces.

Austria, with only the smaller part of the Russian army against her, had a relatively easy task. She would always have forces to spare for the pursuit of her aims in the Balkan peninsula. Germany faced not only the greater part of the Russian army but also, as became soon apparent, the French army.

This disproportion might have been rectified by Italy, which had joined the Alliance. Indeed, in the hope of regaining Nice and Savoy, the latter was intending to cross the Alps and to invade central and southern France, thereby relieving Germany of a great part of the French army. The plan had to be abandoned when France fortified all the Alpine passes. But in order to take part in the expected Franco-German war, Italy was to bring some corps over the Austrian and south German railways to the Upper Rhine, where she would unite with Germany in a common campaign. This plan also was eventually abandoned, because it was thought dangerous to send a large part of the army abroad when the French could cross the Alps and invade the Po valley.

So Italy left the Triple Alliance, at least as a working member. Austria kept far away in a separate theatre. [Germany meanwhile faced the greater part of the Russian, and the whole of the French army, without any support.]

If both her enemies were to advance from east and west, Germany would certainly find herself in a serious situation. But neither dared take the decisive step. Each feared the other would let her down or come too late, and that she alone would be saddled with the whole German army. Secure behind fortresses, rivers, mountains and swamps, both were lying in wait for their unprotected weaker adversary who was entirely on his own.

So it was not the Triple Alliance, but solely the German army which held Russia and France in check, preventing the former from giving Austria, and the latter Italy, a taste of her superiority. Peace was kept in Europe. It mattered little that Italy, prevented by the French Alpine fortifications from attacking France, tried to vent her expansionist desires on Austria. When the Austrians, too, fortified their Alpine passes, the Italians were forced to give up their lust for conquest here as well.

The power and prestige of the German army proved their worth in 1905 and 1909. Neither France nor Russia was willing to take up arms once Germany left no doubt about her determination to fight back. This favourable state of affairs underwent a change in 1911. German resolution was paralysed by England's threat to come to the assistance of France with 100,000 men. In 1911 England would have yielded before Germany's manifest intention of using the army if necessary, as France had done in 1905 and Russia in 1909. But on this occasion it was Germany who yielded, and so the spell was broken which had so far made her army seem invincible. Nor could the lost prestige be restored by the army reform of 1912, which brought little more than changes in organisation—none in power. This time it was not Germany's promise to stand by her Austrian allies which secured peace, but only England's wish, for economic reasons, to avoid a world war.

It is to be hoped that England's will may not for ever be decisive, and that Germany will one day regain the position of power necessary to her economic prosperity. Without a war this will scarcely be possible. How it will come about remains to be seen. How it is to be conducted must be left to Germany. She has done her duty as a member of the Triple Alliance by making an enemy of Russia, from whom she was not divided by any conflicting interests—and off whom she could have won nothing worth while—and by drawing upon herself the greater part of the Russian army. As a result she stands between two powerful enemies. . . .

[THE PLAN OF ATTACK]

The *whole* of Germany must throw itself on *one* enemy—the strongest, most powerful, most dangerous enemy: and that can only be the Anglo-French!

Austria need not worry: the Russian army intended against Germany will not invade Galicia before the die is cast in the West. And Austria's fate will be decided not on the Bug but on the Seine!

Against Germany, the French intend to hold a position extending from the frontier at Belfort along the Upper Moselle as far as Toul, from there following the course of the Meuse to Verdun and leaning on neutral Belgian territory as far as the neighbourhood of Montmédy. In front of this position they will further occupy the passes across the Vosges, the fortified city of Nancy, Manonvillers, the heights right of the Meuse between Toul and Verdun, and also Longwy. Should the Germans succeed in breaking through the left wing of this position, they will still find the enemy behind the Meuse between Verdun and Mézières. Below the latter the river is not easily accessible. The first important crossing, farther north, is blocked by the fortress of Givet. The Germans cannot therefore count on crossing the Meuse without serious fighting so long as it runs through French territory. Beyond the Givet the rivers enter Belgium. This country is regarded as neutral, but in fact it is not. More than thirty years ago it made Liège and Namur into strong fortresses to prevent Germany from invading its territory, but towards France it has left its frontiers open. The French will therefore be free to send as many reinforcements as they wish into the position which the Belgians apparently intend to occupy between these two fortresses. The English may also be present. In 1911 they threatened to land with 180,000 men in Antwerp. On its landward side the latter is heavily fortified. It is unlikely that the Dutch will bring their Scheldt batteries into action against the English, upon whose goodwill they depend for their colonies. Therefore via Antwerp, or if need be Dunkirk, the English can join up with the Belgians and French in the position Liège–Namur. From there the three, or two, of them will be able not only to prevent the Germans crossing the Meuse between Givet and Liège, but also most effectively to flank a German attack on the French position Belfort–Mézières.

Unless, therefore, the Germans are prepared to suffer a serious defeat, they are obliged to attack the offensive flank which the Belgians have added to the French position. This can be done if at an early stage a German army crosses

the Meuse below Liège, wheels left and invades Belgium and France left of the
Meuse and Sambre, while a second army supports the attack between Givet and
[Namur on] the right of those rivers, a third advances on the sector Mézières–
Verdun, and a fourth advances on the front Verdun–Belfort. . . .

A successful march through Belgium on both sides of the Meuse is therefore
the prerequisite of a victory. It will succeed beyond doubt, if it is only the
Belgian army which tries to obstruct it. But it will be very difficult if the
English army, and perhaps even part of the French, is present. The area between Namur and Antwerp is so confined that it can easily be blocked by the
English and Belgian corps, supported if necessary by a few French corps. In
this case, the advance of the second army on the right of the Sambre must create
a breathing space. If they, too, find the Meuse blocked between Namur and
Mézières, help can come only from an attack on the whole front, with a break-
through at some point after large-scale heavy artillery preparation.

But in general we must put our trust in an overwhelming right wing, which
will progressively bring the whole line forward. When the latter reaches the
approximate level Abbeville, St. Quentin, Rethel–Verdun, the French will
slowly evacuate the position Verdun–Toul, Toul–Epinal, etc. Their general
retreat will first be towards the position Rheims–La Fère, then towards Paris.
The first, second and third German armies, joined by the released corps with
strong cavalry on their wings, will follow in a wide arc with the intention of
completely encircling the greatest possible part of the enemy army.

For the occupation of the conquered territory and the covering of the lines
of communication, the Landwehr and Ersatz troops will not be sufficient. The
Landsturm must be mobilised. . . .

THE GREAT WAR

5. COMMUNICATIONS BETWEEN BERLIN, ST. PETERSBURG, AND PARIS ON THE EVE OF WAR*

The assassination of the Archduke Franz Ferdinand, heir to the Austro-
Hungarian thrones, and his wife on June 28, 1914, shocked the courts of Europe.
The Austrian Foreign Minister, Count Leopold Berchtold, believed that the
assassination, perpetrated by a Bosnian student of Serbian extraction, was a
threat to the continued existence of the harried Dual Monarchy. Berchtold
argued that Austria-Hungary could be saved from disintegration only by quick
action that would prove the monarchy's vitality and defeat Serbian nationalistic
ambitions. After receiving a "blank check" from Germany on July 6—indicating
Berlin's support of the Austro-Hungarian position—Berchtold sent Serbia an
ultimatum on July 23. Serbia had twenty-four hours to reply, and when Belgrade
rejected two of the Austrian demands the Dual Monarchy declared war on
July 28.

* "The German White Book" in *Collected Diplomatic Documents Relating to the Outbreak of
the European War* (London: His Majesty's Stationery Office, 1915), pp. 431–34. Reprinted by
permission.

Austrian actions moved the military party in St. Petersburg to press for immediate Russian assistance to the Serbs, and the Tsar authorized mobilization in the southern districts of Russia. Although it was clear that a general mobilization probably meant a European war would follow, Tsar Nicholas II was too weak to withstand the entreaties of his military advisers. Without consulting his French allies, Nicholas took the fatal step on July 31. The German government reacted immediately by demanding cessation of Russia's mobilization within twelve hours, and when the time limit expired without an answer the two nations went to war.

The following selections are eleventh-hour telegrams between Kaiser Wilhelm II and Tsar Nicholas II and between the German Chancellor and his ambassadors in St. Petersburg and Paris. What arguments did the Kaiser use to justify Germany's support of Austrian actions against Serbia? What was the Tsar's response? On what grounds did Wilhelm II issue the following warning to his cousin Nicholas II: "You have to bear the responsibility for war or peace"? At what point was it inevitable that the Schlieffen Plan would be put into practice?

HIS MAJESTY TO THE TSAR

July 28th, 10.45 p.m.

I have heard with the greatest anxiety of the impression which is caused by the action of Austria-Hungary against Servia. The inscrupulous agitation which has been going on for years in Servia, has led to the revolting crime of which Archduke Franz Ferdinand has become a victim. The spirit which made the Servians murder their own King and his consort still dominates that country. Doubtless You will agree with me that both of us, You as well as I, and all other sovereigns, have a common interest to insist that all those who are responsible for this horrible murder shall suffer their deserved punishment.

On the other hand I by no means overlook the difficulty encountered by You and Your Government to stem the tide of public opinion. In view of the cordial friendship which has joined us both for a long time with firm ties, I shall use my entire influence to induce Austria-Hungary to obtain a frank and satisfactory understanding with Russia. I hope confidently that You will support me in my efforts to overcome all difficulties which may yet arise.

Your most sincere and devoted friend and cousin

(*Signed*)   WILHELM.

THE TSAR TO HIS MAJESTY

Peterhof Palace, July 29th, 1 p.m.

I am glad that You are back in Germany. In this serious moment I ask You earnestly to help me. An ignominious war has been declared against a weak country and in Russia the indignation which I fully share is tremendous. I fear that very soon I shall be unable to resist the pressure exercised upon me and that I shall be forced to take measures which will lead to war. To prevent a calamity as a European war would be, I urge You in the name of our old friendship to do all in Your power to restrain Your ally from going too far.

(*Signed*)   NICOLAS.

HIS MAJESTY TO THE TSAR

July 29th, 6.30 p.m.

I have received Your telegram and I share Your desire for the conservation of peace. However: I cannot—as I told You in my first telegram—consider the action of Austria-Hungary as an "ignominious war." Austria-Hungary knows from experience that the promises of Servia as long as they are merely on paper are entirely unreliable.

According to my opinion the action of Austria-Hungary is to be considered as an attempt to receive full guaranty that the promises of Servia are effectively translated into deeds. In this opinion I am strengthened by the explanation of the Austrian Cabinet that Austria-Hungary intended no territorial gain at the expense of Servia. I am therefore of opinion that it is perfectly possible for Russia to remain a spectator in the Austro-Servian war without drawing Europe into the most terrible war it has ever seen. I believe that a direct understanding is possible and desirable between Your Government and Vienna, an understanding which—as I have already telegraphed You—my Government endeavours to aid with all possible effort. Naturally military measures by Russia, which might be construed as a menace by Austria-Hungary, would accelerate a calamity which both of us desire to avoid and would undermine my position as mediator which—upon Your appeal to my friendship and aid—I willingly accepted.

(*Signed*)   WILHELM.

HIS MAJESTY TO THE TSAR

July 30th, 1 a.m.

My Ambassador has instructions to direct the attention of Your Government to the dangers and serious consequences of a mobilisation. I have told You the same in my last telegram. Austria-Hungary has mobilised only against Servia, and only a part of her army. If Russia, as seems to be the case, according to Your advice and that of Your Government, mobilises against Austria-Hungary, the part of the mediator with which You have entrusted me in such friendly manner and which I have accepted upon Your express desire, is threatened if not made impossible. The entire weight of decision now rests upon Your shoulders, You have to bear the responsibility for war or peace.

(*Signed*)   WILHELM.

THE TSAR TO HIS MAJESTY

Peterhof, July 30th, 1914, 1.20 p.m.

I thank You from my heart for Your quick reply. I am sending to-night Tatisheff (Russian honorary aide to the Kaiser) with instructions. The military measures now taking form were decided upon five days ago, and for the reason of defence against the preparations of Austria. I hope with all my heart that these measures will not influence in any manner Your position as mediator which I appraise very highly. We need Your strong pressure upon Austria so that an understanding can be arrived at with us.

NICOLAS.

TELEGRAM OF THE CHANCELLOR TO THE IMPERIAL AMBASSADOR AT
ST. PETERSBURG ON JULY 31ST, 1914. URGENT

In spite of negotiations still pending and although we have up to this hour made no preparations for mobilisation, Russia has mobilised her *entire* army and navy, hence also against us. On account of these Russian measures, we have been forced, for the safety of the country, to proclaim the threatening state of war, which does not yet imply mobilisation. Mobilisation, however, is bound to follow if Russia does not stop every measure of war against us and against Austria-Hungary within 12 hours, and notifies us definitely to this effect. Please to communicate this at once to M. Sasonof and wire hour of communication.

TELEGRAM OF THE CHANCELLOR TO THE IMPERIAL AMBASSADOR IN
PARIS ON JULY 31ST, 1914. URGENT

Russia has ordered mobilisation of her entire army and fleet, therefore also against us in spite of our still pending mediation. We have therefore declared the threatening state of war which is bound to be followed by mobilisation unless Russia stops within 12 hours all measures of war against us and Austria. Mobilisation inevitably implies war. Please ask French Government whether it intends to remain neutral in a Russo-German war. Reply must be made in 18 hours. Wire at once hour of inquiry. Utmost speed necessary.

TELEGRAM OF THE IMPERIAL AMBASSADOR IN PARIS TO THE
CHANCELLOR ON AUGUST 1ST, 1.05 P.M.

Upon my repeated definite inquiry whether France would remain neutral in the event of a Russo-German war, the Prime Minister declared that France would do that which her interests dictated.

6. WORLD WAR I—THE HUMAN PRICE*

From a military standpoint the First World War in western Europe took on the character of a gigantic siege operation. The failure of the Schlieffen Plan to achieve a quick victory over France forced German armies to halt north of Paris, and because Anglo-French forces were unable to break through the German lines a military stalemate resulted. By the fall of 1914, from Switzerland to the English Channel, the war on the western front had settled down to semi-static trench warfare dominated by the spade, barbed wire, and the machine gun. For four years the armies of the belligerent powers attempted numerous mass offensives, exhausting their manpower in vain hopes for a breakthrough and ultimate victory. By 1917 both sides were bled white after fruitless assaults which gained scant yards of terrain. No single engagement was more destructive of human life than the six-month struggle for the French city of Verdun of 1916. What effect did the technological developments of warfare, with the capacity for such wholesale slaughter, have upon the psychology of citizen soldiers?

* Charles F. Horne, ed., *Source Records of the Great War* (7 vols. [New York:] National Alumni, 1923), IV, 221–28.

ACCOUNT OF THE ATTACKS ON LE MORT HOMME FROM MAY 20TH TO 24TH [1916]

Nothing that the manuals say, nothing that the technicians have foreseen, is true to-day. . . . The German bombardments outdid all previsions.

When my battalion was called up as re-enforcements on May 20th, the dugouts and trenches of the first French line were already completely destroyed. The curtain fire of the Germans, which had succeeded their bombardment of the front lines, fell on the road more than two kilometers behind these. Now and then the heavy long-distance guns of the Germans lengthened their fire in an attempt to reach our batteries and their communications. At eight o'clock in the evening, when we arrived in auto-buses behind the second or third lines, several shells reached our wagons, and killed men. . . . I have read a good many stories of battle, and some of their embroideries appear to me rather exaggerated; the truth is quite good enough by itself. . . . The cannonade worked on the ears and the nerves, getting louder with every step nearer the front, till the very earth shook and our hearts jumped in our breasts.

Where we were there were hardly any trenches or communication trenches left. Every half-hour the appearance of the earth was changed by the unflagging shell fire. It was a perfect cataract of fire. We went forward by fits and starts, taking cover in shell-holes, and sometimes we saw a shell drop in the very hole we had chosen for our next leap forwards. A hundred men of the battalion were half buried, and we had scarcely the time to stop and help them to get themselves out. Suddenly we arrived at what remained of our first-line trenches, just as the Boches arrived at our barbed wire entanglements—or, rather, at the caterpillar-like remains of our barbed wire.

At this moment the German curtain fire lengthened, and most of our men buried in shell-holes were able to get out and rejoin us. The Germans attacked in massed formation, by big columns of five or six hundred men, preceded by two waves of sharpshooters. We had only our rifles and our machine guns, because the 75's could not get to work.

Fortunately the flank batteries succeeded in catching the Boches on the right. It is absolutely impossible to convey what losses the Germans must suffer in these attacks. Nothing can give an idea of it. Whole ranks are mowed down, and those that follow them suffer the same fate. Under the storm of machine gun, rifle and 75 fire, the German columns were plowed into furrows of death. Imagine if you can what it would be like to rake water. Those gaps filled up again at once. That is enough to show with what disdain of human life the German attacks are planned and carried out.

In these circumstances German advances are sure. They startle the public, but at the front nobody attaches any importance to them. As a matter of fact, our trenches are so near those of the Germans that once the barbed wire is destroyed the distance between them can be covered in a few minutes. Thus, if one is willing to suffer a loss of life corresponding to the number of men necessary to cover the space between the lines, the other trench can always be reached. By sacrificing thousands of men, after a formidable bombardment, an enemy trench can always be taken.

There are slopes on Hill 304 where the level of the ground is raised several meters by mounds of German corpses. Sometimes it happens that the third German wave uses the dead of the second wave as ramparts and shelters. It was behind ramparts of the dead left by the first five attacks, on May 24th, that we saw the Boches take shelter while they organized their next rush.

We make prisoners among these dead during our counter-attacks. They are men who have received no hurt, but have been knocked down by the falling of the human wall of their killed and wounded neighbors. They say very little. They are for the most part dazed with fear and alcohol, and it is several days before they recover.

ACCOUNT OF THE STRUGGLE FOR FORT DOUAUMONT ON MAY 20TH–23RD [1916]

Verdun has become a battle of madmen in the midst of a volcano. Whole regiments melt in a few minutes, and others take their places only to perish in the same way. Between Saturday morning (May 20th) and noon Tuesday (May 23rd) we estimate that the Germans used up 100,000 men on the west Meuse front alone. That is the price they paid for the recapture of our recent gains and the seizure of our outlying positions. The valley separating Le Mort Homme from Hill 287 is choked with bodies. A full brigade was mowed down in a quarter hour's holocaust by our machine guns. Le Mort Homme itself passed from our possession, but the crescent Bourrus position to the south prevents the enemy from utilizing it.

The scene there is appalling, but is dwarfed in comparison with fighting around Douaumont. West of the Meuse, at least, one dies in the open air, but at Douaumont is the horror of darkness, where the men fight in tunnels, screaming with the lust of butchery, deafened by shells and grenades, stifled by smoke.

Even the wounded refuse to abandon the struggle. As though possessed . . . they fight on until they fall senseless from loss of blood. A surgeon in a frontline post told me that, in a redoubt at the south part of the fort, of 200 French dead, fully half had more than two wounds. Those he was able to treat seemed utterly insane. They kept shouting war cries and their eyes blazed, and, strangest of all, they appeared indifferent to pain. At one moment anesthetics ran out owing to the impossibility of bringing forward fresh supplies through the bombardment. Arms, even legs, were amputated without a groan, and even afterward the men seemed not to have felt the shock. They asked for a cigarette or inquired how the battle was going.

Our losses in retaking the fort were less heavy than was expected, as the enemy was demoralized by the cannonade—by far the most furious I have ever seen from French guns—and also was taken by surprise. But the subsequent action took a terrible toll. Cover was all blown to pieces. Every German rush was preceded by two or three hours of hell-storm, and then wave after wave of attack in numbers that seemed unceasing. Again and again the defender ranks were renewed.

Never have attacks been pushed home so continuously. The fight for Cemetery Hill at Gettysburg was no child's play, nor for Hougoumont at Waterloo, but here men have been flung 5,000 at a time at brief intervals for the last forty-eight hours. Practically the whole sector has been covered by a cannonade, compared to which Gettysburg was a hailstorm and Waterloo mere fireworks. Some shell-holes were thirty feet across, the explosion killing fifty men simultaneously.

Before our lines the German dead lie heaped in long rows. I am told one observer calculated their were 7,000 in a distance of 700 yards. Besides they cannot succor their wounded, whereas of ours one at least in three is removed safely to the rear. Despite the bombardment supplies keep coming. Even the chloroform I spoke of arrived after an hour's delay when two sets of bearers had been killed. . . .

We know . . . the Germans cannot long maintain their present sacrifices. Since Saturday the enemy has lost two, if not three, for each one of us. Every bombardment withstood, every rush checked brings nearer the moment of inevitable exhaustion. Then will come our recompense for these days of horror.

ACCOUNT OF THE ASSAULTS UPON FORT VAUX IN JUNE [1916]

We had scarcely arrived at the right of Fort de Vaux, on the slope of the ravine, when there came an unprecedented bombardment of twelve hours. Alone, in a sort of dugout without walls, I pass twelve hours of agony, believing that it is the end. The soil is torn up, covered with fresh earth by enormous explosions. In front of us are not less than 1,200 guns of 240, 305, 380, and 420 caliber, which spit ceaselessly and all together, in these days of preparation for attack. These explosions stupefy the brain; you feel as if your entrails were being torn out, your heart twisted and wrenched; the shock seems to dismember your whole body. And then the wounded, the corpses!

Never had I seen such horror, such hell. I felt that I would give everything if only this would stop long enough to clear my brain. Twelve hours alone, motionless, exposed, and no chance to risk a leap to another place, so closely did the fragments of shell and rock fall in hail all day long. At last, with night, this diminished a little. I can go on into the woods! The shells still burst all around us, but their infernal din no longer makes any impression on me—a queer trait of the human temperament. After that we are lodged in fortified caves where we pass five days in seclusion, piled on top of each other, without being able to lie down.

I bury three comrades in a shell-hole. We are without water, and, with hands that have just touched the poor mangled limbs, we eat as if nothing were wrong.

We are taken back for two days into a tunnel where the lacrymal shells make us weep. Swiftly we put on our masks. The next day, at the moment of taking supper and retiring to rest, we are hastily called into rank; that's it—we are going to the motion-picture show. We pass through an infernal barrage fire that cracks red all around in the dark. We run with all speed, in spite of our knapsacks, into the smother of broken branches that used to be a forest. Scarcely have we left a hole or a ditch when shells as big as a frying pan fall on the spot. We are laid flat by one that bursts a few yards away. So many of them fall at one time that we no longer pay any attention to them. We tumble into a ravine which we have named Death Ravine. That race over shell-swept open country, without trenches, we shall long remember.

At last we enter the village—without suspecting that the Germans are there! The commanding officer scatters us along the steep hill to the left and says: "Dig holes, quickly; the Boches are forty yards away!" We laugh and do not believe him; immediately, cries, rifle shots in the village; our men are freeing our Colonel and Captain, who were already prisoners. Impossible! Then there are no more Frenchmen there? In two minutes the village is surrounded, while the German batteries get a rude jolt. It was time! All night long you hear tools digging from one end to the other; trenches are being made in haste, but secretly. After that there is a wall, and the Germans will advance no further.

The next morning a formidable rumor—the Boches are coming up to assault Fort de Vaux. The newspapers have told the facts; our 75's firing for six hours, the German bodies piling up in heaps. Horrible! but we applauded. Everybody went out of the trenches to look. The Yser, said the veterans, was nothing beside this massacre.

That time I saw Germans fleeing like madmen. The next day, the same thing over again; they have the cynicism to mount a battery on the slope; the German chiefs must be hangmen to hurl their troops to death that way in masses and in broad daylight. All afternoon, a maximum bombardment; a wood is razed, a hill ravaged with shell-holes. It is maddening; continuous salvos of "big chariots"; one sees the 380's and 420's falling; a continuous cloud of smoke everywhere. Trees leap into air like wisps of straw; it is an unheard-of spectacle. It is enough to make you lose your head. . . .

The barrage fire cuts our communication with the rear, literally barring off the isthmus of Death Ravine. If the attacks on our wings succeed, our two regiments are prisoners, hemmed in, but the veterans (fathers of families) declare that we shall not be taken alive, that we will all fight till we die. It is sublime. . . .

It is magnificent to see that our last recourse is a matter of sheer will; despite this monstrous machinery of modern war, a little moral effort, a will twenty years old that refuses to weaken, suffices to frustrate the offensive! The rifles do not shoot enough, but we have machine guns, the bayonet, and we have vowed that they shall not pass. Twenty times the alarm is given; along the hillside one sees the hands gripping the rifles; the eyes are a little wild, but show an energy that refuses to give way.

Suddenly it is already night. A sentinel runs up to the outposts: "There they are! Shoot!"

A whole section shoots. But are the outposts driven in? Nobody knows. I take my rifle to go and see. . . . I find the sentinels flat on their faces in their holes, and run to the rear gesticulating and crying out orders to cease firing. The men obey. I return to the front, and soon, a hundred yards away, I see a bush scintillate with a rapid line of fire. This time it is they. Ta-ca-ta-ca, bzzi—bzzi. I hold my fire until they approach, but the welcome evidently does not please them, for they tumble back over the ridge leaving some men behind. One wounded cries, "Frenchmen!"

I am drunk, mad. Something moves in the bushes to the right; I bound forward with set bayonet. It is my brave sergeant, who has been out to see whether the Boches have all run away. . . .

The next day we are relieved at last. Another race with death, this time with broad daylight shining upon the horrible chaos, the innumerable dead, and a few wounded here and there. Oh! those mangled bodies, still unburied, abandoned for the moment. . . . A shell falls squarely among us, jarring us and bathing us in flame. My knapsack gets a sliver of shell; I am not touched; it is a miracle. In the evening we arrive at the river ford, and have another race. The next day, at Verdun, the Germans are still shelling us at the moment when we mount the auto trucks. In the course of all these actions our losses certainly have been high, but they are nothing compared with the frightful and unimaginable hecatomb of Germans I have witnessed.

7. GEORG ALEXANDER VON MÜLLER: THE KAISER AND THE WAR*

The declaration of unrestricted submarine warfare by Germany was the single most important event in the chain of occurrences and interlocking interests which brought the United States of America into World War I. The Germans had been fighting a desperate war on two fronts for three years, while shoring up their faltering allies. Toward the end of 1916 pressure began to mount for a great effort to weaken the Allies in order to force a peace before Germany's resources were strained to the breaking point. Since the German High Seas Fleet, the pride of the nation before the war, was powerless to break the Allied naval blockade or to interrupt the shipment of vital war goods and supplies to the Allies from neutral nations and colonies, many influential Germans argued for the unrestricted use of a new naval weapon—the submarine. The drastic and unprecedented decision for unrestricted submarine warfare was taken by the Imperial High Command, the Chancellor, and the Kaiser, after lengthy consideration. In his diaries, Admiral Georg Alexander von Müller, Chief of the German Naval Cabinet from 1914 to 1918, kept a record of events at the Kaiser's court, recording the fatal decision on submarine warfare. Müller's diaries provide a revealing commentary on the important question of whether the Kaiser actually ruled during the war or whether real control of the nation rested in the hands of the army. What was the Kaiser's attitude toward military problems? Why did Germany adopt unrestricted submarine warfare?

30th June, 1916

The news from both the Russo-Austrian and the Italian fronts is again unfavourable. Treutler has asked Falkenhayn and Lyncker whether he can work at Eastern Supreme Command under Hindenburg. . . .

7.0 report by Holtzendorff to the Kaiser to develop his U-boat viewpoint. The most ruthless form of submarine warfare is essential according to him and Falkenhayn. For the moment we must wait until after July because of the situation in America (presidential elections and the Mexican crisis). The Fleet to wage war solely against English warships until July 1st. The Kaiser was in full agreement.

After dinner he went for a memorial on the deciphering of the Hittite language, discussed the subject at length and enquired why this important matter had not been brought to his notice earlier.

When Lyncker remarked that it was believed the Kaiser had more important things to worry about he flew in a rage and said: "What more important things? The breaking of the Hittite script is as important as the whole war. Had the

---

* Walter Görlitz, ed., *The Kaiser and His Court: The Diaries, Note Books and Letters of Admiral Georg Alexander von Müller, Chief of the Naval Cabinet, 1914–1918*, trans. Mervyn Savill (New York: Harcourt, Brace and World, Inc., 1964), pp. 178–79, 187, 190–91, 198–99, 228–30, 234–37. Reprinted by permission.

world busied itself more with the Hittites a war would never have broken out, for France and England would have recognised that the danger always comes from the East and would never have become allied to Russia!"

Lyncker and the rest of us were flabbergasted by this muddled thinking.

Incidentally the Kaiser did not address a word to the intelligent, well-informed Hamann or question him on the many important matters that are in the air.

Further setbacks in the East. The Austrians have abandoned Kolomea.

26th July, 1916

The Chancellor insists that the appointment of Hindenburg as Supreme Commander East must be carried through and has informed His Majesty that the fate of the Hohenzollern dynasty depends upon it. With Hindenburg he could make a face-saving peace, without him he could do nothing. The Kaiser must not leave Pless before confirming Hindenburg in his new appointment.

Archduke Frederick has been summoned for tomorrow afternoon. It is presumed that, unlike his Chief of Staff, he is in favour of Hindenburg, and thus in accord with Vienna and first and foremost the old Emperor, whom Plessen is eventually to visit.

The Kaiser was in a highly nervous state the whole evening. At 10.30 Lyncker advised him to think of other matters and to play a few rounds of *skat*. This proved very successful. The Kaiser remarked to me: "I am spared nothing. Now they expect me to square the circle."

I replied: "I should not worry. The circle has already become a hexagon." Not very witty, but it managed to pacify him.

7th August, 1916

Great indignation with the Kaiser who spends hours supervising the building of a fountain at Homburg, for which a war contractor has raised the money. He went for an excursion to Saalburg and Friedrichshof this afternoon and refused to read a report from Hindenburg on the situation on the Eastern Front because "he had no time".

Talked this evening to the Empress's Cabinet Chief, Freiherr v. Spitzemberg and begged him to persuade her not to keep the Kaiser any longer at Homburg. She is perhaps more aware of the seriousness of the situation than the Kaiser.

8th August, 1916

Spoke with Freiherr v. Grünau on the Roumanian question. [Freiherr v. Grünau had gradually taken the place of Ambassador v. Treutler, then on sick leave, whose deputy he had formerly been. Despite my personal liking for this intelligent and tactful man, I always wondered why the Chancellor had not chosen a higher official who would have had some say with the High Command and with the Kaiser, and more authority in his important position as an intermediary with right of audience. The Kaiser himself was obviously very satisfied with Grünau.] A new war in the East, which would engage the Salonica armies, would create new tasks for our U-boats in the Mediterranean and demand an increase in their numbers there.

Then a long conversation with Reischach, who tried to convince me that if we wished to avoid the Kaiser's complete breakdown His Majesty must be allowed a long convalescence at Homburg "as soon as things quieten down on the Western Front" (?). I stood by my guns and insisted that the Kaiser did not need any physical cure but that we must work on his temperament by giving him some responsible task to do to jolt him out of his lethargy.

Soon after this I was given an audience by His Majesty and I must confess I was horrified to notice how worn and ill he looked.

Violent and unpredictable, dominated by a single thought: "Leave me in peace." Occasionally this changed to: "The Chancellor must make up his own mind." This referred to the as yet undecided use of unrestricted U-boat warfare in the Channel if the English tried to close the Straits to merchant shipping.

The mood at Headquarters is very gloomy. . . . Lyncker confessed to me that the morale of the troops is very low. No wonder! . . .

29th August, 1916

Hindenburg and Ludendorff arrived, followed shortly afterwards by the Empress and Holtzendorff. Hindenburg (today is the anniversary of Tannenberg) was appointed Chief of the General Staff and Ludendorff First Quartermaster-General, with promotion to Infantry General. Falkenhayn left unobtrusively for Berlin. . . .

Holtzendorff proposed both verbally and in a memorandum, unrestricted U-boat warfare. I supported him on three grounds: 1. Thanks to a bumper harvest, we shall be less dependent upon imports in the spring. 2. We have more U-boats available than last spring. 3. The neutrals are resentful of England and are more disposed to our wholesale blockading of Britain. . . .

At 6.0 p.m. I walked with the Chancellor, who discussed with me at great length the whole political situation and the dangers of unrestricted U-boat warfare. He told me incidentally that Falkenhayn had left because he refused to hear the Kaiser asking Hindenburg's advice on the conduct of the war. There was only one adviser to the Kaiser and that was the Chief of the General Staff. If the Kaiser insisted upon receiving Hindenburg he—Falkenhayn—must go! The reply was: "As you wish."

8th January, 1917

Holtzendorff arrived to obtain the Kaiser's decision on the U-boat campaign. A long conversation with me, without his having to convince me, for I have already come to the conclusion that the general war situation now demands this last shot in our locker. After our peace feelers and their curt rejection by the Entente, circumstances, including the improved political situation, warrant the use of this weapon which offers a reasonable chance of success. I told Holtzendorff that he could rely on my support.

Audience this evening at 7 o'clock with the Kaiser, who has suddenly come round to the idea that unrestricted U-boat warfare is now called for, and is definitely in favour of it even if the Chancellor is opposed to it. He voiced the very curious viewpoint that the U-boat war was a purely military affair which did not concern the Chancellor in any way. Moreover, there was no question of a discussion with him.

We (Holtzendorff and I) pointed out to him that it was absolutely essential that the Chancellor remain, even in the event of unrestricted U-boat warfare, for in the eyes of the neutrals it would then appear to be the logical result of the political situation rather than a desperate coup.

This evening Holtzendorff and I dined with Hindenburg. The latter had asked this morning how I stood on the U-boat question and seemed very pleased when Holtzendorff replied: "He is entirely on our side."

After dinner I discussed with the Field-Marshal the question of transferring HQ from Pless and proposed Potsdam (as the next best, since the Kaiser would never have agreed to Berlin), stressing the importance of a closer collaboration between the Army and the political leaders and the Government and the danger of allowing the Kaiser to vegetate in a God-forsaken hole like Pless.

Hindenburg replied: "Your idea has a lot to recommend it, but on the other hand I feel that Potsdam entails the danger of the Kaiser falling into the hands of the duffers."

I dismissed this danger and took the opportunity of breaking a lance for the Chancellor, who was always loyal in a crisis. For example, he had carried through the change—Falkenhayn-Hindenburg—with the Kaiser. He had spoken to his Majesty in a manner he had never been addressed before. . . .

9th January, 1917

My conversation with Hindenburg has been of no avail. At today's audience Kreuznach was chosen as the new HQ.

From a telephone conversation with Bethmann and a telegraphic attempt by him to draw Scheer into the discussions, I felt that the Chancellor was very agitated and depressed; I went early this morning, therefore, to meet him at the station, to pacify him and put him in the picture on the different decisions that lay before us. It was a good idea!

I succeeded in consoling him somewhat and begged him not to reject the idea of unrestricted U-boat warfare out of hand. I may have influenced him slightly by pointing out that for two years I had always been for moderation on this tricky question, but that now, in the altered circumstances, I considered unrestricted warfare to be necessary and that it had a reasonable chance of success. . . .

Six o'clock audience given to the Chancellor, Hindenburg, Ludendorff, Holtzendorff and the three Cabinet Chiefs.

The Chancellor opened the proceedings in a rather rambling tone—not unlike one of his parliamentary speeches—and summed up the situation, saying for some odd reason that Switzerland would be in a very difficult position if by aggravating the whole war by our U-boat campaign we closed all food supplies to the Allies and to her. This would bring pressure to bear on her to enter the war on the side of the Entente or to allow their troops to march through her country.

The crux of the Chancellor's speech was that in view of the opinions of the General Staff and the Admiralty he (the Chancellor) could not oppose unrestricted U-boat warfare. It was not so much approval as an acceptance of the facts.

Holtzendorff then spoke very enthusiastically on the subject, and was followed by the Field-Marshal who stated that the soldier in the trenches was waiting for the U-boat war, that the Army, as a result of the vacillating behaviour of

Denmark and Holland, had troops ready to go over to the offensive within a few months, and that he felt no particular anxieties with regard to Switzerland. An attack on us by Switzerland would have no more effect than the one staged by the Roumanians.

Then His Majesty replied, giving statistics of the corn and shipping markets from a newspaper article by Newman, very much in favour of unrestricted U-boat warfare, and upon this signed the decree that was laid before him. He remarked in passing that he expected a declaration of war by America. If it came—and the Chancellor should if necessary make concessions to American passenger liners to avoid it—so much the better. . . .

28th January, 1917

. . . . Prince Henry with me. . . . The U-boat subject was not broached. Last night the Prince had declared to several gentlemen of his suite—rather disloyally to the Kaiser—that had we embarked on unrestricted U-boat warfare a year ago we should never have had to fight the Battle of the Somme.

The Kaiser told us that a telegram had come in from Washington asking for a few days' postponement of the decision. Zimmermann replied by telegram: "Too late."

In actual fact Wilson's request for a postponement had stemmed from Bernstorff, and Zimmermann's reply had read: "Delay impracticable."

The Kaiser thinks that Wilson only asked for a postponement in the interest of England, knowing of the hardship resulting from her serious food shortage. He is confirmed in his view by a letter received today from the Hamburg corn merchant Newman to the aide Count Moltke, who had shown it to His Majesty. . . .

29th January, 1917

Valentini came to my room to inform me that the Chancellor is on his way here to discuss the news from Washington with His Majesty. It concerns the handing of our peace terms to Wilson. The Kaiser is beside himself because once more he has to make a decision.

I was summoned to His Majesty about 10 o'clock. The Chancellor, Zimmermann, Hindenburg, Ludendorff, Plessen and Lyncker were already there. The Chancellor read the draft of his instructions to our Washington Ambassador in reply to Wilson's communication to Bernstorff asking for our peace terms, so that he can start peace negotiations before the great new Spring Offensives. Bernstorff advises us to comply, for otherwise war with America is inevitable.

The Chancellor's instructions specify unrestricted warfare from February 1st, but requests Wilson to renew his efforts for peace against the day when the Entente's irresponsible will to war will begin to crack.

Finally Wilson is informed confidentially, and for his ears alone, of our peace terms as we stated them on December 12th. . . .

The Chancellor skilfully defended his instructions which, without abandoning U-boat warfare, will make it possible for America not to enter the war immediately. Perhaps, in the meantime the U-boat warfare will have proved so successful that she will think twice before going to war at all.

Hindenburg agreed, as did the Kaiser, but he insisted that the instructions must clearly indicate that Wilson is not himself the mediator.

A hideous evening. The Empress in full regalia. And to think that our sentries are freezing in the Carpathians. . . .

31st January, 1917

Archduke Maximilian, the Emperor of Austria's brother, arrived to announce his ascent to the throne. The usual banquet. His Majesty refused the Court Marshal's proposal that he should reside in Berlin during the next visit of the High Command. He has never agreed. If he says Berlin he means Potsdam. Given the opportunity, Hindenburg will have to draw His Majesty's attention to the fact that he makes life more difficult by residing at Potsdam.

This evening the Kaiser read out a long thesis by Professor Förster of Breslau University on the eagle as a heraldic beast. A gruesome evening!

THE RUSSIAN REVOLUTION

8. GEORGE BUCHANAN: MY MISSION TO RUSSIA*

Sir George Buchanan was the British Ambassador to Petrograd (1910–18) who urged Russia's Provisional Government to fulfill its wartime obligations to Great Britain and France. Military operations had reached a stalemate on the western front, and Britain hoped that renewed Russian offensives would draw German strength to the east. In order to continue receiving Allied aid and assistance, the Provisional Government reluctantly agreed to organize a new offensive. Russia's ill-fated final offensive against German and Austro-Hungarian armies led to the disintegration of Russian military strength and dramatically weakened the tenuous grip of the Provisional Government on the home front.

To what extent did Sir George Buchanan, Prince Lvov (Lvoff), and Alexander Kerensky fail to grasp the realities of Russia's domestic crisis? What was Buchanan's assessment of Kerensky's leadership? How did he assess Lenin's revolutionary potential? In what ways did Allied policy, as expressed by the British Ambassador, complicate the problems faced by the Provisional Government?

April 9, [1917]

The Socialistic propaganda in the army continues, and though I miss no opportunity of impressing on Ministers the disastrous consequences of this subversion of discipline, they appear to be powerless to prevent it. Not only are the relations of officers and men most unsatisfactory, but numbers of the latter are returning home without leave. In some cases they have been prompted to do so by reports of an approaching division of the land and by the desire to be on the spot to secure their share of the spoils. I do not wish to be pessimistic, but unless matters improve we shall probably hear of some serious disaster as soon as the Germans decide to take the offensive.

The Russian idea of liberty is to take things easily, to claim double wages, to demonstrate in the streets, and to waste time in talking and in passing resolutions at public meetings. Ministers are working themselves to death, and have the best intentions; but, though I am always being told that their position is

* George Buchanan, *My Mission to Russia and Other Diplomatic Memories* (2 vols.; Boston: Little, Brown and Co., 1923), II, 110–12, 114–17, 126–28, 147–48, 161–63, 202.

becoming stronger, I see no signs of their asserting their authority. The Soviet continues to act as if it were the Government and has been trying to force Ministers to approach the Allied Governments on the subject of peace.

Kerensky, with whom I had a long conversation yesterday, does not favour the idea of taking strong measures at present, either against the Soviet or the Socialist propaganda in the army. On my telling him that the Government would never be masters of the situation so long as they allowed themselves to be dictated to by a rival organization, he said that the Soviet would die a natural death, that the present agitation in the army would pass, and that the army would then be in a better position to help the Allies to win the war than it would have been under the old régime.

Russia, he declared, was in favour of what he termed a war of defence, as opposed to a war of aggression, though a military offensive might be necessary to secure the objects of such a war. The presence of two great democracies in the war might eventually cause the Allies to modify their ideas about the terms of peace, and he spoke of an ideal peace as one "that would secure to every nation the right to determine its own destiny." I told him that the reply which we had returned to President Wilson's note showed that we were not fighting for conquest, but for principles which ought to appeal to Russian democracy. The question as to whether effect was to be given to the Constantinople agreement—about which he and Miliukoff held such opposite views—was a question for Russia to decide. Kerensky next spoke of the hopes which he entertained of influencing the German Social Democrats through the Russian Socialists, contending that Russia had brought a new force into the war which, by reacting on the internal situation in Germany, might bring about a durable peace. He admitted, however, that if these hopes proved fallacious we should have to fight on till Germany yielded to the will of Europe. . . .

April 16, [1917]

I yesterday went to see Prince Lvoff, whom I found in a very optimistic mood. On my calling his serious attention to the state of the army, he asked me the reasons for my pessimism. I told him that while Ministers were constantly assuring me that the army would now render us far greater services than it had under the Empire, our military attachés, who had visited the Petrograd regiments and talked to officers returned from the front, took the contrary view. From what they told me I feared that, unless steps were at once taken to stop the visits of Socialist agitators to the front, the army would never be able to play an effective part in the war. I was also much preoccupied by the fact that the Government seemed powerless to shake off the control of the Committee of Workmen's and Soldiers' Deputies. Lvoff reassured me by declaring that the only two weak points on the front were Dvinsk and Riga. The army as a whole was sound, and any attempts made by agitators to subvert its discipline would meet with no success. The Government could count on the support of the army, and even the Petrograd garrison had, like the troops at the front, offered to suppress the Workmen's Council. This, he added, was an offer which the Government could not accept without exposing themselves to the charge of planning a counter-revolution.

I cannot share the optimism with which Prince Lvoff and his colleagues regard the situation. The revolution has put the machinery of government temporarily out of gear, and disorganization reigns in many of the administrative services. There is but little enthusiasm for the war, and the Socialist propaganda is being reinforced by the arrival of fresh Anarchists from abroad. I am only speaking of Petrograd, but Petrograd at present rules Russia and is likely to do so for some time to come. . . .

April 23, [*1917*]

On several points on the front the German soldiers are fraternizing with the Russians, and trying to complete the work begun by the Socialists by urging them to kill their officers. But, disquieting as is the state of the army, I fear that, were we to take collective action here and to threaten to stop the despatch of all war material unless the subversive propaganda is at once suppressed, we should only be playing into the hands of the Socialists, who would contend that Russia, being left without munitions by the Allies, had no choice but to make peace.

Kerensky dined at the Embassy last night to meet Thorne and O'Grady, and in a long conversation I told him quite frankly why my confidence in the army, and even in the Provisional Government, was shaken. He admitted the accuracy of the facts which I cited, but said that he knew his people and that he only hoped that the Germans would not delay taking the offensive, as, when once the fighting began, the army would pull itself together. He wanted, he said, to make the war a national one, as it was in England and France. He saw no danger of the Provisional Government being overthrown, as only a small minority of the troops were on the side of the Soviet. He added that the Communistic doctrines preached by Lenin have made the Socialists lose ground.

It will be best for us, at present, to confine our action to individual representations on the part of the Allied Ambassadors. If the results of the fighting show that the army has been demoralized, we must then have recourse to some collective action. . . .

On *May 21* I wrote as follows to the Foreign Office:
The last two weeks have been very anxious ones, as the victory which the Government had won over the Soviet in the matter of the note to the Powers was not nearly so complete as Miliukoff had imagined. So long as the Soviet maintained its exclusive right to dispose of the troops, the Government, as Prince Lvoff remarked, was 'an authority without power,' while the Workmen's Council was 'a power without authority.' Under such conditions it was impossible for Guchkoff, as Minister of War, and for Korniloff, as military governor of Petrograd, to accept responsibility for the maintenance of discipline in the army. They both, consequently, resigned, while the former declared that if things were to continue as they were the army would cease to exist as a fighting force in three weeks' time. Guchkoff's resignation precipitated matters, and Lvoff, Kerensky and Tereschenko came to the conclusion that, as the Soviet was too powerful a factor to be either suppressed or disregarded, the only way of putting an end to the anomaly of a dual Government was to form a Coalition. Though this idea did not at first find favour with the Soviet, it was eventually

agreed that the latter should be represented in the Government by three delegates—Tseretelli, Chernoff and Scobeleff. Miliukoff was at headquarters when
the crisis broke out, and he had on his return to choose between accepting the
post of Minister of Education or leaving the Cabinet. After a vain struggle to
retain charge of the Foreign Office he tendered his resignation.

Though the more moderate section of the Government, with which I am
naturally in sympathy, will be weakened by Miliukoff's and Guchkoff's departure, their loss will, I think, be compensated by gains in other directions. The
former is so obsessed by one idea—Constantinople, which to the Socialists represents the imperialistic policy of the old régime—that he has never voiced the
views of the Government as a whole; and I personally prefer to deal with someone who, even if he does not see eye to eye with us, can speak with authority as
the exponent of the Government's policy. Guchkoff, on the other hand, suffers from a weak heart and is hardly up to his work. His views with regard to
discipline in the army are very sound, but he has been unable to impose them on
his colleagues. He has not, moreover, any hold on the masses—the principal factor—as he lacks Kerensky's gift of personal magnetism. The new Coalition
Government, as I have already telegraphed, offers us the last and almost forlorn
hope of saving the military situation on this front. Kerensky, who assumes
charge of both the War Office and the Admiralty, is not an ideal War Minister,
but he hopes, by going to the front and making passionate appeals to the patriotism of the soldiers, to be able to galvanize the army into new life. He is the
only man who can do it if it can be done, but his task will be a very difficult
one. The Russian soldier of to-day does not understand for what or for whom
he is fighting. He was ready formerly to lay down his life for the Tsar, who in
his eyes impersonated Russia; but now that the Tsar has gone Russia means
nothing to him beyond his own village. Kerensky has begun by telling the army
that he is going to re-establish the strictest discipline, to insist on his orders being
obeyed, and to punish all recalcitrants. He has been going round the barracks
to-day, and to-morrow he leaves for the front to prepare for the coming
offensive. . . .

The internal situation, meanwhile, had undergone but little change. The
Government had dealt firmly with an attempt made by the sailors at Cronstadt
to set up an independent Republic of their own, and had also scored a certain
success by stopping an armed demonstration that had been organized by the
Bolsheviks. In a conversation which I had with him on June 27, Prince Lvoff
assured me that my fears as to Russia being unable to continue the war were
groundless, and that, now that the Government had the requisite forces at their
disposal, they were determined to maintain order. These assurances were discounted by the fact that on the very next day they failed to enforce compliance
with the orders which they had given for the evacuation of two villas which
had been occupied and held by the Bolsheviks, a failure which, as I told
Tereschenko, was tantamount to an abdication of their authority. . . .

August 4, [1917]

I would venture to submit that the time has come for us, in reply to Russia's
appeal for our co-operation, to tell her Government frankly that, while we will

continue to do all that is possible to relieve the pressure on her front by pushing our offensive, we expect her in return to concentrate all her energies on the re-organization of her armies and to re-establish discipline both at the front and in the rear. It would be well were the Allied Ambassadors to be instructed to speak in the above sense to the president of the council as soon as the new Government is formed. . . .

August 11, [1917]

I met Kerensky to-day at a luncheon given by Tereschenko. In the course of our conversation I said that I was much depressed by the fact that everybody seemed to regard the situation entirely from the party point of view, and that political considerations had precedence over military exigencies. Referring next to a request which Korniloff had addressed to us for more guns, I remarked that we had seen the initial success of the July offensive converted into a rout owing to lack of discipline, and that our military authorities were hardly likely to accede to the above request unless assured that Korniloff would be given full powers to restore discipline. It would, I added, help to reassure my Government could I inform them that Petrograd had been included in the front zone and placed under martial law. Kerensky, after declaring that the Government were determined to maintain order, said, somewhat huffily, that if we were going to haggle about guns and would not help Russia, we had better say so at once. I told him that he had misunderstood me, that we had had every desire to help Russia, but that it was no good our sending guns to her front if they were to be captured by the Germans. We had need of every gun we could get on our own front, and by using them there we were rendering her effective assistance. . . .

November 3, [1917]

Verkhovski, the Minister of War, has resigned. He had always contended that if the troops were to be kept in the trenches they must be told what they were fighting for, and that we ought, therefore, to publish our peace terms and to throw the responsibility for the continuance of the war on the Germans. At last night's meeting of the committee of the Provisional Council he seems to have completely lost his head, declaring that Russia must make peace at once, and that, when once peace had been concluded, 'a military dictator must be appointed to ensure the maintenance of order. On Tereschenko, who was supported by all the other members of the committee, demanding the withdrawal of this declaration, he tendered his resignation, which was accepted.

9. V. I. LENIN: STATE AND REVOLUTION*

The Russian Social Democratic Labor party was split into two factions when the Revolution broke out. One faction was led by V. I. Lenin (1870–1924), who had provoked the split in 1903 at the Second Party Congress by insisting that the party be a small, conspiratorial advance guard of the revolution rather than

* V. I. Lenin, "The State and Revolution: The Marxist Theory of the State and the Tasks of the Proletariat in the Revolution" in Stepan Apresyan and Jim Riordan, eds., *Collected Works* (38 vols.; Moscow: Progress Publishers, 1964), XXV, 400, 402–5, 459–69.

a mass party seeking popular support. Lenin and his supporters received a majority of the votes in a ballot pertaining to the control of the party newspaper, and he immediately seized upon the term Bolsheviks (majority-ites) for his faction. Although Lenin's group was only a minority at the Congress, his shrewd action proved decisive. The other faction was promptly dubbed Mensheviks (minority-ites). Lenin urged the Bolsheviks to accept his views completely and poured criticism and scorn on his opponents.

Lenin was both a Marxian scholar and a revolutionary fanatic. His many books and pamphlets were written to explain his interpretations of Marx and to demolish his political and ideological foes. He was not always consistent, except in his goals of world revolution and the overthrow of bourgeois capitalist society. The March Revolution in Russia gave Lenin his opportunity, since it replaced a crumbling monarchy with a feeble bourgeois democratic government. From March to November 1917, Russia was, in Lenin's own words, "the freest, most advanced country in the world."

State and Revolution, which Lenin wrote in 1917 and partially ignored after he seized power in November, remains an important element of Marxist-Leninist philosophy. What, according to Lenin, was a "state"? What was the relationship between social classes and the state? Contrast "capitalist democracy" with the "dictatorship of the proletariat." Why must the state wither away? When would a stateless society be realized? What views on the perfectibility of men and on human psychology were essential for Lenin's assumption that the state would eventually disappear?

We have already said above, and shall show more fully later, that the theory of Marx and Engels of the inevitability of a violent revolution refers to the bourgeois state. The latter *cannot* be superseded by the proletarian state (the dictatorship of the proletariat) through the process of "withering away", but, as a general rule, only through a violent revolution. . . . The necessity of systematically imbuing the masses with *this* and precisely this view of violent revolution lies at the root of the *entire* theory of Marx and Engels. The betrayal of their theory by the now prevailing social-chauvinist and Kautskyite trends expresses itself strikingly in both these trends ignoring *such* propaganda and agitation.

The supersession of the bourgeois state by the proletarian state is impossible without a violent revolution. The abolition of the proletarian state, *i.e.,* of the state in general, is impossible except through the process of "withering away." . . .

Here we have a formulation of one of the most remarkable and most important ideas of Marxism on the subject of the state, namely, the idea of the "dictatorship of the proletariat" (as Marx and Engels began to call it after the Paris Commune); and also, a highly interesting definition of the state, which is also one of the "forgotten words" of Marxism: *"the state, i.e., the proletariat organised as the ruling class".*

This definition of the state has never been explained in the prevailing propaganda and agitation literature of the official Social-Democratic parties. More than that, it has been deliberately ignored, for it is absolutely irreconcilable with reformism, and is a slap in the face for the common opportunist prejudices and philistine illusions about the "peaceful development of democracy".

The proletariat needs the state—this is repeated by all the opportunists, social-chauvinists and Kautskyites, who assure us that this is what Marx taught. But they *"forget"* to add that, in the first place, according to Marx, the proletariat needs only a state which is withering away, *i.e.,* a state so constituted that it begins to wither away immediately, and cannot but wither away. And, secondly, the working people need a "state, *i.e.,* the proletariat organised as the ruling class".

The state is a special organisation of force: it is an organisation of violence for the suppression of some class. What class must the proletariat suppress? Naturally, only the exploiting class, *i.e.,* the bourgeoisie. The working people need the state only to suppress the resistance of the exploiters, and only the proletariat can direct this suppression, can carry it out. For the proletariat is the only class that is consistently revloutionary, the only class that can unite all the working and exploited people in the struggle against the bourgeoisie, in completely removing it.

The exploiting classes need political rule to maintain exploitation, *i.e.,* in the selfish interests of an insignificant minority against the vast majority of the people. The exploited classes need political rule in order to completely abolish all exploitation, *i.e.,* in the interests of the vast majority of the people, and against the insignificant minority consisting of the modern slave-owners—the landowners and capitalists.

The petty-bourgeois democrats, those sham socialists who replaced the class struggle by dreams of class harmony, even pictured the socialist transformation in a dreamy fashion—not as the overthrow of the rule of the exploiting class, but as the peaceful submission of the minority to the majority which has become aware of its aims. This petty-bourgeois utopia, which is inseparable from the idea of the state being above classes, led in practice to the betrayal of the interests of the working classes, as was shown, for example, by the history of the French revolutions of 1848 and 1871, and by the experience of "socialist" participation in bourgeois Cabinets in Britain, France, Italy and other countries at the turn of the century.

All his life Marx fought against this petty-bourgeois socialism, now revived in Russia by the Socialist-Revolutionary and Menshevik parties. He developed his theory of the class struggle consistently, down to the theory of political power, of the state.

The overthrow of bourgeois rule can be accomplished only by the proletariat, the particular class whose economic conditions of existence prepare it for this task and provide it with the possibility and the power to perform it. While the bourgeoisie break up and disintegrate the peasantry and all the petty-bourgeois groups, they weld together, unite and organise the proletariat. Only the proletariat—by virtue of the economic role it plays in large-scale production—is capable of being the leader of *all* the working and exploited people, whom the bourgeoisie exploit, oppress and crush, often not less but more than they do the proletarians, but who are incapable of waging an *independent* struggle for their emancipation.

The theory of the class struggle, applied by Marx to the question of the state and the socialist revolution, leads as a matter of course to the recognition of the *political rule* of the proletariat, of its dictatorship, *i.e.,* of undivided power

directly backed by the armed force of the people. The overthrow of the bourgeoisie can be achieved only by the proletariat becoming the *ruling class,* capable
of crushing the inevitable and desperate resistance of the bourgeoisie, and of
organising *all* the working and exploited people for the new economic system.

The proletariat needs state power, a centralised organisation of force, an
organisation of violence, both to crush the resistance of the exploiters and to
lead the enormous mass of the population—the peasants, the petty bourgeoisie,
and semi-proletarians—in the work of organising a socialist economy.

By educating the workers' party, Marxism educates the vanguard of the
proletariat, capable of assuming power and *leading the whole people* to
socialism, of directing and organising the new system, of being the teacher, the
guide, the leader of all the working and exploited people in organising their
social life without the bourgeoisie and against the bourgeoisie. By contrast, the
opportunism now prevailing trains the members of the workers' party to be the
representatives of the better-paid workers, who lose touch with the masses, "get
along" fairly well under capitalism, and sell their birthright for a mess of
pottage, *i.e.,* renounce their role as revolutionary leaders of the people against
the bourgeoisie.

Marx's theory of "the state, *i.e.,* the proletariat organised as the ruling class",
is inseparably bound up with the whole of his doctrine of the revolutionary role
of the proletariat in history. The culmination of this role is the proletarian
dictatorship, the political rule of the proletariat.

But since the proletariat needs the state as a *special* form of organisation of
violence *against* the bourgeoisie, the following conclusion suggests itself: is it
conceivable that such an organisation can be created without first abolishing,
destroying the state machine created by the bourgeoisie *for themselves?* The
Communist Manifesto leads straight to this conclusion, . . .

Marx continued:

"Between capitalist and communist society lies the period of the revolutionary
transformation of the one into the other. Corresponding to this is also a political
transition period in which the state can be nothing but *the revolutionary
dictatorship of the proletariat."*

Marx bases this conclusion on an analysis of the role played by the proletariat
in modern capitalist society, on the data concerning the development of this
society, and on the irreconcilability of the antagonistic interests of the proletariat
and the bourgeoisie.

Previously the question was put as follows: to achieve its emancipation, the
proletariat must overthrow the bourgeoisie, win political power and establish
its revolutionary dictatorship.

Now the question is put somewhat differently: the transition from capitalist
society—which is developing towards communism—to communist society is
impossible without a "political transition period", and the state in this period
can only be the revolutionary dictatorship of the proletariat.

What, then, is the relation of this dictatorship to democracy?

We have seen that the *Communist Manifesto* simply places side by side the
two concepts: "to raise the proletariat to the position of the ruling class" and

"to win the battle of democracy". On the basis of all that has been said above, it is possible to determine more precisely how democracy changes in the transition from capitalism to communism.

In capitalist society, providing it develops under the most favourable conditions, we have a more or less complete democracy in the democratic republic. But this democracy is always hemmed in by the narrow limits set by capitalist expoitation, and consequently always remains, in effect, a democracy for the minority, only for the propertied classes, only for the rich. Freedom in capitalist society always remains about the same as it was in the ancient Greek republics: freedom for the slave-owners. Owing to the conditions of capitalist exploitation, the modern wage slaves are so crushed by want and poverty that "they cannot be bothered with democracy", "cannot be bothered with politics"; in the ordinary, peaceful course of events, the majority of the population is debarred from participation in public and political life.

The correctness of this statement is perhaps most clearly confirmed by Germany, because constitutional legality steadily endured there for a remarkably long time—nearly half a century (1871-1914)—and during this period the Social-Democrats were able to achieve far more than in other countries in the way of "utilising legality", and organised a larger proportion of the workers into a political party than anywhere else in the world.

What is this largest proportion of politically conscious and active wage slaves that has so far been recorded in capitalist society? One million members of the Social-Democratic Party—out of fifteen million wage-workers! Three million organised in trade unions—out of fifteen million!

Democracy for an insignificant minority, democracy for the rich—that is the democracy of capitalist society. If we look more closely into the machinery of capitalist democracy, we see everywhere, in the "petty"—supposedly petty—details of the suffrage (residential qualification, exclusion of women, etc.), in the technique of the representative institutions, in the actual obstacles to the right of assembly (public buildings are not for "paupers"!), in the purely capitalist organisation of the daily press, etc., etc.—we see restriction after restriction upon democracy. These restrictions, exceptions, exclusions, obstacles for the poor seem slight, especially in the eyes of one who has never known want himself and has never been in close contact with the oppressed classes in their mass life (and nine out of ten, if not ninety-nine out of a hundred, bourgeois publicists and politicians come under this category); but in their sum total these restrictions exclude and squeeze out the poor from politics, from active participation in democracy.

Marx grasped this *essence* of capitalist democracy splendidly when, in analysing the experience of the Commune, he said that the oppressed are allowed once every few years to decide which particular representatives of the oppressing class shall represent and repress them in parliament!

But from this capitalist democracy—that is inevitably narrow and stealthily pushes aside the poor, and is therefore hypocritical and false through and through—forward development does not proceed simply, directly and smoothly, towards "greater and greater democracy", as the liberal professors and petty-bourgeois opportunists would have us believe. No, forward development, *i.e.,* development towards communism, proceeds through the dictatorship of the proletariat, and cannot do otherwise, for the *resistance* of the capitalist exploiters cannot be *broken* by anyone else or in any other way.

And the dictatorship of the proletariat, *i.e.,* the organisation of the vanguard of the oppressed as the ruling class for the purpose of suppressing the oppressors, cannot result merely in an expansion of democracy. *Simultaneously* with an immense expansion of democracy, which *for the first time* becomes democracy for the poor, democracy for the people, and not democracy for the money-bags, the dictatorship of the proletariat imposes a series of restrictions on the freedom of the oppressors, the exploiters, the capitalists. We must suppress them in order to free humanity from wage slavery, their resistance must be crushed by force; it is clear that there is no freedom and no democracy where there is suppression and where there is violence.

Engels expressed this splendidly in his letter to Bebel when he said, as the reader will remember, that "the proletariat needs the state, not in the interests of freedom but in order to hold down its adversaries, and as soon as it becomes possible to speak of freedom the state as such ceases to exist."

Democracy for the vast majority of the people, and suppression by force, *i.e.,* exclusion from democracy, of the exploiters and oppressors of the people—this is the change democracy undergoes during the *transition* from capitalism to communism.

Only in communist society, when the resistance of the capitalists has been completely crushed, when the capitalists have disappeared, when there are no classes (*i.e.,* when there is no distinction between the members of society as regards their relation to the social means of production), *only* then "the state . . . ceases to exist", and "*it becomes possible to speak of freedom*". Only then will a truly complete democracy become possible and be realised, a democracy without any exceptions whatever. And only then will democracy begin to *wither away,* owing to the simple fact that, freed from capitalist slavery, from the untold horrors, savagery, absurdities and infamies of capitalist exploitation, people will gradually *become accustomed* to observing the elementary rules of social intercourse that have been known for centuries and repeated for thousands of years in all copy-book maxims. They will become accustomed to observing them without force, without coercion, without subordination, *without the special apparatus* for coercion called the state.

The expression "the state *withers away*" is very well chosen, for it indicates both the gradual and the spontaneous nature of the process. Only habit can, and undoubtedly will, have such an effect; for we see around us on millions of occasions how readily people become accustomed to observing the necessary rules of social intercourse when there is no exploitation, when there is nothing that arouses indignation, evokes protest and revolt, and creates the need for *suppression*.

And so in capitalist society we have a democracy that is curtailed, wretched, false, a democracy only for the rich, for the minority. The dictatorship of the proletariat, the period of transition to communism, will for the first time create democracy for the people, for the majority, along with the necessary suppression of the exploiters, of the minority. Communism alone is capable of providing really complete democracy, and the more complete it is, the sooner it will become unnecessary and wither away of its own accord.

In other words, under capitalism we have the state in the proper sense of the word, that is, a special machine for the suppression of one class by another, and, what is more, of the majority by the minority. Naturally, to be successful, such an undertaking as the systematic suppression of the exploited majority by the exploiting minority calls for the utmost ferocity and savagery in the matter of suppressing, it calls for seas of blood, through which mankind is actually wading its way in slavery, serfdom and wage labour.

Furthermore, during the *transition* from capitalism to communism suppression is *still* necessary, but it is now the suppression of the exploiting minority by the exploited majority. A special apparatus, a special machine for suppression, the "state", is *still* necessary, but this is now a transitional state. It is no longer a state in the proper sense of the word; for the suppression of the minority of exploiters by the majority of the wage slaves of *yesterday* is comparatively so easy, simple and natural a task that it will entail far less bloodshed than the suppression of the risings of slaves, serfs or wage-labourers, and it will cost mankind far less. And it is compatible with the extension of democracy to such an overwhelming majority of the population that the need for a *special machine* of suppression will begin to disappear. Naturally, the exploiters are unable to suppress the people without a highly complex machine for performing this task, but *the people* can suppress the exploiters even with a very simple "machine", almost without a "machine", without a special apparatus, by the simple *organisation of the armed people* (such as the Soviets of Workers' and Soldiers' Deputies, we would remark, running ahead).

Lastly, only communism makes the state absolutely unnecessary, for there is *nobody* to be suppressed—"nobody" in the sense of a *class,* of a systematic struggle against a definite section of the population. We are not utopians, and do not in the least deny the possibility and inevitability of excesses on the part of *individual persons,* or the need to stop *such* excesses. In the first place, however, no special machine, no special apparatus of suppression, is needed for this; this will be done by the armed people themselves, as simply and as readily as any crowd of civilised people, even in modern society, interferes to put a stop to a scuffle or to prevent a woman from being assaulted. And, secondly, we know that the fundamental social cause of excesses, which consist in the violation of the rules of social intercourse, is the exploitation of the people, their want and their poverty. With the removal of this chief cause, excesses will inevitably begin to *"wither away"*. We do not know how quickly and in what succession, but we do know they will wither away. With their withering away the state will also *wither away*.

Without building utopias, Marx defined more fully what can be defined *now* regarding this future, namely, the difference between the lower and higher phases (levels, stages) of communist society. . . .

It is this communist society, which has just emerged into the light of day out of the womb of capitalism and which is in every respect stamped with the birthmarks of the old society, that Marx terms the "first", or lower, phase of communist society.

The means of production are no longer the private property of individuals. The means of production belong to the whole of society. Every member of society, performing a certain part of the socially-necessary work, receives a certificate from society to the effect that he has done a certain amount of work. And with this certificate he receives from the public store of consumer goods a corresponding quantity of products. After a deduction is made of the amount of labour which goes to the public fund, every worker, therefore, receives from society as much as he has given to it. . . .

The first phase of communism, therefore, cannot yet provide justice and equality: differences, and unjust differences, in wealth will still persist, but the *exploitation* of man by man will have become impossible because it will be impossible to seize the *means of production*—the factories, machines, land, etc. —and make them private property. In smashing Lassalle's petty-bourgeois, vague phrases about "equality" and "justice" *in general,* Marx shows the *course of development* of communist society, which is *compelled* to abolish at first *only* the "injustice" of the means of production seized by individuals, and which is *unable* at once to eliminate the other injustice, which consists in the distribution of consumer goods "according to the amount of labour performed" (and not according to needs). . . .

Marx not only most scrupulously takes account of the inevitable inequality of men, but he also takes into account the fact that the mere conversion of the means of production into the common property of the whole of society (commonly called "socialism") *does not remove* the defects of distribution and the inequality of "bourgeois right," which *continues to prevail* so long as products are divided "according to the amount of labour performed" . . . .

And so, in the first phase of communist society (usually called socialism) "bourgeois right" is *not* abolished in its entirety, but only in part, only in proportion to the economic revolution so far attained, *i.e.,* only in respect of the means of production. "Bourgeois right" recognises them as the private property of individuals. Socialism converts them into *common* property. *To that extent*— and to that extent alone—"bourgeois right" disappears.

However, it persists as far as its other part is concerned; it persists in the capacity of regulator (determining factor) in the distribution of products and the allotment of labour among the members of society. The socialist principle, "He who does not work shall not eat", is *already* realised; the other socialist principle, "An equal amount of products for an equal amount of labour", is also *already* realised. But this is not yet communism, and it does not yet abolish "bourgeois right", which gives unequal individuals, in return for unequal (really unequal) amounts of labour, equal amounts of products.

This is a "defect", says Marx, but it is unavoidable in the first phase of communism; for if we are not to indulge in utopianism, we must not think that having overthrown capitalism people will at once learn to work for society *without any standard of right*. Besides, the abolition of capitalism *does not immediately create* the economic prerequisites for *such* a change.

Now, there is no other standard than that of "bourgeois right". To this extent, therefore, there still remains the need for a state, which, while safeguarding the common ownership of the means of production, would safeguard equality in labour and in the distribution of products.

The state withers away insofar as there are no longer any capitalists, any classes, and, consequently, no *class* can be *suppressed*.

But the state has not yet completely withered away, since there still remains the safeguarding of "bourgeois right", which sanctifies actual inequality. For the state to wither away completely, complete communism is necessary. . . .

Only now can we fully appreciate the correctness of Engels's remarks mercilessly ridiculing the absurdity of combining the words "freedom" and "state". So long as the state exists there is no freedom. When there is freedom, there will be no state.

The economic basis for the complete withering away of the state is such a high stage of development of communism at which the antithesis between mental and physical labour disappears, at which there consequently disappears one of the principal sources of modern *social* inequality—a source, moreover, which cannot on any account be removed immediately by the mere conversion of the means of production into public property, by the mere expropriation of the capitalists.

This expropriation will make it *possible* for the productive forces to develop to a tremendous extent. And when we see how incredibly capitalism is already *retarding* this development, when we see how much progress could be achieved on the basis of the level of technique already attained, we are entitled to say with the fullest confidence that the expropriation of the capitalists will inevitably result in an enormous development of the productive forces of human society. But how rapidly this development will proceed, how soon it will reach the point of breaking away from the division of labour, of doing away with the antithesis between mental and physical labour, of transforming labour into "life's prime want"—we do not and *cannot* know.

That is why we are entitled to speak only of the inevitable withering away of the state, emphasising the protracted nature of this process and its dependence upon the rapidity of development of the *higher phase* of communism, and leaving the question of the time required for, or the concrete forms of, the withering away quite open, because there is *no* material for answering these questions.

The state will be able to wither away completely when society adopts the rule: "From each according to his ability, to each according to his needs", *i.e.,* when people have become so accustomed to observing the fundamental rules of social intercourse and when their labour has become so productive that they will voluntarily work *according to their ability.* . . .

10. V. I. LENIN: APRIL THESES*

The provisional government was unable to solidify its control over Russia and failed to perceive the urgency of land reform and peace. Meanwhile, the German General Staff, determined to force Russia out of the war at all costs, facilitated the travel of Lenin to Petrograd via a sealed railroad car. Lenin, upon his arrival in the turbulent Russian capital, found that even the Bolshevik leaders had not fully understood the potentialities of the revolutionary crisis. In a potent speech Lenin expounded his so-called *April Theses*. He boldly rejected Menshevik assertions that the provisional government, as the embodiment of the "bourgeois revolution," should be tacitly supported until the second, or "proletarian revolution," took place. Not only Mensheviks but also some of the Bolsheviks were puzzled by Lenin's apparent departure from Marxist orthodoxy. His masterful will eventually prevailed, however, and the Bolshevik Central Committee fell into line. Within a matter of months, Lenin was able to marshal his forces, win important allies like Leon Trotsky, and carry out a Bolshevik coup. In what ways did Lenin leave himself open to the charge that his views violated orthodox Marxist doctrines? On what grounds did Lenin demand support for the Soviet? What did he mean by a "democratic peace"?

1) In our attitude towards the war, which under the new government of Lvov and Co. unquestionably remains on Russia's part a predatory imperialist war owing to the capitalist nature of that government, not the slightest concession to "revolutionary defencism" is permissible.

The class-conscious proletariat can give its consent to a revolutionary war, which would really justify revolutionary defencism, only on condition: (a) that the power pass to the proletariat and the poorest sections of the peasants aligned with the proletariat; (b) that all annexations be renounced in deed and not in word; (c) that a complete break be effected in actual fact with all capitalist interests.

In view of the undoubted honesty of those broad sections of the mass believers in revolutionary defencism who accept the war only as a necessity, and not as a means of conquest, in view of the fact that they are being deceived by the bourgeoisie, it is necessary with particular thoroughness, persistence and patience to explain their error to them, to explain the inseparable connection existing between capital and the imperialist war, and to prove that without overthrowing capital *it is impossible* to end the war by a truly democratic peace, a peace not imposed by violence.

The most widespread campaign for this view must be organised in the army at the front. . . .

2) The specific feature of the present situation in Russia is that the country is *passing* from the first stage of the revolution—which, owing to the insufficient class-consciousness and organisation of the proletariat, placed power in the hands of the bourgeoisie—to its *second* stage, which must place power in the hands of the proletariat and the poorest sections of the peasants.

This transition is characterised, on the one hand, by a maximum of legally recognised rights (Russia is *now* the freest of all the belligerent countries in the

*V. I. Lenin, "April Theses" in Bernard Isaacs, ed., *Collected Works* (38 vols.; Moscow: Progress Publishers, 1964), XXIV, 21–26.

world); on the other, by the absence of violence towards the masses, and, finally, by their unreasoning trust in the government of capitalists, those worst enemies of peace and socialism.

This peculiar situation demands of us an ability to adapt ourselves to the *special* conditions of Party work among unprecedentedly large masses of proletarians who have just awakened to political life.

3) No support for the Provisional Government; the utter falsity of all its promises should be made clear, particularly of those relating to the renunciation of annexations. Exposure in place of the impermissible, illusion-breeding "demand" that *this* government, a government of capitalists, should *cease* to be an imperialist government.

4) Recognition of the fact that in most of the Soviets of Workers' Deputies our Party is in a minority, so far a small minority, as against *a bloc of all* the petty-bourgeois opportunist elements, from the Popular Socialists and the Socialist-Revolutionaries down to the Organising Committee (Chkheidze, Tsereteli, etc.), Steklov, etc., etc., who have yielded to the influence of the bourgeoisie and spread that influence among the proletariat.

The masses must be made to see that the Soviets of Workers' Deputies are the *only possible* form of revolutionary government, and that therefore our task is, as long as *this* government yields to the influence of the bourgeoisie, to present a patient, systematic, and persistent *explanation* of the errors of their tactics, an explanation especially adapted to the practical needs of the masses.

As long as we are in the minority we carry on the work of criticising and exposing errors and at the same time we preach the necessity of transferring the entire state power to the Soviets of Workers' Deputies, so that the people may overcome their mistakes by experience.

5) Not a parliamentary republic—to return to a parliamentary republic from the Soviets of Workers' Deputies would be a retrograde step—but a republic of Soviets of Workers', Agricultural Labourers' and Peasants' Deputies throughout the country, from top to bottom.

Abolition of the police, the army and the bureaucracy.[1]

The salaries of all officials, all of whom are elective and displaceable at any time, not to exceed the average wage of a competent worker.

6) The weight of emphasis in the agrarian programme to be shifted to the Soviets of Agricultural Labourers' Deputies.

Confiscation of all landed estates.

Nationalisation of *all* lands in the country, the land to be disposed of by the local Soviets of Agricultural Labourers' and Peasants' Deputies. The organisation of separate Soviets of Deputies of Poor Peasants. The setting up of a model farm on each of the large estates (ranging in size from 100 to 300 dessiatines, according to local and other conditions, and to the decisions of the local bodies) under the control of the Soviets of Agricultural Labourers' Deputies and for the public account.

7) The immediate amalgamation of all banks in the country into a single national bank, and the institution of control over it by the Soviet of Workers' Deputies.

---

1. *I.e.*, the standing army to be replaced by the arming of the whole people.

8) It is not our *immediate* task to "introduce" socialism, but only to bring social production and the distribution of products at once under the *control* of the Soviets of Workers' Deputies.

9) Party tasks:
    (a) Immediate convocation of a Party congress;
    (b) Alteration of the Party Programme, mainly:
        (1) On the question of imperialism and the imperialist war;
        (2) On our attitude towards the state and *our* demand for a "commune state";
        (3) Amendment of our out-of-date minimum programme.
    (c) Change of the Party's name [from "Social-Democrat" to Communist].

10) A new International.

We must take the initiative in creating a revolutionary International, an International against the *social-chauvinists* and against the "Centre". . . .

I write, announce and elaborately explain: "In view of the undoubted honesty of those *broad* sections of the *mass* believers in revolutionary defencism . . . in view of the fact that they are being deceived by the bourgeoisie, it is necessary with *particular* thoroughness, persistence and *patience* to explain their error to them. . . ."

Yet the bourgeois gentlemen who call themselves Social-Democrats, who *do not* belong either to the *broad* sections or to the *mass* believers in defencism, with serene brow present my views thus: "The banner [!] of civil war" (of which there is not a word in the theses and not a word in my speech!) has been planted (!) "in the midst [!!] of revolutionary democracy. . .".

What does this mean? In what way does this differ from riot-inciting agitation, from *Russkaya Volya?*

I write, announce and elaborately explain: "The Soviets of Workers' Deputies are the *only possible* form of revolutionary government, and therefore our task is to present a patient, systematic, and persistent *explanation* of the errors of their tactics, an explanation especially adapted to the practical needs of the masses."

Yet opponents of a certain brand present my views as a call to "civil war in the midst of revolutionary democracy"!

I attacked the Provisional Government for *not* having appointed an early date, or any date at all, for the convocation of the Constituent Assembly, and for confining itself to promises. I argued that *without* the Soviets of Workers' and Soldiers' Deputies the convocation of the Constituent Assembly is not guaranteed and its success is impossible.

And the view is attributed to me that I am opposed to the speedy convocation of the Constituent Assembly!

I would call this "raving," had not decades of political struggle taught me to regard honesty in opponents as a rare exception.

Mr. Plekhanov in his paper called my speech "raving." Very good, Mr. Plekhanov! But look how awkward, uncouth, and slow-witted you are in your polemics. If I delivered a raving speech for two hours, how is it that an audience of hundreds tolerated this "raving"? Further, why does your paper devote a whole column to an account of the "raving"? Inconsistent, highly inconsistent!

It is, of course, much easier to shout, abuse, and howl than to attempt to relate, to explain, to recall *what* Marx and Engels said in 1871, 1872 and 1875 about the experience of the Paris Commune and about the *kind* of state the proletariat needs.

Ex-Marxist Mr. Plekhanov evidently does not care to recall Marxism.

I quoted the words of Rosa Luxemburg, who on August 4, 1914, called *German* Social-Democracy a "stinking corpse". And the Plekhanovs, Goldenbergs and Co. feel "offended". On whose behalf? On behalf of the *German* chauvinists, because they were called chauvinists!

They have got themselves in a mess, these poor Russian social-chauvinists—socialists in word and chauvinists in deed.

11. V. I. LENIN: DECREES ON PEACE AND LAND*

Immediately after the Bolshevik seizure of power in November 1917, Lenin and his followers sought to consolidate their authority inside Russia while implementing their ideological goals. The new Russian government was directed by the *Sovnarkom* (Council of Peoples Commissars or CPC), a group dominated and controlled by the Bolsheviks. Conscious of the deep-seated desire of the Russian people to escape the miseries of war, a force which had weakened the Provisional Government in its desperate effort to continue the struggle, the *Sovnarkom* issued a propaganda Decree on Peace on November 8. Although war weariness was apparent throughout Europe, none of the belligerent powers was prepared to accept peace on Bolshevik terms. Issued the same day, the Decree on Land initiated the Bolsheviks' attempt to reconstruct Russian society in accordance with their philosophy. In what sense was the Decree on Peace idealistic? Why was it unacceptable to both the Central Powers and the Allies? Contrast provision five of the Decree on Land with section one of the Peasant Instructions on the Land. What did these provisions mean for the future of the Russian peasantry?

DECREE ON PEACE

The workers' and peasants' government, created by the Revolution of October 24-25 and basing itself on the Soviets of Workers', Soldiers' and Peasants' Deputies, calls upon all the belligerent peoples and their governments to start immediate negotiations for a just, democratic peace.

By a just or democratic peace, for which the overwhelming majority of the working class and other working people of all the belligerent countries, exhausted, tormented and racked by the war, are craving—a peace that has been most definitely and insistently demanded by the Russian workers and peasants ever since the overthrow of the tsarist monarchy—by such a peace the government means an immediate peace without annexations (*i.e.,* without the seizure of foreign lands, without the forcible incorporation of foreign nations) and without indemnities.

The Government of Russia proposes that this kind of peace be immediately concluded by all the belligerent nations, and expresses its readiness to take all

* V. I. Lenin, "Decree on Peace" and "Decree on Land," trans. Yuri Sdobnikov and George Hanna in George Hanna, ed., *Collected Works* (38 vols.; Moscow: Progress Publishers, 1964), XXVI, 249-53, 258-60.

the resolute measures now, without the least delay, pending the final ratification of all the terms of such a peace by authoritative assemblies of the people's representatives of all countries and all nations.

In accordance with the sense of justice of democrats in general, and of the working classes in particular, the government conceives the annexation or seizure of foreign lands to mean every incorporation of a small or weak nation into a large or powerful state without the precisely, clearly and voluntarily expressed consent and wish of that nation, irrespective of the time when such forcible incorporation took place, irrespective also of the degree of development or backwardness of the nation forcibly annexed to the given state, or forcibly retained within its borders, and irrespective, finally, of whether this nation is in Europe or in distant, overseas countries.

If any nation whatsoever is forcibly retained within the borders of a given state, if, in spite of its expressed desire—no matter whether expressed in the press, at public meetings, in the decisions of parties, or in protests and uprisings against national oppression—it is not accorded the right to decide the forms of its state existence by a free vote, taken after the complete evacuation of the troops of the incorporating or, generally, of the stronger nation and without the least pressure being brought to bear, such incorporation is annexation, *i.e.,* seizure and violence.

The government considers it the greatest of crimes against humanity to continue this war over the issue of how to divide among the strong and rich nations the weak nationalities they have conquered, and solemnly announces its determination immediately to sign terms of peace to stop this war on the terms indicated, which are equally just for all nationalities without exception.

At the same time the government declares that it does not regard the above-mentioned peace terms as an ultimatum; in other words, it is prepared to consider any other peace terms, and insists only that they be advanced by any of the belligerent countries as speedily as possible, and that in the peace proposals there should be absolute clarity and the complete absence of all ambiguity and secrecy.

The government abolishes secret diplomacy, and, for its part, announces its firm intention to conduct all negotiations quite openly in full view of the whole people. It will proceed immediately with the full publication of the secret treaties endorsed or concluded by the government of landowners and capitalists from February to October 25, 1917. The government proclaims the unconditional and immediate annulment of everything contained in these secret treaties insofar as it is aimed, as is mostly the case, at securing advantages and privileges for the Russian landowners and capitalists and at the retention, or extension, of the annexations made by the Great Russians.

Proposing to the governments and peoples of all countries immediately to begin open negotiations for peace, the government, for its part, expresses its readiness to conduct these negotiations in writing, by telegraph, and by negotiations between representatives of the various countries, or at a conference of such representatives. In order to facilitate such negotiations, the government is appointing its plenipotentiary representative to neutral countries.

The government proposes an immediate armistice to the governments and peoples of all the belligerent countries, and, for its part, considers it desirable that this armistice should be concluded for a period of not less than three months, *i.e.,* a period long enough to permit the completion of negotiations for peace with the participation of the representatives of all peoples or nations, without exception, involved in or compelled to take part in the war, and the summoning of authoritative assemblies of the representatives of the peoples of all countries for the final ratification of the peace terms.

While addressing this proposal for peace to the governments and peoples of all the belligerent countries, the Provisional Workers' and Peasants' Government of Russia appeals in particular also to the class-conscious workers of the three most advanced nations of mankind and the largest states participating in the present war, namely, Great Britain, France and Germany. The workers of these countries have made the greatest contributions to the cause of progress and socialism; they have furnished the great examples of the Chartist movement in England, a number of revolutions of historic importance effected by the French proletariat, and, finally, the heroic struggle against the Anti-Socialist Law in Germany and the prolonged, persistent and disciplined work of creating mass proletarian organisations in Germany, a work which serves as a model to the workers of the whole world. All these examples of proletarian heroism and historical creative work are a pledge that the workers of the countries mentioned will understand the duty that now faces them of saving mankind from the horrors of war and its consequences, that these workers, by comprehensive, determined, and supremely vigorous action, will help us to conclude peace successfully, and at the same time emancipate the labouring and exploited masses of our population from all forms of slavery and all forms of exploitation.

The workers' and peasants' government, created by the Revolution of October 24-25 and basing itself on the support of the Soviets of Workers', Soldiers' and Peasants' Deputies, must start immediate negotiations for peace. Our appeal must be addressed both to the governments and to the peoples. We cannot ignore the governments, for that would delay the possibility of concluding peace, and the people's government dare not do that; but we have no right not to appeal to the peoples at the same time. Everywhere there are differences between the governments and the peoples, and we must therefore help the peoples to intervene in questions of war and peace. We will, of course, insist upon the whole of our programme for a peace without annexations and indemnities. We shall not retreat from it; but we must not give our enemies an opportunity to say that their conditions are different from ours and that therefore it is useless to start negotiations with us. No, we must deprive them of that advantageous position and not present our terms in the form of an ultimatum. Therefore the point is included that we are willing to consider any peace terms and all proposals. We shall consider them, but that does not necessarily mean that we shall accept them. We shall submit them for consideration to the Constituent Assembly which will have the power to decide what concessions can and what cannot be made. We are combating the deception practised by governments which pay lip-service to peace and justice, but in fact wage annexationist and predatory wars. No government will say all it thinks. We, however, are opposed to secret diplomacy and will act openly in full view of the whole people. We do not close our eyes to difficulties and never have done. War cannot be ended by refusal, it cannot be ended by one side. We are proposing an armistice for three months, but shall not reject a shorter period, so that the exhausted army may breathe freely, even if only for a little while; moreover, in all the civilised countries national assemblies must be summoned for the discussion of the terms.

In proposing an immediate armistice, we appeal to the class-conscious workers of the countries that have done so much for the development of the proletarian movement. We appeal to the workers of Britain, where there was the Chartist movement, to the workers of France, who have in repeated uprisings displayed the strength of their class-consciousness, and to the workers of Germany, who waged the fight against the Anti-Socialist Law and have created powerful organisations.

In the Manifesto of March 14, we called for the overthrow of the bankers, but, far from overthrowing our own bankers, we entered into an alliance with them. Now we have overthrown the government of the bankers.

The governments and the bourgeoisie will make every effort to unite their forces and drown the workers' and peasants' revolution in blood. But the three years of war have been a good lesson to the masses—the Soviet movement in other countries and the mutiny in the German navy, which was crushed by the officer cadets of Wilhelm the hangman. Finally, we must remember that we are not living in the depths of Africa, but in Europe, where news can spread quickly.

The workers' movement will triumph and will pave the way to peace and socialism.

DECREE ON LAND

(1) Landed proprietorship is abolished forthwith without any compensation.

(2) The landed estates, as also all crown, monastery, and church lands, with all their livestock, implements, buildings and everything pertaining thereto, shall be placed at the disposal of the volost land committees and the uyezd Soviets of Peasants' Deputies pending the convocation of the Constituent Assembly.

(3) All damage to confiscated property, which henceforth belongs to the whole people, is proclaimed a grave crime to be punished by the revolutionary courts. The uyezd Soviets of Peasants' Deputies shall take all necessary measures to assure the observance of the strictest order during the confiscation of the landed estates, to determine the size of estates, and the particular estates subject to confiscation, to draw up exact inventories of all property confiscated and to protect in the strictest revolutionary way all agricultural enterprises transferred to the people, with all buildings, implements, livestock, stocks of produce, etc.

(4) The following peasant Mandate, compiled by the newspaper *Izvestia Vserossiiskogo Soveta Krestyanskikh Deputatov* from 242 local peasant mandates and published in No. 88 of that paper shall serve everywhere to guide the implementation of the great land reforms until a final decision on the latter is taken by the Constituent Assembly.

PEASANT MANDATE ON THE LAND

"The land question in its full scope can be settled only by the popular Constituent Assembly.

"The most equitable settlement of the land question is to be as follows:

"(1) *Private ownership of land shall be abolished forever;* land shall not be sold, purchased, leased, mortgaged, or otherwise alienated.

"All land, whether *state, crown, monastery, church, factory, entailed, private, public, peasant, etc., shall be confiscated without compensation* and become the property of the whole people, and pass into the use of all those who cultivate it.

"Persons who suffer by this property revolution shall be deemed to be entitled to public support only for the period necessary for adaptation to the new conditions of life.

"(2) All mineral wealth—ore, oil, coal, salt, etc., and also all forests and waters of state importance, shall pass into the exclusive use of the state. All the small streams, lakes, woods, etc., shall pass into the use of the communes, to be administered by the local self-government bodies.

"(3) Lands on which *high-level scientific* farming is practised —orchards, plantations, seed plots, nurseries, hothouses, etc.—*shall not be divided up, but shall be converted into model farms,* to be turned over for exclusive use *to the state or to the communes,* depending on the size and importance of such lands.

"Household land in towns and villages, with orchards and vegetable gardens, shall be reserved for the use of their present owners, the size of the holdings, and the size of tax levied for the use thereof, to be determined by law.

"(4) Stud farms, government and private pedigree stock and poultry farms, etc., shall be confiscated and become the property of the whole people, and pass into the exclusive use of the state or a commune, depending on the size and importance of such farms.

"The question of compensation shall be examined by the Constituent Assembly.

"(5) All livestock and farm implements of the confiscated estates shall pass into the exclusive use of the state or a commune, depending on their size and importance, and no compensation shall be paid for this.

"The farm implements of peasants with little land shall not be subject to confiscation.

"(6) The right to use the land shall be accorded to all citizens of the Russian state (without distinction of sex) desiring to cultivate it by their own labour, with the help of their families, or in partnership, but only as long as they are able to cultivate it. The employment of hired labour is not permitted.

"In the event of the temporary physical disability of any member of a village commune for a period of up to two years, the village commune shall be obliged to assist him for this period by collectively cultivating his land until he is again able to work.

"Peasants who, owing to old age or ill-health, are permanently disabled and unable to cultivate the land personally, shall lose their right to the use of it but, in return, shall receive a pension from the state.

"(7) Land tenure shall be on an equality basis, *i.e.,* the land shall be distributed among the working people in conformity with a labour standard or a subsistence standard, depending on local conditions.

"There shall be absolutely no restriction on the forms of land tenure—household, farm, communal, or co-operative, as shall be decided in each individual village and settlement.

"(8) All land, when alienated, shall become part of the national land fund. Its distribution among the peasants shall be in charge of the local and central self-government bodies, from democratically organised village and city communes, in which there are no distinctions of social rank, to central regional government bodies.

"The land fund shall be subject to periodical redistribution, depending on the growth of population and the increase in the productivity and the scientific level of farming.

"When the boundaries of allotments are altered, the original nucleus of the allotment shall be left intact.

"The land of the members who leave the commune shall revert to the land fund; preferential right to such land shall be given to the near relatives of the members who have left, or to persons designated by the latter.

"The cost of fertilisers and improvements put into the land, to the extent that they have not been fully used up at the time the allotment is returned to the land fund, shall be compensated.

"Should the available land fund in a particular district prove inadequate for the needs of the local population, the surplus population shall be settled elsewhere.

"The state shall take upon itself the organisation of resettlement and shall bear the cost thereof, as well as the cost of supplying implements, etc.

"Resettlement shall be effected in the following order: landless peasants desiring to resettle, then members of the commune who are of vicious habits, deserters, and so on, and, finally, by lot or by agreement."

The entire contents of this Mandate, as expressing the absolute will of the vast majority of the class-conscious peasants of all Russia, is proclaimed a provisional law, which, pending the convocation of the Constituent Assembly, shall be carried into effect as far as possible immediately, and as to certain of its provisions with due gradualness, as shall be determined by the uyezd Soviets of Peasants' Deputies.

(5) The land of ordinary peasants and ordinary Cossacks shall not be confiscated.

12. V. I. LENIN: THE DISSOLUTION OF THE CONSTITUENT ASSEMBLY*

The Provisional Government had scheduled for November 25, 1917, the election of a constituent assembly to draft a constitution for Russia. The Bolsheviks, following their seizure of power in Petrograd on November 7, did not feel

* V. I. Lenin, "Draft Decree on the Dissolution of the Constituent Assembly," trans. Yuri Sdobnikov and George Hanna in George Hanna, ed., *Collected Works* (38 vols.; Moscow: Progress Publishers, 1964), XXVI, 434–36.

strong enough to cancel the elections. Moreover, they expected to dominate that body when it met. But Lenin and his supporters were sharply disappointed when, in the only free elections ever held in Russia, his party received only approximately half as many votes as the Social Revolutionaries. When the extent of the Bolshevik defeat became known, Lenin was determined to abolish the Constituent Assembly as soon as it met. The Assembly convened in Petrograd on January 18, 1918, but it was promptly dispersed by Bolshevik troops. How did Lenin justify the dissolution of the Constituent Assembly? In what ways do Lenin's views appear to have been a rationalization for having wrenched historical developments from the course predicted by Marx?

DRAFT DECREE

ON THE DISSOLUTION

OF THE CONSTITUENT ASSEMBLY

At its very inception, the Russian revolution produced the Soviets of Workers', Soldiers' and Peasants' Deputies as the only mass organisation of all the working and exploited classes capable of leading the struggle of these classes for their complete political and economic emancipation.

During the whole of the initial period of the Russian revolution the Soviets multiplied in number, grew and gained strength and were taught by their own experience to discard the illusions of compromise with the bourgeoisie and to realise the deceptive nature of the forms of the bourgeois-democratic parliamentary system; they arrived by practical experience at the conclusion that the emancipation of the oppressed classes was impossible unless they broke with these forms and with every kind of compromise. The break came with the October Revolution, which transferred the entire power to the Soviets.

The Constituent Assembly, elected on the basis of electoral lists drawn up prior to the October Revolution, was an expression of the old relation of political forces which existed when power was held by the compromisers and the Cadets. When the people at that time voted for the candidates of the Socialist-Revolutionary Party, they were not in a position to choose between the Right Socialist-Revolutionaries, the supporters of the bourgeoisie, and the Left Socialist-Revolutionaries, the supporters of socialism. The Constituent Assembly, therefore, which was to have crowned the bourgeois parliamentary republic, was bound to become an obstacle in the path of the October Revolution and Soviet power.

The October Revolution, by giving power to the Soviets, and through the Soviets to the working and exploited classes, aroused the desperate resistance of the exploiters, and in the crushing of this resistance it fully revealed itself as the beginning of the socialist revolution. The working classes learned by experience that the old bourgeois parliamentary system had outlived its purpose and was absolutely incompatible with the aim of achieving socialism, and that not national institutions, but only class institutions (such as the Soviets) were capable of overcoming the resistance of the propertied classes and of laying the foundations of socialist society. To relinquish the sovereign power of the Soviets, to relinquish the Soviet Republic won by the people, for the sake of the bourgeois parliamentary system and the Constituent Assembly, would now be a step backwards and would cause the collapse of the October workers' and peasants' revolution.

Owing to the above-mentioned circumstances, the Party of Right Socialist-Revolutionaries, the party of Kerensky, Avksentyev and Chernov, obtained the majority in the Constituent Assembly which met on January 5. Naturally, this party refused to discuss the absolutely clear, precise and unambiguous proposal of the supreme organ of Soviet power, the Central Executive Committee of the Soviets, to recognise the programme of Soviet power, to recognise the Declaration of Rights of the Working and Exploited People, to recognise the October Revolution and Soviet power. By this action the Constituent Assembly severed all ties with the Soviet Republic of Russia. It was inevitable that the Bolshevik group and the Left Socialist-Revolutionary group, who now patently constitute the overwhelming majority in the Soviets and enjoy the confidence of the workers and the majority of the peasants, should withdraw from such a Constituent Assembly.

The Right Socialist-Revolutionary and Menshevik parties are in fact carrying on outside the Constituent Assembly a most desperate struggle against Soviet power, calling openly in their press for its overthrow and describing as arbitrary and unlawful the crushing of the resistance of the exploiters by the forces of the working classes, which is essential in the interests of emancipation from exploitation. They are defending the saboteurs, the servants of capital, and are going as far as undisguised calls to terrorism, which certain "unidentified groups" have already begun. It is obvious that under such circumstances the remaining part of the Constituent Assembly could only serve as a screen for the struggle of the counter-revolutionaries to overthrow Soviet power.

Accordingly, the Central Executive Committee resolves that the Constituent Assembly is hereby dissolved.

THE PEACEMAKERS AND THE TREATY OF VERSAILLES

13. WOODROW WILSON: THE FOURTEEN POINTS*

World War I began as an old-fashioned nationalistic war, with each belligerent defending what it believed to be its national interest. Ideological unity among the allied powers—democratic France, reactionary tsarist Russia, aristocratic Great Britain—was impossible before 1917. Only after revolution overthrew the monarchy in Russia and the United States joined the Allied camp were the western powers able to outline their victory plans in ideological terms and turn their military effort into a "war to end wars."

The clearest expression of faith in a just peace and a peaceful postwar world was embodied in President Woodrow Wilson's (1856–1924) address to a joint session of the United States Congress on January 8, 1918. The core of the President's message was Fourteen Points which affirmed the principles of democracy and self-determination and urged the establishment of an international organization to preserve the peace. After the war Wilson's proposals still stood as a centerpiece around which the heated debates of the Peace Confer-

* Woodrow Wilson, "Fourteen Points," *Congressional Record*, Vol. LVI (1918), Part I, pp. 680–81.

ence revolved. Other allied national leaders, less idealistic than the American President and bound by prior secret treaties, accepted the Fourteen Points with reservations and applied Wilsonian principles only when they corresponded with national objectives. What, according to Wilson, was "the only possible program" to create a durable peace? What basic alterations did he propose in the map of Europe to redress prewar grievances and recognize the nationalistic aspirations of minorities? In what ways were the Fourteen Points open to interpretation and distortion? What advantages might accrue to a defeated Germany in requesting an armistice on the basis of Wilson's Fourteen Points?

Gentlemen of the Congress:

... What we demand in this war, ... is that the world be made fit and safe to live in; ... All the peoples of the world are in effect partners in this interest, and for our own part we see very clearly that unless justice be done to others it will not be done to us. The program of the world's peace, therefore, is our program; and that program, the only possible program, as we see it, is this:

1. Open covenants of peace, openly arrived at, after which there shall be no private international understandings of any kind but diplomacy shall proceed always frankly and in the public view.

2. Absolute freedom of navigation upon the seas, outside territorial waters, alike in peace and in war, except as the seas may be closed in whole or in part by international action for the enforcement of international covenants.

3. The removal, so far as possible, of all economic barriers and the establishment of an equality of trade conditions among all the nations consenting to the peace and associating themselves for its maintenance.

4. Adequate guarantees given and taken that national armaments will be reduced to the lowest point consistent with domestic safety.

5. A free, open-minded, and absolutely impartial adjustment of all colonial claims, based upon a strict observance of the principle that in determining all such questions of sovereignty the interests of the populations concerned must have equal weight with the equitable claims of the government whose title is to be determined.

6. The evacuation of all Russian territory and such a settlement of all questions affecting Russia as will secure the best and freest co-operation of the other nations of the world in obtaining for her an unhampered and unembarrassed opportunity for the independent determination of her own political development and national policy and assure her of a sincere welcome into the society of free nations under institutions of her own choosing; and, more than a welcome, assistance also of every kind that she may need and may herself desire. The treatment accorded Russia by her sister nations in the months to come will be the acid test of their good will, of their comprehension of her needs as distinguished from their own interests, and of their intelligent and unselfish sympathy.

7. Belgium, the whole world will agree, must be evacuated and restored, without any attempt to limit the sovereignty which she enjoys in common with all other free nations. No other single act will serve as this will to restore confidence among the nations in the laws which they have themselves set and determined for the government of their relations with one another. Without this

healing act the whole structure and validity of international law is forever impaired.

8. All French territory should be freed and the invaded portions restored, and the wrong done to France by Prussia in 1871 in the matter of Alsace-Lorraine, which has unsettled the peace of the world for nearly fifty years, should be righted, in order that peace may once more be made secure in the interests of all.

9. A readjustment of the frontiers of Italy should be effected along clearly recognizable lines of nationality.

10. The peoples of Austria-Hungary, whose place among the nations we wish to see safeguarded and assured, should be accorded the freest opportunity of autonomous development.

11. Rumania, Serbia, and Montenegro should be evacuated; occupied territories restored; Serbia accorded free and secure access to the sea; and the relations of the several Balkan states to one another determined by friendly counsel along historically established lines of allegiance and nationality; and international guarantees of the political and economic independence and territorial integrity of the several Balkan states should be entered into.

12. The Turkish portions of the present Ottoman Empire should be assured a secure sovereignty, but the other nationalities which are now under Turkish rule should be assured an undoubted security of life and an absolutely unmolested opportunity of autonomous development, and the Dardanelles should be permanently opened as a free passage to the ships and commerce of all nations under international guarantees.

13. An independent Polish state should be erected which should include the territories inhabited by indisputably Polish populations, which should be assured a free and secure access to the sea, and whose political and economic independence and territorial integrity should be guaranteed by international covenant.

14. A general association of nations must be formed under specific covenants for the purpose of affording mutual guarantees of political independence and territorial integrity to great and small states alike.

... An evident principle runs through the whole program I have outlined. It is the principle of justice to all peoples and nationalities, and their right to live on equal terms of liberty and safety with one another, whether they be strong or weak. Unless this principle be made its foundation no part of the structure of international justice can stand. ...

14. THE TREATY OF VERSAILLES*

The Treaty of Versailles, between the Allies and Germany, was only one of the several peace settlements developed at Paris in 1919. It was, however, the most extensive of the peace agreements as well as the most difficult to complete, for the terms under which postwar Germany must live were spelled out in detail in the fifteen major parts of the Treaty.

* The Treaties of Peace, 1919-1923 (New York: Carnegie Endowment for International Peace, 1924), I, 10-11, 13-15, 17-21, 32, 59, 61-62, 84, 95-96, 98, 100-101, 111, 121-23, 254-55. Reprinted by permission.

The Covenant of the League of Nations (Part I) reflected the highest ideals of the peacemakers, although it resulted not from the initiative of continental leaders but from the repeated proposals of President Wilson. The reparations clauses of Part VIII were more controversial and reflected the political realities of a battered western Europe. Germany, the loser, was expected to pay the cost of a war, the proportions of which were inconceivable by pre-1914 standards. Germany was also forced to accept sole responsibility for the four-year holocaust in Article 231 of the Treaty.

Contrast the terms of the Treaty of Versailles with the principles and actions stated in the Fourteen Points. What new nations were created in part out of prewar German territory? What disposition was made of Germany's prewar colonies? What limits were placed on German military strength? How much was Germany obliged to pay in reparations? Which articles were likely to prove most offensive to Germany? Which article, or articles, in the Covenant of the League of Nations were most critical to its success in preserving the peace?

THE TREATY OF PEACE BETWEEN THE ALLIED AND ASSOCIATED POWERS AND GERMANY SIGNED AT VERSAILLES, JUNE 28, 1919

PART I. THE COVENANT OF THE LEAGUE OF NATIONS

The High Contracting Parties,

In order to promote international co-operation and to achieve international peace and security

by the acceptance of obligations not to resort to war,

by the prescription of open, just and honourable relations between nations,

by the firm establishment of the understandings of international law as the actual rule of conduct among Governments, and

by the maintenance of justice and a scrupulous respect for all treaty obligations in the dealings of organised peoples with one another,

Agree to this Covenant of the League of Nations. . . .

ARTICLE 3: The Assembly may deal at its meetings with any matter within the sphere of action of the League or affecting the peace of the world. . . .

ARTICLE 8: The Members of the League recognise that the maintenance of peace requires the reduction of national armaments to the lowest point consistent with national safety and the enforcement by common action of international obligations. . . .

ARTICLE 10: The Members of the League undertake to respect and preserve as against external aggression the territorial integrity and existing political independence of all Members of the League. In case of any such aggression or in case of any threat or danger of such aggression the Council shall advise upon the means by which this obligation shall be fulfilled.

ARTICLE 11: Any war or threat of war, whether immediately affecting any of the Members of the League or not, is hereby declared a matter of concern to the whole League, and the League shall take any action that may be deemed wise and effectual to safeguard the peace of nations. . . .

ARTICLE 12: The Members of the League agree that if there should arise between them any dispute likely to lead to a rupture, they will submit the matter either to arbitration or to inquiry by the Council, and they agree in no case to resort to war until three months after the award by the arbitrators or the report by the Council. . . .

ARTICLE 13: The Members of the League agree that whenever any dispute shall arise between them which they recognise to be suitable for submission to arbitration and which cannot be satisfactorily settled by diplomacy, they will submit the whole subject-matter to arbitration. . . .

The Members of the League agree that they will carry out in full good faith any award that may be rendered, and that they will not resort to war against a Member of the League which complies therewith. . . .

ARTICLE 16: Should any Member of the League resort to war in disregard of its covenants under Articles 12 [or] 13, it shall *ipso facto* be deemed to have committed an act of war against all other Members of the League, which hereby undertake immediately to subject it to the severance of all trade or financial relations, the prohibition of all intercourse between their nationals and the nationals of the covenant-breaking State, and the prevention of all financial, commercial, or personal intercourse between the nationals of the covenant-breaking State and the national of any other State, whether a Member of the League or not.

It shall be the duty of the Council in such case to recommend to the several Governments concerned what effective military, naval, or air force the Members of the League shall severally contribute to the armed forces to be used to protect the covenants of the League.

The Members of the League agree, further, that they will mutually support one another in the financial and economic measures which are taken under this Article, in order to minimise the loss and inconvenience resulting from the above measures, and that they will mutually support one another in resisting any special measures aimed at one of their number by the covenant-breaking State, and that they will take the necessary steps to afford passage through their territory to the forces of any of the Members of the League which are co-operating to protect the covenants of the League. . . .

ARTICLE 19: The Assembly may from time to time advise the reconsideration by Members of the League of treaties which have become inapplicable and the consideration of international conditions whose continuance might endanger the peace of the world. . . .

ARTICLE 22: To those colonies and territories which as a consequence of the late war have ceased to be under the sovereignty of the States which formerly governed them and which are inhabited by peoples not yet able to stand by themselves under the strenuous conditions of the modern world, there should be applied the principle that the well-being and development of such peoples form a sacred trust of civilisation and that securities for the performance of this trust should be embodied in this Covenant.

The best method of giving practical effect to this principle is that the tutelage of such peoples should be entrusted to advanced nations who by reason of their resources, their experience or their geographical position can best undertake this responsibility, and who are willing to accept it, and that this tutelage should be exercised by them as Mandatories on behalf of the League. . . .

ARTICLE 23: Subject to and in accordance with the provisions of international conventions existing or hereafter to be agree upon, the Members of the League:

(a) will endeavour to secure and maintain fair and humane conditions of labour for men, women, and children, both in their own countries and in all countries to which their commercial and industrial relations extend, and for that purpose will establish and maintain the necessary international organisations;

(b) undertake to secure just treatment of the native inhabitants of territories under their control;

(c) will entrust the League with the general supervision over the execution of agreements with regard to the traffic in women and children, and the traffic in opium and other dangerous drugs;

(d) will entrust the League with the general supervision of the trade in arms and ammunition with the countries in which the control of this traffic is necessary in the common interest;

(e) will make provision to secure and maintain freedom of communications and of transit and equitable treatment for the commerce of all Members of the League. In this connection, the special necessities of the regions devastated during the war of 1914–1918 shall be borne in mind;

(f) will endeavour to take steps in matters of international concern for the prevention and control of disease. . . .

PART II. BOUNDARIES OF GERMANY

PART III. POLITICAL CLAUSES FOR EUROPE

ARTICLE 42: Germany is forbidden to maintain or construct any fortifications either on the left bank of the Rhine or on the right bank to the west of a line drawn 50 kilometres to the East of the Rhine.

ARTICLE 43: In the area defined above the maintenance and the assembly of armed forces, either permanently or temporarily, and military manocuvres of any kind, as well as the upkeep of all permanent works for mobilization, are in the same way forbidden.

ARTICLE 44: In case Germany violates in any manner whatever the provisions of Articles 42 and 43, she shall be regarded as committing a hostile act against the Powers signatory of the present Treaty and as calculated to disturb the peace of the world.

ARTICLE 80: Germany acknowledges and will respect strictly the independence of Austria, within the frontiers which may be fixed in a Treaty between that State and the Principal Allied and Associated Powers; she agrees that this independence shall be inalienable, except with the consent of the Council of the League of Nations.

ARTICLE 81: Germany, in conformity with the action already taken by the Allied and Associated Powers, recognises the complete independence of the Czecho-Slovak State which will include the autonomous territory of the Ruthenians to the south of the Carpathians. Germany hereby recognises the frontiers of this State as determined by the Principal Allied and Associated Powers and the other interested States.

ARTICLE 86: The Czecho-Slovak State accepts and agrees to embody in a Treaty with the Principal Allied and Associated Powers such provisions as may be deemed necessary by the said Powers to protect the interests of inhabitants of that State who differ from the majority of the population in race, language, or religion. ...

Subsequent agreements will decide all questions not decided by the present Treaty which may arise in consequence of the cession of the said Territory.

PART IV. GERMAN RIGHTS AND INTERESTS OUTSIDE GERMANY

ARTICLE 118: In territory outside her European frontiers as fixed by the present Treaty, Germany renounces all rights, titles and privileges whatever in or over territory which belonged to her or to her allies, and all rights, titles, and privileges whatever their origin which she held as against the Allied and Associated Powers.

ARTICLE 119: Germany renounces in favour of the Principal Allied and Associated Powers all her rights and titles over her overseas possessions.

PART V. MILITARY, NAVAL AND AIR CLAUSES

ARTICLE 159: The German military forces shall be demobilised and reduced as prescribed hereinafter.

ARTICLE 160: By a date which must not be later than March 31, 1920, the German Army must not comprise more than seven divisions of infantry and three divisions of cavalry.

After that date the total number of effectives in the Army of the States constituting Germany must not exceed one hundred thousand men, including officers. ... The Army shall be devoted exclusively to the maintenance of order within the territory and to the control of the frontiers.

The total effective strength of officers, including the personnel of staffs, whatever their composition, must not exceed four thousand. ...

The Great German General Staff and all similar organisations shall be dissolved and may not be reconstituted in any form. ...

ARTICLE 168: The manufacture of arms, munitions, or any war material, shall only be carried out in factories or works the location of which shall be communicated to and approved by the Governments of the Principal Allied and Associated Powers, and the number of which they retain the right to restrict. ...

ARTICLE 173: Universal compulsory military service shall be abolished in Germany.

The German Army may only be constituted and recruited by means of voluntary enlistment.

ARTICLE 177: Educational establishments, the universities, societies of discharged soldiers, shooting or touring clubs and, generally speaking associations of every description, whatever be the age of their members, must not occupy themselves with any military matters. ...

ARTICLE 198: The armed forces of Germany must not include any military or naval air forces. ...

PART VI. PRISONERS OF WAR AND GRAVES

PART VII. PENALTIES

ARTICLE 227: The Allied and Associated Powers publicly arraign William II of Hohenzollern, formerly German Emperor, for a supreme offence against international morality and the sanctity of treaties. ...

ARTICLE 228: The German Government recognises the right of the Allied and Associated Powers to bring before military tribunals persons accused of having committed acts in violation of the laws and customs of war. . . .

PART VIII. REPARATION

ARTICLE 231: The Allied and Associated Governments affirm and Germany accepts the responsibility of Germany and her allies for causing all the loss and damage to which the Allied and Associated Governments and their nationals have been subjected as a consequence of the war imposed upon them by the aggression of Germany and her allies.

ARTICLE 232: The Allied and Associated Governments recognise that the resources of Germany are not adequate, after taking into account permanent diminutions of such resources which will result from other provisions of the present Treaty, to make complete reparation for all such loss and damage.

The Allied and Associated Governments, however, require, and Germany undertakes, that she will make compensation for all damage done to the civilian population of the Allied and Associated Powers and to their property during the period of the belligerency of each as an Allied or Associated Power against Germany by such aggression by land, by sea and from the air, and in general all damage as [hereafter] defined. . . .

ARTICLE 233: The amount of the above damage for which compensation is to be made by Germany shall be determined by an Inter-Allied Commission, to be called the *Reparation Commission.* . . .

The findings of the Commission as to the amount of damage defined as above shall be concluded and notified to the German Government on or before May 1, 1921, as representing the extent of that Government's obligations. . . .

PART IX. FINANCIAL CLAUSES

PART X. ECONOMIC CLAUSES

PART XI. AERIAL NAVIGATION

PART XII. PORTS, WATERWAYS AND RAILWAYS

PART XIII. LABOUR

PART XIV. GUARANTEES

ARTICLE 428: As a guarantee for the execution of the present Treaty by Germany, the German territory situated to the west of the Rhine, together with the bridgeheads, will be occupied by Allied and Associated troops for a period of fifteen years from the coming into force of the present Treaty.

ARTICLE 429: [explains three-stage withdrawal of Allied troops over fifteen year period.]

ARTICLE 430: In case either during the occupation or after the expiration of the fifteen years referred to above the Reparation Commission finds that Germany refuses to observe the whole or part of her obligations under the present Treaty with regard to reparation, the whole or part of the areas specified . . . will be reoccupied immediately by the Allied and Associated forces.

ARTICLE 431: If before the expiration of the period of fifteen years Germany complies with all the undertakings resulting from the present Treaty, the occupying forces will be withdrawn immediately.

PART XV. MISCELLANEOUS PROVISIONS

15. GERMAN AND ALLIED OBSERVATIONS ON THE TREATY OF VERSAILLES*

Despite Wilson's preconference insistence on "open covenants openly arrived at," German representatives were not permitted to participate in the deliberations of the Peace Conference and did not see a full text of the Treaty of Versailles until the lengthy draft was finally completed. The German delegation, prepared beforehand to try to alter any provisions of the peace not consistent with the Fourteen Points, found the victors' terms unacceptable. After careful examination of the Treaty, the German delegation compiled a lengthy series of objections and forwarded them to the president of the Peace Conference. Two weeks later, with equal firmness, the Allies rejected most of the German complaints.

To what extent were the German objections concentrated on specific items, and to what extent were they centered on general principles? On what grounds did the allied powers base their rejection of the German observation? In what ways did both sides base their statements on the contents of the Fourteen Points?

THE PRESIDENT OF THE GERMAN PEACE DELEGATION TO THE
PRESIDENT OF THE PEACE CONFERENCE

May 29, 1919.

MR. PRESIDENT: I have the honour to transmit to you herewith the observations of the German Delegation on the draft Treaty of Peace. We came to Versailles in the expectation of receiving a peace proposal based on the agreed principles. We were firmly resolved to do everything in our power with a view to fulfilling the grave obligations which we had undertaken. We hoped for the peace of justice which had been promised to us. We were aghast when we read in that document the demands made upon us by the victorious violence of our enemies. The more deeply we penetrated into the spirit of this Treaty, the more convinced we became of the impossibility of carrying it out. The exactions of this Treaty are more than the German people can bear.

With a view to the re-establishment of the Polish State we must renounce indisputably German territory, nearly the whole of the province of West Prussia, which is preponderantly German, of Pomerania, Danzig, which is German to the core; we must let that ancient Hanse town be transformed into a free State under Polish suzerainty. We must agree that East Prussia shall be amputated from the body of the State, condemned to a lingering death, and robbed of its northern portion including Memel which is purely German. We must renounce Upper Silesia for the benefit of Poland and Czecho-Slovakia, although it has been in close political connexion with Germany for more than 750 years, is instinct with German life, and forms the very foundation of industrial life throughout East Germany.

Preponderantly German circles (*Kreise*) must be ceded to Belgium without sufficient guarantees that the plebiscite, which is only to take place afterwards, will be independent. The purely German district of the Saar must be detached

---

* United States, Department of State, *Papers Relating to the Foreign Relations of the United States: The Paris Peace Conference, 1919* (Washington: Government Printing Office, 1947), XIII, 39–54.

from our Empire and the way must be paved for its subsequent annexation to France, although we owe her debts in coal only, not in men.

For fifteen years Rhenish territory must be occupied, and after those fifteen years the Allies have the power to refuse the restoration of the country; in the interval the Allies can take every measure to sever the economic and moral links with the mother country and finally to misrepresent the wishes of the indigenous population.

Although the exaction of the cost of the war has been expressly renounced, yet Germany, thus cut in pieces and weakened, must declare herself ready in principle to bear all the war expenses of her enemies, which would exceed many times over the total amount of German State and private assets. Meanwhile her enemies demand in excess of the agreed conditions reparation for damage suffered by their civil population, and in this connexion [sic] Germany must also go bail for her allies. The sum to be paid is to be fixed by our enemies unilaterally and to admit of subsequent modification and increase. No limit is fixed save the capacity of the German people for payment, determined not by their standard of life but solely by their capacity to meet the demands of their enemies by their labour. The German people would thus be condemned to perpetual slave labour.

In spite of these exhorbitant demands, the reconstruction of our economic life is at the same time rendered impossible. We must surrender our merchant fleet. We are to renounce all foreign securities. We are to hand over to our enemies our property in all German enterprises abroad, even in the countries of our allies. Even after the conclusion of peace the enemy States are to have the right of confiscating all German property. No German trader in their countries will be protected from these war measures. We must completely renounce our Colonies, and not even German missionaries shall have the right to follow their calling therein. We must thus renounce the realisation of all our aims in the spheres of politics, economics, and ideas.

Even in internal affairs we are to give up the right of self-determination. The International Reparation Commission receives dictatorial powers over the whole life of our people in economic and cultural matters. Its authority extends far beyond that which the Emperor, the German Federal Council and the Reichstag combined ever possessed within the territory of the Empire. This Commission has unlimited control over the economic life of the State, of communities and of individuals. Further, the entire educational and sanitary system depends on it. It can keep the whole German people in mental thralldom. In order to increase the payments due by the thrall, the Commission can hamper measures for the social protection of the German worker.

In other spheres also Germany's sovereignty is abolished. Her chief waterways are subjected to international administration; she must construct in her territory such canals and railways as her enemies wish; she must agree to treaties, the contents of which are unknown to her, to be concluded by her enemies with the new States on the east, even when they concern her own frontiers. The German people is excluded from the League of Nations to which is entrusted all work of common interest to the world.

Thus must a whole people sign the decree for its own proscription, nay, its own death sentence.

Germany knows that she must make sacrifices in order to attain peace. Germany knows that she has, by agreement, undertaken to make these sacrifices and will go in this matter to the utmost limits of her capacity.

1. Germany offers to proceed with her own disarmament in advance of all other peoples, in order to show that she will help to usher in the new era of the peace of Justice. She gives up universal compulsory service and reduces her army to 100,000 men except as regards temporary measures. She even renounces the warships which her enemies are still willing to leave in her hands. She stipulates, however, that she shall be admitted forthwith as a State with equal rights into the League of Nations. She stipulates that a genuine League of Nations shall come into being, embracing all peoples of goodwill, even her enemies of to-day. The League must be inspired by a feeling of responsibility towards mankind and have at its disposal a power to enforce its will sufficiently strong and trusty to protect the frontiers of its members.

2. In territorial questions Germany takes up her position unreservedly on the ground of the Wilson programme. She renounces her sovereign right in Alsace-Lorraine, but wishes a free plebiscite to take place there. She gives up the greater part of the province of Posen, the districts incontestably Polish in population together with the capital. She is prepared to grant to Poland, under international guarantees, free and secure access to the sea by ceding free ports at Danzig, Königsberg and Memel, by an agreement regulating the navigation of the Vistula and by special railway conventions. Germany is prepared to ensure the supply of coal for the economic needs of France, especially from the Saar region, until such time as the French mines are once more in working order. The preponderantly Danish districts of Sleswig will be given up to Denmark on the basis of a plebiscite. Germany demands that the right of self-determination shall also be respected where the interests of the Germans in Austria and Bohemia are concerned.

She is ready to subject all her colonies to administration by the community of the League of Nations if she is recognized as its mandatory.

3. Germany is prepared to make payments incumbent on her in accordance with the agreed programme of peace up to a maximum sum of 100 milliards of gold marks,—20 milliards by May 1, 1926, and the balance (80 milliards) in annual payments without interest. These payments shall in principle be equal to a fixed percentage of the German Imperial and State revenues. The annual payment shall approximate to the former peace Budget. For the first ten years the annual payment shall not exceed one milliard of gold marks a year. The German taxpayer shall not be less heavily burdened than the taxpayer of the most heavily burdened State among those represented on the Reparation Commission.

Germany presumes in this connexion that she will not have to make any territorial sacrifices beyond those mentioned above and that she will recover her freedom of economic movement at home and abroad.

4. Germany is prepared to devote her entire economic strength to the service of reconstruction. She wishes to cooperate effectively in the reconstruction of the devastated regions of Belgium and Northern France. To make good the loss in production of the destroyed mines in Northern France, up to 20 million tons

of coal will be delivered annually for the first five years and up to 8 million tons for the next five years. Germany will facilitate further deliveries of coal to France, Belgium, Italy and Luxemburg.

Germany is moreover prepared to make considerable deliveries of benzol, coal tar and sulphate of ammonia as well as dye-stuffs and medicines.

5. Finally, Germany offers to put her entire merchant tonnage into a pool of the world's shipping, to place at the disposal of her enemies a part of her freight space as part payment of reparation, and to build for them for a series of years in German yards an amount of tonnage exceeding their demands.

6. In order to replace the river boats destroyed in Belgium and Northern France, Germany offers river craft from her own resources.

7. Germany thinks that she sees an appropriate method for the prompt fulfillment of her obligation to make reparation, by conceding participation in industrial enterprises, especially in coal mines to ensure deliveries of coal.

8. Germany, in accordance with the desires of the workers of the whole world, wishes to see the workers in all countries free and enjoying equal rights. She wishes to ensure to them in the Treaty of Peace the right to take their own decisive part in the settlement of social policy and social protection.

9. The German Delegation again makes its demand for a neutral enquiry into the responsibility for the war and culpable acts in its conduct. An impartial Commission should have the right to investigate on its own responsibility the archives of all the belligerent countries and all the persons who took an important part in the war.

Nothing short of confidence that the question of guilt will be examined dispassionately can put the peoples lately at war with each other in the proper frame of mind for the formation of the League of Nations.

These are only the most important among the proposals which we have to make....

The time allowed us for the preparation of this memorandum was so short that it was impossible to treat all the questions exhaustively. A fruitful and illuminating negotiation could only take place by means of oral discussion. This treaty of peace is to be the greatest achievement of its kind in all history. There is no precedent for the conduct of such comprehensive negotiations by an exchange of written notes only. The feeling of the peoples who have made such immense sacrifices makes them demand that their fate should be decided by an open, unreserved exchange of ideas on the principle: "Open covenants of peace openly arrived at, after which there shall be no private international understandings of any kind, but diplomacy shall proceed always frankly and in the public view."

Germany is to put her signature to the Treaty laid before her and to carry it out. Even in her need, Justice is for her too sacred a thing to allow her to stoop to accept conditions which she cannot undertake to carry out. Treaties of Peace signed by the Great Powers have, it is true, in the history of the last decades again and again proclaimed the right of the stronger. But each of these Treaties of Peace has been a factor in originating and prolonging the World War. Whenever in this war the victor has spoken to the vanquished, at Brest-Litovsk and Bucharest, his words were but the seeds of future discord.

The lofty aims which our adversaries first set before themselves in their conduct of the war, the new era of an assured peace of justice, demand a Treaty instinct with a different spirit. Only the cooperation of all nations, a cooperation of hands and spirits can build up a durable peace. We are under no delusions regarding the strength of the hatred and bitterness which this war has engendered; and yet the forces which are at work for an union of mankind are stronger now than ever they were before. The historic task of the Peace Conference of Versailles is to bring about this union.

Accept, Mr. President, the expression of my distinguished consideration.

BROCKDORFF-RANTZAU

LETTER TO THE PRESIDENT OF THE GERMAN DELEGATION, COVERING THE
REPLY OF THE ALLIED AND ASSOCIATED POWERS

June 16, 1919.

SIR: The Allied and Associated Powers have given the most earnest consideration to the observations of the German Delegation on the Conditions of Peace. The reply protests against the peace both on the ground that it conflicts with the terms upon which the Armistice of November 11th, 1918 was signed, and that it is a peace of violence and not of justice. The protest of the German Delegation shows that they utterly fail to understand the position in which Germany stands to-day. They seem to think that Germany has only to "make sacrifices in order to attain peace", as if this were but the end of some mere struggle for territory and power.

I. The Allied and Associated Powers therefore feel it necessary to begin their reply by a clear statement of the judgment passed upon the war by practically the whole of civilised mankind.

In the view of the Allied and Associated Powers the war which began on August 1st, 1914, was the greatest crime against humanity and the freedom of peoples that any nation, calling itself civilised, has ever consciously committed. For many years the rulers of Germany, true to the Prussian tradition, strove for a position of dominance in Europe. They were not satisfied with that growing prosperity and influence to which Germany was entitled, and which all other nations were willing to accord her, in the society of free and equal peoples. They required that they should be able to dictate and tyrannise to a subservient Europe, as they dictated and tyrannised over a subservient Germany.

In order to attain their ends they used every channel in their power through which to educate their own subjects in the doctrine that might was right in international affairs. They never ceased to expand German armaments by land and sea, and to propagate the falsehood that this was necessary because Germany's neighbours were jealous of her prosperity and power. They sought to sow hostility and suspicion instead of friendship between nations. They developed a system of espionage and intrigue which enabled them to stir up internal rebellion and unrest and even to make secret offensive preparations within the territory of their neighbours whereby they might, when the moment came, strike them down with greater certainty and ease. They kept Europe in a ferment by threats of violence and when they found that their neighbours were resolved to resist their arrogant will, they determined to assert their predominance in Europe by force. As soon as their preparations were complete, they encouraged a subservient ally to declare war against Serbia at 48 hours' notice, knowing full well that a conflict involving the control of the Balkans could not be localised and almost certainly meant a general war. In order to make doubly sure, they refused every attempt at conciliation and conference until it was too late, and the world war was inevitable for which they had plotted, and for which alone among the nations they were fully equipped and prepared.

Germany's responsibility, however, is not confined to having planned and started the war. She is no less responsible for the savage and inhuman manner in which it was conducted.

Though Germany was herself a guarantor of Belgium, the rulers of Germany violated, after a solemn promise to respect it, the neutrality of this unoffending people. Not content with this, they deliberately carried out a series of promiscuous shootings and burnings with the sole object of terrifying the inhabitants into submission by the very frightfulness of their action. They were the first to use poisonous gas, notwithstanding the appalling suffering it entailed. They began the bombing and long distance shelling of towns for no military object, but solely for the purpose of reducing the morale of their opponents by striking at their women and children. They commenced the submarine campaign with its piratical challenge to international law, and its destruction of great numbers of innocent passengers and sailors, in mid ocean, far from succour, at the mercy of the winds and the waves, and the yet more ruthless submarine crews. They drove thousands of men and women and children with brutal savagery into slavery in foreign lands. They allowed barbarities to be practised against their prisoners of war from which the most uncivilised people would have recoiled.

The conduct of Germany is almost unexampled in human history. The terrible responsibility which lies at her doors can be seen in the fact that not less than seven million dead lie buried in Europe, while more than twenty million others carry upon them the evidence of wounds and sufferings, because Germany saw fit to gratify her lust for tyranny by resort to war.

The Allied and Associated Powers believe that they will be false to those who have given their all to save the freedom of the world if they consent to treat this war on any other basis than as a crime against humanity and right. . . .

Justice, therefore, is the only possible basis for the settlement of the accounts of this terrible war. Justice is what the German Delegation asks for and says that Germany had been promised. Justice is what Germany shall have. But it must be justice for all. There must be justice for the dead and wounded and for those who have been orphaned and bereaved that Europe might be freed from Prussian despotism. There must be justice for the peoples who now stagger under war debts which exceed £30,000,000,000 that liberty might be saved. There must be justice for those millions whose homes and land, ships and property German savagery has spoliated and destroyed.

That is why the Allied and Associated Powers have insisted as a cardinal feature of the Treaty that Germany must undertake to make reparation to the very uttermost of her power; for reparation for wrongs inflicted is of the essence of justice. That is why they insist that those individuals who are most clearly responsible for German aggression and for those acts of barbarism and inhumanity which have disgraced the German conduct of the war, must be handed over to a justice which has not been meted out to them at home. That, too, is why Germany must submit for a few years to certain special disabilities and arrangements. Germany has ruined the industries, the mines and the machinery of neighbouring countries, not during battle, but with the deliberate and calculated purpose of enabling her industries to seize their markets before their industries could recover from the devastation thus wantonly inflicted upon them. Germany has despoiled her neighbours of everything she could make use of or carry away. Germany has destroyed the shipping of all nations on the high seas, where there was no chance of rescue for their passengers and crews. It is only justice that restitution should be made and that these wronged peoples should be safeguarded for a time from the competition of a nation whose industries are intact and have even been fortified by machinery stolen from occupied territories. If these things are hardships for Germany, they are hardships which Germany has brought upon herself. Somebody must suffer for the consequences of the war. Is it to be Germany, or only the peoples she has wronged?

Not to do justice to all concerned would only leave the world open to fresh calamities. If the German people themselves, or any other nation, are to be deterred from following the footsteps of Prussia, if mankind is to be lifted out of the belief that war for selfish ends is legitimate to any state, if the old era is to be left behind and nations as well as individuals are to be brought beneath the reign of law, even if there is to be early reconciliation and appeasement, it will be because those responsible for concluding the war have had the courage to see that justice is not deflected for the sake of convenient peace. . . .

II. The Allied and Associated Powers therefore believe that the peace they have proposed is fundamentally a peace of justice. They are no less certain that it is a peace of right fulfilling the terms agreed upon at the time of the armistice. There can be no doubt as to the intentions of the Allied and Associated Powers to base the settlement of Europe on the principle of freeing oppressed peoples, and redrawing national boundaries as far as possible in accordance with the will of the peoples concerned, while giving to each facilities for living an independent national and economic life. These intentions were made clear, not only in President Wilson's address to Congress of January 8, 1918, but in "the principles of settlement enunciated in his subsequent addresses", which were the agreed basis of the peace. . . .

Accordingly the Allied and Associated Powers have provided for the reconstitution of Poland as an independent state with "free and secure access to the sea". All "territories inhabited by indubitably Polish populations" have been accorded to Poland. All territory inhabited by German majorities, save for a few isolated towns and for colonies established on land recently forcibly expropriated and situated in the midst of indubitably Polish territory, have been left to Germany. Wherever the will of the people is in doubt a plebiscite has been provided for. The town of Danzig is to be constituted a free city, so that the inhabitants will be autonomous and not come under Polish rule and will form no part of the Polish state. Poland will be given certain economic rights in Danzig and the city itself has been severed from Germany because in no other way was it possible to provide for that "free and secure access to the sea" which Germany has promised to concede.

The German counter-proposals entirely conflict with the agreed basis of peace. They provide that great majorities of indisputably Polish population shall be kept under German rule. They deny secure access to the sea to a nation of over twenty million people, whose nationals are in the majority all the way to the coast, in order to maintain territorial connection between East and West Prussia, whose trade has always been mainly sea-borne. They cannot, therefore, be accepted by the Allied and Associated Powers. At the same time in certain cases the German Note has established a case for rectification, which will be made; and in view of the contention that Upper Silesia though inhabited by a two to one majority of Poles (1,250,000 to 650,000, 1910 German census) wishes to remain a part of Germany, they are willing that the question of whether Upper Silesia should form part of Germany, or of Poland, should be determined by the vote of the inhabitants themselves.

In regard to the Saar basin the regime proposed by the Allied and Associated Powers is to continue for fifteen years. This arrangement they considered necessary both to the general scheme for reparation, and in order that France may have immediate and certain compensation for the wanton destruction of her Northern coal mines. The district has been transferred not to French sovereignty, but to the control of the League of Nations. This method has the double advantage that it involves no annexation, while it gives possession of the coal field to France and maintains the economic unity of the district, so important to the interests of the inhabitants. At the end of fifteen years the mixed population, who in the meanwhile will have had control of its own local affairs under the governing supervision of the League of Nations, will have complete freedom to decide whether they wish union with Germany, union with France, or the continuance of the regime established by the Treaty.

As to the territories which it is proposed to transfer from Germany to Denmark and Belgium, some of these were forcibly seized by Prussia, and in every case the transfer will only take place as the result of a decision of the inhabitants themselves taken under conditions which will ensure complete freedom to vote.

Finally, the Allied and Associated Powers are satisfied that the native inhabitants of the German colonies are strongly opposed to being again brought under Germany's sway, and the record of German rule, the traditions of the German Government and the use to which these colonies were put as bases from which to prey upon the commerce of the world, make it impossible for the Allied and Associated Powers to return them to Germany, or to entrust to her the responsibility for the training and education of their inhabitants.

For these reasons the Allied and Associated Powers are satisfied that their territorial proposals are in accord both with the agreed basis of peace and are necessary to the future peace of Europe. They are therefore not prepared to modify them except as indicated. . . .

IV. The German Delegation appear to have seriously misinterpreted the economic and financial conditions. There is no intention on the part of the Allied and Associated Powers to strangle Germany or to prevent her from taking her proper place in international trade and commerce. Provided that she abides by the Treaty of Peace and provided also that she abandons those aggressive and exclusive traditions which have been apparent no less in her business than in her political methods, the Allied and Associated Powers intend that Germany shall have fair treatment in the purchase of raw materials and the sale of goods, subject to those temporary provisions already mentioned in the interests of the nations ravaged and weakened by German action. It is their desire that the passions engendered by the war should die as soon as possible, and that all nations should share in the prosperity which comes from the honest supply of their mutual needs. They wish that Germany shall enjoy this prosperity like the rest, though much of the fruit of it must go for many years to come, in making reparation to her neighbours for the damage she has done. In order to make their intention clear, a number of modifications have been made in the financial and economic clauses of the Treaty. But the principles upon which the treaty is drawn must stand.

V. The German Delegation have greatly misinterpreted the Reparation proposals of the Treaty.

These proposals confine the amount payable by Germany to what is clearly justifiable under the terms of armistice in respect of damage caused to the civilian population of the Allies by German aggression. They do not provide for that interference in the internal life of Germany by the Reparation Commission which is alleged.

They are designed to make the payment of that reparation which Germany must pay as easy and convenient to both parties as possible and they will be interpreted in that sense. The Allied and Associated Powers therefore are not prepared to modify them.

But they recognise with the German Delegation, the advantage of arriving as soon as possible at the fixed and definite sum which shall be payable by Germany and accepted by the Allies. It is not possible to fix this sum to-day, for the extent of damage and the cost of repair has not yet been ascertained. They are therefore willing to accord to Germany all necessary and reasonable facilities to enable her to survey the devastated and damaged regions, and to make proposals thereafter within four months of the signing of the Treaty for a settlement of the claims under each of the categories of damage for which she is liable. If within the following two months an agreement can be reached, the exact liability of Germany will have been ascertained. If agreement has not been reached by then, the arrangement as provided in the Treaty will be executed.

VI. The Allied and Associated Powers have given careful consideration to the request of the German Delegation that Germany should at once be admitted to the League of Nations. They find themselves unable to accede to this request.

The German revolution was postponed to the last moments of the war and there is as yet no guarantee that it represents a permanent change.

In the present temper of international feeling, it is impossible to expect the free nations of the world to sit down immediately in equal association with those by whom they had been so grievously wronged. To attempt this too soon would delay and not hasten that process of appeasement which all desire.

But the Allied and Associated Powers believe that if the German people prove by their acts that they intend to fulfill the conditions of the peace, and that they have abandoned those aggressive and estranging policies which caused the war, and have now become a people with whom it is possible to live in neighbourly good fellowship, the memories of the past years will speedily fade, and it will be possible at an early date to complete the League of Nations by the admission of Germany thereto. It is their earnest hope that this may be the case. They believe that the prospects of the world depend upon the close and friendly co-operation of all nations in adjusting international questions and promoting the welfare and progress of mankind. But the early entry of Germany into the League must depend principally upon the action of the German people themselves.

VII. In the course of its discussion of their economic terms and elsewhere the German Delegation has repeated its denunciation of the blockade instituted by the Allied and Associated Powers.

Blockade is and always has been a legal and recognised method of war, and its operation has from time to time been adapted to changes in international communications.

If the Allied and Associated Powers have imposed upon Germany a blockade of exceptional severity which throughout they have consistently sought to conform to the principles of international law, it is because of the criminal character of the war initiated by Germany and of the barbarous methods adopted by her in prosecuting it.

The Allied and Associated Powers have not attempted to make a specific answer to all the assertions made in the German note. The fact that some observations have been passed over in silence does not indicate, however, that they are either admitted or open to discussion.

VIII. In conclusion the Allied and Associated Powers must make it clear that this letter and the memorandum attached constitute their last word.

They have examined the German observations and counter-proposals with earnest attention and care. They have, in consequence, made important practical concessions, but in its principles they stand by the Treaty.

They believe that it is not only a just settlement of the great war, but that it provides the basis upon which the peoples of Europe can live together in friendship and equality. At the same time it creates the machinery for the peaceful adjustment of all international problems by discussion and consent, whereby the settlement of 1919 itself can be modified from time to time to suit new facts and new conditions as they arise.

It is frankly not based upon a general condonation of the events of 1914–1918. It would not be a peace of justice if it were. But it represents a sincere and deliberate attempt to establish "that reign of law, based upon the consent of the governed, and sustained by the organised opinion of mankind" which was the agreed basis of the peace.

As such the Treaty in its present form must be accepted or rejected.

The Allied and Associated Powers therefore require a declaration from the German Delegation within five days from the date of this communication that they are prepared to sign the Treaty as it stands today. . . .

In default of such a declaration, this communication constitutes the notification provided for in article 2 of the Convention of February 16th 1919 prolong-

ing the Armistice which was signed on November 11th 1918 and has already
been prolonged by the agreement of December 13th 1918 and January 16th
1919. The said armistices will then terminate, and the Allied and Associated
Powers will take such steps as they think needful to enforce their Terms.

I have the honor, etc.

CLEMENCEAU

16. JOHN MAYNARD KEYNES: THE ECONOMIC CONSEQUENCES OF THE PEACE*

The Treaty of Versailles came under sharp attack even before it was completed, and through the 1920's demands for a substantial revision of the Treaty
mounted. The most emphatic non-German criticism was developed by the noted
British economist, John Maynard Keynes (1883–1946). Keynes served as a
member of the British delegation to the Peace Conference, but resigned in protest
when the outline of the Treaty became clear.

Keynes indicted both the peacemakers and the Treaty in his *Economic Consequences of the Peace* (1919). He criticized the plans and policies of Allied
leaders and accused the peacemakers of deliberately ignoring Wilson's original
concept of a just peace. Keynes believed that the Treaty would, by its harsh
treatment of Germany, reduce that nation to the position of a second-rate power
and compound the economic dislocation of postwar Europe. Only with the
revival of an aggressive Germany in the 1930's did Keynes' dramatic call for
revision lose its appeal in the Western world. Why, in Keynes' view, were the
French more guilty than the other powers of imposing a harsh and vindictive
peace on Germany? Why did Wilson compromise his idealism? On what
grounds did Keynes hold that the Treaty would create new postwar difficulties?

In those parts of the Treaty with which I am here concerned, the lead was
taken by the French, in the sense that it was generally they who made in the
first instance the most definite and the most extreme proposals. This was partly
a matter of tactics. When the final result is expected to be a compromise, it is
often prudent to start from an extreme position; and the French anticipated at
the outset—like most other persons—a double process of compromise, first of all
to suit the ideas of their allies and associates, and secondly in the course of the
Peace Conference proper with the Germans themselves. These tactics were
justified by the event. Clemenceau gained a reputation for moderation with
his colleagues in Council by sometimes throwing over with an air of intellectual
impartiality the more extreme proposals of his ministers; and much went
through where the American and British critics were naturally a little ignorant
of the true point at issue, or where too persistent criticism by France's allies put
them in a position which they felt as invidious, of always appearing to take
the enemy's part and to argue his case. Where, therefore, British and American
interests were not seriously involved their criticism grew slack, and some provisions were thus passed which the French themselves did not take very

* John Maynard Keynes, *The Economic Consequences of the Peace* (London: Macmillan and
Co., 1920), pp. 25–41, 44–47, 49–50, 211–13, 215–17, 219–23, 232–33, 239–40. Reprinted by
permission of Harcourt, Brace & World, Inc., the Trustees of the Estate of the late Lord Keynes, the
Macmillan Company of Canada Ltd., and Macmillan & Co. Ltd.

seriously, and for which the eleventh-hour decision to allow no discussion with the Germans removed the opportunity of remedy.

But, apart from tactics, the French had a policy. Although Clemenceau might . . . close his eyes with an air of fatigue when French interests were no longer involved in the discussion, he knew which points were vital, and these he abated little. In so far as the main economic lines of the Treaty represent an intellectual idea, it is the idea of France and of Clemenceau.

Clemenceau was by far the most eminent member of the Council of Four, and he had taken the measure of his colleagues. He alone both had an idea and had considered it in all its consequences. His age, his character, his wit, and his appearance joined to give him objectivity and a defined outline in an environment of confusion. One could not despise Clemenceau or dislike him, but only take a different view as to the nature of civilised man, or indulge, at least, a different hope.

The figure and bearing of Clemenceau are universally familiar. . . . His walk, his hand, and his voice were not lacking in vigour, but he bore nevertheless, especially after the [assassination] attempt upon him, the aspect of a very old man conserving his strength for important occasions. He spoke seldom, leaving the initial statement of the French case to his ministers or officials; he closed his eyes often and sat back in his chair with an impassive face of parchment, his grey gloved hands clasped in front of him. . . . But speech and passion were not lacking when they were wanted, and the sudden outburst of words, often followed by a fit of deep coughing from the chest, produced their impression rather by force and surprise than by persuasion. . . .

He felt about France what Pericles felt of Athens—unique value in her, nothing else mattering; but his theory of politics was Bismarck's. He had one illusion—France: and one disillusion—mankind, including Frenchmen, and his colleagues not least. His principles for the Peace can be expressed simply. In the first place, he was a foremost believer in the view of German psychology that the German understands and can understand nothing but intimidation, that he is without generosity or remorse in negotiation, that there is no advantage he will not take of you, and no extent to which he will not demean himself for profit, that he is without honour, pride, or mercy. Therefore you must never negotiate with a German or conciliate him; you must dictate to him. On no other terms will he respect you, or will you prevent him from cheating you. . . . His philosophy had, therefore, no place for "sentimentality" in international relations. Nations are real things, of whom you love one and feel for the rest indifference—or hatred. . . . The politics of power are inevitable, and there is nothing very new to learn about this war or the end it was fought for; . . . Prudence required some measure of lip service to the "ideals" of foolish Americans and hypocritical Englishmen; but it would be stupid to believe that there is much room in the world, as it really is, for such affairs as the League of Nations, or any sense in the principle of self-determination except as an ingenious formula for rearranging the balance of power in one's own interests. . . .

. . . According to this vision of the future, European history is to be a perpetual prize-fight, of which France has won this round, but of which this round is certainly not the last. From the belief that essentially the old order does not change, being based on human nature which is always the same, and from a consequent scepticism of all that class of doctrine which the League of Nations stands for, the policy of France and of Clemenceau followed logically. For a Peace of magnanimity or of fair and equal treatment, based on such "ideology" as the Fourteen Points of the President [Wilson], could only have the effect of shortening the interval of Germany's recovery and hastening the day when she will once again hurl at France her greater numbers and her superior resources and technical skill. . . . Thus, as soon as this view of the world is adopted and the other discarded, a demand for a Carthaginian Peace is inevitable, . . .

So far as possible, therefore, it was the policy of France to set the clock back and to undo what, since 1870, the progress of Germany had accomplished. . . .

This is the policy of an old man, whose most vivid impressions and most lively imagination are of the past and not of the future. He sees the issue in terms of France and Germany, not of humanity and of European civilisation struggling forwards to a new order. The war has bitten into his consciousness somewhat differently from ours, and he neither expects nor hopes that we are at the threshold of a new age.

. . . My purpose in this book is to show that the Carthaginian Peace is not *practically* right or possible. Although the school of thought from which it springs is aware of the economic factor, it overlooks, nevertheless, the deeper economic tendencies which are to govern the future. The clock cannot be set back. You cannot restore Central Europe to 1870 without setting up such strains in the European structure and letting loose such human and spiritual forces as, pushing beyond frontiers and races, will overwhelm not only you . . . but your institutions, and the existing order of your Society. . . .

In November 1918 the armies of Foch and the words of Wilson had brought us sudden escape from what was swallowing up all we cared for. The conditions seemed favourable beyond any expectation. . . . The enemy had laid down his arms in reliance on a solemn compact as to the general character of the Peace, the terms of which seemed to assure a settlement of justice and magnanimity and a fair hope for a restoration of the broken current of life. To make assurance certain the President was coming himself to set the seal on his work.

When President Wilson left Washington he enjoyed a prestige and a moral influence throughout the world unequalled in history. His bold and measured words carried to the peoples of Europe above and beyond the voices of their own politicians. The enemy peoples trusted him to carry out the compact he had made with them; and the allied peoples acknowledged him not as a victor only but almost as a prophet. . . .

The disillusion was so complete, that some of those who had trusted most hardly dared speak of it. Could it be true? they asked of those who returned from Paris. Was the Treaty really as bad as it seemed? What had happened to the President? What weakness or what misfortune had led to so extraordinary, so unlooked-for a betrayal?

Yet the causes were very ordinary and human. The President was not a hero or a prophet; he was not even a philosopher; but a generously intentioned man, with many of the weaknesses of other human beings, and lacking that dominating intellectual equipment which would have been necessary to cope with the subtle and dangerous spellbinders whom a tremendous clash of forces and personalities had brought to the top as triumphant masters in the swift game of give and take, face to face in Council,—a game of which he had no experience at all. . . .

. . . What chance could such a man have against Mr. Lloyd George's unerring, almost medium-like, sensibility to every one immediately round him? To see the British Prime Minister watching the company, with six or seven senses not available to ordinary men, judging character, motive, and subconscious impulse, perceiving what each was thinking and even what each was going to say next, and compounding with telepathic instinct the argument or appeal best suited to the vanity, weakness, or self-interest of his immediate auditor, was to realise that the poor President would be playing blind man's buff in that party. . . . The Old World was tough in wickedness anyhow; the Old World's heart of stone might blunt the sharpest blade of the bravest knight-errant. But this blind and deaf Don Quixote was entering a cavern where the swift and glittering blade was in the hands of the adversary.

But if the President was not the philosopher-king, what was he? . . . The President was like a Nonconformist minister, perhaps a Presbyterian. His thought and his temperament were essentially theological not intellectual, with all the strength and the weakness of that manner of thought, feeling, and expression. . . . He had no plan, no scheme, no constructive ideas whatever for clothing with the flesh of life the commandments which he had thundered from the White House. . . .

He not only had no proposals in detail, but he was in many respects, perhaps inevitably, ill-informed as to European conditions. And not only was he ill-informed—that was true of Mr. Lloyd George also—but his mind was slow and unadaptable. . . . There can seldom have been a statesman of the first rank more incompetent than the President in the agilities of the council chamber. . . . His mind was too slow and unresourceful to be ready with *any* alternatives. The President was capable of digging his toes in and refusing to budge, . . . But he had no other mode of defence, and it needed as a rule but little manœuvring by his opponents to prevent matters from coming to such a head until it was too late. . . .

He did not remedy these defects by seeking aid from the collective wisdom of his lieutenants. . . . His fellow-plenipotentiaries were dummies; and even the trusted Colonel House, with vastly more knowledge of men and of Europe than the President, . . . fell into the background as time went on. . . .

At the crisis of his fortunes the President was a lonely man. . . . And in this drought the flower of the President's faith withered and dried up.

. . . as soon, alas, as he had taken the road of compromise, the defects, already indicated, of his temperament and of his equipment, were fatally apparent. He could take the high line; he could practise obstinacy; he could write Notes from Sinai or Olympus; he could remain unapproachable in the White House or even in the Council of Ten and be safe. But if he once stepped down to the intimate equality of the Four, the game was evidently up.

Now it was that what I have called his theological or Presbyterian temperament became dangerous. . . . He was too conscientious. Although compromises were now necessary, he remained a man of principle and the Fourteen Points a contract absolutely binding upon him. He would do nothing that was not honourable; he would do nothing that was not just and right; he would do nothing that was contrary to his great profession of faith. . . .

The President's attitude to his colleagues had now become: I want to meet you so far as I can; I see your difficulties and I should like to be able to agree to what you propose; but I can do nothing that is not just and right, and you must first of all show me that what you want does really fall within the words of the pronouncements which are binding on me. Then began the weaving of that web of sophistry and Jesuitical exegesis that was finally to clothe with insincerity the language and substance of the whole Treaty. . . .

At last the work was finished; and the President's conscience was still intact. In spite of everything, I believe that his temperament allowed him to leave Paris a really sincere man; . . . in the sweat of solitary contemplation and with prayers to God he had done *nothing* that was not just and right; . . .

. . . If only the President had not been so conscientious, if only he had not concealed from himself what he had been doing, even at the last moment he was in a position to have recovered lost ground and to have achieved some very considerable successes. But the President was set. His arms and legs had been spliced by the surgeons to a certain posture, and they must be broken again before they could be altered. To his horror, Mr. Lloyd George, desiring at the last moment all the moderation he dared, discovered that he could not in five days persuade the President of error in what it had taken five months to prove to him to be just and right. After all, it was harder to de-bamboozle this old Presbyterian than it had been to bamboozle him; . . .

. . . The Treaty includes no provisions for the economic rehabilitation of Europe,—nothing to make the defeated Central Empires into good neighbours, nothing to stabilise the new States of Europe, nothing to reclaim Russia; nor does it promote in any way a compact of economic solidarity amongst the Allies themselves; no arrangement was reached at Paris for restoring the disordered finances of France and Italy, or to adjust the systems of the Old World and the New.

The Council of Four paid no attention to these issues, being preoccupied with others,—Clemenceau to crush the economic life of his enemy, Lloyd George to do a deal and bring home something which would pass muster for a week, the President to do nothing that was not just and right. It is an extraordinary fact that the fundamental economic problem of a Europe starving and disintegrating before their eyes, was the one question in which it was impossible to arouse the interest of the Four. Reparation was their main excursion into the economic field, and they settled it as a problem of theology, of politics, of electoral chicane, from every point of view except that of the economic future of the States whose destiny they were handling. . . .

The essential facts of the situation, as I see them, are expressed simply. Europe consists of the densest aggregation of population in the history of the world. . . . In relation to other continents Europe is not self-sufficient; in particular it cannot feed itself. Internally the population is not evenly distributed, but much of it is crowded into a relatively small number of dense industrial centres. This population secured for itself a livelihood before the War, without much margin of surplus, by means of a delicate and immensely complicated organisation, of which the foundations were supported by coal, iron, transport, and an unbroken supply of imported food and raw materials from other continents. By the destruction of this organisation and the interruption of the stream of supplies, a part of this population is deprived of its means of livelihood. . . . The danger confronting us, therefore, is the rapid depression of the standard of life of the European populations to a point which will mean actual starvation for some (a point already reached in Russia and approximately reached in Austria). Men will not always die quietly. For starvation, which brings to some lethargy and a helpless despair, drives other temperaments to the nervous instability of hysteria and to a mad despair. And these in their distress may overturn the remnants of organisation, and submerge civilisation itself in their attempts to satisfy desperately the overwhelming needs of the individual. This is the danger against which all our resources and courage and idealism must now cooperate. . . .

. . . This is the fundamental problem in front of us, before which questions of territorial adjustment and the balance of European power are insignificant. . . .

The significant features of the immediate situation can be grouped under three heads: first, the absolute falling-off, for the time being, in Europe's internal productivity; second, the breakdown of transport and exchange by means of which its products could be conveyed where they were most wanted; and third, the inability of Europe to purchase its usual supplies from overseas.

The decrease of productivity cannot be easily estimated, and may be the subject of exaggeration. But the *prima facie* evidence of it is overwhelming, . . . A variety of causes have produced it;—violent and prolonged internal disorder as in Russia and Hungary; the creation of new governments and their inexperience in the readjustment of economic relations, as in Poland and Czecho-Slovakia; the loss throughout the Continent of efficient labour; . . . the falling off in efficiency through continued underfeeding in the Central Empires; the exhaustion of the soil from lack of the usual applications of artificial manures throughout the course of the war; the unsettlement of the minds of the labouring classes on the fundamental economic issues of their lives. . . . Many persons are for one reason or another out of employment altogether. According to Mr. [Herbert] Hoover, a summary of the unemployment bureaus in Europe in July 1919, showed that 15,000,000 families were receiving unemployment allowances in one form or another, and were being paid in the main by a constant inflation of currency. In Germany there is the added deterrent to labour and to capital (in so far as the Reparation terms are taken literally), that anything, which they may produce beyond the barest level of subsistence, will for years to come be taken away from them. . . .

What then is our picture of Europe? A country population able to support life on the fruits of its own agricultural production but without the accustomed surplus for the towns, and also (as a result of the lack of imported materials and so of variety and amount in the saleable manufactures of the towns) without the usual incentives to market food in return for other wares; an industrial

population unable to keep its strength for lack of food, unable to earn a livelihood for lack of materials, and so unable to make good by imports from abroad
the failure of productivity at home....

Lenin is said to have declared that the best way to destroy the Capitalist System was to debauch the currency. By a continuing process of inflation, governments can confiscate, secretly and unobserved, an important part of the wealth
of their citizens. By this method they not only confiscate, but they confiscate
arbitrarily; and, while the process impoverishes many, it actually enriches
some.... Those to whom the system brings windfalls, beyond their deserts and
even beyond their expectations or desires, become "profiteers," who are the object of the hatred of the bourgeoisie, whom the inflationism has impoverished,
not less than of the proletariat....

... There is no subtler, no surer means of overturning the existing basis of
society than to debauch the currency. The process engages all the hidden forces
of economic law on the side of destruction, and does it in a manner which not
one man in a million is able to diagnose.

In the latter stages of the war all the belligerent governments practised, from
necessity or incompetence, what a Bolshevist might have done from design.
Even now, when the war is over, most of them continue out of weakness the
same malpractices. But further, the Governments of Europe, being many of
them at this moment reckless in their methods as well as weak, seek to direct
on to a class known as "profiteers" the popular indignation against the more
obvious consequences of their vicious methods. These "profiteers" are, broadly
speaking, the entrepreneur class of capitalists, that is to say, the active and constructive element in the whole capitalist society.... By combining a popular
hatred of the class of entrepreneurs with the blow already given to social security by the violent and arbitrary disturbance of contract and of the established
equilibrium of wealth which is the inevitable result of inflation, these governments are fast rendering impossible a continuance of the social and economic
order of the nineteenth century. But they have no plan for replacing it.

We are thus faced in Europe with the spectacle of an extraordinary weakness on the part of the great capitalist class, which has emerged from the industrial triumphs of the nineteenth century, and seemed a very few years ago
our all-powerful master. The terror and personal timidity of the individuals of
this class is now so great, their confidence in their place in society and in their
necessity to the social organism so diminished, that they are the easy victims of
intimidation.... They allow themselves to be ruined and altogether undone by
their own instruments, governments of their own making, and a press of which
they are the proprietors. Perhaps it is historically true that no order of society
ever perishes save by its own hand. In the complexer world of Western Europe
the Immanent Will may achieve its ends more subtly and bring in the revolution ... of the bloodthirsty philosophers of Russia.

The inflationism of the currency systems of Europe has proceeded to extraordinary lengths. The various belligerent Governments, unable or too timid
or too short-sighted to secure from loans or taxes the resources they required,
have printed notes for the balance....

All these influences combine not merely to prevent Europe from supplying
immediately a sufficient stream of exports to pay for the goods she needs to

import, but they impair her credit for securing the working capital required to re-start the circle of exchange and also, by swinging the forces of economic law yet further from equilibrium rather than towards it, they favour a continuance of the present conditions instead of a recovery from them. An inefficient, unemployed, disorganised Europe faces us, torn by internal strife and international hate, fighting, starving, pillaging, and lying. What warrant is there for a picture of less sombre colours? ...

What then is to be done? ... The opportunity was missed at Paris during the six months which followed the Armistice, and nothing we can do now can repair the mischief wrought at that time. Great privation and great risks to society have become unavoidable. All that is now open to us is to re-direct, so far as lies in our power, the fundamental economic tendencies which underlie the events of the hour, so that they promote the re-establishment of prosperity and order, instead of leading us deeper into misfortune....

I propose ... a programme, for those who believe that the Peace of Versailles cannot stand, under the following heads:

1. The Revision of the Treaty.
2. The settlement of inter-Ally indebtedness.
3. An international loan and the reform of the currency.
4. The relations[hip] of Central Europe to Russia....

Chapter Eight

BETWEEN THE WARS

NO statistical measurement, whether in terms of human sacrifices or property losses, can convey the full impact of World War I on western institutions and society. The old Europe which had lived in a state of sober optimism at the turn of the century died at its own hand between the trenches of northern France and the plains of Russia. Four major empires were erased and the prewar social order in Europe was thoroughly disrupted. The odor of gangrene and poison gas haunted the memories of surviving veterans while Europe experienced for the first time the phenomenon of large numbers of displaced persons.

In an era of confusion, uncertainty, and revolution, middle-class Europeans found it difficult to re-establish the apparent stability of the pre-war decade. Despite sporadic signs of normalcy in the 1920's, Europe's loss of confidence in the future was apparent at almost every level of national activity. The expansion of political democracy reached its zenith in 1919 when the peacemakers reshaped European boundaries, but democracy soon receded in central and eastern Europe. Even before the Great Depression of 1929, Italy, Bulgaria, Poland, and Yugoslavia turned to authoritarianism, and the ability of parliamentary democracies to cope with twentieth-century problems was challenged by dictatorships of the right and the left.

The totalitarian systems of the interwar period—fascism and communism—offered radical but different solutions to the problems of the Western world while utilizing similar techniques of control to realize their goals. Soviet leaders, modifying the theories of Karl Marx to meet practical considerations, attempted to create a new society from the shambles of tsarist Russia, often using force, coercion, and violence to achieve their immediate objectives. Fascism, employing similar tactics to control and exploit the masses, attempted to shore up the existing structure of society while concentrating power in the party itself.

The western democracies generally regarded fascism as a more immediate threat than communism. Fascism was closer geographically, more aggressive in foreign policy, militarily more powerful, and less predictable in its actions. Under opportunistic leaders fascist states seemed dynamic, restless, and filled with unlimited ambition. The ideological foundations of the various fascist movements were rarely precise or uniform. Soviet communism, on the other hand, seemed relatively remote and militarily unimpressive between the wars. Marxian concepts were almost a century old and had been debated intensively by both supporters and opponents long before Lenin's Bolsheviks overturned the Russian Provisional Government in November 1917. Communist political parties existed as a potential threat in the western democracies, but no European state fell under communist domination between 1919 and 1939. Many nations, unable to cope with complex social and economic pressures, turned to fascism, or a modified version of fascism, in their search for a drastic solution to immediate problems.

The legacy of World War I could be seen most completely in the reparations problem and the civil war which raged in Russia until late in 1920. On the assumption that German reparations payments would cover the cost, France began the reconstruction of her devastated northern areas even before the Versailles Treaty had been completed. Across the Rhine, the new German Republic made little attempt to fulfill the' terms of a peace treaty it considered unduly harsh. Attempts to resolve the problem were complicated by the insistence of the United States on collecting allied war debts. Those debts could be paid only through the collection of reparations from Germany, while Germany seemed able to pay only through loans from the United States. Thus, the reparations question and Allied war debts proved a circuitous problem impossible to resolve and served to exacerbate differences among the former wartime Allies while also promoting enmity between France and Germany. A French attempt to force the issue by occupying the Ruhr in 1923 led to a drastic inflation in Germany and to lesser economic difficulties in France. Only when reparations payments were scaled down through the Dawes Plan in 1924 and the Young Plan in 1929 did the issue become less emotional. The stabilization of the franc in 1926 restored confidence in the French economy and helped to create a prosperity that was more apparent than real.

Weimar Germany never enjoyed stability, despite the seeming calm of the Stresemann years between 1924 and 1929. The Republic had not been created through the will of the people, and though most Germans were prepared to tolerate the Weimar constitution in the beginning the nation tended to be impatient with the compromises inherent in a democratic system. Few of Germany's many political parties were committed to the democratic process, and the creation of political democracy in 1919 was not supplemented by comprehensive social and economic reforms. The German army remained a state within a state, and the trade unions were disillusioned after 1920 by the failure of German workers to achieve anticipated material gains under the Republic. The inflation of 1923 wiped out the savings of the German middle class and made the average German burgher susceptible to extremist appeals. Although the economy revived and some small segments of the population prospered through 1929, the achievements of the Republic proved inadequate when confronted with the problems of the world Depression, and Germany drifted toward chaos.

Eastern Europe was the poorhouse of the Continent. Both old and new states, with the exception of Czechoslovakia, lacked a solid industrial base. There was no tradition of representative government to supplement a democratic spirit, and governmental control remained in the hands of an elite while land reform lagged far behind peasant expectations. Minority groups were dissatisfied and were often persecuted in east European states, and the lack of investment in agri-

culture combined with overpopulation in many areas led to serious unemployment and underemployment.

The Soviet Union pursued its own course, attempting to bring a western ideology based upon industrialization into harmony with a Russian agrarian society. Tortured at first by civil war and then by internal feuds among party
leaders, the Soviets experimented with the economy to keep their regime in
power. War communism, the NEP, and Five-Year Plans slowly moved the
Soviet Union from the brink of national famine to the status of a ranking industrial power.

After a decade of peace, every western nation was immersed in its own domestic problems. The League of Nations had not yet faced a decisive challenge to its
presumed authority as the world's peacemaker; prewar production levels had
finally been surpassed; the issue of reparations had eased; and the Western
world seemed capable of stumbling toward security and even prosperity. The
financial crash of 1929 abruptly reshaped the future of Western man. Soaring
unemployment, the recalling of foreign loans, a sharp drop in tourism, and
shrinking world markets saw industrial production indices move steadily downward. Tariff walls were ineffective in preventing goods from being dumped
abroad at increasingly lower prices, while more than half of the world's trade
was destroyed.

Reactions to the depression crisis ranged from uncertainty to panic. In the
western democracies the debate centered on the concepts of deflation and a balanced budget or deliberate inflation to stimulate production. Authoritarian
regimes masked their economic problems more successfully and sometimes
found solutions which gave such states a reputation for efficiency. Soviet leaders
insisted that, with the means of production nationalized, unemployment was
nonexistent, and the trains continued to "run on time" in Fascist Italy. Not until
the mid-1930's was the worst of the Depression past, and by then weaker regimes
had toppled and the more fragile democracies had turned to authoritarian
solutions.

Germany under National Socialist rule was more than just another Fascist
state. The changes which took Mussolini years to effect in Italy were carried out
by the Nazis within months. Almost overnight Germany's destiny rested in the
hands of a minority party, and individual liberty was buried in the same tomb
as the Weimar Republic.

The 1930's continued to be troubled years. The Fascist states, through mobilization of their masses, seemed better able to cope with depression problems. By
1936 the League of Nations had been effectively neutralized by German and Italian aggression, and a "New Order" was promised to the discontented throughout Europe. Neo-Fascist organizations and para-military leagues aping the
brownshirts and blackshirts sprang to life even in the established democracies,
and after 1936 foreign affairs and the threat of war dominated the Western
world.

THE INTELLECTUAL DILEMMA

1. SIGMUND FREUD: CIVILIZATION AND ITS DISCONTENTS*

Sigmund Freud (1856–1939), the founder of psychoanalysis, made original contributions to physiology, anatomy, and neurology, as well as to psychology. Both Darwin and Nietzsche had helped depose man from his proud position as central figure in the universe; Freud continued to emphasize that man is an animal and to insist that the principles of the animal world provide a satisfactory explanation for man's development. Freud's major purpose, in his own words, was "to infer or to guess how the mental apparatus is constructed and what forces interplay and counteract in it." He concluded that the human mental process was governed by three basic forces: the *id,* which constitutes the primordial reservoir of energy derived from the primary senses; the *ego,* a specialized agency derived from the *id* through contact with the outer world; and the *super-ego,* a segment of the *ego* incorporating parental demands and the moral standards and norms of society. The development of "conscience" arises from tensions between *ego* and *super-ego.*

In *Civilization and Its Discontents* (1930) Freud looked back over his long and distinguished career in psychoanalysis and attempted to examine man's chances for happiness. He believed that if the human species were to survive, man's instinct for aggression and self-destruction would have to be curbed. What specific analogies did Freud draw between the development of individuals and the growth of civilizations? What was the role of the super-ego in civilization, and why was the commandment "Love thy neighbor as thyself" a psychological impossibility, according to Freud's analysis? On what grounds did Freud label a civilization "neurotic"? In attempting to explain the sinister aspects of human civilization, to what extent was Freud's thought in the tradition of Machiavelli and Hobbes? Contrast Freud's view of history with the doctrines of eighteenth-century *philosophes,* nineteenth-century Hegelians, and Karl Marx.

The analogy between the process of civilization and the path of individual development may be extended in an important respect. It can be asserted that the community, too, evolves a super-ego under whose influence cultural development proceeds. It would be a tempting task for anyone who has a knowledge of human civilizations to follow out this analogy in detail. I will confine myself to bringing forward a few striking points. The super-ego of an epoch of civilization has an origin similar to that of an individual. It is based on the impression left behind by the personalities of great leaders—men of overwhelming force of mind or men in whom one of the human impulses has found its strongest and purest, and therefore often its most one-sided, expression. In many instances the analogy goes still further, in that during their lifetime these figures were—often enough, even if not always—mocked and maltreated by others and even despatched in a cruel fashion. In the same way, indeed, the primal father did not

* *The Standard Edition of the Complete Psychological Works of Sigmund Freud,* trans. James Strachey (24 vols.; London: The Hogarth Press, 1961), XXI, 141–45. Reprinted by permission of Sigmund Freud Copyrights Ltd., the Estate of Mr. James Strachey, the Hogarth Press Ltd. and W. W. Norton and Co., Inc.

attain divinity until long after he had met his death by violence. The most arresting example of this fateful conjunction is to be seen in the figure of Jesus Christ —if, indeed, that figure is not a part of mythology, which called it into being from an obscure memory of that primal event. Another point of agreement between the cultural and the individual super-ego is that the former, just like the latter, sets up strict ideal demands, disobedience to which is visited with "fear of conscience." Here, indeed, we come across the remarkable circumstance that the mental processes concerned are actually more familiar to us and more accessible to consciousness as they are seen in the group than they can be in the individual man. In him, when tension arises, it is only the aggressiveness of the super-ego which, in the form of reproaches, makes itself noisily heard; its actual demands often remain unconscious in the background. If we bring them to conscious knowledge, we find that they coincide with the precepts of the prevailing cultural super-ego. At this point the two processes, that of the cultural development of the group and that of the cultural development of the individual, are, as it were, always interlocked. For that reason some of the manifestations and properties of the super-ego can be more easily detected in its behaviour in the cultural community than in the separate individual.

The cultural super-ego has developed its ideals and set up its demands. Among the latter, those which deal with the relations of human beings to one another are comprised under the heading of ethics. People have at all times set the greatest value on ethics, as though they expected that it in particular would produce especially important results. And it does in fact deal with a subject which can easily be recognized as the sorest spot in every civilization. Ethics is thus to be regarded as a therapeutic attempt—as an endeavour to achieve, by means of a command of the super-ego, something which has so far not been achieved by means of any other cultural activities. As we already know, the problem before us is how to get rid of the greatest hindrance to civilization— namely, the constitutional inclination of human beings to be aggressive towards one another; and for that very reason we are especially interested in what is probably the most recent of the cultural commands of the super-ego, the commandment to love one's neighbour as oneself. In our research into, and therapy of, a neurosis, we are led to make two reproaches against the super-ego of the individual. In the severity of its commands and prohibitions it troubles itself too little about the happiness of the ego, in that it takes insufficient account of the resistances against obeying them—of the instinctual strength of the id [in the first place], and of the difficulties presented by the real external environment [in the second]. Consequently we are very often obliged, for therapeutic purposes, to oppose the super-ego, and we endeavour to lower its demands. Exactly the same objections can be made against the ethical demands of the cultural super-ego. It, too, does not trouble itself enough about the facts of the mental constitution of human beings. It issues a command and does not ask whether it is possible for people to obey it. On the contrary, it assumes that a man's ego is psychologically capable of anything that is required of it, that his ego has unlimited mastery over his id. This is a mistake; and even in what are known as normal people the id cannot be controlled beyond certain limits. If more is demanded of a man, a revolt will be produced in him or a neurosis, or he will be made unhappy. The commandment, "Love thy neighbour as thyself," is the strongest defence against human aggressiveness and an excellent example of the unpsychological proceedings of the cultural super-ego. The commandment is impossible to fulfil; such an enormous inflation of love can only lower its value, not get rid of the difficulty. Civilization pays no attention to all this; it merely admonishes us that the harder it is to obey the precept the more meritorious it is to do so. But anyone who follows such a precept in present-day civilization only puts himself at a disadvantage *vis-à-vis* the person who disregards it. What a potent obstacle to civilization aggressiveness must be, if the defence against it can cause as much unhappiness as aggressiveness itself! 'Natural' ethics, as it is called, has nothing to offer here except the narcissistic satisfaction of being able to think oneself better than others. At this point the ethics based on religion introduces its promises of a better after-life. But so long as virtue is not rewarded here on earth, ethics will, I fancy, preach in vain. I too think it quite certain that a real change in the relations of human beings to possessions would be of more help in this direction than any ethical commands; but the recognition of this fact among socialists has been obscured and made useless for practical purposes by a fresh idealistic misconception of human nature.

I believe the line of thought which seeks to trace in the phenomena of cultural development the part played by a super-ego promises still further discoveries. I hasten to come to a close. But there is one question which I can hardly evade. If the development of civilization has such a far-reaching similarity to the development of the individual and if it employs the same methods, may we not be justified in reaching the diagnosis that, under the influence of cultural urges, some civilizations, or some epochs of civilization—possibly the whole of mankind—have become "neurotic"? An analytic dissection of such neuroses might lead to therapeutic recommendations which could lay claim to great practical interest. I would not say that an attempt of this kind to carry psycho-analysis over to the cultural community was absurd or doomed to be fruitless. But we should have to be very cautious and not forget that, after all, we are only dealing with analogies and that it is dangerous, not only with men but also with concepts, to tear them from the sphere in which they have originated and been evolved. Moreover, the diagnosis of communal neuroses is faced with a special difficulty. In an individual neurosis we take as our starting-point the contrast that distinguishes the patient from his environment, which is assumed to be "normal." For a group all of whose members are affected by one and the same disorder no such background could exist; it would have to be found elsewhere. And as regards the therapeutic application of our knowledge, what would be the use of the most correct analysis of social neuroses, since no one possesses authority to impose such a therapy upon the group? But in spite of all these difficulties, we may expect that one day someone will venture to embark upon a pathology of cultural communities.

For a wide variety of reasons, it is very far from my intention to express an opinion upon the value of human civilization. I have endeavoured to guard myself against the enthusiastic prejudice which holds that our civilization is the most precious thing that we possess or could acquire and that its path will necessarily lead to heights of unimagined perfection. I can at least listen without indignation to the critic who is of the opinion that when one surveys the aims of cultural endeavour and the means it employs, one is bound to come to the conclusion that the whole effort is not worth the trouble, and that the outcome of it can only be a state of affairs which the individual will be unable to tolerate. My impartiality is made all the easier to me by my knowing very little about all these things. One thing only do I know for certain and that is that man's judgements of value follow directly his wishes for happiness—that, accordingly, they are an attempt to support his illusions with arguments. I should find it very understandable if someone were to point out the obligatory nature of the course of human civilization and were to say, for instance, that the tendencies to a restriction of sexual life or to the institution of a humanitarian ideal at the expense of natural selection were developmental trends which cannot be averted or turned aside and to which it is best for us to yield as though they were necessities of nature. I know, too, the objection that can be made against this, to the effect that in the history of mankind, trends such as these, which were considered unsurmountable, have often been thrown aside and replaced by other trends. Thus I have not the courage to rise up before my fellow-men as a prophet, and I bow to their reproach that I can offer them no consolation: for at bottom that is what they are all demanding—the wildest revolutionaries no less passionately than the most virtuous believers.

The fateful question for the human species seems to me to be whether and to what extent their cultural development will succeed in mastering the disturbance of their communal life by the human instinct of aggression and self-destruction. It may be that in this respect precisely the present time deserves a special interest. Men have gained control over the forces of nature to such an extent that with their help they would have no difficulty in exterminating one another to the last man. They know this, and hence comes a large part of their current unrest, their unhappiness and their mood of anxiety. And now it is to be expected that the other of the two 'Heavenly Powers,' eternal Eros, will make an effort to assert himself in the struggle with his equally immortal adversary. But who can foresee with what success and with what result? . . .

2. FRANZ KAFKA: THE TRIAL*

Franz Kafka (1883–1924) was born to a prosperous Jewish family in Prague. After taking a law degree at the German University in his native city, he secured a minor civil service post and soon began to devote increasing amounts of time to writing. He died from tuberculosis at the age of forty.

Few of Kafka's writings were published during his lifetime, and it was not until the eve of World War II that his highly original novels began to appeal to a wide reading public in Europe and abroad. All of Kafka's work dealt with the experience of man in an unintelligible universe. Reacting to the helplessness of individuals in the face of a mass, technological society, Kafka sensed the ingredients of twentieth-century totalitarianism. How did Kafka's hero in *The Trial* ("K") attempt to maintain his integrity as a human being in the face of

* Franz Kafka, *The Trial*, trans. Willa and Edwin Muir (New York: Alfred A. Knopf, 1957), pp. 279–86. Reprinted by permission.

incomprehensible surroundings? Did he succeed? What apparent meaning did the so-called forces of "law and order" have for Kafka? To what extent can the influence of Freudian ideas be detected in Kafka's views of human psychology?

On the evening before K.'s thirty-first birthday—it was about nine o'clock, the time when a hush falls on the streets—two men came to his lodging. In frock coats, pallid and plump, with top hats that were apparently irremovable. After some exchange of formalities regarding precedence at the front door, they repeated the same ceremony more elaborately before K.'s door. Without having been informed of their visit, K. was sitting also dressed in black in an armchair near the door, slowly pulling on a pair of new gloves that fitted tightly over the fingers, looking as if he were expecting guests. He stood up at once and scrutinized the gentlemen with curiosity. "So you are meant for me?" he asked. The gentlemen bowed, each indicating the other with the hand that held the top hat. K. admitted to himself that he had been expecting different visitors. He went to the window and took another look at the dark street. Nearly all the windows at the other side of the street were also in darkness; in many of them the curtains were drawn. At one lighted tenement window some babies were playing behind bars, reaching with their little hands toward each other although not able to move themselves from the spot. "Tenth-rate old actors they send for me," said K. to himself, glancing round again to confirm the impression. "They want to finish me off cheaply." He turned abruptly toward the men and asked: "What theater are you playing at?" "Theater?" said one, the corners of his mouth twitching as he looked for advice to the other, who acted as if he were a dumb man struggling to overcome a stubborn disability. "They're not prepared to answer questions," said K. to himself and went to fetch his hat.

While still on the stairs the two of them tried to take K. by the arms, and he said: "Wait till we're in the street, I'm not an invalid." But just outside the street door they fastened on him in a fashion he had never before experienced. They kept their shoulders close behind his and instead of crooking their elbows, wound their arms round his at full length, holding his hands in a methodical, practiced, irresistible grip. K. walked rigidly between them, the three of them were interlocked in a unity which would have brought all three down together had one of them been knocked over. It was a unity such as can hardly be formed except by lifeless matter.

Under the street lamps K. attempted time and time again, difficult though it was at such very close quarters, to see his companions more clearly than had been possible in the dusk of his room. "Perhaps they are tenors," he thought, as he studied their fat double chins. He was repelled by the painful cleanliness of their faces. One could literally see that the cleansing hand had been at work in the corners of the eyes, rubbing the upper lip, scrubbing out the furrows at the chin.

When that occurred to K. he halted, and in consequence the others halted too; they stood on the verge of an open, deserted square adorned with flower beds. "Why did they send you, of all people!" he said; it was more a cry than a question. The gentlemen obviously had no answer to make, they stood waiting with their free arms hanging, like sickroom attendants waiting while their patient takes a rest. "I won't go any farther," said K. experimentally. No answer was needed to that, it was sufficient that the two men did not loosen their grip and tried to propel K. from the spot; but he resisted them. "I shan't need my strength much longer, I'll expend all the strength I have," he thought. Into his mind came a recollection of flies struggling away from the flypaper till their little legs were torn off. "The gentlemen won't find it easy."

And then before them Fräulein Bürstner appeared, mounting a small flight of steps leading into the square from a low-lying side-street. It was not quite certain that it was she, but the resemblance was close enough. Whether it were really Fräulein Bürstner or not, however, did not matter to K.; the important thing was that he suddenly realized the futility of resistance. There would be nothing heroic in it were he to resist, to make difficulties for his companions, to snatch at the last appearance of life by struggling. He set himself in motion, and the relief his warders felt was transmitted to some extent even to himself. They suffered him now to lead the way, and he followed the direction taken by the girl ahead of him, not that he wanted to overtake her or to keep her in sight as long as possible, but only that he might not forget the lesson she had brought into his mind. "The only thing I can do now," he told himself, and the regular correspondence between his steps and the steps of the other two confirmed his thought, "the only thing for me to go on doing is to keep my intelligence calm and analytical to the end. I always wanted to snatch at the world with twenty hands, and not for a very laudable motive, either. That was wrong, and am I to show now that not even a year's trial has taught me anything? Am I to leave this world as a man who has no common sense? Are people to say of me after I am gone that at the beginning of my case I wanted to finish it, and at the end of it I wanted to begin it again? I don't want that to be said. I am grateful for the fact that these half-dumb, senseless creatures have been sent to accompany me on this journey, and that I have been left to say to myself all that is needed."

Fräulein Bürstner meanwhile had gone round the bend into a side-street, but by this time K. could do without her and submitted himself to the guidance of his escort. In complete harmony all three now made their way across a bridge in the moonlight, the two men readily yielded to K.'s slightest movement, and when he turned slightly toward the parapet they turned, too, in a solid front. The water, glittering and trembling in the moonlight, divided on either side of a small island, on which the foliage of trees and bushes rose in thick masses, as if bunched together. Beneath the trees ran gravel paths, now invisible, with convenient benches on which K. had stretched himself at ease many a summer. "I didn't mean to stop," he said to his companions, shamed by their obliging compliance. Behind K.'s back the one seemed to reproach the other gently for the mistaken stop they had made, and then all three went on again.

They passed through several steeply rising streets, in which policemen stood or patrolled at intervals; sometimes a good way off, sometimes quite near. One with a bushy mustache, his hand on the hilt of his saber, came up as of set purpose close to the not quite harmless-looking group. The two gentlemen halted, the policeman seemed to be already opening his mouth, but K. forcibly pulled his companions forward. He kept looking round cautiously to see if the policeman were following; as soon as he had put a corner between himself and the policeman he started to run, and his two companions, scant of breath as they were, had to run beside him.

So they came quickly out of the town, which at this point merged almost without transition into the open fields. A small stone quarry, deserted and desolate, lay quite near to a still completely urban house. Here the two men came to a standstill, whether because this place had been their goal from the very beginning or because they were too exhausted to go farther. Now they loosened their hold of K., who stood waiting dumbly, took off the top hats and wiped the sweat from their brows with pocket handkerchiefs, meanwhile surveying the quarry. The moon shone down on everything with that simplicity and serenity which no other light possesses.

After an exchange of courteous formalities regarding which of them was to take precedence in the next task—these emissaries seemed to have been given no specific assignments in the charge laid jointly upon them—one of them came up to K. and removed his coat, his waistcoat, and finally his shirt. K. shivered involuntarily, whereupon the man gave him a light, reassuring pat on the back. Then he folded the clothes carefully together, as if they were likely to be used again at some time, although perhaps not immediately. Not to leave K. standing motionless, exposed to the night breeze, which was rather chilly, he took him by the arm and walked him up and down a little, while his partner investigated the quarry to find a suitable spot. When he had found it he beckoned, and K.'s companion led him over there. It was a spot near the cliffside where a loose boulder was lying. The two of them laid K. down on the ground, propped him against the boulder, and settled his head upon it. But in spite of the pains they took and all the willingness K. showed, his posture remained contorted and unnatural-looking. So one of the men begged the other to let him dispose K. all by himself, yet even that did not improve matters. Finally they left K. in a position which was not even the best of the positions they had already tried out. Then one of them opened his frock coat and out of a sheath that hung from a belt girt round his waistcoat drew a long, thin, double-edged butcher's knife, held it up, and tested the cutting edges in the moonlight. Once more the odious courtesies began, the first handed the knife across K. to the second, who handed it across K. back again to the first. K. now perceived clearly that he was supposed to seize the knife himself, as it traveled from hand to hand above him, and plunge it into his own breast. But he did not do so, he merely turned his head, which was still free to move, and gazed around him. He could not completely rise to the occasion, he could not relieve the officials of all their tasks; the responsibility for this last failure of his lay with him who had not left him the remnant of strength necessary for the deed. His glance fell on the top story of the house adjoining the quarry. With a flicker as of a light going up, the casements of a window there suddenly flew open; a human figure, faint and insubstantial at that distance and that height, leaned abruptly far forward and stretched both arms still farther. Who was it? A friend? A good man? Someone who sympathized? Someone who wanted to help? Was it one person only? Or was it mankind? Was help at hand? Were there arguments in his favour that had been overlooked? Of course there must be. Logic is doubtless unshakable, but it cannot withstand a man who wants to go on living. Where was the Judge whom he had never seen? Where was the High Court, to which he had never penetrated? He raised his hands and spread out all his fingers.

But the hands of one of the partners were already at K.'s throat, while the other thrust the knife deep into his heart and turned it there twice. With failing eyes K. could still see the two of them immediately before him, cheek leaning against cheek, watching the final act. "Like a dog!" he said; it was as if the shame of it must outlive him.

3. T. S. ELIOT: THE WASTE LAND*

Thomas Stearns Eliot (1888–1965), born of New England stock in St. Louis, Missouri, was educated at Harvard, Paris, and Oxford. In 1914 he settled in London and became a British subject in 1927. He contributed to various magazines and, in 1922, established his own literary review, *The Criterion.* In the same year he published *The Waste Land* and dedicated the poem to another American expatriate, Ezra Pound. The poem achieved much of its stylistic force from Pound's criticism.

The Waste Land was composed in five vignettes, or color-flashes, and expressed the disillusionments of the postwar period. How did Eliot manipulate classical and contemporary language to show the postwar disenchantment with traditional education and culture? What strains and stresses in postwar British society were evident in the following selection from Eliot's poem? To what extent did the author share Kafka's attitudes toward life?

II. A GAME OF CHESS

The Chair she sat in, like a burnished throne,
Glowed on the marble, where the glass
Held up by standards wrought with fruited vines
From which a golden Cupidon peeped out
(Another hid his eyes behind his wing)
Doubled the flames of sevenbranched candelabra
Reflecting light upon the table as
The glitter of her jewels rose to meet it,
From satin cases poured in rich profusion;
In vials of ivory and coloured glass
Unstoppered, lurked her strange synthetic perfumes,
Unguent, powdered, or liquid—troubled, confused
And drowned the sense in odours; stirred by the air
That freshened from the window, these ascended
In fattening the prolonged candle-flames,
Flung their smoke into the laquearia,
Stirring the pattern on the coffered ceiling.
Huge sea-wood fed with copper
Burned green and orange, framed by the coloured stone,
In which sad light a carvèd dolphin swam.
Above the antique mantel was displayed

As though a window gave upon the sylvan scene
The change of Philomel, by the barbarous king
So rudely forced; yet there the nightingale
Filled all the desert with inviolable voice
And still she cried, and still the world pursues,
"Jug Jug" to dirty ears.
And other withered stumps of time
Were told upon the walls; staring forms
Leaned out, leaning, hushing the room enclosed.
Footsteps shuffled on the stair.
Under the firelight, under the brush, her hair
Spread out in fiery points
Glowed into words, then would be savagely still.

"My nerves are bad to-night. Yes, bad. Stay with me.
"Speak to me. Why do you never speak. Speak.
   "What are you thinking of? What thinking? What?
"I never know what you are thinking. Think."

I think we are in rats' alley
Where the dead men lost their bones.

"What is that noise?"
                  The wind under the door.
"What is that noise now? What is the wind doing?"
                Nothing again nothing.
                        "Do
You know nothing? Do you see nothing? Do you remember
"Nothing?"

   I remember
Those are pearls that were his eyes.
"Are you alive, or not? Is there nothing in your head?"
                                  But

O O O O that Shakespeherian Rag—
It's so elegant
So intelligent
"What shall I do now? What shall I do?"
"I shall rush out as I am, and walk the street
"With my hair down, so. What shall we do tomorrow?
"What shall we ever do?"
                    The hot water at ten.
And if it rains, a closed car at four.
And we shall play a game of chess,
Pressing lidless eyes and waiting for a knock upon the door.

When Lil's husband got demobbed, I said—
I didn't mince my words, I said to her myself,
HURRY UP PLEASE ITS TIME
Now Albert's coming back, make yourself a bit smart.
He'll want to know what you done with that money he gave you
To get yourself some teeth. He did, I was there.
You have them all out, Lil, and get a nice set,
He said, I swear, I can't bear to look at you.
And no more can't I, I said, and think of poor Albert,
He's been in the army four years, he wants a good time,
And if you don't give it him, there's others will, I said.
Oh is there, she said. Something o' that, I said.
Then I'll know who to thank, she said, and give me a straight look.
HURRY UP PLEASE ITS TIME
If you don't like it you can get on with it, I said.
Others can pick and choose if you can't.
But if Albert makes off, it won't be for lack of telling.
You ought to be ashamed, I said, to look so antique.
(And her only thirty-one.)
I can't help it, she said, pulling a long face,
It's them pills I took, to bring it off, she said.
(She's had five already, and nearly died of young George.)
The chemist said it would be all right, but I've never been the same.
You *are* a proper fool, I said.
Well, if Albert won't leave you alone, there it is, I said,
What you get married for if you don't want children?
HURRY UP PLEASE ITS TIME
Well, that Sunday Albert was home, they had a hot gammon,
And they asked me in to dinner, to get the beauty of it hot—
HURRY UP PLEASE ITS TIME
HURRY UP PLEASE ITS TIME
Goonight Bill. Goonight Lou. Goonight May. Goonight.
Ta ta. Goonight. Goonight.
Good night, ladies, good night, sweet ladies, good night, good night.

4. JOSÉ ORTEGA Y GASSET: THE REVOLT OF THE MASSES*

A leading Spanish intellectual of the twentieth century, José Ortega y Gasset (1883–1955) received his earliest training under Jesuit teachers. Later he studied at the universities of Madrid and Marburg. In 1910 Ortega was appointed Professor of Metaphysics at Madrid. A dedicated opponent of the Spanish monarchy, Ortega was elected a deputy to the republican Cortes in 1931. Early in the Spanish Civil War (1936–39) he concluded that the republican cause was doomed and went into voluntary exile. After teaching in Argentina, Peru, and Portugal, Ortega returned to Spain in 1949.

* José Ortega y Gasset, *The Revolt of the Masses* (New York: W. W. Norton and Co., Inc., 1932), pp. 195–203. Copyright © 1960 by Teresa Carey. Reprinted by permission.

Of Ortega's many books on philosophy, literature, and politics, none was more influential than *The Revolt of the Masses* (1930). Ortega was seriously disturbed by the historical phenomenon of rapid population growth and especially by the seeming impossibility of the masses being able to assimilate traditional cultural values. What was Ortega's solution for the bankruptcy of contemporary European civilization? What was his evaluation of Communism? To what extent did Ortega's fear of "mass man" parallel the earlier views of Friedrich Nietzsche? In what ways did Ortega and Freud agree or disagree in their diagnoses of the dilemma of European civilization?

No one knows towards what centre human things are going to gravitate in the near future, and hence the life of the world has become scandalously provisional. Everything that to-day is done in public and in private—even in one's inner conscience—is provisional, the only exception being certain portions of certain sciences. He will be a wise man who puts no trust in all that is proclaimed, upheld, essayed, and lauded at the present day. All that will disappear as quickly as it came. All of it, from the mania for physical sports (the mania, not the sports themselves) to political violence; from "new art" to sun-baths at idiotic fashionable watering-places. Nothing of all that has any roots; it is all pure invention, in the bad sense of the word, which makes it equivalent to fickle caprice. It is not a creation based on the solid substratum of life; it is not a genuine impulse or need. In a word, from the point of view of life it is false. We are in presence of the contradiction of a style of living which cultivates sincerity and is at the same time a fraud. There is truth only in an existence which feels its acts as irrevocably necessary. There exists to-day no politician who feels the inevitableness of his policy, and the more extreme his attitudes, the more frivolous, the less inspired by destiny they are. The only life with its roots fixed in earth, the only autochthonous life, is that which is made up of inevitable acts. All the rest, all that it is in our power to take or to leave or to exchange for something else, is mere falsification of life. Life to-day is the fruit of an interregnum, of an empty space between two organisations of historical rule—that which was, that which is to be. For this reason it is essentially provisional. Men do not know what institutions to serve in truth; women do not know what type of men they in truth prefer.

The European cannot live unless embarked upon some great unifying enterprise. When this is lacking, he becomes degraded, grows slack, his soul is paralysed. We have a commencement of this before our eyes to-day. The groups which up to to-day have been known as nations arrived about a century ago at their highest point of expansion. Nothing more can be done with them except lead them to a higher evolution. They are now mere past accumulating all around Europe, weighing it down, imprisoning it. With more vital freedom than ever, we feel that we cannot breathe the air within our nations, because it is a confined air. What was before a nation open to all the winds of heaven, has turned into something provincial, an enclosed space.

Everyone sees the need of a new principle of life. But as always happens in similar crises—some people attempt to save the situation by an artificial intensification of the very principle which has led to decay. This is the meaning of the "nationalist" outburst of recent years. And, I repeat, things have always gone

that way. The last flare, the longest; the last sigh, the deepest. On the very eve
of their disappearance there is an intensification of frontiers—military and
economic.

But all these nationalisms are so many blind alleys. Try to project one into the
future and see what happens. There is no outlet that way. Nationalism is always
an effort in a direction opposite to that of the principle which creates nations.
The former is exclusive in tendency, the latter inclusive. In periods of consolidation, nationalism has a positive value, and is a lofty standard. But in Europe
everything is more than consolidated, and nationalism is nothing but a mania, a
pretext to escape from the necessity of inventing something new, some great
enterprise. Its primitive methods of action and the type of men it exalts reveal
abundantly that it is the opposite of a historical creation.

Only the determination to construct a great nation from the group of peoples
of the Continent would give new life to the pulses of Europe. She would start to
believe in herself again, and automatically to make demands on, to discipline,
herself. But the situation is much more difficult than is generally realised. The
years are passing and there is the risk that the European will grow accustomed
to the lower tone of the existence he is at present living, will get used neither to
rule others nor to rule himself. In such a case, all his virtues and higher capacities would vanish into air.

But, as has always happened in the process of nation-forming, the union of
Europe is opposed by the conservative classes. This may well mean destruction
for them, for to the general danger of Europe becoming definitely demoralised
and losing all its historic strength is added another, more concrete and more
imminent. When Communism triumphed in Russia, there were many who
thought that the whole of the West would be submerged by the Red torrent. I
did not share that view; on the contrary I wrote at the time that Russian Communism was a substance not assimilable by the European, a type that has in its
history thrown all its efforts and energies in the scale of individualism. Time
has passed, and the fearful ones of a while since have recovered their tranquillity. They have recovered their tranquillity precisely at the moment when they
might with reason lose it. Because now indeed is the time when victorious, overwhelming Communism may spread over Europe.

This is how it appears to me. Now, just as before, the creed of Russian Communism does not interest or attract Europeans—offers them no tempting future.
And not for the trivial reasons that the apostles of Communism—obstinate,
unheeding, strangers to fact—are in the habit of alleging. The bourgeois of the
West knows quite well, that even without Communism, the days are numbered
of the man who lives exclusively on his income and hands it down to his children. It is not this that renders Europe immune to the Russian creed, still less is
it fear. The arbitrary bases on which Sorel founded his tactics of violence twenty
years ago seem to us stupid enough to-day. The bourgeois is no coward, as Sorel
thought, and at the actual moment is more inclined to violence than the workers. Everybody knows that if Bolshevism triumphed in Russia, it was because
there were in Russia no bourgeois. Fascism, which is a *petit bourgeois* movement, has shown itself more violent than all the labour movement combined. It
is nothing of all this then that prevents the European from flinging himself into

Communism, but a much simpler reason. It is that the European does not see in the Communistic organisation an increase of human happiness.

And still, I repeat, it seems to me quite possible that in the next few years Europe may grow enthusiastic for Bolshevism. Not for its own sake, rather in spite of what it is. Imagine that the "five year plan" pursued with herculean efforts by the Soviet Government fulfils expectations and that the economic situation of Russia is not only restored, but much improved. Whatever the content of Bolshevism be, it represents a gigantic human enterprise. In it, men have resolutely embraced a purpose of reform, and live tensely under the discipline that such a faith instils into them. If natural forces, so responseless to the enthusiasms of man, do not bring failure to this attempt; if they merely give it free scope to act, its wonderful character of a mighty enterprise will light up the continental horizon as with a new and flaming constellation. If Europe, in the meantime, persists in the ignoble vegetative existence of these last years, its muscles flabby for want of exercise, without any plan of a new life, how will it be able to resist the contaminating influence of such an astounding enterprise? It is simply a misunderstanding of the European to expect that he can hear unmoved that call to new *action* when he has no standard of a cause as great to unfurl in opposition. For the sake of serving something that will give a meaning to his existence, it is not impossible that the European may swallow his objections to Communism and feel himself carried away not by the substance of the faith, but by the fervour of conduct it inspires.

To my mind the building-up of Europe into a great national State is the one enterprise that could counterbalance a victory of the "five year plan." Experts in political economy assure us that such a victory has little probability in its favour. But it would be degradation indeed, if anti-Communism were to hope for everything from the material difficulties encountered by its adversary. His failure would then be equivalent to universal defeat of actual man. Communism is an extravagant moral code, but nothing less than a moral code. Does it not seem more worthy and more fruitful to oppose to that Slavonic code, a new European code, the inspiration towards a new programme of life? . . .

This is the question: Europe has been left without a moral code. It is not that the mass-man has thrown over an antiquated one in exchange for a new one, but that at the centre of his scheme of life there is precisely the aspiration to live without conforming to any moral code. Do not believe a word you hear from the young when they talk about the "new morality." I absolutely deny that there exists to-day in any corner of the Continent a group inspired by a new *ethos* which shows signs of being a moral code. When people talk of the "new morality" they are merely committing a new immorality and looking for a way of introducing contraband goods. Hence it would be a piece of ingenuousness to accuse the man of to-day of his lack of moral code. The accusation would leave him cold, or rather, would flatter him. Immoralism has become a commonplace, and anybody and everybody boasts of practising it.

If we leave out of question, as has been done in this essay, all those groups which imply survivals from the past—Christians, Idealists, the old Liberals—there will not be found amongst all the representatives of the actual period, a single group whose attitude to life is not limited to believing that it has all the rights and none of the obligations. It is indifferent whether it disguises itself as reactionary or revolutionary; actively or passively, after one or two twists, its state of mind will consist, decisively, in ignoring all obligations, and in feeling itself, without the slightest notion why, possessed of unlimited rights. Whatever be the substance which takes possession of such a soul, it will produce the same result, and will change into a pretext for not conforming to any concrete purpose. If it appears as reactionary or anti-liberal it will be in order to affirm that the salvation of the State gives a right to level down all other standards, and to manhandle one's neighbour, above all if one's neighbour is an outstanding personality. But the same happens if it decides to act the revolutionary; the apparent enthusiasm for the manual worker, for the afflicted and for social justice, serves as a mask to facilitate the refusal of all obligations, such as courtesy, truthfulness and, above all, respect or esteem for superior individuals. I know of quite a few who have entered the ranks of some labour organisation or other merely in order to win for themselves the right to despise intelligence and to avoid paying it any tribute. As regards other kinds of Dictatorship, we have seen only too well how they flatter the mass-man, by trampling on everything that appeared to be above the common level.

This fighting-shy of every obligation partly explains the phenomenon, half ridiculous, half disgraceful, of the setting-up in our days of the platform of "youth" as youth. Perhaps there is no more grotesque spectacle offered by our times. In comic fashion people call themselves "young," because they have heard that youth has more rights than obligations, since it can put off the fulfilment of these latter to the Greek Kalends of maturity.

The youth, as such, has always been considered exempt from *doing* or *having done* actions of importance. He has always lived on credit. It was a sort of false right, half ironic, half affectionate, which the no-longer young conceded to their juniors. But the astounding thing at present is that these take it as an effective right precisely in order to claim for themselves all those other rights which only belong to the man who has already done something.

Though it may appear incredible, "youth" has become a *chantage;* we are in truth living in a time when this adopts two complementary attitudes, violence and caricature. One way or the other, the purpose is always the same; that the inferior, the man of the crowd, may feel himself exempt from all submission to superiors.

It will not do, then, to dignify the actual crisis by presenting it as the conflict between two moralities, two civilisations, one in decay, the other at its dawn. The mass-man is simply without morality, which is always, in essence, a sentiment of submission to something, a consciousness of service and obligation. But perhaps it is a mistake to say "simply." For it is not merely a question of this type of creature doing without morality. No, we must not make his task too easy. Morality cannot be eliminated without more ado. What, by a word lacking even in grammar, is called *amorality* is a thing that does not exist. If you are unwilling to submit to any norm, you have, *nolens volens,* to submit to the norm of denying all morality, and this is not amoral, but immoral. It is a negative morality which preserves the empty form of the other. How has it been possible to believe in the amorality of life? Doubtless, because all modern culture and civilisation tend to that conviction. Europe is now reaping the painful results of her spiritual conduct. She has adopted blindly a culture which is magnificent, but has no roots.

THE WEARY WEST: VICTORY AND DEPRESSION

5. ANDRÉ TARDIEU: THE POLICY OF FRANCE*

France emerged from the First World War crippled in body but determined to exercise her rights under the provisions of the Treaty of Versailles. Relations between the wartime allies had deteriorated, and the reparations issue was a continuing source of irritation to both France and Germany. The issue finally exploded in 1923 when French troops occupied the industrial Ruhr in an attempt to make Germany pay. Even before the Ruhr crisis, André Tardieu (1876–1945), one of the architects of the peace treaty, had attempted to explain the French attitude toward Germany and the postwar world. What evidence did Tardieu offer to show that victorious France had suffered more than defeated Germany? On what grounds did Tardieu insist that the attitude of the French government reflected a view of the postwar world that was both reasonable and realistic? To what extent was France willing to compromise her demands or to modify the Treaty of Versailles?

During the last half-century France has given the most striking proofs of her love of peace. Invaded and dismembered in 1871, she did not seek revenge. Attacked again in 1914 by an insatiable rival, she defended herself, and in so doing gave time to the free peoples of the world to range themselves by her side in the battle against German militarism. After fifty-two months of a struggle which ravaged her soil, she and her allies and associates were victorious; she did not then demand a peace of violence, nor did she extend her sovereignty over a single human being who had not for years been whole-heartedly French. Seeking only her security and the repair of her ruins, she set herself again to the peaceful labors which Germany had twice in fifty years disturbed.

Here is our starting-point. What France was yesterday, such she is today. But in three years of peace she has been bitterly disillusioned.

France counted on the cooperation of her recent comrades in arms in carrying out the long-term clauses of the just peace which they had signed in common. She counted on it in vain.

In March, 1920, the United States refused to ratify the Treaty of Versailles and the Tripartite Military Guarantee. In 1921 it concluded with Germany a separate peace by which it definitely rejected the mutual engagements implied in the treaty of 1919. From that moment Germany knew that America would not insist on the execution of a peace treaty in which she had no further interest.

In the same way Great Britain has turned her back on her 1919 policy. It was Great Britain who had called for the most draconian clauses—for the punishment of war criminals, for example, and for the repayment of war pensions.

* André Tardieu, "The Policy of France," *Foreign Affairs*, Vol. I, No. 1 (September 1922), pp. 11–13, 15–24, 28. Reprinted by permission. Copyright by the Council on Foreign Relations, Inc., New York.

Less than six months after the ratification of the treaty she repudiated these stipulations, which had been under-written by twenty-seven states.

In his successive conferences Mr. Lloyd George has followed a definite policy of mutilating the peace terms, thus time and again imposing sacrifices on France without granting her any corresponding compensation. So it happens that during the past few months my country has come to feel herself isolated, without feeling that she was responsible for this isolation.

Because she took seriously the signatures of June 28, 1919—signatures in which she has a vital interest—France finds herself in 1922 in the paradoxical position of being denounced everywhere as a trouble-maker. Because she asked what was her due, even though she did not obtain it, she has won the reputation of being nervous, insatiable and imperialistic. This accusation has hurt her to the quick, and out of it grows the dissatisfaction to which she sometimes gives vent. One may approve or disapprove of this dissatisfaction, but one must understand it in order to judge sanely the present tendencies in French policy.

If France insists upon the execution of the treaty it is not solely because it is a contract; it is because its non-execution would very shortly place her in an impasse.

The war bled us terribly. Out of our population of less than 38,000,000 there were mobilized 8,500,000; 5,300,000 of them were killed or wounded (1,500,000 killed, 800,000 *mutilés,* 3,000,000 wounded), not counting 500,000 men who have come back to us from German prisons in very bad physical condition.

Almost 4,000,000 hectares of land were devastated, together with 4,000 towns and villages; 600,000 buildings were destroyed, among them 20,000 factories and work-shops, besides 5,000 kilometers of railroads and 53,000 kilometers of roads. About 1,400,000 head of cattle were carried off. Altogether, a quarter of our productive capital was annihilated.

The financial consequences of the annihilation of all these resources bear down on us heavily today. The war cost us 150 billions of francs. The damage to property and persons comes to 200 billions. Our ordinary budget has increased from 4½ billions to 25 billions; our debt from 36 billions to 330 billions. Since the armistice we have spent on reconstruction and on pensions a total of 90 billions, and we have received from Germany in one form or another less than two billions of gold marks (about six billions of francs), or about six per cent of what we have had to spend on restoring our provinces—a task as yet but half completed.

To measure what we have undergone, suppose that the war had taken place in America and that you had suffered proportionately. You would have had 4,000,000 of your men killed and 10,000,000 wounded. All your industries from Washington to Pittsburgh would have ceased to exist. All your coal mines would have been ruined. That is what the war would have meant to you. That is what it has meant to us.

If you will go back for a moment to the expense figures which I have just cited, you will find that in the last two years France has spent on reconstruction and pensions 7½ billions of dollars, or $5,700 a minute, while in the same period Germany has only spent 500 millions of dollars, or $381 a minute. In other words, we have accumulated a deficit of $5,319 every minute; and it is we who have paid it, in place of Germany who was responsible for creating the damage.

We think that this cannot go on. You would think the same in our place. The interest and amortization on the sums borrowed by us since the armistice to make up for Germany's default have cost us 4½ billions of francs a year. The interest on our debt absorbs 55 per cent of our taxes. We ask that all this be ended. Who can say it is not a legitimate demand?

To these just claims our recent allies and associates have usually replied by recommending that we reduce our bill against Germany. They doubtless forget that what Germany does not pay France will have to pay—France, who did not provoke the ruin wrought by Germany on her soil, whose total working capital Germany has cut down by twenty-five per cent while her own means of production remain intact. We are unanimous in thinking such proposals unjust. . . .

France would never have refused to make Germany's payment easier if Germany, after having given proof of good faith, had found herself in real difficulties. But this is not the case. Forced by the treaty to pay in gold, Germany has done everything possible to bring about the depreciation of her paper money to a point where it has lost all exchange value. The fall of the mark is not the result of Germany's payments in gold, for in thirty months her payments have totaled less than a billion and a half gold marks. The depreciation of the mark is the direct result of Germany's financial policy, a policy which from the very first day has been one of deliberate evasion. . . .

France, therefore, is within her rights in saying that the primary cause of Germany's default is by no means her incapacity to pay, but her determination not to pay. She is equally within her rights in regretting that her Allies have seemed so little interested in preventing Germany from reaching her present state of insolvency. Indeed, she is surprised that although always prepared to grant delays to Germany, the Allies never dream that France deserves help in facing the results of a German crisis which she has in no way provoked.

Until our Anglo-Saxon friends have grasped these essential truths our state of mind will remain a mystery to them, and failing to understand it they will continue attributing to us motives quite different from our real ones; and the misunderstanding will grow worse and worse. One of their unjustified grounds for criticsm is the pretended militarism of France, so frequently denounced in a certain section of the American press. I wish to brand it as one of the most absurd legends which has ever laid hold of the public mind.

If, in speaking of French militarism, one wishes to insinuate that France dreams of adventures and conquests and even of a new war, one has only to re-read my estimate of the crushing burden left on our shoulders by our victorious war. We want only peace, and we want it more intensely than any other people in the world. We have almost died of war.

If on the other hand, as I have read only too often in English and American newspapers, it is claimed that France is militaristic because she is devoting to armaments more money than any other country, I say—and I shall prove—that such a statement is contrary to the truth. No country has since the armistice made such reductions in miltary expenditures as has France. In comparing our war budget of 1918 with that of 1922 we find in the latter a reduction of 31 billions of francs from 36 billions. If we compare the 1913 budget to the 1922 budget, we find in the latter an increase of 266 per cent, or less than the general increase in the cost of living, which is more than 300 per cent. This means that, taking into account the increased cost of living, France in 1922 is spending less on her soldiers than she did in 1913. . . .

When I add that in June, 1922, the Chamber of Deputies reduced the length of military service from three years to eighteen months, I think I may conclude that nothing remains of the myth of an aggressive France, bowed down by the weight of unwarrantable armaments.

Does this mean that France is prepared to disarm completely? No, and she has reasons for not doing so. We do not, for the moment, fear a German attack, but an unprepared and defenceless France would be a real temptation to those Germans who still firmly believe in war. We are convinced of this because the Kaiser's generals are not alone in preaching revenge, because the professors preach it in the universities and the teachers in the schools. We are convinced because every day brings us new proof of the camouflage behind which Germany eludes the rules for her disarmament, hiding arms everywhere, maintaining reserve officers and recruiting bureaus and forming military police corps with machine guns, cannon and aeroplanes. And what becomes of Germany's disarmament after the Treaty of Rapallo, which permits her to manufacture in Russia everything which she is forbidden to produce at home?

All the guarantees and contracts upon which France had the right to rely at the end of 1919 have failed her. The United States refused to ratify the defensive pact embodied in Article 10 of the League of Nations. It also refused to ratify the military guarantee of June 28, 1919, and consequently the Anglo-French agreement went by the board. France today is more alone than she was in 1914, when at least she could count on the Russian alliance.

All that we can now count on are material guarantees, and of these there are but two. One is a military force sufficient to withstand in all circumstances the attack of a people sixty million strong who are disarmed in appearance only. The other consists in the occupation of the left bank of the Rhine, an occupation which the treaty allows us to prolong 15 years because Germany has not fully met her engagements and because we have no other sure guarantee against possible aggression. Twice in fifty years we have been used as a battlefield, and we know what that costs. We know this creditor who repudiates his signature, this aggressor who disavows his responsiblities. At no price will we consent to being exposed to the risk of beginning the struggle over again.

This, then, is the stuff that French militarism is made of! Our precautions are legitimate. Any one who investigates them on the spot will be convinced. . . .

The state of the world is the result of the war. But if, during the last two years, the non-execution of the peace terms has created a general feeling of instability, whose is the fault? Over two years ago a German journalist, Mr. Redlich, editor of the *Gazette de Voss,* said to me: "It is true that we are not carrying out the peace treaty. But lay the blame on your Allies, who show plainly that they are not in the least interested in its execution."

Think just for a moment about this remark, which is in some ways quite fair. Everything that was decided in 1919 has since then been placed in doubt. The close solidarity which made victory possible disappeared in peace. A series of improvisations has taken its place. Can European order be re-established in this haphazard manner? I doubt it, and events are confirming my doubts.

With just what can France be reproached? With intransigeance? Surely not, for during the past thirty months she has patiently accepted all the successive compromises, each more onerous than the last, which her Allies have recommended. Recall the international conferences of 1920, 1921 and 1922. Which of them was broken off by France? And in which one did France not lose either an arm or a leg?

In February, 1920, we gave up our demand for the German war criminals. In April, 1920, we abandoned our mandate over Cilicia and the military command of Constantinople. In July, 1920, we loaned to Germany several hundred million francs in order to get, in greatly reduced amounts, the coal which she owed us. In January, 1921, we renounced our claim for the integral reparation for damages done us. In May, 1921, we gave up the 12 billion gold marks due us on that date. In December, 1921, and in March, 1922, we acted similarly about the already reduced payments which had been fixed by the London Agreement of the preceding May.

Where is there in all this any sign of our famous intransigeance? What solution did we refuse to accept? Everywhere and at all times France has given proof of absolute good will and a fine spirit of conciliation. . . .

Having said all of this I feel in a better position to reply to the question that has been put to me: "What does France want? What is her policy?" My reply lies in a single phrase: "France wants to live."

France want to live. By that I mean she wants not to succumb beneath the burden of her victory—that she wants to rebuild her ruins instead of being crushed beneath them—that she asks for justice and justice only. If she is denied this, then to the economic crisis which now staggers the world will be added the incalculable blow of French bankruptcy, an event which the preachers of economic solidarity should wish to prevent as much as they wish to prevent a German bankruptcy.

France wants to live, and her acts have proved it. The work of reconstruction accomplished since the armistice is the admiration of all who have come to study it. Without any outside assistance we have restored all our railroads and highways, have put back into condition 80 per cent of our devastated fields, have brought home 90 per cent of the people driven away by the war, have rebuilt half of our factories and have put up temporary houses which, whether bad or good, at least will serve until permanent structures can be erected. No one in the wake of such a catastrophe and with the means at our disposal could have done better than France. . . .

Nothing, therefore, is more unjust than to represent France as a nervous, demoralized country, always complaining but never acting. France is in full action, but she wants to have fulfilled the two conditions which will permit her efforts to bear fruit: one, lasting security; two, effective reparations. The pursuit of these two conditions determines her policy. . . .

When Great Britain declared war on Germany in 1914 and when the United States in 1917 declared war, it was because they realized—in the case of the United States the realization came only after three years—that France's danger was their danger also. These two great nations brought inestimable aid to France, but both of them were led to a final decision by national reasons, Great Britain by British reasons, the United States by American reasons. It would be a mistake to think that the factors in the problem have changed At most, one can say that the Rapallo Treaty has made them more real. It is such a self-evident truth that I will not insist upon it.

And so France asks that when one talks of her security one shall not have the appearance of condescending to quiet chimerical fears; she asks that she, with her army on the Rhine, be considered, today as yesterday, the Sentinel of Liberty. The question looked at from this angle, the angle of historic and political reality, becomes easy to settle.

Will France ever be reimbursed by Germany, in conformity with the Treaty of Versailles, for the total cost of reconstruction and war pensions? Since the London agreement of May, 1921, no Frenchman entertains such a hope. But France intends to be paid what was promised her at that time, and if ever she should accept any reduction on the amount it would be only with the absolute certainty of a rapid payment of the reduced sum. I have said, and I repeat, that this condition has never so far been met.

The policy upheld by the 250 Deputies who agree with me is neither absolute nor merely negative. On the contrary we stand resolutely for the doctrine of economic solidarity recommended by Mr. Lloyd George, but we do not want France to be the only country excluded from its benefits. A few examples will make our position more clear.

We are asked to grant Germany a prolonged moratorium. Very well. But what will be done to help us through this period when Germany is paying us nothing? We are asked to consider another reduction in the German debt. Once again, very well. But what is offered us in exchange in the way of a reduction of the French debt? We are asked not to use against our defaulting creditor the military sanctions authorized by the treaty. Once again, very well. But what common means of political and economic pressure is offered us to force Germany to act? We are asked to help float an international loan, which nobody wants more than we ourselves. Agreed. But what will the other powers do to force Germany to produce the yearly interest without which no loan is possible? . . .

On all these points France offers her Allies their choice.

They can agree to follow the course I have outlined or they can refuse. If they agree, success will come surely and rapidly; if they refuse, responsibility for the failure will be on their own heads. . . .

In order that the world may regain its equilibrium France must have the cooperation of those who fought by her side. But Great Britain and the United

States will make no lasting progress in Europe without the cooperation of France. A minute explanation in the interest of a thorough agreement becomes, then, the duty of us all. To fulfill this duty one must escape from the habit of thinking that one's own difficulties are worse than those of one's neighbors. An English minister said to me one day: "You are in luck to have your devastated regions; they are a real guarantee against unemployment." There are things which it is well not to say—or, still better, not to think. . . .

6. LÉON BLUM: FOR ALL MANKIND*

The Popular Front was born in the aftermath of the Depression, the Paris riots of 1934, and the abrupt willingness of Moscow to allow French Communist leaders to cooperate with bourgeois parties. The three major parties of the left (Communist, Socialist, and Radical) campaigned together in 1936, and the election brought Léon Blum (1872–1950) to power as France's first Socialist premier. Blum was the heir to the humanitarian socialism of Jean Jaurès (1859–1914), the French revisionist, and opposed the Marxian concept of violent revolution. After the Bolshevik triumph in Russia he had refused to alter the direction of French socialism and had walked out of the international movement to form a parliamentary Socialist party in 1920.

The Popular Front reform program did not succeed, and Blum was ousted as premier after thirteen months in office. In 1940, after military invasion by Germany, defeated France was divided into two zones—Vichy France in the south and German-occupied France in the north and west. Blum was arrested and wrote the manuscript of *À l'échelle humaine* (*For All Mankind*) while in prison. His notes were smuggled out early in 1942, and parts of the book were printed in the clandestine newspapers of the French Resistance. When Blum and his wife were finally liberated from Buchenwald concentration camp in 1945 the entire book was already in print.

What was Blum's attitude toward the Republic and the French system of government? Why was it improper to place the blame for military defeat in 1940 at the door of democracy? What comparisons did Blum draw between the virtues and vices of democracy and dictatorship?

No one knows better than I that my generation failed in its task. Yet I do not propose to defend it, but rather to try to point out to the rising generation—and to those to whom we shall pass on our burdens tomorrow—what can be learned from our mistakes, our illusions, and our misfortunes. That lesson will be of more use to others than to us. That was, at least, the hope that led me to put down on paper the fruit of my solitary reflections. I wanted, above all, to put young people, and adults as well, on their guard against a feeling in which there is perhaps presumption as well as discouragement.

France today [1941] is faced, not with a vacuum, but with an interregnum. Not everything has been destroyed, not everything needs to be rebuilt. Defeat revealed the collapse of our military machine and the bankruptcy of our ruling class; it discredited in men's minds the political system which that class had created in its own image; it destroyed human lives and wealth. But it did not destroy France's people, her soil, her nature, all the complex of traditions, con-

* Léon Blum, *For All Mankind*, trans. W. Pickles (New York: The Viking Press, 1946), pp. 18–19, 24–30, 33–34, 37–38, 47–49, 55–56, 60. Reprinted by permission.

victions, and aspirations that we call today the spirit of France. Seen from the angle of our military power, the war is, no doubt, over for us; but in terms of our national existence it goes on. France is not yet beaten; her fate is not yet sealed while the war is fought on elsewhere, without her, but on her behalf. I believe that it is not unreasonable to hope that she may yet emerge from it independent, intact, with her moral stature perhaps increased, in a Europe once more free and at peace. . . .

But when war has ended in defeat, and when sudden and total defeat has brought with it humiliation and despair, then a different type of collective feeling appears—a feeling that is probably as old as human society itself, . . .

Nations, like men, are always tempted to believe that what happens to them and affects their existence has never happened before or to others. [But] there are few precedents in history for so deliberate and complacent a cultivation of the idea of sin and redemption as the effort we are witnessing in France today, or for the vitiation of the idea by a mania for self-flagellation carried almost to the point of perversion. Nor has the idea ever before been exploited with greater subtlety or dishonesty. . . .

It is time we stopped beating our breasts so noisily; time we called a halt to this mortification and self-denunciation—or rather to these denunciations of others . . . those who are most arrogantly generous in their dealing out of collective vituperations and maledictions are careful not to begin with a confession of their own sins, a *mea culpa* of their own. . . . What is true and natural is that a nation after a great defeat, . . . should take conscience as its mirror, . . . It is proper too that the self-examination should be severe, and that it should lead perhaps to stern self-criticism, . . .

When a whole nation is shaken by catastrophe, the first instinct of its people —first because it is simplest—is to accuse what is nearest to hand: their responsible leaders, their political system, their institutions. . . . But it went far beyond merely placing responsibility for the catastrophe on the country's political system or its recent leaders; it refused to stop at the mere constitution and personnel of the Republic, but went on to accuse in addition the whole complex structure of public life, its form and its content. The net of accusation was cast wide enough to bring in everything that for a century and a half had given life to political doctrine and habit as well as to institutions. Let us not mince words: what was attempted, in addition to a political revolution, was no less than a counterrevolution in social relations and civic obligations. Responsibility for defeat was laid at the door not only of the Republic but of democracy, of the idea of individual liberty, of the principle of the natural equality of all citizens. . . . To deny them or to ignore them is not enough; we are assured that they have been destroyed, reduced to nothing, by some *reductio ad absurdum* or some evidential proof, and we are invited to look upon their ruin and mock them.

I am aware that exponents of this view make much play of their intention to build afresh from amid the chaos, but I shall waste no time on these attempts at reconstruction even though they be dignified with the name of National

Revolution. Their first inherent vice is their precariousness; they are condemned in advance to survive neither the increasingly probable defeat of Hitler, nor even his final victory. The second is their self-contradiction. The fumbling craftsmen who have taken upon themselves this task of reconstruction are perpetually torn between two patently contradictory concepts—between a return to French traditions and customs of an earlier time and mere imitation of the totalitarian systems built up from nothing by German Nazism and Italian Fascism. The feelings that lie behind these two concepts have in common the proof they offer of the routine thinking, the unimaginative minds, the intellectual poverty of their authors, but beyond that they are in total contradiction with each other. The desire to return to old French traditions is the mark of an overweening nationalistic infatuation with everything that is or was French, while the urge to imitate the totalitarian regimes is evidence rather of a spirit of national self-abasement, of submission to the conqueror, of servility. The two may converge in their common desire to destroy republican France, but there is neither compatibility nor possibility of compromise between them when they turn to the task of construction. . . .

. . . The totalitarian dictatorships, selecting among the fruits of modern civilization only the material achievements of progress, would drive our European societies back into a period of history much more remote than monarchy as we knew it. They go back through the centuries of history to the legends of barbarian kings and elemental tribal rites. Moreover, besides refusing to mix with each other, these two concepts are both in themselves among the emptiest of intellectual aberrations. . . . We can honor the dead, find inspiration in their example, but we cannot resuscitate them. . . . And if we turn to the other concept, what reason is there to believe that the edifices built by Hitler or Mussolini will prove more durable than those of Napoleon? How can we give a European basis to structures that are bound up with the lives of their founders even in their own countries? Scattered elements may survive, but the whole, the essential portion, will not. The truth is that two thousand years of history cannot be reduced to nothing in a decade, for human progress has its own irresistible force. Nothing established by violence and maintained by force, nothing that degrades humanity and is based on contempt for human personality, can endure. . . .

Dictatorship and war, democracy and peace—these, then, are the inevitable concomitants. If you do not deny this—and you dare not—you have no right to throw democracy so casually onto the scrap heap. . . .

I cannot refrain at this point from commenting on one of the peculiarities of these times, though it is perhaps peculiar only in appearance. The men, the parties, the newspapers that preached and made profession of extreme nationalism and distorted to their own uses that grand word "patriotism" all called loudly for the armistice and applauded the capitulation. Today they all advocate collaboration with the conqueror, or, more accurately, with the enemy. And yet during the early months of the war, when almost all Frenchmen looked forward to slow but certain victory, these same people were anxious to lay down in advance peace terms of inflexible harshness. Many wanted to put an end, once and for all, not only to Hitler and his gang, but to the millions of men, women, and children that make up the human reality behind the term "Germany." They demanded not only that Germany should be kept under supervision, but that she be dismembered and large portions of her territory annexed to France, and they were ever ready to accuse Socialists and democrats of lack of patriotism because they asked of victory no other fruit than a "new order" in which the mutual cooperation of peoples would be the guarantee of peace. Today they worship the force that yesterday they were prepared to misuse, and tomorrow they will repeat their crimes. In a France once more free and strong, they will become nationalist and jingo again. They will begin all over again their attacks on the treachery of "pacifists," who refuse to abandon the idea of founding a peace based on human liberty and the fraternal equality of nations; and the men whom they denounced yesterday and will denounce again tomorrow as "pacifists" are those whom today they describe as "warmongers." . . .

. . . Republican and democratic France did *not* want war. From the victory of 1918 she hoped for no other conquest than that of lasting, organic peace. It was toward this that her collective will was turned, that all her aspirations converged. There has probably been no example in history of a nation so generally and so consciously peaceful. No painful uphill effort was required of her, because she had emerged triumphantly from the latest European crisis and because she regarded herself and was regarded by others as the strongest power. Her internal regime required no effort of popularization or revivification, because up to the time of Hitler's accession to power nobody challenged it, except a few negligible groups of conspirators and theorists. In any case, war could have done nothing to popularize a regime in essence pacific. It is, I think, beyond dispute that when Hitler seized power in Germany there was in Europe neither the risk nor any reasonable possibility of war, and history will confirm a fact which two years ago every Frenchman regarded as blindingly self-evident—that it was Hitler who brought war back into the European perspective and Hitler who imposed it on republican France.

I should be the last to deny that from that time onward mistakes were made. But the worst of these was the failure to appreciate or to foresee the danger: the failure to realize quickly and clearly enough the Hitlerite plan of rearmament, revenge, and conquest; the failure to perceive the inexorability of its unfolding. Because she was in essence pacific, France preferred to believe in the possibility of "peaceful co-existence" of the democracies already installed in Europe and the warlike autocracy growing up. . . .

I recognize that there were mistakes of the kind I have just described, wrong attitudes that the French shook off only little by little and one by one, and which many had still failed to shake off when the hour of collapse came. I confess to them, without a blush, because they are the right kind of mistakes. They are not so much mistakes as illusions, testimony to a premature faith in the future of peace, in the inherent virtue of peace itself. . . .

Finally, I should like to remind my readers that the governmental instability of which so much has been made is by no means peculiar to republican democracy. The Republic today has lasted more than four times as long as any other political regime we have had in a century and a half; it was stable for more than sixty years, in the sense that its legality was no longer contested or its existence threatened, and that nobody dared publicly to oppose it. It is still stable today, whatever people may say or do about it, for it is so deeply rooted in popular habit and affection that any effort to get rid of it would be doomed to failure. . . . [As to] why the Third Republic itself had to withstand so many of the kind of shocks that would have shaken or destroyed a less popular regime, I can only recall what so many statesmen of limited vision and so many second-rate polemists seem to be unaware of or to lose sight of—that no government can remain stable in an unstable society and an unstable world. . . .

What nobody has a right to do is to push the conclusion still further and stretch the verdict to cover the essential principles of democracy itself—sovereignty of the people, government of the nation by the people, supervision by the nation of the executive power, recognition and guarantee of the civil and personal rights of the individual. . . .

7. STANLEY BALDWIN: PEACE IN INDUSTRY*

Economic difficulties and working-class unrest characterized Britain's immediate postwar years. A general strike in 1926, stemming from a wage dispute in the coal mines, dramatized labor's real and imagined grievances. Stanley Baldwin (1867–1947) was Prime Minister in the Conservative governments of 1923, 1924–29, and 1935–37. A moderate Conservative, Baldwin was convinced of the long-run moderateness of labor, and he believed that the differences between himself and the parliamentary leader of the Labour party, Ramsay MacDonald (1866–1937), were differences of degree rather than of method.

In 1925 Baldwin attempted to reassure organized labor about his government's attitude and plans. Speaking to workingmen at Birmingham, he urged peace in industry to stimulate the British economy. Did Baldwin present a comprehensive program for the future? What advantages, if any, were promised to the working class? What was Baldwin's attitude toward Labour party leaders?

But what is it that has prevented the recovery of Europe proceeding at a greater speed than it has, and what is it to-day that is the one check and the one blight on an outlook which is beginning to look more hopeful? It is that cursed and diabolic suspicion between man and man and nation and nation that robs Europe of that sense of security that is essential to the unity of spirit which we must have before the world can function aright. . . .

But while in England we can put our finger here and there on the hopeful signs, there are many that cause us anxiety. We have only a very partial prosperity, an industry here and there, sometimes one, sometimes another; but for four years we have hoped against hope that we might be able to show prosperity in all our industries. . . .

If we look at the figures of our foreign trade as a whole, we do indeed find some ground for moderate hopefulness. We find that the balance of imports over exports is not larger proportionately than we are accustomed to, and that

* Stanley Baldwin, *On England and Other Addresses* (London: Philip Allan and Co., Ltd., 1926), pp. 26–28, 30–35, 39–40.

our invisible exports come to our rescue as they did before the War, and we cannot yet say that we have an adverse balance.

But whatever conclusions people may draw from the examination of figures of exports and imports, I never can help translating this story into terms of unemployment. At the end of January there were a million and a quarter on the registers—practically the same as a year ago—no real substantial improvement. . . .

And so it is, seven years nearly after the War, that we yet see this prolonged and intensified depression, and this horrible figure of unemployment. . . .

. . . We stand to-day at a point where, roughly speaking, one out of every ten of the insured population is out of work—a thought sufficient to arrest the imagination of the dullest and the most thoughtless amongst us—and a challenge to all of us to use every power we have to remedy this state of things. But there is no direct remedy from the State alone. There can be no direct remedy by private men alone.

Nothing can be done unless we can all pull together with a will. And I am— and I speak seriously—quite profoundly thankful that the Labour Party have been in office, and for this reason: that they now know that they, no more than any other Government, have been able to produce a panacea that would remedy unemployment. And in their hearts they must admit that they have no remedy which can be guaranteed to cure this disease and at the same time maintain unimpaired the international position and power of the British Empire. . . .

By the natural evolution of our industrial life in England we are confronted to-day, and shall be more and more, with great consolidations of capital managed by small concentrated groups, and by great organisations of Labour led by experienced and responsible leaders. That position must be accepted. It is the natural accompaniment of the large-scale production which is gradually becoming the predominant force in all the industrial countries of the world.

It is perfectly true that if the great trade unions of this country, such as the miners, the transport workers, and the railwaymen, unite on a policy of trying to enforce a demand for higher wages in their own trades by means of a strike, they have it in their power to hold up at the same time many industries in this country, and do them irreparable damage. . . .

Having said that, I want to recognise, in the most generous way that I can, that there have been speeches made amongst the leaders of Labour to-day which would endorse every word that I have uttered; and I recognise the courage of those speeches, because the men who uttered them are trying at the same time to do their duty to those whom they represent and to that greater community, their country.

When a man is in public life, whether he be a Labour leader or the leader of the Tory Party, if he speaks the truth that is in him and that he burns to tell, often enough he will find many who will be ready to deride him for what he has said. I want to endorse the kind of speeches to which I have referred.

I want to plead for a truce. . . .

I want a truce of God in this country, that we may compose our differences, that we may join all our strengths together to see if we cannot pull the country into a better and happier condition.

It is little that a Government can do; these reforms, these revolutions must come from the people themselves.

The organisations of employers and men, if they take their coats off to it, are far more able to work out the solutions of their troubles than the politicians. . . . So let those who represent labour and capital get down to it, and seek and pursue peace through every alley and every corner of this country. . . .

. . . let those who are working for peace in England realise that the breach of the peace in industry can mean nothing more than the prolongation of what is already too much misery among those who are suffering from unemployment to-day. . . .

Look for a moment at the employers' side.

Are the reasons for our failure to compete connected with over-capitalisation, are they connected with defective management, with wasteful use of plant and of material?

Are they due at all to the absence of facilities for economic marketing?

Are State subsidies granted on the Continent?

Is there a freer use abroad of unskilled labour in various processes?

What is the cause?

And on the men's side, should not they look into the question of whether in the allocation to different branches of labour, there is not greater fluidity and absence of demarcation disputes which make it easier for the Continent to compete?

These are questions no Government can settle, that no Government can interfere with, and no Government can solve; but to get a correct answer is life and death to those in industry, whether they be employers or employed. . . .

There may be a better industrial system imaginable than ours, and I hope indeed we may be slowly moving towards something better; but there is no doubt in my mind that if it were possible to destroy the present system in a moment, those who destroyed it would cause a shipwreck, and they would not bring into being a ship in which to take away the survivors.

Short, too, of any deliberate destruction of our industry, such as we have seen advocated in a few quarters, I dread that subtle poison of hatred which is being preached in some quarters, which weakens the faith of men in their own efficient service and sound workmanship—the very things which have built up the reputation of our great country, on which we still live. You may have one of the finest fleets of liners in this world, you may have it owned by the State, and you may have it run by the State; but if you have a crew bent on defying all that makes for co-operation and discipline you will bankrupt that fleet.

It has not come to that in this country, and in my belief it never will. The power of managing our own affairs in our own way is the greatest gift of Englishmen. We have demonstrated that fact in the past, and we shall demonstrate it in the future. . . .

And if I have a message to-night for you and the people of the country, it is just this. I would say:

"England! Steady! Look where you are going! Human hands were given us to clasp, and not to be raised against one another in fratricidal strife."

8. HAROLD LASKI: LETTERS ON BRITISH POLITICS AND SOCIETY*

Oliver Wendell Holmes (1841–1935), a Justice of the United States Supreme Court for thirty years, and Harold J. Laski (1893–1950), a British Socialist and Professor of Political Science at the University of London, were an unlikely pair of friends. Holmes was more than a half-century older than Laski, and their political views rarely pushed toward the same immediate objective. But for nineteen years they exchanged letters regularly, sharing their observations on almost every facet of human activity.

Laski's role within the Labour party gave him access to many British and European leaders, and although he often exaggerated and embellished his tales, his flow of letters to Holmes demonstrated a caustic wit and keen insight into the machinery and personalities of English politics. The following excerpts from Laski's letters provide a cameo portrait, sketched in sharp phrases, of western life and society between the wars. What was Laski's opinion of the political abilities of Stanley Baldwin, Ramsay MacDonald, and Winston Churchill? Why, in Laski's opinion, were western statesmen politically ineffective?

December 13, 1923

The electoral battle is over, and we have won an amazing victory [the Labour party had gained 47 seats in the House of Commons]. Probably within six weeks a Labour ministry will be in power for the first time in English history; and though I do not think the situation will admit of great changes, it will be satisfactory because it will produce on the elector the atmosphere of labour as a government. I wish I could reproduce for you the excitement the new situation has created. The *rentier* is in despair; the trade-unionist holds his head a little higher; the clubs discuss the probable destination of offices with that air of secret knowledge which makes clubs intolerable to me. . . . I hope to heaven we shall go back to a two-party system, for at present the prospects are towards an indefinite series of general elections. The real triumph, I think, is for Sidney Webb who had worked and dreamed and hoped for this for over forty years— another proof, were one needed, of the power of the man of thought. . . .

April 19, 1924

. . . I gather that a general election is probably impending. The liberals are restless, and MacDonald feels that he has exploited all the good there is in this minority situation. Really I think he has done very well; and it is very amusing to watch him being courted by people who two years ago, would not have sat in the same room with him. You must not miss the great joke that Curzon's son-in-law [Sir Oswald Mosely, later the leader of the British Fascist party], a clever and eloquent fellow, has joined the Labour party; so does time bring its revenges. I should dearly like ten minutes of Curzon's undiluted views on that change. Churchill, whom I saw the other day, takes the simple and child-like view that any aristocrat who joins the Labour party is a traitor to his class;

* Mark DeWolfe Howe, ed., *Holmes-Laski Letters, 1916–1935* (2 vols.; Cambridge, Mass.: Harvard University Press, 1953), I, 569–70, 610–11, 664–65, 669; II, 908, 981, 995–96, 1153–54, 1242, 1378–79, 1389, 1408–1409, 1437, 1465–66. Reprinted by permission of Mrs. Harold J. Laski.

and then goes on to denounce the Labour party on the ground, God save the mark, that it is essentially a class-organisation. I wish it were anything so coherent as that would imply. Some people are in it because they really have a considered social philosophy; others because they have a vague pity for the working-class; others again on religious grounds. It is a queer mixture, and I have sat through many a meeting which made me feel with Halifax that "ignorance maketh a man enter into a party, and shame preventeth him from leaving it." But it's the best of the lot and liberalism today in England is so completely void of influence or meaning that to dwell even casually in its halls is like spending your time in the archaeological section of the British Museum. . . .

October 4, 1924

. . . as you will know, we are in the midst of a first-rate political crisis which will, I think, result in a general election [Prime Minister MacDonald requested a general election less than a week later]. So I have been dining on it with Haldane and MacDonald and having the peculiar thrill which comes from knowing news about a day before anyone else. . . . MacDonald is tired, and I imagine that the surrender of responsiblity will not irk him greatly. He asked me quite pathetically about books, and insisted that the life of the thinker is the only one which has really final compensations. . . . On the way back from Haldane's I met Baldwin [Stanley Baldwin, leader of the Conservative Party] and we walked over the Green Park together. He told me that he viewed with horror the prospect of office, and that it would be a happy day for him if MacDonald decided to go on despite defeat. I said that he could always retire from politics. No, he said, its curse is the curse of alcohol; you must go on, and when you are not in office you miss the sense of power. It is only in office that retirement looks attractive. I wish you could meet Baldwin. He isn't a profound person, but he is one of the most loveable people I have met. . . .

November 3, 1924

Well! The thing is over and we have had a damned good licking. As MacDonald said to me on Friday, we have now at least four years to devote ourselves to political science. Yet there are some comforting features. . . . Practically we have wiped out the Liberal party, so that we are back again at the two-party system which I regard as essential to political stability, and our total poll is one million larger than it was a year ago. So that I remain incurably optimistic about the future; for if in 25 years we can increase our [the Labour Party] voting strength from sixty thousand to five and a half millions, it is obvious that the process of political education is slow but sure. . . .

December 29, 1926

Since I wrote last week not much has happened. The most interesting thing was a dinner at Haldane's when he and the Prime Minister and I talked confidentially for a couple of hours. You can't help liking Baldwin. He is far from intellectually first-rate, but he is *good*—a kind of Colonel Dobbin to whom you could turn with your troubles and be comforted. He interested me much by

saying that Churchill was quite the ablest, and Bonar Law the shrewdest,
mind he had encountered in politics. . . .

September 24, 1927

. . . Last night we had MacDonald to dinner and talked over the universe.
He is a fascinating creature. To watch him is like observing a really tempera-
mental prima donna. He is brilliant, jealous, eager for applause, quick, incoherent—the last person who ought ever to lead a party. He dismayed me a
little by his vivid certainty that God is on his side; hardly less by his perception
of politics as a struggle in a theatre between contestants for the limelight.
I was amused, too, by his pose as a connoisseur of the arts—which seemed to
mean legislation against Romneys and Gainsboroughs leaving the country; and
I do not think he appreciated my remark that I rather wanted legislation to
make Goyas and Degas come in. He spoke most warmly about America where
he seems to think the future of culture lies; and with the Calvinist's contempt
for Latin countries. I told him that he would have got on admirably with John
Adams and found Jefferson wanting in delicacy and taste. . . .

November 13, 1927

. . . Lunched yesterday with Churchill. . . . [He] was most amusing. After
three years at the Exchequer he believes himself to be a financier of genius
with a full insight into the great mystery of the gold standard. So I teased him
gloriously by asking with the guile of simpl[icity] all sorts of elementary questions. What did he think would happen if the South African gold mines doubled
their output? Did he approve of Irving Fisher's theory of a compensated dollar?
Didn't he think the burden of proof was on those who accepted the quantity
theory of money? If 4.86 is better than 3.19 for the pound sterling why is not
5 better still? He did not (neither did I) know the answers, but all his satellites
waited for papal bulls which did not come. As all this came on top of a denunciation of the Labour Party for its inability to understand the questions the City
has to face, I am afraid I thoroughly enjoyed it. I add that I like him much;
and I greatly enjoy his unique power of convincing himself as he goes along
by the sheer force of his own eloquence. I was amused too by his obvious
contempt for most of his colleagues . . .; and his pity for Lloyd George as a
fellow adventurer whose boat has missed the tide. . . . It was amusing to see at
that table how much still the English aristocracy is a close corporation. All of
them were in some degree related to each other . . . and they were discussing
the engagement of the Duke of Argyll's heir to the daughter of Beaverbrook,
the great newspaper owner, as a most distressing thing. They make their small
talk charming and very graceful; but their ignorance is really colossal. Churchill
had never heard of Port-Royal; the lady next to me thought that the Richelieu
of Louis XV's reign [the Duc de Richelieu, 1696–1788, was the grand-nephew
of Cardinal Richelieu] was the great Cardinal and was shocked by his *amours*
of which she had just read, as she thought, in reading about his great-nephew;
and another person there when Churchill spoke of a visit he had received from
a descendant of Madame de Staël looked so blank that I had to explain in an
undertone. But they know all the current books, or pictures or plays, about

which there is gossip. They have an absolutely immovable opinion of all the politicians and the novelists and the painters. They are charming people who do not know that other worlds exist, or that any can compete with their own.... One lady said to me that she was so surprised by Ramsay MacDonald's charming manners, "and his father, you know, was only a workman." ...

June 4, 1929

I have, as you can imagine, been swept off my feet in these last three weeks. Thirty speeches, articles innumerable, my school work, and now the amusement of watching *de près* a cabinet in the making—it has been hard but interesting work.... It is amazing to sit with MacDonald and watch what happens. People who hate him like poison send gifts and congratulations. They write pages to insist on their claims. When the leaders meet each has a list of his particular pets who think that they ought not to be overlooked. People who have never been Labour write to offer their help. It is all the most incredible picture of the lust for power that I have ever seen....

... Nor must I forget to tell you of the lady who asked me in Dulwich whether a Labour government would base its legislation on the principles of Jesus Christ. I said that I thought this unlikely in the first five years, but that afterwards anything might happen. I add that one thing that pleases me most in the defeat of Baldwin is the tolerable certainty of an improvement in Anglo-American relations. MacDonald is set on a term to this insane naval competition and a new agreed definition of freedom of the seas. I am hopeful that all this may do immense good to the peace of the world. With England and America in harmony big things can be done. And I see no reason at all for the bickering of the last few years. At the same time I do regret the loss of Baldwin himself, for with many faults, he is a great gentleman and one of the cleanest fighters I have ever met in politics....

April 19, 1930

... I went on Monday to hear Snowden introduce the Budget of which the essential feature was a small but (I think) inevitable increase in the income-tax. I wish you could have seen the House. It was packed like a sardine-tin, with a hum of eager expectancy the like of which one rarely sees as possible. The rich members sat as tho' they were going to hear sentence of death. The Labour people were like hounds in leash ready to dash into cheers at the slightest provocation. And the production of anger, sorrow, temper at a change which I can best express by saying that I shall pay about one hundred dollars more a year was, to me, quite amazing. I put the reflexion that I cannot understand why men are so anxious to die for the State and so angry if they are asked to give money to it, even for objects they know to be essential. Churchill, for instance, spoke to me in the lobby like a man who has heard that London has fallen. A young Tory said to me that four years more of this would ruin the empire. And all I heard was a rather dull and careful speech, with nothing dramatic in it, which made a difference of perhaps three per cent to the expenditure of anyone there with a thousand [pounds] a year. Truly Madison was right when he said that the only durable source of faction is property. I asked Churchill if he thought of taxation as a voluntary offering by the citizen to objects he felt inclined individually to support; certainly that was his attitude. Lady Astor, who is said to have a million dollars a year, was acting like a woman who has just heard that a defaulting solicitor has run off with all her money. . . .

April 23, 1932

As this has been the last week of my vacation I have spent it idling very pleasantly. We went to hear a discussion on the state of the world by eminent economists and business men which amused me greatly. One man read out a programme of the measures necessary for salvation and explained that it was impossible to hope they would be carried out. Another saw the only hope in Russia which he had not visited and did not propose to visit in case he suffered disillusion. Then came the *pièce de résistance* in which a most eminent business man explained that the woes of the world had come because we had forgotten Christianity; by which it appeared, to our astonishment, that he meant the gold standard. Then an eminent economist suggested (I) that America should go Free Trade (II) that the world should disarm and (III) that the working class should accept a thirty per cent cut in wages. At that point we went home feeling, as John Bright once said, that the worst of great thinkers is that they will not think greatly. . . .

May 29, 1932

We are living here through a period of grim pessimism—worse than anything I have known. The dark outlook in Germany, the black prospect in the Danubian states, the failure of America to recover, and the danger of war in the Far East raises awful questions of economic collapse. Our people are making a mess of it. They lack courage and faith in big principle and we seem to be drifting rather helplessly to disaster. No one seems to nail his colours to the mast; and if I had to find a metaphor I should say that statesmen look like nothing so much as squirrels running round a cage. Unless I gravely miss my guess the foundations are being laid of a position out of which, all over the world, there is no egress save through social conflict; and the price we may have to pay for that is hardly likely to be worth the results. . . .

October 9, 1932

. . . Our politics, like yours, go from bad to worse. We ignore common sense in the pursuit of a stupid economic imperialism which denies every rational economic principle; and in matters of social constitution we are now reaping the evil fruit of our class-ridden society. It is becoming terribly true that our governors speak in terms which mean less and less to the multitude. I am finally convinced that a civilisation dominated by business men is incapable of statesmanship. Their habits and motives are not wide enough for the task of a democracy; and the economic world they make gets into relentless contradiction with the political. The result is that the vested interests of the one deny the established expectations of the other; and the thing moves with an almost awe-inspiring determination to catastrophe. I don't say that is for today or tomorrow; I do prophesy that the basis of common agreement is in process of disappearance. It is a tragedy; but it is a tragedy implied logically in the facts. . . .

May 7, 1933

Since I came home ten days ago I have been plunged into a whirlpool of work. Mainly it concerns this quite terrible German situation, and the vast academic problem it has created [a month earlier all Jews in Germany had been ousted from the civil service, the academic world, and professional life by the Nazi Aryan decrees]. It is so large and so tragic that the problem is to know just where one can begin. I have got my colleagues by a unanimous vote to give up five per cent of their salaries for three years to form a fund for endowing fellowships for the dismissed people; and now I am trying, with the assistance of other professors, to get all the British universities to follow the same road. It looks as though we may be successful; and if so I hope that we in England can take care of about one hundred of them. No doubt France and America will take a similar line; and it may well be, if we show energy and resolution, that we can make this German tragedy a turning-point at which men make a determined stand for intellectual freedom indifferently to the views in which it results. The letters I have from Germany are just horrible. It is as though a whole people was luxuriating in sadism. There is neither respect for persons nor for ideas. Mild liberals go out just as much as Jews and socialists. There has been nothing like it since the aftermath of the Revocation of the Edict of Nantes. . . .

January 28, 1934

The atmosphere here is very grim. Hitler grows worse; and it is evident enough that the long-term prospects for peace are bad. He has shown that persecution, ardently enough pursued, can in fact break the spirit of a people, and all its consequences are those pointed out by Aristotle in the fifth book of the Politics. . . . We are in a bad way. There is no energy and no clarity of purpose. The government has nothing to say and its opponents lack the courage to say the things that need to be said. It is a tragedy, because among the masses is a confused stirring of spirit which could be turned to great ends under adequate leadership. As it is one feels drift, complacency and apathy. Great things do not, Micawber-like, turn up in civilisations; you have to go out and search for them in the high-ways and by-ways. But I do not see the politicians who are making the search. . . .

9. JOHN MAYNARD KEYNES: THE WORLD'S ECONOMIC CRISIS*

Few twentieth-century economists have been as generally admired and roundly condemned as John Maynard Keynes (1883-1946). Denounced by many conservatives as a "destroyer of capitalism" because he proposed pump-priming to lift the world out of the Depression, Keynes was viewed with equal distaste by Marxists who saw in him an economist who "purported to make capitalism work." While the world Depression drove western nations to the edge of despair, heated governmental debates failed to provide economic and financial answers to the immediate problems of unemployment, falling levels of production, and declining world trade. What, according to Keynes, was the most pressing prob-

* Sir Arthur Salter, Sir Josiah Stamp, J. Maynard Keynes *et al.*, *The World's Economic Crisis and the Way of Escape* (New York: The Century Co., 1932), pp. 57-65, 67-75. Reprinted by permission of George Allen & Unwin Ltd.

lem of the moment? Why were governmental policies contradictory and generally futile? What areas of hope did Keynes acknowledge, and what additional measures did he insist had to be taken to restore economic stability?

The immediate problem for which the world needs a solution to-day is different from the problem of a year ago. Then it was a question of how we could lift ourselves out of the state of acute slump into which we had fallen, and raise the volume of production and of employment back towards a normal figure. But to-day the primary problem is to avoid a far-reaching financial crisis. There is now no possibility of reaching a normal level of production in the near future. Our efforts are directed towards the attainment of more limited hopes. Can we prevent an almost complete collapse of the financial structure of modern capitalism? With no financial leadership left in the world and profound intellectual error as to causes and cures prevailing in the responsible seats of power, one begins to wonder and to doubt. At any rate, no one is likely to dispute that for the world as a whole the avoidance of financial collapse, rather than the stimulation of industrial activity, is now the front-rank problem. The restoration of industry must come second in order of time.

The immediate causes of the world financial panic—for that is what it is—are obvious. They are to be found in a catastrophic fall in the money value not only of commodities but of practically every kind of asset. The "margins," as we call them, upon confidence in the maintenance of which the debt and credit structure of the modern world depends have "run off." In many countries the assets of banks—perhaps in most countries with the exception of Great Britain —are no longer equal, conservatively valued, to their liabilities to their depositors. Debtors of all kinds find that their securities are no longer the equal of their debts. Few Governments still have revenues sufficient to cover the fixed money-charges for which they have made themselves liable.

Moreover, a collapse of this kind feeds on itself. We are now in the phase where the risk of carrying assets with borrowed money is so great that there is a competitive panic to get liquid. And each individual who succeeds in getting more liquid forces down the price of assets in the process, with the result that the margins of other individuals are impaired and their courage undermined. And so the process continues. . . .

The competitive struggle for liquidity has now extended beyond individuals and institutions to nations and to governments, each of which endeavours to make its international balance sheet more liquid by restricting imports and stimulating exports by every possible means, the success of each one in this direction meaning the defeat of someone else. Moreover, every country discourages capital development within its own borders for fear of the effect on its international balance. . . .

We have here an extreme example of the *disharmony* of general and particular interest. Each nation, in an effort to improve its relative position, takes measures injurious to the absolute prosperity of its neighbours; and since its example is not confined to itself, it suffers more from similar action by its neighbours than it gains by such action itself. Practically all the remedies popularly advocated today are of this internecine character. Competitive wage-reductions, competitive tariffs, competitive liquidation of foreign assets, competitive currency deflations, competitive economy campaigns, competitive contractions of new development—all are of this beggar-my-neighbour description. The modern capitalist is a fair-weather sailor. As soon as a storm rises he abandons the duties of navigation and even sinks the boats which might carry him to safety by his haste to push his neighbours off and himself in.

I have spoken of competitive economy campaigns and competitive contractions of new development. But perhaps this needs a little more explanation. An economy campaign, in my opinion, is a beggar-my-neighbour enterprise, just as much as competitive tariffs or competitive wage-reductions, which are perhaps more obviously of this description. For one man's expenditure is another man's income. Thus whenever we refrain from expenditure, whilst we undoubtedly increase our own margin, we diminish that of someone else; and if the practice is universally followed, everyone will be worse off. An individual may be forced by his private circumstances to curtail his normal expenditure, and no one can blame him. But let no one suppose that he is performing a public duty in behaving in such a way. An individual or an institution or a public body, which voluntarily and unnecessarily curtails or postpones expenditure which is admittedly useful, is performing an anti-social act.

Unfortunately the popular mind has been educated away from the truth, away from common sense. The average man has been taught to believe what his own common sense, if he relied on it, would tell him was absurd. Even remedies of a right tendency have become discredited because of the failure of a timid and vacillating application of them at an earlier stage.

Now, at last, under the teaching of hard experience, there may be some slight movement towards wiser counsels. But through lack of foresight and constructive imagination the financial and political authorities of the world have lacked the courage or the conviction at each stage of the decline to apply the available remedies in sufficiently drastic doses; and by now they have allowed the collapse to reach a point where the whole system may have lost its resiliency and its capacity for a rebound.

Meanwhile the problem of reparations and war debts darkens the whole scene. We all know that these are now as dead as mutton, and as distasteful as stale mutton. There is no question of any substantial payments being made. The problem has ceased to be financial and has become entirely political and psychological. If in the next six months the French were to make a very moderate and reasonable proposal in final settlement, I believe that the Germans, in spite of all their present protestations to the contrary, would accept it and would be wise to accept it. But to all outward appearances the French mind appears to be hardening against such a solution and in favour of forcing a situation in which Germany will default. French politicians are feeling that it will be much easier for them, *vis-à-vis* the home political front, to get rid of reparations by a German default than to reach by agreement a moderate sum, most of which might have to be handed on to the United States. Moreover, this outcome would have what they deem to be the advantage of piling up grievances and a legal case against Germany for use in connection with the other outstanding questions created between the two countries by the Treaty of Versailles. I cannot, therefore, extract much comfort or prospective hope from developments in this sphere of inter-national finance.

Well, I have painted the prospect in the blackest colours. What is there to be said on the other side? What elements of hope can we discern in the surround-ing gloom? And what useful action does it still lie in our power to take?

The outstanding ground for cheerfulness lies, I think, in this—that the system has shown already its capacity to stand an almost inconceivable strain. If anyone had prophesied to us a year or two ago the actual state of affairs which exists to-day, could we have believed that the world could continue to maintain that even degree of normality which we actually have? ... This remarkable capacity of the system to take punishment is the best reason for hoping that we still have time to rally the constructive forces of the world.

Moreover, there has been a still recent and, in my judgment, most blessed event, of which we have not yet had time to gain the full benefit. I mean Great Britain's abandonment of the Gold Standard. ...

This means a very great abatement of the deflationary pressure which was existing six months ago. Over wide areas producers are now obtaining prices in terms of their domestic currencies which are not so desperately unsatisfactory in relation tó their costs of production and to their debts. ...

It would not be true to say, in spite of these favourable developments, that there is as yet in any part of the world an adequate relaxation of the deflationary pressure. But the widespread abandonment of the Gold Standard is preparing the way for the possibility of such a relaxation. ...

But there is a second major consequence of the partition of the countries of the world into two groups on and off the Gold Standard respectively. For the two groups as they now are, or as they soon may be, roughly correspond to those which have been exercising deflationary pressure on the rest of the world by having a *net* creditor position which causes them to draw gold and those which have been suffering this pressure. Now the departure of the latter group from gold means the beginning of a process towards the restoration of economic equilibrium. It means the setting into motion of natural forces which are certain in course of time to undermine and eventually destroy the creditor position of the two leading creditor gold countries. ...

The undermining of the competitive position of the export industries of these gold countries will be, in truth, in response to their own request; or, at any rate, a case of poetic justice. The rest of the world owes them money. They will not take payments in goods; they will not take it in bonds; they have already received all the gold there is. The puzzle which they have set to the rest of the world admits logically of only one solution, namely that some way must be found of doing without their exports. The expedient of continually reducing world prices failed; for prices were dragged down equally everywhere. But the expedient of exchange depreciation relatively to gold will succeed.

Thus a process has been set moving which may relieve in the end the defla-tionary pressure. The question is whether this will have time to happen before financial organization and the system of international credit break under the strain. If they do, then the way will be cleared for a concerted policy, probably under the leadership of Great Britain, of capital expansion and price raising throughout the world. For without this the only alternative solution which I can envisage is one of the general default of debts and the disappearance of the existing credit system, followed by rebuilding on quite new foundations.

The following, then, is the chapter of events which might conceivably—I will not attempt to evaluate the probability of their occurrence—lead us out of the bog. The Financial Crisis might wear itself out before a point of catastrophe and general default had been reached. This is perhaps happening. . . . If and when these things are clearly the case, we shall then enter the cheap money phase. This is the point at which, on the precedent of previous slumps, we might hope for the beginning of recovery. . . . We should use this strength to cheapen money and increase the volume of credit, to restart home activity and to lend abroad to the utmost of our powers. . . .

I am not confident, however, that on this occasion the cheap money phase will be sufficient by itself to bring about an adequate recovery of new investment. Cheap money means that the riskless, or supposedly riskless, rate of interest will be low. But actual enterprise always involves some degree of risk. It may still be the case that the lender, with his confidence shattered by his experiences, will continue to ask for new enterprise rates of interest which the borrower cannot expect to earn. Indeed this was already the case in the moderately cheap money phase which preceded the financial crisis of last autumn.

If this proves to be so, there will be no means of escape from prolonged and perhaps interminable depression except by direct State intervention to promote and subsidize new investment. Formerly there was no expenditure out of the proceeds of borrowing, which it was thought proper for the State to incur, except war. In the past, therefore, we have not infrequently had to wait for a war to terminate a major depression. I hope that in the future we shall not adhere to this purist financial attitude, and that we shall be ready to spend on the enterprises of peace what the financial maxims of the past would only allow us to spend on the devastations of war. At any rate I predict with an assured confidence that the only way out is for us to discover *some* object which is admitted even by the deadheads to be a legitimate excuse for largely increasing the expenditure of someone on something!

In all our thoughts and feelings and projects for the betterment of things, we should have it at the back of our heads that this is not a crisis of poverty but a crisis of abundance. It is not the harshness and the niggardliness of nature which is oppressing us, but our own incompetence and wrong-headedness which hinders us from making use of the bountifulness of inventive science and causes us to be overwhelmed by its generous fruits. The voices which—in such a conjuncture—tell us that the path of escape is to be found in strict economy and in refraining, whenever possible, from utilizing the world's potential production, are the voices of fools and madmen. . . .

Obviously it is much more difficult to solve the problem to-day than it would have been a year ago. But I still believe even now, as I believed then, that we still could be, if we would, the masters of our fate. The obstacles to recovery are not material. They reside in the state of knowledge, judgment, and opinion of those who sit in the seats of authority. Unluckily the traditional and ingrained beliefs of those who hold responsible positions throughout the world grew out of experiences which contained no parallel to the present, and are often the opposite of what one would wish them to believe to-day. . . . In the United States it is almost inconceivable what rubbish a public man has to utter to-day if he is to keep respectable. . . . We must believe that safety lies in boldness and nowhere else. If we lack boldness . . . then I recur to those prognostications of gloom with which I opened my remarks.

THE RISE OF FASCISM IN ITALY AND SPAIN

10. BENITO MUSSOLINI: THE POLITICAL AND SOCIAL DOCTRINE OF FASCISM*

Between 1919 and 1922 Italy suffered from unemployment, political laxity, and civil strife. Particularly in the north the numerical superiority of the Socialist party was challenged by a new nationalist movement led by Benito Mussolini (1883–1945)—fascism. By the fall of 1922 Mussolini's blackshirts had created a condition of near anarchy, and *Il Duce* (The Leader) was invited to form a new government. A twenty-year experiment in authoritarian dictatorship had begun in Italy.

Italian fascism was always opportunistic in nature, appealing to nationalistic feelings and superpatriotism, and promising action and answers to the Italian people. Not until 1925 did Mussolini begin to explain the ideological foundations of his new system. Then, looking back, correlations were found between the ideals of Italian fascism and certain ideas contained in the writings of men like Nietzsche, Sorel, and others. In 1932 the fundamentals of Italian fascism were elaborated in the *Enciclopedia Italiana*. The article, although it appeared under Mussolini's name, was written by the philosopher Giovanni Gentile.

What was the role of the individual and the role of the state in a fascist nation? How much liberty was left to the individual? What rewards could the people expect to receive from fascist rule? What were Mussolini's specific criticisms of liberalism, democracy, and Marxism? In what ways was fascism attempting to turn the clock back while posing as the radical faith of the future?

After the War, in 1919, Socialism was already dead as a doctrine: it existed only as a hatred. There remained to it only one possibility of action, especially in Italy, reprisals against those who had desired the War and who must now be made to "expiate" its results. . . . Fascism was not the nursling of a doctrine worked out beforehand with detailed elaboration; it was born of the need for action and it was itself from the beginning practical rather than theoretical; it was not merely another political party but, even in the first two years, in opposition to all political parties as such, and itself a living movement. The name which I then gave to the organization fixed its character. And yet, if one were to re-read, in the now dusty columns of that date, the report of the meeting in which the *Fasci Italiana di combattimento* were constituted, one would there

---

* Benito Mussolini, *The Political and Social Doctrine of Fascism*, trans. Jane Soames (London: The Hogarth Press, 1933), pp. 8–26. Reprinted by permission.

find no ordered expression of doctrine, but a series of aphorisms, anticipations and aspirations which, when refined by time from the original ore, were destined after some years to develop into an ordered series of doctrinal concepts, forming the Fascist political doctrine—different from all others either of the past or the present day.

. . . I said then, . . . "We want to accustom the working-class to real and effectual leadership, and also to convince them that it is no easy thing to direct an industry or a commercial enterprise successfully. . . . We shall combat every retrograde idea, technical or spiritual. . . . When the succession to the seat of government is open, we must not be unwilling to fight for it. We must make haste; when the present regime breaks down, we must be ready at once to take its place. It is we who have the right to the succession, because it was we who forced the country into the War, and led her to victory. The present method of political representation cannot suffice, we must have a representation direct from the individuals concerned. It may be objected against this programme that it is a return to the conception of the corporation, but that is no matter. . . ."

The years which preceded the march to Rome were years of great difficulty, during which the necessity for action did not permit of research or any complete elaboration of doctrine. The battle had to be fought in the towns and villages. There was much discussion, but—what was more important and more sacred— men died. They knew how to die. Doctrine, beautifully defined and carefully elucidated, with headlines and paragraphs, might be lacking; but there was to take its place something more decisive—Faith. Even so, anyone who can recall the events of the time through the aid of books, articles, votes of congresses and speeches of great and minor importance—anyone who knows how to research and weigh evidence—will find that the fundamentals of doctrine were cast during the years of conflict. It was precisely in those years that Fascist thought armed itself, was refined, and began the great task of organization. The problem of the relation between the individual citizen and the State; the allied problems of authority and liberty; political and social problems as well as those specifically national—a solution was being sought for all these while at the same time the struggle against Liberalism, Democracy, Socialism, and the Masonic bodies was being carried on, contemporaneously with the "punitive expedition." But, since there was inevitably some lack of system, the adversaries of Fascism have disingenuously denied that it had any capacity to produce a doctrine of its own, though that doctrine was growing and taking shape under their very eyes, even though tumultuously; . . .

Fascism is now a completely individual thing, not only as a regime but as a doctrine. And this means that to-day Fascism, exercising its critical sense upon itself and upon others, has formed its own distinct and peculiar point of view, to which it can refer and upon which, therefore, it can act in the face of all problems, practical or intellectual, which confront the world.

And above all, Fascism, the more it considers and observes the future and the development of humanity quite apart from political considerations of the moment, believes neither in the possibility nor the utility of perpetual peace. It thus repudiates the doctrine of Pacifism—born of a renunciation of the struggle and an act of cowardice in the face of sacrifice. War alone brings up to its highest tension all human energy and puts the stamp of nobility upon the peoples who have the courage to meet it. All other trials are substitutes, which never really put men into the position where they have to make the great decision—the alternative of life or death. Thus a doctrine which is founded upon this harmful postulate of peace is hostile to Fascism. And thus hostile to the spirit of Fascism, though accepted for what use they can be in dealing with particular political situations, are all the international leagues and societies which, as history will show, can be scattered to the winds when once strong national feeling is aroused by any motive—sentimental, ideal, or practical. This anti-Pacifist spirit is carried by Fascism even into the life of the individual; the proud motto of the *Squadrista*, . . . written on the bandage of the wound, is an act of philosophy not only stoic, the summary of a doctrine not only political —it is the education to combat, the acceptation of the risks which combat implies, and a new way of life for Italy. Thus the Fascist accepts life and loves it, knowing nothing of and despising suicide: he rather conceives of life as duty and struggle and conquest, life which should be high and full, lived for oneself, but above all for others—those who are at hand and those who are far distant, contemporaries, and those who will come after. . . .

Such a conception of life makes Fascism the complete opposite of that doctrine, the base of so-called scientific and Marxian Socialism, the materialist conception of history; according to which the history of human civilization can be explained simply through the conflict of interests among the various social groups and by the change and development in the means and instruments of production. . . . Fascism, now and always, believes in holiness and in heroism; that is to say, in actions influenced by no economic motive, direct or indirect. And if the economic conception of history be denied, according to which theory men are no more than puppets, carried to and fro by the waves of chance, while the real directing forces are quite out of their control, it follows that the existence of an unchangeable and unchanging class-war is also denied—the natural progeny of the economic conception of history. And above all Fascism denies that class-war can be the preponderant force in the transformation of society. These two fundamental concepts of Socialism being thus refuted, nothing is left of it but the sentimental aspiration—as old as humanity itself—towards a social convention in which the sorrows and sufferings of the humblest shall be alleviated. But here again Fascism repudiates the conception of "economic" happiness, to be realized by Socialism and, as it were, at a given moment in economic evolution to assure to everyone the maximum of well-being. Fascism denies the materialist conception of happiness as a possibility, and abandons it to its inventors, the economists of the first half of the nineteenth century: that is to say, Fascism denies the validity of the equation, well-being-happiness, which would reduce men to the level of animals, caring for one thing only—to be fat and well-fed—and would thus degrade humanity to a purely physical existence.

After Socialism, Fascism combats the whole complex system of democratic ideology, and repudiates it, whether in its theoretical premises or in its practical application. Fascism denies that the majority, by the simple fact that it is a majority, can direct human society; it denies that numbers alone can govern by means of a periodical consultation, and it affirms the immutable, beneficial and fruitful inequality of mankind, which can never be permanently levelled through the mere operation of a mechanical process such as universal suffrage. The democratic regime may be defined as from time to time giving the people the illusion of sovereignty, while the real effective sovereignty lies in the hands of other concealed and irresponsible forces. . . . This explains why Fascism, having first in 1922 (for reasons of expediency) assumed an attitude tending towards republicanism, renounced this point of view before the march to Rome; . . .

Fascism denies, in democracy, the absurd conventional untruth of political equality dressed out in the garb of collective irresponsibility, and the myth of "happiness" and indefinite progress. But, if democracy may be conceived in diverse forms—that is to say, taking democracy to mean a state of society in which the populace are not reduced to impotence in the State—Fascism may write itself down as "an organized, centralized and authoritative democracy."

Fascism has taken up an attitude of complete opposition to the doctrines of Liberalism, both in the political field and the field of economics. There should be no undue exaggeration (simply with the object of immediate success in controversy) of the importance of Liberalism in the last century, nor should what was but one among many theories which appeared in that period be put forward as a religion for humanity for all time, present and to come. Liberalism only flourished for half a century. . . . The era of Liberalism, after having accumulated an infinity of Gordian knots, tried to untie them in the slaughter of the World War—and never has any religion demanded of its votaries such a monstrous sacrifice. Perhaps the Liberal Gods were athirst for blood? But now, to-day, the Liberal faith must shut the doors of its deserted temples, deserted because the peoples of the world realize that its worship—agnostic in the field of economics and indifferent in the field of politics and morals—will lead, as it has already led, to certain ruin. In addition to this, let it be pointed out that all the political hopes of the present day are anti-Liberal, and it is therefore supremely ridiculous to try to classify this sole creed as outside the judgment of history, as though history were a hunting ground reserved for the professors of Liberalism alone—as though Liberalism were the final unalterable verdict of civilization.

But the Fascist negation of Socialism, Democracy and Liberalism must not be taken to mean that Fascism desires to lead the world back to the state of affairs before 1789, the date which seems to be indicated as the opening years of the succeeding semi-Liberal century: we do not desire to turn back; Fascism has not chosen De Maistre for its high-priest. Absolute monarchy has been and can never return, any more than blind acceptance of ecclesiastical authority.

So, too, the privileges of the feudal system "have been," and the division of society into castes impenetrable from outside, and with no intercommunication among themselves: the Fascist conception of authority has nothing to do with such a polity. A party which entirely governs a nation is a fact entirely new to history, there are no possible references or parallels. Fascism uses in its construction whatever elements in the Liberal, Social or Democratic doctrines still have a living value; it maintains what may be called the certainties which we owe to history, but it rejects all the rest—that is to say, the conception that there can be any doctrine of unquestioned efficacy for all times and all peoples. Given that the nineteenth century was the century of Socialism, of Liberalism, and of Democracy, it does not necessarily follow that the twentieth century must also be a century of Socialism, Liberalism and Democracy: political doctrines pass, but humanity remains; and it may rather be expected that this will be a century of authority, a century of the Left, a century of Fascism. For if the nineteenth century was a century of individualism (Liberalism always signifying individualism) it may be expected that this will be the century of collectivism, and hence the century of the State. It is a perfectly logical deduction that a new doctrine can utilize all the still vital elements of previous doctrines.

No doctrine has ever been born completely new, completely defined and owing nothing to the past; no doctrine can boast a character of complete originality; it must always derive, if only historically, from the doctrines which have preceded it and develop into further doctrines which will follow. Thus the scientific Socialism of Marx is the heir of the Utopian Socialism of Fourier, of the Owens and of Saint-Simon; thus again the Liberalism of the eighteenth century is linked with all the advanced thought of the seventeenth century, and thus the doctrines of Democracy are the heirs of the Encyclopedists. Every doctrine tends to direct human activity towards a determined objective; but the action of men also reacts upon the doctrine, transforms it, adapts it to new needs, or supersedes it with something else. A doctrine then must be no mere exercise in words, but a living act; and thus the value of Fascism lies in the fact that it is veined with pragmatism, but at the same time has a will to exist and a will to power, a firm front in face of the reality of "violence."

The foundation of Fascism is the conception of the State, its character, its duty, and its aim. Fascism conceives of the State as an absolute, in comparison with which all individuals or groups are relative, only to be conceived of in their relation to the State. . . . In 1929, at the first five-yearly assembly of the Fascist regime, I said:

"For us Fascists, the State is not merely a guardian, preoccupied solely with the duty of assuring the personal safety of the citizens; nor is it an organization with purely material aims, such as to guarantee a certain level of well-being and peaceful conditions of life; for a mere council of administration would be sufficient to realize such objects. Nor is it a purely political creation, divorced from all contact with the complex material reality which makes up the life of the individual and the life of the people as a whole. The State, as conceived of and as created by Fascism, is a spiritual and moral fact in itself, since its political, juridical and economic organization of the nation is a concrete thing: and such an organization must be in its origins and development a manifestation of the spirit. The State is the guarantor of security both internal and external, but it is also the custodian and transmitter of the spirit of the people, as it has grown up through the centuries in language, in customs and in faith. And the State is not only a living reality of the present, it is also linked with the past and above all with the future, and thus transcending the brief limits of individual life, it represents the immanent spirit of the nation. . . . It is the State which educates its citizens in civic virtue, gives them a consciousness of their mission and welds them into unity; . . . It leads men from primitive tribal life to that highest expression of human power which is Empire: it links up through the centuries the names of those of its members who have died for its existence and in obedience to its laws, it holds up the memory of the leaders who have increased its territory and the geniuses who have illumined it with glory as an example to be followed by future generations. When the conception of the State declines, and disunifying and centrifugal tendencies prevail, whether of individuals or of particular groups, the nations where such phenomena appear are in their decline."

From 1929 until to-day, evolution, both political and economic, has everywhere gone to prove the validity of these doctrinal premises. Of such gigantic importance is the State. It is the force which alone can provide a solution to the dramatic contradictions of capitalism, and that state of affairs which we call the crisis can only be dealt with by the State, as between other States. . . . whoever says Liberalism implies individualism, and whoever says Fascism implies the State. Yet the Fascist State is unique, and an original creation. It is not reactionary, but revolutionary, in that it anticipates the solution of the universal political problems which elsewhere have to be settled in the political field by the rivalry of parties, the excessive power of the Parliamentary regime and the irresponsibility of political assemblies; while it meets the problems of the economic field by a system of syndicalism which is continually increasing in importance, as much in the sphere of labour as of industry: and in the moral field enforces order, discipline, and obedience to that which is the determined moral code of the country. Fascism desires the State to be a strong and organic body, at the same time reposing upon broad and popular support. The Fascist State has drawn into itself even the economic activities of the nation, and, through the corporative social and educational institutions created by it, its influence reaches every aspect of the national life and includes, framed in their respective organizations, all the political, economic and spiritual forces of the nation. A State which reposes upon the support of millions of individuals who recognize its authority, are continually conscious of its power and are ready at once to serve it, is not the old tyrannical State of the medieval lord nor has it anything in common with the absolute governments either before or after 1789. The individual in the Fascist State is not annulled but rather multiplied, just in the same way that a soldier in a regiment is not diminished but rather increased by the number of his comrades. The Fascist State organizes the nation, but leaves a sufficient margin of liberty to the individual; the latter is deprived of all useless and possibly harmful freedom, but retains what is essential; the deciding power in this question cannot be the individual, but the State alone.

The Fascist State is not indifferent to the fact of religion in general, or to that particular and positive faith which is Italian Catholicism. The State professes no theology, but a morality, and in the Fascist State religion is considered as one of the deepest manifestations of the spirit of man, thus it is not only respected but defended and protected. . . .

The Fascist State is an embodied will to power and government: the Roman tradition is here an ideal of force in action. According to Fascism, government is not so much a thing to be expressed in territorial or military terms as in terms of morality and the spirit. It must be thought of as an Empire—that is to say, a nation which directly or indirectly rules other nations, without the need for conquering a single square yard of territory. For Fascism, the growth of Empire, that is to say the expansion of the nation, is an essential manifestation of vitality, and its opposite a sign of decadence. Peoples which are rising, or rising again after a period of decadence, are always imperialist; any renunciation is a sign of decay and of death. Fascism is the doctrine best adapted to represent the tendencies and the aspirations of a people, like the people of Italy, who are rising again after many centuries of abasement and foreign servitude. But Empire demands discipline, the co-ordination of all forces and a deeply-felt sense of duty and sacrifice: this fact explains many aspects of the practical working of the regime, the character of many forces in the State, and the necessarily severe measures which must be taken against those who would oppose this spontaneous and inevitable movement of Italy in the twentieth century, and would oppose it by recalling the outworn ideology of the nineteenth century—repudiated wheresoever there has been the courage to undertake great experiments of social and political transformation: for never before has the nation stood more in need of authority, of direction and of order. If every age has its own characteristic doctrine, there are a thousand signs which point to Fascism as the characteristic doctrine of our time. For if a doctrine must be a living thing, this is proved by the fact that Fascism has created a living faith; and that this faith is very powerful in the minds of men, is demonstrated by those who have suffered and died for it. . . .

11. BENITO MUSSOLINI: THE CORPORATE STATE*

The theory of corporatism did not originate with fascism, but Mussolini's Italy was the first state to attempt to organize its economy according to corporate principles. In theory, a corporate system redefined the economy along functional lines, with labor and management cooperating as partners—reducing class strife and increasing production. But in the Italian experiment labor lost its right to strike and to bargain collectively, while management found it necessary to cooperate with the ruling Fascist party. The selections below include two of Mussolini's speeches on corporatism and the Labor Charter of 1927. To what extent was the state involved in the economy under a corporate system? How free was the individual worker? In what ways did corporatism fit logically with the political and social doctrines elaborated by Mussolini in 1932?

[NOVEMBER 14, 1933]

We can now assert that the capitalistic mode of production has been superseded, and with it the theory of economic liberalism to which it owes its illustration and apology. . . .

When does the capitalistic enterprise cease to be an economic phenomenon? When its very size turns it into a social phenomenon, and it is precisely at this moment that capitalistic enterprise, finding itself in difficulties, falls like a dead weight into the arms of the State.

It is here that State intervention begins, and becomes increasingly necessary.
It is here that those who ignore the State seek it out anxiously.

* Benito Mussolini, *Four Speeches on the Corporate State* (Rome: Laboremus, 1935), pp. 11, 16–17, 19–23, 31–34, 53–55.

Things have now gone so far that if in all the countries of Europe the Government were to sleep 24 hours, this hold-up would be sufficient to produce disaster.

At this stage, there is not a single field of economy in which the State is not forced to intervene.

Were we—it is a mere supposition—to give way to this latest phase of capitalism we would slide into State capitalism which is merely State socialism reversed. By one way or another we shall arrive at the bureaucratisation of national economy.

This is the crisis of the capitalistic system considered in its universal significance....

In my opinion Italy should remain a country with a mixed economic system, with a strong agricultural organisation which is the basis of everything, so much so that the slight revival in industry witnessed lately, is due, in the unanimous opinion of all who are acquainted with these matters, to the fairly good crops of the last few years; a sound small and medium-sized industry; banks which do not speculate; a trade system fulfilling its proper task of supplying commodities rapidly and rationally to consumers.

The statement I submitted yesterday evening outlined the Corporation as we intend and wish to create it, and also defined its purposes and aims. The Corporation, it says, is created with a view to expanding the wealth, political power and well-being of the Italian people. These three objectives are conditional each on the other.

Political power creates wealth, and wealth in its turn strengthens political action.

I should like to call your attention to the third objective expounded: the well-being of the Italian people. It is essential that these institutions we have set up should, at a given moment, be felt and perceived by the masses themselves as instruments, through which those masses improve their standard of life.

At a given moment, the worker, the tiller of the soil, must be able to say for himself and to his family: If I am actually better off today, I owe it to the institutions created by the Fascist Revolution.

In every national society poverty is inevitable.

There is a percentage of people who live on the edge of society; but there are special institutions to look after them. That which should really distress our mind is the poverty of strong, capable men, vainly and feverishly seeking work.

It should be our wish to make the Italian workers, who interest us as Italians, as workers, and as Fascists, realise that we are setting up institutions not only to provide a form of expression for our doctrinal views, but in order that, in due course, they may yield positive, concrete, practical and tangible results. . . .

Our State is an organic, human State, desirous of adhering to the realities of life. . . .

It is quite conceivable that a National Council of Corporations may replace "in toto" the present Chamber of Deputies. I have never liked the Chamber of Deputies. After all, the Chamber of Deputies is now an anachronism in its very name: it is an institution which we found already in existence and which is alien to our mentality and to our creed as Fascists.

The Chamber presupposes the existence of a world we have overturned; it presupposes plurality of parties and not infrequently the hold-up of ministerial activity. From the day on which we annulled this plurality, the Chamber of Deputies has lost the essential reason for which it was formed. . . .

When we dealt a death-blow at all that had been the theory and practice of liberalism by creating the Militia, the armed defence of the party and of the Revolution, and the Grand Council, the supreme organ of the Revolution, we entered definitely upon the road of Revolution.

Today we are burying economic liberalism.

The Corporation operates in the economic field as the Grand Council and the Militia operate in the political field.

Corporations mean regulated economy and therefore also controlled economy, for there can be no regulation without control.

Corporations supersede socialism and supersede liberalism, they establish a new synthesis.

One fact is symptomatic: a fact which has perhaps not been adequately considered, that the decline of capitalism coincides with the decline of socialism.

All the socialist parties in Europe are shattered. . . .

[JANUARY 13, 1934]

In recent times State intervention has occurred in various and sometimes contrasting forms.

There is disorganic intervention, occurring empirically case for case. This has been done in every country, even where the flag of economic liberalism had remained hoisted until very recent times.

There is a form of intervention, communistic intervention, for which I have absolutely no sympathy, not even as regards size. Personally, I exclude that Communism applied in Germany would have yielded different results from those seen in Russia. In any case it is evident that the German people would not have it.

This form of Communism, as we see it in certain of its exasperated Americanised aspects (for the extremes meet) is nothing but a form of State Socialism, meaning the bureaucratisation of economy. I think that none of you wish to bureaucratise, that is to freeze, the tangible facts of the economic life of the nation: complicated and changeable facts, closely bound to all that happens in the world, and above all, of such a nature that if they lead to errors these may bear consequences which are impossible to forestall.

The American experiment should be followed with great attention. Even in America, State intervention in economic matters is direct and sometimes peremptory. The codes enforced are nothing but collective contracts to which the United States President compels both parties to submit.

One should wait a while before passing judgment upon this experiment. Nevertheless, I would like to state my own opinion on the matter, which is that monetary manoeuvres cannot lead to a lasting and effective rise in prices. . . .

In fact who could really believe that the wealth of a people can be increased through the multiplication of coinage? Someone has already quoted the following example, namely, that it would be the same as believing that the photograph of one man reproduced one million times causes the population to increase by one million men.

Have there not been enough experiments? From the "assignats" in France to the German post-war mark?

The [final] experiment is the Fascist one. If liberal economy is the economy of individuals in a condition of more or less absolute freedom, Fascist corporate economy is the economy of individuals as well as of associated groups and of the State.

What are its features? Or rather what are the features of corporate economy?

Corporate economy respects the principle of private property. Private property completes the human personality: it is a right and therefore an obligation. So much so in fact that we think it should be viewed as a social function; not inactive property, therefore, but the reverse; not property which merely enjoys the produce of wealth, but develops, increases and multiplies this produce.

Corporate economy also respects private initiative. It is clearly stated in the Labour Charter that the State shall intervene only when individual economy is deficient, nonexistent or insufficient. . . .

Corporate economy introduces order in the field of economy. If there is a phenomenon that calls for order and should be directed to a definite purpose, it is precisely the economic phenomenon, because it concerns the whole population. It is not only industrial economy that should be disciplined, but also agricultural economy (in easy times agriculturists have been known to go off the beaten track), commercial economy, banking and the arts and crafts.

In what way should this order be enacted? Through self-discipline of the various categories concerned.

It is only when various categories fail to come to an agreement, or to establish the proper balance that the State may intervene, although the State always has undisputed power to do so, because it also represents the other aspect of the phenomenon, which is consumption. The nameless mass which forms the bulk of consumers, not being actually organised into regular bodies, must be protected by some organ voicing their collective interests. . . .

THE LABOUR CHARTER
(PROMULGATED BY THE GRAND COUNCIL OF FASCISM ON APRIL 21, 1927)
THE CORPORATE STATE AND ITS ORGANISATION

I. The Italian Nation is an organism having ends, a life and means superior in power and duration to the single individuals or groups of individuals composing it. It is a moral, political and economic unit which finds its integral realisation in the Fascist State.

II. Work in all its forms—intellectual, technical and manual—both organising or executive, is a social duty. On this score and only on this score, it is protected by the State.

From the national standpoint the mass of production represents a single unit; it has a single object, namely the well-being of individuals and the development of national power.

III. There is complete freedom of professional or syndical organisation. But syndicates legally recognised and subject to State control alone have the right of legal representation of the whole category of employers and workers for which they are constituted; they have the right to protect their interests in their relations with the State or with professional associations; they stipulate collective labour contracts binding on all those belonging to the category; they levy their dues and exercise with regard to them functions of public interest devolved to them. . . .

VI. Legally recognised professional associations ensure legal equality between employers and workers, control the discipline of production and labour, and promote the improvement of both.

Corporations constitute the unitary organisation of all the forces of production and integrally represent their interests.

In virtue of this integral representation, since the interests of production are the interests of the nation, the corporations are recognised by the law as State organs.

As representing the unitary interests of production, corporations may enforce binding regulations for the discipline of labour relations as well as for the co-ordination of production, whenever they are empowered to do so by the affiliated associations. . . .

VIII. Professional associations of employers are required to promote by all possible means the increase and improvement of production and a reduction of costs. Organs representing those who exercise a liberal profession or art, and associations of civil servants should promote the interests of art, science and letters, with a view to improving production and to achieving the moral aims of the syndical system.

IX. State intervention in economic production arises only when private initiative is lacking or insufficient, or when the political interests of the State are involved. This intervention may take the form of control, assistance or direct management. . . .

12. THE SPANISH CIVIL WAR—GENERAL FRANCO ON THE FUTURE OF SPAIN*

In the period between the two world wars Spain was plagued by almost every problem facing twentieth-century European nations. A small industrial base, excessive unemployment, political turmoil, and deep social divisions kept the tradition-bound nation from coming to grips with the present. After a decade of dictatorship through the 1920's, the nation turned to republicanism just as the depression dealt a near-fatal blow to the Spanish economy. By 1936 sporadic bursts of violence wracked the nation, and an electoral triumph by the parties of the left (a popular front coalition of Anarchists, Socialists, Communists, and Republicans) coupled with several political assassinations triggered a revolt in the officer corps of the army. The nationalist revolt began in Spanish Morocco and rapidly spread to the mother country. Supporting the nationalist or rebel cause were elements of the army, most of the large landowners, the Catholic Church, and those who believed in a "traditional" Spain. Italy and Germany quickly lent their prestige and aid to the rebels. The loyalist forces, fighting

* Georges Rotvand, *Franco Means Business,* trans. Reginald Dingle (New York: Devin-Adair Co., [1937]), pp. 49–54, 56–62. Reprinted by permission.

in the name of the Republic, were recruited from the workers, peasants, and the small Spanish middle class. Volunteer forces from around the world added vigor and sometimes idealism to the loyalist cause, and the Soviet Union sent advisers and equipment. As the war ran its bloody course between 1936 and 1939, some observers concluded that they were witnessing a clash between fascism (rebels) and communism (loyalists); others believed that the struggle was a prelude to World War II, with the forces of freedom resisting the scourge of tyranny. In fact, the Spanish conflict was a civil war with foreign powers intervening for their own immediate advantage.

In October 1936, General Francisco Franco (1892–   ) was declared "chief of the Spanish state" by the rebels. The first of the following statements was made immediately after Franco's appointment as chief of state, and the second approximately three months later in January 1937. What did Franco envisage as the "New Spain"? On what basis did he propose to restore national unity? How much freedom was to be left to the individual? Compare Franco's political principles with Mussolini's.

ADDRESS BROADCAST BY GENERAL FRANCO FROM "RADIO CASTILLE," OCTOBER IST, 1936

SPANIARDS:

You, who in your homes listen in to the news of the war, you, who in the front lines await the news from behind the lines, you, who in the zones in possession of the Reds, anxiously await the arrival of our liberating forces, you, who exiled from Spain, follow with anxiety the vicissitudes of the conflict—I salute you all from the microphone of Radio Castille.

I do not intend to address you in a high-flown military speech because the responsibilities of Government make it my duty to tell you all that must be our task in the future

To attempt to divide my time by the discussion of strongly differentiated subjects, without establishing a more or less direct link between them, would be to err on the side of Utopianism.

As soon as we begin to talk of our plans, a brief examination of the past becomes imperative, so that we may, as the result of experience, usefully determine our actions in the future.

So that it is not a question of appealing to a state of things so entirely national as to need no discussion, but it is of the highest importance that we should not allow ourselves to fall into a state of collective amnesia to which we dreaming hidalgos, the sons of Don Quixote, are so prone.

SPAIN, and in invoking that name I do so with all the warmth of my heart, had been suffering for many long years from influences of various sorts, of which not the least dangerous and hurtful was that of a horde of mistaken intellectuals who, despising the true and acknowledged thinkers of our race, were peering over their own frontiers and absorbing everything exotic and destructive to be found in other countries.

In some cases preferences of language, the savouring of decadent literature, admiration of demagogic doctrines, raging rationalism, the distortion of historic truths, which implied that we were not a civilised race—all these things, and many more, ended by effacing in the minds of the teaching classes the sentiment of patriotism. Once this inoculation had taken place it was in no way surprising that it should have followed the channels we shall now describe.

The loss of the most prominent characteristics of our race, shame for our present, forgetfulness of our past, want of confidence in our future, a misgiving that we lacked the modern point of view, would entail the stifling of such ideals as the FLAG, HONOUR and COUNTRY.

Some steeped in error, others having as a foundation the ignorance and want of culture among the masses—all these things led up to a moment in which it was not surprising to find an immediate repercussion of all the forces of hate and every iconoclastic plan for disruption among all the forces which went to make up the glory of our country.

After this, having made sure of the moral assassination of a people which appeared to be sunk in the abyss, it was not difficult to sell and hand it over to the highest foreign bidder; to keep it in control, to make it obey, and to barter its birthright.

In the meantime our former favourable commercial balance was becoming an adverse one, the fruits of our soil depreciated, pseudo-pacifist limitations were imposed, which had for their real object the withholding of a helping hand from the prostrate country. Obstacles were placed in the way of everything that made for the expression of our own personality, which they were deter-mined to destroy. False prophets, by conjuring up glowing visions, managed to stifle the genuine national character, and by means of a communism which promised the land for the peasant, sovereignty for the worker and regional political autonomy, sowed the seeds of hatred and extermination. A triple lie, loaded with cynicism because, on obtaining power its tyrannous rule snatches the land from the peasant, withdraws liberty from the worker and is openly opposed to all autonomous flexibility.

For all the above reasons the new Spain takes note of the magnitude and importance of the whole of this dreadful past, and embarks on the task of liberation, in order to make it clear in a broadminded spirit of social collabora-tion, that the re-establishment of order and legitimate authority, austerely exer-cised, is the unconditional and only way of restoring to the country its own liberty, which because it is its own, will regenerate all co-nationalists within and outside our native land.

SPAIN *is re-organising within a broad totalitarian concept through those na-tural institutions which assure its nationality, its unity and its continuity.* The establishment of a strong principle of authority which is implied in this move-ment, will not have an exclusive military character; rather it is the inauguration of a functional *régime,* through the harmonious action of which all the capa-bility and energy of the nation will manifest itself.

Respect will be shown to regional characteristics and peculiarities in harmony with the ancient national traditions in the best days of our national splendour, but without allowing any harm to be done to the national unity. . . .

Once the moribund suffrage, which was first abused by the local "bosses" and subsequently, under the tyrannical oppression of the Syndicates, made subservient to political interests, is broken up, the national will will in due course express itself by means of those technical institutions and corporations which, proceeding from the very bowels of the country, truly express its needs and ideals.

The greater the strength of the new Spanish State, and the more normal its evolution, the more quickly will it progress to the decentralisation of those functions which do not specifically belong to it; and the districts, municipalities and associations will enjoy more and wider liberties within the supreme governance of the State.

In its social aspect labour will be endowed with absolute guarantees which will do away with its slavery to capitalism; but at the same time, it will not be allowed to organise itself in the modern manner—in that combative and bitter spirit which implies sterile rebellion and renders it incapable of loyal co-operation.

Security for daily labour will be assured and the labourer will participate in the benefits and share in the increase of production, it being understood that he shall not seek to dictate the methods by which these advantages are obtained. Every victory which implies a betterment in the sphere of Spanish economics will be respected.

Side by side with these rights will be the duties and obligations of the worker, especially as regards the performance of his task and his loyal co-operation with the other elements which create wealth. Every Spaniard will be required to work according to his capacity. The new State has no room for parasite citizens.

The State as such will not have any official religion, but will make a concordat with the Catholic Church as to the respective functions of each, thereby respecting our traditions and the religious sentiment of the immense majority of the Spanish people, but allowing of no interference in the specific functions of the State. . . .

In the international sphere we intend to live in harmony with all nations, favouring community of race, language and ideals, but not for that reason disdaining or setting aside those traditional relations which are not incompatible or antithetical to our ample horizon which is always open to the whole world.

We except in no uncertain manner all contacts with Sovietism, which has so pernicious an effect on the cause of humanity and of civilisation.

I feel sure that in this land of heroes and martyrs, which is now spilling its generous blood so that the whole world may see on our Spanish soil the solution of problems which exist on the other side of our frontiers, Spain will discharge an ancient debt, providentially imposed, and will have shown an example to be imitated when it can write on the pages of its history those glorious deeds which are neither from the East nor from the West because they are genuinely Spanish.

Spaniards! Long Live Spain!

ADDRESS BROADCAST BY GENERAL FRANCO ON
JANUARY 19TH, 1937, FROM SALAMANCA

Spain, Spain, Spain!—land of heroic deeds, of heroic greatness, home of ascetics and of Quixotes, land of nobles, has awakened with new vitality and strength. It is a National Movement, this wakening of a people who did not know themselves, and felt strange and out of place. Undermined by the hidden forces of revolution, little by little it was succumbing to the criminal designs of alien Committees that, under the mask of Democracy, and brandishing the strong weapon of materialism, was undermining all there was of nobility and spirituality in our ancient homeland.

Liberty, fettered by the licence of Government partisans; Equality, destroyed by those who in the Government proclaimed themselves to be belligerents; Fraternity, given the lie by daily assassinations of men of the opposition, with the complacency and complicity of the authorities and the Government; these exist again.

Hidden pacts with Russian Communism, secret agreements with foreign nations behind the back of the Constitution and the Laws, persecution without truce of everything representing any spiritual or moral value, or that did not yoke itself to the tumbril of Muscovite revolution—this was the Spain of yesterday; the Spain of workers criminally exploited by their employers, of the tubercular without sanatoriums, of the hearths without fires, of political bosses, of social injustice, of children with no schools, of Spaniards without a Fatherland, of men without a God.

For peace and the country's welfare, for the rational and just betterment of working and middle classes, for liberty of conscience and respect for Religion and Tradition, for the tranquillity and prosperity of the home, for our threatened civilisation, and the prestige of our Flag, for the independence of our country, for a new Spain, a free Spain, a great Spain, our soldiers are fighting to-day this Russo-Communistic invasion.

This new Spain will represent a great national family, one without masters or vassals, without poor or potentate. Social justice will be the basis of our new Empire, without destructive and suicidal class warfare, without meddlesome interferences from abroad that are so incompatible with our national dignity. We want a fraternal Spain, an industrious and working Spain, where parasites can find no lodging. A Spain without chains and tyrannies; a nation without destructive Marxism and Communism; a State for the people and not a people for the State. A Spain without parties in continual conflict, without parliamentary preponderancies or irresponsible assemblies. We want a Spain great, strong and united, one with authority, direction and order. Our progress must be firm and unhesitating; and we must go progressively and constantly on to our goal of a great organic Spain.

With our rapid social improvement we will insure economical conditions of living that will permit the private individual to participate in the realisation of the greatness of the Fatherland.

We must awaken in all Spaniards the love of country, pride in realising their Spanish birth, by creating conditions of life for all social classes that will permit them to appreciate without pain or rancour the political greatness of the new State. . . .

This is our commission—love of our country; honour; love for the people; deep Catholic sentiment, and a complete faith in the destiny of Spain.

In the order of Religion, to the angry persecution of the Marxists and Communists of whatever represents the existence of spirituality, of faith or of religious worship, we oppose the sentiment of a Catholic Spain, with her saints and martyrs, with her secular institutions, her social justice, her Christian charity and that great comprehensive soul which, in the Golden Ages of our history when a vigorous and deep-rooted Catholicism was the reconstructing arm of our historic unity, suffered, under the tolerant guardianship of the Catholic State, the mosques and synagogues to be gathered within the soul of Catholic Spain.

This great National Movement demands of everyone faith and enthusiasm, and includes the sacrifice of everything that in this holocaust of our land can be spared. If we are to make a Spain for everyone, everyone must sacrifice himself for Spain, and put aside shades of difference and details that might roughen the facets that in a new Spain must be limpid and glittering.

Union and collaboration with the State must be disinterested, self-sacrificing, without materialistic aims or self-seeking. Law and the family must be its principal cells. *Family, laws, corporations, municipalities, province, region, will be the principal wheels of progress of this new State.*

Nor need those fear who at first have not been with us, nor those who, misled by propaganda, have been on the side of the Red hordes, or even fought in their ranks.

Those who either by conviction or through being deceived by others are fighting against us have my word of honour that nothing will happen to them if they surrender to our troops. It will be the work of the courts of justice to punish only those who have committed crimes or acts punishable under ordinary law.

We shall forge a new Spain for all, and we will not close the doors of the State to any who come to it frankly and without evil intentions, for we know that of those great numbers who have been exploited and deceived will, one day, become new Spain's most enthusiastic defenders. Peace and Justice we offer and the sooner our offer is accepted the sooner will the land go forward with the rhythmical progress we announce to all. . . .

Whilst our troops follow their path of triumph, the war continues its victorious course, and the men in the front ranks vie with each other in heroism for the National Cause, in the rear we are studying and putting together the basis of our new Spain.

There will be laws for the suppression of strikes, and for helping the workless; for the family budget, and for bettering conditions of life among the poor; for assisting the children of the middle and necessitous cases; for the anti-tubercular League that guarantees medical assistance to the diseased; for the assisting of the families of poor combatants, and many more, of which a list is being prepared, all proving that the points of the programme of new Spain are effective and real.

This is the Spain that, honoured by the recognition of those countries which understand the threat of Communism and the sanctity of our crusade for the defence of Civilisation, salutes the world. Spain which nobly thanks those other nations for their spiritual assistance, those other nations which, without official manifestation, weep for the profanation of Churches and the martyrdom of our brethren at the hands of blood-maddened hordes, as if our churches were the very ones in which they kneel in worship and the blood of our martyred were that of their own.

Spain that unites in intimate communion with the plans of her Chief! Spaniards all: LONG LIVE SPAIN!

13. ARTHUR KOESTLER: DIALOGUE WITH DEATH*

Mercy was conspicuously absent on both sides in the Spanish Civil War. Prisoners were tortured or executed (or both), and civilians fared little better than soldiers. The record of life inside loyalist and rebel prisons was fragmentary and was exaggerated for propaganda purposes during the war, but a few first-hand reports trickled out from survivors. One classic account was written by Arthur Koestler (1905–   ), a journalist and onetime Communist who visited both the nationalist and loyalist zones on different trips. He was expelled by the nationalists in 1936 when his Communist background was discovered, but on a subsequent trip in early February 1937, he was captured after the fall of Malaga. Imprisoned and condemned to death without trial or examination, Koestler spent more than three months in a nationalist prison (two of the months in solitary confinement) before the British Consul in Seville managed to secure his release.

Koestler saw the war, and life and death in prison, in very personal terms. "Dying," he concluded, "is a confoundedly serious thing; one shouldn't make a melodrama out of it." Why, according to the author, did Malaga fall to rebel forces so quickly? What kind of legal procedures existed for captured prisoners? Who, if any, were the "heroes" of the Spanish Civil War in Koestler's view? Contrast Koestler's account with General Franco's promise to loyalist troops who surrendered.

The winter was cold; the wind from the Guadarrama whipped Madrid; the Moors in their trenches caught pneumonia and spat blood. The passes in the Sierra Nevada were blocked, the Republican Militiamen had neither uniforms nor blankets and their hospitals had no chloroform; their frozen fingers and feet had to be amputated without their being put to sleep. At the Anarchist hospital in Malaga a boy sang the Marseillaise while they sawed away two of his toes; this expedient gained a certain popularity.

Then spring came and all was well again; the buds on the trees opened and the tanks started on the roads. Nature's benevolence enabled General Queipo de Llano to launch, as early as mid-January, his long-planned offensive against Malaga.

This was in nineteen hundred and thirty-seven. General Gonzales Queipo de Llano, who not so long ago had conspired against the Monarchy and proclaimed his sympathy with communism to all and sundry in the cafés round the Puerta del Sol, was now in command of the Second Division of the insurgent army. He had a microphone installed in a room at his G.H.Q. in Seville and talked

* Arthur Koestler, *Dialogue with Death*, trans. Trevor and Phyllis Blewitt (New York: The Macmillan Co., 1942), pp. 1–2, 6–7, 40–43, 53–54, 168–71, 175–76. Reprinted by permission.

into it every night for an hour. "The Marxists," he said, "are ravening beasts, but we are gentlemen. Señor Companys deserves to be stuck like a pig."

General Queipo's army consisted of approximately 50,000 Italian troops, three *banderas* of the Foreign Legion and 15,000 African tribesmen. The rest of his men, about ten per cent, were of Spanish nationality.

The offensive began on January 10th.

I was in Paris at the time. I had written a pamphlet on the Spanish War; the French edition was just out. In the preceding months I had worked as a special correspondent for the *News Chronicle,* first with the insurgents and later, after Franco's propaganda department had kicked me out of Nationalist territory, in Catalonia and Madrid. Now the war had shifted to the Andalusian front and it was decided that I should go there.

I left Paris on January 15th, took a train to Toulouse and from there flew to Barcelona. I stayed in Barcelona for only one day. The city presented a depressing picture. There was no bread, no milk, no meat to be had, and there were long queues outside the shops. The Anarchists blamed the Catalan Government for the food shortage and organized an intensive campaign of political agitation; the windows of the trams were plastered with their leaflets. The tension in the city was near danger-point. It looked as though Spain were not only to be the stage for the dress-rehearsal of the second world war, but also for the fratricidal struggle within the European Left.

I was glad not to have to write an article on Barcelona. On the 16th I left by the 4 p.m. train for Valencia. . . .

On the day before I left for Malaga I attended a parade of troops at Castellon, a seaside town not far from Valencia, at the invitation of General Julio.

General Julio had formerly been Julius Deutsch and Minister of War in the Austrian Republic after the collapse of 1918. His aide-de-camp was a certain Count Reventlow, nephew of the Nazi member of the Reichstag; himself, like Deutsch, a member of the Social-Democratic Party. When the Republic was set up in Austria in 1918 and Julius Deutsch was appointed Minister of War, his first act was to dismiss all the reactionary officers of the old army—exactly what the Spanish Republic in 1931 failed to do. Deutsch was one of the very few men of the Left in Europe who knew anything about strategy and military matters. At that time this was looked upon as bad form in Left-wing circles.

Deutsch was an exception. When the situation in Austria became threatening, he organized the Austrian workers' defence corps, the famous *Schutzbund*. The *Schutzbund* was destroyed in February, 1934, by Dollfuss; but Deutsch was and continued to be the most popular figure of the Austrian Left, loved and respected by the rank and file as scarcely any Socialist leader of the post-war era has even been. . . .

So it is all over. Malaga has surrendered.

And I remember Colonel Villalba's last statement before he stepped into his car: "The situation is a critical one, but Malaga will put up a good fight."

Malaga did not put up a good fight.

The city was betrayed by its leaders—deserted, delivered up to the slaughter. The rebel cruisers bombarded us and the ships of the Republic did not come. The rebel 'planes sowed panic and destruction, and the 'planes of the Republic did not come. The rebels had artillery, armoured cars and tanks, and the arms and war material of the Republic did not come. The rebels advanced from all directions and the bridge on the only road connecting Malaga with the Republic had been broken for four months. The rebels maintained an iron discipline and machine-gunned their troops into battle, while the defenders of Malaga had no discipline, no leaders, and no certainty that the Republic was backing them up. Italians, Moors and Foreign Legionaries fought with the professional bravery of mercenaries against the people in a cause that was not theirs; and the soldiers of the people, who were fighting for a cause that was their own, turned tail and ran away.

The guilty leaders of the town, who deserted their men, were court-martialled. The guilty government of Largo Caballero, who left Malaga to her fate, was forced to resign. The guilty governments of the Western Democracies, which left the Spanish Republic to her fate, could neither be court-martialled nor forced to resign; they will be tried by History. But that will not make the dead arise.

The longer one waits for a thing to happen, the more astonished one is when it finally does happen. We had known for days that Malaga was lost, but we had pictured the end differently. Everything had proceeded so terribly silently, noiselessly, undramatically. Events had shown every sign of coming to a head, but we were cheated of the climax. In all secrecy the white flag had been hoisted on the Malaga tower. When, on the morrow, the enemy's cruisers and 'planes arrived, we expected them to open fire, and did not realize that there was no longer an enemy, that we were already living under the domination of the Bourbon flag.

This smooth, slick transition was more terrifying than anything we had feared. Without our knowing it, while we slept, we had been delivered up to the tender mercies of General Franco.

The entry of the rebel troops likewise took place in an uncannily natural and undramatic fashion. My diary runs:

1 p.m. An officer wearing the grey steel helmet of the Italian army appears on the road leading to Colmenar, just opposite our house.

He looks round and fires a revolver shot into the air. Immediately after this about two hundred infantry come marching down the road in perfect formation. They are singing Mussolini's hymn, "Giovinezza."

As they pass by the house they salute us, and the household staff, who only yesterday assiduously raised their clenched fists, now, with equal Spanish effusiveness, raise their arms in the Fascist salute. They seem perfectly at ease, but since they look upon us foreigners as half imbecile, the gardener advises Sir Peter and me to change our demeanour, too, "because we have a new Government now."[1]

1. Koestler was visiting the home of Sir Peter Mitchell, a retired Englishman who resided permanently in Malaga.

After some time, as more and more troops go by and salute us—we are all gathered on the balcony as though reviewing a march past—Sir Peter and I are constrained to raise our arms too. We avoid looking at each other.

I drink a tumblerful of cognac.

2 p.m. A company of Italian infantry occupies the neighbouring hill.

3 p.m. The Italian Lieutenant in command of the company on the hill comes into the garden and asks whether he may wash. He introduces himself courteously, and Sir Peter gives orders for a bath to be got ready for him. A few soldiers follow him down from the hill to get a wash and a drink of water. They do not speak a word of Spanish. They look pretty worn-out; their behaviour is perfectly polite.

Sir Peter and I settle down in our deck chairs on the porch. The sun is shining. We hear the Lieutenant splashing about in the bathtub. We agree that he is a nice fellow. We still avoid looking at each other.

Shame chokes me, is like a dry sponge in my throat.

4 p.m. A storm of hurrahs and clapping is heard coming from the city. The rebels have reached the centre of Malaga.

4.30 p.m. Cars flying the Bourbon flag come driving along the road. Tanks are lumbering down in an endless column from Colmenar. Shots can be heard from the town at regular intervals. One of the household staff volunteers the suggestion that, since the fighting is over, these shots may mean "that the execution of the Red criminals is beginning."

Once more it was evening, and once more we sat opposite one another on high-backed Victorian arm-chairs at the formally laid table.

I had burned all compromising papers: letters of introduction from the Spanish Embassy in Paris, travel-permits issued by the authorities at Valencia, and all the copies of my book except the one which I had dedicated to Sir Peter; but he promised to destroy that too. Then I blotted out all dangerous references in my diary....

Deep down in us, too, on this last evening was that smiling voice that told us that the morrow would be just as yesterday.

The next morning at 11 a.m. we were arrested. . . .

I was led into a vast empty room. In the corner of the room was a stool, upon which I was made to sit down. Two Civil Guards sat down opposite me near the door, their rifles on their knees.

We sat like this for a while.

Then I heard screams coming from the courtyard, and a young man, his naked torso streaming with blood, was led into the room. His face was battered, cut about and slashed; for a moment I thought the man must have been run over by a steam engine. Holding him by the armpits they dragged him across the room. He yelled and whimpered. The Phalangists who were dragging him along spoke to him in honeyed tones: "*Hombre,* we're not going to beat you any more." The door closed after them, and a moment later there were sounds of ringing blows and dull thuds and kicks. The man groaned and cried by turns. He cried at regular intervals.

Then for a few seconds there was silence. All I could hear was quick, stertorous breathing. I don't know what they did to him in those few seconds. Then he screamed again in an unnaturally high-pitched shrill voice, and then at last he was silent. A few moments later the door flew open and they dragged him across the room in which I was sitting into the courtyard. I couldn't make out whether he was dead or merely unconscious. I did not care to look very closely.

Then a second victim was taken through the room to be subjected to the same treatment; and then a third.

Every time they went through the room the Phalangists looked at me as though marking me down as their next victim, but they said nothing. After the third case, no more were brought in; I sat still and waited.

The Civil Guards sitting opposite me seemed to be disagreeably affected by these proceedings. While the tortures were going on in the next room they scrutinized my features keenly to watch my reaction; perhaps, too, with a faint stirring of pity. When the third victim was brought back, dead or unconscious, the elder of the Civil Guards shrugged his shoulders with a glance in my direction; it was an unconscious gesture of apology. In it was expressed the whole attitude towards life of a fifty-year-old gendarme who, on the one hand, had thirty years of service in a medieval country behind him and, on the other, probably had a wife, several underfed children and a pet canary. In it was expressed an entire human philosophy of shame, resignation and apathy. "The world's like that," he seemed to be saying, "and neither I nor you will ever change it." The shrug of the Civil Guard is more vivid in my memory than the screams of the tortured. . . .

I had spent the first two months in the Seville prison in complete isolation. Only now, when I came into contact with the other prisoners, did I learn what was going on around me.

I learned that in the week after my transfer to the prison thirty-seven men from that big patio had been executed.

In the last week of February no executions had taken place; in March, forty-five.

Most of the victims were prisoners of war from the various fronts. . . .

True, not a single man had been shot without trial. But these trials were far more disgraceful than the unceremonious slaughter of prisoners in the front lines, immediately after a battle.

In the case of every single prisoner of war, without exception, the charge was one of "rebelión militar." Those who were defending the legal Government against open rebellion, were condemned for taking part in a rebellion—by an authority that claimed to be a court of law and to pronounce judgment in the name of justice.

The scenario of this sinister comedy was always the same. The proceedings lasted two or three minutes. The so-called Prosecutor demanded the death sentence; always and without exception. The so-called Defending Officer—always and without exception—asked for a life sentence in view of mitigating circumstances. Then the prisoner was marched off. He was never informed of his sentence. Sentence was passed the moment he was out of the door; it was one of death; always and without exception.

The record of the sentence was passed on to the Commander-in-Chief of the Southern Forces, General Queipo de Llano. The sentences were carried out in summary fashion. Twenty to twenty-five per cent of the prisoners—according to Queipo's mood or the situation at the front—were reprieved. The rest were shot. . . .

During March forty-five men were shot.

During the first thirteen days of April there were no executions.

During the night of April 13th to 14th seventeen men were shot, in celebration of the anniversary of the proclamation of the Republic. . . .

Two nights later, the night of Thursday, eight were shot. This was the first time I heard anything.

The proceedings were very subdued; perhaps that explains why I hadn't heard them before. But now I was on the watch.

I had learned that the critical time was between midnight and two o'clock in the morning. For some days I stood from midnight until two o'clock with my ear pressed to the door of my cell.

During the first night of my vigil, the night of Wednesday, nothing happened. During the second night . . .

A feeling of nausea still comes over me when I remember that night.

I had gone to sleep, and I woke up shortly before midnight. In the black silence of the prison, charged with the nightmarish dreams of thirteen hundred sleeping men, I heard the murmured prayer of the priest and the ringing of the sanctus bell.

Then a cell door, the third to the left of mine, was opened, and a name was called out. "*Qué?*"—What is the matter?—asked a sleepy voice, and the priest's voice grew clearer and the bell rang louder.

And now the drowsy man in his cell understood. At first he only groaned; then in a dull voice, he called for help: "*Socorro, socorro.*"

"*Hombre,* there's no help for you," said the warder who accompanied the priest. He said this neither in a hostile nor in a friendly tone; it was simply a statement of fact. For a moment the man who was about to die was silent; the warder's quiet, sober manner puzzled him. And then he began to laugh. He kept slapping his knees with his hands, and his laughter was quiet and subdued, full of little gasps and hiccoughs. "You are only pretending," he said to the priest. "I knew at once that you were only pretending."

"*Hombre,* this is no pretence," said the warder in the same dry tone as before. They marched him off.

I heard him shouting outside. But the sound of the shots came only a few minutes later.

In the meantime the priest and the warder had opened the door of the next cell; it was No. 42, the second to my left. Again, "*Qué?*" And again the prayer and the bell. This one sobbed and whimpered like a child. Then he cried out for his mother: "*Madre, madre!*" . . .

"*Hombre,* why didn't you think of her before?" said the warder.

They marched him off.

They went on to the next cell. When my neighbour was called, he said nothing. Most probably he was already awake, and, like me, prepared. But when the priest had ended his prayer, he asked, as if of himself: "Why must I die?" The priest answered in five words, uttered in a solemn voice but rather hurriedly: "Faith, man. Death means release."

They marched him off.

They came to my cell and the priest fumbled at the bolt. I could see him through the spy-hole. He was a little, black, greasy man.

"No, not this one," said the warder.

They went on to the next cell. He, too, was prepared. He asked no questions. While the priest prayed, he began in a low voice to sing the "Marseillaise." But after a few bars his voice broke, and he too sobbed.

They marched him off. . . .

On the night of Tuesday seventeen were shot.

On Thursday night eight.

On Friday night nine.

On Saturday night thirteen.

I tore strips off my shirt and stuffed my ears with them so as not to hear anything during the night. It was no good. I cut my gums with a splinter of glass, and said they were bleeding, so as to obtain some iodized cotton wool. I stuffed the cotton wool in my ears; it was no good, either.

Our hearing became preternaturally sharp. We heard everything. On the nights of the executions we heard the telephone ring at ten o'clock. We heard the warder on duty answer it. We heard him repeating at short intervals: "ditto . . . ditto . . . ditto. . . ." We knew it was someone at military headquarters reading out the list of those to be shot during the night. We knew that the warder wrote down a name before every "ditto." But we did not know what names they were and we did not know whether ours was among them.

The telephone always rang at ten. Then until midnight or one o'clock there was time to lie on one's bed and wait. Each night we weighed our lives in the balance and each night found them wanting.

Then at twelve or one we heard the shrill sound of the night bell. It was the priest and the firing squad. They always arrived together.

Then began the opening of doors, the ringing of the sanctus bell, the praying of the priest, the cries for help and the shouts of "Mother."

The steps came nearer down the corridor, receded, came nearer, receded. Now they were at the next cell; now they were in the other wing; now they were coming back. Clearest of all was always the priest's voice: "Lord, have mercy on this man, Lord, forgive him his sins, Amen." We lay on our beds and our teeth chattered.

On Tuesday night seventeen were shot.

On Thursday night eight were shot.

On Friday night nine were shot.

On Saturday night thirteen were shot.

Six days shalt thou labour, saith the Lord, and on the seventh day, the Sabbath, thou shalt do no manner of work.

On Sunday night three were shot.

THE WEIMAR REPUBLIC AND THE NAZI STATE

14. ERICH MARIA REMARQUE: THE ROAD BACK*

Born in Osnabrück, Germany, Erich Maria Remarque (1897–   ) completed his education at the University of Münster before being drafted into the army during World War I. He experienced at first hand on the western front the bloody human sacrifices and the mangling effects of artillery barrages in trench warfare. During the postwar decade he tried several occupations before devoting his full energies to writing. His first book, *All Quiet on the Western Front,* was published in 1929. In his novel Remarque sought to present a simple but eloquent story to capture the horror of war for people of all countries. It brought him world fame. A sequel, *The Road Back* (1931), carried on the story as it applied to German veterans trying to readjust to civilian life in the troubled early years of the Weimar Republic. The returning soldier was no longer the fresh optimist who had marched to war singing, and the land to which he returned was something markedly different from the one he had left. The selection which follows describes the first encounter between Remarque's returning rabble and revolutionary activists at home. Months later, while participating in a giant demonstration, the same veterans found themselves at odds with regular troops commanded by their former comrade and sergeant. What was the attitude of the government toward returning veterans who attempted to gain assistance for the wounded and jobs for themselves? What did the conduct of Lieutenant Heel toward his former comrades-in-arms reveal about events in Germany after 1918?

Demonstrations in the streets have been called for this afternoon. Prices have been soaring everywhere for months past, and the poverty is greater even than it was during the war. Wages are insufficient to buy the bare necessities of life, and even though one may have the money it is often impossible to buy anything with it. But ever more and more gin palaces and dance halls go up, and ever more and more blatant is the profiteering and swindling.

Scattered groups of workers on strike march through the streets. Now and again there is a disturbance. A rumour is going about that troops have been concentrated at the barracks. But there is no sign of it as yet.

Here and there one hears cries and counter-cries. Somebody is haranguing at a street corner. Then suddenly everywhere is silence.

A procession of men in the faded uniforms of the front-line trenches is moving slowly toward us.

It is formed up by sections, marching in fours. Big white placards are carried before: *Where is the Fatherland's gratitude?—The War Cripples are starving.*

---

* Erich Maria Remarque, *The Road Back,* trans. A. W. Wheen (Boston: Little, Brown and Co., 1931), pp. 266–69, 271–76. Reprinted by permission of the author.

The men with one arm are carrying the placards, and they look around continually to see if the procession is still coming along properly behind them, for they are the fastest. . . .

It is strange how a face without eyes alters—how in the upper half it becomes extinct, smooth and dead; and how odd the mouth is in comparison, when it speaks! Only the lower half of the face lives. All these have been shot blind; and so they behave differently from men born blind. They are more violent, and at the same time more cautious, in their gestures that have not yet gained the sureness of many years of darkness. The memory of colours, of sky, earth and twilight still lives with them. They move still as if they had eyes; involuntarily they lift and turn their heads to see who it is that speaks to them. Some have black patches or bandages over their eyes, but most go without them, as if by that means they would stand nearer to colours and the light. Their eyelids are withered and closed: only the narrow strip of the lower lid still protrudes a little, blotched, wet and red like a dim, cheerless dawn. Many of them are healthy, powerful fellows with strong limbs that would like well to move freely and have play. The pale sunset of the March sky gleams behind their bowed heads. In shop windows the first lamps are being lighted. But they hardly feel the mild, sweet air of evening on their brow. In their heavy boots they move slowly through the everlasting darkness that stretches about them like a cloud; and troubled and persistent, their thoughts clamber up and down the meagre scale of figures that would mean bread and comfort and life to them, and yet cannot be. Hunger and penury stir idly in the darkened rooms of their mind. Helpless and full of dull fear, they sense their nearness; yet they cannot see them nor do aught against them but to walk slowly in their numbers through the streets, lifting up their dead faces from the darkness toward the light, in dumb appeal to others, who can still see.

Behind the blind come the men with one eye, the tattered faces of men with head wounds: wry, bulbous mouths, faces without noses and without lower jaws, entire faces one great red scar with a couple of holes where formerly were a mouth and a nose. But above this desolation, quiet, questioning, sad human eyes.

On these follow the long line of men with legs amputated. Some already have artificial limbs that spring forward obliquely as they walk and strike clanking on the pavement, as if the whole man were artificial, made up of iron and hinges. Others have their trouser legs looped up and made fast with safety pins. These go on crutches or sticks with black rubber pads.

Then come the shakers, the shell-shocked. Their hands, their heads, their clothes, their bodies quake as though they still shuddered with horror. They no longer have control of themselves; the will has been extinguished, the muscles and nerves have revolted against the brain, the eyes become void and impotent. . . .

The later it gets, the more disturbed the city becomes. I go with Albert through the streets. Men are standing in groups at every corner. Rumours are flying. It is said that the military have already fired on a procession of demonstrating workers.

From the neighbourhood of St. Mary's Church comes suddenly the sound of rifle shots, at first singly, then a whole volley. Albert and I look at each other; without a word we set off in the direction of the shots.

Ever more and more people come running toward us. "Bring rifles! The bastards are shooting!" they shout. We quicken our pace. We wind in and out of the groups, we shove our way through, we are running already—a grim, perilous excitement impels us forward. We are gasping. The racket of rifle fire increases. . . .

The crowd, still shouting, gives way before us. We plough our way through. Women hold their aprons over their faces and go stumbling away. A roar of fury goes up. A wounded man is being carried off.

We reach the Market Square. There the Reichswehr has taken up a position in front of the Town Hall. The steel helmets gleam palely. On the steps is a machine gun ready for action. The square is empty; only the streets that lead into it are jammed with people. It would be madness to go farther—the machine gun is covering the square. . . .

"Comrades, put up your weapons! Would you shoot at your brothers? Put up your weapons and come over to us."

Never was the moon so bright. The uniforms on the Town Hall steps are like chalk. The windows glisten. The moonlit half of the church tower is a mirror of green silk. With gleaming helmets and visors the stone knights by the doorway spring forward from the wall of shadow.

"Back! Or we fire!" comes the command coldly.

I look round at Ludwig and Albert. It was our company commander! That was Heel's voice. A choking tension grips me, as if I must now look on at an execution. Heel will fire—I know.

The dark mass of people moves within the shadow of the houses; it sways and murmurs. An eternity goes by. Two soldiers with rifles detach themselves from the steps and make toward the solitary man in the midst of the square. It seems endlessly long before they reach him, as though they marked time in some grey morass, glittering, tinselled rag puppets with loaded, lowered rifles. The man awaits them quietly. "Comrades—" he says again as they come up.

They grab him by the arms and drag him forward. The man does not defend himself. They run him along so fast that he stumbles. Cries break out behind us. The mob is beginning to move, an entire street moving slowly, irregularly forward.

The clear voice commands, "Quick! Back with him! I fire!"

A warning volley crackles out upon the air. Suddenly the man wrenches himself free. But no, he is not saving himself! He is running toward the machine gun!

"Don't shoot, Comrades!"

Still nothing has happened. But when the mob sees the unarmed man run forward, it advances too. In a thin stream it trickles along the side of the church. The next instant a command resounds over the square. Thundering, the tick-tack of the machine gun shatters into a thousand echoes from the houses, and the bullets, whistling and splintering, strike on the pavement. . . .

"No!" I cry, "No!" The cry goes up shrill between the walls of the houses.

I feel myself pushed aside. Ludwig Breyer stands up and goes out over the square toward the dark lump of death.

"Ludwig!" I shout.

But he still goes on—on——

I stare after him in horror.

"Back!" comes the command once again from the Town Hall steps.

For a moment Ludwig stands still. "Fire away, Lieutenant Heel!" he calls back to the Town Hall. Then he goes forward and stoops down to the thing lying there on the ground.

We see an officer come down the steps. Without knowing quite how, we are suddenly all standing there beside Ludwig, awaiting the coming figure that for a weapon carries only a walking stick. He does not hesitate an instant, though there are now three of us and we could drag him off if we wanted to— his soldiers would not dare to shoot for fear of hitting him.

Ludwig straightens up. "I congratulate you, Lieutenant Heel. The man is dead."

A stream of blood is running from under the dead man's tunic and trickling into the cracks between the cobblestones. Near his right hand that has thrust forward, thin and yellow, out of the sleeve, it is gathering to a pool of blood that reflects black in the moonlight.

"Breyer," says Heel.

"Do you know who it is?" asks Ludwig.

Heel looks at him and shakes his head.

"Max Weil."

"I wanted to let him get away," says Heel after a time, almost pensively.

"He is dead," answers Ludwig.

Heel shrugs his shoulders.

"He was our comrade," Ludwig goes on.

Heel does not answer.

Ludwig looks at him coldly. "A nice piece of work!"

Then Heel stirs. "That does not enter into it," he says calmly. "Only the pur-pose—law and order."

"Purpose—" replies Ludwig contemptuously. "Since when do you offer excuse for yourself? Purpose!—Occupation—That is all that you ask. Withdraw your men, so that there shall be no more shooting!"

Heel makes a gesture of impatience. "My men stay where they are! If they withdrew, they would be attacked to-morrow by a mob ten times as big. You know that yourself. In five minutes I occupy all the road heads. I give you till then to take off this dead man."

"Set to it," says Ludwig to us. Then he turns to Heel once again. "If you withdraw now, no one will attack you. If you stay, more will be killed. And through you! Do you realize that?"

"I realize it," answers Heel coldly.

For a second longer we stand face to face. Heel looks at the row of us. It is a strange moment. Then something snaps.

We take up the limp body of Max Weil and bear him away. The streets are again filled with people. A wide passage opens before us as we come. Cries go up. "Noske bloodhounds!" "Police thugs!" "Murderers!" From Max Weil's back the blood drips. . . .

15. THE GERMAN INFLATION OF 1923*

The German economy was seriously affected by a general disruption of European trade patterns after World War I and impaired by the obligations of the Versailles Treaty as well. The unit of currency, the mark, dropped precipitously in value from its prewar level. When French and Belgian troops occupied the industrial Ruhr early in 1923, the economy of the Weimar Republic suffered another blow.

Chancellor Wilhelm Cuno chose to oppose the French with passive resistance. The decision put further pressure on the German economy and the mark when Berlin undertook to support and supply striking workers in the Ruhr. German Communists attempted to exploit the crisis by means of a general strike and, in some cases, revolt. The German right wing, including National Socialists led by Adolf Hitler, also appeared ready to move against the shaky Republic. Inflation sapped the government's strength, and Chancellor Cuno suddenly resigned. He was replaced by Gustav Stresemann, who capitulated to the French and used emergency powers to rescue the Republic. Although Stresemann ended passive resistance, the mark tumbled to further depths while he was occupied in ousting Communists from governments in Saxony and Thuringia and struggling to defeat reactionary opposition in Bavaria to the central government. In Munich, the Bavarian capital, Hitler unsuccessfully attempted a *putsch* during November of 1923.

By the end of 1923 the Republic seemed to have been saved—but just barely. The inflation of the mark had wiped out the savings of broad segments of the middle class, leading to further disenchantment with the unfortunate Weimar Republic. The following selections are drawn from the pages of *Die Rote Fahne* (*The Red Flag*), official newspaper of the German Communist party. What was the attitude of the German Communists toward the Republic? What comparisons may be drawn between the various events described in this selection and the statements of John Maynard Keynes?

THE RED FLAG

founded by Karl Liebknecht
and Rosa Luxemburg

Central Organ of the Communist Party of Germany (section of the Communist International)

Tuesday, 14 August 1923

Price of this issue 20,000 marks

MILLIONS IN THE STRUGGLE

The lessons of 1918 to 1923 have been learned. This time in spite of the resignation of Chancellor Cuno, the workers will not be calmed by a mere change in the name plate on the door [of the chancellor's office]. The workers of Berlin have left their jobs. The sabotage attempts of the Social Democrats and of the

* *Die Rote Fahne*, August 14, 1923, p. 1; August 21, 1923, p. 1; September 13, 1923, p. 1; September 16, 1923, p. 1; September 18, 1923, pp. 1, 18. Translated by the editors.

reformist union leaders have not worked. The masses want the absolute fulfillment of their demands. Not Cuno, but the capitalist system which he represents, must be removed.

All over the Reich the workers are on the move. Millions have joined the struggle. In Central Germany, in Lausitz, in the greater part of Thuringia, there is a general strike. In Hamburg, Luebeck, Hanover there is general strike. In Bremen, Kiel, Stettin the greater part of the workers have left their plants....

The bourgeoisie is trying to suppress the workers by means of bloody terror. In Hanover, Hamburg, Zeitz, Luebeck, and other places, dozens of workers have been killed and hundreds severely wounded in the last few days. The result of this terror is a rapid growth of the struggle and a measureless embitterment of the workers.

News from the occupied territories reports that the hunger of the workers in the Rhineland and the Ruhr becomes ever more unbearable. . . . In spite of the menace of German and French military power the workers press forward with the general strike. . . .

Tuesday, 21 August 1923   *Price of this issue 50,000 marks*

NEW FASCIST CONCENTRATION

It is reported from parliamentary circles:

The fascist organizations, National Socialists, German Racists, and their armed suborganizations are preparing a new concentrated effort. It is believed that a putsch-atmosphere . . . will be created by September 2, as a consequence of the general indignation over the occupation of the Ruhr and the increasing violence of the French militarists.

Thursday, 13 September 1923   *Price of this issue 300,000 marks*

ONE DOLLAR A WEEK SALARY AT DOLLAR PRICES

The Dollar 125 million   Stocks rise 28 billion   one pound of butter
                                                        50 million

The end of the Mark is here.

One fall of the mark passes the preceding one.

Ten days ago a dollar was barely ten million marks; yesterday [the mark] fell to 125 million marks to the dollar and, owing to strong official intervention, was finally fixed at 96 million marks to the dollar.

In one day wages have fallen 59 per cent....

The price of foodstuffs rose yesterday on the average between 50 and 60 per cent. They will climb higher today and tomorrow. One pound of butter, which for workers is an unattainable luxury, cost yesterday no less than 50 million marks.

The salary of a worker, on his pay day today or tomorrow, will be perhaps not quite enough to buy one pound of butter. Salaries will probably be seventy-five cents to one dollar per week against an average 12 dollars per week which a worker in the United States receives. Therefore the prices in dollars are higher here than in America.

According to our estimate, a worker's family of four would have had to spend 527 million marks in the period from last Thursday to yesterday in order to buy only the most necessary needs. . . .

Sunday, 16 September 1923   *Price of this issue 800,000 marks*

A NEW WAVE OF PRICE RISES!

The Dollar 130 million marks   *Railroad rates*   *New Price*
                                    quadruple   *rise in coal. . . .*

The dollar yesterday. rose to the new rate of 130 million marks. That means a new rise in all prices. Prices also rise when the dollar does not. Last week wholesale prices . . . rose far higher than the course of the dollar. New shocking prices for important services and articles stand ahead of us. . . .

Tuesday, 18 September 1923   *Price of this issue 700,000 marks*

BLOOD BATH IN SORAU

Hungry workers murdered in Sorau   *The Dollar Climbs to 230*
                                        million marks. . . .

The Dollar at 230 million Marks

Yesterday a new horrible collapse of the mark set in. The dollar, which as of the last market quotation was officially noted at 90 million marks and on Sunday stood at 100 million marks, passed beyond the 200 million mark. Yesterday one dollar was worth approximately:

9:30 A.M.	115 million marks
10:00 A.M.	135 million marks
11:00 A.M.	140 million marks
1:00 P.M.	130 million marks
	(owing to efforts by the Reichsbank)
2:00 P.M.	145 million marks
7:00 P.M.	220–230 million marks

The Economy: Rise of the Costs of Living

In the week from the 13th to the 19th of September it was necessary for a married couple with two children of school age to pay the following amounts if they wished to live as well as they did before the war:

For Nourishment	704,559,000 marks
Clothing, Apartment, Commuting	
Expenses, gas and so on	592,250,000 marks
To pay 8% tax	103,745,440 marks
All together a grand total of;	1,400,563,440 marks for one week.

This represents a climb of over 870 million marks or approximately 165.8% above the preceding week.

16. ADOLF HITLER: MEIN KAMPF*

Adolf Hitler (1889-1945) took over the leadership of the tiny National Socialist party shortly after World War I and quickly transformed it into a militant and growing threat to the Weimar Republic. He wrote *Mein Kampf* (*My Struggle*) during 1924 in Landsberg Prison, where he was confined briefly after the failure of his attempted *putsch* against the Bavarian government in November 1923. Hitler's book did not sell very well, partly because of its poor literary style, but circulated widely after the fortunes of his party improved. His hatred of the Jews and of democracy, his ruthlessness, and his dreams of conquest were all spelled out in *Mein Kampf*. What was Hitler's concept of race? What, according to Hitler, was the function of propaganda in his movement? What was his concept of the relationship between the individual and the folk, and the individual and the state? What was the function of the party? What was the relation of the individual to the party? What were Hitler's goals for German foreign policy? Explain the connection between Hitler's racial views and his idea of *Lebensraum* (living space).

Our present current political conception of life is generally based upon the conception that one can ascribe to the State in itself a creative culture-forming force, but that it has nothing to do with racial presumptions, and that it is rather a product of economic necessities, but at best the natural result of the political urge for power. This fundamental view, in its further logical and consequent development, leads not only to a mistaken recognition of racial original forces, but also to an undervaluation of the individual. For the negation of the difference of the several races as regards their general culture-creating forces, must necessarily also transfer this greatest error to the judgment of the individual person. The belief in the equality of the races will then become the basis of an equal manner of observation of the peoples and further for the individual man. Therefore Marxism itself is nothing but the transmission, carried out by the Jew Karl Marx, of a long existing attitude and conception, conditioned by a view of life, to the form of a definite political creed: international Marxism. Without the basis of such a general, previously existing poisoning, the astounding political success of this doctrine would never have been possible. Karl Marx was really the only *one* among millions who, in the swamp of a gradually decomposing world, recognized, with the keen eye of the prophet, the most essential poison elements, took them out, in order to render them, like a magician of the black arts, into a concentrated solution for the quicker destruction of the independent existence of the free nations of this earth. But all this in the service of his race.

The Marxist doctrine is the brief spiritual extract of the view of life that is generally valid today. Merely for this reason every fight by our so-called *bourgeois* world against it is impossible, even ridiculous, as this *bourgeois* world also is essentially interspersed with all these poison elements, and worships a view of life which in general is distinguished from the Marxian view only by

* Adolf Hitler, *Mein Kampf* (New York: Reynal and Hitchcock, 1939), pp. 577-81, 588-89, 669-71, 849-50, 852-53, 888-91. 947-50, 447-51. Reprinted by permission of Houghton Mifflin Co.

degrees of persons. The *bourgeois* world is Marxist, but it believes in the possibility of a domination of certain human groups (*bourgeoisie*), while Marxism itself plans to transmit the world systematically into the hands of Jewry.

In opposition to this, the "folkish" view recognizes the importance of mankind in its racially innate elements. In principle, it sees in the State only a means to an end, and as its end it considers the preservation of the racial existence of men. Thus it by no means believes in an equality of the races, but with their differences it also recognizes their superior and inferior values, and by this recognition it feels the obligation in accordance with the Eternal Will that dominates this universe to promote the victory of the better and stronger, and to demand the submission of the worse and the weaker. Thus in principle it favors also the fundamental aristocratic thought of nature and believes in the validity of this law down to the last individual. It sees not only the different values of the races, but also the different values of individual man. In its opinion, out of the masses emerges the importance of the person, but by this it has an organizing effect, as contrasted with disorganizing Marxism. It believes in the necessity of idealizing mankind, as, in turn, it sees in this the only presumption for the existence of mankind. But it cannot grant the right of existence to an ethical idea, if this idea represents a danger for the racial life of the bearers of higher ethics; for in a hybridized and negrified world all conceptions of the humanly beautiful and sublime, as well as all conceptions of an idealized future of our mankind, would be lost forever.

In this world human culture and civilization are inseparably bound up with the existence of the Aryan. His dying-off or his decline would again lower upon this earth the dark veils of a time without culture.

The undermining of the existence of human culture by destroying its supporters appears, in a folkish view of life, as the most execrable crime. He who dares to lay hand upon the highest image of the Lord sins against the benevolent Creator of this miracle and helps in the expulsion from Paradise.

With this the folkish view of life corresponds to the innermost will of nature, as nature restores that free play of the forces which is bound to lead to a permanent mutual higher breeding, until finally the best of mankind, having acquired the possession of this earth, is given a free road for activity in domains which will lie partly above, partly outside it.

We all sense that in the distant future problems could approach man for the conquest of which only a highest race, as the master nation, based upon the means and the possibilities of an entire globe, will be called upon. . . .

During the past hundred years it was truly a misfortune to be compelled to observe how in these circles, sometimes in the best of faith, one played with the word *"Germanizing."* I myself remember how during my youth this very word led to quite unbelievably wrong conceptions. Even in Pan-German circles one could at that time hear the opinion that Austrian Germanity, with promoting help on the part of the government, could very well succeed in a Germanization of the Austrian Slavs, whereby, however, one did not in the least see clearly the fact that a *Germanization* can only be carried out with the *soil* and never with *men*. For what one generally understood by this word was only the enforced outward acceptance of the German language. But it is a hardly conceivable mistake in thinking to believe that, let us say, a negro or a Chinese would become a German because he learns German and is prepared to speak the German language in the future and perhaps to give his vote to a German political party. It never became clear to our *bourgeois* national world that any Germanization of this kind is in reality a de-Germanization. For if to-day by the enforcement of a general language the differences between various peoples that hitherto caught the eye are bridged and finally wiped out, it would mean the beginning of a hybridization and with this, in our case, not a Germanization but a destruction of the Germanic element. In history it happens only too frequently that the outward means of power of a conquering people succeeds in forcing their language upon the oppressed, but that after a thousand years their language is spoken by a different people and the conquerors thus become actually the vanquished.

As the nationality, or rather the race, is not rooted in the language but in the blood, one could be permitted to speak of a Germanization only if one could succeed in changing, by such a procedure, the blood of the subjugated. But this is impossible. Except, perhaps, if by a blood blending a change were to take place which then, however, would mean the lowering of the standard of the higher race. Therefore the final result of such a procedure would be the destruction of just those qualities which once made the conquering people capable of victory. By a coupling with a lower race, the cultural energies especially would disappear, though the resulting mixture would speak a thousand times the language of the formerly higher race. For some time there will take place a certain wrestling between the various mentalities and it may be that then the more and more sinking people, in a last effort, so to speak, will bring to light astounding cultural values. But they are only the single elements pertaining to the higher race or bastards, in whom after the first crossing the better blood has the upper hand and which now tries to struggle through; but never the final products of cross-breeding. In them a culturally backward movement will always show itself....

The folkish State has to care for the welfare of its citizens by acknowledging the significance of the value of the person in all and everything and thus introducing in all domains that highest degree of productive efficiency which grants the individual also the highest degree of participation.

The folkish State, therefore, has to free the entire leadership—especially the highest, that means the political leadership—from the parliamentary principle of decision by majority, that means decision by the masses, in order to establish firmly in its place the right of the person.

From this results the following conclusion:

The best State constitution and State form is that which, with the most natural certainty, brings the best heads of the national community to leading importance and to leading influence.

But just as in economic life the able personalities cannot be determined from above, but have to wrestle through for themselves, and exactly as here from the smallest shop up to the greatest enterprise, infinite training is given by itself and only life makes the necessary examinations, thus of course the political heads too cannot suddenly be "discovered." Geniuses of an extraordinary kind do not admit consideration of the normal mankind.

The State in its organization, beginning with the smallest cell of the community up to the highest leadership of the entire Reich, must be built upon the principle of personality.

There must be no decisions by majority, but only responsible persons, and the word "council" is once more reduced to its original meaning. At every man's side there stand councillors, indeed, but *one man decides.*

The principle which once made the Prussian army the most marvelous instrument of the German people has to be some day in a transformed meaning the principle of the construction of our whole State constitution: *authority of every leader towards below and responsibility towards above.*

Even then one will not be able to do without those corporations which today we call parliaments. Their councillors will then actually give counsel, but responsibility can and must be borne always only by *one* man and thus he alone can and must have the authority and right of command.

Parliaments in themselves are necessary, because it is above all in them that the heads to whom one can later allot special responsible tasks have the chance to raise themselves gradually.

This gives the following picture:

The folkish State, from the community up to the leadership of the Reich, has no representative body which decides by majority, but only *bodies of councils* who stand at the side of the respective elected leader, receiving their share of work from him, so that, as the circumstances require, they in turn have to assume absolute responsibility in certain domains, exactly as on a large scale has the leader himself or the head of the respective corporation.

The folkish State, in principle, does not tolerate that in concerns of a special kind, for instance of economic nature, people are asked for advice or judgment who, by virtue of their education and activity, are unable to understand anything of the matter. Therefore it divides its representative body from the beginning into *political and professional chambers.*

In order to guarantee a profitable co-operation between them a special selected *senate* is provided above them.

No voting ever takes place in any chamber or senate. They are working institutions and not voting machines. The individual member has an advisory vote but never a deciding one. The latter is the exclusive privilege of the respective responsible chairman.

This principle of unconditional connection of absolute responsibility with absolute authority will gradually breed up a choice of leaders as is inconceivable today, in the era of irresponsible parliamentarianism.

Thus the State constitution of the nation will be brought into harmony with that law to which the nation already owes its greatness in the domains of culture and economics. . . .

If a movement has the intention of pulling down a world and of building a new one in its place, then there must be absolute clarity about the following points in the ranks of its own leaders: *Every movement, at first, will have to divide the human material it has won into two great groups: into followers and members.*

The task of propaganda is to attract followers; the task of organization to win members....

Therefore propaganda will have to see to it that untiringly an idea wins followers, while the organization has to watch most sharply that from the followers only the most valuable ones are made members. Propaganda, therefore, needs not to rack its brain about the importance of each individual it enlightens, about his ability, achievements, and understanding or of his character, while the organization has most carefully to collect from the masses of these elements those who really make possible the victory of the movement.

Propaganda tries to force a doctrine upon an entire people; organization embraces in its frame only those who for psychological reasons do not threaten to become a brake to a further spreading of the idea....

In every really great revolutionary movement propaganda will first have to spread the idea of this movement. That means, it will untiringly try to make clear to the others the new train of thought, to draw them over to its own ground, or at least to make them doubtful of their own previous conviction. Since the propagation of a doctrine—that means this propaganda—has to have a backbone, the doctrine will have to give itself a solid organization. The organization receives its members from the followers in general won by propaganda. The latter will grow the more quickly, the more intensively propaganda is carried out, and the latter in turn is able to work the better, the stronger and the more vigorous the organization is that stands behind it.

The highest task of organization, therefore, is to see to it that no kind of internal disagreements among the members of the movement lead to a cleavage and with it to a weakening of the work in the movement; further, that the spirit of determined aggression does not die out, but that it continuously renews and fortifies itself. The number of members need not grow infinitely, on the contrary; since only a fraction of mankind is energetic and bold, a movement which enlarges its organization *ad infinitum* would necessarily some day be weakened by this procedure. *Organizations—that means numbers of members which grow beyond a certain limit—gradually lose their fighting force and are no longer able to support, or rather to benefit from, the propaganda of an idea by determination and attack.*

The greater and the more revolutionary, essentially, an idea is, the more active will its members become, since for its supporters the revolutionary force of the doctrine involves a danger; which appears suitable for keeping off small and cowardly petty bourgeois. They will quietly consider themselves followers, but they will decline to manifest this publicly by membership. *Through this, however, the organization of a truly revolutionary idea receives as members only the most active followers, won by propaganda.* In this very activity of the membership of a movement—guaranteed by natural selection—lies the presumption for an equally active further propagation of the movement, as well as for the successful fight for the realization of the idea. . . .

If, before the War, the task of German foreign policy was to guarantee the sustenance of our nation and its children on this globe through the preparation of ways which could lead to this goal, as well as the winning of the auxiliary forces necessary thereto in the form of suitable allies, then today it is the same, with only one difference: *Before the War it was necessary to serve the preservation of the German nationality, having in mind a certain available force of the independent, free power State; today it is imperative first to restore to the people, in the form of the free power State, that strength which is the presumption for the later carrying-out of a practical foreign policy signifying the maintenance, promotion, and sustenance of our people for the future.*

In other words: *The goal of a German foreign policy of today must be the preparation of the reconquest of freedom for tomorrow.*

Moreover, one thing above all must be kept in mind as a directive: *A nation's chance of reconquering its independence is not absolutely bound up with the integrity of a State territory, but rather with the existence of a never so small remnant of this nation and State which, having the necessary freedom, has it in its power to be not only the bearer of the spiritual communion of the entire nationality, but also the preparer of the military struggle for freedom.*

If a people of one hundred million men, to protect the State's integrity, jointly tolerates the yoke of slavery, then that is worse than if such a State and such a people had been demolished and only a part of it could remain in possession of full freedom, of course on condition that this last remnant were filled with the sacred mission not only constantly to proclaim spiritual and cultural inseparability, but also to achieve the armed preparation for final liberation and the reuniting of the unhappy oppressed portions with the motherland.

It should be further noted that the question of the regaining of lost portions of territory of a people and State is always in the first instance the question of regaining the political power and independence of the motherland; that consequently in such a case the interests of the lost regions as compared with the sole interest of the regaining of the freedom of the main territory must be unhesitatingly set aside. For the liberation of oppressed, since separated splinters of a nationality or province of a realm takes place, not on the basis of a desire of the oppressed or a protest of those remaining behind, but through the instruments of power of those remnants of the former common fatherland which have remained more or less sovereign.

Consequently, the premise for the winning of lost territories is the intensive advancement and strengthening of the remaining remnant State as well as the unshakable decision, slumbering in the heart, to consecrate at the given moment to the service of the liberation and unification of the whole nation that new force, forming itself through this process: that is, *setting aside* the interests of the separated regions as opposed to the sole interest of winning for the remaining remnant that measure of political power and strength which is the premise for a rectification of the will of a hostile victor. *For oppressed countries will*

*not be brought back into the bosom of a common Reich by means of fiery pro-
tests, but by a mighty sword.*

*To forge this sword is the task of the domestic political leadership of a people;
to guard the work of forging and to seek comrades in arms is the task of the
foreign-policy leadership....*

If, however, one professes the conviction that the German future, one way or
another, calls forth the supreme risk, one must, entirely aside from all considerations of political intelligence in itself, for the very sake of this risk, pose
and fight for a goal worthy of it.

The frontiers of the year 1914 signify nothing at all for the future of the German nation. They embodied neither a protection in the past, nor would they
embody strength for the future. The German nation will neither maintain its
internal integrity through them, nor will its sustenance be guaranteed by them,
nor do these frontiers appear appropriate or even satisfactory from a military
viewpoint, ...

As opposed to this, we National Socialists must cling unflinchingly to our
foreign-policy aims, that is to guarantee the *German nation the soil and territory
to which it is entitled on this earth.* And this is the only action which, before
God and our German posterity, would seem to justify an investment of blood:
before God, since we are placed in this world on condition of an eternal struggle
for daily bread, as beings to whom nothing shall be given and who owe their
position as lords of the earth only to the genius and courage with which they
know how to struggle for and defend it: before our German posterity, however,
in so far as we spill no citizen's blood except that out of it a thousand others
are bequeathed to posterity. The soil and territory on which a race of German
peasants will some day be able to beget sons sanction the investment of the sons
of today, and will some day acquit the responsible statesmen of blood and guilt
and national sacrifice, even though they be persecuted by their contemporaries....

State frontiers are man-made and can be altered by man.

The reality of a nation having managed a disproportionate acquisition of territory is no superior obligation for its eternal recognition. It proves at most the
might of the conqueror and the weakness of the victim. And, moreover, this
might alone makes right. If the German people today, penned into an impossible area, face a wretched future, this is as little Fate's command as its rejection
would constitute a snub to Fate. Just as little as some superior power has promised another nation more soil and territory than the German, or would be
insulted by the fact of this unjust division of territory. Just as our forefathers did
not get the land on which we are living today as a gift from Heaven, but had to
conquer it by risking their lives, so no folkish grace but only the might of a triumphant sword will in the future assign us territory, and with it life for our
nation. ...

We National Socialists, however, must go further: *the right to soil and territory can become a duty if decline seems to be in store for a great nation unless it
extends its territory.* Even more especially if what is involved is not some little
negro people or other, but the German mother of all life, which has given its

cultural picture to the contemporary world. *Germany will be either a world power or will not be at all.* To be a world power, however, it requires that size which nowadays gives its necessary importance to such a power, and which gives life to its citizens. . . .

The ignorance of the great masses about the inner nature of the Jew, the lack of instinct and narrow-mindedness of our upper classes, make the people easily fall victim to the Jewish campaign of lies.

While the upper classes, out of their inborn cowardice, turn from a man who is attacked by the Jew in such manner with lie and calumny, the great masses, out of stupidity or simplicity, usually believe everything. But the State authorities either wrap themselves in silence, or, as is mostly the case, they persecute him who is unjustly attacked, in order to make an end to the nuisance of the Jewish press, something which then, in the eyes of such an official idiot, appears as the preservation of State authority and as safeguarding peace and order.

Slowly the fear of the Marxist weapon of Jewry sinks into the brains and souls of decent people like a nightmare.

One begins to tremble before the terrible enemy, and thus one has become his final victim.

The Jew's rule in the State now appears secured to such an extent that he may not only again call himself Jew, but ruthlessly admits his final thoughts as regards nationality and politics. A part of his race even admits quite openly that it is a foreign people, however, not without again lying in this respect. For while Zionism tries to make the other part of the world believe that the national self-consciousness of the Jew finds satisfaction in the creation of a Palestinian State, the Jews again most slyly dupe the stupid *goiim*. [Jewish colloquial expression: Gentile men or women.] They have no thought of building up a Jewish State in Palestine, so that they might perhaps inhabit it, but they only want a central organization of their international world cheating, endowed with prerogatives, withdrawn from the seizure of others: a refuge for convicted rascals and a high school for future rogues.

But it is the sign, not only of their rising confidence, but also their feeling of safety, that now, at a time when one part of them still mendaciously plays the German, the Frenchman, or the Englishman, the other part impudently and openly documents itself as the Jewish race.

How far they keep the approaching victory before their eyes is seen from the terrible manner which their intercourse with the members of other peoples assumes.

For hours the black-haired Jew boy, diabolic joy in his face, waits in ambush for the unsuspecting girl whom he defiles with his blood and thus robs her from her people. With the aid of all means he tries to ruin the racial foundations of the people to be enslaved. Exactly as he himself systematically demoralizes women and girls, he is not scared from pulling down the barriers of blood and race for others on a large scale. It was and is the Jews who bring the negro to the Rhine, always with the same concealed thought and the clear goal of destroying, by the bastardization which would necessarily set in, the white race which they hate, to throw it down from its cultural and political height and in turn to rise personally to the position of master.

For a racially pure people, conscious of its blood, can never be enslaved by the Jew. It will forever only be the master of bastards in this world.

Thus he systematically tries to lower the racial level by a permanent poisoning of the individual.

In the political sphere, however, he begins to replace the idea of democracy by that of the dictatorship of the proletariat.

In the organized mass of Marxism he has found the weapon which makes him now dispense with democracy and which allows him, instead, to enslave and to "rule" the people dictatorially with the brutal fist.

He now works methodically towards the revolution in a twofold direction: economically and politically.

Thanks to his international influence, he ensnares with a net of enemies those peoples which put up a too violent resistance against the enemy from within, he drives them into war, and finally, if necessary, he plants the flag of revolution on the battlefield.

In the field of economics he undermines the States until the social organizations which have become unprofitable are taken from the State and submitted to his financial control.

Politically he denies to the State all means of self-preservation, he destroys the bases of any national self-dependence and defense, he destroys the confidence in the leaders, he derides history and the past, and he pulls down into the gutter everything which is truly great.

In the domain of culture he infects art, literature, theater, smites natural feeling, overthrows all conceptions of beauty and sublimity, of nobility and quality, and in turn he pulls the people down into the confines of his own swinish nature.

Religion is ridiculed, customs and morality are presented as outlived, until the last supports of a nationality in the fight for human existence in this world have fallen.

(e) [sic] Now begins the great, final revolution. The Jew, by gaining the political power, casts off the few cloaks which he still wears. The democratic national Jew becomes the blood Jew and the people's tyrant. In the course of a few years he tries to eradicate the national supporters of intelligence, and, while he thus deprives the people of their natural spiritual leaders, he makes them ripe for the slave's destiny of permanent subjugation.

The most terrible example of this kind is offered by Russia where he killed or starved about thirty million people with a truly diabolic ferocity, under inhuman tortures, in order to secure to a crowd of Jewish scribblers and stock exchange robbers the rulership over a great people.

But the end is not only the end of the freedom of the peoples oppressed by the Jew, but also the end of these peoples' parasites themselves. With the death of the victim this peoples' vampire will also die sooner or later. . . .

17. A NAZI PARTY DIRECTIVE AGAINST THE JEWS*

Hitler moved quickly to consolidate his power after he was appointed Chancellor of the Reich in January 1933; and within a few months the Reichstag became a mere rubber stamp for Nazi decrees. By the middle 1930's the Reichstag, purged of all opposition, had authorized extensive race laws "for the protection of German blood and honor." Any marriages between Jews and "citizens having German or related blood lineage" were strictly forbidden. The following directive to officials of Hitler's NSDAP (National Socialist German Workers' Party), issued three short months after the Führer came to power, served as a model for all anti-Jewish legislation later imposed by the Nazis. What organizational procedures were required of party members in their campaign against the Jews? To what extent did the following party directive embody Hitler's racial views as stated in *Mein Kampf?*

In each local group and division of the NSDAP, Action Committees are to be formed immediately to accomplish a practical and orderly boycott of Jewish business goods, Jewish physicians and lawyers. It is the responsibility of these Action Committees to see that the boycott does not affect the innocent, but that the guilty are rigorously treated. . . .

The Action Committees have the responsibility to make the boycott popular through propaganda and through public enlightenment. Maxim: No German will buy goods from a Jew or his employees nor will he recommend their services to others. This boycott must be all-inclusive. . . .

The Action Committees have the responsibility of observing newspapers very closely to determine how actively they are participating in the campaign to enlighten people about the atrocious provocations perpetuated by the Jews abroad. If newspapers do not participate at all or only to a limited degree, the Committee must see to it that these papers are immediately removed from any house in which Germans live. No German person or business is permitted to place advertising in such newspapers. . . . Such newspapers may continue to be published for their Jewish compatriots, but not for the German people.

The Action Committees, in conjunction with the Party cells organized in industry, must transmit clarifying propaganda into the business world about the results of the atrocious provocations perpetuated by the Jews upon German industry and thereby upon the worker. This must be done in order to make clear the necessity of a national boycott as a means of protecting *German* labor.

Action Committees must be formed even in the smallest farming village in order to counteract the Jewish peddler in the low land areas. Basically it must be emphasized that we are concerned with a protective measure which has been forced upon us.

The boycott must not be instituted piece-meal, but completely and instantaneously. All preparations must be immediately arranged with this in mind. Orders have been issued to the S.A. [Sturmabteilung or Storm-Troopers] and

* *Völkischer Beobachter*, March 30, 1933, in *Dokumente der Deutschen Politik und Geschichte*, Band IV, *Die Zeit der nationalsozialistischen Diktaten, 1933–1938*, ed. Dr. Johannes Hohlfeld, rev. by Dr. Klaus Hohlfeld (Berlin: Dokumenten-Verlag, Dr. Herbert Wendler & Co., n.d.), pp. 45–47. Translated for this volume by E. Bernell McIntire.

the S.S. [the Nazi Elite Corps] that the public be warned against entering Jewish businesses after the start of the boycott which begins on the first of April at 10:00 A.M. The boycott must continue until an order cancelling it is issued from Party headquarters.

The Action Committees are to organize tens of thousands of mass meetings immediately, extending into the smallest villages. Through these meetings the introduction of a relative percentage limiting the participation of Jews in all professions to the actual proportion of Jews per thousand of population in Germany must be accomplished. . . .

Furthermore, the Action Committees have the task of assuring that every German who has any connections abroad utilizes these connections to transmit by letter, by telegram, and by telephone the truth that quiet and order prevail in Germany, that Germans are motivated solely by an intense desire to go about their work in peace and to live in peace with the rest of the world, and that the battle against the Jews is purely a defensive measure.

The Action Committees are responsible that this whole offensive be conducted in absolute quiet and under the most intensive discipline. Do not touch the hair of the head of a Jew! We will get rid of this rabble simply through the incisive force of these regulations! More than ever before it is necessary for the whole Party to stand united behind its leaders in absolute obedience.

National Socialists, you have accomplished a wonderful thing by destroying the government which was in power last November with a single attack. You will also be able to fulfill this second task in a like manner. International world Jewry must learn that the National Revolutionary Government of Germany does not exist in a vacuum; it is the representative of the industrious German people. Whoever attacks it attacks Germany. Whoever maligns it maligns the nation. Whoever attacks it has thrown down a challenge to 65 million people. We are finished with the Marxist rabble in Germany. They will never conquer us even though they continue their traitorous actions from abroad. National Socialists! Saturday at 10:00 a.m. sharp the Jews will know whom they have challenged!

18. MARTIN BORMANN: ON CHRISTIANITY AND NATIONAL SOCIALISM*

The National Socialist regime attempted to root out all sources of potential opposition including religious organizations. Protestant churches were expected to accept the direction of the new "German Christian Church" under Nazi control and headed by Reich Bishop Mueller. The Nazi party attempted to dominate the Catholic Church through Hitler's concordat with the Papacy in 1933. Nevertheless, party members found it increasingly difficult to tolerate Christianity in any form, and the following document explains Nazi attitudes toward Christian churches.

Martin Bormann (1900–45?), author of this letter to Alfred Rosenberg, one of the party "intellectuals," was a brutal party manipulator who had succeeded in becoming the second most powerful man in Germany by 1945. He enjoyed

* Office of the United States Chief of Counsel for Prosecution of Axis Criminality, *Nazi Conspiracy and Aggression* (Washington, 1946), III, 152–57.

Hitler's confidence and was a clear rival to Heinrich Himmler, head of the SS. Why, according to Bormann, were Nazism and Christianity incompatible? Compare Bormann's views with the ideas expressed in *Mein Kampf.*

NATIONAL SOCIALIST GERMAN LABOR PARTY

Munich, 33, Brown house
at present Berlin, 22 Feb [19]40

Deputy of the Fuehrer
Staff Leader

Mr. Reich leader Alfred Rosenberg
Berlin W 35
Margareten Str. 17

Subject: Directions for the administration of classes in religion

Dear Party Member Rosenberg:

The deputy of the Fuehrer has heard from different sources, that Reich Bishop Mueller tells everywhere, that he received a commission from you to work out directions for formulating the teaching of religion for the schools. . . .

The ministry for education of the Reich has repeatedly indicated its desire in the course of the past few years for new directions for formulating the teaching of religion, which would also be acceptable to the NSDAP.

With your agreement, this request has repeatedly been refused by the Fuehrer's deputy. Just as your ministry did, so the deputy of the Fuehrer took the position based on the assumption, that it could not be the task of the party to give directions for the instruction of the teachings of Christian religions.

Christianity and National Socialism are phenomona which originated from entirely different basic causes. Both differ fundamentally so strongly, that it will not be possible to construct a Christian teaching which would be completely compatible with the point of view of the national socialist ideology; just as the communities of Christian faith would never be able to stand by the ideology of national socialism in its entirety. The issuing of national socialist directions for the teaching of religious classes would however be based on a synthesis of national socialism and Christianity which I find impossible.

If the directions should really be permeated by the spirit of national socialism, some very fundamental articles of faith of the Christian teachings could not be recognized. I am referring here only to the position of the Christian churches to the race question, to the question of hindrance or destruction of life not valuable, its position to marriage, which speaks for the celibacy of priests and the toleration and furtherance of orders for monks and nuns, the teaching, contradictory to German feeling, of the immaculate conception of Mary, etc.

No matter how these directions may be formulated, in no case will they ever simultaneously find the approval of the church and the party.

In addition to this, the religions themselves cannot agree on the contents of the Christian teachings; as far as the Protestants themselves are concerned, there are not only the followers of the confessional church in the Reich and the German Christians, but also the adherents of a teaching, which is endeavoring to create a new Lutheran Christendom of a particular kind approximately in the shape which seems desirable to the Reich Minister of churches, party member Kerrl. The party thus would have to decide first which of these directions of faith it would give preference, or if it should even decide for a fourth. I do not think it entirely impossible that the Reich Bishop may take this latter road, since according to his last publication he himself has already turned sharply away from conceptions which up to now have been part of the faith of the German Christians.

But if directions for the instruction of religion should ever be worked out, it will not be enough, to my mind, to make them for Protestants only; respective directions should also be worked out for Catholics. To work out directions for instructions of Catholic faith, the Reich Bishop is hardly the suitable person, and one would probably have to choose a Catholic. Of course the directions for both faiths would differ in fundamental questions, each, however, would lay claim to the fact that it really contained the truly authentic interpretation of article 24 of the party program.

By issuing directions nothing would therefore be improved in the present situation in the field of the churches. The fight between the faiths would be carried on in the old form and spread into the lines of the party. Yes, all faiths and Christian groups would attack state and party, because they had assumed to encroach upon their own territory, that of teaching the Christian faith and to try to reform it.

The churches cannot be conquered by a compromise between national socialism and Christian teachings, but only through a new ideology, whose coming you yourself have announced in your writings. Because of this conviction we have always been careful, not to exert a reforming influence on the Christian dogma in any shape nor to exert any influence on the church directives for religious teachings. In complete mutual agreement we have rejected the intention of the Reich Minister for churches who, against the objection of the party, always tried anew to renew the church life in the frame of national socialist spirit, in searching for a compromise between Christian teachings and the ideology of national socialism.

Should, however, any one personality emanating from the life of the church, be charged now to work out directions for the teaching of the Christian religion, the party would thereby basically approve and accept for itself the position of the Reich Minister for the churches previously opposed by it as there is no basic difference between a position which wants to reform and reorganize the church life in its entirety, and one which aims at this goal solely in the realm of the education of youth.

So far we have always been in accord, that by taking such a step the party would leave the soil on which it is firmly planted and would step on the swaying ground of the controversial Christian doctrines. It would enter into the domain of the interpretation of the teachings of Jesus, and there would doubtless be subordinate to those who for centuries have done nothing but interpret and rewrite the words and deeds of Jesus of Nazareth as written in the old books about the actual wording of which the scientists fight even today. When in later decades and centuries the German people's soul liberated by national socialism should once again be choked and crippled by Christian doctrines, it could be possible that it may have been caused by today's attempt to effect a synthesis between national socialism and Christianity.

On the other hand, of course I am also of the opinion that it is not possible to eliminate the religous instruction in schools without replacing it with something better for the moral education of youth.

Religious instruction as given in schools today does not only comprise the instruction in the Christian doctrines of faith, the teachings of the creation of the world and of the life thereafter; besides, the children receive also instructions in the ten commandments, which for most comrades of the people to this day still are the only directives for their moral behavior and for an orderly collective life in the people's community. If this instruction is taken from the children without replacing it with something better, the objection can be made—in my estimation not without reason, that, as many contend, the present degradation of youth is in part caused by the lack of religious instruction in schools.

What, in my opinion, is therefore necessary is the preparation of a short directive about a national socialist life formulation. We need for the work of education in the party, especially also in the Hitler Youth a short resume in which the ethical principles are documented, to respect which each German boy and girl, who at one time will be representatives of the national socialistic Germany, must be educated. In such a directive for instance belongs the law of bravery, the law against cowardness, the commandment of love for the soulful nature in which God makes himself apparent also in the animal and the plant, a commandment to keep the blood pure; many principles also belong here which are for instance also contained in the decalogue of the Old Testament, as far as they can be regarded as moral principles of all people's life.

The publication of such a directive can and must only come out of our national socialist conduct of life. Its commandments of customs need to be explained by reference to any doctrines of faith about the creation of life and about life of the soul after death.

They can and must originate beyond any confessional discussions.

I take the publication of such a directive to be of utmost importance, because the German boys and girls must once be told what they can and must do, and what is forbidden for them to do. I don't even think it necessary to introduce this directive immediately into the schools as a text; it would be sufficient if for the time being it would be introduced into the party and its affiliations. Later it could also be taken over by the schools just as the little Catechism also was not created by the school boards, but first taught by the Church and later taken over by the schools.

As far as the religious instructions in the schools is concerned, I do not think that anything has to be changed in the present situation. No fault can be found with any national socialist teacher, who after the unmistakenly clear instructions of the Fuehrer's deputy, is ready to give school instructions in the Christian religion. For the contents of this instruction, however, the directives should still be binding which have in former years been made by the churches themselves. In the circular of the Fuehrer's deputy No. 3/39 of 4 Jan 1939 it is stated explicitly that the teachers charged with religious instruction are not to choose from the material on biblical history at their own discretion, but have the obligation to teach the entire biblical instruction material. Interpretations, explanations and separations in the sense of several attempts of particular church directions have to be omitted. The pupils must be given the entire picture of the biblical instruction material.

However, the teachers have the right to present this material as property of biblical thought and not as that of Germany or national socialism. If thus in some cases comparison will be drawn, this, according to the circular, corresponds only to the duties of the educator. Against such instruction of religion the churches cannot have any objections.

When, sometime later, the proposed directive for a new German conduct of life first to be used in this educational work of the party, will have found entry into the schools, it shall in no way supplant classes in religion. It may perhaps be used as a foundation for some classes in German and must have validity for all pupils, without consideration of their religious affiliations. Against such educational procedure the churches could not object, either because it would really be a matter of additional education, which would take place next to the religious instruction and without any connection with it. On the contrary, the churches would have reason to be thankful to the state because it is not satisfied with the religious instruction according to the very insufficient moral education based on the ten commandments, but that it is giving youth an additional Education, which makes much higher demands on its moral conduct.

Parallel to that the desire of the parents for the instruction in the doctrines of faith may thus well go on. The stronger and more fertile our *positive* educational work in the schools will be formulated, however, the more certain it is that instruction of religions will be losing in importance.

If the youth which is now being educated according to our moral laws will later have to decide if it is still willing to have its children brought up in the far inferior Christian doctrines, the decision will in most cases be negative.

I would think that today, seven years after taking over the power, it should be possible to set up principles for a national socialist conduct of life. They have long been apparent to the people from the numerous early fighters for the national socialist idea.

As long as we do not master this task, however, it will always be pointed out from various sides, and rightly so, that children, not taking part in religious instruction, are no longer taught even the most simple moral laws which are a standard for the communal life of all nations.

The Fuehrer's deputy finds it necessary that all these questions should be thoroughly discussed in the near future in the presence of the Reich leaders, who are especially affected by them. I would appreciate it very much if you would let me know your position in this matter before the discussion.

Heil Hitler!
/s/ M. Bormann

THE SOVIET STATE

19. V. I. LENIN: REPORT ON THE NEW ECONOMIC POLICY*

Russia, reeling and beaten in the First World War, and severely damaged in the Revolution, barely survived the civil war that raged between Whites and Reds through 1921. The new Communist government applied "war communism," a system of armed confiscation, requisition, and pillage in order to keep factories running and farms producing. That policy left Russia starving, her farms and factories in peril, and her workers dismayed. In mid-1921 Lenin became convinced that the world revolution the Bolsheviks had expected would not arrive immediately and that a partial and temporary return to a form of capitalism was necessary to revive his country. Accordingly, he pressed his colleagues to accept the New Economic Policy, which he hoped to introduce at once. The NEP was contrary to Communist theory and principles, necessitating a retreat from ideology, but the party accepted Lenin's direction.

Lenin explained his attitude in the following report, delivered to the All-Russian Congress of Political Education Departments on October 17, 1921. How did Lenin justify the NEP? What was the function of capitalists under the NEP in the path toward communism?

At the beginning of 1918 we expected a period in which peaceful construction would be possible. When the Brest peace was signed it seemed that danger had subsided for a time and that it would be possible to start peaceful construction. But we were mistaken, because in 1918 a real military danger overtook us in the shape of the Czechoslovak mutiny and the outbreak of civil war, which dragged on until 1920. Partly owing to the war problems that overwhelmed us and partly owing to the desperate position in which the Republic found itself when the imperialist war ended—owing to these circumstances, and a number of others, we made the mistake of deciding to go over directly to communist production and distribution. We thought that under the surplus-food appropriation system the peasants would provide us with the required quantity of grain, which we could distribute among the factories and thus achieve communist production and distribution.

I cannot say that we pictured this plan as definitely and as clearly as that; but we acted approximately on those lines. That, unfortunately, is a fact. I say unfortunately, because brief experience convinced us that that line was wrong, that it ran counter to what we had previously written about the transition from capitalism to socialism, namely, that it would be impossible to bypass the period of socialist accounting and control in approaching even the lower stage of communism. Ever since 1917, when the problem of taking power arose and the Bolsheviks explained it to the whole people, our theoretical literature has been definitely stressing the necessity for a prolonged, complex transition through socialist accounting and control from capitalist society (and the less developed it is the longer the transition will take) to even one of the approaches to communist society.

* V. I. Lenin, "The New Economic Policy and the Tasks of the Political Education Departments" in David Skvirsky and George Hanna, eds., *Collected Works* (38 vols.; Moscow: Progress Publishers, 1966), XXXIII, 62–66, 69.

A STRATEGICAL RETREAT

At that time, when in the heat of the Civil War we had to take the necessary steps in economic organisation, it seemed to have been forgotten. In substance, our New Economic Policy signifies that, having sustained severe defeat on this point, we have started a strategical retreat. We said in effect: "Before we are completely routed, let us retreat and reorganise everything, but on a firmer basis." If Communists deliberately examine the question of the New Economic Policy there cannot be the slightest doubt in their minds that we have sustained a very severe defeat on the economic front. In the circumstances it is inevitable, of course, for some people to become very despondent, almost panic-stricken, and because of the retreat, these people will begin to give way to panic. That is inevitable. When the Red Army retreated, was its flight from the enemy not the prelude to its victory? Every retreat on every front, however, caused some people to give way to panic for a time. But on each occasion—on the Kolchak front, on the Denikin front, on the Yudenich front, on the Polish front and on the Wrangel front—once we had been badly battered (and sometimes more than once) we proved the truth of the proverb: "A man who has been beaten is worth two who haven't." After being beaten we began to advance slowly, systematically and cautiously.

Of course, tasks on the economic front are much more difficult than tasks on the war front, although there is a general similarity between the two elementary outlines of strategy. In attempting to go over straight to communism we, in the spring of 1921, sustained a more serious defeat on the economic front than any defeat inflicted upon us by Kolchak, Denikin or Pilsudski. This defeat was much more serious, significant and dangerous. It was expressed in the isolation of the higher administrators of our economic policy from the lower and their failure to produce that development of the productive forces which the Programme of our Party regards as vital and urgent.

The surplus-food appropriation system in the rural districts—this direct communist approach to the problem of urban development—hindered the growth of the productive forces and proved to be the main cause of the profound economic and political crisis that we experienced in the spring of 1924. That was why we had to take a step which from the point of view of our line, of our policy, cannot be called anything else than a very severe defeat and retreat. Moreover, it cannot be said that this retreat is—like retreats of the Red Army—a completely orderly retreat to previously prepared positions. True, the positions for our present retreat were prepared beforehand. That can be proved by comparing the decisions adopted by our Party in the spring of 1921 with the one adopted in April 1918, which I have mentioned. The positions were prepared beforehand; but the retreat to these positions took place (and is still taking place in many parts of the country) in disorder, and even in extreme disorder.

PURPORT OF THE NEW ECONOMIC POLICY

It is here that the task of the Political Education Departments to combat this comes to the forefront. The main problem in the light of the New Economic Policy is to take advantage of the situation that has arisen as speedily as possible.

The New Economic Policy means substituting a tax for the requisitioning of food; it means reverting to capitalism to a considerable extent- -to what extent we do not know. Concessions to foreign capitalists (true, n y very few have been accepted, especially when compared with the number we have offered) and leasing enterprises to private capitalists definitely mean restoring capitalism, and this is part and parcel of the New Economic Policy; for the abolition of the surplus-food appropriation system means allowing the peasants to trade freely in their surplus agricultural produce, in whatever is left over after the tax is collected—and the tax takes only a small share of that produce. The peasants constitute a huge section of our population and of our entire economy, and that is why capitalism must grow out of this soil of free trading.

That is the very ABC of economics as taught by the rudiments of that science, and in Russia taught, furthermore, by the profiteer, the creature who needs no economic or political science to teach us economics with. From the point of view of strategy the root question is: who will take advantage of the new situation first? The whole question is—whom will the peasantry follow? The proletariat, which wants to build socialist society? Or the capitalist, who says, "Let us turn back; it is safer that way; we don't know anything about this socialism they have invented"?

WHO WILL WIN, THE CAPITALIST OR SOVIET POWER?

The issue in the present war is—who will win, who will first take advantage of the situation: the capitalist, whom we are allowing to come in by the door, and even by several doors (and by many doors we are not aware of, and which open without us, and in spite of us), or proletarian state power? What has the latter to rely on economically? On the one hand, the improved position of the people. In this connection we must remember the peasants. It is absolutely incontrovertible and obvious to all that in spite of the awful disaster of the famine—and leaving that disaster out of the reckoning for the moment—the improvement that has taken place in the position of the people has been due to the change in our economic policy.

On the other hand, if capitalism gains by it, industrial production will grow, and the proletariat will grow too. The capitalists will gain from our policy and will create an industrial proletariat, which in our country, owing to the war and to the desperate poverty and ruin, has become declassed, i.e., dislodged from its class groove, and has ceased to exist as a proletariat. The proletariat is the class which is engaged in the production of material values in large-scale capitalist industry. Since large-scale capitalist industry has been destroyed, since the factories are at a standstill, the proletariat has disappeared. It has sometimes figured in statistics, but it has not been held together economically.

The restoration of capitalism would mean the restoration of a proletarian class engaged in the production of socially useful material values in big factories employing machinery, and not in profiteering, not in making cigarette-lighters for sale, and in other "work" which is not very useful, but which is inevitable when our industry is in a state of ruin.

The whole question is who will take the lead. We must face this issue squarely —who will come out on top? Either the capitalists succeed in organising first—

in which case they will drive out the Communists and that will be the end of it. Or the proletarian state power, with the support of the peasantry, will prove capable of keeping a proper rein on those gentlemen, the capitalists, so as to direct capitalism along state channels and to create a capitalism that will be subordinate to the state and serve the state. The question must be put soberly. All this ideology, all these arguments about political liberties that we hear so much of, especially among Russian émigrés, in Russia No. 2, where scores of daily newspapers published by all the political parties extol these liberties in every key and every manner—all these are mere talk, mere phrase-mongering. We must learn to ignore this phrase-mongering. . . .

WE MUST NOT COUNT
ON GOING STRAIGHT TO COMMUNISM

We must not count on going straight to communism. We must build on the basis of peasants' personal incentive. We are told that the personal incentive of the peasants means restoring private property. But we have never interfered with personally owned articles of consumption and implements of production as far as the peasants are concerned. We have abolished private ownership of land. Peasants farmed land that they did not own—rented land, for instance. That system exists in very many countries. There is nothing impossible about it from the standpoint of economics. The difficulty lies in creating personal incentive. We must also give every specialist an incentive to develop our industry.

Have we been able to do that? No, we have not! We thought that production and distribution would go on at communist bidding in a country with a declassed proletariat. We must change that now, or we shall be unable to make the proletariat understand this process of transition. No such problems have ever arisen in history before. We tried to solve this problem straight out, by a frontal attack, as it were, but we suffered defeat. Such mistakes occur in every war, and they are not even regarded as mistakes. Since the frontal attack failed, we shall make a flanking movement and also use the method of siege and undermining. . . .

20. JOSEPH STALIN: ON THE FIRST FIVE-YEAR PLAN*

After years of struggle among the party leaders Joseph Stalin (1879–1953) emerged supreme in 1929. He shunted aside his rivals and used his post as General Secretary of the Communist Party to achieve absolute control. Since the party ruled the Soviet Union, Stalin's power was unchallenged. Lenin often had to convince his colleagues to follow him, but Stalin needed only to give commands. Believing that his task was to propel the Soviet Union toward communism, Stalin had already launched the first Five-Year Plan in October 1928. The plan called for a total mobilization of the economy under state control, direction, and planning, the collectivization of all Soviet agriculture, and progress toward industrialization at breakneck speed, whatever the cost.

* J. V. Stalin, "The Fundamental Task of the Five-Year Plan and the Way to Its Fulfilment" in *Works* (Moscow: Foreign Languages Publishing House, 1955), XIII, 174–75, 177–83, 193–95, 211–16.

The following selection presents the core of a report delivered by Stalin to the Central Committee of the Communist Party in January 1933. Stalin had received his education at the theological seminary of Tiflis in Russian Georgia. What marks of his early theological training are evident in his style of writing and his method of presenting ideas? What were the various goals of the Five-Year Plan? Compare the roles of the party, the state, and the individual in the completion of the Five-Year Plan. What, for Stalin, was "the basic revolutionary law," and what justification for the existence of a secret police force was evident? What happened to the theory of the "withering away of the state" in Stalin's arguments?

What was the fundamental task of the five-year plan?

The fundamental task of the five-year plan was to transfer our country, with its backward, and in part medieval, technology, on to the lines of new, modern technology.

The fundamental task of the five-year plan was to convert the U.S.S.R. from an agrarian and weak country, dependent upon the caprices of the capitalist countries, into an industrial and powerful country, fully self-reliant and independent of the caprices of world capitalism.

The fundamental task of the five-year plan was, in converting the U.S.S.R. into an industrial country, to completely oust the capitalist elements, to widen the front of socialist forms of economy, and to create the economic basis for the abolition of classes in the U.S.S.R., for the building of a socialist society. . . .

The fundamental task of the five-year plan was to transfer small and scattered agriculture on to the lines of large-scale collective farming, so as to ensure the economic basis of socialism in the countryside and thus to eliminate the possibility of the restoration of capitalism in the U.S.S.R.

Finally, the task of the five-year plan was to create all the necessary technical and economic prerequisites for increasing to the utmost the defence capacity of the country, enabling it to organise determined resistance to any attempt at military intervention from abroad, to any attempt at military attack from abroad. . . .

That is how matters stand with regard to the fundamental task of the five-year plan.

But the execution of such a gigantic plan cannot be started haphazardly, just anyhow. In order to carry out such a plan it is necessary first of all to find its main link; for only after finding and grasping this main link could a pull be exerted on all the other links of the plan.

What was the main link in the five-year plan?

The main link in the five-year plan was heavy industry, with machine building as its core. For only heavy industry is capable of reconstructing both industry as a whole, transport and agriculture, and of putting them on their feet. It was necessary to begin the fulfilment of the five-year plan with heavy industry. Consequently, the restoration of heavy industry had to be made the basis of the fulfilment of the five-year plan. . . .

But the restoration and development of heavy industry, particularly in such a backward and poor country as ours was at the beginning of the five-year plan period, is an extremely difficult task; for, as is well known, heavy industry calls for enormous financial expenditure and the existence of a certain minimum of experienced technical forces, without which, generally speaking, the restoration of heavy industry is impossible. Did the Party know this, and did it take this into account? Yes, it did. Not only did the Party know this, but it announced it for all to hear. The Party knew how heavy industry had been built in Britain, Germany and America. It knew that in those countries heavy industry had been built either with the aid of big loans, or by plundering other countries, or by both methods simultaneously. The Party knew that those paths were closed to our country. What, then, did it count on? It counted on our country's own resources. It counted on the fact that, with a Soviet government at the helm, and the land, industry, transport, the banks and trade nationalised, we could pursue a regime of the strictest economy in order to accumulate sufficient resources for the restoration and development of heavy industry. The Party declared frankly that this would call for serious sacrifices, and that it was our duty openly and consciously to make these sacrifices if we wanted to achieve our goal. The Party counted on carrying through this task with the aid of the internal resources of our country—without enslaving credits and loans from abroad. . . .

To change from the muzhik horse of poverty to the horse of large-scale machine industry—such was the aim of the Party in drawing up the five-year plan and striving for its fulfilment.

To establish a regime of the strictest economy and to accumulate the resources necessary for financing the industrialisation of our country—such was the path that had to be taken in order to succeed in creating heavy industry and in carrying out the five-year plan. . . .

What are the results of the five-year plan in four years in the sphere of *industry*? . . .

We did not have an iron and steel industry, the basis for the industrialisation of the country. Now we have one.

We did not have a tractor industry. Now we have one.

We did not have an automobile industry. Now we have one.

We did not have a machine-tool industry. Now we have one.

We did not have a big and modern chemical industry. Now we have one.

We did not have a real and big industry for the production of modern agricultural machinery. Now we have one.

We did not have an aircraft industry. Now we have one.

In output of electric power we were last on the list. Now we rank among the first.

In output of oil products and coal we were last on the list. Now we rank among the first.

We had only one coal and metallurgical base—in the Ukraine—and it was with difficulty that we made do with that. We have not only succeeded in improving this base, but have created a new coal and metallurgical base—in the East—which is the pride of our country.

We had only one centre of the textile industry—in the North of our country. As a result of our efforts we shall have in the very near future two new centres of the textile industry—in Central Asia and Western Siberia.

And we have not only created these new great industries, but have created them on a scale and in dimensions that eclipse the scale and dimensions of European industry.

And as a result of all this the capitalist elements have been completely and irrevocably ousted from industry, and socialist industry has become the sole form of industry in the U.S.S.R.

And as a result of all this our country has been converted from an agrarian into an industrial country; for the proportion of industrial output, as compared with agricultural output, has risen from 48 per cent of the total in the beginning of the five-year plan period (1928) to 70 per cent at the end of the fourth year of the five-year plan period (1932).

And as a result of all this we have succeeded by the end of the fourth year of the five-year plan period in fulfilling the total programme of industrial output, which was drawn up for five years, to the extent of 93.7 per cent, thereby raising the volume of industrial output to more than *three times* the pre-war output, and to more than *double* the level of 1928. As for the programme of output for heavy industry, we have fulfilled the five-year plan by 108 per cent.

It is true that we are 6 per cent short of fulfilling the total programme of the five-year plan. But that is due to the fact that in view of the refusal of neighbouring countries to sign pacts of non-aggression with us, and of the complications that arose in the Far East, we were obliged, for the purpose of strengthening our defence, hastily to switch a number of factories to the production of modern defensive means. And owing to the necessity of going through a certain period of preparation, this switch resulted in these factories suspending production for four months, which could not but affect the fulfilment of the total programme of output for 1932, as fixed in the five-year plan. As a result of this operation we have completely filled the gaps with regard to the defence capacity of the country. But this was bound to affect adversely the fulfilment of the programme of output provided for in the five-year plan. It is beyond any doubt that, but for this incidental circumstance, we would almost certainly not only have fulfilled, but even overfulfilled the total production figures of the five-year plan.

Finally, as a result of all this the Soviet Union has been converted from a weak country, unprepared for defence, into a country mighty in defence, a country prepared for every contingency, a country capable of producing on a mass scale all modern means of defence and of equipping its army with them in the event of an attack from abroad.

Such, in general terms, are the results of the five-year plan in four years in the sphere of industry. . . .

In this connection, the task of the five-year plan in the sphere of agriculture was to unite the scattered and small, individual peasant farms, which lacked the possibility of using tractors and modern agricultural machinery, into large collective farms, equipped with all the modern implements of highly developed agriculture, and to cover unoccupied land with model state farms.

The task of the five-year plan in the sphere of agriculture was to convert the U.S.S.R. from a small-peasant and backward country into one of large-scale agriculture organised on the basis of collective labour and providing the maximum output for the market.

What has the Party achieved in carrying out the programme of the five-year plan in four years in the sphere of agriculture? Has it fulfilled this programme, or has it failed?

The Party has succeeded in the course of some three years in organising more than 200,000 collective farms and about 5,000 state farms devoted to grain growing and livestock raising, and at the same time it has succeeded during four years in expanding the crop area by 21,000,000 hectares.

The Party has succeeded in getting more than 60 per cent of the peasant farms to unite into collective farms, embracing more than 70 per cent of all the land cultivated by peasants; this means that we have *fulfilled* the five-year plan *three times over*.

The Party has succeeded in making possible its procurement of 1,200 million to 1,400 million poods of marketable grain annually, instead of the 500,000,000–600,000,000 poods that were procured in the period when individual peasant farming predominated.

The Party has succeeded in routing the kulaks as a class, although they have not yet been dealt the final blow; the labouring peasants have been emancipated from kulak bondage and exploitation, and the Soviet regime has been given a firm economic basis in the countryside, the basis of collective farming.

The Party has succeeded in converting the U.S.S.R. from a country of small-peasant farming into a country of the largest-scale agriculture in the world. . . .

Now, after all this, judge for yourselves what worth there is in the talk in the bourgeois press about the "collapse" of collectivisation, about the "failure" of the five-year plan in the sphere of agriculture.

And what is the position of agriculture in the *capitalist* countries, which are now passing through a severe agricultural crisis?

Here are the generally known official data.

In the principal grain-producing countries the crop area has been reduced by 8–10 per cent. The area under cotton in the United States has been reduced by 15 per cent; the area under sugar-beet in Germany and Czechoslovakia has been reduced by 22–30 per cent; the area under flax in Lithuania and Latvia has been reduced by 25–30 per cent.

According to the figures of the United States Department of Agriculture, the value of the gross output of agriculture in the U.S.A. *dropped* from $11,000 million in 1929 to $5,000 million in 1932. The value of the gross output of grain in that country *dropped* from $1,288 million in 1929 to $391,000,000 in 1932. The value of the cotton crop in that country *dropped* from $1,389 million in 1929 to $397,000,000 in 1932.

Do not all these facts testify to the superiority of the Soviet system of agriculture over the capitalist system? Do not these facts go to show that collective farms are a more efficient form of farming than individual and capitalist farms? . . .

As a result of the fulfilment of the five-year plan in regard to industry, agriculture and trade, we have established the principle of socialism in all spheres of the national economy and have expelled the capitalist elements from them.

What should this have led to in relation to the capitalist elements; and what has it actually led to?

It has led to this: the last remnants of the moribund classes—the private manufacturers and their servitors, the private traders and their henchmen, the former nobles and priests, the kulaks and kulak agents, the former whiteguard officers and police officials, policemen and gendarmes, all sorts of bourgeois intellectuals of a chauvinist type, and all other anti-Soviet elements—have been thrown out of their groove.

Thrown out of their groove, and scattered over the whole face of the U.S.S.R., these "have-beens" have wormed their way into our plants and factories, into our government offices and trading organisations, into our railway and water transport enterprises, and, principally, into the collective farms and state farms. They have crept into these places and taken cover there, donning the mask of "workers" and "peasants," and some of them have even managed to worm their way into the Party.

What did they carry with them into these places? Of course, they carried with them a feeling of hatred towards the Soviet regime, a feeling of burning enmity towards the new forms of economy, life and culture.

These gentlemen are no longer able to launch a frontal attack against the Soviet regime. They and their classes made such attacks several times, but they were routed and dispersed. Hence, the only thing left them is to do mischief and harm to the workers, to the collective farmers, to the Soviet regime and to the Party. And they are doing as much mischief as they can, acting on the sly. They set fire to warehouses and wreck machinery. They organise sabotage. They organise wrecking activities in the collective farms and state farms, and some of them, including certain professors, go to such lengths in their passion for wrecking as to inject plague and anthrax germs into the cattle on the collective farms and state farms, help to spread meningitis among horses, etc.

But that is not the main thing. The main thing in the "work" of these "have-beens" is that they organise mass theft and plundering of state property, co-operative property and collective-farm property. Theft and plundering in the factories and plants, theft and plundering of railway freight, theft and plundering in warehouses and trading enterprises—particularly theft and plundering in the state farms and collective farms—such is the main form of the "work" of these "have-beens." Their class instinct, as it were, tells them that the basis of Soviet economy is public property, and that it is precisely this basis that must be shaken in order to injure the Soviet regime—and they try indeed to shake the foundations of public ownership, by organising mass theft and plundering.

In order to organise plundering they play on the private-property habits and survivals among the collective farmers, the individual farmers of yesterday who are now members of collective farms. You, as Marxists, should know that in its development man's consciousness lags behind his actual position. The position of the members of collective farms is that they are no longer individual farmers, but collectivists; but their consciousness is as yet still the old one—that of private property owners. And so, the "have-beens" from the ranks of the exploiting classes play on the private-property habits of the collective farmers in order to organise the plundering of public wealth and thus shake the foundation of the Soviet system, viz., public property.

Many of our comrades look complacently upon such phenomena and fail to understand the meaning and significance of this mass theft and plundering. They remain blind to these facts and take the view that "there is nothing particular in it." But these comrades are profoundly mistaken. The basis of our system is public property, just as private property is the basis of capitalism. If the capitalists proclaimed private property sacred and inviolable when they were consolidating the capitalist system, all the more reason why we Communists should proclaim public property sacred and inviolable in order to consolidate the new socialist forms of economy in all spheres of production and trade. To permit theft and plundering of public property—no matter whether it is state property or co-operative or collective-farm property—and to ignore such counter-revolutionary outrages means to aid and abet the undermining of the Soviet system, which rests on public property as its basis. It was on these grounds that our Soviet Government passed the recent law for the protection of public property. This enactment is the basis of revolutionary law at the present time. And it is the prime duty of every Communist, of every worker, and of every collective farmer strictly to carry out this law.

It is said that revolutionary law at the present time does not differ in any way from revolutionary law in the first period of NEP, that revolutionary law at the present time is a reversion to revolutionary law of the first period of NEP. That is absolutely wrong. The sharp edge of revolutionary law in the first period of NEP was directed mainly against the excesses of war communism, against "illegal" confiscation and imposts. It guaranteed the security of the property of the private owner, of the individual peasant and of the capitalist, provided they strictly observed the Soviet laws. The position in regard to revolutionary law at the present time is entirely different. The sharp edge of revolutionary law at the present time is directed, not against the excesses of war communism, which have long ceased to exist, but against thieves and wreckers in public economy, against rowdies and pilferers of public property. The main concern of revolutionary law at the present time is, consequently, the protection of public property, and not something else.

That is why it is one of the fundamental tasks of the Party to fight to protect public property, to fight with all the measures and all the means placed at our command by our Soviet laws.

A strong and powerful dictatorship of the proletariat—that is what we need now in order to scatter to the winds the last remnants of the dying classes and to frustrate their thieving designs.

Some comrades have interpreted the thesis about the abolition of classes, the creation of a classless society, and the withering away of the state as a justification of laziness and complacency, a justification of the counter-revolutionary theory of the extinction of the class struggle and the weakening of the state power. Needless to say, such people cannot have anything in common with our Party. They are either degenerates or double-dealers, and must be driven out of the Party. The abolition of classes is not achieved by the extinction of the class struggle, but by its intensification. The state will wither away, not as a result of weakening the state power, but as a result of strengthening it to the utmost, which is necessary for finally crushing the remnants of the dying classes and for organising defence against the capitalist encirclement, which is far from having been done away with as yet, and will not soon be done away with.

As a result of fulfilling the five-year plan we have succeeded in finally ejecting the last remnants of the hostile classes from their positions in production; we have routed the kulaks and have prepared the ground for their elimination. Such are the results of the five-year plan in the sphere of the struggle against the last detachments of the bourgeoisie. . . .

We must bear in mind that the growth of the power of the Soviet state will intensify the resistance of the last remnants of the dying classes. It is precisely because they are dying and their days are numbered that they will go on from one form of attack to another, sharper form, appealing to the backward sections of the population and mobilising them against the Soviet regime. There is no mischief and slander that these "have-beens" will not resort to against the Soviet regime and around which they will not try to rally the backward elements. This may provide the soil for a revival of the activities of the defeated groups of the old counter-revolutionary parties: the Socialist-Revolutionaries, the Mensheviks, and the bourgeois nationalists of the central and border regions, it may also provide the soil for a revival of the activities of the fragments of counter-revolutionary elements among the Trotskyists and Right deviators. Of course, there is nothing terrible in this. But we must bear all this in mind if we want to have done with these elements quickly and without particular sacrifice.

That is why revolutionary vigilance is the quality that Bolsheviks especially need at the present time.

21. JOSEPH STALIN: ON THE DRAFT CONSTITUTION OF 1936*

The Soviet Constitution of 1936 appeared democratic at first glance. But self-determination, elections, and federalism were all defined in Stalinist terms. The Communist party alone was recognized, and elections could only return candidates nominated by the party. The federal structure of the Soviet Union was itself a thin façade for the total control that remained in the hands of the party.

The following selection is Stalin's report to the Extraordinary Eighth Congress of Soviets of the U.S.S.R. on November 25, 1936, explaining the new constitution. As Stalin interpreted Marx, what distinction did he draw between socialism and communism, and how did that distinction apply to Russia? What were Stalin's views on bourgeois democracy? How did Stalin describe the role of the party in the government and the role of the government in the state? Compare Stalin's political goals with the political philosophies of Mussolini and Hitler.

What are the changes in the life of the U.S.S.R. that have been brought about in the period from 1924 to 1936 and which the Constitution Commission was to reflect in its Draft Constitution?

What is the essence of these changes?

What was the situation in 1924?

* "Stalin: On the Draft Constitution" in James H. Meisel and Edward S. Kozera, eds., *Materials for the Study of the Soviet System* (2d ed., rev.; Ann Arbor, Mich.: The George Wahr Publishing Co., 1953), pp. 231–37. Reprinted by permission.

At that time we were in the first period of the New Economic Policy, the beginning of NEP, the period of a certain revival of capitalism; now, however, we are in the last period of NEP, the end of NEP, the period of the complete liquidation of capitalism in all spheres of the national economy.

And what does this mean?

It means that the exploitation of man has been abolished, eliminated, while the Socialist ownership of the implements and means of production has been established as the unshakable foundation of our Soviet society. [Prolonged applause.]

As a result of all these changes in the sphere of the national economy of the U.S.S.R., we now have a new, Socialist economy, which knows neither crises nor unemployment, which knows neither poverty nor ruin, and which provides our citizens with every opportunity to lead a prosperous and cultured life.

In conformity with these changes in the economic life of the U.S.S.R., the class structure of our society has also changed.

The landlord class, as you know, had already been eliminated as a result of the victorious conclusion of the civil war. As for the other exploiting classes, they have shared the fate of the landlord class. The capitalist class in the sphere of industry has ceased to exist. The kulak class in the sphere of agriculture has ceased to exist. And the merchants and profiteers in the sphere of trade have ceased to exist. Thus all the exploiting classes have now been eliminated.

There remains the working class.

There remains the peasant class.

There remains the intelligentsia.

But it would be a mistake to think that these social groups have undergone no change during this period, that they have remained the same as they were, say, in the period of capitalism.

Take, for example, the working class of the U.S.S.R. By force of habit, it is often called the proletariat. But what is the proletariat? The proletariat is a class bereft of the instruments and means of production, under an economic system in which the instruments and means of production have been taken for the capitalists and transferred to the state, of which the leading force is the working class. Consequently, there is no longer a capitalist class which would exploit the working class. . . . This being the case, can our working class be called the proletariat? Clearly, it cannot. . . . And what does this mean? This means that the proletariat of the U.S.S.R. has been transformed into an entirely new class, into the working class of the U.S.S.R., which has abolished the capitalist economic system, which has established the Socialist ownership of the instruments and means of production and is directing Soviet society along the road to Communism.

. . . Let us pass on to the question of the peasantry. . . . In our country there are no longer any landlords and kulaks, merchants and usurers who could exploit the peasants. Consequently, our peasantry is a peasantry emancipated from exploitation. Further. Our Soviet peasantry, its overwhelming majority is a collective farm peasantry, i.e., it bases its work and wealth not on individual labour and on backward technical equipment, but on collective labour and up-to-date technical equipment. Finally, the economy of our peasantry is based, not on private property, but on collective property, which has grown up on the basis of collective labour.

Lastly, let us pass on to the question of the intelligentsia, to the question of engineers and technicians, of workers on the cultural front, of employees in general, and so on. The intelligentsia, too, has undergone great changes during this period. It is no longer the old hidebound intelligentsia which tried to place itself above classes, but which actually, for the most part, served the landlords and the capitalists. Our Soviet intelligentsia is an entirely new intelligentsia, bound up by its very roots with the working class and the peasantry. In the first place, the composition of the intelligentsia has changed. People who come from the aristocracy and the bourgeoisie constitute but a small percentage of our Soviet intelligentsia; 80 to 90 per cent of the Soviet intelligentsia are people who have come from the working class, from the peasantry, or from other strata of the working population. Finally, the very nature of the activities of the intelligentsia has changed. Formerly it had to serve the wealthy classes, for it had no alternative. Today it must serve the people, for there are no longer any exploiting classes. And that is precisely why it is now an equal member of Soviet society, in which, side by side with the workers and peasants, pulling together with them, it is engaged in building the new, classless, Socialist society.

What do these changes signify?

Firstly, they signify that the dividing lines between the working class and the peasantry, and between these classes and the intelligentsia, are being obliterated, and that the old class exclusiveness is disappearing. This means that the distance between these social groups is steadily diminishing.

Secondly, they signify that the economic contradictions between these social groups are declining, are becoming obliterated.

And lastly, they signify that the political contradictions between them are also declining and becoming obliterated.

Such is the position in regard to the changes in the class structure of the U.S.S.R.

How are all these changes in the life of the U.S.S.R. reflected in the draft of the new Constitution?

... In drafting the new Constitution, the Constitution Commission proceeded from the proposition that a constitution must not be confused with a program. ... Whereas a program speaks of that which does not yet exist, of that which has yet to be achieved and won in the future, a constitution, on the contrary, must speak of that which already exists, of that which has already been achieved and won now, at the present time. A program deals mainly with the future, a constitution with the present.

Two examples by way of illustration.

Our Soviet society has already, in the main, succeeded in achieving Socialism; it has created a Socialist system, i.e., it has brought about what Marxists in other words call the first, or lower, phase of Communism. Hence, in the main, we have already achieved the first phase of Communism, Socialism. The fundamental principle of this phase of Communism is, as you know, the formula: "From each according to his abilities, to each according to his work." Should our Constitution reflect this fact, the fact that Socialism has been achieved? Should it be based on this achievement? Unquestionably, it should. It should, because for the U.S.S.R. Socialism is something already achieved and won.

But Soviet society has not yet reached the higher phase of Communism, in which the ruling principle will be the formula: "From each according to his abilities, to each according to his needs," although it sets itself the aim of achieving the higher phase of Communism in the future. Can our Constitution be based on the higher phase of Communism, which does not yet exist and which has still to be achieved? No, it cannot, because for the U.S.S.R. the higher phase of Communism is something that has not yet been realized, and which has to be realized in the future. It cannot, if it is not to be converted into a program or a declaration of future achievements.

Such are the limits of our Constitution at the present historical moment.

Further. The constitutions of bourgeois countries usually proceed from the conviction that the capitalist system is immutable.

Unlike these, the draft of the new Constitution of the U.S.S.R. proceeds from the fact that the capitalist system has been liquidated, and that the Socialist system has triumphed in the U.S.S.R. The main foundation of the draft of the new Constitution of the U.S.S.R. is the principles of Socialism, whose main pillars are things that have already been achieved and realized: the Socialist ownership of the land, forests, factories, works and other instruments and means of production; the abolition of exploitation and of exploiting classes; the abolition of poverty for the majority and of luxury for the minority; the abolition of unemployment; work as an obligation and an honorable duty for every able-bodied citizen, in accordance with the formula; "He who does not work, neither shall he eat"; the right to work, *i.e.,* the right of every citizen to receive guaranteed employment; the right to rest and leisure; the right to education, etc. The draft of the new Constitution rests on these and similar pillars of Socialism. It reflects them, it embodies them in law.

Such is the second specific feature of the draft of the new Constitution.

Further. Bourgeois constitutions tacitly proceed from the premise that society consists of antagonistic classes, of classes which own wealth and classes which do not own wealth; that no matter what party comes into power, the guidance of society by the state (the dictatorship) must be in the hands of the bourgeoisie; that a constitution is needed for the purpose of consolidating a social order desired by and beneficial to the propertied classes.

Unlike bourgeois constitutions, the draft of the new Constitution of the U.S.S.R. proceeds from the fact that there are no longer any antagonistic classes in society; that society consists of two friendly classes, of workers and peasants; that it is these classes, the labouring classes, that are in power; that the guidance of society by the state (the dictatorship) is in the hands of the working class, the most advanced class in society; that a constitution is needed for the purpose of consolidating a social order desired by and beneficial to the working people.

Such is the third specific feature of the draft of the new Constitution.

Further. Bourgeois constitutions tacitly proceed from the premise that nations and races cannot have equal rights, that there are nations with full rights and nations without full rights, and that in addition, there is a third category of nations or races, for example in the colonies, which have even fewer rights than the nations without full rights. This means that, at bottom, all these constitutions are nationalistic, *i.e.,* constitutions of ruling nations.

Unlike these constitutions, the draft of the new Constitution of the U.S.S.R. is, on the contrary, profoundly internationalistic. It proceeds from the proposition that all nations and races have equal rights. It proceeds from the fact that neither difference in colour or language, cultural level, or level of political development, nor any other difference between nations and races, can serve as grounds for justifying national inequality of rights. It proceeds from the proposition that all nations and races, irrespective of their past and present position, irrespective of their strength or weakness, should enjoy equal rights in all spheres of the economic, social, political and cultural life of society.

Such is the fourth specific feature of the draft of the new Constitution.

The fifth specific feature of the draft of the new Constitution is its consistent and thorough going democratism. From the standpoint of democratism bourgeois constitutions may be divided into two groups: One group of constitutions openly denies, or actually nullifies, the equality of rights of citizens and democratic liberties. The other group of constitutions readily accepts, and even advertises, democratic principles, but at the same time it makes reservations and provides for restrictions which utterly mutilate these democratic rights and liberties. They speak of equal suffrage for all citizens, but at the same time limit it by residential, educational, and even property qualifications. They speak of equal rights for citizens, but at the same time they make the reservation that this does not apply to women, or applies to them only in part. And so on and so forth.

What distinguishes the draft of the new Constitution of the U.S.S.R. is the fact that it is free from such reservations and restrictions. For it, there exists no division of citizens into active and passive ones; for it, all citizens are active. It does not recognize any difference in rights as between men and women. "residents" and "non-residents," propertied and propertyless, educated and uneducated. For it, all citizens have equal rights. It is not property status, not national origin, not sex, nor office, but personal ability and personal labour, that determines the position of every citizen in society.

Lastly, there is still one more specific feature of the draft of the new Constitution. Bourgeois constitutions usually confine themselves to stating the formal rights of citizens, without bothering about the conditions for the exercise of these rights, about the opportunity of exercising them, about the means by which they can be exercised.

What distinguishes the draft of the new Constitution is the fact that it does not confine itself to stating the formal rights of citizens, but stresses the guarantees of these rights, the means by which these rights can be exercised. It does not merely proclaim equality of rights for citizens, but ensures it by giving legislative embodiment to the fact that the regime of exploitation has been abolished, to the fact that the citizens have been emancipated from all exploitation. It does not merely proclaim the right to work, but ensures it by giving legislative embodiment to the fact that there are no crises in Soviet society, and that unemployment has been abolished. It does not merely proclaim democratic liberties, but legislatively ensures them by providing definite material resources.

I must admit that the draft of the new Constitution does preserve the regime of the dictatorship of the working class, just as it also preserves unchanged the present leading position of the Communist Party of the U.S.S.R. [Loud applause.] If the esteemed critics regard this as a flaw in the Draft Constitution, that is only to be regretted. We Bolsheviks regard it as a merit of the draft Constitution. [Loud applause.]

As to freedom for various political parties, we adhere to somewhat different views. A party is a part of a class, its most advanced part. Several parties, and, consequently, freedom for parties, can exist only in a society in which there are antagonistic classes whose interests are mutually hostile and irreconcilable—in which there are, say, capitalists and workers, landlords and peasants, kulaks and poor peasants, etc. But in the U.S.S.R. there are no longer such classes as the capitalists, the landlords, the kulaks, etc. In the U.S.S.R. there are only two classes, workers and peasants, whose interests—far from being mutually hostile —are, on the contrary, friendly. Hence, there is no ground in the U.S.S.R. for the existence of several parties, and, consequently, for freedom for these parties. In the U.S.S.R. there is ground only for one party, the Communist Party. In the U.S.S.R. only one party can exist, the Communist Party, which courageously defends the interests of the workers and peasants to the very end. . . .

They talk of democracy. But what is democracy? Democracy in capitalist countries, where there are antagonistic classes, is, in the last analysis, democracy for the strong, democracy for the propertied minority. In the U.S.S.R., on the contrary, democracy is democracy for the working people, *i.e.,* democracy for all. But from this it follows that the principles of democratism are violated, not by the draft of the new Constitution of the U.S.S.R., but by the bourgeois constitutions. That is why I think that the Constitution of the U.S.S.R. is the only thoroughly democratic Constitution in the world.

22. ANDREI A. ZHDANOV: SOVIET LITERATURE*

In the 1920's and 1930's the Soviet Union was intent upon building not only an industrial base but a new society as well. This aim was in conformity with Communist ideology, and the regime bent every effort to rid Russia of remnants of its feudal or bourgeois past. All aspects of state power and all elements of life were to be meshed into the all-inclusive philosophy that Lenin had believed to be the wave of the future. Basic instruments for the construction of a new society were education, literature, and the arts. In literature and the arts, Socialist Realism was expected to replace former patterns in use in bourgeois countries.

In the following selection, Andrei Zhdanov (1896–1948), later one of Stalin's chief lieutenants, discussed Soviet literature. Why, according to Zhdanov, was

* A. A. Zhdanov, "Soviet Literature: The Richest in Ideas" in A. Zhdanov, Narim Gorky, M. Bukharin, K. Radek, and A. Stetsky, *Problems of Soviet Literature, Reports and Speeches at the First Soviet Writers Congress* (Moscow: Cooperative Publishing Society of Foreign Workers in the U.S.S.R., 1935), pp. 17–22.

bourgeois society "no longer able to produce great works of art"? What did Stalin and Zhdanov mean when they insisted that Soviet writers must be "engineers of human souls"? What specific contrasts did Zhdanov draw between Soviet literature and the literature of other countries? What was his ultimate test in determining the validity of all art forms?

The key to the success of Soviet literature is to be sought for in the success of socialist construction. Its growth is an expression of the successes and achievements of our socialist system. Our literature is the youngest of all literatures of all peoples and countries. And at the same time it is the richest in ideas, the most advanced and the most revolutionary literature. Never before has there been a literature which has organized the toilers and oppressed for the struggle to abolish once and for all every kind of exploitation and the yoke of wage slavery. Never before has there been a literature which has based the subject matter of its works on the life of the working class and peasantry and their fight for socialism. Nowhere, in no country in the world, has there been a literature which has defended and upheld the principle of equal rights for the toilers of all nations, the principle of equal rights for women. There is not, there cannot be in bourgeois countries a literature which consistently smashes every kind of obscurantism, every kind of mysticism, priesthood and superstition, as our literature is doing.

Only Soviet literature, which is of one flesh and blood with socialist construction, could become, and has indeed become, such a literature—so rich in ideas, so advanced and revolutionary.

Soviet authors have already created not a few outstanding works, which correctly and truthfully depict the life of our Soviet country. Already there are several names of which we can be justly proud. Under the leadership of the Party, with the thoughtful and daily guidance of the Central Committee and the untiring support and help of Comrade Stalin, a whole army of Soviet writers has rallied around the Soviet power and the Party. And in the light of our Soviet literature's successes, we see standing out in yet sharper relief the full contrast between our system—the system of victorious socialism—and the system of dying, mouldering capitalism.

Of what can the bourgeois author write, of what can he dream, what source of inspiration can he find, whence can he borrow this inspiration, if the worker in capitalist countries is uncertain of the morrow, if he does not know whether he will have work the next day, if the peasant does not know whether he will work on his plot of ground tomorrow or whether his life will be ruined by the capitalist crisis, if the brain worker has no work today and does not know whether he will receive any tomorrow?

What can the bourgeois author write about, what source of inspiration can there be for him, when the world is being precipitated once more—if not today, then tomorrow—into the abyss of a new imperialist war?

The present state of bourgeois literature is such that it is no longer able to create great works of art. The decadence and disintegration of bourgeois literature, resulting from the collapse and decay of the capitalist system, represent a characteristic trait, a characteristic peculiarity of the state of bourgeois culture and bourgeois literature at the present time. Gone never to return are the times when bourgeois literature, reflecting the victory of the bourgeois system over feudalism, was able to create great works of the period when capitalism was flourishing. Everything now is growing stunted—themes, talents, authors, heroes.

In deathly terror of the proletarian revolution, fascism is wreaking its vengeance on civilization, turning people back to the most hideous and savage periods of human history, burning on the bonfire and barbarously destroying the works of humanity's best minds.

Characteristic of the decadence and decay of bourgeois culture are the orgies of mysticism and superstition, the passion for pornography. The "illustrious persons" of bourgeois literature—of that bourgeois literature which has sold its pen to capital—are now thieves, police sleuths, prostitutes, hooligans.

All this is characteristic of that section of literature which is trying to conceal the decay of the bourgeois system, which is vainly trying to prove that nothing has happened, that all is well in the "state of Denmark," that there is nothing rotten as yet in the system of capitalism. Those representatives of bourgeois literature who feel the state of things more acutely are absorbed in pessimism, doubt in the morrow, eulogy of darkness, extolment of pessimism as the theory and practice of art. And only a small section—the most honest and far-sighted writers—are trying to find a way out along other paths, in other directions, to link their destiny with the proletariat and its revolutionary struggle.

The proletariat of capitalist countries is already forging the army of its writers, of its artists—the revolutionary writers whose representatives we are glad to welcome here today at the first Congress of Soviet Writers. The detachment of revolutionary writers in capitalist countries is not large as yet, but it is growing and will continue to grow every day, as the class struggle becomes more intense, as the forces of the world proletarian revolution grow stronger.

We firmly believe that these few dozens of foreign comrades who are here today represent the nucleus, the core of a mighty army of proletarian writers which will be created by the world proletarian revolution in capitalist countries.

That is how matters stand in capitalist countries. Not so with us. Our Soviet writer derives the material for his works of art, his subject-matter, images, artistic language and speech, from the life and experience of the men and women of Dnieprostroy, of Magnitostroy. Our writer draws his material from the heroic epic of the Chelyuskin expedition, from the experience of our collective farms, from the creative action that is seething in all corners of our country.

In our country the main heroes of works of literature are the active builders of a new life—working men and women, men and women collective farmers, Party members, business managers, engineers, members of the Young Communist League, Pioneers. Such are the chief types and the chief heroes of our Soviet literature. Our literature is impregnated with enthusiasm and the spirit of heroic deeds. It is optimistic, but not optimistic in accordance with any "inward," animal instinct. It is optimistic in essence, because it is the literature of the rising class of the proletariat, the only progressive and advanced class. Our Soviet literature is strong by virtue of the fact that it is serving a new cause —the cause of socialist construction.

Comrade Stalin has called our writers engineers of human souls. What does this mean? What duties does the title confer upon you?

In the first place, it means knowing life so as to be able to depict it truthfully in works of art, not to depict it in a dead, scholastic way, not simply as "objective reality," but to depict reality in its revolutionary development.

In addition to this, the truthfulness and historical concreteness of the artistic portrayal should be combined with the ideological remoulding and education of the toiling people in the spirit of socialism. This method in *belles lettres* and literary criticism is what we call the method of socialist realism.

Our Soviet literature is not afraid of the charge of being "tendencious." Yes, Soviet literature is tendencious, for in an epoch of class struggle there is not and cannot be a literature which is not class literature, not tendencious, allegedly non-political.

And I think that every one of our Soviet writers can say to any dull-witted bourgeois, to any philistine, to any bourgeois writer who may talk about our literature being tendencious: "Yes, our Soviet literature is tendencious, and we are proud of this fact, because the aim of our tendency is to liberate the toilers, to free all mankind from the yoke of capitalist slavery."

To be an engineer of human souls means standing with both feet firmly planted on the basis of real life. And this in its turn denotes a rupture with romanticism of the old type, which depicted a non-existent life and non-existent heroes, leading the reader away from the antagonisms and oppression of real life into a world of the impossible, into a world of utopian dreams. Our literature, which stands with both feet firmly planted on a materialist basis, cannot be hostile to romanticism, but it must be a romanticism of a new type, revolutionary romanticism. We say that socialist realism is the basic method of Soviet *belles lettres* and literary criticism, and this presupposes that revolutionary romanticism should enter into literary creation as a component part, for the whole life of our Party, the whole life of the working class and its struggle consist in a combination of the most stern and sober practical work with a supreme spirit of heroic deeds and magnificent future prospects. Our Party has always been strong by virtue of the fact that it has united and continues to unite a thoroughly business-like and practical spirit with broad vision, with a constant urge forward, with a struggle for the building of communist society. Soviet literature should be able to portray our heroes; it should be able to glimpse our tomorrow. This will be no utopian dream, for our tomorrow is already being prepared for today by dint of conscious planned work.

One cannot be an engineer of human souls without knowing the technique of literary work, and it must be noted that the technique of the writer's work possesses a large number of specific peculiarities.

You have many different types of weapons. Soviet literature has every opportunity of employing these types of weapons (genres, styles, forms and methods of literary creation) in their diversity and fullness, selecting all the best that has been created in this sphere by all previous epochs. From this point of view, the mastery of the technique of writing, the critical assimilation of the literary heritage of all epochs, represents a task which you must fulfil without fail, if you wish to become engineers of human souls.

Comrades, the proletariat, just as in other provinces of material and spiritual culture, is the sole heir of all that is best in the treasury of world literature. The bourgeoisie has squandered its literary heritage; it is our duty to gather it up carefully, to study it and, having critically assimilated it, to advance further. . . .

Chapter Nine

THE SECOND WORLD WAR
AND AFTER

THE aftermath of World War I witnessed a sharp contrast between the hopes of the 1919 peacemakers and the realities of a world which was unable to return to "normalcy." Instead of peace, security, and international cooperation, a battered Europe was confronted with economic distress and continued national rivalries and suspicions in the interwar years. The reparations struggle embittered relations between France and Germany, while Britain was sorely pressed by internal problems and Soviet Russia remained locked in its ideological prison. The new states of Europe faced almost impossible social and economic problems in their search for stability.

By the mid-1920's a mood of reconciliation seemed nevertheless to gather strength in the West. Although Frenchmen and Germans still refused to trust each other completely, statesmen of the two countries were able to achieve a nebulous *détente*. A reduction in the scale of German reparation payments was accompanied by Germany's admission to the League of Nations and successful negotiation of the Locarno Pact, wherein Germany acknowledged the permanence of her western frontiers as established in the Treaty of Versailles. International disarmament discussions generally proved futile, but in 1928 more than a dozen world powers signed the Kellogg-Briand Treaty to outlaw war. In the long run, the Kellogg-Briand agreement merely constituted an idealistic symbol, and the League of Nations failed in its declared purpose of preserving world peace.

The failure of democracy in Italy, Germany, and many other European states resulted from internal difficulties and postwar dislocations. Adolf Hitler began the rearmament of Germany soon after he became chancellor in 1933 and withdrew Germany from the disarmament conference and the League of Nations. For six years the western democracies failed to grasp the aggressive nature of Hitler's policies and permitted him to violate the provisions of the Versailles Treaty and the Locarno Pact. The German Führer remilitarized the Rhineland in 1936 and annexed Austria in 1938. The somnolent West protested, but failed to take effective steps to combat German ambitions. British Prime Minister Neville Chamberlain hoped to appease Hitler's designs by further acceding to his demands in 1938 at the Munich Conference. Chamberlain was anxiously applauded by an English public strongly influenced by pacifism and unwilling to go to war for the Sudentenland portion of Czechoslovakia, and France declined to challenge Hitler's claims without the full support of the British.

Only when the remainder of independent Czechoslovakia disappeared from the map early in 1939, despite the Munich accord, was the futility of appeasement fully recognized by the western democracies. Chamberlain quickly guaranteed Poland against German aggression, but Hitler was not to be stopped by words. A non-aggression pact with the Soviet Union simplified the German invasion of Poland on September 1, 1939. Britain and France responded with declarations of war, and the Second World War had begun.

The new world war surpassed the first in horror and destruction. After smashing through eastern and western Europe, German armies attacked the Soviet Union in 1941. From the Bay of Biscay to the outskirts of Moscow, from Norway to North Africa, Germany seemed triumphant. Only Britain and the Soviet Union held out. Germany's Japanese ally, at war with China since 1937, also expanded her goals of Asian conquest and attacked the United States in December 1941, at Pearl Harbor. When Germany and Italy also declared war on the United States the Second World War became a titanic global struggle.

Nazi Germany maintained concentration camps during the war, in part to keep its own political prisoners in close confinement, but mainly as a means of exterminating millions of human beings. Six million Jews and uncounted others were systematically murdered. Nazi brutality intensified as Germany strove for total victory in Europe; forced-labor camps in Germany were packed with millions of Slavic Europeans, as well as hapless citizens deported from other German-occupied lands. Termed subhumans in accordance with Nazi ideology, the Slavs were brutally abused, although the full dimension of Nazi terror and inhumanity did not become clear to the West until the end of the war. Hitler's frustrations increased when his armies failed to achieve their final objectives. As American, British, and Russian troops converged on his shrinking empire in 1945, the Führer hysterically proclaimed that the Germans were unworthy of his struggle and vowed to see Germany itself destroyed in the final holocaust of war.

Toward the end of the war, the United States, fighting in Europe, Africa, and Asia, developed what seemed to be the ultimate weapon—the atomic bomb. Perfected at the moment of German defeat, the bomb was used twice against Japan, and led to Japan's unconditional surrender.

The ideological gap between the western allies and the Soviet Union was masked by the necessities of military victory but reappeared when postwar questions were considered. Even before the end of the war, Winston Churchill of Great Britain, Franklin Roosevelt of the United States, and Joseph Stalin of the Soviet Union met to discuss the future of the postwar world. The final defeat of Germany, Italy, and Japan saw no general agreement, however. Soviet armies occupied war-torn eastern Europe and facilitated Communist control in all the nations of that area between 1945 and 1948, while the United States helped to rescue western and southern Europe through massive economic and political aid. Thus, Europe was again divided in the postwar years, and peace turned into cold war.

After 1945 western Europe began to draw closer together, a process climaxed by the successes of the European Economic Community. Even Britain, long tied to her Commonwealth and enjoying a close relationship with the United States, bid to join the Common Market of continental states. Eastern Europe remained Communist, but Russian control became less effective and less direct after the death of Stalin in 1953.

Despite a gradual thaw in relations between East and West, world affairs continued to be dominated by what the German philosopher Karl Jaspers has called "the tension between the impossibility of an atomic world war and the danger, constantly kindled by small wars, that the impossible will happen." The emerging states of Asia and Africa, in seeking their own national identities amid staggering economic, social, and political problems and the pressures of population explosion, have produced a fertile field for local conflicts which threaten to upset the balance between the two superpowers—Soviet Russia and the United States. Man's opportunity for future life on this planet clearly depends upon the effective employment of some new political and psychological approach which can achieve a world-wide reconciliation of interests. It no longer seems possible for one power to pursue a completely independent course of action without jeopardizing the existence of humanity.

To many observers, the major question of our age is whether life under the constant threat of total annihilation can in fact impel men toward some form of stable world community. Under the pressure of modern civilization, must man, in the words of Jean Paul Sartre, simply "act without hope," or will he, with Albert Camus, find the strength to assert and act upon the principle that there is "only one kind of inevitability in history, that which we ourselves create"?

THE SECOND WORLD WAR

1. THE KELLOGG-BRIAND PACT*

Many people across the world, and especially in Europe, hoped that war could be banished from the globe forever by the League of Nations. The arms race had been an important factor in bringing on the First World War, and attempts were made to limit armaments even among the victors.

Trusting that France and Germany could live together in peace, French Foreign Minister Aristide Briand (1862–1932) and German Foreign Minister Gustav Stresemann strove for reconciliation after the disastrous French occupation of the Ruhr in 1923. The United States of America, wishing to avoid another European conflict, encouraged their efforts and sent Secretary of State Frank B. Kellogg (1856–1937) to Europe. Finally, in August 1928, fifteen nations, including the United States, Great Britain, France, Italy, Germany, and Japan, signed the Kellogg-Briand Pact—a treaty to outlaw war. Why were the provisions of the pact unrealistic in the face of postwar problems? What machinery for the enforcement of its provisions and for a settlement of disputes was provided under the terms of the pact?

* *United States Statutes at Large* (Washington, 1931), Vol. XLVI, Pt. 2, pp. 2343–2347.

The President of the German Reich, the President of the United States of America, His Majesty the King of the Belgians, the President of the French Republic, His Majesty the King of Great Britain, Ireland and the British Dominions Beyond the Seas, Emperor of India, His Majesty the King of Italy, His Majesty the Emperor of Japan, the President of the Republic of Poland, the President of the Czechoslovak Republic,

Deeply sensible of their solemn duty to promote the welfare of mankind;

Persuaded that the time has come when a frank renunciation of war as an instrument of national policy should be made to the end that the peaceful and friendly relations now existing between their peoples may be perpetuated;

Convinced that all changes in their relations with one another should be sought only by pacific means and be the result of a peaceful and orderly process, and that any signatory Power which shall hereafter seek to promote its national interests by resort to war should be denied the benefits furnished by this Treaty;

Hopeful that, encouraged by their example, all the other nations of the world will join in this humane endeavor and by adhering to the present Treaty as soon as it comes into force bring their peoples within the scope of its beneficent provisions, thus uniting the civilized nations of the world in a common renunciation of war as an instrument of their national policy; . . .

ARTICLE I: The High Contracting Parties solemnly declare in the names of their respective peoples that they condemn recourse to war for the solution of international controversies, and renounce it as an instrument of national policy in their relations with one another.

ARTICLE II: The High Contracting Parties agree that the settlement or solution of all disputes or conflicts of whatever nature or of whatever origin they may be, which may arise among them, shall never be sought except by pacific means.

ARTICLE III: The present Treaty shall be ratified by the High Contracting Parties named in the Preamble in accordance with their respective constitutional requirements, and shall take effect as between them as soon as all their several instruments of ratification shall have been deposited at Washington.

This Treaty shall, when it has come into effect as prescribed in the preceding paragraph, remain open as long as may be necessary for adherence by all the other Powers of the world. Every instrument evidencing the adherence of a Power shall be deposited at Washington and the Treaty shall immediately upon such deposit become effective as between the Power thus adhering and the other Powers parties hereto.

It shall be the duty of the Government of the United States to furnish each Government named in the Preamble and every Government subsequently adhering to this Treaty with a certified copy of the Treaty and of every instrument of ratification or adherence. It shall also be the duty of the Government of the United States telegraphically to notify such Governments immediately upon the deposit with it of each instrument of ratification or adherence.

IN FAITH WHEREOF the respective Plenipotentiaries have signed this Treaty in the French and English languages both texts having equal force, and hereunto affix their seals.

DONE at Paris, the twenty-seventh day of August in the year one thousand nine hundred and twenty-eight.

2. MAXIM LITVINOV: THE ETHIOPIAN CRISIS*

Benito Mussolini hoped to promote Italy's role as a dominant power in the Mediterranean. In his view it was essential for Italy to expand its African empire. In 1935 Italian forces invaded Ethiopia and produced an international crisis. Although the League of Nations imposed minor economic sanctions on Italy, no embargo was placed on oil and Mussolini's ambitions were not severely curbed by the League's action. Before the international organization could apply more substantial economic pressures, Ethiopia had been conquered. Within months, the League recognized the *fait accompli,* and Adolf Hitler used the international crisis to remilitarize the Rhineland in contravention of the Versailles Treaty.

The following selection is from a speech of July 1, 1936, by the Soviet Foreign Minister, Maxim Litvinov (1876–1951), to the League of Nations Assembly. Why were the sanctions imposed by the League ineffective, and what sanctions did Litvinov advocate? Which members of the League did Litvinov imply were especially to blame for the failure of collective security in the Ethiopian crisis? What proposals did Litvinov offer to make the future conduct of the League effective?

We have met here to complete a page in the history of the League of Nations, a page in the history of international life which it will be impossible for us to read without a feeling of bitterness. We have to liquidate a course of action which was begun in fulfilment of our obligations as Members of the League to guarantee the independence of one of our fellow-Members, but which was not carried to its conclusion. Each of us must feel his measure of responsibility and of blame, which is not identical for all, and which depends, not only on what each of us did in fact, but also on the measure of our readiness to support every common action required by the circumstances....

However, sooner than might have been expected, the moment came when the necessity for reconsidering the measures adopted at Geneva, from the angle of their serving any useful purpose, became absolutely clear. That moment was when the resistance of the valiant Ethiopian troops was broken, when the Emperor and Government of Ethiopia left their territory, and when a considerable portion of their territory was occupied by the Italian army. It appeared then indubitable that, by economic sanctions alone, it would be impossible to drive the Italian army out of Ethiopia and restore the independence of that country, and that such an objective could only be attained by more serious sanctions, including those of a military nature.

* "Extracts from a Statement by Litvinov at the League of Nations Assembly on the Italo-Abyssinian Dispute" in Jane Degras, ed., *Soviet Documents on Foreign Policy* (3 vols.; London: Oxford University Press, 1953), III, 194–99. Reprinted by permission.

Such measures could only be considered if one or several States could be found which, in virtue of their geographical position and special interests, would agree to bear the main brunt of a military encounter. Such States were not to be found among us; and even if they had been found, the other States, before deciding on any particular degree of co-operation in serious measures, would require guarantees that similar co-operation could also be counted upon in other cases of opposing the aggressor. Such guarantees were all the more necessary because some actions and statements of one European State, whose aggressive intentions leave no room for doubt—indeed, are openly proclaimed by that State itself—indicated an accelerated rate of preparations for aggression in more than one direction. The attitude of some countries to these actions, and the lenient treatment accorded to their authors, shook the belief that those guarantees which I have just mentioned could be immediately secured. In view of these circumstances, I came to the conclusion, even during the May session of the Council of the League, that the further application of economic sanctions was useless, and that it was impossible to afford any practical aid to Ethiopia in this way. It seems that this conclusion was reached by nearly all Members of the League.

I speak of the necessity for every Member of the League now to realise its individual responsibility for the lack of success of the common action undertaken in defence of the independence of a fellow-Member of the League, because, both inside the League and outside it, there have been attempts to ascribe this lack of success to the League Covenant, to its defects and to the present composition of the League. From this are drawn far-reaching conclusions, which may lead to the result that, together with Ethiopian independence, the League itself may turn out to have been buried as well. Such attempts and conclusions must be decisively rejected.

We find ourselves face to face with the fact that the League of Nations has proved unable to secure for one of its Members the territorial integrity and political independence provided for by Article 10 of the Covenant, and today is able only to express to that Member its platonic sympathy. We cannot tranquilly and indifferently pass by this crying fact; we must analyse it, and draw from it all the lessons requisite to prevent similar cases for the future. . . .

I assert that Article 16 equipped the League of Nations with such powerful weapons that, in the event of their being fully applied, every aggression can be broken. Moreover, the very conviction that they may be applied may rob the aggressor of his zeal to put his criminal intentions into practice.

The melancholy experience of the Italo-Ethiopian conflict does not contradict this assertion: on the contrary. In this particular case, whether because this was the first experiment in the application of collective measures; whether because some considered that this case has particular characteristics; whether because it coincided with the preparations elsewhere for aggression on a much larger scale, to which Europe had to devote special attention; whether for these or other reasons, it is a fact that not only was the whole terrible mechanism of Article 16 not brought into play, but from the very outset there was a manifest striving to confine the action taken to the barest minimum. Even economic sanctions were limited in their scope and their function, and even in this limited scope sanctions were not applied by all Members of the League. . . .

Given all these restrictions, sanctions could have been effective only in the event of their more prolonged application side by side with the military resistance of Ethiopia herself. The latter, however, was broken down much sooner than our most authoritative sources of information anticipated.

In such circumstances, it may be said that Members of the League of Nations, for one reason or another, refrained from bringing Article 16 completely into play. But it does not follow from this that Article 16 itself is a failure.

Some are inclined to attribute the failure of League action to the absence from it of some countries, or its insufficiently universal character. We see, however, that not every Member of the League took part in sanctions. There is no reason to believe that sanctions would have been endorsed by those States which left the League, since they rejected the very foundations of the League, and particularly the presence of Articles 10 and 16 in the Covenant. Their membership of the League would only have facilitated the still further disorganisation of our ranks, and would have acted rather as a demoralising factor than otherwise. On the other hand, we see from the example of the United States of America that the League of Nations may reckon on non-members of the League in applying Article 16, and reckon with them all the more, the more energetically it acts itself. Thus we see that it is not in the imperfections of the League Covenant that we must seek the causes of the failure to grant adequate aid to Ethiopia, nor yet in the lack of universality in the League. . . .

We are asked at all cost to restore to the League States which have left it only because they see obstacles to the fulfilment of their aggressive intentions in the Covenant, in Articles 10 and 16, in sanctions. We are told: "Throw Article 10 out of the Covenant, throw out Article 16, renounce sanctions, reject collective security, and then former Members of the League may return to our ranks, and the League will become universal." In other words: "Let us make the League safe for aggressors."

I say that we don't need such a League, we don't need a League which, with all its universality, is safe for aggressors, since such a League, from an instrument of peace, will turn into its very opposite. At best, by depriving the League of the functions of collective security, we should be turning it into a debating society or a charitable institution unworthy of the name of League of Nations, unworthy of the resources spent on it, and not answering to those hopes and anticipations which are centred upon it.

For my part, I would propose that the Covenant be adapted, not to the frame of mind of any particular category of people, any particular statesmen or temporary rulers, but to the frame of mind of the millions of people in all countries and in all continents—those who are rightly called humanity and who demand the maintenance of peace at all cost and its defence by all means. It is not the Covenant which we have to degrade, but people whom we have to educate and bring up to the level of its lofty ideas. We must strive for the universality of the League, but not make it safe for the aggressor for the sake of that universality. On the contrary, every new Member, every old Member wishing to return to it, must read over its doorway, "All hope of aggression with impunity abandon, ye who enter here."

Let us be frank. The League of Nations is not going through its first reverse by any means. There have been not less, but even more striking cases of military attacks by one Member of the League on another when the League did not react at all and left the victim of aggression face to face with the aggressor in an unequal struggle. There was no question then of the Covenant being unsuitable, or of revising it. If there were no grounds for such actions then, there are still less today. For my part, I prefer the League which attempts to afford even some kind of aid to the victim of aggression, albeit unsuccessfully, to a League which shuts its eyes to aggression and calmly passes by.

I consider that the League made a tremendous step forward when the overwhelming majority of its Members, regardless of substantial material sacrifices, came to the assistance—even unsuccessfully—of a fellow-Member who was attacked, instead of busying itself solely with sending the dispute from committee to sub-committee, and despatching commissions of enquiry, as has happened in other cases. In other words, the frame of mind of the Member States has been improved considerably, and this justifies our hope that next time it will rise to the full level of League ideas, and the victim will be saved from the aggressor altogether.

I am far from idealising the Covenant. Its imperfections consist, not so much in its articles as in its omissions and obscurities. Therefore, one has to speak, not of reforming the Covenant, but of making it more precise and of reinforcing it. I consider it, for instance, a serious omission that a definition of aggression is absent from the Covenant, a fact which, in the Italo-Ethiopian conflict, enabled some Members of the League to refuse to participate in sanctions at the very beginning. There is no clarity on the question of what organ of the League registers the fact of aggression. There is no clarity as to the binding character of decisions taken by League organs in the matter of sanctions.

We must put an end to the situation in which references to sovereignty and constitutional formalities serve as obstacles to the execution of international undertakings. Article 16 must remain untouched. Economic sanctions must remain obligatory for all Members of the League. Only when sanctions are obligatory will be removed the apprehension and mistrust that if, in a certain case, certain States which have no direct interest in the conflict undergo considerable sacrifices, in another case other disinterested States will act with less idealism.

What is necessary is confidence that in all cases of aggression, independent of the degree of interest in the particular conflict, sanctions will be applied by all, and this can be attained only when sanctions are obligatory. I consider this circumstance to be the principal cause of the reverse sustained by the League in the Italo-Ethiopian conflict. It may be possible to conceive of individual cases—very rare, it is true—when aggression may be stopped by economic sanctions alone; but I recognise that, in the majority of cases, economic sanctions must march parallel with military action. In the ideal League of Nations, military sanctions as well as economic sanctions ought to be binding on all.

But, if we cannot as yet rise to such heights of international solidarity, we ought to see that every continent, and Europe, if only as a beginning, should be covered with a net work of regional pacts, in virtue of which individual groups of States would undertake to defend particular regions from the aggressor, and the fulfilment of these regional obligations would be considered equivalent to the fulfilment of obligations under the Covenant and would have the full support of all the Members of the League. These regional pacts should not replace, but should supplement the League Covenant, otherwise they would amount in effect to the pre-war military alliances.

These are the directions in which I conceive of the perfection and reinforcement of the League of Nations, and my Government is ready to co-operate to the utmost with other Members of the League in achieving this. . . .

3. THE HOSSBACH MEMORANDUM*

The postwar trial of Nazi war criminals at Nürnberg, beginning in 1946, sought to establish an accurate picture of the background and causes of the Second World War. One of the most significant pieces of evidence about the designs and plans of Adolf Hitler was the so-called Hossbach Memorandum. This document recorded the course of a special conference called by the Führer in the Reich Chancellery on November 10, 1937, and was drawn up by the secretary of the meeting, Colonel Hossbach.

According to Hitler, what were the goals of German foreign policy in the immediate future? What efforts must be made to achieve those goals? How correct was Hitler's analysis of British and French policy?

Berlin, 10 Nov 1937

Notes on the Conference in the Reichskanzlei
on 5 Nov 37 from 1615—2030 hours

Present: The Fuehrer and Reich Chancellor
The Reichsminister for War, Generalfeldmarschall
v. Blomberg
The C-in-C Army, Generaloberst Freiherr von
Fritsch
The C-in-C Navy, Generaladmiral Dr. h. c. Raeder
The C-in-C Luftwaffe, Generaloberst Goering
The Reichsminister for Foreign Affairs Freiherr v.
Neurath
Oberst Hossbach

The Fuehrer stated initially that the subject matter of today's conference was of such high importance, that its further detailed discussion would probably take place in Cabinet sessions. However, he, the Fuehrer, had decided NOT to discuss this matter in the larger circle of the Reich Cabinet, because of its importance. His subsequent statements were the result of detailed deliberations and of the experiences of his 4½ years in Government; he desired to explain to those present his fundamental ideas on the possibilities and necessities of expanding our foreign policy and in the interests of a far-sighted policy he requested that

* Office of United States Chief of Counsel for Prosecution of Axis Criminality, *Nazi Conspiracy and Aggression* (Washington, 1946) III, 295–305.

his statements be looked upon in the case of his death as his last will and testament.

The Fuehrer then stated:

The aim of German policy is the security and the preservation of the nation, and its propagation. This is, consequently, a problem of space.

The German nation is composed of 85 million people, which, because of the number of individuals and the compactness of habitation, form a homogeneous European racial body which cannot be found in any other country. On the other hand, it justifies the demand for larger living space more than for any other nation. If no political body exists in space, corresponding to the German racial body, then that is the consequence of several centuries of historical development, and should this political condition continue to exist, it will represent the greatest danger to the preservation of the German nation [Volkstum] at its present high level. An arrest of the deterioration of the German element in Austria and Czechoslovakia is just as little possible as the preservation of the present state in Germany itself. Instead of growth, sterility will be introduced, and as a consequence, tensions of a social nature will appear after a number of years, because political and philosophical ideas are of a permanent nature only as long as they are able to produce the basis for the realization of the actual claim of existence of a nation. The German future is therefore dependent exclusively on the solution of the need for living space. Such a solution can be sought naturally only for a limited period, about 1-3 generations.

Before touching upon the question of solving the need for living space, it must be decided whether a solution of the German position with a good future can be attained, either by way of an autarchy or by way of an increased share in universal commerce and industry.

Autarchy [National Sovereignty]: Execution will be possible only with strict National-Socialist State policy, which is the basis; assuming this can be achieved the results are as follows:

A. In the sphere of raw materials, only limited, but NOT total autarchy can be attained:

1. Wherever coal can be used for the extraction of raw materials autarchy is feasible.

2. In the case of ores the position is much more difficult. Requirements in iron and light metals can be covered by ourselves. Copper and tin, however, can NOT.

3. Cellular materials can be covered by ourselves as long as sufficient wood supplies exist. A permanent solution is not possible.

4. Edible fats—possible.

B. In the case of foods, the question of an autarchy must be answered with a definite "NO".

The general increase of living standards, compared with 30-40 years ago, brought about a simultaneous increase of the demand for an increase of personal consumption even among the producers, the farmers, themselves. The proceeds from the production increase in agriculture have been used for covering the increase in demands, therefore they represent no absolute increase in production. A further increase in production by making greater demands on the soil is *not* possible because it already shows signs of deterioration due to the use of artificial fertilizers, and it is therefore certain that, even with the greatest possible increase in production, participation in the world market could NOT be avoided.

The considerable expenditure of foreign currency to secure food by import, even in periods when harvests are good, increases catastrophically when the harvest is really poor. The possibility of this catastrophe increases correspondingly to the increase in population, and the annual 560,000 excess in births would bring about an increased consumption in bread, because the child is a greater bread eater than the adult.

Permanently to counter the difficulties of food supplies by lowering the standard of living and by rationalization is impossible in a continent which had developed an approximately equivalent standard of living. As the solving of the unemployment problem has brought into effect the complete power of consumption, some small corrections in our agricultural home production will be possible, but NOT a wholesale alteration of the standard of food consumption. Consequently autarchy becomes impossible, specifically in the sphere of food supplies as well as generally.

Participation in World Economy. There are limits to this which we are unable to transgress. The market fluctuations would be an obstacle to a secure foundation of the German position; international commercial agreements do NOT offer any guarantee for practical execution. It must be considered on principle that since the World War (1914–18) an industrialization has taken place in countries which formerly exported food. We live in a period of economic empires, in which the tendency to colonize again approaches the condition which originally motivated colonization; in Japan and Italy economic motives are the basis of their will to expand, the economic need will also drive Germany to it. Countries outside the great economic empires have special difficulties in expanding economically.

The upward tendency, which has been caused in world economy, due to armament competition, can never form a permanent basis for an economic settlement, and this latter is also hampered by the economic disruption caused by Bolshevism. It is a pronounced military weakness of those States who base their existence on export. As our exports and imports are carried out over those sea lanes which are ruled by Britain, it is more a question of security of transport rather than one of foreign currency, and this explains the great weakness in our food situation in wartime. The only way out, and one which may appear imaginary, is the securing of greater living space, an endeavor which at all times has been the cause of the formation of states and of movements of nations. It is explicable that this tendency finds no interest in Geneva and in satisfied States. Should the security of our food position be our foremost thought, then the space required for this can only be sought in Europe, but we will not copy liberal capitalist policies which rely on exploiting colonies. It is NOT a case of conquering people, but of conquering agriculturally useful space. It would also be more to the purpose to seek raw material producing territory in Europe directly adjoining the Reich and not overseas, and this solution would have to be brought into effect in one or two generations. What would be required at a later date over and above this must be left to subsequent generations. The development of great world-wide national bodies is naturally a slow process and the

German people, with its strong racial root, has for this purpose the most favorable foundations in the heart of the European Continent. The history of all times—Roman Empire, British Empire—has proved that every space expansion can only be effected by breaking resistance and taking risks. Even setbacks are unavoidable; neither formerly nor today has space been found without an owner; the attacker always comes up against the proprietor.

The question for Germany is where the greatest possible conquest could be made at lowest cost.

German politics must reckon with its two hateful enemies, England and France, to whom a strong German colossus in the center of Europe would be intolerable. Both these states would oppose a further reinforcement of Germany, both in Europe and overseas, and in this opposition they would have the support of all parties. Both countries would view the building of German military strongpoints overseas as a threat to their overseas communications, as a security measure for German commerce, and retrospectively a strengthening of the German position in Europe.

England is NOT in a position to cede any of her colonial possessions to us owing to the resistance which she experiences in the Dominions. After the loss of prestige which England has suffered owing to the transfer of Abyssinia to Italian ownership, a return of East Africa can no longer be expected. Any resistance on England's part would at best consist in the readiness to satisfy our colonial claims by taking away colonies which at the present moment are NOT in British hands, e.g. Angola. French favors would probably be of the same nature.

A serious discussion regarding the return of colonies to us could be considered only at a time when England is in a state of emergency and the German Reich is strong and well-armed. The Fuehrer does not share the opinion that the Empire is unshakable. Resistance against the Empire is to be found less in conquered territories than amongst its competitors. The British Empire and the Roman Empire cannot be compared with one another in regard to durability; since the Punic Wars the latter did not have a serious political enemy. Only the dissolving effects which originated in Christendom, and the signs of age which creep into all states, made it possible for the Ancient Germans to subjugate Ancient Rome.

Alongside the British Empire today a number of States exist which are stronger than it. The British Mother Country is able to defend its colonial possessions only allied with other States and NOT by its own power. How could England alone, for example, defend Canada against an attack by America or its Far Eastern interests against an attack by Japan.

The singling out of the British Crown as the bearer of Empire unity is in itself an admission that the universal empire cannot be maintained permanently by power politics. The following are significant pointers in this respect.

a. Ireland's tendency for independence.

b. Constitutional disputes in India where England, by her half-measures, left the door open for Indians at a later date to utilize the nonfulfillment of constitutional promises as a weapon against Britain.

c. The weakening of the British position in the Far East by Japan.

d. The opposition in the Mediterranean to Italy which—by virtue of its history, driven by necessity and led by a genius—expands its power position and must consequently infringe British interests to an increasing extent. The outcome of the Abyssinian War is a loss of prestige for Britain which Italy is endeavoring to increase by stirring up discontent in the Mohammedan world.

It must be established in conclusion that the Empire cannot be held permanently by power politics by 45 million Britons, in spite of all the solidity of her ideals. The proportion of the populations in the Empire, compared with that of the Motherland is 9:1, and it should act as a warning to us that if we expand in space, we must NOT allow the level of our population to become too low.

France's position is more favorable than that of England. The French Empire is better placed geographically, the population of its colonial possessions represents a potential military increase. But France is faced with difficulties of internal politics. At the present time only 10 per cent approximately of the nations have parliamentary governments whereas 90 per cent of them have totalitarian governments. Nevertheless we have to take the following into our political considerations as power factors: Britain, France, Russia and the adjoining smaller States.

The German question can be solved only by way of force, and this is never without risk. The battles of Frederick the Great for Silesia, and Bismarck's wars against Austria and France had been a tremendous risk and the speed of Prussian action in 1870 had prevented Austria from participating in the war. If we place the decision to apply force with risk at the head of the following expositions, then we are left to reply to the questions "when" and "how". In this regard we have to decide upon three different cases.

Case 1. Period 1943–45. After this we can only expect a change for the worse. The re-arming of the Army, the Navy and the Air Force, as well as the formation of the Officers' Corps, are practically concluded. Our material equipment and armaments are modern, with further delay the danger of their becoming out-of-date will increase. In particular the secrecy of "special weapons" cannot always be safeguarded. Enlistment of reserves would be limited to the current recruiting age groups and an addition from older untrained groups would be no longer available.

In comparison with the re-armament, which will have been carried out at that time by the other nations, we shall decrease in relative power. Should we not act until 1943/45, then, dependent on the absence of reserves, any year could bring about the food crisis, for the countering of which we do NOT possess the necessary foreign currency. This must be considered as a "point of weakness in the regime". Over and above that, the world will anticipate our action and will increase counter-measures yearly. Whilst other nations isolate themselves we should be forced on the offensive.

What the actual position would be in the years 1943–1945 no one knows today. It is certain, however, that we can wait no longer.

On the one side the large armed forces, with the necessity for securing their upkeep, the aging of the Nazi movement and of its leaders, and on the other side the prospect of a lowering of the standard of living and a drop in the birth rate, leaves us no other choice than to act. If the Fuehrer is still living, then it will be his irrevocable decision to solve the German space problem no later than 1943–45. The necessity for action before 1943–45 will come under consideration in cases 2 and 3.

Case 2. Should the social tensions in France lead to an internal political crisis of such dimensions that it absorbs the French Army and thus renders it incapable for employment in war against Germany, then the time for action against Czechoslovakia has come.

Case 3. It would be equally possible to act against Czechoslovakia if France should be so tied up by a war against another State, that it cannot "proceed" against Germany.

For the improvement of our military political position it must be our first aim, in every case of entanglement by war, to conquer Czechoslovakia and Austria simultaneously, in order to remove any threat from the flanks in case of a possible advance Westwards. In the case of a conflict with France it would hardly be necessary to assume that Czechoslovakia would declare war on the same day as France. However, Czechoslovakia's desire to participate in the war will increase proportionally to the degree to which we are being weakened. Its actual participation could make itself felt by an attack on Silesia, either towards the North or the West.

Once Czechoslovakia is conquered—and a mutual frontier, Germany-Hungary is obtained—then a neutral attitude by Poland in a German-French conflict could more easily be relied upon. Our agreements with Poland remain valid only as long as Germany's strength remains unshakable; should Germany have any setbacks then an attack by Poland against East Prussia, perhaps also against Pomerania, and Silesia, must be taken into account.

Assuming a development of the situation, which would lead to a planned attack on our part in the years 1943–45, then the behavior of France, Poland and Russia would probably have to be judged in the following manner:

The Fuehrer believes personally that in all probability England and perhaps also France have already silently written off Czechoslovakia, and that they have got used to the idea that this question would one day be cleaned up by Germany. The difficulties in the British Empire and the prospect of being entangled in another long-drawn-out European War, were decisive factors in the non-participation of England in a war against Germany. The British attitude would certainly NOT remain without influence on France's attitude. An attack by France without British support is hardly probable assuming that its offensive would stagnate along our Western fortifications. Without England's support, it would also NOT be necessary to take into consideration a march by France through Belgium and Holland, and this would also not have to be reckoned with by us in case of a conflict with France, as in every case it would have as consequence the enmity of Great Britain. Naturally, we should in every case have to bar our frontier during the operation of our attacks against Czechoslovakia and Austria. It must be taken into consideration here that Czechoslovakia's defence measures will increase in strength from year to year, and that a consolidation of the inside values of the Austrian army will also be effected in the course of years. Although the population of Czechoslovakia in the first place is not a thin one, the embodiment of Czechoslovakia and Austria would nevertheless constitute the conquest of food for 5–6 million people, on the basis that a compulsory emigration of 2 million from Czechoslovakia and of 1 million from Austria could be carried out. The annexation of the two States to Germany militarily and politically would constitute a considerable relief, owing to shorter and better frontiers, the freeing of fighting personnel for other purposes and the possibility of re-constituting new armies up to a strength of about 12 Divisions, representing a new division per 1 million population.

No opposition to the removal of Czechoslovakia is expected on the part of Italy; however, it cannot be judged today what would be her attitude in the Austrian question since it would depend largely on whether the Duce were alive at the time or not.

The measure and speed of our action would decide Poland's attitude. Poland will have little inclination to enter the war against a victorious Germany, with Russia in its rear.

Military participation by Russia must be countered by the speed of our operations; it is a question whether this need be taken into consideration at all in view of Japan's attitude.

Should Case 2 occur—paralyzation of France by a Civil War—then the situation should be utilized *at any time* for operations against Czechoslovakia, as Germany's most dangerous enemy would be eliminated.

The Fuehrer sees Case 3 looming nearer; it could develop from the existing tensions in the Mediterranean, and should it occur he has firmly decided to make use of it any time, perhaps even as early as 1938.

Following recent experiences in the course of the events of the war in Spain, the Fuehrer does NOT see an early end to hostilities there. Taking into consideration the time required for past offensives by Franco, a further three years duration of war is within the bounds of possibility. On the other hand, from the German point of view a 100 per cent victory by Franco is not desirable; we are more interested in a continuation of the war and preservation of the tensions in the Mediterranean. Should Franco be in sole possession of the Spanish Peninsula it would mean the end of Italian intervention and the presence of Italy on the Balearic Isles. As our interests are directed towards continuing the war in Spain, it must be the task of our future policy to strengthen Italy in her fight to hold on to the Balearic Isles. However, a solidification of Italian positions on the Balearic Isles can NOT be tolerated either by France or by England and could lead to a war by France and England against Italy, in which case Spain, if entirely in white (*i.e.* Franco's) hands, could participate on the side of Italy's enemies. A subjugation of Italy in such a war appears very unlikely. Additional raw materials could be brought to Italy via Germany. The Fuehrer believes that Italy's military strategy would be to remain on the defensive against France on the Western frontier and carry out operations against France from Libya against North African French colonial possessions.

As a landing of French-British troops on the Italian coast can be discounted, and as a French offensive via the Alps to Upper Italy would be extremely difficult and would probably stagnate before the strong Italian fortifications, French lines of communication by the Italian fleet will to a great extent paralyze the transport of fighting personnel from North Africa to France, so that at its frontiers with Italy and Germany France will have at its disposal solely the metropolitan fighting forces.

If Germany profits from this war by disposing of the Czechoslovakian and the Austrian questions, the probability must be assumed that England—being at war with Italy—would not decide to commence operations against Germany. Without British support a warlike action by France against Germany is not to be anticipated.

The date of our attack on Czechoslovakia and Austria must be made dependent on the course of the Italian-English-French war and would not be simultaneous with the commencement of military agreements with Italy, but of full independence and, by exploiting this unique favorable opportunity he wishes to begin to carry out operations against Czechoslovakia. The attack on Czechoslovakia would have to take place with the "speed of lightning" [blitzartig schnell].

Feldmarschall von Blomberg and Generaloberst von Fritsch in giving their estimate on the situation, repeatedly pointed out that England and France must not appear as our enemies, and they stated that the war with Italy would NOT bind the French army to such an extent that it would NOT be in a position to commence operations on our Western frontier with superior forces. Generaloberst von Fritsch estimated the French forces which would presumably be employed on the Alpine frontier against Italy to be in the region of 20 divisions, so that a strong French superiority would still remain on our Western frontier. The French would, according to German reasoning, attempt to advance into the Rhineland. We should consider the lead which France has got in mobilization, and quite apart from the very small value of our then existing fortifications —which was pointed out particularly by Generalfeldmarschall von Blomberg— the four motorized divisions which had been laid down for the West would be more or less incapable of movement. With regard to our offensive in a South-Easterly direction, Feldmarschall von Blomberg draws special attention to the strength of the Czechoslovakian fortifications, the building of which had assumed the character of a Maginot line and which would present extreme difficulties to our attack.

Generaloberst von Fritsch mentioned that it was the purpose of a study which he had laid on for this winter to investigate the possibilities of carrying out operations against Czechoslovakia with special consideration of the conquest of the Czechoslovakian system of fortifications; the Generaloberst also stated that owing to the prevailing conditions he would have to relinquish his leave abroad, which was to begin on 10 November. This intention was countermanded by the Fuehrer who gave as a reason that the possibility of the conflict was not to be regarded as being so imminent. In reply to the remark by the Minister for Foreign Affairs, that an Italian-English-French conflict be not as near as the Fuehrer appeared to assume, the Fuehrer stated that the date which appeared to him to be a possibility was summer 1938. In reply to statements by Generalfeldmarschall von Blomberg and Generaloberst von Fritsch regarding England and France's attitude, the Fuehrer repeated his previous statements and said that he was convinced of Britain's non-participation and that consequently he did not believe in military action by France against Germany. Should the

Mediterranean conflict already mentioned lead to a general mobilization in Europe, then we should have to commence operations against Czechoslovakia immediately. If, however, the powers who are not participating in the war should declare their disinterestedness, then Germany would, for the time being, have to side with this attitude.

In view of the information given by the Fuehrer, Generaloberst Goering considered it imperative to think of a reduction or abandonment of our military undertaking in Spain. The Fuehrer agreed to this in so far as he believed this decision should be postponed for a suitable date.

The second part of the discussion concerned material armament questions.

(Signed) HOSSBACH

4. MUNICH—TWO EDITORIALS FROM "THE TIMES"*

Although a union of Germany and Austria was forbidden by the Versailles Treaty, Hitler forced the resignation of Chancellor Kurt von Schuschnigg (1897–   ) in March 1938 and annexed Austria to Germany. The western powers contented themselves with protests and rationalized that Austria was a German state which had always desired an *Anschluss.* Within months, Hitler began pressing the Czechoslovakian government to accept the extreme demands of the German minority in the Sudentenland. Britain and France were concerned that Hitler would resort to force and send the German army against Czechoslovakia, initiating a general war. Although France had an alliance with the Czechs, the French were unwilling to move without British help. Neville Chamberlain (1869–1940), the British Prime Minister, met with Hitler, who continually expanded his original demands. Chamberlain finally agreed to urge Czechoslovakia to cede the Sudetenland, inhabited largely by Germans but containing most of Czechoslovakia's defenses, to Germany. Britain, France, Italy, and Germany—but not Czechoslovakia—met at Munich in September 1938, to solemnize the appeasement of the German dictator, an act which many Europeans believed would preserve peace. A few months later, in violation of the Munich agreements, Hitler startled the West by helping destroy the remnants of Czechoslovakian independence.

The following selection consists of two editorials from *The Times* (London) just after Chamberlain's return from Munich. What concessions had Hitler made to Chamberlain, according to *The Times* editorial? Why did *The Times* urge the British public to support the partition of Czechoslovakia in the absence of consultations with the Czech government? What, according to *The Times,* were the best procedures for enabling "democracy to survive in a world of dictatorships"? Why did *The Times* insist that "the policy of international appeasement must of course be pressed forward"?

A NEW DAWN

No conqueror returning from a victory on the battlefield has come home adorned with nobler laurels than MR. CHAMBERLAIN from Munich yesterday: and KING and people alike have shown by the manner of their reception their sense

* "A New Dawn," *The Times* (London), October 1, 1938, p. 13; "Munich and After," October 3, 1938, p. 11. Reprinted by permission.

of his achievement. The terms of settlement in the Czech-German dispute, reached in the small hours of the morning and published in the latter issues of *The Times* of yesterday, had been seen to deliver the world from a menace of extreme horror while doing rough-and-ready justice between the conflicting claims. Yet even this great service to humanity was already beginning to appear as the lesser half of the PRIME MINISTER's work in Munich. He himself announced it as the prelude to a larger settlement. He had not only relegated an agonizing episode to the past; he had found for the nations a new hope for the future. The joint declaration made by HERR HITLER and MR. CHAMBERLAIN proclaims that "the desire of the two peoples never to go to war with one another again" shall henceforth govern the whole of their relationships. There have been times when such a manifesto could be dismissed as a pious platitude, likely to be forgotten long before an occasion could arise for it to be practically tested. The present, it is fair to think is not such a time. The two statesmen plainly recognize in their declaration that there are still sources of difference between Great Britain and Germany, which for the sake of the peace of Europe must be settled at an early date; it is in direct relation to these that they pledge themselves to the methods of peaceful consultation, and so demonstrate that they expect to be taken at the full value of their word. By inserting a specific reference to the Anglo-German Naval Agreement, as well as to the negotiations so happily concluded at Munich, the FÜHRER reminds us of an earnest of his good intentions, which the British people, in the new atmosphere, will readily acknowledge.

Civilization had been so near to the brink of collapse that any peaceful issue from the dispute of the last months would have been an overwhelming relief; but close examination of the Munich terms, in particular of the geographical adjustments, shows that they constitute not only a settlement but a hopeful settlement. That they should be bitterly resented in Czechoslovakia must add to the profound sympathy which has always been felt in England with one of the smaller and, as it seemed to many, the more promising countries emerging from the Peace Treaties. Yet the loss of the Sudeten territories had long been unavoidable, nor was it desirable that it should be avoided. That was the opinion not only of all who believed in the theory of self-determination, but of LORD RUNCIMAN, who had acquired, from a position of unique and informed detachment, an intimate knowledge of the whole problem in practice. At any rate—the Prague Government, the only dissentient, having been induced to acquiesce in secession—the issue was narrowed down to finding the means for an orderly execution of an agreed plan. That on such an issue the whole world should be plunged into war was the monstrous prospect that had to be contemplated until less than three days ago. It would inevitably have been realized if HERR HITLER had insisted on a spectacular "conquest" of the Sudetenland by German troops. The Czechs would certainly have resisted in arms, nor would any Power have had the right to attempt to dissuade them. France would have been drawn in by direct obligations to Czechoslovakia: Great Britain and the Soviet Union would have been certain to come to the help of France; and so the widening conflict would have involved all those peoples throughout the world who had watched with ever-increasing revulsion the development of brutal methods of national aggrandisement, and thought that the time had come to make a stand against them.

These methods have been publicly renounced by their principal exponents, to whom the peace loving peoples should be ready to give full credit for their professions. But, at the moment when the current racing towards the precipice seemed irresistible, it was the leadership of the BRITISH PRIME MINISTER that showed how immense were the forces ranged on the side of reason against violence. The gathering urgency of persuasion was reinforced by unmistakable proofs of resolution for defence. France mobilized her army and manned her impregnable lines. Preparation in England, though slower in starting, as is the national habit, became at the crucial moment universal and formidable. The Fleet was mobilized; the anti-aircraft forces were brought into readiness; and civilians, taking post for emergency under voluntary as well as official schemes, showed plainly that the nation would not flinch. The Dominions were prompt to affirm their unanimity with the Mother Country. These things were not a threat, nor is it to be supposed that the GERMAN CHANCELLOR would yield to threats, but there is no doubt that the evidence that MR. CHAMBERLAIN offered concession from strength and not from weakness won him a respect that might not otherwise have been accorded. Meanwhile other authoritative voices were uplifted for peace: the PRESIDENT of the UNITED STATES spoke out for humanity, and the ITALIAN DUCE, responding to the PRIME MINISTER's leadership, acknowledged that peace is a supreme interest to dictators as to other national rulers. HERR HITLER deferred, as no man need be ashamed of doing, to the protest of the whole world against war.

This was the crucial moment. That peace would follow the Munich negotiations was almost a foregone conclusion once a dictator had made the difficult renunciation of consenting to treat after he had announced his last word. The message so dramatically brought to MR. CHAMBERLAIN in the House of Commons marked the true claims and ended the threat of war. In the upshot both sides have made concessions. HERR HITLER has yielded important points of substance, consenting, it seems, to modify in a number of places the new frontiers that he claimed in the Godesberg memorandum. A dictator could hardly recede from the intention so loudly proclaimed of at least entering his new territories to-day; but the German troops will make a "token" entry, and only move by defined stages occupying several days, up to the limits agreed. By granting so much the Czechs suffer no practical loss, and they gain much by the acceptance of international control for the plebiscites that are to be held in areas of mixed race.

By the terms thus concluded the most dangerous threat of war in Europe is at last removed, and by the joint declaration we are given the hope that others will be peacefully eliminated. That twofold achievement, by common consent, we owe first and foremost to the PRIME MINISTER. Had the Government of the United Kingdom been in less resolute hands it is as certain as it can be that war, incalculable in its range, would have broken out against the wishes of every people concerned. The horror of such a catastrophe was not least in Germany. So much is clear from the immense popular enthusiasm with which MR. CHAMBERLAIN was greeted on each of his three visits; a crowd of that disciplined nation does not break through a police cordon to acclaim a foreign statesman

out of conventional politeness. Indeed these visits seem to have increased the
FÜHRER's understanding of his own people's sentiments, with a definite effect
upon his policy. Let us hope that he may go on to see the wisdom of allowing
them at all times to know the sentiments of other peoples instead of imposing
between them a smoke-screen of ignorance and propaganda. For our own nation
it remains to show our gratitude to MR. CHAMBERLAIN, chiefly by learning the
lessons taught by the great dangers through which we have been so finely led—
that only a people prepared to face the worst can through their leaders cause
peace to prevail in a crisis; but that the threat of ruin to civilization will recur
unless injustices are faced and removed in quiet times, instead of being left to
fester until it is too late for remedy. If these manifest truths, always recognized
yet so seldom applied, are allowed to guide the diplomacy of the coming
months, then we may at last expel from men's minds the deadly doctrine of
preventive war and labour with confidence for a preventive peace.

MUNICH AND AFTER

The message addressed by the KING to the nation this morning closes in the
right mood of reverent thanksgiving a period of incalculable peril. And a week
end that has brought seclusion even to the PRIME MINISTER, who was able to
escape for a few hours to Chequers on Saturday, has given the whole country a
pause for reflection, the results of which will find their most important expression in Parliament this afternoon and thereafter. This period of more leisurely
consideration has certainly not diminished the importance of the events that
culminated at Munich on Thursday night. The volume of applause for MR.
CHAMBERLAIN, which continues to grow throughout the globe, registers a popular
judgment that neither politicians nor historians are likely to reverse. Meanwhile
German troops have crossed and obliterated a part of the frontier created at
Versailles. Their token entry into the Sudetenland has been orderly in manner
and limited in extent; since they have entered only the country of their kinsmen,
they have been received with popular acclamation. The Czech troops and
officials who withdrew before their coming did so with sullen resignation, as
was natural. But even the universal sympathy for a people who have made a
great sacrifice of pride and some surrender of material interest must not omit
to contrast this bloodless transfer of authority with what might have been the
alternative—a savage swarming of armies over a country that war could not
have saved and even a victorious peace would never have reconstituted in its
old form. Much as the Czechs have sacrificed, they also share in the universal
deliverance.

After so great an outpouring of thankfulness as filled the first hours after
the settlement was announced, some reaction was only to be expected. The
removal of the threat of war has already released controversy on the platform,
nor was it ever to be supposed that the unanimity of the people would be maintained at its recent level of enthusiasm and completeness. In Parliament to-day
there will certainly be abundant criticism: the Houses would be failing in their
function if there were not. There are still lacunae in the story of the last weeks
to be filled in; its manifold implications for the future must needs cause divergence of opinion. The resignation of a Minister shows that another side of the

question has been raised even within the Cabinet. But, if Parliament is truly to represent the people, there can surely be nothing like a vote of censure—and certainly not from the Labour Party. The peace concluded at Munich is a peace dictated at bottom by the peoples who would have suffered in case of war; and not least insistent, though with difficulty articulate, were the German people. One fundamental truth that MR. CHAMBERLAIN's daring diplomacy brought into the light was this—that even in a totalitarian State the people will have their influence in the last resort upon the party. The man who has arrested universal destruction by appealing to that truth need not fear that in his own country the cavillings of party will outweight the people's gratitude.

But, even if there is the inevitable reaction, there must be no retrograde step. Relief from intolerable strain cannot be followed by mere relapse into inertia. The lessons of the crisis are plain and urgent. The policy of international appeasement must of course be pressed forward, working through the peoples, who have shown that they desire it, and whose life depends on it. There must be appeasement not only of the strong but of the weak—of the State that has allowed itself to be weakened for the common good. Czechoslovakia has desired well of humanity, and it should be a first international responsibility not only to guarantee the contracted frontiers, but also to assist in solving the new problems that the settlement has imposed upon her. As between the greater Powers the field for necessary appeasement is wide. It may be hoped that there is truth in the rumours, first that the breach between France and Italy will shortly be closed, and afterwards that Great Britain, France, and Italy together may settle the other perilous problems concerning their interests and activities in the Mediterranean. If at the same time the declaration of MR. CHAMBERLAIN and HERR HITLER, at present bilateral, can be expanded to become in effect multi-lateral, the peoples of Western and Central Europe, for what declarations are worth, may have a new peace treaty without a new war.

But with the policy of appeasement must go the policy of preparation—preparation not so much for war as against war, since no nation can afford to be without its essential shield so long as other nations remain heavily armed. So much is clear from the movement of last week's negotiations—that the scale did not begin to tip in favour of peace until MR. CHAMBERLAIN was able to point with one hand to a mobilized Navy and a nation aroused to defence while he offered conciliation with the other. This awakening of the national spirit in the last fortnight has unquestionably been another determining factor in the crisis. Not only the universal rally to the call of authority in matters of self-defence, but the queues of young men at the recruiting stations of every branch of the fighting Services, have been worthy of the tradition of 1914. These things are taken for granted by our own people, having been repeated as a matter of course at every crisis that required them; but they always come as a surprise to foreign nations. In case of war we know—but the rest of the world does not know—that the entire people, with insignificant exceptions, will wish to serve the State. Having lived through the last month, they will surely be ready to give expression to this spirit lest a similar emergency should recur.

There is now, for example, time and opportunity to work out in practice to the fullest possible extent the ideal of National Service. Had war broken out last Saturday, then one of the first steps Parliament would have had to take would certainly have been to call on every subject, according to his capacity, to place his services at the disposal of his country. These services would have been given cheerfully; but it might have been too late. What is now required, as an essential precaution on which peace may some day depend, is such an organization of the man-power and woman-power of the nation as will enable us all to know in advance, and prepare for, the part that we shall play in emergency. To undertake some service should be compulsory; within such a scheme the tradition, rightly cherished, of the volunteer system should survive even the strain of war. The popular response last week to the call of the A.R.P. service was admirable, but it seemed a little to overshadow the rest. There is a vast complexity of other duties for civilians, as we learnt twenty years ago; our organization should provide for them all, and A.R.P. would fall into its proper place among them. Members of Parliament—and particularly those who are most ardent for "standing up to the dictators"—have an opportunity now, which they cannot in logic reject, of translating their professions into practice. It is not words alone, but hard work and self-sacrifice that will enable democracy to survive in a world of dictatorships, which have proved themselves at least to be capable of achieving their ends by different methods. And it is only through these same qualities of hard work and self-sacrifice that the world will reach the further goal, which is known to be MR. CHAMBERLAIN's dearest ambition, of an era when the race in armaments will be seen for the madness that it is and will be abandoned because it has ceased even to be profitable.

5. THE NAZI-SOVIET PACT*

Shortly before the First World War, Count von Schlieffen had meticulously prepared a plan of operations in the event of war. Assuming that Germany would be faced with a war on two fronts, Schlieffen had planned to secure a rapid initial victory in the west. But Schlieffen's timetable for the rapid capture of Paris failed, and German armies found themselves bogged down on both the eastern and western fronts. Adolf Hitler resolved not to be caught in a two-front war, and he was able to negotiate a non-aggression pact with the Soviet Union on August 23, 1939. What advantages did the Soviet Union gain by signing a ten-year non-aggression pact with Nazi Germany? What concessions did Hitler require from the Russians both in the pact itself and in the accompanying secret protocol? What "further political events" did Hitler clearly have in mind when he negotiated the second clause of the secret protocol?

TREATY OF NON-AGGRESSION BETWEEN GERMANY AND
THE UNION OF SOVIET SOCIALIST REPUBLICS

The Government of the German Reich and the Government of the Union of Soviet Socialist Republics, desirous of strengthening the cause of peace between Germany and the U.S.S.R., and proceeding from the fundamental provisions of the Treaty of Neutrality, which was concluded between Germany and the U.S.S.R. in April 1926, have reached the following agreement:

* "Treaty of Non-Aggression between Germany and the Union of Soviet Socialist Republics" in *Documents on German Foreign Policy, 1918–1945* (Publications of the Department of State, No. 6462; Washington, 1956), Series D, VII, 245–47.

ARTICLE I: The two Contracting Parties undertake the refrain from any act of violence, any aggressive action and any attack on each other either severally or jointly with other Powers.

ARTICLE II: Should one of the Contracting Parties become the object of belligerent action by a third Power, the other Contracting Party shall in no manner lend its support to this third Power.

ARTICLE III: The Governments of the two Contracting Parties will in future maintain continual contact with one another for the purpose of consultation in order to exchange information on problems affecting their common interests.

ARTICLE IV: Neither of the two Contracting Parties will join any grouping of Powers whatsoever which is aimed directly or indirectly at the other Party.

ARTICLE V.: Should disputes or conflicts arise between the Contracting Parties over questions of one kind or another, both Parties will settle these disputes or conflicts exclusively by means of a friendly exchange of views or if necessary by the appointment of arbitration commissions.

ARTICLE VI: The present Treaty shall be concluded for a period of ten years with the proviso that, in so far as one of the Contracting Parties does not denounce it one year before the expiry of this period, the validity of this Treaty shall be deemed to be automatically prolonged for another five years.

ARTICLE VII: The present treaty shall be ratified within the shortest possible time.[1] The instruments of ratification will be exchanged in Berlin. The treaty shall enter into force immediately upon signature.

Done in duplicate in the German and Russian languages.

Moscow, August 23, 1939.

For the Government   With full power of the
of the German Reich: Government of the U.S.S.R.
v. RIBBENTROP   V. MOLOTOV

SECRET ADDITIONAL PROTOCOL

On the occasion of the signature of the Non-Aggression Treaty between the German Reich and the Union of Soviet Socialist Republics, the undersigned plenipotentiaries of the two Parties discussed in strictly confidential conversations the question of the delimitation of their respective spheres of interest in Eastern Europe. These conversations led to the following result:

1. In the event of a territorial and political transformation in the territories belonging to the Baltic States (Finland, Estonia, Latvia, Lithuania), the northern frontier of Lithuania shall represent the frontier of the spheres of interest both of Germany and the U.S.S.R. In this connection the interest of Lithuania in the Vilna territory is recognized by both Parties.

2. In the event of a territorial and political transformation of the territories belonging to the Polish State, the spheres of interest of both Germany and the U.S.S.R. shall be bounded approximately by the line of the rivers, Narev, Vistula, and San.

The question whether the interests of both Parties make the maintenance of an independent Polish State appear desirable and how the frontiers of this State

1. Instruments of ratification were exchanged on September 24, 1939.

should be drawn can be definitely determined only in the course of further political developments.

In any case both Governments will resolve this question by means of a friendly understanding.

3. With regard to South-Eastern Europe, the Soviet side emphasizes its interest in Bessarabia. The German side declares complete political *désintéressement* in these territories.

4. This Protocol will be treated by both parties as strictly secret.

Moscow, August 23, 1939.

For the Government of the German Reich: v. RIBBENTROP	With full power of the Government of the U.S.S.R. V. MOLOTOV

6. HITLER'S SECRET CONVERSATIONS*

During the war, Adolf Hitler held supreme civil and military power in Germany. All subordinates, government officials, party leaders, and military officers acted in his name. A partial record of his wartime conversations with military and civilian personnel has been preserved, and excerpts from those conversations compose the following selection. What were Hitler's plans for Germany? What destiny did he plan for nations and peoples conquered by the "master race"? In what specific ways did Hitler propose to achieve "a collective harnessing of the efforts of the entire German people" for the building of a Thousand Year Reich? Compare the views expressed in his secret conversations with the doctrines which Hitler defended in *Mein Kampf*.

It's very important for the future that the Germans don't mingle with the Poles, so that the new Germanic blood may not be transmitted to the Polish ruling class. Himmler is right when he says that the Polish generals who genuinely put up a serious resistance in 1939 were, so to speak, exclusively of German descent. It's an accepted fact that it's precisely the best elements of our race who, as they lose awareness of their origin, add themselves to the ruling class of the country that has welcomed them. As for the elements of less value, they retain the characteristics of their ethnic group and remain faithful to their Germanic origin. The same caution is necessary towards the Czechs. They're skilled at not awakening the distrust of their occupiers, and are wonderful at playing the rôle of subjects. It's true they've had five centuries' experience of it! I saw them at work in Vienna during my youth. Arriving penniless and dragging their worn-out shoes over the streets of the city, they quickly acquired the Viennese accent —and one fine day one was quite surprised to see them installed in the key-positions.

We shall not win the peace, on the racial level, unless the Reich knows how to maintain a certain stature. Confronted with the United States, whose population is scarcely greater than ours, our strength lies in the fact that four-fifths of our people are of Germanic race. . . .

* *Hitler's Secret Conversations, 1941–1944*, trans. Norman Cameron and R. H. Stevens (New York: Farrar, Straus and Young, 1953), pp. 329, 344–45, 399–400, 445, 477. Reprinted by permission of Farrar, Straus & Giroux, Inc., and Weidenfeld & Nicolson Ltd.

One thing which it is essential to organise in the Russian territories is an efficient system of communications, which is vital both to the rational economic exploitation of the country and to the maintenance of control and order. The local inhabitants must be taught our highway code, but beyond that I really do not see the need for any further instruction.

In the field of public health there is no need whatsoever to extend to the subject races the benefits of our own knowledge. This would result only in an enormous increase in local populations, and I absolutely forbid the organisation of any sort of hygiene or cleanliness crusades in these territories. Compulsory vaccination will be confined to Germans alone, and the doctors in the German colonies will be there solely for the purpose of looking after the German colonists. It is stupid to thrust happiness upon people against their wishes. Dentistry, too, should remain a closed book to them; but in all these things prudence and commonsense must be the deciding factors, and if some local inhabitant has a violent tooth-ache and insists on seeing a dentist—well, an exception must be made in his particular case!

The most foolish mistake we could possibly make would be to allow the subject races to possess arms. History shows that all conquerors who have allowed their subject races to carry arms have prepared their own downfall by so doing. Indeed, I would go so far as to say that the underdog is a *sine qua non* for the overthrow of any sovereignty. So let's not have any native militia or police. German troops alone will bear the sole responsibility for the maintenance of law and order throughout the occupied Russian territories, and a system of military strong-points must be evolved to cover the entire occupied country.

All Germans living in territories must remain in personal contact with these strong-points. The whole must be most carefully organised to conform with the long-term policy of German colonisation, and our colonising penetration must be constantly progressive, until it reaches the stage where our own colonists far outnumber the local inhabitants. . . .

Once the war is over, and I am less absorbed in military problems, I shall make it my particular business to develop in our youth this type of man—wide-awake, intelligent, self-assured— . . . This will allow me to oppose foreigners, whose manhood appears to be composed either of degenerates or of brute beasts or some such sort of extremes, with fine lads of the kind that defended Narvik and Cholm.

Exactly in the same way as the war of 1870–71 was the melting-pot of the old Reich, the battlefields of this war will be the cement which will bind into one indissoluble whole all the races of the Greater German Reich. Not one of them will come into the confederation feeling like a whipped hound, for each and every one of them will come with the pride born of the knowledge that each and every one has shed his blood and played his part in the greatest struggle for freedom in the history of the German race.

As I expect everyone to give of his best, I shall adhere to the principle that all Germans, whatever their origin, must be represented in the Party Chancellery at Munich. In the same way, when it is a question of major undertakings such as buildings, autobahnen, canals, or indeed anything which calls for a determined effort on the part of the whole nation, I wish everyone to play their part. Dispersal of effort spells merely dissipation of force. Just as intervention in great numbers by the Air Arm is decisive in an operation in war, to know how to concentrate the efforts of the entire nation on the important objective is the decisive factor in great undertakings in times of peace. Munich, for example, can only acquire the great central railway station which it requires, if the power of the whole Reich is behind the undertaking. For the future, therefore, reasoned planning by the German Government is essential; plans must be drawn up for the undertaking, year by year, of some great enterprise, and these plans must be attacked and brought to fruition at all costs.

This sort of collective harnessing of the efforts of the entire German people cannot but have its influence on the individual participant. He will come to feel that nothing is impossible and, as the young Briton of to-day serves his apprenticeship in India, the young German will learn his lessons, looking round the most easterly territories of the Reich, in Norway, or on some other frontier of our land. He will realise, too, thanks to his personal experiences, that, although some sort of hierarchy is necessary in the homeland, abroad there must be no differences at all between German and German. To the last man, too, the Germans must have the conviction as a matter of course that the youngest of German apprentices, the most humble of German mechanics, stands closer to him than the most important British Lord.

The measure of the importance of the revolution we have accomplished in the abolition of social differences can be well gauged if one recalls that German princes in the old days preferred to go off and play the Nabob in some tinpot Balkan State, rather than remain and earn their living in their own country, in however humble a manner—even as a crossing sweeper. If only we can succeed in inculcating into the German people, and above all into the German youth, both a fanatical team spirit and a fanatical devotion to the Reich, then the German Reich will once again become the most powerful State in Europe, as it was a thousand years after the collapse of the Roman Empire. Such a spirit would be a guarantee, once and for all, that never again would the German Reich split up into a number of little States, with mutual diplomatic representatives, and each with its diplomats abroad, stirring up trouble for German unity—as did, not so very long ago, a certain French Ambassador to Munich. A Reich whose component entities are moulded in fanatic solidarity will soon find, too, a solution to the Czech problem—as Hacha himself well knows. As a lawyer of the old Austrian State he must feel that the setting up of an independent Czech State was a mistake; for never in the course of history have the Czechs shown themselves capable of solving their own political problems, and even in their cultural development leant heavily on the German culture of the Hapsburg State. The right, and, indeed, for the German Reich the obvious, policy is firstly to purge the country of all dangerous elements, and then to treat the Czechs with friendly consideration. If we pursue a policy of this sort, all the Czechs will follow the lead of President Hacha. In any case, a certain feeling of guilt, coupled with the fear of being compelled to evacuate their homes, as the result of the transfer of population we are undertaking, will persuade them that it will be in their best interests to emerge as zealous co-operators of the Reich. It is this fear which besets them that explains why the Czechs at the moment—and particularly in the war factories—are working to our complete satisfaction, doing their utmost under the slogan: "Everything for our Fuehrer, Adolf Hitler!" . . .

I have just read a report by Gauleiter Frauenfeld on the South Tyrol. In it he proposes that the South Tyrolese should be transplanted *en masse* to the Crimea, and I think the idea is an excellent one. There are few places on earth in which a race can better succeed in maintaining its integrity for centuries on end than the Crimea. The Tartars and the Goths are the living proof of it. I think, too, that the Crimea will be both climatically and geographically ideal for the South Tyrolese, and in comparison with their present settlements it will be a real land of milk and honey.

Their transfer to the Crimea presents neither physical nor psychological difficulty. All they have to do is to sail down just one German waterway, the Danube, and there they are. . . .

I recently read an article from the pen of some Herr Doktor advocating the prohibition of the sale in the occupied territories of contraceptives. If any criminal lunatic should really try to introduce this measure I'd soon have his head off! In view of the extraordinary fertility of the local inhabitants, we should be only too pleased to encourage the women and the girls to practise the arts of contraception at all times. Far from prohibiting the sale of contraceptives, therefore, we should do our utmost to encourage it. We should call on the Jews for help! With their unrivalled sense of commerce, they are the very people for the job!

In all seriousness, however, there is a very real danger that these local inhabitants will increase too rapidly under our care and domination. Their conditions of life will inevitably improve under our jurisdiction, and we must take all the measures necessary to ensure that the non-German population does not increase at an excessive rate. In these circumstances, it would be sheer folly to place at their disposal a health service such as we know it in Germany; and so—no inoculations and other preventative measures for the natives! We must even try to stifle any desire for such things, by persuading them that vaccination and the like are really most dangerous! . . .

7. THE YALTA CONFERENCE*

As the war in Europe neared a close the Big Three—Franklin D. Roosevelt of the United States, Winston Churchill of Great Britain, and Joseph Stalin of the U.S.S.R.—met at Yalta in the Crimea for a series of important discussions about the future of eastern Europe, the structure of the United Nations, and the occupation of Germany. What special position in the United Nations did the U.S.S.R. achieve under the Yalta agreements? What guarantees of free, popular government did the western powers receive from Stalin with regard to occupied eastern Europe? What machinery for the fulfillment of those guarantees did the Yalta accord provide? To what extent did the West recognize the Polish provisional government, formed under Russian auspices by Polish Communists?

* "Protocol of the Proceedings of the Crimea Conference" in *Foreign Relations of the United States: The Conferences at Malta and Yalta, 1945* ("Publications of the Department of State," No. 6199; Washington, 1955), pp. 975–982.

PROTOCOL OF THE PROCEEDINGS OF THE CRIMEA CONFERENCE

The Crimea Conference of the Heads of the Governments of the United States of America, the United Kingdom, and the Union of Soviet Socialist Republics which took place from February 4th to 11th came to the following conclusions.

I. *World Organisation*

It was decided:

(1) that a United Nations Conference on the proposed world organisation should be summoned for Wednesday, 25th April, 1945, and should be held in the United States of America.

(2) the Nations to be invited to this Conference should be:

(*a*) the United Nations as they existed on the 8th February, 1945 and

(*b*) such of the Associated Nations as have declared war on the common enemy by 1st March, 1945. (For this purpose by the term "Associated Nation" was meant the eight Associated Nations and Turkey). When the Conference on World Organization is held, the delegates of the United Kingdom and United States of America will support a proposal to admit to original membership two Soviet Socialist Republics, i. e. the Ukraine and White Russia.

(3) that the United States Government on behalf of the Three Powers should consult the Government of China and the French Provisional Government in regard to the decisions taken at the present Conference concerning the proposed World Organisation.

(4) that the text of the invitation to be issued to all the nations which would take part in the United Nations Conference should be as follows:

INVITATION

"The Government of the United States of America, on behalf of itself and of the Governments of the United Kingdom, the Union of Soviet Socialist Republics, and the Republic of China and of the Provisional Government of the French Republic, invite the Government of ——— to send representatives to a Conference of the United Nations to be held on 25th April, 1945, or soon thereafter, at San Francisco in the United States of America to prepare a Charter for a General International Organisation for the maintenance of international peace and security.

"The above named governments suggest that the Conference consider as affording a basis for such a Charter the Proposals for the Establishment of a General International Organisation, which were made public last October as a result of the Dumbarton Oaks Conference, and which have now been supplemented by the following provisions for Section C of Chapter VI:

" 'C. *Voting*

'1. Each member of the Security Council should have one vote.

'2. Decisions of the Security Council on procedural matters should be made by an affirmative vote of seven members.

'3. Decisions of the Security Council on all other matters should be made by an affirmative vote of seven members including the concurring votes of the permanent members; provided that, in decisions under Chapter VIII, Section A and under the second sentence of paragraph 1 of Chapter VIII, Section C, a party to a dispute should abstain from voting'.

"Further information as to arrangements will be transmitted subsequently.

"In the event that the Government of ——— desires in advance of the Conference to present views or comments concerning the proposals, the Government of the United States of America will be pleased to transmit such views and comments to the other participating Governments".

TERRITORIAL TRUSTEESHIP

It was agreed that the five Nations which will have permanent seats on the Security Council should consult each other prior to the United Nations Conference on the question of territorial trusteeship.

The acceptance of this recommendation is subject to its being made clear that territorial trusteeship will only apply to (a) existing mandates of the League of Nations; (b) territories detached from the enemy as a result of the present war; (c) any other territory which might voluntarily be placed under trusteeship; and (d) no discussion of actual territories is contemplated at the forthcoming United Nations Conference or in the preliminary consultations, and it will be a matter for subsequent agreement which territories within the above categories will be placed under trusteeship.

II. *Declaration on Liberated Europe*

The following declaration has been approved:

"The Premier of the Union of Soviet Socialist Republics, the Prime Minister of the United Kingdom and the President of the United States of America have consulted with each other in the common interests of the peoples of their countries and those of liberated Europe. They jointly declare their mutual agreement to concert during the temporary period of instability in liberated Europe the policies of their three governments in assisting the peoples liberated from the domination of Nazi Germany and the peoples of the former Axis satellite states of Europe to solve by democratic means their pressing political and economic problems.

"The establishment of order in Europe and the re-building of national economic life must be achieved by processes which will enable the liberated peoples to destroy the last vestiges of Nazism and Fascism and to create democratic institutions of their own choice. This is a principle of the Atlantic Charter—the right of all peoples to choose the form of government under which they will live—the restoration of sovereign rights and self-government to those peoples who have been forcibly deprived of them by the aggressor nations.ᶾ

"To foster the conditions in which the liberated peoples may exercise these rights, the three governments will jointly assist the people in any European liberated state or former Axis satellite state in Europe where in their judgment conditons require (a) to establish conditions of internal peace; (b) to carry out emergency measures for the relief of distressed peoples; (c) to form interim governmental authorities broadly representative of all democratic elements in the population and pledged to the earliest possible establishment through free elections of governments responsive to the will of the people; and (d) to facilitate where necessary the holding of such elections.

"The three governments will consult the other United Nations and provisional authorities or other governments in Europe when matters of direct interest to them are under consideration.

"When, in the opinion of the three governments, conditions in any European liberated state or any former Axis satellite state in Europe make such action necessary, they will immediately consult together on the measures necessary to discharge the joint responsibilities set forth in this declaration.

"By this declaration we reaffirm our faith in the principles of the Atlantic Charter, our pledge in the Declaration by the United Nations, and our determination to build in co-operation with other peaceloving nations world order under law, dedicated to peace, security, freedom and general well-being of all mankind.

"In issuing this declaration, the Three Powers express the hope that the Provisional Government of the French Republic may be associated with them in the procedure suggested."

III. *Dismemberment of Germany*

It was agreed that Article 12 (a) of the Surrender Terms for Germany should be amended to read as follows:

"The United Kingdom, the United States of America and the Union of Soviet Socialist Republics shall possess supreme authority with respect to Germany. In the exercise of such authority they will take such steps, including the complete disarmament, demilitarisation and the dismemberment of Germany as they deem requisite for future peace and security."

The study of the procedure for the dismemberment of Germany was referred to a Committee, consisting of Mr. Eden (Chairman), Mr. Winant and Mr. Gousev. This body would consider the desirability of associating with it a French representative.

IV. *Zone of Occupation for the French and Control Council for Germany*

It was agreed that a zone in Germany, to be occupied by the French Forces, should be allocated to France. This zone would be formed out of the British and American zones and its extent would be settled by the British and Americans in consultation with the French Provisional Government.

It was also agreed that the French Provisional Government should be invited to become a member of the Allied Control Council for Germany.

V. *Reparation*

The following protocol has been approved:

1. Germany must pay in kind for the losses caused by her to the Allied nations in the course of the war. Reparations are to be received in the first instance by those countries which have borne the main burden of the war, have suffered the heaviest losses and have organised victory over the enemy.

2. Reparation in kind is to be exacted from Germany in three following forms:

a) Removals within 2 years from the surrender of Germany or the cessation of organised resistance from the national wealth of Germany located on the territory of Germany herself as well as outside her territory (equipment, machine-tools, ships, rolling stock, German investments abroad, shares of industrial, transport and other enterprises in Germany etc.), these removals to be carried out chiefly for purpose of destroying the war potential of Germany.

b) Annual deliveries of goods from current production for a period to be fixed.

c) Use of German labour.

3. For the working out on the above principles of a detailed plan for exaction of reparation from Germany an Allied Reparation Commission will be set up in Moscow. It will consist of three representatives—one from the Union of Soviet Socialist Republics, one from the United Kingdom and one from the United States of America.

4. With regard to the fixing of the total sum of the reparation as well as the distribution of it among the countries which suffered from the German aggression the Soviet and American delegations agreed as follows:

"The Moscow Reparation Commission should take in its initial studies as a basis for discussion the suggestion of the Soviet Government that the total sum of the reparation in accordance with the points (*a*) and (*b*) of the paragraph 2 should be 20 billion dollars and that 50% of it should go to the Union of Soviet Socialist Republics."

The British delegation was of the opinion that pending consideration of the reparation question by the Moscow Reparation Commission no figures of reparation should be mentioned.

The above Soviet-American proposal has been passed to the Moscow Reparation Commission as one of the proposals to be considered by the Commission.

VI. *Major War Criminals*

The Conference agreed that the question of the major war criminals should be the subject of enquiry by the three Foreign Secretaries for report in due course after the close of the Conference.

VII. *Poland*

The following Declaration on Poland was agreed by the Conference:

"A new situation has been created in Poland as a result of her complete liberation by the Red Army. This calls for the establishment of a Polish Provisional Government which can be more broadly based than was possible before the recent liberation of the Western part of Poland. The Provisional Government which is now functioning in Poland should therefore be reorganised on a broader democratic basis with the inclusion of democratic leaders from Poland itself and from Poles abroad. This new Government should then be called the Polish Provisional Government of National Unity.

"M. Molotov, Mr. Harriman and Sir A. Clark Kerr are authorised as a commission to consult in the first instance in Moscow with members of the present Provisional Government and with other Polish democratic leaders from within Poland and from abroad, with a view to the reorganisation of the present Government along the above lines. This Polish Provisional Government of National Unity shall be pledged to the holding of free and unfettered elections as soon as possible on the basis of universal suffrage and secret ballot. In these elections all democratic and anti-Nazi parties shall have the right to take part and to put forward candidates.

"When a Polish Provisional Government of National Unity has been properly formed in conformity with the above, the Government of the U.S.S.R., which now maintains diplomatic relations with the present Provisional Government of Poland, and the Government of the United Kingdom and the Government of the U. S. A. will establish diplomatic relations with the new Polish Provisional Government of National Unity, and will exchange Ambassadors by whose reports the respective Governments will be kept informed about the situation in Poland.

"The three Heads of Government consider that the Eastern frontier of Poland should follow the Curzon Line with digressions from it in some regions of five to eight kilometres in favour of Poland. They recognise that Poland must receive substantial accessions of territory in the North and West. They feel that the opinion of the new Polish Provisional Government of National Unity should be sought in due course on the extent of these accessions and that the final delimitation of the Western frontier of Poland should thereafter await the Peace Conference."

VIII. *Yugoslavia*

It was agreed to recommend to Marshal Tito and to Dr. Subasic:

(*a*) that the Tito-Subasic Agreement should immediately be put into effect and a new Government formed on the basis of the Agreement.

(*b*) that as soon as the new Government has been formed it should declare:

(i) that the Anti-Fascist Assembly of National Liberation (AUNOJ) will be extended to include members of the last Yugoslav Skupstina who have not compromised themselves by collaboration with the enemy, thus forming a body to be known as a temporary Parliament and

(ii) that legislative acts passed by the Anti-Fascist Assemb[l]y of National Liberation (AUNOJ) will be subject to subsequent ratification by a Constituent Assembly;

and that this statement should be published in the communique of the Conference.

IX. *Italo-Yugoslav Frontier*
Italo-Austria Frontier

Notes on these subjects were put in by the British delegation and the American and Soviet delegations agreed to consider them and give their views later.

X. *Yugoslav-Bulgarian Relations*

There was an exchange of views between the Foreign Secretaries on the question of the desirability of a Yugoslav-Bulgarian pact of alliance. The question at issue was whether a state still under an armistice regime could be allowed to enter into a treaty with another state. Mr. Eden suggested that the Bulgarian and Yugoslav Governments should be informed that this could not be approved. Mr. Stettinius suggested that the British and American Ambassadors should discuss the matter further with M. Molotov in Moscow. M. Molotov agreed with the proposal of Mr. Stettinius.

XI. *South Eastern Europe*

The British Delegation put in notes for the consideration of their colleagues on the following subjects:

(*a*) the Control Commission in Bulgaria.

(*b*) Greek claims upon Bulgaria, more particularly with reference to reparations.

(*c*) Oil equipment in Roumania.

XII. *Iran*

Mr. Eden, Mr. Stettinius and M. Molotov exchanged views on the situation in Iran. It was agreed that this matter should be pursued through the diplomatic channel.

XIII. *Meetings of the Three Foreign Secretaries*

The Conference agreed that permanent machinery should be set up for consultation between the three Foreign Secretaries; they should meet as often as necessary, probably about every three or four months.

These meetings will be held in rotation in the three capitals, the first meeting being held in London.

XIV. *The Montreux Convention and the Straits*

It was agreed that at the next meeting of the three Foreign Secretaries to be held in London, they should consider proposals which it was understood the Soviet Government would put forward in relation to the Montreux Convention and report to their Governments. The Turkish Government should be informed at the appropriate moment.

The foregoing Protocol was approved and signed by the three Foreign Secretaries at the Crimean Conference, February 11, 1945.

> E R STETTINIUS, JR
> B. MOЛOTOB. [V. MOLOTOV]
> ANTHONY EDEN

THE POSTWAR WORLD

8. THE TRUMAN DOCTRINE*

American and British hopes that the Soviet Union would respect the Yalta agreements and permit free elections in eastern Europe vanished during 1945 and 1946. Winston Churchill, no longer British Prime Minister after the election of 1945, pointedly declared in a speech at Fulton, Missouri in March 1946:

---

* "Recommendations on Greece and Turkey (Truman Doctrine)" in *A Decade of American Foreign Policy: Basic Documents, 1941–1949* (United States Senate Committee on Foreign Relations, Senate Document No. 123; Washington, 1950), pp. 1253–1257.

"From Stettin in the Baltic to Trieste in the Adriatic, an iron curtain has descended across the continent." Britain's financial inability to support the non-Communist nations of the eastern Mediterranean, however, threw the burden of aid on the United States. Although many Americans had assumed that the United States could disassociate itself from postwar European problems, President Harry S Truman, in a message to the Congress on March 12, 1947, enunciated what has been called the Truman Doctrine of aid to Greece and Turkey. Why was existing economic aid to Greece and Turkey insufficient to prevent a collapse of their governments? Why did Truman assert that "the United Nations and its related organizations are not in a position to extend the kind of help that is required"? How did the President rationalize American support of a Greek government which was not as democratically chosen as his own?

MESSAGE OF THE PRESIDENT TO THE CONGRESS, MARCH 12, 1947

Mr. President, Mr. Speaker, Members of the Congress of the United States:

The gravity of the situation which confronts the world today necessitates my appearance before a joint session of the Congress.

The foreign policy and the national security of this country are involved.

One aspect of the present situation, which I wish to present to you at this time for your consideration and decision, concerns Greece and Turkey.

The United States has received from the Greek Government an urgent appeal for financial and economic assistance. Preliminary reports from the American Economic Mission now in Greece and reports from the American Ambassador in Greece corroborate the statement of the Greek Government that assistance is imperative if Greece is to survive as a free nation.

I do not believe that the American people and the Congress wish to turn a deaf ear to the appeal of the Greek Government.

Greece is not a rich country. Lack of sufficient natural resources has always forced the Greek people to work hard to make both ends meet. Since 1940 this industrious and peace-loving country has suffered invasion, four years of cruel enemy occupation, and bitter internal strife.

When forces of liberation entered Greece they found that the retreating Germans had destroyed virtually all the railways, roads, port facilities, communications, and merchant marine. More than a thousand villages had been burned. Eighty-five per cent of the children were tubercular. Livestock, poultry, and draft animals had almost disappeared. Inflation had wiped out practically all savings.

As a result of these tragic conditions, a militant minority, exploiting human want and misery, was able to create political chaos which, until now, has made economic recovery impossible.

Greece is today without funds to finance the importation of those goods which are essential to bare subsistence. Under these circumstances the people of Greece cannot make progress in solving their problems of reconstruction. Greece is in desperate need of financial and economic assistance to enable it to resume purchases of food, clothing, fuel, and seeds. These are indispensable for the subsistence of its people and are obtainable only from abroad. Greece must have help to import the goods necessary to restore internal order and security so essential for economic and political recovery.

The Greek Government has also asked for the assistance of experienced American administrators, economists, and technicians to insure that the financial and other aid given to Greece shall be used effectively in creating a stable and self-sustaining economy and in improving its public administration.

The very existence of the Greek state is today threatened by the terrorist activities of several thousand armed men, led by Communists, who defy the Government's authority at a number of points, particularly along the northern boundaries. A commission appointed by the United Nations Security Council is at present investigating disturbed conditions in northern Greece and alleged border violations along the frontier between Greece on the one hand and Albania, Bulgaria, and Yugoslavia on the other.

Meanwhile, the Greek Government is unable to cope with the situation. The Greek Army is small and poorly equipped. It needs supplies and equipment if it is to restore authority to the Government throughout Greek territory.

Greece must have assistance if it is to become a self-supporting and self-respecting democracy.

The United States must supply that assistance. We have already extended to Greece certain types of relief and economic aid, but these are inadequate.

There is no other country to which democratic Greece can turn.

No other nation is willing and able to provide the necessary support for a democratic Greek Government.

The British Government, which has been helping Greece, can give no further financial or economic aid after March 31. Great Britain finds itself under the necessity of reducing or liquidating its commitments in several parts of the world, including Greece.

We have considered how the United Nations might assist in this crisis. But the situation is an urgent one requiring immediate action, and the United Nations and its related organizations are not in a position to extend help of the kind that is required.

It is important to note that the Greek Government has asked for our aid in utilizing effectively the financial and other assistance we may give to Greece, and in improving its public administration. It is of the utmost importance that we supervise the use of any funds made available to Greece, in such a manner that each dollar spent will count toward making Greece self-supporting, and will help to build an economy in which a healthy democracy can flourish.

No government is perfect. One of the chief virtues of a democracy, however, is that its defects are always visible and under democratic processes can be pointed out and corrected. The Government of Greece is not perfect. Nevertheless it represents 85 per cent of the members of the Greek Parliament who were chosen in an election last year. Foreign observers, including 692 Americans, considered this election to be a fair expression of the views of the Greek people.

The Greek Government has been operating in an atmosphere of chaos and extremism. It has made mistakes. The extension of aid by this country does not mean that the United States condones everything that the Greek Government has done or will do. We have condemned in the past and we condemn now, extremist measures of the right or the left. We have in the past advised tolerance, and we advise tolerance now.

Greece's neighbor, Turkey, also deserves our attention.

The future of Turkey as an independent and economically sound state is clearly no less important to the freedom-loving peoples of the world than the future of Greece. The circumstances in which Turkey finds itself today are considerably different from those of Greece. Turkey has been spared the disasters that have beset Greece. And during the war the United States and Great Britain furnished Turkey with material aid.

Nevertheless, Turkey now needs our support.

Since the war Turkey has sought additional financial assistance from Great Britain and the United States for the purpose of effecting that modernization necessary for the maintenance of its national integrity.

That integrity is essential to the preservation of order in the Middle East.

The British Government has informed us that, owing to its own difficulties, it can no longer extend financial or economic aid to Turkey.

As in the case of Greece, if Turkey is to have the assistance it needs, the United States must supply it. We are the only country able to provide that help.

I am fully aware of the broad implications involved if the United States extends assistance to Greece and Turkey, and I shall discuss these implications with you at this time.

One of the primary objectives of the foreign policy of the United States is the creation of conditions in which we and other nations will be able to work out a way of life free from coercion. This was a fundamental issue in the war with Germany and Japan. Our victory was won over countries which sought to impose their will, and their way of life, upon other nations.

To insure the peaceful development of nations, free from coercion, the United States has taken a leading part in establishing the United Nations. The United Nations is designed to make possible lasting freedom and independence for all its members. We shall not realize our objectives, however, unless we are willing to help free peoples to maintain their free institutions and their national integrity against aggressive movements that seek to impose upon them totalitarian regimes. This is no more than a frank recognition that totalitarian regimes imposed upon free peoples, by direct or indirect aggression, undermine the foundations of international peace and hence the security of the United States.

The peoples of a number of countries of the world have recently had totalitarian regimes forced upon them against their will. The Government of the United States has made frequent protests against coercion and intimidation, in violation of the Yalta agreement, in Poland, Rumania, and Bulgaria. I must also state that in a number of other countries there have been similar developments.

At the present moment in world history nearly every nation must choose between alternative ways of life. The choice is too often not a free one.

One way of life is based upon the will of the majority, and is distinguished by free institutions, representative government, free elections, guaranties of individual liberty, freedom of speech and religion, and freedom from political oppression.

The second way of life is based upon the will of a minority forcibly imposed upon the majority. It relies upon terror and oppression, a controlled press and radio, fixed elections, and the suppression of personal freedoms.

I believe that it must be the policy of the United States to support free peoples who are resisting attempted subjugation by armed minorities or by outside pressures.

I believe that we must assist free peoples to work out their own destinies in their own way.

I believe that our help should be primarily through economic and financial aid which is essential to economic stability and orderly political processes.

The world is not static, and the *status quo* is not sacred. But we cannot allow changes in the *status quo* in violation of the Charter of the United Nations by such methods as coercion, or by such subterfuges as political infiltration. In helping free and independent nations to maintain their freedom, the United States will be giving effect to the principles of the Charter of the United Nations.

It is necessary only to glance at a map to realize that the survival and integrity of the Greek nation are of grave importance in a much wider situation. If Greece should fall under the control of an armed minority, the effect upon its neighbor, Turkey, would be immediate and serious. Confusion and disorder might well spread throughout the entire Middle East.

Moreover, the disappearance of Greece as an independent state would have a profound effect upon those countries in Europe whose peoples are struggling against great difficulties to maintain their freedoms and their independence while they repair the damages of war.

It would be an unspeakable tragedy if these countries, which have struggled so long against overwhelming odds, should lose that victory for which they sacrificed so much. Collapse of free institutions and loss of independence would be disastrous not only for them but for the world. Discouragement and possibly failure would quickly be the lot of neighboring peoples striving to maintain their freedom and independence.

Should we fail to aid Greece and Turkey in this fateful hour, the effect will be far-reaching to the West as well as to the East.

We must take immediate and resolute action.

I therefore ask the Congress to provide authority for assistance to Greece and Turkey in the amount of $400,000,000 for the period ending June 30, 1948. In requesting these funds, I have taken into consideration the maximum amount of relief assistance which would be furnished to Greece out of the $350,000,000 which I recently requested that the Congress authorize for the prevention of starvation and suffering in countries devastated by the war.

In addition to funds, I ask the Congress to authorize the detail of American civilian and military personnel to Greece and Turkey, at the request of those countries, to assist in the tasks of reconstruction, and for the purpose of supervising the use of such financial and material assistance as may be furnished. I recommend that authority also be provided for the instruction and training of selected Greek and Turkish personnel.

Finally, I ask that the Congress provide authority which will permit the speediest and most effective use, in terms of needed commodities, supplies, and equipment, of such funds as may be authorized.

If further funds, or further authority, should be needed for purposes indicated in this message, I shall not hesitate to bring the situation before the Congress. On this subject the Executive and Legislative branches of the Government must work together.

This is a serious course upon which we embark.

I would not recommend it except that the alternative is much more serious.

The United States contributed $341,000,000,000 toward winning World War II. This is an investment in world freedom and world peace.

The assistance that I am recommending for Greece and Turkey amounts to little more than one-tenth of one per cent of this investment. It is only common sense that we should safeguard this investment and make sure that it was not in vain.

The seeds of totalitarian regimes are nurtured by misery and want. They spread and grow in the evil soil of poverty and strife. They reach their full growth when the hope of a people for a better life has died.

We must keep that hope alive.

The free peoples of the world look to us for support in maintaining their freedoms.

If we falter in our leadership, we may endanger the peace of the world—and we shall surely endanger the welfare of our own Nation.

Great responsibilities have been placed upon us by the swift movement of events.

I am confident that the Congress will face these responsibilities squarely.

9. THE MARSHALL PLAN*

A few months after the announcement of the Truman Doctrine, American Secretary of State George C. Marshall (1880–1959) proposed a European Recovery Program. In a speech at Harvard University on June 5, 1947, Marshall proposed a vast system of economic aid which was promptly termed the Marshall Plan. Why did Marshall suggest such a sweeping measure of economic support? What advantages would the United States gain from the realization of the Marshall Plan? What restrictions were imposed upon governments which chose to participate in the plan? What connection was there between the Marshall Plan, the Truman Doctrine, and the Cold War?

THE EUROPEAN RECOVERY PROGRAM

REMARKS BY SECRETARY MARSHALL, JUNE 5, 1947

I need not tell you gentlemen that the world situation is very serious. That must be apparent to all intelligent people. I think one difficulty is that the problem is one of such enormous complexity that the very mass of facts presented to the public by press and radio make it exceedingly difficult for the man in the street to reach a clear appraisement of the situation. Furthermore, the people of this country are distant from the troubled areas of the earth and it is hard for them to comprehend the plight and consequent reactions of the long-suffering peoples, and the effect of those reactions on their governments in connection with our efforts to promote peace in the world.

In considering the requirements for the rehabilitation of Europe, the physical loss of life, the visible destruction of cities, factories, mines, and railroads was

* "The European Recovery Program," pp. 1268–1270; "A Proposal for Interim Aid," pp. 1270–1271, 1277, in *A Decade of American Foreign Policy: Basic Documents, 1941–1949* (United States Senate Committee on Foreign Relations, Senate Document No. 123; Washington, 1950).

correctly estimated, but it has become obvious during recent months that this visible destruction was probably less serious than the dislocation of the entire fabric of European economy. For the past 10 years conditions have been highly abnormal. The feverish preparation for war and the more feverish maintenance of the war effort engulfed all aspects of national economies. Machinery has fallen into disrepair or is entirely obsolete. Under the arbitrary and destructive Nazi rule, virtually every possible enterprise was geared into the German war machine. Long-standing commercial ties, private institutions, banks, insurance companies, and shipping companies disappeared, through loss of capital, absorption through nationalization, or by simple destruction. In many countries, confidence in the local currency has been severely shaken. The breakdown of the business structure of Europe during the war was complete. Recovery has been seriously retarded by the fact that two years after the close of hostilities a peace settlement with Germany and Austria has not been agreed upon. But even given a more prompt solution of these difficult problems, the rehabilitation of the economic structure of Europe quite evidently will require a much longer time and greater effort than had been foreseen.

There is a phase of this matter which is both interesting and serious. The farmer has always produced the foodstuffs to exchange with the city dweller for the other necessities of life. This division of labor is the basis of modern civilization. At the present time it is threatened with breakdown. The town and city industries are not producing adequate goods to exchange with the food-producing farmer. Raw materials and fuel are in short supply. Machinery is lacking or worn out. The farmer or the peasant cannot find the goods for sale which he desires to purchase. So the sale of his farm produce for money which he cannot use seems to him an unprofitable transaction. He, therefore, has withdrawn many fields from crop cultivation and is using them for grazing. He feeds more grain to stock and finds for himself and his family an ample supply of food, however short he may be on clothing and the other ordinary gadgets of civilization. Meanwhile people in the cities are short of food and fuel. So the governments are forced to use their foreign money and credits to procure these necessities abroad. This process exhausts funds which are urgently needed for reconstruction. Thus a very serious situation is rapidly developing which bodes no good for the world. The modern system of the division of labor upon which the exchange of products is based is in danger of breaking down.

The truth of the matter is that Europe's requirements for the next three or four years of foreign food and other essential products—principally from America—are so much greater than her present ability to pay that she must have substantial additional help or face economic, social, and political deterioration of a very grave character.

The remedy lies in breaking the vicious circle and restoring the confidence of the European people in the economic future of their own countries and of Europe as a whole. The manufacturer and the farmer throughout wide areas must be able and willing to exchange their products for currencies the continuing value of which is not open to question.

Aside from the demoralizing effect on the world at large and the possibilities of disturbances arising as a result of the desperation of the people concerned, the consequences to the economy of the United States should be apparent to all. It is logical that the United States should do whatever it is able to do to assist in the return of normal economic health in the world, without which there can be no political stability and no assured peace. Our policy is directed not against any country or doctrine but against hunger, poverty, desperation, and chaos. Its purpose should be the revival of a working economy in the world so as to permit the emergence of political and social conditions in which free institutions can exist. Such assistance, I am convinced, must not be on a piecemeal basis as various crises develop. Any assistance that this Government may render in the future should provide a cure rather than a mere palliative. Any government that is willing to assist in the task of recovery will find full cooperation, I am sure, on the part of the United States Government. Any government which maneuvers to block the recovery of other countries cannot expect help from us. Furthermore, governments, political parties, or groups which seek to perpetuate human misery in order to profit therefrom politically or otherwise will encounter the opposition of the United States.

It is already evident that, before the United States Government can proceed much further in its efforts to alleviate the situation and help start the European world on its way to recovery, there must be some agreement among the countries of Europe as to the requirements of the situation and the part those countries themselves will take in order to give proper effect to whatever action might be undertaken by this Government. It would be neither fitting nor efficacious for this Government to undertake to draw up unilaterally a program designed to place Europe on its feet economically. This is the business of the Europeans. The initiative, I think, must come from Europe. The role of this country should consist of friendly aid in the drafting of a European program and of later support of such a program so far as it may be practical for us to do so. The program should be a joint one, agreed to by a number, if not all, European nations.

An essential part of any successful action on the part of the United States is an understanding on the part of the people of America of the character of the problem and the remedies to be applied. Political passion and prejudice should have no part. With foresight, and a willingness on the part of our people to face up to the vast responsibility which history has clearly placed upon our country, the difficulties I have outlined can and will be overcome.

PROPOSAL FOR INTERIM AID

STATEMENT OF SECRETARY MARSHALL BEFORE THE JOINT SESSION OF THE SENATE COMMITTEE ON FOREIGN RELATIONS AND THE HOUSE COMMITTEE ON FOREIGN AFFAIRS, NOVEMBER 10, 1947

The Congress in the coming session will be called upon to make decisions which, although less spectacular and dramatic, will be no less important for the future of our country and the world than those of the war years. Your responsibilities as members of the committees directly concerned with our foreign relations are accordingly very great.

It appears unnecessary to elaborate for you on the somber picture of the world situation. You all, I am sure, are fully aware of its gravity and the immense responsibility which the course of events has placed upon our country

The President will lay before the Congress the program of his administration for aid to Europe. My duty as Secretary of State is to present the reasons for this program; the reasons why I profoundly believe that the vital interest of the United States is directly involved.

In concentrating upon the problem of aid to Europe I do not ignore the fact that there are other areas of the world beset by economic problems of tremendous gravity. But the very magnitude of the world problem as a whole requires a careful direction of our assistance to the critical areas where it can be most immediately effective.

The need for our assistance in the European area is real and it is urgent. The report of the 16 nations represented on the Committee of European Economic Cooperation sets this forth, I think, in a convincing manner.

As a result of the war, the European community which for centuries had been one of the most productive and indeed creative portions of the inhabited world was left prostrate. This area, despite its diversity of national cultures and its series of internecine conflicts and wars, nonetheless enjoys a common heritage and a common civilization.

The war ended with the armies of the major Allies meeting in the heart of this community. The policies of three of them have been directed to the restoration of that European community. It is now clear that only one power, the Soviet Union, does not for its own reasons share this aim.

We have become involved in two wars which have had their origins in the European continent. The free peoples of Europe have fought two wars to prevent the forcible domination of their community by a single great power. Such domination would have inevitably menaced the stability and security of the world. To deny today our interest in their ability to defend their own heritage would be to disclaim the efforts and sacrifices of two generations of Americans. We wish to see this community restored as one of the pillars of world security; in a position to renew its contribution to the advancement of mankind and to the development of a world order based on law and respect for the individual.

The record of the endeavors of the United States Government to bring about a restoration of the whole of that European community is clear for all who wish to see. We must face the fact, however, that despite our efforts, not all of the European nations have been left free to take their place in the community of which they form a natural part.

Thus the geographic scope of our recovery program is limited to those nations which are free to act in accordance with their national traditions and their own estimates of their national interests. If there is any doubt as to this situation, a glance at the present map of the European continent will provide the answer.

The present line of division in Europe is roughly the line upon which the Anglo-American armies coming from the west met those of the Soviet Union coming from the east. To the west of that line the nations of the continental European community have been grappling with the vast and difficult problem resulting from the war in conformity with their own national traditions without pressure or menace from the United States or Great Britain. Developments in the European countries to the east of that line bear the unmistakable imprint of an alien hand. All the nations of Europe, 16 in number, which were in a position to exercise free choice gave a prompt and energetic response to the simple suggestion made at Harvard on June 5 last and thereby an impressive demonstration of the continuing vitality of European civilization.

It would be well, therefore, to deal briefly with what the area encompassed by those 16 nations plus western Germany has meant to us and has meant to the world. This community before the war accounted for nearly one-half of the world's trade. They owned nearly two-thirds of the world's shipping. Their industrial production in terms of the basic commodities of coal, steel, and chemicals was before the war slightly greater than that of the United States. Their economy was highly integrated, each part depending upon the efficient working of the other.

I think that the figures cited will indicate the importance, even from a purely economic point of view, of the 16 nations who have joined together to develop a program for their mutual recovery. Their response to our suggestion of June 5 was a remarkable cooperative effort in a postwar world in which that element has hitherto been distressingly lacking.

Congress will wish to go into the objectives and the details of the European recovery program at some length, but I feel that a brief summary of the tentative conclusions we have reached may serve the useful purpose of making clear the distinction between the long range recovery program and the stop-gap program, which we refer to as interim aid. . . .

[*Marshall proceeded to request prompt support from the Senate and House Committees on Foreign Relations for an initial foreign aid appropriation of 1.5 billion dollars and prepared them for a total expenditure of $20 billion or more.*]

The automatic success of the program cannot be guaranteed. The imponderables are many. The risks are real. They are, however, risks which have been carefully calculated, and I believe the chances of success are good. There is convincing evidence that the peoples of western Europe want to preserve their free society and the heritage we share with them. To make that choice conclusive they need our assistance. It is in the American tradition to help. In helping them we will be helping ourselves—because in the larger sense our national interests coincide with those of a free and prosperous Europe.

We must not fail to meet this inspiring challenge. We must not permit the free community of Europe to be extinguished. Should this occur it would be a tragedy for the world. It would impose incalculable burdens upon this country and force serious readjustments in our traditional way of life. One of our important freedoms—freedom of choice in both domestic and foreign affairs—would be drastically curtailed.

Whether we like it or not, we find ourselves, our Nation, in a world position of vast responsibility. We can act for our own good by acting for the world's good.

10. FERENC NAGY: THE STRUGGLE BEHIND THE IRON CURTAIN*

The pattern of Communist seizure of power was roughly similar throughout eastern Europe. "United front" governments were installed with Communists in key positions while other political parties were hamstrung by Soviet pressure. Elections, when held, reinforced Communist strength, and non-Communists or anti-Communists were removed from positions of power.

An exception to the pattern seemed to occur when the independent Small-holders party in Hungary won a majority in the election of 1945. Ferenc Nagy (1903-   ), leader of the Smallholders party, became Premier and attempted to resist Russian pressures. In 1947, while on a trip outside of Hungary, Nagy was suddenly informed that it was dangerous for him to return. He was deposed and the Communists seized power.

The following selection is from the memoirs of Ferenc Nagy. What electoral procedures were employed by the Soviets in the towns and villages of occupied Hungary in order to assure paramount Communist influence? What caliber of local citizens did the Soviets select as police officers, and what tactics did the Russians employ to muzzle freedom of the press? Why did Marshal Voroshilov object to a new government ministry to represent cooperatives and insist that a "ministry for propaganda to aid the growth of democracy" be set up instead? Why did Hungarian Communists demand possession of the Ministry of the Interior in the new government?

COMEDY OF THE FIRST NATIONAL COUNCIL

Béla Kovács, Stephen Vásáry, and Stephen B. Szabó told me in Debrecen how the temporary National Council and its temporary government were formed. It is worth while to deal with each separately, as their method of creation throws light on preliminary political tactics of the Soviet in the different occupied countries.

When the Russians had taken the region beyond the river Tisza, Red army and Communist leaders announced that the political reorganization of the country should begin. The Communists dashed about in Red army cars, looking for collaborators to represent the other parties. From the Peasant party they secured Francis Erdei, author of books on Hungarian social conditions with which they were very familiar. John Gyöngyösi was asked to represent the Smallholders party. They visited Stephen Balogh, priest of a country parish near Szeged. Father Balogh, until then an independent, decided to join the group under the Smallholders' colors. Francis Takács, stalwart Social Democratic leader in Hódmezövásárhely, and Austin Valentini, a lawyer of Szeged, were recruited to join the Social Democrats. This group became the political executive committee of the region beyond the Tisza. They were advised by the Soviet to organize some kind of national council, to pass new laws, and "elect" a temporary government. The group was supplemented by Béla Dálnoki Miklós, John Vörös, and Gabriel Faraghó, generals who had gone over to the Russians in the last weeks of the war, and by Count Géza Teleki, who had been in Moscow with Faraghó in October to sign the temporary armistice.

* Ferenc Nagy, *The Struggle Behind the Iron Curtain*, trans. Stephen K. Swift (New York: Macmillan Co., 1948), pp. 73-75, 95-99, 159-63. Reprinted by permission.

It was decided to call a national council. The more difficult the convocation of such a council appeared, the more willing the Communists were to concern themselves with it, since they would be bound by fewer procedural rules. Since it was impossible to elect representatives, because there was no way of registering the electorate within a reasonable length of time, they simplified the whole matter by making a list of the towns and villages of the liberated territories and arbitrarily fixing the number of representatives that each might send to the assembly. The Communists, being well informed as to the political leanings of each district, determined the number of representatives accordingly. Towns where large numbers of left-wing workers and landless peasants lived were assigned many representatives, while communities favoring liberal democracy received correspondingly fewer. For example, the leftist town of Orosháza, with its population of 30,000, was assigned fourteen representatives while Pécs with 80,000 and the surrounding county of Baranya with 300,000 were allowed only seven representatives between them.

As soon as the convocation of the council was decided upon, four Communist-driven cars set out from Debrecen to arrange the election. A single representative of some other party was permitted to go along in each car. Upon arriving in a community, they called together the party and trade union to nominate representatives. Just proportions were out of the question; the Communists said that since no one as yet knew the relative strength of the parties, an equal number of representatives should be chosen for the Communists, Social Democratic, and Smallholders parties. Only the Peasant party was given smaller representation. As soon as the flying squad of nominators agreed on the nominees, they announced mass meetings in the cinema, theater, or village square and told the people that a new political life was about to begin, calling upon them to elect by acclamation the candidates chosen. The unfortunate citizens, who had lived through the oppression of the German occupation and were now experiencing the terrors of Russian occupation, cheered the speakers and unanimously accepted the nominees in the hope that a national council would bring a desperately needed change for the better.

After staging this comedy throughout the liberated territories, the Communists at once convoked the National Council at Debrecen. Soviet trucks transported the "elected" representatives to the meeting, and during the few days that the assembly was in session the representatives were lodged and fed by the Russians.

The Communists wanted to elect as president of the council a certain Béla Szentpéteri-Kun. Someone, however, yelled, "Why, that's the same gentleman who was a Rightist during the war!" The Communists, caught short, were nonplused; they could hardly begin by saying that they would forget the past of any reactionary who joined the party. Their nominee was dropped.

During further consultations, the distinguished figure of Béla Zsedényi, old-time democrat and professor of law in Miskolc could be seen in the middle of the auditorium. Someone cried out, "Béla Zsedényi will do!"

It was thus that Béla Zsedényi became president of the National Council. Later, he proved to be a man of courage and determination in the face of Communist terror.

Assuming that the Soviet had no selfish motives in helping to start Hungarian political life, we were moved by these signs of support. How often we praised

the leaders of the army of occupation for their generosity, and how often did
I state that the Red army had come, not as a victor, but as a friend ready to help!
Under what an obligation this Soviet aid placed the later development of Hungarian politics! And how often the Soviet carried through its one-sided directives on the ground that, after all, it was Russia that had made new political
life in Hungary possible! . . .

PENETRATION THROUGH DEMOCRATIC INSTITUTIONS

The disintegration of the government of the country opened the way for
Communist penetration. None of the old town councils or municipal assemblies
remained; the new political order substituted for them transitory administrative
bodies called "national committees," with unlimited power. Assuming control
of the municipalities, townships, and even cities, they appointed their own
men as elders, councilors, and committeemen to pass judgment upon the political past and present of each citizen. The national committees managed the
scant food supply; few aspects of daily life escaped their control.

This situation was not peculiar to Hungary; the Communists acted similarly
in Rumania, Poland, Bulgaria, and Czechoslovakia.

These committees were not elected by the people but were formed by the
delegates of the political parties. The Communists repeated the dubious argument they had used during the formation of the National Council: because the
strength of the parties was unknown each party would have equal representation on the committees.

Thus, for example, a town with a thousand Smallholders and possibly half a
dozen members of other parties sent four delegates from each party to the national committees. Naturally the Communists and the Peasant party were in no
position to select outstanding, respected citizens; they had to delegate anyone
available. While the Smallholders party was able to select respectable citizens,
the Communists and the Peasant party were often forced to pluck vagrants,
radicals, ex-convicts, and drunks off the streets to represent them.

The standards of these national committees were dismally low. The leftist
parties naturally voted *en bloc,* preventing the Smallholders representatives from
promulgating or enforcing any worth-while decision. The people of the village
were horrified at the ineptitude of the men who managed their affairs. It was
not unusual for a one-time convict to find himself police captain of an entire
district.

It was lucky that only Smallholders could be found in many of the hamlets;
the party appointed its best men to the national committees. Admittedly, the
committees accomplished some good. There was leadership of a sort, and something like a communal assembly. If the national committees had been elected by
the local citizenry, they could have served adequately as a revolutionary body
during the transition. The committees, blamed for every crisis and every crime,
had many enemies among the people.

If, for instance, the policemen pillaged, the people of the village immediately
blamed the national committee. Frequently stolen goods were found in the
homes of the policemen; art treasures belonging to Jews who had returned from
deportation were often seen on the living-room walls of police officers. The

reputation of law enforcement officers, and indirectly of the national committees, suffered.

Later, agricultural production committees were formed in exactly the same fashion. No one could expect increased production from leftist members who hated work; in some villages the worst farmer, who neglected both his fields and his animals, became chairman of the committee.

The stewardship of the village wealth was in the hands of its least competent citizen—generally the first to offer himself for public service. Many circumstances prevented the return of peace of mind and a stable economy; one was the denunciations. Malfeasants with the right party affiliations started to denounce any who stood in their way, particularly the former respected and sure-handed leaders of the community. The new police force needed no proof; without warning they arrested and tortured anybody marked by a Communist party member. Many of these high-principled men were interned by police authorities who were on a moral level with the denouncer, and spent months in detention camps for the offense of performing their duties well in the past.

It was a sorry state of affairs when former Gestapo quislings switched their allegiance to the Communist-controlled police. In most cases the victims were respected, responsible members of the community.

We made efforts to advance consolidation, but increasing abuses forced us to complain to the Soviet authorities and the leaders of the Communist party. Since in those days it was still impossible to check on the execution of any orders, it frequently took us months to find out that no directives had been issued which would have helped correct injustices. Thus consolidation seemed to march steadily backward, but we blamed the revolutionary conditions for everything; later we realized that all these excesses had been part of a set plan, for it was essential to Communist and Soviet aims that scourging hordes should make respectable people tremble with fear.

We saw the necessity for an informed public opinion; the people of Hungary had awaited democracy for a long time but had to be taught its application. For this we needed a press. As there was little newsprint in the country and both manufacturing and importing had stopped, the Communists proposed that all parties should unite in publishing a single newspaper in each of the cities. Conditions forced us to agree. Suddenly we awoke to the fact that our joint newspapers were attacking us, and the Communists were maligning the leadership of the Smallholders in the press in which we owned an equal share. Paying no heed to the paper shortage, we requested publishing permits and put out our own newspaper. We learned from our nonpartisan publishing effort that anyone allied in any Communist enterprise will be pushed out sooner or later. It happened, too, when we tried to govern with them.

UNIONS BECOME A POLITICAL TOOL

As soon as the old leaders of the Smallholders party emerged from their prisons and hide-outs and began to work for the party and exert their influence on national politics, the political scale approached a balance. Against the original advantages of the Communist party, the importance of the Smallholders party continually increased. The Smallholders actions moved us further along on the road to consolidation, its strength growing not only on the national political stage but in the hamlets and cities. As the well-meaning Social Democratic and other liberty-loving representatives in the national committees began to accept the opinions of the wise and experienced Smallholders, order began to evolve.

Naturally the Soviet wished to offset the influence of the Smallholders party, using as a tool the promotion of an organization to which, because of its honest and blameless past, no one could object. This was the Federation of Hungarian Labor. These workers' groups were for decades under the leadership of the Social Democratic party. They were respected institutions of the laboring class, credited with many advances against selfish capitalism and responsible for welfare institutions for the workingman.

This determinedly socialistic organization of the working class came, soon after the liberation, under the influence of Communist laborers who had exchanged their Arrow Cross membership cards for the current variety of absolutism. Naturally the Communist party did not neglect the Federation; to lead it, they brought along from Moscow a well trained former streetcar conductor of Budapest, Stephen Kossa. This terroristic, uncouth, and one-sided individual became a prisoner of the Russians in the early stages of the war. They discovered a good Communist in him, and put him through the political education mill. Returned as a star union leader, he became a blind tool of Russia and the Communists.

Kossa worked fast. He reorganized the Federation of Hungarian Labor and appointed himself executive secretary. Next to the weak president, Edwin Kisházi, he became practically dictator of union life. Seizing its leading positions from the hands of the Social Democrats, he soon divided the leadership within the unions equally between the Communists and the Social Democrats—which is to say that the Communists planned the orders while the Socialists obediently executed them.

This union organization was sent by the Communists to dam the rising Smallholders tide. First they demanded that unions get the same rights as political parties, then asked for membership in the national committees, and city and municipal governments.

The union member regarded these demands as the rightful aims of labor and, in the beginning, backed up the moves of the leaders with mass demonstrations. Later, naturally, the leaders never troubled to ask the workers to approve their actions, but meanwhile the Socialists backed Kossa. Either they did not recognize the machinations of the Communists, or they dared not oppose them.

There was not even a debate about giving the unions equal status with the political parties; Zoltán Tildy, who was at Debrecen at the time, granted the demands of the unions but argued that Rákosi promised the same status and rights to our Peasant Alliance. The net result was that, while the unions achieved political equality, the promise regarding the Peasant Alliance was forgotten. Openly the Communists agreed to equalize the status of the Peasant Alliance; actually they sent out confidential instructions to their local leaders to refuse admittance of representatives of the Peasant Alliance to the national or production committees. In some villages, where a few sensible men represented the non-Communist parties, the Peasant Alliance was seated, but in most instances the secret orders were followed. The Peasant Alliance could not offset the advantage gained by the Communists through political representation of the unions.

A handy political tool for the labor unions developed with the establishment of "political clearance" committees. In all Soviet-controlled countries, every public servant, professional worker, clerk, and laborer had his political past scrutinized by these clearance committees, on which, next to the representatives of the political parties, sat a union man with equal voice. They usually voted the straight Communist line, and a great number of persons lost their livelihood through the rulings promulgated. The clearance committees urged the public to report on anyone who appeared before them, and a flood of accusations engulfed all who were not members of the Communist party.

These clearance committees used great pressure against government employees: any mistake would be reprimanded, and a man with a tainted past could be transferred or forcibly retired. Against the decision of the clearance committees an appeal could be made to the Peoples' Court, which was the only recourse for old-time, reliable public servants with no unsavory political past. Thus a few were saved from dismissal despite the radical methods of these clearance committees.

As every individual appearing before these panels knew that the Communist party had the majority vote, many accepted the hint that clearance would proceed smoothly for party members.

Thus the respected, long-standing institutions of labor became tools of the Communists, halting the advancing consolidation and serving as springboards for the onsurge of the united forces of the Soviet and local Communists. . . .

COMMUNIST CONNIVANCE FOR POLICE POWER

The elections initiated a new chapter in post-liberation politics. After the elections, the temporary government naturally resigned. After heading the government for ten and a half months, Prime Minister Béla Miklós handed his resignation to the National Council of Three. It should be stated that the temporary government, despite its inexperience, had accomplished worthy results in a chaotic situation. With honesty and good will it had laid the foundations for the constitutional government which was to follow.

Party leaders assembled to discuss the formation of a new cabinet. We could not dream of running the government on the basis of majority rule; one-party administration could not have carried the burden of so many difficult tasks in the face of the minority opposition by the leftist parties. Besides, Voroshilov had told us, in a way not to be misunderstood, that the Allied Control Commission would not approve of such a government. A coalition was the only solution.

Many of our newly elected deputies were in favor of our requesting a 57.5 per cent share of governmental power, in accordance with the election returns. Tildy's opinion was that we should not accept more than 50 per cent; if we did, we should be held responsible for every single step forced upon us by the occupying power. Moreover, according to his information, the Communist party would refuse to join a government in which we had an absolute majority. I too leaned toward this solution, and finally it was decided that the Smallholders should ask for 50 per cent and the rest should be divided among the other three parties. This proposition was accepted by all parties of the coalition.

Next came the choice of a prime minister. All agreed that he should be a Smallholder, and the choice quickly fell on Zoltán Tildy. In Hungary, tradition has it that the leader of the party in power shall hold the post of premier. I then urged that Rákosi and Szakasits, Communist and Social Democrat leaders, be given posts in the cabinet. It would have been most unfortunate to leave these two leaders free to play politics without shouldering responsibility, and to allow them to bring pressure to bear on the government from the outside. Because neither was willing to accept a portfolio under any circumstances, we agreed to let them join the cabinet as vice premiers.

Until now the Smallholders had had the Ministries of Finance, Foreign Affairs, and Reconstruction; the Communists had had the Ministries of Commerce, Agriculture, and Social Welfare; the Social Democrats, the Ministries of Industry, Justice, and Supply; and the Ministry of the Interior had been in the hands of the Peasant party.

At the opening of the interparty discussions, it was found only natural that the Smallholders should have the Ministry of Agriculture in the new government. Nor were there any objections to its having the Ministries of Foreign Affairs and Finance. But beyond this the other parties would have liked us to satisfy ourselves with unimportant portfolios.

Tildy had presided at the discussions until he was appointed Prime Minister. Then I took over, and found it extremely difficult to harmonize the divergent viewpoints. There were days when it seemed as though the conference would be profitless and either the parties of the left or the Smallholders would have to be left out.

The great struggle was for the Ministry of the Interior. In Hungary as in most European countries, the Minister of the Interior is responsible for the administration and for the public security, and internments are decided at his discretion. His office has exceptional significance in times of turbulence when the police and other authorities are greatly concerned with political issues. He has power to favor certain parties and interfere with others. Even in normal times, when the country has a regular army, the police are a strong armed force. After the collapse, the Hungarian army was weakened by Russian obstruction and by the lack of funds and equipment. In consequence, the police were stronger than the army.

Naturally every party sought the Ministry of the Interior, so that it might control the police. First the Peasant party wanted it, because it had already held it during the temporary government. Then the Social Democrats claimed it, asserting that they alone, in the middle ground between Smallholders and Communists, could keep the Interior portfolio neutral. The real struggle, however, developed between the Smallholders and Communists. Both were aware that, despite the tendency toward coalition, they polarized Hungary's political life.

All sorts of arguments were brought up by both sides, and the talks were without results for days at a time. Party leaders would leave the discussion table daily to consult with their directorate. The Smallholders would not yield. We had already decided to name to this post Béla Kovács, the hard-fisted peasant who, until recently, had been Undersecretary of the Interior.

After resisting stubbornly for days, the Communists finally agreed to let the Smallholders name the Minister of the Interior. The leftist parties were to have the undersecretaryships.

That night I invited our parliamentary deputies to dinner and announced that the Ministry of the Interior was ours. There was an ovation for the success in the discussions and for Béla Kovács, the minister elect.

The discussions continued on the next day, and it was then that the incident occurred which showed that the Soviet Union meant to have a hand in determining the composition of the coalition government.

The leftist parties insisted that in the interests of arithmetical distribution, the number of portfolios should be set at eighteen. Of these, nine belonged to the Smallholders, four each to the Communists and Social Democrats, and one to the Peasant party. In the temporary cabinet there had been twelve, and so six new portfolios had to be created. The parties had received three portfolios which went under the title of Minister of State—including Rákosi's and Szakasits' posts of vice premier and a state ministership of the Smallholders. Three additional portfolios had to be created, either by dividing up the functions of existing ones, or by creating new departments. The Smallholders also had to accept one of these newly created portfolios, and I thought we should set up a portfolio for cooperatives, to be headed by a Smallholder minister.

I recognized that Hungarian agriculture, which had been broken up into small units, could prosper only by founding strong cooperatives. I also knew that a federated peasantry, supplemented by a ministry for cooperatives, would have a great influence upon economic life.

Marshal Voroshilov, president of the Allied Control Commission, asked to be continually informed about our discussions. That afternoon I went to him and told him that, inasmuch as it was necessary to create a new portfolio, I wished to set up a ministry for cooperatives headed by a Smallholder. It seems that Voroshilov had received, by then, the Communists' report on my intention.

"I don't approve of setting up such a ministry. The cooperatives should remain independent," said Voroshilov with a hypocritical regard for constitutionality.

"They will remain independent, even if a ministry is established. We want a ministry to represent cooperatives in the government, not to oppress them," I replied.

"But the cooperatives must not be organized by a ministry. They must organize independently," said Voroshilov, as though in Russia the cooperatives were free of governmental control.

"Yes, the cooperatives are to organize themselves; but their activity will be more widespread than in the past. The distribution of the goods produced by those who have received land must be organized. The joint use of the machines of former large estates, can only be arranged for on cooperative lines. Only through cooperatives is it possible to convert Hungarian agriculture to small-farm production. Cooperatives must be prepared to overcome marketing difficulties in the years to come. In short, they will have many tasks to fulfill, and it is only fair that they should be represented in the cabinet."

"No," countered Voroshilov. "This decision is not justifiable. The affairs of the cooperatives fit well into the Ministry of Commerce. You people have greater need for a ministry of propaganda to aid the growth of democracy and publicize its achievements. You must drop the idea of a ministry for cooperatives and set up a ministry for propaganda."

Obviously Voroshilov, in order to give support to the Communists, infringed the armistice terms with this obdurate request.

I argued for a while, pointing out that the public relations division of the Prime Ministry would suffice for the popularization of democracy. But Voroshilov remained adamant and I returned empty-handed to the interparty discussions.

The conference between the parties lasted another few days. The distribution of all the portfolios was decided upon, and we set the day for the official appointment of the cabinet.

The day before the official appointment, the Communists requested an immediate interparty conference. When it assembled, Rákosi asked to be heard.

"The Communist party," announced Rákosi, "must insist on the modification of the interparty agreement. Our party must receive the post of the Minister of Interior. Otherwise, it can take no share in the government."

I reproached the Communists sharply for creating this sudden break. It was quite evident that if the Communists withdrew from the government, the Social Democrats and the Peasant party would follow, leaving the Smallholders to form the cabinet. Our party membership would have favored such a solution, but we, who knew that Voroshilov would only approve a coalition, realized that it was unwise. I asked Rákosi to explain this unwarranted demand.

"The Communist party must lead the fight against reaction," said Rákosi. "For this reason it needs the Ministry of the Interior. Besides, after the elections, crowds of Smallholders began to terrorize the Communist party. We need protection. Though we regret to disturb the discussions with this request, we must nevertheless insist on getting the Interior."

"The Smallholders have proven themselves in the fight against reaction," said I. "Terrorization of Communists by Smallholders is an entirely sporadic phenomenon, by no means it be compared with the terrorism of the Communist party up to now. We guarantee that Smallholders will not harm Communists, and must insist on retaining the portfolio."

"You don't seem to realize! Look around in southeastern Europe, and see if you can find a country where the Ministry of Interior isn't in the hands of the Communist party," said Rákosi.

We were to understand from this pronouncement that the Communists made this sudden demand in accordance with Soviet instructions.

Smallholder leaders were assembled for a special meeting, where Béla Kovács said:

"If, with the Ministry of the Interior in its possession, our party were to seek to right every wrong suffered until now, it would be impossible to uphold the coalition. In a practical sense the Ministry of the Interior would not represent the power it symbolically holds. Let us not disrupt the formation of a government by demanding the Ministry of the Interior, but let us give this portfolio to the Communists and appoint a strong undersecretary to head the police."

We had no choice but to surrender the Ministry of the Interior. . . .

11. NIKITA KHRUSHCHEV: THE CRIMES OF STALIN*

After the death of Joseph Stalin in 1953 a struggle for power took place behind the scenes in the Kremlin. Although no party functionary was able to secure the absolute power which had been held by the late dictator, Nikita Khrushchev (1894–   ) gradually rose to a position of leadership. In October 1956, Khrushchev delivered an important speech before the Twentieth Congress of the Communist Party of the Soviet Union. To the great surprise of the assembled delegates and the world, Khrushchev criticized and debunked the Stalin regime. According to Khrushchev, what was the "cult of the individual," and why was collective leadership more satisfactory? How, in Khrushchev's view, had Stalin used the formula "enemy of the people" to pervert the proper course of Leninist communism?

The objective of the present report is not a thorough evaluation of Stalin's life and activity. Concerning Stalin's merits, an entirely sufficient number of books, pamphlets and studies had already been written in his lifetime. The role of Stalin in the preparation and execution of the Social Revolution, in the Civil War, and in the fight for the construction of socialism in our country, is universally known. Everyone knows this well.

At present, we are concerned with a question which has immense importance for the party now and for the future—with how the cult of the person of Stalin has been gradually growing, the cult which became at a certain specific stage the source of a whole series of exceedingly serious and grave perversions of the party principles, of party democracy, of revolutionary legality.

Because of the fact that not all as yet realize fully the practical consequences resulting from the cult of the individual, the great harm caused by the violation of the principle of collective direction of the party and because of the accumulation of immense and limitless power in the hands of one person, the Central Committee of the party considers it absolutely necessary to make the material pertaining to this matter available to the 20th Congress of the Communist Party of the Soviet Union. . . .

Allow me first of all to remind you how severely the classics of Marxism-Leninism denounced every manifestation of the cult of the individual. In a letter to the German political worker, Wilhelm Bloss, Marx stated: "Because of my antipathy to any cult of the individual, I never made public during the existence of the International the numerous addresses from various countries which recognized my merits and which annoyed me. I did not even reply to them, except sometimes to rebuke their authors. Engels and I first joined the secret society of Communists on the condition that everything making for superstitious worship of authority would be deleted from its statute. [Ferdinand] Lassalle subsequently did quite the opposite." . . .

Underlining the role of the Central Committee of the party and its authority, Vladimir Ilyich pointed out: "Our Central Committee constituted itself as a closely centralized and highly authoritative group."

During Lenin's life the Central Committee of the party was a real expression

* *New York Times*, June 5, 1956, pp. 13–16. Reprinted by permission.

of collective leadership of the party and of the nation. Being a militant Marxist-revolutionist, always unyielding in matters of principle, Lenin never imposed by force his views upon his co-workers. He tried to convince, he patiently explained his opinions to others. Lenin always diligently observed that the norms of party life were realized, that the party statute was enforced, that the party congresses and the plenary sessions of the Central Committee took place at the proper intervals.

In addition to the great accomplishments of V. I. Lenin for the victory of the working class and of the working peasants, for the victory of our party and for the application of the ideas of scientific Communism to life, his acute mind expressed itself also in this—that he detected in Stalin in time those negative characteristics which resulted later in grave consequences.

Fearing the future fate of the party and of the Soviet nation, V. I. Lenin made a completely correct characterization of Stalin, pointing out that it was necessary to consider the question of transferring Stalin from the position of the Secretary General because of the fact that Stalin is excessively rude, that he does not have a proper attitude toward his comrades, that he is capricious and abuses his power.

In December 1922, in a letter to the Party Congress, Vladimir Ilyich wrote: "After taking over the position of Secretary General, Comrade Stalin accumulated in his hands immeasurable power and I am not certain whether he will be always able to use this power with the required care." . . .

Stalin acted not through persuasion, explanation and patient cooperation with people, but by imposing his concepts and demanding absolute submission to his opinion. Whoever opposed this concept or tried to prove his viewpoint and the correctness of his position was doomed to removal from the leading collective and to subsequent moral and physical annihilation. This was especially true during the period following the 17th Party Congress, when many prominent party leaders and rank-and-file party workers, honest and dedicated to the cause of Communism, fell victim to Stalin's despotism. . . .

It was precisely during this period (1935–1937–1938) that the practice of mass repression through the Government apparatus was born, first against the enemies of Leninism—Trotskyites, Zinovievites, Bukharinites, long since politically defeated by the party—subsequently also against many honest Communists, against those party cadres who had borne the heavy load of the Civil War and the first and most difficult years of industrialization and collectivization, who actively fought against the Trotskyites and the rightists for the Leninist party line.

Stalin originated the concept "enemy of the people." This term automatically rendered it unnecessary that the ideological errors of a man or men engaged in a controversy be proven; this term made possible the usage of the most cruel repression, violating all norms of revolutionary legality, against anyone who in any way disagreed with Stalin, against those who were only suspected of hostile intent, against those who had bad reputations.

This concept "enemy of the people" actually eliminated the possibility of any kind of ideological fight or the making of one's views known on this or that issue, even those of a practical character. In the main, and in actuality, the only proof of guilt used, against all norms of current legal science, "confessions" were acquired through physical pressures against the accused.

This led to glaring violations of revolutionary legality and to the fact that many entirely innocent persons, who in the past had defended the party line, became victims.

We must assert that, in regard to those persons who in their time had opposed the party line, there were often no sufficiently serious reasons for their physical annihilation. The formula "enemy of the people" was specifically introduced for the purpose of physically annihilating such individuals. . . .

Lenin's wisdom in dealing with people was evident in his work with cadres.

An entirely different relationship with people characterized Stalin. Lenin's traits—patient work with people, stubborn and painstaking education of them, the ability to induce people to follow him without using compulsion, but rather through the ideological influence on them of the whole collective—were entirely foreign to Stalin. He discarded the Leninist method of convincing and educating, he abandoned the method of ideological struggle for that of administrative violence, mass repressions and terror. He acted on an increasingly larger scale and more stubbornly through punitive organs, at the same time often violating all existing norms of morality and of Soviet laws. . . .

The majority of the Central Committee members and candidates elected at the 17th Congress and arrested in 1937-1938 were expelled from the party illegally through the brutal abuse of the party statute, because the question of their expulsion was never studied at the Central Committee plenum.

Now, when the cases of some of these so-called "spies" and "saboteurs" were examined, it was found that all their cases were fabricated. Confessions of guilt of many arrested and charged with enemy activity were gained with the help of cruel and inhuman tortures. . . .

The way in which the former NKVD workers manufactured various fictitious "anti-Soviet centers" and "blocs" with the help of provocatory methods is seen from the confession of Comrade Rozenblum, party member since 1906, who was arrested in 1937 by the Leningrad NKVD.

During the examination in 1955 of the Komarov case Rozenblum revealed the following fact: When Rozenblum was arrested in 1937, he was subjected to terrible torture during which he was ordered to confess false information concerning himself and other persons. He was then brought to the office of Zakovsky, who offered him freedom on condition that he make before the court a false confession fabricated in 1937 by the NKVD concerning "sabotage, espionage and diversion in a terroristic center in Leningrad." With unbelievable cynicism, Zakovsky told about the vile "mechanism" for the crafty creation of fabricated "anti-Soviet plots."

"In order to illustrate it to me," stated Rozenblum, "Zakovsky gave me several possible variants of the organization of this center and of its branches. After he detailed the organization to me, Zakovsky told me that the NKVD would prepare the case of this center, remarking that the trial would be public. Before the court were to be brought 4 or 5 members of this center: Chudov, Ugarov, Smorodin, Pozern, Shapeshnikova (Chudov's wife) and others together with 2 or 3 members from the branches of the center. . . .

". . . The case of the Leningrad center has to be built solidly, and for this reason witnesses are needed. Social origin (of course, in the past) and the party standing of the witness will play more than a small role.

"You, yourself," said Zakovsky, "will not need to invent anything. The NKVD will prepare for you a ready outline for every branch of the center; you will have to study it carefully and to remember well all questions and answers which the Court might ask. This case will be ready in four–five months, or perhaps a half year. During all this time you will be preparing yourself so that you will not compromise the investigation and yourself. Your future will depend on how the trial goes and on its results. If you begin to lie and to testify falsely, blame yourself. If you manage to endure it, you will save your head, and we will feed and clothe you at the Government's cost until your death."

This is the kind of vile things which were then practiced.

Facts prove that many abuses were made on Stalin's orders without reckoning with any norms of party and Soviet legality. Stalin was a very distrustful man, sickly suspicious; we knew this from our work with him. He could look at a man and say: "Why are your eyes so shifty today?" or "Why are you turning so much today and avoiding to look me directly in the eyes?" The sickly suspicion created in him a general distrust even toward eminent party workers whom he had known for years. Everywhere and in everything he saw "enemies," "two-facers" and "spies."

Possessing unlimited power, he indulged in great willfulness and choked a person morally and physically. A situation was created where one could not express one's own will.

When Stalin said that one or another should be arrested, it was necessary to accept on faith that he was an "enemy of the people." Meanwhile, Beria's gang, which ran the organs of state security, outdid itself in proving the guilt of the arrested and the truth of materials which it falsified. . . .

Comrades: The cult of the individual acquired such monstrous size chiefly because Stalin himself, using all conceivable methods supported the glorification of his own person. This is supported by numerous facts. One of the most characteristic examples of Stalin's self-glorification and of his lack of even elementary modesty is the edition of his *Short Biography*, which was published in 1948. . . .

In the situation which then prevailed I have talked often with Nikolai Alexandrovich Bulganin; once when we two were traveling in a car, he said, "It has happened sometimes that a man goes to Stalin on his invitation as a friend. And, when he sits with Stalin, he does not know where he will be sent next—home or to jail." . . .

Comrades! We must abolish the cult of the individual decisively, once and for all; we must draw the proper conclusions concerning both ideological-theoretical and practical work.

It is necessary for this purpose:

First, in a Bolshevik manner to condemn and to eradicate the cult of the individual as alien to Marxism-Leninism and not consonant with the principles of party leadership and the norms of party life, and to fight inexorably all attempts at bringing back this practice in one form or another. . . .

Secondly, to continue systematically and consistently the work done by the party's Central Committee during the last years, a work characterized by minute observation in all party organizations, from the bottom to the top, of the Leninist principles of party leadership, characterized, above all, by the main principles of collective leadership, characterized by the observance of the norms of party life described in the statutes of our party, and, finally, characterized by the wide practice of criticism and self-criticism.

Thirdly, to restore completely the Leninist principles of Soviet socialist democracy, expressed in the Constitution of the Soviet Union, to fight willfulness of individuals abusing their power. The evil caused by acts violating revolutionary socialist legality which have accumulated during a long time as a result of the negative influence of the cult of the individual has to be completely corrected. . . .

. . . And the fact that we present in all their ramifications the basic problems of overcoming the cult of the individual which is alien to Marxism-Leninism, as well as the problem of liquidating its burdensome consequences, is an evidence of the great moral and political strength of our Party.

We are absolutely certain that our party, armed with the historical resolutions of the 20th Congress, will lead the Soviet people along the Leninist path to new victories.

Long live the victorious banner of our party—Leninism!

12. MILOVAN DJILAS: THE NEW CLASS*

The first Communist state to break away from the Soviet bloc in eastern Europe was Yugoslavia. The Yugoslav Communist leader, Marshal Tito (Josip Broz, 1893–   ) had a considerable popular following and was able to resist Soviet threats and pressures. Although Yugoslavia remained a Communist state, a pragmatic domestic policy was maintained and a new relationship between Yugoslavia and the West was developed. Domestic criticism of the Tito regime was not permitted, but in 1957 Milovan Djilas (1911–   ), a high-ranking associate of Tito and long-time Communist philosopher, succeeded in publishing *The New Class*. The reaction of the Yugoslav government was swift. Djilas was arrested and imprisoned.

The New Class presented a devastating attack on the new elite groups which had appeared in Communist states. According to Djilas, who constituted the new class of "owners and exploiters," and how did they differ from all other classes? What distinctions did Djilas draw between the Communist party and the new class? Why was Stalin "the real and direct originator" of the new class? How could a new class exist in a classless society? What historical significance lies behind the appearance of a new class in Communist societies?

Everything happened differently in the U.S.S.R. and other Communist countries from what the leaders—even such prominent ones as Lenin, Stalin, Trotsky, and Bukharin—anticipated. They expected that the state would rapidly wither away, that democracy would be strengthened. The reverse happened.

* Milovan Djilas, *The New Class: An Analysis of the Communist System* (New York: Frederick A. Praeger, 1957), pp. 37–42, 44–46, 48–50, 52–54, 59. Reprinted by permission.

They expected a rapid improvement in the standard of living—there has been scarcely any change in this respect and, in the subjugated East European countries, the standard has even declined. In every instance, the standard of living has failed to rise in proportion to the rate of industrialization, which was much more rapid. It was believed that the differences between cities and villages, between intellectual and physical labor, would slowly disappear; instead these differences have increased. Communist anticipations in other areas—including their expectations for developments in the non-Communist world—have also failed to materialize.

The greatest illusion was that industrialization and collectivization in the U.S.S.R., and destruction of capitalist ownership, would result in a classless society. In 1936, when the new Constitution was promulgated, Stalin announced that the "exploiting class" had ceased to exist. The capitalist and other classes of ancient origin had in fact been destroyed, but a new class, previously unknown to history, had been formed.

It is understandable that this class, like those before it, should believe that the establishment of its power would result in happiness and freedom for all men. The only difference between this and other classes was that it treated the delay in the realization of its illusions more crudely. It thus affirmed that its power was more complete than the power of any other class before in history, and its class illusions and prejudices were proportionally greater.

This new class, the bureaucracy, or more accurately the political bureaucracy, has all the characteristics of earlier ones as well as some new characteristics of its own. Its origin had its special characteristics also, even though in essence it was similar to the beginnings of other classes.

Other classes, too, obtained their strength and power by the revolutionary path, destroying the political, social, and other orders they met in their way. However, almost without exception, these classes attained power *after* new economic patterns had taken shape in the old society. The case was the reverse with new classes in the Communist systems. It did not come to power to *complete* a new economic order but to *establish* its own and, in so doing, to establish its power over society.

In earlier epochs the coming to power of some class, some part of a class, or of some party, was the final event resulting from its formation and its development. The reverse was true in the U.S.S.R. There the new class was definitely formed after it attained power. Its consciousness had to develop before its economic and physical powers, because the class had not taken root in the life of the nation. This class viewed its role in relation to the world from an idealistic point of view. Its practical possibilities were not diminished by this. In spite of its illusions, it represented an objective tendency toward industrialization. Its practical bent emanated from this tendency. The promise of an ideal world increased the faith in the ranks of the new class and sowed illusions among the masses. At the same time it inspired gigantic physical undertakings.

Because this new class had not been formed as a part of the economic and social life before it came to power, it could only be created in an organization of a special type, distinguished by a special discipline based on identical philosophic and ideological views of its members. A unity of belief and iron discipline was necessary to overcome its weaknesses.

The roots of the new class were implanted in a special party, of the Bolshevik type. Lenin was right in his view that his party was an exception in the history of human society, although he did not suspect that it would be the beginning of a new class.

To be more precise, the initiators of the new class are not found in the party of the Bolshevik type as a whole but in that stratum of professional revolutionaries who made up its core even before it attained power. It was not by accident that Lenin asserted after the failure of the 1905 revolution that only professional revolutionaries—men whose sole profession was revolutionary work—could build a new party of the Bolshevik type. It was still less accidental that even Stalin, the future creator of a new class, was the most outstanding example of such a professional revolutionary. The new ruling class has been gradually developing from this very narrow stratum of revolutionaries. These revolutionaries composed its core for a long period. Trotsky noted that in pre-revolutionary professional revolutionaries was the origin of the future Stalinist bureaucrat. What he did not detect was the beginning of a new class of owners and exploiters.

This is not to say that the new party and the new class are identical. The party, however, is the core of that class, and its base. It is very difficult, perhaps impossible, to define the limits of the new class and to identify its members. The new class may be said to be made up of those who have special privileges and economic preference because of the administrative monopoly they hold. . . .

The party makes the class, but the class grows as a result and uses the party as a basis. The class grows stronger, while the party grows weaker; this is the inescapable fate of every Communist party in power.

If it were not materially interested in production or if it did not have within itself the potentialities for the creation of a new class, no party could act in so morally and ideologically foolhardy a fashion, let alone stay in power for long. Stalin declared, after the end of the First Five-Year Plan: "If we had not created the apparatus, we would have failed!" He should have substituted "new class" for the word "apparatus," and everything would have been clearer.

It seems unusual that a political party could be the beginning of a new class. Parties are generally the product of classes and strata which have become intellectually and economically strong. However, if one grasps the actual conditions in pre-revolutionary Russia and in other countries in which Communism prevailed over national forces, it will be clear that a party of this type is the product of specific opportunities and that there is nothing unusual or accidental in this being so. Although the roots of Bolshevism reach far back into Russian history, the party is partly the product of the unique pattern of international relationships in which Russia found itself at the end of the nineteenth and the beginning of the twentieth century. Russia was no longer able to live in the modern world as an absolute monarchy, and Russia's capitalism was too weak and too dependent on the interests of foreign powers to make it possible to have an industrial revolution. This revolution could only be implemented by a new class, or by a change in the social order. As yet, there was no such class.

In history, it is not important who implements a process, it is only important that the process be implemented. Such was the case in Russia and other countries in which Communist revolutions took place. The revolution created forces, leaders, organizations, and ideas which were necessary to it. The new class came into existence for objective reasons, and by the wish, wits, and action of its leaders. . . .

The movement of the new class toward power comes as a result of the efforts of the proletariat and the poor. These are the masses upon which the party or the new class must lean and with which its interests are most closely allied. This is true until the new class finally establishes its power and authority. Over and above this, the new class is interested in the proletariat and the poor only to the extent necessary for developing production and for maintaining in subjugation the most aggressive and rebellious social forces.

The monopoly which the new class establishes in the name of the working class over the whole of society is, primarily, a monopoly over the working class itself. This monopoly is first intellectual, over the so-called *avant-garde* proletariat, and then over the whole proletariat. This is the biggest deception the class must accomplish, but it shows that the power and interests of the new class lie primarily in industry. Without industry the new class cannot consolidate its position or authority.

Former sons of the working class are the most steadfast members of the new class. It has always been the fate of slaves to provide for their masters the most clever and gifted representatives. In this case a new exploiting and governing class is born from the exploited class. . . .

As in other owning classes, the proof that it is a special class lies in its ownership and its special relations to other classes. In the same way, the class to which a member belongs is indicated by the material and other privileges which ownership brings to him.

As defined by Roman law, property constitutes the use, enjoyment, and disposition of material goods. The Communist political bureaucracy uses, enjoys, and disposes of nationalized property.

If we assume that membership in this bureaucracy or new owning class is predicated on the use of privileges inherent in ownership—in this instance nationalized material goods—then membership in the new party class, or political bureaucracy, is reflected in a larger income in material goods and privileges than society should normally grant for such functions. In practice, the ownership privilege of the new class manifests itself as an exclusive right, as a party monopoly, for the political bureaucracy to distribute the national income, to set wages, direct economic development, and dispose of nationalized and other property. This is the way it appears to the ordinary man who considers the Communist functionary as being very rich and as a man who does not have to work. . . .

Other systems, too, have their professional politicians. One can think well or ill of them, but they must exist. Society cannot live without a state or a government, and therefore it cannot live without those who fight for it.

However, there are fundamental differences between professional politicians in other systems and in the Communist system. In extreme cases, politicians in other systems use the government to secure privileges for themselves and their cohorts, or to favor the economic interests of one social stratum or another.

The situation is different with the Communist system where the power and the government are identical with the use, enjoyment, and disposition of almost all the nation's goods. He who grabs power grabs privileges and indirectly grabs property. Consequently, in Communism, power or politics as a profession is the ideal of those who have the desire or the prospect of living as parasites at the expense of others. . . .

Although he did not realize it, Lenin started the organization of the new class. He established the party along Bolshevik lines and developed the theories of its unique and leading role in the building of a new society. This is but one aspect of his many-sided and gigantic work; it is the aspect which came about from his actions rather than his wishes. It is also the aspect which led the new class to revere him.

The real and direct originator of the new class, however, was Stalin. He was a man of quick reflexes and a tendency to coarse humor, not very educated nor a good speaker. But he was a relentless dogmatician and a great administrator, a Georgian who knew better than anyone else whither the new powers of Greater Russia were taking her. He created the new class by the use of the most barbaric means, not even sparing the class itself. It was inevitable that the new class which placed him at the top would later submit to his unbridled and brutal nature. He was the true leader of that class as long as the class was building itself up, and attaining power.

The new class was born in the revolutionary struggle in the Communist Party, but was developed in the industrial revolution. Without the revolution, without industry, the class's position would not have been secure and its power would have been limited.

While the country was being industrialized, Stalin began to introduce considerable variations in wages, at the same time allowing the development toward various privileges to proceed. He thought that industrialization would come to nothing if the new class were not made materially interested in the process, by acquisition of some property for itself. Without industrialization the new class would find it difficult to hold its position, for it would have neither historical justification nor the material resources for its continued existence.

The increase in the membership of the party, or of the bureaucracy, was closely connected with this. In 1927, on the eve of industrialization, the Soviet Communist Party had 887,233 members. In 1934, at the end of the First Five-Year Plan, the membership had increased to 1,874,488. This was a phenomenon obviously connected with industrialization: the prospects for the new class and privileges for its members were improving. What is more, the privileges and the class were expanding more rapidly than industrialization itself. It is difficult to cite any statistics on this point, but the conclusion is self-evident for anyone who bears in mind that the standard of living has not kept pace with industrial production, while the new class actually seized the lion's share of the economic and other progress earned by the sacrifices and efforts of the masses. . . .

Lenin's revolutionary epoch was replaced by Stalin's epoch, in which authority and ownership, and industrialization, were strengthened so that the much desired peaceful and good life of the new class could begin. Lenin's *revolutionary* Communism was replaced by Stalin's *dogmatic* communism, which in turn was replaced by *non-dogmatic* Communism, a so-called collective leadership or a group of oligarchs.

These are the three phases of development of the new class in the U.S.S.R. or of Russian Communism (or of every other type of Communism in one manner or another). . . .

Lenin too was a dogmatist, and Stalin too was a revolutionary, just as collective leadership will resort to dogmatism and to revolutionary methods when necessary. What is more, the non-dogmatism of the collective leadership is applied only to itself, to the heads of the new class. On the other hand, the people must be all the more persistently "educated" in the spirit of the dogma, or of Marxism-Leninism. By relaxing its dogmatic severity and exclusiveness, the new class, becoming strengthened economically, has prospects of attaining greater flexibility.

The heroic era of Communism is past. The epoch of its great leaders has ended. The epoch of practical men has set in. The new class has been created. It is at the height of its power and wealth, but it is without new ideas. It has nothing more to tell the people. The only thing that remains is for it to justify itself. . . .

No class is established by its own action, even though its ascent is organized and accompanied by a conscious struggle. This holds true for the new class in Communism.

The new class, because it had a weak relationship to the economy and social structure, and of necessity had its origin in a single party, was forced to establish the highest possible organizational structure. Finally it was forced to a deliberate and conscious withdrawal from its earlier tenets. Consequently the new class is more highly organized and more highly class-conscious than any class in recorded history.

This proposition is true only if it is taken relatively; consciousness and organizational structure being taken in relation to the outside world and to other classes, powers, and social forces. No other class in history has been as cohesive and singleminded in defending itself and in controlling that which it holds—collective and monopolistic ownership and totalitarian authority.

On the other hand, the new class is also the most deluded and least conscious of itself. Every private capitalist or feudal lord was conscious of the fact that he belonged to a special discernible social category. He usually believed that this category was destined to make the human race happy, and that without this category chaos and general ruin would ensue. A Communist member of the new class also believes that, without his party, society would regress and founder. But he is not conscious of the fact that he belongs to a new ownership class, for he does not consider himself an owner and does not take into account the special privileges he enjoys. He thinks that he belongs to a group with prescribed ideas, aims, attitudes, and roles. That is all he sees. He cannot see that at the same time he belongs to a special social category: the *ownership* class. . . .

13. THE WARSAW SECURITY PACT*

As the Cold War intensified in the late 1940's and East and West drew farther apart, the United States encouraged the creation of a military defensive-alliance system to embrace the non-Communist nations of Europe and North America. The North Atlantic Treaty Organization (NATO) was formed to provide for defense in a possible "hot" war with the Communist world. The success of NATO in coordinating and unifying military plans produced a reaction in eastern Europe. In 1955 the Soviet Union sponsored an eastern military alliance through the Warsaw Security Pact. What reasons did the parties to the Warsaw Pact give for the formation of a military alliance? What were the essential terms of the treaty, and in what ways did it reflect the Cold War ideological differences between East and West?

TREATY OF FRIENDSHIP, COOPERATION AND MUTUAL ASSISTANCE BETWEEN THE PEOPLE'S REPUBLIC OF ALBANIA, THE PEOPLE'S REPUBLIC OF BULGARIA, THE HUNGARIAN PEOPLE'S REPUBLIC, THE GERMAN DEMOCRATIC REPUBLIC, THE POLISH PEOPLE'S REPUBLIC, THE RUMANIAN PEOPLE'S REPUBLIC, THE UNION OF SOVIET SOCIALIST REPUBLICS AND THE CZECHOSLOVAK REPUBLIC, MAY 14, 1955

The Contracting Parties,

reaffirming their desire for the establishment of a system of European collective security based on the participation of all European states irrespective of their social and political systems, which would make it possible to unite their efforts in safeguarding the peace of Europe;

mindful, at the same time, of the situation created in Europe by the ratification of the Paris agreements, which envisage the formation of a new military alignment in the shape of "Western European Union," with the participation of a remilitarized Western Germany and the integration of the latter in the North-Atlantic bloc, which increased the danger of another war and constitutes a threat to the national security of the peaceable states;

being persuaded that in these circumstances the peaceable European states must take the necessary measures to safeguard their security and in the interests of preserving peace in Europe;

guided by the objects and principles of the Charter of the United Nations Organization;

being desirous of further promoting and developing friendship, cooperation and mutual assistance in accordance with the principles of respect for the independence and sovereignty of states and of non-interference in their internal affairs,

have decided to conclude the present Treaty of Friendship, Cooperation and Mutual Assistance and have for that purpose appointed as their plenipotentiaries: . . .

who, having presented their full powers, found in good and due form, have agreed as follows:

ARTICLE 1: The Contracting Parties undertake, in accordance with the Charter of the United Nations Organization, to refrain in their international relations

* "The Warsaw Security Pact" in *American Foreign Policy, 1950–1955* (Department of State, General Foreign Policy Series, No. 117, 2 vols.; Washington, 1957). I, 1239–1242.

from the threat or use of force, and to settle their international disputes peacefully and in such manner as will not jeopardize international peace and security.

ARTICLE 2: The Contracting Parties declare their readiness to participate in a spirit of sincere cooperation in all international actions designed to safeguard international peace and security, and will fully devote their energies to the attainment of this end.

The Contracting Parties will furthermore strive for the adoption, in agreement with other states which may desire to cooperate in this, of effective measures for universal reduction of armaments and prohibition of atomic, hydrogen and other weapons of mass destruction.

ARTICLE 3: The Contracting Parties shall consult with one another on all important international issues affecting their common interests, guided by the desire to strengthen international peace and security.

They shall immediately consult with one another whenever, in the opinion of any one of them, a threat of armed attack on one or more of the Parties to the Treaty has arisen, in order to ensure joint defence and the maintenance of peace and security.

ARTICLE 4: In the event of armed attack in Europe on one or more of the Parties to the Treaty by any state or group of states, each of the Parties to the Treaty, in the exercise of its right to individual or collective self-defence in accordance with Article 51 of the Charter of the United Nations Organization, shall immediately, either individually or in agreement with other Parties to the Treaty, come to the assistance of the state or states attacked with all such means as it deems necessary, including armed force. The Parties to the Treaty shall immediately consult concerning the necessary measures to be taken by them jointly in order to restore and maintain international peace and security.

Measures taken on the basis of this Article shall be reported to the Security Council in conformity with the provisions of the Charter of the United Nations Organization. These measures shall be discontinued immediately the Security Council adopts the necessary measures to restore and maintain international peace and security.

ARTICLE 5: The Contracting Parties have agreed to establish a Joint Command of the armed forces that by agreement among the Parties shall be assigned to the Command, which shall function on the basis of jointly established principles. They shall likewise adopt other agreed measures necessary to strengthen their defensive power, in order to protect the peaceful labours of their peoples, guarantee the inviolability of their frontiers and territories, and provide defence against possible aggression.

ARTICLE 6: For the purpose of the consultations among the Parties envisaged in the present Treaty, and also for the purpose of examining questions which may arise in the operation of the Treaty, a Political Consultative Committee shall be set up, in which each of the Parties to the Treaty shall be represented by a member of its Government or by another specifically appointed representative.

The Committee may set up such auxiliary bodies as may prove necessary.

ARTICLE 7: The Contracting Parties undertake not to participate in any coalitions or alliances and not to conclude any agreements whose objects conflict with the objects of the present Treaty.

The Contracting Parties declare that their commitments under existing international treaties do not conflict with the provisions of the present Treaty.

ARTICLE 8: The Contracting Parties declare that they will act in a spirit of friendship and cooperation with a view to further developing and fostering economic and cultural intercourse with one another, each adhering to the principle of respect for the independence and sovereignty of the others and non-interference in their internal affairs.

ARTICLE 9: The present Treaty is open to the accession of other states, irrespective of their social and political systems, which express their readiness by participation in the present Treaty to assist in uniting the efforts of the peaceable states in safeguarding the peace and security of the peoples. Such accession shall enter into force with the agreement of the Parties to the Treaty after the declaration of accession has been deposited with the Government of the Polish People's Republic.

ARTICLE 10: The present Treaty is subject to ratification, and the instruments of ratification shall be deposited with the Government of the Polish People's Republic.

The Treaty shall enter into force on the day the last instrument of ratification has been deposited. The Government of the Polish People's Republic shall notify the other Parties to the Treaty as each instrument of ratification is deposited.

ARTICLE 11: The present Treaty shall remain in force for twenty years. For such Contracting Parties as do not at least one year before the expiration of this period present to the Government of the Polish People's Republic a statement of denunciation of the Treaty, it shall remain in force for the next ten years.

Should a system of collective security be established in Europe, and a General European Treaty of Collective Security concluded for this purpose, for which the Contracting Parties will unswervingly strive, the present Treaty shall cease to be operative from the day the General European Treaty enters into force.

Done in Warsaw on May 14, 1955, in one copy each in the Russian, Polish, Czech and German languages, all texts being equally authentic. Certified copies of the present Treaty shall be sent by the Government of the Polish People's Republic to all the Parties to the Treaty.

In witness whereof the plenipotentiaries have signed the present Treaty and affixed their seals.

14. WALTER HALLSTEIN: THE EUROPEAN ECONOMIC COMMUNITY*

The contrast between Europe after World War I and contemporary Europe is characterized by economic progress and self-confidence. The continuing integration of economic functions in western Europe has created new attitudes, increased prosperity, and raised production levels. Beginning in 1950 with the proposal of a French economist, Jean Monnet, for a European coal and steel community, the drive for integration has led to the signing of the Treaty of Rome in 1957 and the creation of Euratom. With all three programs under a

* "The Dynamics of the European Community" in *European Community*, No. 103 (June 1967), pp. 10–12. Reprinted by permission.

single authority, the Common Market nations—Belgium, the Netherlands, Luxemburg, France, West Germany, and Italy—progressively reduced internal tariffs to allow the freer flow of goods between member states, and the resulting prosperity led to numerous applications for membership from non-members.

One of the architects of the Common Market, and a leading exponent of the European community, has been Walter Hallstein (1901–   ), past president of the EEC's Commission. On what grounds, in the following article, did Hallstein characterize the European Economic Community as "political, democratic, and dynamic"? Why did he applaud the British government's recognition that membership in the Common Market would constitute "a political decision first of all, and . . . an economic decision secondarily"? What facts did he muster to support his assertion that "our young people will live to see a political map of Europe that does not look like a patchwork quilt"? Why, in his view, did European unification threaten "neither the Soviet Union nor anyone else"?

Just a few weeks ago we celebrated the tenth anniversary of the Treaty of Rome—more than commercial treaty—and of the European Economic Community—more than a free trade area. This point must be made clear. Sometimes those in constant touch with world trade may underestimate the need for the hand of State to guide economic activity (a single hand, not a new one at every hundred kilometers).

Because Europe is not a federal State today, we do not yet have a European internal market. But we can build this market by bringing the elements together, one by one. This process started 10 years ago when the Treaty of Rome called into being a community of States, one type of economic federation. This Economic Community is political, democratic, and dynamic. . . .

The political foundation of the Community is expressed most strongly in its institutions. Through them, the Community releases the dynamic power inherent in the integration process. On their inter-action, the outcome of European integration depends.

The Council of Ministers, composed of representatives of the six Governments, makes the most important decisions and is, therefore, first and foremost, the Community's legislature. The Commission, the independent executive branch, is invested with the exclusive right to initiate legislation, without instructions from the Governments. Responsible only to the European Parliament, the Commission represents the interests of the Community. Finally, the Court of Justice protects the Community order against infringements and ensures that all—the six European States and their citizens—shall obey the law and enjoy its protection.

In the European Parliament the Community will of the six peoples finds free and independent expression. Thus, the Community has the basic attributes of democratic legitimacy. Although the Parliament still lacks real law-making powers and sovereignty in budgetary matters, the Treaty does contain strict provisions under which it must be consulted and its Committees have come to form an important instrument of surveillance. The Parliament's powers of control culminate in a vote of no confidence. The Parliament—and only the Parliament —has the power to dismiss the members of the Commission.

Our European work by pre-empting the future, also reflects the political nature of the Community. Every policy is only as strong as the hope it embodies.

The Treaty of Rome is no pandect, no legal code, no guarantee of the *status quo*. European integration is a process. It is movement wherever we come into contact with it. Everything we do is done with an eye on the year 2000, when the world and the conditions of our individual and collective lives will be fundamentally different. Our young people will live to see a political map of Europe that does not look like a patchwork quilt.

But how do we assure movement towards a future situation? There are four main lines of advance.

The Community can only be built in stages. The vast field covered by the Rome Treaty and its nature as an outline treaty necessitate the constant search for agreement on matters not covered when the Treaty was negotiated; when it was completely impossible to make final arrangements for every field of integration. As an outline treaty, the Treaty of Rome differs appreciably from earlier integration treaties such as the one for the Coal and Steel Community. From the very first day there has been a strict legal obligation to apply the Treaty of Rome, but its implementation has more often than not required a political choice.

A second dynamic element is the dialogue between the institutionalized common interest, the Commission, and the federal organ, the Council of Ministers. The privilege, the monopoly, and indeed the duty to initiate this dialogue belong to the Commission. It opens when the Commission submits a proposal to the Council of Ministers. In addition to supporting the proposal in Council meetings, the Commission must occasionally act as the intermediary for compromise.

A third dynamic element is the conflict of special interests built into the integration process. Like the weights of a clock, they keep it in perpetual movement as different economic sectors bring their views to the attention of the institutions involved.

A fourth dynamic element is the logic of the facts. How, for example, can capital movements be fully liberalized without common concepts in the monetary and currency fields? We have made a pact with the frightening and irresistible power of logic. The material logic of the facts of integration urges us relentlessly on from one step to the next, from one field to another.

Because economic integration is an autonomous process, its success does not necessarily depend on merging the Community members' foreign and defense policies, still hidebound by historical particularism. However, it does influence these areas of policy by creating a "bias" in favor of political union, a "bias of reason." Although a politically united Europe, the European federation, will not just "happen" upon the completion of economic integration (There aren't any automatic developments in politics), economic integration will help attain this objective.

A common trade policy will influence areas of non-economic foreign policy remaining within the national competence. The effects of common European initiatives to promote scientific research and technological development will be limited if they exclude the extensive and complex armaments industry. This in turn will influence the defense policies of the member states.

Even in the economic sphere, Europe's role in the world depends on its unity. The Community made great concessions to align its position with the wishes of its partners in the Kennedy Round. Without our unified economic policy and without our great new bargaining power, fully reciprocal comprehensive liberal-ization of world trade would be impossible. The acid test of the Kennedy Round will not be forgotten.

The geographical extension of European integration, another product of the Community's dynamics, also confirms its course as the right one. The historically significant decisions of the British Government and the Governments of Denmark and Ireland to negotiate again for admission find us prepared. The negotiations of 1961–63 are fresh in our memories although a great deal has changed since then.

Community structures have solidified during and because of crises. The common agricultural policy no longer exists only on paper. The common external tariff is complete. The customs union will be an accomplished fact in 14 months. Today, membership in the Community means accepting not only the spirit and the letter of the Rome Treaty with its ultimate political goals, but also the laws of its institutions.

We are pleased to see that the British Government also accepts this viewpoint and is prepared to base its negotiations on it. (By this I do not mean to exclude the possibility of transitional arrangements.) No longer does the British Government face a united opposition in its own country. The Government recognizes accession to the European Community as a political decision, first of all, and as an economic decision, secondarily. The British Government's emphasis on the political nature or its decision in encouraging.

Equally clear is the interest in a unified, large European commercial market, expressed in the European Free Trade Association *communiqué* of April 28, 1967. Today, more distinctly than in 1962, there are two lines of thinking on European integration, so that it may be possible to deal with them more adequately in the future. One group of states wants to overcome vested interests in the area of commercial policy and achieve political fusion. On the other side, we see a line of development directed more by economic and, especially, commercial policy.

These applications put the spotlight again on the question of what kind of Community we want. Once again, Europe stands at a fork in the road. The right road will exact dogged patience and constructive optimism of every one of us. Admittedly, no cut-and-dried formula yet exists on how to establish political union, no specific method of integration on which the member states agree. But a fund of constitutional experience does exist, built up by the European Communities.

This experience shows that only an independent embodiment of the Community interest, vested with real powers, can prevent cooperation from running into a dead end. The driving force of economic unification has been the European Commission's right of initiative. By its presence at negotiations between the Governments, the Commission has acted in the important role of mediator. Another equally important part of this constitutional experience is the realization that only the equality of all Europeans and their states can guarantee long-term stability and continuity.

The Europe of the European Community has proven its value as the nucleus of European unification. The influence of that Europe extends beyond the Yalta line which divides all of Europe. Once the customs and agricultural unions are complete, the European Economic Community will become a factor impossible to ignore in economic relations with Eastern Europe. By hard, intensive and resourceful work to remove the many small and large obstacles hampering the development of these economic relations, the European Economic Community will be able to contribute towards easing tensions in Europe. European unification threatens neither the Soviet Union nor anyone else. Every step toward European unity could achieve what no bi-polarization of world power, no disarmament conference, and no "European security system" can bring about: exorcism of the dangers inherent in frontiers and the establishment of true peace in troubled Europe.

President Kennedy once described European integration as the most constructive political achievement in our century. It has made an unparalleled contribution to the material well-being of the peoples of Europe, and proven that even after two catastrophic wars even in so complicated and interest-ridden sphere as socio-economic activity, unity is possible in Europe. After nearly ten years of practical experience, the European Community stands as an example of an organizational principle demonstrably appropriate for the unity of peoples. It provides new evidence daily that there can be a European Community and that it works.

We do not know whether man's age-old dream of "one world" will ever be realized, or whether national frontiers can or should be eliminated. We know only that to keep the peace and make it strong we must deprive national frontiers of their power to harm. Our work to unite Europe is a mighty work of peace, our deepest satisfaction, and our greatest pride.

15. ALBERT CAMUS: THE REBEL*

Albert Camus (1913–60)—French journalist, novelist, and playwright—was born in Mondovi, Algeria, and studied philosophy at the University of Algiers. He lived in Paris during World War II where, as a writer for the underground newspaper *Combat*, he became a leading journalist of the Resistance. After the war he produced a series of plays, novels, and essays, all of which emphasized the dilemma of human existence in an irrational universe. Insisting that he was a moralist and not a philosopher, Camus continually raised the question of how individual self-fulfillment was possible in a world of confused and conflicting values. In 1957 he was awarded the Nobel Prize in literature for the "clearsighted earnestness" with which he had "illuminated the problems of the human conscience in our time."

In *L'homme révolté* (*The Rebel*), 1951, Camus presented an analysis of the human quest for individuality and self-expression in a seemingly meaningless stream of history. What values or purposes did he see in the penchant of each individual to rebel against society? In view of Camus' assertion that "the twentieth century revolution . . . is first of all a politics and an ideology," why did he insist that concentration upon politics and ideologies was futile and unrealistic? Compare Camus' opinions on man's potential for self-expression with Kafka's views in *The Trial*.

* Albert Camus, *The Rebel*, trans. Anthony Bower (New York: Alfred A. Knopf, 1957), pp. 21–22, 101–102, 251–252, 296–298, 300–301. Reprinted by permission of Alfred A. Knopf, Inc., and Hamish Hamilton Ltd.

... The rebel is a man who is on the point of accepting or rejecting the sacred and determined on laying claim to a human situation in which all the answers are human—in other words, formulated in reasonable terms. From this moment every question, every word, is an act of rebellion while in the sacred world every word is an act of grace. It would be possible to demonstrate in this manner that only two possible worlds can exist for the human mind: the sacred (or, to speak in Christian terms, the world of grace) and the world of rebellion. The disappearance of one is equivalent to the appearance of the other, despite the fact that this appearance can take place in disconcerting forms. There again we rediscover the *All or Nothing*. The present interest of the problem of rebellion only springs from the fact that nowadays whole societies have wanted to discard the sacred. We live in an unsacrosanct moment in history. Insurrection is certainly not the sum total of human experience. But history today, with all its storm and strife, compels us to say that rebellion is one of the essential dimensions of man. It is our historic reality. Unless we choose to ignore reality, we must find our values in it. Is it possible to find a rule of conduct outside the realm of religion and its absolute values? That is the question raised by rebellion. . . .

Man's solidarity is founded upon rebellion, and rebellion, in its turn, can only find its justification in this solidarity. We have, then, the right to say that any rebellion which claims the right to deny or destroy this solidarity loses simultaneously its right to be called rebellion and becomes in reality an acquiescence in murder. In the same way, this solidarity, except in so far as religion is concerned, comes to life only on the level of rebellion. And so the real drama of revolutionary thought is announced. In order to exist, man must rebel, but rebellion must respect the limit it discovers in itself—a limit where minds meet and, in meeting, begin to exist. Rebellious thought, therefore, cannot dispense with memory: it is a perpetual state of tension. In studying its actions and its results, we shall have to say, each time, whether it remains faithful to its first noble promise or if, through indolence or folly, it forgets its original purpose and plunges into a mire of tyranny or servitude.

Meanwhile, we can sum up the initial progress that the spirit of rebellion provokes in a mind that is originally imbued with the absurdity and apparent sterility of the world. In absurdist experience, suffering is individual. But from the moment when a movement of rebellion begins, suffering is seen as a collective experience. Therefore the first progressive step for a mind overwhelmed by the strangeness of things is to realize that this feeling of strangeness is shared with all men and that human reality, in its entirety, suffers from the distance which separates it from the rest of the universe. The malady experienced by a single man becomes a mass plague. In our daily trials rebellion plays the same role as does the *"cogito"* in the realm of thought: it is the first piece of evidence. But this evidence lures the individual from his solitude. It founds its first value on the whole human race. I rebel—therefore we exist. . . .

. . . Essentially, then, we are dealing with a perpetual demand for unity. The rejection of death, the desire for immortality and for clarity, are the mainsprings of all these extravagances, whether sublime or puerile. Is it only a cowardly and personal refusal to die? No, for many of these rebels have paid the ultimate price in order to live up to their own demands. The rebel does not ask for life, but for reasons for living. He rejects the consequences implied by death. If nothing lasts, then nothing is justified; everything that dies is deprived of meaning. To fight against death amounts to claiming that life has a meaning, to fighting for order and for unity.

The protest against evil which is at the very core of metaphysical revolt is significant in this regard. It is not the suffering of a child, which is repugnant in itself, but the fact that the suffering is not justified. After all, pain, exile, or confinement are sometimes accepted when dictated by good sense or by the doctor. In the eyes of the rebel, what is missing from the misery of the world, as well as from its moments of happiness, is some principle by which they can be explained. The insurrection against evil is, above all, a demand for unity. The rebel obstinately confronts a world condemned to death and the impenetrable obscurity of the human condition with his demand for life and absolute clarity. He is seeking, without knowing it, a moral philosophy or a religion. Rebellion, even though it is blind, is a form of asceticism. Therefore, if the rebel blasphemes, it is in the hope of finding a new god. He staggers under the shock of the first and most profound of all religious experiences, but it is a disenchanted religious experience. It is not rebellion itself that is noble, but its aims, even though its achievements are at times ignoble.

At least we must know how to recognize the ignoble ends it achieves. Each time that it deifies the total rejection, the absolute negation, of what exists, it destroys. Each time that it blindly accepts what exists and gives voice to absolute assent, it destroys again. Hatred of the creator can turn to hatred of creation or to exclusive and defiant love of what exists. But in both cases it ends in murder and loses the right to be called rebellion. One can be nihilist in two ways, in both by having an intemperate recourse to absolutes. Apparently there are rebels who want to die and those who want to cause death. But they are identical, consumed with desire for the true life, frustrated by their desire for existence and therefore preferring generalized injustice to mutilated justice. At this pitch of indignation, reason becomes madness. If it is true that the instinctive rebellion of the human heart advances gradually through the centuries toward its most complete realization, it has also grown, as we have seen, in blind audacity, to the inordinate extent of deciding to answer universal murder by metaphysical assassination. . . .

. . . "Obey," said Frederick the Great to his subjects; but when he died, his words were: "I am tired of ruling slaves." To escape this absurd destiny, the revolution is and will be condemned to renounce, not only its own principles, but nihilism as well as purely historical values in order to rediscover the creative source of rebellion. Revolution, in order to be creative, cannot do without either a moral or metaphysical rule to balance the insanity of history. Undoubtedly, it has nothing but scorn for the formal and mystifying morality to be found in bourgeois society. But its folly has been to extend this scorn to every moral demand. At the very sources of its inspiration and in its most profound transports is to be found a rule that is not formal but that nevertheless can serve as a guide. Rebellion, in fact, says—and will say more and more explicitly—that revolution must try to act, not in order to come into existence at some future date in the eyes of a world reduced to acquiescence, but in terms of the obscure existence that is already made manifest in the act of insurrection. This rule is neither formal nor subject to history, it is what can be best described by examining it in its pure state—in artistic creation. Before doing so, let us only note that to the "I rebel, therefore we exist" and the "We are alone" of metaphysical rebellion, rebellion at grips with history adds that instead of killing and dying in order to produce the being that we are not, we have to live and let live in order to create what we are....

. . . Virtue cannot separate itself from reality without becoming a principle of evil. Nor can it identify itself completely with reality without denying itself. The moral value brought to light by rebellion, finally, is no farther above life and history than history and life are above it. In actual truth, it assumes no reality in history until man gives his life for it or dedicates himself entirely to it. Jacobin and bourgeois civilization presumes that values are above history, and its formal virtues then lay the foundation of a repugnant form of mystification. The revolution of the twentieth century decrees that values are intermingled with the movement of history and that their historical foundations justify a new form of mystification. Moderation, confronted with this irregularity, teaches us that at least one part of realism is necessary to every ethic: pure and unadulterated virtue is homicidal. And one part of ethics is necessary to all realism: cynicism is homicidal. That is why humanitarian cant has no more basis than cynical provocation. Finally, man is not entirely to blame; it was not he who started history; nor is he entirely innocent, since he continues it. Those who go beyond this limit and affirm his total innocence end in the insanity of definitive culpability. Rebellion, on the contrary, sets us on the path of calculated culpability. Its sole but invincible hope is incarnated, in the final analysis, in innocent murders.

At this limit, the "We are" paradoxically defines a new form of individualism. "We are" in terms of history, and history must reckon with this "We are," which must in its turn keep its place in history. I have need of others who have need of me and of each other. Every collective action, every form of society, supposes a discipline, and the individual, without this discipline, is only a stranger, bowed down under the weight of an inimical collectivity. But society and discipline lose their direction if they deny the "We are." I alone, in one sense, support the common dignity that I cannot allow either myself or others to debase. This individualism is in no sense pleasure; it is perpetual struggle, and, sometimes, unparalleled joy when it reaches the heights of proud compassion....

. . . The revolution of the twentieth century claims to base itself on economics, but is primarily political and ideological. It cannot, by its very function, avoid terror and violence done to the real. Despite its pretensions, it begins in the absolute and attempts to mold reality. Rebellion, inversely, relies on reality to assist it in its perpetual struggle for truth. The former tries to realize itself from top to bottom, the latter from bottom to top. Far from being a form of romanticism, rebellion, on the contrary, takes the part of true realism. If it wants a revolution, it wants it on behalf of life, not in defiance of it. That is why it relies primarily on the most concrete realities—on occupation, on the village, where the living heart of things and of men is to be found. Politics, to satisfy the demands of rebellion, must submit to the eternal verities. Finally, when it causes history to advance and alleviates the sufferings of mankind, it does so without terror, if not without violence, and in the most dissimilar political conditions. . . .

But historical absolutism, despite its triumphs, has never ceased to come into collision with an irrepressible demand of human nature, of which the Mediterranean, where intelligence is intimately related to the blinding light of the sun, guards the secret. Rebellious thought, that of the commune or of revolutionary trade-unionism, has not ceased to deny this demand in the presence of bourgeois nihilism as well as of Cæsarian socialism. Authoritarian thought, by means of three wars and thanks to the physical destruction of a revolutionary elite, has succeeded in submerging this libertarian tradition. But this barren victory is only provisional; the battle still continues. Europe has never been free of this struggle between darkness and light. It has only degraded itself by deserting the struggle and eclipsing day by night. The destruction of this equilibrium is today bearing its bitterest fruits. Deprived of our means of mediation, exiled from natural beauty, we are once again in the world of the Old Testament, crushed between a cruel Pharaoh and an implacable heaven.

In the common condition of misery, the eternal demand is heard again; nature once more takes up the fight against history. Naturally, it is not a question of despising anything, or of exalting one civilization at the expense of another, but of simply saying that it is a thought which the world today cannot do without for very much longer. There is, undoubtedly, in the Russian people something to inspire Europe with the potency of sacrifice, and in America a necessary power of construction. But the youth of the world always find themselves standing on the same shore. Thrown into the unworthy melting-pot of Europe, deprived of beauty and friendship, we Mediterraneans, the proudest of races, live always by the same light. In the depths of the European night, solar thought, the civilization facing two ways awaits its dawn. But it already illuminates the paths of real mastery.

Real mastery consists in refuting the prejudices of the time, initially the deepest and most malignant of them, which would reduce man, after his deliverance from excess, to a barren wisdom. It is very true that excess can be a form of sanctity when it is paid for by the madness of Nietzsche. But is this intoxication of the soul which is exhibited on the scene of our culture always the madness of excess, the folly of attempting the impossible, of which the brand can never be removed from him who has, once at least, abandoned himself to it? Has Prometheus ever had this fanatical or accusing aspect? No, our civilization survives in the complacency of cowardly or malignant minds—a sacrifice to the vanity of aging adolescents. Lucifer also has died with God, and from his ashes has arisen a spiteful demon who does not even understand the objects of his venture. In 1950, excess is always a comfort, and sometimes a career. Moderation, on the one hand, is nothing but pure tension. . . .

The real madness of excess dies or creates its own moderation. It does not cause the death of others in order to create an alibi for itself. In its most extreme manifestations, it finds its limit, on which it sacrifices itself if necessary. Moderation is not the opposite of rebellion. Rebellion in itself is moderation, and it

demands, defends, and re-creates it throughout history and its eternal disturbances. The very origin of this value guarantees us that it can only be partially
destroyed. Moderation, born of rebellion, can only live by rebellion. It is a perpetual conflict, continually created and mastered by the intelligence. It does not
triumph either in the impossible or in the abyss. It finds its equilibrium through
them. Whatever we may do, excess will always keep its place in the heart of
man, in the place where solitude is found. We all carry within us our places of
exile, our crimes and our ravages. But our task is not to unleash them on the
world; it is to fight them in ourselves and in others. Rebellion, the secular will
not to surrender, is still today at the basis of the struggle. Origin of form, source
of real life, it keeps us always erect in the savage, formless movement of history. . . .

16. KARL JASPERS: THE FUTURE OF MANKIND*

   Karl Jaspers (1883–   ) attracted world-wide attention when he published
a profoundly personal volume which raised *The Question of German Guilt*
in 1946. The author had served as Professor of Philosophy at the University of Heidelberg since 1920, but was dismissed by the Nazis in 1937 because
of his refusal to subscribe to party doctrines. Jaspers was reinstated in his pro-
fessorship at Heidelberg in 1945 and accepted a chair in philosophy at Basel in
1948. A trained psychologist as well as a philosopher, Jaspers has applied his
sensitive intellect to the problem of survival in an atomic age. The following
selections are taken from his speculations upon *The Future of Mankind*, published in 1958.
   According to Jaspers' analysis, what is the political and psychological basis of
our "present world-wide confusion"? On what basis does he assert that a new
world order which will permit the survival of humanity "cannot be symbolized
either by an idea of empire or by the idea of a universal church"? Why, in its
past historical conduct, has the West been "no better or politically wiser than the
great Asian civilizations"? What is Jaspers' formula for reducing "the hatred
which more than half of mankind harbors against the West"? What "new
politics" does Jaspers advocate to afford man a brighter future?

Today . . . politics has two sources: the two superpowers and the special
interests of the many small nations. The latter, as in the past, use all means to
get what they want by the old methods, acting on the most varied national,
social, religious motives. They want status, independence, more power, a chance
to form new states. Yet none of these wars is like earlier ones. The difference is
that all ventures are undertaken with a glance at the two superpowers, with
their help or permission, and with the idea of gaining advantages from them
and playing one against the other. And the interest of both great powers is
involved in all wars. They have a hand in every one. Neither of them wants
to see its influence in the world decline; each wants to extend it.
   The present situation is governed by the tension between the "impossibility"
of an atomic world war and the danger, constantly kindled by small wars, that
the impossible will happen. For the time being, the age of a "new politics" manifests itself in the fact that since 1945 all small wars and conflicts have ended not

* Karl Jaspers, *The Future of Mankind*, trans. E. B. Ashton (Chicago: University of Chicago
Press, © 1961), pp. 63–65, 71–72, 74–79, 329–35. Reprinted by permission.

in decisions but in armistices. When Russia herself, in the Berlin blockade, risked an attempt to use force beyond the limits of her territorially secured power, America beat it off peacefully, at immense cost, with the unexpected airlift. When the Israelis, abandoned by the British withdrawal, rose in 1948 to defend their new state against the attacks that were launched from all sides to destroy them, the conclusion of the struggle—which would have been the wholly unexpected, hard-earned, but overwhelming victory of Israel—was cut short by the British threat of aerial bombardment; the result was not a peace such as used to follow upon a victorious war, but an armistice. In the Korean and Indonesian wars the outcome was similar: an armistice, not peace. "Armistices" are the hallmark of this new politics in our world. Each time, world war threatens; each time, the possibility is nipped in the bud at the expense of some small nation. Again and again, the actions, the events, the words are such that world war should be expected at once, by all previous standards. The tension of such moments is repeated, and one is never quite sure that there will be no total disaster. But when world war really seems imminent, both superpowers have so far called a halt.

Thus the extremes of atomic war and world peace are parted by a wide range of wars with conventional weapons. What matters here is to bring the scale of realities, of contemporary facts, into proper perspective. We must not fail to prepare for dangers near at hand because we see only the extreme danger. The extreme may happen any day, but it need never happen. It is a limit to all possibilities of action, but within this limit lie the concrete tasks we must perform.

Small nations—and today all are small, except for the two superpowers—must reckon with wars. Political changes can be brought about by small wars if the great powers do not interfere, or if they want the changes. Those who wish to preserve themselves, their way of life, their identity as a people, their form of the principle of political freedom, must be ready for small wars—small in comparison with total atomic wars, but as terrible as ever for whole nations. Those who cannot maintain themselves in small wars are lost in this transitional period which determines what nations and territorial boundaries will survive in a totally different future. Hence the general apprehension of being totally menaced by the shadow of the bomb, even if it is not used. Politics has not replaced war by any means, and stocks of "old weapons" and soldierly valor in "small wars" are by no means immaterial.

Let me restate the present military situation. America and the West are far inferior to Russia in conventional arms; Russia is catching up with America in nuclear arms, and in missiles to deliver them she is at the moment superior. The total war potential of the West would today—given time to bring it into play in case of war—still exceed Russia's considerably. If Russia should start the war —by crossing her western boundaries, for example—her immense armies could quickly conquer Europe with conventional weapons and would probably be met at once with atomic weapons. America would thus commit the first act with such weapons but would suffer retaliation within the hour. Russian politicians have said that they would never be the first to use the bomb, but would use it only in retaliation—statements which carry scarcely more weight than their pledges of peace, long refuted by actual deeds of violence. American politicians have made no such pronouncements, saying only that they would never use atomic weapons except as a last resort; but American military men have declared that these weapons would come into play at once against a Russian attack on Europe. Such statements do carry weight, for they would scarcely be made if they were not meant seriously.

It would be self-deception to distinguish between tactical and strategic bombs, or generally between types of nuclear weapons. The use of "atomic artillery" would instantly result in total atomic war. This has been expressly stated by the Russians and has the same weight as the American statement; it would not be said if it were not meant seriously.

In this presently world-wide confusion, the power of leadership appears to be declining everywhere. More and more of the men we see coming to the top seem to be merely drifting. If no leader follows a simple line derived from his thinking, from the logic of his position—whether in totalitarian fashion, like Stalin, or by means of reasons convincing to his people and by the power of his personality, as in Churchill's or Roosevelt's case—we get an ersatz leadership by a phantom, a pseudo-leadership.

The result is helplessness in a collective leadership that hides from the public. A world war might be decided upon because no one dares any longer to say no, because all agree, although they are against it. Each fears the others, and each thinks the other wants what he himself does not want but must agree to, if he is to keep his miserable bit of power. If no one dares any more, on his own responsibility, against the welter of opinions, prevailing or otherwise, to carry all others along on the path of righteousness, the disaster will come—with all disclaiming responsibility. But their evasion makes all of them jointly guilty. There could be, in intensified form, a repetition of 1914, when a war which nobody wanted came, and in which no one, or all, shared the guilt.

Matters are becoming less and less predictable. We used to have Stalin and Truman, and although one employed pitiless terror while the other was anxious but firm in defense, both were acting from a rationale: a reasoning attitude that knows what it sees and what it wants. You could figure out their intentions, whether reprehensible or desirable. There was then still something like leadership in the world, but at the time of this writing it appears more leaderless than ever. We no longer seem to see anything but doctrinaire notions on one side and momentary moves, skilful or blundering, on the other; we sense nothing simple and constant. Thus begins the drifting and the rule of accident, which will no longer serve a flexible leadership as an eminently history-making force. . . .

The age of colonialism is at an end. Europe's rule of the world is shattered, her world position in ruins, her pre-eminence a thing of the past, her own future gravely imperiled. What will happen? If the world's population grows from two billion to three billion and more; if the Westerners, already outnumbered, continue to fall behind; if the vast colored masses, possessing most of the world's area and the bulk of its resources, become the technological equals of the West— will this human majority, not yet free from the hatred begotten by four centuries, not turn against the West? Is there a chance for a community of all nations?

With the collapse of colonial rule, technology has conquered the world and made history, for the first time, world history. Is this a triumph of the European mind—not only in science and technology but in its thinking processes, in Anglo-Saxon enlightenment, in Marxism, in nationalist oratory, in the whole rationale of organization, of planning, of calculating? A common knowledge and know-how covers the world. Whether received with the delight of children who suddenly discover an undreamed-of skill or with the reluctance of one who adopts what he feels will lead to his destruction—it is always the same irresistible development of the technological age.

It is no European triumph. What came into the world by means of Europe, historically speaking, is valid in itself, independently of its origin. It is not a unique culture but the property of man as such, of man as a rational being. It is identically transferable. Where it has once been acquired, it can, with more or less talent, be cultivated—whether for mere use, for participation in further scientific research, or for technical inventions. The necessary talent is no basic trait or permanent condition of nations. For example, the number of patent applications is today a sort of yardstick of national inventiveness, and it varies enormously. In the nineteenth century, France marched in the van of progress, but today new French patents are scarce, and we find the highest number in America. Among the men active in the immensely difficult construction of the American atom bomb were a large number of European immigrants from Germany, Italy, and Hungary. What we have in common is the technological age of history; the talent for it is scattered at random and attracted by challenges and opportunities. It no longer belongs to a few privileged nations. . . .

A common concern, therefore, unites the nations today: can technology be subordinated as a tool? As yet no one knows how. Will the deeper source, dried up at first, well up again with new vigor, in new forms; will it master technology and convert it into the mere management of life? We see no sign of this, but we must expect it if we are conscious of our human roots. Or will technology become absolute and destroy man—a notion easy to throw out but impossible to think through?

We are looking for outlines of political thought that would aim, in the breathing spell before the threatening end, at two inseparable objectives: true humanity and the preservation of existence. Let us try to draft such a kind of new politics for our situation at the end of the colonial age. It will be governed by two basic, closely related problems.

One concerns *liberation and self-preservation*. Peace can be served only by truth, not by lies in points of principle. From the Western point of view, honesty requires, first, the actual and unqualified liberation of all colonial areas, and second, in view of the dangers arising therefrom, the accompanying defensive self-preservation of the West.

As to the first, there is no more stopping the non-European peoples' march to freedom. It is futile to maintain domination anywhere, in any past forms, with no matter how many concessions. The withdrawal from all colonial areas demands a simultaneous reversal of the colonial idea into its opposite, a will to leave the existence of others to their own responsibility.

As to the second, the vast dangers arising from racial hatred; from shortsighted, confused actions of the liberated; from their frequent incompetence in making their way in the technological age; from the incalculable consequences of the violence they employ toward each other—these dangers can be met only by a defensive union of the West. This calls for substantial economic sacrifices, for giving up ingrained feelings of national power, and for a transformation of technological, economic, and social ways of life. Only thus can we preserve ourselves reliably and non-aggressively.

The second problem concerns the direction *toward a world order*. In liberation and self-preservation, the prevailing mood is still one of hostility. The final stage of peace cannot be mere juxtaposition, cannot involve constant threats and the constant danger of explosions. The grand objective of politics must be a world order—starting out, to be sure, from the given states, territories, and power relationships. We must envision possible ways, as well as seemingly insuperable obstacles, to such an order.

Both aspects of the new politics are problems of mankind. They outrank all special national problems and pervade all politics not thoughtlessly confined to local interests of the moment. Yet both, today, differ from the analogous conceptions of past ages. They are not to be imagined after the pattern of the former European community; they must come into being in the framework of the one, globe-wide humanity, not in the framework of a European world. We cannot seek order by means of the communion of any single faith, only by means of a future communion of reason. Therefore, this new world order cannot be symbolized either by an idea of empire or by the idea of a universal church. These could only be deceptive stage props of a global despotism. If freedom is to be saved—that is to say, if man is to be saved—he will have to keep struggling for himself in a process of self-education that can never end. What remains—in constant danger, based on historical premises, never lastingly terminable—will be an unstable situation that must always be realized and secured again.

A fundamental fact is that the conflict between the West and its former colonies cuts across another conflict: between Russia and the West, between totalitarianism and freedom. Both Russia and America support anticolonialism. Russia foments hatred and offers herself and her communism as useful allies, but America also offers herself and her freedom. Neither is acting unselfishly, for they vie for influence abroad. Each stresses her anticolonialism and accuses the other of colonialism; each wants to increase her own power and to contain the other's. It is in the shadow of this struggle over the vast formerly colonial areas that we must see the possibilities of liberation and self-preservation. On the one hand, the interplay of the two conflicts—West versus former colonies, and America versus Russia—promotes the rapid but still quite external liberation of all colored nations; but, on the other hand, it beclouds the liberation issue that might otherwise be clear.

Descriptions of the colonial age sound either like indictments or like vindications. In view of this whole four-hundred-year process that made the European technological era a global era, and thus made the world one and let history become world history, indictments and vindications seem rather inappropriate, unless we speak in terms of original sin. Still, it was we of the West who wrought this evil.

Particular indictments and vindications always bear on common human traits. Terrible, merciless, treacherous actions mark the history of China and India no less than ours. Indeed, it is to the credit of Europe that in her case self-criticism of colonial activities set in early and persisted. Nor was it quite ineffective. The motives of the Europeans active in colonialism were varied: adventure; love of danger and violence, of discovery and exploration; missionary zeal; self-sacrifice in the service of God; greed; the search, on foreign soil, for a freedom suppressed at home; or the will to create new political forms. This great process was a terrible outbreak of human passions. But its greatness lies on the dreadful side of world history, beyond good and evil. No one intended this dreadful greatness; no one may cite it either for vindication or complaint.

We may doubt the desirability of freeing peoples who have never known inner political freedom. Their liberation has thrown mankind into chaos. Were not all nations happier—as far as men can be happy—before the end of colonial rule? Was the world peace about 1900, the world communion under British dominance, not a great and singular moment in world history? Yet we are deceiving ourselves if we give in to this idea. If the Westerners' political wisdom and moral purity had entitled them to rule and educate mankind until their guidance, respecting the spiritual roots of others, would have nurtured the slow growth of world-wide political freedom—then such colonial rule would have been preferable. But the West, in its actual conduct, has been no better or politically wiser than the great Asian civilizations, even though individual thinkers and statesmen realized what was happening and tried to do better—as the British, at times, did in India. In fact, the combination of common human cruelty, of negligence and sloth, of the enjoyment of fruits reaped by adventurers, of ambiguous administration and imperialistic ambition—the combination of these blazed a trail unfit to be the high road of humanity. For a moment, the West had a task. It failed. The results are final.

Yet the non-Westerners are no better. Those who have obtained freedom from us are men, not angels. The freedom that all but fell into their laps in the technological age—thanks, above all, to Anglo-Saxon initiative—confronts them with a task which they must now solve for themselves. No one can guide or teach them. They have forgotten their own traditional wisdom—and again it is frightening how much they seem like the natural prey of totalitarian rule. But not inevitably.

As yet, no one blames us for our most dubious achievement: having dragged down all mankind to a technological fate. What is resented is not technology but dependence upon the white man; his technological world, and all that it implies, is exactly what all seem to want. On grounds of religious tradition, some nations were initially averse and later reluctant, but now all accept with enthusiasm. It is like a conquest—not by human beings, not by a foreign culture, not by Europeans, but by the thing itself which belongs to man as an intellectual being, to all men alike, challenging all to make of it what they can.

The liberation of nations from colonial rule is governed not only by an elemental urge for independence but by ideas introduced by colonization itself. In liberating themselves, they continue what colonial rule began. Without England, for example, there would today be no large, unified India with rudiments of common education, of a common law, and of industrial development. Everywhere intellectuals educated in or by the West are leading the way. The nations themselves are still largely in the dreamlike hold of newly questioned traditions. But no country seeks to return to its condition before colonial rule. China and India deal with their historic substance—the very thing that so greatly distinguishes them in our eyes—as if it were of no account.

To achieve world peace, to reduce the hatred which more than half of mankind harbors against the West, it is essential for the West to acknowledge honestly and unreservedly that colonialism is finished. We must think through the consequences of this situation and outline the principles of the resulting political actions. That is easy to say, but for Westerners, and for all others, it is hard to find the right and effective way to peace in the world chaos left behind by colonialism—and this world peace alone can save us from the atom bomb.

The first step is a great renunciation. The Western powers must withdraw to their own territories. They must grant others the full independence they seek. In large measure this has already been done. Where it has not yet been done, there is constant unrest—in the Near East, in North Africa, in the African territories. The renunciation must be simultaneously political and economic, to establish political and economic relations on a new basis of free reciprocity. Why and to what end is this renunciation necessary for world peace?

First: expansion has come to an end because the world has been distributed. As the globe at large has no more free space, the self-restriction of all to their own territories must follow.

Second: people resent not only the political power of the West but its economic power. Their experience with this strikes them, often justly, as exploitation, oppression, fraud. Taxation seems like tribute to them, the procurement of raw materials from their territories, with the help of freely hired and paid native labor, like robbery and enslavement. Economic thinking, tied to legal warrants and calculable sureties, is foreign to them. This attitude is fostered by transferring Marxist notions of the entrepreneur-worker relationship to that of colonial powers and natives. The existence of this attitude is a powerful fact, a fact surmountable only if the liberated will have their own experience of freedom, and if the economic ethics of a technologically unified world will draw upon a new source for the binding force of equality.

Third: granting that all achievements of the colonial powers—of the British in India, the Dutch in Indonesia, the Germans in their former African colonies and in Chinese Kiao-Chou—testified to technological skill and economic efficiency and benefited the natives, they still were not motivated by the natives' interest, even if this was subsequently considered. The motives were self-interest and delight in achievement as such, and these have no absolute value that would justify placing them above everything else. We must restore the true hierarchy of values, which technological and economic progress has obscured for both colonial powers and natives.

Withdrawal to one's own territory has taken economic sacrifices and will take more. Moreover, its inescapable consequence is a change in the principle of the industrial age. In this age industry lived by expansion, by the extension of markets, by the steadily increased procurement of raw materials wherever they were made cheapest by organized Western exploitation, and by the export of capital for the establishment of enterprises abroad. The result of all this was direct or indirect economic expropriation, secured by the power of governments assuming the protection of business transactions and agreements. Now, external expansion must yield to inner intensification.

If this alone can pave the way to world peace, the greatest sacrifices would be minor in comparison with the alternative. The new principle, which seems absurd to our economic and technological thinking, must at least be thought through. This is a matter for the energies of economic analysis—which is not my field—in conjunction with a new moral will. . . .

A sense of stability marked most historical ages. There were great events, dangers, adventures, but in a changeless, valid world order that kept men safe. Today we feel caught up in an all-consuming motion to which we contribute, unintentionally or intentionally, by what we do and what we are. As the pace quickens, everyone is swept along willy-nilly. We keep trying for temporary stabilizations, but an absolute one is futile. In the past, the movement of history was dispersed and unconscious; now it has become one global, conscious process of mankind.

Three basic political approaches to this movement have emerged and failed.

The first says: I will have no part in the course of calamity. I want to keep myself pure, and I can do so only by excluding myself, ready to bear what the course of events may bring, and to perish in it. There have been such ways of life since time immemorial. Ascetics live in the world that tolerates them, feeds them, wants them at times, but does not concern them; they do not intervene in it, ask nothing, suffer everything—they live as if the world did not exist. Today, however, such a life is hardly possible. Wherever modern civilization penetrates, man is compelled to work, to assume some function in the totality of labor. There is little room for the contemplative life. On the other hand, this life of "count me out" is actually quick to turn impure, inconsistent, and contemptible. It becomes either skeptical indifference or outraged acceptance in a still uninjured personal position. This leads to the confusion of condemning what I live by—and wanted to hold aloof from. It should not concern me, yet I am entangled in it by my life and judgment.

The second approach says: I want to be in on it. This is a world process; what does not go along is annulled or annihilated by irresistible fate. I can be either nothing or part of the substance of things, so whatever enters with the iron tread of necessity will lead me. I am not only with it—I am it, if I hear and obey. My fate is one with the world's; I see and welcome the wave of the future. I become a Nazi; I become a Communist; I obediently apply the force I share in to those who resist or who do not belong, to those of ill will or to those naturally unfit for what I know to be truth as well as reality. Whatever cruelty, seeming injustice, and coercion is committed by the force I live by, the force that carries me, is the destined course of salvation. This force does only what must happen in any case. I know the world spirit, the course of history—the why and how of the struggle of classes or races, for instance—and I do what I have come to know. My sense of existence is powerfully enhanced, proving that I am on the right track. And if things go wrong, I mull over the dark destiny of being; I extract, experience, excogitate that there is such a thing, that it was hidden and will appear, and I stand ready to follow. . . . It is this pliant thinking that makes men ready to go along with each new despotism, without any faith but that in their own knowledge of historic destiny.

The third approach is that of defiant independence. I cannot be indifferent to this chaotic world, this conglomeration of stupidity and malice, for I am outraged. There is no other world; but this one, as it is, is not for me. My reality is negation—in general, and consequently in every particular. I defy this nonsense. I take what personal happiness comes my way, against the general trend, and I perish senselessly, but in possession of my inner independence.

Yet in so doing I involve myself in contradictions. I am outraged, but I cannot remain guiltless. Under the Nazis, life in negation was still carried on in Nazi terms; I was, in fact, living by the Nazis and sharing their guilt if my "No" did not extend to the instant risk and sacrifice of my life. So it is with every negation of things at large. The man who says "No"—whether audibly, as in the free world where any nonsense may be uttered, or inaudibly—still goes on living. He thinks he is being different in this life, an exception, a case of resistance on the smallest scale, a private individual, an outsider. Yet everything tends to entangle him in the reality he rejects.

All three approaches—worldlessness, complicity, defiance—are inadequate to the problem. Each time, the solution seems clear but is unclear and biased in practice, in relation to the whole. All three miss the existential situation. They lose sight of the measure of man; they miss the human opportunities of reason. The ascetic is ineffectual; he seems to vanish in his solitude. The joiner surrenders to the evil of violence. The stubborn independent does not get beyond saying "No" to an evil for which he, too, bears the guilt. These three approaches do not tell us what to do; they show only what does not help.

The basic question is what makes life worth living.

To achieve a life that is worthy of him, man must survive—but he will survive only if he achieves that life. This is a circle that we cannot break out of merely to stay alive. Now, at the brink, mere life depends on worthy living. This alone leads to the actions that would bar atomic doom.

For such a life it cannot suffice to be safe, peaceful, and prosperous. There are ambiguities in praising, respecting, worshipping life as such. The faith in life is truthful when it explores the mystery of living; it is truthful when it protects the human body—even a legally imprisoned criminal's—from physical violation by the state; it is still truthful when it shudders to kill in war. But it is not the last thing. It becomes untruthful, untrue, and ruinous when life as such is made the sole, the absolutely highest good. Then man takes the place of Transcendence, expressing an actual lack of faith.

Besides, it is a vain endeavor to stem the march to the abyss by proclaiming the sanctity of life, for this kindles only inconsequential emotions, not a revival of the ethos itself.

The life worship becomes untrue wherever it forgets that man is superior to his life. He can sanctify it only by fulfilling his task. The conditions of a life worthy of man, the premises of finding the road to salvation, are the risk and the sacrifice of life—not in themselves, but as moments of human reason and love.

The questions are always the same. What makes life worth living? What do I want in the face of extremity? What will I do, what will I be, how will I live in awareness of my humanity and our common peril? Is there a truth that makes the ultimate effort and, if it fails, lets us meet the end without fear?

This is where ends and means and plans and achievements cease. What makes life worth living has consequences in action and in the conduct of life, but it cannot be willed—for it is the source of our will. Man's present reality must show what is, and what he is, but it can show this only on the premise and in the fulfilment of his way of life. I live in order to manifest it, and this kind of life is already the manifestation.

The threat of doom will not be banished by measures confined to the atom bomb, nor by measures designed merely to prevent a new war; what is required is that all particular actions, purposes, plans, agreement, or institutions issue from the entirety of human life. What is done in any of these directions will be lastingly, constructively successful only if all of them, without exception, work together. The result would be a new politics.

At first, the new politics would have to move in the tracks of the old politics that is still with us but must be overcome. What the change in individuals can sometimes accomplish cannot be done at once in the community of all. Attempts at instant reformation would quickly produce total anarchy and despotism. The political change must let the new grow in the framework of the old; it must fill the old track with new meanings, until it can be left for a new track. Individual decisions make this a common process, with large areas still in darkness as the light starts shining here and there.

The old politics acts on the principles of present enmity and future war; the new politics will act on the principle that there can be honest, rational communication and peace. What matters in the old politics is neither to be fooled by your opponent nor to fool yourself; each jeopardizes self-preservation. But what matters further, to make the new politics possible, is to drum the reality and the meaning of all those activities into the general consciousness, to strip the camouflage from what goes on not only among our enemies but among ourselves—for it is only then that man can come out of his drifting, that ethos, reason, and self-sacrifice can awaken and find both the valor of self-preservation and the turn to a true will to peace in a new politics. The old politics sees everything in the reality of friend and foe, with reference to war. The new politics will search in this reality for the premises of peace.

To the old politics, which ultimately relates all things to the Cold War and the impending hot one, all spheres of life turn into "theaters of war." In present world strategy we find not only a military theater, but economic, cultural, ideological, religious theaters of war—effects upon all of which are carefully considered and psychologically calculated in the propaganda effort to sway opinions, motives, ways of action. Our time will make the choice between this refinement of the old politics and its transformation. If the change occurs, the question will be not only where violent struggle shall cease, but where and how struggles that are not naturally violent shall be divorced from violence and retained. Every step toward pure, non-violent struggle is a step in the conquest of war.

While the threat of war exists, reason would be weakened if a statesman, or a nation, abolished all indirect, war-related methods at one stroke. But everyone today can know about these methods and be aware of the unnatural, poisonous, ruinous abuse they constitute. The question now is when it will be politically possible to venture into the new politics—to stop the abuse of economics as a political weapon, for instance, because the inner self-preservation of the Western world (as discussed in our chapter on the end of colonialism) has developed far enough to permit it.

The old politics does not recognize any act that does not benefit its own state power. Even "cultural policy" is part of power politics. When it communicates its own national spirit, its language, its works, its way of life, it is thinking of national prestige, not of humanity—except, perhaps, when it fancies its nation as humanity's perfect embodiment, a model of human excellence which all the rest should join for their own salvation.

The new politics will be able to proceed with candor, because its self-preservation is strictly defensive and without expansionist aims. It gives up any claims to totality; it grants freedom; it allows ideas to be communicated regardless of their political consequences. It dares to promote its own way as a common way for all, by relinquishing the power potentials of the old politics. It frankly shows both its self-interest, if any, and its disinterestedness. Thus it can stimulate forces that agree with it.

The passage from the old politics to the new would be the passage from falsehood to truth. Today, the old "sophistical maxims" are still as effective as when Kant exposed them. *Fac et excusa*—do it when you have the chance, and explain later; the very brazenness of the deed lends it a certain glow of inner conviction, because success is the best advocate. *Si fecisti, nega*—if you did it, deny that you are at fault; blame others or human nature. *Divide et impera*—set the rulers against the people or against each other; by seeming to side with the underdog you will subject them all, one by one. Kant says that these maxims, being generally known, do not fool anyone, and that no one is ashamed of being found out, only of having failed—for aggrandizement of power, however accomplished, is the only honor in politics.

The new politics would make men ashamed of following these maxims. They would no longer win appreciative smiles from the knowing and unsmiling applause from masses that do not believe in man because they do not believe in themselves. Not until men are changed can they frankly resolve to discard the sophistical maxims, the principle of falsehood in politics, in word and deed.

The old politics culminates, on the one hand, in the frankly ruthless will to power that exterminates the enemy who does not submit and, on the other hand, in the disingenuous, deceiving, and self-deceiving vindication of war by the sole guilt of the enemy, whom the victor calls to account. In the case of naked force there is the chance of mercy; in the case of hypocritical justification, the chance of merciless exploitation of victory by imposing intolerable burdens upon the vanquished.

The new politics, resting on the political ethos that regards peace as the now definitive premise of any human existence, will press for firm moral judgments, but the essence of evil, in its eyes, is the lie—above all, the hypocritical lie—including the grain of falsehood in a true accusation. It will end the most diabolical, though seemingly unbloody, type of combat: the tallying-up of one another's guilt by every means at hand. Instead, like a rational individual, it seeks to preserve itself by finding its own faults first. Where the fault lies with the other side, where a principle (and not, therefore, its every human representative!) seems morally and politically evil, the new politics will show concretely what is going on, will analyze, illuminate, expose the noxious principle —but it will do so, first, without abandoning its own truthfulness at any point of the exposure, and second, without censoriousness, intending, rather, to convince.

This struggle never ceases. To let it go on in the light of full publicity is the beginning of peace. In this true battle of minds—which today, in the framework of the old politics, is often so obscured as to be imperceptible—the point is to know the facts and to impart ideas. It is to cut to the root of the matter, to find the simplest forms in which men can absorb ideas and be convinced—not to falsify truth and conviction with suggestive slogans that will substitute for understanding. We cannot elaborate here, but ahead of us lies a great new world of intellectual struggle, distinguished by breadth, abundance, and precision, and inspired by the ethos of a true polemics that no longer wants to hoodwink men with sophisms but will seek truth together.

Violent war will cease once the battle of minds has shown it up, with all its premises, as a thing we cannot want any more. War will cease when men are no longer fooled, when they sense the power of conviction in their own thinking, and when they understand that they themselves are responsible for the evil if they promote it by their untruthfulness.

In foolishly idealistic politics we act as if the condition we want had been attained already. In foolishly realistic politics we act as if it were unattainable. Both ways are irresponsible. The responsible way is to foster each rudiment, to nurture each germ, to take up each good impulse, to see the chances of the future in the facts of the present and to think and act with these chances in mind. This is not a middle way between extremes; it is the high road above the two abysmal benightments that we call idealism and realism.

78 79 9 8 7 6

Praise for *The Journeyer*

"Astonishing and titillating." —*Chicago Tribune*

"Fabulous . . . Sumptuous and exceedingly bawdy."
  —*The Washington Post*

"Pound for pound, *The Journeyer* is a classic."
  —Gene Lyons, *Newsweek*

"Perfect entertainment." —*The Philadelphia Inquirer*

"Employing both great sweep and meticulous detail, Gary Jennings has produced an impressively learned gem of the astounding and the titillating." —*Chicago Tribune Book World*

"Relentlessly gripping." —*Publishers Weekly*

"Remarkable . . . Extraordinary . . . Re-creates a whole lost civilization." —*The Miami Herald*

FORGE BOOKS BY GARY JENNINGS

Aztec
Aztec Autumn
Aztec Blood
Aztec Rage
The Journeyer

Visit Gary Jennings at www.garyjennings.net.

THE
JOURNEYER

GARY JENNINGS

A Tom Doherty Associates Book

New York

THE JOURNEYER

Copyright © 1984 by Gary Jennings

First published in the United States by Atheneum and
published simultaneously in Canada by McClelland and Stewart Ltd.

A Forge Book
Published by Tom Doherty Associates, LLC
175 Fifth Avenue
New York, NY 10010

www.tor-forge.com

Forge® is a registered trademark of Tom Doherty Associates, LLC.

ISBN 978-0-7653-2349-1

First Forge Trade Paperback Edition: March 2010

Printed in the United States of America

0 9 8 7 6 5 4 3 2 1

FOR GLENDA

When Marco Polo lay on his deathbed,
his priest, his friends and relations
clustered around him to plead that he
at last renounce the countless lies he
had related as his true adventures, so his
soul would go cleansed to Heaven. The
old man raised up, roundly damned them
all and declared, "I have not told
the half of what I saw and did!"

ACCORDING TO
FRA JACOPO D'ACQUI,
MARCO POLO'S CONTEMPORARY
AND HIS FIRST BIOGRAPHER

THE
JOURNEYER

CY APRES COMMENCE
LE LIURE DE
MESSIRE MARC PAULE
DES DIUERSES
ET GRANDISMES
MERUEILLES DU MONDE

Come hither, great princes! Come hither,
emperors and kings, dukes and marquises,
knights and burgesses! Come hither, you people of
all degrees, who wish to see the many faces of mankind
and to know the diversities of the whole world!
Take up this book and read it, or have it read to you.
For herein you will find all the greatest wonders
and most marvelous curiosities. . . .

AH, LUIGI, LUIGI! In the worn and wrinkled fustian of those old pages I hear your very voice again.

It had been many years since I last looked into our book, but when your letter came I fetched it out once more. I can still smile at it and admire it simultaneously. The admiration is for its having made me famous, however little I may deserve that fame, and the smile is for its having made me notorious. Now you say that you wish to write another work, an epic poem this time, again incorporating the adventures of Marco Polo—if I will grant that liberty—but attributing them to an invented protagonist.

I cast back in my memory to our first meeting, in the cellars of that

Genoa palazzo where we prisoners of war were lodged. I remember how diffidently you approached me, and with what reticence you spoke:

"Messer Marco, I am Luigi Rustichello, late of Pisa, and I have been a captive here since long before you arrived. I have listened to you telling that hilariously ribald story of the Hindu with his *ahem* caught in the holy rock hole. I have heard you tell it three times now. Once to your fellow prisoners, again to the warder, and yet again to the visiting almoner of the Brotherhood of Justice."

I inquired, "Are you weary of hearing it, Messere?"

And you said, "Not at all, Messere, but you will soon be weary of the telling. Many more persons will want to hear that tale, and all the other tales you have told, and any others which perhaps you have not told yet. Before you tire of the telling, or of the stories themselves, why do you not simply tell to *me* all your recollections of your travels and adventures? Tell them only the once and let me set them down on paper. I am a writer of some facility and much experience. Your tales could make a considerable book, Messer Marco, and multitudes of people then can read it for themselves."

And so I did, and so you did, and so the multitudes have done. Though many other journeyers before me had written of their travels, none of those works ever enjoyed the immediate and continuing popularity of our *Description of the World*. Perhaps, Luigi, it was because you chose to transcribe my words in French, the most widely known Western language. Or perhaps you made my stories better in the writing than I could do in the telling. At any rate, somewhat to my surprise, our book became much read and talked of and sought after. It was copied and recopied, and by now has been translated into every other language of Christendom, and of those versions, too, countless copies have been taken and circulated.

But none of them tells the singular story of the anguished Hindu and his rape of a rock.

When I sat in that clammy Genoa prison, recounting my reminiscences, and you sat putting them into proper words, we decided that they would be told in *only* the most proper words. You had your reputation to consider, and I had my family name. You were the Rustichello of Pisa, and I was a Polo of Venice. You were the romancier courtois, already known for your retellings of the classic tales of chivalry—of Tristan and Isolde, of Lancelot and Ginevra, of Amys and Amyllion. I was, as you described me in the book, representative of the "sajes et nobles citaiens de Venece." So we agreed that our pages would contain only those of my adventures and observations which we could publish without a blush or a qualm, and which could be read without offending the Christian sensibilities even of maiden ladies or nuns.

Further, we determined to leave out of the book anything which might strain the credence of any stay-at-home reader. I recall that we even debated before we included my encounters with the stone that burns and the fabric that will not. Thus many of the most marvelous incidents of my travels were, so to speak, abandoned by the wayside of my wanderings. We left out the unbelievable and the bawdy and the scandalous. But now, you tell me, you want to mend those gaps—though still without hazarding my good name.

So your new protagonist will be called Monsieur Bauduin, not Messer Marco, and he will hail from Cherbourg, not Venice. But in all else he will be me. He will experience, enjoy, endure all that I did—*and all that I left untold heretofore*—if I will refresh your memory by telling those many stories to you again.

It is a great temptation, certainly. It would be like living those days anew—and those nights—and that is a thing I have long yearned to do. I always intended, you know, to journey again to the far eastward. But no, you could not have known. I have not spoken of that even in my family circle. It has been a dream I treasured too much to share. . . .

Yes, I meant to go again sometime. But when I was freed from Genoa and returned to Venice, the family business demanded my attention, and so I hesitated to depart. And then I met Donata, and she became my wife. So I hesitated again a while, and then there was a daughter. Naturally that gave me cause to hesitate, and there came a second daughter, and then there were three. So, for one reason and another, I kept on hesitating, and suddenly one day I was old.

Old! It is inconceivable! When I look into our book, Luigi, I see myself there a boy, and then a youth, and then in my manhood, and even at the book's very end I am still a stalwart. But when I look into a glass, I see there an aged stranger, sapped and sagged and blemished and enfeebled by the corroding rusts of five and sixty years. I murmur, "*That* old man cannot go again a-journeying," and then I realize: that old man is Marco Polo.

So your letter came to me at a vulnerable moment. And your suggestion that I contribute to a new book is an opportunity I will not let pass. If I cannot do again the things I once did, at the least I can remember them and take relish in them while I relate them, since I can now do that with the impunity of your Bauduin disguise. You may wonder at my so welcoming that disguise, as you may also have wondered at my remark that the earlier book earned me both undeserved renown and undeserved notoriety. I shall explain.

I never claimed to have been the first man to travel from the West into the far East, and you did not put any such boast into our book. Nevertheless, that seems to have been the impression produced upon most of its readers—or those readers living elsewhere than Venice, where no such illusion obtains. After all, my own Venetian father and uncle had gone to and returned from the East before they retraced their journey and that time took me with them. Also, in the East itself I met many other Westerners, of all nations from England to Hungary, who had arrived there before me, and some of whom stayed there longer than I did.

But long previous to them, many other Europeans had traversed the same Silk Road I trod. There was the Spanish rabbi Benjamin of Tudela, and the Franciscan friar Zuàne of Carpini, and the Flemish friar Guillaume of Rubrouck—and, like me, all those men published accounts of their travels. As far back as seven or eight hundred years ago, there were missionaries of the Nestorian Christian Church penetrating into Kithai, and there are many laboring there today. Even before Christian times, there must have been Western traders wandering to and from the East. It is known that the Pharaones of ancient Egypt wore the silk of the Orient, and silk is thrice mentioned in the Old Testament.

Numerous other things and the words describing them were, long before my time, made part of our Venetian language. Several of our city's buildings are decorated, inside or out, with that sort of filigree fancywork we adopted from the Arabs and have long called arabesco. The murderous sassìn gets his name from the hashishiyin of Persia, men who kill at the instigation of a religious fervor induced by the drug hashish. The making of that cheap glazed fabric called indiana was learned in India, where that cloth is called chint, and where the inhabitants also inspired our Venetian expression "far l'Indiàn," meaning to behave utterly stupidly.

No, I was not the first to go East or to return from there. Insofar as my fame rests on the misapprehension that I was, it is indeed unmerited. But my notoriety is even less deserved, for it depends on the widespread assumption of my dishonesty and untruthfulness. You and I, Luigi, put into our book only those observations and experiences we judged believable, but even so I am disbelieved. Here in Venice I am jeeringly called Marco Millions—an epithet implying not any wealth of ducats, but my supposed store of lies and exaggerations. That amuses me more than it annoys me, but my wife and daughters are exceedingly vexed at being known as the Dona and Damìne Milioni.

Hence my willingness to put on the mask of your fictional Bauduin as I commence to tell everything that has not until now been told. Let the world, if the world chooses, think it *all* a fiction. It is better to be disbelieved in such matters than to remain forever mute about them.

But first, Luigi:

From the sample of manuscript you sent with your letter, to show me how you propose to open Bauduin's story, I gather that your command of French has considerably improved since you set down our *Description of the World.* I am emboldened to make another small comment on that earlier book. A reader of those pages might think that Marco Polo had been a man of sober age and judgment through all his traveling days—and that he had somehow done that traveling through the sky, so high aloft that he could see all at once the entire breadth of our earth, and point to one and then another land and say with certainty, "Herein this one differs from that." True, I was forty when I came home from my journeying. I hope I came back a little more wise and discerning than when I went, for I was then only a wide-eyed adolescent— ignorant, inexperienced, foolish. Also, like any journeyer, I had to see all lands and the contents of them, not from the hindsight vantage of some twenty-five years later, but in the order in which I came upon them in my travels. It was kind and flattering of you, Luigi, to portray me in that earlier book as having been always a man all-seeing and all-knowing, but your new work might benefit if you made its narrator somewhat more true to life.

I would further suggest, Luigi, if you truly intend to cut your Monsieur Bauduin to the pattern of Marco Polo, that you commence his career by giving him a misspent youth of reckless abandon and misbehavior. That is one thing which I am here telling for the first time. I did not depart from Venice merely because I was eager for new horizons. I left Venice because I had to—or, at any rate, because Venice decreed that I had to.

Of course I cannot know, Luigi, *how* closely you wish to make your Bauduin's history parallel my own. But you did say "tell all," so I will begin even before the beginning.

VENICE

. 1 .

ALTHOUGH the Polo family has been Venetian, and proud of it, for perhaps three hundred years now, it did not originate on this Italian peninsula, but on the other side of the Adriatic Sea. Yes, we were originally from Dalmatia, and the family name would then have been something like Pavlo. The first of my forebears to sail to Venice, and stay here, did so sometime after the year 1000. He and his descendants must have risen rather quickly to prominence in Venice, for already in the year 1094 a Domènico Polo was a member of the Grand Council of the Republic, and in the following century so was a Piero Polo.

The most remote ancestor of whom I have even a dim recollection was my grandfather Andrea. By his time, every man of our house of Polo was officially designated an Ene Aca (meaning N.H., which in Venice means Nobilis Homo or gentleman), and was addressed as Messere, and we had acquired the family arms: a field argent bearing three birds sable with beaks gules. This is actually a visual play on words, for that emblematic bird of ours is the bold and industrious jackdaw, which is called in the Venetian tongue the pola.

Nono Andrea had three sons: my uncle Marco, for whom I was

named, my father Nicolò and my uncle Mafìo. What they did when they were boys I do not know, but when they grew up, the eldest son, Marco, became the Polo trading company's agent in Constantinople in the Latin Empire, while his brothers remained in Venice to manage the company's headquarters and keep up the family palazzo. Not until after Nono Andrea's death did Nicolò and Mafìo scratch the itch to go traveling themselves, but when they did they went farther than any Polo before them had gone.

In the year 1259, when they sailed away from Venice, I was five years old. My father had told my mother that they intended to go only as far as Constantinople, to visit their long-absent elder brother. But, as that brother eventually reported to my mother, after they had stayed with him there for a time, they took a notion to go on eastward. She never heard another report of them, and, after a twelvemonth, she decided they must be dead. That was not just the vaporings of an abandoned and grieving woman; it was the most likely possible surmise. For it was in that year of 1259 that the barbarian Mongols, having conquered all the rest of the Eastern world, pushed their implacable advance to the very gates of Constantinople. While every other white man was fleeing or quailing before "the Golden Horde," Mafìo and Nicolò Polo had gone marching foolhardily right into their front line—or, considering how the Mongols were then regarded, better say: into their slavering and champing jaws.

We had reason to regard the Mongols as monsters, did we not? The Mongols were something more and something less than human, were they not? More than human, in their fighting ability and physical endurance. Less than human, in their savagery and lust for blood. Even their everyday food was known to be reeking raw meat and the rancid milk of mares. And it was known that, when a Mongol army ran out of those rations, it would unhesitatingly cast lots to choose every tenth man of its ranks to be slaughtered for food for the others. It was known that every Mongol warrior wore leather armor only on his breast, not his back; so that, if he ever *did* feel cowardice, he could not turn and run from an opponent. It was known that the Mongols polished their leather armor with grease, and they procured that grease by boiling down their human victims. All those things were known in Venice, and were repeated and retold, in hushed voices of horror, and some of those things were even true.

I was just five years old when my father went away, but I could share the universal dread of those savages from the East, for I was already familiar with the spoken threat: "The Mongols will get you! The orda will get you!" I had heard that all through my childhood, and so had every other little boy whenever he required admonishment. "The orda will get you if you do not eat up all your supper. If you do not go straight to bed. If you do not cease your noise." The orda was wielded by mothers and governesses, in those times, as they had earlier threatened their misbehaving children with "The orco will get you!"

The orco is the demon giant that mothers and nursemaids have forever kept on call, so it was no strain for them to substitute the word orda: the horde. And the Mongol horde was assuredly the more real and believable monster; the women invoking it did not have to feign the fright in their voices. The fact that they even knew that word is evidence that they had reason to fear the orda as much as any child did. For it was the Mongols' own word, yurtu, originally meaning the great pavilioned tent of the chieftain of a Mongol encampment, and it was adopted, only slightly changed, into all the European languages, to mean what Europeans thought of when they thought of Mongols—a marching mob, a teeming mass, an irresistible swarm, a horde.

But I did not much longer hear that threat from my mother. As soon as she decided that my father was dead and gone, she commenced to languish and dwindle and weaken. When I was seven years old, she died. I have only one recollection of her, from a few months before that. The last time she ventured outside our Casa Polo, before she took to her bed and never got up again, was to accompany me on the day I was enrolled in school. Indeed, although that day was in another century, nearly sixty years ago, I recall it quite clearly.

At that time, our Ca' Polo was a small palazzo in the city's confino of San Felice. In the bright morning hour of mezza-terza, my mother and I came out the house door onto the cobbled street alongside the canal. Our old boatman, the black Nubian slave Michièl, was waiting with our batèlo moored to its striped pole, and the boat was freshly waxed for the occasion, gleaming in all its colors. My mother and I got into it and seated ourselves under the canopy. Also for the occasion, I was dressed in new and fine raiment: a tunic of brown Lucca silk, I remember, and hose soled with leather. So, as old Michièl rowed us down the narrow Rio San Felice, he kept exclaiming things like "Che zentilòmo!" and "Dassèno, xestu, Messer Marco?"—meaning "Quite the gentleman!" and "Truly, is that you, Master Marco?"—which unaccustomed admiration made me feel proud and uncomfortable. He did not desist until he turned the batèlo into the Grand Canal, where the heavy boat traffic required all his attention.

That day was one of Venice's best sort of days. The sun was shining, but its light lay on the city in a manner more diffused than sharp-edged. There was no sea mist or land haze, for the sunlight was by no means diminished. Rather, the sun seemed to shine not in direct beams, but with a more subtle luminosity, the way candles glow when they are set in a many-crystaled chandelier. Anyone who knows Venice has known that light: as if pearls had been crushed and powdered—pearl-colored pearls and the pale pink ones and the pale blue—and that powder ground so fine that its particles hung in the air, not dimming the light but making it more lustrous yet soft at the same time. And the light came from other places than the sky alone. It was reflected from the canals' dancing waters, so it put dapples and spangles and roundels of that pearl-powder light bouncing about on all the walls of old wood and brick and stone, and softened their rough textures as well. That day had a gentling bloom on it like the bloom on a peach.

Our boat slid under the Grand Canal's one bridge, the Ponte Rialto —the old, low, pontoon bridge with the swing-away center section; it had not then been rebuilt as the arched drawbridge it is now. Then we passed the Erbarìa, the market where young men, after a night of wine, go strolling in the early morning to clear their heads with the fragrance of its flowers and herbs and fruits. Then we turned off the canal again into another narrow one. A little way up that, my mother and I debarked at the Campo San Todaro. Around that square are situated all the lower-grade schools of the city, and at that hour the open space seethed with boys of all ages, playing, running, chattering, wrestling, while they waited for the school day to begin.

My mother presented me to the school maistro, presenting him also with the documents pertaining to my birth and to my registry in the Libro d'Oro. ("The Golden Book" is the popular name for the Register of Protocol in which the Republic keeps the records of all its Ene Aca families.) Fra Varisto, a very stout and forbidding man in voluminous robes, appeared less than impressed by the documents. He looked at them and snorted, "Brate!" which is a not very polite word meaning a Slav or Dalmatian. My mother countered with a ladylike sniff, and murmured, "Veneziàn nato e spuà."

"Venetian spawned and born, perhaps," rumbled the friar. "But Venetian *bred*, not yet. Not until he has endured proper schooling and the stiffening of school discipline."

He took up a quill and rubbed the point of it on the shiny skin of his tonsure, I suppose to lubricate its nib, then dipped it in an inkwell and opened a tremendous book. "Date of Confirmation?" he inquired. "Of First Communion?"

My mother told him and added, with some hauteur, that I had not, like most children, been allowed to forget my Catechism as soon as I had been confirmed, but could still say it and the Creed and the Commandments on demand, as facilely as I could say the Our Father. The maistro grunted, but made no additional notation in his big book. My mother then went on to ask some questions of her own: about the school's curriculum and its examinations and its rewards for achievement and its punishments for failure and . . .

All mothers take their sons to school for the first time with a considerable pride, I suppose, but also, I think, with an equal measure of wariness and even sadness, for they are relinquishing those sons to a mysterious realm they never can enter. Almost no female, unless she is destined for holy orders, ever gets the least bit of formal schooling. So her son, as soon as he learns just so much as to write his own name, has vaulted somewhere beyond her reach forever after.

Fra Varisto patiently told my mother that I would be taught the proper use of my own language and of Trade French as well, that I would be taught to read and to write and to figure in numbers, that I would learn at least the rudiments of Latin from the *Timen* of Donadello, and the rudiments of history and cosmography from Callisthenes' *Book of Alexander*, and religion from Bible stories. But my mother persisted with so many other anxious questions that the friar finally said, in a voice mingling compassion and exasperation, "Dona e Madona, the boy is merely being enrolled in school. He is not taking the veil. We will immure him merely during the daylight hours. You will still have him the rest of the time."

She had me for the rest of her life, but that was not long. So thereafter I heard the threat that "the Mongols will get you if" only from Fra Varisto at school, and at home from old Zulià. This was a woman who really was a Slav, born in some back corner of Bohemia, and clearly of peasant stock, for she always walked like a washerwoman waddling with a full wash bucket dangling from either hand. She had been my mother's personal maid since before I was born. After my mother's death, Zulià took her place as my nurse and monitor, and took the courtesy title of Aunt. In assuming the task of raising me up to be a decent and responsible young man, Zia Zulià did not exert much strictness—apart from frequently invoking the orda—nor did she, I must confess, have much success in her self-appointed task.

In part, this was because my namesake Uncle Marco had not come back to Venice after the disappearance of his two brothers. He had for too long made his home in Constantinople, and was comfortable there, although by this time the Latin Empire had succumbed to the Byzantine. Since my other uncle and my father had left the family business in the keeping of expert and trustworthy clerks, and the family palazzo in the keeping of similarly efficient domestics, Zio Marco left them so. Only the most weighty but least urgent matters were referred to him, by courier vessel, for his consideration and decision. Managed in that manner, both the Compagnia Polo and the Ca' Polo went on functioning as well as ever.

The one Polo property that misfunctioned was myself. Being the last and sole male scion of the Polo line—the only one in Venice, anyway—I had to be tenderly preserved, and I knew it. Though I was not of an age to have any say in the management of either the business or the house (fortunately), neither was I answerable to any adult authority for my own actions. At home I demanded my own way, and I got it. Not Zia Zulià, nor the maggiordomo, old Attilio, nor any of the lesser servants dared to raise a hand against me, and seldom a voice. My Catechism I never again recited, and soon forgot all the responses. At school I began to shirk my lessons. When Fra Varisto despaired of wielding the Mongols and resorted to wielding a ferrule, I simply stayed away from school.

It is a small wonder that I got as much formal education as I did. But I remained in school long enough to learn to read and write and do arithmetic and speak the Trade French of commerce, mainly because I knew I should need those abilities when I grew old enough to take over the family business. And I learned what history of the world, and what description of it, is supplied by *The Book of Alexander*. I absorbed all of that, mainly because the great Alexander's journeys of conquest had taken him eastward, and I could imagine my father and uncle having followed some of the same trails. But I saw little likelihood of my ever needing a knowledge of Latin, and it was when my school class had its collective nose forced into the boring rules and precepts of the *Timen* that I pointed my nose elsewhere.

Though my seniors loudly lamented and predicted dire ends for me, I really do not think that my willfulness signified that I was an evil child. My chief besetting sin was curiosity, but of course that *is* a sin by our Western standards. Tradition insists that we behave in conformity with our neighbors and peers. The Holy Church demands that we believe and have faith, that we stifle any questions or opinions derived from our own reasoning. The Venetian mercantile philosophy decrees that the only palpable truths are those numerated on the bottommost ledger line where debits and credits are balanced.

But something in my nature rebelled against the constraints accepted by all others of my age and class and situation. I wished to live a life beyond the rules and the ruled ledger lines and the lines written in the Missal. I was impatient and perhaps distrustful of received wisdom, those morsels of information and exhortation so neatly selected and prepared and served up like courses of a meal, for consumption and assimilation. I much preferred to make my own hunt for knowledge, even if I found it raw and unpalatable to chew and nauseating to swallow, as often I would do. My guardians and preceptors accused me of lazy avoidance of the hard work required to gain an education. They never realized that I had chosen to follow a far harder path, and would follow it—wherever it led—from that childhood time through all the years of my manhood.

On the days when I stayed away from the school and could not go home, I had to idle the days away somewhere, so sometimes I loitered about the establishment of the Compagnia Polo. It was situated then, as now, on the Riva Ca' de Dio, the waterfront esplanade which looks directly out onto the lagoon. On the water side, that esplanade is fringed with wooden quays, between which are ships and boats moored stem to stern and side by side. There are vessels of small and medium size: the shallow-draft batèli and gòndole of private houses, the bragozi fishing boats, the floating saloons called burchielli. And there are the much grander seagoing galleys and galeazze of Venice, interspersed with English and Flemish cogs, Slavic trabacoli and Levantine caïques. Many of those ocean vessels are so large that their stems and bowsprits overhang the street, and cast a latticed shadow on its cobbles, almost all the way to the variegated building fronts that line the esplanade's landward side. One of those buildings was (and still is) ours: a cavernous warehouse, with one little interior space of it partitioned off for a counting room.

I liked the warehouse. It was aromatic of all the smells of all the countries of the world, for it was heaped and piled with sacks and boxes and bales and barrels of all the world's produce—everything from Barbary wax and English wool to Alexandria sugar and Marseilles sardines. The warehouse workers were heavily muscled men, hung about with hammers, fist-hooks, coils of rope and other implements. They were forever busy, one man perhaps wrapping in burlap a consignment of Cornish tinware, another hammering the lid on a barrel of Catalonia olive oil, yet another shouldering a crate of Valencia soap out to the docks, and every man seeming always to be shouting some command like "logo!" or "a corando!" at the others.

But I liked the counting room, too. In that cramped coop sat the director of all that business and busy-ness, the old clerk Isidoro Priuli. With no apparent exertion of muscle, no rushing about or bellowing, no tools but his abaco, his quill and his ledger books, Maistro Doro controlled that crossroads of all the world's goods. With a little clicking of the abaco's colored counters and a scribble of ink in a ledger column, he could send to Bruges an ànfora of Corsican red wine and to Corsica, in exchange, a skein of Flanders lace, and, as the two items passed each other in our warehouse, dip off a metadella measure of the wine and snip off a braccio length of the lace to pay the Polos' profit on the transaction.

Because so many of the warehouse's contents were flammable, Isidoro did not allow himself the aid of a lamp or even a single candle to light his working space. Instead, he had arranged on the wall above and behind his head a large concave mirror made of real glass, which scooped in what light it could from the day outside and directed it down onto his high table. Seated there at his books, Maistro Doro looked like a very small and shriveled saint with an oversized halo. I would stand peering over the edge of that table, marveling that just the twitch of the maistro's fingers could exercise so much authority, and he would tell me things about the work in which he took such pride.

"It was the heathen Arabs, my boy, who gave the world these curlicue marks representing numbers, and this abaco for counting them with. But it was Venice that gave the world this system of *keeping* account—the books with facing pages for double entry. On the left, the debits. On the right, the credits."

I pointed to an entry on the left: "to the account of Messer Domeneddio," and asked, just for instance, who that Messere might be.

"Mefè!" the maistro exclaimed. "You do not recognize the name under which our Lord God does business?"

He flipped over the pages of that ledger to show me the flyleaf in the front, with its inked inscription: "In the name of God and of Profit."

"We mere mortals can take care of our own goods when they are secure here in this warehouse," he explained. "But when they go out in flimsy ships upon the hazardous seas, they are at the mercy of—who else but God? So we count Him a partner in our every enterprise. In our books He is allotted two full shares of every transaction at venture. And if that venture succeeds, if our cargo safely reaches its destination and pays us the expected profit, why then those two shares are entered to il conto di Messer Domeneddio, and at the end of each year, when our dividends are apportioned, they are paid to Him. Or rather, to His factor and agent, in the person of Mother Church. Every Christian merchant does the same."

If all my days stolen from school had been passed in such improving conversations, no one could have complained. I probably would have had a better education than I could ever have got from Fra Varisto. But inevitably my loitering about the waterfront brought me into contact with persons less admirable than the clerk Isidoro.

I do not mean to say that the Riva is in any sense a low-class street.

While it teems with workmen, seamen and fishermen at all hours of the day, there are just as many well-dressed merchants and brokers and other businessmen, often accompanied by their genteel wives. The Riva is also the promenade, even after dark on fine nights, of fashionable men and women come merely to stroll and enjoy the lagoon breeze. Nevertheless, among those people, day or night, there lurk the louts and cutpurses and prostitutes and other specimens of the rabble we call the popolàzo. There were, for example, the urchins I met one afternoon on that Riva dockside, when one of them introduced himself by throwing a fish at me.

. 2 .

I T was not a very large fish, and he was not a very large boy. He was of about my own size and age, and I was not hurt when the fish hit me between my shoulder blades. But it left a smelly slime on my Lucca silk tunic, which was clearly what the boy had intended, for he was clad in rags already redolent of fish. He danced about, gleefully pointing at me and singing a taunt:

> Un ducato, un ducatòn!
> Bùtelo . . . bùtelo . . . zo per el cavròn!

That is merely a fragment of a children's chant, meant to be sung during a throwing game, but he had changed the last word of it into a word which, though I could not then have told you its meaning, I knew to be the worst insult one man can fling at another. I was not a man and neither was he, but my honor was obviously in dispute. I interrupted his dance of mockery by stepping up to him and striking him in the face with my fist. His nose gushed bright red blood.

In the next moment, I was flattened under the weight of four other rascals. My assailant had not been alone on that dockside, and he was not alone in resenting the fine clothes Zia Zulià made me don on schooldays. For a while, our struggles made the dock planks rattle. Numerous of the passersby stopped to watch us, and some of the rougher sorts shouted things like "Gouge him!" and "Kick the beggar in his baggage!" I fought valiantly, but I could strike back at only one boy at a time, while they all five were pummeling me. Before long, I had the wind knocked out of me and my arms pinned down. I simply lay there being beaten and kneaded like pasta dough.

"Let him up!" said a voice from outside our entangled heap.

It was only a piping falsetto of a voice, but it was loud and commanding. The five boys stopped pounding on me, and one after another, although reluctantly, peeled off me. Even when I was unencumbered, I still had to lie there for a bit and get my breath back before I could stand.

The other boys were shuffling their bare feet and sullenly regarding the owner of the voice. I was surprised to see that they had obeyed a mere girl. She was as ragged and aromatic as they were, but smaller and younger than any of them. She wore the short, tight, tubelike dress worn by all Venetian girl children until about the age of twelve—or I should say she wore the remains of one. Hers was so tattered that she would have been quite indecently exposed, except that what showed of her body was the same dingy gray color as her frock. Perhaps she derived some authority from the fact that she, alone of the urchins, wore shoes—the cloglike wooden tofi of the poor.

The girl came close to me and maternally brushed at my clothes, which were now not very disparate from her own. She also informed me that she was the sister of the boy whose nose I had bloodied.

"Mama told Boldo never to fight," she said, and added, "Papà told him always to fight his own fights without help."

I said, panting, "I wish he had listened to one of them."

"My sister is a liar! We do not have a mama or a papà!"

"Well, if we did, that is what they would tell you. Now pick up that fish, Boldo. It was hard enough to steal." To me she said, "What is your name? He is Ubaldo Tagiabue and I am Doris."

Tagiabue means "built like an ox," and I had learned in school that Doris was the daughter of the pagan god Oceanus. This Doris was too pitifully skinny to merit the surname, and far too dirty to resemble any water goddess. But she stood staunch as the ox, imperious as the goddess, as we watched her brother obediently go to pick up the discarded fish. He could not exactly pick it up; it had several times been stepped on during the brawl; he had more or less to gather it up.

"You must have done something terrible," Doris said to me, "to have made him throw our supper at you."

"I did nothing at all," I said truthfully. "Until I hit him. And that was because he called me a cavròn."

She looked amused and asked, "Do you know what that means?"

"Yes, it means one must fight."

She looked even more amused and said, "A cavròn is a man who lets his wife be used by other men."

I wondered why, if that was all it meant, the word should be such a deadly insult. I knew of several men whose wives were washerwomen or seamstresses, and those women's services were used by many other men, and that excited no public commotion or private vendèta. I made some remark to that effect, and Doris burst out laughing.

"Marcolfo!" she jeered at me. "It means the men put their candles into the woman's scabbard and together they do the dance of San Vito!"

No doubt you can divine the street meaning of her words, so I will not tell you the bizarre picture they brought to my ignorant mind. But some respectably merchant-looking gentlemen were strolling nearby at that moment, and they recoiled from Doris, their various mustaches and beards bristling like quills, when they heard those obscenities shouted by so small a female child.

Bringing the mangled corpse of his fish cradled in his grimy hands,

Ubaldo said to me, "Will you share our supper?" I did not, but in the course of that afternoon he and I forgot our quarrel and became friends.

He and I were perhaps eleven or twelve years old then, and Doris about two years younger, and during the next few years I spent most of my days with them and their somewhat fluid following of other dockside brats. I could easily have been consorting in those years with the well-fed and well-dressed, prim and priggish offspring of the lustrìsimi families, such as the Balbi and the Cornari—and Zia Zulià used every effort and persuasion to make me do so—but I preferred my vile and more vivacious friends. I admired their pungent language, and I adopted it. I admired their independence and their fichèvelo attitude to life, and I did my best to imitate it. As could be expected, since I did not slough off those attitudes when I went home or elsewhere, they did not make me any better beloved by the other people in my life.

During my infrequent attendances at school, I began calling Fra Varisto by a couple of nicknames I had learned from Boldo—"il bel de Roma" and "il Culiseo"—and soon had all the other schoolboys doing the same. The friar-maistro put up with that informality, even seemed flattered by it, until gradually it dawned on him that we were not likening him to the grand old Beauty of Rome, the Colosseum, but were making a play on the word culo, and in effect were calling him the "landmark of buttocks." At home, I scandalized the servants almost daily. On one occasion, after I had done a thing reprehensible, I overheard a conversation between Zia Zulià and Maistro Attilio, the maggiordomo of the household.

"Crispo!" I heard the old man exclaim. That was his fastidious way of uttering a profanity without actually saying the words "per Cristo!" but he managed, anyway, to sound outraged and disgusted. "Do you know what the whelp has done now? He called the boatman a black turd of merda, and now poor Michièl is dissolving in tears. It is an unforgivable cruelty to speak so to a slave, and remind him that he is a slave."

"But Attilio, what can I do?" whimpered Zulià. "I cannot beat the boy and risk injuring his precious self."

The chief servant said sternly, "Better he be beaten young, and here in the privacy of his home, than that he grow up to earn a public scourging at the pillars."

"If I could keep him always under my eye . . ." sniffled my nena. "But I cannot chase him throughout the city. And since he took to running with those popolàzo boat children . . ."

"He will be running with the bravi next," growled Attilio, "if he lives long enough. I warn you, woman: you are letting that boy become a real bimbo viziato."

A bimbo viziato is a child spoiled to rottenness, which is what I was, and I would have been delighted with a promotion from bimbo to bravo. In my childishness, I thought the bravi were what their name implies, but of course they are anything but brave.

The skulking bravi are the modern Vandals of Venice. They are young men, sometimes of good family, who have no morals and no useful employment, and no ability except low cunning and perhaps some swordsmanship, and no ambition except to earn an occasional ducat for committing a sneak murder. They are sometimes hired for that purpose by politicians seeking a short road to preferment, or merchants seeking to eliminate competition by the easiest means. But, ironically, the bravi are more often utilized by *lovers*—to dispose of an impediment to their love, like an inconvenient husband or a jealous wife. If, in daytime, you should see a young man swaggering about with the air of a cavaliere errante, he is either a bravo or wishes to be mistaken for one. But if you should meet a bravo by night, he will be masked and cloaked, and wearing modern chain mail under his cloak, and lurking furtively far from any lamplight, and when he stabs you with sword or stilèto, it will be in the back.

This is no digression from my history, for I did live to become a bravo. Of sorts.

However, I was speaking of the time when I was still a bimbo viziato, when Zia Zulià complained of my being so often in the company of those boat children. Of course, considering the foul mouth and abominable manners I acquired from them, she had good reason to disapprove. But only a Slav, not Venice-born, would have thought it unnatural that I should loiter about the docks. I was a Venetian, so the salt of the sea was in my blood, and it urged me seaward. I was a boy, so I did not resist the urge, and to consort with the boat children was as close as I could then get to the sea.

I have, since then, known many seaside cities, but I have known none that is so nearly a part of the sea as is this Venice. The sea is not just our means of livelihood—as it is also for Genoa and Constantinople and the Cherbourg of the fictional Bauduin—here it is indissoluble from our lives. It washes about the verge of every island and islet composing Venice, and through the city's canals, and sometimes—when the wind and the tide come in from the same quarter—it laps at the very steps of the Basilica of San Marco, and a gondolier can row his boat among the portal arches of Samarco's great piazza.

Only Venice, of all the world's port cities, claims the sea for its bride, and annually affirms that espousal with priests and panoply. I watched the ceremony again just last Thursday. That was Ascension Day, and I was one of the honored guests aboard the gold-encrusted bark of our Doge Zuàne Soranzo. His splendid buzino d'oro, rowed by forty oarsmen, was but one of a great fleet of vessels, crowded with seamen and fishermen and priests and minstrels and lustrìsimi citizens, going in stately procession out upon the lagoon. At the Lido, the most seaward of our islands, Doge Soranzo made the ages-old proclamation, "Ti sposiamo, O mare nostro, in cigno di vero e perpetuo dominio," and threw into the water a gold wedding ring, while the priests led our waterborne congregation in a prayer that the sea might, in the coming twelvemonth, prove as generous and submissive as a human bride. If the tradition is true—that the same ceremony has been performed on every Ascension Day since the year 1000—then there is a considerable fortune of more than three hundred gold rings lying on the sea bottom off the beaches of the Lido.

The sea does not merely surround and pervade Venice: it is within every Venetian; it salts the sweat of his laboring arms, and the weeping or laughing tears of his eyes, and even the speech of his tongue. Nowhere else in the world have I heard men meet and greet each other with the glad cry of *"Che bon vento?"* That phrase means "What good wind?" and to a Venetian it means "What good wind has wafted you across the sea to this happy destination of Venice?"

Ubaldo Tagiabue and his sister Doris and the other denizens of the docks had an even more terse greeting, but the salt was in that one, too. They said simply, "Sana capàna," which is short for a salute "to the health of our company," and assumes the understanding that what is meant is the company of boat people. When, after we had been acquainted for some time, they began to salute me with that phrase, I felt included, and proud to be so.

Those children lived, like a swarm of dock rats, in a rotting hulk of a tow barge mired in a mud flat off the side of the city that faces the Dead Lagoon and, beyond that, the little cemetery isle of San Michièl, or Isle of the Dead. They really spent only their sleeping hours inside that dark and clammy hull, for their waking hours had to be mainly devoted to scavenging bits of food and clothing. They lived almost entirely on fish because, when they could steal no other nutriment, they could always descend on the Fish Market at the close of each day, when, by Venetian law—to prevent any stale fish from ever being vended—the fishmongers have to scatter on the ground whatever stock is left unsold. There was always a crowd of poor people to scramble and fight for those leavings, which seldom consisted of anything tastier than molefish.

I did bring to my new friends what scraps I could save from the table at home, or pilfer from the kitchen. At least that put some vegetables in the children's diet when I fetched something like kale ravioli or turnip jam, and some eggs and cheese when I brought them a maccherone, and even good meat when I could sneak a bit of mortadella or pork jelly. Once in a while I provided some viand they found most marvelous. I had always thought that, on Christmas Eve, Father Baba brought to all Venetian children the traditional torta di lasagna of the season. But when, one Christmas Day, I carried a portion of that confection to Ubaldo and Doris, their eyes widened in wonder, and they exclaimed with delight at every raisin and pine-nut and preserved onion and candied orange peel they found among the pasta.

I also brought what clothing I could—outgrown or worn-out garb of my own for the boys and, for the girls, articles that had belonged to my late mother. Not everything fit everybody, but they did not mind. Doris and the other three or four girls paraded about, most proudly, in shawls and gowns so much too big for them that they tripped on the dragging ends. I even brought along—for my own wear when I was with the boat children—various of my old tunics and hose so derelict that Zia Zulià had consigned them to the household bin of dust rags. I would remove whatever fine attire I had left my house in, and leave that wedged among the barge's timbers, and dress in the rags and look just like another boat urchin, until it was time to change again and go home.

You might wonder why I did not give the children money instead of my meager gifts. But you must remember that I was as much of an orphan as any of them were, and under strict guardianship, and too young to make any dispensation from the Polo family coffers. Our household's money was doled out by the company, meaning by the clerk Isidoro Priuli. Whenever Zulià or the maggiordomo or any other servant had to buy any sort of supplies or provender for the Ca' Polo, he or she went to the markets accompanied by a page from the company. That page boy carried the purse and counted out the ducats or sequins or soldi as they were spent, and made a memorandum of every one. If there was anything I personally needed or wanted, and if I could put up a good argument, that thing would be bought for me. If I contracted a debt, it would be paid for me. But I never possessed, at any one time, more than a few copper bagatini of my own, for jingling money.

I did manage to improve the boat children's existence at least to the extent of improving the scope of their thievery. They had always filched from the mongers and hucksters of their own squalid neighborhood; in other words, from petty merchants who were not much less poor than they were, and whose goods were hardly worth the stealing. I led the children to my own higher-class confino, where the wares displayed for sale were of better quality. And there we devised a better mode of theft than mere snatch-and-run.

The Mercerìa is the widest, straightest and longest street in Venice, meaning that it is practically the *only* street that can be called wide or straight or long. Open-fronted shops line both sides of it and, between them, long ranks of stalls and carts do an even brisker business, selling everything from mercery to hourglasses, and all kinds of groceries from staples to delicacies.

Suppose we saw, on a meat man's cart, a tray of veal chops that made the children's mouths water. A boy named Daniele was our swiftest runner. So he it was who elbowed his way to the cart, seized up a handful of the chops and ran, nearly knocking down a small girl who had blundered into his path. Daniele continued running, stupidly it seemed, along the broad, straight, open Mercerìa where he was visible and easily pursued. So the meat man's assistant and a couple of outraged customers took out after him, shouting "alto!" and "salva!" and "al ladro!"

But the girl who had been shoved was our Doris, and Daniele had in that scuffling moment, unobserved, handed to her the stolen veal chops. Doris, still unnoticed in the commotion, quickly and safely disappeared down one of the narrow, twisty side alleys leading off the open area. Meanwhile, his flight being somewhat impeded by the crowds on the Mercerìa, Daniele was in peril of capture. His pursuers were closing in on him, and other passersby were clutching at him, and all were bellowing for a "sbiro!" The sbiri are Venice's apelike policemen, and one of them, heeding the call, was angling through the crowd to intercept the thief. But I was nearby, as I always contrived to be on those occasions. Daniele stopped running and I started, which made me seem the quarry, and I ran deliberately right into the sbiro's ape arms.

After being soundly buffeted about the ears, I was recognized, as I always was and expected to be. The sbiro and the angry citizens hauled me to my house not far from the Mercerìa. When the street door was hammered on, the unhappy maggiordomo Attilio opened it. He heard out the people's babble of accusation and condemnation and then wearily put his thumbprint on a pagherò, which is a paper promising to pay, and thereby committed the Compagnia Polo to reimburse the meat man for his loss. The sbiro, after giving me a stern lecture and a vigorous shaking, let go of my collar, and he and the crowd departed.

Though I did not have to interpose myself every time the boat children stole something—more often it was deftly managed, with both the grabber and the receiver getting clean away—nevertheless I was dragged to the Ca' Polo more times than I can remember. That did not much lessen Maistro Attilio's opinion that Zia Zulià had raised the first black sheep in the Polo line.

It might be supposed that the boat children would have resented the participation of a "rich boy" in their pranks, and that they would have resented the "condescension" implicit in my gifts to them. Not so. The popolàzo may admire or envy or even revile the lustrìsimi, but they keep their active resentment and loathing for their fellow poor, who are, after all, their chief competitors in this world. It is not the rich who wrestle with the poor for the discarded molefish at the Fish Market. So when I came along, giving what I could and taking nothing, the boat people tolerated my presence rather better than if I had been another hungry beggar.

· 3 ·

J u s t to remind myself now and again that I was *not* of the popolàzo, I would drop in at the Compagnia Polo to luxuriate in its rich aromas and industrious activity and prosperous ambience. On one of those visits, I found on the clerk Isidoro's table an object like a brick, but of a more glowing red color, and lighter in weight, and soft and vaguely moist to the touch, and I asked him what it was.

Again he exclaimed, "My faith!" and shook his gray head and said, "Do you not recognize the very foundation of your family's fortune? It was built on those bricks of zafràn."

"Oh," I said, respectfully regarding the brick. "And what is zafràn?"

"Mefè! You have been eating it and smelling it and wearing it all your life! Zafràn is what gives that special flavor and yellow color to rice and polenta and pasta. What gives that unique yellow color to fabrics. What gives the women's favorite scent to their salves and pomades. A mèdego uses it, too, in his medicines, but what it does there I do not know."

"Oh," I said again, my respect somewhat less for such an everyday article. "Is that all?"

"All!" he blurted. "Hear me, marcolfo." That word is not an affectionate play on my name; it is addressed to any exceedingly stupid boy.
"Zafràn has a history more ancient and more noble even than the history
of Venice. Long before Venice existed, zafràn was used by the Greeks
and Romans to perfume their baths. They scattered it on their floors to
perfume whole rooms. When the Emperor Nero made his entry into
Rome, the streets of *the entire city* were strewn with zafràn and made
fragrant."

"Well," I said, "if it has always been so commonly available . . ."

"It may have been common then," said Isidoro, "in the days when
slaves were numerous and cost nothing. Zafràn is not common today. It
is a scarce commodity, and therefore of much value. That one brick you
see there is worth an ingot of gold of almost equal weight."

"Is it indeed?" I said, perhaps sounding unconvinced. "But why?"

"Because that brick was made by the labor of many hands and
immeasurable zonte of land and a countless multitude of flowers."

"Flowers!"

Maistro Doro sighed and said patiently, "There is a purple flower
called the crocus. When it blooms, it extends from that blossom three
delicate stigmi of an orange-red color. Those stigmi are ever so carefully
detached by human hands. When some millions of those dainty and
almost impalpable stigmi are collected, they are either dried to make
loose zafràn, what is called hay zafràn, or they are what is called
'sweated' and compressed together to make brick zafràn like this one.
The arable land must be devoted to nothing but that crop, and the
crocus blooms only once a year. That blooming season is brief, so many
gatherers must work at the same time, and they must work diligently. I
do not know how many zonte of land and how many hands are required
to produce just one brick of zafràn in a year, but you will understand
why it is of such extravagant value."

I was by now convinced. "And where do we buy the zafràn?"

"We do not. We grow it." He put on the table beside the brick
another object; I would have said it was a bulb of ordinary garlic. "That
is a culm of the crocus flower. The Compagnia Polo plants them and
harvests from the blossoms."

I was astonished. "Not in Venice, surely!"

"Of course not. On the teraferma of the mainland southwest of here.
I told you it requires innumerable zonte of terrain."

"I never knew," I said.

He laughed. "Probably half the people of Venice do not even know
that the milk and eggs of their daily meals are extracted from animals,
and that those animals must have dry land to live on. We Venetians are
inclined to pay little attention to anything but our lagoon and sea and
ocean."

"How long have we been doing this, Doro? Growing crocuses and
zafràn?"

He shrugged. "How long have there been Polos in Venice? That was
the genius of some one of your long-ago ancestors. After the time of the
Romans, zafràn became too much of a luxury to cultivate. No one farmer

could grow enough of it to make it worth his while. And even a land-owner of great estates could not afford all the paid laborers that crop would require. So zafràn was pretty well forgotten. Until some early Polo remembered it, and also realized that modern Venice has almost as big a supply of slaves as Rome had. Of course, we now have to buy our slaves, not just capture them. But the gathering of crocus stigmi is not an arduous labor. It does not require strong and expensive male slaves. The puniest women and children can do it; weaklings and cripples can do it. So that was the cheap sort of slaves your ancestor bought; the sort the Compagnia Polo has been acquiring ever since. They are a motley sort, of all nations and colors—Moors, Lezghians, Circassians, Russniaks, Armeniyans—but their colors blend, so to speak, to make that red-gold zafràn."

"The foundation of our fortune," I repeated.

"It buys everything else we sell," said Isidoro. "Oh, we sell the zafràn too, for a price, when the price is right—to be used as a foodstuff, a dye, a perfume, a medicament. But basically it is our company's capital, with which we barter for all our other articles of merchandise. Everything from Ibiza's salt to Còrdoba's leather to Sardinia's wheat. Just as the house of Spinola in Genoa has the monopoly of trading in raisins, our Venetian house of Polo has the zafràn."

The only son of the Venetian house of Polo thanked the old clerk for that edifying lesson in high commerce and bold endeavor—and, as usual, sauntered off again to partake of the easy indolence of the boat children.

As I have said, those children tended to come and go; there was seldom the same lot living in the derelict barge from one week to the next. Like all the grown-up popolàzo, the children dreamed of some-where finding a Land of Cockaigne, where they could shirk work in luxury instead of squalor. So they might hear of some place offering better prospects than the Venice waterfront, and they might stow away aboard an outbound vessel to get there. Some of them would come back after a while, either because they could not reach their destination or because they had and were disillusioned. Some never came back at all, because—we never knew—the vessel sank and they drowned, or because they were apprehended and thrown into an orphanage, or maybe be-cause they did find "il paese di Cuccagna" and stayed there.

But Ubaldo and Doris Tagiabue were the constants, and it was from them that I got most of my education in the ways and the language of the lower classes. That education was not force-fed to me in the way Fra Varisto stuffed Latin conjugations into his schoolboys; rather, the brother and sister parceled it out to me in fragments, as I required it. Whenever Ubaldo would jeer at some backwardness or bewilderment of mine, I would realize that I lacked some bit of knowledge, and Doris would supply it.

One day, I remember, Ubaldo said he was going to the western side of the city, and going by way of the Dogs' Ferry. I had never heard of that, so I went along, to see what strange kind of boat he meant. But we crossed the Grand Canal by the quite ordinary agency of the Rialto Bridge, and I must have looked either disappointed or mystified, for he scoffed at me, "You are as ignorant as a cornerstone!" and Doris explained:

"There is only one way to get from the eastern to the western side of the city, no? That is to cross the Grand Canal. Cats are allowed in boats, to catch the rats, but dogs are not. So the dogs can cross the canal only on the Ponte Rialto. So that is the Dogs' Ferry, no xe vero?"

Some of their street jargon I could translate without assistance. They spoke of every priest and monk as le rigioso, which could mean "the stiff one," but it did not take me long to realize that they were merely twisting the word religioso. When, in fine summer weather, they announced that they were moving from the barge hulk to La Locanda de la Stela, I knew that they were not going to reside in any Starlight Inn; they meant that they would be sleeping outdoors for a season. When they spoke of a female person as una largazza, they were playing on the proper term for a girl, la ragazza, but coarsely suggesting that she was ample, even cavernous, in her genital aperture. As a matter of fact, the greater part of the boat people's language—and the greater part of their conversations, and their interests—dealt with such indelicate topics. I absorbed a lot of information, but it sometimes did more to confuse than to enlighten me.

Zia Zulià and Fra Varisto had taught me to refer to those parts between my legs—if I had to refer to them at all—as le vergogne, "the shames." On the docks I heard many other terms. The word baggage for a man's genital equipment was clear enough; and candelòto was an apt word for his erect organ, which is like a stout candle; and so was fava for the bulbous end of that organ, since it does somewhat resemble a broad bean; and so was capèla for the foreskin, which does enclose the fava like a little cloak or a little chapel. But it was a mystery to me why the word lumaghèta was sometimes spoken in reference to a woman's parts. I understood that a woman had nothing but an opening down there, and the word lumaghèta can mean either a small snail or the tiny peg with which a minstrel tunes each string of his lute.

Ubaldo and Doris and I were playing on a dock one day when a greengrocer came pushing his cart along the esplanade, and the boat wives ambled over to paw through his produce. One of the women fondled a large yellowish cucumber, and grinned and said, "Il mescolòto," and all the women cackled lasciviously. "The stirrer"—I could make out the implications of that. But then two lissome young men came strolling along the esplanade, arm in arm, walking with a sort of springiness in their step, and one of the boat women growled, "Don Meta and Sior Mona." Another woman glanced scornfully at the more delicate of the two young men and muttered, "That one wears a split seat in his hose." I had no notion of what they were talking about, and Doris's explanation did not tell me much:

"Those are the sorts of men who do with each other what a real man does only with a woman."

Well, there was the main flaw in my comprehension: I had no very clear idea of what a man did with a woman.

Mind you, I was not entirely benighted in the matter of sex, any more than other upper-class Venetian children are—or, I daresay, upper-class children of any other European nationality. We may not consciously remember it, but we have all had an early introduction to sex, from our mothers or our nursemaids, or both.

It seems that mothers and nurses have known, from the beginning of time, that the best way to quiet a restless baby or put it easily to sleep is to do for it the act of manustupraziòn. I have watched many a mother do that to an infant boy whose bimbìn was so tiny that she could only just manipulate it with her finger and thumb. Yet the wee organ lifted and grew, though not in proportion as a man's does, of course. As the woman stroked, the baby quivered, then smiled, then squirmed voluptuously. He did not ejaculate any spruzzo, but there was no doubt that he enjoyed a climax of release. Then his little bimbìn shrank again to its littlest, and he lay quiet and soon he slept.

Assuredly my own mother often did that for me, and I think it is good that mothers do so. That early manipulation, besides being an excellent pacifier of the infant, clearly stimulates development in that part of him. The mothers in the Eastern countries do not engage in that practice, and the omission is sadly evident when their babies grow up. I have seen many Eastern men undressed, and almost all had organs pitifully minute in comparison to mine.

Although our mothers and nursemaids gradually leave off doing that, when their children are about two years old—that is, at the age when they are weaned from the breast milk and introduced to wine— nevertheless, every child retains some dim recollection of it. Therefore a boy is not puzzled or frightened when he grows to adolescence and that organ seeks attention of its own accord. When a boy wakes in the night with it coming erect under his hand, he knows what it wants.

"A cold sponge bath," Fra Varisto used to tell us boys at school. "That will quell the upstart, and avert the risk of its shaming you with the midnight stain."

We listened respectfully, but on our way home we laughed at him. Perhaps friars and priests do endure involuntary and surprising spruzzi, and feel embarrassed or somehow guilty on that account. But no healthy boy of my acquaintance ever did. And none would choose a cold douche in place of the warm pleasure of doing for his candelòto what his mother had done for it when it was just a bimbìn. However, Ubaldo was contemptuous when he learned that those night games were the total extent of my sexual experience to date.

"What? You are still waging the war of the priests?" he jeered. "You have never had a girl?"

Once again uncomprehending, I inquired, "The war of the priests?"

"Five against one," Doris said, without a blush. She added, "You must get yourself a smanza. A compliant girl friend."

I thought about that and said, "I do not know any girls I could ask. Except you, and you are too young."

She bridled and said angrily, "I may not have hair on my artichoke yet, but I am twelve, and that is of marrying age!"

"I do not wish to marry anybody," I protested. "Only to—"

"Oh, no!" Ubaldo interrupted me. "My sister is a *good* girl."

You might smile at the assertion that a girl who could talk as she did could be a "good" girl. But there you have evidence of one thing our upper and lower classes have in common: their reverent regard for a maiden's virginity. To the lustrìsimi and the popolàzo alike, that counts for more than all other feminine qualities: beauty, charm, sweetness, demureness, whatever. Their women may be plain and malicious and ill-spoken and ungracious and slovenly, but they must retain unbroken that little tuck of maidenhead tissue. In that respect at least, the most primitive and barbarous savages of the East are superior to us: they value a female for attributes other than the bung in her hole.

To our upper classes, virginity is not so much a matter of virtue as of good business, and they regard a daughter with the same cool calculation as they would a slave girl in the market. A daughter or a slave, like a cask of wine, commands a better price if it is sealed and demonstrably untampered with. Thus they barter their daughters for commercial advantage or social enhancement. But the lower classes foolishly think that their betters have a high *moral* regard for virginity, and they try to imitate that. Also, they are more easily frightened by the thunders of the Church, and the Church demands the preservation of virginity as a sort of negative show of virtue, in the same way that good Christians show virtue by abstaining from meat during Lent.

But even in those days when I was still a boy, I found reason to wonder just how many girls, of any class, really were kept "good" by the prevailing social precepts and attitudes. From the time I was old enough to sprout the first fuzz of "hair on my artichoke," I had to listen to lectures from Fra Varisto and Zia Zulià on the moral and physical dangers of consorting with bad girls. I listened with close attention to their descriptions of such vile creatures, and their warnings about them, and their inveighings against them. I wanted to make sure I would recognize any bad girl at first sight, because I hoped with all my heart that I would soon get to meet one. That seemed quite likely, because the main impression I got from those lectures was that the bad girls must considerably outnumber the good ones.

There is other evidence for that impression. Venice is not a very tidy city, because it does not have to be. All of its discards go straight into the canals. Street garbage, kitchen trash, the wastes from our chamber pots and licet closets, all gets dumped into the nearest canal and is soon flushed away. The tide comes in twice daily, and surges through every least waterway, roiling up whatever matter lies on the bottom or is crusted on the canal walls. Then the tide departs and takes all those substances with it, through the lagoon, out past the Lido and off to sea. That keeps the city clean and sweet-smelling, but it frequently afflicts fishermen with unwelcome catches. There is not one of them who has not many times found on his hook or in his net the glistening pale blue and purple cadaver of a newborn infant. Granted, Venice is one of the three most populous cities of Europe. Still, only half of its citizens are female, and of those perhaps only half are of childbearing age. So the fishermen's annual catch of discarded infants would seem to indicate a scarcity of "good" Venetian girls.

"There is always Daniele's sister Malgarita," said Ubaldo. He was not enumerating good girls, but quite the contrary. He was counting those females of our acquaintance who might serve to wean me from the war of the priests to a more manly diversion. "She will do it with anybody who will give her a bagatìn."

"Malgarita is a fat pig," said Doris.

"She is a fat pig," I concurred.

"Who are you to sneer at pigs?" said Ubaldo. "Pigs have a patron saint. San Tonio was very fond of pigs."

"He would not have been fond of Malgarita," Doris said firmly.

Ubaldo went on, "Also there is Daniele's mother. She will do it and not even ask a bagatìn."

Doris and I made noises of revulsion. Then she said, "There is someone down there waving at us."

We three were idling the afternoon away on a rooftop. That is a favorite occupation of the lower classes. Because all the common houses of Venice are one story high, and all have flat roofs, their people like to stroll or loll upon them and enjoy the view. From that vantage, they can behold the streets and canals below, the lagoon and its ships beyond, and Venice's more elegant buildings that stand above the mass: the domes and spires of churches, the bell towers, the carved facades of palazzi.

"He is waving at me," I said. "That is our boatman, taking our batèlo home from somewhere. I might as well ride with him."

There was no necessity for me to go home before the bells began ringing the nighttime coprifuoco, when all honest citizens who do not retire indoors are supposed to carry lanterns to show that they are abroad on honest errands. But, to be truthful, I was at that moment feeling a bit apprehensive that Ubaldo might insist on my immediately coupling with some boat woman or girl. I did not so much fear the adventure, even with a slattern like Daniele's mother; I feared making a fool of myself, not knowing what to *do* with her.

From time to time, I tried to atone for my being so often rude to poor old Michièl, so that day I took the oars from him and myself rowed us homeward, while he took his ease under the boat canopy. We conversed as we went, and he told me that he was going to boil an onion when he got to the house.

"What?" I said, unsure I had heard him right.

The black slave explained that he suffered from the bane of boatmen. Because his profession required him to spend most of his time with his backside on a hard and damp boat thwart, he was often troubled by bleeding piles. Our family mèdego, he said, had prescribed a simple allevement for that malady. "You boil an onion until it is soft, and you wad it well up in there, and you wind a cloth around your loins to hold it there. Truly, it does help. If you ever have piles, Messer Marco, you try that."

I said I would indeed, and forgot about it. I arrived home to be accosted by Zia Zulià.

"The good friar Varisto was here today, and he was so angry that his dear face was bright red, clear to his tonsure."

I remarked that that was not unusual.

She said warningly, "A marcolfo with no schooling should speak with a smaller mouth. Fra Varisto said you have been shirking your classes again. For more than a week this time. And tomorrow your class must be heard in recitation, whatever that is, by the Censori de Scole, whoever they are. It is required that you participate. The friar told me—and I am telling you, young man—you *will be* in school tomorrow."

I said a word that made her gasp, and stalked off to my room to sulk. I refused to come out even when called to supper. But by the time the coprifuoco was rung, my better instincts had begun to overcome my worse ones. I thought to myself: today when I behaved with kindness to old Michièl it gratified him; I ought to say a kindly word of apology to old Zulià.

(I realize that I have characterized as "old" almost all the people I knew in my youth. That is because they seemed so to my young eyes, though only a few of them really were. The company's clerk Isidoro and the chief servant Attilio were perhaps as old as I am now. But the friar Varisto and the black slave Michièl were no more than middle aged. Zulià of course seemed old because she was about the same age as my mother, and my mother was dead; but I suppose Zulià was a year or two younger than Michièl.)

That night, when I determined to make amends to her, I did not wait for Zia Zulià to do her customary before-bedtime rounds of the house. I went to her little room and rapped on the door and opened it without waiting for an avanti. I probably had always assumed that servants did nothing at night except sleep to restore their energies for service the next day. But what was happening in that room that night was not sleep. It was something appalling and ludicrous and astounding to me—and educational.

Immediately before me on the bed was a pair of immense buttocks bouncing up and down. They were distinctive buttocks, being as purple-black as aubergines, and even more distinctive because they had a strip of cloth binding a large, pale-yellow onion in the cleft between them. At my sudden entrance, there was a squawk of dismay and the buttocks bounded out of the candlelight into a darker corner of the room. This revealed on the bed a contrastingly fish-white body—the naked Zulià, sprawled supine and splayed wide open. Her eyes were shut, so she had not noticed my arrival.

At the buttocks' abrupt withdrawal, she gave a wail of deprivation, but continued to move as if she were still being bounced upon. I had never seen my nena except in gowns of many layers and floor length, and of atrociously garish Slavic colors. And the woman's broad Slavic face was so very plain that I had never even tried to imagine her similarly broad body as it might look undressed. But now I took avid notice of everything so wantonly displayed before me, and one detail was so eminently noticeable that I could not restrain a blurted comment:

"Zia Zulià," I said wonderingly, "you have a bright red mole down there on your—"

Her meaty legs closed together with a slap, and her eyes flew open almost as audibly. She grabbed for the bed covers, but Michièl had taken those along in his leap, so she seized at the bed curtains. There was a moment of consternation and contortion, as she and the slave fumbled to swaddle themselves. Then there was a much longer moment of petrified embarrassment, during which I was stared at by four eyeballs almost as big and luminous as the onion had been. I congratulate myself that I was the first to regain composure. I smiled sweetly upon my nena and spoke, not the words of apology I had come to say, but the words of an arrant extortioner.

With smug assurance I said, "I will *not* go to school tomorrow, Zia Zulià," and I backed out of the room and closed the door.

· 4 ·

B E C A U S E I knew what I *would* be doing the next day, I was too restless with anticipation to sleep very well. I was up and dressed before any of the servants awoke, and I broke my fast with a bun and a gulp of wine as I went through the kitchen on my way out into the pearly morning. I hurried along the empty alleys and over the many bridges to that northside mud flat where some of the barge children were just emerging from their quarters. Considering what I had come to ask, I probably should have sought out Daniele, but I went instead to Ubaldo and put my request to him.

"At this hour?" he said, mildly scandalized. "Malgarita is likely still asleep, the pig. But I will see."

He ducked back inside the barge, and Doris, who had overheard us, said to me, "I do not think you ought to, Marco."

I was accustomed to her always commenting on everything that everybody did or said, and I did not always appreciate it, but I asked, "Why ought I not?"

"I do not want you to."

"That is no reason."

"Malgarita is a fat pig." I could not deny that, and I did not, so she added, "Even I am better looking than Malgarita."

Impolitely I laughed, but I was polite enough not to say that there was small choice between a fat pig and a scrawny kitten.

Doris kicked moodily at the mud where she stood, and then said in a rush of words, "Malgarita will do it with you because she does not care what man or boy she does it with. But I would do it with you because I do care."

I looked at her with amused surprise, and perhaps I also looked at her for the first time with appraisal. Her maidenly blush was perceptible even through the dirt on her face, and so was her earnestness, and so was a dim prefiguring of prettiness. At any rate, her undirtied eyes were of a nice blue, and seemed extraordinarily large, though that was probably because her face was somewhat pinched by lifelong hunger.

"You will be a comely woman someday, Doris," I said, to make her feel better. "If you ever get washed—or at least scraped. And if you grow more of a figure than a broomstick. Malgarita already is grown as ample as her mother."

Doris said acidly, "Actually she looks more like her father, since she also grew a mustache."

A head with frowzy hair and gummy eyelids poked out through one of the splintery holes in the barge hull, and Malgarita called, "Well, come on then, before I put on my frock, so I do not have to take it off!"

I turned to go and Doris said, "Marco!" but when I turned back impatiently, she said, "No matter. Go and play the pig."

I clambered inside the dark, dank hull and crept along its rotting plank decking until I came to the hold partition where Malgarita squatted on a pallet of reeds and rags. My groping hands encountered her before I saw her, and her bare body felt as sweaty and spongy as the barge's timbers. She immediately said, "Not even a feel until I get my bagatìn."

I gave her the copper, and she lay back on the pallet. I got over her, in the position in which I had seen Michièl. Then I flinched, as there came a loud *wham!* from the outside of the barge hull, but just beside my ear, and then a *screech!* The boat boys were playing one of their favorite games. One of them had caught a cat—and that is no easy feat, although Venice does teem with cats—and had tied it to the barge side, and the boys were taking turns running and butting it with their heads, competing to see who would first mash it to death.

As my eyes adapted to the darkness, I noted that Malgarita was indeed hairy. Her palely shining breasts seemed the only hairless part of her. In addition to the frowze on her head and the fuzz on her upper lip, she was shaggy of legs and arms, and a large plume of hair hung from either armpit. What with the darkness in the hold and the veritable bush on her artichoke, I could see considerably less of her female apparatus than I had seen of Zia Zulià's. (I could smell it, however, Malgarita being no more given to bathing than were any of the boat people.) I knew that I was expected to insert myself somewhere down there, but . . .

Wham! from the hull, and a yowl from the cat, further confounding me. In some perplexity, I began to feel about Malgarita's nether regions.

"Why are you playing with my pota?" she demanded, using the most vulgar word for that orifice.

I laughed, no doubt shakily, and said, "I am trying to find the—er—your lumaghèta."

"Whatever for? That is of no use to you. Here is what you want." She reached down one hand to spread herself and the other to guide me in. It was easily done, she was so well reamed.

Wham! Squawl!

"Clumsy, you jerked it out again!" she said peevishly, and did some brisk rearranging.

I lay there for a moment, trying to ignore her piggishness and her aroma and the dismal surroundings, trying to enjoy the unfamiliar, warm, moist cavity in which I was loosely clasped.

"Well, get on with it," she whined. "I have not yet peed this morning."

I commenced to bounce as I had seen Michièl do, but, before I could get fairly started, the barge hold seemed to darken still more before my eyes. Though I tried to restrain and savor it, my spruzzo gushed unbidden and without any sensation of pleasure whatever.

Wham! Yee-oww!

"Oh, che braga! What a lot of it!" Malgarita said disgustedly. "My legs will be sticking together all day. All right, get off, you fool, so I can jump!"

"What?" I said groggily.

She wriggled out from under me, stood up, and took a jump backward. She jumped forward, then backward again, and the whole barge rocked. "Make me laugh!" she commanded, between jumps.

"What?" I said.

"Tell me a funny story! There, that was seven jumps. I said make me laugh, marcolfo! Or would you rather make a baby?"

"What?"

"Oh, never mind. I will sneeze instead." She grabbed a lock of her hair, stuck the frowzy ends of it up one of her nostrils, and sneezed explosively.

Wham! Rowr-rr-rrr . . . The cat's complaint died off as, evidently, the cat died, too. I could hear the boys squabbling about what to do with the carcass. Ubaldo wanted to throw it in onto me and Malgarita, Daniele wanted to throw it in some Jew's shop door.

"I hope I have jarred it all out," said Malgarita, wiping at her thighs with one of her bed rags. She dropped the rag back on her pallet, moved to the opposite side of the hold, squatted down and began copiously to urinate. I waited, thinking that one of us ought to say something more. But finally I decided that her morning bladder was inexhaustible, and so crept out of the barge the way I had come in.

"Sana capàna!" shouted Ubaldo, as if I had just then joined the company. "How was it?"

I gave him the jaded smile of a man of the world. All the boys whooped and hooted good-naturedly, and Daniele called, "My sister is good, yes, but my mother is better!"

Doris was nowhere about, and I was glad I did not have to meet her eyes. I had made my first journey of discovery—a short foray toward manhood—but I was not disposed to preen myself on that accomplishment. I felt dirty and I was sure I smelled of Malgarita. I wished I had listened to Doris and not done it. If that was all there was to being a man, and doing it with a woman, well, I had done it. From now on, I was entitled to swagger as brashly as any of the other boys, and swagger

I would. But I was privately determining, all over again, to be kind to
Zia Zulià. I would not tease her about what I had found in her room, or
despise her, or tell on her, or wrest concessions with the threat of telling.
I was sorry for her. If I felt soiled and wretched after my experience
with a mere boat girl, how much more miserable my nena must feel,
having no one willing to do it with her but a contemptible black man.

However, I was to have no opportunity to demonstrate my noble-
mindedness. I got home again to find all the other servants in a turmoil,
because Zulià and Michièl had disappeared during the night.

The sbiri had already been called in by Maistro Attilio, and those
police apes were making conjectures typical of them: that Michièl had
forcibly abducted Zulià in his batèlo, or that the two of them had for
some reason gone out in the boat in the night, overturned it, and
drowned. So the sbiri were going to ask the fishermen on the seaward
side of Venice to keep a close eye on their hooks and nets, and the
peasants on the Vèneto mainland to keep a lookout for a black boatman
conveying a captive white damsel. But then they thought to investigate
the canal right outside the Ca' Polo, and there lay the batèlo innocently
moored to its post, so the sbiri scratched their heads for new theories. In
any event, if they could have caught Michièl even without the woman,
they would have had the pleasure of executing him. A runaway slave is
ipso facto a thief, in that he steals his master's property: his own living
self.

I kept silent about what I knew. I was convinced that Michièl and
Zulià, alarmed by my discovery of their sordid connection, had eloped
together. Anyway, they were never apprehended and never heard from
again. So they must have made their way to some back corner of the
world, like his native Nubia or her native Bohemia, where they could live
squalidly ever after.

· 5 ·

I was feeling so guilty, for so many different reasons, that I did something unprecedented for me. Of my own accord, not impelled by any
authority, I betook myself to church to make my confession. I did not go
to our confino's San Felice, for its old Pare Nunziata knew me as well as
the local sbiri did, and I desired a more disinterested auditor. So I went
all the way to the Basilica of San Marco. None of the priests there knew
me, but the bones of my namesake saint lay there, and I hoped they
would be sympathetic.

In that great vaulted nave, I felt like a bug, diminished by all the
glowing gold and marble and the holy notables aloft and aloof in the
ceiling mosaics. Everything in that most beautiful building is bigger than
real life, including the sonorous music, which brays and bleats from a
rigabèlo that seems too small to contain so much noise. San Marco's is
always thronged, so I had to stand in line before one of the confessionals.

Finally, I got in and got launched on my purgation: "Father, I have too freely followed where my curiosity has led me, and it has led me astray from the paths of virtue. . . ." I went on in that vein for some time, until the priest impatiently requested that I not regale him with *all* the circumstances preliminary to my misdemeanors. So, albeit reluctantly, I fell back on formula—"have sinned in thought and word and deed"—and the pare decreed some number of Paternosters and Avemarìas, and I left the box to begin on them, and I got hit by lightning.

I mean that almost literally, so vivid was the shock I felt when I first laid eyes on the Dona Ilaria. I did not then know her name, of course; I knew only that I was looking at the most beautiful woman I had yet seen in my life, and that my heart was hers. She was just then coming out of a confessional herself, so her veil was up. I could not believe that a lady of such radiant loveliness could have had anything more than trivial to confess, but, before she lowered her veil, I saw a sparkle as of tears in her glorious eyes. I heard a creak as the priest shut the slide in the box she had just quitted, and he too came out. He said something to the other supplicants waiting in line there, and they all mumbled grouchily and dispersed to other lines. He joined the Dona Ilaria and both of them knelt in an empty pew.

In a sort of trance, I moved closer and slid into the pew across the aisle from them, and fixed my gaze sideways on them. Though they both kept their heads bent, I could see that the priest was a young man and handsome in an austere kind of way. You may not credit this, but I felt a twinge of jealousy that my lady—*my lady*—had not chosen a drier old stick to tell her troubles to. Both he and she, as I could tell even through her veil, were moving their lips prayerfully, but they were doing so alternately. I supposed he must be leading her in some litany. I might have been consumed with curiosity to know what she could have said in the confessional to require such intimate attention from her confessor, but I was too much occupied with devouring her beauty.

How do I describe her? When we view a monument or an edifice, any such work of art or architecture, we remark on this and that element of it. Either the combination of details makes it handsome, or some particular detail is so noteworthy as to redeem the whole from mediocrity. But the human face is never viewed as an accretion of details. It either strikes us immediately as beautiful in its entirety, or it does not. If we can say of a woman only that "she has nicely arched eyebrows," then clearly we had to look hard to see that, and the rest of her features are little worth remarking.

I can say that Ilaria had a fine and fair complexion and hair of a glowing auburn color, but many other Venetian women do, too. I can say that she had eyes so alive that they seemed to be lighted from within instead of reflecting the light without. That she had a chin one would want to cup in the palm of a hand. That she had what I have always thought of as "the Verona nose," because it is seen most often there— thin and pronounced, but shapely, like a sleek boat's fine prow, with the eyes deepset on either side.

I could praise her mouth especially. It was exquisitely shaped and gave promise of being soft if ever other lips should press upon it. But more than that. When Ilaria and the priest rose together after their orisons and genuflected, she curtsied again to him and said some few words in a soft voice. I do not recall what they were, but let me suppose that they were these: "I will join you behind the chantry, Father, after the compline." I do recall that she concluded by saying "Ciao," because that is the languid Venetian way of saying *schiavo*, "your slave," and I thought it an oddly familiar way of saying goodbye to a priest. But all that mattered then was the manner in which she spoke: "I will j-join you behind the ch-chantry, Father, after the compline. Ci-ciao." Each time she pouted her lips to form the *ch* or *j* sound, she stammered ever so slightly and thus prolonged the pout. It made her lips look ready and waiting for a kiss. It was delicious.

I instantly forgot that I was supposed to be petitioning for absolution of other misdeeds, and tried to follow her when she left the church. She could not possibly have been aware of my existence, but she departed from San Marco's in a way that almost seemed intended to discourage pursuit. Moving more swiftly and adroitly than I could have done even if chased by a sbiro, she flickered through the crowd in the atrium and vanished from my sight. Marveling, I went all the long way around the basilica's outside, then up and down all the arcades surrounding the vast piazza. Mystified, I several times crisscrossed the piazza itself, through clouds of pigeons—then the smaller piazzetta, from the bell tower down to the two pillars at the waterfront. Despairing, I returned to the great church and looked in every last chapel and the sanctuary and the baptistery. Desolated, I even went up the stairs to the loggia where the golden horses stand. At last, heartbroken, I went home.

After a tormented night, I went again the next day to comb the church and its environs. I must have looked like a wandering soul seeking solace. And the woman might have been a wandering angel who had alighted only the once; she was not to be found. So I made my mournful way to the neighborhood of the boat people. The boys gave me a cheery salute, and Doris gave me a glance of disdain. When I responded with a forlorn sigh, Ubaldo was solicitous and asked what ailed me. I told him—I had lost my heart to a lady and then lost my lady—and all the children laughed, except Doris, who looked suddenly stricken.

"You have largazze on your mind these days," Ubaldo said. "Do you intend to be the cock of every hen in the world?"

"This is a full-grown woman, not a girl," I said. "And she is too sublime even to be thought of as . . .."

"As a pota!" several of the boys chorused.

"Anyway," I said, in a bored drawl, "as regards the pota, all women are alike." Man of the world, I had now seen a grand total of two females in the nude.

"I do not know about that," one boy said ruminatively. "I once heard a much-traveled mariner tell how to recognize a woman of the most utterly desirable bedworthiness."

"Tell us! Tell!" came the chorus.

"When she stands upright, with her legs pressed together, there should be a little, a tiny little triangle of daylight between her thighs and her artichoke."

"Does your lady show daylight?" someone asked me.

"I have seen her the once, and that was in church! Do you suppose she was undressed in church?"

"Well, then, does Malgarita show daylight?"

I said, and so did several other boys, "I did not think to look."

Malgarita giggled, and giggled again when her brother said, "You could not have seen, anyway. Her bottom hangs down too far behind, and her belly in front."

"Let us look at Doris!" someone shouted. "Olà, Doris! Stand with your legs together and raise your skirt."

"Ask a real woman!" Malgarita sneered. "That one would not know whether to lay eggs or give milk."

Instead of lashing back with some retort, as I would have expected of her, Doris sobbed and ran away.

All the chaffering was amusing enough, and maybe even educational, but my concern was elsewhere. I said, "If I can find my lady again, and point her out to you fellows, perhaps you could manage to follow her better than I did, and tell me where she lives."

"No, grazie!" Ubaldo said firmly. "To molest a highborn lady is to gamble between the pillars."

Daniele snapped his fingers. "That reminds me. I heard that there is to be a frusta at the pillars this very afternoon. Some poor bastard who gambled and lost. Let us go and see it."

And so we did. A frusta is a public scourging and the pillars are those two I have mentioned, near the waterfront in Samarco's piazzetta. One of the columns is dedicated to my namesake saint and the other to Venice's earlier patron saint Teodoro, called Todaro here. All public punishments and executions of malefactors are carried out there—"between Marco and Todaro," as we say.

The centerpiece that day was a man we boys all knew, though we did not know his name. He was universally called only Il Zudìo, which means either the Jew or the usurer, or more commonly both. He resided in the burghèto set aside for his race, but the narrow shop in which he changed money and lent money was on the Mercerìa, where we boys lately did most of our thieving, and we had often seen him huddled at his counting table. He had hair and beard like a sort of curly red fungus going gray; he wore on his long coat the round yellow patch proclaiming him a Jew and the red hat that proclaimed him a Western Jew.

There were numerous others of his race in the crowd that afternoon, most in red hats, but some in the yellow head-wrappings signifying their Levantine origin. They would probably not have come of their own will to see a fellow Jew whipped and humiliated, for which reason Venetian law makes it mandatory for all adult male Jews to attend on such occasions. Of course, the crowd consisted mostly of non-Jews, gathered just for the sport, and an unusually high proportion were female.

The zudìo had been convicted of a fairly common offense—the gouging of excessive interest on some loan—but gossip had him guilty of more spicy intrigues. There was a widespread rumor that he, unlike any sensible Christian pawnbroker who dealt only in jewels and plate and other valuables, would take in pawn and lend good money for letters of mere paper, though they had to be letters of an indiscreet or compromising nature. Since so many Venetian women employed scribes to write for them letters of just that nature, or to read to them the letters of that nature which they received, perhaps the women wanted to look at the zudìo and speculate on whether he held incriminating copies of their correspondence. Or maybe, as so many women so often do, they simply wished to see a man flogged.

The usurer was accompanied to the flogging post by several uniformed gastaldi guards and his assigned comforter, a member of the lay Brotherhood of Justice. The brother, to remain anonymous in that degrading capacity of comforter to a Jew, wore a full gown and a hood over his head with eyeholes cut in it. A preco of the Quarantia stood where I had stood on the day before—high above the crowd on San Marco's loggia of the four horses—and read in a ringing voice:

"Inasmuch as the convict Mordecai Cartafilo has behaved very cruelly, against the peace of the State and the honor of the Republic and the virtue of its citizens . . . he is sentenced to endure thirteen vigorous strokes of the frusta, and thereafter to be confined in a pozzo of the Palace Prison while the Signori della Notte make inquiry of him into further particulars of his crimes. . . .".

The zudìo, when by custom he was asked if he had any complaint to make of the judgment, merely growled uncaringly, "Nè tibi nè catabi." The wretch may have shrugged coolly enough before he felt the scourge, but he did other things during the next several minutes. First he grunted, then he cried out, and then he howled. I glanced around at the crowd—the Christians were all nodding approvingly and the Jews were trying to look elsewhere—and my glance stopped at a certain face, and locked there, and I began sidling through the pack of people to get nearer to my lost lady found.

There came a shriek from behind me, and Ubaldo's voice calling, "Olà, Marco, you are not listening to the music of the sinagòga!"

But I did not turn around. I was taking no chance of letting the woman slip from my sight this time. She was again unveiled, the better to watch the frusta, and again I feasted my eyes on her beauty. As I got closer I saw that she stood next to a tall man who wore a cloak with a hood closely drawn about his face; he was nearly as anonymous as the Brother of Justice at the flogging post. And when I stood very close I heard that man murmur to my lady, "Then it was you who spoke to the snout."

"The J-Jew deserved it," she said, the delicious pout lingering briefly on her lips.

He murmured, "A chicken before a tribunal of foxes."

She laughed lightly but without humor. "Would you have preferred that I let the ch-chicken go to the confessional, Father?"

I wondered if the lady was younger than she looked, that she addressed every man as father. But then I sneaked a look up into the man's hood, I being shorter than he was, and saw that it was the San Marco priest of the day before. Wondering why he should be going about with his vestments hidden, I listened some more, but their disjointed conversation gave me no hint.

He said, still in a murmurous voice, "You fixed on the wrong victim. The one who might talk, not the someone who might listen."

She laughed again and said archly, "You never speak the name of that someone."

"Then you speak it," he murmured. "To the snout. Give the foxes a goat instead of a chicken."

She shook her head. "That someone—that old goat—has friends among the foxes. I require a means even more secret than the snout."

He was silent for a time. Then he murmured, "Bravo."

I assumed that he was murmurously applauding the performance of the frusta, which, after one last loud and piercing screech, was just then ending. The crowd began to mill about in preparation for dispersal.

My lady said, "Yes, I will inquire into that possibility. But now"—she touched his cloaked arm—"that someone approaches."

He clasped the hood still closer about his face and moved off with the crowd, away from her. She was joined by another man, this one gray-haired, red-faced, dressed in clothes as fine as hers—perhaps her real father, I thought—who said, "Ah, there you are, Ilaria. How did we get separated?"

That was the first time I heard her name. She and the older man strolled off together, she chattering brightly about "how well the frusta was done, what a nice day for it," and other such typically feminine remarks. I hung far enough behind them not to be noticeable, but I followed as if I were being tugged on a string. I feared that they would walk only as far as the waterfront and there step into the man's batèlo or gòndola. In that case I should have had a hard time following them. Everyone in the crowd who did not have a private craft was competing for the boats for hire. But Ilaria and her companion turned the other way and walked up the piazzetta toward the main piazza, skirting the crowd by staying close to the wall of the Doge's Palace.

Ilaria's rich robe flicked the very muzzles of the lionlike marble masks which protrude from the palace wall at waist level. Those are what we Venetians call the musi da denonzie secrete, and there is one of them for each of several sorts of crime: smuggling, tax evasion, usury, conspiracy against the State, and so on. The snouts have slits for mouths and on the other side of them, inside the palace, the agents of the Quarantia squat like spiders waiting for a web to twitch. They do not have to wait long between alarms. Those marble slits have been worn ever wider and smoother over the years, by the countless hands slipping into them unsigned messages imputing crimes to enemies, creditors, lovers, neighbors, blood relations and even total strangers. Because the accusers remain unknown and can accuse without proof, and because the law makes little allowance for malice, slander, frustration and spite, it is the accused who must disprove the accusations. That is not easy, and it is seldom done.

The man and woman circled around two sides of the arcaded square, with me close enough behind to overhear their desultory talk. Then they entered one of the houses there on the piazza itself, and, from the demeanor of the servant who opened the door, it was evident that they lived there. Those houses of the innermost heart of the city are not elaborately decorated on the outside, and so are not called palazzi. They are known as the "mute houses" because their outward simplicity says nothing about the wealth of their occupants, who comprise the oldest and noblest families of Venice. So I will be likewise mute about which house I followed Ilaria to, and not risk casting shame on that family name.

I learned two other things during that brief surveillance. From the bits of conversation, it became apparent even to my besotted self that the gray-haired man was not Ilaria's father but her husband. That caused me some hurt, but I salved it with the thought that a young woman with an old husband ought to be readily susceptible to the attentions of a younger man, like myself.

The other thing I overheard was their talk of the festa to be celebrated the next week, the Samarco dei Bòcoli. (I should have mentioned that the month was April, of which the twenty-fifth is the day of San Marco, and in Venice that day is always a feast of flowers and gaiety and masquerade dedicated to "San Marco of the Buds." This city loves feste, and it welcomes that day because it comes around each year when there has been no festa since Carnevale, perhaps two months agone.)

The man and woman spoke of the costumes they were having made, and the several balls to which they had been invited, and I felt another heart pang because those festivities would be held behind doors closed to me. But then Ilaria declared that she was also going to mingle in the outdoor torchlight promenades of that night. Her husband made some remonstrance, grumbling about the crowds and the crush to be endured "among the common herd," but Ilaria laughingly insisted, and my heart beat with hope and resolve again.

Directly they disappeared inside their casa muta, I ran to a shop I knew near the Rialto. Its front was hung with masks of cloth and wood and cartapesta, red and black and white and face-colored, in forms grotesque and comic and demonic and lifelike. I burst into the shop, shouting to the maskmaker, "Make me a mask for the Samarco festa! Make me a mask that will make me look handsome but old! Make me look more than twenty! But make me look well preserved and manly and gallant!"

. 6 .

S o it was that, on the morning of that late-April festa day, I dressed in my best without having to be bidden to do so by any of the servants. I put on a cerise velvet doublet and lavender silk hose and my seldom worn red Còrdoba shoes, and over all a heavy wool cloak intended to disguise the slenderness of my figure. I hid my mask beneath the cloak, and left the house, and went to try my masquerade on the boat children. As I approached their barge, I took out and put on the mask. It had eyebrows and a dashing mustache made of real hair, and its face was the craggy, sun-browned visage of a mariner who had sailed far seas.

"Olà, Marco," said the boys. "Sana capàna."

"You *recognize* me? I look like *Marco*?"

"Hm. Now that you mention it . . .," said Daniele. "No, not much like the Marco we know. Who do you think he looks like, Boldo?"

Impatient, I said, "I do not look like a seafarer more than twenty years old?"

"Well . . .," said Ubaldo. "Sort of a *short* seafarer . . ."

"Ship's food is sometimes scanty," Daniele said helpfully. "It could have stunted your growth."

I was much annoyed. When Doris emerged from the barge and immediately said, "Olà, Marco," I wheeled to snarl at her. But what I saw gave me pause.

She too appeared to be in masquerade in honor of the day. She had washed her formerly nondescript hair, revealing it to be of a nice straw-gold color. She had washed her face clean and powdered it attractively pale, as grown-up Venetian women do. She was also wearing womanly garb, a gown of brocade cut down and remade from one that had been my mother's. Doris spun around to make the skirts whirl, and said shyly, "Am I not as fine and beautiful as your lustrìsima lady love, Marco?"

Ubaldo muttered something about "all these dwarf ladies and gentlemen," but I only stared through the eyes of my mask.

Doris persisted, "Will you not walk out with me, Marco, on this day of festa? . . . What are you laughing at?"

"Your shoes."

"What?" she whispered, and her face fell.

"I laugh because no *lady* ever wore those awful wooden tofi."

She looked inexpressibly hurt, and retired again inside the barge. I loitered long enough for the boys to assure me—and make me half believe—that nobody would recognize me as a mere boy except those who already knew me to be a mere boy. Then I left them, and went to the piazza San Marco. It was far too early for any ordinary celebrants to be yet abroad, but the Dona Ilaria had not described her costume while I was eavesdropping. She might be as heavily disguised as I was, so to recognize her I had to be lurking outside her door when she departed for the first of her balls.

I might have attracted some unwelcome attention, idling about that one end of one arcade like a novice cutpurse of extreme stupidity, but fortunately I was not the only person in the piazza already strikingly attired. Under almost every arch, a costumed matacìn or a montimbanco was setting up his platform and, long before there was really enough of a crowd to play to, they were displaying their talents. I was glad, for they gave me something to look at besides the doorway of the casa muta.

The montimbanchi, swathed in robes like those of physicians or

astrologers, but more extravagantly spangled with stars and moons and
suns, did various conjuring tricks or cranked music from an ordegnogor-
gia to attract attention, and, when they had caught the eye of any
passerby, began vociferously to hawk their simples—dried herbs and
colored liquids and moon-milk mushrooms and the like. The matacìni,
even more resplendent in gaudy face paint and costumes of checks and
diamonds and patches, had nothing to peddle but their agility. So they
bounded up and down on their platforms, and onto and off them, doing
energetic acrobatics and sword dances, and they contorted themselves
into fantastic convolutions, and they juggled balls and oranges and each
other, and then, when they paused to take breath, they passed their hats
around for coins.

As the day went on, more entertainers came and took up stands in
the piazza, also the sellers of confèti and sweets and refreshing drinks,
and more commonfolk strolled through, too, though not yet wearing
their own festa finery. Those would congregate about a platform and
watch the tricks of a montimbanco or listen to a castròn singing bar-
carole to lute accompaniment, and then, as soon as the artist began passing his hat or peddling his wares, would move on to another platform.
Many of those people ambled from one performer to another until they
came to where I lurked in my mask and cloak, and they would stand
stolidly and ogle me and expect me to do something entertaining. It was
slightly distressing, as I could do nothing but sweat at them—the spring
day had become most unseasonably warm—and try to look as if I were a
servant posted there, waiting patiently for my master.

The day wore on and on interminably, and I wished fervently that
I had worn a lighter cloak, and I wished I could kill every one of the
million nasty pigeons in the piazza, and I was grateful for every new
diversion that came along. The first citizens arriving in anything but
everyday raiment were the arti guilds wearing their ceremonial clothes.
The arte of physicians, barber-surgeons and apothecaries wore high con-
ical hats and billowing robes. The guild of painters and illuminators
wore garments that may have been of mere canvas, but were most
fancifully gold-leafed and colored over. The arte of tanners, curriers and
leatherworkers wore hide aprons with decorative designs not painted or
sewn but branded onto them. . . .

When all the many guilds were assembled in the piazza, there came
from his palace the Doge Ranieri Zeno, and, though his public costume
was familiar enough to me and everybody else, it was sufficiently lavish
for any festive day. He had the white scufieta on his head and the ermine
cape over his golden gown, the train of which was carried by three
servants clad in the ducal livery. Behind them emerged the retinue of
Council and Quarantia and other nobles and officials, all likewise richly
attired. And behind them came a band of musicians, but they held their
lutes and pipes and rebecs silent while they moved with measured pace
down to the waterfront. The Doge's forty-oared buzino d'oro was just
gliding up against the mole, and the procession marched aboard. Not
until the gleaming bark was well out upon the water did the musicians
begin to play. They always wait like that, because they know how the

music gains a special sweetness when it skips across the wavelets to us listeners on the land.

About the hour of compieta the twilight came down, and the lampaderi moved about the piazza, setting alight the torch baskets bracketed above the arches, and I was still hovering within sight of the Lady Ilaria's door. I felt as if I had been there all my life, and I was getting faint with hunger—for I had not even gone as far from it as a fruit peddler's stand—but I was prepared to wait all the rest of my life if that should be necessary. At least by that hour I was not so conspicuous, for the square was well populated, and almost all the promenaders were in some kind of costume.

Some of them danced to the distant music of the Doge's band, some sang along with the warbling castròni, but most simply paraded about to show off their own regalia and admire that of others. The young people pelted each other with confèti, which are the little sprinkles of sweets and the eggshells filled with perfumed waters. The older girls carried oranges and waited to catch a glimpse of some favorite gallant at whom they could throw one. That custom is supposed to commemorate the wedding-gift orange of Jupiter and Juno, and a young man can boast himself an especially favored Jupiter if his Juno throws the orange hard enough to give him a black eye or knock out a tooth.

Then, as the twilight deepened, there came in from the sea the caligo, the briny mist that so often envelops Venice by night, and I began to be glad for my woolen cloak. In that fog, the hanging torches changed from iron baskets of curly flames into soft-edged globes of light magically suspended in space. The people in the piazza became merely darker and more coherent blobs of mist moving through the mist, except when they passed between me and one of the blurs of torchlight. Then they radiated extravagant spokes and wedges of shadow that flickered like black swordblades slashing at the gray fog. Only when some stroller passed quite near me did he or she briefly become solid, then in the next moment dissolve again. Like something out of a dream, an angel would take substance: a girl of tinsel and gauze and laughing eyes, and she would melt into something out of a nightmare: a Satan with varnished red face and horns.

Suddenly the door behind me opened and the gray fog was gashed by bright lamplight. I turned and saw two shadows against the dazzle, and they resolved themselves into my lady and her husband. Truly, if I had not been posted at the door, I could not have recognized either of them. He was totally transformed into one of the standard characters of masquerade, the comic physician, Dotòr Balanzòn. But Ilaria was so much changed that I could not immediately determine into what she was changed. A white and gold miter concealed her bronze hair, a brief dòmino mask hid her eyes, and layers of alb, chasuble, cope and stole made a dumpy dome shape of her fine figure. Then I realized that she was adorned as the long-ago female Pope Zuàna. Her costume must have cost a fortune, and I feared that it would cost her a heavy penance if any real cleric caught her dressed as that legendary lady Pope.

They crossed the square through the porridge of people, and them-

selves immediately entered into the festa spirit: she scattering confèti
in the manner of a priest aspersing holy water, and he tossing them in
the manner of a mèdego dispensing dosages. Their gòndola was waiting
at the lagoon-side, and they stepped into it, and it pushed off toward the
Grand Canal. After a moment's thought, I did not bother to hail a boat
in which to follow them. The caligo was by then so thick that all the
vessels on the water were moving with extreme caution, close to the
banks. It was easier for me to keep my quarry in sight, and to pursue it,
by trotting along the canalside streets and occasionally waiting on a
bridge to see which canal it would take when the waterways diverged. I
did a good deal of trotting that night, as Ilaria and her consort went
from one grand palazzo and casa muta to another. But I did a lot more
of waiting outside those places, in the company of only prowling cats,
while my lady enjoyed the feste within.

I lurked in the salt-smelling fog, which was now so heavy that it
collected and dripped from eaves and arches and the end of my mask's
nose, and I listened to the muffled music from indoors and I imagined
Ilaria dancing the furlàna. I leaned against slippery, streaming stone
walls and I enviously eyed the windowpanes where the candlelight
glowed through the murk. I sat on cold, wet bridge balustrades and
heard my stomach growling and envisioned Ilaria daintily nibbling at
scalete pastries and bignè buns. I stood and stamped my gradually
numbing feet, and I again cursed my cloak as it weighed ever more
heavy and dank and cold and dragged at my ankles. Notwithstanding
my sodden misery, I perked up and tried to look like an innocent merry-
maker whenever other masqueraders loomed out of the caligo and
shouted tipsy greetings at me—a cackling bufòn, a swaggering corsàro,
three boys capering in company as the three Ms: mèdego, musician and
madman.

The city does not sound the coprifuoco on feste nights, but, when
we had arrived at the third or fourth palazzo of that night and I was
waiting soggily outside it, I heard all the church bells ringing the compline. As if that had been a signal, Ilaria slipped away from the ballroom
and came outdoors and came straight to where I crouched in an alcove
of the house wall, my hood and cloak clasped close about me. She was
still in her papal vestments, but she had taken off the dòmino.

She said softly, "Caro là," the greeting used only between lovers,
and I was struck stiff as a statue. Her breath smelled sweetly of bevarìn
hazelnut liqueur when she whispered to the folds of my hood, "The old
goat is drunk at last, and will not be ch-chasing after—*Dio me varda!*
Who are you?" And she shrank back from me.

"My name is Marco Polo," I said. "I have been following—"

"I am discovered!" she cried, so shrilly that I feared a sbiro might
hear. "You are his bravo!"

"No, no, my lady!" I stood up and threw back my hood. Since my
seafarer mask had so affrighted her, I slipped that off, too. "I am
nobody's but yours only!"

She backed farther away, her eyes wide in disbelief. "You are a
boy!"

I could not deny that, but I could qualify it. "Of a man's experience," I said quickly. "I have loved you and sought you since first I saw you."

Her eyes narrowed to examine me more closely. "What are you doing here?"

"I was waiting," I babbled, "to put my heart at your feet and my arm in your service and my destiny in your keeping."

She looked nervously about her. "I have page boys enough. I do not wish to hire—"

"Not for hire!" I declared. "For love of my lady I shall serve her forever!"

I may have hoped for a look of melting surrender. The look she gave me conveyed more of exasperation. "But it is the hour of compline," she said. "Where is—? I mean, have you seen no one else hereabout? Are you alone?"

"No, he is not," said another voice, a very quiet one.

I turned about and realized that a sword's point had been very near the back of my neck. It was just then withdrawing into the fog, and it glinted a gleam of cold, bedewed steel as it vanished beneath the cloak of its wielder. I had thought the voice was that of Ilaria's priest acquaintance, but priests do not carry swords. Before I or she could speak, the hooded figure murmured again:

"I see by your raiment tonight, my lady, that you are a mocker. So be it. Now is the mocker mocked. This young intruder desires to be a lady's bravo, and will serve for no hire but love. Let him, then, and let that be your penance for mockery."

Ilaria gasped and started to say, "Are you suggesting—?"

"I am absolving. You are already forgiven whatever must be done. And when the greater obstacle has been removed, a smaller one will be more easily dismissed."

With that, the shape in the fog moved farther back in the fog and blended into the fog and was gone. I had no idea what the stranger's words had meant, but I did perceive that he had spoken in my behalf, and I was grateful. I turned again to Ilaria, who was regarding me with a sort of rueful appraisal. She put one slim hand inside her robe and brought out the dòmino and raised it before her eyes as if to mask something there.

"Your name is . . . Marco?" I bowed my head and mumbled that it was. "You said you followed me. You know my house?" I mumbled yes. "Come there tomorrow, Marco. To the servants' door. At the hour of mezza-vespro. Do not fail me."

· 7 ·

I did not fail her, at least in the matter of promptness. The next afternoon, I presented myself as commanded, and the servants' door was opened by an ancient hag. The hag's little eyes were as mistrustful as if she knew every shameful thing about Venice, and she admitted me to the house as distastefully as if I had been one of the worst. She led me upstairs, along a hall, pointed a withered finger at a door, and left me. I knocked at the panel and the Dona Ilaria opened it. I stepped inside and she secured the latch behind me.

She bade me be seated, and then she walked up and down before my chair, regarding me speculatively. She wore a dress covered with gold-colored flakes that shimmered like a serpent's scales. It was a close-fitting dress and her walk was sinuous. The lady would have looked rather reptilian and dangerous, except that she kept wringing her hands the while, and thus betrayed her own uncertainty at our being alone together.

"I have been thinking about you ever since last night," she said. I started to echo that, wholeheartedly, but I could not make my voice work, and she went on. "You say you ch-choose to serve me, and there is indeed a service you could do. You say you would do it for love, and I confess that arouses my . . . my curiosity. But I think you are aware that I have a husband."

I swallowed loudly and said yes, I was aware.

"He is much older than I, and he is embittered by age. He is j-jealous of my youth and envious of all things youthful. He also has a violent temper. Clearly I cannot enlist the service of a—of a young man—not to mention enjoy the love of one. You understand? I might wish to, even yearn to, but I cannot, being a married woman."

I gave that some thought, then cleared my throat and said what seemed to me obvious, "An old husband will die and you will still be young."

"You do understand!" She stopped wringing her hands and clapped them, applauding. "You are quick of intellect for such a—such a young man." She cocked her head, the better to look admiringly at me. "So he must die. Yes?"

Dejectedly I stood up to go, supposing that we had agreed that any yearned-for connection between us must simply wait until her bad-natured old husband was dead. I was not happy at that postponement, but, as Ilaria said, we both were young. We could restrain ourselves for a while.

Before I could turn to the door, though, she came and stood very close to me. She pressed herself against me, in fact, and looked down into my eyes and very softly inquired, "How will you do it?"

I gulped and said hoarsely, "How will I do what, my lady?"

She laughed a conspiratorial laugh. "You are discreet besides! But I think I will have to know, because it will require some prior planning to ensure that I am not. . . . However, that can wait. For now, pretend that I asked how you will—love me."

"With all my heart!" I said in a croak.

"Oh, with that, too, let us hope. But surely—do I shock you, Marco? —with some other part of you as well?" She laughed merrily at what must have been the expression on my face.

I made a strangled noise and coughed and said, "I have been taught by an experienced teacher. When you are free and we can make love, I will know how to do that. I assure you, my lady, I will not make a fool of myself."

She lifted her eyebrows and said, "Well! I have been wooed with promises of many different delights, but never quite that one." She studied me again, through eyelashes that were like talons reaching for my heart. "Show me, then, how you do not make a fool of yourself. I owe you at least an earnest payment for your service."

Ilaria raised her hands to her shoulders and somehow unfastened the top of her gold-serpent gown. It slipped down to her waist, and she undid the bustenca underneath, and let that drop to the floor, and I was gazing upon her breasts of milk and roses. I think I must have tried simultaneously to grab for her and to peel off my own clothes, for she gave a small shriek.

"Who was it taught you, boy? A goat? Come to the bed."

I tried to temper my boyish eagerness with manly decorum, but that was even more difficult when we were on the bed and both of us were totally unclad. Ilaria's body was mine to savor in every inviting detail, and even a stronger man than myself might have wished to abandon all restraint. Tinted of milk and roses, fragrant of milk and roses, soft as milk and roses, her flesh was so beautifully different from the gross meat of Malgarita and Zulià that she might have been a woman of a new and superior race. It was all I could do to keep from nibbling her to see if she tasted as delectable as she looked and smelled and felt to the touch.

I told her that, and she smiled and stretched languorously and closed her eyes and suggested, "Nibble, then, but g-gently. Do to me *all* the interesting things you have learned."

I ran one tremulous finger along the length of her—from the fringe of closed eyelashes down her shapely Verona nose, across the pouted lips, down her chin and her satin throat, over the mound of one firm breast and its pert nipple, down her smoothly rounded belly to the feathering of fine hair below—and she squirmed and mewed with pleasure. I remembered something that made me halt my tracing finger there. To demonstrate that I knew very well how to do things, I told her with suave assurance, "I will not play with your pota, in case you have to pee."

Her whole body jerked and her eyes flew open and she exploded, "*Amoredèi!*" and she flailed angrily out from under my hand and well away from me.

She knelt at the far edge of the bed and stared as if I were something that had just emerged from a crack in the floor. After vibrating at me for a moment, she demanded, "Who *was* it taught you, asenazzo?"

I, the ass, mumbled, "A girl of the boat people."

"Dio v'agiuta," she sighed. "Better a goat."

She lay down again, but on her side, with her head propped on a hand so she could go on staring at me. "Now I really am curious," she said. "Since I do not have to—excuse myself—what do you do next?"

"Well," I said, disconcerted. "I put my. You know, my candle. Into your uh. And move it. Back and forth. And, well, that is it." A wondering and terrible silence ensued, until I said uncomfortably, "Is it not?"

"Do you truly believe that is all there is to it? A melody on one string?" She shook her head in slow marveling. I began miserably to collect myself. "No, do not go away. Do not move. Stay where you are and let me teach you properly. Now, to begin with . . ."

I was surprised, but pleasantly so, to learn that making love should be rather like making music, and that "to begin with," both players should commence the playing so far away from their main instruments—instead, using lips and eyelashes and earlobes—and that the music could be so enjoyable even in its pianìsimo beginning. The music swelled to vivace when Ilaria introduced for instruments her full breasts and softly rigid nipples, and teased and coaxed me into using my tongue instead of fingers to pluck the notes from them. At that pizzicato, she literally gave voice and sang in accompaniment to the music.

In a brief interval between those choruses, she informed me, in a voice gone whispery, "You have now heard the hymn of the convent."

I also learned that a woman really does possess such a thing as the lumaghèta of which I had heard, and that the word is correct in both its meanings. The lumaghèta is indeed a thing somewhat resembling a small snail, but in function it is more like the tuning key that a lutist employs. When Ilaria showed me, by doing it first herself, how to manipulate the lumaghèta delicately and adroitly, I could make her, like a veritable lute herself, hum and twang and ring delightfully. She taught me how to do other things, too, which she could not do to herself, and which would never have occurred to my imagination. So at one moment I would be twiddling with my fingers as on the frets of a viella, and the next I would be using my lips in the manner of playing a dulzaina, and the next I would be flutter-tonguing in the way a flutist blows his flute.

It was not until well along in that afternoon's divertimento that Ilaria gave the cue for us to join our main instruments, and we played all'unisono, and the music rose in crescendo to an unbelievable climax of tuti fortìsimi. Then we kept on bringing it back up to that peak, again and again, during most of the rest of the afternoon. Then we played several codas, each a little more diminuendo, until we were both fairly drained of music. Then we lay quietly side by side, enjoying the waning tremolo after-echoes . . . dolce, dolce . . . dolce . . .

When some time had passed, I thought to make gallant inquiry: "Do you not want to jump around and sneeze?"

She gave a slight start, looked sideways at me, and muttered something I could not hear. Then she said, "No, grazie, I do not, Marco. I wish now to talk of my husband."

"Why darken the day?" I objected. "Let us rest a little longer and then see if we cannot play another tune."

"Oh, no! As long as I remain a married woman, I shall remain a ch-chaste one. We do not do this again until my husband is dead."

I had acquiesced when she earlier set that condition. But now I had sampled the ecstasy that awaited, and the thought of waiting was insupportable. I said, "Even though he is old, that might take years."

She gave me a look and said sharply, "Why should it? What means do you propose using?"

Bewildered, I said, "I?"

"Did you intend j-just to go on following him, as you did last night? Until perhaps you *annoy* him to death?"

The truth finally began to filter through my density. I said in awe, "Do you seriously mean he is to be killed?"

"I mean he is to be killed seriously," she said, with flat sarcasm. "What did you think we have been talking about, asenazzo, when we talked of your doing me a service?"

"I thought you meant . . . this." And I shyly touched her there.

"No more of that." She wriggled a little away from me. "And by the way, if you must use vulgar language, try at least to call that my mona. It sounds a *little* less awful than that other word."

"But am I never to touch your mona again?" I said wretchedly. "Not until I do that other service for you?"

"To the victor the spoils. I have enjoyed polishing your stilèto, Marco, but another bravo might offer me a sword."

"A bravo," I reflected. "Yes, such a deed would make me a real bravo, would it not?"

She said persuasively, "And I would much rather love a dashing bravo than a furtive despoiler of other men's wives."

"There is a sword in a closet at home," I muttered to myself. "It must have belonged to my father or one of his brothers. It is old, but it is kept honed and bright."

"You will never be blamed or even suspected. My husband must have many enemies, for what important man has not? And they will be of his own age and standing. No one would think to suspect a mere—I mean a younger man who has no discernible motive for taking his life. You have only to accost him in the dark, when he is alone, and make sure of your strike so he does not linger long enough to give any description—"

"No," I interrupted her. "Better if I could find him among a gathering of his peers, those who include his actual enemies. If in those circumstances I could do it unobserved . . . But no." I suddenly realized that I was contemplating murder. I concluded lamely, "That would probably be impossible."

"Not for a g-genuine bravo," Ilaria said, in the voice of a dove. "Not for one who will be rewarded so bounteously."

She moved against me again, and continued to move, tantalizing with the promise of that reward. This aroused in me several conflicting emotions, but my body recognized only one of them and raised a baton to play a fanfare of salute.

"No," said Ilaria, fending me off and becoming very businesslike. "A music maistra may give the first lesson free, to indicate what can be learned. But if you wish further lessons in more advanced execution, you must earn them."

She was clever, to send me away not completely satiated. As it was, I left the house—again by the servants' door—throbbing almost painfully and lusting as if I had not been satisfied at all. I was being led and directed, so to speak, by that baton of mine, and its inclination was to lead me back to Ilaria's bower, whatever that might require of me. Other events seemed also to be conspiring toward that end. When I came around from the back of the block of houses, I found the Samarco piazza full of people in a buzzing commotion, and a uniformed banditore was crying the news:

The Doge Ranieri Zeno had been stricken by a sudden seizure that afternoon in his palace chambers. The Doge was dead. The Council was being summoned to start voting for a successor to the ducal crown. The whole of Venice was bidden to observe a three-day period of mourning before the funeral of the Doge Zeno.

Well, I thought as I went on my way, if a great Doge can die, why cannot a lesser noble? And, it occurred to me, the funeral ceremonies would entail more than one assemblage of those lesser nobles all together. Among them would be my lady's husband and undoubtedly, as she had suggested, some of his enviers and enemies.

. 8 .

F o R the next three days, the late Doge Zeno lay in state in his palace, being visited by respectful citizens during the days and being watched over by the professional vigil-keeper during the nights. I spent most of that time in my room, practicing with the old but still worthy sword until I became quite adept at slashing and stabbing phantom husbands. What I had the most trouble with was simply carrying the sword about, because it was nearly as long as my leg. I could not just slip it naked under my belt or else, when I walked, I might impale my own foot. To carry the thing anywhere, I should have to carry it in its scabbard, and that made it even more unwieldy. Also, for concealment of it, I should have to wear my all-enveloping long cloak, which would not permit any quick draw-and-lunge.

Meanwhile, I made cunning plans. On the second day of vigil, I wrote a note, most carefully drawing the characters in my schoolboy hand: "Will he be at both the Funeral and the Installation?" I regarded that critically, then underscored the *he* so that there should be no mistaking whom I meant. I painstakingly drew my name underneath, so that there should be no mistaking the note's author. Then I did not entrust it to any servant, but carried it myself to the casa muta, and waited for another interminable time until I saw the *he* leave the house, dressed in dark mourning clothes. I went around to the back door, gave the note to the old hag doorkeeper, and told her I would wait for a reply.

After another while, she returned. She bore no reply but beckoned me with a gnarled finger. Again I followed her to Ilaria's suite of rooms, and found my lady studying the paper. She looked flustered, somehow, and neglected to give me any fond greeting, saying only, "I can read, of course, but I cannot make out your wretched writing. Read this to me."

I did, and she said yes, her husband, like every other member of the Venetian Grand Council, would be attending both the funeral rites for the late Doge and the installation ceremonies of the new one when he had been selected. "Why do you ask?"

"It gives me two opportunities," I said. "I shall try to—accomplish my service—on the funeral day. If that proves impossible, I will at least have a better idea of how to go about it at the next gathering of nobles."

She took the paper from me and looked at it. "I do not see my name on this."

"Naturally not," I said, the experienced conspirator. "I would not compromise a lustrìsima."

"Is your name on it?"

"Yes." I pointed with pride. "There. That is my name, my lady."

"I have learned that it is not always wise to commit things to paper." She folded and tucked the paper into her bodice. "I will keep this safe." I started to tell her just to tear it up, but she went on, sounding peevish, "I hope you realize that you were very foolish to come here unbidden."

"I waited to make certain *he* left."

"But if someone else—if one of his relatives or friends was here? Listen to me now. You are never to come here again until I summon you."

I smiled. "Until we are free of—"

"*Until I summon you.* Now go, and go quickly. I am expecting—I mean, *he* may come back any minute."

So I went home and practiced some more. And the next day, when at sundown the pompe funebri began, I was among the spectators. Even the least commoner's burial in Venice is always dignified by as much pageantry as his or her family can afford, so the Doge's was splendid indeed. The dead man lay not in a coffin but on an open litter, dressed in his finest robes of state, his stiff hands clasping his mace of office, his face fixed by the pomp-masters in an expression of serene sanctimony. The widowed Dogaressa stayed always beside it, so draped in veils that only her white hand was visible where it rested on her late husband's shoulder.

The litter was first laid on the roof of the Doge's great buzino d'oro, at the prow of which the gold-and-scarlet ducal flag hung at half staff. The bark was rowed with solemn slowness—the forty oars seeming scarcely to move—up and down the main canals of the city. Behind it and around it were grouped black funeral gòndole and crape-hung batèli and burchielli, bearing the members of the Council and the Signoria and the Quarantia and the city's chief priests and the confratèli of the arti guilds, the whole retinue alternately singing hymns and chanting prayers.

When the dead man had been sufficiently paraded on the waterways, his litter was lifted off the bark and onto the shoulders of eight of his nobles. Because the corteggio then had to wind up and down all the main streets of the central city, and because so many of the pallbearers were elderly, they changed places frequently with new men. And the litter was again followed by the Dogaressa and all the other court mourners, now on foot, and by bands of musicians playing doleful slow music, and contingents from the flagellant brotherhoods lethargically pretending to whip themselves, and finally by every other Venetian not too young or old or crippled to walk.

I could do nothing during the water-borne procession except watch it from the banks with the rest of the citizens. But by the time it came ashore, I decided that good fortune was attending my scheme. For there also came in from the water the twilight caligo again, and the obsequies became even more melancholy and mysterious, shrouded by fog, the music muffled and the chants lugubriously hollow.

Bracket torches were lighted along the route, and most of the marchers took out and lighted candles. For a while I walked among the common herd—or limped, rather, since the sword along my left leg forced me to swing it stiffly—and gradually eased myself to the forefront of that throng. From there I could verify that almost every official mourner was cloaked and hooded, except the priests. So was I well covered, and in the thick mist I could be taken for one of the guilds' artists or artisans. Even my size was not conspicuous; the procession included numerous veiled women no bigger than I was, and a few cowled dwarfs and hunchbacks smaller than I was. So I edged my way imperceptibly among the court mourners, and ever farther forward, being challenged by nobody at all, until I was separated from the litter and its pallbearers only by a rank of priests yammering their ritual pimpirimpàra and swinging censers to add smoke to the fog.

I was not the only inconspicuous marcher in the procession. What with everybody being so shrouded in cloth and in the almost equally woolly mist, I had a hard time picking out my quarry. But the street march was long enough that, by moving cautiously from side to side and peering sharply at the little of each man's profile that protruded beyond his cowl, I at last was able to perceive which was Ilaria's husband, and thereafter I kept my eye on him.

My chance came when the corteggio finally debouched from a narrow street onto the cobbled embankment of the city's north shore—on the Dead Lagoon, not far from where the boat children's barge lay, though that was invisible in the fog and the now near-dark. Alongside the embankment was the Doge's bark, which had circled the city to get ahead of us, waiting to ferry him on his last voyage—to the Isle of the Dead, also invisible far offshore. There was a milling of the mourners, as all the men nearest the litter tried to help its bearers hoist it aboard the bark, and that gave me the opportunity to mingle in with them. I elbowed until I was right beside my quarry, and in all the shoving and bustling no one remarked the struggle I had to make to unsheathe my sword. Fortunately, Ilaria's husband did not manage to get his shoulder under the litter—or the dispatching of him might have meant the Doge's getting dropped into the Dead Lagoon.

What did get dropped was my heavy scabbard; somehow my fumbling had unhooked it from my tunic belt. It clattered heavily onto the cobblestones and kept on noisily proclaiming itself as the many shuffling feet kicked it about. My heart bounded into my throat and then almost popped out of my mouth as Ilaria's husband bent down to pick up the scabbard. But he made no outcry; he handed it back to me with the kindly comment, "Here, young fellow, you dropped this." I was still right next to the man, and both of us were still being buffeted by the movement of the crowd around us, and my sword was in my hand beneath my cloak, and that was the moment to strike, but how could I? He had saved me from immediate discovery; could I stab him in return for the favor?

But then another voice spoke, hissing beside my ear, "You stupid asenazzo!" and something else made a rasping noise, and something metallic glinted in the torchlight. It happened at the edge of my vision, so my impressions were fragmentary and confused. But it appeared to me that one of the priests who had been swinging a golden censer had abruptly swung something silvery instead. And then Ilaria's husband leaned into my view, and opened his mouth and belched a substance that looked black in that light. I had done nothing to him, but *something* had happened to him. He tottered and jostled against the other men in the bunched group, and he and at least two others fell down. Then a heavy hand clutched at my shoulder, but I yanked away from it, and the recoil took me out of the center of the tumult. As I struggled through the outer fringe of people, and caromed off a couple of them, I again dropped my scabbard and then the sword as well, but I did not pause. I was in panic and I could think of nothing but to run fast and far. Behind me I heard exclamations of astonishment and outrage, but by then I was well away from the massed torch and candlelight and well away into the blessed darkness and fog.

I kept on running along the embankment until I saw two new figures taking form before me in the misty night. I might have shied away, but I saw they were children's figures and, after a moment, they resolved themselves into Ubaldo and Doris Tagiabue. I was ever so relieved to see someone familiar—and small. I tried to put on a glad face and probably put on a ghastly one, but I hailed them jollily:

"Doris, you are still scrubbed and clean!"

"You are not," she said, and pointed.

I looked down at myself. The front of my cloak was wet with more than a soaking of caligo. It was splotched and spattered with glistening red.

"And your face is as pale as a tombstone," said Ubaldo. "What happened, Marco?"

"I was . . . I was almost a bravo," I said, my voice gone suddenly unsteady. They stared at me, and I explained. It felt good to tell it to somebody unconcerned in the matter. "My lady sent me to slay a man. But I think he died before I could do it. Some other enemy must have intervened, or hired a bravo to do it."

Ubaldo exclaimed, "You *think* he died?"

"Everything happened all at once. I had to flee. I suppose I will not know what really happened until the banditori of the night watch cry the news."

"Where was this?"

"Back yonder, where the dead Doge is being put aboard his bark. Or maybe he is not yet. All is turmoil."

"I could go and see. I can tell you sooner than a banditore."

"Yes," I said. "But be careful, Boldo. They will be suspecting every stranger."

He ran off the way I had come, and Doris and I sat down on a waterside bollard. She regarded me gravely, and after a while said, "The man was the lady's husband." She did not frame it as a question, but I nodded numbly. "And you hope to take his place."

"I already have," I said, with as much of boastfulness as I could muster. Doris seemed to wince, so I added truthfully, "Once, anyway."

That one afternoon now seemed long in the past, and at the moment I felt no arousal of the urge to repeat it. Curious, I thought to myself, how anxiety can so diminish a man's ardor. Why, if I were in Ilaria's room right now, and she was naked and smiling and beckoning, I could not . . .

"You may be in terrible trouble," said Doris, as if to shrivel my ardor utterly.

"I think not," I said, to convince myself rather than the girl. "I did nothing more criminal than to be where I did not belong. And I got away without being caught or recognized, so no one knows I did even that much. Except you, now."

"And what happens next?"

"If the man is dead, my lady will soon summon me to her grateful embrace. I will go slightly shamefaced, for I had hoped to go to her as a gallant bravo, the slayer of her oppressor." A thought came to me. "But now at least I can go to her with a clear conscience." The thought brought a little cheer with it.

"And if he is not dead?"

The cheer evaporated. I had not yet considered that eventuality. I said nothing, and sat trying to think what I might do—or might have to do.

"Perhaps then," Doris ventured in a very small voice, "you might take me instead of her for your smanza?"

I ground my teeth. "Why do you keep on making that ridiculous proposal? Especially now, when I have so many other problems to think about?"

"If you had accepted when I first offered, you would not now have so many problems."

That was either female or juvenile illogic, and palpably absurd, but there was just enough truth in it to make me respond with cruelty, "The Dona Ilaria is beautiful; you are not. She is a woman; you are a child. She merits the Dona to her name, and I also am of the Ene Aca. I could never take for my lady anyone not nobly born and—"

"She has not behaved very nobly. Neither have you."

But I careered on, "She is always clean and fragrant; you have only just discovered washing. She knows how to make love sublimely; you will never know more than the pig Malgarita—"

"If your lady knows how to fottere so well, then you must have learned, too, and you could teach me—"

"There you are! No lady would use a word like *fottere*! Ilaria calls it musicare."

"Then teach me to talk like a lady. Teach me to musicare like a lady."

"This is insupportable! With everything else on my mind, why am I sitting here arguing with an imbecile?" I stood up and said sternly, "Doris, you are supposed to be a good girl. Why do you keep offering not to be?"

"Because . . ." She bowed her head so that her fair hair fell like a casque around her face and hid her expression. "Because that is all I can offer."

"Olà, Marco!" called Ubaldo, solidifying out of the fog and coming up to us, panting from his run.

"What did you find out?"

"Let me tell you one thing, zenso. Be glad you are *not* the bravo who did that."

"Who did what, exactly?" I asked apprehensively.

"Killed the man. The man you spoke of. Yes, he is dead. They have the sword that did it."

"They do not!" I protested. "The sword they have must be mine, and there is no blood on it."

Ubaldo shrugged. "They found a weapon. They will assuredly find a sassìn. They will have to find somebody to blame, because of who it was he assassinated."

"Only Ilaria's husband—"

"The next Doge."

"*What?*"

"The same man. But for this, the banditori would have been proclaiming him Doge of Venice tomorrow. Sacro! That is what I overheard, and I heard it several times repeated. The Council had elected him to succeed the Serenità Zeno, and were only waiting until after the pompe funebri to make the announcement."

"Oh, Dio mio!" I would have said, but Doris said it for me.

"Now they must start the voting all over again. But not before they find the bravo who is guilty. This is not just another back-alley knifing. From the way they were talking, this is something that has never before occurred in the history of the Republic."

"Dio mio," Doris breathed again, then asked me, "What will you do now?"

After some thought, if my mind's perturbation could be called thinking, I said, "Perhaps I ought not go to my house. Can I sleep in a corner of your barge?"

· 9 ·

S o that is where I passed the night, on a pallet of smelly rags—but not in sleep; in staring, glaring wakefulness. When, at some small hour, Doris heard my restless tossing and came creeping to ask if I would like to be held and soothed, I simply snarled, and she crept away again. She and Ubaldo and all the other boat children were asleep when the dawn began to poke its fingers through the many cracks in the old barge hull, and I got up, leaving my blood-stained cloak, and slipped out into the morning.

The city was all fresh pink and amber in color, and every stone sparkled with dew left by the caligo. By contrast, I felt anything but sparkly, and an over-all drab brown in color, even to the inside of my mouth. I wandered aimlessly through the awakening streets, the turnings of my path determined by my veering away from every other person out walking that early. But gradually the streets began to fill with people, too many for me to avoid them all, and I heard the bells ringing the terza, the start of the working day. So I let myself drift lagoonward, to the Riva Ca' de Dio and into the warehouse of the Compagnia Polo. I think I had some dim notion of asking the clerk Isidoro Priuli if he could quickly and quietly arrange for me the berth of cabin boy on some outbound vessel.

I trudged into his little counting room, so sunk in my morosity that it took me a moment to notice that the room was more than usually cramped and that Maistro Doro was saying to a crowd of visitors, "I can only tell you that he has not set foot in Venice in more than twenty years. I repeat, the Messer Marco Polo has long lived in Constantinople and still lives there. If you refuse to believe me, here is his nephew of the same name, who can vouch—"

I spun on my heel to go out again, having recognized the crowd in the room as no more than two, but extremely burly, uniformed gastaldi of the Quarantia. Before I could escape, one of them growled, "Same name, eh? And look at the guilty face on him!" and the other reached out to clamp a massive hand around my upper arm.

Well, I was marched away, while the clerk and the warehouse men goggled. We had no great distance to go, but it seemed the longest of all the journeys I have ever made. I struggled feebly in the iron grip of the gastaldi and, more like a bimbo than a bravo, pleaded tearfully to know of what I was accused, but the stolid bailiffs never replied. As we tramped along the Riva, through crowds of passersby also goggling, my mind was a tumult of questions: Was there a reward? Who turned me in? Did Doris or Ubaldo somehow send word? We crossed over the Bridge of the Straw, but did not continue as far as the piazzetta entrance to the Doge's Palace. At the Gate of the Wheat, we turned in to the Torresella, which stands adjacent to the palace and is the last remainder of what was in ancient times a fortified castle. It is now officially the State Prison of Venice, but its inmates have another name for it. The prison is called by the name our ancestors called the fiery pit before Christianity taught them to call it Hell. The prison is called Vulcano.

From the bright pink and amber morning outside, I found myself suddenly thrust into an orbà, which might not sound like much unless you know that it means "blinded." An orbà is a cell just big enough to contain one man. It is a stone box, totally unfurnished and absolutely without any opening for light or air. I stood in a darkness unrelieved, suffocatingly close, foul with stench. The floor was thick with some gluey mess that sucked at my feet when I moved them, so I did not even try to sit down, and the walls were spongy with some slime that seemed to crawl when I touched it, so I did not even lean; when I tired of standing, I squatted. And I shook with an ague as I slowly comprehended the full horror of where I was and what had become of me. I, Marco Polo, son of the Ene Aca house of Polo, bearer of a name inscribed in the Libro d'Oro—so recently a free man, a carefree youth, free to wander where I would in the whole wide world—I was in *prison*, disgraced, despised, shut up in a box that no rat would willingly inhabit. Oh, how I wept!

I do not know how long I stayed in that blind cell. It was at least the remainder of that day, and it may have been two or three days, for, although I tried hard to control my fright-churned bowels, I several times contributed to the mess on the floor. When finally a guard came to let me out, I assumed I had been freed as innocent, and I exulted. Even had I been guilty of killing the Doge-elect, I was sure I had suffered punishment enough for it, and had felt enough remorse and sworn enough repentance. But of course my exultation was dashed when the guard told me that I had endured only the first and probably least of my punishments—that the orbà is only the temporary cell where a prisoner is held until time for his preliminary examination.

So I was brought before the tribunal called the Gentlemen of the Night. In an upstairs room of the Vulcano, I was stood in front of a long table behind which sat eight grave and elderly men in black gowns. I was not positioned too close to their table, and the guard on either side of me did not stand too close to me, for I must have smelled as terrible as I felt. If I also looked as terrible, I must have appeared the very portrait of a low and brutish criminal.

The Signori della Notte began by taking turns at asking me some innocuous questions: my name, my age, my residence, particulars of my family history and the like. Then one of them, referring to a paper before him, told me, "Many other questions must be asked before we can determine on a bill of indictment. But that interrogation will be postponed until you have been assigned a Brother of Justice to act as your advocate, for you have been denounced as the perpetrator of a crime which is capitally punishable. . . ."

Denounced! I was so stunned that I missed most of the man's subsequent words. The denouncer had to be either Doris or Ubaldo, for only they knew that I had even been near the murdered man. But how could either of them have done it so quickly? And who did they get to write for them the denunciation to be slid into one of the snouts?

The gentleman concluded his speech by asking, "Have you any comment to make on these most serious charges?"

I cleared my throat and said hesitantly, "Who—who denounced me, Messere?" It was an inane thing to ask, since I could not reasonably expect an answer, but it was the question uppermost in my mind. And much to my surprise, the examiner did answer:

"You denounced yourself, young Messere." I must have blinked at him stupidly, for he added, "Did you not write this?" and read from a piece of paper: "Will *he* be at both the Funeral and the Installation?" I am sure I blinked at him stupidly, for he added, "It is signed Marco Polo."

Walking like a sleepwalker, I was taken by my guards down the stairs again, and then down another flight of stairs into what they called the wells, the deepest part of the Vulcano. Even that, they told me, was not the real dungeon of the prison; I could look forward, when I had been properly convicted, to being shifted into the Dark Gardens reserved for the keeping of condemned men until their execution. Laughing coarsely, they opened a thick but only knee-high wooden door in the stone wall, pushed me down and shoved me through it, and gave the door a slam like the knell of Doomsday.

This cell was at least considerably larger than the orbà and had at least a hole in the low door. The hole was too small to permit me to shake a fist through it at the departing jailers, but it did admit a trace of air and enough light to keep the cell from being utterly dark. When my eyes had adjusted to the murk, I could see that the cell was furnished with a lidded pail for a pissòta and two bare plank shelves for beds. I could see nothing else except what looked like a tumbled heap of bedclothes in one corner. However, when I approached it, the heap heaved and stood up and was a man.

"Salamelèch," he said hoarsely. The greeting sounded foreign. I squinted at him and recognized the red-gray, fungoid hair and beard. It was the zudìo whose public scourging I had witnessed on a day memorable for much else.

. 10 .

"MORDECAI," he introduced himself. "Mordecai Cartafilo." And he asked the question that all prisoners ask each other at first meeting: "What are you in for?"

"Murder," I said with a sniffle. "And I think treason and lesa-maestà and a few other things."

"Murder will suffice," he said drily. "Not to worry, lad. They will overlook those trifling other items. You cannot be punished for them once you have been punished for murder. That would be what is called double jeopardy, and that is forbidden by the law of the land."

I gave him a sour look. "You are jesting, old man."

He shrugged. "One lightens the dark as best one can."

We sat gloomy in the gloom for a while. Then I said, "You are in here for usury, are you not?"

"I am not. I am in here because a certain lady *accused* me of usury."

"That is a coincidence. I am also in here—at least indirectly—because of a lady."

"Well, I only said lady to indicate the gender. She is really"—he spat on the floor—"a shèquesa kàrove."

"I do not understand your foreign words."

"A gentile putana cagna," he said, as if still spitting. "She begged a loan from me and pledged some love letters as security. When she could not pay, and I would not return the letters, she made sure I would not deliver them to anyone else."

I shook my head sympathetically. "Yours is a sad case, but mine is more ironic. My lady begged a service from me and pledged herself as reward. The deed was done, but not by me. Nevertheless, here I am, rather differently rewarded, but my lady probably does not even know of it yet. Is that not ironic?"

"Hilarious."

"Yes, Ilaria! Do you know the lady?"

"What?" He glared at me. "Your kàrove is named Ilaria, too?"

I glared at him. "How dare you call my lady a putana cagna?"

Then we ceased glaring at each other, and we sat down on the bed shelves and began comparing experiences, and alas, it became evident that we had both known the same Dona Ilaria. I told old Cartafilo my whole adventure, concluding:

"But you mentioned love letters. I never sent her any."

He said, "I am sorry to be the one to tell you. They were not signed with your name."

"Then she was in love with someone else all the time?"

"So it would seem."

I muttered, "She seduced me only so I would play the bravo for her. I have been nothing but a dupe. I have been exceptionally stupid."

"So it would seem."

"And the one message that I did sign—the one the Signori now have—*she* must have slipped it into the snout. But why should she do that to me?"

"She has no further use for her bravo. Her husband is dead, her lover is available, you are but an encumbrance to be shed."

"But I did not kill her husband!"

"So who did? Probably the lover. Do you expect her to denounce him, when she can offer you up instead and thereby keep him safe?" I had no answer to that. After a moment he asked, "Did you ever hear of the lamia?"

"Lamia? It means a witch."

"Not exactly. The lamia can take the form of a very *young* witch, and very beautiful. She does that to entice young men to fall in love with her. When she has snared one, she makes love to him so voluptuously and industriously that he gets quite exhausted. And when he is limp and helpless, she eats him alive. It is only a myth, of course, but a curiously pervasive and persistent myth. I have encountered it in every country I have visited around the Mediterranean Sea. And I have traveled much. It is strange, how so many different peoples believe in the bloodthirstiness of beauty."

I considered that, and said, "She did smile while she watched you flogged, old man."

"I am not surprised. She will probably reach the very height of venereal excitement when she watches you go to the Meatmaker."

"To the what?"

"That is what we old prison veterans call the executioner—the Meatmaker."

I cried, distraught, "But I cannot be executed! I am innocent! I am of the Ene Aca! I should not even be shut up with a Jew!"

"Oh, excuse me, your lordship. It is that the bad light in here has dimmed my eyesight. I took you for a common prisoner in the pozzi of the Vulcano."

"I am not *common!*"

"Excuse me again," he said, and reached a hand across the space between our bed shelves. He plucked something off my tunic and regarded it closely. "Only a flea. A common flea." He popped it between his fingernails. "It appeared as common as my own."

I grumbled, "There is nothing wrong with your eyesight."

"If you really are a noble, young Marco, you must do what all the noble prisoners do. Agitate for a better cell, a private one, with a window over the street or the water. Then you can let down a string, and send messages, or haul up delicacies of food. That is not supposed to be allowed, but in the case of nobility the rules are winked at."

"You make it sound as if I will be here a long time."

"No." He sighed. "Probably not long."

The import of that remark made my hair prickle. "I keep telling you, old fool. *I am innocent!*"

And that made him reply, just as loudly and indignantly, "Why tell me, unhappy mamzar? Tell it to the Signori della Notte! I am innocent, too, but here I sit and here I will rot!"

"Wait! I have an idea," I said. "We are both here because of the Lady Ilaria's wiles and lies. If together we tell that to the Signori, they ought to wonder about her veracity."

Mordecai shook his head doubtfully. "Whom would they believe? She is the widow of an almost Doge. You are an accused murderer and I am a convicted usurer."

"You may be right," I said, dispirited. "It is unfortunate that you are a Jew."

He fixed me with a not at all dim eye and said, "People are forever telling me that. Why do you?"

"Oh . . . only that the testimony of a Jew is naturally suspect."

"So I have frequently noticed. I wonder why."

"Well . . . you did kill our Lord Jesus. . . ."

He snorted and said, "I, indeed!" As if disgusted with me, he turned his back and stretched out on his shelf and drew his voluminous robe about him. He muttered to the wall, "I only spoke to the man . . . only two words . . ." and then apparently went to sleep.

When a long and dismal time had passed, and the door hole had darkened, the door was noisily unlocked and two guards crawled in dragging a large vat. Old Cartafilo stopped snoring and sat up eagerly. The guards gave him and me each a wooden shingle, onto which they spooned from the vat a lukewarm, glutinous glob. Then they left for us a feeble lamp, a bowl of fish oil in which a scrap of rag burned with much smoke and little light, and they went away and slammed the door. I looked dubiously at the food.

"Polenta gruel," Mordecai told me, avidly scooping his up with two fingers. "A holòsh, but you had better eat it. Only meal of the day. You will get nothing else."

"I am not hungry," I said. "You may have mine."

He almost snatched it, and ate both portions with much lip smacking. When he had done, he sat and sucked his teeth as if unwilling to miss a particle, and peered at me from under his fungus eyebrows, and finally said:

"What would you ordinarily be eating for supper?"

"Oh . . . perhaps a platter of tagiadèle with persuto . . . and a zabagiòn to drink . . ."

"Bongusto," he said sardonically. "I cannot pretend to tempt such a refined taste, but perhaps you would like some of these." He rummaged inside his robe. "The tolerant Venetian laws allow me some religious observance, even in prison." I could not see how that accounted for the square white crackers he brought out and handed to me. But I ate them gratefully, though they were almost tasteless, and I thanked him.

By the next day's suppertime, I was hungry enough not to be fastidious. I would probably have eaten the prison gruel just because it meant a break in the monotony of doing nothing but sitting, and sleeping on the coverless hard bench, and walking the two or three steps the cell permitted, and occasionally making conversation with Cartafilo. But that is how the days went on, each of them marked off only by the lightening and darkening of the door hole, and the old zudìo's praying three times a day, and the evening arrival of the horrid food.

Perhaps it was not such a dreadful experience for Mordecai, since, to the best of my knowledge, he had spent all of his prior days huddled in his cell-like money shop on the Mercerìa, and this could not be a much different confinement. But I had been free and untrammeled and convivial; being immured in the Vulcano was like being buried alive. I realized that I ought to be grateful for having some company in my untimely grave, even if it was only a Jew, and even if his conversation was not always buoyant. One day I mentioned to him that I had seen several sorts of punishment administered at the pillars of Marco and Todaro, but never an execution.

He said, "That is because most of them are done here inside the walls, so that not even the other prisoners are aware of them until they are over. The condemned man is put into one of the cells of the Giardini Foschi, so called, and those cells have barred windows. The Meatmaker waits outside the cell, and waits patiently, until the man inside, moving about, moves before that window and with his back to it. Then the Meatmaker whips a garrotta through the bars and around the man's throat, so that either his neck snaps or he strangles to death. The Dark Gardens are on the canal side of this building, and there is a removable stone slab in the corridor there. In the night, the victim's body is slid through that secret hole and into a waiting boat, and it is conveyed to the Sepoltùra Pùblica. Not until it is all finished is the execution announced. Far less fuss that way. Venice does not care to have it widely known that the old Roman lege de tagiòn is still so often exercised here. So the *public* executions are few. They are inflicted only on those convicted of really heinous crimes."

"Crimes like what?" I asked.

"In my time, one man has died so for having raped a nun, and another for having told a foreigner some of the secrets of the Murano art of glassworking. I daresay the murder of a Doge-elect will rank with those, if that is what you are wondering."

I swallowed. "What is—how is it done—in public?"

"The culprit kneels between the pillars and is beheaded by the Meatmaker. But before that, the Meatmaker has cut off whatever part of him was guilty of the crime. The nun raper, of course, had his gid amputated. The glassworker had his tongue cut out. And the condemned man marches to the pillars with the guilty piece of him suspended from a string around his neck. In your case, I suppose it will be only your hand."

"And only my head," I said thickly.

"Try not to laugh," said Mordecai.

"Laugh?!" I cried in anguish—and then I did laugh, his words were so preposterous. "You are jesting again, old man."

He shrugged. "One does what one can."

One day, the monotony of my confinement was interrupted. The door was unlocked to let a stranger come stooping in. He was a fairly young man who wore not a uniform but the gown of the Brotherhood of Justice, and he introduced himself to me as Fratello Ugo.

"Already," he said briskly, "you owe a considerable casermagio of room and board in this State Prison. If you are poor, you are entitled to the assistance of the Brotherhood. It will pay your casermagio for as long as you are incarcerated. I am a licensed advocate, and I will represent you to the best of my ability. I will also carry messages to and from the outside, and procure some few small comforts—salt for your meals, oil for your lamp, things like that. I can also arrange for you"—he glanced over at old Cartafilo and sniffed slightly—"a private cell."

I said, "I doubt that I would be any less unhappy elsewhere, Fra Ugo. I will stay in this one."

"As you wish," he said. "Now, I have been in communication with the house of Polo, of which it seems you are the titular head, albeit still a minor. If you prefer, you can well afford to pay the prison casermagio, and also to hire an advocate of your own choice. You have only to write out the necessary pagherì and authorize the company to pay them."

I said uncertainly, "That would be a public humiliation to the company. And I do not know if I have any right to squander the company's funds. . . ."

"On a lost cause," he finished for me, nodding in agreement. "I quite understand."

Alarmed, I started to remonstrate, "I did not mean—that is, I would hope. . . ."

"The alternative is to accept the help of the Brotherhood of Justice. For its reimbursement, the Brotherhood is then allowed to send upon the streets two beggars, asking alms of the citizens for pity of the wretched Marco P—"

"Amoredèi!" I exclaimed. "That would be infinitely more humiliating!"

"You do not have to decide your choice this instant. Let us discuss your case instead. How do you intend to plead?"

"Plead?" I said, indignant. "I shall not plead, I shall protest! I am innocent!"

Brother Ugo looked over at the Jew again, and distastefully, as if he suspected that I had already been receiving counsel. Mordecai only pulled a face of skeptical amusement.

I went on, "For my first witness I shall call the Dona Ilaria. When she is compelled to tell of our—"

"She will not be called," the Brother interrupted. "The Signori della Notte would not allow it. That lady has been recently bereaved and is still prostrate with grief."

I scoffed, "Are you trying to tell me that she grieves for her husband?"

"Well . . .," he said, with deliberation. "If not that, you can be sure that she exhibits some extreme emotion because she is not now the Dogaressa of Venice."

Old Cartafilo made a noise like a smothered snicker. Maybe I made a noise, too—of dismay—for that aspect of the situation had not before occurred to me. Ilaria must be seething with disappointment and frustration and anger. When she sought her husband's removal, she had not dreamed of the honor he was about to be accorded, and she with him. So now she would be inclined to forget her own involvement; she would be consumed with a desire to exact revenge for her forfeited title. It would not matter on *whom* she vented her rage, and who was an easier target than myself?

"If you are innocent, young Messer Marco," said Ugo, "who did murder the man?"

I said, "I think it was a priest."

Brother Ugo gave me a long look, then rapped on the cell door for a guard to let him out. As the door creaked open at his knee level, he said to me, "I suggest that you do choose to hire some other advocate. If you intend to accuse a reverend father, and your prime witness is a woman bent on vendèta, you will need the best legal talent there is in the Republic. Ciao."

When he had gone, I said to Mordecai, "Everyone takes it for granted that I am doomed, whether I am guilty *or not*. Surely there must be some law to safeguard the innocent against unjust conviction."

"Oh, almost surely. But there is an old saying: the laws of Venice are supremely fair and they are sedulously obeyed . . . for a week. Do not let your hopes get too high."

"I would have more hope if I had more help," I said. "And you could help us both. Let the Brother Ugo have those letters you hold, and let him show them in evidence. They would at least cast a shadow of suspicion on the lady and her lover."

He gazed at me with his blackberry eyes and scratched reflectively in his fungus beard, and said, "You think that would be the Christian thing to do?"

"Why . . . yes. To save my life, to set you free. I see nothing *un*-Christian about it."

"Then I am sorry that I adhere to a different morality, for I cannot do it. I did not do that to save myself from the frusta, and I will not do it for both of us."

I stared, unbelieving. "Why in the world not?"

"My trade is founded on trust. I am the only moneylender who takes such documents in pawn. I can do that only if I trust my clients to repay their loans and the accrued interest. The clients pledge such papers only because they can trust me to keep their contents inviolable. Do you think women would otherwise hand over *love letters*?"

"But I told you, old man, no human being trusts a Jew. Look how the Lady Ilaria repaid you with treachery. Is that not proof enough that she thought you untrustworthy?"

"It is proof of something, yes," he said wryly. "But if even once I should fail my trust, even on the most dire provocation, I must abandon my chosen trade. Not because others would think me contemptible, but because *I* would."

"What trade, you old fool? You may be in here the rest of your life! You said so yourself. You cannot conduct any—"

"I can conduct myself according to my conscience. It may be small comfort, but it is my only comfort. To sit here and scratch my flea and bedbug bites, and see my once prosperously fat flesh shrinking gaunt, and feel myself superior to the Christian morality that put me here."

I snarled, "You could preen yourself just as well *outside*—"

"Zito! Enough! The instruction of fools is folly. We will not speak of it further. Look here on the floor, my boy, here are two large spiders. Let us race them against each other and wager incalculable fortunes on the outcome. You may choose which spider will be yours. . . ."

. 11 .

M O R E time passed, in dismalness, and then Brother Ugo came again, stooping in through the low door. I waited glumly for him to say something as disheartening as he had the other time, but what he said was astounding:

"Your father and his brother have returned to Venice!"

"What?" I gasped, unable to comprehend. "You mean their bodies have been returned? For burial in their native land?"

"I mean they are here! Alive and well!"

"Alive? After almost ten years of silence?"

"Yes! All their acquaintances are as amazed as you are. The entire community of merchants is talking of nothing else. It is said that they bear an embassy from Far Tartary to the Pope at Rome. But by good fortune—*your* good fortune, young Messer Marco—they came home to Venice before going to Rome."

"Why my good fortune?" I said shakily.

"Could they have come at a more opportune time? They are even now petitioning the Quarantia for permission to visit you, which is not normally allowed to anyone but a prisoner's advocate. It may just be that your father and uncle can influence some lenity in your case. If nothing else, their presence at your trial ought to give you some moral support. And some stiffness to your spine when you walk to the pillars."

On that equivocal note, he departed again. Mordecai and I sat talking with animated speculation far into the night, even after the copri-fuoco had rung and a guard growled through the door hole for us to extinguish the dim light of our rag lamp.

Another four or five days had to pass, fretful ones for me, but then the door creaked open and a man came in, a man so burly he had to struggle through it. Inside the cell he stood up, and he seemed to keep *on* standing up, so tall was he. I had no least recollection of being related to a man so immense. He was as hairy as he was big, with tousled black locks and a bristling blue-black beard. He looked down at me from his intimidating great height, and his voice was disdainful when he boomed loudly:

"Well! If this is not pure merda with a piecrust on it!"

I said meekly, "Benvegnùo, caro pare."

"I am not your dear father, young toad! I am your uncle Mafìo."

"Benvegnùo, caro zio. Is not my father coming?"

"No. We could get permission for only one visitor. And he should rightly be secluded in mourning for your mother."

"Oh. Yes."

"In truth, however, he is busy courting his next wife."

That rocked me on my heels. "What? How could he do such a thing?"

"Who are you to sound disapproving, you disreputable scagaròn? The poor man comes back from abroad to find his wife long buried, her maid-servant disappeared, a valuable slave lost, his friend the Doge dead—and his son, the hope of the family, in prison charged with the foulest murder in Venetian history!" So loudly that everybody in the Vulcano must have heard, he bellowed, "Tell me the truth! Did you do the deed?"

"No, my lord uncle," I said, quailing. "But what has all that to do with a new wife?"

My uncle said more quietly, with a snort of deprecation, "Your father is an uxorious man. For some reason, he likes being married."

"He chose an odd way to demonstrate it to my mother," I said. "Going away and staying as he did."

"And he will be going away again," said Uncle Mafio. "That is why he must have someone with good sense to leave in charge of the family interests. He has not time to wait for another son. Another wife will have to do."

"Why another anything?" I said hotly. "He *has* a son!"

My uncle did not reply to that with words. He merely looked me up and down, with scathing eyes, and then let his gaze roam around the constricted, dim, fetid cell.

Again abashed, I said, "I had hoped he could get me out of here."

"No, you must get yourself out," said my uncle, and my heart sank. But he continued to look about the room and said, as if thinking aloud, "Of all the kinds of disaster that can befall a city, Venice has always most feared the risk of a great fire. It would be especially fearsome if it threatened the Doge's Palace and the civic treasures contained in it, or the Basilica of San Marco and its even more irreplaceable treasures. Since that palace is next door to this prison on one side, and that church adjoining on the other side, the guards here in the Vulcano used to take particular precautions—I imagine they do still—that any smallest lamp flame in these cells is carefully monitored."

"Why, yes, they—"

"Shut up. They do that because if in the nighttime such a lamp were to set fire to, say, these wooden bed planks, there would be urgent outcry and much running about with pails of water. A prisoner would have to be let out of his burning cell so the fire could be extinguished. And then, if, in the smoke and turmoil, that prisoner could get as far as the corridor of the Giardini Foschi on the canal side of the prison, he might think to slide away the moveable stone panel in the wall there, which leads to the outside. And if he contrived to do that, say, tomorow night, he would probably find a batèlo idling about on the water immediately below."

Mafio finally brought his eyes around to me again. I was too busy contemplating the possibilities to say anything, but old Mordecai spoke up unbidden:

"That has been done before. And because of that, there is now a law that any prisoner attempting such an arson—no matter how trivial his original offense—will be himself condemned to burn. And from that sentence there is no appeal."

Uncle Mafìo said sardonically, "Thank you, Matùsalem." To me he said, "Well, you have just heard one more good reason to make not a try but a success of it." He kicked at the door to summon the guard. "Until tomorrow night, nephew."

I lay awake most of that night. It was not that the escape required much planning; I simply lay awake to enjoy the prospect of being free again. And old Cartafilo roused up suddenly out of an apparently sound sleep to say:

"I hope your family know what they are doing. Another law is that a prisoner's closest relation is responsible for his behavior. A father for a son—khas vesholem—a husband for a female prisoner, a master for a slave. If a prisoner does escape by arson, that one responsible for him will be burned instead."

"My uncle does not appear to be a man much concerned about laws," I said, rather proudly, "or even much afraid of burning. But Mordecai, I cannot do it without your participation. We must make the break together. What say you?"

He was silent for a while, then he mumbled, "I daresay burning is preferable to a slow death from the pettechie, the prison disease. And I long ago outlived every last one of my relations."

So the next night came, and when the coprifuoco tolled and the guards commanded us to put out our lamp, we only shaded its light with the pissòta pail. When the guards had gone on by, I spilled most of the fish oil from the lamp onto my bed planks. Mordecai contributed his outer robe—it was quite green with mold and mildew and would make the blaze smokier—and we bundled that under my bed and lighted it from the lamp's rag wick. In just moments the cell was clouded black and the wood had begun to flicker with flames. Mordecai and I fanned our arms to help the smoke out through the door hole, and clamored loudly, "Fuoco! Al fuoco!" and heard running feet in the corridor.

Then, as my uncle had predicted, there was commotion and confusion, and Mordecai and I were ordered out of the cell so the men with water buckets could crawl in. Smoke billowed out with us, and the guards shoved us out of their way. There was quite a number of them in the passage, but they paid us little heed. So, aided by the concealing smoke and darkness, we sneaked farther down the corridor and around a bend in it. "Now this way!" said Mordecai, and he set off at a speed remarkable for a man of his age. He had been in the prison long enough to have learned its passages, and he led me this way and that, until we glimpsed light at the end of one long hall. He stopped there at a corner, peered around it and waved me on. We turned into a shorter corridor furnished with two or three wall lamps, but otherwise empty.

Mordecai knelt, motioned for me to help, and I saw that one large square stone in the bottom of the wall had iron grips bolted to it. Mordecai seized one, I the other, and we heaved and the stone came away, revealing itself to be shallower than the others around it. Wonderfully fresh air, damp and smelling of salt, swept in through the opening. I stood up straight to take a gratefully deep inhalation, and in the next instant I was knocked down. A guard had sprung from somewhere and was shouting for help.

There was a moment of even more confusion than before. The guard threw himself upon me and we thrashed about on the stone floor, while Mordecai crouched by the hole and regarded us with open mouth and wide eyes. I found myself briefly on top of the guard, and took advantage of it. I knelt so that he had my full weight on his chest and my knees pinned his arms to the floor. I clamped both hands over his loudly flapping mouth, turned to Mordecai and gasped, "I cannot hold—for long."

"Here, lad," he said. "Let me do that."

"No. One can escape. You go." I heard more running feet somewhere in the corridors. "Hurry!"

Mordecai stuck his feet out through the hole, then turned to ask, "Why me?"

Between grapplings and thrashings, I got out a few last words in spurts, "You gave—my choice—of spiders. Get out!"

Mordecai gave me a wondering look, and he said slowly, "The reward of a mitzva is another mitzva," and he slid out through the opening and vanished. I heard a distant splash out there beyond the dark hole, and then I was overwhelmed.

I was roughly manhandled along the passages and literally thrown into a new cell. I mean another very ancient cell, of course, but a different one. It had only a bed shelf for furniture, and no door hole and not so much as a candle stub for light. I sat there in the darkness, my bruises aching, and reviewed my situation. In attempting the escape, I had forfeited all hope of ever proving my innocence of the earlier charge. In failing to escape, I had doomed myself to burn. I had just one reason to be thankful: I now had a private cell. I had no cellmate to watch me weep.

Since the guards, for a considerable while thereafter, spitefully refrained from feeding me even the awful prison gruel, and the darkness and monotony were unrelieved, I have no idea how long I was alone in the cell before a visitor was admitted. It was the Brother of Justice again.

I said, "I assume that my uncle's permission to visit has been revoked."

"I doubt that he would willingly come," said Brother Ugo. "I understand he became quite irate and profane when he saw that the nephew he hauled from the water had turned into an elderly Jew."

"And, since there is no further need for your advocacy," I said resignedly, "I assume you have come only in the guise of prisoner's comforter."

"At any rate, I bring news you should find comforting. The Council this morning elected a new Doge."

"Ah, yes. They were postponing the election until they had the sassìn of Doge Zeno. And they have me. Why should you think I find that comforting?"

"Perhaps you forget that your father and uncle are members of that Council. And since their miraculous return from their long absence, they are quite the most popular members of the community of merchants. Therefore, in the election, they could exert noticeable influence on the votes of all the merchant nobles. A man named Lorenzo Tiepolo was eager to become Doge, and in return for the merchants' bloc of votes, he was prepared to make certain commitments to your father and uncle."

"Such as what?" I asked, not daring to hope.

"It is traditional that a new Doge, on his accession, proclaims some amnesties. The Serenità Tiepolo is going to forgive your felonious commission of arson, which permitted the escape of one Mordecai Cartafilo from this prison."

"So I do not burn as an arsonist," I said. "I merely lose my hand and my head as a murderer."

"No, you do not. You are right that the sassìn has been captured, but you are wrong about its being you. Another man has confessed to the sassinàda."

Fortunately the cell was small or I should have fallen down. But I only reeled and slumped against the wall.

The Brother went on, at an infuriatingly slow pace. "I told you I brought news of comfort. You have more advocates than you know, and they have all been busy in your behalf. That zudìo you freed, he did not just keep on running, or take ship to some distant land. He did not even hide in the warrens of the Jews' burghèto. Instead, he went to visit a priest—not a rabìno, a real Christian priest—one of the under-priests of the San Marco Basilica itself."

I said, "I tried to tell you about that priest."

"Well, it seems the priest had been the Lady Ilaria's secret lover, but she turned bitter toward him when she so nearly became our Dogaressa and then did not. When she put away the priest from her affections, he became remorseful of having done such a vile deed as murder, and to no profitable end. Of course, he might still have kept silent, and kept the matter between himself and God. But then Mordecai Cartafilo called on him. It seems the Jew spoke of some papers he holds in pawn. He did not even show them, he had only to mention them, and that was enough to turn the priest's secret remorse into open repentance. He went to his superiors and made full confession, waiving the privilege of the confessional. So he is now under house arrest in his canònica chambers. The Dona Ilaria is also confined to her house, as an accomplice in the crime."

"What happens next?"

"All must await the new Doge's taking office. Lorenzo Tiepolo will not wish the very start of his Dogato made notorious, for this case now involves rather more prominent persons than just a boy playing bravo. The lady widow of the murdered Doge-elect, a priest of San Marco . . . well, the Doge Tiepolo will do everything possible to minify the scandal. He will probably allow the priest to be tried in camera by an ecclesiastical court, instead of the Quarantia. My guess is that the priest will be exiled to some remote parish in the Vèneto mainland. And the Doge will probably command the Lady Ilaria to take the veil in some remote nunnery. There is precedent for such procedure. A hundred or so years ago, in France, there was a similar situation involving a priest and a lady."

"And what happens to me?"

"As soon as the Doge dons the white scufieta, he proclaims his amnesties, and yours will be among them. You will be pardoned of the arson, and you have already been acquitted of the sassinàda. You will be released from prison."

"Free!" I breathed.

"Well, perhaps a trifle more free than you might wish."

"What?"

"I said the Doge will arrange that this whole sordid affair be soon forgotten. If he simply turned you loose in Venice, you would be an ever present reminder of it. Your amnesty is conditional upon your banishment. You are outcast. You are to leave Venice forever."

During the subsequent days that I remained in the cell, I reflected on all that had come to pass. It was hurtful to think of leaving Venice, la serenisima, la clarisima. But that was better than dying in the piazzetta or staying in the Vulcano, which provided neither serenity nor brightness. I could even feel sorry for the priest who had struck the bravo's blow in my stead. As a young curate in the Basilica, he had doubtless looked forward to high advancement in the Church, which he could never hope for in backwoods exile. And Ilaria would endure an even more pitiable exile, her beauty and talents to be forever useless to her now. But maybe not; she had managed to lavish them rather prodigally when she was a married woman; she might also manage to enjoy them as a bride of Christ. She would at least have ample opportunity to sing the hymn of the nuns, as she had called it. All in all, compared to our victim's irrevocable fate, we three had got off lightly.

I was released from the prison even less ceremoniously than I had been bundled into it. The guards unlocked my cell door, led me along the corridors and down stairs and through other doors, unlocking the final one to let me out into the courtyard. There I had only to walk through the Gate of the Wheat onto the sunlit lagoonside Riva, and I was as free as the countless wheeling sea gulls. It was a good feeling, but I would have felt even better if I had been able to clean myself and don fresh raiment before emerging. I had been unwashed and clad in the same clothes all this time, and I stank of fish oil, smoke and pissòta effluvium. My garments were torn, from my struggle on the night of the aborted escape, and what was left of them was dirty and rumpled. Also, in those days I was just sprouting my first down of beard; it may not have been very visible, but it added to my feeling of scruffiness. I could have wished for better circumstances in which to meet my father for the first time in my memory. He and my uncle Mafìo were waiting on the Riva, both dressed in the elegant robes they had probably worn, as members of the Council, at the new Doge's accession.

"Behold your son!" bellowed my uncle. "Your arcistupendonazzìsimo son! Behold the namesake of our brother and our patron saint! Is this not a wretched and puny meschìn, to have caused so much ado?"

"Father?" I said timorously to the other man.

"My boy?" he said, almost as hesitantly, but opening his arms.

I had expected someone even more overwhelming than my uncle, since my father was the elder of the two. But he was actually pale alongside his brother; not nearly so big and burly, and much softer of voice. Like my uncle, he wore a journeyer's beard, but his was neatly trimmed. His beard and hair were not of a fearsome raven black, but a decorous mouse color, like my own hair.

"My son. My poor orphan boy," said my father. He embraced me, but quickly put me away at arm's length, and said worriedly, "Do you always smell like that?"

"No, Father. I have been locked up for—"

"You forget, Nico, that this is a bravo and a bonvivàn and a gambler between the pillars," boomed my uncle. "A champion of ill-married matrons, a lurker in the night, a wielder of the sword, a liberator of Jews!"

"Ah, well," said my father indulgently. "A chick must stretch his wings farther than the nest. Come, let us go home."

. 12 .

T H E house servants were all moving with more alacrity and more cheerful demeanor than they had shown since my mother died. They even seemed glad to see me home again. The maid hastened to heat water when I asked, and Maistro Attilio, at my polite request, lent me his razor. I bathed several times over, inexpertly scraped the fuzz off my face, dressed in clean tunic and hose, and joined my father and uncle in the main room, where the tile stove was.

"Now," I said, "I want to hear about your travels. All about everywhere you have been."

"Dear God, not again," Uncle Mafìo groaned. "We have been let talk of nothing else."

"Time enough for that later, Marco," said my father. "All things in their time. Let us speak now of your own adventures."

"They are over now," I said hastily. "I would rather hear of new things."

But they would not relent. So I told them, fully and frankly, everything that had happened since my first glimpse of Ilaria in San Marco's— only omitting the amatory afternoon she and I had spent together. Thus I made it seem that mere mooncalf chivalry had impelled me to make my calamitous try at bravura.

When I was done, my father sighed. "Any woman could give pointers to the devil. Ah, well, you did what seemed best to you. And he who does all he can, does much. But the consequences have been tragic indeed. I had to agree to the Doge's stipulation that you leave Venice, my son. He could, however, have been much harder on you."

"I know," I said contritely. "Where shall I go, Father? Should I go seeking a Land of Cockaigne?"

"Mafìo and I have business in Rome. You will go with us."

"Do I spend the rest of my life in Rome, then? The sentence was banishment forever."

My uncle said what old Mordecai had said, "The laws of Venice are obeyed . . . for a week. A Doge's forever is a Doge's lifetime. When Tiepolo dies, his successor will hardly prevent your returning. Still, that could be a good while from now."

My father said, "Your uncle and I are bearing to Rome a letter from the Khakhan of Kithai—"

I had never heard either of those harsh-sounding words before, and I interrupted to say so.

"The Khan of All Khans of the Mongols," my father explained. "You may have heard him titled the Great Khan of what is here miscalled Cathay."

I stared at him. "You met the Mongols? And you survived?"

"Met and made friends among them. The most powerful friend possible—the Khan Kubilai, who rules the world's widest empire. He asked us to carry a request to Pope Clement. . . ."

He went on explaining, but I was not hearing. I was still staring at him in awe and admiration, and thinking—this was my father, whom I had believed long dead, and this very ordinary-looking man claimed to be a confidant of barbarian Khans and holy Popes!

He concluded, ". . . And then, if the Pope lends us the hundred priests requested by Kubilai, we will lead them east. We will go again to Kithai."

"When do we depart for Rome?" I asked.

My father said bashfully, "Well . . ."

"After your father marries your new mother," said my uncle. "And that must wait for the proclamation of the bandi."

"Oh, I think not, Mafìo," said my father. "Since Fiordelisa and I are hardly youngsters, both of us widowed, Pare Nunziata will probably dispense with all three cryings of the bandi."

"Who is Fiordelisa?" I asked. "And is this not rather abrupt, Father?"

"You know her," he said. "Fiordelisa Trevan, mistress of the house three doors down the canal."

"Yes. She is a nice woman. She was Mother's best friend among all our neighbors."

"If you are implying what I think you are, Marco, I remind you that your mother is in her grave, where there is no jealousy or envy or recrimination."

"Yes," I said. And I added impertinently, "But you are not wearing the luto vedovile."

"Your mother has been *eight years* in her grave. I should wear black now, and for another twelvemonth? I am not young enough to sequester myself in mourning for a year. Neither is the Dona Lisa any bambina."

"Have you proposed to her yet, Father?"

"Yes, and she has accepted. We go tomorrow for our pastoral interview with Pare Nunziata."

"Is she aware that you are going away immediately after you marry her?"

My uncle burst out, "What is this inquisition, you saputèlo?"

My father said patiently, "I am marrying her, Marco, *because* I am going away. Needs must when the devil drives. I came home expecting to find your mother still alive and still head of the house of Polo. She is not. And now—through your own fault—I cannot leave you entrusted with the business. Old Doro is a good man, and needs no one peering over his shoulder. Nevertheless, I prefer to have someone of the name of Polo standing as the figurehead of the company, if nothing more. Dona Fiordelisa will serve in that capacity, and willingly. Also, she has no children to compete for your inheritance, if that is what concerns you."

"It does not," I said. And again I spoke impertinently, "I am only concerned for the seeming disrespect to my own mother—and to the Dona Trevan as well—in your haste to marry solely for mercenary reasons. She must know that all Venice will be whispering and snickering."

My father said mildly, but with finality, "I am a merchant and she is the widow of a merchant and Venice is a merchant city, where all know that there is no better reason for doing *anything* than a mercenary reason. To a Venetian, money is the second blood, and you are a Venetian. Now, I have heard your objections, Marco, and I have dismissed them. I wish to hear no more. Remember, a closed mouth says nothing wrong."

So I kept my mouth closed and said nothing more on the subject, wrong or otherwise, and on the day my father married the Dona Lisa I stood in the confino church of San Felice with my uncle and all the free servants of both households and numerous neighbors and merchant nobles and their families, while the ancient Pare Nunziata tremblingly conducted the nuptial mass. But when the ceremony was over and the Pare pronounced them Messere e Madona and it was time for my father to lead his bride to her new dwelling, together with all the reception guests, I slipped away from the happy procession.

Although I was dressed in my best, I let my feet take me to the neighborhood of the boat people. I had only infrequently and briefly visited the children since my release from prison. Now that I was an ex-convict, the boys all seemed to regard me as a grown man, or maybe even a person of celebrity; anyway, there had come a sort of distance between us that had not existed before. However, on that day I found no one at the barge except Doris. She was kneeling on the planking inside its hull, wearing only a skimpy shift, and lifting wet wads of cloth from one pail to another.

"Boldo and the others begged a ride on a garbage scow going out to Torcello," she told me. "They will be gone all day, so I am taking the opportunity to wash everything not being worn by somebody."

"May I keep you company?" I asked. "And sleep here again in the barge tonight?"

"Your clothes will also need laundering, if you do," she said, eyeing them critically.

"I have had worse accommodations," I said. "And I own other clothes."

"What are you running away from this time, Marco?"

"This is my father's wedding day. He is bringing home a marègna for me, and I do not particularly want one. I have already had a real mother."

"I must have had one, too, but I would not mind having a marègna." She added, sighing like an exasperated grown woman, "Sometimes I feel I *am* one, to all this crowd of orphans."

"This Dona Fiordelisa is a nice enough woman," I said, sitting down with my back against the hull. "But I somehow do not wish to be under the same roof on my father's wedding night."

Doris looked at me with evident surmise, dropped what she was doing, and came to sit beside me.

"Very well," she whispered into my ear. "Stay here. And pretend that it is your own wedding night."

"Oh, Doris, are you starting that again?"

"I do not know why you should refuse. I am accustomed now to keeping myself clean, as you told me a lady ought to do. I keep myself clean all over. Look."

Before I could protest, she stripped off her one garment in one lithe movement. She was certainly clean, even to being totally hairless of body. The Lady Ilaria had not been quite so smooth and glossy all over. Of course, Doris was also lacking in feminine curves and rotundities. Her breasts were only just beginning to be distinct from her chest, and their nipples were only a faintly darker pink than her skin, and her flanks and buttocks were but lightly padded with womanly flesh.

"You are still a zuzzurullona," I said, trying to sound bored and uninterested. "You have a long way to go to become a woman."

That was true, but her very youth and smallness and immaturity had their own sort of appeal. Though all boys are lecherous, they usually lust for real women. Any girl of their own age, they tend to regard as only another playmate, a tomboy among the boys, a zuzzurullona. However, I was somewhat more advanced in that respect than most boys; I had already had the experience of a real woman. It had given me a taste for musical duets—and I had for some time been without that music— and here was a pretty novice pleading to be introduced to it.

"It would be dishonorable of me," I said, "even to pretend a wedding night." I was arguing with myself more than with her. "I have told you that I am going far away to Rome in a few days."

"So is your father. But it has not prevented his getting *really* married."

"True, and we quarreled about that. I did not think it right. But his new wife seems perfectly content."

"And so would I be. For now, let us pretend, Marco, and afterward I will wait, and you will come back. You said so—when there is another change of Doge."

"You look ridiculous, little Doris. Sitting here naked and talking of Doges and such." But she did not look ridiculous; she looked like one of the pert nymphs of old legend. I truly tried to argue. "Your brother always talks of what a good girl his sister—"

"Boldo will not be back until tonight, and he will know nothing of what happens between now and then."

"He would be furious," I went on, as if she had not interrupted. "We should have to fight again, the way we fought after he threw that fish so long ago."

Doris pouted. "You do not appreciate my generosity. It is a pleasure I offer you at the cost of pain to myself."

"Pain? How so?"

"The first time is always painful for a virgin. And unsatisfying. Every girl knows that. Every woman tells us so."

I said reflectively, "I do not know why it should be painful. Not if it is done the way my—" I decided it would be maladroit of me to mention my Lady Ilaria at this moment. "I mean, the way I have learned to do it."

"If that is true," said Doris, "you could earn the adoration of many virgins in your lifetime. Do show me this way you have learned."

"One begins by doing—certain preliminary things. Like this." I touched one of her diminutive nipples.

"The zizza? That only tickles."

"I believe the tickling changes to another sensation very soon."

Very soon she said, "Yes. You are right."

"The zizza likes it, too. See, it lifts to ask for more."

"Yes. Yes, it does." She slowly lay back, supine on the deck, and I followed her down.

I said, "A zizza likes even more to be kissed."

"Yes." Like a lazing cat, she stretched her whole little body, voluptuously.

"Then there is this," I said.

"That tickles, too."

"It also gets better than tickling."

"Yes. Truly it does. I feel . . ."

"Not pained, surely."

She shook her head, her eyes now closed.

"These things do not even require the presence of a man. It is called the hymn of the convent, because girls can do this for themselves." I was being scrupulously fair, giving her the opportunity to send me away.

But she said only, and breathlessly, "I had no idea . . . I do not even know what I *look* like down there."

"You could easily see your mona with a looking glass."

She said faintly, "I do not know anyone who owns a looking glass."

"Then look at—no, she is all hairy down there. Yours is still bare and visible and soft. And pretty. It looks like . . ." I reached for a poetic comparison. "You know that kind of pasta shaped like a folded little shell? The kind called ladylips?"

"You make it feel like lips being kissed," she said, as if talking in her sleep. Her eyes were closed again and her small body was moving in a slow squirm.

"Kissed, yes," I said.

From the slow squirm, her body seemed to clench briefly, then to relax, and she made a whimpering noise of delight. As I continued to play musically upon her, she made that slight convulsion again and again, each time lasting longer, as if she was learning through practice to prolong the enjoyment. Not ceasing my attentions to her, but using only my mouth, I had my hands free to strip off my own clothes. When I was naked against her, she appeared to enjoy her gentle spasms all the more, and her hands fluttered eagerly over my body. So I went on for quite a while, making the music of the convent, as Ilaria had taught me. When finally Doris was shiny with perspiration, I stopped and let her rest.

Her breathing slowed from its rapid pace, and she opened her eyes, looking dazed. Then she frowned, because she felt me hard against her, and she shamelessly moved a hand to take hold of me, and she said with surprise, "You did all that . . . or you made me do all that . . . and you never . . ."

"No, not yet."

"I did not know." She laughed in great good humor. "I could not have known. I was far away. In the clouds somewhere." Still holding me in one hand, she felt herself with the other. "All that . . . and I am still a virgin. It is miraculous. Do you suppose, Marco, that is how Our Blessed Virgin Lady—?"

"We are already sinning, Doris," I said quickly. "Let us not add blasphemy."

"No. Let us sin some more."

And we did, and I soon had Doris cooing and quivering again—in the clouds somewhere, as she had said—enjoying the hymn of the nuns. And finally I did what no nun can do, and that happened not roughly or forcibly, but easily and naturally. Doris, sleek with perspiration, moved without friction in my arms, and that part of her was even more moist. So she felt no violation, but only a more intense sensation among the many new ones she had been experiencing. She opened her eyes when that happened, and her eyes were brimming with pleasure, and the whimper she gave was merely in a different musical register from the previous ones.

It was a new sensation for me, too. Inside Doris, I was held as tightly as in a tender fist, far more tightly than I had been in either of the other two females with whom I had lain. Even in that moment of high excitement, I realized that I was disproving my onetime ignorant assertion that all women are alike in their private parts.

For the next while, both Doris and I made many different noises. And the final sound, when we stopped moving to rest, was her sigh of commingled wonder and satisfaction: "Oh, my!"

"I think it was not painful," I said, and smiled at her.

She shook her head vehemently, and returned the smile. "I have dreamt of it many times. But I never dreamed it would be so . . . And I never heard any woman recall her first time as so . . . Thank you, Marco."

"I thank you, Doris," I said politely. "And now that you know how—"

"Hush. I do not wish to do anything like that with anyone but you."

"I will soon be gone."

"I know. But I know you will be back. And I will not do that again until you come back from Rome."

However, I did not get to Rome. I have never been there yet. Doris and I went on disporting ourselves until nightfall, and we were dressed again and behaving most properly when Ubaldo and Daniele and Malgarita and the others returned from their day's excursion. When we retired into the barge to sleep, I slept alone, on the same pallet of rags I had used once before. And we were all awakened in the morning by the bawling of a banditore, making unusually early rounds because he had unusual news to cry. Pope Clement IV had died in Viterbo. The Doge of Venice was proclaiming a period of mourning and of prayer for the Holy Father's soul.

"Damnation!" bellowed my uncle, slapping the table and making the books on it jump. "Did we bring bad luck home with us, Nico?"

"First a Doge dies, and now the Pope," my father said sadly. "Ah, well, all psalms end in glory."

"And the word from Viterbo," said the clerk Isidoro, in whose counting room we were gathered, "is that there may be a long deadlock in the Conclave. It seems there are many feet twitching with eagerness to step into the Fisherman's shoes."

"We cannot wait for the election, soon or late," my uncle muttered, and he glowered at me. "We must get this galeotto out of Venice, or we may all go to prison."

"We need not wait," my father said, unperturbed. "Doro has most capably purchased and collected all the travel gear we will need. We only lack the hundred priests, and Kubilai will not care if they are not chosen by a Pope. Any high prelate can provide them."

"To what prelate do we apply?" demanded Mafìo. "If we asked the Patriarch of Venice, he would tell us—and with reason—that to lend us one hundred priests would empty every church in the city."

"And we would have to take them the extra distance," my father mused. "Better we seek them closer to our destination."

"Forgive my ignorance," said my new marègna, Fiordelisa. "But why on earth are you recruiting priests—and so many priests—for a savage Mongol warlord? Surely he cannot be a Christian."

My father said, "He is of no discernible religion, Lisa."

"I would have thought not."

"But he has that virtue peculiar to the ungodly: he is tolerant of what other people choose to believe. Indeed, he wishes his subjects to have an ample array of beliefs from which to choose. There are in his lands many preachers of many pagan religions, but of the Christian faith there are only the deluded and debased Nestorian priests. Kubilai desires that we provide adequate representation for the true Christian Church of Rome. Naturally, Mafìo and I are eager to comply—and not alone for the propagation of the Holy Faith. If we can accomplish this mission, we can ask the Khan's permission to engage in missions more profitable."

"Nico means to say," my uncle said, "that we hope to arrange to trade between Venice and the Eastern lands—to start again the flow of commerce along the Silk Road."

Lisa said wonderingly, "There is a road laid of silk?"

"Would that it were!" said my uncle, rolling his eyes. "It is more tortuous and terrible and punishing than any pathway to Heaven. Even to call it a road is an extravagance."

Isidoro begged leave to explain to the lady: "The route from the Levantine shores across the interior of Asia has been called the Silk Road since ancient times, because the silk of Cathay was the most costly merchandise carried along it. In those days, silk was worth its weight in gold. And perhaps the road itself, being so precious, was better maintained and easier to travel. But in more recent times it fell into disuse—partly because the secret of silkmaking was stolen from Cathay, and today silk is cultivated even in Sicily. But also those Eastern lands became impossible to traverse, what with the depredations of Huns, Tartars, Mongols, marauding back and forth across Asia. So our Western traders abandoned the overland route in favor of the sea routes known to the Arab seafarers."

"If you can get there by sea," Lisa said to my father, "why suffer all the rigors and dangers of going by land?"

He said, "Those sea routes are forbidden to our ships. The once pacific Arabs, long content to live meekly in the peace of their Prophet, rose up to become the warrior Saracens, who now seek to impose that religion of Islam on the entire world. And they are as jealous of their sea lanes as they are of their current possession of the Holy Land."

Mafìo said, "The Saracens are willing to trade with us Venetians, and with any other Christians from whom they can make a profit. But we would deprive them of that profit if we sent fleets of our own ships to trade in the East. So the Saracen corsairs are on constant patrol in the seas between, to make sure we do not."

Lisa looked primly shocked, and said, "They are our enemies, but we trade with them?"

Isidoro shrugged. "Business is business."

"Even the Popes," said Uncle Mafìo, "have never been unwilling to deal with the heathen, when it has been profitable. And a Pope or any other pragmatist ought to be eager to institute trade with the even farther East. There are fortunes to be made. We know; we have seen the richness of those lands. Our former journey was mere exploration, but this time we will take along something to trade. The Silk Road is awful, but it is not impossible. We have now traversed those lands twice, going and coming. We can do it again."

"Whoever is the new Pope," said my father, "he should give his blessing to this venture. Rome was much affrighted when it looked as if the Mongols would overrun Europe. But the several Mongol Khans seem to have extended their Khanates as far westward as they intend to encroach. That means the Saracens are the chief threat to Christianity. So Rome ought to welcome this chance for an alliance with the Mongols against Islam. Our mission on behalf of the Khan of All Khans could be of supreme importance—to the aims of Mother Church as well as the prosperity of Venice."

"And the house of Polo," said Fiordelisa, who was now of our house.

"That above all," said Mafìo. "So let us stop beating our beaks, Nico, and get on with it. Shall we go again by way of Constantinople and collect our priests there?"

My father thought it over and said, "No. The priests there are too comfortable—all gone soft as eunuchs. The gloved cat catches no mice. However, in the ranks of the Crusaders are many chaplain priests, and they will be hard men accustomed to hard living. Let us go to the Holy Land, to San Zuàne de Acre, where the Crusaders are presently encamped. Doro, is there a ship sailing eastward that can put us in Acre?"

The clerk turned to consult his registers, and I left the warehouse to go and tell Doris of my new destination and to say, to her and to Venice, goodbye.

It was to be a quarter of a century before I saw either of them again. Much would have changed and aged in that time, not least myself. But Venice would still be Venice, and—strangely—so would Doris somehow still be the Doris I had left. What she had said: that she would not love again until I came back—those words could have been a magic charm that preserved her unchanged by the years. For she would still, that long time later, be so young and so pretty and so vibrantly still Doris that I would recognize her on sight and fall instantly enamored of her. Or so it would seem to me.

But that story I will tell in its place.

THE LEVANT

.I.

At the hour of vespro on a day of blue and gold, we departed from the basin of Malamoco on the Lido, the only paying passengers in a great freight galeazza, the *Doge Anafesto*. She was carrying arms and supplies to the Crusaders; after unloading those things and us in Acre, she would go on to Alexandria for a cargo of grain to bring back to Venice. When the ship was outside the basin, on the open Adriatic, the rowers shipped their oars while the seamen stepped the two masts and unfurled their graceful lateen sails. The spreads of canvas fluttered and snapped and then bellied full in the afternoon breeze, as white and billowy as the clouds above.

"A sublime day!" I exclaimed. "A superb ship!"

My father, never inclined to rhapsodize, replied with one of his ever ready adages: "Praise not the day until night has brought its close; praise not the inn until the next day's awakening."

But even on the next day, and on succeeding days, he could not deny that the ship was as decent in its accommodations as any inn on the land. In earlier years, a vessel that touched at the Holy Land would have been crowded with Christian pilgrims from every country of Europe, sleeping in rows and layers on the deck and in the hold, like sardines in a butt. However, by that time of which I am telling, the port of San Zuàne de Acre was the last and only spot in the Holy Land not yet over-whelmed by the Saracens, so all Christians except Crusaders were staying at home.

We three Polos had a cabin all to ourselves, right under the captain's quarters in the sterncastle. The ship's galley was provided with a live-stock pen, so we and the seamen had meals of fresh meat and fowl, not salted. There was pasta of all varieties, and olive oil and onions, and good Corsican wine kept cool in the damp sand the ship carried for ballast at the bottom of the hold. All we missed was fresh-baked bread; in its place we were served hard agiàda biscuits, which cannot be bitten or chewed but have to be sucked, and that was the only fare of which we might have complained. There was a medegòto on board, to treat any ailments or injuries, and a chaplain, to hear confessions and hold masses. On the first Sunday, he preached on a text from Ecclesiasticus: "The wise man shall pass into strange countries, and good and evil shall he try in all things."

"Tell me, please, about the strange countries yonder," I said to my father after that mass, for he and I had really not had much time in Venice to talk just between ourselves. His reply told me more about him, however, than about any lands beyond the horizon.

"Ah, they brim with opportunities for an ambitious merchant!" he said exultantly, rubbing his hands. "Silks, jewels, spices—even the dullest tradesman dreams of those obvious things—but there are many more possibilities for a clever man. Yes, Marco. Even in coming with us only as far as the Levant, you can, if you keep your eyes open and your wits about you, perhaps begin the making of a fortune of your very own. Yes, indeed, all the lands yonder are lands of opportunity."

"I look forward to them," I said dutifully. "But I could learn of commerce without leaving Venice. I was thinking more of . . . well, adventure . . ."

"Adventure? Why, my boy, could there ever be any more satisfying adventure than the descrying of a commercial opportunity not yet glimpsed by others? And the seizing advantage of it? And the taking of a profit from it?"

"Of course, most satisfying, those things," I said, not to dampen his ebullience. "But what of excitement? Exotic things seen and done? Surely in all your travels there have been many such."

"Oh, yes. Exotic things." He scratched meditatively in his beard. "Yes, on our way back to Venice, through Cappadocia, we came upon one instance. There grows in that land a poppy, very like our common red field poppy, but of a silvery-blue color, and from the milk of its pod can be decocted a soporific oil that is a most potent medicine. I knew it would be a useful addition to the simples employed by our Western physicians, and I foresaw a good profit to our Compagnia from that. I sought to collect some of the seeds of that poppy, intending to sow them among the crocuses in our Vèneto plantations. Now, that was an exotic thing, no xe vero? And a grand opportunity. Unfortunately, there was a war going on in Cappadocia at the time. The poppy fields were all devastated, and the populace in such disarray that I could find no one who could provide me with the seeds. Gramo de mi, an opportunity lost."

I said, with some amazement, "You were in the middle of a war, and all that concerned you was poppy seeds?"

"Ah, war is a terrible thing. A disruption of commerce."

"But, Father, you saw in it no opportunity for adventure?"

"You keep on about *adventure*," he said tartly. "Adventure is no more than discomfort and annoyance recollected in the safety of reminiscence. Believe me, an experienced traveler makes plans and takes pains *not* to have such adventures. The most successful journey is a dull journey."

"Oh," I said. "I was rather looking forward to—well, hazards overcome . . . hidden things discovered . . . enemies bested . . . maidens rescued . . ."

"There speaks the bravo!" boomed Uncle Mafìo, joining us just then. "I hope you are disabusing him of such notions, Nico."

"I am trying," said my father. "Adventure, Marco, never put a bagatìn in anybody's purse."

"But is the purse the only thing a man is to fill?" I cried. "Should not he seek something else in life? What of his appetite for wonders and marvels?"

"No one ever found marvels by seeking them," my uncle grunted. "They are like true love—or happiness—which, in fact, are marvels themselves. You cannot say: I will go out and have an adventure. The best you can do is put yourself in a place where it may occur."

"Well, then," I said. "We are bound for Acre, the city of the Crusaders, fabled for daring deeds and dark secrets and silken damsels and the life voluptuous. What better place?"

"The Crusaders!" snorted Uncle Mafìo. "Fables, indeed! The Crusaders who survived to come home had to pretend to themselves that their futile missions had been worthwhile. So they bragged of the wonders they had seen, the marvels of the far lands. About the only thing they brought back was a case of the scolamento so painful they could hardly sit a saddle."

I said wistfully, "Acre is not a city of beauty and temptation and mystery and luxury and—?"

My father said, "Crusaders and Saracens have been fighting over San Zuàne de Acre for more than a century and a half. Imagine for yourself what it must be like. But, no, you need not. You will see it soon enough."

So I left them, feeling rather dashed in my expectations, but not demolished. I was privately coming to the conclusion that my father had the soul of a line-ruled ledger, and my uncle was too blunt and gruff to contain any finer feelings. They would not recognize adventure if it was thrust upon them. But I would. I went and stood on the foredeck, not to miss seeing any mermaids or sea monsters that might swim by.

A sea voyage, after the first exhilarating day or so, becomes mere monotony—unless a storm enlivens it with terror, but the Mediterranean is stormy only in winter—so I occupied myself with learning all I could about the workings of a ship. In the absence of bad weather, the crew had nothing but routine work to do, so everyone from the captain to the cook willingly let me watch and ask questions and even occasionally lend a hand with the work. The men were of many different nationalities, but all spoke the Trade French—which they called Sabir—so we were able to converse.

"Do you know anything at all about sailing, boy?" one of the seamen asked me. "Do you know, for instance, which are the liveworks of a ship, and which are the deadworks?"

I thought about that, and looked up at the sails, spread out on either side of the ship like a living bird's wings, and guessed that they must be the liveworks.

"Wrong," said the mariner. "The liveworks are every part of a ship that is in the water. The deadworks are everything above water."

I thought about that, and said, "But if the deadworks were to plunge under water, they could hardly then be called live. We should all be dead."

The seaman said quickly, "Do not speak of such things!" and crossed himself.

Another said, "If you would be a seafarer, boy, you must learn the seventeen names of the seventeen winds that blow over the Mediterranean." He began ticking them off on his fingers. "At this moment, we are sailing before the etesia, which blows from the northwest. In winter, the ostralada blows fiercely from the south, and makes storms. The gregalada is the wind that blows out of Greece, and makes the sea turbulent. From the west blows the maistràl. The levante blows out of the east, out of Armeniya—"

Another seaman interrupted, "When the levante blows, you can smell the Cyclopedes."

"Islands?" I asked.

"No. Strange people who live in Armeniya. Each of them has only one arm and one leg. It takes two of those people to use a bow and arrow. Since they cannot walk, they hop on the one leg. But if they are in a hurry, they go spinning sideways, wheeling on that hand and foot. That is why they are called the Cyclopedes, the wheel-feet."

Besides telling me of many other marvels, the seamen also taught me to play the guessing and gambling game called venturina, which was devised by mariners to while away long and boring voyages. They must endure many such voyages, for venturina is an exceedingly long and boring game, and no player can win or lose more than a few soldi in the course of it.

When I later asked my uncle if, in his travels, he had ever encountered curiosities like the wheel-feet Armeniyans, he laughed and sneered. "Bah! No seaman ever ventures farther into a foreign port than the nearest dockside wineshop or whorehouse. So when he is asked what sights he saw abroad, he must invent things. Only a marcolfo who would believe a woman would believe a seaman!"

So from then on I listened only tolerantly, with half an ear, when the mariners told of landward wonders, but I still gave full attention when they spoke of things to do with the sea and sailing. I learned their special names for common objects—the small sooty bird called in Venice a stormbird is at sea called petrelo, "little Pietro," because, like the saint, it seems to walk on the water—and I learned the rhymes which seamen use when talking of the weather—

> Sera rosa e bianco matino:
> Alegro il pelegrino

—which is to say that a red sky in the evening or a white sky in the morning foretells good weather in the offing, hence the pilgrim is pleased. And I learned how to toss the scandàgio line, with its little ribbons of red and white at intervals along its length, to measure the depth of water under our keel. And I learned how to speak to other vessels we passed—which I was allowed to do two or three times, for there were many ships asea upon the Mediterranean—shouting in Sabir through the trumpet:

"A good voyage! What ship?"

And the reply would come hollowly back: "A good voyage! The *Saint Sang*, out of Bruges, homeward bound from Famagusta! And you, what ship are you?"

"The *Anafesto*, of Venice, outward bound for Acre and Alexandria! A good voyage!"

The ship's steerer showed me how, through an ingenious arrangement of ropes, he single-handedly controlled both the immense steering oars, one raked down either side of the ship to the stern. "But in heavy weather," he said, "a steerer is required on each, and they must be masters of dexterity, to swing the tillers separately and variously, but always in perfect concert, at the captain's calls."

The ship's striker let me practice pounding his mallets when none of the rowers was at the oars. They seldom were. The etesia wind was so nearly constant that the oars were not often needed to help the ship make way, so the rowers had their only sustained work on that voyage in taking us out of the Malamoco basin and into the harbor of Acre. At those times they took their places—"in the mode called *a zenzile*," the striker told me—three men to each of the twenty benches along each side of the vessel.

Each rower worked an oar that was separately pivoted to the ship's outriggers, so that the shortest oars rowed inboard, the longest outboard and the medium-length oars between them. And the men did not sit, as oarsmen do, for example, in the Doge's buzino d'oro. They stood, each with his left foot on the bench before him, while they swept the oars forward. Then they all fell back supine on the benches when they made their powerful strokes, propelling the ship in a sort of series of rushing leaps. This was done in time to the striker's striking, a tempo that began slow, but got faster as the ship did, and the two mallets made different sounds so the rowers on one side would know when they had to pull harder than the others.

I was never let to row, for that is a job requiring such skill that apprentices are made to practice first in mock galleys set up on dry land. Because the word galeotto is so often used in Venice to mean a convict, I had always assumed that galleys and galeazze and galeotte were rowed by criminals caught and condemned to drudgery. But the striker pointed out that freight ships compete for trade on the basis of their speed and efficiency, for which they would hardly depend on reluctant forced labor. "So the merchant fleet hires only professional and experienced oarsmen," he said. "And war ships are rowed by citizens who choose to do that service as their military obligation, instead of taking up the sword."

The ship's cook told me why he baked no bread. "I keep no flour in my galley," he said. "Fine ground flour is impossible to preserve from contamination at sea. Either it breeds weevils or it gets wet. That is why the Romans first thought of making the pasta we enjoy today— because it is well-nigh imperishable. Indeed, it is said that a Roman ship's cook invented that foodstuff, volente o nolente, when his stock of flour got soaked by an errant wave. He kneaded the mess into pasta to save it, and he rolled it thin and he cut it into strips so it would more quickly dry solid. From that beginning have come all the numerous sizes and shapes of vermicelli and maccheroni. They were a godsend to us mariner cooks, and to the landbound as well."

The ship's captain showed me how the needle of his bussola pointed always to the North Star, even when that star is invisible. The bussola, in those times, was just beginning to be regarded as a fixture almost as necessary for sea voyages as a ship's San Cristoforo medal, but the instrument was yet a novelty to me. So was the periplus, which the captain also showed me, a sheaf of charts on which were drawn the curly coastlines of the whole Mediterranean, from the Levant to the Pillars of Hercules, and all its subsidiary seas: the Adriatic, the Aegean and so on. Along those inked coastlines, the captain—and other captains of his acquaintance—had marked the land features visible from the sea: lighthouses, headlands, standing rocks and other such objects which would help a mariner to determine where he was. On the water areas of the charts, the captain had scribbled notations of their various depths and currents and hidden reefs. He told me that he kept changing those notations according as he found, or heard from other captains, that those depths had changed through silting up, as often happens off Egypt, or through the activity of undersea volcanoes, as often happens around Greece.

When I told my father about the periplus, he smiled and said, "Almost is better than nothing. But we have something much better than a periplus." He brought out from our cabin an even thicker sheaf of papers. "We have the Kitab."

My uncle said proudly, "If the captain possessed the Kitab, and if his ship could sail overland, he could go clear across Asia, to the eastern Ocean of Kithai."

"I had this made at great expense," said my father, handing it to me. "It was copied for us from the original, which was done by the Arab mapmaker al-Idrisi for King Ruggiero of Sicily."

Kitab, I later discovered, means in Arabic only "a book," but then so does our word Bible. And al-Idrisi's Kitab, like the Holy Bible, is much more than just a book. The first page was inscribed with its full title, which I could read, for it was rendered in French: *The going out of a Curious Man to explore the Regions of the Globe, its Provinces, Islands, Cities and their Dimensions and Situation; for the Instruction and Assistance of him who desires to Traverse the Earth.* But all the many other words on the pages were done in the execrable worm-writing of the infidel Arab countries. Only here and there had my father or uncle penned in a legible translation of this or that place-name. Turning the pages so I could read those words, I realized something and I laughed.

"Every chart is upside down. Look, he has the foot of the Italian peninsula kicking Sicily *up* toward Africa."

"In the East, everything is upside down or backward or contrary," said my uncle. "The Arab maps are all made with south at the top. The people of Kithai call the bussola the *south*-pointing needle. You will get accustomed to such customs."

"Aside from that peculiarity," said my father, "al-Idrisi has been amazingly accurate in representing the lands of the Levant, and beyond them as far as Middle Asia. Presumably he himself once traveled those regions."

The Kitab comprised seventy-three separate pages which, laid side by side (and upside down), showed the entire extent of the world from west to east, and a goodly part of it north and south, the whole divided by curving parallels according to climatic zones. The salt sea waters were painted in blue with choppy white lines for the waves; inland lakes were green with white waves; rivers were squiggly green ribbons. The land areas were painted dun yellow, with dots of gold leaf applied to show cities and towns. Wherever the land rose in hills and mountains, those were represented by shapes rather like caterpillars, which were colored purple, pink, and orange.

I asked, "Are the highlands of the East really so vividly colored? Purple mountaintops and—?"

As if in reply, the lookout shouted down from his basket atop the ship's taller mast, "Terra là! Terre là!"

"You can look and see for yourself, Marco," said my father. "The shore is in sight. Behold the Holy Land."

· 2 ·

OF course, I eventually discovered that the coloring on al-Idrisi's maps was to indicate the height of the land, with purple representing the highest mountains, pink those of moderate altitude, and orange the lowest, and yellow land of no particular elevation. But there was nothing in the vicinity of Acre to prove this discovery by, that part of the Holy Land being an almost colorless country of low sand dunes and even lower sand flats. What color there was to the land was a dirty gray-yellow, not even a vestige of green growing there, and the city was a dirty gray-brown.

The oarsmen swept the *Anafesto* around the base of a lighthouse and into the meager harbor. It was awash with every sort of garbage and offal, its waters slimy and greasy, stinking of fish, fish guts and decayed fish. Beyond the docks were buildings that appeared to be made of dried mud—they were all inns and hostels, the captain told us, there being nothing in Acre that could be termed a private residence—and above those low buildings, here and there, stood the taller stone edifices of churches, monasteries, a hospital and the city's castle. Farther landward beyond that castle was a high stone wall, stretching in a semicircle from the harbor to the sea side of the city, with a dozen towers upjutting from it. To me it looked like a dead man's jawbone sparsely studded with teeth. On the other side of that wall, said the captain, was the encampment of the Crusader knights, and beyond that yet another and even stouter wall, fencing Acre's point of land off from the mainland where the Saracens held sway.

"This is the last Christian holding in the Holy Land," the ship's priest said sadly. "And it will fall, too, whenever the infidels choose to overrun it. This eighth Crusade has been so futile that the Christians of Europe have lost their fervor for crusading. The newly arriving knights are fewer and fewer. You notice that we brought none on this passage. So Acre's force is too small to do anything but make occasional skirmishes outside the walls."

"Humph," said the captain. "The knights seldom even bother to do that any more. They are all of different orders—Templars and Hospitalers and whatnot—so they much prefer to fight among themselves . . . when they are not scandalously disporting themselves with the Carmelitas and Clarissas."

The chaplain winced, for no reason I could see, and said petulantly, "Sir, have a regard for my cloth."

The captain shrugged. "Deplore it if you will, Pare, but you cannot refute it." He turned to speak to my father. "Not only the troops are in disarray. The civilian population, what there is of it, consists entirely of suppliers and servitors to the knights. Acre's native Arabs are too venal to be inimical to us Christians, but they are forever at odds with Acre's native Jews. The remainder of the population is a shifting motley of Pisans and Genoese and your fellow Venetians—all rivals and all quarrelsome. If you wish to conduct your business here in peace, I suggest that you go straight to the Venetian quarter when we debark, and take lodgings there, and try not to get involved in the local discords."

So we three gathered our belongings from the cabin and prepared to debark. The quay was crowded with ragged and dirty men, pressing close around the ship's gangplank and waving their arms and jostling each other, crying their services in Trade French and any number of other languages:

"Carry your bags, monsieur! Lord merchant! Messere! Mirza! Sheikh khaja! . . ."

"Lead you to the auberge! The inn! Locanda! Karwansarai! Khane! . . ."

"Provide for you horses! Asses! Camels! Porters! . . ."

"A guide! A guide speaking Sabir! A guide speaking Farsi! . . ."

"A woman! A beautiful fat woman! A nun! My sister! My little brother! . . ."

My uncle demanded only porters, and selected four or five of the least scabrous of the men. The rest drifted away, shaking their fists and shouting imprecations:

"May Allah look upon you sideways!"

"May you choke while eating pig meat!"

". . . Eating your lover's zab!"

". . . Your mother's nether parts!"

The seamen unloaded our portion of the ship's cargo, and our new porters slung our bundles on their backs or shoulders or perched them atop their heads. Uncle Mafio commanded them, first in French, then in Farsi, to take us to the part of the city reserved for Venetians, and to the best inn there, and we all moved off along the quay.

I was not much impressed by Acre—or Akko, as its native inhabitants call it. The city was no cleaner than the harbor, being mostly of squalid buildings with the widest streets between them no wider than the narrowest alleys of Venice. In its most open areas, the city stank of old urine. Where walls closed it in, it smelled even worse, for the alleys were sinks of sewage and swill, in which gaunt dogs competed for the pickings with monster rats, abroad even in full daylight.

More overpowering than Acre's stink was its noise. In every alley wide enough for a sitting rug to be spread, there were vendors, shoulder to shoulder, squatting behind little heaps of trashy merchandise—scarves and ribbons, shriveled oranges, overripe figs, pilgrims' shells and palm leaves—every man of them bellowing to be heard above the others. Beggars, legless or blind or leprous, whined and sniveled and clawed at our sleeves as we passed. Asses, horses and mangy-furred camels—the first camels I had ever seen—shouldered us out of their way as they shuffled through the garbage of the narrow lanes. They all looked weary and miserable under their heavy loads, but they were driven by the drumming sticks and bawled curses of their herders. Groups of men of all nations stood about conversing at the top of their lungs. I suppose some of their talk dealt with mundane matters of trade, or the war, or maybe just the weather, but their conversations were so clamorous as to be indistinguishable from raging quarrels.

I said to my father, when we were in a street wide enough for us to walk abreast, "You said that you were bringing trade goods on this journey. I did not see any merchandise put aboard the *Anafesto* in Venice, and I do not see anything of that nature now. Is it still on the ship?"

He shook his head. "To have brought a pack train's load of goods would have been to tempt the innumerable bandits and thieves between us and our destination." He hefted the one small pack he was carrying at that moment, having refused to relinquish it to any of the porters. "Instead, we are carrying something light and inconspicuous, but of great trading value."

"Zafràn!" I exclaimed.

"Just so. Some in pressed bricks, some in loose hay. And also a good number of the culms."

I laughed. "Surely you will not stop to plant them, and wait a whole year for the harvest."

"If circumstances require, yes. One must try to be prepared against all contingencies, my boy. Who has, God helps. And other journeyers have traveled on the three-bean march."

"What?"

My uncle spoke. "The famed and feared Chinghiz Khan, grandfather of our Kubilai, conquered most of the world in exactly that slow-marching manner. His armies and all their families had to cross the entire vast extent of Asia, and they were far too numerous to have lived off the land, whether by pillaging or scavenging. No, they carried seeds for planting, and animals fit for breeding. Whenever they had marched to the limit of their rations, and beyond the reach of their supply trains, they simply stopped and settled. They planted their grains and beans, bred their horses and cattle, and waited for the harvest and the calving. Then, again well fed and well provisioned, they moved on toward the next objective."

I said, "I heard that they ate every tenth man of their own men."

"Nonsense!" said my uncle. "Would any commander decimate his fighting men? He might as sensibly command them to eat their swords and spears. And the weapons would be about equally edible. I doubt that even a Mongol has teeth capable of chewing another warrior Mongol. No, they stopped and planted and harvested, and moved again, and stopped again."

My father said, "They called that the three-bean march. And it inspired one of their war cries. Whenever the Mongols fought their way into an enemy city, Chinghiz would shout, 'The hay is cut! Give your horses fodder!' And that was the signal for the horde to go wild, to plunder and rape and ravage and slaughter. Thus they laid waste Tashkent and Bukhara and Kiev and many another great city. It is said that when the Mongols took Herat, in India Aryana, they butchered every last one of its inhabitants, to the number of nearly *two million*. Ten times the population of Venice! Of course, of Indians such a diminution is hardly worth remark."

"The three-bean march sounds efficient enough," I conceded, "but intolerably slow."

"He who endures, wins," said my father. "That slow march took the Mongols all the way to the borders of Poland and Romania."

"And all the way to here," added my uncle. We were just then passing two swarthy men in clothing that appeared to be made of hides, much too heavy and hot for the climate. To them Uncle Mafio said, "Sain bina."

They both looked slightly startled, but one of them responded, "Mendu, sain bina!"

"What language was that?" I asked.

"Mongol," said my uncle. "Those two are Mongols."

I stared at him, then turned to stare at the men. They were also walking with their heads turned, looking wonderingly back at us. The streets of Acre teemed with so many people of exotic features and complexions and raiment that I could not yet distinguish one kind of foreigner from another. But those were *Mongols*? The orda, the orco, the bogle, the terror of my childhood? The bane of Christianity and menace to all Western civilization? Why, they might have been merchants of Venice, exchanging a "bon zorno" with us as we all promenaded on the Riva Ca' de Dio. Of course, they did not *look* like merchants of Venice. Those two men had eyes like slits in faces like well-tanned leather. . . .

"Those are Mongols?" I said, thinking of the miles and the millions of corpses they must have tramped across to get to the Holy Land. "What are they doing here?"

"I have no idea," said my father. "I daresay we will find out in good time."

"Here in Acre," said my uncle, "as in Constantinople, there seem to be at least a few persons of every nationality on earth. Yonder goes a black man, a Nubian or an Ethiope. And that woman there is certainly an Armeniyan: each of her breasts is exactly as large as her head. The man with her I would say is a Persian. Now, the Jews and Arabs I can never tell apart, except by their garb. That one yonder has on his head a white tulband, which Islam forbids to Jews and Christians, so he has to be a Muslim. . . ."

His speculations were interrupted because we were almost run down by a war horse ridden at an uncaring canter through the tangled streets. The eight-pointed cross on the rider's surcoat identified him as a Knight of the Order of the Hospital of San Zuàne of Jerusalem. He went past with a noise of jingling chain mail and creaking leather, but with no apology for his rudeness and not even a nod to us brother Christians.

We came to the square of buildings set aside for Venetians, and the porters led us to one of the several inns there. Its landlord met us at the entrance, and he and my father exchanged some deep bows and flowery greetings. Though the landlord was an Arab, he spoke in Venetian: "Peace be upon you, my lords."

My father said, "And on you, peace."

"May Allah give you strength."

"Strong have we become."

"The day is blessed which brings you to my door, my lords. But Allah has led you to choose well. My khane has clean beds, and a hammam for your refreshment, and the best food in Akko. Even now, a lamb is being stuffed with pistachios for the evening meal. I have the honor to be your servant, and my miserable name is Ishaq, may you speak it with not too much contempt."

We introduced ourselves, and each of us thereafter was addressed by the landlord and servants as Sheikh Folo, because the Arabs have no *p* in their own language, and find it difficult to make the sound when speaking any other. As we Folos were disposing our belongings about our room, I asked my father and uncle, "Why is a Saracen so hospitable to us, his enemies?"

My uncle said, "Not all Arabs are engaged in this jihad—which is their name for a holy war against Christianity. The ones here in Acre are profiting too much from it to take sides, even with their fellow Muslims."

"There are good Arabs and there are bad," said my father. "The ones now fighting to oust all Christians from the Holy Land—from the entire eastern Mediterranean—are actually the Mamluks of Egypt, and they are very bad Arabs indeed."

When we had unpacked the things necessary for our stay in Acre, we went to the inn's hammam. And the hammam, I think, must rank with those other great Arabian inventions: arithmetic and its numbers and the abaco for counting. Essentially a hammam is only a room full of steam, generated by throwing water on fire-hot stones. But after we had sat for a time on benches in that room, sweating copiously, half a dozen menservants came in and said, "Health and delight to you, lords, from this bath!" and directed us to lie prostrate on the benches. Then, two men to each of us, their four hands wearing gloves made of coarse hemp, they rubbed us all over, briskly and for a long time. As they rubbed, the accumulated salt and dirt of our voyage was scraped off our skin in long gray rolls. We might have deemed that sufficient for cleanliness, but they kept on rubbing, and more dirt came out of our pores, like thin gray worms.

When we were exuding no more grayness, and were steamed and rubbed to redness, the men offered to depilate us of our body hair. My father declined that treatment, and so did I. I had already that day shaved off what skimpy whiskers I had, and I wished to keep what other hair I possessed. Uncle Mafìo, after a moment's consideration, told the servants to remove his artichoke escutcheon, but not to tamper with his beard or chest hair. So two of the men, the two youngest and most handsome, hastened to the task. They applied a dun-colored ointment to his crotch area, and the thick thatch of hair there began to disappear like smoke. Almost immediately, he was as bald in that place as was Doris Tagiabue.

"That salve is magical," he said admiringly, looking down at himself.

"In truth it is, Sheikh Folo," said one of the young men, smiling so that he leered. "The removal of the hair makes your zab more visible, as prominent and as pretty as a war lance. A veritable torch to guide your lover to you in the night. It is a pity that the Sheikh is not circumcised, so that his zab's bright plum might be more readily observed and admired and—"

"Enough of that! Tell me, can this ointment be purchased?"

"Certainly. You have but to order me, Sheikh, and I will run to the apothecary for a fresh jar of the mumum. Or many jars."

My father said, "You see it as a commodity, Mafìo? But there would be scant market for it in Venice. A Venetian treasures every least bloom on the peach."

"But we are going eastward, Nico. Remember, many of those Eastern peoples regard body hair as a blemish on either sex. If this mumum is not too costly here, we could turn a considerable profit there." He said to his rubber, "Please stop fondling me, boy, and get on with the bathing."

So the men washed us all over, using a creamy sort of soap, and washed our hair and beards in fragrant rose water, and dried us with great fleecy, musk-scented towels. When we were dressed again, they gave us cool drinks of sweetened lemon-juice sharbat, to restore our internal moisture, which by then had been depleted by all the heat. I left the hammam feeling cleaner than I had ever felt before, and I was grateful for the Arabs' invention of that facility. I made frequent use of that one, and others thereafter, and the only complaint I might ever have had was that so many of the Arab people themselves preferred filth and fetor to the cleanness available in the hammam.

The landlord Ishaq had spoken the truth about the khane's food being good, though of course we were paying enough that he could profitably have fed us on ambrosia and nectar. That first night's meal was the lamb stuffed with pistachios, also rice and a dish of cucumbers sliced and dripped with lemon juice, and afterwards a confection of sugared pomegranate pulp mixed with grated almonds and delicately perfumed. It was all delicious, but I was most taken by the accompanying beverage. Ishaq told me it is an infusion from ripe berries in hot water, and is called qahwah. That Arabic word means "wine," which qahwah is not, for the Arabs' religion forbids them wine. Only in color is the qahwah winelike, a deep garnet-brown, rather resembling a Barolo of the Piedmont, but it does not have Barolo's strong flavor or its faint aftertaste of violets. Neither is it sweet or sour, like some other wines. Neither does it intoxicate like wine, or make the head to ache the next day. But it does gladden the heart and enliven the senses and—so said Ishaq—a few glasses of qahwah enable a traveler or a warrior to march or fight untiringly for hours on end.

The meal was served upon a cloth around which we sat on the floor, and it was served without any table implements. So we used our belt knives for cutting and slicing, as we would have employed table knives at home, and used the knife points to spear our bits of meat, in place of the little metal skewers we would have had at home. Lacking skewers or spoons, we ate the lamb's stuffing and the rice and the sweet with our fingers.

"Only the thumb and first two fingers of the right hand," my father cautioned me in a low voice. "The left hand's fingers are considered by the Arabs nasty, for they are reserved to the wiping of one's behind. Also, sit only upon your left haunch, take only small portions of the food with your fingers, chew well each mouthful, and look not at your fellow diners while they eat, lest you embarrass them and make them lose their appetite."

There is much to be read in an Arab's use of his hands, as I gradually learned. If, while he is speaking, he strokes his beard, his most precious possession, then he is swearing by his beard that his words are truthful. If he puts his index finger to his eye, it is his sign of assent to your words or consent to your command. If he puts his hand to his head, he is vowing that his head will answer for any disobedience. If, however, he makes any of those gestures with his *left* hand, he is merely mocking you, and if he touches you with that left hand, it is the direst insult.

· 3 ·

S O M E days later, when we had ascertained that the commander of the Crusaders was in the city's castle, we went to pay our courtesy call upon him. The forecourt of the castle was full of knights of the various orders, some merely lounging about, others gambling with dice, others chatting or quarreling, still others quite visibly drunk for that early in the day. None seemed to be about to dash out and do battle with the Saracens, or eager to do so, or sorry that he was not doing so. When my father had explained our mission to the two drowsy-looking knights guarding the castle door, they said nothing, but only jerked their heads for us to enter. Inside, my father explained our business to one lackey and squire after another, in one hall after another, until we were ushered into a room hung with battle flags and told to wait. After a time, a lady entered. She was about thirty years of age, not pretty but gracious of demeanor, and wearing a gold coronet. She said, in Castilian-accented French, "I am Princess Eleanor."

"Nicolò Polo," said my father, bowing. "And my brother Mafìo and my son Marco." And for the sixth or seventh time, he told why we were seeking audience.

The lady said, with admiration and a little apprehension, "Going all the way to Cathay? Dear me, I hope my husband will not volunteer to go with you. He does love to travel, and he does abhor this dismal Acre." The room door opened again, admitting a man of about her age. "Here he is now. Prince Edward. My love, these are—"

"The Polo family," he said brusquely, with an Anglo accent. "You came in on the supply ship." He too wore a coronet, and a surcoat emblazoned with the cross of San Zorzi. "What can I do for *you*?" He stressed the last word as if we were only the latest in a long procession of appellants.

For the seventh or eighth time, my father explained, concluding, "We merely ask Your Royal Highness to introduce us to the chief prelate among your Crusader chaplains. We would ask him for the loan of some of his priests."

"You may have all of them, as far as I am concerned. And all the Crusaders as well. Eleanor, my dear, would you ask the Archdeacon to join us?"

As the Princess left the room, my uncle said boldly, "Your Royal Highness appears less than pleased with this crusade."

Edward grimaced. "It has been one disaster after another. Our latest best hope was the leadership of the pious French Louis, since he was so successful with the previous Crusade, but he sickened and died on his way here. His brother took his place, but Charles is only a politician, and spends all his time negotiating. For his own advantage, I might add. Every Christian monarch embroiled in this mess is seeking only to advance his own interests, not those of Christianity. Small wonder the knights are disillusioned and lackadaisical."

My father remarked, "Those outside do not look particularly enterprising."

"What few have not gone home in disgust, I can only seldom pry from their wenches' beds, to make a sally among the foe. And even in the field, they prefer bed to battle. One night not long ago, they slept while a Saracen hashishi slipped through the pickets and into my tent, can you imagine that? And I do not wear a sword under my nightshirt. I had to snatch up a pricket candlestick and stab him with that." The Prince sighed profoundly. "As the situation stands, I must resort to politicking myself. I am presently treating with an embassy of Mongols, hoping to enlist their alliance against our common enemy of Islam."

"So that is it," said my uncle. "We had marveled to see a couple of Mongols in the city."

My father began hopefully, "Then our mission closely accords with the aims of Your Royal—"

The door opened again and the Princess Eleanor returned, bringing with her a tall and quite old man wearing a splendidly embroidered dalmatic. Prince Edward made the introductions:

"The Venerable Tebaldo Visconti, Archdeacon of Liège. This good man despaired of the impiety of his fellow churchmen in Flanders, and applied for a papal legacy to accompany me hither. Teo, these are some near countrymen of your own Piacenza. The Polos of Venice."

"Yes, indeed, i Pantaleoni," said the old man, calling us by the sneering nickname with which the citizens of rival cities refer to Venetians. "Are you here to further your vile republic's trade with the enemy infidels?"

"Come now, Teo," said the Prince, looking amused.

"Really, Teo," said the Princess, looking embarrassed. "I told you: the gentlemen are not here to trade at all."

"To do what wickedness, then?" said the Archdeacon. "I will believe anything but good of Venice. Liège was evil enough, but Venice is notorious as the Babylon of Europe. A city of avaricious men and salacious women."

He seemed to be glaring straight at me, as if he knew of my recent adventures in that Babylon. I started to protest in my defense that I was not avaricious, but my father spoke first, and placatively:

"Perhaps our city is rightly so known, Your Reverence. Tuti semo fati de carne. But we are not traveling on behalf of Venice. We bear a request from the Khan of All Khans of the Mongols, and it can only redound to the good of all Europe and Mother Church." He went on to explain why Kubilai had asked for missionary priests. Visconti heard him out, but then asked haughtily:

"Why do you apply to me, Polo? I am only in deacon's orders, an appointed administrator, not even an ordained priest."

He was not even polite, moreover, and I hoped my father would tell him so. But he said only, "You are the highest ranking Christian church-man in the Holy Land. The Pope's legate."

"There is no Pope," Visconti retorted. "And until an apostolic authority is chosen, who am I to delegate a hundred priests to go into the far unknown, at the whim of a heathen barbarian?"

"Come now, Teo," said the Prince again. "I think we have in our entourage more chaplains than we have fighting men. Surely we can spare some of them, for a good purpose."

"If it *is* a good purpose, Your Grace," said the Archdeacon, scowling. "Remember, these are Venetians proposing it. And this is not the first such proposal. Some twenty-five years ago, the Mongols made a similar overture, and directly to Rome. One of their Khans, one named Kuyuk, a cousin to this Kubilai, sent a letter to Pope Innocent asking—no, demanding—that His Holiness and all the monarchs of the West come to him, in a body, to render homage and submission. Naturally he was ignored. But *that* is the kind of invitation the Mongols proffer, and when it comes by the agency of a Venetian . . ."

"Despise our provenance, if you will," said my father, still equably. "If there were no fault in the world, there could be no pardon. But please, Your Reverence, do not despise this opportunity. The Khakhan Kubilai asks nothing but that your priests come and preach their religion. I have here the missive written by the Khan's scribe at the Khan's dictation. Does Your Reverence read Farsi?"

"No," said Visconti, adding a snort of exasperation. "It will require an interpreter." He shrugged his narrow shoulders. "Very well. Let us retire to another room while it is read to me. No need to waste the time of Their Graces."

So he and my father adjourned for their conference. Prince Edward and Princess Eleanor, as if to make up for the Archdeacon's bad manners, stayed long enough to make some conversation with me and Uncle Mafio. The Princess asked me:

"Do *you* read Farsi, young Marco?"

"No, my Lady—Your Royal Highness. That language is written in the Arabic alphabet, the fish-worm writing, and I cannot make sense of it."

"Whether you read it or not," said the Prince, "you had better learn to speak Farsi, if you are going eastward with your father. Farsi is the common trade tongue of all of Asia, just as French is in the Mediterranean lands."

The Princess asked my uncle, "Where do you go from here, Monsieur Polo?"

"If we get the priests we want, Your Royal Highness, we will lead them to the court of the Khakhan Kubilai. Which means we must some-how make our way past the Saracens inland."

"Oh, you should get the priests," said Prince Edward. "You could probably have nuns, too, if you want them. Teo will be glad to rid himself of all of them, for they are the cause of his ill humor. You must not let his behavior dismay you. Teo is from Piacenza, so you can hardly be surprised by his attitude toward Venice. He is also a godly and pious old gentleman, staunch in his disapproval of sin. So, even in the best of humors, he is a trial to us mere mortals."

I said impertinently, "I was hoping that my father would talk back to him, just as ill-humoredly."

"Your father may be wiser than you are," said Princess Eleanor. "The rumor is that Teobaldo may be the next Pope."

"What?" I blurted, so surprised that I forgot to use her due address. "But he just said that he is not even a priest!"

"Also he is a very old man," she said. "But that seems to be his chief qualification. The Conclave is at a standstill because, as usual, every faction has its own favorite candidate. The laity are growing clamorous; they demand a Pope. Visconti would be at least acceptable to them, and to the cardinals as well. So, if the Conclave remains much longer at impasse, it is expected to choose Teo because he *is* old. Thus there will be a Pope at Rome, but not for too long. Just long enough for the various factions to do their secret maneuvers and machinations and settle which favorite will don the beehive tiara when our Visconti dies under it."

Prince Edward said mischievously, "Teo will die in a hurry, of an apoplexy, if he finds Rome to be anything like Liège or Acre—or Venice."

My uncle said, smiling, "Babylonian, you mean?"

"Yes. That is why I think you will get the priests you want. Visconti may make a show of grumbling, but he will not grieve at seeing these Acre priests go far, far away from him. All the monastic orders are in residence here to serve the needs of the fighting men, of course, but they have taken a rather liberal view of that duty. In addition to their hospital ministrations and spiritual solacements, they are providing some services that would dismay the saintly founders of their orders. You can imagine which of the men's needs the Carmelitas and Clarissas are taking care of, and most lucratively, too. Meanwhile, the monks and friars are getting rich by trading illicitly with the natives, even peddling the provisions and medical supplies donated to their monasteries by the good-hearted Christians back in Europe. Meanwhile, also, the priests are selling indulgences and trafficking in absurd superstitions. Have you seen one of these?"

He took out a slip of scarlet paper and handed it to Uncle Mafio, who unfolded it and read aloud:

" 'Bless, O God, sanctify this paper that it may frustrate the work of the Devil. He who upon his person carries this paper writ with Holy Word shall be free from the visitation of Satan.' "

"There is a ready market for such daubs, among men going into battle," the Prince said drily. "Men of both sides, since Satan is the adversary of Muslims as well as Christians. The priests will also, for a price—for an English groat or an Arabian dinar—treat a wound with holy water. Any man's wound, and no matter if it is the gash of a sword or a sore of the venereal pox. The latter is the more frequent."

"Be glad you will soon get out of Acre," sighed the Princess. "Would that we could."

Uncle Mafio thanked them for our audience, and he and I took our leave. He told me he was going back to the khane, for he wished to learn more about the availability of the mumum ointment. I set out merely to wander about the city, in hope of hearing some Farsi words and memorizing them, as Prince Edward had recommended. As it happened, I learned some that the Prince might not have approved of.

I fell in with three native boys of about my own age, whose names were Ibrahim, Daud and Naser. They did not have much grasp of French, but we managed to communicate—boys always will—in this case with gestures and facial expressions. We roamed together through the streets, and I would point to this or that object and speak the name by which I knew it, in French or Venetian, and then ask, "Farsi?" and they would tell me its name in that language, sometimes having to consult among themselves as to what that name was. Thus I learned that a merchant or a trader or a vendor is called a khaja, and all young boys are ashbal or "lion cubs," and all young girls are zaharat or "little flowers," and a pistachio nut is a fistuk, and a camel is a shutur, and so on: Farsi words that would be useful anywhere in my Eastern journeying. It was later that I learned the others.

We passed a shop where an Arab khaja offered writing materials for sale, including fine parchments and even finer vellums, and also papers of various qualities, from the flimsy Indian rice-made to the Khorasan flax-made to the expensive Moorish kind called cloth parchment because it is so smooth and elegant. I chose what I could afford, a medium grade but sturdy, and had the khaja cut it into small pieces that I could easily carry or pack. I also bought some rubric chalks to write with when I had no time to prepare pen and ink. And I began then to set down my first lexicon of unfamiliar words. Later, I would begin to make note of the names of places I passed through and people I met, and then incidents which occurred, and in time my papers came to constitute a log of all my travels and adventures.

It was by then past midday, and I was bareheaded in the hot sun, and I began to perspire. The boys noticed and, giggling, suggested by gesture that I was warm because of my comical clothing. They seemed to find particularly funny the fact that my spindly legs were exposed to public view but tightly enclosed in my Venetian hose. So I indicated that I found equally risible their baggy and voluminous robes, and suggested that they must be more uncomfortably warm than I was. They argued back that theirs was the only practical dress for that climate. Finally, to test our arguments, we went into a secluded alley cul-de-sac and Daud and I exchanged clothes.

Naturally, when we stripped down to the skin, another disparity between Christian and Muslim became evident, and there was much mutual examination and many exclamations in our different languages. I had not known before exactly what mutilation was involved in circumcision, and they had never before seen a male over the age of thirteen with his fava still wearing its capèla. We all minutely scrutinized the difference between me and Daud—how his fava, because it was always exposed, was dry and shiny and almost scaly, and stuck with bits of lint and fluff; while mine, enclosable or exposable at my whim, was more pliant and velvety to the touch, even when, because of all the attention it was getting, my organ rose erect and firm.

The three Arab boys made excited remarks which seemed to mean "Let us try this new thing," and that made no sense to me. So the naked Daud sought to demonstrate, reaching behind him to take my candelòto in his hand, then directing it toward his scrawny backside which, bending over, he wiggled at me, meanwhile saying in a seductive voice, "Kus! Baghlah! Kus!" Ibrahim and Naser laughed at that and made poking gestures with their middle fingers and shouted, "Ghunj! Ghunj!" I still comprehended nothing of the words or byplay, but I resented Daud's taking liberties with my person. I loosed his hand and shoved it away, then hurried to cover myself by getting into the clothes he had doffed. The boys all shrugged good-naturedly at my Christian prudery, and Daud put on my clothes.

The nether garment of an Arab is, like the hose of a Venetian, a forked pair of leg-envelopers. They go from the waist, where they tie with a cord, down to the ankles, where they are snug, but in between they are vastly capacious instead of tight. The boys told me that the Farsi word for that garment is pai-jamah, but the best they could do by way of a French translation was troussés. The Arab upper garment is a long-sleeved shirt, not much different from ours except in its loose and blousy fit. And over that goes an aba, a sort of light surcoat with slits for the arms to go through, and the rest of it hanging loose around the body, almost to the ground. The Arab shoes are like ours, except that they are made to fit any foot, being of considerable length, the unoccupied portion of which curls up and backward over the foot. On the head goes a kaffiyah, a square of cloth large enough to hang well below the shoulders at the sides and back, and it is held on with a cord loosely bound around the head.

To my surprise, I did feel cooler in that ensemble. I wore it for some while before Daud and I exchanged again, and I continued to feel cooler than in my Venetian garb. The many layers of the clothing, instead of being stifling to the skin as I would have expected, seem somehow to entrap what cool air there is and to be a barrier against the sun's warming it. The clothes, being loose, are quite comfortable and not constrictive.

Because those clothes are so loose, and so easily made looser yet, I could not understand why the Arab boys—and all Arab males of every age—urinate as they do. They squat when they make water, in the same way women do. And furthermore they do it just anywhere, as blandly regardless of the people passing as those passersby are of them. When I expressed curiosity and distaste, the boys wanted to know how a Christian makes water. I indicated that we do it standing up, and preferably invisible inside a licet closet. They made me understand that such a vertical position is called unclean by their holy book, the Quran—and further, that an Arab dislikes to go inside a privy, or mustarah, except when he has to do the more substantial evacuation of his bowels, because privies are dangerous places. On learning that, I expressed still more curiosity, so the boys explained. Muslims, like Christians, believe in devils and demons that emanate from the underworld—beings called jinn and afarit—and those beings can most easily climb up from the underworld by way of the pit dug under a mustarah. It sounded reasonable. For a long time afterward, I could not crouch comfortably over a licet hole for dread of feeling the clutch of talons from underneath.

The street clothes of an Arab man may be ugly to our eyes, but they are less so than the street clothes of an Arab woman. And hers are uglier because they are so unfemininely indistinguishable from his. She wears identically voluminous troussés and shirt and aba, but instead of a kaffiyah headcloth she wears a chador, or veil, which hangs from the crown of her head almost to her feet, before and behind and all around her. Some women wear a black chador thin enough so that they can see dimly through it without being seen themselves; others wear a heavier chador with a narrow slit opening in front of their eyes. Swathed in all those layers of clothes and veil, a woman's form is only a sort of walking heap. Indeed, unless she *is* walking, a non-Arab can hardly tell which is her front and which her back.

With grimaces and gestures, I managed to convey a question to my companions. Suppose that, in the manner of Venetian young men, they should go strolling about the streets to ogle the beautiful young women —how would they know if a woman *was* beautiful?

They gave me to understand that the prime mark of beauty in a Muslim woman is not the comeliness of her face or her eyes or her figure in general. It is the massive amplitude of her hips and her behind. To the experienced eye, the boys assured me, those great quivery rotundities are discernible even in a woman's street garb. But they warned me not to be misled by appearances; many women, they indicated, falsely padded out their haunches and buttocks to a counterfeit immensity.

I put another question. Suppose that, in the manner of Venetian young men, Ibrahim and Naser and Daud wished to strike up an acquaintance with a beautiful stranger—how would they go about it?

That inquiry seemed to puzzle them slightly. They asked me to elaborate. Did I mean a beautiful strange *woman*?

Yes. Certainly. What else should I mean?

Not, perchance, a beautiful strange man or boy?

I had earlier suspected, and now I was becoming sure, that I had fallen in with a troop of fledgling Don Metas and Sior Monas. I was not unduly surprised, for I knew that the site of the erstwhile city of Sodom was not far distant to the east of Acre.

The boys were again giggling at my Christian naïveté. From their pantomime and their rudimentary French, I gathered that—in the view of Islam and its holy Quran—women had been created solely so that men could beget male children upon them. Except for the occasional wealthy ruling sheikh, who could afford to collect and keep a whole hive of certified virgins, to be used one time apiece and then discarded, few Muslim men utilized women for their sexual enjoyment. Why should they? There were so many men and boys to be had, more plump and

beautiful than any woman. Other considerations aside, a male lover was
preferable to a female simply because he *was* male.

There, for an example of the worth intrinsic in the male—they
pointed out to me a walking heap of clothing that was a woman, carrying a baby in an extra looped swath of cloth—they could ascertain that
the child was a boy baby, because its face was entirely obscured by a
crawling swarm of flies. Did I not wonder, they inquired, why the
mother did not shoo away the flies? I might have suggested "sheer sloth,"
but the boys went on to explain. The mother *liked* having the flies cover
the baby's face *because* it was a male infant. Any malicious jinn or afarit
hovering about would not easily see that the baby was a valuable male
child, hence would be less likely to attack it with a disease or a curse or
some other affliction. If the baby had been a girl child, the mother would
uncaringly flick the flies away, and let the evil beings see it unobscured,
because no demons would bother to molest a female, and the mother
would not greatly care even if they did.

Well, fortunately being a male myself, I supposed I had to concur in
the prevailing opinion that males were vastly superior to females, and
infinitely more to be treasured. Nevertheless, I had had some small sexual experience, which had led me to conclude that a woman or girl was
useful and desirable and functional in that respect. If she was or could
be nothing else in the world, as a *receptacle* she was incomparable, even
necessary, even indispensable.

Not a bit of it, the boys indicated, laughing yet again at my simplemindedness. Even as a receptacle, any Muslim male was far more sexually responsive and delightful than any Muslim female, whose parts had
been properly deadened by circumcision.

"Wait a moment," I conveyed to the boys. "You mean the males'
circumcision somehow causes . . . ?"

No, no, no. They shook their heads firmly. They meant the circumcision of the females. I shook my own head. I could not imagine how
such an operation could be performed on a creature that possesses no
Christian candelòto or Muslim zab or even an infantile bimbìn. I was
thoroughly mystified, and I told them so.

With an air of amused indulgence, they pointed out—pointing
toward their own truncated organs—that the trimming of a boy's foreskin was done merely to mark him as a Muslim. But, in every Muslim
family of better than beggar or slave status, every female infant was
subjected to an equivalent trimming in the cause of feminine decency.
To illustrate: it was a terrible revilement to call another man the "son of
an uncircumcised mother." I was still mystified.

"Toutes les bonnes femmes—tabzir de leurs zambur," they repeated
over and over. They said that the tabzir, whatever that was, was done to
divest a baby girl of her zambur, whatever that was, so that when she
was grown to womanhood she would be devoid of unseemly yearnings,
hence disinclined to adultery. She would be forever chaste and above
suspicion, as every bonne femme of Islam should be: a passive pulp with
no function but to dribble out as many male children as possible in her
bleak lifetime. No doubt that was a commendable end result, but I still

did not understand the boys' attempted explication of the tabzir means that effected it.

So I changed the subject and put another question. Suppose that, in the manner of Venetian young men, Ibrahim or Daud or Naser *did* want a woman, not a man or boy—and a woman not condemned to numbness and torpor—how would they go about finding one?

Naser and Daud snickered contemptuously. Ibrahim raised his eyebrows in disdainful inquiry, and at the same time raised his middle finger and moved it up and down.

"Yes," I said, nodding. "That sort of woman, if that is the only sort with any life left in her."

Though limited in their means of communication, the boys made it all too plain that, to find such a shameful woman, I should have to seek among the Christian women resident in Acre. Not that I should have to seek very strenuously, for there were many of those sluts. I had only to go—they pointed—to that building directly across the market square we stood in at that moment.

I said angrily, "That is a convent! A house of Christian nuns!"

They shrugged and stroked imaginary beards, asserting that they had spoken truly. And just then the door of the convent opened and a man and a woman came out into the square. He was a Crusader knight, wearing the surcoat insigne of the Order of San Làzaro. She was unveiled, obviously not an Arab woman, and she wore the white mantle and brown habit of the Order of Our Lady of Mount Carmel. Both of them were flushed of face and reeling with wine.

Then, of course, but only then, did I recall having heard two previous mentions of the "scandalous" Carmelitas and Clarissas. I had ignorantly assumed that the references were to the names of particular women. But now it was clear that what had been meant were the Carmelite sisters and those other nuns, the Minoresses of the Order of San Francesco, affectionately nicknamed Clarissas.

Feeling as if I had been personally disgraced in the eyes of the three infidel boys, I abruptly said goodbye to them. At that, they clamored and gestured insistently for me to join them soon again, indicating that then they would show me something *really* marvelous. I gave them a noncommittal reply, and made my way through the streets and alleys back to the khane.

· 4 ·

I arrived there at the same time my father was returning from his conference with the Archdeacon at the castle. As we aproached our chamber, a young man came out of it, the hammam rubber who had attended Uncle Mafìo on our first day at the khane. He gave us a radiant smile and said, "Salaam aleikum," and my father properly responded, "Wa aleikum es-salaam."

Uncle Mafìo was in the room, apparently just in the process of putting on fresh clothes for the evening meal. In his hearty way, he began talking as soon as we entered:

"I had the boy bring me a new jar of the depilatory mumum, for determination of its constituents. It consists only of orpiment and quicklime, pounded together in a little olive oil, with a touch of musk added to make its aroma more pleasant. We could easily compound it ourselves, but its price here is so cheap that that is hardly worth our while. I told the boy to fetch me four dozen of the little jars. What of our priests, Nico?"

My father sighed. "Visconti seems ready enough to delegate every priest in Acre to go away with us. But he feels that, in fairness, they themselves should have something to say about making such a long and arduous journey. So he will only exert himself to the extent of asking for volunteers. He will let us know how many or how few they will be."

On one of the subsequent days, it happened that we were the only guests in residence at the khane, so my father genially asked the proprietor if he would do us the honor of joining us at our supper cloth.

"Your words are before my eyes, Sheikh Folo," said Ishaq, arranging his vast troussés so he could fold his legs to sit.

"And perhaps the Sheikha, your good wife, would join us?" said my uncle. "That is your wife, is it not, in the kitchen?"

"She is indeed, Sheikh Folo. But she would not offend the decencies by presuming to eat in the company of men."

"Of course," said my uncle. "Forgive me. I was forgetting the decencies."

"As the Prophet has said (may blessing and peace be upon him): 'I stood at the gate of Heaven and saw that most of its inhabitants were paupers. I stood at the gate of Hell and saw that most of its inhabitants were women.'"

"Um, yes. Well, perhaps your children might join us, then, as company for Marco here. If you have children."

"Alas, I have none," Ishaq said dolefully. "I have only three daughters. My wife is a baghlah, and barren. Gentlemen, will you permit me humbly to petition grace upon this supper?" We all bowed our heads, and he muttered, "Allah ekber rakmet," adding in Venetian, "Allah is great, we thank Him."

We began helping ourselves to the mutton slices cooked with tomatoes and pearl onions, and to the baked cucumbers stuffed with rice and nuts. As we did so, I said to the landlord, "Excuse me, Sheikh Ishaq. May I ask you a question?"

He nodded affably. "Pleasure me with some command, young Sheikh."

"That word you used in speaking of your lady wife. Baghlah. I have heard it before. What does it mean?"

He looked a trifle discomfited. "A baghlah is a female mule. The word is also used to speak of a woman likewise infertile. Ah, I perceive that you think it a harsh word for me to use of my wife. And you are right. She is, after all, an excellent woman in other respects. You gentlemen may have noticed how magnificently moonlike is her behind. Wonderfully big and ponderously heavy. It forces her to sit down when she would stand up, and to sit up when she would lie down. Yes, an excellent woman. She also has beautiful hair, though you cannot have seen that. Longer and more luxuriant than my beard. No doubt you are aware that Allah appointed one of His angels to do nothing but stand by His throne and praise Him on that account. The angel has no other employment. He simply and constantly praises Allah for His having dispensed beards to men and long tresses to women."

When he paused for a moment in his prattle, I said, "I have heard another word. Kus. What is that?"

The servant who was waiting upon us made a strangled noise and Ishaq looked even more discomfited. "That is a very low word for—this is hardly a topic fit for mealtime discussion. I will not repeat the word, but it is a low term for the even lower parts of a woman."

"And ghunj?" I asked. "What is ghunj?"

The waiter gasped and hurriedly left the room, and Ishaq looked discomfited to the point of distress. "Where have you been spending your time, young Sheikh? That is also a low word. It means—it means the movement a woman makes. A woman or a—that is to say, the passive partner. The word refers to the movement made during—Allah forgive me—during the act of sexual congress."

Uncle Mafìo snorted and said, "My sapùtelo nephew is eager to acquire new words, that he may be more useful when he travels with us into far regions."

Ishaq murmured, "As the Prophet has said (peace be upon him): 'A companion is the best provision for the road.' "

"There are a couple of other words—" I began.

"And, as the saying goes on," Ishaq growled, " 'Even bad company is better than none.' But really, young Sheikh Folo, I must decline to translate any more of your acquisitions."

My father spoke then, and changed the subject to something innocuous, and our meal progressed to the sweet, a conserve of crystallized apricots, dates and citron rind, perfumed with amber. So I did not find out the meaning of those mysterious words tabzir and zambur until a long time afterward. When the meal ended, with qahwah and sharbat to drink, Ishaq again said the grace—unlike us Christians, the infidels do that at the close of a meal as well as at the beginning—"Allah ekber rakmet" and, with an air of relief, left our company.

When, some days later, my father, my uncle and I went again to Acre castle at the summons of the Archdeacon, he met us in assemblage with the Prince and Princess, and also two men wearing the white habits and black mantles of the Order of Friars Preachers of San Domènico. When we had all exchanged greetings, the Archdeacon Visconti introduced the newcomers:

"Fra Nicolò of Vicenza and Fra Guglielmo of Tripoli. They have volunteered to accompany you, Messeri Polo."

Whatever disappointment he may have felt, my father dissembled, saying only, "I am grateful to you, Brothers, and I welcome you to our party. But may I inquire why you have volunteered to join our mission?"

One of them said, in rather a petulant voice, "Because we are disgusted with the behavior of our Christian fellows here in Acre."

The other said, in the same tone, "We look forward to the cleaner and purer air of Far Tartary."

"Thank you, Brothers," my father said, still politely. "Now, would you excuse our having a private word with His Reverence and Their Royal Highnesses?"

The two friars sniffed as if offended, but left the room. To the Archdeacon, my father then quoted the Bible, "The harvest indeed is great, but the laborers are few."

Visconti countered with the quotation, "Where there are two or three gathered together in My name, there am I in the midst of them."

"But, Your Reverence, I asked for priests."

"And no priest volunteered. These two, however, are Preaching Friars. As such, they are empowered to undertake practically any ecclesiastical task—from founding a church to settling a matrimonial dispute. Their powers of consecration and absolution are somewhat limited, of course, and they cannot confer ordination, but you would have to take along a bishop for that. I am sorry for the fewness of the volunteers, but I cannot in conscience conscript or compel any others. Have you any further complaint?"

My father hesitated, but my uncle boldly spoke up, "Yes, Your Reverence. The friars admit they are not going for any positive purpose. They wish simply to get away from this dissolute city."

"Just like Saint Paul," the Archdeacon said drily. "I refer you to the Book of Acts of the Apostles. This city was in those times called Ptolemais, and Paul once set foot here, and evidently he could stand the place for only a single day."

Princess Eleanor said fervently, "Amen!" and Prince Edward chuckled in sympathy.

"You have your choice," Visconti said to us. "You can apply elsewhere, or you can await the election of a Pope and apply to him. Or you can accept the services of the two Dominican brothers. They declare that they will be ready and eager to leave on the morrow."

"We accept them, of course, Your Reverence," said my father. "And we thank you for your good offices."

"Now," said Prince Edward. "You must get beyond the Saracen lands in order to go eastward. There is one best route."

"We would be gratified to know it," said Uncle Mafio. He had brought with him the Kitab of al-Idrisi, and he opened it to the pages showing Acre and its environs.

"A good map," the Prince said approvingly. "Look you, then. To go east from here, you must first go north, to skirt around the Mamluks inland." Like every other Christian, the Prince held the pages upside down to put north at the top. "But the major ports nearest to the northward: Beirut, Tripoli, Latakia . . ."—he tapped the gilded dots on the map which represented those seaports—"if they have not already fallen to the Saracens, they are heavily under siege. You must go—let me calculate: more than two hundred English miles—north along the coast. To this place in Lesser Armeniya." He tapped a spot on the map which apparently did not merit a gilded dot. "There, where the Orontes River debouches into the sea, is the old port of Suvediye. It is inhabited by Christian Armeniyans and peaceable Avedi Arabs, and the Mamluks have not yet got near it."

"That was once a major port of the Roman Empire, called Selucia," said the Archdeacon. "It has since been called Ayas and Ajazzo and many other names. Of course, you will go to Suvediye by sea, not along the coast itself."

"Yes," said the Prince. "There is an English ship leaving here for Cyprus on tomorrow's evening tide. I will instruct the captain to go by way of Suvediye, and to take you and your friars along. I will give you a letter to the Ostikan, the governor of Suvediye, bidding him see to your safe conduct." He directed our attention again to the Kitab. "When you have procured pack animals in Suvediye, you will go inland through the river pass—here—then east to the Euphrates River. You should have an easy journey down the Euphrates valley to Baghdad. And from Baghdad, there are diverse routes to the farther eastward."

My father and uncle stayed on at the castle while the Prince wrote the letter of safe conduct. But they let me make my farewells to His Reverence and Their Royal Highnesses, so that I might take my leave and spend that last day in Acre as I pleased. I did not see the Archdeacon or the Prince and Princess again, but I did hear news of them. My father, my uncle and I had not been long gone from the Levant when we got word that the Archdeacon Visconti had been elected Pope of the Church of Rome, and had taken the papal name of Gregory X. About the same time, Prince Edward gave up the Crusade as a lost cause, and sailed for home. He had got as far as Sicily when he too received some news: that his father had died and that he was King of England. So, all unknowing, I had been acquainted with two of the men of highest eminence in Europe. But I have never much preened in that brief acquaintance. After all, I was later to meet men in the East whose eminence made midgets of Popes and kings.

When I left the castle that day, it was at one of the five hours when Arabs pray to their god Allah, and the beadles whom they call muedhdhin were perched on every tower and high rooftop, loudly but monotonously intoning the chants that announce those hours. Everywhere—in shops and doorways and in the dusty street—men of the Islamic faith were unfolding tatty little rugs and kneeling on them. Turning their faces to the southeast, they pressed those faces to the ground between their hands, while they elevated their rear ends in the air. At those hours, any man you could look in the face instead of the rump had to be a Christian or a Jew.

As soon as everyone in Acre was vertical again, I spotted my three acquaintances of a week or so before. Ibrahim, Naser and Daud had seen me go into the castle and had waited near its entrance for me to emerge. They were all shiny-eyed with eagerness to show me the great marvel they had promised. First, they conveyed to me, I must eat something they had brought. Naser was carrying a little leather bag, which proved to contain a quantity of figs preserved in sesame oil. I liked figs well enough, but these were so oil-soaked that they were pulpy and slimy and disagreeable in the mouth. Nevertheless, the boys insisted that I must ingest them as preparation for the revelation to come, so I forced myself to swallow four or five of the dreadful things.

Then the boys led me on a roundabout way through the streets and alleys. It began to seem a very long way, and I began to feel very weary in my limbs and addled in my mind. I wondered if the hot sun was affecting my bare head or if the figs had been somehow tainted. My vision was disturbed; the people and buildings about me seemed to sway and distort themselves in odd ways. My ears sang as if I were beset by swarms of flies. My feet stumbled on every least irregularity in our path, and I pleaded with the boys to let me stop and rest for a bit. But they, still insistent and excited, took my arms and helped me plod along. I understood from them that my muzziness was indeed an effect of the specially pickled figs, and that it was necessary to what was to come next.

I found myself dragged to an open but very dark doorway, and I started obediently to enter. But the boys set up an angry uproar, and I interpreted it to mean something like "You stupid infidel, you must take off your shoes and enter barefooted"—from which I assumed the building must be one of the houses of worship the Muslims call a masjid. Since I was not wearing shoes, but soled hose, I had to strip myself naked from the waist down. I clutched my tunic and stretched it as far down over my exposed self as I could, meanwhile wondering woozily why it should be more acceptable to enter a masjid with one's privates bare than with one's feet shod. Anyway, the boys did not hesitate, but propelled me through the doorway and inside the place.

Never having been in a masjid, I did not know what to expect, but I was vaguely surprised to find it absolutely unlighted and empty of worshipers or anybody else. All I could see in the dim interior was a row of immense stoneware jars, nearly as tall as I was, standing against one wall. The boys led me to the jar at the end of the row and bade me get into it.

I had been slightly apprehensive—being outnumbered and half nude and not in full command of myself—that the juvenile Sodomites perhaps had designs upon my body, and I was prepared to fight. But what they proposed struck me as more hilarious than outrageous. When I asked for an explanation, they simply continued to motion at the massive jar, and I was too fuddled to balk. Instead, even while laughing at the preposterousness of what I was doing, I let the boys boost me up to a sitting position on the lip of the jar, and swung my feet over and let myself down into it.

Not until I was inside it did I perceive that the jar contained a fluid, because there was no splash or sudden feeling of coldness or wetness. But the jar was at least half filled with oil, so nearly at body warmth that I hardly felt it until my immersion raised its level to my throat. It really felt rather pleasant: emollient and enveloping and smooth and soothing, especially around my tired legs and my sensitively exposed private parts. That realization roused me a little. Was this a prelude peculiar to some strange and exotic sexual rite? Well, thus far at least, it felt good and I did not complain.

Only my head protruded from the collar of the jar, and my fingers still rested on its rim. The boys laughingly pushed my hands inside with me, and then produced something they must have found nearby: a large disk of wood with hinges, rather like a portable pillory. Before I could protest or dodge, they fitted the thing around my neck and closed it shut. It made a lid for the jar I stood in, and, though it was not uncomfortably constrictive around my neck, it somehow had clamped onto the jar so securely that I could not dislodge or lift it.

"What is this?" I demanded, as I sloshed my arms around inside the jar and vainly shoved upward against the wooden lid. I could slosh and shove only slowly, as sometimes one moves in a dream, because of the warm oil's viscosity. My confused senses finally registered the sesame smell of that oil. Like the figs I had earlier been made to eat, I had apparently been put to steep in sesame oil. "What is this?" I shouted again.

"Va istadan! Attendez!" commanded the boys, making gestures for me to stand patient in my jar and wait.

"Wait?" I bellowed. "Wait for what?"

"Attendez le sorcier," said Naser with a giggle. Then he and Daud ran out through the gray oblong that was the door to the outside.

"Wait for the wizard?" I repeated in mystification. "Wait for how long?"

Ibrahim lingered long enough to hold up some fingers for me to count. I peered through the gloom and saw that he had splayed the fingers of both hands.

"Ten?" I said. "Ten what?" He too edged backward toward the door, meanwhile closing his fingers and flicking them open again—four times. "Forty?" I said desperately. "Forty what? Quarante à propos de quoi?"

"Chihil ruz," he said. "Quarante jours." And he disappeared out the door.

"Wait for forty *days*?" I wailed, but got no answer.

All three boys were gone and, it seemed evident, not just to hide from me for a while. I was left alone in my pickling jar in the dark room, with the smell of the sesame oil in my nose, and the loathsome taste of figs and sesame in my mouth, and still a whirl of confusion in my mind. I tried hard to think what all this meant. Wait for the wizard? No doubt it was a boyish prank, something to do with Arab custom. The khane landlord Ishaq would probably explain it to me, with many a laugh at my gullibility. But what kind of prank could keep me immured for forty days? I would miss tomorrow's ship and be marooned in Acre, and Ishaq would have ample time to explain Arab customs to me at leisure. Or would I have vanished in the clutches of the wizard? Did the infidel Muslim religion, unlike the rectitudinous Christian, allow wizards to practice their evil arts unmolested? I tried to imagine what a Muslim wizard would want with a bottled Christian. I hoped I would not find out. Would my father and uncle come looking for me before they sailed? Would they find me before the wizard did? Would anybody?

Just then somebody did. A shadowy shape, larger than any of the boys, loomed in the gray doorway. It paused there, as if waiting for its eyes to adjust to the darkness, and then moved slowly toward my jar. It was tall and bulky—and ominous. I felt as if I were contracting, or shriveling, inside the jar, and wished I could retract my head below the lid.

When the man got close enough, I saw that he wore clothes of the Arab style, except that he had no cords binding his headcloth. He had a curly red-gray beard like a sort of fungus, and he stared at me with bright blackberry eyes. When he spoke the traditional greeting of peace-be-with-you, I noticed even in my befuddlement that he pronounced it slightly differently from the Arab manner: "Shalom aleichem."

"Are you the wizard?" I whispered, so frightened that I said it in Venetian. I cleared my throat and repeated it in French.

"Do I look like a wizard?" he demanded in a rasping voice.

"No," I whispered, though I had no idea what a wizard ought to look like. I cleared my throat again and said, "You look more like someone I used to know."

"And you," he said scornfully, "seem to seek out smaller and ever smaller prison cells."

"How did you know—?"

"I saw those three little mamzarim manhandle you in here. This place is well and infamously known."

"I meant—"

"And I saw them leave again without you, just the three of them. You would not be the first fair-haired and blue-eyed lad to come in here and never come out again."

"Surely there are not many hereabouts with eyes and hair not black."

"Precisely. You are a rarity in these parts, and the oracle must speak through a rarity."

I was already confused enough. I think I just blinked at him. He bent down out of my sight for a moment, and then reappeared, holding the leather bag that Naser must have dropped when he departed. The man reached into it and took out an oil-dripping fig. I nearly retched at sight of it.

"They find such a boy," he said. "They bring him here and soak him in sesame oil, and they feed him only these oil-soaked figs. At the end of forty days and nights, he has become macerated as soft as a fig. So soft that his head can be easily lifted off his body." He demonstrated, twisting the fig in his fingers so that, with a squishy noise just barely audible, it came in two.

"Whatever for?" I said breathlessly. I seemed to feel my body softening below the wooden lid, becoming waxy and malleable like the fig, already sagging, preparing to part from my neck stump with a squishy noise and sink slowly to rest on the bottom of the jar. "I mean, why kill a perfect stranger, and in such a way?"

"It does not kill him, so they say. It is an affair of black sorcery." He dropped the bag and the pieces of fig and wiped his fingers on the hem of his gown. "At any rate, the head part of him goes on living."

"What?"

"The wizard props the severed head in that niche in the wall yonder, on a comfortable bed of olivewood ashes. He burns incense before it, and chants magic words, and after a while the head speaks. On command, it will foretell famines or bounteous harvests, forthcoming wars or times of peace, all manner of useful prophecies like that."

I began to laugh, at last realizing that he was merely joining in the prank that had been played on me, and prolonging it.

"Very well," I said between laughs. "You have paralyzed me with terror, old cellmate. I am uncontrollably pissing and adulterating this fine oil. But now, enough. When I last saw you, Mordecai, I did not know you would flee this far from Venice. But you are here, and I am glad to see you, and you have had your joke. Now release me, and we will go and drink a qahwah together and talk of our adventures since last we met." He did not move; he simply stood and looked sorrowfully at me. "Mordecai, enough!"

"My name is Levi," he said. "Poor lad, you are already ensorceled to the point of derangement."

"Mordecai, Levi, whoever you are!" I ranted, beginning to feel a touch of panic. "Lift this accursed lid and let me out!"

"I? I will not touch that terephah uncleanness," he said, fastidiously taking a step backward. "I am not a filthy Arab. I am a Jew."

My disquiet and anger and exasperation were beginning to clear my head, but they were not influencing me to be tactful. I said, "Did you come here, then, only to entertain me in my confinement? Are you going to leave me here for the idiot Arabs? Is a Jew as idiotically superstitious as they are?"

He grunted, "Al tidàg," and left me. He trudged across the chamber and out through the gray doorway opening. I looked after him, appalled. Did al tidàg mean something like be-damned-to-you? He was probably my only hope of rescue, and I had insulted him.

But he came back almost immediately, and he was carrying a heavy bar of metal. "Al tidàg," he said again, and then thought to translate: "Do not worry. I will get you out, as I am bidden, but I must do it without touching the uncleanness. Happily for you, I am a blacksmith, and my smithy is just across the way. This bar will do it. Stand firm, now, young Marco, so you do not fall when it breaks."

He swung the bar and, at the moment it crashed against the jar, he leapt well to one side, so that his garments would not be defiled by the resultant cascade of oil. The jar shattered with a great noise, and I swayed unsteadily, as the pieces and all the oil fell away from me. The wooden lid suddenly weighed heavily on my neck. But, since I could now reach my hands to the upper surface of it, I quickly found and undid the catches that held it closed, and I dropped the wooden disk in the spreading pool of oil at my feet.

"Will you not get into trouble over this?" I asked, indicating the mess all about us. Very elaborately, Levi shrugged his shoulders, his hands and his fungoid eyebrows. I went on, "You called me by name, and you said something about having been bidden to rescue me from this danger."

"Not from this danger specifically," he said. "The word was merely to try to keep Marco Polo out of trouble. There were also some words of description—that you could easily be recognized by your proximity to the nearest available trouble."

"That is interesting. The word from whom?"

"I have no idea. I gather that you once helped some Jew get out of a bad spot. And the proverb says that the reward of a mitzva is another mitzva."

"Ah, as I suspected: old Mordecai Cartafilo."

Levi said, almost peevishly, "That could be no Jew. Mordecai is a name from ancient Babylon. And Cartafilo is a gentile name."

"He said he was a Jew, and so he seemed to be, and that was the name he used."

"Next you will say that he wandered, as well."

Puzzled, I said, "Well, he did tell me that he had traveled extensively."

"Khakma," he said, which rasping noise I took to be a word of derision. "That is a fable concocted by fabulists of the goyim. There is not one immortal wandering Jew. The Lamed-vav are mortal, but there are always thirty-six of them going secretly and helpfully about the world."

I was disinclined to linger in that dark place while Levi argued about fables. I said, "You are a fine one to sneer at fabulists, after your ludicrous tale of wizards and talking heads."

He gave me a long look, and scratched thoughtfully in his curly beard. "Ludicrous?" He held out to me his metal bar. "Here. I do not wish to put my feet in the oil. You break the next jar in the row."

I hesitated for a moment. Even if this place was just an ordinary masjid house of worship, we had already considerably desecrated it. But then I thought: one jar, two jars, what matter? And I swung the bar as hard as I could, and the second jar broke with a brittle smash, and loosed its surge of sesame oil with a splash, and something else hit the ground with a thick, moist thud. I bent over to see it better, and then hastily recoiled, and said to Levi, "Come, let us go away."

On the threshold I found my hose where I had discarded them, and I gratefully put them on again. I did not mind that they got instantly soaked with the oil clinging to me; the rest of my garb already was sopping and clammy. I thanked Levi for his having rescued me, and for his explication of Arabian sorcery. He bade me "lechàim and bon voyage," and cautioned me not to depend on the relayed word of a nonexistent Jew to keep me forever out of *every* trouble. Then he went off to his forge and I hastened back toward the inn, looking repeatedly over my shoulder in case I should be seen and pursued by the three Arab boys or the wizard for whom they had captured me. I no longer believed the adventure to have been a prank, and I no longer contemned the sorcery as a fable.

When Levi watched me break that second jar, he did not ask me what it was I bent to peer at among its shards, and I did not try to tell him, and I cannot tell it clearly even yet. The place was very dark, as I have said. But the object that fell onto the ground with that sickening wet plop was a human body. What I saw and can tell about it is that the corpse was naked, and had been a male, not full grown to manhood. Also it lay oddly on the ground, like a sack made of skin, a sack that had been emptied of its contents. I mean it looked more than soft, it looked flaccid, as if somehow all its bones had been extracted, or dissolved. The only other thing I could see was that the body had no head. I have never since that time been able to eat figs or anything flavored with sesame.

· 5 ·

T H E next afternoon, my father paid our bill to landlord Ishaq, who accepted the money with the words, "May Allah smother you with gifts, Sheikh Folo, and repay every generous act of yours." And my uncle distributed to the khane servants the gratuities of smaller money, which are in all the East called by the Farsi word bakhshish. He gave the largest amount to the hammam rubber who had introduced him to the mumum ointment, and that young man thanked him with the words, "May Allah conduct you through every hazard and keep you ever smiling." And all the staff, Ishaq and the servants together, stood in the inn door to wave after us with many other cries:

"May Allah flatten the road before you!"

"May you travel as upon a silken carpet!" and the like.

So our expedition proceeded northward up the Levantine coast, and I congratulated myself on having got out of Acre intact, and I trusted that I had had my one and last encounter with sorcery.

That short sea voyage was unremarkable, as we stayed in sight of the shore the whole way, and that shore is everywhere much the same to look at: dun-colored dunes with dun-colored hills behind them, the occasional dun-colored mud hut or village of mud huts almost imperceptible against the landscape. The cities we sailed past were slightly more distinguishable, since each was marked by a Crusaders' castle. The most noticeable from the sea was the city of Beirut, it being sizable and set upon an outjutting point of land, but I judged it to be inferior, as a city, even to Acre.

My father and uncle occupied themselves on shipboard with making lists of the equipment and supplies they should have to procure in Suvediye. I occupied myself mainly in chatting with the crew; although most of them were Englishmen, they of course spoke the Sabir of travelers and traders. The Brothers Guglielmo and Nicolò occupied themselves in talking to each other, and talking endlessly, about the iniquities of Acre and how thankful they were to God for His having let them decamp from there. Of all the complaints they might have aired in regard to Acre, they seemed most exercised about the unchaste and licentious behavior of the resident Clarissas and Carmelitas. But, from what I overheard of their lamentations, they sounded more like hurt husbands or rejected suitors of those nuns than like their brothers in Christ. Lest I sound disrespectful of a noble calling, I will say no more about my impressions of the two friars. For they deserted our expedition before we got any farther than Suvediye.

That city was a poor and small place. To judge from the ruins and remains of a much larger city standing around it, Suvediye had gradually been reduced from what grandeur it may have had in Roman times, or perhaps earlier, when Alexander had come its way. The reason for its diminishment was not far to seek. Our own ship, not a large one, had to anchor well out in the little bay, and we passengers had to be brought ashore in a skiff, because the harbor was so badly silted and shallowed by the outflow of the Orontes River there. I do not know if Suvediye still is a functioning seaport, but at that time it clearly did not have very many more years in which to be so.

For all the city's puniness and poor prospects, Suvediye's inhabitant Armeniyans seemed to regard it as the equal of a Venice or a Bruges. Though only one other ship was anchored there when ours arrived, the port officials behaved as if their harbor roads were thronged with vessels, and all requiring the most scrupulous attention. A fat and greasy Armeniyan inspector came bustling aboard, his arms laden with papers, while we five passengers were in the process of debarking. He insisted on counting us—five—and all our packs and bundles, and entered the numbers in a ledger. Then he let us go, and began to pester the English captain for the information with which to fill out innumerable other manifests of cargo, origin, destination and so forth.

There was no Crusaders' castle in Suvediye, so we five—pushing our way through the city's throngs of beggars—went directly to the palace of the Ostikan, or governor, to present our letters from Prince Edward. I charitably call the Ostikan's residence a palace; it was in fact a rather shabby building, but it was respectable in extent and two stories in height. After numerous entry guards and reception clerks and under-officials had severally demonstrated their importance, each of them delaying us with an officious show of fuss, we were finally conducted into the palace throne room. I charitably call it a throne room, for the Ostikan sat on no imposing throne, but lolled on what is called a daiwan, which is only a heap of cushions. In spite of the day's warmth, he repeatedly rubbed his hands over a brazier of coals before him. In a corner, a young man sat on the floor, using a large knife to cut his toenails. Those nails must have been exceedingly horny; each gave a loud thwack as it was cut off, and then went *whiz* and fell elsewhere in the room with an audible click.

The Ostikan's name was Hampig Bagratunian, but his name was the only wonderful thing about him. He was small and wizened and, like all Armeniyans, he had no back to his head. It was flat there, as if his head had been designed to hang on a wall. He did not look at all like a governor of anything, and he was as clerkly as his clerks in tongue-clucking fussiness. Unlike an Arab or a Jew, who obey their religions' injunctions to entertain strangers with a good grace, the Christian Armeniyan received us with unconcealed annoyance.

When he had read the letter, he said in Sabir, "Just because I am a fellow monarch"—casually inflating his rank to regality—"any other prince seems to think he can rid himself of a bother by shunting it on to me."

We politely said nothing. A toenail went *thwack*, whiz, *click*.

Ostikan Hampig continued, "Here you arrive on the very eve of my son's wedding"—he indicated the toenail cutter—"when I have countless other things to attend to, and guests coming from all over the Levant, trying not to get themselves slaughtered by the Mamluks on their way, and all the festivities to arrange, and . . ." He went on listing the botherations to which our arrival had added another.

His son carved off a final clamorous toenail, then looked up and said, "Wait, Father."

The Ostikan, interrupted in his recital, said, "Yes, Kagig?"

Kagig got up from where he sat, but did not quite rise erect. Instead, he began to roam about the room, bent over, as if to give us a good view of the flat back of his head. He picked up something, and I realized that he was for some reason retrieving his pared bits of toenail. While he worked, he said over his shoulder to the Ostikan, "These strangers brought two churchmen with them."

"Yes, so they did," his father said impatiently. "What of it?"

One of the toenail crescents had landed near my own foot; I picked it up and gave it to Kagig. He nodded and, seeming satisfied that he had all the bits, he sat down beside his father on the daiwan, brushing the horny scraps from his hand into the brazier. "There," he said. "No sorcerer will use those to conjure against me." The toenails seemed still determined not to die quietly: they sizzled and popped among the coals.

"What about these churchmen, my boy?" Hampig inquired again, paternally stroking his son's backless head.

"Well, we have old Dimirjian to conduct my nuptial mass," Kagig said languidly. "But every common peasant has *one* priest to do the marrying of him. Suppose I had three . . ."

"Hm," said his father, turning his eyes to the Brothers Nicolò and Guglielmo; they stared haughtily back at him. "Yes, that would add to the pomp of the occasion." To my father and uncle he said, "You may not be unwelcome, after all. Are these clerics empowered to confer the sacrament of matrimony?"

"Yes, Your Excellency," said my father. "These are Friars Preachers."

"They could serve the mass as acolytes suffragan to the Metropolitan Dimirjian. And they should feel honored to participate. My son is marrying a pshi—a Princess—of the Adighei. What you call the Circassians."

"A people famous for their beauty," said Uncle Mafìo. "But . . . Christian?"

"My son's betrothed has taken instruction from the Metropolitan

Dimirjian himself, and Confirmation and First Communion. The Princess Seosseres is now a Christian."

"And a beautiful Christian indeed," said Kagig, smacking his liver-like lips. "People stop in their footsteps when they see her—even Muslims and other infidels—and bow their heads and thank the Creator for having created the Pshi Seosseres."

"Well?" Hampig said to us. "The wedding is tomorrow."

My father said, "I am sure the frati will be honored to participate. Your Excellency has only to bid me, and I will bid them serve."

The two frati looked somewhat indignant at not having been personally consulted during the conversation, but they raised no objection.

"Good," said the Ostikan. "We shall have three ecclesiastics at the nuptials, and two of them foreigners from afar. Yes, that will impress my guests and my subjects. On that condition, then, messieurs, you will—"

"We will remain here in Suvediye for the royal wedding," said Uncle Mafio, smoothly dropping in the adjective. "Of course, we will desire to continue our journey immediately afterward. And so, of course, Your Excellency will meantime have helped to expedite our procurement of mounts and supplies."

"Er . . . yes . . . of course," said Hampig, looking fussed at having been given some conditions in return. He rang a bell by his hand, and one of the under-officials entered. "This is my palace steward, messieurs. Arpad, you will show these gentlemen to quarters here in the palace, then introduce the friars to the Metropolitan, then accompany the gentlemen to the market and render whatever assistance they may require." He turned again to us. "Very well, then, I welcome you to Suvediye, messieurs, and I formally invite you to the royal wedding and all the attendant festivities."

So Arpad led us to two chambers on the upper floor, one for us and one for the friars. As soon as we had unpacked enough of our belongings for a brief stay, we went downstairs again and handed the Brothers over to the Metropolitan Dimirjian. He was a large old man, the backlessness of whose head was less remarkable than what could be seen on the forward side of it: a massive nose, a weighty underslung jaw, overslung eyebrows and long fleshy ears. When he had taken the friars off to rehearse them in the morrow's ritual, my father, my uncle and I went with Steward Arpad to the Suvediye marketplace.

"You might as well get used to calling it the bazàr," he said helpfully. "That is the Farsi word used from here to the eastward. You are buying at a good time, for the wedding has attracted vendors from everywhere, hawking every conceivable thing, so you will have ample choice of goods. But I beg that you will let me assist you in the bargaining for your selections. Gods knows the Arab merchants are tricksters and swindlers, but the Armeniyans are so much shiftier that only a fellow Armeniyan dares deal with them. The Arabs would merely cheat you naked. The Armeniyans would flay you of your very skins."

"The chief thing we need is riding animals," said my uncle. "They can carry us and what goods we have, as well."

"I suggest horses," said Arpad. "You may wish to change them later for camels, when you have much desert to cross. But for now, since your next destination is Baghdad, no hard journey, horses will be more speedy, and much more easy to handle than camels. Mules would be even better, but I doubt that you wish to spend what they would cost."

In much of the East, as in civilized Europe, the mule, because it is so gentle and amenable and intelligent, is the preferred mount of men and ladies of high degree—meaning the very rich—so a mule breeder unblushingly asks exorbitant prices for his animals. My father and uncle agreed that they did not care to pay such prices, that horses would have to do for us.

So we visited the several rope corrals set up around the outskirts of the bazàr, where could be bought all sorts of riding and pack animals: mules, asses, horses of every breed from the exquisite Arabian to the heftiest drafter, and also camels and their cousins, the sleek racing dromedaries. After examining many horses, my father and uncle and the steward settled on five—two geldings and three mares—of good appearance and conformation, not so heavy as the draft animals but nowhere near so elegant as the fine-boned Arabians.

Buying five horses meant five separate dickerings. So there in the Suvediye bazàr, for the first time, I witnessed a procedure that I was eventually to become weary of, for I had to endure it in every bazàr of the East. I mean the curious Eastern manner of transacting a purchase. Although the steward Arpad kindly did it for us that time, it was a prolonged and tedious affair.

Arpad and the horse trader each extended a hand to the other, letting their long sleeves drape over the meeting hands to make them invisible to anyone looking on—and in any bazàr there are always countless loiterers with nothing better to do than to watch other people's business dealings. Then Arpad and the trader each wiggled and tapped his hidden fingers against the other's hidden hand, the trader signaling the price he wanted, Arpad the price he would give. Although I learned the signals and remember them well, I will not set them out in all their intricacy. Suffice it to say that one man first taps to indicate either single digits or tens or hundreds, and thus, by subsequently tapping thrice, say, indicates either three or thirty or three hundred. And so on. The system allows the signaling even of fractions, and even of the different values when buyer and merchant must deal in different currencies, say dinars and ducats.

By exchanging the taps, the horse trader gradually reduced his demand, and the steward gradually increased his offer. In this way, they worked their way through all the reasonable prices and unreasonable extortions conceivable. In the East, the various sorts of prices even have names: the great price, the small price, the city price, the beautiful price, the fixed price, the good price—and an infinity of others. When they reached a mutually acceptable deal for the first horse, they had to repeat the process for each of the four others, and in each case the steward had to consult at intervals with us, not to exceed his authority or our purse.

Any of those sessions could easily have been conducted in spoken words, but that is never done, for the secrecy of the hand-and-sleeve method benefits both buyer and seller, since no one else ever knows the original asking price or the final price agreed on. Thus a buyer sometimes can drive a merchant down to a figure the merchant would be ashamed to speak aloud, but he may finally sell at that price, knowing that any next prospective buyer will not know of it and cannot take advantage of it. Or a buyer, so eager to acquire some item that he will not haggle much over the price, can pay it knowing that he will not be jeered by the bystanders for a spendthrift fool.

Our five transactions were not completed until the sun was almost down, leaving us not time enough that day even to buy saddles for the horses, not to mention the many other necessities on our lists. We had to return to the palace, to visit its hammam and get thoroughly clean before donning our best clothes for the evening meal. For it was to be a banquet, Arpad told us, the traditional all-male celebration on the eve of a wedding. While we were being rubbed and pummeled in the hammam, my father said anxiously to my uncle:

"Mafìo, we must present some sort of celebratory gift to the Ostikan or his son or his son's bride, if not a gift to each of them. I cannot think what might be suitable. Worse, I cannot think what we might afford. Our budget was much depleted by the purchase of those mounts, and we have many other things yet to buy."

"No fear. I had already given that some thought," said my uncle, sounding confident as usual. "I looked into the kitchen where the banquet is being prepared. For color and condiment, the cooks are using what they told me was safflower. I tasted it and—can you imagine?—it is nothing but common càrtamo, bastard zafràn. They have none of the real thing. So we will give the Ostikan a brick of our good golden zafràn, and it should delight him more than the golden trinkets everyone else will be giving."

For all its decrepitude, the palace had a commendably large dining hall, and that night it needed it, because just the males among the Ostikan's guests made a tremendous crowd. They were mostly Armeniyans and Arabs—the former including the "royal" Bagratunian family and its relations, from close to remote; plus the palace and government officials; plus what I suppose passed for the nobility of Suvediye; plus legions of visitors from elsewhere in Lesser Armeniya and the rest of the Levant. The Arabs seemed all to be of the Avedi tribe, which must have been a huge tribe, for all the Arabs claimed to be sheikhs of high or lower degree. My father, my uncle, the two Dominicans and myself were not the only foreigners, for all of the bride's Circassian family had come south from the Caucasus Mountains for the occasion. I might say that they were—as is reputed of all Circassians—a strikingly handsome people, and by far the best looking men in the company that night.

The banquet actually consisted of two separate meals, served simultaneously, each meal comprising numberless courses. Those courses served to us and the Armeniyan Christians were the most various, because they were not limited by any infidel superstitions. The courses set before the Muslim guests had to exclude the many foods their Quran forbids them to eat—pork, of course, and shellfish, and every meat from every sort of creature that lives in a hole, whether a hole in the ground, a hole in a tree or a hole in the underwater mud.

I paid no particular attention to what the Arab guests were given to eat, but I recall that our Christian main course was a young camel calf stuffed with a lamb which was stuffed with a goose which was stuffed with minced pork, pistachios, raisins, pine seeds and spices. There were also stuffed aubergines and stuffed marrows and stuffed vine leaves. For drink, there were sharbats made with still-frozen *snow*, brought from God knows where and by God knows what swift means and at God knows what cost. The sharbats were of different flavors—lemon, rose, quince, peach—and all perfumed with nard and frankincense. For sweets, there were pastries rich with butter and honey and as crisp as honeycombs, and a paste called halwah, made of powdered almonds, and lime tarts, and little cakes unbelievably made of rose petals and orange blossoms, and a conserve of dates stuffed with almonds and cloves. There was also the uniquely wonderful qahwah. There were wines of many different colors, and other intoxicating liquors.

The Christians speedily got drunk on those drinks, and the Arabs and Circassians were not far behind them. It is well known that the Muslims' Quran forbids them to drink wine, but it is not so well known that many Muslims observe that stricture *precisely* to the letter of the law. I will explain. Since wine must have been the only intoxicant in the world at the time the Prophet Muhammad wrote the Quran, it did not occur to him to proscribe every inebriating substance that might subsequently be discovered or invented. Thus many Muslims, even the most rigidly religious in other respects, feel at liberty—especially on festive occasions—to drink any intoxicant not, like wine, made from grapes, and also to chew the herb they variously call hashish, banj, bhang and ghanja, which is quite as potently deranging as any wine.

Since that night's banquet was well provided with vivacious drinks never dreamed of by the Prophet—a sparkling urine-colored liquid called abijau, which is brewed from grain, and araq, which is wrung from dates, and something called medhu, which is an essence of honey, and also gummy wads of hashish for chewing—the Arabs and Circassians, except for a few elderly holy men among them, became just as addled and jolly and argumentative and lachrymose as did all the Christians. Well, not all the Christians; my uncle got notably bleary and inclined to sing, but my father and I and the friars abstained.

There was a band of musicians—or acrobats, it was hard to say which, for they did the most astonishing capers and tricks and contortions *while they played*. Their instruments were bagpipes and drums and long-necked lutes, and I would have called their music a dreadful caterwauling, except that I suppose it was admirable that they could play at all while they were doing somersaults and walking on their hands and bounding on and off each other's shoulders.

The guests knelt or squatted or half-reclined on daiwan pillows around the dining cloths which covered every square inch of the floor, except in the narrow aisles where the servers and servants moved about in a sort of crouch. The guests got up, one or a group of them after another, to carry to the Ostikan and his son, who sat on a dais raised a little above the rest of the company, the gifts they had brought for the occasion. They knelt and bowed their heads and raised up in their hands ewers and platters and dishes of gold and silver, and jeweled brooches and tiaras and tulband medallions, and fabrics of silk threaded with gold, and many other fine things.

I discovered that night that, in the lands of the East, the recipient of a gift must give in return not just thanks but a gift at least as rich as that which he is given. I was to see that exchange take place often and often thereafter, and to see many a donor walk away with something incalculably more valuable than what he gave. But that night I was more amused than impressed by the practice. For the Ostikan Hampig, having the soul of a clerk, complied with the custom simply by giving to each new donor some object from the pile of valuables he had been given by earlier givers. It amounted to nothing more than a brisk shuffle of the gifts, so that, in effect, the guests would all go home with the same goods they had brought—only each would go home with someone else's.

Hampig made only one departure from that routine, when it came our turn to get up and advance to the dais. As my uncle had predicted, the Ostikan was so overjoyed to receive our brick of zafràn that he bade his son Kagig get up and run to fetch something extraordinary to give in return. Kagig came back with three objects that looked—as a brick of zafràn does at first glance—rather commonplace. They appeared to be merely three small leather purses. But when Hampig handed them reverently to my father, we saw that they were the cods of musk deer, tightly packed with the precious grains of musk obtained from those deer. The three deer scrota were provided with long rawhide strings, for a reason which Hampig explained:

"If you know the value of these cods, messieurs, you will tie them behind your own testicles, and wear them there, hidden for safekeeping during your journey."

My father gave sincere thanks for the gift, and my uncle made a drunkenly fulsome speech of gratitude that might have gone on endlessly, except that he got to coughing. I did not realize how really precious that gift was, and how untypical of the clerkly Hampig, until my father told me later that the value of the three cods full of musk was easily equal to what we had spent that day in the bazàr.

When we made our last bows to the Ostikan and left the dais, his son came lurching along, to join us at our cloth. It was of course quite far from the dais of honor, down among some barbarous-looking lesser guests, perhaps some poor country relations. Kagig, who was by then as drunk as anyone else in the hall, told us he wished to sit with us for a while, because his soon-to-be bride resembled us more than she did him or any of his people. Being a Circassian, Seosseres was fair of skin, he said, with chestnut hair and features of incomparable beauty. He went on at great length about her beauty: "More beautiful than the moon!" and her gentleness: "Gentler than the west wind!" and her sweetness: "Sweeter than the fragrance of the rose!" and her various other virtues:

"She is fourteen years of age, which may be somewhat overripe for marriage, but she is as virgin as any unpierced and unstrung pearl. She is educated and can talk well on a number of subjects about which I, even I, know nothing. Philosophy and logic, the canons of the great physician ibn Sina, the poems of Majnun and Laila, the mathematics called geometry and al-jebr . . ."

I think we listeners were rightly doubtful that the Pshi Seosseres could be so sublime. If so, why would she be willing to marry an uncouth Armeniyan with liver lips and no back to his head and a dedication to keeping his toenails safe from sorcerers? And I think our dubiety must have shown in our faces, and Kagig must have seen it, for he finally got up, staggered from the hall and clumped upstairs to fetch the Princess from her sequestered chamber. When he dragged her down, hauling on one of her wrists, she was trying maidenly to hold back, yet trying also not to put up an unwifely show of fight. He brought her into the hall and stood her in front of the company, and stripped off the chador that covered her face.

If all the guests had not been occupied with the viands before them, and most of them sodden with drink, probably someone would have prevented Kagig's act of boorishness. The girl's forced entry certainly caused a muttering in the hall, loudest and angriest among her male relations. Several Muslim holy men covered their faces, and several Christian elders averted theirs. But the rest of us, while we might deplore Kagig's breach of good behavior, were able to be pleasured by the result of it. For the Pshi Seosseres was indeed an outstanding representative of her famously handsome people.

Her hair was long and wavy, her figure breathtakingly superb, her face so lovely that its light adornments of al-kohl around the eyes and red berry juice on the lips were quite unnecessary. The girl's fair skin blushed pink in her embarrassment, and she only briefly let us see her qahwah-brown eyes before she lowered them and kept them lowered. Still we could gaze upon her unblemished brow and long lashes and perfect nose and winsome mouth and delicate chin. Kagig held her standing there for at least a full minute, while he made clownish bows and gestures of presentation. Then, as soon as he let go her wrist, she fled the hall and disappeared from our sight.

The Armeniyans, it is said, were once good men and valiant, and did dauntless deeds of arms. But in our time they are but poor simulacra of men, and good at nothing, unless it be drinking and bazàr-cheating. So I had heard, and so the Ostikan's son demonstrated. I do not mean his exposure to the male banqueters of his bride-to-be; I mean what happened afterward.

When Seosseres had gone, Kagig flopped down again at our cloth, between me and my father, and looked around with a self-satisfied smirk, and asked of all within hearing, "What did you think of her, eh?" The girl's male relations sitting nearby responded only with black looks; other men in our vicinity merely murmured respectful remarks of praise. Kagig preened as if they had been complimenting *him*, and proceeded to get even more drunk and even more vile. His continued eulogies on his

Princess began to dwell less on the beauty of her face than on the attractiveness of some other parts of her, and his smirks became open leers, and his liver lips drooled. Before long, he was so besotted with wine and lust that he was muttering, "Why wait? Why should I wait for old Dimirjian to croak words over us? I am her husband in all but title. Tonight, tomorrow night, what difference . . . ?"

And suddenly he unfolded himself from the pillows and staggered again out of the hall and lumbered loudly up the stairs. As I have said, the palace was of no very sturdy construction. So anyone in the hall who bothered to direct an ear—as I did—could hear what happened next. However, none of the other guests, not even the Ostikan or the Circassians who might have been most interested, seemed to notice Kagig's abrupt departure or the subsequent sounds. I did, and so did my still sober father and our two frati. Listening carefully, I heard distant thumps and little cries and indistinct commands and thin protests and then some more thumps that became a regular and insistent pulse of thumps. My father and the friars rose up from the cloth, and so did I, and we all helped Uncle Mafio get up, and the five of us made our salutations to the host Hampig—who was drunk and quite uncaring if we left or stayed—and we departed to our own quarters.

We Polos spent the next morning in the bazàr again, and again accompanied by the steward Arpad. It was heroic of him to be still assisting us, for he clearly was suffering from the bibulous night before. But, headache notwithstanding, he performed capably as our hand-and-sleeve bargainer in another tedious series of interminable transactions. We bought saddles and saddle panniers and bridles and blankets, and had them and our horses delivered by bazàr boys to the palace stables, to be ready for our decamping. We bought leather water bags, and many sacks of dried fruits and raisins, and large goat cheeses sheathed against spoilage by heavy wax coatings. At Arpad's suggestion, we bought a thing called a kamàl. It was only a palm-sized rectangle of wood strips, like a small and empty picture frame, with a long string depending from it.

"Any journeyer," said Arpad, "can determine from the sun or the stars the directions of north, east, west and south. You are going eastward, and you will be able to judge each day's progress eastward by your traveling pace. But it will sometimes be difficult to judge how far north or south of due east you have gone, and that is what the kamàl can tell you."

My father and uncle made noises of surprise and interest. Arpad tenderly held his head in both hands, for it evidently hurt him when noises were made.

"The Arabs are infidels," he said, "and unworthy of respect or admiration, but they did invent this useful device. Here, you will have the use of it, young Monsieur Marco, and I will show you how. Tonight, when the stars come out, you face north and hold the kamàl up at arm's length. Move it back and forth from your face until the lower edge of the frame rests on the northern horizon and the North Star sits just on top of the frame. Then tie a knot in the string so that when you hold the knot in your teeth the string is at such a length that you always hold the rectangle out at that same distance from your eye."

"Very well, Steward Arpad," I said obediently. "Then what?"

"As you travel eastward from here, the land is almost all flat, so you will always have a more or less level horizon. Each night, hold the kamàl out to the length of the string's knot and position the rectangle's lower bar on the northern horizon. If the North Star is still on the upper bar, you are due east of Suvediye here. If the star is perceptibly above the wooden bar, you have veered to the north of east. If the star is below that bar, you have wandered to the south."

"Cazza beta!" my uncle exclaimed in admiration.

"The kamàl can do even more," said the steward. "Put a tag marked Suvediye on that first knot you make, young Marco. Then, when you reach Baghdad, do the same positioning of the rectangle away from or closer to your face, so that it just fits between the northern horizon and the North Star, and tie another knot in the string at that distance, and mark the knot Baghdad. If you continue to do that, making and marking a new horizon-knot for each destination as you reach it, you will always know—as you go on eastward—whether you are north or south of your last stopping place, or any of your previous stopping places."

Deeming the kamàl a most useful addition to our equipment, we gladly paid for it—after Arpad and the merchant had done their long bargaining and set the price at a laughably few copper shahis. We went on to buy numerous other things we thought we would need on the road. And, thanks to the Ostikan's musk-cod replenishment of our budget, we even bought a few extra comforts and small luxuries that we might otherwise have done without.

Not until that afternoon did we see again any of the other participants in the previous night's banquet. That was when we all gathered in Suvediye's Church of San Gregorio for the nuptial mass. To judge from the haggard faces in the congregation, and an occasional subdued groan, most of the men were, like Arpad, still feeling the effects of their indulgence at that banquet. The bridegroom-to-be looked worst of all. I might have expected him to look satisfied or smug or guilty, but he merely looked more lumpish than usual. The bride-to-be was so heavily veiled that I could not see her expression, but her handsome mother and the various other female relations all exhibited extremely angry eyes glaring through the slits of their chador veils.

The wedding went off without incident, and our two frati, almost unrecognizable in the garish vestments of the Armeniyan Church, ably supported the Metropolitan in his conduct of the service. Afterwards, the wedding party and the whole congregation trooped from the church to the palace again for another banquet. This time, of course, the female guests—all of them except the female Muslims—also were allowed to partake. Again there were entertainments: the tumblers with their music, and conjurers and singers and dancers. While the evening was yet young, the newly married couple—he looking pained and she looking more woebegone than even a bride of that lout should have looked—had their hands joined by the Metropolitan and, after he said an Armeniyan prayer over them, trudged away upstairs to their bridal chamber, trailed by some halfhearted rude jesting and cheering from the guests.

This time there was enough noise in the hall—the musicians and dancers making most of it—that not even my inquisitive ear could catch any sounds identifiable as denoting the consummation of the marriage. But after a while there came a number of heavy thuds and something suspiciously like a distant scream, audible even above the music. And suddenly, there came Kagig again, his clothes disheveled, as if they had been once doffed and then thrown on again just anyhow. He came stamping angrily down the stairs and into the hall. He strode straight to the nearest jar of wine and, disdaining a cup, drained it to the vertical.

I was not the only one who watched his entrance. But I think the other guests, astounded at seeing a husband deserting his bride on their wedding night, at first tried to pretend he was not there among them. However, he began loudly to curse and swear—or that is what the Armeniyan words sounded like to me—and none could ignore his presence. The Circassians again began to growl, and the Ostikan Hampig cried anxiously something like, "What on earth is wrong, Kagig?"

"Wrong!" the young man exclaimed—or so I was told later; he was too distraught to speak anything but Armeniyan. "My new wife is revealed to be a harlot, that is what is wrong!"

Several people ejaculated protests and refutations, and the Circassians exclaimed what was probably "Liar!" and "How dare you?"

"Do you think I could not tell?" Kagig raged, as I was later told. "She wept all during the ceremony, behind her veil, for she knew what I was soon to discover! She wept when we went together to our chamber, for the moment of revelation was at hand! She wept as she and I undressed, for she was at the brink of her perfidy's disclosure! She wept even more loudly when I embraced her. And at the crucial moment, *she did not give the cry that must be cried!* So I investigated, and I could feel no maidenhead in her, and I saw no spot of blood upon the bed, and—"

One of Seosseres' male relatives interrupted him, shouting, "Oh, mongrel dog of an Armeniyan, do you not *remember*?"

"I remember that I was promised a virgin! Not your shouting nor her weeping can change the fact that she had been had by some man before me!"

"You accursed defamer! You nothing!" shouted the Circassians, frothing from the lips. "Our sister Seosseres has never been near a man before!" They were all trying to get at Kagig, but other guests were holding them back.

"Then she has made love to a phallocrypt!" Kagig shouted wildly. "A tent peg or a cucumber or one of those haramlik carvings! But that is the only kind of thing that will ever love her again!"

"Oh, putridity! Oh, spew!" the Circassians bellowed, struggling against the holders-back. "Have you harmed our sister?"

"I should have!" he grumbled. "I should have cut out her duplicious tongue and thrust it up between her legs. I should have boiled oil and poured it into the defiled hole. I should have nailed her alive to the palace gate."

At that, several of his own relatives seized him and shook him roughly, demanding, "Never mind that! What *did* you do?"

He fought loose of them, and petulantly shrugged his clothes back into an approximation of place. "I did only what a cuckolded husband is entitled to do, and I shall sue for annulment of this mock marriage!"

Not just the Circassians, but also the Arabs and Armeniyans shouted at him every kind of filthy name and revilement. There was so much commotion and tearing of hair and beards and rending of garments that it was several minutes before anyone could collect himself to speak coherently and tell the detestable husband what, in his drunkenness, he had done and then forgotten. It was his father, the Ostikan Hampig, who, weeping, told him:

"Oh, unfortunate Kagig, it was *you* who deflowered the maiden! Last night, on your wedding eve. You thought it would be clever and amusing to anticipate your husbandly rights. You went upstairs and forced her to bed, and you boasted of it afterward in this very room. It cost me dearly to persuade these her people not to slay you and anticipate her widowhood. The Princess is guiltless of any sin. It was you! You yourself!"

The cries in the hall redoubled:

"Pig!"

"Carrion!"

"Putrescence!"

And Kagig turned pale and his thick lips twitched, and for the first time in my knowledge of him he acted like a man. He showed genuine chagrin and he called for retribution as if he meant it, crying, "May the coals of Hell lie hot upon my head! I truly loved the beautiful Seosseres, and I have cut off her nose and her lips!"

. 6 .

M Y father plucked at my sleeve, and he and I and my uncle slipped discreetly through the roiling crowd and out of the dining hall.

"This is not bread to my teeth," said my father, frowning. "The Ostikan is in bad trouble, and any sovereign in trouble can make things trebly troublous for everyone around him."

I said, "Surely he cannot blame us for anything."

"When the head hurts, the whole body may suffer. I think it best that we get our horses loaded for a departure at first light. Let us go to our chamber and start packing."

There we were joined by the two Dominicans, who spoke loudly of their nausea and disgust at what Kagig had done, as if only they of us all had sensibilities to be offended.

"Ho ho," said Uncle Mafio without humor. "These are fellow Christians. You have yet to meet some real barbarians."

"That is what most disturbs us," said Brother Guglielmo. "We understand that such horrendous cruelties are common practices in farther Tartary."

My father remarked placidly that he had known of atrocities having been committed in the West, as well.

"Nevertheless," said Brother Nicolò, "we fear that we could not competently minister to such monsters as you would have us go among. We wish to be excused from our preaching mission."

"Would you now?" My uncle coughed and hawked and spat. "You wish to desert before we are even underway? Well, wish all you like. We have committed ourselves, and so have you."

Brother Guglielmo said frostily, "Perhaps Fra Nico did not put it strongly enough. We are not asking your permission, Messeri, we are telling you our decision. The conversion of such raw savages would require more more authority than we possess. And the Scriptures say: Turn away thy foot from evil. He that touches pitch shall be defiled with it. We decline to accompany you any farther."

"You could not have supposed that this would be an easy or enjoyable mission," said my father. "As the old saying has it, nobody goes to Heaven on a cushion."

"A cushion? Fichèvelo!" boomed my uncle, thereby suggesting a unique use for a cushion. "We have paid good money to buy horses for these two manfroditi!"

"Calling us filthy names is not likely to persuade us," said Brother Nicolò with hauteur. "In the manner of the Apostle Paolo, we do shun profane and vain babblings. The ship which brought us here is now preparing to sail on to Cyprus, and we will be aboard."

My uncle would have blustered on, probably using still more words that sacerdoti seldom get to hear, but my father gestured him to silence, saying:

"We wanted emissaries of the Church to prove to Kubilai Khan the worth and superiority of Christianity over other religions. These sheep in priestly clothing would hardly be the best examples to show him. Go to your ship, Brothers, and God go with you."

"And God and you go quickly!" snarled my uncle. When they had gathered up their belongings and left the chambers, he grumbled, "Those two merely seized upon our venture as an excuse to get away from the wicked women of Acre. Now they welcome this ugly incident here as an excuse to get away from us. We were bidden to bring a hundred priests, and we got two spineless old zitelle. Now we do not even have them."

"Well, it is less hurtful losing the two than a hundred," said my father. "The proverb says it is better to fall from a window than from the roof."

"I can bear losing those two," said Uncle Mafio. "But now what? Do we go on? Without any clerics for the Khan?"

"We promised him we would return," said my father. "And we have already been long away. If we do not go back, the Khan will lose faith in any Westerner's word. He may bar the gates against all traveling merchants, including us, and we are merchants before anything else. We have no priests to take, but we do have enough capital—our zafràn and Hampig's musk—that we can multiply it yonder into an estimable fortune. I say yes, let us go on. We shall simply tell Kubilai that our Church was in disarray during this papal interregnum. It is true enough."

"I concur," said Uncle Mafìo. "We go on. But what about this sprout?"

They both looked at me.

"He cannot return yet to Venice," my father mused. "And the English ship is sailing on to England. But he could change at Cyprus to some vessel headed for Constantinople. . . ."

I said quickly, "I will not sail even to Cyprus with those two poltroon Dominicans. I might be tempted to do them some injury, and that would be a sacrilege, and that would imperil my hope of Heaven."

Uncle Mafìo laughed and said, "But if we leave him here, and those Circassians start a blood feud with the Armeniyans, Marco may get to Heaven sooner than one might have hoped."

My father sighed and said to me, "You will come with us as far as Baghdad. There we will seek out a merchant train headed westward by way of Constantinople. You will go to visit your Uncle Marco. You can either stay with him until we return or, if you hear that a new Doge has succeeded Tiepolo, you can take ship for Venice."

I think only we, of all the people then inhabiting Hampig's palace, even tried to sleep that night. And we slept but little, for the whole building kept shaking to the tread of heavy feet and the shouting of angry voices. The Circassian guests had all put on clothes of the sky-blue color they affect for mourning, but evidently they were unmournfully storming about the building, threatening to wreak some vengeance for the mutilation of their Seosseres, and the Armeniyans were as loudly trying to placate them, or at least shout them down. The turmoil was still undiminished when we rode out of the palace stable yard, eastward into the dawn. I do not know what finally became of the people we left behind there: whether the two craven friars got safely away to Cyprus, or whether the wretched Bagratunians ever did suffer any retaliation from the Princess's people. I have never heard of any of them since that day. And on that day I truthfully was not worrying about them, but about staying in my saddle.

I had never in my life been transported by any conveyance other than water craft. So my father bridled and saddled my mare for me, and made me watch the procedure, telling me that I should have to do that job myself thereafter. Then he showed me how to mount, and the proper side of the animal from which to do it. I imitated his demonstration. I put my left foot into the stirrup, bounced briefly on my right foot, bounded high with enthusiasm, swung my right leg over, came down with a smack astride the hard seat, and gave a wild ululation of pain. Each of us was, as instructed by the Ostikan, wearing one of the leather cods of musk tied so that it hung under our crotch, and it was *that* that I thumped down on—and I thought for an agonized and writhing few minutes that it had cost me my own personal cod.

My father and uncle abruptly turned away, their shoulders shaking, to attend to their own mounts. I gradually recovered, and rearranged the musk pouch so it would not again endanger my vitals. Realizing that I was for the first time perched atop an animal, I rather wished that I had commenced with one not so tall, an ass perhaps, for I seemed to be teetering very high and insecurely far above the ground away down there. But I stayed in the saddle while my father and uncle also mounted, and each of them took the lead rope of one of the two extra horses, on which we had loaded all our packs and traveling gear. We rode out of the yard and toward the river, just as the day was breaking.

At the bank, we turned upriver toward the cleft in the hills where it came from inland. Very soon the troubled city of Suvediye was behind us, and then so were the ruins of earlier Suvediyes, and we were in the Orontes valley. It was a lovely warm morning, and the valley was lush with vegetation   green orchards of fruit trees separating extensive fields of spring-sown barley, now golden ripe for harvesting. Even that early in the day, the women workers were out and cutting the grain. We could see only a few of them, bent over their knives, but we knew that many were working there, from the multitudinous clicking noise. Because in Armeniya all the field hands are female, and because barley stalks are coarse and rough and injurious to their skin, the women wore wooden tubes on their fingers while they worked. In their numbers and their busyness, those fingers made a pervasive rattle that could have been mistaken for a fire crackling through the grain.

When we got beyond the cultivated lands, the valley was still verdant and colorful and full of life. There were the vast, spreading, dark-green plane trees, called hereabouts chinar trees, of welcome deep shade; and vividly green tiger-thistles; and the bountiful, silver-leaved, thorny trees called zizafun, from which a traveler can pluck the plumlike golden jujube fruit, good to eat whether fresh or dried. There were herds of goats munching the tiger-thistles; and on every goatherd's mud hut there was the scraggly rooftop nest of a stork; and there were whole nations of pigeons, in every flock as many of them as in all of Venice; and there were the golden eagles, almost always on the wing, because they are so clumsy and vulnerable when they light, having to run and struggle and beat their pinions for a long way before they can get aloft again.

In the East, an overland journey is called by the Farsi word karwan. We were on one of the principal east–west karwan routes, so at easy intervals of about every sixth farsakh—which is to say about every fifteen miles—there stood one of the stopping places called a karwansarai. Although we rode leisurely, not pushing ourselves or our horses, we could always depend on finding, about sundown, one of those places on the Orontes riverside.

I do not remember the first of them very well, for that night I was mainly occupied with my own discomfort. During our first day on the trail we had not made our horses move faster than a walking gait, and I had thought I was enjoying a comfortable ride, and I several times dismounted and mounted again without noticing that the ride was affecting me in the least. However, at the karwansarai, when I finally got down from the saddle for the night, I found that I was sore and suffering. My backside hurt as if it had been thrashed, the inner sides of my legs were chafed and burning, the thews inside my thighs were so stretched and aching that I felt as if I would forever after walk bowlegged. But the discomfort gradually ebbed, and in a few days I could ride my horse at a walk and at intermittent canters and gallops—or even at the trot, which is the roughest gait—all the day long, if necessary, without feeling any ill effect. That was a pleasing development, except that, no longer being intent on my own misery, I could take more notice of the miseries of putting up each night at a karwansarai.

It is a sort of combination inn for traveling people and stable or corral for their animals, though the accommodations for men and animals are not, in their comfort and cleanliness, easily distinguishable. No doubt that is because each such establishment must be of a size and readiness to receive and provide for a hundred times more people and beasts than we comprised. On several nights, indeed, we shared a karwansarai with a veritable throng of merchants, Arabs or Persians, traveling in karwan with countless horses, mules, asses, camels and dromedaries, all heavy laden, hungry, thirsty and sleepy. Nevertheless, I would as soon eat the dry fodder stocked for the animals as the meals set before the humans, and rather sleep in the stable straw than on one of the webbed-rope affairs called a bed.

The first two or three such places we came to had signboards identifying each as a "Christian rest house." They were run by Armeniyan monks, and were filthy and verminous and smelly, but the meals at least had the virtue of variety in their composition. Farther eastward, each karwansarai was run by Arabs and bore a signboard announcing, "Here, the true and pure religion." Those establishments were a trifle cleaner and better kept, but the Muslim meals were monotonously unvarying—mutton, rice, a bread the exact size and shape and texture and taste of a wicker chair seat, and weak, warm, much-watered sharbats for drink.

Only a few days out of Suvediye, we came to the riverside town of Antakya. When one is making a journey across country, any community appearing on the horizon ahead is a welcome sight, and even a beautiful one from a distance. But that beauty lent by distance is all too often dispelled by closer approach. Antakya was, like every other town in those regions, ugly and dirty and dull and swarming with beggars. But it had the one distinction of having given its name to the surrounding land: Antioch, as it is called in the Bible. In other times, when the region was a part of Alexander's empire, that land was called Syria. At the time of our passing through, it was an adjunct of the Kingdom of Jerusalem, or what still remained of that kingdom, which has since fallen entirely under the rule of the Mamluk Saracens. Anyway, I tried to look at Antakya and all of Antioch, or Syria, as Alexander might have regarded it, for I was mightily excited to be traveling one of the karwan trails that Alexander the Great once had trodden.

There at Antakya, the Orontes River bends due south. So we left it at that point and kept on bearing east, to another and much larger town, but also a dreary one—Haleb, called Aleppo by Westerners. We stayed the night in a karwansarai there and, because the landlord strongly advised that we would ride more comfortably if we changed our traveling costume, we bought from him Arab garments for each of us. When we left Aleppo, and for a long time afterward, we wore the full garb, from kaffiyah headcloth to the baggy leg coverings. That costume really is more comfortable for a man riding horseback than a tight Venetian tunic and hose. And from a distance at least, we looked like three of the nomad Arabs who call themselves the empty-landers, or bedawin.

Since most of the karwansarai keepers in those regions are Arabs, I of course learned many Arab words. But those landlords also spoke the universal trade language of Asia, which is Farsi, and we were getting nearer every day to the land of Persia, where Farsi is the native tongue. So, to help me more quickly pick up that language, my father and uncle did their best to converse always in what they knew of Farsi, instead of our own Venetian or the other jargon of Sabir French. And I did learn. In truth, I found Farsi considerably less difficult than some of the other tongues I had to contend with later on. Also, it must be supposed that young people acquire new languages more easily than do their elders, for it was not long before I was speaking Farsi far more fluently than either my father or my uncle did.

Somewhere east of Aleppo, we came to the next river, the Furat, which is better known as the Euphrates, named in the Book of Genesis as one of the four rivers of the Garden of Eden. I do not dispute the Bible, but I saw little that was gardenlike along the entire great length of the Furat. Where we joined it, to follow it downstream to the southeastward, that river does not, like the Orontes, flow through a pleasant valley; it merely wanders vagrantly through a flat country which is one immense pasture of grass for herds of goats and sheep. That is a useful enough function for a country, but it makes an extremely uninteresting terrain to travel across. One rejoices to see the occasional grove of olive trees or date palms, and one can see even a single isolated tree from a great distance before reaching it.

Over that level land a breeze blows almost constantly from the east, and, there being deserts far to the eastward, even that light breeze comes heavily freighted with a fine gray dust. Since only the far-apart trees and the infrequent travelers stick up above the low grass, it is on those things that the drifting dust collects. Our horses put their muzzles down and drooped their ears and closed their eyes and kept their direction by keeping the breeze on their left shoulders as they ambled along. We riders wrapped our abas tightly about our bodies and our kaffiyahs across our faces, and still we had dust making our eyelids gritty and our skins scratchy, clogging our nostrils and crunching between our teeth. I realized why my father and uncle and most other journeyers let their beards grow, for to shave each day in such conditions is a painful drudgery. But my own beard was yet too scanty to grow out handsomely. So I tried Uncle Mafio's depilatory mumum, and it worked well, and I continued to use the salve in preference to a razor.

But I think my most enduring recollection of that dust-laden Eden was the sight of a pigeon one day lighting in a tree there: when the bird touched the branch it puffed up a cloud of dust as if it had lighted in a flour barrel.

I will set down here two other things that came into my mind during that long ride down the River Furat:

One is that the world is large. That may seem no very original observation, but it had just then begun to dawn upon me with the awesomeness of revelation. I had heretofore lived in the constricted city of Venice, which in all of history has never sprawled beyond its seawalls and never can—so it gives us Venetians a sense of being enclosed in safety and snugness; in coziness, if you will. Although Venice fronts upon the Adriatic, the sea's horizon seems not impossibly far away. Even aboard ship, I saw that horizon staying fixed on every side; there was no sense of progression toward it or away from it. But traveling overland is different. The contour of the horizon changes constantly, and one is always moving toward or away from some landmark. In just the early weeks of our riding, we approached and arrived at and traversed and left again several different towns or villages, several contrasting kinds of countryside, several separate rivers. And always we realized that there was more beyond: more countries, more cities, more rivers. The world's land is *visibly* bigger than any empty ocean. It is vast and diverse, and always promising yet more vastness and diversity to come, and then producing them and promising more. The overland journeyer knows the same sensation that a man feels when he is stark naked—a fine sense of unfettered freedom, but also a sense of being vulnerable, unprotected and, compared to the world about him, very small.

The other thing I wish to say here is that maps lie. Even the best of maps, those in the Kitab of al-Idrisi, are liars, and they cannot help being liars. That is because everything shown on a map appears measurable by the same standards, and that is a delusion. For one instance, suppose your journey must take you over a mountain. The map can warn you of that mountain before you get to it, and even indicate more or less how high and wide and long it is, but the map cannot tell you what will be the conditions of terrain and weather when you get there, or what condition *you* will be in. A mountain that can be easily scaled on a good day in high summer by a young man in prime health may be a mountain considerably more forbidding in the cold and gales of winter, to a man enfeebled by age or illness and wearied by all the country he has already traversed. Because the limited representations of a map are thus deceptive, it may take a journeyer longer to travel the last little fingerbreadth of distance across a map than it took him to travel all the many handspans previous.

Of course, we had no such difficulties on that journey to Baghdad, since we had only to follow the River Furat downstream through the flat grassland. We did get out the Kitab at intervals, but just to see how its maps conformed to the actuality about us—and they did, with commendable accuracy—and sometimes my father or uncle would add markings to them to indicate useful landmarks which the maps omitted:

bends of the river, islands in it, things like that. And every few nights, though it was not then needed, I would get out the kamàl we had bought. Extending it toward the North Star at the length of the knot I had tied in the string at Suvediye, and laying the lower bar of the wooden rectangle on the flat horizon, I saw each time that the star was farther down below the upper bar of the frame. It indicated what we knew: that we were moving south of east.

Everywhere in that country, we were continually crossing the invisible borders of one little nation after another, the nations being likewise invisible except in name. It is the same in all the Levant lands: the larger expanses are labeled on maps as Armeniya, Antioch, the Holy Land and so on, but within those areas the local folk recognize innumerable smaller expanses, and give them names and call them nations and dignify their paltry chieftains with resounding titles. In my childhood Bible classes, I had heard of such Levantine kingdoms as Samaria and Tyre and Israel, and I had envisioned them as mighty lands of awesome extent, and their kings Ahab and Hiram and Saul as monarchs over vast populations. And now I was learning, from the natives we met along our way, that I was traversing such self-proclaimed nations as Nabaj and Bishri and Khubbaz, ruled by various kings and sultans and atabegs and shcikhs.

But any of those nations could be crossed in a ride of a day or two, and they were drab and featureless and poor and full of beggars and otherwise scantily populated, and the one "king" we encountered there was merely the oldest goatherd in a bedawi tribe of goatherding Arabs. Not a single one of all those crammed together fragment kingdoms and sheikhdoms in that part of the world is larger than the Republic of Venice. And Venice, though thriving and important, occupies but a handful of islands and a meager portion of the Adriatic coast. I gradually came to realize that all those biblical kings, too—even the great ones like Solomon and David—had ruled domains that in the Western world would be called only confini or counties or parishes. The great migrations recorded in the Bible must really have been negligible wanderings like those of the modern goatherding tribes I had seen. The great wars of which the Bible tells must really have been trifling skirmishes between puny armies to settle insignificant disputes between those petty kings. It made me wonder why the Lord God had bothered, in those olden times, to send fires and tempests and prophets and plagues to influence the destinies of such fence-corner nations.

· 7 ·

O N two nights in that country, we deliberately skirted the nearest karwansarai and camped outdoors on our own. It was something we would later have to do, when we got into even less populous regions, so my father and uncle thought I should start having the experience in an easy terrain and clement weather. Also, all three of us were by then getting extremely tired of filth and mutton. So, on each of those nights, we made pallets of our blankets, with our saddles for pillows, and laid a fire for cooking, and turned our horses free to graze, hobbling their front legs together so they could not wander far.

I had already learned from my much-traveled father and uncle some of the tricks of traveling. For example, they had taught me always to carry my bedding in one saddle pannier and my clothing in another, and always to keep the two apart. Since a traveler has to use his own blankets at every karwansarai, they inevitably get full of fleas and lice and bedbugs. Those vermin are a torment even when one sleeps the usual deep sleep of exhaustion, but they would be intolerable when one is dressed and awake and about. So, getting naked out of bed each morning, I would pick myself clean of the accumulated bugs, and then, having carefully kept my clothing apart from the bedding, I could put on either used or clean garments without their having been contaminated. When we did not stay at a karwansarai, but made our own camp, I learned other things. I remember, the first night we camped, I started to tilt one of the water bags for a good long drink, but my father stopped me.

"Why?" I said. "We have one of the blessed rivers of Eden with which to refill it."

"Better get used to thirst when it is not necessary," he said, "for you will have to when it is. Just wait and I will show you something."

He built a fire of branches hacked with his belt knife from a convenient zizafun tree, the thorny wood of which burns hot and quickly, and he let it burn until the wood was all charcoal but not yet ashes. Then he scraped most of the charcoal to one side, and laid new branches on what was left, to make up the fire again. He let the removed charcoal cool, then crushed it to powder and heaped that onto a cloth and put the cloth like a sieve over the mouth of one of the pottery bowls we had brought. He handed me another bowl and bade me go and fill it from the river.

"Taste that Eden water," he said, when I fetched it.

I did and said, "Muddy. Some insects. But not bad water."

"Watch. I will make it better." He poured it slowly through the charcoal and cloth into the other bowl.

When it had finished its slow trickling, I tasted it again from that bowl. "Yes. Clear and good. It even tastes cooler."

"Remember that trick," he said. "Many times your only source of water will be putrid or vile with salts or even suspect of poison. That trick will render it potable at least, and harmless, if not delicious. However, in the deserts where the water is worst, there is usually no wood to burn. Therefore, try always to carry a supply of charcoal with you. It can be used over and over again before it gets saturated and ineffectual."

The reason we made our outdoor camp only twice during the journey down the Furat was that, while my father could strain insects and impurities out of the water, he could not remove the birds from the air, and I have mentioned that that country abounds in golden eagles.

On that day of which I speak, my uncle had, by good luck, come upon a large hare in the grass, and it stood immobile and trembling in that moment of surprise, and he whipped out and threw his belt knife, and killed the creature. It was on that account—having our own provender for a non-mutton meal—that we decided to make the first camp. But when Uncle Mafìo skewered the skinned hare on a zizafun stick and hung it over the fire, and it began to sizzle and its aroma rose with the smoke into the air, we got as much of a surprise as the hare had got.

There came a loud, rustling, swooshing noise from out of the night sky above us. Before we could even look up, a blur of brown flashed in an arc down between us, through the firelight and upward into the darkness again. At the same instant, there was a sound like *klop!* and the fire flew all apart in a spray of sparks and ashes, and the hare was gone, complete with its stick, and we heard a triumphant barking yell, "*Kya!*"

"Malevolenza!" exclaimed my uncle, picking up a large feather from the remains of the fire. "A damned thieving eagle! Acrimonia!" And that night we had to make our meal on some hard salt pork from our packs.

The same thing, or very near it, happened the second time we stayed outdoors. That camping was occasioned by our having bought, from a passing family of bedawin Arabs, a haunch of fresh-killed camel calf. When we put that on the fire, and the eagles espied it, another of them came in a rush. The moment my uncle heard the first rustle of its pinions in the air, he made a dive to throw himself protectively over the cooking meat. That saved our meal for us, but nearly lost us Uncle Mafìo.

A golden eagle has wings that spread wider than a man's outstretched arms, and it weighs about as much as a fair-sized dog, so when it comes plummeting down—when it stoops, as the hawkers say—it is a formidable projectile. That one hit the back of my uncle's head, fortunately only with its wing and not with its talons, but that was a blow heavy enough to knock him sprawling across the fire. My father and I dragged him out, and beat the sparks out of his smoldering aba, and he had to shake his head for a time to get his senses back, and then he cursed magnificently, until he went into a fit of coughing. Meanwhile, I stood over the spitted meat, ostentatiously swinging a heavy branch, and the eagles stayed away, so we did manage to cook and eat the meal. But we decided that, as long as we were in eagle country, we would stifle our revulsions and spend each night in a karwansarai from then on.

"You are wise to do so," said the next night's landlord to us, as we ate yet another nasty meal of mutton and rice. We were the only guests that night, so he conversed while he swept the day's collected dust out the door. His name was Hasan Badr-al-Din, which did not suit him at all, for it means Beauty of Faith's Moon. He was wizened and gnarled, like an old olive tree. He had a face as leathery and wrinkled as a cobbler's apron, and a wispy beard like a nimbus of wrinkles that could not find room on his face. He went on, "It is not good to be out of doors and unprotected at night in the lands of the Mulahidat, the Misguided Ones."

"What are the Misguided Ones?" I asked, sipping a sharbat so bitter that it must have been made of green fruit.

Beauty of Faith's Moon was now going about the room, sprinkling water to lay the remaining dust. "You perhaps have heard them called hashishiyin. The killers who kill for the Old Man of the Mountain."

"What mountain?" growled my uncle. "This land is flatter than a halycon sea."

"He has always been called that—the Sheikh ul-Jibal—though no one knows really where he lives. Whether his castle is really on a mountain or not."

"He does not live," said my father. "That old nuisance was slain by the Ilkhan Hulagu when the Mongols came this way fifteen years ago."

"True," said the aged Beauty. "Yet not true. That was the Old Man Rokn-ed-Din Kurshah. But there is always another Old Man, you know."

"I did not know."

"Oh, yes, indeed. And an Old Man still commands the Mulahidat, though some of the Misguided must be old men themselves by now. He hires them out to the faithful who have need of their services. I hear that the Mamluks of Egypt paid high to have a hashishi slay that English Prince who leads the Christian Crusaders."

"Then they wasted their money," said Uncle Mafìo. "The Englishman slew the sassìn."

Beauty shrugged and said, "Another will try, and another, until it is done. The Old Man will command, and they will obey."

"Why?" I asked, and swallowed a wad of rice that tasted of taint. "Why should any man risk his own life to kill at the behest of another man?"

"Ah. To understand that, young Sheikh, you must know something of the Holy Quran." He came and sat down at our cloth, as if pleased to explain. "In that Book, the Prophet (blessing and peace be upon him) makes a promise to the men of the Faith. He promises to every man that, if he is unswervingly devout, then once in his life he will enjoy one miraculous night, the Night of the Possible, in which he will be granted his every desire." The old man arranged his wrinkles in a smile, a smile that was half happy and half melancholy. "A night replete with ease and luxury, with marvelous food and drink and banj, with beautiful and compliant haura women and boys, with renewed youth and virility for the zina enjoyment of them. Thus, every man who believes will live his life in fierce devoutness, and hope for that Night of the Possible."

He stopped, and seemed to lose himself in contemplation. After a moment, Uncle Mafìo said, "It is an appealing dream."

Beauty said distantly, "Dreams are the painted pictures in the book of sleep."

Again we waited, then I said, "But I do not see what that has to do with—"

"The Old Man of the Mountain," he said, as if coming abruptly awake. "The Old Man *gives* that Night of the Possible. Then he holds out promise of still other such nights."

My father, my uncle and I exchanged glances of amusement.

"Do not doubt it!" the landlord said testily. "The Old Man, or one of his Mulahidat recruiters, will find a qualified man—a strong and bold man—and will slip a potent bit of banj into his food or drink. When the man swoons to sleep, he is spirited away to the Castle ul-Jibal. He wakes to find himself in the most lovely garden imaginable, surrounded by comely lads and ladies. Those haura feed him rich viands and more of the hashish and even forbidden wines. They sing and dance enchantingly, and reveal their nippled breasts, their smooth bellies, their inviting bottoms. They seduce him to such raptures of lovemaking that at last he swoons again. And again he is spirited away—back to his former place and life, which is humdrum at best, and more probably dismal. Like the life of a karwansarai keeper."

My father yawned and said, "I begin to comprehend. As the saying goes, he has been given cake and a kick."

"Yes. He has now partaken of the Night of the Possible, and he yearns to do so again. He wishes and begs and prays for that, and the recruiters come and tantalize him until he promises to do *anything*. He is set a task—to slay some enemy of the Faith, to steal or rob for the enrichment of the Old Man's coffers, to waylay infidels intruding on the lands of the Mulahidat. If he successfully performs that task, he is rewarded with another Night of the Possible. And after each subsequent deed of devotion, another night and another."

"Each of which," said my skeptical uncle, "is really nothing but a hashish dream. Misguided, indeed."

"Oh, unbeliever!" Beauty chided him. "Tell me, by your beard, can *you* distinguish between the memory of a delightful dream and the memory of a delightful occurrence? Each exists only in your memory. Telling of them to another, how could you prove which happened when you were awake and which when you were asleep?"

Uncle Mafio said affably, "I will let you know tomorrow, for I am sleepy now." He stood up, with a massive stretch and a gaping yawn.

It was rather earlier in the night than we were accustomed to go to bed, but I and my father also were yawning, so we all followed Beauty of Faith's Moon as he led us down a long hall and—because we were the only guests—allotted us each a separate room, and quite clean, with clean straw on the floor. "Rooms deliberately well apart from each other," he said, "so that your snores will not disturb each other, and your dreams will not get intertangled."

Nevertheless, my own dream was tangled enough. I slept and dreamed that I awoke from my sleep, to find myself, like a recruit of the Misguided Ones, in a dreamlike garden, for it was full of flowers I had never seen when awake. Among the sunlit flower beds danced dancers so dreamily beautiful that one could not say, or care, whether they were girls or boys. In a dreamy languor, I joined the dance and found, as often happens in dreams, that my every step and prance and movement was dreamily slow, as if the air were sesame oil.

That thought was so repugnant—even in my dream I remembered my experience with sesame oil—that the sunlit garden instantly became a bosky palace corridor, down which I was dancing in pursuit of a dancing girl whose face was the face of the Lady Ilaria. But when she pirouetted into a room and I followed through the only door and caught

her there, her face got old and warty and sprouted a red-gray beard like
a fungus. She said, "Salamelèch" in a man's deep voice, and I was not in
a palace chamber, or even a bedroom of a karwansarai, but in the dark,
cramped cell of the Venice Vulcano. Old Mordecai Cartafilo said, "Misguided One, will you never learn the bloodthirstiness of beauty?" and
gave me a square white cracker to eat.

Its dryness was choking and its taste was nauseous. I retched so
convulsively that I woke myself up—really awoke this time, in the
karwansarai room, to find that I was not dreaming the nausea. Evidently
our meal's mutton or something *had* been tainted, for I was about to be
violently sick. I scrambled out of my blankets and ran naked and barefoot down the midnight hall to the little back room with the hole in the
ground. I hung my head over it, too wretched to recoil from the stink or
to fear that a demon jinni might reach up out of the depths and snatch at
me. As quietly as I could, I vomited up a vile green mess and, after
wiping the tears from my eyes and getting my breath back, I padded
quietly toward my room again. The hall took me past the door of the
chamber my uncle had been given, and I heard a muttering behind it.

Giddy anyway, I leaned against the wall there and gave ear to the
noise. It was partly my uncle's snoring and partly a sibilant low speaking
of words. I wondered how he could snore and talk at the same time, so
I listened more intently. The words were Farsi, so I could not make out
all of them. But when the voice, sounding astonished, spoke louder, I
clearly heard:

"Garlic? The infidels pretend to be merchants, but they carry only
worthless *garlic?*"

I touched the door of the room, and it was unlatched. It swung
easily and silently open. Inside, there was a small light moving, and
when I peered I could see that it was a wick lamp in the hand of Beauty
of Faith's Moon, and he was bending over my uncle's saddle panniers,
piled in a corner of the room. The landlord was obviously seeking to
steal from us, and he had opened the packs and found the precious
culms of zafràn and had mistaken them for garlic.

I was more amused than angry, and I held my tongue, so as to see
what he would do next. Still muttering, telling himself that the unbeliever probably had taken his purse and true valuables to bed with
him, the old man sidled over beside the bed and, with his free hand,
began cautiously groping about beneath Uncle Mafìo's blankets. He
encountered something, for he gave a start, and again spoke aloud in
astonishment:

"By the ninety-nine attributes of Allah, but this infidel is hung like
a horse!"

Sick though I still felt, I very nearly giggled at that, and my uncle
smiled in his sleep as if he enjoyed the fondling.

"Not only an untrimmed long zab," the thief continued to marvel,
"but also—praise Allah in His munificence even to the unworthy—*two*
sacks of balls!"

I might really have giggled then, but in the next moment the situation ceased to be amusing. I saw in the lamplight the glint of metal, as

old Beauty drew a knife from his robes and lifted it. I did not know whether he intended to trim my uncle's zab or to amputate his supernumerary scrotum or to cut his throat, and I did not wait to find out. I stepped forward and swung my fist and hit the thief hard in the back of his neck. I might have expected the blow to incapacitate such a fragile old specimen, but he was not so delicate as he looked. He fell sideways, but rolled like an acrobat and came up from the floor slashing the blade at me. It was more by happenstance than by deftness that I caught his wrist. I twisted it, and wrenched at his hand, and found the knife in my own hand, and used it. At that, he did fall down and stay down, groaning and burbling.

The scuffle had been brief, but not silent, yet my uncle had slept through it, and he still slept, still smiling in his sleep. Appalled by what I had just done, as well as by what had almost been done, I felt very alone in the room and badly needed a supporting ally. Though my hands were trembling, I shook Uncle Mafìo, and had to shake him violently to bring him to consciousness. I realized now that the more than ordinarily nasty evening meal had been heavily laced with banj. We would all three have been dead but for the dream that had wakened me to the danger and made me disgorge the drug.

My uncle finally, unwillingly, began to come awake, smiling and murmuring, "The flowers . . . the dancers . . . the fingers and lips playing on my flute . . ." Then he blinked and exclaimed, "Dìo me varda! Marco, that was not *you*?"

"No, Zio Mafìo," I said, in my agitation speaking Venetian. "You were in peril. We are still in peril. Please wake up!"

"Adrìo de vu!" he said crossly. "Why have you snatched me from that wondrous garden?"

"I believe it was the garden of the hashishiyin. And I have just stabbed a Misguided One."

"Our host!" cried my uncle, sitting up and seeing the crumpled form on the floor. "Oh, scagaròn, what have you done? Are you playing bravo again?"

"No, Zio, look. That is his own knife sticking in him. He was about to kill you for your cod of musk." As I related the circumstances, I began to weep.

Uncle Mafìo bent over the old man and examined him, growling, "Right in the belly. Not dead, but dying." Then he turned to me and said kindly, "There, there, boy. Stop slobbering. Go and wake your father."

Beauty of Faith's Moon was nothing to weep over, alive or dead or dying. But he was the first man I ever slew with my own hand, and the killing of another human being is no trivial milestone in a man's career. As I went to fetch my father out of the hashish garden, I was thinking how more than ever I was glad that, back in Venice, another hand had thrust the sword into my guiltless earlier prey. For I had just learned one thing about killing a man, or at least about killing him with a blade. It slides into the victim's belly easily enough, almost eagerly, almost of its own accord. But there it is instantly seized by the violated muscles, held as tightly as another tool of mine had once been clasped in the virgin flesh of the girl Doris. I had pushed the knife into old Beauty with no effort whatever, but I could not withdraw it again when I had done so. And in that instant I had known a sickening realization: that a deed so ugly and so easily done cannot thereafter be undone. It made killing seem rather less gallant and dashing and bravìsimo than I had imagined it to be.

When I had, with difficulty, roused my father, I took him to the scene of the crime. Uncle Mafìo had laid the landlord on his own pallet of blankets, despite the flow of blood, and had composed Beauty's limbs for death, and the two of them were conversing, it seemed companionably. The old man was the only one of us who had any clothes on. He looked up at me, his murderer, and he must have seen the traces of tears on my face, for he said:

"Do not feel bad, young infidel. You have slain the most Misguided One of all. I have done a terrible wrong. The Prophet (peace and blessing be upon him) enjoins us to treat a guest with the most reverent care and respect. Though he be the lowliest darwish, or even an unbeliever, and though there be only one crumb in the house, and though the host's family and children go hungry, the guest must be given that crumb. Be he a sworn enemy, he must be accorded every hospitality and safeguard while he is under one's roof. My disobedience to that holy law would have deprived me of my Night of the Possible, even did I live. In my avarice, I acted hastily, and I have sinned, and for that sin I beg forgiveness."

I tried to say that I gave the forgiveness, but I choked on a sob, and in the next moment I was glad of that, for he continued:

"I could as easily have drugged your breakfast meal in the morning, and let you get some way upon the road before you fell. Then I could have robbed and murdered you under the open sky instead of under my roof, and it would have been a deed of virtue, and pleasing to Allah. But I did not. Though in all my lifetime before now I have lived devoutly in the Faith and have slain many other infidels to the greater glory of Islam, this one impiety will cost me my eternity in the Paradise of Djennet, with its haura beauties and perpetual happiness and unfettered indulgence. And for that loss, I grieve sincerely. I should have killed you in fitter fashion."

Well, those words at any rate stopped my weeping. We all stared stonily at the landlord as again he went on:

"But you have yourselves a chance at virtue. When I am dead, do me the kindness of wrapping me in a winding sheet. Take me to the main room and lay me in the middle of it, in the prescribed position. Wind my tulband over my face, and place me so my feet are turned to the south, toward the Holy Kaaba in Mecca."

My father and uncle looked at each other, and they shrugged, but we were all glad they made no promise, for the old fiend now spoke his last words:

"Having done that, vile dogs, you will die virtuous, when my brothers of the Mulahidat come and find me here dead with a knife wound in

my gut, and they follow the tracks of your horses and hunt you down
and do to you what I failed to do. Salaam aleikum."

His voice had not at all weakened, but, after perversely calling
peace upon us, Beauty of Faith's Moon closed his eyes and died. And,
that being the first deathbed I had ever stood close to, I first learned then
that most deaths are as ugly as most killings. For in dying, Beauty
unbeautifully and copiously evacuated both his bladder and his bowels,
befouling his garments and the blankets and filling the room with a
ghastly stench.

A disgusting indignity is not what any person would wish to be last
remembered for. But I have since attended many dyings and—except
in the rare case when there has been opportunity of a purge aforetime—
that is how all human beings make their farewell to life; even the strongest and bravest of men, the fairest and purest of women, whether they
die a violent death or go serenely in their sleep.

We stepped outside the room to breathe clean air, and my father
sighed. "Well. Now what?"

"First of all," said my uncle, untying the thongs of his musk cod, "let
us relieve ourselves of these uncomfortable danglers. It is clear that they
will be as safe inside our packs—or no less safe—and anyway I would
rather lose the musk than again imperil my own dear cod."

My father muttered, "Worry about balls when we may be about to
lose our heads?"

I said, "I am sorry, Father, Uncle. If we are to be hunted by the
surviving Misguided Ones, then I did wrong to kill that one."

"Nonsense," said my father. "Had you not awakened and acted with
celerity, we would not even have lived to be hunted."

"It is true that you are impetuous, Marco," said Uncle Mafìo. "But if
a man stopped to consider all the consequences of his every action before
he acted, he would be a very old man before he ever did any damned
thing at all. Nico, I think that we might keep this fortunately impetuous
young man as our companion. Let him not be tucked safe away in
Constantinople or Venice, but let him come with us clear to Kithai.
However, you are his father. It is for you to say."

"I am inclined to concur, Mafìo," said my father. And to me, "If you
wish to come along, Marco . . ." I grinned broadly at him. "Then you
come. You deserve to come. You did well this night."

"Perhaps better than well," said my uncle thoughtfully. "That bricòn
vechio called himself the most Misguided One of all. Is it not possible he
meant also the chief one of them all? The latest and reigning Sheikh ul-
Jibal? An old man he certainly was."

"The Old Man of the Mountain?" I exclaimed. "I slew *him*?"

"We cannot know," said my father. "Not unless the other hashishiyin
tell us when they catch up to us. I am not that eager to know."

"They must not catch us," said Uncle Mafìo. "We have already been
remiss, coming this far into alien country with no weapons but our work
knives."

My father said, "They will not catch us if they have no reason to chase after us. We have only to remove the reason. Let the next comers find the karwansarai deserted. Let them presume that the landlord is afield on an errand—killing a sheep for the larder, perhaps. It could be days before those next guests come, and days more before they begin to wonder where the landlord is. By the time any of the Misguided Ones get involved in the search for him, and by the time they give up looking for him and start to suspect foul play, we shall be long gone and far away and beyond their tracing."

"Take the old Beauty with us?" asked my uncle.

"And risk an embarrassing encounter before we have gone far at all?" My father shook his head. "Nor can we just drop him down the well here, or hide him or bury him. Any arriving guest will go first to the water. And any Arab has a nose like a staghound, to sniff out a hiding place or fresh-turned earth."

"Not on land, not in water," said my uncle. "There is only one alternative. I had better do it before I put any clothes on."

"Yes," said my father, and he turned to me. "Marco, go through this whole establishment and search out some blankets to replace those of your uncle. While you are at it, see if you can find any sort of weapons we can carry when we go."

The command was obviously given just to get me out of the way while they did what they did next. And it took me quite a while to comply, for the karwansarai was old, and must have had a long succession of owners, each of whom had built and added on new portions. The main building was a warren of hallways and rooms and closets and nooks, and there were also stables and sheds and sheep pens and other outbuildings. But the old man, evidently having felt secure in his drugs and deceits, had not taken much trouble to hide his possessions. To judge from the armory of weapons and provisions, he *had* been, if not the veritable Old Man, at least a main supplier of the Mulahidat.

I first selected the best two woolen blankets from the considerable stock of traveling gear. Then I searched among the weapons and, though I could not find any straight swords of the type we Venetians were accustomed to, I picked out the shiniest and sharpest of the local sort. This was a broad and curved blade—more of a saber, since it was sharp only on the outcurved edge—called the shimshir, which means "silent lion." I took three of them, one for each of us, and belts with loops from which to hang them. I could have further enriched our purses, for Beauty had secreted a small fortune in the form of bags of dried banj, bricks of compacted banj, and flagons of oil of banj. But I left all that where it was.

The dawn was breaking outdoors when I brought my acquisitions to the main room, where we had dined the night before. My father was preparing a breakfast meal at the brazier, and being most carefully selective of the ingredients. Just as I entered the room, I heard a series of noises from the yard outside: a long, rustling whistle, a loud *klop!* and a screeching yell of *kya!* Then my uncle came in from that yard, still naked, his skin spattered with blood spots, his beard smelling of smoke, and he saying with satisfaction:

"That was the last of the old devil, and it went as he wished. I have burned his garments and the blankets, and dispersed the ashes. We can depart as soon as we have dressed and eaten."

I realized, of course, that Beauty of Faith's Moon had been given no laying-out, but an extremely un-Muslim obsequy, and that made me curious as to what Uncle Mafìo meant by "went as he wished." I asked him, and he chuckled and said:

"The last of him went flying southward. Toward Mecca."

BAGHDAD

. 1 .

WE kept on downstream along the Furat, still southeastward, now traversing a particularly unappealing stretch of country where the river had cut its channel through solid basalt rock—a land bleak and black and barren even of grass, pigeons and eagles—but we were not pursued by the Misguided Ones or anyone else. And gradually, as if in celebration of our deliverance from danger, the countryside became more pleasant and hospitable. The terrain began perceptibly to rise up on either side of the river, until it was flowing through a wide and verdant valley. There were orchards and forests, pastures and farms, flowers and fruits. But the orchards were as shaggy and untended as the native forests, the farms as overgrown and weedy as the fields of wild flowers. The land's owners had all gone away, and the only people we met in that valley were nomad families of bedawin shepherds, the landless and rootless roamers, roaming in that valley as they roamed in the grasslands. There were nowhere any settled folk, nobody working to keep the once domesticated land from reverting to wilderness.

"It is the doing of the Mongols," said my father. "When the Ilkhan Hulagu—that is to say, the Lesser Khan Hulagu, brother to our friend

Kubilai—when he swept through this land and overthrew the Persian Empire, most of the Persians fled or fell before him, and the survivors have not yet returned to rework their lands. But the nomad Arabs and Kurdi are like the grass on which they live and in search of which they wander. The bedawin bend uncaringly before any wind that blows— whether it be a gentle breeze or the fierce simùm—but they rebound as does the grass. To the nomads it matters not who rules the land, and it never will matter to them until the end of time, as long as the land itself remains."

I turned in my saddle, looking at the land all about us, the richest, most fertile, most promising land we had yet seen in our journey, and I asked, "Who does rule Persia now?"

"When Hulagu died, his son Abagha succeeded as Ilkhan, and he has established a new capital in the northern city of Maragheh instead of in Baghdad. Although the Persian Empire is now a part of the Mongol Khanate, it is still divided into Shahnates, as before, for convenience of administration. But each Shah is subordinate to the Ilkhan Abagha, just as Abagha is subordinate to the Khakhan Kubilai."

I was impressed. I knew we were yet many months of hard travel distant from the court city of that Khakhan Kubilai. But already, here in the western reaches of Persia, *already* we were within the borders of the domain of that far distant Khan. In school, I had bent my most admiring and enthusiastic study on *The Book of Alexander*, so I knew that Persia was once a part of that conqueror's empire, and his empire was so extensive as to earn him the sobriquet of "the Great." But the lands won and held by that Macedonian comprised a mere fragment of the world, compared to the immensities conquered by Chinghiz Khan, and further enlarged by his conqueror sons, and still further enlarged by his conqueror grandsons, into the unimaginably immense Mongol Empire over which the grandson Kubilai now reigned as Khan of All Khans.

I believe that not the ancient Pharaones nor the ambitious Alexander nor the avaricious Caesars could have dreamed that so much world existed, so they could hardly have dreamed of acquiring it. As for all the later Western rulers, their ambitions and acquisitions have been even more paltry. Alongside the Mongol Empire, the entire continent called Europe seems merely a small and crowded peninsula, and all its nations, like those of the Levant, only so many peevishly self-important little provinces. From the eminence on which the Khakhan sits enthroned, my native Republic of Venice, proud of its glory and grandeur, must appear as trivial as the Suvediye cranny of the Ostikan Hampig. If the history keepers will continue to dignify Alexander as the Great, surely they ought to acknowledge Kubilai as the immeasurably Greater. That is not for me to say. But what I can say is that, on my entrance into Persia, I was thrilled to realize that I, mere Marco Polo, was setting foot in the most far-flung empire ever ruled by one man in all the years in which the world of men has existed.

"When we get to Baghdad," my father went on, "we will show to the current Shah, whoever he may be, the letter we carry from Kubilai. And the Shah will have to make us welcome, as accredited ambassadors of his overlord."

So we proceeded on down the Furat, watching the valley get ever more marked with the traces of civilization, for hereabouts it was criss-crossed by many irrigation canals branching off the river. However, the towering wooden wheels in the canals were not being turned by men or animals or any other agency; they stood still, the clay jugs around their rims not lifting and pouring any water. In the widest and most verdant part of that valley, the Furat makes its nearest approach to the other great south-running river of that country, the Dijlah, sometimes called Tigris, which is supposedly one of the other rivers of the Garden of Eden. If that is so, then the land between the two rivers would pre sumably be the site of that biblical garden. And if *that* is so, then the garden, when we saw it, was as empty of resident men and women as it was immediately after the expulsion of Adam and Eve.

In that vicinity, we turned our horses eastward from the Furat and rode the intervening ten farsakhs to the Dijlah, and crossed that river on the bridge there—made of empty boat hulls supporting a plank roadway —to Baghdad on the eastern bank.

The city's population, like that of the surrounding countryside, had been grievously diminished during Hulagu's siege and capture of it. But in the fifteen or so ensuing years, much of its populace had returned and repaired what damage it had suffered. City merchants, it seems, are more resilient than country farmers. Like the primitive bedawin, civ-ilized tradesmen seem to recover quickly from the prostrations of dis-aster. In the case of Baghdad, that may have been because so many of its merchants were not passive and fatalistic Muslims, but irrepressibly energetic Jews and Christians—some of them having come originally from Venice and even more of them from Genoa.

Or perhaps Baghdad recovered because it is such a *necessary* city, at an important crossroads of trade. Besides being a western terminus of the Silk Road which comes overland, it is a northern terminus of the sea route from the Indies. The city is not itself on the seaside, of course, but its Dijlah River bears a heavy traffic of large river boats, sailing down-stream with the current or being poled upriver against it, going to and coming from Basra in the south, on the Persian Gulf, where the seagoing Arab ships make landfall. Anyway, whatever the beneficent reason, Baghdad was, when we arrived there, what it had been before the Mongols came: a rich and vital and busy trading center.

It was as beautiful as it was busy. Of the Eastern cities I had seen so far, Baghdad was the most reminiscent of my native Venice. Its Dijlah waterfront was as thronged and tumultuous and littered and odorous as the Riva of Venice, though the vessels to be seen here—all of them built and manned by Arabs—were nowise comparable to ours. They were alarmingly shoddy craft to be entrusted to the water, built entirely with-out pegs or nails or iron fastenings of any fashion, their hull planking instead *stitched* together by ropes of some coarse fiber. Their seams and interstices were not plugged watertight with pitch, but with a sort of lard

made from fish oil. Even the biggest of those boats had only a single
steering oar, and it was not very manipulable since it was firmly hinged
at mid-stern. Another deplorable thing about those Arab boats was the
unfastidious way their cargoes were stored. After filling the hold with a
load of, as it may be, all foodstuffs—dates and fruits and grains and
such—the Arab boatmen might then crowd the deck above the hold with
a herd of livestock. That frequently consisted of fine Arabian horses, and
they are beauteous beasts, but they evacuate themselves as often and as
hugely as any other horses, and their droppings would dribble and seep
between the planks onto the cargo of edibles belowdecks.

Baghdad is not, like Venice, interlaced with canals, but its streets
are constantly sprinkled with water to lay the dust, so they have a humid
fragrance reminiscent to me of canals. And the city has a great many
open squares equivalent to Venice's piazze. Some are bazàr market-
places, but most are public gardens, for the Persians are passionately
fond of gardens. (I learned there that the Farsi word meaning garden,
pairi-daeza, became our Bible's word Paradise.) Those public gardens
have benches for passersby to rest on, and streamlets running through,
and many birds in residence, and trees and shrubs and perfumed plants
and luminous flowers—roses especially, for the Persians are passionately
fond of roses. (They call any and every flower a gul, though that Farsi
word means specifically a rose.) Likewise, the palaces of noble families
and the larger houses of rich merchant families are built around private
gardens as big as the public ones, and as full of roses and birds, and as
nearly like earthly Paradises.

I suppose I had got it into my head that the words Muslim and Arab
were interchangeable, and therefore that any Muslim community must
be indistinguishable—in matters of filth and vermin and beggars and
stench—from the Arab cities, towns and villages I had passed through. I
was agreeably surprised to find that the Persians, although their religion
is Islam, are more inclined to keep their buildings and streets and garments and persons clean. That, with the abundance of flowers everywhere, and a comparative fewness of beggars, made Baghdad a most
pleasant and even nice-smelling city—except, of necessity, around the
waterfront and the bazàr markets.

Although much of Baghdad's architecture was of course peculiarly
Eastern, even that was not entirely exotic to my Western eyes. I saw a
great deal of that lacy filigree "arabesco" stonework which Venice has
also adopted for some of its building fronts. Baghdad being still a Muslim city, even after its absorption into the Khanate—for the Mongols,
unlike most conquerors, do not anywhere impose any change of religion
—it was studded with those great Muslim masjid temples of worship.
But their immense domes were not much different from the domes of
San Marco and the other churches of Venice. Their slender manarat
towers were not too dissimilar to the campanili of Venice, only being
generally round instead of square in cross-section, and having little bal-
conies at their tops, from which the muedhdhin beadles shouted at intervals to announce the hours of prayer.

Those muedhdhin in Baghdad, incidentally, were all blind men. I inquired whether that was a necessary qualification for the post, something demanded by Islam, and was told it was not. Blind men were engaged as the prayer-calling beadles for two pragmatic reasons. Being unfit for most other employments, they could not demand much pay for the work. And they could not take sinful advantage of their literally high position: they could not look down to ogle any decent woman who ascended to her rooftop to doff her veil—or more of her coverings—for a private sunbath.

In their interiors, the masjid temples differ notably from our Christian churches. In none of them, anywhere, is there ever to be found any statue or painting or other recognizable image. Though Islam recognizes, I think, as many angels and saints and prophets as Christianity does, it will allow no representation of them, or of any other creature alive or which ever has lived. Muslims believe that their Allah, like our Lord God, created all things living. But, unlike us Christians, they maintain that all creation, even in paint or wood or stone imitation of life, must be forever reserved to Allah. Their Quran warns them that on Judgment Day any maker of any such image will be commanded to bring that image to life; if the maker cannot do that, and of course he cannot, he will be damned to Hell for his presumption in having made it. Therefore, although a Muslim masjid—or palace or home—is always rich in decoration, those decorations are never pictures of anything; they consist only of patterns and colors and intricate arabeschi. Sometimes, though, the patterns are discernible as being woven of the Arabic fish-worm letters and spelling out some phrase or verse from the Quran.

(I learned these several uncommonly odd things about Islam—and I learned many other uncommonly odd things besides—because, during my stay in Baghdad, I acquired first one and then another uncommonly odd teacher, and I will tell of them in their turn.)

I was particularly taken with one form of decoration I saw in the interior rooms of every public and private building in Baghdad. I should say that I first saw it there, but afterward I saw it in other palaces, homes and temples throughout Persia and throughout much of the rest of the East. I should think it might be advantageously adopted by any people anywhere which loves a garden, and what people does not love a garden?

What it is, is a way to bring a garden *indoors*, though never having to tend or weed or water it. Called in Persia a qali, it is a sort of carpet or tapicierie made to lie on a floor or hang on a wall, but it is unlike any such work we know in the West. The qali is colored in all the colors of a bounteous garden, and its figures form the shapes of multitudes of flowers, vines, trellises, leaves—everything to be found in a garden—all disposed in pleasing designs and arrangements. (In keeping with the Quran's ban on images, however, a Persian qali is made so that the flowers are not recognizable as any known existing flowers.) At first sight of a qali, I thought the garden must be painted or embroidered upon it. But, on examination, I found that all that intricacy was *woven into it*. I marveled that any tapicier could contrive such a fanciful thing with mere warp and weft of dyed yarns, and it was some while before I learned the marvelous manner in which it is done.

But I have already got ahead of my chronicle.

We three led our five horses across the wobbling and undulating boat bridge which spanned the Dijlah River. At the Baghdad waterfront, teeming with men of all complexions and costumes and languages, we accosted the first one we saw wearing Western clothes. He was a Genoan, but I should remark that, out East, all Westerners get along convivially enough—even Genoans and Venetians, albeit they are rivals in trade and even though their home republics may be embroiled in one of their frequent sea wars. The Genoan merchant amiably told us the name of the incumbent Shah—he gave it as "Shahinshah Zaman Mirza" —and directed us to the palace "in the Karkh quarter, which is the exclusively royal quarter of the city."

We rode thither, and found the palace in a gated garden, and made ourselves known to the guards at the gate. Those guards wore helmets that seemed to be of solid gold—but could not have been, or their weight would have been intolerable—and, even if only of plated wood or leather, were objects of great value. They were also objects of interest, being fashioned to give their wearers a wealth of curly golden hair and side whiskers. One of the guards went inside the gate and through the garden to the palace. When he returned and beckoned to us, another guard took charge of our horses, and we entered.

We were led to a chamber richly hung and carpeted with brilliant qali, where the Shahinshah half-sat and half-reclined on a heap of daiwan cushions of equally vivid colors and fine fabrics. He himself was not gaudily garbed; from tulband to slippers, his dress was a uniform pale brown. That is the Persian color of mourning, and the Shah always wore pale brown now in mourning for his lost empire. We were somewhat surprised—this being a Muslim household—to see that a woman occupied another heap of pillows beside him, and there were also two other females in the room. We made the proper bows of salaam and, still bowed down, my father greeted the Shahinshah in the Farsi tongue, then raised up upon his two hands the letter of Kubilai Khan. The Shah took it and read aloud its salutation:

" 'Most Serene, most Puissant, most High, Noble, Illustrious, Honorable, Wise and Prudent Emperors, Ilkhani, Shahi, Kings, Lords, Princes, Dukes, Earls, Barons and Knights, as also Magistrates, Officers, Justicians and Regents of all good cities and places, whether ecclesiastic or secular, who shall see these patents or hear them read . . .' "

When he had perused the whole thing, the Shahinshah bade us welcome, addressing each of us as "Mirza Polo." That was a little confusing, as I had understood Mirza to be one of *his* names. But I gradually gathered that he was using the word as a respectful honorific, as the Arabs use Sheikh. And eventually I realized that Mirza before a name means only what Messer does in Venice; when it is appended after the name, it signifies royalty. The Shah's name was actually and simply Zaman, and his full title of Shahinshah meant Shah of All Shahs, and he

introduced the lady beside him as his Royal First Wife, or Shahryar, by
the name of Zahd.

That was very nearly all he got to say that day, because, once she
was introduced into the conversation, the Shahryar Zahd proved to be
effusively and endlessly talkative. First interrupting, then overriding her
husband, she gave us her own welcome to Persia and to Baghdad and to
the palace, and she sent our accompanying guard back to the gate, and
she hammered a little gong at her side to summon a palace maggiordomo
whom she told us was called a wazir, and she instructed the wazir to
prepare quarters for us in the palace and assign palace servants to us,
and she introduced us to the other two females in the room: one her
mother, the other the eldest daughter of herself and the Shah Zaman,
and she informed us that she herself, Zahd Mirza, was a direct descendant of the fabled Balkis, Queen of Sabaea—and, of course, so were
her mother and daughter—and she reminded us that the famous encounter of Queen Balkis with the Padshah Solaiman was recorded in
the annals of Islam as well as those of Judaism and Christianity (which
remark enabled me to recognize the biblical Queen of Sheba and King
Solomon), and she further informed us that the Sabaean Queen Balkis
herself was a jinniyeh, descended from a demon named Eblis, who was
chief jinni of all the demon jinn, and furthermore . . .

"Tell us, Mirza Polo," the Shah said, almost desperately, to my
father, "something of your journey thus far."

My father obligingly began an account of our travels, but he had
not even got us out of the Venice lagoon when the Shahryar Zahd
pounced in with a lyrical description of some pieces of Murano glass she
had recently bought from a Venetian merchant in downtown Baghdad,
and that reminded her of an old but little-known Persian tale of a glass-
blower who, once upon a time, fashioned a horse of blown glass and
persuaded a jinni to make some magic by which the horse was enabled
to fly like a bird, and . . .

The tale was interesting enough, but unbelievable, so I let my attention wander to the other two females in the room. The women's very
presence in a meeting of men—not to mention the Shahryar's unquench-
able garrulity—was evidence that the Persians did not shield and sequester and stifle their womenfolk as most other Muslims do. Each
woman's eyes were visible above a mere half-veil of chador, which was
diaphanous anyway and did not conceal her nose and mouth and chin.
On their upper bodies they wore blouse and waistcoat, and on their
lower limbs the voluminous pai-jamah. However, those garments were
not thick and many-layered as on Arab women, but gossamer light and
translucent, so the shapes of their bodies could be easily discerned and
appreciated.

I gave only one look at the aged grandmother: wrinkled, bony,
hunched, almost bald, toothlessly champing her granulated lips, her eyes
red and gummy, her withered paps flapping against slatted ribs. One
look at the crone was enough for me. But her daughter, the Shahryar
Zahd Mirza, was an exceptionally handsome woman, anyway when she
was not talking, and *her* daughter was a superbly beautiful and shapely

girl about my own age. She was the Crown Princess or Shahzrad, and named Magas, which means Moth, and subtitled with the royal Mirza. I have neglected to say that the Persians are not, like Arabs, of dark and muddy complexion. Though they all have blue-black hair, and the men wear blue-black beards like Uncle Mafio's, their skin is as fair as any Venetian's, and many have eyes of lighter color than brown. The Shahzrad Magas Mirza was at that moment taking my measure with eyes of emerald green.

"Speaking of horses," said the Shah, seizing on the tail of the flying-horse tale, before his wife could be reminded of some other story. "You gentlemen should consider trading your horses for camels before you leave Baghdad. Eastward of here you must cross the Dasht-e-Kavir, a vast and terrible desert. Horses cannot endure the—"

"The Mongols' horses did," his wife sharply contradicted him. "A Mongol goes everywhere on a horse, and no Mongol would ever bestride a camel. I will tell you how they despise and mistreat camels. While they were besieging this city, the Mongols captured a herd of camels somewhere, and they loaded them with bales of dry grass, and set that hay afire, and stampeded the poor beasts into our streets. The camels, their own fur and humps of fat burning as well, ran mad in agony and could not be caught. So they careered up and down our streets, setting fire to much of Baghdad, before the flames ate into them and reached their vitals, and they collapsed and died."

"Or," said the Shah to us, when the Shahryar paused to take a breath, "your journey could be much shortened if you went part way by sea. You might wish to go southeast from here, to Basra—or even farther down the Gulf, to Hormuz—and take passage on some ship sailing to India."

"In Hormuz," said the Shahryar Zahd, "every man has only a thumb and the two outer fingers on his right hand. I will tell you why. That seaport city has for ages treasured its importance and its independence, so its every adult male citizen has always been trained as an archer to defend it. When the Mongols under the Ilkhan Hulagu laid seige to Hormuz, the Ilkhan made an offer to the city fathers. Hulagu said he would let Hormuz stand, and retain its independence, and keep its citizen archers, if only the city fathers would *lend* him those bowmen for long enough to help him conquer Baghdad. Then, he promised, he would let the men come home to Hormuz and be its staunch defense again. The city fathers agreed to that proposal, and all its men—however reluctantly—joined Hulagu in his siege of this city, and fought well for him, and eventually our beloved Baghdad fell."

She and the Shah both sighed deeply.

"Well," she went on, "Hulagu had been so impressed by the valor and prowess of the Hormuz men that he then sent them to bed with all the young Mongol women who always accompany the Mongol armies. Hulagu wished to add the potency of the Hormuz seed to the Mongol birthlines, you see. After a few nights of that enforced cohabitation, when Hulagu presumed his females had been sufficiently impregnated, he kept his promise and freed the archers to go home to Hormuz. But before he let them depart, he had every man's two bowstring fingers amputated. In effect, Hulagu took the fruit from the trees and then felled the trees. Those mutilated men could make no defense of Hormuz at all, and of course that city soon became, like our dear defeated Baghdad, a possession of the Mongol Khanate."

"My dear," said the Shah, looking flustered. "These gentlemen are emissaries of that Khanate. The letter they showed me is a ferman from the Khakhan Kubilai himself. I very much doubt that they are amused to hear tales of the Mongols'—cr—misbehavior."

"Oh, you can freely say *atrocities*, Shah Zaman," my uncle boomed heartily. "We are still Venetians, not adoptive Mongols nor apologists for them."

"Then I should tell you," said the Shahryar, again leaning eagerly forward, "the ghastly way Hulagu treated our Qalif al-Mustasim Billah, the holiest man of Islam." The Shah breathed another sigh, and fixed his gaze on a remote corner of the room. "As perhaps you know, Mirza Polo, Baghdad was to Islam what Rome is to Christianity And the Qalif of Baghdad was to Muslims what your Pope is to you Christians. So, when Hulagu laid siege here, it was to the Qalif Mustasim that he proposed surrender terms, not to the Shah Zaman." She flicked a disparaging glance at her husband. "Hulagu offered to lift the siege if the Qalif acceded to certain demands, among them the handing over of much gold. The Qalif refused, saying, 'Our gold sustains our Holy Islam.' And the reigning Shah did not overrule that decision."

"How could I?" that Shah said weakly, as if it was an argument much argued previously. "The spiritual leader outranks the temporal."

His wife went implacably on. "Baghdad might have withstood the Mongols and their Hormuz allies, but it could not withstand the hunger imposed by a siege. Our people ate everything edible, even the city rats, but the people got weaker and weaker, and many died and the rest could fight no longer. When the city inevitably fell, Hulagu imprisoned the Qalif Mustasim in solitary confinement, and let him get even hungrier. At last the holy old man had to beg for food. Hulagu with his own hands gave him a plate full of gold coins, and the Qalif whimpered, 'No man can eat gold.' And Hulagu said, 'You called it sustenance when I asked for it. Did it sustain your holy city? Pray, then, that it will sustain you.' And he had the gold melted, and he poured that glowing-hot liquid metal down the old man's throat, killing him horribly. Mustasim was the last of the Qalifate, which had endured for more than five hundred years, and Baghdad is no longer the capital either of Persia or of Islam."

We dutifully shook our heads in commiseration, which encouraged the Shahryar to add:

"As an illustration of how low the Shahnate has been brought: this my husband, Shah Zaman, who was once Shahinshah of all the Empire of Persia, is now a pigeon keeper and cherry picker!"

"My dear . . . ," said the Shah.

"It is true. One of the lesser Khans—somewhere to the eastward; we have never even met this Ilkhan—has a taste for ripe cherries. He is also a fancier of pigeons, and his pigeons are trained always to fly home to him from wherever they may be transported. So there are now some hundred of those feathered rats in a dovecote behind the palace stables, and for each there is a tiny silken bag. My Emperor husband has instructions. Next summer when our orchards ripen, we are to pick the cherries, put one or two of them into each of those little bags, fasten the bags to the legs of the pigeons and let the birds free. Like the rukh bird carrying off men and lions and princesses, the pigeons will carry our cherries to the waiting Ilkhan. If we do not pay that humiliating tribute, he will doubtless come rampaging from out of the east and lay our city waste again."

"My dear, I am sure the gentlemen are now weary of—of traveling hither," said the Shah, sounding weary himself. He struck the gong to summon the wazir once more, and said to us, "You will wish to rest and refresh yourselves. Then, if you will do me the honor, we will foregather again at the evening meal."

The wazir, a middle-aged and melancholy man named Jamshid, showed us to our chambers, a suite of three rooms with doors between. They were well furnished, with many qali on the floors and walls, and windows of stone tracery inset with glass, and soft beds of quilts and pillows. Our packs had already been removed from our horses and brought there.

"And here is a manservant for each of you," said the Wazir Jamshid, producing three lissome, beardless young men. "They are all expert in the Indian art of champna, which they will perform for you after you have been to the hammam."

"Ah, yes," said Uncle Mafio, sounding pleased. "We have not enjoyed a shampoo, Nico, since we came through Tazhikistan."

So again we had the thorough cleansing and refreshment of a hammam, an elegantly appointed one this time, in which our three young men served as our rubbers. And afterward we lay nude on our separate beds in our separate rooms for what was called the champna—or shampoo, as my uncle had pronounced it. I had no idea what to expect; it had sounded like a dance performance. But it proved to be a vigorous rubbing and pummeling and kneading of my entire body, more energetically done than the hammam rubbing, and with the intent not of extruding dirt from the skin, but of exercising every part in a manner to make one feel even healthier and more invigorated than a hammam bath can do.

My young servant, Karim, pounded and pinched and tweaked me, and at first it was painful. But after a while, my muscles and joints and sinews, stiffened by long riding, began to uncoil and unknot under that assault, and gradually I lay at ease and enjoyed it, and felt myself beginning to tingle with vitality. As a matter of fact, one impertinent part of me became obtrusively alive, and I was embarrassed. Then I was startled, for Karim with an evidently practiced hand started to exercise that also.

"I can do that for myself," I snapped, "if I deem it necessary."

He shrugged delicately and said, "As the Mirza commands. When the Mirza commands," and concentrated on less intimate parts of me.

He finished the mauling at last, and I lay half wanting to doze, half wanting to leap up and do athletic feats, and he asked to be excused.

"To attend the Mirza your uncle," he explained. "For such a massive man, it will require all three of us to give him an adequate champna."

I graciously gave him leave, and abandoned myself to my drowsiness. I think my father also slept the afternoon away, but Uncle Mafìo must have had a most thorough working-over, for the three young men were just leaving his room when Jamshid came to see us dressed for the evening meal. He brought for us new and myrrh-scented clothing of the Persian style: the lightweight pai-jamah, and loose shirts with tight cuffs, and, to wear over the shirts, beautifully embroidered short waistcoats, and kamarbands to go tightly about our waists, and silk shoes with upturned, curly, pointed toes, and tulbands instead of hanging kaffiyah headcloths. My father and uncle each proficiently and neatly wound his tulband around his head, but young Karim had to instruct me in the winding and tucking of mine. When we were dressed, we all looked exceptionally handsome and nobly Mirza and genuinely Persian.

. 2 .

WAZIR Jamshid led us to a large but not overpowering dining hall, lighted with torches and ringed about with servants and attendants. They were all males, and only the Shah Zaman joined us at the sumptuously laid dining cloth. I was rather relieved to see that the palace household was not so unorthodox that females were allowed to violate Muslim custom and routinely sit down to eat with men. We and the Shah had a meal uninterrupted by the facundities of the Shahryar, and he only once referred to her:

"The First Wife, being of royal Sabaean blood, has never reconciled herself to the fact that this Shahnate was heretofore subordinate to the Qalif and now is subordinate to the Khanate. Like a fine-bred Arabian mare, the Shahryar Zahd bucks at being harnessed. But otherwise she is an excellent consort, and more tender than the tail of a fat-tailed sheep."

His barnyard similes perhaps explained, but to my mind did not excuse, her seeming to be the cock of that yard, and he the much-pecked hen. Nevertheless, the Shah was a congenial fellow, and he drank with us like a Christian, and he was a knowledgeable conversationalist when he was unencumbered of his wife. At my remark that I was thrilled to be following the trails which Alexander the Great had trodden, the Shah said:

"Those trails of his ended not far from here, you know, after Alexander had returned from his conquest of India's Kashmir and Sind and the Panjab. Only fourteen farsakhs south of here are the ruins of Babylon, where he died. Of a fever brought on, it is said, by his having drunk too much of our wine of Shiraz."

I thanked the Shah for the information, but I privately wondered how anyone could drink a killing amount of that sticky liquid. Even in Venice I had heard travelers extol their remembrance of the wine of Shiraz, and it is much praised in song and fable, but we were drinking it at that very meal, and I thought it fell far short of its reputation. That wine is an unappetizing orange in color, and cloyingly sweet, and thick as treacle. A man would have to be determined on drunkenness, I decided, to drink very much of it.

The other elements of the meal, though, were unqualifiedly superb. There was chicken cooked in pomegranate juice, and lamb cubed and marinated and broiled in a manner called kabab, and a rose-flavored sharbat cold with snow, and a billowy, trembling confection like a fluffed-up nougat, made of fine white flour, cream, honey, daintily flavored with oil of pistachio, and called a balesh. After the meal, we lolled among our cushions and sipped an exquisite liqueur expressed from rose petals, while we watched two court wrestlers, naked and shiny and slippery with almond oil, try to bend each other double or break each other in half. Then, when they had escaped the performance unharmed, we listened to a court minstrel play on a stringed instrument called al-ud, very like a lute, while he recited Persian poems, of which I can recall only that their every line ended in a mouselike squeak or a mournful sob.

When that torment was concluded, I was given leave by the elder men to go and amuse myself, if I wished. I did so, leaving my father and uncle discussing with the Shah the various land and water routes they might take after Baghdad. I left the room and walked down a long corridor, where were many closed doors guarded by giant men holding spears or shimshir sabers. They all wore the sort of helmet I had seen at the palace gates, but some of the guards had faces of African black or Arab brown, ill according with the helmets' gold-sculptured tresses.

At the end of the corridor was an unguarded archway giving onto the outdoor garden, and I went there. The smooth gravel pathways and lush flower beds were softly illuminated by a full moon that was like a great pearl displayed on the black velvet of the night. I wandered idly about, admiring the unfamiliar blooms made even more new to me by the pearl light shining on them. Then I came to something so novel as to be astonishing: a flower bed that was visibly and all on its own *doing* something. I stopped to watch and ponder what appeared to be an unvegetably deliberate behavior. The flower bed was a tremendous circular area, divided piewise into twelve slices, each segment planted densely with a different variety of flowers. All of them were at the blooming stage, but in ten of the slices the flowers had closed their blossoms, as many flowers do at night. However, in one segment, some pale pink flowers were just then folding their petals, and in the adjoining segment some large white flowers were at the same time just opening their blossoms and loosing on the night a heady perfume.

"It is the gulsa'at," said a voice that might also have been perfumed. I turned to see the young and comely Shahzrad and, standing some way behind her, the aged grandmother. Princess Moth went on, "Gulsa'at means the flower dial. In your country, you have sand glasses and water glasses to tell the hours, do you not?"

"Yes, Shahzrad Magas Mirza," I said, taking care to use her whole regalia of address.

"You may call me Moth," she said, with a sweet smile visible through her sheer chador. She indicated the gulsa'at. "This flower dial also tells the hours, but it never has to be turned or refilled. Each kind of flower in that round bed naturally opens at a certain hour of the day or night, and closes at another. They are selected for their regularity of habit, and planted here in proper sequence and—lo! They silently announce each of the twelve hours we count from sunset to sunset."

I said daringly, "It is a thing as beautiful as you are, Princess Moth."

"My father the Shah takes a delight in measuring time," she said. "Yonder is the palace masjid in which we worship, but it is also a calendar. In one wall it has openings so the sun in its rounds shines its light each dawn through one after another to tell the day and the month."

Somewhat similarly, I was sidling around the girl, to put her between me and the moon, so its light shone through her filmy garments and outlined her delectable body. The old grandmother evidently perceived my intention, for she grinned her gums evilly at me.

"And yonder, beyond," the Princess continued, "is the anderun where reside all my father's other wives and concubines. He has more than three hundred, so he can have a different one almost every night of the year if he chooses. However, he prefers my mother, the First Wife, except that she talks all night. So he only takes one of the others to bed when he wishes to have a good night's sleep."

Looking at the Shahzrad's moon-revealed body, I felt my own body again stirring as vivaciously as it had done during the champna. I was glad I was not wearing tight Venetian hose, or I would have bulged them most disgracefully. Dressed as I was in ample pai-jamah, I did not think my arousal could have been visible. But the Princess Moth must have sensed it anyway, for to my shocked amazement she said:

"You would like to take *me* to bed and make zina, would you not?"

I stammered and stuttered, and managed to say, "Surely you should not speak so, Princess, in the presence of your royal grandmother! I assume she is your"—I did not know the Farsi word, so I said it in French—"your chaperon?"

The Shahzrad made an airy gesture. "The old woman is as deaf as that gulsa'at. Be not concerned, but answer me. You would like to put your zab into my mihrab, no?"

I swallowed and gulped. "I could hardly be so presumptuous . . . I mean, a Royal Highness . . ."

She nodded and said briskly, "I believe we can arrange something of the sort. No, do not grab at me. The grandmother can see, if she cannot hear. We must be discreet. I will ask my father's permission to be your guide while you are here, to show you the delights of Baghdad. I can be a very good guide to those delights. You will see."

And with that, she drifted away down the moonlit garden, leaving me shaken and shaking. I might say vibrant. When I tottered to my room, Karim was waiting to help me doff the unfamiliar Persian clothes, and he laughed and made noises of admiration and said:

"Surely now the young Mirza will allow me to complete the relaxing champna!" and he poured almond oil into his hand, and he did so with expertness, and I fell languidly into sleep.

The next day I slept late, and so did my father and uncle, for their consultation with Shah Zaman had lasted well into the night. As we ate our breakfast meal, brought by the servants to our suite, they told me that they were contemplating the Shah's suggestion that we go by sea as far as the Indies. But they would first have to find out if it was practicable. They would each go to one of the Gulf ports—my father to Hormuz, my uncle to Basra—and see if, as the Shah believed, an Arab trader-captain could be persuaded to allow passage to us rival Venetian traders.

"When we have investigated," said my father, "we will regather here in Baghdad, because the Shah will be wanting us to carry many gifts from him to the Khakhan. So you, Marco, can come along with either one of us to the Gulf, or you can await our return here."

Thinking of the Shahzrad Magas, but having the good sense not to mention her, I said I thought I would stay. I would take the opportunity to get better acquainted with Baghdad.

Uncle Mafìo snorted. "In the way that you got so well acquainted with Venice when we were last away? Truly, not so very many Venetians get to know the interior of the Vulcano." To my father he said, "Is it prudent, Nico, to leave this malanòso alone in an alien city?"

"Alone?" I protested. "I have the servant Karim and"—I again refrained from mentioning the Princess Moth—"and the whole palace guard."

"They are responsible to the Shah, not to you or us," said my father. "If you should get into trouble again . . ."

I indignantly reminded him that my most recent trouble had involved my saving them from being slaughtered in their sleep, and they had praised me for it, and that was why I was still in their company, and—

My father sternly interrupted with a proverb, "One sees better backwards than forwards. We are not going to set a warden over you, my boy. But I think it would be a good idea to buy a slave to be your personal servant and see to your best interests. We will go to the bazàr."

The melancholy Wazir Jamshid walked with us, to interpret for us if our command of Farsi should prove inadequate. Along the way he explained several curious things I was seeing for the first time. For example, in eyeing the other men on the streets, I observed that they did not allow their blue-black beards to go gray or white as they aged. Every elderly man I saw had a beard of a violent pink-orange color, like Shiraz wine. Jamshid told me that it was done with a dye made from the leaves of a shrub called hinna, and he said the hinna was also much used by women as a cosmetic and by carters to adorn their horses. I should mention that the horses used in Baghdad for carriage and cartage are not the fine Arabians used for riding. They are tiny little ponies, not much bigger than mastiff dogs, and they do look very pretty with their flowing manes and tails dyed that brilliant pink-orange color.

There were, on the Baghdad streets, men of many other nations than Persia. Some wore Western clothes and had faces, like ours, that would have been white had they not been sun-darkened. Some had black faces, some brown, some a sort of tan-yellow hue, and there were many whose faces were like weathered leather. Those were the Mongols of the occupying garrison, all dressed in armor of varnished hides or metal chain mail, and striding contemptuously through the street crowds, shoving aside anybody who stepped in their way. Also on the streets were many women, also of various complexions, the Persians only lightly veiled, and others not wearing chador at all, a strange thing to see in a Muslim city. But, even in liberal Baghdad, no woman walked alone; whatever her race or nationality, she was attended either by one or several other women or by a male attendant of considerable bulk and beardless face.

I was so bedazzled by the Baghdad bazàr that I could hardly believe the city had been conquered and plundered and held to tribute by the Mongols. It must have recovered commendably from its recent impoverishment, for it was the richest and most thriving center of commerce I had yet seen, far surpassing every marketplace of Venice in the variety and abundance and value of the goods for sale.

The cloth merchants stood proudly among bales and bolts of fabrics woven of silk and wool and Ankara-goat hair and cotton and linen and fine camel hair and sturdier camelot. There were more exotic Eastern fabrics like mussoline from Mosul and dungri from India and bokhram from Bukhara and demesq from Damascus. The book merchants displayed volumes of fine vellum and parchment and paper, gorgeously engrossed in many colors and gold leaf besides. Most of the books, being copies of the works of Persian authors like Sadi and Nimazi, and of course written in Farsi and rendered in the convulsed-worm Arabic lettering, were incomprehensible to me. But one of them, titled *Iskandarnama*, I could recognize from its illuminations as being a Persian version of my favorite reading, *The Book of Alexander*.

The bazàr's apothecaries stocked jars and phials of cosmetics for men and women: black al-kohl and green malachite and brown summaq and red hinna and eye-brightening collyrium washes, and perfumes of nard and myrrh and frankincense and rose attar. There were tiny bags of an almost impalpably fine grit which Jamshid said was fern seed, to be employed by those who knew the proper accompaniment of magical incantations, to make their corporeal persons invisible. There was an oil called teryak, expressed from the petals and pods of poppy flowers, which Jamshid said physicians prescribed for the relief of cramps and other pains, but which any person depressed by age or misery could buy and drink as an easy way out of an unbearable life.

The bazàr was also shiny and glittering and coruscating with precious metals and gems and jewelry. But of all the treasures for sale there, I was most taken with a particular sort. There was a merchant who dealt exclusively in sets of a certain board game. In Venice it is unimaginatively called the Game of Squares, and it is played with cheap pieces carved of ordinary woods. In Persia that game is called the War of the

Shahi, and the playing sets are works of art, priced beyond the reach of all but a real Shah or someone of equal wealth. A typical board offered for sale by that Baghdad merchant was of alternate ebony and ivory squares, expensive all by itself. The pieces on one side of it—the Shah and his General, the two elephants, the two horsemen, the two rukhi warriors and the eight peyadeh foot soldiers—were made of gem-encrusted gold, the sixteen facing pieces across the board being of gem-encrusted silver. The price asked for that set I cannot remember, but it was staggering. He had other Shahi sets variously fashioned of porcelain and jade and rare woods and pure crystal, and all of those pieces were sculptured as exquisitely as if they had been miniature statues of living monarchs and generals and their men at arms.

There were merchants of livestock—of horses and ponies and asses and camels, of course, but also of other beasts. Some of them I had known only by repute and never seen before that day, such as a big and shaggy bear, which I thought resembled my Uncle Mafìo; a delicate kind of deer called a qazèl, which people bought to grace their gardens; and a yellow wild dog called a shaqàl, which a hunter could tame and train to stop and kill a charging boar. (A Persian hunter will go alone and with only a knife to challenge a savage lion, but he is timid of meeting a wild pig. Since a Muslim recoils even from speaking of pig meat, he would deem it a death horrific beyond imagination if he should die at the tusks of a boar.) Also in the livestock market was the shuturmurq, which means "camel-bird," and it certainly did look like a mongrel offspring of those two different creatures. The camel-bird has the body and feathers and beak of a giant goose, but its neck is unfeathered and long, like a camel's, and its two legs are ungainly long, like a camel's four, and its splayed feet are as big as a camel's pads, and it can no more fly than a camel can. Jamshid said the shuturmurq was caught and kept for the one pretty thing it can supply: the billowy plumes it grows on its rump. There were also apes for sale, of the sort which uncouth seamen some-times bring to Venice, where they are called simiazze: those apes as big and ugly as Ethiope children. Jamshid called that animal nedjis, which means "unspeakably unclean," but he did not tell me why it was so named or why anyone, even a seaman, would buy such a thing.

In the bazàr were many fardarbab, or tomorrow-tellers. They were shriveled, orange-bearded old men who squatted behind trays of care-fully smoothed sand. A client who paid a coin would shake the tray and the sand would ripple into patterns which the old man would read and interpret. There were also many of the darwish holy beggars, as ragged, scabby, filthy and evil-looking as those in any other Eastern city. Here in Baghdad they had an additional attribute: they danced and skipped and howled and whirled and convulsed as violently as any epilept in a seizure. It was, I suppose, at least some entertainment in return for the bakhshish they beseeched.

Before we could even inspect any of the bazàr's wares, we had to be interviewed by a market official called the revenue-farmer, and satisfy him that we possessed both the means to buy and also the means to pay the jizya, which is a tax levied on non-Muslim sellers and buyers alike.

Wazir Jamshid, although he was himself a court official, privately confided to us that all such petty officials and civil servants were despised by the people and were called batlanim, which means "the idle ones." When my father produced for that idle one a cod of musk, surely wealth enough to pay for a Shahi set at least, the revenue-farmer grumbled suspiciously:

"Got it from an Armeniyan, you say? Then it probably contains not the deer's musk, but his chopped liver. It must be tested."

The idle one took out a needle and thread and a clove of garlic. He threaded the needle and ran it several times through and through the garlic, until the thread was reeking with the garlic odor. Then he took the musk cod and ran the needle and thread just once through it. He sniffed at the thread and looked surprised.

"The smell is all gone, totally absorbed. Verily, you have genuine musk. Where on this earth did you meet an honest Armeniyan?" And he gave us a ferman, a paper authorizing us to trade in the Baghdad bazàr.

Jamshid took us to the slave pen of a Persian dealer who he said was trustworthy, and we stood among the crowd of other prospective purchasers and mere lookers-on, while the dealer detailed the lineage, history, attributes and merits of each slave brought to the block by his burly assistants.

"Here is a standard eunuch," he said, presenting an obese and shiny black man, who looked quite cheerful for a slave. "Guaranteed placid and amenable to orders and never known to steal more than the allowable. He would make an excellent servant. However, if you seek a veritable Keeper of the Keys, here is a perfect eunuch." He presented a young white man, blond and muscular, who was quite handsome but who looked as melancholy as a slave might be expected to look. "You are invited to examine the merchandise."

My uncle said to the wazir, "I know, of course, what a eunuch is. We have castròni in our own country, sweet-singing boys neutered so they will always sing sweetly. But how can a totally sexless creature be differentiated as standard and perfect? Is it because one is an Ethiope and the other a Russniak?"

"No, Mirza Polo," said Jamshid, and he explained in French, so we would not be confounded by unfamiliar Farsi words. "The eunuque ordinaire is deprived of his testicles when he is yet a baby, to make him grow up docile and obedient and not contrary of nature. It is easily done. A thread is tied tightly around the roots of a boy infant's scrotum, and in a matter of weeks that cod withers, turns black and drops off. That is quite enough to make him become a good servant of general utility."

"What more could a master want?" said Uncle Mafìo, perhaps sincerely, perhaps sarcastically.

"Well, to be a Keeper of the Keys, the eunuque extraordinaire is preferred. For he must live in and watch over the anderun, the quarters in which reside his master's wives and concubines. And those women, especially if they are not often favored in the matter of the master's bed, can be most enterprising and inventive, even with inert male flesh. So that sort of slave must be shorn of *all* his equipment—the rod as well as the stones. And that removal is a serious operation, not so easily done. Look yonder and observe. The merchandise is being examined."

We looked. The dealer had directed the two slaves to drop their paijamah, and they stood with their crotches exposed to the scrutiny of an elderly Persian Jew. The fat black man was hairless down there, and bagless, but he did have a member of respectable size, though of a repellent black and purple color. I supposed that a woman of the anderun, if she was so desperate for a man and so depraved as to want that thing inside her, might contrive some kind of splint to stiffen it. But the far more presentable young Russniak had not even a flaccid appendage. He showed only a growth of blond artichoke hair, and something like the tip of a small white stick grotesquely protruding from the hair, and otherwise his groin was as featureless as a woman's.

"Bruto barabào!" grunted Uncle Mafìo. "How *is* it done, Jamshid?"

As expressionlessly as if he was reading from a medical text, the wazir said, "The slave is taken into a room dense with the smoke of smoldering banj leaves, and he is set in a hot bath and he is given teryak to sip, all that done to dull his sense of pain. The hakim doing the operation takes a long ribbon and winds it tightly about him, starting at the tip of the slave's penis and wrapping inward to the roots, bundling in with it the cod of testicles, so that the organs make a single package. Then, using a keenly sharp blade, the hakim removes that whole beribboned package with a single slicing stroke. He immediately applies to the wound a styptic of powdered raisins, puffball fungus and alum. When the bleeding stops, he inserts a clean quill, which will stay there during the slave's whole life. For the chief danger of the operation is that the urinary passage may close in the healing. If, by the third or fourth day afterward, the slave has not passed water through the quill, he is certain to die. And sad to say, that does occur in perhaps three out of five cases."

"Capòn mal caponà!" exclaimed my father. "It sounds gruesome. You have actually witnessed such a procedure?"

"Yes," said Jamshid. "I watched with some interest when it was done to me."

I should have realized that that accounted for his always melancholy aspect, and I should have kept silent. Instead I blurted, "But you are not fat, Wazir, and you have a full beard!"

He did not rebuke my impertinence. He replied, "Those who endure castration in infancy never grow a beard, and their bodies grow corpulent and feminine of contour, often even growing heavy breasts. But when the operation is done after a slave's passing puberty, he remains masculine, at least in outward appearance. I was a full-grown man, with a wife and son, when our farm was raided by Kurdi slave-takers. The Kurdi sought only robust worker slaves, so my wife and little boy were spared. They were merely raped several times apiece, and then slain."

An appalled silence ensued and might have got uncomfortable, but Jamshid added, almost offhandedly, "Ah, well, can I complain? I might have been a mere millet farmer to this day. But having been relieved of a man's natural desires—to sow and cultivate land and lineage—I was freed to cultivate my intellect instead. Now I have risen to become Wazir to the Shahinshah of Persia, and that is no small attainment."

Having so graciously dismissed the subject, he summoned the slave dealer to come and give ear to our requirements. The dealer left his assistants to oversee the inspection of the two slaves already on display, and came smiling and rubbing his hands together.

I had half hoped that my father would buy for me a comely girl slave, who could be more than a servant, or at least a young man of my own age, who would be a congenial companion. But of course he told the dealer not what I might want, but what he wanted for me:

"An older man, well versed in travel, but still agile enough to travel farther yet. Wise in the ways of the East, so that he can both safeguard and instruct my son. And I think"—he flicked a sympathetic glance at the wazir—"not a eunuch. I had rather not help to perpetuate that practice."

"I have the very man, messieurs," said the dealer, speaking good French. "Mature but not old, wily but not willful, experienced but not inflexible to command. Now, where has he got to? He was here just moments ago. . . ."

We followed him about through his herd—or herds, I should say, for there were a considerable number of slaves in the pen, and also a number of the tiny hinna'ed Persian horses which drew his wagons from town to town. The pen was partly fenced and partly enclosed by those canvas-hooped wagons, in which he and his assistants and his merchandise traveled by day and slept by night.

"The ideal slave for you, messieurs, this man," the dealer went on, as he kept looking around. "He has belonged to numerous masters, hence has traveled widely and knows many lands. He speaks several tongues, and has a vast repertoire of useful talents. But where is he?"

We continued circulating among the men and women slaves, who had lengths of light chain connecting their ankle rings, and among the midget horses, which were not fettered. The dealer began to look slightly embarrassed at having misplaced the very slave he was trying to peddle.

"I had loosed him from the skein," he muttered, "and shackled him to one of my mares, which he was currying for me—"

He was interrupted by a loud, piercing, prolonged equine whinny. With a ripple of orange mane and tail, a little horse came flying out through the front flaps of one of the covered wagons. Literally, it was in flight for a moment, like the magic glass horse of which the Shahryar Zahd had told us, for it had to bound from the interior of the wagon bed and clear the driver's bench and the dashboard to get to the ground below. As it made that high arcing bound, a chain attached to its rear leg came trailing in the same looping arc, and at the other end of the chain a man popped out legs-first through the canvas flaps, like a stopper yanked from a bottle. The man also flew over the front of the wagon and hit the ground in a thump of dust. Because the horse tried to flee farther yet, the man got dragged about and raised quite a cloud of dust before the slave dealer could catch the frightened animal's bridle and bring that brief entertainment to a halt.

The little horse's orange mane was silkily combed, but its orange tail was disheveled. So were the man's nether regions, for his pai-jamah were down around his feet. He sat for a moment, too winded to do anything but make several faint exclamations in several languages. Then he hastily rearranged his garments, as the slave dealer came and stood over him and bellowed imprecations and kicked him until he got upright. The slave was about my father's age, but his scruffy beard appeared to be only about two weeks' growth and did not adequately conceal a receding chin. He had bright, shifty pig's eyes and a large fleshy nose that drooped over fleshy lips. He was no taller than I, but much thicker, with a paunch that drooped as did his nose. All in all, he looked something like a camelbird.

"My newly acquired mare!" the dealer was raging, in Farsi, still kicking the slave. "You indescribable wretch!"

"The mischievous horse was wandering, master," whined the wretch, his arms raised protectively around his head. "I had to follow—"

"The horse wandered *up*? And climbed into a *wagon*? You lie to me as readily as you lie with innocent animals! You execrable pervert!"

"But give me due credit, master," whimpered the pervert. "Your mare could have gone farther, and been lost. Or I could have gone with her, and escaped."

"Bismillah, I wish you had! You are an insult to the noble institution of slavery!"

"Then sell me, master," sniveled the insult. "Foist me onto some unsuspecting purchaser and get me out of your sight."

"Estag farullah!" the dealer prayed toward Heaven at the top of his voice. "Allah pardon me my sins, I thought I had done just that. These gentlemen might have bought you, abomination, but now they have seen you caught in the act of raping my best mare!"

"Oh, I dispute that accusation, master," said the abomination, daring to speak with an air of righteous indignation. "I have known much better mares."

Speechless of words, the dealer clenched his fists and teeth and roared, "Arrrgh!"

Jamshid interrupted this singular colloquy, saying sternly, "Mirza Dealer, I assured the messieurs that you were a trustworthy seller of dependable merchandise."

"Before Allah, that I am, Wazir! I would not sell, I would not *give* them this walking pustule! I would not sell him to the harridan wife Awwa of the Devil Shaitan, I swear it, now that I know his true nature. I sincerely apologize to you, messieurs. And so will this creature apologize. You hear me? Apologize for that disgraceful exhibition. Abase yourself! Speak, Nostril!"

"*Nostril?*" we all exclaimed.

"It is my name, good masters," said the slave, unapologetically. "I have other names, but I am most often called Nostril, and for a reason."

He put a grimy finger to his blob of nose and pushed up the tip of it so we could see that instead of two nostrils he had only one large one. It would have been a sight repulsive enough, but was made more so by the profusion of snotty hair growing out of it.

"A minor punishment I once incurred for an even more minor misdemeanor. But be not prejudiced against me on that account, kind masters. As you can perceive, I am otherwise a distinguished figure of a man, and I have countless virtues besides. I was by profession a seaman, before I fell into slavery, and I have traveled *everywhere*, from my native Sind to the farthermost shores of—"

"Gèsu Marìa Isèpo," said Uncle Mafìo, marveling. "The man's tongue is as limber as his middle leg!"

We all stood fascinated and let Nostril babble on. "I would still be traveling, but for my misfortunate seizure by slavers. I was making love to a female shaqàl when the slave-raiders attacked, and you gentlemen doubtless know how a bitch's mihrab enclasps the loving zab and holds it trapped. So I could not run very fast, with the shaqàl bitch dangling from my front and bouncing and squawling. So I was caught, and my sea career ended and my slave career began. But I say in all modesty that I quickly became a nonpareil slave. You will have remarked that I am now speaking in Sabir, your trade language of the West—and now hearken, auspicious masters, I am speaking in Farsi, the trade language of the East. I am also fluent in my native Sindi, in Pashtun, in Hindi and Panjabi. I speak also a passable Arabic, and can get along in several of the Turki dialects and—"

"Do you never shut up in any of them?" asked my father.

Nostril went on, unheeding. "And I have many more qualities and talents of which I have not begun yet to speak. I am good with horses, as you must have noticed. I grew up with horses and—"

"You just said you were a seaman," my uncle pointed out.

"That was after I grew up, perspicacious master. I am also an expert with camels. I can cast and divine horoscopes in the Arab manner or the Persian or the Indian. I have refused offers from the most exclusive hammams to hire them my services as a rubber unsurpassed. I can dye gray beards with hinna, or remove wrinkles by applying quicksilver salve. With my single nostril I can play a flute more sweetly than any musician with his mouth. Also, employing that orifice in a certain other fashion—"

In unison, my father and uncle and the wazir severally exclaimed:

"Dio me varda!" and

"This man would disgust a maggot!" and

"Remove him, Mirza Dealer! He is a blot on Baghdad! Stake him out somewhere for the vultures!"

"I hear and obey, Wazir," said the dealer. "After I have shown you some other wares, perhaps?"

"It is late," said Jamshid, instead of what he might have said about the dealer and his wares. "We are expected back at the palace. Come, messieurs. There is always tomorrow."

"And tomorrow will be a cleaner day," said the dealer, glaring vengefully at the slave.

So we left the slave pen and the bazàr and wended our way through the streets and garden squares. We were nearly back at the palace before Uncle Mafìo thought to remark:

"You know? That despicable scoundrel Nostril never *did* apologize."

· 3 ·

AGAIN we had our servants dress us in our best new raiment, and again we joined the Shah Zaman for the evening meal, and again it was a delicious repast, again excepting the Shiraz wine. I remember that the concluding course was a confection of sheriye, which are a sort of pasta ribbons like our fetucine, these cooked in cream with almonds and pistachios and tiny slivers of gold and silver foil so very thin and dainty that they were to be eaten along with the rest of the sweet.

While we dined, the Shah told us that his Royal First Daughter, the Shahzrad Magas, had asked his permission, and he had given it, to act as my companion and guide, to show me the sights of the city and its environs—with of course the additional company of a lady chaperon—as long as I should be in Baghdad. My father gave me a sidelong glance, but thanked the Shah for his and the Princess's kindness. My father further declared that, since I would obviously be in good hands, it would be unnecessary to buy a slave to look after me. So he would head southward the very next morning toward Hormuz, and Mafìo toward Basra.

I saw them off at dawn, each of them riding away in the company of a palace guard assigned by the Shah to be their servants and protectors on the journey. Then I went to the palace garden, where the Shahzrad Magas waited, again with her grandmother discreetly shadowing, to give me my first day of sightseeing under her tutelage. I made her a very formal greeting of salaam, and said nothing of what else she had hinted at giving me, and neither did she speak of it for a while.

"Dawn is a good time to see our palace masjid," she said, and escorted me to that temple of worship, where she bade me admire the exterior of it, which was admirable indeed. The immense dome was covered with a mosaic of blue and silver tiles and topped with a golden knob, all shining in the sunrise. The manaret spire was like an elaborate giant candlestick, richly chased and engraved and inlaid with glowing gemstones.

At that moment I formed a private surmise, and I would speak of it here.

I already knew that Muslim men are bidden to keep their women sequestered and useless and mute and veiled from all eyes—in pardah, as the Persians call that lifelong suppression of their females. I knew that, by decree of the Prophet Muhammad and the Quran he wrote, a woman is merely one of a man's chattels, like his sword or his goats or his wardrobe, and she differs only in being the one of his chattels with which he occasionally couples, and that with the sole purpose of siring children, and those valued only when they are male, like him. The majority of devout Muslims, men and women alike, must not speak of sexual relations between them, or even the relation of mutual companionship, though a man might be leeringly frank about his relations with other men.

But I decided, on that morning when I gazed at the palace masjid, that Islam's strictures against the normal expression of normal sexuality has not been able to stifle *all* expression of it. Look at any masjid and you will see each dome copied from the female human breast, its aroused nipple erect to the sky, and in each manaret a representation of the male organ, likewise joyously erect. I might be mistaken in discerning those similarities, but I do not think so. The Quran has decreed inequality between men and women. It has made indecent and unmentionable the natural relation between them, and distorted it most shamefully. But Islam's own temples bravely declare that the Prophet was wrong, and that Allah made man and woman to cleave to each other and to be of one flesh.

The Princess and I went inside the masjid's wonderfully high and broad central chamber, and it was beautifully decorated, though of course entirely with patterns, not pictures or statues. The walls were covered with mosaic designs made of blue lapis lazura alternating with white marble, so the chamber was a soft and restful pale-blue place.

Just as there are no images in Muslim temples, there also are no altars, no priests, no musicians or choristers, no apparatus of the ceremonial, like censers and fonts and candelabra. There are no masses or communions or other such rites, and a Muslim congregation observes only one ritual rule: in praying, they all prostrate themselves in the direction of the holy city Mecca, birthplace of their Prophet Muhammad. Since Mecca lies southwest of Baghdad, that masjid's farther wall was to the southwest, and in the center of it was a shallow niche, a little taller than a man, also tiled blue and white.

"That is the mihrab," said Princess Moth. "Though Islam has no priests, we are sometimes addressed by a visiting wise man. Perhaps an imam, one whose deep study of the Quran has made him an authority on its spiritual tenets. Or a mufti, who is similarly an expert on the temporal laws laid down by the Prophet (peace and blessing be upon him). Or a hajji, one who has made the long hajj pilgrimage to Holy Mecca. And to lead our devotions, the wise man takes position yonder in the mihrab."

I said, "I thought the word mihrab meant—" and then I stopped, and the Princess smiled naughtily at me.

I was about to say that I had thought the word mihrab meant a woman's most private part, what a Venetian girl had once vulgarly called her pota, and a Venetian lady had more fastidiously called her mona. But then I took notice of the shape of that mihrab niche in the masjid wall. It was shaped exactly like a woman's genital orifice, slightly oval in outline and narrowing at the top to close in a pointed arch. I have been inside many another masjid, and in every one that niche is so shaped. I believe it to be an additional corroboration of my theory that human sexuality has influenced Islamic architecture. Of course I do not know—

and I doubt that any Muslim knows—which use of the word mihrab came first: the ecclesiastical or the bawdy.

"And there," said Princess Moth, pointing upward, "are the windows which make the sun tell the passing days."

Sure enough, there were openings carefully spaced about the upper periphery of the dome, and the new-risen sun was sending a beam across to the dome's opposite inner side, where there were inset slabs with Arabic writings entwined in their mosaics. The Princess read aloud the words where the beam rested. According to that evidence, the present day was, in the Muslim reckoning, the third day of the month Jumada Second in the 670th year of Muhammad's Hijra, or, in the Persian calendar, the 199th year of the Jalali Era. Then Princess Moth and I together, with much muttering and counting on our fingers, did the calculations necessary to convert the date to the Christian reckoning.

"Today is the twentieth of the month September!" I exclaimed. "It is my birthday!"

She congratulated me and said, "You Christians sometimes are given gifts on your birthdays, are you not, as we are?"

"Sometimes, yes."

"Then I will give you a gift this very night, if you are brave enough to run some risk in receiving it. I will give you a night of zina."

"What is zina?" I asked, though I suspected I knew.

"It is illicit intercourse between a man and a woman. It is haram, which means forbidden. If you are to receive the gift, I must sneak you into my chamber in the anderun of the palace women, which is also haram."

"I will brave any risk!" I cried wholeheartedly. Then I thought of something. "But . . . excuse me for asking, Princess Moth. But I have been informed that Muslim women are somehow deprived of—of their enthusiasm for zina. I have been told that they are, well, somehow circumcised, though I cannot imagine how."

"Oh, yes, tabzir," she said casually. "That is done to the general run of women, yes, when they are infants. But not to any infants of royal blood, or any who could in future become the wives or concubines of a royal court. It was certainly not done to me."

"I am happy for you," I said, and meant it. "But what *is* done to those unfortunate females? What *is* tabzir?"

"Let me show you," she said.

I was startled, expecting her to undress, right then and there, so I made a cautionary gesture at the lurking grandmother. But Moth only grinned at me and stepped to the preacher's niche in the masjid wall, saying, "Are you much acquainted with the anatomy of a female person? Then you know that here"—she pointed at the top of the arch—"toward the front of her mihrab opening, a woman has a tender buttonlike protrusion. It is called the zambur."

"Ah," I said, enlightened at last. "In Venice it is called the lumaghèta." I tried to sound as clinical as a physician, but I know I blushed as I spoke.

"The exact position of the zambur may vary slightly in different women," Moth went on, herself unblushingly clinical. "And the size of it may vary considerably. My own zambur is commendably large, and in arousal it extends to the length of my little finger's first joint."

Just the thought of it made *me* arouse and extend. Since the grandmother was present, I was again grateful for my voluminous nether garments.

The Princess blithely continued, "So I am much in demand by the other women of the anderun, because my zambur can service them almost as well as a man's zab. And women's play is halal, which means allowable, not haram."

And if my face had been pink before, it must have been maroon by now. But if Princess Moth noticed, it did not deter her.

"In every woman, that is her most sensitive place, the very nub of her sexual excitability. Without the arousal of her zambur, she is unresponsive in the sexual embrace. And lacking any enjoyment of that act, she does not yearn for it. That of course is the reason for the tabzir—the circumcision, as you called it. In a grown woman, until she is very much aroused, the zambur is modestly hidden between the closed lips of her mihrab. But in an infant female, that zambur protrudes beyond the little baby lips. An attending hakim can very easily snip it off with just a scissors."

"Dear God!" I exclaimed, my own arousal going instantly limp from horror. "That is not circumcision. That is the making of a female eunuch!"

"Very like it," she agreed, as if it were not horrible at all. "The child grows up to be a woman virtuously cold and devoid of sexual response, or even any desire for it. The perfect Muslim wife."

"Perfect?! What husband would want such a wife?"

"A Muslim husband," she said simply. "That wife will never commit adultery and make him a cuckold. She is incapable of contemplating an act of zina, or anything else haram. She will not even tease her husband to anger by flirting with another man. If she correctly keeps pardah, she will never even *see* another man—until she gives birth to a man-child. You understand, tabzir does not hamper her function of maternity. She can become a mother, and in that she is superior to a eunuch, who cannot become a father."

"Even so, it is a ghastly fate for a woman."

"It is the fate decreed by the Prophet (may blessing and peace be upon him). Nevertheless, I am thankful that we upper classes are exempted from many such inconveniences visited upon the common folk. Now, about your birthday gift, young Mirza Marco . . ."

"I wish it was already night," I said, glancing up at the slow-creeping sunbeam. "This will be the longest birthday of my life, waiting for night and zina with you."

"Oh, not with *me!*"

"What?"

She giggled. "Well, not exactly with me."

Bewildered, I said again, "What?"

"You distracted me, Marco, asking about the tabzir, so I did not explain the gift I am giving you. Before I explain, you must bear in mind that I am a virgin."

I started pettishly to say, "You have not been talking like—" but she laid a finger across my lips.

"True, I am not tabzir and I am not cold and perhaps you would call me not entirely virtuous, since I am inviting you to do something haram. It is true, too, that I have a most charming zambur, and I dearly love to exercise it, but only in ways halal which will not diminish my virginity. In addition to my zambur, you see, I have *all* my parts, including my sangar. That maiden membrane has not been breached, and never will be until I wed some royal Prince. It must not be breached, or no Prince would have me. I should be lucky if I were not beheaded for letting myself be despoiled. No, Marco, do not even dream of consummating the zina with me."

"I am confused, Princess Moth. You distinctly said you would sneak me into your chamber. . . ."

"And so I shall. And I shall remain with you there to assist you in zina with my sister."

"With your *sister?!*"

"Hush! The old grandmother is deaf, but sometimes she can read simple words from the lips. Now keep silent and listen. My father has many wives, so I have many sisters. One of them is amenable to zina. In fact, she can never get enough of it. And it is she who will be your birthday gift."

"But if she is also a royal Princess, why is her virginity not equally—?"

"I said keep silent. Yes, she is as royal as I, but there is a reason why she does not treasure maidenhood as I do. You will know everything tonight. But until tonight I will say no more, and if you pester me with questions I will rescind the gift. Now, Marco, let us enjoy the day. Let me command a coachman to take us for a ride about the city."

The coach, when it came for us, was really only a dainty cart on two high wheels, drawn by a single midget Persian horse. Its driver helped me hoist the infirm old grandmother up to sit beside him at the front, and the Princess and I sat on the inside seat. As the cart rolled down the garden drive and out through the palace gates into Baghdad, Moth remarked that she had not yet had anything of breakfast to eat, opened a cloth bag, took from it some greenish-yellow fruits, and bit into one and offered another to me.

"Banyan," she called it. "A variety of fig."

I winced at the word fig, and politely declined, not bothering to mention my Acre misadventure that had made figs repulsive to me. Moth looked sulky when I refused, and I asked her why.

"Do you know," she said, leaning close and whispering so the coachman would not hear, "that this is the forbidden fruit with which Eve seduced Adam?"

I whispered back, "I prefer the seduction without the fruit. And speaking of which—"

"I told you not to speak of it. Not until tonight."

Several other times during the morning's ride, I tried to broach that subject, but every time she ignored me, speaking only to call my attention to this or that point of interest and to tell me informative things about it.

She said, "Here we are in the bazàr, which you have already visited, but perhaps you do not recognize it now, all empty and deserted and silent. That is because today is Jumè—Friday, as you call it—which Allah appointed to be the day of rest, and there is no doing of trade or business or labor."

And she said, "That grassy parkland which you see yonder is a graveyard, which we call a City of the Silent."

And she said, "That large building is the House of Delusion, a charitable institution founded by my father the Shah. In it are confined and cared for all the persons who go insane, as many persons do in the hot summertime. They are regularly examined by a hakim, and if they ever regain their reason, they are set free again."

In the outer skirts of the city, we crossed a bridge over a small stream, and I was struck by the color of that water, which was a most unusually deep blue for mere water. Then we crossed another stream, and it was a most unwaterly vivid green. But not until we had crossed yet another, and it was as red as blood, did I make any comment.

The Princess explained, "The waters of all the streams out here are colored by the dyes of the makers of qali. You have never seen a qali made? You must see." And she gave directions to the coachman.

I would have expected to be taken back into Baghdad, and to some city workshop, but the cart went farther still into the countryside, and came to a stop beside a hill that had a low cave entrance halfway up it. Moth and I got down from the cart, climbed the hill and ducked our heads to go into the hole.

We had to go crouching through a short, dark tunnel, but then we came out inside the hill, and into a vastly wide and high rock cavern, full of people, its floor cluttered with work tables and benches and dye vats. The cavern was dark until my eyes got accustomed to its half-light, cast by innumerable candles and lamps and torches. The lamps were set on the various pieces of furniture, the torches were ensconced at intervals around the rock walls, some of the candles were stuck to the rocks by their own drip, and other candles were carried about in the hands of the multitude of workers.

I said to the Princess, "I thought this was a day of rest."

"For Muslims," she said. "These are all slaves, Christian Russniaks and Lezghians and such. They are allowed their due sabbath on Sundays."

Only a few of the slaves were grown men and women, and they worked at various tasks, like the stirring of the dye vats, on the floor of the cavern. All the rest were children, and they worked while floating high in the air. That may sound like one of the Shahryar Zahd's stories of magic, but it was a fact. From the high dome of the cavern hung a giant comb of strings, hundreds of strings, parallel and close together, a vertical web as high and as wide as the entire cavern's height and width. It was obviously the weft for a qali which, when finished, would carpet some immense palace chamber or ballroom. High up against that wall of weft, hung in loops of rope that depended from somewhere even higher in the roof darkness, dangled a crowd of children.

The little boys and girls were all naked—because of the heat of the air up there, Princess Moth told me—and they were suspended across the width of the work, but at various levels, some higher and some lower. Up there, the qali was partially completed, from its hem at the top of the weft down to those levels where the children worked, and I could see that it was, even at that early stage of progress, a qali of a most intricate and varicolored flower-garden design. Each of the dangling children had a candle stuck on its head with the wax, and all were busily engaged, but at what I could not discern; they seemed to be plucking with their little fingers at the unfinished lower edge of the qali.

The Princess said, "They are weaving the warp threads through the weft. Each slave holds a shuttle and a hank of thread of a single color. He or she weaves it through and makes it tight, in the order required by the design."

"How in the world," I asked, "can one child know when and where to contribute his bit, among so many other slaves and threads, and in such a complex work?"

"The qali master sings to them," she said. "Our arrival interrupted him. There, he begins again."

It was a wonderful thing. The man called the qali master sat before a table on which was spread a tremendous sheet of paper. It was ruled in countless neat little squares, over which was superimposed a drawing of the qali's entire intended design, with the innumerable different colors indicated. The qali master read aloud from that design, singing something on this order:

"One, red! . . . Thirteen, blue! . . . Forty-five, brown! . . ."

Except that what he chanted was far more complicated than that. It had to be audible away up there near the cavern roof, and it had to be unmistakably understood by each boy and girl it called upon, and it had to have a cadence that kept them all working in rhythm. While the *words* addressed one slave child after another, out of the great many of them, and told each one when to bring in his individual shuttle, the *singing* of the words either in a high tone or a low tone told that slave how far across the weft to warp his thread and when to knot it. In that marvelous manner of working, the slaves would bring the qali, thread by thread, line by line, all the way down to the cavern floor, and when it was finished it would be as perfect in execution as if it had been painted by a single artist.

"Just that one qali can eventually cost many slaves," said the Princess, as we turned to leave the cavern. "The weavers must be as young as possible, so they are light of weight and have tiny, agile fingers. But it is not easy to teach such demanding work to such young boys and girls. Also, they frequently swoon from the heat up yonder, and fall and break and die. Or, if they live long enough, they are almost sure to go blind from the close work and poor light. And for every one lost, another slave child must be already trained and standing by."

"I can understand," I said, "why even the smallest qali is so valuable."

"But just imagine what one would cost," she said, as we emerged again into the sunlight, "if we had to employ real people."

· 4 ·

T H E cart took us back to the city, and through it, and again into the palace gardens. Once or twice more I tried to pry from the Princess some hint of what would happen in the nighttime, but she remained adamant against my curiosity. Not until we got down from the cart, and she and her grandmother were leaving me to go to their anderun quarters, did she refer to our rendezvous.

"At moonrise," she said. "By the gulsa'at again."

I had a minor ordeal to go through before then. When I got to my room, the servant Karim informed me that I was to be accorded the honor of dining that evening with the Shah Zaman and his Shahryar Zahd. It was no doubt a signal kindness on their part, considering my youth and my insignificance in the absence of my ambassadorial father and uncle. But I confess that I did not much esteem the honor, and I sat wishing that the meal would hasten to its conclusion. For one reason, I felt slightly uncomfortable in the presence of the parents of the girl who had invited me to zina later that night. (Of the other girl, who would somehow share in the zina, I knew the Shah had to be the father, but I could not guess who might be her mother.) Also, I was literally salivating at the prospect of that which was to occur, even though I did not know exactly what *was* to occur. With my tongue glands thus uncontrollably gushing, I could hardly eat of the fine meal, let alone make sustained conversation. Fortunately, the Shahryar's loquacity precluded my having to say more than an occasional "Yes, Your Majesty" and "Is that a fact?" and "Do tell." For she did tell; nothing could have stopped her telling; but she told not many facts, I think.

"So," she said, "today you visited the makers of qali."

"Yes, Your Majesty."

"You know, in olden times there were magic qali which were capable of carrying a man through the air."

"Is that a fact?"

"Yes, a man could step onto a qali and command it to take him to some far, far distant part of the world. And off it would fly, over mountains and seas and deserts, whisking him there in the twinkling of an eyelid."

"Do tell."

"Yes. I will tell you the story of a Prince. His Princess lover was abducted by the giant rukh bird, and he was desolate. So he procured from a jinni one of the magic qali and . . ."

And finally the story was over, and finally so was the meal, and finally so was my impatient waiting, and, like the story Prince, I hurried to my Princess lover. She was at the flower dial, and for the first time she was unaccompanied by her crone chaperon. She took my hand and led me along the garden paths and around the palace to a wing of it I had not known existed. Its doors were guarded like all the other palace entrances, but Princess Moth and I merely had to wait in the conceal-ment of a flowery shrub until both the guards turned their heads. They did so in unison, and almost as if they were doing it on command, and I wondered if Moth had bribed them. She and I flitted inside unseen, or at least unchallenged, and she led me along several corridors oddly empty of guards, and around corners, and finally through an unguarded door.

We were in her chambers, a place hung with many splendid qali and with filmy, transparent curtains and draperies in the many colors of sharbats, looped and swathed and swagged in a delicious confusion, but all carefully kept clear of the lamps burning among them. The room was carpeted almost from wall to wall with sharbat-colored cushions, so many that I could not tell which were daiwan and which composed the Princess's bed.

"Welcome to my chambers, Mirza Marco," she said. "And to this."

And somehow she undid what must have been a single knot or clasp sustaining all her clothes, for they all dropped away from her at once. She stood before me in the warm lamplight, garbed only in her beauty and her provocative smile and her seeming surrender and one ornament, one only, a spray of three brilliant red cherries in the elaborately ar-ranged black hair of her head.

Against the pale sharbat colors of the room, the Princess stood out vividly red and black and green and white: the cherries red upon her black tresses, her eyes green and their long lashes black and her lips red in her ivory face, her nipples red and her nether curls black against the ivory body. She smiled more broadly as she watched my gaze wander down her naked body and up again, to rest on the three living ornaments in her hair, and she murmured:

"As bright as rubies, are they not? But more precious than rubies, for the cherries will wither. Or will they instead"—she asked it seduc-tively, running the red tip of her tongue across her red upper lip—"will they be eaten?" She laughed then.

I was panting as if I had run all the way across Baghdad to that enchanted chamber. Clumsily I moved toward her, and she let me ap-proach to her arm's length, for that was where her hand stopped me, reaching out to touch my foremost approaching part.

"Good," she said, approving what she had touched. "Quite ready and eager for zina. Take off your clothes, Marco, while I attend to the lamps."

I obediently disrobed, though keeping my fascinated eyes on her the while. She moved gracefully about the room, snuffing one wick after another. When for a moment Moth stood before one of the lamps, though she stood with her legs neatly together, I could see a tiny triangle of lamplight shine like a beckoning beacon between her upper thighs and her artichoke mount, and I remembered what a Venetian boy had said long ago: that such was the mark of "a woman of the most utterly desirable bedworthiness." When all the lamps were extinguished, she came back through the darkness to me.

"I wish you had left the lamps alight," I said. "You are beautiful, Moth, and I delight in looking at you."

"Ah, but lamp flames are fatal to moths," she said, and laughed. "There is enough moonlight coming through the window for you to see me, and see nothing else. Now—"

"Now!" I echoed in total and joyful accord, and I lunged, but she dodged adroitly.

"Wait, Marco! You forget, I am not your birthday gift."

"Yes," I mumbled. "I was forgetting. Your sister. I remember now. But why are you stripped naked, Moth, if it is she who — ?"

"I said I would explain tonight. And I will, if you will restrain your groping. Hear me now. This sister of mine, being also a royal Princess, did not have to endure the mutilation of tabzir when she was a baby, because it was expected that she would someday marry royalty. There-fore, she is a complete female, unimpaired in her organs, with all of a female's needs and desires and capabilities. Unfortunately, the dear girl grew up to be ugly. Dreadfully ugly. I cannot tell you how ugly."

I said wonderingly, "I have seen no one like that about the palace."

"Of course not. She would not wish to be seen. She is excruciatingly ugly, but tender of heart. So she keeps forever to her chambers here in the anderun, not to chance meeting even a child or a eunuch and fright-ening the wits out of such a one."

"Mare mia," I muttered. "Just how is she ugly, Moth? Only in the face? Or is she deformed? Hunchbacked? What?"

"Hush! She waits just outside the door, and she might hear."

I lowered my voice. "What is this thing's—what is this girl's name?"

"The Princess Shams, and that is also a pity, for the word means Sunlight. However, let us not dwell on her devastating ugliness. Suffice it to say that this poor sister long ago gave up hope of making any sort of marriage, or even of attracting a transient lover. No man could look at her in the light, or feel her in the dark, and still keep his lance atilt for zina."

"Che braga!" I muttered, feeling a frisson of chill. If Moth had not been still visible to me, only dimly but alluringly, my own lance might have drooped then.

"Nevertheless, I assure you that her feminine parts are quite normal. And they quite normally wish to be filled and fulfilled. That is why she and I contrived a plan. And, because I love my sister Shams, I conspire with her in that plan. Whenever she espies from her hiding place a man who wakens her yearning, I invite him here and—"

"You have done this before!" I bleated in dismay.

"Imbecile infidel, of course we have! Many and many a time. That is why I can promise you will enjoy it. Because so many other men have."

"You said it was a birthday gift—"

"Do you disdain a gift because it comes from a generous giver of gifts? Be still and listen. What we do is this. You lie down, on your back. I lie across your waist, staying always in your view. While you and I fondle and frolic—and we will do everything but the ultimate thing—my sister creeps quietly in and contents herself with your lower half. You never see Shams or touch her, except with your zab, and it encounters nothing repugnant. Meanwhile, you see and feel only me. And you and I will excite each other to a delirium, so that when the zina is accomplished down there, you will never know it is *not* me you are having it with."

"This is grotesque."

"You may of course decline the gift," she said coldly. But she moved close, so that her breast touched me, and it was anything but cold. "Or you can give me and yourself a delight, and at the same time do a good deed for a poor creature doomed always to darkness and nonentity. Well . . . do you decline it?" Her hand reached for the answer. "Ah, I thought you would not. I knew you for a kindly man. Very well, Marco, let us lie down."

We did so. I lay on my back, as instructed, and Moth draped her upper body across my waist, so I could not see below it, and we commenced the preludes of music-making. She lightly stroked her fingertips over my face and through my hair and over my chest, and I did the same to her, and every time we touched, everywhere we touched, we felt the sort of tingling shock one can feel by briskly rubbing a cat's fur the wrong way. But there *was* no wrong way she could have fondled me—or I her, as I discovered. Her nipples got perkily swollen under my touch, and even in the dim light I could see the dilation of her eyes, and I could taste that her lips were engorged with passion.

"Why do you call it music-making?" she softly asked at one point. "It is far nicer than music."

"Well, yes," I said, after thinking about it. "I had forgotten the kind of music you have here in Persia. . . ."

Now and then, she would extend a hand behind her, to stroke the part of me she was shielding from my sight, and each time that gave me a deliciously urgent start, and each time she withdrew her hand just in time, or I should have made spruzzo into the air. She let me reach a hand down to her own parts, only whispering in a quaver, "Careful with the fingers. Only the zambur. Not inside, remember." And that fondling made her several times come to paroxysm.

And later she was straddling my chest, her body upright, her nether curls soft against my face, so that her mihrab was within reach of my tongue, and she whispered, "A tongue cannot break the sangar membrane. You may do with your tongue all you can do." Though the Princess wore no perfume, that part of her was coolly fragrant, like fresh fern or lettuce. And she had not exaggerated in speaking of her zambur; it was like having the tip of another tongue meet mine there, and lick and flick and probe in response to mine. And that sent Moth into a constant paroxysm, only waxing and waning slightly in intensity, like the wordless singing she did in accompaniment.

Delirium, Moth had said, and delirium it became. I truly believed, when I made spruzzo the first time, that I was somehow doing it inside her mihrab, even though the mihrab was still close and warm and wet against my mouth. Not until my wits began to collect again did I realize that another female person had to be astride my lower body, and it had to be the seclusive sister Shams. I could not see her, and I did not try to or want to, but from her light weight upon me I could deduce that the other Princess must be small and fragile. I turned my mouth from Moth's avidly thrusting mount to ask, "Is your sister much younger than you are?"

As if coming reluctantly back from far distances, she paused in her ecstasy just long enough to say, in a breathless small voice, "Not . . . very much . . ."

And then she dissolved into her distances again, and I resumed doing my best to send her ever farther and higher, and I repeatedly joined her in that soaring exultation, and I made my subsequent several spruzzi into the alien mihrab, not really caring whose it was, but retaining enough consciousness to hope vaguely that the younger and ugly Princess Sunlight was enjoying her employment of me as much as I was enjoying it.

The tripartite zina went on for a long time. After all, the Princess Moth and I were in the springtime of our youth, and we could keep on exciting each other to renewed flowerings, and the Princess Shams gleefully (I assumed) gathered in my every bouquet. But at last even the seemingly insatiable Moth seemed sated, and her tremors dwindled, and so did my zab finally dwindle and sink to weary rest. That member felt quite raw and chafed by then, and my tongue ached at its roots, and my whole body felt empty and expended. Moth and I lay still for a while of recuperation, she limp upon my chest, with her hair disposed across my face. The three ornamenting cherries had long before been shaken loose and lost. While we lay there, I was conscious of a smeary wet kiss being bestowed upon my belly skin, and then there was a brief rustling sound as Shams scuttled unseen out of the room.

I got up and dressed, and Princess Moth slipped into a scanty little tunic that did nothing really to cover her nakedness, and she led me again through the anderun corridors and out into the gardens. From a manaret somewhere, the day's first muedhdhin was warbling the call to the hour-before-sunrise prayer. Still unchallenged by any guards, I found my own way through the gardens to the palace wing where my chamber was. The servant Karim was conscientiously waiting awake for me. He helped me undress for bed, and he made some awed exclamations when he saw my extremely spent condition.

"So the young Mirza's lance found its target," he said, but he did not ask any audacious questions. He only sniffled a bit, seeming aggrieved that I would not be having further need for his small ministrations, and he went to his own bed.

My father and uncle were absent from Baghdad for three weeks or more. During that time, I spent almost every day being escorted about and shown interesting things by the Shahzrad Magas, with her grandmother trailing, and almost every night I spent indulging in zina with both of the royal sisters, Moth and Sunlight.

In the daytime, the Princess and I did such things as going to the House of Delusion, that building which combined a hospital and a prison. We went there on a Friday, the day of rest when the place was much frequented by citizens at leisure, and also by foreign visitors from elsewhere, as one of the chief amusements of Baghdad. People came in families and in groups shepherded by guides, and at the door everyone was given by the doorkeeper a large smock to cover his clothes. Then all would stroll through the building, being lectured by the guides on the several kinds of madness exhibited by the men and women inmates, all of us laughing at their antics or commenting on them. Some of those antics were truly risible, and some were pitiable, and others were entertainingly lewd, but other doings were merely dirty. For example, a number of the deranged men and women appeared to resent us visitors, and pelted us with anything that came to their hand. Since all those inmates were sensibly kept naked and empty-handed, their only available missiles were their own body wastes. That was the reason for the doorman's distribution of smocks, and we were glad to be wearing them.

Sometimes in the nights in the Princess's chamber, I felt like some kind of inmate myself, subjected to supervision and exhortation. On perhaps the third or fourth of those occasions, early in the night's proceedings, before the sister crept in, when Moth and I had just disrobed and were enjoying our preliminary play, she stopped her roving hands to hold my roving own, and said:

"My sister Shams would beg a favor of you, Marco."

"I was afraid of this," I said. "She wishes to dispense with you as intermediary, and take your place up front."

"No, no. She would never. She and I are both happy with the arrangement as it is. Except for one small detail."

I only grunted, being wary.

"I told you, Marco, that Sunlight has had zina often and often. So often and so vigorously that, well, the poor girl's mihrab opening has been quite enlarged by that indulgence. To speak frankly, she is as open down there as a woman who has borne many children. Her pleasure in our zina would be much increased if your zab were in a sense enlarged by—"

"No!" I said firmly, and began to wriggle, trying to move crabwise out from under Moth. "I will not submit to any tampering—"

"Wait!" she protested. "Hold still. I suggest no such thing."

"I do not know what you have in mind, or why," I said, still wriggling. "I have seen the zab of numerous Eastern men, and my own is already superior. I refuse any—"

"I said be still! You have an admirable zab, Marco. It quite fills my hand. And I am sure that in length and girth it satisfies Shams. She suggests only a refinement of performance."

Now that was vexatious. "No other woman ever complained of my performance!" I shouted. "If this one is as ugly as you say she is, I suggest that she is hardly in a position to be critical of whatever she can get!"

"Hark to who is being critical!" Moth mocked me. "Have you any notion how many men dream, and dream fruitlessly, of ever lying with a royal Princess? Ever even once seeing a Princess with her *face* unveiled? And here you have *two* of them lying with you absolutely naked and compliant each night! You would presume to deny one of them a small whim?"

"Well . . . ," I said, chastened. "What is the whim?"

"There is a way to heighten the pleasure of a woman who has a large orifice. It enhances not the zab itself, but the—what do you call the blunt head of it?"

"In Venetian it is the fava, the broad bean. I think in Farsi that is the lubya."

"Very well. Now, I noticed of course that you are uncircumcised, and that is good, for this refinement cannot be accomplished with a circumcised zab. All you do is this." And she did it, tightening her hand around my zab and pulling the capèla skin back as far as it would go, and then a trifle farther. "See? It makes the broad bean bulge more grandly broad."

"And it is uncomfortable, almost to hurting."

"Only briefly, Marco, and bearably. Just do that as you first insert it. Shams says it gives to her mihrab lips that fine first feeling of being spread apart. Sort of a welcome violation, she says. Women enjoy that, I think, though of course I cannot know until I am married."

"Dio me varda," I muttered.

"And of course *you* do not have to do it, and risk touching Sunlight's ugly body. She will do that little stretching and broadening for you, with her own hand. She merely wished your permission."

"Would Shams wish anything further?" I asked acidly. "For a monster, she seems uncommonly finicking."

"Hark at you!" Moth mocked me again. "Here you are, in company that any other man would envy you. Being taught by royalty a trick of sex that most men never learn. You will be grateful, Marco, someday when you desire to give pleasure to a woman of large or slack mihrab, you will be grateful that you learned how. And so will she be grateful. Now, before Sunlight arrives, make *me* grateful a time or two, in other ways. . . ."

· 5 ·

O N some days, for entertainment and edification, Moth and I attended the sittings of the royal court of justice. It was called simply the Daiwan, from its profusion of daiwan pillows on which sat the Shah Zaman and the Wazir Jamshid and various elderly muftis of Muslim law, and sometimes some visiting Mongol emissaries of the Ilkhan Abagha. Before them were brought criminals to be tried, and citizens with complaints to be heard or boons to be asked, and the Shah and his wazir and the other officials would listen to the charges or pleas or supplications, and then would confer, and then would render their judgments or devisements or sentences.

I found the Daiwan instructive, as a mere onlooker. But had I been a criminal, I would have dreaded being hauled there. And had I been a citizen with a grievance, it would have had to be a towering grievance before I should have dared to take it to the Daiwan. For on the open terrace just outside that room stood a tremendous burning brazier, and on it was a giant cauldron of oil heated to bubbling, and beside it waited a number of robust palace guards and the Shah's official executioner, ready to put it to use. Princess Moth confided to me that its use was sanctioned, not only for convicted evildoers, but also for those citizens who brought false charges or spiteful complaints or gave untruthful testimony. The vat guards looked fearsome enough, but the executioner was a figure calculated to inspire terror. He was hooded and masked and garbed all in a red as red as Hell fire.

I saw only one malefactor actually sentenced to the vat. I would have judged him less harshly, but then I am not a Muslim. He was a wealthy Persian merchant whose household anderun consisted of the allowable four wives and the usual numerous concubines besides. The offense with which he was charged was read aloud: "Khalwat." That means only "compromising proximity," but the details of the indictment were more enlightening. The merchant was accused of having made zina with two of his concubines at the same time, while his four wives and a third concubine were let to watch, and all together those circumstances were haram under Muslim law.

Listening to the charges, I felt distinctly sympathetic to the defendant, but distinctly uneasy in my own person, since I was almost every night making zina with two women not my wives. But I stole a look at my companion Princess Moth, and saw in her face neither guilt nor apprehension. I gradually learned from the proceedings that even the most vilely haram offense is not punishable by Muslim law unless at least four eyewitnesses testify to its having been committed. The merchant had willingly, or pridefully, or stupidly, let five women observe his prowess and later, out of pique or jealousy or some other feminine reason, they had brought the khalwat complaint against him. So the five women also got to observe his being taken, kicking and screaming, out to the terrace and pitched alive into the seething oil. I will not dwell on the subsequent few minutes.

Not all the punishments decreed by the Daiwan were so extraordinary. Some were nicely devised to fit the crimes involved. One day a baker was hauled before the court and convicted of having given his customers short weight of bread, and he was sentenced to be crammed into his own oven and baked to death. Another time, a man was brought in for the singular offense of having stepped on a scrap of paper as he walked along the street. His accuser was a boy who, walking behind the man, had picked up that paper and discovered that the name of Allah was among the words written on it. The defendant pleaded that he had only unwittingly committed that insult to almighty Allah, but other witnesses testified that he was an incorrigible blasphemer. They said he had often been seen to lay other books atop his copy of the Quran, and had sometimes even held the Holy Book below his waist level, and once had held it *with his left hand.* So he was sentenced to be trodden, like the piece of paper, by the executioner and the guards until he was dead.

But only during the Daiwan sittings was the Shah's palace a place of pious dread. On more frequent religious occasions, the palace was the scene of galas and gaiety. The Persians recognize some seven thousand old-time prophets of Islam, and accord to every one of them a day of celebration. On the dates honoring the more major prophets, the Shah would give parties, usually inviting all the royalty and nobility of Baghdad, but sometimes throwing open the palace grounds to all comers.

Though I was not royal or noble, and not Muslim, I was a palace resident, and I attended several of those feste. I recall one night's holiday celebration of some long-defunct prophet, which celebration was held outdoors in the palace gardens. Every guest was given not the usual pile of daiwan cushions to sit or recline upon, but an individual, high-heaped mound of fresh and fragrant rose petals. Every branch of every tree was outlined in candles affixed to the bark, and that candlelight shone through the leaves in every shade and hue of green. Every flower bed was full of candelabra, and their candles' light shone through the multitudes of different blossoms in every shade and hue of every color. All those candles were sufficient to make the garden almost as bright and colorful as it was in daytime. But, in addition, the Shah's servants had beforehand collected every little tortoise and turtle to be bought in the bazàr or caught by children in the countryside, and had affixed a candle to the carapace of each one, and had let all those thousands of creatures loose to crawl about the gardens as moving points of illumination.

As always, there was more and richer food and drink provided than I had ever seen laid out at any Western festa. Among the entertainments there were players of musical instruments, many of which I had never seen or heard before, and to their music dancers danced and singers sang. The male dancers re-created, with lances and sabers and much foot stamping, famous battles of famous Persian warriors of the past, like Rustam and Sohrab. The female dancers scarcely moved their feet at all, but convulsed their breasts and bellies in a manner to make a watcher's eyeballs spin. The singers sang no songs of a religious nature—Islam frowns on that—but quite the other sort; I mean exceedingly bawdy songs. There were also bear trainers with agile and acrobatic bears, and snake charmers making the hooded snakes called najhaya to dance in their baskets, and fardarbab telling the tomorrows in their trays of sand, and shaukhran clowns comically garbed and capering and reciting or acting out lewd jests.

When I had got quite addled on the date liquor araq, I dismissed my Christian scruples against divination, and applied to one of the fardarbab, an old Arab or Jew with a funguslike beard, and asked what he could see in my future. But he must have recognized me for a good Christian unbeliever in his sorcerous art, for he only looked once into the shaken sand and growled, "Beware the bloodthirstiness of the beautiful," which told me nothing of my future at all, though I recalled having heard something like that before, in the past. So I laughed jeeringly at the old fraud, and stood up and twirled and pirouetted away from him, and fell down, and Karim came and supported me to my bedchamber.

That was one of the nights on which the Princesses Moth and Sunlight and I did not convene. On another occasion, Moth told me to find something else to do with my next few nights, because she was enduring her moon curse.

"Moon curse?" I echoed.

She said impatiently, "The female bleeding."

"And what is that?" I asked, truly never having heard of it before then.

Her green eyes gave me a sidelong look of amused exasperation, and she said fondly, "Fool. Like all young men, you perceive a beautiful woman as a pure and perfect thing—like the race of little winged beings called the peri. The delicate peri do not even eat, but live on the fragrance they inhale from flowers, and therefore they never have to urinate or defecate. Just so, you think a beautiful woman can have none of the imperfections or nastinesses common to the rest of humankind."

I shrugged. "Is it bad to think that way?"

"Oh, I would not say that, for we beautiful women often take advantage of that masculine delusion. But a delusion it is, Marco, and I will now betray my sex and disabuse you of it. Hear me."

She explained what happens to a girl child at about the age of ten, which turns her into a woman, and goes on happening to her thereafter, once in every moon of the year.

"Really?" I said. "I never knew. All women?"

"Yes, and they must bear that moon curse until they get old and dry up in every respect. The curse is also accompanied by cramps and backaches and ill temper. A woman is morose and hateful during that time, and a wise woman keeps herself away from other people, or drugged to stupefaction with teryak or banj, until the curse passes."

"It sounds frightful."

Moth laughed, but without humor. "Far more frightful for the woman if there comes a moon when she is not cursed. For that means she is pregnant. And of the damps and leaks and disgusts and embarrassments which then ensue, I will not even begin to speak. I am feeling morose and ill-tempered and hateful, and I will betake myself to seclusion. You go away, Marco, and make merry and enjoy your body's freedom, like all damned disencumbered men, and leave me to my woman's misery."

Despite the Princess Moth's depiction of the weaknesses of her sex, I could not then, or ever since then, think of a beautiful woman as being inherently flawed or faulty—or at least not until she proved herself to be so, as the Lady Ilaria once had done, and thereby had lost all my esteem.

Out here in the East, I was still learning new ways to appreciate beautiful women, and still making new discoveries about them, and I was disinclined to disparage them.

To illustrate: when I was younger, I had believed that the physical beauty of a woman resided only in such easily observable features as her face and breasts and legs and buttocks, and in less easily observable ones like a pretty and inviting (and accessible) artichoke mound and medallion and mihrab. But by this time, I had had enough women to realize that there were more subtle points of physical beauty. To mention just one: I am particularly fond of the delicate sinews that extend from a woman's groin along the inner sides of her thighs when she opens them apart. I also had come to realize that, even in the features common to all beautiful women, there are differences which are discernible, and exciting for being so. Every beautiful woman has beautiful breasts and nipples, but there are innumerable variations in size and shape and proportions and coloration, all beautiful. Every beautiful woman has a beautiful mihrab, but oh, how delectably different each is from another: in its placement forward or underneath, in its tint and downiness of the outer lips, in its purse-likeness and purse-tightness of closure, in its zambur's position and size and erectability. . . .

Perhaps I make myself sound more lecherous than gallant. But I only wish to emphasize that I never could and never did and never will disprize the beautiful women of this world—not even then, in Baghdad, when the Princess Moth, although herself one of them, did her best to show me their worst. For instance, one day she arranged for me to sneak into the palace anderun, not for our nighttime frolic, but in the afternoon, because I had said to her:

"Moth, do you remember that merchant whom we saw executed for his haram method of making zina? Is that the sort of thing that usually goes on in an anderun?"

She gave me one of her green looks and said, "Come and see for yourself."

On that occasion, indubitably, she had to have bribed the guards and eunuchs to look the other way, for she did not merely get me unseen into that wing of the palace, but also put me into a corridor wall's closet which had two peepholes drilled to look into either of two large and voluptuously furnished chambers. I peeped through one hole and then the other; both rooms were empty at the moment.

Moth said, "Those are communal rooms, where the women can congregate when they weary of being alone in their separate quarters. And this closet is one of the many watch places throughout the anderun where a eunuch takes station at intervals. He watches for quarrels or fights among the women, or other sorts of misbehavior, and reports them to my mother, the Royal First Wife, who is responsible for order being kept. The eunuch will not be in here today, and I will now go and let the women know that. Then we shall watch together and see what advantage they may take of the warder's absence."

She went away and then returned, and we stood back to back in the close space, each with an eye to one of the holes. For a long time nothing happened. Then four women came into the room I was watching, and disposed themselves here and there on the daiwan cushions. They were all about the age of the Shahryar Zahd, and about equally as handsome. One woman was apparently a native Persian, for she had ivory skin and night-black hair, but eyes as blue as lapis lazura. Another I took to be an Armeniyan, for each of her breasts was exactly the size of her head. Another was a black woman, Ethiope or Nubian, and she of course had paddle feet and spindly calves and a behind like a balcony, but she was otherwise fairly comely: pretty face with not too-everted lips, shapely bosom and fine long hands. And the fourth woman was so dusky of skin and dark of eyes that she must have been an Arab.

But the women's believing themselves to be not under scrutiny, and free to do what they liked, did not provoke any libertine throwing off of restraint or modesty. Except that none wore the chador, they were all fully clothed, and remained so, and they were not joined by any sneaked-in lovers. The black woman and the Arab had brought with them some kind of hand-held needlework, and occupied themselves with that lethargic pastime. The Persian sat with pots and brushes and little implements, and painstakingly manicured the finger and toe nails of the Armeniyan, and when that was done, both the women began coloring the palms of their hands and soles of their feet with hinna dye.

I was very soon bored to apathy, and so were the four women—I could see them yawn and hear them belch and smell them breaking wind—and I wondered why I had entertained any spicy suspicions of Babylonian orgies in a house full of women, just because all the women belonged to one man. Clearly, when so many women had nothing to do but wait for a summons from their master, there literally *was* nothing else for them to do. They could only loll about, no more enterprising or vivacious than vegetables, until the infrequent calls for the exercise of their animal parts. I might as well have been watching a row of cabbages going to seed, and I turned in the closet to say something like that to the Princess.

But she was grinning lasciviously, and she put a cautionary finger to her lips, then pointed it at her peephole. I leaned over and looked through, and barely suppressed an exclamation of surprise. That room had two occupants, one of them female, a girl considerably younger than any of my room's four—and also much prettier, perhaps because more of her was visible. She had taken off her pai-jamah and anything else she wore under that garment, and was bare from the waist down. She was another dusky-skinned Arab, but her pretty face was now pink with exertion. The male occupant of the room was one of those child-sized simiazze apes, so hairy all over that I would not have known it for a male, except that the girl was fervently working with one hand to encourage the animal's maleness. She eventually accomplished that, but the ape only looked stupidly at the upright small evidence, and the girl had to work just as strenuously to show him what to do with it, and where. But eventually that too was accomplished, while Moth and I took turns observing through the peephole.

When the ridiculous performance was concluded, the Arab girl wiped herself with a cloth, and then wiped at some scratches her partner had inflicted on her. Then she pulled on her pai-jamah and led the ape shuffling and hopping out of the room. Moth and I struggled from our closet, which had got quite warm and humid, out into the corridor where we could talk unheard by the four women still in the other room.

I said, "No wonder the wazir told me that animal is called the unspeakably unclean."

"Oh, Jamshid is just envious," the Princess said lightly. "It can do what he cannot."

"But not very well. Its zab was even smaller than an Arab's. Anyway, I should think a decent woman would rather employ the finger of a eunuch than the zab of an ape."

"Indeed, some do. And also you know now why my zambur is so much in demand. There are many women here who must wait a long and hungry time between summonses from the Shah. That is why the Prophet (peace and blessing be upon him) long ago instituted the tabzir. So that decent women should not be urged by their yearnings to unwifely resorts."

"I think, if I were Shah, I should much prefer my women's resorting to each other's zambur than to a random zab. Why, suppose that Arab girl gets pregnant by that ape! What revolting kind of offspring would she have?" The awful thought brought an even more awful one to my mind. "Per Cristo, suppose your gruesome sister Shams gets pregnant by me! Would I have to marry her?"

"Be not alarmed, Marco. Every woman here, of whatever nation, has her own native specific against such an occurrence."

I stared. "They know how to prevent conception?"

"With varying degrees of success, but all better than relying on chance. An Arab woman, for example, before making zina, pushes inside herself a plug of wool soaked in the juice of weeping willow. A Persian woman lines her inner self with the delicate white membrane from under the rind of a pomegranate."

"How abominably sinful," I said, as a Christian should. "Which works better?"

"Surely the Persian way is preferable, if only because it is more comfortable for both partners. Shams uses it, and I will wager that you never have felt it."

"No."

"But imagine ramming your tender lubya against that thick woolen plug inside an Arab woman. Anyway, I should distrust the efficacy of that method. What would an Arab woman know about preventing conception? Unless an Arab man *wants* to make a baby, he never does zina with his woman except through her rear entrance, as he is accustomed to using other men and boys, and they him."

I was relieved to learn that the Princess Shams was not going to be fruitful and multiply her ugliness, thanks to her pomegranate preventive, though by rights I should have been disquieted, because I was thereby participating in one of the most abhorrent and mortal sins a Christian can commit. At some time in my travels, or when I returned home to

Venice, I should again be in the vicinity of a Christian priest, and I should be obliged to make confession. Of course the priest would belabor me with penances for my having fornicated with two unmarried women at one time, but that was only a venial sin in comparison to the other. I could well foresee his horror when I confessed that, through the wicked arts of the East, I had been enabled to copulate for the sheer enjoyment of the act, with no Christian intention or expectation of progeny resulting from it.

Needless to say, I went on sinfully enjoying it. If there was any slight thing that hampered my total and complete enjoyment, it was not any nagging sense of guilt. It was my natural wish that each of my zina consummations could take place inside the Princess Moth to whom I was making love, and not in the unloved, unlovely Princess Shams. However, when Moth sternly repulsed my few tentative hints in that regard, I had the good sense to stop making them. I would not risk losing a happy situation out of greed for an unattainable happier one. What I did instead, I invented for myself a story, of a kind that might have been told by the story-telling Shahryar Zahd.

In my mind's story, I made Sunlight not what she was, the ugliest female person in Persia, but *the most gloriously beautiful*. I made her *so beautiful* that Allah in His wisdom decreed: "It is unthinkable that the divine beauty and the blessed love of the Princess Shams should be limited to the enjoyment of any one man alone." And *that* was why Shams was not married, and never would be. In obedience to almighty Allah, she was constrained to dispense her favors to all good and deserving suitors, and that was why I was currently the favored one. For a while, I utilized that story only when necessary. During most of each night's zina, I had no need of anything more than the real loveliness and closeness of the Princess Moth to stir and sustain my ardor. But then, when our mutual play had made the delicious pressure mount inside me until it could no longer be contained, and I had to let it go, then I brought to mind my invented, alternate, imaginary, unreally sublime Princess Sunlight, and made her the receptacle of my surge and my love.

As I say, that sufficed me for a while. But after that while, I gradually fell prey to a sort of mild lunacy; I began to wonder if my story might not be something near *the truth*. Getting increasingly demented, I began to suspect a deep secret here, and to suspect that, by the workings of my subtle mind, I had been the first and only to uncover that secret. Eventually, I had got so deranged that I began making new hints to Moth: hinting that I really would like to see her unseeable sister. Moth looked worried and agitated when I did that, and even more so when I daringly began mentioning her sister's name on occasions when we were in the presence of her parents and grandmother.

"I have had the honor of meeting most of your royal family, Your Majesty," I would say to the Shah Zaman or the Shahryar Zahd, and then add in an offhand manner, "Except, I think, the estimable Princess Shams."

"Shams?" he or she would say guardedly, and would look about in a shifty sort of way, and Moth would begin talking volubly to distract us all, while she rudely and almost literally elbowed me out of whatever room we were in.

God knows where that behavior might finally have got me—perhaps committed to the House of Delusion—but then my father and uncle returned to Baghdad, and it was time for me to say farewell to all three of my zina partners: to Moth and Shams and my story-made Shams.

. 6 .

M Y father and uncle returned together, having met somewhere on the roads north from the Gulf. On first setting eyes on me, before we even exchanged a greeting, my uncle jovially roared out:

"Ecco Marco! For a wonder, still alive and still vertical and still at liberty! Are you not in any trouble then, scagaròn?"

I replied, "Not yet, I think," and went to make sure I would not be. I sought out the Princess Moth and told her that our liaisons were at an end. "I can no longer stay out at night without causing suspicion."

"It is too bad," she pouted. "My sister has by no means tired of our zina."

"Nor have I, Shahzrad Magas Mirza. But in truth I am much weakened by it. And now I must regain my strength for the rest of our journey."

"Yes, you do look somewhat strained and haggard. Very well, I give you leave to desist. We will say our formal farewells before you depart."

So my father and uncle and I sat down with the Shah, and they told him they had decided against taking the sea route to shorten our way eastward.

"We thank you sincerely, Shah Zaman, for having made the suggestion," my father said. "But there is an old Venetian proverb. Loda el mar e tiente a la tera."

"Which means—?" the Shah said affably.

"Laud the sea and attend to the land. In more general application it means: Praise the mighty and the dangerous, but cling to the small and secure. Now, Mafìo and I have done much sailing on mighty seas, but never aboard such ships as those of the Arab traders. No overland route could be less safe or more risky."

"The Arabs," said my uncle, "build their ocean-going ships in exactly the same slipshod way they build their ramshackle river boats, which Your Majesty sees here at Baghdad. All tied and fish-glued together, not a bit of metal in the construction. And deckloads of horses or goats dropping their merda into the passenger cabins below. Maybe an Arab is ignorant enough to venture to sea in such a squalid and rickety cockleshell, but we are not."

"You are perhaps wise not to do so," said the Shahryar Zahd, coming into the room at that moment, although we were a gathering of men. "I will tell you a tale. . . ."

She told several, and all of them concerned a certain Sindbad the Sailor, who had suffered a series of unlikely adventures—with a giant rukh bird, and with an Old Sheikh of the Sea, and with a fish as big as an island, and I do not remember what else. But the point of her recitation was that Sindbad's every adventure had proceeded from his repeatedly taking passage on Arab ships, and each of those craft getting wrecked at sea, and his surviving to drift alone onto some uncharted shore.

"Thank you, my dear," said the Shah, when she had concluded the sixth or seventh of the Sindbad tales. Before she might begin another, he said to my father and uncle, "Was your trip to the Gulf entirely unprofitable, then?"

"Oh, no," said my father. "There was much of interest to see and to learn and to procure. For example, I bought this fine and keen new shimshir saber in Neyriz, and its artificer told me it was made of steel from Your Majesty's iron mines nearby. His words bewildered me. I said to him, 'Surely you mean steel mines.' And he said, 'No, we take the iron from the mines and put it into an ingenious sort of furnace, and the iron becomes steel.' And I said, 'What? You would have me believe that if I put an ass into a furnace it will come out a horse?' And the artificer had to make much explanation to convince me. In solemn truth, Your Majesty, I and all of Europe have always believed that steel was a totally different and much superior metal to mere iron."

"No," said the Shah, smiling. "Steel is but iron much refined by a process which perhaps your Europe has not yet learned."

"So I improved my education there in Neyriz," said my father. "Also, my trip took me through Shiraz, of course, and its extensive vineyards, and I sampled all the famous wines in the very wineries where they are produced. I also sampled—" He paused, and glanced at the Shahryar Zahd. "Also, there are in Shiraz more comely women, and more of them, than in any city I have visited."

"Yes," said the lady. "I was born there myself. It is a proverb of Persia that if you seek a beautiful woman, look in Shiraz; if you seek a beautiful boy, look in Kashan. You will be passing through Kashan as you go on eastward."

"Ah," said Uncle Mafìo. "And for my part, I found a new thing in Basra. The oil called naft, which comes not from olives or nuts or fish or fat, but seeps from the very ground. It burns more brightly than other oils, and for a longer time, and with no suffocating odor. I filled several flasks with it, to light our journey's nights, and perhaps also to astonish others like myself who never saw such a substance before."

"Regarding your journey," said the Shah. "Now that you have decided to continue overland, remember my warning of the Dasht-e-Kavir, the Great Salt Desert to the eastward. This late autumn season is the best time of year in which to cross it, but truthfully there is no good time. I have suggested camels for your karwan, and I suggest five of them. One for each of you and your personal panniers, one for your puller, one for the burden of your main packs. The wazir will go with you tomorrow to the bazàr and help you choose them, and he will pay for them, and I will accept your horses in exchange for that payment."

"That is kind of Your Majesty," said my father. "Just one thing—we have no camel-puller."

"Unless you are well versed in the management of those beasts, you will need one. I probably can help you with that item, too. But first get the camels."

So the next day, we three went again to the bazàr in company with Jamshid. The camel market was an extensive square area set off by itself, and it had a raised skirting of stone laid around it. The camels for sale were all arrayed standing with their forefeet on that shelf of stone, to make them seem to stand taller and prouder. That market was vastly more noisy than any other part of the bazàr, for to the customary shouting and quarreling of buyers and sellers were added the angry bellowing and mournful groans of the camels, as their muzzles were repeatedly seized and twisted to make them demonstrate their agility in kneeling and rising. Jamshid made that test and many others. He tweaked the camels' humps and felt up and down their legs and peered into their nostrils. After examining almost every full-grown beast on sale that day, he had five of them led apart, a bull and four cows. To my father he said:

"See if you agree with my selection, Mirza Polo. You will note that all have much larger forefeet than rear feet, a sure sign of superior staying power. Also they are all clean of nose worms. Always keep a watch for that infestation, and if you ever see worms, dust the nostrils well with pepper."

Since my father and uncle owned to no expertness in camel trading, they were pleased to concur in the wazir's selections. The merchant sent an assistant to lead the camels, hitched together in single file, to the palace stables, and we followed at our leisure.

At the palace, the Shah Zaman and Shahryar Zahd were waiting for us, in a room well heaped with gifts they wished us to convey for them to the Khakhan Kubilai. There were tightly rolled qali of the highest quality, and caskets of jewels, and platters and ewers of exquisitely worked gold, and shimshirs of Neyriz steel in gem-encrusted scabbards, and for the Khakhan's women polished looking glasses also of Neyriz steel, and cosmetics of al-kohl and hinna, and leather flasks of Shiraz wine, and tenderly wrapped cuttings of the palace garden's most prized roses, and also cuttings of seedless banj plants and of the poppies from which teryak is made. The most striking of all the gifts was a board on which some court artist had painted the portrait of a man, a man grim and ascetic of mien, but blind, his eyeballs being all white. It was the only delineation of any animate being I had ever seen in a Muslim country.

The Shah said, "It is a likeness of the Prophet Muhammad (peace and blessing be upon him). There are many Muslims in the Khakhan's realms, and many have no idea what the Prophet (blessing and peace be his) looked like in life. You will take this to show them."

"Excuse me," said Uncle Mafìo, with uncharacteristic hesitancy. "I thought lifelike images were forbidden by Islam. And an image of the very Prophet himself . . . ?"

The Shahryar Zahd explained, "It does not live until the eyes are painted in. You will engage some artist to do that just before you present the picture to the Khan. It requires only two brown dots painted onto the eyeballs."

The Shah added, "And the picture itself is painted in magic tinctures which in a few months will begin to fade, until the picture totally disappears. Thus it cannot become an image of worship, like those you Christians revere, which are forbidden because they are unnecessary to our more civilized religion."

"The portrait," said my father, "will be a gift unique among all the gifts the Khan is forever receiving. Your Majesties have been more than generous in your tribute."

"I should have liked to send him also some virgin Shiraz girls and Kashan boys," mused the Shah. "But I have tried to do that before, and somehow they never arrive at his court. Virgins must be difficult of transport."

"I just hope we can transport all *this*," said my uncle, gesturing.

"Oh, yes, with no trouble," said the Wazir Jamshid. "Any one of your new camels will easily carry all that burden, and carry it at the pace of eight farsakhs in a day, and for three days between drinks of water, if that be necessary. Assuming, of course, that you have a competent camel-puller."

"Which now you do have," said the Shah. "Another gift of mine, and this one is for you, gentlemen." He signaled to the guard at the door and the guard went out. "A slave which I myself only recently acquired, bought for me by one of my court eunuchs."

My father murmured, "Your Majesty's generosity continues to abound, and to astound."

"Ah, well," said the Shah modestly. "What is one slave between friends? Even a slave which cost me five hundred dinars?"

The guard returned with that slave, who immediately fell to the floor in salaam, and cried shrilly, "Allah be praised! We meet again, good masters!"

"Sia budelà!" exclaimed Uncle Mafìo. "That is the reptile *we* recoiled from buying!"

"The creature Nostril!" exclaimed the wazir. "Really, my Lord Shah, how did you come to acquire this excrescence?"

"I think the eunuch fell enamored of him," the Shah said sourly. "But I have not. So he is yours, gentlemen."

"Well . . . ," said my father and uncle, uncomfortable and unwilling to give offense.

"I have never known a slave more rebellious and odious," said the Shah, dropping any pretense of lauding his gift. "He curses and reviles me in half a dozen languages which I do not comprehend, except that the word pork occurs in all of them."

"He has also been insolent to me," said the Shahryar. "Fancy a slave criticizing the sweetness of his mistress's voice."

"The Prophet (on whom be all peace and blessing)," said the creature Nostril, as if ruminating aloud to himself. "The Prophet called that house accursed where a woman's voice could be heard outside its doors."

The Shahryar glared venomously at him, and the Shah said, "You hear? Well, the eunuch who bought him unbidden has been pulled asunder by four wild horses. The eunuch was expendable, having been born under this roof to one of my other slaves, and having cost nothing. But this son of a bitch shaqàl cost five hundred dinars, and should be more usefully disposed of. You gentlemen need a camel-puller, and he claims to be one."

"Verily!" cried the son of a bitch shaqàl. "Good masters, I grew up with camels, and I love them like my sisters—"

"That," said my uncle, "I believe."

"Answer me this, slave!" Jamshid barked at him. "A camel kneels to be loaded. It groans and complains mightily at each new weight of the loading. How do you know when to load it no further?"

"That is easy, Wazir Mirza. When it ceases to grumble, you have laid upon it the last straw it will bear."

Jamshid shrugged. "He knows camels."

"Well . . . ," mumbled my father and uncle.

The Shah said flatly, "You take him with you, gentlemen, or you stand by and watch while he goes to the vat."

"The vat?" inquired my father, who knew not what that was.

"Let us take him, Father," I said, speaking up for the first time. I did not say it with enthusiasm, but I could not have watched again an execution by boiling oil, even of this obnoxious vermin.

"Allah will reward you, young Master Mirza!" cried the vermin. "Oh, ornament upon perfection, you are as compassionate as the old-time darwish Bayazid, who while traveling found an ant caught in the lint of his navel, and went hundreds of farsakhs back to his starting place, to return that abducted ant to its home nest, and—"

"Be silent!" bellowed my uncle. "We will take you, for we would rid our friend the Shah Zaman of your reeking presence. But I warn you, putridity, you will enjoy precious little compassion!"

"I am content!" cried the putridity. "The words of vituperation and beatings bestowed by a sage are more to be valued than the flattery and flowers lavished by the ignorant. And furthermore—"

"Gèsu," my uncle said wearily. "You will be beaten not on your buttocks but on your clattering tongue. Your Majesty, we will depart at dawn tomorrow, and take this stench speedily out of your vicinity."

Early the next morning, Karim and our other two servants dressed us in good sturdy traveling garb in the Persian style, and helped us pack our personal belongings, and presented us with a large hamper of fine foods and wines and other delicacies, prepared by the palace cooks so that the viands would keep well and sustain us for a good part of our way. Then all three servants indulged in a performance of wild grief, as if we had been their lifelong beloved masters and were leaving them forever. They prostrated themselves in salaams and tore off their tulbands and beat their bare heads on the floor, and did not desist until my father distributed bakhshish among them, at which they saw us off with broad smiles and commendations to the protection of Allah.

At the palace stable, we found that Nostril had, without command or beating or supervision, got our riding camels saddled and the pack camel loaded. He had even carefully wrapped and arranged all the gifts being sent by the Shah, so they would not fall or jar against each other or be dirtied by the dust of the road, and, so far as we could determine, he had not stolen a single item from among them.

Instead of complimenting him, my uncle said sternly, "You scoundrel, you think to please us now and cozen us into leniency, so that we will be easygoing when you regress into your natural sloth. But I warn you, Nostril, we will *expect* this sort of efficiency, and—"

The slave interrupted, but obsequiously. "A good master makes a good servant, and gets from him service and obedience in direct proportion to the respect and trust accorded him."

"From all report," said my father, "you have not very well served your recent owners—the Shah, the slave dealer . . ."

"Ah, good Master Mirza Polo, I have been too long pent in cities and households, and my spirit gets crabbed by confinement. I was made by Allah to be a wanderer. Once I learned that you gentlemen are journeyers, I bent every effort to get myself expelled from this palace and attached to your karwan."

"Hm," said my father and uncle, skeptically.

"In so doing, I knew I risked an even more immediate release—like a dunking in the oil vat. But this young Mirza Marco saved me from that, and he will never regret it. To you elder masters, I will be the obedient servant, but to him I will be the devoted mentor. I will stand between him and harm, as he did for me, and I will sedulously instruct him in the wisdoms of the road."

So here was the second of the uncommon teachers I acquired in Baghdad. I heartily wished that it could have been another as comely and companionable and desirable as the Princess Moth. I was not much pleased at the prospect of being the ward of this scruffy slave, and possibly having some of his nasty attributes rub off on me. But I was disinclined to wound him by saying those things aloud, and I responded merely by making a face of tolerant acceptance.

"Mind, I do not claim to be a good man," said Nostril, as if he had overheard my thoughts. "I am a man of the world, and not all my tastes and habits are acceptable in polite society. Doubtless you will have frequent occasion to chide me or beat me. But a good traveler, *that* I am. And now that I shall be again upon the open road, you will appreciate my usefulness. You will see!"

So we three went to make our final and formal leavetakings of the Shah and the Shahryar and her old mother and the Shahzrad Magas. They had all risen early on purpose, and they said their farewells as feelingly as if we had been real guests instead of merely bearers of the Khakhan's ferman who had to be accommodated.

"These are the papers of ownership of that slave," said the Shah

Zaman, giving them to my father. "You will cross many borders from here eastward, and the border guards may require to know the identities of all in your karwan. Now goodbye, good friends, and may you walk always in the shadow of Allah."

Princess Moth said to us all, but with a special smile for me, "May you never meet an afriti or an evil jinni on the way, but only the sweet and perfect peri."

The grandmother nodded a mute goodbye, but the Shahryar Zahd said a leavetaking almost as long as one of her stories, concluding fulsomely, "Your departure leaves all of us here bereft."

At that, I made bold to say to her, "There is one here in the palace to whom I would like my personal regards conveyed." I confess, I was still slightly bemazed by my own made-up story about the Princess Sunlight, and by my delusion that I had almost uncovered some long-kept secret regarding her. Anyway, whether or not she was as sublimely beautiful as I had made her in my mind, she *had* been my unflagging lover, and it was only politeness to make especial farewell to her. "Would you give her my fond goodbye, Your Lady Majesty? I do not think the Princess Shams is your own daughter, but   "

"Really," said the Shahryar, with a giggle. "My daughter, indeed. You jest, young Mirza Marco, to leave us all laughing in good humor. I am sure you must be aware that the Shahrpiryar is the only Persian Princess named Shams."

I said uncertainly, "I have never heard that title before." I was puzzled, having noticed that the Princess Moth had retreated to a corner of the room and muffled her face in the qali draperies, only her green eyes visible and sparkling naughtily, as she tried to contain the laughter that was nearly doubling her over.

"The title Shahrpiryar," said her mother, "means the Dowager Princess Shams, the Venerable Royal Matriarch." She gestured. "My mother here."

Speechless with astonishment and horror and revulsion, I stared at the Shahrpiryar Shams, the wrinkled, balding, mottled, shrunken, moldy, decrepit, unspeakably old grandmother. She responded to my eye-extruding stare with a lascivious and gloating smile that bared her withered gray gums. Then, as if to make sure I did not fail of realization, she slowly ran the tip of her mossy tongue across her granulated upper lip.

I think I may have reeled where I stood, but somehow I followed my father and uncle out of the room without falling unconscious or vomiting on the alabaster floor. I only vaguely heard the cheery, laughing, mocking goodbyes Moth called after me, for I was hearing inside my head other mocking noises—my own fatuous query, "Is your sister much younger than you are?" and my imagined Allah's decree about "the divine beauty of the Princess Shams" and the fardarbab's sand reading, "Beware the bloodthirstiness of the beautiful . . ."

Well, this latest encounter with beauty had cost me no blood, and I daresay no one ever died of disgust or humiliation. If anything, the experience served to keep my blood long astir and red and vigorous afterward, for my every recollection of those nights in the anderun of the palace of Baghdad made my blood suffuse me with a blazing red blush.

· 7 ·

THE wazir, riding a horse, accompanied our little camel train for the isteqbal—the half a day's journey—which the Persians traditionally perform as a courteous escort for departing guests. During that morning's ride, Jamshid several times solicitously remarked on my mien of glazed eyes and slack jaw. My father and uncle and the slave Nostril also several times inquired if I was being made ill by the rolling gait of my camel. To each I made some evasive reply; I could not admit that I was simply stunned by the knowledge that for the past three weeks or so I had been blissfully coupling with a drooling hag some sixty years older than myself.

However, because I *was* young, I was resilient. After a while, I convinced myself that no real harm had been done—except perhaps to my self-esteem—and that neither of the Princesses was likely to gossip and make me a universal laughingstock. By the time Jamshid gave us his final "salaam aleikum" and turned his horse back for Baghdad, I was able again to look about me and see the country through which we were riding. We were then, and would be for some time, in a land of pleasantly green valleys winding among cool blue hills. That was good, for it enabled us to get used to our camels before we should reach the harder going in the desert.

I will mention that riding a camel is no more difficult than riding a horse, once one has acquired a head for the much higher altitude where one is perched. A camel walks with a mincing gait and wears a supercilious sneer, exactly like certain men of a certain sort. That gait is easy for even a new rider to adjust to, and the riding is easiest done with both legs on the same side, in the way a woman rides a horse sidesaddle, one's forward leg crooked around the saddle bow. The camel is reined, not with a bridle, but with a line tied to a wooden peg permanently fixed in its snout. The camel's sneer gives it a look of haughty intelligence, but that is entirely spurious. One must constantly be aware that a camel is among the most stupid of beasts. An intelligent horse may take a notion to play pranks, to vex or unseat its rider. A camel would never be capable of such an idea, but neither does it have a horse's good sense to watch its way and sidestep avoidable hazards. A camel's rider must stay alert and guide it even around obvious rocks and holes, lest it fall or snap a leg.

As we had been doing ever since Acre, we were still traveling through country that was as new to my father and uncle as it was to me, because they had earlier crossed Asia, both going eastward and returning home, by a much more northerly route. Therefore, with whatever misgivings, they left our direction to the slave Nostril, who claimed to have traversed this country many times in his life of wandering. And so he must have done, for he confidently led us along, and did not pause at the frequent branchings of the trail, but always seemed to know which fork to take. Precisely at that first day's sundown, he brought us to a comfortably appointed karwansarai. By way of rewarding Nostril's good conduct, we did not make him put up in the stable with the camels, but paid for him to eat and sleep in the main building of the establishment.

As we sat about the dining cloth that night, my father studied the papers the Shah had given us, and said:

"I remember your telling us, Nostril, that you have borne other names. It appears from these documents that you have served each of your previous masters under a different one. Sindbad. Ali Babar. Ali-ad-Din. They are all nicer sounding names than Nostril. By which would you prefer that we call you?"

"By none of them, if you please, Master Nicolò. They all belong to past and forgotten phases of my life. Sindbad, for example, refers only to the land of Sind where I was born. I long ago left that name behind."

I said, "The Shahryan Zahd told us some stories about the adventures of another habitual journeyer who called himself Sindbad the Sailor. Could that possibly have been you?"

"Someone very like me, perhaps, for the man was clearly a liar." He chuckled at his own self-deprecation. "You gentlemen are from the marine republic of Venice, so you must know that no seaman ever calls himself a sailor. Always seaman or mariner, sailor being a landsman's ignorant word. If that Sindbad could not get his own by-name correct, then his stories must be suspect."

My father persisted, "I must inscribe on this paper some name for you under our ownership. . . ."

"Put down Nostril, good master," he said airily. "That has been my name ever since the contretemps which earned it for me. You gentlemen might not believe it, but I was a surpassingly handsome man before that mutilation of my nose ruined my looks."

He went on at great length about how handsome he had been when he still had two nostrils, and how sought after by women enamored of his manly beauty. In his early days, as Sindbad, he said, he had so entranced a lovely girl that she had risked her life to save him from an island peopled by winged and wicked men. Later, as Ali Babar, he had been captured by a band of thieves and thrust into a jar of sesame oil, and would have had his talking head pulled off his softened neck but that another lovely girl, beguiled by his charm, had rescued him from the jar and the thieves. As Ali-ad-Din, he with his handsome looks had emboldened yet another comely girl to save him from the clutches of an afriti commanded by an evil sorcerer. . . .

Well, the tales were as implausible as any told by the Shahryar Zahd, but no more implausible than his assertion that he had once been a good-looking man. No one could have believed that. Had he had the normal two nostrils, or three, or none, it would not have improved his resemblance to a large-beaked, chinless, pot-bellied shuturmurq camel-bird, made even more comical by a stubble of beard under its beak. He went on even more incredibly, embellishing his claim of physical appeal by claiming to have done exploits of bravery and ingenuity and fortitude. We listened politely, but we knew all his rodomontata to be—as my father said later—"All vine and no grapes."

Some days afterward, when my uncle compared our eastward progress against the maps in the Kitab of al-Idrisi, he announced that we had arrived at a historic place. According to his calculations, we were somewhere very near the spot, recorded in *The Book of Alexander*, where, during the conqueror's march across Persia, the Amazon Queen Thalestris had come with her host of warrior women to greet and pay homage to him. We could only take Uncle Mafìo's word, for there was in that place no monument to commemorate the occasion.

In after years, I have often been asked whether I in my journeyings ever found the nation of Amazonia, or, as some call it, the Land of Femynye. Not there in Persia, I did not. Later, in the Mongol domains, I met many warrior women, but they were all subservient to their menfolk. I have also been often asked whether, out yonder in those far lands, I ever met the Prete Zuàne, called in other languages Presbyter Johannes and Prester John, that reverend and mighty man so shrouded in myth and fable and legend and enigma.

For more than a hundred years, the Western world has been hearing rumor and report of him: a direct descendant of the royal Magi who first worshiped the Christ child, hence himself royal and devoutly Christian, and furthermore wealthy and powerful and wise. As the Christian monarch of a reputedly immense Christian realm, he has been a figure to tantalize Western imagination. Given our fragmented West, of many and little nations, ruled by comparatively petty kings and dukes and such, forever warring against each other—and a Christianity continually sprouting new and schismatic and antagonistic sects—we needs must look with wistful admiration on a vast congeries of peoples all peaceably united under one ruler and one supreme pontiff, and both of those embodied in one majestic man.

Also, whenever our West has been beleaguered by heathen savages swarming out of the East—Huns, Tàtars, Mongols, the Muslim Saracens —we have fervently hoped and prayed that the Prete Zuàne would emerge from his still farther East and come up *behind* the invaders with his legions of Christian warriors, so that those heathens would be caught and crushed between his armies and ours. But the Prete Zuàne never *has* ventured out of his mysterious fastnesses, neither to help the Christian West in its recurrent times of need nor even to make demonstration of his existence in reality. Does he then exist, and if so, who is he? Does he really hold sway over a far-off Christian empire, and if so, where is it?

I have already speculated, in my earlier published chronicle of my travels, that the Prete Zuàne did exist, *in a sense*, and in that sense may still exist, but he is not and never was a Christian potentate.

Back when the Mongols were only separate and disorganized tribes, they called each tribal chief a Khan. When the many tribes united under the fearsome Chinghiz, he became the only Eastern monarch ruling over an empire resembling the one rumored to belong to the Prete Zuàne. Since the time of Chinghiz, that Mongol Khanate was ruled in part or in whole by various of his descendants, before his grandson Kubilai became Khakhan and enlarged it even further and consolidated it more firmly. All of those Mongol rulers down the years had different names, but all were titled Khan or Khakhan.

Now, I invite you to notice how easily the spoken or written word Khan or Khakhan could be misread or misheard as Zuàne or John or Johannes. Suppose a long-ago Christian traveler in the East misheard it so. He naturally would be reminded of the sainted Apostle of that name. It would be no small wonder if he thereafter believed he had heard mention of a priest or bishop named for the Apostle. He had only to mingle the misapprehension with the reality—the extent and power and wealth of the Mongol Khanate—and by the time he went home to the West he would have been eager to tell of an imaginary Prete Zuàne ruling an imaginary Christian empire.

Well, if I am right, the Khans probably did inspire the legend, through no doing of their own, but they are not Christians. And they never have owned any of the fabulous possessions ascribed to that Prete Zuàne—the enchanted mirror in which he spies on the distant doings of his enemies, the magic medicaments with which he can cure any mortal ill, his man-eating warriors who are invincible because they can subsist only on the enemies they vanquish—all those other fanciful marvels so reminiscent of the Shahryar Zahd's stories.

This is not to say that there are no Christians in the East. There are, and many of them, individuals and groups and entire communities of Christians, to be found everywhere from the Mediterranean Levant to the farther shores of Kithai, and they are of all colors, from white to dun and brown and black. Unfortunately, they are all communicants of the Eastern Church, which is to say followers of the doctrines of the fifth-century schismatic Abbot Nestorius, which is to say heretics in the eyes of us Christians of the Roman Church. For the Nestorians deny the Virgin Mary the title of Mother of God, they do not allow a crucifix in their churches, and they revere the despised Nestorius as a saint. They practice many other heresies besides. Their priests are not celibate, many of them are married, and all are simoniacs, for they will not administer any of the sacraments except for a fee of money paid. The Nestorians' only tie with us real Christians is that they worship the same Lord God, and recognize Christ as His Son.

That at least made them seem more kin to me and my father and uncle than did the far more numerous surrounding worshipers of Allah or Buddha or even more alien divinities. So we tried not to abhor the Nestorians too much—even while we disputed their doctrines—and they were usually hospitable and helpful to us.

If indeed the Prete Zuàne existed in actuality, not just in the Western imagination—and if, as rumored, he were a descendant of one of the Magi kings—then we ought to have found him during our traverse of Persia, for that is where the Magi lived, and it was from Persia that they followed the Nativity star to Bethlehem. However, that would have made the Prete Zuàne a Nestorian, since those are the only sorts of Christians existing in those parts. And in fact we did find among the Persians a Christian elder of that name, but he could hardly have been the Prete Zuàne of the legend.

His name was Vizan, which is the Persian rendition of the name rendered elsewhere Zuàne or Giovanni or Johannes or John. He had been born into the royalty of Persia—had indeed been born a Shahzadè, or Prince—but in his youth he had embraced the Eastern Church, which meant renouncing not only Islam, but also his title and heritage and wealth and privilege and right to succession in the Shahnate. All of that he had forsworn, to join a roving tribe of Nestorian bedawin. Now a very old man, he was that tribe's elder and leader and acknowledged Presbyter. We found him to be a good man and a wise man, and altogether an admirable man. In those particulars he well fit the character of the fabled Prete Zuàne. But he reigned over no broad and rich and populous domain, only a ragtag tribe of some twenty impoverished and landless shepherd families.

We encountered that bunch of sheep herders on a night when there was no karwansarai nearby, and they invited us to share their camping ground in the middle of their herd, and so we spent that evening in the company of their Presbyter Vizan.

While he and we made our simple meal around a small fire, my father and uncle engaged him in a theological discussion, and they ably discredited and demolished many of the old bedawi's most cherished heresies. But he seemed not in the least dismayed or ready to discard the shreds they left of his beliefs. Instead, he cheerfully turned the conversation to the Baghdad court we had recently inhabited, and asked after all there, who were of course his royal relatives. We told him that they were well and thriving and happy, although understandably chafing under the overlordship of the Khanate. Old Vizan seemed pleased with the news, though no whit nostalgic for that life of courtly ease he had long ago given up. Only when Uncle Mafìo chanced to mention the Shahrpiryar Shams—making me inwardly flinch—did the ancient shepherd-bishop heave a sigh that might have denoted regret.

"The Dowager Princess still lives, then?" he said. "Why, she would be nearly eighty years of age by now, as I am." And I flinched again.

He was silent for a time, and he took a stick and stirred the fire, and stared thoughtfully into its heart, and then he said, "Doubtless the Shahrpiryar Shams no longer shows it—and you good brethren may not credit my telling of it—but that Princess Sunlight in her youth was the most beautiful woman in Persia, perhaps the most beautiful of all time."

My father and uncle murmured noncommittally. I was still flinching at my all too vivid recollection of the wrecked and ravaged crone.

"Ah, when she and I and the world were young," said old Vizan, dreamily. "I was then still Shahzadè of Tabriz and she was the Shahzrad, first daughter of the Shah of Kerman. The report of her loveliness brought me from Tabriz, and brought innumerable other princes from as far away as Sabaea and the Kashmir, and none was disappointed when he saw her."

Under my breath, I made an impolite noise of scoffing incredulity, not loud enough for him to hear.

"I could tell you of that maiden's radiant eyes and rose lips and willow grace, but that would not begin to picture her for you. Why, just to look at her could heat a man to fever and yet refresh him at the same time. She was like—like a field of clover that has been warmed in the sun and then washed by a gentle rain. Yes. That is the sweetest-scented thing God ever put on this earth, and always when I come upon that fragrance I remember the young and beautiful Princess Shams."

Comparing a woman to clover: how like a rustic and unimaginative shepherd, I thought. Surely the old man's wits had been dulled if not scrambled by his decades of association with nothing but greasy sheep and greasier Nestorians.

"There was not a man in all Persia who would not have risked a drubbing from the Kerman palace guards, just to sneak near and steal a glimpse of Princess Sunlight walking in her garden. To have seen her uncovered of her chador veil, a man would have given his very life. In the remote hope of a smile from her, why, a man would have relinquished his immortal soul. As for any further intimacy, that would have been an unthinkable thought, even for the multitude of princes already hopelessly in love with her."

I sat staring at Vizan, amazed and unbelieving. The old hag I had spent so many nights naked with—a vision unattainable and inviolable? Impossible! Ludicrous!

"There were so many suitors, and all so anguished in their yearning, that the tender-hearted Shams could not or would not choose from among them, and thus blight the lives of all the rest. Neither could her father the Shah, for a long time, choose for her; he was so besieged by so many, each imploring more eloquently, each pressing upon him more precious gifts. That tumult of courtship went on literally for years. Any other maiden would have fretted at the passing of her springtime, and she not yet wed. But Shams only grew the more rose-beautiful and willow-graceful and clover-sweet as the time went on."

I still sat and stared at him, but my skepticism was slowly giving way to wonder. My lover had been all *that*? So exquisitely desirable to this man and to other men in that long-gone time, so exquisitely memorable that she was not yet forgotten, by this one at least, even now at the approaching end of his life?

Uncle Mafìo went to speak, and got to coughing, but at last cleared his throat and asked, "What was the outcome of that crowded courtship?"

"Oh, it had to come to a conclusion at last. Her father the Shah—with her approval, I trust—finally chose for her the Shahzadè of Shiraz. He and Shams were wed, and the whole Persian Empire—all but the rejected suitors—celebrated with joyous holiday. However, for a long time the marriage had no issue. I strongly suspect that the bridegroom was so overwhelmed by his good fortune, and by the pure beauty of his bride, that it was a long time before he could perform the consummation. It was not until after his father died, and he had succeeded as Shah in Shiraz, and Shams was thirty or older, that she gave birth to their only child, and then only a daughter. She was also handsome, so I have heard, but nothing like her mother. That was Zahd, who is now Shahryar of Baghdad, and I think has a nearly grown daughter of her own."

"Yes," I said faintly.

Vizan went on, "Had it not been for those events I have recounted—had the Princess Shams chosen otherwise—I might still be . . ." He poked at the fire again, but it was now only embers fast fading. "Ah, well. I was inspired to go away into the wilderness, and to seek. And I sought, and I found the true religion, and these my wandering brethren, and with them a new life. I think I have lived it well, and have been a good Christian. I have some small hope of Heaven . . . and in Heaven, who knows . . . ?"

His voice seemed to fail him. He said no more, not even a good-night, and got up from among us and walked away—wafting his smell of sheep wool and sheep dip and sheep manure—and disappeared into his much-weathered, many-patched little tent. No, I never did take him to be the Prete Zuàne of the legends.

When my father and uncle had also gone to roll into their blankets, I sat on by the darkening embers of the fire, thinking, trying to reconcile in my mind the derelict old grandmother and she who was the Princess Sunlight, unsurpassable in beauty. I was confused. If Vizan saw her now, would he see the aged and ugly crone, or the glorious maiden she once had been? And I, should I keep on feeling disgust because, in her old age, hardly even recognizable as female, she still felt feminine hungers? Or should I pity her for the deceit she had to employ now to slake them, when once she could have had any prince for the beckoning?

To look at it another way, should I congratulate myself and delight in the knowledge that I had enjoyed the Princess Sunlight for whom a whole generation of men had yearned in vain? But, trying to think along that line, I found myself wrenching present time into past time, and past into present, and confronting even more insubstantial questions—I was led to wonder: does immortality reside in memory?—and with such deep metaphysic my mind was incapable of grappling.

My mind still is, as most minds are. But I know one thing now which I did not then. I know it from my own experience and knowledge of myself. A man stays always the same age, somewhere down inside himself. Only the outside of him grows older—his wrapping of body, and *its* integument, which is the whole world. Inwardly he attains to a certain age, and stays there throughout his whole remaining life. That perpetual inner age may vary, I suppose, with different individuals. But in general I suspect that it gets fixed at early maturity, when the mind has reached adult awareness and acuity, but has not yet been calloused by habit and disillusion; when the body is newly full-grown and feeling the fires of life, but not yet any of life's ashes. The calendar and his glass and the solicitude of his juniors may tell a man that he is old, and he can see for himself that the world and all around him have aged, but secretly he knows that *he* is still a youth of eighteen or twenty.

And what I have said of a man, I have said because a man is what I am. It must be even more true of a woman, to whom youth and beauty

and vitality are so much more to be treasured and conserved. I am sure
there is not anywhere a woman of advanced age who has not inside her a
maiden of tender years. I believe that the Princess Shams, even when I
knew her, could see in her glass the radiant eyes and rose lips and willow
grace that her suitor Vizan still could see, more than half a century after
parting from her, and could smell the fragrance of clover after rain, the
sweetest-scented thing God ever put on this earth.

THE GREAT
SALT

· 1 ·

K A S H A N was the last city we came to in the habitable green part of
Persia; eastward beyond it lay the empty wasteland called the Dasht-e-
Kavir, or Great Salt Desert. On the day before we arrived in that city,
the slave Nostril said:

"Observe, my masters, the pack camel has begun to limp. I believe
he has suffered a stone bruise. Unless it is relieved, that could cause us
bad trouble when we get into the desert."

"You are the camel-puller," said my uncle. "What is your professional advice?"

"The cure is simple enough, Master Mafìo. A few days of rest for the
animal. Three days should do it."

"Very well," said my father. "We will put up in Kashan, and we can
make use of the delay. Replenish our traveling rations. Get our clothes
cleaned, and so on."

During the journey from Baghdad to this point, Nostril had behaved
so efficiently and submissively that we had quite forgotten his penchant
for devilry. But soon I, at least, had reason to suspect that the slave had
deliberately inflicted the camel's minor injury just to provide himself
with a holiday.

Kashan's foremost industry (and the source of the city's name) has for centuries been the manufacture of kashi, or what we would call mosaic, those artfully glazed tiles which are used throughout Islam for the decoration of masjid temples, palaces and other fine buildings. The kashi manufacture is done inside enclosed workshops, but Kashan's second most valuable article of commerce was more immediately visible to us as we rode into the city: its beautiful boys and young men.

While the girls and women to be seen on the streets—as well as could be seen through their chador veils—were of the usual mix, ranging from plain to pretty, with here and there one really worth noticing, *all* the young males were of strikingly handsome face and physique and bearing. I do not know why that should have been so. Kashan's climate and foods and water did not differ from those we had encountered elsewhere in Persia, and I could see nothing extraordinary in those local folk who were of an age to be mothers and fathers. So I have no least idea why their male offspring should have been so superior to the boys and young men of other localities—but they undeniably were.

Of course, being a young male myself, I should have preferred to be riding into Kashan's counterpart city, Shiraz, reportedly just as full of beautiful females. Nevertheless, even my uncaring eye had to admire what it saw in Kashan. The boys and youths were not dirty or pimply or spotty; they were immaculately clean, with glossy hair, brilliant eyes, clear and almost translucent complexions. They were not sullen of demeanor or slouching of posture; they stood straight and proud, and their gaze was forthright. They were not mumbly and slovenly of speech; they spoke articulately and intelligently. One and all, and of whatever class, they were as comely and attractive as girls—and girls of high birth, well cared for, well brought up and well mannered. The smaller boys were like the exquisite little Cupids drawn by Alexandrian artists. The larger lads were like the angels pictured in the panels of the San Marco Basilica. Though I was honestly impressed, and even a little envious of them, I made no vocal acknowledgment of that. After all, I flattered myself that *I* was no inferior specimen of my sex and age. But my three companions did exclaim.

"Non persiani, ma prezioni," my uncle said admiringly.

"A precious sight, yes," said my father.

"Veritable jewels," said Nostril, casting a leer about.

"Are they all young eunuchs?" asked my uncle. "Or fated to be?"

"Oh, no, Master Mafìo," said Nostril. "They can give as good as they get, if you take my meaning. Far from being impaired in their virile parts, they are *improved* in their other nether region. Made more accessible and hospitable, if you take my meaning. Do you comprehend the words fa'il and mafa'ul? Well, al-fa'il means 'the doer' and al-mafa'ul means 'the done-to.' These Kashan boys are bred to be beautiful and trained to be obedient and they are physically, er, modified—so that they perform equally delightfully as fa'il or mafa'ul."

"You make them sound far less angelic than they look," said my father, with distaste. "But the Shah Zaman said it was from Kashan that he procures virgin boys to distribute as gifts to other monarchs."

"Ah, the virgins, now, they are something else. You will not see the virgin boys on the streets, Master Nicolò. They are kept confined in pardah as strict as that of virgin Princesses. For they are reserved to become the concubines of those Princes and other rich men who maintain not just one anderun but two: one of women and one of boys. Until the virgin lads are ripe for presentation, their parents keep them in perpetual indolence. The boys do nothing but loll about on daiwan cushions, while they are force-fed on boiled chestnuts."

"Boiled chestnuts! Whatever for?"

"That diet makes their flesh get immensely plump and pale and so soft you can dent it with a fingertip. Boys of that maggot appearance are especially esteemed by the anderun procurers. There is no accounting for taste. I myself prefer a boy who is sinewy and sinuous and athletic in the act, not a sulky lump of suet that—"

"There is evidently lewdness enough here," my father said. "Spare us yours."

"As you command, master. I will only remark further that the virgin boys are vastly expensive to buy, and cannot be hired. On the other hand, observe! Even the street urchins here are beautiful. They can be cheaply bought for keeping, or even more cheaply hired for a quick—"

"I said be silent!" snapped my father. "Now, where shall we seek lodging?"

"Is there such a thing as a Jewish karwansarai?" said my uncle. "I should like to eat properly for a change."

I must explain that remark. During the past weeks, we had found most of the wayside inns run by Muslims, of course, but several of them had been the property of Nestorian Christians. And the degenerate Eastern Church foolishly observes so many fast days and feast days that *every* day is one or the other. So in those places we were either piously starved or piously glutted. Also, we were now in the month the Persian Muslims call Ramazan. That word means "the hot month," but, because the Islamic calendar follows the moon, its Hot Month occurs variously in each year, and can fall in August or January or any other time, and this year it came in late autumn. Whenever it comes, it is the month ordained for Muslims to fast. On each of the thirty days of Ramazan, from that morning hour when there is light enough to distinguish a white thread from a black one, a Muslim cannot partake of food or drink—or sex between man and woman—until the fall of night. Neither can he serve any comestible to his guests, whatever their religion. So in the daytimes we journeyers had not been able to beg even a dipper of well water from any Muslim establishment, while in every one of them, every day after sundown, we were absolutely gorged to stupefaction. For some time, then, we had all been suffering miseries of indigestion, and Uncle Mafio's suggestion was no expression of idle whim.

I need hardly remark that Jews in the East seldom engage in such an occupation as renting bed and board to passing strangers—any more than they do in the West—no doubt because it is less profitable and more laborious than moneylending and other such forms of usury. However, our slave Nostril was a most resourceful person. After only a little inquiry of passersby, he learned of an elderly Jewish widow whose house adjoined a stable which she no longer used. Nostril led us there, and got himself admitted to audience with the widow, and proved himself to be also a most persuasive envoy. He came out of her house to report that she would let us house our camels in her stable and ourselves in the hayloft above it.

"Furthermore," he said, as we towed the beasts in there and began to unload them, "since all the household servants are Kashan Persians and therefore bound by the strictures of Ramazan, the Almauna Esther has agreed to prepare and serve you gentlemen your meals with her own hands. So again you will be eating at your accustomed hours, and she assures me she is a good cook. The payment she asks for our stay is also most reasonable."

My uncle frankly gaped at the slave, and said in awe, "You are a Muslim, the thing most despised by a Jew, and we are Christians, the next-most despised things. If that were not enough to make this Widow Esther spurn us from her door, you must be the most repulsive creature she has ever set eyes on. How in God's name did you accomplish all this?"

"I am only a Sindi and a slave, master, but I am not ignorant or lacking in initiative. Also I can read and I can observe."

"I congratulate you. But that does not answer my question or lessen your ugliness."

Nostril scratched thoughtfully in his meager beard. "Master Mafio, in the holy books of your religion and of mine and of the Almauna Esther's religion, you will find the word beauty often mentioned, but never the word ugliness, not in any of those scriptures. Perhaps our several gods are not offended by the physical ugliness of mere mortals, and perhaps the Almauna Esther is a godly woman. Anyway, before those holy books were written, we were of one religion—my ancestors, the almauna's, perhaps yours as well—all were of the old Babylonian religion that is now abhorred as pagan and demonic."

"Impertinent upstart! How dare you suggest such a thing?" my father demanded.

"The almauna's name is Esther," said Nostril, "and there are Christian ladies also of that name, and it derives from the demon goddess Ishtar. The almauna's late husband, she tells me, was named Mordecai, which name comes from the demon god Marduk. But long before those gods existed in Babylon, there existed Noah and his son Shem, and the almauna and I are Shem's descendants. Only the later difference of our religions divides us Semites, and that should not have been too severely divisive. Muslims and Jews, we both eschew certain foods, we both seal our sons in the Faith with circumcision, we both believe in heavenly angels and loathe the same adversary, whether he is called Satan or Shaitan. We both revere the holy city of Jerusalem. Perhaps you did not know that the Prophet (may peace and blessing be upon him) originally bade us Muslims bow to Jerusalem, not to Mecca, when we make our devotions. The language originally spoken by the Jews and that spoken by the Prophet (all blessing and peace be his) were not greatly dissimilar, and—"

"And Muslims and Jews alike," my father said drily, "have tongues hinged in the middle, to wag at both ends. Come, Mafìo, Marco. Let us go and pay our own respects to our hostess. Nostril, you finish unloading the animals and then procure feed for them."

The Widow Esther was a white-haired and sweet-faced little woman, and she greeted us as graciously as if we had not been Christians. She insisted that we sit down and drink what she called her "restorative for travelers," which turned out to be hot milk flavored with cardamom. The lady prepared it herself, since it was not yet sundown and none of her Muslim servants could do so much as heat the milk or pulverize the seeds.

It seemed that the Jew lady did have, as my father had supposed, a tongue hinged in the middle, for she kept us in conversation for some while. Rather, my father and uncle conversed with her; I looked about me. The house clearly had been a fine one, and richly appointed, but— after the death of its Master Mordecai, I guessed—had got somewhat dilapidated and its furnishings threadbare. There was still a full staff of servants, but I got the impression that they remained not for wages but out of loyalty to their Mistress Esther and, unbeknownst to her, took in washing at the back door, or through some such genteel subterfuge supported themselves and her as well.

Two or three of the servants were as old and unremarkable as the mistress, but three or four others were the supernally handsome Kashan boys and young men. And one servant, I was pleased to note, was a female as pretty as any of the males, a young woman with dark-red hair and a voluptuous body. To pass the time while the Widow Esther prattled on, I made the cascamorto at that maidservant, giving her languishing looks and suggestive winks. And she, when her mistress was not observing, smiled encouragingly back at me.

The next day, while the lame camel rested, and so did the other four, we travelers all went separately out into the city. My father went seeking a kashi workshop, expressing a wish to learn something about the manufacture of those tiles, for he deemed it a useful industry that he might introduce to the artisans of Kithai. Our camel-puller Nostril went out to buy some kind of salve for the camel's bruised foot, and Uncle Mafìo went to get a new supply of the mumum depilatory. As it turned out, none of them found what he sought, because no one in Kashan was working during Ramazan. Having no errands of my own, I simply strolled and observed.

As I was to see in every city from there eastward, the sky over Kashan was constantly awhirl with the big, dark, fork-tailed scavenger kites circling and swooping. As also in every city from there eastward, the other most prevalent bird seemed to spend all its time scavenging on the ground. That was the mynah, which strutted aggressively about with its lower beak puffed out like the pugnacious underjaw of a little man looking for a quarrel. And of course the next most visible denizens of

Kashan were the pretty boys at play in the streets. They chanted their ball-bouncing songs and their hide-and-seek songs and their whirling-dance songs, just as Venetian children do, except that these songs were of the cat-screech variety. So was the music played by the street enter-tainers soliciting bakhshish. They seemed to own no instruments except the changal, which is nothing but a guimbarde or Jew's harp, and the chimta, which is nothing but iron kitchen tongs, so their music was nothing but a horrid cacophony of twang and clatter. I think the passerby who tossed them a coin or two did so not out of thanks for the entertainment but to interrupt it, however briefly.

I did not wander far that morning, for my stroll brought me around through the streets in a circle, and I soon found myself again approaching the widow's house. From a window the pretty maidservant beckoned, as if she had been waiting there just to see me pass. She let me into the house, into a room furnished with slightly shabby qali and daiwan pillows, and confided to me that her mistress was occupied elsewhere, and told me that her name was Sitarè, which means Star.

We sat down together on a pile of pillows. Being no longer a callow and inexperienced stripling, I did not set upon her with clumsy juvenile avidity. I began with soft words and sweet compliments, and only gradually moved closer until my whispers tickled her dainty ear and made her wriggle and giggle, and only then raised her chador veil and moved my lips to hers and tenderly kissed her.

"That is nice, Mirza Marco," she said. "But you need not waste time."

"I count it no waste," I said. "I enjoy the preliminaries as much as the fulfillment. We can take the whole day if—"

"I mean you need not do anything with me."

"You are a considerate girl, Sitarè, and kind. But I must tell you that I am not a Muslim. I do not abstain during Ramazan."

"Oh, your being an infidel does not matter."

"I rejoice to hear it. Then let us proceed."

"Very well. Loose your embrace of me and I will fetch him."

"What?"

"I told you. There is no need to continue in pretense with me. He is already waiting to come in."

"*Who* is waiting?"

"My brother Aziz."

"Why the devil would we want your brother in here with us?"

"Not we. You. I will go away."

I loosed my hold on her, and sat up and looked at her. "Excuse me, Sitarè," I said warily, not knowing any better way to ask it than to ask it: "Are you perhaps, er, divanè?" Divanè means crazy.

She looked genuinely puzzled. "I assumed you took notice of our resemblance when you were here last evening. Aziz is the boy who looks like me, and has red hair like mine, but is much prettier. His name means Beloved. Surely that was why you winked and leered at me?"

Now I was the one puzzled. "Even if he were as pretty as a peri, why would I wink at *you*—except that you were the one I—?"

"I tell you no pretext is necessary. Aziz saw you also, and was also instantly enthralled, and he already is waiting and eager."

"I do not care if Aziz is eternally adrift in Purgatory!" I cried in exasperation. "Let me put this as plainly as I know how. I am at this moment trying to seduce you into letting me have my way with you."

"Me? You wish to make zina with me? Not with my brother Aziz?"

I briefly pounded my fists on an unoffending pillow, and then said, "Tell me something, Sitarè. Does every girl in all of Persia misspend her energies in acting as procurer for someone else?"

She thought about that. "All of Persia? I do not know. But here in Kashan, yes, that is often the case. It is the result of established custom. A man sees another man, or a boy, and is smitten with him. But he cannot pay court to him outright, for that is against the law laid down by the Prophet."

"Peace and blessing be upon him," I muttered.

"Yes. So the man pays court to the other man's nearest woman relative. He will even marry her, if necessary. So that then he has excuse to be near his true heart's desire—the woman's brother perhaps, or maybe her son if she is a widow, or even her father—and has every opportunity to make zina with him. That way, you see, the proprieties are not openly flouted."

"Gèsu."

"That is why I supposed you were paying court to me. But of course, if you do not want my brother, you cannot have me."

"Whyever not? You seemed pleased to learn that I wanted you and not him."

"Yes, I am. Both surprised and pleased. That is an unusual preference; a Christian eccentricity, I daresay. But I am a virgin, and I must remain so, for my brother's sake. You have by now crossed many Muslim lands; surely you have comprehended. That is why a family keeps its maiden daughters and sisters in strict pardah, and jealously guards their virtue. Only if a maiden remains intact or a widow chaste can she hope to make a good marriage. At least, so it is here in Kashan."

"Well, it is the same where I come from . . . ," I had to admit.

"Yes, I shall seek to make a good marriage to a good man who will be a good provider and a good lover to us both, for my brother Aziz is all the family I have."

"Wait a moment," I said, scandalized. "A Venetian female's chastity is often an item of barter, yes, and often traded for a good marriage, yes. But only for the commercial or social advancement of her whole family. Do you mean the women here willingly endorse and connive in the lust of one man for another? You would deliberately become the wife of a man just so you could share him with your brother?"

"Oh, not just any man who comes along," she said airily. "You should feel flattered that both Aziz and I found you to our liking."

"Gèsu."

"To couple with Aziz commits you to nothing, you see, since a male has no sangar membrane. But if you wish to be the breaker of mine, you must wed me and take us both."

"Gèsu." I got up from the daiwan.

"You are going? Then you do not want me? But what of Aziz? You will not have him even once?"

"I think not, thank you, Sitarè." I slouched toward the door. "I simply was ignorant of local custom."

"He will be desolated. Especially if I have to tell him it was me you desired."

"Then do not," I mumbled. "Just tell him I was ignorant of local custom." And I went on out the door.

. 2 .

B E T W E E N the house and the stable was a little garden plot planted with kitchen herbs, and the Widow Esther was out there. She was wearing only one slipper, her other foot was bare, and she had the removed slipper in her hand, beating with it at the ground. Curious, I approached her, and saw that she was pounding at a large black scorpion. When it was pulped, she moved on and turned over a rock; another scorpion sluggishly crawled into view and she squashed that one, too.

"Only way to get the nasty things," she said to me. "They do their prowling at night, when they are impossible to see. You have to turn them up in daylight. This city is infested with them. I do not know why. My late dear husband Mordecai (alav ha-sholom) used to grumble that the Lord erred miserably in sending mere locusts upon Egypt, when He could have sent these venomous Kashan scorpions."

"Your husband must have been a brave man, Mirza Esther, to criticize the Lord God Himself."

She laughed. "Read your scriptures, young man. The Jews have been giving censure and advice to God ever since Abraham. You can read in the Book of Genesis how Abraham first argued with the Lord and then proceeded to haggle Him into a bargain. My Mordecai was no less hesitant to cavil at God's doings."

I said, "I once had a friend—a Jew named Mordecai."

"A Jew was your friend?" She sounded skeptical, but I could not tell whether she doubted that a Christian would befriend a Jew, or a Jew a Christian.

"Well," I said, "he was a Jew when I first met him, when he called himself Mordecai. But I seem to keep on meeting him under other names or in other guises. I even saw him once in one of my dreams."

And I told her of those various encounters and manifestations, each of them evidently intended to impress upon me "the bloodthirstiness of beauty." The widow stared at me as I talked, and her eyes widened, and when I was done she said:

"Bar mazel, and you a gentile! Whatever he is trying to tell you, I suggest that you take it to heart. Do you know who that is you keep meeting? That must be one of the Lamed-vav. The thirty-six."

"The thirty-six what?"

"Tzaddikim. Let me see—saints, I suppose a Christian would call them. It is an old Jewish belief. That there are always in the world just thirty-six men of perfect righteousness. No one ever knows who they are, and they themselves do not realize they are tzaddikim—or else, you see, that self-consciousness would impair their perfection. But they go constantly about the world, doing good deeds, for no reward or recognition. Some say the tzaddikim never die. Others say that whenever one tzaddik dies, another good man is appointed by God to that office, without his knowing he has been so honored. Still others say that there is really only one tzaddik, who can be in thirty-six places simultaneously, if he chooses. But all who believe in the legend agree that God will end this world if ever the Lamed-vav should cease doing their good works. I must say, though, that I never heard of one of them extending his good offices to a gentile."

I said, "The one I met in Baghdad may not even have been a Jew. He was a fardarbab tomorrow-teller. He could have been an Arab."

She shrugged. "The Arabs have an identical legend. They call the righteous man an abdal. The true identity of each of them is known only to Allah, and it is only on their account that Allah lets the world go on existing. I do not know if the Arabs borrowed the legend of our Lamed-vav, or if it is a belief which they and we have shared ever since the long-ago time when we were mutually the children of Shem. But whichever yours is, young man—an abdal bestowing his favor on an infidel or a tzaddik on a gentile—you are highly favored and you should pay heed."

I said, "They seem never to speak to me of anything but beauty and bloodthirstiness. I already seek the one and shun the other, insofar as I can. I hardly need further counsel in either of those respects."

"Those sound to me like the two sides of a single coin," said the widow, as she slapped with her slipper at another scorpion. "If there is danger in beauty, is there not also beauty in danger? Or why else does a man so gladly go a-journeying?"

"Me? Oh, I journey just out of curiosity, Mirza Esther."

"*Just* curiosity! Listen to him! Young man, do not ever deprecate the passion called curiosity. Where would danger be without it, or beauty either?"

I failed to see much connection among the three things, and again began to wonder if I was talking to someone slightly divanè. I knew that old people could sometimes get wonderfully disjointed in their conversations, and so this one seemed when she said next:

"Shall I tell you the saddest words I ever heard?"

In the manner of all old people, she did not wait for me to say yes or no, but went right on:

"They were the last words spoken by my husband Mordecai (alav ha-sholom). It was when he lay dying. The darshan was in attendance, and other members of our little congregation, and of course I was there, weeping and trying to weep with quiet dignity. Mordecai had made all his farewells, and he had said the Shema Yisrael, and he was composed for death. His eyes were closed, his hands folded, and we all thought he was peacefully slipping away. But then, without opening his eyes or addressing anybody in particular, he spoke again, quite clearly and distinctly. And what he said was this . . ."

The widow pantomimed the deathbed occasion. She closed her eyes and crossed her hands on her bosom, one of them still holding her dirty slipper, and she leaned her head back a little, and she said in a sepulchral voice, "I always wanted to go there . . . and do that . . . but I never did."

Then she stayed in that pose; evidently I was expected to say something. I repeated the dying man's words, "I always wanted to go there . . . and do that . . ." and I asked, "What did he mean? Go where? Do what?"

The widow opened her eyes and shook her slipper at me. "That was what the darshan said, after we had waited for some moments to hear more. He leaned over the bed and said, 'Go to what place, Mordecai? To do what thing?' But Mordecai said no more. He was dead."

I made the only comment I could think to make. "I am sorry, Mirza Esther."

"So am I. But so was he. Here was a man in the very last flicker of his life, lamenting something that had once piqued his curiosity, but he had neglected to go and see it or do it or have it—and now he never could."

"Was Mordecai a journeyer?"

"No. He was a cloth merchant, and a very successful one. He never traveled farther from here than to Baghdad and Basra. But who knows what he would have liked to be and do?"

"You think he died unhappy, then?"

"Unfulfilled, at least. I do not know what it was he spoke of, but oh! how I wish he *had* gone there while he was alive, wherever it was, and done whatever it was."

I tried tactfully to suggest that it could not matter to him now.

She said firmly, "It mattered to him when it mattered most. When he knew the chance was gone forever."

Hoping to make her feel better, I said, "But if he had seized the chance, you might be sorrier now. It may have been something—something less than approvable. I have noticed that sinful temptations abound in these lands. In all lands, I suppose. I myself once had to confess to a priest for having too freely followed where my curiosity led me, and—"

"Confess it, if you must, but do not ever abjure it or ignore it. That is what I am trying to tell you. If a man is to have a fault, it should be a passionate one, like insatiable curiosity. It would be a pity to be damned for something paltry."

"I hope not to be damned, Mirza Esther," I said piously, "as I trust the Mirza Mordecai was not. It may well have been out of virtue that he let that chance go by, whatever it was. Since you cannot know, you need not weep for—"

"I am not weeping. I did not broach the matter to sniffle over it."

I wondered why, then, she had bothered to broach it. And, as if in reply to my silent question, she went on:

"I wanted you to know this. When you come at last to die, you may be devoid of all other urges and senses and faculties, but you will still possess your passion of curiosity. It is something that even cloth merchants have, perhaps even clerks and other such drudges. Certainly a journeyer has it. And in those last moments it will make you grieve—as Mordecai did—not for anything you have done in your lifetime, but for the things you never got to do."

"Mirza Esther," I protested. "A man cannot live always in dread of missing something. I fully expect never to be Pope, for instance, or Shah of Persia, but I hope that lack will not blight my life. Or my deathbed either."

"I do not mean things unattainable. Mordecai died lamenting something that had been within his reach, within his capability, within his having, and he let it go by. Imagine yourself pining for the sights and delights and experiences you could have had, but missed—or even just one single small such experience—and pining too late, when it *is* forever unattainable."

Obediently, I did try to imagine that. And young though I was, remote though I assumed that prospect to be, I felt a faint chill.

"Imagine going into death," she went on implacably, "without having tasted everything in this world. The good, the bad, the indifferent even. And to know, at that final moment, that it was no one but you who deprived yourself, through your own careful caution or careless choice or failure to follow where your curiosity led. Tell me, young man, could there be any more hurtful pang on the *other* side of death? Even damnation itself?"

After the moment it took me to shake off the chill, I said, as cheerfully as I could, "Well, with the help of those thirty-six you spoke of, maybe I can avoid both deprivation in my lifetime and damnation after it."

"Aleichem sholem," she said. But, as she was swatting with her slipper at another scorpion at that moment, I was not sure if she was wishing peace to me or to it.

She moved on down the garden, turning over rocks, and I idly ambled into the stable to see if any of our party had returned from wandering about town. One of them had, but not alone, and the sight brought me up short, with a gasp.

Our slave Nostril was there, with a stranger, one of the gorgeous young Kashan men. Perhaps my conversation with the maidservant Sitarè had made me temporarily impervious to disgust, for I did not make violent outcry or retreat from the scene. I looked on as indifferently as did the camels, which only shuffled and mumbled and munched. Both of the men were naked, and the stranger was on his hands and knees in the straw, and our slave was hunched over his backside, bucking like a camel in rut. The lewdly coupling Sodomites turned their heads when I entered, but only grinned at me and kept on with their indecency.

The young man had a body that was as handsome to look upon as his face was. But Nostril, even when fully clothed, was of a repellent appearance, as I have already described. I can only say further that his paunchy torso and pimply buttocks and spindly limbs, when totally exposed, were a sight to make most onlookers retch up their most recent meal. I was amazed that such a revolting creature could have persuaded anyone the least bit less revolting to play al-mafa'ul to his al-fa'il.

Nostril's fa'il implement was invisible to me, being inserted where it was, but the young man's organ was visible below his belly, and stiffened into its candelòto aspect. I thought that somewhat odd, since neither he nor Nostril was manipulating it in any way. And it seemed even more odd, when he and Nostril finally groaned and writhed together, to see his candelòto—still without benefit of touch or fondling—squirt spruzzo into the straw on the floor.

After they had briefly rested and panted, Nostril heaved his sweat-shiny bulk off the young man's back. Without dipping a wash of water from the camel trough, without even wadding some straw to wipe his extremely wee little organ, he began putting his clothes back on, and humming a merry tune as he did so. The young stranger more indolently and slowly began to get dressed, as if he frankly enjoyed displaying his nude body even under such disgraceful circumstances.

Leaning against a stall partition, I said to our slave, as if we had all the while been chatting companionably, "You know something, Nostril? There are many rascals and scamps portrayed in song and story—characters like Encolpios and Renart the Fox. They live a gay vagabond life, and they live by their foxy wits, but somehow they are never guilty of crime or sin. They commit only pranks and jests. They steal from none but thieves, their amatory exploits are never sordid, they drink and carouse without ever getting drunk or foolish, their swordplay never causes more than a flesh wound. They have winning ways and twinkling eyes and a ready laugh, even on the scaffold, for they never hang. Whatever the adventure, those adventurous scoundrels are always charming and dashing, clever and amusing. Such stories make one want to *meet* such a brave, bold, lovable rascal."

"And now you have," said Nostril. He twinkled his piggy eyes and smiled to show his stubble teeth and struck a pose that he probably thought was dashing.

"Now I have," I said. "And there is nothing lovable or admirable about you. If you are the typical rascal, then all the stories are lies, and a rascal is a swine. You are filthy of person and of habit, loathsome in appearance and character, cloacal in your proclivities. You are altogether deserving of that seething oil vat from which I too indulgently argued for your rescue."

The handsome stranger laughed coarsely at that. Nostril sniffled and muttered, "Master Marco, as a devout Muslim I must object to being likened to a swine."

"I hope you would also balk at coupling with a sow," I said. "But I doubt it."

"Please, young master. I am devoutly keeping Ramazan, which prohibits intercourse between Muslim men and women. I must also admit that, even in the permissible months, women are sometimes hard for me to come by, ever since my pretty face was disfigured by my nose's misfortune."

"Oh, do not exaggerate," I said. "There is always somewhere a woman desperate enough for anything. In my lifetime, I have seen a Slavic woman couple with a black man and an Arab woman couple with an actual ape."

Nostril said loftily, "I hope you do not suppose that I would condescend to a woman as ugly as I am. Ah, but Jafar here—Jafar is as comely as the comeliest woman."

I growled, "Tell your comely wretch to hurry with his dressing and get out of here, or I will feed him to the camels."

The comely wretch glared at me, then gave a melting look of entreaty to Nostril, who immediately insulted me with an impertinent question: "You would not like to try him yourself, Master Marco? The experience might broaden your mind."

"I will broaden your one nose-hole!" I snarled, taking the dagger from my belt. "I will open it all the way around your ugly head! How dare you speak so to a master? What do you take me for?"

"For a young man with much yet to learn," he said. "You are a journeyer now, Master Marco, and before you get home again you will have traveled much farther yet, and seen and experienced much more. When you do arrive home at last, you will be rightfully scornful of men there who call mountains high and swamps deep, without their ever having scaled a mountain or plumbed a swamp—men who have never ventured beyond their narrow streets and their commonplace routines and their cautious pastimes and their pinched little lives."

"Perhaps so. But what has that to do with your galineta whore?"

"There are other journeys that can take a man beyond the ordinary, Master Marco, not in distance of travel but in breadth of understanding. Consider. You have reviled this young man as a whore, when he is only what he was bred and developed and trained and expected to be."

"A Sodomite, then, if you prefer. To a Christian, that is a sinful thing to be—a sinner and a sin to be abhorred."

"I ask you, Master Marco, to make only a short journey into the world of this young man." Before I could object, he said, "Jafar, tell the foreigner of your upbringing."

Still clutching his lower garment in his hand, and glancing uneasily at me, Jafar began. "Oh, young Mirza, reflection of the light of Allah—"

"Never mind that," said Nostril. "Just tell of your body's preparation for sexual commerce."

"Oh, blessing of the world," Jafar began again. "From the earliest years I can remember, always while I slept I wore inserted into my nether aperture a golulè, which is an implement made of kashi ceramic, a sort of small tapered cone. Every time my bedtime toilet was completed, the golulè was put into me, well greased with some drug to stimulate the development of my badàm. My mother or nurse would at intervals ease it farther inside me, and when I could accommodate it all, a larger golulè was substituted. Thus my opening gradually grew more ample, but without impairing the muscle of closure which surrounds it."

"Thank you for the story," I said to him, but coldly, and to Nostril I said, "Born so or made so, a Sodomite is still an abomination."

"I think his story is not finished," said Nostril. "Bear with the journey only a little farther."

"When I was perhaps five or six years old," Jafar went on, "I was relieved of having to wear the golulè, and instead my next older brother was encouraged to use me whenever he had an urge and an erected organ."

"Adrìo de vu!" I gasped, compassion getting the better of my revulsion. "What a horrible childhood!"

"It could have been worse," said Nostril. "When a bandit or slave-taker captures a boy, and that boy has not been thus carefully prepared, the captor brutally impales him there with a tent peg, to make the opening fit for subsequent use. But that tears the encircling muscle, and the boy can never thereafter contain himself, but excretes incontinently. Also, he cannot thereafter utilize that muscle to give pleasurable contractions during the act. Go on, Jafar."

"When I had got accustomed to that brother's usage, my next older and better-equipped brother helped my further development. And when my badàm was mature enough to let me begin to *enjoy* the act, then my father . . ."

"Adrìo de vu!" I exclaimed again. But now curiosity had got the better of both my revulsion and my compassion. "What do you mean about the badàm?" I could not comprehend that detail, for the word badàm means an almond.

"You did not know of it?" said Nostril with surprise. "Why, you have one yourself. Every male does. We call it the almond because of its shape and size, but physicians sometimes refer to it as the third testicle. It is situated behind the other two, not in the bag, but hidden up inside your groin. A finger or, ahem, any other object inserted far enough into your anus rubs against that almond and stimulates it to a pleasurable excitement."

"Ah," I said, enlightened. "So that is why, just now, Jafar made spruzzo seemingly without any caress or provocation."

"We call that spurt the almond milk," Nostril said primly. He added, "Some women of talent and experience know of that invisible male gland. In one way or another, they tickle it while they are coupling with a man, so that when he ejaculates the almond milk his enjoyment is blissfully heightened."

I wagged my head wonderingly, and said, "You are right, Nostril. A man can learn new things from journeying." I slid my dagger back into its sheath. "This time at least, I forgive the brash way you spoke to me."

He replied smugly, "A good slave puts utility before humility. And now, Master Marco, perhaps you would like to slip your other weapon into another sheath? Observe Jafar's splendid scabbard—"

"Scagaròn!" I snapped. "I may tolerate such customs of others while

I am in these regions, but I will not partake of them. Even if Sodomy were not a vile sin, I should still prefer the love of women."

"Love, master?" echoed Nostril, and Jafar laughed in his coarse way, and one of the camels belched. "No one spoke of love. The love between a man and a man is another thing entirely, and I believe that only we warmhearted warrior Muslims can know that most sublime of all emotions. I doubt that any cold-blooded and peace-preaching Christian could be capable of that love. No, master, I was suggesting merely a matter of convenient release and relief and satisfaction. For that, what difference what sex?"

I snorted like a supercilious camel. "Easy for you to say, slave, since to you it makes no difference what *animal*. As for me, I am happy to say that as long as there are women in the world I shall have no yearning for men to couple with. I am a man myself, and I am too familiar with my own body to have the least interest in that of any other male. But women—ah, women! They are so magnificently different from me, and each so exquisitely different from another I can never value them enough!"

"Value them, master?" He sounded amused.

"Yes." I paused, then said with due solemnity, "I once killed a man, Nostril, but I could never bring myself to kill a woman."

"You are young yet."

"Now, Jafar," I said to the young man, "put on the rest of your clothes and go, before my father and uncle get back here."

"I saw them arrive just now, Master Marco," said Nostril. "They went with the Almauna Esther into her house."

So I went over there, too, and was again waylaid by the maidservant Sitarè, as she let me in the door. I would have gone on by her unheeding, but she took me by the arm and whispered, "Do not speak loudly."

I said, not whispering, "I have nothing to speak to you about."

"Hush. The mistress is inside, and your father and uncle are with her. So do not let them hear, but answer me. My brother Aziz and I have discussed the matter of you and—"

"I am not a matter!" I said testily. "I do not much like my being discussed."

"Oh, do please hush. Are you aware that the day after tomorrow is the Eid-al-Fitr?"

"No. I do not even know what that is."

"Tomorrow at sundown Ramazan ends. At that moment begins the month of Shawal, and its first day is the Feast of Fast-Broken, when we Muslims are released from abstinence and restriction. Any time after sundown tomorrow, you and I can licitly make zina."

"Except that you are a virgin," I reminded her. "And must stay that way, for your brother's sake."

"That is what Aziz and I discussed. We have a small favor to ask of you, Mirza Marco. If you will consent to it, I will consent—and I have my brother's consent—to make zina with you. Of course, you can have him too, if you like."

I said suspiciously, "Your offer sounds like a considerable return for

a small favor. And your beloved brother sounds brotherly indeed. I can
hardly wait to meet this pimping and simpering lout."

"You have met him. He is the kitchen scullion, with hair dark red
like mine, and—"

"I do not remember." But I could imagine him: the twin to Nostril's
stable mate Jafar, a muscular and handsome hulk of a man, with the
orifice of a woman, the wits of a camel and the morals of a jack weasel.

"When I say a small favor," Sitarè went on, "I mean a small one for
me and Aziz. For yourself it will be a greater favor, since you will profit
by it. Actually earn money from it."

Here was a beautiful chestnut-haired maiden, offering me herself
and her maidenhead and a monetary return as well—plus, if I wanted
him, her reputedly even more beautiful brother into the bargain. Naturally this brought to my recollection the phrase I had several times
heard, "the bloodthirstiness of beauty." And naturally that made me
cautious, but not so cautious that I would flatly refuse the offer without
hearing more.

"Tell me more," I said.

"Not now. Here comes your uncle. Hush."

"Well, well!" boomed Uncle Mafìo, approaching us from the darker
interior of the house. "Collecting *fiame*, are we?" And his black beard
split in a bright white grin, as he shouldered past us and went out the
door toward the stable.

The remark was a play on the word fiame, since in Venice "flames"
can mean—in addition to fire—either red-headed persons or secret lovers. So I assumed that my uncle was jocosely twitting what he took to be
a boy-and-girl flirtation.

As soon as he was out of hearing, Sitarè said to me, "Tomorrow. At
the kitchen door, where I let you in before. At this same hour." And then
she too was gone, somewhere into the back parts of the house.

I strolled on along the front passage, into the room from which I
heard the voices of my father and the Widow Esther. As I entered, he
was saying, in a muted and serious tone, "I know it was your good heart
that proposed it. I only wish you had asked me first, and me alone."

"I never would have suspected," she said, also in a hushed tone.
"And if, as you say, he has nobly exerted himself to reform, I would not
wish to be the provocation of a relapse."

"No, no," said my father. "No blame can be laid to you, even if the
good deed should turn out ill. We will talk it over, and I will ask flatly
whether this would be an irresistible temptation, and on that basis we
will decide."

Then they noticed my presence, and abruptly dropped whatever it
was they were privily discussing, and my father said, "Yes, it was as well
that we stopped these few days. There are several items we need which
are unobtainable in the bazàr during this holy month. When the month
ends tomorrow, they will be purchasable, and by then the lame camel
will be healed, and we will aim at departure the day after. We cannot
thank you enough for the hospitality you have shown us during our
stay."

"Which reminds me," she said. "I have your evening meal almost done. I will bring it out to your quarters as soon as it is."

My father and I went together to the hayloft, where we found Uncle Mafìo perusing the pages of our Kitab. He looked up from it and said, "Our next destination, Mashhad, is no easy one to get to. Desert all the way, and the very widest extent of that desert. We will be dried and shriveled like a bacalà." He broke off to scratch vigorously at the inside of his left elbow. "Some damned bug has bitten me, and I itch."

I said, "The widow told me that this city is infested with scorpions."

My uncle gave me a scornful look. "If you ever get stung by one, asenazzo, you will learn that scorpions do not *bite*. No, this was a tiny fly, perfectly triangular in shape. It was so tiny that I cannot believe this tormenting itch it left."

The Widow Esther made several crossings of the yard, bringing out the dishes of our meal, and we three ate while bent together over the Kitab. Nostril ate apart, in the stable below, among the camels, but he ate almost as audibly as a camel eats. I tried to disregard his noises and concentrate on the maps.

"You are right, Mafìo," said my father. "The broadest part of the desert to cross. God send us good."

"Still, an easy route to keep to. Mashhad is just a little north of east from here. At this season, we will only have to take aim at the sunrise each morning."

"And I," I put in, "will frequently verify our course with our kamàl."

"I notice," said my father, "that al-Idrisi shows not a single well or oasis or karwansarai in that desert."

"But some such things must exist. It is a trade route, after all. Mashhad, like Baghdad, is a major stop on the Silk Road."

"And as big a city as Kashan, the widow told me. Also, thank God, it is in the cool mountains."

"But beyond it, we will come to genuinely cold ones. We shall probably have to lay up for the winter somewhere."

"Well, we cannot expect to go through the world with the wind always astern."

"And we will not be on territory familiar to you and me, Nico, until we get all the way to Kashgar, in Kithai itself."

"Distant from the eye, Mafìo, is distant from the heart. Sufficient the evils of the day, and all that. For the time being, let us not plan or worry beyond Mashhad."

· 3 ·

T H E next day, the last day of Ramazan, we spent mostly in just lazing about the widow's property. I think I have neglected to mention that, in Muslim countries, a day's beginning is not counted from dawn, as one might expect, or from the midnight hour, as it is in civilized countries, but from the moment of the sun's setting. Anyway, there was no point in our haunting the Kashan bazàr, as my father had remarked, until it should be again fully stocked with goods for purchase. We had no other tasks except to feed and water the camels and shovel their manure out of the stable. Of course, Nostril attended to that—and at the widow's request he spread the manure on her herb garden. Now and again, I or my father or uncle would go out for a stroll in the streets. And so did Nostril, in the intervals between his chores, and in the process, I have no doubt, managed to consummate some more of his nasty liaisons.

When I went walking out into the city in the late afternoon, I found a crowd of people standing at a corner where two streets intersected. Most of them were young—good-looking males and nondescript females. I would have assumed that they were merely engaged in the favorite occupation of the East, which is standing and staring—or, in the case of Eastern men, standing and staring and scratching their crotches—except that I heard a droning voice proceeding from the center of the group. So I stopped and joined the audience, and gradually worked my way through them until I could see the object of their attention.

It was an old man seated cross-legged on the ground: a sha'ir, or poet, and he was entertaining the people by telling a story. From time to time, evidently whenever he spoke an especially poetic and felicitous phrase, one of the bystanders would drop a coin into the begging bowl on the ground beside the old man. My grasp of Farsi was not good enough to enable me to appreciate anything of that sort, but it was good enough at least to follow the thread of the tale, and it was an interesting tale, so I stood and listened. The sha'ir was telling how dreams came to be.

In the Beginning, he said, among all the kinds of spirits which exist—the jinn and the afarit and the peri and so on—there was a spirit named Sleep. He had charge then, as he has now, of that dormant condition in all living creatures. Now, Sleep had a whole swarm of children, who were called Dreams, but in that far-off time neither Sleep nor his children had ever thought of the Dreams getting inside people's heads. But one day, it being a nice day, and Sleep not having much to do during the daytime, that good spirit decided to take all his boys and girls for a holiday at the seashore. And there he let them get into a little boat they found, and fondly watched as they paddled out upon the water a short way.

Unfortunately, said the old poet, the spirit Sleep had earlier done something to offend the mighty spirit called Storm, and Storm had been waiting an opportunity for revenge. So when Sleep's little Dreams ventured upon the sea, the malevolent Storm whipped the sea into a frothing fury, and blew a driving wind, and washed the frail boat far out into the ocean and wrecked it on the rocky reefs of a desert island called Boredom.

Ever since that time, said the sha'ir, all the Dream boys and girls have been marooned on that bleak island. (And you know, he said, how restless children become when subjected to idleness in Boredom.) During the days, the poor Dreams must endure that monotonous exile from the living world. But every night—al-hamdo-lillah!—the spirit Storm must wane in power, because the kindlier spirit Moon has charge of the night. So that is when the Dream children can most easily escape for a while from their Boredom. And they do. That is when they leave the island and go about the world and occupy themselves by entering the heads of sleeping men and women. That is why, said the sha'ir, on any night, any sleeper may be entertained or instructed or warned or frightened by a Dream, depending on whether that particular Dream on that particular night is a beneficent little-girl Dream or a mischievous little-boy Dream, and depending on his or her mood that night.

The listeners all made gratified noises at the tale's conclusion, and fairly showered coins into the old man's bowl. I tossed in a copper shahi myself, having found the story amusing—and not incredible, like so many of the more foolish Eastern myths. I found quite logical the poet's notion of innumerable Dream children of both sexes and mercurial temperaments and meddlesome ways. That notion could even suggest an acceptable explanation of certain phenomena frequently occurring in the West, and well attested but never before explicable. I mean the dreaded nighttime visitations of the incubo which seduces otherwise chaste women and the succubo which seduces otherwise chaste priests.

When sundown marked the close of Ramazan, I was at the back door of the Widow Esther's house, and Sitarè let me into the kitchen. She and I were its only occupants, and she seemed in a state of barely suppressed excitement: her eyes sparkled and her hands fluttered. She was dressed in what must have been her very best garments, and she had put al-kohl around her eyelids and berry juice on her lips, but the pink flush on her cheeks had not come out of a cosmetic jar.

"You are attired for the feast day," I said.

"Yes, but to please you, too. I will not dissemble, Mirza Marco. I said I was glad to be the object of your ardor, and I truly am. Look, I have spread a pallet for us yonder in the corner. And I have made sure that the mistress and the other servants are all occupied elsewhere, so we will not be interrupted. I am frankly eager for our—"

"Now wait," I said, but feebly. "I have acceded to no bargain. You are a beauty to make a man's mouth water, and mine does, but I must know first. What is this favor for which you wish to trade yourself?"

"Indulge me only for a moment, then I will tell you. I should like to set you a riddle beforehand."

"Is this another local custom?"

"Just sit on this bench here. Keep your hands at your sides—hold onto the bench—so you are not tempted to touch me. Now close your eyes. Tight. And keep them closed until I tell you."

I shrugged, and did as I was bidden, and heard her briefly moving about. Then she kissed me on my lips, in a shy and inexpert and maidenly way, but most deliciously, and for a long time. It so stimulated me that I was made quite dizzy. If I had not been holding onto the bench, I might actually have rocked from side to side. I waited for her to speak.

Instead, she kissed me again, and as if practice was making her enjoy it more, and for even a longer time. There was another pause, and I waited for another kiss, but now she said, "Open your eyes."

I did, and smiled at her. She was standing directly before me, and the flush of her cheeks had suffused her whole face, and her eyes were bright, and her rosebud lips were merry, and she asked, "Could you tell the kisses apart?"

"Apart? Why, no," I said gallantly. I added, in what I imagined might be the style of a Persian poet, "How can a man say, of equally sweet perfumes or equally intoxicating flavors, that one is better than another? He simply wants more. And I do, I do!"

"And more you shall have. But of me? It was I who kissed you first. Or of Aziz, who kissed you next?"

At that, I did rock upon my bench. Then she reached a hand around behind her and drew him into my view, and I wobbled even more unsteadily.

"He is only a child!"

"He is my little brother Aziz."

No wonder I had failed to notice him among the household servants. He could have been no older than eight or nine, and was small even for his age. But, once noticed, Aziz would have been hard to overlook again. Like all the local boy-children I had seen, he was an Alexandrian Cupid, but even more beautiful than the Kashan standard, just as his sister was superior to all the other Kashan girls I had seen. Ìncubo and sùccubo, I thought wildly.

I being still seated on the low bench, my eyes and his were at the same level. And his blue eyes were clear and solemn, seeming, in his small face, even bigger and more luminous than his sister's. His mouth was a rosebud identical to hers. His body was perfectly formed, right down to his tapering tiny fingers. His hair was the same deep chestnut-red as his sister's, and his skin the same ivory. The boy's beauty was further adorned by an application of al-kohl around the eyelids and berry juice on his lips. I thought them unnecessary additions, but, before I could say so, Sitarè spoke.

"Whenever, in my hours off from attendance on the mistress, I am allowed to wear cosmetics"—she talked rapidly, as if to ward off my saying anything—"I like to do the same decoration of Aziz." Again forestalling my comment, she said, "Here, let me show you something, Mirza Marco." With hurried and fumbling fingers, she undid and took off the blouse her brother wore. "Being a boy, of course he has no breasts, but regard his delicately shaped and prominent nipples." I stared at them, for they were tinted bright red with hinna. Sitarè said, "Are they not very similar to my own?" My eyes widened further, for she had whipped off her own upper garment, and was presenting her hinna-nippled bosom for my comparison. "See? His get aroused and erect, just like my own."

Still she chattered on, though I was already incapable of interrupting. "Also, being a boy, Aziz of course has something I do not have." She undid the string of his pai-jamah, and let the garment fall to the floor, and knelt beside him. "Is it not a perfect zab in miniature? And watch, when I stroke. Just like a little man's. Now look at this." She turned the boy around, and with her hands spread his dimpled pink buttocks apart. "Our mother always was punctilious about using the golulè, and after she died so was I, and you see the superb result." In another quick movement, and without any maidenly coyness, she let drop her own pai-jamah. She turned and bent far over, so that I could observe the under part of her that was not veiled by dark-red fluff. "Mine is two or three fingers' breadth farther forward, but could you truly distinguish between my mihrab and his—?"

"Stop this!" I managed at last to say. "You are trying to importune me into sin with this boy-child!"

She did not deny it, but the boy-child did. Aziz turned to face me again and spoke for the first time. His voice was the musical small voice of a songbird, but firm. "No, Mirza Marco. My sister does not importune, nor do I. Do you really think I would ever have to?"

Taken aback by the direct question, I had to say, "No." But then I rallied my Christian principles and said accusingly, "Flaunting is as reprehensible as importuning. When I was your age, child, I barely knew the *normal* purposes that my parts were for. God forbid I should have exposed them so consciously and wickedly and—and vulnerably. Just standing there like that, you are a sin!"

Aziz looked as hurt as if I had slapped him, and knit his feathery brows in seeming perplexity. "I am still very young, Mirza Marco, and perhaps ignorant, for no one has yet taught me how to be a sin. Only how to be al-fa'il or al-mafa'ul, as the occasion requires."

I sighed, "Alas, I was again forgetting the local customs." So I momentarily dismissed my principles in favor of honesty, and said, "As the doer or the done-to, you probably could make a man forget it *is* a sin. And if to you it is not, then I apologize for castigating you unjustly."

He gave me such a radiant smile that his whole naked little body seemed to glow in the darkening room.

I added, "I apologize also for having thought other unjust things about you, Aziz, without knowing you. Beyond a doubt, you are the most bewitchingly beautiful child I have ever seen, of either sex, and more tantalizing than many grown women I have seen. You are like one of the Dream children of whom I have recently heard. You would be a tempta-tion even to a Christian, in the absence of your sister here. Alongside *her* desirability, you understand, you must take only second place."

"I understand," the boy said, still smiling. "And I agree."

Sitarè, also a figure of glowing alabaster in the twilight, regarded me with some amazement. She breathed almost unbelievingly, "You still want *me*?"

"Very much. So much, indeed, that I am now praying that the favor you desire is something within my power to grant."

"Oh, it is." She picked up her discarded clothes and held them bunched in front of her, that I should not be distracted by her nudity. "We ask only that you take Aziz along in your karwan, and only as far as Mashhad."

I blinked. "Why?"

"You said yourself that you have never seen a more beautiful or more winning child. And Mashhad is a convergence of many trade routes, a place of many opportunities."

"I myself do not much want to go," said Aziz. His nudity was also a distraction, so I picked up his clothes and gave them to him to hold. "I do not wish to leave my sister, who is all the family I have. But she has convinced me that it is for the best."

"Here in Kashan," Sitarè went on, "Aziz is but one of countless pretty boys, all competing for the notice of any anderun purveyor who passes through. At best, Aziz can hope to be chosen by one of those, to become the concubine of some nobleman, who may turn out to be an evil and vicious person. But in Mashhad he could be presented to and appreciated by and acquired by some rich traveling merchant. He may start his life as that man's concubine, but he will have the opportunity to travel, and in time he can hope to learn his master's profession, and he can go on to make something much better of himself than a mere anderun plaything."

Playing was much on my own mind at that moment. I would have been happy to conclude the talking and start doing other things. Never-theless, I was also at that moment realizing a truth that I think not many journeyers ever do.

We who wander about the world, we pause briefly in this com-munity or that, and to us each is but one flash of vague impression in a long series of such forgettable flashes. The people there are only dim figures looming momentarily out of the dust clouds of the trail. We travelers usually have a destination and a purpose in aiming for it, and every stop along the way is merely one more milestone in our progress. But in actuality the people living there had an existence before we came, and will have after we leave, and they have their own concerns—hopes and worries and ambitions and plans—which, being of great moment to them, might sometimes be worth remarking also by us passersby. We might learn something worth knowing, or enjoy a laugh of amusement, or garner a sweet memory worth treasuring, or sometimes even improve our own selves, by taking notice of such things. So I paid sympathetic attention to the wistful words and glowing faces of Sitarè and Aziz, as they spoke of their plans and their ambitions and their hopes. And ever since that time, in all my journeyings, I have tried always to see in its entirety every least place I have passed through, and to see its humblest inhabitants with an unhurried eye.

"So we ask only," said the girl, "that you take Aziz with you to Mashhad, and that in Mashhad you seek out a karwan merchant of wealth and kindly nature and other good qualities. . . ."

"Someone like yourself, Mirza Marco," suggested the boy.

". . . And sell Aziz to him."

"Sell your brother?" I exclaimed.

"You cannot just take him there and abandon him, a little boy in a strange city. We would wish you to place him in the keeping of the best possible master. And, as I said, you will realize a profit on the transac-tion. For your trouble of transporting him, and your taking pains to find the right sort of buyer for him, you may keep the entire amount you get for him. It ought to be a handsome price for such a fine boy. Is that not fair enough?"

"More than fair," I said. "It may sway my father and uncle, but I cannot promise. After all, I am just one of three in our party. I must put the proposition to them."

"That should suffice," said Sitarè. "Our mistress has already spoken to them. The Mirza Esther also wishes to see young Aziz set upon a better road in life. I understand that your father and uncle are considering the matter. So, if you are agreeable to taking Aziz, yours should be the persuading voice."

I said truthfully, "The widow's word probably carries more weight than mine does. That being so, Sitarè, why were you prepared to"—I gestured, indicating her state of undress—"to go to such lengths to cajole me?"

"Well . . . ," she said, smiling. She moved aside the clothes she held to give me another unimpeded look at her body. "I hoped you would be *very* agreeable . . ."

Still being truthful, I said, "I would be, anyway. But there are some other aspects you ought to consider. For one thing, we must cross a perilous and uncomfortable desert. It is no fit place for any human being, not to mention a small boy. As is well known, the Devil Satan is most evident and most powerful in the desert wastes. It is into deserts that saintly Christians go, simply to test their strength of faith—and I mean the most sublimely devout Christians, like San Antonio. Unsaintly mortals go there only at great hazard."

"Perhaps so, but they do go," said young Aziz, sounding unperturbed by the prospect. "And since I am not a Christian, I may be in less danger. I may even be some protection for the rest of you."

"We have another non-Christian in the party," I said sourly. "And that is a thing I would have you also consider. Our camel-puller is a beast, who habitually consorts and couples with the vilest of other beasts. To tempt his bestial nature with a desirable and accessible little boy . . ."

"Ah," said Sitarè. "That must be the objection your father raised. I knew the mistress was concerned about something. Then Aziz must promise to avoid the beast, and you must promise to watch over Aziz."

"I will stay always by your side, Mirza Marco," declared the boy. "By day and by night."

"Aziz may not be chaste, by your standards," his sister went on. "But neither is he promiscuous. As long as he is with you, he will be yours only, not lifting his zab or his buttocks or even his eyes to any other man."

"I will be yours only, Mirza Marco," he affirmed, with what might have been charming innocence, except that he held aside the garments in his hands, as Sitarè had done, to let me look my fill.

"No, no, no," I said, in some agitation. "Aziz, you are to promise not to tempt *any* of us. Our slave is only a beast, but we other three are Christians! You are to be *totally* chaste, from here to Mashhad."

"If that is what you wish," he said, though he appeared crestfallen. "Then I swear it. On the beard of the Prophet (peace and blessing be upon him)."

Skeptical, I asked Sitarè, "Is that oath binding on a beardless child?"

"Indeed it is," she said, regarding me askance. "Your dreary desert journey will not be at all enlivened. You Christians must take some morbid pleasure in the denial of pleasure. But so be it. Aziz, you may put on your clothes again."

"You too, Sitarè," I said, and if Aziz had looked crestfallen, she looked thunderstruck. "I assure you, dear girl, I say that unwillingly, but with the best of will."

"I do not understand. When you take responsibility for my brother, my virginity is worth nothing toward his advancement. So I give it to you, and thankfully."

"And with all thanks I decline it. For a reason I am sure you are aware of, Sitarè. Because, when your brother departs, what becomes of you?"

"What matter? I am only a female person."

"In a person most *beautifully* female. Therefore, once Aziz is provided for, you can offer yourself for your own advancement. A good marriage, or concubinage, or whatever you can attain to. But I know that a woman cannot attain to much unless she is virginally intact. So I will leave you that way."

She and Aziz both stared at me, and the boy murmured, "Verily, Christians are divanè."

"Some, no doubt. Some try to behave as Christians should."

Sitarè's stare turned to a softer look, and she said in a soft voice, "Perhaps some few succeed." But again, provocatively, she moved the screening clothes aside from her fair body. "You are sure you decline? You are steadfast in your kindly resolve?"

I laughed shakily. "Not at all steadfast. For that reason, let me go quickly from here. I will consult with my father and uncle about taking Aziz with us."

The consultation did not take long, for they were in the stable talking it over at that very time.

"So there," said Uncle Mafìo to my father. "Marco is also in favor of letting the boy come along. That makes two of us voting yes, against one vote wavering."

My father frowned and tangled his fingers into his beard.

"We will be doing a good deed," I said.

"How can we refuse to do a good deed?" demanded my uncle.

My father growled an old saying, "Saint Charity is dead and her daughter Clemency is ailing."

My uncle retorted with another, "Cease believing in the saints and they will cease doing miracles."

They then looked at each other in a silence of impasse, until I ventured to break it.

"I have already warned the lad about the likelihood of his being molested." They both swiveled their gaze to me, looking astonished.

"You know," I mumbled uncomfortably, "Nostril's propensities for, er, making mischief."

"Oh, that," said my father. "Yes, there is that."

I was glad that he seemed not unduly concerned about it, for I did not wish to be the one to tell of Nostril's most recent indecency, and probably earn the slave a belated beating.

"I made Aziz promise," I said, "to be wary of any suspicious advances. And I have promised to watch over him. As for his transportation, the pack camel is not at all heavily laden, and the boy weighs very little. His sister offered to let us pocket whatever money we can sell him for, which should be a substantial amount. But I rather think we ought merely to subtract from it the cost of his keep, and let the boy have the rest. As a sort of legacy, to start his new life with."

"So there!" said Uncle Mafìo again, scratching at his elbow. "The lad has a mount to ride and a guardian to protect him. He is paying his own way to Mashhad, and earning himself a dowry as well. There can be no further possible objection."

My father said solemnly, "If we take him, Marco, he will be your responsibility. You guarantee to keep the child from harm?"

"Yes, Father," I said, and put my hand significantly on my belt knife. "Any harm must take me before it takes him."

"You hear, Mafìo."

I perceived that I must be making a weighty vow indeed, since my father was commanding my uncle to bear witness.

"I hear, Nico."

My father sighed, looked from one to the other of us, clawed in his beard some more, and finally said, "Then he comes with us. Go, Marco, and tell him so. Tell his sister and the Widow Esther to pack whatever belongings Aziz is to take."

So Sitarè and I took the opportunity for a flurry of kisses and caresses, and the last thing she said to me was, "I will not forget, Mirza Marco. I will not forget you, or your kindness to us both, or your consideration of my fortunes hereafter. I should very much like to reward you—and with that which you have so gallantly forgone. If ever you should journey this way again . . ."

· 4 ·

We had been told that we were crossing the Dasht-e-Kavir at the best time of the year. I should hate to have to cross it at the worst. We did it in the late autumn, when the sun was not infernally hot, but, even without incident, that would by no means have been a pleasant trip. I had hitherto supposed that a long sea voyage was the most unvarying and boring and interminable and monotonous sort of travel possible, at least when not made terrible by storm. But a desert crossing is all of that, and besides is thirsty, itchy, scratchy, rasping, scraping, parching—the list of hateful adjectives could go on and on. And the list does go on, like a chant of curses, through the morose mind of the desert journeyer, as he endlessly trudges from one featureless horizon across a featureless flat surface toward the featureless skyline ever receding ahead of him.

When we left Kashan, we were again dressed for hard traveling. No longer did we wear the neat Persian tulbands on our heads and the gorgeously embroidered body garments. We were again loosely en-wrapped in the Arabs' hanging kaffiyah headcloths and ample aba cloaks, that less handsome but more practical attire which does not cling about a person but billows free, so it allows the dissipation of body heat and sweat, and affords no folds in which the drifting sand can accumu-late. Our camels were hung all about with leather bags of good Kashan water and sacks of dried mutton and fruits and the brittle local bread. (It was to procure these foodstuffs that we had had to wait for the bazàr to restock after Ramazan.) We had also acquired in Kashan some new items to carry with us: smooth round sticks and lengths of light fabric with their hems sewn to form sheaths. By inserting the sticks into those sheaths, we could quickly shape the cloths into tents, each just of a size to shelter one man comfortably, or, if necessary, to accommodate two persons in rather less comfortable intimacy.

Before we even got out of Kashan, I warned Aziz never to let our slave Nostril tempt him inside a tent or anywhere else out of sight of the rest of us, and to report to me any other sorts of advances the camel-puller might make to him. For Nostril, on first seeing the boy among us, had widened his piggy eyes almost to human size and dilated his single nostril as if he scented prey. That first day, also, Aziz had been briefly naked in our company—and Nostril had hung about, ogling—while I helped the boy doff the Persian garb his sister had dressed him in, and showed him how to put on the Arab kaffiyah and aba. So I gave Nostril some stern warnings, too, and toyed significantly with my belt knife while I was haranguing him, and he made insincere promises of obedi-ence and good behavior.

I would hardly have trusted Nostril's promises, but, as things turned out, he never did molest the little boy, or even try to. We were not many days into the desert when Nostril began noticeably to suffer from some painful ailment in his under parts. If, as I suspected, the slave had deliberately made one of the camels lame to make us stop in Kashan, then another of the beasts was now exacting revenge. Every time Nos-tril's camel made a misstep and jounced him, he would cry out sharply. Soon he had his saddle pillowed with everything soft he could find among our packs. But then, every time he went away from our camp fire to make water, we could hear him groaning and thrashing about and cursing vehemently.

"One of the Kashan boys must have clapped him with the scola-mento," said Uncle Mafìo derisively. "Serves him right, for being un-virtuous—and indiscriminate."

I had not then and indeed never have been similarly afflicted myself, for which I give more thanks to my good fortune than to my virtue or my discrimination. Nevertheless, I might have shown more comradely sympathy to Nostril, and laughed less at his predicament, if I had not been thankful that his zab was giving him other concerns than trying to put it into my young ward. The slave's ailment gradually abated and finally went away, leaving him apparently no worse for the experience, but by that time other events had occurred to put Aziz beyond threat of his lechery.

A tent, or some shelter like a tent, is an absolute necessity in the Dasht-e-Kavir, for a man cannot just lie down in his blankets to sleep, or he would be covered by sand before he woke. Most of that desert can be likened to the giant tray of a giant fardarbab tomorrow-teller. It is a flat expanse of smooth, dun-colored sand, a sand so fine that it flows through one's fingers like water. In the intervals between winds, that sand lies as virginally unmarked as the sand in the tomorrow-teller's tray. So fine and so smooth is it that the least passing insect—a centipede, a grasshopper, a scorpion—leaves a trail visible from afar. A man could, if he got bored enough by the tedium of desert traveling, find distraction by following the meandering track of a single ant.

However, in the daytime, it was seldom that a wind was not blowing, stirring that sand and picking it up and carrying it and throwing it. Since the winds of the Dasht-e-Kavir blow always from the same direction, from the southwest, it is easy to tell in which direction a stranger is traveling—even if you meet him camped and immobile—simply by seeing which flank of his mount is the most heavily coated with blown sand. In the nighttime, the desert wind drops, and lets drop from the air the heavier particles of sand. But the finer particles hang in the air like dust, and hang there so densely as to constitute a dry fog. It blots out whatever stars there may be in the sky, sometimes obscures even a full moon. In the combined darkness and fogginess, one's vision may be limited to just a few arm-lengths. Nostril told us that there were creatures called Karauna which took advantage of that dark fog—according to Persian folk legend the Karauna create it, said Nostril, by some dark magic—in which to do dark deeds. More usually, the chief danger of that fog is that the suspended dust sifts imperceptibly down from the air during the stillness of night, and a traveler not sheltered under a tent could be quietly, stealthily buried and smothered to death in his sleep.

We had still the greater part of Persia to cross, but it was the empty part—perhaps the emptiest part of the entire world—and we did not meet a single Persian along our way, or much of anything else, or see in the sand the tracks of anything larger than insects. In other regions of Persia, similarly unoccupied and uncultivated by man, we journeyers might have had to be on our guard against predatory prides of lions, or scavenging packs of shaqàl dogs, or even flocks of the big flightless shuturmurq camel-birds, which, we had been told, can disembowel a man with a kick. But none of those hazards had to be feared in the desert, for no wild thing lives in it. We saw an occasional vulture or kite, but they stayed high in the windy sky above and did not tarry in their passing. Even vegetable plants seem to shun that desert. The only green thing I saw growing there was a low shrub with thick and fleshy-looking leaves.

"Euphorbia," Nostril said it was. "And it grows here only because Allah put it here to be a help to the journeyer. In the hot season, the euphorbia's seed pods grow ripe and burst and fling out their seeds. They begin to pop when the desert air gets exactly as hot as a human's blood. Then the pods burst with increasing frequency as the air gets even hotter. So a desert wanderer can tell, by listening to the loudness of the popping of the euphorbia, when the air is getting so perilously hot that he *must* stop and put up a shelter for shade, or he will die."

That slave, for all his squalid person and sexual erethism and detestable character, was an experienced traveler, and told us or showed us many things of use or interest. For example, on our very first night in that wasteland, when we stopped to camp, he got down from his camel and stuck his prodding pole into the sand, pointed in the direction we were going.

"It may be needful in the morning," he explained. "We have determined to go always toward the spot where the sun rises. But if the sand is blowing at that hour, we may not be able otherwise to fix on the spot."

The treacherous sands of the Dasht-e-Kavir are not its only menace to man. That name, as I have said, means the Great Salt Desert, and for a reason. Vast extents of it are not of sand at all; they are immense reaches of a salty paste, not quite wet enough to be called mud or marsh, and the wind and sun have dried the paste to a surface of caked solid salt. Often a traveler must cross one of those glittering, crunching, quivering, blindingly white salt crusts, and he must do it gingerly. The salt crystals are more abrasive than sand; even a camel's callused pads can quickly be worn to bleeding rawness, and, if the rider has to dismount, his boots can be likewise shredded, and then his feet. Also, the salt surfaces are of uneven thickness, making of those areas what Nostril called "the trembling lands." Sometimes the weight of a camel or a man will break through the crust. If that happens, the animal or the man falls into the pasty muck beneath. From that salt quicksand it is impossible to climb out unaided, or even to stay put and wait for help to come. It slowly but ineluctably draws down whatever falls into it, and sucks the fallen creature under the surface, and closes over it. Unless a rescuer is nearby, and on firmer ground, the unfortunate fallen one is doomed. According to Nostril, entire karwan trains of men and animals have thus disappeared and left no trace.

So, when we came to the first of those salt flats, though it looked as innocuous as a layer of hoarfrost unseasonably on the ground, we halted and studied it with respect. The white crust gleamed out before us, clear to the skyline, and away as far as we could see to either side.

"We could try going around," said my father.

"The maps of the Kitab show no such details as this," said my uncle, scratching meditatively at his elbow. "We have no way of knowing its extent, or of guessing whether a north or a south detour would be shorter."

"And if we are going to skirt every one of these," said Nostril, "we will be in this desert forever."

I said nothing, being totally ignorant of desert travel, and not ashamed to leave the decisions to the more expert. So we four sat our camels and looked out over the sparkling waste. But the boy Aziz, behind us, prodded his pack camel and made it kneel, and he dismounted. We did not notice what he was doing until he walked out from among us and walked onto the salt crust. He turned and looked up at us, and smiled prettily, and said in his little bird voice:

"Now I can repay your kindness in bringing me along. I shall walk ahead, and I can tell from the trembling underfoot how strong is the surface. I will keep to the firmest ground, and you have only to follow."

"You will cut your feet!" I protested.

"No, Mirza Marco, for I am of light weight. Also, I took the liberty of extracting these plates from the packs." He held up two of the golden dishes the Shah Zaman had sent. "I shall strap them under my boots as an extra protection."

"It is dangerous nonetheless," said my uncle. "You are brave to volunteer, lad, but we have sworn that no harm must come to you. Better one of us—"

"No, Mirza Mafìo," said Aziz, still staunchly. "If by chance I should fall through, it would be easier for you to pluck me out than any larger person."

"He is right, masters," said Nostril. "The child has good sense. And, as you remark, a good heart for courage and initiative."

So we let Aziz precede us, and we followed at a discreet distance. It was slow going, keeping to his shuffle pace, but that made the walking less painful for the camels. And we did cross that trembling land in safety, and before nightfall had come to an area of more trustworthy sand on which to camp.

Only once that day did Aziz misjudge the crust. With a sharp crackle, it broke like a sheet of glass, and he plummeted waist-deep into the muck under it. He did not exclaim in fright when it happened, nor did he make so much as a whimper during the time it took for Uncle Mafìo to get down from his camel and make a loop in his saddle rope and cast it over the boy and draw him gently back above ground and onto a firmer place. But Aziz had known very well that he was, for that while, precariously suspended over a bottomless abyss, for his face was very pale and his blue eyes very big when we all clustered solicitously around him. Uncle Mafìo embraced the boy and held him, murmuring inspiriting words, while my father and I brushed the fast-drying salt mud from his garments. By the time that was done, the boy's courage had returned, and he insisted on going ahead again, to the admiration of us all.

In the days thereafter, each time we again came upon a salt flat, we could do no more than make guesses or take a vote to determine whether we should venture upon it at once, or camp there at its near edge and wait to start upon it early the next morning. We were always apprehensive that we might find ourselves still in the middle of a trembling land at nightfall, and therefore have to take one of two equally unappealing alternatives: try to press on, braving the night's dark and its dry fog, which could be much more nerve-racking than making such a crossing by day; or camp upon the salt flat and have to do without a fire, for we feared that laying a fire upon such a surface might melt it, and drop ourselves, our animals and all our packs into the quicksand. Surely it was only through good fortune—or Allah's blessing, as our two Muslims would have put it—certainly not through any wisdom informing our guesses, but each time we guessed right, and each time got across the salt to safe sand by nightfall.

So we never had to make a cold camp on the dreaded trembling lands, but making camp anywhere in that desert, even on the sand which we could trust not to dissolve from under us, was no holiday treat. Sand, if you look closely enough at it, is nothing but an infinite multitude of little tiny rocks. Rocks do not hold heat, and no more does sand. The desert days were comfortable enough, even warm, but when the sun went down the nights were cold, and the sand under us even colder. We always needed a fire just to keep us warm until we crawled into our blankets inside our tents. But many nights were so very cold that we would rake the fire into five separate fires, well apart, and let them burn a while to warm those separate plots of sand, and only then spread our blankets and raise our tents on top of the warmed places. Even so, the sand did not for long hold that heat either, and by morning we would be chilled and stiff, in which unjoyous condition we would have to rise and face another day of the joyless desert.

The nightly camp fires served for warmth, and for some illusion of homelikeness in the middle of that empty, lonely, silent, dark wasteland, but they were not much use for cookery. Wood being nonexistent in the Dasht-e-Kavir, we used dried animal dung for fuel. The animals of countless generations of earlier desert crossers had dropped easily found supplies of it, and our own camels contributed their deposits for the benefit of future wayfarers. Our only comestibles, however, were several varieties of dried meats and fruits. A hunk of cold dry mutton might be rendered more palatable by soaking it and then broiling it over a fire, but *not* over a fire built of camel dung. Though we ourselves already reeked of the smoke of those fires, we could not bring ourselves to eat something similarly impregnated. When we felt we could spare the water, we sometimes heated it and steeped our meat in it, but that did not make a very tasty dish either. When water has been carried for a long time in a hide bag, it begins to look and smell and taste rather like the water a man carries in his bladder. We had to drink it to survive, but we less and less desired to cook our foods in it, preferring to gnaw them dry and cold.

Each night we also fed the camels—a double handful of dried peas apiece, and then a fair drink of water to make the peas swell inside their bellies and simulate a hearty meal. I will not say the beasts enjoyed those scant rations, but then camels have never been known to enjoy anything. They would not have muttered and grumbled less if we had been feeding them banquets of delicacies, and they would not, out of gratitude, have performed any better at their labors the next day.

If I sound unloving of camels, it is because I am. I think I have straddled or perched upon every sort of transport animal there is in the world, and I would prefer any other to a camel. I grant that the two-humped camel of the colder lands of the East is somewhat more intelligent and tractable than the single-humped camel of the warm lands. And that lends some credibility to the belief of some people that the camel's brains are in its hump, if it has any anywhere. A camel whose hump has diminished from thirst and starvation is even more sullen, irritable and unmanageable than a well-fed camel, but not much more.

The camels had to be unloaded each night, as would any other karwan animals, but no other animals would have been so maddeningly difficult to reload in the morning. The camels would bawl and back away and roar and prance about and, when those tricks only exasperated but did not dissuade us, they would spit on us. Also, once on the trail, no other animals are so devoid of a sense of direction, or self-preservation. Our camels would have walked indifferently, and one after another, into every quicksand hole in those salt flats if we riders or our puller had not taken pains to steer them around. Camels are also, more than any other animals, devoid of a sense of balance. A camel, like a man, can lift and carry about one-third of its own weight for a whole day and a goodly distance. But a man, with only two legs, is not so teetery as a camel with four. One or another of ours would frequently slip in the sand, even more often on the salt, and grotesquely collapse sideways, and be impossible to raise again until it was entirely unloaded and loudly encouraged and powerfully assisted by our combined strength. At which it would give thanks by spitting on us.

I have used the word "spit" because, even back home in Venice, I had heard far-travelers speak of camels doing that, but in fact they do not. I wish they did. What they actually do is to hawk up from their nethermost cud an awfulness of regurgitated matter to spew. In the case of our camels, that was a substance compounded of peas first dried, then eaten, then soaked and swollen and made gaseous, then half-digested and half-fermented, then—at that substance's peak of noxiousness—churned together with stomach juices, vomited up, collected in the camel's mouth, aimed through pouted lips and ejected with all possible force at some one of us, and preferably into his eye.

There is of course no such thing as a karwansarai anywhere in the Dasht-e-Kavir, but on two occasions in the month or more that it took us to cross it, we had the blessedly good fortune to come upon an oasis. This is a spring which wells up from underground, only God or Allah knows why. Its waters are fresh, not salt, and around it has sprung up an area of vegetation, several zonte in extent. I never could discover anything edible growing there, but the very greenness of the scrub trees and stunted bushes and sparse grass was a refreshment as welcome as fresh fruit or vegetables. On both those occasions, we were pleased to halt our journey for a while before moving on. During that time, we dipped up water from the spring to bathe our dust-coated and salt-encrusted and dung-smoke-smelling bodies, and water to fill the camels' bowel tanks, and water to be boiled—and sieved through the charcoal my father always carried—to flush out and refill our water bags.

Those labors done, we just lay about to enjoy the novel sensation of resting in a green shade.

I noticed, at the first oasis halt, how we all soon separated and drew apart and found separate shade trees under which to loll, and later put up our individual tents at a considerable distance from each other. None of us had recently quarreled, and we had no definable reason for shunning each other's company—except that for so long we *had been* in each other's company, and now it was pleasant to have some privacy for a change. I might have kept Aziz protectively close to me, but the slave Nostril was at that time all too plainly preoccupied with his shameful private affliction, and I deemed him incapable of molesting the little boy. So I let Aziz also go off to be by himself.

Or so I thought. But, after we had been luxuriating in the oasis for a day and a night, I took a notion on the succeeding night to go for a stroll through the surrounding grove. I pretended that I was in a less constricted garden, perhaps the environs of the Baghdad palace, where I had walked so often with the Princess Moth. It was easy enough to pretend, for that night had brought the dry fog, making it impossible for me to see anything but the trees closest about me. Even sounds were muffled by that fog, so I must have been almost stepping on Aziz when I heard him laugh his musical laugh and say:

"Harm? But *that* is no harm to me. Or to anybody. Let us do it."

A deeper voice responded, but in a murmur, so its words were indistinguishable. I was about to shout in outrage, and seize Nostril and drag him off the boy, but Aziz spoke again, and in a voice of marveling:

"I never saw one like that before. With a sheath of skin that encloses it . . ."

I stood where I was, unmoving, stupefied.

". . . Or can be pulled back at will." Aziz still sounded awed. "Why, it is like having your own private mihrab always tenderly enveloping your zab."

Nostril possessed no such apparatus. He was a Muslim, and circumcised, like the boy. I began to back away from that place, being careful to make no noise.

"It must make for a blissful sensation, even without a partner," the little bird voice went on, "when you move the sheath back and forth like that. May I do it for you . . .?"

The fog closed around his voice, as I got farther away. But I was waiting, awake and watchful outside his tent, when he eventually returned to it. He came like a stray moonbeam out of the darkness, radiant, for he was entirely naked and carrying his clothes.

"Look at you!" I said sternly, but keeping my voice low. "I swore a binding oath that no harm would come to you—"

"None has, Mirza Marco," he said, blinking, all innocence.

"And you swore on the Prophet's beard not to tempt any of us—"

"I have not, Mirza Marco," he said, looking hurt. "I was fully dressed when he and I chanced to meet in the grove yonder."

"And to be totally chaste!"

"And I have been, Mirza Marco, all the way from Kashan. No one has penetrated me, and I no one. All we did was kiss." He came close and sweetly kissed me. "And this . . ." He demonstrated, and after a moment insinuated his little self into my hand, and breathed, "To each other we did it . . ."

"Enough!" I said hoarsely. I let go of him and put his hand away from me. "Go to sleep now, Aziz. We ride again at sunrise."

I myself did not get to sleep that night until I acknowledged the excitement Aziz had raised in me, and manually relieved myself of it. But my sleeplessness was also partly on account of my new view of my uncle, and the disillusionment it caused me, and the tinge of disdain that now colored my feelings toward him. It was no trivial disappointment, to have learned that Uncle Mafio's bold, bluff, black-bearded and hearty aspect was a mask he wore, and that behind it he was only a simpering and sly and despicable Sodomite.

I knew I was no saint, and I tried hard not to be a hypocrite. I could frankly admit that I, too, was susceptible to the charms of the boy Aziz. But that was because he was here, near at hand, and no woman was, and he was as comely and seductive as a woman, and he was freely amenable to being used as a substitute for a woman. But Uncle Mafio, I now realized, must see him differently; he must see Aziz as an available and beautiful and beddable *boy*.

I recalled previous events involving other males: hammam rubbers, for instance—and previous words spoken: that furtive exchange between my father and the Widow Esther, for instance. The inference was unavoidable: Uncle Mafio was a lover of persons of his own sex. A man of that bent was no curiosity here in the Muslim lands, where almost every male seemed similarly warped. But I knew very well that, in our more civilized West, his kind was laughed at and sneered at and cursed at. I suspected that the same situation must obtain in the totally uncivilized nations farther east. At any rate, it appeared that *somewhere* my uncle's depravity had caused problems in the past. I gathered that my father had already had reason to try breaking his brother of his perversion, and Mafio himself had apparently made some attempt to suppress the urges. If that was so, I reflected, then he was not entirely detestable, and perhaps there was hope for him.

Very well. I would lend my own best efforts to help his reformation and redemption. When we rode on, I would not ride reproachfully far apart from him, or avoid his eye, or refuse to speak to him. I would say nothing of what had occurred. I would give no hint that I was privy to his shameful secret. What I *would* do was resume keeping a close watch on Aziz, and not again let the child run at liberty under cover of night. Especially would I be paternally careful and strict if we should come upon another green oasis. In such a place, there was a tendency to let discipline lapse, and self-restraints, just as we let our weary muscles relax. If we again found ourselves in that ambience of comparative ease and abandon, my uncle might find the temptation irresistible: to enjoy more of Aziz than he had already sampled.

The next day, as we proceeded once more northeastward into the ungreen wasteland, I was as affable as usual to all in the party, Uncle

Mafìo included, and I think no one could have discerned my inner
feelings. Nevertheless, I was glad that the burden of conversation that
day was taken by the slave Nostril. Possibly to get his own mind off his
own problems, he began expatiating on one subject, then veered onto
others, and I, at least, was content to ride silent and listen and let him
ramble.

What started him off was that, during our loading of the camels, he
had found a small snake coiled asleep in one of our pack hampers. He
had let out a screech at first, but then he said, "We must have brought
the poor thing all the way from Kashan," and, instead of killing the
thing, he had tipped it out onto the sand and let it slither away. As we
rode, he told us why.

"We Muslims do not abhor and loathe serpents as you Christians do.
Oh, we are not particularly fond of them, but neither do we fear and
hate them as you do. According to your Holy Bible, the snake is the
incarnation of the Devil Satan. And in your legends, you have inflated
the snake to the monster called a dragon. All our Muslim monsters take
the form of human beings—the jinn and afarit—or a bird, in the case
of the giant rukh, or combinations like the mardkhora. That is a monster
comprising the head of a man, the body of a lion, the quills of a porcu-
pine and the tail of a scorpion. Notice, there is no snake included."

My father said mildly, "The serpent has been accursed ever since
that unfortunate affair in the Garden of Eden. It is understandable that
Christians should fear it, and right that they should hate it and kill it at
every opportunity."

"We Muslims," said Nostril, "give credit where credit is due. It was
the serpent of Eden who bequeathed to Arabs the Arabic language, for
he contrived that language in which to speak to Eve and seduce her,
because Arabic, as every man knows, is the most subtle and suasive of
languages. Of course, Adam and Eve spoke Farsi when they were alone
together, for the Persian Farsi is the loveliest of all languages. And the
avenging angel Gabriel always speaks Turki, for that is the most menacing of all languages. However, that is by the way. I was speaking of
serpents, and it must be obvious that it was the snake's sinuosity and
convolutions which inspired the writing of characters, the Arabic alphabet which is also employed for the transcription of Farsi, Turki, Sindi
and all other civilized languages."

My father spoke again. "We Westerners have always called it the
fish-worm writing, and never knew how nearly right we were."

"And the serpent gave us more than that, Master Nicolò. His mode
of progression along the ground, by bending and straightening himself—
that inspired some ingenious one of our ancestors to invent the bow and
arrow. The bow is thin and sinuous, like a snake. The arrow is thin and
straight, like a snake, and it has a killing head. We have good reason to
honor the serpent, and we do. For example, we call the rainbow the
celestial snake, and that is a compliment to them both."

"Interesting," my father murmured, with a tolerant smile.

"By contrast," Nostril went on, "you Christians liken the snake to
your own zab, and assert that the serpent of Eden introduced sexual

pleasure into the world, and that therefore sexual pleasure is wrong and ugly and abominable. We Muslims put the blame where it belongs. Not on the inoffensive snake, but on Eve and all her female descendants. As the Quran says in the fourth sura, 'Woman is the source of all evil on the earth, and Allah only made this monster that the man should be repelled, and turn away from earthly—"

"Ciacche-ciacche!" said my uncle.

"Pardon, master?"

"I said *nonsense!* Sciocchezze! Sottise! Bifam ishtibah!"

Looking shocked, Nostril exclaimed, "Master Mafio, you call the Holy Book a bifam ishtibah?"

"Your Quran was written by a man, you cannot deny it. So were the Talmud and the Bible written by men."

"Come now, Mafio," my pious father put in. "They only transcribed the words of God. And the Savior."

"But they were men, indisputably men, with the minds of men. All the prophets and apostles and sages have been men. And what sort of men did the writing of the holy books? Circumcised men!"

"I beg to suggest, master," said Nostril, "that they did not write with their—"

"In a sense, they did exactly that. All those men were religiously mutilated in their infant organs. When they grew to manhood, they found themselves diminished in their sexual pleasure, to the degree they had been diminished in their parts. *That* is why they made their holy books decree that sex should be not for delight, but solely for procreation, and in all other respects a matter for shame and guilt."

"Good master," Nostril persisted. "We are only divested of foreskin, we are not pruned to eunuchs."

"Any mutilation is a deprivation," Uncle Mafio retorted. He dropped his camel's rein to scratch his elbow. "The sages of ancient days, realizing that the trimming of their members had blunted their sensations and their enjoyment, were envious and fearful that others might find more pleasure in sex. Misery loves company, so they wrote their scriptures in a way to ensure that they had company. First the Jews, then the Christians—for the Evangelists and the other early Christians were only converted Jews—and then Muhammad and the subsequent Muslim sages. All of those having been circumcised men, their disquisitions on the subject of sex are akin to the singing of the deaf."

My father looked as shocked as Nostril did. "Mafio," he cautioned, "on this open desert we are terribly exposed to thunderbolts. Your criticism is a novel one in my experience, perhaps even original, but I suggest you temper it with discretion."

Unheeding, my uncle went on, "Their putting fetters on human sexuality was like cripples writing the rules for an athletic contest."

"Cripples, master?" Nostril inquired. "But how could they have known they were cripples? You contend that my sensations have been blunted. Since I myself have no exterior standard alongside which to measure my own enjoyments, I wonder how anyone else could possibly do so. I can think of only one sort who might qualify to judge even himself. That would be a man who has had experience, so to speak, before and after. Excuse my impertinence, Master Mafìo, but were you perhaps not circumcised until midway in your adult life?"

"Insolent infidel! I never have been!"

"Ah. Then, excepting such a man, it seems to me that no one could adjudicate the matter but a *woman*. A woman who has given joy to both sorts of men, the circumcised and the uncircumcised, and paid close heed to their comparative heights of enjoyment."

I winced at that. Whether Nostril spoke in snide malice or sheer ingenuousness, his words hit very close to Uncle Mafìo's true nature and probable experience. I glanced at my uncle, fearing he would blush or bluster or maybe knock Nostril's head off, and thereby confess what he had so far kept concealed. But he bore the seeming insinuation as if he had not noticed it, and only continued to muse aloud:

"If the choice were mine, I should seek out a religion whose scriptures were not written by men already ritually maimed in their manhood."

"Where we are going," my father remarked, "there are several such religions."

"As I well know," said my uncle. "That is what makes me wonder how we Christians and Jews and Muslims dare to speak of the more Eastern peoples as barbarians."

My father said, "The traveled man can look with a pitying smile at the crude pebbles still treasured by his home folk, yes, for he has seen real rubies and pearls in far places. Whether that also holds true for the home-kept religions, I cannot say, not being a theologian." He added, rather sharply for him, "But this I do know: we are at present still under the Heaven of those religions you so openly disprize, and vulnerable to heavenly rebuke. If your blasphemies provoke a whirlwind, we may not get any farther. I strongly recommend a change of subject."

Nostril obliged. He reverted to his earlier topic and told us, at stupefying length, how each letter of the Arabic fish-worm writing is permeated by a certain specific emanation from Allah, and therefore, as the letters squirm into the shape of words and the words into reptilian sentences, any piece of Arabic writing—even something as mundane as a signpost or a landlord's bill—contains a beneficent power which is greater than the sum of the individual characters, and therefore is efficacious as a talisman against evil and jinn and afarit and the Devil Shaitan . . . and so on and on. To which the only rejoinder was made by one of our bull camels. He unfurled his underworks as he strode along, and copiously made water.

· 5 ·

WELL, we did not get annihilated by any thunderbolt or whirlwind, and I cannot recall that anything else of significance happened on that journey until, as I have remarked, we did come to a second green oasis in that dun dreariness, and again made camp, intending to luxuriate there for two or even three days. In keeping with my resolve, I did not this time let Aziz out of my arm's reach while we drank our fill of the good water and watered the camels and topped up our water bags and—especially—while we bathed our bodies and laundered our clothes, during which time he and all the rest of us were necessarily naked. And when again we were disposed to pitch our tents privily apart from each other, I made sure that his and mine were side by side.

We did, however, all cluster together around the camp fire for our evening meal. And I recollect, as if it were yesterday, every trivial incident of that night. Aziz took his seat across the fire from me and Nostril, and first my uncle sat companionably close beside him, and then my father plumped down on his other side. While we gnawed gristly mutton and munched moldy cheese and dipped shriveled jujubes into our water cups to soften them, my uncle gave arch sidewise looks at the boy, and I and my father cast wary looks at both of them. Apparently unaware of any tension in the group, Nostril casually remarked to me:

"You are beginning to look like a real journeyer, Master Marco."

He was referring to my new grown beard. In the desert, no man would be fool enough to waste water on shaving, or vain enough to endure a lather that must get mixed with abrasive sand and salt. My own beard was by then of a manly density, and I had ceased even to use the easy depilatory of the mumum salve, letting the beard grow as a protection for the skin of my face. I took only the trouble to keep it clipped to a tidy and comfortable shortness, and I have worn it so ever since.

"Now you may realize," Nostril chatted on, "how merciful it was of Allah to give whiskers to men, but not to women."

I thought about that. "It is clearly good that men have beards, for they may have to go into the scouring desert sands. But why is it a mercy that women have them not?"

The camel-puller raised up his hands and his eyes, as if in consternation at my ignorance. But before he could reply, little Aziz laughed and said:

"Oh, let me tell him! Think, Mirza Marco! Was it not considerate of the Creator? He did not put a beard upon that creature who could never keep it shaven clean or even trimmed to neatness, because *her jaw waggles so!*"

I laughed, too, and so did my father and uncle, and I remarked, "If that is the reason, then I am glad for it. I would recoil from a whiskered woman. But would it not have been wiser of the Creator to create females less inclined to wag the jaw?"

"Ah," said my father, the proverbialist. "Wherever there are pots, they will rattle."

"Mirza Marco, here is another riddle for you, Mirza Marco!" chirruped Aziz, merrily bouncing where he sat. The boy was admittedly a soiled angel, and in many respects more worldly-wise than any adult Christian, but he was, after all, still a child. His words almost tumbled over each other, he was so eager to get them out. "There are few animals in this desert. But there is one to be found here which unites in itself the natures of *seven different beasts*. What is it, then, Marco?"

I knit my brow and pretended to think ponderously, and then said, "I give it up."

Aziz crowed with triumphant laughter, and opened his mouth to speak. But then his mouth opened wider, and his big eyes got bigger. So did the eyes and mouths of my father and uncle. Nostril and I had to spin about to see what they were staring at.

Three shaggy brown men had materialized out of the night's dry fog, and were regarding us with slit eyes in expressionless faces. They wore skins and leathers, not Arab garments, and they must have ridden far and fast, for they were coated with dust caked by perspiration, and they stank even from the distance where they stood.

"Sain bina," said my uncle, the first to recover from his surprise, and he slowly got to his feet.

"Mendu, sain bina," said one of the strangers, looking faintly surprised himself.

My father also stood up, and he and Uncle Mafio made gestures of welcome, and they went on speaking to the intruders in a language I did not comprehend. The shaggy men drew three horses by their reins out of the fog behind them, and led the animals to the spring. Not until the horses had been watered did the men take a drink.

Nostril, Aziz and I got up from the fire, and let the strangers take our places. My father and uncle sat down with them, and got out food from our packs and offered it, and continued sitting and talking while the visitors ate voraciously. I scrutinized the newcome three as well as I could while standing discreetly apart from the confabulation. They were of short but sturdy stature. Their faces were the color and texture of tanned kid leather, and two of them had long but wispy mustaches; none wore a beard. Their coarse black hair was womanly long, and plaited into numerous braids. Their eyes, I repeat, were mere slits, so very narrowly slitted that I wondered how they could see out of them. Each man carried a short and sharply curved-and-recurved bow slung on his back, with its bowstring across his chest, and a quiver of short arrows for it, and at his waist what was either a short sword or a long knife.

I recognized, now, that the men were Mongols, for I had seen the occasional Mongol by this time, and this land was, although nominally Persia, a province of the Mongol Khanate. But why were three Mongols prowling out here in the wilderness? They did not seem to be bandits or to mean us any harm—or at least my father and uncle had quickly talked them out of any such notion. And why were they in such an apparent hurry? In the everlasting desert, no man hurries.

But these men stayed in the oasis only long enough to eat to repletion. And they might not have halted for even that long, except that our foodstuffs, unappealing though they were, must have seemed real viands and delicacies to the Mongols, for these men carried no traveling rations at all except strips of jerked horsemeat like rawhide bootlaces. My father and uncle, to judge from their gesturings, were cordially and almost insistently inviting the newcomers to rest for a while, but the Mongols only shook their shaggy heads and grunted as they devoured mutton and cheese and fruits. Then they rose, belched appreciatively, gathered up the reins of their horses and remounted.

The horses rather resembled the men, being exceptionally shaggy and wild-looking and almost as small as the hinna'ed horses of Baghdad, but much more stocky and muscular. They were crusted with dried foam and dust, from having been hard ridden, but they acted as eager as their riders to be off and going again. One of the Mongols, from his saddle, jabbered to my father a lengthy speech that sounded monitory. Then they all tugged their mounts' heads around, and cantered off southwestward, and almost instantly they were gone from our sight into the foggy dark, and the creak and jingle of their arms and harness was as instantly gone from our hearing.

"That was a military patrol," my father made haste to tell us, perceiving that Nostril and Aziz looked quite frightened. "It seems that some bandits have lately been, er, active in this desert, and the Ilkhan Abagha desires to have them brought quickly to justice. Mafio and I, being naturally concerned for the safety of us all, tried to persuade them to stay and guard us, or even to travel for a time in our company. But they prefer to keep on the trail of the bandits, and press them hard, hoping to wear them down by thirst and hunger."

Nostril cleared his throat and said, "Excuse me, Master Nicolò. I would of course never eavesdrop on a master, but I heard some of the conversation. Turki is one of the languages known to me, and the Mongols speak a variant of the Turki tongue. May I ask—when those Mongols mentioned bandits, did they actually say *bandits*?"

"No, they used a name. A tribal name, I assume. Karauna. But I take them to be—"

"Ayee, that is what I thought I heard!" Nostril keened. "And that is what I feared I heard! May Allah preserve us! *The Karauna!*"

Let me say here that almost all the languages I heard spoken from the Levant eastward, no matter how disparate they were in other respects, contained a word or word-element that was the same in all, and that was *kara*. It was variously pronounced: kara, khara, qara or k'ra, and in some languages kala, and it could have various meanings. Kara could mean black or it could mean cold or it could mean iron or it could mean evil or it could mean death—or kara could mean all those things at the same time. It might be spoken in admiration or deprecation or revilement, as for instance the Mongols were pleased to call their onetime capital city Karakoren, meaning Black Palisade, while they called a certain large and venomous spider the karakurt, meaning evil or deadly insect.

"Karauna!" Nostril repeated, almost gagging on the word. "The Black Ones, the Cold Hearts, the Iron Men, the Evil Fiends, the Death Bringers! The name is of no tribe, Master Nicolò. It was bestowed on them as a curse. The Karauna are the outcasts of other tribes—of the Turki and Kipchak of the north, the Baluchi of the south. And *those* peoples are bandits born, so imagine how terrible a man has to be, that he is expelled from such a tribe. Some of the Karauna are even former

Mongols, and you *know* they must be loathly indeed, to be outcast by the Mongols. The Karauna are the soulless men, the most cruel and bloodthirsty and feared of all predators in these lands. Oh, my lords and masters, we are in awful danger!"

"Then let us extinguish the fire," said Uncle Mafìo. "In truth, Nico, we have been sauntering rather blithely through this desert. I will break out swords from the packs, and I suggest we begin tonight to take turns at guard."

I volunteered to take the first watch awake, and asked Nostril how I should recognize the Karauna if they came.

Somewhat sarcastically he said, "You may have noticed that the Mongols fastened their coats on their right side. The Turki and Baluchi and such, they lap their coats to the left." Then his sarcasm dissolved in his dread, and he cried, "Oh, Master Marco, if you even have a chance to see them before they strike, you will have no doubt whatever. Ayee, bismillah, kheli zahmat dadam . . ." and, praying at the top of his lungs, he made an astonishing number of deep salaam prostrations before crawling into his tent.

When all my companions were abed, I walked, with my shimshir sword in hand, twice or thrice around the entire perimeter of the oasis, peering out as far as I could into the surrounding thick, black, foggy night. Since that darkness was so impenetrable, and since I could not possibly stand athwart all the approaches to our camp, I decided to post myself at my own tent, beside that of Aziz. The night being one of the more chilly nights of the journey, I lay prone inside my tent, under the blankets, and let just my head protrude beyond the flaps. Either Aziz was lying sleepless or I waked him with the noise of my getting settled, for he also stuck his head out, and whispered, "I am frightened, Marco, and I am cold. May I sleep next to you?"

"Yes, it is cold," I agreed. "I am shivering even with all my clothes on. I would go and fetch more blankets, but I dislike to rouse the camels. Here, you bring your covers, Aziz, and I will take down your tent as well, to use for an extra cover. If you lie close to me, and we pile all the fabrics on us, we ought to be snug enough."

That is what we did. Aziz wriggled out of his tent, like a little naked newt, and into mine. Working quickly in the cold, I shook the supporting rods out of his tent's hems, and bundled the cloth in on top of him. I burrowed in beside him, leaving only my head still out, and my hands and the shimshir. Very soon I had stopped shivering, but inwardly I felt quivery in a different way, not from the chill, but from the warmth and nearness and softness of the little boy's body. He was pressed against me in a most intimate embrace, and I suspected he had done that deliberately. In a moment I was sure of it, for he loosed the cord of my paijamah, and nestled his bare body against my bare bottom, and then he did something even more intimate. It made me gasp, and I heard him whisper, "Does this not warm you even more?"

Warm was not the word for it. His sister Sitarè had boasted that Aziz was expert at his art, and he clearly knew how to excite the thing that Nostril had called "the almond inside," for my member came erect as quickly and as stiffly as a tent cloth does when the rod is slid inside its hem sheath. What would have occurred next, I do not know. It might be asserted that I was grievously neglecting my guard watch, but I think the Karauna would have approached and struck unseen, even if I had been more attentive. Something struck the back of my head, so hard that the black night around me went even blacker, and when I was next conscious of anything, it was of being painfully dragged by my hair across the grass and sand.

I was dragged to where the camp fire was being rekindled, but not by any of us. The intruders were men to make the earlier visiting Mongols look like elegant and polished court gentlemen by comparison. There were seven of these, and they were filthy and ragged and ugly and somehow, though they never smiled, they kept their snaggle teeth always bared. They each had a horse, a small one like a Mongol horse, but bony and ribby and pustular with sores. One other thing I noticed about those horses, even in my dazed condition: they had no ears.

One of the marauders was making up the fire, the others were dragging my companions to it, and all of them were babbling in a high voice another language new to me. Nostril alone seemed to understand it, and he, though also having been knocked about and yanked from his bed and consumed with terror, took the pains to translate and shout to us all:

"These are the Karauna! They are mortally hungry! They say they will not kill us if we feed them! Please, my masters, in the name of Allah, get busy and show them food!"

The Karauna dumped us all beside the fire and then began frantically scooping up water from the spring with their hands and dashing it down their throats. My father and uncle obediently hurried to get out the food stores. I still lay on the ground, shaking my head, striving to get the pain and darkness and buzzing out of it. Nostril, trying to look properly and obsequiously busy, and doubtless half scared to death, nevertheless kept shouting:

"They say they will not rob or kill *the four of us*! Of course they are lying, and they will, but not until after *the four of us* have fed them. So, please Allah, let us keep on feeding them as long as there is food to feed! *All four of us!*"

Mainly concerned with the havoc inside my head, I dimly supposed that he was urging me, too, to show some life and activity. So I struggled upright and bestirred myself to pour some dried apricots into a pot of water to soften. I heard Uncle Mafio also shouting:

"We must comply, *the four of us*! But then, while they are gorging themselves, *the four of us* may see a chance to retrieve our swords and to fight."

I finally caught the message he and Nostril were trying to impart. Aziz was not among us. When the Karauna swooped down, they had seen four tents, had dragged four men out of them, and now had four captives dutifully scurrying at their command. It was because I had taken down Aziz's tent. When they plucked me from mine, Aziz might have come along, attached, but he had not. And he must have realized what was happening, so he would stay hidden, unless. . . . The boy was brave. He might try some desperate expedient. . . .

One of the Karauna roared at us. His thirst quenched, he seemed delighted to see us slaving for him. Like a victorious conqueror, he thumped his chest with his fists, and bellowed quite a long narrative, which Nostril translated in a quaver:

"They have been so hotly pursued that they were near dead of thirst and starvation. They several times opened the veins of their horses to drink their blood for sustenance. But the horses got so weak that they desisted from that, but at last cut off and ate the horses' ears. Ayee, mashallah, che arz konam? . . ." and he tailed off into another spate of praying.

The confusion also diminished, as the seven Karauna ceased to mill about the spring, and let their mistreated horses get to it, and came to where we had laid all our food around the fire. With bared teeth and guttural growls, they indicated that we should all stand aside, well out of range to interfere. The four of us backed away, and the Karauna fell slavering upon the provender, and in the next moment there was confusion confounded. Three more horses came plunging suddenly out of the darkness, bearing three howling riders swinging swords.

The Mongol patrol had returned! I might better say, the Mongols had all the while been lurking somewhere nearby, and not even I, the camp guard, had suspected it. They had known that we would be an irresistible bait to the Karauna, and simply had waited for the bandits to walk into the trap.

But the Karauna, although taken unawares and unmounted and with their attention fixed upon the food before them, neither surrendered on the instant nor fell before the flashing swords. Two or three of the dirty brown men magically turned bright red before our eyes, as blood spurted from the cuts given them by the Mongols. But they, like the not immediately wounded others, whipped out swords of their own.

The Mongols, having leapt in on horseback, could make only that one flailing slash before their mounts carried them a little way past the fray. Not turning their horses, they slid from their saddles to continue the fight on foot. But the Karauna, in their avidness to feed, had not tethered or hobbled or unsaddled their own mounts. They must have been mightily tempted to stand and fight, with the food all laid out for them, and they being seven against three. Probably only because they *were* weak with hunger—and knowing that three well-fed Mongols were their fighting equal—they bounded astride their pitiful horses and, beating their blades down on the swords of the Mongols now afoot, put spurs to their horses and surged out of the firelight in the direction from which they had dragged me.

The Mongols considerately hesitated long enough to glance around at us, and ascertain that we were not visibly injured, before they caught their own horses, vaulted to their saddles, and were off in hot pursuit. Everything had happened in such a furious tumult—from the moment I had been clouted to this sudden quiet fallen on the oasis—that it might

have been a simùm desert storm that had swept down and embroiled us
and swept on past.

"Gèsu . . . ," my father breathed.

"Al-hamdo-lillah . . . ," prayed Nostril.

"Where is the boy Aziz?" Uncle Mafìo asked me.

"He is safe," I said loudly, to be heard above the ringing still going
on in my head. "He is in my tent." And I gestured toward where the dust
of the horses' departure was hanging in the air.

As soon as he could get some clothes on, my uncle went running off
in that direction. My father saw me rubbing my head, and came and felt
of it. He remarked that I had a palpable knot there, and told Nostril to
put a cup of water to heat.

Then my uncle came running back, out of the darkness, shouting,
"Aziz is not there! His clothes are, but he is not!"

Leaving Nostril to bathe my head and bind a poultice of salve about
it, my father and uncle went to beat the bushes for the boy. They did not
find him. Nor did any of us, when Nostril and I joined them, and we did
a methodical back-and-forth pacing of the entire oasis. Consulting together, we tried to reconstruct what must have happened.

"He would have left the tent. Even undressed and in this cold."

"Yoo, he would have known they would loot it soon or later."

"So he sought a safer place to hide."

"More likely he was creeping close, to see if he could aid us."

"Anyway, he was in the open when the Karauna suddenly fled."

"And they saw him and snatched him up and took him with them."

"At the first opportunity, they will kill him." It was Uncle Mafìo who
said that, and he said it in the voice of one bereaved. "They will kill him in
some bestial manner, for they must be furious, thinking we arranged that
ambuscade."

"They may have no opportunity. The Mongols are close behind."

"The Karauna will not kill the boy, but hold him hostage. A shield to
ward off the Mongols."

"And if the Mongols hold off, which they may not," said my uncle,
"think what the Karauna will be doing to that little boy."

"Let us not weep until someone is hurt," said my father. "But whatever the outcome, we must be there. Nostril, you stay. Mafìo, Marco,
mount up!"

We laid the sticks to our camels. Since we had never pressed them
before, the beasts were so startled that they did not think to complain or
balk, but went at a stretch-out gallop, and maintained it. The movement
made my head seem to pound upon the neck-top of my spine with an
excruciating beat, but I said nothing.

On sand, camels run faster than horses can, so we caught up to the
Mongols well before dawn. We would eventually have met them in any
case, as they were leisurely returning toward the oasis. The dry fog
having settled to the ground by then, we saw them at some distance in
the starlight. Two of them were walking and leading the horses, and
supporting the third in his saddle, where he sagged and wobbled, being

evidently badly hurt. The two called something to us as we approached, and waved their hands to indicate where they had come from.

"A miracle! The boy lives!" said my father, and lashed his camel harder.

We did not pause to speak to the Mongols, but kept on going, until we saw far off a scattering of dark, motionless shapes on the sand. They were the seven Karauna and their horses, all dead and much hacked and arrow-punctured, and some of the men lay separate from their severed sword hands. But we paid them no mind. Aziz was sitting on the sand, in a large puddle of blood from one of the fallen horses, his back propped against its saddle. He had covered his bare body with a blanket he must have pulled from the saddle pannier, and it was drenched with gore. We jumped off our camels before they had entirely knelt, and ran to him. Uncle Mafìo, with tears pouring down his face, fondly rumpled the child's hair, and my father patted him on the shoulder, and we all exclaimed in wonder and relief:

"You are all right!"

"Praise the good San Zudo of the Impossible!"

"What happened, dear Aziz?"

He said, his little bird voice even quieter than usual, "They passed me from one to another as we rode, so each could take a turn, and so they did not have to slow their pace."

"And you are unhurt?" my uncle asked.

"I am cold," Aziz said listlessly. Indeed, he was shivering violently under the threadbare old blanket.

Uncle Mafìo persisted anxiously, "They did not—abuse you? Here?" He laid a hand on the blanket between the boy's thighs.

"No, they did nothing like that. There was no time. And I think they were too hungry. And then the Mongols caught us up." He puckered his pale face as if to cry. "I am so *cold* . . ."

"Yes, yes, lad," said my father. "We will set you soon to rights. Marco, you stay by him and comfort him. Mafìo, help me look about for dung to make a fire."

I took off my aba and spread it over the boy for an extra cover, uncaring about the blood that soaked into it. But he did not hug the covers about him. He only sat where he was, against the sideways saddle, his little legs stuck out in front of him and his hands lying limp alongside. Hoping to cheer and enliven him, I said:

"All this time, Aziz, I have been wondering about the curious animal you challenged me to guess."

A faint smile came briefly to his lips. "I did riddle you to puzzlement, Marco, did I not?"

"Yes, you did. How does it go again?"

"A desert creature . . . that unites in itself . . . the natures of seven different beasts." His voice was fading again to listlessness. "Can you still not divine it?"

"No," I said, frowning as before, and pretending to delve deep in my mind. "No, I confess I cannot."

"It has the head of a horse . . ." he said slowly, as if he were having trouble remembering, or having trouble speaking. "And the neck of a bull . . . the wings of a rukh . . . belly of a scorpion . . . feet of a camel . . . horns of a qazèl . . . and the . . . and the hindquarters . . . of a serpent . . ."

I was worried by his uncharacteristic lack of vivacity, but I could discern no cause for it. As his voice dwindled, his eyelids drooped. I squeezed his shoulder encouragingly, and said:

"That must be a most marvelous beast. But what is it? Aziz, unriddle the riddle. What is it?"

He opened his beautiful eyes and gazed at me, and he smiled and he said, "It is only a common grasshopper." Then he fell abruptly forward, his face hitting the sand between his knees, as if he had been loosely hinged at the waist. There was a sudden, noticeable increase in the prevailing stench of blood and body odors and horse manure and human excrement. Aghast, I leaped up and called for my father and uncle. They came running, and stared down at the boy, unbelieving.

"No living human being ever bent over flat like that!" my uncle exclaimed in horror.

My father knelt and took one of the boy's wrists and held it for a moment, then looked up at us and somberly shook his head.

"The child has died! But of what? Did he not say he was unhurt? That they only handed him back and forth as they rode?"

I helplessly raised my hands. "We spoke for a little. Then he fell over like that. Like a sawdust doll from which all the sawdust is gone."

My uncle turned away, sobbing and coughing. My father gently took the boy's shoulders and lifted him, and laid the lolling head back against the saddle, and with one hand held him sitting up while with the other he pulled down the gory covers. Then my father made a retching noise and, repeating what the boy had told us, he muttered, "The Karauna were hungry," and he backed away in sick revulsion, letting the body topple forward flat again, but not before I also saw. What had happened to Aziz—I could liken it to nothing except an ancient Greek tale I had once been told in school, about a stalwart boy of Sparta and a voracious fox cub he hid beneath his tunic.

. 6 .

WE left the dead Karauna where they lay, carrion for the beaks of any scavenger vultures that might find them. But we took with us the already bitten and gouged and partially devoured little corpse of Aziz, as we headed back for the oasis. We would not leave him on the surface of the sand, or even bury him under it, for nothing can be so deeply buried in the sand but the wind will continually cover and uncover it again, as indifferently as it does the karwan leavings of camel dung.

On our way forth from the oasis, we had passed the white fringe of a minor salt flat, so we stopped there on our return. We carried Aziz out upon the trembling land, wrapped in my aba for a shroud, and we found a place where we could break through the glittering crust, and we laid Aziz on the quaggy quicksand under it. We said our farewells and some prayers during the time it took the small bundle to sink from our sight.

"The salt slab will soon re-form over him," mused my father. "He will rest under it undisturbed, even by corruption, for the salts will permeate his body and preserve him."

My uncle, scratching absentmindedly at his elbow, said with resignation, "It may even be that this land, like others I have seen, will in time heave and break and rearrange its topography. Some future journeyer may find him, centuries hence, and gaze upon his sweet face, and wonder how it came to pass that an angel fell from Heaven to be interred here."

That was as fine a valedictory as could be pronounced over any departed one, so we left Aziz then and remounted and rode on. When we arrived again at the oasis, Nostril came running, all worry and concern, and then all lamentation when he saw there were still only the three of us. We told him, in as few words as possible, how we had been deprived of the smallest member of our party. Looking properly grieved and woebegone, he muttered some Muslim prayers, and then he spoke to us a typically fatalistic Muslim condolence:

"May your own spans be lengthened, good masters, by the days which the boy has lost. Inshallah."

The day was at its noon by then, and anyway we were weary and my head was near to splitting with pain and we had no heart for hastening to resume our journey, so we prepared to spend another night in the oasis, even though it was no longer any happy place for us. The three Mongols had preceded us there, and Nostril went on with what he had been doing when we came: helping those men clean and anoint and bind up their wounds.

Those wounds were many, but none very serious. The man we had thought worst hurt had only had his brains temporarily scrambled when he was kicked in the head by a horse during the final affray with the Karauna; he had considerably recovered. Even so, all three of the men bore numerous sword cuts and had lost much blood and must have been much weakened, and we would have expected them to remain in the oasis for some days while they recuperated. But no, they said, they were Mongols, indestructible, unstoppable, and they would ride on.

My father asked where they would go. They said they had no assigned destination, only a mandate to go and seek and chase and destroy the Karauna of the Dasht-e-Kavir, and they wanted to get on with that job. So my father showed them our passepartout signed by the Khakhan Kubilai. For certain, none of those men could read, but they easily recognized the distinctive seal of the Khan of All Khans. They were agog at our possession of it, as they had earlier been impressed to hear my father and uncle speaking their tongue, and they inquired if we wished to give them any orders in the name of the Khakhan. My father suggested that, since we were carrying rich gifts for their great lord, the men might help ensure the delivery of them by riding as our escort as far as Mashhad, and they readily agreed to do so.

The next day, we were seven when we moved on northeastward. Since the Mongols disdained conversing with a lowly camel-puller, and since Uncle Mafìo seemed indisposed to speak to anybody, and since my head still hurt whenever I jarred it by talking, only my father and our three new companions talked as we rode, and I was satisfied to ride close to them and listen, and thereby begin learning yet another new language.

The first thing I learned was that the name Mongol does not connote a race or a nation of people—the name derives from the word *mong*, meaning brave—and similar though our three escorting Mongols appeared to my unaccustomed eye, they were in fact as disparate as if they had been Venetian, Genoan and Pisan. One was of the Khalkas tribe, one was of the Merkit and one was of the Buriat—which tribes, I gathered, originally hailed from widely separated parts of those lands that the mighty Chinghiz (himself a Khalkas) long ago first united and so began building the Mongol Khanate. Also, one of the men was of the Buddhist faith, another of the Taoist—religions of which I then knew nothing— and the third was, of all things, a Nestorian Christian. But I learned at the same time that, whatever a Mongol's tribal origin or his religious affiliation or his soldierly occupation, he is never to be referred to as a Khalkas or a Christian or even as a bowman or an armorer or any other such applicable appellation. He calls himself only a Mongol—and proudly, thus: *"Mongol!"*—and he must be spoken of only as a Mongol, for his being a Mongol supersedes anything else he may be, and that name of Mongol takes precedence over all other names.

However, long before I could make the least conversation with our three escorts, I had discerned from their behavior some of the Mongols' curious ways and customs—or, I might better say, their barbaric superstitions. While we were still in the oasis, Nostril had suggested to them that they might like to wash the blood and sweat and long-accumulated dirt out of their clothes, and so have them fresh and clean for the next stage of traveling. The men declined, giving as a reason that it was unwise to launder any article of apparel when abroad from one's home camp, because that would raise a thunderstorm. *How* it would do that, they could not say, and would not demonstrate. Now, any man of ordinary good sense, in the middle of a parched and bleached desert, would scarcely object to any kind of wet storm, however mysteriously produced. But the Mongols, who fear nothing else under Heaven, are as terrified of thunder and lightning as is the most timid child or woman.

Also, while still in that abundantly watered oasis, the three Mongols never once treated themselves to a thorough and refreshing bath, though God knows they needed one. They were so crusty they almost creaked, and their aroma would have gagged a shaqàl. But they washed no more of themselves than their heads and hands, and did that little washing most miserly. One of them would dip a gourd in the spring, but use not even the dipper's amount of water. He would slurp from the gourd only a single mouthful, and hold it in his mouth, then spit the water into his cupped hands, a little at a time, and with one spurt wet his hair, with the next his ears, and so on. Granted, that may not have been a matter of superstition, but of conservation, a custom decreed by a people who spend so much of their time in arid lands. But I did think they would have been a more socially acceptable people if they had relaxed that stringency when it was not needful.

Another thing. Those three men had been traveling from out of the northeast when they first came upon us. Now that we were proceeding in that direction, and perforce so were they, the men insisted that we ride a farsakh or so to one side of their prior trail, because, they assured us, it was unlucky to return over the exact same route by which one has gone out.

It was also extremely unlucky, they remarked, during the first night we all camped together on the trail, for any member of a party to sit with his head hanging as in sorrow, or to lean his cheek or chin on his hand as an aid to cogitation. That, they said, could bring sadness on the entire company. And they said it while glancing uneasily at Uncle Mafìo, who was sitting just that way, and looking mournful indeed. My father or I might jolly him into sociability for a while, but he soon would lapse into gloom again.

For a very long time after the death of Aziz, my uncle spoke seldom and sighed often and looked miserably bereft. Where earlier I had tried to take a tolerant attitude toward his unmanly nature, I was now more inclined to an amused and exasperated contempt. No doubt a man who can find sensual pleasure only with one of his own sex can also find a deep and lasting love for one of them, and such a true ardor—like the more conventional instances of true love—can be esteemed and admired and commended. However, Uncle Mafìo had had only a single and insignificant sexual encounter with Aziz, and otherwise he had been no closer to the boy than any of the rest of us. We all grieved for Aziz, and felt sorrow at his loss. But for Uncle Mafìo to carry on, in the way that another man might grieve for a wife lost after many years of happy marriage—that was lugubrious and farcical and unworthy. He was still my uncle, and I would continue to treat him with all due respect, but I had come privately to conclude that his big and burly and strong outer semblance had not much inside it.

No one could have been sorrier for the death of Aziz than I was, but I realized that my reasons were mainly selfish, and gave me no right to make loud lamentation. One reason was that I had promised both Sitarè and my father that I would keep the boy from harm, and I had not. So I could not be sure whether I was feeling more sorry for his death or for my failure as a guardian. Another of my selfish reasons was that I was grieving because someone worth keeping had been snatched out of my world. Oh, I know that all people grieve so, on the occasion of a death, but that makes it no less a selfish reason. We survivors are deprived of that one person newly dead. But he or she is deprived of everything—of all other persons, of all things worth keeping, of the entire world and every least thing in it, all in an instant—and such a loss deserves a lamentation so loud and vast and lasting that we who stay are incapable of expressing it.

I had yet another selfish reason for lamenting the death of Aziz. I could not help recalling the Widow Esther's admonition: that a man should avail himself of everything life offers, lest he die repining for those opportunities he neglected to seize. It was perhaps virtuous of me, and laudable, that I had declined what Aziz offered me, and so left his chastity unsmirched. It would perhaps have been sinful of me, and reprehensible, if I had accepted, and so despoiled his chastity. But, I asked myself now, since Aziz would have gone so soon to his grave in either case, what difference could it have made? If we had embraced, it might have meant one last pleasure for him, and a unique one for me: what Nostril had called "a journey beyond the ordinary"—and whether it had been innocuous or iniquitous, it would have left no trace on the all-covering quicksand. But I had refused, and in all the rest of my life, if any such chance ever came again, it could not come from the beautiful Aziz. He was gone, and that opportunity was lost, and now—not on some putative future deathbed—*now* I was sorry.

But I was alive. And I and my uncle and my father and our companions journeyed on, for that is all that the living can do to forget death, or defy it.

We were not accosted by any more Karauna, or any other sorts of lurkers, and we did not even meet any other fellow travelers during the rest of our desert crossing. Either our Mongol escort had been unnecessary or its presence had discouraged any further molestation. We came finally out of the lowland sands at the Binalud Mountains, and up through that range to Mashhad. It was a fair and pleasant city, somewhat larger than Kashan, and its streets were lined with chinar and mulberry trees.

Mashhad is one of the very holy cities of Persian Islam, because a highly revered martyr of olden time, the Imam Riza, is entombed in an ornate masjid there. A Muslim's worshipful visit to Mashhad earns him the prefix of Meshadi to his name, as a pilgrimage to Mecca earns him the right to be addressed as Hajji. So the greater part of the city's population consisted of transient pilgrims and, because of that, Mashhad had very good and clean and comfortable karwansarai inns. Our three Mongols led us to one of the best, and themselves spent a night there before turning back to resume their patrol of the Dasht-e-Kavir.

There at the karwansarai, the Mongols demonstrated yet another of their customs. While my father, my uncle and I gratefully took lodging inside the inn, and our camel-puller Nostril gratefully took lodging in the stable with his animals, the Mongols insisted on laying their bedrolls outside in the center of the courtyard, and staked their horses to the ground about them. The Mashhad landlord indulged them in that eccentricity, but some landlords will not. As I later discovered, when a Mongol party is commanded by the innkeeper to lodge indoors like civilized folk, the Mongols will grudgingly comply, but they still will not depend on the karwansarai kitchen. They will lay a fire in the middle of their chamber floor, put a tripod over it and do their own cooking. Come night, they will not repose on the beds provided, but will unroll their own carpets and blankets and sleep on the floor.

Well, I could now sympathize in some measure with the Mongols'
reluctance to reside under a fixed roof. Myself, my father and my uncle,
after our long crossing of the Great Salt, had also developed a taste for
unconfined spaces and unrestricted elbow room, and the limitless silence
and clean air of the outdoors. Though at first we exulted in the refreshment of a hammam bath and rubbing, and were pleased to have our
meals cooked and presented to us by servants, we soon found ourselves
vexed by the noise and agitation and turmoil of indoor living. The air
seemed close and the walls even closer and the other karwansarai guests
a terribly talkative crowd. The all-pervading smoke especially tormented
Uncle Mafìo, who was troubled by intermittent coughing spells. So, for
all that the inn was well appointed and Mashhad an estimable city, we
stayed only long enough to exchange our camels again for horses, and
to replenish our traveling gear and rations, and we moved on.

BALKH

.1.

W E went now a little south of east, to skirt the Karakum, or Black Sands, which is another desert lying due eastward of Mashhad. We chose a route across the Karabil, or Cold Plateau, which is a long shelf of more solid and verdant land extending like a coastline between the bleak dry ocean of Black Sands to the north and the bleak escarpment of the treeless Paropamisus Mountains to the south.

It would have made a shorter journey to go straight across the Karakum desert, but we were weary of desert. And it would have been a more easeful journey if we had gone farther to the southward, through the valleys of the Paropamisus, for there we would have found accommodation in a succession of villages and towns and even cities of respectable size, such as Herat and Maimana. But we preferred to take the middle course. We were well accustomed to camping out of doors, and that high Karabil plateau must have got its name only by comparison to lower and warmer lands, for it was not terribly cold even then in early wintertime. We simply added layers of shirts and pai-jamah and abas as we needed them, and found the weather tolerable enough.

The Karabil consisted mostly of monotonous grassland, but there were also stands of trees—pistachio, zizafun, willow and conifers. We had seen many greener and more pleasant lands, and would see many others, but, after having endured the Great Salt, we found even the dull gray grass and scanty foliage of the Karabil a delight to our eyes, and our horses found it adequate for forage. After the lifeless desert, that plateau seemed to us to teem with wildlife. There were coveys of quail, and flocks of a red-legged partridge, and everywhere marmots peeking from their burrows and whistling peevishly at our passing. There were migrant geese and ducks wintering there, or at least passing through: a kind of goose with a barred head-feathering, and a duck of lovely russet and gold plumage. There were multitudes of brown lizards, some of them so immense—longer than my leg—that they frequently startled our horses.

There were herds of several different sorts of delicate qazèl, and of a large and handsome wild ass, called in that region the kulan. When we first saw it, my father said that he almost wished we could stop and capture some, and tame them, and take them back to the West for sale, as they would fetch a far better price than the mules which noblemen and ladies buy for their mounts. The kulan is veritably as big as a mule, and has the same jug head and short tail, but it is of an extraordinarily rich dark-brown coat with a pale belly, and it is beautiful. A man can never tire of watching the herds of them swiftly running and frisking and wheeling in unison. But the Karabil natives told us the kulan cannot be tamed and ridden; they value it only for its edible flesh.

We ourselves, and Uncle Mafìo especially, did much hunting on that stage of our journey, to supplement our travel rations. In Mashhad we had each procured a compact Mongol-style bow and the short arrows for it, and my uncle had practiced until he was expert with that weapon. As a rule, we tried to shy clear of the herds of qazèl and kulan, for we feared they might be attended by other hunters: wolves or lions, which also abound in the Karabil. But we did occasionally risk stalking a herd, and several times brought down a qazèl, and once a kulan. Almost every day we could count on getting a goose or duck or quail or partridge. That fresh meat would have been eminently enjoyable, except for one thing.

I forget what was the first creature we brought down with an arrow, or which of us it was who got it. But when we started to carve it for spitting over our fire, we discovered that it was riddled with some kind of small blind insects, dozens of them, alive and wriggling, snugged between the skin and flesh. Disgusted, we flung it aside and made do that night with a desert-type dried-food meal. But the very next day, we brought down some other sort of game, and found it identically infested. I do not know what demon afflicts every living wild creature of the Karabil. The natives we asked could not tell us, and seemed not to care, and even expressed disdain of our queasiness. So, since all our subsequently bagged game was similarly crawly, we forced ourselves to pick out the vermin and cook and eat the meat, and it did not make us ill, and eventually we came to regard the matter as commonplace.

Another thing we might have thought bothersome—but which, after

the desert, we found rather exhilarating—was that three times during
our traverse of the Karabil we had to cross a river. As I recall, their
names were the Tedzhen, the Kushka and the Takhta. They were not
wide waters, but they were cold and deep and fast-running, tumbling
down from the Paropamisus heights to the Karakum flats, where eventually they would seep into the Black Sands and disappear. At each riverside we found a karwansarai, and each provided a ferry service, of a sort
I found amusing. Our horses we simply unsaddled and unloaded and let
swim across the rivers, which they did with aplomb. But we travelers
were taken across, one at time, with our packs, by a ferryman plying a
peculiar kind of raft called a masak. Each of those craft was not much
bigger than a tub and consisted of a light framework of wood, supported
by a score or so of inflated goatskins.

A masak was ludicrous looking, with all the tied-off stumps of goat
legs poking up among its framing poles, but I learned that there was a
reason for that. Those rivers ran briskly, and the men paddling had little
control over something as awkward as a masak, so it yawed and rocked
and revolved and pitched wildly as it went careening on a long diagonal
from one shore to the other. Each crossing took quite a while, during
which time the inflated goatskins leaked and bubbled and whistled.
When the masak began to get alarmingly low in the water, the ferryman
would stop paddling, untie the goat legs and vigorously blow into the
hide bags, one after another, until they were buoyant again, and then
deftly retie them. I should amend my earlier remark and say I found that
an amusing mode of ferriage *after* I was on each occasion put safely
aground on the other side. During the turbulent crossings, I had other
feelings—compounded of giddiness, wetness, coldness, sea-sickness and
expectation of imminent drowning.

At the Kushka ferry, I remember, another karwan party was preparing to cross, and we watched and wondered how it would manage, for
it was traveling in a number of horse-drawn carts. But that did not deter
the ferrymen. They unhitched the horses and sent them swimming for
the far bank, and made several raft trips to transport the occupants and
contents of the wagons. Then, as each cart was emptied, they eased it
down the riverbank until its four wheels rested one apiece in four of the
tubby little masaks, and they rowed it across in quaternion. That made a
sight to see: each wagon dipping and dancing and whirling down the
river, and its raftmen at each of its corners alternately paddling like
Charon to make headway and puffing like Aeolus to keep the goatskins
inflated.

I must remark that the riverside inns in the Karabil provided better
ferriage than forage for their guests. At only one karwansarai did we
have a decent meal, in fact something unique in our experience thus far:
huge and tasty steaks carved from a fish caught in the river outside the
door. The steaks were so tremendous that we marveled and asked permission to go into the kitchen for a look at the fish they had been cut
from. It was called an ashyotr, and it was bigger than a big man, bigger
than Uncle Mafio, and instead of scales it had a shell of bony plates, and
beneath its long snout it had barbels like whiskers. In addition to giving

edible flesh, the ashyotr yielded a black roe, each egg of seed-pearl size, and we ate some of that too, salted and pressed to make a relish called khavyah.

But at the other inns the food was awful, and there was no reason for it to be, given the abundance of game in that country. Every landlord of a karwansarai seemed to think that he must serve his guests something they had not lately been eating. Since we had been dining on such delicacies as game birds and wild qazèl does, the innkeepers fed us the mutton of domestic sheep. The Karabil is not sheep country, meaning that the meat had probably traveled as far from its point of origin as we had, to get to the karwansarai. Mutton had long since ceased to delight me, and this was dried and salted and tough, and there was no oil or vinegar or anything else to season it with, only pungent red meleghèta pepper, and it was invariably accompanied by beans boiled in sugar water. After enough such gaseous meals, we could probably have served instead of the goatskins to support the masak rafts. But, to say one good thing about the inns in the Karabil, they charged only for their human patrons, not for the karwan animals. That was because wood was hard to come by, and the beasts paid their own way by leaving their dung to be dried for fuel.

The next city of any consequence to which we came was Balkh, and in times past that had been a city of truly great consequence: the site of one of Alexander's main encampments, a major station for karwan traders traveling the Silk Road, a city of crowded bazàrs and majestic temples and luxurious karwansarais. But it had stood in the path of the first waves of Mongols rampaging out of the fastnesses to the east—meaning that earliest Mongol Horde commanded by the invincible Chinghiz Khan—and in the year 1220 the Horde had stamped upon Balkh as a booted foot might stamp upon an ant nest.

It was more than half a century later that my father, my uncle, our slave and I arrived in Balkh, but the city had not even yet recovered from that disaster. Balkh was a grand and noble ruin, but it was still a ruin. It was perhaps as busy and thriving as of old, but its inns and granaries and warehouses were only slatternly buildings thrown together of the broken bricks and planks left after the ruination. They looked even more dingy and pathetic, standing as they did among the stumps of once towering columns, the tumbled remains of once mighty walls and the jagged shells of once perfect domes.

Of course, few of Balkh's current inhabitants were old enough to have been there when Chinghiz sacked the city, or before, when it had been far-famed as Balkh Umn-al-Bulud, the "Mother of Cities." But their sons and grandsons, who were now the proprietors of the inns and counting houses and other establishments, appeared as dazed and miserable as if the devastation had occurred only yesterday, and in their own seeing. When they spoke of the Mongols, they recited what must have been a litany committed to memory by every Balkhite: "Amdand u khandand u sokhtand u kushtand u burdand u raftand," which means, "They came and they slew and they burned and they plundered and they seized their spoils and they went on."

They had gone on, yes, but this whole land, like so many others, was still under tribute and allegiance to the Mongol Khanate. The glum demeanor of the Balkhites was understandable, since a Mongol garrison was still encamped nearby. Armed Mongol warriors strode through the bazàr crowds, remindful that the grandson of Chinghiz, the Khakhan Kubilai, still held his heavy boot poised over the city. And his appointed magistrates and tax collectors still peered watchfully over the shoulders of the Balkhites in their market stalls and money-changing booths.

I could say, as I have said before, and say it truthfully, that everywhere east of the Furat River basin, away back at the far western beginning of Persia, we journeyers had been traversing the lands of the Mongol Khanate. But if we had thus simplistically marked our maps—writing nothing but "Mongol Khanate" over that whole vast area of the world—we might as well not have kept up our maps at all. They would have been of little use to us or anyone else without more detail than that. We did expect to retrace our trail someday, when we returned home again, and we also hoped that the maps would be of use even after that, for the guidance of whole streams of commerce flowing back and forth between Venice and Kithai. So, every day or so, my father and uncle would get out our copy of the Kitab and, only after deliberation and consultation and final agreement, they would inscribe upon it the symbols for mountains and rivers and towns and deserts and other such landmarks.

That had now become a more necessary task than before. From the shores of the Levant all the way across Asia, to Balkh or hereabouts, the Arab mapmaker al-Idrisi had proved a dependable guide for us. As my father had long ago remarked, al-Idrisi himself must at some time have traveled through all those regions and seen them with his own eyes. But, from the vicinity of Balkh on eastward, al-Idrisi seemed to have relied on hearsay information from other travelers, and not very observant travelers at that. The Kitab's more easterly map pages were notably empty of landmarks, and what major things it did show—things like rivers and mountain ranges—frequently turned out to be incorrectly located.

"Also, the maps from here on seem exceedingly *small*," said my father, frowning at those pages.

"Yes, by God," said my uncle, scratching and coughing. "There is an almighty lot more land than he indicates, between here and the eastern ocean."

"Well," said my father. "We must be that much more assiduous in our own mapping."

He and Uncle Mafio could usually agree, without long debate, on the penning-in of mountains and waters and towns and deserts, because those were things we could see and judge the measure of. What required deliberation and discussion, and sometimes sheer guesswork, was the drawing-in of invisible things, which is to say the borders of nations. That was maddeningly difficult, and only partly because the spread of the Mongol Khanate had engulfed so many once-independent states and nations and even whole races as to render immaterial—except to a mapmaker—the question of where they had been, and where they had abutted, and where the lines between them had lain. It would have been difficult even if some native of each nation had come with us to pace off the bounds of it for us. I daresay that would be a troublesome job on our own Italian peninsula, where no two city-states can yet agree on each other's limits of ownership and authority. But in central Asia the extents of the nations and their frontiers and even their names have been in flux since long before the Mongols made those matters moot.

I shall illustrate. Somewhere during our long traverse from Mashhad to Balkh, we had crossed the invisible line which, in Alexander's time, marked the division between two lands known as Arya and Bactria. Now it marks—or at least it did until the Mongols came—the division between the lands of Greater Persia and Greater India. But let me pretend for a moment that the Mongol Khanate does not exist, and try to give some idea of the confusion attendant throughout history on that imprecise border.

India may once have been inhabited in all its vastness by the small, dark people we now know as the Indians. But long ago the incursions of more vigorous and courageous peoples pushed those original Indians into a smaller and smaller compass of land, so that nowadays the Hindu India lies far distant to the south and east of here. This northern India Aryana is the habitat of the descendants of those long-ago invaders, and they are not of the Hindu but of the Muslim religion. Every least tribe calls itself a nation and gives its nation a name and asserts that its nation has mappable borders. Most of the names hereabout end in -stan, which signifies "land of"—Khaljistan, meaning Land of the Khalji, and Pakhtunistan and Kohistan and Afghanistan and Nuristan and I disremember how many others.

In olden time, it was somewhere in this area, in either the then-Arya or the then-Bactria, that Alexander the Great, during his eastward march of conquest, met and fell enamored of and took to wife the Princess Roxana. Nobody can say exactly where that happened, or of what tribe's "royal family" Roxana was a member. But nowadays and hereabout, every one of the local tribes—Pakhtuni, Khalji, Afghani, Kirghiz and every other—claims descent from, first, the royal line which produced Roxana and, also, the Macedonians of Alexander's army. There may even be some cause for those claims. Although the greater number of people one sees in Balkh and its environs possess dark hair and skin and eyes, which presumably Roxana also had, there are among them many persons of fair complexion and blue or gray eyes and reddish or even yellow hair.

However, each tribe purports to be the *only* true descendants, and on that basis claims sole sovereignty over all these lands now constituting India Aryana. To me, that seemed a devious sort of reasoning, since even Alexander was a latecomer here, and an unwelcome marauder, so all the natives here—except perhaps the Princess Roxana—should have felt about the Macedonians as they now feel about the Mongols.

The one thing we found common to all the peoples in these regions was the still later come religion of Islam. In accord with Muslim custom, then, we never got to converse with any but the *male* persons, and that

made Uncle Mafio skeptical of their boasts of their lineage. He quoted
an old Venetian couplet:

> La mare xe segura
> E'l pare de ventura.

Which is to say that, while a father may claim to know, only a mother
can know for certain who sired each of her children.

I have recounted this tangled and disjointed bit of history merely to
indicate how it added to the other frustrations of us would-be map-
makers. Whenever my father and uncle sat down together to decide the
designations to ink onto our map pages, hoping to do that tidily, the
discussion might go untidily thus:

"To begin with, Mafio, this land is in the portion of the Khanate
governed by the Ilkhan Kaidu. But we must be more specific."

"How specific, Nico? We do not know what Kaidu or Kubilai or any
other Mongol officially calls this region. All the Western cosmographers
call it merely the India Aryana of Greater India."

"They have never set foot upon it. The Westerner Alexander did,
and he called it Bactria."

"But most of the local folk call it Pakhtunistan."

"On the other hand, al-Idrisi has it marked as Mazar-i-Sharif."

"Gèsu! It occupies only a thumb span of the map. Is it worth this
fuss?"

"The Ilkhan Kaidu would not maintain a garrison here if the land
were worthless. And the Khakhan Kubilai will wish to see how accurately we have done our maps."

"All right." Sigh of exasperation. "Let us give it a good thinking
over. . . ."

. 2 .

W E dawdled in Balkh for a time, not because it was an attractive city, but
because there were high mountains to the eastward, on the way we had
yet to go. And now there was snow thick on the ground even here in the
lower lands, so we knew the mountains would be impassable until perhaps late in the spring. Since we had to wait out the winter somewhere,
we decided that our Balkh karwansarai was a comfortable enough place
to spend at least part of it.

The food was good and ample and fairly various, as it should have
been, at such a crossroads of commerce. There were excellent breads,
and several sorts of fish, and the meat, though it was mutton, was broiled
in a tasty brochette manner called shashlik. There were savory winter
melons and well-kept pomegranates, besides all the usual dried fruits.
There was no qahwah in those parts, but there was another hot beverage
called cha, made of steeped leaves, almost as vivifying as qahwah and

equally fragrant, though in a different way, and much thinner in consistency. The staple vegetable was still beans and the only other accompaniment to the meals was the everlasting rice, but we contributed a fragment of a brick of zafràn to the kitchen, and so made the rice palatable and won those cooks the praise of every other patron of that karwansarai.

Since zafràn was as much of a novelty and a nonesuch in Balkh as it had been in other places, our budgets were ample for buying anything we needed or wanted. My father traded bits of the brick and hay zafràn for coin of the realm and, when an occasional merchant pleaded eloquently enough, would even deign to sell him a culm or two or three, so the khaja could start growing his own crocus crop. For each culm, my father demanded and got a number of gems of beryl or lapis lazura, of which stones this land is the chief source in all the world, and those were worth a great deal of coin indeed. So we were nicely well-to-do, and had not yet so much as opened our cods of musk.

We bought for ourselves heavy winter clothing, wools and furs, made in the local style. In that locality, the main garment was the chapon, which, as need required, could serve either for an overcoat or for a blanket or for a tent. When worn as a coat, it hung to the ground all around and its capacious sleeves hung a good foot-length beyond the fingertips. It looked ungainly and comical, but what people really looked at was not the fit but the color of one's chapon, for that told one's wealth. The lighter the color of the chapon, the harder it was to keep clean, and the more frequently it had to be cleaned, and the more it cost for that cleaning, and so it signified that the man wearing it cared little for that cost, and a chapon of pure snow-white color meant that its wearer was a man so rich he could be criminally spendthrift. My father and uncle and I each settled for a chapon of a medium tan color, indicating something modestly between opulence and the dark-brown of the chapon we bought for our slave Nostril. We also donned the local style of boot, called the chamus, which had a tough but flexible leather sole, bound to a soft leather upper which reached to the knee, and was held on by thongs wrapped around the calf. We also traded our flatland saddles, and paid a goodly sum of coin besides, to buy new saddles with high pommels and cantles that would seat us more securely during upland riding.

What time we were not buying or trading in the bazàr, we put to other uses. The slave Nostril fed and curried and combed our horses to prime condition, and we Polos made conversation with other karwan journeyers. We gave them our observations on the routes to the westward of Balkh, and those of them who had come from the east told us news of the routes and travel conditions out there. My father painstakingly wrote a letter of several pages to the Dona Fiordelisa, recounting our travels and progress and assuring her of our wellbeing, and gave it to the leader of a westbound train, to start it on the long way back to Venice. I remarked that a letter might have had a better prospect of getting there if he had posted one on the other side of the Great Salt.

"I did," he said. "I gave one to a train going west from Kashan."

I also remarked, without rancor, that he might have apprised my mother in the same way.

"I did," he said again. "I wrote a letter every year, to her or to Isidoro. I had no way of knowing that they never arrived. But in those days the Mongols were still actively conquering new territories, not just occupying them, and the Silk Road was an even less reliable post route than it is now."

In the evenings, he and my uncle put much devoted labor, as I have said, into bringing our maps up to date and place, and I did the same with my log papers of notes taken so far.

While doing that, I came upon the names of the Princesses Moth and Sunlight, away back in Baghdad, and I was made acutely aware that I had not lain with a woman since that long ago. Not that I really needed reminding; I had got quite tired of the only substitute: waging a war of the priests in the middle of every other night or so. But I have mentioned that the Mongols, having no perceptible organized religion of their own, do not interfere with the religions practiced by their tributary peoples, neither do they interfere with the laws observed by those peoples. So Balkh was still of Islam, and still abided by the sharaiyah, the law of Islam, and all of Balkh's resident females either stayed at home in close pardah or walked abroad only in chador-muffled invisibility. For me to have brashly approached one would have meant, first, chancing the possibility that she was an aged crone like Sunlight, and worse, chancing the likely wrath of her menfolk or the imams and muftis of Islamic law.

Nostril, of course, had found one of his usual perverse (but lawful) outlets for his animal urges. In every karwan train that stopped at Balkh, each Muslim man who did not have an accompanying wife or concubine, or two or three of each, had his kuch-i-safari. That term also signifies "traveling wives," but those really were boys, carried along to be used for wifely purposes, and there was no sharaiyah prohibition against strangers paying for a share of their favors. I knew that Nostril had hastened to do just that, for he had wheedled from me the money for it. But I was not tempted to emulate him. I had seen the kuch-i-safari, and had seen none among them to compare even remotely with the late Aziz.

So I went on wanting and wishing and lusting, and finding nothing to lust for. I could only stare hard at every walking heap I passed on the streets, and try in vain to descry what sort of female was inside that bale of clothing. Even doing no more than that, I was risking the outrage of the Balkhites. They call that idle ogling "Eve-baiting," and condemn it as vicious.

Meanwhile, Uncle Mafìo was also being celibate, almost ostentatiously so. For a while, I assumed it was because he was still grieving for Aziz. But it was soon evident that he was simply becoming too physically weak to engage in any dalliance. His persistent cough had been for some time past getting insistent. Now it would come upon him in such racking spells as to leave him feeble afterwards, and compel him to take bed rest. He looked hale enough, and he seemed still as robust as ever, and his color was good. But now, when he began to find it intolerably tiring just to walk from our karwansarai to the bazàr and back, my father and I overrode his protestations and called in a hakim.

Now, that word hakim merely means "wise," not necessarily educated in medicine or professionally qualified or experienced, and it may be given as a title to one who deserves it—say, the trusted physician to a palace court—or to one who may not, like a bazàr tomorrow-teller or an old beggar who gathers and sells herbs. So we were a trifle apprehensive about finding in these parts a person of real mèdego skill. We had seen many Balkhites with all too obvious afflictions—the most numerous being men with dangling goiters, like scrotums or melons, under their jawline—and that did not much inspire us with confidence in the local medicinal arts. But our karwansarai keeper fetched for us a certain Hakim Khosro, and we put Uncle Mafìo in his hands.

He *seemed* to know what he was doing. He had to make only a brief examination diagnostic to tell my father, "Your brother is suffering from the hasht nafri. That means one-of-eight, and we call it that because one of eight will die of it. But even those mortally stricken do not often die until after a long time. The jinni of that disease is in no hurry. Your brother tells me he has had this condition for some while, and it has worsened only gradually."

"The tisichezza it is, then," said my father, nodding solemnly. "Where we come from, it is sometimes also called the subtle sickness. Can it be cured?"

"Seven times out of eight, yes," said Hakim Khosro cheerfully enough. "To begin, I will need certain things from the kitchen."

He called on the landlord to bring him eggs and millet seed and barley flour. Then he wrote some words on a number of bits of paper— "powerful verses from the Quran," he said—and stuck those papers onto Uncle Mafìo's bare chest with dabs of egg yolk into which he had mixed the millet seed—"the jinni of this ailment seems to have some affinity to millet seeds." Then he had the innkeeper help him sprinkle and rub flour all over my uncle's torso, and rolled a number of goatskins tightly around him, explaining that this was "to promote the active sweating-out of the jinni's poisons."

"Malevolenza," growled my uncle. "I cannot even scratch my itching elbow."

Then he began coughing. Either the flour dust or the excessive heat inside the goatskins sent him into a fit of coughing that was worse than ever. His arms being pinioned by the wrapping, he could not pummel his chest for relief, or even cover his mouth, so the coughing went on until it seemed he would strangle, and his ruddy face got more red, and he sprayed little flecks of blood onto the hakim's white aba. After some time of that agony, he turned pale and swooned dead away, and I thought he *had* strangled.

"No, be not alarmed, young man," said Hakim Khosro. "This is nature's means of cure. The jinni of this disease will not trouble a victim when he is not conscious of being troubled. You notice, when your uncle is in the faint, he does not cough."

"He has only to die, then," I said skeptically, "and he is permanently cured of coughing."

The hakim laughed, unoffended, and said, "Be not suspicious either. The hasht nafri can only be arrested in nature's good time, and I can but lend assistance to nature. See, he wakes now, and the fit has passed."

"Gèsu," Uncle Mafìo muttered weakly.

"For now," the hakim went on, "the best prescriptive is rest and perspiration. He is to stay in bed except when he must go to the mustarah, and that he will do frequently, for I am also giving him a strong purgative. There are always jinn hiding in the bowels, and it does no harm to get rid of them. So, each time the patient returns from the mustarah to bed, one of you —since I will not always be here—must dust him with a new coating of barley flour and rewrap the skins about him. I will look in from time to time, to write new verses to be pasted on his chest."

So my father and I and the slave Nostril took turns tending Uncle Mafìo. But that was no onerous duty—except for having to listen to his continuous grumbling about his enforced prostration—and after a while my father decided he might as well make another use of our stay in Balkh. He would leave Mafìo in my keeping, and he and Nostril would travel to the capital city of these regions, to pay our respects to the local ruler (whose title was Sultan) and make us known to him as emissaries of the Khakhan Kubilai. Of course, that city was only nominally a capital, and its sovereign Sultan was, like the Shah Zaman of Persia, only a token ruler, subordinate to the Mongol Khanate. But the journey would also enable my father to embellish our maps with further details and modern designations. For example, our Kitab gave the name of that city as Kophes, and it was Nikaia in Alexander's time, but nowadays and hereabout we heard it always called Kabul. So my father and Nostril saddled two of our horses and prepared to ride there.

The evening before they departed, Nostril sidled up to me. He had apparently taken notice of my lovelorn and forlorn condition, and perhaps he hoped to keep me out of trouble while I was left on my own in Balkh. He said:

"Master Marco, there is a certain house here in this city. It is the house of a Gebr, and I would have you look at it."

"A Gebr?" I said. "Is that some sort of rare beast?"

"Not all that rare, but bestial, yes. A Gebr is one of the unregenerate Persians who never accepted the enlightenment of the Prophet (blessing and peace be upon him). Those people still worship Ormuzd, the discredited old-time god of fire, and engage in many wicked practices."

"Oh," I said, losing interest. "Why should I look at the house of yet another misbegotten heathen religion?"

"Because this Gebr, not being bound by Muslim law, expectably flouts all decencies. In front, his building is a shop vending articles made of amianthus, but in the rear it is a house of assignation, let by the Gebr to illicit lovers for their clandestine meetings. By the beard, it is an abomination!"

"What would you have me do about it? Go yourself and report it to a mufti."

"No doubt I should, being a devout Muslim, but I will not yet. Not until you have verified the Gebr's abomination, Master Marco."

"I? What the devil do I care about it?"

"Are not you Christians even more scrupulous about other people's decencies?"

"I do not abominate lovers," I said, with a self-pitying sniffle. "I envy them. Would that I had one of my own to take to the Gebr's back door."

"Well, he also perpetrates another offense against morality. For those who do not have a convenient lover, the Gebr keeps two or three young girls in residence and available for hire."

"Hm. This does begin to sound like a matter for reprobation. You did right to bring it to my attention, Nostril. Now, if you could point out that house, I would suitably reward your almost Christian vigilance. . . ."

And so the next day, a day when snow was falling, after he and my father had ridden off to the southeastward, and after I had made sure Uncle Mafìo was well snugged in his goatskins, I walked into the shop Nostril had shown me. There was a counter piled with bolts and swatches of some heavy cloth, and also on it was a stone bowl of naft oil feeding a wick burning with a bright yellow flame, and behind the counter stood an elderly Persian with a red-hinna'ed beard.

"Show me your softest goods," I said, as Nostril had instructed me to say.

"Room on the left," said the Gebr, jerking his beard at a beaded curtain at the back of the shop. "One dirham."

"I should like," I specified, "a beautiful piece of goods."

He sneered. "You show me a beautiful one among these country rustics, I will pay *you*. Be glad the goods are clean. One dirham."

"Oh, well, any water to put out a fire," I said. The man glowered as if I had spat at him, and I realized that was not the most tactful thing to say to a person who allegedly worshiped fire. I hastily laid my coin on the counter and pushed through the rattling curtain.

The little room was hung all about with locust twigs, for their sweet scent, and was furnished only with a charcoal brazier and a charpai, which is a crude bed made of a wooden frame laced crisscross with ropes. The girl was no prettier of face than the only other female I had paid to use, that boat girl Malgarita. This one was plainly of some local tribe, for she spoke the prevailing Pashtun tongue, and had a woefully scant vocabulary of Trade Farsi. If she told me her name, I did not catch it, because anybody speaking Pashtun sounds as if he or she is rapidly and repeatedly and simultaneously clearing the throat, spitting and sneezing.

But the girl was, as the Gebr had claimed, rather more cleanly of person than Malgarita had been. In fact, she made unmistakable complaint that I was *not*, and with some reason. In coming here, I had not worn my new-bought clothes; they were too bulky and difficult to get out of and into. I was wearing the garments I had worn while crossing the

Great Salt and the Karabil, and I daresay they were markedly odoriferous. They were certainly so caked with dust and sweat and dirt and salt that they could almost stand upright even when I got out of them.

The girl held them at arm's length, by her fingertips, and said, "dirty-dirty!" and "dahb!" and "bohut purana!" and several other gargled Pashtun noises indicative of revulsion. "I send yours, mine together, be clean."

She swiftly took off her own clothes, bundled them with mine, bawled what was evidently a call for a servant, and handed the bundle out the door. I confess that my attention was mainly on the first naked female body I had seen since Kashan; nevertheless, I noticed that the girl's clothing was made of a material so coarse and thick that, though cleaner than mine, it also could almost have stood alone.

The girl's body was more fetching than her face, it being slim but bearing amazingly large, round, firm breasts for such a slender figure. I assumed that that was one reason why the girl had chosen a career in which she would cater mainly to transient infidels. Muslim men are better attracted by a big fundament, and do not much admire women's breasts, regarding them only as milk spouts. Anyway, I hoped the girl would make her fortune in her chosen career while she was still young and shapely. Every woman of those "Alexandrine" tribes, well before middle age, grows so gross in the rest of her physique that her once-splendid bosom becomes just one of a series of fleshy shelves descending from her several chins to her several rolls of abdomen.

Another reason why I hoped the girl would make a fortune was that her chosen career was clearly no pleasure to her. When I attempted to share with her the enjoyment of the sexual act, by arousing her with fondling of her zambur, I found she had none. At the arch tip of her mihrab, where the tiny tuning key should have been, there was no slightest protrusion. For a moment I thought she was pathetically deformed, but then I realized that she was tabzir, as Islam demands. She had nothing there but a fissure of soft scar tissue. That lack may have diminished my own delight in my several ejaculations, because every time I approached spruzzo and she cried, "Ghi, ghi, ghi-ghi!"—meaning "Yes, yes, yes-yes!"—I was aware that she was only feigning an ecstasy of her own, and I thought it sad. But who am I to call criminal other people's religious observances? Besides, I soon discovered that I had a lack of my own to worry about.

The Gebr came and banged on the outside of the door, shouting, "What do you want for a single dirham, eh?"

I had to concede that I had had my money's worth, so I let the girl get up. She went, still naked, out the door to fetch a pan of water and a towel, meanwhile calling down the corridor for the return of our laundered clothes. She set the pan of tamarind-scented water on the room's brazier to warm, and was using it to wash my parts when the next knock came on the door. But the servant handed in only the girl's garments, with a long spate of Pashtun that must have been an explanation. The girl came back to me, an unreadable expression on her face, and said tentatively, as if asking a question, "Your clothes burn?"

"Yes, I suppose they would. Where are they?"

"No got," she said, showing me that she had only her own.

"Ah, you do not mean burn. You mean dry. Is that it? Mine are not dry yet?"

"No. Gone. Your clothes all burn."

"What does that mean? You said they would be washed."

"Not wash. Clean. Not in water. In fire."

"You put my clothes in a *fire*? They have *burned*?"

"Ghi."

"Are you a fire worshiper too, or are you just divanè? You sent them to be washed in fire instead of water? Olà, Gebr! Persian! Olà, whoremaster!"

"No make trouble!" the girl pleaded, looking scared. "I give you dirham back."

"I cannot wear a dirham across the city! What kind of lunatic place is this? Why did you people burn my clothes?"

"Wait. Look." She snatched up a piece of unburned charcoal from the brazier and gave it a swipe across a sleeve of her own tunic to make a black mark. Then she held the sleeve over the burning coals.

"You are divanè!" I exclaimed. But the cloth did not take fire. There was only a single flash as the black mark burned away. The girl took the sleeve from the fire to show me how it was suddenly spotless, and babbled a mixture of Pashtun and Farsi, of which I gradually got the import. That heavy and mysterious fabric was always cleaned in that manner, and my clothes had been so crusty that she had taken them to be of the same material.

"All right," I said. "I forgive you. It was a well-intentioned mistake. But I am still without anything to wear. Now what?"

She indicated that I could choose which of two things I would do. I could lodge a complaint with the Gebr master, and demand that he procure new raiment for me, which would cost the girl her day's wages and probably a beating besides. Or I could put on what clothes were available—meaning some of hers—and go across the city of Balkh in feminine masquerade. Well, that meant no choice at all; I must be a gentleman; therefore I must play the lady.

I scuttled out through the shop as fast as I could, but I was still adjusting my chador veil, and the old Gebr behind the counter raised his eyebrows, exclaiming, "You took me seriously! You are showing me a beautiful one among these country rustics!"

I snarled at him one of the few Pashtun expressions I knew: "Bahi chut!" which is a directive to do something to one's own sister.

He guffawed and called after me, "I would, if she were as pretty as you!" while I scurried out into the still falling snow.

Except for stumbling now and then, because I could see the ground only dimly through the obscuring snow and my chador, and also because I frequently stepped on my own hems, I got back to the karwansarai without incident. That disappointed me a little, for I had gone the whole way with my teeth and fists clenched and my temper seething, hoping to be rudely addressed or winked at by some Eve-baiting oaf, so I could kill him. I slipped into the inn by a rear door, unobserved, and hurried to put on clothes of my own, and started to throw away the girl's. But then I reconsidered, and cut from her gown a square of the cloth to keep for a curiosity, and with it I have since astonished many persons disinclined to believe that any cloth could be proof against fire.

Now, I had *heard* of such a substance long before I left Venice. I had heard priests tell that the Pope at Rome kept among the treasured relics of the Church a sudarium, a cloth which had been used to wipe the Holy Brow of Jesus Christ. The cloth had been so sanctified by that use, they said, that it could nevermore be destroyed. It could be thrown into a fire, and left there for a long time, and taken out again miraculously entire and unscorched. I also had heard a distinguished physician contest the priestly claim that it was the Holy Sweat which made the sudarium impervious to destruction. He insisted that the cloth must be woven of the wool of the salamander, that creature which Aristotle averred lives comfortably in fire.

I will respectfully contradict both the reverent believers and the pragmatic Aristotelian. For I took the trouble to inquire about that unburnable fabric woven by the Gebr fire worshipers, and eventually I was shown how it is made, and the truth of the matter is this. In the mountains in the region of Balkh is found a certain rock of palpable softness. When that rock is crushed, it comes apart not in grains, as of sand, but in fibers, as of raw flax. And those fibers, after repeated mashing and drying and washing and drying again and carding and spindling, are spun together into thread. It is clear that of any thread a cloth can be woven, and it is equally clear that a cloth made of earth's rock ought not burn. The curious rock and the coarse fiber and the magical material woven of it, all are regarded by the Gebr as sacred to their fire god Ahura Mazda, and they call that substance by a word meaning "unsoilable stone," which I take the liberty of rendering in a more civilized tongue as amianthus.

· 3 ·

M y father and Nostril were gone for some five or six weeks, and, because Uncle Mafìo required my attendance only intermittently, I had a good deal of spare time on my hands. So I went back several times to the house of the Gebr Persian—each time taking care to wear clothes that would not need "laundering." And every time I spoke the password, "Show me your softest goods," the old man would convulse with amusement and roar, "Why, *you* were the softest and most appealing piece that ever passed through this shop!" and I would have to stand and endure his guffaws until he finally subsided into giggles and took my dirham and told me which room was available.

At one time or another, I sampled all three of his back-room wares. But all the girls were Pakhtuni Muslims and tabzir, meaning that I found only release with them, not any satisfaction worth mentioning. I could have done that with the kuch-i-safari, and more cheaply. I did not even learn more than a few words of Pashtun from the girls, deeming it too slovenly a language to be worth learning. Just for example, the sound *gau*, when spoken normally on an exhaled breath, means "cow," but the same gau, spoken while breathing in, means "calf." So imagine what the simple sentence "The cow has a calf" sounds like in Pashtun, and then try to imagine conducting a conversation of any more complexity.

On my way out through the amianthus-cloth shop, though, I would pause to exchange some few words in Farsi with the Gebr proprietor. He would usually make some further mocking remarks about the day I had had to masquerade as a woman, but he would also condescend to answer my questions about his peculiar religion. I asked because he was the only devotee of that old-time Persian religion I had ever met. He admitted that there were few believers left in these days, but he maintained that the religion once had reigned supreme, not only in Persia but west and east of there as well, from Armeniya to Bactria. And the first thing he told me about it was that I should not call a Gebr a Gebr.

"The word means only 'non-Muslim' and it is used by the Muslims derisively. We prefer to be called Zarduchi, for we are the followers of the prophet Zaratushtra, the Golden Camel. It was he who taught us to worship the god Ahura Mazda, whose name is nowadays slurred to Ormuzd."

"And that means fire," I said knowledgably, for Nostril had told me that much. I nodded toward the bright lamp that always burned in the shop.

"*Not* fire," he said, sounding annoyed. "It is a stupid misbelief that we worship fire. Ahura Mazda is the God of Light, and we merely keep a flame burning as a reminder of His beneficent light which banishes the darkness of his adversary Ahriman."

"Ah," I said. "Not too different, then, from our own Lord God, Who contends against the adversary Satan."

"No, not different at all. Your Christian God and Satan you got from the Jews, as the Muslims derived their Allah and Shaitan. And the God and the Devil of the Jews were frankly patterned on our Ahura Mazda and Ahriman. So were your God's angels and your Satan's demons copied from our celestial malakhim messengers and their daeva counterparts. So were your Heaven and Hell copied from Zaratushtra's teachings about the nature of the afterlife."

"Oh, come now!" I protested. "I hold no brief for the Jews or the Muslims, but the True Religion cannot have been a mere imitation of somebody else's—"

He interrupted, "Look at any picture of a Christian deity or angel or saint. He or she is portrayed with a glowing halo, is that not so? It is a pretty fancy, but it was our fancy first. That halo imitates the light of our ever-burning flame, which in turn signifies the light of Ahura Mazda forever shining on His messengers and holy ones."

That sounded likely enough that I could not dispute it, but neither would I concede it, of course. He went on:

"That is why we Zardushi have for centuries been persecuted and derided and dispersed and driven into exile. By Muslims and Jews and Christians alike. A people who pride themselves on possessing the only true religion must pretend that it came to them through some exclusive revelation. They do not like to be reminded that it merely derives from some other people's original."

I went back to the karwansarai that day, thinking: the Church is perhaps wise to demand faith and forbid reason in Christians. The more questions I ask, and the more answers I get, the less I seem to know of anything for certain. As I walked along, I scooped up a handful of snow from a snowbank I was passing, and I wadded it to a snowball. It was round and solid, like a certainty. But if I looked at it closely enough, its roundness really was a dense multitude of points and corners. If I held it long enough, its solidity would melt to water. That is the hazard in curiosity, I thought: all the certainties fragment and dissolve. A man curious enough and persistent enough might find even the round and solid ball of earth to be not so. He might be less proud of his faculty of reasoning when it left him with nothing whereon to stand. But then again, was not the truth a more solid foundation than illusion?

I forget whether it was on that day or another that I got back to the karwansarai to find that my father and Nostril had returned from their journey. The Hakim Khosro was there, too, and they were gathered about the sickbed of Uncle Mafio, all talking at once.

". . . Not in the city called Kabul. The Sultan Kutb-ud-Din now has a capital far to the southeast of there, a city called Delhi. . . ."

"No wonder you were gone so long," said my uncle.

". . . Had to cross the vasty mountains, through a pass called the Khaibar . . ."

". . . Then clear across the land called Panjab . . ."

"Or properly Panch Ab," the hakim put in, "meaning Five Rivers."

". . . But worth the effort. The Sultan, like the Shah of Persia, was eager to send gifts of tribute and fealty to the Khakhan. . . ."

". . . So we now have an extra horse, laden with objects of gold and Kashmir cloth and rubies and . . ."

"But more important," said my father, "how fares our patient Mafio?"

"Empty," growled my uncle, scratching his elbow. "From one end I have coughed out all my sputum, from the other I have spewed out every last turd and fart, and in between I have sweated out every last bead of perspiration. I am also infernally tired of being stuck all over wih paper charms and powdered all over like a bignè bun."

"Otherwise, his condition is unchanged," the Hakim Khosro said soberly. "My efforts to assist nature in a cure have not availed much. I am happy you are all together again, for I now wish you all to go from this place, and take the patient even closer to nature. Up, into the high mountains to the east, where the air is more clear and pure."

"But cold," my father objected. "As cold as charity. Can that be good for him?"

"Cold air is the cleanest air," said the hakim. "I have determined that, by close observation and professional study. Witness: people who live in always cold climates, like the Russniaks, are a clean white of skin color; in hot climates, like the Indian Hindus, dirty brown or black. We Pakhtuni, living midway, are a sort of tan color. I urge you to take the patient, and take him soon, to those cold, clean, white mountain heights."

When the hakim and we helped Uncle Mafìo get up and get out of the goatskin wrappings and get dressed for the first time in weeks, we were dismayed to see how thin he had become. He looked even taller in his suddenly oversized clothes than he had seemed before, when his burliness had strained his clothes at the seams. He was also pale instead of ruddy, and his limbs were tremulous from disuse, but he proclaimed himself tremendously glad to be up and about. And later, in the hall of the karwansarai, when we dined that night, he bellowed to the other diners, in a voice as stentorian as ever, asking for the latest word on the mountain trails to the eastward.

Men from several other karwan trains responded, and told us of current conditions, and gave us much advice relevant to mountain travel. Or we hoped the advice was relevant, but we could not be sure, since no two of our informants seemed to agree on even the name of those mountains east of here.

One man said, "Those are the Himalaya, the Abode of the Snows. Before you go up into them, buy a phial of poppy juice to carry. In case of snowblindness, a few drops in the eyes will relieve the pain."

And another man said, "Those are the Karakoram, the Black Mountains, the Cold Mountains. And the snow-fed waters up there are cold at all seasons of the year. Do not let your horses drink, except from a pail in which you have warmed the water a little, or they will be convulsed by cramps."

And another said, "Those are the mountains called Hindu Kush, the Hindu Killers. In that hard terrain, a horse sometimes gets rebellious and unmanageable. Should that occur, simply tie the hair of the horse's tail to its tongue, and it will quieten on the instant."

And another said, "Those mountains are the Pai-Mir, meaning the Way to the Peaks. The only forage your horses will find yonder is the slate-colored, strong-smelling little shrub called burtsa. But your horses *will* always find it for you, and it is also good fuel for a fire, being naturally full of oil. Oddly enough, the greener it looks, the better the burtsa burns."

And another said, "Those mountains are the Khwaja, the Masters. And up there the Masters make it impossible for you to lose your direction, even in the thickest storm. Just remember that every mountain is barren on its south face. If you see any trees or shrubs or growth at all, it is on the mountain's north face."

And another said, "Those mountains are the Muztagh, the Keepers. Try to get completely through and out of them before spring becomes summer, for then begins the Bad-i-sad-o-bist, the terrible Wind of One Hundred and Twenty Days."

And yet another man said, "Those mountains are Solomon's Throne, the Takht-i-Sulaiman. If you should encounter a whirlwind up there, you may be sure it issues from some cavern nearby, the den of one of the demons banished into that exile by the good King Solomon. Simply find that cavern and stop it with boulders, and the wind will die."

So we packed and we paid for our keep and we said some goodbyes to those with whom we had got acquainted and again we moved on, my father and uncle and Nostril and I, riding our four mounts and leading a packhorse and two extra packhorses loaded with a princely amount of valuables. We went straight east from Balkh, through villages named Kholm and Qonduz and Taloqan, which seemed to exist only as market-places for the horse breeders who inhabit that grassy region. Everybody thereabout raises horses and is continually trading breed stallions and brood mares with his neighbors at the markets. The horses are fine ones, comparable to Arabians, though not so dainty in the shape of the head. Every breeder claims that his stock are descended from Alexander's steed Bucephalas. Every breeder makes that claim for his stock only, which is ridiculous, with all the trading that goes on. Anyway, I never saw any horses there that had the peacock tail worn by Bucephalas in the il luminations to *The Book of Alexander* that I had pored over in my youth.

At this season, the grazing lands were covered by snow, so we could not see how the verdure thinned out as we went eastward. But we knew it did so, because the ground under the snow got pebbly, then rocky, and the villages ceased to be, and there was only an infrequent and inade-quate karwansarai along the trail. After we had passed the last village, a cluster of piled-stone huts which called itself Keshem, in the foothills preceding the mountains, we had to make our own stopping places per haps three nights out of four. That was not an idyllic way to live, sleep-ing under tents and under our chapons in snow and chill and wind, and generally having to dine on dried or salted travel rations.

We had worried that the outdoor life would be especially hard on Uncle Mafio. But he made no complaint even when we healthier ones did. He maintained that he *was* feeling better in that sharp, cold air, as the Hakim Khosro had predicted, and his cough had lessened and did not lately bring up any blood. He allowed the rest of us to take over what heavy work had to be done, but he would not let us shorten the marches on his account, and each day he sat his saddle or, on the rougher stretches, walked beside his horse, as indefatigably as any of us. We were not hurrying, anyway, for we knew we would have to halt for the rest of the winter as soon as we came up against the mountain ramparts. Also, after a while on that hard trail, living on hard rations, the rest of us were nearly as gaunt as Uncle Mafio was, and not eager to exert ourselves. Only Nostril kept his paunch, but it looked now less integral to him, like a separate melon he was carrying under his clothes.

When we came to the Ab-e-Panj River, we followed its broad valley upstream to the eastward, and from then on we were going uphill, ever higher above the level of the rest of the world. To speak of a valley ordinarily brings to mind a depression in the earth, but that one is many farsakhs wide and is lower only in relation to the mountains that rise far off on either side of it. If it were anywhere else in the world, that valley would not be *on* the world, but immeasurably far above it, high among the clouds, unseeable by mortal eyes, unattainable, like Heaven. Not that the valley resembles Heaven in any way, I hasten to say, it being cold and hard and inhospitable, not balmy and soft and welcoming.

The landscape was unvarying: the wide valley of tumbled rocks and scrub growth, all humped under quilts of snow; the white-water river running through; and far away on both sides the tooth-white, tooth-sharp mountains. Nothing ever changed there but the light, which ranged from sunrises colored like gilded peaches to sunsets colored like roses on fire, and, in between, skies so blue they were near to purple, except when the valley was roofed by clouds of wet gray wool wringing out snow or sleet.

The ground was nowhere level, being all a clutter of boulders and rocks and talus that we had to thread our way around or gingerly make our way across. But, apart from those ups and downs, our continuous climb was imperceptible to our sight, and we might almost have supposed that we were still on the plains. For, each night when we stopped to camp, the mountains on either horizon seemed identically high to those of the night before. But that was only because the mountains were getting higher, the farther we climbed that up-sloping valley. It was like going up a staircase where the banister always keeps pace with you and, if you do not look over, you do not realize that everything beyond is dropping down and away from you.

Nevertheless, we had various means of knowing that we were climbing all the time. One was the behavior of our horses. We two-legged creatures, when we occasionally dismounted to walk for a while, might not have been physically aware that each step forward was also a trifle higher, but the animals with legs fore and aft knew well that they always stood or moved at an incline. And, horses having good sense, they slyly exaggerated their trudging walk to make it seem a plodding labor, so that we would not press them to move faster.

Another indicator of the climb was the river running the length of the valley. The Ab-e-Panj, we had been told, is one of the headwater sources of the Oxus, that great river which Alexander crossed and recrossed, and in his *Book* it is described as immensely broad and slow-running and tranquil. However, that is far to the west and downhill of where we were now. The Ab-e-Panj alongside our trail was not wide nor deep, but it raced through that valley like an endless stampede of white horses, tossing white manes and tails. It even sounded sometimes more like a stampede than a river, the noise of its cascading water being often lost in the scrape and grate and rumble of the sizable boulders it rolled and jostled along its bed. A blind man could have told that the Ab-e-Panj was hurtling downhill and, for it to have such momentum, the river's uphill end had to be somewhere far higher yet. In this winter season, certainly, the river could not for a moment have slowed its tumultuous pace, or it would have frozen solid, and there might not have existed any Oxus downstream. This was apparent, because every splash and spatter and lick of the water on the rock banks instantly turned to blue-white ice. Since that made the footing close to the river even more treacherous than the snow-covered ground—and also because every splash of the water that reached us froze on our horses' legs and flanks, or on ours—we kept our trail well to one side of the river wherever we could.

Still another indicator of our continuous climb was the noticeable thinning of the very air. Now, I have been often disbelieved, and even jeered, when I have told of this to non-journeyers. I know as well as they do that air is weightless at all times, impalpable except when it moves as wind. When the disbelievers demanded to know *how* an element without the least weight can have less weight yet, I cannot tell them how, or why; I only know it does. It gets less and less substantial in those upland heights, and there are evidences to show it.

For one, a man has to breathe deeper to fill his lungs. This is not the panting occasioned by fast movement or brisk exercise; a man standing still has to do it. When I exerted myself—loading a horse's packsaddle, say, or clambering over a boulder blocking the trail—I had to breathe so fast and hard and deep that it seemed I never would get enough air into me to sustain me. Some disbelievers have dismissed that as a delusion fostered by tedium and hardship, of which God knows we had enough to contend with, but I maintain that the insubstantial air was a very real thing. I will additionally adduce the fact that Uncle Mafio, though he like all of us had to breathe deep, was not so frequently or painfully afflicted by the need to cough. Clearly, the thin air of the heights lay not so heavily in his lungs and did not so often have to be forcibly expelled.

I have other evidence. Fire and air, both being weightless, are the closest-related of the four elements; everybody will concede that. And in the high lands where the air is feebler, so is fire. It burns more blue and dim than yellow and bright. This was not just a result of our having to burn the local burtsa shrub for fuel; I experimented with burning other and more familiar things, like paper, and the resultant flame was equally debile and languid. Even when we had a well-fueled and well-laid camp fire, it took longer to char a piece of meat or to boil a pot of water than it had done in lower lands. Not only that, the boiling water also took longer than customary to cook something put into it.

In that winter season, there were no great karwan trains on the trail, but we did meet an occasional other traveling party. Most of these were hunters and trappers of furs, moving from place to place in the mountains. The winter was their working season, and in the clement springtime they would take their accumulated stores of hides and pelts down to market in one of the lowland towns. Their shaggy little pack-horses were heaped with the baled pelts of fox, wolf, pard, the urial, which is a wild sheep, and the goral, which is something between a goat and a qazèl. The hunter-trappers told us that this valley which we were climbing was called the Wakhàn—or sometimes the Wakhàn Corridor, because many mountain passes open off it on all sides, like doors off a corridor, and the valley constitutes both the border between and the access to all the lands beyond. To the south, they said, were passes leading out of the Corridor to lands called Chitral and Hunza and Kashmir, in the east leading to a land called To-Bhot, and in the north to the land of Tazhikistan.

"Ah, Tazhikistan is yonder?" said my father, turning to gaze to the north. "Then we are not too far now, Mafìo, from the route we took homeward."

"True," said my uncle, sounding tired and relieved. "We have only to go through Tazhikistan, then a short way east to the city of Kashgar, and we are again in Kubilai's Kithai."

On their packhorses, the hunter-trappers also carried many horns which they had taken from a kind of wild sheep called the artak, and I, having so far seen only the lesser horn-racks of such animals as the qazèl and cows and domestic sheep, was mightily impressed by those horns. At their root end they were as big around as my thigh, and from there they spiraled tightly to points. On the animal's head, the points would be easily a man's length apart; but if the spirals could have been unwound and stretched out straight, *each* of the horns must have measured a man's length. They were such magnificent things that I supposed the hunters took them and sold them for ornaments to be admired. No, they said, laughing; those great horns were to be cut and fashioned into all manner of useful articles: eating bowls and drinking cups and saddle stirrups and even horse shoes. They averred that a horse shod with such horn shoes would never slip on the most slippery road.

(Many months later, and higher in the mountains, when I saw some of those artak sheep alive and at liberty in the wild, I thought them so splendidly beautiful that I deplored the killing of them for merely utile purposes. My father and uncle, to whom utility meant commerce and commerce meant everything, laughed as the hunters had done, and chided my sentimentality, and from that time on referred sarcastically to the artak as "Marco's sheep.")

As we went on up the Wakhàn, the mountains on either side remained as awesomely high as ever, but now, each time the snowfall let up enough for us to raise our eyes to the mountains' immensity, they stood perceptibly closer to us. And the banks of ice on either side of the Ab-e-Panj River built up thicker and bluer, and constricted the racing water to an ever narrower stream between them, as if vividly to illustrate how the winter was closing its grip on the land.

The mountains kept shouldering in on us day by day, and finally others reared up in front of us as well, until we had those Titans standing close all around us except at our backs. We had come to the head end of that high valley, and the snowfall ceased briefly and the clouds cleared, for us to see the white mountain peaks and the cold blue sky magnificently reflected in a tremendous frozen lake, the Chaqmaqtin. From under the ice at its western end spilled the Ab-e-Panj we had been following, so we took the lake to be the river's source, hence also the ultimate headwater of the fabled Oxus. My father and uncle marked it so, according to their practice, on the Kitab's otherwise imprecise map of that region. I was not any help in locating our position, as the horizon was much too high and jagged for me to make use of the kamàl. But, when the night sky was clear, I could at least tell, from the height of the North Star, that we were now a far way north of where we had begun our overland march at Suvediye on the Levant shore.

At the northeastern end of Lake Chaqmaqtin stood a community that called itself a town, Buzai Gumbad, but it really comprised only a single extensive karwansarai of many buildings, and roundabout it a tent city and the corrals of karwan trains encamped for the winter. It was evident that, come better weather, almost the entire population of Buzai Gumbad would get up and vacate the Wakhàn Corridor by way of its various passes. The landlord of the karwansarai was a jolly and expansive man named Iqbal, which means Good Fortune, and the name was apt for one who prospered richly by owning the only karwan stopping place on that stretch of the Silk Road. He was a native Wakhani, he said, born right there in the inn. But, as the son and grandson and great-grandson of previous generations of Buzai Gumbad's innkeepers, he of course spoke Trade Farsi, and had, if not experience, good hearsay knowledge of the world beyond the mountains.

Spreading his arms wide, Iqbal welcomed us most cordially to "the high Pai-Mir, the Way to the Peaks, the Roof of the World," and then confided that his extravagant words were no exaggeration. Here, he said, we were exactly one farsakh straight up—that is, two and a half miles—above the level of the earth's seas and such sea-level cities as Venice and Acre and Basra. Landlord Iqbal did not explain how he could know so *exactly* the local altitude. But, assuming he spoke true—and because the mountain peaks around us visibly stood as high again—I would not dispute his claim that we had come to the Roof of the World.

THE ROOF OF
THE WORLD

. 1 .

W E engaged a room for ourselves, including Nostril as one of us, in the main building of the inn, and corral space for our horses outside, and prepared to stay in Buzai Gumbad until the winter broke. The karwansarai was no very elegant place, and, because all its appurtenances and most of its supplies had to be imported from beyond the mountains, Iqbal charged his guests high for their keep. But the place was actually more comfortable than it had to be, considering the circumstance that it was all there was, and that neither Iqbal nor his forebears need ever have bothered to provide any more than the most rudimentary shelter and provender.

The main building was of two stories—the first karwansarai I had seen built so—the bottom half being a commodious stable for Iqbal's own cattle and sheep, which constituted both his life savings and his inn's larder. The upstairs was for people, and was encircled by an open portico which had, outside each sleeping chamber, a privy hole cut in its floor, so that the guests' droppings fell into the inn yard for the benefit of a flock of scrawny chickens. The lodgings being upstairs over the stable meant that we enjoyed the warmth wafting upward from the animals, but we did not much enjoy the smell of them. Still, that was not so bad as the smell of us and the other long-unwashed guests and our unwashed garments. The landlord would not squander precious dried-dung fuel on anything like a hammam or hot water for washing clothes.

He preferred, and so did we guests, to use the fuel to keep our beds warm at night. All of Iqbal's beds were of the style called in the East the kang, a hollow platform of piled-up stones covered with boards supporting a heap of camel-hair blankets. Before retiring, one lifted the planks, spread some dry dung inside the kang and placed on that a few burning coals. The newcome traveler usually did it inexpertly at first, and either froze all night or set the planks afire under him. But with practice one learned to lay the fire so that it smoldered all night at an even warmth, and did not make quite enough smoke to suffocate everybody in the room. Each guest chamber also had a lamp, handmade by Iqbal himself, and the like of which I never saw elsewhere. To make one, he would take a camel's bladder, blow it up to a sphere, then paint it with lacquer to make it hold that shape and to give it a bright design of many colors. With a hole cut out of it so it could be positioned over a candle or an oil lamp, that big globe gave a varicolored and most radiant glow.

The inn's everyday meals were the usual Muslim monotony: mutton and rice, rice and mutton, boiled beans, big rounds of a thin-rolled, chewy bread called nan, and, for drink, a green-colored cha that always had an inexplicable slight taste of fish. But good host Iqbal did his best to vary the monotony whenever he had an excuse: on every Muslim Sabbath Friday and on the various Muslim feste days which occurred during that winter. I do not know what the days celebrated—they had names like Zu-l-Heggeh and Yom Ashura—but on such occasions we were served beef instead of mutton, and a rice called pilaf, colored red or yellow or blue. There were also sometimes fried meat tarts called samosa, and a sort of sharbat confection of snow flavored with pistachio or sandalwood, and once—once only, but I think I still can taste it—for a sweet, we were served a pudding made of crushed ginger and garlic.

There was nothing to prevent our eating the various foods of other nationalities and religions, and we frequently did. In the lesser outbuildings of the karwansarai, and in tents all around it, were camped the people of many karwan trains, and they were people of many different countries and customs and languages. There were Persian and Arab merchants and Pakhtuni horse traders who had come, like us, from the west, and big blond Russniaks from the far north, and shaggy, burly Tazhiks from the nearer north, and flat-faced Bho from the easterly land called the High Place of the Bho, or To-Bhot in their language, and dark-skinned little Hindus and Tamil Cholas from southern India, and gray-eyed, sandy-haired people called Hunzukut and Kalash from the nearer south, and some Jews of indeterminate origin, and numerous others. This was the commingled population which made of Buzai Gumbad a town-sized community—in the wintertime, anyway—and they all exerted themselves to make it a well-run and livable town. Indeed, it was a much more neighborly and friendly community than many settled and permanent ones I have been in.

At any mealtime, anybody could sit down at any family's cook fire and be made welcome—even if he and they could not speak a mutually comprehensible language—the understanding being that his next cook fire would be equally hospitable to any comer. By the end of that winter, I think we Polos had sampled every kind of food that was served in Buzai Gumbad, and, since we did there no cooking of our own, had treated as many strangers to meals in Iqbal's dining hall. Besides offering a variety of eating experiences—some memorable for their deliciousness, a few memorable for their awfulness—the community provided other diversions. Almost every day was a festa day for some group of people, and they were pleased to have everybody else in the encampment come and watch or join in their music making and singing and dancing and games of sport. All the doings in Buzai Gumbad were not festive, of course, but the diversity of people managed to unite in more solemn matters, too. Because they observed among them so many different codes of law, they had elected one man of every color, tongue and religion gathered there, to sit together as a court for hearing complaints of pilferage and trespass and other disturbances of the peace.

I have mentioned the law court and the festivities in the same breath, as it were, because they figured together in one incident I found amusing. The handsome people called the Kalash were a quarrelsome sort, but only among themselves, and not ferociously so; their quarrels usually ended in laughter all around. They were also a merry and musical and graceful sort; they had any number of different Kalash dances, with names like the kikli and the dhamal, and they danced them almost every day. But one of their dances, called the luddi, remains unique in my experience of dances.

I saw it performed first by a Kalash man who had been hailed before the motley court of Buzai Gumbad, accused of having stolen a set of camel bells from a Kalash neighbor. When the court acquitted him, for lack of evidence, the entire contingent of Kalash folk—including his accuser—set up a squalling and clattering music of flutes and chimta tongs and hand drums, and the man began to dance the flailing, flinging luddi dance, and eventually his whole family joined him in it. I saw the luddi performed next by the other Kalash man, the one who had lost the camel bells. When the court was unable to produce either the bells or a punishable culprit, it ordered that a collection be taken up from every head of household in the encampment to recompense the victim. This meant only a few coppers from every contributor, but the total was probably more than the purloined bells had been worth. And when the man was handed the money, the entire contingent of Kalash folk—including the accused but acquitted thief—again set up a screechy, rackety music of flutes and tongs and hand drums, and *that* man began to dance the flailing, flinging luddi dance, and eventually *his* whole family joined him in it. The luddi, I learned, is a Kalash dance which the happily quarrelsome Kalash dance only and specifically to celebrate a victory in litigation. I wish I could introduce to litigious Venice something of the sort.

I thought the composite court had judged wisely in that case, as I thought they did in most cases, considering what a touchy job they had.

Of all the peoples gathered in Buzai Gumbad, probably no two were accustomed to abiding by (or disobeying) the same set of laws. Drunken rape seemed to be a commonplace among the Nestorian Russniaks, as Sodomite sex was among the Muslim Arabs, while both those practices were regarded with horror by the pagan and irreligious Kalash. Petty thievery was a way of life for the Hindus, and that was tolerantly condoned by the Bho, who regarded anything not tied down as ownerless, but theft was condemned as criminal by the dirty but honest Tazhiks. So the members of the court had to tread a narrow course, trying to dispense acceptable justice while not insulting any group's accepted customs. And not every case brought to trial was as trivial as the affair of the stolen camel bells.

One that had come to court before we Polos arrived was still being recounted and discussed and argued over. An elderly Arab merchant had charged the youngest and comeliest of his four wives with having abandoned him and eloped to the tent of a young and good-looking Russniak. The outraged husband did not want her back; he wanted her and her lover condemned to death. The Russniak contended that under the law of his homeland a woman was as fair game as any forest animal, and belonged to the taker. Besides, he said, he truly loved her. The errant wife, a woman of the Kirghiz people, pleaded that she had found her lawful husband repugnant, in that he never entered her except in the foul Arab manner, by the rear entrance, and she felt entitled to a change of partners, if only to get a change of position. But besides that, she said, she truly loved the Russniak. I asked our landlord Iqbal how the trial had come out. (Iqbal, being one of the few permanent inhabitants of Buzai Gumbad, hence a leading citizen, was naturally elected to every winter's new court.)

He shrugged and said, "Marriage is marriage in any land, and a man's wife is his property. We had to find for the cuckolded husband in that aspect of the case. He was given permission to put his faithless wife to death. But we denied him any part in deciding the fate of her lover."

"What was his punishment?"

"He was only made to stop loving her."

"But she was dead. What use—?"

"We decreed that his love for her must die, too."

"I—I do not quite understand. How could that be done?"

"The woman's dead body was laid naked on a hillside. The convicted adulterer was chained and staked just out of reach of her. They were left that way."

"For him to starve to death beside her?"

"Oh, no. He was fed and watered and kept quite comfortable until he was released. He is free now, and he still lives, but he no longer loves her."

I shook my head. "Forgive me, Mirza Iqbal, but I really do not understand."

"A dead body, lying unburied, does not just lie there. It changes, day by day. On the first day, only some discoloration, wherever there was last a pressure on the skin. In the woman's case, some mottling about the throat, where her husband's fingers had strangled her. The lover had to sit and see those blotches appearing on her flesh. Perhaps they were not too gruesome to look at. But a day or so later, a cadaver's abdomen begins to swell. In another little while, a dead body begins to belch and otherwise expel its inner pressures in manners most unmannerly. Later, there come flies—"

"Thank you. I begin to understand."

"Yes, and he had to watch it all. In the cold here, the process is slowed somewhat, but the decay is inexorable. And as the corpse putrefies, the vultures and the kites descend, and the shaqàl dogs come boldly closer, and—"

"Yes, yes."

"In ten days or thereabouts, when the remains were deliquescing, the young man had lost all love for her. We believe so, anyway. He was quite insane by then. He went away with the Russniak train, but being led on a rope behind their wagons. He still lives, yes, but if Allah is merciful, perhaps he will not live long."

The karwan trains wintering there on the Roof of the World were laden with all sorts of goods and, while I found many of them worth admiring—silks and spices, jewels and pearls, furs and hides—most of those were no great novelty to me. But some of the trade items I had never even heard of before. A train of Samoyeds, for instance, was bringing down from the far north baled sheets of what they called Muscovy glass. It looked like glass cut into rectangular panes, and each sheet measured about my arm's length square, but its transparency was marred by cracklings and webbings and blemishes. I learned that it was not real glass at all, but a product of another strange kind of rock. Rather like amianthus, which comes apart in fibers, this rock peels apart like the pages of a book, yielding the thin, brittle, blearily transparent sheets. The material was far inferior to real glass, such as that made at Murano, but the art of glassworking is unknown in most of the East, so the Muscovy glass was a fairly adequate substitute and, said the Samoyeds, fetched a good price in the markets.

From the other end of the earth, from the far south, a train of Tamil Cholas was transporting out of India toward Balkh heavy bags of nothing but salt. I laughed at the dark-skinned little men. I had seen no lack of salt in Balkh, and I thought them stupid to be lugging such a common commodity across whole continents. The tiny, timid Cholas begged my indulgence of their obsequious explanation: it was "sea salt," they said. I tasted it—no different from any other salt—and I laughed again. So they explained further: there was some quality inherent to sea salt, they claimed, that is lacking in other sorts. The use of it as a seasoning for foods would prevent people's being beset by goiters, and for that reason they expected the sea salt to sell in these lands for a price worth their trouble of bringing it so far. "Magic salt?" I scoffed, for I had seen many of those ghastly goiters, and I knew they would require more than the eating of a sprinkling of salt to remove. I laughed again at the Cholas' credulity and folly, and they looked properly chastened, and I went on my way.

The riding and pack animals corraled about the lakeside were almost as various as their owners. There were whole herds of horses and asses, of course, and even a few fine mules. But the many camels there were not the same sort that we had formerly seen and used in the lowland deserts. These were not so tall or long-legged, but bulkier of build, and made to look even more ponderous by their long, thick hair. They also wore a mane, like a horse, except that the mane depended from the bottom, not the top, of their long necks. But the chief novelty of them was that they all had two humps instead of one; it made them easier to ride, since they had a natural saddle declivity between the two humps. I was told that these Bactrian camels were best adapted to wintry conditions and mountainous terrain, as the single-humped Arabian camels are to heat and thirst and desert sands.

Another animal new to me was the pack-carrier of the Bho people, called by them an yyag and by most other people a yak. This was a massive creature with the head of a cow and the tail of a horse, at opposite ends of a body resembling a haystack in shape and size and texture. The yak may stand as high as a man's shoulder, but its head is carried low, at about a man's knee level. Its shaggy, coarse hair—black or gray or mixed dark and white in patches—hangs all the way to the ground, obscuring hoofs that look too dainty for its great bulk, but those hoofs are astonishingly precise of step and placement on narrow mountain trails. A yak grunts and grumbles like a pig, and continuously gnashes its millstone teeth as it shambles along.

I learned later that yak meat is as good to eat as the best beef, but no yak-herder in Buzai Gumbad had occasion to slaughter one of the animals while we were there. The Bho did, however, milk the cow yaks of their herds, a procedure which takes some daring, given the immense size and unpredictable irritability of those animals. That milk, of which the Bho had so much that they gave it freely to others, was delicious, and the butter which the Bho made from it would have been a praiseworthy delicacy if only it had not always had long yak hairs embedded in it. The yak gives other useful products: its coarse hair can be woven into tents so sturdy that they will stand against mountain gales, and its much finer tail hairs make excellent fly whisks.

Among the smaller animals at Buzai Gumbad, I saw many of the red-legged partridges I had in other places seen wild, these having their wings clipped so they could not fly. Since the camp children were forever playing hide-and-seek with the bird, I took them to be kept for either pets or pest catchers—every tent and building being infested with insect vermin. But I soon learned that the partridges had another and peculiar utility for the Kalash and Hunzukut women.

They would chop the red legs off those birds, keep the flesh for the pot, and burn the legs to a fine ash, which came out of the fire as a purple powder. That powder they used, as other Eastern women use al-kohl, as a cosmetic for ringing and enhancing their eyes. The Kalash women also painted their faces all over with a cream made from the yellow seeds of flowers called bechu, and I can attest that a woman with a face entirely bright yellow, except for the great, purple-masked eyes, is a sight to see. No doubt the women deemed that it made them sexually attractive, because their other favorite ornamentation was a cap or hood and a cape made of innumerable little shells called kauri, and a kauri shell is easily seen as a perfect human female sex organ in miniature.

Speaking of which, I was pleased to hear that Buzai Gumbad offered a sexual outlet other than drunken rape, Sodomy and hideously punishable adultery. It was Nostril who nosed it out, when we had been in the community only a day or two, and again he sidled up to me as he had done in Balkh, pretending disgust at the discovery:

"A foul Jew this time, Master Marco. He has taken the small karwansarai building farthest from the lake. In front, it pretends to be a grinding shop for the sharpening of knives and swords and tools. But in the rear he keeps a variety of females of varied race and color. As a good Muslim, I should denounce this carrion bird perched on the Roof of the World, but I will not unless you bid me to, after you have cast a Christian eye upon the establishment."

I told him I would, and I did, a few days later, after we were unpacked and well settled in residence. In the shop at the front of the building, a man sat hunched, holding a scythe blade to a grinding wheel that he was turning with a foot treadle. Except that he wore a skullcap, he would have resembled a khers bear, for he was very hairy of face, and those locks and whiskers seemed to merge into the great furry coat he wore. I took note that the coat was of costly karakul, an elegant garment for the mere knife grinder he pretended to be. I waited for a pause in the gritty whir of the spinning stone wheel and the rain of sparks it was spraying all about.

Then I said, as Nostril had instructed, "I have a special tool I wish pointed and greased."

The man raised his head, and I blinked. His hair and eyebrows and beard were like a curly red fungus going gray, and his eyes were like blackberries, and his nose like a shimshir blade.

"One dirham," he said, "or twenty shahis or a hundred kauri shells. Strangers coming for the first time pay in advance."

"I am no stranger," I said warmly. "Do you not know me?"

Less than warmly, he said, "I know no one. That is how I stay in business in a place rife with contradictory laws."

"But I am Marco!"

"Here, you drop your name when you drop your lower garment. If I am questioned by some meddling mufti, I can say truthfully that I know no names except my own, which is Shimon."

"The Tzaddik Shimon?" I asked impudently. "One of the Lamed-vav? Or all thirty-six of them?"

He looked either alarmed or suspicious. "You speak the Ivrit? You are no Jew! What do you know of the Lamed-vav?"

"Only that I seem to keep meeting them." I sighed. "A woman named Esther told me what they are called and what they do."

He said disgustedly, "She could not have told you very accurately, if you can mistake a brothel keeper for a tzaddik."

"She said the tzaddikim do good for men. So does a brothel, in my opinion. Now—are you not going to warn me, as always before?"

"I just did. The karwan muftis can often be meddlesome. Do not go braying your name around here."

"I mean about the bloodthirstiness of beauty."

He snorted. "If at your age, Nameless, you have not yet learned the danger of beauty, I will not attempt to instruct a fool. Now, one dirham or the equivalent, or begone."

I dropped the coin into his callused palm and said, "I should like a woman who is not Muslim. Or at least not tabzir in her parts. Also, if possible, I should like one I can talk to for a change."

"Take the Domm girl," he grunted. "She never stops talking. Through that door, second room on the right." He bent again to the scythe and the wheel, and the rasping noise and the flying sparks again filled the shop.

The brothel consisted, like the one in Balkh, of a number of rooms that would better have been called cubicles, opening off a corridor. The Domm girl's cubicle was sketchily furnished: a dung-fired brazier for warmth and light—and smoke and smell—and, for the business transaction, the sort of bed called a hindora. This is a pallet that does not stand on legs, but is hung from a ceiling beam by four ropes, and adds some movement of its own to the movements that go on in it.

Never having heard the word Domm before, I did not know what sort of girl to expect. The one sitting and swinging idly on the hindora turned out to be something new in my experience, a girl so dark-brown she was almost black. Apart from that, though, she was sufficiently pleasing of face and figure. Her features were finely shaped, not Ethiope gross, and her body was small and slight but well formed. She spoke several languages, among them Farsi, so we were able to converse. Her name, she told me, was Chiv, which in her native Romm tongue meant Blade.

"Romm? The Jew said you were Domm."

"Not the Domm!" she protested fiercely. "I am a Romni! I am a juvel, a young woman, of the *Romm!*"

Since I had no idea what either a Domm or a Romm was, I avoided argument by getting on with what I had come for. And I soon discovered that, whatever else the juvel Chiv might be—and she claimed to be of the Muslim religion—she was anyhow a *complete* juvel, not Muslimly deprived of any of her female parts. And those parts, once I got past the dark-brown entryway, were as prettily pink as those of any other female. Also, I could tell that Chiv was not feigning delight, but truly did enjoy the frolic as much as I did. When, afterward, I lazily inquired how she had come to this brothel occupation, she did not spin me any tale of having been brought low by woe, but said blithely:

"I would be doing zina anyway, what we call surata, because I like to. Getting paid for making surata is an extra bounty, but I like that, too. Would you refuse a wage, if it were offered, for every time you have the pleasure of making water?"

Well, I thought, Chiv might not be a girl of flowery sentiments, but she was honest. I even gave her a dirham that she would not have to share with the Jew. And, on my way out through the grinding shop, I was pleased to be able to make a snide remark to that person:

"You were mistaken, old Shimon. As I have found you to be on other occasions. The girl is of the Romm."

"Romm, Domm, those wretched people call themselves anything they take a mind to," he said uncaringly. But he went on, more amiably talkative than he had been when I came in. "They were originally the Dhoma, one of the lowest classes of all the Hindu jati of India. The Dhoma are among the untouchables, the loathed and detested. So they are continually seeping out of India to seek better situations elsewhere. God knows how, since they have no trades but dancing and whoring and tinkering and thieving. And dissimulation. When they call themselves Romm, it is to pretend descent from the Western Caesars. When they call themselves Atzigàn, it is to pretend descent from the conqueror Alexander. When they call themselves Egypsies, it is to pretend descent from the ancient Pharaones." He laughed. "They descended only from the swinish Dhoma, but they are descending on all the lands of the earth."

I said, "You Jews have also dispersed widely about the world. Who are you to look down on others for doing the same?"

He gave me a look, but he answered with deliberation, as if I had not spoken spitefully. "True, we Jews adapt to the circumstances in which our dispersal puts us. But one thing the Domm do which we never will. And that is to seek acceptance by cravenly adopting the prevailing local religion." He laughed again. "You see? Any despised people can always discern some more lowly people to look down on and despise."

I sniffed and said, "It follows, then, that the Domm also have someone to look down on."

"Oh, yes. Everyone else in creation. To them, you and I and all others are the Gazhi. Which means only 'the dupes, the victims,' those who are to be cheated and swindled and deceived."

"Surely a pretty girl, like your Chiv yonder, need not deceive—"

He gave an impatient shake of his head. "You walked in here yammering about beauty as a basis for suspicion. Were you carrying any valuables when you came?"

"Do you take me for an ass, to carry anything of worth into a whorehouse? I brought only a few coins and my belt knife. Where *is* my knife?"

Shimon smiled pityingly. I brushed past him, stormed into the back room and found Chiv happily counting a handful of coppers.

"Your knife? I already sold it, was that not quick of me?" she said, as I stood over her, fuming. "I did not expect you to miss it so soon. I sold it to a Tazhik herdsman just now passing at the back door, so it is gone. But do not be angry with me. I will steal a better blade from someone else, and keep it until you come again, and give it to you. This I will do—out of my great esteem for your handsomeness and your generosity and your exceptional prowess at surata."

Being so liberally praised, I of course stopped being angry, and said

I would look forward to visiting her soon again. Nevertheless, in making my second departure from the place, I slunk past Shimon at his wheel, much as I had slunk from another brothel at another time in female raiment.

. 2 .

I think Nostril could have produced for us, if we had required it, a fish in a desert. When my father asked him to seek out a physician to give us an opinion on the seeming improvement of Uncle Mafìo's tisichezza, Nostril had no trouble in finding one, even on the Roof of the World. And the elderly, bald Hakim Mimdad impressed us as being a competent doctor. He was a Persian, and that alone certified him as a civilized man. He was traveling as karwan keeper-of-the-health in a train of Persian qali merchants. In just his general conversation, he gave evidence of having more than just routine knowledge of his profession. I remember his telling us:

"Myself, I prefer to prevent afflictions, rather than have to cure them, even though prevention puts no money in my purse. For example, I instruct all the mothers here in this encampment to boil the milk they give their children. Whether it be yak milk, camel milk, whatever, I urge that it first be boiled, and in a vessel of iron. As is known to all people, the nastier jinn and other sorts of demons are repelled by iron. And I have determined by experiment that the boiling of milk liberates from the vessel its iron juice, and mixes that into the milk, and thereby fends off any jinni that might lurk in readiness to inflict some childhood disease."

"It sounds reasonable," said my father.

"I am a strong advocate of experiment," the old hakim went on. "Medicine's accepted rules and recipes are all very well, but I have often found by experiment new cures which do not accord with the old rules. Sea salt, for one. Not even the greatest of all healers, the sage ibn Sina, seems ever to have noticed that there is some subtle difference between sea salt and that obtained from inland salt flats. From none of the ancient treatises can I divine any reason for there being such a difference. But *something* about sea salt prevents and cures goiters and other such tumorous swellings of the body. Experiment has proven it to me."

I made a private resolve to go and apologize to the little Chola salt merchants I had laughed at.

"Well, come then, Dotòr Balanzòn!" my uncle boomed, mischievously calling him by the name of that Venetian comic personage. "Let us get this over with, so you can tell me which you prescribe for my damned tisichezza—the sea salt or the boiled milk."

So the hakim proceeded to his examination diagnostic, probing here and there at Uncle Mafìo and asking him questions. After some while he said:

"I cannot know how bad was the coughing before. But, as you say, it is not very bad now, and I hear little crepitation inside the chest. Do you have any pain there?"

"Only now and then," said my uncle. "Understandable, I suppose, after all the hard coughing I have done."

"But allow me a guess," said Hakim Mimdad. "You feel it only in one place. Under your left breastbone."

"Why, yes. Yes, that is so."

"Also, your skin is quite warm. Is this fever constant?"

"It comes and goes. It comes, I sweat, it goes away."

"Open your mouth, please." He peered inside it, then lifted the lips away to look at the gums "Now hold out your hands." He looked at them front and back. "Now, if I may pluck just one hair of your head?" He did, and Uncle Mafio did not wince, and the physician scrutinized the hair, bending it in his fingers. Then he asked, "Do you feel a frequent need to make kut?"

My uncle laughed and rolled his eyes bawdily. "I feel many needs, and frequently. How does one make kut?"

The hakim, looking tolerant, as if he were dealing with a child, significantly patted a hand on his own backside.

"Ah, kut is *merda!*" roared my uncle, still laughing. "Yes, I have to make it frequently. Ever since that earlier hakim gave me his damned purgative, I have been afflicted with the cagasangue. It keeps me trotting. But what does all this have to do with a lung ailment?"

"I think you do not have the hasht nafri."

"Not the tisichezza?" my father spoke up, surprised. "But he was coughing blood at one time."

"Not from the lungs," said Hakim Mimdad. "It is his gums exuding blood."

"Well," said Uncle Mafio, "a man can hardly be displeased to hear that his lungs are not failing. But I gather that you suspect some other ailment."

"I will ask you to make water into this little jar. I can tell you more after I have inspected the urine for signs diagnostic."

"Experiments," my uncle muttered.

"Exactly. In the meantime, if the innkeeper Iqbal will bring me some egg yolks, I would have you allow the application of more of the little Quran papers."

"Do they do any good?"

"They do no harm. Much of medicine consists of precisely that: not doing harm."

When the hakim departed, carrying the small jar of urine with his hand capping it to prevent any contamination, I also left the karwan-sarai. I went first to the tents of the Tamil Cholas and said words of apology and wished those men all prosperity—which seemed to make them even more nervous than they always were anyway—and then wended my way to the establishment of the Jew Shimon.

I asked again to have my tool greased, and asked to have Chiv do it again, and I got her, and as she had promised, she did present me with a fine new knife, and to show my gratitude I tried to outdo my former prowess in the performance of surata. Afterward, on my way out, I paused to chide old Shimon yet again:

"You and your nasty mind. You said all those belittling things about the Romm people, but look what a splendid gift the girl just gave me in exchange for my old blade."

He humphed indifferently and said, "Be glad she has not yet given you one between your ribs."

I showed him the knife. "I never saw one like this before. It resembles any ordinary dagger, yes? A single wide blade. But watch. When I have stabbed it into some prey, I squeeze the handle: so. And that wide blade separates into two, and they spring apart, and this third, hidden, inner blade darts out from between them, to pierce the prey even more deeply. Is it not a marvelous contrivance?"

"Yes. I recognize it now. I gave it a good sharpening not long ago. And I suggest, if you keep it, that you keep it handy. It formerly belonged to a very large Hunzuk mountain man who drops in here occasionally. I do not know his name, for everyone calls him simply the Squeeze Knife Man, because of his proficiency with it and his ready employment of it when his temper is. . . . Must you dash off?"

"My uncle is ailing," I said, as I went out the door. "I really should not stay away too long at a time."

I did not know if the Jew was just making a crude jest, but I was not confronted by any large and ill-tempered Hunzik man between Shimon's place and the karwansarai. To avoid any such confrontation, I stayed prudently close to the inn's main building for the next few days, listening, in company with my father or uncle, to the various bits of advice dispensed by the landlord Iqbal.

When we loudly praised the good milk given by the cow yaks, and loudly marveled at the bravery of the Bho who dared to milk those monsters, Iqbal told us, "There is a simple trick to milking a cow yak without hazard. Only give her a calf to lick and nuzzle, and she will stand still and serene while it is being done."

But not all the information we got at that time was welcome. The Hakim Mimdad came again to confer with Uncle Mafìo, and began by suggesting gravely that it be done in private. My father and Nostril and I were present, and we got up to leave the chamber, but my uncle stopped us with a peremptory flap of his hand.

"I do not keep secret any matters that may eventually concern my karwan partners. Whatever you have to tell, you may tell us all."

The hakim shrugged. "Then, if you will drop your pai-jamah . . ."

My uncle did, and the hakim eyed his bare crotch and big zab. "The hairlessness, is that natural or do you shave yourself there?"

"I take it off with a salve called mumum. Why?"

"Without the hair, the discoloration is easy to see," said the hakim, pointing. "Look down at your abdomen. You see that metallic gray tinge to the skin there?"

My uncle looked, and so did all of us. He asked, "Caused by the mumum?"

"No," said Hakim Mimdad. "I noticed the lividity also on the skin of your hands. When next you remove your chamus boots, you will see it on your feet as well. These manifestations tend to confirm what I suspected from my earlier examination and from observation of your urine. Here, I have poured it into a white jar so you may observe for yourself. The smoky color of it."

"So?" said Uncle Mafìo, as he reclothed himself. "Perhaps I had been dining on the colored pilaf that day. I do not remember."

The hakim shook his head, slowly but positively. "I have seen too many other signs, as I said. Your fingernails are opaque. Your hair is brittle and breaks easily. There is only one other confirming sign I have not seen, but you must have it somewhere on your body. A gummatous small sore that refuses to heal."

Uncle Mafìo looked at him as if the hakim had been a sorcerer, and said in awe, "A fly bite, away back in Kashan. A mere fly bite, no more."

"Show me."

My uncle rolled up his left sleeve. Near his elbow was an angry and shiny red spot. The hakim leaned to peer at it, saying, "Tell me if I am wrong. Where the fly first bit, the bite healed and a small scar formed, in the natural manner. But then the sore erupted anew beyond the scar, and then healed again, and then erupted again, always beyond the old scar . . ."

"You are not wrong," my uncle said weakly. "What does it mean?"

"It confirms my conclusion diagnostic—that you are suffering from the kala-azar. The black sickness, the evil sickness. It does indeed proceed from the bite of a fly. But that fly is, of course, the incarnation of an evil jinni. A jinni who cunningly takes the form of a fly so small that it would hardly be suspected of bearing so much harm."

"Oh, not so much that I cannot bear it. Some mottled skin, some coughing, a little fever, a little sore . . ."

"But unhappily it will not for long be not so much. The manifestations will multiply, and worsen. Your brittle hair will break and you will go bald all over. The fever will bring emaciation and asthenia and lassitude, until you have no will to move at all. The pain below your breast bone proceeds from the organ called your spleen. That will hurt even more, and begin to bulge frighteningly outward, as it hardens and loses all function. Meanwhile, the lividity will spread over your skin, and it will darken to black, and it will pouch out into gummata and blebs and furuncles and squamations until your entire body—including your face—resembles one great bunch of black raisins. By then, you will be ardently wishing to die. And die you will, when your splenic functions fail. Without immediate and continuing treatment, you are sure to die."

"But there is a treatment?"

"Yes. This is it." Hakim Mimdad produced a small cloth sack. "This medicament consists principally of a fine-powdered metal, a trituration of the metal called stibium. It is a sure vanquisher of the jinni and a sure cure for the kala-azar. If you start now to take this, in exceedingly minute amounts, and go on taking it as I prescribe, you will soon start to improve. You will regain the weight you have lost. Your strength will return. You will be again in the best of health. But this stibium is the only cure."

"Well? Only one cure is needed, surely. I will gladly settle for the one."

"I regret to tell you that the stibium, while it arrests the kala-azar, is itself physically harmful in another particular." He paused. "Are you sure you would not prefer to continue this consultation in private?"

Uncle Mafìo hesitated, glancing about at us, but squared his shoulders and growled, "Whatever it is, tell it."

"Stibium is a heavy metal. When it is ingested, it settles downward from the stomach into the splanchnic area, working its beneficial effects as it goes, subduing the jinni of the kala-azar. But being heavy, it precipitates into the lower part of the body, which is to say the bag containing the virile stones."

"So my cod dangles heavier. I am strong enough to carry it."

"I assume that you are a man who enjoys, er, exercising it. Now that you are afflicted with the black sickness, there is no time to waste. If you do not yet have a lady friend in this locality, I recommend that you hie yourself to the local brothel maintained by the Jew Shimon."

Uncle Mafìo barked a laugh, which perhaps I or my father could better interpret than the Hakim Mimdad. "I fail to see the connection. Why should I do that?"

"To indulge your virile capability while you can. Were I you, Mirza Mafìo, I should hasten to make all the zina I could. You are doomed either to be horribly disfigured by the kala-azar, and eventually to die of it—or, if you are to be cured and kept alive, you must begin immediately taking the stibium."

"What do you mean, *if*? Of course I want to be cured."

"Think on it. Some would rather die of the black sickness."

"In the name of God, why? Speak plainly, man!"

"Because the stibium, settling in your scrotum, will instantly start exercising its other and deleterious effect—of petrifying your testicles. Very soon, and for the rest of your life, you will be totally impotent."

"Gèsu."

No one else said anything. There was a terrible silence in the room, and it seemed that no one wished to brave the breaking of it. Finally Uncle Mafìo spoke again himself, saying ruefully:

"I called you Dotòr Balanzòn, little realizing how truly I spoke. That you would indeed present me with a mordant jest. Giving me such a comical choice: that I die miserably or I live unmanned."

"That is the choice. And the decision cannot be long postponed."

"I will be a eunuch?"

"In effect, yes."

"No capability?"

"None."

"But . . . perhaps . . . dar mafa'ul be-vasilè al-badàm?"

"Nakher. The badàm, the so-called third testicle, also gets petrified."

"No way at all, then. Capòn mal caponà. But . . . desire?"

"Nakher. Not even that."

"Ah, well!" Uncle Mafìo surprised us all by sounding as jovial as ever. "Why did you not say that at the first? What matter if I cannot function, if I shall not even want to? Why, think of it! No desire—therefore no need, therefore no nuisance, therefore no complicated aftermath. I ought to be the envy of every priest ever tempted by a woman or a choirboy or a sùccubo." I decided that Uncle Mafìo was not really so jovial as he was trying to sound. "And after all, not many of my desires could ever have been realized, anyway. My most recent one dwindled away in a trembling land. So it is fortunate that this jinni of castration assailed only me and not someone of worthier desires." He barked another laugh, with that horrid false joviality. "But listen to me raving and maundering. If I am not careful, I may even become a moral philosopher, the last refuge of eunuchdom. God forfend. A moralist is more to be shunned than a sensualist, no xe vero? By all means, good hakim, I shall choose to live. Let us commence the medication—but not until tomorrow, eh?" He picked up and put on his voluminous chapon overcoat. "As you have also prescribed, while I still have desires, I ought to squander them. While I still have juices, wallow in them, yes? So excuse me, gentlemen. Ciao." And he left us, slamming vigorously out the door.

"The patient puts a brave face on it," murmured the hakim.

"He may honestly mean it," my father said speculatively. "The most dauntless mariner, after having many ships sink under him, may be thankful when he is finally beached on a placid strand."

"I hope not!" blurted Nostril. He added hastily, "Only my own opinion, good masters. But no mariner should be grateful for being dismasted. Especially not one of Master Mafìo's age—which is approximately the same as my own. Excuse me, Hakim Mimdad, but is this grisly kala-azar possibly . . . infectious?"

"Oh, no. Not unless you also should be bitten by the jinni fly."

"Still and all," Nostril said uneasily, "one feels compelled to . . . to make sure. If you masters have no commands for me, I too will ask to be excused."

And off he went, and shortly so did I. Probably the fearful and superstitious slave had not believed the physician's assurance. I did, but even so. . . .

When one attends a dying, as I have said before, one of course comes away grieving for the loss of the dead one, but even more—even if only secretly, even if only unconsciously—rejoicing at being oneself still alive. Having just now attended what might be called a partial dying, or a dying by parts, I rejoiced in still possessing those parts, and, like Nostril, I was anxious to verify that I did still possess them. I went straight to Shimon's establishment.

I did not meet Nostril or my uncle there; most likely the slave had gone in search of some accessible boy of the kuch-i-safari, and possibly so had Uncle Mafìo. I again asked the Jew for the dark-brown girl Chiv, and got her, and had her, so energetically that she gasped Romm words of astonished pleasure—"yilo!" and "friska!" and "alo! alo! alo!"—and I felt sadness and compassion for all the eunuchs and Sodomites and castròni and every other sort of cripple who would never know the delight of making a woman sing that sweet song.

· 3 ·

O N my every subsequent visit to Shimon's place of business—and they were fairly frequent, once or twice a week—I asked for Chiv. I was quite satisfied with her performance of surata, and had almost ceased to notice her skin's qahwah color, and was not at all disposed to try the other colors and races of females the Jew kept in his stable, for they were all inferior to Chiv in face and figure. But surata was not my only diversion during that winter. There was always something happening in Buzai Gumbad that was of novelty and interest to me. Whenever I heard a burst of noise that was either someone stepping on a cat or someone starting to play the native music, I always assumed it was the latter, and went to see what kind of entertainment it promised. I might find just a mirasi or a najhaya malang, but it would as often be something more worth observing.

A mirasi was only a male singer, but of a special sort: he sang nothing but family histories. On request, and on payment, he would squat before his sarangi—which was an instrument rather like a viella, played with a bow, but laid flat on the ground—and he would saw at its strings, and to that wailing accompaniment he would warble the names of all the forebears of the Prophet Muhammad or Alexander the Great or any other historical personage. But not many requested that sort of performance; it seemed that everybody already knew by heart the genealogies of all the accepted notables. A mirasi was oftenest hired by a family to sing *its* history. Sometimes, I suppose, they indulged in the expense just to enjoy hearing their family tree set to music, and perhaps sometimes just to impress all their neighbors within hearing. But usually they engaged a mirasi when a matrimonial match was contemplated with some other family, and so would set forth, at the top of the mirasi's lungs, the estimable heritage of the boy or girl about to be betrothed. The family's head would write down or recite that entire genealogy to the mirasi, who would then arrange all the names into rhyme and rhythm—or so I was told; I never could preceive much other than monotonous noise—the singing and sarangi sawing of which could occupy hours. I assume this took a considerable talent, but after one stint of hearing how "Reza Feruz begat Lotf Ali and Lotf Ali begat Rahim Yadollah" and so on, from Adam to date, I did not exert myself to attend any other such performances.

The doings of a najhaya malang did not pall *quite* so quickly. A malang is the same thing as a darwish, a holy beggar, and even up on top of the Roof of the World there were beggars, both native and

transient. Some of these offered entertainment before demanding
bakhshish. A malang would sit down cross-legged in front of a basket
and tweedle on a simple wood or clay pipe. A najhaya snake would raise
its head from the basket, spread its hood and gracefully sway, seeming to
dance in time to the raucous tweedling. The najhaya is a fearsomely
cross and venomous snake, and every malang maintained that none but
he had such power over the serpent—a power acquired in occult ways.
For instance, the basket was a special sort called a khajur, and could be
woven only by a man; the cheap pipe had to be mystically sanctified; the
music was a melody known only to the initiated. But I soon perceived
that every snake had had its fangs drawn and was harmless. It was also
apparent, since snakes have no ears, that the najhaya was simply swaying back and forth to keep its impotent aim fixed on the wiggling pipe
end. The malang could have played a melodious Venetian furlàna and
got the same effect.

But sometimes I would hear a sudden burst of music and follow it to
its source and find a group of handsome Kalash men chanting in bari-
tone, "Dhama dham mast qalandar . . ." as they put on their red shoes
called utzar, which they donned only when they were about to charge
into the stamping, kicking, pounding dance they called the dhamal. Or I
might hear the rumbling drumbeat and wild piping that accompanied an
even more frenzied, furious, whirling dance called the attan, in which
half the camp, men and women alike, might join.

Once, when I heard music swelling forth in the darkness of night, I
followed it to a Sindi train's encampment of wagons in a circle, and
found the Sindi women doing a dance for women only, and singing as
they danced, "Sammi meri warra, ma'in wa'ir. . . ." I found Nostril also
looking on, smiling and beating time with his fingers on his paunch, for
these were women of his own native land. They were rather too brawny
for my taste, and inclined to mustaches, but their dance was pretty,
being done by the light of the moon. I sat down beside Nostril, where he
sat propped against a wheel of one of the covered wagons, and he
interpreted the song and dance for me. The women were recounting a
tragic love story, he said—the story of a Princess Sammi, who was a girl
much in love with a boy Prince named Dhola, but when they grew up he
went away and forgot her and never came back. A sad story, but I could
sympathize with Prince Dhola, if his little Princess Sammi had grown
meaty and mustached as she matured.

Every woman in the train must have been recruited into the dance,
because, inside the wagon against which Nostril and I leaned, an unattended and restive baby was bellowing loud enough to drown out even
the sonorous Sindi music. I endured it for some time, hoping the child
would eventually doze—or strangle, I did not much care which. When
after a long time it did neither, I grumbled irascibly.

"Allow me to hush it, master," said Nostril, and he got up and
climbed inside the wagon.

The child's wails subsided to gurgles and then to silence. I was
grateful, and bent all my attention on the dance. The infant remained
blessedly quiet, but Nostril stayed in there for some time. When at last

he climbed down to sit beside me again, I thanked him and said in jest, "What did you do? Kill and bury it?"

He replied complacently, "No, master, I had an inspiration of the moment. I delighted the child with a fine new pacifier to suck, and a creamier milk than its mother's."

It took me a little while to realize what he had said. Then I recoiled from him and exclaimed, "Good God! You did not!" He looked not at all ashamed, only mildly surprised at my outburst. "Gèsu! That miserable little thing of yours has been foully diseased, and filthily inserted in animals and backsides and—and now a baby! Of your own people!"

He shrugged. "You wished the infant quieted, Master Marco. Behold, it still sleeps the sleep of contentment. And I do not feel half bad myself."

"Bad! Gèsu Marìa Isèpo, but you are the worst—the most vile and loathsome excuse for a human being that I have ever met!"

He deserved at least to be beaten bloody, and surely he would have got worse than that from the baby's parents. But, since I had in a way incited him, I did not strike the slave. I merely scolded and reviled him and quoted to him the words of Our Lord Jesus—or Nostril's Prophet Isa—that we should always treat tenderly little children, "for of such is the kingdom of God."

"But I *did* it tenderly, master. Now you have peace in which to enjoy the rest of the dancing."

"I will not! Not in your company, creature! I could not meet the eyes of the dancing women, knowing that one of them is the mother of that wretched innocent." So I went away before that performance was concluded.

But happily, most such occasions were not spoiled for me by any such incident. Sometimes, when I heeded the call of music, it led me not to a dance but to a game. There were two kinds of outdoor sport popular at Buzai Gumbad, and neither could have been played in a much smaller area, for both involved a considerable number of men on horseback, riding hard.

One game was played only by the Hunzukut men, because it had been originally invented in their home valley of Hunza, somewhere to the south of these mountains. In that game, the men swung heavy sticks, like mallets, batting at an object they called the pulu, a rounded-off knot of willow wood which rolled on the ground like a ball. Each team comprised six mounted Hunzukut, who tried to strike that pulu with their sticks—meanwhile often and enthusiastically striking their opponents, their horses and their own teammates—in order to drive the pulu past the six opponents' flailing defense until it rolled or flew beyond a winning line at the far end of the field.

I often lost track of a game's progress because I had a hard time telling the members of the two teams apart. They all wore heavy garments of fur and hide, plus the typical Hunzuk hat, which makes a man look as if he is balancing two thick pies atop his head. The hat actually consists of a long tube of coarse cloth rolled from both ends until the two rolls meet, and the whole then plopped onto the head. For a contest of the pulu, the six men on one team would don red pie-hats and the other six put on blue ones. But, after a very short time of play, the colors would be almost indistinguishable.

I also often lost sight of the wooden pulu itself, among the horses' forty-eight pounding hoofs and the thrown-about snow and mud and sweat, and the intermixed clashing mallets and, not infrequently, some unhorsed players being whacked and kicked about as well. But the more experienced game-watchers, meaning almost everybody else in Buzai Gumbad, were keener of eye. Every time they saw the pulu bounce past the winning line at one or the other end of the field, the whole crowd would shout, "Gol! Go-o-o-ol!"—a Hunzuk word signifying that one team had tallied a point toward winning the game—and simultaneously a band of musicians would pound drums and blow flutes in a cacophony of celebration.

A game did not end until one team had nine times put the pulu past the opposing gol line. So that herd of twelve horses might spend a whole day thundering up and down the increasingly sloppy and treacherous field, with the players bellowing and cursing and the spectators roaring encouragement, and the sticks waving and crashing and often splintering, and the churned-up terrain plastering the players and horses and watchers and musicians, and the riders falling from their saddles and trying to scurry to safety and being cheerfully ridden down by their fellows, and, toward the end of the day, when the field was a mere swamp of mud and slime, the horses also slipping and slewing and falling down. It was a splendid kind of sport, and I never missed a chance to watch it.

The other game was similar, in that it was played by many men on horseback. But in that sport it did not matter how many, for there were no teams; each rider played for himself, against all the others. It was called bous-kashia, and I think that is a Tazhik term, but the game was not the specialty of any one people or tribe, and all the men joined in it on one occasion or another. Instead of a pulu, the central object in bous-kashia was the cadaver of a goat from which the head had just been severed.

The newly dead thing was simply tossed onto the ground among the horses' legs, and the many riders all spurred close around it and wrestled and shoved and pummeled one another, each striving to reach down and snatch up the goat from the ground. He who finally succeeded in that, next had to gallop and carry it across a line at the end of the field. But of course he was pursued by all the others, snatching at his trophy and trying to trip or swerve his horse or knock him out of the saddle. And whoever did seize the contested cadaver himself became the prey of all the other riders. So the game really amounted to not much more than a wrestling and grabbing match on horseback and at the gallop. It was furious and exciting, and few players emerged from it in good health, and many a spectator got trodden on by the herd of horses, or got knocked insensible by a flying goat, or a ripped-loose bloody haunch of it.

During those long winter months on the Roof of the World, besides the time I spent watching games and dances, and in the hindora bed with Chiv, and in other diversions, I also spent some less frivolous whiles in conversation with the Hakim Mimdad.

Uncle Mafìo invited no comment on his ailment or the other troubles it had brought upon him. He was taking the powdered stibium as prescribed, and we could see that he was putting on the weight he had lost, and getting stronger day by day, but we restrained any curiosity we might have had as to exactly when the medicine turned him into a eunuch, and he did not volunteer the information. Since I never encountered him in company with a boy or any other sort of partner while we stayed in Buzai Gumbad, I could not say when he may finally have desisted from such partnerships. Anyway, the hakim still called on us at regular intervals, to make a routine examination of Uncle Mafìo's progress and to increase or decrease by minute amounts the stibium he was taking. After the physician's sessions with the patient, he and I would often sit and talk together, for I found him to be a most interesting old fellow.

Like every other mèdego I have ever known, Mimdad regarded his everyday medical practice only as a necessary drudgery by which he had to earn his living, and preferred to concentrate most of his energies and devotions on his private studies. Like every other mèdego, he dreamed of discovering something new and medically miraculous, to astound the world and to enshrine his name forever alongside those of physician deities like Asklepios and Hippocrates and ibn Sina. However, most doctors of my acquaintance—in Venice, anyway—pursue studies sanctioned or at least tolerated by Mother Church, such as the seeking of new ways to expel or expunge the demons of disease. Mimdad's studies and experiments, I learned, were less in the realm of the healing arts than in the realm of Hermes Trismegistus, which arts verge on sorcery.

Because the Hermetic arts were originally and for so long practiced by pagans like Greeks and Arabs and Alexandrians, Christians are naturally forbidden to delve into them. But every Christian has heard of them. I, for one, knew that the Hermetics ancient and modern—the adepts, as they like to be called—have almost always and to a man been seeking to discover one of two arcane secrets: the Elixir of Life or the Universal Touchstone that will change base metals into gold. So I was surprised when the Hakim Mimdad scoffed at both of those aims as "unrealistic prospects."

He admitted that yes, he too was an adept of the age-old and occult art. He called it al-kimia, and claimed that Allah had first taught it to the prophets Musa and Haroun, meaning Moses and Aaron, whence it had been passed down through the years to such other famous experimenters as the great Arab sage Jabir. And Mimdad admitted that yes, like every other adept, he was chasing an elusive quarry, but one less grandiose than immortality or untold wealth. All he hoped to discover—or rediscover, rather—was what he called "the philter of Majnun and Laila." One day when the upland winter had begun to ease its clamp, and the karwan leaders were studying the sky to decide when they would start downhill from the Roof of the World, Mimdad told me the history of that remarkable philter.

"Majnun was a poet and Laila a poetess, and they lived long ago and far away. No one knows where or when. Except for the poems that have survived them, all that is known about Majnun and Laila is this: they had the power of changing their forms at will. They could become younger or older, more handsome or more ugly, and of whichever sex they chose. Or they could change their persons entirely, becoming giant rukh birds or mighty lions or terrible mardkhora. Or, in a lighter mood, they could become gentle deer or beautiful horses or pretty butterflies. . . ."

"A useful talent," I said. "Their poetry then could depict those alien ways of life more accurately than any other poet had done."

"No doubt," said Mimdad. "But they never sought to make capital or renown of their peculiar power. They used it only for sport—and their favorite sport was love. The physical act of making love."

"Dio me varda! They liked making love to horses and such? Why, our slave must have the blood of a poet in his veins!"

"No, no, no. Majnun and Laila made love only to each other. Consider, Marco. What need had they of anyone or anything else?"

"Hm . . . yes," I mused.

"Imagine the variety of experiences available to them. She could become the male and he the female. Or she could be Laila and he could mount her as a lion. Or he could be Majnun and she a delicate qazèl. Or they could both be other people entirely. Or they could both be dewy children, or both men, or both women, or one an adult and the other a child. Or both of them freaks of grotesque configuration."

"Gèsu . . ."

"When they tired of making human love, however various or capricious, they could sample the even more different pleasures that must be known to beasts and serpents and the demon jinn and the fair peri. They could be two birds, doing it in midair, or two butterflies, doing it within the embrace of a fragrant flower."

"What a pleasant thought."

"Or they could even take the form of hermaphrodite humans, and both Majnun and Laila could be simultaneously al-fa'il and al-mafa'ul to each other. The possibilities would have been infinite, and they must have tried every one, for that was their lifelong occupation—except when they were momentarily sated, and paused to write a poem or two."

"And you hope to emulate them."

"I? Oh, no, I am old, and long past all venereal yearning. Also, an adept must not do al-kimia for his own advantage. I hope to make the philter and its power accessible to all men and women."

"How do you know it was a philter they employed? Suppose it was a spell or a poem they recited before each change."

"In that case, I am confounded. I cannot write a poem, or even recite one with any eloquence. Please do not make discouraging suggestions, Marco. A philter I *can* concoct, with liquids and powders and incantations."

It sounded to me a slim hope, seeking the power in a philter because a philter was all he could make. But I asked, "Well? Have you had any success?"

"Some, yes. Back home in Mosul. One of my wives died after trying one of my preparations, but she died with a blissful smile on her lips. A variant of that preparation gave another of my wives an eminently vivid dream. In her sleep she began fondling and pawing and even clawing at her private parts, and that was a good many years ago, and she has not left off yet, for she has never awakened from that dream. She lives now in a cloth-walled room at Mosul's House of Delusion, and every time I travel there to inquire of her condition, my hakim colleague there tells me she is still interminably performing her interminable self-arousal. I wish I could know what she is dreaming."

"Gèsu. You call that *success*?"

"Any experiment is a success when one learns something from it. So I have since deleted the heavy metallic salts from my recipe, having concluded that those are what cause the deep coma or death. Now I lean to the postulates of Anaxagoras, and employ only organic and homoeomeric ingredients. Yohimbinum, cantharis, the phalloid mushroom, things like that. Oysters pulv., Nux v., Onosm., Pip. nig., Squilla . . . There is no longer any danger of the subjects' not awakening."

"I rejoice to hear it. And now?"

"Well, there was a childless couple, who had given up all hope of a family. They now have four or five fine boys, and I think they never counted the number of girl progeny."

"That does sound like success of a sort."

"Of a sort, yes. But all the children are human. And normal. They must have been conceived in the ordinary way."

"I see what you mean."

"And those were my last volunteers to try the philter. I think the hakim of that House of Delusion has perhaps been spreading gossip around Mosul, in violation of the physicians' oath. So my chief difficulty is not in making new variants of the philter, it is the finding of test subjects. I am too old for the purpose, and my two remaining wives would refuse, anyway, to join me in the experiments. As you must appreciate, it is best to try the philter on a man and a woman at the same time. Preferably a young and vital man and woman."

"Yes, clearly. A Majnun and a Laila, so to speak."

There was a long silence.

Then he said quietly, shyly, tentatively, hopefully, "Marco, do you perchance have access to a complaisant Laila?"

The beauty of danger.

· 4 ·

T H E danger of beauty.

"I suggest you leave your knife out here," said Shimon, as I came through his shop. "That Domm female is in a vile humor today. But perhaps you would like one of the others this time? Now that the camp is starting to break up, I suppose your party too will soon be gone. Now at the last, perhaps you would like a change? A girl other than the Domm?"

No, I wanted Chiv for the playing of Laila to my Majnun. However, considering the unpredictable nature of that play, I did take the Jew's advice and left my squeeze knife on his counter. I also left there a small stack of dirhams, to pay for however long I might stay, and avert his interrupting us to say my time was up. Then I went on into Chiv's room, saying as I entered:

"I have something for you, my girl."

"I have something for you, too," she said. She was sitting naked on the hindora, and she was making the bed sway slightly on its ropes as she rubbed oil onto her round dark-brown breasts and her flat dark-brown belly to make them shine. "Or I will have something, before too long."

"Another knife?" I asked idly, starting to undress.

"No. Have you lost the other already? It appears that you have. No, this will be something you cannot disown so easily. I am going to have a baby."

I stopped moving, standing stockstill and probably looking silly, for I was half out of my pai-jamah and standing like a stork on one leg. "What do you mean, I cannot disown? Why tell me?"

"Whom else should I tell?"

"Why not that Hunzuk mountain man? To mention just one other."

"I would, if it were another's doing. It is not."

I had weathered the first astonishment by now and was again in command of my faculties. I resumed my undressing, but not so eagerly as before, and I said reasonably, "I have been coming here for only three months or so. How could you possibly know?"

"I know. I am a Romni juvel. We of the Romm have ways of knowing such things."

"Then you also ought to know how to prevent such things."

"I do. I usually insert beforehand a plug made of sea salt moistened with walnut oil. If I neglected the precaution, it was because I was overwhelmed by your vyadhi, your impetuous desire."

"Do not blame me, or flatter me, whichever you think will win me over. I do not want any dark-brown offspring."

"Oh?" was all she said to that, but she narrowed her eyes as she regarded me.

"Anyway, I refuse to believe you, Chiv. I see absolutely no change in your body. It is still very nice and trim."

"It is, yes, and my occupation depends on my keeping it that way. Not deformed by pregnancy and useless for surata. So why do you not believe me?"

"I think you are only pretending. To keep me by you. Or to make me take you along when I leave Buzai Gumbad."

Quietly, "You are so desirable."

"I am at least not a simpleton. I am surprised that you would think me gullible by such an old and common woman's trick."

Quietly, "Common woman, is it?"

"Anyway, if you are with child, surely an experienced—surely a clever Romni juvel knows how to get rid of it."

"Oh, yes. There are various ways. I only thought you ought to have some say in the matter of disowning it."

"Then what are we quarreling about? We are in complete accord. Now, in the meantime, I have something for you. For both of us."

As I dropped the last of my garments, I tossed onto the hindora a paper-wrapped packet and a small clay phial.

She opened the paper and said, "This is only common bhang. What is in the little bottle?"

"Chiv, have you ever heard of Majnun the poet and Laila the poetess?"

I sat down beside her and related to her what the Hakim Mimdad had told me about the long-ago lovers and their facility at being so many other kinds of lovers. I did not, however, repeat what the hakim had said when I volunteered myself and Chiv as test subjects for his latest version of the philter. He had looked dubious and he had muttered, "A girl of the Romm? Those people claim to know sorceries of their own. It could conflict with al-kimia." I concluded my account with the instructions he had given me. "We share the drink from the phial. Then, while we wait for it to take effect, we set the hashish burning. The bhang, as you call it. We inhale the smoke and that exhilarates us and suspends our wills, and makes us more receptive to the powers of the philter."

She smiled, as if quietly amused. "You would try a Gazho magic on a Romni? There is a saying, Marco. About a fool's taking the trouble to lay sticks on the devil's fire."

"This is not some foolish magic. This is al-kimia, carefully concocted by a sage and studious physician."

The smile stayed on her face, but it lost its amusement. "You said you saw no change in my body, but now you would change both our bodies. You scolded me for what you called pretending, but now you would have us both pretend."

"This is not a pretense, this is an *experiment*. Look, I do not expect a mere—I do not expect you to comprehend Hermetic philosophy. Just take my word that this is something much loftier and finer than any barbaric superstition."

She unstopped the phial and sniffed at it. "This smells sick-making."

"The hakim said that the hashish fumes will quell any nausea. And he told me all the ingredients of the philter. Fern seed, dodder leaves, the chob-i-kot root, powdered antler, goat wine—other innocuous things, none of them noxious. I certainly would not swallow the stuff myself, or ask you to, if it were otherwise."

"Very well," she said, her smile becoming a rather wicked grin, and she tilted the phial and took a sip. "I will spread the bhang on the brazier."

She had left most of the philter for me—"Your body is larger than mine, perhaps harder to change"—and I drank it down. The little room quickly filled with the thick, blue, cloyingly sweet smoke of the hashish, as Chiv stirred it into the brazier coals, meanwhile muttering to herself in what I took to be her native tongue. I lay back at full length on the hindora, and closed my eyes, the better to be surprised when I opened them to see what I had changed into.

Maybe I fell into a hashish-drugged sleep, but I do not think so. The last time I had done that, the dream occurrences had been mixed and swimmy and confused. This time, all the consequent events seemed very real and sharp-edged and *happening*.

I lay with my eyes closed, feeling all over my naked body the heat from the stirred brazier, and I vigorously inhaled its sweet smoke, and I waited to feel some difference in myself. I do not know what I expected: perhaps the unfolding at my shoulder blades of bird wings or butterfly wings or peri wings; or perhaps the unfurling of my virile member, which was already erect in anticipation, to the massive size of a bull's. But all I felt was a gradual and unpleasant increase of the room's thick heat, and then a definite need to void my bladder. It was like that common morning phenomenon, when you wake with your member in candelòto stiffness, but only gorged by vulgar urine, which makes it an embarrassment for employment in either of its normal functions. You do not then want to utilize it sexually, but you also dislike to disengorge it by urination, because in that erection it always pees upward and you usually make a mess.

This was not at all a promising beginning to my amatory expectations, so I continued to lie still, with my eyes closed, and hoped the sensation would go away. It did not. It increased, and so did the room's heat, until I was annoyed and uncomfortable. Then a pain suddenly went through my groin, as it sometimes does when micturition is too long withheld, but so intensely hurtfully that, not meaning to, I let at least a brief spurt of urine. For another moment, I only lay there feeling ashamed of myself and hoping that Chiv had not noticed. But then I realized that I had felt no sprinkle on my bare belly, as I should have done if my erect organ had peed into the air. Instead, I felt the wetness down the inside of my legs. Unusual. A small puzzlement. I opened my eyes. All around me there was nothing but the blue smoke haze; the walls of the room, the brazier, the girl, all were invisible in it. I cast my glance downward, to see why my candelòto had behaved so oddly, but my view of it was impeded by my breasts.

Breasts! I had the breasts of a woman, and very fine ones they were, too: shapely, upthrusting, ivory-skinned, with nicely large, fawn-colored areole around tumescent nipples, the whole array shining with sweat and a trickle meandering down the cleft between. The philter was working! I was changing! I was embarked upon the most bizarre journey of discovery I had ever undertaken!

I raised my head to see how my candelòto accorded with these new additions. But I still could not see it, for I also had an immense rounded belly, like a mountain to which my breasts were the foothills. I began to sweat in earnest. It should be a novel experience to be a woman for a while—but an obesely *fat* woman? Maybe I was even a deformed woman, for my navel, which had always before been nothing but an insignificant dimple depression, was now a protrusion, perched like a little lighthouse atop my mountain stomach.

Unable to see my member, I groped for it with a hand. All I encountered was the hair on my artichoke, but it was rather more luxuriant and kinky than I was accustomed to feeling. When I reached down past it, I discovered—no great surprise now—that my candelòto was gone, and so was my cod. In their place I had the organs of a woman.

I did not leap up screaming. After all, I had been inviting and expecting a change. To have changed into something like a rukh would probably have been more of a shock and dismay to me. Anyway, I was confident that the change was not going to be permanent. But I was not entirely happy, either. The organs of a woman should have felt familiar enough to my inquiring hand, but they too had a disturbing difference about them. To my fingers, they felt tight and hard and hot, and nastily clammy from my involuntary micturition. They did not, to my touch, resemble the soft and darling and hospitable purse—the mihrab, the kus, the pota, the mona—into which I had so often put fingers and other things.

Besides that, to my *self* they felt . . . how do I put this?

I would have expected, if I were a woman being fingered in my private parts, even if by my own fingers, to feel some pleasurable sensation or an intimate tickle or at least a comfortable old acquaintance. But now I *was* a woman, and I perceived only the prod of fingers, and it made me feel only molested, and my only internal response was a surge of irritability. I slowly slid a finger inside myself, but it did not go far before it was blocked, and then the soft sheathing around it rejected it—I could almost say *spat* it out. There was something up there inside me. Perhaps a precautionary plug of sea salt? But my probing aroused in me more revulsion than curiosity, and I was disinclined to probe again. Even when I deliberately let a finger lightly flick my zambur, my lumaghèta—that tenderest part of my new parts, as sensitive as an eyelash to any touch—I felt nothing but an intensification of my peevishness and a wish to be let alone.

I wondered: does a woman when fondled never experience anything nicer than this? Surely not, I told myself. Then maybe a fat woman never experiences anything? I had yet to fondle a really fat woman, but I doubted that. Anyway, in my new womanly incarnation, *was* I a fat woman? I sat up to see.

Well, I still had that grossly swollen abdomen, and now I could see that it was made even uglier by a discoloration marring the taut ivory skin, a brown line that extended from my protuberant navel down to my artichoke. But the belly seemed to be the only fat thing about me. My legs were slim enough, and hairless, and would have been pretty, except that the veins of them were all raised and visible and squirmy-looking, like a net of worm burrows just under the skin. My hands and arms also looked slim enough, and girlishly soft. But they did not feel soft to me; they felt gnarled and painful. Even as I looked at them and flexed them, both of my hands crooked in a cramp that made me groan.

The groan was loud enough to have brought some response from Chiv, but she did not materialize out of the blue smoke around me, even when I several times called her name. What had the philter made of her? I would have supposed, just on the principle of turnabout, that if I had become female, Chiv would have become male. But the hakim had said that Majnun and Laila sometimes disported themselves as both of the same sex. And sometimes one or both of them had availed themselves of invisibility. Still, the philter's main purpose was to enhance the partners' lovemaking, and in that I judged this trial philter to be a failure. No kind of partner—male, female, invisible—was likely to want to couple with a creature as grotesque as what I had turned into. Nevertheless, what *had* become of Chiv? I called her again and again . . . and then I screamed.

I screamed because another sensation had shaken my body, a sensation more gruesome than mere pain. Something had *moved*, something that was not me, but it had moved *inside me*, inside that monstrous bloat that was my belly. I knew it was not just unsettled food in my stomach, for it happened somewhere below my stomach. And it was not ill-digested food making wind in my lower gut, for I had known that sensation before. That can be unpleasant enough, and sometimes startling, even when it is not noisy or noisome. But this was something different, something I had never experienced before. It felt as if I might have swallowed some small sleeping animal, and it had been digested well down into my bowels, and there it had suddenly awakened and stretched and yawned. My God, I thought, suppose it tries to fight its way out!

Just then it moved again, and I shrieked again, for it seemed about to do exactly that. But it did not. The movement quickly abated, making me ashamed of having shrieked. The animal might only have turned about a bit in its snuggery, as if to judge how inextricaby it was held there. I felt renewed wetness between my legs, and thought I had once more soiled myself in my fright. But when I put a hand down there I felt something awfuller than urine. I brought my hand up into my view, and my fingers were webbed with a viscous substance that clung in strings between hand and groin, moistly stretching and sagging and soggily breaking. The substance was wet but not liquid; it was a gray slime, like nose-blown mucus, and it was streaked with blood. I began to curse the Hakim Mimdad and his unholy philter. Not only had he and it given me an ugly woman's body, and evidently one with defective female parts, there was also something ailing this body and causing a nauseous discharge from those parts.

If my new integument was indeed ill or injured, I thought, I had better not risk standing it up and taking it to look for Chiv. I had better remain lying where I was. So I called for her some more, still without result. I even began calling for Shimon, though I could imagine how the Jew would sneer and snicker, seeing me in a woman's form. He did not come, either, and now I regretted having paid him in advance for a long stay. Whatever noises or cries he might hear from in here, he would probably take for boisterous lovemaking, and not intrude.

For a long time, I lay supine there, and nothing further happened except that the room got more and more hot, and I got sweatier, and my need to urinate became also a need to defecate. It might have been that the imagined small animal inside me was pressing its weight against my bladder and my bowels and squeezing them intolerably. I had to make a determined effort not to let go, but I did resist, not wanting to spew between my legs and all over the bed. Then suddenly, as if a door had been opened to the thawing snows outside, I was blasted by a chill. The film of sweat on my body became icy, I shook in every limb, my teeth chattered, my skin turned all to gooseflesh, my already prominent nipples stood up like sentries. There was nothing for me to cover myself with; if my discarded clothes were still on the floor, they were out of my sight and reach, and I was afraid to get up and look for them. But then the chill was as suddenly gone again, and the room was as muggy as before and my sweat started out afresh and I panted for breath.

Not having much else to meditate on, I tried to take stock of my feelings. They were numerous and various. I felt a measure of excitement: the philter had worked, at least partway. I felt a measure of anticipation: the philter was bound to do something more, and it might be interesting. But most of my emotions were not at all pleasant. I felt discomfort: my hands kept cramping, and my need to evacuate my bowels was becoming extreme. I felt disgust: there was still a seepage of that puslike stuff from my mihrab. I felt indignation: being put in this situation—and I felt self-pity: being left all alone to endure this situation. I felt guilt: by rights, I should be at the karwansarai, helping my companions pack and prepare to take the trail again, not here indulging my demon curiosity. I felt fear: not really knowing what the philter might have yet in store for me—and I felt apprehension: whatever happened next might be no improvement on what already had.

Then, in one paralyzing instant, all other feelings went away, abolished, demolished by the one feeling that takes precedence over everything else, and that is pain. It was a tearing pain that tore through my lower vitals, and I might have thought I heard the sound of it, like the ripping of sturdy cloth, except that I could hear only my agonized cry. I would have clawed at my betrayer belly, but I was so shaken by the pain that I had to clutch the sides of the swaying hindora to keep from pitching out of it.

In any access of agony, one instinctively tries to move, hoping that some movement might alleviate it, and the only movement I could make was to draw up my legs. That abruptness broke my control of my more intimate muscles, and my urine gushed out in a sudden wet warmth, down and about my buttocks. Instead of quickly abating, the pain made a leisurely departure, merging into an alternation of heat and chill. I jolted as each flush of fever gave way to a clamp of cold and that to heat once more. When those pulses finally, gradually subsided, leaving me awash in sweat and urine, I lay weak and flaccid and gasping as if I had been scourged, and now that I could make words I cried aloud, *"What is happening to me?"*

And then I knew. Look: here on this pallet lies a woman, flat on her back, and most of her body is flat, too, only curved and shaped as a woman's body ought to be, except for that horrendous bulge of distended abdomen. She lies with her legs drawn up and apart, exposing a mihrab that is tight and numb with tension. Something is up in there, inside her. It is what makes the belly big, and it is alive, and she has felt it move in there, and she has felt the first pangs of its wanting to get out of there, and where shall it come out except through that mihrab canal between her legs? This is obviously a woman in advanced pregnancy and about to give birth.

All very well, that lofty and cool and detached view. But I was not any viewer looking on; I was *it*. The pitiful, slow-writhing object on the pallet, in the absurd posture and semblance of a frog flipped underside up, was *me*.

Gèsu Marìa Isèpo, I thought—and loosed one hand from gripping the bedside to cross myself—how could the philter have made two beings of me, and put one inside the other? Whatever that was inside me, must I go through the whole process of birthing it? How long does that take? What does one do to help it along? In addition to thinking those things, I was thinking some less repeatable things about the Hakim Mimdad, recommending him to eternity in Hell. That was perhaps unwise of me, for if ever I needed a hakim it was now. The nearest I had ever been to childbirth was the time or two I had seen a pale blue and purple, flayed-looking newborn infant dredged dead from the waters of Venice. I had never been present while even a street cat actually gave birth. The more knowledgeable Venetian boat children had occasionally discussed the subject, but all I could remember was their mention of "labor pains," and in those I now required no instruction. I knew, too, that women often perished of their childbed travail. Suppose I died in this alien body! No one would even know who I was. I would be buried as a nameless, unclaimed, probably unwed wench who had been killed by her own bastard. . . .

But I had more immediate concerns than the disposition of my inglorious remains. The tearing pain came again, and it was as rippingly severe as before, but I gritted my teeth and did not cry out, and even tried to examine the pain. It seemed to start deep in my abdomen, somewhere back toward my spine, and to wrench its way around to my front. Then I had a respite in which to breathe again before the pain made a new onslaught. With each succeeding wave, though the pain did not lessen, I seemed a little better able to stand it. So I tried to take a measure of the pains and the intervals between them. Each seizure lasted while I could count slowly to thirty or forty, but when I tried to time the intervening lulls I counted so high that I became confused and lost count.

There were other afflictions contributing to my confusion. Either the room or myself was still alternating between fever and chill, and I was alternately roasted to limpness or frozen to a clench. My belly, somewhere among its other troubles, found room for nausea; I burped and belched repeatedly, and several times had to fight against vomiting. I was still incontinently urinating each time the pain struck, and only by determined muscular contraction not emptying my bowels as well. The spilled urine might have been a caustic; it made my thighs and my groin and my underneath feel raw and chafed and sore. I had developed a maddening thirst, probably because I had sweated and peed out so much of my internal moisture. My hands continued spasmodically to cramp, and now so did my legs, from the ungainly position I kept them in. The contact of the bed against my back was an irritation. In truth, I was hurting everywhere, even at the mouth; it was locked open in such a distorted rictus that my very lips hurt. I could almost be glad when the labor pains rasped through my gut; they were so terribly much worse that they took my mind off the lesser hurts.

I had resigned myself to the realization that my drinking of the philter was not going to bring me any enjoyment. Now, as the endless hours ground on and on, I tried to resign myself to enduring what the philter had brought instead—thirst and nausea and self-pollution and general misery, varied by intermittent jolting pain—either until its power wore off and I was restored to being myself again, or until it besieged me with some new and different miseries.

Which is what it did. When the pains were squeezing out of me no more spurts of urine, I thought my body had finally been emptied of all its fluids. But suddenly I felt my lower self washed by more wetness than I had yet ejected, a flood of wetness, as if someone had upended a pitcher between my legs. It was warm like urine, but when I raised up to look, I could see that the spreading puddle was colorless. I realized also that the water had not come from my bladder, by way of the little female peeing hole, but out of the mihrab canal. I had to suppose that this mess signaled some new and messier stage in the exceedingly messy process of giving birth.

The abdominal pains were now coming at intervals closer together, barely giving me time to get my breath after each onslaught, and to stiffen my preparedness, before the next was upon me. It made me think to myself: perhaps it is your bracing yourself against each pain, and trying to flinch away from it, that makes them hurt so much. Maybe if you bravely met each pain and bore down against it . . . So I tried that, but "bearing down" in this situation meant exerting the same muscular push as is involved in defecation, and it had the same result. When that particular grinding pain briefly let up again, I discovered that I had extruded onto the bed between my legs a considerable mess of stinking merda. But I was really beyond caring by this time. I merely thought to myself: you already knew that human life ends with merda; now you know that human life also begins in merda.

"Of such is the kingdom of God." I suddenly recollected having preached that to the slave Nostril, not long ago. "Suffer the little children to come unto me," I recited, and laughed ruefully.

I did not laugh for long. Though it is hardly believable, things now got even worse. The pains were coming not in waves or pulses, but in fast succession, and each lasting longer, until they became just one constant agony in my belly, unremitting, rising in intensity until I was unashamedly sobbing and whimpering and moaning, and I feared I could not stand it, and I wished mightily for a merciful faint. If someone had leaned over me then and said, "This is nothing. You can hurt worse than this, and you will," I might, even in that excruciation, have got out another laugh among my sobs. But the someone would have been right.

I felt my mihrab begin to open and stretch, like a mouth yawning, and the lips of it continued to gape wider, until they must have made the orifice a full circle, like a mouth screaming. And, as if that was not torment enough, the entire round of the circle seemed suddenly to have been painted with liquid fire. I put a hand down there, to pat desperately at the blaze. But it felt no burning, only a crumbly something. I brought the hand back to my streaming eyes and saw through my tears that the fingers were smeared with a cheesy, pale green substance. How could that burn so?

And even then, besides the rampaging pain in my belly and the searing fire at the bottom, I could sense other awful things. I could taste the sweat running from my face into my mouth, and the blood from where I had by now gnawed my lips raw. I could hear my grunts and moans and racking gasps. I could smell the stench of my squalidly spilled body wastes. I could feel the creature inside me moving again, and apparently tumbling and kicking and flailing, as it edged its ponderous way through the belly pain toward the blaze below. As it moved, it pressed still more intolerably upon my bladder and bowels in there, and somehow they found more contents to void. And out, through that last extrusion of urine and turds, the creature began to come. And *ah, God!* when God decreed, "In sorrow shalt thou bring forth," God did make it so. I had known trivial pains in earlier times, and I had known real pain throughout these hours, and I have known other pains since, but I think there must be no pain in all the world like the pain I felt now. I have seen torture done, by men expert in torture, but I think no man is so cruel and inventive and accomplished in pain as God is.

The pain was compounded of two different sorts of pain. One was that of my mihrab flesh tearing, front and back. Take a piece of skin and rip it, ruthlessly but slowly, and try to imagine how that feels to the skin, and then imagine that it is the skin between your own legs, from artichoke to anus. While that was happening to me, and making me scream, the head of the creature inside me was butting its way through the enclosing bones down there, and that made me bellow between my screams. The bones of that place are close together; they must be shoved apart and aside, with a grinding and grating like that of a boulder going implacably through a too narrow cleft of rocks. That is what I felt, and what I felt all at the same time: the sickening movement and pain inside me, the crunching and buckling of all the bones between my legs, the tearing and burning of the outside flesh. And God allows, even in that extremity, only screaming and bellowing; no swooning to get away from the unbearable agony.

I did not faint until after the creature came out, with a final brutal bulge and billow and rasp of pain like an audible screech—and the dark-brown head raised up between my thighs, slimy with blood and mucus, and said in Chiv's voice, maliciously, "Something you cannot disown so easily . . ." Then I seemed to die.

· 5 ·

WHEN I came back to myself, I was myself. I was still naked and supine on the hindora bed, but I was a male again, and the body appeared to be my own. I was scummed with dried sweat and my mouth was terribly dry and thirsty and I had a pounding headache, but I felt no pains anywhere else. There was not any mess of my body wastes on the pallet; it looked as clean as it ever looked. The room was very nearly clear of the smoke, and I saw my discarded clothes on the floor. Chiv was also there, and fully dressed. She was hunkered down, wrapping a small something, pale blue and purple, in the paper I had brought the hashish in.

"Was it all a dream, Chiv?" I asked. She did not speak or look up, but went on with what she was doing. "What happened to you in the meantime, Chiv?" She did not reply. "I thought I had a baby," I said, with a dismissive laugh. No response. I added, "You were there. You were it."

At that, she raised her head, and her face wore much the same expression it had worn in the dream or whatever that had been. She asked, "I was dark brown?"

"Why, er, yes."

She shook her head. "Babies of the Romm do not get dark brown until later. They are the same color as white women's babies when they are born."

She stood up and carried her little package out of the room. When the door opened, I was surprised to see the brightness of daylight. Had I been here all through the night and into the next day? My companions would be much annoyed at my leaving them all the work to do. I began hurriedly putting on my clothes. When Chiv came back to the room, without her bundle, I said conversationally:

"For the life of me, I cannot believe that any sane woman would ever *want* to go through that horror. Would you, Chiv?"

"No."

"Then I was right? You were only pretending before? You are really not with child?"

"I am not." For a normally talkative person, she was being very brusque.

"Have no fear. I am not angry with you. I am glad, for your sake. Now I must get back to the karwansarai. I am going."

"Yes. Go."

She said it in a way that implied "do not come back." I could not see any reason for her surliness. It was I who had done all the suffering, and I strongly suspected that she had contributed in some cunning way to the philter's miscarriage of purpose.

"She is in a vile humor, as you said, Shimon," I told the Jew, on my way out. "But I suppose I owe you more money, anyway, for all the time I spent."

"Why, no," he said. "You were not long. In conscience—here—I give you a dirham back. Here also is your squeeze knife. Shalom."

So it was still the same day, then, and not really far into the afternoon, at that, and my travail had only seemed much, much longer. I got back to the inn to find my father and uncle and Nostril still collecting and packing our possessions, but having no immediate need of my assistance. I went down to the lakeside, where the washerwomen of Buzai Gumbad kept always a patch of water cleared of ice. The water was so blue-cold that it seemed to bite, so my bath was perfunctory—my hands and face, and then I briefly took off my upper garments to dash some few drops at my chest and armpits. That wetting was the first I had had all winter; I would probably have been revolted by my own smell, except that everyone else smelled the same or worse. At least it made me feel a trifle cleaner of the sweat that had dried on me in Chiv's room. And, as the sweat got diluted, so did my worst recollections of my experience. Pain is like that; it is excruciating to endure, but easy to forget. I daresay that is the only reason why any woman, after having been agonized and riven by the extrusion of one child, can even contemplate chancing the ordeal of another.

On the eve of our departure from the Roof of the World, the Hakim Mimdad, whose own karwan train would also be leaving, but in a different direction, came to the karwansarai to say his goodbyes to us all, and to give Uncle Mafìo a traveling supply of his medicine. Then, while my father and uncle looked rather agog, I told the Hakim how his philter had failed—or else had succeeded wildly far beyond his intent. I told him graphically what had happened, and I told it not at all enthusiastically, and not a little accusingly.

"The girl must have meddled," he said. "I was afraid of that. But no experiment is a total failure if something can be learned from it. Did you learn anything?"

"Only that human life begins and ends in merda, or kut. No, one other thing: to be careful when I love in future. I will never condemn any woman I love to such a hideous fate as motherhood."

"Well, there you are, then. You learned something. Perhaps you would like to try again? I have here another phial, another slight variant on the recipe. Take it along with you, and try it with some female who is not a Romni sorceress."

My uncle grumbled ruefully, "There is a Dotòr Balanzòn for you. Gives me a stunting potion and, to level the scales, gives an enhancer to one too young and brisk to need it."

I said, "I will take it, Mimdad, as a keepsake curiosity. The notion is appealing—to sample lovemaking in a multitude of shapes. But I have a long way to go before I exhaust all the possibilities of this body, and I will remain in it for now. Doubtless, when you have finally refined your philter to perfection, the word of it will be noised all about the world, and by then I may be jaded with my own possibilities, and I will seek you out and ask then to try your perfected potion. For now, I wish you success and salaam and farewell."

I did not get to say even that much to Chiv, when that same evening I went to Shimon's place.

"Earlier this afternoon," he told me indifferently, "the Domm girl asked for her share of her income to date, and resigned from this establishment, and joined an Uzbek karwan train departing for Balkh. The Domm do things like that. When they are not being shiftless, they are being shifty. Ah, well. You still have the squeeze knife to remember her by."

"Yes. And to remind me of her name. Chiv means blade."

"Does it now. And she never stuck one into you."

"I am not so sure of that."

"There are still the other females. Will you have one, this last night?"

"I think not, Shimon. From the glances I have had of them, they are exceedingly unbeautiful."

"By your reckoning as once expressed, then, they are nicely undangerous."

"You know something? Old Mordecai never said so, but that may be a count *against* unbeautiful people, not in their favor. I think I will always prefer the beautiful, and take my chances. Now I thank you for your good offices, Tzaddik Shimon, and I bid you farewell."

"Sakanà aleichem, nosèyah."

"That sounded different from the usual peace-go-with-you."

"I thought you would appreciate it." He repeated the Ivrit words, then translated them into Farsi: "Danger go with you, journeyer."

Although there was still plenty of snow about Buzai Gumbad, the whole of Lake Chaqmaqtin had gradually exchanged its cover of blue-white ice for a multicolored cover of waterfowl—numberless flocks of ducks and geese and swans that had flown in from the south, and continued to come. The noise of their contented honks and quacks was a continuous clamor, and they would make a rustling rumble like a windstorm in a forest whenever a thousand of them suddenly vaulted from the water all at once for a joyous flight around the lake. They provided a welcome addition to our diet, and their arrival had been the signal for the karwan trains to begin packing their gear, harnessing and herding their animals, forming up their wagons in line, and one after another plodding off for the horizon.

The first trains to leave had been those headed westward, to Balkh or farther, because the long decline of the Wakhàn Corridor was the easiest route down from the Roof of the World, and the earliest to become negotiable in the spring. The journeyers bound for the north or east or south prudently waited a while longer, because to go in any of those directions meant first climbing the mountains surrounding this place on those three sides, and descending through their high passes only to climb the next mountains beyond, and the ones beyond them. To the north, east and south of here, we were informed, the high passes never completely shed their snow and ice even in midsummer.

So we Polos, having to go north and having no experience of travel in such terrain and conditions, had waited for the prudent others. We might really have hesitated longer than we needed to, but one day there had come to us a delegation of the little dark Tamil Chola men at whom I had once laughed and to whom I had later apologized. They told us, speaking the Trade Farsi very badly, that they had decided not to carry their cargo of sea salt to Balkh, for they had heard reliable report that it would fetch a much better price in a place called Murghab, which was a trading town in Tazhikistan, on the east-west route between Kithai and Samarkand.

"Samarkand is far to the northwest of here," Uncle Mafio remarked.

"But Murghab is directly to the north," said one of the Cholas, a spindly little man named Talvar. "It is on your way, O twice-born, and you will have crossed the worst of the mountains when you get there, and the mountain journey from here to Murghab will be easier for you if you travel in karwan with us, and we wish only to say that you would be welcome to join us, for we have been much impressed by the good manners of this twice-born Saudara Marco, and we believe you will be congenial companions for the trail."

My father and uncle, and even Nostril, looked slightly bemazed at being called twice-born, and at my being praised by strangers for my good manners. But we all concurred in accepting the Cholas' invitation, expressing gratitude and thanks, and it was in their train that we rode our horses out of Buzai Gumbad and up into the forbidding mountains to the northward.

This was a small train compared to some we had seen in the encampment, trains comprising scores of people and hundreds of animals. The Cholas numbered only a dozen, all men, no women or children, with only half a dozen small and scrawny saddle horses, so they took turns riding and walking. For vehicles they had only three rickety, two-wheeled carts, each drawn by a small harness horse, in which carts they hauled their bedding, provender, animal feed, smithy and other traveling necessities. They had brought their sea salt as far as Buzai Gumbad on twenty or thirty pack asses, but had there effected a trade for a dozen yaks, which could carry the same load but were better suited to the more northerly terrain.

The yaks were good trailbreakers. They were uncaring of snow and cold and discomfort, and they were sure of foot, even when heavy laden. So, as they trudged at the head of our train, they not only picked the best trail, but also plowed it clean of snow and tramped it firm for us who followed. In the evenings, when we made camp and staked the animals roundabout, the yaks showed the horses how to paw down through the snow to find the dingy and shriveled but edible burtsa shrubs left from the last growing season.

I imagine the Cholas had invited us to accompany them only because we were big men—at least in comparison to them—and they must have supposed that we would be good fighters if the train should encounter bandits on the way to Murghab. We did not meet any, so our muscularity was not required for that contingency, but it did come in useful on the frequent occasions when a cart overturned on the rugged trail, or a horse fell into a crevice, or a yak scraped off one of its pack sacks when squeezing past a boulder. We also helped in preparing the meals at evening, but that we did more out of self-interest than affability.

The Cholas' way of preparing every meat dish was to drench it with a sauce of gray color and mucoid consistency, compounded of numerous different and pungent spices, a sauce called by them kàri. The effect was that, whatever one ate, one could taste only kàri. This was admittedly a blessing when the dish was a tasteless knob of dried or salted meat, or was high on its way toward green putrefaction. But we non-Cholas soon got tired of tasting only kàri and never knowing whether the substance underneath was mutton or fowl or, as it could have been, hay. We first asked permission to improve the sauce, and added to it some of our zafràn, a condiment hitherto unknown to the Cholas. They were much pleased by the new flavor and the new golden color it added to the kàri, and my father gave them a few culms of the zafràn to take back to India with them. When even the improved sauce began to weary us, I and Nostril and my father volunteered to alternate with the Cholas as cooks of the camp-time meals, and Uncle Mafìo got from our packs his bow and arrows and began to supply us with fresh-killed game. It was usually small things like snow hares and red-legged partridges, but once in a while something larger, like a goral or an urial, and we cooked plain and simple meals of boiled or broiled meat, served blessedly sauceless.

The Cholas' addiction to kàri excepted, those men were good traveling companions. In fact, they were so retiring, and so shy of speaking until they were spoken to, and so reticent of seeming obtrusive, that we others could have journeyed all the way to Murghab without much awareness of their presence. Their timidity was understandable. Although the Cholas spoke Tamil, not Hindi, they were of the Hindu religion and they came from India, so they had to endure the contempt and derision with which all other nations rightly regard the Hindus. Our slave Nostril was the only non-Hindu person I knew who had bothered to learn the lowly Hindi language, and not even he had ever learned the Tamil. So none of us could converse with these Cholas in their own tongue, and they were very imperfect in the Trade Farsi. However, when we made it clear to them that we were not going to shun and scorn them overtly, or laugh at their halting speech, they became almost fawningly friendly to us and exerted themselves to tell us things of interest about this part of the world and things of usefulness on our way through it.

This is the land which most Westerners call Far Tartary and think of as the uttermost eastern end of the earth. But the name is doubly mistaken. The world extends far eastward beyond this Far Tartary, and the word Tartary is even more of a misnomer. A Mongol is called a Tàtar in the Farsi language of Persia, which is where Westerners first heard mention of the Mongol people. Later, when the Mongols-called-Tàtars rampaged across the borders of Europe, and all Europe trembled with fear and hatred of them, it was perhaps natural that many Westerners confused the word Tàtar with the ancient classical name for the infernal regions, which was Tartarus. So the Westerners came to speak of "the Tartars from Tartary," much as they would speak of "the demons from Hell."

But even Eastern men who should have known the proper names hereabout, the veterans of many karwan journeys across this land, had told us several different names for the mountains we were now making our way through—the Hindu Kush, the Himalaya, the Karakoram and so on. I can attest that there are indeed enough individual mountains and entire ranges of mountains and whole nations of mountains to justify and support any number of appellations. However, for the sake of our map-making, we asked our Chola companions if they could clarify the matter. They listened as we repeated all the various names we had heard, and they did not deride the men who had told them to us—because no man, they affirmed, could possibly say precisely where one range and one name left off and another began.

But, to locate us as accurately as possible, they said we were currently forging northward through the ranges called the Pai-Mir, having left behind us the Hindu Kush range to the southwest, and the Karakoram range to the south, and the Himalaya range somewhere far off to the southeast. The other names which we had been told—the Keepers, the Masters, Solomon's Throne—the Cholas said were probably local and parochial names bestowed by and used only by the folk living among the various ranges. So my father and uncle marked the maps of our Kitab accordingly. To me, the mountains all looked very much alike: great high crags and sharp-edged boulders and sheer cliffs and the tumbled detritus of rock slides—all of rock that would have been gray and brown and black if it had not been so heavily quilted with snow and festooned with icicles. In my opinion, the name of Himalaya, Abode of the Snows, could have served for any and every range in Far Tartary.

For all its bleakness and the lack of lively color, however, this was the most magnificent landscape I have seen in all my travels. The Pai-Mir mountains, immense and massive and awesome, stood ranked and ranged and towering heedless above us few fidgety creatures, us insignificant insects twitching our way across their mighty flanks. But how can I portray in mere insect words the overwhelming majesty of these mountains? Let me say this: the fact of the highness and the grandeur of the Alps of Europe is known to every traveled or literate person in the West. And let me add this: if there could be such a thing as a world made entirely of Alps, then the peaks of the Pai-Mir would be the Alps of that world.

One other thing I will say about these Pai-Mir mountains, a thing I have never heard remarked by any other journeyer returned from them. The karwan veterans who had told us so many different names for this region had also been free with advice about what we could expect to experience when we got here. But not one of those men spoke of the aspect of the mountains that I found most distinctive and memorable. They talked of the Pai-Mir's terrible trails and punishing weathers, and told us how best a traveler could survive those rigors. But the men never mentioned the one thing I remember most vividly: the unceasing *noise* these mountains make.

I do not mean the sound of wind or snowstorm or sandstorm raging through them, though God knows we heard those sounds often enough. We were frequently breasting a wind into which a man could literally let himself fall, and not hit the ground but hang atilt, held up by the blast. And to that wind's bawling noise would be added the seethe of wind-blown snow or the sizzle of windblown dust, according as we were in the heights where winter still held sway or in the deep gorges where it was now late springtime.

No, the noise I remember so well was the sound of the mountains' decay. It was a surprise to me, that mountains so titanic could be falling to pieces all the time, falling apart, falling down. When I first heard the sound, I thought it was thunder rolling among the crags, and I marveled, for there were no clouds anywhere in the pure blue sky that day, and anyway I could not imagine a thunderstorm occurring in such crystalline cold weather. I reined my mount to a halt, and sat still in the saddle, listening attentively.

The sound began as a deep-throated rumble somewhere out ahead of us, and it loudened to a distant roar, and then that sound was compounded by its echoes. Other mountains heard it and repeated it, like a choir of voices taking up, one after another, the theme from a solo singer singing bass. The voices enlarged on that theme and amplified it and added to it the resonances of tenors and baritones, until the sound was coming from over there and from over yonder and from behind me and from all around me. I remained transfixed by the thrumming reverberation, while it dwindled from a thunder to a mutter and a mumble and faded away diminuendo. The mountains' voices only lingeringly let go, one after another, so that my human ear could not discern the moment when the sound died into silence.

The Chola named Talvar rode up beside me on his scraggly little horse, and gave me a look and broke my enthrallment by saying in his Tamil tongue, "Batu jatuh," and in Farsi, "Khak uftadan," both of which said, "Avalanche." I nodded as if I had known it all the while, and kneed my horse to move on.

That was only the first of innumerable occasions; the noise could be heard almost any time of day or night. Sometimes it would come from so near our trail that we would hear it above the creak and clatter of our harness and cartwheels and the grumbling and tooth-gnashing of our yak herd. And if we looked up quickly, before the echoes confused the direction, we would see rising into the sky from behind some ridge a smoke-like plume of dust or a glittering billow of snow particles, marking the place where the slide had occurred. But I could hear the noise of more distant rockfalls whenever I chose to listen for them. I had only to ride ahead of the train or dawdle behind its racket, and wait for not long. I would hear, from one direction or another, a mountain groaning in the agony of losing a part of itself, and then the echoes overlapping from every other direction: all the other mountains joining in a dirge.

The slides were sometimes of snow and ice, as can happen also in the Alps. But they more often marked the slow corruption of the mountains themselves, for these Pai-Mir, though infinitely bigger than the Alps, are notably less substantial. They appear steadfast and eternal from a distance, but I have seen them close. They are made of a rock much veined and cracked and flawed, and the mountains' very loftiness contributes to their instability. If the wind nudges a single pebble from a high place, its rolling can dislodge other fragments, and their movement shoves loose other stones until, all rolling together, their ever more rapid downhill progress can topple huge boulders, and those in falling can sheer the lip off a vast cliff, and that in coming down can cleave away the whole side of a mountain. And so on, until a mass of rocks, stones, pebbles, gravel, earth and dust, usually mushed with snow, slush and ice—a mass perhaps the size of a minor Alp—sluices down into the narrow gorges or even narrower ravines that separate the mountains.

Any living thing in the path of a Pai-Mir avalanche is doomed. We came upon much evidence—the bones and skulls and splendid horn racks of goral, urial and "Marco's sheep," and the bones and skulls and pathetically broken belongings of men—the relics of long-dead wild flocks and long-lost karwan trains. Those unfortunates had heard the mountains moan, then groan, then bellow, and they had never since heard anything at all. Only chance preserved us from the same fate, for there is no trail or camping spot or time of day that is exempt from avalanche. Happily, none fell on us, but on many occasions we found the trail absolutely obliterated, and had to seek a way around the interruption. This was trouble enough when the slide had left in our path an unclimbable barrier of rubble. It was much harder on the frequent trail that was nothing but a narrow shelf chiseled from the face of a cliff, and an avalanche had broken it with an unvaultable void. Then we would have to retrace our steps for many farsakhs backward, and trudge many, many weary farsakhs circuitously roundabout before we were headed north again.

So my father and uncle and Nostril all cursed bitterly and the Cholas whimpered miserably every time they heard the rumble of rockfall, from whatever direction. But I was always stirred by the sound, and I cannot understand why other travelers seem to think it not worth mentioning in their reminiscences, for what the noise means is that these great mountains will not last forever. The crumbling of them will of course take centuries and millennia and eons before the Pai-Mir crumble down even to the still-grand stature of the Alps—but crumble they will, and eventually to a featureless flat land. Realizing that, I wondered why, if God intended only to let them fall, He had piled them so extravagantly high as they are now. And I wondered too, and I wonder still, how immeasurably, stupendously, unutterably high these mountains must have been when God made them in the Beginning.

All the mountains being of unvarying colors, the only changes we could see in their appearance were those made by weather and time of day. On clear days, the high peaks caught the brilliance of dawn while we were still benighted, and they held the glow of sunset long after we had camped and supped and bedded down in darkness. On days when there were clouds in the sky, we would see a white cloud trail across a bare brown crag and hide it. Then, when the cloud had passed, the pinnacle would reappear, but now as white with snow as if it had shredded off rags of the cloud in which to drape itself.

When we ourselves were high up, climbing an upward trail, the high light up there played tricks with our eyesight. In most mountain country there is always a slight haze which renders each farther object a little dimmer to the eye, so one can judge which objects are near and which far. But in the Pai-Mir there is no trace of haze, and it is impossible to reckon the distance or even the size of the most common and familiar objects. I would often fix my gaze on a mountain peak on the far horizon, then be startled to see our pack yaks scrambling over it, a mere rock pile and only a hundred paces distant from me. Or I would glimpse a hulking surragoy—one of the wild mountain yaks, like a fragment of mountain himself—lurking just to one side of our trail, and I would worry that he might lure our tame yaks to run away from us, but then realize that he was actually standing a farsakh away, and there was a whole valley between us.

The high air was as tricksome as the light. As it had done in the Wakhàn (which we now regarded as a mere lowland), the air refused to support the flames of our cook fires more than meagerly, and they burned only pale and blue and tepid, and our water pots took an eternity to come to a boil. Up here, somehow, the thin air also affected the heat of the very sunshine. The sunny side of a boulder would be too uncomfortably hot to lean against, but its shady side would be too uncomfortably cold. Sometimes we would have to doff our heavy chapon overcoats because the sun made them so swelteringly hot, but not a crystal of the snow all about us would be melting. The sun would fire icicles into blindingly bright and iridescent rainbows, but never make them drip.

However, that was only in clear and sunny weather on the heights, when the winter briefly slept. I think these heights are where the old man winter goes to mope and sulk when all the rest of the world spurns him and welcomes warmer seasons. And in here, perhaps in one or another of the many mountain caves and caverns, old winter retires to doze from time to time. But he sleeps uneasily and he continually reawakens, yawning great gusts of cold and flailing long arms of wind and from his white beard combing cascades of snow. Often and often, I watched the snowy high peaks blend into a fresh fall of snow and vanish in its whiteness; then the nearer ridges would disappear, and then the yaks leading our train, and then the rest of it, and finally everything beyond my horse's wind-whipped mane would disappear in whiteness. In some of those storms the snow was so thick and the gale so fierce that we riders could progress best by turning and sitting backward on our saddles, letting our mounts pick their onward way, tacking like boats against the blast.

Since we were constantly going uphill and down, that iron weather would soften every few days, when we descended into the warm, dry, dusty gorges where young lady spring had arrived, then would harden around us again when we ascended once more into the domains still held by old man winter. So we alternated: plodding through snow above, slogging through mud below; half frozen by a sleet storm above, half suffocated by a whirling dust-devil below. But as we progressed ever northward, we began to see in the narrow valley bottoms bits of living green—stunted bushes and sparse grasses, then small and timid patches of meadow; an occasional greening-out tree, then stands of them. Those fragmentary verdant areas looked so new and alien, set among the snow-white and harsh-black and arid-dun heights, that they might have been snippets of faraway other countries cut out with scissors and inexplicably scattered through this wasteland.

Still farther north, the mountains were farther apart, allowing for wider and greener valleys, and the terrain was even more remarkable for its contrasts. Against the mountains' cold white background shone a hundred different greens, all warm with sunlight—voluminous dark-green chinar trees, pale silver-green locust trees, poplars tall and slender like green feathers, aspens twinkling their leaves from the green side to the gray-pearl side. And under and among the trees glowed a hundred different other colors—the bright yellow cups of the flowers called tul-bands, the bright reds and pinks of wild roses, the radiant purple of the flower called lilak. That is a tall-growing shrub, so the lilak's purple plumes looked even more vivacious for our seeing them always from below, against the stark white snowline, and its perfume—one of the most delicious of all flower fragrances—smelled the sweeter for being borne on the absolutely odorless and sterile wind from the snowfields.

In one of those valleys we came to the first river we had encountered since leaving the Ab-e-Panj, this one the Murghab by name, and beside it was the town of the same name. We took the opportunity to rest for two nights in a karwansarai there, and to bathe ourselves and wash our clothes in the river. Then we bade goodbye to the Cholas and kept on northward. I hoped that Talvar and his comrades did get much coin for their sea salt, because Murghab had not much else to offer. It was a shabby town and its Tazhik inhabitants were distinctive only for their exceptional resemblance to their co-inhabitants, the yaks—men and women alike being hairy, smelly, broad of face and features and torso, bovine in their impassivity and incuriosity. Murghab was empty of enticements to linger there, but the Cholas would leave it having nothing better to look forward to, only the grueling journey back across the high Pai-Mir and all of India.

Our own journey, from Murghab on, was not too arduous, we having got well used to traveling in these highlands. Also, the farther-north ranges were not so high or wintry, their slopes were not so steep, the passes were not so far to climb up to and over and down from, and the intervening valleys were broad and green and flowery and pleasant. According to what calculations I could make with our kamàl, we were now much farther north than Alexander had ever penetrated into central Asia, and, according to our Kitab maps, we were now squarely in the center of that largest land mass on earth. So we were astonished and bewildered one day to find ourselves on the shore of a *sea*. From the shore where the wavelets lapped at our horses' fetlocks, the waters stretched away to the west as far as the eye could see. We knew, of course, that a mighty inland sea does exist in central Asia, the Ghelan or Caspian by name, but we had to be far, far east of that one. I briefly felt sorry for our recent companions, the Cholas, thinking they had fetched all their sea salt to a land already provided with a more than ample salt sea.

But we tasted the water, and it was fresh and sweet and crystal clear. This was a lake, then, but that was not much less astounding—to encounter a vastly big and deep lake situated as high as an Alp above the bulk of the world. Our northward route took us up its eastern shore, and we were many days in passing it. On every one of those days, we made excuse to camp early in the evening, so we could bathe and wade and disport ourselves in those balmy, sparkling waters. We found no towns on the lake shore, but there were the mud-brick and driftwood huts of Tazhik shepherds and woodcutters and charcoal burners. They told us that the lake was called Karakul, which is to say Black Fleece, which is the name of that breed of domestic sheep raised by all the shepherds in the vicinity.

That was one more oddity about the lake: that it should have the name of an animal; but that animal is admittedly not a common one. In fact, looking at a herd of those sheep, one might wonder why they are called kara, since the adult rams and ewes are mostly of varying shades of gray and grayish-white, only a few of them being black. The explanation is in the much-prized fur for which the karakul is noted. That costly pelt, of tight and kinky black curls, is not just a shearing of the sheep's fleece. It is a lamb skin, and all the karakul lambs are born black, and the pelt is obtained by killing and flaying a lamb before it is three days old. A day older, and the pure black color loses some of its black intensity, and no fur trader will accept it as karakul.

A week's journey north of the lake, we came to a river flowing from west to east. It was called by the local Tazhiks the Kek-Su, or Passage River. The name was fitting, for its broad valley did constitute a clear passage through the mountains, and we gladly followed it eastward, down and down from the highlands we had been among for so long. Even our horses were grateful for that easier passage; the rocky mountains had been hard on both their bellies and their hoofs; down here was ample grass for feed and it was soft under their feet. Curiously, at every single village and even isolated hut we came to, my father or uncle asked again the name of the river, and every time were told, "Kek-Su." Nostril and I wondered at their insistently repeated question, but they only laughed at our puzzlement and would not explain why they needed so many reassurances that we were following the Passage River. Then one day we came upon the sixth or seventh of the valley villages and, when my father asked a man there, "What do you call the river?" the man politely replied, "Ko-tzu."

The river was the same as yesterday, the terrain was no different from yesterday's, the man looked as yaklike as any other Tazhik, but he had pronounced the name differently. My father turned in his saddle to shout back to Uncle Mafio, riding a little way behind us—and he shouted it triumphantly—"We have arrived!" Then he dismounted, picked up a handful of the road's yellowish dirt and regarded it almost fondly.

"Arrived where?" I asked. "I do not understand."

"The river's name is the same: the Passage," said my father. "But this good fellow spoke it in the Han language. We have crossed the border from Tazhikistan. This is the stretch of the Silk Road by which your uncle and I went westward home. The city of Kashgar is only two days or so ahead of us."

"So we are now in the province of Sin-kiang," said Uncle Mafio, who had ridden up to us. "Formerly a province of the Chin Empire. But now Sin-kiang, and everything east of here, is a part of the Mongol Empire. Nephew Marco, you are finally in the heartland of the Khanate."

"You are standing," said my father, "upon the yellow earth of Kithai, which extends from here to the great eastern ocean. Marco, my son, you have come at last to the domain of the Khakhan Kubilai."

KITHAI

. I .

THE city of Kashgar I found to be of respectable size and of sturdy-built inns and shops and residences, not the mud-brick shacks we had been seeing in Tazhikistan. Kashgar was built for permanence, because it is the western gateway of Kithai, through which all Silk Road trains coming from or going to the West must pass. And we found that no train could pass without challenge. Some farsakhs before we got to the city walls, we were waved down by a group of Mongol sentries at a guard-post on the road. Beyond their shelter we could see the countless round yurtu tents of what appeared to be an entire army camped around Kashgar's approaches.

"Mendu, Elder Brothers," said one of the sentries. He was a typical Mongol warrior of forbidding brawn and ugliness, hung all about with weapons, but his salute was friendly enough.

"Mendu, sain bina," said my father.

I could not then understand all the words which were spoken, but my father later repeated the conversation to me, in translation, and told me it was the standard sort of exchange between parties meeting any-where in Mongol country. It was odd to hear such gracious formalities spoken by a seeming brute, for the sentry went on to inquire politely, "From under what part of Heaven do you come?"

"We are from under the skies of the far West," my father replied. "And you, Elder Brother, where do you erect your yurtu?"

"Behold, my poor tent stands now among the bok of the Ilkhan Kaidu, who is currently encamped in this place, while surveying his dominions. Elder Brother, across what lands have you cast your beneficent shadow on your way hither?"

"We come most recently from the high Pai-Mir, down this Passage River. We wintered in the estimable place called Buzai Gumbad, which is also among your master Kaidu's territories."

"Verily, his dominions are far-flung and many. Has peace accompanied your journey?"

"So far we have traveled safely. And you, Elder Brother, are you at peace? Are your mares fruitful, and your wives?"

"All is prosperous and peaceful in our pastures. Whither does your karwan party proceed, then, Elder Brother?"

"We plan to stop some days in Kashgar. Is the place wholesome?"

"You can there light your fire in comfort and tranquillity, and the sheep are fat for eating. Before you proceed, however, this lowly minion of the Ilkhan would be pleased to know your ultimate destination."

"We are bound eastward, for the far capital Khanbalik, to pay our respects to your very highest lord, the Khakhan Kubilai." My father took out the letter we had carried for so long. "Has my Elder Brother stooped to learn the clerk's humble art of reading?"

"Alas, Elder Brother, I have not attained to that high learning," said the man, taking the document. "But even I can perceive and recognize the Great Seal of the Khakhan. I am desolated to realize that I have impeded the peaceful passage of such dignitaries as you must be."

"You are but doing your duty, Elder Brother. Now, if I may have the letter back, we will proceed."

But the sentry did not give it back. "My master Kaidu is but a miserable hut to a mighty pavilion alongside his Elder Cousin the high lord Kubilai. For that reason he will yearn for the privilege of seeing his cousin's written words, and reading them with reverence. No doubt my master will also wish to receive and greet his lordly cousin's distinguished emissaries from the West. So, if I may, Elder Brother, I will show him this paper."

"Really, Elder Brother," my father said, with some impatience, "we require no pomp or ceremony. We would be pleased just to go straight on through Kashgar without causing any fuss."

The sentry paid no heed. "Here in Kashgar, the various inns are reserved to various sorts of guests. There is a karwansarai for horse traders, another for grain merchants. . . ."

"We already knew that," growled Uncle Mafio. "We have been here before."

"Then I recommend to you, Elder Brothers, the one that is reserved for passing travelers, the Inn of the Five Felicities. It is in the Lane of Perfumed Humanity. Anyone in Kashgar can direct—"

"We know where it is."

"Then you will be so kind as to lodge there until the Ilkhan Kaidu requests the honor of your presence in his pavilion yurtu." He stepped back, still holding the letter, and waved us on. "Now go in peace, Elder Brothers. A good journey to you."

When we had ridden out of the sentry's hearing, Uncle Mafìo grumbled, "Merda with a piecrust on it! Of all the Mongol armies, we ride into Kaidu's."

"Yes," said my father. "To have come all this way through his lands without incident, only to come up against the man himself."

My uncle nodded glumly and said, "This may be as far as we get."

To explain why my father and uncle voiced annoyance and concern, I must explain some things about this land of Kithai to which we had come. First, its name is universally pronounced in the West "Cathay," and there is nothing I can do to change that. I would not even try, because the rightly pronounced "Kithai" is itself rather an arbitrary name, bestowed by the Mongols, and only comparatively recently, only some fifty years before I was born. This land was the first the Mongols conquered in their rampage across the world, and it is where Kubilai chose to set his throne, and it is the hub of the many spokes of the Mongols' widespread empire—just as our Venice is the holding center of our Republic's many possessions: Thessaly and Crete and the Vèneto mainland and all the rest. However, just as the Vèneti people originally came to the Venetian lagoon from somewhere out of the north, so did the Mongols come to Kithai.

"They have a legend," said my father, when we all were comfortably settled in Kashgar's karwansarai of the Five Felicities, and were discussing our situation. "It is a laughable legend, but the Mongols believe it. They say that once upon a time, long ago, a widow woman lived alone and lonely in a yurtu on the snowy plains. And out of loneliness, she befriended a blue wolf of the wild, and eventually she mated with it, and from their coupling sprang the first ancestors of the Mongols."

That legendary start of their race occurred in a land far north of Kithai, a land called Sibir. I have never visited there, nor ever wanted to, for it is said to be a flat and uninteresting country of perpetual snow and frost. In such a harsh land, it was perhaps only natural that the various Mongol tribes (one of which called itself "the Kithai") should have found nothing better to do than to fight among themselves. But one man of them, Temuchin by name, rallied together several tribes and, one by one, subdued the others, until all the Mongols were his to command, and they called him Khan, meaning Great Lord, and they gave him a new name, Chinghiz, meaning Perfect Warrior.

Under Chinghiz Khan, the Mongols left their northland and swept southward—to this immense country, which was then the Empire of Chin—and they conquered it, and called it Kithai. The other conquests made by the Mongols, in the rest of the world, I need not recount in series, since they are too well known to history. Suffice it to say that Chinghiz and his lesser Ilkhans and later his sons and grandsons extended the Mongol domains westward to the banks of the River Dnieper in the Polish Ukraine, and to the gates of Constantinople on the Sea of Marmara—which sea, incidentally, like the Adriatic, we Venetians regard as our private pond.

"We Venetians made the word 'horde' from the Mongol word yurtu," my father reminded me, "and we called the marauders collectively the Mongol Horde." Then he went on to tell me something I had not known. "In Constantinople I heard them called by a different name: the *Golden* Horde. That was because the Mongol armies invading that region had come originally from this region, and you have seen the yellowness of the soil hereabout. They always colored their tents yellow like the earth, for partial concealment. So—yellow yurtu: Golden Horde. However, the Mongols who marched straight west out of their native Sibir were accustomed to coloring their yurtus white, like the Sibir snows. So those armies, invading the Ukraine, were called by their victims the White Horde. I suppose there may yet be Other-Colored Hordes."

If the Mongols had never conquered more than Kithai, they would have had much to boast about. The tremendous land stretches from the mountains of Tazhikistan eastward to the shores of the great ocean called the Sea of Kithai, or by some people the Sea of Chin. To the north, Kithai abuts on the Sibir wasteland where the Mongols originated. In the south—in those days, when I had first arrived in the country—Kithai bordered on the Empire of Sung. However, as I shall tell in its place, the Mongols later conquered that empire, too, and called it Manzi, and absorbed it into Kubilai's Khanate.

But even in those days of my first arrival, the Mongol Empire was so immense that—as I have repeatedly indicated—it was divided into numerous provinces, each under the sovereignty of a different Ilkhan. Those provinces had been parceled out with no particular attention paid to any previous map-drawn borders observed by former rulers now overthrown. The Ilkhan Abagha, for example, was the lord of what had been the Empire of Persia, but his lands also included much of what had been Greater Armenia and Anatolia to the west of Persia and, on the east, India Aryana. There, Abagha's domain bordered on the lands apportioned to his distant cousin, the Ilkhan Kaidu, who reigned over the Balkh region, the Pai-Mir, all of Tazhikistan and this western Sin-kiang Province of Kithai where my father, my uncle and I now lodged.

The Mongols' accession to empire and power and wealth had not lessened their lamentable propensity for quarreling among themselves. They quite frequently fought each other, just as they had used to do when they were only ragged savages in the wastes of Sibir, before Chinghiz unified them and impelled them to greatness. The Khakhan Kubilai was a grandson of that Chinghiz, and all the Ilkhans of the outlying provinces were likewise direct descendants of that Perfect Warrior. It might be supposed that they should have constituted a close-knit royal family. But several were descended from different sons of Chinghiz, and had been distanced from each other by two or three generations of the family tree's branchings apart, and not all were satisfied that they had inherited their fair share of the empire bequeathed by their mutual progenitor.

This Ilkhan Kaidu, for instance, whose summons to audience we were now awaiting, was the grandson of Kubilai's uncle, Okkodai. That Okkodai, in his time, had himself been the ruling Khakhan, the second after Chinghiz, and evidently his grandson Kaidu resented the fact that the title and throne had passed to a different branch of the line. Evidently he felt, too, that he deserved more of the Khanate than he presently held. Anyway, Kaidu had several times made incursions on the lands given to Abagha, which was tantamount to insubordination against the Khakhan, for Abagha was Kubilai's nephew, son of his brother, and his close ally in the otherwise disputatious family.

"Kaidu has never yet rebelled openly against Kubilai," said my father. "But, besides harassing Kubilai's favorite nephew, he has disregarded many court edicts, and usurped privileges to which he is not entitled, and in other ways has flouted the Khakhan's authority. If he deems us friends of Kubilai, then he must regard us as enemies of himself."

Nostril, sounding woeful, said, "I thought we were only having a trivial delay, master. Are we instead in danger again?"

Uncle Mafio muttered, "As the rabbit said in the fable: 'If that is not a wolf, it is a damned big dog.' "

"He may snatch for himself all the gifts we are carrying to Khanbalik," said my father. "Out of envy and spite, as much as rapacity."

"Surely not," I said. "That would most certainly be flagrant lesa maestà, defying the Khakhan's letter of safe conduct. And Kubilai would be furious, would he not, if we arrived empty-handed at his court, and told him why?"

"Only if we did arrive there," my father said ominously. "Kaidu is presently the gatekeeper of this stage of the Silk Road. He holds the power of life and death here. We can only wait and see."

We were kept waiting for some days before we were bidden to our confrontation with the Ilkhan, but no one hindered our freedom of movement. So I spent some of that time in wandering about within the walls of Kashgar. I had long ago learned that crossing a border between two nations is not like going through a gate between two different gardens. Even in the far countries, all so exotically different from Venice, to go from one land into the next usually brought no more surprise than one finds, say, in crossing from the Vèneto into the Duchy of Padua or Verona. The first commonfolk I had seen in Kithai looked just like those I had been seeing for months, and at first glimpse the city of Kashgar might have been only a much bigger and better-built version of the Tazhik trade town of Murghab. But on closer acquaintance I did find Kashgar different in many respects from anywhere I had visited before.

In addition to the Mongol occupiers and settlers in the vicinity, the population included Tazhiks from across the border, and people of various other origins, Uzbek and Turki and I know not how many others. All of those the Mongols lumped under the name of Uighur, a word which means only "ally," but signified more. The various Uighurs were not just allied to the Mongols, they were all in some measure related by racial heritage, language and customs. Anyway, except for some variation in their dress and adornments, they all *looked* like Mongols—berry-brown of complexion, slit-eyed, notably hairy, big-boned, burly and squat and rough-hewn. But the population also included persons who were totally distinct—from me as well as from the Mongoloid peoples—in appearance, language and comportment. Those were the Han people, I learned, the aboriginal inhabitants of these lands.

Most of them had faces paler than mine, of a delicate ivory tint, like the best grade of parchment, and bearing little or no facial hair. Their eyes were not narrowed by heavily pouched lids, like the Mongols', but were nevertheless so very slitlike as to appear slanted. Their bodies and limbs were fine-boned, slim and seeming almost fragile. If, when one looked at a shaggy Mongol or one of his Uighur relatives, one thought at once, "That man has lived always out of doors," then one was inclined to think, when looking at a Han, even a wretched farmer hard at work in his field, filthy with mud and manure, "That man was born and raised indoors." But one did not have to look; a blind man would perceive a Han to be unique, merely hearing him talk.

The Han language resembles no other on this earth. While I had no trouble learning to speak Mongol, and to write with its alphabet, I never learned more than a rudimentary comprehension of Han. The Mongol speech is gruff and harsh, like its speakers, but it at least employs sounds not too different from those heard in our Western languages. The Han, by contrast, is a speech of staccato syllables, and they are *sung* rather than spoken. Evidently the Han throat is incapable of forming more than a very few of the sounds that other people make. The sound of *r*, for one, is quite beyond them. My name in their speech was always Mah-ko. And, having so very few noises to work with, the Han must sound them on different tones—high, mid, low, rising, falling—to make a sufficient variety for compiling a vocabulary. It is like this: suppose our Ambrosian plainsong *Gloria in excelsis* had that meaning of "glory in the highest" *only* when sung to its traditional up and down neumes, and, if the syllables were sung in different ups and downs, were to change its meaning utterly—to "darkness in the lowest" or "dishonor to the basest" or even "fish for the frying."

But there were no fish to be had in Kashgar. Our Uighur innkeeper almost proudly explained why. Here in this place, he said, we were as far inland as a person could get from any sea on the earth—the temperate oceans to the east and west, the tropic seas to the south, the frozen white ones in the north. Nowhere else in the world, he said, as if it were a thing to boast about, was there any spot farther from the sea. Kashgar had no freshwater fish either, he said, for the Passage River was too much befouled by the city's effluxions to support any. I was already aware of the effluxions, having noticed one sort here that I had never seen before. Every city spews out sewage and garbage and smoke, but the smoke of Kashgar was peculiar. It came from the stone that burns, and this was the first place I saw it.

In a sense, the burnable rock is the exact opposite of that rock I earlier saw in Balkh, which produces the cloth that will not burn. Many of my untraveled fellow Venetians have derided both stones as unbelievable, when I have spoken of them. But other Venetians—mariners in the English trade—tell me that the burning rock is well known and commonly used for fuel in England, where it is called kohle. In the Mongol lands it was called simply "the black"—kara—for that is its color. It occurs in extensive strata just a little way under the yellow soil, so it is easily got at with simple picks and spades, and, being rather crumbly, the stone is easily broken into wieldy chunks. A hearth or brazier heaped with those chunks requires a kindling fire of wood, but once the kara is alight it burns much longer than wood and gives a greater heat, as does naft oil. It is abundant and free for the digging and its only fault is its dense smoke. Because every Kashgar household and workshop and karwansarai used it for fuel, a pall hung perpetually between the city and the sky.

At least the kara did not, like camel or yak dung, give a noxious flavor to the food cooked over it, and the food served us in Kashgar was already dismally familiar of flavor. There were flocks of goats as well as sheep, and herds of cows and domestic yaks all over the landscape, and pigs and chickens and ducks in every backyard, but the staple meat at the Five Felicities was still the everlasting mutton. The Uighur peoples, like the Mongol, have no national religion, and I could not then make out whether the Han did. But Kashgar, as a trade crossroads, represented in its permanent and transient population just about every religion that exists, and the sheep is the one animal edible by communicants of all of them. And the aromatic, weak, not intoxicating, hence not religiously objectionable cha was still the staple beverage.

Kithai did introduce one pleasing improvement to our meals. Instead of rice, we got a side dish called miàn. That was not exactly new to us, as it was only a pasta of the vermicelli string sort, but it was a welcome old acquaintance. Usually it was served boiled al dente, just as Venetian vermicelli is, but sometimes it was cut into small bits and fried to crunchy kinks. What *was* new about it—to me, anyway—was that it was served with two slender sticks for the eating of it. I stared at this curiosity, nonplussed, and my father and uncle laughed at the expression on my face.

"They are called kuài-zi," said my father. "The nimble tongs. And they are more practical than they look. Observe, Marco."

Holding both of his sticks in the fingers of one hand, he began most adroitly to pick up bits of meat and skeins of the miàn. It took me some fumbling minutes to learn the use of the nimble-tong sticks, but, when I had, I found them to be notably neater than the Mongol fashion of eating with the fingers, and indeed more efficacious for twirling up strings of pasta than our Venetian skewers and spoons.

The Uighur landlord smiled approvingly when he saw me begin to pick and peck and spool with the sticks, and informed me that the nimble tongs were a Han contribution to fine dining. He went on to assert that the miàn-vermicelli was a Han invention, too, but I contested that. I told him that pasta of every variety had been on every table of the Italian peninsula ever since a Roman ship's cook fortuitously conceived the making of it. Perhaps, I suggested, the Han had learned of it during some Caesarean era of trade between Rome and Kithai.

"No doubt it happened so," said the innkeeper, he being a man of impeccable politeness.

I must say that I found all the commonfolk of Kithai, of every race—when they were not bloodily engaged in feud, revenge, banditry, rebellion or warfare—to be exceptionally courteous of address and comportment. And that gentility, I believe, *was* a contribution of the Han.

The Han language, as if to make up for its many inherent deficiencies, is replete with flowery expressions and ornate turns of phrase and intricate formalities, and the Han's manners are also exquisitely refined. They are a people of a very ancient and high culture, but whether their elegant speech and graces impelled their civilization or simply grew out of it, I have no idea. However, I do believe that all the other nations in proximity to the Han, though woefully inferior in culture, acquired from them at least those outward trappings of advanced civilization. Even in Venice, I had seen how people ape their betters, in appearance if not in substance. No shopkeeper is ever anything loftier than a shopkeeper, but he who purveys to fine ladies will converse better than the one who sells only to boat wives. A Mongol warrior may be by nature an uncouth barbarian, but when he chooses—as witness the first sentry who had challenged us—he can speak as politely as any Han, and exhibit manners suitable for a court ballroom.

Even in this rough frontier trade town, the Han influence was evident. I walked through streets with names like Flowery Benevolence and Crystallized Fragrance and, in a market square called Productive Endeavor and Fair Exchange, I saw lumpish Mongol soldiers buying caged bright songbirds and bowls of shiny tiny fish to adorn their rude army quarters. Every stall in the market had a sign, a long, narrow board hung vertically, and passersby helpfully translated for me the words inscribed in the Mongol alphabet or the Han characters. Besides giving notice of what the stall sold: "Pheasant Eggs for Making Hair Pomade" or "Spicy-Odored Indigo Dye," each board added a few words of advice: "Loitering and Gossiping Are Not Conducive to Good Business" or "Former Customers Have Induced the Sad Necessity of Denying Credit" or something of the sort.

But if there was one aspect of Kashgar that first told me Kithai was different from other places I had been, it was the endless variety of smells. True, every other Eastern community had been odorous, but chiefly and awfully of old urine. Kashgar was not free of that stale smell, but it had many and better others. Most noticeable was the odor of kara smoke, which is not unpleasant, and into that were blended countless and fragrant incenses, which the people burned in their houses and shops as well as in places of worship. Also, at all hours of the day and night, one could smell foodstuffs cooking. That was sometimes familiar: the simple, good, mouth-watering aroma of pork chops frying in some non-Muslim kitchen. But the scent was often otherwise: the smell of a pot of frogs being boiled or a dog being stewed defies description. And sometimes it was an exotically nice smell: that of burned sugar, for example, when I watched a Han vendor of sweets melt bright-colored sugars over a brazier and then, as magically as a sorcerer, somehow blow and spin that fondant into delicate shapes of floss—a flower with pink petals and green leaves, a brown man on a white horse, a dragon with many wings of different colors.

In baskets in the market were more kinds of cha leaves than I had known existed, all aromatic and no two smelling alike; and jars of spices of pungencies new to me; and baskets of flowers of shapes and colors and perfumes I had never encountered before. Even our Inn of the Five Felicities smelled different from all the others we had inhabited, and the landlord told me why. In the plaster of the walls was mixed red meleghèta pepper. It discouraged insects, he said, and I believed him, for the place was singularly clean of vermin. However, this being early summer, I could not verify his other claim: that the hot red pepper made the rooms warmer in winter.

I saw no other Venetian traders in the city, or Genoese or Pisan or any other of our commercial rivals, but we Polos were not the only white men. Or white men, so-called; I remember being asked by a Han scholar, many years later:

"Why are you people of Europe called white? You have more of a brick-red complexion."

Anyway, there were a few other whites in Kashgar, and their brick-redness was easily visible among the Eastern skin colors. During my first day's stroll through the streets, I saw two bearded white men deep in conversation, and one of them was Uncle Mafìo. The other wore the vestments of a Nestorian priest, and had a flat-backed head that identi-fied him as an Armeniyan. I wondered what my uncle could have found to discuss with a heretic cleric, but I did not intrude, only waved a greeting as I went by.

. 2 .

ON one of the days of our enforced idleness, I went outside the city walls to view the camp of the Mongols—what they called their bok—and to exercise what Mongol words I knew, and to learn some new ones.

The first new words I learned were these: "Hui! Nohaigan hori!" and I learned them in a hurry, for they mean "Olà! Call off your dogs!" Packs of large and truculent mastiffs prowled freely through the whole bok, and every yurtu had two or three chained at its entrance. I learned also that I was wise to be carrying my riding quirt, as the Mongols always do, for beating off the curs. And I early learned to leave the quirt outside whenever I entered a yurtu, for to carry it inside would be unmannerly, would offend the human occupants, being an implication that they were no better than dogs.

There were other niceties of behavior to be observed. A stranger must approach a yurtu by walking first between two of the camp fires outside, thus properly purifying himself. Also, one never steps upon the threshold of a yurtu when entering or leaving it, and never whistles while inside it. I learned those things because the Mongols were eager to receive me and to instruct me in their ways and to query me about mine. Indeed, they were almost overwhelmingly eager. If the Mongols have one trait exceeding the ferocity they show to inimical outsiders, it is the inquisitiveness they show about peaceable ones. The single most frequent sound in their speech is "uu," which is not a word but a vocal question mark.

"Sain bina, sain urkek! Good meeting, good brother!" a group of warriors greeted me, and then immediately inquired, "From under what skies do you come, uu?"

"From under the skies of the West," I said, and they widened their eyes as much as those slits would widen, and they exclaimed:

"Hui! Those skies are immense, and they shelter many lands. In your Western country, did you dwell beneath a roof, uu, or a tent, uu?"

"In my native city, a roof. But I have been long upon the road, and living under a tent, when not the open sky."

"Sain!" they cried, smiling broadly. "All men are brothers, is that not true, uu? But those men who dwell beneath tents are even closer brothers, as close as twins. Welcome, twin brother!"

And they bowed and gestured me into the yurtu belonging to one of them. Except for its being portable, it bore little relation to my flimsy sleeping tent. Its interior was only a single round room, but it was a commodious six paces in diameter and its top was well above a standing man's head. The walls were of interlaced wooden laths, vertical walls from ground level to shoulder height, then curving inward to form a dome. At its top center was an open roundel, whence the smoke from the room's heating brazier escaped. The lath framework supported the yurtu's outer covering: overlapping sheets of heavy felt, colored yellow with clay, lashed to the frame by crisscrossed ropes. The furnishings were few and simple, but of good quality: floor carpets and couches of cushions, also all made of brightly colored felt. The yurtu was as sturdy and warm and weather-repellent as any house, but it could be dismantled in an hour and compacted into bundles small and light enough to be carried on a single pack saddle.

My Mongol greeters and I entered the yurtu through the felt-flapped opening which, as in all Mongol edifices, was on its southern side. I was motioned to take a seat on the "man's bed" of the establishment, the one on the north side of the yurtu, where I could sit facing the good-omened south. (Beds for women and children were ranged around the less-auspicious other sides.) I sank down on the felt-covered cushions, and my host pressed into my hand a drinking vessel that was simply a ram's horn. Into it, he poured from a leather bag a rank-smelling and bluish-white thin liquid.

"Kumis," he said it was.

I waited politely until all the men held full horns. Then I did as they did, which was to dip fingers into the kumis and flick a few drops in each direction of the compass. They explained, well enough for me to comprehend, that we were saluting "the fire" to the south, "the air" to the east, "the water" to the west and "the dead" to the north. Then we all raised our horns and drank deeply, and I committed a bad breach of manners. Kumis, I would learn, is to the Mongols a drink as beloved and sacrosanct as qahwah is to the Arabs. I thought it was awful and, unpardonably, I let my face express my opinion. The men all looked distressed. One of them said hopefully that I would grow to like the taste in time, and another said I would like the exhilarating effect of it even more. But my host took my horn and drank it empty, then refilled it from a different leather bag and handed the vessel back to me, saying, "This is arkhi."

The arkhi had a better smell, but I sipped at it cautiously, for it looked just like the kumis. I was gratified that it tasted much better, rather like a wine of medium quality. I nodded and smiled and asked the source of their beverages, for I had seen no vineyards in the vicinity. I was astonished when my host said proudly:

"From the good milk of healthy mares."

Except for their weapons and armor, the Mongols manufacture two things, and only two, and those are made by the Mongol women, and I had just encountered both of them. I was seated on felt-covered pillows in a felt-covered tent, and I was drinking a beverage made from mare's milk. I think the Mongol females are not ignorant of the arts of spinning and weaving, but scorn them as basely effeminate, for these women are veritable Amazons. Anyway, the woven fabrics they wear they buy from other peoples. But they are most expert in beating and matting together the hairs of animals into felts of every weight, from the heavy yurtu coverings to a cloth that is as soft and fine as Welsh flannel.

The Mongol women also disdain every kind of milk except the equine. They do not even give their children to suck from their own breasts, but nourish them from infancy on mare's milk. They do some uncommon things with that fluid, and it did not take me long to overcome my repugnance and become an enthusiastic partaker of all the Mongol milk products. The most prevalent is the mildly intoxicating kumis. It is made by putting fresh mare's milk into a great leather sack, which the women beat with heavy clubs until butter forms. They scoop off the butter and leave the fluid residue to ferment. That kumis then is pungent and sharp to the tongue, with an aftertaste rather like almonds, and a man who drinks enough of it can get estimably drunk. If the sack of milk is beaten longer, until both butter and curds are separated, and the very thin remaining liquid left to ferment, it becomes the more agreeably sweet and wholesome and effervescent sort of kumis called arkhi. And a man can get drunk on that without drinking a very great deal of it.

Besides making use of the butter acquired from the milk, the Mongol women make an ingenious use of the curds. They spread them in the sun and let them dry to a hard cake. That substance, called grut, they crumble into pellets which can be kept indefinitely without spoiling.

Some of it is set aside for the wintertime, when the herd mares give no milk, and some is put into pouches to be carried as emergency rations by men going on the march. The grut has only to be dissolved in water to make a quick and nourishing thick drink.

The actual milking of the herd mares is done by the Mongol men; it constitutes some kind of masculine prerogative and is forbidden to the women. But the subsequent making of kumis and arkhi and grut, like the making of felt, is women's work. In fact, *all* the work in a Mongol bok is done by the women.

"Because the only proper concern of men is the making of war," said my host that day. "And the only proper concern of women is the tending of their men. Uu?"

It cannot be denied that, since a Mongol army goes everywhere accompanied by all the warriors' wives, and extra women for the unmarried men, and the offspring of all those women, the men seldom have to give attention to anything but the fighting. A woman unaided can take down or put up a yurtu, and do all the necessary chores of keeping it supplied and maintained and clean and in good repair, and keeping her man fed and clothed and in fighting humor and cosseted when he is wounded, and keeping his war gear in ready condition, and his horses as well. The children also work, collecting dung or kara for the bok fires, doing herdsman and guard duty. On the few occasions when a battle has gone against the Mongols, and they have had to call up their encamped reserves, the women have been known to seize up weapons and go themselves into the fray, and give good account of themselves.

I regret to say that the Mongol females do not resemble the warrior Amazons of antiquity as portrayed by Western artists. They could almost be mistaken for Mongol males, because they have the same flat face, the broad cheekbones, the leathery complexion, the puffed eyelids making slits of eyes that, when visible, are always redly inflamed. The women may be less burly than the men, but they do not appear so, because they wear equally bulky clothes. Like the men, accustomed to riding for most of their lives, and riding astride, they have the same shambling horseman's gait when afoot. The women do differ in not wearing a wispy beard or mustache, which some of the men do. The men also have their hair hanging long and braided behind, and sometimes shaven on the crown like a priest's tonsure. The women pile their hair up on top of their head in an elaborate fashion—and perhaps they do this just once in a lifetime, because they then varnish it in place with the sap of the wutung tree. And on top of that, they fix a high headpiece called a gugu, a thing made of bark, decorated with bits of colored felt and ribbons. Her cemented hair and her gugu together make a woman some two feet taller than a man, so cumbrously tall that she can enter a yurtu only by bowing her head.

While I sat conversing with my hosts, the woman of the yurtu several times came in and went out, and she had to bend like that every time. But the bending was not a genuflection, and she showed no other signs of servility. She simply bustled about at her work, fetching fresh flagons of kumis and arkhi for us, taking out the emptied ones, and otherwise seeing to our comfort. The man who was her husband addressed her as Nai, which just means Woman, but the other men said courteously Sain Nai. I was interested to see that a Good Woman, although she works like a slave, does not behave like a slave and is not treated as a slave. A Mongol woman does not, like a Muslim woman, have to hide her face behind a chador or hide her whole self in pardah or endure any of the other female humiliations of Islam. She is expected to be chaste, at least after marriage, but no one is appalled if she uses immodest language or laughs at a bawdy story—or tells one, as this Sain Nai did.

She had, unbidden, laid a meal for us on the felt carpet in the middle of the yurtu. And then, equally unbidden, she squatted down to eat with us—and was not forbidden—which surprised and delighted me almost as much as the meal did. She had served a sort of Mongol version of the Venetian scaldavivande: a bowl of boiling-hot broth, a smaller bowl of red-brown sauce and a platter of strips of raw lamb. We all took turns dipping pieces of meat into the scalding broth, cooking it to our taste, dipping it into the piquant sauce and then eating it. The Sain Nai, like the men, dipped her bits of meat barely long enough to warm them, and ate them nearly raw. Any doubts about Mongol women being as robust as their men were dispelled by the sight of that one tearing at the hunks of meat, her hands and teeth and lips all bloodied. One difference: the men ate without talking, giving all their attention to the food; the woman, in the intervals between her devourings, was most voluble.

I gathered that she was making fun of the newest wife her husband had acquired. (There was no limit to the number of women a Mongol man could wed, so long as he could afford to set up each one in a separate yurtu.) The woman acidly remarked that he had been dead drunk when he asked for the hand of this latest one. All the men chuckled, the husband included. And they all snickered and giggled as she listed the new wife's shortcomings, evidently in ribald terms. And they absolutely guffawed and fell about on the carpet when she concluded by suggesting that the new wife probably urinated standing up, like a man.

That was not the most comical thing I had ever heard, but it was certain evidence that the Mongol women enjoy a freedom denied to almost all other females in the East. Except in comeliness, they are more like Venetian women: full of liveliness and good cheer, because they know they are the equals and comrades of their men, only having different functions and responsibilities in life.

The Mongol males do not simply sit idle while their women drudge, or at least do not all the time. After our meal, my hosts walked with me about the bok, showing me the work of men variously occupied at fletching, armoring, currying, cutling and other military crafts. The fletchers, having already laid up a good store of ordinary arrows, were that day forging special arrowheads pierced with holes in a way that, they told me, would make the arrows whistle and shriek in their flight, thereby putting fear in the heart of an enemy. Some of the armorers were thunderously hammering sheets of red-hot iron into the form of breastplates for men and horses, and others were more quietly doing the same with cuirbouilli, heavy leather boiled to softness, then shaped and let dry, when it gets almost as hard as iron. The curriers were making wide waist belts ornamented with colored stones—not to be worn for mere decoration, they told me, but to protect the wearers against thunder and lightning. The cutlers were making wicked shimshirs and daggers, and putting new edges onto old blades, and fitting helves to battle axes, and one of them was forging a lance that had a curious hook projecting from the blade—to yank an enemy from his saddle, the maker told me.

"A fallen foe can be more neatly skewered," added one of my guides. "The earth makes a firmer stop than the air, to pin him against."

"However, we disdain too easy a stroke," said another. "When the foe is unhorsed, we ride back a way from where he lies, and wait for him to cry defiance—or mercy."

"Yes, and then plunge the lance point through his open mouth," said another. "That is a fine feat of aim when done at the gallop."

Those remarks put my hosts in a mood of happy reminiscence, and they went on to recount for me various stories of their people's wars and campaigns and battles. None of those engagements seemed ever to have ended in a defeat for the Mongols, but always a victory and a conquest and a profitable pillage afterward. Of the many tales they told, I recall two with special clarity, for in them the Mongols contended, not just with other men, but with fire and ice.

They told how, once upon a time, during their siege of some city in India, the cowardly but cunning Hindu defenders had tried to rout them by sending against them a cavalry troop of unusual composition. The horses bore riders made of hammered copper in the shape of men, and each of those charging riders was in reality a mobile furnace, the copper shell being filled with burning coals and flaming oil-soaked cotton. Whether the Hindus intended to spread conflagration among the Mongol Horde, or merely consternation, never was known. For the furnace-warriors so singed their own mounts that the horses sensibly bucked them off, and the Mongols rode unimpeded into the city, and slaughtered all its less-incandescent defenders, and made the city their own.

Again, the Mongols waged a campaign against a savage tribe of Samoyeds in the cold far north. Before the battle began, the men of that tribe ran to a nearby river and plunged into it, and then, on emerging, rolled in the dust of the riverbank. They let that coating freeze upon their bodies, then repeated the process several more times, until they were armored all over with thick mud-ice, and judged themselves safe against the Mongols' arrows and blades. Perhaps they were, but the frozen armor made the Samoyeds so thick and clumsy that they could neither fight nor dodge, and the Mongols simply trampled them under the hoofs of their steeds.

So fire and ice had unsuccessfully been used against them, but the Mongols themselves had occasionally used water, and successfully. In the Kazhak country, for example, the Mongols once besieged a city called Kzyl-Orda, and it long held out against them. The word Kazhak means "man without a master," and the Kazhak warriors, whom we in the West call Cossacks, are very nearly as formidable as the Mongols. But the besiegers did not simply sit encircling the city and waiting for it to surrender. They made use of their wait by digging a new channel for the nearby Syr-Daria River. They diverted its course and let it flood Kzyl-Orda and drown every person in it.

"Flooding is a good way of taking a city," said one of the men. "Better than pitching in big boulders or fire arrows. Another good way is the catapulting into it of diseased dead bodies. Kills all the defenders, you see, but leaves the buildings intact for new occupants. The only bad thing about those methods is that they cheat our leaders of their favorite enjoyment—making their celebration banquet on human tables."

"Human tables?" I said, thinking I must have misheard. "Uu?"

They laughed as they explained. The tables were heavy planks supported on the bent backs of kneeling men, the vanquished officers of whatever army they defeated. And they laughed right heartily as they imitated the moans and sobs of those hungry men bowed under the weight of planks laden with high-heaped trenchers of meat and brimming jugs of kumis. And they positively guffawed as they imitated the even more piteous cries of those table-men when the feasting was done, when the Mongol celebrants vaulted onto the tables to do their furious, stamping, leaping victory dances.

In telling their war stories, the men mentioned various leaders under whom they had served, and the leaders all seemed to have had a confusing variety of titles and ranks. But I gradually divined that a Mongol army is really not a shapeless horde, but a model of organization. Of every ten warriors, the strongest and fiercest and most war-experienced is made captain. Similarly, of every ten captains, one is chief, thereby having command of a hundred men. And the ordering continues to progress by tens. Of every ten chief-captains, one is flag-captain, with fully a thousand men rallying to his pennant. Then, of every ten flag-captains, one is the sardar, having command of ten thousand men. The word for "ten thousand" is toman, and that word also means "yak's tail," so the sardar's standard is a plume of yak tail on a pole instead of a flag.

It is a superbly efficient system of command, since any officer at any level from captain up to sardar need confer with only nine other equals when making his plans and decisions and dispositions. There is only one rank higher than sardar. That is orlok, meaning roughly a commander-in-chief, who has under him at least ten sardars and their tomans, making a tuk of a hundred thousand warriors, sometimes more. His power is so awesome that the rank of orlok is seldom given to any man but an actual ruling Ilkhan of the Chinghiz family line. The army then camped in bok about Kashgar was a part of the forces commanded by the Orlok-and-Ilkhan Kaidu.

Any Mongol officer, besides being a good leader in combat, must at other times be what Moses was to the Israelites on the move. Whether he is the captain of ten men or the sardar of ten thousand, he is responsible for the movement and the provisioning of them and their wives and their women and their children and many other camp followers—such as the aged veterans who have no usefulness whatever, but who have the right to refuse retirement into garrison inactivity. The officer is also responsible for the herds of livestock that go afield with his troops: the horses for riding, the beasts for butchering, the yaks or asses or mules or camels for pack carrying. To count just the horses, every Mongol man travels with a string of war steeds and kumis-milk mares that number, on the average, eighteen all together.

Of the various leading officers mentioned by my hosts, the only name I recognized was that of the Ilkhan Kaidu. So I asked if they had ever been led in battle by the Khakhan Kubilai whom I hoped to meet in the not too distant future. They said they had never had the high honor to be directly under his command, but had been fortunate enough to glimpse him once or twice at some remove. They said he was of manly beauty and soldierly bearing and statesmanlike wisdom, but that the most impressive of his qualities was his much-feared temper.

"He can be more fierce even than our fierce Ilkhan Kaidu," said one of them. "No man is eager to raise the wrath of the Khakhan Kubilai. Not even Kaidu."

"Nor the very elements of the earth and sky," said another. "Why, people call out the name of the Khakhan when it thunders—'Kubilai!'— so the lightning will not strike them. I have heard even our fearless Kaidu do that."

"Truly," said another, "in the presence of the Khakhan Kubilai, the wind does not presume to blow too strongly, or the rain to fall harder than a drizzle, or to splash up any mud on his boots. Even the water in his pitcher shrinks fearfully from him."

I commented that that must be rather a nuisance when he was thirsty. That was a sacrilegious remark to make about the most powerful man in the world, but no one present raised an eyebrow, for we were all quite drunk by then. We were seated again in the yurtu, and my hosts had gone through several flagons of kumis, and I had imbibed a goodly amount of their arkhi. The Mongols will not ever constrain themselves to have just one drink, or let a guest have just one, for when the one is downed they exclaim:

"A man cannot walk on one foot!" and they pour another. And *that* one foot requires another, and that another, and so on. The Mongols go even into death still drinking, so to speak. A slain warrior is always buried on the battlefield under a cairn of stones, and he is interred in a seated position, holding his drinking horn in his hand at waist level.

The day had given way to darkness when I decided that I had better stop drinking or risk qualifying for interment myself. I climbed to my feet and thanked my hosts for their hospitality and made my farewells and took my leave of them, while they cried cordially after me, "Mendu, sain urek! A good horse and a wide plain to you, until we meet again!"

I was not on a horse, but afoot, and therefore staggered somewhat. But that excited no comment from anybody, as I weaved through the

bok and back through the Kashgar gate and through the scented streets
to the karwansarai of the Five Felicities. I lurched into our chamber, and
stopped short, staring. A large, black-garbed, black-bearded priest stood
there. It took me a moment to recognize him as my Uncle Mafìo and, in
my fuddled condition, all I could think was, "Dear God, what depth of
depravity has he sunk to now? Uu?"

<h1 style="text-align:center">· 3 ·</h1>

I slumped onto a bench and sat grinning as my uncle preened piously in
his cassock. My father, sounding peeved, quoted an old saying: "The
clothes make the man, but a habit does not make a monk. Let alone a
priest, Mafìo. Where did you get it?"

"I bought it from that Father Boyajian. You remember him, Nico,
from when we were here last."

"Yes. An Armeniyan would probably peddle the Host. Why did
you not make him an offer for that?"

"A sacramental wafer would mean nothing to the Ilkhan Kaidu, but
this disguise will. His own chief wife, the Ilkhatun, is a converted
Christian—at least a Nestorian. So I am trusting that Kaidu will respect
this cloth."

"Why? You do not. I have heard you criticize the Church in utterances that verge on heresy. And now this. It is blasphemy!"

Uncle Mafìo protested, "The cassock is not in itself a liturgical garment. Anybody can wear one, as long as he does not pretend to its
sanctity. I do not. I could not, if I wanted to. Deuteronomy, you know:
'An eunuch, whose testicles are broken, shall not enter into the Church of
the Lord.' Capòn mal caponà."

"Mafìo! Do not try to justify your impiety with self-pity."

"I am only saying that if Kaidu mistakes me for a priest, I see no
need to correct him. Boyajian gives it as his opinion that a Christian may
employ any subterfuge in dealing with a heathen."

"I do not accept a Nestorian reprobate as an authority on Christian
behavior."

"Had you rather accept Kaidu's decree? Confiscation, or worse?
Look, Nico. He has Kubilai's letter; he knows that we were bidden to
bring priests to Kithai. Without any priests, we are mere vagrants wandering through Kaidu's domain with a most tempting lot of valuables. I
will not claim that I am a priest, but if Kaidu supposes it—"

"That white collar never protected anybody's neck from a heads-
man's ax."

"It is better than nothing. Kaidu can do as he pleases to ordinary
travelers, but if he slays or detains a priest, the ripples will eventually
reach Kubilai's court. And a priest whom Kubilai sent for? We know that
Kaidu is temerarious, but I doubt that he is suicidally so." Uncle Mafìo

turned to me. "What do you say, Marco? Observe your uncle as a reverend father. How do I look?"

"Magnissifent," I said thickly.

"Hm," he murmured, regarding me more closely. "It will help, yes, if Kaidu is as drunk as you are."

I started to say that he probably would be, but I fell suddenly asleep where I sat.

The next morning, my uncle was again wearing the cassock when he came to the karwansarai's dining table, and my father again began berating him. Nostril and I were present, but did not participate in the dispute. To the Muslim slave it was, I suppose, a matter of total unconcern. And I stayed silent because my head was hurting. But both the argument and our breaking of our fast were interrupted by the arrival of a Mongol messenger from the bok. The man, dressed in splendid war regalia, swaggered into the inn like a newcome conqueror, strode directly to our table and, without any courtesy of greeting, said to us—in Farsi to make sure we all understood:

"Arise and come with me, dead men, for the Ilkhan Kaidu would hear your last words!"

Nostril gasped so that he choked on whatever he was eating, and began to cough, meanwhile goggling his eyes with terror. My father pounded him on the back and said, "Be not alarmed, good slave. That is the usual wording of a summons from a Mongol lord. It portends no harm."

"Or it does not necessarily," my uncle amended. "I am still glad that I thought of this disguise."

"Too late to make you doff it now," muttered my father, for the messenger was pointing imperiously toward the outer door. "I just hope, Mafìo, that you will temper your profane performance with priestly decorum."

Uncle Mafìo raised his right hand to each of the three of us in the sign of benediction, smiled beatifically and said with utmost unction, "Si non caste, tamen caute."

The mock-pious gesture and the mock-solemn Latin play on words were so typical of my uncle's mischievously cheerful bravado that I—even feeling as sour as I did—had to laugh aloud. Granted, Mafìo Polo had some lamentable shortcomings as a Christian and as a man, but he was a good companion to have standing by in an uneasy situation. The Mongol messenger glowered at me when I laughed, and he barked his command at us again, and we all got up and followed him from the building at a quick march.

It was raining that day, which did not do much to lighten my mal di capo, or to make more cheerful our trudge through the streets and beyond the city wall and through the packs of yapping and snarling dogs of the Mongol bok. We hardly raised our heads to look around until the messenger shouted, "Halt!" and directed us to pass between the two fires burning before the entrance to Kaidu's yurtu.

I had not been near it on my previous visit to the camp, and now I realized that *this* was the sort of yurtu which must have inspired the

Western word "horde." It would indeed have encompassed a whole
horde of the ordinary yurtu tents, for this was a grand pavilion. It was
almost as high and as big around as the karwansarai in which we were
residing; but that was a solidly built edifice, and this was entirely of
yellow-clayed felt, supported by tent poles and stakes and braided horse-
hair ropes. Several mastiffs roared and lunged against their chains at the
south-facing entrance, and on either side of that flapped opening hung
elaborately embroidered felt panels. The yurtu was no palace, but it
certainly overshadowed the lesser ones of the bok. And next to it rested
the wagon which transported it from place to place, for Kaidu's pavilion
was usually moved intact, not dismantled and bundled. The wagon was
the most huge I have ever seen anywhere: a flat bed of planks, as big as
a meadow, balanced on an axle like a tree trunk and with wheels like
mill wheels. The drawing of it, I learned later, required fully twenty-two
yaks hitched in two wide spans of eleven abreast. (The drafters had to
be placid yaks or oxen; no horses or camels would have worked in such
close proximity.)

The messenger ducked under the yurtu's flap to announce us to his
lord, emerged again and jerked his arm to order us inside. Then, as we
passed him, he barred Nostril's way, growling, "No slaves!" and kept him
outside. There was a reason for that. The Mongols regard themselves as
naturally superior to all other freemen in the world, even kings and such,
so any man who is held inferior by *their* inferiors is considered unworthy
even of contempt.

The Ilkhan Kaidu regarded us in silence as we crossed the brilliantly
carpeted and pillow-furnished interior, to where he sat sprawled on a
heap of furs—all gorgeously striped and spotted: evidently the pelts of
tigers and pards—on a dais that set him above us. He was dressed in
battle armor of polished metals and leathers, and wore on his head an
earflapped hat of karakul. He had eyebrows that looked like detached
bits of the kinky black karakul, and not small bits either. Under them, his
slit eyes were red-shot, seemingly inflamed by rage at the very sight of
us. On his either side stood a warrior, as handsomely caparisoned as the
man who had fetched us. One held a lance erect, the other held a sort of
canopy on a pole over Kaidu's head, and both stood as rigid as statues.

We three made a slow approach. In front of the furry throne, we
made a dignified slight bow, all together, as if we had rehearsed it, and
looked up at Kaidu, waiting for him to make the first indication of the
mood of this meeting. He continued for some moments to stare at us, as
if we were vermin that had crawled out from under the yurtu's carpet-
ings. Then he did something disgusting. He made a hawking noise from
deep in his throat, bringing up a great wad of phlegm into his mouth.
Then he languidly unsprawled himself from his couch and stood upright
and turned to the guardsman at his right, and with his thumb pressed
the man's chin so that his mouth opened. Then Kaidu spat his hawked-
up gob of substance directly into the man's mouth and thumbed it shut
again—the warrior's expression and rigidity never changing—and languidly resumed his seat, his eyes again on us and glittering evilly.

It had clearly been a gesture intended to awe us with his power and arrogance and uncordiality, and it would have served to cow me, I think. But at least one of us—Mafìo Polo—was not impressed. When Kaidu spoke his first words, in the Mongol language and in a harsh voice: "Now, interlopers—" he got no further, for my uncle daringly interrupted, in the same language:

"First, if it please the Ilkhan, we will sing a praise to God for having conducted us safely across so many lands into the Lord Kaidu's august presence." And, to the astonishment of myself—probably also of my father and the Mongols—he began bawling out the old Christmas hymn:

> A solis orbu cardine
> Et usque terre limitem . . .

"It does *not* please the Ilkhan," Kaidu said through his teeth, when my uncle drew breath at that point. But my father and I, emboldened, had joined in for the next two lines:

> Christum canamus principem
> Natum Maria virgine . . .

"*Enough!*" bellowed Kaidu, and our voices trailed off. Fixing his red eyes on Uncle Mafìo, the Ilkhan said, "You are a Christian priest." He said it flatly—loathingly, in fact—so my uncle did not have to take it as a question, which would have required him to deny it.

He said only, "I am here at the behest of the Khan of All Khans," and indicated the paper Kaidu was holding clenched in one hand.

"Hui, yes," said Kaidu, with an acid smile. He unfolded the document in a manner suggesting that it was filthy to the touch. "At the behest of my esteemed cousin. I notice that my cousin wrote this ukaz on yellow paper, as the Chin emperors used to do. Kubilai and I conquered that decadent empire, but he more and more imitates its effete customs. Vakh! He has become no better than a Kalmuk! And our old war god Tengri is no longer good enough for him, either, it seems. Now he must import womanish Ferenghi priests."

"Merely to enlarge his knowledge of the world, Lord Kaidu," said my father, in a conciliatory voice. "Not to propagate any new—"

"The only way to know the world," Kaidu said savagely, "is to seize it and wring it!" He flicked his lurid gaze from one to another of us. "Do you dispute that, uu?"

"To dispute the Lord Kaidu," murmured my father, "would be like eggs attacking stones, as the saying goes."

"Well, at least you manifest some good sense," the Ilkhan said grudgingly. "I trust you also have the sense to realize that this ukaz is dated some years ago and some seven thousand li distant from here. Even if cousin Kubilai has not totally forgotten it by now, I am in no way bound to honor it."

My uncle murmured, even more meekly than my father had done, "It is said: How can a tiger be subject to the law?"

"Exactly," grunted the Ilkhan. "If I choose, I can regard you as mere trespassers. Ferenghi interlopers with no good intent. And I can condemn you to summary execution."

"Some say," murmured my father, more meekly yet, "that tigers are really the agents of Heaven, appointed to chase down those who have somehow eluded their deserved date with death."

"Yes," said the Ilkhan, looking slightly exasperated by all this agreement and mollification. "On the other hand, even a tiger can sometimes be lenient. Much as I detest my cousin for abandoning his Mongol heritage—much as I despise the increasing degeneracy of his court—I would let you go there and join his retinue. I could, if I so choose."

My father clapped his hands, as if in admiration of the Ilkhan's wisdom, and said with delight, "Clearly the Lord Kaidu remembers, then, the old Han story of the clever wife Ling."

"Of course," said the Ilkhan. "It was in my mind as I spoke." He unbent enough to smile frigidly at my father. My father smiled warmly back. There was an interval of silence. "However," Kaidu resumed, "that story is told in many variations. In which version did you hear it, uu, trespasser?"

My father cleared his throat and declaimed, "Ling was wife to a rich man who was overfond of wine, and was forever sending her to the wine shop to fetch bottles for him. The lady Ling, fearing for his health, would deliberately prolong the errands, or water the wine, or hide it, to keep him from drinking so much. At which her husband would be wroth and would beat her. Finally, two things happened. The lady Ling fell out of love with her husband, although he was rich, and she noticed how handsome was the wine-shop clerk, although he was a humble trades man. Thereafter, she willingly bought wine at her husband's command, and even poured it for him, and urged it on him. Eventually the husband died in a drunkard's convulsions, and she inherited all his wealth, and she married the wine-shop clerk, and they both were rich and happy ever after."

"Yes," said the Ilkhan. "That is the correct story." There was another silence, and a longer one. Then Kaidu said, more to himself than to us, "Yes, the drunkard caused his own rot, and others helped it along, until he rotted through and fell, and was supplanted by a better. It is legendary, and it is salutary."

Just as quietly, my uncle said, "Also legendary is the tiger's patience in the tracking of his prey."

Kaidu shook himself, as if awakening from a reverie, and said, "A tiger can be lenient as well as patient. I have already said so. I shall therefore let you all proceed in peace. I will even give you an escort against the hazards of the road. And you, priest, for all I care, you may convert cousin Kubilai and his entire court to your enfeebling religion. I hope you do. I wish you success."

"One nod of the head," my father exclaimed, "is heard farther than a thunderclap. You have done a good thing, Lord Kaidu, and its echoes will long resound."

"Just one thing," said the Ilkhan, again using a tone of severity. "I am told by my Lady Ilkhatun, who is a Christian and should know, that

Christian priests maintain a vow of poverty, and possess nothing of material value. But I am also informed that you men travel with horses heavy-laden with treasure."

My father threw my uncle a look of annoyance, and said, "Some baubles, Lord Kaidu. They belong to no priest, but are destined for your cousin Kubilai. They are tokens of tribute from the Shah of Persia and the Sultan of India Aryana."

"The Sultan is my liege subject," said Kaidu. "He has no right to give away what belongs to me. And the Shah is a subject of my cousin the Ilkhan Abagha, who is no friend to me. Whatever he sends is contraband, subject to confiscation. Do you understand me, uu?"

"But, Lord Kaidu, we have promised to deliver—"

"A broken promise is no more than a broken pot. The potter can always make more. Have no concern for your promises, Ferenghi. Just bring your packhorses at this hour tomorrow, here to my yurtu, and let me see which of the baubles catch my fancy. I may let you keep some few of them. Do you understand, uu?"

"Lord Kaidu—"

"*Uu! Do you understand?*"

"Yes, Lord Kaidu."

"Since you understand, then obey!" He abruptly stood up, signaling the end of the audience.

We bowed our way out of the great yurtu, and collected Nostril from where he waited outside, and we started back through the rain and the mud underfoot, this time unaccompanied, and my uncle said to my father:

"I think we did rather well, Nico, in concert there. Especially adroit of you to remember that Ling story. I never heard it before."

"Neither did I," my father said drily. "But surely the Han have some such instructive tale, among the many they do have."

I opened my mouth for the first time. "Something else you said, Father, gave me an idea. I will meet you back at the inn."

I parted from them, to go and call on my Mongol hosts of the day before. I requested an introduction to one of their armorers, and got it, and asked the man at the forge if I might borrow for a day one of his yet-unhammered sheets of metal. He graciously found for me a piece of copper that was long and broad, but thin, so it wobbled and rippled and thrummed as I carried it to the karwansarai. My father and uncle paid no attention as I carried it into our room and leaned it against the wall, for they were again arguing.

"All the fault of that cassock," said my father. "Your being an impoverished priest gave Kaidu the notion of impoverishing us."

"Nonsense, Nico," said my uncle. "He would have found some other excuse, if that had not occurred to him. What we must do is offer him freely something from our hoard, and hope he will ignore the rest."

"Well . . . ," said my father, thinking. "Suppose we give him our cods of musk. At least they are ours to give."

"Oh, come, Nico! To that sweaty barbarian? Musk is for making fine perfume. You might as well give Kaidu a powder puff, for all the use he would have of it."

They kept on like that, but I stopped listening, for I had my own idea, and I went to explain to Nostril the part he would play in it.

The next day, a day of only drizzling rain, Nostril loaded two of the three packhorses with our cargo of valuables—we of course always kept them safe inside our chambers whenever we lodged in a karwansarai—and also roped my sheet of metal onto one of the horses, and led them for us to the Mongol bok. There, when we entered the Ilkhan's yurtu, he stayed outside to unload the goods, and Kaidu's guardsmen began carrying them in and stripped off their protective wrappers.

"Hui!" Kaidu exclaimed, as he started to inspect the various objects. "These engraved golden platters are superb! A gift from the Shah Zaman, you said, uu?"

"Yes," my father said coldly, and my uncle added, in a melancholy voice, "A boy named Aziz once strapped them on his feet to cross a quicksand," and I took out a kerchief and loudly blew my nose.

There came from outside a low, mumbling, bumbling mutter of sound. The Ilkhan looked up, surprised, saying, "Was that thunder, uu? I thought there was only a sprinkle of rain. . . ."

"I beg to inform the Great Lord Kaidu," said one of his guardsmen, bowing low, "that the day is gray and wet, but there are no thunderclouds to be seen."

"Curious," Kaidu muttered, and put down the golden dishes. He rummaged among the many other things accumulating in the tent and, finding a particularly elegant ruby necklace, again exclaimed, "Hui!" He held it up to admire it. "The Ilkhatun will thank you personally for this."

"Thank the Sultan Kutb-ud-Din," said my father.

I blew my nose into my kerchief. The rippling rumble of thunder came again from outside, and somewhat louder now. The Ilkhan started so that he dropped the string of rubies, and his mouth closed and opened soundlessly—but framing a word I could read from his lips—and then said aloud, "There it is again! But thunder without thunderclouds . . . uu . . . ?"

When a third item caught his greedy eye, a bolt of fine Kashmir cloth, I barely gave him time to cry "Hui!" before I blew my nose, and the thunder gave a menacing grumble, and he jerked his hand away as if the cloth had burned him, and again he mouthed the word, and my father and uncle gave me an odd look.

"Pardon, Lord Kaidu," I said. "I think this thunder weather has given me a head cold."

"You are pardoned," he said offhandedly. "Aha! And this, is this one of those famous Persian qali carpets, uu?"

Nose blow. Veritable clamor of thunder. His hand again jerked away and his lips convulsively made the word, and he glanced fearfully skyward. Then he looked around at us, his slit eyes almost opened to roundness, and he said:

"I was but toying with you!"

"My lord?" inquired Uncle Mafìo, whose own lips were twitching now.

"Toying! Jesting! Teasing you!" Kaidu said, almost pleadingly. "A tiger sometimes toys with his quarry, when he is not hungry. And I am not hungry! Not for tawdry acquisitions. I am Kaidu, and I own countless mou of land and innumerable li of the Silk Road and more cities than I have hairs and more subject people than a gobi has pebbles. Did you really think I lack for rubies and gold dishes and Persian qali, uu?" He feigned a hearty laugh, "Ah, ha, ha, ha!" even bending double to pound his meaty fists on his massive knees. "But I had you worried, did I not, uu? You took my toying in earnest."

"Yes, you truly fooled us, Lord Kaidu," said my uncle, managing to subdue his own incipient merriment.

"And now the thunder has ceased," said the Ilkhan, listening. "Guards! Wrap up all these things again and reload them on the horses of these elder brothers."

"Why, thank you, Lord Kaidu," said my father, but his twinkling eyes were on me.

"And here, here is my cousin's letter of ukaz," said the Ilkhan, pressing it into my uncle's hand. "I return it to you, priest. Take yourself and your religion and these paltry baubles to Kubilai. Perhaps he is a collector of such trinkets, but Kaidu is not. Kaidu does not take, he gives! Two of the best warriors of my personal pavilion guard will attend you to your karwansarai, and they will ride with you whenever you are ready to continue your journey eastward. . . ."

I slipped out of the yurtu as the guardsmen began to carry out the rejected goods, and slipped around to the back side of it, where Nostril stood holding the metal sheet by one edge and waiting to flap it again whenever he heard me blow my nose. I gave him the signal employed throughout the East to mean "purpose accomplished"—showing him my fist with upraised thumb—took the piece of copper from him and trotted across the bok to return it to the armorer, and got back to the Ilkhan's yurtu by the time the horses were reloaded.

Kaidu stood in the entrance of his pavilion, waving and shouting, "A good horse and a wide plain to you!" until we were out of earshot.

Then my uncle said, in Venetian, not to be overheard by the two Mongol escorts leading our horses and theirs, "Verily, we have all done well in concert. Nico, you only invented a good story. Marco invented a thunder god!" and he flung his arms about my shoulders and Nostril's, and gave us both a hearty squeeze.

· 4 ·

WE had now come so far around the world, and into lands so very little known, that our Kitab was no longer of the slightest use to us. Clearly, the mapmaker al-Idrisi had never ventured into these regions, and apparently never had met anyone who had, from whom he could ask even hearsay information. His maps rounded off the eastern edge of Asia much too shortly and abruptly at the great ocean called the Sea of Kithai. Thus they gave the false impression that Kashgar was at no enormous distance from our destination, Kubilai's capital city of Khanbalik, which itself lies well inland of that ocean. But, as my father and uncle warned me, and as I wearily verified for myself, Kashgar and Khanbalik in fact are a whole half a continent apart—half of a continent immeasurably bigger than al-Idrisi had imagined it to be. We journeyers had almost exactly as far yet to go *as we had already come* from Suvediye away back on the Levant shore of the Mediterranean.

Distance is distance, no matter whether it is calculated in the number of human footsteps or the number of days on horseback required to get over it. Nevertheless, here in Kithai, any distance always *sounded* longer, because here it was counted not in farsakhs but in li. The farsakh, comprising about two and a half of our Western miles, was invented by Persians and Arabs who, having always been far travelers, are accustomed to think in expansive terms of measurement. But the li, which is only about one-third of a mile, was invented by the Han, and they are for the most part homebodies. The common Han peasant in his lifetime probably never ventures more than a few li away from the farm village where he was born. So I suppose, to his mind, a third of a mile is a far distance. Anyway, when we Polos left Kashgar, I was still accustomed to calculating in farsakhs, so it did not much dismay me to say to myself that we had only some eight or nine hundred of them to go to Khanbalik. But when I gradually got used to calculating in li, the number of them was appalling, some six thousand seven hundred from Kashgar to Khanbalik. If I had not previously appreciated the vastness of the Mongol Empire, I surely did now, as I contemplated the vastness of just its central nation of Kithai.

There were two ceremonies attendant on our departure from Kashgar. Our Mongol escorts insisted that our horses—now numbering six mounts and three pack animals—must be treated to a certain ritual for protection against the "azghun" of the trail. Azghun means "desert voices," and I gathered that those were some sort of goblins which infest the wilderness. So the warriors brought from their bok a man called a shamàn—what they would describe as a priest and we would describe as a sorcerer. The wild-eyed and paint-daubed shamàn, who looked rather like a goblin himself, mumbled some incantations and poured some drops of blood on the heads of our horses and pronounced them protected. He offered to do the same for us unbelievers, but we politely declined on the ground that we had our own accompanying priest.

The other ceremony was the settling of our bill with the landlord of the karwansarai, and that involved more time and fuss than the sorcery had. My father and uncle did not simply accept and pay the innkeeper's account, but haggled with him over every single item. And the bill did include every single item of our stay—the space we had occupied in the inn and our beasts had occupied in the stable, the quantity of food eaten

by ourselves and grain eaten by our horses, the amounts of water we and
they had swallowed, and the cha leaves steeped in ours, the kara fuel
that had been burned for our comfort, the amount of lamplight we had
enjoyed and the measures of oil required for that—everything but the air
we had breathed. As the discussion heated up, it was joined by the inn's
cook, or Governor of the Kettle, as he styled himself, and the man who
had served our meals, or the Steward of the Table, and they two began
vociferously adding up the number of paces they had walked and the
weights they had carried and the amounts of efficiency and sweat and
genius they had expended in our behalf. . . .

But I soon realized that this was not a contest of larceny on the
landlord's part versus outrage on ours. It was merely an expected
formality—another custom derived from the complicated comportment
of the Han people—a ceremony that is so enjoyed by both creditor and
debtor that they can string it out to hours of eloquent argument, mutual
abuse and reconciliation, claim and denial, refusal and compromise, until
eventually they agree to agree, and the account is paid, and they emerge
better friends than they were before. When we finally rode away from
the inn, the landlord, the Kettle Governor, the Table Steward and all the
other servants stood at the door, waving and calling after us the Han
farewell: "Man zou," which means, "Leave us only if you must."

The Silk Road forks into two as it goes eastward from Kashgar. This
is because there is a desert directly to the east of the city, a dry, peeling,
curling desert, like a plain of shattered yellow pottery, a desert as big as
a nation, and just the name of it gives good reason to avoid it, for its
name is Takla Makan, meaning "once in, never out." So a traveler on the
Silk Road can choose the branch which loops northeasterly around that
desert or the one looping southeast of it, which is the one we took. The
road led us from one to the next of a chain of habitable oases and small
farm villages, about a day's journey apart. Always off to our left were the
lion-tawny sands of the Takla Makan and, to our right, the snow-topped
Kun-lun mountain range, beyond which, to the south, lies the high land
of To-Bhot.

Although we were skirting clear of the desert, along its pleasantly
verdant and well-watered rimlands, this was high summertime, so we
had to endure a lot of desert weather that edged over from it. The only
really tolerable days were those on which a wind blew down from the
snowy mountains. Most frequently the days were windless, but not still,
for on those days the nearness of the smoldering desert made the air
about us seem to tremble. The sun might have been a blunt instrument,
a brass bludgeon, beating on the air so that it rang shrill with heat. And
when occasionally there came a wind from the desert, it brought the
desert with it. The Takla Makan then stood on end—making moving
towers of pale-yellow dust, and those towers gradually turned brown,
getting darker and heavier until they toppled over onto us, turning high
noon to an oppressive dusk, seething viciously and stinging the skin like
a beating with twig brooms.

That dun-colored dust of the lion-colored Takla Makan is known
everywhere in Kithai, even by untraveled people who have no least

suspicion of the desert's existence. The dust rustles through the streets of Khanbalik, thousands of li away, and powders the flowers in the gardens of Xan-du, farther yet, and scums the lake waters of Hang-zho, farther yet, and is cursed by the tidy housekeepers of every other Kithai city I ever was in. And once, when I sailed in a ship far upon the Sea of Kithai, not just out of touch but out of sight of the shore, I found that same dust sifting down upon the deck. A visitor to Kithai might later lose his memory of everything else he saw and experienced there, but he will forever feel the pale dun dust settling on him, never letting him forget that once he walked that lion-colored land.

The buran, as the Mongols call a dust storm of the Takla Makan, has a curious effect which I never encountered in any such storm in any other desert. While a buran was buffeting us, and for a long while after it had blown on past, it somehow made the hair of our heads stand fantastically on end, and the hairs of our beards bristle like quills, and our clothes crackle as if they had turned to stiff paper, and if we chanced to touch another person we saw a snapping spark and felt a small jolt like that from cat fur briskly rubbed.

Also, the buran's passing, like the passing of a celestial broom, would leave the night air immaculately clean and clear. The stars came out in multitudes untellable, infinitely more of them than I ever saw elsewhere, every tiniest one as bright as a gem and the familiar bigger stars so big that they looked globular, like little moons. Meanwhile, the actual moon up there, even if it was in the phase we would ordinarily call "new"—only a fragile fingernail crescent of it lighted—was nevertheless visible in its whole roundness, a bronze full moon cradled in the new moon's silver arms.

And on such a night, if we looked out over the Takla Makan from our camping or lodging place, we could see even stranger lights, blue ones, bobbing and dipping and twinkling over the surface of the desert, sometimes one or two, sometimes whole bevies of them. They might have been lamps or candles carried about by persons in a distant karwan camp out there, but we knew they were not. They were too blue to be flames of fire, and they winked on and off too abruptly to have been kindled by any human agency, and their presence, like that of the day's buran, made our hair and beards stir uneasily. Besides all that, it was well-known that no human beings ever traveled or camped in the Takla Makan. Not living human beings. Not willingly.

The first time we saw the lights, I inquired of our escorts what they might be. The Mongol named Ussu said, in a hushed voice, "The beads of Heaven, Ferenghi."

"But what makes them?"

The one named Donduk said curtly, "Be silent and listen, Ferenghi."

I did, and, even as far from the desert as we were standing, I heard faint sighs and sobs and soughings, as if small night winds were fitfully blowing. But there was no wind.

"The azghun, Ferenghi," Ussu explained. "The beads and the voices always come together."

"Many an inexperienced traveler," added Donduk, in a supercilious way, "has seen the lights and heard the cries, and thought them to be a fellow traveler in trouble, and gone seeking to help, and been lured by them away, not ever to be seen again. They are the azghun, the desert voices, and the mysterious beads of Heaven. Hence the desert's name—once in, never out."

I wish I could claim that I divined the cause of those manifestations, or at least a better explanation of them than wicked goblins, but I did not. I knew that the azghun and the lights occurred only after the passing of a buran, and a buran was only a mighty mass of dry sand blowing about. I wondered, did that friction have something in common with the rubbing of a cat's fur? But out there in the desert, the sand grains had nothing to rub against except each other. . . .

So, baffled by that mystery, I applied my mind to a smaller but more accessible one. Why did Ussu and Donduk, though they knew all our names and had no trouble saying them, always address us Polos indiscriminately as Ferenghi? Ussu spoke the word amiably enough; he seemed to enjoy traveling with us, as a change from boring garrison duty back at Kaidu's bok. But Donduk spoke the word distastefully, seeming to regard this journey as a nursemaid attention to us unworthy persons. I rather liked Ussu, and did not like Donduk, but they always were together, so I asked them both: why Ferenghi?

"Because you *are* Ferenghi," said Ussu, looking puzzled, as if I had asked a witless question.

"But you also call my father Ferenghi. And my uncle."

"He and he is Ferenghi also," said Ussu.

"But you call Nostril Nostril. Is that because he is a slave?"

"No," said Donduk scornfully. "Because he is not Ferenghi."

"Elder Brothers," I persisted. "I am trying to find out what Ferenghi means."

"Ferenghi means only Ferenghi," snapped Donduk, and threw up his hands in disgust, and so did I.

But that mystery I finally *did* figure out: Ferenghi was only their pronunciation of Frank. Their people must first have heard Westerners call themselves Franks eight centuries ago, in the time of the Frankish Empire, when some of the Mongols' own ancestors, then called Bulgars and Hiung-nu, or Huns, invaded the West and gave their names to Bulgaria and Hungary. Ever since then, apparently, the Mongols have called any white Westerner a Ferenghi, no matter his real nationality. Well, it was no more inaccurate than the calling of all Mongols Mongols, though they were really of many different origins.

Ussu and Donduk told me, for instance, how their Mongol cousins the Kirghiz had come into existence. The name derived from the Mongol words kirk kiz, they said, meaning "forty virgins," because sometime in the remote past there had existed in some remote place that many virgin females, unlikely though it might seem to us moderns, and all forty of them had got impregnated by the foam blown from an enchanted lake, and from the resultant miraculous mass birth had descended all the people now called Kirghiz. That was interesting, but I found more interesting another thing Ussu and Donduk told me about the Kirghiz. They

lived in the perpetually frozen Sibir, far north of Kithai, and perforce had
invented two ingenious methods of getting about those harsh lands.
They would strap to the bottom of their boots bits of highly polished
bone, on which they could glide far and fast upon the ice of frozen
waters. Or they would similarly strap on long boards like barrel staves, to
skim far and fast over the snowy wastes.

The very next farm village on our way was populated by yet another breed of Mongols. Some of the communities on that stretch of the
Silk Road were peopled by Uighurs, those nationalities "allied" to the
Mongols, and others were peopled by Han folk, and Ussu and Donduk
had not made any comment about them. But when we came to this
particular village, they told us the people were Kalmuk Mongols, and
they spat the name, thus: "Kalmuk! Vakh!"—*vakh* being a Mongol noise
to register sheer disgust, and the Kalmuk were disgusting, right enough.
They were the filthiest human creatures I ever saw outside of India. To
depict just one aspect of their filthiness, let me say this: not only did they
never wash their bodies, they never even took off their clothes, day or
night. When a Kalmuk's outer garment got too worn to be serviceable,
he or she did not discard it, but simply donned a new one over it, and
continued wearing layers upon layers of ragged clothes until the under-
most gradually rotted and shredded away from underneath, like a sort of
ghastly scurf of the crotch. I will not attempt to say how they smelled.

But the name Kalmuk, I learned, is not a national or tribal designation. It is only the Mongol word meaning one who stays, or one who settles down in any place. All normal Mongols being nomads, they have a
deep disdain for any of their race who ceases roaming and takes up a
fixed abode. In the majority opinion, any Mongol who becomes a Kalmuk
is doomed to degeneracy and depravity, and if the Kalmuk people I saw
and smelled were typical, then the majority have good reason to despise
them. And now I recalled having heard the Ilkhan Kaidu speak slight-
ingly of the Khakhan Kubilai as "no better than a Kalmuk." Vakh, I
thought, if I find that he is, I shall turn around and go straight back to
Venice.

However, despite my awareness that the word Mongol was a too
general term for a multiplicity of peoples, I found it convenient to go on
using the name. I soon realized also that the other, the original, inhabitants of Kithai were not all Han, either. There were nationalities called
Yi and Hui and Naxi and Hezhe and Miao and God knows how many
others, of skin colors ranging from ivory to bronze. But, as with the
Mongols, I continued to think of all those other nationalities as Han. For
one reason, their languages all sounded very much alike to me. For
another, every one of those races regarded every other as inferior, and so
called each other by their various words meaning Dog People. For still
another reason, they all called any foreigner, including me, a name even
less deserved than Frank. In Han and in every other of their singsong
languages and dialects, any outlander is a Barbarian.

As we rode farther and farther along the Silk Road, it became
increasingly crowded with traffic—groups and trains of traveling traders
like ourselves, individual farmers and herders and artisans taking their

wares to market towns, Mongol families and clans and whole boks on the move. I remembered how Isidoro Priuli, our clerk of the Compagnia Polo, had remarked, just before we left Venice, that the Silk Road had been a busy thoroughfare from the most ancient times, and now I saw reason to believe him. Over the years and centuries and maybe millennia, the traffic on that road had worn it down far below the level of the surrounding terrain. In places it was a broad trench so deep that a farmer in his nearby bean patch might see no more of the passing processions than the flick of a cart driver's upraised whip. And down inside that trench, the cartwheels' ruts had worn so deep that every cart now had to go where the ruts went. A carter never had to worry about his vehicle's overturning, but neither could he pull it to one side when he needed to relieve himself. To change direction on the road—say, to turn off to some side-village destination—a driver had to keep going until he came to a junction where there were diverging ruts in which to set his wheels.

The carts used in that region of Kithai were of a peculiar type. They had immensely big wheels with knobbed rims, standing so high that they often reached above the wooden or canvas cart roof. Perhaps the wheels had had to be built bigger and bigger over the years just so their axles would clear the hump of ground between the road ruts. Each such wagon also had an awning projecting from its top front, to cover the driver from inclement weather, and that awning was considerately extended on poles far enough so that it also sheltered the team of horses, oxen or asses pulling the wagon.

I had heard much about the cleverness and inventiveness and ingenuity of the inhabitants of Kithai, but I now had cause to wonder if those qualities might be overrated. Very well, every cart had an awning to shelter its draft animals as well as its driver, and maybe that was a clever invention. But every wagon also had to carry several sets of spare axles for its wheels. That was because every separate province of Kithai has its own idea of how far apart a cart's wheels should be, and of course its local wagons have long ago put the roads' ruts that far apart. So the distance between the ruts is wide, for example, on the stretch of Silk Road that goes through Sin-kiang, but narrow on the road through the province of Tsing-hai, wide again but not quite so wide in Ho-nan, and so on. A carter traversing any considerable length of the Silk Road must stop every so often, laboriously take the wheels and axles off his wagon, put on axles of a different breadth and replace the wheels.

Every draft animal wore a bag slung under its tail by a webbing around its hindquarters, to collect its droppings while on the move. That was not to keep the road clean or to spare annoyance to people coming along behind. We were by now out of the region where the earth was full of burnable kara rock, free for the taking, so every carter carefully hoarded his animals' dung to fuel the camp fire on which he would prepare his mutton and miàn and cha.

We saw many herds of sheep being driven to market or to pasture, and the sheep too wore peculiar backside appendages. The sheep were of the fat-tailed breed, and that breed is to be seen all over the East, but

I had never seen any so fat-tailed as these. A sheep's clublike tail might weigh ten or twelve pounds, nearly a tenth of its whole body weight. It was a genuine burden to the creature, and also that tail is considered the best part of the animal for eating. So each sheep had a light rope harness to drag a little plank behind it, and on that trailing shelf its tail rode safe from being bruised or unnecessarily dirtied. We saw also many herds of swine being driven, and it seemed to me that they could have used some expenditure of inventiveness, too. The pigs of Kithai are also a distinctive breed, being long in the body and ludicrously swaybacked, so that their bellies actually drag the ground, and I wondered why their herders had not considerately provided something like belly wheels.

Our escorts Ussu and Donduk were contemptuous of the wheeled vehicles and slow-plodding herds on the road. They were Mongols, and they thought all rights of way should be reserved to horseback riders. They grumbled that the Khakhan Kubilai had not yet kept a promise he had made some time ago: to level every least obstruction on every plain in Kithai, so that a horseman could canter across the entire country, even in darkest night, and never fear his horse's stumbling. They were naturally impatient of our having to lead packhorses and proceed at a sedate pace instead of galloping headlong. So they now and then found a way to enliven what to them was a boring journey.

At one of our night stops, when we camped by the road instead of pushing on to a karwansarai, Ussu and Donduk bought from a nearby camp of drovers one of their fat-tailed sheep and some doughy ewe cheese. (I should probably say they *procured* those things, for I doubt that they paid anything to the Han shepherds.) Donduk unslung his battle-ax, sliced away the sheep's tail-drag harness and in almost the same single motion cut off the animal's head. He and Ussu sprang onto their horses, and one of them reached down to catch up by the club tail the sheep's still-twitching and blood-spouting carcass, and the two riders began a gleefully galloping game of bous-kashia. They thundered back and forth between our camp and that of the sheepherders, wrenching the trophy animal from one another, slinging it about, dropping it frequently, trampling over it. Which of them won the game, or how they could tell, I do not know, but they tired at last and flung down at our feet the limp and gory thing, all covered with dust and dead leaves.

"Tonight's meal," said Ussu. "Good and tender now, uu?"

Somewhat to my surprise, he and Donduk volunteered to do the skinning and butchering and cooking themselves. It seems that Mongol men do not mind doing woman's work when there are no women about to do it. The meal they made was one to remember, but not with bon-gusto. They began by retrieving the sheep's lopped-off head, and it was spitted with the rest of the animal over our fire. A whole sheep should have sufficed to gorge several families of hearty eaters, but Ussu and Donduk and Nostril, with not much help from us other three, consumed that entire animal from nose to fat tail. The eating of the head was the least appetizing to watch and listen to. One of the gourmands would slice off a cheek from it, another an ear, the other a lip, and they would dip those awful fragments in a bowl of peppered juice from the meat, and chew and slurp and slobber and swallow and belch and fart. Since Mongols consider it bad manners for men to talk while they dine, that succession of good-mannered noises was not varied until they got down to the body bones and added the sound of sucking out the marrow.

We Polos ate only the meat sliced from the sheep's loins—well-beaten by the bous-kashia and admittedly most tender. Or we would have preferred to eat only that, but Ussu and Donduk kept carving and pressing on us the real delicacies: pieces of the tail, meaning blobs of yellow-white fat. They quivered and trembled repulsively in our fingers, but we could not in politeness refuse, so we somehow managed to gag them down, and I can still feel the way those ghastly gobbets went slimily palpitating down my gullet. After the first dreadful mouthful, I tried to clean my palate with a hearty swig of cha—and nearly strangled. Too late I discovered that Ussu, after brewing the cha leaves with boiling water, had not stopped there as civilized cooks do, but had melted into the drink chunks of mutton fat and ewe cheese. That Mongol-style cha would make a nourishing full meal all by itself, I suppose, but I must say that it was downright revolting.

We ate other meals on the Silk Road that are more pleasant to recall. This far into the interior of Kithai, the Han and Uighur karwan-sarai landlords did not limit their fare to only the things a Muslim can eat, so we found a good diversity of meats—including that of the illik, which is a tiny roe deer that barks like a dog, and of a lovelily golden-feathered pheasant, and steaks cut from yaks, and even the meat of black bears and brown bears, which abound here. When we camped in the open, Uncle Mafìo and the two Mongols vied at providing game for the pot: ducks and geese and rabbits and once a desert qazèl, but more usually they sought ground squirrels to shoot, because those little creatures thoughtfully provide the fuel for their own cooking. A hunter knows that, when he has no kara or wood or dried dung to make a fire with, he has only to look for the ground squirrels and their holes; even in a desert barren, they somehow contrive to put a weather-protective dome over their holes, of laced twigs and grass, well dried for the burning.

There were many other wild creatures in that region, not for eating but interesting to observe. There were black vultures with wings so broad that a man would have to take three paces to walk from tip to tip; and a snake so much resembling yellow metal that I would have sworn it was made of molten gold, but, having been informed that it was deadly venomous, I never touched one to find out. There was a little animal called a yerbò, like a mouse but with extravagantly long hind legs and tail, upon which three appendages it hopped about upright; and a magnificently beautiful wild cat called a palang, which I once saw making a meal of a wild ass it had downed, and which was like the heraldic pard, only not yellow of coat, but silvery gray with black rosettes spotted all over it.

The Mongols taught me to pick various wild plants as vegetable dishes for our meals—wild onions, for example, which go so well with any venison meat. There was a growth that they called the hair plant, and it did look exactly like a shock of black human hair. Neither its name nor its appearance was very appetizing, but when boiled and seasoned with a bit of vinegar, it made a delicate pickle condiment. Another oddity was what they called the vegetable lamb; they averred that it was indeed a mongrel creature bred from a mating of animal and plant, and said they preferred eating it to eating real lamb. It was tasty enough, but it was really only the woolly rootstalk of a certain fern.

The one ravishingly delicious novelty I found on that stage of the journey was the wonderful melon called the hami. Even the method of its growing was a novelty. When the vines started forming their fruit buds, the melon farmers paved over the whole field with slabs of slate for the vines to lie on. Instead of the melons' getting sunshine only on their upper sides, those slates reflected the sun's heat so that the hami ripened evenly all the way around. The hami had flesh of a pale greenish-white, so crisp that it crackled when bitten, dripping with juice, of a cool and refreshing flavor, not cloying but *just* the right sweetness. The hami had a taste and a fragrance different from all other fruits, and was almost as good when dried into flakes for travel rations, and has never been surpassed in my experience by any other garden sweet.

When we had been traveling for two or three weeks, the Silk Road abruptly turned northward for a little way, the only time it touched the Takla Makan, making a very short traverse across that desert's eastern-most edge, then turning directly east again toward a town named Dun-huang. That northward jink of the road took us through a pass that twined among some low mountains—really they were extremely high sand dunes—called the Flame Hills.

There is a legend to account for every place-name in Kithai, and according to legend these hills once were lushly forested and green, until they were set afire by some malicious kwei, or demons. A monkey god came along and kindly blew out the flames, but there was nothing left except these mountainous heaps of sand, still glowing like embers. That is the legend. I am more inclined to think that the Flame Hills are so called because their sands are a sort of burnt ocher color, and are wind-swept into flame-shaped furrows and wrinkles, and they perpetually shimmer behind a curtain of hot air, and—especially at sunset—they do glow a truly fiery red-orange color. But the most curious thing about them was a nest of four eggs which Ussu and Donkuk uncovered from the sand at the base of one of the dunes. I would have thought the objects were only large stones, perfectly oval and smooth and about the size of hami melons, but Donduk insisted:

"These are the abandoned eggs of a giant rukh bird. Such nests can be found all along the Flame Hills here."

When I held one, I realized that it was indeed too light for a stone of that size. And when I examined it, I saw that it did have a porous surface, exactly as do the eggs of hens or ducks or any other bird. These were eggs, all right, and far bigger even than those of the camel-bird, which I had seen in Persian markets. I wondered what kind of a for-tagiona these would make if I broke them and scrambled them and fried them for our evening meal.

"These Flame Hills," said Ussu, "must have been the rukh's favored nesting place in times past, Ferenghi, do you not think so, uu?"

"Times *very* long past," I suggested, for I had just tried to crack one of the eggs. Although it was not of stonelike weight, it had long ago aged and petrified to stonelike solidity. So the things were both uneatable and unhatchable, and they were too unwieldy for me to carry one off for a memento. They were most certainly eggs, and of a size that could have been laid only by a monster bird, but whether in truth that bird had been a rukh, I cannot say.

· 5 ·

D U N - H U A N G was a thriving trade town, about as big and as populous as Kashgar, sitting in a sandy basin ringed by camel-colored rock cliffs. But where Kashgar's inns had catered to Muslim travelers, those of Dun-huang made special provision for the tastes and customs of Buddhists. This was because the town had been founded, some nine hundred years ago, when a traveling trader of the Buddhist faith was beset, somewhere on the Silk Road hereabout, by bandits or the azghun voices or a kwei demon or something, and was somehow miraculously saved from those malign clutches. So he paused here to give thanks to the Buddha, and he did that by making a statue of that deity and placing it in a niche in one of the cliffs. In the nine centuries since, every other Buddhist traveler on the Silk Road has added an adornment to another of those caves. And now the name of Dun-huang, though it really means only Yellow Cliffs, is sometimes translated as the Caves of the Thousand Buddhas.

The designation is too modest. I would call these the Caves of the Million Buddhas, at the very least. For there are now some hundreds of caves pocking the cliffs, some natural, some hewn out by hand, and in them are perhaps two thousand statues of the Buddha, large and small, but on the cave walls are painted frescoes displaying at least a thousand *times* that many images of the Buddha, not to mention lesser divinities and worthies of the Buddha's retinue. I could discern that most of the images were male, and some just as clearly female, but a goodly number were indistinct as to sex. However, all had one feature in common: they all had tremendously elongated ears with lobes dangling to their shoulders.

"It is a common belief," said the old Han caretaker, "that a person born with large ears and well-defined earlobes is destined for good fortune. Since the most fortunate of all humans were the Buddha and his disciples, we assume that they had such ears, and we depict them so."

That aged ubashi, or monk, was pleased to conduct me on a tour of the caves, and he spoke Farsi for the occasion. I followed him from niche to cavern to grotto, and in all of them were statues of the Buddha, standing or lying peacefully asleep or, most often, sitting cross-legged on a giant lotus blossom. The monk told me that Buddha is an ancient

Indian word meaning the Enlightened One, and that the Buddha had been a Prince of India before his apotheosis. So I might have expected the statues to be all of a black and runty man, but they were not. Buddhism long ago spread from India to other nations, and evidently every devout traveler who paid to put up a statue or a painting had envisioned the Buddha as looking like *him*. Some of the older images were indeed dark and scrawny like Hindus, but others could have been Alexandrine Apollos or hawklike Persians or leathery Mongols, and the most recently done all had unlined faces with waxy complexions and placid expressions and slanted slit eyes; that is to say, they were pure Han.

It was also evident that, in the past, Muslim marauders had often swept through Dun-huang, for many of the statues were in ruins, hacked apart, revealing their simple construction of gesso molded onto cane and reed armatures, or at the least were cruelly disfigured. As I have told, the Muslims detest any portrayal of a living being. So here, when they had not had time to destroy a statue utterly, they had chopped the head off it (the head being the abode of life) or, in even more haste, they had been satisfied to gouge out the eyes from it (the eyes being the expression of life). The Muslims had taken the trouble to scratch out even the tiny eyes of many thousands of miniature painted images on the walls—even those of delicate and pretty female figures.

"And the females," said the old monk mournfully, "are not even divinities at all." He pointed to one lively little figure. "She is a Devatas, one of the celestial dancing girls who entertain the blessed souls in the Sukhavati, the Pure Land between lives. And this one"—he pointed to a girl who was painted in the act of flying, in a swallowlike swirl of skirts and veils—"she is an Apsaras, one of the celestial temptresses."

"There are temptresses in the Buddhist Heaven?" I asked, intrigued.

He sniffed and said, "Only to prevent an overcrowding of the Pure Land."

"Indeed? How?"

"The Apsarases have the duty of seducing holy men here on earth, so their souls get damned to the Awful Land of Naraka between lives, instead of the blissful Sukhavati."

"Ah," said I, to show that I comprehended. "An Apsaras is a sùccubo."

Buddhism has certain other parallels to our True Faith. Its devotees are adjured not to kill, not to tell untruths, not to take what is not given, not to indulge in sexual misbehavior. But in other respects, it is very different from Christianity. Buddhists are also adjured not to drink intoxicants, not to eat after the noon hour, not to attend entertainments, not to wear bodily adornments, not to sleep or even rest on a comfortable mattress. The religion does have the equivalents of our monks and nuns and priests, called ubashi and ubashanza and lamas, and Buddha enjoined them to live lives of poverty, as ours also are admonished, but few of them comply.

For example, Buddha told his followers to wear nothing but "yellowed garments"—by which he meant mere rags discolored by mold and decay. But the Buddhist monks and nuns obey that instruction only to the letter, not the spirit, for they are now arrayed in robes of the costliest fabrics, gaudily dyed in hues from brilliant yellow to fiery orange. They also have grand temples, called potkadas, and monasteries, called lamasarais, richly endowed and furnished. Also, I suspect that every Buddhist owns many more personal possessions than the few that Buddha specified: a sleeping mat, three rags for garments, a knife, a needle, a begging bowl with which to solicit one meager meal a day, and a water strainer with which to dip out from one's drinking water any incautious insects or fry or tadpoles, lest they get swallowed.

The water strainer illustrates Buddhism's foremost rule: that no creature alive, however humble or minute, shall ever be killed, deliberately or even accidentally. However, this has nothing in common with a Christian's wish to be good so as to go to Heaven after death. A Buddhist believes that a good man dies only to be reborn as a better man, further on his way to Enlightenment. And he believes that a bad man dies only to be reborn as a lesser grade of creature: an animal, bird, fish or insect. That is why a Buddhist must not kill anything. Since every least speck of life in Creation is presumably a soul trying to clamber up the ladder of Enlightenment, a Buddhist dares not squash so much as a louse, for it could be his late grandfather, demoted after death, or his future grandson on the way to being born.

A Christian might admire a Buddhist's reverence for life, no matter the ludicrous illogic behind it, except for two inevitable results of it. One is that every Buddhist man, woman and child is a seething nest of lice and fleas, and I found those vermin all too ready to risk their Enlightenment by emigrating onto Christian unbelievers like me. Also, a Buddhist of course cannot eat animal flesh. The devout confine themselves to boiled rice and water, and the most liberal will not eat anything more daring than milk and fruit and vegetables. So that is what we journeyers got in the Dun-huang inn: at mealtime, boiled fronds and tendrils and weak cha and bland custards, and at bedtime, fleas and ticks and bedbugs and lice.

"There was formerly here in Dun-huang a very holy lama," said my Han monk, in a voice of reverence, "so holy that he ate only *raw* rice, uncooked. And to further his humility even more, he wore an iron chain clenched about his shrunken belly. The chafing of the rusty chain made a sore, and it became quite putrid, generating a quantity of maggots. And if one of those munching maggots chanced to fall to the ground, the lama would lovingly pick it up, saying, 'Why do you flee, beloved? Did you not find enough to eat?' and he would tenderly replace it in the juiciest part of the sore."

That instructive tale may not have furthered my own humility, but it did diminish my appetite so that, when I got back to the inn, I was easily able to forgo that night's meal of pallid pap. Meanwhile, the monk went on:

"That lama eventually became a walking sore, and was consumed by it, and died of it. We all admire and envy him, for he surely moved far along the way to Enlightenment."

"I sincerely hope so," I said. "But what happens at the end of that way? Does the Enlightened One finally get to Heaven then?"

"Nothing so crass," said the ubashi. "One hopes, by means of sequacious rebirths and lifetimes of striving upward, eventually to be freed of having to live at all. To be liberated from the bondage of human needs and desires and passions and griefs and miseries. One hopes to achieve Nirvana, which means 'the blowing-out.' "

He was not jesting. A Buddhist has not the aim, as we do, of meriting for his soul an eternity of glad existence in the mansions of Heaven. A Buddhist yearns only for absolute extinction, or, as the monk put it, "a merging with the Infinite." He did admit that his religion makes provision for several heavenly Pure Lands and hellish Awful Lands, but they are—something like our Purgatory or Limbo—only way stations between a soul's successive rebirths on the way to Nirvana. And at that ultimate destination a soul gets snuffed out, as a candle flame is snuffed, nevermore to enjoy or endure not earth nor Heaven nor Hell nor anything.

I had cause to reflect on those beliefs, as our company continued eastward from Dun-huang, on a day that was marvelously full of things to reflect on.

We departed the inn at sunrise, when all the just-waking birds were uttering their morning chirps and cheeps and twitters, so many and so loud that they sounded like grease sizzling in a great pan. Then the later-rousing doves awoke, to murmur their discreet plaints and regrets, but in such numbers that their low warbling was near a roar. A considerable karwan train was also leaving the inn yard that morning, and in these regions the camels wore their bells not on a neckband, but on their front knees. So they strode out jingling and clanging and bonging as if they musically rejoiced in being on the move. I rode my horse alongside one of that train's wagons for a space, and one of its massive wheels had caught up somewhere a spray of jasmine in its spokes, and every time that high wheel revolved it brought the blossoms past my face and wafted their sweet scent to my nose.

The route out of the Dun-huang basin took us through a cleft in the cave-pocked cliffs, and that opened into a valley verdant with trees and fields and wildflowers, the last such oasis we would see for a while. As we rode through that valley I saw something so beautiful that I still can see it in my memory. Some way ahead of us, a plume of golden-yellow smoke rose up on the morning breeze, and we all remarked on it and wondered at it. Perhaps it came from a fire in a karwan camp, but what could the campers be burning to make such a distinctively colored cloud? The smoke continued to rise and billow, and eventually we came up to it and saw that it was not smoke at all. On the left side of the valley there was a meadow totally covered with golden-yellow flowers, and all those numberless flowers were exultantly freeing their golden-yellow pollen to let the breeze carry it across the Silk Road and away to the other slopes of the valley. We rode through that cloud of seeming smoke, and we came out the other side of it, and we and our horses shimmered in the sunlight as if we had been freshly plated with pure gold.

Another thing. From the valley, we emerged into a land of undulant sand dunes, but the sand was no longer the color of camels or lions, it was a dark silvery gray, like a powdered metal. Nostril got down from his horse to relieve himself, and climbed over a dune of the gray sand, seeking privacy, and to his surprise—and mine—the sand *barked* like a peevish dog at each of his footsteps. It made no particular noise when Nostril wetted on it, but, as he turned to descend the dune, his foot slipped and he slid the whole way down from the crest, and his slide was accompanied by a lovely loud musical note, vibrato, as if a string on the world's biggest lute had been thrummed.

"Mashallah!" Nostril blurted fearfully, as he picked himself up. He ran all the way from the sand to the firmer surface of the road before pausing to dust himself off.

My father and uncle and the two escorts were all laughing at him. One of the Mongols said, "These sands are called the lui-ing."

"The thunder voices," Uncle Mafio translated for me. "Nico and I have heard them when we passed this way before. They will cry also if the wind blows hard, and they cry loudest in winter, when the sands are cold."

Now, that was a thing most marvelous. But it was only a thing of this earth, as were the sunrise birdsongs and the common camel bells and the perfumed jasmine and the golden wild flowers so determined to flourish that they flung their seed haphazard to the wind.

This world is fair, I thought, and life is good, no matter whether one is certain of Heaven or apprehensive of Hell at the end of it. I could only pity such pathetic persons as Buddhists, deeming the earth and their existence on it so ugly and miserable and repugnant that their highest yearning was to flee into sheer oblivion. Not I, not ever I. If I might accept any of the Buddhist beliefs, it would be that of rebirth over and over into this world, though it mean coming back sometimes as a lowly dove or a sprig of jasmine between my human incarnations. Yes, I thought, if I could I would go on living forever.

. 6 .

THE land continued gray, but that color got darker as we went eastward, darkening to veritable black—black grit and black gravel drifting over black bedrock—for we had come now to another desert, one too broad and extensive for the Silk Road to skirt around. It was called by the Mongols the Gobi, and by the Han the Sha-mo, both words meaning a desert of that peculiar composition: one from which all the sand had long ago blown away, leaving only the heavier particles, and they all black. It made for an unearthly landscape, appearing to be not of pebbles and stones and rocks, but of even harder metal. In the sun, every black hill and boulder and ridge glittered with a sharp bright rim as if it had been honed on a whetstone. The only growing things were the colorless plumes of camel-weed and some tufts of colorless grass like fine metal wires.

The Gobi is also called by travelers the Great Silence, because any conversation softer than a shout goes unheard there, and so does the clatter of black stones rolling and shifting underfoot, and so do the piteous whinnies of sore-footed horses, and so do the whines and grumbles of a complainer like Nostril, all such noises blotted out by the everlasting wail of the wind. Over the Gobi the wind blows ceaselessly through three hundred and sixty days of the year, and, in the late summer days of our crossing, it blew as hot as a blast from the opened doors of the fearsome ovens of the vasty kitchens of the nethermost levels of Satan's fiercest Inferno.

The next town we came to, Anxi, must be the most desolately situated community in all Kithai. It was a mere cluster of shacky shops peddling karwan necessities, and some travelers' inns and stables, all of unpainted wood and mud-brick much pitted and eroded by wind-blown grit. The town had come into being there on the edge of the dreary Gobi only because at this point the two branches of the Silk Road came together again—the southerly one by which we arrived in town, and the other route that had circled around north of the Takla Makan—and at Anxi they merged into the single road that goes on, without again dividing, over the interminable more li to the Kithai capital of Khanbalik. At this convergence of roads, there was of course an even more bustling traffic of individual traders and groups and families and karwan trains. But one procession of mule-drawn wagons made me ask our escorts:

"What kind of train is that? It moves so slowly and so quietly."

All the wheels of the wagons had their rims tied about with bunched hay and rags, to muffle the sound of them, and the mules had their hoofs tied in bags of wadding for the same purpose. That did not make the train entirely noiseless, for the wheels and hoofs still made a rumbling and clumping sound, and there was much creaking of the wooden wagon beds and leather harness, but its progress was quieter than that of most trains. Besides the Han men driving the wagon mules, other Han were mounted on mules as outriders and, as they accompanied the train through Anxi, they rode like an honor guard, shouldering a path through the crowded streets, but never using their voices to demand clear passage.

The street folk moved obligingly aside and silenced their own chatter and averted their faces, as if the train were that of some grand and haughty personage. But there was no one in the procession *except* those drivers and escorts; no one rode in any of the several score wagons. They were occupied only by heaps of what might have been rolled tents or rugs, many hundreds of them, cloth-wrapped long bundles, piled like cordwood in the wagon beds. Whatever those objects were, they looked very old, and they gave off a dry, musty smell, and their cloth wrappings were all tattered and shredded and flapping. When the wagons jounced on the rutted streets, they shed bits and flakes of cloth.

"Like shrouds decaying," I remarked.

To my astonishment, Ussu said, "That is what they are." In a hushed voice, he added, "Show respect, Ferenghi. Turn away and do not stare as they go by."

He did not speak again until the muffled train had passed. Then he told me that all Han people have a great desire to be buried in the places where they were born, and their survivors bend every effort to have that done. Since most of the Han who keep inns and shops on the far western reaches of the Silk Road had come originally from the more populous eastern end of the country, that was where they wished their remains to rest. So any Han who died in the west was only shallowly buried, and when—after many years—a sufficiency of them had died, their families in the east would organize a train and send it west. All those bodies would be dug up and collected and transported together back to their native regions. It happened perhaps only once in a generation, said Ussu, so I could count myself unique among Ferenghi, to have glimpsed one of the karwans of the corpses.

All along the Silk Road from Kashgar, we had been fording the occasional minor river—meager streams trickling down from the mountain snows in the south and quickly soaking into the desert to the north. But some weeks eastward of Anxi we found a more considerable river going easterly with us. In its beginnings, it was a merrily tumbling clear water, but every time the road brought us again alongside it, we saw that it was wider and deeper and more turbulent and turning dun-yellow with its accumulation of silt; hence the name given it, Huang, the Yellow River. Swooping throughout the whole breadth of Kithai, the Huang is one of the two great river systems of these lands. The other is far to the south of this, an even mightier water—called Yang-tze, meaning simply Tremendous River—traversing the land of Kithai.

"That Yang-tze and this Huang," my father said instructively, "they are, after the historic Nile, the second and third longest rivers in all the traveled world."

I might facetiously have remarked that the Huang must be the *tallest* river on earth. What I mean—and I am seldom believed when I say this—is that through much of its length the Huang River stands *above* the land surrounding it.

"But how can that be?" people protest. "A river is not independent of the earth. If a river should rise, it would merely overflow onto the land about."

But the Yellow River does not, except at disastrous intervals. Over the years and generations and centuries, the Han farmers along the river have built up earthen levees to reinforce its banks. But, because the Huang carries such quantities of silt, and continuously deposits that on its bed, its surface level also continuously goes up. So the Han farmers, over generations and centuries and eons, have had to keep building the levees higher. Thus, between those artificial banks, the Yellow River literally does stand higher than the land. In some places, if I had wished to jump into the river, I would have had to climb a bank higher than a four-storied building.

"But big as they are, those levees are only of packed earth," said my father. "In one very rainy year while we were last here, we saw the Huang get so full and boisterous that it broke those banks."

"A river held up in the air and then let fall," I mused. "It must have been something to see."

Uncle Mafìo said, "Like watching Venice and the whole mainland Vèneto submerge beneath the lagoon, if you can imagine such a thing. A flood of unbelievable extent. Entire villages and towns dissolved. Whole nations of people drowned."

"It happens not every year, God be thanked," said my father. "But often enough to have given the Yellow River its other name—the Scourge of the Sons of Han."

However, as long as the river runs tame, the Han make good use of it. Here and there along the banks, I saw the biggest wheels in the world: waterwheels of wood and cane as high as twenty men standing atop one another. Around the wheels' rims were multitudes of buckets and scoops, which the river considerately filled and lifted and spilled into irrigation canals.

And in one place, I saw a boat beside the bank that had immense, revolving paddlewheels on either side. On first seeing it, I thought it was some kind of Han invention to replace man-worked oars for propulsion. But again I was disillusioned of the vaunted Han inventiveness, for I realized that the craft was only moored to the bank and the paddle-wheels were merely turned by the river current. They in turn rotated axles and spokes inside the vessel to make millstones grind grain. So the whole thing was nothing but a water mill, novel only in that it was not stationary, but could be moved up and down the river, to any place where there was a harvest of grain to be ground into flour.

There were innumerable other kinds of vessels, for the Yellow River was more crowded with traffic than was the Silk Road. The Han people, having such tremendous distances over which to freight their goods and produce, prefer to use their waterways rather than overland methods of transport. It is really a sensible practice, however much their Mongol masters ridicule the Han's disregard for horses. A horse or any other pack animal, over any distance, will eat more grain than it can carry, but the river boatmen consume very little man-fueling food to accomplish each li of travel. So the Han rightfully respect and revere their rivers; they even give the name of River of Heaven to what we Westerners call the Milky Way.

On the Yellow River there were many shallow scows, called san-pan, and each scow's crew was a family, to whom the boat was simul-taneously home, transport and livelihood. The males of the family did the san-pan's rowing or towing upstream, and the steering downstream, and the loading and unloading of the cargo. The females did what seemed to be perpetual cooking and laundering. And among them played a multitude of smaller boys and girls, all blithely naked except for a large gourd tied at the waist, to help them float when they fell over-board, which they did with regularity.

There were many larger craft propelled by sails. When I asked our escorts what they were called, the Mongols indifferently said what sounded like "chunk." The correct Han word, I learned, is chuan, but that means only sailing vessels in general; I never did learn the thirty-eight different names of the thirty-eight different kinds of rivergoing and seagoing "chunks."

Anyway, the smallest of them was as big as a Flemish cog, but of shallow draft, and looked to me ridiculously cumbersome, like an immense floating wooden shoe. But I gradually perceived that the chuan's shape is not patterned on a fish, as most Western vessels are, for a fishlike celerity. It is patterned on a duck, for stability on the water, and I could see that it floated serenely over the Yellow River's most tumultuous whirlpools and whitecaps. Perhaps because the chuan is slow and sturdy, it has only a single rudder for steering, not two as on our vessels, and it is set amidship at the stern and requires no more than a single steersman. A chuan's sails are also odd, not being let to belly in the wind, but latticed by slats at intervals, so they look rather like ribbed bat wings. And when it is necessary to shorten sail, they are not reefed like ours, but are folded, slat by slat, like a griglia of persiana window blinds.

Of all the craft I saw on that river, though, the most striking was a small oared skiff called a hu-pan. It was ludicrously unsymmetrical, being bent in a sideways arc. Now, a Venetian gòndola is also built with a touch of camber to allow for the fact that the gondolier paddles always on the right side, but a gòndola's keel bend is so slight as to be unnoticeable. These hu-pan were as skewed as a shimshir sword laid on its side. Again, it was a matter of practicality. A hu-pan always travels close against the riverbank, and as its oarsman variously keeps its concave or convex side to the bending shore, it more easily slips around the river bends. Of course, the rower must keep switching stern for bow as the river twists this way and that, so his progress resembles that of an agitated water-strider insect.

Before long, however, I had something even more strange to wonder at—on the land, not on the river. Near a village called Zong-zhai, we came to a deserted and tumbledown ruin that must once have been a substantial stone edifice with two stout watchtowers. Our escort Ussu told me that it had in olden time been a Han fortress of some long-past dynasty, and was still called by its old name: the Gates of Jade. The fortress was not actually a gate, and certainly not made of jade, but it constituted the western end of a massively thick and impressively high wall stretching northeastward from this point.

The Great Wall, as foreigners call it, is more colorfully called by the Han the "Mouth" of their land. In times past, the Han spoke of themselves as the People Within the Mouth, meaning this wall, and spoke of all other nations to the north and westward as the People Outside the Mouth. Whenever a Han criminal or traitor was condemned to exile, he was said to have been "spat beyond the Mouth." The wall was built to *keep* all but the Han outside it, and it is unquestionably the longest and strongest defensive barrier ever built by human hands. How many hands, or how long they labored, no one can say. But the construction of it must have consumed the entire lives of many generations of whole populations of men.

According to tradition, the wall follows the wandering course laid out by a favorite white horse of a certain Emperor Chin, the Han ruler who commenced its construction in some distantly ancient time. But I doubt that story, for no horse would willingly have taken such a difficult route along mountaintop ridges, as much of the wall does. Certainly we and our horses did not. Though the remaining weeks of our seemingly never-to-end journey across Kithai required us generally to follow the course of that seemingly never-to-end wall—and while we were seldom out of sight of it from then on—we could usually find lower and easier ground downhill of it.

The Great Wall winds sinuously across Kithai, sometimes uninterruptedly from horizon to horizon, but in other places it takes advantage of natural ramparts like peaks and cliffs, and incorporates them into its length, then resumes again on more vulnerable ground beyond. Also, it is not everywhere just a single wall. In one region of eastern Kithai, we found that there were three parallel walls, one behind another, at intervals some hundred li apart.

The wall is not everywhere of the same composition. Its more easterly stretches are built of great squared rocks, neatly and firmly mortared together—as if in those places it was built under the Emperor Chin's stern eye—and is to this day still staunch and unbroken: a great, high, thick, solid bulwark, its top wide enough for a troop of horsemen to ride abreast, and with embrasured battlements on either side of that walltop roadway, and with bulky watchtowers jutting up even higher at intervals. But in some of its western lengths—as if the Emperor's subjects and slaves did only perfunctory work, knowing he would never come to inspect—the wall was built only shoddily, of stones and mud slapped together in a structure not so high nor thick, and consequently has been much crumbled and interrupted by gaps over the centuries.

Nevertheless, in sum, the Great Wall is a majestic and awesome thing, and I am not easily able to describe it in terms comprehensible to a Westerner. But let me put it this way. If the wall could somehow be transported intact out of Kithai, and all its numerous segments laid end to end, starting from Venice, thence going northwestward over the continent of Europe, across the Alps, over the meadows and rivers and forests and everything else, clear to the North Sea at the Flemish port of Bruges, there would yet be enough of the wall to *double back again* that same tremendous distance to Venice, and *still* there would be enough of the wall left over to extend from Venice westward to the border of France.

Considering the undeniable grandeur of the Great Wall, why did my father and uncle, who had seen it before, not ever mention it to me, to excite my anticipation of seeing it? And why did I myself not tell of such a marvel in that earlier book recounting my journeys? It was not, in this case, an omission of something which I judged people would refuse to believe. I neglected to mention the wall because—for all its prodigiousness—I deemed it a trivial achievement of the Han, and I still do. It seemed to me one more disavowal of the reputed genius of the natives of Kithai, and it still does. For this reason:

As we rode along beside the Great Wall, I remarked to Ussu and Donduk, "You Mongols were People Outside the Mouth, but now you are inside it. Did your armies have no trouble breaching that barrier?"

Donduk sneered. "Since the wall was first built, in times before history, no invader has ever had any trouble getting over it. We Mongols and our ancestors have done it again and again over the centuries. Even a puny Ferenghi could do it."

"Why is that?" I asked. "Were all other armies always better warriors than the Han defenders?"

"What defenders, uu?" Ussu said contemptuously.

"Why, the sentries on the parapets. They must have been able to see any enemy approaching from afar. And surely they had legions to summon for the repelling of enemies."

"Oh, yes, that is true."

"Well, then? Were they so easy to defeat?"

"Defeat!" they said together, their voices still heavy with disdain. Ussu explained the reason for their scorn. "No one ever had to defeat them. Any outsider who ever wished to cross the wall had merely to bribe the sentries with a bit of silver. Vakh! No wall is any taller or stronger or more forbidding than the men behind it."

And I saw that it was so. The Great Wall, built with God knows what expenditure of money and time and labor and sweat and blood and lives, has never been any more a deterrent to invaders than has the merest boundary line casually drawn on a map. The Great Wall's only real claim to notability is in its being the world's most stupendous monument to futility.

As witness: we came at last, some weeks later, to the city which that wall enwraps most securely, where the wall is highest and thickest and best preserved. The city there behind the wall has been known through the ages by many different names: Ji-cheng and Ji and Yu-zho and Chung-tu and other names—and at one time or another it has been the capital of many different empires of the Han people: the Chin and the Chou and the Tang dynasties, and no doubt others. But what availed the enormous wall? Today that city into which we rode is named Khanbalik, "City of the Khan"—commemorating the latest invader to cross the Great Wall and conquer this land, and by my reckoning the grandest of them: the man who resoundingly but justifiably titled himself Great Khan, Khan of All Khans, Khan of the Nations, son of Tulei and brother of Mangu Khan, grandson of Chinghiz Khan, Mightiest of the Mongols, the Khakhan Kubilai.

KHANBALIK

. 1 .

To my surprise, when we entered Khanbalik—that is to say, when we came in the twilight of a fading day to the place where the dusty road became a broad, paved, clean avenue leading into the city—our little train was met by a considerable reception party.

First there was waiting a band of Mongol foot soldiers wearing dress armor of highly polished metal and gleaming oiled leathers. They did not step out to impede our way, as Kaidu's road guards at Kashgar had done. With unanimous precision, they presented their glittering lances at a slant of salute, then formed a hollow square about our train and marched with us along the avenue, between crowds of the city's everyday inhabitants, who paused in their occupations to ogle us curiously.

The next waiting greeters were a number of distinguished-looking, elderly gentlemen—some Mongols, some Han, some evidently Arab and Persian—wearing long silk robes of various vivid colors, each man attended by a servant holding over him a fringed canopy on a tall pole. The elders strode out to march on our either flank, their servants scurrying to keep the canopies in place over them, and all smiled at us and made sedate gestures of welcome and called in their several languages: "Mendu! Ying-jie! Salaam!"—though those words were quickly drowned out by a troop of musicians joining the procession with an unearthly screech and clangor of horns and cymbals. My father and uncle smiled and nodded and bowed from their saddles, appearing to have expected this extravagant reception, but Nostril and Ussu and Donduk looked as astonished as I was.

Ussu said to me, over the noise, "Of course, your party has been watched all along the road, as is every traveler, and post riders will have kept the Khanbalik authorities informed of your approach. No one arrives at the City of the Khan unobserved."

"But," said Donduk, in a newly respectful voice, "usually it is only the city's Wang who keeps account of visitors' comings and goings. You Ferenghi"—he pronounced the word benignly for a change—"seem to be known to the very palace, and warmly awaited, and exceptionally welcome. Those elders marching alongside, I believe they are courtiers of the Khakhan himself."

I was looking from side to side of the avenue, eager to get some idea of the city's appearance, but suddenly the view was obscured and my attention diverted elsewhere. There came a noise like a crack of thunder and a light like a lightning flash, not high in the sky but frighteningly close overhead. It made me start and made my horse shy, so violently that I lost my stirrups. I curbed the animal before he could bolt, and held him to a skittish dance, while the terrific noise banged again and again, each time with a flare of light. I saw that all our other horses had also shied, and all our party were occupied in keeping them under control. I would have expected every one of the city folk in the avenue to be running for cover, but all seemed not only composed but actually to be enjoying the tumult and the brightening of the dusk. My father and uncle and the two Mongols were equally tranquil; they even grinned broadly as they sawed on the reins of the plunging horses. It seemed that the flicker and the racket were a bewilderment only to me and to Nostril —I could see his eyeballs protruding whitely from his head as he looked wildly about for the source of the commotion.

It came from the curly-eaved rooftops along both sides of the avenue. Blobs of bright light, like great sparks—or more like the desert's mysterious "beads of Heaven"—went lofting upward from those roofs and arcing into the air overhead. Directly above us, they burst asunder, making that ear-clapping thump of sound, and became whole constellations of different-colored sprinkles and streaks and splinters of light that drifted down and dwindled and died before they reached the street pavement, leaving a trail of sharp-smelling blue smoke. So many were going up from the roofs and bursting at such close intervals that their flares made an almost constant glow, abolishing the natural twilight, and their bangs concerted in such a roar that our accompanying band was inaudible. The musicians, trudging unconcerned through the clouds of blue smoke, appeared to be only pantomiming the play of their instruments. Though also inaudible, the crowds of city folk along each side of our line of march seemed, from their jumpings and arm wavings and wagging mouths, to be cheering exuberantly at every new burst and blast.

It may be that my own eyes were bulging at sight of that strange and unaccountable flying fire. For, when we had proceeded farther along the avenue, and the smoke and the artificial lightning storm were behind us, Ussu again brought his horse close beside mine and spoke loudly to be heard above the again rambunctious band music:

"You never saw such a show before, Ferenghi? It is a toy devised by the childish Han people. They call it huo-shu yin-hua—fiery trees and sparkling flowers."

I shook my head and said, "Toy, indeed!" but managed to smile as if I too had enjoyed it. Then I resumed my glancing about to see what the fabled city of Khanbalik looked like.

I will speak later of that. For now, let me just say that the city, which I suppose had suffered much ruination in the Mongols' taking of it, sometime before I was born, had ever since been in the process of rebuilding from the ground up. These many years later, it was still being added to and refined and embellished and made as grand as the capital of the world's greatest empire rightly ought to be. The broad avenue led us and our procession of troops and elders and musicians straight on for quite a long way, between the fronts of handsome buildings, until it ended at a towering, south-facing gateway in a wall that was almost as high and thick and impressive as the best-built stretches of the Great Wall out in the countryside.

We went through that gateway and we were in one of the courtyards of the Khakhan's palace. But palace is a word not comprehensive enough. That was more than a palace; it was a fair-sized city within the city; and it also was still a-building. The courtyard was full of the wagons and carts and draft animals of stonemasons and carpenters and plasterers and gilders and such, and the conveyances of farmers and tradesmen purveying provender and necessities to the inhabitants of the palace city, and the mounts and carriages and porter-borne palanquins of other visitors come on other business from near and far.

From the group of courtiers who had accompanied us through the city, one stepped forward, a quite old and fragile-appearing Han, saying in Farsi, "I shall summon servants, my lords." He only gently clapped his pallid, papery hands, but somehow that imperceptible command carried through the confusion of the courtyard and he was instantly obeyed. Out of somewhere came half a dozen stable grooms, and he instructed them to take charge of our mounts and packhorses, also to lead Ussu and Donduk and Nostril to quarters in the palace guard barracks. He clapped his hands almost soundlessly again, and three female servants just as magically appeared.

"These maids will attend you, my lords," he said to my father and uncle and me. "You will lodge temporarily in the pavilion of honored guests. I will come on the morrow and conduct you to the Khakhan, who is most eager to greet you, and at that time doubtless he will appoint more permanent quarters for you."

The three women bowed four times before us in the abjectly humble

Han salute called the ko-tou, which is a prostration so low that the bowing forehead actually is supposed to knock the ground. Then the women smilingly beckoned and, with curiously birdlike, tripping little steps, led us across the courtyard, and the crowd made way before us. We went another considerable distance through the twilit palace city— along galleries and through cloisters and across other open courtyards and down corridors and over terraces—until the women again did the ko-tou at the guest pavilion. It had a seemingly blank wall of translucent oiled paper in frames of wood filigree, but the women easily opened it by sliding two panels apart and aside, and bowed us in. Our chambers were three bedrooms and a sitting room, en suite, lavishly decorated and ornamented, with an ornate brazier already alight—burning clean charcoal, not animal dung or the smoky kara coals. One of the women began turning down our beds—real beds, high standing and piled higher with downy quilts and pillows—while another set water to heat on the brazier for our baths and the third began bringing in trays of already hot food from some kitchen somewhere.

We fell first on the food, almost snatching and stabbing with our nimble-tong sticks, for we were hungry and it was fine fare: bits of steamed shoat in a garlic sauce, pickled mustard greens cooked with broad beans, the familiar miàn pasta, a porridge very like our Venetian chestnut-meal polenta, a cha flavored with almonds and, for the sweet, red-candied little crabapples impaled on twigs for ease of eating. Then, in our separate rooms, we bathed all over—or got bathed, I should say. My father and uncle seemed to accept those ministrations as indifferently as if the young women had been male rubbers in a hammam. But it was the first time I had been so served by a female since the long-ago days of Zia Zulià, and I felt both embarrassment and titillation.

To distract myself, I watched the maid instead of what she was doing to me. She was a young woman of the Han, perhaps a little older than I, but at that time I knew not how to gauge the age of such alien beings. She was far better dressed than any Western servant would have been, but also was much more meek and docile and solicitous than any Western servant.

She had face and hands of ivory tint, an upswept mass of blue-black hair, barely perceptible eyebrows, no apparent eyelashes, and eyes also invisible because their opening was so narrow and she kept them always downcast. She had rosebud lips, red and dewy-looking, but a nose almost nonexistent. (I was beginning to resign myself to never seeing a shapely Verona-style nose in these lands.) Her ivory face was at the moment marred by a smudge on her forehead, from her ko-tou in the courtyard. However, a small imperfection in a woman can sometimes be a most appealing feature. I began to wish very much that I could see what the rest of the young woman looked like, under her many layers of brocade —stole and robe and gown and sashes and ties and other furbelows.

I was tempted to suggest that, as soon as she had me clean all over, she might serve me in other ways. But I did not. I could not speak her language, and the necessary gestures of suggestion might have been taken as more offensive than inviting. Also, I did not know how liberal or how strict the local conventions might be in regard to such things. So I decided prudence was called for, and, when she finished my bath and made the ko-tou, I let her depart. The hour was still early, but the day had been a tiring one. My combined fatigue of traveling, excitement at having finally arrived, and languor induced by the bath put me immediately to sleep. I dreamed that I was undressing the Han maidservant like a toy doll, layer by layer, and when the last garment was peeled away she suddenly became that other toy: that bursting, blazing display called fiery trees and sparkling flowers.

In the morning, the same three women brought trays of food which they served upon our laps while we still lay in bed, and, while we broke our fast, prepared hot water to give us each another bath. I endured it without complaint, though I did think that two all-over bathings in the course of a single day was rather excessive. Then Nostril came, leading some of the stable hands carrying our travel packs. So, after the baths, we donned the finest and least worn clothes we owned. Those were our dashing Persian costumes—tulbands on our heads, embroidered waistcoats over loose shirts with tight cuffs, kamarbands around our middles, and ample pai-jamah tucked into well-cut boots. Our three maids giggled, and nervously put their hands over their mouths, as Han women always do when they laugh, but they hastened to indicate that they were tittering in admiration of our handsomeness.

Then arrived our elderly Han guide of the evening before—this time he introduced himself: Lin-ngan, the Court Mathematician—and led us from the pavilion. Now, in full morning light, I could better appreciate our surroundings, as we went along arcades and colonnades and through vine-trellised bowers and along porticoes overhung by curly-edged roof caves and along terraces that overlooked flower-filled gardens and over high-arched bridges that spanned lotus ponds and little streams in which golden fish swam. In every place and passage we saw servants, most of them Han, male and female, richly garbed but timorously hastening on their errands, and many Mongol guardsmen in dress uniforms, standing rigid as statues but holding weapons which they looked ready to use, and we saw the occasional strolling noble or elder or courtier, as dignified and sumptuously robed and important-appearing as our guide Lin-ngan, with whom they exchanged ceremonious nods in passing.

All the unwalled passages open to the air had intricately carved and fretted balustrades and exquisitely sculptured pillars and hanging, tinkling wind chimes and silk tassels swishing like horses' tails. All the enclosed passages where the sun did not enter were lighted by tinted Muscovy-glass lanterns like soft-colored moons, and they glowed with a lovely diffuse light, because every such passage was misted by the fragrant smoke of burning incense. And all the passages, open or enclosed, were decorated with standing objects of art: elegant marble sundials and lacquered screens and figured gongs and images of lions and horses and dragons and other animals which I could not recognize, and great urns of bronze and vases of porcelain and jade, overflowing with cut flowers.

We crossed again the gateside courtyard by which we had entered on the previous evening, and it was again or still thronged with saddle horses and pack asses and camels and carts and wagons and palanquins and people. Among that press, I happened to see two Han men just dismounting from mules and, though they were but two faces in an innumerable crowd, I had a vague sense of having seen those men before. After leading us some way farther, old Lin-ngan brought us finally to a south-facing pair of immense doors, chased and gilded and lacquered in many colors, doors so massive in size and so weighty with metal studs and bosses that they might have been intended to keep giants out—or in. Pausing with his wisp of a hand on one of the formidable wrought-dragon handles, Lin-ngan said in his whisper of a voice:

"This is the Cheng, the Hall of Justice, and this is the hour of the Khakhan's dispensing judgment to plaintiffs and supplicants and miscreants. If you will but attend until that is concluded, my Lords Polo, he wishes to make his greetings immediately afterward."

The frail old man, with no apparent effort, swung open the ponderous doors—they must have been cleverly counterpoised and on well-oiled hinges—and bowed us inside. He followed us in and closed the door behind us, and remained standing with us to provide helpful interpretations of what was going on in the hall.

The Cheng was a tremendous and lofty chamber, fully as big as an indoor courtyard, its ceiling held up by carved and gilded columns, its walls paneled with red leather, but its floor space empty of furniture. At the far end was a raised platform and on that a substantial thronelike chair, flanked by rows of lower and less elegantly upholstered chairs. There were dignitaries occupying all those seats, and in the shadows behind the dais were other figures standing and moving about. Between us and the platform knelt a great crowd of petitioners, enough to fill the chamber from wall to wall, most of them in coarse peasant dress but others in noble raiment.

Even from the distance at which we stood, I knew the man seated centrally on the dais. I would have known him even if he had been shabbily clothed and crammed ignominiously among the ranks of commoners on the chamber floor. The Khan Kubilai needed not his elevated throne nor his gold-threaded, fur-trimmed silk robes to proclaim himself; his sovereignty was implicit in the upright way he sat, as if he still were astride a battle charger, and in the strength of his craggy face and in the forcefulness of his voice, though he spoke only infrequently and in low tones. The men in the chairs to either side of him were almost as well dressed, but their manner made evident that they were subordinates. Our guide Lin-ngan, pointing discreetly and murmuring quietly, explained who they all were.

"One is the official called Suo-ke, which means the Tongue. Four are the Khakhan's secretary scribes who record on scrolls the proceedings here. Eight are ministers of the Khakhan, two each of four ascending degrees. Behind the dais, those running about are relays of clerks who fetch documents from the Cheng archives, when any are needed for reference."

The one called Tongue of the Cheng was continuously occupied, leaning down from the platform to hear a petitioner, then turning to converse with one or another of the ministers. And those eight ministers also were continuously busy, consulting with the Tongue, bidding clerks bring them documents, peering into those papers and scrolls, consulting among themselves and occasionally with the Khakhan. But the four secretaries seemed only now and then to bestir themselves to write anything on their papers. I commented that it seemed odd: the lordly ministers of the Cheng working harder than the mere secretaries.

"Yes," said Master Lin-ngan. "The scribes do not trouble to write down anything of these proceedings except the words spoken by the Khan Kubilai himself. Everything else is but preliminary discussion, for the Khakhan's words sum up and distill and supersede all other words spoken."

Such a vast room with so many people in it might have been cacophonous and echoing, but the crowd was quiet and orderly, like a congregation in church. Only one person at a time went up to the dais, and he spoke only to the official called the Tongue, and in a murmur so respectful or fearful that we in the back of the room could hear nothing that passed until, after all the deliberations, the Tongue announced the judgment for all to know.

Lin-ngan said, "During the Cheng, no one but the Tongue ever addresses the Khan Kubilai directly, nor ever is directly addressed by him. A supplicant or prosecutor puts his case to the Tongue—who, incidentally, is so called because he is fluent in all the languages of the realm. The Tongue then puts the case to one of the two ministers of least degree. If that official deems it a subject of sufficient importance, he will refer it upward. At whatever level, and after whatever precedents are consulted, an adjudication is suggested and told to the Tongue, who then tells it to the Khakhan. He may give assent, or make some slight change in the ruling, or controvert it completely. Then the Tongue pronounces aloud that final decree to the persons concerned and to all within hearing —damages to be paid to a plaintiff, or to be exacted from a defendant, or a punishment laid on, or sometimes a dismissal of the whole affair—and the case is closed forever."

I perceived that this Cheng of Khanbalik was not like the Daiwan of Baghdad, where every case had been a matter for discussion and mutual agreement among the Shah and his wazir and an assortment of officious Muslim imams and muftis. Here, the cases might be argued first among the ministers, but every single verdict was finally at the sole discretion of the Khan Kubilai, and his pronouncement was not to be disputed or appealed. I also perceived that his verdicts were sometimes witty or whimsical, but sometimes appalling in their cruel inventiveness.

Old Lin-ngan was at that moment saying, "The farmer who just petitioned the Cheng is a delegate sent by a whole district of farmers in the province of Ho-nan. He brings word that the rice fields have been chewed clean by a plague of locusts. A famine is on the land and the farm families are starving. The delegate asks relief for the people of Ho-nan and inquires what might be done. Regard, the ministers have discussed the problem and referred it to the Khakhan, and now the Tongue will deliver the Khakhan's decree."

The Tongue did, in a bellow of Han that I could not understand, but Lin-ngan translated:

"The Khan Kubilai speaks thus. With all that rice inside them, the locusts should be delicious. The families of Ho-nan have the Khakhan's permission to eat the locusts. The Khan Kubilai has spoken."

"By God," muttered Uncle Mafìo, "the old tyrant is just as flippantly imperious as I had remembered him."

"Honey in his mouth and a dagger at his belt," my father said admiringly.

The next case was that of a provincial notary named Xen-ning, responsible for recording deeds of land transfer and testaments of bequest and such things. He was accused, and found guilty, of having falsified his ledgers for his own aggrandizement, and the Tongue proclaimed and Lin-ngan translated the sentence accorded him:

"The Khan Kubilai speaks thus. You have lived all your life by words, Notary Xen-ning. Henceforth you shall live *on* them. You are to be imprisoned in a solitary cell, and at every mealtime you will be served pieces of paper inscribed 'meat' and 'rice' and 'cha.' Those will be your food and drink for as long as you can survive on them. The Khan Kubilai has spoken."

"Truly," said my father, "he has a tongue of scissors."

The next and last case that morning was the matter of a woman taken in adultery. It would have been a thing too trivial for the Cheng's consideration, said old Lin-ngan, except that she was a Mongol woman, and wife to a Mongol functionary of the Khanate, a certain Lord Amursama; therefore her crime was more heinous than if she had been a mere Han. Her outraged husband had stabbed her lover to death at the moment of discovery, said Lin-ngan, meaning that the miscreant had died too mercifully quickly and without the torment he deserved. So now the husband was petitioning the Cheng to decide a more salutary fate for his unfaithful wife. The cuckold's petition was duly granted, and I trust it satisfied him. Lin-ngan translated:

"The Khan Kubilai speaks thus. The guilty Lady Amursama will be delivered to the Fondler—"

"The Fondler?" I exclaimed, and I laughed. "I thought she had just been delivered *from* one of those."

"The Fondler," the old man said stiffly, "is our name for the Court Executioner."

"In Venice we more realistically call him the Meatmaker."

"It so happens that in the Han language the term for physical torture, dong-xing, and the term for sexual arousal, dong-qing, are, as you have just heard, very similar in pronunciation."

"Gèsu," I muttered.

"I resume," said Lin-ngan. "The wife will be delivered to the Fondler, accompanied by her betrayed husband. In the presence of the Fondler, and if necessary employing his assistance, the husband will with his teeth and fingernails tear out his wife's pudendal sphincter, and with that he will strangle her to death. The Khan Kubilai has spoken."

Neither my father nor my uncle saw fit to comment on that decree, but I did. I scoffed knowingly:

"Vakh! This is pure show. The Khakhan is well aware that we are present. He is only making such eccentric judgments to impress and confound us. Just as the Ilkhan Kaidu did when he spat in his guardsman's mouth."

My father and the Mathematician Lin-ngan gave me looks askance, and my uncle growled, "Brash upstart! Do you really think that the Khan of All Khans would exert himself to impress any human being alive? Least of all, some unimportant wretches from an inconsiderable cranny of the world far beyond his domains?"

I made no reply, but neither did I put on a contrite look, being sure that my disparaging opinion would eventually be confirmed. But it never was. Uncle Mafio was right, of course, and I was wrong, and I would soon know how foolishly I had misread the Khakhan's temperament.

But at that moment the Cheng was emptying. The huddled ruck of petitioners humped to their feet and shuffled out through the door by which we had entered, and the presiding justices at the dais, all except the Khakhan, disappeared through some doorway at that end of the hall. When there was no one left between him and us except his ring of guards, Lin-ngan said, "The Khakhan beckons. Let us approach."

Following the Mathematician's example, we all knelt to make the ko-tou obeisance to the Khakhan. But before we had folded far enough to put our foreheads to the floor, he said in a boomingly hearty voice:

"Rise! Stand! Old friends, welcome back to Kithai!"

He spoke in Mongol, and I never afterwards heard him speak anything else, so I do not know if he was acquainted with Trade Farsi or any others of the multifarious languages employed in his realm, and I never heard anyone else address him in anything but his native Mongol. He did not embrace my father or uncle in the fashion of Venetian friends meeting, but he did clap each of them on the shoulder with a big, heavily beringed hand.

"It is good to see you again, Brothers Polo. How fared you in the journeying, uu? Is this the first of my priests, uu? How young he looks, for a sage cleric!"

"No, Sire," said my father. "This is my son Marco, also now an experienced journeyer. He, like us, puts himself at the service of the Khakhan."

"Then welcome is he, as well," said Kubilai, nodding amiably to me. "But the priests, friend Nicolò, do they follow behind you, uu?"

My father and uncle explained apologetically, but not abjectly, that we had failed to bring the requested one hundred missionary priests—or any priests at all—because they had had the misfortune to return home during the papal interregnum and the consequent disarray of the Church hierarchy. (They did not mention the two faint-hearted Friars Preachers who had come no farther than the Levant.) While they explained, I took the opportunity to look closely at this most powerful monarch in the world.

The Khan of All Khans was then just short of his sixtieth birthday, an age which in the West would have counted him an ancient, but he was still a hale and sturdy specimen of mature manhood. For a crown, he wore a simple gold morion helmet, like an inverted soup bowl, with nape and jugular lappets depending from its back and sides. His hair, what I could see of it under the morion, was gray but still thick. His full mustache and his beard, which was close-trimmed in the style worn by shipwrights, were more pepper than salt. His eyes were rather round, for a Mongol, and bright with intelligence. His ruddy complexion was weathered but not wrinkled, as if his face had been carved from well-seasoned walnut. His nose was his only unhandsome feature, it being short like those of all Mongols, but also bulbous and quite red. His garments were all of splendid silks, thickly brocaded with figures and patterns, and they covered a figure that was stout but nowise suety. On his feet were soft boots of a peculiar leather; I learned later that they were made from the skin of a certain fish, which is alleged to allay the pains of gout, the only affliction I ever heard the Khakhan complain of.

"Well," he said, when my father and uncle had finished, "perhaps your Church of Rome shows a cunning wisdom in keeping close its mysteries."

I was still holding my newly formed opinion that the Khan Kubilai was like any other mortal—as evidenced by his posturings for our benefit during the proceedings of the Cheng—and now he seemed to validate that opinion, for he went on talking, as chattily as any ordinary man making idle conversation with friends.

"Yes, your Church may be right *not* to send missionaries here. When it comes to religion, I often think that none is better than too much. We already have Nestorian Christians, and they are ubiquitous and vociferous, to the point of pestilence. Even my old mother, the Dowager Khatun Sorghaktani, who long ago converted to that faith, is still so besotted with it that she harangues me and every other pagan she meets. Our courtiers are lately desperate to avoid meeting her in the corridors. Such fanaticism defeats its own aims. So, yes, I believe your Roman Christian Church may well attract more converts if it pretends to stand aloof from the herd. That is the way of the Jews, you know. Thus the few pagans who do get accepted into Judaism can feel flattered and honored by the fact."

"Oh, please, Sire," my father said anxiously. "Do not compare the True Faith with the heretic Nestorian sect. And do not equate it with the despised Judaism. Blame me and Mafio, if you will, for our error of timing. But at any and all other times, I sincerely assure you, the Church of Rome holds open its warm embrace to enfold all who desire salvation."

The Khakhan said sharply, "Why, uu?"

That was my first experience of that particular one of Kubilai's attributes, but I was often to remark it thereafter. The Khakhan could be as congenial and discursive and loquacious as an old woman, when it suited his mood and purpose. But when he wanted to know something, when he wanted an answer, when he sought a particle of information, he could suddenly emerge from the clouds of garrulity—his own or a whole roomful of other people's—and swoop like a falcon to strike to the meat of a matter.

"Why?" echoed Uncle Mafio, taken aback. "Why does Christianity seek to save all mankind?"

"But we told you years ago, Sire," said my father. "The faith which preaches love and which was founded on Jesus, the Christ and Savior, is the only hope of bringing about perpetual peace on earth, and plenty, and ease of body and mind and soul, and good will among men. And after life, an eternity of bliss in the Bosom of Our Lord."

I thought my father had put the case for Christianity as well as any ordained cleric could have done. But the Khakhan only smiled sadly and sighed.

"I had hoped you would bring learned men of persuasive arguments, good Brothers Polo. Fond as I am of you, and much as I respect your own convictions, I fear that you—like my dowager mother and like every missionary I have ever met—offer only unsupported asseveration."

Before my father or uncle could profess further, Kubilai launched into another of his periphrases:

"I do indeed remember your telling me how your Jesus came to earth, with His message and His promise. That was more than one thousand and two hundred years ago, you said. Well, I myself have lived long, and I have studied the histories of times before my own. In all ages, it seems, all sorts of religions have held out promises of worldwide peace and bounty and good health and brotherly love and pervading happiness—and some kind of Heaven hereafter. About the hereafter I know nothing. But of my own knowledge, most of the people on this earth, including those who pray and worship with sincerest faith and devotion, remain poor and sickly and unhappy and unfulfilled and in utter detestation of each other—even when they are not actively at war, which is seldom."

My father opened his mouth, perhaps to comment on the incongruity of a Mongol deploring war, but the Khakhan went on:

"The Han people tell a legend about a bird called the jing-wei. Since the beginning of time, the jing-wei has been carrying pebbles in its beak, to fill in the limitless, bottomless Sea of Kithai and make solid land of it, and the jing-wei will continue that futile endeavor until the other end of time. So it must be, I think, with faiths and religions and devotions. You can hardly deny that your own Christian Church has been playing the jing-wei bird for twelve whole centuries now—forever futile, forever fatuously promising what it can never provide."

"Never, Sire?" said my father. "Enough pebbles *will* fill a sea. Even the Sea of Kithai, in time."

"Never, friend Nicolò," the Khakhan said flatly. "Our learned cosmographers have proved that the world is more sea than land. There do not exist enough pebbles."

"Facts cannot prevail against faith, Sire."

"Nor against adamant folly, I fear. Well, well, enough of this. You are men in whom we placed our trust, and you have failed that trust in not fetching the priests requested. However, it is a custom here: never to dispraise men of good breeding in the presence of others." He turned to the Mathematician, who had been listening to those exchanges with an expression of polite boredom. "Master Lin-ngan, will you kindly retire, uu? Leave me alone with these Masters Polo while I chastise them for their nonfeasance."

I was startled and angry and a little uneasy. So that was why he had had us present in the Cheng to observe his capricious judgments—to have us already fearful and trembling even before we heard his judgment on us. Had we come all this weary way only for some frightful punishment? But he surprised me again. When Lin-ngan had gone, he chuckled and said:

"There. All the Han are notorious for their swift conveyance of gossip, and Lin-ngan is a true Han. The whole court already knew of your priestly mission, and now it will be told that our conversation concerned nothing else. Therefore, let us proceed to the nothing-else."

Uncle Mafio said, smiling, "There are numerous nothing-elses to speak of, Sire. Which first?"

"I am told that your road brought you right into the hand of my cousin Kaidu, and that he closed his fist on you for a time."

"A brief delay only, Sire," said my father, and waved toward me. "Marco yonder most ingeniously aided us to elude him, but we will tell you of that another time. Kaidu wished to plunder the gifts we have brought you from your liege subjects the Shah of Persia and the Sultan of India Aryana. Your cousin might have confiscated everything, but for Marco."

The Khakhan nodded again to me, only briefly, before he swung back to my father and uncle. "Kaidu took nothing from you, uu?"

"Nothing, Sire. At your command, we will have servants bring in and display for you the wealth of gold and jewels and finery—"

"Vakh!" the Khakhan interrupted. "Never mind the trinkets. What of the maps, uu? Besides the wretched priests, you promised to bring maps. Did you make them, uu? Did Kaidu filch them from you, uu? I would gladly have had him steal everything else but those!"

I was understandably bewildered by the several and rapid changes of topic under discussion. The Khakhan was not chastising us, but interrogating us, and on a matter until now unsuspected by me. I might have been sufficiently astonished to hear a man say *vakh* to a gift of trinkets that would purchase any duchy in Europe. But I was more astonished to learn that my father and uncle had all this time been engaged on a project more secret and important than just the procurement of missionaries.

"The maps are safe, Sire," said my father. "It never occurred to Kaidu to think of any such things. And Mafio and I believe we have compiled the best maps yet done of the western and central regions of this continent—especially those regions held by the Ilkhan Kaidu."

"Good . . . good . . . ," murmured Kubilai. "The maps drawn by the Han are unsurpassable, but they confine themselves to the Han lands. Those maps we captured from them in earlier years much aided the

Mongol conquest of Kithai, and they will be of equal use as we march south against the Sung. But the Han have always ignored everything beyond their own borders as unworthy of consideration. If you have done your work well, then for the first time I have maps of the entire Silk Road into the farther reaches of my empire."

· Beaming with satisfaction, he looked about him and caught sight of me. Perhaps he took my vapid gawking for a look of stricken conscience, for he beamed even more broadly and spoke directly to me. "I have already promised, young Polo, never to use the maps in any Mongol campaign against the territory or the holdings of the Dogato of Venice."

Then, turning again to my father and uncle, he said, "I will later arrange a private audience for us to sit together and examine the maps. In the meantime, a separate chamber and staff of servants have been appointed for each of you, conveniently close to my own in the main palace residence." He added, rather as an afterthought, "Your nephew may reside in either suite, as you choose."

(It is a curious thing, but for all Kubilai's acuity in every other area of human knowledge and experience, he never, through all the years I knew him, bothered to remember of which elder Polo I was the son and of which the nephew.)

"For tonight," he went on, "I have ordered a banquet of welcome, at which you will meet two other visitors newly come from the West, and we will all together discuss the vexing question of my insubordinate cousin Kaidu. Now Lin-ngan waits outside to escort you to your new quarters."

We all began a ko-tou, and again as he always would do—he bade us rise before we had prostrated ourselves very deeply, and he said, "Until tonight, friends Polo," and we took our leave.

. 2 .

As I say, that was my first realization that my father and uncle, in their assiduous making of maps, had been working at least partly for the Khan Kubilai—and this is the first time I have ever publicly revealed that fact. I did not mention it in the earlier chronicle of my travels and theirs, because at that time my father was still alive, and I hesitated to impute any suspicion that he might have served the Mongol Horde in ways inimical to our Christian West. However, as all men know, the Mongols never again have invaded or threatened the West. Our foremost enemies for many years have continued to be the Muslim Saracens, and the Mongols have frequently been our friendly allies against them.

Meanwhile, as my father and uncle all along intended, Venice and the rest of Europe have profited from increased trade with the East, a trade much facilitated by the copies of all our maps of the Silk Road which we Polos brought home from there. So I no longer see any need to maintain the slightly preposterous fiction that Nicolò and Mafìo Polo crossed and recrossed the whole extent of Asia simply to herd a flock of priests with them. And not in that other book, or ever, have I tried to keep secret the fact that I, Marco Polo, also became an agent and journeyer and observer and mapmaker for the Khan Kubilai. But I will here tell the beginning of my becoming so well regarded by the Khakhan that he entrusted me with such missions.

It was at that night's welcoming banquet that I first attracted his notice. But it could have happened—and almost did—that Kubilai's first attention to me might have been a command that I deliver myself to the Fondler, with my neck in my sphincter.

The banquet was laid in the largest hall of the main palace building, a hall which, one of the table servants boasted to me, would accommodate six thousand diners at a single seating. The high ceiling was held up on pillars that seemed made of solid gold, twisted and convoluted, inset with gems and jade. The walls were paneled alternately in rich carved woods and fine embossed leathers, and hung with Persian qali and Han scroll paintings and Mongol trophies of the hunt. Those included the mounted heads of snarling lions and spotted pards and great-horned artak ("Marco's sheep") and large bearlike creatures called da-mao-xiong, the mounted heads of which were startlingly snow-white except for black ears and black masks about the eyes.

The trophies were probably of the Khakhan's own hunts, for he was famous for his love of the chase, and spent every spare day in forest or field. Even here in the banquet hall, his affection for that manliest of sports was evident, for the guests seated closest to him were his dearest hunting partners. On either arm of his thronelike chair was perched a hooded hunting falcon, and to each of the chair's two front legs was tethered a hunting cat called a chita. The chita resembles a spotted pard, but is much smaller in size and proportionately much longer in the legs. It is different from all other cats in that it cannot climb a tree, and is even more different in that it will willingly chase and pull down game at its master's bidding. Here, however, the chitas and the falcons sat quietly, now and then politely accepting tidbits which Kubilai fed to them with his own fingers.

There were not six thousand persons present on that particular night, so the hall was partitioned by screens of black and gold and red lacquer, to make a more intimate enclosure for rather fewer people. Still, there must have been close on two hundred of us, plus as many servants and a constantly changing crew of musicians and entertainers. That many people breathing and sweating, and the savory steams from the hot foods served, should have made even that huge hall rather warm on that late-summer night. But, although we were screened about and all the outer doors were shut, the hall had a cool breeze mysteriously blowing through it. Not until some while later did I learn by what ingeniously simple means that coolness was effected. But there were other mysteries in that dining hall which made me goggle and thrill and wonder, and for them I never did manage to find adequate explanation.

For example, in the middle of all the many tables stood a tall artificial tree, crafted of silver, its multiple limbs and branches and twigs hung with beaten-silver leaves that fluttered gently in the hall's artificial breeze. Around the tree's silver-barked trunk were coiled four golden serpents. Their tails were twined among the upper branches and their heads snaked downward to poise, open-mouthed, above four immense porcelain vases. The vases were molded in the shape of fantastic lions with their heads thrown back and their mouths also wide. There were some other artificial creatures in the room; on several tables, including the one at which we guest Polos sat, was a life-sized peacock made of gold, its tail feathers finely articulated and colored by inlaid enamels. Now, the mystery about those objects was this. When the Khan Kubilai called for drink—and only when *he* called aloud, not when anyone else did—those several animals of precious metals did wondrous things. I will tell what they did, though I scarcely expect to be believed.

"Kumis!" Kubilai would bellow, and one of the golden serpents coiled about the silver tree would suddenly gush from its mouth a flow of pearly liquid into the mouth of the lion vase set below. A servant would bring the vase to the Khakhan's table and pour the beverage into his jewel-encrusted goblet and the goblets of other guests. They would sip and verify that it was indeed the mare's-milk kumis, and they would all clap their hands in applause of that marvel, and immediately another marvelous thing would occur. The golden peacock on the table—and every golden peacock in the room—would likewise applaud, raising and beating its golden wings, erecting and fanning out its splendid tail.

"Arkhi!" the Khakhan would shout next, and the second serpent on the tree would disgorge its measure into the second lion vase, and a servant would bring the drink and we all would find it to be that finer and tastier grade of kumis called arkhi. And we would applaud and so would the peacocks. And those animated creatures, the liquor-spouting serpents and the exuberant birds, they worked, mind you, without any human agency. I several times went close to observe them, both while they were performing and while they were at rest, and I could find no wires or strings or levers that might have been manipulated from a distance.

"Mao-tai!" the Khakhan would shout next, and the whole activity would be repeated, from serpent spout to lion vase to peacock fanning. The liquor dispensed by the third serpent, mao-tai, was new to me: a yellowish, slightly syrupy beverage of a tingling flavor. The Mongol diner at my elbow cautioned me to beware of its potency, which he demonstrated. He took a tiny porcelain cup of the liquor and applied to it the flame of one of the table candles. The mao-tai caught fire with a sizzling blue flame and burned like naft oil for a good five minutes before it was consumed. I understand that mao-tai is a Han concoction somehow expressed from common millet, but it is an uncommon beverage—as fiery a fuel to the belly and the brain as it is to any open flame.

"Pu-tao!" was the fourth command the Khakhan shouted to the serpent tree; the word pu-tao means grape wine. But to the consternation of all us guests, *nothing happened*. The fourth serpent simply hung there, sullenly dry, and we sat gaping, almost fearful, wondering what had gone wrong. The Khakhan, though, sat grinning with secret glee, enjoying the air of suspense, until he demonstrated the last and most magical magic of the apparatus. Not until he shouted "Pu-tao!" and then added a shout of either "hong!" or "bai!" would the fourth serpent begin to gush, and according to Kubilai's command it would dispense red (hong) or white (bai) wine, at which we guests erupted in a storm of cheers and applause, and the golden peacocks beat their wings and fanned their tails so wildly that they shed flakes of golden feathers.

The banquet guests that night, except for the visitors being welcomed, comprised the highest lords and ministers and courtiers of the Khanate, plus some women whom I took to be their wives. The lords were a mixture of nationalities and complexions: Arabs and Persians as well as Mongols and Han. But of course the women present were the non-Muslim Mongol and Han wives; if the Arabs and Persians had wives, they were not permitted to dine in mixed company. All the men were finely garbed in brocaded silks, some wearing robes, as did the Khakhan and other Mongols and the native Han, some wearing their silks in the form of Persian pai-jamah and tulband, and others wearing their silks as Arab aba and kaffiyah.

But the women were even more gorgeously arrayed. The Han ladies all had powdered their already ivory faces to the whiteness of snow, and wore their blue-black hair in voluminous piles and swirls atop their heads, pinned up there by long jeweled implements they called hair-spoons. The Mongol ladies were of slightly darker complexion, a sort of fawn color, and I was much interested to see that these women, unlike their plains-dwelling nomad sisters, were not coarsened to leather by sun and wind, nor were they bulkily muscular of body. Their coiffures were even more complex than that of the Han women. Their hair, ruddy-black instead of blue-black, was braided onto a framework to make it swoop in a wide crescent at either side of the head, rather like sheep horns, and those crescents were festooned with dangling brilliants. Also, though they wore the same simple, flowing gowns as the Han women, the Mongol ladies added to the shoulders of them some curious high fillets of padded silk that stood up like fins.

At the Khakhan's table with him sat members of his immediate family. Five or six of his twelve legitimate sons were ranged at his right. On his left sat his first and chief wife, the Khatun Jamui, then his aged mother, the Dowager Khatun Sorghaktani, then his three other wives. (Kubilai had also a considerable and constantly varying consort of concubines, all younger than his wives. The current contingent sat at a separate table. By his concubines, Kubalai had another twenty-five sons, and God knows how many legitimate and bastard daughters besides, from all his women.)

The whole dining area was divided so that the male guests occupied the tables to Kubilai's right and the females those to his left. Closest to the Khakhan's table, within easy speaking distance, was the table appointed for us Polos, and with us was seated a Mongol dignitary to converse with us, interpret for us when necessary, explain to us the unfamiliar dishes and drinks served, and so on. He was a fairly young man—exactly ten years older than myself, it turned out—who introduced himself as Chingkim, saying he held the office of Wang of Khanbalik, which was to say the Chief City Officer or Magistrate. That office being equivalent to a European city's mayor—or podestà, in the Venetian term —I gathered that we Polos were entitled to only a minor functionary as our table companion.

The Khakhan more formally introduced us to others of his lords and ministers seated at nearby tables. I will not attempt to list them all, for they included so many persons of so many different degrees of authority, and so many bore titles which I had never heard in any other court, or ever even heard *of*—the Master of the Black-Ink Arts (nothing but the Court Poet), the Master of the Mastiffs, Hawks and Chitas (the Khakhan's Chief Huntsman), the Master of the Boneless Colors (nothing but the Court Artist), the Chief of Secretaries and Scribes, the Archivist of Marvels and Wonders, the Recorder of Things Strange. But I *will* mention by name some lords who seemed to me curiously out of place in a supposedly Mongol court—for example, Lin-ngan, whom we already knew, was one of the supposedly conquered Han, but held the fairly important post of Court Mathematician.

The young man Chingkim appeared to hold the grandest title assigned by Kubilai to any of his fellow Mongols, and Chingkim claimed to be only a mere city Wang. By contrast, the Khakhan's Chief Minister, whose office was called by the Han title of Jing-siang, was neither a conqueror Mongol nor a subject Han. He was an Arab named Achmad-az-Fenaket, and he himself preferred to be called by the Arab title signifying his office, which is Wali. By whatever honorific he was addressed—Jing-siang or Chief Minister or Wali—Achmad was the second most powerful man in the entire Mongol hierarchy, subordinate only to the Khakhan himself, for he also held the office of Vice-Regent, meaning that he literally ruled the empire whenever Kubilai was out hunting or making war or otherwise occupied, and Achmad also held the office of Finance Minister, meaning that at all times he controlled the purse strings of the empire.

It seemed equally odd to me that the Mongol Empire's Minister of War—war being the activity in which the Mongols most excelled and exulted—was *not* a Mongol but a Han gentleman named Chao Meng-fu. The Court Astronomer was a Persian named Jamal-ud-Din, a native of far-off Isfahan. The Court Physician was a Byzantine, a native of even farther-off Constantinople, the Hakim Gansui. The palace staff included other persons, not present at that banquet, of even more surprising alien origins, and I would eventually come to know them all.

The Khakhan had promised that we Polos would that night meet "two other visitors newly come from the West," and they were present, seated at a table within speaking distance of his table and ours. They were not Westerners, but Han, and I recognized them as the two men I had seen dismounting from mules in the palace courtyard on the evening of our arrival, and I still had the feeling that I had seen them somewhere else even before that.

The tables at which we all sat were surfaced with a pinkish-lavender

inlay of what looked to me like precious stones. And so they were, said
our tablemate Chingkim:

"Amethyst," he told me. "We Mongols have learned much from the
Han. And the Han physicians have concluded that tables made of purple
amethyst prevent drunkenness in those who sit drinking at them."

I thought that interesting, but I should also have been interested to
see how much drunker the company might have got without the countering influence of the amethyst. Kubilai was not alone in bellowing for
kumis and arkhi and mao-tai and pu-tao, and ingesting quantities of all
those beverages. Even of the resident Arabs and Persians, the only one
who stayed Muslimly sedate and sober all night was the Wali Achmad.
And the guzzling was not confined to the male guests; the female Mongols put away their share, too, and gradually got quite raucous and
bawdy. The Han females kept to wine only, and only infrequent sips of
it, and maintained their ladylike propriety.

But the company did not get drunk immediately, or all at once. The
banquet began at what is in Kithai known as the Hour of the Cock, and
the first guests did not stagger from the hall or slide insensible under the
amethyst tables until well into the Hour of the Tiger, which is to say that
the feasting and talking and laughing and entertainment lasted from
early evening until just before dawn the next morning, and the general
inebriation was not too evident until the tenth or eleventh hour of that
twelve-hour festa.

"Onyx," said Chingkim to me, and he pointed at the open area of
the floor around the drink-pouring serpent tree, where at the moment
two monstrously stout and sweatily naked Turki wrestlers were trying to
dismember each other for our amusement. "The Han physicians have
concluded that the black onyx stone imparts strength to those in contact
with it. So the wrestling floor is paved with onyx to enliven the com-
batants."

After the two Turki had crippled each other to the company's satisfaction, we were regaled by a troupe of Uzbek girl singers, wearing gold-
embroidered gowns of ruby red and emerald green and sapphire blue.
The girls had rather pretty but exceptionally flat faces, as if their features
were only painted on the fronts of their heads. They screeched for us
some incomprehensible and interminable Uzbek ballads, in voices like
ungreased wheels on a runaway wagon. Then some Samoyed musicians
performed pieces of similar cacophony on an assortment of instruments
—hand drums and finger cymbals and pipes resembling our fagotto and
dulzaina.

Then there came Han jugglers who were far more entertaining,
since they performed in silence as well as with incredible dexterity. It
was astounding to see the tricks they could do with swords and rope
loops and blazing torches, and how many such objects they could keep
flying or spinning or suspended in the air at one time. But I really
thought I could no longer trust my eyes when the jugglers began tossing
into the air and to one another wine cups *full of wine*, and never spilling
a drop! In the intervals between those performances, there wandered
about the hall a tulhulos, which is a Mongol minstrel, sawing on a sort of

three-stringed viella and dolefully wailing chronicles of battles and victories and heroes past.

Meanwhile, we all ate. And how we ate! We ate from paper-thin porcelain plates and bowls and platters, some softly colored in brown and cream colors, others blue with plum-color mottlings. I did not know then but later was told that those porcelains, called Chi-zho and Jen ware, were Han works of art, worthy of being treasured in collections, and not even the emperors of the Han would have dreamed of employing them for mere tableware. But, just as Kubilai had appropriated those art objects for his guests' convenience, so had he acquired for his palace kitchens the foremost cooks of all Kithai, and those, more than the Chi-zho and Jen porcelain, were loudly appreciated by us guests. As we were served with each new course of the meal, and sampled it, the whole room would breathe "Hui!" and "Hao!" in approval, and the cook responsible for that particular dish would emerge from the kitchens and smile and ko-tou, and we would applaud him by clicking together our nimble tongs, making a cricket crepitation. I might remark that we guests were supplied with eating tongs of intricately carved ivory, but those used by Kubilai—so I was told by Chingkim—were made from the forearm bones of a gibbon ape, because such tongs will turn black if they touch poisoned food.

Our tablemate also explained each dish that came to our table, because almost every one was of Han origin and had a Han name that was most intriguing but gave no hint of the dish's content, and I could not always determine what it was I was eating and applauding. Of course, at the start of the feasting, when the first dish was announced as Milk and Roses, I had no trouble seeing that those were simply white grapes and pink grapes. (A meal in the Han style goes contrary to ours; it begins with fruits and nuts and ends with a soup.) But when I was presented with a dish called Snow Babies, Chingkim had to explain that it was made of bean curd and the cooked flesh of frogs' legs. And the dish called Red-Beaked Green Parrot with Gold-Trimmed Jade was a sort of multicolored custard containing the boiled and pulverized leaves of a Persian plant called aspanakh, creamed mushrooms and the petals of various flowers.

When the servants set before me One-Hundred-Year Eggs, I nearly declined them, for they were only hens' and ducks' eggs, hard-boiled, but the whites of them were a ghastly green and the yolks were black, and they *smelled* a hundred years old. However, Chingkim assured me that they were really only pickled, and only for sixty days, so I ate them and found them tasty. There were stranger things—the meat of bear paws, and fish lips, and a broth made of the saliva with which a certain bird glues its nest together, and pigeons' feet in jelly, and a blob of substance called go-ba, which is a fungus that grows on ricestalks—but I valiantly partook of them all. There were also more recognizable foods—the miàn pasta in numerous shapes and sauces, dumplings stuffed and steamed, the familiar aubergine in an unfamiliar fish gravy.

The banquet, like the banqueters and the banquet hall, gave ample evidence that the Mongols had climbed a fair way from barbarism toward civilization, and had done it mainly by adopting so much of the Han people's culture, from their foods to their costumes to their bathing habits to their architecture. But the banquet's main culinary treat—the piatanza di prima portata—Chingkim said was a dish long ago devised by the Mongols, and only recently but happily adopted by the Han. They called it Windblown Duck, and Chingkim told me the complicated process of its preparation.

A duck, he said, came from egg to kitchen in exactly forty-eight days, then required forty-eight hours for the proper cooking. Its brief lifetime included three weeks of being force-fed (in the way that the Strasbourgeois of the Lorraine stuff their geese). The well-fatted fowl was killed and plucked and cleaned, and its body cavity was blown full of air and distended, and it was hung outdoors in a south wind. "Only a south wind will do," said Chingkim. Then it was glazed by being smoked over a fire in which camphor burned. Then it was roasted over an ordinary fire, meanwhile being basted with wine and garlic and bead molasses and a fermented-bean sauce. Then it was cut up and served in bite-sized pieces—the flakes of crisp black skin being the most prized part—with lightly cooked onion greens and water chestnuts and a transparent miàn vermicelli, and if there was anything to make the Han people less resentful of their Mongol conquerors, in my opinion it must be Windblown Duck.

After a confection of sugared lotus petals and a clear soup made from hami melons, the very last dish was placed upon each table: a huge tureen of plain boiled rice. This was purely symbolic, and no one partook of it. Rice is the staple of the diet of the Han people—in truth, in the southern Han realms, rice is almost the whole of the people's diet—and it therefore merits a place of honor on every table, even a rich man's table. But a rich man's guests will refrain from eating it, for to do so would insult the host, implying that all the foregoing delicacies had been insufficient.

Then, while the servants cleared the tables for the serious business of drinking, Kubilai and my father and uncle and some others began to converse. (As I have told, Mongol men do not customarily talk during a meal, and the other men in the hall had also observed that custom. It had, however, not at all deterred the Mongol women, who had cackled and shrieked all through the dinner.) Kubilai said to my father and uncle:

"These men, Tang and Fu"—he indicated the two Han I had already noticed—"came from the West about the same time that you did. They are spies of mine, clever and adept and unobtrusive. When I got word that a Han wagon train was going into the lands of my cousin Kaidu, to bring back Han cadavers for burial, I had Tang and Fu join that karwan." Aha, I thought, so that explained my having seen them before, but I made no comment. Kubilai turned to them. "Tell us then, honorable spies, what secrets you ferreted out from Sin-kiang Province."

Tang spoke, and as if he were reciting from a written list, though he used no such thing: "The Ilkhan Kaidu is orlok of a bok comprising an entire tuk, of which he can instantly put six tomans into the field."

The Khakhan did not look much impressed, but he translated that for my father and uncle: "My cousin commands a camp containing one hundred thousand horse warriors, of whom sixty thousand stand always ready for battle."

I wondered why the Khan Kubilai had had to employ professional spies to get such information by stealth, when I had learned as much simply by sharing a meal in a yurtu.

Fu spoke in his turn: "Each warrior goes into battle with one lance, one mace, his shield, at least one sword and dagger, one bow and sixty arrows for it. Thirty arrows are light, with narrow heads, for long-range use. Thirty are heavy, with broad heads, for use at close quarters."

I knew that much, too, and more: that some of the arrowheads would scream and whistle furiously as they flew.

Tang took a turn again: "To be independent of the bok supplies, each warrior also carries one small earthenware pot for cooking, a small folding tent and two leather bottles. One is full of kumis, the other of grut, and on those he can subsist for a long time without weakening."

Fu added: "If he haply procures a piece of meat, he need not even pause to cook it, but tucks it between his saddle and his mount. As he rides, the pounding and the heat and the sweat cure the meat and make it edible."

Tang again: "If a warrior has no other nutriment, he will nourish himself and quench his thirst by drinking the blood of the first enemy he slays. He will also use that body's fat to grease his tack and weapons and armor."

Kubilai compressed his lips and fingered his mustache, in evident impatience, but the two Han said no more. With a trace of exasperation he muttered, "Numbers and details are all very well. But you have told me little that I have not known since I first straddled my own horse at the age of four. What of the mood and temper of the Ilkhan and his troops, uu?"

"No need to inquire privily into that, Sire," said Tang. "All men know that all Mongols are forever ready and eager to fight."

"To fight, yes, but to fight *whom*, uu?" the Khakhan persisted.

"At present, Sire," said Fu, "the Ilkhan uses his forces only for putting down bandits in his own Sin-kiang Province, and for petty skirmishes against the Tazhiks to secure his western borders."

"Hui!" said Kubilai, in a sort of pounce. "But is he doing those things merely to keep his fighting men occupied, uu? Or is he honing their skill and spirit for more ambitious undertakings, uu? Perhaps a rebellious thrust at *my* western borders, uu? Tell me that!"

Tang and Fu could only make respectful noises and shrugs to excuse their ignorance. "Sire, who can examine the inside of an enemy's head? Even the best spy can but observe the observable. The facts we brought we have gleaned with much perseverance, and much care that they be accurate, and at much hazard of our being discovered, which would have meant our being tied spread-eagle among four horses, and they whipped toward the four horizons."

Kubilai gave them a look of some disdain, and turned to my father and uncle. "You at least came face to face with my cousin, friends Polo. What did you make of him, uu?"

Uncle Mafìo said thoughtfully, "Certain it is that Kaidu is greedy for more than he has. And he is patently a man of bellicose temper."

"He is, after all, of the Khakhan's own family lineage," said my father. "It is an ancient truth: that a she-wolf does not drop lambs."

"Those things, too, I know very well," growled Kubilai. "Is there *no one* who has perceived more than the flagrantly obvious, uu?"

He had not put that "uu?" directly to me, but the question emboldened me to speak. Granted, I could more gracefully have imparted what I wanted to tell him. But I was still being scornful of what I took to have been his pose of cruel caprice when he made sure we heard his harsh sentences in the Cheng—hence I was still under the misapprehension that the Khan Kubilai was, in fondo, only an ordinary man. Perhaps also I had already imbibed rather too freely of the drinks dispensed by the serpent tree. Anyway, I spoke, and spoke somewhat more loudly than I need have done:

"The Ilkhan Kaidu called you decadent and effete and degenerate, Sire. He said that you have become no better than a Kalmuk."

Every person present heard me. Every person present must have known what a squalid thing a Kalmuk is. An instant and vast and appalled hush fell upon the whole banquet hall. Every man stopped talking, and even the strident Mongol women seemed to suffocate in midgabble. My father and uncle covered their faces with their hands, and the Wang Chingkim stared at me in utter horror, and the Khakhan's sons and wives all gasped, and Tang and Fu put trembling hands to their mouths, as if they had untimely laughed or belched, and all the other varicolored faces within my view went uniformly pale.

Only the face of the Khan Kubilai did not go ashen. It went maroon and murderous, and it began to contort as he started framing words of condemnation and command. Had he ever got those words out, I know now, he never would have retracted them, and nothing would have mitigated my gross offense or moderated my condign sentence, and the guards would have hauled me off to the Fondler, and the manner of my execution must have become a legend in Kithai forevermore. But Kubilai's face kept on working, as he evidently discarded one set of words as too mild, and substituted another and another more terribly damnatory, and that gave me time to finish what I wished to say:

"However, when it thunders, Sire, the Ilkhan Kaidu invokes your name for protection against the wrath of Heaven. He does it silently, under his breath, but I have read your name upon his lips, Sire, and his own warriors confided the same to me. If you doubt it, Sire, you could ask the two of Kaidu's personal guardsmen that he sent as our escort, the warriors Ussu and Donduk . . ."

My voice trailed off into the dreadful hush that still prevailed. I could hear droplets of kumis or pu-tao or some other of the liquids dripping, plink, plunk, from a serpent spout into a lion vase beneath. In that breathless, monumental quiet, Kubilai kept his black eyes impaling me, but his face slowly ceased its contortions and became still as stone,

and the violent color slowly ebbed from it, and at last he said, only in
a murmur, but again all present heard:

"Kaidu invokes my name when he is affrighted. By the great god
Tengri, that single observation is worth more to me than six tomans of
my best and fiercest and most loyal horsemen."

· 3 ·

I awoke the next day, in the afternoon, in a bed in my father's chambers,
with a head that I almost wished *had* been lopped off by the Fondler.
The last thing that I clearly remembered of the banquet was the
Khakhan's roaring to the Wang Chingkim, "See to this young Polo!
Appoint him separate quarters of his own! And servants of twenty-two
karats!" That had sounded fine, but to be given immobile metal servants,
even of nearly pure gold, did not make much sense, so I assumed that
Kubilai had been as drunk as was I at the time, and Chingkim, and
everybody else.

However, after my father's two women servants had helped him and
me to get up and get bathed and get dressed, and had brought us each a
potion to clear the head—a spicy and aromatic drink, but so heavily
laced with mao-tai that I could not force it down—Chingkim came
calling, and father's servants fell down in ko-tou to him. The Wang,
looking as if he felt much the way I did, gently booted the two prostrate
bodies out of his way, and told me he had come, as ordered, to conduct
me to the new suite prepared for my occupancy.

As we went there—no far distance along the same hall that my
father's and uncle's quarters opened onto—I thanked Chingkim for the
courtesy and, seeking to be polite even to a minor functionary assigned
to serve me, I added, "I do not know why the Khakhan should have
ordered you to see to my comfort. After all, you are the Wang of the city,
and an official of some small importance. Surely the palace guests should
be a steward's responsibility, and this palace has as many stewards as a
Buddhist has fleas."

He gave a laugh, only a small one, not to jar his own head, and said,
"I do not object to being given a trivial duty now and then. My father
believes that a man can only learn to command others by learning himself to obey the least command."

"Your father seems to lean as heavily on wise proverbs as mine
does," I said companionably. "Who is your father, Chingkim?"

"The man who gave me the order. The Khakhan Kubilai."

"Oh?" I said, as he bowed me through the doorway of my new
quarters. "One of the bastards, are you?" I said offhandedly, as I might
have spoken to the son of a Doge or a Pope, nobly born, but on the
wrong side of the blanket. I was looking with appreciation at the doorway, for it was not rectangular in the Western style or peaked to an arch
in the Muslim fashion. It and the others between my various rooms were

called variously Moon Gate and Lute Gate and Vase Gate, because their openings were contoured in the outlines of those objects. "This is a sumptuous apartment."

Chingkim was regarding me with somewhat the same appraisal I was giving to the suite's luxurious appointments. He said quietly, "Marco Polo, you do have your own peculiar way of speaking to your elders."

"Oh, you are not that much older than I, Chingkim. How nice, these windows open onto a garden." Truly I was being very dense, but my head, as I have said, was not at its best. Also, at the banquet, Chingkim had not sat at the head table with Kubilai's legitimate sons. That recollection made me think of something. "I saw none of the Khakhan's concubines who looked old enough to have a son your age, Chingkim. Which of last night's women was your mother?"

"The one who sat nearest the Khakhan. Her name is Jamui."

I paid little attention, being occupied in the admiration of my bedchamber. The bed was most lovelily springy, and it had a Western style pillow for me. Also—apparently in case I should invite a court lady to bed—it had one of the Han-style pillows, a sort of shallow pedestal of porcelain, itself molded in the form of a reclining woman, to prop up a lady's neck without disarranging her coiffure.

Chingkim went on chatting idly, "Those of Kubilai's sons who sat with him last night are Wangs of provinces and ortoks of armies, things like that."

For summoning my servants, there was a brass gong as big around as a Kashgar wagon wheel. But it was fashioned like a fish with a great round head, mostly a vast mouth, and only a stumpy brass body, for resonance, behind its wide opening.

"I was appointed Wang of Khanbalik," Chingkim prattled on, "because Kubilai likes to keep me near him. And he sat me at your table to do honor to your father and uncle."

I was examining a most marvelous lamp in my main room. It had two cylindrical paper shades, one inside the other, both fitted with paper blades inside their circumference, so that somehow the heat of the lamp flame made the shades slowly turn in opposite directions. They were painted with various lines and spots, and were translucent, so that their movement and the light within made the paints intermittently resolve themselves into a recognizable picture—and the picture *moved*. I later saw other such lamps and lanterns displaying different scenes, but this one of mine showed, over and over, a mule kicking up its heels and catching a little man in his backside and sending him flying. I was entranced.

"I am not Kubilai's eldest son, but I am the only son born to him by his premier wife, the Khatun Jamui. That makes me Crown Prince of the Khanate and Heir Apparent to my father's throne and title."

By that time, I was down on my knees, puzzling over the composition of the strange, flat, pale carpet on the floor. After close scrutiny, I determined that it was made of long strips of thin-peeled ivory, woven together, and I had never before seen or heard of any such wondrous artisanry as *woven ivory*. Since I was already kneeling—when Chingkim's words at last penetrated into my dismally dimmed mind—it was easy for me to slide prostrate and make ko-tou at the feet of the next Khan of All Khans of the Mongol Empire, whom I had a moment ago addressed as Bastard.

"Your Royal Highness . . . ," I began to apologize, speaking to the woven ivory on which my aching and now sweating forehead was pressed.

"Oh, get up," the Crown Prince said affably. "Let us continue to be Marco and Chingkim. Time enough for titles when my father dies, and I trust that will not be for many years yet. Get up and greet your new servants. Biliktu and Buyantu. Good Mongol maidens, whom I selected for you personally."

The girls made ko-tou four times to Chingkim and then four times to us both and then four times to me alone. I mumbled, "I expected to get statues."

"Statues?" echoed Chingkim. "Ah, yes. Twenty-two karat, these maidens. That grading system is of my father's devising. If you will command for me a goblet of head-clearing potion, we can sit down and I will explain about the karats."

I gave the command, and ordered cha for myself, and the two girls bowed their way backwards out of the room. From their names, and from what little I had glimpsed of them, Buyantu and Biliktu were sisters. They were about my own age, and far prettier than the other Mongol females I had seen so far—certainly much prettier than the middle-aged women who had been assigned to my father and uncle. When they came back with our drinks, and Chingkim and I sat down on facing benches, and the maids brought fans to fan us, I could see that they were twins, identical in comeliness and wearing identical costumes. I would have to direct them to dress differently, I thought, so I could tell them apart. And when they were undressed? That thought, too, came naturally to my mind, but I dismissed it, to listen to the Prince, who, after taking a long draft from his goblet, had begun to talk again.

"My father, as you know, has four wedded wives. Each in her turn receives him in her own separate yurtu, but—"

"Yurtu!" I interrupted.

He laughed. "So it is called, though no Mongol plainsman would recognize it. In the old nomad days, you see, a Mongol lord kept his wives dispersed about his territory, each in her own yurtu, so that wherever he rode he never had to endure a wifeless night. Now, of course, each wife's so-called yurtu is a splendid palace here in these grounds— and a populous place, more like a bok than a yurtu. Four wives, four palaces. And my mother's alone has a permanent staff of more than three hundred. Ladies-in-waiting and attendants and physicians and servants and hairdressers and slaves and wardrobe mistresses and astrologers . . . But I started out to tell you about the karats."

He broke off to touch a hand tenderly to his head, and swigged again from his goblet before going on:

"I think my father is now of an age that a mere four women in rotation would suffice him, even well-worn wives who are also getting on in years. But it is an ancient custom for all his subject lands—as far away as Poland and India Aryana—to send him each year the finest of their newly nubile maidens. He cannot possibly take them all as concubines, or even as servants, but neither can he disappoint his subjects by refusing their gifts outright. So he now has those annual crops of girls weeded down at least to a manageable number."

Chingkim emptied his goblet and handed it, without looking, over his shoulder, where Biliktu-or-Buyantu took it and scurried off.

"Each year," he resumed, "as the maidens are delivered to the various Ilkhans and Wangs in the various lands and provinces, those men examine the girls and assay them like so much gold bullion. Depending on the quality of a maiden's facial features and bodily proportions and complexion and hair and voice and grace of gait and so on, she is rated at fourteen karats—or sixteen or eighteen, as the case may be, and so on up. Only those above sixteen karats are sent on here to Khanbalik, and only those assayed at the fineness of pure unalloyed gold, twenty-four karats, have any hope of getting near the great Khakhan."

Though Chingkim could not have heard my maid's silent approach, he put up his hand and she arrived just in time to place the refilled goblet in his grasp. He appeared not at all surprised to receive it—as if he had naturally assumed it would be there—and he gulped from it and went on:

"Even those comparatively few maidens of twenty-four karats must first live for a while with older women here in the palace. The old women inspect them even more closely, especially their behavior in the nighttime. Do the girls snore in their sleep, or toss restlessly in the bed? Are their eyes bright and their breath sweet when they awaken in the morning? Then, on the old women's recommendations, my father will take a few of the girls as his concubines for the next year, others to be his maidservants. The rest of them he apportions out, according to their karat grade, to his lords and ministers and court favorites, according to their rank. Congratulate yourself, Marco, that you suddenly rank high enough to merit these twenty-two-karat virgins."

He paused, and laughed again. "I do not quite know *why* you do—unless it is your propensity for reviling your betters as Kalmuks and bastards. I hope all the other courtiers do not start imitating your style of address, and expect to emulate your rise to favor."

I cleared my throat and said, "You mentioned that the girls come from all lands. Had you any particular reason for selecting Mongols for me?"

"Again, my father's instructions. You already speak our tongue very well, but he desires that you achieve impeccable fluency. And it is a known fact that pillow talk is the best and quickest way to learn a language. Why do you ask? Would you have preferred some other breed of women?"

"No, no," I said hastily. "The Mongol is one breed of woman I have not yet had an opportunity to—er—assay. I look forward to the experience. I am honored, Chingkim."

He shrugged. "They are twenty-two karat. Near perfect." He sipped again at his drink, then leaned toward me to say seriously, speaking now in Farsi, that the maids might not eavesdrop, "There are many lords here, Marco, and older ones, and very high-ranking ones, who have never yet received better than a sixteen-karat regard from the Khan Kubilai. I suggest you keep that in mind. Any palace community is an anthill teeming with intrigues and plots and conspiracies, even at the level of page boys and kitchen scullions. It will rankle many in this court, that a young man like you is *not* consigned to that grub-ant level of pages and scullions. You are a newcomer and a Ferenghi, which would make you suspect enough, but abruptly and incomprehensibly you have been exalted. Overnight, you have become an interloper, a target for envy and spite. Believe me, Marco. No one else would give you this friendly warning, but I do, because I am the only one who can. Second only to my father, I am the one man in the entire Khanate who need not be fearful and jealous of his position. Everyone else must be—and so must see you as a threat. Be always on your guard."

"I believe you, Chingkim, and I thank you. Can you suggest any way I might make myself less of a target?"

"A Mongol horseman takes care never to ride on the skyline of the hills, but always a little way below the crest."

I sat and considered that advice. Just then, there came a scratching noise from the hall door, and one of the maids glided away to answer it. I could not quite determine how I might stay off the skyline while resident inside a palace, unless perhaps I went about in a permanent posture of ko-tou. The maid came back into the room.

"Master Marco, it is a caller who gives his name as Sindbad, and urgently entreats audience."

"What?" I said, preoccupied with skylines. "I am acquainted with no person named Sindbad."

Chingkim looked at me and raised his eyebrows, as if to say, "Already come the enemies?"

Then I shook my head and got it to working again, and said, "Oh, of course I know the man. Bid him come in."

He did, and rushed straight to me, looking distraught, wringing his hands, his eyes and central orifice wildly dilated. Without ko-tou or salaam, he bleated in Farsi, "By the seven voyages of my namesake, Master Marco, but this is a terrible place!"

I held up a hand to stop his saying something as indiscreet as I had several times done lately, and turned to say to Chingkim in the same language, "Allow me, Royal Highness, to introduce my slave Nostril."

"Nostril?" Chingkim murmured wonderingly.

Taking my hint, Nostril made a perfect ko-tou to the Prince and then to me, and said meekly, "Master Marco, I would beg a boon."

"You may speak in the Prince's presence. He is a friend. But why are you going about under an assumed name?"

"I have been seeking you everywhere, master. I used all my names, a different one to every person I asked. I thought it prudent, since I go in fear for my life."

"Why? What have you done?"

"Nothing, master! I swear it! I have been so well behaved for so long that Hell itches with impatience. I am spotless as a new-dropped lamb. But so were Ussu and Donduk. Master, I beg that you rescue me from that sty called a barrack. Let me come and lodge in your quarters. I ask not even a pallet. I will lay me down across your threshold like a watchdog. For the sake of all the times I saved your life, Master Marco, now save mine!"

"What? I do not recall your ever saving my life."

Chingkim looked amused and Nostril looked befuddled.

"Did I not? Some earlier master, perhaps. Well, if I have not, it was only for lack of opportunity. However, if and when some such dread opportunity occurs, it is best that I be near at hand and—"

I interrupted, "What about Ussu and Donduk?"

"That is what has terrified me, master. The frightful fate of Ussu and Donduk. They did nothing wrong, did they? Only escorted us from Kashgar to here, did they not, and performed capably in that duty?" He did not wait for a reply, but babbled on. "This morning a squad of guards came and manacled Donduk and dragged him away. Ussu and I, certain that some terrible mistake had been made, inquired around the barracks, and were told that Donduk was being *questioned*. After a while of worrying, we inquired again, and were told that Donduk had not satisfactorily answered the questions, so he was at that moment being *buried*."

"Amoredèi!" I cried. "He is dead?"

"One hopes so, master; otherwise an even more terrible mistake has been made. Then, master, after a while the guards came again and manacled Ussu and dragged *him* away. After another while of wringing my hands, I inquired again about the two of them, and I was rudely told to inquire no more about matters of *torture*. Well, Donduk had been taken and slain and buried, and Ussu had been taken, and who else was there to torture but *me*? So I fled the barrack to come looking for you and—"

"Hush," I said. I turned to look a query at Chingkim.

He said, "My father is anxious to know all he can learn about his eternally restive cousin Kaidu. It was you who mentioned to him last night that your escorts were men of Kaidu's personal guard. No doubt my father assumes them to be well informed about their master—about any possible insurrection Kaidu may be planning." He paused and looked down into his goblet and said, "It is the Fondler who does the questioning."

"The Fondler?" Nostril murmured wonderingly.

I pondered, which hurt my head, and after a moment said to Chingkim, "It would be obtrusive of me to interfere in Mongol affairs that involve Mongols only. But I do feel in a measure responsible. . . ."

Chingkim drained his cup and stood. "Let us go and see the Fondler."

I would much rather have stayed in my new quarters all day, and nursed my head, and got acquainted with the twins Buyantu and Biliktu, but I went, and made Nostril come with us.

We went a long way, through enclosed passages and open areas and more passages, and then down some stairs that led underground, and then another long way through subterranean workshops full of busy artisans, and through storage cellars and lumber rooms and wine cellars. When Chingkim was leading us through a series of torch-lit but unpeopled chambers, their rock walls damp with slime and mottled with fungus, he paused to say in an undertone to Nostril, though surely meaning the advice for me, too:

"Do not again use the word torture, slave. The Fondler is a sensitive man. He resents and recoils from such rough terms. Even when a matter of importance necessitates his plucking out a person's eyeballs and putting hot coals in the sockets, it is never torture. Call it questioning, call it caressing, call it tickling—call it anything but torture—lest someday it is required that you be fondled by the Fondler and he remembers your disrespect of his profession."

Nostril only gulped loudly, but I said, "I understand. In Christian dungeons the practice is formally known as the Asking of the Question Extraordinaire."

Chingkim finally led us into a room that, except for its torch light and beslimed rock walls, might have been a counting room in a prosperous mercantile establishment. It was full of counting desks at which stood clerks busy with ledgers and documents and abachi and the petty routine of any well-run institution. This might be a human abattoir, but it was an orderly abattoir.

"The Fondler and all his staff are Han," Chingkim said to me aside. "They are so much better at these things than we."

Evidently even the Crown Prince did not demand entry straightaway into the Fondler's domain. We all waited until one of the Han clerks, the tall and austerely expressionless chief of those clerks, deigned to approach us. He and the Prince spoke for a time in the Han language, then Chingkim translated to me:

"The man called Donduk was first questioned, and with propriety, but declined to betray anything he knew of his master Kaidu. So then he was questioned extraordinarily, as you put it, to the limits of the Fondler's ingenuity. But he remained obdurate and so—as is my father's standing order in such cases—he was relinquished to the Death of a Thousand. Then the man Ussu was brought in. He also has resisted both the questioning and the questioning extraordinary, and will also be accorded the Death of a Thousand. They deserve it, of course, being traitors to their ultimate ruler, my father. But"—he said this with some pride—"they are loyal to their Ilkhan, and they are stubborn and they are brave. They are true Mongols."

I said, "Pray, what is the Death of a Thousand? A thousand what?"

Chingkim said, again in an undertone, "Marco, call it the death of a thousand caresses, a thousand cruelties, a thousand endearments, what matter? Given a thousand of *anything*, a man will die. The name only signifies a death long drawn out."

He was plainly urging that I not pursue the matter, but I did. I said, "I never held any affection for Donduk. Ussu, though, was a more congenial companion on the long trail. I should like to know how his long trail ends."

Chingkim made a face, but he turned to speak again to the chief clerk. The man looked surprised and doubtful, but he went out of the room by an iron-studded door.

"Only my father or I could even contemplate doing this," muttered Chingkim. "And even I must convey to the Fondler most fulsome compliments and abject apology for interrupting him when he is actually engaged in his work."

I expected the chief clerk to come back bringing a monstrous, shaggy brute of a man, broad of shoulder, brawny of arm, beetling of brow, black-garbed like the Meatmaker of Venice or all in Hellfire-red like the executioner of the Baghdad Daiwan. But if the chief clerk had looked the picture of a clerk, the man who returned with him was the very essence of clerkness. He was gray-haired and pale and frail, fussy and fidgety of manner, prissily dressed in mauve silks. He tripped across the room with small, precise steps, and he looked at us, despite his diminutive Han nose, very much de haut en bas. He was a man born to be a clerk. Surely, I thought, he cannot be other than that. But he spoke in the Mongol tongue, and said:

"I am Ping, the Fondler. What wish you of me?" His voice was tight, with the barely controlled and not at all concealed indignation that is the natural speech of a clerk interrupted in his clerking.

"I am Chingkim, the Crown Prince. I should like you, Master Ping, to explain to this honored guest of mine the manner of giving the Death of a Thousand."

The creature sniffed clerkishly. "I am not accustomed to requests of that indelicate nature, and I do not grant them. Also, the only honored guests here are my own."

Chingkim perhaps stood in awe of the Fondler's title of office, but he himself was entitled Prince. More than that, he was a Mongol being affronted by a mere Han. He drew himself up tall and rigid, and snarled:

"You are a public servant and we are the public! You are a civil servant and you will be civil! I am your Prince and you have arrogantly neglected to make ko-tou! Do so at once!"

The Fondler Ping flinched back as if we had pelted him with some of his own hot coals, and obediently fell down and did the ko-tou. All the other clerks in the chamber peered awestricken over their counting desks at what must have been a first-ever occurrence. Chingkim smoldered down at the prostrate man for some moments before bidding him to rise. When Ping did, he was suddenly all conciliation and solicitude, as is the way of clerks when someone has the temerity to bark at them. He fawned on Chingkim and expressed himself willing, nay, avid to fulfill the Prince's every least whim.

Chingkim said grumpily, "Just tell the Lord Marco here how the Death of a Thousand is administered."

"With pleasure," said the Fondler. He turned on me the same benign smile he had bestowed on Chingkim, and spoke in the same unctuous voice, but his eyes on me were snake cold and malevolent.

"Lord Marco," he began. (Actually he said Lahd Mah-ko, in the Han manner, but I eventually got so used to not hearing *r*'s when a Han spoke that I will henceforth forbear from remarking on the fact.)

"Lord Marco, it is named the Death of a Thousand because it re-, quires one thousand small pieces of silk paper, folded and tossed haphazard in a basket. Each paper bears a word or two, no more than three, signifying some part of the human body. Navel or right elbow or upper lip or left middle toe or whatever. Of course, there are not one thousand parts to the human body—at any rate, not one thousand capable of feeling sensation, like a fingertip, say, or being caused cessation of function, like a kidney. To be precise, there are, by the traditional Fondler's Count, only three hundred and thirty-six such parts. So the inscribed papers are almost all in triplicate. That is to say, three hundred and thirty-two parts of the body are thrice written on separate papers, making a total of nine hundred and ninety-six. Are you following this, Lord Marco?"

"Yes, Master Ping."

"Then you will have noted that there are four parts of the body not inscribed thrice on the papers. Those four are written only once apiece, on the four papers remaining of the thousand. I will later explain why—if you have not guessed by then. Very well, we have one thousand inscribed and folded little papers. Every time a man or woman is sentenced to the Death of a Thousand, before I commence my attentions to the Subject, I have my assistants newly mix and toss and tumble those papers in the basket. I do that mainly to reduce the likelihood of repetition in the Fondling, which might be unnecessarily distressing to the Subject or boring to me."

He really was a clerk at heart, I thought, with his finicking numbers and his calling the victim the Subject and his lofty condescension to my interest in the matter. But I was not fool enough to say so. Instead, I remarked respectfully:

"Excuse me, Master Ping. But all of this—this writing and folding and tossing of papers—what has this to do with death?"

"Death? It has to do with *dying!*" he said sharply, as if I had strayed into irrelevance. Flicking a sly glance sideways at Prince Chingkim, he said, "Any crude barbarian can kill a Subject. But artfully to lead and guide and beckon and cajole a man or woman through the dying—ah, for that, the Fondler!"

"I see," I said. "Please do go on."

"After having been purged and evacuated, to avert unseemly accidents, the Subject is securely but not uncomfortably tied erect between two posts, so that I can easily do the Fondling at his or her front or back or side, as required. My work tray has three hundred and thirty-six compartments, each neatly labeled with the name of a bodily part, and in each reposes one or several instruments exquisitely designed to be used on that certain part. Depending on whether the part is of flesh or sinew or muscle or membrane or sac or gristle, the implements may be knives of certain shapes, or awls, probes, needles, tweezers, scrapers. The instruments are newly whetted and polished, and my assistants are ready

—my Blotters of Fluids and Retrievers of Pieces. I commence by doing the traditional Fondler's Meditations. Thereby I attune myself not only to the Subject's fears, which are usually apparent, but also to his inmost apprehensions and deepest levels of response. The artful Fondler is the man who can very nearly feel the same sensations as his Subject. According to legend, the most perfect of all Fondlers was a long-ago *woman*, who could so closely attune herself that she would actually cry out and writhe and weep in unison with her Subject, and even plead with herself for mercy."

"Speaking of women—" said Nostril. All this time he had been standing, almost huddling for invisibility, behind me. But his ever lewd inquisitiveness must have overcome his timorousness. He spoke in Farsi to the Prince, "Women and men do differ, Prince Chingkim. You know . . . in their bodily parts . . . here and there. How do the Master Fondler's labels and implements reconcile those differences?"

The Fondler took a step backward and said, "Who . . . is . . . *this?*" with dainty revulsion, as he might have done if he had stepped on a street turd and it had had the effrontery to protest aloud.

"Forgive the slave's impertinence, Master Ping," Chingkim said smoothly. "But the question had occurred to me, too." He repeated it in Mongol.

The executioner sniffed clerkishly again. "The differences between male and female, as regards the Fondling, are merely superficial. If the folded paper reads 'red jewel,' that means the frontmost genital organ, of which there is a large one in the male, a tiny one in the female. If the paper reads 'jade gland,' left or right, it means the man's testicle or the woman's internal gonad. If it reads 'deep valley,' that literally means the woman's womb, but in the case of a man can be taken to mean his internal almond gland, the so-called third testicle."

Involuntarily, Nostril made an "ooh!" noise of pain. The Fondler glared at him.

"Now, *may* I proceed? After my Meditations, the proceeding goes thus. I select a paper from the basket, at random, and unfold it, and it tells me the part of the Subject destined for the first Fondling. Suppose it says left little finger. Do I simply step up to the Subject, as a butcher would do, and saw off his left little finger? No. Or what would I do if the identical paper came up again later? So the first time I may merely drive a needle deep under that finger's nail. The second time perhaps slice the finger to the bone all along its length. Only if it came up a third time would I lop the finger off entirely. Usually, of course, the second paper I select will direct me to a different part of the Subject—another extremity, or the nose, or the jade gland perhaps. However, given the triplication of the papers and the randomness of choice, it can occasionally happen that the same part will be called for twice in succession, but that does not occur too boringly often. And in all my career there has been just one single occasion when three papers in a row all named the exact same part of the Subject's body. Most unusual, that. Memorable. I later asked the Mathematician Lin-ngan to calculate for me the rarity of that having happened. As I remember, he said something like one chance in three million. Years ago, that was. Her left nipple, it was . . ."

There he seemed to drift off into a blissful contemplation of that time past. Then, after a moment, he came abruptly back to us.

"Perhaps you have begun to perceive the expertness required in the Fondling. One does not simply run back and forth, snatching up papers and then slicing bits off the Subject. No, I proceed only leisurely—very leisurely—back and forth, for the Subject must have ample time to appreciate each individual pain. And they must vary in nature—this time an incision, next a piercing, then a rasping, a burning, a mashing, and so on. Also, the wounds must vary in keenness, so that the Subject experiences not just an overall agony, but a multitude of separate pains that he can differentiate and *locate*. Here, an upper molar slowly wrenched out and a nail driven where it had been, up into the frontal sinus. There, his elbow joint cracking and crumbling in an ingenious slow vise of my own invention. Yonder, a red-hot metal probe inserted down his red jewel's inner canal—or delicately and repeatedly applied to the tender little bulb at the opening of *her* red jewel. And in between, perhaps, the skin flayed from the chest and peeled loose and hanging down like an apron."

I swallowed and asked, "How long does this go on, Master Ping?"

He gave a fastidious small shrug. "Until the Subject perishes. It is, after all, called the *Death* of a Thousand. But no one has ever died of dying, if you take my meaning. Therein lies my greatest art—the prolongation of that dying, and the ever increasing excruciation of it. To put it another way, no one has ever died of sheer pain. Even I am sometimes astonished at how much pain can be borne, and for how long. Also, I was a physician before I became the Fondler, so I never inadvertently inflict a mortal injury, and I know how to prevent a Subject's untimely death from blood loss or shock to his constitution. My assistant Blotters are adept at stanching blood flow and, if I am required to puncture a troublesome organ like the bladder, early on in the Fondling, my Retrievers are competent at replacing any plugs I have to take out."

"To put it another way, then," I said, mimicking his own words, "how long until the Subject perishes of those attentions?"

"It depends mainly on chance. On which of the folded papers, and in which order, chance puts into my hand. Do you believe in some god or gods, Lord Marco? Then presumably the gods regulate the papers' chance according to the magnitude of the Subject's crime and the severity of punishment it merits. Chance, or the gods, can guide my hand at any time to one of those four papers I earlier mentioned."

He raised his thin eyebrows at me. I nodded and said:

"I think I have guessed. There must be four vital parts of the body where a wound would cause quick death instead of slow dying."

He exclaimed, "The indigo dye is bluer than the indigo plant! Which is to say: the pupil exceeds the master." He smiled thinly at me. "An apt student, Lord Marco. You yourself would make a good—" I expected him to say Fondler, of course. I would not wish to be a Fondler, good or not. I was perversely gratified when he said, "—a good Subject, because all your apprehensions and perceptions would be heightened by your intimate knowledge of the Fondling. Yes, there are four spots—the heart, naturally, and also one place in the spinal column and two places in the brain—where an inserted blade or point causes death quite instantaneously and, as far as one can tell, quite painlessly. That is why they are written on only one paper apiece, for if and when one of those papers comes to my hand, the Fondling is finished. I always instruct the Subject to pray that it comes soon. He or she always does pray, and eventually out loud, and sometimes very loudly indeed. The Subject's fond entertainment of that hope—really a rather meager hope: four chances out of the thousand—seems to add a certain extra refinement to his or her agonies."

"Excuse me, Master Ping," Chingkim put in. "But you still have not said how long the Fondling lasts."

"Again, it depends, my Prince. Aside from the incalculable factors of gods and chance, the duration depends on me. If I am not overpressed by other Subjects waiting their turn, if I can proceed at leisure, I may take an hour between picking up one paper and the next. If I put in a respectable working day of, say, ten hours, and if chance dictates that we must go through almost every one of the thousand folded papers, then the Death of a Thousand can last for very near a hundred days."

"Dio me varda!" I cried. "But they tell me that Donduk is already dead. And you only got him this morning."

"That Mongol, yes. He went deplorably quickly. His constitution had been rather impaired by the preliminary questioning. But no need to commiserate with me, though I thank you, Lord Marco. I am not unduly chagrined. I have the other Mongol already secured for Fondling." He sniffed once more. "Indeed, if you seek reason for commiseration, do so because you interrupted my Meditations."

I turned to Chingkim and, speaking Farsi for privacy, demanded of him, "Does your father really decree these—these hideous tortures? To be performed by this—this simpering enjoyer of other people's torments?"

Nostril, at my side, began to make meaningful and urgent plucks at my sleeve. The Fondler was at my other side, so I did not see, as Nostril did, the man's glower of loathing, boring into me like one of his ghastly probes.

Chingkim manfully tried to subdue his own anger at me. Through clenched teeth he said, "Elder Brother," in the formal style of address, though he was the elder of us two. "Elder Brother Marco, the Death of a Thousand is prescribed only for a few of the most serious crimes. And of all capital crimes, treason leads the list."

I was hastily revising my estimate of his father. If Kubilai could decree such an unspeakable end for two of his fellow Mongols—two good warriors whose only crime had been loyalty to the Khakhan's own underchief Kaidu—then obviously I was wrong when I took his behavior in the Cheng to have been mere posturing to impress us visitors. Evidently Kubilai did not mean for the sentences he handed down to be cautionary or exemplary to others. He did not care one whit whether anyone else ever took note of them or not. (I might never have known the gruesome fate of Ussu and Donduk, so *this* was certainly not being done to impress our party.) The Khakhan simply exercised his absolute power absolutely. To criticize or question or deride his motives was suicidal—happily, I had done so only in the privacy of my head—and even to commend his actions would be needless and futile and ignored. Kubilai would do what he would do. Well, for me at least, this episode had been an exemplary one. From now on, as long as I was in the realms of the Khan of All Khans, I would walk lightly and speak softly.

But just this once, before I subsided into docility, I would make one attempt to change one thing.

"I told you, Chingkim," I said to him, "Donduk was no friend of mine, and he is gone in any case. But Ussu—I liked him, and it was my incautious words that put him down here, and he still lives. Can nothing be done to moderate his punishment?"

"A traitor must die the Death of a Thousand," Chingkim said stonily. But then he relented enough to say, "There is only one possible amelioration."

"Ah, you know of it, of course, my Prince," said the Fondler, with a smirk. To my surprise and horror, he spoke in perfect Farsi. "And you know the manner of arranging the amelioration. Well, my chief clerk handles that sort of transaction. If you will excuse me, Prince Chingkim, Lord Marco . . ."

He minced away across the room again, motioning for his chief clerk to attend upon us, and went out through the iron-studded door.

"What will be done?" I asked Chingkim.

He growled, "A bribe that is paid now and then, in these cases. Though never before by me," he added disgustedly. "Usually it is done by the Subject's family. They may bankrupt themselves and mortgage their whole future lives to scrape together the bribe. Master Ping must be one of the richest officials in Khanbalik. I hope my father never hears of this folly of mine; he would laugh me to scorn. And you, Marco, I suggest that you do not ask this sort of favor ever again."

The chief clerk sauntered over to us and raised his eyebrows in inquiry. Chingkim dug into a purse at his waist, and said in the round-about Han way:

"For the Subject Ussu, I would pay the balance weight for the scales, to make the four papers ascend." He took out some gold coins and slipped them into the clerk's discreetly cupped hand.

I asked, "What does that mean, Chingkim?"

"It means that the four papers naming vital parts will be moved to the top of the basket, where the Fondler's hand is likely to pick them up soonest. Now come away."

"But how—?"

"It is all that *can* be done!" he gritted at me. "Now come, Marco!"

Nostril was tugging at me, too, but I persisted. "How can we be sure it will be done? Can we trust the Fondler to do all that work—all those folded papers to be unfolded and read first—and all alike—"

"No, my lord," said the chief clerk, unbending for the first time, almost kindly, and speaking in Mongol for my benefit. "All the others of the thousand papers are colored red, which is the Han color signifying good fortune. Only those four papers are purple, which is the Han color of mourning. The Fondler always knows where those four papers lurk."

· 4 ·

DURING the next several days, I was left on my own. I got unpacked and settled into my private quarters—with the help of Nostril, for I let the slave move in and lay his pallet in one of my more commodious closets—and I began to get acquainted with the twins Biliktu and Buyantu, and I began to learn my way around that central palace building and the rest of the edifices and gardens and courtyards that constituted the palace city-within-a-city. But I will speak later of how I spent my private time, because my working time also soon began.

One day a palace steward came to bid me attend upon the Khan Kubilai and the Wang Chingkim. The Khakhan's suite was not far from my own, and I went there with celerity, but not with much alacrity, for I assumed that he had learned of our visit to the dungeons and was going to castigate me and Chingkim for our having meddled in the Fondler's business. However, when I got there, and was bowed through a succession of luxurious chambers by a succession of attendants and secretaries and armed guards and beautiful women, and arrived at last in the Khakhan's innermost sitting room, and started my ko-tou, and was bidden to take a seat, and was offered my choice of beverages from a maid's tray laden with decanters, and took a goblet of rice wine, the Khakhan began the interview amiably enough, inquiring:

"How go your language lessons, young Polo?"

I tried not to blush, and murmured, "I have acquired numerous new words, Sire, but not of the kind I could speak in your august presence."

Chingkim said drily, "I did not think there were any words, Marco, that you would hesitate to speak in any place."

Kubilai laughed. "I had intended to converse politely for a while in the Han manner, rambling only indirectly to the subject at hand. But my rude Mongol son comes straight to the point."

"I have already made a vow to myself, Sire," I said, "that I will henceforth be careful of my too ready tongue and too abrupt opinions."

He considered that. "Well, yes, you might be more respectfully circumspect in your choice of words before you blurt them out. But I shall want your opinions. It is for those that I would have you become fluent and precise in our language. Marco, look yonder. Do you know what that thing is?"

He indicated an object in the center of the room. It was a giant bronze urn, standing some eight feet high and about half that in diameter. It was richly engraved, and on the outside of it clung eight lithe and elegant bronze dragons, their tails curled at the top rim of the urn, their heads downward near its base. Each one held in its toothed jaws an immense and perfect pearl. There were eight bronze toads squatting around the urn's pedestal, one under each dragon, its mouth gaping as if eager to snatch the pearl above.

"It is an impressive work of art, Sire," I said, "but I have no idea of its function."

"That is an earthquake engine."

"Sire?"

"This land of Kithai is now and again shaken by earth tremors. Whenever one occurs, that engine informs me of it. The thing was designed and cast by my clever Court Goldsmith, and only he fully understands the workings of it. But somehow an earthquake, even if it is so far away from Khanbalik that none of us here can feel it, makes the jaws of one of the dragons to open, and he drops his pearl into the maw of the toad beneath. Tremors of other sorts have no effect. I have stamped and jumped and danced all about that urn—and I am no butterfly—but it ignores me."

I saw in my mind the majestic Great Khan of All Khans bouncing about the chamber like an inquisitive boy, his rich robes billowing and his beard wagging and his helmet-crown askew, and probably all his ministers goggling. But I remembered my vow, and I did not smile.

He said, "According to which pearl drops, I know the direction where the earth shook. I cannot know how distant it was, or how devastating, but I can dispatch a troop at the gallop in that direction, and eventually they will bring me word of the damage and casualties incurred."

"A miraculous contrivance, Sire."

"I could wish that my human informants were as succinct and reliable in reporting the occurrences in my domains. You heard those Han spies of mine, that night at the banquet, rattling off numbers and items and tabulations, and telling me nothing."

"The Han are infatuated with numbers," said Chingkim. "The five constant virtues. The five great relationships. The thirty positions of the sex act, and the six ways of penetration and the nine modes of movement. They even regulate their politeness. I understand they have three hundred rules of ceremony and three thousand rules of behavior."

"Meanwhile, Marco," said Kubilai, "my other informants—my Muslim and even Mongol officials—they tend to leave out of their reports any fact they think I might find inconvenient or distressing. I have a large realm to administer, but I cannot personally be everywhere at once. As a wise Han counselor once said: you can conquer on horseback, but to rule you must get down from the horse. So I depend heavily on reports from afar, and they too often contain everything but the necessary."

"Like those spies," Chingkim put in. "Send them to the kitchen to see about tonight's dinner soup, and they would report its quantity and density and ingredients and coloration and aroma and the volume of steam it throws off. They would report everything except whether it tastes good or not."

Kubilai nodded. "What struck me at the banquet, Marco—and my son agrees—is that you appear to have a talent for discerning the taste of things. After those spies had talked interminably, you said only a few words. True, they were not very tactful words, but they told me the taste of the soup brewing in Sin-kiang. I should like to verify that seeming talent of yours, in order to make further use of it."

I said, "You wish me to be a spy, Sire?"

"No. A spy must blend into the locality, and a Ferenghi could hardly do that anywhere in my domains. Besides, I would never ask a decent man to take up the trade of sneak and tattler. No, I have other missions in mind. But to undertake them you must first learn many things besides fluency of language. They will not be easy things. They will demand much time and effort."

He was looking keenly at me, as if to see whether I flinched from the prospect of hard work, so I made bold to say:

"The Khakhan does me great honor if he asks only drudgery of me. So much greater the honor, Sire, if the drudgery is a preparation for some task of significance."

"Be not too eager to accede. Your uncles, I hear, are planning some trading enterprises. That should be easier work, and profitable, and probably more safe and secure than what I may require of you. So I give you permission to stay in association with your uncles, if you prefer."

"Thank you, Sire. But if I valued only safety and security I would not have left home."

"Ah, yes. It is truly said: He who would climb high must leave much behind."

Chingkim added, "It is also said: For a man of fortitude there are nowhere any walls, only avenues."

I decided I would ask my father if it was here in Kithai that he had got crammed so full of proverbs that he continually overflowed.

"Let me say this, then, young Polo," Kubilai went on. "I would not ask you to puzzle out for me how that earthquake engine performs its function—and that would be a difficult task enough—but I will ask of you something even harder. I wish you to learn as much as you can about the workings of my court and my government, which are infinitely more intricate than the insides of that mysterious urn."

"I am at your command, Sire."

"Come here to this window." He led the way to it. Like those in my quarters, it was not of transparent glass, but of the shimmery, only translucent Muscovy glass, set in a much curlicued frame. He unlatched it, swung it open and said, "Look there."

We were looking down onto a considerable extent of the palace grounds which I had not yet visited, for this part was still under construction, only an expanse of yellow earth littered with piles of wall stones and paving stones and barrows and tools and gangs of sweating slaves and—

"Amoredèi!" I exclaimed. "What are those gigantic beasts? Why do their horns grow so oddly?"

"Foolish Ferenghi, those are not horns, those are the tusks from which come ivory. That animal, in the southern tropics where it comes from, is called a gajah. There is no Mongol word for it."

Chingkim supplied the Farsi word, "Fil," and I knew that one.

"Elephants!" I breathed, marveling. "Of course! I have seen a drawing of one, but the drawing cannot have been very good."

"Never mind the gajah," said Kubilai. "Do you see what they are piling up?"

"It looks like a great mountain of kara blocks, Sire."

"It is. The Court Architect is building for me an extensive park out there, and I instructed him to put a hill in it. I have also instructed him to plant much grass on it. Have you seen the grass in my other courtyards?"

"Yes, Sire."

"You remarked nothing distinctive about it?"

"I fear not, Sire. It looked just like the same grass we have traveled through, for countless thousands of li."

"That is its distinction—that it is not an ornamental garden growth. It is the simple, ordinary, sweet grass of the great plains where I was born and grew up."

"I am sorry, Sire, but if I am supposed to draw some lesson from this . . ."

"My cousin the Ilkhan Kaidu told you that I had degenerated to something less than a Mongol. In a sense, he was right."

"Sire!"

"In a sense. I did get down from my horse to do the ruling of these domains. In doing so, I have found admirable many things of the cultured Han, and I have embraced them. I try to be more mannerly than uncouth, more diplomatic than demanding, more of an ordained emperor than an occupying warlord. In all those ways, I have changed from being a Mongol of Kaidu's kind. But I do not forget or repudiate my origins, my warrior days, my Mongol blood. That hill says it all."

"I regret, Sire," I said, "that the example still eludes my understanding."

He said to his son, "Explain it, Chingkim."

"You see, Marco, the hill will be a pleasure park, with terraces and walks and willowed waterfalls and comely pavilions cunningly set here and there. The whole thing will be an ornament to the palace grounds. In that, it is very Han, and reflects our admiration of Han art. But it will be more. The Architect could have mounded it of the local yellow earth, but my Royal Father commanded kara. The burnable rock will probably never be needed, but just in case this palace should ever come under siege, we will have there an unlimited supply of fuel. That is a warrior's thinking. And the whole hill, roundabout the buildings and streams and flower beds, will be greened over by plains grass. A living reminder to us of our Mongol heritage."

"Ah!" I said. "Now it all is clear."

"The Han have a concise proverb," said Kubilai. "Bai wen buru yi jian. To hear tell a hundred times is not as good as once seeing. You have seen. So now let me speak of another aspect of rulership."

We returned to our seats. In response to some inaudible summons, the maidservant glided in and refilled our goblets.

The Khakhan resumed, "There are times when I, too—like you, Marco Polo—can taste the attitudes of other people. You have expressed your willingness to join my retinue, but I wonder if I taste in you a lingering trace of your disapprobation."

"Sire?" I said, quite jolted by his bluntness. "Who am I, Sire, to disapprove of the Khan of All Khans? Why, even for me to approve would be presumptuous."

He said, "I was informed of your visit to the Fondler's cavern." I must have cast an involuntary glance, for he went on, "I am aware that Chingkim was with you, but it was not he who told. I gather that you were dismayed by my treatment of Kaidu's two men."

"I might have hoped, Sire, that their treatment had been a little less extreme."

"You do not tame a wolf by pulling one of his teeth."

"They had been my companions, Sire, and they did nothing lupine during that time."

"On arrival here, they were hospitably quartered with my own palace guards. A Mongol trooper is not ordinarily garrulous, but those two asked a great many and very searching questions of their barrackmates. My men answered only evasively, so those two would not have taken much intelligence home with them, anyway. You knew that I had sent spies into Kaidu's lands. Did you think him incapable of doing the same?"

"I did not know—" I gasped. "I did not think—"

"As ruler of a far-spread empire, I must rule over a considerable diversity of peoples, and try to bear in mind their peculiarities. The Han are patient and devious, the Persians are couched lions and all other Muslims are rabid sheep, the Armeniyans are blustering grovelers, and so on. I may not always deal with all of them as I ought. But the Mongols I understand ⋯⋯⋯ There I must rule with an iron hand, for in them I rule an iron ⋯

"Yes, ⋯

"Hav⋯⋯⋯⋯⋯⋯⋯⋯⋯⋯tment of any others?"

"We⋯⋯⋯⋯⋯⋯⋯ly knew, "I thought—that day in the ⋯⋯⋯⋯⋯⋯rving Ho-nan farmers rather brusqu⋯

J⋯⋯⋯⋯⋯⋯⋯⋯do not help those in trouble who snive⋯⋯⋯⋯⋯⋯se who survive the trouble. Any man⋯⋯⋯⋯⋯ally not worth the keeping. When peo⋯⋯⋯⋯⋯dden calamity or a long siege of mi⋯⋯⋯⋯hwhile will survive. The remainder a⋯

⋯⋯⋯or, Sire, or only a fair chance?"

⋯⋯⋯unt piglet squeals for a fair chance at ⋯⋯art. Think about it."

⋯⋯ghts took me a long way back in time— ⋯⋯trying to help the survival of the boat ⋯⋯ce of little Doris came to my memory.

I said, "Sire, when you speak of feckless, sniveling men and women, no one could disagree. But starving children?"

"If they are the offspring of the dispensable, they too are dispensable. Realize this, Marco Polo. Children are the most easily and cheaply renewed resource in the world. Cut down a tree for timber; it takes nearly a lifetime to replace. Dig kara from the ground for burning; it is gone forever. But if a child is lost in a famine or flood, what is required for its replacement? A man and a woman and less than a year's time. If the man and woman are the strong and capable who have defied the disaster, the better the replacement child is likely to be. Have you ever killed a man, Marco Polo?"

I blinked and said, "Yes, Sire, I have."

"Good. A man better deserves the space he occupies on this earth if he has cleared that space for his occupancy. There is only *so much* space on this earth, only so much game to hunt and grass for pasturage and kara to burn and wood to build with. Before we Mongols took Kithai, there were one hundred million people living here, the Han and their related races. Now there are only half that many, according to my Han counselors, who are anxious for their countrymen to multiply again. If I will relax some of my strictures, they say, the population will soon again be what it was. They assure me that a single mou of land is sufficient to feed and support an entire Han family. To which I retort: would that family not feed better if it had two mou of land? Or three, or five? The family would be better nourished, healthier, probably happier. The sad fact is that the fifty or so million who perished in the years of conquest were mostly the best of the Han—the soldiers, the young and strong and vital. Should I now let them be replaced with mere indiscriminate *spawning*? No, I will not. I think the former rulers here liked to count heads only, and boast that they ruled great swarming numbers. I had rather boast that I rule a populace of quality, not quantity."

"You would be envied by many other rulers, Sire," I murmured.

"As to my manner of ruling them, let me say this. I am again unlike Kaidu in that I can recognize some limitations in us Mongols, and some superiorities in other nationalities. We Mongols excel in action, in ambition, in the dreaming of bold dreams and the making of grand plans— and in military affairs, most certainly. So for my ministers of overall administration I have mostly Mongols. But the Han know their own country and countrymen best, so I have recruited many Han for my ministries dealing with Kithai's internal management. The Han are also incredibly adept in matters mathematical."

"Like the regulation of the thirty sexual postures," said Chingkim, with a laugh.

"However," Kubilai went on, "the Han would naturally cheat me if I put them in charge of revenues. So for those offices I have Muslim Arabs and Persians, who are almost the equal of the Han when it comes to finances. I have let the Muslims establish what they call an Ortaq, a net of Muslim agents dispersed over all Kithai to supervise its trade and commerce. They are very good at exploiting the material resources of this land and the talents of its natives. So I let the Muslims do the squeezing and I take a specified share of the Ortaq's profits. That is much easier for me than to levy a multitude of separate taxes on separate products and transactions. Vakh, I have enough trouble collecting the simple land and property taxes due me from the Han."

I asked, "Do not the natives chafe at having outlanders supervising them?"

Chingkim said, "They have always had outlanders over them, Marco. The Han emperors long ago devised an admirable system. Every magistrate and tax collector, every provincial official of every sort, was always sent to serve somewhere other than his birthplace, to ensure that in his duties and dealings and gouges he would not favor his relatives. Also, he was never let to serve more than three years in any post before being moved on somewhere else. That was to ensure his not making close friends and cronies whom he might favor. So in any province, town or village, the natives always had outsiders governing. Probably they find our Muslim minions only a trifle more foreign."

I said, "Besides Arabs and Persians, I have seen men of other nationalities around the palace."

"Yes," said the Khakhan. "For lesser officers of the court—the Winemaster, the Firemaster, the Goldsmith and such—I simply install the men who perform those functions most ably, whether they be Han, Muslims, Ferenghi, Jews, whatever."

"It all sounds most sensible and efficient, Sire."

"You are to ascertain whether that is so. You are to do it by exploring the chambers and halls and counting rooms from which the Khanate is administered. I have instructed Chingkim to introduce you to every official and courtier of every degree, and he will instruct them to speak freely to you of their offices and duties. You will be paid a liberal stipend, and I will set an hour each week when you will report to me. Thus I will judge how well you are learning and, more important, how well you are perceiving the *taste* of things."

"I will do my best, Sire," I said, and Chingkim and I made the perfunctory ko-tou we were permitted, and we left the room.

I had already determined that, with my first report to the Khakhan after my very first week of employment, I would make sure to astonish him—and I did. When I called upon him the next time, a week or so later, I said:

"I will show you, Sire, how the earthquake engine works. You see—here—suspended down the throat of the vase is this heavy pendulum. It is daintily hung, but it does not move, no matter how much jumping or banging goes on in this room. Only if the whole great urn trembles, which is to say the whole ponderous weight of this palace building, then does that trembling make the pendulum *seem* to move. In reality, it hangs steady and still, and its apparent slight displacement is caused by the imperceptible quiver of its container. Thus, when a remote earthquake sends the least tremor through the earth and the palace and the floor and the vase, that tremor leans the pendulum's pressure against one of these delicate linkages—you see, there are eight—and thereby loosens the hinged jaw of one of the dragons sufficiently that it lets go of its pearl."

"I see. Yes. Very clever, my Court Goldsmith. And you, too, Marco Polo. You apprehended that the haughty Khakhan would never demean himself to confess ignorance to a mere smith and plead for an explanation. So you did it in my stead. Your taste perception is still very good."

· 5 ·

B u t those gratifying words came later. On the day Chingkim and I left his Royal Father's presence, the Prince said cheerfully to me, "Well? Which high or lowly courtier would you like to interrogate first?" And when I requested audience with the Court Goldsmith, he said, "Curious choice, but very well. That gentleman is often in his noisy forge, which is no place for talking. I will see that he awaits us in his quieter studio workshop. I will call for you in an hour."

So I went then to the suite of my own father, to tell him of my new situation. I found him sitting and being fanned by one of his women servants. He waved toward an inner room and said, "Your Uncle Mafìo is in yonder, closeted with some Han physicians we knew when we were here before. Having them appraise his physical condition."

I sat down to share the being fanned, and I told him all that had transpired during my interview with the Khan Kubilai, and asked if I had his parental permission to turn courtier instead of trader for a while.

"By all means," he said warmly. "And I congratulate you on having won the Khakhan's esteem. Your new situation, far from depriving me and your uncle of your active partnership, should redound to our good. A very apt illustration of the old proverb: chi fa per sè fa per tre."

I echoed, "Do for myself and I will do for all three? Then you and Uncle Mafìo plan to stay in Kithai for a time?"

"Indeed, yes. We are traveling traders, but we have been traveling for long enough; now we are eager to start trading. We have already applied to the Finance Minister Achmad for the necessary licenses and franchises to deal with the Muslims' Ortaq. In that and other matters, Mafìo and I may benefit from having you now as a friend at court. Surely you did not think, Marco, that we came all this way to turn right around."

"I thought your prime concern was to take back to Venice the maps of the Silk Road and start to spur the East–West trade in general."

"Ah, well, as to that, we believe our Compagnia Polo ought to enjoy first advantage of the Silk Road before we throw it open to competition. Also, we ought to set a good example, to fire enthusiasm in the West. So we will stay here while we earn an estimable fortune, and send it home as it accumulates. With those riches, your Marègna Fiordelisa can dazzle the stay-at-homes and whet their appetite. Then, when we finally do go home, we will freely proffer our maps and experience and advice to all our confratelli in Venice and Constantinople."

"A fair plan, Father. But is it not likely to take a long time—to work up to a fortune from a very meager beginning? You and Uncle Mafìo have no trading capital except our cods of musk and whatever zafràn still remains."

"The most fortunate of all merchants in the legends of Venice, the Jew Nascimbene, set forth with nothing to his name but a cat he picked up from the street. The fable tells that he landed in a kingdom overrun with mice, and by hiring out his cat he founded his fortune."

"There may be plenty of mice here in Kithai, Father, but there are also plenty of cats. Not least among the cats, I think, are the Muslims of the Ortaq. From what I have heard, they may be voracious."

"Thank you, Marco. As the saying goes, a man warned is already armed. But we are not starting quite so small as did Nascimbene. In addition to our musk, Mafìo and I have also the investment we left on deposit here during our earlier visit."

"Oh? I did not know."

"Quite literally on deposit—planted in the ground. You see, we brought crocus culms on that journey, too. Kubilai kindly granted us a tract of farmland in the province of Ho-pei, where the climate is benign, and a number of Han slaves and overseers, whom we instructed in the methods of cultivation. According to report, we have now a quite extensive crocus plantation and already a fair stock of zafràn pressed into bricks or dried into hay. That commodity being still a novelty throughout the East, and we having a monopoly—well!"

I said admiringly, "I should have known better than to worry about your prospects. God help the Muslim cats if they try to pounce upon Venetian mice."

He smiled and oozed another proverb, "It is better to be envied than consoled."

"*Bruto scherzo!*" came a bellow from the inner room, and our colloquy was interrupted. We heard several raised voices, loudest among them Uncle Mafìo's, and other noises, from which it seemed that furniture and things were being thrown about and smashed, to the accompaniment of my uncle's shouted curses in Venetian, Farsi, Mongol and perhaps some other languages. "Scarabazze! Badbu qassab! Karakurt!"

As if they had been flung, three elderly Han gentlemen flew out through the curtains of the room's Vase Gate. Without a nod to me or my father, they continued their rapid progress across the room, running for dear life, and on out of the suite. After their swift passage, Uncle Mafìo burst out through the curtains, still erupting scandalous profanity. His eyes were glaring, his beard bristling like quills, and his clothes were disarranged where evidently the physicians had been examining him.

"Mafìo!" my father said in alarm. "What in the world has happened?"

Alternately shaking his fist and stabbing the vulgar gesture of the figa in the direction of the already departed doctors, my uncle continued roaring epithets of description and suggestion. "Fottuti! Pedarat namard! Che ghe vegna la giandussa! Kalmuk, vakh!"

My father and I took hold of the agitated man and gently eased him down to a seat, saying, "Mafìo!" and "Uncle!" and "Ste tranquilo!" and "What in God's name has happened?"

He snarled, "I do not wish to speak of it!"

"Not speak?" my father said mildly. "You have already waked echoes as far as Xan-du."

"Merda!" my uncle grunted, and sulkily began rearranging his clothes.

I said, "I will see if I can catch the doctors and ask them."

"Oh, never mind!" growled Uncle Mafìo. "I might as well tell." He did, and interspersed the explanation with exclamations. "You recall the malady with which I was afflicted? Dona Lugia!"

"Yes, of course," said my father. "But I believe it was called the kala-azar."

"And you remember the Hakim Mimdad's prescription of stibium, which would save my life but cost my balls? Which it did, sangue de Bacco!"

"Of course," said my father again. "What is it, Mafìo? Did the physicians find that you have taken a turn for the worse?"

"Worse, Nico? What could be *worse*? No! The damned scataroni have just informed me, in honeyed words, that I never had to take the damned stibium at all! They say they could have cured the kala azar simply by having me eat mildew!"

"Mildew?"

"Well, some kind of green mold that grows in empty old millet bins. That treatment would have restored me to health, they say, with no ugly side effect. I need never have shriveled my pendenti! Is it not nice to hear this *now*? Mildew! Porco Dio!"

"No, it cannot be very pleasant to hear."

"Need the the damned scataroni have told me at all? Now that it is too late? Mona Merda!"

"It was not very tactful of them."

"The damned saputèli simply wanted me to know that they are superior to the backwoods charlatan who castrated me! Aborto de natura!"

"There is an old saying, Mafìo. This world is like a pair of shoes that—"

"Bruto barabào! *Shut up, Nico!*"

Looking pained, my father withdrew into the other room. I could hear him picking up and straightening things in there. Uncle Mafìo sat and simmered and fizzed like a kettle on slow boil. But finally he looked up, caught my eye, and said more calmly:

"I am sorry, Marco, for the display of temper. I know I said once that I would regard my predicament with resignation. But now to learn that the predicament was unnecessary . . ." He ground his teeth. "I hope I may rot if I can decide which is worse, being a eunuch or knowing I need not have been."

"Well . . ."

"If you tell me a proverb, I will break your neck."

So I sat silent for a while, wondering how best to express my sympathy and at the same time suggest that his diminishment might not be totally deplorable. Here among the manly Mongols, his formerly perverse tendencies would not be so tolerantly accepted as they had been, for example, in the Muslim countries. If he were still subject to the urge to fondle some man or boy, he might well find himself being caressed by the Fondler. But how was I to say so? Prepared to dodge a blow of his still-knotted fist, I cleared my throat and tried:

"It seems to me, Uncle Mafìo, that almost every time I have strayed into serious trouble or embarrassment, it was my candelòto that lit the way. I would not, on that account, willingly forfeit the candelòto and the pleasures it more often affords me. But I think, if I were deprived of it, I could more easily be a good man."

"You think that, do you?" he said sourly.

"Well, of all the priests and monks I have known, the most admirable were those who took seriously their vow of celibacy. I believe it was because they had closed their senses to the distractions of the flesh that they could concentrate on being good."

"O merda o beretta rossa. You believe that, do you?"

"Yes. Look at San Agostino. In his youth he prayed, 'Lord, make me chaste, but not just yet.' He knew very well where evil lay lurking. So he was anything *but* a saint, until finally he did renounce the temptations of—"

"*Chiava el santo!*" raged Uncle Mafìo, the most terrible thing he had yet uttered.

After a moment, when no thunderbolt had sizzled down at us, he said in a more temperate but still grim voice:

"Marco, I will tell you what I believe. I believe that your beliefs, if not puling hypocrisy, are exactly backward. There is no difficulty in being good. Every man and woman of mankind is as evil as he or she is capable of being and dares to be. It is the less capable, more timorous persons who are called good, and then only by default. The least capable, most fainthearted of all are called saints, and then usually first by themselves. It is easier to proclaim, 'Look at me, I am a saint, for I have fastidiously withdrawn from striving with bolder men and women!' than to say honestly, 'I am incapable of prevailing in this wicked world and I fear even to try.' Remember that, Marco, and be bold."

I sat and tried to think of an adequate riposte that would not sound simply sanctimonious. But, seeing that he had subsided into muttering to himself again, I rose and quietly took my leave.

Poor Uncle Mafìo. He seemed to be arguing, first, that his abnormal nature had been no infirmity, but a superiority merely unrecognized in a mediocre world and, second, that he might have made the purblind world acknowledge that superiority, if only he had not been untimely cheated of it. Well, I have known many people, unable to hide some gross deficiency or imperfection, try instead to flaunt it as a blessing. I have known the parents of a deformed or witless child to drop its baptismal name and call it "Christian," in the pathetic pretense that the Lord predestined it for Heaven and so deliberately made it ill-equipped for life. I could be sorry for cripples, but I would never believe that giving a blemish a noble name made it either an ornament or a noble blemish.

I went to my own chambers, and found the Wang Chingkim already waiting, and he and I went together to the distant palace building where was the studio of the Court Goldsmith.

"Marco Polo—the Master Pierre Boucher," said Chingkim, introducing us, and the Goldsmith smiled cordially and said, "Bon jour, Messire Paule," and I do not recall what I said, for I was much surprised. The young man, no older than myself, was the first real Ferenghi I had met since leaving home—I mean to say, a genuine Frank, a Frenchman.

"Actually, I was born in Karakoren, the old Mongol capital," he told me, speaking an amalgam of Mongol and half-forgotten French, as he showed me about the workshop. "My parents were Parisians, but my father Guillaume was Court Goldsmith to King Bela of Hungary, so he and my mother were taken prisoner by the Mongols when the Ilkhan Batu conquered Bela's city of Buda. They were brought captive to the Khakhan Kuyuk at Karakoren. But when the Khakhan recognized my father's talent, alors, he entitled him Maître Guillaume and raised him to the court, and he and my mother lived happily in these lands for all the rest of their lives. So have I, having been born here, during the reign of the Khakhan Mangu."

"If you are so well regarded, Pierre," I said, "and a freeman, could you not resign from the court and go back to the West?"

"Ah, oui. But I doubt that I could live as well there as here, for my talent is somewhat inferior to my late father's. I am competent enough in the arts of gold and silver work and the cutting of gemstones and the fabrication of jewelry, mais voilà tout. It was my father who made most of the ingenious contrivances you will see around the palace here. When I am not making jewelry, my chief responsibility is to keep those engines in good repair. So the Khakhan Kubilai, like his predecessor, favors me with privilege and largesse, and I am comfortably situated, and I am about to marry an estimable Mongol lady of the court, and I am quite content to abide."

At my request, Pierre explained the workings of the earthquake engine in the Khakhan's chambers—which, as I have told, enabled me later to impress Kubilai. However, Pierre refused, with good humor but with firmness, to satisfy my curiosity about the banquet hall's drink-dispensing serpent tree and animated gold peacocks.

"Like the earthquake urn, they were invented by my father, but they are considerably more complex. If you will forgive my obstinacy, Marco—and Prince Chingkim"—he made a little French bow to each of us—"I will keep secret the workings of the banquet engines. I like being the Court Goldsmith, and there are many other artisans who would like to take my place. Since I am only an outlander, vous savez, I must guard what advantage I possess. As long as there are at least a few contrivances which only I can keep in operation, I am safe against usurpers."

The Prince smiled understandingly and said, "Of course, Master Boucher."

So did I, and then I added, "Speaking of the banquet hall, I wondered at another thing there. Though the hall was crowded, the air never got stale, but stayed cool and fresh. Is that done by some other apparatus of yours, Pierre?"

"Non," he said. "That is a very simple affair, devised long ago by the Han, and presently in the charge of the Palace Engineer."

"Come, Marco," said Chingkim. "We can pay him a visit. His workshop is very near."

So we said au revoir to the Court Goldsmith, and went on our way, and I was next introduced to one Master Wei. He spoke only Han, so Chingkim repeated my query about the banquet hall's ventilation, and translated to me the Engineer's explanation.

"A very simple affair," he said also. "It is well-known that cool air from below will always displace warm air above. There are cellars beneath all the palace buildings, and passages connecting them. Under each building is a cellar room used only as a repository for ice. We are continuously supplied with ice blocks cut by slaves in the ever cold northern mountains, wrapped in straw and brought here by swift-traveling trains. At any time, by the judicious opening of doors and passages here and there, I can make breezes waft the ice stores' coolness wherever it is wanted, or shut it off when it is not."

Without my asking, Master Wei went on to boast of some other devices under his control.

"By the agency of a waterwheel of Han design, some of the water from the gardens' decorative streams is diverted and forced into tanks under the peaks of all the palace buildings' roofs. From each tank the water can be loosed, at my direction, to flow through pipes over the ice rooms or over the kitchen ovens. Then, when it has been cooled or warmed, I can command it to make artificial weather."

"Artificial weather?" I said, marveling.

"In every garden are pavilions in which the lords and ladies take their leisure. If a day is very warm, and some lord or lady wishes the refreshment of a rain, without getting rained on—or if some poet merely wishes to meditate in a mood of melancholy—I have only to twist a wheel. From the roof eaves of the pavilion a curtain of rain will fall gently all around the outside. Also in the garden pavilions, there are seats that appear to be of solid stone, but they are hollow. By directing cool water through them in summer, or warm water in spring or fall, I make the seats more comfortable to the august rumps that repose on them. When the new Kara Hill is completed, I shall install in the pavilions there some even more pleasurable devices. The piped waters will move linkages to wave cooling fans, and will bubble through jug flutes to play a warbling soft music."

And they did. I know they did, for in after years I passed many a dreamy afternoon with Hui-sheng in those pavilions, and I translated the murmurous music for her into gentle touches and soft caresses. . . . But that was in after years.

I have so far mentioned only a very few of the novelties and marvels I encountered in Kithai and in Khanbalik and within the confines of the Khakhan's palace—perhaps insufficiently to illustrate how different Kithai was from any other place I had known. But different it was; I should like to emphasize that difference. Be it remembered that the Khan Kubilai owned an empire comprising all sorts of peoples and communities and terrains and climates. He could have made his residence in the Mongols' earlier, far-northern capital of Karakoren, or in the Mongols' original, very-far-north homeland of Sibir, or he could have chosen to locate his habitation anywhere else on the continent. But of all his lands he deemed Kithai the most appealing, and so did I, and so it was.

I had been seeing exotic countries and cities all the long way from Acre, but their differences were mainly in the *foreground* of them. By that I mean: whenever I entered a new city, my eye naturally lighted first on the things closest. They would be people of strange complexions and comportment, wearing strange costumes, and behind them would be buildings of unfamiliar architecture. But at ground level would always be street dogs and cats, no different from those anywhere else, and overhead would be the trash-picker birds—pigeons or gulls or kites or whatever—as in any other city in the world. And around the outskirts of the city would stretch humdrum hills or mountains or plains. The countryside and its wildlife might sometimes, at first, be striking—like the mighty snowclad crags of the high Pai-Mir and the magnificent "Marco's sheep"—but after long journeying, one finds repetition and familiarity even in most landscapes and their fauna and flora.

By contrast, almost anywhere in Kithai, not only was the foreground of interest to an observer, but so also was the least glimpse of things going on at the corner of one's eye, and the sounds at the edge of one's hearing, and the smells wafting from all sides. On a walk through the streets of Khanbalik, I might fix my gaze anywhere, from the swooping, curly-eaved rooflines to the multifarious faces and garments of the passersby, and still be conscious that much else worth notice was awaiting my glance.

If I dropped my gaze to street level, I would see cats and dogs, but I would not mistake them for the scavengers of Suvediye or Balkh or anywhere else. Most of the Kithai cats were small and handsomely colored, all-over dun except for brown ears and paws and tail, or silvery-gray with extremities almost indigo-blue, and the cats' tails were oddly short and even more oddly kinked at the very tip, like hooks for hanging them up with. Some of the dogs running about resembled tiny lions, bushy-maned, with pushed-in muzzles and bulging eyes. Another breed looked like no thing ever seen before on this earth, except maybe an ambulatory tree stump, if there ever was such a thing. Indeed, that kind of dog was called shu-pei, meaning "loose-barked," for its skin was so voluminously too large for it that none of the dog's features was perceptible, nor even its shape; it was only a grotesque, waddling heap of wrinkles.

Yet another breed of dog I saw employed in a way I almost hesitate to tell, for I would probably not believe anyone else telling of it. That dog was large, of a reddish and bristly pelt, and was called xiang-gou. Every one wore a harness like a pony, and walked with great care and dignity, because its harness had an upstanding handle, by which the dog led a man or woman. The person holding to the handle was blind—not a beggar, but a man or woman going forth on business or to the market or just for a stroll. It is true. The xiang-gou, meaning "leader-dog," was bred and trained to lead a blind master about his own premises, without a stumble or collision, and just as confidently through teeming crowds and clashing cart traffic.

Besides the sights, there were the sounds and smells, which sometimes proceeded from the same source. On every corner was a stall or handcart selling hot cooked foods for the outdoor workers or busy passersby who had to eat on the run. So the smell of fish or meat morsels frying came to one's nose simultaneously with the sizzle coming to one's ears. Or the faint garlicky smell of miàn boiling was accompanied by the slurping of its eaters shoveling the pasta from bowl to mouth with nimble tongs. Khanbalik being the Khan's own city, it was continuously patrolled by street cleaners wielding brooms and buckets. So it was generally free of noxious odors like that of human excrement— more so than any other Kithai city, and ineffably more so than cities elsewhere in the East. The basic odor of Khanbalik was a mingled smell of spices and frying oil. To that, as I walked by different shops and market stalls, were variously added the smells of jasmine, cha, brazier smoke, sandalwood, fruits, incense, occasionally the fragrance of a passing lady's perfumed hand-fan.

Most of the street noises went on incessantly, day and night: the chatter and jabber and singsong of the constantly talking street people, the rumble and clatter of wagon and cart wheels—and as often the jingly music of them, for many carters strung little bells to slide along the spokes of their wheels—the thud of horse and yak hoofs, the lighter patter of asses' hoofs, the shuffle of camels' big pads, the rustle of the straw sandals worn by the ceaselessly scampering porters. That continuous blend of noise was frequently punctuated by the wail of a fish vendor, or the howl of a fruit vendor, or the *thwock-thwock* of a poultry vendor pounding on his hollow wooden duck, or the reverberating *boom-boom-boom* that was one of the city drum towers sounding the alarm of a fire somewhere. Only now and again would the street noise diminish to a respectful hush—when a troop of palace guards came trotting through, one of the men playing a fanfare by beating on a sort of lyre of brass rods, the others swinging quarterstaffs to clear the way for the noble lord coming behind them on horseback or being carried in a palanquin.

Sometimes, above the street noise—literally above it—could be heard a thin melodious fluting in the air. The first few times, I was puzzled by it. But then I realized that at least one in every flock of the city's common pigeons had been banded with a little whistle that sang as it flew. Also, among the more ordinary pigeons was a very fluffy sort I have never seen anywhere else. In its flight it would suddenly pause in midair and somehow, like a tightrope tumbler but without a tightrope, it would topple end for end, merrily making a perfect somersault in the air, and then fly on as sedately as if it had done nothing wonderful.

And if I lifted my gaze even higher above the city roofs, on any breezy autumn day I would see flocks of feng-zheng flying. These were not birds, though some were shaped and painted like birds; others were made to resemble immense butterflies or small dragons. The feng-zheng was a construction of light sticks and very thin paper, and to it a string from a reel was tied. A man would run with the feng-zheng and let the breeze take it, and then, by subtle twitches at his end of the string, he could make it ascend and fly and swoop and curvet in the sky. (Myself, I never could master the art of it.) The height of its ascent was limited only by the amount of string on the flyer's reel, and sometimes one would go up almost out of sight. Men liked to engage in feng-zheng battles. They would glue on their string an abrasive grit of powdered porcelain or Muscovy glass and then let their feng-zheng fly, and try to guide them so that one's string would saw and cut another's, and make that contraption come tumbling down from the sky. The flyers and other men would make heavy wagers on the battle's outcome. But women and children liked to fly the feng-zheng just for enjoyment.

In the nighttimes, I did not have to make any special effort to observe the peculiar things that happened in the Kithai sky—for my head would be jerked up, volente o nolente, by the noises of those things. I mean the violent booms and bangs and sputters of the artificial lightnings and thunders, the so-called fiery trees and sparkling flowers. As in so many other Eastern countries, in Kithai too every day seemed to mark some folk holiday or anniversary requiring celebration. But only in Kithai did the festivities go on into the night, so there would be reason to send those curious fires flying skyward to burst into brighter fires and then into corpuscles of multicolored fire drifting down to the ground. I regarded the displays with admiration and awe, which was not lessened when later I discovered how those marvels were effected.

Outside the cities, Kithai's variegated landscape also differed from those of other countries. I have already described a few of Kithai's distinctive terrains, and will speak of others in their turn. But let me here say this. While I lived in Khanbalik I could, whenever I wished to spend a day in the country, command a horse from the palace stables and in just a morning's ride go to look at something to be seen in no other landscape on this earth. It may be a relic of total uselessness and vainglory, but the Great Wall, that monster serpent petrified in the act of wriggling from horizon to horizon, is still a fantastic feast for the eyes.

I do not mean to give the impression that everything in Kithai, or even within the Khan's capital city, was all beautiful, easy, rich and sweet. I would not have wished things so, for an unrelieved niceness can be as tiresome as the monotonously grand landscape of the Pai-Mir. Kubilai could have located his capital in a city of more temperate climate, for instance—there were places to the south that enjoyed perpetual springtime, and some much farther south that basked in perpetual summer. But the people who lived in such places, I found when I visited them, also were boringly bland. The climate of Khanbalik was very like that of Venice: springtime rains, winter snows and a sometimes oppressive summer heat. While its inhabitants did not have to contend with the mildewing dampness of Venice, their houses and clothes and furnishings were pervaded by the yellow dust forever being blown from the western deserts.

Like the seasons and the weathers, Khanbalik was ever changing and various and invigorating, never cloying. For one reason, besides such splendors and happy novelties as I have cited, there were dark and not so happy aspects as well. Beneath the Khan's magnificent palace crouched the dungeons of the Fondler. The gorgeous robes of nobles and courtiers sometimes cloaked men of mean ambitions and base designs. Even my own two pretty maidservants evinced some not so pretty turns of temperament. And outside the palace, in the streets and markets, not everybody in those throngs was a prosperous merchant or an opulent purchaser. There were poor people, too, and wretched ones. I remember seeing a market stall that sold meat to the poor, and someone translated its signboard for me: "Forest shrimp, household deer, brushwood eels"— then told me those were only high-flown Han names. The meats for sale were really grasshoppers and rats and the tripes of snakes.

. 6 .

F o r many months, my workdays consisted of talking to and asking respectful questions of one after another of the many lords-ministers and administrators and accountants and courtiers responsible for the smooth functioning of the entire Mongol Khanate and this land of Kithai and this city of Khanbalik and this palace court. Chingkim introduced me to most of them, but he had his own work to do as Wang of Khanbalik, so he then left it to me and them to arrange our meetings at our mutual convenience. Some of the men, including lords of high position, were most hospitable to my interest and forthcoming in their explications of their offices. Others, including some mere palace stewards of laughably low degree, regarded me as a prying busybody and would talk only grudgingly. But all, by their Khakhan's command, had to receive me. So I did not neglect to visit any of them, and did not let even the unfriendly ones put me off with scanty or evasive interviews. I must admit, though, that I found some of the men's work more interesting than others', and so spent more time with some than with others.

My colloquy with the Court Mathematician was particularly brief. I have never had much of a head for arithmetic, as my old teacher Fra Varisto could have attested. Although Master Lin-ngan was friendly— having been the first courtier I had met on arrival in Khanbalik—and was proud of his duties and eager to explain them, I fear that my lackluster responses rather dampened his enthusiasm. We did not get any further, in fact, than his showing me a nan-zhen, a Kithai-style instrument for marine navigation.

"Ah, yes," I said. "The north-pointing needle. Venetian ships' captains have them, too. It is called a bussola."

"We call it the south-riding carriage, and I submit that it cannot be compared to your crude Western versions. You in the West are still dependent on a circle divided into only three hundred and sixty degrees. That is but a clumsy approximation of the truth, arrived at by some of your primitive forebears, who could not count the days of the year any better than that. The true span of the solar year was known to us Han three thousand years ago. You will notice that our circle is divided into the accurate number of three hundred and sixty-five and one-quarter degrees."

I looked, and it was so. After contemplating the circle for some moments, I ventured to say, "A perfect count, certainly. A perfect division of the circle, undoubtedly. But what good is it?"

He stared at me, aghast. "What *good* is it?"

"Our outmoded Western circle is at least easily divisible into fourths. How could a man using this one ever mark off a right angle?"

His serenity somewhat ruffled, he said, "Marco Polo, honored guest, do you not realize what genius is represented here? What patient observation and refined calculation? And how sublimely superior to the slapdash mathematics of the West?"

"Oh, I freely concede that. I merely remark on the impracticality of it. Why, this would drive a land-surveyor mad. It would make hash of all our maps. And a builder could never erect a house with true corners or square rooms."

His serenity totally flown, he snapped in exasperation, "You Westerners are concerned only with amassing knowledge. You have no concern at all for acquiring wisdom. I speak to you of pure mathematics and you speak to me of carpenters!"

Humbly I said, "I am ignorant of philosophies, Master Lin-ngan, but I have known a few carpenters. This circle of Kithai, they would laugh at."

"*Laugh?!*" he cried, in a strangled voice.

For someone usually so wise and remote and dispassionate, he worked himself into quite a decent fury. Being not entirely unwise myself, I made my adieux and respectfully backed out of his chambers. Well, it was just one more of my encounters with Han ingenuity that made me dubious of their renown for ingenuity.

But in a somewhat similar interview, at the palace Observatory of the Astronomers, I managed better to hold my own, with self-assurance and aplomb. The Observatory was an unroofed upper terrace of the palace, cluttered with immense and complex instruments: armillary spheres and sundials and astrolabes and alidades, all beautifully made of marble and brass. The Court Astronomer, Jamal-ud-Din, was a Persian, by reason of the fact that all those instruments, he told me, had been invented and designed ages ago in his native land, so he knew best how to operate them. He was chief of half a dozen Under Astronomers, and they were all Han, because, said Master Jamal, the Han had been keeping scrupulous records of astronomical observations longer than any other people. Jamal-ud-Din and I conversed in Farsi, and he interpreted the comments made by his colleagues.

I began by admitting frankly, "My lords, the only education I ever had in astronomy was the Bible's account of how the Prophet Joshua, in order to prolong a battle for an extra day, made the sun to stand still in its course across the sky."

Jamal gave me a look, but repeated my words to the six elderly Han gentlemen. They seemed to get extremely excited, or confounded, and chattered among themselves, and then put a question to me, saying politely:

"Stopped the sun, did he, this Joshua? Most interesting. When did this occur?"

"Oh, a long, long time ago," I said. "When the Israelites strove against the Amorrhites. Several books before Christ was born and the calendar began."

"This is most interesting," they repeated, after some more consultation among themselves. "Our astronomical records, the Shu-king, go back more than three thousand five hundred and seventy years, and they contain no least mention of the occurrence. One would imagine that a cosmic event of that nature would have occasioned some comment even from the man in the street, let alone the astronomers of the time. Would it have been longer ago than that, do you suppose?"

The solemn old men were clearly trying to dissemble their consternation at my knowing more of historical astronomy than they did, so I graciously changed the subject.

"Though I lack formal education in your profession, my lords, I do possess some curiosity, and have frequently myself observed the sky, and therefrom have conceived some theories of my own."

"Indeed?" said Master Jamal, and, after consulting the others, "We would be honored to hear them."

So, with due modesty but with no paltering equivocation, I told them one of the conclusions I had come to: that the sun and the moon are closer to the earth in their orbits at morning and evening than at other hours.

"It is easy to see, my lords," I said. "Merely observe the sun at its rise or setting. Or better, observe the full moon rising, since it can be looked at without paining the eyes. As it ascends from the other side of the earth, it is immense. But as it rises it dwindles, until at its zenith it is only a fraction of its earlier size. I have remarked that phenomenon many times, watching the moon rise from beyond the Venetian lagoon. Obviously that heavenly body is getting farther from the earth as it proceeds in its orbit. The only other explanation for its diminishment would be that it *shrinks* as it goes, and that would be too foolish to credit."

"Foolish, truly," muttered Jamal-ud-Din. He and the Under Astronomers soberly shook their heads, seeming much impressed, and there was more muttering. Finally one of the sages must have determined to test the extent of my astronomical knowledge, for he put another question, by way of Jamal:

"What is your opinion, Marco Polo, of sun spots?"

"Ah," I said, pleased to be able to answer promptly. "A most damaging disfigurement, those. Terrible things."

"Say you so? We have been divided, among ourselves, as to whether, in the universal scheme of things, they mean good or evil."

"Well, I do not know that I would say *evil*. But ugly, yes, most certainly. For a long time, I mistakenly believed that all Mongol women were ugly, until I saw the ones here at the palace."

The gentlemen looked blank, and blinked at me, and Master Jamal said uncertainly, "What has that to do with the topic?"

I said, "I realized that it was only the *nomad* Mongol women, those who spend all their lives out of doors, who are sun-spotted and blotched and tanned like leather. These more civilized Mongol ladies of the court, by contrast, are—"

"No, no, no," said Jamal-ud-Din. "We are speaking of the spots *on the sun*."

"What? Spots on the sun?"

"Verily. The desert dust ever blowing hereabouts is usually a pestilence, but it has at least one good property. At times it veils the sun sufficiently that we can gaze directly at it. We have seen—severally and independently, and often enough to be in no doubt—that the sun occasionally is marred by dark spots and speckles on its otherwise luminous face."

I smiled and said, "I see," and then began laughing as expected. "You make a jest. I am amused, Master Jamal. But I do think, in all humanity, that you and I should not laugh at the expense of these hapless Han."

He looked even more blank and confounded than before, and he said, "What are we talking about *now*?"

"You make fun of their eyesight. Sun spots, indeed! Poor fellows, it is not their fault that they are constructed so. Having to peer all their lives from between those constricted eyelids. No wonder they have spots before their eyes! Nevertheless, a good jest, Master Jamal." And, bowing in the Persian fashion, still laughing, I took my departure.

The palace's Master Gardener and Master Potter were Han gentlemen, each supervising whole legions of young Han apprentices. So when I called on them I was again treated to a typically Han spectacle— of ingenuity being lavished on the inconsequential. In the West, such occupations are relegated to menials who do not care how dirty their hands get, not to men of intellect who can be better employed. But the Palace Gardener and Palace Potter seemed proud to be putting their wit and devotion and inventiveness at the service of garden manure and potter's clay. They seemed no less proud to be training a new generation of youngsters for a similar lifetime of mean and mucky manual labor.

The Palace Gardener's workshop was a vast hothouse built entirely of panes of Muscovy glass. At its several long tables his numerous apprentices sat hunched over boxes full of what looked like the culms of crocus flowers, doing something to them with very tiny knives.

"Those are bulbs of the celestial lily, being readied for planting."

said the Master Gardener. (When later I saw them in bloom, I recognized the flower as what we in the West call the narcissus.) He held up one of the dry bulbs and pointed and said, "By making two very precise, minute incisions in the bulb, it will grow in the shape we deem most attractive for this flower. Two stems will spring from the bulb, sideways and apart. But then, as the stems leaf out, they will curve inward again. So the lovely flowers, when they bloom, will bend toward each other like arms about to embrace. To the beauty of the flower we add grace of line."

"A remarkable art," I murmured, refraining from saying that I considered it also a negligible one to occupy so many people.

The Palace Potter's workshop, equally vast, was in the cellars underground and was lighted by lamps. His shop did not make crude table pottery, but the finest porcelain works of art. He showed me his bins of various clays and the mixing vessels and wheels and kilns and jars of colors and glazes which, he assured me, were "of most secret composition." Then he took me to a table where some dozen of his apprentices were working. They each had a finished porcelain bud vase, elegant little things of bulbous body and high narrow neck, but still of raw clay color. The apprentices were painting them preparatory to their firing.

"Why are all the boys' brushes broken?" I asked, for each young man was wielding a fine-haired brush that had a definite kink in its long handle.

"They are not broken," said the Master Potter. "The brushes are specially angled. These apprentices are painting the designs of flowers, birds, reeds, whatever—purely by feel and instinct and art—onto the *inside* of the vases. When the article is finished, its decoration will be invisible except when it is set before a light, and then the paper-thin white porcelain will allow the colorful picture to be delicately, mistily, subtly seen."

He led me to another table and said, "These are the newest and youngest apprentices, just learning their art."

"What art?" I said. "They are playing with eggshells."

"Yes. Porcelain objects of great value sometimes unfortunately get broken. These lads are learning to repair them. But naturally they do not practice on valuable articles. I take blown eggs and shatter their shells and give to each boy the commingled shards of two eggs. He must pick out and separate the fragments to reconstruct the two. That he does, putting each shell back together with those tiny brass rivets you see there. Not until an apprentice can rebuild an entire egg, so artfully that it appears never to have been broken, is he trusted to work on actual porcelain objects."

Nowhere else in the world had I seen so many instances of capable men devoting their lives to such minikin pursuits, and high intelligence dedicated to trivial ends, and stupendous skill and labor expended on paltry endeavors. And I do not mean just among the court craftsmen. I saw much the same sort of thing even among the lofty ministers at the uppermost levels of the Khanate's administration.

The Minister of History, for example, was a Han gentleman who looked ever so scholarly, and was fluent in many languages, and seemed to have memorized all of Western history as well as the Eastern. But his employment consisted only in being very busy at doing nothing worthwhile. When I asked what he was engaged upon at the moment, he got up from his big writing desk, opened a door of his chamber and showed me a much bigger chamber beyond. It was full of small writing desks very close together, and bent over each one was a scribe hard at work, almost hidden behind the books and rolled scrolls and sheaves of documents piled at his place.

Speaking perfect Farsi, the Minister of History said, "The Khakhan Kubilai decreed four years ago that his reign will commence a Yuàn Dynasty comprising all subsequent reigns of his successors. The title he chose, Yuàn, means 'the greatest' or 'the principal.' Which is to say, it must eclipse the lately extinguished Chin Dynasty, and the Xia before that, and every other dynasty dating back to the beginning of civilization in these lands. So I am compiling, and my assistants are writing, a glowing history to assure that future generations will recognize the supremacy of the Yuàn Dynasty."

"A deal of writing is being done, certainly," I said, looking at all the bowed heads and twitching ink brushes. "But how much can there be to write, if the Yuàn Dynasty is only four years old?"

"Oh, the recording of current events is nothing," he said dismissively. "The difficult part is rewriting all the history that has gone before."

"What? But how? History is history, Minister. History is what has happened."

"Not so, Marco Polo. History is what is remembered of what has happened."

"I see no difference," I said. "If, say, a devastating flood of the Yellow River occurred in such and such a year, whether or not anyone made written record of the event, it is likely that the flood will be remembered and so will the date."

"Ah, but not all the attendant circumstances. Suppose the then-emperor came promptly to the aid of the flood victims, and rescued them and fetched them to safe ground, and gave them new land and helped them again to prosperity. If those beneficent circumstances were to stay in the archives as part of the history of that reign, then this Yuàn Dynasty might, by comparison, appear deficient in benevolence. So we change the history just slightly, to record that earlier emperor as having been callous to his people's suffering."

"And the Yuàn seems kind by comparison? But suppose Kubilai and his successors prove to be *truly* callous in such calamities?"

"Then we must rewrite again, and make the earlier rulers *more* hardhearted. I trust you perceive now the importance of my work, and the diligence and creativeness required. It is no job for a lazy man, or a stupid one. History is not just a daily setting down of events, like keeping a ship's log. History is a fluid process, and the work of a historian is never done."

I said, "Historical events may be variously rendered, but current ones? For instance, in the Year of Our Lord one thousand two hundred seventy-five, Marco Polo arrived in Khanbalik. What more could be said of such a trifle?"

"If it is indeed a trifle," said the Minister, smiling, "then it need not be mentioned in history at all. But it could prove later to be significant. So I make a note of even such a trifle, and wait to see if it should be inscribed in the archives as an occasion to be treasured or regretted."

He went back to his writing desk, opened a large leather folder and riffled through the papers inside it. He picked out one and read from it:

"At the hour of Xu in the sixth day of the seventh moon, in the Year of the Boar, the year three thousand nine hundred seventy-three of the Han calendar, the year four of Yuàn, there returned from the Western city of Wei-ni-si to the City of the Khan the two foreigners, Po-lo Ni-klo and Po-lo Mah-fyo, bringing with them a third and younger Po-lo Mah-ko. It remains to be seen whether this young man will make Khanbalik better for his presence"—he threw me a mischievous side glance, and I could tell that he was no longer reading from the paper—"or whether he will be merely a nuisance, inflicting himself upon busy officials and inter-rupting them in their pressing duties."

"I will go away," I said, laughing. "Just one last question, Minister. If you can write a whole new history, cannot someone else rewrite yours?"

"Of course," he said. "And someone will." He looked surprised that I had even asked. "When the late Chin Dynasty was new, its first Minister of History rewrote everything that had gone before. And Chin historians continued so to write, to make the Chin period appear the Golden Age of all time. But dynasties come and go; the Chin lasted only a hundred and nineteen years. It could well happen that the Yuàn Dynasty and all I accomplish here"—he waved an arm to indicate his chamber and the other full of scribes—"may not outlast my own lifetime."

So I went away, resisting the temptation to suggest to the Minister that instead of exerting his scholarship and erudition, he might better employ his muscles, helping to pile up the kara blocks for the new hill being built in the palace gardens. That hill would less likely be disman-tled by future generations than would the pile of falsehoods he was building in the capital archives.

The conclusion I was coming to—that a great many men were en-gaged in doing very little of moment—I did not immediately confide to the Khakhan during my audience that week. But he himself began talk-ing of a matter rather similar. It seemed that he had recently had a count made of the various and numerous holy men currently habitant in Kithai, and was disgruntled by it.

"Priests," he growled. "Lamas, monks, Nestorians, malangs, imams, missionaries. All looking to accrete a congregation on which they can batten. I would not mind so much if they only preached sermons and then held out their begging bowls. But as soon as they do accumulate a few believers, they command the deluded wretches to despise and detest everyone who prefers some other faith. Of all the religions being propa-gated, only the Buddhists are tolerant of every other. I do not wish either to impose or oppose any religion, but I am seriously considering an edict against the *preachers*. My ukaz would command that what time the preachers now spend on petty ritual and ranting and prayer and evangelism and meditation be spent instead with a fly whisk, swatting flies. What do you think, Marco Polo? They would do incalculably more than they are doing now to make this world a better place."

"I think, Sire, the preachers are chiefly concerned with the next world."

"Well? Making this one better should earn them high credit in the next one. Kithai is overrun with pestiferous flies and with self-proclaimed holy men. I cannot abolish the flies by ukaz. But would you not agree that it would be good use of the holy men to kill the flies?"

"I have lately reflected, yes, Sire, that a large proportion of men are misemployed."

"*Most* men are misemployed, Marco," he said emphatically, "and do no manly work. To my mind, only warriors, laborers, explorers, craftsmen, artists, cooks and physicians are worth esteem. They do things or they discover things or they make things or they preserve things. All other men are scavengers and parasites dependent on the doers and the makers. Government functionaries, counselors, tradesmen, astrologers, money changers, factors, scribes, priests, clerks, they perform activity and call it action. They do nothing but move things about—and usually nothing weightier than bits of paper—or they exist only to proffer commentary or advice or criticism to the doers and the makers of things."

He paused and frowned, and then almost spat. "Vakh! What am I, since I got down from my horse? I lift no lance any longer, only a yin seal to stamp approval or disapproval. In honesty, I must include myself among the busy men who do nothing. Vakh!"

In that, of course, he was dead wrong.

I was no expert on monarchs, but I had long ago, from my reading in *The Book of Alexander*, taken that great conqueror as my ideal of what a sovereign should be. And I had by now met quite a number of real, living, ruling rulers, and I had formed some opinions of them: Edward, now King of England, who had seemed to me only a good soldier dutifully playing at princedom; and the miserable Armeniyan governor Hampig; and the Persian Shah Zaman, a henpecked zerbino of a husband inhabiting royal robes; and the Ilkhan Kaidu, not even pretending to be other than a barbarian warlord. Only this most recently met ruler, the Khakhan Kubilai, came anywhere near my imagined ideal.

He was not beautiful, as Alexander is portrayed in the *Book*'s illuminations, and not as young. The Khakhan was near twice the age Alexander had been when he died; but, by the same token, he held an empire some three times the size of that won by Alexander. And in other respects Kubilai came close to resembling my classical ideal. Though I early learned awe and dread of his tyrant power and his penchant for sudden, sweeping, unqualified, irrevocable judgments and decisions (his every published decree concluded thus: "The Khakhan has spoken; tremble, all men, and obey!"), it must be granted that such limitless power and the impetuous exercise of it are, after all, attributes to be expected of an absolute monarch. Alexander exhibited them, too.

In after years, some have called me "a posturing liar," refusing to believe that mere Marco Polo could ever have been more than remotely acquainted with the most powerful man in the world. Others have called me "a slavish sycophant," contemning me as an apologist for a brutal dictator.

I can understand why it is hard to believe that the high and mighty Khan of All Khans should have lent a moment of his attention to a lowly outsider like me, let alone his affection and trust. But the fact is that the Khakhan stood so high above *all* other men that, in his eyes, lords and nobles and commoners and maybe even slaves seemed of the same level and of indistinguishable characteristics. It was no more remarkable that he should deign to notice me than that he should give regard to his closest ministers. Also, considering the humble and distant origin of the Mongols, Kubilai was as much an outsider as I was in the exotic purlieus of Kithai.

As for my alleged sycophancy, it is true that I never personally suffered from any of his whims and caprices. It is true that he became fond of me, and entrusted me with responsibilities, and made me a close confidant. But it is not on that account that I still defend and praise the Khakhan. It was because of my closeness to him that I could see, better than some, that he wielded his vast authority as wisely as he knew how. Even when he did so despotically, it was always as a means to an end he thought right, not just expedient. Contrary to that philosophy expressed by my Uncle Mafio, Kubilai was as evil as he had to be and as good as he could be.

The Khakhan had layers and circles and envelopes of ministers and advisers and other officers about him, but he never let them wall him off from his realm, his subjects or his scrupulous attention to the details of government. As I had seen him do in the Cheng, Kubilai might delegate to others some minor matters, even the preliminary aspects of some major matters, but in everything of importance he always had the last word. I might liken him and his court to the fleets of vessels I first saw on the Yellow River. The Khakhan was the chuan, the biggest ship on the water, steered by a single firm rudder gripped by a single firm hand. The ministers in attendance on him were the san-pan scows that did the ferrying of cargoes to and from the master chuan vessel, and ran the lesser errands in shallower waters. Just one there was among the ministers—the Arab Achmad, Chief Minister, Vice-Regent and Finance Minister—who could be likened to the lopsided hu-pan skiff, cunningly designed to skirt curves, forever turning end for end, while always staying in safe water close to shore. But of Achmad, that man as warped as the hu-pan boat, I will tell in due time.

Kubilai, like the fabled Prete Zuàne, had to rule over a conglomeration of diverse nations and disparate peoples, many of them hostile to each other. Like Alexander, Kubilai sought to meld them by discerning the most admirable ideas and achievements and qualities in all those varied cultures, and disseminating them broadcast for the good of all his different peoples. Of course, Kubilai was not saintly like Prete Zuàne, nor even a Christian, nor even a devotee of the classical gods, like

Alexander. As long as I knew him, Kubilai recognized no deity except the Mongol war god Tengri and some minor Mongol idols like the household god Nagatai. He was *interested* in other religions, and at one time or another studied many of them, in hope of finding the One Best, which could be another benefit to his subjects and another unifying force among them. My father and uncle and others repeatedly urged Christianity upon him, and the swarms of Nestorian missionaries never ceased preaching at him their heretic brand of Christianity, and other men championed the oppressive religion of Islam, the godless and idolatrous Buddhism, the several religions peculiar to the Han, even the nauseous Hinduism of India.

But the Khakhan never could be persuaded that Christianity is the one True Faith, and never found any other he favored. He said once—and I do not remember whether at the time he was amused or exasperated or disgusted—"What difference what god? God is only an excuse for the godly."

He may ultimately have become what a theologian would call a skeptic Pyrrhonist, but even his disbeliefs he did not force upon anyone. He remained always liberal and tolerant in that respect, and let every man believe in and worship what he would. Admittedly, Kubilai's lack of any religion at all left him without any guidance of dogma and doctrine, free to regard even the basic virtues and vices as narrowly or liberally as he saw fit. So his notions of charity, mercy, brotherly love and other such things were often at dismaying variance with those of men of ingrained orthodoxy. I myself, though no paragon of Christian principle, often disagreed with his precepts or was aghast at his applications of them. Even so, nothing that Kubilai ever did—however much I may have deplored it at the time—ever diminished my admiration of him, or my loyalty to him, or my conviction that the Khan Kubilai was the supreme sovereign of our time.

· 7 ·

I N subsequent days and weeks and months, I was granted audience with every one of the Khakhan's ministers and counselors and courtiers of whose offices I have earlier spoken in these pages, and with numerous others besides, of high and low degree, whose titles I may not yet have mentioned—the three Ministers of Farming, Fishing and Herding, the Chief of Digging the Great Canal, the Minister of Roads and Rivers, the Minister of Ships and Seas, the Court Shamàn, the Minister of Lesser Races—and ever so many others.

From every audience I came away knowing new things of interest or usefulness or edification, but I will not here recount them all. From one of the meetings I came away embarrassed, and so did the minister concerned. He was a Mongol lord named Amursama, and he was Minister of Roads and Rivers, and the embarrassment arose most unexpectedly, while he was discoursing on a really prosaic matter: the post service he was putting into effect all across Kithai.

"On every road, minor as well as major, at intervals of seventy-five li, I am building a comfortable barrack, and the nearest communities are responsible for keeping it supplied with good horses and men to ride them. When a message or a parcel must be swiftly conveyed in either direction, a rider can take it at a stretch-out gallop from one post to the next. There he flings it to a new rider, ready saddled and waiting, who rides to the next post, and so on. Between dawn and dawn, a succession of riders can transport a light load as far as an ordinary karwan train could take it in twenty days. And, because bandits will hesitate to attack a known emissary of the Khanate, the deliveries arrive safely and reliably."

I was later to know that that was true, when my father and Uncle Mafìo began to prosper in their trading ventures. They would usually convert their proceeds into precious gems that made a small, light packet. Utilizing the Minister Amursama's horse post, they would send the packets from Kithai all the way to Constantinople, where my Uncle Marco would deposit them in the coffers of the Compagnia Polo.

The Minister went on, "Also, because occasionally something unusual or important may occur in the regions between the horse posts—a flood, an uprising, some marvel worth reporting—I am establishing, every ten li or so, a lesser station for foot runners. So, from anywhere in the realm, there is a run of less than an hour to the next station, and the runners continue by relays until one gets to the nearest horse post, whence the news can be conveyed farther and more quickly. I am just now getting the system organized throughout Kithai, but eventually I will have it operating across the entire Khanate, to bring news or important burdens even from the farthermost border of Poland. Already I have the service so efficient that a white-flag porpoise caught in Tung-ting Lake, more than two thousand li south of here, can be cut up and packed in saddlebags of ice and hurried here to the Khakhan's kitchen while it is still fresh."

"A fish?" I respectfully inquired. "Is that an important burden?"

"That fish lives only in one place, in that Tung-ting Lake, and is not easily caught, so it is reserved for the Khakhan. It is a great table delicacy in spite of its great ugliness. The white-flag porpoise is as big as a woman, has a head like a duck, with a snout like a duck's beak, and its slanted eyes are sadly blind. But it is a fish only by enchantment."

I blinked and said, "Uu?"

"Yes, each is a royal descendant of a long-ago princess, who was changed by enchantment into a porpoise after she drowned herself in that lake, because . . . because of a . . . a tragic love affair. . . ."

I was surprised that a typically brisk and brusque Mongol should begin stammering like a schoolboy. I looked up at him, and saw that his formerly brown face had flushed red. He avoided my eye and clumsily fumbled to turn our conversation to something else. Then I remembered who he was, so I—probably also reddening in sympathy—made some excuse to terminate the interview, and I withdrew. I had totally forgotten, you see, that that Minister Amursama was the lord who, after his lady was taken in adultery, had been ordered to strangle her with her own sphincter. Actually, a great many of the palace residents were curious to know the grisly details of Amursama's compliance with that order, but were shy of bringing up the matter in his presence. However, they said, he himself seemed somehow always to be stumbling onto reminders of the subject, and then getting tongue-tied and uncomfortable, and making everybody around him just as uncomfortable.

Well, I could understand that. But I could not understand why another minister, likewise discoursing on a prosaic subject, should have seemed equally distraught and evasive. He was Pao Nei-ho and he was the Minister of Lesser Races. (As I have told, the Han people are everywhere in the majority, but in Kithai and in the southerly lands which were then the Sung Empire, there are some sixty other nationalities.) Minister Pao told me, at tedious length, how it was his responsibility to ensure that all of Kithai's minority peoples enjoyed the same rights as the Han majority. It was one of the duller disquisitions I had so far endured, but Minister Pao told it in Farsi—in his position, he had to be multilingual—and I could not see why the telling of it made him so nervously falter and fidget and sprinkle his speech with er and uh and ahem.

"Even the er conqueror Mongols are uh few compared to us Han," he said. "The ahem lesser nationalities are fewer still. In the er western regions, for example, the uh so-called Uighur and the ahem Uzbek, Kirghiz, Kazhak and er Tazhik. Here in the uh north we find also the ahem Manchu, the Tungus, the Hezhe. And when the er Khan Kubilai completes his uh conquest of the ahem Sung Empire, we will absorb all the other er nationalities down there. The uh Naxi and the Miao, the Puyi, the Chuang. Also ahem the obstreperous Yi people who populate the er entire province of Yun-nan in the uh far southwest . . ."

He went on and on like that, and I might have dozed, except that my mind was busy sieving out the ers and uhs and ahems. But even when I had done that, I found the speech still a dry one. It seemed to contain nothing shameful or sinister that would require concealment in a lot of vocal weeds. I did not know why Minister Pao should be speaking so haltingly. Neither did I know why I was being suspicious of that fractured oratory. But I was. He was saying *something* that I was not supposed to grasp. I was sure of it. And, as it turned out, I was right.

When I finally got loose of him that day, I went to my own rooms and to the closet which I let Nostril use for his pallet chamber. He was sleeping at that moment, though it was only midafternoon. I shook him and said:

"You have not enough work to do, slovenly slave, so I have thought of a job for you."

In truth, the slave was lately having quite an indolent life. My father and uncle, having no need for him, had relinquished his services entirely to me. But I was so well served by the maids Buyantu and Biliktu that I employed Nostril only for such things as buying me a wardrobe of suitable Kithai-style clothing, and keeping it well stocked and in good order, and occasionally to groom and saddle a horse for me. Between times, Nostril did not do much roaming about or mischief making. He seemed to have subdued his former nasty habits and natural inquisitiveness. He spent most of his time in his closet, except when he ventured as far as the palace kitchens to seek a meal, or, when I invited him, to dine with me in my chambers. I did not allow that often, for the girls were clearly repelled by his appearance and uncomfortable in the role of Mongols waiting upon a mere slave.

Now he came awake, grumbling, "Bismillah, master," and yawning so that even his dreadful nose hole seemed to gape wider.

I said sternly, "Here am I, busy all the day, while my slave slumbers. I am supposed to be evaluating the Khakhan's courtiers by talking to them face to face, but you could do even better behind their backs."

He mumbled, "I gather, master, that you wish me to snoop about among their servants and attendants. But how? I am an outlander and a newcomer, and my grasp of the Mongol tongue is still imperfect."

"There are many outlanders among the domestic staff. Prisoners taken from every land. The servants' talk belowstairs must be a Babel of languages. And I know very well that your one nostril is adept at sniffing out gossip and scandal."

"I am honored that you ask me, master, but—"

"I am not asking. I am commanding. You are henceforth to spend all your spare time, of which you have an ample measure, mingling with the servants and your fellow slaves."

"Master, to be honest, I am fearful of wandering about these halls. I might blunder into the Fondler's precincts."

"Do not talk back or I will take you there myself. Hear me. Every evening from now on, you and I will sit down and you will repeat to me every least morsel of tattle and tale you have heard."

"About anything? Everything? Most of the talk is trivial."

"Everything. But right now I am interested to know all I can find out about the Minister of Lesser Races, the Han lord named Pao Nei-ho. Whenever you can subtly turn the conversation to that subject, do so. But *subtly*. Meanwhile, I shall want everything else you hear, as well. There is no foretelling what tidbit may be of value to me."

"Master Marco, I must make some respectful demur in advance. I am not so handsome now as I once was, when I could beguile even princesses to blurt their innermost—"

"Oh, that imbecilic old lie again! Nostril, you and all the world know that you have always been damnably ugly, and you never once so much as touched the hem of a princess's gown!"

Undeterred, he persisted, "On the other hand, you have at your command two pretty maids who could easily employ their comeliness for come-hitherness. They are far better fitted for wheedling secrets out of—"

"Nostril," I said patiently. "You will spy for me because I tell you to, and I need give no other reason. However, I will mention just this. It apparently has not occurred to you, but it has to me, that those two maids are very likely spying on *my* doings. Watching my every move and reporting it. Remember, it was the son of the Khakhan, on the orders of the Khakhan, who gave me the girls."

I always spoke of them as "the girls" when speaking to others, because to use both their names every time would have been unwieldy, and I did not speak of them as "the servants" because they were rather more than that to me, but I would not speak of them as "the concubines" because that seemed to me a slightly derogatory term. In private, however, I addressed them separately as Buyantu and Biliktu, for I had early learned to tell them apart. Although when dressed they were identical, I now knew their individualities of expression and gesture. Undressed, although still identical even to the dimples in their cheeks, the dimples at their elbows and those especially winsome dimples on either side of the base of their spines, the twins were more easily identifiable. Biliktu had a sprinkle of freckles on the underswell of her left breast, and Buyantu had a tiny scar on her upper right thigh from some childhood mishap.

I had taken note of those things on our very first night together, and of some other things as well. The girls were both nicely shaped and, not being Muslims, were complete in all their private parts. In general, they were built like other mature females I had known, except that they were a trifle shorter in the leg and a trifle less indented at the waistline than, say, Venetian and Persian women are. But their one most intriguing difference from women of other races was the matter of their inguinal hair. They had the usual dark triangle in the usual place—the han-mao, they called it, their "little warmer"—but it was not a curly or bushy tuft. Through some quirk of nature, Mongol women—at least those I have known—have an exceptionally smooth escutcheon; the hair lies as flat and neat there as on the pelt of a cat. When earlier lying with a woman, I had sometimes amused myself (and her) by twining and twiddling my fingers in her little warmer; with Buyantu or Biliktu, I stroked and petted it as I would a kitten (and made her purr like one).

On my first night in my private apartments, the twins had made it plain that they expected me to take one of them to bed with me. When they bathed me, they also stripped and bathed themselves, and most fastidiously washed my and their dan-tian, our "pink places," our private parts. When they had dusted me and themselves with fragrant powders, they slipped into dressing gowns of silk so sheer that their little warmers were still quite visible, and the girl I would come to recognize as Buyantu asked me, straight out:

"Will you be desiring children of us, Master Marco?"

Involuntarily I blurted, "Dio me varda, no!" She could not have understood the words, but evidently could not mistake the meaning, for she nodded and went on:

"We have procured fern seed, which is the best preventive of conception. Now, as you know, master, we are both of twenty-two-karat quality, and of course are virgins. So we have been speculating all afternoon as to which of us will have the honor of being first qing-du chu-kai—awakened to womanhood—by our handsome new master."

Well, I was pleased that they were not, like so many virgins, dreading the event. Indeed, they seemed to have been, in a sisterly way, contending for precedence, for Buyantu added, "As it happens, master, I am the elder of the two."

Biliktu laughed and told me, "By a matter of minutes only, according to our mother. But all our lives, Elder Sister has been claiming privilege on that account."

Buyantu shrugged and said, "One of us must have the first night, and the other wait for the second. If you would prefer not to make the choice yourself, master, we could draw straws."

I said airily, "Far be it from me to leave delight to chance. Or to discriminate between two such compelling attractions. You will both be first."

Buyantu said chidingly, "We are virgins, but we are not ignorant."

"We helped raise our two younger brothers," said Biliktu.

"So, while bathing you, we saw that you are normally equipped in your dan-tian," said Buyantu. "Bigger than boys in that respect, of course, but not *multiplied*."

"Therefore," said Biliktu, "you can be in only one place at a time. How can you pretend that we both could be first?"

"The bed is beautifully commodious," I said. "We will all three lie together and—"

"That would be indecent!"

They both looked so shocked that I smiled. "Come, come. It is well-known that men sometimes disport themselves with more than one woman at a time."

"But—but those are concubines of long experience, long past modesty, and of no embarrassing relation. Master Marco, we are *sisters*, and this is our first jiao-gou, and we will . . . that is to say, we cannot . . . in each other's presence . . ."

"I promise," I said, "you will find it no less sisterly than bathing in each other's presence. Also, that you will soon cease to fret about proprieties. Also, that you will both so enjoy the jiao-gou that you will not notice which of you was first. Or ever care."

They hesitated. Buyantu frowned prettily in contemplation. Biliktu meditatively bit her lower lip. Then they looked shyly sideways at each other from the corners of their eyes. When their glances met, they blushed—so extensively that their sheer gowns turned pink all down the breast. Then they laughed, a little shakily, but they made no further objection. Buyantu got from a drawer a phial of fern seed, and she and Biliktu turned their backs on me while each of them took a pinch of that fine, almost powdery seed and, with a finger, inserted it deep inside themselves. Then they let me take them each by a hand and let me lead them to the inviting bed, and let me go on leading from there.

Harking back to my youthful experience in Venice, I put to use the modes of music making I had learned from the Lady Ilaria and then had refined by practicing on the little maiden Doris. Thus I was able to make the initiation of these virgins, too, an occasion for them to remember, not just without wincing, but with genuine joy. At first, as I turned or moved from Buyantu to Biliktu and back again, they kept their eyes not on me but sideways on each other, and were obviously trying not to make any visible or audible responses to my ministrations, lest the other consider her immodest. But as I worked delicately with fingers and lips and tongue and even my eyelashes, they eventually closed their own eyes and ignored each other and gave themselves up to their own feelings.

I might remark that that night's jiao-gou, my first such activity in Kithai, was endowed with a special piquancy, just because of the fanciful Han terms which were employed there for all parts of the human body. As I had already learned, the name "red jewel" can mean either the male or female parts in general. But it is usually reserved for the male's organ, while the female's is the "lotus" and its lips are its "petals" and what I had formerly called the lumaghèta or zambur is the "butterfly between the petals of the lotus." The female posterior is her "calm moon" and its dainty valley is the "rift in the moon." Her breasts are her "flawless jade viands" and her nipples are her "small stars."

So, by variously and adroitly touching, caressing, teasing, tasting, fondling, tickling, nibbling jade viands and flowers and petals and moons and stars and butterflies, I succeeded marvelously in making both the twins achieve their first peak of jiao-gou simultaneously. Then, before they could realize how much unabashed singing and thrashing they had done on the way there, and perhaps get mutually embarrassed, I did other things to urge them up again to the peaks. They were quick learners and eager to partake again of those heights, so I kept my mind off my own urgent yearnings and devoted myself entirely to their enjoyments. At times, one girl would be up among the peaks by herself, and her sister would regard her—and my ministrations to her—with a wondering and marveling smile. Then it would be her turn, while the other watched and approved. Not until both the girls were dazed and delighted with their new-discovered sensations, and well moistened by their own secretions, did I play them both at once to a veritable frenzy. While both were oblivious to everything but their ecstasy, I penetrated first one, then the other—easily and pleasurably for me and them, too—and continued giving myself into one and the other, so that even I do not remember in which order, or in which twin I first made spruzzo.

After that first and musically perfect triad, I let the girls rest and pant and perspire happily for a while, and smile at me and each other, until, when they had regained their breath, Biliktu and Buyantu were joking aloud and laughing at their earlier silliness about modesty and decorum. So then, free of restraints, we did many other things, and more leisurely, so that when one girl was not actively participating she could get a vicarious enjoyment by watching and assisting the other two of us. But I did not neglect either of them for very long. I had, after all, learned from the Persian Princesses Moth and Shams how two females could be thoroughly pleasured at once, and myself with them. The doing of that was of course far nicer with these Mongol twins, since neither of them had to remain invisible during the proceedings. Indeed, before the night was over, they had shed all vestiges of prudery, and were quite ready for their innermost dan-tian to be seen by me or each other, and for their and my pink places to do or be done to, in every variation I and they could think of.

So our first night together was an unqualified success, and the precursor of many other such nights, during which we became ever more inventive and acrobatic. It surprised even me: how many more combinations can be made of three than of two. But we did not always frolic in a threesome. The twins, otherwise so identical, were dissimilar in one physiological respect: they got their jing-gi, their monthly affliction, in a tidy alternation. Hence, for a few days every two weeks or so, I enjoyed an ordinary coupling with just a single female, while the other slept apart and jealously sulked.

However, young and lusty as I was, I did have some physical limits, and I also had other occupations that required my strength and stamina and alertness. After a couple of months, I began to find rather debilitating what the twins called their xing-yu or "sweet desires"—and what I called their insatiable appetites. So I suggested to them that my participation was not *always* necessary, and I told them about the "hymn of the convent," as the Lady Ilaria had named it. At the notion of a woman's manipulating her own petals and stars and so on, Buyantu and Biliktu looked as shocked as they had on our first night of acquaintance. When I went on to tell them what the Princess Moth had once confided to me—how she relieved and gratified the neglected women of the Shah Zaman's anderun, the twins looked even more shocked, and Buyantu exclaimed:

"That would be indecent!"

I said mildly, "You complained about indecency once before, and I think I proved you mistaken."

"But—a woman doing to another woman! An act of gua-li! That *would* be indecent!"

"I daresay it would, if one or both of you were old or ugly. But you are both beautiful and desirable women. I see no reason why you could not find as much pleasure in each other as I find in you."

Again the girls looked askance at each other, and again that caused them to blush, and that made them giggle—a trifle naughtily, a trifle guiltily. Still, it took some persuasion on my part before they would lie down naked together, without me between them, and let me remain fully clothed while I instructed and guided their movements. They were tense and reticent to do to each other what they let me do with no reticence whatever. But as I took them through the nuns' hymn, note by note, so to speak—gently moving Buyantu's fingertip to caress Biliktu here, gently moving Biliktu's head so that her lips pressed Buyantu there —I could see them get aroused in spite of themselves. And after some time of play under my guidance, they began to forget about me. When their small stars twinkled erect, the girls did not need me to show them how they could employ those darling protrusions to good effect on each other. When first Biliktu's lotus began to unfold its petals, Buyantu needed no one to show her how to gather its dew. And when both their butterflies were aroused and fluttering, the girls twined together as naturally and passionately as if they had been born to be lovers instead of sisters.

I must confess that, by this time, I had myself become aroused, and had forgotten whatever debility I had earlier felt, and so doffed my own garments and joined in the play.

That happened quite often, from then on. If I came to my chambers weary from a day's work, and the twins were itching with xing-yu, I would give them leave to begin on their own, and they would do so with alacrity. I might go on down the hall to Nostril's closet and sit with him for a time, listening to his day's gleanings of gossip from the servants' quarters. Then I would return to my bedroom, and perhaps pour a goblet of arkhi, and sit down and take my ease while I watched the girls frolicking together. After a while, my fatigue would abate and my normal urges would come alive and I would ask the girls' permission to join them. Sometimes they would mischievously make me wait until they had fully enjoyed and exhausted their sisterly ardors. Only then would they let me onto the bed with them, and sometimes they would mischievously pretend that I was unneeded, unwanted, an intruder—and would mischievously pretend reluctance to open their pink places to me.

After some more time, it began to happen that I would come home to my chambers to find the twins already abed, and doing vigorous jiao-gou in their fashion. They laughingly referred to their style of coupling as chuai-sho-ur, a Han term which translates as "tucking the hands into opposite sleeves." (We Westerners would speak of "folding our arms," but that gesture is done by Eastern folk *inside* their capacious sleeves.) I thought the twins were clever to adopt that term to describe the way two women make love.

When I joined them, it would often happen that Biliktu would profess herself already quite emptied of joys and juices—she was less robust than her sister, she said; perhaps from being a few minutes the younger—and she would ask to be allowed just to sit by and admire while Buyantu and I cavorted. And on those occasions, Buyantu would sometimes pretend that she found me and my equipment and my performance deficient in comparison to what she had just been enjoying, and she would laugh derisively and call me gan-ga, which means awkward. But I always played along with the pretense, and pretended to be insulted by her pretended disdain, so she would laugh more loudly and give herself to me with passionate abandon, to show that she had only been jesting. And if I asked Biliktu, after she had rested for a while, to come and join me and her sister, she might sigh, but she would usually accede, and she would give good account of herself.

So, for a long time, the twins and I enjoyed a cozy and convivial ménage à trois. That they were almost certainly spies for the Khakhan, and probably reporting to him everything including our bedtime diversions, did not worry me, because I had nothing to hide from him. I was ever loyal to Kubilai, and faithful in his service, and doing naught that could be reported as contrary to his best interests. My own small spying —Nostril's nosing about among the palace servants—I was doing in the Khakhan's behalf, so I took no great pains to conceal even that from the girls.

No, there was at that time only one thing that troubled me about Buyantu and Biliktu. Even when we were all three in the rapturous throes of jiao-gou, I could never cease remembering that these girls, according to the prevailing system of grading females, were of *only* twenty-two-karat quality. Some conventicle of old wives and concubines and senior servants had discovered in them some trace of base alloy. To me, the twins seemed excellent specimens of womanhood, and indubitably they were nonpareil servants, in bed or out, and they did not snore or have bad breath. What, then, did they lack that they fell short of the twenty-four-karat perfection? And why was that lack imperceptible to me? Any other man would doubtless have rejoiced to be in my situation, and would cheerfully have brushed aside any such finical reservations. But then as always my curiosity never would rest until it was satisfied.

.8.

A F T E R that uninformative interview in which the Minister of Lesser Races had been so reserved and uneasy, my next, with the Minister of War, was refreshingly open and candid. I would have expected a holder of such an important office to be quite the opposite, but then there were a lot of anomalies about the Minister of War. As I have said, he was unaccountably a Han and not a Mongol. Also, the Minister Chao Meng-fu looked to me exceedingly young to have been given such high office.

"That is because the Mongols do not *need* a Minister of War," he said cheerfully, bouncing a round ball of ivory in one hand. "They make war as naturally as you or I would make jiao-gou with a woman, and they are probably better at doing war than jiao-gou."

"Probably," I said. "Minister Chao, I would be grateful if you would tell me—"

"Please, Elder Brother," he said, raising the hand which held the ivory ball. "Ask me nothing about war. I can tell you absolutely nothing about war. If, however, you require advice on the making of jiao-gou . . ."

I looked at him. It was the third time he had spoken that slightly indelicate term. He looked placidly back at me, squeezing and revolving the carved ivory ball in his right hand. I said, "Forgive my persistence, Minister Chao, but the Khakhan has enjoined me to make inquiry of every—"

"Oh, I do not *mind* telling you anything. I mean only that I am totally ignorant of war. I am much better informed about jiao-gou."

That made the fourth mention. "Could I be mistaken?" I asked. "Are you not the Minister of War?"

Still cheerfully, he said, "It is what we Han call passing off a fish eye for a pearl. My title is an empty one, an honor conferred for other functions I perform. As I said, the Mongols *need* no Minister of War. Have you yet called on the Armorer of the Palace Guard?"

"No."

"Do so. You would enjoy the encounter. The Armorer is a handsome woman. My wife, in fact: the Lady Chao Ku-an. That is because the Mongols no more require an adviser on armaments than they require advice on making war."

"Minister Chao, you have me quite confounded. You were drawing at that table when I came in, drawing on a scroll. I assumed you were making a map of battle plans, or something of the sort."

He laughed and said, "Something of the sort. If you consider jiao-gou as a sort of battle. Do you not see me palpating this ivory ball, Elder Brother Marco? That is to keep my right hand and fingers supple. Do you not know why?"

I suggested feebly, "To be deft in the caresses of jiao-gou?"

That sent him into a real convulsion of laughter. I sat and felt like a fool. When he recovered, he wiped his eyes and said, "I am an artist. If you ever meet another, you will find him also playing with one of these hand balls. I am an artist, Elder Brother, a master of the boneless colors, a holder of the Golden Belt, the highest accolade bestowed upon artists. More to be desired than an empty Mongol title."

"I still do not understand. There is already a Court Master of the Boneless Colors."

He smiled. "Yes, old Master Chien. He paints *pretty* pictures. Little flowers. And my dear wife is famous as the Mistress of the Zhu-gan Cane. She can paint just the shadows of that graceful cane, and make you see it entire. But I " He stood tall, and thumped his chest with his ivory ball, and said proudly, "I am the Master of the Feng-shui, and feng-shui means 'the wind, the water'—which is to say, I paint that which cannot be grasped. *That* is what won me the Golden Belt from my artist peers and elders."

I said politely, "I should like to see some of your work."

"Unfortunately, I now have to paint the feng-shui on my own time, if ever. The Khan Kubilai gave me my bellicose title just so I could be installed here in the palace to paint another sort of thing. My own fault. I was incautious enough to reveal to him that other talent of mine."

I tried to return to the subject that had brought me. "You have nothing to do with war, Master Chao? Not in the least?"

"Well, the least possible, yes. That cursed Arab Achmad would probably withhold my wages if I did not make some pretense at fulfilling my titular office. Therefore, with my unsupple left hand, so to speak, I keep records of the Mongols' battles and casualties and conquests. The orloks and sardars tell me what to write, and I write it down. Nobody ever looks at the records. I might as well be writing poetry. Also, I set little flags and simulated yak tails on a great map to keep visible account of what the Mongols have conquered, and what yet remains to be conquered."

Chao said all of that in a very bored voice, unlike the happy fervor with which he had spoken of his feng-shui painting. But then he cocked his head and said, "You also spoke of maps. You are interested in maps?"

"I am, yes, Minister. I have assisted in the making of some."

"None like this, I wager." He led me to another room, where a vast table, nearly as big as the room, was covered by a cloth, lumped and peaked by what it protected. He said, "Behold!" and whisked off the cloth.

"Cazza beta!" I breathed. It was not just a map, it was a work of art. "Did you make this, Minister Chao?"

"I wish I could say yes, but I cannot. The artist is unknown and long dead. This sculptured model of the Celestial Land is said to date back to the reign of the First Emperor Chin, whenever that was. It was he who commanded the building of the wall called the Mouth, which you can see there in miniature."

Indeed I could. I could see everything of Kithai, and the lands around it as well. The map was, as Chao said, a model, not a drawing on a sheet of paper. It appeared to have been molded of gesso or terracotta, flat where the earth was in fact flat, raised and convoluted and serrated where the earth actually rose in hills and mountains—and then the whole of it had been overlaid with precious metals and stones and colored enamels. To one side lay a turquoise Sea of Kithai, its curving shores and bays and inlets all carefully delineated, and into that sea ran the land's rivers, done in silver. All the mountains were gilded, the highest of them tipped with diamonds to represent snow, and the lakes were little pools of blue sapphires. The forests were done, almost to the individual *tree*, in green jade, and farmlands were a brighter green enamel, and the major cities were done, almost to the individual *house*, in white alabaster. Hither and yon ran the wavery line of the Great Wall—or Walls, as it is in places—done in rubies. The deserts were sparkling flats of powdered pearl. Across the whole great table-sized landscape were lines inlaid in gold, appearing squiggly where they undulated over mountains and highlands, but when I looked directly down on them, I could see that the lines were straight—up and down the model, back and forth, making an overlay of squares. The east–west lines were clearly the climatic parallels, and the north–south lines the longitudes, but from what meridian they measured their distances I could not discern.

"From the capital city," said Chao, having noticed my scrutiny. "In those times it was Xian." He pointed to the tiny alabaster city, far to the southwest of Khanbalik. "That is where this map was found, some years ago."

I noticed also the additions Chao had made to the map—little paper flags to represent the battle standards of orloks, and feathers to represent the yak tails of sardars—outlining what the Khan Kubilai and his Ilkhans and Wangs held of the lands represented.

"Not all of the map, then, is within the empire," I observed.

"Oh, it will be," said Chao, in the same bored voice with which he talked of his office. He began to point. "All of this, here, to the south of the River Yang-tze, is still the Empire of Sung, with its capital over here in the beautiful coast city of Hang-zho. But you can see how closely the Sung Empire is pressed about by our Mongol armies on its borders. Everything north of the Yang-tze is what used to be the Empire of Chin and is now Kithai. Over yonder, the entire west is held by the Ilkhan Kaidu. And the high country of To-Bhot, south of there, is ruled by the Wang Ukuruji, one of Kubilai's numerous sons. The only battles being waged at the moment are down here—in the southwest—where the Orlok Bayan is campaigning in the province of Yun-nan."

"I have heard of that place."

"A rich and fertile country, but inhabited by the obstreperous Yi people," Chao said indifferently. "When the Yi finally have the good sense to succumb to Bayan, and we have Yun-nan, then, you see, we will have the remaining Sung provinces so tightly encircled that they are bound to surrender, too. The Khakhan has already picked out a new name for those lands. They will be called Manzi. The Khan Kubilai will then reign over everything you see on this map, and more. From Sibir in the frozen north to the borders of the hot jungle lands of Champa in the south. From the Sea of Kithai on the east to far, far beyond the western extent of this map."

I said, "You seem to think that will not be enough to satisfy him."

"I know it will not. Only a year ago, he ordered the Mongols' first venture ever *eastward*. Yes, their first foray upon the sea. He sent a fleet of chuan out across the Sea of Kithai, to the islands called Jihpen-kwe, the Empire of the Dwarfs. That tentative probe was repulsed by the dwarfs, but Kubilai is certain to try again, and more energetically." The Minister stood for a moment, looking over the immense and beautiful map model, then said, "What matter what more he takes? When Sung falls, he has all the Celestial Land that once was Han."

He sounded so uncaring about it that I remarked, "You can say it more emotionally, if you like, Minister. I would understand. You are, after all, a Han."

"Emotion? Why?" He shrugged. "A centipede, even when it dies, does not fall. Being likewise many-legged, the Han have always endured and always will." He began replacing the cloth cover on the table. "Or, if you prefer a more vivid image, Elder Brother: like a woman in jiao-gou, we simply envelop and absorb the impaling lance."

I said—and not critically, for I had become fond of the young artist in just this short time—"Minister Chao, the matter of jiao-gou seems rather to tincture all your thoughts."

"Why not? I am a whore." He sounded cheerful again, and led me back into his main room. "On the other hand, it is said that, of all women, a whore most resents being raped. Here, look at what I was painting when you arrived." He unrolled the silk scroll on the drawing board, and again I breathed an exclamation:

"Porco Dio!"

I had never seen a picture like it. And I mean that in more than one sense. Not in Venice, where there are many works of art to be seen, nor in any of the countries I had come through, in some of which also were many works of art, had I ever seen a picture so exquisitely drawn and tinted that it was veritable *life* captured in the round; so lighted and shaded that it seemed my fingers could stroke its rotundities and delve into its recesses; so sinuous in its forms that they seemed to move before my eyes; yet at the same time a picture—well, there it lay, easily to be seen—done, like any other, *on a flat surface*.

"Observe the likenesses," said Master Chao, droning in the manner of a San Marco docent showing the Basilica's mosaic saints. "Only an artist capable of painting the impalpable feng-shui could so perfectly render, as well, substantial flesh and meat."

Indeed, the six persons depicted in Master Chao's painting were instantly and unmistakably recognizable. I had seen every one of them in this very palace, alive and breathing and moving about. Yet here they were on silk—from the hairs of their head and the hues of their skin to the intricate brocaded designs on their robes and the tiny glints of light that gave animation to their eyes—all six alive still, but frozen in their movement, and each person magically reduced to the size of my hand.

"Observe the composition," said Master Chao, still good-humoredly sounding humorless. "All the curves, the directions of movement, they beguile the eye to the main subject and what he is doing."

And therein the picture was egregiously different from any other I had ever seen. The main subject referred to by Master Chao was his and my liege lord, the Khan of All Khans—Kubilai, no doubt about it— though the picture's only intimation of his regnancy was the gold morion helmet he wore, that being *all* he was wearing. And what he was doing in the picture he was doing to a young lady who was lying back on a couch with her brocade robes shamelessly caught up above her waist. I recognized the lady (from her face, which was all I had ever before seen of her) as one of Kubilai's current concubines. Two additional concubines, also considerably dishevelled in their garments and exposed in their persons, were pictured as assisting in the coupling, while the Khatun Jamui and one other of Kubilai's wives stood by, fully and modestly clothed, but looking not at all disapproving.

Master Chao, still playing the dullard docent, said, "This one is entitled 'The Mighty Stag Mounts the Third of His Yearning Does.' You will observe that he has already had two—you can see the pearly drop-lets of his jing-ye dribbling down their inner thighs—and there are two more yet to be enjoyed. Correctly, in the Han, this one's title would be 'Huang-se Gong-chu—' "

"This one?" I gasped. "You have made other pictures like this?"

"Well, not identical to this. The last one was entitled 'Kubilai Is Mightiest of Mongols Because He Partakes of Yin to Augment His Yang.' It showed him on his knees before a very young, naked girl, his tongue lapping from her lotus the pearly droplets of her yin juices, while she—"

"*Porco Dio!*" I exclaimed again. "And you have not yet been dragged off to the Fondler?"

Mimicking my outcry, he said cheerfully, "Porco Dio, I hope not to be. Why do you suppose I continue in this artistic whoredom? As we Han say, it is my wineskin and my rice bag. It was to have such pictures that the Khakhan honored me with this ministry-in-name-only."

"He *wants* these made?"

"He must have whole galleries hung with my scrolls by now. I also do hand-fans. My wife paints on a fan a superb design of zhu-gan cane or peony flowers and, if the fan is unfolded in the usual direction, that is all you see. But if the fan is flirtatiously flicked open the other way, you glimpse an erotic bit of dalliance."

"So this—this sort of thing is really your main work for Kubilai."

"Not only for Kubilai, curse it. By his decree, I am as biddable as the banquet-hall jugglers. My talent is at the command of all my fellow ministers and courtiers. Even you, I should not be surprised. I must remember to inquire."

"Imagine . . . ," I marveled. "The Khanate's Minister of War . . . spending his time painting vile pictures. . . ."

"Vile?" He pretended to recoil in horror. "Really, you wound me. Subject matter aside, they are, after all, from the supple hand of Chao Meng-fu, Golden Belt Master of Feng-shui."

"Oh, I do not denigrate the expertness of them. The artistry of this one is impeccable. Except—"

"If this one distresses you," he said, "you should see what I have to paint for that degenerate Arab, Achmad. But go on, Elder Brother. Except, what?"

"Except—no man, not even the great Khakhan, ever possessed a masculine red jewel like that one in the picture. You certainly made it vividly red enough—but the size and the veining of it! It looks like he is ramming a rough-barked log into her."

"Ah, that. Yes. Well. Of course he does not pose for these portrayals, but one must flatter one's patron. The only male model I employ is myself, in a looking glass, to get the anatomical articulations correct. However, I must confess that the virile member of any male Han—myself unhappily included—would hardly be worth a viewer's looking at. If it could be discerned at all in a picture of that size."

I started to say something condoling, but he raised his hand.

"Please! Do not offer. Go and show yours, if you must, to the Armorer of the Palace Guard. She might appreciate its contrast to her husband's. But I have already been shown one Westerner's gross organ, and that will suffice. I was nauseated to see that the Arab's unwholesome red jewel, even in repose, is bald-headed!"

"Muslims are circumcised; I am not," I said loftily. "And I was not about to volunteer. But you might sometime like to paint my twin maid-servants, who do some wondrous—" I paused there, and frowned, and inquired, "Master Chao, did you mean to say that the Minister Achmad *does* pose for the pictures you paint of him?"

"Yes," he said, making a face of disgust. "But I would never show to you or to anyone any of those, and I am certain Achmad will not. As soon as a painting is finished, he even sends away the other models employed—away to far corners of the empire—so they cannot make gossip or complaint hereabout. But this I will wager: however far they go, they never forget him. Or me. For my having seen what happened, and having made permanent record of their shame."

Chao's former cheerfulness had all dissipated, and he seemed disinclined to talk further, so I took my leave. I went to my chambers, thinking deeply—and not about erotic paintings, much as that work had impressed me, nor about the Chief Minister Achmad's secret diversions, much as they had interested me. No, I went pondering on two other things Chao had mentioned while he was speaking as Minister of War:

Yun-nan Province.

The Yi people.

The evasive Minister of Lesser Races, Pao Nei-ho, had also touched briefly on those subjects. I wanted to know more about them, and about him. But I did not learn anything further that day. Though Nostril was waiting for me, returned from his latest foraging among the domestic staff, he could not yet tell me anything concerning the Minister Pao. We sat down together, and I bade Biliktu bring us each a goblet of good pu-tao white wine, and she fanned us with a perfumed fan while we talked. Nostril, pridefully showing off how much his grasp of Mongol had lately improved, said in that language:

"Here is a juicy bit, Master Marco. When it was confided to me that the Armorer of the Palace Guard is a most promiscuous voluptuary, it did not at first intrigue me. After all, what soldier is not a fornicator? But that officer, it transpires, is a young *woman*, a Han lady of some degree. Her whorishness is evidently notorious, but is not punished, because her lord husband is such a poltroon that he condones her indecent conduct."

I said, "Perhaps he has other worries that trouble him more. Let us then, in compassion, you and I, not add our voices to the general tattling. Not about that poor fellow, anyway."

"As you command, master. But I have nothing to tell about anyone else . . . except the servants and slaves themselves, in whom you surely have no interest."

True, I had not. But I got the feeling that Nostril wanted to say something more. I studied him speculatively, then said:

"Nostril, you have been extraordinarily well behaved for quite a while now. For you, that is. I recollect only one recent misdemeanor— when I caught you peeping that night at me and the girls—and I cannot recall any outright felony in ever so long. There are other things different about you lately. You are dressing as finely as all the other palace servants and slaves. And you are letting your beard grow. I always wondered how you managed to keep it forever looking like a scruffy two weeks' growth. But now it looks a respectable beard, though much grayer than it used to be, and your receding chin is no longer so noticeable. Why the turnout of whiskers? Are you hiding from somebody?"

"Not exactly, master. As you say, slaves here at this resplendent palace are encouraged not to look like slaves. And, as you say, I simply wished to appear more respectable. More like the handsome man I used to be." I sighed. But he did not elaborate in his usual braggart way; he added only, "I have recently espied someone in the slave quarters. Someone I think I knew long ago. But I hesitate to approach, until I can be sure."

I laughed heartily. "Hesitate? *You*? Reticent of being thought forward? And to another slave? Why, even the kitchen's trash-pile pigs do not hesitate to approach a slave."

He winced slightly, but then drew himself up as tall as he could.

"The pigs are not also slaves, Master Marco. And we slaves were not always so. There used to be some social distinctions among some of us, when we were free. The one dignity we can exercise now is to observe those bygone distinctions. If this slave is who I believe her to be, then she was once a high-born lady. I was a freeman in those days, but only a drover. I would ask, master, if you would do me the favor of ascertaining who she is, before I make myself known to her, that I may do so with the appropriate formality of address."

For a moment I almost felt ashamed of myself. I had commanded compassion for the cuckold Master Chao, yet laughed heartlessly at this poor wretch. Was I, like him, so ready to make ko-tou to class distinctions? But in the next moment I reminded myself that Nostril really *was* a wretch, of repellent nature and, as long as I had known him, doing none but revolting deeds.

I snapped, "Do not play the noble slave at me, Nostril. You live a life far better than you deserve. However, if you merely wish me to corroborate someone's identity, I will. What do I ask, and of whom?"

"Could you just inquire, master, whether the Mongols have ever taken prisoners from a kingdom called Cappadocia in Anatolia? That will tell me what I wish to know."

"Anatolia. That is north of the route by which we came from the Levant into Persia. But my father and uncle must have traveled through it on their earlier journeys. I will ask them, and perhaps I will not need to ask anyone else."

"May Allah smile ever on you, kind master."

I left him to finish his wine, though Biliktu sniffed with disapproval of his continuing to loll in her presence. I went along the palace corridors to my father's chambers, and found my uncle also there, and said I had a question to ask of them. But first my father informed me that they were contending with some problems of their own.

"Obstacles," he said, "being thrown in the way of our mercantile ventures. The Muslims are proving less than eager to welcome us into their Ortaq. Delaying issuance of permits for us even to sell our accumulated stock of zafràn. Clearly they are reflecting some jealousy or spitefulness on the part of the Finance Minister Achmad."

"We have two options," muttered my uncle. "Bribe the damned Arab or put pressure on him. But how do you bribe a man who already has everything, or can easily get it? How do you influence a man who is the second most powerful in the realm?"

It occurred to me that if I told them what hints I had had of Achmad's private life, they might profitably wield a threat to expose him. But on second thought I did not mention it. My father would refuse to stoop to any such tactic, and would forbid my uncle to do so. Also, I suspected that my hearsay knowledge was a dangerous thing even for me to have acquired, and I would not hand on the risk of danger to them. I made only one mild suggestion:

"Can you perhaps employ, as they say, the devil that tempted Lucifer?"

"A woman?" grunted Uncle Mafìo. "I doubt it. There seems to be a deal of mystery about Achmad's tastes—whether he prefers women or men or children or ewes or what. In any case, he could take his pick from the whole empire, excepting only the Khakhan's prior choices."

"Well," said my father, "if he truly does have everything he could possibly want, there is an old proverb that applies. Ask favors of the man with a full stomach. Let us cease quibbling with the petty underlings of the Ortaq. Go direct to Achmad and put our case before him. What can he do?"

"From what little I know of him," growled Uncle Mafìo, "that man would laugh at a leper."

My father shrugged. "He will tergiversate for a time, but he will eventually concede. He knows we stand well with Kubilai."

I said, "I would be happy to put in a word with the Khakhan when I call on him next."

"No, Marco, do not you fret about this. I would not wish you to compromise your own standing on our account. Perhaps later, when you have been longer in the Khakhan's confidence, and when perhaps we have real need of your intercession. But with this situation, Mafìo and I will cope. Now, you wished to ask a question?"

I said, "You first came here to Kithai and went home again by way of Constantinople, so you must have gone through the lands of Anatolia. Did you happen to traverse a place there called Cappadocia?"

"Why, yes," said my father. "Cappadocia is a kingdom of the Seljuk Turki people. We stopped briefly in its capital city of Erzincan on our way back to Venice. Erzincan is very nearly directly north of Suvediye—where you have been, Marco—but a long way to the north of it."

"Were those Turki ever at war with the Mongols?"

"Not then," said Uncle Mafìo. "Not yet, as far as I know. But there was some trouble there, which involved the Mongols, because Cappadocia abuts on the Persian realm of the Ilkhan Abagha. The trouble occurred while we were passing through, as a matter of fact. That was what, Nico—eight, nine years ago?"

"And what was it that happened then?" I asked.

My father said, "The Seljuk King Kilij had an overly ambitious Chief Minister—"

"As Kubilai has the Wali Achmad," grumbled Uncle Mafìo.

"And that Minister secretly connived with the Ilkhan Abagha, promising to make the Cappadocians vassals of the Mongols if Abagha would help him depose the King. And that is what happened."

"How did it come about?" I asked.

"The King and the whole royal family were assassinated, right there in his Erzincan palace," said my uncle. "The people knew it was the doing of the Chief Minister, but none dared denounce him, for fear that Abagha would take advantage of any internal dispute, to march his Mongols in and ransack the country."

"So," my father concluded the tale, "the Minister put his own infant son on the throne as King—with himself as ruling Regent, of course—and what few survived of the royal family, he handed over to Abagha for disposal as he wished."

"I see," I said. "And presumably they are now dispersed all over the Mongol Khanate. Would you know, Father, if there were any women among them?"

"Yes. The survivors may *all* have been female. The Chief Minister was a practical man. He probably slew every one of the King's male descendants, so there could be no legitimate claimant to the throne he had won for his own son. The females would not have mattered."

"The survivors were mostly cousins and such," said Uncle Mafìo. "But there was at least one of the King's daughters among them. She was said to be beautiful, and it was said that Abagha would have taken her for his concubine, except—he found some fault with her. I forget. Anyway, he simply gave her to the slave traders, with the others."

"You are right, Mafìo," said my father. "There was at least that one royal daughter. Mar-Janah was her name."

I thanked them and returned to my own suite. Nostril, in his sly way, had made capital of my generosity, and was still being wined and fanned by a scowling Biliktu. Exasperated, I said, "Here you sprawl like a lordly courtier, you sloth, while I run about on your errands."

He grinned drunkenly and in a slurred voice inquired, "With any success, master?"

"This slave you think you recognized. Could it have been a woman of the Seljuk Turki people?"

His grin evaporated. He bounded to his feet, spilling his wine and making Biliktu squeal in complaint. He stood almost trembling before me and waited for my next words.

"By any chance, could it be a certain Princess Mar-Janah?"

However much he had drunk, he was suddenly sober—and also stricken speechless, it seemed, for perhaps the first time in his life. He only stood and vibrated and stared at me, his eyes as wide as his nostril.

I said, "That speculation I got from my father and uncle." He made no comment, still standing transfixed, so I said sharply, "I take it that *is* the identity you wished confirmed?"

He whispered, so low that I barely heard, "I did not really know . . . whether I wished it to be so . . . or I dreaded that it was so. . . ." Then, without ko-tou or salaam or even a murmur of thanks for my pains, he turned away and, very slowly, like an aged man, he shuffled off to his closet.

I dismissed the matter from my mind and I also went to bed—with only Buyantu, because Biliktu had been for some nights indisposed for that service.

· 9 ·

I had been in residence at the palace for a long time before I had the opportunity to meet the courtier whose work most fascinated me: the Court Firemaster responsible for the so-called fiery trees and sparkling flowers. I was told that he was almost continuously traveling about the country, arranging those displays wherever and whenever this town or that had some festa to celebrate. But one winter day, Prince Chingkim

came to tell me that the Firemaster Shi had returned to his palace
quarters, to begin his preparations for Khanbalik's biggest annual celebration—the welcoming-in of the New Year, which was then imminent—
and Chingkim took me to call on him. The Master Shi had an entire
small house for his residence and workshop, and it was situated—for the
sake of the palace's safety, said Chingkim—well apart from the other
palace buildings, in fact on the far side of what was now the Kara Hill.

The Firemaster was bent over a littered work table when we entered, and from his garb I took him first to be an Arab. But when he
turned to greet us, I decided he had to be a Jew, for I had seen those
lineaments before. His blackberry eyes looked haughtily but good-
humoredly at me down a long, hooked nose like a shimshir, and his hair
and beard were like a curly fungus, gray but showing still a trace of
red.

Chingkim said, speaking in Mongol, "Master Shi Ix-me, I would
have you meet a Palace guest."

"Marco Polo," said the Firemaster.

"Ah, you have heard of his visit."

"I have heard of him."

"Marco is much interested in your work, and my Royal Father
would have you tell him something of it."

"I will attempt to do so, Prince."

When Chingkim had gone, there was a brief silence, myself and the
Firemaster eyeing each other. At last he said, "Why are you interested
in the fiery trees, Marco Polo?"

I said simply, "They are beautiful."

"The beauty of danger. That attracts you?"

"You know it always has," I said, and waited.

"But there is also danger in beauty. That does not repel you?"

"Aha!" I crowed. "Now I suppose you are going to tell me that your
name is not really Mordecai!"

"I was not going to tell you anything. Except about my work with
the beautiful but dangerous fires. What would you wish to know, Marco
Polo?"

"How did you get a name like Shi Ix-me?"

"That has nothing to do with my work. However . . ." He shrugged.
"When the Jews first came here, they were allotted seven Han surnames
to apportion among them. Shi is one of the seven, and was originally
Yitzhak. In the Ivrit, my full name is Shemuel ibn-Yitzhak."

I asked, "When did you come to Kithai?" expecting him to say that
he had arrived only shortly before me.

"I was born here, in the city of Kai-feng, where my forebears settled
some hundreds of years ago."

"I do not believe it."

He snorted, as Mordecai had done so often at my comments. "Read
the Old Testament of your Bible. Chapter forty-nine of Isaiah, where the
prophet foresees a regathering of all the Jews. 'Behold, these shall come
from afar, and behold these from the north, and from the sea, and these
from the land of Sinim.' This land of Kithai is still in Ivrit called Sina. So

there were Jews here in Isaiah's time, and that was more than one thousand eight hundred years ago."

"Why would Jews have come *here*?"

"Probably because they were unwelcome somewhere else," he said wryly. "Or perhaps they took the Han to be one of their own lost tribes, wandered away from Israel."

"Oh, come now, Master Shi. The Han are pork eaters, and always have been."

He shrugged again. "Nevertheless, they have things in common with the Jews. They slaughter their animals in a ceremonial manner almost kasher, except that they do not remove the terephah sinews. And they are even more than Jewishly strict in the customs of dress, never wearing garments mixed of animal and vegetable fibers."

Stubbornly I maintained, "The Han could never have been a lost tribe. There is no least physical resemblance between them and the Jews."

Master Shi laughed and said, "But there is now—between the Jews and the Han. Do not judge by my looks. It only happens that the Shi family never much intermarried here. Most others of the seven names did. So Kithai is full of Jews with ivory skins and squinty eyes. Only sometimes by their noses shall you know them. Or a man by his gid." He laughed again, then said more seriously, "Or you may know a Jew because, wherever he wanders, he still observes the religion of his fathers. He still turns toward Jerusalem to pray. Also, wherever he wanders, he still keeps the memory of old Jewish legends—"

"Like the Lamed-vav," I interrupted. "And the tzaddikim."

"—and, wherever he wanders, he continues to share with other Jews what things he remembers of the old, and what worthwhile new things he learns along his way."

"*That* is how you knew of me! One telling another. Ever since Mordecai escaped from the Vulcano—"

He gave no sign of having heard a single word I had interposed, but went right on, "Happily, the Mongols do not discriminate among us lesser races. So I, albeit a Jew, am the Court Firemaster to the Khan Kubilai, who respects my artistry and cares not at all that I bear one of the seven surnames."

"You must be very proud, Master Shi," I said. "I should like to hear how you came to take up this extraordinary profession, and how you became so successful in it. I have always thought of Jews as being money-lenders and pawnbrokers, not as artists or seekers of success."

He snorted again. "When did you ever hear of an inartistic money-lender? Or an unsuccessful pawnshop?"

I could give no answer to that, and he seemed to expect none, so I inquired, "How did you come to invent the fiery trees?"

"I did not. The secret of making them was discovered by a Han, and that was ages ago. My contribution has been to make that secret more easy of application."

"And what is the secret, Master Shi?"

"It is called huo-yao, the flaming powder." He motioned me to the work table and, from one of the many jars and phials thereon, he took a pinch of dark-gray powder. "Observe what happens when I place this very little bit of huo-yao on this porcelain plate, and touch it with fire— so." He picked up a stick of already smoldering incense and applied its spark end to the powder.

I started as, with a quick, angry, fizzing noise, the huo-yao burned away in a brief, intense flash, leaving a puff of the blue smoke whose acrid smell I had come to recognize.

"Essentially," said the Firemaster, "all that the powder does is to burn with the fiercest rapidity of any substance. But when it is confined in a fairly tight container, its burning bursts that confinement, making a loud noise and much light as it does so. Adding to the basic huo-yao other powders—metallic salts of one kind or another—makes it burn in different colors."

"But what makes it fly?" I asked. "And sometimes explode in sequacious bursts of those different colors?"

"For such an effect, the huo-yao is packed into a paper tube like this one, with a small opening at one end." He showed me such a tube, made of stiff paper. It looked like a large, hollow candle, with a hole where the wick would have been. "When touched with a spark at that hole, the powder burns and the intense flame spurting from that aperture at the nether end throws the whole tube forward—or upward, if it is pointed that way."

"I have seen it do so," I said. "But *why* should it do so?"

"Come, come, Polo," he chided me. "We have here one of the first principles of natural philosophy. *Everything* flinches away from fire."

"Of course," I said. "Of course."

"This being the fiercest of fires, the container flinches away most energetically. So violently that it recoils to a great distance or a great altitude."

"And," I said, to show how well I understood, "having the fire in its own vitals, it perforce takes the fire with it."

"Exactly so. And takes with it more than the fire, in fact, for I have previously attached other tubes around the one that flies. When the first has consumed itself—and I can predetermine how long that will take—it ignites the other tubes. Depending on what sorts I have used, they either explode at that instant, scattering fire of one color or another, or they go flinging off on their own, to explode at another distance. By combining in one engine a number of flying tubes and explosive tubes, I can contrive a fiery tree that sprouts upward to any height, and then bursts into one of various patterns of the sparkling flowers in many different colors. Peach blossoms, poppy flowers, tiger lilies, whatever I choose to make bloom in the sky."

"Ingenious," I said. "Fantastic. But the main ingredient—the huo-yao—of what magical elements is it compounded?"

"It was indeed an ingenious man who first compounded them," the Firemaster concurred. "But the constituent elements are the simplest imaginable." From each of three other jars he took a pinch of powder and dropped them on the table; one powder was black, one yellow, one white. "Tan-hua, liu and tung-bian. Taste them and you should know them."

I licked a fingertip and picked up a few grains of the fine black powder and touched my tongue, then said, wondering, "Nothing but charcoal of wood." Of the yellow powder, I said, "Only common sulphur." Of the white powder, I said thoughtfully, "Hm. Salty, bitter, almost vinegary. But what . . . ?"

Master Shi grinned and said, "The crystallized urine of a virgin boy."

"Vakh," I grunted, and rubbed my sleeve across my mouth.

"Tung-bian, the autumn stone, so the Han call it," he said, wickedly enjoying my discomfiture. "The sorcerers and wizards and practitioners of al-kimia deem it a precious element. They employ it in medicines, love philters and the like. They take the urine of a boy no older than twelve, filter it through wood ash, then let it solidify into crystals. Rather difficult of procurement, you see, and in only trifling amounts. But it was specified in the original recipe for making the flaming powder: charcoal, sulphur and the autumn stone—and that recipe was handed unchanged down through the ages. Charcoal and sulphur have always been plentiful, but the third ingredient was not. So there simply *was* not much making of the flaming powder, until my lifetime."

"You found some way to procure maiden boys in quantity?"

He snorted, very Mordecai-like. "Sometimes there are benefits in coming from a humble family. When I first tasted the element, as you just did, I recognized it as another and much less exquisite substance. My father was a fish peddler, and to make the fillets of cheap fish look more delectably pink, he soaked them in a brine of the lowly salt called saltpeter. That is all the autumn stone is—saltpeter. I do not know why it should be present in boys' urine, and I do not care, for I have no need of boys to make it. Kithai is abundantly supplied with salt lakes, and they are abundantly rimmed with crusts containing saltpeter. So, these many centuries after the flaming powder was first compounded by some Han genius of al-kimia, I, merely the inquisitive son of the Jewish fish peddler Shi, am the first to make it in vast quantities, and to make the glorious displays of its fiery trees and sparkling flowers enjoyable by all men everywhere."

"Master Shi," I said diffidently. "In addition to my admiration of the beauty of those works, I have been struck by the thought of turning them to more useful account. The thought came to me when my own horse shied and bucked at first seeing a display of the fiery trees. Could not these engines of yours be used as weapons of war? To break up a cavalry charge, for example?"

He snorted yet again. "A good idea, yes, but you are more than sixty years late with it. In the year when I was born—let me see, that would have been by your Christian count the year one thousand two hundred fourteen—my native city of Kai-feng was first besieged by the Mongols of the Khan Chinghiz. His horse troops were affrighted and dispersed by balls of fire which flew into their midst, trailing sparks and whistling and banging. The Mongols were not stopped for long, needless to say, and they eventually took the city, but that valiant defense contrived by the

Kai-feng Firemaster became legendary. And, as I told you, we Jews are great rememberers of legends. Thus it was that I grew up enthralled by the subject, and finally myself became a Firemaster. That employment of the flaming powder at Kai-feng was its first recorded use in warfare."

"Its first," I echoed. "Then it has been used since?"

"Our Khan Kubilai is not a warrior likely to ignore any promising tool of war," said Master Shi. "Even if I were not personally interested in trying new applications of my art, and I am, he has charged me with investigating every possible use of the huo-yao for war missiles. And I have had some partial successes."

I said, "I should be gratified to hear of them."

The Firemaster seemed hesitant to confide. He looked from under his fungoid eyebrows at me and said, "The Han have a story. Of the master archer Yi, all his life prevailing over every foe, until he taught all his skills to an eager pupil, and that man finally slew him."

"I do not seek to appropriate any of your ideas," I said. "And I will freely tell you any that might occur to me. They could be of some small worth."

"The danger of beauty," he mumbled. "Well, are you acquainted with the large, hairy nut called the India nut?"

Wondering what that had to do with anything, I said, "I have eaten its meat in certain confections served at table here."

"I have taken hollowed-out India nuts and packed them full of the huo-yao, and inserted wicks to supply the spark after a suitable interval. I have done the same with joints of the stout zhu-gan cane. Those objects can be thrown by a man or a simple catapult into an enemy's defenses and—when they work properly—they let loose their energy with such explosive force that a single nut or cane would well nigh wreck this whole house."

"Marvelous," I said.

"When they work. I have also used cylinders of larger zhu-gan cane in another manner. By inserting one of my flying engines into a long empty cane before lighting its wick, a warrior can literally aim the missile like an arrow, and send it flying toward a target, more or less straightly."

"Ingenious," I said.

"When it works. I have also made missiles in which the huo-yao is compounded with naft oil, with kara dust, even with barnyard dung. When they are hurled into an enemy's defenses, they spread an almost inextinguishable fire, or a dense, stinking, choking smoke."

"Fantastic," I said.

"When they work. Unfortunately, there is one flaw in the huo-yao that renders it totally impractical for military use. Its three component elements, as you have seen, are finely ground powders. But each of those powders has a different inherent density, or weight. Therefore, no matter how tightly the huo-yao is packed into a container, the three elements gradually separate out from one another. The least movement or vibration of the container makes the heavier saltpeter discombine and sift down to the bottom, so the huo-yao becomes inert and impotent. Thus it is impossible to make and store any supply of any of my inventions. The mere movement of them into a storehouse, not to mention out of it, causes them to become absolutely useless."

"I see," I said, sharing his air of deep disappointment. "That is why you are perpetually on the road, Master Shi?"

"Yes. To arrange a fiery-tree display in any city, I must go there and make the things on the spot. I travel with a supply of paper tubes, wicks, barrels of each of the constituent powders, and it is no great chore to mix the huo-yao and charge my various engines. That is obviously what the Kai-feng Firemaster did, when my city was besieged. But can you imagine doing all that in wartime, *in the field*, in the midst of battle? Every company of warriors would have to have its own separate Firemaster, and he to have at hand all his supplies and equipment, and he would have to be inhumanly quick and proficient. No, Marco Polo, I fear that the huo-yao will forever be only a pretty toy. There seems no hope of its military application, except in the occasional case of a city under siege."

"A pity," I murmured. "But the only problem is the powder's tendency to separate?"

"That is the *only* problem," he said, with heavy irony, "just as the only impediment to a man's flying is that he has no wings."

"Only the separation . . . ," I said to myself, several times, then I snapped my fingers and exclaimed, "I have it!"

"Have you now?"

"Dust blows about, but mud does not, and hardened clods do not. Suppose you wetted the huo-yao into mud? Or baked it into a solid?"

"Imbecile," he said, but with some amusement. "Wet the powder and it does not burn at all. Put a baking fire to it and it may blow up in your face."

"Oh," I said, deflated.

"I told you, there is danger in this stuff of beauty."

"I am not over timid of danger, Master Shi," I said, still pondering the problem. "I know you are busy preparing for the New Year celebrations, so I would not obtrude my company upon you. But, while you are occupied, would you let me have some jars of the huo-yao, so that I could speculate on ways and means—"

"Bevakashà! This is nothing to play with!"

"I will be most careful, Master Shi. I will not ignite so much as a pinch of it. I will but study its properties and try to think of a solution to the problem of its sifting down—"

"Khakma! As if I and every other Firemaster have not devoted our lives to that, ever since the flaming powder was first compounded! And you, who never even saw the stuff before—you truly are suggesting that I play the master archer Yi!"

I said, with insinuation, "So might have spoken, once upon a time, the Firemaster of Kai-feng." There was a short silence, and I said, "The inquisitive son of a Jewish fish peddler might not have been trusted, either, to bring a new idea to the art."

There was another and longer silence. Then Master Shi sighed and said, evidently to his deity:

"Lord, I am committed. I hope You see that. This Marco Polo must once have done something right, and the proverb instructs us that one mitzva deserves another."

From under the work table, he picked up two tightly woven cane baskets and thrust them into my arms. "Here, estimable fool. In each, fifty liang measures of huo-yao. Do as you will, and l'chaim to you. I hope the next I hear of Marco Polo is not his thunderous departure from this world."

I took the baskets back to my apartment, intending to start my essay at al-kimia straight away. But I found Nostril again waiting for me, so I asked if he had brought any information.

"Precious little, master. Only a salacious small item about the Court Astrologer, if you are interested. It seems he is a eunuch, and for fifty years he has kept his spare parts pickled in a jar that stands beside his bed. He intends to have them buried with him, so that he will go entire to the afterworld."

"That is all?" I said, wanting to get to work.

"Elsewhere, all is preparation for the New Year. Every courtyard is strewn with dry straw, so that any approaching evil kwei spirits will be frightened off by the crackling noise when they tread on it. The Han women are all cooking the Eight-Ingredient Pudding, which is a holiday treat, and the men are making the many lanterns to light the festivities, and the children are making little paper windmills. It is said that some families spend their entire year's savings on this celebration. But not everybody is exhilarated; a good many of the Han are committing suicide."

"Whatever for?"

"It is their custom that all outstanding debts be settled at this season. The creditors are going about knocking on doors, and many a desperate debtor is hanging himself—to save his face, as the Han say—from the shame of not being able to pay. Meanwhile, the Mongol folk, who do not care much about face, are smearing molasses on the faces of their kitchen gods."

"What?"

"They have the quaint belief that the idol they keep over the kitchen hearth, the house god Nagatai, ascends to Heaven at this time to report their year's behavior to the great god Tengri. So they feed molasses to Nagatai in the quaint belief that thus his lips are sealed, and he cannot tattle anything detrimental."

"Quaint, yes," I said. Biliktu came into the room just then and took the baskets from me. I motioned for her to set them on a table. "Anything else, Nostril?"

He wrung his hands. "Only that I have fallen in love."

"Oh?" I said, immersed in my own thoughts. "With what?"

"Master, do not mock me. With a woman, what else?"

"What *else*? To my own knowledge, you have previously had congress with a Baghdad pony, with a young man of Kashan, with a Sindi baby of indeterminate sex—"

He wrung his hands some more. "Please, master, do not tell her."

"Tell whom?"

"The Princess Mar-Janah."

"Oh, yes. That one. So you have now fixed your regard on a princess, have you? Well, I give you credit for craving wide variety. And I will not tell her. Why should I tell her anything at all?"

"Because I would beg a boon, Master Marco. I would ask you to speak to her in my behalf. To tell her of my virtues and uprightness."

"Upright? Virtuous? You? Por Dio, I have never even been sure that you are human!"

"Please, master. You see, there are certain palace rules regarding the marriage of slaves to one another—"

"Marriage!" I gasped. "You are contemplating marriage?"

"It is true, as the Prophet declares, that women are all stones," he said meditatively. "But some are millstones hung about our neck, and some are gemstones hung about our heart."

"Nostril," I said, as kindly as I could be. "This woman may have come down in the world, but not—" I stopped myself. I could not say "as low down as you." I began again, "She may be now a slave, but she was once a princess, and you said you were only a drover then. Also, from what I have heard, she is handsome, or she once was."

"She is," he said, and added feebly, "So was I . . . once."

Exasperated anew by his persistence in that old fiction, I said, "Has she seen you lately? Look at yourself! There you stand, as graceless as a camel-bird, pot-bellied, pig-eyed, with your finger picking your one nose hole. Tell me truthfully, since you spied out her identity have you made yourself known to this Princess Mar-Janah? Did she recognize you? Did she flee in revulsion, or merely burst out laughing?"

"No," he said, hanging his head. "I have not introduced myself. I have only worshiped her from afar. I was hoping that you would first say some words to her . . . to prepare her . . . to make her desire to know me. . . ."

At which, it was I who burst out laughing. "It needed but this! I have never heard such effrontery. Asking me to pimp between one slave and another. What am I to tell her, Nostril?" I put on a wheedling voice, as if I were addressing the princess: "So far as I know, Your Highness, your adoring suitor does not at this moment suffer any shameful disease of his amative parts." Then I said sternly, "What could I possibly tell, without such lying as to imperil my immortal soul, that could possibly make any female—let alone a former princess—look favorably on such a creature as I know you to be?"

With preposterous dignity for such a creature, he said, "If the master would have the goodness to listen for just a little, I would tell some of the history of this affair."

"Tell, then, but make haste. I have things to do."

"It began twenty years ago in the Cappadocian capital city of Erzincan. True, she was a Turki princess, the daughter of King Kilij, and I was only a Sindi drover of horses in his employ. Neither he nor she knew it, probably, since I was only one of many stable servants they would have seen, whenever they called for a mount or a carriage. But I saw *her*, and then as now I worshiped her dumbly from afar. Nothing would ever have come of it, of course. Except that Allah caused both her and me to fall among Arab bandits—"

"Oh, Nostril, no!" I pleaded. "Not another account of your heroics. I have had my laugh for the day."

"I will not dwell on the abduction episode, master. Sufficient to say that the princess had cause to notice me, then, and she regarded me with melting eyes. But when we had escaped from the Arabs and returned to Erzincan, her father rewarded me with a higher position in his service, which sent me into the countryside at a considerable remove from the palace."

"That," I murmured, "I believe."

"And unhappily I once more fell among marauders. Kurdi slave-takers, this time. I was borne away, and I never saw Cappadocia or the princess again. I kept an ear open for every rumor and gossip from that part of the world, and I never heard of her marrying, so I still had some small cause for hopefulness. But then I heard of the wholesale slaughter of that Seljuk royal family, and I supposed she had died with the rest. Who knows, if I had been still at the palace when that occurred, what might not—?"

"Please, Nostril."

"Yes, master. Well, if Mar-Janah was dead, I cared no longer what became of me. I was a slave—the lowest form of life—so I would *be* the lowest form of life. I endured every kind of humiliation, and I did not care. I invited humiliation. I even began to humiliate myself. I wallowed in humiliation. I would be the worst thing in the world, because I had lost the best. I became a wretch degraded and contemptible. I did not care that it cost me my handsomeness and my self-respect and the respect of all other men. I would not even have cared if it had cost me my vital parts, but, for some reason, none of my many masters ever thought to make me a eunuch. So I was still a man, but, having no hope of love, I abandoned myself to lust. I took anyone or anything accessible to a slave—and not many but vile things are. Thus I was when you found me, Master Marco, and thus I continued to be."

"Until now," I said. "Let me finish for you, Nostril. Now that long lost love has reentered your life. Now you are going to *change*."

He surprised me by saying, "No. No, master, too many men have too often said that. None but a fool would believe that, and my master is no fool. So I will say instead that I wish only to change *back*. Back to what I was before I became . . . this Nostril."

I looked long at him, and I considered long before I spoke.

"None but a wicked master would refuse a man the chance at that much, and I am not wicked. Indeed, I should be interested to see what it was that you once were." I was also a little interested to see the draggled sloven he had set his heart on. She had to be a pitiful drab, of course, after eight or nine years of slavery among the Mongols, whatever she had begun as. "Very well. You wish me to apprise this Mar-Janah that her onetime hero still exists. I will do that much. How do I do it?"

"I shall simply pass the word in the slave quarters that the Master

Marco wishes to speak with her. And then, if you could find it in your compassionate generosity to say—"

"I will tell no lies for you, Nostril. I promise only to skirt the nastier truths, insofar as I can."

"It is all I could ask. May Allah ever bless—"

"Now I have other things to think about. Do not have her come here until after the New Year doings are done with."

When he had gone, I sat down to gaze at the huo-yao I had brought, and occasionally I dabbled my fingers in it, and now and again I shook one of the baskets, to see for myself how readily the white grains of saltpeter separated from among the black specks of charcoal and the yellow sulphur, and sank out of sight. That day—and for many days afterward, because other things took precedence—I did not do anything else with the flaming powder.

That night, when I went to bed, and only Buyantu joined me, I grumbled, "What is this indisposition Biliktu is suffering? I saw her only hours ago in these rooms, and she appeared perfectly healthy. But it must be more than a month now since she has slept in this bed with me or with us. Is she avoiding me? Have I somehow displeased her?"

Buyantu made only a teasing reply: "Do you miss her? Am I not enough for you? After all, my sister and I are identical. Hold me and see." She snuggled into my arms. "There. You cannot complain that you yearn for what you are this moment holding. But, if you like, I give you leave to pretend that I am Biliktu, and I challenge you to tell me in what respect I am not."

She was right. When, in the dark, I pretended that she was her sister, she very well could have been, and I could hardly claim that I was being deprived.

. 10 .

IN Venice, we do not take much account of any new year's coming. It is merely the first day of March, on which we begin the next year's calendar, and it is no cause for celebration unless it chances to fall on the day of Carnevale. But in Kithai every New Year was regarded as portentous, and had to be fittingly welcomed. So it was the excuse for festivities that consumed an entire month, lapping over from the old year into the new one. Like our Christian movable holy days, the entire Kithai calendar depends on the moon, so its First Day of the First Moon can fall any time between mid-January and mid-February. The celebrations commenced on the seventh night of the old year's Twelfth Moon, when families sat down to partake of the traditional Eight-Ingredient Pudding, then exchanged gifts among themselves, their neighbors and friends and relatives.

From that time on, there seemed to be some kind of observance every day and night. On the twenty-third day of that Twelfth Moon, for example, everyone set up a clamor to wish "bon viazo" to their kitchen god Nagatai, as he ostensibly ascended to Heaven to make his report on the household of which he was overseer. Since he allegedly does not return to his place over the hearth until the eve of the New Year, the people all took advantage of his absence to indulge in libertine feasting and drinking and gambling and other things they would be afraid or ashamed to do under Nagatai's scrutiny.

The final day of the old year was the most frenetic of the whole season, that being the last day on which debts were to be collected and accounts settled. Every street leading to a pawnshop was clogged with people pledging, for a pitiful few tsien, their valuables, furniture, even the clothes they wore. Every other street was similarly crowded and turmoiled by the creditors dashing about in search of their debtors and the debtors dashing about in desperate search of some means either to pay them or avoid them. Everybody was chasing somebody, and himself was being chased by somebody else. There was much vociferation and loud abuse and blows exchanged and even, as Nostril had told me, the occasional self-immolation of a debtor no longer able to hold up his head—or his face, as the Han say.

As that last day of the old year turned into night and became the eve of the First Day of the First Moon, it turned also into a night-long display of Master Shi's fiery trees and sparkling flowers, in wondrous variety, accompanied by parades and street dances and tumultuous noise and the music of chimes and gongs and trumpets. When the New Year day dawned, the interminable festivities were tempered by their only token touch of a Lenten abstention, that being the one day of the year when all were forbidden to eat meat. And on the subsequent five days, no one was allowed to throw away anything at all. Even for a scullion to throw out the kitchen's waste water would risk throwing out the household's good fortune for the next year. Apart from those two gestures of austerity, the celebrating went on unceasingly, right through the fifteenth day of the First Moon.

The common people put up new pictures of all their old gods, ceremoniously pasting them over the tattered old ones that had hung for the past year on their house doors and walls. Every family that could afford it paid a scribe to compose for them a "spring couplet," likewise to be pasted up somewhere. The streets perpetually teemed with acrobats, masquers, stiltwalkers, storytellers, wrestlers, jugglers, hoop twirlers, fire eaters, astrologers and fortune-tellers, purveyors of every sort of food and drink, even "dancing lions"—each consisting of two extremely agile men inside a costume of gilt plaster and red cloth, doing some unbelievable and most unleonine contortions.

In their temples, the Han priests of every religion rather unreligiously presided over public games of chance. These were attended by multitudes of players—creditors squandering their new gains, I assumed, and debtors trying to recoup their losses—and, most of them being drunk and wagering heavily and playing ineptly, their contributions no doubt supported all the temples and priests for the entire year to come. One game was merely the familiar throwing of dice. Another, called majiang, was played with little bone tiles. Another game was played with stiff paper cards called zhi-pai.

(I myself later got intrigued by the intricacies of the zhi-pai and learned to play all the games—for there are innumerable gambling pastimes possible with a pack of seventy-eight cards divided into orders of hearts, bells, leaves and acorns, and they subdivided into cards of points and coats and emblems. But, since I brought back a pack of the cards to Venice, and they have been so much admired and copied and, now called tarocchi, are so well and widely known, I need not expatiate on the zhi-pai.)

The weeks of celebration concluded with the Feast of Lanterns, on the fifteenth day of the First Moon. In addition to everything else that was still going on in the streets of Khanbalik, every family vied that night to see which could flaunt the most marvelously made lantern. They paraded with their creations, of paper or silk or translucent horn or Muscovy glass, in shapes of balls, cubes, fans, little temples, all illuminated by candles or wick lamps inside.

Toward midnight occurred the romping through the streets of a wonderful dragon. More than forty paces long, it was constructed of silk stiffened with ribs of cane, the ribs outlined in little stuck-on candles, and was carried by some fifty men, of whom only their dancing feet were visible, shod with shoes made to look like great claws. The head of the dragon was of plaster and wood, gilded and enameled, with flaring gold-and-blue eyes, silver horns, a green floss beard under its chin, a red velvet tongue lolling from its fearsome mouth. The head alone was so big and heavy that it required four men to carry, and to make it lunge at the people in the streets and champ its jaws at them. The whole dragon pranced and undulated and curvetted most realistically as it wound up one street and down another. And finally, when the last late reveler went off to bed or fell drunkenly unconscious in the open, the weary dragon also slithered back to its lair, and the New Year had officially begun.

The city folk of Khanbalik had enjoyed a whole month of freedom from their more usual occupations. But the work of public servants, like the work of farmers, does not abate just because the calendar declares a holiday. The palace courtiers and government ministers, except for occasional ventures outside to watch the people's enjoyments, went right on working through the whole festive season. I continued making my calls upon one after another of them, and every week having my audience with the Khan Kubilai, that he might judge the progress of my education. At every visit, I tried either to impress or astonish him with whatever new things I had learned. Sometimes, of course, I had nothing to report but a trifle like, "Did you know, Sire, that the eunuch Court Astrologer keeps his cast-off equipment preserved in a jar?"

To which he replied, with some asperity, "Yes. It is rumored that, in doing his predictions, the old fool consults those pickles oftener than he does the stars."

But usually we talked of weightier matters. In one of our meetings, sometime after that New Year season, and after I had spent the foregoing week interviewing the eight Justices of the Cheng, I made so bold as to discuss with the Khakhan the laws and statutes by which his domain was regulated. The mode of that conversation was as interesting as its content, because we talked outdoors and in singular circumstances.

The Court Architect and his slaves and his elephants had, by then, finished piling up the Kara Hill, and had covered it with soft turf, and the Master Gardener and his men had planted its lawns and flowers and trees and shrubs. None of those things was yet flourishing, so the hill still was quite bald. But many of its architectural additions were already done, and they, being in the Han style, gave the hill color enough. The Khakhan and Prince Chingkim were that day inspecting the latest work completed, and they invited me to accompany them. The hill's newest adornment was a round pavilion about ten paces across, an edifice that was all curlicues: swooping roof and convoluted pillars and filigreed balustrades, not a single straight line about it. It was encircled by a tiled terrace, as wide across as the pavilion's diameter, and that was encircled by a solid wall about twice man-high, its entire inner and outer surface a mosaic of gems, enamels, gilt, tesserae of jade and porcelains.

The pavilion was sufficiently striking to the eye, but it had one feature apparent only to the ear. I do not know if the Court Architect had planned it so, or if it came about merely fortuitously. Two or more persons could stand anywhere within that encircling wall, at any distance apart, and, speaking even in a whisper, be able to hear each other perfectly well. The place later became known to all as the Echo Pavilion, but I believe the Khakhan, the Prince and I were the first to amuse ourselves with its peculiar property. We conversed by standing at three points equidistant inside the wall, some eighty feet from each other, none of us able to see each other around the pavilion in the middle, but all speaking in normal tones, and we conversed as easily as if we had been seated about a table indoors.

I said, "The Justices of the Cheng read to me Kithai's current code of laws, Sire. I thought some of them severe. I remember one which commanded that, if a crime is committed, the magistrate of the prefecture must find and punish the guilty party—or himself suffer the punishment specified by law for that crime."

"What is so severe about that?" asked Kubilai's voice. "It only ensures that no magistrate shirks his duty."

"But is it not likely, Sire, that an innocent person is often punished, simply because *somebody* must be?"

"And so?" said Chingkim's voice. "The crime is requited, and all people know that any crime always will be. So the law tends to make all people shun all crime."

"But I have noticed," I said, "that the Han people, when left to themselves, seem adequately to rely on their traditions of good manners to guide their behavior in all things, from everyday matters to those of the greatest gravity. Take common courtesy, for example. If a carter were to be so rude as to ask directions of a passerby without politely getting down from his wagon, he would at the least be told a wrong direction, if not reviled for his bad behavior."

"Ah, but would that reform him?" asked Kubilai's voice. "As a good whipping would do?"

"He need not be reformed, Sire, because he would never do such an unmannerly thing in the first place. Take another example: simple honesty. If a man walking along the road discovers an object someone has lost, he will not appropriate it, but stand guard over it. He will relinquish that guard duty to the next comer, and he to the next. That object will be sedulously kept safe until its loser comes back looking for it."

"You are talking now of happenstance," said the Khakhan's voice. "You began with crimes and laws."

"Very well, Sire, consider an actual tort. If one man is wronged by another, he does not run to a magistrate and demand forced redress. Indeed, the Han have a proverb: advising the dead to avoid damnation and the living to avoid the law court. If a man of the Han disgraces himself, he will take his own life in expiation, as I have seen often happen during the past New Year. If another man does him a grievous wrong, and *his* conscience does not soon resolve the matter, the *victim* will go and hang himself outside the guilty man's door. The disgrace thus conferred on the transgressor is considered far worse than any revenge that could have been inflicted."

Kubilai inquired drily, "Would you say that that fact gives much satisfaction to the dead man? You call that redress?"

"I am told, Sire, that the malefactor can only remove the taint of that shame by making restitution to the hanged man's surviving family."

"So does he under the Khanate's code of law, Marco. But if anybody has to get hanged, it is *he*. You may call that severity, but I see nothing unfair about it."

"Sire, I once remarked that you were rightly to be admired and envied—for the quality of your subjects in general—by every other ruler in the world. But I wonder: how are you regarded by the people themselves? Might you not better secure their affection and fealty if you were not quite so strict in your standards for them?"

"Define that," he said sharply. " 'Not quite so strict.' "

"Sire, regard my native Republic of Venice. It is patterned on the classical republics of Rome and Greece. In a republic, the citizen has the liberty to be an individual, to shape his own destiny. There are slaves in Venice, true, and class levels. But in theory a stalwart man can rise above his class. On his own, he can climb from poverty and misery to prosperity and ease."

Chingkim's quiet voice said, "Does that happen often in Venice?"

"Well," I said, "I remember one or two who took calculated advantage of their good looks, and thereby married above their station."

"You call that being stalwart? Here it would be called concubinage."

"It is only that offhand I cannot think of other instances to cite. But—"

"In Rome or Greece," said Kubilai, "were there any such instances? Your Western histories, do they record any instances?"

"I honestly cannot say, Sire, not being a scholar of history."

Chingkim spoke again. "Do you believe it could happen, Marco? That all men could and would make themselves equal and free and rich, if only they were given the liberty to do so?"

"Why not, my Prince? Some of our foremost philosophers have believed it."

"A man will believe anything that does not cost him anything," said Kubilai's voice. "That is another proverb of the Han. Marco, I know what happens when people are set free—and I did not get that knowledge from reading history. I know because I have done that for people myself."

Some moments passed. Then Chingkim said in an amused tone, "Marco is shocked to silence. But it is true, Marco. I saw my Royal Father employ that tactic one time to conquer a province in the land of To-Bhot. The province resisted our frontal attacks, so the Khakhan simply made announcement to the Bho people: 'You are free of your former tyrant rulers and oppressors. And I, being a liberal ruler, I give you license to take your rightful places in the world as you deserve.' And do you know what happened?"

"I hope, my Prince, it made them happy."

Kubilai gave a laugh that resounded around the wall like the noise of an iron cauldron being pounded with a mallet. He said:

"What happens, Marco Polo, is this. Tell a poor man that he has free permission to rob the rich he has envied for so long. Does he sally forth and ransack the gilded mansion of some lord? No, he seizes the pig owned by his peasant neighbor. Tell a slave that he is set free at last and made the equal of all other men. Perhaps his first display of equality is to murder his former master, but the second thing he does: he acquires a slave. Tell a troop of soldiers, unwillingly impressed into military service, that they may freely desert and go home. Do they, as they go, assassinate the lofty generals who drafted them? No, they butcher the man who was promoted from among them to be their troop sergeant. Tell *all* the downtrodden that they have free permission to rise up against their most brutal oppressor. Do they march in grand array against their tyrant Wang or Ilkhan? No, they go in a mob and tear to pieces the village moneylender."

There was another silence. I could think of no comment to make. Finally Chingkim spoke again:

"The ruse worked there in To-Bhot, Marco. It threw the whole province into chaos, and we took it quite easily, and my brother Ukuruji is now Wang of To-Bhot. Of course, nothing is changed for the Bho people, as regards class and privilege and prosperity and liberty. Life goes on there as before."

I still could think of no comment to make, for the Khakhan and the Prince were obviously not talking just of some ignorant rustics in the backward land of To-Bhot. The opinion they had of the common folk was of all common folk everywhere, and it was no high opinion, but I had no argument with which to controvert it. So we three moved from our places around the Echo Pavilion and went back inside the palace and drank mao-tai together and talked of other things. And I did not again suggest any moderations of the Mongol code of laws, and to this day the decrees proclaimed throughout the Khanate conclude as they did then: "The Khakhan has spoken; tremble, all men, and obey!"

Kubilai never made any comment on the order in which I was calling upon his various ministers, though he might have supposed that I should rightly have commenced with his highest of all: that Chief Minister Achmad-az-Fenaket of whom I have by now so often spoken. But I would have been glad to omit the Arab entirely, especially after I heard so many unpleasant things about him. In fact, I never did seek audience with him, and it was Achmad who impelled our meeting at last. He sent a servant to me with a testy message, requiring me to appear before him and collect my wages from his own hand, in his capacity as Finance Minister. I gathered that he had got annoyed by the money's having accumulated untouched, and by my having let the New Year season go past without a settling of account. Ever since my being taken into employment by the Khakhan, I had not bothered to inquire by whom I was to be paid, or even how much, for I had so far had no need of a single bagatìn—or tsien, as the smallest unit of Kithai currency was called. I was elegantly housed and fed and supplied with everything, and could not imagine how I would spend any money if I had any.

Before I obeyed Achmad's summons, I went to ask my father if the Compagnia Polo's enterprises were still being thwarted, and, if so, whether he would like me to broach the subject with the obstructive Arab. Failing to find my father in his suite, I went to my uncle's. He was reclining on a couch, being shaved by one of his women servants.

"What is this, Uncle Mafìo?" I exclaimed. "Getting rid of your journeyer's beard! Why?"

Through the lather he said, "We shall be dealing mainly with Han merchants, and the Han despise hairiness as a mark of the barbarian. Since all the Arabs of the Ortaq are bearded, I thought Nico and I might enjoy some advantage if one of us was clean-shaven. Also, to be frank, it troubled my vanity that my older brother's beard is still its natural color, while mine has gone as gray as Nostril's."

My uncle, I assumed, was also still keeping his crotch hairless, so I remarked, somewhat waspishly, "Many of the Han shave their heads as well. Are you going to do that, too?"

"And many of them let their hair grow as long as a woman's," he said equably. "I may do that. Did you come in here just to criticize my toilet?"

"No, but I think you have answered what I was going to ask. When you say you will be dealing with merchants, I gather it means that you and Father have resolved your differences with the evil Arab Achmad."

"Yes, and quite pleasantly. He has conceded all the necessary permits. Do not speak of the Chief Minister in such a tone, Marco. He turns out to be—not so bad, after all."

"I am pleased to hear it," I said, though not much believing it. "I have to go and see him right now."

Uncle Mafìo sat up from his recumbent position. "Did he bid you stop to see me—for any reason?"

"No, no. I merely must collect from him some money that I do not know what to do with."

"Ah," said my uncle, lying back again. "Give it to Nico to invest in the Compagnia. You could not make any better investment."

I said, after some hesitation, "I must remark, uncle, that you seem in a much better humor now than when we last spoke in private."

"E cussì? I am back in business again."

"I was not referring to—well, material things."

"Ah, my famous *condition*," he said wryly. "You would prefer to see me drooped and draped in melancholy."

"I would not, uncle. I am delighted if you have in some measure made peace with yourself."

"That is kind of you, nephew," he said in a more gentle voice. "And in truth I have. I discovered that a man who cannot any longer be given pleasure can yet find considerable pleasure in *giving* pleasure."

"Whatever that means, I am glad for you."

"You may not believe this," he said, almost shyly.. "But, in a mood to experiment, I found I could even give pleasure to this one who is shaving me. Yes—do not look so startled—to a female. And in return she taught me some feminine arts of giving pleasure." He seemed suddenly embarrassed by his own air of embarrassment, and gave a loud laugh to blow it away. "I may have a whole new career ahead of me. Thank you for inquiring, Marco, but spare me my blushes. If Achmad is expecting you, you had best run along."

When I entered the sumptuously appointed sanctum of the Chief Minister, the Vice-Regent, the Finance Minister, he did not rise or salute me. Instead, unlike the Khan of All Khans, he obviously expected me to make ko-tou, and waited for me to do it, and when I stood up again he did not offer me a seat. The Wali Achmad looked like any other Arab—hawk-beak nose, stiff black beard, dark and grainy complexion— except that he was cleaner than most Arabs I had seen in Arab lands, he having adopted the Kithai custom of frequent bathing. Also, he had the coldest eyes I ever saw in an Arab or any other Easterner. Brown eyes are usually as warm as qahwah, but his looked more like chips of the Mukha agate stone. He wore Arab aba and kaffiyah, but not of flimsy cotton; of silks colored like a rainbow.

"Your wages, Folo," he said ungraciously, and shoved across his table no purse of money, but an untidy pile of slips of paper.

I picked them up and examined them. The slips were all alike: made of dark and durable mulberry paper, decorated on both sides with complex designs and a multitude of words both in Han characters and Mongol alphabet, done in black ink, over which a large and intricate seal mark had been added in red ink. I did not say thank you. I had taken an instant, instinctive dislike to the man, and was quite prepared to suspect chicanery. So I said:

"Excuse me, Wali Achmad, but am I being paid in pagherì?"

"I do not know," he said languidly. "What does the word mean?"

"Pagherì are papers promising to repay a loan, or to pay in the future some pledge made. They are a convenience of the commerce of Venice."

"Then I suppose you could call these pagherì, for they are also a convenience, being the legal tender of this realm. We took over the system from the Han, who call it 'flying money.' Each of those papers you hold is worth a liang of silver."

I pushed the little pile back across the table toward him. "If it please the Wali, then, I should prefer to take the silver."

"You have the equivalent," he snapped. "That much silver would make your purse drag the floor. It is the beauty of the flying money that large sums, even immense sums, can be exchanged or transported without weight or bulk. Or hidden away in your mattress, if you are a miser. Also, when you pay for a purchase, the merchant need not every time weigh the currency and verify its metal's purity."

"You mean," I said, unconvinced, "I could go into the market and buy a bowl of miàn to eat and the vendor would accept one of these pieces of paper in payment?"

"Bismillah! He would give you his whole market-stall for it. Probably his wife and children as well. I told you: each of those is worth a whole liang. A liang is one thousand tsien, and for one tsien you could buy twenty or thirty bowls of miàn. If you have need of small change—here." He took from a drawer several packets of smaller sized papers. "How do you want it? Notes of half a liang each? A hundred tsien? What?"

Marveling, I said, "The flying money is made in all denominations? And the common folk accept them like real money?"

"It is real money, unbeliever! Cannot you read? Those words on the paper attest its realness. They proclaim its face value, and appended are the signatures of all the Khakhan's numerous officers and bursars and clerks of the imperial treasury. My own name is among them. And over all is stamped in red ink a much bigger yin—the great seal of Kubilai himself. Those are guarantees that at any time the paper can be exchanged for its face amount in actual silver from the treasury stores. Thus the paper is as real as the silver it represents."

"But if," I persisted, "someday someone should wish to redeem one of these papers, and it were repudiated . . .?"

Achmad said drily, "If the time ever comes when the Khakhan's yin evokes disrespect, you will have many more urgent things to worry about than your wages. We all will."

Still examining the flying money, I mused aloud, "Nevertheless, I should think it would be less trouble for the treasury simply to issue the bits of silver. I mean, if there are sheaves of these little papers circulating throughout the realm, and if every official must write his name on every last one—"

"We do not write our names over and over again," said Achmad, beginning to sound very annoyed. "We write them only once, and from that signature the palace Master Yinmaker makes a yin, which is a backward-written word like an engraved seal, and can be inked and stamped on paper innumerable times. Surely even you uncivilized Venetians are familiar with seals."

"Yes, Wali Achmad."

"Very well. For the making of a piece of money, all the necessary separate yin for words and characters and letters are arranged and locked together into a form of the proper size. The form is repeatedly inked and the papers pressed onto it one by one. It is a process the Han call zi-shu-ju, which means something like 'the gathered writing.' "

I nodded. "Our Western monks will often cut a backward block of wood for the big initial letter of a manuscript, and impress several pages with it, for the several Friars Illuminators to color and elaborate in their individual styles, before proceeding to write the rest of the page by hand."

Achmad shook his head. "In the gathered writing the impression need not be limited to the initial letter, and no hand writing need be done at all. By the molding in terra-cotta of many identical yin of every character in the Han language—and now having yin of every letter of the Mongol alphabet—this zi-shu-ju can combine any number of yin into any number of words. Thus can be composed whole pages of writing, and those combined into whole books. Zi-shu-ju can produce them in great quantities, every copy alike, far more quickly and perfectly than any scribes can indite by hand. If provided with yin of the Arabic alphabet and of the Roman alphabet, the process could produce books in any known language, equally easily and abundantly and cheaply."

"Say you so?" I murmured. "Why, Wali, that is an invention more to be admired even than the advantages of the flying money."

"You are right, Folo. I perceived that myself, the first time I saw one of the gathered-writing books. I thought of sending some of the Han experts westward to teach the doing of the zi-shu-ju in my native Arabia. But fortunately I learned in time that the zi-shu-ju forms are inked with brushes made of the bristles of swine. So it would be unthinkable to suggest the process to the nations of holy Islam."

"Yes, I can see that. Well, I thank you, Wali Achmad, both for the instruction and for the wages." I began to put the papers away in my belt purse.

"Allow me," he said casually, "to proffer one or two other bits of instruction. There are some places you *cannot* spend the flying money. The Fondler, for example, will take bribes only in solid gold. But I think you already knew that."

Taking care to make my face expressionless, I raised my eyes from my purse to his cold agate gaze. I wondered how much else he knew about my doings, and obligingly he told me:

"I would not dream of suggesting that you disobey the Khakhan. He did instruct you to make inquiries. But I will suggest that you confine your inquiries to the upper stories of the palace. Not down in Master Fing's dungeons. Not even in the servants' quarters."

So he knew that I had put an ear belowstairs. But did he know why? Did he know that I was interested in the Minister of Lesser Races, and, if he did, why should he care? Or did he fear that I might hear something damaging to Achmad the Chief Minister? I kept my face expressionless and waited.

"Cellar dungeons are unhealthy places," he went on, as indifferently as if he were warning me against rheumatic damp. "But tortures can happen aboveground as well, and far worse ones than anything the Fondler inflicts."

I had to correct him there. "I am sure there could be nothing worse than the Death of a Thousand. Perhaps, Wali Achmad, you are unacquainted with—"

"I am acquainted with it. But even the Fondler knows how to inflict a death worse than that one. And I know several." He smiled—or his lips did; his stone eyes did not. "You Christians think of Hell as the most terrible torture there can be, and your Bible tells you that Hell consists of pain. 'To be cast into the Hell of fire, where their worm dieth not, and the fire is not extinguished.' So spoke your gentle Jesus, at Capharnaum, to His disciples. Like your Jesus, I warn you not to flirt with Hell, Marco Folo, and not to pursue any temptations that might put you there. But I will tell you something more about Hell than your Christian Bible does. Hell is not necessarily an ever burning fire or a gnawing worm or a physical pain of any sort. Hell is not necessarily even a place. Hell is whatever hurts worst."

. 11 .

I went from the chambers of the Chief Minister directly to my own, intending to tell Nostril to cease his spy activities—at least until I could give some serious cogitation to the Wali's warnings and threats. But Nostril was not there; another slave was. Biliktu and Buyantu met me in the vestibule, their eyebrows haughtily aloft, to inform me that a slave, a stranger, had come calling and had begged leave to stay and wait my return. The twins, not being owned by me or anybody, were always disdainful of their inferiors, but they seemed even more than usually bothered by this one. Rather curious to see what had provoked them, I went into my main room. A woman was seated on a bench there. When I came in, she swept down to the floor in a graceful ko-tou, and stayed kneeling until I bade her rise. She stood up, and I looked at her, and I looked with wide eyes.

The palace slaves, when their errands brought them from their cellars or kitchens or stables up among their betters, were always well dressed, to reflect credit on their masters, so it was not the woman's fine garb that made me stare. What struck me was that she wore it as if she *deserved* nothing but the best, and was used to it, and was aware that no richest raiment would ever outshine her own radiance.

She was not a girl; she must have been about the same age as Nostril or my Uncle Mafio. But her face was unlined, and the years had marked her beauty only with dignity. If any youthful brook-twinkle had gone from her eyes, it had been replaced by forest-pool depth and placidity. There were some threads of silver in her hair, but it was mostly a warm, ruddy black, and not Kithai-straight, but a tumble of curls. Her figure was erect and, as far as I could make out through the brocade robes, still firm and nicely shaped.

When I continued to greet her only with a gawk, she said, in a velvet voice, "You are, I believe, the master of the slave Ali Babar."

"Who?" I said stupidly. "Oh, him. Yes, Ali Babar belongs to me."

To cover my momentary confusion, I mumbled an excuse-me, and went to peer into a jar to see how my flaming powder was doing. So this was the Turki Princess Mar-Janah! A day or two ago, I had poured the huo-yao from one of the two baskets into a sturdier jar. No wonder Nostril had been enamored once before, and was now again. Then I had poured some water into that portion of the powder. No wonder Nostril was ready to promise an extravagant change in himself, to win this woman. Despite the Firemaster's skepticism, I had wanted to see whether I could make the powder more stable in the form of a thick mud. Any man would make that extravagant promise, and probably *would* change, too, or die trying. But it seemed the Firemaster had been right to scoff at my suggestion. How in God's name had a buffoon like Nostril ever got even remotely acquainted with such a woman as this? The wet powder was only a morose, dark-gray sludge, and showed no sign of ever becoming anything else. A woman such as this ought to laugh at a thing like Nostril—or jeer. The powder might be stable in the form of muck, but it would never ignite. Or retch violently. Vakh!

"Tell me if I have guessed right, Master Marco," said Mar-Janah. She sounded amused, but was obviously trying to help me compose my scattered wits. "You asked me here to regale me with praises of your slave Ali Babar."

I coughed a few times, and tried: "Nost—" I coughed again and tried again: "Ali can boast of a good many virtues and talents and attainments."

That much I could say without a blush, and without speaking one word of falsehood, for if any true thing could be said about Nostril it was, by God, that he could boast.

Mar-Janah smiled slightly and said, "As I have it from our fellow slaves, they cannot decide which is greater: Ali Babar's monumental self-admiration or the windiness with which he expresses it. But all agree that those are traits to be commended in a man who has so abjectly failed at everything else."

I stared at her, and I think my mouth hung open. Then I said, "Wait a moment. You evidently know a great deal about Nost—about Ali. Yet you are not even supposed to know he is in residence here."

"I know more than that. I know that the other slaves are wrong in their mocking appraisal of him. When I first met Ali Babar, he was everything that he now only pretends he is."

"I do not believe it," I said flatly. Then I more courteously put a question, "Will you take cha with me?"

I clapped my hands and Buyantu appeared so promptly that I suspected she had been jealously lurking and listening just outside the curtained doorway. I ordered cha for the visitor and pu-tao for myself, and Buyantu went out again.

I turned back to Mar-Janah. "I would be interested to know more—about you and Ali Babar."

"We were young then," she said reminiscently. "The Arab bandits galloped out of the hills, down on my carriage, and they killed the coachman, but Ali was riding postilion, and they took him alive. They bore us away to their caves in the hills, and Ali was to be the messenger who would carry their ransom demand to my father. But I bade him refuse, and he did. At which, they laughed and they beat him most cruelly and they sealed him into a great jar of sesame oil. It would soften his obduracy, they said."

I nodded. "It is a thing the Arabs do. It softens more than obduracy."

"But Ali Babar did not soften. I did, or I pretended to. I feigned an infatuation for the bandit leader, though it was the staunch and loyal Ali with whom I had fallen in love. My pretense won me some measure of freedom, and one night I contrived to free Ali from the big jar, and to procure for him a sword."

Buyantu returned, and Biliktu with her, each of them carrying a drink. They gave Mar-Janah her cup, and me my goblet, lingering to get a good look at the handsome visitor, as if they feared that I was recruiting an unwelcome fourth for our ménage. I waved them out, and prompted Mar-Janah to continue: "Well?"

"All went well. On Ali's instructions, I pretended further. I feigned submission to the chieftain's lust that night, and, as planned, when I had him most vulnerable, Ali Babar leapt through the bed curtains and slew him. Then Ali bravely slashed our way through the other bandits, as they awakened and converged, and we got to the horses. By Allah's mercy, we got safe away."

"This is all very hard to believe."

"The only disadvantage to our plan was that I had to make my escape stark naked." She modestly turned her face away from me. "But that made it sublimely easy for me—when we lay down for the rest of the night in a friendly forest glade—to reward Ali as he deserved."

"A better reward—or so I understand—than your father the King gave him."

She sighed. "He promoted Ali to Chief Drover, and sent him far away from the palace. A royal father prefers a royal son-in-law. He never got one, though. Much to his vexation, I spurned all later suitors, even after I heard that Ali Babar had been taken in slavery. My spinsterhood probably saved my life when, some years afterward, our royal house was overthrown."

"I know about that, yes."

"I was left my life, but not much else. Allah's ways are sometimes inscrutable. When I was handed over to the Ilkhan Abagha, he thought he was getting a royal concubine. He was outraged to find I was not a virgin, and he gave me to his Mongol troops. They cared nothing about virginity and were much amused to have a royal plaything. When they had had their sport, the remains of me were sold in the slave market. I have passed through many hands since then."

"I am sorry. What can one say? It must have been terrible."

"Not so very." Like a spirited mare, she tossed her mane of dark curls. "I had learned how to pretend, you see. I pretended that every man was my handsome, brave Ali Babar. And now I hope Allah has brought me near to my own reward. If you had not summoned me to this meeting, Master Marco, I should have sought audience—to ask if you will assist our reunion. Will you tell Ali that I yearn to be his again, and that I hope we will be allowed to marry?"

I coughed some more, uncertain of how to proceed. "Ahem— Princess Mar-Janah . . ."

"Slave Mar-Janah," she corrected me. "There are even stricter marriage rules for slaves than for royalty."

"Mar-Janah, the man you remember so fondly—I assure you he remembers you the same way. But he believes you have not yet recognized him. Frankly, I am amazed that you could have done."

She smiled again. "You see him, then, as his fellow slaves do. From what they tell me, he has changed most markedly."

"From what they—? Then you *have* not seen him."

"Oh, of course I have. But I do not know what he looks like. I still see the champion who battled for me against the Arab abductors, twenty years ago, and made tender love to me that night. He is young, and as straight and slender as the written letter alif, and beautiful in a manly way. Much as you are, Master Marco."

"Thank you," I said, but faintly, for I was still bemused. Had she not even noticed the one outstanding unbeautifulness that had earned him the name of Nostril? I said, "Far be it from me to disillusion a lovely lady of her lovely imaginings, but—"

"Master Marco, no woman can ever be disillusioned about the man she truly loves." She set down her cup and came close to me and shyly put out a hand to touch my face. "I am near old enough to be your mother. May I tell you a motherly thing?"

"Please do."

"You too are handsome, and young, and someday soon a woman will truly love you. Whether Allah grants that you and she live together all your lives—or requires, as happened to Ali Babar and me, that you be not united until a long time after your first meeting—you will grow older, and so will she. I cannot predict whether you will grow feeble and bent, or gross, or bald, or ugly, but it will not matter. This I can say with certainty: she will see you always as you were when you met. To the very end of your days. Or hers."

"Your Highness," I said, and with feeling, for if ever anyone merited a lofty title, it was she. "God grant that I find a woman of such loving heart and eye as you possess. But, in conscience, I must remark that a man can change in ways that cannot be seen."

"You feel you must inform me that Ali Babar has not remained a good man during all these years? Not a steadfast or faithful or admirable or even a manly man? I know that he has been a slave, and I know that slaves are expected to be creatures less than human."

"Well, yes," I muttered. "He said something of the same sort. He said he tried to become the worst thing in the world, because he had lost the best."

She thought about that, and said pensively, "Whatever he and I have been, he will more readily see the marks on me than I on him."

It was my turn to correct her. "That is flagrantly untrue. To say that you have survived beautifully would be to say the least. When I first heard of Mar-Janah, I expected to see a pitiable ruin, but I see a princess still."

She shook her head. "I was a maiden when Ali Babar knew me, and I was entire. That is to say, although I was born a Muslim, I was of royal blood and so had not been deprived of my bizir in infancy. I had then a body to be proud of, and Ali exulted in it. But since then, I have been the toy of half a Mongol army, and of as many men afterward, and some men mistreat their toys." She looked away from me once more, but went on: "You and I have spoken frankly; I will continue to do so. My meme are ringed with the scars of teethmarks. My bizir has been stretched to flaccidity. My göbek is slack and loose-lipped. I have miscarried three times and now can never conceive again."

I had to guess the meaning of the Turki words she had used, but I could not mistake the sincerity with which she concluded:

"If Ali Babar can love what is left of me, Master Marco, do you think I cannot love what is left of him?"

"Your Highness," I said again, and again with feeling, though my voice was a little choked, "I stand abashed and ashamed—and enlightened. If Ali Babar can deserve a woman like you, he is more of a man than I ever suspected. And I should be less the man if I did not exert myself to see you wed to him. So that I may start immediately to make arrangements, tell me: what are the palace rules regarding slave marriages?"

"That the owners of both parties must give permission, and must concur in the matter of where the couple shall reside. That is all, but not every master is so lenient as you."

"Who is your master? I will send to ask audience with him."

Her voice faltered a bit. "My master, I am sorry to say, has little mastery in his household. You will have to address his wife."

"Singular household," I observed. "But that need not complicate matters. Who is she?"

"The Lady Chao Ku-an. She is one of the court artists, but by title she is the Armorer of the Palace Guard."

"Oh. Yes. I have heard of her."

"She is—" Mar-Janah paused, to choose carefully the description. "She is a strong-willed woman. The Lady Chao desires that her slaves be entirely hers, and commandable at all hours."

"I am not exactly weak-willed, myself," I said. "And I have promised that your twenty-year separation is to end here and now. As soon as the arrangements are made, I will see you and your champion reunited. Until then . . ."

"May Allah bless you, good master and friend Marco," she said, with a smile as bright as the tears in her eyes.

I called for Buyantu and Biliktu, and told them to see the visitor to the door. They accompanied her ungraciously, with frowning brows and curled lips, so, when they returned, I spoke to them severely.

"Your superiority of manner is less than mannerly, and it ill becomes you, my dears. I know you to be of only twenty-two-karat valuation. The lady you have so grudgingly attended is, in my estimation, of a perfect twenty-four. Now, Buyantu, you go and present my compliments to the Lady Chao Ku-an, and say that Marco Polo requests an appointment to call upon her."

When she left, and Biliktu flounced off to sulk in some other room, I went and took one more disappointed look at my jar full of huo-yao sludge. Clearly, those fifty liang of the flaming powder were now ruined beyond salvage. So I set the jar aside, picked up the remaining basket and contemplated the contents of that. After a while, I began very carefully to pick out from the mixture some grains of the saltpeter. When I had a dozen or so of the white specks, I lightly moistened the end of an ivory fan handle. I picked up the saltpeter with that, and idly held it in the flame of a nearby candle. The grains instantly melted into a glaze on the ivory. I gave that some thought. The Firemaster had been right about wetting the powder, and he had warned me not to try baking it. But suppose I set a pot of the huo-yao on a low fire, not very hot, so that its integral saltpeter *melted* and thereby held the whole together . . . ? My meditations were interrupted by the return of Buyantu, reporting that the Lady Chao would see me that very moment.

I went, and I introduced myself, "Marco Polo, my lady," and I made a proper ko-tou.

"My lord husband has spoken of you," she said, indicating that I should rise by giving me a playful nudge with a bare foot. Her hands were occupied in playing with an ivory ball, as her husband had done, for the suppling of the fingers.

As I stood, she went on, "I wondered when you would deign to call upon this lowly female courtier." Her voice was as musical as wind chimes, but seemed somehow just as devoid of any human agency in the making of that music. "Would you wish to discuss my titular office, or my real work? Or my pastimes in between?"

That last was said with a leer. Lady Chao evidently and correctly assumed that, like everyone else, I had heard of her gluttonous appetite for men. I will confess that I was briefly tempted to join her cupboard of morsels. She was about my own age and would have been fetchingly beautiful if she had not had her eyebrows plucked entirely off and her delicate features coated with a dead-white powder. I was, as always, curious to discover what was beneath the rich silk robes—in this case, especially, because I had not yet lain with a woman of the Han race. But I restrained my curiosity and said:

"None of those today, my lady, if you please. I come on a different—"

"Ah, a bashful one," she said, and changed her leer to a simper. "Let us begin, then, by talking of *your* favorite pastimes."

"On some other occasion, perhaps, Lady Chao. I would speak today of your female slave named Mar-Janah."

"Aiya!" she exclaimed, which is the Han equivalent of "vakh!" She sat abruptly upright on her couch, and she frowned—and a frown is very unpleasant to look at when it is done without eyebrows—and she snapped, "You find that Turki wench more appealing than I am?"

"Why, no, my lady," I lied. "Having been nobly born in my native land, I would never—there or here—even consider admiring any but a woman of perfect pedigree, such as yourself." I tactfully did not point out that she was only nobility and Mar-Janah was royalty.

But she seemed mollified. "That is well said." She leaned voluptuously back again. "On the other hand, I have sometimes discovered that a grimy and sweaty soldier can be appealing. . . ."

She trailed off, as if inviting comment, but I did not care to be drawn into a contest of comparing our experiences of perversity. So I attempted to continue, "Regarding the slave—"

"The slave, the slave . . ." She sighed, and pouted, and petulantly tossed and caught the ivory ball. "For a moment there, you were well spoken, as a gallant should be when calling on a lady. But you prefer to talk of slaves."

I reminded myself that any business with a Han ought to be approached roundabout, only after long exchanges of trivialities. So I said gallantly, "I would much rather talk of my Lady Chao, and her surpassing beauty."

"That is better."

"I am a little surprised that, with such a choice model so conveniently at hand, the Master Chao has not made many paintings of her."

"He has," she said, and smirked.

"I regret that he showed me none."

"He would not if he could, and he cannot. They are in the possession of the various other lords who were portrayed in the same pictures. And those lords are not likely to show them to you, either."

I did not have to ponder on that remark to realize what it meant. I would defer making judgment on Master Chao—whether I felt sympathy for his predicament or disgust for his pliant complicity in it—but I knew that I did not much like his young lady, and I would be glad to quit her company. So I made no further attempt at small talk.

"I beg that my lady will forgive my persistence in the subject of the slave, but I seek to right a wrong of long duration. I entreat the Lady Chao's permission for her slave Mar-Janah to marry."

"Aiya!" she exclaimed again, and loudly. "That aging slut is pregnant!"

"No, no."

Unhearing, she went on, while her nonexistent eyebrows writhed.

"But that does not obligate you! No man weds a slave just because he has impregnated her."

"I did not!"

"The embarrassment is slight, and easily disposed of. I will call her in and kick her in the belly. Concern yourself no further."

"My concern is not—"

"It is, however, a matter for speculation." Her little red tongue came out and licked her little red lips. "The physicians all pronounced that woman barren. You must be exceptionally potent."

"Lady Chao, the woman is *not* pregnant and it is *not* I who would marry her!"

"What?" For the first time, her face lost all expression.

"It is a man slave of my own who has been long enamored of your Mar-Janah. I merely entreat your concurrence in my permission for them to wed and live together."

She stared at me. Ever since I had come in, the young lady had been assuming one expression after another—of invitation, of coyness, of petulance—and now I saw why she had kept her features so much in motion. That white face, without some conscious contortion, was as empty as a sheet of unwritten paper. I wondered: would the rest of her body be as unexciting? Were Han women all blanks that only sporadically assumed human semblance? I was almost grateful when she put on a look of annoyance and said:

"That Turki woman is my dresser and applier of cosmetics. Not even my lord husband infringes on her time. I do not see why I should share her with a husband of her own."

"Then perhaps you would sell her outright? I can pay a sum that will purchase an excellent replacement."

"Are you now trying to insult me? Do you imply that I cannot afford to give away a slave, if I so choose?"

She bounded up from the couch and, her little bare feet twinkling, her robes and ribbons and tassels and perfumed powder swirling in her wake, she left the room. I stood and wondered if I had been summarily dismissed or if she had gone for a guardsman to take me in charge. The young woman was as exasperatingly changeable as her inconstant face. In just our brief conversation, she had managed to accuse me in quick succession of being bashful, presumptuous, salacious, meddlesome, gullible and finally offensive. I was not surprised that such a woman required an endless supply of lovers; she probably forgot each one in the moment that he slunk from her bed.

But she came tripping into the room again, unaccompanied, and flung at me a piece of paper. I snatched and caught it before it drifted to the floor. I could not read the Mongol writing on it, but she told me what it was, saying contemptuously:

"Title to the slave Mar-Janah. I give it to you. The Turki is yours to do with as you please." In its fickle way, her face went from contempt to a seductive smile. "And so am I. Do what you will—to render me proper thanks."

I might have had to, and I could probably have nerved myself to do

it, if she had commanded it earlier. But she had incautiously given me
the paper now, before setting a price on it. So I folded it into my purse,
and bowed, and said with all the floweriness I could muster:

"Your humble supplicant does indeed most fervently thank the gracious Lady Chao Ku-an. And, I am sure, so will the lowly slaves likewise
honor and bless your name, as soon as I inform them of your bountiful
goodness, which I shall this minute go and do. Until we meet again,
then, noble lady—"

"What?" she screeched, like a wind chime being blown to pieces.
"You would simply turn and walk away?"

I was inclined to say no, that I would run if it were not undignified.
However, having told her I was well born, I maintained my courteous
manner and bowed repeatedly as I backed toward the door, murmuring
things like "most benevolent" and "undying gratitude."

Her paper face was now a palimpsest written over with disbelief,
shock and outrage, all at once. She was holding the ivory ball as if about
to throw it at me. "Many men have regretted my sending them away,"
she said menacingly, through clenched teeth. "You will be the first to
regret having gone away unbidden."

I had bowed my way out into the corridor by then, but I heard her
shriek a few words as I turned to flee for my own chambers.

"And I promise! That you will! Regret it!"

I have to say that it was not any sudden access of rectitude that
made me run from the Lady Chao's proffered embrace, nor any concern
I felt for her husband's sensibilities, nor any fear of compromising consequences that might ensue. It seemed likelier that consequences would
ensue from my *not* having ravished her. No, it was none of those things,
and it was not even the general repugnance she inspired in me. To be
perfectly honest, I had been mainly repelled by her feet. I must explain
about that, because many other Han women had the same sort of feet.

They were called "lotus points," and the incredibly tiny shoes for
them were called "lotus cups." Not until later did I learn that the Lady
Chao—apart from her other immodesties which I easily recognized—had
been lascivious beyond the bounds of harlotry just in letting me see her
feet bare of their lotus cups. The lotus points of a woman were deemed
by the Han her most intimate parts, to be kept more carefully covered
than even the pink parts between her legs.

It seems that, many years ago, there lived a Han court dancer who
could dance on her toes, and that posture—her seeming to be balanced
on points—excited every man who saw her dance. So other women, ever
since, had enviously been trying to emulate that fabled seductress. Her
contemporary sister dancers must have tried various ways to diminish
their already woman-sized feet, and not too successfully, for the women
of later days went further. By the time I came to Khanbalik, there were
many Han women who had had their feet compressed by their mothers
from their infancy, and had grown up thus crippled, and were carrying
on the gruesome tradition by binding their own daughters' feet.

What a mother would do was take her girl-child's foot and double it
under, the toes as near to the heel as possible, and tie it so, until it stayed

that way, and then double it even more tightly, and tie it so. By the time
a girl reached womanhood, she could wear lotus cups that were literally
no bigger than drinking cups. Naked, those feet looked like the claws of
a small bird just yanked from its grip on a twig perch. A lotus-pointed
woman had to walk with mincing, precarious steps, and only seldom
walked at all, because that gait was regarded by the Han as other people
would regard a woman's most flagrantly provocative gesture. Just to say
certain words—feet or toes or lotus points or walking—in reference to a
woman, or in the presence of a decent woman, would cause as many
gasps as shouting "pota!" in a Venetian drawing room.

I grant that the lotus crippling of a Han woman constituted a less
cruel mutilation than the Muslim practice of snipping off the butterfly
from between the petals of her lotus higher up her body. Nevertheless, I
winced at sight of such feet, even when they were modestly shod, for the
lotus-cup shoes resembled the leather pods with which some beggars
cover the stumps of their amputations. My detestation of the lotus points
made me something of a curiosity among the Han. All the Han men with
whom I became acquainted thought me odd—or maybe impotent, or
even depraved—when I averted my eyes from a lotus-pointed woman.
They frankly confessed that they got aroused by the glimpse of a woman's nether extremities, as I might by a glimpse of her breast. They
proudly averred that their little virile organs actually came erect whenever they heard an unmentionable word like "feet," or even when they
let their minds imagine those unrevealable parts of a female person.

At any rate, the Lady Chao that afternoon had so dampened my
natural ardors that, when Buyantu undressed me at bedtime, and insinuated into the act some suggestive fondling, I asked to be excused. So she
and Biliktu lay down together on my bed and I merely sat drinking arkhi
and looking on, while the naked girls played with each other and with a
su-yang. That was a kind of mushroom native to Kithai, shaped exactly
like a man's organ, even to having a reticulation of veins about it, but
somewhat smaller in length and girth. However, as Buyantu demonstrated, when she gently slid it in and out of her sister a few times, and
Biliktu's yin juices began to flow, the su-yang somehow absorbed those
juices and got bigger and firmer. When it had attained a quite prodigious
size, the twins had themselves a joyous time, using that phallocrypt on
each other in various and ingenious ways. It was a sight that should have
been as rousing to me as feet to a Han man, but I only smiled on them
tolerantly and, when they had exhausted each other, I lay down between
their warm, moist bodies and went to sleep.

. 12 .

T H E twins, fatigued, were still sleeping when I eased out from between
them the next morning. Nostril had not been anywhere in evidence the
night before, and was not in his closet when I went to look for him. So,

being temporarily without any servants at all, I stirred up the embers of the brazier in my main room and brewed myself a pot of cha with which to break my fast. While I sipped at it, I bethought myself of trying the experiment I had been contemplating the previous day. I put just enough charcoal on the brazier to keep it burning, but at a very low flame. Then I rummaged about my chambers until I found a stoneware pot with a lid, and I poured into that my remaining fifty-liang measure of flaming powder, lidded it securely and set it on the brazier. At that moment, Nostril came in, looking rather rumpled and seedy, but pleased with himself.

"Master Marco," he said, "I have been up all night. Some of the menservants and horse herders started a gambling game of zhi-pai cards in the stable, and it is still going on. I watched the play for some hours until I grasped the rules of the game. Then I wagered some silver, and I won, too. But when I scooped in my winnings I was dismayed to see that I had won only this sheaf of dirty papers, so I quit in disgust at men who play only with worthless vouchers."

"You ass," I said. "Have you never seen flying money before? As well as I can tell, you are holding there the equivalent of a month of my wages. You should have stayed, as long as you were doing so well." He looked bewildered, so I said, "I will explain later. Meanwhile, I rejoice to see that one of us can squander his time in frivolity. The slave plays the prodigal while his master labors and scurries about on the slave's errands. I have had a visit from your Princess Mar-Janah and—"

"Oh, master!" he exclaimed, and turned colors, as if he had been an adolescent boy and I were twitting him on his first mooncalf love.

"We will speak later of that also. I will just say that your gambling earnings should serve you and her to set up housekeeping together."

"Oh, master! Al-hamdo-lillah az iltifat-i-shoma!"

"Later, later. Right now, I must bid you to cease your spying activities. I have heard intimations of displeasure, from a lord whom I think we would be wise not to displease."

"As you command, master. But it may be that I have already procured a trifle of information that may interest you. That is why I stayed sleepless and absent from my master's quarters all the night long, being not frivolous but assiduous in my master's behalf." He put on a look of self-sacrifice and self-righteousness. "Men get as talkative as women when they play at cards. And these men, for mutual comprehension, all talked in the Mongol tongue. When one of them made a passing reference to the Minister Pao Nei-ho, I thought I ought to linger. Since I was instructed by my master to make no overt inquiries, I could only listen. And my devoted patience kept me there all night, never drowsing, never getting drunk, never even departing to relieve my bladder, never—"

"No need to beat me over the head with hints, Nostril. I accept that you were working while you played. Come to the point."

"For what it is worth, master, the Minister of Lesser Races is himself of a lesser race."

I blinked. "How say you?"

"He evidently passes here for a Han, but he is really of the Yi people of Yun-nan Province."

"Who told you so? How reliable is this information?"

"As I said, the game was played in the stables. That is because a stud of horses was yesterday brought in from the south, and their drovers are at leisure until they are dispatched on another karwan. Several of them are natives of Yun-nan, and one of them said, offhand, that he had glimpsed the Minister Pao here at the palace. And later another said yes, he had recognized him also, as a former petty magistrate of some little Yun-nan prefecture. And later another said yes, but let us not give him away. If Pao has escaped from the backwoods and prospers by passing as a Han here in the great capital, let us let him go on enjoying his success. Thus they spoke, Master Marco, and not falsely but credibly, it seemed to me."

"Yes," I murmured. I was remembering: the Minister Pao had indeed spoken of "us Han" as if he belonged among that people, and of "the obstreperous Yi" as if he concurred in regarding that people as distasteful. Well, I mused, the Chief Minister Achmad may have warned me too late to cease my covert investigations. But, if he was to be angry because I had learned this much of a secret, I must risk making him angrier still.

The twins had waked, perhaps from hearing us talking, and Buyantu came into the main room, looking rather prettily tousled. To her I said, "Run straight to the chambers of the Khan Kubilai, and present to his attendants the compliments of Marco Polo, and inquire if an early appointment can be fixed for me to see the Khakhan on a matter of some urgency."

She started to go back into the bedroom to arrange her dress and hair more orderly, but I said, "Urgency, Buyantu, is urgency. Go as you are, and go quickly." To Nostril I said, "You go to your closet and catch up on your sleep. We will discuss our other concerns when I return."

If I return, I thought, as I went into my bedchamber to dress in my most formal court costume. For all I knew, the Khakhan might, like the Wali Achmad, disapprove of my having taken it upon myself to ferret out secrets, and might express his disapproval in some violent manner not at all to my liking.

Biliktu was just then making up the very disordered bed, and she grinned impishly at me when she found among the covers the su-yang phallocrypt, now as small and limp as any real organ would have been after the exercise it had enjoyed. Seeing it, I decided to take this opportunity for some similar exercise of my own, since there was no knowing whether it might not be my last opportunity for a while. So, being at that moment undressed, I took gentle hold of Biliktu and began to undress her.

She seemed faintly startled. It had, after all, been a long time since she and I had indulged. She struggled a little and murmured, "I do not think I should, Master Marco."

"Come," I said heartily. "You cannot be still indisposed. If you could employ that"—I nodded at the discarded su-yang—"you can employ a real one."

And she did, with no further demur except an occasional whimper, and a tendency to keep moving away from my caresses and thrusts, as if to prevent my penetrating her very deeply. I assumed that she was merely still weary, or perhaps a little sore, from the preceding night, and her maidenly show of reluctance did not prevent my enjoying myself. Indeed, my enjoyment may have been keener than it had been for some while past, from the realization that I was inside Biliktu for a change, and not her twin.

I had finished, and most delightfully, but still had my red jewel inside Biliktu, relishing the final few diminishing squeezes of her lotus-petal muscles, when a voice said harshly, "The Khakhan will see you as soon as you can get there."

It was Buyantu, standing over the bed, glowering fiercely at me and her sister. Biliktu gave another whimper that was almost a whinny of fright, wriggled out of my embrace and out of the bed. Buyantu spun on her heel and stamped from the room. I also got up and got dressed, taking great care with my appearance. Biliktu dressed at the same time, but seemed to be dawdling, as if deliberately to make sure that I was the first to confront Buyantu.

That one stood waiting in the main room, with her arms folded tight inside her sleeves and a thundercloud expression on her face, like a schoolmistress waiting to chastise a naughty pupil. She opened her mouth, but I raised a masterly hand to stop her.

"I had not realized until now," I said. "You are displaying jealousy, Buyantu, and I think that is most selfish of you. For months now, it is clear, you have been gradually weaning me away from Biliktu. I ought to be flattered, I suppose, that you want me all for yourself. But I really must protest. Any such unsisterly jealousy could disturb the peace our little domicile has heretofore enjoyed. We will all continue to share, and share alike, and you must simply resign yourself to sharing with your sister my affection and attentions."

She stared at me as if I had uttered pure gibberish, and then she burst into a laughter that did not signify amusement.

"Jealous?" she cried. "Yes, I have grown jealous! And you will regret having taken that sordid advantage of my absence. You will regret that furtive quick frolic! But you think I am jealous of *you*? Why, you blind and strutting fool!"

I rocked with astonishment, never in my life having been so addressed by any servant. I thought she must have lost her senses. But in the next instant, I was even more severely shaken, for she raged on:

"You conceited goat of a Ferenghi! Jealous of you? It is *her* love I want! And for me alone!"

"You have it, Buyantu, and you know you have it!" cried Biliktu, hastening into the room and laying a hand on her sister's arm.

Buyantu shrugged the hand away. "That is not what I saw."

"I am sorry that you saw. And I am sorrier for having done it." She glanced hatefully at me, where I stood stunned. "He took me unaware. I did not know how to resist."

"You must learn to say no."

"I will. I have. I promise."

"We are twins. Nothing should ever come between us."

"Nothing ever will, dearest, not ever again."

"Remember, you are *my* little one."

"Oh, I am! I am! And you are mine!"

Then they were in each other's arms, and weeping lovers' tears down each other's necks. I stood shifting foolishly from one foot to the other, and finally cleared my throat and said:

"Well . . ."

Biliktu gave me a wet-eyed look of hurt and reproach.

"Well . . . uh . . . the Khakhan is waiting for me, girls."

Buyantu gave me a look brimming with massacre.

"When I come back, we will . . . that is, I will be glad to hear suggestions . . . that is, somehow to rearrange . . ." I gave it up, and said instead, "Please, my dears. Until I return, if you can leave off groping at each other, I have a small chore for you. Do you see this pot on this brazier?"

They turned their heads to cast an indifferent regard on it. The pot had got quite hot, so I used a corner of my robe to lift its lid and look in. The contents emitted a thin, peevish sort of smoke, but showed no sign of having melted at all. I set the lid securely on it again and said, "Keep up the fire under it, girls, but keep it a very low fire."

They unwound from each other, and dutifully came to the brazier, and Biliktu laid a few new chips of charcoal on the embers.

"Thank you," I said. "It will require no other attendance than that. Simply stay close by it and keep it at a simmering heat. And when I return . . ."

But they had already dismissed me and were gazing soulfully at each other, so I went on my way.

Kubilai received me in his earthquake-engine chamber, and with no one else present, and he greeted me cordially but not effusively. He knew that I had something to say, and he was ready for me to say it at once. However, I did not wish just to blurt out the information I had brought, so I began circumspectly.

"Sire, I am desirous that I do not, in my ignorance, give undue weight or impetuosity to my small services. I believe I bring news of some value, but I cannot properly evaluate it without knowing more than the little I now know of the Khakhan's disposition of his armies, and the nature of their objectives."

Kubilai did not take affront at my presumption or tell me to go and inform myself from his underlings.

"Like any conqueror, I must hold what I have won. Fifteen years ago, when I was chosen Khan of All Khans of the Mongols, my own brother Arikbugha challenged my accession, and I had to put him down. More recently, I have several times had to stifle similar ambitions on the part of my cousin Kaidu." He waved a dismissal of such trifles. "The mayflies continually plot to topple the cedar. Nuisances only, but they require my keeping portions of my troops on all the borders of Kithai."

"May I ask, Sire, about those on the march, not in garrison?"

He gave me another summary, just as succinct. "If I am to keep secure this Kithai I won from the Chin, I must also have the southern lands of the Sung. I can best conquer them by encirclement, taking first the province of Yun-nan. So that is the only place where my armies are actively campaigning right now, under my very capable Orlok Bayan."

Not to impugn the capability of his Orlok Bayan, I chose my next words with care.

"He has been engaged in that for some while now, I understand. Is it possible, Sire, that he is finding the conquest of Yun-nan more difficult than expected?"

Kubilai regarded me narrowly. "He is not about to be defeated, if that is what you mean. But neither is he having an easy victory. His advance had to be made from the land of To-Bhot, meaning that he had to come down into Yun-nan through the steeps of the Hang-duan Mountains. Our horse armies are better suited and more accustomed to fighting on flat plains. The Yi people of Yun-nan know every crevice of those mountains, and they fight in a shifty and cunning way—never facing us in force, but sniping from behind rocks and trees, then running to hide somewhere else. It is like trying to swat mosquitoes with a hod of bricks. Yes, you could fairly say that Bayan is finding it no easy conquest."

I said, "I have heard the Yi called obstreperous."

"Again, a fair enough description. From their safe concealments, they shout taunts of defiance. They evidently hold the delusion that they can resist long enough to make us go away. They are wrong."

"But the longer they resist, the more men dead on both sides, and the land itself made poorer and less worth the taking."

"Again, true enough. Unfortunately."

"If they were disabused of their delusion of invincibility, Sire, might not the conquest be easier? With fewer dead and less ravagement of the province?"

"Yes. Do you know some way to dissolve that delusion?"

"I am not sure, Sire. Let me put it this way. Do you suppose the Yi are bolstered in their resistance by knowing that they have a friend here at court?"

The Khakhan's gaze became that of a hunting chita. But he did not roar like a chita, he said as softly as a dove, "Marco Polo, let us not dance around the subject, like two Han in the market. Tell me who it is."

"I have information, Sire, apparently reliable, that the Minister of Lesser Races, Pao Nei-ho, though posing as a Han, is really a Yi of Yun-nan."

Kubilai sat pensive, though the blaze in his eyes did not abate, and after a while he growled to himself, "Vakh! Who can tell the damnable slant-eyes apart? And they are all equally perfidious."

I thought I had better say, "That is the only information I have, Sire, and I accuse the Minister Pao of nothing. I have no evidence that

he has spied for the Yi, or even been in communication with them in
any way."

"Sufficient is it that he misrepresented himself. You have done well,
Marco Polo. I will call Pao in for questioning, and I may later have reason to speak to you again."

When I left the Khakhan's suite, I found a palace steward waiting
for me in the corridor, with a message that the Chief Minister Achmad
would have me call upon him that moment. I went to his chambers, not
gleefully, thinking: How could he have heard already?

The Arab received me in a room decorated with a single massive
piece of—I suppose it would be called a sculpture made by nature. It
was a great rock, twice as tall as a man and four times as big around, a
tremendous piece of solidified lava that looked like petrified flames, all
gray twists and convolutions and holes and little tunnels. Somewhere in
the base of it a bowl of incense smoldered, and the perfumed blue smoke
rose and coiled through the sculpture's sinuosities and seeped out from
some apertures and in through others, so that the whole thing seemed to
writhe in a slow, ceaseless torment.

"You disobeyed and defied me," Achmad said immediately, with no
greeting or other preliminary. "You kept listening until you heard something damaging to a high minister of this court."

I said, "It was a piece of news that came to me before I could
withdraw the ear." I offered no further apology or extenuation, but
boldly added, "I thought it had come only to me."

"What is spoken on the road is heard in the grass," he said indifferently. "An old Han proverb."

Still boldly, I said, "It requires a listener in the grass. All this time, I
had assumed that my maidservants were reporting my doings to the
Khan Kubilai or the Prince Chingkim, and I accepted that as reasonable.
But all this time they have been your spies, have they not?"

I do not know whether he would have bothered to lie and deny it,
or would even have bothered to confirm the fact, for at that moment
came a slight interruption. From an adjoining room, a woman started in
through the curtained doorway, and then, perceiving that Achmad had
company, abruptly swished back through them again. All I saw of her
was that she was a strikingly large woman, and elegantly garbed. From
her behavior, it was evident that she did not wish to be seen by me, so I
supposed that she was somebody else's wife or concubine engaging in an
illicit adventure. But I could not recall ever having seen such a tall and
robust woman anywhere about the palace. I reflected that the painter,
Master Chao, in speaking of the Arab's depraved tastes, had not said
anything about the objects of his tastes. Did the Wali Achmad have a
special liking for women who were larger than most men? I did not
inquire, and he paid no attention to the interruption, but said:

"The steward found you at the Khakhan's chambers, so I take it that
you have already imparted to him your information."

"Yes, Wali, I have. Kubilai is summoning the Minister Pao to interrogate him."

"A fruitless summons," said the Arab. "It seems that the Minister has made a hasty departure, destination unknown. Lest you be so brash as to accuse me of having connived in his flight, let me suggest that Fao probably recognized the same visitors from the southland who recognized him, and whose indiscreet gossip your ear overheard."

I said, and truthfully, "I am not brash to the extreme of being suicidal, Wali Achmad. I would accuse you of nothing. I will only mention that the Khakhan seemed gratified to have the information I brought him. So, if you deem that a disobedience to you, and punish me for it, I imagine Kubilai will wonder why."

"Impertinent piglet of a sow mother! Are you daring me to punish you, with a threat of the Khakhan's displeasure?"

I made no reply to that. His black agate eyes got even stonier, and he went on:

"Get this clear in your mind, Folo. My fortunes are dependent on the Khanate of which I am Chief Minister and Vice-Regent. I would be not only traitorous—I would be imbecilic—if I did anything to undermine the Khanate. I am as eager as Kubilai that we take Yun-nan, and then the Sung Empire, and then all the rest of the world as well, if we can do so and if Allah wills it so. I do not berate you for having discovered, before I did, that the Khanate's interests may have been imperiled by that Yi impostor. But get this also clear in your mind. *I am the Chief Minister.* I will not tolerate disobedience or disloyalty or defiance from my inferiors. Especially not from a younger man who is an inexperienced outsider in these parts and a despicable Christian and a rank newcomer to this court and, for all that, an impudent upstart of overweening ambition."

I started angrily to say, "I am no more an outsider here than—" but he imperiously raised his hand.

"I will not utterly demolish you for this instance of disobedience, since it was not to my disservice. But I promise that you will regret it, Folo, sufficiently that you will not be inclined to repeat it. Earlier, I only *told* you what Hell is. It seems you require a demonstration." Then, perhaps reflecting that his lady visitor might be within hearing, he lowered his voice. "In my own good time, I will provide that demonstration. Go now. And go well away from me."

I went, but not too far, in case I should be wanted again by the Khakhan. I went outdoors and through the palace gardens and up the Kara Hill to the Echo Pavilion, to let the clear breezes of the heights blow through my cluttered mind. I strolled around the promenade within the mosaic wall, mentally sorting among all the numerous things I had recently been given or had taken upon myself to worry about: Yun-nan and the Yi, Nostril and his lady lost and found, the twins Buyantu and Biliktu, now revealed as more than sisters to each other and less than faithful to me. . . .

Then, as if I had not enough to concern me, I was suddenly given a new thing. A voice whispered in my ear, in the Mongol tongue, "Do not turn. Do not move. Do not look."

I froze where I was, expecting next to feel a stabbing point or a slashing blade. But there came only the voice again:

"Tremble, Ferenghi. Dread the coming of what you have deserved. But not now, for the waiting and the dread and the not knowing are part of it."

By then, I had realized that the voice was not really at my ear. I turned and looked all about me, and I saw no one, and I said sharply, "What have I deserved? What do you want of me?"

"Only expect me," whispered the voice.

"Who? And when?"

The voice whispered just seven more words—seven short and simple words, but words freighted with a menace more chilling than the most fearsome threat—and it never spoke again afterward. It said only and flatly and finally:

"Expect me when you least expect me."

· 13 ·

I waited for more, and, when I heard no more, I asked another question or two, and got no answer. So I ran around the terrace to my right, and got to the Moon Gate in the wall without having seen anyone, so I continued to run all the way around the Echo Pavilion, back to the Moon Gate again, and still had seen no one. There was only that one entranceway in the wall, so I stood in it and looked down the Kara Hill. There were several lords and ladies also taking the air that day, strolling about in ones and twos on lower levels of the hill. Any one of them could have been the person who had invisibly accosted me—could have run that far, then slowed to a walk. Or the whisperer could have run another way. The flagstone pathway from the Moon Gate descended only a short distance before forking in two, and one of the paths circled around behind the pavilion to descend the back slope of the hill. Or the whisperer could still be right inside the wall with me, and could easily keep the pavilion between us, no matter how speedily I ran or how stealthily I prowled around the promenade. It was useless to search, so I simply stood there in the entranceway and pondered.

The voice could have been that of either a man or a woman, and of any of several people who had lately had cause to wish me hurt. Just since this hour yesterday, I had been told by three people that I would "regret" some action of mine: the icy Achmad, the irate Buyantu and the outraged Lady Chao. I could also assume that the fugitive Minister Pao was not now any friend of mine, and might still be within the palace confines. And, if I were to count all the palace people whom I had alienated since coming here, I would have to include Master Ping, the Fondler. All of those persons spoke Mongol, as had the whisperer.

There were even other possibilities. The immense lady lurking in Achmad's chambers might think that I had recognized her, and resent me for it. Or the Lady Chao could have told her lord husband some lie about my visit to her, and he might now be as angry at me as she was. I had repeated nasty gossip about the eunuch Court Astrologer, and eunuchs were notoriously vindictive. For that matter, I had once remarked to Kubilai that I thought most of his ministers were misemployed, and that word could have got back to them, and every single one of them might be mortally peeved at me.

I was casting my gaze back and forth over the curly-eaved roofs of the many palace edifices, as if trying to see through their yellow tiles to identify my accoster, when I saw a vast cloud of smoke erupt abruptly from the main building. The smoke was too much to have come from a brazier or a kitchen hearth, and was too sudden to have come from a room caught fire or anything of that sort. The black cloud seemed to *boil* as it billowed, and it appeared to have fragments of the building and the roof mixed into it. A fraction of an instant later, the sound of it reached me—a thunderclap so loud and slapping that it actually stirred my hair and the loose folds of my robes. I saw the other few persons on the hill also wince at the sound, and turn to look, and then we were all running down the slope toward the scene.

I did not have to get very close before I recognized that the eruption had come from my own chambers. In fact, the main room of my suite had burst its walls and roof, and was now laid open to the sky and the view of the gathering crowd, and what few of its contents had not disintegrated outright were now burning. The black cloud of the initial blast, still quite intact and still writhing in its slow boil, was now drifting out over the city, but the lesser smoke from the room's burning was yet dense enough to keep most of the onlookers at a respectful distance. Only a number of palace servants were scuttling in and out of the smoke, carrying buckets of water and dashing them into the burning remains. One of them dropped his bucket when he saw me, and came running—tottering, rather—to meet me. He was so blackened by smoke and singed of garments that it was a moment before I recognized Nostril.

"Oh, master, come no closer! It is a frightful destruction!"

"What happened?" I asked, though I had already guessed.

"I do not know, master. I was asleep in my closet when all of a sudden—bismillah!—I found myself awake and floundering here on the grass of this garden court, my clothes all a-smolder, and shards of broken furniture falling all about me."

"The girls!" I said urgently. "What of the girls?"

"Mashallah, master, they are dead, and in a most horrible manner. If this was not the doing of a vengeful jinni, it was the attack of a fire-breathing dragon."

"I think not," I said miserably.

"Then it must have been a rukh, insanely tearing with its beak and talons, for the girls are not just dead—they no longer exist, not as separate girls. They are nothing but a spatter on the remaining walls. Bits of flesh and blobs of gore. Twins they were in life, and twinned they have gone into death. They will be inseparable forever, since no funeral practitioner could possibly sort out the fragments and say which were of whom."

"Bruto barabào," I breathed, appalled. "But it was not any rukh or jinni or dragon. Alas, it was *I* who did this."

"And to think, master, you once told me that you could never kill a woman."

"Unfeeling slave!" I cried. "I did not do it deliberately!"

"Ah, well, you are young yet. Meanwhile, let us be thankful that those two did not keep any pet dog or cat or ape, to be intermingled also with them in the afterlife."

I swallowed sickly. Whether this was my fault or God's doing, it was a terrible loss of two lovely young women. But I had to reflect that, in a very real sense, to me they had been lost already. One or both of them had been betraying me to the inimical Achmad, and I had entertained suspicion of Buyantu as the secret whisperer at the Echo Pavilion. Whoever that was, though, it evidently had not been she. But just then I jumped, as another voice spoke in my ear:

"Lamentable mamzar, what have you done?"

I turned. It was the Court Firemaster, who no doubt had come at a run because he had known the distinctive noise of his own product.

"I was trying an experiment in al-kimia, Master Shi," I said, contrite. "The girls were instructed to keep the fire very low, but they must have—"

"I told you," he said through his teeth. "The flaming powder is not a thing to play with."

"No one can tell Marco Polo anything," said Prince Chingkim, who, as Wang of Khanbalik, had come apparently to see what havoc had been visited upon his city. He added drily, "Marco Polo must be shown."

"I would rather not have been shown this," I mumbled.

"Then do not look, master," said Nostril. "For here come the Court Funeralmaster and his assistants, to gather the mortal remains."

The fire had been damped down, by now, to wisps of smoke and occasional little sizzles of steam. The spectators and the water-carrying servants all went away, for people naturally disliked to linger in the vicinity of the funeral preparers. I remained, out of respect for the departed, and so did Nostril, to keep me company, and so did Chingkim, in his capacity as Wang, to see that all was properly concluded, and so did the Master Shi, out of a professional desire to examine the wreckage and make notes for future reference in his work.

The purple-garbed Funeralmaster and his purple-garbed men, although they must have been accustomed to seeing death in many forms, clearly found this job distasteful. They took a look about, then went away, to return with some black leather containers and wooden spatulas and cloth mops. With those objects, and with expressions of revulsion, they went through my rooms and the garden area outside, scraping and swabbing and depositing the results in the containers. When finally they were done, we other four went in and examined the ruins, but only cursorily, for the smell was dreadful. It was a stink compounded of smoke, char, cooked meat and—though it is ungallant to say of the beautiful young departed—the stench of excrement, for I had given the girls no opportunity that morning to make their toilet.

"To have done all this damage," said the Firemaster, as we were glumly poking about in the main room, "the huo-yao must have been tightly confined at the moment it ignited."

"It was in a securely lidded stoneware pot, Master Shi," I said. "I would have thought no spark could have got near it."

"The pot itself only had to get hot enough," he said, with a glower at me. "And a stoneware pot? More explosive potential than an Indian nut or a heavy zhu-gan cane. And if the women were huddled over it at the time . . ."

I moved away from him, not wanting to hear any more about the poor girls. In a corner, to my surprise, I found one undestroyed thing in that destroyed room. It was only a porcelain vase, but it was entire, unbroken, except for some chips lost from its rim. When I looked into it, I saw why it had survived. It was the vase into which I had poured the first measure of huo-yao, and then poured in water. The powder had dried to a solid cake that nearly filled the vase, and so had made it impervious to damage.

"Look at this, Master Shi," I said, taking it to show to him. "The huo-yao can be a preservative as well as a destroyer."

"So you first tried wetting it," he said, looking into the vase. "I could have told you that it would dry solid and useless like that. As a matter of fact, I believe I *did* tell you. Ayn davàr, but the Prince is right. You cannot be told anything by anybody. . . ."

I had stopped listening, and went away from him again, for a dim recollection was stirring in my mind. I took the vase out into the garden, and pried up a stone from a whitewashed ring of them around a flower bed, and used it for a hammer to shatter the porcelain. When all the fragments fell away, I had a heavy, gray, vase-shaped lump of the solid-caked powder. I regarded it, and the dim memory came clearer in my mind. What I remembered was the making of that foodstuff the Mongols called grut. I remembered how the Mongol women of the plains would spread milk curd in the sun, and let that dry to a hard cake, then crumble it into pellets of grut, which would keep indefinitely without spoiling, until someone wished to make an emergency meal of it. I took up my stone again, and hammered on the lump of huo-yao until a few pellets, the size and appearance of mouse droppings, crumbled off from it. I regarded them, then went once again to the Firemaster and said diffidently:

"Master Shi, would you look at these and tell me if I am wrong—"

"Probably," he said, with a contemptuous snort. "They are mouse turds."

"They are pellets broken from that lump of huo-yao. It appears to me that these pellets hold in firm suspension the correct proportions of the three separate powders. And, being now dry, they should ignite just as if—"

"Yom mekhayeh!" he exclaimed huskily, in what I took to be the Ivrit language. Very, very slowly and tenderly, he picked the pellets from my palm, and held them in his, and bent to peer closely at them, and again huskily exclaimed, in what I recognized as Han, several other words like "hao-jia-huo," which is an expression of amazement, and "jiao-hao," which is an expression of delight, and "chan-juan," which is a term usually employed to praise a beautiful woman.

He suddenly began dashing about the ruined room, until he found a splinter of wood still smoldering. He blew that into a glow, and ran out into the garden. Chingkim and I followed him, the Prince saying, "What now?" and "Not again!" as the Firemaster touched the ember to the pellets and they went off with a bright flare and fizz, just as if they had been in their original finely powdered form.

"Yom mekhayeh!" Master Shi breathed once more, and then turned to me and, wide-eyed, murmured, "Bar mazel!" and then turned to Prince Chingkim and said in Han, "Mu bu jian jie."

"An old proverb," Chingkim told me. "The eye cannot see its own lashes. I gather that you have discovered something new about the flaming powder that is new even to the experienced Firemaster."

"It was just an idea that came to me," I said modestly.

Master Shi stood looking at me, still saucer-eyed, and shaking his head, and muttering words like "khakhem" and "khalutz." Then again he addressed Chingkim:

"My Prince, I do not know if you were contemplating a prosecution of this incautious Ferenghi for the damage and casualties he has caused. But the Mishna tells us that a thinking bastard, even, is more highly to be regarded than a high priest who preaches by rote. I suggest that this one has accomplished something worth more than any number of women servants and bits of palace."

"I do not know what the Mishna is, Master Shi," grumbled the Prince, "but I will convey your sentiments to my Royal Father." He turned to me. "I will convey you, too, Marco. He had already sent me looking for you when I heard the thunder of your—accomplishment. I am glad I do not have to carry you to him in a spoon. Come along."

"Marco," said the Khakhan without preamble, "I must send a messenger to the Orlok Bayan in Yun-nan, to apprise him of the latest developments here, and I think you have earned the honor of being that messenger. A missive is now being written for you to take to him. It explains about the Minister Pao and suggests some measures that Bayan may take, now that the Yi are deprived of their secret ally in our midst. Give Bayan my letter, then attend upon him until the war is won, and then you will have the honor of bringing me the word that Yun-nan at last is ours."

"You are sending me to war, Sire?" I said, not quite sure that I was eager to go. "I have had no experience of war."

"Then you should have. Every man should engage in at least one war in his lifetime—else how can he say that he has savored all the experiences which life offers a man?"

"I was not thinking of life, Sire, so much as death." And I laughed, but not with much merriment.

"Every man dies," Kubilai said, rather stiffly. "Some deaths are at least less ignominious than others. Would you prefer to die like a clerk, dwindling and wilting into the boneyard of a secured old age?"

"I am not afraid, Sire. But what if the war drags on for a long time? Or never *is* won?"

Even more stiffly, he said, "It is better to fight in a losing cause than to have to confess to your grandchildren that you never fought at all. Vakh!"

Prince Chingkim spoke up. "I can assure you, Royal Father, that this Marco Polo would never dodge any confrontation imaginable. He is, however, at the moment a trifle shaken by a recent calamity." He went on to tell Kubilai about the accidental—he stressed accidental—devastation of my ménage.

"Ah, so you are bereft of women servants and the services of women," the Khakhan said sympathetically. "Well, you will be traveling too rapidly on the road to Yun-nan to have need of servants, and you will be too fatigued each night to yearn for anything more than sleep. When you get there, of course, you will do your share of the pillage and rape. Take slaves to serve you, take women to service you. Behave like a Mongol born."

"Yes, Sire," I said submissively.

He leaned back and sighed, as if he missed the good old days, and murmured in reminiscence·

"My esteemed grandfather Chinghiz, it is said, was born clutching a clot of blood in his tiny fist, from which the shamàn foretold for him a sanguinary career. He lived up to the prophecy. And I can still remember him telling us, his grandsons, 'Boys, a man can have no greater pleasure than to slay his enemies, and then, besmeared and reeking with their blood, to rape their chaste wives and virgin daughters. There is no more delightful sensation than to spurt your jing-ye into a woman or a girl-child who is weeping and struggling and loathing you and cursing you.' So spake Chinghiz Khan, the Immortal of Mongols."

"I will bear it in mind, Sire."

He sat forward again and said, "No doubt you have arrangements to make before your departure. But make them as expeditiously as possible. I have already sent advance riders to ready your route. If, on your way along it, you can sketch for me maps of that route—as you and your uncles did of the Silk Road—I shall be grateful and your reward will be handsome. Also, if in your travels you should catch up to the fugitive Minister Pao, I give you leave to slay him, and your reward for that would also be handsome. Now go and prepare for the journey. I will have fast horses and a trustworthy escort ready when you are."

Well, I thought, as I went to my chambers, this would at least put me out of reach of my court adversaries—the Wali Achmad, the Lady Chao, the Fondler Ping, whoever else that whisperer might have been. Better to fall in open warfare than to someone sneaking up behind me.

The Court Architect was in my suite, making measurements and muttering to himself and snapping orders to a team of workmen, who were commencing the replacement of the vanished walls and roof. Happily, I had kept most of my personal possessions and valuables in my bedroom, which had been unravaged. Nostril was in there, burning incense to clear the air. I bade him lay out a traveling wardrobe for me and to make a light pack of other necessities. Then I gathered up all the journal notes I had written and accumulated since leaving Venice, and carried them to my father's chambers.

He looked a little surprised when I dropped the pile on a table beside him, for it was an unprepossessing mound of smudged and wrinkled and mildewed papers of all different sizes.

"I would be obliged, Father, if you would send these to Uncle Marco, the next time you entrust some shipment of goods to the Silk Road horse post, and ask him to send them on to Venice for safekeeping by Marègna Fiordelisa. The notes may be of interest to some future cosmographer, if he can decipher them and arrange them in order. I had intended to do that myself—someday—but I am bidden to a mission from which I may not return."

"Indeed? What mission?"

I told him, and with dramatic somberness, so I was taken aback when he said, "I envy you, doing something I have never done. You should appreciate the opportunity Kubilai is giving you. Da novèlo tuto xe belo. Not many white men have watched the Mongols make war— and lived to remember it."

"I only hope I do," I said. "But survival is not my sole consideration. There are other things I had rather be doing. And I am sure that there are more profitable things I could be doing."

"Now, now, Marco. To a good hunger there is no bad bread."

"Are you suggesting, Father, that I should *enjoy* wasting my time in a war?"

He said reprovingly, "It is true that you were trained for trade, and you come from a merchant lineage. But you must not look at everything with a tradesman's eye, always asking yourself, 'What is this good for? What is this worth?' Leave that grubby philosophy to the tradesmen who never step beyond their shop doors. You have ventured out to the farthest edge of the world. It would be a pity if you take home only profit, and not at least a little of poetry."

"That reminds me," I said. "I turned a profit yesterday. May I borrow one of your maidservants for an errand?"

I sent her to fetch from the slave quarters the Turki woman called Mar-Janah, formerly the possession of the Lady Chao Ku-an.

"Mar-Janah?" my father repeated, as the servant departed. "And a Turki . . . ?"

"Yes, you know of her," I said. "We have spoken of her before." And I told him the whole story, of which he had so long ago heard only a part of the beginning.

"What a wondrously intricate web!" he exclaimed. "And to have been at last unraveled! God does not always pay His debts just on Sundays." Then, as I had done on first seeing her, he widened his eyes when the lovely woman came smiling into the chamber, and I introduced him to her.

"My Mistress Chao did not seem pleased about it," she said shyly to me, "but she tells me that I am now your property, Master Marco."

"Only briefly," I said, taking the paper of title from my purse and holding it out to her. "You are your own property again, as you should be, and I will hear you call no one Master any more."

With a tremulous hand she accepted the paper, and with her other hand she brushed tears from her long eyelashes, and she seemed to have trouble finding words to speak.

"Now," I went on, "I doubt not that the Princess Mar-Janah of Cappadocia could take her pick of men from this court or any other. But, if Your Highness still has her heart set on Nost—on Ali Babar, he awaits you in my chambers down the hall."

She started to kneel in ko-tou, but I caught her hands, raised her, turned her to the door, said, "Go to him," and she went.

My father approvingly followed her with his gaze, then asked me, "You will not wish to take Nostril with you to Yun-nan?"

"No. He has waited twenty years or more for that woman. Let them be married as soon as can be. Will you tend to those arrangements, Father?"

"Yes. And I will give Nostril his own certificate of title as a wedding present. I mean Ali Babar. I suppose we ought to accustom ourselves to addressing him more respectfully, now that he will be a freeman and consort to a princess."

"Before he is entirely free, I had better go and make sure he has packed for me properly. So I will say goodbye now, Father, in case I do not see you or Uncle Mafio before I leave."

"Goodbye, Marco, and let me take back what I said before. I was wrong. You may *never* make a proper tradesman. You just now gave away a valuable slave for no payment at all."

"But, Father, I got her free of payment."

"What better way to turn a clear profit? Yet you did not. You did not even set her free with fanfare and fine words and noble gesticulations, letting her kiss and slobber over your hands, while a numerous audience applauded your liberality and a palace scribe recorded the scene for posterity."

Mistaking the tenor of his words, I said in some exasperation, "To quote one of your own adages, Father: one minute you are lighting torches and the next you are counting candle wicks."

"It is poor business to give things away, and worse business to get not even praise for doing so. Clearly you know the value of nothing— except perhaps a human being or two. I despair of you as a tradesman. I have hope of you as a poet. Goodbye, Marco, my son, and come back safe."

I got to see Mar-Janah one more time. The next morning, she and Nostril-now-Ali came to wish me "salaam aleikum" before my departure, and to thank me again for having helped to bring them together. They had risen early, to make sure of catching me—and evidently had got up from a shared bed, for they were disheveled and sleepy-eyed. But they were also smiling and blithesome, and, when they tried to describe to me their rapturous reunion, they were quite rapturously and absurdly inarticulate.

He began, "It was almost as if—"

"No, it *was* as if—" said she.

"Yes, it was *indeed* as if—" he said. "All the twenty years since we last knew each other—it was as if they, well—".

"Come, come," I said, laughing at the foolish locutions. "Neither of you used to be such an inept teller of tales."

Mar-Janah laughed too, and finally said what was meant: "The twenty intervening years might never have been."

"She still thinks me handsome!" exclaimed Nostril. "And she is more beautiful than ever!"

"We are as giddy as two youngsters in first love," she said.

"I am happy for you," I said. Though they were both perhaps forty-five years old, and though I still could not help feeling that a love affair between persons nearly old enough to be my parents was a quaint and risible thing, I added, "I wish you joy forever, young lovers."

I went then to call on the Khakhan, to collect his letter for the Orlok Bayan—and found that he already had visitors: the Court Firemaster, whom I had seen only the day before, the Court Astronomer and the Court Goldsmith, whom I had not seen for quite some time. They all three looked curiously bloodshot, but their red eyes gleamed with something like excitement.

Kubilai said, "These gentlemen courtiers wish you to carry to Yunnan something of theirs also."

"We have been up all night, Marco," said the Firemaster Shi. "Now that you have devised a way to make the flaming powder transportable, we are eager to see it employed in combat. I have spent the night wetting quantities of it and drying it into cakes and then pulverizing it into pellets."

"Et voilà, I have been making new containers for it," said the Goldsmith Boucher, displaying a shiny brass ball, about the size of his head. "Master Shi told us how you destroyed half the palace with just a stoneware pot."

"It was not half the palace," I protested. "It was only—"

"Qu'importe?" he said impatiently. "If a mere lidded pot could do that, we reckoned that an even stouter confinement of the powder should make it trebly powerful. We decided on brass."

"And I worked out, by comparison with the planetary orbs," said the Astronomer Jamal-ud-Din, "that a globular container would be best. It can be most accurately and farthest thrown by hand or by catapult, or can even be rolled among the enemy, and its shape—inshallah!—will most effectually disperse its destructive forces in all directions."

"So I made balls like this, in sections of two hemispheres," said Master Boucher. "Master Shi filled them with the powder pellets, and then I brazed them together. Nothing but their internal force will ever break them apart. But when it does—les diables sont déchaînés!"

"You and the Orlok Bayan," said Master Shi, "will be the first to put the huo-yao to practical use in field warfare. We made a dozen of the balls. Take them with you and let Bayan use them as he will, and they ought to work without fail."

"So it sounds," I said. "But how do the warriors ignite them?"

"You see this string like a wick sticking out? It was inserted before the halves were brazed together. It is actually of cotton twisted around a core of the huo-yao itself. Only touch a spark to it—a smoldering stick of incense will serve—and it will give a long count of ten before the spark reaches the charge inside."

"Then they cannot discharge accidentally? I am disinclined to devastate some innocent karwansarai before I even get there."

"No fear," said Master Shi. "Just please do not let any women play with them." He added drily, "It is not for nothing that my people's morning thanksgiving prayer contains the words 'Blessed art Thou, O Lord our God, Who hath not made me a woman.'"

"Is that a fact?" said the Master Jamal, sounding interested. "Our Quran says likewise, in the fourth sura: 'Men are superior to women on account of the qualities with which Allah has gifted the one above the other.'"

I decided the old men must be lightheaded from lack of sleep, to be starting a discussion of the demerits of women, so I cut it short by saying, "I will gladly take the things, then, if the Khan Kubilai is in favor."

The Khakhan made a gesture of assent, and the three courtiers hurried off to load the dozen balls onto my train's pack horses. When they had gone, Kubilai said to me:

"Here is the letter to Bayan, sealed and chained for carrying safely about your neck, under your clothes. Here also is my yellow-paper letter of authority, as you have seen your uncles carry. But you should not often have to show it, for I am giving you also this more visible pai-tzu. You have only to wear it on your chest or hung on your saddle, and at sight of it anyone in this realm will do you ko-tou and accord you every hospitality and service."

The pai-tzu was a tablet or plaque, as broad as my hand and nearly as long as my forearm, made of ivory with an inset silver ring for hanging it by, and inlaid gold lettering, in the Mongol alphabet, instructing all men to welcome and obey me, under pain of the Khakhan's displeasure.

"Also," Kubilai went on, "since you may have to sign vouchers of expenses, or messages, or other documents, I had the Court Yinmaster engrave this personal yin for you."

It was a small block of smooth stone, a soft gray in color with blood-red veinings through it, about an inch square and a finger-length long, rounded at one end for comfortable holding in the hand. The squared-off front end of it was intricately incised, and Kubilai showed me how to stamp that end on an inked pad of cloth and then onto any paper that required my signature. I never would have recognized the imprint it made—as *being* my signature, I mean—but it looked nicely impressive, and I commented admiringly on the fineness of the work.

"It is a good yin, and it will last forever," said the Khakhan. "I had the Yinmaster Liu Shen-dao make it of the marble which the Han call chicken-blood stone. As to the fineness of the engraving, that Master Liu is so expert that he can inscribe an entire prayer on a single human hair."

And so I left Khanbalik for Yun-nan, carrying, besides my own pack and clothes and other necessities, the twelve brass balls of flaming powder, the sealed letter to the Orlok Bayan, my own letter of authority and the confirming pai-tzu plaque—and my very own personal yin, with which I could leave my name stamped, if I chose, all across Kithai. This is what my name looks like, in the Han characters, for I still have the little stone yin:

I was not sure, when I set out to war, how long I would last. But, as the Khan Kubilai had said, my yin could last forever, and so might my name.

TO-BHOT

.I.

I T was a long journey from Khanbalik to the Orlok Bayan's site of operations, nearly as many li as from Khanbalik to Kashgar, but my two escorts and I rode light and fast. We carried only essential traveling gear—no food or cookware or bedding—and the heaviest items, the powder-charged brass balls, were divided among our three extra horses. Those were also fleet steeds, not the usual trudging pack animals, so all six horses were capable of proceeding at the Mongols' war-march pace of canter and walk and canter. Whenever any horse began to show signs of wearying, we had only to pause at the nearest of the Road Minister's horse posts and demand six fresh ones.

I had not known what Kubilai had meant when he said that he had already sent advance riders to "ready the route." But I learned that that was an arrangement made whenever the Khakhan or any of his impor-tant emissaries made a long cross-country journey. Those riders went ahead to announce the journeyer's imminent approach, and every Wang of every province, every prefect of every prefecture, even the elders of every least village, were expected to prepare for the passing-through. So there were always comfortable beds waiting in the best possible accommodations, good cooks waiting to prepare the best available fare, even new wells dug if necessary to supply sweet water in arid regions. That is why we were enabled to carry only the lightest of packs. Every night, too, there were women supplied for our enjoyment, but, as Kubilai had also said, I was too fatigued and saddle sore to make use of them. Instead, I spent each night's short interval between table and bed in scribbling down on paper what details and landmarks I had noticed during that day's travel.

We rode in a southwestering arc from Khanbalik, and I cannot remember how many villages, towns and cities we passed through or spent a night in, but only two of them were of estimable size. One was Xian, which the War Minister Chao had pointed out to me on his great map and told me had once been the capital city of the First Emperor of these lands. Xian had dwindled considerably in the centuries since, and, though still a busy and prosperous crossroads city, possessed none of the finery of an imperial capital. The other big city was Cheng-du—in what was called the Red Basin country, because the earth there is not yellow, as in most of the rest of Kithai. Cheng-du was the capital city of the province called Si-chuan, and its Wang inhabited a palace city-within-a-city almost as grand as that of Khanbalik. The Wang Mangalai, another of Kubilai's sons, would gladly have had me stay a long time as his honored guest, and I was much tempted to rest there for a least a while. But, mindful of my mission, I made my excuses, and of course Mangalai accepted them, and I spent only a single night in his company.

From Cheng-du, my escorts and I turned directly west—into the mountainous border country where the Kithai province of Si-chuan and the Sung province of Yun-nan and the land of To-Bhot all mingled together—and our pace slowed as we began a long climb that soon became a steep climb. The mountains were not so sky-reaching as, for instance, the Pai-Mir of High Tartary. These had much more forest growth on them and no snow, and even in deep winter, I was told, the snow never clung to them for long, except on their very tops. But these mountains, if less high than others I had seen, were much more vertical in their general configuration. Except for the wooded slopes, they were mostly monstrous slabs set on end, separated by narrow, deep, dark ravines. But at least they were solid mountains; we did not have to dodge any avalanches, and I did not ever hear any of them booming roundabout. The country was called by its inhabitants the Land of the Four Rivers, those four streams being locally named the N'mai, the Nu, the Lan-kang and the Jin-sha. But those waters, said the natives, broadened and deepened as they flowed out of the mountains, to become the four greatest rivers of that part of the world, better known by their downstream names of Irawadi, Sal-win, Me-kong and Yang-tze. The first three of those, when they got beyond Yun-nan Province, ran southward or southeastward into the tropical lands called Champa. The fourth would become that Yang-tze of which I have earlier spoken—the Tremendous River—which runs eastward clear to the Sea of Kithai.

But I and my escorts were crossing those rivers far upstream of where they became only four—in the highlands where the rivers began

as a multitude of tributary streams. There were so many that they did
not all have names, but none was contemptible on that account. Every
single stream was a rushing white water which, through the ages, had
worn its own individual channel through the mountains, and every single
channel was a slab-sided gorge that might have been cleft by the downward slash of some jinni's giant shimshir sword. The only way along and
across those precipitous gashes in the mountains was by way of what the
local people proudly called their Pillar Road.

Calling it a road at all was a considerable exaggeration, but it did
stand on pillars—or, more accurately, corbels—logs driven and wedged
into cracks and crannies in the cliffsides, and planks laid across them,
and layers of earth and straw piled on. It could better have been called
the Shelf Road. Or even better, the Blind Road, because I traveled most
of it with my eyes shut, trusting in the surefootedness and imperturbability of my horse, and hoping it was shod with the never-slip shoes made
of the "Marco's sheep" horn. To open my eyes and look up, down, ahead,
behind or sideways made me equally giddy. Glancing upward or downward gave much the same sight: two walls of gray rock converging with
distance to a narrow, bright, green-edged crack—up there the sky between two fringes of trees, down yonder the water that looked like a
moss-lined brook, but was really a rushing river between two belts of
forest. Ahead or behind was the vertiginous view of the Pillar Road shelf
that looked too fragile to bear its own weight, never mind a horse and
rider, or a train of them. Looking to one side, I would see the cliff that
brushed my stirrup and seemed to threaten to give me a sudden shove.
Looking the other way, I would see the farther cliff, which appeared to
stand so close that I was tempted to reach out and touch it—and to lean
was to risk toppling from my saddle and falling forever.

The only thing more dizzying than following the Pillar Road along
the cliffsides was the crossing from one side of a gorge to the other, on
what the mountain folk, without exaggeration, called the Limp Bridges.
Those were made of planks and thick ropes of twisted cane strips, and
they swayed in the winds that blew ceaselessly through the mountains,
and they swayed worse when a man stepped out onto them, and they
swayed even worse when he led his horse out behind him, and during
those crossings I think even the horses shut their eyes.

Though Kubilai's advance riders had made sure that all the mountain inhabitants expected the arrival of me and my escorts, and we got
the best hospitality those people could give us, it was not exactly of royal
quality. Only occasionally did we come to a place in the mountains flat
and habitable enough to support even a meager village of woodcutters'
huts. More often we spent the night in a cliff niche where the road was
built wide enough for travelers going in opposite directions to edge past
each other. At those places there was a group of rough men stationed,
waiting to receive us, having erected a yak-hair tent for us to sleep in,
and having brought some meat or killed a mountain sheep or goat to
cook for us over an open camp fire.

I well remember the first time we stopped in such a place, when the
day was just darkening to dusk. The three mountain men awaiting us

made salutations and ko-tou and—since we could not converse; they knew no Mongol, and spoke some tongue which was not even Han—they immediately set about making our evening meal. They built up a good fire, and spitted some cutlets of musk deer over it, and hung a pot of water to heat. I noticed that the men had made the fire of wooden branches—which must have required much labor of clambering up and down the steep ravine sides to collect—but also had a small pile of pieces of zhu-gan cane lying beside it. The dusk had deepened to full darkness by the time the food was ready, and, while two of the men served us, the other tossed one of those bits of cane onto the fire.

The deer meat was better than the usual mountain fare of mutton or goat, but the accompaniments were ghastly. The meat was handed to me in a hunk, for me to hold while I tore at it with my teeth. The only implement provided me was a shallow wooden bowl, into which one of the servers poured hot green cha. But I had taken only a couple of sips before the other server politely took it from me, to add to it. He held a platter of yak butter, all stuck about with hairs and lint and road dust, and grooved by the fingers of those who had dug at it previously, and with his own black fingernails raked off a lump and dropped it into my cha to melt. The dirty yak butter would have been repellent enough, but then he opened a filthy cloth sack and poured into the cha bowl something that looked like sawdust.

"Tsampa," he said.

When I only peered at the mess with disgust and bewilderment, he demonstrated what was to be done with it. He stuck his grimy fingers into my bowl and worked the sawdust and butter together until it became a paste, then a doughy lump when it had absorbed all the cha in the bowl. Then, before I could move to prevent it, he pinched off a wad of that tepid, dirty dough and poked it into my mouth.

"Tsampa," he said again, and chewed and swallowed as if to show me how.

I could now taste—apart from the bitter green cha and the rancid, cheesy yak butter—that the apparent sawdust was really barley meal. But I do not know if I would voluntarily have swallowed the wad, except that I was abruptly startled into doing so. The camp fire gave a sudden, tremendous *bang!* and threw up a constellation of sparks into the darkness—and I gulped my tsampa and leaped to my feet, and so did my two escorts, while the noise echoed and reechoed from all the mountains around. Two things went through my mind in that instant. One was the dreadful thought that one of the charged brass balls had somehow fallen into the fire. The other was a recollection of words once heard: "Expect me when you least expect me."

But the mountain men were laughing at our surprise, and making gestures to calm us and explain what had happened. They held up one of the pieces of zhu-gan cane and pointed to the fire and jumped about and bared their teeth and growled. They made it clear enough. The mountains were full of tigers and wolves. To keep them off, it was their practice to toss into the camp fire every so often a joint of zhu-gan. The heat evidently made its inner juices seethe until the steam burst the cane apart—quite like a charge of the flaming powder—with that enormous noise. I had no doubt that it would keep predators at bay; it had made me swallow the awful stuff called tsampa.

Later on, I got so I could eat tsampa, never with enjoyment, but at least without violent repugnance. A man's body requires other nourishment than meat and cha, and barley was the only domestic vegetable grown in those highlands. Tsampa was cheap and easily transportable and sustaining, if nothing else, and could be made a trifle more appetizing by the addition of sugar or salt or vinegar or the fermented bean sauce. I never got as fond of it as were the natives, who, after making the dough at mealtime, would tuck balls of the stuff inside their clothes and *wear* the tsampa all night and next day, so it got salted by their sweat, and they would pluck out a bit whenever they felt like having a snack.

I also got better acquainted with the zhu-gan cane. In Khanbalik, I had known it only as a graceful floral subject for painters like the Lady Chao and the Master of the Boneless Colors. But in these regions it was such a staple of life that I believe the people could not have existed without it. The zhu-gan grew wild, everywhere in the lowlands, from the Si-Chuan–Yun-nan border country southward throughout the tropics of Champa—where it was variously named in the various languages: banwu and mambu and other names—and everywhere it was used for many more purposes than frightening off tigers.

The zhu-gan would resemble any ordinary reed or cane, at least when it is young and only as thick as a finger, except that at intervals it has—very like a finger—nodes or knuckles along its length. Those mark little walls inside the cane, which interrupt its tubular length into separate compartments. For some uses—such as being thrown into a fire to burst—a single joint-length of the cane is employed, the wall intact at either end. For other purposes, the walls inside are punched through to make the cane a long tube. When the zhu-gan is no bigger around than a finger, it is easily cut with a knife. As it grows—and a single cane can get as tall and as big around as any tree—it must be laboriously sawed, for then it is almost as rigid as iron. But big or small, the zhu-gan is a beautiful plant, the cane part of it a golden color, the nodes sprouting withes with delicate green leaves at the ends; an immense clump of zhu-gan, all gold and green and catching the sun in its fronds, is a subject worthy of any painter.

In one of the few lowland places we crossed in that region, we came to a village built entirely of zhu-gan, and furnished with it, and totally dependent on it. The village, called Chieh-chieh, sat in a wide valley, through which ran one of the innumerable rivers of that country, and the whole valley bottom was thick with groves of the zhu-gan, and Chieh-chieh looked as if it too had grown there. Its houses were all made of the golden cane. Their walls were composed of arm-thick stalks of it, stood up side by side and lashed together; thicker lengths of zhu-gan were the posts and columns that held up roofs of split-cane segments laid over-and-underlapping like curved tiles. Inside each house, the furniture of tables and couches and floor mats was woven of slender strips peeled from the zhu-gan, as also were things like boxes, bird cages and baskets.

Because the river was bordered by extensive marshes, Chieh-chieh was situated several li distant from it, but the river's water was brought all that way through a pipe made of waist-thick canes joined end to end, and in the village square that water spilled into a trough made of half a log-sized zhu-gan. From the trough, the village boys and girls carried water to their cane-built homes in buckets and pots and bottles, all of which were joints of zhu-gan of various sizes. In the homes, the women used splinters of the cane for pins and needles, and the unraveled fiber of it for thread. The menfolk made from split lengths of the cane both their hunting bows and the arrows for them, and carried the arrows in a quiver that was only a big joint of zhu-gan. They used tree-sized stalks of the cane as the masts for their fishing boats and, with ropes braided of zhu-gan fibers, hung from those masts sails of lattice-worked zhu-gan strips. The village's headman probably had little writing to do, but he did it with a pen made of cane strip, split at one end, and wrote on paper made from the pulp scraped from the soft interior walls of the cane, and kept his written scrolls in a vase-sized joint of zhu-gan.

When my escorts and I dined that night in Chieh-chieh, the meal was served in bowls that were halved joints of big zhu-gan, and the nimble tongs were slender sticks of zhu-gan, and the meal included—besides river fish fresh-caught with a zhu-gan fiber net and broiled over a fire of burning zhu-gan scraps—the soft-boiled and succulent shoots of new-sprouted zhu-gan, and some of the same shoots pickled for a condiment, and some more of them candied for a sweet. None of us visitors was ill or injured, but, if we had been, we might have been doctored with tang-zhu, which is a liquid that fills the hollow joints of the zhu-gan when it has just come to maturity, and that tang-zhu has many medicinal uses.

I learned all those things about the zhu-gan from Chieh-chieh's elderly headman, one Wu. He was the only villager who spoke Mongol, and in consequence he and I sat up talking quite late, while my two escorts, one after the other, wearied of listening to us and went off to their allotted bedchambers. Old Wu and I were at last interrupted by a young woman coming into the cane-walled room where we sat on cane couches, to make what sounded like a whine of complaint.

"She wishes to know if you are never coming to bed," said Wu. "This is the prime female of Chieh-chieh, chosen from all the others to make your night here memorable, and she is eager to get on with it."

"Hospitable of her," I said, and regarded her with speculation.

The people in that Land of the Four Rivers, men and women alike, wore clothing that was lumpy and shapeless: a hat like a sort of pod for the head, robes and wraps and shawls layered from shoulders to feet, clumsy boots with upturned toes. The body garments were all patterned in broad stripes of two different colors, and everybody in a village wore the same two colors, and the colors of each village were different—so a "foreigner" from the next village down the road could be instantly recognized—and the colors were always dark and dingy ones (in Chieh-chieh they were brown and gray) so they would not show the ingrained dirt of them. In the mountain communities, that costume made the people blend into their background, which may have been useful for hunting or hiding. But in Chieh-chieh, against the background of bright gold and green, it made them obtrusively unsightly.

Since the men and women were indistinguishably garbed, indistinguishably hairless of face, flat of features, ruddy-brown of complexion, they had to show—even for their own convenience, I would suppose—something to mark their sex. So the stripes of a woman's garments went up and down, the stripes of a man's from side to side. A real foreigner like myself, not immediately perceiving that subtle difference of costume, could only tell them apart when they took off their pod hats. The men could then be seen to have their heads shaven and a gold or silver ring in the left ear. The women had their hair twisted into a multitude of thin, spiky braids—to be specific, exactly one hundred and eight braids, that being the number of books in the Kandjur, the Buddhist scriptures, and these people being all Buddhists.

Since my journey that day had not been a punishing one, and since the prettiness of the cane-built village had relaxed and rested me, I was inclined to indulge my curiosity as to what other evidences of femininity might lurk beneath this young woman's graceless garments. I noticed that she was wearing an ornament: a neck chain from which depended a fringe of jingling silver coins—and, assuming that they also numbered one hundred and eight, I said to old Wu:

"When you call her the village's prime female, do you refer to her wealth or her piety?"

"Neither," he said. "The coins attest to her female charms and desirability."

"Indeed?" I said, and stared at her. The neck chain was attractive enough, but I could not see how it made *her* any more so.

"In this land, our young women compete," he explained, "as to which of them can lie with the most men—those of their own village, or other villages, or casual passersby, or the men of trains traveling through—and require of each man a coin in token of the coupling. Clearly, the girl who amasses the most coins has attracted and satisfied the most men, and is preeminent among women."

"You mean marked an outcast, surely."

"I mean preeminent. When she finally is ready to marry and settle down, she can take her pick of husbands. Every eligible young man vies for her hand."

"Her hand no doubt being the least used-up part of her," I said, slightly scandalized. "In civilized lands, a man marries a virgin whom he knows is his alone."

"That is all that *can* be known of a virgin," said old Wu, with a disparaging sniff. "A man wedding a virgin risks getting a fish less warm than the one you ate at dinner. A man wedding any of our women gets credentials of her desirability and experience and talents. He also gets, not incidentally, a fair dowry of coins. And this young lady is most eager now to add your coin to her string, for she has never had one from a Ferenghi."

I was not averse to lying with nonvirgins, and it might have been instructive to lie with one who brought credentials to the encounter. But the young woman *was* most regrettably plain, and I did not much like being regarded as just one more of a string. So I mumbled some excuse about being on a pilgrimage, and bound by a vow of the Ferenghi religion. I gave her a coin anyway, as recompense for my spurning of her well-attested charms, and escaped to my bed. It was a bedstead woven of strips of zhu-gan and it was very comfortable, but it creaked all night, with just me alone in it, and must have waked the whole village if I had availed myself of Chieh-chieh's prime female. So I decided that the zhu-gan cane, for all its marvelous usefulness to mankind, was not ideal for every human purpose.

. 2 .

M y escorts and I rode on, through the alternation of mountains, ravines and valleys, sometimes up on the stark heights of the Pillar Road, occasionally down in the bright zhu-gan lowlands. That terrain did not change noticeably, but we realized that we had reached the High Land of To-Bhot when the people we met began to greet us by uncovering their heads, scratching the right ear, rubbing the left hip, and sticking out their tongues at us. That absurd salute—signifying that the greeter intends to think, hear, do or speak no evil—was peculiar to the people called Drok and Bho. Actually, they were the same people, only the nomads were called Drok and the settled ones Bho. The herder-and-hunter Drok lived like the plains-dwelling Mongols, and might have been indistinguishable from them except for their style of tent, which was black instead of yellow and was not supported by an interior lattice, as was the yurtu. A Drok tent had its walls pegged to the ground and its top hung up by long ropes which ran over high poles propped some distance away, then down to ground pegs farther off. That gave the tent the appearance of a black karakurt spider, crouched among its skinny, high-kneed legs.

The farmer-and-merchant Bho, though they had settled in communities, lived even more uncomfortably than the nomad Drok. They had tucked their villages and towns into high cliff crannies, which required them to pile their houses one atop another and another. That was contrary to what I knew of the Buddhist religion, which holds that the human head is the residence of the soul, so that a mother will not even pat the head of her own child. Yet here were the Bho living in such a manner that everybody dumped his wastes and trash and excretions on his neighbor's plot and rooftop, and often enough in his very hair. That custom of building as high up as possible, I learned, dated from some long-ago time when the Bho worshiped a god called Amnyi Machen, or "Old Man Great Peacock," who was believed to live in the highest peaks, and everyone tried to reside close to the god.

But now all the Bho were Buddhists, so on top of every community was perched a lamasarai, called by its inhabitants the Pota-lá. (Lá meant mount, and Pota was the Bho pronunciation of Buddha. And I will not make ribald word-play on that fact, from the indecorous meaning of "pota" in the Venetian tongue. No one has any need to *invent* derisions of the Bho and their religion.) The Pota-lá being the topmost and most populous building in every community, the result was that the priests and monks—here called lamas and trapas—excreted copiously on all their lay congregation downhill. I was to find that Buddhism, in its To-Bhot form of Potaism, was dismally degraded by even stranger lunacies.

A Bho town might look charming when we saw it from afar—say, across the landscape of the huge blue-and-yellow poppies unique to To-Bhot, and the "Pota's hair" willow trees hung with yellow bloom, and the clear blue sky speckled pink and black with rose finches and ravens. Any cliffside town was a vertical jumble of cliff-colored houses, distinguishable from the cliff because they oozed smoke from their little windows—curiously shaped windows, wider at the top than at the bottom—and that clutter of houses was overtopped by the even more jumbled Pota-lá, all turrets and gilded roofs and promenades and outside staircases and varicolored pennants flapping in the breeze, and dark-robed trapas pacing sedately about the terraces. But when we got closer, what had appeared from a distance comely, serene, even holy of aspect, was revealed to be ugly, torpid and squalid.

The quaint little windows of the town's residences were set only in the upper stories, to be above the ghastly mess and smell of the streets. The populace at first seemed to consist only of wandering goats and fowl and skulking yellow mastiffs, and the steep, narrow, twisty alleys were thick with droppings we assumed to be theirs. But then we would begin to meet people, and wish we had been satisfied with the cleaner animals, because when the people stuck out their tongues in greeting, we could see that their tongues were the only un-dirt-caked things about them. They wore robes as drab and grimy as had the people in the lowlands; if males and females wore differing patterns of the drabness and griminess, I could not discern them. There were very few men, and a great many women, but I could tell the sexes apart because the men took the trouble to open their long robes when they urinated in the street; the women simply squatted; they wore nothing under their outer robes, or I hoped they did not. Sometimes a larger than ordinary heap of dung in the street would stir feebly, and I would see that it was a human being laid out to die, usually a very old man or woman.

My Mongol escorts confided to me that the Bho, in former times, disposed of their old folks by eating their corpses—on the theory that the dead could wish no finer resting place than the guts of their own get—and had discontinued that practice only after Potaism became the prevailing religion, because the Pota-Buddha had frowned on the eating of meat. The only relic of the former custom was that families now conserved the skulls of their dead and made them into drinking bowls or little drums, so that the departed could still partake of holiday feasts and music making. Nowadays the Bho observed four other methods of sepulture. They burned the dead on mountaintops, or left them there for the birds, or they threw them into the rivers and ponds from which they got their drinking water, or they cut the corpses into pieces and fed them to dogs. The latter was the method most preferred, because that hastened the dissolution of the flesh, and until the old flesh was gone, its habitant soul was marooned in a sort of Purgatory between death here and rebirth elsewhere. The bodies of the poor were merely thrown to the packs of street curs, but the bodies of the rich were conveyed to special lamasarais which maintained kennels of sanctified mastiffs.

Those practices doubtless accounted for To-Bhot's teeming population of scavenger vultures and ravens and magpies and dogs, but they also accounted for more humans' dying than necessary. The dogs were so many that they were exceedingly liable to the canine madness, and in their fits they bit people as well as each other. More of the Bho were slain by the canine infection than by all the vile diseases engendered by their own squalor. Often, the heap in the street would be not just feebly stirring, but writhing and contorting and howling like a dog, in the terrible death agonies of that madness.

Because I had no wish to be bitten, and because I was on my way to war, I procured a bow and arrows and began to improve my aim and my arm by shooting every stray dog that came within range. That earned me black looks from the religious and the lay Potaists alike, who would rather that people die for no reason than that people should kill for good reason. However, since I carried the Khakhan's plaque, no one dared to do more than scowl and mutter, and I became quite proficient with both the broad-head and narrow-head arrows, and I hope I effected some small improvement in that wretched land, but I doubt it. I doubt that anyone or anything could.

On our arrival in any Bho community, my escorts and I climbed as quickly as we could to the Pota-lá on top, where we honored visitors were always put up, it affording the best of local accommodations. That meant only that we did not get excreted on from above—though, if we had, it could not have made the rooms and the bedding and the food and the company much filthier. Before leaving Kithai, I had heard a Han gentleman quote a contemptuous saying of his people—that the three national products of To-Bhot were lamas, women and dogs—and now I believed him. It was apparent that the disproportionate number of women in the town down the hill was owing to the fact that at least a third of their men had taken holy orders and residence in some lamasarai. Having seen the Bho women, I could not much fault the Bho men for having fled, but I did think that they might have fled to some existence better than a living embalmment.

Entering a Pota-lá courtyard, we were greeted first by the creaking, fluttering and clattering of prayer mills, prayer flags and prayer bones, then by the roars and snarls of the savage yellow To-Bhot mastiffs, which in those places were at least kept chained to the walls. Also along those walls, in every least niche, there was incense or a juniper sprig burning, but its perfume was insufficient to mask the overall miasma of yak-dung fires, putrid yak butter and unwashed religiosity. After meeting the noise and the stench, we met a number of monks and a few priests plodding majestically toward us, each of them holding out across his palms the khata, the pale blue silk scarf with which (instead of his tongue) every upper-class Bho salutes an equal or superior. They addressed me as Kungö, which means "Highness," and I properly addressed each lama as Kundün, "Presence," and each trapa as Rimpoche, "Treasured One"— though it nearly gagged me to utter such honorific lies. I could see nothing treasurable about any of them. Their robes, which had first seemed to be of ecclesiastically sedate colors, could be seen up close to have been originally bright red, and were dark only from years of accumulated dirt. Their faces, hands and shaved heads were blotched with a brown plant-sap they daubed on their various skin diseases, and their chins and chops were shiny with the yak butter that drenched everything they ate.

In the matter of foods at the lamasarais, we were most often served Potaist vegetable meals, of course—tsampa, boiled nettles, ferns—and a strange, stringy, slimy, bright-pink stalk of some plant unknown to me. I suspect that the holy men ate it only because it made one's urine pink for days afterward, and that effluent trickle no doubt awed the people downhill of the lamasarai. But the Bho had a peculiar selectivity about the Potaist injunction against eating meat. They would not slaughter domestic fowl or cattle, but would allow the slaying of game pheasants and antelope. So the lamas and trapas sometimes provided those venisons for us, as an excuse for them to enjoy the meats as well. (I am not unjustly scoffing at their hypocrite austerities. One lama was introduced to me as "a most holy of holy men" because he subsisted on "absolutely no nourishment except a few bowls of cha a day." Out of skeptic curiosity, I kept a close eye on that lama, and eventually caught him in the preparation of his mealtime bowl. It was not cha leaves he used in the steeping, but cha-like shreds of dried meat.)

However un-Potaistly lavish our meals sometimes were, they were never very elegant. We being honored guests, we were always seated to dine in the Pota-lá's "chanting hall," so we had the mealtime entertainment of several dozen trapas dolefully chanting while they ·thumped skull drums and rattled prayer bones. Among the serving platters and eating bowls, the banquet table bore an array of spittoons, and the holy men used them to the point of overflow. All about the dark hall stood statues of the Pota and his numerous disciple godlings and the numerous adversary demons, and every one of them was visible even in the gloom, because it gleamed with its slathering of yak butter. Where we Christians would light a candle to a saint, or perhaps leave with him a taolèta, it was the Bho's practice to smear their idols with yak butter, and the thick and ancient layers reeked of rancid decay. Whether the Pota and the other images were gratified by that, I do not know, but I can attest that the local vermin were. Even when the hall was full of noisy diners and chanters, I could hear the squeaks and snickers of mice and rats as they—plus cockroaches, centipedes and God knows what else—scurried foraging up and down the statues. Most nauseating of all, we and our dinner hosts always sat on what I at first took to be a low dais built up above the floor level. It felt rather spongy under me, so I furtively

investigated to see what it was made of—and discovered that we were
seated atop nothing but a mound of compacted food droppings, the
detritus of decades or maybe centuries of the holy men's slovenly drool-
ings and slobberings of their meals.

When their mouths were not masticating or otherwise occupied, the
holy men chanted almost continuously, in concert at the top of their
lungs, in solitude under their breaths. One chant went like this: "Lha so
so, khi ho ho," which meant more or less, "Come gods, begone demons!"
A shorter one went like this: "Lha gyelo," meaning "The gods are victorious!" But the chant that was heard most often and interminably and
everywhere in To-Bhot went like this: "Om mani pémé hum." The opening and closing noises of it were always intoned in a drawn-out manner,
so: "O-o-o-om" and "Hu-u-u-um," and they constituted just a sort of
"amen." The other two words meant, literally, "the jewel in the lotus," in
the same sense that those terms are used in the Han lexicon of sex. In
other words, the holy men were chanting, "Amen, the male organ is
inside the female's! Amen!"

Now, one of the Han religions prevailing back in Kithai, the one
they call Tao, "the Way," has an unashamed connection with sex. In
Taoism, the male essence is called yang and the female's is yin, and
everything else in the universe—whether material, intangible, spiritual,
whatever—is regarded as being either yang or yin, hence totally discrete
and opposite (as men and women are) or complementary and necessary
to each other (as men and women are). Thus active things are called
yang, passive ones yin. Heat and cold, the heavens and the earth, sun
and moon, light and darkness, fire and water, they are all respectively
yang and yin, or, as anyone can recognize, inextricably yang-yin. At the
most basic level of human behavior, when a man couples with a woman
and absorbs her female yin by means of his male yang, he is not in any
sense tinged with effeminacy, but becomes more of a *complete man*,
stronger, more alive, more aware, more worthwhile. And just so, the
woman becomes more of a woman by accepting his yang with her yin.
From that elementary foundation, Tao proceeds up to metaphysical
heights and abstractions that I cannot pretend to grasp.

It may be that some Han Taoist, wandering into To-Bhot long ago,
when the natives still worshiped the Old Peacock, kindly tried to explain
to them his amiable religion. The Bho could hardly have misunderstood
the universal act of putting male organ into female—or jewel into lotus,
as the Han would have expressed it—or mani into pémé, in their language. But such oafs would have been baffled by the higher significances
of yang and yin, so all they ever retained of Tao was that preposterous
chant of "Om mani pémé hum." Still, not even the Bho could have built
much of a religion on a prayer that had no loftier meaning than "Amen,
stick it in her! Amen!" So, as they later and gradually adopted Buddhism
from India, they must have adapted the chant to fit that religion. All they
had to do was construe the "jewel" as Buddha, or Pota, because he is so
often portrayed as sitting in meditation on a large lotus blossom. So the
chant came to mean something like "Amen, Pota is in his place! Amen!"
And then, no doubt, some later lamas—in the way that self-appointed

sages always complicate even the purest faith with their unsolicited commentaries and interpretations—decided to festoon the simple chant with more abstruse aspects. So they decreed that the word mani (jewel, male genitals, Pota) would henceforth signify The Means, and the word pémé (lotus, female genitals, Pota's place) would henceforth refer to Nirvana. Thus the chant became a prayer beseeching The Means to achieve that Nirvana oblivion which Potaists deem the highest end of life: "Amen, blot me out! Amen!"

Certainly, Potaism no longer had any laudable connection with sexual relations between men and women, because at least one of every three Bho males, at puberty or even younger, fled from the prospect of ever having to endure sex with any Bho female, and took the red robe of religion. So far as I could tell, that vow of celibacy was the only qualification necessary for entrance into a Pota-lá and eventual elevation through the ascending degrees of monkhood and priesthood. The chabis, or novices, were given nothing like a secular education or seminary instruction, and I encountered only three or four of the oldest and highest-grade lamas who could even read and write the "Om mani pémé hum," let alone the one hundred and eight books of the Kandjur scriptures, let alone the two hundred and twenty-five Tengyur books of commentary on the Kandjur. In speaking of the holy men's celibacy, however, I should rightly have said celibacy in regard to females. Many of the lamas and trapas flagrantly flaunted their amorousness toward each other, to leave no doubt that they had forsworn sordid, ordinary, normal sex.

Potaism, however it developed, was a religion demanding only sheer quantity of devotion, not any quality of it. By that I mean a seeker of oblivion simply had to repeat "Om mani pémé hum" *enough times* during his life and he expected that would take him to Nirvana when he died. He did not even have to speak the words, or repeat them in any way requiring his own volition. I have mentioned prayer mills; they were everywhere in the lamasarais, and in every house, and even to be found standing in empty countryside. They were drumlike cylinders within which were wound paper scrolls on which the mani chant was written. A man had only to give the cylinder a spin with his hand and those "repetitions" of the prayer counted to his credit. Sometimes he rigged it like a waterwheel, so that a stream or cascade kept it turning and praying constantly. Or he could hoist a flag inscribed with the prayer, or a whole line of them—those were far more frequently to be seen in To-Bhot than any lines of washing hung out—and every flap the wind gave every flag was credited to him. Or he could run his hand along a line of dangling sheep shoulder blades, each bone inscribed with the mani, strung like wind chimes, and they prayed for him as long as they went on clattering.

I once came upon a trapa crouched beside a creek, flinging into it and hauling out again a tile attached to a string. He had been doing that, he said, all his adult life, and would go on doing it until he died.

"Doing *what*?" I asked, thinking that perhaps, in some idiotic Bho way, he was trying to emulate San Piero as a fisher of souls. The monk showed me his tile; it was engraved with the mani prayer, in the fashion of a yin seal. He explained that he was "imprinting" the prayer on the running water, stamping it there over and over again, and he was accruing piety with every invisible "impression."

Another time, in a Pota-lá courtyard, I saw two trapas come to violent blows because one of them had given a twirl to a prayer mill and then, glancing back as he walked on, saw a brother monk stop the mill and spin it in the other direction to pray for *him*.

Atop one of the major towns on our way was an especially large lamasarai, and there I made bold to seek audience of its venerable and filthy and sap-daubed Grand Lama.

"Presence," I addressed the old abbot, "I seldom observe anything going on in any Pota-lá that looks like ecclesiastical activity. Aside from twirling prayer mills or shaking prayer bones, what exactly are your religious duties?"

In a voice like the rustle of far-off leaves, he said, "I sit in my cell, my son Highness, or sometimes in a remote cave, or on a lonely mountaintop, and I meditate."

"Meditate on what, Presence?"

"On my once having laid eyes on the Kian-gan Kundün."

"And what would that be?"

"The Sovereign Presence, the Holiest of Lamas, he who is an actual reincarnation of the Pota. He resides in Lha-Ssa, the City of the Gods, a long, long journey from here, where the people are building for him a Pota-lá worthy of his occupancy. They have been building on it for more than six hundred years now, but they expect to have it completed in only four or five hundred more. The Holiest will be pleased to grace it with his Sovereign Presence, for it will be a palace most magnificent when it is finally done."

"Are you saying, Presence, that this Kian-gan Kundün has been alive and waiting for six hundred years? And he will still be alive when the palace is finished?"

"Assuredly so, my son Highness. Of course you, being ch'hipa— outside the belief—might not see him so. His corporeal integument dies from time to time, and then his lamas must cast about the land and find the infant boy into whom his soul has transmigrated. So the Sovereign Presence looks physically different, from lifetime to lifetime. But we nang-pa—we within the belief—we know him to be always the same Holiest of Lamas, and the Pota reincarnated."

It seemed to me somewhat unfair that the Pota, having created and prescribed Nirvana for his devotees, evidently never got to rest obliviously there himself, but had to keep on being fetched back to Lha-Ssa, a town doubtless as awful as any other in To-Bhot. But I refrained from remarking on that, and gently prompted the old abbot:

"So you made the far journey to Lha-Ssa, and you saw the Holiest of Lamas . . . ?"

"Yes, my son Highness, and that event has occupied my meditations and contemplations and devotions ever since. You may not believe this, but the Holiest actually opened his own rheumy old eyes and looked at *me.*" He put on a wrinkled smile of rapt reminiscence. "I think, if the Holiest had not been then so ancient and approaching his next transmigration, he might almost have summoned up his strength and *spoken* to me."

"You and he only looked at each other? And that has furnished you with meat for meditation ever since?"

"Ever since. Just that one bleared glance from the Holiest was the commencement of my wisdom. Forty-eight years ago, that was."

"For nearly half a century, Presence, you have done nothing but contemplate that single fleeting occurrence?"

"A man blessed with the beginning of wisdom is obligated to let it ripen without distraction. I have forgone all other interests and pursuits. I do not interrupt my meditation even to take meals." He arranged his wrinkles and blotches in a look of blissful martyrdom. "I subsist on only an occasional bowl of weak cha."

"I have heard of such wondrous abstentions, Presence. Meanwhile, I suppose you share with your underlamas the fruits of your meditations, for their instruction."

"Dear me, no, young Highness." His wrinkles rearranged into a startled and slightly offended look. "Wisdom cannot be taught, it must be learned. The learning to be done by others is up to them. Now, if you will excuse me for saying so, this brief audience with you has constituted the longest distraction of my meditative life. . . ."

So I made my obeisances and left him, and sought out a lama of fewer pustules and less exalted degree, and inquired what *he* did when he was not churning prayers out of a mill.

"I meditate, Highness," he said. "What else?"

"Meditate on what, Presence?"

"I fix my mental regard on the Grand Lama, for he once visited Lha-Ssa and looked upon the visage of the Kian-gan Kundün. From that, he acquired great holiness."

"And you hope to absorb some holiness from meditating on him?"

"Dear me, no. Holiness cannot be taken, only bestowed. I can, however, hope from that meditation to extract some small wisdom."

"And that wisdom you will impart to whom? To your junior lamas? To the trapas?"

"Really, Highness! One never casts one's regard downward, only upward! Where else is wisdom? Now, if you will excuse me. . . ."

So I went and found a trapa, recently accepted into monkhood after a long novitiate as a chabi, and asked what *he* contemplated while awaiting elevation to the priesthood.

"Why, the holiness of my elders and superiors, of course, Highness. They are the receptacles containing all the wisdom of all the ages."

"But, if they never teach you anything, Treasured One, whence comes that knowledge to you? You all claim to be eager to acquire it, but what is the source of it?"

"Knowledge?" he said, with lofty contempt. "Only worldly creatures like the Han fret about knowledge. *We* wish to acquire *wisdom.*"

Interesting, I thought. That same disdainful estimate had once been made of me—and by a Han. Nevertheless, I was not prepared to believe, then or now, that inertness and torpor represent the highest attainment humanity can aspire to. In my opinion, stillness is not always evidence of intelligence, and silence is not always evidence of a mind at work. Most vegetables are still and silent. In my opinion, meditation is not infallibly productive of profound ideas. I have seen vultures meditate on a full belly, and then do nothing more profound than regurgitate. In my opinion, inarticulate and obscure pronouncements are not always expressive of a wisdom so mystically sublime that only sages can comprehend it. The mouthings of the Potaist holy men were inarticulate and obscure, but so were the yappings of their lamasarai curs.

I went and found a chabi, the lowest form of life in a Pota-lá, and asked how *his* time was spent.

"My admission here was granted on condition that I apprentice as a cleaning orderly," he said. "But of course I pass most of my time meditating on my mantra."

"And what is that, boy?"

"A few syllables from the Kandjur of holy scripture, assigned to me for my contemplation. When I have meditated long enough upon the mantra—some years perhaps—and it has expanded my mind sufficiently, I may be considered fit to rise to the status of trapa, and then begin to contemplate larger bits of the Kandjur."

"Did it ever occur to you, boy, actually to spend your time in cleaning this sty, and studying ways to clean it better?"

He stared at me as if I had been rendered rabid by a dog bite. "Instead of my mantra, Highness? Whatever for? Cleaning is the lowliest of occupations, and he who would rise should look upward, not downward."

I snorted. "Your Grand Lama does nothing but squat and contemplate the Holiest of Lamas, while his underlamas do nothing but squat and contemplate *him*. All the trapas do nothing but squat and contemplate the lamas. I would wager that the first apprentice who ever actually learned cleanliness could overthrow the whole regime. Become the master of this Pota-lá, and then the Pope of Potaism, and eventually the Wang of all To-Bhot."

"You have been grievously mad-bit by a dog, Highness," he said, looking alarmed. "I will run and fetch one of our physicians—the pulse-feeler or the urine-smeller—that he may attend you in your affliction."

Well, so much for the holy men. The influence of Potaism on the lay population of To-Bhot was about equally elevating. The men had learned to twirl any prayer mill they encountered, and the women had learned to screw up their hair into one hundred and eight braids, and both men and women were careful always, when walking past any holy edifice, to walk to the left of it and keep it always on their right hand. I do not know exactly why, except that there was a saying, "Beware the demons on the left," and there were to be found in the countryside a great many stone walls and piled-up heaps of stone that had some indiscernible religious significance, and the road always divided around them, so that a traveler from either direction could keep the holiness on his right.

At every twilight, all the men, women and children of every community would leave off their day's occupations, if any, and squat in the town streets or on their own rooftops, while they were led by the lamas and trapas of the Pota-lá overhead, in chanting their evening appeal for oblivion, "Om mani pémé hum," over and over again. I might have been impressed by what was at least an example of popular solidarity and unabashed religiosity—in contrast to Venice, say, where my sophisticated townsfolk would blush to make even the sign of the cross in any gathering more public than a church service—but I simply could not admire a people's devotion to a religion that did no good for them, or anyone.

Presumably it prepared them for the oblivion of Nirvana, but it made them so phlegmatic in this life, and so oblivious to this world, that I could not imagine how they would recognize the other oblivion when they got there. Most religions, I think, inspire their followers to an occasional activity and enterprise. Even the detestable Hindus sometimes bestir themselves, if only to butcher each other. But the Potaists had not enough initiative to kill a rabid dog, or even bother to step out of its way when it lunged. As well as I could tell, the Bho evinced one sole ambition: to break out of their constitutional torpor only long enough to advance into absolute and eternal coma.

Regard just one example of Bho apathy. In a land where so many men had retreated into celibacy and there was a consequent abundance of women, I would have expected to find the normal men enjoying a paradise: taking their pick of the females and taking as many as they wished. Not so. It was the females who did the picking and collecting. The women followed the custom I had earlier encountered: casually coupling before marriage with as many passersby as possible, and extorting a memento coin from each, so that, at marriageable age, the female laden with the most coins was the most desirable wife-to-be. But she did not simply take for husband the most eligible man in her community; she took *several* of them. Instead of each man being the Shah of a whole anderun of wives and concubines, every marriageable woman possessed a whole anderun of men, and the legions of her less comely sisters were doomed to spinsterhood.

One might say, well, that at least showed some enterprise on the part of at least a few women. But it was a poor showing, because what sort of eligible men could a woman choose her consorts *from*?

All those males with enough ambition and energy to walk uphill had done exactly that, and vanished into the Pota-lá. Of the remainder, the only ones with any verifiable manhood and livelihood were usually those committed to the carrying-on of an established family farm or herd or trade. So a woman who could take her pick of men did so, not by marrying *into* one of those "best families," but by marrying the *whole family*—anyway, the male members of it. That made for some complex conjugalities. I met one woman who was married to two brothers and to a son of each of them, and had children by all. Another woman was married to three brothers, while her daughter by one of them was married to the two others of them, plus another man she had procured somewhere outside the house.

How anybody in those tangled and inbred unions ever knew whose children were whose, I have no notion, and I suspect that none of them cared to know. I have concluded that the Bho people's atrocious marital customs accounted for their general feeblemindedness, and also for their Potaist travesty of the Buddhist religion, and their continued sapless adherence to it, and their laughable belief that Potaism represented the accumulation of "all the wisdom of all the ages." I came to that conclusion when, much later, I talked about the Bho to some distinguished Han physicians. They told me that generations of close inbreeding—common to mountain communities, and inevitable in those fanatically faith-bound —must produce a people of physical lethargy and diminished brain. If that is true, and I am convinced it is, then Potaism represents To-Bhot's accumulation of all the imbecility of all the ages.

· 3 ·

"Your Royal Father Kubilai prides himself on ruling peoples of quality," I said to the Wang Ukuruji. "Why did he ever trouble to conquer and annex this miserable land of To-Bhot?"

"For its gold," said Ukuruji, without great enthusiasm. "Gold dust can be panned from almost any river or creek bed in this country. We could get a lot more of it, of course, if I could make the wretched Bho dig and mine the sources of it. But they have been persuaded by their cursed lamas that gold nuggets and veins are the *roots* of the metal. Those must be left undisturbed, or they will not produce the gold dust, which is their *pollen*." He laughed, and ruefully wagged his head. "Vakh!"

"One more evidence of the Bho intellect," I said. "The land may be worth something, but the people are not. Why did Kubilai condemn his own son to govern them?"

"Somebody has to," he said, with a resigned shrug. "The lamas would probably tell you that I must have committed some vile crime in some former existence, to deserve being made ruler of the Drok and the Bho. They might be right."

"Perhaps," I said, "your father will give you Yun-nan to rule instead —or in addition to To-Bhot."

"That is what I devoutly hope," he said. "Which is why I removed my court from the capital to this garrison town, to be close to the Yun-nan war zone, and await here the war's outcome."

This garrison town, actually a trade-route market city named Ba-Tang, was where my escorts and I had ended our long journey from Khanbalik, and found the Wang Ukuruji, alerted by our advance riders, awaiting our arrival. Ba-Tang was in To-Bhot, but was the largest city conveniently close to the Yun-nan frontier of the Sung Empire. So this was where the Orlok Bayan had chosen to set his headquarters, and from which he repeatedly led or sent incursions southward against the Yi people. Ba-Tang had not been evacuated of its Bho inhabitants, but they were almost outnumbered by the Mongols occupying the city and its outskirts and the valley roundabout—five tomans of troops and their camp-follower women, the Orlok and his numerous staff, the Wang and his courtiers.

"I am ready and eager to move on again at a moment's notice," Ukuruji continued, "if ever Bayan succeeds in taking Yun-nan, and if my father gives me leave to go there. The Yi people will naturally be inimical to a Mongol overlord at first, but I had rather go among raging enemies than stay among the blighted Bho."

"You mentioned your capital, Wang. I assume you mean the city of Lha-Ssa."

"No. Why?"

"I was told that there dwells the Holiest of Lamas, the Sovereign Presence. I took it to be the chief city of the nation."

He laughed. "Yes, there is the Holiest of Lamas at Lha-Ssa. There is another Holiest of Lamas at a place called Dri Kung, and another at Pak-Dup, and another at Tsal, and others in other places. Vakh! You must understand that there is not just a single noxious Potaism, but innumerable rival sects of it, no one to be any more admired or abominated than another, and every one recognizing a different Holiest Lama at its head. For convenience, I recognize a Holiest Lama named Phags-pa, whose lamasarai is at the city of Shigat-Se, so that is where I have located the capital. Nominally at least, the venerable Phags-pa and I are co-governors of the country, he of its spiritual aspects, I of the temporal. He is a despicable old fraud, but no worse than any of the other Holiest Lamas, I suspect."

"And Shigat-Se?" I asked. "Is it as fine a city as I have heard Lha-Ssa to be?"

"Probably," he grunted. "Shigat-Se is a dunghill. And so, no doubt, is Lha-Ssa."

"Well," I said, as cheerfully as I could, "you must be grateful to be residing for a while in this more beautiful place."

Ba-Tang was situated on the east bank of the river Jin-sha, which was here a white-water stream tumbling down the middle of a broad valley plain, but downstream in Yun-nan it would collect other tributary waters and widen and eventually become the mighty river Yang-tze. The Ba-Tang valley, in this season of summer, was gold and green and blue, with bright touches of other colors. The blue was the high, windswept sky. The gold was the color of the Bho's barley fields and zhu-gan groves and the countless yellow yurtu tents of the Mongol bok. But beyond the cultivated and camped-on areas, the valley was the rich green of forests —elms and junipers and pines—besprinkled with the colors of wild roses, bluebells, anemones, columbine, irises and, over all, morning glories of every hue, wreathing every tree and bush.

In such a setting, any town would have been as obtrusive as an ulcer on a beautiful face. But Ba-Tang, since it had the whole valley to spread out in, had set its buildings side by side, not atop each other, and not squashed close together, and the river disposed of most of its wastes, so it was not quite so ugly and filthy as most Bho communities. The inhabitants even dressed better than other Bho. At any rate, the upper-class folk among them could be recognized by their garnet-colored robes and gowns, nicely trimmed with fur of otter, pard or tiger, and an upper-class woman's hundred-and-eight braids of hair were adorned with kauri shells, bits of turquoise and even coral from some far distant sea.

"Can it be that these Bho here are superior to those elsewhere in To-Bhot?" I asked hopefully. "They at least appear to have different customs. As I rode into the town, the people were commencing their New Year celebration. Everywhere else, the year begins in midwinter."

"So it does here. And there is no such thing as a superior Bho, not anywhere in the world. Do not deceive yourself."

"I could not have been deceived about the festivities, Wang. A parade—with the dragons and the lanterns and all—it was clearly in honor of the New Year. Listen, you can hear the gongs and drums from here." He and I were seated, drinking from horns of arkhi, on a terrace of his temporary palace, some way upriver of Ba-Tang.

"Yes, I hear them. The poor sheep-wits." He shook his head in deprecation. "It is indeed a New Year festivity, but not to welcome a real new year. It seems there has been an outbreak of sickness in the town. Only the flux, which is a common summertime affliction of the bowels, but no Potaist can be convinced that anything ever happens normally. The local lamas, in their wisdom, decided that the flux was the doing of demons, and they decreed a New Year celebration, so the demons will think they were mistaken in the season, and will go away and take their summer sickness with them."

I said with a sigh, "You are right. To find a Bho with good sense would be as unlikely as finding a white crow."

"However, the lamas being furious with me, they may also have intended the celebration to drive the bowel demons upriver to here, and flush me out of this Pota-lá."

For his temporary palace, Ukuruji had commandeered the town's lamasarai, and had summarily evicted its entire population of lamas and trapas, and kept only the chabi novices to be servants to him and his courtiers. The holy men, he told me—jolted out of their stupor for once in their lives—had departed shaking their fists and invoking every curse the Pota could inflict. But the Wang and his court had now been for some months ensconced and comfortable. He had allotted me a whole suite of rooms on my arrival and, because my Mongol escorts desired to join our advance riders and their other fellows in the Orlok's bok, had assigned me a retinue of chabis also.

Ukuruji went on, "Still, we ought to be thankful for the unseasonal New Year. Only on that holiday do the Bho clean their abodes or wash their garments or bathe themselves. So this year the Bho of Ba-Tang have twice got clean."

"No wonder I took the town and the people to be out of the ordinary," I muttered. "Well, as you say, let us be thankful. And let me laud you, Wang Ukuruji, for being perhaps the first man ever to have taught something more useful than religion to these folk. You have certainly made them transform this Pota-lá. I have lodged in lamasarais all across To-Bhot, but to see a clean chanting hall—or to see it at all—is something of a revelation."

I looked from the terrace into that hall. No longer a gloomy cavern layered with stinking yak butter and ancient food droppings, it had been unshuttered to the sunlight, and the whole place scraped clean, and the encrusted images removed, and now it could be seen to have a floor of fine marble slabs. A chabi servant, at Ukuruji's command, had just spread candle grease on that floor and was now polishing it by shuffling about wearing sheep-fleece hats on his feet.

"Also," said the Wang, "as soon as the people washed themselves and their faces were discernible, I was able to cull out a few good-looking females. Even I, a non-Bho, think them almost worthy of the many coins they wear. Shall I send two or three tonight for your selection?" When I did not immediately accept, he said, "Surely you would not prefer one of the gaping leather bags of the bok!" Then he thought to add, delicately, "There are, among the chabis, two or three pretty boys."

"Thank you, Wang," I said. "I prefer women, but I prefer to be a woman's first coin, so to speak, not her latest. Here in To-Bhot, that would mean coupling with a woman ugly and undesirable. So I shall decline, with thanks, and continue in chastity until perhaps I can get down south into Yun-nan, and hope the Yi women there are more to my taste."

"I have been hoping the same," he said. "Well, old Bayan is due to return any day from his latest foray down there. So you can present to him my Royal Father's missive, and I will be greatly gratified if it contains orders for me to proceed southward with the armies. Until we convene, then, make yourself free of what comforts this place affords."

That most hospitable young Wang must have gone straightaway to see if he could find for me a female who had not yet conferred her favors, but would merit a coin for them when she did. For, when I retired to my chambers at bedtime, my chabis proudly ushered forth two small persons. They had smiling, un-sap-splotched faces and were clad in clean, fur-trimmed, garnet-colored gowns. Like all the Bho, these small persons wore no underclothes, as I saw when the chabis whisked the gowns off them to show me that they were females. The chabis also made gestures and noises to acquaint me with the little girls' names— Ryang and Odcho—and made further gestures to indicate that they were to be my bedmates. I could not speak the language of the chabis and the girls, but I managed, also with gestures, to inquire their age. Odcho was ten years old and Ryang was nine.

I could not help bursting into laughter, though it seemed to bewilder the chabis and offend the girls. Clearly, to find a passably good-looking virgin in To-Bhot, one had to rummage among the very children.

I found that amusing, but also slightly frustrating to my curiosity for pertinent details. Since females of that tender age are so formless and so nearly devoid of sexual characteristics, Ryang and Odcho gave no indication of how they would look or perform when they grew up. Thus I cannot claim that I ever enjoyed a real Bho woman, or even examined one unclothed, and so am unable to report—as I have sedulously tried to report of women of other races—what physical attributes or interesting bodily features or copulative eccentricities may be noticed in the adult females of the Bho.

The only peculiarity I saw in the two girl children was that each of them bore a discoloration, like a birthmark, on her lower back just above the buttock cleft. It was a purplish spot on the creamy skin, about the size of a saucer, somewhat darker on the nine-year-old Ryang than on the older girl. Since the children were not sisters, I wondered at the coincidence, and one day asked Ukuruji if all Bho females had that blemish.

"All children, male as well as female," he said. "And not just those of the Bho and Drok. The Han, the Yi, even Mongol infants are born with it. Your Ferenghi babies are not?"

"I never saw any such thing, no. Nor among the Persians, the Armeniyans, the Semitic Arabs and Jews. . . ."

"Indeed? We Mongols call it the 'deer dapple,' because it slowly fades and disappears—like the spots on a fawn—as a child grows older. It is usually gone by the age of ten or eleven. Another difference between us and you Westerners, eh? But a trifling one, I suppose."

Some days later, the Orlok Bayan returned from his expedition, at the head of several thousand mounted warriors. The column looked travel-weary, but not much decimated by combat, as it included only a few dozen horses with empty saddles. When Bayan had changed into clean clothes at his yurtu pavilion in the bok, he came to the Pota-lá palace, accompanied by some of his sardars and other officers, to pay his respects to the Wang and to meet me. We three sat around a table on the terrace, and the lesser officers sat at a distance apart, and all were attended by chabis dispensing horns and skulls of kumis and arkhi and some native Bho beverage brewed from barley.

"The Yi did their usual cowardly evasions," Bayan grumbled, by way of report on his foray. "Hide and snipe and run away. I would chase the cursed runaways clear to the jungles of Champa, but that is what they hope for—that I will expose my flanks and outrun my supply lines. Anyway, a rider brought me word that a message from my Khakhan was on the way to here, so I broke off and turned back. Let the misbegotten Yi think they repulsed us; I do not care; I will savage them yet. I hope, Messenger Polo, you bring some good advice from Kubilai on how to do that."

I handed over the letter, and the rest of us sat silent while he broke its waxen yin seals and unfolded it and read it. Bayan was a man of late middle age, sturdy and swarthy and scarred and ferocious-looking as any other Mongol warrior, but he also had the most fearsome teeth I ever saw in a human mouth. I watched him champ them as he perused the letter, and for a while I was more fascinated by his mouth than by the words that came out of it.

After some time of watching closely, I made out that the teeth were not his. That is to say, they were imitation teeth, made of heavy porcelain. They had been constructed for him—he told me later—after he lost all his real ones when a Samoyed foeman hit him in the mouth with an iron mace. I eventually saw other Mongols and Han wearing artificial teeth—they were called kin-chi by the Han physicians who specialized in the making of them—but Bayan's were the first I ever saw, and the worst, evidently having been made for him by a physician not very fond of him. They looked as ponderous and granitic as roadside milestones, and they were held together and held in place by an elaborate grid of garish, glittering goldwork. Bayan himself told me that they were painfully uncomfortable, so he only wedged them between his gums when he had to call upon some dignitary, or had to eat, or wished to seduce a woman with his beauty. I did not say so, but it was my opinion that his kin-chi must have revolted every dignitary he champed them at, and every servant who waited upon him at table—and their effect upon a woman I did not wish even to speculate on.

"Well, Bayan," Ukuruji was saying eagerly, "does my Royal Father command that I am to follow you into Yun-nan?"

"He does not say that you are not to," Bayan replied diplomatically, and handed the document to the Wang for him to read for himself. Then the Orlok turned to me. "Very well. As Kubilai suggests, I will cause a proclamation to be made, loud and within hearing of the Yi, that they no longer have a secret friend in the Khanbalik court. Is that supposed to make them surrender on the spot? It seems to me that they would fight the harder, out of sheer peevishness."

I said, "I do not know, Orlok."

"And why does Kubilai suggest that I do the very thing I have tried to avoid doing? Penetrate so far into Yun-nan that my flanks and my rear are vulnerable?"

"I really do not know, Orlok. The Khakhan did not confide to me his ideas for either strategy or tactics."

"Humph. Well, you must know this much, Polo. He appends a postscript—something about you having brought me some new weapon."

"Yes, Orlok. It is a device that might help prosecute a war without too many soldiers being killed."

"Being killed is what soldiers are for," he said decisively. "What is this device?"

"A means by which to employ in combat the powder called huo-yao."

He erupted, rather like the flaming powder himself, "Vakh! That again?" He gnashed his ghastly teeth and bellowed what I took to be a terrible profanity: "By the smelly old saddle of the sweaty god Tengri! Every year or so, another lunatic inventor proposes to replace cold steel with hot smoke. It has never worked yet!"

"This time it might, Orlok," I said. "It is a totally new kind of huo-yao." I beckoned to a hovering chabi and sent him running to my chambers to fetch one of the brass balls.

While we waited, Ukuruji finished reading the letter and said, "I think, Bayan, I perceive the intent in my Royal Father's tactical proposal. So far, your troops have failed to close with the Yi in a decisive battle, because they continually melt away before you into the mountain recesses. But if your columns were to proceed far enough—so that the Yi saw an opportunity of utterly surrounding you—why, then they would have to trickle down from their hideaways and collect in mass at your flanks and rear." The Orlok appeared both bored and exasperated by this explication but, out of respect for rank, he let him go on: "Thus, for the first time, you would have all the Yi foemen gathered and exposed, and distant from their bolt holes, and engageable in close combat. Well?"

"If my Wang will permit me," said the Orlok. "That is all very likely true. But my Wang has himself mentioned the egregious flaw in that argument. I *would* be utterly surrounded. If I may draw a parallel, I submit that the most practical way of extinguishing a fire is *not* to plump one's bare rump down on it."

"Hm," said Ukuruji. "Well . . . suppose you ventured only a portion of your troops, and held others in reserve . . . to swoop down when the Yi had collected behind the first columns . . . ?"

"Wang Ukuruji," the Orlok said patiently. "The Yi are shifty and elusive, but they are not stupid. They know how many men and horses I have at my disposal, and probably even how many women usable for warriors. They would not be drawn into such a trap unless they could see and count that I had committed my entire force. And then—who is in the trap?"

"Hm," Ukuruji murmured again, and subsided into a thoughtful silence.

The chabi returned, bringing the brass ball, and I explained to the Orlok all the incidents leading up to its contrivance, and how the Firemaster Shi had seen in it a new potential for military usefulness. When I had done, the Orlok champed his teeth some more, and gave me much the same look with which he had received the Wang's tactical advice.

"Let me see if I understand you correctly, Polo," he said. "You have brought me twelve of these elegant baubles, right? Now, correct me if I am wrong. From your own experience, you can assure me that each of the twelve will effectually demolish *two* persons—*if* they are both standing closely over it when it ignites—and *if* they are both unarmored, delicate, incautious and unsuspecting *women*."

I mumbled, "Well, true, it happened that the two I spoke of were women, but—"

"Twelve balls. Each capable of killing two defenseless women. Meanwhile, down the farther valleys to the south, there are some fifty thousand staunch Yi *men*—warriors encased in leather armor stout enough to turn a blade. I cannot really expect them to huddle close when I roll a ball among them. Even if they did, let me think, fifty thousand minus, um, twenty-four . . . leaves, um. . . . "

I coughed and cleared my throat and said, "On my way hither, along the Pillar Road, I was struck by a notion for a different use of the balls than just to project them among the enemy. I perceived that the mountains hereabout are not much subject to landslides or rockslides—like the Pai-Mir, say—and these mountain people are evidently unwary of any such occurrences."

For a change, he did not munch his teeth at me, but regarded me narrowly. "You are right. These mountains are reliably solid. So?"

"So if the brass balls were to be securely tucked into tight crevices of the high peaks along both crests above a valley, and all ignited at the same and proper moment, they should set loose a mighty avalanche. It would thunder down from both sides and completely fill the valley and mash and bury every living thing in it. To a people who have for so long felt safe among these mountains, even sheltered and protected by them, it would be a cataclysm immense and unexpected and inescapable. The avalanche would come down upon them like God's boot heel. Of course, as the Wang has said, it would be necessary to arrange that all the foe be congregated in that one valley. . . ."

"Hui! That is it!" Ukuruji exclaimed. "First, Bayan, you have heralds make that proclamation proposed by my Royal Father. Then, as if that had given you mandate for a full-scale assault, you send your whole force into the likeliest valley, the mountains alongside it having previously been seeded with the huo-yao balls. The Yi will think you have taken leave of your senses, but they will take advantage of it. They will filter down from their hiding places and collect and cluster and prepare to assault from your sides and rear. And then—"

"Honorable Wang!" the Orlok bleated, almost pleadingly. "I should *have* to take leave of my senses! Not enough that I commit my entire five tomans—half a tuk—to be surrounded by the enemy. Now you wish me to condemn my fifty thousand men as well to a devastating avalanche! What good for us to wipe out the Yi warriors and have all Yun-nan prostrate before us, if we have no troops of our own left alive to take it and hold it?"

"Hm," said Ukuruji yet again. "Well, our troops would at least be expecting the avalanche. . . ."

The Orlok refrained even from dignifying that with a comment. Just then, one of the serving chabis came out of the Pota-lá onto the terrace, bringing a leather flask of arkhi to refill our drinking horns and skull cups. Bayan, Ukuruji and I were sitting now with our eyes pensively fixed on the tabletop, so my gaze was caught by the bright garnet sleeves of that young Bho man dispensing the liquor. Then my eyes, idling on those movements of color, caught the similarly idling gaze of Ukuruji, and I saw his eyes quicken with light, and I think the garnet sleeves inspired in both of us the same outrageous idea at the same instant, but I was glad to let him do the expressing of it. He leaned urgently toward Bayan and said:

"Suppose we do not risk our own men to bait the trap. Suppose we send the worthless and expendable Bho. . . ."

YUN-NAN

.1.

I т had to be done either quickly or in a secrecy so strict that it would have been almost impossible to sustain. So it was done quickly.

The first thing done was the posting of pickets all around the Ba-Tang valley, alert day and night to stop any Yi scouts from sneaking into the area, or any already planted Yi spies from sneaking out with word of what we were up to.

I have seen animal flocks march willingly to a slaughter pen when led by a Judas goat, but the Bho required not even that much cajolery or duress. Ukuruji merely outlined our plan to the lamas he had evicted from the Pota-lá. Those selfish and heartless holy men were all too anxious to do anything that would get the Wang and his court out of their lamasarai and themselves back into it—and the Bho would do anything their holy men told them to do. So the lamas, evincing no fatherly concern for their Potaist followers, no feeling for their fellows, no loyalty to their own country or reluctance to aid their Mongol over-lords, showing no qualms or scruples whatever, made proclamation to the people of Ba-Tang that they must obey every order the Mongol officers gave them, and go anywhere they might be sent—and the mind-less Bho complied.

Bayan immediately had his warriors begin corralling every able-bodied Bho in the city and environs—men, women, boys and girls of sufficient size—and begin outfitting them with cast-off Mongol arms and armor, giving them the more worn horses for mounts, and forming them into columns complete with pack animals and yurtu-carrier wagons, Bayan's own orlok flag, the yak tails of his sardars, other suitable pennants and guidons. Except for the lamas and trapas and chabis, only the very oldest, youngest and frailest Bho were spared to be left behind—plus a few others. Ukuruji kindly excepted the several culled-out women he had been keeping for the enjoyment of himself and his courtiers, and I likewise sent Ryang and Odcho safely to their homes, each with a necklace of coins to help her further her career of bedding toward a prospect of wedding.

Meanwhile, Bayan sent heralds under white flags of truce riding southward to bellow over and over, in the Yi language, something like this: "Your traitor spy in the capital of Kithai has been exposed and overthrown! You have no more hope of standing under siege! Therefore this province of Yun-nan is declared annexed to the Khanate! You are to throw down your arms and welcome the conquerors when they come! The Khan Kubilai has spoken! Tremble, all men, and obey!" Of course, we did not expect the Yi either to tremble or to obey. We merely trusted that they would be enough bemused and distracted by those heralds arrogantly riding through the valleys that they would not notice the other men flitting furtively along the mountaintops—engineers finding the best places to secrete the brass balls, and then hiding near them, ready to fire their wicks on a signal from me.

In case the Yi had any watchers of excellent eyesight posted far beyond our pickets surrounding Ba-Tang, the whole bok was struck and the yurtu tents collapsed, and all that equipment and the wagons and animals not going with the pretended invasion were hidden away. All the thousands of real Mongol men and women moved into the evacuated buildings of the city. But they did not don the drab and dirty civilian clothing of the displaced Bho. They—and I and Ukuruji and his courtiers as well—stayed clad in battle dress and armor and accouterments, ready to move out on the track of the doomed columns as soon as we got word that the trap was sprung.

It was necessary to send some real Mongols along with those decoy columns of mock Mongols, but Bayan only had to call for volunteers and he got them. The men knew they were volunteering to commit suicide, but these were warriors who had bested death so often that they firmly believed their long service under the Orlok had imbued them with some power always to do so. Any few who survived this latest perilous mission would simply rejoice in Bayan's having once again proved their indestructibility, and the dead would not reproach him. So a band of the men rode at the front of the simulated invasion army, playing on musical instruments the Mongols' war anthems and marching music (which the Bho, for all their willingness, would not have known how to play), and, with that music, setting the alternate canter-walk-canter pace for the thousands behind. At the tail end of that army had to ride another troop of real Mongols, to keep the columns from straggling, and also to send couriers back to us when the Yi—as we hoped—began to congregate for their assault.

The Bho knew very well that they were posing as Mongols, and their lamas had commanded them to do so with a will—though I doubt that the lamas had told them it was probably the last thing they would ever do—and they entered into the pretense most heartily. When they learned that they would be led by a band of military musicians, some of them asked Bayan and Ukuruji, "Lords, should not we chant and sing, as real Mongols do on the march? What should we chant? We know nothing but the 'om mani pémé hum.' "

"Anything but that," said the Orlok. "Let me think. The capital of Yun-nan is named Yun-nan-fu. I suppose you could go clamoring, 'We march to seize Yun-nan-fu!' "

"Yun-nan-pu?" they said.

"No," said Ukuruji, laughing. "Forget about shouting or chanting." He explained to Bayan, "The Bho are incapable of enunciating the sounds of *v* and *f*. Better have them not voice anything at all, or the Yi may recognize that deficiency." He paused, struck by a new idea. "One other thing we might have them do, though. Tell the leaders always to lead the column to the right around any holy structure, like a mani wall or a ch'horten stone pile, leaving that on their *left* hand."

The Bho made a feeble wail of protest at that—it would be an insult to those monuments to the Pota—but their lamas quickly stepped in and bade them obey, and even took the pains to say a hypocritical prayer giving the people special dispensation on this occasion to insult the almighty Pota.

The preparations took only a few days, while the heralds and the engineers went on ahead, and the columns moved out as soon as they were finally formed up, on a beautiful morning of bright sunshine. I must say that even that mock army made a magnificent sight and sound as it left Ba-Tang. Up front, the band of Mongol musicians led with an unearthly but blood-stirring martial music. The trumpeters sounded the great copper trumpets called karachala, which name could rightly translate as "the hellhorns." The drummers had tremendous copper and hide drums like kettles, one slung on either side of the saddle, and they did marvels of twirling and flailing their mallets and crossing and uncrossing their arms as they hammered the thunderous beat for the march. Cymbalists clashed immense brass platters that flashed a flare of sunlight with every stunning ring of sound. Bell players beat a sort of scampanio —metal tubes of various sizes arranged in a lyre-shaped frame. Between and among the louder, blaring noises could be heard the sweeter string music of lutes made with specially short necks for playing while riding.

The music moved on and gradually diminished as it blended into the sound of the thousands of hoofs clip-clopping along behind, and the heavy rumble of wagon wheels, and the creak and jingle of armor and harness. The Bho, for once in their lives, looked not pathetic or contemptible, but as proud and disciplined and determined as if they had actually been going out to war, and on their own account. The horsemen rode rigidly upright in their saddles and facing sternly forward, except to do a very respectable eyes-right when they passed the reviewing Orlok Bayan and his sardars. As the Wang Ukuruji remarked, the decoy men and women did indeed resemble genuine Mongol warriors. They had even been persuaded to ride using the long Mongol stirrups— which enable a hard-riding bowman to stand for better aim with his arrows—instead of the short, cramped, knees-up stirrups favored by the Bho and the Drok and the Han and the Yi.

When the last column's last rank and its rear guard of real Mongols had disappeared downriver, there was nothing for the remainder of us to do except wait and, while waiting, try to maintain, for the benefit of any putative keen-eyed watchers from afar, the illusion that Ba-Tang was an ordinary, nasty Bho city going about its ordinary, nasty Bho business. In the daytimes, our people thronged the market areas and, at twilights, gathered on rooftops as if praying. Whether we ever really were spied upon, I do not know. But if we were, our stratagem could not have been discovered by the Yi down south, for it worked exactly as planned— up to a point, anyway.

About a week after the leavetaking, one of the rear-guard Mongols came galloping to report that the decoy army had got well within Yun-nan, and was still proceeding forward, and the Yi apparently had been fooled by the imposture. Scouts, he said, had seen the scattered individual snipers in the mountains, and outpost groups of them, beginning to collect together and to move downhill like tributary streams converging to become a river. We waited some more, and in another few days another rider came galloping to report that the Yi were unmistakably massing in force behind and on both rear quarters of our mock army— that, in fact, he had had to ride most evasively to get around the gathering Yi and get out of Yun-nan with that information for us.

So now the real army rode forth, and—though it moved as discreetly as possible, with no marching music—that must have been a *really* magnificent sight to see. The entire half a tuk surged out of the Ba-Tang valley like an elemental force of nature on the move. The fifty thousand troops were divided into tomans of ten thousand, each led by a sardar, and those divided into the flag-captains' thousands, and those into the chiefs' hundreds—each riding in broad ranks of ten in files of ten—and each hundred riding far enough apart not to be suffocated by the dust kicked up by those ahead. I say the departure must have made a magnificent spectacle, because I did not get to see it go past me. I rode out well ahead of it, in company with Bayan, Ukuruji and a few senior officers. The Orlok, of course, had to go first, and Ukuruji was in the forefront because he wished to be, and I was there because Bayan ordered me to be there. I had been provided with a special, immense banner of brilliant yellow silk, and I was to unfurl that at the proper moment to signal for the avalanche. Any trooper could have done the signaling, but Bayan insisted on regarding the brass balls as "mine," and their employment as my responsibility.

So we cantered a good many li in advance of the tuk, following the river Jin-sha and the broad, trampled track beside it that was the spoor of the mock army. After only a few days of hard riding and spartan camping, the Orlok grunted, "Here we are crossing the border into Yun-nan Province." A few days farther on, we were intercepted by a Mongol sentry, one of that army's rear guard set to wait for us, and he led us off the river route, taking us to one side of the line of march and around a hill. At the far side of that hill, in late afternoon, we came upon eight more of the Mongol rear guard, where they had made a fireless camp. The captain of the guard respectfully invited us to dismount and share some of their cold rations of dried meat and tsampa balls.

"But first, Orlok," he said, "you may wish to climb to the top of this hill and look over. It will give you a view down this valley of the Jin-sha, and I think you will recognize that you have come just in time."

The captain led the way, as Bayan, Ukuruji and I all made the climb on foot. We did it rather slowly, being stiff from our long ride. Toward the top, our guide motioned for us to crouch and then to crawl, and at last we only cautiously poked our heads over the grass at the crest. We could see that it was well we had been intercepted. Had we followed the river and the tracks for a few hours more, we should have rounded the other side of this hill and entered the long but narrow valley opening before us, in which our mock army was camped. The Bho, as instructed, were behaving more like an occupying force than an invading one. They had not erected any tents, but they had camped this evening as non-chalantly as if they had been invited by the Yi to Yun-nan and were welcome there—with innumerable camp fires and torches twinkling throughout the twilit valley, and only a few guards negligently posted around the camp perimeter, and much movement and noise going on.

"We would have ridden right into the camp," said Ukuruji.

"No, Lord Wang, you would not," said our guide. "And I respect-fully suggest that you subdue your voice." Keeping his own voice low, the captain explained, "All down the other side of this hill are the Yi, lurking in force, and at the entrance to the valley, and on the farther slopes—in fact, everywhere between us and that camp, and beyond. You would have ridden right into their rear, and been seized. The foe are massed in a great horseshoe, around this end and both valley sides of the decoy camp. You cannot see the Yi because, like us, they have lighted no fires and they are concealed in every available cover."

Bayan asked, "They have done so every night the army has camped?"

"Yes, Lord Orlok, and each time increasing in their numbers. But I think tonight's camp will be the last that mock army will make. I might be wrong. But, as best I could count, today was the first day the foe have not added to their numbers. I think every fighting man in this area of Yun-nan is now congregated in this valley—a force of some fifty thou-sand, about equal to our own. And, if I were commanding the Yi, I should deem this rather narrow defile the perfect place to make a crush-ing assault on what appears to be a singularly unapprehensive invader. As I say, I might be wrong. But my warrior instinct tells me the Yi will attack at tomorrow's dawn."

"A good report, Captain Toba." I think Bayan knew by name every man of his half a tuk. "And I am inclined to share your intuition. What of the engineers? Have you any idea of their disposition?"

"Alas, no, Lord Orlok. Communication with them would be impossible without revealing them to the enemy. I have had to assume and trust that they have been keeping pace along the mountain crests, and each day newly placing and readying their secret weapons."

"Let us trust they did it this day, anyway," said Bayan. He lifted his head enough to make a slow scan of the mountains ringing the valley.

So did I. If the Orlok was going to persist in holding me responsible for the secret weapons, it was to my best interest that the things do what I hoped they would. If they did, some fifty thousand Bho were going to perish, and about that many Yi as well. It was a considerable responsibility, indeed, for a noncombatant and a Christian. But it would mean winning the war for my chosen side, and a victory would show that God was also on our side, and that would allay any Christian qualms about wholesale slaughter. If the brass balls did not perform as warranted, the Bho would die anyway, but the Yi would not. The war would have to go on, and that might cause me some Christian pangs of conscience—killing so many people, even if they were only Bho, to no purpose at all.

But what mainly concerned me, I must confess, was the satisfaction of my curiosity. I was interested to see if the flaming-powder balls *did* work, and how well. Certainly, I said to myself, I could see a dozen vantage points on the mountains where, if I had been doing the placing, I would have laid the charges. Those were outcrops of bare rock, like Crusader castles towering up from the forest growth, and showing clefts and checkerings where they had been split by time or weather, and where, if they were suddenly split farther asunder, the slabs ought to topple and fall and, in falling, take other chunks of their mountains with them. . . .

Bayan grunted a command, and we slithered down the hill the way we had come. At the bottom, he gave orders to the waiting men:

"The real army should be about forty or fifty li behind us, and also preparing to stop for the night. Six of you start riding toward it, this instant. One of you pull off to the trailside every ten li, and wait there, so your horses will be fresh tomorrow. The sixth rider should reach there before sunrise. Tell the sardars not to start marching again. Tell them to wait where they are, lest the dust of their march be visible from here, and spoil all our plans. If all goes as planned tomorrow, I will send Captain Toba riding next and riding hard, and you will rush the word on in relays to the tuk. The word will be for the sardars to bring the whole army on, at a stretch-out gallop, to do the mopping up of any remnants of the enemy that might be left alive in this valley. If things go wrong here, well . . . I will send Captain Toba with different orders to impart. Now go. Ride."

The six men left, leading their horses until they should be well out of hearing. Bayan turned to the rest of us.

"Let us eat a little and sleep a little. We must be watching from the hilltop before first light."

. 2 .

A N D we were there: the Orlok Bayan and his accompanying officers, the Wang Ukuruji, myself, Captain Toba and the remaining two men of his troop. The others were each carrying a sword, a bow and a quiver of arrows, and Bayan—ready for combat, not parade—was toothless. I, since I had the unwieldy flag-lance to handle, had no other weapon but my belt knife. We lay in the grass and watched as the scene before us slowly became visible. The morning would have to be well advanced before the sun would show itself above the mountaintops, but its rise lightened the cloudless blue sky, and that light gradually reflected down into the black bowl of the valley, and it sucked a mist up off the river. At first, that was the only movement we could see, a milky luminescence drifting against the blackness. But then the valley assumed shape and color: misty blue at its mountain edges, dark green of forests, paler green of the grass and undergrowth in the clearings, silver glitter of the river as the obscuring mist evaporated. With shape and color came movement also: the horse herd began to stir and mill a little, and we could hear an occasional distant whicker and neigh. Then the women of the bok began to arise from their bedrolls and move about, blowing the banked camp fires into flame and setting water to heat for cha—we heard the distant clink of kettles—before waking the menfolk.

The Yi had often enough, by now, watched that camp awaken to know its routine. And they chose this moment for their assault: when there was light enough for them to see their objective clearly, but only the women were astir and the men still asleep. I do not know how the Yi signaled for the attack; I saw no banner waved and heard no trumpet blown. But the Yi warriors moved all in an instant and all together, with admirable precision. One moment, we watchers were looking down an empty hill slope at the bok in the valley; we might have been at the top of an empty amphitheater, looking down the unpeopled seat-shelves at a tableau on the distant stage. The next moment, our view was blocked by the slope's being no longer empty, as if all the amphitheater's shelves had magically and silently sprouted a vast audience in tier upon tier. Out of the grass and weeds and bushes downhill of us, there sprang erect a taller growth—leather-armored men, each with a bow already bent and an arrow already nocked to the string. So abruptly did it happen that it seemed to me that some of them had arisen from right before my face; I fancied I could *smell* the half dozen nearest; and I think I was not the only one of us lurkers who did not have to repress an impulse to start up, too. But I only widened my eyes and moved my head enough to gaze about, seeing all around the valley amphitheater that suddenly visible and menacing audience, standing in thousands, in horseshoe rows and tiers—man-sized where they were near me, doll-sized farther away, insect-sized on the more distant valley slopes—all those ranks quilled and fringed

and fuzzed with arrows aimed at a central point that was the stage-
tableau encampment.

That had all happened in near silence, and far more quickly than it
takes to tell. The next thing that happened—the first sound made by the
Yi—was not a concerted, ululating battle cry, as a Mongol army would
have made. The sound was only the weird, whishing, slightly whistling
noise of all their arrows loosed at once, the thousands of them making all
together a sort of fluttering roar, like a wind soughing along the valley.
Then the sound, as it diminished away from us, was repeated, but fragmented and doubled into an overlapping noise of whish-whish-whish as
the Yi, with great rapidity but no longer simultaneity, plucked from their
quivers more arrows—while the first were still in flight—and nocked
them and loosed them, meanwhile running full tilt toward the bok. The
arrows went high against the sky and briefly darkened the blue of it,
even as they dwindled in size from discernible sticks to twigs to slivers to
toothpicks to whiskers, and then arced lazily over to become a dim,
shady haze that drizzled down on the camp, looking no more dreadful
than a gray patter of early morning rain. We watchers, being out behind
and near to the archers, had seen and heard that first movement of the
assault. But its targets—the standing women and horses and recumbent
men in the bok—would probably have noticed nothing until the thousands of arrows began showering down and among and around and into
them. No mere haze or fuzz at that extremity of their flight, the arrows
were sharp-pointed and heavy and moving fast from their long fall, and
many must have fallen upon flesh and struck to the bone.

And by then the ranks of the Yi nearest to the camp were running
into the outskirts of it, still making no warning outcry and heedless of
their own fellows' arrows still falling, their swords and lances already
flashing and stabbing and slashing. All the time, up where we were, we
watched the Yi warriors still new-sprouting from our hillside and all the
mountainsides around, as if the valley greenery was incessantly blooming
over and over again into dark flowers that were standing archers, then
shedding those and letting them run down toward the bok, then blos-
soming with more of them. Now there was also noise, louder than the
wind-and-rain sound of the arrows—shouts of alarm and outrage and
fright and pain from the people in the camp. When that noise began and
surprise was no longer enjoined, the Yi also began to bellow battle cries
as they ran and converged on their objective, now at last allowing themselves the yells that raise a warrior's courage and ferocity and, he hopes,
strike terror into his foe.

When all was clamor and confusion down in the valley, Bayan said,
"I think now is the time, Marco Polo. The Yi are all running for the bok,
and no more are springing up, and I see none held in reserve outside the
combat area."

"Now?" I said. "Are you sure, Orlok? I will be highly visible, standing here and waving a flag. It may give the Yi reason for suspicion and
pause. If they do not drop me with an immediate arrow."

"No fear," he said. "No advancing warrior ever looks back. Get up
there."

So I clambered to my feet, expecting any moment to feel a thumping puncture of my leather cuirass, and hurriedly unfurled the silk from my lance. When nothing struck me down, I gripped the lance in both hands, raised the banner as high as I could, and began waving it from left to right and back again, the yellow shining bright in the morning light and the silk snapping briskly. I could not just wave it once or twice and then again drop prone, on the assumption that it had been seen from afar. I had to stand there until I *knew* that the distant engineers had seen the signal and acted on it. I was mentally calculating:

How long will it take? They must be already looking this way. Yes, they would have known where we had to come from, at the rear of the enemy. So, from their hiding places, the engineers are peering in this direction. They are scanning this end of the valley, alert for a moving dot of yellow among all the ambient greenery. Now—hui! alalà! evviva!— they see the distant, tiny, wagging banner. Now they scramble back from their lookout positions to wherever they earlier secreted the brass balls. That may take them some moments. Allow a few moments for that. Very well, now they pick up their smoldering incense sticks and blow on them—*if* they had the good sense to have them already alight and waiting. Perhaps they did not! So now they must fumble with flint and steel and tinder. . . .

Allow a few more moments for that. God, but the banner was getting heavy. Very well, so *now* they have their tinder glowing, and now they are wheedling into flame a pile of dry leaves or something. Now they have each got a twig or an incense stick afire, and now they are bearing those over to the brass balls. Now they are touching the fire to the wicks. Now the wicks are burning and sputtering and the engineers are leaping up and running hard for safe distance. . . .

I wished them good luck and much distance and safe shelter, for I myself was feeling exceptionally exposed and visible and vulnerable. I seemed to have been flaunting my flag and my bravata and my person for an eternity already, and the Yi must be blind not to have spotted me. Now—how long had the Firemaster said?—a slow count of ten after the wicks were lit. I counted ten slow wags of my big, rippling yellow banner. . . .

Nothing happened.

Caro Gèsu, what had gone wrong? Could it be that the engineers had misunderstood? My arms were weary of the waving, and I was sweating profusely, though the sun was still behind the mountains and the morning was not yet warm. Could it be that the engineers had waited to see my signal before even *placing* the balls? Why had I entrusted this enterprise—and now my very life—to a dozen thickheaded Mongol rankers? Would I have to stand here, waving more and more feebly, for another eternity or two, while the engineers leisurely did what should have been done already? And how long after that would it be before they even began lackadaisically to rummage around in their belt purses for flint and steel? And during all that time, must I stand here flailing this extremely eye-inviting yellow flag? Bayan might be convinced that no warrior ever looked back *voluntarily*, but any of those Yi had only to stumble and fall, or be knocked sprawling, so that his head turned this way. He could hardly fail to see such an uncommon battle-field sight as I presented. He would yell to his companion warriors, and they would come pelting toward me, loosing arrows as they came. . . .

The green landscape was blurred by sweat running into my eyes, but I saw a brief flicker of yellow at the corner of my vision. Maledetto! I was letting the banner sag; I must hold it higher. But then, where the flick of yellow had been, there was now a puff of blue against the green. I heard a chorus of "Hui!" from my fellows still prone in the grass, and then they leapt up to stand beside me, cheering "Hui!" again and again. I let the flag and its lance drop, and I stood panting and sweating and watching the yellow flashes and blue smokes of the huo-yao balls doing what they had been intended to do.

The whole center of the valley, where now the Yi and the Bho mock-Mongols were intimately commingled, was clouded by the dust raised by their fierce confusion. But the flashes and smokes were high above that dome of dust, and not obscured by it. They were up where I would have put them myself, twinkling and puffing from those crevices in the castle-like rock outcrops. They did not all ignite at once, but flared by ones and twos, from one mountain height and then another. I was pleased that the engineers had placed them where I would have done, and I was pleased when I counted twelve ignitions; every single ball had performed as warranted—but I was dismayed by the apparent puniness of them. Such tiny flashes of fire, and so soon extinguished—and leaving only such insignificant plumes of blue smoke. The sound of them came much later and, though the noises were loud enough to be heard above the clamor of shouting and scuffling down in the valley, they were no such thunder-ous roar as I had heard when my palace chamber was demolished. These noises of ignition were only sharp slaps of sound—as might have been produced by a Yi warrior yonder hitting the flat of his sword on a horse's flank—one and two slapping sounds, and then several together in a sustained crackle of slaps, and then the final few separate again.

And then nothing more happened, except that the furious but futile battle continued unabated down in the valley, where none of the com-batants seemed to have noticed our byplay in the heights. The Orlok turned and gave me a lacerating look. I shrugged my eyebrows help-lessly at him. But suddenly all the other men were murmuring "Hui!" in a wondering way, and they were all pointing, and most of them in different directions. Bayan and I looked first where one was pointing, and then where another was, and another. Over here, high up, the cleft gashed in a wall-like rock was perceptibly widening. Over there, high up, two great slabs of rock that had been side by side were gradually leaning apart. Over yonder, high up, a pinnacle of rock like a castle keep was toppling over, and breaking into separate rocks as it did so, and spraying those rocks apart, and doing all those things as slowly as if it had been under water.

If those mountains truly never had suffered an avalanche before, then *because* they never had, they may have been ready and poised for one. I think we could have accomplished our intentions with just three or

four of the brass balls lodged on either side of the valley; we had put six
on each side, and all had done their work. And, puny as was the commencement of the performance, the conclusion was spectacular. I can
best describe it thus: consider the high rocks to have been a few exposed
knobs of the backbones of the mountains, and consider our charges to
have been hammer blows that broke the bones. As the mountains' spines
crumbled, their earth cover began to peel away here and there, like a
hide being skinned piecemeal off an animal. And as the hide wrinkled
and folded, the forests began to shed and shred off it, as a camel's fur
does in summertime, in unsightly tufts and patches.

As early as the breaking-away of the first rocks, we watchers could
feel the hill under us tremble, though we were many li distant from the
very nearest of those rockslides. The valley floor had to be quivering
then, too, but the two armies conjoined in battle still took no notice; or, if
they did, every man and woman no doubt believed it to be only his or
her own personal quaking of fear and rage. I remember thinking: that
must be the way we mortals will ignore the first tremors of Armageddon,
continuing to pursue our trivial and pitiful and spiteful little strifes even
while God is loosing the unimaginable devastation that will end the
world and all.

But a goodly piece of the world was being devastated right here.
The falling rocks dislodged other rocks below them and, rolling and
sliding, they gouged up great swathes and whole zonte of earth and
then, rocks and earth together, they scoured their various mountainsides
of their vegetation, the trees toppling and colliding and heaping up and
overlying and splintering, and then the surface of each mountain and
everything that grew upon it or was contained within it boulders,
rocks, stones, clods, loose earth, meadow-sized pieces of rumpled turf,
trees, bushes, flowers, probably even the forest creatures caught unawares—all came *down*, down into the valley, in a dozen or more separate avalanches, and the noise of them, until now delayed by distance,
finally began to batter our ears. It was a mutter that grew to a growl that
grew to a roar that grew to a thunder, but a thunder like I never heard
before—not even in the unstable heights of the Pai-Mir, where the noises
had often been loud, but never for longer than a few minutes. This
thunder here continued to grow in volume and to create echoes and to
collect and absorb the echoes, and to bellow ever louder, as if it never
would reach its loudest. Now the hill on which we stood was quivering
like a jelly—the noise alone might have been enough to shake it—so that
we could scarcely keep our feet, and all the trees nearby us were rustling
so they shed many of their leaves, and birds were bursting up everywhere, squawking and screeching, and the very air around us seemed to
quake.

The rumblings of the several avalanches would have overwhelmed
the noise of battle in the valley, but there was no more of that shouting
and war-crying and clinking together of sword blades. The poor people
had at last perceived what was happening, and so had the camp's herds
of horses, and the people and horses were scurrying hither and thither.
Being myself in a state of some agitation, I could not too well discern

what the people were doing individually. I saw them rather as an indistinct mass—like the blurred masses of landscape coming down the mountains roundabout—the thousands of people and horses all running in a tremendous, untidy bunch. The way they were moving, I might have thought the whole valley floor was tilting back and forth and sloshing them from side to side of it. Except for the numbers already struck down in combat, lying motionless or moving only feebly, the people and horses seemed first, and all at the same time, to glimpse the havoc hurtling toward them down the western slopes, and they all ran in a body away from there, only to see the other calamity coming down the eastern slopes, and all in a body they surged back again to the middle of the valley floor, all but a few who jumped into the river, as if they were fleeing a forest fire and might find safety in the cool water. Some two or three dozen individuals—I did make out that much—were running straight down the valley's middle, toward us, and probably others were scampering up it in the other direction. But the avalanches were moving faster than any mere human could.

And down they came. Though the swooping blurs of brown and green contained whole forests of full-sized trees and countless boulders as big as houses, they looked, from where we stood, like cascades of dirty, gritty, lumpy tsampa porridge being poured down the sides of a giant tureen to puddle in its bottom, and the towering clouds of dust they raised on the way looked like the steam rising from that tsampa porridge. When the several separate slides reached the lower skirts of their mountains, they coalesced on either side into a single stupendous avalanche roaring into the valley—one from the east, one from the west —to meet in the middle. Rasping across the flat valley floor, they must have slowed their rush to some slight degree, but not so I could see it, and the front face of each cataract was still as high as a three-story wall when they came together. And when they did that, it made me remember once having seen two great mountain rams, in the season of rut, gallop at each other and butt their huge horned heads together with a shock that made my own teeth shake.

I would have expected to hear a similarly teeth-rattling crash when the two monster avalanches met head on, but their thunder climaxed instead with a sort of cosmically loud kissing noise. The Jin-sha River, on its way through this valley, ran along its eastern edge. So the landslide sluicing down from the east simply scooped up a considerable length of that river as it careered across it, and, as it continued on, must have churned that water into its forward content so that its front became a wall of sticky muck. When the two careening masses came together, then, it was with a loud, slapping, moist *slurp!*, suggesting that the avalanches were cemented there to be the valley's new and higher floor for all time to come. Also, at the instant of their collision, the sun bounded into view beyond the eastern mountains, but the sky was so thick with dust that its disk was discolored. The sun came up as suddenly and as brassy of hue and as blurred around the rim as if it had been a cymbal thrown up there to ring the finale to all the commotion in the valley. And, while the trailing rubble skirts of the slides continued to sweep down from the heights, the noise did indeed die down, not all at once, but with the kind of wobbling, clashing, diminishing clangor that a cymbal makes as its blur slows to stillness.

In the sudden hush—it was not a total silence, for many boulders were still thudding and bouncing down from the heights, and trees still crunching and skidding down, and patches of turf still skittering down, and unidentifiable other things still caroming about in the distance—the first words I heard were the Orlok's:

"Ride now, Captain Toba. Fetch our army."

The captain went back the way we had come. Bayan leisurely took out from a purse the great gleaming device of gold and porcelain that was his teeth, and forced it into his mouth, and gnashed it a few times to settle its jaws to his own. Looking now a proper Orlok, ready for his triumphal parade, he strode off down the hill in the direction we were facing. When he dimmed into the cloud of dust, the rest of us followed after him. I did not know why we were doing that, unless to gloat on the completeness of our unusual victory. But there was nothing to be seen of it, or of anything really, in that dense and stifling pall. When we had gone only as far as the bottom of the hill, I had lost sight of my companions, and only heard Bayan's muffled voice, off to my right somewhere, saying to somebody, "The troops will be disappointed when they get here. No battlefield loot to pick over."

The enormous cloud of dust thrown up by the avalanches had, by the time the two masses met, entirely obscured our view of the valley and its ultimate devastation. So I cannot say that I actually witnessed the annihilation of something like a hundred thousand people. Nor, in all the noise, did I hear their last hopeless screams or the snapping of their limbs. But they were now gone, together with all the horses, weapons, their personal belongings and other equipment. The valley had been resurfaced, and the people had been wiped out as if they had been no bigger or more worth keeping than the crawling ants and beetles that had inhabited the old ground.

I remembered the bleached bones and skulls I had seen lying about the Pai-Mir, the remains of animal herds and karwan trains that had encountered other avalanches. There would not be even that much trace left here. None of the Ba-Tang Bho we had excused from the march— little Odcho and Ryang, for instance—if they journeyed here to visit the place where their city's population was last seen, would ever find the skull of a father or brother to fashion into a sentimental keepsake like a drinking bowl or a festa drum. Maybe some Yi farmer tilling this valley in some far distant century would turn up with his digging stick a fragment of one of the less deeply buried corpses. But, until then. . . .

It occurred to me that, of all the men and women who had been so frantically running about, and those who had crouched pathetically in the river, and those who had been already lying wounded or unconscious or dead, only the insensible had been the fortunate few. The others had had to endure at least one terrible last moment of knowing that they were about to be stamped on like insects or, even worse, buried alive. Maybe some of them were *yet* alive, uncrushed, still conscious, trapped underground in dark, tight, contorted little graves and tunnels and pockets of air that would persist until the great weight of earth and rocks and rubble had finished shifting and settling in its new location.

It would take some while for the valley to accommodate itself to its changed topography. I could tell that because, even while I groped about and coughed and sneezed in the cloud of dry dust, I found that I was sloshing about in muddy water that had not been there before. The Jin-sha River was nuzzling and probing at the barrier that had so abruptly impeded its flow, and was having to spread out sideways beyond what had formerly been its banks. Evidently, in my trudging about in the dimness, I had veered over to the left, to the eastward. Not wanting to walk any deeper into the gathering water, I turned right and, my boots alternately sucking and slipping in the new mud, went to rejoin the others. When a human shape loomed up before me in the murk, I called to him in the Mongol language, and that was an almost fatal mistake.

I never had a chance to inquire how he had survived the catastrophe —whether he was one of those who had gone running the length of the valley instead of back and forth, or whether he had simply and inexplicably been lifted up by the avalanche instead of crushed beneath it. Maybe he could not have told me, for maybe he did not know himself how he had been spared. It seems that there are always at least a few survivors of even the worst disaster—perhaps there will even be a few after Armageddon—and in this case we would discover that there were about four score still alive of the hundred thousand. Half of those were Yi, and about half of the Yi were quite undamaged and ambulatory— and at least two of them were still armed and brimming with a rage for immediate revenge—and I had had the misfortune to meet one of those.

He may have believed himself to be the *only* Yi left alive, and may have been startled to encounter another human form in the dust cloud, but I gave him the advantage when I spoke in Mongol. I did not know what he was, but he knew instantly that I was an enemy—one of the enemy that had just swept away his army and his companions in arms and probably close friends, even brothers of his. With the instinctive action of an angered hornet, he made a swipe at me with his sword. Had it not been for the new mud in which we stood, I should have perished at that moment. I could not have consciously dodged the sudden blow, but my involuntary flinch made me slip in the mud, and I fell down as the sword went *whish!* where I had been.

I still did not know who or what had attacked me—one thing went through my mind: "Expect me when you least expect me"—but there was no mistaking the attack. I rolled away from his feet and grabbed for the only weapon I carried, my belt knife, and tried to stand, but got only to one knee before he lunged again. We were both still only indistinct figures in the dust, and his footing was as slippery as mine, so his second swing also missed me. That blow brought him close enough to me that I made a dart with my knife point, but it fell short when I slid again in the mud.

Let me say something about close combat. I had earlier, in Khanbalik, seen the imposing map of the Minister of War, with its little flags and yak tails marking the positions of armies. At other times, I have watched high officers plotting out battle tactics and following the progress of them, using a tabletop and colored blocks of different sizes. Such exercises make battle look neat and tidy and perhaps, to a remote officer or an observer not involved, even predictable in the outcome. Back home in Venice, I had seen pictures and tapestries depicting famous Venetian victories on land and sea—over here Our fleet or cavalry, over yonder Theirs, the combatants always facing each other squarely and loosing arrows or aiming lances with precision and assuredness and even a calm look of equanimity. A viewer of such pictures would take a battle to be a thing as orderly and trim and methodical as a Game of Squares, or Shahi, played on a flat board in a well-lighted, comfortable room.

I doubt that any battle has ever been like that, and I know that close combat cannot be. It is a flailing, messy, desperate confusion, usually on wretched terrain and in vile weather, one man against another, both of them having forgotten in their rage and terror everything they ever were taught about how to fight. I suppose every man has learned the rules of swordplay and knifeplay, do thus and so to parry your opponent's offense, move like this to get past his guard, execute these other feints to expose the weak places in his defense and the gaps in his armor. Perhaps those rules apply when two masters stand toe to toe in a gara di scherma, or when two duelists politely face off in a pleasant meadow. It is quite different when you and your opponent are grappling in a mud puddle with dense cloud all about, when both of you are dirty and sweaty, when your eyes are gritty and watering so you can barely see.

I will not try to describe our struggle, blow by blow. I do not remember the sequence. All I recall is that it was a time of grunting, panting, squirming, thrashing desperation—a very long time, it seemed —with me trying to get close enough to him to stab with my knife, and he trying to keep enough distance to swing his sword. We were both body-armored in leather, but differently, so that we each had an advantage over the other. My cuirass was of supple hides, allowing me freedom to move and dodge. His was of cuirbouilli so stiff that it stood out around him like a barrel; it hampered his agility, but made an effective barrier against my short, wide-bladed knife. When at last, more by chance than skill, I struck at his chest and the blade went in, I realized that it had penetrated the cuirass, and was stuck there, but could only lightly have pricked his rib cage. So in that moment he had me at his mercy, my knife wedged in his leather, I clinging to its handle, while he was free to wield his sword.

He took that moment to laugh derisively, triumphantly before he struck, and that was *his* mistake. My knife was the one I had long ago been given by a Romm girl whose name meant Blade. I squeezed its haft in the proper way, and I felt the wide blades jar apart, and I knew the inner, slim, third blade had leapt out from between them, for my foe bulged his eyes in unbelieving surprise. He gave a snarling gasp and his mouth stayed open, and his back-flung hand let drop his sword, and he belched blood all over me, and he toppled away from me and fell. I yanked my knife loose of him and wiped it clean and closed it up again, and I stood up, thinking: now I have slain two men in my lifetime. Not to mention the twin women in Khanbalik. Do I also take credit for the whole victory here, and count my lifetime kill as one hundred thousand and four? The Khan Kubilai ought to be proud of me, having cleared such ample room for myself on the overcrowded earth.

· 3 ·

M y companions, I saw when I located and rejoined them, had also encountered a vengeful enemy in the fog, but had not fared so well as I. They were grouped around two figures stretched on the ground, and Bayan whirled with his sword in his hand as I approached.

"Ah, Polo," he said, relaxing as he recognized me, though I must have been bloody all over. "Looks as if you met one, too—and dispatched him. Good man. This one was insanely fierce." He pointed his blade at one of the supine figures, a Yi warrior, much hacked about and obviously dead. "It took three of us to slay him, and not before he had got one of us." He indicated the other figure.

I exclaimed, "A tragedy! Ukuruji has been hurt!" The young Wang was lying with his face screwed up in pain, and his own two hands clutched around his neck. I cried, "He seems to be strangling!" and bent to loosen his hands and examine the injury to his throat. But when I raised the clenched hands, his head came along in their grasp. It had been completely severed from his body. I grunted and recoiled, then stood looking sadly down at him, and murmured, "How terrible. Ukuruji was a good fellow."

"He was a Mongol," said one of the officers. "Next to killing, dying is what Mongols do best. It is nothing to weep over."

"No," I agreed. "He was eager to help win Yun-nan, and he did."

"He will not govern it, unfortunately," said the Orlok. "But his last sight was of our total victory. That is no bad moment to die."

I asked, "You regard Yun-nan as ours, then?"

"Oh, there will be other contested valleys. And cities and towns to take. We have not annihilated every last one of the foe. But the Yi will be demoralized by this crushing defeat, and will be putting up only token resistance. Yes, I can safely say that Yun-nan is ours. That means we will next be battering at the back door of the Sung, and the whole empire must fall very soon. That is the word you will take back to Kubilai."

"I wish I were taking him the good news unalloyed with bad. It cost him a son."

One of the officers said, "Kubilai has many other sons. He may even adopt you, Ferenghi, after what you did for him here. Behold, the dust is settling. You can see what you accomplished with your ingenious brass engines."

We all turned from contemplating Ukuruji's body, and looked down the valley. The dust was finally sifting out of the air and laying itself like a soft, gentle, age-yellowed shroud on the tormented and tumbled landscape. The mountain slopes on both sides, which earlier in the morning had been thickly forested, now had trees and greenery only fringing the edges of their open wounds—great gouged-out gullies and gorges of raw brown earth and new-broken rock. There was just enough foliage left on the mountains that they looked like matronly women who had been stripped and violated, and now were clutching to themselves the vestiges of their finery. Down in the valley, some few living people were picking their way through the last shreds of dust fog, across the jumble of rubble and rocks and tree limbs and upended tree roots. They had apparently espied us, gathered at this clear end of the valley, and decided this was the place to regroup.

They kept plodding and hobbling up to us during the rest of that day, singly and in little groups. Most of them, as I have said, were Bho and Yi survivors of the devastation—with no idea how they had lived through it—some injured or crippled, but some entirely unscathed. Most of the Yi, even the unhurt ones, had lost all will to fight, and approached us with the resignation of prisoners of war. Some of them might have come running and frothing and swinging steel, as two of them already had done, but they came in custody of Mongol warriors who had disarmed them on the way. The Mongols were the volunteers who had accompanied the mock army as musicians and rear guards. Since they had been at the leading and trailing ends of the march, hence at the farther ends of the camp, and had had foreknowledge of our plans, they had had the best chance to run out of the way of the avalanches. Though they were only a score or two in number, those men were loud with congratulations on the success of our stratagem, and with self-congratulation on their own escape from it.

Even more to be congratulated—and I made sure to give each of them a comradely embrace—were the Mongol engineers. They were the last survivors to join us, for they had to come all the way down the ravaged mountain slopes. They arrived looking justifiably proud of what they had done, but looking also rather stunned, some of them because they had been standing close to the concussion when their engines ignited, but some because of the sheer awesomeness of what had then occurred. But I told every one of them, and sincerely, "I could not have done the positioning better myself!" and took his name, to praise him personally to the Khakhan. I must remark, though, that I collected only eleven names. Twelve men had gone up into the mountains, and twelve balls had done what they were supposed to do, but we never learned what happened to the man who did not return.

It was the middle of the night when Captain Toba returned, in company with the leading columns of the authentic Mongol army, but I was still awake at that hour and glad to see them. Some of the blood with which I was caked was my own, and some of it was still flowing, for

I had not emerged entirely undamaged from my private contest with the Yi. That warrior had given me some cuts on the hands and forearms, which I had hardly noticed at the time, but by now were quite painful. The first thing the army troops did was to erect a small yurtu for a hospital tent, and Bayan made sure that I was the first casualty attended by the shamàn physician-priest-sorcerers.

They cleaned my cuts and anointed them with vegetable salves and bandaged them, which would have sufficed me. But then they had to engage in some sorcery to divine whether I might have sustained internal injuries not visible. The chief shamàn set upright before me a knotted bunch of dried herbs that he called the chutgur, or "demon of fevers," and read aloud to it from a book of incantations, while all the lesser physicians made an infernal noise with little bells and drums and sheep's-horn trumpets. Then the head shamàn tossed a sheep's shoulder bone onto the brazier burning in the middle of the tent and, when it had charred black, raked it out and peered at it to read the cracks the heat had produced. He finally adjudged me to be internally intact, which I could have told him with a lot less fuss, and let me leave the hospital. The next casualty brought in was the Wang Ukuruji, to be sewn back together and made presentable for his funeral the next day.

Outside the yurtu, the darkness of the night had been considerably abolished by the light of many tremendous camp fires. Around them, the troops were doing their stamping, leaping, pounding victory dances, and yelling "Ha!" and "Hui!" and liberally sloshing all onlookers with arkhi and kumis from the cups they held while they danced. They were all rapidly getting quite drunk.

I found Bayan and a couple of the just-arrived sardars, still fairly sober, waiting to present me with a gift. On the army's march south from Ba-Tang, they told me, its advance scouts had routinely swept every town and village and isolated building, to rout out any suspicious persons who might be Yi soldiers passing as civilians to get behind the Mongol lines as spies or agents of random destruction. And, in a run-down karwansarai on a back road, they had found a man who could not give a satisfactory account of himself. They produced him for me, with the air of giving me a great prize, but he looked no such thing. He was just another dirty, smelly Bho trapa with his head shaven and his face clotted with that medicinal brown plant-sap.

"No, a Bho he is not," said one of the sardars. "A question was put to him which contained the name of the city Yun-nan-fu, in such a way that he had to repeat the name in his reply. And he said *fu*, not Yun-nan-pu. Further, he claims his own name to be Gom-bo, but he was carrying in his loincloth this signature yin."

The sardar handed the stone seal to me, and I duly examined it, but it could equally well have said Gom-bo or Marco Polo, as far as I could tell. I asked what it did say.

"Pao," said the sardar. "Pao Nei-ho."

"Ah, the Minister of Lesser Races." Now that I knew who he was, I could recognize him despite the disguise. "I remember once before, Minister Pao, you had trouble speaking out plain and clear."

He only shrugged and did not speak at all.

I said to the sardar, "The Khan Kubilai commanded that, if this man was found, I was to slay him. Will you have someone see to that for me? I have already done enough killing for one day. I will keep this yin to show to the Khakhan as evidence that his order was obeyed." The sardar saluted, and began to lead the prisoner away. "One moment," I said, and again addressed Pao. "Speaking of speaking—did you ever have occasion to whisper the words, 'Expect me when you least expect me'?"

He denied it, as he probably would have done in any case, but his expression of genuine surprise and bafflement convinced me that he had not been the whisperer in the Echo Pavilion. Very well, one after another, I was diminishing my list of suspects: the servant girl Buyantu, now this Minister Pao. . . .

But the next day I found that Pao was still alive. The whole bok woke late, and most of its people with aching heads, but all of them immediately set to preparing for Ukuruji's sepulture. Only the shamàns seemed to be taking no part in the preparations, now that they had readied the funeral's centerpiece. They sat apart, in a group, with the condemned Minister Pao among them, and they appeared to be solicitously feeding him his breakfast meal. I went in search of the Orlok Bayan, and asked in annoyance why Pao had not been slain.

"He is being slain," said Bayan. "And in a particularly nasty way. He will be dead by the time the tomb is dug."

Still somewhat testily, I inquired, "What is so nasty about letting him eat himself to death?"

"The shamàns are not feeding him, Polo. They are spooning quicksilver into him."

"Quicksilver?"

"It kills with cruelly agonizing cramps, but it is also a most efficacious embalming agent. When he is dead, he will keep. And he will retain the color and freshness of life. Go look at the Wang's corpse, which the shamàns also filled with quicksilver. Ukuruji looks as healthy and rosy as any bouncing babe, and will look so throughout eternity."

"If you say so, Orlok. But why accord the same funerary rites to the treacherous Pao?"

"A Wang must go to his grave attended by servants for the afterlife. We will also be killing and entombing with him all the Yi who emerged from the disaster yesterday—and a couple of Bho women survivors, too, for his afterlife enjoyment. They may get handsomer in the afterlife; one never knows. But we are giving special attention to Pao. What better servant could Ukuruji take into death than a former Minister of the Khanate?"

When the shamàns adjudged the hour to be auspicious, the troops did a lot of marching about the catafalque on which Ukuruji lay, some afoot and others on horseback, with commendable dash and precision, and with much martial music and doleful chanting, and the shamàns lit many fires making colored smokes, and wailed their foolish incantations. Those performances were all recognizably funerary of aspect, but some other details of the ceremony had to be explained to me. The troops had dug for Ukuruji a cave in the ground, right at the edge of the avalanche rubble. Bayan told me the position was chosen so it would be unnotice-able to any potential grave robbers.

"We will eventually erect a properly grandiose monument over it. But while we are still occupied with the war, some Yi might sneak back into this valley. If they cannot find the Wang's resting place, they can-not loot his belongings or mutilate his corpse or desecrate the tomb by making water and excrement in it."

Ukuruji's body was reverentially laid in the grave, and about it were laid the fresher cadavers of the newly slaughtered Yi prisoners and the two unfortunate Bho females, and close beside Ukuruji was laid the body of the Minister of Lesser Races. Pao had so contorted himself in his death agonies that the proceedings had to be briefly delayed while the shamàns broke numerous of his bones to straighten him out decently. Then the burial detail of troops set up a wooden rack between the bodies and the cave entrance, and began to affix to it some bows and arrows. Bayan explained that for me:

"It is an invention of Kubilai's Court Goldsmith Boucher. We mili-tary men do not always scorn inventors. Regard—the arrows are strung so they aim at the entrance, and the bows are hard bent, and that rack holds them so, but on a sensitive arrangement of levers. If grave robbers ever should find the place and dig into it, their opening the tomb will trip those levers, and they will be met by a killing barrage of arrows."

The gravediggers closed the entrance with earth and rocks so delib-erately untidy that the tomb was indistinguishable from the nearby rub-ble, at which I inquired:

"If you take such pains to make the tomb undiscoverable, how will *you* find it when the time comes to build the monument?"

Bayan merely glanced to one side, and I looked over there. Some troopers had brought one of their herd mares on a lead rein, closely accompanied by her nursling foal. Some of the men held to the lead rein while the others dragged the little infant horse away from its mother and over to the grave site. The mare began to plunge and whinny and rear, and did so even more frantically when the men holding the foal raised a battle-ax and brained it. The mare was led kicking and neighing away, while the buriers scraped earth over the new body, and Bayan said:

"There. When we come this way again, even if it is two or three or five years hence, we have only to let the same mare loose and she will lead us to this spot." He paused, and champed his great teeth thought-fully, and said, "Now, Polo, although you deserve much credit for the victory here, you did it so thoroughly that there is no plunder for you to share in, and I think that deplorable. However, if you care to continue riding with us, we shall next assail the city of Yun-nan-fu, and I promise that you will be among the high officers who are let to take first choice of the loot. Yun-nan-fu is a large city, and respectably rich, I am told, and the Yi women are not at all repulsive. What say you?"

"It is a generous offer, Orlok, and a tempting one, and I am honored by your kind regard. But I think I had best resist the temptation, and hurry back to tell the Khakhan all the news, good and bad, of what has occurred here. By your leave, I shall depart tomorrow, when you march on southward."

"I thought as much. I took you to be a dutiful man. So I have already dictated to a yeoman scribe a letter for you to carry to Kubilai. It is properly sealed for his eyes only, but I make no secret of its highly praising you and suggesting that you deserve more praise than only mine. I will go now to detach two advance riders to leave immediately and start making ready your route for you. And when you depart tomorrow, I will provide two escorts and the best horses."

So that was all I got to see of Yun-nan, and that was my only experience of war on land, and I took no plunder, and I had no chance to form any opinion of the Yi women. But those who had observed my brief military career—the survivors of it, anyway—seemed to agree that I had acquitted myself well. And I had ridden with the Mongol Horde, which was something to tell my grandchildren, if I ever had any. So I turned again for Khanbalik, feeling quite the seasoned old campaigner.

XAN-DU

. 1 .

IT was again a long ride, and again my escorts and I rode hard. But, when we were yet some two hundred li southwest of Khanbalik, we found our advance riders waiting at a crossroads to intercept us. They had already been to Khanbalik, and had ridden back along the route to inform us that the Khan Kubilai was not presently in residence there. He was out enjoying the hunting season, meaning that he was staying at his country palace of Xan-du, to which the riders would lead us instead. Waiting with them was another man, and he was so richly attired, in Arab-style garments, that at first I mistook him for some gray-bearded Muslim courtier unknown to me. He waited for the riders to give me their message, and then addressed me exuberantly:

"Former Master Marco! It is I!"

"Nostril!" I exclaimed, surprised that I was glad to see him. "I mean Ali Babar. It is good to see you! But what do you out here, so far from city comforts?"

"I came to meet you, former master. When these men brought word of your imminent return, I joined them. I have been given a missive to deliver to you, and it seemed a good excuse to take a holiday from toil and care. Also, I thought you might have some use for the services of your former slave."

"That was thoughtful of you. But come, we will make holiday together."

The Mongols led the way, the two advance riders and my two escorts, and Ali and I rode side by side behind them. We turned more northerly than we had been traveling, because Xan-du is up in the Da-ma-qing Mountains, a considerable distance directly north of Khanbalik. Ali groped about under his embroidered aba and brought out a paper, folded and sealed, with my name written on the outside in Roman letters and also in the Arabic and Mongol letters and in the Han character.

"Someone wanted to make sure I got it," I muttered. "From whom did it come?"

"I know not, former master."

"We are equally freemen now, Ali. You may call me Marco."

"As you will, Marco. The lady who gave me that paper was heavily veiled, and she accosted me in private and in the nighttime. Since she spoke no word, neither did I, taking her probably to be—ahem—some secret friend of yours, and maybe the wife of some other. I am far more discreet and less inquisitive than perhaps I used to be."

"You have the same perfervid imagination, however. I was conducting no such intrigue at court. But thank you, anyway." I tucked the paper away to read that night. "But now, what of you, old companion? How fine you do look!"

"Yes," he said, preening. "My good wife Mar-Janah insists that I dress and comport myself now like the affluent proprietor and employer I have become."

"Indeed? Proprietor of what? Employer of whom?"

"Do you remember, Marco, the city called Kashan in Persia?"

"Ah, yes. The city of beautiful boys. But surely Mar-Janah has not let you open a male brothel!"

He sighed and looked pained. "Kashan is also famous for its distinctive kashi tiles, you may recall."

"I do. I remember that my father took an interest in the process of their manufacture."

"Just so. He thought there might be a market here in Kithai for such a product. And he was right. He and your Uncle Mafio put up the capital for the establishment of a workshop, and helped teach the art of kashi-making to a number of artificers, and put the whole enterprise in the charge of Mar-Janah and myself. She designs the patterns for the kashi and supervises the workshop, and I do the peddling of the product. We have done very well, if I may say so. The kashi tiles are much in demand as an adornment for rich men's houses. Even after paying the share of the profits owed to your father and uncle, Mar-Janah and I have become eminently affluent. We are all still learning our trade—she and I and our artificers—but earning while we do so. Prospering to such an extent that I could well afford to take some time off to do this bit of journeying with you."

He chattered on for the rest of the day, telling me every last detail

of the business of making and selling tiles—not all of which I found
compellingly interesting—and occasionally imparting other news of
Khanbalik. He and the beautiful Mar-Janah were blissfully happy. He
had not seen my father in some time, the elder Polo being also out
traveling on some mercantile venture, but he had glimpsed my uncle
about the city, now and then of late. The beautiful Mar-Janah was more
beautiful than ever. The Wali Achmad was holding the Vice-Regency
and the reins of government in the Khan's absence. The beautiful Mar-
Janah was still as loving of Ali Babar as he of her. Many courtiers had
accompanied Kubilai to Xan-du for the autumn hunting, including several of my acquaintances: the Wang Chingkim, the Firemaster Shi and
the Goldsmith Boucher. The beautiful Mar-Janah agreed with Ali that
the time they had so far spent in wedlock had been, though coming late
in life, the best time of both their lives, and worth having waited all their
lives to attain. . . .

We put up that night at a comfortable Han karwansarai in the
shadow of the Great Wall, and when I had bathed and dined, I sat down
in my room to open the missive Ali had brought me. It did not take me
long to read it—though I had to spell it out letter by letter, being still not
very accomplished at the Mongol alphabet—for it consisted of only a
single line, translating as: "Expect me when you least expect me." The
words had lost none of their chill, but I was getting rather more weary of
their refrain than apprehensive of their threat. I went to Ali's room and
demanded:

"The woman who gave you this for me. Surely you would have
recognized her, even veiled, if she had been the Lady Chao Ku-an. . . ."

"Yes, and she was not. Which reminds me: the Lady Chao is dead. I
only heard of it myself a day or two ago, from a courier riding the horse-
post route. It happened since I left Khanbalik. An unfortunate accident.
According to the courier, it is believed that the lady must have been
chasing from her chambers some lover who had displeased her, and in
running after him—you know she had the lotus feet—she tripped on the
staircase and fell headlong."

"I regret to hear it," I said, though I really did not. One more off my
list of suspect whisperers. "But about the letter, Ali. Was the lady who
brought it perhaps a very *large* lady?" I was remembering the extraordinary female I had briefly seen in the chambers of the Vice-Regent
Achmad.

Ali thought about it, and said, "She may have been taller than I
am, but most people are. No, I would not say she was notably large."

"You said she did not speak. It suggests that you would have known
her by her voice, does it not?"

He shrugged. "How do I answer that? Since she did not, I did not.
Does the letter contain bad news, Marco, or some other cause for
despondency?"

"I could better decide that if I knew where it came from."

"All I can tell you is that your advance riders arrived in the city on a
day some days ago, heralding your imminent return, and—"

"Wait. Did they announce anything else?"

"Not really. When people asked how went the war in Yun-nan, the two would say nothing—except that *you* were bringing the official word —but their swaggering implied that the word would be of some Mongol victory. Anyway, it was in the night of that day that the veiled lady came to me with that missive for you. So, with Mar-Janah's blessing, when the two men left again the next morning to ride back to you, I rode with them."

He could add nothing more, and I truly could not think of any females who might be nursing a grudge against me, what with the Lady Chao and the twins Buyantu and Biliktu all dead. If the veiled woman had been someone else's agent, I had no idea whose. So I said no more about the matter, and tore up the vexing letter, and we continued on our journey, reaching Xan-du without anything dreadful happening to us, of either unexpected or expectable nature.

Xan-du was just one of four or five subsidiary palaces that the Khakhan maintained in places outside Khanbalik, but it was the most sumptuous of those. In the Da-ma-qing Mountains, he had had an extensive hunting park laid out, and stocked with all manner of game, and staffed with expert huntsmen and gamekeepers and beaters, who lived there the year around, in villages on the park's outskirts. In the center of the park stood a marble palace of goodly size, containing the usual halls for gathering and dining and entertaining and holding court, plus ample quarters for any number of the royal family and their courtiers and guests, and for all the numerous servants and slaves they would require, and for all the musicians and mountebanks brought along to enliven the nighttime hours. Every room, down to the smallest bedchamber, was decorated with wall paintings done by the Master Chao and other court artists, depicting scenes of the chase and the course and the hunt, and all marvelously done. Outside the main palace building were grand stables for the mounts and the pack animals—elephants as well as horses and mules—and mews for the Khan's hawks and falcons, and kennels for his dogs and chita cats, and all those buildings were as finely built and adorned and as spotlessly clean as the palace itself.

The Khakhan had also at Xan-du a sort of portable palace. It was like a tremendous yurtu pavilion, only so *very* tremendous that it could not have been constructed of cloth or felt. It was mostly made of the zhu-gan cane and palm leaves, and was supported on wooden columns carved and painted and gilded to seem dragons, and was held together by an ingenious webbing of silk ropes. Although of great size, it could be taken apart and carried about and put up again as easily as a yurtu. So it was continually being moved about the Xan-du parkland and the surrounding countryside—a train of elephants was reserved for the task of transporting its components—to wherever the Khakhan and his company chose to hunt on any day.

Every time Kubilai went out to hunt, he did it in consummate style. He and his guests would depart from the marble palace in a numerous and colorful and glittering train. Sometimes the Khan rode on one of his "dragon steeds"—the milk-white horses specially bred for him in Persia—

and sometimes in the little house called a hauda, rocking atop an elephant's high shoulders, and at other times in a lavishly ornamented, two-wheeled chariot, drawn by either horses or elephants. When he went on horseback, he always carried one of the sleek chita cats draped elegantly across the horse's withers in front of his saddle, and would loose it whenever some small animal started up in his path. The chita could run down anything that moves, and would always dutifully fetch its catch back to the train, but, since a chita always mangled its prey considerably, a huntsman would toss that game into a separate bag and later mince it for feed for the birds in the palace mews. When Kubilai rode out in a hauda or his chariot, he always had two or more of his milk-white gerfalcons perched on its rim and would start them at sight of small game running or flying.

Behind the Khakhan's chariot or steed or elephant would come the train of his company, all lords and ladies and distinguished guests mounted only a little less royally than the Khan himself, and all—depending on the game to be sought that day—carrying hooded hawks on their gauntleted wrists, or accompanied by servants carrying their lances or bows or leading on leash their chase dogs. Out ahead of the train, earlier in the day, would have gone the many beaters, to form up in three sides of a vast square and, at the proper time, to start flushing the game—stags or boars or otters or whatever—out the fourth side of the square, toward the approaching hunters.

Whenever Kubilai's train passed through or by one of the villages situated around his parkland, all the families of women and children living there would run outdoors to cry "Hail!" They also kept welcome fires always burning, in case the Khan should come that way, and would cast into the flames spices and incense to perfume the air as the Khakhan went by. At midday, the hunting party would repair to the zhu-gan palace, always set up at a convenient place, for food and drink and soft music and a brief nap before going afield again in the afternoon. And when the day's hunt was done, depending on how tired they all might be, or how far from the main palace, they would either return there or stop the night in the zhu-gan palace, for it had copious room and comfortable bedding.

I and Ali and our four Mongols reached Xan-du in the middle of a morning, and were told by a steward where to find the Khakhan's portable palace, and arrived there at midday, when the whole party was lolling over its meal. Several people recognized me and hailed me, including Kubilai. I introduced Ali Babar to him as "a citizen of Khanbalik, Sire, one of your rich merchant princes," and Kubilai received him cordially, not having noticed Ali in my company in the days when he had been the lowly slave Nostril. Then I started to say, "I bring from Yunnan both good and bad news, Sire—" but he held up his hand to stop me.

"Nothing," he said firmly. "Nothing is important enough to interrupt a good hunt. Hold your news until we return to the Xan-du palace this evening. Now, are you hungry?" He clapped for a servant to bring food.

"Are you fatigued? Would you rather precede us to the palace and rest while you wait, or would you take a lance with us? We have been starting some admirably big and vicious boar hogs."

"Why, thank you, Sire. I should like to join the hunt. But I have little experience with a lance. Can boar be killed with bow and arrow?"

"Anything can be killed with anything, including bare hands. And those you may have to use, to finish a boar." He turned and called, "Hui! Mahawat, make ready an elephant for Marco Polo!"

It was my first ride aboard an elephant, and it was most pleasant, infinitely more so than riding a camel, and very different from riding a horse. The hauda was made like a basket, of woven zhu-gan strips, with a little bench on which I sat beside the elephant driver, who is properly called a mahawat. The hauda had high sides to protect us from flicking tree branches, and a roof canopy over us, but was open in the front, so the mahawat could direct the elephant by prodding it with a stick, and so I could let fly my arrows. At first I was a little dizzied by my great height above the ground, but I soon got used to that. And when the animal first stepped out on the march through the park, I did not immediately realize that it was walking rather faster than a horse or camel does. Also, when it came time to chase a fleeing boar, it took me a while to realize that the elephant, for all its immense bulk, was running as fast as a galloping horse.

The mahawat took great pride in his great charges, and bragged about them, and I found his bragging informative. Only cow elephants, he told me, were used as working beasts. The bulls being not very amenable to training, only a few of those were kept in any domestic herd, as company for the cows. The elephants all wore bells, big chunky things carved of wood, that sounded with a hollow thunking noise instead of a jangle. The mahawat said that if I ever heard a clanging metal bell, I had better move in a hurry, because metal bells were hung only on elephants that had misbehaved and so could not any longer be trusted— in other words, those elephants most resembling people: usually a cow maddened, like any human mother, by the loss of a calf, or a bull gone grumpy and mean and irascible with age, like any old man.

An elephant, said the mahawat, was more intelligent than a dog, and more obedient than a horse, and more adept with its trunk and tusks than a monkey with its paws, and could be taught to do many things both useful and entertaining. In the timber forests, two elephants could work a saw between them to cut down a tree, then pick up and stack the giant logs or drag them to a log road, with the attendance of only a single human logger to select the trees to be cut. As a beast of burden, the elephant was incomparable to any others—being able to carry as much of a load as three strong oxen, and carry it for a distance of thirty to forty li in an ordinary working day, or more than fifty li in an emergency. The elephant was not at all shy of water, as a camel is, for it is a good swimmer, and a camel cannot swim at all.

I do not know if an elephant could have negotiated a precarious trail like the Pillar Road, but that animal carried us swiftly and surely across a variety of Da-ma-qing terrain. Since my elephant was just one in a line of them, the Khan's and several others ahead of me, my mahawat did not have to do much directing. But when he wished the elephant to turn, he merely had to touch one or the other of the door-sized ears. When we were traveling among trees, the animal would, unbidden, use its trunk to move aside any impeding limbs, and the more whippy branches it would even break off to ensure that they did not swipe back at us riders. It went sometimes between trees that looked too close together to allow passage, and did that so sinuously and smoothly as not to scrape the belts that held our hauda on its shoulders. When we came to the wet clay bank of a small stream, the elephant, almost as playfully as a child, put its four tree-trunk feet close together and *slid* down the slope to the water's edge. At that place, the river was laid with stepping-stones for crossing. Before venturing out onto them, the elephant first gently tested its weight on one, and sounded with its trunk the depth of the water roundabout. Then, seeming satisfied, it stepped out onto the stones and from one to the next, never hesitating, but treading as delicately and precisely as a fat man who has drunk a drop too much.

If the elephant has one unlovely trait, it is one that is common to all creatures, but is amplified to a prodigious degree by the animal's size. That is to say that the elephant I rode frequently and appallingly broke wind. Other animals do that—camels, horses, even human beings, God knows—but no other animal in God's Creation can do it so thunderously and odoriferously as an elephant, which produces a noxious miasma almost as visible as it is audible. With heroic effort, I pretended not to notice those lapses of manners. But I did make some small complaint of another trait: the elephant several times coiled its trunk back over its head and *sneezed* in my face—so windily as to rock me on my seat, and so wetly that I was soon damp all over. When I voiced my vexation at the sneezing, the mahawat said loftily:

"Elephants do not sneeze. The cow is just blowing your aroma away from her."

"Gèsu," I muttered. "*My* aroma is bothering *her*?"

"It is only that you are a stranger, and she is unaccustomed to you. When she gets to know you, she will put up with your smell and will moderate her behavior."

"I rejoice to hear it."

So we rollicked along, rhythmically swaying in the high hauda, and the mahawat told me other things. Down in the jungles of Champa, he said, where the elephants came from, there were such things as white elephants.

"Not *really* white, of course, like the Khakhan's snow-white horses and hawks. But a paler gray than ordinary. And because they are rare, like albinos among humans, they are held to be sacred. They are often employed for revenge against an enemy."

"Sacred," I repeated, "but instruments of revenge? I do not understand."

He explained. When a white elephant was caught, it was always presented to the local king, because only a king could afford to keep one. Being sacred, the elephant could never be put to labor, but had to be pampered with a fine stable and dedicated attendants and a princely diet, and its only function was to march in religious processions, when it had to be festooned with gold-threaded blankets and jeweled chains and baubles and such. That was a burdensome expense even for a king. However, said the mahawat, suppose a king got displeased with some one of his lords, or feared his rivalry, or simply took a dislike to him. . . .

"In the old days," he said, "a king would have sent him poisoned sweetmeats, so that the recipient would die when he ate them—or a beautiful slave girl poisoned in her pink places, so that the noble would die after he lay with her. But those stratagems are now too well-known. So the king nowadays simply sends the noble a white elephant. He cannot refuse a sacred gift. He can make no profit from it. But he has the ruinous expense of maintaining it in proper style, so he is soon bankrupted and broken—if he waits to be. Most commit suicide on first receiving the white elephant."

I refused to believe such a story, and accused the mahawat of inventing it. But then he told me something else unbelievable—that he could calculate for me the exact height of any elephant without even seeing it—and when at the close of the day we got down from ours, he demonstrated that ability, and even I could do it. So, being forced to believe him about that, I ceased scoffing at his white elephant story. Anyway, the measurement is done thus. You simply find an elephant's track and pick out the print of one of its forefeet and measure the circumference of that. Everyone knows that a perfectly proportioned woman has a waist exactly twice the circumference of her neck, and her neck twice that of her wrist. Just so, the elephant's height at the shoulder is exactly twice the circumference of its forefoot.

When we heard the beaters hooting and thrashing up ahead of us, I nocked an arrow to my bowstring. And when a spiny black shape shouldered its way through a thicket and snorted at us, and clashed its yellow tusks as if it would challenge those of my elephant, I let fly the arrow. I hit the boar; I could hear the *thwock* and see the puff of dust go up from the coarse-haired hide. I believe he would have gone down on the instant if I had chosen one of the heavy, broad-headed arrows. But I had expected it to be a long shot, and it had been, so I had used one of the narrow-headed, long-range arrows. It pierced the boar clean and deep, but only made him turn and run.

Without waiting for the goad, my elephant ran after him, following as closely on his jinks and curvettings as a trained boar-hound, while I and the mahawat bounced about in the jouncing hauda. It was impossible for me to nock another arrow, let alone shoot it and hope to hit anything. But the wounded boar soon realized that it was fleeing into the line of beaters. It skidded awkwardly to a stop in a dry creek bed, and turned at bay, and lowered its long head, its red eyes blinking angrily above and behind the four upcurved tusks. My elephant also slid to a halt, which must have made a humorous sight to see, if I had been elsewhere looking on. But the mahawat and I were pitched out of the hauda's open front to sprawl atop the elephant's great head, and would have gone on falling, if we had not been clutching at each other and the beast's big ears and the straps holding the hauda and anything else in reach.

When the elephant again curled her trunk backward over her head, I confusedly wished she had thought of something better to do than sneeze—but it turned out that she had. She curled the trunk around my waist and, as if I had been no weightier than a dry leaf, lifted me off her head, twirled me in midair and set me down on my feet—between her and the enraged, pawing, snorting boar. I did not know whether the elephant maliciously intended that I, the new-smelling stranger, should suffer the brunt of the boar's charge, or whether she was trained to do that in order to give a hunter a second shot at the quarry. But if she thought she was being helpful, she was mistaken, for she had put me down without my bow and arrows, still up in the hauda. I could have turned to see whether the little eyes among her wrinkles were bright with mischief or solemn with concern—elephants' eyes are as expressive as women's—but I dared not turn my back to the wounded boar.

From where I now stood, it looked bigger than a barnyard brood sow, and inexpressibly more savage. It stood with its black snout close to the ground, above it the four wicked tusks curling up and out, above them the blazing red eyes, the tufty ears twitching and, behind them, the powerful black shoulders hunching for a lunge. I threw my hand to my belt knife, yanked it out and in front of me, and flung myself headlong toward the boar in the same moment that it charged. Had I waited a breath longer, I should have moved too late. I fell atop the boar's long snout and high-humped back, but the beast did not jerk its tusks upward into my groin, for it died too quickly. My knife went through the hide and deep into flesh, and I squeezed its handle in the instant of thrust, so that I struck with all three blades at once. The boar's dying plunge carried me with it for some way, then its legs crumpled and we came down in a heap.

I scrambled up quickly, fearful that the animal might still have one last convulsion left in it. When it only lay still and bled, I plucked out my knife and then the arrow, and wiped them clean on the quill-like black hairs. Closing the trusty squeeze-knife and putting it back into its sheath, I mentally sent another thank-you into the far away and long ago. Then I turned and gave a not-so-thankful look at the elephant and the mahawat. He sat up there gawking with awe and perhaps some admiration. But the elephant only stood rocking gently from foot to foot, her eye regarding me with self-complacent feminine composure, as if to say, "There. You did it just as I expected you to," which no doubt was the offhand remark made by the liberated princess to San Zorzi after he slew her dragon captor.

. 2 .

B A C K at the Xan-du palace, Kubilai took me walking with him in the gardens while we waited for the cooks to prepare a dinner of the boars— my own trophy and the several others brought in by other hunters of the party (who had speared theirs from the more usual and safer distances). The afternoon was waning into twilight as the Khakhan and I stood on an inverted bridge and looked out over an artificial lake of some size. That lake was fed by a small waterfall, and the bridge was built in front of it, not arching over it, but in the form of a letter U, with stairs going down from one bank and upward to the other, so that at the middle of the bridge one stood at the foaming foot of the little cascade.

I admired it for a time, then turned to look at the lake, while Kubilai perused the letter from the Orlok Bayan, which I had given him to read before the light was gone. It was a lovely and peaceful autumn evening. There were flaming sunset clouds high in the sky above the lake, and then a patch of clear ice-blue sky between them and the black serration of the farther lakeside's treetops, which looked as flat as if they had been cut from black paper and pasted there. The mirror-smooth lake reflected only the black trees and the clear blue of the lower sky, except where a few ornamental ducks were leisurely paddling across it. They rumpled the water behind them just enough that it reflected there the high sunset clouds, so each duck was trailing a long wedge of warm flame across the ice-blue surface.

"So Ukuruji is dead," sighed Kubilai, folding the paper. "But a great victory has been accomplished, and all of Yun-nan will soon capitulate." (Neither the Khan nor I could have known it at that moment, but the Yi had by then already laid down their arms, and another messenger was riding hard from Yun-nan-fu to bring the news.) "Bayan says that you can tell me the details, Marco. Did my son die well?"

I told him all the how and where and when of it—our employment of the Bho as an expendable mock army, the laudable efficacy of the brass balls, the dwindling of the battle into two final skirmishes, man against man, one of which I had survived, the other which Ukuruji had not, and I concluded with the capture and execution of the treacherous Pao Nei-ho. I had meant to show Kubilai the yin seal of the Minister Pao, but I realized as I spoke that I had left it in my saddlebags, which were now in my palace chamber, so I did not mention it, and of course the Khakhan demanded no such proof.

I added, perhaps a little wistfully, "I must apologize, Sire, that I neglected to follow the noble precepts of your grandfather Chinghiz."

"Uu?"

"I left Yun-nan at once, Sire, to bring you the news. So I took no opportunity to ravish any chaste Yi wives or virgin Yi daughters."

He chuckled and said, "Ah, well. Too bad you had to forgo the handsome Yi women. But when we have taken the Sung Empire, perhaps you will have occasion to travel to the Fu-kien Province there. The females of the Min people of Fu-kien are so gloriously beautiful, it is said, that parents will not send a daughter out of the house even to fetch water or cut firewood, for fear that she will be abducted by slave hunters or the emperor's concubine collectors."

"I shall look forward to my first meeting with a Min girl, then."

"Meanwhile, it appears that your prowess in other aspects of warfare would have pleased the warrior Khan Chinghiz." He indicated the letter. "Bayan here gives you much of the credit for the Yun-nan victory. You evidently impressed him. He even makes the brash suggestion that I might console myself for the loss of Ukuruji by making you an honorary son of mine."

"I am flattered, Sire. But please to reflect that the Orlok wrote that while he was flushed with triumphal enthusiasm. I am sure he meant no disrespect."

"And I still have a sufficiency of sons," said the Khan, as if he were reminding himself, not me. "On the son Chingkim, of course, I long ago settled the mantle of heir apparent. Also—you would not yet have heard this, Marco—Chingkim's young wife Kukachin has recently been delivered of a son, my premier grandson, so the continued succession of our line is assured. They have named him Temur." He went on, as if he had forgotten my presence, "Ukuruji most earnestly desired to become Wang of Yun-nan. A pity he died. He would have been a capable viceroy for a newly conquered province. I think now . . . I will award that Wangdom to his half-brother Hukoji . . ." Then he turned abruptly to me again. "Bayan's suggestion that I insinuate a Ferenghi into the Mongol royal dynasty is unthinkable. However, I agree with him that such good blood as yours should not be ignored. It might profitably be infused into the lesser Mongol nobility. There is precedent, after all. My late brother, the Ilkhan Hulagu of Persia, during his conquest of that empire, was so impressed by the valor of the foemen of Hormuz that he put them to stud with all his camp-following females, and I believe that the get was worthwhile."

"Yes, I heard that bit of history, Sire, while I was in Persia."

"Well, then. You have no wife, I know that. Are you bound or vowed to any other woman or women at present?"

"Why . . . no, Sire," I said, suddenly apprehensive that he was thinking of marrying me off to some spinster Mongol lady or minor princess of his choosing. I was not yearning to be married, and certainly not to una gata nel saco.

"And if you neglected to take advantage of the Yi women, you must by now be aching for an outlet for your ardors."

"Well . . . yes, Sire. But I can myself seek—"

He waved me to silence and nodded decisively. "Very well. Shortly before I brought the court from Khanbalik, there arrived this year's accumulation of presentation maidens. I brought here to Xan-du some two score of them whom I have not yet covered. Among them are about a dozen choice Mongol girls. They may not be up to the Min standard of beauty, but they are all of twenty-four-karat quality, as you will see. I will send them to your chambers, one a night, first bidding them not to employ any fern seed, that they may readily be impregnated. You will do me and the Mongol Khanate the favor of servicing them."

"A dozen, Sire?" I said, with some incredulity.

"Surely you do not demur. The last command I gave you was that you go to war. A command to go to bed—with a succession of prime Mongol virgins—is rather more eagerly to be obeyed, is it not?"

"Oh, assuredly, Sire."

"Be it done, then. And I shall expect a good crop of healthy Mongol-Ferenghi hybrids. Now, Marco, let us wend our way back to the palace. Chingkim must be apprised of his half-brother's death so that, as Wang of Khanbalik, he can order his city draped in purple mourning. Meanwhile, the Firemaster and the Goldsmith are in a fever to hear exactly how you utilized their brass-ball invention. Come."

The dining hall of the Xan-du palace was an imposing chamber, hung with painted scrolls and stuffed animal-head trophies of the hunt, but dominated by a sculpture of fine green jade. It was a single, solid piece of jade that must have weighed five tons, and God knows what it was worth in gold or flying money. It was carved into the semblance of a mountain very like those I had helped destroy in Yun-nan—complete with cliffs and crags and forests of trees and winding steep paths like the Pillar Road, being toilsomely climbed by little carved peasants and porters and horse carts.

The boar meat made a tasty meal, and I ate it sitting at the high table with the Khan, the Prince Chingkim, the Goldsmith Boucher and the Firemaster Shi. I tendered Chingkim my condolences on his brother's demise and my congratulations on his son's birth. The other two courtiers alternated between plying me with intense questions about the successful working of the huo-yao balls and fulsomely praising me and each other for having invented a true invention, one that would be imitated throughout the world, and would endure down the ages, changing the whole face of war, and making forever famous the names Shi and Polo and Boucher.

"For shame!" I chided. "You said yourself, Master Shi, that the flaming powder was invented by some unknown Han."

"Peu de chose!" cried Boucher. "It was nothing but a toy until its full potential was realized by a wily Venetian, a renegade Jew and a brilliant young Frenchman!"

"Gan-bei!" cried old Shi. "L'chaim!" as he toasted us all with a goblet of mao-tai, and then downed it in a gulp. Boucher emulated him, but I took only a sip of mine. Let my fellow immortals get drunk; I would not, for I expected later to have need of my faculties.

Some Uighur musicians played during the meal—mercifully softly —and after it we were entertained by jugglers and funambulists and then a company performing a play which, for all its foreignness, I found familiar. A Han storyteller droned and yammered and bellowed the tale, and the conversations occurring in it, while his associates worked the strings of marionettes acting out the various roles. I could not understand a word, but found it perfectly comprehensible, because the Han characters—Aged Cuckold and Comic Physician and Sneering Villain and Bumbling Sage and Lovelorn Maiden and Valiant Hero and so on—were so recognizably similar to those of any Venetian puppet show: our fuddled Pantaleone and inept physician Dotòr Balanzòn and rascal Pulcinella and dim-witted lawyer Dotòr da Nulla and coquette Colombina and dashing Trovatore and so on. But Kubilai seemed not much to enjoy the show, grumbling to us near him, "Why use puppets to portray people? Why not have people portray people?" (And obediently, in after years, all the player companies did exactly that: dispensed with the narrator and the marionettes, and presented human players each speaking his or her own part in the story.)

Most of the court was still loudly making merry when I retired to my chambers. But evidently Kubilai had given his instructions some while earlier, for I had just got into bed and not yet blown out the bedside lamp when there was a scratching at my door and a young woman came in, bearing what looked like a small white chest.

"Sain bina, sain nai," I said politely, but she made no response, and when she came into the lamplight I saw that she was not a Mongol, but a Han or one of the related races.

She was obviously just a maid preparing for the entry of her lady, for now I discerned that the white object she carried was only an incense burner. I hoped that her lady would prove to be as comely and as exquisitely delicate as the servant. She set down the burner near my bed, a lidded porcelain box, shaped like a jewel chest and embossed with intricate raised designs. Then she took up my lamp, shyly smiling a silent request for permission and, when I nodded, used the lamp's flame to set smoldering a stick of incense, lifted the burner's lid and carefully placed the incense inside. I took note that it was the purple tsan-xi-jang, which is the very finest incense, compounded of aromatic herbs, musk and gold dust, to give a room not a heavy, spicy, closed-in smell, but the scent of summer fields. The servant girl sank down to sit meek and silent beside my bed, her eyes discreetly lowered, while the fragrant and calming perfume permeated my room. It did not calm me quite enough; I felt almost as nervous as if I had been really a bridegroom. So I tried to make small talk with the maid, but either she was well trained to imperturbability or was totally ignorant of Mongol, for she never even raised her eyes. Finally there was another scratching at the door, and her lady came proudly in. I was pleased to see that she *was* handsome—exceptionally so, for a Mongol—if not so tiny and dainty and porcelain-lovely as her servant.

I said again in Mongol, "Good meeting, good woman," and this one murmured back, "Sain bina, sain urkek."

"Come! Do not call me brother," I said, with a shaky laugh.

"It is the accepted salutation."

"Well, at least try not to think of me as a brother."

And she and I continued to make such small talk—very small talk, indeed, quite inane—as the maid helped her unpeel and get out of her considerable nuptial finery. I introduced myself, and she responded, in a

sort of cascade of words, that she was called Setsen, and she was of the
Mongol tribe called Kerait, and she was a Nestorian Christian, all the
Kerait having been converted, in a bunch, by some long-ago wandering
Nestorian bishop, and she had never set foot outside her nameless village
in the far-northern fur-trapping country of Tannu-Tuva until she was
selected for concubinage and transported to a trading town called Urga,
where, to her surprise and delight, the provincial Wang had graded her
at twenty-four karats and sent her on south to Khanbalik. Also, she said,
she had never before laid eyes on a Ferenghi, and excuse her impudence,
but were my hair and beard really naturally pale of color or had they
simply gone gray with age? I told Setsen that I was not a great deal
older than she, and still far from senile, as she ought to have descried
from my rising excitement while I watched her disrobe. I would offer
further evidence of my youthful vigor, I promised, as soon as the maidservant quitted the room. However, that girl, after tucking her naked
lady in beside me, sank down again beside the bed as if to stay there,
and did not even put out the light. So the subsequent conversation
between me and Setsen got worse than inane, it got ridiculous.

I said, "You may dismiss your servant."

She said, "The lon-gya is not a servant. She is a slave."

"Whatever. You may dismiss her."

"She is commanded to attend my qing-du chu-kai—my defloration."

"I undo the command."

"You cannot, Lord Marco. She is my attendant."

"I do not care, Setsen, if she is your Nestorian bishop. I would prefer
that she attend elsewhere."

"I cannot send her away and neither can you. She is here by order of
the Court Procurer and the Lady Matron of Concubines."

"I take precedence over matrons and procurers. I am here by order
of the Khan of All Khans."

Setsen looked hurt. "I thought you were here because you wanted to
be."

"Well, that, too," I said, instantly contrite. "But I did not expect to
have an audience to cheer my endeavors."

"She will not cheer. She is a lon-gya. She will not say anything."

"Perdiziòn! I do not care if she sings an inno imeneo, only she must
do it somewhere else!"

"What is that?"

"A wedding song. A hymeneal hymn. It celebrates the—well, the
breaking of the—that is to say, the defloration."

"But that is exactly what she is here for, Lord Marco!"

"To *sing*?"

"No, no, as a witness. She will depart as soon as you—as soon as she
sees the stain on the bedsheet. Then she goes to report to the Lady
Matron that all is as it should be. You comprehend?"

"Protocol, yes. Vakh."

I glanced over at the girl, who seemed to be occupied in studying
the white convolutions of the incense burner, and paying no least heed to
our squabble. I was glad I was not a real bridegroom, or the circum-

stances would have stopped my living up to my earlier braggery. However, since I was only a sort of surrogate bridegroom and since neither
the bride nor the bride's maid found the situation embarrassing, why
should I find it inhibiting? So I proceeded to provide the evidence the
slave was waiting to get, and Setsen amiably if inexpertly cooperated,
and during those exertions, so far as I noticed, the slave paid no more
attention than if we had been as inert as her incense burner. But, after
some while, Setsen leaned out from the bed and shook the girl by the
shoulder, and she got up and helped Setsen untangle the bedclothes, and
they found the small red smear. The slave nodded and smiled brightly
at us, bent and blew out the lamp and left the room and left us to
any nonobligatory consummations we might care to make for ourselves.

Setsen left me at morning, and I joined the Khan and his courtiers
for a day of hawking. Even Ali Babar came along, after I had assured
him that falconry involved no such risks to the hunter as did the more
strenuous veneries, like boar-sticking. We started much game that day,
and the sport was good. Since the sharp-eyed falcons could see to wait
on and stoop and strike well into the twilight, our whole company stayed
out that night in the zhu-gan field palace. We returned to Xan-du the
next day, with an abundance of game birds and hares for the kitchen
pots, and that night, after a good dinner of venison, I received the
second of Kubilai's contributions to the improvement of the Mongol
race.

However, she also was preceded by a slave bringing the white
porcelain incense burner and, when I saw that it was the *same* pretty
slave girl, I tried to convey to her my discomfiture at her having to
attend *two* of these nuptial nights. But she only smiled winningly, and
either failed or refused to comprehend me. So, when the Mongol maiden
finally arrived and introduced herself as Jehol, I said:

"Forgive my unmanly agitation, Jehol, but I find it more than a little
disquieting that the same monitor must twice oversee my nighttime
doings."

"Do not concern yourself with the lon-gya," said Jehol indifferently.
"She is only a slave girl of the lowly Min people of the Fu-kien Province."

"Is she indeed?" I said, interested to hear that. "Of the Min, is she?
Nevertheless, I do not care to have my successive performances
compared—in their degree of prowess or stupration or efficacy or whatever other aspect."

Jehol only laughed and said, "She will make no comparisons, neither
here nor in the concubine quarters. She cannot do any such thing."

By this time, with the slave girl's assistance, Jehol had undressed to
an extent that took my mind off other matters. So I said, "Well, if you do
not care, I suppose I need not," and the night proceeded as had the other
one.

But, when came the night for the next Mongol maiden—her name
was Yesukai—and she was preceded by that same Min slave girl bearing
that same incense burner, I once more raised objections. Yesukai only
shrugged and said:

"When we were at the palace in Khanbalik, we had a numerous complement of servants and slaves. But when the Lady Matron brought us out here to Xan-du for the season, we came with only a few domestics, and this slave is the only lon-gya among them. If we girls must make do with her, you must get used to her."

"She may be admirably reticent about what goes on in this chamber," I grumbled. "But I have ceased to fret that she may indiscreetly talk. Now I fear that, after many more such nights as this, she will start *laughing*."

"She cannot laugh," said Cheren, who was the next of the Mongol maidens to visit me. "No more than she can talk or hear. The slave is a lon-gya. You do not know the word? It means a deaf-mute."

"Is that a fact?" I murmured, regarding the slave with more compassion than I had done. "No wonder she has never answered when I railed at her. All this time, I thought lon-gya was her name."

"If she ever had a name, she cannot tell it," said Toghon, who was the next of the Mongol maidens. "In the concubine quarters, we call her Hui-sheng. But that is only our feminine malice, when we make sport of her."

"Hui-sheng," I repeated. "What malice in that? It is a most mellifluous name."

"It is a most unfitting name, for it means Echo," said Devlet, the next of the Mongol maidens. "But no matter. She neither hears it nor answers to it."

"A soundless Echo," I said, and smiled. "An unfitting name, perhaps, but a pleasing paradox. Hui-sheng. Hui-sheng. . . ."

To Ayuka, the seventh or eighth of the Mongol maidens, I said, "Tell me, does your Lady Matron deliberately seek deaf-mute slaves for the duty of overseeing the nuptial nights?"

"She does not seek them. She makes them so from childhood. Incapable either of eavesdropping or of gossiping. They cannot gasp in surprise or disapproval if they see strange sights in the bedchamber, or afterward prattle of perverse things they have witnessed. If they do ever misbehave and must be beaten, they cannot scream."

"Bruto barabào! *Makes* them so? How?"

"Actually, the Lady Matron has a shamàn physician do the silencing operation," said Merghus, who was the eighth or ninth of the Mongol maidens. "He puts a red-hot skewer down each ear and through the neck into the gullet. I cannot tell you exactly what is done, but look at Hui-sheng—you can see the tiny scar on her throat."

I looked, and it was so. But I saw more than that when I gazed upon Hui-sheng, for Kubilai had spoken truly when he said that the girls of the Min were unsurpassably beautiful. At least this one was. Being a slave, she wore not the blank white-powdered face of the other women native to these lands, nor the elaborate stiff hairdos of her Mongol mistresses. Her pale-peach skin was her own, and her hair was but simply piled in soft billows on her head. Except for the little crescent scar on her throat, she bore not a blemish, which was not true of the noble maidens she attended. They, having grown up mostly outdoors, in rude living conditions, among horses and such, had many nicks and pocks and abrasions marring even the more intimate areas of their flesh.

Hui-sheng was at that moment seated in the most graceful and endearing posture a woman can ever unconsciously assume. Quite unaware of anyone's regard, she was fixing a flower in her soft black hair. Her left hand held the pink blossom above her left ear, and she had her right hand arched over her head to assist in the arranging. That particular placement of the head and hands and arms and upper torso makes of any woman, clothed or naked, a poem of curves and gentle angles— her face turned a little downward and to one side, her arms framing it in harmonious composition, her neck line flowing smoothly to the bosom, her breasts sweetly uplifted by the raised arms. In that posture even an old woman looks young, a fat one looks lithe, a gaunt one looks sleek, and a beautiful woman is never more beautiful.

I remember also noticing that Hui-sheng had, in front of each ear, a fluff of very fine black hair growing as far down as her jaw line, and another feathery floss growing down the back of her neck into her collar. They were winsome details, and they made me wonder if a Min woman might be exceptionally furry in more private places. The Mongol maidens, I might mention, all had in their most private places those peculiarly Mongol "little warmers" of smooth, flat hair like small swatches of cat pelt. But, if I have uncharacteristically said little else about their charms, or about my nights of frolicking with them, it is owing to no sudden access of modesty or reserve on my part; it is only that I do not too well remember those girls. I have even forgotten now whether I was visited by an even dozen of them, or eleven, or thirteen, or some other number.

Oh, they were handsome, enjoyable, competent, satisfying, but they were that and no more. I recall them as just a succession of fleeting incidents, a different one each night. My consciousness was more impressed by the small, unobtrusive, silent Echo—and not simply for the reason that she was present every night, but because she outshone all the Mongol maidens together. Had she not been a distracting influence, I probably would not have found them so forgettable. They were, after all, the pick of Mongol womanhood, of twenty-four-karat quality, eminently well suited to their function of bed partnership. But, even while I enjoyed the sight of them being undressed by the lon-gya slave, I could not help observing how unnecessarily over-sized they seemed alongside the diminutive, dainty Hui-sheng, and how coarse of complexion and physiognomy, alongside her peach-blossom skin and exquisite features. Even their breasts, which in other circumstances I would have adored as beautifully voluptuous, I thought somehow too aggressively mammalian, compared to the almost childlike slimness and fragility of Hui-sheng's body.

In honesty, I will say that the Mongol maidens must have found me not their ideal, either, and they must have been less than overjoyed to be mating with me. They had been recruited, and had survived a rigorous system of selection, to be bedded with the Khan of All Khans. He was an old man, and perhaps also not the dream man of a young woman, but he *was* the Khakhan. It must have been a considerable disappointment for them to be allotted to a foreigner instead—a Ferenghi, a nobody—and worse yet, to be commanded not to take the fern-seed precaution before lying with me. They were, presumably, of twenty-four-karat fecundity, meaning that they had to expect impregnation by me, and the consequent bearing not of noble Mongol descendants of the Chinghiz line, but of half-breed bastards, who were bound to be regarded askance by the rest of the Kithai population, if not actively despised.

I had doubts of my own about the wisdom of Kubilai's having set me and the concubines to this conjoining. It was not that I felt myself either superior or inferior to them, for I was aware that they and I and all other folk in the world are of the same single human race. I had been taught that from my earliest years, and I had in my travels seen ample evidence of it. (Two small examples: all men everywhere, except sometimes the holy and the hermit, are ever ready to get drunk; all women everywhere, when they run, run as if their knees are hobbled together.) Clearly, all people are descendants of the same original Adam and Eve, but it is just as clear that the progeny have diverged widely in the generations since the expulsion from Eden.

Kubilai called me a Ferenghi, and he meant no offense by it, but the word lumped me into a mistakenly undifferentiated mass. I knew that we Venetians were quite distinct from the Slavs and Sicilians and all others of the Western nationalities. While I could not perceive as much variety among the numerous Mongol tribes, I knew that every person took pride in his own, and regarded it as the foremost breed of Mongols, even while asserting that all Mongols were the foremost of mankind.

In my travels, I did not always conceive an affection for every new people I met, but I did find them all of interest—and the interest was in their differences. Different skin colors, different customs, foods, speech, superstitions, entertainments, even interestingly different deficiencies and ignorances and stupidities. Some while after this time at Xan-du, I would visit the city of Hang-zho, and I would see that it, like Venice, was a city all of canals. But in every other respect, Hang-zho was not at all like Venice, and it was the variances, not the similarities, that made the place lovely in my eyes. So is Venice still lovely and dear to me, but it would cease to be if it were not unique. In my opinion, a world of cities and places and views all alike would be the dullest world imaginable, and I feel much the same way about the world's peoples. If all of them— white and peach and brown and black and whatever other colors exist— were stirred together into a bland tan, every other of their jagged and craggy differences would flatten down into featurelessness. You can walk confidently across a tan sand desert because it is not fissured by any chasms, but neither does it have any high peaks worth looking at. I realized that my contribution to the blending of Ferenghi and Mongol bloodlines would be negligible. Still I was reluctant that people so distinct should be blended at all—by fiat, deliberately, not even by casual encounter—and thereby made in any degree less various, and therefore less interesting.

I was first attracted to Hui-sheng at least partly by her differences from all other women I had so far known. To see that Min slave girl among her Mongol mistresses was like seeing a single spray of pink-ivory peach blossom in a vase of shaggy, spiky, brass- and copper- and bronze-colored chrysanthemums. However, she was beautiful not only in comparison with those less so. Like a peach blossom, she was comely all by herself, and she would have stood out even among a whole flowering peach orchard of her comely sisters of the Min. There were reasons for that. Hui-sheng lived in a perpetually silent world, so her eyes were full of dreaming even when she was wide awake. Yet her deprivation of speech and hearing was not a total handicap, nor even very noticeable to others—I myself had not realized, until I was told, that she was a deaf-mute—for she had evolved a liveliness of facial expression and a vocabulary of small gestures that communicated her thoughts and feelings without a sound but without any mistaking them. In time, I learned to read at a glance her every infinitesimal movement of qahwah-colored eyes, rose-wine lips, feathery brows, twinkling dimples, willow hands and frond fingers. But that was later.

Inasmuch as I had become enthralled of Hui-sheng under the worst possible circumstances—while she was seeing me shamelessly cavort with her dozen or so Mongol mistresses—I could hardly commence any courtship of her, without risking her derisive repulsion, until some time had passed and, I would hope, blurred her memory of those circumstances. I determined that I would delay a decent while before beginning any overtures, and in the meantime I would arrange to put some distance between her and those concubines, while not distancing her from me. To do those things, I needed the help of the Khakhan himself.

So, when I was sure there were no more Mongol maidens forthcoming, and when I knew Kubilai to be in a good mood—the messenger had recently arrived to tell him that Yun-nan was his and that Bayan was forging into the heartland of the Sung—I requested audience with him and was cordially received. I told him that I had accomplished my service to the maidens, and thanked him for giving me that opportunity to leave some trace of myself in the posterity of Kithai, and then said:

"I think, Sire, now that I have enjoyed this orgy of unrestrained pleasure, it might stand as the capstone to my bachelor career. That is to say, I believe I have attained to an age and maturity where I ought to cease the prodigal squandering of my ardors—the filly-chasing, as we call it in Venice, or the dipping of the ladle, as you say in these parts. I think it would be fitting for me now to contemplate a more settled conjugality, perhaps with an especially favored concubine, and I ask your permission, Sire—"

"Hui!" he exclaimed, with a smile of delight. "You were captivated by one of those twenty-four-karat damsels!"

"Oh, by *all* of them, Sire, it goes without saying. However, the one I would have for my keeping is the slave girl who attended them."

He sat back and grunted, with rather less delight, "Uu?"

"She is a girl of the Min, and—"

"Aha!" he cried, smiling broadly again. "Tell me no more. That captivation I can appreciate!"

"—and I would ask your leave, Sire, to purchase the slave's freedom, for she serves your Lady Matron of Concubines. Her name is Hui-sheng."

He waved a hand and said, "She will be deeded to you as soon as we get back to Khanbalik. Then she will be your servant or slave or consort, whatever you and she may choose. She is my gift to you in return for your help in acquiring Manzi for me."

"I thank you, Sire, most sincerely. And Hui-sheng will thank you, too. Are we returning soon to Khanbalik?"

"We will leave Xan-du tomorrow. Your companion Ali Babar has already been informed. He is probably in your chambers packing for you at this moment."

"Is this an abrupt departure, Sire? Has something happened?"

He smiled more broadly than ever. "Did you not hear me mention the acquisition of Manzi? A messenger just rode up from the capital with the news."

I gasped, "Sung has fallen!"

"The Chief Minister Achmad sent the word. A company of Han heralds rode into Khanbalik to announce the imminent arrival of the Sung's Dowager Empress Xi-chi. She is coming herself to surrender that empire and the Imperial Yin and her own royal person. Achmad could receive her, of course, as my Vice-Regent, but I prefer to do that myself."

"Of course, Sire. It is an epochal occasion. The overthrow of the Sung and the creation of a whole new Manzi nation for the Khanate."

He sighed comfortably. "Anyway, the cold weather is upon us, and the hunting here will be less enjoyable. So I shall go and take an Empress trophy instead."

"I did not know that the Sung Empire was ruled by a woman."

"She is only Regent herself, mother to the Emperor who died a few years ago, and died young, leaving only infant sons. So the old Xi-chi was reigning until her first grandson should grow up and take the throne. Which now he will not. Go then, Marco, and make ready to ride. I return to Khanbalik to rule an expanded Khanate, and you to start putting down roots. May the gods give wisdom to us both."

I hurried to my chamber, and burst in shouting, "I have momentous news!"

Ali Babar was helpfully gathering up the traveling things I had brought with me to Xan-du, and the few new things I had acquired while in residence—the tusks of my first-killed boar, for example, to keep as mementos—and was packing them into saddlebags.

"I have heard already," he said, with not much enthusiasm. "The Khanate is bigger and greater than ever."

"More amazing news than that! I have met the woman of my life!"

"Let me think if I can guess which. There has lately been quite a procession through this room of yours."

"You would never guess!" I said gleefully, and started to extol the charms of Hui-sheng. But then I checked myself, for Ali was not rejoicing with me. "You look unusually glum, old companion. Has something cast you down?"

He mumbled, "That rider from Khanbalik brought other news, not so inspiriting. . . ."

I looked more attentively at him. If he had had a chin under that gray beard, it would have been quivering. "What other news?"

"The messenger said that, when he was leaving the city, he was intercepted by one of my kashi artisans, who asked him to tell me that Mar-Janah has gone away."

"What? Your good wife Mar-Janah? Gone away? Gone where?"

"I have not the least idea. My shop man said that, some while back—it must be a month ago, by now, or more—two palace guards called at the kashi shop. Mar-Janah departed with them, and has not been seen or heard of since. The workers are consequently in some confusion and disarray. My man told the messenger no more than that."

"Palace guards? Then it must have been official business. I will run again to Kubilai and ask—"

"He professes to know nothing of the matter. I naturally went to inquire of him. That is when he told me to pack for us. And, since we are going back to Khanbalik immediately, I have made no great outcry. I suppose, when we get there, I will learn what has occurred. . . ."

"This is most strange," I murmured.

I said no more than that, though a recollection had come suddenly and unbidden into my mind—the message Ali had brought: "Expect me when you least expect me." I had not shown it to Ali or told him what it said. I had seen no need to burden him with my troubles—or what I then assumed were my troubles only—and I had torn up and thrown away the missive. Now I wished I had not. As I have said, Mongol writing was not easy for me to unravel. Could I perhaps have misread it? Could it, this time, have said something slightly different? "Expect me *where* you least expect me," perhaps? Had it been given to Ali Babar to deliver, not only to threaten and alarm me again, but also to get *him* out of the city while dirty deeds were being done?

Whoever in Khanbalik wished me evil must have been aware that—when I was absent from the city—I was vulnerable only vicariously, through the few persons I held dear there. A mere three persons, in fact. My father and uncle were two. But they were grown men, and strong, and anyone who harmed them would have to answer to an irate Khakhan. The third, however, was the good and beauteous and sweet Mar-Janah, who was only a weakling woman, and an insignificant former slave, and treasured by none but me and *my* former slave. With a pang, I remembered her saying, "I was left my life, but not much else . . ." and wistfully, "If Ali Babar can love what is left of me. . . ."

Had my unknown enemy, the lurking, sneaking whisperer, abducted that blameless woman for no reason but to hurt me? If so, the enemy was loathsomely vile, but clever in his choice of surrogate victim. I had helped to rescue the fallen Princess Mar-Janah from a life of abuse and degradation, and had helped her at last to safe and happy harbor—I remembered her saying, "The intervening twenty years might never have been"—and if I should now be the cause of her enduring yet another kind of misery, it would be a bitter hurt to me indeed.

Well, we would know when we got to Khanbalik. And I had a strong apprehension: if we were ever to find the vanished Mar-Janah, we should have first to find the veiled woman who had given Ali that missive for me. But, for the time being, I said nothing of that to him; he was already worried enough. I also ceased to exult over my newfound Hui-sheng, out of regard for his concern for his own darling, so long lost before and now lost again.

"Marco, could we not ride out ahead of this slow cortege?" he asked anxiously, when we and the whole Xan-du court had been on the road for two or three days. "You and I could be in Khanbalik much sooner if we could put spurs to our horses."

He was right, of course. The Khakhan traveled with much ceremony and no haste at all, holding the whole train to a stately slow march. It would not have been seemly for him to travel otherwise, especially when this was something in the nature of a triumphal procession. All his people in towns and villages along the way—having heard of the Sung war's successful conclusion—were eager to gather along the roadside and cheer and wave and throw flowers as he passed.

Kubilai rode in a majestic, thronelike, canopied carriage adorned with jewels and gilding, drawn by four immense elephants likewise much bedizened. Kubilai's carriage was followed by others carrying a number of his wives and many more of his other women, including those maidens he had lent to me, and servants and slaves and so forth. Variously before and behind and beside the carriages rode Prince Chingkim and all the other courtiers on horses gorgeously arrayed. Behind the carriages came wagons loaded with luggage and equipment and hunting arms and trophies of the season and traveling provender of wines and kumis and viands; one wagon was occupied by a band of musicians and their instruments, to play for us at our nighttime stops. A troop of Mongol warriors rode one day's journey ahead of us, to trumpet our approach to each community, so that its inhabitants could prepare to light their incense-fires and, if we arrived in twilight, to ignite the fiery trees and sparkling flowers (stores of which the Firemaster Shi had deposited with them on the outward march), and another troop of horsemen followed a day behind us, to retrieve any broken-wheeled wagons or lamed horses that had to fall out of the train. Also, the Khakhan, as usual in this season, had two or three brace of white gerfalcons riding on the sideboards of his carriage, and the whole procession would have to halt whenever we started some game that he wished to fly the falcons at.

"Yes, Ali, we could make better time on our own," I replied to his query. "But I think we ought not. For one reason, it would appear disrespectful of the Khakhan, and we may have need of his continued warm friendship. For another reason, if we stay with the train, anyone who has any news of Mar-Janah will have no trouble finding us to tell us."

That was quite true, though I did not confide to Ali all my reasoning in that regard. I had convinced myself that Mar-Janah had been abducted by my whisperer enemy. Since I knew not who that was, I saw no use in our riding furiously to the city just to cast about in desperation. It was more logical to assume that the whisperer would be keeping an eye out for me, and would the sooner see me if I arrived in conspicuous pomp, and could the sooner deliver his next message, or his ransom demand for Mar-Janah's deliverance, or just another taunting threat. It was our best hope for making contact with him, or at least with his veiled woman courier, and eventually with Mar-Janah.

My staying with the Khakhan's entourage also enabled me to keep a protective watch over Hui-sheng, but that had no influence on my decision not to hurry ahead. Hui-sheng was still traveling in company with her Mongol mistresses, and had no knowledge of my interest in her or the arrangements I had made for her future. I did pay her some occasional little attentions, just so she would not forget me—helping her climb in or out of the concubines' carriage when we stopped at a karwansarai or some provincial official's country mansion, fetching her a dipper of water from an inn-yard well, gathering a posy of a village's thrown flowers and presenting it to her with a gallant bow—trifles like that. I wished her to think well of me, but I had now more reason than before not to force my suit upon her.

I had earlier decided to wait a decent interval; now I *had* to. It seemed to me that my whisperer enemy knew always where I was and what I was doing. I dared not risk that enemy's learning that I had any special attachment to Hui-sheng. If he was malicious enough to strike at me through a dearly esteemed friend like Mar-Janah, God only knew what he might do to someone he thought *really* dear to me. It was hard for me to keep my gaze from lingering on her and to resist doing little services for the reward of her dimpled smile. I would have had an easier time of it if Ali and I had ridden on ahead, as he wanted to do. But, for his sake and Mar-Janah's, I stayed with the train, trying not to stay always near Hui-sheng.

KHANBALIK
AGAIN

. 1 .

I N addition to the troop of horsemen staying a day ahead of us, there
were other riders continually galloping off to Khanbalik or galloping up
to us, ostensibly to keep the Khakhan informed of developments there.
Ali Babar anxiously questioned each arriving courier, but none had any
further word of his missing wife. In fact, the riders' only function was to
keep track of the train of the Dowager Empress of the Sung, which was
also approaching the city. That enabled Kubilai to set our rate of march
so that our procession finally swept down the great central avenue of
Khanbalik on the same day—at the same hour—that hers entered from
the south.

The entire populace of the city, and probably of the whole province
for hundreds of li around, was jammed along the sides of the avenue and
clogging every fringe street and dangling from windows and clinging to
roof eaves, to greet the triumphant Khakhan with roars of approval, with
flapping banners and swirling pennants, with the booming and flaring
overhead of the fiery trees and sparkling flowers, with a ceaseless and ear-
thumping fanfare of trumpets and gongs and drums and bells. The people continued to carry on as the only slightly less splendiferous train of

the Sung Empress came up the avenue and halted respectfully on meeting ours. The crowds muted their clamor a little when the Khakhan got
chivalrously down from his throne-carriage and advanced to take the old
Empress's hand. He gently helped her down from her carriage to the
street, and enfolded her in a brotherly embrace of welcome, at which the
people bellowed and blared a really deafening uproar of noise and music.

After the Khan and the Empress had both got into his throne-
carriage, there was a period of confused milling, as the contingents of the
two trains churned about to coalesce and march all together to the
palace, where would begin the many days required for the ceremonies of
formal surrender: the conferences and discussions, the drafting and in-
diting and signing of documents, the handing over to Kubilai of Sung's
great seal of state or Imperial Yin, the public readings of proclamations,
the balls and banquets mingling celebration of victory and condolence of
defeat. (So condolent was Kubilai's chief wife, the Khatun Jamui, that
she settled a generous pension on the deposed Empress and granted that
she and her two grandsons be let to live out their lives in religious
retirement, the old woman in a Buddhist nunnery, the boys in a lamasarai.)

I held my horse back in the less congested rear of the procession as
it moved toward the palace, and motioned for Ali to do the same. When
I had the opportunity, I reined my mount alongside his and leaned close
so he could hear me over the ambient tumult without my having to
shout: "You see now why I wanted us to arrive with the Khakhan.
Everybody in the city is congregated here today, including any who
know where Mar-Janah is, and so now they know we are here, too."

"It would seem so," he said. "But no one has plucked at my stirrup
to volunteer any word."

"I think I know where the word will be volunteered," I said. "Stay
with me as far as the palace courtyard and then, when we dismount, let
us seem to separate, for I am sure we are being watched. Then this is
what we will do." And I gave him certain instructions.

The untidy procession went shouldering and elbowing and nudging
its way through the pressing onlookers and well-wishers, so slowly that
the day was ending when we finally reached the palace, and Ali and I
entered the stable court as we had done on our very first arrival at
Khanbalik, in a deepening twilight. The courtyard was a turmoil of
people and animals and noise and confusion; if anyone was watching us,
he could not have had a very clear view. Nevertheless, when we got
down from our horses and handed them over to stable hands, we made a
distinct show of waving farewells and going off in opposite directions.

Walking as tall and visibly as I could, I went to a horse trough and
splashed water at my dusty face. When I straightened up, I looked about
and made faces expressive of distaste at the surrounding commotion. I
started jostling through the mob toward the nearest palace portal, then
stopped and made flagrant gestures of repugnance—not worth the effort
—and plowed my way out of the crowd to where I was conspicuously
alone and apart. Keeping my distance from everyone I met, I sauntered
slowly across uncovered walks and through gardens and over streamlet

bridges and along terraces until I came to the newer parkland on the other side of the palace. I stayed always in the open, out from under roofs or trees, so that anyone who wanted to could see me and follow me. On the farther side of the palace grounds, there were fewer people, but still there were people about—minor functionaries trotting here and there on court business, servants and slaves scurrying about at their chores—for the Khakhan's arrival naturally caused a beehive stir.

However, when I came to the Kara Hill and began idly to climb its path, as if I were only seeking to get away from the crush of people below, I really did. There was no one else in sight up there. So I strolled on uphill to the Echo Pavilion, and first walked around its entire outside perimeter, to give my putative pursuer a chance to dodge inside the wall. Finally, as if paying no least attention to where I was or what I was doing, I ambled through the Moon Gate in the wall and around the inside terrace. When I was at the farthest remove from the Moon Gate, the pavilion squarely between me and it, I leaned back against the ornamental wall and contemplated the stars coming out one by one in the plum-colored sky above the pavilion's dragon-ridge roof. I had moved only leisurely the whole way from the entry courtyard to here, but my heart was beating as if I had run hard, and I feared that its thumping must be audible all around the pavilion precincts. But I had not long to worry about that. The voice came, as it had come before: a whisper in the Mongol tongue, low and sibilant and unidentifiable even as to gender, but as clearly as if the whisperer were right at my side, whispering the words I expected:

"Expect me when you least expect me."

I immediately bellowed, *"Now, Nostril!"*—in my excitement forgetting his new name and estate.

So did he, for he bellowed back, *"I have him, Master Marco!"*

And then I heard the grunts and gasps of a scuffle, as clearly as if it were being fought right at my feet, though I had to run all the way around the pavilion before I found the two rolling and struggling together on the very jamb of the Moon Gate. One of them was Ali Babar. The other I could not recognize; he appeared to be just a shapeless welter of robes and scarves. But that one I seized and tore away from Ali and held while Ali got to his feet. Panting, he pointed and said, "Master —it is no man—it is the veiled woman."

I realized then that I was clutching a not very big or muscular body, but I did not lessen my grip. I held on, and the body writhed fiercely, while Ali reached out and yanked the veils off her.

"Well?" I snarled. "Who is the bitch?" All I could see was the back of her dark hair and, past that, Ali's face, which got very round of eye and dilated of nostril and astonished and almost comically frightened.

"Mashallah!" he gasped. "Master—it is the dead come alive! It is your onetime maidservant—Buyantu!"

At that exclamation of her name she ceased to struggle and stood slumped in sullen resignation. So I eased my tight grasp of her, and turned her around to scrutinize her in what remained of the twilight. She did not look as if she had ever been dead, but her face was much harder and tight-skinned and colder than I remembered it, and her dark hair had much silver in it, and her eyes were defiant slits. Ali was still regarding her with wary consternation, and my voice was not entirely steady when I said:

"Tell us everything, Buyantu. I am glad to see you still among the living, but by what miracle did you survive? Is it possible that Biliktu lives, too? *Somebody* died in that calamity in my chambers. And what do you here, whispering in the Echo Pavilion?"

"Please, Marco," said Ali, in an even more trembly voice. "First things first. Where is Mar-Janah?"

Buyantu snapped, "I will not talk to a lowly slave!"

"He is no longer a slave," I said. "He is a freeman who has been bereft of his wife. She is a freewoman besides, so her abductor faces execution as a felon."

"I do not choose to believe a word you say. And I will not talk to a slave."

"Talk to me, then. You had best unburden yourself, Buyantu. I can promise no pardon for a felony but, if you tell us all—and if Mar-Janah is safely restored to us—the penalty may be something more lenient than execution."

"I spit on your pardon and leniency!" she said wildly. "The dead cannot be executed. I *did* die in that calamity!"

Ali's eyes and nostril widened again, and he took a step backward from her. I almost did, too, her words sounded so dreadfully sincere. But I stood my ground, and grasped her again and shook her and said menacingly, "Talk!"

Still stubborn, she said only, "I will not talk before a slave."

I could have wrung her until she did, but it might have taken all night. I turned to Ali and suggested:

"This may go more quickly if you absent yourself, and quickness may be vital." Either he saw the sense of that or he was not unwilling to leave the vicinity of one apparently come alive from the dead. Anyway, he nodded, so I told him, "Wait for me in my chambers. You can make sure for me that I do have those chambers again, and that they are habitable. I will come for you as soon as I know anything useful. Trust me."

When he had gone down the hill, out of hearing, I said again to Buyantu, "Talk. Is the woman Mar-Janah safe? Is she alive?"

"I do not know and I do not care. We dead care nothing. For the living *or* the dead."

"I have no time to hear your philosophies. Just tell me what happened."

She shrugged and said sullenly, "That day . . ." I did not have to inquire what day she meant. "On that day I first began to hate you, and I continued to hate you, and I hate you still. But on that day I also died. Dead bodies cool, and I suppose burning hatreds do, too. Anyway, I do not mind now, letting you know of my hatred and how I manifested it. That can make no difference now."

She paused, and I prodded, "I know you were spying on me for the Wali Achmad. Start with that."

"That day . . . you sent me to request audience for you with the Khakhan. When I returned, I found you and my—you and Biliktu in bed together. I was enraged, and I let you see *some* of how enraged I was. You left me and Biliktu to tend the brazier fire under a certain pot. You did not tell us it was dangerous, and I did not suspect. Being still in a rage and wishing you harm, I left Biliktu to watch the brazier, and I went to the Minister Achmad, who had long been paying me to inform him of your doings."

Even though I had known about that, I must have made a noise of displeasure, for she shrieked at me:

"Do not sniff! Do not pretend it is a practice beneath your high principles. You used a spy, too. That slave yonder." She waved in the direction Ali had gone. "And you paid him, too, by *pimping* for him! You paid him with the female slave Mar-Janah."

"Never mind that. Go on."

She paused to recollect her thoughts. "I went to the Minister Achmad, for I had much to tell him. I had, that very morning, overheard you and the slave talking of the Minister Pao, a Yi passing as a Han. It was that morning, too, that you promised the slave he would wed that woman Mar-Janah. I told those things to the Minister Achmad. I told him that you were at that moment impeaching the Minister Pao to the Khan Kubilai. The Minister Achmad immediately wrote a message and sent it by a servant to that Minister Pao."

"Aha," I muttered. "And Pao made a timely escape."

"Then the Minister Achmad sent another steward to fetch you to him when you left the Khakhan. He bade me wait, meanwhile, and I did. When you came, I was hiding in his private quarters."

"And not alone," I interrupted. "There was someone else in there that day. Who was she?"

"She?" echoed Buyantu, as if puzzled. Then she gave me a calculating look from her slit eyes.

"The large woman. I know she was there, for she almost came out into the room where the Arab and I were talking."

"Oh . . . yes . . . the large woman. That exceptionally large woman. We did not speak. I assumed that person to be merely some new fancy of the Minister Achmad. Perhaps you are aware that he has some eccentric fancies. If that person had a woman's name, I did not ask it, and do not know it. We merely sat in each other's company, looking sidelong at each other, until you departed again. Are you much interested in learning the identity of that large woman?"

"Perhaps not. Surely not *everyone* in Khanbalik was involved in these devious plots. Go on, Buyantu."

"As soon as you left his chambers, the Minister Achmad came for me again and took me to the window. He showed me—you were wandering up the Kara Hill—up here, to this Echo Pavilion. He told me to run after you, but unseen, and whisper the words you heard. I was pleased to make secret threats against you, even though I did not know what was threatened, for I hated you. *Hated you!*"

She choked on her rabid words, and stopped. I could not help feeling some compassion, so I said, "And a few minutes later, you had even more reason for hating me."

She nodded wretchedly, and swallowed, and got her voice working again. "I was returning to your chambers when they flew all apart, before my eyes, with that terrible noise and flame and smoke. Biliktu died then—and so did I, in everything but body. She had long been my sister, my twin, and we had long loved each other. I might have felt wrath enough if I had lost only my twin sister. But it was *you* who made us more than sisters. You made us *lovers*. And then you destroyed my loved one. *You!*"

That last word burst out in a spray of spittle. I prudently said nothing, and again it took her a moment before she could go on.

"I would happily have killed you then. But too many things were happening, too many people about. And then you went suddenly away. I was left alone. I was as alone as a person can be. The only one I loved in the world was dead, and everyone else thought I was, too. I had no employment to occupy me, no one to answer to, no place I was expected to be. I felt quite thoroughly dead, myself. I still do."

She fell morosely silent again, so I prodded. "But the Arab found employment for you."

"He knew I had not been in the room with Biliktu. He was the only one who knew. No one else suspected my existence. He told me he might have use for such an invisible woman, but for a long time he did not. He paid me wages, and I lived alone in a room down in the city, and I sat and looked at the walls of it." She sighed deeply. "How long has it been?"

"Long," I said sympathetically. "It has been a long time."

"Then one day he sent for me. He said you were on your way back, and we must prepare a suitable surprise with which to welcome you home. He wrote out two papers, and had me heavily veil myself—even more of an invisible woman—and I delivered them. One I gave to your slave to give to you. If you have seen it, you know it was not signed. The other paper he did sign, but not with his own yin, and that one I delivered some while later to the Captain of the Palace Guard. It was an order to arrest the woman Mar-Janah and take her to the Fondler."

"Amoredèi!" I exclaimed in horror. "But . . . but . . . the guardsmen do not arrest and the Fondler does not punish just on someone's whim! What was Mar-Janah charged with? What did the paper say? And how did the vile Wali sign it, if not with his own name?"

While Buyantu had been telling of occurrences, her voice had had some spirit in it, if only the spirit of a venomous snake taking satisfaction in malevolent accomplishment. But when I began demanding details, the spirit went out of her, and her voice got leaden and lifeless.

She said, "When the Khan is away from the court, the Minister Achmad is Vice-Regent. He has access to all the yins of office. I suppose he can use whichever he pleases, and sign it to any paper. He used the yin of the Armorer of the Palace Guard, who was the Lady Chao Ku-an, who was the former owner of the slave Mar-Janah. The order charged that the slave was a runaway, passing as a freewoman of property. The guardsmen would not question the written word of their own Armorer, and the Fondler questions nobody but his victims."

I was still sputtering in appalled bewilderment. "But . . . but . . . even the Lady Chao—she is no paragon of virtue, but even she would refute an untrue charge illicitly made in her name."

Buyantu said dully, "The Lady Chao died very shortly thereafter."

"Oh. Yes. I had forgotten."

"She probably never knew of the misuse of her official yin. In any case, she did not halt the proceedings, and now she never will."

"No. How very convenient for the Arab. Tell me, Buyantu. Did he ever confide to you why he was taking so much trouble, and involving so many people—or eliminating them—on my account?"

"He said only 'Hell is what hurts worst,' if that means anything to you. It does not to me. He said it again this evening, when he sent me again to follow you up here and whisper that threat once more."

I said between my teeth, "I think it is time I spread some of that Hell around." Then a chilling realization struck me, and I exclaimed, "Time! How much time? Buyantu—quick, tell me—what punishment would the Fondler inflict for Mar-Janah's alleged crime?"

She said, with indifference, "A slave posing as a free subject? I do not really know, but—"

"If it is not too severe, we still have hope," I breathed.

"—but the Minister Achmad said that such a crime is tantamount to treason against the state."

"Oh, dear God!" I groaned. "The penalty for treason is the Death of a Thousand! How—how long ago was Mar-Janah taken?"

"Let me think," she said languidly. "It was after your slave had gone to catch up to you and give you the unsigned message. So it has been . . . about two months . . . two and a half. . . ."

"Sixty days . . . seventy-five . . ." I tried to calculate, though my mind was in a ferment. "The Fondler once said he could stretch out that punishment, when he had the leisure and was in the mood, to near a hundred days. And a beautiful woman in his clutches ought to put him in a most leisurely mood. There might yet be time. I must run!"

"Wait!" said Buyantu, seizing my sleeve. Again there came a trace of life into her voice, though not very fittingly, for what she said was, "Do not go until you have slain me."

"I will not slay you, Buyantu."

"You must! I have been dead all this long time. Now kill me, so I can lie down at last."

"I will not."

"You would not be punished for it, since you could justify it. But you will not even be charged—for you are slaying an invisible woman, nonexistent, already attested dead. Come! You must feel the same rage that I felt when you slew my love. I have been long working to your hurt, and now I have helped to send your lady friend to the Fondler. You have every reason to slay me."

"I have more reason to let you live—and atone. You will be my proof of Achmad's involvement in these filthy doings. There is no time now to explain. I must run. But I need you, Buyantu. Will you just stay here until I return? I will be as quick as I can."

She said wearily, "If I cannot lie in my grave, what matter where I am?"

"Only wait for me. Try to believe that you owe me that much. Will you?"

She sighed and sank down, her back bowed against the inner curve of the Moon Gate. "What matter? I will wait."

I went down the hill in long bounds, asking myself whether I ought first accost the instigating Achmad or the perpetrating Fondler. Better hasten first to the Fondler, and hope I could stay his hand. But would he still be working at this late hour? As I scurried through the subterranean tunnels toward his cavern chambers, I groped in my purse and tried to count my money by feel. Most of it was paper, but there were some coins of good gold. The Fondler might be wearying of his enjoyment by now, and be cheaply bribable. As it turned out, he was still at his labors, and was surprisingly amenable to my appeal—but not from either boredom or avarice.

I had to do a lot of shouting and pounding of my fist on a table and shaking of it at the austere and aloof chief of the chambers clerks, but he finally unbent and went to interrupt his master at his work. The Fondler came mincing out through the iron-studded door, fastidiously wiping his hands on a silk cloth. Restraining my impulse to throttle him then and there, I upended my purse on the table between us, and poured out all its contents, and said breathlessly, "Master Ping, you hold a Subject woman named Mar-Janah. I have this moment learned that she was unjustly condemned to you. Does she still live? Can I request a temporary cessation of due process?"

His eyes glittered as he studied me. "I have a warrant for her execution," he said. "Do you bring a revoking warrant?"

"No, but I will get one."

"Ah. When you do, then. . . ."

"I ask only that the proceedings be suspended until I can do so. That is—if the woman still lives. Does she?"

"Of course she lives," he said haughtily. "I am not a butcher." He even laughed and shook his head, as if I had foolishly disparaged his professional skill.

"Then do me the honor, Master Ping, of accepting this token of my appreciation." I indicated the litter of money on the table. "Will that requite your kindness?"

He only grunted a noncommittal "Humpf," but began swiftly picking out the gold coins from the pile, without seeming to look at what he was doing. For the first time, I noticed that his fingers had nails incredibly long and curved, like talons.

I said anxiously, "I understand that the woman was sentenced to the Death of a Thousand."

Contemptuously disregarding the paper money, he scooped the coins into his belt purse, and said, "No."

"No?" I echoed, hopefully.

"The warrant specified the Death Beyond a Thousand."

I was briefly stunned, and then afraid to ask for elucidation. I said, "Well, can that be suspended for a time? Until I can fetch a revocation order from the Khakhan?"

"It can," he said, rather too readily. "If you are certain that that is what you want. Mind you, Lord Marco—that is your name? I thought I remembered you. I am honest in my transactions, Lord Marco. I do not sell goods sight unseen. You had best come and take a look at what you are buying. I will refund your—token of appreciation—if you ask it."

He turned and tripped across the chamber to the iron-studded door, and held it open for me, and I followed him into the inner chamber, and—dear God—I wish I had not.

However, in my desperate urgency to rescue Mar-Janah, I had neglected to bear in mind certain things. She, simply in being a beautiful female Subject, would have inspired the Fondler to inflict his most infernal tortures, and to drag them out as cruelly long as possible. But more than that. The warrant would have told him that Mar-Janah was the spouse of one Ali Babar, and it would have been an easy matter for Master Ping to discover that Ali was the onetime slave who had visited these very chambers, to the Fondler's extreme disgust. (He had said in revulsion, "Who . . . is . . . this?") And Ping would have remembered that that slave was *my* slave, and that I had been an even more obnoxious visitor. (I had, not knowing that he understood Farsi, called him "this simpering enjoyer of other people's torments.") So he would have had every excuse for exerting himself to the utmost in his attentions to the condemned Subject, who was wife to the lowly slave of Marco Polo, who had once so brashly insulted him. And now he had the very same Marco Polo before him, abjectly suppliant and pleading and cringing. The Fondler was not just willing, but fiendishly eager and proud, to show me the handiwork he had wrought—and to let me realize that it had resulted, in no small part, from my own foolhardy impertinence.

In the stone-walled, torch-lighted, blood-warmed, gore-spattered, nauseously reeking inner chamber, Master Ping and I stood side by side and looked at the room's central object, red and shiny and dripping and ever so slightly steaming. Or rather, I looked at it, and he looked sideways at me, gloating and waiting for my comment. I said nothing for a while. I could not have done, for I was repeatedly swallowing, determined not to let him hear me retch or see me vomit. So, probably to goad me, he began pedantically to explain the scene before us:

"You realize, I trust, that the Fondling has been going on for some time now. Observe the basket, and in it the comparatively few papers still unpicked from it and unfolded. Only those eighty-seven papers are left, because I had this day got to the nine hundred and thirteenth of them. You may believe it or not, but just that single paper has occupied my entire afternoon, and kept me working this late into the evening. That was because, when I unfolded it, it was the third directive to the Subject's 'red jewel,' which was somewhat hard to find in all that mess down there between the thigh stumps, and which of course had already received attention twice before. So it required all my skill and concentration to—"

I was able finally to interrupt him. I said harshly, "You told me this was Mar-Janah, and she was still living. This thing is not she, and it cannot conceivably be alive."

"Yes, it is, and yes, it is. Furthermore, she is capable of *staying* alive, too, with proper treatment and care—if anyone were unkind enough to want her to. Step closer, Lord Marco, and see for yourself."

I did. It was alive and it was Mar-Janah. At the top end of it, where must have been the head, there hung down, from what must have been the scalp, a single matted lock of hair not yet torn out by the roots, and it was long—a woman's hair—and it was still discernibly ruddy-black in color, and curly—Mar-Janah's hair. Also the thing made a noise. It could not have seen me, but it might dimly have heard my voice, through the remaining aperture where an ear had been, and perhaps even recognized my voice. The noise it made was only a faint bubbling blubber of sound, but it seemed feebly to say, "Marco?"

In a controlled and level voice—I would not have believed that I could manage that—I remarked to the Fondler, almost conversationally:

"Master Ping, you once described to me, in loving detail, the Death of a Thousand, which is what this seems to me to be. But you called this one by another name. What is the difference?"

"A trivial one. You could not be expected to notice. The Death of a Thousand, as you know, consists of the Subject's being gradually reduced —by the cutting off of bits, and slicings and probings and gougings and so on—a process prolonged by intervals of rest, during which the Subject is given sustaining food and drink. The Death Beyond a Thousand is much the same, differing only in that the Subject is given nothing but the bits of herself to eat. And to drink, only the—*what are you doing?*"

I had taken out my belt knife and plunged it into the glistening red pulp that I took to be the remains of Mar-Janah's breast, and I gave the haft the extra squeeze to ensure that all three blades stabbed deep. I could only hope that the thing was more certainly dead than before, but it did seem to slump a little more limply, and it did not make any more utterances. In that moment, I remembered how I had protested to Mar-Janah's husband, a long time ago, that I could never knowingly kill a woman, and he had said casually, "You are young yet."

Master Ping was speechlessly grinding his teeth at me, and glaring at me with furious eyes. But I coolly reached out and took from him the silk cloth with which he had wiped his hands. I used it to clean my knife, and rudely tossed it back at him as I closed up the knife and returned it to my belt sheath.

He sneered hatefully and said, "An utter waste of the most refined finishing touches yet to come. And I was going to accord you the privilege of looking on. What a waste!" He replaced the sneer with a mocking smile. "Still, an understandable impulse, I daresay, for a layman and a barbarian. And you had, after all, paid for her."

"I have not done paying for her, Master Ping," I said, and shoved past him and went out.

· 2 ·

I was anxious to get back to Buyantu, worried that she might have got restless by now, and I would gladly have put off telling Ali Babar the sad news. But I could not leave him wringing his hands in the Purgatory of not knowing, so I went to my old chambers, where he was waiting. In a pretense of cheerfulness, he made a sweeping gesture and said:

"All restored and refurnished and redecorated. But no one thought to assign you new servants, it seems. So I will stay tonight, in case you should need——" His voice faltered. "Oh, Marco, you look stricken. Is it what I fear it is?"

"Alas, yes, old comrade. She is dead."

Tears started in his eyes, and he whispered, "Tanha . . . hamishè. . . ."

"I know no easier way to tell it. I am sorry. But she is free of captivity and free of pain." Let him, at least for now, think that she had had an easy death. "I will tell you, another time, the how and the why of it, for it was an assassination, and unnecessary. It was done only to hurt you and me, and you and I will avenge it. But tonight, Ali, do not question me and do not stay. You will wish to go and grieve by yourself, and I have many things to do—to set our vengeance in train."

I turned and went out abruptly, for if he had asked me anything I could not have lied to him. But just the telling of that much had made me more angry and determined and bloodthirsty than before, so, instead of going directly to the Echo Pavilion for Buyantu, I went first to the chambers of the Minister Achmad.

I was briefly impeded by his sentries and servants. They protested that the Wali had endured a hectic day of making preparations for the Khakhan's return and the reception of the Dowager Empress, that he was much fatigued and had gone already to bed, and that they dared not announce a visitor. But I snarled at them—"Do not announce me! Admit me!"—so ferociously that they moved out of my way, muttering fearfully, "On your head be it, then, Master Polo," and I slammed unannounced and ungentlemanly through the door of the Arab's private apartments.

I was immediately reminded of Buyantu's words about Achmad's "eccentric fancies" and similar words spoken by the artist Master Chao long before. As I burst into the bedroom, I surprised a very large woman already there, and she whisked out through another door. I got only a glimpse of her, voluptuously gowned in filmy, flimsy, fluttering robes the color of the flower called lilak. But I had to assume that she was the same tall and robust woman I had seen in these chambers before. This particular one of Achmad's fancies, I thought, seemed to have lasted for some while; but then I gave it no more thought. I confronted the man who lay in the vast, lilak-sheeted bed, propped against lilak-colored pillows. He regarded me calmly, his black stone-chip eyes not flinching from the storm he must have seen in my face.

"I trust you are comfortable," I said, through clenched teeth. "Enjoy your swinishness. You will not for long."

"It is not mannerly to speak of swine to a Muslim, pork eater. You are also addressing the Chief Minister of this realm. Have a care how you do it."

"I am addressing a disgraced and deposed and dead man."

"No, no," he said, with a smile that was not a pleasant smile. "You may be Kubilai's current great favorite, Folo—even invited to share his concubines, I hear—but he will never let you lop off his good right hand."

I considered that remark, and said, "You know, I should never have thought myself a very important personage in Kithai—certainly not any rival to you, or any danger to you—were it not that you have so plainly thought me so. And now you mention the Mongol maidens I enjoyed. Are you resentful that *you* never have? Or that you never *could?* Was that the latest corrosive to eat at your good sense?"

"Haramzadè! *You* important? A rival? A danger? I have only to touch this bedside gong and my men will mince you in an instant. Tomorrow morning, I should have only to explain to Kubilai that you had spoken to me as you have just done. He would make no least fuss or comment, and your existence would be forgotten as readily as the ending of it."

"Why do you not do that, then? Why have you never done that? You said you would make me regret my having once flouted your express command—but why do so by attrition? Why have you only furtively and indolently made threats and menaces, while destroying instead the innocent folk around me?"

"It amused me to do so—Hell is what hurts worst—and I can do as I please."

"Can you? Until now, perhaps. Not any more."

"Oh, I think so. For my next amusement, I think I will make public some paintings the Master Chao did for me. The very name of Folo will be a laughingstock throughout the Khanate. Ridicule hurts worst of all." Before I could demand to know what he was talking about, he had gone on to another subject. "Are you really aware, Marco Folo, of who this Wali is that you presume to challenge? It was many years ago that I started serving as an adviser to the Princess Jamui of the Kungurat tribe of the Mongols. When the Khan Kubilai made her his first wife, and she therefore became the Khatun Jamui, I accompanied her to this court. I have served Kubilai and the Khanate ever since, in many capacities. Most recently, for many years, in this next-highest office of all. Do you really think you could topple an edifice of such firm foundation?"

Again I considered, and said, "It may surprise you, Wali, but I believe you. I believe that you have been dedicated in your service. I will

probably never know why, at this late date, you have let an unworthy
jealousy corrupt you into malversation."

"So say you. In all my career, I have done nothing wrong."

"Nothing wrong? Shall I enumerate? I do not think you conspired to
put the Yi named Pao in a ministerial office. I do not think you even
knew of his subversive presence. But you most certainly connived in his
escape when he was revealed. I call that treasonous. You have misused
another courtier's yin to your private purpose, and I call that mal-
feasance of office, if nothing worse. You have most foully murdered the
Lady Chao and the woman Mar-Janah—one a noble, one a worthy
subject of the Khan—all for no reason but to afflict me. You have done
nothing wrong?"

"Wrong must be proven," he said, in a voice as stony as his eyes.
"Wrong is an abstract word of no independent existence. Wrong is, like
evil, only a matter of other people's judgment. If a man do a deed and
none call it wrong, then he did no wrong."

"You did, Arab. Many wrongs. And so they will be adjudged."

"Take murder now . . . ," he went on, as if I had not interrupted.
"You have imputed to me murder. However, if some woman named Mar-
Janah *is* truly dead, and wrongfully, there is a reputable witness to her
last hours. He can testify that the Wali Achmad never once laid eyes on
the woman, let alone murderous hands. That witness can testify that
the woman Mar-Janah died from a knife wound administered by a certain Marco Folo." He turned on me a gaze of arch and mocking good
humor. "Why, Marco Folo, how you do look! Is that a look of astonishment or guilt or shame at being found out? Did you suppose I have been
tucked abed here all the night? I have been going about, cleaning up
after you. I was only just now able to lay my weary self down to rest,
and in you come, to annoy me yet further."

But I was not discomfited by his sarcasm. I simply shook my head
and said, "I will freely confess the knife wound, when we are on trial in
the Hall of Justice."

"This will never get to the Cheng. I have just told you that a wrong
must be proven. But, before that, the wrongdoer must be accused. Could
you do such a reckless and profitless thing? Would you really dare to lay
charges against the Chief Minister of the Khanate? The word of an
upstart Ferenghi against the reputation of the longest-serving and
highest-ranking courtier of the court?"

"It will not be only my word."

"There is no other to speak against me."

"There is the woman Buyantu, my former maidservant."

"Are you sure you wish to bring that up? Would it be wise? She also
died by your doing. The whole court knows that, and so will every
justice of the Cheng."

"You know different, damn you. She spoke to me this very evening,
and told me everything. She waits for me now on the Kara Hill."

"There is no one on the Kara Hill."

"This once, you are mistaken," I said. "There is Buyantu." And I
may even have smiled smugly at him.

"There is no one on the Kara Hill. Go and see. It is true that earlier this evening I sent a servant up there. I disremember her name, and now I cannot even recollect on what errand I sent her. But when she did not return after a time, I went to look for her. Most considerate of me, to do that personally, but Allah bids us be considerate of our underlings. Had I found her, it might have been she who told me you had gone running to visit the Fondler. However, I regret to report that I did not find her. Nor will you. Go and see."

"You murdering monster! Have you slain yet another—?"

"Had I found her," he went on implacably, "she might also have told me that you refused her exactly that consideration. But Allah bids us be more considerate than you heartless Christians. So—"

"Dio me varda!"

He dropped the mocking tone and snapped, "I begin to tire of this jousting. Let me say just one thing more. I foresee that it will raise some eyebrows, Folo, if you start claiming publicly to have heard disembodied voices in the Echo Pavilion, especially if you insist that you have heard the voice of a person known by all to be long defunct, and she a person slain in a misadventure of which you were the cause. The most charitable interpretation of your babblings will be that you are woefully demented by grief and guilt arising from that incident. Anything else you may babble—such as accusations against important and well-esteemed courtiers—will be similarly regarded."

I could only stand there and seethe at him, impotently.

"Mind you," he went on, "your pitiable affliction may redound to the public good, after all. In civilized Islam, we have institutions called Houses of Delusion, for the safe confinement of those persons possessed by the demon of insanity. I have long pressed Kubilai to establish the same hereabout, but he stubbornly maintains that no such demon infests these more wholesome regions. Your obviously troubled mind and troublesome behavior may convince him otherwise. In which event, I shall order the commencement of construction of Kithai's first House of Delusion, and I leave you to guess the identity of its first occupant."

"You—you—!" I might have lunged across the lilak bed at him, but he was stretching a hand toward the bedside gong.

"Now, I have told you to go and look and satisfy yourself that there is no one on the Kara Hill—no one anywhere to substantiate your demented imaginings. I suggest you go. There or somewhere. But go!"

What could I do but go? I went, miserably disheartened, and I plodded hopelessly up the Kara Hill to the Echo Pavilion once more, though knowing it would be as the Arab had said, barren of people, and it was. There was no least trace of Buyantu's ever having been there, or ever having been anything but dead. I came with dragging steps down the hill again, even more dejected and demolished, "with my bagpipes turned inside their sack," as the old Venetian phrase—and my father—would express it.

The sardonic thought of my father put me in mind of him and, having now no other destination, I trudged off to his chambers to pay a homecoming call. Maybe he would have some sage advice for me. But one of his maidservants answered to my scratch at the portal, and told me that her Master Polo was out of the city—still or again, I did not ask which. So I moped on farther along the corridor to Uncle Mafìo's suite. The maidservant there told me that yes, her Master Polo was in residence, but that he did not always spend the night in his chambers, and sometimes, not to disturb his servants unnecessarily, he came and went by a back door he had had cut in a rear wall of the suite.

"So I never know, at night, whether he is in his bedroom or not," she said, with a slightly sad smile. "And I would not intrude upon him."

I remembered that Uncle Mafìo had once claimed to have "given pleasure" to this servant woman, and I had been glad for him. Perhaps it had been only a brief foray into normal sexuality, and he had since found it unsatisfactory, and desisted, and that was why she looked a little sad, and why she would not "intrude upon him."

"But you are his family, no intruder," she said, bowing me in the door. "You may go and see for yourself."

I went through the rooms to his bedchamber, and it was dark and the bed was unoccupied. He was not there. My homecoming, I thought wryly, was not exactly being greeted with open arms and shouts of joy, not by anybody. In the lamplight spilling in from the main room, I began feeling about for a piece of paper and something to write with, to leave a note saying at least that I was back in residence. When I groped in the drawer of a cabinet, my fingernails snagged in some curiously filmy and flimsy cloth goods. Wondering, I held them up in the half-light; they seemed hardly garments sturdy enough for a man's wear. So I went back to the main room and brought a lamp, and held them up again. They were indisputably feminine gowns, but of voluminous size. I thought: Dear God, is he nowadays disporting himself with some female giant? Was that why the maidservant seemed sad: because he had discarded her for something grotesque and perverse? Well, at least it was female. . . .

But it was not. I lowered the robes to fold them away again, and there stood Uncle Mafìo, who had evidently that moment come sidling in through his new back door. He looked startled, embarrassed and angry, but that was not what I noticed first. What I saw immediately was that his beardless face was powdered blank white all over, even over his eyebrows and lips, and his eyes were darkened and lengthened with an application of al-kohl rimming the eyelids and extending out from them, and a little puckered rosebud mouth had been painted in the middle of where his wide mouth should have been, and his hair was elaborately skewered by hair-spoons, and he was dressed all in gossamer robes and wispy scarves and fluttering ribbons the color of the flower called lilak.

"Gèsu . . ." I breathed, as my initial shock and horror gave way to realization—or as much of realization as I needed, and more than I wanted. Why had it not dawned on me long ago? I had heard from enough people, God knows, about the Wali Achmad's "eccentric tastes," and I had long known of my uncle's desperate clutchings, like those of a man adrift on an outgoing tide, at one crumbling anchorage after another. Just tonight, Buyantu had looked puzzled when I mentioned

Achmad's "large woman," and then she had said evasively, "If that person had a woman's name. . . ." *She* had known, and she had probably decided, with female cunning, to save the knowledge for bargaining with, later on. The Arab had more forthrightly threatened, "I will make public some paintings . . ." and I should have remembered then the kind of pictures the Master Chao was forced to paint in private. "The very name of Polo will be a laughingstock. . . ."

"Gèsu, Uncle Mafìo . . ." I whispered, with pity, revulsion and disillusionment. He said nothing, but he had the good grace to look now ashamed instead of angry at being discovered. I slowly shook my head, and considered several things I might say, and at last said:

"You once preached to me, uncle, and most persuasively, on the profitable uses of evil. How it is only the boldly evil person who triumphs in this world. Have you followed your own preachings, Uncle Mafìo? Is this"—I gestured at his squalid disguise, his whole aspect of degradation—"is this the triumph it won for you?"

"Marco," he said defensively, and in a husky voice. "There are many kinds of love. Not all of them are nice. But no kind of love is to be despised."

"Love!" I said, making of it a dirty word.

"Lust, lechery . . . last resort . . . call it what you will," he said bleakly. "Achmad and I are of an age. And both of us, feeling much apart from other people . . . outcasts . . . uncommon. . . ."

"Aberrant, I would call it. And I would think you both of an age to subdue your more egregious urges."

"To retire to the chimney corner, you mean!" he flared, angry again. "To sit quiet there and decay, and gum our gruel and nurse our rheumatics. Do you think, because you are younger, that you have a monopoly on passion and longing? Do I look decrepit to you?"

"*You look indecent!*" I shouted back at him. He quailed and covered his horrible face with his hands. "At least the Arab does not parade his perversions in gossamer and ribbons. If he did, I should only laugh. When you do it, I weep."

He almost did, too. Anyway, he began sniffling pitifully. He sank down on a bench and whimpered, "If you are fortunate enough to enjoy whole banquets of love, do not ridicule those of us who must make do with the leavings and droppings from the table."

"Love again, is it?" I said, with a scathing laugh. "Look, uncle, I grant that I am the last man qualified to lecture on bedroom morality and propriety. But have you no sense of discrimination? Surely you know how vile and wicked that man Achmad is, *outside* the bedroom."

"Oh, I know, I know." He flapped his hands like a woman in distress, and gave a sort of womanish squirm. It was ghastly to see. And it was ghastly to hear him gibber, like a woman agitated beyond coherence, "Achmad is not the best of men. Moody. Fearsome temper. Unpredictable. Not admirable in all his behavior, public or private. I have realized that, yes."

"And did nothing?"

"Can the wife of a drunkard stop him drinking? What could I do?"

"You could have ceased whatever it is that you *have* been doing."

"What? Loving? Can the wife of a drunkard cease loving him just because he is a drunkard?"

"She can refuse submission to his embrace. Or whatever you two— never mind. Please do not try to tell me. I do not want even to imagine it."

"Marco, be reasonable," he whined. "Would you give up a lover, a loving mistress, simply because others found her unlovable?"

"Per dio, I hope I would, uncle, if her unlovable characteristics included a penchant for cold-blooded murder."

He appeared not to hear that, or veered away from it. "All other considerations aside, nephew, Achmad is the Chief Minister, and the Finance Minister, hence he is head of the mercantile Ortaq, and on his permission has depended our success as traders here in Kithai."

"Was that permission contingent on your crawling like a worm? De-meaning and debasing yourself? Dressing up like the world's largest and least beautiful whore? Having to flit through back halls and back doors in that ridiculous garb? Uncle, I will not excuse depravity as *good business.*"

"No, no!" he said, squirming some more. "Oh, it was far more than that to me! I swear it, though I can hardly expect you to understand."

"Sacro, I do not. If it were only the casual experiment in curiosity, yes, I have done some such things myself. But I know how long you have persisted in this folly. How could you?"

"He wanted me to. And after a time, even degradation becomes habitual."

"You never felt the least impulse to break the habit?"

"He would not let me."

"Not *let* you! Oh, uncle!"

"He is a . . . wicked man, perhaps . . . but a masterful one."

"So were you, once. Caro Gèsu, how far you have fallen. However, since you spoke of this as a business affair—tell me, I must know—has my father been aware of this development? This entanglement?"

"No. Not this one. Not this time. No one knows, except you. And I wish you would put it out of your mind."

"Be sure I will," I said acidly, "when I am dead. I trust you know that Achmad is bent on my destruction. Have you known it all this time?"

"No, I have not, Marco. That, too, I swear."

Then, in the manner of a woman—who, in any conversation, is always eager to turn it down some avenue where she can run without check or hindrance or contradiction—he began to prattle most fluently:

"I know it now, yes, because tonight when you came there and I fled from the room, I put my ear to the door. But only once before was I in his chambers when you and he had words, and that time I took mannerly pains not to overhear. He never otherwise disclosed to me the full extent of his animosity toward you, or the clandestine moves he was making to harm you. Oh, I did know—I confess this much—that he was no friend of yours. He often made disparaging remarks to me about 'that pestiferous nephew of yours,' and sometimes facetious references to 'that *pretty* nephew of yours,' and sometimes, when we were every close, he would even say 'that provocative nephew of *ours*.' And lately, after a messenger from Xan-du confided to him that Kubilai had rewarded your war service by letting you play stud to a string of Mongol mares, Achmad began speaking of you as 'our wayward warrior nephew' and 'our misguided voluptuary nephew.' And recently, in our most intimate moments, when we were . . . when he was . . . well, he would do it uncommonly hard and deep, as if to hurt, and he would moan, 'Take *that*, nephew, and *that!*' And at the surge, he would almost shriek, saying—"

He stopped, for I had clapped my hands over my ears. Sounds can sicken, as well as sights. And I felt nearly as nauseated as I had felt earlier, when I had to look upon the flayed and limbless meat that had been Mar-Janah.

"But no," he said, when I would listen again, "I did not know until tonight how much he really hates you. How he has been impelled by that passion to do so many dreadful things—and how he still seeks to discredit and destroy you. Of course, I knew him to be a passionate man. . . ." And the nausea rose in me again, as he once more lapsed into broken sniveling. "But to threaten to use even *me* . . . the paintings of us. . . ."

I barked harshly at him, "Well, then? It was some while ago that you heard those threats. What have you been doing since? Did you linger in his company—I devoutly hope—to *kill* the son of a bitch shaqàl?"

"Kill my—kill the Chief Minister of the Khanate? Come, come, Marco. You had as much opportunity as I, and more reason, but you did not. Would you have your poor old uncle do the deed instead, and doom him to the fondling of the Fondler?"

"Adrìo de vu! I have known you to kill before, and without such womanly compunction. In this instance, you would have had at least more chance than I to escape undetected. I presume Achmad has a back door for sneaking through, as you do."

"Whatever else he is, Marco, he is the Chief Minister of this realm. Can you imagine the hue and cry? Can you believe that his slayer would go undiscovered? How long would it have been before I was revealed, not only as his murderer but—but—so much else revealed besides?"

"There. You almost said it. It is not the murder that you shy from, nor the penalty for it. Well, neither do I fear killing or death. So this I promise you: I will get Achmad before he gets me. You can tell him so, next time you cuddle together."

"Marco, I beg you—as I begged him—consider! He at least told you the truth. There exists no single witness or slightest evidence with which to impugn him, and his word will carry more weight than yours. If you contend with him, you are bound to lose."

"And if I do not, I lose. So the only matter still in doubt—and all you care about—is whether you lose your unnatural lover. Whoever is with him is against me. You and I are of a blood, Mafìo Polo, but if you can forget that, so can I."

"Marco, Marco. Let us discuss this like rational men."

"*Men*?" My voice cracked on the word, out of sheer fatigue and confusion and grief. I had been used to feeling, in the presence of my uncle, that I had grown up not at all from the boy I was when we first began our journeying together. Now suddenly, in the presence of this travesty of him, I felt much older than he was, and much the stronger of us two. But I was not sure that I was strong enough to endure this new conflict of feelings—in addition to all the other emotions that had been provoked in me this day—and I feared that I might myself break down into sobs and snivelings. To avert that, I raised my voice to a shout again. "*Men*? Here!" I seized up a shiny brass hand mirror from his bedside table. "Look at yourself, *man*!" I flung it into his silken and matronly lap. "I will converse no more with a painted drab. If you would speak again, let it be tomorrow—and come to me with a clean face. I am going to bed now. This has been the hardest day of all my life."

And indeed it had been, and it was not over yet. I tottered to my chambers like a hard-hunted and much-torn hare getting to its burrow just one jaw snap ahead of the hounds. The rooms were dark and empty, but I did not mistake them for any safe burrow. The Wali Achmad could very well know that I was alone and unattended—he might even have had the palace stewards arrange it so—and I decided to sit up all night, awake and full-dressed. I was too utterly tired to disrobe, in any case, but so very drowsy that I wondered how I could fend off sleep.

I had no sooner sunk down on a bench than I was jolted wide awake, to hunted-hare awareness, as my door silently swung open and a dim light shone in. My hand was already on my knife when I saw that it was only a maidservant, unarmed, no menace. Servants usually coughed politely or made some premonitory noise before entering a room, but this one had not because she could not. She was Hui-sheng, the silent Echo. The palace stewards might have neglected to provide attendants for me, but the Khan Kubilai never neglected or forgot anything. Even with all his press of other concerns, he had remembered his latest promise to me. Hui-sheng came in carrying a candle in one hand and cradled in the other arm—perhaps she worried that I would not recognize her without it—that white porcelain incense burner.

She set it down on a table and came across the room, smiling, to me. The burner was already charged with that finest quality tsan-xi-jang incense, and she brought with her the fragrance of its smoke, the scent of clover fields that have been warmed in the sun and then washed by a gentle rain. I was immediately, blessedly refreshed and heartened, and I would always thereafter associate Hui-sheng and that aroma inseparably. Long years afterward, the very thought of Hui-sheng reminds me of the incense, or the actual smell of such a fragrant field reminds me of her.

She took from her bodice a folded paper and handed it to me, and held the candle so I could read. I had been so nicely calmed and newly invigorated, by the sweet sight of her and the sweet scent of clover, that I opened the paper without hesitation or apprehension. It bore a thicket of black-inked Han characters, incomprehensible to me, but I recognized the big seal of Kubilai stamped in red over much of the writing. Hui-sheng raised an ivory small finger and pointed to another word or two, then tapped her own breast. I understood that—her name was on the paper—and I nodded. She pointed to another place on the paper—I recognized the character; it was the same as on my own personal yin— and she shyly tapped my chest. The paper was the deed to ownership of the slave girl Hui-sheng, and the Khan Kubilai had transferred that title to Marco Polo. I nodded vigorously, and Hui-sheng smiled, and I laughed aloud—the first joyful noise I had made in ever so long—and I caught her to me in an embrace that was not passionate or even amorous, but only glad. She let me hug her small self, and she actually hugged back with her free arm, for we were celebrating the event of our first communication.

I sat down again and sat her beside me, and went on holding her close like that—probably to her extreme discomfort and bewilderment, but she never once wriggled in complaint—all through that long night, and it seemed not long at all.

· 3 ·

I was eager to make my next communication to Hui-sheng—actually to make a gift to her—which meant waiting for daylight when I could see what I was doing. But, by the time the first light of dawn shone upon the translucent windowpanes, she had fallen fast asleep in my arms. So I simply sat still and held her, and took the opportunity to look closely and admiringly and affectionately at her.

I knew that Hui-sheng was rather younger than I, but by how many years I never would know, for she herself had no idea of her exact age. Neither could I divine whether it was owing to her youth or her race—or just her personal perfection—but her face did not loosen and sag in sleep as I had seen other women's faces do. Her cheeks, lips, jaw line, all remained firm and composed. And her pale-peach complexion, seen close, was the clearest and most finely textured I ever saw, even on statues of polished marble. The skin was so clear that, at her temples and just under either ear, I could trace the faint-blue hint of delicate veins beneath, glowing through the skin the way the Master Potter's paper-thin porcelain vases showed their inside-painted designs when held to a light.

Another thing I realized while I had this chance to examine her features so closely. I had previously believed that all the men and women of these nations had narrow, slitlike eyes—*slant eyes*, Kubilai had once called them—barren of eyelashes, expressionless and inscrutable. But now I could see that it was only a matter of their having just a tiny extra inner corner to their upper eyelids that made the eyes look so, and then only from a distance. Up close, I could see that Hui-sheng's eyes were most gorgeously equipped with perfect fans of perfectly fine, long, gracefully curved black lashes.

And when the increasing daylight in the room finally roused her and she opened her eyes, I could see that they were, if anything, even larger and more brilliant than those of most Western women. They were a rich, dark, qahwah brown, but with tawny glints inside them, and the whites around them were so pure-white that they had almost a blue sheen. Hui-sheng's eyes, when first opened, were perceptibly brimming with leftover dreams—as anyone's are at waking—but as they took cognizance of the real and daytime world, her eyes became lively and expressive of mood and thought and emotion. They were different from Western women's eyes only in that they were not so readily readable; not inscrutable at all, merely requiring of a looker some attention and some *caring* to see what message they held. What a Western woman's eyes have to tell, they usually tell to anyone who will look. What was in Hui-sheng's eyes was ever discernible only to one—like me—who really wanted to know, and took the trouble to gaze deep and see it.

By the time she woke, the morning was full upon us, and it brought a scratching at my outer door. Hui-sheng of course did not hear it, so I went to open the door—with some caution, being still apprehensive of who might be calling. But it was only a matched pair of Mongol maid-servants. They made ko-tou and apologized for not having been earlier in attendance, and explained that the palace's Chief Steward had only belatedly realized that I was without servants. So now they had come to inquire what I would eat to break my fast. I told them, and told them to bring enough for two, and they did. Unlike my earlier servants, the twins, these maids seemed to have no objection to serving a slave in addition to myself. Or maybe they took Hui-sheng to be a visiting concubine, and possibly of noble blood, she was pretty enough, and noble enough in her bearing. Anyway, the maids served us both without demur, and hovered solicitously nearby while we dined.

When we were done, I made gestures to Hui-sheng. (I did this most awkwardly, with broad and unnecessary flourishes, but in time she and I would get so accomplished in sign language, and so well attuned, that we could make each other understand even complex and subtle communications, and with movements so slight that people around us seldom noticed them, and marveled much that we could "talk" in silence.) On this occasion, I wished to tell her to go and bring to my chambers—if she wished to do so—all her wardrobe and personal belongings. I clumsily ran my hands up and down my own costume, and pointed to her, and pointed to my closets, and so on. To a less perceptive person, it might have seemed that I was directing her to go and garb herself, as I was dressed at the time, in Persian-style male attire. But she smiled and nodded her understanding, and I sent the two maids with her to help carry her things.

While they were gone, I got out the paper Hui-sheng had brought me: the formal title to possession of her, relinquished by Kubilai to me. This was the gift I wanted to give her—namely, herself. I would sign the paper over to her, thereby manumitting her to the full status of free-woman, belonging to nobody, beholden to nobody. I had several reasons for wanting to do so, and to do it right away. For one, if I was likely soon to be condemned by the Arab to the cavern of the Fondler or the cell of a House of Delusion, I should have to flee or fight my way out, or fall in the fight—and so I wanted Hui-sheng to be in no way involved with me. But if I should live and keep my freedom and my courtier status, I hoped that eventually I would have possession of Hui-sheng in a different relation than master-and-slave. If it was to come about, it had to be of her own bestowing, and she could bestow herself only if she was at full liberty to do so.

I got from my bedroom the packs I had most recently carried and turned them out on the floor, looking for the little chicken-blood stone yin seal for affixing my signature firmly on the paper. When I found it, I also found the yellow-paper letter of authority and the large pai-tzu plaque Kubilai had given me to carry on my mission to Yun-nan. I probably ought to return those things to him, I thought. And that reminded me of something else I had brought for him: the paper on which I had scrawled the names of Bayan's engineers who had placed the brass balls, and whom I had promised to praise by name to the Khakhan. I found that, too, and it in turn made me recollect many other mementos I had picked up during even earlier journeying.

For all I knew, I might never have another chance to review my past, since I might not have any future to look forward to. So I went and rummaged among the older packs and saddlebags I had carried, and got out all those items and regarded them fondly. All my notes and partial maps I had given to my father to tend for me, but I had quite a few other things—dating clear back to the wood-and-string kamàl that a man named Arpad had given me in Suvediye to track our wanderings north and south . . . and a now rather rusty shimshir sword I had taken from the store of an old man named Beauty of Faith's Moon, and. . . .

There was another scratching at the door, and this time it was Mafìo. I was not overjoyed to see him, but at least he was dressed in man's clothes, so I let him come in. As if the change of raiment had restored some of his manhood, he spoke in the gruff voice of old, and even seemed emboldened to bluster. After giving me a perfunctory "Bondì," he began a harangue:

"I have lain awake all night, Neodo Marco, worrying over your situation—our several situations—and I came straight here without even taking time to break my fast, to tell you—"

"No!" I snapped. "I am long past being a little nephew boy, and you will do no *telling* to me. I also sat up all night, determining what I must do, though I have not yet determined exactly how I will do it. So, if you have any ideas, I shall be willing to hear them. But I will hear no telling of instructions or ultimatums."

He immediately pleaded, "Adasio, adasio," and raised his hands appeasingly, and let his shoulders slump as if he were enduring a lash. I was almost sorry to see him so quickly cowed by my strong rejoinder, so I said less harshly, "If you have not yet broken fast, yonder is a pot of cha still hot."

"Thank you," he said meekly, and sat down and poured a cup, and began again. "I came only to say, Marco—to suggest, that is—that you not embark on any drastic plan of action until I can talk again to the Wali Achmad."

Since I had in fact no plan of action, drastic or otherwise, I only shrugged and sat down on the floor to continue sorting through my keepsakes. He went on:

"As I tried to tell you last night, I have already petitioned Achmad to consider a truce between him and you. Mind you, I hold no brief for the atrocities he has committed. But, as I pointed out to him, in the doing of those things, he has bereft you of supporting witnesses, so he need not fear your crying calumny against him. At the same time, as I also pointed out, he has sufficiently punished you for having angered him in the first place." Mafio sipped at his cup of cha, then leaned down to see what I was doing. "Cazza beta! The relics of our journeys. I had forgotten some of those things. Arpad's kamàl. And there, a jar of the mumum shaving ointment. And that phial, is that not a memento of the charlatan Hakim Mimdad? And a pack of the zhi-pai playing cards. Olà, Marco, but you and I and Nico were once a carefree threesome of journeyers, were we not?" He sat back again. "So my argument is this. If Achmad has no reason to pursue his campaign against you, and you have no weapons against him, then a declaration of truce between you—"

"Would mean," I said scornfully, "that nothing disrupts your cozy affair with your masterful lover. Dolce far niente. That is all you care about."

"That is not true. And if necessary, I am prepared to prove my caring for—for all concerned. But even if you deplore that side result, there is much else to be said for a truce. No one gets hurt and all are benefited."

"It does not much benefit the slain Mar-Janah and Buyantu and Lady Chao. Achmad slew them all, and all were innocent of any harm or wrong to him, and Mar-Janah was a friend of mine."

"What *would* benefit the dead?" he cried. "Nothing you could do would bring them back alive!"

"I am still alive, and I must live with my conscience. You just now mentioned us three carefree journeyers, forgetting that for most of our journeys we were four. Nostril was one of us. And later, as Ali Babar, he was Mar-Janah's devoted husband, and on my account he has lost her. Your conscience may be infinitely pliable, but I will not be able to look Ali in the eye again until I avenge Mar-Janah."

"But how? Achmad is too powerful—"

"He is only a human being. He can die, too. I tell you honestly that I do not know how I shall do it, but I swear to you that I will kill the Wali Achmad-az-Fenaket."

"You would die for doing it."

"Then I die, as well."

"And what of me? What of Nicolò? What of the Compagnia—?"

"If you suggest *good business* to me again—" I began, but I strangled on it.

"Look, Marco. Do only what I asked a moment ago. Do not so rashly commit yourself until I have talked again with Achmad. I shall go immediately and plead with him. He may offer a palliative to your anger. Something you would accept. A new wife for Ali, perhaps."

"Gèsu," I said, with the deepest disgust I had felt yet. "Go away, you creature. Go and crawl before him. Go and do whatever sordid things you do with him. Get him so delirious with love that he promises anything. . . ."

"I can do that!" he said eagerly. "You think you make only a cruel jest, but I can do that!"

"Enjoy the doing, then, for it will probably be the last time. I will see Achmad dead, and as soon as I can arrange it."

"You really mean that, I think."

"Yes! *How can I make you understand?* I care not what it costs me—or you—or the Compagnia or the Khanate or the Khan Kubilai himself. I shall seek only to shield my innocent father from the repercussions of my act, so I must do it before he returns. And I will. Achmad will die, and by my doing."

He must have been at last convinced, for he only said dully, "There is nothing I can say to dissuade you? Nothing I can do?"

I shrugged again. "If you are going to him now, you could kill him yourself."

"I love him."

"Kill him lovingly."

"I think I could not live, now, without him."

"Then die with him. Must I say it to you straight—to you who were my uncle and companion and trusted ally? I say it then: the friend of my enemy is as much my enemy!"

I did not even see him leave the room, because Hui-sheng and the two maids came back just then, and I was briefly occupied in showing them where to stow her little stock of clothes and belongings. Then, during another little while, I managed totally to forget the evil Achmad and my pitifully decayed Uncle Mafio and all the other cares that weighed upon me and all the hazards that waited for me beyond this place and this moment—for I was happily engaged in giving to Hui-sheng the deed to herself.

I motioned for her to sit down at a table, which had on it the brushes and arm rest and ink block that the Han use for writing. I unfolded the title paper and laid it before her. I wetted the block to make ink, and brushed some of that onto the engraved surface of my yin, then pressed that firmly on a clear space on the paper, and showed her the mark. She looked at it and then at me, her lovely eyes striving to comprehend what I meant by those actions. I pointed to her, to the mark on the paper, to myself, then made dismissing gestures—the paper is no longer mine, *you* are no longer mine—and thrust the paper at her.

A great light came into her face. She imitated my gestures of dismissal, and looked questioningly at me, and I nodded definitely. She held the paper, still gazing at me, and made as if to tear it up—though she did not—and I nodded even more definitely, to assure her: that is correct, the slave deed no longer exists, you are a free woman. Tears came into her eyes, and she stood up and let go the paper and let it flutter to the floor, and gave me one last questioning look: there is no mistake? I made a wide, sweeping motion to indicate: the world is yours, you are free to go. There ensued one frozen moment, during which I held my breath, and we simply stood and regarded each other, and it seemed an interminably long moment. All she had to do was gather up her belongings again and take her leave; I could not have prevented her. But then the frozen moment fractured. She made two gestures that I *hoped* I understood—putting one hand to her heart, the other to her lips, then extending both to me. I smiled uncertainly, and then I gave a happy laugh, for she threw her small self against me, and we were embracing as we had done the night before—not passionately or even amorously, but gladly.

I silently thanked and blessed the Khan Kubilai for having given me that yin seal. This was the first time I had ever used it, and behold, it had put this darling girl in my arms. It was truly amazing, I thought, what the simple impress of a mere carved stone on a piece of paper could accomplish. . . .

And then, abruptly, I let go of Hui-sheng and turned away from her and threw myself on the floor.

On the way down, I had a flashing glimpse of her startled little face, but there was no time to explain or apologize for my rudeness. I had been suddenly possessed of an idea—an outrageous and maybe even a lunatic idea, but a most enthralling one. It might have been Hui-sheng's own refreshing touch that had stimulated my wits to think of it. If it was, I would thank her later. Right now, sprawled on the floor, I ignored what must have been her great astonishment, and anxiously began pawing through the litter of oddments I had emptied from my packs. I found the pai-tzu plaque I had decided to return to Kubilai, and the list of engineers' names I wanted to give him, and—yes! there it was!—the yin seal engraved Pao Nei-ho, which I had taken from the Minister of Lesser Races just before his execution, and kept ever since. I seized upon it and gleefully regarded it and stood up clutching it, and I think I sang some song words and danced a few steps. I desisted when I realized that Hui-sheng and my two new servants were staring at me with wonder and dubiety.

One of the maids waved toward the door and said hesitantly, "Master Marco, a caller asking to see you."

I sobered immediately, for it was Ali Babar. I felt ashamed that he had found me capering, as if I were light of heart when he was bereaved and grieving. But it could have been worse; I should have felt more guilty if he had entered while I was embracing Hui-sheng. I strode to him and clasped his hand and drew him in, murmuring words of greeting and condolence and friendship. He looked terrible. His eyes were red from weeping, his great nose seemed to droop even more than usual, and he was wringing his hands, but that did not keep them from trembling.

"Marco," he said in a quaver. "I have just been to the Court Funeralmaster, seeking to look one last time at my dear Mar-Janah. But he says he has, among his store of the departed, not any such person!"

I should have anticipated that, and averted his going, and saved him the bewilderment of that announcement. I knew that executed felons did not go to the Funeralmaster; the Fondler disposed of them himself, without sacrament or ceremony. But I said nothing of that, only said soothingly, "Doubtless some confusion caused by the turmoil of the court's return from Xan-du."

"Confusion," mumbled Ali. "I am *much* confused."

"Leave everything to me, old friend. I will make all straight. I was just this moment about to do that. I am on my way to make various arrangements pertaining to this matter."

"But wait, Marco. You said you would tell me . . . all the how and the why of her dying. . . ."

"I will, Ali. As soon as I return from this errand. It is urgent, but it will not take long. Do you rest here, and let my ladies attend you." To the maids I said, "Prepare for him a hot bath. Rub him with balms. Fetch for him food and drink. Every kind of drink, and as much as he will take." I started out, but then thought of something else, and commanded most strictly, "Admit no one else to these chambers until I am back again."

I went, almost running, to call upon the Minister of War, the artist Master Chao, and by good fortune found him not occupied with either war or art so early in the day. I commenced by saying that I had heard of the accident which had taken his lady, and that I was sorry for it.

"Why?" he said languidly. "Were you among her stable of stallions?"

"No. I am merely observing the decencies."

"I must thank you. It is more than she ever did. But I imagine you did not come visiting for that only."

"No," I said again. "And if you prefer bluntness, so do I. Are you aware that the Lady Chao died by no accident? That it was so arranged by the Chief Minister Achmad?"

"I must thank him. It is more than he ever did for me before. Have you any notion why he took such an abrupt interest in tidying up the disarray of my small household?"

"He did not, Master Chao. It was purely in his own interest." I went on to tell of Achmad's use of the Lady Chao's official yin for the disposal of Mar-Janah, and the several preceding and subsequent events. I did not mention Mafìo Polo, but I did conclude by saying, "Achmad has threatened also to make public certain paintings done by you. I thought you might be averse to that."

"It would be embarrassing, yes," he murmured, still languidly, but his keen glance told me that he knew what paintings I referred to, and that they would be embarrassing to the Famiglia Polo as well. "I take it that you would like to interrupt the Jing-siang Achmad's suddenly head-long career of destruction."

"Yes, and I believe I know how. It occurred to me that if he could employ someone else's signature to covert purpose, so could I. And I also happen to be in possession of another courtier's yin."

I handed the stone to him, and I did not have to tell him whose it was, for he was able to read the name from it. "Pao Nei-ho. The former and impostor Minister of Lesser Races." He looked up at me and grinned. "Are you suggesting what I think you are?"

"The Minister Pao is dead. No one really knows why he had insinuated himself into this court, or whether he ever really used his office to the subversion of the Khanate. But if, all at once, a letter or a memorandum were found, bearing his signature, concerning some nefarious intention—say, a conspiracy somehow to defame the Khan and upraise the Chief Minister—well, Pao is not around to disown it, and Achmad might have a hard time refuting it."

Chao exclaimed delightedly, "By my ancestors, Polo, but you show certain ministerial talents yourself!"

"One talent I do not possess is an ability to write in the Han character. You do. There are others I could have applied to, but I took you to be no friend of the Arab Achmad."

"Well, if all you say is true, he did relieve me of one burden. But I still groan under his lading of others. You are right: I would happily join in deposing that son of a turtle. Except, you overlook one detail. You are proposing a *real* conspiracy. If it fails, you and I have an early appointment with the Fondler. If it succeeds—even worse—you and I are in each other's power forever after."

"Master Chao, I desire only vengeance against the Arab. If I can hurt him in the least degree, I care not if it costs me my head—tomorrow or some years hence. Simply by proposing this action, I have already put myself in your power. I can offer you no other surety of my bona fides."

"It is enough," he said with decision, and got up from his work table. "In any case, this is so wondrously grand a jest that I could not refuse. Come here." He led me into the next room, and whisked the cover off the tremendous map table. "Let us see. The Minister Pao was a Yi of Yun-nan, which was then under siege. . . ." We stood and looked at Yun-nan, which now was dotted with Bayan's flags. "Suppose the Minister Pao was trying to aid his home province . . . and the Minister Achmad was hoping to dethrone the Khan Kubilai. . . . We need something to link those two ambitions . . . some third component . . . I have it! Kaidu!"

"But the Ilkhan Kaidu rules way over yonder in the northwest," I said dubiously, pointing to the Sin-kiang Province. "Is he not rather remote to be involved in the conspiracy?"

"Come, come, Polo," he chided me, but with high good humor. "In this sin of perpetrating a lie, I am incurring the wrath of my revered ancestors, and you are putting at peril your immortal soul. Would you go to Hell for a merely feeble and pusillanimous lie? Have you no artistry, man? No sweeping scope of vision? Let us make it a *thundering* lie, and a sin to scandalize all the gods!"

"It should at least be a believable lie."

"Kubilai will believe anything of his barbarian cousin Kaidu. He loathes the man. And he knows Kaidu to be reckless and voracious enough to enter into any wildest scheme."

"That is true enough."

"So there we have it. I shall concoct a missive in which the Minister Pao privily discusses with the Jing-siang Achmad their mutual and secret and culpable conspiracy with the Ilkhan Kaidu. Those are the picture's main outlines. Leave the details of its composition to a master artist."

"Gladly," I said. "God knows you paint believable pictures."

"Now. How will you have come to be in possession of this highly volatile document?"

"I was one of the last to see the Minister Pao alive. I shall have discovered the paper while searching him. As I really did find the yin."

"You never found the yin. Forget that altogether."

"Very well."

"You found on him only an old and much-creased paper. I shall make it a letter which, here in Khanbalik, Pao wrote to Achmad but had no chance to deliver, because he was forced to flee. So he simply and foolishly carried it with him. Yes. I shall rumple and dirty it a bit. How soon do you want this?"

"I *should* have given it to the Khan back when I first arrived at Xandu."

"Never mind. You had no way of recognizing its significance. You have just now found it while unpacking your travel gear. Give it to Kubilai, saying most ingenuously, 'Oh, by the way, Sire. . . .' The very offhandedness will lend verisimilitude. But the sooner the better. Let me get right at it."

He sat down to his work table again, and began busily to get out papers and brushes and ink blocks of red and black and other appurtenances of his art, saying meanwhile:

"You applied to the right man for your conspiracy, Polo, though I would wager much money that you do not even realize why. To you, no doubt, any two pages of Han characters look alike, so you are unaware that not every scribe can counterfeit another's writing. I must now try to remember Pao's hand, and practice until I can fluently imitate it. But that should not take me too long. Go now and leave me to it. I will have the paper in your hands as soon as I can."

As I moved toward the door, he added, in a voice combining cheer and rue, "Do you know something else? This may be the crowning effort of my whole career, the masterpiece of my entire life." And as I went out, he was saying, though still cheerfully enough, "Why could you not have conceived a work to which I could sign Chao Meng-fu? Curse you, Marco Polo."

· 4 ·

"I F all goes well," I told Ali, "the Arab will be flung to the Fondler. And, if you like, I will petition permission for you to be present and *help* the Fondler put Achmad to the Death of a Thousand."

"I should like to help put him to death," mumbled Ali. "But help the hateful Fondler? You said it was he who did the actual ravagement of Mar-Janah."

"That is true, and God knows he is hateful in the extreme. But in this case he was acting at the Arab's bidding."

I had returned to my chambers to find, as I had hoped, that the maidservants had plied Ali Babar with enough liquor to numb him somewhat. So, although he variously had gasped with horror, wailed with grief and moaned with regret, as I told him all the circumstances attendant on Mar-Janah's demise, he had not indulged in the extravagant thrashing about and howling which most Muslims consider the only proper form of lamentation. Of course, I had not dwelt in detail on what last remnants I had found of Mar-Janah, or her last minutes of life.

"Yes," said Ali, after a long, pensive silence. "If you can arrange it, Marco, I *would* like to be present at the Arab's execution. Without Mar-Janah, I have not any other desires or anticipations to be realized. If only that wish is granted, it will suffice."

"I shall see to it—if all does go well. You might sit there and beseech Allah that all does go well."

Saying which, I got out of my own chair and knelt down on the floor again, to pick up and put away the litter of keepsakes. As I collected the various things—Arpad's kamàl, the pack of zhi-pai cards, and so on—I got the curious impression that something was gone from among them. I sat back and wondered, what could that be? I was not missing the Minister Pao's yin, for I had taken that away myself. But something was gone that had been there when I first emptied my packs. Suddenly I realized what it was.

"Ali," I said. "Did you perhaps pick up something from among this mess while I was absent?"

"No, nothing," he said, with an air of not even having noticed the litter on the floor, which in his stunned and preoccupied condition he probably had not.

I asked the two Mongol maids, and they denied having touched anything. I went and got Hui-sheng, who was in the bedroom putting her own few belongings carefully away in closets and drawers. I smiled at that; it indicated that she planned to stay, and for more than a brief while. I took her hand and drew her into the main room, and indicated the goods on the floor, and made questioning gestures. Evidently she comprehended, for she replied with a shake of her pretty head.

So only Mafìo could have taken it. What was missing was the small clay phial at which he had exclaimed, "Is that not a memento of the charlatan Hakim Mimdad?"

It was. It was the love philter the Hakim had given me on the Roof of the World, the potent potion allegedly employed by the long-ago poet Majnun and his poetess Laila to enhance their making of love. Mafìo knew exactly what it was, and he knew it was unpredictably dangerous, for he had heard me berating Mimdad after my one horrible experience with the stuff, and he had seen me only warily accept from the Hakim a second little bottle to carry away with me. Now he had filched that phial. What could he want it for?

There came to me, with a jolt, some other words he had spoken this morning: "If necessary, I am prepared to prove my caring . . ." And when I jeered, "Go and get the Arab delirious with love!" he had said: "I can do that!"

Dio le varda! I must run and find him and stop him! God knows I had ample reason to be disillusioned and disgusted with Mafìo Polo, and not to care a bagatìn what became of him, but still . . . he was blood of my blood. And any self-pitying or self-glorifying act of self-sacrifice he might make now was futile and unnecessary, for I already had a trap in preparation for the damnable Arab Achmad. So I scrambled to my feet —causing Hui-sheng again to regard me with mild wonderment. But I got only as far as the door, for there stood the happily beaming Master Chao.

"It is accomplished," he said. "And so is your vengeance, the moment you show this to Kubilai."

He glanced past me and saw the others in the room, and tugged me by my sleeve out of their hearing down the corridor. He took out from some recess of his robes a folded, wrinkled, smudged paper that truly looked as if it had had a hard journey from Khanbalik to Yun-nan and back again. I opened it and gazed at what looked to me—as all Han documents looked to me—like a garden plot much tracked over by a flock of chickens.

"What does it say?"

"Everything necessary. Let us not take time for a translation. I hurried with it, and so must you. The Khan is right now on his way to the Hall of Justice, where he is about to declare the Cheng in session. Many matters of litigation have accumulated to await his judgment. He is conscientious about such things, even to the delaying of his acceptance of Sung's surrender. But if you do not catch him before the Cheng convenes, he will be occupied there, and later in negotiations with the Sung Empress. It may be days before you can get to him again, and in that time Achmad could be busy to your detriment. Go quickly."

"The moment I do this," I said, "I am putting not just Achmad's fate, but mine also, irrevocably in your hands, Master Chao."

"And I mine, Polo, in yours. Go."

I went, after running into my rooms again to gather up the other things I had for the Khakhan. And I did catch him, just as he and the lesser justices and the Tongue were taking their seats on the dais of the Cheng. He motioned amiably for me to approach the dais, and, when I gave him the items I had brought, he said, "There was no hurry about returning these things, Marco."

"I had already kept them longer than I should have done, Sire. Here is the ivory pai-tzu plaque, and your yellow-paper letter of authority, and a paper the late Minister Pao was carrying at the time of his capture, and this note of mine, which lists those engineers who so capably positioned the huo-yao balls. Since I set down their names in Roman letters, Sire, perhaps you would listen as I read them. I hope I can pronounce them correctly, and that you can comprehend them, for you may wish to reward those men with some mark of—"

"Read, read," he said indulgently.

I did so, while he idly laid aside the plaque and the letter he had given me to carry, and idly opened and glanced at the paper the Master Chao had forged. When he saw that it was written in Han, he idly handed it to the many-tongued Tongue, and went on listening to me. I was struggling to comprehend my own not clearly legible list of scrawls, reading aloud, "A man named Gegen, of the Kurai tribe . . . a man named Jassak, of the Merkit tribe . . . a man named Berdibeg, also of the Merkit—" when the Tongue suddenly leapt to his feet and, for all his grasp of many languages, gave a cry that was entirely inarticulate.

"Vakh!" exclaimed the Khakhan. "What ails you, man?"

"Sire!" the Tongue gasped excitedly. "This paper—a matter of the utmost importance! It must take precedence over all else! This paper—brought by that man yonder."

"Marco?" Kubilai turned back to me. "You said it was taken from the late Minister Pao?" I said it was. He turned again to the Tongue. "Well?"

"You might prefer, Sire—" said the Tongue, looking pointedly at me, at the other justices and the guards. "You might prefer to clear the hall before I divulge the contents."

"Divulge them," growled the Khan, "and then I will decide if the hall is to be cleared."

"As you command, Sire. Well, I can give you a word by word translation at your leisure. But suffice it now to say that this is a letter signed with the yin Pao Nei-ho. It hints—it implies—no, it bluntly reveals—a treacherous conspiracy between your cousin the Ilkhan Kaidu and—and one of your most trusted ministers."

"Indeed?" said Kubilai frostily. "Then I think it best that *no one* leave this hall. Go on, Tongue."

"In brief, Sire, it appears that the Minister Pao, whom we all now know to have been a Yi impostor here, hoped to avert the total devastation of his native Yun-nan. It appears that Pao had persuaded the Ilkhan Kaidu—or perhaps bribed him; money is mentioned—to march south and fling his forces upon the rear of ours then invading Yun-nan. It would have been an act of rebellion and civil war. In that event, it was expected that you yourself, Sire, would take the field. In your absence and the ensuing confusion, the—the Vice-Regent Achmad was to proclaim himself Khakhan—"

The assembled Cheng justices all cried "Vakh!" and "Shame!" and "Aiya!" and other expressions of horror.

"—upon which," the Tongue resumed, "Yun-nan would declare its surrender and fealty to the new Khakhan Achmad, in return for an easy peace. Next, it seems also to have been agreed, the Yi would join with Kaidu in falling upon the Sung, and help to conquer that empire. And after all was done, Achmad and Kaidu would divide and rule the Khanate between them."

There were more exclamations of "Vakh!" and "Aiya!" Kubilai had yet made no comment, but his face was like the black buran sandstorm rising over the desert. While the Tongue waited for some command, the ministers began passing the letter around among them.

"Is it truly Pao's hand?" asked one.

"Yes," said another. "He always wrote in the grass stroke, not the formal upright character."

"And there, see?" said another. "To write money, he used the character for kauri-shell, which is currency among the Yi."

Another asked, "What of the signature?"

"It looks to be genuinely his."

"Send for the Yinmaster!"

"No one is to leave this room."

But Kubilai heard and nodded, and a guard went running out. In the meantime, the ministers kept up a muted hubbub of argument and expostulation, and I heard one say solemnly, "It is too outrageous to be believed."

"There is precedent," said another. "Remember, some years ago, our Khanate acquired the land of Cappadocia by a similar ruse. A likewise trusted Chief Minister of the Seljuk Turki enlisted the covert aid of our Ilkhan Abagha of Persia to help him overthrow the rightful King Kilij. And, once the treachery was accomplished, the upstart allied Cappadocia to our Khanate."

"Yes," remarked another. "But happily there was a difference in those circumstances. Abagha conspired not for his own aggrandizement, but for the benefit of his Khakhan Kubilai and the whole Khanate."

"Here comes the Yinmaster."

Hurried along by the guardsman, old Master Yiu came shuffling into the Cheng. He was shown the paper, and had to squint at it only briefly before he pronounced:

"I cannot mistake my own work, my lords. That is indeed the yin I cut for the Minister of Lesser Races, Pao Nei-ho."

"There!" said several of them, and "It is all true!" and "It is beyond question now!" and they all looked to Kubilai. He inhaled a great breath of air, and slowly sighed it out, and then said in a doomful voice, "Guards!" Those men snapped to rigid attention, and thumped their lances on the floor in unison. "Go and demand the presence here of the Chief Minister Achmad-az-Fenaket." They thumped their lances again, and wheeled to march out, but Kubilai halted them for a moment and turned to me.

"Marco Polo, it seems that you have once again been of service to our Khanate—albeit inadvertently this time." The words were commendatory enough, but, from the expression on his face, one would have thought I had tracked into the hall on my boots some dog dirt from the outdoors. "You may see it through to the close, Marco. Go with the guards and yourself utter to the Chief Minister the formal command: 'Arise and come, dead man, for Kubilai the Khan of All Khans would hear your last words.'"

So I went, as instructed. But the Khakhan had not ordered me to return to the Cheng in company with the Arab, and, as it happened, I did not. I and my troop of guards arrived at Achmad's chambers to find its outer doors unguarded and wide open. We went inside, and found his own sentries and all his servants gathered in attitudes of anxious listening and hand-wringing indecision outside his closed bedroom door. When they saw our arrival, the servants raised a clamor of greeting, and thanked Tengri and praised Allah that we had come, and it was some time before we could quiet them down and get a coherent account of what was going on.

The Wali Achmad, they said, had been in his bedchamber all day. That was not an uncommon occurrence, they said, because he often took work with him at night and continued, after awakening and breaking his fast, to deal with it while lying comfortably abed. But this day, there had begun to proceed from inside the bedroom some extraordinary noises and, after some understandable hesitation, a maidservant had pecked at the door to inquire if all was well. She had been answered by a voice recognizably the Wali's, but in an unnaturally high and nervous tone, commanding, "Leave me be!" The unaccountable sounds had then resumed and continued: giggles rising to wild laughter, squeaks and sobs increasing to moans and groans, laughter again, and so on. The listeners —by then comprising Achmad's whole staff clustered against the door— had been unable to decide whether the noises expressed pleasure or distress. In the course of what had now been some hours, they had frequently called out to their master and knocked on the door and tried to open it and peer in. But the door was fastened tight shut, and they were debating the propriety of breaking through it when fortunately we arrived and saved them having to decide.

"Listen for yourselves," they said, and I and the corporal of the guard pressed our ears to the panels.

After an interval, the corporal said wonderingly to me, "I never heard anything like it."

I had, but it had been a long time ago. In the anderun of the palace of Baghdad, I had once watched through a peephole as a young girl inmate seduced an ugly, hairy simiazza ape. The sounds I now heard through this door were much like the sounds I had heard then—the girl's murmured endearments and encouragements, the ape's puzzled gibbering, his grunts and her moans of consummation, all mingled with little yips and squeaks of pain, because the ape, in clumsily satisfying her, had also clumsily given her many small bites and scratches.

I said nothing of that to the corporal, saying only, "I suggest that you have your men clear all these servants away from here, away to their quarters. We must arrest the Minister Achmad, but we need not humiliate him before his staff. Get rid of his guards, too. We have enough of our own."

"We go in, then?" asked the corporal, as that was being done. "Even if he is indisposed?"

"We go in. Whatever is happening in there, the Khakhan wants that man and wants him now. Yes, force the door."

I had ordered the onlookers removed, not because I was concerned for Achmad's feelings, but for my own, since I expected to find my uncle conspicuously present in there. To my considerable relief, he was not, and the Arab was in no condition to care about humiliation.

He lay naked on the bed, his scrawny and sweaty brown body squirming in a welter of his own secretions. The bedclothes today were of pale-green silk, but much slimed and crusted with white and also with pink, for it appeared that, after many emissions, Achmad's later ones had been streaky with blood. He was still uttering the gibberish noises, though only in a muffled voice, for he had in his mouth one of those su-yang mushroom phallocrypts, moisture-bloated to such a bigness that it stretched his lips and cheeks. There was another pretend-organ protruding from his backside, but that was made of fine green jade. At his front, his own true organ was invisible inside something that looked like a Mongol warrior's wintertime fur hat, and with both hands he was frantically jerking it back and forth to fricate himself. His agate eyes were wide open, but their stoniness looked blurred, as if by moss, and, whatever he was seeing, it was not us.

I gestured to the guards. A couple of them bent over the Arab and began plucking the various devices off him and out of him. When the su-yang was withdrawn from his sucking mouth, his whimpered utterances got louder, but were still only senseless noises. When the jade cylinder was yanked out of him, he moaned lasciviously and his body briefly convulsed. When the furry thing was taken off him, he feebly continued moving his hands, though they had not much left to play with down there, for he was rubbed raw and bloody and small. The corporal of the guard turned the hatlike object over and over, curiously examining it, and I observed that it was hairy only in part, but then I averted my eyes, as a quantity of white substance and stringy blood oozed out of it.

"By Tengri!" growled the corporal to himself. "Lips?" Then he flung it down and said loathingly, "Do you know what that *is*?"

"No," I said. "And I do not wish to know. Stand the creature on his feet. Throw cold water on him. Wipe him down. Get some clothes on him."

As those things were done to him, Achmad seemed to revive to some degree. At first he was utterly limp, and the guards attending him had to hold him upright. But gradually, after much wobbling and teetering, he was able to stand alone. And, after several drenchings with cold water, he began to make comprehensible words of his whimpers, though they were still disjointed.

"We were both dewy children . . . ," he said, as if repeating some poetry that only he could hear. "We fitted well together. . . ."

"Oh, shut up," grunted the grizzled soldier who was swabbing the sweat and scum off him.

"Then I grew up, but she stayed small . . . with only tiny apertures . . . and she cried. . . ."

"Shut up," grunted the other leathery veteran who was trying to get an aba onto him.

"Then she became a stag . . . and I a doe . . . and it was I who cried. . . ."

The corporal snapped, "You have been told to be silent!"

"Let him talk and clear his head," I said indulgently. "He will have need of it."

"Then we were butterflies . . . embracing inside a fragrant flower blossom. . . ." His rolling eyes momentarily steadied on me, and he said quite distinctly, "Folo!" But the eyes' stone hardness was still mossed over, and so were his other faculties, for he added only a mumble: "Make that name a laughingstock. . . ."

"You may try," I said indifferently. "I am commanded to speak to you thus: Go with these guards, dead man, for Kubilai the Khan of All Khans would hear your last words." I motioned one more time and said, "Take him away."

I had let Achmad continue babbling just to prevent the guards' noticing another sound I had heard in that room—a faint but persistent and musical sort of noise. As the guards left with their prisoner, I stayed behind to investigate the source of that sound. It did not come from anywhere in the room itself, nor from outside either of the room's two doors, but from behind some one of the walls. I listened closely and traced it to one particularly garish Persian qali hanging opposite the bed, and I swept that aside. The wall behind it looked solid, but I had only to lean on it and a section of the paneling swung inward like a door, giving on a dark stone passage, and I could make out now what the noise was. It was a strange sound to be hearing in a secret corridor in the Mongol palace of Khanbalik, for it was an old Venetian song being sung. And it was most exceedingly strange in these circumstances, for it was a simple song in praise of Virtue—something notably lacking in the Wali Achmad and his vicinity and everything to do with him. Mafìo Polo was singing, in a low quaver:

> La virtù te dà grazia anca se molto
> Vechio ti fussi e te dà nobil forme. . . .

I reached back into the bedroom for a lamp to light my way, and went into the darkness and swung the secret door shut behind me, trusting that the qali would fall and cover it. I found Mafìo sitting on the cold, damp stone floor, not far along the passage. He was again costumed in the ghastly "large woman" raiment—this time all in pale green —and he looked even more dazed and deranged than the Arab had done. But at least he was not smeared or caked with blood or any other body fluids. Evidently, whatever part he had played in the love-philter orgy, it had not been a very active one. He showed no recognition of me, but he made no resistance when I took him by the arm and stood him up and began walking him farther along the passage. He only went on singing quietly:

> La virtù te fa belo anca deforme,
> La virtù te fa vivo anca sepolto.

Though I had never been in that secret walkway before, I was well enough acquainted with the palace to have a general idea of where the passage's twists and turns were taking us. The whole way, Mafìo went on murmurously singing the virtues of Virtue. We passed numerous other closed doors in the wall, but I took us a considerable distance before choosing one door to open just a crack and peep out.

It gave on a small garden not far from the palace wing where we were quartered. I tried to hush Mafìo as I drew him outdoors, but to no avail. He was abiding in some other world, and would have taken no notice if I had dragged him through the garden's lotus pond. However, by good fortune, there was no one about, and I think no one at all saw us as I hurried him the rest of the way to his chambers. But there, since I did not know how to find *his* back door, I had to take him in through the usual one, and we were met there by the same woman servant who had admitted me the night before. I was somewhat surprised but much pleased when she evinced no shock or horror at seeing her master and onetime paramour so grotesquely attired. She only looked sad again, and pitying, as he crooned to her:

> La virtù è un cavedàl che sempre è rico,
> Che no patisse mai rùzene o tarlo. . . .

"Your master is taken ill," I told the woman, that being the only explanation I could think of—and it was true enough.

"I will attend him," she said, with calm compassion. "Do not worry."

> . . . Che sempre cresce e no se pol robarlo,
> E mai no rende el possessòr mendico.

I gladly left him in her care. And I might as well tell, here, that it was in her tender and solicitous care that Mafìo remained long afterward, for he never recovered his reason.

It had already been quite an arduous day, and the one before had been even worse, and I had passed a sleepless night between. So I dragged myself to my own chambers, to rest and myself enjoy some solicitude from my servants and pretty Hui-sheng, while I kept Ali Babar company and watched him drink himself unconscious of his own misery.

I never saw Achmad again. He was accused and tried and judged and convicted and sentenced, all in that same day, and I will tell of it just as quickly. I have no wish to dwell on the subject, because it happened that, even in winning my vengeance, I had to suffer one more loss.

In all the long time since then, I have felt no least remorse for having destroyed Achmad-az-Fenaket through the agency of a forged letter, nor for its having implicated him in a crime which was never committed. He was guilty of enough other crimes and vices. Indeed, the false letter might easily have failed in its purpose, but for the Arab's truly perverted nature, which had led him to indulge in the love philter with Mafìo. From that experiment in hallucination, he emerged with his shrewd mind addled and his sharp wits blunted and his serpent tongue knotted. Perhaps he had been less severely impaired by the experience than had my uncle—the Arab at least briefly recognized me afterward, and Mafio did not, ever again—and perhaps Achmad would have recovered after a time, but he did not get that time.

When he was dragged before the irate Khakhan that day and confronted with the really flimsy evidence of his "treason," he could readily have talked his way out of the predicament. All he had to do was invoke the privilege of office and request an adjournment of the Cheng until an embassy could be sent to the Ilkhan Kaidu, the other of the alleged triumvirate of conspirators. Kubilai and the justices could hardly have refused to wait and hear what word Kaidu might send back. But Achmad never asked for that or for anything else, according to those who were present. He was unprepared to defend himself at all, they said, they not being aware that he was *unable* to defend himself, incapable of it. They said he only gibbered and ranted and twitched, giving the unmistakable impression of a culprit felon deranged by his guilt and his having been apprehended and his dread of the penalty. Then and there, the assembled justices of the Cheng found against him, and the still outraged Kubilai did not overrule them. Achmad was adjudged guilty of treason, and the punishment for that was the Death of a Thousand.

The whole affair had blown up as suddenly as a summer storm, but it constituted the most serious and spectacular scandal in the memory of the oldest courtier. People talked of nothing else, and were avid to hear or to recount any least detail of news or rumor, and anyone who had a juicy tidbit to impart was a center of a crowd. The greatest celebrity accrued to the Fondler, who had been given the most illustrious Subject of his career, and Master Ping reveled in that celebrity. Contrary to his usual dark secrecy, he boasted openly that he was stocking his cavern dungeon with provender to last for a hundred days, and that he was dismissing all his assistants and clerks on holiday—even his Blotters and Retrievers—so that he could give this distinguished Subject his undivided and *unshared* attention.

I went to call on Kubilai. By then, he had calmed somewhat and resigned himself to the defection and loss of his Chief Minister, and he no longer looked at me the way ancient kings used to look at the bearers of ill tidings. I told him, without going into unnecessary detail, that Achmad had been responsible for the inexcusable murder of Ali Babar's blameless wife. I asked, and got, the Khakhan's permission for Ali to attend the execution of his wife's executioner. The Fondler Ping was aghast at this, of course, but he could not countermand the permission, and he did not even dare make any loud complaint, lest a closer look be given to his own willing part in Mar-Janah's murder.

So, on the appointed day, I went with Ali to the underground cavern, and bade him be manfully stalwart as he witnessed the piecemeal reduction of our mutual enemy. Ali looked pale—he had never had stomach for bloodshed—but he looked determined, even while he said his salaams and farewells to me as solemnly as if he himself were going to the Death of a Thousand. Then he and the Master Ping, who was still grumbling at this unwelcome intrusion, went through the iron-studded door to where Achmad was already dangling and waiting, and closed the door behind them. I came away with only one regret at the time: that the Arab, from what I had heard, was still numb and bemazed. If it was true, as Achmad had once told me, that Hell is what hurts worst, then I regretted that he might not feel the hurts as keenly as I would have wished.

Since the Fondler had given notice that this Fondling might occupy a full hundred days, everyone naturally expected that it would. So not until the expiration of that time did his clerks and assistants return to congregate in the outer chamber and await their master's triumphant emergence. When several more days passed, they began to fidget, but dared not intrude. Not until I sent one of my maidservants, seeking word of Ali Babar, was the chief clerk emboldened to open the iron-studded door a crack. He was met by a charnel-house stench that sent him reeling backward. Nothing else came out of the inner room, and no one could even peek in without fainting dead away. The Palace Engineer had to be sent for and asked to direct his artificial breezes through the underground tunnels. When the chambers had been blown clean enough to be bearable, the Fondler's chief clerk ventured in and came out, looking stunned, to report what he had found.

There were three dead bodies, or the constituents and remains of three bodies. That of the ex-Wali Achmad was a mere shred, obviously having endured at least a Death of Nine Hundred and Ninety-nine. As well as could be ascertained, Ali Babar had watched that entire dissolution, had then seized and bound *the Fondler,* and proceeded to imitate, on his sacrosanct and inviolate person, the whole process of the Fondling. However, the chief clerk reported, it had not gone much beyond a Death of Perhaps One or Two Hundred. The supposition was that Ali had got too ill—from the miasma of Achmad's decay and all the other accumulated gore and carnage and excrement—to persevere to the end. He had left the only partially dismembered Master Ping hanging to die at his leisure, and had taken up one of the longer knives and plunged it into his own breast, and died himself.

So Ali Babar, Nostril, Sindbad, Ali-ad-Din, whom I had scorned and derided as a coward and an empty braggart all the time I had known him, at the very last was impelled by the one praiseworthy motive of his life—his love for Mar-Janah—to do something eminently courageous and laudable. He took revenge on both of her slayers, the instigator and the perpetrator, and then took his own life, so that none other (meaning myself) could be blamed for the deed.

The palace population, and the city of Khanbalik, and probably all of Kithai, if not the whole of the Mongol Empire, were still buzzing and twittering with the scandal of Achmad's precipitous downfall. The new scandal from underground provided still more fodder for the gossips to chew—and set Kubilai to regarding me again with stern exasperation. But this latest news contained one revelation so macabre, so almost risible, that even the Khakhan was bemused and distracted from any inclination to vindictiveness. What happened was that, when the Fondler's assistants collected and reassembled his cadaver for decent burial, they discovered that the man had all his life had *lotus feet,* bound since infancy, warped and contorted to dainty points, like those of a Han noblewoman. So the resultant mood of everybody, including Kubilai, was not so much glowering: "Now who should pay for *this* outrage?"— but speculative and almost amused, people asking each other: "What awful kind of mother must the Master Ping have had?"

My own mood, I have to say, was less frivolous. My vengeance had been accomplished, but at the cost of a long-time companion, and I was melancholy. That depression was not alleviated when I went to Mafìo's chambers, as I did every day or so, to regard what was left of *him*. That devoted woman servant kept him clean and nicely dressed (in proper men's clothes), and she kept neatly trimmed the gray beard that was growing in again. He appeared well-fed and healthy enough, and he might have been taken for the hearty and blustering Uncle Mafìo of old, except that his eyes were vacant and he was again singing, in a sort of cow-moo voice, his litany to Virtue:

> La virtù è un cavedàl che sempre è rico,
> Che no patisse mai rùzene o tarlo. . . .

I was contemplating him morosely and feeling very low indeed when another visitor unexpectedly arrived, finally come back from his latest trading karwan around the country. I had never—not even on his first arrival in Venice when I was a boy—been so glad to see my bland and gentle and dull and benign and colorless old father.

We fell into each other's arms and made the Venetian abrazzo, and then stood side by side while he looked sadly at his brother. He had, on the roads hither, heard in broad outline of all the events that had occurred during his journeying: the end of the Yun-nan war, my return to court, the surrender of Sung, the death of Achmad and the Master Ping, the suicide of his once-slave Nostril, the unfortunate indisposition of the Ferenghi Polo, his brother. Now I told him all the facts of those events which only I could tell. I omitted nothing but the most vile details and, when I had done, he looked again at Mafìo and shook his head, fondly, ruefully, regretfully, murmuring, "Tato, tato . . ." the diminutive and affectionate way of saying, "Brother, brother. . . ."

". . . Belo anca deforme," Mafìo mooed, in seeming response. "Vivo anca sepolto. . . ."

Nicolò Polo mournfully shook his head again. But then he turned and clapped a comradely hand on my sagging shoulders, and squared his own, and perhaps for the very first time I was grateful to hear one of his stock encouragements:

"Ah, Marco, sto mondo xe fato tondo."

Which is to say that, whatever happens, good or bad, cause for rejoicing or lament, "the world will still be round."

MANZI

. 1 .

T H E storm of scandal gradually abated. The Khanbalik court, like a ship that had been dangerously careened, gradually came upright again and steadied on its keel. As far as I know, Kubilai never tried to call his cousin Kaidu to account for his presumed part in the recent outrages. Kaidu being still far away in the west, and all danger of his involvement being now past, the Khakhan was content to leave him there, and instead devoted his energies to cleaning up the mess on his own doorstep. He sensibly began by dividing the late Achmad's three different offices among three different men. To his son Chingkim's duties as Wang of the city, he added the responsibility to serve as Vice-Regent during the Khakhan's absences. He promoted my old battlefield companion Bayan to the rank of Chief Minister, but, since Bayan preferred to stay in the field as an active orlok, that office too devolved onto Prince Chingkim. Kubilai might have desired another Arab to replace Achmad as Finance Minister—or a Persian or a Turki or a Byzantine—since he had such a high opinion of Muslims' financial abilities, and since that ministry had charge of the Muslim Ortaq of merchants and traders. However, the settling of the late Achmad's estate produced another revelation that soured the Khakhan on Muslims forever after. It was the rule in Kithai, as in Venice and elsewhere, that a traitor's belongings be confiscated by the state. And it was discovered that the Arab's estate consisted of a vast amount of wealth he had fraudulently appropriated and embezzled and extorted during his official career. (Some others of his belongings— including his hoard of paintings—never did come to light.)

The irrefutable evidence of Achmad's longtime duplicity so enraged Kubilai, all over again, that he appointed as Finance Minister the elderly Han scholar of my acquaintance, the Court Mathematician Lin-ngan. In his new detestation of Muslims, Kubilai went further, proclaiming new laws that severely abridged the freedom of Kithai's Muslims, and limited the extent of their mercantile activities, and forbade them to practice usury as heretofore, and diminished their exorbitant profits. He also made all Muslims publicly forswear that part of their Holy Quran which permits them to dupe, cheat and kill all who are not of Islam. He even passed a law requiring Muslims to *eat pork*, if it were served to them by a host or innkeeper. I think that law was never much obeyed or stringently enforced. And I know that the other laws envenomed many already rich and powerful Muslims resident in Khanbalik. I know because I heard them muttering imprecations, not against Kubilai, but against us "infidel Polos" whom they held to blame for inciting him to the persecution of Muslims.

Ever since my return from Yun-nan to Khanbalik, I had been finding the city not a very hospitable or pleasant place. Now the Khakhan, occupied with so many other things, including the posting of a Wang and magistrates and prefects in the newly acquired Manzi, assigned me no work to do for him, and the Compagnia Polo likewise had no need of me. The appointment of our old acquaintance Lin-ngan as Finance Minister had caused no interference in my father's trading activities. If anything, the new suppression of Muslim business had meant an increase in his own, but he was capable of handling it all by himself. He was currently engaged in picking up the reins of what ventures Mafio had guided, and in training new overseers for the kashi works Ali Babar and Mar-Janah had headed. So I was at loose ends anyway, and it occurred to me that by leaving Khanbalik for a while I might allay some of the local unrest and grievances still smoldering. I went to the Khakhan and asked if he had any mission abroad that I could undertake for him. He studied on the matter and then said, with a trace of malicious amusement:

"Yes, I have, and I thank you for volunteering. Now that Sung has become Manzi, it is a part of our Khanate, but it is not yet subscribing any funds to our treasury. The late Finance Minister would already have flung his Ortaq net over that whole land, and would by now be seining rich tribute out of it. Since he is not, and since you contributed to the fact that he is not, I think it only right that you volunteer to take on the task in his place. You will go to the Manzi capital of Hang-zho and inaugurate some system of tax collection that will satisfy our imperial treasury and not too seriously dissatisfy the Manzi population."

It was rather more of a mission than I had meant to volunteer for. I said, "Sire, I know nothing about taxation—"

"Then call it something else. The former Finance Minister called it a tariff on trade transactions. You can call it impost or levy—or involuntary benevolence, if you like. I will not ask you to bleed those newly annexed subjects of every drop in their veins. But I shall expect a respectable amount of tribute paid by every head of household in all the provinces of Manzi."

"How many heads are there, Sire?" I was sorry I had ever come calling on him. "How much would you deem a respectable amount?"

He said drily, "I daresay you can count the heads yourself, when you get there. As to the amount, I will let you know very promptly if it is not to my liking. Now do not stand there gulping at me like a fish. You requested a mission. I have given you one. All the necessary documents of appointment and authority will be ready by the time you are ready to leave."

I set off for Manzi not much more enthusiastically than I had set off for the war in Yun-nan. I could not know that I was setting forth upon the happiest and most satisfying years of my whole life. In Manzi, as in Yun-nan, I would successfully accomplish the mission set me, and again win the plaudits of the Khan Kubilai, and become quite legitimately wealthy—in my own right, by my own doing, not merely as a sharer in the Compagnia Polo—and I would be entrusted with other missions, and would accomplish them as well. But when I now say "I" it should be taken as "I and Hui-sheng," for the silent Echo was now my traveling partner and my wise adviser and my steadfast comrade, and without her beside me I could not have accomplished what I did in those years.

The Holy Bible tells us that the Lord God said, "It is not good for man to be alone: let Us make him a help like unto himself." Well, even Adam and Eve were not entirely like unto each other—a fact for which I, all these generations later, have never ceased thanking God—and Hui-sheng and I were physically different in many other ways. But more of a help no man could ever have asked, and many of our unlikenesses consisted, I must honestly say, in her being superior to me: in calm temperament, in tenderness of heart, in a wisdom that was something deeper than mere intelligence.

Even had she continued as a slave, doing nothing but serve me, or become my concubine, doing nothing but satisfy me, Hui-sheng would have been a valuable and welcome addition to my life, and an ornament to it, and a delight. She was beautiful to look at, and delicious to love, and a high-spirited joy to have around. Unbelievable as it may seem, her *conversation* was a pleasure to be enjoyed. As the Prince Chingkim had once remarked to me, pillow talk is the very best way to learn any language, and that was just as true for a language of signs and gestures, and no doubt our loving closeness on the pillow made our mutual learning quicker and our invented mutual language more fluent. When we got adept at that method of communication, I found that Hui-sheng's conversation was rich with meaning and good sense and nuances of real wittiness. All in all, Hui-sheng was far too bright and too talented to have been relegated to any of the underling positions where most women belong and are pleased to be and are best useful.

Hui-sheng's deprivation of sound had made all her other senses superlatively keen. She could see or feel or smell or *somehow* detect things that would have gone by me unnoticed, and she would direct my notice to them, so that I was perceiving more than I ever had before. For a very trivial example, she would sometimes dart from my side, when we were out walking, and run to what looked to me like a distant bank of nothing but weeds. She would kneel and pluck something unremarkably weed-looking, and bring it to show me that it was a flower not yet even budded, and she would keep that sprig and tend it until it bloomed and was beautiful.

Once, in the early days when we were still inventing our language, we were idling away an afternoon in one of those garden pavilions where the Palace Engineer had so miraculously piped water to play jug flutes positioned under the eaves. I awkwardly managed to convey to Hui-sheng how those things worked, though I assumed she had not the least idea what music *was*, and I waved my hands about in time to that murmurous warbling. She nodded brightly, and I supposed she was pretending to comprehend, to please me. But then she caught one of my hands and put it against one of the carved side columns, and held it there, and signed for me to be very, *very* still. Perplexed but fondly amused, I did so, and after a moment I realized, with vast amazement, that I was feeling the very, *very* faintest vibration—from the jug flute overhead, down through the wood and so to my touch. My silent Echo had shown me an echo in silence, indeed. She was capable of appreciating and even enjoying the rhythms of that unhearable music—perhaps even better than I could, *hearing* it—so delicate were her hands and her skin.

Those extraordinary faculties of hers were of incalculable value to me in my travels and my work and my dealings with others. That was especially true in Manzi, where I was naturally regarded with distrust as an emissary of the conquerors, and where I had to do business with resentful former overlords and grasping merchant chiefs and reluctant hirelings. Just as Hui-sheng could discern a flower invisible to others, so could she often discern a person's unvoiced thoughts and feelings and motives and intentions. She could reveal them to me, too—sometimes in private, sometimes while that very person sat talking with me—and on many occasions that gave me a notable advantage over other folk. But even more often, I had an advantage in her merely being at my side. The men of Manzi, nobles and commoners alike, were unused to women sitting in on masculine conferences. If mine had been an ordinary woman—plain, voluble, strident—they would have disdained me as an uncouth barbarian or a henpecked capon. But Hui-sheng was such a charming and attractive adornment to any gathering (and so blessedly silent) that every man put on his most courtly manners, and spoke most chivalrously, and postured and almost pranced for her admiration, and many times—I know for a fact—deferred to my demands or acceded to my instructions or gave me the better of a bargain, just to earn Hui-sheng's look of approbation.

She was my fellow journeyer, and she adopted a costume that en-

abled her to ride a horse astride, and she rode always beside me. She was
my capable companion, my trusted confidante and, in everything but
title, my wife. I would have been ready at any time for us to have
"broken the plate," as the Mongols called it (because their ceremony of
wedding, performed by a shamàn-priest, culminated in the ceremonial
smashing of a piece of fine porcelain). But Hui-sheng, again unlike the
commonalty of women, attached no importance to tradition or formality
or superstition or ritual. She and I made what vows we wished to make,
and made them in private, and that sufficed us both, and she was happy
to forgo any public trumpeting and trumpery exhibition.

Kubilai advised me once, when the subject came up, "Marco, do not
break the plate. So long as you have not yet taken a First Wife, you will
find pliant and conciliatory every man with whom you have to deal, in
matters of commerce or treaty negotiation or whatever. He will seek
your good regard and he will not obstruct your good fortune, because he
will be nursing the secret hope of making his daughter or niece your
First Wife and mother of your principal heir." That advice might well
have made me hasten immediately to break a plate with Hui-sheng, for I
scorned ever to order my life according to the dictates of "good business." But Hui-sheng pointed out, with some vigor, that as my wife she
would *have* to observe some traditions—at least those enjoining wifely
subordination—and so could not any longer ride joyously at my side,
but, if she was allowed to go anywhere at all, would have to travel in a
closed palanquin, and she could not any longer assist me in my working
conferences with other men, and tradition would forbid her to—

"Enough, enough!" I said, laughing at her agitation. I caught and
stopped her flickering fingers, and promised that *nothing* would make
me marry her, *ever*.

So we remained lovers only, which may be the very best sort of
marriage there could be. I did not treat her as a wife, an inferior, but
accorded her—and insisted that all others accord her—full equality with
myself. (That may not have been so liberal of me as it sounds, since I
well recognized her many points of superiority, and so perhaps did some
cognitive others.) But I did treat her as a wife, a most noble wife, in
regaling her with gifts of jewelry and jade and ivory, and the richest
and most becoming garments for her to wear, and, for her personal
mount, a superb white mare of the Khan's own "dragon horses." Only
one husbandly rule did I lay down: she was never to mask her beauty
with cosmetics, in the Khanbalik fashion. She complied, and so her
peach-bloom complexion was never slathered rice-white, her rose-wine
lips were not discolored or redrawn with garish paint, her feathery brows
were not plucked bald. That made her unfashionable, and so radiantly
lovely that all other women cursed the fashion, and their own slavishness
to it. I did allow Hui-sheng to dress her hair as she liked, since she
never did it any way I did not like, and I bought her jeweled combs and
hair-spoons for it.

Of jewels and gold and jade and such, she eventually owned a trove
that a Khatun might envy, but she always treasured one thing most of
all. So did I, really, though I often pretended to consider it trash and

urged her to throw it away. It was a thing I had not given her, but one of the pathetically few belongings she had brought when she first came to me: that plain and inelegant white porcelain incense burner. She lovingly bore it everywhere we journeyed and, in palace or karwansarai or yurtu or on open camp ground, Hui-sheng made sure that the sweet scent of warm clover after a gentle rain was the accompaniment of all our nights.

All our nights . . .

We were lovers only, never wedded man and wife. Nevertheless, I will invoke the privacy of the marriage bed and decline to relate the particulars of what she and I did there. In recalling others of my intimate relationships, I have spoken without reserve, but I prefer to keep some things private to me and Hui-sheng.

I will make only some general observations on the subject of anatomy. That will not violate the privacy of Hui-sheng, and would not cause her any blushes, for she often maintained that she was physically no different from any other female of the Min, and that those women were no different from the Han or any other race native to Kithai and Manzi. I beg to differ with her. The Khan Kubilai himself had once observed that the Min women were above all others in beauty, and Hui-sheng was outstanding even among the Min. But when she insisted, with modest and self-deprecatory gestures, that she was only ordinary of features and figure, I sensibly made no demur—for the most beautiful woman is the woman who does not realize she is.

And Hui-sheng was beautiful all over. That would adequately describe her, but I must go into some detail, to correct a few misapprehensions I myself had earlier entertained. I have mentioned the fine floss of hair that grew in front of her ears and at her nape, and I said then that I wondered if it implied an abundant hairiness in other places on her body. I could not have been more mistaken in that expectation. Hui-sheng was totally hairless on her legs and arms, under her arms, even on her artichoke. She was as clean and silkily smooth in that place as had been the child Doris of my youth. I did not mind that at all—an organ so accessible permits of various close attentions that a furred one does not—but I made mild inquiry. Was the hairlessness peculiar to her, or did she perhaps use a mumum to achieve it? She replied that no women of the Min (or the Han or the Yi or other such races) had hair on their bodies, or, if they did, had but the merest trace.

Her whole body was similarly childlike. Her hips were narrow and her buttocks small, just right for cupping in my hands. Her breasts were also small, but perfectly shaped and distinctly separate. I had long ago conceived a private belief that women with large nipples and a considerable dark halo around them were far more sexually responsive than women with small and pale ones. Hui-sheng's nipples were minute by comparison with other women's, but not when regarded in proportion to her porcelain-cup breasts. They were neither dark nor pale, but bright, as pink as her lips. And they indicated no lack of responsiveness, because Hui-sheng's breasts, unlike those of larger women which are ticklish only at the extremity, were marvelously sensitive over their whole hemispheres. I had but to caress them anywhere, and their "small stars" pouted out as perkily as little tongues there. The same below. Perhaps because of the hairlessness, her lower belly and adjacent thighs were sensitive all over. Caress her anywhere there, and from her maidenly modest cleft would slowly emerge her pink and pretty "butterfly between the petals," the more appreciable and enticing for its not being concealed within any tuft.

I never knew, and refrained from ever asking, whether Hui-sheng had been a virgin when she first came to me. One reason that I never knew was that she was so *perpetually* virginal, which I will explain in a moment. Another reason was that—as she told me—women of those races *never* came to marriage with a maidenhead. They were accustomed to being bathed in infancy, and later bathing themselves, several times a day, and not only on the outside but—with dainty fluids made of flower juices—inside as well. Their fastidiousness went far beyond that of even the most civilized, refined, high-born Venetian ladies (at least until I later dictated that the custom be adopted by the women of my own Venetian family). One result of that scrupulous cleanliness was that a young girl's maidenhead got gradually, painlessly dilated and folded away to nonexistence. So she came to her nuptial bed with no fear of the first penetration, and no least twinge of hurt when it happened. And, in consequence, those races of Kithai and Manzi made no such fuss as other peoples do, about the sheet-stain certification of defloration.

While I am speaking of other peoples, let me remark that men of the Muslim countries treasure a certain belief. They believe that, when they die and go to the Heaven they call Djennet, they will disport themselves throughout eternity with whole anderuns of heavenly women called haura, who have, among their many other talents, the ability continually to renew their virginity. Buddhist men believe the same about the Devatas women they will enjoy in their heavenly Pure Land between lives. I do not know whether any such supernatural females exist in any afterlife, but I can testify that the Min women right here on earth possessed that wondrous quality of never getting slack and flaccid in their parts. Or at least Hui-sheng did.

Her opening was not just childishly small on the outside—the shyest and dearest dimple—but inside as well, most thrillingly tight and close-clasping. Yet it was mature, too, in that it was somehow delicately muscular all up along its inside length, so that it imparted not a constant squeeze but a repetitive rippling sensation from one end to the other. Aside from the other delicious effects produced by her smallness, my every entering of Hui-sheng was like a first time. She was haura and Devatas: perpetually virginal.

Some of her anatomical uniqueness I recognized on our very first night in bed together, and even before we coupled. I should also say of that first coupling that it occurred not from my taking of Hui-sheng, but from her giving herself to me. I had resolutely kept my resolve not to urge or press her, and instead had courted her with all the genteel gallantries and flourishes of a trovatore minstrel demonstrating his affection for a lady high above his humble station. During that time, I ignored all other women and every other sort of distraction, and spent every possible moment with Hui-sheng or nearby, and she slept in my chambers, but we slept always apart. What attraction or attention of mine finally won her, I do not know, but I know when it happened. It was the day she showed me, in the jug-flute pavilion, how to feel music as well as hear it. And that night, for the first time in my chambers, she brought the incense burner and set it alight beside my bed, and got into the bed with me, and—let me put it this way—she allowed me again to feel music as well as hear it and see it and taste it (and smell it, too, in that sweet incense aroma of warm clover after gentle rain).

There was yet another smell and taste perceptible in my making love to Hui-sheng. That first night, before we began, she inquired timidly whether I would desire children. Yes, truly I would have, from one as precious as she—but, because she *was* precious to me, I would not subject her to the horrors of childbirth—so I said a definite no. She looked a trifle downcast at that, but immediately took precautions against the eventuality. She went and got a very small lemon, and peeled it to the white and cut it in half. I expressed some disbelief that anything as simple and common as a lemon could do something as difficult as preventing conception. She smiled assurance and showed me how it was employed. In fact, she gave me the piece of lemon and let me do the applying. (In fact, she let me do that every night we slept together, ever after.) She lay back and spread her legs, baring the creased little peach-hued purse down there, and I gently parted its cleft and eased the bit of lemon inside. That was when I first realized how *very* small and virginally tight she was, a snug fit even for my one finger, as it carefully, tremulously, worked the lemon up along the warm channel to the firm, smooth nub of her womb, where the lemon almost eagerly and lovingly cupped over it.

As I withdrew my hand, Hui-sheng smiled again—perhaps at the expression on my flushed face, or my breathlessness—and perhaps she mistook my excitement for concern, because she hastened to assure me that the lemon cap was a sure and certain preventive of accidents. She said it was provably superior to any other means, such as the Mongol women's fern seed, or the Bho women's insertion of a jagged nugget of rock salt, or the witless Hindu women's puffing of wood smoke inside themselves, or the Champa women's making their men clamp onto their organ a little hat of tortoise-shell. Most of those methods I had never heard of, and I cannot comment on the practicality of them. But I later had proof of the lemon's efficacy in that respect. And I also discovered, that same night, that it was a much more *pleasing* method than most, because it added a fresh, tart, bright scent and taste to Hui-sheng's already impeccably clean and fragrant parts and their emanations and essences. . . .

But there. I said I would not dwell on the particulars of our bedtime enjoyments.

. 2 .

W H E N we departed for Hang-zho, our karwan train consisted of four horses and ten or twelve asses. One horse was Hui-sheng's own high-stepping white mare; the other three, not quite so handsome, were for me and two armed Mongol escorts. The asses carried all our traveling packs, a Han scribe (to interpret and write for me), one of my Mongol maidservants (brought along to attend Hui-sheng), two nondescript male slaves to do the camping chores and any other hard labor.

I had another of Kubilai's gold-inscribed ivory plaques hanging at my saddle horn, but not until we were on the road did I open the documents of authority he had given me. They were of course written in Han, for the convenience of the Manzi officials to whom I would be showing them, so I ordered my scribe to tell me what they said. He reported, in tones of some awe, that I had been appointed an agent of the imperial treasury, and accorded the rank of Kuan, meaning that all the magistrates and prefects and other governing officers, everyone except the Wang overlord, would be required to obey me. The scribe added, as a point of information, "Master Polo—I mean Kuan Polo—you will be entitled to wear the coral button." He said it as if that would be the greatest honor of all, but it was not until later that I found out what that meant.

It was an easy, leisurely, pleasant and mostly level ride southward from Khanbalik through the province of Chih-li—the Great Plain of Kithai—which was one vast farmland from horizon to horizon, except that it was crazily fenced into minuscule family holdings of just a mou or two apiece. Since no two adjoining farm families seemed to agree on the ideal crop for the land and the season, one plot would be of wheat, the next of millet, the next of clover or garden truck or something else. So that whole nation of greenery actually comprised a checkering and speckling of every different hue and tint and shade of green. After Chih-li came the province of Shan-dong, where the farms gave way to groves of mulberry trees, the leaves of which are sustenance for silk-worms. It was from Shan-dong that came the heavy, nubbed, much-prized silk fabric also called shan-dong.

One thing I noticed on all the main roads in this southern region of Kithai: they were posted at intervals with informative signboards. I could not read the Han writing, but my scribe translated them for me. There would be a column erected at the roadside, with a board sticking out from it each way, and on one might be painted: "To the North to Gai-ri, nineteen li," and on the other: "To the South to Zhen-ning, twenty-eight li." So a traveler always knew where he was, and where he was going, and where (if he had forgotten) he had just come from. The signposts were especially informative at crossroads, where a whole thicket of them would list every city and town in every direction from

there. I made a note of that very helpful Han contrivance, thinking it
could well be recommended for adoption in all the rest of the Khanate—
and, for that matter, all over Europe—where there were no such things.

Most of the way southward through Kithai, we were either riding
close beside the Great Canal, or within sight of it, and it teemed with
water traffic, so, whenever we were any distance from it, we had the odd
view of boats and ships apparently sailing seas of grain fields and navi-
gating among orchard trees. That canal was inspired, or made necessary,
by the fact that the Huang or Yellow River had so often changed its
channel. Within recorded history, the eastern length of the river had
whipped back and forth across the land like a snapped rope—though of
course not so rapidly. In one century or another, it had emptied into the
Sea of Kithai way up north of the Shan-dong Peninsula, just a couple of
hundred li south of Khanbalik. Some centuries later, its immense and
serpentine length had wriggled down the map to flow into the sea far
south of the Shan-dong Peninsula, fully a thousand li distant from its
earlier outlet. To envision that, try to imagine a river flowing through
France and at one time spilling into the Bay of Biscay at the English port
of Bordeaux, then squirming across that whole breadth of Europe to
empty into the Mediterranean at the Republic of Marseilles. And the
Yellow River, at other times in history, had pushed out to the Sea of
Kithai at various shore points intermediate between those northernmost
and southernmost reaches.

The river's inconstancy had left many lesser streams and isolated
lakes and ponds all across the lands where it used to run. Some of the
earlier ruling dynasties cunningly took advantage of that, to dig a canal
interconnecting and incorporating the existent waters and make a nav-
igable waterway running roughly north and south, inland of the sea. I
believe it was, until recently, only a desultory and fragmentary canal,
connecting just two or three towns in each stretch. But Kubilai, or rather
his Chief of Digging the Great Canal, with armies of conscript labor, had
done more trenching and dredging, and done it better. So the canal was
now broad and deep and permanent, its banks neatly beveled and faced
with stone, with locks and hoisting engines provided wherever it had to
vault intervening highlands. It enabled vessels of every size, from san-
pan scows to seagoing chuan ships, to sail or row or be towed all the way
from Khanbalik to the southern border of Kithai, where the delta of the
other great river, the Yang-tze, fanned out into the Sea of Kithai. And
now that Kubilai's realm extended south of the Yang-tze, the Great
Canal was being pushed clear to Manzi's capital city of Hang-zho. It was
a modern-day accomplishment nearly as grand and sightly and awesome
as the ancient Great Wall—and far more useful to mankind.

When our little karwan train was ferried across the Yang-tze, the
Tremendous River, it was like crossing a dun-colored sea, so broad that
we could barely distinguish the darker dun line on the far side that was
the shore of Manzi. I had some difficulty in reminding myself that this
was the water I had been able to throw a stone across, away to the
west and upriver in Yun-nan and To-Bhot where it was called the Jin-
sha.

Until now, we had been traversing a country inhabited mostly by Han, but a country that had been for many years under Mongol domination. Now here, in what had until very recently been the Sung Empire, we were among Han peoples whose ways of life had not yet been in the least impressed or overlaid by the more robust and vigorous Mongol society. To be sure, Mongol patrols roamed hither and yon, to preserve order, and every community had a new headman who, though usually a Han, had been imported from Kithai and installed by the Mongols. But those had not had time to make any changes in what the country had been. Also, because Sung had surrendered to become Manzi without any struggle, the land had not been fought over or ravaged or blighted in any way. It was peaceful and prosperous and pleasing to the eye. So, from the moment of our landing on the Manzi shore, I began to take an even keener interest in our surroundings, eager to see what the Han were like in their natural state, so to speak.

The most noticeable aspect of them was their incredible ingenuity. I had been inclined in the past to denigrate that much-vaunted quality of theirs, having so often found their inventions and discoveries to be as impractical as, for instance, their circle divided into three hundred sixty-five and a quarter segments. But I was more taken with the cleverness of the Han in Manzi, and it was never better demonstrated than by a prosperous landowner who took me on a tour of his holdings, just outside the city of Su-zho. I was accompanied by my scribe, who translated for me.

"A vast estate," said our host, waving at it expansively.

Perhaps it was, in a country where the average farmer owned a miserable mou or two of land. But it would have been accounted ridiculously tiny anywhere else—say, in the Vèneto, where the properties are measured in sweeps of zonte. All I could see here was a plot of ground just barely big enough to contain the owner's one-room shack—his "country house"; he had a substantial mansion in Su-zho—and a cramped truck garden beside the shack, a single trellis thickly grown with grapevine, some rickety pig sties, a pond no bigger than the smallest in a Khanbalik palace garden, and a sparse grove of trees which, from their gnarled fistlike limbs, I took to be mere mulberries.

"Kan-kàn! Behold! My orchard, my piggery, my vineyard and my fishery!" he boasted, as if he were describing an entire and fertile and thriving prefecture. "I harvest silk and pork and zu-jin fish and grape wine, four staples of gracious living."

That they were, I agreed, but remarked that there seemed little room here to harvest any profitable quantity of any of them, and that they struck me, besides, as a strangely assorted quartet of crops.

"Why, they all support and increase one another," he said, with some surprise. "So they do not require much space to produce a bountiful harvest. You have seen my abode in the city, Kuan Polo, so you know I am wealthy. My wealth came all from this estate."

I could not gainsay him, so I asked politely if he would explain his farming methods, for they must be masterful. He began by telling me that in the skimpy garden plot he grew radishes.

That sounded so trifling that I murmured, "You failed to mention that staple of gracious living."

"No, no, not for the table, Kuan, nor for marketing. The radishes are only for the grapes. If you bury your grapes among a bin of radish roots, the grapes will stay fresh and sweet and delicious for months, if necessary."

He continued. The radish tops, the greens, he fed to the pigs in the sties. The sties were uphill of the mulberry grove, and tiled channels were laid between, so the pigs' offal sluiced downhill to fertilize the trees. The trees' green summer leaves nourished the silkworms, and, in autumn when the leaves turned brown, they too were fodder for the pigs. Meanwhile, the excreta of the silkworms was the favorite food of the zu-jin fish, and the fishes' excrement enriched the pond bottom, the silt of which was dredged up at intervals to nourish the grape arbor. And so—kan-kàn! ecco! behold!—in this miniature universe, every living thing was interdependent, and flourished by being so, and made him wealthy.

"Ingenious!" I exclaimed, and sincerely meant it.

The Han of Manzi were clever in other, less striking ways, too, and not just 'the upper classes, but the least of them. A Han farmer, when he judged the time of day by glancing at the altitude of the sun, was of course doing nothing that any Vèneto peasant could not. However, *indoors*, that farmer's wife at home in their hut could tell precisely when it was time to start making her man's evening meal—merely by glancing at the eyes of the family cat and judging how much its pupils had dilated in the waning light. The commonfolk were diligent, too, and thrifty and unbelievably patient. No farmer ever bought a pitchfork, for example. He would find a tree limb terminating in three pliable twigs, tie those twigs parallel, wait years until they grew into sturdy branches, saw off the limb, and he would have a tool that would serve him and probably his grandsons as well.

I was much impressed by the ambition and perseverance of one farm boy I met. The majority of the Han country folk were illiterate and content to remain so, but this one lad had somehow learned to read, and was determined to rise above his poverty, and had borrowed books to study. Since he could not neglect his farm work—being the only stay of aged parents—he would tie a book to the horns of his ox and read while he led the beast about in tilling the field. And at night, because the household could not afford even a grease wick-lamp, he would read by the light of glowworms which he plucked from the farm furrows during the day.

I do not mean to assert that every Han in Manzi was the embodiment of virtues and talents and no less worthy attributes. I saw also some egregious evidences of fatuity and even lunacy. One night we came to a village where a religious festa of some sort was going on. There was music and song and dance and merry fires burning all about, and every so often the night was rent by the thunder and flash of the fiery trees and sparkling flowers. The center of all the celebration was a table set up in the village square. It was piled with offerings to the gods: samples of the finest local farm produce, flasks of pu-tao and mao-tai, slaughtered piglet and lamb carcasses, fine cooked viands, beautifully arranged vases of flowers. There was a gap among all that bounty, where a hole was cut in the middle of the table, and one villager after another would crawl under the table, put his head up through the hole, pose that way for a time, then remove himself to make way for another. When I inquired in amazement what that was meant to signify, my scribe asked about and then reported:

"The gods look down and see the sacrifices heaped up for them. Among the offerings, the heads. So each villager goes away confident that the gods, having seen him already dead, will take his name off their list of local mortals to be afflicted with ills and sorrows and death."

I might have laughed. But it occurred to me that, however simple-mindedly those people were behaving, at least they were being *ingeniously* simpleminded. After some time in Manzi, and after admiring innumerable instances of the Han's intelligence, and after deploring as many instances of witlessness, I eventually came to a conclusion. The Han possessed prodigious intellect and industry and imagination. They were mainly flawed in this respect: they too often wasted their gifts in fanatic observance of their religious beliefs, which were flagrantly fatuous. If the Han had not been so preoccupied with their notions of godliness, and so bent on seeking "wisdom instead of knowledge" (as one of them had once expressed it to me), I think those people, as a people, could have done great things. If they had not forever lain worshipfully prostrate—a position which invited their being trodden on by one oppressive dynasty after another—they might themselves by now be rulers of the whole world.

That farm boy I earlier spoke of, whose initiative and assiduity I found admirable, forfeited some of my regard as we talked further and he told me, by way of my scribe:

"My passion for reading and my yearning for learning might distress my aged parents. They might decry my ambition as an overweening arrogance, but—"

"Why on earth should they?"

"We follow the Precepts of Kong Fu-tze, and one of his teachings was that a low-born person should not presume above his ordained station in life. But I was about to say that my parents do *not* object, for my reading affords me opportunity also to manifest my filial piety, and another of the Precepts is that parents be honored above all else. So, since each night I am so eager to get to my books and my glowworms, I am the first of us to retire. I can lie on my pallet and force myself to lie perfectly still while I read, so that all the mosquitoes in the house can freely suck my blood."

I blinked and said, "I do not understand."

"By the time my aged parents stretch their old bodies on their pallets, you see, the mosquitoes are gorged and sated, and do not molest them. Yes, my parents often boast of me to our neighbors, and I am held an example to all sons."

I said unbelievingly, "This is something marvelous. The old fools boast of you letting yourself be eaten alive, but not of your striving to better yourself?"

"Well, doing the one is being obedient to the Precepts, while the other. . . ."

I said, "Vakh!" and turned and went away from him. A parent too apathetic to swat his own mosquitoes seemed not much worth honoring, or humoring with attention—or preserving, for that matter. As a Christian, I believe in devotion to one's father and mother, but I think that not even the Commandment enjoins abject filiality to the exclusion of everything else. If that were so, no son would ever have time or opportunity to produce a son to honor *him*.

That Kong Fu-tze, or Kong-the-Master, of whom the boy had spoken, was a long-ago Han philosopher, the originator of one of the three chief religions of those people. The three faiths all were fragmented into numerous contradictory and antagonistic sects, and all three were much intermingled in popular observance, and they were interlarded with traces of ever so many lesser cults—worship of gods and goddesses, demons and demonesses, nature spirits, ancient superstitions —but in the main there were three: Buddhism, the Tao and the Precepts of Kong Fu-tze.

I have already mentioned Buddhism, holding out to man a salvation from the rigors of this world by means of continual rebirths ascending to the nothingness of Nirvana. I have also mentioned the Tao, the Way by which a man could hope to harmonize and live happily with all the good things of the world around him. The Precepts dealt less with the here or the hereafter than with all-that-has-gone-before. To put it simplistically, a practitioner of Buddhism looked to the empty void of the future. A follower of the Tao did his best to enjoy the teeming and eventful present. But a devotee of the Precepts was concerned mostly with the past, the old, the dead.

Kong Fu-tze preached respect for tradition, and tradition is what his Precepts became. He ordained that younger brothers must revere the older, and a wife revere her husband, and all revere the parents, and they the community elders, and so on. The result was that the greatest honor accrued not to the best, but to the oldest. A man who had heroically prevailed against fierce odds—to win some notable victory or attain to some notable eminence—was accounted less worthy than some human turnip who had merely sat inert and *existed* and survived to a venerable age. All the respect rightly owed to excellence was bestowed upon vegetable antiquity. I did not think that reasonable. I had known enough old fools—and not just in Manzi—to know that age does not, as a matter of inevitability, confer wisdom, dignity, authority or worth. Years do not do that by themselves; the years must have contained experience and learning and achievement and travail overcome; and most people's years do not.

Worse yet. If a living grandfather was to be venerated, well, *his* father and grandfather, though dead and gone, were even older—no xe vero?—and even more highly to be venerated. Or so the Precepts were interpreted by their devotees, and those Precepts had permeated the consciousness of all the Han, including those who professed faith in Buddhism or the Tao or the Mongols' Tengri or the Nestorian version of Christianity or some one of the lesser religions. There was a general attitude of "Who knows? It may not help, but it does no harm, to burn a bit of incense to the next fellow's deity, however absurd." Even the most nearly rational persons, those Han who had converted to Nestorian Christianity—who would never have made ko-tou to the next fellow's absurd fat idol, or a shamàn's divining bones, or a Taoist's advice-giving sticks, or whatever—saw no harm, and possible benefit, in making ko-tou to his own ancestors. A man may be poor in all material assets, but even the most impoverished wretch has whole nations of ancestors. Paying the requisite reverence to all of them kept every living person of the Han perpetually prone—if not in physical fact, certainly in his outlook on life.

The Han word mian-tzu meant literally "face," the face on the front of one's head. But, because the Han seldom let their faces show much surface expression of their feelings, the word had come to mean the feelings going on *behind* those faces. To insult a man or humiliate him or best him in a contest was to cause him to "lose face." And the vulnerability of his feeling-face persisted beyond the grave, into uttermost eternity. If a son dared not behave in any way to shame or sadden the feeling-faces of his living elders, how much more reprehensible it would have been to hurt the disembodied feeling-faces of the dead. So all the Han ordered their lives as if they were being watched and scrutinized and judged by all their forebear generations. It might have been a worth while superstition, if it had spurred all men to attempt feats that their ancestors would applaud. But it did not. It made them only anxious to evade their ancestors' disapproval. A life entirely devoted to the avoidance of wrong seldom achieves anything exceptionally right—or anything at all.

Vakh.

·3·

THE city named Su-zho, through which we passed on our way south, was a lovely city, and we were almost loath to leave it. But when we reached our destination, Hang-zho, we found it an even more beautiful and gracious place. There is a rhyming adage which is known even to faraway Han who have never visited either of the cities:

> Shang ye Tian tang,
> Zhe ye Su, Hang!

Which could be translated thus:

Heaven is far from me and you,
But here for us are Hang and Su!

As I have said, Hang-zho was like Venice in one respect, being girt
all about by water and riddled by waterways. It was both a riverside and
a seaside city, but not a port city. It was situated on the north bank of a
river called the Fu-chun, which here widened and shallowed and fanned
out, eastward of the city, into many separate runnels across a vast,
spreading, flat delta of sand and pebbles. That empty delta extended for
some two hundred li, from Hang-zho to what was, most of the time, the
distant edge of the Sea of Kithai. (I will shortly make plain what I mean
by "most of the time.") Since no seaborne vessels could cross that immense sandy shoal, Hang-zho had no port facilities, except what docks
were necessary to handle the comparatively few and small boats that
plied the river inland from the city.

All the many main avenues of Hang-zho were canals running from
the riverside into the city and through it and round about it. At places
those canals broadened out into wide, serene, mirror-smooth lakes, and
in those were islands that were public parks, all flowers and birds and
pavilions and banners. The lesser streets of the city were neatly cobbled,
and they were broad but tortuous and twisty, and they humped themselves over the canals on ornate, high-arched bridges, more of them than
I could ever count. At every bend in every street or canal, one had a
view of one of the city's many high and elaborate gates, or a tumultuous
marketplace, or a palatial building or temple, as many as ten or twelve
stories high, with the distinctive curly Han eaves projecting from every
single story.

The Court Architect of Khanbalik had once told me that Han cities
never had straight streets because the Han commonfolk foolishly believed that demons could travel only in straight lines, and foolishly believed that they were thwarting the demons by putting kinks in all their
streets. But that was nonsense. In truth, the streets of any Han city—
including both the paved and the watery ones of Hang-zho—were laid
out in deliberate emulation of the Han style of writing. The city's
marketplace—or each of the marketplaces, in a city like Hang-zho that
had so many—was a straight-edged square, but all the surrounding
streets would have bends and curves and sinuosities, gentle or abrupt,
just as do the brush strokes of a written Han word. My own personal yin
signature could very well be the street plan of some walled Han town.

Hang-zho was, as befits a capital city, very civilized and refined, and
it exhibited many touches of good taste. At intervals along every street
were tall vases in which the householders or shopkeepers put flowers for
the delight of the passersby. At this season they were all brimming with
glowing, dazzling chrysanthemums. That flower, incidentally, was the
national symbol of Manzi, reproduced on all official signboards and documents and such, revered because the exuberant florets of its blossom are
so reminiscent of the sun and its sunbeams. Also at intervals along the
streets were posts bearing boxes labeled—so my scribe told me—
"Receptacle for the respectful deposit of sacred paper." That meant, he

told me, any piece of paper with writing on it. Ordinary litter was simply swept up and removed, but the written word was held in such high regard that all such papers were taken to a special temple and ritually burned.

But Hang-zho also was, as befits a prosperous trading city, rather gaudily voluptuous in other respects. It seemed that every last person on the streets, except for travel-dusted new arrivals like us, was luxuriously garbed in silks and velvets, and jingling with jewelry. Although admirers of Hang-zho called the city a Heaven on earth, people in other cities enviously called it "the Melting-Pot of Money." I also saw on the streets, in full daylight, numbers of the sauntering young women-for-hire whom the Han called "wild flowers." And there were many open-fronted little wine shops and cha shops—with names like the Pure Delight and the Fount of Refreshment and the Garden of Djennet (that one patronized by Muslim residents and visitors)—some of which shops, said my scribe, actually dispensed wine and cha, but all of which mainly traded in wild flowers.

The names of Hang-zho's streets and landmarks, I suppose, ranked somewhere between the tasteful and the voluptuous. Many of them were nicely poetic: one park island was called the Pavilion from Which the Herons Take Flight at Dawn. Some names seemed to record some local legends: one temple was the Holy House That Was Borne Here Through the Sky. Some were tersely descriptive: a canal known as Ink to Drink was not inky, but clear and clean; it was lined with schoolhouses, and when a Han spoke of drinking ink, he was referring to scholastic study. Some names were more lavishly descriptive: the Lane of Flowers Worked with Colorful Birds' Feathers was a short street of shops where hats were made. And some names were simply unwieldy: the main road going from the city inland was labeled the Paved Avenue Which Winds a Long Way Between Gigantic Trees, Among Streams Falling in Cascades, and Upward at Last to an Ancient Buddhist Temple on a Hilltop.

Hang-zho was again like Venice in not allowing large animals into the center of the city. In Venice, a rider coming from Mestre on the mainland must tether his horse in a campo on the northwest side of the island, and go by gòndola the rest of the way. We, arriving at Hang-zho, left our mounts and pack asses at a karwansarai on the outskirts, and went leisurely on foot—the better to examine the place—through the streets and over the many bridges, our slaves carrying our necessary luggage. When we came to the Wang's immense palace, we even had to leave our boots and shoes outside. The steward who met us at the main portal advised us that that was the Han custom, and gave us soft slippers to wear indoors.

The recently appointed Wang of Hang-zho was another of Kubilai's sons, Agayachi, a little older than myself. He had been informed by an advance rider of our approach, and he greeted me most warmly, "Sain bina, sain urkek," and Hui-sheng too, addressing her respectfully as "sain nai." When she and I had bathed and changed into presentable attire, and sat down with Agayachi to a welcoming banquet, he seated me on his right and Hui-sheng at his left, not at a separate women's table. Few people had given much notice to Hui-sheng in the days when she had been a slave, because, although she had been then no less comely, and had dressed as well as all court slaves were made to do, she had cultivated the slave's demeanor of unobtrusiveness. Now, as my consort, she dressed as richly as any noblewoman, but it was her letting her radiant personality shine forth that made people notice her—and approvingly, and admiringly.

The table fare of Manzi was opulent and delicious, but somewhat different to what was popular in Kithai. The Han, for some reason, did not care for milk and milk products, of which their neighbor Mongols and Bho were so fond. So we had no butter or cheeses or kumis or arkhi, but there were enough novelties to make up for the lack. When the servants loaded my plate with something called Mao-tai Chicken, I expected to get drunk from it, but it was not spirituous, only delightfully delicate. The dining hall steward told me that the chicken was not cooked in that potent liquor, but killed with it. Giving a chicken a drink of mao-tai, he said, made it as limp as it would make a man, relaxing all its muscles, letting it die in bliss, so it cooked most tenderly.

There was a tart and briny dish of cabbage, shredded and fermented to softness, which I praised—and got myself laughed at—my table companions informing me that it was really a peasant food, and had first been concocted, ages ago, as a cheap and easily portable provender for the laborers who built the Great Wall. But another dish with a genuinely peasant-sounding name, Beggar's Rice, was not likely ever to have been available to many peasants. It got the name, said the steward, because it had originated as a mere tossing together of kitchen scraps and oddments. However, at this palace table, it was like the most rich and various risotto that ever was. The rice was but a matrix for every kind of shellfish, and bits of pork and beef, and herbs and bean sprouts and zhu-gan shoots and other vegetable morsels, and the whole tinted yellow—with gardenia petals, not with zafràn; our Compagnia had not yet started selling in Manzi.

There were crisp, crunchy Spring Rolls of egg batter filled with steamed clover sprigs, and the little golden zu-jin fish fried whole and eaten in one bite, and the miàn pasta prepared in various ways, and sweet cubes of chilled pea paste. The table also was laden with salvers of delicacies peculiar to the locality, and I took at least a taste of all of them—tasting first and *then* inquiring their identity, lest their names make me reluctant. They included ducks' tongues in honey, cubes of snake and monkey meat in savory gravy, smoked sea slugs, pigeon eggs cooked with what looked like a sort of silvery pasta, which was really the tendons from the fins of sharks. For sweets, there were big, fragrant quinces, and golden pears the size of rukh's eggs, and the incomparable hami melons, and a soft-frozen, fluffy confection made, said the steward, of "snow bubbles and apricot blossoms." For drink there was amber-colored kao-liang wine, and rose wine the exact color of Hui-sheng's lips, and Manzi's most prized variety of cha, which was called Precious Thunder Cha.

After we had concluded the meal with the soup, a clear broth made from date plums, and after the soup cook had emerged from the kitchen for us all to applaud him, we repaired to another hall to discuss my business here. We were a group of a dozen or so, the Wang and his staff of lesser ministers, all of whom were Han, but only a few of them locals retained from the Sung administration; most had come from Kithai and so could converse in Mongol. All of them, including Agayachi, wore the floor-sweeping, straight-lined but elegantly embroidered Han robes, with ample sleeves for tucking the hands in and carrying things in. The first order of business was the Wang's remarking to me that I was at liberty to wear any costume I pleased—I was then wearing, and had long been partial to, the Persian garb of neat tulband and blouse with tight sleeve cuffs, and a cape for outdoors—but he suggested that, for official meetings, I ought to replace the tulband with the Han hat, as worn by himself and his ministers.

That was a shallow, cylindrical thing like a pillbox, with a button on its top, and the button was the only indication of rank among all those in the room. There were, I learned, nine ranks of ministers, but all were dressed so finely and looked so distinguished that only by the discreet insignia of the buttons could they be told apart. Agayachi's hat button was a single ruby. It was big enough to have been worth a fortune, and it betokened his being of the very highest rank possible here, a Wang, but it was much less conspicuous than, say, Kubilai's gleaming gold morion or a Venetian Doge's scufieta. I was entitled to a hat with a coral button, indicating the next-most rank, a Kuan, and Agayachi had such a hat all ready to present to me. The other ministers variously wore the buttons of descending rank: sapphire, turquoise, crystal, white shell, and so on, but it would be a while before I learned to sort them out at a glance. I unwound my tulband and perched the pillbox on my head, and all said I looked the very picture of a Kuan, all but one aged Han gentleman, who grumbled:

"You ought to be more fat."

I asked why. Agayachi laughed and said:

"It is a Manzi belief that babies, dogs and government officials ought to be fat, or else they are assumed to be ill-tempered. But never mind, Marco. A fat official is assumed to be filching from the treasury and taking bribes. Any government official—fat, thin, ugly or handsome —is always an object of revilement."

But the same old man grumbled, "Also, Kuan Polo, you ought to dye your hair black."

Again I asked why, for his own hair was a dusty gray. He said:

"All Manzi loathes and fears the kwei—the evil demons—and all Manzi believes the kwei to have reddish fair hair, like yours."

The Wang laughed again. "It is we Mongols who are to blame for that. My great-grandfather Chinghiz had an orlok named Subatai. He did many depredations in this part of the world, so he was the Mongol general most hated by the Han, and he had reddish fair hair. I do not know what the kwei were supposed to look like in earlier times, but ever since Subatai's day, they have looked like *him*."

Another man chuckled and said, "Keep your kwei hair and beard,

Kuan Polo. Considering what you are here to do, it may *help* if you are feared and hated." He spoke Mongol well enough, but it was obviously a newly acquired language for him. "As the Wang has remarked, all government officials are reviled. You can imagine that, of all officials, tax collectors are the most detested. And I hope you can imagine how a *foreign* tax collector, collecting for a conqueror government, is going to be regarded. I propose that we spread the word that you really *are* a kwei demon."

I gave him a look of amusement. He was a plump, pleasant-faced Han of middle age, and he wore a wrought-gold button on his hat, identifying him as being of the seventh rank.

"The Magistrate Fung Wei-ni," Agayachi introduced him. "A native of Hang-zho, an eminent jurist and a man much esteemed by the people for his fairness and acumen. We are fortunate that he has consented to keep the same magistracy he held under the Sung. And I am personally pleased, Marco, that he has agreed to serve as your adjutant and adviser while you are attached to this court."

"I am also much pleased, Magistrate Fung," I said, as he and I both made the sedate, hands-together bow that passes for a ko-tou between men of near equal rank. "I will be grateful for any assistance. In undertaking this mission of collecting taxes in Manzi, I am ignorant of two things only. I know nothing whatever about Manzi. And I know nothing whatever about tax collecting."

"Well!" grunted the grumbly gray-haired man, this time grudgingly complimentary. "Well, frankness and a lack of self-importance are at least refreshingly new qualities in a tax collector. I doubt, however, that they will help you in your mission."

"No," said the Magistrate Fung. "No more than getting fat or blacking your hair, Kuan Polo. I will be frank, also. I see no way for you to extract taxes from Manzi for the Khanate, except by going yourself from door to door and demanding, or having a whole army of men to do it for you. And even at starvation wages, an army would cost more than you would collect."

"In any case," said Agayachi, "I have no army of men to delegate to you. But I *have* provided—for you and your lady—a fine house in a good quarter of the city, well staffed with domestics. When you are ready, my stewards will show you to the place."

I thanked him and then said to my new adjutant, "If I cannot immediately start learning my job, perhaps I can start learning of my surroundings. Would you accompany us to our house, Magistrate Fung, and on the way show us something of Hang-zho?"

"With pleasure," he said. "And I will show you first the single most spectacular sight of our city. This is the phase of the moon and—yes— the very hour is at hand for the appearance of the hai-xiao. Let us go at once."

There was no clock of sand or water in the room, and not even a cat about, so I did not know how he could be so precise about the hour, or what the time had to do with seeing a hai-xiao, or what a hai-xiao *was*. But Hui-sheng and I made our good nights to the Wang and his staff, and we and our little company of scribe and slaves left the palace with the Magistrate Fung.

"We will take boat from here to your residence," he said. "There is a royal barge waiting on the canal side of the palace. But first, let us walk up the promenade here, along the riverside."

It was a fine night, balmy, softly lighted by a full moon, so we had a good view. From the palace, we went along a street that paralleled the river. It had a waist-high balustrade on that side, mainly constructed of some curiously shaped stones. They were circular, each with a hole in its center, and they were as big around as my encircled arms and as thick as my waist. They were too small to have been millstones, but too heavy to have been wheels. Whatever they had once been used for, they had been retired to serve here, set on edge, rim to rim, and the spaces between filled in with smaller stones, to make the balustrade a solid wall and flat on top. I looked over, and saw that the parapet fell away on the other side, a vertical wall of stone, some two house-stories' distance to the river surface below.

I said, "I take it that the river rises considerably in flood season."

"No," said Fung. "The city is built high above the water on this side to allow for the hai-xiao. Fix your eyes yonder, eastward, toward the ocean."

So he and I and Hui-sheng stood leaning against the parapet and gazed out toward the sea, across the flat, moonlit plain of delta sand that stretched featurelessly to the black horizon. Of course, there was no ocean to be seen; it was some two hundred li away beyond that shoal. Or it usually was. For now I began to hear, from that far distance, a murmur of sound, like a Mongol army on horseback galloping toward us. Hui-sheng tugged at my sleeve, which surprised me, for she could not have heard anything. But she indicated her other hand, which rested on the parapet, and she gave me a querying look. Hui-sheng, I realized, was again *feeling* the sound. However far away it was, I thought, it must be a veritable thunder to be vibrating a stone wall. I could only give her a shrug, no explanation. Fung evidently expected whatever was coming, and without misgivings.

He pointed again, and I saw a line of bright silver suddenly split the darkness of the horizon. Before I could ask what it was, it was close enough for me to make out: a line of sea foam, brilliant in the moonlight, coming toward us across the desert of sand, as rapidly as a line of charging, silver-armored horsemen. Behind it was the whole weight of the Sea of Kithai. As I have said, that shoal was fan-shaped—a hundred li broad out where it met the ocean, narrow here at the river mouth. So the inrushing sea came into the delta as a tumbling sheet of water and spume, but was rapidly constricted as it came, and compressed and piled up, and all its dark color was churned into white. The hai-xiao happened too quickly for me even to exclaim in astonishment. There, pounding toward us, was a wall of water as wide as the delta and as high as a house. But for its foamy glitter, it looked like the avalanche that had scoured across the Yun-nan valley, and rumbled very like it, too.

I glanced down at the river below us. Like a small animal emerging from its burrow and encountering a foam-muzzled rabid dog, it was flowing *backward*, recoiling, trying to vacate its invaded burrow mouth and retreat back toward the mountains it had come from. The next moment, that vast roaring wall of water surged by us, just below the level of the parapet, a welter and tumult of foam, and flecks of it spattered up upon us. I had been transfixed by the spectacle, but at least I had seen seawater before; I think Hui-sheng never had, so I turned to see if she was frightened. She was not. She was bright-eyed and smiling, and moon-glowing spindrift was in her hair like opals. To someone in a soundless world, I suppose, more than to the rest of us, it must be a delight to *see* splendid things, especially when they are so splendid as to be feelable. And even I had felt the stone balustrade beside us and the night all about us tremble under that impact. The rumbling, fizzing, sizzling sea continued to seethe past and upstream, the bright white of it getting streaked with black-green, and finally the black-green predominating, until it was all an unfoamed choppy sea occupying the whole river breadth beneath us.

When I could make myself heard, I said to Fung, "What in the name of all the gods *is* it?"

"Newcomers usually are impressed," he said, as if he had done it all himself. "It is the hai-xiao. The tidal bore."

"Tidal!" I exclaimed. "Impossible! Tides come and go with stately decorum."

"The hai-xiao is not always so dramatic," he conceded. "Only when the season and the moon and the time of day or night properly coincide. On those occasions, as you just saw, they bring the sea across those sands at the pace of a galloping horse—across two hundred li in no longer than it takes a man to eat a leisurely meal. The river boatmen learned, ages ago, to take advantage of it. They cast off from here at just the right moment, and the hai-xiao takes them upriver, hundreds of li, without their having to stroke an oar."

I said politely, "Forgive my doubting you, Magistrate Fung. But I come from a sea city myself, and I have seen tides all my life. They move the sea perhaps an arm's-reach up and down. This was a *mountain* of sea!"

He said politely, "Forgive my contradicting you, Kuan Polo. But I must presume that your native city is on a *small* sea."

I said loftily, "I never thought of it as small. But yes, there are greater ones. Beyond the Pillars of Hercules is the limitless Ocean Sea Atlantic."

"Ah. Well. So is this one a great sea. Beyond this coast there are islands. Many of them. To the north of east, for example, the islands called Jihpen-kwe, which compose the Empire of the Dwarfs. But go east far enough, and the islands thin out, become sparse, are left behind. And *still* goes on the Sea of Kithai. On and on."

"Like our Ocean Sea," I murmured. "No mariner has ever crossed it, or knows its end, or what lies there, or if it *has* an end."

"Well, this one does," said Fung, very matter of fact. "Or at least there is one record of its having been crossed. Hang-zho now is sep-

arated from the ocean by that two-hundred-li delta. But you see these
stones?" He indicated the rounds that constituted most of the balustrade.
"They are anchors for mighty seagoing vessels, and the counterweights
for those vessels' boom ends. Or they were."

"Then Hang-zho was once a seaport," I said. "And it must have been
a busy one. But a long time ago, or so I judge from the extent that the
delta has silted over."

"Yes. Nearly eight hundred years ago. There is in the city archives a
journal written by a certain Hui-chen, a Buddhist trapa, and it is dated—
by our count—in the year three thousand one hundred, or thereabout. It
tells how he was aboard a seagoing chuan which had the misfortune to
be blown from this coast by the tai-feng—the great storm—and kept on
going eastward and at long last made landfall somewhere yonder. By the
trapa's estimate, a distance of more than twenty-one thousand li to there.
Nothing but water all the way. And another twenty-one thousand li back
again. But he did come back from wherever he went, for the journal
exists."

"Hui! Twenty-one thousand li! Why, that is as far as from here
overland all the way back to Venice." A thought came to me, and it was
an excitingly beguiling one. "If there is land that far from here to the
eastward across this sea, it must be my own continent of Europe! This
continent of Kithai and Manzi must be the far side of our own Ocean
Sea! Tell me, Magistrate, did the monk mention cities on the other side?
Lisboa? Bordeaux?"

"No cities, no. He called the land Fu-sang, which means nothing
more than the Place We Drifted To. The natives, he said, resembled
Mongols or Bho rather than Han, but were even more barbaric, and
spoke an uncouth tongue."

"It must have been Iberia . . . or Morocco . . . ," I said thoughtfully.
"Both full of Muslim Moors even that long ago, I think. Did the monk
say anything else of the place?"

"Very little. The natives were hostile, so it was only with hazard and
difficulty that the mariners managed to restock the chuan with food and
water. They cast off in a hurry, to come west again. The only other thing
that seems to have impressed Hui-chen was the vegetation. He described
the trees of Fu-sang as being very odd. He said they were not of wood
and leafy branches, but of green flesh and wicked thorns." Fung made a
face of amused disbelief. "That signifies little. I think all holy men tend
to see flesh and thorns everywhere."

"Hm. I do not know what kind of trees grow in Iberia or Morocco,"
I muttered, unable to cease speculating. "But it is awesome even to think
that—just possibly—one could *sail* from here to my homeland."

"Better not try it," Fung said offhandedly. "Not many men since Hui-
chen have encountered a tai-feng on the open sea and lived to tell of it.
That storm rages frequently, between here and the Jihpen-kwe islands.
The Khan Kubilai has twice now attempted to invade and conquer that
empire, sending fleets of chuan full of warriors. The first time, he sent
too few, and the dwarfs repulsed them. The last time, he sent hundreds
of ships and nearly an entire tuk of men. But the tai-feng came up and

ravaged the fleet, and that invasion failed also. I hear that the dwarfs, grateful to the storm, have named the tai-feng the kamikaze, which in their uncouth language means Divine Wind."

"However," I said, still ruminating, "if the storm rages only *between* here and Jihpen-kwe, then—if Kubilai ever does take those islands—one might be able to sail safely eastward from *there.* . . ."

But Kubilai never made another sortie against them, and never took those islands, and I never got to them, or any farther eastward. I was several times upon the Sea of Kithai, but never for long out of sight of the mainland. So I do not know whether that far-off Fu-sang was, as I suspected, the western shores of our known Europe, or if it was some new land, still undiscovered to this day. I am sorry for having failed, in that instance, to satisfy my curiosity. I should very much have liked to go there and see that place, and I never did.

· 4 ·

HUI-SHENG and I and the Magistrate Fung and our servants stepped from the palace dock into an intricately carved teakwood san-pan, and sat under a stretched-silk canopy as ornate and curly-edged as any Han roof. A dozen oarsmen, naked to the waist and their bodies oiled so they gleamed in the moonlight, rowed us from there, along a winding canal route, to our new abode, and along the way Fung pointed out various things worth our notice.

He said, "That short street you see going off on our left is the Lane of Sweet Breezes and Stroking Airs. In other words, the lane of the fanmakers. Hang-zho's fans are prized throughout the land—this is where the folding fan was invented—some having as many as fifty sticks, and all being painted with the most exquisite pictures, often naughty ones. Nearly a hundred of our city's families have been engaged in the making of fans for generations, father to son to grandson."

And he said, "That building on our right is the biggest in the city. Only eight stories high, so it is not our tallest, but it extends from street to street in one direction, and canal to canal in the other. It is Hang-zho's permanent indoor marketplace, and I believe the only one in Manzi. In its hundred or more rooms are displayed for sale those wares too precious or too fragile to be outdoors in the weather of the open markets— fine furnishings, works of art, perishable goods, child slaves and the like."

And he said, "Here, where the canal has broadened out so expansively, this is called Xi Hu, the West Lake. You see the brightly lighted island in the middle? Even at this hour, there are barges and san-pans moored all around it. Some of the people may be visiting the temples on the island, but most are making merry. You hear the music? The inns there stay open all night long, dispensing food and drink and good cheer. Some of the inns are hospitable to all comers, others are for hire to wealthy families for their private celebrations and weddings and banquets."

And he said, "That street going off to our right, you will note, is hung all with lanterns of red silk over the doors, marking that as one of the streets of brothels. Hang-zho regulates its prostitutes most strictly, grading them into separate guilds, from grand courtesans down to riverboat drabs, and they are periodically examined to make sure they maintain good health and cleanliness."

I had so far been making only murmurs of acknowledgment and appreciation of Fung's remarks, but when he touched on the matter of prostitutes, I said:

"I noticed quite a number of them actually strolling the streets in daylight, something I never saw in any other city. Hang-zho seems quite tolerant of them."

"Ahem. Those abroad in daylight would have been the male prostitutes. A separate guild, but also regulated by statute. If you ever are solicited by a whore, and are inclined to use her, first examine her bracelets. If one among them is copper, she is not a female, however feminine her attire. That copper bracelet is dictated by the city—to prevent the male whores, poor wretches, from passing themselves off as what they are not."

Unpleasurably recollecting that I was the nephew of just such a wretch, I said, perhaps a little peevishly, "Hang-zho seems quite tolerant in many respects, and so do you."

He only said affably, "I am of the Tao. Each of us goes his own Way. A male lover of his own sex is, by choice, only what a eunuch is involuntarily. Both of them being a reproach to their ancestors, in not continuing their line, they require no additional rebuke from me. Now yonder, on our right, that high drum tower marks the center of the city, and is our tallest structure. It is manned day and night to drum the alarm of any fire. And Hang-zho does not depend on passersby and volunteers to quench any fires. There are one thousand men employed and paid to do nothing else but stand ready for that duty."

The barge eventually deposited us at the dock of our own house, just as if we had been in Venice, and the house was quite a palazzo. A sentry was posted on either side of the main portal, each man holding at attention a lance that had an ax blade as well as a point, and both the men were the biggest Han I had ever seen.

"Yes, good robust specimens," said Fung, when I admired them. "Each, I would say, easily sixteen hands tall."

"I think you are mistaken," I said. "I myself am seventeen handspans high, and they are half a head taller than I." I added jestingly, "If you are so inept at counting, I wonder if you are really suited to the arithmetical work of tax collecting."

"Oh, eminently so," he said, in an equally cheerful way, "for I know the Han methods of counting. A man's height is ordinarily reckoned to the top of his head, but a soldier's is measured only to his shoulders."

"Cazza beta! Why?"

"So they can be assigned in pairs to the carrying poles. Being foot soldiers, not horsemen, they are their own load bearers. But also it is taken for granted that a good and obedient soldier has no need for a mind, or a head to carry it in."

I shook my own head in admiring amazement, and apologized to the magistrate for having even mildly disparaged his knowledge. Then, when we had again exchanged our shoes for slippers, he accompanied me and Hui-sheng on a tour of the house. While servants in one room after another fell down in ko-tou to us, he pointed out this and that facility provided for our comfort and pleasure. The house even had its own garden, with a lotus pond in the middle and a flowering tree over-hanging that. The gravel of the winding paths was not just raked smooth, but raked into graceful patterns. I was particularly taken by one ornament there: a carving of a large seated lion that guarded the door-way between house and garden. It was sculptured from a single im-mense piece of stone, but done so cleverly that the lion had a stone ball in its half-open mouth. The ball could, with a finger, be rolled back and forth in there, but could never be pried out from behind the lion's teeth.

I think I slightly impressed the Magistrate Fung with my eye for artwork when, admiring the painted scrolls on the walls of our bedroom, I remarked that those pictures of landscapes were done differently here than by the artists of Kithai. He gave me a sidewise look and said:

"You are right, Kuan. The northern artists think of all mountains as resembling the rugged and craggy peaks of their Tian Shan range. The artists here in Sung—Manzi, I mean; excuse me—are better acquainted with the soft, lush, rounded, woman's-breast mountains of our south."

He took his departure, declaring himself ready to be with me again at the instant of my summons, whenever I should feel like starting work. Then Hui-sheng and I strolled about the new residence by ourselves, dismissing one servant after another to their quarters, and getting ac-quainted with the place. We sat for a while in the moonlit garden while, with gestures, I apprised Hui-sheng of what details of the day's various events and comments she might have failed to comprehend on her own. I concluded by conveying the general impression I had got: that no one seemed to hold very high hopes of my success as a tax gouger. She nodded her understanding of each of my explications and, in the tactful way of a Han wife, made no comment on my fitness for my work or my prospects in it. She asked only one question:

"Will you be happy here, Marco?"

Feeling a truly hai-xiao surge of affection for her, I gestured back, "I *am* happy—here!" making it plain that I meant "with you."

We allowed ourselves a holiday week or so to get settled into our new surroundings, and I learned quickly to leave all the multitudinous details of housekeeping to Hui-sheng's supervision. As she had earlier done with the Mongol maid who came with us, she seemed easily to establish some imperceptible mode of communication with the new Han servants, and they leaped to obey her every whim, and usually did so to perfection. I was not so good a master as she was a mistress. For one thing, I could no more talk in Han than she could. But also I had been long accustomed to having Mongol servants, or servants trained by Mongols, and these of Manzi were different.

I could recite a whole catalogue of differences, but I will mention just two. One was that, owing to the Han reverence for antiquity, a servant could never be dismissed or retired on the mere ground of his or her getting old, useless, senile, even immobile. And, as servants got older, they got cranky and crafty and impudent, but they could not be discharged for that, either, or even beaten. One of ours was an ancient crone whose only duty was to make up our bedroom each morning after we arose. Whenever she smelled the scent of lemon on me or Huisheng or the bedclothes, she would cackle and whinny most abominably, and I would have to grit my teeth and bear it.

The other difference had to do with the weather, of all unlikely things. Mongols were indifferent to weather; they would go about their occupations in sunshine, rain, snow—probably in the chaos of a tai-feng, if they were ever to encounter one. And God knows, after all my journeying, I was as impervious to cold or heat or wet as any Mongol. But the Han of Manzi, for all their devotion to bathing at every opportunity, had a catlike aversion to rain. When it rained, *nothing* that involved going outdoors ever got done—and I do not mean just by servants; I mean by *anybody*.

Agayachi's ministers mostly resided in the same palace that he did, but those who lived elsewhere stayed at home when it rained. The marketplaces of the city, on rainy days, were vacant of both buyers and sellers. So was the vast indoor market, though it was under shelter, because people would have had to endure the rain to get there. Though I went about as I had always done, I had to do it on foot. There was not a palanquin to be found, nor even a canal boat. Though the boatmen spent all their lives on the water, most of the time soaked with water, they would not go out in the water that fell from the sky. Even the male prostitutes did not parade the streets.

Even my so-called adjutant, the Magistrate Fung, had the same eccentricity. He would not come across the city to my house on rainy days, and would not even make his appointed judicial sittings at the Cheng. "Why bother? No litigants would be there." He expressed sympathy at my annoyance over the many wasted wet days and evinced a mild amusement at his own and his countrymen's peculiarity, but he never tried to cure himself of it. Once, when I had not seen him during a whole week of rain, and railed at him indignantly, "How am I supposed to get anything done, when I have only a fair-weather adjutant?" he sat down, got out a paper and brushes and ink block, and wrote for me a Han character.

"That says 'an urgent action not yet taken,' " he informed me. "But see: it is composed of two elements. This one says 'stopped' and this one 'by rain.' Clearly, a trait enshrined in our writing must be ingrained in our souls."

But on clement days, anyway, we sat in my garden and had many long talks about my mission and about his own magistracy. I was interested to hear some of the local laws and customs, but, as he explained them, I gathered that in his judicial practice he relied more on his people's superstitions and his own arbitrary caprices.

"For example, I have my bell which can tell a thief from an honest man. Suppose something has been stolen, and I have a whole array of suspects. I bid each of them reach through a curtain and touch the hidden bell, which will ring at the guilty man's touch."

"And does it?" I asked skeptically.

"Of course not. But it is smeared with ink-powder. Afterward, I examine the men's hands. The man with clean hands is the thief, the one who feared to touch the bell."

I murmured, "Ingenious," a word I found myself often uttering here in Manzi.

"Oh, judgments are easy enough. It is the sentences and penalties that require ingenuity. Suppose I sentence that thief to wear the yoke in the jail yard. That is a heavy wooden collar, rather like the stone anchors, which gets locked around his neck, and he must sit in the jail yard while he wears it, to be jeered at by passersby. Suppose I judge that his crime merits his suffering that discomfort and humiliation for, say, two months. However, I know very well that he or his family will bribe the jailers, and they will only put him into the yoke at times when they know I will be passing in and out of the yard. Therefore, to make sure he is properly chastised, I sentence him to *six* months in the yoke."

"Do you," I said hesitantly, "do you employ a Fondler for the more felonious culprits?"

"Yes, indeed, and a very good one," he said cheerfully. "My own son, in preparation for the study of law, is currently apprenticed to our Fondler. By way of teaching him the trade, the Master has had young Fung beating a pudding for some weeks now."

"What?"

"There is a punishment called chou-da, which is to whip a felon with a zhu-gan cane split at the end into a many-thonged scourge. The object is to inflict the most terrible pain and rupture all the internal organs without causing visible mutilation. So, before he is permitted to wreak chou-da on a human, young Fung must learn to pulverize a pudding without breaking its surface."

"Gèsu. I mean interesting."

"Well, there are punishments more popular with the crowds that come to look on—and some less so, of course. They depend on the severity of the crime. Simple branding on the face. A stay in the cage. The kneeling on sharp-linked chains. The medicine that bestows instant old age. Women especially like to watch that one inflicted on other women. Another one popular with the women is to see an adultress upended and poured full of boiling oil or molten lead. And there are the punishments with self-descriptive names: the Bridal Bed, the Affectionate Snake, the Monkey Sucking a Peach Dry. I must say modestly that I myself recently invented rather an interesting new one."

"What was that?"

"It was done to an arsonist who had burned down the house of an enemy. He failed to get the enemy, who had gone on a journey, but burned to death the wife and children. So I decreed a punishment to fit the crime. I directed the Fondler to pack the man's nostrils and mouth with huo-yao powder, and seal him tightly with wax. Then, before he could suffocate or strangle, the wicks were ignited and his head was blown to pieces."

"While we are on the subject of meet punishments, Wei-ni"—we were by this time informally using first names—"what do you predict the Khakhan will inflict on you and me, for indigence in office? We have not got very far with our strategies for tax imposition. I do not believe Kubilai will accept rainy weather as an excuse."

"Marco, why weary ourselves with the making of plans that cannot be put into practice?" he said lazily. "And today is not rainy. Let us just sit here and enjoy the sun and the breeze and the tranquil sight of your lovely lady gathering flowers from the garden."

"Wei-ni, this is a rich city," I persisted. "The only marketplace under roof I ever saw, and ten more market squares outdoors. All of them teeming—except when it rains, anyway. Pleasure pavilions on the lake islands. Prosperous families of fanmakers. Thriving brothels. Not a single one of them yet paying a single tsien to the new government's treasury. And if Hang-zho is so wealthy, what must the rest of Manzi be like? Are you asking me to sit still and let *no one* in the nation *ever* pay a head tax or a land tax or a trade tax or a—?"

"Marco, I can only tell you—as both I and the Wang have told you repeatedly—every last tax record maintained by the Sung regime disappeared *with* the Sung regime. Perhaps the old Empress ordered them destroyed, out of female malice. More likely her subjects invaded the halls of records and the Cheng archives, the moment she left for Kahnbalik to surrender her crown, and *they* destroyed the records. It is understandable. It is expectable. It happens in every newly conquered place, before the conquerors march in, so that—"

"Yes, yes, I have accepted that as a fact. But I am not interested in knowing who paid how much to the late Sung's tax officers! What do I care about a lot of old ledgers?"

"Because without them—look." He leaned forward and held three fingers in front of my face. "You have three possible courses of action. Either you go yourself into every single market stall, every inn on every island, every whore's working cubicle—"

"Which is impossible."

"—or you have an army of men to do it for you."

"Which you have declared impractical."

"Yes. But, just for argument, say that you go to a market stall where a man is peddling mutton. You demand the Khan's share of the value of that mutton. He says, 'But Kuan, I am not the owner of this stall. Speak to the master yonder.' You accost the other man and he says, 'I am master here, yes, but I only manage this stall for its owner, who lives in retirement in Su-zho.' "

"I would refuse to believe either of them."

"But what do you do? Wring money from one? From both? From whom you would get only a dribble. And perhaps overlook the real owner—perhaps the purveyor of all the mutton in Manzi—who really is luxuriating beyond your grasp in Su-zho. Also, do you go through the same fuss at every market stall at every tax time?"

"Vakh! I would never get out of the one market!"

"But if you had the old ledgers, you would *know* who was obligated and where to find him and how much he paid last time around. So there is your third course of action, and the only practical one: compile new records. Even before you begin dunning, you must have a list of every going business and shop and whorehouse and property and plot of land. *And* the names of all their owners and proprietors and heads of household. *And* an estimate of what their holdings are worth and what their annual profits amount to and—"

"Gramo mi! That alone would take my lifetime, Wei-ni. And meanwhile I am collecting nothing!"

"Well, there you are." He sat indolently back again. "Enjoy the day and the view of the eye-soothing Hui-sheng. Salve your conscience with this consideration. The Sung dynasty had existed here for three hundred and twenty years before its recent fall. It had had that long to collect and codify its records and make its taxation methods workable. You cannot expect to do the same thing overnight."

"No, I cannot. But the Khan Kubilai can expect just that. What do I do?"

"Nothing, since anything you did do would be futile. Do you hear that cuckoo in the tree yonder? 'Cu-cu . . . cu-cu . . .' We Han like to think that the cuckoo is saying 'pu-ju ku-ei.' That means 'why not go home?' "

"Thank you, Wei-ni. I expect I will go home, someday. *All* the way home. But I will not go, as we Venetians say, with my bagpipes turned inside their sack."

There was some while of peaceful silence, except for the cuckoo's reiterated advice. At last Fung resumed:

"Are you happy here in Hang-zho?"

"Exceptionally so."

"Then be happy. Try to regard your situation like this. It may be a long and pleasant time before the Khakhan even remembers he sent you here. When he does, you may still evade his inquisition for a long and pleasant time. When he finally does demand an accounting, he may accept your explanation of your delinquency. If he does not, then he may or may not put you to death. If he does, your worries are all over. If he does not, but only has you broken by the chou-da scourge, well, you can live out your life as a crippled beggar. The market stallkeepers will be kind and let you have a begging station in the market square—*because* you never harried and hounded them for taxes, do you see?"

I said rather sourly, "The Wang called you an eminent jurist, Wei-ni. Is that a sample of your jurisprudence?"

"No, Marco. That is Tao."

Some while later, after he had departed for his own dwelling, I said again, "What do I do?"

I said it again in the garden, but now it was the cool of the early evening, and the cuckoo had taken its own advice and gone home, too, and I was sitting with Hui-sheng after our dinner. I had related to her all that Fung and I had said about my predicament, and now appealed for her advice.

She sat pensive for a time, then signaled, "Wait," and got up and went to the house kitchen. She came back with a bag of dry beans and indicated that I was to sit with her on the ground among a bed of flowers. In a bare patch of earth there, she traced with her slim fore-finger the figure of a square. Then she traced a line down the center of that and another across it, to divide the square into four smaller ones. Inside one of those she scratched a single little line, in the next two lines, in the next three, and in the last a sort of squiggle, then looked up at me. I recognized the marks as Han numerals, so I nodded and said, "Four little boxes, numbered one, two, three and four."

While I wondered what this had to do with my current and pressing and frustrating problems, Hui-sheng took out of the bag one bean, showed it to me and placed it on box number three. Then, without looking, she reached into the bag, took out a casual handful of beans and spread them beside the square. Very rapidly, she flicked out four beans from that spread, and four more, shoving them to one side, and kept on separating out four beans at a time from that spread. When they had all, by fours, been moved apart, there remained two beans over. She pointed to those two, pointed to the empty number-two box drawn on the ground, snatched up the bean from the box numbered three, added it to the ones she still had, grinned impishly at me, and made a gesture signifying "too bad."

"I understand," I said. "I wagered on box number three, but number two won, so I lost my bean. I am desolated."

She scooped all the beans back into the bag, took one out, ostenta-tiously put it on a number for me again—this time number four. She started to reach into the bag again, but stopped, and motioned for me to do that. I understood: the game was totally fair, the counting beans were grabbed up at random. I took a considerable handful from the bag and spread them beside her. She rapidly flicked them aside again, four at a flick, and this time they happened to be divisible by four. There were none left to one side at the finish.

"Aha," I said. "That means my number four wins. *What* do I win?"

She held up four fingers, pointed to my wager, added to it three beans more, and shoved them all toward me.

"If I lose, I lose my bean. If my numbered box is the winner, I get my bean back fourfold." I made a face of toleration. "It is a simple game, a childish game, no more complex than the old mariners' game of ven-turina. But if you are suggesting that we play at it for a while—very well, my dear, let us play. I assume you are trying to convey something more than boredom."

She gave me an ample stock of beans to wager with, and indicated that I could risk as many as I liked, and on as many boxes as I chose. So I piled ten beans in each of them, all four boxes, to see what would happen. With an impatient look at me, and without even delving into her bag to ascertain the winning number, she simply gave me forty beans from it, then scooped up the forty on the ground. I realized that, by such a system of play, I could do no more than stay even. So I began trying varieties of play—leaving one box empty, piling different numbers of beans on the other boxes, and so on. The game became a puzzle in arithmetical terms. Sometimes I would win a whole handful of beans, and Hui-sheng would retain only a few. Sometimes the favor of chance went the other way: I would heavily augment her supply and diminish my own.

I perceived that, if a man were seriously playing this game, he could, by one lucky win, come out of it much richer in beans—*if* he got up with his winnings, and went away, and could refuse the temptation to try again. But there was always the urge, especially when one was ahead, to try for more yet. I could also imagine, if one player were vying with three others, plus the banker with the bean bag, it could get absorbing, challenging, tantalizing. But, as well as I could gauge the probabilities, the banker would be getting richer all the time, and any winning player would be enriching himself mainly at the expense of the other three.

I gestured for Hui-sheng's attention. She raised her eyes from the playing ground, and I pointed to myself, to the game, to my money purse, indicating: "If a man were playing for money instead of beans, this could be an expensive sport."

She smiled, and her eyes danced, and she nodded emphatically: "That is what I was trying to convey." And she swept an arm to indicate all of Hang-zho—or maybe all of Manzi—completing the sweep by pointing to the room in our house that I and my scribe used for our working quarters.

I stared at her eagerly glowing little face, then at the beans on the ground. "Are you suggesting this as a *substitute* for tax collecting?"

Emphatic nodding: "Yes." And a spreading of hands: "Why not?"

What a ridiculous idea, was my first thought, but then I reflected. I had seen Han men risking their money on the zhi-pai cards, on the majiang tiles, even on the feng-zheng flying toys—and doing it avidly, feverishly, madly. Could they possibly be enticed into a madness for this simpleminded game? And with me—or rather, the imperial treasury—holding the bank?

"Ben trovato!" I muttered. "The Khakhan said it himself: involuntary benevolence!" I sprang up and raised Hui-sheng from the flower bed and embraced her enthusiastically. "You may have provided my succor and salvation. Tell me, did you learn this game as a child?"

Yes, she had. Some years ago—after a Mongol band of marauders torched her village and slew all the adults, and took her and the other children as slaves, and she was chosen to be raised as a lon-gya of concubines, and a shamàn did the cutting that made her and the whole world silent—the old woman who tended her convalescence had kindly taught her that game, because it was one that could be played without words spoken or heard. Hui-sheng thought she had been about six years old at the time.

I tightened my embrace of her.

· 5 ·

WITHIN three years, I was accounted the richest man in Manzi. Of course, I really was not, because I scrupulously and punctiliously sent on all my profits to the imperial treasury in Khanbalik, by trustworthy Mongol carriers with heavily armed outriders. Over the years, they transported a fortune in paper money and coins, and, for all I know, they still are transporting more.

Hui-sheng and I between us decided on the name for the game— Hua Dou Yin-hang, which means roughly "Break the Bean Bank"—and it was a success from the very start. The Magistrate Fung, though at first incredulous, was soon enchanted with the idea, and convened a special session of his Cheng just to put the seal of legality on my venture and issue to me letters of patent and entitlement—all embossed with the Manzi chrysanthemum—so that no others could copy the idea and set up in competition to me. The Wang Agayachi, though at first dubious of the propriety of my venture—"Who ever heard of a *government* sponsoring a game of chance?"—soon was praising it, and me, and declaring that I had made Manzi the most lucrative of all the Khanate's acquired lands. To every accolade, I said modestly and truthfully, "It was not my doing, but that of my intelligent and talented lady. I am only the harvester. Hui-sheng is the gardener with the golden touch."

She and I commenced the venture with an investment so trivial and meager that it would have shamed a fishmonger outfitting a poor stall in the marketplace. Our equipment consisted of nothing but a table and a tablecloth. Hui-sheng procured a piece of brilliant vermilion red cloth— the Han color signifying good fortune—and embroidered on it in black the quartered square, and in gold the four numbers inside the boxes, and we spread that cloth over a stone table in our garden, and we sent all our servants out to cry along the streets and canals and the riverfront: "Come one, come all venturesome souls! Wager a tsien and win a liang! Come and Break the Bean Bank! Make your dreams come true and your ancestors raise their hands in wonderment! Quick fortune awaits at the establishment of Polo and Echo! Come one and all!"

They came. Perhaps some people came just to steal a close look at me, the demon-haired Ferenghi. Perhaps some came out of actual avarice to win an easy fortune, but most seemed merely curious to see what we were offering, and some simply idled in on their way to some-where else. But they came. And, although some jested and jeered—"A game for children!"—all made at least one play at it. And, although they tossed their tsien or two onto the red cloth in front of Hui-sheng as if they were only humoring a pretty child, they waited to see if they had won or lost. And, although many then just laughed good-humoredly and left the garden, some got intrigued and stayed to play again. And again. And, because only four could play at once, there was some mild wrangling and pushing among them, and those who could not play stayed to watch enthralled. And by the end of the day, when we declared the game over, it was quite a crowd our servants ushered out of the garden. Some of the players went away with more money than they had brought, and went rejoicing that they had found "an unguarded money vault," and vowed to keep coming back and plundering it. And some went away rather lighter in the purse than when they had come, and they went berating themselves for having been bested by "such a juvenile sport," and vowed to come back for retaliation on the Bean Bank table.

So that night Hui-sheng embroidered another cloth, and our servants nearly ruptured themselves manhandling another stone table into the garden. And the next day, instead of just standing about to keep order while Hui-sheng played banker, I took the other table. I was not so swift at the play as she, and did not collect as much money, but we both were hard worked all the day and fatigued by the end of it. Most of the winners of the day before had come back again—and the losers, as well—and more people besides, who had heard of this unheard-of new establishment in Hang-zho.

Well, I need hardly go on. We never again had to send our servants out crying in public, "Come all!" The house of Polo and Echo had overnight become a fixture, and a popular one. We taught the servants— the brighter ones—how to act as bankers, so Hui-sheng and I could take a rest now and then. It was not long before Hui-sheng had to make more of the black-gold-and-red tablecloths, and we purchased all the stone tables in the stock of a neighbor mason, and we set the servants at them as permanent bankers. Curiously enough, our aged crone who always got so gleeful at the smell of lemon turned out to be the best of our apprentice bankers, as swift and accurate as Hui-sheng herself.

I suppose I did not fully realize what a *grand* success we had made of our venture until one day the sky drizzled rain, and no one fled from the garden, and still more patrons arrived, having come through the rain, and they all went on playing all day, oblivious to the wet! No man of the Han would previously have let himself get rained on, even for the sake of visiting Hang-zho's most legendary courtesan. When I realized that we had contrived a diversion more compelling than sex, I went out and about the city and took hire of other disused gardens and empty plots, and instructed our neighbor stonemason to start chiseling more tables for us in a hurry.

Our patronage came from all levels of Hang-zho society—rich nobles retired from the old regime, prosperous and oily-looking merchants, harassed-looking tradesmen, starved-looking porters and palanquin carriers, smelly fishermen and sweaty boatmen—Han, Mongols, a scattering of Muslims, even some men I took to be native Jews. The few fluttery and twittery players who looked at first to be women turned out to be wearing copper bracelets. I do not recall a genuine woman ever coming to our establishment, except to look on with supercilious amusement, as I have seen the visitors do in a House of Delusion. The Han women simply had no wagering instinct, but with the Han men it was more of a passion than drinking to excess or exercising their wee masculine organs.

The men of lower classes, who came desperately hoping to improve their lot, wagered usually only the little center-punched tsien coins that were the currency of the poor. Men of the middle classes usually risked flying money, but of small face-value (and often tattered paper). The already rich men who came, thinking they could Break the Bean Bank by heavy siege or long attrition, would thump down large wads of the more valuable notes of flying money. But a man, whether he wagered a single tsien or a heap of liang, had the same chance of winning when the banker's counting beans were flicked aside, four by four, to disclose the winning box number. What exactly the chance of anyone's making a fortune *was*, I never even troubled to calculate. All I know is that about the same number of patrons went home richer as went home poorer, but it was their own money they had exchanged, and an appreciable portion of it had remained with our Bean Bank. My scribe and I spent much of every night sorting the paper money into sheaves of the same face values, and threading the little coins into strings of hundreds and skeins of thousands.

Eventually, of course, the business got too big and complex for me and Hui-sheng to be personally involved at all. After we had established many Bean Banks all over Hang-zho, we did the same in Su-zho, and then in other cities, and within a few years there was not a single least village in Manzi that did not have one in operation. We employed only tested and trusted men and women to act as the bankers of them, and my Adjutant Fung, for his contribution, put into every establishment a sworn officer of the law to act as general overseer and auditor of accounts. I promoted my scribe to be my manager of the entire wide-flung operation, and thereafter I had nothing to do with the business except to keep tally of the receipts from all over the nation, pay expenses out of that amount, and send on the considerable residue—the eminently considerable residue—to Khanbalik.

I took nothing of the profits for myself. Here in Hang-zho, as in Khanbalik, Hui-sheng and I had an elegant residence and plenty of servants and we dined from an opulent table. All of that was provided to us by the Wang Agayachi—or rather, by his government, which, since it shared in the imperial revenue, was largely supported by our Bean Banks. For indulgence in any additional luxuries or follies I might desire for myself and Hui-sheng, I had my income from my father's Compagnia Polo, still thriving and now sending zafràn and other commodities for trade here in Manzi. So, from the Bean Banks' receipts, I regularly deducted only enough to pay the rentals and maintenance of the banks' gardens and buildings, the wages of the bankers and overseers and couriers, and the ludicrously small costs of equipment (nothing much beyond tables and tablecloths and supplies of dried beans). What went every month to the treasury was, as I have said, a fortune. And, as I have also said, it is probably still a continuing stream.

Kubilai had cautioned me not to bleed every drop from the veins of his Manzi subjects. It might seem that I was contravening his orders and doing precisely that. But I was not. Most players ventured at our Bean Banks the money they had already earned and hoarded and could afford to risk. If they lost it, they were impelled to work harder and earn some more. Even those who injudiciously impoverished themselves at our tables did not simply slump into hopeless idleness and beggary, as they would have done if they had lost their all to a tax collector. The Bean Banks offered always a hope of recovering one's losses—a tax collector never lets *anything* be retrieved—so even the very bankrupts had reason to work their way up again from nothing toward a prosperity that would enable them to return to our tables. I am happy to say that our system did not—as the old tax systems had done—force anyone to the desperate expedient of borrowing at usurious terms and getting into the dire clutches of deep debt. But I take no credit for that; it was thanks to the Khakhan's strictures against the Muslims; there simply were no longer any usurers to borrow from. So in sum, as well as I could see, our Bean Banks—far from bleeding Manzi—gave it new drive and industry and productiveness. They benefited all concerned, from the Khanate as a whole, to the working population at large (not to forget the many people who found steady employment *in* our banks), and so on down to the poorest peasant in the farthest corner of Manzi, to whom the lure of easy fortune gave at least an aspiration.

Kubilai had threatened that he would let me know promptly if he was dissatisfied with my performance as his treasury's agent in Hang-zho. Of course, he never had reason to do any such thing. Quite to the contrary, he eventually sent the highest possible dignitary, the Crown Prince and Vice-Regent Chingkim, to convey to me his heartiest regards and congratulations on the exceptional job I was doing.

"Anyway, that is what he told me to tell you," said Chingkim, in his usual lazily humorous way. "In truth, I think my Royal Father wanted me to spy about and see if you were actually leading bandits in plundering the whole countryside."

"No need to plunder," I said airily. "Why bother to rob what people are eager to bestow?"

"Yes, you have done well. The Finance Minister Lin-ngan tells me that this Manzi is pouring more wealth into the Khanate even than my cousin Abagha's Persia. Oh, speaking of family, Kukachin and the children also send their greetings to you and Hui-sheng. And so does your own estimable father Nicolò. He said to let you know that your uncle Mafìo's condition has improved enough that he has learned several new songs from his lady attendant."

Chingkim, instead of putting up at his half-brother Agayachi's palace, had done me and Hui-sheng the high honor of lodging with us during his visit. Since she and I had long ago delegated the management of our Bean Banks to our hirelings, we were now nobles of unlimited leisure, so we were able to devote all our time and attention to entertaining our royal guest. This day, the three of us, without any servants in attendance, were enjoying a merenda in the open country. Hui-sheng had with her own hands prepared a basket of food and drink, and we had got horses from the karwansarai where we kept them, and we had

ridden out of Hang-zho along that Paved Avenue Which Winds a Long
Way Between Gigantic Trees, Eccètera, and, well away from the city,
we had spread a cloth and dined under those trees, while Chingkim told
me of other things going on here and there in the world.

"We are now waging war in Champa," he said, as idly as a non-
Mongol might remark, "We are building a lotus pond in our back
garden."

"So I gathered," I said. "I have seen the troops moving overland,
and transports of men and horses coming down the Great Canal. I take it
that your Royal Father, balked of expanding eastward to Jihpen-kwe,
has determined to expand southward instead."

"Actually it came about rather fortuitously," he said. "The Yi people
of Yun-nan have accepted our sovereignty there. But there is a lesser
race in Yun-nan, a people called the Shan. Unwilling to be ruled by us,
they have been emigrating southward into Champa in great numbers. So
my half-brother Hukoji, the Wang of Yun-nan, sent an embassy into
Champa, to suggest to the King of Ava that he might obligingly turn
those refugees around and send them back to us, where they belong.
However, our ambassadors had not been warned that all persons, when
calling on the King of Ava, are expected to remove their shoes, and they
did not, and he was insulted, and he ordered his guards, 'Remove their
feet instead!' So, of course, having our ambassadors mutilated *was* an
insult to us, and ample incentive for the Khanate to declare war on Ava.
Your old friend Bayan is on the march again."

"Ava?" I inquired. "Is that another name for Champa?"

"Not exactly. Champa refers to that whole tropical land, the country
of jungles and elephants and tigers and heat and humidity. The people
down there are of—who knows?—ten or twenty separate races, and
almost every one has its own midget kingdom, and every kingdom has
various names, depending on who is speaking of it. Ava, for example, is
also known as Myama and Burma and Mien. The Shan people fleeing
from our Yun-nan are seeking refuge in a kingdom that earlier Shan
emigrants established in Champa a long time ago. It is variously known
as Sayam and Muang Thai and Sukhothai. There are other kingdoms
down there—Annam and Cham and Layas and Khmer and Kambuja—
and maybe many more." Again offhandedly, he said, "While we are
taking Ava, we may well take two or three of the others."

Like a proper merchant, I remarked, "It would save our paying the
exorbitant prices they demand for their spices and woods and elephants
and rubies."

"I had intended," said Chingkim, "to proceed southward from here
and follow Bayan's route of march and have a look for myself at those
tropical lands. But I really do not feel up to making such a rigorous
journey. I shall simply rest here for a while with you and Hui-sheng, and
then return to Kithai." He sighed and said, a little wistfully, "I am sorry
not to be going there. My Royal Father is getting old, and it cannot be
too long before I must succeed him as Khakhan. I should have liked to
do a lot more traveling before I got permanently stabled in Khanbalik."

Such an air of lassitude and resignation was not usual to the Prince

Chingkim, and now I took notice that he was indeed looking rather worn and weary. A little later, when he and I walked a way into the wood to make water in private, I noticed something else, and commented lightly on it:

"At some inn on the road hither, you must have dined on that slimy red vegetable called dai-huang. You did not eat it at our table, for I do not care for it."

"Neither do I," he said. "And neither have I taken a fall from any horse lately, which might account for my pissing pink like this. But I have been doing it for some time. The Court Physician has been treating me for it—in the Han manner, by sticking pins in my feet and burning little heaps of moxa fluff up and down my spine. I keep telling the idiot old Hakim Gansui that I do not piss through my feet or—" He stopped and looked up into the trees. "Listen, Marco. A cuckoo. Do you know what the Han believe the cuckoo is saying?"

Chingkim did go home, as the cuckoo advised, but not until he had spent a month or so enjoying our company and the restful ambience of Hang-zho. I am glad he had that month of simple pleasure, far from the cares of office and state, for when he went home, he went to a much more distant home than Khanbalik. It was not long before the couriers came galloping to Hang-zho, on horses blanketed in purple and white, to tell the Wang Agayachi to drape his city in those Han and Mongol colors of mourning, for his brother Chingkim had arrived home only to die.

As it happened, our city had no more than finished the term of mourning for the Crown Prince, and started to take down the crape bunting, than the couriers came again, with orders to leave it hanging. Now it was in mourning for the Ilkhan Abagha of Persia, who had died also—and also not in battle, but of some illness. The loss of a nephew was of course not so terrible a tragedy to Kubilai as the loss of his son Chingkim, and it did not cause the same widespread murmurs of specu- lation about future succession. Abagha had left a full-grown son, Arghun, who immediately assumed the Ilkhanate of Persia—and even married one of his late father's Persian wives, to further secure his claim to that throne. But Chingkim's son Temur, the next heir apparent to the whole Mongol Empire, was still under-age. Kubilai was well along in years, as Chingkim had remarked. The people worried that, if he were soon to die, the Khanate might be much riven and convulsed by claimants older than Temur, the many uncles and cousins and such, eager to oust him and make the Khanate theirs.

But, for the time being, we suffered nothing worse than grief from Chingkim's untimely demise. Kubilai did not let his sorrow distract him from the affairs of state, and I did not let mine interfere with my regular transmittal of Manzi's tribute to the treasury. Kubilai continued to prose- cute the war against Ava, and even extended the Orlok Bayan's mission —as Chingkim had predicted—to seize, as well, any of Ava's neighbor nations in Champa that might be ripe for conquest.

It made me restless, to know that so much was happening in the world outside, while I simply lolled in luxury in Hang-zho. My restlessness was irrational, of course. Look at all I had. I was quite an esteemed personage in Hang-zho. No one even looked askance at my kwei-colored hair any more when I walked the streets. I had many friends, and I was ever so comfortable, and I was blissfully content with my loving and lovely consort. Hui-sheng and I might have lived—as is said of the lovers at the concluding page of a roman courtois—happily ever after, just as we were. I possessed everything that any rational man could desire. All those most precious things were mine then, at that high moment, that skyline crest of my lifetime. Furthermore, I was no longer the reckless stripling I once had been, with only tomorrows stretching out before me. There were a lot of yesterdays behind me now. I was past thirty years of age, and I found an occasional gray hair among the demon-colored, and I might sensibly have been giving thought to making the downhill slope of my life a soft and easy glide.

Nevertheless, I was restless, and the restlessness inexorably became dissatisfaction with myself. I had done well in Manzi, yes, but was I to bask in the reflected glow of that for the remainder of my days? Once the great thing had been accomplished, it was no great thing merely to perpetuate it. That required no more than my stamping my yin signature on papers of receipt and dispatch, and waving my couriers off to Khanbalik once a month. I was no better than a roadside postmaster of the horse relay stations. I decided I had for too long now enjoyed too much of *having*; I wanted something to *want*. I flinched at the vision of myself growing old in Hang-zho, like a vegetable Han patriarch, and having nothing to take pride in except my survival to old age.

"You will never get old, Marco," Hui-sheng told me when I broached the subject. She looked affectionately amused, but sincere, as she conveyed that pronouncement.

"Old or not," I said, "I think we have luxuriated in Hang-zho long enough. Let us move on."

She concurred: "Let us move on."

"Where would you like to go, my dearest?"

Simply: "Wherever you go."

. 6 .

So my next northbound courier took a message from me to the Khakhan, respectfully requesting that I be relieved of my long-since accomplished mission and my Kuan title and my coral hat button; that I be given permission to return to Khanbalik, where I could cast about for some new venture to occupy me. The courier returned with Kubilai's amiable acquiescence, and it took me and Hui-sheng not long to make ready to depart from Hang-zho. Our native servants and slaves all wept and agonized and fell about in frequent ko-tou, but we assuaged their bereavement by making gifts to them of many things we decided not to

take with us. I made other parting gifts—and rich ones—to the Wang
Agayachi and my Adjutant Fung Wei-ni and my manager-scribe and
other worthies who had been our friends.

"The cuckoo calls," they all said sadly, one after another, as they
toasted us with their wine goblets at the countless farewell banquets and
balls given in our honor.

Our slaves packed into bales and crates our personal belongings and
our wardrobes and our many Hang-zho acquisitions—furnishings,
painted scrolls, porcelains, ivories, jades, jewelry and such—that we were
taking with us. Taking also the Mongol maid we had brought from
Khanbalik, and Hui-sheng's white mare (now somewhat silvery about
the muzzle), we went aboard a sizable canal barge. Only one of our
possessions would Hui-sheng not let be crated and stowed in the hold:
she herself carried her white porcelain incense burner.

During our residence, the Great Canal had been completed all the
way to Hang-zho's riverside. But because we had already covered the
canal route before, following it on our way south, we had decided to
take a very different way home. We stayed on the barge only as far as
the port of Zhen-jiang, where the Great Canal met the Yang-tze River.
There, for the first time (for either me or Hui-sheng), we boarded a
gigantic oceangoing chuan, and sailed down the Tremendous River and
out into the boundless Sea of Kithai and northward up the coast.

That chuan made the good ship *Doge Anafesto*, the galeazza in
which I had crossed the Mediterranean, seem like a gòndola or a san-
pan. The chuan—I cannot call it by name, because it purposely had no
name, so it could not be cursed by rival shipowners, who might persuade
the gods to send it contrary winds or other misfortune—had *five masts*,
each like a tree. From them depended sails as big as some towns' market
squares, made of slats of the zhu-gan cane, and employed as I have
described elsewhere. The bigness of the chuan's duck-shaped hull was in
proportion to its sky-scraping upper works. On the deck and in the
passenger quarters below were more than one hundred cabins, each
comfortably adequate for six persons. That is to say, the ship could carry
more than six hundred passengers *in addition to* its crew, which totaled
fully four hundred men, of several different races and languages. (There
were only a few passengers on this short trip. Besides Hui-sheng, myself
and the maid, there were some traveling merchants, some minor government officials, and a number of other ships' captains, idle between
voyages, aboard just for a seaman's holiday.) In the chuan's holds was
loaded a variety of goods, seeming enough to stock a city. But, simply for
a measure of the holds' capacity, I would say the ship could have carried
two thousand Venetian butts.

I have said "holds" advisedly, instead of hold, because every chuan
was ingeniously built with bulkheads dividing the hull's interior into
numerous compartments, end to end, and they were tarred watertight, so
that if the chuan should strike a reef or otherwise hole itself below the
waterline, only that one compartment would flood, while the others
stayed dry and kept the ship afloat. However, it would have required a
sharp and solid reef to hole that chuan. Its entire hull was triply planked,

actually built three times over, one shell enveloping another. The Han captain, who spoke Mongol, took great pride in showing me how the innermost hull had its planking set vertically, from keel to deck, and the next was planked at an angle diagonal to that, and the outermost was laid in horizontal strakes, stem to stern.

"Solid as rock," he boasted, slamming his fist into a bulwark and producing a sound as of a rock hit with a mallet. "Good Champa teak-wood, held with good iron spikes."

"We do not have teakwood in the West where I come from," I said, almost apologetically. "Our shipbuilders rely on oak. But we do use iron spikes."

"Foolish Ferenghi shipbuilders!" he roared, with a mighty laugh. "Have they not yet realized that oak wood exudes an acid which cor-rodes the iron? Teak, on the other hand, contains an essential oil which preserves iron!"

So I had once again been presented with an example of ingenious Eastern artistry that made my native West seem backward. Somewhat spitefully, I hoped for an example of Eastern simplemindedness to bal-ance the scales, and I expected I would encounter one before the voyage was over—and I thought I had when one day, well out of sight of the safe shore, we sailed into a rather nasty thunderstorm. There was wind and rain and lightning, and the sea got choppy, and the ship's masts and yards got all laced with flickering blue Santermo's fire, and I heard the captain shouting to his crew, in various languages:

"Prepare the chuan for sacrifice!"

It seemed a shockingly unnecessary early surrender, when the chuan's ponderous bulk was barely rocking to the storm. I was only a "sweet-water seaman"—as real Venetian mariners derisively say—and such are supposed to be overly apprehensive of danger on the sea. But I saw no danger here that called for more than a simple shortening of sail. Certainly this was not the fierce storm that merited the dread name of tai-feng. However, I was seaman enough to know better than to volunteer advice to the captain, or to show any contempt of his appar-ently over-extreme agitation.

I am glad I did not. For, as I started glumly below to prepare my womenfolk to abandon ship, I met two seamen coming not fearfully but gaily up the companionway, carrying with care a ship made all of paper, a toy ship, a miniature replica of ours.

"The chuan for sacrifice," the captain told me, quite unperturbed, as he tossed it over the side. "It deceives the sea gods. When they see it dissolve in the water, they think they have sunk our real ship. So they let the storm abate instead of making it more troublesome."

It was just one more reminder to me that even when the Han did something simpleminded, they did it ingeniously. Whether or not the paper-ship sacrifice had any effect, the storm did soon abate, and a few days later we made landfall at Qin-huang-dao, which was the coast city nearest Khanbalik. From there we proceeded overland, with a small train of carts carrying our goods.

When we got to the palace, Hui-sheng and I naturally went first to make ko-tou to the Khakhan. At his royal chambers, I noticed that the elderly stewards and women servants formerly in attendance seemed to have been replaced by some half a dozen young page boys. They were all much of an age, and all handsome, and all had uncommonly light hair and eyes, rather like those tribesmen in India Aryana who had claimed to be descended from Alexander's soldiers. I vaguely wondered if Kubilai, in his old age, was developing a perverse affection for pretty boys, but then I gave it no further mind. The Khakhan greeted us most warmly, and he and I exchanged mutual condolences on the loss of his son and my friend, Chingkim. Then he said:

"I must congratulate you again, Marco, on the splendid success you made of your mission to Manzi. I believe you did not take a single tsien of the tribute for yourself during all these years? No, I thought not. It was my own fault. I neglected to tell you, before you left here, that a tax collector customarily gets no wage, but earns his keep by taking a twentieth part of what he collects. It makes him work more diligently. I have no complaint, however, about the diligence of your own work. Therefore, if you will call upon the Minister Lin-ngan, you will find that he has, all this while, been putting aside your share, and it is a respectable amount."

"Respectable!" I gasped. "Why, Sire, it must amount to a fortune! I cannot accept it. I was not working for gain, but for my Lord Khakhan."

"All the more reason why you deserve it, then." I opened my mouth again, but he said sternly, "I will hear no dispute about it. However, if you would care to demonstrate your gratitude, you might take on one more charge."

"Anything, Sire!" I said, still gasping at the magnitude of the surprise.

"My son and your friend Chingkim wished most earnestly to see the jungles of Champa, and he never got there. I have messages for the Orlok Bayan, currently campaigning in the land of Ava. They are only routine communications, nothing urgent, but they would give you reason to make the journey which Chingkim did not. And your going as surrogate for him might be a consolation to his spirit. Will you go?"

"Without hesitation or delay, Sire. Is there anything else I can do for you down there? Dragons I might slay? Captive princesses I could rescue?" I was only halfway being facetious. He had just made me a wealthy man.

He chuckled appreciatively, but a little sadly. "Bring me back some small memento. Something that a fond son might have brought home to his aged father."

I promised I would seek for something unique, something never before seen in Khanbalik, and Hui-sheng and I took our departure. We went next to greet my father, who embraced us both, and wept a little for joy, until I stopped his tears by telling him of the great beneficence just bestowed on me by the Khakhan.

"Mefè!" he exclaimed. "That is no hard bone to gnaw! I always thought of myself as a good businessman, but I swear, Marco, you could sell sunshine in August, as they say on the Rialto."

"It was all Hui-sheng's doing," I said, giving her an affectionate squeeze.

"Well . . . ," said my father thoughtfully. "This . . . on top of what the Compagnia has already sent home by way of the Silk Road . . . Marco, it may be time we started thinking of going home ourselves."

"What?" I said, startled. "Why, Father, you have always had another saying. To the right sort of man, the whole world is home. As long as we continue to prosper here—"

"Better an egg today than a chicken tomorrow."

"But our prospects all are still rosy. We are still in the Khakhan's high regard. The whole empire is at its richest, ripe for our exploitation. Uncle Mafio is being well attended, and—"

"Mafio is four years old again, so he cares not where he is. But I am touching sixty, and Kubilai is at least ten years older."

"You look nowhere near senility, Father. True, the Khakhan shows his age—and some despondency—but what of that?"

"Have you thought what our position would be if he should die suddenly? Just *because* he favors us, others resent us. Only furtively now, but they are likely to manifest that resentment when his protecting hand falls away. The very rabbits dance at the funeral of a lion. Also, there will be a resurgence of the Muslim factions he suppressed, and they love us not at all. I hardly need mention the likelihood of even worse troubles —upheavals from here to the Levant—if there should be a war of succession. But I am increasingly glad that I have all these years been sending our profits west to your Uncle Marco in Constantinople. I shall do the same with this new fortune of yours. However, anything else we shall have accrued at the moment of Kubilai's death is bound to be sequestered here."

"Can we really gnash our teeth if that happens, Father, considering all the wealth we have already taken out of Kithai and Manzi?"

He shook his head somberly. "What good our fortune waiting in the West, if we are marooned here? If we are dead here? Suppose, of all the claimants to the Khanate succession, it should be Kaidu who won!"

"Verily, we should be at hazard," I said. "But need we abandon ship right now, so to speak, when there is not yet any cloud in the sky?" With some amusement, I realized that, as usual in my father's presence, I was beginning to talk like him, in parables and metaphors.

"The hardest step is the one across the threshold," he said. "However, if your reluctance signifies a concern for your sweet lady here, I hope you do not think I am suggesting her abandonment. Sacro, no! Of course you will bring her with you. She may be a curiosity in Venice, for a little while, but she will be a beloved one. Da novèlo xe tuto belo. You would not be the first to come home with a foreign wife. I recall, there was a ship's captain, one of the Doria, who brought home a Turki wife when he retired from the sea. Tall as a campanile, she was. . . ."

"I take Hui-sheng everywhere," I said, and smiled at her. "I should be lost without her. I will be taking her on this journey to Champa. We will not even stop to unpack the household goods we brought from Manzi. And I have *always* intended to take her home to Venice. But,

Father, you are not recommending, I trust, that we slip away this very day?"

"Oh, no. Only that we make plans. Be ready to go. Keep one eye on the frying pan and the other on the cat. It would take me some time, in any event, to close or dispose of the kashi works—to tidy up many other loose ends."

"There should be ample time. Kubilai looks old, but not moribund. If he has the vivacity, as I suspect, to be playing with boys, he is not apt to drop dead as suddenly as Chingkim did. Let me comply with this latest mission he has set me, and when I return . . ."

He said portentously, "No one, Marco, can foretell the day."

I almost snapped an exasperated reply. But it was impossible for me to feel exasperation at him, or share his morbidity, or work myself into a mood of apprehension. I was a new-made wealthy man, and a happy one, and about to go journeying into new country, and with my dearest companion at my side. I merely clapped an assuring hand on my father's shoulder and said, not with resignation but with genuine jollity, "Let come the day! Sto mondo xe fato tondo!"

CHAMPA

.1.

I T was again the Orlok Bayan I was off to find, and this time he was much farther away, but this time I had no need to get to him in a hurry. So I again arranged that Hui-sheng and I travel with attendants and supplies—her Mongol maid, two slaves for any necessary camping chores, Mongol escorts for protection, and a string of pack animals. But I also laid out each day's march so that we traveled not arduously, and frequently got fresh mounts at the horse posts, and arrived each night at some decent karwansarai or some sizable town or even some provincial palace. In all, we had to cover about seven thousand li of every kind of terrain—plains, farmlands, mountains—but by doing it slowly and leisurely, we managed to sleep comfortably every night while we traversed more than five thousand of those long li. Going southwest from Khanbalik, we were, for much of the way, following the same course I had previously taken to Yun-nan, and so we stopped in many places I had stayed before—the cities of Xian and Cheng-du, for example—and only when we got beyond Cheng-du were we in territory I had not seen before.

From Cheng-du we did not, as I had had to do before, turn west into the highlands of To-Bhot. We continued southwest, directly into the province of Yun-nan, and to its capital, Yun-nan-fu, the last big city on our route, where we were royally received and entertained by the Wang Hukoji. I had one private reason for being eager to see Yun-nan-fu, but it was a reason I did not mention to Hui-sheng. When I had been last in these regions, I had finished my part in the Yun-nan war and taken myself out of it before Bayan besieged the capital city, not availing myself of his invitation to be among the privileged first looters and rapers. Having forgone that opportunity to "behave like a Mongol born," I now looked about me with a special interest—to see what I had missed —and I took notice that the Yi women were indeed handsome, as reported. No doubt I would have enjoyed disporting myself with Yun-nan-fu's "chaste wives and virgin daughters," and no doubt would have believed I was enjoying some of the most comely women in the East. But I had since had the great good fortune to discover Hui-sheng, so now the Yi women looked to me distinctly inferior, and far less desirable than she was, and I felt no deprivation at never having had any of them.

From Yun-nan-fu onward, bearing ever southwest, we were traveling what had been called, from ancient times, the Tribute Road. It was so named, I learned, because the several nations of Champa had, since earliest history, at one time or another all been vassal states of the powerful Han dynasties to the north—the Sung and its predecessors— and that road had been tramped hard and smooth by the traffic of elephant trains bearing to those masters Champa's tribute of everything from rice to rubies, slave girls to exotic apes.

From the last mountains of Yun-nan, the Tribute Road brought us down into the nation of Ava at a river plain and a place called Bhamo, which was only a chain of rather primitively constructed forts. They were also apparently ineffectual forts, for Bayan's invaders had easily overwhelmed their defending forces, and taken Bhamo and gone on past. We were received by a captain commanding the few Mongols left to garrison the place, and he informed us that the war was already concluded, the King of Ava in hiding somewhere, and Bayan now celebrating his victory in the capital city of Pagan, a long way downriver. The captain suggested that we could get there more comfortably and quickly by river barge, and gave us one, and Mongol crewmen for it, and a Mongol yeoman scribe named Yissun, who knew the Mien language of the country.

So we left our other attendants there at Bhamo, and Hui-sheng and her maid and I had a slow river voyage for the last thousand li or more of our journey. That river was the Irawadi, which had begun as a tumbling torrent called the N'mai, away up in the Land of the Four Rivers, high in To-Bhot. Down in this flatter country, the river was as broad as the Yang-tze, and flowed sedately southward in great swooping bends. It was full of so much silt, perhaps carried all the way down from To-Bhot, that its water was nearly viscous, like a thin glue, and unpleasantly tepid. It was a sickly tan color across its immense sunlit breadth, and brown in the deep shade on both extremes, where an almost unbroken forest of giant trees overhung the distant banks.

Even the enormous width and endless length of the Irawadi River must have looked, to the numberless birds flying overhead, like a mere insignificant gap meandering through the greenery that covered the land. Ava was almost entirely overgrown with what we would call jungle, and the jungle natives called the Dong Nat, or Forest of the Demons. The local nat, I gathered, were similar to the kwei of the north: demons of varying degrees of badness, from mischief to real evil, and usually invisible but capable of assuming any form, including the human. I privately imagined that the nat seldom put on corporeality, because in the dense tangle of that Dong jungle there was scarcely *room* for them to do so. Beyond the muddy riverbanks, there was no ground to be seen, only a welter of ferns and weeds and vines and flowering shrubs and thickets of zhu-gan cane. Out of that confusion towered the trees, rank on rank, shouldering and elbowing each other. At their tops, their crowns of leaves merged together high in the air to make a veritable thatch over the whole land, a thatch so thick that it was equally impervious to rainstorm and sunlight. It seemed permeable only by the creatures that lived up there, for the treetops continuously rustled and shook to the coming and going of gaudy birds and the leaps and swings of chattering monkeys.

Each evening, when our barge steered for the shore to make camp—unless we happened on a clearing with a cane-built Mien village in it—Yissun and the boatmen would have to get out first and, each wielding a broad, heavy blade called a dah, hack out a place sufficient for us to spread our bedrolls and lay our fire. I always had the impression that, on the next day, we would have got only around the next bend downstream before the rank, greedy, fervid jungle closed over the little dimple we had made in it. That was not an unlikely notion. Whenever we camped near a grove of zhu-gan cane, we could hear it crackling, even when there was not a breath of wind; that was the sound of it *growing*.

Yissun told me that sometimes the fast-growing, very hard cane would rub against a soft-wooded jungle tree, and the heat of friction would start a blaze and—damp and sticky though the vegetation always was—it could blaze up and burn for hundreds of li in all directions. Only those inhabitants and denizens able to reach the river would survive the terrible fire, and they would likely fall victim to the ghariyals which always converged on any scene of disaster. The ghariyal was a tremendous and horrible river serpent which I took to be related to the dragon family. It had a knobby body as big as a cask, eyes like upstanding saucers, dragon jaws and tail, but no wings. The ghariyals were everywhere along the riverbanks, usually lurking in the mud like logs with glaring eyeballs, but they never molested us. Evidently they subsisted mostly on the monkeys which, in their antics, frequently fell shrieking into the river.

We were not molested by any of the other jungle creatures, either, although Yissun and the Mien villagers along the way warned us that the Dong Nat was the habitat of worse things than the nat and the ghariyal. Fifty different kinds of venomous snakes, they said, and tigers and pards and wild dogs and boars and elephants, and the wild ox called the seladang. I remarked lightly that I should not care to meet a wild ox; the domestic kind I saw in the villages looked vicious enough. It was as big as a yak, a sort of blue-gray in color, with flat horns swooping in a crescent backward from its brow. Like the serpent ghariyal, it liked to lie wallowing in a mudhole, with only its snout and eyes above the surface, and when the huge beast lumbered loose from the mud, there was a noise like huo-yao exploding.

"That animal is only the karbau," Yissun said indifferently. "No more dangerous than a cow. The little children herd them. But a seladang stands higher at the shoulder than the top of your head, and even the tigers and elephants move out of its way when it walks through the jungle."

We could always tell from afar when we were approaching a riverside village, because it always had what looked like a cloud of rusty-black smoke hovering over it. That was actually a canopy of crows—called by the Mien "the feathered weeds"—raucously rejoicing over the village's rich litter of garbage. Besides the crows overhead and the swill underfoot, every village had also a span or two of the karbau draft oxen, and some scrawny black-feathered chickens running about, and a lot of those pigs with long bodies that sagged in the middle and dragged in the swill, and an incredible lot of naked children that very much resembled the pigs. Every village had also a span or two of tame cow elephants. That was because the jungle Mien's only trade and craft was the taking of timber and other tree products out of this wilderness, and the elephants did most of the work.

The jungle trees were not all ugly and useless, like the riverside draggles of mangrove, or pretty and useless, like the one called the peacock's tail, a solid mass of flame-colored flowers. Some gave edible fruits and nuts, and others were hung with pepper vines, and the one called chaulmugra gave a sap which is the only medicine known for leprosy. Others yielded good hardwood lumber—the black abnus, the speckled kinam, the golden saka which, when the wood has seasoned to a rich, mottled brown, is known as teak. I might record that teakwood looks much more handsome in the form of a ship's decking and planking than it does in its natural state. The teak trees were tall and as straight as ledger lines, but dingy gray of bark, with only scraggly branches and sparse and untidy leaves.

I might also remark that the Mien people were no adornment to the landscape, either. They were ugly, squat and dumpy, most of the men being a good two handspans shorter than myself, and the women a hand or so shorter than that. Even in their daily toil, as I said, the men put most of the labor onto their elephants, and at all other times the men were idle slovens and the women limp slatterns. In Ava's tropical climate, they had no real need of clothes, but they could have contrived some costume more comely than they had done. Both sexes wore woven-fiber hats like large mushroom tops, but were otherwise bare from the waist up and the knees down, wearing a drab cloth wrapped around them like a skirt. The women, indifferent to their flapping dugs, did add one article for modesty's sake. Each wore a sash with long ends, weighted with beads and hanging front and rear, so that it dangled to screen her private parts when she sat in a squat, which was her customary position. Both sexes would put cloth sleeves on their calves when they had to wade in the river, as protection against the leeches. But they always went barefoot, their feet having got so horny-hard that they were proof against any irritant. As I recall, I saw just two men in that whole region who owned shoes. They wore them slung on a string around their neck, for preservation of such rarities.

The men of the Mien were unlovely enough as they stood, but they had devised a means of making themselves even more so. They smirched their skin with colored pictures and patterns. I do not mean paint, but a coloring pricked into and under the skin, and ineradicable ever after. It was done with a sharp sliver of zhu-gan and the soot from burned sesame oil. The soot was black, but put under the skin it showed as blue dots and lines. There were so-called artists in that craft, who traveled from village to village, and were welcome everywhere, for a Mien man would be considered effeminate if he were not decorated like a qali carpet. The pricking was begun in boyhood and, with time off for rest between the painful sessions, was continued until he was latticed with blue patterns from knees to waist. Then, if he was really vain, and could afford the artist's further ministrations, a man would have other designs done, in some kind of red pigment, in among the blue, and was considered handsome indeed.

That ugliness was reserved to the males, but they generously let the females share in another one: the unsightly habit of constantly chewing. Indeed, I believe the jungle Mien did their forestry work only so they could afford to purchase another tree product—a chewable one— that they could not grow, but had to import. It was the nut of a tree called the areca, which was found only in seacoast regions. The Mien bought those nuts, boiled them, sliced them and let them dry black in the sun. Whenever they felt like having a treat—which was all the time— they would take a slice of the areca nut, dab a little lime on it, roll it in a leaf of a vine called the betel, pop that wad into the mouth and chew it—or rather, chew a constant succession of wads—the whole day long. It was to the Mien what the cud is to cows: their only diversion, their only enjoyment, the only activity they engaged in that was not absolutely necessary to existence. A village full of Mien men, women and children was not pretty. It was not made prettier by the sight of all of them champing their jaws up and down and about.

Even that was not the extremity of their deliberate self-defilement. The chewing of a wad of areca and betel had the further effect of making the chewer's saliva bright red. Since a Mien child began chewing as soon as it was off the teat, it grew up to have gums and lips as red as open sores, and teeth as dark and corrugated as teak bark. Just as the Mien accounted handsome a man who elaborated on his already awful body colors, they accounted beautiful a woman who put a coat of lacquer on her already teak-bark teeth and thereby colored them absolutely dead black. The first time a Mien beauty gave me a smile all tar-black and ulcer-red, I reeled backward in revulsion. When I recovered, I asked

Yissun the motive for that ghastly disfigurement. He asked the woman, and relayed to me her haughty response:

"Why, *white* teeth are for dogs and monkeys!"

Speaking of whiteness, I would have expected those people to show some surprise or even fright at my approach—since I must have been the first white man ever seen in the Ava nation. But they evinced no emotion whatever. I might have been one of the less fearsome nat, and an inept one, which had chosen to appear in a defectively colorless human-body disguise. But neither did the Mien show any resentment, fear or loathing of Yissun and our boatmen, though they were all aware that the Mongols had recently conquered their country. When I remarked on their lackadaisical attitude, they only shrugged and repeated—and Yissun translated—what I took to be a Mien peasant proverb:

"When the karbau fight, it is the grass that gets trampled."

And when I inquired if they were not dismayed because their king had fled into hiding, they only shrugged and repeated what they said was a traditional peasant prayer: "Spare us the five evils," and then enumerated the five: "Flood, fire, thieves, enemies and kings."

When I inquired of one village's headman, who seemed a degree more intelligent than the village's karbau oxen, what he could tell me of the history of his Mien people, this is what Yissun relayed to me:

"Amè, U Polo! Our great people once had a splendid history and a glorious heritage. It was all written down in books, in our poetic Mien language. But there came a great famine, and the books were boiled and sauced and eaten, so now we remember nothing of our history and know nothing of writing."

He did not elucidate further, and neither can I, except to explain that "amè!" was the Mien's favorite exclamation and expletive and profanity (though it meant nothing but "mother") and "U Polo" was their way of addressing me respectfully. They entitled me "U" and Hui-sheng "Daw," which was their equivalent of saying Messere e Madona Polo. As for the story of the history books' having been "sauced and eaten," I can verify at least this much. The Mien did have a sauce that was their favorite food—they used it as often as they uttered "amè!"—and it was a stinking, revolting, absolutely nauseous liquid condiment which they expressed from *fermented fish*. The sauce was called nuoc-mam, and they slathered it on their rice, their pork and chicken, their vegetables, on everything they ate. Since nuoc-mam made everything taste ghastlily like itself, and since the Mien would eat any ghastlily thing if it had nouc-mam poured on it, I did not for a moment disbelieve that they could have "sauced and eaten" all their historical archives.

We came one evening to a village where the inhabitants were, most unnaturally, *not* being phlegmatic and idle, but were leaping about in great excitement. They were all women and children, so I bade Yissun inquire what was happening and where all the men had gone to.

"They say the men have caught a badak-gajah—a unicorn—and should shortly be fetching it in."

Well, that news excited even me. As far away as Venice, unicorns were known by repute, and some people believed in their existence, and others regarded them as mythical creatures, but all thought fondly and admiringly of the *idea* of unicorns. In Kithai and Manzi, I had known many men—usually those well along in years—to ingest a medicine made of powdered "horn of unicorn," as an enhancer of virility. The medicine was scarce and only seldom available, and prodigiously costly, so that gave some evidence that unicorns really existed, and were as rare as the legends said they were.

On the other hand, the legends told in Venice and Kithai alike, and the pictures artists drew, depicted the unicorn as a beautiful, graceful, horse- or deerlike animal with a long, sharp, twisted, single golden horn springing from its forehead. Somehow I had doubts that this Ava unicorn could be the same. For one thing, it was hard to conceive of such a dreamlike creature living in these nightmarish jungles, and letting itself be caught by the dullard Mien. For another, that local name, badak-gajah, translated only as "an animal as big as an elephant," which did not sound right at all.

"Ask them, Yissun, if they take the unicorn by setting out a virgin maiden to entice it to capture."

He asked, and I could see the blank looks with which that query was received, and several of the women murmured "amè!" so I was not surprised when he reported that no, they had never had opportunity to try that method.

"Ah," I said. "The unicorns are that scarce, are they?"

"The virgins are that scarce."

"Well, let us see how they do take the creature. Can someone show us where it is now?"

A little naked boy, running almost energetically ahead of us, led me and Hui-sheng and Yissun there, to a mud flat near the river. Unaccountably, a vast pile of rubbish was burning furiously in the very middle of the mud, and all the village men, exhibiting none of their usual torpor, were actually dancing around the fire. There was no sign of any unicorn, or any other animal, caught or not. Yissun asked about and reported to me:

"The badak-gajah, like the karbau ox and the ghariyal serpent, likes to sleep in the coolness of the mud. These men, early this dawn, found one here asleep, only its horn and nostrils visible above the surface. They took it in their usual manner. Moving quietly, they piled over the spot reeds and cane and dry grass, and set it afire. The beast awoke, of course, but could not wallow loose of the mud before the fire began to crust it, and the smoke quickly rendered the unicorn unconscious."

I exclaimed, "What a dreadful way to treat an animal of so many pretty legends! So then they made it captive, I suppose. Where is it?"

"Not captive. It is still under there. In the mud under the fire. Baking."

"What?" I cried. "They are *baking* the *unicorn*?"

"These people are Buddhists, and Buddhism forbids their hunting and killing any wild animal. But their religion cannot hold them to account if the animal simply suffocates and then cooks, all by itself. They then can eat it without committing any sacrilege."

"*Eat a unicorn?* I cannot conceive of a worse sacrilege!"

However, when the sacrilege was finally concluded, and the middle of the mud flat had baked to pottery hardness, and the Mien chipped it apart and revealed the cooked animal, I saw that it was not a unicorn— anyway, not the unicorn of legend. The only thing it had in common with the stories and the pictures was its single horn. But that grew not from its forehead, it grew out of an ugly long snout. The rest of the animal was just as ugly and, though nowhere near as big as an elephant, at least as big as a karbau. It did not resemble a horse or a deer, or my image of a unicorn, or anything else I had ever seen. It had a leathery skin that was all in plates and folds, rather like cuirbouilli armor. Its feet were vaguely elephantine in shape, but its ears were only little tufts, and the long snout had an overhanging upper lip, but no trunk.

The whole animal had been cooked quite black by the mud baking, so I could not say what its original color was. But the single horn had never been golden. In fact, as I could see when the Mien carefully sawed it off the animal's casklike head, it was not really made of horn substance at all, nor of ivory, like a tusk. It seemed merely a compaction of long hairs all grown in a hard, heavy clump that rose to a blunt point. But the Mien assured me, with much exuberance at their good fortune, that this really was the source of the "horn of unicorn" virility enhancer, and they would receive much payment for it—by which I daresay they meant an ample exchange in areca nuts.

Their headman took possession of the precious horn, and the others began to skin off the heavy hide and cut up the carcass and bear the steaming portions back to the village. One of the men handed to me and Hui-sheng and Yissun each a piece of the meat—straight from the oven, so to speak—and we all found it tasty, though somewhat stringily fibrous. We looked forward to sharing the Mien's evening meal, but we returned to the village to find that every last morsel of the unicorn meat had been drenched in the reeking nuoc-mam sauce. So we declined to join in, and instead that night ate some fish our boatmen had caught from the river.

Although the Mien claimed to be Buddhists, the only remotely religious behavior we saw for a long time was their fearful and fretful concern about the surrounding nat demons. The Mien addressed their children, whatever their names, as "Worm" and "Pig," so the nat would deem them beneath notice. Although there was plenty of oil locally available—oil of fish and sesame and even naft oil seeping from the jungle ground in places—the Mien would never grease their elephants' harness or their cart and barrow wheels. They said the squeaking kept the nat away. In one village, where I saw that the women had to carry water from a distant spring, I suggested building a conduit of split zhu-gan cane to bring the water right into the village. "Amè!" cried the villagers; that would bring the spring's resident "water nat" too dangerously close to human habitation. The first time the Mien saw Hui-sheng light her incense burner in our camp at bedtime, they muttered "amè!" and got Yissun to tell us that they never employed incense or perfumes— as if we needed to be told that—for fear sweet smells might attract the nat.

However, as our company got farther down the Irawadi, into more populous country, we began to find in many villages a mud-brick temple. It was called a p'hra, and it was circular, shaped like a large hand bell with its mouth on the ground and its steeple-handle sticking up in the air, and in each p'hra lived a Buddhist lama, here called a pongyi. Each was shaven-headed and yellow-robed, each was disapproving of this world and his fellow Mien and life in general, and was morosely impatient to get out of Ava and on to Nirvana. But I met one who was at least convivial enough to converse with Yissun and me. That pongyi proved to be so educated that he could even write, and he showed me how the Mien writing was done. He could not add anything to the tale I had heard—that the Mien's earlier history had ended in their bellies—but he did know that writing had been nonexistent in Ava until less than two hundred years ago, when the nation's then King Kyansitha, all by himself, invented an alphabet.

"The good king was careful," he said, "not to make any of the letters angular in shape." He drew them for us with a finger in the dusty yard of his p'hra. "Our people have nothing to write on but leaves, and only sticks to scratch on them with, and angular characters might tear the leaves. So, you see, all the letters are rounded and easy-flowing."

"Cazza beta!" I blurted. "Even the *language* is lazy!"

Until now, I had been blaming the Mien people's lassitude and slovenliness on the Ava climate, which God knows was oppressive and enervating. But the friendly pongyi volunteered the real and astonishing and terrible truth about the Mien. They had taken that name, he said, when they first came to Champa and settled this country that was now the Ava nation—and that had happened, he said, only about four hundred years ago.

"Who were they originally?" I asked. "Where did they come from?"

He said, "From To-Bhot."

Well, that explained the Mien! They were really nothing but a displaced overflow of To-Bhot's wretched Bho. And if the Bho could be lethargic of both intellect and energy, up in the bracing clean air of their native highlands, it was no wonder that, down here in the vigor-sapping hot low country, they should have degenerated even further—to where their only willful exertion was a bovine chewing and their most strenuous profanity was a milk-mild "mother!" and even their king's writing was limp.

In all charity, I have to say that not much ambition and vitality can rightly be expected of any people who live in a tropical climate and jungle conditions. It must take all their will just to exist at all. I myself was not usually a sluggard, but in Ava I felt always drained of strength and purpose, and even my usually pert and lively Hui-sheng got quite languid in her movements. I had known heat in other places, but never such a damp, heavy, dragging-down heat as I felt in Ava. I might as well have wrung a blanket in hot water, then flung it over my head so that I had both to wear it and try to breathe through it.

The cloacal climate would have been affliction enough, but it bred various other torments, chief among them the jungle vermin. During the daytimes, our barge went downriver in a thick accompanying cloud of mosquitoes. We could reach out and catch them by handfuls, and their massed buzzing was as loud as the snores of the ghariyal serpents on the mudbanks, and their biting was so continuous that it eventually and blessedly induced a sort of numb indifference. When any of our men stepped into the river shallows while beaching the barge at evening, he stepped out again with his legs and garments striped black and red, the black being long, slimy, clinging leeches that had fastened to him, right through the fabric of his clothes, sucking so avidly that they drooled streaks of his blood. Then, on land, we might be attacked either by enormous red ants or by darting oxflies, either insect's bite so painful that, we were told, they could drive even elephants to mad rampage. Nighttime brought little respite, because all the ground was infested with a breed of fleas so tiny they could hardly be seen and never be caught, but whose bite raised an enormous welt. Hui-sheng's incense smoke gave us some relief from the night-flying insects, and we did not care how many nat it might attract.

I do not know whether it was because of the heat, the humidity or the insects, or all those miseries, but many people in that jungle suffered from illnesses that seemed never to conclude either in death or recovery. (The people of Yun-nan referred to the whole of Champa as "the Valley of Fever.") Two of our sturdy Mongol boatmen fell to one of those maladies, or maybe several, and Yissun and I had to take over their chores. The men's gums bled almost as red as those of a Mien cud-chewer, and much of their hair fell out. Under their arms and between their legs the skin began to rot, getting green and crumbly, like cheese going bad. Some kind of fungus attacked their fingers and toes, so that their fingernails and toenails got soft and moist and painful, and often bled.

Yissun and I asked a Mien village headman for advice from his own experience, and he told us to rub pepper into the men's sores. When I protested that that was bound to cause excruciating pain, he said, "Amè, of course, U Polo. But it will hurt the disease nat even worse, and the demon may depart."

Our Mongols bore that treatment stoically enough, but so did the nat, and the men stayed ill and prostrate all the way downriver. At least they, and we other men, did not contract another jungle affliction I heard about. Numerous Mien men confided dolefully to us that they suffered from it, and always would. They called it koro, and they described its very terrible effect: a sudden and dramatic and irreversible shrinking of the virile organ, a retraction of it up into the body. I did not inquire for further details, but I could not help wondering if the jungle koro was related to the fly-borne kala-azar that had commenced my Uncle Mafìo's pathetic dissolution.

For a time, Yissun and Hui-sheng and her Mongol maid and I took turns tending our two sick men. From our experience and observation so far, we had got the impression that the jungle's diseases troubled only the male sex, and Yissun and I were not much inclined to worry about ourselves. But when the maidservant also started to show signs of illness, I made Hui-sheng leave off her nursing, and confine herself to the farthest end of the barge, and sleep well apart from the rest of us at night. Meanwhile, our best efforts did not improve the condition of the two men. They were still ill and flaccid and gaunt when we finally reached Pagan, and they had to be carried ashore to be put in the care of their army's shamàn-physicians. I do not know what became of them after that, but at least they survived to get that far. Hui-sheng's maid did not.

Her ailment had seemed identical to that of the men, but she had been much more troubled and dismayed by it. I suppose, being a female, she was naturally more frightened and embarrassed when she began to rot at her extremities and under her arms and between her legs. However, she also began to complain, which the men had not, of itching all over her body. Even *inside* it, she said, which we took to be delirium. But Yissun and I gently undressed her and found, here and there, what looked like grains of rice stuck to her skin. When we tried to pick them off, we discovered that they were only the protruding ends—heads or tails, we could not tell—of long, thin worms that had burrowed deep into her flesh. We tugged, and they came out reluctantly, and kept coming, span after span, as we might have unspooled a web-thread from the spinneret of a spider's body.

The poor woman wept and shrieked and weakly writhed during most of the time we were doing that. Each worm was no thicker than a string, but easily as long as my leg, greenish-white in color, slick to our touch, hard to grasp and resisting our pull, and there were many of them, and even the hardened Mongol Yissun and I could not help retching violently while we did that hand-over-hand hauling out of the worms and throwing them overboard. When we had done, the woman was no longer squirming, but lay still in death. Perhaps the worms had been coiled around organs inside her, and our pulling had disarranged those parts and thereby killed her. But I am disposed to believe that she died from the sheer horror of the experience. Anyway, to spare her any further miseries—because we had heard that the funeral practices of the Mien were barbaric—we rowed ashore at a deserted spot, and buried her deep, well out of reach of the ghariyals or any other jungle predators.

. 2 .

I was glad to see the Orlok Bayan again. I was even glad to see his teeth. Their garish glare of porcelain and gold was far more sightly than the snaggled and blackened teeth of the Mien I had been seeing all the way down the Irawadi. Bayan was somewhat older than my father, and he had lost some hair and added some girth since our campaign together, but he was still as leathery and supple as his own old armor. He was also, at the moment, slightly drunk.

"By Tengri, Marco, but *you* have put on great beauty since I saw you last!" He bawled that at me, but he was ogling Hui-sheng at my side. When I introduced her, she smiled a little nervously at him, for Bayan was on the throne of the King of Ava, in the throne room of the palace of Pagan, but he was not looking very kinglike. He was half-lying asprawl on the throne, guzzling from a jeweled cup, and his eyes were vividly bloodshot.

"Found the king's wine cellar," he said. "No kumis or arkhi, but something called choum-choum. Made of rice, they tell me, but I think it is really compounded of earthquake and avalanche. Hui, Marco! Remember our avalanche? Here, have some." He snapped his fingers, and a barefoot, bare-chested servant hurried to pour me a cup.

"What has become of the king, then?" I asked.

"Threw away his throne, his people's respect, his name and his life," said Bayan, smacking his lips. "He was King Narasinha-pati until he fled. Now his former subjects all call him contemptuously Tayok-pyemin, which means the King Who Ran Away. By comparison, they almost like having us here. The king fled west as we approached, over to Akyab, the port city on the Bay of Bangala. We thought he would escape by ship, but he just stayed there. Eating and calling for more and more food. He ate himself to death. A singular way to go."

"That sounds like a Mien," I said disgustedly.

"Yes, it does. But he was not a Mien. The royal family was of Bangali stock, originally from India. That is why we thought he would escape to there. Anyway, Ava is now ours, and I am Acting Wang of Ava until Kubilai sends a son or something to be my permanent replacement. If you see the Khakhan before I do, tell him to send somebody of frosty blood who can endure this infernal climate. And tell him to hurry. My sardars are now fighting over east, in Muang Thai, and I want to join them."

Hui-sheng and I were given a grand suite in the palace, together with some of the late royal family's exceptionally obsequious servants. I asked Yissun to take one of our many bedrooms and stay nearby as my interpreter. Hui-sheng, being now bereft of a personal maid, chose a new one from the staff given us, a girl of seventeen, of the race sometimes called Shan and sometimes Thai. Her name was Arùn, or Dawn, and she was almost as comely of face as was her new mistress.

In our bathing chamber, which was as big and as well-equipped as a Persian hammam, the maid helped Hui-sheng and me, together, to bathe several times over, until we felt clean of our encrustation of jungle, and then helped us dress. For me, there was just a length of brocade silk to be wrapped around me, skirt fashion. Hui-sheng's costume was much the same, except that it wrapped high enough to cover her breasts. Arùn, without shyness, opened and rewrapped her own single garment several times, not to show us that it was all she wore, but to show us how to wrap ours so they would stay on. Nevertheless, I took the opportunity to admire the girl's body, which was as fair as her name, and Hui-sheng made a face at me when she noticed, and I grinned and Arùn giggled. We were given no shoes or even slippers; everyone in the palace went barefoot, except the heavy-booted Bayan, and I later put on boots only when I went outdoors. Arùn did bring one other item of dress; earrings for both of us. But, since our ears were not bored for them, we could not wear them.

When Hui-sheng had, with Arùn's help, fetchingly arranged her hair and fixed flowers in it, we went downstairs again, to the palace's dining hall, where Bayan had commanded a welcoming feast for us. We were not much accustomed to eating at midday, which it then was, but I was looking forward to some decent food after our hard rations on the voyage, and I was a trifle dismayed to see what was set before us—black meat and purple rice.

"By Tengri," I growled to Bayan. "I knew the Mien blacked their teeth, but I never noticed that they also blacked the food to go between their teeth."

"Eat, Marco," he said complacently. "The meat is chicken, and the chickens of Ava have not only black plumage, but black skin, black flesh, black everything except their eggs. Never mind how the bird looks, it is cooked in the milk of the India nut, and is delicious. The rice is only rice, but in this land it grows in gaudy colors—indigo, yellow, bright red. Today we have purple. It is good. Eat, Drink." And with his own hand, he poured a brimming beaker of the rice liquor for Hui-sheng.

We did eat, and the meal was very good. In that country, even at the Pagan palace, there were no such things as nimble tongs or any other table implements. Eating was done with the fingers, which is how Bayan would have done it anyway. He sat taking alternately handfuls of the flamboyant food and great drafts of choum-choum—Hui-sheng and I only sipped at ours, for it was highly potent—while I told of our adventures on the Irawadi, and the considerable distaste I had developed for the inhabitants of Ava.

"In the river plain, you saw only the misbegotten Mien," said Bayan. "But you might think more kindly even of them, if you had come through the hill country, and seen the real aboriginal natives of these lands. The Padaung, for instance. Their females start in childhood to wear a brass ring around the neck, and add another above that, and another and another, until in womanhood they have a brass-ringed neck as long as a camel's. Or the Moi people. *Their* women bore holes in their earlobes and put increasingly large ornaments in the holes, until the lobes are distended to hoops that can hold a platter. I saw one Moi woman with earlobes she had to put her arms through, to keep them out of her way."

I assumed Bayan was only drunkenly babbling, but I listened respectfully. And I later realized, when I saw actual specimens of those barbarian tribes on the streets of Pagan itself, that he had been telling only sober truth.

"All those are country folk," he went on. "The city dwellers are a

better mixture. Some visiting aborigines and Mien, a few Indian immigrants, but mostly the more civilized and cultured people called Myama.
They have long been the nobility and upper classes of Ava, and they are
far superior to all the others. The Myama have even had the good sense
not to take their inferior neighbors as servants or slaves. They have always gone afield and got Shan for those purposes, the Shan—or Thai, if
you prefer—being notably more handsome and cleanly and intelligent
than any of the lesser local races."

"Yes, I have just now encountered one Thai," I said, and added,
since Hui-sheng could not hear and object, "a Thai girl who is indeed a
superb creature."

"It was on account of them that I came to Ava," said Bayan. I
already knew that, but I did not interrupt. "They *are* worthy people.
People worth keeping. And too many of them had been deserting our
dominions, fleeing to the nation they call Muang Thai, Land of the Free.
The Khanate wishes them to remain Shan, not turn Thai. That is, not go
free, but remain subjects of the Khanate."

"I understand the Khanate's view," I said. "But if there really is a
whole land full of such beautiful people, I should wish that it could go
on existing."

"Oh, it can go on existing," said Bayan, "as long as it is ours. Let me
but take the capital, a place called Chiang-Rai, and accept their king's
surrender, and I will not lay waste the rest of the country. That way it
will be a permanent source of the finest slaves, to serve and to adorn the
rest of the Khanate. Hui! But enough of politics." He shoved aside his
still-heaped plate and licked his lips most slaveringly and said, "Here
comes our sweet to conclude our meal. The durian."

That was another dubious surprise. The sweet looked to be a melon
with a spikily armored rind, but, when the table steward cut it, I saw
that it had large seeds inside, like chicken's eggs, and the odor that
erupted from it nearly made me shove back from the table.

"Yes, yes," Bayan said testily. "Before you complain, I already know
about the stink. But this is durian."

"Does the word mean carrion? That is what it smells like."

"It is the fruit of the durian tree. It has the most repellent smell of
any fruit, and the most captivating taste. Ignore the stench and eat."

Hui-sheng and I looked at each other, and she looked as distressed
as I probably did. But the male must show courage before his female. I
took up a slice of the cream-colored fruit and, trying not to inhale, took a
bite of it. Bayan was right again. The durian had a taste unlike anything
I ever ate, before or since. I can taste it yet, but how do I describe it?
Like a custard made of cream and butter, and flavored with almonds—
but with that taste came hints of other flavors, most unexpected: wine
and cheese and even shallots. It was not sweet and juicy, like a hami
melon, nor a tart refreshment, like a sharbat, but it partook of those
qualities and—providing one could persevere past the rank odor of it—
the durian was a most delightful novelty.

"Many people get addicted to the eating of durian," said Bayan. He
must have been one of them, for he was gorging on it, and talking with

his mouth full. "They loathe the hideous climate of Champa, but they stay for the durian alone, because it grows nowhere except in this corner of the world." And again he was right. Both Hui-sheng and I would become ardent enthusiasts of the fruit. "And it is more than refreshing and delicious," he went on. "It incites and excites other appetites. There is a saying here in Ava: when the durian falls, the skirts go up." That was true, too, as Hui-sheng and I would later prove.

When we were all at last satiated with the fruit, Bayan leaned back and wiped his mouth on his sleeve and said, "So. It is good to have you here, Marco, especially when you come so handsomely accompanied." He reached out to pat Hui-sheng's hand. "But how long will you and she stay? What are your plans?"

"I have none at all," I said, "now that I have delivered the Khakhan's letters to you. Except that I did promise Kubilai I would bring him a memento from this new province of his. Something unique to this place."

"Hm," Bayan said reflectively. "Offhand, I can think of nothing better than a gift basket of durian, but they would spoil on the long road. Well, now. The day is getting on for evening, and that is the coolest time for walking. Take your good lady and your interpreter and stroll about Pagan. If anything strikes your fancy, it is yours."

I thanked him for the generous offer. As Hui-sheng and I got up to go, he added, "When it is dark, come back here to the palace. The Myama are great devotees of play-acting, and very good at it, and a troupe of them have been putting on a most beguiling play for me in the throne room each night. I do not understand a bit of it, of course, but I can assure you it is no trivial story. It is now in its eighth night, and the actors eagerly anticipate getting to the crucial scenes of it in just two or three nights more."

When Yissun joined us, he had with him the yellow-robed chief pongyi of the palace. That elderly gentleman kindly walked with us and, speaking through Yissun, explained many things that I might not otherwise have comprehended, and I was able to relay the explanations to Hui-sheng. The pongyi began by directing our attention to the exterior of the palace itself. That was an agglomeration of two- and three-storied buildings, almost equal in extent and splendor to the palace of Khanbalik. It was built somewhat in the Han style of architecture but, I might say, in a very refined essence of the Han style. All the buildings' walls and columns and lintels and such were, like those of the Han, much carved and sculptured and convoluted and filigreed, but in a manner more delicate. They reminded me of the reticella lace of Venice's Burano. And the dragon-ridge roof lines, instead of curving upward in a gentle swoop, soared more sharply and pointedly toward the sky.

The pongyi laid his hand on one finely finished outer wall and asked if we could tell what it was made of. I said, marveling, "It appears to have been worked from one vast piece of stone. A piece the size of a cliff."

"No." Yissun translated the explanation. "The wall is of brick, a multitude of separate bricks, but no one nowadays knows how it was done. It was made long ago, in the days of the Cham artisans, who had a secret process of somehow baking the bricks *after* they were laid in courses, to give this effect of one smooth and uninterrupted stone face."

Next he took us to an inner garden court, and asked if we could tell what it represented. It was square, as big as a market square, and bordered with flower banks and beds, but the whole interior of it was a lawn of well-kept grass. I should say a lawn of two different varieties of grass, one pale green, one very dark, and the two seeded in alternate smaller squares, in a checkered effect. I could only venture, "It is for ornament. What else?"

"For a purpose of utility, U Polo," said the pongyi. "The King Who Ran Away was an avid player of the game called Min Tranj. Min is our word for king and Tranj means war, and—"

"Of course!" I exclaimed. "The same as the War of the Shahi. So this is an immense outdoor playing board. Why, the king must have had playing pieces as large as himself."

"He did. He had subjects and slaves. For everyday games, he himself would represent one Min and a favorite courtier would be the opposing other. Slaves would be made to put on the masks and costumes of the various other pieces—the General on either side, and each side's two elephants, horsemen and warriors and foot soldiers. Then the two Min would direct the play, and each piece that was lost was literally lost. Amè! Removed from the board and beheaded—yonder, among the flowers."

"Porco Dio," I murmured.

"However, if the Min—the real king, that is—got displeased with some courtier or some number of them, he would make *them* put on the costumes of the foot soldiers in the front ranks. It was, in a way, more merciful than simply ordering their decapitation, since they could have some hope of surviving the game and keeping their heads. But, sad to say, on those occasions the king would play most recklessly, and it was seldom—amè!—that the flower beds did not get well watered with blood."

We spent the rest of that afternoon wandering among Pagan's p'hra temples, those circular buildings like set-down hand bells. I daresay a really devout explorer could have spent his whole lifetime wandering among them, without ever getting to see them all. The city might have been the workshop of some Buddhist deity who was charged with the making of those odd-shaped temples, for there was a whole forest of their steeple-handles sticking up from the river plain there, stretching some twenty-five li up and down the Irawadi and extending six or seven li inland on both sides of the river. Our pongyi guide said proudly that there were more than one thousand three hundred of the p'hra, each crammed with images and each surrounded by a score or more of lesser monuments, idol statues and sculptured columns he called thupo.

"Evidence," he said, "of the great holiness of this city and the piety of all its inhabitants, past and present, who built these edifices. The rich people pay for their erection, and the poor find gainful employment in doing so, and both classes earn eternal merit. Which is why, here in

Pagan, one cannot move a hand or foot without touching some sacred thing."

But I could not help noticing that only about a third of the buildings and monuments appeared in good repair, and all the remainder were in various stages of decrepitude. Indeed, as the brief tropical twilight came on, and temple bells rang out across the plain, calling to Pagan's worshipers, the people filed into only the better-kept few p'hra, while out of the many broken and crumbling ones came long skeins of flittering bats, like plumes of black smoke against the purpling sky. I remarked that the local piety did not seem to extend to the preservation of holiness.

"Well, really, U Polo," the old pongyi said, with a touch of asperity. "Our religion confers great merit on those who build a holy monument, but little on those who merely repair one. So, even if a wealthy noble or merchant cared to waste his merit on such an activity, the poor would be unwilling to do the work. Naturally, all would rather build even a very small thupo than tend to the repair of even the largest p'hra."

"I see," I said drily. "A religion of good business practices."

We wended our way back to the palace as the night came swiftly down. We had done our wandering, as Bayan had said, at the time of day that was cool by Ava standards. Nevertheless, Hui-sheng and I felt again rather sweaty and dusty by the time we got back, and so decided to forgo Bayan's invitation to join him at the night's session of the interminable play that was being performed for him. Instead, we went directly to our own suite, and told the Thai maidservant Arùn to draw us another bath. When the immense teak tub was full of water, perfumed with miada grass and sweetened with gomuti sugar, we both stripped off our silks and got into it together.

The maid, while getting in hand her washcloths and brushes and unguents and little crock of palm-oil soap, pointed to me and smiled and said, "Kaublau," then smiled again and pointed to Hui-sheng and said, "Saongam." I later learned, by inquiry of others who spoke Thai, that she had called me "handsome" and Hui-sheng "radiantly beautiful." But right then, I could only raise my eyebrows, and so did Hui-sheng, for Arùn took off her own wrapping and prepared to get into the warm water with us. Seeing us exchange looks of some surprise and perplexity, the maid paused to do an elaborate pantomime of explanation. That might have been incomprehensible to most foreigners, but Hui-sheng and I, being ourselves adept at gesture language, managed to understand that the girl was apologizing for not having disrobed with us during our earlier bath. She conveyed that we then had been simply "too dirty" for her to attend us in the nude, as she was supposed to do. If we would forgive her for that earlier evasion of her due participation, she would now attend us in the proper manner. So saying, she slid down into the tub, with her bath equipment, and began to soap Hui-sheng's body.

We had both been often attended in the bath by servants of Hui-sheng's sex, and of course I had often been bathed by servants of my own sex, but this was our first experience of a servant bathing *with* us. Well, other countries, other customs, so we merely exchanged a look of amiable amusement. What harm in it? There was certainly nothing unpleasant about Arùn's participation—quite the contrary, to my mind, for she was a comely person, and I had no objection whatever to being in the company of two beautiful and naked females of different races. The girl Arùn was about the same size as the young woman Hui-sheng, and of very similarly childish figure—budlike breasts and small neat buttocks and so on—differing mainly in that her skin was more of a cream-yellow color, the color of durian flesh, and her "little stars" were fawn-colored instead of rose-colored, and she had the merest feathering of body hair, just along the line where the lips of her pink parts joined.

Since Hui-sheng could not speak, and I could think of nothing pertinent to say, we both were silent, and I simply sat soaking in the perfumed water while, at the other side of the tub, Arùn washed Hui-sheng, and chattered merrily as she did so. I suppose she had not yet realized that Hui-sheng was mute and deaf, for it became apparent that Arùn was taking this opportunity to try teaching us a few rudiments of her own language. She would touch Hui-sheng here, then there, with a dab of soft suds, and pronounce the Thai words for those parts of the body, then touch herself in the same places and repeat the words.

Hui-sheng's hand was a mu, and each finger a niumu, and so were Arùn's. Hui-sheng's shapely leg was a khaa, and her slim foot a tau, and each pearly toe a niutau, and so were Arùn's. Hui-sheng only smiled tolerantly as the girl touched her pom and kiu and jamo—her hair and eyebrows and nose—and she made a silent laugh of appreciation as Arùn touched her lips—baà—and then puckered her own in a kissing way and said, "Jup." But Hui-sheng's eyes widened a bit when the girl touched her breasts and nipples with bubbly suds and identified them as nom and kwanom. And then Hui-sheng blushed most beautifully, because her little stars twinkled erect from the bubbles, as if rejoicing in their new name of kwanom. Arùn laughed aloud when she saw that, and companionably twiddled her own kwanom until they matched Hui-sheng's in prominence.

Then she pointed out the difference between their bodies which I had already noticed. She indicated that she had a very scant trace of hair—this kind called moè—there where Hui-sheng had none. However, she went on, they did have one thing in common thereabouts, and she touched first her own pink parts and then Hui-sheng's, in a lightly lingering way, and said softly, "Hìi." Hui-sheng gave a small jump that rippled the water in the tub, and turned a wondering look on me, and then turned it on the girl, who met it with a smile that was openly provocative and challenging. Arùn sloshed around to face me, as if asking for my approval of her impudence, and pointed to my corresponding organ and laughed and said, "Kwe."

I think Hui-sheng had earlier been only amused, not affronted, by Arùn's irrepressibly jaunty behavior. Perhaps at that latest and frankly fondling touch, she had seemed a little apprehensive of its portent. But now she joined the girl in pointing gleefully at me, and it was my turn to blush, for my kwe had got vigorously aroused by the foregoing events, and was most flagrantly in evidence. I started guiltily to cover it with a washcloth, but Arùn reached over, gently took hold of it with a soapy hand, saying "kwe" again, while, with her other hand under water, continuing to caress Hui-sheng's counterpart and saying again "hìì." Hui-sheng only went on silently laughing, not minding at all, seeming to have begun to take pleasure in the situation. Then Arùn briefly let go of both of us, said joyously, "Aukàn!" and clapped her hands together to show us what she was suggesting.

Hui-sheng and I had had no opportunity to enjoy each other during the voyage from Bhamo to Pagan, and not much inclination either, in the circumstances. We were more than ready to make up for that lost time, but we would never have dreamed of asking for assistance in doing so. We had never required any help before, and we did not now, but we let ourselves accept it—and revel in it. Perhaps it was simply because Arùn was so vivaciously eager to be of service. Or perhaps it was because we were in a new and exotic land, and amenable to the new experiences it offered. Or perhaps the durian and its alleged properties had something to do with it.

I have not before spoken, as I said I would not, of any of the activities private to Hui-sheng and myself, and I will not now. I will only remark that this night we did not exactly comport ourselves in the manner which, long ago, I and the Mongol twins had done. In this event, the extra girl's participation was mainly that of a very busy matchmaker and instructor and manipulator of our various parts, during which she showed us a number of things that were evidently accepted practice among her own people, but new to us. I remember thinking that it was no wonder her people were called Thai, meaning Free. However, either Hui-sheng or I, and usually both of us, always had some part of us otherwise unoccupied, with which to give Arùn pleasure, too, and she clearly found it pleasant, for she was frequently either crooning or exclaiming, "Aukàn! Aukàn!" and "Saongam!" and "Chan pom rak kun!" which means "I love you both!" and "Chakatì pasad!" which I will not tell the meaning of.

We did aukàn again and again, the three of us, on most of the nights Hui-sheng and I remained in the Pagan palace, and often during the days, too, when the weather was too hot for doing anything outdoors. But I best remember that first night—including every least Thai word Arùn taught me—not so much because of what we did, but because, a long while afterward, I had cause to remember one thing I failed to do that night.

· 3 ·

S o m e days later, Yissun came to tell me that he had just discovered the late King of Ava's royal stables, at a distance from the palace, and asked if I would like to visit them. Early the next morning, before the day got hot, he and I and Hui-sheng went there in palanquins borne by slaves. The stable steward and his workers were fond and proud of their kuda and gajah wards—the royal horses and elephants—and eager to show them off to us. Since Hui-sheng was well acquainted with horses, we only admired the fine kuda steeds as we passed through their sumptuous quarters, but spent more time at the gajah stable yard, for she had never before been very close to an elephant.

Evidently the great cow elephants had not been much exercised since the king had run away on one of their sisters, so the stable men were pleased and acquiescent when we inquired, through Yissun, if we might ride a gajah.

"Here," they said, as they brought out a towering one. "You may have the rare honor of riding a sacred *white* elephant."

It was splendidly attired in silk blanket and jeweled head cap and pearl-bedizened harness and a richly carved and gilded teak hauda, but, as I had long ago been told, the white elephant was not at all white. It did have some vaguely human-flesh-colored patches on its wrinkled pale-gray hide, but the steward and the mahawats told us that "white" referred not even to that—"white" when spoken of elephants meant only "special, distinctive, superior." They pointed out some of the features of this one, which, to elephant-men, marked it as well above the ordinary run of elephants. Notice, they said, the pretty way her front legs bowed outward, and how her crupper slanted low behind, and how ponderous was the dewlap hanging from her breast. But here, they said, taking us to view the animal's tail, here was the unmistakable indication that it was worthy of being treated as a holy white elephant. This animal, besides having the usual bristly tuft of hairs at the end of her tail, had also a fringe of hair up both sides of that appendage.

To show off my experience and ease with these beasts, in the way of any man posturing before his mate, I stood Hui-sheng to one side and bade her watch. I borrowed from one of the mahawats his ankus hook, and reached up with it and tapped the elephant in the proper place on her trunk, and she obediently bent it for a stirrup and lowered it for me, and I stepped onto that and was hoisted up to the nape of her neck. Down below, Hui-sheng danced and applauded admiringly, like an excited little girl, and Yissun more sedately cheered, "Hui! Hui!" The steward and the mahawats looked approving of my management of the sacred elephant, and gave waves of their hands to indicate that I might take it away unsupervised. So I beckoned to Hui-sheng, and had the elephant make a stirrup again, and Hui-sheng, with only some pretty flutters of pretended anxiety, was hoisted aboard with me. I helped her into the hauda and turned the elephant by touching an ear with the ankus, then tapped the go-ahead place on the shoulder. And off we went for a swift-striding, pleasantly swaying ride out beyond the innumerable riverside p'hra, along the banyan-lined avenues beside the Irawadi, and some distance out of the city.

When the elephant began to make snuffling and whoofing noises, I guessed that it was scenting ghariyals basking in the river shallows, or perhaps a tiger lurking among the serpentine tangles of banyan trees. I was disinclined to put a sacred white elephant to any risk, and besides the day was heating up, so I turned back for the stables, and we covered

the last several li at an exhilarating full-out run. As I helped Hui-sheng
down from the hauda, I was loud in my thanks to the elephant-men, and
bade Yissun translate my words most fulsomely. Hui-sheng thanked the
men in silence, but with consummate grace, making to each of them the
wai—the gesture of palms together, brought to the face, the head given a
slight nod—which Arùn had taught her.

On the way back to the palace, Yissun and I discussed the notion of
my taking a white elephant back to Khanbalik, to be the unique gift I
had promised to the Khakhan. We agreed that it was a memento distinctive of the Champa lands, and rare even here. But then it occurred to me
that the task of getting an elephant across seven thousand li of difficult
terrain was best left to heroes like Hannibal of Carthage, so I readily
abandoned the notion after Yissun remarked:

"Frankly, Elder Brother Marco, I would never be able to tell a white
elephant from any other, and I doubt that the Khan Kubilai could, and
he already has plenty of other elephants."

It was only midday, but Hui-sheng and I returned to our suite and
directed Arùn to draw us a bath, to get the smell of elephant off us.
(Actually, that is far from being an unpleasant smell; imagine the aroma
of a good leather bag stuffed with sweet hay.) The maid went with
delighted alacrity to fill the teak tub, and got undressed as we did. But,
when Hui-sheng and I were in the water, and Arùn was perched on the
rim of the tub, about to slide in between us, I stopped her there for a
moment. I only wished to make a small jest, for the three of us had got
quite free and easy in each other's presence by this time, and even had
begun to communicate with some facility. I gently parted the girl's
knees, and reached between her legs and ran my fingertip lightly down
the soft trace of hair that fringed the closure of her pink parts, and
called Hui-sheng's attention to it, telling her: "Look—the tail of the
sacred white elephant!"

Hui-sheng dissolved in silent laughter, causing Arùn to look rather
worriedly down to see what might have gone wrong with her body. But
when, with rather more difficulty, I had translated the jest for her, Arùn
too crowed with appreciative laughter. It was probably the first time in
human history, and maybe the last, that a woman good-humoredly took
as flattery her being compared to an elephant. In return, Arùn began
calling me, instead of U Marco as heretofore, U Saathvan Gajah. That, I
finally figured out, meant "U Sixty-Year-Old Elephant." But I took that
good-humoredly, too, when she made me understand that it was the
highest sort of compliment. Everywhere in Champa, she said, a bull
elephant of sixty years was taken to represent the very peak of strength,
virility and masculine powers.

A few nights later, Arùn brought some things to show to us—"mata
ling," she called them, which meant "love bells," and she also said, with a
mischievous grin, "aukàn"—so I gathered that she was suggesting these
things as an addition to our nighttime diversions. She held out a handful
of the mata ling, which looked like tiny camel bells, each about the size
of a hazelnut, made of a good gold alloy. Hui-sheng and I each took one
and shook it, and some kind of pellet inside rang or rattled softly. How-

ever, the things had no openings that would enable their being fastened onto garments or camel harness or anything else, and we could not discern the purpose of them, so we merely regarded Arùn with bewilderment and waited for further explanation.

That took quite a while, with many repetitions and numerous bafflements to be resolved. But Arùn finally explained—mainly by several times uttering the word "kwe" with various gestures—that the mata ling were designed for implantation under the skin of the masculine organ. When I grasped that much, I laughed at what I took to be a jest. But then I grasped that the girl was serious, and I made loud noises of appalled indignation and horror. Hui-sheng motioned for me to hush and be calm, and let Arùn go on explaining. She did—and I think, of all the curiosities I encountered on my journeys, the mata ling must have been the most curious.

They had been invented, said Arùn, by a long-ago Myama Queen of Ava, whose king-husband had been woefully inclined to prefer the company of small boys. The queen made mata ling of brass and—Arùn did not say how—secretly slit the skin of the king's kwe, put in a number of the little bells and sewed him up again. Thereafter, he had not been able to penetrate the small orifices of small boys with his newly massive organ, and had had to make do with the more hospitable hiì receptacle of his queen. Somehow—again Arùn did not say how—the other women of Ava heard of that, and persuaded their own men to follow the royal precedent. At which, both the men and women of Ava found that they were not only being fashionable, but also had infinitely increased their mutual pleasures, the men being prodigiously bigger of circumference than before, and the vibration of the mata ling affording an ineffably new sensation to both partners in the act of aukàn.

The mata ling were still made in Ava, said Arùn, and only in Ava, and only by certain old women who knew how to do the implanting of them safely and painlessly and in the most effective places on the kwe. Every man who could afford one had at least one implanted, and those who could afford more might eventually have a kwe worth more than their money purse, and weighing more. She herself, said Arùn, had formerly had a Myama master whose kwe was like a knotted wooden club, even in repose, and when it was aroused: "Amè!" She added that the love bells had undergone some improvement over the centuries since the queen invented them. For one thing, the Ava physicians had decreed that they be made of incorruptible gold instead of brass, so they would not cause infection under the delicate kwe skin. Also, the old women bellmakers had invented a whole new and exceedingly piquant capability for the mata ling.

Arùn demonstrated for us. Some of the little things were *only* bells or rattles, as we had perceived, their inside pellets vibrating only when they were shaken. Some others, Arùn showed us, lay equally inert when she put them on a table. But then she put one in each of our palms, and closed our hands around them. Hui-sheng and I both started in astonishment when, after a moment, the warmth of our hands seemed to confer life on the little gold objects, as if they had been eggs about to hatch, and they began quivering and twitching *all by themselves.*

That new and improved kind of mata ling, said Arùn, contained some never-dying tiny creature or substance—the old women never would reveal what it was—which ordinarily slept quietly in its little gold shell underneath a man's kwe skin. But when his kwe was inserted in a woman's hìi, the secret sleeper came awake and active and—she solemnly asserted—the man and woman could lie together unmoving, totally still, and yet enjoy, through the agency of that busy little love bell, all the sensations and the mounting excitement and finally the bursting pleasure of consummation. In other words, they could perform aukàn, and over and over again, without the least exertion on their part.

When Arùn had concluded, quite out of breath from her own exertions of explaining, I found her and Hui-sheng regarding me speculatively. I said loudly, "No!" I said it several times and in several different languages, including that of emphatic gestures. The idea of utilizing the mata ling in aukàn was an intriguing one, but I was not going to sneak to some back door in some Pagan back alley and let some hag sorceress meddle with my person, and I made that as plain as I knew how.

Hui-sheng and Arùn pretended to look at me with disappointment and disdain, but really they were trying not to laugh at the vehemence of my refusal. Next, they exchanged a glance, as if to say to each other, "Which of us should speak?" and Arùn gave a slight nod, as if to say that Hui-sheng could more easily communicate with me. So Hui-sheng did, pointing out that the only function of the mata ling was to be put inside the female hìi *with* the male kwe, not necessarily as *part* of it. Would I care to try the experience, she inquired with great delicacy (and no small amusement), by doing only what we did normally, but allowing herself and Arùn to put the little love bells inside themselves beforehand?

Well, of course I could have no objection to that, and before the night was out I had developed a great fondness and enthusiasm for the mata ling, and so had Hui-sheng and Arùn. But again I will draw the curtain of privacy here. I will confide only that I found the love bells such a worthwhile contrivance—and Hui-sheng and Arùn concurred in my opinion—that I naturally thought of making *those* things the "unique gift" I would carry back to Kubilai. But I hesitated to decide definitely on that. One can hardly approach the Khan of All Khans, the most puissant sovereign in all the world, and he a dignified elderly gentleman besides, with the suggestion that he submit to an "improvement" of his venerable organ. . . .

No, I really could not think of any way to present the gift of mata ling that would not cause instant affront, resentment and perhaps an outraged reprisal. However, the very next day, I was relieved to receive an alternative idea, a most appealing one, and I proceeded to act upon it straightaway. A thing unique is one of a kind, and therefore it is an impossibility for anything to be "more unique" than something else. But if the durian fruit was unique in its way, and so was a white elephant, and so were the mata ling love bells, then this new idea was unique among uniquities.

It was the aged palace pongyi who put the idea in my head. He and I and Hui-sheng and Yissun were again strolling about Pagan, while he expatiated on this and that sight we saw. On this day, he led us to the most substantial and holiest and highest regarded p'hra in all of Ava. It was not just one of those hand-bell-shaped affairs, but an enormous and beautiful and really magnificent temple, dazzlingly white, like an edifice built of foam, if it is possible to imagine a pile of foam as big as the Basilica of San Marco, and intricately carved and roofed with gold. It was called Ananda, a word meaning "Endless Bliss," which also had been the name of one of the Buddha's disciples during his lifetime. Indeed, said the pongyi as he showed us around the temple's interior, Ananda had been the Buddha's best-beloved disciple, as John was Jesus's.

"This was the reliquary of the Buddha's tooth," said the pongyi, as we passed a golden casket on an ivory stand. "And here is a statue of the dancing deity Nataraji. The sculpture was originally so perfectly made that *it* began dancing, and when a god dances the earth shudders. Our city was nearly shaken asunder, until the dancing image chipped off a finger in its cavorting, at which it quieted and became only a statue again. Therefore, to this day, all religious images are made with a single deliberate flaw. It will be so trivial that you may never see it, but it is there—just for safety's sake."

"Excuse me, Reverend Pongyi," I said. "But did you, in passing, say that the casket yonder held the Buddha's tooth?"

"It used to," he said sadly.

"A real tooth? Of the Buddha himself? A tooth preserved for seventeen centuries?"

"Yes," he said, and opened the casket to show us the velvet socket where it had lain. "A pilgrim pongyi from the island of Srihalam brought it here, some two hundred years ago, for the dedication of this Ananda temple. It was our most treasured relic."

Hui-sheng expressed surprise at the large size of the tooth's vacated resting place, and conveyed to me that the tooth must have been of a size to occupy the Buddha's whole head. I relayed that rather irreverent remark to Yissun and he to the pongyi.

"Amè, yes, a mighty tooth," said the old gentleman. "Why not? The Buddha was a mighty man. On that same island of Srihalam is still to be seen a footprint he made in a rock. From his foot size, the Buddha is calculated to have been nine forearms tall."

"Amè," I echoed. "That is forty hands. Thirteen feet and a half. The Buddha must have been of the race of Goliath."

"Ah, well, when he comes to earth again, in seven or eight thousand years, we expect him to be *eighty* forearms tall."

"His devotees should have no trouble recognizing him, as we might with Jesus," I said. "But what became of this sacred tooth?"

The pongyi sniffled slightly. "The King Who Ran Away purloined it as he went, and absconded with it. An execrable sacrilege. No one knows why he did it. He was presumed to be fleeing to India, and in India the Buddha is no longer worshiped."

"But the king got only as far as Akyab, and died there," I murmured. "So the tooth might still be among his effects."

The pongyi gave a shrug of hopeful resignation, and went on to show us some more of the Ananda's admirable treasures. But I had already conceived my idea and, as soon as I could politely do so, I terminated our tour for the day, and thanked the pongyi for his kind attentions, and hurried Hui-sheng and Yissun back to the palace, telling them of my idea as we went. At the palace, I asked an immediate audience with the Wang Bayan, and told him, too.

"If I can retrieve the tooth, *that* will be my gift to Kubilai. Though the Buddha is not a god he reveres, still the tooth of a god ought to be a keepsake no other monarch has ever owned. Even in Christendom, though various relics exist—bits of the True Cross, the Holy Nails, the Holy Sudarium—nothing remains of the Corpus Christi except some drops of the Holy Blood. The Khakhan should be most pleased and proud to have the Buddha's very own tooth."

"If you can retrieve it," said Bayan. "Me, I never even got any of my *own* back, or I would not have to wear this torture device in my mouth. How do you intend to go about it?"

"With your permission, Wang Bayan, I shall proceed from here to the seaport of Akyab, and examine the place where the late king died, go through his belongings, interrogate any surviving family. It ought to be there somewhere. Meanwhile, I should like to leave Hui-sheng here, under your protection. I know now that travel through these lands is arduous, and I will not subject her to any more of that until we are ready to return to Khanbalik. She is well attended by her maid and our other servants, if you will give her leave to stay in residence here. I should like to ask the further favor of keeping Yissun with me as my interpreter still. I need only him, and a horse for each of us. I will ride light, that I may ride swiftly."

"You know you need not have asked, Marco, for you carry the Khakhan's pai-tzu plaque, which is all the authority you need. But I thank you for the courtesy of asking, and of course you have my permission, and my promise to see that no harm comes to your lady, and my best wishes for your success in your quest." He concluded with the traditional Mongol farewell: "A good horse to you, and a wide plain, until we meet again."

· 4 ·

My quest turned out to be not easily or quickly accomplished, although I enjoyed generally good fortune and ample assistance. To begin with, I was received at the squalid seaside city of Akyab by the sardar Bayan had set in command of the Mongol occupation forces there, one Shai-

bani. He received me cordially, almost eagerly, at the house he had
appropriated for his residency. It was the best house in Akyab, which
is not to say much for it.

"Sain bina," he said. "It is good to greet you, Elder Brother Marco
Polo. I see that you carry the Khakhan's pai-tzu."

"Sain bina, Sardar Shaibani. Yes, I come on a mission for our mutual Lord Kubilai."

Yissun led our horses around to the stable that occupied the rear
half of the house. Shaibani and I went into the front half, and his aides
set out a meal for us. While we ate, I told him that I was on the trail of
Ava's late King Narasinha-pati, and why I was, and that I sought to
examine the fugitive's remaining effects and to speak with any still-living
members of his entourage.

"It shall be as you desire," said the Sardar. "Also, I am overjoyed to
see you carrying the pai-tzu, for it gives you the authority to settle a
vexatious dispute here in Akyab. It is a question that has caused much
uproar, and divided the çitizenry into opposing factions. They have been
so embroiled in this local fuss that they scarcely paid any attention to our
marching in. And until it is settled, I am balked of imposing any orderly
administration. My men spend all their time breaking up street fights. So
I am very glad you have arrived."

"Well," I said, a little mystified. "Whatever I can do, I will. But my
business concerning the late king must come first."

"This does concern the late king," he said, and added in a growl,
"May the worms gag on his cursed remains! The dispute is over those
very effects and survivors you wish to get hold of—or what is left of
them, anyway. May I explain?"

"I wish you would."

"This Akyab is a wretched and dismal city. You look to be a sensible
man, so I assume you will leave here as soon as you can. I am assigned
here, so I must stay, and I shall try to make it a useful addition to the
Khanate. Now, wretchedness aside, this is a seaport, and in that it is like
all seaport cities. Which is to say, it has two industries to justify its
existence and support its citizens. One is the provision of port facilities—
docks and chandlers and warehouses and such. The other industry, as in
every port city, is the pandering to the appetites of ships' crews while
they lay over here. That means whorehouses, wineshops and games of
chance. But most of Akyab's trade is done with India across the Bay of
Bangala yonder, so most of the visiting mariners are miserable Hindus.
They have no stomach for strong drink and they have not much vigor
between the legs, so they spend all their shore time at the games of
chance. For that reason, the whorehouses and wineshops here are few
and small and poor—and vakh! the whores and the drinks are vile. But
Akyab has several halls of games, and they are the most thriving establishments of this city, and their proprietors are the leading citizens."

"This is all very interesting, Sardar, but I fail to—"

"Only allow me, Elder Brother. You will understand. That King
Who Ran Away—his cowardly action did not make him much loved by
his former subjects. Or by anyone. I am informed that he left Pagan with

a substantial train of elephants and pack animals and wives and children and courtiers and servants and slaves—and all the treasure they all could carry. But every night, on the road, that train dwindled. Under cover of darkness, his courtiers stole away with much of the looted treasure. Servants departed, with whatever they could pilfer. Slaves ran away to freedom. Even the king's wives—including even his Queen First Wife— took their princeling children and vanished. Probably to change their names and hope to start a new life unblemished."

"I almost feel sorry for the poor coward king."

"Meanwhile, just to buy an occasional meal and bed on the road, the fugitive king had to pay heavily to village headmen, innkeepers, everybody, all of them surly and inimical and eager to take advantage of him. I am told that he arrived here in Akyab nearly impoverished and nearly alone, with only one of his lesser and younger wives, a few loyal old servants and a not very heavy purse. This city did not receive him very hospitably, either. He managed to find lodging for himself and his remaining goods and retinue at a waterfront inn. But, if he was to survive, he had to go on farther, over the bay to India, which meant buying passage for himself and his little company. Naturally, any ship's captain demands a stiff price to transport any fugitive, but especially such a desperate one as he—a fleeing king, with the conquering Mongols close behind him. I do not know what price was asked, but it was more than he had."

I nodded. "So he tried to multiply what little he had. He resorted to the halls of games of chance."

"Yes. And, as is well known, misfortune likes to dog the already unfortunate. The king played at dice and, over a matter of some few days only, he lost every last thing he owned. Gold, jewels, wardrobe, belongings. Among them, I imagine, that sacred tooth you are chasing, Elder Brother. His losses were profligate and promiscuous. His crown, his old servants, the relic you speak of, his royal robes—there is no knowing which were won by residents of Akyab here, and which by mariners who have since sailed away."

"Vakh," I said glumly.

"At last the King of Ava was reduced to his own person, and the clothes in which he stood in that hall of games, and one wife waiting forlorn in their waterfront lodgings. And on that last desperate day of play, the king offered to wager *himself*. To become, if he lost, the slave of the winner. I do not know who accepted the wager, or how much wealth he staked against the winning of a king."

"But of course the king lost."

"Of course. All in the hall were already despising him, though he had enriched them no little, and now they despised him even more— they must have curled their lips—when the desolate man said, 'Hold. I have one last property besides myself. I have a beautiful Bangali wife. Without me, she will be destitute. She might as well chance having a master to care for her. I will stake my wife, the Lady Tofaa Devata, on one last throw of the dice.' The wager was taken, the dice were rolled, and he lost."

"Well, that was that," I said. "All gone. A misfortune for me, too. But where was there any cause for dispute?"

"Bear with me, Elder Brother. The king asked one last favor. He begged that, before he surrender himself into slavery, he be let to go and tell the sad news himself to his lady. Even wagering men are men of some compassion. They let him go, by himself, to the waterfront inn. And he was honorable enough to tell the Lady Tofaa bluntly what he had done, and he commanded her to present herself to her new master at the hall of games. She obediently set forth, and the king sat down to table, to have one last meal as a freeman. He gorged and guzzled, to the amazement of the innkeeper, and kept calling for more food, more drink. And finally he turned purple and toppled over in an apoplexy and died."

"So I had heard. But what, then? That was no ground for dispute. The man who won him still owned him, whatever his condition."

"Bear with me still. The Lady Tofaa, as ordered by her husband, presented herself at the hall. They say the winner's eyes lighted up when he saw what a choice slave he had won. She is a young woman, a fairly recent acquisition of the king's, neither a titled queen nor yet mother of any heirs, so she is hardly a valuable property just for her innate royalty. And this city's standards of beauty are not my own, but some men call her beautiful, and all call her cunning, and with that I must agree. For when Tofaa's new master reached to take her hand, she withheld it, long enough to speak to all in the hall. She spoke just one sentence, asked just one question: 'Before my husband wagered me, had he first wagered and lost his own self?' "

Shaibani finally fell silent. I waited a moment and then prodded, "Well?"

"Well, there you are. That was the start of the dispute. Since then, the question has echoed and reechoed all over this misbegotten city, and no two citizens can agree on the answer to it, and one magistrate argues with the next, and even brother has turned against brother, and they fight in the streets. I and my troops marched in not long after the events I have described, and all the litigants keep clamoring at me to settle the contention. I cannot, and frankly I am sick of it, and I am ready to put the whole foul city to the torch, if you cannot resolve it."

"What is to resolve, Sardar?" I said patiently. "You already *said* the king had wagered and lost his own person before he put his wife up at stake. So they both were fairly lost. And dead or alive, willing or unwilling, they belong to their winners."

"Do they? Or rather—since he already went to his funeral pyre— does *she*? That is what you must decide, but you must hear all the arguments. I took the lady into custody, pending resolution of the case. I have her in a room upstairs. I can fetch her down and also send for all the men who were gaming in the hall that day. If you will consent, Elder Brother, to be a one-man Cheng this once, it will at the same time give you your best opportunity for inquiring into the whereabouts of that tooth you seek."

"You are right. Very well, bring them on. And please send in my man Yissun to interpret for me."

The Lady Tofaa Devata, though her name meant Gift of the Gods, was not beautiful by my standards, either. She was about Hui-sheng's age, but she was ample enough to have made two of Hui-sheng. Shaibani had called her a Bangali, and evidently the King of Ava had imported her from that Indian state of Bangala, for she was typically Hindu: an oily brown skin that was almost black, and indeed *was* black in a semicircle under each of her eyes. I thought at first that she had misapplied her al-kohl eyelid-darkening cosmetic, but I was later to see that almost all Hindus, men as well as women, naturally had that unsightly discoloration of each eye pouch. The Lady Tofaa also had a red measle of paint on her forehead between her eyes, and a hole in one nostril where presumably she had worn a bauble before it was lost by her dicing husband. She wore a costume that appeared to be (and was, I discovered) a single length of cloth wound several times about her amplitude in such a way that her arms, one shoulder and a roll of unctuous dark-brown flesh around her waist were left bare. It was not a very seductive baring, and the cloth was a garish fabric of many blatant colors and metallic threads. The lady and her attire gave a general impression, besides, of being somewhat unwashed, but I gallantly attributed that to the hard times she had suffered lately. I might find her unappealing, but I would not prejudge her case on that account.

Anyway, the other claimants and witnesses and counselors in the Sardar's main room were considerably less prepossessing. They were of various races—Mien, Hindu, some Ava aborigines, maybe even some of the higher-class Myama—but hardly choice specimens of any. They were the usual assortment of layabouts that wait to prey on seamen in the waterfront alleys of any port city. Again I felt almost sorry for the pusillanimous King Who Ran Away, having pitched himself from a throne down among such base company as this. But neither would I prejudge this case because I found *all* the participants so unappealing.

I was acquainted with one rule of law in these regions: that a woman's testimony was to be far less regarded than a man's. So I motioned for the men first to have their say, and Yissun translated, as one ugly man stepped forward and deposed:

"My Lord Justice, the late king wagered his person, and I hazarded a stake he accepted, and the dice rolled in my favor. I won him, but he later cheated me of my winnings when—"

"Enough," I said. "We are concerned here only with the events in the hall of games. Let speak next the man who played next against the king."

An even uglier one stepped forth. "My Lord Justice, the king said he had one last property to offer, which was this woman here. I took that wager and the dice rolled in my favor. There has since been much foolish argument—"

"Never mind the since," I said. "Let us continue with the events in sequence. I believe, Lady Tofaa Devata, that next you presented yourself at the hall."

She took a heavy step forward, revealing that she was barefoot and dirty about the ankles, just like the nonroyal waterfront denizens in the room. When she began to speak, Yissun leaned over to me and muttered, "Marco, forgive me, but I do not speak any of the Indian languages."

"No matter," I said. "I understand this one." And I did, for she was speaking not any Indian tongue, but the Farsi of the trade routes.

She said, "I presented myself at the hall, yes—"

I said, "Let us observe protocol. You will address me as your Lord Justice."

She bridled in obvious rancor at being so bidden by a pale-skinned and untitled Ferenghi. But she contented herself with a regal sniff, and began again:

"I presented myself at the hall, Lord Justice, and I asked the players, 'Before my dear husband wagered me, had he first wagered and lost himself?' Because, if he had, you see, my lord, then he was already a slave himself, and by law slaves can own no property. Therefore I was not his to hazard in the play, and I am not bound to the winner, and—"

I stopped her again, but only to ask, "How is it that you speak Farsi, my lady?"

"I am of the nobility of Bangala, my lord," she said, standing very erect and looking as if I had sought to cast doubt on that. "I come from a noble merchant family of Brahman shopkeepers. Of course, being a lady, I have never stooped to clerk's learning—of reading or writing. But I speak the trade tongue of Farsi, besides my native Bangali, and also most of the other major tongues of Greater India—Hindi, Tamil, Telugu. . . ."

"Thank you, Lady Tofaa. Let us now proceed."

After having spent so long in the far eastern parts of the Khanate, I had quite forgotten how prevalent in the rest of the world was the Trade Farsi. But clearly most of the men in the room, because they dealt always with the mariners of the sea trade, also knew the tongue. For several of them inmediately spoke up, and in a vociferous clamor, but what they had to say, in effect, was this:

"The woman cavils and equivocates. It is a husband's legal right to venture any of his wives in a game of chance, just as it is his right to sell her or put her body out to hire or divorce her utterly."

And others, equally loudly, said in effect:

"No! The woman speaks true. The husband had forfeited himself, therefore all his husbandly rights. He was at that moment a slave himself, illegally venturing property he did not own."

I held up a magisterial hand and the room quieted, and I leaned my chin on my hand in a pose of thinking deeply. But I really was not doing any such thing. I did not pretend, even to myself, to be a Solomon of juridical wisdom, or a Draco or a Khan Kubilai of impulsive decision. But I had spent my boyhood reading about Alexander, and I well remembered how he opened the unopenable Gordian knot. However, I would at least pretend to ponder. While I did so, I said casually to the woman:

"Lady Tofaa, I have come here in search of something your late husband was carrying. The tooth of the Buddha that he took from the Ananda temple. Are you acquainted with it?"

"Yes, Lord Justice. He wagered that away, too, I am sorry to say. But I am pleased to say that he did it before he wagered me, plainly valuing *me* more than even that sacred relic."

"Plainly. Do you know who won the tooth?"

"Yes, my lord. The captain of a Chola pearl-fisher boat. He took it away rejoicing that it should bring good fortune to his divers. That boat sailed weeks ago."

"Do you have any idea where it sailed to?"

"Yes, Lord Justice. Pearls are fished in only two places. Around the island of Srihalam and along the Cholamandal coast of Greater India. Since the captain was of the Chola race, he undoubtedly returned to that coast of the mainland mandal, or region, inhabited by the Cholas."

The men in the room were muttering dourly at this seemingly irrelevant exchange, and the Sardar Shaibani sent me an imploring look. I ignored them and said to the woman:

"Then I must pursue the tooth to the Cholamandal. If you would be pleased to come with me as my interpreter, I will afterward assist you to make your way to your people's home in your native Bangala."

The men's muttering got mutinous at that. The Lady Tofaa did not like it, either. She flung her head back, so she could look down her nose at me, and she said frostily, "I would remind my *Lord* Justice that I am not of a station to accept menial employment. I am a noblewoman born, and the widow of a king, and   "

"And the slave of that ugly brute yonder," I said firmly, "if I should find in his favor in this proceeding."

She swallowed her pomposity—actually gulped aloud—and instantly went from arrogant to servile. "My Lord Justice is as masterful a man as my late dear husband. How could a mere fragile young woman resist such a dominant man? Of course, my lord, I will accompany you and work for you. *Slave* for you."

She was anything but fragile, and I was not complimented by being compared to the King Who Ran Away. But I turned to Yissun and said, "I have made my decision. Publish it to all here. This argument turns on the precedence of the late king's wagers. Therefore the whole matter is moot. From the moment King Narasinha-pati abdicated his throne in Pagan, he had surrendered all his rights and properties and holdings to the new ruler, the Wang Bayan. Whatever that late king spent or squandered or lost here in Akyab was and still is the rightful property of the Wang, who is here represented by the Sardar Shaibani."

When that was translated, everyone in the room, including Shaibani and Tofaa, gave a gasp, all of astonishment, but variously also of chagrin, relief and admiration. I went on:

"Each man in this room will be accompanied by a guard patrol back to his residence or business establishment, and all those plundered treasures will be retrieved. Any person of Akyab refusing to comply, or later found to be hoarding any such property, will be summarily executed. The emissary of the Khan of All Khans has spoken. Tremble, all men, and obey."

As the guards herded the men out, wailing and lamenting, the Lady

Tofaa fell down flat on her face, totally prone before me, which is the abject Hindu equivalent of the more sedate salaam or ko-tou, and Shaibani regarded me with a sort of awe, saying:

"Elder Brother Marco Polo, you are a real Mongol. You put this one to shame—for not himself having thought of that master stroke."

"You can make up for it," I said genially. "Find me a trusty ship and crew that will take me and my new interpreter immediately across the Bay of Bangala." I turned to Yissun. "I will not drag you there, for you would be as speechless as I. So I relieve you from that duty, Yissun, and you may report back to Bayan or to your former commander at Bhamo. I shall be sorry not to have you with me, for you have been a staunch companion."

"It is I who should be sorry for you, Marco," he said, and pityingly shook his head. "To be on duty in Ava is a dreadful enough fate. But *India . . .?*"

INDIA

N o sooner had our vessel cast off from the Akyab dock than Tofaa
Devata said to me, very primly, "Marco-wallah," and began to lay down
rules for our good behavior while we traveled together.

Since I was no longer being a Lord Justice, I had given her leave to
address me less formally, and she told me that the -wallah was a Hindu
suffixion which denoted both respect and friendliness. I had not given
her leave, as well, to preach at me. But I listened politely and even
managed not to laugh.

"Marco-wallah, you must realize that it would be a grave sin for us
to lie together, and exceedingly wicked in the sight of both men and
gods. No, do not look so stricken. Let me explain, and you will be less
heartbroken by your unrequited yearning. You see, your judicial decision
resolved that dispute back yonder in Akyab, but without deciding on the
merits of the opposing arguments, so those arguments must still be taken
into account in our relationship. On the one hand, if my dear late husband was still my husband at his death, then I am still sati, unless and
until I remarry, so you would be committing the very worst of sins when
you lay with me. If, for example, over yonder in India, we were caught

in the act of surata, you would be sentenced to do surata with a fire-filled, incandescent brass statue of a woman, until you scorched and shriveled horribly to death. And then, after death, you would have to abide in the underworld called Kala, and suffer its fires and torments, for as many years as there are pores on my body. On the other hand, if I am now technically the slave of that Akyab creature who won me at dice, then your lying with me, his slave woman, would make you also legally his slave. In any event, I am of the Brahman jati—the highest of the four jati divisions of Hindu humankind—and you are of no jati at all, and therefore inferior. So, when we lay together, we would be defying and defiling the sacred jati order, and in punishment we would be thrown to those dogs trained to eat such heretics. Even if you were gallantly willing to risk that frightful death by raping me, I am still held to be an equal defiler and subject to the same grisly punishment. If it is ever known in India that you put your linga into my yoni, whether I actively engulf it or only passively spread myself for it, we are both in terrible disgrace and peril. Of course I am not a kanya, a green and unripe and flavorless virgin. Since I am a widow of some experience, not to say talent and ability and a capacious, warm, well-lubricated zankha, there would be no physical evidence of our sin. And I daresay these barbarian sailors would take no notice of what we civilized persons might do in private. So it would probably never be known in my homeland that you and I had reveled in ecstatic surata out here on the gentle ocean waters under the caressing moon. But we must desist as soon as we touch my native land, for all Hindus are most adept at scenting the least whiff of scandal, and crying shame and jeering nastily, and demanding bribes to keep silent about it, and then gossiping and tattling anyway."

She had exhausted either her breath or the myriad aspects of the subject, so I said mildly, "Thank you for the useful instruction, Tofaa, and set your mind at ease. I will observe all the proprieties."

"Oh."

"Let me suggest just one thing."

"*Ah!*"

"Do not call the crewmen sailors. Call them seamen or mariners."

"Ugh."

The Sardar Shaibani had gone to some trouble to find for us a good ship, not a flimsy Hindu-built coasting dinghi, but a substantial lateen-rigged Arab qurqur merchant vessel that could sail straight across the vast Bay of Bangala instead of having to skirt around its circumference. The crew was composed entirely of some very black, wiry, extraor-dinarily tiny men of a race called Malayu, but the captain was a genuine Arab, sea-wise and capable. He was taking his ship to Hormuz, away west in Persia, but had agreed (for a price) to take me and Tofaa as far as the Cholamandal. That was an open-sea, no-sight-of-land crossing of some three thousand li, about half as far as my longest voyage to date: the one from Venice to Acre. The captain warned us, before departure, that the bay could be a boat-eater. It was crossable only between the months of September and March—we were doing it in October—because only in that season were the winds right and the weather not

murderously hot. However, during that season, when the bay had got
itself nicely provided with a copious meal of many vessels bustling east
and west across its surface, it would frequently stir up a tai-feng storm
and capsize and sink and swallow them all.

But we encountered no storm and the weather stayed fine, except at
night, when a dense fog often obscured the moon and stars, and
wrapped us in wet gray wool. That did not slow the qurqur, since the
captain could steer by his bussola needle; but it must have been miserably uncomfortable for the half-naked black crewmen who slept on the
deck, because the fog collected in the rigging and dripped down a constant clammy dew. We two passengers, however, had a cabin apiece, and
were snug enough, and we were given food enough, though it was not
viand dining, and we were not attacked or robbed or molested by the
crew. The Muslim captain naturally despised Hindus even more than
Christians, and stayed aloof from our company, and he kept the seamen
forever busy, so Tofaa and I were left to our own diversions. That we
had none—beyond idly watching the flying fish skimming over the waves
and the porkfish frolicking among the waves—did not discourage Tofaa
from prattling about what diversions we must *not* succumb to.

"My strict but wise religion, Marco-wallah, holds that there is more
than one sinfulness involved in lying together. So it is not just the sweet
surata that you must put out of your mind, poor frustrated man. In
addition to surata—the actual physical consummation—there are eight
other aspects. The very least of them is as real and culpable as the most
passionate and heated and sweaty and enjoyable embrace of surata. First
there is smarana, which is *thinking* of doing surata. Then there is kir-
tana, which is speaking of doing it. Speaking to a confidant, I mean, as
you might discuss with the captain your barely controllable desire for
me. Then there is keli, which is flirting and dallying with the man or woman of one's affection. Then there is prekshana, which means peeping
secretly at his or her kaksha—the unmentionable parts—as for example
you frequently do when I am bathing over the bucket back yonder on the
afterdeck. Then there is guyabhashana, which is conversing on the subject, as you and I are so riskily doing at this moment. Then there is
samkalpa, which is *intending* to do surata. Then there is adyavasaya,
which is resolving to do it. Then there is kriyanishpati, which is . . . well
. . . doing it. Which we must not."

"Thank you for telling me these things, Tofaa. I shall manfully
endeavor to restrain myself even from the wicked smarana."

"Oh."

She was right about my having frequently glimpsed her unmentionable kaksha, if that was what it was called, but I could hardly have
avoided it. The wash bucket for us passengers was, as she had said, on
the high afterdeck of the ship. All she had to do, for a measure of privacy
while she sponged her nether parts, was to squat facing astern. But she
seemed always to face the bow, and even the timorous Malayu crewmen
would discover chores needing doing amidships, so they could peep
upward when she opened the drapery of her sari garment and spread her
thick thighs and mopped water up from the bucket to her wide-open and

unclothed crotch. It bore a bush as black and thick as that on the black men's heads, so maybe it inspired lustful smarana in them, but not in me. Anyway, though repellent itself, that thicket at least concealed whatever was within it. All I knew of that was what Tofaa insisted on telling me.

"Just in case, Marco-wallah, you should fall enamored of some pretty nach dancing girl when we get to Chola, and should wish to make conversation with her as flirtatiously and naughtily as you do with me, I will tell you the words to say. Pay attention, then. Your organ is called the linga and hers is called the yoni. When that nach girl excites you to ravening desire, that is called vyadhi, and your linga then becomes sthanu, 'the standing stump.' If the girl reciprocates your passion, then her yoni opens its lips for you to enter her zankha. The word *zankha* means only 'shell,' but I hope your nach girl's is something better than a shell. My own zankha, for example, is more like a gullet, ever hungry, near to famishment, and salivating with anticipation. No, no, Marco-wallah, do not beseech me to let you feel with your trembling finger its eagerness to clasp and suck. No, no. We are civilized persons. It is good that we can stand close together like this, watching the sea and amiably conversing, with no compulsion to roll and thrash in surata on the deck, or in your cabin or mine. Yes, it is good that we can keep tight rein on our animal natures, even while discoursing so frankly and provocatively as we do, about your ardent linga and my yearning yoni."

"I like that," I said thoughtfully.

"*You do?!*"

"The words. Linga *sounds* sturdy and upright. Yoni *sounds* soft and moist. I must confess that we of the West do not give those things such nicely expressive names. I am something of a collector of languages, you see. Not in a scholarly way, only for my own use and edification. I like your teaching me all these new and exotic words."

"Oh. Only words."

However, I could not endure too many of hers at a time. So I went and sought out the reclusive Arab captain and asked him what he knew of the pearl fishers of the Cholamandal—whether we would be encountering them along the coast.

"Yes," he said, and snorted. "According to the Hindus' contemptible superstition, the oysters—the reptiles, as they call them—rise to the surface of the sea in April, when the rains begin to fall, and each reptile opens its shell and catches a raindrop. Then it settles to the sea bottom again, and there slowly hardens the raindrop into a pearl. That takes until October, so it is now that the divers are going down. You will arrive right when they are collecting the reptiles and the solidified raindrops."

"A curious superstition," I said. "Every educated person knows that pearls accrete around grains of sand. In fact, in Manzi, the Han may soon cease diving for the sea pearls, for they have recently learned to grow them in river mussels, by introducing into each mollusc a grain of sand."

"Try telling that to the Hindus," grunted the captain. "They have the *minds* of molluscs."

It was impossible, aboard a ship, to evade Tofaa for very long. The next time she found me idling at the rail, she leaned her considerable bulk to wedge me there while she continued my education in things Hindu.

"You should also learn, Marco-wallah, how to look with knowing eyes at the nach dancing girls, and compare their beauty, so that you fall enamored only of the most beautiful. You might best do that by comparing them in your mind with what you have seen of me, for I fulfill all the standards of beauty for a Hindu woman. As it is set down: the three and the five, five, five. Which is to say, in order of specification, that three things of a woman should be deep. Her voice, her understanding and her navel. Now, of course I am not so talkative as most—giddy girls who have not yet attained to dignity and reserve—but on the occasions when I do speak, I am sure you have taken note that my voice is not shrill, and that my utterances are full of deep feminine understanding. As for my navel . . ." She pushed down the waistband of her sari, and lifted up the billow of dark-brown flesh there. "Regard! You could hide your heart in that profound navel, could you not?" She plucked out some matted old fluff that had already hidden there, and went on:

"Then there are five things that should be fine and delicate: a woman's skin, her hair, her fingers, toes and joints. Surely you can find no fault with any of those attributes of mine. Then there are the five things that should be healthily bright pink: the woman's palms and soles and tongue and nails and the corners of her eyes." She went through quite an athletic performance: sticking out her tongue, flexing her talons, exhibiting her palms, tugging at the sooty pouches around her eyes to show me the red corner dots, and picking up each of her grimy feet to show me their leathery but rather cleaner undersides.

"Last, there are the five things that should be high-arched: the woman's eyes, nose, ears, neck and breasts. You have seen and admired all of those except my bosom. Regard." She unwound the top part of her sari, and bared her pillowlike dark-brown breasts, and somewhere down the deck a Malayu uttered a sort of anguished whinny. "High-arched they are indeed, and set close together, like nestling hoopoe birds, no gap between. The ideal Hindu breasts. Slide a sheet of paper in that tight cleft and it will stay there. As for putting your linga there, well, do not even consider it, but imagine the sensation of that close, soft, warm envelopment of it. And behold the nipples, like thumbs, and their halos, like saucers, and all black as night against the golden fawn skin. When examining your nach girl, Marco-wallah, be sure to look closely at her teats, and give them a wet lick with your tongue, for many women try to deceive by darkening theirs with al-kohl. Not I. These exquisite paps are natural, given me by Vishnu the Preserver. It was not casually that my noble parents named me Gift of the Gods. I budded at the age of eight, and was a woman at ten, and a married woman at twelve. Ah, just see the nipples, how they expand and writhe and stand, even though touched only by your devouring gaze. Think how they must behave when actually touched and fondled. But no, no, Marco-wallah, do not dream of touching them."

"Very well."

Rather sulkily, she covered herself again, and the numerous Malayu who had congregated behind nearby deckhouses and things dispersed again about their business.

"I will not," Tofaa said stiffly, "enumerate the Hindu qualifications for beauty in the male, Marco-wallah, since you fall lamentably short of them. You are not even handsome. A handsome man's eyebrows meet above the bridge of his nose, and his nose is long and pendulous. My dear late husband's nose was as long as his royal pedigree. But as I say, I will not list your shortcomings. It would not be ladylike of me."

"By all means, Tofaa, be ladylike."

She may have been a beauty by Hindu standards—in truth, she was, as I later was often told by admiring Hindu men, openly envying me my companion—but I could think of no other people that would have judged her even passable, except possibly the Mien or the Bho. Despite Tofaa's daily and highly visible and well-attended ablutions, she somehow never got quite clean. There was always that measle on her forehead, of course, and always a gray scurf about her ankles and a darker gray curd between her toes. But while I cannot say that the rest of her, from the measle down to the curd, was ever actually, in the Mien and Bho manner, encrusted, it *was* always just perceptibly dingy.

Back in Pagan, Hui-sheng had gone always barefoot in the Ava fashion, and Arùn had done so all her life, and even after a day of padding about the dusty city streets, their feet had always been, even before bath time, kissably clean and sweet. I honestly could not understand how Tofaa always managed to have such dirty feet, especially out here on the sea, where there was nothing to smirch them but fresh breezes and sparkling spindrift. It might have had something to do with the India-nut oil with which she coated all her exposed skin after each day's washing. Her late dear husband had left her with very little in the way of personal possessions: not much but a leather flask of the nut oil and a leather bag that contained a quantity of wood chips. As her employer, I had voluntarily bought her a new wardrobe of the sari fabrics and other necessities. But she had regarded the leather containers as necessities, too, and brought them along. I had known that the oil of India-nut was to keep herself glistening in that unattractively greasy way. But I had no notion of what the wood chips were for—until one day, when she did not emerge from her cabin at mealtime, I tapped on her door and she bade me come in.

Tofaa was squatting in her immodest bathing position, and facing me, but her thicket was hidden by a small ceramic pot she was pressing to her crotch. Before I could make my excuses and step back out of the cabin, she calmly lifted the pot away from herself. It was the sort of pot used for brewing cha, and the spout of it came sliding, slick with secretions, out from among the hair. That would have been surprising enough, but even more so was the fact that the spout was emitting blue smoke. Tofaa had evidently put into the pot some of those wood chips, and set them smoldering, and stuck the smoking spout up inside herself. I had seen women play with themselves before, and with a variety of playthings, but never with *smoke*, and I told her so.

"Decent women do not play with themselves," she said reprovingly. "That is what men are for. No, Marco-wallah, daintiness of the *inside* of one's person is more to be desired than any merely exterior *appearance* of being clean. The application of nim-wood smoke is an age-old and cleanly practice of us fastidious Hindu women, and I do this for your sake, though little you appreciate it."

I frankly saw little there to appreciate: a plump, greasy, dark-brown female squatting on the cabin floor, with her legs shamelessly apart, and the entrapped blue smoke oozing lazily up through her dense bush. I could have remarked that *some* exterior daintiness might have improved her chances of attracting someone nearer to her interior, but I chivalrously refrained.

"Nim-wood smoke is a preventive of unexpected pregnancy," she went on. "It also makes the kaksha parts fragrant and tasty, should anyone happen to nuzzle or browse there. That is why I do this. Just in case you should sometime be overwhelmed by your brute passions, Marco-wallah, and seize me against my will, despite my pleas for mercy, and fling yourself upon me without giving me time to make ready, and force your rigid sthanu through my chaste but soft defenses, I take this precaution of administering the nim-wood smoke every day."

"Tofaa, I wish you would stop."

"You *want* me to?" Her eyes widened, and so must her yoni have done, for a voluminous puff of the blue smoke came suddenly up from there. "You *want* me to bear your children?"

"Gèsu. I want you to cease this everlasting preoccupation with matters below the waist. I engaged you to be my interpreter, and I am already shuddering for fear of what words you are likely to speak, ostensibly mine. But right now, Tofaa, our rice and goat meat are getting wet with salt spray. Come and put something in your other end."

I really believed, at that time, that in choosing a Hindu woman for my translator in India, I had unfortunately chosen a particularly unlovely and witless and pathetic specimen. How she had come to be the consort of a king was beyond my comprehension, but I sympathized more than ever with that wretched man, and thought I better understood now why he had thrown away a kingdom and his life. But I have here recounted a few of Tofaa's charmless attributes—only a few of them—and have repeated some of her fatuous garrulity—only some of it—by way of making her both visible and audible in all her awfulness. I do that because, on arriving in India, I discovered to my horror that Tofaa was *not* an anomaly. She was an unexceptional and purely typical adult Hindu female. From a crowd of Hindu women, whatever the assortment of classes, or jati, I could hardly have picked out Tofaa. Worse yet, I found the women to be immeasurably superior to the Hindu men.

In my journeying I had got acquainted with numerous other races and nations before visiting those of India. I had concluded that the Mien droppings of the Bho of To-Bhot had to be the lowest breed of mankind, and I had been mistaken. If the Mien represented humanity's ground level, then the Hindus were its worm burrows. In some of those countries

I had earlier inhabited or visited, I could not help seeing that some of the people despised and detested other people—for their different language or their lesser refinement or their lower class in society or their peculiar ways of life or their choice of religion. But in India I could not help seeing that *everybody* despised and detested everybody else, and for all those reasons.

Let me be as fair as I can. Let me say that I was in some small error from the start, in thinking of all Indians as Hindus. Tofaa informed me that "Hindu" was only a variant of the name "Indian," and properly referred only to those Indians who practiced the Hindu religion of Sanatana Dharma, or Eternal Duty. Those preferred to be dignified by the name of "Brahmanists," after the chief god (Brahma the Creator) of the three chief gods (the other two being Vishnu the Preserver and Siva the Destroyer) of their numberless multitude of gods. Other Hindus had picked out some lesser god from that mob—Varuna, Krishna, Hanuman, whoever—and gave more devotion to that one, and thereby rated themselves superior to the greater ruck of Hindus. Many others of the population had adopted the Muslim religion seeping in from the north and west. A very few Indians still practiced Buddhism. That religion, after originating in India and spreading afar, had almost died out in its homeland, possibly because it enjoined cleanliness. Still other Indians followed other religions or sects or cults: Jain, Sikh, Yoga, Zarduchi. In all their teeming diversity and jumble and overlap of faiths, however, the Indian people maintained one holy attribute in common: the adherents of every religion despised and detested the adherents of every other.

The Indians did not much like, either, to be lumped all together as "Indians." They were a seething and still unmixed caldron of different races, or so they claimed. There were the Cholas, the Aryans, Sindi, Bhils, Bangali, Gonds . . . I do not know how many. The lighter brown Indians called themselves *white*, and claimed they were descended from fair-haired, pale-eyed ancestors who came from somewhere far to the north. If that was ever true, then there had since been so much intermingling that, over the centuries, the darker browns and blacks of the southern races had predominated—as mud does when poured into milk —and all the Indians were now but shades and tints of muddy brown. None was of any color worth boasting about, and the insignificant differences of hue served only as one more basis for their abhorring each other. The lighter brown ones could sneer at the darker brown, and they at the indisputably black.

Also, depending on their race, tribe, family lineage, place of original origin and place of current habitation, the Indians spoke *one hundred seventy-nine* different languages, hardly any two of them mutually comprehensible, and every one was deemed by its speakers the One True and Holy Tongue (though few of them ever bothered to learn to read and write it, if indeed it had a script or character or alphabet to be written in, which not many did), and the speakers of every True Tongue scorned and reviled those who spoke any False Tongue, which meant any of the one hundred and seventy-eight others.

Whatever their race, religion, tribe, or tongue, *all* the Indians spinelessly submitted to a social order imposed by the Brahmanists. That was the order of jati, which divided the people into four rigid classes and an overflow of discards. Jati having been first devised by some long-ago Brahman priests, their own descendants naturally constituted the highest class, called Brahman. Next were the descendants of long-ago warriors— *very* long ago, I surmised; I saw no man of the present day who could conceivably be imagined as a warrior—next, the descendants of long-ago merchants, and last the descendants of long-ago humble artisans. Those would have been the bottommost order, but there were also the discards, the paraiyar, or "untouchables," who could claim no jati at all. A man or woman born into any of the jati could not associate with anyone born into a higher, and of course would not with anyone of a lower. Marriages and alliances and business transactions were done only between matching jati, so the classes were eternally perpetuated, and a person could no more ascend to a higher one than he could ascend to the clouds. Meanwhile, the paraiyar dared not even let their defiling shadow fall on anyone of jati.

No person in India—except, I suppose, a Hindu of the Brahman class—was pleased with the jati he found himself born into. Every lower-jati person I met was anxious to tell me how his forebears had, in the long-ago, occupied a much nobler class, and had been undeservedly debased through the influence or trickery or sorcery of some enemy. Nevertheless, all preened in the fact that they were of higher order than *somebody* else, even if only the vile paraiyar. And any of the paraiyar could always point derisively to some still more miserable paraiyar to whom *he* was superior. What was most contemptible about the jati order was not that it existed, and had existed for ages, but that all the people caught in its toils—not just Hindus, but every single soul in India— willingly let it go on existing. Any other people, with the least scintilla of courage and sense and self-respect would long ago have abolished it, or died trying. The Hindus never had even tried, and I saw no sign that they ever would.

It is not impossible that even a people as degenerate as the Bho and Mien may have improved in the years since I was last among them, and made something halfway decent of themselves and their country. But, from what travelers' report I have had of India in these later years, nothing has changed there. To this day, if a Hindu ever feels bad about his being one of the dregs of humankind, he has only to look about for some other Hindu he feels better than, and he can feel good. And that satisfies him.

Since it would have been unwieldy for me to try to identify every person I met in India according to all his entitlements of race, religion, jati and language—one man might be simultaneously a Chola, a Jain, a Brahman and a Tamil-speaker—and since the whole population, in any event, was under the sway of the Hindu jati order, I continued to think indiscriminately of them all as Hindus, and to call them all Hindus, and I still do. If the fastidious Lady Tofaa considered that an improper or derogatory appellation I did not and do not care. I could think of numerous epithets more fitting and a lot worse.

. 2 .

T H E Cholamandal was the most dreary and uninviting shore I ever sailed to. All along it, the sea and land merely and indistinctly blended, in coastal flats that were nothing but reedy, weedy, miasmal marshes created by a multitude of creeks and rivulets flowing sluggishly out from India's distant interior. The merging of land and water was so gradual that vessels had to anchor three or four li out in the bay, where there was keel room. We made landfall off a village called Kuddalore, where we found a motley fleet of fishing and pearl-fishing boats already riding at anchor, with little dinghis ferrying their crewmen and cargoes back and forth from the anchorage to the almost invisible village far inland across the mud flats. Our captain adroitly maneuvered our qurqur among the fleet, while Tofaa leaned over the rail and peered at the Hindus aboard the other vessels and occasionally shouted queries at them.

"None of these," she finally reported to me, "is the pearl-fisher boat that was at Akyab."

"Well," said the captain, also to me, "this Cholamandal pearl coast is a good three hundred farsakhs from north to south. Or, if you prefer, more than two thousand li. I hope you are not going to suggest that I cruise up and down its whole length."

"No," said Tofaa. "I think, Marco-wallah, we ought to go inland to the nearest Chola capital, which is Kumbakonam. Since all pearls are royal property, and go ultimately to the Raja, he can probably easiest direct us to the fisher we seek."

"Very well," I said, and to the captain, "If you will hail a dinghi to take us ashore, we will leave you here, and we thank you for the safe crossing. Salaam aleikum."

While a scrawny little black dinghi-man rowed us across the brackish bay water, then poled us through the fetid marshes toward the distant Kuddalore, I asked Tofaa, "What is a Raja? A king, a Wang, what?"

"A king," she said. "Two or three hundred years ago reigned the best and fiercest and wisest king the Chola kingdom ever had, and his name was King Rajaraja the Great. So ever since, in tribute to him and in hope of emulating him, the rulers of Chola—and most other Indian nations, as well—have taken his name as their title of majesty."

Well, that was no uncommon sort of appropriation even in our Western world. Caesar had originally been a Roman family name, but became a title of office, and in the form of Kaiser remains so for the rulers of the more recent Holy Roman Empire, and in the form of Czar is used by the petty rulers of the many trivial Slavic nations. But I was to discover that the Hindu monarchs were not satisfied just to appropriate the former Raja's name—that was not pretentious enough, all by itself—

they had to elaborate and embroider upon it, to affect even more royalty and majesty.

Tofaa went on, "This Chola kingdom was formerly immense and great and unified. But the last high Raja died some years back, and it has since fragmented into numerous mandals—the Chola, the Chera, the Pandya—and their lesser Rajas are all contending for possession of the whole of the land."

"They are welcome to it," I grumbled, as we stepped onto the dock at Kuddalore. We might have been stepping from the Irawadi River into a Mien village. I need not describe Kuddalore further.

On that dock a group of men were jabbering and gesticulating, as they stood around a large wet object lying on the boards. I took a look at it and saw that it was evidently some fisherman's catch. It was a dead fish, or at least it stunk like a fish, though I might better call it a sea creature, for it was bigger than I was, and like nothing I ever saw before. From midway down its body, it was definitely fishlike, terminating in a crescent fish tail. But it did not have fins or scales or gills. It was covered with a leathery skin, like that of a pork-fish, and the upper body was very curious. Instead of pork-fish flippers, it had stubby things like arms, ending in appendages like webbed paws. Even more remarkable, it had on its chest two immense but unmistakable *breasts*—very similar to Tofaa's—and its head was vaguely like that of an extremely ugly cow.

"What in God's name is it?" I asked. "If it were not so appallingly hideous, I should almost believe it a mermaid."

"Only a fish," said Tofaa. "We call it the duyong."

"Then why all the fuss about a fish?"

"Some of the men are the crew of the boat that speared it and brought it in. The others are fishmongers who wish to buy portions of it to sell. The one well-dressed man is the village magistrate. He is demanding oaths and affidavits."

"Whatever for?"

"It happens every time one is caught. Before the duyong is allowed to be sold, the fishermen must swear that none of them did surata with the duyong on their way to shore."

"You mean . . . sexually coupled with it? With a *fish*?"

"They always do, though they always swear they did not." She shrugged and smiled indulgently. "You men."

There would be many later occasions and reasons for me to resent and lament my being included in the gender that also included male Hindus, but that was the first time. I walked in a wide circle around the duyong and the men, and proceeded on along Kuddalore's main street. All the plump women villagers wore the wrap-around sari which adequately covered most of their body dirt, except where the belly roll of flesh was exposed. The skinny men, having less to expose, exposed it, wearing nothing but a messily wound tulband and a loose, large, baggy diaper called a dhoti. The children wore nothing but the measle painted on the forehead.

"Is there a karwansarai?" I asked Tofaa. "Or whatever you call it, where we can take lodging while we make ready to journey on?"

"Dak bangla," she said. "Traveler's rest house. I will inquire."

She abruptly reached out and seized the arm of a passing man, and snapped a question at him. He did not, as a man of any other country would have done, take offense at being so brazenly accosted by a mere woman. Instead, he almost quailed, and spoke meekly in response. Tofaa said something that sounded very nearly accusing, and he replied even more feebly. The conversation went back and forth like that, she almost snarling, he finally almost whimpering. I regarded them with amazement, and at last Tofaa reported the result.

"There is no dak bangla in Kuddalore. So few strangers ever come here, and fewer care to stay as long as a night. It is typical of the lowly Cholas. In my native Bangala, now, we would have been most hospitably received. However, the wretch offers us lodging in his own house."

"Well, that is hospitable enough, certainly," I said.

"He asks that we follow him there, and wait until he is inside for a few moments. Then we are to knock at the door and he will open it, and we are to request a bed and a meal, and he will rudely refuse us."

"I do not understand."

"It is usual. You will see."

She spoke again to the man, and he went off at an anxious trot. We followed, picking our way among the pigs and fowl and infants and excrement and other litter on the streets. Considering what the residents of Kuddalore had to live in—no house being any more substantial or elegant than a hut of the Ava jungle Mien—I was rather grateful that there was *not* a dak bangla for us, since anything maintained only for the occasional transient would have had to be a sty indeed. Our host's residence was not much more—built of mud bricks and plastered with cow dung—as we saw when we halted outside and he disappeared into the dark interior of it. After a brief wait, as commanded, Tofaa and I went up to the shack and she knocked on the rickety doorjamb. What happened thereafter I relate as Tofaa later translated it all to me.

The same man appeared in the doorway, and reared his head back to look down his nose at us. This time, Tofaa addressed him only in an obsequious mumble.

"*What? Strangers?*" he bawled, loudly enough to have been heard down at the bayside dock. "Pilgrim wayfarers? No, indeed, not here! I do not care, woman, if you *are* of Brahman jati! I do not give shelter to just any caller, and I do not allow my wife—"

He not only broke off in mid-bellow, he totally vanished, whisking sideways beyond the door opening, as a meaty brown-black arm thrust him aside. A meaty brown-black woman appeared in his place, and smiled out at us, and she said, syrup sweetly:

"Wayfarers, are you? And seeking a bed and a meal? Well, do come in. Pay no heed to this worm of a husband. In his speech, but in his speech alone, he plays the great lord. Come in, come in, do."

So Tofaa and I lugged our packs inside the house and were shown the bedchamber in which to stow them. The cow-dung-plastered room was entirely occupied by four beds, somewhat like the hindora bed I had encountered in other places, but not quite as good. A hindora was a pallet hung on ropes from a ceiling, but this kind, called a palang, was no more than a sort of slit cloth tube, like a sack opened lengthwise, roped at each end to the walls and swinging free in between. Two of the palangs held a swarm of naked brown-black children, but the woman swept them away as unceremoniously as she had done her husband, and made it plain that Tofaa and I would sleep there in the same room with her and him.

We went back to the other of the hut's two rooms, and the woman swept the children farther, outside onto the street, while she made a meal for us. When she handed us each a slab of wood, I recognized the food on it—or rather, I recognized that it was mostly the mucous kàri sauce I had, a long time ago, eaten in the Pai-Mir mountains. Kàri was the only native word I could remember from that long-ago journey in company with other men of the Chola race. As I remembered, those other brown-black men had shown at least a trifle more manly spirit than my present host. But then, they had had no Chola women with them.

This man and I, since we could not converse, simply squatted together and ate our unappetizing meal and occasionally nodded companionably to each other. I must have seemed as much a flattened and trampled zerbino as he was, both of us mute and mousily nibbling, while the two women chattered vociferously, trading comments—as Tofaa later informed me—on the general worthlessness of men.

"It is well said," remarked the woman of the house, "that a man is a man only when he is filled with angry passion, when he bears no vexation submissively. But is there anything more contemptibly pitiful"—she waved her food slab to indicate her husband—"than a weak man being angry?"

"It is well said," Tofaa volunteered, "that a small pond is easily filled, and the forepaws of a mouse, and likewise a man of no account is easily satisfied."

"I was first married to this one's brother," said the woman. "When I was widowed, when my husband's fellow fishermen brought him home dead—crushed on the very deck, they said, by a newly caught duyong flailing about—I should have behaved like a proper sati, and thrown myself on his funeral pyre. But I was still young, and childless, so the village sadhu urged me to marry this brother of my husband, and have children to carry on the family line. Ah, well, I was still young."

"It is well said," Tofaa remarked, with a salacious giggle, "that a woman never grows old below the girdle."

"True, indeed!" said the woman, with a lubricous giggle. "It is also well said: A fire cannot be laid with too many logs, nor a woman with too many sthanu."

They both giggled lasciviously for a time. Then Tofaa said, waving her food slab to indicate the children swarming on the doorstep, "At least he is fruitful."

"So is a rabbit," grunted the woman. "It is well said: A man whose life and deeds are not outstanding above those of his fellows, he does but add to the heap."

I finally got tired of seeming submissively to share my host's cowed silence. In an attempt to make some communication with him, I indicated my still-heaped food slab and made insincere lip-smackings, as if I had enjoyed the slop, and then made gestures of asking what was the meat under the kàri. He comprehended, and told me what it was, and I realized that I did know one other word of the native language:

"Duyong."

I got up and left the hut to inhale deeply of the evening air. It reeked of smoke and fish and garbage and fish and unwashed people and fish and pukey children, but it helped some. I kept on walking the Kuddalore streets, both of them, until well after dark, and returned to the hut to find all the children asleep on the front-room floor, among the detritus of our used food slabs, and the adults all asleep, fully dressed, in their palangs. With some difficulty at first try, I got into mine, and found it more comfortable than it had appeared, and fell asleep. But I was awakened at some dark hour, by scuffling noises, and determined that the man had climbed into his wife's palang and was noisily doing surata, though she kept snarling and hissing something at him. Tofaa had waked and heard it, too, and later told me what the wife had been saying:

"You are only brother to my late husband, remember, even after all these years. As the sadhu commanded, you are forbidden to enjoy yourself while performing your seed function. No passion, do you hear? *Do not enjoy yourself!*"

I had by now rather come to the opinion that I had at last found the true homeland of the Amazons, and the source of all the legends about them. One of the legends was that they kept only some rather vestigial men about, to impregnate them when it was necessary to make more Amazons.

The next day, our host kindly went out and inquired among his neighbors and found one who was driving his ox cart to the next village inland, and would take me and Tofaa along. We thanked our host and his wife for their hospitality, and I gave the man a bit of silver in payment for our lodging, and his wife instantly snatched that for herself. Tofaa and I perched on the rear of the ox cart, and jostled a good deal as it lumbered off through the flat and feculent marshland. To pass the time, I asked her what that woman had meant when she spoke of sati.

"It is our old custom," said Tofaa. "Sati means a faithful wife. When a man dies, if his widow is properly sati, she will fling herself on the pyre consuming his body, and die herself."

"I see," I said thoughtfully. Perhaps I had been wrong in thinking of the Hindu women as all being overbearing Amazons, of no uxorial qualities. "It is not entirely a grotesque idea. Almost winsome in a way. That a faithful wife accompanies her dear husband to the afterworld, wanting them to be together forever."

"Well, not exactly," said Tofaa. "It is well said: The highest hope of a woman is to die *before* her husband. That is because the plight of a widow is unthinkable. Her husband is probably worthless, but what does she do without one? So many females are constantly ripening to the marriageable age of eleven or twelve, what chance does a used and worn and not-young widow have of marrying again? Left alone and undefended and unsupported in the world, she is an object of uselessness, scorned and reviled. Our word for widow means literally a dead-woman-waiting-to-die. So, you see, she might as well jump in the fire and get it over with."

That somewhat took the luster of lofty sentiment off the practice, but I remarked that still it took some courage, and was not devoid of a certain proud dignity.

"Well, actually," said Tofaa, "the custom originated because some wives *did* plan to remarry, and had their next husbands already picked out, and so poisoned their current ones. The practice of sati-sacrifice was mandated by the rulers and religious leaders, just to avert those frequent murders of husbands. It was made the law that, if a man died for whatever reason, and his wife was not demonstrably innocent of causing his death, she was to leap onto the pyre, and if she did not, the dead man's family were to throw her onto it. So it made wives think twice before poisoning their husbands, and even made them solicitous about *keeping* their men alive, when they fell ill or got old."

I decided I *had* been mistaken. This was not the homeland of the Amazons. It was the homeland of the Harpies.

That latest opinion was not shaken by what next transpired. We got to the village of Panruti well after sunset and found it also lacking any dak bangla, and Tofaa again snatched at a man in the street, and we went through the same performance as yesterday. He went home, we followed him, he loudly refused us entrance and was immediately over-ridden by a blustering female. The only difference in this case was that the henpecked husband was quite young and the hen was not.

When I thanked her for inviting us in, and Tofaa translated my thank-you, it came out something of a stammer. "We are grateful to you and your . . . uh . . . husband? . . . son?"

"He was my son," said the woman. "He is now my husband." I must have gaped, or blinked, for she went on to explain. "When his father died, he was our only child, and he would soon have been of an age to inherit this house and all its contents, and I would then have been a dead-woman-waiting-to-die. So I bribed the local sadhu to marry me to the boy—he being too young and ignorant to object—and thereby main-tained my share in the property. Unhappily, he has not been much of a husband. So far, he has sired on me only these three: my daughters, his sisters." She indicated the slack-jawed and witless-looking brats sitting lumpishly about. "If they are all I have, their eventual husbands will inherit next. Unless I give the girls to be devadasi temple whores. Or perhaps, since they are woefully deficient in their mentality, I could donate them to the Holy Order of Crippled Mendicants. But they may be even too imbecile to make proper beggars. Anyway, I am naturally anxious, and naturally trying mightily every night, to produce another son, and so keep the family property in the direct family line." Briskly, she set before us some wood slabs of kàri-sauced food. "Therefore, if you do not mind, we will all eat in a hurry, so he and I can get to our palang."

And again that night I overheard the moist noises of surata going on in the same room, this time accompanied by urgent whispers, which Tofaa repeated to me the next morning—"Harder, son! You must strive harder!" I wondered whether the avaricious woman planned next to marry her grandson, but I did not really care, and I did not ask. Nor did I bother remarking to Tofaa that all she had told me during our voyage —regarding the Hindu religion's concern about sin, and strictures against it, and dire punishments for it—seemed to have had little elevating effect on Hindu morality in general.

Our destination, the capital city called Kumbakonam, was not impossibly far from where we had landed on the coast. But no Hindu peasant had any riding mounts to sell us, and not many men were willing to take us for hire to the next village or town down the road—or more likely, their wives would not let them—so Tofaa and I had to proceed by exasperatingly slow stages, whenever we could find a carter or a drover going our way. We rode jouncing in ox carts, and splayed across the sharp spine ridges of oxen, and dragged along on stone sledges, and straddling the rumps of pack asses, and once or twice riding real saddle horses, and many times we just set out walking, which usually meant we had to sleep in the roadside hedgerows. That was no intolerable hardship for me, except that on every one of those nights Tofaa gigglingly pretended I was bedding us down in the wilderness only to rape her, and when I did no such thing, she grumbled long into the night about the ungallant way I was treating a nobly born Lady Gift of the Gods.

The last outlying village on our way had a name that was bigger than its total population—Jayamkondacholapuram—and was otherwise remarkable only for something that happened, while we were there, to diminish its populace even further. Tofaa and I were again squatting in a cow-dung hut and supping on some mystery substance disguised in kàri, when there arose a rumbling sound like distant thunder. Our host and hostess immediately sprang erect and shrieked in unison, "Aswamheda!" and ran out of the house, kicking aside several of their children littered about the floor.

"What is aswamheda?" I asked Tofaa.

"I have no idea. The word means only a running away."

"Perhaps we ought to emulate our hosts and run away."

So she and I stepped over the children and went out into the single village street. The rumbling was nearer now, and I could tell that it was a herd of animals coming at a gallop from somewhere to the south. All of the Jayamkondacholapuramites were runing away from the noise, in a panicked and headlong mob, heedlessly trampling under their feet the numerous very young and very old persons who fell down. Some of the more spry villagers climbed up trees or onto the thatched roofs of their dwellings.

I saw the first of the herd come galloping into the southern end of the street, and saw that they were horses. Now, I know horses, and I know that, even among animals, they are not the most intelligent of creatures, but I also know that they have more sense than Hindus. Even a wild-eyed and foam-flecked running herd of them will not step on a fallen human being in its path. Every horse will leap over, or swerve aside, or if necessary execute a tumbler's somersault, to avoid a fallen man or woman. So I simply threw myself prone in the street and dragged Tofaa with me, though she squealed in mortal terror. I held us both lying still and, as I expected, the maddened herd diverged around us and thundered past on our either side. The horses also took care to avoid the inert bodies of aged and infant Hindus already mashed by their own relatives and friends and neighbors.

The last of the horses disappeared on up the road to the northward, and the dust began to settle, and the villagers began to clamber down from roofs and trees and to amble back from whatever distances they had run to. They immediately commenced a concerted keening of grief and lament, as they peeled up their flattened dead, and they shook their fists at the sky and squawled imprecations at the Destroyer God Siva for having so unfeelingly taken so many of the innocent and infirm.

Tofaa and I went back to our meal, and eventually our host and hostess also returned, and counted their children. They had not lost any, and had trodden on only a few, but they were as sorrow-stricken and distraught as all the rest of the village—she and he did not even, after we all went to bed, perform surata for us that night—and they could not tell us anything more about the aswamheda except that it was a phenomenon which occurred about once a year, and was the doing of the cruel Raja of Kumbakonam.

"You would be well advised, wayfarers, not to go to that city," said the woman of the house. "Why not settle down here in tranquil and civilized and neighborly Jayamkondacholapuram? There is ample room for you, now that Siva has destroyed so many of our people. Why persist in going to Kumbakonam, which is called the Black City?"

I said we had business there, and asked why it was so called.

"Because black is the Raja of Kumbakonam, and black his people, and black the dogs, and black the walls, and black the waters, and black the gods, and black the hearts of the people of Kumbakonam."

· 3 ·

UNDETERRED by the warning, Tofaa and I went on southward, and eventually crossed a running sewer that was dignified with the name of Kolerun River, and on the other side of it was Kumbakonam.

The city was much larger than any community we had yet come through, and it had filthier streets bordered with deeper ditches full of stagnant urine, and a greater variety of garbage rotting in the hot sun, and more lepers clicking their warning sticks, and more carcasses of dead dogs and beggars decaying in public view, and it was more rancid with the odors of kàri and cooking grease and sweat and unwashed feet. But the city really was no blacker of color or layered no thicker with surface dirt than any lesser community we had seen, and the inhabitants were no darker of skin and layered no thicker with accumulated grime. There were a great many more people, of course, than we had seen in one place before, and, like any city, Kumbakonam had attracted many eccentric types that had probably left their home villages in search of wider opportunity. For example, among the street crowds I saw quite a few individuals who wore gaudy feminine saris, but had on their heads the untidy tulbands usually worn by men.

"Those are the ardhanari," said Tofaa. "What would you call them? Androgynes. Hermaphrodites. As you can see, they have bosoms like women. But you cannot see, until you pay for the privilege, that they have the nether organs of both men and women."

"Well, well. I had always supposed them mythical beings. But I daresay, if they had to exist anywhere, it would be here."

"We being a very civilized people," said Tofaa, "we let the ardhanari parade freely about the streets, and openly ply their trade, and dress as elegantly as any women. The law requires only that they also wear the headdress of a man."

"Not to deceive the unwary."

"Exactly. A man who seeks an ordinary woman can hire a devanasi temple whore. But the ardhanari, although unsanctioned by any temple, are kept far more busy than the devanasi, since they can serve women as well as men. I am told they can even do both at once."

"And that other man, yonder?" I asked, pointing. "Is he also peddling his nether parts?"

If he was, he could have sold them by bulk weight. He was carrying them before him in a tremendous basket which he held by both hands. Although the parts were still attached to his body, his dhoti diaper could not have contained them. The basket was completely filled by his testicular sac, which was leathery and wrinkled and veined like an elephant's hide, and the testicles inside it must each have been twice the size of the man's head. Just to see the sight made my own parts hurt in sympathy and revulsion.

"Look below his dhoti," said Tofaa, "and you will see that he also has legs of elephant thickness and elephant skin. But do not feel sorry for him, Marco-wallah. He is only a paraiyar afflicted with the Shame of Santomè. Santomè is our name for the Christian saint you call Thomas."

The explanation was even more astounding than the sight of the pitiable man-elephant. I said unbelievingly, "What would this benighted land know of Saint Thomas?"

"He is buried somewhere near here, or so it is said. He was the first Christian missionary ever to visit India, but he was not well received, because he tried to minister to the vile paraiyar outcasts, which disgusted and offended the good jati folk. So they paid Santomè's own congregation of paraiyar converts to slay him, and—"

"His own congregation? And they did it?"

"The paraiyar will do anything for a copper coin. Dirty work is what they are for. However, Santomè must have been a powerfully holy man, albeit a heathen. The men who slew him, and their paraiyar descendants ever since, have been cursed with the Shame of Santomè."

We pressed on to the center of the city, where stood the Raja's palace. To get to it we had to cross a commodious market square, as crowded as all market squares, but on this day not with commerce. There was some kind of festa in progress, so Tofaa and I made our way across it leisurely, to let me see how the Hindus celebrated a joyous occasion. They seemed to be doing it more dutifully than joyously, I decided, for I could not see a happy or animated face anywhere. In fact, the faces, besides having a more than usually ornate measle painted on the forehead, were smeared with what looked like mud, but smelled worse.

"Dung of the sacred cattle," said Tofaa. "First they wash their faces in the cows' urine, then put the dung on their eyes, cheeks and breast."

I refrained from any comment except, "Why?"

"This festival is in honor of Krishna, the God of Many Mistresses and Lovers. When Krishna was only a lad, you see, he was a simple cowherd, and it was in the cowshed that he did his first seductions of the local milkmaids and his fellow cowherds' wives. So this festival, in addition to being a blithe celebration of high-spirited lovemaking, also has its aspect of solemnity in honoring Krishna's sacred cows. That music the musicians are playing, you hear it?"

"I hear it. I did not know it was music."

The players were grouped about a platform in the middle of the square, wringing noises from an assortment of devices—cane flutes, hand drums, wooden pipes, stringed things. In all that concert of strident screeching and twanging and squawking, the only perceptibly sweet notes came from a single instrument like a very long-necked lute with a gourd body, having three metal strings played with a plectrum on the musician's forefinger. The Hindu audience sweatily massed roundabout looked as morosely unmoved by the music and as barely enduring of it as I imagine I did.

"What the musicians are playing," said Tofaa, "is the kudakuttu, the pot-dance of Krishna, based on an ancient song the cowherds have always sung to their cows while milking them."

"Ah. Yes. If you had given me time, I should probably have guessed something like that."

"Here comes a lovely nach girl. Let us stay and watch her dance Krishna's pot-dance."

A brown-black and substantial female, lovely perhaps by the standards Tofaa had previously recited to me, and properly mammalian for the cow-worship occasion, got laboriously onto the platform, carrying a large clay pot—symbolic of Krishna's milking pot, I assumed—and began limbering up by doing various poses with it. She tried shifting it from one arm's crook to the other, and put it on top of her head a few times, and occasionally stamped a broad foot, evidently clearing the platform of ants.

Tofaa confided to me, "The worshipers of Krishna are the most lighthearted and blithesome of all the Hindu sects. Many condemn them for preferring gaiety to gravity and vivacity to meditation. But, as you see, they imitate the carefree Krishna, and they maintain that enjoyment of life gives bliss, and bliss gives serenity, and serenity gives wisdom, all together making for wholeness of soul. That is what the nach girl's pot-dance conveys."

"I should like to see that. When does she commence?"

"What do you mean? You *are* seeing that."

"I mean the dance."

"That *is* the dance!"

We continued on across the square—Tofaa seeming exasperated, but I not feeling much chastened—through the crowd of woebegone and nearly inanimate celebrants, and to the palace gates. I was carrying Kubilai's ivory plaque slung on my chest, and Tofaa explained to the two gate guards what it represented. They were clad in not very military-looking dhotis and holding their spears at lazily disparate angles, and they shrugged as if disinclined either to bow us in or to take the trouble to keep us out. We went through a dusty courtyard and into a palace which was at least palatially built of stone, not the mud-and-dung that constituted most of Kumbakonam.

We were received by a steward—perhaps of some rank, since he wore a clean dhoti—and he did seem impressed by my pai-tzu and Tofaa's explanation of it. He fell flat on his face, and then scrabbled off like a crab, and Tofaa said we should follow him. We did, and found ourselves in the throne room. By way of describing the richness and magnificence of that hall, I will only say that the four legs of the throne stood in tureens full of oil, to keep the local kaja snakes from climbing up into the seat and to keep the local white ants from gnawing and col-lapsing the whole thing. The steward motioned for us to wait, and scut-tled off through another door.

"Why does that man go about on his belly?" I asked Tofaa.

"He is being respectful in the presence of his betters. We too must do so, when the Raja joins us. Not fall down, but make sure your head is never higher than his. I will nudge you at the proper moment."

Half a dozen men came in just then, and stood in a line and re-garded us impassively. They were as nondescript in person as any of the celebrants out in the square, but they were gorgeously attired in gold-threaded dhotis, and even fine jackets to cover their torsos, and almost neatly wound tulbands. For the first time in India, I supposed I was meeting some people of upper class, probably the Raja's retinue of minis-ters, so I began a speech for Tofaa to translate, addressing them as "My lords," and starting to introduce myself.

"Hush," said Tofaa, tugging at my sleeve. "Those are only the Raja's shouters and congratulators."

Before I could ask what that meant, there was a stir at the door again, and the Raja strode ceremonially in at the head of another group of courtiers. Instantly, the six shouters and congratulators bellowed—and believe this or not, they bellowed in unison:

"All hail His Highness the Maharajadhiraj Raj Rajeshwar Narendra Karni Shriomani Sawai Jai Maharaja Sri Ganga Muazzam Singhji Jah Bahadur!"

I later had Tofaa repeat all that for me, slowly and precisely, so I could write it down—not just because the title was so marvelously grandiose, but also because it was so ludicrous a title for a small, black, elderly, bald, paunchy, oily Hindu.

It seemed for a moment to perplex even Tofaa. But she poked me with an elbow and she knelt—and, because she was no small woman, she discovered that even kneeling she was still a fraction taller than the little Raja, so she lowered herself still deeper, into an abject squat, and began falteringly, "Your Highness . . . Maharajadhiraj . . . Raj . . ."

"Your Highness is sufficient," he said expansively.

The shouters and congratulators roared, *"His Highness is the very Warden of the World!"*

He made a genial and modest gesture for them to be silent. They did not bellow again for a while, but neither were they ever entirely silent. Every time the little Raja did anything, they would comment on it, in a murmur, but somehow still in unison, things like: *"Behold, His Highness seats himself upon the throne of his dominion,"* and: *"Behold, how gracefully His Highness pats a hand upon his yawn . . ."*

"And *who,*" said the little Raja to Tofaa, "is *this?*" turning a very haughty look upon me, for I had not knelt or bent at all.

"Tell him," I said in Farsi, "that I am called Marco Polo the Insignificant and Unsung."

The little Raja's look of hauteur became displeasure, and he said, also in Farsi, "A fellow white man, eh? But a white-skinned one. If you are a Christian missionary, go away."

"His Highness bids the lowly Christian go away," murmured the shouters and congratulators.

I said, "I am a Christian, Your Highness, but—"

"Then go away, lest you suffer the fate of your long-ago predecessor Santomè. He had the outrageous nerve to come here preaching that we should worship a carpenter whose disciples were all fishermen. Disgusting. Carpenters and fishermen are of the lowest jati, if not downright paraiyar."

"His Highness is rightly and righteously disgusted."

"I am indeed on a mission, Your Highness, but not to preach." I decided to temporize for a while. "Mainly, I wished to see something of your great nation and"—it cost me an effort, but I lied—"and to admire it." I waved toward the windows, whence came the mournful music and the sullen muttering of the festival, so called.

"Ah, you have seen my people making merry!" the little Raja exclaimed, looking not so petulant. "Yes, one tries to keep the people happy and content. Did you enjoy the exhilarating Krishna frolic, Polo-wallah?"

I tried hard to think of something enjoyable about it. "I was much—much entertained by the music, Your Highness. One instrument in particular . . . a sort of long-necked lute . . ."

"Say you so?" he cried, seeming unaccountably pleased.

"His Highness is royally pleased."

"That is an entirely new instrument!" he went on, excitedly. "It is called a sitar. It was invented by my very own Court Musicmaster!"

It appeared that I had, all fortuitously, melted any incipient frost between us. Tofaa gave me an admiring look as the little Raja bubbled enthusiastically, "You must meet the instrument's inventor, Polo-wallah. May I call you Marco-wallah? Yes, let us dine together, and I will bid the Musicmaster join us. It is a pleasure to welcome such a discerning guest, of such good taste. Shouters, command that the dining hall be prepared."

The six men trotted off down a corridor, bellowing the command, still in concert, and even trotting in step together. I discreetly gestured a suggestion to Tofaa, and she comprehended, and timidly asked the little Raja, "Your Highness, might we wash off some of our travel dust before we are honored by joining you at table?"

"Oh, yes. By all means. Forgive me, lovely lady, but your charms would distract any man from noticing any trivialities. Ah, Marco-wallah, again your good taste is evident. It is also evident that you have admired our country and our people, seeing that you have taken a lady wife from among them." I gasped. He added, archly, "But did you have to take the most beauteous, and thereby so sorely deprive us poor natives?" I tried to make an instant correction of that horrific misapprehension, but he went to where the steward was still lying on his face, and kicked the man and snarled, "Misbegotten wretch! Never to be twice-born! Why did you not lead these eminent guests immediately to a state apartment and see them cared for? Do so! Prepare for them the bridal suite! Assign them servants! Then see to the banquet and the entertainers!"

When I saw that the bridal suite had two separate beds, I decided it would not be necessary to demand other quarters. And when a number of stout dark women dragged in a tub and filled it, I found it not inconvenient for me and Tofaa to have the same bathing chamber. I took the masculine prerogative of bathing first, then stayed to oversee Tofaa's ablutions and direct the women servants—causing some incredulity among them at my insistent thoroughness—so that, for once, Tofaa got well washed. When we put on the best clothes we carried and went downstairs to the dining hall, even her bare feet were clean.

And I made certain, before indulging in any small table talk, to inform the little Raja and all others present, "The Lady Tofaa Devata is not my wife, Your Highness." That sounded brusquely uncomplimentary of the lady, so, to maintain his estimation of her importance, I added, "She is one of the noble widows of the late King of Ava."

"Widow, eh?" grunted the little Raja, as if instantly losing all interest in her.

I continued, "The Lady Gift of the Gods most graciously consented to accompany me on my journey through your fair land, and to interpret for me the wit and wisdom of the many fine people we have met along the way."

He grunted again, "Companion, eh? Well, to each his custom. A sensible and tasteful Hindu, going on a journey, takes not a female Hindu, but a Hindu boy, for his temper is not so like a kaja snake's, and his hole not so like a cow's."

To change the subject, I turned to the fourth at our table, a man of my own age, bearded like me, and seeming more tan than black of complexion behind the beard. "You would be the inventive musician, I believe, Master . . ."

"Musicmaster Amir Khusru," said the little Raja proprietorially. "Master of melodies, and also dances, and also poetry, being an accomplished composer of the licentious ghazal poems. A credit to my court."

"His Highness's court is blessed," crooned the shouters and congratulators, standing against the wall, *"and blessed most by the presence of His Highness"*—during which the Musicmaster only smiled self-deprecatingly.

"I never before saw a musical instrument with strings made of metal," I said, and Tofaa—now subdued to meekness—translated as I went on, "Indeed, I had never before thought of Hindus as inventors of anything so good and useful."

"You Westerners," the little Raja said peevishly, "are always looking to do good. We Hindus seek to *be* good. An infinitely superior attitude to life."

"Nevertheless," I said, "that new Hindu sitar is a doing of good. I congratulate Your Highness and your Master Khusru."

"Except that I am not a Hindu," the Musicmaster said in Farsi, with some amusement. "I am of Persian birth. The name I gave the sitar is from the Farsi, as you may have perceived. Si-tar: three-stringed. One string of steel wire and two of brass."

The little Raja looked still more peeved at my having learned that the sitar was no Hindu achievement. I wished to put him in a good mood again, but I was beginning to wonder if there was any subject that could be discussed without its blatantly or subtly denigrating the Hindus. In mild desperation, I turned to praising the food we had been served. It was some kind of venison, drowned as usual in the kàri sauce, but this kàri was at least colored a sightly yellow-gold and a little enhanced in its flavor, though only with turmeric, which is an inferior substitute for zafràn.

"Meat of the four-horned deer, this is," said the little Raja, when I complimented it. "A delicacy we reserve for only the most favored guests."

"I am honored," I said. "But I thought your Hindu religion forbade the hunting of wild game. Doubtless I was misinformed."

"No, no, you were rightly informed," said the little Raja. "But our religion also bids us be clever." He gave a broad wink. "So I ordered all the people of Kumbakonam to take holy water from the temples and go into the forests and sprinkle that holy water about, loudly declaring that all the forest animals were henceforth sacrifices to the gods. That makes our hunting of them quite permissible, you see—each killing being a tacit offering—and of course our hunters always give a haunch or something to the temple sadhus, so they will not inconveniently decide that we are misinterpreting any sacred text."

I sighed. It really was impossible to light on an innocuous subject. If it did not explicitly or implicitly denigrate the Hindus, it made them impugn themselves. But I tried again:

"Do Your Highness's hunters hunt on horseback? I ask because I wonder if some horses might have been lost from your royal stables. The Lady Tofaa and I encountered quite a herd running loose on the other side of the river."

"Ah, you met my aswamheda!" he cried, sounding now most jovial again. "The aswamheda is another cleverness of mine. A rival Raja, you see, holds that province beyond the Kolerun River. So every year, I have my drovers deliberately whip a horse herd over to there. If that Raja resents the trespass and keeps possession of the horses, then I have excuse for declaring war on him and invading and seizing his lands. However, if he rounds them up and returns them to me—which he has done every year so far—then it betokens his submission to me, and all the world knows I am his superior."

If this little Raja was the superior, I decided, as the meal concluded, then I was glad not to have encountered the other. Because this one marked the close of the banquet by leaning to one side, raising one little buttock and gustily, audibly, odoriferously passing wind.

"*His Highness farts!*" bellowed the shouters and congratulators, making me flinch even more than I had already done. "*The food was good, and the meal acceptable, and His Highness's digestion is still superb, and his bowels an example to us all!*"

I really had not much hope that this posturing monkey could be of any help in my current quest. However, as we sat on at the table, drinking tepid cha from elaborately jeweled but slightly misshapen cups, I recounted to the little Raja and the Master Khusru the events that had brought me hither, and the object of my pursuit, concluding, "I understand, Your Highness, that a pearl-fisher subject of yours was the man who acquired the Buddha's tooth, hoping that it would confer good fortune on his pearl fishing."

The little Raja, as I might have expected, responded by taking my story as a reflection on himself, on Hinduism and on Hindus in general.

"I am distressed," he muttered. "You imply, Marco-wallah, that some one of my subjects imputed supernatural power to that fragment of an alien god. Yes, I am distressed that you could believe that any Hindu has so little faith in his own stalwart religion, the religion of his fathers, the religion of his benevolent Raja."

I said placatively, "Doubtless the new possessor of the tooth has by now realized his error, and found the thing not at all magical, and repented his acquisition of it. He, being a good Hindu, would probably throw it in the sea, except that it cost him some time and perhaps some uncertainty in the winning of it. So, for a suitable exchange, he would probably be glad to give it up."

"Give it up he most certainly will!" snapped the little Raja. "I shall make proclamation that he come forward and surrender it—and surrender himself to the karavat!"

I did not know what a karavat was, but evidently Master Khusru did, for he remarked mildly, "That, Your Highness, is not likely to make anyone come hastening forward with the object."

"Please, Your Highness," I said. "Do not make demand or threat, but publish only a persuasive request and my offer of reward."

The little Raja grumbled for a while, but then said, "I am known as a Raja who always keeps his word. If I offer a reward, it will be paid." He eyed me sidewise. "You will pay it?"

"Assuredly, Your Highness, and most liberally."

"Very well. And then I will keep *my* word, which I have already spoken. The karavat." I did not know whether I should remonstrate on behalf of some unsuspecting pearl fisherman. But anyway, before I could, the little Raja summoned his steward and spoke rapidly to him. The man scuttled from the hall, and the Raja turned again to me. "The proclamation will immediately be cried throughout my realm: bring the heathen tooth and receive a munificent reward. It will bring the desired result, I promise you that, for all my people are honest and responsible and devout Hindus. But it may take a while, because the pearl fishers are constantly sailing back and forth between their coastal villages and the reptile beds."

"I understand, Your Highness."

"You will be my guest—your female, too—until the relic is retrieved."

"With gratitude, Your Highness."

"Then let us now cast off all dull business and sober care," he said, dusting his little hands to demonstrate, "and let mirth and joy reign in here as it does in the square outside. Shouters, bring on the entertainers!"

This was the first entertainment: an aged and very dirty, brown-black man, so ragged of dhoti that he was quite indecent, shuffled woefully into the room and fell prostrate before the little Raja. Master Khusru helpfully murmured to me:

"What we call in Persia a darwish, a holy mendicant, here called a naga. He will perform to earn his supper crust and a few coppers."

The old beggar went to a cleared space in the room and gave a hoarse call, and an equally ragged and filthy young boy came in bearing a roll of what seemed to be cloth and rope. When the two of them unrolled the bundle, it proved to be one of the swing-style palang beds, its two ropes terminating in little brass cups. The boy lay down in the palang on the floor. The ancient naga knelt and slipped the two brass cups onto his eyeballs, and pulled down his wrinkled black eyelids over them. Very slowly, he stood erect, lifting the boy in the palang off the floor—not using his hands or teeth or anything but his eyeballs—then swinging the boy from side to side until the little Raja felt moved to applaud. Khusru and Tofaa and I politely did, too, and we men threw the old beggar some coppers.

Next came into the dining hall a portly, squat, dark-brown nach girl, who danced for us, about as listlessly as the woman I had seen dancing at the Krishna festa. Her only accompanying music was the jingling of a column of gold bracelets which she wore from wrist to shoulder of just one arm, and she wore nothing else at all. I was not much enthralled—it might have been Tofaa stamping her familiar soiled feet and undulating her familiar bushy kaksha—but the little Raja giggled and snorted and slavered throughout, and applauded wildly as the woman withdrew.

Then the tattered and filthy old mendicant returned. Rubbing his eyes, which had got bulged and reddened by his performance with the palang, he made a brief speech to the little Raja, who turned and told me:

"The naga says he is a Yogi, Marco-Wallah. The followers of the Yoga sect are accomplished in many strange and secret arts. You will see. If you truly harbor any belief, as I suspect you do, that we Hindus are backward or lacking in aptitude, then you are about to be convinced otherwise, for you will now witness a wonder that *only* a Hindu could show you." He called to the waiting beggar, "Which Yoga miracle will you show us, Oh Yogi? Will you be buried for a month underground and come up still alive? Will you make a rope stand erect and climb it and disappear into the heavens? Will you carve your boy assistant into pieces and then restore him whole? Will you at least levitate for us, Oh holy Yogi?"

The decrepit old man began to speak in a creaking small voice, but sounding earnest, as if making a momentous announcement, and doing much gesticulation. The little Raja and the Musicmaster leaned forward to listen intently, so now it was Tofaa who explained to me what was going on. She seemed pleased to do so, saying eagerly:

"It will be a wonder which you may wish to observe closely, Marco-wallah. The Yogi says he has discovered a revolutionary new way to do surata with a woman. Instead of his linga gushing out its juice at the climactic moment, as a man's customarily does, *his* gives a great inhaling suck *inward*. Thereby he ingests the life-force of the woman without expending any of his own. He says his discovery not only provides a fantastic new sensation, its continual practice could accrue to a man so much life-force that he might live forever. Would not you like to learn that ability, Marco-wallah?"

"Well," I said, "it sounds like an interestingly novel variation on the ordinary."

"Yes! Show us, Oh Yogi!" the little Raja called to him. "Show us this instant. Shouters, bring back the nach girl. She is already undressed and ready for use."

The six men went trotting out in lock step. But the Yogi held up a cautionary hand and declaimed some more.

"He says he dare not do it with a valuable dancing girl," Tofaa translated, "because any woman must wither to some degree when his linga does its sucking inside her. Instead, he requests a yoni with which he can demonstrate."

The six shouters trotted back in again, bringing the naked girl, but at another command from the little Raja they ran out once more.

I asked, "How can the Yogi be provided with a yoni without a woman attached?"

"A yoni stone," said Tofaa. "Around every temple you will see standing carved linga stone columns, which are representative of the god Siva, and also open-holed yoni stones, representative of his consort goddess Parvati."

The six men came back, one of them bringing a stone like a small wheel, with an oval opening cut through it, roughly resembling a woman's yoni, even having the kaksha hair carved around it.

The Yogi did a number of preparatory gesticulations, and spoke what sounded like solemn incantations, then parted his dhoti rags and unashamedly pulled out his linga, which was like a black-barked twig. With more incantations and gestures of demonstration—this is how it is done, gentlemen—he pushed his limp organ through the yoni hole in the stone. Then, holding the heavy stone against his crotch, he beckoned to the nach girl, who was also standing watching. He bade her take his linga in her fingers and bring it to arousal.

The girl did not recoil or complain, but she did not appear delighted with the idea. Nevertheless, she took hold of what protruded beyond the stone, and began working it, rather as if she were milking a cow. Her own udder bounced and all her bracelets jingled in rhythm to the motion. The old mendicant chanted down at the yoni and at the girl's hand yanking at him, and he narrowed his red eyes in intense concentration, and rivulets of sweat began to course down the dirt of his face. After some while, his linga grew enough to protrude farther past the stone, and we could even see its brown bulbous head creeping out a little beyond the nach girl's fricating fist. Finally the Yogi said something to her and she let go of him and stepped away.

Presumably the old beggar had stopped her just before she brought him to spruzzo. The stone was held to him now simply by the stiffness of his organ. He stared down at that peg and its constricting hoop, and so did the by now slightly breathless nach girl, and so did we at the table, and the shouters against the wall, and all the servants in the dining room. The Yogi's linga had attained to a respectable size, considering the man's age and general scrawniness and beggarly debilitude. But it looked somehow strained and inflamed, bulging as it did from the narrow yoni of the stone it held firmly at his crotch.

The Yogi made several more gesticulations, but in a rather hurried and sketchy manner, and yammered a whole string of incantations, but in a rather strangled voice. Nothing happened that we could see. He glanced about at all of us, looking somewhat abashed, and glowered really hatefully at the nach girl, who was now humming indifferently and examining her fingernails, as if to say, "See? You should have used me." The Yogi yelled some more at his linga and borrowed yoni, as if cursing them, and made some more violent gestures, including shaking his fist. Still nothing happened, except that he sweated more copiously, and his tightly pinched organ was adding a distinct purple hue to its brown-black. The nach girl gave an audible snicker, and the Musicmaster an amused chuckle, and the little Raja began drumming his fingers on the tabletop.

"Well?" I said aside to Tofaa.

She whispered, "The Yogi appears to be having some difficulty."

Indeed he did. He was now dancing in place, more vigorously than the professional dancing girl had done, and his eyes were more redly extruded than they had been after the palang-swinging performance, and his vociferations were no longer incantatory, but recognizable even to me as cries of pain. His ragged boy assistant came running, and tugged at the imprisoning stone, at which his master gave a frightful screech. The six shouters then also dashed forward to help, and there was a confusion of hands at that empurpled center of attention, until the agonized Yogi reeled wailing away from them and fell down, writhing and hammering his fists on the floor.

"Take him away!" the little Raja commanded, in a disgusted voice. "Take the old fraud to the kitchen. Try an application of grease."

The Yogi was carried from the room, not without some trouble, for he was contorting like a gaffed fish and trumpeting like a speared elephant. The entertainment appeared to be over. We four sat on at the table, in a mutually embarrassed silence, listening to the shrieks gradually diminishing down the corridors. I was the first to speak. I naturally did not remark on this having been one more affirmation of my opinion of Hindu foolishness and futility. Instead I said, by way of graciously excusing it:

"That happens all the time, Your Highness, to all the lower animals. Everyone has seen a dog and a bitch stuck together until the bitch's clasping yoni relaxes and the dog's swollen linga wilts."

"It may take some time for the Yogi," said Master Khusru, still with amusement. "The stone yoni will not relax and his linga's swelling therefore cannot go down."

"Bah!" exclaimed the little Raja, in furious exasperation. "I should have insisted that he levitate, not try something new. Let us go to bed." And he stamped out of the room, with no shouters present to congratulate himself and the world on the grace of his gait.

· 4 ·

"I have your Buddha's tooth, Marco-wallah."

That was the very first thing the little Raja said to me when we first met the next day, and he said it about as cheerfully as he might have said, "I have a murderously *aching* tooth."

"Already, Your Highness? Why, that is wonderful. You said it might take some while to find."

"I thought it *would*," he said pettishly.

I understood his rancorous demeanor when he shoved at me a basket and I looked in. It was piled half full of teeth, most of them yellowed and mossy and carious, quite a few of them still bloody at the root, and some of them identifiably not even human—dogs' fangs and pigs' tushes.

"More than two hundred there," the little Raja said sourly. "And people are still arriving with more, from all points of the horizon. Men, women, even holy naga mendicants, even one temple sadhu. Gr-r-r. You can present a Buddha's tooth not only to your Raja Khakhan. You can give one to every Buddhist of your acquaintance."

I tried not to laugh, for his anger was justified. He had boasted of his people's honesty and of their devotion to their Hindu faith, and here they came in flocks to confess that they possessed a relic of the discredited Buddhist religion—meaning they had to *lie* about it, besides.

Holding my face impassive, I inquired, "Am I expected to pay a reward for every one of these?"

"No," he said, gritting his own teeth. "*I* am doing that. The cursed reprobates come in the front door, hand their counterfeit tooth to the steward, and are passed on out the back door to where the Court Executioner is rewarding them with fervent enthusiasm in the rear courtyard."

"Your Highness!" I exclaimed.

"Oh, I am not according them the karavat," he hastened to assure me. "That is reserved for men who have done crimes of some account. Also it takes a bit of time, and we would never have done with this procession."

"Adrio de mi. I can hear the wretches screaming from here."

"No, you cannot," he growled. "They are being very quietly dispatched with a wire loop whipped around the throat and yanked. What you hear is that *other* fraud—that degenerate old Yogi, still screeching in the kitchen. No one has yet been able to get him loose from his clinging rock yoni. We have tried greasing him with cooking fats, softening him with sesame oil, shrinking him with boiling water, wilting him by various natural means—surata by the nach girl, buccal blandishment by his boy assistant—nothing works. We may have to break the sacred yoni stone, and what revenge the goddess Parvati will inflict, I dare not think about."

"Well, I will not sympathize with the Yogi. But the tooth bringers, Your Highness—it really is a trivial misdemeanor they have tried to commit, and in a trivially witless way. These teeth they brought would not fool even me, let alone a Buddhist."

"That is what is especially deplorable! My people's imbecility! That they would shame their Raja and insult their religion, and with trickery so transparent. They are incapable even of a decent crime. Dying is too good for them! They will only be reborn immediately in some lesser form—if there is any."

I frankly believed that any depletion of the Hindus could only improve the planet, but I did not want the little Raja later to realize how severely he had depopulated his realm, and be dismayed, and maybe hold me to blame for it. I said:

"Your Highness, as your guest I formally request that the surviving imbeciles be spared, and any newcomers turned away before they also can perjure themselves. This was, after all, the fault of an apparent omission in Your Highness's proclamation."

"Mine? An omission? Are you suggesting *I* am at fault? That a Brahman *and* a Maharajadhiraj Raj can *have* a fault?"

"I think it was only an understandable oversight. Since Your Highness is of course aware that the Buddha was a man nine forearms tall, and that any tooth of his must have been as big as a drinking cup, Your Highness no doubt assumed that all your people likewise knew that."

"Hm. You are right, Marco-wallah. I did take for granted that my subjects would remember that detail. Nine forearms, eh?"

"Perhaps an amended proclamation, Your Highness . . ."

"Hm. Yes. I will issue one. And I will mercifully pardon the dolts already here. A good Brahman kills no living thing, however lowly, unless it is necessary or expedient."

He called for his steward, and gave the instructions for the proclamation, and commanded also an end to the procession through the rear courtyard. When he returned to me, he was restored to quite good humor.

"There. It is done. A good Brahman host acquiesces in his guest's wishes. But enough of dull business and sober care! You are a guest, and you are not being entertained!"

"Oh, but I am, Your Highness. Constantly."

"Come! You shall admire my zenana."

I half expected him to fling open his dhoti diaper and expose something nasty, but he only reached up and took my arm and began walking me toward a far wing of the palace. As he escorted me through a succession of sumptuously furnished rooms, inhabited by females of various ages and various hues of brown, I realized that zenana must be the local word for an anderun—the apartments of his wives and concubines. The women of mature age I found no more attractive than I had Tofaa or the nach dancers, and they were mostly surrounded by swarms of children of all sizes. But some of the little Raja's consorts were mere girls themselves, and not yet gross of flesh or vulturine of eye or corvine of voice, and some were delicately pretty in a dark-skinned way.

"I am frankly a bit surprised," I remarked to the little Raja, "that Your Highness has so many wives. From your evident aversion to the Lady Tofaa, I had rather assumed . . ."

"Ah, well, if she had been your wife, as I first thought, I should have plied you with concubines and nach girls to distract you, while I seduced that lady to surata. But a widow? What man wishes to couple with a cast-off husk—a dead-woman-waiting-to-die—when there are so many still-juicy wives of one's own and of others to be had, and also so many newly-budding virgins?"

"Yes. I see. Your Highness is a manly man."

"Aha! You took me for a gand-mara, did you? A man-lover and a woman-hater? For shame, Marco-wallah! I grant you that, like any sensible man, for longtime companionship I prefer a quiet and mannerly and compliant boy. But one has one's duties and obligations. A Raja is expected to maintain a teeming zenana, so I do. And I dutifully service them in regular rotation, even the youngest, as soon as they have had their first flow."

"They are married to Your Highness before their first menstruum?"

"Why, not just my wives, Marco-wallah. Every girl in India. The parents of any daughter are anxious to get her married off before she is a woman, and before any mishap to her virginity, which would make her unmarriageable. For another reason, every time a daughter has her flow, her parents are guilty of the hideous crime of letting die an embryo that might prolong the family line. It is well said: If a girl is unwed by the age of twelve, her ancestors in the other world are mournfully drinking the blood she sheds every month."

"Well said, yes."

"However, to return to the subject of my own wives. They enjoy all the traditional wifely rights, but those do not include any queenly rights, as in less civilized and more debile monarchies. The women take no part in my court or my rule. It is well said: What man would heed the crowing of a hen? This one here, for instance, this is my premier wife and my titular Maharani, but she never presumes to sit on a throne."

I bowed politely to the woman and said, "Your Highness." She only gave me the same look of dull detestation she had given her Raja husband. Still trying to be polite, I indicated the dark-brown swarm about her, and added, "Your Highness has some handsome princes and princesses."

She still said nothing, but the little Raja growled, "They are not princes and princesses. Do not give the woman ideas."

I said, in some wonderment, "The royal line is not of patrilineal primogeniture?"

"My dear Marco-wallah! How do I know if any of these brats are mine?"

"Well, er . . . really . . . ," I mumbled, embarrassed to have broached the subject right in front of the woman and her brood.

"Do not cringe, Marco-wallah. The Maharani knows I am not insulting her specifically. I do not know if *any* of my wives' offspring are of my begetting. I cannot know that. *You* cannot know that, if you ever marry and have children. That is a fact of life."

He waved around at the various other wives whose rooms we were strolling through, and repeated:

"That is a fact of life. No man can ever know, *for certain*, that he is the father of his wife's child. Not even of a seemingly loving and faithful wife. Not even a wife so ugly a paraiyar would shun her. Not even a wife so crippled she cannot possibly stray. A woman can always find a way and a lover and a dark place."

"But surely, Your Highness—the young little girls you wed before they could possibly be fecundated—"

"Who knows, even then? I cannot always be on the spot the instant they first flow. It is well said: If a woman sees even her father or brother or son in secret, her yoni grows moist."

"But you must bequeath your throne to *somebody*, Your Highness. To whom, then, if not your presumed son or daughter?"

"To the firstborn son of my sister, as all Rajas do. Every royal line in India descends sororially. You see, my sister is indisputably of my own blood. Even if our royal mother was promiscuously unfaithful to our royal father, and no matter if my sister and I were sired by different lovers, we did drop from the same womb."

"I understand. And then, no matter who sires her firstborn . . ."

"Well, of course, I hope it was I. I took my eldest sister for one of my early wives—fifth or sixth, I forget—and she has borne I think seven children, presumably mine. But the oldest boy, even if *not* my son, is still my nephew, and the royal bloodline remains intact and inviolate, and he will be the next Raja here."

We emerged from the zenana quite near to the part of the palace where the kitchen was, and we could still hear from in there moans and whimpers and sounds of thrashing about. The little Raja asked me if I could amuse myself for a while, since he had to attend to some royal duties.

"Go back to the zenana, if you like," he suggested. "Although I am careful to marry none but wives of my own white race, they keep producing children of disappointingly dark skin. A sprinkling of your seed, Marco-wallah, might lighten the strain."

Not to be discourteous, I murmured something about having taken a vow of continence, and said I would find something else to occupy me. I watched the little Raja strut away, and I quite pitied the man. He was a sovereign of sorts, holding the power of life and death over his people, and he was the tiny cock of a whole hen yard—and he was infinitely poorer and weaker and less contented than I, a mere journeyer with only one woman to love and cherish and keep for the rest of my life; but that one was Hui-sheng.

That reminded me: I could now dispense with my temporary co-journeyer. I went in search of Tofaa, who had been stertorously snoring when I left our chambers that morning. I found her on a palace terrace, gloomily watching the gloomy Krishna celebration still going on in the square below.

She immediately and accusingly said, "I smell the pachouli on you, Marco-wallah! You have been lying with perfumed women. Alas, and after such an admirably sinless long time of behaving gentlemanly with me."

I ignored that, and said, "I came to tell you, Tofaa, that you may resign your menial position of interpreter, whenever you wish, and—"

"I knew it! I was too demure and ladylike. Now you have been beguiled by some shameless and forward palace wench. Ah, you men."

I ignored that, too. "And, as I promised, I will arrange for your safe journey back to your homeland."

"You are eager to be rid of me. My genteel chastity is a reproach to your goatishness."

"I was thinking of you, ungrateful woman. I have nothing to do now but wait here until the proper Buddha's tooth is found and delivered. In the meantime, if I need anything translated, both the Raja and the Musicmaster are fluent in Farsi."

She sniffled noisily, and wiped her nose on her bare arm. "I am in no hurry to go back to Bangala, Marco-wallah. I would be only a widow there, too. In the meantime, the Raja and the Master Khusru have occupations of their own. They will not take time to lead you about and show you the splendid sights of Kumbakonam, as I can do. I have already inquired and sought them out, just for your benefit."

So I did not compel her to leave. Instead, on that day and during the days thereafter, I let her take me about and show me the splendid sights of the city.

"Yonder, Marco-wallah, you see the holy man Kyavana. He is the holiest inhabitant of Kumbakonam. It was many years ago that he determined to stand still, like a tree stump, to the greater glory of Brahma, and he is doing it yet. That is he."

"I see three aged women, Tofaa, but no man. Where is he?"

"There."

"There? That is only an enormous white-ant hill, with a dog wetting on it."

"No, that is the holy man Kyavana. So still did he stand that the white ants used him as framework for their clay hill. It gets bigger every year. But that is he."

"Well . . . if he is in there, he is dead, surely?"

"Who knows? What does it matter? He stood just as immobile when he was alive. A most holy man. Pilgrims come from everywhere to admire him, and parents show their sons that example of high piety."

"This man did nothing but stand still. So very still that no one could tell if he was alive—or if now he may be dead. And that is called holy? That is an example to be admired? Emulated?"

"Do lower your voice, Marco-wallah, or Kyavana may manifest his great holy power at you, as he did at the three girls."

"What three girls? What did he do?"

"You see that shrine a little way beyond the anthill?"

"I see a mud shack, with those three old hags slumped in the doorway, scratching themselves."

"That is the shrine. Those are the girls. One is sixteen years old, the others seventeen, and—"

"Tofaa, the sun is very hot here. Perhaps we should go back to the palace so you can lie down."

"I am showing you the sights, Marco-wallah. When those girls were about eleven and twelve years old, they were as irreverent as you. They decided, for a frolic, to come here and open their garments and reveal their pubescent charms to the holy man Kyavana, and tempt at least one part of him out of immobility. You see what happened. They were instantly struck old and wrinkled and white-haired and haggard, as you see them now. The city built the shrine for them to live out their few remaining years in. The miracle has become famous all over India."

I laughed. "Is there any proof of this absurd story?"

"Indeed, yes. For a copper apiece, the girls will show you the very kaksha parts, once fresh and young, that were so suddenly made old and sour and stinking. See, they are already spreading their rags for you to—"

"Dio me varda!" I stopped laughing. "Here, throw them these coins and let us depart. I will take the miracle on faith."

"Now," said Tofaa, on another day, "here is a special sort of temple. A storytelling temple. You see the marvelously detailed carvings all over its exterior? They illustrate the many ways a man and a woman can do surata. Or a man and several women."

"Yes," I said. "Are you suggesting *this* is holy?"

"Very holy. When a girl is about to marry, it is assumed—because she is still a child—that she does not yet know how a marriage is consummated. So her parents bring her here, and leave her with the wise and kindly sadhu. He walks the girl about the outside of the temple, pointing to this sculpture and that, and gently explaining to her, so that, whatever her husband may do on the wedding night, she will not be terrified. Here is the good sadhu now. Give him some coppers, Marcowallah, and he will take us about, and I will repeat in Farsi what he tells us."

To my eye, the priest was just another black, dirty, scrawny Hindu, in the usual dingy dhoti and tulband and nothing else. I would hardly have asked road directions of such a one. I would certainly never have entrusted a small and apprehensive child bride to his attentions. She was bound to be more repelled by him than by anything that could happen on her wedding night.

But perhaps not. According to the temple sculptures, some astonishing things could happen on her wedding night. As the sadhu pointed out this and that, and snickered and leered and rubbed his hands together, I saw depictions of acts that I had not known were possible until I myself was well along in years and experience. The stone men and women were conjoining in every conceivable position and combination and contortion, and in several ways that—even at my present age—I would not have thought of trying. Almost any one of those sculptured acts, if performed in a Christian land, even by a legitimately wedded man and wife, would have required their going immediately afterward to a confessor. And if the performance could be accurately described and related to that priest, *he* would doubtless stagger away to seek shrift from a superior confessor.

I said, "I will accept, Tofaa, that a girl barely out of childhood might be required to submit to the natural act of surata with her new husband. But are you telling me that she is required to be versed in all these wild variations?"

"Well, she makes a better wife, if she is. But in any case, she should be prepared for whatever tastes her husband might manifest. She is a child, yes, but he may be a mature and lusty and experienced man. Or even a very old man, who has long been surfeited by the natural act, and now requires novelty."

Having myself been all my life led about by my insatiable curiosity, and led into some curious situations, I was hardly one to point an accusing or ridiculing finger at the private practices of any other person or people. So I merely followed the smirking sadhu around the temple as he gesticulated and jabbered, and I made no surprised or scandalized outcries as Tofaa explained, "This is the adharottara, the upside-down act . . . this is the viparita surata, the perverse act. . . ." I was, in fact, regarding the sculptures from a different point of view, and pondering on a different aspect of them.

The carvings might well horrify a prudish spectator, but even the most censorious could not deny that they were fine art, beautifully and intricately done. The acts so explicitly portrayed were bawdy, God knows, even obscene, but the men and women involved were all smiling happily, and they were spirited and vivacious in their attitudes. They were enjoying themselves. So the sculptures expressed both a superb craftsmanship and a wonderful verve for life. They did not at all accord with the Hindus as I knew them: inept in everything they did, and doing everything with joyless sniveling, and doing very little.

As an example of their backwardness: in contrast to the Han, whose historians had been minutely recording every least event in their dominions for thousands of years, the Hindus possessed not one written book recounting any of their history. They had only some "sacred" collections of unbelievable legends—unbelievable because, in them, all the Hindu men were tiger-brave and resourceful, and all the Hindu women angel-sweet and lovable. For another example: the Hindu garments called sari and dhoti were only swathings of fabric. That was because, although the most primitive people elsewhere had long ago invented the needle and the craft of sewing, the Hindus had not yet learned to use a needle and had not any word for "tailor" in any of their multitude of languages.

How, I asked myself, could a people ignorant even of *sewing* have envisioned and crafted these delicate, artful temple carvings? How could a people so slothful and furtive and woeful have portrayed here men and women joyous and nimble, inventive and adroit, lively and carefree?

They could not have done. I decided that these lands must have been inhabited, ages before the Hindus came, by some other and very different race, one with talent and vivacity. God knows where that superior people had gone, but they had left a few artifacts like this splendidly crafted temple, and that was all. They had left no trace of themselves in the later-come, usurper Hindus. That was deplorable, but hardly surprising. Would any such people have interbred with *Hindus*?

"Now here, Marco-wallah," Tofaa said instructively, "this carven couple are entwined in what is called the kaja posture, named for the hooded snake with which you are acquainted."

It looked snaky enough, and it was a position new to me. The man appeared to be sitting on the side of a bed. The woman lay upon and against him, head down, her torso between the man's legs, her hands on the floor, her legs about the man's waist, her buttocks held caressingly by his hands, and presumably his linga inside her (upside-down) yoni.

"A very useful position," the sadhu recited, Tofaa translating. "Say, for instance, if you wish to make surata with a humpbacked woman. As you must know, you simply cannot put a humpbacked woman on a bed in the usual supine position, or she teeters and rocks on her hump, most inconveniently, and—"

"Gèsu."

"You no doubt lust to try that kaja position, Marco-wallah," said Tofaa. "But please do not affront me by asking *me* to do it with you. No, no. However, the sadhu says he has, inside the temple, an exceedingly capable, exceedingly humpbacked devadasi woman who, for a trifle of silver . . ."

"Thank you, Tofaa, and thank the sadhu for me. But I will take this one, too, on faith."

· 5 ·

"I have your Buddha's tooth, Marco-wallah!" said the little Raja. "I rejoice in the happy conclusion of your quest!"

Some three months had gone by since his previous similar announcement, during which time no other teeth, small or large, had been brought to the palace. I had contained my impatience, assuming that a pearl fisher *was* an elusive quarry. But I was glad to have the real thing at last. I was by now very weary of India and of Hindus, and the little Raja had also begun to make plain that he would not weep loudly when I departed. He seemed not to be tiring of my visit, exactly, but getting suspicious of it. Apparently his little mind had conceived the notion that I might be using my tooth quest as a disguise for a real mission of spying out the local terrain in advance of a Mongol invasion. Well, I knew that the Mongols would not have had this dismal land even if it were freely donated to their Khanate, but I was too polite to tell that to the little Raja. I could better allay his suspicions by merely taking the tooth and going, and I would.

"It is a magnificent tooth, indeed," I said, with unfeigned awe. It was certainly no counterfeit. It was a yellowish molar, rather oblong from front to back, and the grinder surface of it was bigger than my hand, and its roots nearly as long as my forearm, and it weighed almost as much as a stone of equal dimensions. I asked, "Was it the pearl fisher who brought it? Is he here? I must give him his reward."

"Ah, the pearl fisher," said the little Raja. "The steward took the good man to the kitchen to give him a meal. If you would care to let me have the reward, Marco-wallah, I will see that he gets it." His eyes widened as I jingled half a dozen gold coins into his hand. "Ach-chaa, so much?!"

I smiled and said, "It is worth it to me, Your Highness"—not adding that I was beholden to the fisherman, not only for the tooth, but also for my release from this place.

"Overgenerous, but he shall have it," said the little Raja. "And I will bid the steward find for you a nice box to put the relic in."

"May I request also, Your Highness, a pair of horses for me and my interpreter, that we may ride back to the coast and seek sea transport from there?"

"You shall have them, first thing in the morning, and likewise a stalwart pair of my palace guards for your escort."

I hurried off to start my packing for departure, and told Tofaa to do the same, and she complied, though not very cheerfully. We were still at it when the Musicmaster stopped by our chambers to say his farewells. He and we exchanged compliments and good wishes and salaam aleikum, and then his eye chanced to fall on the things laid out on my bed to be packed, and he remarked:

"I see you are taking with you an elephant's tooth as a memento of your stay."

"What?" I said. He was regarding the Buddha's tooth. I laughed at his jest and said, "Come, come, Master Khusru. You cannot fool me. An elephant's tusk is taller than I am, and I could probably not lift one."

"A tusk, yes. But do you think an elephant chews its fodder with its tusks? For that, it has ample tiers of molars. Like this one. You have never looked into an elephant's mouth, I take it."

"No, I have not," I muttered, quietly gnashing my own molars. I waited until he had made his last salaam and left us, and then I burst out, "A caval donà no se ghe varda in boca! Che le vegna la cagasangue!"

"What are you shouting, Marco-wallah?" asked Tofaa.

"May the bloody gripes take that cursed Raja!" I raged. "The little wart was worried by my continued presence here, and evidently he despaired of anybody ever coming with another Buddha's tooth, real or false. So he provided one himself. And took my reward for it! Come, Tofaa, let us go and revile him to his face!"

We went downstairs and found the chief steward, and I demanded audience with the little Raja, but the man said apologetically:

"The Raja went out, borne in his palanquin, to ride through the city and grant his subjects the privilege of observing him and admiring him and cheering at him. I was just explaining that to this importunate caller who insists he has come a far distance to see the Raja."

As Tofaa translated that, I glanced only impatiently at the caller—just another Hindu man in a dhoti—but my eye caught on an object he was carrying, and at the same moment Tofaa cried excitedly:

"It is he, Marco-wallah! It is the very pearl fisher whom I remember from Akyab!"

And indeed the man was carrying a tooth. It was another immense one, and quite similar to my own latest acquisition, except that it was cupped in a mesh of gold tracery, like a stone set in a jewel, and the whole had a patina of unmistakable great age. Tofaa and the man jabbered together, then she turned to me again.

"It is truly he, Marco-wallah. The man who gamed with my late dear husband in the Akyab hall. And this is the relic he won with the dice that day."

"How many did he win?" I said, still skeptical. "He has already delivered one."

Jabber, jabber, and Tofaa spoke to me once more. "He knows nothing of any other. He has only this moment arrived, having trudged on foot all the way from the coast. This tooth is the only tooth he has ever had, and he is sad to part with it, for it much increased his crop of pearls in the season past, but he is dutifully heeding his Raja's proclamation."

"What a happy coincidence," I said. "This seems to be a day for teeth." I added, as I heard a commotion in the courtyard outside, "And here the Raja returns now, just in time to greet the one honest Hindu in his realm."

The little Raja strutted in, trailed by his fawning entourage of courtiers and congratulators and other toadies. He halted in some surprise at seeing our group waiting in the entry hall. Tofaa and the steward and the fisherman all collapsed to lower themselves below the Raja's head level, but, before any of them could speak, I addressed the little Raja in Farsi, and said silkily:

"It appears, Your Highness, that the good pearl fisher was so pleased with the reward for the first tooth—and the meal to which you treated him—that he has brought another."

The little Raja looked startled and bewildered for a moment, but he quickly comprehended the situation, and realized that I had caught him out in his chicanery. He did not act guilty or abashed, of course, but only indignant, and flashed a look of pure venom at the innocent fisherman, and contributed another blatant lie:

"The greedy wretch is only trying to take advantage of you, Marco-wallah."

"Perhaps he is, Your Highness," I said, continuing to pretend that I was believing his farce. "But I will gratefully accept this new relic, as well. For now I can make this one a gift to my Khakhan Kubilai, and leave the other as my parting gift to Your Gracious Highness. Your Highness deserves it. There is only the question of the reward I have already paid. Do I give the fisher an equal amount for this new delivery?"

"No," the little Raja said coldly. "You have already paid most generously. I shall persuade the man to be satisfied with that. Believe me, I shall persuade him."

He snapped instructions to the steward to take the man to the kitchen for a meal—*another* meal, he thought to add—and went stamping furiously off to his quarters. Tofaa and I returned to our own to finish packing. I carefully wrapped the new, gold-meshed tooth for safe carrying, but left the other for whatever disposition the little Raja might wish to make of it.

I never saw the man again. Perhaps he could not face me, realizing that I was leaving Kumbakonam with my never very high opinion of him lowered even further, now knowing him to be not only a posturing travesty of a sovereign, but also a giver of false gifts, a cheater of his own people, an embezzler of another's rightful recompense and—worse than all that—a man incapable ever of admitting error or wrong or fault. Anyway, he did not say goodbye or even get out of bed to see us off, when at dawn we took our leave.

Tofaa and I, in the rear courtyard, were standing about while our two assigned escorts saddled our horses and strapped our packs on the cantles, when I saw two other men emerge from a back door of the palace. In the early half-light, I could not see who they were, but one of them sat down on the ground while the other stood over him. Our escorts paused in their work and muttered uneasily, and Tofaa translated for me:

"Those are the Court Executioner and a condemned prisoner. He must be guilty of some noteworthy crime, for he is being accorded the karavat."

Curious, I went a little closer to them, but not close enough to interfere. The karavat, I finally could see, was a peculiar sort of sword blade. It had no handle, but was simply a crescent of sharp steel, like a new moon, each of its points ending in a short chain, and each chain ending in a sort of metal stirrup. The condemned prisoner—not in any hurry, but not too reluctantly either—himself put the crescent blade at the back of his neck, with the chains draped over his shoulders in front. Then he bent his knees and drew up his feet to where he could put a foot in each of the stirrups. Then, after the briefest moment to take a last deep breath, he leaned his neck back against the blade and kicked both feet out straight. The karavat very neatly, and by his own unaided action, sliced his head from his body.

I went closer yet and, while the executioner relieved the body of the karavat, I looked down at the head, which was still opening and shutting its eyes and mouth in a surprised kind of way. It was the pearl fisher who had brought the real Buddha's tooth, the only enterprising and honorable Hindu I had encountered in India. The little Raja had rewarded him, as he had said he would.

As we rode away, I reflected that I had at last seen something which the Hindus could be proud of calling their own. They had nothing else. They had long ago disowned their native-born Buddha and relinquished him to alien lands. The few splendors they could boastfully display to visitors had, in my opinion, been crafted by some different and vanished race. The Hindus' customs and morals and social order and personal habits had, in my opinion, been taught to them by the monkeys. Even their distinctive musical instrument, the sitar, was the contribution of a foreigner. If the karavat *was* the Hindus' own invention, then it had to be their only one, and I was willing to concede them that one—a lazy way of letting the condemned kill themselves—as the highest achievement of their race.

We could have ridden straight east from Kumbakonam to the Cholamandal coast, to seek the nearest village where the bay-crossing vessels put in. But Tofaa suggested, and I agreed, that we might best return the way we had come, to Kuddalore, since we knew from experience that considerable numbers of vessels called there. It was as well that we did, because, when we arrived and Tofaa began inquiring for a ship that we might engage, the local seamen told her there was already a ship there looking for *us*. That puzzled me, but only briefly, for the word of our presence quickly circulated about Kuddalore, and a man who was no Hindu came running and calling, "Sain bina!"

To my great surprise, it was Yissun, my former interpreter, whom I had last seen starting on his way from Akyab back through Ava toward Pagan. We pummeled each other and shouted salutations, but I cut them short to inquire, "What are you doing in this forsaken place?"

"The Wang Bayan sent me looking for you, Elder Brother Marco. And, because Bayan said, 'Bring him *quickly*,' the Sardar Shaibani this time did not just engage a ship, but commandeered one, with all its crew, and put aboard Mongol warriors to urge the mariners on. We ascertained that you had made landfall here at Kuddalore, so this is where I came. But frankly, I was wondering where to look next. These stupid villagers told me you had gone inland only to the next village of Panrati, but that was many months ago, and I knew you must have gone farther than that. So it is a blessing that we have met by accident. Come, we will set sail for Ava at once."

"But why?" I asked. This worried me. Yissun's spate of words seemed intended to tell me everything but why. "What need has Bayan of me, and in such hurry? Is it war, insurrection, what?"

"I am sorry to say no, Marco, nothing natural and normal like that. It seems that your good woman Hui-sheng is in poor health. As best I can tell you—"

"Not now," I said instantly, feeling even on that hot day a cold wind blow. "Tell me on board. As you say, let us sail at once."

He had a dinghi and a Hindu boatman waiting at his service, and we went immediately out to the anchored ship, another good substantial qurqur, this one captained by a Persian and crewed by an assortment of races and colors. They were quite willing to hurry back across the bay, for the month was now March, and the winds would soon drop and the heat worsen and the drenching rains come. We took Tofaa with us, since her destination was Chittagong, and that chief port of Bangala was on the same eastern side of the bay as Akyab, and not far up that coast, so the ship could readily take her there after dropping me and Yissun.

When the qurqur had weighed anchor and was under way, Yissun and I and Tofaa stood at the stern rail—he and I thankfully watching India disappear behind us—and he told me about Hui-sheng.

"When your lady first discovered she was with child—"

"With child!" I cried in consternation.

Yissun shrugged. "I repeat only what I have been told. I am told that she was both overjoyed at the fact and worried that you might disapprove."

"Dear God! She did not try to expel it, and hurt herself?"

"No, no. I think the Lady Hui-sheng would not do anything, Marco, without your approval. No, she did nothing, and I gather she did not even realize that anything might be wrong."

"Well, vakh, man! What is wrong?"

"When I left Pagan, nothing—nothing that anyone could see. The lady appeared to me to be in perfect health, and radiant with expectation, and more beautiful even than before. There was nothing visibly amiss. What it is, I gather, is something that cannot be seen. Because, at the very beginning, when she first confided to her maidservant that she was pregnant, that servant—Arùn, you remember her—took it upon herself to approach the Wang Bayan and inform him that she had misgivings. Now remember, Marco, I am only telling you what Bayan told me the servant told him, and I am no shamàn or physician, and I am not much knowledgeable about the internal workings of women, and—"

"Do get to it, Yissun," I pleaded.

"The girl Arùn informed Bayan that, in her opinion, your Lady Hui-sheng is not physically well adapted for childbearing. Something about the shape of the bones of her pelvic cradle, whatever that is. You must excuse my mentioning intimate details of anatomy, Marco, but I am only reporting. And evidently the servant Arùn, being your lady's chamber attendant, is well acquainted with her pelvic cradle."

"So am I," I said. "And I never noticed anything wrong with it."

At that point, Tofaa spoke up, in her know-everything way, and inquired, "Marco-wallah, is your lady extremely obese?"

"Impudent woman! She is not at all obese!"

"I only asked. That is the most usual cause of difficulty. Well, then, tell me this. Is your lady's mount of love—you know, that little frontal cushion, where the hair grows—is it perhaps delightfully protrusive?"

I said coldly, "For your information, women of her race are not matted with sweaty hair there. However, now that you mention it, I would say yes—that frontal place on my lady is a trifle more prominent than I have seen on other women."

"Ah, well, there you are, then. A woman of that conformation is sublimely sweet and deep and enfolding in the act of surata—as no doubt you are well aware—but it can ill suit her for childbearing. It indicates that her pelvic bones are shaped in such a way that the opening of her pelvic cradle is heart-shaped instead of oval. Clearly, that distortion is what her maid servant recognized, and was worried by. But surely, Marco-wallah, your lady herself should have been aware. Her mother must have told her, or her nursemaid, at the time she became a woman and was sat down for her woman-to-woman counseling."

"No," I said, reflecting. "She could not have been told. Hui-sheng's mother died in her childhood, and she herself . . . well, thereafter she heard no counseling, she had no confidantes. But never mind that. What should she have been told?"

Tofaa said flatly, "Never to have children."

"Why? What does it mean, this pelvic conformation? Is she in great danger?"

"Not while she is pregnant, no. There would be no difficulty in carrying the baby through all the nine months, if she is otherwise healthy. It should be an uneventful pregnancy, and a pregnant woman is always a happy woman. The problem comes at the time for delivery."

"And then?"

Tofaa looked away from me. "The hardest part is the extrusion of the infant's head. But its head is oval, and so is the normal pelvic opening. Whatever the labor and pain involved, it does get out. However, if that passage is constricted, as in the case of a heart-shaped pelvis . . ."

"Then?"

She said evasively, "Imagine that you are pouring grain from a sack that has a narrow neck, and a mouse has got into the grain, and it stops the neck. But the grain has to be emptied, so you press and wring and squeeze. Something must give."

"The mouse will burst. Or the neck will split asunder."

"Or the whole sack."

I moaned, "God, let it be the mouse!" Then I whirled on Yissun and demanded, "What is being done?"

"Everything possible, Elder Brother. The Wang Bayan well remembers that he promised you he would see to her safekeeping. All the physicians of the court of Ava are in attendance, but Bayan was not satisfied to trust in them. He sent couriers galloping to Khanbalik to apprise the Khakhan of the situation. And the Khan Kubilai dispatched his own personal court physician, the Hakim Gansui. That aged man was himself nearly dead by the time he was hauled all the way south to Pagan, but he will wish he *were* dead if anything happens to the Lady Hui-sheng."

Well, I thought, after Yissun and Tofaa had gone away and left me to brood alone, I could hardly blame Bayan or Gansui or anyone else for whatever might happen. It was I who had put Hui-sheng in this peril. It had to have happened on that first night she and I and Arùn frolicked together, so excitedly that I had neglected what was my responsibility and my pleasure—the nightly emplacing of the preventive lemon cap. I tried to calculate when that had been. Right after our arrival in Pagan, so that was how long ago? Gèsu, at least eight months and perhaps nearly nine! Hui-sheng must by now be almost at term. No wonder Bayan was anxious for me to be found and brought to her bedside.

He was no more anxious than I. If my darling Hui-sheng were in the least difficulty, I wanted to be beside her. Now she was in the worst possible trouble, and I was unforgivably far away. In consequence, this crossing of the Bay of Bangala seemed excruciatingly slower and longer than the first traverse, outward bound. The captain and crew did not find me a very agreeable passenger to be transporting on their ship, and my two fellow passengers did not find me a very agreeable companion. I snapped and snarled and fretted and paced the deck, and I cursed the mariners every time they did not have every single scrap of sail stretched to the mast top, and I cursed the uncaring immensity of the bay, and I cursed the weather every time the least cloud appeared in the sky, and I cursed the unfeeling way time was behaving—passing so slowly out here, but elsewhere hastening Hui-sheng toward the day of reckoning.

And mostly I cursed myself, because, if there was one man in the world who knew what he was inflicting on a woman when he made her pregnant, it was I. That time on the Roof of the World when, under the influence of the love philter, I briefly had *been* a woman in the throes of childbirth—whether it was fancy or reality, a drug-caused delusion in my mind or a drug-caused transfiguration of my body—I most definitely *had* experienced every ghastly moment and hour and lifetime of the birthing process. I knew it better than any man, better even than a male physician could know it, however many births he had attended. I knew there was nothing pretty or dulcet or felicitous about it, as all the myths of sweet maternity would have us believe. I knew it to be a filthy business, nauseous, humiliating, terrible torture. I had seen a Fondler do vile things to human Subjects, but even he could not do them *from the inside out*. Childbirth was more terrible, and the Subject could do nothing but scream and scream until the torment ended in the final agonizing extrusion.

But poor Hui-sheng could not even scream.

And if the groping, raging, tearing thing inside her could not *ever* get out . . . ?

I was to blame. I had neglected, on just one occasion, to take the proper precaution. But actually I had been more culpably neglectful than that. Ever after my own horrendous childbed experience, I had said, "I will never subject any woman I love to such a fate." So, if I had rightly loved Hui-sheng, I would never have lain with her and never have put her even remotely at risk. It was hard to regret all the lovely times she and I had engaged in the act of love, but now I did regret them, for even with precautions there was no certainty, and she had every time been in danger. Now I swore to myself and to God that if Hui-sheng survived this peril, I would never lie with her again. I loved her that much, and we would simply have to find other ways of mutually demonstrating our love.

That bitter decision made, I tried to bury my apprehensions in happier recollections, but their very sweetness made them bitter, too. I remembered the last time I had seen her, when Yissun and I rode away from Pagan. Hui-sheng could not have heard or responded to my calling as I went, "Goodbye, my dear one." But she had heard, with her heart. And she had spoken, too, with her eyes: "Come back, my dear one." And I remembered how, bereft of ever hearing music, she had so often felt it instead, and seen it, and sensed it in other ways. She had even made music, though unable to do it herself, for I had known other people—even dour servants engaged in uncongenial labor—often to hum or sing happily, just because Hui-sheng was in the room. I remembered one occasion, one summer day, when we had been caught outdoors in a sudden thundershower, and all the Mongols about us were quaking uneasily and muttering their Khakhan's protecting name. But Hui-sheng had only smiled at the displays of lightning, unafraid of the menacing noise it made; to her, a storm was only another beautiful thing. And I remembered how often, on our walks together, Hui-sheng had run to pluck some flower my unimpaired but duller senses had failed to perceive. Still, I was not totally insensitive to beauty. Whenever she dashed away on one of those forays, I had to smile at the awkward, knee-tied way a woman runs, but it was a fond smile and, every time she ran, my heart went tumbling after. . . .

After another eternity or two, the voyage was done. As soon as we raised Akyab on the horizon, I had my packs ready and said my farewells and thanks to the Lady Tofaa, so that Yissun and I were able to leap from the deck to the dock even before the ship's plank was down. With only a wave to the Sardar Shaibani, we vaulted onto the horses he had brought to the bayside, and we put the spurs to them. Shaibani must also, as soon as our vessel was sighted in the distance, have sent an advance courier riding hard for Pagan, because, as swiftly as Yissun and I covered the four-hundred-li distance, the Pagan palace was expecting us. The Wang Bayan was not waiting to be the first to greet us; no doubt he had decided he was too gruff for such a delicate duty. He had posted instead the old Hakim Gansui and the little maidservant Arùn to receive us. I got down from my mount, trembling, as much from inner palpitation as from the muscular strain of the long gallop, and Arùn came running to take my hands in hers, and Gansui approached more sedately. They did not need to speak. I saw from their faces—his grave, hers grieving—that I had arrived too late.

"All that could have been done was done," said the hakim when, at his insistence, I had taken a bracing drink of the fiery choum-choum. "I did not get here to Pagan until well along in the lady's term, but I could yet have easily and safely made her miscarry. She would not let me. Insofar as I could comprehend her, through the medium of this servant girl, your Lady Hui-sheng insisted that that decision was not hers to make."

"You should have overruled her," I said huskily.

"The decision was not mine to make, either." He kindly refrained from saying that the decision should have been made by me, and I merely nodded.

He went on, "I had no recourse but to await the confinement. And in fact I was not without some hope. I am not one of the Han physicians, who do not even touch their female patients, but instead let them modestly point out on an ivory figurine the spots where they hurt. I insisted on making a full examination. You say you have only recently learned that your lady's pelvic cavity was constricted. I found that its oblique diameters were diminished by the sacral column's forward intrusion and the pubic extremity's being more pointed than rounded, giving the cavity a triradiate instead of oval shape. That is not usually any impediment to a woman—in her walking, riding, whatever—*until* she contemplates becoming a mother."

"She never knew," I said.

"I believe I managed to convey it to her, and to warn her of the possible consequences. But she was stubborn—or determined—or brave. And in truth I could not tell her that the birth was impossible, that it *must* be terminated. In my time, I have attended several African concubines, and of all races the black women have the most narrow pelvic passages, but they have children nonetheless. An infant's head is quite malleable and pliable, so I was not without hope that this one could effect its egress without too much trouble. Unfortunately, it could not."

He paused, to choose his next words carefully. "After some time of labor, it became evident that the fetus was inextricably impacted. And at that point, the decision *is* the physician's to make. I rendered the lady insensible with oil of teryak. The fetus was dissected and extracted. A full-term male infant of apparently normal development. But there already had been too much strain on the mother's internal organs and vessels, and bleeding was occurring in places where it is impossible to stanch. The Lady Hui-sheng never awoke from the teryak coma. It was an easy and a painless death."

I wished he had stopped short of the last words. However compassionately intended, they were an outright lie. I have seen too many deaths to believe that any is ever "easy." And "painless," this one? I knew, better than he did, what "some time of labor" was like. Before he mercifully granted her oblivion, and minced the baby and plucked it out piecemeal, Hui-sheng had endured hours indistinguishable from Hell's own eternity. But I only said dully:

"You did what you could, Hakim Gansui. I am grateful. Can I see her now?"

"Friend Marco, she died four days ago. In this climate . . . Well, the ceremony was simple and dignified, not one of the local barbarities. A pyre at sunset, with the Wang Bayan and all the court as mourners . . ."

So I would not even see her one last time. It was hard, but perhaps it was best. I could remember her, not as a motionless and forever silent Echo, but as she once had been, alive and vibrant, as I last had seen her.

I went numbly through the formalities of greeting Bayan and hearing his rough condolences, and I told him I would depart again as soon as I was rested, to bear the Buddha relic to Kubilai. Then I went with Arùn to the chambers where Hui-sheng and I had last lived together, and where she had died. Arùn emptied closets and chests, to help me pack, though I selected only a few keepsakes to take with me. I told the girl she might have the clothes and other feminine things Hui-sheng no longer had any use for. But Arùn insisted on showing me every single item and asking my permission each time. I might have found that unnecessarily hurtful, but really the clothes and jewels and hair ornaments meant nothing to me without Hui-sheng the wearer of them.

I had determined that I would not weep—at least not until I reached some lonely place on the trail northward, where I could do so in seclusion. It required some exertion, I confess, not to let the tears flow, not to fling myself on the vacant bed we had shared, not to clutch her empty garments to me. But I said to myself, "I will bear this like a stolid Mongol—no, like a practical-minded merchant."

Yes, best to be like a merchant, for he is a man accustomed to the transitoriness of things. A merchant may deal in treasures, and he may rejoice when an exceptional treasure comes to hand, but he knows that he has it for only a while before it must go to other hands—or what is he a merchant for? He may be sorry to see that treasure go, but if he is a proper merchant he will be the richer for having possessed it even briefly. And I was, I was. Though she was gone from me now, Hui-sheng had immeasurably enriched my life, and left me with a store of memories beyond price, and perhaps even made me a better man for having known her. Yes, I had profited. That very practical way of regarding my bereavement made it easier for me to contain my grief. I congratulated myself on my stony composure.

But then Arùn inquired, "Will you be taking this?" and what she held was the white porcelain incense burner, and the stone man broke.

HOME

. I .

M Y father greeted me with joy, and then with condolence when I told him why I had returned to Khanbalik without Hui-sheng. He started somberly to tell me that life was like a something or other, but I interrupted the homily.

"I see we are no longer the most recently arrived Westerners in Kithai," I said, for there was a stranger sitting with my father in his chambers. He was a white man, a little older than myself, and his garb, though travel-worn, identified him as a cleric of the Franciscan order.

"Yes," said my father, beaming. "At long last, a real Christian priest comes to Kithai. And a near countryman of ours, Marco, from the Campagna. This is Pare Zuàne—"

"Padre Giovanni," said the priest, pettishly correcting my father's Venetian pronunciation. "Of Montecorvino, near Salerno."

"Like us, some three years on the road," said my father. "And very nearly our same route."

"From Constantinople," said the priest. "Down into India, where I established a mission, then up through High Tartary."

"I am sure you will be welcome here, Pare Zuàne," I said politely.

"If you have not yet been presented to the Khakhan, I am having audience with him shortly, and—"

"The Khan Kubilai has already most cordially received me."

"Perhaps," said my father, "if you asked, Marco, the Pare Zuàne would consent to say a few words in memory of our dear departed Huisheng . . ."

I would not have asked him anyway, but the priest said stiffly, "I gather that the departed was not a Christian. And that the union was not according to the Sacrament."

So I rudely turned my back on him and rudely said, "Father, if these once remote and unknown and barbaric lands are now attracting civilized arrivisti like this one, the Khakhan should not feel too forlorn when we few pioneers take our departure. I am ready to leave whenever you are."

"I expected you would be," he said, nodding. "I have been converting all the holdings of the Compagnia into portable goods and currencies. Most has already gone westward by horse post along the Silk Road. And the rest is all packed. We need only to decide on our mode of travel and the route we shall take—and get the Khakhan's consent, of course."

So I went to get that. First I presented to Kubilai the Buddha relic I had brought, at which he expressed pleasure and some awe and many thanks. Then I presented a letter which Bayan had given me to carry, and I waited while he read it, and then I said:

"I also brought back with me, Sire, your personal physician, the Hakim Gansui, and I am eternally grateful for your having sent him to care for my late lady consort."

"Your *late* lady? Then Gansui could not have cared for her very effectively. I am desolated to hear it. He has always done well enough in treating my ever afflicting gout, and my more recent ills of old age, and I should be sorry to lose him. But ought he be executed for this lamentable dereliction?"

"Not at my behest, Sire. I am satisfied that he did what he could. And putting him to death would not bring back my lady or my unborn son."

"I commiserate, Marco. A lovely and beloved and loving lady is indeed irreplaceable. But sons?" He gave a casual wave, and I thought he was referring to his own considerable brood of progeny. But he made me start when he said, "You already have these half a dozen. And, I believe, three or four daughters besides."

For the first time, I realized who were the page boys that had replaced his former elderly stewards. I was speechless.

"Most handsome lads," he went on. "A great improvement in the sightliness of my throne room. Visitors can rest their gaze on those comely young men, instead of this aged hulk on the throne."

I looked around at the pages. The one or two within earshot, who had probably overheard that astonishing revelation—astonishing to me, anyway—gave me back timid and respectful smiles. Now I knew where they had got their lighter-than-Mongol complexions and hair and eyes, and I even fancied I could see a vague resemblance to myself. Still, they were strangers to me. They had not been conceived in love, and I would probably not recognize their mothers if we passed in a palace corridor. I set my jaw and said:

"My only son died in childbirth, Sire. The loss of him and his mother has left me sore of soul and heart. For that reason, I ask my Lord Khakhan's permission to make my report on this latest mission of mine, and then to request a favor."

He studied me for a time, and the age-eroded wrinkles and channels of his leather face seemed to deepen perceptibly, but he said only, "Report."

I did it briefly enough, since I had really had no mission except to observe. So I gave my impressions of what I had seen: that India was a country totally worthless of his acquisition or least attention; that the lands of Champa offered the same resources—elephants, spices, timber, slaves, precious gems—and much nearer at hand.

"Also, Ava is already yours, of course. However, I have one observation to make, Sire. Like Ava, the other nations of Champa may be susceptible to easy conquest, but I think the holding of them will be hard. Your Mongols are northern men, accustomed to breathing freely. In those tropical heats and damps, no Mongol garrison can endure for long without falling prey to fevers and diseases and the ambient indolence. I suggest, instead of actual occupation, Sire, that you simply install submissive natives as your Champa administrators and overseeing forces."

He nodded and again picked up the letter I had brought from Bayan. "The King Rama Khamhaeng of Muong Thai is already proposing just such an arrangement, as alternative to our demanding his unconditional surrender. He offers all the produce of his country's tin mines in continuing tribute. I think I shall accept those terms, and leave Muong Thai nominally an independent nation."

I was pleased to hear that, having conceived a real fondness for the Thai people. Let them have their Land of the Free.

Kubilai went on, "I thank you for your report, Marco. You have done well, as always. I should be an ungrateful lord were I to refuse any favor in my granting. Make your request, then."

He knew what I was going to ask. Nevertheless, I did not care to ask it baldly and abruptly: "Give me leave to leave you." So I began in the Han manner, with circumlocution.

"A long time ago, Sire, I had occasion to say, 'I could never slay a woman.' And when I said that, a slave of mine, a man wiser than I realized, said, 'You are young yet.' I could not then have believed it, but I have recently been the cause of the dying of the woman most dear to me in all the world. And I am no longer young. I am a man of middle age, well along in my fourth decade. That death has caused me much hurt and, like a wounded elephant, I should like to limp away to the seclusion of my home ground, there to recover from my wound or to languish of it. I ask your permission, Sire—and I hope your blessing—for the departure from your court of myself and my father and my uncle. If I am no longer young, they are already old, and their dying should also be done at home."

"And I am older yet," said Kubilai, with a sigh. "The scroll depicting my life has been wound much farther from the one hand to the other. And every turn of the scroll's rods reveals a picture with fewer friends standing about me. Someday, Marco, you will envy your lost lady. She died in the summer of her life, not having to see all that was flowery and green about her turn brown and dwindle and blow away like autumn leaves." He shivered as if he felt already the gusts of winter. "I shall be sorry to see my friends Polo depart, but I should be ill repaying your family's long service and companionship if I whined for its continuance. Have you yet made any travel arrangements?"

"Of course not, Sire. Not without your permission."

"You have it, certainly. But now I should like to ask a favor. One last mission for you, which you can perform on your way, and it will make easier your way."

"You have only to command it, Sire."

"I would ask if you and Nicolò and Mafìo could deliver a certain valuable and delicate cargo to my grandnephew Arghun in Persia. When Arghun succeeded to that Ilkhanate, he took a Persian wife as a politic gesture to his subjects. He doubtless has other wives, as well, but now he wishes to have for his premier wife and Ilkhatun a woman of pure Mongol blood and upbringing. So he sent envoys to ask me to procure such a bride for him, and I have chosen a lady named Kukachin."

"The widow of your son Chingkim, Sire?"

"No, no. She has the same name, but she is no relation, and you have never met her. A young maiden straight from the plains, from the tribe called Bayaut. I have provided for her an ample dowry and the usual rich bridal furnishings and a retinue of servants and maids, and she is ready to journey to Persia to meet her pledged husband. However, to send her overland would mean her having to traverse the territories of the Ilkhan Kaidu. That dastardly cousin of mine is as unruly as ever, and you know how inimical he always has been to his cousins who hold the Ilkhanate of Persia. I would not put it past Kaidu to capture the Lady Kukachin on her way and hold her—either to demand a ransom payment from Arghun or just to enjoy the spitefulness of the deed."

"You wish us to escort her through that unsafe territory?"

"No. I had rather she avoided it altogether. My notion is to send her the whole way by sea. However, all my ships' captains are of the Han, and vakh!—the Han mariners performed so disappointingly during our attempted invasions of Jihpen-kwe that I hesitate to trust them with this mission. But you and your uncles are also of a seafaring people. You are familiar with the open sea and with the handling of ships."

"True, Sire, but we have never actually *sailed* one."

"Oh, the Han can do that well enough. I should ask you only to be in command. To keep a stern eye on the Han captains, so *they* do not run off with the lady, or sell her to pirates, or lose her along the way.

And you would keep an eye on the course, so the captains do not sail the whole fleet off the edge of the world."

"Yes, we could see to those things, Sire."

"You would again carry my pai-tzu, and have unquestioned and unlimited authority, both on the sea and at every landfall you may have to make. It would mean comfortable traveling for you, from here to Persia, in good shipboard accommodations, with good food and good servants all the way. Especially it would mean easy travel for the invalid Mafìo, and attendants to care for him. You would be met in Persia by a train sent to fetch the Lady Kukachin, and you would be well and comfortably transported to wherever Arghun is currently making his capital. And surely he would see that you have good transport from there onward. So, Marco, that is the mission. Would you confer with your uncles and consider undertaking it?"

"Why, Sire, I am certain that I can speak now for all of us. We would not only be honored to do it, and eager, we are obligated to you for making the journey so easy for us."

And so, while the bridal fleet was being assembled and provisioned, my father did the final clearing up of some loose ends of our Compagnia's business, and I attended to some loose ends of my own affairs. I dictated to Kubilai's court scribes a letter to be enclosed with the next official dispatch the Khakhan sent to the Wang Bayan in Ava. I sent warm greetings and regards and farewells to my old friend, and then suggested that, since the nation of Muong Thai was to be left free and uninvaded, I would take it as a personal favor if Bayan would see to it that the little Pagan maidservant Arùn was given her liberty and conveyed safely to that land of her own people.

Then, from the last Kithai gains of the Compagnia Polo, which my father had converted into portable goods for us to carry home, I took my share—a parcel of fine rubies—and carried it only as far as the chambers of the Finance Minister Lin-ngan. He was the first Khanbalik courtier I had met, and the first to whom I now said my goodbyes in person. I gave him the parcel of gems and asked him to use their value to make payment of a bequest to the Khakhan's page boys, as each of them reached manhood, so they would have a start when they set out to seek their own fortunes.

Then I went about the palace, saying my farewells to other people. Some of my calls were for duty's sake: on such dignitaries as the Hakim Gansui and the Khatun Jamui, Kubilai's aged premier wife. And some of my calls were less formal, but still brief: on the Court Astronomer and the Court Architect. And one call I made—on the Palace Engineer Wei —was just to thank him for having constructed that garden pavilion in which Hui-sheng had enjoyed the warbling water-piped music. And one call I made—on the Minister of History—was just to tell him:

"Now you can write in your archives another trifle. In the Year of the Dragon, by the Han count the year three thousand nine hundred ninety, the foreigner Po-lo Mah-ko finally left the City of the Khan to return to his native Wei-ni-si."

He smiled, remembering our one conversation so long ago, and said, "Do I record that Khanbalik was made better by his presence here?"

"That is for Khanbalik to say, Minister."

"No, that is for history to say. But here—see—" He took up a brush, wetted his ink block and wrote, on a paper already crowded with writing, a vertical line of characters. Among them I recognized the character that was on my yin seal. "There. The trifle is mentioned. Come back in a hundred years, Polo, or in a thousand, and see if this trifle is still remembered."

Others of my farewell visits were more warm and lingering. In fact, three of them—my calls on the Court Firemaster Shi Ix-me and the Court Goldsmith Pierre Boucher and especially my call on Chao Meng-fu, War Minister, Court Artist, once fellow conspirator—each lasted long into the night and concluded only when we were too drunk to drink more.

When word came that the ships were ready and waiting for us at the port of Quan-zho, my father and I led Uncle Mafìo to the Khakhan's chambers for our introduction to our lady charge. Kubilai first presented to us the three envoys who had come to procure her for the Ilkhan Arghun—their names were Uladai, Koja and Apushka—and then the Lady Kukachin, who was a girl of seventeen, as pretty as any Mongol female I had ever seen, dressed in finery designed to dazzle all Persia. But the young lady was not haughty and imperious, as might have been expected in a noblewoman on her way to become an Ilkhatun, heading an entourage of nearly six hundred, counting all her servants, maids, noble courtiers-to-be and escorting soldiers. As befitted a girl so suddenly promoted from a plains tribe—where probably her entire court had consisted of a horse herd—Kukachin was forthright and natural and pleasant of manner.

"Elder Brothers Polo," she said to us, "it is with the utmost trust and confidence that I put myself in the keeping of such renowned journeyers."

She and the leading nobles of her company and the three envoys from Persia and we three Polos and most of the Khanbalik court all sat down with Kubilai to a farewell banquet in the same vast chamber where we had enjoyed our welcoming banquet so long before. It was a sumptuous feast, and even Uncle Mafìo appeared to enjoy it—he being fed by his constant and faithful woman servant, who would remain with him as far as Persia—and the night was riotous with many and varied entertainments (Uncle Mafìo at one point rising to sing to the Khakhan a verse or two of his well-worn "Virtue" song) and everyone got exceedingly drunk on the liquors which the gold-and-silver serpent tree still dispensed on call. Before we got quite unconscious, my father and I and Kubilai made our mutual leavetakings, a process as lengthy and emotional and replete with embraces and fulsome toasts and speeches as a Venetian wedding.

But Kubilai also managed one private short colloquy with me. "Although I have known your uncles longer, Marco, I have known you best, and I shall be sorriest for your going. Hui, I remember, the first words

you ever spoke to me were insulting." He laughed in recollection. "That
was not wise of you, but it was brave of you, and it was right of you to
speak so. Ever since then, I have relied much on your words, and I shall
be the poorer for hearing no more of them. I will hope that you may
come this way again. I will not be here to greet you. But you would be
doing me a service still, if you befriended and served my grandson
Temur with the same dedication and loyalty you have shown to me." He
laid a heavy hand on my shoulder.

I said, "It will always be my proudest boast, Sire, and my only claim
to having lived a useful life, that once, for a while, I served the Khan of
All Khans."

"Who knows?" he said jovially. "The Khan Kubilai may be remembered only because he had for good adviser a man named Marco Polo."
He gave my shoulder a companionable shake. "Vakh! Enough of sentiment. Let us drink and get drunk! And then"—he raised to me a jeweled
beaker brimming with arkhi—"a good horse and a wide plain to you,
good friend."

"Good friend," I dared to echo, raising my goblet, "a good horse and
a wide plain to you."

And the next morning, with heavy heads and not entirely light
hearts, we took our departure. Just getting that populous train out of
Khanbalik was a tactical problem very nearly on the order of the Orlok
Bayan's moving his tuk of warriors about in the Ba-Tang valley—and
this was a herd consisting mostly of civilians not trained in military
discipline. So, the first day, we did not get farther than the next village to
the south, where we were received with cheers and thrown flowers and
hosannahs and incense and bursts of the fiery trees. We did not make
much better progress on the succeeding days, either, because of course
every least village and town wanted to display its enthusiasm. Even after
we got our company accustomed to forming up and moving out each
morning, the train was so immense—my father and I and the three
envoys, like most of the servants and all the escort troops, mounted on
horses; the Lady Kukachin and her women and my Uncle Mafio riding
in horse-borne palanquins; a number of Khanbalik nobles riding elephant haudas; plus all the pack animals and drovers necessary for the
luggage of six hundred persons—that we made a procession sometimes
stretching the entire length of the road between the community where
we had just spent the night and the next one we were bound for. Our
final destination, the port of Quan-zho, was much farther south than I
had ever been in Manzi—very far south of Hang-zho, my onetime city of
residence—so the journey took an unconscionably long time. But it was
an enjoyable journey because, for a change, the column was not of
soldiers going to war, and we were welcome everywhere we arrived.

. 2 .

A t last we got to Quan-zho, and some of our escorting troops and nobles and the pack train turned back for Khanbalik, and the rest of us filed on board the great chuan ships, and at the next tide we put out into the Sea of Kithai. We made a water-borne procession even more imposing than our land parade had been, for Kubilai had provided an entire fleet: fourteen of the massive four-masted vessels, each crewed by some two hundred mariners. We had apportioned our company among them, my father and uncle and I and the envoy Uladai aboard the one carrying the Lady Kukachin and most of her women. The chuan vessels were good and solid, of the triple-planked construction, and our cabins were luxuriously furnished, and I think every one of us passengers had four or five servants from the lady's entourage to wait upon us, in addition to the sea stewards and cooks and cabin boys also seeing to our comfort. The Khakhan had promised good accommodations and service and food, and I will give just one instance to illustrate how the ships lived up to that promise. On each of the fourteen vessels there was one seaman detailed to a single job throughout the voyage: he kept forever paddling and stirring the water in a deck tank the size of a lotus pool, in which swam *freshwater* fish for our tables.

My father and I had little to do in the way of command or supervision. The captains of the fourteen vessels had been sufficiently impressed and awed, to see us white men striding magisterially aboard with the Khakhan's pai-tzu tablets slung on our chests, that they were commendably sedulous and punctilious in all their responsibilities. As for making sure that the fleet did not wander about, I would from time to time stand conspicuously on deck at night, eyeing the horizon through the kamàl I had kept ever since Suvediye. Though that little wooden frame told me nothing except that we were bearing constantly south, it always brought our ship's captain scurrying to assure me that we were unswervingly keeping proper course.

The only complaint we passengers might have voiced was about the slowness of our progress, but that was caused by our captains' devotion to their duty and our comfort. The Khakhan had chosen the ponderous chuan vessels especially to ensure for the Lady Kukachin a safe and smooth voyage, and the very stability of the big ships made them exceedingly slow in the water, and the necessity for all fourteen to stay together imposed even more slowness. Also, whenever the weather looked at all threatening, the captains would steer for a sheltered cove. So, instead of making a straight southward run across the open sea, the fleet followed the far longer westering arc of the coastline. Also, though the ships were lavishly provisioned with food and other supplies for fully two years' sailing, they could not carry enough drinking water for more than a month or so. To replenish those supplies, we had to put in at intervals, and those were lengthier stops than the occasional shelterings. Just the heaving-to and anchoring of such a numerous fleet of such leviathan ships occupied most of a day. Then the rowing back and forth of barrels in the ships' boats took another three or four days, and the weighing of anchor and setting sail again took yet another day. So every watering stop cost us about a week's progress. After leaving Quan-zho, I remember, we stopped for water at a great island off Manzi, called Hainan, and at a harbor village on the coast of Annam in Champa, called Gai-dinh-thanh, and at an island as big as a continent, called Kaliman-tan. In all, we were three months making just the southward leg of our voyage down the coast of Asia before we could turn westward in the direction of Persia.

"I have watched you, Elder Brother Marco," said the Lady Kukachin, coming up to me on deck one night, "standing here from time to time, manipulating a little wooden device. Is that some Ferenghi instrument of navigation?"

I went and fetched it, and explained to her its function.

"It might be a device unknown to my pledged husband," she said. "And I might gain favor in his eyes if I introduced him to it. Would you show me how to employ it?"

"With pleasure, my lady. You hold it at arm's length, like this, toward the North Star—" I stopped, appalled.

"What is the matter?"

"The North Star has vanished!"

It was true. That star had, every night lately, been lower toward the horizon. But I had not sought it for several nights, and now I was aghast to see that it had sunk entirely out of view. The star which I had been able to see almost every night of my life, the steadfast beacon which throughout history had guided all journeyers on land and sea, had totally *gone from the sky.* That was frightening—to see the one constant, immutable, fixed thing in the universe disappear. We might really have sailed over some farthest edge of the world, and fallen into some unknown abyss.

I frankly confess that it made me uneasy. But, for the sake of Kukachin's confidence in me, I tried to dissemble my anxiety as I summoned the ship's captain to us. In as steady a voice as possible, I inquired what had become of the star, and how he could keep a course or know his position without that fixed point of reference.

"We are now below the bulge of the world's waist," he said, "where the star is simply not visible. We must rely on other references."

He sent a cabin boy running to the ship's bridge to bring him back a chart, and he unrolled it for me and Kukachin. It was not a depiction of the local coasts and landmarks, but of the night sky: nothing but painted dots of different sizes indicating stars of different luminosities. The captain pointed upward, showing us the four brightest stars in the sky—positioned as if marking the arms of a Christian cross—and then pointed to their four dots on the paper. I recognized that the chart was an accurate representation of those unfamiliar skies, and the captain assured us that it was sufficient for him to steer by.

"The chart appears as useful as your kamàl, Elder Brother," Kukachin said to me, and then to the captain, "Would you have a copy made for me—for my Royal Husband, I mean, in case he should ever wish to campaign southward from Persia?"

The captain obligingly and immediately set a scribe to doing that, and I voiced no more misgivings about the lost North Star. However, I still felt a little uneasy in those tropic seas, because even the sun behaved oddly there.

What I had always thought of as "sunset" might have been better called "sunfall" there, for the sun did not ease itself down from the sky each evening and gently settle beneath the sea—it made a sudden and precipitous *plunge*. There was never a flamboyant sunset sky to admire, nor any gradual twilight to soothe the way from day to night. One moment we would be in bright daylight, and in little more than an eye blink we would be in dark night. Also, there was never any perceptible change in the length of day and night. Everywhere from Venice to Khanbalik, I had been accustomed to the long days and short nights of summertime, and the opposite in wintertime. But, in all the months we spent making our way through the tropics, I never could notice any seasonal lengthing of either day or night. And the captain verified that: he told me that the difference between the tropics' longest day of the year and the shortest was only three-quarters of an hour's trickle of sand in the glass.

Three months out from Quan-zho, then, we came to our farthest southern reach, in the archipelago of the Spice Islands, where we would alter course to the westward. But first, since our water needed replenishment again, we made landfall at one of the islands, called Jawa the Greater. From the moment we first saw it on the horizon until we reached it, a good half a day later, we passengers were already saying among ourselves that this must be a most felicitous place. The airs were warm and so laden with the heady aromas of spices that we were almost made giddy, and the island was a tapestry of rich greens and flower colors, and the sea all about was the soft, translucent, glowing color of milk-green jade. Unfortunately, our first impression of having found an island of Paradise did not endure.

Our fleet anchored in the mouth of a river called Jakarta, offshore of a port called Tanjung Priok, and my father and I went ashore with the water-barrel boats. We discovered the so-called seaport to be only a village of zhu-gan cane houses built on high stilts because all the land was quagmire. The community's grandest edifices were some long cane platforms, with palm-thatch roofs but no walls, piled with bags of spices —nuts and barks and pods and powders—waiting for the next passing trade ship. What we could see of the island beyond the village was only dense jungle growing out of more quagmire. The warehouses of spices did provide an aroma that overwhelmed the jungle's miasmic smell and the stench common to all tropical villages. But we learned that this island of Jawa the Greater was only by courtesy called one of the Spice Islands, for nothing more valuable than pepper grew here, and the better spices—nutmeg and clove and mace and sandal and so on—grew on more remote islands of the archipelago and were merely collected in this place because it was more convenient to the sea lanes.

We also soon discovered that Jawa had no Paradise climate, for we had no sooner got ashore than we were drenched by a thunderstorm. Rain falls on that island one day of every three, we were told, and usually in the form of a thunderstorm which, we did not have to be told, was a fair imitation of the end of the world. I trust that, after our eventual departure, Jawa enjoyed an uncommonly long spell of fine weather, because we had nothing but bad. That first storm simply continued, day and night, for weeks, the thunder and lightning taking a rest now and then, but the rain falling interminably, and we rode it out there at anchor in the river mouth.

Our captains had intended to go west from this place through the narrow passage called the Sunda Strait, which separates Jawa the Greater from the next westward island, Jawa the Lesser, also called Sumatera. They said that strait allowed the easiest run to India, but they also said the strait could only be negotiated in calm seas and unimpeded visibility. So our fleet stayed in the Jakarta River mouth, where the downpour was so continuous and so heavy that Jawa was not even visible through it. But we knew the island was still there, because we were waked at every dawn by the howling and whistling of the gibbon apes in the jungle treetops. It was not really an uncomfortable place to be marooned—our boatmen brought from shore fresh pork and fowl and fruits and vegetables to augment our stores of smoked and salted foods, and we had a plenitude of spices to enhance our meals—but the waiting got extremely tiresome.

Whenever I got insupportably weary of seeing nothing but the harbor water jumping up to meet the rain, I would go ashore, but the view there was not much better. The Jawa people were quite comely of appearance—small and neatly proportioned and of golden skin, and the women as well as the men went bare to the waist—but the entire populace of Jawa, whatever religion it had originally espoused, had long ago been converted to Hinduism by the Indians who were the chief spice buyers. Inevitably, the Jawa people had adopted everything else that seems to go with the Hindu religion, meaning squalor and torpor and reprehensible personal habits. So I found the people no more appealing than any other Hindus, and Jawa no more appealing than India.

Some of the others of our company tried to alleviate their boredom in other ways, and came to grief by it. All the Han crewmen of our fleet, like mariners of every race and nationality, were mortally terrified of getting into water. But the Jawa people were quite at home on it and in it as well. A Jawa fisherman would skim about on even a turbulent sea in a craft called a prau, so small and flimsy that it would have been careened by the waves except that it was balanced by a log carried at some distance alongside on long cane spars. And even the Jawa women and children swam considerable distances from the shore through quite fearsome surf. So a number of our Mongol male passengers, and a few venturesome females, all of them inland-born and therefore incautious about large bodies of water, decided to emulate the Jawa folk and frolic in that warm sea.

Though the ambient air, full of the downpouring rain, was almost as liquid as the sea, the Mongols stripped down to a minimum of clothing and slid overboard to splash about. As long as they held onto the many rope ladders dangling overside, they were in no great danger. But many got overdaring, and tried swimming at liberty, and of every ten of them who vanished beyond the curtain of rain, perhaps seven would reappear. We never knew what happened to the missing ones, but the attrition kept on. It did not frighten others from venturing out, and we must have lost at least twenty men and two women from Kukachin's retinue.

We did know what happened to two of our casualties. One man who had been swimming climbed back onto the ship, cursing "Vakh!" to himself and shaking drops of blood from one hand. As the ship's Han physician salved it and bound it up, the man reported that he had rested his hand on a rock, and a fish had been clinging to it, a fish mottled with algae and looking just like the rock, and its dorsal spines had stung him. He said that much, and then screamed, "Vakh! Vakh! Vakhvakhvakh!" and went into insane paroxysms, thrashing all about the deck, foaming at the mouth, and when he finally slumped in a heap, we found that he was dead.

A Jawa fisherman, who had just brought his catch to sell to us, regarded that performance without emotion, and then said—a Han crewman translating—"The man must have touched a stonefish. It is the most venomous creature in any sea. Touch it, you endure such terrible agony that you go mad before you die. If that happens to any-one else, split a ripe durian and apply it to his wound. It is the only remedy."

I knew that the durian had many praiseworthy qualities—I had been voraciously eating of them ever since I discovered that they grew in profusion here—but I would never have suspected that the fruit had medicinal qualities. However, soon afterward, one of Kukachin's hair-dressing women also went for a swim, and came back weeping from the pain of a spine-stung arm, and the physician tried the durian remedy. To everyone's pleased surprise, it worked. The girl suffered no more than a swollen and painful arm. The physician made a careful note for his collection of materia medica, saying in some amazement, "As nearly as I can judge, the durian pulp somehow *digests* the stonefish poison before it can take dire effect."

And we also saw what accounted for the loss of another two of our company. The rain had finally stopped, and the sun had come out, and our captains were all standing on their decks, scrutinizing the sky and waiting to see if the weather might continue fine, long enough for us to up anchor and be away, and they were muttering Han incantations to make it so. The jade-green Jawa Sea that day looked so pretty as almost to tempt *me* into it—a gentle chop, fish-scaled with glittering lunettes of light—and did tempt two other men, Koja and Apushka, two of the three envoys of the Ilkhan Arghun. They challenged each other to a water race to a distant reef, and plunged from the chuan's side and went flailing and splashing away, and we all gathered at the rail to cheer them on.

Then down from the sky swooped a number of albatrosses. The birds, I suppose, had been balked in their usual fishing by the long spell of rain, and were weary of scavenging our ships' garbage and wanted some fresh meat. They began making dives at the two swimmers, stabbing their long hooked beaks at whatever parts of the men showed above the water, which was their heads. Koja and Apushka stopped swimming, trying to fend off the clustering birds and stay above water at the same time. We could hear them shouting, then cursing, then screaming, and see the blood running down their faces. And, when the albatrosses had plucked the eyes out of both of them, the men in desperation sank under water. They tried to rise up for a gasp of air a time or two, but the birds were waiting. And finally the two men simply let themselves drown, in preference to being torn to pieces. But, of course, as soon as their bodies floated limply and soggily on the surface, the albatrosses settled on them and peeled and shredded them for all the rest of that day.

It was sad, that Apushka and Koja had come safely through the countless hazards of journeying overland from Persia to Kithai, and then the long sea way to here, to die so abruptly and in such an un-Mongollike way. We were all, Kukachin especially, much grieved by the loss. We did not think to take it as a premonition of any future and perhaps more grievous loss—my father did not even murmur about "bad things always happening in threes"—though, as events turned out, we might well have seen an omen in it.

When the weather had kept bright and clear for two more days, our captains decided to trust that it would go on holding. The crews were set to their immense oar beams, and rowed our ponderous ships slowly out of the river mouth to the open sea, and the vast slatted sails were raised, and we again were taken by the wind, and turned westward toward home. But when we had rounded a high headland and turned southwest into a channel narrow enough that we could see another distant coast on our other side, a mast-top lookout on the leading ship called down. He did not cry one of the usual curt sea calls, like "Ship in sight!" or "Reefs ahead!"—no doubt because there *was* no accepted and abbreviated call for what he saw. He only shouted down, in a voice of wonderment, "Look how the sea boils!"

All of us on the decks went to look overside—and that is exactly what the Sunda Strait seemed to be doing: boiling and bubbling, like a pot of water set on a brazier to make cha. And then, right in the middle of the fleet, the sea heaved up in a hump, opened like a monster mouth and exhaled a great gust of steam. The plume kept spewing upwards for several minutes, and the steam drifted all among the ships. We passengers had been making exclamations of one kind or another, but when the cloud of steam enveloped us we began to cough and sputter, for it had the suffocating stench of rotten eggs. And when the steam had passed over us, we were all dusted with a fine yellow powder on our skin and clothes. I wiped the dust from my stinging eyes and licked it from my lips, and tasted the distinctive musty taste of sulphur.

The captains were shouting to their crews, and there was a deal of running about and shifting of sail spars, and all our ships turned about and fled the way they had come. When the boiling and belching patch of sea was safely behind us, our vessel's captain told me, apologetically:

"Farther along the strait lies the brooding black ring of sea mountains called the Pulau Krakatau. Those peaks are actually the tops of undersea volcanoes, and they have been known to erupt with devastating effect. Making waves as high as mountains, waves that scour the strait clean of every living thing, from end to end. Whether that boiling of the water yonder presaged an eruption I cannot know, but we cannot take the risk of sailing through."

So the fleet had to double back through the Jawa Sea and then turn northwestward up the Malacca Strait between Jawa the Lesser, or Sumatera, and the land of the Malayu. That was a reach of water three thousand li long and so broad I might have taken it for a sea, except that circumstances forced us to carom back and forth from one side of it to the other, so I knew well that there was extensive land on both verges of it, and got to know those lands rather better than I would have wished. What happened was that the weather turned foul again, and perniciously stayed so, harrying us constantly from the swampy western Sumatera side to the forested eastern Malayu side of the strait and back again, and making us take shelter in bays or coves on one shore or the other—and put in for water and fresh foods at wretched little cane villages too negligible to deserve names, though they all had names: Muntok and Singapura and Melaka and many others I have forgotten.

It took us fully five months to beat our way up the Malacca Strait. There was open sea at the northern end, where we might have turned due west, but our captains kept on northwestward, sailing us in prudent short lunges from one island to the next of a long string of islands called the Necuveram and Angamanam archipelago, using them in the manner of stepping-stones. Finally we came to the island that they said was the farthermost of the Angamanam, and there we anchored offshore and passed enough time to fill all our water tanks and take on all the fruits and vegetables we could wheedle out of the inhospitable natives.

Those were the smallest people I ever saw, and the ugliest. Men and women alike went about stark naked, but the sight of an Angamanam female would arouse no least lust even in a mariner long at sea. Men and women alike were squat and chunky of form, with enormous protruding underjaws, and skin blacker and glossier than any African's. I could easily have rested my chin atop the head of the tallest person among them—except that I would not have done any such thing, because their hair was their most repellent feature: merely random tufts of reddish fuzz. One would expect a people so grotesquely ugly to try to make up for it by cultivating a gracious nature, but the Angamanam folk were uniformly scowling and surly. That was because, a Han seamen told me, they were disappointed and irate that we had not wrecked a vessel or two of our fleet on the island's coral reefs, for the people's only occupation and only religion and only joy was the plundering of grounded ships and the slaughter of their crews and the ceremonial eating of them.

"Eating them? Why?" I asked. "Surely no inhabitants of a tropic isle, with all the provender of sea and jungle, can lack for food to eat."

"They do not eat the shipwrecked mariners for nourishment. They believe that the ingestion of an adventurous seafarer makes *them* as bold and venturesome as he was."

But we were too many and too well armed for the black dwarfs to make any assault on us. Our only problem was persuading them to part with their water and vegetables, for of course such people had no interest in gold or any other sort of monetary recompense. They did, however, like so many hopelessly ugly folk, have a high vanity. So, by doling out among them bits of trumpery cheap jewelry and ribbons and other fripperies with which they could adorn their unspeakable selves, we got what we required, and we sailed away.

From there, our fleet had an uneventful westward run across the Bay of Bangala, which is the only foreign sea that I have now traversed three times, and I will be gratified if I never have to do so again. This crossing was somewhat more to the southerly than my other two had been, but the view was the same: an infinite expanse of azure water with little white trapdoors of foam opening and closing here and there, as if mermaids were taking peeps at the upper world, and herds of pork-fish frisking about our hulls, and so many flying-fish hurtling aboard that our cooks, having long since depleted our tanks of Manzi freshwater fish, periodically collected them from the decks and made us meals of them.

The Lady Kukachin humorously inquired, "If those Angamanam people acquired courage by eating courageous people, will these meals make us able to fly like flying-fish?"

"More likely make us smell like them," grumbled the maid who attended her bathing chamber. She was disgruntled because, on this long run across the bay, the captains had commanded that we could bathe only in sea water dipped up in buckets, not to waste the fresh. Salt water gets one clean enough, but it leaves one cursedly gritty and scratchy and uncomfortable afterward.

· 3 ·

A T the western side of the great bay, we made landfall on the island of Srihalam. That was not far south of the Cholamandal of India, where I had earlier made sojourn, and the islanders were physically very similar to the Cholas and, like the Cholas, the island's coastal residents were mainly engaged in the trade of fishing for pearls. But there the similarity ended.

The Srihalam islanders had adhered to the religion of Buddha, hence were vastly superior to their mainland Hindu cousins in morals and customs and vivacity and personal appeal. Their island was a lovely place, tranquil and lush and of generally balmy weather. I have often noticed that the most beautiful places are given a multiplicity of names:

witness the Garden of Eden, which is also variously called Paradise and Arcadia and Elysium and even Djennet by the Muslims. Just so, Sriha-lam has been severally named by every people who ever admired it. The ancient Greeks and Romans called it Taprobane, meaning Lotus Pond, and the early Moorish seafarers called it Tenerisim, or Isle of Delight, and nowadays Arab mariners call it Serendib, which is only their faulty pronunciation of the islanders' own name for the place, Srihalam. That name, Place of Gems, is variously translated in other languages: Ilanare by the mainland Cholas, Lanka by other Hindus, Bao Di-fang by our Han captains.

Though we had put into Srihalam of necessity, for water and other supplies, our captains and crews and Lady Kukachin and her retinue and I and my father were not a bit reluctant to tarry there for a while. My father even did some trading—the name Place of Gems being descriptive as well as poetic—and acquired some sapphires of a fineness we had never seen elsewhere, including some immense, deep-blue stones with starlike rays coruscating in their depths. I did not engage in any business, but merely wandered about to see the sights. Those included some ancient cities, deserted and abandoned to the jungle, but still displaying a beauty of architecture and adornment that made me wonder if these people of Srihalam could be the remnants of the admirable race that had inhabited India before the Hindus, and had built the temples which the Hindus now pretended were their own.

Our ship's captain and I, glad to be stretching our legs after so long on shipboard, spent a couple of days climbing all the way to the shrine at the top of a mountain peak where, as I had once been told by a pongyi in Ava, the Buddha had left his footprint. I should say that *Buddhists* call it the imprint of the Buddha. Hindu pilgrims aver that it is the print of their god Siva, and Muslim pilgrims insist that it was made by Adam, and some Christian visitors have surmised that it must have been done by San Tommaso or Prete Zuàne, and my Han companion gave it as his opinion that it had been put there by Pan-ku, the Han ancestor of all mankind. I am no Buddhist, but I am inclined to think that the oblong indentation in the rock there—nearly as long and as broad as I am— must have been done by the Buddha, because I have seen his tooth and I *know* him to have been a giant, and I have never personally beheld any evidence pertaining to the other claimants.

To be honest, I was less interested in the footprint than in a story told to us by the shrine's attendant bhikku (as a pongyi was called in Srihalam). He said the island was rich in gems *because* the Buddha had spent time there, and had wept for the wickedness of the world, and each of his holy tears had congealed into a ruby, an emerald or a sapphire. But, said the bhikku, those gems could not just be picked up from the ground. They had all washed into valleys in the interior of the island, and those chasms were unapproachable because they teemed and squirmed with venomous snakes. So the islanders had had to contrive an ingenious method for harvesting the precious stones.

In the mountain crags about the valleys nested eagles which preyed on the serpents. So the islanders would sneak at night among those crags and throw cuts of raw meat down into the chasms, and when the meat hit the ground down there, some few gems would stick to it. Next day, the foraging eagles would pick up and eat the meat in preference to the snakes. Then, whenever an eagle was absent from its nest, a man could climb up there and finger through the bird's droppings and pick out the undigested rubies, sapphires and emeralds. I not only thought that an ingenious method of mining, I also thought it must be the origin of all the legends about the monster rukh bird, which allegedly snatches up and flies off with even bigger meats, includings persons and elephants. When I got back to our ship, I told my father he ought to treasure his newly acquired sapphires for more than their inherent value—for their having been got for him by the fabled rukh.

We might have stayed on longer yet in Srihalam, but one day the Lady Kukachin remarked, rather wistfully, "We have been journeying for a whole year now, and the captain tells me that we are only about two-thirds of the way to our destination."

I knew the lady well enough by this time to know that she was not being sordidly greedy for her entitlement as Ilkhatun of Persia. She merely was eager to meet her betrothed and marry him. She was, after all, a year older now and still a spinster.

So we called an end to our tarrying, and pushed off from the pleasant island. We sailed northward, close along the western coast of India, and made the best time possible, for none of us had any desire to visit or explore any part of that land. We put in to shore only when our water barrels absolutely had to be replenished—at a fair-sized port called Quilon, and at a river-mouth port called Mangalore, where we had to anchor far offshore of the delta flats, and at a settlement scattered over seven pimples of land called the Bombay islets, and at a dismal fishing village called Kurrachi.

Kurrachi at least had good fresh water, and we made sure our tanks were topped full, because from that point we were sailing directly west again, and for some two thousand li—or I should say, now that I was back again where Persian measurements were used, about three hundred farsakhs—we were skirting the dry, dun-colored, baking, thirsty desert coast of the empty land called Baluchistan. The view of that sere coastline was only occasionally enlivened by two things peculiar to it. All year round, a south wind blows from the sea into Baluchistan, so wherever we saw a tree it was always grown in a contorted arc, bending inland, like an arm beckoning us to come ashore. The other peculiarity of that coast was its mud volcanoes: dumpy cone-shaped hills of dried mud, every so often spewing a gush of new, wet mud from the top, to slither down and slowly bake and await a new gush and a new layer. It was a most uninviting land.

But, following that drear shore, we did at last enter the Strait of Hormuz, and that led us to the city of that name, and once again I was in Persia. Hormuz was a very big and bustling city, so populous that some of its residential quarters were spilling from the mainland city center over to the islands offshore. It was also Persia's busiest port, a forest of masts and spars, a tumult of noise and a medley of smells, most of them not nice. The ships tied up or coming and going were, of course, mostly Arab qurqurs and falukahs and dhaos, the biggest of them looking like dinghis and praus alongside our massive vessels. No doubt an occasional trading chuan had been seen here before, but surely never such a fleet as we now brought into the harbor roads. As soon as a pilot boat had fussily led us to anchorage, we were surrounded by the skiffs and scows and barges of every kind of vendor, guide, pimp and water-front beggar, all of them screeching solicitations. And what appeared to be the entire remainder of the population of Hormuz was collected along the dockside, gawking and jabbering excitedly. However, among that mob we could see nothing like what we had expected—a resplendent gathering of nobles to welcome their new Ilkhatun-to-be.

"Curious," muttered my father. "Surely the word of our coming raced ahead of us along the coast. And the Ilkhan Arghun must by now have been getting mightily impatient and eager."

So, while he turned to the daunting job of commanding the debark-ation of all our company and our gear, I hailed a karaji ferry skiff and, fending off the solicitors, was the first to go ashore. I accosted an in-telligent-looking citizen and made inquiry. Then I immediately had myself rowed back to our ship, to tell my father and the envoy Uladai and the anxious-eyed Kukachin:

"You may wish to postpone the debarkation until we have held conference. I am sorry to be the one to bring this news, but the Ilkhan Arghun died of an illness, many months ago."

The Lady Kukachin burst into tears, as sincerely as if the man had been her long-wedded and much-loved husband, instead of just a name to her. As the lady's maids helped her away to her suite of cabins, and my father thoughtfully chewed on a corner of his beard, Uladai said, "Vakh! I will wager that Arghun died at the very moment my fellow envoys Koja and Apushka perished in Jawa. We should have suspected something dire."

"We could not have done much about it, if we had," said my father. "The question is: what do we do now about Kukachin?"

I said, "Well, there is no Arghun waiting for her. And they told me ashore that his son Ghazan is still under age to succeed to the Khanate."

"That is correct," said Uladai. "I suppose his Uncle Kaikhadu is ruling as Regent in the meantime."

"So they say. And either this Kaikhadu knew nothing of his late brother's having sent for a new wife, or he is not at all interested in exercising any levirate right to take her for himself. Anyway, he has sent no embassy to meet her and no transport for her."

"No matter," said Uladai. "She comes from his Lord Khakhan, so he is obliged to relieve you of her care and take her into his own. We shall take her to the capital at Maragheh. As for transportation, you carry the Khakhan's pai-tzu. We have only to command the Shah of Hormuz to supply us with everything we require."

And that is what we did. The local Shah received us not just duti-fully but hospitably, and lodged us all in his palace—though we filled it nearly to bursting—while he assembled all his own camels and probably every other one within his domain, and loaded them with provisions and water bags, and marshaled camel-pullers for them, and also troops of his own to augment ours, and in a few days we were journeying overland, northwest toward Maragheh.

It was a traverse as long as the one my father and uncle and myself had previously made across Persia from west to east. But this time, going south to north, we had no very terrible terrain to cross, for our route took us well west of the Great Salt Desert, and we had good riding camels and copious supplies, and plenty of attendants to do every bit of work for us, and a formidable guard against any possible molesters. So it was a fairly comfortable trip, if not a very merry one. The Lady Kukachin did not wear any of the bridal finery she had brought, but every day wore brown, the Persian color of mourning, and on her pretty face wore a look that was partly apprehensive of what her fate might now be, and partly resigned to it. Since all the rest of us had got very fond of her, we worried with her, but did everything we could to make the journey easy and interesting for her.

Our route did take us through a number of places where I or my father or my uncle—or all of us together—had been before, so my father and I were constantly looking to see what changes, if any, had occurred in the years since then. Most of our stops along the way were only for a night's sleep, but when we got to Kashan, my father and I commanded an extra day's stay, so we could stroll about that city where we had rested before our plunge into the forbidding Dasht-e-Kavir. We led Uncle Mafio walking with us, in a sort of meager hope that those scenes of long ago might jar him back to a semblance of what he had been long ago. But nothing in Kashan woke any glimmer in his dulled eyes, not even the "prezioni" boys and young men who were still the city's most visible asset.

We went to the house and stable where the kindly Widow Esther had given us lodging. The place was now in the possession of a man, a nephew who had inherited it years ago, he said, when that good lady died. He showed us where she was buried—not in any Jewish cemetery but, at her own deathbed insistence, in the herb garden behind her own abode. That was where I had watched her pounding scorpions with her slipper, while she exhorted me never to neglect any opportunity to "taste everything in this world."

My father respectfully crossed himself, and then went on along the street, leading Uncle Mafio, to go and look again at Kashan's kashi-tile workshops, the which had inspired him to set up the same in Kithai, and from which our Compagnia had realized such handsome profits. But I stayed on with the widow's nephew for a while, looking pensively down at her herb-grown grave and saying (but not aloud):

"I followed your advice, Mirza Esther. I let no chance go by untaken. I never hesitated to follow where my curiosity beckoned. I willingly went where there was danger in beauty and beauty in danger. As you foretold, I had experiences in plenty. Many were enjoyable, some were instructive, a few I would rather have missed. But I had them, and I have them still in memory. If, as soon as tomorrow, I go to *my* grave, it will be no black and silent hole. I can paint the darkness with vivid colors, and fill it with music both martial and languorous, with the flicker of swords and the flutter of kisses, with flavors and excitements and sensations, with the fragrance of a field of clover that has been warmed in the sun and then washed by a gentle rain, the sweetest-scented thing God ever put on this earth. Yes, I can enliven eternity. Others may have to endure it; I can enjoy it. For that I thank you, Mirza Esther, and I would wish you shalom . . . but I think that you, too, would not be happy in an eternity of nothing but peace. . . ."

A black Kashan scorpion came scrabbling along the garden path, and I stepped on it for her. Then I turned to the nephew and said, "Your aunt once had a house maid named Sitarè . . ."

"Another of her deathbed dispositions. Every old woman is a matchmaker at heart. She found for Sitarè a husband, and had them married in this house before she died. Neb Efendi was a cobbler, a good craftsman and a good man, though a Muslim. He was also an immigrant Turki, which made him not very popular hereabout. But it also made him not a pursuer of boys, and I trust he was a good husband to Sitarè."

"Was?"

"They moved away from here shortly afterward. He was a foreigner, and evidently folk prefer to have their shoes made and mended by their home folk, even if they are inept in their work. So Neb Efendi picked up his awls and his lasts and his new wife and departed—to his native Cappadocia, I believe. I hope they are happy there. It was a long time ago."

Well, I was a little disappointed not to get to see Sitarè again, but only a little. She would be a matron now, of about my own middle age, and to see her might be even more of a disappointment.

So we pushed on, and eventually arrived at Maragheh. The Regent Kaikhadu did receive us, not grudgingly but not with wild enthusiasm either. He was a typical, shaggy Mongol man at arms, who clearly would have been more comfortable astride a horse, hacking with a blade at some battlefield opponent, than he was on the throne to which his brother's death had shoved him.

"I truly did not know of Arghun's embassy to the Khakhan," he told us, "or you may be sure I would have had you escorted hither in great pomp and ceremony, for I am a devoted subject of the Khakhan. Indeed, it is because I have spent all my time afield, fighting the Khanate's campaigns, that I was unaware of Arghun's canvass for a new wife. Right this minute, I should properly be putting down a band of brigands that are rampaging over in Kurdistan. Anyway, I do not know quite what to do with this woman you have brought."

"She is a handsome one, Lord Kaikhadu," said the envoy Uladai. "And a good-natured one."

"Yes, yes. But I already have wives—Mongol, Persian, Circassian, even one frightful Armeniyan—in yurtus scattered from Hormuz to Azerbaizhan." He threw up his hands distractedly. "Well, I suppose I can inquire among my nobles. . . ."

"We will stay," my father said firmly, "until we see the Lady Kukachin settled according to her station."

But the lady took care of that herself, before we had been many days in residence at the Maragheh palace. My father and I were airing Uncle Mafio in a rose garden one afternoon when she came running up to us, smiling for the first time since our arrival at Hormuz. She also had someone in tow: a boy, very short and ugly and pimply, but in courtier's rich attire.

"Elder Brothers Polo," she said breathlessly. "You need fret over me no longer. By good fortune, I have met a most wonderful man, and we plan shortly to announce our betrothal."

"Why, that is stupendous news," said my father, but cautiously "I do hope, my dear, that he is of suitably high birth and position and prospects. . . ."

"The highest!" she said happily. "Ghazan is the son of the man I came here to wed. He will be Ilkhan himself in two years."

"Mefè, you could not have done better! Lassar la strada vechia per la nova. Is this his page? Can he fetch the good fellow for us to meet?"

"But this is he. This is the Crown Prince Ghazan."

My father had to swallow before he could say, "Sain bina, Your Royal Highness," and I bowed deeply to give myself time to compose my face to sobriety.

"He is two years younger than myself," Kukachin chattered on, not giving the boy much chance to speak for himself. "But what is two years in a lifetime of happy marriage? We will be wed as soon as he ascends to the Ilkhanate. In the meantime, you dear devoted Elder Brothers can leave me in good conscience, knowing I am in good hands, and go on about your own affairs. I shall miss you, but I shall not be lonely or despondent any more."

We made the proper congratulations and good wishes, and the boy grinned like an ape and mumbled acknowledgment, and Kukachin beamed as if she had just won an unimaginably great trophy, and the two of them went off hand in hand.

"Well," said my father with a shrug, "better the head of a cat than the tail of a lion."

But Kukachin must have seen in the boy what we could not. God knows he could never have been better than a goblin for looks and physical stature—he was afterward styled in all the Mongol chronicles "Ghazan the Ugly"—but the fact that he did make history is proof that he was more than he appeared to be. He and the lady were wed when he replaced Kaikhadu as Ilkhan of Persia, and then he went on to become the ablest Ilkhan and warrior of his generation, making many wars and winning many new lands for the Khanate. Unhappily, his loving Ilkhatun Kukachin did not live to share all his triumphs and celebrity, for she died in childbirth two years or so after their marriage.

· 4 ·

S o, having completed our last mission for the Khan Kubilai, my father and uncle and I pressed onward. We left at Maragheh the populous company we had so far been traveling with, but Kaikhadu generously gave us good horses and remounts and packhorses and ample provisions and an escort of a dozen mounted men of his own palace guard, to see us safely through all the Turki lands. However, as things turned out, we would have traveled more safely without that Mongol troop.

From the capital, we circled around the shores of a sea-sized lake named Urumia, which was also called the Sea of the Sunset. Then we climbed up and over the mountains which marked the northwestern frontier of Persia. One of the mountains in that range, said my father, was the biblical Mount Ararat, but it was too far off our route for me to go and climb it to see if any trace of the Ark was still there. Anyway, having recently scaled another mountain to see a footprint that might well have been Adam's, I was now inclined to think of Noah as rather a latecomer in history. On the other side of the mountains, we descended into the Turki lands at another sea-sized lake, this one named Van, but called the Sea Beyond the Sunset.

The country hereabout, and the nations composing it, and the borders thereof, were all in flux and had been for many years. What had formerly been part of the Byzantine Empire under Christian rulers was now the Seljuk Empire under rulers of the Turki race and Muslim religion. But these eastern parts of it were also known by older names, bestowed by peoples who had inhabited these lands since time before time, who had never conceded that they were not still the rightful owners of them, and who recognized none of the vagaries of modern claimants and modern boundary lines. Thus, at the point where we emerged from Persia, we came down from the mountains into a country which could equally well be named Turki, after the race of its rulers, or the Seljuk Empire, as those Turki called it, or Cappadocia, which was its name on older maps, or Kurdistan, for the Kurdi people who populated it.

The land was a green and pleasant one, the wildest parts of it seeming hardly wild at all, but looking almost neatly cultivated, with rolling hills of meadow grass tidily separated by clumps of forest, so that the whole countryside was as trim as an artificial parkland. There was plenty of good water, in sparkling streams as well as immense blue lakes. The people here were all Kurdi, some of them farmers and villagers, but most of them nomad families following flocks of sheep or goats. They were as handsome a race as I have seen in any Islamic land. They had very black hair and eyes, but a complexion as fair as my own. The men were large and solidly built, and wore great black mustaches, and were famously fierce fighters. The Kurdi women were not particularly delicate, either, but withal were well formed and good-looking—and independent; they scorned to wear the veil or live hidden in the pardah imposed on most other women of Islam.

The Kurdi received us journeyers cordially enough—nomads usually are hospitable to other seeming nomads—but they cast unloving looks at our Mongol escorts. There were reasons for that. Besides all the other complications of national names and dominions and boundary lines, this Seljuk Empire was also in enforced vassalage to the Ilkhanate of Persia. That situation dated from the time when a traitorous Turki minister had foully murdered the King Kilij—he who was the father of my one-time princess friend Mar-Janah—and usurped the throne by promising to lay it under subjection to the then Ilkhan Abagha. So this Seljuk Empire, though nominally ruled now by a King Masud in the capital city of Erzincan, was really subordinate to Abagha's surviving son, the Regent Kaikhadu, whose Maragheh court we had just come from and whose palace guards were accompanying us. We journeyers were welcome here; the warriors with us were not.

One might have supposed that the Kurdi—rebellious throughout history against *every* non-Kurdi ruler ever imposed upon them—would have cared little whether Erzincan or Maragheh was the real ruling capital, because out here, a hundred farsakhs or more from either city, they were pretty much left unruled by anybody. But they seemed to regard the Mongols as a tyranny inflicted on top of the Turki tyranny they already chafed under, and the one to be even more hotly resented and hated. We learned how well the Kurdi could hate when, one afternoon, we stopped at an isolated hut to buy a sheep for our evening meal.

The evident proprietor of the hut was sitting in the doorway of it, holding his sheepskin robes around him as if he had a chill. My father and I and just one of our Mongols rode into the dooryard and politely dismounted, but the shepherd impolitely did not stand up. The Kurdi had a language of their own, but almost all of them spoke Turki as well, and so did our Mongol escorts, and in any case the Turki tongue was similar enough to the Mongol that I could usually understand any over-heard conversation. Our Mongol asked the man if we might buy a sheep. The man, still seated, his eyes glumly on the ground, refused us.

"I think I ought not to trade with our oppressors."

The Mongol said, "No one is oppressing you. These Ferenghi way-farers ask a favor of you, and will pay for it, and your Allah enjoins hospitality toward wayfarers."

The shepherd said, not in an argumentative way, but in seeming melancholy, "But the rest of you are Mongols, and you will also eat on the sheep."

"What of that? Once you sell the animal to the Ferenghi, what matter to you what becomes of it?"

The shepherd sniffled and said, almost tearfully, "I did a favor to a passing Turki not long since. Helped him change a broken shoe on his horse. And for that I have been chastised by the Chiti Ayakkabi. A small favor for a mere Turki. Estag farullah! What will the Chiti do to me if he hears I did a favor for a *Mongol*?"

"Come!" snapped our escort. "Will you sell us a sheep?"

"No, I cannot."

The Mongol sneered down at him. "You do not even stand like a man when you speak defiance. Very well, cowardly Kurdi, you refuse to sell. Then would you care to stand up and try to prevent my *taking* a sheep?"

"No, I cannot. But I warn you. The Chiti Ayakkabi will make you regret the robbery."

The Mongol laughed harshly and spat in the dust in front of the seated man, then remounted and rode to cut a fat ewe out of the flock grazing in the meadow beyond the hut. I remained there, curious, staring down at the slumped and defeated-looking shepherd. I knew that Chiti meant a brigand and, as best I knew, Ayakkabi meant a shoe. I wondered what kind of bandit would style himself "the Shoe Brigand" and would occupy himself in punishing his own fellow Kurdi for giving aid and comfort to their presumed oppressors.

I managed to inquire of the man, "What did this Chiti Ayakkabi do to chastise you?"

He did not speak a reply, but showed me, lifting the skirts of his sheepskins to reveal his feet. It was evident why he had not stood to greet us, and I got some idea of why the Kurdi bandit had such a strange name. Both of the shepherd's feet, otherwise bare, were clotted with dried blood and studded with nails—not nail heads but the upthrusting points of nails—where both his feet had been shod with iron horseshoes.

Two or three nights later, near a village called Tunceli, the Chiti Ayakkabi made us regret our robbery of the sheep. Tunceli was a village of the Kurdi, and it had only one karwansarai, and that very small and dilapidated. Since our company of fifteen riders and thirty-odd horses would have crowded it intolerably, we rode on through the village and made camp in a grassy glade beyond, convenient to a clear-flowing brook. We had eaten and rolled ourselves in our blankets and gone to sleep, leaving just one Mongol on guard, when the night erupted with bandits.

Our lone sentry had only time to bellow "*Chiti!*" before he was brained with a battle-ax. The rest of us thrashed free of our bedrolls, but the brigands were among us, with blades and cudgels, and all was a confused turbulence in the dim remaining firelight. My father and I had Uncle Mafìo to thank that we were not slain as abruptly as all our Mongol troop. Those warriors thought first to snatch for their weapons, so the bandits flew first at them. But my father and I both saw Mafìo standing by the fire, looking about him in numb bemusement, and we both at the same moment threw ourselves toward him, and seized him and dragged him to the ground, so he made not such a prominent target. The next moment, something clouted me above the ear and, for me, the night went totally dark.

I woke, lying on the ground with my head cradled in a soft lap, and as my vision cleared I looked up into a female face illumined by the now built-up fire. It was not the square, strong face of a Kurdi woman, and it was framed by a tumble of hair that was not black, but dark-red. I labored to collect my wits, and said in Farsi, in a voice that croaked:

"Am I dead, and are you a peri now?"

"You are not dead, Marco Efendi. I saw you just in time to cry to the men to desist."

"You used to call me Mirza Marco, Sitarè."

"Marco Efendi means the same. I am more of a Kurdi now than a Persian."

"What of my father? My uncle?"

"They are not even bruised. I am sorry you had to take a blow. Can you sit up?"

I did, though the movement threatened to make my head roll off my shoulders, and I saw my father sitting with a group of the black-mustached bandits. They had made qahwah, and he and they were drinking and chatting amiably together, with Uncle Mafìo sitting placidly by. It would have looked quite a civilized scene, except that others of the brigands were stacking the bodies of our dead Mongols like cordwood off to one side of the glade. The largest and most fiercely mustached of the newcomers, seeing me stir, came over to me and Sitarè.

She said, "This is my husband, Neb Efendi, known also as Chiti Ayakkabi."

He spoke Farsi as well as she did. "I apologize to you, Marco Efendi. I would not knowingly have attacked the man who made possible the treasure of my life."

I was still addled in my wits, and did not know what he was talking about. But as I drank bitter black qahwah and my head gradually cleared, he and Sitarè explained. He was the Kashan cobbler whom the Almauna Esther had introduced to her maidservant Sitarè. He had loved her at first sight, but their marriage would of course have been unthinkable had Sitarè not been a virgin, and Sitarè had told him frankly that her being still intact was thanks to a certain gentlemanly Mirza Marco's having declined to take advantage of her. I felt more than a little uncomfortable, listening to a rough and murderous bandit expressing his indebtedness for my not having preceded him in making "sikis," as he called it, with his bride. But also, if I was ever grateful for my onetime constraint, it was now.

"Qismet, we call it," he said. "Destiny, fate, chance. You were good to my Sitarè. Now I am being good to you."

It further transpired that Neb Efendi, having been balked of prospering as a cobbler in Kashan—where the people did not know the difference between a noble Kurdi and a vile Turki, but would have despised him in any event—had brought his wife back here to his native Kurdistan. But here he felt also estranged, a vassal to the Turki regime which was in turn vassal to the Mongol Ilkhanate. So he had given up his trade entirely, keeping only the name of it, and turned to insurrection as the Shoe Brigand.

"I have seen some of your cobblery," I told him. "It was—distinctive."

He said modestly, "Bosh," which is a Turki word meaning "you flatter me overmuch."

But Sitarè nodded proudly. "You mean the shepherd. It was he who set us on your trail to Tunceli here. Yes, Marco Efendi, my dear and valorous Neb is determined to rouse up all Kurdi against the oppressors, and to discourage any weaklings who truckle to them."

"I had rather divined that."

"Do you know, Marco Efendi," he said, thumping a fist loudly against his broad chest, "that we Kurdi are the oldest aristocracy in the world? Our tribal names go back to the days of Sumer. And all that time we have been fighting one tyranny after another. We battled the Hittites, the Assyrians, we helped Cyrus overthrow Babylon. We fought with Salah-ed-Din the Great against the first marauding Crusaders. Not forty years ago, unaided, we slaughtered twenty thousand Mongols at the battle of Arbil. But still we are not free and independent. So now it is my mission—first to throw off from Kurdistan the Mongol yoke and then the Turki."

"I wish you success, Chiti Ayakkabi."

"Well, my band and I are poor and ill-equipped. But your Mongols' weapons and your good horses and the considerable treasure in their packs will help us immensely."

"You are going to rob us? You call that being good to us?"

"I could have been less good." He waved casually at the bloody heap of dead Mongols. "Be glad your qismet decreed otherwise."

"Speaking of qismet," Sitarè said brightly, to distract me, "tell me, Marco Efendi. What of my darling brother Aziz?"

We were in a precarious enough situation, I decided, that I would not hazard making it more so. Neither she nor her ferocious mate would be overjoyed to hear that her little brother had been dead for more than twenty years, that we had let him be slain by a robber band very like their own. Anyway, I was loath to sadden an old friend unnecessarily. So I lied, and lied loudly enough that my father could overhear, and not later contradict me.

"We carried Aziz to Mashhad, as you desired, Sitarè, and we guarded his chastity the whole way. There, he was fortunate enough to catch the admiring eye of a fine and prosperously fat merchant prince. We left them together, and they seemed more than fond of each other. As far as I know, they are still trading together, up and down the Silk Road between Mashhad and Balkh. Aziz would by now be a well-grown man, but I have no doubt he is still as beautiful as he was then. And as you are, Sitarè."

"Al-hamdo-lillah, I hope so," she sighed. "I saw much resemblance to Aziz in my own two sons, as they grew up. But my manly Neb, not being a Kashanite, would not let me insert the golulè in our boys, or show them how to use cosmetics, in preparation for their someday securing male lovers. So they have grown up to be most manly men themselves, and they sikismek only with women. Those are the boys, over yonder, Nami and Orhon, stripping the boots off those dead Mongols. Would you believe, Marco Efendi, that my sons are both older than *you* were when last I saw you? Ah, well, it is good to have news of dear Aziz after all these years, and to know that he made as glowing a success of his life as I have made of mine. We owe it all to you, Marco Efendi."

"Bosh," I said modestly.

I could have suggested that we might be owed our own possessions, but I did not. And my father, when he too realized that we were to be plundered, merely sighed in resignation and said, "Well, when there is no banquet, at least the candles are happy."

True, our lives had been spared. And of our portable valuables I had already dispensed with a third part before we left Khanbalik, and anyway they represented only a trifle compared to what our Compagnia had earlier sent home from Kithai. And the brigands took only the things they could easily spend, sell or trade, meaning that they left us our clothes and personal belongings. So, while we could hardly rejoice at being robbed at this late stage in our long journeying—we especially regretted the loss of the magnificent star sapphires acquired in Srihalam —we neither of us repined too much.

Neb Efendi and his band did allow us to ride our own horses as far as the coast city of Trebizond, and even rode that far with us as a protection against any further Kurdi assault, and they courteously refrained from slaughtering or shoeing anyone else along the way. When we dismounted at the outskirts of Trebizond, the Chiti Ayakkabi gave us back a handful of our own coin, sufficient to pay for our transport and sustenance the rest of the way to Constantinople. So we and they parted in a friendly enough way, and the Shoe Brigand did not strike me dead when Sitarè, as she had done twenty-some years before, kissed me a voluptuous and lingering goodbye.

At Trebizond, on the shore of the Euxine or Kara or Black Sea, we were still more than two hundred farsakhs east of Constantinople, but we were glad to be standing again on Christian ground for the first time since we had left Acre in the Levant. My father and I decided against the purchase of new horses, not out of dread of the overland journey, but out of concern that it might be too hard on Uncle Mafìo, with none but us now to take care of him. So, carrying what was left of our packs, we went to the Trebizond waterfront and, after some search, found a barge-like gektirme fishing boat whose Christian Greek captain—he was captain of a crew consisting of his four loutish sons—would, with Christian goodness, sail us to Constantinople, and would feed us on the way and, with Christian goodness, would charge us only all we had.

It was a tediously slow and miserable voyage, for the gektirme was netting all the way, and netting only anchovies, so anchovies were what we were fed all the way, with pilaf of rice cooked in anchovy oil, and we lived in, slept in, breathed in the smell of anchovies all the way. Besides us and the Greeks, there was a mangy dog aboard, for no discernible reason, and I frequently wished we had not already paid over every coin we possessed, so that I could have bought the dog and offered him up to be cooked, just for a change from the anchovies. But just as well. The dog had been aboard for so long that I suppose he would have tasted no different.

After nearly two dismal months aboard our floating anchovy-cask, we finally made our way into the strait called Bosphorus, and along it to where it met the estuary called the Golden Horn, and there we raised the great city of Constantinople—but on a day of such dense fog that I could not see and appreciate the city's magnificence. The fog did permit me, however, to learn the reason for the gektirme's resident dog. One of the sons beat it regularly with a stick as we crept cautiously through the fog, so that the dog barked and snarled and cursed continuously. I could hear other invisible dogs similarly yowling all about us, and our captain at the steering oar kept his ear cocked to the noises, so I perceived that dog-beating—instead of bell-ringing, as in Venice—was the locally accepted fog warning device.

Our ungainly gektirme groped its way without collision across the Horn and under the walls of the city. Our captain told us he was heading for the Sirkeci dock allocated to fishing boats, but my father prevailed on him to take us instead to the Phanar quarter, which was the Venetian section of the city. And somehow, in that thick fog and after not having seen Constantinople for some thirty years, he managed to direct the captain there. Meanwhile, somewhere behind the fog, the sun was setting, and my father was in a fever of impatience, grumbling, "If we do not get there before dark, we must sleep another night on this wretched scow." We and the nightfall, about simultaneously, touched a wooden dock, and he and I said hasty farewells to the Greeks, helped Uncle Mafìo ashore, and my father led us at an old man's trot through the fog, through a gate in the high wall and then through a labyrinth of sinuous, cramped streets.

We came at last to one of many identical narrow-fronted buildings, this one with a shop at the street level, and my father gave a glad cry—"Nostra compagnia!"—at seeing still a light within. He flung the door open and ushered me and Mafìo inside. A white-bearded man was bent over an open ledger at a table piled with many ledgers, writing in the light of a candle at his elbow. He looked up and growled:

"Gèsu, spuzzolenti sardòni!"

They were the first Venetian words I had heard from anyone except Nicolò and Mafìo Polo in twenty-three years. And thus—as "stinking anchovies"—we were greeted by my Uncle Marco Polo.

But then, marveling, he recognized his brothers—"Xestu, Nico? Mafìo? Tati!"—and he bounded up most spryly from his chair, and the company clerks at counting tables roundabout looked on in wonder at our flurry of abrazzi and backslappings and handshakings and laughs and tears and exclamations.

"Sangue de Bacco!" he bellowed. "Che bon vento? But you have both gone gray, my Tati!"

"And you have gone white, Tato!" my father bellowed back.

"And what took you so long? Your last consignment brought your letter that you were on your way. But that was nearly three years ago!"

"Ah, Marco, do not ask! We have had the wind at our front the whole way."

"E cussì? But I expected you on jeweled elephants—I Re Magi, coming out of the East in a triumphal parade, with Nubian slaves beating drums. And here you creep in from a foggy night, smelling like the crotch of a Sirkeci whore!"

"From shallow waters, insignificant fish. We come penniless, marooned, derelict. We are castaways washed up on your doorstep. But we will talk of that later. Here, you have never yet met your namesake nephew."

"Neodo Marco! Arcistupendonazzìsimo!" So I got a hearty embrace too, and a benvegnùo, and my back pounded. "But our tonazzo Tato Mafìo, usually so loud. Why so silent?"

"He has been ill," said my father. "We will also talk of that. But come! For two months we have been eating nothing but anchovies, and   "

"And they have given you a powerful thirst! Say no more!" He turned to his clerks and bellowed for them to go home, and not to come in to work the next day. They all stood and gave us a rousing cheer— whether for our safe return or for their getting an unexpected holiday, I do not know   and we went out again into the fog.

Uncle Marco took us to his villa on the Marmara seaside, where we spent our first night, and the subsequent week or more, in swilling down good wines and rich viands—none of which was fish—and being bathed and scrubbed and rubbed in my uncle's private hammam—here called a humoun—and sleeping long hours in luxurious beds, and being waited on, hand and foot, by his numerous house servants. Meanwhile, Uncle Marco sent a special courier vessel hastening to Venice to apprise Dona Fiordelisa of our safe arrival here.

When I felt rested and well-fed enough, and looked and smelled presentable, I was introduced to Uncle Marco's son and daughter, Nicolò and Maroca. They were both about my own age, but Cousin Maroca was still a spinster, and kept giving me looks half speculative, half suggestive. I was not interested in responding; I was much more interested in sitting with my father and Uncle Marco as we bent our attention on the books of the Compagnia Polo. They quickly reassured us that we were anything but penniless. We were more than respectably wealthy.

Some of the shipments of goods and valuables my father had entrusted to the Mongol horse post had failed to make it the whole way along the Silk Road, but that was only to have been expected; what was more remarkable was that so many *had* got through to Constantinople. And here Uncle Marco had variously banked and invested and traded most shrewdly with those goods, and by his advice Dona Fiordelisa in Venice had been able to do the same. So by now our Compagnia Polo ranked with the mercantile houses of Spinola of Genoa and Carrara of Padua and Dandolo of Venice as a prima di tuto in the world of commerce. I was especially pleased that, among the consignments which had arrived intact, were those which had contained all the maps my father and Uncle Mafìo and I had made, and all the notes I had jotted down in all those years. Since the Shoe Brigand at Tunceli had not relieved me of my journal notes scribbled since leaving Khanbalik, I now possessed at least a fragmentary record of every one of my journeys.

We stayed on at the villa until spring, so I had time to get well acquainted with Constantinople. And that made for an easy transition between our long sojourn in the East and our return to the West, for Constantinople itself was a blend of both those ends of the earth. It was Eastern of architecture and bazàr markets and variegated races and complexions and costumes and languages and such. But its guazzabuglio of nationalities included some twenty thousand Venetians, about a tenth as many as in Venice itself, and the city had many other similarities to Venice—including its being overrun with cats. Most of the Venetians resided and did business in the Phanar quarter of the city allotted to them, and across the Golden Horn, in the so-called New City, about an equal number of Genoans occupied the Galata quarter.

The exigencies of commerce necessitated daily transactions between Venetians and Genoans. Nothing would ever stop them doing business. But they did their mutual dealings very coolly, at arm's length, so to speak, and were not mingling sociably or friendlily, because back home —as so often before—their native republics were again at war. I mention that because I was later to have some minor involvement in it. But I will not describe all the aspects of Constantinople, or dwell on our stay there, for it was really only a recuperative and resting place in our journey, and our hearts were already in Venice, and we were eager to follow them there.

So it was that, on a blue and gold May morning, twenty-four years after we had left La Città Serenissima, our galeazza tied up at the dock of our company warehouse, and my father and Uncle Mafìo and I walked down the plank and stepped again upon the cobblestones of the Riva Ca' de Dio, in the Year of Our Lord one thousand two hundred ninety-five, or, as it would have been counted in Kithai, the Year of the Ram, three thousand nine hundred ninety-three.

· 5 ·

T H E story of the Prodigal Son notwithstanding, I maintain that there is nothing like coming home *successful* to make the homecoming warm and tumultuous and welcoming. Of course, Dona Fiordelisa would have welcomed us happily, however we had arrived. But if we had slunk into Venice the way we had done at Constantinople, I wager we would have been contemptuously received by our merchant confratelli and the citizenry at large, and they would have cared nothing for the greater fact that we had made such journeys and seen such things as none other of them had ever done. However, since we *did* come home rich and well-dressed and walking tall, we were greeted like champions, like victors, like heroes.

For weeks after our arrival, there came so many people calling at the Ca' Polo that we hardly had time of our own to get reacquainted with Dona Lisa and other relatives and friends and neighbors, or to catch up on family news, or to learn the names of all our new servants and slaves and company workers. The old maggiordomo Attilio had died during our absence, and the old chief clerk Isidoro Priuli—and also our aged parish priest, Pare Nunziata—while other house servants, slaves and working men had departed our employ or been dismissed or been freed or been sold, and we had to meet and get to know their successors.

The converging crowds of visitors included some whom we knew from years past, but many others were total strangers. Some came just to fawn on us newly rich arrichisti and seek some advantage from us, the men bringing schemes and projects and soliciting our investment, the women bringing nubile daughters to present for my delectation. Others came with the obvious and venal hope of prying from us information and maps and advice that would enable them to emulate us. Some few came to say sincere congratulations on our safe return, many came to ask inane questions like, "How does it feel to be back?"

To me, at least, it felt good. It was good to walk about the dear old city and glory in the perpetually changing, lapping, liquid mirror light of Venice, so different from the infernal blaze of deserts and the harsh glare of mountain heights and the abrupt white sun and black shade of Eastern bazàrs. It was good to stroll through the piazza and hear all about me the softly inflected cantilena speech of Venice, so different from the rapid jabber of Eastern throngs. It was good to see that Venice was much as I had remembered it. The piazza campanile had been built somewhat taller, some few old buildings had been torn down and new ones put in their places, the interior of San Marco had been adorned with many new mosaics. But nothing was jarringly changed, and that was good.

And still the callers kept coming to the Ca' Polo. Some of them were agreeable to receive, some were nuisances, some were crass annoyances, and one of them, a fellow merchant, came to cast a pall on our homecoming. He told us, "Word has just arrived from the East, by way of my factor in Cyprus. The Great Khan is dead." When we pressed for details, we determined that the Khakhan must have died about the time we were making our way through Kurdistan. Well, it was saddening news, but not unexpected: he had been then seventy-eight years old, and simply had succumbed to the ravages of time. Some while later, we got further news: that his death had not precipitated any wars of succession; his grandson Dona Temur had without opposition been elevated to the throne.

There had been changes of sovereignty here in the West, too, while we had been away. That Doge Tiepolo who banished me from Venice had died, and the scufieta was now worn by a Piero Gradenigo. Also long dead was His Holiness Pope Gregory X, whom we had known in Acre as the Archdeacon Visconti, and there had been a number of other Popes of Rome since then. Also, that city of Acre had fallen to the Saracens, so the Kingdom of Jerusalem was no more, and the whole of the Levant was now held by the Muslims—and appears likely to be theirs forever. Since I had been in Acre to witness briefly that eighth Crusade being desultorily directed by Edward of England, I think I can say that, among all the other things I saw during my journeyings, I saw the very last of the Crusades.

Now my father and stepmother—possibly impelled to the idea by the visitors thronging our Ca' Polo, or perhaps thinking we ought to start living up to our new prosperity, or perhaps deciding that we could now at last afford to live like the Ene Aca nobility we Polos always had been—began talking of building a new and grander Casa Polo. So to the streams of visitors were now added architects and stonemasons and other aspiring artisans, all eagerly bringing with them sketches and proposals and suggestions that would have had us building something to rival the Doge's palazzo. That reminded me of something, and I reminded my father:

"We have not yet made our courtesy call upon the Doge Gradenigo. I realize that the moment we give official notice of our being in residence in Venice again, we subject ourselves to inquisition by the Dogana tax collectors. They will no doubt find some trinket among all our imports over the years on which Zio Marco failed to pay some trifling duty, and they will insist on wringing every possible bagatìn out of us. Nevertheless, we cannot postpone forever the paying of our respects to our Doge."

So we made formal request for a formal audience, and on the appointed day we took Zio Mafìo with us, and when, as custom dictates, we made gifts to the Doge, we presented some in Mafìo's name as well as ours. I have forgotten what he and my father presented, but I gave to Gradenigo one of the gold and ivory pai-tzu plaques we had carried as emissaries of the Khan of All Khans, and also the three-bladed squeeze knife which had served me so well so often in the East. I showed the Doge how cleverly it worked, and he played with it for a while, and asked me to tell him about the occasions of my employment of the knife, and I did, in brief.

Then he put some polite questions to my father, relevant mainly to East-West trade affairs, and Venice's prospects for an increase of that traffic. Then he expressed his delight that we—and through us, Venice—had prospered so richly by our sojourn abroad. Then, as expected, he said he hoped we would satisfy the Dogana that the proper share of all our successful enterprises had been duly paid into the coffers of the Republic. We said, as expected, that we looked forward to the tax collectors' scrutiny of our Compagnia's unfaultable books of account. Then we stood up, expecting to be dismissed. But the Doge raised one of his heavily beringed hands and said:

"Just one thing more, Messeri. Perhaps it has escaped your recollection, Messer Marco—I know you have had many other things on your mind—but there is the minor matter of your banishment from Venice."

I stared at him, dumbfounded. Surely he was not going to resurrect that old charge against a now most respectable and esteemed (and heavily tax-paying) citizen. With an air of offended hauteur I said, "I assumed, So Serenità, that the statute of enforcement had expired with the Doge Tiepolo."

"Oh, of course I am not *obliged* to respect the judgments made and sentences imposed by my predecessor. But I too like to keep my books unfaultable. And there *is* that little blot upon the pages of the archives of the Signori della Notte."

I smiled, thinking I understood now, and said, "Perhaps a suitable fine would pay for the blot's erasure."

"I was thinking rather of an expiation in accordance with the old Roman lege de tagiòn."

I was again dumbfounded. "An eye for an eye? Surely the books show that I was never guilty of the killing of that citizen."

"No, no, of course you were not. Nevertheless, that sad affair involved a passage at arms. I thought you might atone by engaging in another. Say, in our current war with our old enemy Genoa."

"So Serenità, war is a game for young men. I am forty years old, which is somewhat over-age for wielding a sword, and—"

Snick! He squeezed the knife and made its inner blade dart forth.

"By your own account, you wielded this one not too many years since. Messer Marco, I am not suggesting that you lead a frontal assault on Genoa. Only that you make a token appearance of military service. And I am not being despotic or spiteful or capricious. I am thinking of the future of Venice and the house of Polo. That house has now been raised among the foremost of our city. After your father, you will be the head of it, and your sons after you. If, as seems likely, the house of Polo keeps its commanding position through the generations, I believe the family arms should be totally senza macchia. Wipe off the blot now, lest it embarrass and trouble all your posterity. It is easily accomplished. I have only to write against that page: 'Marco Polo, Ene Aca, loyally served the Republic in her war against Genoa.' "

My father nodded his agreement and contributed, "What is well closed is well kept."

"If I must," I said with a sigh. I had thought my war service was all behind me. However, I must confess, I thought it perhaps *would* look fine in the family history: that Marco Polo in his lifetime fought both with the Golden Horde and with the War Fleet of Venice. "What would you have me do, So Serenità?"

"Serve only as a gentleman at arms. Say, in supernumerary command of a supply ship. Make one sally with the fleet, out to sea and back to port, and then you retire—with new distinction and with old honor preserved."

Well, that is how, when a squadra of the Venetian fleet sailed out some months later under Almirante Dandolo, I came to be aboard the galeazza *Doge Particiaco*, which was actually only the victualler vessel to the squadra. I bore the courtesy rank of Sopracomito, meaning that I had approximately the same function I had had on the chuan that carried the Lady Kukachin—to look commanding and warlike and knowledgeable, and to stay out of the way of the Comito, the real master of the vessel, and the mariners who took his orders.

I do not aver that I could have done any better if I *had* been in command—of the galeazza or of the whole squadra—but I could hardly have done any worse. We sailed down the Adriatic and, near the island of Kurcola off the Dalmatia coast, we encountered a squadra of Genoan ships, flying the ensign of their great Almiranet Doria, and he demonstrated to us why he was called great. Our squadra, we could see from a distance, outnumbered the Genoans, so our Almirante Dandolo commanded that we surge forward in immediate attack. And Doria let our ships close with and disable some nine or ten of his, a deliberate sacrifice, just so our squadra would be enticed inextricably in amongst his own. And then, out of nowhere—or rather, out from behind the island of Peljesac, where they had been concealed—came ten or fifteen *more* fleet Genoan warships. The two-day battle cost many slain or wounded on both sides, but the victory was Doria's, for by sunset of the second day, the Genoans had taken our entire squadra and some seven thousand Venetian seamen prize of war, and I was one of them.

The *Doge Particiaco,* like all the other Venetian galleys, was sailed —still by its prize crew, but under command of a captor Genoan Comito —around the foot of Italy and up through the Tyrrhenian and Ligurian seas to Genoa. From the water, that looked no bad city in which to be interned: its palazzi like layered cakes of alternate black and white marble stacked up the slopes from the harbor. But when we were marched ashore, we found Genoa to be sadly inferior to Venice: all cramped streets and alleys and meager little piazze, and very dirty, not having canals to flush away its effluents.

I do not know where the ordinary seamen and rowers and archers and balestrieri and such were imprisoned, but, if tradition was observed, they no doubt sat out the war in misery and deprivation and squalor. The officers and gentlemen at arms like myself were considerably better treated, and put only under house arrest in the abandoned and run-down palazzo of some defunct religious order, in the Piazza of the Five Lanterns. The building was very little furnished, and very cold and dank—I have suffered worsening twinges of backache in chill weather ever since —but our jailers were courteous and they fed us adequately, and we were allowed to give money to the visiting Prisoners' Friends of the Brotherhood of Justice, to buy for us any extra comforts and refinements we might wish. All in all, it was a more tolerable confinement than I had once endured in the Vulcano prison of my own native Venice. However, our captors told us that they were breaking with tradition in one respect. They would not allow the ransoming of prisoners by their families back home. They said they had learned that it was no profit to profit from ransom payments, only to have to face the same officers again, a little while later, across some other contested piece of water. So we would stay in internment until this war was concluded.

Well, I had not lost my life by going to war, but it appeared that I was going to lose a substantial piece of it. I had carelessly squandered months and years before, making my way across interminable barren deserts or mountain snowfields, but at least I had been in the healthy open air during those journeys, and perhaps had learned something along the way. There was not much to be learned while languishing in prison. I had no Mordecai Cartafilo for cellmate this time.

As well as I could ascertain, all my fellow prisoners were either dilettanti like myself—noblemen who had been only desultorily whiling away their military service obligation—or professional men of war. The dilettanti were devoid of conversation except whines and yearnings to get back to their feste and ballrooms and dancing partners. The officers at least had some war stories to tell. But each such story gets very like every other story after a telling or two, and the rest of their conversation had all to do with rank and promotions and seniority of service, and how unappreciated by their superiors they were. I gather that every military man in Christendom is undeservedly ranked at least two stripes below the grade he ought to have.

So, if I could learn nothing here in prison, perhaps I could instruct, or at least amuse. When the dull conversations threatened to get absolutely stultifying, I might venture a remark like:

"Speaking of stripes, Messeri, there is in the lands of Champa a beast called the tiger, which has stripes all over it. And curiously enough, no two tigers are striped exactly the same. The natives of Champa can recognize one tiger from another by the distinctive striping of its face. They call the beast Lord Tiger, and they say that by drinking a decoction made from the eyeballs of a dead one, you can always see My Lord Tiger before he sees you. Then, by the striping of his face, you can tell if he is a known man-eater or a harmless hunter of only lesser animals."

Or, when one of our jailers brought us our tin supper dishes and the meal was as unsavory as usual, and we greeted him with our usual taunts, and he complained that we were a troublesome bunch, that he wished he had volunteered for duty elsewhere, I might suggest to him:

"Be glad, Genovese, you are not on duty in India. When the servants brought me dinner there, they had to enter the dining room crawling on their bellies and pushing the trays of food before them."

At first, my unsolicited contributions to the barrack conversations were sometimes received with strange and wondering looks, as when, for instance, two foppish gentlemen might be discussing, in high-flown language, the comparative virtues and charms of their lady loves back home, and I might venture:

"Have you yet determined, Messeri, whether your maidens are winter or summer women?" I would be regarded blankly, so I would explain: "The men of the Han say that a woman whose intimate aperture is situated unusually near the front of her artichoke is most suitable for cold winter nights, because you and she must closely intertwine to effect penetration. But a woman whose orifice is situated farther back between her legs is better for summertime. She can sit on your lap in a cool and breezy outdoor pavilion, while you enter her from the rear."

The two elegant gentlemen might then reel away in horror, but less dandified sorts would come congregating to hear more such revelations. And it was not long before, every time I opened my mouth, I would have more listeners than any expounder of ballroom manners or sea-war logistics, and they would listen raptly. Not only did my fellow Venetians cluster about me when I spun my tales, but also the Genoan warders and guards, and the visiting Brothers of Justice, and also Pisan and Corsican and Paduan prisoners taken by the Genoans in other wars and battles. And one day I was approached by one who said:

"Messer Marco, I am Luigi Rustichello, late of Pisa . . ."

And you introduced yourself as a scrivener, a fableor, a romancier, and you asked my permission to write down my stories in a book. So we sat down together and I told my tales to you, and, through the agency of the Brotherhood of Justice, I was enabled to send a request to Venice, and my father dispatched to Genoa my collection of notes and scraps and journals, which added to my recollection many things that I myself had forgotten. Thus our year of confinement passed not wearisomely but busily and productively. And when the war was finally over, and a new peace signed between Venice and Genoa, and we prisoners were released to go home, I could say that the year had not been a wasted time, as I had feared. Indeed, it may have been the most fruitful year of my entire life, in that I accomplished one thing that has lasted, and gives promise of lasting longer than I shall. I mean our book, Luigi, the *Description of the World*. Certainly, in the score or so of years that now have passed since we said goodbye outside that Genoa palazzo, I have accomplished nothing that gave me comparable satisfaction.

So here we are, Luigi. I have once more recounted my life from childhood to the end of my journeying. I have told again many of the tales you heard that long time ago, and many of those in more detail, and I have retold some others which you and I decided not to put into the earlier book, and I think many other stories besides, which I never did confide to you before. Now I give you leave to take any or all of my adventures, and ascribe them to the fictional hero of your latest work in progress, and make of them what you will.

There is not much more to tell of myself, and probably none of it would you find of any application to your new work, so I will tell it briefly.

. 6 .

I got back to Venice to find that my father and Marègna Lisa were well along in the building of our luxurious new Casa Polo—or rather, the making new of an old palazzo they had bought. It was on the Corte Sabionera, in a much more fashionable confino than our previous residence. It was also nearer to the Rialto, where, now that I was the recognized head of the Compagnia Polo, I was expected by tradition to mingle and converse with my fellow merchants twice a day, each morning just before noon and each evening at the close of the working day. That was and still is a pleasant custom, and I have often picked up the odd bit of useful information that might not have come to me in the ordinary course of business. I did not at all mind being respectfully addressed there as Messere, and respectfully listened to when I gave my sage opinion on this or that question of statutes or tariffs or whatever. I also did not *too much* mind being now head of the Compagnia Polo, though I had arrived at that eminence rather by default.

My father never did actually resign in my favor. He merely, from this time on, paid less and less attention to the company and more to other interests. For a while, he gave all his energies to supervision of the building and furnishing and decoration of the new Ca' Polo. On several occasions during its construction, he pointed out to me that this new palazzo was ample enough for many more people than we were preparing to put into it.

"Remember what the Doge said, Marco," he reminded me. "If there is to be a Compagnia Polo and a house of Polo after you, there must be sons."

"Father, you of all people must know how I feel on that subject. I should not mind paternity, but maternity has cost me more than I can ever count."

"Nonsense!" my stepmother put in sternly, but then she softened. "I do not mean to deprecate what you lost, Marco, but I must protest. When you told that tragic story, you were telling of a frail foreign woman. Venetian women are born and bred to breed. They enjoy being 'pregnant to the ears,' as the vulgar describe it, and they keenly feel the lack when they are not. Find yourself a good, wide-hipped Venetian wife, and leave the rest to her."

"Or," said my practical father, "find yourself a wife you can love sufficiently to want to have children with, but one you can love lightly enough that her loss would not be insupportable."

When the Ca' Polo was finished and we had moved in, my father turned his attention to a project even more novel and extraordinary. He founded what I might call a School for Merchant Adventurers. In actuality, it never had a name and it was not any academy of formal study. My father simply offered his experience and advice and access to our map collection, to any who might care to seek their fortune on the Silk Road. It was mostly young men who applied to him for schooling, but a few were as old as myself. For a stipulated percentage of the profit from a student's putative first successful trading expedition—to Baghdad, Balkh, anywhere else in the East, even all the way to Khanbalik—Nicolò Polo would impart to the apprentice adventurer all the useful information at his command, let the apprentice copy the route from our own maps, teach the apprentice some necessary phrases of Trade Farsi, even give the apprentice the names he remembered of native merchants, camel-pullers, guides, drovers and such, all along the route. He guaranteed nothing—since, after all, much of his knowledge had to be out of date by now. But neither did the apprentice journeyers have to pay him anything for their schooling, until and unless they profited from it. As I recall, many novices did set out in the direction Maistro Polo had twice gone, and some came safely back from as far away as Persia, and one or two of them came back prosperous, and paid their dues. But I think my father would have continued in that whimsical occupation even if it had never paid him a bagatìn, for in a sense it kept him still journeying afar—and even into his last years.

However, the consequence was that I, who had been a vagabond as carefree and wandersome and willful as any wind, now found my once wide horizons narrowed down to daily attendance at the company counting house and warehouse, with twice-a-day intervals of conviviality and gossip on the Rialto. It was my obligation; somebody had to keep up the Compagnia Polo; my father had in effect retired from it, and Zio Mafìo was still and forever a housebound invalid. In Constantinople, my eldest uncle also gradually edged out of the business (and died, I think of boredom, not long after). So there my cousin Nicolò and here myself found ourselves inheriting the full responsibility of our separate branches of the company. Cuzìn Nico actually seemed to enjoy being a merchant prince. And I? Well, it was honest and useful and not onerous work I was doing, and I had not yet got bored with the humdrum sameness of it day after day, and I had more or less resigned myself to this being *all* of my life. But then two new things happened.

The first was your sending me, Luigi, my copy of your just-completed *Description of the World*. I immediately gave over every spare moment to reading our book and savoring it and, as I finished each sheet, giving it to a copyist to make additional manuscripts. I found it in all ways admirable, with only a few errors, which were no doubt to be blamed on my pace of narration while you set down the words, and my neglect to read over your original draft with a critical eye.

The errors consisted only in an occasional misdating of this or that event, an occasional adventure set down out of sequence, an occasional one of the difficult Eastern place-names misheard or misspelled—your writing Saianfu, for example, where it should have been Yun-nan-fu, and Yang-zho for Hang-zho (which would have put me and my Manzi tax-collector career in a quite different city and distant from the one where I actually served). However, I never earlier bothered to point out those minor errors to you, and I hope my doing so now does not distress you. They could mean nothing to anyone but me—who else in this Western world would know there *is* any difference between Yang-zho and Hang-zho?—and I did not even trouble to have my scribe correct them while making his copies.

I made formal presentation of one of the copies to the Doge Gradenigo, and he must immediately have circulated it among his Council of nobles, and they to all their families and even servants. I presented another copy to the priest of our new parish of San Zuàne Grisostomo, and he must have circulated it among all his clergy and congregation, because in no time I was famous again. With even more avidity than they had shown when I first came home from Kithai, people began seeking to scrape my acquaintance, accosting me at public functions, pointing at me in the street, on the Rialto, from passing gòndole. And your own copies, Luigi, must have proliferated and scattered like dandelion seeds, for merchants and travelers visiting Venice from abroad said they came as much for a look at me as to see the San Marco Basilica and other notable sights of the city. If I received them, many told me they had read the *Description of the World* in their home country, already translated into their native language.

As I have said, Luigi, it did us little good to omit from that narrative many things we thought too marvelous to be believed. Some of the

enthusiasts seeking to meet me were seeking to meet what they properly
considered a Far Journeyer, but a great many wished to meet a man they
mistakenly considered Un Grand Romancier, author of an imaginative
and entertaining fiction, and others clearly wished only to ogle a Prodigious Liar, as they might have flocked to watch the frusta of some
eminent criminal at the piazzetta pillars. It seemed that the more I
protested—"I told nothing but the truth!"—the less I was believed, and
the more humorously (but fondly) I was regarded. I could hardly complain of being the cynosure of all eyes, and all those eyes warmly admiring, but I should have preferred that they admired me as something
other than a fablemaker.

I earlier said that our family's new Ca' Polo was situated in the
Corte Gabionera. It was, yes, and of course it still is, physically, and I
suppose even the latest street map of Venice gives the official name of
that little square as Ships-Ballast Court. But no resident of the city
called it that any more. It was known to everybody as the Corte del
Milione—in my honor—for I was now known as Marco Milione, man of
the million lies and fictions and exaggerations. I had become both
famous and notorious.

In time, I learned to live with my new and peculiar reputation, and
even to disregard the troops of urchins who sometimes followed me on
my walks from the Corte to the Compagnia or the Rialto. They would
brandish stick swords and prance in a sort of gallop gait, and spank their
own behinds while they did so, and shout things like "Come hither, great
princes!" and "The orda will get you!" Such constant attention was a
nuisance, and enabled even strangers to recognize me and greet me at
times when I might have preferred anonymity. But it was partly on
account of my being now conspicuous that another new thing occurred.

I forget where I was walking that day, but, on the street, I came
face to face with the little girl Doris who had been my childhood playmate and had in those days so much adored me. I was astonished. By
rights, Doris should have been nearly as old as I was—in her early
forties—and probably, she being of the lower class, already a gray and
wrinkled and worn-out drudge of a maràntega. But here she was, grown
only to young womanhood—in her middle twenties, no more—and decently attired, not in the shapeless black of old street women, and just as
golden blonde and fresh-faced and pretty as she had been when I last saw
her. I was more than astonished, I was thunderstruck. I so far forgot my
manners as to blurt her name, right there on the street, but at least I
thought to address her respectfully:

"Damìna Doris Tagiabue!"

She might have bridled at my effrontery and swept her skirts aside
and stalked on past me. But she saw my trailing retinue of urchins
playing Mongols, and she had to suppress a smile, and she said amiably
enough:

"You are Messer Marco of the—I mean—"

"Marco of the Millions. You can say it, Doris. Everyone does. And
you used to call me worse things. Marcolfo and such."

"Messere, I fear you have mistaken me. I assume you must once have known my mother, whose maiden name was Doris Tagiabue."

"Your mother!" For a moment I forgot that Doris must by now be a matron, if not a crone. Perhaps because this girl was so like my memory of her, I remembered only the unformed and untamed little zuzzurrullona I had known. "But she was just a child!"

"Children grow up, Messere," she said, and added mischievously, "Even yours will," and she indicated my half-dozen miniature Mongols.

"Those are not mine. *Beat the retreat, men!*" I shouted at them, and with much rearing and wheeling of their imaginary steeds they retired to a distance.

"I was but jesting, Messere," said the so-familiar stranger, smiling openly now, and even more resembling the merry sprite of my recollection. "Among the things well-known in Venice is that the Messer Marco Polo is still a bachelor. My mother, however, grew up and married. I am her daughter and my name is Donata."

"A pretty name for a pretty young lady: the given one, the gift." I bowed as if we had been formally introduced. "Dona Donata, I would be grateful if you would tell me where your mother lives now. I should like to see her again. We were once—close friends."

"Almèi, Messere. Then I regret to tell you that she died of an influenza di febbre some years ago."

"Gramo mi! I lament to hear it. She was a dear person. My condolences, Dona Donata."

"Damìna, Messere," she corrected me. "My mother was the Dona Doris Loredano. I am, like you, unmarried."

I started to say something outrageously daring—and hesitated—and then said it:

"Somehow I cannot condole on your being unmarried." She looked faintly surprised at my boldness, but not scandalized, so I went on, "Damìna Donata Loredano, if I sent acceptable sensàli to your father, do you think he might be persuaded to let me call at your family residence? We could talk of your late mother . . . of old times. . . ."

She cocked her head and regarded me for a moment. Then she said forthrightly, without archness, as her mother might have done:

"The famous and esteemed Messer Marco Polo surely is welcome everywhere. If your sensàli will apply to the Maistro Lorenzo Loredano at his place of business in the Merceria . . ."

Sensàli can mean business brokers or marriage brokers, and it was the latter kind I sent, in the person of my staid and starched stepmother, together with a formidable maid or two of hers. Marègna Lisa returned from that mission to report that the Maistro Loredano had acceded most hospitably to my request for permission to pay a series of calls. She added, with a noticeable elevation of her eyebrows:

"He is an artisan of leather goods. Evidently an honest and respectable and hardworking currier. But, Marco, *only* a currier. Morel di mezo. You could be paying calls on the daughters of the sangue blo. The Dandolo family, the Balbi, the Candiani . . ."

"Dona Lisa, I once had a Nena Zulià who likewise complained of my tastes. Even in my youth I was contrary, preferring a savory morel to one with a noble name."

However, I did not swoop upon the Loredano household and abduct Donata. I paid court to her as properly and ritually and for as long a time as if she had been of the very bluest blood. Her father, who gave the impression of having been assembled from some of his own tanned hides, received me cordially and made no comment on the fact that I was nearly as old as he. After all, one of the accepted ways for a daughter of the "middle mushroom" class to sprout higher in the world was for her to make an advantageous May-December marriage, usually to a widower with numerous children. On that scale, I was really no older than November, and I came unencumbered with any step-brood. So the Maistro Lorenzo merely mumbled some of the phrases traditionally spoken by an unmoneyed father to a wealthy suitor, to dispel any suspicion that he was voluntarily surrendering his daughter to the diritto di signoria:

"I must make known my reluctance, Messere. A daughter should not aspire to higher station than life gave her. To the natural burden of her low birth she risks adding a heavier servitude."

"It is I who aspire, Messere," I assured him. "I can only hope that your daughter will favor my aspirations, and I promise that she would never have cause to regret having done so."

I would bring flowers, or some small gift, and Donata and I would sit together, always with an accompagnatrice—one of Fiordelisa's iron-corseted maids—sitting nearby to make sure we behaved with rigid respectability. But that did not prevent Donata's speaking to me as freely and frankly as Doris had been wont to do.

"If you knew my mother in her youth, Messer Marco, then you know that she began life as a poor orphan. Literally of the low popolàzo. So I shall put on no false airs and graces in her behalf. When she married a prospering currier, owner of his own workshop, she did marry above her class. But no one would ever have known it, if she had not chosen to make no secret of it. There was never anything coarse or vulgar about her during all the rest of her life. She made a good wife to my father and a good mother to me."

"I would have made wager on it," I said.

"I think she was a credit to her higher station in life. I tell you this, Messer Marco, so that if you—if you should have any doubts about my own qualifications for moving higher yet . . ."

"Darling Donata, I have had no least doubt at all. Even when your mother and I were children together, I could see the promise in her. But I will not say 'like mother, like daughter.' Because, even if I had never known her, I should quickly have recognized your own promise. Shall I, like a mooning and courting trovatore, sing your qualities? Beauty, intelligence, good humor—"

"Please do not omit honesty," she interrupted. "For I would have you know everything there is to know. My mother never whispered any hint of this to me, and I should certainly never breathe it in my good father's hearing, but—but there are things a child gets to know, or at least suspect, without being told. Mind you, Messer Marco, I admire my mother for having made a good marriage. But I might be less admiring of the way she must have done it, and so might you. I have an unshakable suspicion that her marriage to my father was impelled by their having—how do I say?—their having *anticipated the event* to some degree. I fear that a comparison of the date written on their consenso di matrimonio and that written on my own atta di nascita might prove embarrassing."

I smiled at young Donata's thinking she might shock someone as inured and impervious to shock as I was. And I smiled more broadly at her innocent simplicity. She must be quite unaware, I thought, that a great many marriages among the lower classes never were solemnized by *any* document or ceremony or sacrament. If Doris had indeed, by the oldest of feminine ruses, exalted herself from the popolàzo to the morel di mezo, it did not lessen my regard for her—or for this pretty product of her ruse. And if that was the only impediment Donata could fear as a possible interference to our marriage, it was a trifling one. I made two promises at that moment. One was only to myself, and unspoken: I took oath that never during our married lifetime would I reveal any of the secrets of my past or the skeletons in my own cupboard. The other promise I made aloud, after smoothing away my smile and assuming a very solemn face:

"I swear, dearest Donata, that I shall never hold it against you—that you were prematurely born. There is no disgrace in that."

"Ah, you older men are so commendably tolerant of human frailty." I may have winced at that, for she added, "You are a good man, Messer Marco."

"And your mother was a good woman. Do not think ill of her for having been a determined woman, as well. She knew how to get her own way." I remembered, somewhat guiltily, one instance of that. The recollection made me say, "I take it that she never mentioned having been acquainted with me."

"Not that I recall. Should she have?"

"No, no. I was nobody worth mentioning in those days. But I should confess—" I stopped, for I had just sworn not to confess anything that had happened in my past life. And I could hardly confess that Doris Tagiabue had come to Lorenzo Loredano no virgin as a consequence of her having first practiced her wiles on me. So I merely repeated:

"Your mother knew how to get her own way. If I had not had to leave Venice, it could very well have happened that she would have married *me* when we were a little older."

Donata pouted prettily. "What an ungallant thing to say, even if it is true. Now you make me seem like a second choice."

"And now you make *me* seem like someone browsing in a market. I did not choose you by volition, dear girl. I had no part in it. When I first saw you, I said to myself, 'She must have been put on this earth for me.' And when you spoke your name, I *knew* it. I knew that I had been given a gift."

And that pleased her, and made things right again.

On another occasion during our courtship, when we sat together, I put to her this question: "What of children when we are married, Donata?"

She blinked at me in perplexity, as if I had asked whether she intended to go on breathing after we were married. So I went on:

"A married couple are of course expected to have children. It is the natural thing. It is expected by their families, the Church, the Lord God, the community. But despite those expectations, there must be some people who do not wish to conform."

"I am not among them," she said, like a response to a catechism.

"And there are some who simply cannot."

After a moment of silence, she said, "Are you intimating, Marco—?" She had by this time eased into addressing me informally. Now she said, choosing her words with delicacy, "Are you intimating, Marco, that perhaps you were, um, during your journeying, um, injured in some way?"

"No, no, no. I am whole and healthy, and competent to be a father. As far as I know, I mean. I was rather referring to those unfortunate women who are, for one reason or another, barren."

She looked away from me, and blushed as she said, "I cannot protest 'no, no, no,' for I have no way of knowing. But I think, if you were to count the barren women you have heard of, you would find that they are mostly pale and fragile and vaporish noblewomen. I come of good, solid, redblooded peasant stock and, like any Christian woman, I *hope* to be the mother of multitudes. I pray to the good Lord that I will. But if He in His wisdom should somehow choose to make me barren, I would try with fortitude to bear the affliction. However, I have confidence in the Lord's goodness."

"It is not always of the good Lord's doing," I said. "In the East there are known various ways to prevent conception—"

Donata gasped and crossed herself. "Never say such a thing! Do not even speak of such a dreadful sin! Why, what would the good Pare Nardo say, if he even dreamed you had imagined such things? Oh, Marco, do assure me that you put no mention *in your book* of anything so criminal and sordid and un-Christian. I have not read the book, but I have heard some people call it scandalous. Was that the scandal they spoke of?"

"I really do not remember," I said placatively. "I think that was one of the things I left out. I merely wished to tell you that such things are possible, in case—"

"Not in Christendom! It is unspeakable! Unthinkable!"

"Yes, yes, my dear. Forgive me."

"Only if you promise me," she said firmly. "Promise me you will forget that and *all other* vile practices you may have witnessed in the East. That our good Christian marriage will never be tainted by anything un-Christian you learned or saw or even heard of in those pagan lands."

"Well, not everything pagan is vile. . . ."

"Promise me!"

"But, Donata, suppose I should have another opportunity or occasion to go eastward, and wished to take you with me. You would be the first Western woman, to my knowledge, ever to—"

"No. I will never go, Marco," she said flatly, and her blush had gone now. Her face was very white and her lips set. "I should not wish you to go. There. I have said it. You are a wealthy man, Marco, with no need to increase your wealth. You are famous for your journeying already, with no need to increase that fame or to journey ever again. You have responsibilities, and will shortly have me for another, and I hope we will both have others. You are no longer—you are no longer the boy you were when you set out before. I should not have wished to marry that boy, Marco, not then or now. I want a mature and sober and dependable man, and I want him at home. I took you to be that man. If you are not, if you still harbor a restless and reckless boy inside you, I think you had better confess it now. We will have to put on a good face for our families and friends and all the gossips of Venice, when we announce the dissolution of our betrothal."

"You are indeed very like your mother." I sighed. "But you are young. In time to come, you might even *desire* to journey—"

"Not outside Christendom," she said, still in that flat voice. "Promise me."

"Very well. I shall never take you outside Chris—"

"Nor will you go."

"Now that, Donata, I could not swear in good faith. My very business may require at least a return visit to Constantinople on occasion, and all around that city are un-Christian lands. My foot might slip, and—"

"This much, then. Promise me you will not go away until our children, if God gives us children, are grown to a responsible age. You have told me how your own father left his son to run wild among the street folk."

I laughed. "Donata, *they* were not all vile, either. One of them was your mother."

"My mother raised me to be better than my mother. My own children are not to be abandoned. Promise me."

"I promise," I said. I did not pause then to calculate that, if our marriage produced a son in the ordinary interval, I would be something like sixty-five years old before he had reached his majority. I was only thinking that Donata, still young herself, might have many changes of mind during our life together. "I promise, Donata. As long as there are children at home, and unless you decree otherwise, so will I be at home."

And in the first year of the new century, in the year one thousand three hundred and one, we were married.

All was done with punctilious observance of the proprieties. When our period of courtship was deemed suitably long enough, Donata's father and mine and a notary convened at the Church of San Zuàne Grisostomo for the ceremony of impalmatura, and they severally perused and signed and affirmed the marriage contract, just as if I had been some shy and awkward and adolescent bridegroom—when in fact it was I who had seen to the drawing up of the contract, with the counsel of my Compagnia attorneys-at-law. At the conclusion of the impalmatura, I put the betrothal ring on Donata's finger. On subsequent Sundays, Pare Nardo proclaimed from the pulpit the bandi, and posted them on the church door, and no one came forward to dispute the proposed marriage. Then Dona Lisa engaged a friar-scribe with an excellent hand to write the partecipazioni di nozze, and sent them, each with the traditional gift parcel of confèti almonds, by liveried messenger to all the invited guests. They included everyone of any consequence in Venice, for, although there were sumptuary laws limiting the extravagance of most families' public ceremonies, the Doge Gradenigo graciously granted us exemption. And, when the day came, it was a celebration on the scale of a citywide festa—after the nuptial mass, the banquet and feasting, the music and song and dancing, the drinking and brindisi and tipsy guests falling into the Corte canal, the confèti and coriàndoli thrown. When all that required the participation of Donata and myself was over, her bridal maids gave her the donora: setting in her arms for a moment a borrowed baby and tucking in her shoe a gold sequin coin, symbols of her being evermore blessed with fecundity and richness—and then we left the still uproarious festa and betook ourselves inside the Ca' Polo, deserted of all but servants, the family to stay with friends during our luna di miele.

And in our bedchamber, in private, in Donata I discovered Doris all over again, for her body was the same milk-white, adorned with the same two small shell-pink points. Except that Donata was a grown woman and fully developed in womanhood, with a golden floss to prove it, she was the image of her mother, even to the identical appurtenance that I had once likened to the morsel called ladylips. Much else of the night was a repetition of a stolen afternoon long years ago. As I had taught then, so I taught now, beginning with the turning of Donata's shell-pink points to a blushing and eager coral-pink. But here I will again draw the curtain of connubial privacy, though a little belatedly, for I have already told it all—the events of this night being very nearly the same as on that long-ago afternoon. And this time, too, it delighted us both. At risk of sounding disloyal to olden time, I might even say that this occasion was more delicious than the earlier, because this time we were not sinning.

· 7 ·

W H E N Donata came to her confinement, I was there at home, in the house, close at hand, partly in compliance with my promise to her and our then-unarrived family, partly in memory of another time when I had so unforgivably been absent. They would not let me into Donata's chamber for the event, of course, and I had no desire to be there. But I had done everything possible to prepare for the event, including the engagement of the sage physician Piero Abano, whom I paid lavishly to bequeath all his other patients to another mèdego and do nothing but attend Donata throughout her pregnancy. He early inculcated what he called his Six-Element Regimen: proper diet and drink, properly alternating periods of motion and rest, sleep and waking, evacuation and retention, fresh air during the day and close air at night, and "assuagement of the passions of the mind." Whether that regimen was the more to be credited, or Donata's "good peasant stock," there was no childbed difficulty. Dotòr Abano and his two midwives and my stepmother came, in a bunch, to tell me that Donata's labor had been easy and the birth like the squirting of an orange pip. They had to shake me awake to tell me, for I had again been reliving my own onetime experience of such travail and, to ameliorate it, had drunk three or four bottles of Barolo and succumbed into blessed oblivion.

"I am sorry she is not a boy," murmured Donata, when they let me into the chamber to view our daughter for the first time. "I should have known. The carrying and the labor were too easy. Next time I shall pay heed to what the old women say: Labor a little longer, and give birth to a male child."

"Hush, hush," I said. "Now I am the happy recipient of two gifts."

We named her Fantina.

Although Donata was from our earliest acquaintance wary of having me introduce any "un-Christian ideas" into our household, I was able to convince her of the worthiness of *some* alien customs. I do not mean any of the things I taught her in bed. Donata was a virgin when we wed, so she had no way of distinguishing the practices Venetian or exotic, universal or especial. But I also taught her, for instance, what I knew of the way the Han women kept themselves clean inside and out. I very delicately imparted that information to her, early in our marriage, and she saw the merit in that un-Christian bathing habit, and adopted it. After Fantina's birth I insisted that she be likewise frequently bathed on the outside and, when she was older, on the inside as well. Donata briefly balked, saying:

"Bathed, yes. But the inner irrigation? That is all very well for a woman already married, but it would efface Fantina's maidenhead. She would never have proof of her virginity."

I said, "In my opinion, purity is best detected in the wine, not in the waxen seal on the flask. Teach Fantina to keep her body clean and sweet, and I believe her morals are likely to remain so, as well. Any future husband will recognize that quality in her, and require no mere physical token of it."

So Donata complied, and instructed Fantina's nurse to bathe her frequently and thoroughly, and so instructed every subsequent nena we had in the house. Some were at first amazed and critical, but they gradually came to approve, and I think spread the word among their servant circles that an un-Christian cleanliness was not, as commonly believed, debilitating, for in time the Venetians of both sexes and all ages got noticeably cleaner than in the olden days. By introducing just that one custom of the Han, I may have done much to improve the entire city of Venice—from the skin out, so to speak.

Our second child was born almost exactly a year later, and also without difficulty, but not in the same place. The Doge Gradenigo had summoned me one day and asked if I would accept a consular post abroad, the one in Bruges. It was an honor to be invited to that civic duty, and I had by then trained up a good staff of assistants who could look after the Compagnia Polo during my absence, and in Bruges I could accomplish many things to the company's advantage. But I did not say yes on the spot. Although the post was in good Christian Flanders, I thought I ought to confer first with Donata.

She agreed with me that she should at least once in her lifetime see *something* outside her native Venice, so I accepted the posting. Donata was already big with child when we sailed, but we took our sage Venetian physician along and, the voyage being made on a heavy, rock-solid Flemish cog, it caused no distress to either her or our infant Fantina, but Dotòr Abano was seasick all the way. Happily, he was well recovered by the time Donata came to term, and again it was an easy birth, and again Donata complained only that it had been *too* easy, for it produced another daughter.

"Hush, hush," I said. "In the lands of Champa a man and woman do not even get married until after they have produced two children. So, in effect, we are just getting started."

We named that one Bellela.

Venice maintained a permanent consulate in Bruges—and favored its more distinguished Ene Aca citizens with the opportunity to serve there in rotation—because twice a year a numerous fleet of Venetian galleys sailed from Bruges's harbor suburb of Sluys, laden with the produce of all northern Europe. So Donata and I and Fantina—and shortly little Bellela—spent a most enjoyable year or so in the fine consular residence on the Place de la Bourse, a house luxuriously furnished with every convenience, including a permanent staff of servants. I was not overburdened with work, not having much to do except look over the shipping manifests of the bi-yearly fleet, and decide whether this time it would sail direct to Venice, or whether it had hold room for other goods, in which case I might route some or all of the ships by way of London or Southampton across the Channel, or by way of Ibiza or Majorca in the Mediterranean, to pick up some of the produce of those places.

Most of that consular year Donata and I spent being royally entertained by other consular delegations and by Flemish merchant families, at balls and banquets and local feste like the Procession of the Holy Blood. Many of our hosts had read the *Description of the World*, in one language or another, and all had heard about it, and all spoke the Sabir trade tongue, so I was much questioned on this or that of the book's contents, and encouraged to elaborate on this and that aspect of it. An evening's entertainment would often go on late into the night, because the company would keep me talking, and Donata would sit and smile proprietorially. While there were ladies present, I would confine myself to innocuous subjects.

"Our fleet was today loading your good North Sea herring, my lords merchants. They are excellent fish, but I myself prefer to dine on fresh, as we did tonight, not salted or smoked or pickled fish. I suggest you consider marketing them fresh. Yes, yes, I know; fresh fish do not travel. But I *have* seen them do so in the north of Kithai, and your climate here is very similar. You might speculate on adopting the method used there, or some variant of it. In the north of Kithai, the summer is only three months long, so the fishermen plunder the lakes and rivers with all their energy, taking far more fish than they can sell in the same time. They toss the surplus fish into a shallow reservoir of water and keep them alive there until wintertime. Then they break the ice on the reservoir and take the fish out singly, at which exposure to the winter air the fish freeze solid. They are packed like kindling logs, in bundles on pack asses, and are sent thus to the cities, where the rich folk pay exorbitant prices for such delicacies. And when the fish are thawed and cooked, they taste as fresh as any caught in the summertime."

Such remarks would often inspire two or three of the more ambitious merchants present to call for a servant to carry an urgent message to their place of business: I suppose something on the order of "Let us try this man's preposterous notion." But the merchants themselves would not leave the gathering because, when the ladies had betaken themselves elsewhere to chat of feminine things, I would regale the men with more piquant tales.

"My personal traveling physician, the Dotòr Abano, pronounces himself dubious of this, Messeri, but I brought back from Kithai a prescription for long life, and I will share it with you. The men of the Han who profess the religion called Tao have a firm belief that the exhalations of all things contain particles so tiny they are invisible, but have a potent effect nonetheless. For example, the rose particles we call the fragrance of a rose make us feel benign when we inhale them. The meat particles given off as scent by a good roast of meat make our mouths water. Just so, the Taoists profess that the breath passing through the lungs of a young girl gets charged with particles of her young, fresh body and then, when she exhales, imbue the ambient air with vigorous and invigorating qualities. Thus the prescription: if you would live a long time, surround yourself with vivacious young maidens. Stay as close to them as you can. Inhale their sweet exhalations. They will enhance your blood and humors and other juices. They will strengthen your health and lengthen your life. It goes without saying that, if you should meanwhile find other employment for the delicious young virgins . . ."

Raucous laughter, loud and prolonged, and one old Fleming pounded a bony hand on his spiky knee and cried, "Damn your personal physician, Mynheer Polo! I think it a damned fine prescription! I would resort to the young girls in an instant, damn me if I would not, except that my damned old wife would think of some objection to make."

Louder laughter, over which I called to him, "Not if you go about it cunningly, Messere. The prescription for elderly women is, of course, young boys."

Louder laughter yet, and boisterous jests shouted, and the handing around of pitchers of the strong Flemish ale, and often, when Donata and I departed the company, I was glad I had a consular palanquin to ride home in.

Having less to do in the daytime, and Donata being then usually occupied as a mother to our daughters, I applied myself to what I believed would be a project beneficial to trade in general and Venice in particular. I decided to institute here in the West something I had found eminently useful in the East. I established a horse post in imitation of that devised so long ago by the Khan Kubilai's Minister of Roads and Rivers. It took some time and labor and argument to accomplish, since in these lands I had no absolute authority, as I would have had anywhere in the Khanate. I had to overcome a good deal of government torpor, timidity and opposition. And those difficulties were multiplied by the number of governments involved Flanders, Lorraine, Swabia and so on—every suspicious, narrow-minded duchy and principality between Bruges and Venice. But I was determined and stubborn, and I did it. When I had that post-chain of riders and relay stations established, I could send to Venice the cargo manifests of the fleet as soon as it sailed from Sluys. The post would convey the papers those seven hundred miles in seven days, or one-quarter of the best time the fleet could make, so the recipient merchants in Venice often had every item of the cargo sold at a profit before it even reached them.

When it came time for me and my family to quit Bruges, I was much tempted to try posting *us* home the same swift way. But two of the family consisted of infant children, and Donata was pregnant again, so the idea was impractical. We came home as we had gone, by ship, and arrived in good time for our third daughter, Morata, to be born in Venice.

The Ca' Polo was still a place of pilgrimage for visitors wishing to meet and converse with Messer Marco Milione. During my stay in Flanders, my father had been receiving them. But he and Dona Lisa were wearying of that obligation, both of them being now very old and failing in health, and they were glad to have me assume the duty again.

There came to see me, during the years, besides mere gapers and gawkers, some distinguished and intelligent men. I remember a poet, Francesco da Barberino, who (like you, Luigi) wished to know some things about Kithai for a chanson de geste he was writing. And I remember the cartographer Marino Sanudo, who came asking to incorporate some of our maps into a great Map of the World he was compiling. And there came several friars-historians, Jacopo d'Acqui and Francesco Pipino and one from France, Jean d'Ypres, who were severally writing Chronicles of the World. And there came the painter Giotto di Bondone, already famous for his O and his chapel frescoes, who wished to know something of the illustrative arts as practiced by the Han, and seemed impressed by what I could tell him and show him, and went away saying he was going to try some of those exotic effects in his own paintings.

There came also, during the years, from my many correspondents in countries East and West, news of people and places I had known. I heard of the death of Edward, King of England, whom I had known as a

Crusader prince in Acre. I heard that the priest Zuàne of Montecorvino, whom I had known just long enough to detest, had been appointed by the Church its first Archbishop of Khanbalik, and had been sent a number of under-priests to minister to the missions he was establishing in Kithai and Manzi. I heard of the many successful wars waged by the once insignificant boy Ghazan. Among his several triumphs, he swallowed the Seljuk Empire wholly into his Ilkhanate of Persia, and I wondered what became of the Kurdi Shoe Brigand and my old friend Sitarè, but I never heard. I learned of other expansions of the Mongol Khanate —in the south it took Jawa, both the Greater and the Lesser, and in the west moved into Tazhikistan—but, as I had advised Kubilai not to do, none of his successors ever bothered to invade India.

Things happened closer to home, too, not all of them joyous things. In fairly close succession, my father and then my Zio Mafìo and then my Marègna Fiordelisa died. Their funerals were of such splendid pomp and thronged attendance and citywide mourning as almost to overshadow the obsequies for the Doge Gradenigo, who died shortly afterward. About the same time, we here in Venice were set aghast when the Frenchman who had become Pope Clement V summarily removed the Apostolic See from Rome to Avignon in his native France, so that His Holiness might remain near to his mistress, who, being the wife of the Count of Périgord, could not conveniently visit him in the Eternal City. We might have looked tolerantly on that as a temporary aberrancy, typical of a Frenchman, except that, three years ago, Clement was succeeded by another Frenchman, and John XXII seems satisfied that the papal palace remain in Avignon. My correspondents have not kept me well informed of what the rest of Christendom thinks of this sacrilege, but, to judge from the tempest it has raised here in Venice—including some not at all frivolous suggestions that we Venetian Christians contemplate shifting our allegiance to the Greek Church—I must surmise that poor San Piero is raging in his Roman catacomb.

The Doge succeeding Gradenigo was only briefly in office before he too died. The current Doge Zuàne Soranzo is a younger man and should be with us for a while. He has also been a man of innovations. He instituted an annual race of gòndole and batèli on the Grand Canal, and called it the Regata, because prizes were awarded to the winners. In each of the four years since, the Regata has got more lively and colorful and popular—being now a day-long festa, with races for boats of one oar, of two oars, even boats rowed by women, and the prizes have got ever richer and more sought after—until the Regata has become as much of a yearly spectacle as the Wedding of the Sea.

Another thing the Doge Soranzo did was to ask me to assume civic office again, as one of the Proveditori of the Arsenàl, and I still continue in that post. It is purely a ceremonial duty, like being supracomito of a warship, but I do go out to that end of the island once in a while, to pretend that I really am supervising the shipyard. I enjoy being out there in the eternal aroma of boiling pitch, watching a galley begin life at one corner of the yard as just a single keel timber—then take shape as it moves along the ways, from one team of workers to the next, getting ribs and planking and, still slowly moving all the time, goes on through the sheds where workers on both sides stock its hull and holds with every necessity, from cordage and spare sails to armaments and staple provisions, while its decking and upper works are still being finished by other arsenaloti—until it floats out into the Arsenàl basin, a complete new vessel ready for auction to some buyer, ready to dip oars or hoist sail and go a-journeying. It is a poignant sight to one who will journey no more.

I shall not be going away again, not anywhere, and in many respects I might almost never have been away. I am still esteemed in Venice, but as a fixture now, not a novelty, and children do not prance behind me in the streets any more. An occasional visitor from some foreign country, where the *Description of the World* has just made its first appearance, still comes seeking to meet me, but my fellow Venetians have tired of hearing my reminiscences and they do not thank me for my contributions of ideas I picked up in far places.

Not long ago, at the Arsenàl, the Master Shipwright got quite red in the face when I told, at some length, how the Han mariners somehow guide their massive chuan vessels more deftly—with only a single, centered steering oar—than do the helmsmen of our smaller galeazze with their double oars, one on each side. The Master Shipwright listened patiently while I discoursed, but he went away grumbling audibly about "dilettanti disrespectful of tradition." Only a month or so afterward, though, I saw a new galley come down the ways, not with the usual lateen sail but square-rigged in the manner of a Flemish cog, and with only a single, centered, stern-mounted steering oar. I was not invited aboard for that ship's trial voyage, but it must have handled well, for the Arsenàl has since been turning out more and more of the same design.

Also not long ago, when I was honored with an invitation to dine at the palazzo of the Doge Soranzo, the dinner was accompanied by muted music from a band of players in the gallery overlooking the chamber. At a lull in the conversation, I remarked to the table at large:

"Once upon a time, in the palace of Pagan, in the nation of Ava, in the lands of Champa, we were entertained at dinner by a troupe of musicians who were all blind men. I inquired of a steward if blind men in that country found easiest employment as musicians. The steward told me, 'No, U Polo. If a child shows a talent for music, he is deliberately blinded by his parents, so that his hearing will sharpen and he will concentrate his attention only on perfecting his music, so that someday he may be accorded a place as a palace musician.'"

There was a general silence. Then the Dogaressa said crisply, "I do not think that a fit story for the dining table, Messer Marco." And I have not been invited there since.

When a young man named Marco Bragadino, who has lately been making the cascamorto at my eldest daughter Fantina, lavishing on her languishing looks and heartfelt sighs, finally took his courage in both hands and came to me to inquire if he might commence formal calls of courtship, I tried to put him at ease by saying jovially:

"That reminds me, young Bragadino, of an occurrence in Khanbalik once upon a time. There was hauled into the Cheng—into the court of justice—a man accused of beating his wife. The Tongue of the Cheng asked the man if he had good reason for this behavior, and the wretch said yes, he was beating his wife for her having suffocated their baby daughter immediately after its birth. The wife was asked if she had anything to say, and she cried, 'It was only a daughter, my lords. There is no crime in disposing of excess daughters. Anyway, that happened fifteen years ago.' The Tongue then asked the man, 'Man, why in the world are you beating your wife for that *now*?' And the man said, 'My lords, fifteen years ago it did not matter. But recently a plague of some female disease has killed off almost all the other young maidens in our district. Brides are now at a premium, and the few available are fetching princess prices!' "

After a while, young Bragadino cleared his throat and asked, "Er, is that all, Messere?"

"That is all," I said. "I do not remember how the Cheng ruled in that case."

When young Bragadino had departed, looking confused and shaking his head, my wife and Fantina stormed into the room and began berating me. They had evidently both been listening behind the door.

"Papà, what have you done? Gramo mi, you have repulsed my best hope of marriage! I shall be a lonely and despised zitella all my life! I shall die with the jewel! What have you done?"

"Marcolfo vechio!" said Donata, in the memorable style of her own mother. "We have no scarcity of daughters in this house! You can ill afford to turn away any of their suitors!" She spared Fantina none of her frankness, either. "It is not as if they were sensational beauties, much sought after!" Fantina gave a despairing wail and flung herself out of the room. "Can you not curb your everlasting old reminiscences and your wandering old wits?"

"You are right, my dear," I said contritely. "I know better. One of these days I shall *do* better."

She *was* right, too. I concede that. In the matter of children, Donata had reposed her confidence in her Lord's goodness, but, after giving us three daughters, evidently her good Lord despaired of ever providing a son and heir to the Venetian house of Polo. That I had no male issue did not crushingly disappoint me or blight my life. It is not very Christian of me to say so, I know, but I do not believe that when my own life is over I shall be taking much interest in the affairs of this world, or wringing the pale hands of my soul because I left no Marcolino Polo in charge of all the warehouse goods and zafràn plantations I could not take with me. I did not confess this recusancy of mine to old Pare Nardo before he died (and that clement old man would probably have given me small penance for it)—and I shall not confess it to the grim-lipped young Pare Gasparo (who would be righteously severe)—but I am inclined to believe that if there is a Heaven I have not much hope of it; if there is a Hell, I daresay I will have other things to worry about than how my progeny are faring on the Rialto.

I may be less than a model Christian, but neither am I like those Eastern fathers whom I have heard say such things as: "No, I have no children. Only three daughters." I have never been prejudiced against daughters. Of course, I might have hoped for daughters with better looks and brighter wits. I am perhaps overparticular in that regard, having myself been blessed with the knowing of so many extraordinarily beautiful and intelligent women in my younger days. But Donata was one of those, in *her* younger days. If she could not replicate herself in her daughters, the fault must be mine.

The little Raja of the Hindus once harangued me about no man's ever knowing with surety who is the father of any of his children, but I have never had the least cause for anxiety. I have only to look at any one of them—Fantina, Bellela or Morata—they all look too exactly like me for there to be any doubt. Now, I hasten to asseverate that Marco Polo has all his life been no bad-looking man. But I should not wish to be a nubile young maiden and look like Marco Polo. If I was, and did, I should hope at least to have a bright intelligence by way of compensation. Unfortunately, my daughters have been scanted in that respect, as well. I do not mean to say that they are drooling imbeciles; they are no worse than unperceptive and lackluster and charmless.

But they are of my making. Should the potter despise the only pots he will ever produce? And they are good girls, with good hearts, or so I am repeatedly and consolingly told by my acquaintances who possess comely daughters. All I can say, from my own knowledge, is that my girls are cleanly of person and smell good. No, I can also say that they are fortunate in having a Papà who can dower them with the attractions of affluence.

Young Bragadino was not so repulsed by my dithering that day as to stay away forever, and the next time he called I confined my disquisition to topics like bequests and prospects and inheritances. He and Fantina are now formally betrothed, and Bragadino the Elder and I will shortly be convening with a notary for the impalmatura. My second daughter, Bellela, is being sedulously courted by a young man named Zanino Grioni. Morata will have someone, too, in due time. I have no doubt that all three girls will be grateful to be known no longer as the Damìne Milione, and I have no overwhelming regrets that the Compagnia and the fortune and the house of Polo will henceforth percolate down through the generations as the Compagnie and houses of Bragadino, Grioni, Eccètera. If the precepts of the Han are true, this may cause consternation among my ancestors, from Nicolò all the way back to the Dalmatian Pavlo, but it causes not much to me.

. 8 .

I F I had any real lament to make about our lack of sons, it would be a lament for what that did to Donata. She was only about thirty-two years old when Morata was born, but the birth of a third daughter clearly convinced her that she was incapable of male issue. And, as if to avert any hazard of producing yet another daughter, Donata thereafter began to discourage our further indulgence in conjugal relations. She never, by word or gesture, *refused* my amorous overtures, but she began to dress and look and comport herself in a manner calculated to diminish her appeal for me and dampen my ardor for her.

At thirty-two she began to let her face lose its radiance and her hair its luster and her eyes their lively sparkle, and she started dressing in the black bombazine and shawls of an old woman. At thirty-two! I was then fifty years old, but I was still straight and slim and strong, and I wore the rich garb to which my station entitled me and my taste for color inclined me. My hair and beard were still more life-colored than gray, and my blood was still unthinned, and I still had all my lusty appetites for life and pleasure, and my eyes still kindled when I glimpsed a lovely lady. But I have to say that they glazed when I looked at Donata.

Her posturing as an old woman *made* her an old woman. She is younger today than I was when Morata was born. But over these ensuing fifteen years, she has put on all the unsightly lineaments and contours of a woman many years older—the sagging facial features, the stringed and corded throat and that old-woman's hump at the back of the neck, and those tendons that operate the fingers are visible through the spotted skin of her hands, and her elbows have become like old coins, and the meat of her upper arms hangs loose and wobbly, and when she raises her skirt to hobble and lurch from the Corte landing down the steps to one of our boats, I can see that her ankles lop over her shoes. What has become of the milk-white and shell-pink and golden-flossed body, I do not know; I have not seen it in a long time.

During these years, I repeat, she never denied me any of my conjugal rights, but she always moped afterward, until the moon came round again and relieved her of the fear that she might again be pregnant. After a while, of course, that became nothing to fear, and anyway by then I was not giving her any cause to fear it. By then, too, I was occasionally spending an afternoon or a whole night away from home, but she never even required from me a mendacious excuse, let alone castigated me for my pecatazzi. Well, I could not complain of her forbearance; there are many husbands who would be glad to have themselves such a lenient and unshrewish wife. And if today, at the age of forty-seven, Donata is woefully and prematurely ancient, I have caught up to her. I am now in my sixty-fifth year, so there is nothing premature or extraordinary in my looking as old as she does, and I no longer spend nights away from home. Even if I wished to wander, I do not get many alluring invitations to do so, and I should regretfully have to decline them if I did.

A German company has recently opened a branch manufactory here in Venice, producing a newly perfected sort of looking glass, and they sell every one they make, and no fashionable Venetian household, including ours, can be without one or two of those. I admire the lucent mirrors and the undistorted reflections they provide, but I consider them also a mixed blessing. I should prefer to believe that what I see when I look into a glass *is* blamable on imperfection and distortion, rather than have to concede that I am seeing what I really look like. The now totally gray beard and the thinning gray hair, the wrinkles and liverish skin splotches, the dispirited pouches under eyes that are now bleared and dimmed . . .

"No need to have dim eyes, friend Marco," said Dotòr Abano, who has been our family physician all these years, and who is as old as I am. "Those ingenious Germans have created another marvel of glass. They call this device the Brille—occhiale, if you prefer. The two glass pieces in it do wonders for the eyesight. Merely hold the thing up before your face and look at this page of writing. Is it not clearer to read? Now look at yourself in the mirror."

I did, and murmured, "Once, in a harsh wintertime, at a place called Urumqi, I saw some savage-looking men come out of the frozen Gobi, and they frightened me to terror, for they all had great gleaming *eyes of copper*. When they got nearer, I saw that they were each wearing a device rather like this. A sort of dòmino mask made of thin copper and pierced with many pinholes A man could not see very well through the thing, but they said it protected them from going blind in the snow glare."

"Yes, yes," Abano said impatiently. "You have told me more than once about the men with the copper eyes. But what do you think of the occhiale? Cannot you see more vividly?"

"Yes," I said, but not very enthusiastically, for what I was seeing was myself in the mirror. "I am noticing something I never noticed before. You are a mèdego, Abano. Is there a medical reason to account for my losing the hair from the top of my head but simultaneously growing bristles on *the point of my nose?*"

Still impatiently, he said, "The recondite medical term for that is 'old age.' Well, what of the occhiale? I can order a device made especially for you. Plain or ornate, made for holding in the hand or strapping around the head, gem-inlaid wood or tooled leather—"

"Thank you, old friend, but I think not," I said, laying down the mirror and giving him back the apparatus. "I have seen much in my lifetime. It might be a mercy now not to see all the signs of decay."

Just today, I realized that this is the twentieth day of the month of September. My birthday. I am no longer in my sixty-fifth year. I have this day tottered across the invisible but all too distinct line into my sixty-sixth. The realization bowed me down for a moment, but I raised myself to my fullest height—ignoring the twinge in my lower back—and squared my shoulders. Determined not to wallow in a maudlin mood of self-pity, thinking to cheer myself up, I ambled into the kitchen and leaned on the chopping block while our cook bustled about at her work, and I said conversationally:

"Nastàsia, I will tell you an improving and edifying tale. About this time every year, in the Kithai and Manzi lands, the Han people celebrate what they call the Moon Cake Festa. It is a warm and loving family holiday, nothing grandiose. The families simply gather affectionately together and enjoy the eating of Moon Cakes. Those are small, round pastries, heavy with richness and very tasty. I will tell you how they are made, and perhaps you would oblige me by making some, and the Dona and the Damìne and I could pretend we are celebrating in the Han manner. You take nuts and dates and cinnamon and—"

And almost immediately I was out of the kitchen and careering about the house in search of Donata. I found her in her dressing chamber, doing needlework, and I bellowed:

"I have just been expelled from my own kitchen by my own cook!"

Donata, not looking up, said with mild reproof, "Have you been bothering Nata again?"

"Bothering her, indeed! Is she employed to serve us or is she not? The woman had the effrontery to complain that she is tired of hearing of the sumptuous viands I used to enjoy abroad, and she will hear not another word about them! Che braga! Is that any way for a domestic to speak to her own master?"

Donata clucked sympathetically. I stumped about the room for a bit, peevishly kicking things that got in my way. Then I resumed, and tragically:

"Our domestics, the Dogaressa, even my fellows on the Rialto, they all seem disinclined nowadays to *learn* anything. They wish only to stagnate, and not to be stirred or leavened out of their stagnation. Mind you, Donata, I do not much care about outsiders, but *my own daughters!* My own daughters heave sighs and drum their fingers and look out the window when I try to relate some improving and edifying tale from which they might derive great benefit. Are you by any chance encouraging this disrespect for the patriarch of the family? I think it is reprehensible. I begin to feel like that prophet of whom Jesus spoke—the one who was *not* without honor, save in his own country and in his own house."

Donata sat smiling through my tirade, and imperturbably plying her needle, and when I was out of breath she said, "The girls are young. Young folk often find us older folk tiresome."

I roved about the room some more, until my wheezing abated. Then I said, "Old. Yes. Behold us dismal old folk. At least I can claim that I got old in the ordinary way, through the accumulation of years. But you did not have to, Donata."

"Everybody gets old," she said placidly.

"You are just about exactly the same age now, Donata, as I was on our wedding day. Was I old then?"

"You were in your prime of life. Stalwart and handsome. But women age differently than men do."

"Not if they do not wish to. You only desired to hasten past the childbearing years. And you need not have done. I told you long ago that I knew simple things that would prevent—"

"Things not fit to be mentioned by a Christian tongue, or heard by Christian ears. I do not wish to hear them now, any more than I did then."

"If you had listened then," I said accusingly, "you would not now be an Autumn Fan."

"A what?" she said, looking up at me for the first time.

"It is a very descriptive term the Han have. An Autumn Fan means a woman past her years of appeal and attractiveness. You see, in the autumn the air is cool and there is no *necessity* for a fan. It becomes an object without use or purpose or reason for existence. Just so, a woman who has ceased to be womanly, as you deliberately did, solely to avoid having more children—"

"All these years," she interrupted, but in a very soft voice. "All these years, have you thought that was why?"

I stopped, with my mouth still open. She laid down her needlework on her black bombazine lap, and folded her yellowed hands atop it, and fixed me with the faded eyes that had once been bright blue, and said:

"I ceased being a woman when I could no longer deceive myself. When I wearied of pretending to myself that you loved me."

I blinked in bewilderment and disbelief, and had to grope for my voice. "Donata, was I ever anything but tender and caring? Did I fail you in any way? Was I ever less than a good husband?"

"There. Even now you do not speak the word."

"I thought it was implicit. I am sorry. Very well, then. I did love you."

"There was something or someone you loved more, and always have. At our closest, Marco, we were never close. I could look into your face and see only distance, far distance. Was it farness of miles or of years? Was it another woman? God forgive me for believing this, but . . . was it not my mother?"

"Donata, she and I were *children.*"

"Children who are parted forget each other when they are grown. But you mistook me for her when we first met. On our wedding night, I was still wondering if I might not be just a substitute. I was a virgin, yes, and innocent. All I knew to expect was what I had been told by older confidantes, and you made it much better than what I had expected it to be. Nevertheless, I was not oblivious and obtuse, as one of our empty-headed daughters might be. In our cleaving together, Marco, there seemed to be . . . something . . . not quite right. That first time and every time afterward."

Justifiably affronted, I said stiffly, "You never made complaint."

"No," she said, looking pensive. "And that was part of the seeming wrongness: that I *did* enjoy it—always—and somehow felt I should not. I cannot explain it to you, any more than I could explain it to myself. All I ever could think was: it must be that I am enjoying what should rightly have been my mother's."

"How ridiculous. Whatever in your mother I was fond of, I have found also in you. And more. You have been much more to me, Donata —and much more dear to me—than she ever was."

Donata moved her hand across her face, as if brushing away a cobweb that had fallen there. "If it was not she, if it was not some other woman, then it must have been the sheer distance that I felt always between us."

"Come, my dear! I have scarcely been out of your sight since our wedding day, and never out of your reach."

"Not in your physical person, no. But yes, in the parts of you I could not see or reach. You have been ever in love with distance. You never really came home at all. It was unfair of you, to ask a woman to vie for your love with a rival she never could best. The distance. The far horizons."

"You exacted a promise about those far horizons. I made the promise. I kept to it."

"Yes. In your physical person, you kept to it. You never went away again. But did you ever once talk or think of anything but journeying?"

"Gèsu! Who is being unfair now, Donata? For nearly twenty years I have been as passive and compliant as that zerbino by the door yonder. I gave you possession of me, and the saying of where I should be and what I should do. Are you now complaining that I gave you no authority over my memory, my thoughts, my sleeping or waking dreams?"

"No, I am not complaining."

"That does not exactly answer the question I asked."

"You have left a few unanswered yourself, Marco, but I shall not pursue them." She finally took her mourning eyes off me, and picked up her needlework again. "After all, what are we arguing about? None of it matters anymore."

Again I was stopped with my mouth open and words unsaid—words unsaid by both of us, I imagine. I took another ruminative turn or two about the room.

"You are right," I said at last, and sighed. "We are old. We are past passion. Past striving and past strife. Past the beauties of danger and the dangers of beauty. Whatever we did right, whatever we did wrong, none of it matters any more."

She sighed also, and bent again to her sewing. I stood for a while in thought, watching her across the room. She sat in a shaft of September afternoon sunlight, where she could see best to work. The sun did not much enliven her sober attire, and her face was downcast, but the light did play in her hair. There was a time when that sunshine would have made her tresses gleam as golden bright as summer grain. Now her bowed head had more the sweetly melancholy glow of grain in the sheaf, a quiet, drowsy dun color, rimed with the first frost of autumn.

"September," I mused, not realizing that I said it aloud.

"What?"

"Nothing, my dear." I crossed the room to her and bent and, not amorously but only in a fond fatherly sort of way, kissed the top of her dear head. "What are you working on?"

"Parechio. Trifles of apparel for the wedding, for the luna di miele. No harm in getting started on them well ahead of time."

"Fantina is a fortunate girl, to have such a thoughtful mother."

Donata looked up and gave me a wan, shy smile. "You know, Marco . . . I was just thinking. That promise you made—it has been well kept, but it is near its expiration. I mean—Fantina about to be married and gone, Bellela betrothed, Morata nearly full grown. If you did still yearn to begone somewhere . . ."

"You are right again. I had not been counting, but I *am* very nearly at liberty again, am I not?"

"I freely give you leave. But I would miss you. Whatever I said before, I would miss you dreadfully. Still, I keep my promises, too."

"You do, yes. And now you mention it, I might just give the matter some thought. After Fantina's wedding, I could go abroad for—oh, no more than a short journey, to be back in time for Bellela's wedding. Maybe go only as far as Constantinople, see old Cuzìn Nico. Yes, I might do that. As soon as my back is better, anyway."

"Your back is ailing you again? Oh, my dear."

"Niente, niente. A twinge now and then, no more. Nothing to fret about. Why, my dear girl, one time in Persia, and again in Kurdistan, I had to get on a horse—no, the first time it was a camel—and ride despite having had my head near broken by the cudgels of brigands. I may have told you of those occurrences, and the—"

"Yes."

"Yes. Well. I do thank you for the suggestion, Donata. Journeying again. I will indeed give it some thought."

I went into the next room, which was my working chamber for when I brought home work to do, and she must have heard me rummaging about, for she called through the door:

"If you are looking for any of your maps, Marco, I think you have them all stored at the Compagnia fondaco."

"No, no. Merely getting some paper and a quill. I thought I would finish this latest letter to Rustichello."

"Why do you not do it in the garden? It is a tranquil and pleasant afternoon. You should be outside enjoying it. There will not be many more such days before winter."

As I started downstairs, she said, "The young men are coming to dinner tonight. Zanino and Marco. That is why Nata was so busy in the kitchen, and probably why she spoke rudely to you. Since we will be having guests, can we make a small pact? Not to bring any of our quarreling to the table?"

"No more quarreling, Donata, not tonight or ever. I am heartily sorry for whatever cause for quarrel I ever gave. As you say, let us tranquilly enjoy the remaining days. All that went before—none of it matters any more."

So I brought my writing materials out here to the little canalside courtyard we call our garden. It is planted now with chrysanthemums, the flower of Manzi, from seeds I brought from there, and the gold and fire and bronze colors make a gallant show in the mellow September sun. The occasional gòndola going by on the canal steers close here, so its occupants can admire my exotic blossoms, for most of the other gardens and window boxes in Venice contain summer flowers that have gone brown and limp and sad by this time of year. I sat myself down on this bench—slowly and carefully, not to rouse the twinge in my lower back—

and I wrote down the conversation just concluded, and now for some time I have only sat here, thinking.

There is a word, *asolare*, that was first minted here in Venice but has now, I believe, been appropriated into every language of the Italian peninsula. It is a good and useful word, *asolare*—it means to sit in the sun and do absolutely nothing—all that in one word. I would not have thought it could ever in my whole life apply to me. For most of my life, God knows, it did not. But now, as I think back—over those busy years, the ceaseless journeying, the eventful miles and li and farsakhs, the friends and enemies and loved ones who journeyed too for a while and then were lost along the way—of all those things, I remember now a rule my father taught me long ago, when I first strode out as a journeyer. He said, "If ever you are lost in a wilderness, Marco, go always downhill. Always downhill, and eventually you will come to water, and where there is water there will also be provender and shelter and companionship. It may be a long way, but go always downhill and you will come at last to some place safe and warm and secure."

I have come a long, long way, and here is the foot of the hill at last, and here am I: an old man sunning himself in the last beams of an afternoon late in a waning month of the season of the falling leaf.

Once, when I rode with the Mongol army, I noticed a war horse galloping along in one of the columns, neatly keeping gait and place with the troops, handsomely caparisoned in leather body armor, with sword and lance in scabbard—but the horse's saddle was empty. The Orlok Bayan told me, "That was the steed of a good warrior named Jangar. It bore him into many battles in which he fought bravely, and into his last battle, in which he perished. Jangar's horse will continue to ride with us, fully armed, as long as its heart calls it to battle."

The Mongols knew well that even a horse would prefer to fall in combat, or run until its heart failed, than be retired to lush pasture and uselessness and the idle waiting, waiting, waiting.

I think back on everything I have chronicled here, and everything that was written in the earlier book, and I wonder if I might not have put it all into just seven small words: "I went away and I came back." But no, that would not be quite true. It is never the same man who comes home, whether he be returning from a humdrum day's labor at his counting house, or returning after many years in the far places, the long ways, the blue distances, in lands where magic is no mystery but an everyday occurrence, in cities fit to have poems made about them:

> Heaven is far from me and you,
> But here for us are Hang and Su!

For a while when I came home—before I was relegated to a commonplace, and ignored—I was derided as a liar and a braggart and a fableor. But those who derided me were wrong. I came back with not nearly so many lies as I took with me when I went away. I departed Venice shining-eyed with expectation of finding those Cockaigne-dream lands described by the earlier Crusaders and the biographers of Alexander and all the other mythmakers—expecting unicorns and dragons and the legendary king-saint Prete Zuàne and fantastic wizards and mystical religions of enviable wisdom. I found them, too, and if I came back to tell that not all of them were what legend has made us believe, was not the truth about them just as wonderful?

Sentimental people speak of heartbreak, but those people are wrong, too. No heart ever really breaks. I know it well. When my heart leans eastward, as it does so often, it bends most poignantly, but it does not break.

Up there in Donata's chamber, I let her believe that she was pleasantly surprising me with the news that my long bondage to Home was finally over. I pretended I had not for years been thinking, "Shall I go now?" and each time deciding, "No, not now"—deferring to my responsibilities, to my promise to stay, to my aging wife and my three unexceptional daughters—every time saying to myself, "I will wait for a more propitious occasion to take my leave." Up there in Donata's chamber, I pretended also to receive her news gladly, that now I *could* go. And, just to appear properly grateful for her having volunteered that news, I pretended also that yes, I *might* now go again a-journeying. I know I will not. I was deceiving her when I implied that, but it was only a small deception of her, and I meant it kindly, and she will not be displeased when she realizes that I was deceiving her. But I cannot deceive myself. I waited too long, I am now too old, the time has come too late.

Old Bayan was still a fighting man at about the age I am now. And, at about this same age, my father and even my sleepwalking uncle made the long and rigorous return journey from Khanbalik to Venice. Old as I am, I am no more derelict than they were. Perhaps even my backache would benefit from being jolted by a long saddle ride. I do not believe it to be physical debility that dissuades me now from journeying again. Rather, I have the melancholy suspicion that I have seen all the best and worst and most interesting there *was* to see, and wherever I might go now would prove a disappointment by comparison.

Of course, if I could have the least hope that on some street in some city in Kithai or Manzi, I might astonishingly meet again a beautiful woman—as here in Venice I met Donata—who would remind me irresistibly of yet another beautiful woman long gone . . . Ah, for that chance I would journey, on hands and knees if necessary, to the ends of the earth. But that is an impossibility. And however much a new-met woman might resemble my remembered one, it would not be she.

So I go no more. *Io me asolo.* I sit in the last sunlight, here on the last slope of my life's long hill, and I do absolutely nothing . . . except remember, for I have much to remember. As I long ago remarked at someone else's graveside, I possess a treasure trove of memories with which to enliven eternity. I can enjoy those mementos through all the dying afternoons like this one, and then through the endless dead night underground.

But I also said once, maybe more than once, that I should like to live forever. And a lovely lady once told me that I would never get old. Well, thanks to you, Luigi, both those marvelous things may come to pass. Whether the fictional and disguised Marco Polo of your new work will be well received, I cannot predict, but the earlier book which you and I compiled together seems to have made its place secure in the libraries of many countries, and appears likely long to endure. In those pages I was not old, and in them I will go on living as long as the pages are read. I am grateful to you for that, Luigi.

Now the sun is setting, and the golden light fades, and the flowers of Manzi begin to fold their petals, and the blue mist rises from the canal, as blue as reminiscence, and now I would go to an old man's sleep, a young man's dreams. I bid you farewell, Rustichello of Pisa, and I subscribe myself

MARCO POLO OF VENICE
AND THE WORLD, HIS YIN:

set down this 20th day
of September in the
Year of Our Lord 1319,
by the Han count 4017,
the Year of the Ram.

AFTERWORD

There are in existence today only a very few relics of the journeyer Marco Polo. But one thing he brought back from his journeys is in the Céramique Chinoise collection of the Louvre. It is a small incense burner of white porcelain.

ABOUT THE AUTHOR

Gary Jennings led a paradoxically picaresque life. On one hand, he was a man of acknowledged intellect and erudition. His novels were international bestsellers, praised around the world for their stylish prose, lively wit, and adventurously bawdy spirit. They were also massive—often topping 500,000 words—and widely acclaimed for the years of research he put into each one, both in libraries and in the field.

Where the erudition came from, however, was something of a mystery.

Born in the little city of Buena Vista, Virginia, the son of Glen E. and Vaughnye Bayes Jennings, nothing in his upbringing suggested a belletristic future. The story was his birth occurred on the second floor of a movie theater that his parents owned. The theater burned down—and so it went.

The family moved to New Jersey in the early '40s and he graduated from Eastside High School (of *Lean on Me* fame) in Paterson, New Jersey. He attended the Art Students League in Manhattan, but from that point all formal education ceased. Jennings was completely self educated.

Responding to an ad in a New York newspaper at age seventeen, he was hired as an office boy in an advertising firm. It was a steady climb up the ladder in advertising; he thought he might use his artistic talent, but ended up as an account executive.

After a break to serve in the Korean War, where he was awarded the Bronze Star Medal—a decoration rarely given to soldier-reporters—and a personal citation by South Korean President Syngman Rhee for his efforts on behalf of war orphans, he returned briefly to advertising. It was during this period that he met Bill W.

The desire to write was so great that he decided to cut the strings and write full time. New York was not an affordable place and he had always wanted to go to Mexico . . . so he did. He left everything and moved to San Miguel de Allende. There he continued his freelance writing, wrote ten children's books, edited *Gent and Dude* magazine, and wrote two novels.

During his twelve-year stint in Mexico, Gary became fascinated with the Aztecs. He learned Spanish, haunted archaeological digs, and immersed himself in the Aztec history and culture. There he wrote *Aztec,* his break-through novel. He wrote about the Aztec world with vivid intimacy, with an unprecedented authenticity, and with literary grace. He brought something more to that story, something that would inform all four of his subsequent novels: an exotic, often erotic wit, based on characters possessed by an irrepressible Rabelaisian lust for life, stylish charm, and zany joie de vivre. His men and women were eccentric, roguish, and unabashedly bawdy. Jennings enlivened their adventures with an energetic prose, an electrifying power, and a narrative drive that many believed unique to historical fiction.

After leaving Mexico, he stayed briefly in Texas, then in Marin County, California, and finally back home to the Shenandoah Valley in Buena Vista, Virginia. He stayed there until the mid '90s and then returned to New Jersey to be near his oldest friends.

Gary Jennings literally roamed the world in the course of researching *The Journeyer,* for which he faithfully duplicated the travels of his hero Marco Polo. He did the same in the process of researching *Spangle,* during which he traveled with a circus troupe. He went back to Europe to continue his research and finished *Raptor,* a book on the Goths. Demand for more of *Aztec* finally convinced him to write *Aztec Autumn* and to prepare the material for then-unnamed books on the Aztecs.

During 1998 and 1999 Gary collaborated with a composer and lyricist and wrote a musical play based on the life of Joe Hill, a union organizer his father had met in Paterson, New Jersey. He also compiled research for a book set amid the hanging gardens of Babylon and was putting together a book of his short stories.

Gary died on Friday the 13th of February 1999, passing quietly while watching late-night television. He had had a dinner party planned for the next evening with his agent, his doctor, and his two best friends. He is greatly missed by friends and fans alike.